NINTH EDITION, COMPLETELY REVISED

GUIDE TO
AMERICAN
GRADUATE
SCHOOLS

Harold R. Doughty

PENGUIN BOOKS

PENGUIN BOOKS
Published by the Penguin Group
Penguin Group (USA) Inc., 375 Hudson Street, New York, New York 10014, U.S.A.
Penguin Group (Canada), 90 Eglinton Avenue East, Suite 700, Toronto, Ontario,
Canada M4P 2Y3 (a division of Pearson Penguin Canada Inc.)
Penguin Books Ltd, 80 Strand, London WC2R 0RL, England
Penguin Ireland, 25 St Stephen's Green, Dublin 2, Ireland
(a division of Penguin Books Ltd)
Penguin Group (Australia), 250 Camberwell Road, Camberwell,
Victoria 3124, Australia (a division of Pearson Australia Group Pty Ltd)
Penguin Books India Pvt Ltd., 11 Community Centre,
Panchsheel Park, New Delhi – 110 017, India
Penguin Group (NZ), cnr Airborne and Rosedale Roads, Albany,
Auckland 1310, New Zealand (a division of Pearson New Zealand Ltd)
Penguin Books (South Africa) (Pty) Ltd, 24 Sturdee Avenue,
Rosebank, Johannesburg 2196, South Africa

Penguin Books Ltd, Registered Offices:
80 Strand, London WC2R 0RL, England

First edition published in the United States of America by
The Viking Press 1967
Published in a Viking Compass edition 1967
Second edition published 1970
Third edition published 1975
Published in Penguin Books 1976
Fourth edition published 1982
This ninth edition published 2004

5   7   9   10   8   6   4

ISBN 978-0-14-200397-8

Printed in the United States of America
Set in Times Roman

CONTENTS

Preface to the Ninth Edition   v

Introduction   vii

  THE GRADUATE SCHOOL, vii

  THE PROFESSIONAL SCHOOL, xv

Understanding the Entries   xix

Key to Abbreviations   xxv

The Graduate/Professional School Entries   1

Indexes

  LOCATION OF INSTITUTIONS, BY STATE, 725

  INSTITUTIONAL ABBREVIATIONS, 730

  INDEX TO FIELDS OF STUDY, 736

PENGUIN BOOKS

GUIDE TO AMERICAN GRADUATE SCHOOLS

Harold R. Doughty is currently a Management and Educational Consultant. He was formerly a Human Resource Staffing Specialist and Recruiter for J.P. Morgan Chase & Company; Executive Vice President and Chief Operating Officer at American Commonwealth University; Vice President for Admissions, Financial Aid, and Enrollment Services at United States International University; Director of Admissions and Summer Sessions at New York University; and Director of Admissions and Freshmen Development at Adelphi University. He is also the author of *The Penguin Guide to American Business Schools*, *The Penguin Guide to American Law Schools*, and *The Penguin Guide to American Medical and Dental Schools*.

PREFACE TO THE NINTH EDITION

"Crisis" is a word grown impotent from overuse.

That sentence has opened every edition of this *Guide* since it was first published in 1967. Many of the traumata that inspired the remark are now so dated as to seem almost quaint. Some remain, festering. And still others, thought to be in remission, have returned to haunt us. The original observation continues to be valid, then, both for the American educational system and the larger society that supports it and receives its benefits.

Yet, despite a lingering propensity to react to challenges, rather than to anticipate them, our colleges and universities have managed to transform themselves in meaningful ways. This is specially true of the postbaccalaureate. From 1975 to 1998 the number of women enrolled in graduate programs increased 150 percent and total minority group registrations more than tripled. Since 1998 where the number of doctorates awarded reached an all-time high of 42,654 the number of doctorates received since has fallen by one or two percent each year through the year 2001. However, the number of doctorates awarded to women has increased slightly and those granted to minorities has leveled off. These extraordinary advances for minorities in the past may now be showing some signs of leveling or even reversing, possibly the result of the recent widely publicized legal suits alleging reverse discrimination.

Problems persist, of course. Task forces of educators doggedly debate overproduction of doctorates, although the much-bemoaned "Ph.D. glut" is still confined primarily to the humanities, and demand is still high for the products of most other disciplines. Complicating the anxieties of those same graduate faculties is the slowdown in the rate of increase of students pursuing advanced study. There is no *decline* in graduate enrollments, it must be understood. But after doubling every ten years since the turn of the century and tripling in the 1960s, graduate enrollments increased "only" from 985,000 in 1970 to 1,680,000 in 1979 and leveled off at 2,100,000 in 1994. The rush to advanced education has cooled, it is true, but it long threatened to boil over, so the results are not entirely negative. Unrestricted growth has been curtailed, costs are being contained, and some marginal academic operations are being eliminated or absorbed by those in which demand remains high. Under such circumstances— which should prevail throughout this decade—the quality of facilities and instruction should improve as universities learn to live within their means and focus on those areas in which they can best serve their client students.

Despite these contractions, applications for admission in most fields have remained constant. As education beyond high school has become a commonplace expectation, the demand for further training intensifies, if only to give a competitive edge in an ever-more-credentialed and specialized marketplace now being governed by consumer-oriented licensure requirements and regulations. That this is true is exemplified by the marked upswing in candidates for the master's degree, especially in business administration, computer application, and other narrowly defined and specialized programs. In spite of this, the current graduate student is being torn between the perceived need for graduate study and the immediate desire for career or job and instant financial gratification. The burdensome overabundance of applications of the past, which swamped understaffed administrative offices, has been greatly reduced. Higher application fees, earlier and earlier deadlines, and more stringent entrance standards, long a hallmark of the oversubscribed, have given way to the need for many graduate schools to market programs via the Internet, use direct mail solicitations, and actively recruit students in order to maintain an adequate applicant pool. Full-time study has given way to part-time. Indeed, full-time faculty has in many cases had to give way to more specialized part-time or adjunct associates. It is fair to say that only a few prestigious institutions can hold to and enforce the high academic requirements of just a few years ago.

Those full-time applicants who gain entrance to the fabled colleges of their choice are now confronted by financial difficulties substantially greater than those experienced in their undergraduate years. The belief that ample financial aid funds await the use of every graduate student is quickly dispelled. Inflation, tight money, and parents who often are unable or just unwilling to subsidize further education force many students to assume staggering financial burdens just when he or she is least able to afford them. This may be the first confrontation with the practical reality that graduate students must have alternative financial means in order to afford the graduate education they desire. This scenario further reinforces the belief that to find employment now will give the needed direction to pursue graduate study on one's own, the direction that is so often missing in undergraduate study.

Although college guidance is fully developed at the high-school level, no equivalent counseling structure exists for the potential graduate student. Such advisement as is available is provided by a small number of placement officers and faculty members concerned that able students realize their full potential. Unfortunately, no single individual can keep abreast of current offerings at even the major institutions. Indeed, it is difficult to keep track of developments within a single large university. Despite these obstacles, it remains true that most students who hold bachelor's degrees can gain admission to some graduate school in any section of the country.

This volume is designed to provide the kind of basic information students need to reach sound decisions in the selection of appropriate institutions at which to continue their education. It describes more than thirteen hundred institutions throughout the United States providing graduate and professional study. All have been reviewed once again for this ninth edition of the *Guide to American Graduate Schools,* and still more complete information has been sought from their Web sites.

Listed are programs in all areas of the liberal arts and sciences, education, medicine, dentistry, veterinary medicine, pharmacy, nursing, law, social work, agriculture, theology, the applied arts, engineering, and business. Admission and degree requirements, standards, enrollment and faculty figures, tuition charges, financial aid opportunities, and research and housing facilities are given whenever possible. While this book has been prepared with the student in mind, it is hoped that counselors, faculty, and administrative officers will find it of value, as well.

It should be noted that the *Guide to American Graduate Schools* is intended only as a first source of information. Careful use of the data summarized should enable the student to become more fully aware of the opportunities available and then to narrow selections to the geographical area and then the institutions he or she is likely to find most suitable. The student is encouraged to seek the advice of undergraduate faculty, especially those who teach in the proposed field of graduate study. Catalogues, bulletins, departmental brochures, and Web sites should be used when possible. Most important, the applicant must be brutally frank in self-appraisal of his or her ability, objectives, and motives for undertaking graduate study.

The author wishes to express his indebtedness to the graduate deans, admission officers, their assistants, and the Web masters in the nation's colleges and universities who provided the information presented. Further revisions of this volume are planned, and corrections and suggestions are welcomed.

H.R.D

INTRODUCTION

The Graduate School

Many students believe graduate study to be essentially an extension of undergraduate work, "only harder." On the contrary, the basic character and objectives of graduate and undergraduate study differ in many important particulars. The doctorate, and to a certain extent the master's degree, signifies the attainment of a high level of expertise in a given academic or professional field as well as the mastery of the investigative techniques of the scholar. Achievement of these goals relies upon the cultivation of habits of rigorous self-discipline and diligent thoroughness of mind.

The ensuing pages attempt to outline in forthright terms what a student can anticipate in graduate school, what will be demanded of him or her, and what he or she can expect in return. Since graduate education in the United States is simultaneously the target of severe criticism and the recipient of bountiful favor, the following remarks attempt to offer a balanced view of both the strengths and deficiencies of the system. This is not meant to suggest that these words constitute a complete analysis of graduate study. It is hoped, however, that these notes will help the student approach the decisions that face him or her with realism and some precision.

THE FIRST ONE HUNDRED TWENTY-FIVE YEARS

Graduate education in the United States is barely seven generations old. The attitudes and social conditions that characterized this predominantly rural young nation in the first half of the nineteenth century simply were not favorable to the extension of education beyond the college years. Despite the encouragement of many leaders, among them George Washington and Thomas Jefferson, several attempts to establish graduate education failed. The start of a tragic war sped the development of national maturity, and with it the first formal graduate program. Yale awarded three doctorates to students of its Scientific School in 1861.

Resistance to the founding of graduate programs dwindled as concern mounted over the numbers of American students flocking to German universities for postbaccalaureate study. Harvard announced in 1872 the availability of work leading to the Master of Arts, Doctor of Science, and Doctor of Philosophy. With the establishment of Johns Hopkins in 1876, and that university's avowed mission to bring its substantial resources to bear upon its graduate programs, higher education made its first firm commitment to advanced study beyond college.

With this recognition of responsibility, graduate education grew rapidly. By the end of the century, dozens of public and private universities enrolled graduate students. Soon the American penchant for standardization led quite naturally to the formation of the Association of American Universities. Harvard, Princeton, Columbia, Chicago, Johns Hopkins, California, Catholic, Pennsylvania, Michigan, Wisconsin, Clark, Cornell, and Yale were the charter members. As conceived, the organization was to encourage greater uniformity of conditions for successful work leading to higher degrees, to make representations to foreign universities regarding their admission of American students, and to improve European opinion of American degrees. Inevitably, since its membership included many of the most highly regarded universities, the Association became a prestigious organization into which invitation was eagerly sought. By World War I, ten additional institutions had been admitted.

After a period of stabilization in enrollment, during which acceptable standards for graduate study were defined, rapid growth resumed. Graduate enrollments, more than doubling every decade, went from 5800 in 1900 to 106,000 in 1940. World War II brought the demands for trained scientists and attendant governmental support that remain with us today, and the booming college enrollments of the 1950s intensified the need for college teachers. As a result of these and other pressures, graduate enrollment had surpassed the one-million mark by the mid-seventies and now the two-million mark.

Although the prestige of the Ph.D. and the other badges of completion of programs of graduate study has grown steadily over the last century, the increase in stature has been accompanied by rising criticism. The graduate school is often named as the assassin of the liberal arts college, and is said to have promoted professional proficiency at the expense of scholarship. Many critics feel that the value of the Ph.D. is demeaned by the practice of conferring this degree in fields other than those traditionally felt to be worthy of serious study. The graduate school is also accused, with justice, of enforcing archaic degree requirements simply because they have become the "keys to the club" of scholars.

Others have attacked graduate schools for emphasizing research over the training of college teachers (and vice versa), for promoting academic snobbery, and for adopting allegedly second-rate "professional" or "specialized" master's and doctoral degrees. Undoubtedly, debate will continue in the years to come, and along essentially the same lines as in the past. Witness this warning from the North Central Association: "The crowding of graduate schools has become so great as to raise some question as to the quality of work done and the value of the degree." This statement was issued in 1926.

Criticism notwithstanding, it is evident that increasing proportions of college graduates will seek the prestige of graduate degrees and the advantages, both intellectual and material, which accrue to those fortunate enough to be able to add those magic letters to their names.

SELECTING A GRADUATE SCHOOL

Once the student decides that graduate study will be of sufficient value to justify one or more years of hard work, major expenses, and the possible delay of personal plans or obligations, he or she must begin the often torturous task of making a choice of schools and opportunities. Once the choice of the proposed field of study is made, a number of considerations assume importance.

COST, SIZE, LOCATION. Contrary to widely held beliefs, financial aid for graduate students is by no means ample. Most students have to manage their support through means other than fellowships or similar awards. The most common solution is part-time study while employed full-time outside the graduate school. Whatever the method, the cost of attending graduate school is a primary factor in most students' deliberations. Fortunately, at least half of the most highly regarded institutions are publicly supported. Tuition costs therefore remain affordable, although usually somewhat higher than on the undergraduate level. Even the substantially higher charges normally set for out-of-state students at public universities are customarily less than the charges at private institutions. Furthermore, some public institutions are permitted to waive tuition and fees for nonresident graduate students under certain circumstances, or a student can establish residency in a relatively short period of time, thereby reducing tuition enormously, and these features should be checked.

Annual fees or tuition for residents in public institutions range from about $2200 to $7500, and from about $4000 to $21,000 for nonresidents. At most private colleges and universities the student can expect tuition charges of from $6000 to $31,000, although some church-related schools may be less expensive. Private institutions rarely make distinctions between resident and nonresident students. Housing expenses vary widely, of course, depending upon sections of the country, rural or urban location, and the student's accustomed standard of living. Very roughly, married students can anticipate rents of from $3200 to $15,000 annually, while single students will usually be charged between $3100 and $7000 for institutional housing, exclusive of board.

Size of a graduate school is an important factor, but caution must be observed in weighing this consideration.

Even in a graduate school with a very large enrollment, students in many fields can enjoy the advantages of small classes and close faculty–student rapport. Since graduate study is pursued primarily in a single field of study, the size of the major department may determine the closeness of faculty–student relationships as well as class enrollments. This is not meant to suggest that departments with large enrollments do not offer these benefits, but rather to warn against the assumption that large enrollments mean an impersonal, factory-like atmosphere in contrast to the presumed warmth and individual attention of smaller schools. It must be remembered, too, that larger institutions generally offer the extensive facilities required for many fields of study, while smaller institutions are more likely to specialize in fewer areas to permit them to provide equivalent research opportunities. In either case, care must be exercised in selecting not only a graduate school, but also the individual department in question.

Geographical location and type of environment can significantly influence choice of school. Institutions in urban centers offer distinct advantages, including cultural resources and greater research and employment opportunities than may customarily be found in rural locations. On the other hand, students who have spent most of their lives in nonurban environments may well find the tensions of the city too difficult, living costs too high, and distractions too numerous. The study of many fields is enhanced in obvious ways by the environment and by the availability of raw material for research. Sociology can have either an urban or rural emphasis, but other fields, such as public administration and art history, or animal husbandry and geology, are clearly oriented to specific environments. The student must weigh both his own background and preferences. Graduate study is demanding enough without the additional stress of unfamiliar surroundings or inadequate research opportunities.

THE QUESTION OF QUALITY. By the time a student is ready to consider graduate study, he or she knows that no thoroughly reliable measure of quality in education has been devised, including the latest attempts by *U.S. News & World Report*. Viewed through this screen of healthy cynicism, the selection of a graduate school can prove to be a less agonizing task than one might imagine. Recognizing that no two students can be equally served by one institution or program, the potential graduate student is nevertheless in a position to make certain basic judgments that will strengthen his or her chances for a satisfactory experience in graduate school.

The five factors most likely to influence estimations of quality are faculty resources, facilities, student body, reputation, and placement success. The question of reputation is most subject to challenge and yet apparently is most unshakable as it is assigned to particular institutions. This fact is evidenced in several evaluations of quality in graduate education dating from 1925 to the most recent in 2003. In these compilations of academic opinion, the same twenty to twenty-five graduate schools have appeared consistently as the most distinguished institutions. While schools within this group shift position somewhat in each new study, and occasionally a newer school makes the grade, this cluster of top-rated schools varies only slightly.

A relationship clearly exists between *perceived* quality and prestige. For many reasons, however, these listings of academic departments in order of presumed merit inevitably favor the older institutions. Most of the individuals queried in these surveys of opinion are senior professors or deans, for the quite logical reason that they possess sufficient experience to enable them to draw distinctions between departments. On the other hand, it must be remembered that until 1970 only twenty graduate schools gave over half the doctorates awarded annually. Since it can be assumed that most faculty members participating in these studies received their doctorates from these same twenty schools, some narrowness in scope of representation persists as a result of institutional background and loyalties.

Despite these and other limitations, these studies, undertaken by reputable agencies, serve as valuable guides to students seeking strong programs in certain fields. Other criteria for assessing quality are available, however. School catalogues, departmental brochures, or Web sites are valuable sources of information. Many graduate schools list the institutions that awarded the highest degrees held by each member of the faculty. It is often possible to discover the number and kind of publications produced and the professional honors and awards received by a professor by referring to such volumes as *Who's Who in America,* the *Directory of American Scholars,* and reports provided by the professional associations representing each academic field. Since the most distinguished members of every faculty are eagerly sought by industry, government, and other institutions, the catalogue often states whether professors are on leave or sabbatical, and, of course, whether they are still employed by the university. Since graduate students often seek the opportunity to study under noted scholars, it should be determined whether particular faculty members are to be available during the student's period of attendance. This is particularly true of students taking only the master's degree.

Examination of the catalogue or Web site also reveals the number of courses in each department that are open to undergraduate as well as graduate students. While course requirements often differ in such cases, depending upon the status of each student, effectiveness and content of a course may be impaired because of disparities in student backgrounds. Further, the number of courses and breadth of material covered can be important, allowing for the tendency to offer too many courses that might overlap.

Reports in general and academic news media are additional sources of information. These list the institutions attended by the recipients of the many prestigious fellowships, such as the National Science Foundation Fellowship program, as well as the grants of federal and state governments. Since the competition for these awards is keen, the institutions selected by these honored few can be assumed to offer well-regarded programs in specific fields. The simple fact that clusters of fellowship recipients attend specific schools at the very least reflects favorably upon the composition of their student bodies.

Most graduate students agree that the capability of their colleagues is very important in their assessments of the effectiveness of their programs. In fact, many observers suggest that it is difficult to determine whether a school or department is good because the training is better than elsewhere or because the students enrolled are stronger. This suggests a relationship between competitiveness of admission standards and quality of program. The potential graduate student can indeed reach valid conclusions about the makeup of a school's student body by determining the levels of competition resulting from admission policies.

It must be emphasized, however, that difficulty of admission *cannot be equated* with quality of program. As observed elsewhere, students exercise self-selection in applying to the more prestigious institutions, but often little restraint is evident in applications to more lightly regarded schools. This may result in the former group of schools accepting more than two-thirds of their applicants, while the latter rejects a much larger percentage. Also, small departments with excellent faculties and facilities sometimes find they must employ "soft" admission policies to build their enrollments, and thus their contribution to institutional budgets, while larger departments in more popular fields often must restrict admission because of limited faculties and facilities.

Availability and scope of research facilities provide another clue to the quality of individual schools. The nature and breadth of facilities can be indicative of a school's commitment to serious research and of its ability to attract support. The manner in which funds are allocated suggests something of the priorities established by an institution. Elaborate stadia and athletic arenas casting shadows across aging classroom buildings may not only be symptoms of the enthusiasms of misguided alumni, but the situation may also be evidence of misplaced emphasis by the administration.

The size of an institution's library holdings and the manner in which these resources are made available to students can be assumed to have considerable bearing upon quality. Virtually all of the highly regarded universities have library holdings well in excess of two million volumes, and several have more than three million. The only significant exceptions are a few leading technological institutions. Large numbers of volumes, microforms, and periodicals do not in themselves insure the quality of library resources, of course. A major portion of the collections should be on open stacks, or at least permission for access should be easily obtainable. Ideally, individual alcoves or carrels and research databases and Internet access are made available to graduate students. Students are wise to seek information about the nature of specialized collections in their particular fields of interest. Older institutions with large libraries may have weaker collections in the modern disciplines, while newer universities often possess holdings of less breadth. Institutional resources are often supplemented by nearby public libraries and research institutes, and this is to be borne in mind when considering graduate schools. Finally, some groups of institutions have arrangements pooling their libraries for the common use of their combined student bodies.

Other criteria are useful in assessing quality, though perhaps not as important as those discussed above. Among these are faculty salaries, eminence of alumni, number of recipients of major fellowships among both the graduate students and the faculty, number of Nobel Prize winners on the faculty, and institutional rank in production of doctorates and in size of annual gifts. Most of these factors are weighted in favor of the larger institutions, which makes it again necessary to stress the importance of investigating individual departments within graduate schools as well as the schools themselves.

GUIDANCE. Counseling services for prospective graduate students are largely informal and unorganized at most undergraduate colleges, with the exception of a few insti-

tutions that send large percentages of their graduates on to advanced study. Some universities have established regular series of interviews for those undergraduates who have demonstrated particular promise for graduate work. In addition, representatives of professional schools, especially those offering study in law and business administration, often visit colleges and universities as part of recruitment efforts. Unfortunately, this practice is rare on the part of graduate schools.

The best sources of specialized information about graduate study continue to be the members of the faculty in the student's proposed field of graduate study or current graduate students. Most professors can readily list the five to ten graduate schools offering what they believe to be the strongest programs in their disciplines. They can also aid the student in planning for financial aid and in discussing career opportunities. If the student is able to obtain some consensus on these matters from several faculty members, so much the better.

Some college placement offices make efforts to gather material about opportunities for graduate study and financial aid, and libraries and admissions offices generally keep files of graduate catalogues.

ADMISSION

It may be reassuring to know at the outset that most college graduates can gain admission to some graduate school somewhere in the section of the country they prefer. There are, of course, exceptions to this rule in some fields of specialization, but the statement remains valid for the vast majority of applicants. The reason this is true is the tendency on the part of most graduate schools to screen students more vigorously *following* entrance rather than before. This results in the common distinction made between admission to study and admission to candidacy. The latter procedure is typical on the doctoral level, and preliminary or qualifying examinations are usually employed to determine eligibility for continuance toward the degree. Applicants for the master's degree often are expected to meet requirements for formal candidacy, but the practice is less standard at this level.

Although admission policies and procedures vary widely from school to school and between departments, there are general requirements that have become fairly standard.

PREPARATION. Graduate schools of arts and science, education, business, and the like nearly always expect applicants to possess an appropriate bachelor's degree at the time of entrance. Although it is occasionally possible to gain admission without this degree, compensatory strength in previous academic performance or experience is customarily demanded.

The specific kind of undergraduate preparation necessary for individual fields of graduate study is much less subject to uniformity. Some social science departments are willing to consider applicants who do not present undergraduate majors in a particular social science discipline, but who have accumulated course work in several social science fields. While sociology departments are often liberal on this point, economics departments generally demand full undergraduate preparation. Because of the often greater-than-usual curricular requirements on the

graduate level in psychology, many psychology departments accept applications from students with as few as twelve semester hours of undergraduate study in psychology, assuming substantial work was completed in the natural and social sciences. While it is not possible to note all these variations here, it is usually true that natural and physical science departments demand extensive undergraduate preparation in the proposed field of graduate study, and departments of business, political science, sociology, and education place less emphasis on specific training on the college level. The humanities and older social sciences are likely to fall somewhere in the middle range in this regard.

CREDENTIALS. Every graduate institution requires that at least one official transcript of the undergraduate record be provided in support of the application for admission. If a student has attended more than one college or university, a single official transcript from the institution conferring the baccalaureate, showing courses accepted in transfer, is often adequate. More often, graduate schools request submission of transcripts from *each* undergraduate institution attended. Since admission procedures on the graduate level are often coordinated efforts between the offices of the dean, the departments, and/or admissions, it is not unusual for two or even three copies of each transcript to be required. Applicants are of course expected to provide official transcripts of any graduate study completed elsewhere, in addition to undergraduate records.

Letters of recommendation are typically required, usually from one to three persons, but often from as many as four or five. Generally, the letters are to be provided by members of the applicant's faculty who are in a position to assess his aptitude and motivation for graduate study. In the case of elementary and secondary teachers seeking further study, references may be required from a school supervisor. While potential for graduate study is customarily the basis for the letter of recommendation, some graduate schools desire evaluations of the character of the applicant as well.

Special departmental applications must be submitted on occasion if it is felt that a particular area of specialization is not adequately served by the general graduate school application. This is characteristically true of departments or schools offering programs of a more professional nature within larger graduate divisions empowered to grant all or most graduate degrees. This might include majors in social work, business administration, education, urban planning, or architecture, among others.

ENTRANCE EXAMINATIONS. Contrary to widely held opinion, the submission of results of entrance examinations is by no means a standard graduate school admission requirement. Accordingly, a student should ascertain whether he or she must meet this entrance requirement for the specific department of the particular graduate school in which he or she is interested. Those who intend to apply for national fellowships must also determine whether an examination is required for consideration.

Very few graduate schools have flat, divisionwide entrance exam requirements. Individual departments may specify single parts of exams, such as the general or appropriate subject test of the Graduate Record Examination. Others accept either the GRE or the Miller Analogies Test or require both. Many departments have no stated exam requirement but *strongly recommend* submission of test results. (In this case, the prudent applicant will take the suggested exams.) In still other schools, there is a minimum test requirement for all applicants, with the departments stipulating additional exams when felt to be appropriate.

It must be noted that the reason for this lack of uniformity in entrance exam requirements is the divergence of opinion on the relative value of these tests as predictors of success in graduate study. Many graduate schools and departments use the tests essentially as a screening device when confronted with the problem of selecting a limited number of students from a much larger group of highly qualified applicants. It is further suspected that some schools utilize the tests more to satisfy notions of status or prestige than to measure aptitude.

The examinations most commonly used are the Graduate Record Examination (referred to here as the GRE), the Miller Analogies Test (MAT), and the Graduate Management Admissions Test (GMAT). On occasion, individual schools supplement or replace these exams with tests of their own creation. Arrangements often can be made to take the exam at the applicant's present institution if it is inconvenient to travel to the school requiring the special exam.

The Graduate Record Examination has a general test plus subject tests in eight fields of graduate study. The general test has verbal, quantitative, and analytical writing sections, scored separately, and is designed to determine scholastic ability in those three general areas. The general test is two and one-half hours long, the subject test in each field takes three hours. While there is no minimum "passing" score, scores below 450 on the 200 to 800 scale are rarely considered adequate by most graduate schools with this requirement.

The Miller Analogies Test attempts to measure verbal and reasoning ability and takes only fifty minutes to complete.

The Graduate Management Admissions Test measures abilities and skills developed over a long period of time. It requires you to think clearly and systematically.

Information about these examinations may be obtained from graduate admissions offices, their Web sites, or from the Psychological Corporation, 7500 Old Oak Blvd., Cleveland, Ohio 44130 (MAT), and the Educational Testing Service in Princeton, N.J., or Los Angeles, Calif. (GRE and GMAT). Both examinations are given at colleges and universities across the country.

OTHER REQUIREMENTS. Some departments offering certain forms of advanced study set additional admission requirements. Applicants for graduate study in music are usually expected to audition for performance and music education programs or to provide samples of work for composition programs. Creative art majors typically are asked to supply either portfolios or photographs of finished work. Other departments or schools require statements of purpose for graduate study, which may include projected plans for the thesis or final project. Interviews are often requested, either for students with marginal records or for entrance to certain departments.

STANDARDS. Although graduate schools commonly specify a minimum "B–" average for entrance, the manner in which this standard is interpreted or applied varies substantially. It may refer to the cumulative grade average of all four years of undergraduate study, or to just the junior and senior years. The school may have in mind the average for all study completed, or only the courses in the proposed field of graduate study. Still another distinction is in the degree of rigidity with which the stated minimum average is observed. Some schools make no exceptions to the minimum, others regard the average as simply a point of guidance and regularly admit students whose records fall below it.

Further, some schools interpret the "B" as "B–." In other words, "B" to one school may be a 3.0 average on the customary four-point scale (A = 4, B = 3, C = 2), while another school might regard a 2.5 as essentially a "B" average. In practice, therefore, the "B" average stipulation can mean either the admission of virtually any college graduate or of a limited number of superior applicants. Despite the elusive manner in which this standard is interpreted, specific minimum grade point averages are listed, when available, for each graduate institution in this revised *Guide.* Due caution should be exercised in interpreting this information.

Most schools give greatest weight to the undergraduate performance in the proposed field of graduate study, assuming the total average is not significantly out of line with that in the courses in the major area of concentration.

The reputation of the undergraduate college undeniably has some bearing upon admission to the more highly selective graduate schools. It is not unusual for departments to offer admission more readily to graduates of institutions of substantial national prestige than to students applying from little-known colleges. Unhappy experiences with graduates of particular colleges often cause departmental suspicion of subsequent applicants. Some graduate departments are known to deny admission even to honors graduates of colleges they view with disfavor. Generally, however, applicants are judged upon the merits of their individual records. Among the students of the most highly regarded graduate schools are found many alumni of obscure colleges.

DEADLINES. Students are urged to make their inquiries about admission and financial aid at least a year in advance of the date of anticipated enrollment. While closing dates for receipt of applications for admission are rarely as early as for undergraduate colleges, the deadlines for financial aid applications for the more selective institutions are generally set for midwinter, and some fall as early as December 1. Schools state their closing dates in different ways. Some of the highly selective schools simply give the date by which applications for financial aid *and* admission must be filed, indicating that applications solely for admission are considered after that date as long as spaces continue to exist. Most graduate schools give separate closing dates for each type of application, noting that those applying for particular forms of aid must file both applications by the same stated deadline.

Since the award of most assistantships and some service fellowships depends upon vacancies created by the anticipated graduation of present recipients, departments may accept applications later in the spring for these particular awards than for scholarships and most fellowships.

The fragmented organizational structure of graduate schools often makes it difficult to determine to which office inquiries should be directed. Most often, requests for information are answered by the office of the dean of the graduate school or by the admissions office of the school or university. Sometimes the head of the proposed major department is the proper person to query about assistantships as well as admission. Students are advised to contact the specific individuals or offices noted in the institutional entries of this book as an initial resource or visit the individual school's Web site to obtain current information.

FINANCIAL ASSISTANCE

Many types of financial assistance are available through federal and state governmental agencies, private foundations, and civic organizations. While space does not permit a listing here of specific grants and awards, the following paragraphs should enable students to identify sources for further exploration.

The customary distinction drawn between fellowships and scholarships is that the former type of grant often requires some service in exchange for a stipend, while the latter carries no obligation other than satisfactory academic performance. Increasingly, however, graduate schools use the term "fellowship" to cover both outright awards and service grants, since "fellowships" are more readily associated with graduate study. Whatever label is used, it is worth noting that grants that require no service function are tax-free, while those demanding some form of work must be reported on income tax forms. However, IRS regulations and the interpretation of the regulations sometimes change the way income is reported and therefore all students receiving some type of stipend should verify how this remuneration will be reported for tax purposes.

Traineeships, assistantships, and internships provide stipends for performance of a variety of tasks. These include classroom teaching, proctoring in residence halls, laboratory research, and duties of a more or less clerical nature, such as grading undergraduate test papers or gathering and filing research materials.

An aura of status often surrounds the fellowship, and this characteristic may be enhanced by larger stipends and perhaps more engaging tasks than are normally associated with assistantships. Fellowship stipends range on the average from $12,000 to $15,000, and in private institutions carry tuition remission privileges as well. Allowances for dependents of married fellows may range from $1000 to $3500. Assistantships normally carry grants on a somewhat lower scale than fellowships, from perhaps $4500 to $10,000 plus free tuition or tuition waivers. Stipends for some fellowships and/or for married students with two or more dependents occasionally reach highs of over $23,000. At the other end of the scale, awards of an essentially honorary nature may pay as little as $100. Fellowships, assistantships, traineeships, and similar grants are available through the graduate schools or through individual departments, either from their own funds or from outside funds administered by them.

Although fellowships traditionally were reserved for doctoral candidates, many of those mentioned above and those available from other sources are open to students seeking the master's degree. Further information can be obtained through the office of the dean of the graduate school or designated members of the faculty representing various agencies. Students should also note the announcements of fellowships and other forms of assistance customarily posted on bulletin boards at central points in most colleges.

Students should not forget the possibility of full-time employment in the administrative offices of the institution in which they wish to study. Clerical positions are usually available in the offices of the Registrar, Dean of Admissions, Student Housing, Personnel, and others, and often carry a limited tuition remission privilege for part-time graduate study.

Most students must continue to find their solutions in combinations of outside employment, part-time study, loans, and support by parents or working spouses. This situation continues to run counter to the generally accepted conviction that graduate work is best accomplished through full-time study, but it does recognize the practical reality that graduate students must have alternative financial means in order to afford the graduate education they desire.

A note should be made at this point: the Internet has become a potential graduate student's best source of information for both university and nonuniversity financial assistance. Among the most noteworthy nonuniversity Web sites are the Council of Graduate Schools site (www.cgsnet.edu) and the National Association of Graduate Professional Students site (www.nagps.org). Obviously one should consider that the best source for institutional financial assistance is always the individual College's or University's financial aid site. However, one word of caution: always check for the date the Web site was last modified to ensure you are getting the most current information. The author found that some institutional sites were quite out of date; in fact, some sites observed had not been updated in the last two years.

THE STRUCTURE OF GRADUATE STUDY

Anxiety and doubt often attend a student's embarkation on the path to the master's and doctoral degrees. The candidate is confronted by a maze of course options, language and research tool requirements, oral and written examinations, thesis proposals and faculty committees, and academic standards. While no one is likely to suggest that successful negotiation of these obstacles can be accomplished with ease, certain patterns of expected performance can be anticipated prior to entrance.

THE PROGRAMS. Perhaps the first surprise for the beginning student is the realization that graduate study, especially on the master's level, is not necessarily a series of intimate seminars conducted by brilliant scholars and famous professors. In many universities, a number of courses are open to both graduate and undergraduate students, and these are likely to be conducted as lectures rather than discussion groups. In the more popular majors or in classes taught by senior members of the faculty, more than half the courses for the master's may have enrollments in excess of one hundred students. Even courses billed as seminars may have twenty or thirty students, which makes the free-discussion format difficult, or the professor may simply choose to conduct the class on a lecture basis.

For most master's degrees, the customary course requirement is the equivalent of two semesters (or three quarters) of full-time study. In some cases, however, the professional master's extends over two academic years; this is true of the Master of Fine Arts and the Master of Business Administration, for example. In the data disciplines, the necessary time for the master's often includes a full year of course work plus up to one additional year for research for the thesis. A great many graduate schools have two plans for the master's degree, one including the thesis or final project, the other without a thesis.

The candidate planning to continue to the doctorate is wise to make his preliminary decision for his doctoral dissertation early in the master's program. The exercise of this foresight may permit him to accomplish basic research for the dissertation while working on the master's thesis.

Although some cross-disciplinary programs are available for both the master's and doctorate, permitting some flexibility in course work, the graduate student must realize that he or she is subject to what might be described as "instant commitment"; that is, all or nearly all of his or her courses will be in one area of specialization or in fields bearing directly upon his or her major field of study. Interdepartmental programs such as American Studies or biochemistry allow somewhat more latitude in course work, but a common objective serves to emphasize a particular aspect of even the broadest interdisciplinary study. Students cannot expect, therefore, to make decisions about their majors following entrance, as may have been the case when they began undergraduate study.

In the second or third years of study, course work becomes more advanced than in the first year of essentially introductory work. Seminars in more specialized areas are increasingly the rule, and large lecture classes are generally less common. The doctoral candidate can expect to be required to complete a minimum of two years of course work beyond the master's, in full-time attendance or the equivalent in part-time study.

EXAMINATIONS, CANDIDACY, AND RESIDENCE. Some departments conduct placement exams at the time of initial registration for the master's program. This is characteristic of chemistry and music departments, among others, and the test is used essentially for guidance purposes. Others set the exam later in the first semester of registration and use it for the dual purpose of placement and formal matriculation. In either case, the test varies greatly in duration, content, and format from school to school. It may measure general English usage, or knowledge in specific areas of the major field, or simply aptitude for graduate study. The requirement is often waived altogether if the student presents acceptable results of the GRE, MAT, or GMAT taken prior to entrance. Only a few departments or schools make this requirement for the master's, however.

An exam after the initial stages of doctoral study is much more common, although not universal. Again, the test may simply determine the student's acceptability for advanced doctoral study, in which case it is usually referred to as a "preliminary" examination. An exam more comprehensive in content is generally required following completion of a majority of formal course work for the doctorate. Satisfactory performance on this test often precedes admission to doctoral candidacy. At many schools, these tests are combined in a variety of ways, and in form they can be written, oral, or both. Terminology is also mixed, even between departments within schools. As a result, exams may be labeled as "qualifying," "candidacy," or "comprehensive."

In any event, a student can anticipate at least one examination before he or she is admitted to formal candidacy for the doctorate. Less standard is an exam for master's degree candidacy. Candidacy may be withheld further, especially on the doctoral level, until satisfaction of the language or research tool requirements, submission of an acceptable dissertation proposal, and/or appointment of a dissertation advisory committee.

Finally, presentation of the master's thesis or doctoral dissertation is usually followed by an oral and/or written examination, the oral portion of which is customarily a defense of the thesis or dissertation itself. A final written exam is typically required if the "candidacy" or "comprehensive" was oral in form.

Potential students should determine prior to entrance the graduate school's interpretation of the term "residence." At minimum, it refers to the number of semester or quarter hours which must be completed at the school itself, exclusive of advanced standing awarded for work completed at other graduate schools. However, "residence" is sometimes interpreted to mean only work completed while in *full-time* attendance at the institution awarding the degree. Graduate schools are often rather obscure in their explanations of this requirement. An impression may be given in their catalogues that only full-time study is permitted, but the qualification "or its equivalent" may be found tucked away in the text.

Most master's programs demand that at least 24 semester hours of a 30-hour requirement (or 36 *quarter* hours of a 45-hour total) be completed at the institution granting the degree. If the thesis or final project is included in the total credit-hour requirement, the stated residence still applies. Some schools expect only one summer session in full-time attendance, so the attendance and residence requirements obviously differ. Schools or departments requiring full-time residence for the master's during the regular academic year are in the minority. Periods of full-time attendance are increasingly expected for the Ph.D., less commonly for "professional" doctorates such as the Ed.D., Psy.D., and D.B.A.

It is difficult to make definitive statements regarding residence requirements for the doctorate. However, while the trend toward increased full-time residence is clear in the most prestigious schools, most graduate schools still permit students to complete most or all course work while in attendance as part-time students. A number of schools refuse to make flat statements about the doctoral credit-hour requirement, preferring instead to state this in terms of total semesters, quarters, term units, or years. In general, students are expected to complete at least three years of full-time study or its equivalent beyond the bachelor's, including course work applied toward the master's. Time needed for the writing of the dissertation usually extends beyond this minimum period of course work. Indeed, the average total period of work for recipients of the Ph.D. is estimated to be well over six years. This includes, of course, time for the master's degree, research for the dissertation, and interruptions in attendance. It might be noted that this "Ph.D. stretch-out" is a subject of much academic controversy, since lingering students tie up faculty and facilities, cause substantial administrative problems, and contribute to the oversupply of ABDs.

THE LANGUAGE REQUIREMENT. Perhaps ten percent of the nation's graduate schools require some sort of ability in at least one foreign language for the master's degree. A diminishing number of schools, however, demand knowledge of at least one language, and sometimes two, for the doctorate. The language requirement has evolved from the traditional French, German, and/or Russian of the early years of graduate study in the United States to a variety of present forms.

For the master's degree, the language requirement is generally stated as a "reading knowledge of one modern foreign language, usually French, German, or Russian." The requirement is usually not schoolwide, but some departments may stipulate a reading knowledge when their schools do not. On the doctoral level, two of the above-named languages may be specified. Several variations of this customary requirement for the doctorate have cropped up in recent years, however. These include (1) a reading, speaking, and writing knowledge of one foreign language, *or* reading knowledge only of two languages; (2) a proficiency in one foreign language or in two languages; (3) a reading knowledge of one language plus proven ability to use another appropriate research tool such as statistical methods; and (4) reading knowledge of only one language.

Although some graduate schools adhere to the traditional French, German, or Russian requirement for the doctorate, most now permit substitution of another language deemed appropriate for a particular area of specialization for at least one of the two languages. A substantial number of graduate schools, responding to the criticism that the language requirement is no longer justifiable as a research tool in most fields, have either eliminated the language requirement altogether or have reduced it for the doctorate to one language, permitting individual departments to set additional requirements as they feel appropriate. This trend appears to be accelerating. Thus, three or more languages may be stipulated for the Ph.D. in the art history or comparative literature departments, while only one language may be mandatory for the history department; or appropriate languages may be required for particular specializations within a single academic discipline and not for others.

While the language requirement, in its various forms, remains a part of most Ph.D. programs in the arts and sciences, other doctoral programs, notably in education, business, and psychology, have reduced or eliminated the requirement. In these cases, additional course work and a research tool/computer literacy have become acceptable substitutes.

Criticisms of the foreign language requirement are many—that it is no longer a functional tool, that the "general culture" justification is out-of-date, that it serves to discourage able students—and modifications will continue to be made. The admonition to examine departmental rather than institutional standards thus gains strength.

THE THESIS, PROJECT, AND DISSERTATION. When a thesis is required for the master's degree, its purpose is often described as a "comprehensive survey of a specific area of knowledge." The doctoral thesis or dissertation, on the other hand, is typically expected to be the result of substantial research in an area of interest providing an "original contribution to the advancement of knowledge" in a given discipline. The distinction is essentially in the "original contribution" stipulation of the dissertation as compared to the "survey" nature of the master's thesis.

As with all other graduate degree requirements, however, variety abounds. The master's thesis may actually be an essay or an essay-length report of a research or creative project, or a recital, or an exhibition of art works, or a musical composition, or a combination of almost any of these. Schools which use the terms "essay," "paper," or "report" are generally implying a more limited length or depth of content than suggested by the term "thesis." As indicated above, the thesis or similar requirement is made only by some schools and departments, and nonthesis options of additional course work are usually available. As a rule, the thesis is included in total credit-hour requirements; that is, three to six semester hours (or the equivalent in quarter hours) are given for the completed thesis toward the thirty-two hours customarily required. Exceptions are theses or projects for the two-year professional master's degrees, where more credit is typically assigned toward the total semester or quarter-hour requirement.

The length of a master's thesis may be anywhere from fifty to three hundred and fifty pages, but the average is probably around one hundred pages. The doctoral dissertation is rarely less than one hundred pages and ranges up to five hundred pages or more. Although some professors are fond of relating stories about superb dissertations ten pages long, the student is advised not to cling to such fragile hopes.

With diligence and careful planning, the dissertation can be written in less than a year, especially if research material is gathered and sorted while the candidate is still engaged in course work. Unfortunately, the temptation to delay commencement of research or writing until completion of other degree requirements is strong, obviously resulting in increased difficulty when the project is finally begun.

The "contribution to knowledge" aspect of the doctoral dissertation has been increasingly diluted in favor of "significance and relevance." This trend is intended to counter the tendency to seek novelty of concept or subject matter, a practice that often leads to dissertations that are "islands of minutiae in a sea of trivia." To compensate for the peripheral quality of many dissertation topics, departments may emphasize the interpretive and critical approach in preference to pure research.

Whatever the faults or virtues of the master's thesis and doctoral dissertation, there is little doubt that it is for most students the single most satisfying experience in graduate study.

SIXTH-YEAR PROGRAMS. Some mention must be made of the certificates of advanced study available in certain professional fields, notably education and engineering, but occasionally in other areas. These programs fill the need for refresher training beyond the master's, and, it must be said, salary increments often reward those who complete this additional work.

The sixth-year certificate/diploma customarily requires at least one year of full-time study in residence, or the equivalent in part-time attendance. There is usually no language or thesis requirement, but a final project of a type promoting professional proficiency in specific areas is often required. The certificate of advanced study does not attempt to replace the doctorate, but is instead an intermediate program of graduate training.

The Professional School

All study beyond the undergraduate college is essentially "professional" in nature. The graduate school of arts and science was created primarily to train college teachers and scholars, even though most of those who hold master's and doctoral degrees do not enter higher education. But graduate training in fields other than the humanities and sciences is clearly designed for readily identifiable occupations.

Although there are no agreed demarcations, it can be fairly stated that some sixteen disciplines are the predominant arenas of postbaccalaureate professional study: architecture, business, dentistry, education, engineering, forestry, law, library science, medicine, nursing, optometry, pharmacy, public health, social work, theology, and veterinary medicine. Cases can be made for including under this label such fields as journalism and physical therapy, but for the purposes at hand these sixteen are most relevant.

Even this list could be winnowed further. The origins of formal education for just three professions predate those of all others by many decades. Training for these—law, medicine, theology—has developed independently of most forms of graduate study. Indeed, law schools still speak of work for the first law degree as "undergraduate," as if candidates could enter directly from high school. Many of the other programs still struggle for acceptance to fully recognized professional status for themselves, but remain as mere departments of larger divisions.

And make no mistake—the designation of an academic subdivision as a department or institute or school or college is a distinction important beyond simple academic snobbery. Professional "schools" within broader institutions have more stature than departments. They have more independent administrations and faculties, sometimes even their own boards of trustees. Often, they are able to detach their fund-raising activities from their parent institutions and thus have greater latitude in distribution of moneys separated from contributors. There is greater unity of purpose in, say, a graduate school of business administration than in a graduate school of arts and science, which is more often a collection of thirty or more mini-colleges pulling in separate directions. Faculties of *schools* are typically better paid than those of *departments* in the same fields. There is less jockeying for internal political advantage, because academic apples are not thrown together with professional oranges.

And in the current atmosphere of student specialization and vocationalism, professional schools have the upper hand in determining the direction of their institutions, while many liberal arts programs struggle with enrollment and fiscal problems. The following pages outline these schools and programs and briefly survey factors to be considered in selection, admission and degree requirements, and sources of financial aid. Much of the descriptive material contained in the previous section applies to professional schools as well, so these remarks are concerned only with the distinctive characteristics of these programs.

SELECTING A PROFESSIONAL SCHOOL

Professional schools often have been accused of unduly restricting enrollments at times of expanding need. Now, having rushed to meet urgently expressed national needs, educational institutions find themselves the targets of the reverse criticism: they went too far.

There are now oversupplies of teachers in some areas of the country; some say two for every job. New members of the bar are encountering stiffer competition, and there looms the previously unbelievable prospect of a surplus of doctors and dentists. According to one estimate, if the United States merely sustains current output, by 2001 there will be half again as many doctors as in 1980, and a slight decrease in dentists. In a nation headed toward zero population growth, this prediction has been used as justification by federal agencies to attempt to limit aid for professional education to just loan programs.

The result of these trends will be to make professional study even more difficult to undertake than it is already. Medical schools, for example, are talking tentatively about charging tuition that actually covers instructional expenses, meaning annual tuition could soon reach as high as $40,000 at some private institutions! This, not even counting living expenses, and when financial aid is far from munificent and federal cutbacks can be anticipated. Admission standards, too, may escalate still further, putting even the least glossy law and medical schools out of reach of all but the most capable applicants.

In the very short-lived meantime, students of above-average, if unspectacular, aptitude and credentials have reason to be hopeful about gaining entrance to some school in their chosen fields—as long as they are not unrealistically fussy about location and "image."

COST, SIZE, LOCATION. As with graduate schools of arts and science, costs for professional study vary widely, depending principally upon the field and the type of institutional or state support. Nearly all schools of veterinary medicine and forestry are affiliated with public institutions, so tuition expenses are correspondingly lower for state residents in those majors. The other professional schools are as likely to be under private sponsorship as public, so costs can differ substantially. Annual tuition ranges from about $4180 to $23,600 at publicly supported schools, from $20,500 to $38,300 at private schools, all escalating at an average rate of nearly 5 percent a year. The exceptions are the theological seminaries and schools of divinity. These are all privately controlled, yet tuitions may be as little as $2200 or as much as $9000. In general, tuition has been increasing by 6 to 7 percent each year. Always check with the institution in question regarding current tuition charges.

Student bodies of professional schools are customarily in the 200 to 500 range, but some exceed 1000 in enrollment and some seminaries have as few as 25 students. The great majority of professional schools are affiliated with universities, but divinity schools are more frequently parts of colleges or are autonomous. Increasingly, formerly independent law and medical schools are being absorbed into larger institutions or are joining with other institutions to form new entities.

Only the most populous states have schools offering all sixteen types of professional study. There are law schools in forty-nine states, medical, dental, and osteopathic schools in forty-six, and veterinary schools in twenty-seven. On the other hand, there is at least one graduate school of education and one theological school in every state. Under the circumstances, most full-time professional students can expect to enroll at institutions at much greater distance from their homes than their undergraduate colleges.

ADMISSION

The professional schools of law, medicine, dentistry, and veterinary medicine set rigorous entrance requirements and thus avoid the separate step of "admission to candidacy," not to mention the high attrition rate, of most graduate schools. It is not possible, therefore, to suggest that *any* college graduate can gain admission to some professional school in his or her chosen field. Nevertheless, admission is not always as difficult as is commonly supposed, if students are willing to consider professional schools without regard to location or to presumed reputation. (Since most types of professional schools must meet fairly high minimum criteria to retain accreditation by appropriate professional associations, it is probably safe to say that few truly "bad" schools exist.) Several factors influence the decisions of admission committees, and these should be understood by the potential applicant.

PREPARATION. Some professional schools are willing to consider applicants who do not hold a bachelor's degree certifying completion of a four-year undergraduate program. Schools of veterinary medicine and dentistry, for example, sometimes admit students with as little as two years of undergraduate study, though nearly all medical and law schools now require the bachelor's degree.

Undergraduate preparation need not have followed the curricula laid down in preprofessional programs. However, applicants to schools of medicine, dentistry, public health, engineering, nursing, osteopathy, pharmacy, and veterinary medicine should have completed programs that permitted substantial emphasis upon the natural and/or physical sciences. This does not mean, of course, that the diversity of background provided by study in the humanities and social sciences is to be minimized. In fact, basic work in English, humanities, and the social sciences are required for medical school admission nearly as often as biology, chemistry, and physics.

Schools of law, business, social work, and theology are less likely to require specific undergraduate preparation. These schools emphasize in their catalogues that general liberal arts studies are more important for their students than specialized majors in fields thought to be closely related to the professions in question. Applicants to a law school, for example, might hold majors in economics, history, English, sociology, or even business administration.

CREDENTIALS. In addition to transcripts of undergraduate study completed, applicants to the types of professional schools discussed here are nearly always expected to provide one to four letters of recommendation and the scores on the standard tests available for each professional field (except theology). In many cases, the letters of recommendation may be replaced totally or in part by the recommendations of the undergraduate preprofessional faculty committees. Professional schools, particularly those in theology, often request character references as well as estimations of potential for study in the particular field.

Nearly all schools of dentistry, medicine, law, business, nursing, osteopathy, and veterinary medicine demand the results of the appropriate entrance examinations prepared and/or administered by the professional associations. These are as follows:

Dental Aptitude Test (DAT)—applications available from either the chosen dental school or from the Department of Testing Services, American Dental Association, 211 East Chicago Avenue, Suite 1840, Chicago, Ill. 60611-2678; (312)440-2500. Web site: www.ada.org.

Graduate Management Admission Test (GMAT)—applications available from Graduate Management Admissions Test, P.O. Box 6101, Princeton, NJ 08541-6101; (601)771-7330. Web site: www.gmac.com. Beginning January 1, 2006, Pearson VUE and ACT, Inc., will develop and administer the GMAT.

Graduate Record Examination (GRE)—application available from Graduate Record Examination Testing Service, P.O. Box 6000, Princeton, NJ 08541-6000; (609)771-7670. Web site: www.gre.org.

Law School Admission Test (LSAT)—applications available from Law School Council, Box 2000, Newtown, PA 18940; (215)968-1001. Web site: www.lsac.edu.

Medical College Admission Test (MCAT)—applications available from MCAT Program Office, P.O. Box 4056, Iowa City, IA 52243; (319)337-1357. Web site: www.aamc.org.

Miller Analogies Test (MAT)—applications available from The Psychological Corporation, 19500 Bulverde Road, San Antonio, TX 78259; (800)622-3231 or (210)339-8710. Web site: www.tpcweb.com/mat.

Optometry Admission Test (OAT)—applications available from Optometric Admission Testing Program, 211 East Chicago Avenue, Suite 1846, Chicago, IL 60611-2678; (312)4409-2693. Web site: www.opted.org.

Pharmacy College Admission Test (PCAT)—applications available from The Psychological Corporation, 19500 Bulverde Road, San Antonio, TX 78259; (800)622-3231 or (210)339-8710. Web site: www.tpcweb.com/pse/PCAT.

Praxis Series Tests—applications available from the Praxis Series, P.O. Box 6051, Educational Testing Service, Princeton, NJ 08541-6051; (800)772-9476 or (609)771-7395. Web site: www.ets.org/praxis.

Test of English as a Foreign Language, Test of Written English, Test of Spoken English (TOEFL, TWE, TSE)—applications available from TOEFL, P.O. Box 6151, Princeton, NJ 08541-6151; (609)771-7100. Web site: www.toefl.org.

Veterinary College Admission Test (VCAT)—application available from The Psychological Corporation, 19500 Bulverde Road, San Antonio, TX 78259. Web site: www.tpcweb.com/pse/VCAT.

A majority of professional schools required a qualifying interview by invitation for the semifinalist applicants, but this is not universal. For dental, medical, and osteopathy school, the interview usually follows preliminary screening of applications.

DEADLINES. Medical and dental schools customarily accept applications for admission starting in June of the year preceding the proposed term of entrance. Most medical schools set closing dates for receipt of completed applications in October or November, although these dates are now often flexible. Dental schools accept applications as late as May. Preliminary applications are sometimes required, followed by formal applications from those who pass the initial screening.

The other types of professional schools generally accept applications well into the summer preceding the term of entrance, although some of the more prestigious law and business schools have deadlines in January. It is to be remembered that most professional schools restrict entrance for beginning full-time students to the Fall term, or occasionally to the Summer and Fall terms.

COMMON APPLICATION SERVICES. In an effort to ease the burden on students intent on applying for admission—and to cut their own clerical cost—most law, medical, osteopathic, and dental schools have subscribed to the services of centralized processing agencies. These offices accept academic credentials and other data from applicants, summarizing them in uniform formats and passing them on to the designated schools. The clearinghouses do not offer advisement and do not make admission decisions; that remains the province of the schools themselves. After ascertaining whether the schools in which the student is interested employ the relevant service, he or she should write to it as follows:

American Association of Colleges of Osteopathic Medicine Application Service (AACOMAS)—for application information contact AACOMAS, 5550 Friendship Blvd., Suite 310, Chevy Chase, MD 20815; (301)968-4190. Web site: www.aacom.org.

American Association of Dental Schools Applications Service (AADSAS)—for application information contact AADSAS, 1625 Massachusetts Avenue, NW, Suite 600, Washington, DC 20036; (202)667-9433. Web site: www.adea.org.

American Medical College Application Service (AMCAS)—for application information contact AMCAS, Section for Student Service, AAMC, 2501 "M" Street, NW, Washington, DC 20037-1306; (202)828-0600. Web site: www.aamc.org.

Law School Data Assembly Service (LSDAS)—for application information contact the Law School Admissions Council, Box 2000-M, 661 Penn Street, Newtown, PA 18940-0993; (215)968-1314. Web site: www.lsac.org.

Veterinary Medical College Application Service (VMCAS)—for application information contact VMCAS, 1101 Vermont Avenue, NW, Suite 411, Washington, DC 20005-3521; (202)682-0750. Web site: www.AAVMC.org.

There is a fee associated with these applications, usually escalating with the number of schools to which the materials are to be sent. Some of the schools require supplementary materials and/or an interview. A few expect payment of additional application fees.

STANDARDS. It is probably safe to say that at least between 40% and 50% of the applicants to professional schools are accepted for admission, a little less than that for law, medicine, and dentistry, and higher for the other professional schools. Allowing for duplication of applications, available statistics suggest that an even larger percentage of students eventually gain entrance to some school, perhaps as many as two-thirds of all applicants.

Most professional schools seek students with undergraduate grade point averages of "B." Depending on the degree of competition created by numbers of applicants, this may be interpreted to mean an average as low as "C plus" or as high as "A minus." It is generally agreed, in any event, that the grade average is the single most reliable predictor of success in postbaccalaureate professional studies. While the scores on the various entrance exams are undeniably important in the deliberations of admissions committees, students should not expect strong scores to outweigh mediocre grades in undergraduate course work, even if the degree is from a prestigious institution.

FINANCIAL ASSISTANCE

Professional study is expensive and although various forms of aid are available, most students must plan to meet their costs through loans or their own resources. Most financial assistance is based on demonstrated and documented need. Some schools provide limited numbers of scholarships, fellowships, grants, and tuition waivers from institutional funds; the size of these awards is generally tied to the student's academic achievement. However, the basic component in all financial aid packages will be loans. In addition to the loan resources of the schools themselves, low-cost loans are widely available through government agencies, some banks, private lending groups, professional associations, and private or community groups.

Students apply for the Government sponsored loans and scholarships through the individual schools to which they seek admission or through the parent institution's financial aid office. In general, all financial aid applicants must use FAFSA (Free Application for Federal Student Aid).

Most professional schools assist the spouses of their students in obtaining local or institutional employment. Although part-time employment is usually discouraged for first-year students, this possibility should still be explored. Finally, some schools have teaching or research assistantships or fellowships for advanced students.

THE STRUCTURE OF PROFESSIONAL STUDY

Programs leading to first degrees require four years of full-time study for the medical, osteopathy, veterinary, and dental professions, three years of full-time study or the equivalent in part-time attendance (when permitted) for law, and usually two years for the other fields.

Since practice in the medical/osteopathy/veterinary/dental professions demands both clinical skills and thorough understanding of the physical and natural sciences, students in these fields can expect balanced study in both these aspects of training. The first two years are spent in work in the basic and preclinical sciences, while the last two are devoted largely to clinical work. There are no language or thesis requirements as in the graduate school, and summers are usually free.

Law students can anticipate a beginning year of introductory work, usually conducted in lecture classes. The following two years permit more latitude in course selection, and seminars are more commonly available. Course work is generally supplemented by tutorial work emphasizing training in research and various forms of legal writing. First professional degrees in religion usually follow this same pattern, but variations are many.

In the other professions, a full-time two-year program (or its equivalent) is the norm, with the exception of those fields in which graduate study is primarily a continuation of undergraduate work, as in architecture and pharmacy. In many areas, undergraduate study in the field will reduce credit requirements for the graduate degree.

Most medical, osteopathy, dental, and veterinary schools offer advanced study beyond the first degree in both clinical and research specializations. Graduate study in law and religion is also available, though proportionally less common. Such programs are generally administered by the graduate schools of the institutions with which the professional schools are affiliated, and students usually must meet admission and degree requirements established by both the graduate and professional divisions. Sometimes graduate work is given through the professional school itself, especially if the school is located at a medical center separated from the main campus of the institution.

Programs leading to professional degrees are demanding, and standards of performance are rigorous, but the rewards are substantial. If the potential student is realistic in selecting a school consistent with his or her interests and aptitudes, the experience will test his or her mind and spirit and lead to the kind of lifelong fulfillment few others are fortunate to enjoy.

UNDERSTANDING THE ENTRIES

The information on the following pages describes the structure and content of the institutional entries that make up the main portion of this volume. For the entries to be of maximum value, it is important that the reader properly interpret the data provided.

The entries contain the kinds of basic information a potential applicant is likely to seek in choosing a graduate school. Careful examination of the school descriptions should aid the student in reaching realistic preliminary decisions. Since admission standards and requirements, course offerings, and financial aid opportunities are subject to frequent revision, it is not to be assumed that the entries can replace individual school bulletins or their Web sites.

All institutions in this *Guide* are accredited by the appropriate national, regional, and/or professional accrediting associations. Although no agency is specifically charged with the accreditation of graduate schools, those schools which are part of properly approved colleges and universities are all included. Among the associations that assign accreditation of independent professional schools as well as those affiliated with larger institutions are the Liaison Committee on Medical Association, the Commission on Accreditation of the Council on Social Work Education, the American Dental Association, and the American Veterinary Medical Association.

Every effort has been made to render these data understandable without reference to elaborate indexes of codes and abbreviations. However, one symbol, other than abbreviations for degrees and commonly required entrance examinations, has been used throughout this book: the "diagonal" or "slash" mark, as in "teaching/research." As employed here, the slash means *only* "and/or."

The following pages describe in detail the kinds of information to be found under each entry, in the same order. The items listed below are not included in every entry, either because they are not relevant or because specific data were not available.

GENERAL CHARACTERISTICS OF THE INSTITUTION

Name of the institution. The colleges and universities are arranged in alphabetical order according to the most important word in the title. Separate institutional entries are provided for individual university centers that are either autonomously administered or distinct in character or offerings. An institutional index for further assistance is at the back of the book.

Mailing address of the main campus. The name of the city and state in which the main campus offering graduate study is located, plus the zip code. When individual graduate or professional departments or schools are located in other towns or cities, that fact is noted in the body of the text. Internet Web sites are also included when available.

Founding date. Usually the year the institution was chartered, but sometimes the year classes were started or the year of the opening of another institution from which the present one developed.

Location in direction and miles from nearest major city.

Direction from nearest major city is given in appropriate capital letters (NW, SE). The mileage given is approximate road distance. Often the city named is relatively small but sufficiently well known, and is given only to establish the location of the main campus.

Institutional membership. There are many prestigious organizations that institutions can join or are invited to join. Two of the more important ones are Council of Graduate Schools and the Association of American Universities, and if the institution holds membership in either, it is noted in this section.

Coed, men only, or women only. Relatively few institutions limit their graduate enrollments to students of one sex. When the undergraduate program is thus restricted, and the graduate programs are not, it is stated: "Coed on the graduate level."

Type of control. If the institution is supported primarily by public funds, the level of government is specified, whether state, county, or municipal. Occasionally, institutions receive substantial amounts of financial support from the state or city government but decision-making powers are retained by the board of trustees. In other cases, individual divisions of universities are totally or mostly supported by public funds. In these instances, control is often shared. When appropriate, these situations are noted.

Many private institutions are sponsored by religious denominations, and this affiliation is mentioned. Although few such colleges and universities restrict their enrollments to members of the sponsoring churches, students may be expected to adhere to certain basic social or curricular requirements. Institutions that are open only to members of particular denominations or to the clergy are not listed in this book unless they are divisions of larger institutions that are not otherwise restricted. This is also true of colleges offering training only for the clergy of particular churches.

Semester, quarter, or trimester system. The semester system provides study during two terms of a nine-month academic year and, usually, during one or more summer sessions. The quarter system divides the calendar year into four equal terms, the trimester into three. Under all three systems, students typically attend classes for about nine months. For no apparent historical reason, Western colleges and universities most often operate on the quarter system, those in the East on the semester. The trimester is still relatively uncommon but has met favor in some sections.

Major research facilities. Special institutes, laboratories, interdepartmental and interinstitutional programs and resources are mentioned. The list is not intended to be exhaustive, but only to note distinctive offerings or equipment and to suggest their scope. Since this information is not always available, its absence does not necessarily mean that special facilities do not exist at any given institution.

Library. This figure is the total number of bound volumes in the institution's collections; current periodicals are also included when available. When special collections or several libraries at different centers are available, the figure represents the combined number of volumes. If the term "capacity" is used, it can be assumed that fewer volumes are actually in stock and that this figure is not available. If "items" is used instead of "volumes," the figure includes periodicals and similar materials in addition to books.

National Institutes of Health ranking. This ranking information was obtained from NIH Web site and it includes the top 200 institutions/organizations receiving research awards or grants in the year 2000–2001. This information gives a potential applicant an indication of the recognized quality of the research being undertaken at the institution he or she may be considering, as well as the probability for doctoral funding available at the institution.

Annual tuition charges for full-time students. Many public institutions use the term "fees" rather than "tuition," often with additional "tuition" for out-of-state students. This semantic distinction is often employed to maintain the il-lusion of tuition-free institutions. As used here, "fees" refers only to basic expense of course work and does not include the additional charges for use of laboratory and similar facilities. Generally, the cost of tuition and/or fees at public institutions is greater for nonresidents than for residents, while there is usually no such distinction at private colleges and universities. On occasion, still a third level of tuition is charged foreign students. When no flat-rate tuition is set for full-time students, the per hour charge is given.

Throughout this book, "annual" refers to the academic, not the calendar, year. It also should be remembered that tuition charges are constantly on the rise, increasing at a 5% annual rate at most institutions. This fact has been anticipated when possible, and the charges indicated are customarily for the 2002–03 year.

Part-time tuition charges. Schedules of charges are either per credit (or semester or quarter) hour, or according to varying ranges of hours, *i.e.,* $100 for 1–4 hours, $200 for 5–8 hours, and so on. As above, charges are indicated for both resident and nonresident students, when appropriate. Charges indicated are for graduate or professional students only. Tuition scales for undergraduate students sometimes differ and are not listed. If charges are mainly the same for most divisions of a university, any specific difference is noted under this heading *or* under the divisional heading. Unless so indicated, the tuition stated in the general institutional paragraph applies to all divisions.

On-campus housing available. Many institutions are unable to provide separate statistics for housing available to graduate students only. Therefore, unless noted as "for 100 graduate men," the figures given are for all students, both undergraduate and graduate. In this event, it may be assumed that graduate students are eligible for such housing. The figure given for married student housing should be interpreted as family units, while the figure for men and women refers to individual spaces only. "On-campus housing" means institutionally owned or controlled housing and does not include private accommodations. Only one or two colleges indicate that nearby privately owned, off-campus housing is *not* available. Graduate students who choose to live in institutional housing must remember that they are usually expected to observe the restrictions in force for all residents.

Average academic year housing cost. This is for the academic year only. When housing is available to graduate students only during the summer, the summer housing cost is provided. These figures relate only to the cost of university-owned or operated housing, not to private accommodations. The cost described is generally for the middle range, and variations depend upon the nature of accommodations. Unless otherwise specified, figures are for rent or room charges only, not board.

Title of housing officer. This notes the titles of the officers or office to contact for on- and off-campus housing information. If only one officer or office is named, he or she provides information for both institutional and private accommodations unless otherwise indicated.

GRADUATE AND PROFESSIONAL DIVISION REQUIREMENTS AND OFFERINGS

Name of division. The full proper name is usually given. If there is no separate graduate or professional school within the institution, this section is simply headed "Graduate Study" or "Graduate Program."

Founding date. The year graduate study began or when the division was established or affiliated may be given.

Location if other than main campus. In the case of professional schools, graduate study may be offered at two or more centers or in a different city.

Tuition and housing. These are given only if they are different from those indicated in the general institutional paragraph. This is most often true of professional schools.

Enrollment. Figures are for graduate or postbaccalaureate students only, if the division offers undergraduate courses as well. In rare cases, the statistics are for all enrolled students in the division, both graduate and undergraduate. If so, this fact is noted. The figures are usually broken down into full- and part-time enrollments, and the percentages of men and women for the combined total. On occasion, the latter figures refer either to the full- or part-time figure.

Faculty. This is the total number of faculty teaching graduate courses on a full- and/or part-time basis. This is often the least reliable statistic of all, for it is not always possible for institutions to make cut-and-dried distinctions between faculty members teaching primarily graduate or undergraduate students. Where possible, some clarification has been noted.

Types of degrees conferred. All master's, sixth-year, and doctoral level degrees are listed. Abbreviations often differ for the same degree, as in M.A. or A.M., D.Sc. or Sc.D. In the engineering master's degree, the subject field is often part of the formal title, such as "M.S. in Chemical Engineering." To conserve space when many such master's degrees are offered, the subject field has been deleted. Abbreviations have been used wherever possible, such as C.A.S. (Certificate of Advanced Standing); consult the list beginning on page xxv.

ADMISSION REQUIREMENTS

Credentials required in support of application. This paragraph lists all documents, entrance examinations, interviews, and other requirements for admission to all programs and degrees. Since virtually all graduate schools expect applicants to hold a bachelor's degree, only exceptions to this normal requirement are mentioned. Professional schools, on the other hand, may admit students with fewer than four years of undergraduate study. The minimum number of preprofessional years is usually indicated in law, medical, dental, osteopathy, and veterinary school entries. Transcripts of previous undergraduate and graduate study (when applicable) are always required in support of applications for admission. Generally, applicants must submit one transcript from each college or university attended. In some cases, however, transcripts must be provided in duplicate. The opening words "Two official transcripts . . ." refer to this requirement.

Many schools request one or more letters of recommendation. Ordinarily, the applicant is asked to have the letters sent directly to the school. In other cases, the names of the persons willing to send recommendations are requested in the application, and the school takes the responsibility of obtaining the letters.

When the Graduate Record Examination (GRE) is required, the specific test, whether General and/or Subject, is noted wherever possible.

Many graduate schools accept students in special or nonmatriculant categories without prior submission of these credentials. In this *Guide,* degree and admission requirements refer only to those students intending to seek degrees.

Additional requirements for admission. Individual programs, schools, or departments sometimes request supplementary credentials in addition to those mentioned above. This is generally due to the professional nature of the program in question or to the need to have more data available. Entrance examinations such as the Miller Analogies Test (MAT) or the Graduate Management Admissions Test (GMAT) are typical of these extra requirements. Potential art majors often must submit portfolios of their work, and music majors may have to audition. Mention is made of additional requirements only if they pertain to two or more departments. Otherwise, special notice is made in the appropriate departmental listing under the *Fields of Study* section.

Transfer applicants. Most graduate and professional schools accept transfer applicants from similar institutions. Generally speaking, no more than 20 to 25 percent of the total course work for the master's degree is allowed for work completed at other graduate schools. The amount of advanced standing permitted toward the doctorate varies widely, but usually at least the equivalent of the master's degree is granted as transfer credit. Some schools are willing to consider transfer applicants, but not with advanced standing. Graduate schools often give advanced standing only after a student has completed study in residence.

Graduates of unaccredited institutions. Most graduate schools are willing to consider applicants from colleges or universities that do not hold approval from one of the six regional accrediting associations. Therefore, *only* those graduate schools that do *not* consider such applicants have statements to that effect. Special testing is often demanded of graduates of unaccredited colleges, or formal admission may be conditional upon satisfactory performance in residence.

Restrictions upon terms of entrance. Individual departments of graduate schools may restrict entrance to only the Fall semester, or to the Fall and Summer terms. Medical and dental schools nearly always admit only for the Fall, whereas some law schools permit initial entrance to other terms as well. It is usually preferable to begin in the Fall, whether or not such restrictions are set.

Title of admitting officer or office and dates of application. This refers to the officer or office of the college from which application forms can be obtained. The completed forms and supporting documents are customarily returned to the same officer or office. Closing dates for filing applications follow, and should be carefully observed. These dates are generally final, and all supporting credentials must be received with the application by these deadlines for the terms indicated. In some cases, no firm deadlines are set but *preferred* dates are suggested. The applicant is advised to apply well in advance in any event, and both the appli-

cations for admission *and* financial aid should be submitted by the date indicated in the *Financial Aid* section. Information on closing dates for all terms is not always available, so it should not be implied that no summer term exists simply because no closing date is mentioned for that term.

Application fee. This information is not always available. Its absence here does not necessarily mean that no fee is required.

Telephone and fax numbers and e-mail addresses. The number listed in both the Admission Requirements and the Financial Aid sections is a general contact number and is being supplied for a preliminary applicant's convenience only.

ADMISSION STANDARDS, RANKINGS, AND RECOGNITION

A college's/school's/university's quality, strengths, and academic position may be assessed or interpreted in a variety of ways. Accrediting bodies fiercely resist any rating/ranking of their accredited programs beyond a simple statement of accreditation. Qualities that make a graduate/professional school desirable to one student may not be as important to another student. The quality of credentials of the groups of applicants to different institutions varies widely and the degree of difficulty of admission must be interpreted accordingly. In other words, the most highly regarded institutions naturally attract applications from superior students in greater numbers than the less favored colleges/schools.

Therefore, prospective students should consider a variety of factors in making their choice among schools/universities. This section attempts to present factors that may assist the reader in determining the appropriate institutional fit. Among these factors are the selectivity level (very competitive, competitive, very selective, selective, or relatively open); the usual minimum required UGPA and test score; mean GPA and mean test scores of entering class; and several rating or ranking sources.

Since selectivity may vary from department to department within a graduate school, this item may be stated, for example, "Very competitive for some departments, competitive for the others," or some similarly appropriate combination. Some institutions overestimate their selectivity; others receive most applications from colleges with very difficult grading systems. Thus, it is possible to be described as "Selective" (accepting up to 75% of all appli-

cants) and have a 3.0 minimum grade point average, or be "Competitive" with a 2.25 required grade point average.

The UGPA minimum averages were converted to the most widely used 4-point system (A = 4.0, B = 3.0, C = 2.0, D = 1.0). Normally, graduate departments expect somewhat higher averages in the proposed field of graduate study. It must be remembered that grade point average stated here is not necessarily the absolute "Floor" but that typically required for unconditional matriculation. Many schools offer limited matriculation to students below the reported grade point average. As with the characterization of admissions policy above, this information is offered merely as a guide.

Mean GPAs and test score information should be viewed with a discriminating eye as well. It is not a cutoff score but should be viewed as roughly the middle of the class with half the scores below that number.

The rating/ranking sources may include some of or all of the following: The Gourman Report: A Rating of Graduate and Professional Programs in American and International Universities with its rating score (scale: very strong 4.51–4.99; strong 4.01–4.49; good 3.61–3.99; acceptable plus 3.01–3.59; adequate 2.51–2.99; marginal 2.01–2.49); *U.S. News & World Report's America's Best Graduate Schools,* which also ranks a number of programs and professional schools; *Business Week's Guide to the Best Business Schools.* There are other rating/ranking guides available on-line and in book form. The above was included to give additional information for an applicant to use to form some sense of institutional perspective.

FINANCIAL AID

Types of aid other than loans. Scholarships, fellowships, internships, assistantships, tuition waivers, grants, and traineeships are the most common forms of aid available. As given here, they are grants offered from institutional funds or from aid programs administered by the college or university in question. This line also specifies the type of service required of the recipient, when appropriate. Scholarships rarely have service requirements, and the term "fellowship" is often used in lieu of "scholarship." Thus, an entry reading "Scholarships, fellowships, teaching/research assistant-

ships" means that no service is required in exchange for the first two forms of aid, while those who hold assistantships are expected to assume either teaching or research responsibilities, or both. Duties may involve direct assistance in research to a particular faculty member, or general responsibilities within a department, such as grading papers or assisting in laboratory experiments or demonstrations. Fellowships and assistantships typically carry a tuition remission privilege plus an annual stipend. Since fellowships are generally regarded as the more prestigious of the two types of award, the stipend is often larger than for assistantships and the tasks assigned may be more challenging in nature. This is subject to broad variations between departments and schools, however. In medical and dental schools, scholarships are usually the only form of aid other than loans available during the academic year. Many of these schools also award research fellowships for intervening summer sessions when regular classes are not in session.

To whom to apply, and the closing date. It is often necessary to apply to different persons or offices for the kinds of aid available. If no deadline date is set, it is wise to apply by February 1 or earlier to receive maximum consideration. Scholarships and fellowships are often awarded through a central committee of a graduate school, while assistantships are typically granted by the department offering study in the proposed major field. As a result, it may be necessary to contact as many as three or four persons or offices to obtain information about various forms of aid. All graduate and professional schools require interested students to apply for financial aid using the Free Application for Federal Student Aid (FAFSA).

Percentage of students receiving aid other than loans. The percentage given here relates to the number of students awarded scholarships, fellowships, assistantships, and other grants (but not loans) from *both* internal *and* external sources. The latter includes grants provided by private and governmental agencies. Unfortunately, it is not always possible to determine whether the percentages refer to the total graduate enrollment, both full- and part-time, or solely to the full-time student body. Normally, however, the figures are for the entire student group, regardless of full- or part-time status. In any event, this factor changes so rapidly from year to year that the percentages must be considered only as rough estimates.

Aid available to part-time students. It is by no means universal practice to make aid, even loans, available to part-time students. This line states whether or not such aid, including loans, is offered.

DEGREE REQUIREMENTS

For master's degrees. This section begins with the minimum total number of credit (or semester or quarter) hours that must be completed for the master's, followed by the minimum number of hours to be completed in residence at the institution granting the degree. As used here, and throughout this book, "residence" refers to *credit hours completed while in full- or part-time attendance at the institution granting the degree.* Therefore, the difference in credit hour requirements between the minimum number for the degree and the number to be completed "in residence" is the number of hours accepted in transfer from other graduate or professional schools. In those cases where residence credit hours must be completed while in attendance as a full-time student, the entry reads "at least 24 in full-time residence." If the residence and full-time attendance requirements differ, this is normally stated as "at least 24 in residence and 18 in full-time attendance."

If a student may elect whether or not to complete a thesis in partial fulfillment of degree requirements, both options are stated in terms of minimum total and residence credit hours. For example: "24 credit hours plus thesis, at least 18 in residence, *or* 30 hours without thesis, at least 24 in residence." These options are stated in different ways, generally in accordance with the terminology of the school being reported.

Listed next are additional degree requirements: qualifying, candidacy, or final exams; thesis or final projects; language or other research tools. If any of these requirements are only for particular majors or departments, this fact is noted: "thesis for most departments; final oral exam for some departments," etc. Most graduate schools stress that the requirements specified are minimums only, and that additional credit hours, exams, or the like may be stipulated, depending upon the candidate's previous background, his or her performance in, or the special nature of, a particular program. In practice, such variations are more likely to occur at the doctoral rather than the master's level.

Schools always point out that admission to study does not imply automatic admission to candidacy. Advancement to formal candidacy for the degree depends upon successful completion of a variety of requirements, such as the filing of an acceptable thesis plan, appointment of a faculty thesis committee, and/or language tests or candidacy exams. This is true for both the master's and doctoral degrees.

For sixth-year degrees or certificates. The number of credit hours required is generally given as a minimum total "beyond the bachelor's" *or* "beyond the master's." Ordinarily, there are relatively few requirements other than course work, but a thesis or project and/or final exam may be expected. Sixth-year certificates are given primarily in the fields of education, music, and engineering.

For doctoral degrees. As with the sixth-year certificate, the number of hours is given as a minimum total beyond the bachelor's or master's. However, many institutions do not specify a set number of credits for the doctorate, choosing instead to state the residence requirements in terms of semesters or years. (This is occasionally true of the master's as well.) In this case, it can be assumed that the years or semesters of residence required may be completed in equivalent part-time attendance, unless otherwise specified. As mentioned above, "residence" refers to hours completed while in full- *or* part-time attendance at the institution granting the degree. In those cases where residence credit must be completed while in full-time attendance, the entry specifies "in full-time residence." Further, the number of hours (or semesters or years) to be completed in residence is the total required for the doctorate minus maximum possible transfer credit beyond the master's or bachelor's, as indicated.

The nature and scope of the doctoral dissertation and/or project vary for each type of degree. The dissertation for the Ph.D. is normally expected to show technical mastery of the major field and to offer an original contribution to the existing body of knowledge in the field. For the Ed.D. and other professional doctorates, the dissertation is likely to be based upon a specific project designed to fully develop research skills and to contribute new knowledge to the professional field.

FIELDS OF STUDY

Areas of concentration or academic departments. These are arranged alphabetically, usually in the manner listed in the school bulletin; that is, if several divisions contribute programs to the graduate school, the fields of study are noted under each division. Since titles of major fields or departments vary from school to school, the reader should look carefully for the programs that interest him or her. For instance, various engineering majors are listed *either* individually *or* under one department heading. This is often true of education programs as well. To take another example, a biological sciences department may include majors in biochemistry, microbiology, zoology, or these may be in a variety of other combinations. "Art history" is sometimes called "history of art" or "fine arts"; "political science" might be "government" or simply "politics." Further, the Ph.D. in a particular field might be offered by one division while the master's in the same field is offered by another school within the university. Still another complication is the fact that some majors are offered by more than one school or department or even at two or more centers of an institution.

Special majors. Following each departmental listing, if necessary, is a clarification of available majors. The name of the department may not be self-explanatory, so it might be stated, for example: *"Art.* Includes studio art, art history, art education," or *"Modern Languages.* Includes French, German, Spanish." In other cases, special notice is made of unusual majors or of majors not ordinarily found under a particular departmental heading. This is then stated: *"English.* Includes creative writing." The "includes" gives notice that the other more common majors of the field are available. It is important to remember that only fields which offer programs leading to at least one degree are listed. Departments that simply contribute courses to degrees are not mentioned.

Special degree or admission requirements. Notation is made of degree or admission requirements which deviate from those outlined in the general paragraphs, whether in addition to, or in lieu of, those stated above. This can include special entrance examinations, such as the MAT, or extra credit hours for the degree. If no such mention is made, it can be assumed that the general requirements apply.

Types of degrees awarded. This is stated only if appropriate degrees are not awarded in particular departments on all levels conferred by the school. For example, if both master's and doctoral degrees are granted by the school, but the Music Department offers only the M.F.A., the listing reads *"Music.* M.F.A. only." Without this notation, it can be assumed the department offers all the degrees appropriate to the field in question. Occasionally, an additional degree not listed under the general headings is mentioned here, but only if of a special nature.

KEY TO ABBREVIATIONS

MASTER'S DEGREES

A.M.	Master of Arts
E.M.B.A.	Executive Master of Business Administration
LL.C.M.	Master of Comparative Law
LL.M.	Master of Law
M.A.	Master of Arts, Master of Administration
M.A.A.	Master of Applied Art, Master of Administrative Arts, Master of Aeronautics and Astronautics, Master of Applied Anthropology
M.A.A.A.	Master of Arts in Arts Administration
M.A.A.B.S.	Master of Arts in Applied Behavioral Sciences
M.A.A.E.	Master of Arts in Applied Economics, Master of Aeronautical and Astronautical Engineering, Master of Arts in Art Education
M.A.Am.St.	Master of Arts in American Studies
M.A.A.O.M.	Master of Arts in Applied Organizational Management
M.A.A.T.	Master of Arts in Art Therapy
M.Acc.	Master of Accounting
M.Accy.	Master of Accountancy
M.A.B.S.	Master of Arts in Behavior Science
M.A.C.	Master of Arts in Communications, Master of Arts in Counseling
M.A.C.A.	Master of Arts in Computer Applications
M.A.C.C.S.	Master of Arts in Cross-Cultural Studies
M.A.C.E.	Master of Arts in Computer Education
M.A.C.P.	Master of Arts in Community Psychology, Master of Arts in Counseling Psychology
M.A.C.T.A.	Master of Arts in Computer Teaching Applications
M.A.C.C.T.	Master of Arts in Community College Teaching
M.Ad.	Master of Administration
M.A.Ad.Ed.	Master of Arts in Adult Education
M.A.C.P.	Master of Arts in Counseling Psychology
M.A.C.T.	Master of Arts in College Teaching
M.A.E.	Master of Agricultural Extension, Master of Agricultural Engineering, Master of Aerospace Engineering, Master of Architectural Engineering, Master of Economics
M.A.Ed.	Master of Arts in Education
M.A.E.S.	Master of Arts in Environmental Sciences
M.Ag.	Master of Agriculture
M.Ag.Ed.	Master of Agricultural Education
M.Ag.Ext.	Master of Agricultural Extension
M.Aq.	Master of Aquacultures
M.A.F.	Master of Arts in Finance
M.A.F.C.	Master of Arts in Family Counseling
M.A.H.	Master of Arts in Humanities
M.A.H.E.	Master of Arts in Human Ecology
M.A.H.E.& F.E.	Master of Arts in Home Economics and Family Ecology
M.A.H.R.M.	Master of Arts in Human Resource Management
M.A.H.S.	Master of Arts in Human Services
M.A.H.S.M.	Master of Arts in Human Service Management
M.A.I.A.	Master of Arts in International Affairs
M.A.I.B.	Master of Arts in International Business
M.A.I.C.	Master of Arts in International Communication
M.A.I.D.	Master of Arts in International Diplomacy, Master of Arts in Interior Design
M.A.I.R.	Master of Arts in Industrial Relations, Master of Arts in International Relations
M.A.I.S.	Master of Arts in International Studies, Master of Arts in Interdisciplinary Studies, Master of Accounting and Information Systems
M.A.J.	Master of Arts in Journalism
M.A.L.A.	Master of Arts in Liberal Arts
M.A.L.A.S.	Master of Arts in Latin American Studies
M.A.L.D.	Master of Arts in Law and Diplomacy
M.A.L.S.	Master of Arts in Library Science, Master of Arts in Liberal Studies
M.A.L.T.	Master of Arts in Language Teaching
M.A.M.	Master of Arts Management, Master of Animal Medicine, Master of Aviation Management, Master of Arts in Management, Master of Agriculture and Management, Master of Acquisition Management, Master of Applied Mathematics
M.A.M.B.	Master of Arts in Molecular Biology
M.A.M.C.	Master of Arts in Mass Communication
M.A.M.F.C.	Master of Arts in Marriage and Family Counseling
M.A.M.F.C.C.	Master of Arts in Marriage, Family, and Child Counseling
M.A.M.F.T.	Master of Arts in Marriage and Family Therapy
M.A.M.R.D.	Master of Agricultural Management and Resource Development

M.A.M.S.	Master of Applied Mathematical Sciences
M.A.O.M.	Master of Aerospace Operations Management, Master of Arts in Organizational Management
M.A.P.A.	Master of Arts in Public Administration, Master of Arts in Public Affairs
M.A.P.E.	Master of Arts in Physical Education, Master of Arts in Political Economy
M.Appl.M.	Master of Applied Mathematics
M.Ap.Sc.	Master of Applied Science
M.A.P.P.	Master of Arts in Public Policy
M.A.P.R.S.	Master of Arts in Pacific Rim Studies
M.A.P.S.	Master of Arts in Pastoral Studies
M.A.Psych.	Master of Arts in Psychology
M.A.R.	Master of Arts in Religion, Master of Arts in Research
M.Arch.	Master of Architecture
M.Arch.E.	Master of Architectural Engineering
M.Arch.H.	Master of Architectural History
M.Arch.U.D.	Master of Architecture in Urban Design
M.A.S.	Master of Accounting Science, Master of Actuarial Science, Master of Aeronautical Science, Master of American Studies, Master of Applied Statistics, Master of Archival Studies
M.A.S.A.C.	Master of Arts in Substance Abuse Counseling
M.A.S.P.	Master of Applied Social Psychology
M.A.T.	Master of Arts in Teaching
M.A.T.M.	Master of Arts in Teaching Mathematics
M.A.U.A.	Master of Arts in Urban Affairs
M.A.U.D.	Master of Arts in Urban Design
M.A.U.R.P	Master of Arts in Urban and Regional Planning
M.A.W.	Master of Arts in Writing
M.B.	Master of Bioninformatics
M.B.A.	Master of Business Administration
M.B.A.I.B.	Master of Business Administration in International Business
M.B.A.I.M.	Master of Business Administration in International Management
M.B.E.	Master of Bilingual Education, Master of Biomedical Engineering, Master of Business Education, Master of Business Economics
M.B.I.	Master of Biological Illustration
M.Biorad.	Master of Bioradiology
M.B.M.	Master of Brand Management
M.B.S.	Master of Basic Science, Master of Behavioral Science, Master of Building Science, Master of Biological Science, Master of Biomedical Sciences
M.B.T.	Master of Business Taxation
M.C.	Master of Commerce, Master of Counseling, Master of Communication
M.C.A.M.	Master of Computational and Applied Mathematics
M.C.S.	Master of Computer Science
M.C.D.	Master of Communication Disorders, Master of Community Development
M.C.E.	Master of Chemical Engineering, Master of Civil Engineering, Master of Computer Engineering
M.C.H.	Master of Community Health
M.C.I.S.	Master of Communication and Information Studies, Master of Computer Information Systems
M.C.J.	Master of Comparative Jurisprudence, Master of Criminal Justice
M.C.J.A.	Master of Criminal Justice Administration
M.C.L.	Master of Comparative Law, Master of Civil Law
M.C.M.	Master of Church Music
M.C.M.S.	Master of Clinical Medical Science
M.C.P.	Master of City Planning, Master of Community Planning, Master of Counseling Psychology
M.C.R.P.	Master of City and Regional Planning
M.C.S.	Master of Computer Science
M.C.Sc.	Master of Commercial Science
M.C.S.E.	Master of Computer Science and Engineering
M.Des.	Master of Design
M.Des.S.	Master of Design Studies
M.Div.	Master of Divinity
M.D.S.	Master of Dental Science, Master of Decision Sciences
M.E.	Master of Engineering
M.E.A.	Master of Engineering Administration, Master of Engineering Architecture
M.E.C.E.	Master of Electrical and Computer Engineering
M.Ed.	Master of Education
M.E.D.	Master of Environmental Design, Master of Education of the Deaf
M.E.D.S.	Master of Environmental Design Studies
M.E.E.	Master of Electrical Engineering
M.E.H.W.E.	Master of Engineering in Hazardous Waste Engineering
M.E.M.	Master of Engineering Management, Master of Environmental Engineering
M.E.M.S.	Master of Engineering in Manufacturing Systems
M.Eng.	Master of Engineering
M.E.P.	Master of Environmental Planning
M.E.P.C.	Master of Environmental Pollution Control
M.E.S.	Master of Engineering Science, Master of Environmental Science, Master of Environmental Studies
M.Ex.St.	Master of Experimental Statistics
M.Ext.Ed.	Master of Extension Education
M.E.R.	Master of Energy Resources
M.E.T.	Master of Education in Teaching, Master of Engineering Technology
M.F.	Master of Forestry, Master of Finance
M.F.A.	Master of Fine Arts
M.F.E.	Master of Forest Engineering
M.F.R.	Master of Forest Resources
M.F.S.	Master of Family Studies, Master of Foreign Service, Master of Forest Science, Master of Forensic Science
M.F.T.	Master of Family Therapy
M.G.A.	Master of Government Administration
M.G.E.	Master of Geological Engineering, Master of Geotechnical Engineering
M.G.S.	Master of Gerontological Studies
M.G.T.	Master of Gas Technology
M.H.	Master of Humanities
M.H.A.	Master of Health Administration, Master of Healthcare Administration, Master of Hospital Administration
M.H.A.M.S.	Master of Historical Administration and Museum Studies
M.H.C.A.	Master of Health Care Administration
M.H.E.	Master of Health Education, Master of Higher Education, Master of Home Economics
M.H.E.Ed.	Master of Home Economics Education
M.H.H.S.	Master of Health and Human Service
M.H.C.M.	Master of Health Care Management
M.H.K.	Master of Human Kinetics
M.H.M.	Master of Hospitality Management
M.H.P.	Master of Heritage Preservation, Master of Historical Preservation
M.H.R.	Master of Human Resources

M.H.R.D.	Master of Human Resource Development
M.H.S.	Master of Health Services, Master of Human Services
M.H.S.A.	Master of Health Services Administration, Master of Human Services Administration
M.I.	Master of Insurance
M.I.A.	Master of International Affairs
M.I.B.	Master of International Business
M.I.B.A.	Master of International Business Administration
M.I.D.	Master of Industrial Design, Master of Interior Design
M.I.E.	Master of Industrial Engineering
M.I.L.R.	Master of Industrial and Labor Relations
M.I.L.S.	Master of Information and Library Science
M.I.M.	Master of Industrial Management, Master of International Management
M.I.P.A.	Master of International Public Administration
M.I.P.P.	Master of International Public Policy
M.I.R.	Master of Industrial Relations
M.I.S.	Master of Individualized Studies, Master of Information Services, Master of Interdisciplinary Studies
M.I.T.	Master of Industrial Technology, Master of Information Technology, Master of Internet Technology
M.J.	Master of Journalism
M.J.N.M.M.	Master of Journalism in New Media Management
M.J.A.	Master of Justice Administration
M.J.S.	Master of Judicial Science
M.L.A.	Master of Landscape Architecture, Master of Liberal Arts
M.L.A.U.D.	Master of Landscape Architecture in Urban Development
M.L.H.R.	Master of Labor and Human Resources
M.L.I.R.	Master of Labor and Industrial Relations
M.L.I.S.	Master of Library and Information Science
M.Lit.M.	Master of Liturgical Music
M.L.L.	Master of Law Librarianship
M.L.S.	Master of Legal Studies, Master of Liberal Studies, Master of Library Science, Master of Life Science
M.L.S.P.	Master of Law and Social Policy
M.L.&T.	Master of Law and Taxation
M.M.	Master of Music, Master of Management, Master of Mathematics
M.M.A.	Master of Marine Affairs, Master of Medical Art, Master of Musical Art
M.M.B.	Master of Medical Biochemistry
M.M.C.	Master of Mass Communication
M.M.E.	Master of Manufacturing Engineering, Master of Material Engineering, Master of Mechanical Engineering, Master of Mineral Engineering
M.M.Ed.	Master of Music Education
M.M.F.C.C.	Master of Marriage, Family, and Child Counseling
M.M.F.T.	Master of Marriage and Family Therapy
M.M.I.S.	Master of Management Information Systems
M.M.M.	Master of Manufacturing Management
M.M.M.E.	Master of Metallurgical and Materials Engineering
M.M.P.	Master of Marine Policy, Master of Museum Practice
M.M.R.	Master of Marketing Research
M.M.S.	Master of Management Science, Master of Marine Science, Master of Materials Science
M.Mu.	Master of Music
M.Mus.	Master of Music
M.M.T	Master of Movement Therapy, Master of Music Teaching
M.N.	Master of Nursing
M.N.A.	Master of Nursing Administration, Master of Nonprofit Administration, Master of Nurse Anesthesia
M.Nat.Sci.	Master of Natural Science
M.N.E.	Master of Nuclear Engineering
M.N.Ed.	Master of Nursing Education
M.N.S.	Master of Nursing Science, Master of Nutritional Sciences, Master of Natural Sciences, Master of Nuclear Science
M.Nuc.Sc.	Master of Nuclear Science
M.O.B.	Master of Organizational Behavior
M.Oc.E.	Master of Oceanographic Engineering
M.Opt.	Master of Optometry
M.O.D.	Master of Organizational Development
M.O.E.	Master of Ocean Engineering
M.O.H.	Master of Organizational Health
M.O.T.	Master of Occupational Therapy
M.P.	Master of Planning
M.P.A.	Master of Physician Assistant, Master of Public Administration, Master of Public Affairs, Master of Professional Accounting
M.P.Acc.	Master of Public Accounting,
M.P.A.S.	Master of Physician Assistant Science, Master of Physician Assistant Studies
M.P.C.	Master of Professional Counseling, Master of Personnel Counseling
M.P.D.	Master of Product Design
M.P.D.S.	Master of Planning and Development Studies
M.P.E.	Master of Physical Education
M.P.E.M.	Master of Project Engineering and Management
M.P.E.R.	Master of Personnel and Employee Relations
M.Pet.E.	Master of Petroleum Engineering
M.P.H.	Master of Public Health
M.P.H.Ed.	Master of Public Health Education
M.P.H.T.M.	Master of Public Health and Tropical Medicine
M.Pharm.	Master of Pharmacy
M.Phil.	Master of Philosophy
M.P.I.A.	Master of Public and International Affairs, Master of Pacific International Affairs
M.P.M.	Master of Personnel Management, Master of Project Management, Master of Public Management
M.P.M.&P.H.	Master of Preventive Medicine and Public Health
M.P.N.A.	Master of Public and Nonprofit Administration
M.P.O.T.	Master in Psychiatric Occupational Therapy
M.P.P.	Master of Public Policy
M.P.P.A.	Master of Public Policy Administration
M.Prof.Acc.	Master of Professional Accounting
M.P.P.P.M.	Master of Plant Protection and Pest Management
M.Pr.Met.	Master of Professional Meteorology
M.P.R.T.M.	Master of Park, Recreation, and Tourism Management
M.Ps.Sc.	Master of Psychological Science
M.P.S.	Master of Personnel Service, Master of Political Science, Master of Policy Studies, Master of Preservation Studies, Master of Public Service
M.P.S.L.	Master of Public Safety Leadership
M.P.T.	Master of Physical Therapy
M.P.V.M.	Master of Preventive Veterinary Medicine
M.Q.F.	Master of Quantitative Finance
M.Q.M.	Master of Quality Management
M.Q.S.	Master of Quantitative Systems, Master of Quality Systems

M.R.A.	Master of Recreation Administration, Master of Rehabilitation Administration, Master of Resource Administration
M.R.C.	Master of Rehabilitation Counseling
M.R.C.P.	Master of Regional and Community Planning
M.R.D.	Master of Rural Development
M.R.E.	Master of Religious Education
M.R.Ed.	Master of Recreation Education
M.Rel.Ed.	Master of Religious Education
M.R.E.C.M.	Master of Real Estate and Construction Management
M.R.E.D.	Master of Real Estate Development
M.R.M.	Master of Rehabilitation Medicine, Master of Resource Management
M.R.P.	Master of Regional Planning
M.R.P.A.	Master of Recreation and Parks Administration
M.R.T.P.	Master of Rural and Town Planning
M.S.	Master of Science
M.S.A.	Master of Science in Accounting, Master of Science in Administration, Master of Sport Administration
M.S.A.A.E.	Master of Science in Aeronautical and Astronautical Engineering
M.S.A.E.	Master of Science in Aerospace Engineering
M.S.Ag.	Master of Science in Agriculture
M.S.A.I.	Master of Science in Artificial Intelligence
M.S.Ap.Sc.	Master of Science in Applied Science
M.S.Arch.	Master of Science in Architecture
M.S.A.S.	Master of Science in Architectural Studies
M.S.B.A.	Master of Science in Business Administration
M.S.B.E.	Master of Science in Biomedical Engineering
M.S.C.	Master of Speech Communication, Master of Science in Counseling
M.Sc.A.	Master of Social Administration
M.S.Ch.E.	Master of Science in Chemical Engineering
M.S.Chem.	Master of Science in Chemistry
M.S.C.E.	Master of Science in Civil Engineering, Master of Science in Computer Engineering
M.Sc.D.	Master of Science in Dentistry
M.S.C.Ed.	Master of Science in Continuing Education
M.S.Ch.E.	Master of Science in Chemical Engineering
M.S.Cer.E.	Master of Science in Ceramic Engineering
M.S.C.J.	Master of Science in Criminal Justice
M.S.Econ.	Master of Science in Economics
M.Sc.T.	Master of Science Teaching, Master of Science in Teaching
M.S.D.	Master of Science in Dentistry
M.S.E.	Master of Science Education, Master of Science in Education, Master of Science in Engineering, Master of Software Engineering
M.Sec.Sch.Sci.	Master of Secondary School Science
M.S.Ed.	Master of Science Education, Master of Science in Education
M.S. in Ed.	Master of Science in Education
M.S.E.E.	Master of Science in Electrical Engineering, Master of Science in Environmental Engineering
M.S.Eng.	Master of Science in Engineering
M.S.Engr.	Master of Science in Engineering
M.S.E.M.	Master of Science in Engineering and Mining
M.S.E.Mgt.	Master of Science in Engineering Management
M.S.E.R.	Master of Science in Energy Resources
M.S.Envr.E.	Master of Science in Environmental Engineering
M.S.E.S.S.	Master of Science in Exercise and Sport Studies
M.S.F.	Master of Science in Finance, Master of Science in Forestry
M.S.F.S.	Master of Science in Financial Services, Master of Science in Forensic Science, Master of Science in Foreign Service
M.S.G.	Master of Science in Gerontology
M.S.G.C.	Master of Science in Genetic Counseling
M.S.G.L.	Master of Science in Global Leadership
M.S.H.A.	Master of Science in Health Administration
M.S.H.C.A.	Master of Science in Health Care Administration
M.S.H.E.	Master of Science in Health Education
M.S.H.R.	Master of Science in Human Resources
M.S.I.A.	Master of Institutional Administration, Master of Science in International Affairs
M.S.I.E.	Master of Science in Industrial Engineering
M.S.I.E.O.R.	Master of Science in Industrial Engineering and Operations Research
M.S.I.M.	Master of Science in Information Management
M.S.I.M.C.	Master of Science in Information Management and Communication, Master of Science in Integrated Marketing Communication
M.S.I.R.	Master of Science in Industrial Relations
M.S.I.S.	Master of Science in Information Science, Master of Science in Information Systems, Master of Science in Interdisciplinary Studies
M.S.J.	Master of Science in Journalism
M.S.J.A.	Master of Science in Judicial Administration
M.S.J.P.S.	Master of Science in Justice and Public Safety
M.S.K.	Master of Science in Kinesiology
M.S.L.	Master of Science in Limnology
M.S.L.S.	Master of Science in Library Science, Master of Science in Logistic Systems
M.S.M.	Master of Sacred Music, Master of Science in Management
M.S.Mat.S.E.	Master of Science in Materials Science Engineering
M.S.M.C.	Master of Science in Mass Communication, Master of Science in Marketing Communication
M.S.M.E.	Master of Science in Mechanical Engineering
M.S.Met.E.	Master of Science in Metallurgical Engineering
M.S.Mgt.	Master of Science in Management
M.S.M.I.	Master of Science in Medical Illustration
M.S.M.O.T.	Master of Science in Management of Technology
M.S.M.S.Ed.	Master of Science in Mathematics and Science Education
M.S.M.T.	Master of Science in Medical Technology
M.S.N.	Master of Science in Nursing
M.S.N.A.	Master of Science in Nursing Administration, Master of Science in Nurse Anesthesia
M.S.N.E.	Master of Science in Nuclear Engineering
M.S.N.S.	Master of Science in Natural Science
M.S.O.	Master of Science in Orthodontics
M.S.O.D.	Master of Science in Organizational Development
M.S.O.M.	Master of Science in Organization and Management
M.S.O.R.	Master of Science in Operations Research
M.S.O.T.	Master of Science in Occupational Therapy, Master of Science in Occupational Technology
M.S.P.A.	Master of Science in Public Administration, Master of Science in Professional Accounting
M.S.Pet.E.	Master of Science in Petroleum Engineering
M.S.P.Ex.	Master of Science in Physiology of Exercise
M.S.P.H.	Master of Science in Public Health
M.S.P.H.N.	Master of Science in Public Health Nursing
M.S.P.N.G.E.	Master of Science in Petroleum and Natural Gas Engineering
M.S.Poly.	Master of Science in Polymers
M.S.P.S.	Master of Science in Pharmaceutical Science, Master of Science in Psychological Services
M.S.P.T.	Master of Science in Physical Therapy

M.S.Psy.	Master of Science in Psychology	M.T.	Master of Taxation, Master of Teaching, Master of Technology
M.S.R.	Master of Rehabilitation Sciences		
M.S.R.E.D.	Master of Science in Real Estate Development	M.T.A.	Master of Tax Accounting, Master of Teaching Arts
M.S.R.T.M.	Master of Science in Resort and Tourism Management	M.Tech.	Master of Technology
M.S.S.	Master of Science in Software, Master of Social Service, Master of Sport Science, Master of Stategic Studies	M.Th.	Master of Theology
		M.T.H.M.	Master of Tourism and Hospitality Management
M.S.S.A.	Master of Science in Social Administration	M.T.M.	Master of Tourism Management
M.S.S.E.	Master of Science in Software Engineering	M.T.P.W.	Master of Technical and Professional Writing
M.S.S.P.A.	Master of Speech Pathology and Audiology, Master of Student Personnel Administration	M.T.S.	Master of Teaching of Science
		M.T.S.C.	Master of Teaching Speech Communication, Master of Technical and Scientific Communication
M.S.Stat.	Master of Science in Statistics		
M.S.S.T.	Master of Science in Science Teaching		
M.S.S.W	Master of Science in Social Work	M.U.A.	Master of Urban Affairs, Master of Urban Architecture
M.S.T.	Master of Sacred Theology, Master of Secondary Teaching, Master of Science in Taxation, Master of Science in Teaching, Master of Science in Technology, Master of Science in Tourism, Master of Speech Therapy	M.U.D.	Master of Urban Design
		M.U.P.	Master of Urban Planning
		M.U.P.P.	Master of Urban Planning and Policy
		M.U.R.P.	Master of Urban and Regional Planning, Master of Urban and Rural Planning
M.S.T.E.	Master of Science in Technical Education, Master of Science in Transportation Engineering	M.U.S.	Master of Urban Studies
		M.Vet.Sc.	Master of Veterinary Science
		M.V.T.E.	Master of Vocational Technical Education
M.S.T.Ed.	Master of Science in Technical Education	M.W.P.S.	Master of Wood and Paper Science
M.S.Text.	Master of Science in Textiles	M.W.S.	Master of Women's Studies
M.S.T.M.	Master of Science in Technology Management, Master of Science in Technical Management	Phil.M.	Master of Philosophy
		P.M.B.A.	Professional Master of Business Adminstration
M.S.T.S.L.	Master of Science in Teaching a Second Language	S.M.	Master of Science
		S.T.M.	Master of Sacred Theology
		Th.M.	Master of Theology
M.S.U.D.	Master of Science in Urban Design	W.E.M.B.A.	Weekend Executive Master of Business Administration
M.S.V.C.	Master of Vocational Counseling		
M.S.W.	Master of Social Work	X.M.B.A.	Executive Master of Business Administration

SIXTH-YEAR DEGREES

A.C.	Advanced Certificate	G.D.M.	Graduate Diploma in Management
A.D.	Artist's Diploma	G.D.P.A.	Graduate Diploma in Public Administration
A.G.C.	Advanced Graduate Certificate	G.D.T.	Graduate Diploma in Taxation
A.G.S.C.	Advanced Graduate Specialist Certificate	G.P.D.	Graduate Performance Diploma
C.A.G.S.	Certificate of Advanced Graduate Studies	P.D.	Professional Diploma
C.A.G.S.B.	Certificate in Advanced Study in Business	Psy.S.	Specialist in Psychology
C.A.M.S.	Certificate of Advanced Management Studies	S.C.C.T.	Specialist in Community College Teaching
C.A.P.S.	Certificate of Advanced Professional Studies	S.C.G.	Specialist Certificate in Gerontology
C.A.S.	Certificate of Advanced Study	S.L.S.	Specialist in Library Science
C.E.	Civil Engineer	Sp.C.	Specialist in Counseling
Ch.E.	Chemical Engineer	Sp.Ed.	Specialist in Education
E.E.	Electrical Engineer	S.P.A.	Specialist in Public Administration
Ed.S.	Specialist in Education	S.S.A.	Specialist in School Administration
Eng.	Engineer	S.S.P.	Specialist in School Psychology
Engr.	Engineer	S.T.L.	Licentiate in Sacred Theology

DOCTORAL DEGREES

A.Mus.D.	Doctor of Musical Arts	D.E.	Doctor of Engineering
Au.D.	Doctor of Audiology	D.Eng.	Doctor of Engineering
D.A.	Doctor of Arts	D.E.D.	Doctor of Environmental Design
D.A.I.S.	Doctor of Arts in Information Science	D.Ed.	Doctor of Education
		D.Eng.Sc.	Doctor of Engineering Science
D.Arch.	Doctor of Architecture	D.Env.Des.	Doctor of Environmental Design
D.B.A.	Doctor of Business Administration	D.E.S.	Doctor of Engineering Science
D.C.L.	Doctor of Comparative Law, Doctor of Civil Law	D.F.	Doctor of Forestry
		D.F.A.	Doctor of Fine Arts
D.C.S.	Doctor of Computer Science	D.F.E.S.	Doctor of Forestry and Environmental Systems
D.Chem.	Doctor of Chemistry	D.H.S.	Doctor of Health and Safety, Doctor of Human Services
D.D.S.	Doctor of Dental Surgery		

D.I.B.A.	Doctor of International Business Administration	Dr.P.H.	Doctor of Public Health
D.I.T.	Doctor of Industrial Technology	D.R.E.	Doctor of Recreation Education
D.L.I.S.	Doctor of Library and Information Sciences	D.Sc.	Doctor of Science
D.L.S.	Doctor of Library Science	D.Sc.D.	Doctor of Science in Dentistry
D.M.	Doctor of Management, Doctor of Music	D.Sc.V.M.	Doctor of Science in Veterinary Medicine
D.M.A.	Doctor of Musical Arts	D.S.M.	Doctor of Sacred Music, Doctor of Sport Management
D.M.D.	Doctor of Medical Dentistry, Doctor of Dental Medicine	D.S.Sc.	Doctor of Social Science
D.M.Ed.	Doctor of Music Education	D.S.W.	Doctor of Social Work
D.M.F.T.	Doctor of Marriage and Family Therapy	D.Th.	Doctor of Theology
D.Min.	Doctor of Ministry	D.V.M.	Doctor of Veterinary Medicine
D.M.Sc.	Doctor of Medical Science	Ed.D.	Doctor of Education
D.M.L.	Doctor of Modern Languages	J.D.	Doctor of Jurisprudence
D.Mus.	Doctor of Music	J.S.D.	Doctor of Judicial Science
D.Mus.Ed.	Doctor of Music Education	L.L.D.	Doctor of Laws
D.N.	Doctor of Nursing	Ph.D.	Doctor of Philosophy
D.N.Sc.	Doctor of Nursing Science	Pharm.D.	Doctor of Pharmacy
D.O.	Doctor of Osteopathy	Psy.D.	Doctor of Psychology
D.P.A.	Doctor of Public Administration	Re.D.	Doctor of Recreation
D.P.D.S.	Doctor of Planning and Development Studies	Rh.D.	Doctor of Rehabilitation
D.P.E.	Doctor of Physical Education	Sc.D.	Doctor of Science
D.P.H.	Doctor of Public Health	S.J.D.	Doctor of Judicial Science

EXAMINATIONS AND OTHER ABBREVIATIONS

AACOMAS	American Association of Colleges of Osteopathic Medicine Application Service	MAT	Miller Analogies Test
		MCAT	Medical College Admissions Test
AADSAS	American Association of Dental Schools Application Service	MELAB	Michigan English Language Assessment Battery
AACSB	American Assembly of Collegiate Schools of Business—The American Association of Management Education	MMPI	Minnesota Multiphasic Personality Inventory
		MSTP	Medical Scientist Training Program
		NCATE	National Council for Accreditation of Teacher Education
AAU	Association of American Universities		
AAUW	American Association of University Women	NIH	National Institutes of Health
AMCAS	American Medical College Application Service	NLNGNE	National League of Nursing Graduate Nursing Examination
AOA	American Optometric Association		
CGS	Council of Graduate Schools	NTE	National Teaching Examination
COPA	Council on Postsecondary Accreditation	OAT	Optometry Admissions Test
DAT	Dental Aptitude Test	PAEG	Prueba de Admisiones para Estudios Graduados
DSTP	Dental Scientist Training Program		
ED	Education Department	PAT	Perceptual Ability Test
EDP	Early Decision Program	PCAT	Pharmacy College Admissions Test
EMSAP	Early Medical School Acceptance Program	PHEAA	Pennsylvania Higher Education Assistance Agency
ETS	Educational Testing Service		
FAF	Financial Aid Form	SAAC	Student Aid Application for California
FAFSA	Free Application for Federal Student Aid	SREB	Southern Regional Education Board
FAT	Financial Aid Transcript	TOEFL	Test of English as a Foreign Language
FFS	Family Financial Statement	TSE	Test of Spoken English
GMAC	Graduate Management Admission Council	TWE	Test of Written English
GMAT	Graduate Management Admissions Test	UGPA	Undergraduate Grade Point Average
GPA	Grade Point Average	USMLE	U.S. Medical Licensing Examination
GRE	Graduate Record Exam	VA	Veterans Administration
HEAL	Health Education Assistance Loan	VMAT	Veterinary Medicine Aptitude Test
IELTS	International English Language Testing Systems	WAMI	Wyoming, Alaska, Montana, Idaho
		WES	World Education Service
IIE	Institute of International Education	WICHE	Western Interstate Commission for Higher Education
LSAT	Law School Aptitude Test		
LSDAS	Law School Data Assembly Service	WWAMI	Washington, Wyoming, Alaska, Montana, Idaho

GUIDE TO
AMERICAN GRADUATE SCHOOLS

ABILENE CHRISTIAN UNIVERSITY
Abilene, Texas 89699
Web site: www.acu.edu

Coed. Independent/religious. Semester system. CGS member. Library: more than 500,000 items. Special facilities: Center for Restoration Studies, Center for Aging, Center for Adolescent Studies. More than 650 computers available on campus.

Tuition: per credit $347. On-campus rooms and apartments available. Annual room and board expenses: single students $4420, married students $4000 (room only). Apply to the Graduate Housing Office by May 11. Phone: (915)674-2066. Day-care facilities available.

Graduate School
E-mail: gradinfo@acu.edu

Enrollment: full- and part-time 525. University faculty teaching graduate students: full- and part-time 131. Degrees conferred: M.A., M.Acc., M.B.A., M.Div., M.Ed., M.L.A., M.M.F.T., M.P.A., M.S., M.S.N., D.Min.

ADMISSION REQUIREMENTS. Transcripts, GRE/MAT/GMAT, personal interview, three letters of recommendation (license to practice nursing in Texas for nursing) required in support of application. TOEFL or other evidence of English ability required of foreign students. Accepts transfer applicants. Apply to Office of University Admission by April 1 (Summer and Fall admission), November 1 (Spring). Application fee $25, $45 for international students. Phone: (915)674-2355.

ADMISSION STANDARDS. Selective for most departments. Usual minimum average: 2.75 (A = 4).

FINANCIAL AID. Annual awards from institutional funds: scholarships, research/teaching assistantships, internships, Federal W/S, loans. Apply to the University of Financial Aid by April 1. Use FAFSA. Aid available for part-time students.

DEGREE REQUIREMENTS. For M.A., M.Acc., M.S., M.L.A.: 30–42 credit hours depending upon program; thesis/nonthesis option/professional paper/synthesis project, depending upon major; comprehensive exam; reading knowledge of one foreign language for some majors; practicum (M.S.). For M.A. (Psychology), M.M.F.T.: 45 credit program; practicum; thesis. For M.B.A.: 33 credit hour program for students holding undergraduate degrees in business, other students may need to enroll in up to 39 additional credits; no comprehensive exam. For M.P.A.: 42 credit hour program; internship; comprehensive exam. For D.Min.: 45–72 credit hours beyond master's depending upon program; reading knowledge of at least two foreign languages; preliminary exam; dissertation; final oral/written exam.

FIELDS .OF STUDY.

COLLEGE OF ARTS AND SCIENCES:
Communication.
Communication Science and Disorders.
Digital Media.
Education. Includes educational diagnostician, elementary school teacher, reading specialist, school administrator and superintendent, school counselor, school supervisor, secondary school teacher.
English.
Family Studies.
Gerontology.
Human Communication.
Liberal Arts. M.L.A. only.
Marriage and Family Therapy.
Organizational and Human Resource Development.
Psychology. Includes clinical, counseling and school.

COLLEGE OF BIBLICAL STUDIES:
Missions. 54 credit M.A. program and a 84 credit, nonthesis D.Min. program.

COLLEGE OF BUSINESS ADMINISTRATION:
Accounting. M.Acc.
Business Administration. GMAT for admission. M.B.A. only.

GRADUATE SCHOOL OF THEOLOGY:
Christian Ministry. M.A.
History and Theology. M.A.
New Testament. M.A.
Old Testament. M.A.
Theological Education. M.Div.

SCHOOL OF NURSING:
Nursing. M.S.N. only.

ADAMS STATE COLLEGE
Alamosa, Colorado 81102
Web site: www.adams.edu

Founded 1921. Located 220 miles SW of Denver. Coed. State control. Semester system. Special facilities: Luther Bean Historical Museum, Hatfield Art Gallery, Zachers Observatory. Library: 466,351 volumes.

Tuition: per credit $262, nonresident $314. On-campus housing for 114 married students, 170 single graduate students. Average annual housing cost: $6000 for married students, $5240 (including board) for single students. Apply to Director of Housing by May 1. Phone: (719)589-7522.

School of Education and Graduate Studies

Enrollment: full-time 46, part-time 426, summer 1106. Degree conferred: M.A.

ADMISSION REQUIREMENTS. Transcripts, GRE/MAT, a letter of intent required in support of application. TOEFL required for international applicants. Accepts transfer applicants. Apply to Office of the Dean at least two weeks prior to registration. Application fee $25. Phone: (800)662-3382.

ADMISSION STANDARDS. Selective. Usual minimum average: 2.75 (A = 4), MAT score: 37, GRE combined score: 1250.

FINANCIAL AID. Annual awards from institutional funds: graduate assistantships, internship, Federal W/S, loans. Approved for VA benefits. Apply by March 1 to Dean for assistantships; to Financial Aid Office for all other programs. Use FAFSA. Phone: (800)824-6494 or (719)587-7306. About 10% of students receive aid other than loans from College and outside sources.

DEGREE REQUIREMENTS. For M.A.: 30–36 semester hours, at least 24–30 in residence; thesis/nonthesis option/creative project; final comprehensive exam; no language requirement.

FIELDS OF STUDY.
Community Counseling. Autobiographical essay for admission.
Education. Includes literacy, language and culture; educational leadership.
Elementary Education.
Health and Physical Education. Autobiographical statement for admission.
School Counseling. Autobiographical essay for admission. Includes elementary and secondary.

Secondary Education. Active teaching license, two letters of recommendation for admission. Includes art, business, English, health, physical education, recreation, history, government, industrial arts, science.

Special Education, Teacher I—Moderate Need. Active teaching license, two letters of recommendations for admission. Includes bilingual education, ESL.

ADELPHI UNIVERSITY

Garden City, New York 11530
Web site: www.adelphi.com

Founded 1896. Located 20 miles E of New York City. Coed. Private control. Semester system. Library: 630,000 volumes, 1750 subscriptions. Special facilities: Hy Weinberg Center for Communicative Disorders, Adelphi Institute for Prevention of Drug Abuse, Center for Social Policy. More than 950 computers available on campus, 100 in library.

Tuition: per credit $540. No on-campus housing. Annual room and board expenses: $7450. Apply to Director of Housing for off-campus housing information. Phone: (516)877-3650. Daycare facilities available.

Graduate School of Arts and Sciences

Enrollment: full- and part-time 50 (men 30%, women 70%). University faculty teaching graduate students: full- and part-time 19. Degrees conferred: M.A., M.S., D.A.

ADMISSION REQUIREMENTS. Transcripts, two letters of recommendation required in support of application. GRE required by some departments. TOEFL (score of 550/213 or better required of foreign students. Interview by invitation. Accepts transfer applicants. Apply to Graduate Office of Admission at least two months prior to registration. Foreign students must apply by February 1 (Fall admission only). Application fee $50. Phone: (516)877-3050.

ADMISSION STANDARDS. Selective for most departments. Usual minimum average: 2.75 (A = 4).

FINANCIAL AID. Annual awards from institutional funds: partial scholarships, research/teaching assistantships, internships, Federal W/S, loans. Apply to the University Office of Financial Aid by February 15. Use FAFSA. About 50% of full-time students receive aid other than loans from University and outside sources.

DEGREE REQUIREMENTS. For M.A., M.S.: 30–36 credit hours depending upon program; thesis optional, depending upon major; reading knowledge of one foreign language for some M.S. majors. For D.A.: 45–72 credit hours beyond master's depending upon program; reading knowledge of at least two foreign languages for mathematics and language majors, one language or knowledge of computer programming for psychology majors; preliminary exam; dissertation; final oral/written exam.

FIELDS OF STUDY.
Art, Studio. 33 credits for M.A.
Art History.
Biology. 33 hours for M.S.
English. M.A. only.
Environmental Studies.
Mathematics and Computer Sciences. M.S., D.A.
Physics. M.S. only.

Gorden F. Derner Institute of Advanced Psychological Studies

Founded 1951.
Enrollment: full- and part-time 301 (men 50%, women 50%). Institute faculty teaching graduate students: about 100 full- and part-time. Degrees conferred: M.A., Ph.D.

ADMISSION REQUIREMENTS: Transcripts, GRE, two letters of recommendation required in support of application. TOEFL (minimum scores of 550/213) required of foreign students. Interview by invitation. Accepts transfer applicants. For M.A.: rolling admissions, apply to Office of Graduate Admission at least two months prior to registration. Admits Fall, Spring, and Summer. For Ph.D: Apply by January 15; admits Fall only. Foreign students must apply by February 1 (Fall admission only). Application fee $50. Phone: (516)877-3050.

ADMISSION STANDARDS. Selective. Usual minimum average: 3.0 (A = 4).

FINANCIAL AID. Annual awards from institutional funds: scholarships and fellowships (New York State residents), clinical/research/teaching assistantships, internships, paid field placements, Federal W/S, loans. Apply to the University Financial Aid Office by February 15. Use FAFSA. About 70% of full-time students receive aid other than loans from University and outside sources.

DEGREE REQUIREMENTS. For M.A.: 36 credit hours program, no thesis or 18 core credits and thesis. For Ph.D: five-year program, four years in full-time study on campus; weekly colloquia, clinical practicum; second-year research project; clerkship; internship in fifth year; dissertation; final oral exam.

FIELDS OF STUDY.
Clinical Psychology. Ph.D. only.
General Psychology. M.A. only.
Postdoctoral Diplomas.

School of Business and Management

Tuition: per credit $540.
Enrollment: full-time 36, part-time 200 (men 60%, women 40%). Graduate faculty: full-time 20, part-time 18. Degrees conferred: M.B.A., M.S.

ADMISSION REQUIREMENTS. Transcripts, three recommendations, GMAT required in support of application. TOEFL required for foreign applicants. Accepts transfer applicants. Admits Fall and Spring semester. Apply to the University's Office of Graduate Admissions at least one month prior to semester of registration. Application fee $50. Phone: (516)877-3050.

ADMISSION STANDARDS. Selective. Usual minimum average: 2.75 (A = 4).

FINANCIAL AID. Annual awards from institutional funds: assistantships, Federal W/S, loans. Apply to the Financial Aid Office by March 1 (Fall and Spring). Use FAFSA. Phone: (516)877-3364. About 5% of students receive aid other than loans from School and outside sources.

DEGREE REQUIREMENTS. For M.B.A.: 33–66 credit hour program. For M.S.: 30–51 credit hour program. For M.B.A.-M.S. (Nursing): 72–74 credit hour program.

FIELDS OF STUDY.
Business Administration. M.B.A. only.
Finance. M.S. only.

Human Resource Management. Certificate only.
Management for Non-Business Majors. Certificate only.

School of Education

Tuition: per credit $540.

Enrollment: full- and part-time 1500 (men 30%, women 70%). University faculty teaching graduate students: full- and part-time 60. Degrees conferred: M.A., M.S., P.D., D.A.

ADMISSION REQUIREMENTS. Transcripts, three letters of recommendation required in support of School's application. MAT required by some departments. TOEFL required of international applicants. Interviews encouraged. Accepts transfer applicants. Apply to Office of Graduate Admission at least two months prior to registration. Foreign students must apply by February 1 (Fall admission only). Application fee $50. Phone: (516)877-3050.

ADMISSION STANDARDS. Selective for most departments. Usual minimum average: 2.75 (A = 4).

FINANCIAL AID. Annual awards from institutional funds: fellowships, tuition waivers, partial scholarships, research/teaching assistantships, Federal W/S, loans. Apply to the Office of Financial Aid by February 15. Use FAFSA. About 20% of full-time students receive aid other than loans from University and outside sources. Aid available for part-time students.

DEGREE REQUIREMENTS. For M.A., M.S.: 30–36 credit hours depending upon program; thesis/nonthesis option, depending upon the program. For M.S. (Communication Disorders): 53–56 credit program; clinical practica; departmental final comprehensive exam. For D.A.: 60 credit hours beyond master's; candidacy; preliminary exam; dissertation; final oral exam.

FIELDS OF STUDY.
Art Education.
Communicative Disorders. Includes specializations in special/language, pathology, audiology. M.S., D.A.
Community Health Education.
Deaf Studies. M.S. only.
Early Childhood.
Educational Leadership and Technology.
Elementary Education.
Health Education.
Literacy. M.S. only.
Physical Education. Includes specializations in adapted physical education, exercise physiology, sport management.
Secondary Education. Includes biology, chemistry, English, mathematics, physics, social studies.
Special Education for School-Age Learners.
TESOL.

School of Nursing—Graduate Division

Graduate study since 1949. Tuition: per credit $520. On-campus housing available. Enrollment: full- and part-time 110. Graduate Faculty: full-time 15, part-time 7. Degrees conferred: M.S., M.S.-M.B.A.

ADMISSION REQUIREMENTS. Transcripts, two years experience in nursing, GRE, letters of reference required in support of application. TOEFL required for foreign applicants. Accepts transfer applicants. Apply to Office of Graduate Admissions by May 1 (Fall), November 1 (Spring). Application fee $50. Phone: (516)877-3050.

ADMISSION STANDARDS. Selective. Usual minimum average: 3.0 (A = 4).

FINANCIAL AID. Annual awards from institutional funds: Federal Nursing traineeships, Federal W/S, loans. Apply to Director, Graduate Studies by February 15. Use FAFSA. Phone: (516)877-4545. About 75–90% of students receive aid other than loans from all sources.

DEGREE REQUIREMENTS. For M.S.: 45–48 credit hours minimum; master's project. For M.S.-M.B.A.: 69–71 credit hours minimum.

FIELDS OF STUDY.
Nursing. Includes adult health, advanced nursing practice, nursing service administration.

School of Social Work

Founded 1949. Annual tuition: $18,000; per credit $520. On-campus housing available. Contact Director of Housing. Phone: (516)877-3650.
Enrollment: full-time 177, part-time 500. Faculty: full-time 28, part-time 35. Degrees conferred: M.S.W., D.S.W.

ADMISSION REQUIREMENTS. Transcript, three professional references, minimum of twenty semester hours in social sciences required in support of application. Interview sometimes required. TOEFL score of 585 required for foreign applicants. Accepts transfer applicants. Apply to Director of Admissions. Rolling admissions process. Application fee $50. Phone: (516) 877-3020; fax: (516)877-3039.

ADMISSION STANDARDS. Competitive. Usual minimum average: 3.0 (A = 4).

FINANCIAL AID. Annual awards from institutional funds: assistantships, Federal W/S, loans. Apply to Director of Admissions by February 15. Phone: (516)877-3080; fax: (516)877-3380. Use FAFSA. About 20% of students receive aid other than loans from School and outside sources.

DEGREE REQUIREMENTS. For M.S.W.: 64 credit hours minimum, at least one year in full-time residence; internship; capstone seminar. For D.S.W.: 48 doctoral-level credits beyond master's degree; candidacy exam; dissertation; oral exam.
Note: Accelerated one-year program available for qualified applicants with undergraduate Social Work degree; 16-month accelerated M.S.W. also available.

FIELDS OF STUDY.
Social Welfare. M.S.W. only.
Social Work. D.S.W. only.

AIR FORCE INSTITUTE OF TECHNOLOGY
Dayton, Ohio 45433-7765
Web site: www.afit.edu

Founded 1919 as the Air School of Application to provide education and research to meet Air Force requirements. Located adjacent to Dayton. Coed. Federal control. Graduate only. Quarter system. Library: 110,000 volumes, 1100 subscriptions. More than 200 computers available.
Tuition paid by U.S. Government. Air Base has facilities for limited number of single and married students.
Enrollment: full- and part-time 450. Participation in Institute by military personnel and Federal Civil Service employees is on a voluntary basis. Faculty: full-time 96, part-time 4. Degrees conferred: M.S., Ph.D.

ADMISSION REQUIREMENTS. Transcripts, GRE/GMAT required in support of application. Apply to the Director of Admission/Registrar by March 1. Application fee: none. Applications processed on a rolling basis. Phone: (937)255-7168.

ADMISSION STANDARDS. Very selective for most majors, competitive for others. Usual minimum average: for M.S. in management programs: 2.5, for M.S. in engineering/technical: 3.0, for Ph.D.: 3.5 (A = 4).

FINANCIAL AID. All students are military officers or Federal or Civil Service employees drawing full pay.

DEGREE REQUIREMENTS. For M.S.: 48 quarter hours, 36 in residence; thesis. For Ph.D.: 3 consecutive quarters of full-time course work, 48 quarter hours residence; dissertation; final oral exam.

FIELDS OF STUDY.

GRADUATE SCHOOL OF ENGINEERING AND MANAGEMENT:
Aeronautical Engineering.
Applied Mathematics.
Astronautical Engineering.
Computer Engineering.
Computer Systems/Science.
Electrical Engineering.
Electro-Optics.
Engineering and Environmental Management.
Engineering Management.
Engineering Physics.
Meteorology.
Nuclear Engineering.
Operations Research.
Space Operations.
System Engineering.

UNIVERSITY OF AKRON

Akron, Ohio 44325-0001
Web site: www.uakron.edu

Founded 1870 by the Unitarians. Located about 45 miles S of Cleveland, Ohio. Coed. State supported. Semester system. About 1,000,000 volumes, 6000 subscriptions. 1200 computers on campus. Special facilities: Akron Polymer Training Center, Ray C. Bliss Institute of Applied Politics, Institute for Biomedical Engineering Research, Center for Economic Education, Center for Environmental Studies, Center for Family Business, Institute for Health and Social Policy, Center for Nursing, Center for Conflict Management, Center for Small Business, Center for Urban Studies, Fisher Institute for Professional Selling, William and Rita Fitzgerald Institute for Entrepreneurial Studies, Institute for Future Studies, Institute for Global Business, Institute for Life-Span Development and Gerontology, Center for Organizational Research, Center for Policy Studies, Institute for Polymer Engineering, The Maurice Morton Institute of Polymer Science, Microscale Physiochemical Engineering Center, Training Center for Fire and Hazardous Materials, Institute for Teaching and Learning. Total University enrollment: 23,000.

Tuition: per credit, resident $200, nonresident $364. Limited on-campus housing available. Annual housing costs: $5420 (including board). For off-campus housing contact the Off-Campus Housing Office. Phone: (330)972-6936.

Graduate School

First graduate degree conferred 1880. Enrollment: full-time 1563, part-time 1882. University faculty teaching graduate students: full-time 532, part-time 124. Degrees conferred: M.A., M.A.Ed., M.A.H.E.&F.E., M.P.A., M.S., M.S.Ed., M.S.A., M.S.M., M.B.A., M.T., M.S.T.Ed., M.S.E., M.S.E.E., M.S.C.E., M.S.M.E., M.S.Ch.E., M.S.N., M.M., Ed.D., Ph.D.

ADMISSION REQUIREMENTS. Transcripts, departmental exam may be required in support of application. TOEFL (scores of 550/213 preferred) for foreign students. Accepts transfer applicants. Graduates of unaccredited institutions not considered. Apply to Graduate School at least six weeks prior to registration. Rolling admissions process. Application fee $40, International application fee $50. Phone: (330)972-7663; fax: (330)972-7663; International Students: (330)972-6349.

ADMISSION STANDARDS. Selective for most departments. Usual minimum average: 2.75 (A = 4).

FINANCIAL AID. Annual awards from institutional funds: fellowships, research assistantships, teaching assistantships, Federal W/S, loans. Approved for V.A. benefits. Apply to Office of Student Financial Aid by March 1. Phone (330)972-7032. About 60% of full-time students receive aid other than loans from both University and outside sources.

DEGREE REQUIREMENTS. For master's: 30–36 semester hours minimum; thesis required by some departments; advancement to candidacy; final/cumulative exams for most departments. For M.B.A.: 58 credit hour program; some foundation courses may be waived. For M.P.A.: 40 credit hour program. For Ph.D.: at least two academic years beyond the master's; one year minimum in full-time residence; reading knowledge of two languages or comprehensive knowledge of one language; or language option in selected departments; preliminary/cumulative exams for many departments; advancement to candidacy; dissertation; final oral exam. For Ed.D.: essentially the same as for Ph.D. except no language requirement.

FIELDS OF STUDY.

BUCHTEL COLLEGE OF ARTS AND SCIENCES:
Applied Mathematics. Thesis optional. Master's only.
Applied Politics.
Biology. Thesis for master's.
Chemistry. Includes analytical, inorganic, organic, physical. Thesis for master's.
Computer Science. M.S. only.
Counseling Psychology.
Earth Science. Thesis. Master's only.
Economics. M.A. only.
English. Thesis or two essays for master's. Master's only.
French. Thesis/nonthesis options for master's. Master's only.
Geography/Urban Planning. Thesis for M.A. Master's only.
Geology. Thesis. Master's only.
Geophysics. Thesis. Master's only.
History. Master's, Ph.D.
Industrial/Organizational Psychology.
Mathematical Sciences. Thesis optional. Master's only.
Physics. Thesis optional. Master's only.
Political Science. Thesis for master's. Master's only.
Psychology. Includes industrial, general; M.A., Ph.D.
Public Administration.
Sociology. Thesis for master's.
Spanish. Thesis/nonthesis option for master's. Master's only.
Statistics. Final paper of thesis for master's. Master's only.
Urban Studies. Includes urban studies; urban studies/urban planning 45 credits. Ph.D.

COLLEGE OF BUSINESS ADMINISTRATION:
Accounting. Master's only.
Business Administration. Master's only.

Business Administration/Law. J.D./M.B.A.
Entrepreneurship.
Finance. Master's only.
International Business.
Management. Master's only.
Management-Human Resources.
Management of Technology.
Marketing. Master's only.
Quality Management.
Taxation. Master's only.
Taxation/Law. J.D.-M.Tax.

COLLEGE OF EDUCATION:
Athletic Training for Sports. M.A.Ed.
Classroom Guidance for Teachers. M.A., M.S.
Community Counseling.
Counseling Psychology. Ph.D.
Educational. M.A.Ed.
Elementary Administration. M.A., M.S., Ed.D.
Elementary Education.
Elementary School Counseling. M.A., M.S.
Health and Physical Education. M.A.Ed., M.S.Ed.
Higher Educational Administration. M.A., M.S.
Marriage and Family Therapy. M.A., M.S.
Outdoor Education. M.A.Ed., M.S.Ed.
Physical Education. K–12.
Reading Supervisor. M.A.Ed., M.S.Ed.
School Psychology. M.A., M.S.
Secondary School Administration. M.A.Ed., M.S.Ed.
Secondary School Education. M.A.Ed., M.S., Ph.D.
Special Education.
Sports Science/Coaching.
Technical Education.

COLLEGE OF ENGINEERING:
Biomedical Engineering.
Chemical Engineering.
Civil Engineering.
Electrical Engineering.
Engineering. Includes specializations in management, polymer.
   M.S. only.
Engineering-Applied Mathematics. Ph.D. only.
Mechanical Engineering.

COLLEGE OF FINE AND APPLIED ARTS:
Arts Management.
Audiology.
Child Development.
Child Life.
Clothing, Textile, and Interior.
Communication.
Composition.
Family Development.
Food Science.
Music Education.
Music History and Literature.
Music Technology.
Performance.
Speech Pathology.
Social Work.
Theater.
Theory.

COLLEGE OF NURSING:
Nursing.
Public Health.

COLLEGE OF POLYMER SCIENCE AND POLYMER ENGINEERING:
Polymer Engineering.
Polymer Science.

School of Law (2901)

Founded 1921. Merged with University of Akron 1959. Located in downtown Akron. ABA approved 1961. AALS member. Semester system. Full- and part-time study; both day and evening available. Special facilities: Center for Intellectual Property. Law library: 264,909 volumes; 3325 periodicals/subscriptions; has LEXIS, NEXIS, WESTLAW, OhioLINK; is a Federal Government Depository. The law student's microcomputer network has 66 workstations with complete Internet access.

Annual tuition: resident full-time $7884, part-time $5711; nonresident full-time $12,938, part-time $9321. Limited on-campus housing for single students, none for married students. Affordable housing opportunities within walking distance of campus available.

Enrollment: first-year class 167 day and evening; total day and evening 520 (men 60%, women 40%).

Faculty: full-time 20, part-time 27; 40% female; 15% minority; student to faculty ratio 19 to 1.

Degrees conferred: J.D., J.D.-M.B.A., J.D.-M.P.A., J.D.-M.TAX., LL.M. (Intellectual Property).

ADMISSION REQUIREMENTS FOR FIRST-YEAR APPLICANTS. LSDAS Law School report, LSAT, two recommendations, bachelor's degree from accredited institution, personal statement required with application. Applicants must have received bachelor's degree prior to enrollment. In addition, international applicants must submit TOEFL and TSE before application can be considered. Interview not required. Apply to Admission Director as early as possible after September 1, before March 1 (priority deadline). Applicants admitted Fall semester only (mid-August). Rolling admissions process; notification begins in late November/early December. Application fee $35. Phone: (330)972-7331, 7334; fax (330)258-2343. Acceptance of offer and first deposit due in April.

ADMISSION REQUIREMENTS FOR TRANSFER APPLICANTS. Accepts transfer applicants from other ABA accredited schools on a space available basis. At least one year of enrollment, letter from current Dean indicating applicant is in good standing, LSAT, LSDAS report (photocopy of original acceptable), personal statement, current Law School transcript required in support of School's application. Submit course descriptions/syllabi for all courses taken at current law school. Apply to Admission Director by May 1 (decision made by mid-July). Application fee $35. Will consider visiting/transient students.

ADMISSION STANDARDS. Number of full-time applicants 870, part-time 280; number accepted 310 full-time, 160 part-time; enrolled 102 full-time, 71 part-time. LSAT: 151 (75% of full-time class have a score at or above 151 and 75% of part-time class have a score at or above 150); GPA: 2.96 (A = 4) (75% of full-time class have a GPA at or above 2.96, 75% of part-time class have a score at or above 2.75). Gourman rating: 2.89. *U.S. News & World Report* ranking is in the fourth tier of all U.S. law schools.

FINANCIAL AID. Scholarships, need- and merit-based loans. Assistantships available for upper divisional joint degree candidates. Apply after January 1, but prior to May 1 (priority deadline) to the University's Office of Student Financial Aid. Phone: (800)621-3847 or (330)972-7331. Use FAFSA (School code: 003123). Information from the College Scholarship Service regarding the applicant's financial need must be received before a Financial Aid offer can be extended. About 30% of students receive full or partial scholarships; merit- and need-based loans available. Financial assistance available for part-time students. Average grant full-time $7873, part-time $3300.

DEGREE REQUIREMENTS. For J.D.: 88 credits (44 required credits) with a 2.0 (A = 4) GPA, plus an upper divisional writing requirement; three-year day program, four-year evening program; accelerated J.D. program available. On-campus summer sessions available. Upper divisional students may attend an ABA accredited law school's "Summer Abroad Program" as long as it does not effect the J.D. degree residency requirements. For J.D.-M.B.A.: total 103 credits (J.D. 78 credits, M.B.A. 25 credits). For J.D.-M.P.A.: total 109 credits (J.D. 77 credits, M.P.A. 32 credits). For J.D.-M.Tax.: total 98 (J.D. 78 credits, M.Tax. 20 credits). For LL.M. (Intellectual Property): one-year program beyond the J.D.

ALABAMA AGRICULTURAL AND MECHANICAL UNIVERSITY
Normal, Alabama 35762
Web site: www.aamu.edu

Founded 1875. Located in Huntsville. Coed. State control. Semester system. Library: 396,000 volumes, 528,000 microforms. Special facilities: Optics Center, Agriculture Research Center, Biological Research Center, Remote Sensor Center.

Tuition: per semester hour residents $265, nonresidents $415. Limited on-campus housing available for single graduate students, none for married students. Average annual housing cost: $2450–3200 (including board) for single students. Apply to Director of Housing. Phone: (256)851-5797.

School of Graduate Studies

Enrollment: full- and part-time 1499 (men 36%, women 64%). Graduate faculty: full-time 59. Degrees conferred: M.S., M.Ed., M.B.A., Ed.S., Ph.D.

ADMISSION REQUIREMENTS. Transcripts, evaluation or recommendations, GRE, GMAT (business) required in support of application. TOEFL and statement of financial support required for international applicants. Admits Spring, Fall, Summer. Apply two months prior to registration. International students must apply six months in advance. Application fee $25. Phone: (256)859-7415; fax: (256)859-3641.

ADMISSION STANDARDS. Selective. Usual minimum average: 2.5 (A = 4).

FINANCIAL AID. Annual awards from institutional funds: research fellowships, internships, Federal W/S, loans. Apply to Office of Financial Aid by February 15. Use FAFSA. Phone: (256)851-5400; fax: (256)851-5407. About 10% of students receive aid other than loans from University and outside sources.

DEGREE REQUIREMENTS. For master's: 39–48 semester hours minimum; thesis, or 6 additional hours and research paper; comprehensive exam for some programs. For Ed.S.: 30 semester hours beyond the master's; thesis. For M.S.W.: 60 semester hour program. For Ph.D.: at least 45 credits beyond the master's degree; preliminary exam; reading knowledge of two foreign languages or one language and approved appropriate research technique substitution; dissertation; final oral exam.

FIELDS OF STUDY.
Agribusiness. M.S. only.
Agriscience Technology.
Art Education. M.Ed.
Biology. M.S. only.
Business Administration. Includes accounting, economics, finance, human resource management, logistics, management, MIS, marketing.
Clinical Psychology.
Communicative Sciences and Disorders.
Computer Science.
Counseling Psychology.
Early Childhood Education.
Economics.
Educational Administration.
Elementary Education.
Food Science and Animal Industry.
Guidance Counseling.
Home Economics.
Industrial Technology.
Music Education.
Personnel Administration.
Physical Education.
Physics. Includes material science, optics/lasers.
Psychometry.
Reading.
School Psychology.
School Psychometry.
Secondary Education. Includes biology, business education, chemistry, English, family and consumer sciences, general science, home economics, education, industrial arts, language arts, mathematics, physics, technical, technology.
Social Work. Includes community mental health, family and child welfare, policy, planning and administration.
Soil and Plant Science. Includes plant physiology, remote sensing, soil physics, biotechnology.
Urban and Regional Planning.

ALABAMA STATE UNIVERSITY
Montgomery, Alabama 36101-0271
Web site: www.alasu.edu

State control. Semester system. Library 395,000 volumes, 1299 subscriptions. 350 computer stations on campus.

Tuition: part-time per semester hour residents $120, nonresidents $240. On-campus housing available on a first-come, first-served basis for single graduate students, none for married students. Average annual housing cost: $1750 (including board) for single students. Apply to Director of Housing by July 15.

School of Graduate Studies

Enrollment: full- and part-time 911 (men 30%, women 70%). Graduate faculty: full- and part-time 56. Degrees conferred: M.A., M.B.A., M.Ed., M.M.E., M.S., Ed.S.

ADMISSION REQUIREMENTS. Transcripts, GRE, GMAT (business) required in support of application. TOEFL, financial statement and all foreign transcripts (must be translated/interpreted course-by-course by WES or AACRAO) required for foreign applicants. Admits Spring, Fall, Summer. Apply at least two months prior to registration. International students must apply six months in advance. Applications fee $10. Phone: (334)229-4275, fax: (334)229-4928.

ADMISSION STANDARDS. Selective. Usual minimum average: 2.5 (A = 4).

FINANCIAL AID. Annual awards from institutional funds: research assistantships, Federal W/S, grants, loans. Apply to Office of Financial Aid. Use FAFSA. Aid available for part-time students.

DEGREE REQUIREMENTS. For master's: 30 semester hours minimum; foreign language proficiency for most degrees, a computer language may be substituted in some programs; thesis, or 6 additional hours and research paper. For Ed.S.: 30 semester hours beyond the master's; thesis.

FIELDS OF STUDY.
Accountancy. M.S.
Administration and Supervision. M.Ed., Ed.S.
Biology. M.Ed., M.S., Ed.S.
Collaborative Teacher (Special Education). M.Ed.
Early Childhood Education. M.Ed., Ed.S.
Elementary Education. M.Ed., Ed.S.
English Language Arts. M.Ed.
General Counseling. M.A.
Health Education. M.Ed.
History. M.A., M.Ed., Ed.S.
Library Education Media. M.Ed., Ed.S.
Mathematics. M.S., M.Ed., Ed.S.
Music—Instrumental. M.M.E.
Music—Vocal/Choral. M.M.E.
Physical Education. M.Ed.
Physical Therapy. M.S.
School Counseling. M.Ed., Ed.S.

UNIVERSITY OF ALABAMA

Tuscaloosa, Alabama 35487
Web site: www.ua.edu

Founded 1831. Main campus located 50 miles SW of Birmingham. Coed. State control. Semester system. CGS member. 1450 computers for campus use. Special facilities: Alabama Business Research Council, Alabama Law Institute, Alabama Museum of Natural History, Alabama Oil and Gas Board, Belser-Parton Reading Laboratory, Brewer-Porch Children's Center, Bureau of Education Services and Research, Bureau of Engineering, Research Bureau of Legal Research, Capstone International Program Center, Cartographic Laboratory Center for Administrative and Policy Studies, Center for Alcohol and Drug Education, Center for Business and Economic Research, Center for Communication Research and Service, Center for Developmental and Learning Disorders, Center for Economic Education, Center for Government and Public Service, Center for Law and Public Policy, Center for Southern Regional Folk Life Studies, Center for the Study of Aging, Center for the Study of Southern History and Culture, Child Development Laboratories, Computer Center, Early Childhood Day Care Center, Electron Microscope Laboratory, Evaluation and Assessment Laboratory, Geological Survey of Alabama, Herbarium, Human Development Laboratory, Human Resources Institute, Institute of Higher Education Research and Services, Inter-University Consortium for Political Research, J. Nicholene Bishop Biological Station, Legal Aid Clinic, Marine Environmental Services Consortium Incorporated, Mineral Resources Institute—State Mine Experimental Station, Minority Culture Archives, Mound State Monument, Museum of Natural History, Natural Resources Center, Office for Archeological Research, Office of Education Media, Psychological Clinic, Remote Sensing Laboratory, Research Laboratory of Human Nutrition, Ridgecrest Center, Rochester Products Applied Research Facility, Rose Tower Learning Center, School of Mines and Energy Development, Speech and Hearing Center, Teaching and Learning Center, Transportation Research Group, Tuscaloosa Metallurgical Laboratory, U.S. Bureau of Mines, University of Alabama Arboretum, University of Alabama Art Gallery, University of Alabama Icthyological Collection, University of Alabama Press, University of Alabama Theatre, University of Alabama Television Service, William B. Bennett International Trade Center. Library: 3,400,000 volumes, 17,788 subscriptions, plus access to on-line retrievals services. Total University enrollment: approximately 13,000.

Annual tuition: full-time, resident $3014, nonresident $8162. On-campus housing for 300 married students, 500 men, 500 women. Average housing cost: $350 monthly for married students, $1680 per semester for single students. Apply to Director of Housing by March 1. Phone: (205)348-6676. Day-care facilities available.

Graduate School

Organized 1924. Enrollment: full-time 2000, part-time 1375. Graduate faculty: full-time 450, part-time 274. Degrees conferred: M.A., M.S., M.B.A., M.C.R., M.F.A., M.L.S., M.P.A., M.S.W., Ed.S., D.M.A., D.P.A., Ed.D., D.S.W., Ph.D.

ADMISSION REQUIREMENTS. Two transcripts, references, GRE required in support of application. GRE Subject Test required by many departments. GMAT required for Manderson Graduate School of Business. GRE or MAT or NTE for College of Education. GRE or MAT for School of Human Environmental Sciences. GRE for College of Engineering. Interview sometimes required. Accepts transfer applicants. TOEFL, financial statement, and all foreign transcripts (must be translated/interpreted course-by-course by WES or AACRAO) required for international applicants. Apply to Dean of the Graduate School six weeks prior to registration. Application fee $25. Phone: (205)348-5921.

ADMISSION STANDARDS. Very selective for some departments, selective for the others. Usual minimum average: 3.0 (A = 4). Usual minimum test score, 50th percentile.

FINANCIAL AID. Annual awards from institutional funds; graduate council fellowships, departmental teaching and research assistantships, Federal W/S, loans, tuition waivers. All full-time fellowships and departmental assistantships accompanied by full-tuition scholarships. Apply to Dean of the Graduate School by March 1. Phone: (205)348-6756. Use FAFSA. About 30% of the students receive aid other than loans from University and outside sources.

DEGREE REQUIREMENTS. For master's: Plan I—24 semester hours minimum; reading knowledge of one foreign language for some departments; thesis; final written/oral exam. Plan II—30 semester hours minimum; reading knowledge of one foreign language for some departments; no thesis; final written/oral exam. For Ed.S.: 30 semester hours minimum beyond master's. For Ph.D.: 48 semester hours minimum beyond the bachelor's, at least 18 in full-time residence; preliminary exam; dissertation; reading knowledge of two foreign languages or one language and appropriate research technique/tool or other approved substitution; final written/oral exam. For other doctoral programs: 90 semester hours minimum beyond the bachelor's, at least 45 in residence; preliminary exam; final oral exam; no language requirement; dissertation.

FIELDS OF STUDY.

COLLEGE OF ARTS AND SCIENCES:
American Studies. M.A.
Anthropology. M.A.
Art. M.A., M.F.A.
Audiology. M.S.
Biology. Includes ecology and systematics, molecular and cellular biology. M.S., Ph.D., Ed.S.
Chemistry. M.S. Ph.D., Ed.S.
Communicative Disorders. M.S.
Creative Writing. M.F.A.
Criminal Justice. M.S., M.C.J.
English. M.A.
French. M.A.
Geography. M.S.
Geology. M.S., Ph.D.
German. M.A.
History. M.A., Ph.D.
Latin American Studies. M.A.

Mathematics. M.A., Ph.D.
Music. M.M.
Music (Applied). M.M.
Music Management. M.M.
Music (Performance and Composition). M.M.
Physics. M.S., Ph.D.
Political Science. M.S., Ph.D.
Psychology. M.A., Ph.D., Psychological Spec.
Public Administration. M.P.A., D.P.A.
Romance Languages. M.A., Ph.D.
Spanish. M.A.
Theatre. M.A., M.F.A.
Women's Studies. M.A.

COLLEGE OF COMMERCE AND BUSINESS ADMINISTRATION:
Accounting. M.A., M.Acct., M.S.C., Ph.D.
Applied Statistics. M.A., M.S.C., Ph.D.
Business Administration. M.B.A.
Economics. M.A., M.S.C., Ph.D.
Finance. M.A., M.S.C., Ph.D.
Human Resource Management. M.S., M.S.C., Ph.D.
Management Science. M.A., M.S.C., Ph.D.
Marketing. M.A., M.S.C., Ph.D.
Tax Accounting. M.T.A.

SCHOOL OF COMMUNICATION AND INFORMATION SCIENCES:
Advertising and Public Relations. M.A.
Broadcast and Film Communication. M.A.
Journalism. M.A.
Library and Information Studies. M.A., M.F.A., M.L.I.S., Ph.D.
Mass Communication. Ph.D.
Speech Communication. M.A.
Telecommunications. M.A.

COLLEGE OF COMMUNITY HEALTH SCIENCES:
Community Health Sciences.

COLLEGE OF EDUCATION:
Art Education. M.A.
Business Education. M.A.
Counselor Education. M.A. in community, elementary, rehabilitation, secondary, student personnel counseling. Ed.D., Ph.D., Ed.S.
Early Childhood Education. M.A.
Educational Leadership: Higher Education. M.A., Ed.D., Ph.D.
Educational Psychology. M.A., Ed.D., Ph.D., Ed.S.
Educational Research. Ed.D., Ph.D., Ed.S.
Elementary Education. M.A., Ed.D., Ph.D., Ed.S.
Health, Physical and Recreation Education. M.A., Ed.D., Ed.S.
Instructional Leadership. M.A., Ed.D., Ph.D., Ed.S.
Middle School Education. Includes biology, chemistry, earth and space science, economics, English, French, general science, geography, history, language arts, mathematics, physics, political science, sociology, Spanish, speech communication/theater. M.A., Ed.S.
Music Education. M.A.
School Psychology. M.A., Ph.D.
Secondary Education. M.A., Ed.D., Ph.D., Ed.S. offered in all areas except as indicated: anthropology, M.A. only; art, Ed D., Ph.D., Ed.S.; biology, business education, Ed.D., Ph.D., Ed.S.; chemistry, earth science, M.A., Ed.S.; economics, English, French, geography, German, M.A. only; history, home economics, Ed.D., Ph.D., Ed.S.; language arts, M.A., Ed.S.; Latin American studies, mathematics, music, Ed.D., Ph.D., Ed.S.; physics, political science, psychology, M.A., Ed.S.; social science, sociology, Spanish, rhetoric and speech communication.
Speech Education. Ed.D., Ed.S.; M.A. in emotional conflict, gifted and talented, learning disabilities, mental retardation, multiple disabilities, special education administration.
Supervision of Health Education. M.A., Ed.S.
Supervision of Physical Education. M.A., Ed.S.

Supervision of Reading. M.A., Ed.S.
Supervision of Special Education. M.A., Ed.S.
Teaching of Reading. M.A., Ed.S.
Trade and Industrial Education. M.A.

COLLEGE OF ENGINEERING:
Aerospace Engineering and Mechanics. M.S.
Chemical Engineering. M.S., Ph.D.
Civil Engineering. M.S., Ph.D.
Computer Engineering. M.S.
Computer Science. M.S.
Electrical Engineering. M.S., Ph.D.
Engineering. M.S.
Engineering (Coastal). M.S.
Engineering (Environmental). M.S.
Engineering Hydrology. M.S.
Engineering Mechanics. M.S., Ph.D.
Industrial Engineering. M.S.
Materials Engineering. M.S.
Mechanical Engineering. M.S., Ph.D.
Metallurgical Engineering. M.S.

COLLEGE OF HUMAN ENVIRONMENTAL SCIENCES:
Clothing, Textiles and Interior Design. M.S.
Consumer Sciences. M.S.
General Human Environmental Sciences. M.S.
Health Sciences. M.S.
Human Development and Family Life. M.S.
Human Nutrition and Hospitality. M.S.

CAPSTONE COLLEGE OF NURSING:
Nursing. Includes case management for rural populations. M.S., M.S.-M.A., M.S.-M.B.A.

SCHOOL OF SOCIAL WORK:
Social Work. M.S.W., Ph.D.

School of Law (35487-0382)
Web site: www.law.ua.edu

Established 1872. Located at Tuscaloosa. ABA approved since 1926. AALS member. Semester system. Full-time, day study only. Law library: 388,300 volumes; 3259 subscriptions; has LEXIS, NEXIS, WESTLAW, DIALOG, OCLC, Dialog; is a Federal Government Depository. Special programs: summer study abroad at University of Fribourg, Switzerland and Australia National University in Camberra, Australia.

Annual tuition: resident $5112, nonresident $10,798. On-campus housing available for both single and married students. Annual on-campus housing cost: $8776. Law students tend to live off-campus. Off-campus housing cost: approximately $9260.

Enrollment: first-year class 177; total full-time 524 (men 63%, women 37%); no part-time students.

Faculty: full-time 29, part-time 25; 25% female; 20% minority; student to faculty ratio 17.5 to 1.

Degrees conferred: J.D., J.D.-M.B.A., LL.M. (Tax), LL.M. (International Lawyers for persons who have completed a basic legal education and received a university degree in law in another country).

ADMISSION REQUIREMENTS FOR FIRST-YEAR APPLICANTS. LSDAS Law School report, LSAT (not later that December test date; if more than one LSAT, highest is used), bachelor's degree from an accredited institution, transcripts (must show all schools attended and at least three years of study) required in support of application. Applicants must have received bachelor's degree prior to entrance. Interview not required but may be requested by School. In addition, international applicants must submit TOEFL (not older than two years). Apply to Admission Coordinator after September 1, before March 1. First-year students admitted Fall only. Rolling admissions process, notification starts in November and is finished by late April. Acceptance of offer and first deposit deadline May 1. School does maintain a waiting list. Application fee $25. Phone: (205)348-5440; e-mail: admissions@law.ua.edu. Admission deadline for LL.M. February 1.

ADMISSION REQUIREMENTS FOR TRANSFER APPLICANTS. Accepts transfers from other ABA accredited schools. Admission limited to space available. At least one year of enrollment, in good standing, prefer applicants in the top quarter of first-year class, LSAT, LSDAS, personal statement regarding reason for transfer request. Apply to Admission coordinator by June 1. Application fee $25.

ADMISSION STANDARDS. Number of full-time applicants 931; number of accepted 344; number enrolled 177; LSAT (75% of class have a score at or above 157); GPA (75% of class have a GPA at or above 2.99). Gourman rating: 3.24. *U.S. News & World Report* ranking is in the top tier, tied for 47th.

FINANCIAL AID. Scholarships, merit scholarships; loans and Federal WS offered through University's Financial Aid Office. For scholarships (selection criteria places heavy reliance on LSAT and undergraduate GPA) apply to Assistant Dean of School after January 1 before May 1; phone: (205)348-4508; use School's FAF. For all other programs apply to Director of Student Financial Services, University of Alabama, P.O. Box 870162, phone: (205)348-6756. Use FAFSA (School code: 001051). Approximately 25% receive scholarships. Average scholarship grant $2000.

DEGREE REQUIREMENTS. For J.D.: 90 credits (36 credits required) with a GPA of at least 2.0 (A = 4), plus completion of upper divisional writing course; three-year program. Accelerated J.D. with one summer of course work. For J.D.-M.B.A.: total 118 credits (J.D. approximately 80 credits, M.B.A. approximately 38). For LL.M. (Tax): 24 credits. For LL.M. (International Lawyers): 24 credits; at least two semesters in residence; a GPA of 2.5 (A = 4) required.

UNIVERSITY OF ALABAMA AT BIRMINGHAM

Birmingham, Alabama 35294-1203
Web site: www.uab.edu

Founded 1966. Coed. Semester system. CGS member. 400 computers on campus for general use. Libraries: 1,450,000 volumes, 5250 subscriptions, plus access to on-line data retrieval services. Special facilities: Center for Urban Affairs, Small Business Development Center. University's ranking by NIH in domestic higher educational institutions was 21st with 505 grants, total dollars awarded $189,833,497.

Tuition: per credit hour, residents $112, nonresidents $224. Limited on-campus housing for married and single students. Average housing cost: single students $6471 (including board); married students $2536. Contact UAB Student Housing and Residential Life Office, 1604 Ninth Ave., South Birmingham, AL 35294-1230. Phone: (205)934-2092. Day-care facilities available.

Graduate School

Enrollment: full-time 3110, part-time 886. Faculty: full- and part-time 1200. Degrees conferred: M.S.N.A., M.P.A., M.S.O.T., M.S.H.A., M.S.F.S., M.A., M.Ac., Ph.D., M.S., M.B.A., M.S.C.L.S., M.S.C.J., M.A.Ed., Ed.S., Ed.D., M.S.B.E., M.S.C.E., M.S.E.E., M.S.Mte., M.S.M.E., M.S.H.I., D.S.N., M.S.N.

ADMISSION REQUIREMENTS. Two transcripts, three evaluations, GRE (some UAB graduate programs require, or are willing to accept, other recognized national tests) required in support of application. TOEFL and TWE required of foreign students. Interview required for some departments. Accepts transfer applicants. Apply to Dean of the Graduate School at least six weeks prior to registration; some graduate programs admit only at certain times of the year and have specific deadlines. Application fee $35, international applicants $60. Phone: (205)934-8243, or (800)975-GRAD.

ADMISSION STANDARDS. Competitive for most departments.

FINANCIAL AID. Partial tuition waivers, assistantships, fellowships, Federal W/S, loans. Financial Aid Office administers loan, grant, and work-study programs, students in certain programs may participate in UAB's Coop Ed program. Contact Office of Student Financial Aid. Phone: (205)934-8223; fax: (205)934-8941. Apply to the specific graduate program director for assistantships and fellowships.

DEGREE REQUIREMENTS. For master's: Plan I—24 hours minimum, at least 18 in major and 6 in related minor; thesis; reading knowledge of one foreign language for some departments; candidacy; final written/oral exam. Plan II—30 hours minimum, at least 18 in major; no thesis; reading knowledge of one foreign language for some departments; candidacy; final written/oral exam for some programs. For Ed.S.: 30 hours beyond the master's; final oral/written exam. For doctoral programs: preliminary exam; candidacy; dissertation; reading knowledge of one language, a research tool, or computer technique; research project for some programs; final oral exam.

FIELDS OF STUDY.

ADMINISTRATION AND BUSINESS:
Accounting. M.Ac.
Administration—Health Services. Ph.D.
Business Administration. M.B.A.
Health Administration. M.S.H.A.
Health Informatics. M.S.H.I.
Public Administration. M.P.A.

ALLIED HEALTH SCIENCES:
Dentistry. M.S.
Nurse Anesthesia. M.N.A.
Nursing. Ph.D.
Nutrition, Clinical. M.S.
Nutrition Sciences. Ph.D.
Occupational Therapy. M.S.
Oral Biology. M.S.
Physical Therapy. M.S.

BASIC LIFE AND BIOMEDICAL SCIENCES:
Biochemistry. Ph.D.
Biology. M.S., Ph.D.
Cell Biology. Ph.D.
Clinical Laboratory Sciences. M.S.C.L.S.
Medical Genetics. Ph.D.
Microbiology. Ph.D.
Neurobiology. Ph.D.
Pathology. Ph.D.
Pharmacology. Ph.D.
Physiology and Biophysics. Ph.D.
Vision Science. M.S., Ph.D.

COORDINATED DEGREES:
D.M.D.-Ph.D.
M.S.-M.D. & Ph.D.-M.D.
O.D.-M.S. & O.D.-Ph.D.
M.D.-M.S.B.M.S.

M.B.A.-M.P.H.
M.S.H.A.-M.B.A.
M.P.A.-M.P.H.
M.P.A.-J.D.
Ph.D.-M.B.A.

EDUCATION:
Education, Arts. M.A.Ed., Ed.S.
Education, Counseling. M.A., Ed.S.
Education, Early Childhood. M.A.Ed., Ed.S., Ph.D.
Education, Elementary. M.A.Ed., Ed.S.
Education, Health. M.A.Ed., Ed.S.
Education, High School. M.A.Ed., Ed.S.
Education, Physical. M.A.Ed., Ed.S.
Education, Special. M.A.Ed., Ed.S.
Educational Leadership. Ed.D., M.A.Ed., Ph.D., Ed.S.

ENGINEERING:
Biomedical Engineering. M.S.B.M.E., Ph.D.
Civil Engineering. Ph.D., M.S.C.E.
Computer Engineering. Ph.D.
Electrical Engineering. M.S.E.E.
Environmental Health Engineering. Ph.D.
Materials Engineering. M.S.Mt.E., Ph.D.
Mechanical Engineering. M.S.M.E.

PHYSICAL AND MATHEMATICAL SCIENCES:
Chemistry. M.S., Ph.D.
Computer and Information Science. M.S., Ph.D.
Forensic Science. M.S.F.S.
Materials Science. Ph.D.
Mathematics. M.S.
Mathematics, Applied. Ph.D.
Physics. M.S., Ph.D.

PUBLIC HEALTH:
Biostatistics. M.S., Ph.D.
Environmental Health Sciences. Ph.D.
Epidemiology. Ph.D.
Health Education/Health Promotion. Ph.D.

SOCIAL SCIENCES, ART, AND HUMANITIES:
Anthropology. M.A.
Art History. M.A.
Criminal Justice. M.S.C.J.
English. M.A.
History. M.A.
Medical Sociology. Ph.D.
Psychology. Ph.D.

FIFTH-YEAR PROGRAMS–EDUCATION:
Arts.
Counseling.
Early Childhood.
Elementary.
Health.
High School.
Physical.
Special.

School of Dentistry
(Box 16-SDB)

Established 1945. Located in Birmingham (35294-0007). Special facility: Research Center for Oral Biology. Library (combined with School of Medicine) 240,000 volumes. Tuition: resident $6276, nonresident $18,828. Housing: very limited. Total average cost for all other first-year expenses $5800.

Enrollment: first-year class 56; total full-time 285 (men 162, women 63). Faculty: full-time 76, part-time 78. Degree con-

ferred: D.M.D., M.S. (Oral Biology), D.M.D.-M.P.H., D.M.D.-Ph.D.

ADMISSION REQUIREMENTS. For D.M.D.: AADSAS transcripts showing completion of at least three years of undergraduate study, DAT, four recommendations required in support of School's application. Interview by invitation only. Accepts transfer applicants for second and third years only. Preference given to Alabama and SREB residents. Graduates of unaccredited colleges not considered. For M.S., M.P.H., Ph.D.: students may apply after completion of second year of program. Apply to AADSAS after June 1 and before April 1. Acceptance fee $50. Phone: (205)934-3387.

ADMISSION STANDARDS. Competitive. Admits 40% of total annual applicants. Mean DAT: 17.8; mean GPA: 3.68 (A = 4). Approximately 80% are state residents.

FINANCIAL AID. Scholarships, minority scholarships, grants, HEAL, DEAL, HPSL, loans. Apply to School's Office of Financial Aid; no specified closing date. For need based programs use FAFSA (School code: 001052). About 79% of students receive aid other than loans from School.

DEGREE REQUIREMENTS. For D.M.D.: satisfactory completion of four-year program. For M.S., M.P.H., Ph.D.: see Graduate School listing above.

FIELDS OF GRADUATE STUDY.
Anatomy. Ph.D.
Biochemistry. Ph.D.
Dentistry. M.S.
Microbiology. Ph.D.
Oral Biology. M.S.
Pharmacology. Ph.D.
Physiology and Biophysics. Ph.D.
Public Health. M.P.H.

School of Medicine
(Box 100-UAB Station)

Founded 1859 in Mobile; located in Birmingham (35294) since 1945. Branch campuses created in 1969 at Huntsville and Tuscaloosa. Medical library 240,000 volumes. Annual tuition: resident $7564, nonresident $22,692; student fees $927. Very limited on-campus housing available. Contact Admissions office for both on- and off-campus availability.

Enrollment: first-year class 161 (8 were M.D.-Ph.D.); approximately 12 EDP; total full-time 684 (men 70%, women 30%). Faculty: full-time 314, part-time 80. Degrees conferred: M.D., M.D.-Ph.D. The Ph.D. conferred through the Graduate School.

ADMISSION REQUIREMENTS. AMCAS report, transcripts, MCAT, recommendations, interview required in support of application. Has EDP preference given to Alabama residents. Graduates of unaccredited institutions not considered. For EDP, apply to Director of Admissions after June 15, before November 1. Secondary applications sent to all residents and selected nonresidents. Dual degree candidates must be accepted by both schools. Application fee $65. Phone: (205)934-2333; fax: (205)934-8724; e-mail: admissions@uasom.meis.4ab.edu.

ADMISSION STANDARDS. Competitive. Accepts about 20% of total annual applicants. Approximately 80% of class are state residents. Gourman rating: 3.67. *U.S. News & World Report* ranks school in top 30 of all schools and top 30 of all primary-care schools.

FINANCIAL AID. Scholarships, summer stipends, summer fellowships, loans grants, HEAL, NIH stipends. Assistantship may be available for dual degree candidates. Apply to Director of Financial Aid after acceptance; no specified closing date. Phone: (205)934-4384. 67% of students receive financial aid.

DEGREE REQUIREMENTS. For M.D.: satisfactory completion of four-year program. For Ph.D., see Graduate School listing above.

FIELDS OF GRADUATE STUDY.
Anatomy.
Biochemistry.
Biophysics.
Cell Biology.
Genetics.
Immunology.
Microbiology.
Neurosciences.
Pathology.
Pharmacology.
Physiology.

UNIVERSITY OF ALABAMA IN HUNTSVILLE
Huntsville, Alabama 35899
Web site: www.uah.edu

Established 1950. Coed. Public control. Semester system. CGS member. There are 520 computers available on campus for student use. Special facilities: Alabama Solar Research Center, Center for Applied Optics, Johnson Research Center, Center for Microgravity and Materials Research, Center for Robotics, Center for Space Plasma and Aeronomic Research. Library: 627,000 volumes, 1668 subscriptions.

Annual tuition: resident $4088, nonresident $8394. On-campus housing available for 160 married students, for 700 single graduate students. Average academic year housing costs: $3500 (including board) for single students, $4920 for married students. Contact Director of University Housing for both on- and off-campus housing information. Phone: (205)895-6108. Day-care facilities available.

School of Graduate Studies

Enrollment: full-time 470, part-time 686. Faculty: full-time 211, part-time 50. Degrees conferred: M.A., M.Acc., M.S., M.S.E., M.S.M.I.S., M.S.M., M.S.N., M.S.O.R., Ph.D.

ADMISSION REQUIREMENTS. Two official transcripts, bachelor's degree, GRE (subject for some departments)/GMAT/MAT, three recommendations required in support of School's application. TOEFL required for international applicants. Accepts transfer applicant. Graduates of unaccredited institutions not considered. Apply to Graduate Office by July 1 (Fall), December 1 (Spring); international students must apply three months prior to registration. Rolling admissions process. Application fee $35. Dean's office: (256)824-6002; fax: (256)824-6349; e-mail: deangrad@uah.edu. Admissions office: (256)824-6198.

ADMISSION STANDARDS. Selective. Usual minimum average: 3.0 (A = 4).

FINANCIAL AID. Annual awards from institutional funds: scholarships, tuition waivers, fellowships, research assistantships, teaching assistantships, Federal W/S, loans. Approved for VA benefits. Apply to the Office of Financial Aid. Phone: (256)824-6241. Use FAFSA. About 36% of students receive aid other than loans from both University and outside sources.

DEGREE REQUIREMENTS. For master's: 24 semester hours minimum plus thesis; or 36 semester hours without thesis; final comprehensive exam. For Ph.D.: three years of study beyond the bachelor's, at least one year in full-time residence; qualifying exam; dissertation; final exam; additional requirements determined by appropriate department adviser.

FIELDS OF STUDY.

COLLEGE OF ADMINISTRATIVE SCIENCE:
Accounting. M.Acc.
Management. M.S.M.
Management of Information Systems. M.S.M.I.S.

COLLEGE OF ENGINEERING:
Chemical and Material Engineering. M.S.E.
Civil and Environmental Engineering. M.S.E.
Computer Engineering. M.S.E., Ph.D.
Electrical Engineering. M.S.E., Ph.D.
Industrial and Systems Engineering. M.S.E., Ph.D.
Mechanical Engineering. M.S.E., Ph.D.
Operations Research. M.S.O.R.

COLLEGE OF LIBERAL ARTS:
English. M.A.
History. M.A.
Psychology. M.A.
Public Affairs. M.A.

COLLEGE OF NURSING:
Nursing. M.S.N.

COLLEGE OF SCIENCE:
Applied Mathematics. Ph.D.
Atmospheric Science. M.S.
Biological Sciences. M.S.
Chemistry. M.S.
Computer Science. M.S.
Mathematics. M.A.
Physics. M.A.

INTERDISCIPLINARY PROGRAMS:
Biotechnology Science and Engineering. Ph.D.
Materials Science. Ph.D.
Optical Science and Engineering. Ph.D.

FIFTH-YEAR PROGRAMS—EDUCATION:
Biology.
Chemistry.
English.
History.
Mathematics.
Physics.

UNIVERSITY OF ALASKA FAIRBANKS
Fairbanks, Alaska 99775-0820
Web site: www.uaf.edu

Founded 1917. Located 4 miles NW of Fairbanks. Coed. State control. Semester system. CGS member. More than 500 computers on campus. Special research units: Alaska Cooperative Wildlife Research Unit, Alaska Coop Fisheries Research Unit; Center for Cross-Cultural Studies, Institute of Arctic Biology, Geophysics Institute, Marine Science, Water Resources, and Institute of Northern Engineering; Mineral Industry Research Laboratory, Petroleum Development Laboratory. State and federal agencies on campus include the Branch of Alaskan Geology of the U.S. Geological Survey, Alaska Division of Geological and

Geophysical Survey, Institute of Northern Forestry (U.S. Forest Service), and College Observatory (U.S. Dept. of Commerce). Library: 586,000 volumes, 6825 subscriptions, plus access to on-line data retrieval services.

Semester tuition/fees: full-time, resident $4128, per credit $150; nonresident $8064, per credit $300. On-campus housing for 180 married students, housing available as needed for single graduate students. Average academic-year housing cost: $7000 for married students, $4760 for single students. Apply to Director of Housing by March 15. Phone: (907)474-7247. Day-care facilities available.

Graduate School

Graduate study since 1950. Enrollment: full-time 507, part-time 266 (men 378, women 395). Faculty teaching graduate students: full-time 300, part-time 111. Degrees conferred: M.A., M.A.T., M.B.A., M.F.A., M.Ed., M.M.E., M.C.E., M.E.E., M.S., Ph.D.

ADMISSION REQUIREMENTS. Transcripts, résumé/vitae, Statement of Academic Goals, three letters of recommendation required in support of application. GRE/GMAT required. TOEFL required for all foreign students; TSE and TWE may be requested. Interview not required. Accepts transfer applicants. Apply to Director of Admissions and Records; apply by August 1 (Fall), December 1 (Spring). Application fee $50. Phone: (907)474-7500; fax: (907)474-5379; e-mail: byapply@uaf.edu.

ADMISSION STANDARDS. Selective for most departments. Usual minimum average: 3.0 (A = 4).

FINANCIAL AID. Annual awards from institutional funds: scholarships, fellowships, assistantships, grants, Federal W/S, loans. Apply to Dean of the appropriate College for assistantships; closing date early Spring; for all other aid apply by February 15 for Fall semester. Phone: (907)474-7256. Use FAFSA (University code: 001063) and institutional FAF. About 50% of students receive aid other than loans from University and outside sources. Aid sometimes available for part-time students.

DEGREE REQUIREMENTS. For master's: 30–33 semester credits minimum, at least 21 in residence; candidacy; thesis or project for most departments; final written/oral exam. For Ph.D.: number of credits determined by the advisory committee, but usually at least two years beyond the master's; minimum 18 credit thesis; written comprehensive exam; reading knowledge of one foreign language or other research-tool competence for most programs; dissertation; final oral exam.

FIELDS OF STUDY.
Anthropology. M.A., Ph.D.
Art. M.F.A.
Atmospheric Sciences. M.S., Ph.D.
Biochemistry/Molecular Biology. M.S., Ph.D.
Biological Sciences. Includes biology, botany, wildlife biology, zoology. Ph.D. only.
Biology. M.S., M.A.T.
Botany. M.S.
Business Administration. M.B.A.
Chemistry. M.A., M.S.
Civil Engineering. M.C.E., M.S.
Community Psychology. M.A.
Computational Physics. M.S.
Computer Science. M.S.
Creative Writing. M.F.A.
Cross-Cultural Studies. M.A.
Economics, Resources and Applied Economics. M.S.
Education. Includes cross-cultural, curriculum and instruction, educational leadership, language and literacy. M.Ed.
Electrical Engineering. M.E.E., M.S.

Engineer of Mines. E.M.
Engineering. Includes arctic, civil, electrical, engineering management environmental, mechanical. Ph.D.
Engineering Management. M.S.
English. M.A.
Environmental Chemistry. M.S., Ph.D.
Environmental Engineering and Environmental Quality Science. M.S.
Fisheries. M.S., Ph.D.
General Science. M.S.
Geological Engineering. M.S.
Geology. Includes economic, general, petroleum, quaternary, remote sensing, volcanology. M.S., Ph.D.
Geophysics. Includes remote sensing, snow, ice and permafrost, solid-earth. M.S., Ph.D.
Guidance and Counseling. Includes elementary, secondary. M.Ed.
Interdisciplinary Studies. M.A., M.S., Ph.D.
Justice. M.A.
Marine Biology. M.S., Ph.D.
Mathematics. M.S., M.A.T., Ph.D.
Mechanical Engineering. M.S.
Mineral Preparation Engineering. M.S.
Mining Engineering. M.S.
Music. Includes conducting, music education, music history, performance, theory/composition. M.A.
Natural Resource Management. M.S.
Northern Studies. M.A.
Oceanography. Includes biological, chemical, fisheries, geological, physical. M.S., Ph.D.
Petroleum Engineering. M.S.
Physics. M.S., M.A.T., Ph.D.
Professional Communication. Includes communication, journalism. M.A.
Rural Development. M.A.
Science Management. M.S.
Space Physics. M.S., Ph.D.
Wildlife Biology. M.S.
Zoology. M.S.

ALBANY LAW SCHOOL OF UNION UNIVERSITY
Albany, NY 12208-3494
Web site: www.als.edu

Founded 1851. Semester system. There are 98 computers available on campus for student use. Special facilities: Government Law Center, Science and Technology Center. Law library: 250,000 volumes, 1491 subscriptions; has LEXIS, NEXIS, WESTLAW, DIALOG, VU TEST, WILSONLINE.

Annual tuition: full-time $21,495, part-time $16,121. No on-campus housing available. Off-campus cost approximately $6000.

Enrollment: first-year class full-time 275, part-time 31; full-time 744 (men 50%, women 50%). Faculty: full-time 42, part-time 27. Degrees conferred: J.D., J.D.-M.B.A. (Union College, R.P.I., St. Rose College), J.D.-M.P.A. (University at Albany).

ADMISSION REQUIREMENTS. LSDAS Law School report, Bachelor's degree, transcripts, LSAT (prior to March 15), two letters of recommendation required in support of application. Interview not required. Accepts transfer applicants on a space-available basis. Graduates of unaccredited colleges not considered. Apply to School by March 15. Fall admission only. Application fee $50. Phone: (518)445-2326; fax: (518)445-2369; e-mail: admissions@mail.als.edu.

ADMISSION STANDARDS. Selective. Accepts 60% of total applicants.

FINANCIAL AID. Scholarships, partial tuition waiver, assistantships, Federal W/S, loans. Apply to Financial Aid Director by April 15. Use FAFSA and institutional request for Financial Assistance form. Aid available for part-time students. About 85% of students receive aid other than loans from School.

DEGREE REQUIREMENTS. For J.D.: satisfactory completion of three-year program; 87 credits hour program.

ALBANY MEDICAL COLLEGE

Albany, New York 12208-3479
Web site: www.amc.edu

Founded 1839. College is part of Union University. One of the oldest medical schools in the country. Medical school is attached to Albany Medical Center Hospital. Library: 124,000 volumes, 2563 subscriptions.

Annual tuition: M.D. program resident $33,954, graduate study, full-time $14,035. Limited on-campus housing available. Total average figure for all other expenses: $7500.

Enrollment: M.D. program, first-year class 107; total 450 (men 52%, women 48%); graduate study, full-time 136, part-time 3. Faculty: M.D., full-time 54, part-time 35; Graduate Study, full-time 631, part-time 39. Degrees conferred: B.A.-M.D., B.S.-M.D. (with Union College, Siena College, and RPI), M.D., M.D.-Ph.D., Ph.D.

ADMISSION REQUIREMENTS. For M.D. program: AMCAS report, transcripts, MCAT required in support of application. Interview by invitation only. Applicants must have completed at least three years of college study. Preference given to state residents. Does not have EDP. Apply to Secretary of Admissions after June 15, before November 15 (Fall). Application fee $75. Phone: (518)445-5521; fax: (518)445-5887. For graduate study: transcripts, two letters of recommendation, interview required in support of application. GRE recommended. Accepts transfer applicants. Apply to Office of Admissions at least forty-five days prior to registration. Application fee $75. Office of Minority Affairs: (518)262-5824.

ADMISSION STANDARDS. Very competitive. Mean GPA: 3.4 (A = 4). Accepts 3–4% total annual applicants. Approximately 47% are state residents.

FINANCIAL AID. For M.D. program: scholarships. Apply to Financial Aid Committee on Scholarships and Loans by January 15. For graduate study: research fellowships/assistantships. Apply to Office of Admissions, Graduate School; no specified closing date. Use FAFSA. About 85% of medical students, 35% of graduate students receive some aid from College.

DEGREE REQUIREMENTS. For M.D.: satisfactory completion of four-year program. For M.D.-Ph.D.: Completion of 6-year program. For Ph.D.: 90 hours minimum beyond the bachelor's; preliminary exam; dissertation; final oral/written exam.

FIELDS OF GRADUATE STUDY.
Biochemistry.
Cell Biology.
Immunology.
Microbiology.
Molecular Biology.
Neurosciences.
Pathology.
Pharmacology.
Physiology.

UNIVERSITY AT ALBANY, STATE UNIVERSITY OF NEW YORK

Albany, New York 12222-0001
Web site: www.albany.edu

Founded 1844. Coed. State control. Semester system. CGS member. More than 500 computers on campus for general use. Special facilities: Albany Center for Learning Disabilities, Atmospheric Sciences Research Center, Center for Biological Macromolecules, Child Research and Study Center, Hindelang Criminal Justice Center, Center for Molecular Genetics, Center for Neuro-Biological Research, Center for Executive Development, Instructional Resources Center, Local Government Studies Center, New York State Writer's Institute, Performing Arts Center, Center for Social and Demography Analysis, Center for Stress and Anxiety Disorders, Dudly Observatory, Wadsworth Center for Laboratories and Research. Library: 1,100,000 volumes, 16,103 subscriptions, 87 PCs in all libraries.

Annual tuition; resident full-time $5100, per credit $213; non-resident full-time $8416, per credit $351. On-campus housing for 100 graduate men, 100 graduate women; none for married students. Average annual housing cost: $5872 (including board). Contact Housing Office for both on- and off-campus housing information. Phone: (518)442-5875. Day-care facilities available.

School of Graduate Studies

Graduate study since 1913. Enrollment: full-time 2265, part-time 1838 (men 40%, women 60%). University faculty: full-time 558, part-time 328. Degrees conferred: M.A., M.S., M.B.A., M.L.S., M.P.A., M.P.H., M.F.A., M.R.P., M.S.W., C.A.S., Dr.P.H., D.A., Ed.D., D.P.A., Ph.D., Psy.D.

ADMISSION REQUIREMENTS. Official transcripts required in support of School's application. GRE General/Subject Tests required for University Certificate and doctoral applicants, GMAT for business applicants. Interview required by some departments. TOEFL required for international applicants. Accepts transfer applicants. Graduates of unaccredited institutions not considered. Master's applicants apply to appropriate School or College by August 15 (Fall), January 1 (Spring), April 15 (Summer). Doctoral and University Certificate applicants apply to Office of Graduate Studies by April 30 (Fall), November 15 (Spring), March 1 (Summer). International applicants apply to School of Graduate Studies by February 1 (Fall). Application fee $50. Phone: (518)442-3980; fax: (518)442-3922; e-mail: graduate@uamail.albany.edu.

ADMISSION STANDARDS. Competitive for most departments, selective for the others. Usual minimum average: 3.0 (A = 4).

FINANCIAL AID. Annual awards from institutional funds: external assistantships, internal assistantships, internal fellows, external fellows, Federal W/S, loans. Approved for VA benefits. Apply by February 15 to appropriate department chair for fellowships, assistantships; to Financial Aid Office for all other programs. Phone: (518)442-5757. Use FAFSA. About 35% of students receive aid other than loans from School and outside sources. No aid for part-time students.

DEGREE REQUIREMENTS. For M.A., M.S.: 30 semester hours minimum, at least 24 in residence; reading knowledge of one foreign language required by some departments; thesis/non-thesis option for some departments; comprehensive exam required by some departments. For M.B.A.: 30–60 semester hours, depending on previous preparation. For M.L.S.: 36 semester hours minimum. For M.F.A.: 48 credits minimum, at least 40 in residence. For M.P.H.: 51 semester hours, at least 30 in residence; two internships required. For M.P.A.: 12 graduate courses minimum; comprehensive exam. For M.S.W.: 60 semester hours minimum, at least 30 in residence, one year in full-time attendance; research project. For C.A.S.: 48 semester hours minimum, at least 30 in residence, one semester or equivalent in full-time attendance; comprehensive exam. For Ed.D.: 75 semester hours minimum, at least 38 in residence, one year in full-time attendance; qualifying exam; dissertation. For D.P.A.: 60 credit hours minimum beyond the bachelor's; dissertation. For Ph.D.: 60 semester hours minimum, at least 30 in residence, one year in full-time attendance; competency in one or two research tools; qualifying exam; dissertation. For D.A.: 60 semester hours minimum, at least 30 in residence; research project; supervised college teaching internship; research tool; written/oral comprehensive exam.

FIELDS OF STUDY.

COLLEGE OF ARTS AND SCIENCE:
Africana Studies.
Anthropology.
Art Studio.
Atmospheric Sciences.
Biopsychology.
Cellular and Developmental Biology.
Chemistry.
Classics.
Clinical Psychology.
Cognitive Psychology.
Communication.
Computer Science.
Demography.
Ecology and Animal Science.
Economics.
English.
French Studies.
General/Experimental Psychology.
Geography.
Geological Sciences.
History.
Humanistic Studies.
Industrial/Organizational Psychology.
Italian.
Latin American and Caribbean Studies.
Liberal Studies.
Mathematics.
Molecular Biology.
Neurobiology.
Philosophy.
Physics.
Public History.
Regional Planning.
Russian.
Social Psychology.
Sociology.
Spanish.
Statistics.
Theater.
Urban Policy.
Women's Studies.

SCHOOL OF BUSINESS:
Accounting.
Business Administration. Weekend program in Saratoga, NY.
Finance.
Human Resources Information Systems.
Management.
Management Information Systems.

Organizational Studies.
Taxation.

SCHOOL OF CRIMINAL JUSTICE:
Criminal Justice. Includes nature of crime, law and social justice, administration, planned change.

SCHOOL OF EDUCATION:
Counseling Psychology.
Curriculum and Instruction.
Curriculum Planning and Development.
Educational Administration.
Educational Communication.
Educational Psychology.
Educational Psychology and Statistics.
Measurement and Evaluation.
Reading.
Rehabilitation Counseling.
School Psychology.
Special Education.
Statistic and Research Design.

SCHOOL OF INFORMATION SCIENCE AND POLICY:
Information Science.
Information Science and Policy.
Library Science.

NELSON A. ROCKEFELLER COLLEGE OF PUBLIC AFFAIRS AND POLICY:
Administrative Behavior.
Comparative and Development Administration.
Human Resource.
Information Science and Policy.
Legislative Administration.
Planning and Policy Analysis.
Political Science.
Program Analysis and Evaluation.
Public Administration.
Public Affairs and Policy.
Public Finance.
Public Management.

SCHOOL OF PUBLIC HEALTH:
Behavior Science.
Biochemistry, Molecular and Genetics.
Biostatistics.
Cell and Molecular Structure.
Environmental Chemistry.
Environmental Health.
Epidemiology.
Health Administration.
Immunobiology and Immunochemistry.
Molecular Pathogenesis.
Neurosciences.
Public Health.
Toxicology.

SCHOOL OF SOCIAL WELFARE:
Social Welfare.

ALFRED UNIVERSITY
Alfred, New York 14802
Web site: www.alfred.edu

Founded 1836. Located 70 miles S of Rochester. Coed. Private control. CGS member. These are 390 computers on campus for student use. The New York State College of Ceramics is located on campus. Special facility: College of Ceramics Library, Center for Advanced Ceramics Technology, Center for Glass Research. Library: 350,000 volumes, 1500 subscriptions.

Annual tuition: full-time $22,444. For College of Ceramics, annual tuition: $14,500. On-campus housing available on a first-come, first-served basis. Contact Assistant Dean for Student Life for on- and off-campus housing information. Phone: (607)871-2186. Total annual average housing costs: $7582.

Graduate School

Graduate study since 1947. Enrollment: full-time 189, part-time 159. University faculty teaching graduate students: full-time 72, part-time 17. Degrees conferred: M.A., M.S. in Ed., M.P.S., M.S., M.F.A., Ph.D.

ADMISSION REQUIREMENTS. Transcripts, GRE/GMAT, personal statement of objectives, two letters of recommendation required in support of application. Art portfolio required for M.F.A. and M.S.Ed. (Art). TOEFL required of foreign students. Interview required for some Programs. Accepts transfer applicants. Apply to Office of Graduate Admissions, rolling admissions process. Application fee $50. Phone: (607)871-2141, (800)541-9229; fax: (607)871-2198.

ADMISSION STANDARDS. Very selective for some departments, selective for the others. Usual minimum average: 3.0 (A = 4).

FINANCIAL AID. Annual awards from institutional funds: scholarships, full and partial tuition grants, research assistantship, teaching assistantships, Federal W/S, loans. Apply to the Graduate Admissions Office. Phone: (607)871-2159. Use FAFSA. About 80% of students receive aid from University and outside sources.

DEGREE REQUIREMENTS. For M.A. (Psychology): 52 hours minimum; oral/written qualifying exam, thesis. For M.B.A.: 55 hours minimum. For M.S. in Ed., M.P.S.: 30–36 hours minimum; thesis or master's project or final oral/written comprehensive exam.

College of Ceramics. For M.S.: 30 hours minimum; thesis; comprehensive exam. For M.F.A.: 60 hours minimum, at least two years in residence; thesis. For Ph.D.: 90 hours minimum beyond the bachelor's, at least two years in residence (105 hours for Psy.D.); qualifying exam; doctoral thesis; final oral exam.

FIELDS OF STUDY.
Art. M.F.A., M.S. in Ed.
Biomedical Materials Engineering Science. M.S.
Business Administration. M.B.A.
Ceramic Art. M.F.A.
Ceramic Engineering. M.S.
Ceramics. Ph.D.
Community Services Administration. M.P.S.
Counseling. M.S. in Ed.
Electrical Engineering. M.S.
Electronic Integrated Arts. M.F.A.
Elementary Education. M.S. in Ed.
Glass Art. M.F.A.
Glass Science. M.S., Ph.D.
Industrial Engineering. M.S.
Literacy Teacher. M.S. in Ed.
Materials Science and Engineering. M.S.
School Psychology. M.A., Psy D.
Sculpture. M.F.A.
Secondary Education. Includes art, biology, business, chemistry, earth science, English, mathematics, physics, social studies. M.S. in Ed.

ALLIANT INTERNATIONAL UNIVERSITY
San Diego, California 92131-1799
Web site: www.alliant.edu

Founded 1924. Private control. Quarter system. Multicampus institution: graduate study at Fresno, Irvine, Los Angeles, San Diego, San Francisco, Nairobi, Kenya, Mexico City, Mexico campuses. Library in San Diego about 205,000 volumes, 1200 subscriptions. Total University enrollment: 6,200.

Tuition: per unit $295–460 depending on program and location. On-campus housing available in San Diego. Average academic year housing costs: $8025 (private room), $6180 (double occupancy). Contact Director of Housing for both on- and off-campus housing information. Phone: (858)635-4592.

Graduate Programs

Enrollment (San Diego): full-time 487, part-time 336 (men 40%, women 60%). University faculty teaching graduate students: full-time 53, part-time 69. Degrees conferred: M.A., M.A.O.B., M.A.O.P., M.B.A., M.I.B.A., D.B.A., Ed.D., Psy.D.

ADMISSION REQUIREMENTS. Official transcripts, references, personal essay, GRE or MAT or GMAT required in support of School's application. On-line application available. Interview not required. International applicants must also submit evidence of proficiency in English or TOEFL and a financial statement. Accepts transfer applicants. Graduates of unaccredited institutions not considered. Apply to Director of Admissions at least six weeks prior to registration. Application fee $40. Phone: (858)635-4772; fax (858)635-4739.

ADMISSION STANDARDS. Selective. Usual minimum average: 3.0 master's; 3.2 doctorate (A = 4). TOEFL minimum score: 500.

FINANCIAL AID. Scholarships, research assistantships, internships, Federal W/S, loans. Apply to individual schools for fellowships, assistantships; to Financial Aid Office for federal programs. Phone: (858)635-4558. Use FAFSA and institutional FAF.

DEGREE REQUIREMENTS. For master's: 45 quarter units minimum, at least 35 in residence; thesis; final written exam. For D.B.A., Ed.D., Psy.D.: at least 105 quarter units beyond the master's; dissertation; final oral exam.

FIELDS OF STUDY.

CALIFORNIA SCHOOL OF ORGANIZATIONAL STUDIES:
Change Leadership. M.A., Ph.D.
Consulting Psychology. M.A., Ph.D.
Industrial/Organization Psychology. M.A., Ph.D.
Organizational Behavior. M.A.O.B.
Organizational Consulting. Psy.D.
Organizational Development. M.A., Psy D.
Organizational Psychology. M.A.O.P., Ph.D.
Organizational Studies. Psy.D.

CALIFORNIA SCHOOL OF PROFESSIONAL PSYCHOLOGY:
Clinical Psychology. M.A., Ph.D., Psy.D.
Counseling Psychology. M.A.
Marital and Family Therapy. M.A., Psy.D.
Psychopharmcology (Post-Doctoral). M.S.

COLLEGE OF ARTS AND SCIENCE:
International Relations. M.A.

GRADUATE SCHOOL OF EDUCATION:
Cross-Cultural Studies. M.A.
Educational Administration. M.A.
Educational Leadership. Ed.D.
Educational Psychology. M.A.
Teaching. M.A.
Technology and Learning. Ed.D.
TESOL. M.A., Ed.D.

SCHOOL OF SOCIAL AND POLICY STUDIES:
Culture and Human Behavior. Psy.D.
Forensic Psychology. Ph.D., Psy.D.

UNITED STATES INTERNATIONAL COLLEGE OF BUSINESS:
Business Administration. M.B.A., D.B.A.
International Business Administration. M.I.B.A.
Management and Organizational Development. M.S.

THE AMERICAN UNIVERSITY

Washington, D.C. 20016-8111
Web site: www.american.edu

Founded 1893 by an act of Congress. Located 3 miles W of downtown. CGS member. More than 600 computers on campus for student use. Coed. Private control, Methodist affiliation. University participates in Joint Graduate Consortium with Catholic, Georgetown, George Washington, Howard Universities. Special facilities: American University of Sharjah, Center for Asian Studies, Center for Congressional and Presidential Studies, Center for Global Peace, Center for the Global South, Center for Islamic Peace, Center of Slavic and Related Studies, Graduate Research Center in Europe, Intercultural Management Institute, International Institute for Health Promotion, Kogod's Center for Information, Technology and Economy, National Center for Health and Fitness. Transnational Crime and Corruption Center, Women and Politics Institute. Library: 850,000 volumes, 3600 subscriptions, plus access to on-line data retrieval services. Total enrollment: 10,000.

On-campus housing available for single and married students. Average annual cost: $7000–11,000. Apply to Housing Office. Phone: (202)885-3370. Day-care facilities available.

College of Arts and Sciences—Graduate Division

Annual tuition: $14,886. Enrollment: full-time 494, part-time 737. Faculty: full-time and part-time 235. Degrees conferred: M.A., M.S., M.F.A., Ph.D.

ADMISSION REQUIREMENTS. Transcripts, two letters of recommendation required in support of application. GRE, interview for some departments. TOEFL required of foreign students. Accepts transfer applicants. Apply to Office of Graduate Admissions by August 1 (Fall), December 1 (Spring), April 15 (Summer). Application fee $50. Phone: (202)885-1098, (202)885-6000; fax: (202)885-6014.

ADMISSION STANDARDS. Selective for most departments. Usual minimum average: 3.0 (A = 4). Accepts about 60% of applicant pool.

FINANCIAL AID. Annual awards from institutional funds: scholarships, fellowships, assistantships, grants, tuition waivers, Federal W/S, loans. Apply by January 15 to Financial Aid Office. Phone: (202)885-1098. About 60% of students receive aid other than loans from College and outside sources.

DEGREE REQUIREMENTS. For master's: 30 hours minimum, at least 24 in residence; reading knowledge of one foreign language for some departments; thesis or nonthesis option for some departments; written comprehensive exam. For Ph.D.: 72 hours minimum beyond the bachelor's, at least 42 in residence; two languages or one language and statistical or computer analysis as a research tool; three to four written comprehensives; one oral comprehensive; dissertation; final oral defense.

FIELDS OF STUDY.
Anthropology. Thesis, oral exam for M.A. M.A., Ph.D.
Art. Thesis/final project for M.A., M.F.A. Includes painting, sculpture, printmaking, art history.
Biology. Thesis, oral exam for M.S. M.A.
Chemistry. One language, thesis, oral exam for M.S. M.S., Ph.D.
Computer Science and Information Systems. M.S. only. Weekend option.
Creative Writing. M.F.A.
Economics. Includes applied, development, finance and banking, financial economics for public policy. M.A., Ph.D.
Education. M.A.T. (includes elementary, secondary, TESOL); M.A. (includes eduational leadership, educational technology, learning disabilities); Ph.D.
Environmental Science. M.S.
Ethics and Peace. M.A.
Health/Fitness Management. M.S.
History. One language for M.A. M.A., Ph.D.
Language and Foreign Studies. Includes French, Russian, Spanish, foreign language, Latin American studies, media, TESOL. M.A.
Literature. Includes literary studies. M.A.
Mathematics. Includes mathematics education, statistics, statistics for policy analysis. M.A., M.S., Ph.D.
Performing Arts. Includes dance, arts management. M.A.
Philosophy. M.A.
Philosophy and Social Policy. M.A. only.
Physics. Thesis, oral exam for M.S. M.A., M.S., Ph.D.
Psychology. M.A., Ph.D.
Sociology. Includes international training and education. Thesis, oral exam for M.A. M.A., Ph.D.
Toxicology. M.A.

Kogod College of Business Administration

Web site: www.kogod.american.edu

Established 1955. Special programs: foreign study Tokyo Keizai University, the Netherlands International Institute of Management, Université Paris Dauphine, École Supèrieure de Commerce de Nantes. Enrollment: full-time 313, part-time 268. Graduate faculty: full-time 53, part-time 37.

Tuition: fewer than 9 credit hours: $827 per credit hour; 9–13 credit hours: $851 per credit hour; 13.5–17 credit hours: $11,466 per semester. Housing is available for single and married students. Degrees conferred: M.A., M.B.A., M.S. (Acc.), M.S.T., M.B.A.-J.D., M.B.A.-M.A.I.A., M.B.A.-M.S.

ADMISSION REQUIREMENTS. Transcripts, GMAT required in support of application. TOEFL recommended for international students. Graduates of unaccredited institutions not considered. Apply to the Director of Graduate Admissions and Financial Aid by February 1. Application fee $50. Phone: (202)885-1319; fax: (202)885-1078.

ADMISSION STANDARDS. Selective. Accepts about 60% of total annual applicant pool.

FINANCIAL AID. Annual awards from institutional funds: research assistantships, scholarships, fellowships, internships, partial tuition waivers, loans. Apply to the Director of Financial Aid by February 1. Phone: (202)985-6000; fax: (202)885-6014. Use FAFSA. Aid available for part-time students. About 40% of students receive aid other than loans from School and outside sources.

DEGREE REQUIREMENTS. For M.B.A.: 54 semester hour program. For M.A., M.S., M.S.T.: 30–33 semester hour programs.

FIELDS OF STUDY.
Accounting. M.B.A., M.S.
Business Administration. M.B.A.
Business Management Information Systems.
Entrepreneurship and Management.
Finance.
Human Resource Management.
International Business. Tracks in finance, marketing, and management.
Management of Global Information Technology.
Marketing Management.
Real Estate and Urban Development.
Taxation. M.S.

School of Communication

Special programs: Center for Social Media, Film and Video Institute. Annual tuition: $14,886.

Enrollment: full- and part-time 331. Faculty: full-time 34, part-time 40. Degrees conferred: M.A., M.F.A.

ADMISSION REQUIREMENTS. Offical transcripts, GRE, 1000-word Statement of Purpose, résumé, two letters of recommendation, 3.0 GPA (A = 4), in last 60 credits required in support of application. TOEFL (minimum score 600, or 250 on computer-based version) required of international students. Accepts transfer applicants. Graduates of unaccredited institutions not considered. Apply to the Office of Admissions by November 15 (Spring), June 1 (Fall). Application fee $50. Phone: (202)885-1098.

ADMISSION STANDARDS. Selective. Usual minimum average: 2.75, 3.0 average last 60 credits (A = 4).

FINANCIAL AID. Merit-based financial aid awards available including fellowships, scholarships, assistantships; Federal W/S, loans. Approved for VA benefits. Apply by February 1 to School for merit-based aid, assistantships, fellowships; to Financial Aid Office for all other programs. Phone: (202)885-6100. Use FAFSA for all need based programs. Aid available for part-time students.

DEGREE REQUIREMENTS. For M.A.: 30–33 semester hours minimum, at least 24 in residence; written general communication and journalism comprehensive exams; thesis or two research papers.

FIELDS OF STUDY.
Broadcast Journalism.
Communication.
Film and Video Production.
Multimedia Development.
News Media Studies.
Print Journalism.
Public Communication.
Screenwriting.

School of International Service

Established 1958. Annual tuition: $14,886. On-campus housing available. Contact Director, Residential Life. Phone: (202)885-3370. Day-care facilities available.

Enrollment: full-time 540, part-time 293. Faculty: full-time 55, part-time 34. Degrees conferred: M.A., M.S., Ph.D., M.A.-M.B.A., M.A.-J.D., M.A.-M.T.S. (Wesley Theological Seminary).

ADMISSION REQUIREMENTS. Transcripts, two letters of recommendation, GRE required in support of application. TOEFL required for non-English-speaking foreign students. Graduates of unaccredited institutions not considered. Apply to the Office of Admissions by January 15 (Fall), October 1 (Spring). Rolling admissions process. Application fee $50. Phone: (202)885-6000; fax: (202)885-6014.

ADMISSION STANDARDS. Selective. Usual minimum average: 3.45, 3.0 average last 60 credits (A = 4).

FINANCIAL AID. Scholarships, fellowships, research and teaching assistantships, all federal financial aid programs. Apply to Dean of the School before March 1 for all non-Federal programs; to the Financial Aid Office before April 1 for all Federal programs. Use FAFSA. No aid for part-time students.

DEGREE REQUIREMENTS. For master's: 36–42 semester hours minimum, at least 24 in residence; proficiency in one foreign language; written comprehensive exams; thesis or two research papers. For Ph.D.: 72 semester hours, at least 30 in residence; proficiency in one foreign language; oral and written exams; dissertation; final oral exam. For M.B.A., M.T.S., J.D.: see degree requirements listed in the other graduate schools.

FIELDS OF STUDY.
Comparative and Regional Studies. M.A.
Development Management. Forty-two semester hours for M.S.
Global Environmental Policy. M.A.
International Communication. M.A.
International Development. Forty-three semester hours for M.A. M.A., Ph.D.
International Economic Policy. M.A.
International Law and Organization. J.D.-M.A.
International Politics. M.A.
International Relations. Ph.D. only.
Peace and Conflict Resolution. M.A.
U.S. Foreign Policy. M.A.
Note: Dual degrees available with Ritsuoneikan University (Kyoto, Japan), Korea University (Seoul, Korea).

School of Public Affairs

Established 1958. Annual Tuition: $14,866. Enrollment: full-time 206, part-time 239. Faculty: full-time 53, part-time 32. Degrees conferred: M.A., M.P.A., M.P.P., Ph.D.

ADMISSION REQUIREMENTS. Official transcripts, GRE, two letters of recommendation (three letters for Ph.D. applicants) required in support of application. TOEFL required of international students. GRE General/Subject Tests recommended for those who desire consideration for financial aid. Accepts transfer applicants. Graduates of unaccredited institutions not considered. Apply to the Office of Admissions by February 1 (Fall), October 1 (Spring). Application fee $55. Phone: (202)885-6000. School Contact: Phone: (202)885-6202.

ADMISSION STANDARDS. Selective. Usual minimum average: 2.75, 3.0 average last 60 credits (A = 4).

FINANCIAL AID. Fellowships, scholarships, research and teaching assistantships, tuition waivers, Federal W/S, loans. Approved for VA benefits. Apply by February 1 to School for assistantships, fellowships; to Financial Aid Office for all other programs. No aid for part-time students.

DEGREE REQUIREMENTS. For M.A.: 33 semester hours minimum, at least 24 in residence; written comprehensive exams; thesis or two research papers. For M.P.A.: 42 semester hours minimum, at least 33 in residence; written comprehensive exam. For M.P.P.: 36 credit hour program; written comprehensive exam; thesis/nonthesis option. For Ph.D.: 60–72 semester hours, at least 30 in residence; proficiency in one foreign language or proficiency in statistics, computer science; written exam; dissertation; final oral exam.

FIELDS OF STUDY.
American Politics.
Comparative Politics.
Human Resource Management. M.S.
Justice, Law and Society. M.S., Ph.D.
Policy Analysis.
Political Science. M.A., Ph.D.
Public Administration. Ph.D.
Public Policy. M.P.P.

Washington College of Law

Web site: www.wcl.american.edu

Founded 1896. ABA approved since 1940. AALS member. Semester system. Full- and part-time evening study. Law library: 462,373 volumes, 6736 subscriptions. Library has LEXIS, WESTLAW.

Annual tuition: full-time $25,312; part-time $17,797. On-campus housing limited. Total annual additional expense $13,771.

Enrollment: first-year full-time 296, part-time 96; total full-time 1006, part-time 479 (men 52%, women 48%). Faculty: full-time 51, part-time 80 (men 70%, women 30%). Degrees conferred: J.D., J.D.-M.A. (International Service), J.D.-M.B.A. (Kogod College), J.D.M.S. (Justice), LL.M. (International Legal Studies, one-year program for both U.S. and internationally trained attorneys), L.L.M. (Law and Government).

ADMISSION REQUIREMENTS. LSDAS Law School report, transcripts, LSAT, bachelor's degree required in support of application. Interview not required. Accepts transfer applications. Graduates of unaccredited colleges not considered. Apply to Director of Admission of the College after October 1, before March 1. Fall admission only. Application fee $55. Phone: (202)274-4101; fax: (202)274-4107; e-mail: wcladmit@american.edu.

ADMISSION STANDARDS. Selective. Accepts approximately 30% of total annual applicants. Gourman rating: 3.84. *U.S. News & World Report* ranking in first tier of all law schools at 49th.

FINANCIAL AID. Scholarships, fellowships loans. Apply to Director of Financial Aid by February 15. Phone: (202)885-6100. Use FAFSA. About 5% of students receive aid other than loans from College. Aid available for part-time students.

DEGREE REQUIREMENTS. For J.D.: 86 semester hours minimum, at least 28 in residence. Transfer credit individually considered. For LL.M.: at least 24 graduate credits beyond J.D. For M.A., M.B.A., M.S.: see Graduate School listing above.

ANDREWS UNIVERSITY

Berrien Springs, Michigan 49104
Web site: www.andrews.edu

Founded 1874. Located 25 miles N of South Bend, Indiana. CGS member. Coed. Private control. Seventh-Day Adventist. Semester system. Special facilities: Center for Caring, Center for College Faith, Center for Global Urban Mission, Global Church Growth Research Center, Greek Manuscript Research Center, Horn Archaeological Museum, Institute for Prevention of Addictions, Institute of Archaeology, Institute of Church Ministry, Institute of Hispanic Ministry. Library: about 684,600 volumes, 3000 subscriptions.

Tuition: per hour $525 (master's), $610 (doctoral and Ed.S). On-campus housing for 460 married students, 100 graduate men, 100 graduate women. Annual housing costs: per month $355–624. Efficiency and one-bedroom apartments for single students only. Apply to Housing Manager. Phone: (616)471-6979. Day-care facilities available.

School of Graduate Studies

Coordinates programs for College of Arts and Sciences, College of Technology, School of Business, School of Education, and SDA Theological Seminary. Enrollment: full-time 491, part-time 365. University faculty teaching graduate: full-time 162, part-time 20. Degrees conferred: M.A., M.Mus., M.S., M.S.C.L.S., M.S.M.T., M.S.P.T., M.A.T., M.B.A., M.Div., Ed.S., Ed.D., Ph.D., D.Min., Th.D.

ADMISSION REQUIREMENTS. Transcripts, GRE, recommendations required in support of application. GMAT required for business programs. TOEFL/MELAB required for foreign applicants. Accepts transfer applicants. Apply to Supervisor of Admissions at least one month prior to registration. Application fee $30. Phone: (616)471-3490 or (800)253-2874; fax: (616)471-3228; e-mail: graduate@andrews.edu.

ADMISSION STANDARDS. Selective. Usual minimum average: 2.6 (A = 4); doctoral: 3.5 (A = 4).

FINANCIAL AID. Annual awards from institutional funds: scholarships, research/teaching fellowships, Federal W/S, loans. Apply to Office of Financial Aid; no specified closing date. Phone: (616)471-3334. Use FAFSA and institutional FAF.

DEGREE REQUIREMENTS. For master's: 30–48 quarter credits minimum, at least 35 in residence; candidacy; thesis; comprehensive exam/project paper, depending upon major and degree. For doctoral degrees: 64 credit program, at least three years of study beyond bachelor's, at least three semesters in residence; candidacy; appropriate research tool; comprehensive exam; dissertation; final oral defense.

FIELDS OF STUDY.
Biology. M.S.
Business Administration. M.B.A.
Church Administration. M.S.A.
Clinical Laboratory Science. M.S.C.L.S.
Communication Interdisciplinary Studies. M.A.
Community Counseling. M.A.
Community Development. M.S.A.
Counseling Psychology. Ph.D.
Curriculum & Instruction. M.A., Ed.S., Ed.D., Ph.D.
Educational Administration & Leadership. M.A., Ed.S., Ed.D., Ph.D.
Educational & Developmental Psychology. M.A., Ed.D., Ph.D.
Elementary Education. M.A.T.
Engineering Management. M.S.A.
English. M.A.
History. M.A.
Human Nutrition. M.S.
International Development. M.S.A.
Leadership. M.A., Ed.D., Ph.D.
Ministry. M.Div., D.Min.
Music. M.A., M.Mus.
Nursing. M.S.
Pastoral Ministry. M.A.
Physical Therapy. M.S.P.T., M.P.T.
Reading Education. M.A.
Religion. M.A., Ph.D., Th.D.
Religious Education. M.A., Ed.S., Ed.D., Ph.D.
School Counseling. M.A.

School Psychology. Ed.S.
Social Work. M.S.W.
Secondary Education. M.A.T.
Software Engineering. M.S.
Theology. M.Th.
Youth Ministry. M.A.

Kinesiology.
Nursing.
Physical Therapy.
Public Administration.
Reading Specialist.
School Administration.

ANGELO STATE UNIVERSITY
San Angelo, Texas 76909
Web site: www.angelo.edu

Formerly Angelo State College, created in 1963. CGS member. 325 computers on campus for student use. Coed. Semester system. Library: 452,200 volumes, 1850 subscriptions, 37 PCs.

Annual tuition: resident $1672, nonresident $5542. Housing available for 82 married, single graduate students. Annual housing cost: $6640 (including board). Apply by July 15. Phone: (915)942-2035. Some day-care facilities available.

Graduate School
Web site: www.angelo.edu/grad/

Graduate study since 1970. Enrollment: full-time 109, part-time 302. Faculty: full-time 109, part-time 18. Degrees conferred: M.A., M.A.T., M.B.A., M.Ed., M.M.Ed., M.M.E., M.P.A., M.P.T., M.S., M.S.N.

ADMISSION REQUIREMENTS. Official transcripts, GRE/GMAT required in support of School's application. Nursing students can substitute MAT for GRE. TOEFL required for international applicants. Accepts transfer applicants. Graduates of unaccredited institutions not considered. Apply to Coordinator of Graduate Admissions by August 15 (Fall), January 5 (Spring). Application fee, $25; $50 for international applicants. Phone: (915)942-2169; fax: (915)942-2194.

ADMISSION STANDARDS. Selective. Usual minimum average: 2.5 (A = 4); or 3.0 for last 60 semester hours.

FINANCIAL AID. Fellowships, research and teaching assistantships, tuition waivers, Federal W/S, loans. Approved for VA benefits. Apply by July 15 to Dean of Graduate School for fellowships, assistantships; to Financial Aid Office for all other programs. Phone: (915)942-2246. Use FAFSA and University's FAF. Aid available for part-time students.

DEGREE REQUIREMENTS. For master's: 30–36 semester hours minimum; written/oral comprehensive exam; thesis/nonthesis option in some programs. For M.B.A.: Plan I—39 semester hours minimum; capstone course; Plan II—36 semester hours (accounting concentration).

FIELDS OF STUDY.
Animal Science.
Biology.
Business Administration. Includes accounting, computer science, management.
Communication.
Counseling Psychology.
Curriculum and Instruction.
Educational Diagnostician.
Educational Guidance and Counseling.
English.
General Psychology.
History.
Interdisciplinary Studies.
International Studies.

ANTIOCH UNIVERSITY MCGREGOR
Yellow Springs, Ohio 45387
Web site: www.mcgregor.edu

Founded 1852. Located 20 miles E of Dayton. Coed. Private control. Quarter system. Library: over 285,000 volumes, 1000 subscriptions. University has graduate campuses in Keene, New Hampshire; Los Angeles and Santa Barbara, California; Seattle, Washington.

Tuition: full-time per quarter: liberal studies $2291, conflict resolution $2678; per credit, management $317, leadership $268. No campus housing available.

The McGregor School

Graduate study since 1964. Enrollment: full- and part-time 375 (men 136, women 239). Graduate faculty: full-time 13, part-time 31. Degrees conferred: M.A., M.Ed.

ADMISSION REQUIREMENTS. Two transcripts, three letters of recommendation, goal statement, résumé, interview required in support of application. Apply to Director of Admissions at least one month prior to quarter of registration. Admits to Fall (September 1), Winter (December 1), and Summer (June 1) quarters. Application fee $25. Phone: (937)769-1818; fax: (937)769-1805; e-mail: admiss@mcgregor.edu.

ADMISSION STANDARDS. Selective. Usual minimum average: 2.5 (A = 4).

FINANCIAL AID. Scholarships, assistantships, Federal W/S, loans. Apply to Director of Admissions and Financial Aid: no specified closing date. Use FAFSA.

DEGREE REQUIREMENTS. For M.A. (Management): two years in full-time residence; program offered on Saturdays only. For other M.A.: 45–60 quarter hours; residency requirements vary by program. For M.Ed.: 45 quarter hours; internship; professional portfolio.

FIELDS OF STUDY.
Conflict Resolution. M.A.
Educational Leadership. M.Ed.
Individualized Study. M.A.
Intercultural Relations. M.A.
Liberal and Professional Studies. M.A.
Liberal Studies. M.A.
Management. M.A.
Management for Community College Professionals. M.A.

ANTIOCH LOS ANGELES
Marina del Rey, California 90292
Web site: www.antiochla.edu

Established 1972. Coed. Private control. Semester and quarter system. Library: access to on-line bibliographic databases, union catalogs, and interlibrary loan networks. The main University campus is located in Yellow Springs, Ohio. It also has graduate campuses in Keene, New Hampshire; Santa Barbara, California; Seattle, Washington.

Tuition: per credit $350. Only off-campus housing is available.

Graduate School

Enrollment: full-time 270, part-time 153. Graduate faculty: full-time 14, part-time 76. Degrees conferred: M.A.E., M.F.A., M.A.O.M., M.A.P.

ADMISSION REQUIREMENTS. Transcripts, two letters of recommendation, goal statement, interview (except Creative Writing) required in support of application. GRE/MAT may be submitted. Passing CBEST required for M.A.E. TOEFL required for all international applicants. Apply to Director of Admissions by August 4 (Fall); rolling for other quarters. Admits Fall, Winter, Spring, and Summer. Application fee $60. Phone: (310)578-1080, ext. 100; fax: (310)822-4824.

ADMISSION STANDARDS. Selective. Usual minimum average: 2.5 (A = 4).

FINANCIAL AID. Scholarships, Federal W/S, loans. Apply to Director of Financial Aid by August 4. Phone: (310)578-1080; fax: (310)822-4824. Use FAFSA.

DEGREE REQUIREMENTS. For M.A.E.: 45 quarter hour program. For M.A.P.: 72 quarter units; thesis/nonthesis option or special project. For M.A.O.M.: 60 credit program; field study project. For M.F.A.: 48–60 semester units; five-month project; teaching; final manuscript.

FIELDS OF STUDY.
Creative Writing. M.F.A.
Education. M.A.E.
Organizational Management. Includes specializations in organizational development, human resources management, leadership. M.A.O.M.
Psychology. Includes specializations in applied community psychology, child studies. M.A.P.

ANTIOCH NEW ENGLAND GRADUATE SCHOOL
Keene, New Hampshire 03431-3516
Web site: www.antiochne.ed

Coed. Private control. Three semester system. Graduate only institution. Library: 30,864 volumes, 1100 subscriptions, 23 PCs, and access to on-line bibliographic databases, union catalogs, and interlibrary loan networks. The main University campus is located in Yellow Springs, Ohio. It also has graduate campuses in Los Angeles and Santa Barbara, California; Seattle, Washington.

Tuition: per semester master's $2600–4800, doctoral program $3200–3800. Only off-campus housing is available. Average academic year housing costs: $1100 per month.

Graduate School

Enrollment: full- and part-time 820. Graduate faculty: full-time 36, part-time 89. Degrees conferred: M.A., M.Ed., M.S.H.A., M.S., Psy.D.

ADMISSION REQUIREMENTS. Two transcripts, three letters of recommendation, goal statement, interview required in support of application. Accepts transfer applicants. Graduates of unaccredited institutions not considered. Apply to Director of Admissions by December 31 (Winter), August 31 (Fall); January

15 for doctoral programs. Admits Winter, Summer, Fall for master's; Fall only for doctoral programs. Application fee $40. Phone: (603)357-6265, ext. 287; fax: (603)357-0718; e-mail: admissions@antiochne.edu.

ADMISSION STANDARDS. Selective. Usual minimum average: 2.5 (A = 4).

FINANCIAL AID. Annual awards from institutional funds: fellowships, research and teaching assistantships, traineeships, scholarships for ethnic and racial groups which are historically underrepresented, Federal W/S, loans, institutional interest-free loans. Apply to Director of Financial Aid by April 1. Use FAFSA. Aid available for part-time students.

DEGREE REQUIREMENTS. For master's: 40–60 credits, at least 30 in residence; thesis/nonthesis option or special project. For Psy.D.: 60 credits beyond an approved master's; qualifying exam; advancement to candidacy; dissertation; final oral exam.

FIELDS OF STUDY.
Administration and Supervision. M.S. only.
Applied Psychology.
Clinical Psychology. Psy.D. only.
Counseling Psychology. Includes substance abuse and addiction, marriage and family therapy, dance/movement therapy. M.A. only.
Elementary/Early Childhood Education. Includes integrated day, Waldorf, science. M.Ed.
Environmental Studies. M.S.
Foundation of Education for Experienced Educators. M.Ed.
Human Services Administration. M.H.S.A. only.
Interdisciplinary Studies. M.A. only.
Management. M.S. only.
Marriage and Family Therapy. M.A.
Resource Management and Administration. M.S. only.
Substance Abuse Counseling. M.A.

ANTIOCH SANTA BARBARA
Santa Barbara, California 93101
Web site: www.antiochsb.edu

Coed. Private control. Quarter system. Library: access to on-line bibliographic databases, union catalogs, and interlibrary loan networks. The main University campus is located in Yellow Springs, Ohio. It also has graduate campuses in Keene, New Hampshire; Los Angeles, California; and Seattle, Washington.

Tuition: full-time $4000, half-time $2400 per quarter. Only off-campus housing is available.

Graduate School

Enrollment: full-time 118, part-time 32. Graduate faculty: full-time 13, part-time 19. Degrees conferred: M.A.C.L., M.A.E., M.A.O.M., M.A.P.

ADMISSION REQUIREMENTS. Transcripts, two letters of recommendation, admissions dialogue, interview required in support of application. TOEFL (minimum score 600) required of international applicants. Accepts transfer applicants. Apply to Director of Admissions for M.A.C.L. August 1 (Fall), November 12 (Winter); for M.A.E. April 1 (Summer); for M.A.O.M. September 1 (Fall), December 1 (Winter), March 1 (Spring), June 1 (Summer); for M.A.P. in Professional Development and Career Counseling November 12 (Winter), for M.A.P. in Family and Child Studies August 1 (Fall), November 12 (Winter); rolling admissions process. Application fee $60. Phone: (805)962-8179, ext. 113; fax: (805)962-4786; e-mail: admissions@antiochsb.edu.

ADMISSION STANDARDS. Selective. Usual minimum average: 2.5 (A = 4).

FINANCIAL AID. Scholarship, tuition grants, Federal W/S, loans. Approved for VA benefits. Apply to Director of Financial Aid by August 1. Use FAFSA (School code: E00556). About 70% of students receive some sort of financial assistance.

DEGREE REQUIREMENTS. For M.A.E.: 45 credit program. For M.A.O.M.: 56–60 quarter units; thesis/nonthesis option, or special project. For M.A.C.L.: 72 quarter units; internship. For M.A.P.: 60 credit program; project.

FIELDS OF STUDY.
Clinical Psychology. M.A.C.L.
Education. Includes emphasis in social justice and educational leadership. Teaching credential or equivalent required for admission. M.A.E.
Organizational Management. M.A.O.M.
Psychology. Includes professional development, career counseling, family and child studies. M.A.P.

ANTIOCH UNIVERSITY SEATTLE
Seattle, Washington 98121
Web site: www.antiochsea.edu

Coed. Private control. Quarter system. Library: 5130 volumes, 70 subscriptions, and has access to on-line bibliographic databases, union catalogs, and interlibrary loan networks. Special program: study abroad in Egypt, Bali. The main University campus is located in Yellow Springs, Ohio. It also has graduate campuses in Keene, New Hampshire; Los Angeles, and Santa Barbara, California.
Tuition: per credit $450; $380 for Whole System Design. Only off-campus housing is available.

Graduate Programs

Enrollment: full-time 419, part-time 242. Graduate faculty: full-time 32, part-time 39. Degrees conferred: M.A., M.A.Ed., M.S.

ADMISSION REQUIREMENTS. Two transcripts, three letters of recommendation, goal statement, interview required in support of application. TOEFL (minimum score 600 or 250 on computer-based version) required for all international applicants. Accepts transfer applicants. Apply to Director of Admissions by August 16 (Fall); rolling for other semesters. Admits Winter, Spring, Summer, Fall. Application fee $60. Phone: (206)441-5352; e-mail: admissions@antiochsea.edu.

ADMISSION STANDARDS. Selective. Usual minimum average: 2.5 (A = 4).

FINANCIAL AID. Limited to Federal W/S, loans. Apply by June 15 to Director of Financial Aid. Use FAFSA.

DEGREE REQUIREMENTS. For master's: 48–70 credits, at least 30 in residence; thesis/nonthesis option or special project. For M.S.: two-year program; personal excellence project.

FIELDS OF STUDY.
Education. M.A.Ed. 48 credit program.
Environment and Community. M.A. 66 credits for degree.
Management. M.S.
Organizational Psychology. M.A. 62 credit program.
Psychology.

Whole System Design. Includes individualized degree. M.A. 70 credit minimum for degree.

APPALACHIAN STATE UNIVERSITY
Boone, North Carolina 28607
Web site: www.appstate.edu

Founded 1899. Located 120 miles NW of Charlotte. CGS member. Coed. State control. Semester system. Special facilities: Dark Sky Observatory, Center for Appalachian Studies, Early Childhood Learning Center, Center for Management Development, Western Carolina Research Center. Library: 780,000 volumes, 5000 subscriptions.
Tuition: resident per semester full-time $576, nonresident per semester full-time $4211. On-campus housing available for both single and married students. Average academic year housing cost $2340–$3100. Contact Director of Residential Life for both on- and off-campus housing information. Phone: (828)262-2160.

Cratis D. Williams Graduate School

Graduate study since 1948. Enrollment: full-time 600, part-time 514 (men 35%, women 65%). Graduate faculty: full-time 437. Degrees conferred: M.A., M.S., M.M., M.L.S., M.B.A., M.P.A., Ed.S., Ed.D.

ADMISSION REQUIREMENTS. Transcripts, three letters of recommendation, GRE/GMAT/MAT required in support of the School's application. Interview required by some departments. TOEFL required for international applicants. Accepts transfer applicants. Graduates of unaccredited institutions not considered. Apply to the Office of the Dean of Graduate Studies by August 1 (Fall), November 1 (Spring); international applicants apply by April 1 (Fall). Application fee $35. Phone: (828)262-2130; fax: (828)262-2709.

ADMISSION STANDARDS. Selective. Use 2,000 point formula (Undergraduate GPA × 400)+GRE – V + GRE – Q = 2000. Use 1050 point formula for M.B.A. (Undergraduate GPA × 200) + GMAT=Total. MAT minimum score is 41. TOEFL minimum score 550 or 233 for computer-based score.

FINANCIAL AID. Scholarships, fellowships, assistantships, grants, Federal W/S, loans. Approved for VA benefits. Apply by March 31 (Fall); October 31 (Spring) to Office of the Dean of Graduate Studies for fellowships, assistantships; to Director of Student Financial Aid for all other programs. Phone: (825)262-2190. Use FAFSA. About 60% of students receive aid other than loans from University and outside sources.

DEGREE REQUIREMENTS. For M.A.: 30–37 semester hours, exclusive of the thesis, 24 in residence; thesis/nonthesis option; written and oral comprehensive exam. For M.B.A., M.P.A.: 36 semester hour program. For M.L.S.: 37–42 credit program. For M.S.: 30 credit hours minimum with thesis. For Ed.S.: 30–36 hours beyond the master's degree. For Ed.D.: 60 hours beyond master's, one year of full-time study; comprehensive exam; internship; dissertation; oral/written exam.

FIELDS OF STUDY.
Accounting. M.S.
Appalachian Studies. M.A.
Applied Physics. M.S.
Biology. M.A.
Biology Education. M.A.
Business Administration. M.B.A.
Child Development, Birth through Kindergarten. M.A.
College Student Development. M.A.

Communication Disorders. M.A.
Community Counseling. M.A.
Computer Science. M.S.
Curriculum Specialist. M.A.
Educational Leadership. Ed.D.
Educational Media. M.A.
Elementary Education. M.A.
English. M.A.
English Education. M.A.
Exercise Science. M.A.
Family and Consumer Sciences. M.A.
Family and Consumer Sciences Education. M.A.
Geography. M.A.
Gerontology. M.A.
Higher Education. M.A., Ed.S.
History. M.A.
History Education. M.A.
Industrial Technology. M.A.
Library Science. M.L.S.
Marriage and Family Therapy. M.A.
Mathematics. M.A.
Mathematics Education. M.A.
Media Literacy. M.A.
Middle Grades Education. M.A.
Music. Includes music composition, music performance. M.M.
Music Education. M.M.
Physical Education. M.A.
Political Science. M.A.
Psychology. Includes clinical, general experimental, health, industrial/organizational and human resource management, school. Admits Fall only. M.A.
Public Administration. M.P.A.
Public History. M.A.
Reading Education. M.A.
Romance Languages. M.A.
School Administration. M.S.A.
School Counseling. M.A.
Social Science. M.S.
Special Education. M.A.
Sports Management. M.A.
Technology Education. M.A.

ARIZONA STATE UNIVERSITY

Tempe, Arizona 85287-1003
Web site: www.asu.edu

Founded 1885. Located 10 miles E of Phoenix. CGS member. Coed. State control. Semester system. Special facilities: Architecture Library, Bureau of Broadcasting with Public Broadcasting Station KAET, Center for Asian Studies, Center for Executive Development, Center for Latin American Studies, Center for Medieval and Renaissance Studies, Institute for Studies in the Arts, Cancer Research Institute, Center for Research in Engineering and Applied Sciences, Center for Environmental Studies, Exercise and Sport Research Center, Center for Meteorite Studies with Miniger Meteorite Collection, Center for Solid State Science, Fine Arts Center, Grady Gammage Center for the Performing Arts, Law Library, Music Library, Research Park, University Art Collection Library: 2,712,000 volumes; 28,100 subscriptions. Total university enrollment: 42,100.

Tuition: per credit resident $119, nonresident $405. On-campus housing for 98 graduate men and 98 graduate women; none for married students. Housing cost: per semester $1700–2400. Apply to Residential Life. Phone: (480)965-1532.

Graduate College

Organized 1937. Enrollment: full-time 4801, part-time 2132. Faculty: full-time 1831, part-time 134. Degrees conferred: M.A., M.S., M.Acc., M.Arch., M.Ed., M.E.P., M.T., M.B.A., M.C., M.C.S., M.F.A., M.H.S.A., LL.M., M.M., M.M.C., M.N.S., M.P.A., M.S.D., M.S.E., M.S.W., M.Tax., M.T.E.S.L., Ed.D., Ph.D., D.M.A., D.P.A.

ADMISSION REQUIREMENTS. Official application, two official transcripts, letters of recommendation required in support of application. Some academic departments may require additional information, e.g., GRE, GMAT, MAT. TOEFL and Financial Guarantee form required for international applicants. Accepts transfer students. Apply to the Admissions Office, Graduate College at least two months prior to registration, earlier for international applicants. Deadlines vary by degree program. Application fee $45. Phone: (480)965-6113; fax: (480)965-5158; e-mail: asugrad@asu.edu.

ADMISSION STANDARDS. Selective to very competitive. Generally students must have a minimum junior/senior average: 3.0 (A = 4). Some academic departments may require higher averages. TOEFL minimum score 550 or 213 on computer-based version required.

FINANCIAL AID. Annual awards from institutional funds: scholarships, fellowships, assistantships, grants, tuition waivers, Federal W/S, loans. Approved for VA benefits. Apply to Director of Financial Aid by July 15. Phone: (480)965-3355. Use FAFSA.

DEGREE REQUIREMENTS. For most master's: 30 semester hours minimum, at least 24 in residence; reading knowledge of one foreign language for some departments; thesis often required; final written/oral exam. For Ph.D.: normally 84 hours minimum beyond the bachelor's, at least 30 in residence, plus 24 hours dissertation and two semesters in continuous full-time attendance; comprehensive oral/written exams; dissertation; final oral exam.

FIELDS OF STUDY.
Accountancy and Information Systems. M.A.I.S.
Aerospace Engineering. M.S., M.S.E., Ph.D.
Agribusiness. Includes agribusiness management and marketing, food quality assurance. M.S. only. (Courses offered at ASU East Site.)
Anthropology. Includes archaeology, bioarchaeology, linguistic, medical anthropology, museum studies, physical anthropology, social-cultural anthropology. M.A., Ph.D.
Architecture. M.Arch. only.
Art. Includes art education, art history, ceramics, drawing, fibers, intermedia, painting, photography, printmaking, sculpture, wood. M.A., M.F.A.
Asian Languages and Civilization—Chinese/Japanese. M.A.
Bioengineering. M.S., Ph.D.
Biological Sciences. M.S. only.
Building Design. Includes computer-aided design, energy performance of buildings, facilities development and management, solar architecture. M.S. only.
Business Administration. M.B.A., Ph.D.
Chemical Engineering. Includes biomedical and clinical, chemical processing, chemical reactor, energy and material conversion, environmental control, solid state processing, transport phenomena. M.S., M.S.E., Ph.D.
Chemistry. Includes analytical, biochemistry, geochemistry, inorganic, organic, physical, solid state. M.S., M.N.S., Ph.D.
Civil Engineering. Includes environmental/sanitary, geotechnical/soil mechanics, structure, transportation, water resources/hydraulics. M.S., M.S.E., Ph.D.
Communication. M.A., Ph.D.
Communication Disorders. M.S. only.
Computer Science. M.C.S., M.S., Ph.D.

Construction. Includes facilities, management. M.S. only.

Counseling. M.C. only.

Counseling Psychology. Ph.D. only.

Counselor Education. M.Ed., Ed.D. only.

Creative Writing. M.F.A. only.

Curriculum and Instruction. M.A., M.Ed., Ed.D., Ph.D.

Dance. M.F.A. only.

Design. Includes graphics, industrial, interior. M.S.D. only.

Economics. M.S., Ph.D. only.

Educational Administration and Supervision. M.Ed., Ed.D.

Educational Leadership and Policy Studies. Ph.D. only.

Educational Psychology. M.A., M.Ed., Ph.D.

Educational Technology. Ph.D.

Electrical Engineering. M.S., M.S.E., Ph.D.

Elementary Education. Includes bilingual, educational media and computers, ESL, reading. M.Ed.

Engineering Sciences. M.S., M.S.E., Ph.D.

English. Includes comparative literature, English linguistics, literature and language, rhetoric and composition. M.A., Ph.D.

Environmental Design and Planning. Ph.D. only.

Environmental Planning. Includes landscape ecological planning, urban and regional development. M.E.P. only.

Environmental Resources. M.S. only.

Exercise Science. Includes biomechanics, physiology of exercise, psychology of exercise and sport. Ph.D. only.

Exercise Science/Physical Education. M.S. only.

Family Resources and Human Development. M.S. only.

Family Science. Ph.D. only.

French. Includes comparative literature, language and culture, literature. M.A. only.

Geography. M.A., Ph.D.

Geological Studies. M.S., M.N.S., Ph.D.

German. M.A. only.

Health Services Administration. M.H.S.A. only.

Higher and Postsecondary Education. M.Ed., Ed.D. only.

History. Includes Asian, British, European, Latin, Public, United States, U.S./Western. M.A., Ph.D.

History and Theory of Art. Ph.D. only.

Humanities. M.A. only.

Industrial Engineering. Includes human factor, information systems, operations research, organization control, quality control/reliability. M.S., M.S.E., Ph.D.

Information Management. M.S.

Justice Studies. M.S., Ph.D.

Learning and Instructional Technology. M.A., M.Ed., Ed.D., Ph.D.

Mass Communication. M.M.C. only.

Materials Engineering. M.S., M.S.E.

Materials Science. M.S.

Mathematics. M.A., M.N.S., Ph.D.

Mechanical Engineering. M.S., M.S.E., Ph.D.

Microbiology. M.S., M.N.S., Ph.D.

Molecular and Cellular Biology. M.S., Ph.D.

Music. Includes education, ethnomusicology, history, choral, instrumental, performance, theory and composition. M.A., M.M., D.M.A.

Natural Science. Includes biology, chemistry, geological mathematics, microbiology, physics, plant biology. M.N.S.

Nursing. Includes administration, adult health, community health, community mental health/psychiatric, parent–child nursing, women's health. M.S. only.

Philosophy. M.A., Ph.D.

Physical Education. M.P.E.

Physics. M.S., M.N.S., Ph.D.

Political Science. Includes American politics, comparative politics, international relations, political theory. M.A., Ph.D.

Psychology. Includes clinical, developmental, environmental, experimental, physiological, social. Ph.D. only.

Public Administration. M.P.A., D.P.A.

Public Health. M.P.H.

Recreation. Includes outdoor, administration, social/psychological aspects of leisure, tourism, and commercial. M.S. only.

Religious Studies. M.A. only.

School Library Sciences. M.A., M.Ed.

Secondary Education. Includes educational media and computers. M.Ed.

Social and Philosophical Foundations of Education. M.A. only.

Social Work. Includes advanced direct practice, planning, administration, community practice. M.S.W., Ph.D.

Sociology. M.A., Ph.D.

Spanish. Includes comparative literature, language and culture, linguistics, literature. M.A., Ph.D.

Special Education. M.Ed. only.

Speech and Hearing Sciences. Includes developmental neurolinguistic disorders, neuroauditory processes, neurogerontologic communication disorders. Ph.D. only.

Statistics. M.S. only.

Taxation. M.Tax. only.

Teaching English as a Second Language. M.TESL only.

Technology. Includes aeronautical engineering, aeronautical management, electronics engineering, graphic communication, industrial management and supervision, manufacturing engineering, mechanical engineering, welding engineering. M.S.T. only. (Courses offered at ASU East site.)

Theater. Includes scenography, theater for youth. M.A., M.F.A., Ph.D.

Zoology. M.S., M.N.S., Ph.D.

CONCURRENT AND DUAL DEGREE PROGRAMS:

M.B.A.-M.A.I.S, M.B.A.-M.Arch., M.B.A.-M.S.A., M.B.A.-M.I.M., M.B.A.-M.S. (Economics), M.B.A.-M.S. (Information Management), M.B.A.-M.Tax., M.S.E.-M.I.M.T. (Thunderbird), M.S. (Justice)-M.A. (Anthropology), M.S.N.-M.H.S.A.

College of Law (85287-7906)

Web site: www.law.asu.edu

Established 1966. ABA approved since 1974. AALS member since 1969. Semester system. Full-time day only. Special facilities: Center for the Study of Law, Science and Technology; Indian Legal Program. Library: 386,800 volumes, 3900 subscriptions. Library has LEXIS, WESTLAW.

Tuition: per semester, resident $5096, nonresident $12,552. On- and off-campus housing available for single graduate students. Total annual cost for all other expenses: $9500–11,400.

Enrollment: first year 202; full-time 501 (men 57%, women 43%). Faculty: full-time 32, part-time 20; student to faculty ratio 13.6 to 1. Degrees conferred: J.D., J.D.-M.B.A., J.D.-M.H.S.A. (Health Services Administration), J.D.-M.S. (Economics), J.D.-Ph.D. (Justice Studies).

ADMISSION REQUIREMENTS. LSDAS Law School report, transcripts, LSAT, bachelor's degree required in support of application. Interview not required. Preference given to state residents. Accepts transfer applicants on a space-available basis. Graduates of unaccredited colleges not considered. Apply to Office of Admissions after September 1, before March 1. Applicants admitted Fall only. Application fee nonresident $45. Phone (480)965-1474; fax: (480)965-7930.

ADMISSION STANDARDS. Selective. Accepts 15% of total annual applicants. Nonresidents are 24% of entering class. Gourman rating: 3.3. *U.S. News & World Report* ranking in the second tier of law schools.

FINANCIAL AID. Scholarships, grants, fellowships, assistantship, Federal W/S, state grants, loans. Median grant $3000. About 36% of student receive aid other than loans from College funds. Apply to Financial Aid Office by March 1.

DEGREE REQUIREMENTS. For J.D.: 87 semester hours minimum; transfer credit individually considered. For M.B.A., M.H.S.A., Ph.D.: see Graduate College listing above.

Graduate School of Social Work

Created 1961. Tuition: residents $99 per credit, nonresident $330 per credit. Enrollment: full-time 345, part-time 123 (men 16%, women 84%). Faculty: full-time 28, part-time 25. Degrees conferred: M.S.W., M.S.D., Ph.D.

ADMISSION REQUIREMENTS. Two transcripts, three letters of reference, GRE/MAT required in support of application. Accepts transfer applicants. TOEFL required of international applicants. Graduates of unaccredited institutions not considered. Apply to both the School of Social Work and the Graduate College by March 1; February 1 (priority deadline). Fall admission only. Application fee $45. Phone: (480)965-6081.

ADMISSION STANDARDS. Very selective. Usual minimum average: 3.0 (A = 4).

FINANCIAL AID. Annual awards from University funds: scholarships, research assistantships, teaching assistantships, out-of-state waivers, Federal W/S, loan. Apply to Graduate College by March 1. Use FAFSA. No aid for part-time students. Phone: (480)695-3355.

DEGREE REQUIREMENTS. For M.S.W.: 60 semester hours minimum, at least 30 (the second year) in full-time residence; comprehensive exam or thesis. For Ph.D.: 3–4 year full-time program; comprehensive oral/written exams; dissertation; final oral defense.

FIELDS OF STUDY
Advanced Direct Practice. M.S.W.
Planning, Administration, and Community Practice. M.S.D.
Social Work. GRE for admission. Ph.D.

ARIZONA STATE UNIVERSITY WEST
Box 37100
Phoenix, Arizona 85069-7100
Web site: www.west.asu.edu

Founded 1984. Located in northwest Phoenix. Coed. State control. Semester system. Library: 300,000 volumes; 3429 current periodicals; has links to all other ASU libraries.

Annual tuition: full-time resident $2508, nonresident $11,028; part-time six credits per semester resident $786, nonresident $2760. No on-campus housing available.

Graduate College

Enrollment: full-time 145, part-time 471. University faculty: full-time 56, part-time 44. Degrees conferred: M.A., M.B.A., M.Ed.

ADMISSION REQUIREMENTS. Official application, two official transcripts. GRE/GMAT required for some departments. TOEFL and Financial Guarantee form required for international applicants. Accepts transfer students. Apply to the Admissions Office, Graduate College at least two months prior to registration, earlier for international applicants. Application fee $45. Phone: (602)543-4567; fax: (602)543-4561; e-mail: asuwgrad@asu.edu.

ADMISSION STANDARDS. Selective. Generally students must have a minimum junior/senior average: 2.75 (A = 4). Some departments may require higher averages.

FINANCIAL AID. Annual awards from institutional funds: scholarships, assistantships, full and partial tuition waivers, Fed-

eral W/S, loans. Apply to Financial Aid Services Office by July 15. Phone: (602)543-8178. Use FAFSA.

DEGREE REQUIREMENTS. For M.A., M.Ed.: 30–36 semester hours minimum, at least 24 in residence; thesis/nonthesis option; final written/oral exam. For M.B.A.: 45 semester hour program.

FIELDS OF STUDY.
Business Administration. M.B.A.
Communication Studies. M.A.
Criminal Justice. M.A.
Educational Administration. M.Ed.
Elementary Education. Includes bilingual, educational media and computers, ESL, reading. M.Ed.
Interdisciplinary Studies. M.A.
Secondary Education. Includes educational media and computers. M.Ed.
Social Work. M.S.W.
Special Education. M.A.

THE UNIVERSITY OF ARIZONA
Tucson, Arizona 95721
Web site: www.arizona.edu

Founded 1885. Located 100 miles SW of Phoenix. CGS and AAU member. Coed. State control. Semester system. Special facilities: Agricultural Experiment Station, Arizona Arthritis Center, Arizona Cancer Center, Arizona Center on Aging, Arizona Center for Mathematical Sciences, Arizona Cooperative Fish and Wildlife Research Unit, Arizona Cooperative National Park Resources Studies Unit, Arizona Emergency Medicine Research Center, Arizona Institute for Neurogenic Communication Disorders, Arizona Poison and Drug Information Center, Arizona Remote Sensing Center, Arizona Research Laboratories, Arizona State Museum, Arizona Transportation and Traffic Institute, Arizona Veterinary Diagnostic Laboratory, Boyce Thompson Southwestern Arboretum, Bureau of Applied Research in Anthropology, Bureau of Mineral Technology, Center for Computing and Information Technology, Center for Creative Photography, Center for Electronic Packaging Research, Center for Insect Science, Center for Microcontamination Control, Center for Middle Eastern Studies, Center for Pharmaceutical Economics, Center for the Management of Information, Center for the Study of Complex Systems, Center for the Study of Higher Education, Center for Toxicology, Cooperative Extension System, Division of Economic and Business Research, Division of Neural Systems, Memory and Aging, Division of Neurobiology, Division of Social Perspectives in Medicine, Economic Science Laboratory, Engineering Experiment Station, Flandrau Science Center and Planetarium, Institute for the Study of Planet Earth, Institute of Atmospheric Physics, Jeffrey M. Golding Clinical Research Unit, Karl Eller Center for the Study of the Private Market Economy, KUAT Communications Group, Laboratory of Tree-Ring Research, Latin American Area Center, Lunar and Planetary Laboratory, Mexican American Studies and Research Center, Mineral Museum, Office of Arid Land Studies, Optical Sciences Center, Respiratory Sciences Center, Ruth E. Golding Clinical Pharmacokinetics Laboratory, Sematech Center of Excellence for Contamination/Defect Control and Assessment, Social and Behavioral Sciences Research Institute, Southwest Center, Southwest Institute for Research on Women, Southwest Retail Center, Steele Memorial Children's Research Center, Steward Observatory, USDA Forest Service Cooperative Research Unit, University Animal Care, University Heart Center, University of Arizona Museum of Art, University of Arizona Press, Water Resources Research Center, Extended University, Summer Sessions, Guadalajara Summer School in Mexico. The University Library System, 7,000,000 catalogued volumes consisting of the Main Library,

Science Library, Music Collection, the Center for Creative Photography, the Library Science Collection, College of Law Library, Health Sciences Center Library, and several others; 26,900 subscriptions. Total University enrollment: 35,000.

Tuition: resident $126 per unit; nonresident $412 per unit. On-campus housing for a limited number of graduate students, some housing for married students. Average annual (9 month) housing cost: $3000–$5200 for married students or single students. Apply to Director of Resident Life. Phone: (520)621-6500.

Graduate College

Graduate study since 1898. Enrollment: full-time 4681, part-time 1269, Graduate faculty, teaching and research: 1402. Degrees conferred: M.A., M.S., M.Acc., M.Ag.Ed., M.H.E.Ed., M.Arch., M.B.A., M.Ed., M.F.A., M.L.S., M.M., M.P.A., M.T., Ed.S., Ed.D., Ph.D.

ADMISSION REQUIREMENTS. One transcript from each institution attended required in support of application. GRE General/Subject Tests/GMAT, interview required for some majors. TOEFL required of all non-English-speaking international applicants. Graduates of unaccredited colleges not considered. Accepts transfer applicants. Apply to the Dean of Graduate College at least by June 1 (Fall), considerably earlier for most departments. Application fee for degree program $35, nondegree status $10. Phone: (520)621-3132; fax: (520)621-7112; e-mail: gradadm@lorax.admin.arizona.edu.

ADMISSION STANDARDS. Selective. Usual minimum average: 3.0 (A = 4).

FINANCIAL AID. Annual awards from institutional funds: academic scholarships, teaching assistantships, research assistantships, unspecified assistantship, Federal W/S, loans. Approved for VA benefits. Apply to appropriate department head by February 1. Phone: (520)621-1858. Use FAFSA and University FAF. About 33% of students receive aid other than loans from University and outside sources. Aid sometimes available for part-time students.

DEGREE REQUIREMENTS. For M.A., M.S.: 30 units minimum, at least 15 in residence; thesis required by many departments; reading knowledge of one or more foreign language(s) in some departments (options available in lieu of second language in some cases); final exam. For M.Acc.: 30 units minimum, at least 15 in residence; thesis optional; GMAT required. For M.Ag.Ed., M.H.E.Ed.: 32 units minimum; final research problem. For M.Arch.: 32 units minimum; three-part thesis; final oral exam. For M.B.A.: 60 units minimum, at least 30 units in residence; research project instead of thesis. Prerequisites are Mathematics 119 (Finite Mathematics) and Mathematics 123 (Elements of Calculus) or the equivalent. For M.Ed.: 32 units minimum; final exam may be written, oral, or both. For M.F.A.: major in Art—60 units minimum; thesis or original work or group of such work presented to the public. For major in Creative Writing—36 units minimum; original book-length work of fiction or poetry; final exam. For major in Drama—60 units minimum, in lieu of thesis, monograph/rehearsal, performance journal/original designer production project; final oral exam. For M.L.Arch.: 30 units minimum; thesis. For M.P.H.: a minimum of 33 units including a minimum of 3 units of internships. For M.M.: 30 units minimum; public recital for Applied Music Majors only; reading knowledge of German or French for Music History majors. For M.P.A.: 54 units minimum; optional internship or thesis. For M.T.: 32 units minimum; final written exam. For Ph.D.: 6 semesters minimum beyond bachelor's; at least 2 semesters and 30 units in full-time residence; qualifying exam; language requirement varies; pre-

liminary and oral exam; dissertation; final oral exam. For Ed.D.: essentially the same as for the Ph.D.; reading knowledge of one foreign language is required only when deemed necessary. For A.Mus.D.: essentially the same as for the Ed.D. For Ed.S.: 60 units minimum; GRE General required.

FIELDS OF STUDY.

Accounting. GMAT for admission. M.Acc., Ph.D. (Management).

Aerospace Engineering. Thesis optional for M.S.

Agricultural and Biosystems Engineering.

Agricultural and Resource Economics. Thesis for M.S. M.S. only.

Agricultural Education. One year's teaching experience for admission. M.S., M.Ag.Ed. only.

Animal Science. Thesis for M.S. M.S. only.

Anthropology. GRE for admission.

Applied and Industrial Physics. M.S.P.

Applied Biosciences. M.S.B.

Applied Mathematics.

Architecture. Bachelor's degree in architecture for admission; three-part thesis for M.Arch. M.Arch. only.

Arid Lands Resource Sciences. Ph.D. only.

Art. Portfolio for admission; thesis optional. M.A. only.

Art Education. Portfolio for admission; thesis optional. M.A. only.

Art History. One language for M.A. M.A. only.

Astronomy. GRE/Subject (Physics) for admission; written document for M.S.

Atmospheric Sciences. GRE admission. Thesis for M.S.

Bilingual/Bicultural Education. M.A., M.Ed.

Biomedical Engineering.

Botany. GRE/Subject for admission.

Business Administration. GMAT or GRE for admission.

Cancer Biology.

Chemical and Environmental Engineering. Thesis for M.S.

Chemistry. Thesis for M.S.; reading knowledge of one foreign language and thesis for M.S.

Civil Engineering. Thesis or Engineering Report for M.S.

Classics. M.A. only.

Communication. GRE for admission.

Comparative Cultural and Literary Studies.

Computer Science.

Dance. M.A., M.F.A.

Drama. Thesis for theater history and criticism. M.A., M.F.A.

East Asian Studies. M.A. only.

Ecology and Evolutionary Biology. GRE/Subject for admission.

Economics. GRE/Subject for admission.

Educational Administration/Leadership. Thesis for M.A.; GRE General/ Subject for Ph.D., Ed.D., Ed.S.

Educational Media. MAT for M.Ed., GRE for Ed.S.

Educational Psychology. GRE for admission.

Electrical and Computer Engineering. Thesis option for M.S. M.S., M.S.E., Ph.D.

Elementary Education. M.T.

Engineering Mechanics. Thesis or Engineering Report for M.S.

English. GRE/Subject for admission.

English as a Second Language. Language proficiency required for admission. M.A. only.

Entomology. GRE/Subject for admission. Thesis for M.S.

Environmental Education. M.A. only.

Epidemiology. M.S., M.P.H.

Family and Consumer Resources. M.S., Ph.D. only.

Finance. GMAT for admission; thesis or report for M.S. M.S. only.

French. GRE/Subject for admission.

Genetics. Thesis for M.S.

Geography. GRE/Subject for admission; thesis option for M.S.

Geological and Geophysical Engineering. GRE/Subject for admission; thesis for M.S.

Geosciences. GRE/Subject for admission; thesis/nonthesis optional for M.A.

German Studies. M.A., M.Ed. only.

Gerontology. M.S. only.

Higher Education. MAT or GRE for admission to doctoral programs.

History. GRE Subject for admission; one language; thesis optional for M.A.

Hydrology. Thesis for M.S.

Immunology. M.S., Ph.D.

Industrial Engineering. M.S. only.

Information Resources and Library Science. M.A. only.

Insect Science. Interdisciplinary. Ph.D. only.

Journalism. M.A. only.

Landscape Architecture. Thesis for M.L.Arch. M.L.Arch. only.

Latin American Studies. GRE Subject for admission; oral and written proficiency in Spanish/Portuguese. M.A. only.

Management. Ph.D.

Management Information Systems. GMAT or GRE for admission; proficiency in programming language. M.S. only.

Marketing. GMAT for admission. M.S. only.

Materials Science and Engineering.

Mathematical Sciences. M.S.M. only.

Mathematics. Computer programming exam for master's.

Mechanical Engineering. Thesis optional for M.S.

Media Arts. M.A. only.

Mexican American Studies. M.S.

Microbiology. GRE for admission; thesis for M.S.

Mining Engineering. GRE/Subject (Engineering); thesis for M.S.

Molecular and Cellular Biology. GRE/Subject for admission.

Music. Includes applied music, theory, music education, musicology, composition; conducting large-scale composition for A.Mus.D. in composition; three years' experience for admission to A.Mus.D. in music education; four recitals in lieu of dissertation for A.Mus.D. in performance and conducting.

Near Eastern Studies. M.A., Ph.D.

Neuroscience. M.S., Ph.D. only.

Nuclear Engineering. Thesis for M.S.

Nursing. GRE for admission.

Nutritional Sciences. M.S. only.

Nutrition and Food Sciences. M.S., Ph.D.

Optical Sciences. GRE for admission; thesis for M.S.

Pathobiology.

Pharmaceutical Sciences.

Pharmacology. GRE for admission; thesis for M.S.

Philosophy. GRE/Subject for admission.

Physics. GRE/Subject for admission; thesis for M.S.

Physiological Sciences. GRE for admission.

Planetary Sciences. GRE/Subject for admission; thesis for M.S.

Planning. M.S. only.

Plant Pathology. Thesis for M.S.

Plant Sciences.

Political Science. GRE for admission.

Psychology. GRE for admission.

Public Administration. GRE for admission; thesis or internship for M.P.A. M.P.A. only.

Public Health. Interuniversity and interdisciplinary. M.P.H.

Range Management. GRE for admission.

Reliability and Quality Engineering. M.S. only.

Renewable Natural Resources.

Resource Studies.

Russian. M.A., M.Ed. only.

School Psychology.

Second Language Acquisition and Teaching.

Sociology. GRE/Subject for admission.

Soil and Water Science. Thesis for M.S.

Spanish. GRE/Subject for admission.

Special Education and Rehabilitation. GRE/Subject for Ph.D., Ed.D., Ed.S.; thesis for M.A.

Speech and Hearing Sciences. GRE for admission.

Systems and Industrial Engineering. Ph.D. only.

Systems Engineering. Thesis for M.S. M.S. only.

Teaching and Teacher Education.

Theatre. Includes theatre studies, education (M.A.); acting, directing, design/technical (M.F.A.).

Toxicology. GRE for admission; thesis for M.S. M.S. only.

Water Resources Administration. Thesis for M.S.

Watershed Management. GRE for admission; thesis for M.S.

Wildlife and Fisheries Science. GRE/Subject for admission; thesis or professional paper for M.S. M.S., Ph.D.

Women's Studies. M.A. only.

James E. Rogers College of Law

Web site: www.law.arizona.edu

Law instruction since 1915. ABA approved since 1930. AALS member since 1931. Semester system. Full-time study only. Library: 382,000 volumes, 4449 subscriptions. Library has LEXIS, NEXIS, WESTLAW, DIALOG, OCLC.

Annual tuition: resident $5098, nonresident $12,554. On-campus housing available for single graduate students. Total annual cost for all other expenses: single students $9000, married students $12,501.

Enrollment: first-year 154; full-time 457 (men 50%, women 50%). Faculty: full-time 27, part-time 24. Student to faculty ratio 14 to 1. Degrees conferred: J.D., J.D.-M.A. (Economics, American Indian Studies, Latin American Studies, Women's Studies), J.D.-M.B.A., J.D.-M.P.H., J.D.-Ph.D. (Philosophy, Psychology, Economics), LL.M. (International Trade, Indigenous People Law and Policy).

ADMISSION REQUIREMENTS. LSDAS Law School report, transcripts, LSAT, bachelor's degree, two letters of recommendation required in support of application. Interview not required. Preference given to state residents. Accept transfer applicants. Graduates of unaccredited colleges not considered. Apply to Admissions Office after September 1, before March 1. Beginning and nonresident applicants admitted Fall only. Application fee $45. Phone (520)621-3477 fax: (520)621-9140; e-mail: admissions@law.arizona.edu.

ADMISSION STANDARDS. Selective. Accepts 25% of total annual applicants. Gourman rating: 3.3. *U.S. News & World Report* ranking in the top 40 of all law schools.

FINANCIAL AID. Scholarships, cash awards, fellowships, research assistantships, partial tuition waivers, loans. Apply to Financial Aid Office by March 1. Phone: (520)621-3477. Use FAFSA (College code: 001083). Some preference given to minority group students. About 17% of students receive aid other than loans from College funds.

DEGREE REQUIREMENTS. For J.D.: 6 semester minimum, at least the final 2 semesters in residence; 85 units. For LL.M.: at least 24 units beyond J.D. For M.A., M.B.A., M.P.A., Ph.D.: see Graduate School listing above.

College of Medicine (58724)

P.O. Box 245075

Web site: www.medicine.arizona.edu

First class entered 1967. Library: 70,000 volumes. Annual tuition: resident $9660. On-campus housing for 480 married students, for single students very limited. Average figure for all other expenses $8250.

Enrollment: first-year class, 100; total 390 (men 50%, women 50%). School faculty: full-time 247, part-time 642. Degrees conferred: M.D., M.D.-Ph.D., M.D.-M.P.H.

ADMISSION REQUIREMENTS. AMCAS report, transcripts, MCAT, Preprofessional committee evaluation, letters of recommendation, interview required in support of application. Applicants must have completed at least ninety semester units of college study. All candidates must be residents of Arizona or WICHE certified residents. Graduates of unaccredited institutions not considered. Does not have EDP. Apply to College Admissions Office after June 1, before November 1. Application fee, none. Phone: (520)626-6214; fax: (520)626-3777.

ADMISSION STANDARDS. Competitive. Accepts 41% of total resident applicants. All are state residents or certified WICHE funded residents. Gourman rating: 3.42. University's ranking by NIH was 54, total dollars awarded $89,403,532.

FINANCIAL AID. Scholarships, miniority scholarships, loans; assistantships may be available for dual degree programs. About 87% of students receive aid other than loans from College. Apply after acceptance, before May 15, to Financial Aid Office. Phone: (520)626-7145. Use FAFSA (College code: 001083).

DEGREE REQUIREMENTS. For M.D.: satisfactory completion of four-year program. For Ph.D., M.P.H.: see degree requirements above.

FIELDS OF GRADUATE STUDY.
Anatomy.
Biochemistry.
Cell Biology.
Genetics.
Immunology.
Microbiology.
Molecular Biology.
Neurosciences.
Pharmacology.
Physiology.

ARKANSAS STATE UNIVERSITY
Jonesboro, State University, Arkansas 72467
Web site: www.astate.edu

Founded 1909. CGS member. Located 60 miles NW of Memphis, Tennessee. Coed. State control. Semester system. Library: 596,300 volumes; 1775 subscriptions. There are 500 computers on campus for student use.

Annual tuition: resident $3192, per credit $133, nonresident $8040, per credit $335. On-campus housing for 217 married students, 1000 men, 1000 women. Average annual housing cost: $2750 for married students, $3030 for single students (including housing). Apply to Director of Housing. Phone: (870)972-2042.

Graduate School

Graduate study since 1995. Enrollment: full-time 244, part-time 896 (men 35%, women 65%). College faculty: full-time 269, part-time 9. Degrees conferred: M.A., M.S.A., M.S.E., M.M.E., M.M., M.R.C., M.B.A., M.P.A., M.S.Agric., M.S.M.C., M.S.N., M.C.D., S.C.C.T., Ed.S., Ed.D., Ph.D.

ADMISSION REQUIREMENTS. Transcripts required in support of application. MAT/GRE/GMAT required by some departments or programs. Interview required for Specialist and Doctoral programs. TOEFL required for international applicants. Accepts transfer applicants. Apply to Graduate Dean at least six weeks prior to registration. Application fees: $15, for international applicants $25, for doctoral applicants $35. Phone: (870)972-3209, 877-278-4723.

ADMISSION STANDARDS. Selective. Usual minimum average: 2.5 overall or 2.75 last 60 hours.

FINANCIAL AID. Annual awards from institutional funds: fellowships, research and teaching assistantships, internships, Federal W/S, loans. Apply to Dean six weeks prior to registration. Use FAFSA. Phone: (870)972-2310. About 60% of full-time students receive aid loans from other than University funds. Aid available for part-time students.

DEGREE REQUIREMENTS. For M.A.: 30 semester hours minimum, at least 24 residence; thesis for 6 semester hours; reading knowledge of one foreign language; comprehensive exam. For M.S.M.C.: same as M.A., except no language requirement. For M.S.: 30–36 semester hours minimum including thesis; reading knowledge of one foreign language or research tool; final written/oral exam. For M.B.A.; M.M., M.M.E., M.S.A., M.S.E., M.S.N., M.C.D.: 30–39 hours minimum, at least 24 in residence; thesis optional; no language requirement. For M.R.C.: 48–54 hours. For M.P.A.: 42 hours. For Ed.S., S.C.C.T.: 30 hours beyond the master's including internship or field study; admission to candidacy; final written comprehensive. For Ed.D.: 99 credit program beyond bachelor's; comprehensive exam; admission to candidacy; dissertation; oral defense. For Ph.D.: 90 credit program beyond bachelor's; one year full-time residency; qualifying exam; admission to candidacy; comprehensive exam; dissertation; oral defense.

FIELDS OF STUDY.
Agricultural Education. M.S.A.
Agriculture. M.S.A.
Art. M.A.
Biology. M.S.
Business. M.B.A.
Chemistry. M.S.
Communicative Disorders. M.C.D.
Computer Science. M.S.
Counselor Education. M.S.E.
Early Childhood Education. M.S.E., M.S.
Educational Administration. M.S.E., Ed.S.
Elementary Education. M.S.E.
English. M.A.
Environmental Sciences. Ph.D.
Exercise Science. M.S.
Health Sciences. M.S.H.S.
Heritage Studies. Ph.D.
History. M.A.
Mass Communications. M.S.M.C.
Mathematics.
Music. M.M.
Music Education. M.M.E.
Nursing. M.S.N.
Physical Therapy. M.P.T.
Political Science. M.A.
Psychology and Counseling. M.S.
Public Administration. M.P.A.
Public History. M.A.
Reading. M.S.E.
Rehabilitation Counseling. M.R.C.
Secondary Education. Most subject fields.
Sociology. M.A.
Special Education. Includes grades P–4, grades 4–12, emotionally disturbed. M.S.E.
Speech Communication and Theater Arts. M.A.
Vocational-Technical Administration. M.S.

UNIVERSITY OF ARKANSAS
Fayetteville, Arkansas 72701-1201
Web site: www.uark.edu

Founded 1871. Main campus at Fayetteville, 200 miles NW of Little Rock. In Little Rock (72201): University of Arkansas for

Medical Sciences, includes College of Health-Related Professions, Medicine, Nursing, Pharmacy, Graduate Institute of Technology (72203). CGS member. Coed. State control. Semester system. Special facilities: Agricultural Experiment Station, Engineering Experiment Station, Bureau of Business and Economic Research, Water Resources Research Center. Sponsoring University of the Oak Ridge Institute of Nuclear Studies in Tennessee. Library: 1,400,000 volumes, 16,000 subscriptions, 150 PCs in all libraries, plus access to on-line data retrieval services. More than 1400 PCs on campus for student use.

Annual tuition: full-time, resident $3384, nonresident $8010; per credit, resident $188, nonresident $445. On-campus housing for 334 married students, unlimited for single graduate students. Average annual housing cost: $4258 (including board) for single students, $3000 for married students. Contact the Residence Life and Dining services for both on- and off-campus housing information. Phone: (501)575-3951.

Graduate School

Web site: www.uark.edu/depts/gradinfo

Graduate study since 1927. Enrollment: full-time 1432, part-time 1412 (men 60%, women 40%). University faculty: full-time 844, part-time 137. Degrees conferred: M.A., M.Acc., M.A.T., M.B.A., M.F.A., M.M., M.Ed., M.S., M.S.C.E., M.S.Ch.E., M.S.E.E., M.S.I.E., M.S.M.E., M.P.A., M.T.L.M., Ed.S., Ed.D., Ph.D.

ADMISSION REQUIREMENTS. Official transcripts, three letters of recommendation required in support of School's application. GRE for marginal applicants. Interview not required. TOEFL required for international applicants. Accepts transfer applicants. Graduates of unaccredited institutions not considered. Apply to Office of Graduate Admissions; no specified closing dates. Application fee $40; $50 for international applicants. Phone: (501)575-4401; fax: (501)575-5908; e-mail: gradinfo@cavern.uark.edu.

ADMISSION STANDARDS. Selective for most departments. Usual minimum average: 2.75 (A = 4).

FINANCIAL AID. Annual awards from institutional funds: scholarships, fellowships, teaching/research assistantships, Federal W/S, loans. Approved for VA benefits. Apply to appropriate department head, normally before April 1 for assistantships; to Financial Aid Office for all other programs. Phone: (501)575-3806; fax: (501)575-7790. Use FAFSA. About 35% of students receive aid other than loans from University and outside sources. Aid available for part-time students.

DEGREE REQUIREMENTS. For M.A., M.S., M.M.: 24 semester hours minimum and thesis, or 30 hours minimum, without thesis, at least 30 weeks in residence; final written/oral exam; no language requirement in most cases. For M.B.A.: 30 hours minimum, at least 30 weeks in residence, final exam. For M.Ed.: 33 hours minimum, at least 30 weeks in residence, final exam. For M.F.A.: 60 hours minimum in residence; thesis and creative project; final written/oral exam. For Ed.S.: 60 hours minimum beyond bachelor's, 30 weeks in residence. For Ed.D.: at least three years of full-time residence beyond bachelor's or the equivalent; preliminary written/oral exam; dissertation; final oral exam. For Ph.D.: same as for Ed.D., except reading knowledge of two foreign languages required by some departments.

FIELDS OF STUDY.
Accounting. M.Acc. only.
Adult Education.
Agricultural and Extension Education. M.S. only.
Agricultural Economics. M.S. only.
Agricultural Education. M.A.T. only.
Agronomy. M.S., Ph.D. only.

Anatomy. At U. of A. M.S., Ph.D.
Animal Science. M.S., Ph.D. only.
Anthropology. M.A. only.
Applied Physics. M.S. only.
Art. M.F.A.
Biological and Agricultural Engineering. M.S., Ph.D.
Biology. M.A., M.S., Ph.D.
Business Administration. M.B.A., Ph.D. (finance, management).
Chemical Engineering. M.S., Ph.D.
Chemistry. M.S., Ph.D.
Childhood Education. M.A.T. only.
Civil Engineering. M.S., Ph.D.
Communication. M.A. only.
Communicative Disorders. M.S. only.
Comparative Literature. M.A., Ph.D.
Computer Science. M.S., Ph.D.
Computer Systems Engineering. M.S., Ph.D.
Counseling. M.S.
Counselor Education. Ph.D. only.
Creative Writing. M.F.A. only.
Curriculum and Instruction. Ph.D. only.
Drama. M.A., M.F.A.
Economics. M.A. only.
Educational Administration. M.Ed. only.
Educational Technology. M.Ed. only.
Electrical Engineering. M.S., Ph.D.
Elementary Education. M.Ed., Ed.S. only.
English. M.A., Ph.D.
Entomology. M.A. only.
Environmental Dynamics. Ph.D.
Environmental Engineering. M.S.
Food Science. M.S., Ph.D.
Foreign Languages and Literature. Includes French, German, Spanish. M.A. only.
Geography. M.A. only.
Geology. M.S. only.
Health Science. M.S. only.
Higher Education. M.Ed., Ed.S., Ed.D.
History. M.A., Ph.D.
Horticulture. M.S. only.
Human Environmental Sciences. M.S.
Industrial Engineering. M.S., Ph.D.
Information Systems. M.I.S.
Journalism. M.A.
Kinesiology. M.S., Ph.D.
Mathematics. M.A., M.S., Ph.D.
Mechanical Engineering. M.S., Ph.D.
Microelectronics-Photonics. M.S. only.
Music. M.M. only.
Operational Research. M.S. only.
Operations Management. M.S. only.
Philosophy. M.A., Ph.D.
Physical Education. M.A.T. only.
Physics. M.A., M.S., Ph.D.
Plant Pathology. M.S. only.
Plant Science. Ph.D. only.
Political Science. M.A. only.
Poultry Science. M.S., Ph.D.
Psychology. M.A., Ph.D.
Public Administration. M.P.A. only.
Public Policy. Ph.D. only.
Recreation. M.Ed. only.
Rehabilitation Counseling. M.S. only.
Secondary Education. M.Ed. only.
Sociology. M.A. only.
Special Education. M.A.T., M.Ed.
Statistics. M.S. only.
Translation. M.F.A. only.
Transportation and Logistics Management. M.T.L.M.
Transportation Engineering. M.S. only.
Vocational Education. M.A.T. only.

Robert A. Leflar Law Center
Web site: www.law.uark.edu

Established 1924. Located on main campus. ABA approved since 1926. AALS member since 1927. Semester system. Full-time day only. Library: 296,800 volumes, 2200 subscriptions. Library has LEXIS, WESTLAW. Annual tuition: resident $5752, nonresident $11,536. On- and off-campus housing available. Total annual cost for all other expenses: $11,273.

Enrollment: first-year 113; full-time 352 (men 60%, women 40%), Faculty: full-time 21, part-time 8; student to faculty ratio 14.7 to 1. Degrees conferred: J.D., J.D.-M.B.A., J.D.-M.P.A., LL.M. (Agricultural Law).

ADMISSION REQUIREMENTS. LSDAS Law School report, transcripts, LSAT (no later than February) required in support of application. Interview not required. International applicants submit TOEFL. Preference given to state residents. Accepts transfer applicants. Graduates of unaccredited colleges not considered. Apply to Director of Admissions after September 1, before April 1. Applicants admitted Fall only. Application fee: none. Phone: (501)575-3102. For LL.M.: Apply to Director of Graduate Programs.

ADMISSION STANDARDS. Selective. Accepts 50% of total annual applicants. Gourman rating: 2.86. *U.S. News & World Report* ranking is in the third tier of all law schools.

FINANCIAL AID. Scholarships, minority scholarships, grants, Federal W/S, loans. Apply by April 1 to the University's Office of Student Financial Aid. Phone: (501)575-3806. Use FAFSA. About 70% of students receive aid other than loans from School.

DEGREE REQUIREMENTS. For J.D.: satisfactory completion of three-year program: 90 semester hours; transfer credit individually considered. For LL.M.: at least 24 credits beyond the J.D. For M.B.A., M.P.A.: see Graduate School listing above.

William H. Bowen School of Law (72202-5142)
Web site: www.valr.edu

Established 1965. Located in Little Rock. ABA approved since 1969. AALS member since 1970. Semester system. Full- and part-time study. Law library: 269,900 volumes, 3536 subscriptions. Library has LEXIS, NEXIS, WESTLAW, DIALOG.

Annual tuition: resident $3718, nonresident $8424; per credit, resident $143, nonresident $324. No on-campus housing.

Enrollment: first-year class 130, total 385 (men 55%, women 45%). Faculty: full-time 21, part-time 11; student to faculty ratio 13.5 to 1. Degrees conferred: J.D., J.D.-M.B.A., J.D.-M.P.A.

ADMISSION REQUIREMENTS. LSDAS Law School report, LSAT, transcripts, bachelor's degree, three recommendations required in support of applications. Preference given to state residents. Accepts transfer applicants. Graduates of unaccredited colleges not considered. Apply to the Director of Admissions by April 1. Admits to Fall semester only. Application fee $40. Phone: (501)324-9439; fax: (501)324-9433.

ADMISSION STANDARDS. Accepts 55% of total annual applicants. Gourman rating: 2.47. *U.S. News & World Report* ranking is in the third tier.

FINANCIAL AID. Scholarships available to second- and third-year students, Federal W/S, loans. Apply to Director of Financial Aid by March 1. Phone: (501)569-3130. Use FAFSA. About 65% of full-time and 30% of part-time students receive some financial assistance.

DEGREE REQUIREMENTS. For J.D.: 87 semester hours, at least two years in residence. For M.B.A., M.P.A.: see Graduate School listing above.

College of Medicine
Web site: www.uams.edu

Established 1879. Located in Little Rock (72205-7199) and is part of the University of Arkansas for Medical Sciences. The University's NIH ranking is 98 with total dollars awarded $39,274,308. Library: 183,000 volumes, 1567 subscriptions.

Annual tuition: residents $10,080, nonresidents, $20,160. Average figure for all other expenses $10,000. On-campus housing available. Phone: (501)686-5850.

Enrollment: first-year class 144; total full-time 465 (men 57%, women, 43%). Faculty: full-time 190, part-time 190. Degrees conferred: M.D., M.D.-Ph.D. The M.S. and Ph.D. are offered through the Graduate School.

ADMISSION REQUIREMENTS. AMCAS, transcripts, MCAT, interview (all state residents), recommendations required in support of application. Admission to first-year class given almost exclusively to state residents. Apply to the Dean or AMCAS after June 1, before November 1. Does not have EDP. Application fee $50. Phone: (501)686-5354; fax: (501)686-5873.

ADMISSION STANDARDS. Selective. Accepts 30–40% of total annual applicants. Approximately 97% are state residents. Gourman rating: 3.45.

FINANCIAL AID. Scholarships, minority scholarships, loans, grants. Assistantships may be available for dual degree applicants. Apply to Dean after notification of acceptance. Use FAFSA (School code: E00600). About 85% of students receive aid other than loans from School.

DEGREE REQUIREMENTS. For M.D.: satisfactory completion of four-year program. For M.S., Ph.D.: see Graduate School listing above.

FIELDS OF GRADUATE STUDY.
Anatomy.
Biochemistry.
Microbiology.
Molecular Biology.
Neurosciences.
Pharmacology.
Physiology.

ARMSTRONG ATLANTIC STATE UNIVERSITY
Savannah, Georgia 31419
Web site: www.armstrong.edu

Founded 1935. CGS member. Public control. Semester system. Coed. Library: 187,000 volumes, 2684 subscriptions. About 160 PCs on campus for student use.

Annual tuition: full-time resident $2618, nonresident $9376; per credit, resident $94, nonresident $282. On-campus housing available for single graduate students. Average academic year housing costs: $5300 (includes board). Contact Office of Student Affairs for both on- and off-campus housing information. Phone: (912)927-5271. Total University enrollment 5500.

School of Graduate Studies

Graduate study since 1971. Enrollment: full-time 139, part-time 317. College faculty: full- and part-time 158. Degrees conferred: M.A., M.Ed., M.S.C.J., M.H.S.A., M.S.N., M.S.N.-M.H.S.A., M.S.P.T.

ADMISSION REQUIREMENT. Two official transcripts, GRE/MAT/GMAT, letter of intent required in support of application. TOEFL required for international applicants. Accepts transfer applicants. Graduates of unaccredited institutions not considered. Apply to Admissions Office at least one month prior to registration. Application fee $15. Phone: (912)927-5377; fax: (912)921-5586; e-mail: graduate@mail.armstrong.edu.

ADMISSION STANDARDS. Relatively open. Usual minimum average: 2.5 (A = 4). Minimum scores GRE 900, MAT 44, GMAT 450.

FINANCIAL AID. Regent's Opportunity grants, fellowships, assistantships, grants, out-of-state tuition waivers, Federal W/S, loans. Approved for VA benefits. Apply to the Dean's Office for assistantships; to Financial Aid Office for all other programs. Use FAFSA. Phone: (912)927-5272; fax: (912)921-7357.

DEGREE REQUIREMENTS. For master's: 30–45 semester hours minimum; at least 24–36 in residence; candidacy; thesis; comprehensive exam. For M.S.N.-M.H.S.A.: 54 credit program.

FIELDS OF STUDY.
Computer Science.
Criminal Justice.
Elementary Education.
Health Services Administration. Includes long-term care emphasis.
History.
Middle Grades Education.
Nursing. Includes adult health clinical nurse specialist, adult nurse practitioner, nursing administration.
Physical Therapy.
Public Health.
Secondary Education.
Special Education. Includes behavior disorders, learning disabilities, speech/language pathology.
Sports Medicine.

ARMSTRONG UNIVERSITY
Berkeley, California 94704-1489
Web site: www.armstrong-u.edu

Founded 1918. Located 10 miles NE of San Francisco. Coed. Private control. Semester system. Library: 24,000 volumes, 5000 microforms, 170 periodicals, 20 PCs.
Tuition: per quarter hour $325. No on-campus housing available. Contact the Student Services Office for off-campus housing information. Phone: (510)848-2500.

Graduate School of Business Administration

Enrollment: full-time 150, part-time 5. Graduate faculty: full-time 6, part-time 15. Degree conferred: M.B.A.

ADMISSION REQUIREMENTS. Official transcripts, interview required in support of School's application. TOEFL (minimum score 525) required for international applicants. Accepts transfer applicants. Apply to Director of Admissions, preferably one month prior to registration. Rolling admissions process. Application fee $35 domestic, $50 international. Phone: (510)848-7900; fax: (510)848-8935; e-mail: info@armstrong-u.edu.

ADMISSION STANDARDS. Relatively open. Usual minimum average: 2.5 (A = 4).

FINANCIAL AID. Limited loans. Approved for VA benefits. Contact the Financial Aid Office for current information. Phone: (510)848-2500; fax: (510)848-9438.

DEGREE REQUIREMENTS. For M.B.A.: 36 units minimum with an undergraduate degree in business, all in residence; final written exam.

THE SCHOOL OF THE ART INSTITUTE OF CHICAGO
Chicago, Illinois 60603-3103
Web site: www.artic.edu/saic

Founded 1866. Coed. Private control. Semester system. Associated with The Art Institute of Chicago, the Ryerson and Burnham libraries. Special facilities: Museum of the Art Institute, Center for Advanced Studies in Art and Technology. Library: 216,000 volumes, 2225 current periodicals.
Tuition: per credit $840. On-campus housing available for single students only, average cost from $6825–$8200. Contact the Student Affairs Office for off-campus housing information. Phone: (312)345-3527.

Graduate Program

Enrollment: full-time 342, part-time 133. School faculty: full-time 41, part-time 30. Degrees conferred: M.F.A., M.A.A.H., M.A.A.T., M.A.T., P.B.C., M.A.A.E., M.S.H.P., M.A.A.A.

ADMISSION REQUIREMENTS. Official transcripts, three letters of recommendation, portfolio (preferably 20 pieces, on slides), statement of purpose required in support of application. GRE required for Art History applicants. Photographs, videocassette, film for Time Arts, Video and Filmmaking. Interview and résumé required for several programs. TOEFL (TWE is required for several degree programs) required for international applicants. Apply to Office of Admission by March 1 for M.F.A. (Studio); at least two months prior to registrations for all other programs. Application fee $55. Phone: (800)232-7242.

ADMISSION STANDARDS. Very selective. Decision based primarily on general creativity and visual perception displayed in portfolio.

FINANCIAL AID. Scholarship, grants, Federal W/S, loans. Approved for VA benefits. Apply to the Director of Financial Aid by March 15. Phone: (312)899-5106; e-mail: finaid@artic.edu. Use FAFSA. About 65% of students receive aid other than loans from Institute.

DEGREE REQUIREMENTS. For the M.F.A., M.A.A.T., M.S.H.P.: 60 semester hours minimum, at least 30 in full-time residence (programs worked out with adviser); 48 semester hours in studio work, and 12 semester hours in advanced art history; thesis for M.S.H.P. For M.A.A.H., M.A.A.E.: 36 semester hours. For M.A.A.A., M.A.T.: 48 semester hours; thesis for M.A.T. For P.B.C.: 30 semester hours.

FIELDS OF STUDY.
Art and Technology. M.F.A.
Art Education. M.A.A.E.
Arts Administration. M.A.A.A.
Art Therapy. Master's only.
Ceramics. M.F.A.
Fiber and Materials Studies. M.F.A.
Film, Video and New Media. M.F.A.
Historic Preservation. M.S.H.P.
Interior Architecture. M.F.A.
Modern Art History, Theory and Criticism. M.A.
Painting and Drawing. M.F.A.
Performance Art. M.F.A.

Photography. M.F.A.
Printmedia. M.F.A.
Sculpture. Includes electronics, kinetics, holography, laser.
M.F.A.
Visual Communication. M.F.A.
Writing. M.F.A.

ASSUMPTION COLLEGE
Worcester, Massachusetts 01615-0005
Web site: www.assumption.edu.

Established 1904. Private control. Roman Catholic. Semester system. Library: 240,000 volumes, 1119 subscriptions. Tuition: per credit $352. No on-campus housing. Apply to Director of Residential Life for off-campus housing information. Phone (508)767-7505.

Graduate School

Established 1951. Enrollment: full-time 60, part-time 213. Graduate faculty: full-time 37, part-time 37. Degrees conferred: M.A., M.B.A., C.A.G.S., C.A.P.S., C.P.S.

ADMISSION REQUIREMENTS. Transcripts, two letters of recommendation (three for Psychology), personal essay, required in support of application. TOEFL (minimum score 500) required for international applicants. Graduates of unaccredited colleges not considered. Accepts transfer applicants. Rolling admissions policy. Apply to Director of Graduate Enrollment at least one month prior to registration. Application fee $30, Phone: (508)767-7365; fax: (508)799-4412.

ADMISSION STANDARDS. Selective. Usual minimum average: 2.75 overall, last 60 credits 3.0 (A = 4).

FINANCIAL AID. Fellowships, traineeships, assistantships, loans. Approved for VA benefits. Use FAFSA. Apply for assistantships to the department chair by July 1. Phone: (508)767-7387.

DEGREE REQUIREMENTS. For M.A. (Counseling Psychology): 60 credit program; internship; oral exam. For M.A. (Special Education): 30 credit program. For M.A. (Rehabilitation Counseling): 62–68 credit program; internship. For M.B.A.: 36 credits minimum, with undergraduate degree in business. For C.A.G.S., C.A.P.S.: 30 credits beyond the master's. For C.P.S.: 15 credits beyond master's.

FIELDS OF STUDY.
Business Administration. GMAT for admission. M.B.A.
Counseling Psychology. M.A.
Rehabilitation Counseling. Includes substance abuse, guidance, psychiatric rehabilitation, supervision of rehabilitation personnel and programs. M.A.
Special Education. M.A.

AUBURN UNIVERSITY
Auburn University, Alabama 36849-5122
Web site: www.auburn.edu

Founded 1856. Located 60 miles NE of Montgomery. CGS member. Coed. State control. Semester system. Special facilities: Alabama Microelectronics Science and Technology Center, Advanced Manufacturing Technology Center, Scott-Ritchey Small Animal Research Facility, The Center for the Arts and Humani-

ties, Center for Aging Studies, National Center for Asphalt Technology, Space Power Institute, Truman Pierce Institute for the Advancement of Teacher Education, Institute for Biological Detection Systems, Pulp and Paper Research and Education Center, Dauphin Island Sea and Gulf Coast Research Laboratories, International Center for Aquaculture. Library: 2,500,00 volumes, 18,919 subscriptions. Total University enrollment: 22,000.

Annual tuition: full-time resident $3050, nonresident $9150. On-campus housing for 384 married students, 700 men, 2500 women. Average annual housing cost: $5000 for married students, $2090 ($4500 including board) for single students. Apply to Director of Housing. Phone: (334)844-4580.

Graduate School

Graduate study since 1870. Enrollment: full-time 1384, part-time 1437. Graduate faculty: 993. Degrees Conferred: M.S., M.A., M.Acc., M.Ag., M.A.C.T., M.A.E., M.B.A., M.B.C., M.C., M.C.D., M.Ch.E., M.C.E., M.C.P., M.Ed., M.E.E., M.F.A., M.F., M.F.S., M.H.S., M.I.D., M.I.E., M.Mat.E., M.M.E., M.M.I.S., M.Mu., M.P.S., M.Z.S., Au.D., Ed.S., Ed.D., Ph.D.

ADMISSION REQUIREMENTS. Transcripts, GRE required in support of application. GRE Subject Test required for some master's applicants, for most doctoral applicants. GMAT required for M.B.A. Letters of recommendation required by some departments. Accepts transfer applicants. Apply to Graduate School at least six weeks prior to first day of class. Application fee $25. Phone: (334)844-4700; fax: (334)844-4348; e-mail: gradadm@auburn.edu.

ADMISSION STANDARDS. Selective; competitive for some departments.

FINANCIAL AID. Scholarships, fellowships, teaching assistantships, research assistantships, Federal W/S, loans. Apply by February 15 to Dean of the Graduate School for fellowships, to appropriate department head for assistantships. Use FAFSA. About 50% of students receive aid other than loans from University and outside sources. Aid available for part-time students.

DEGREE REQUIREMENTS. For master's: 30–45 hours, at least one semester in residence; thesis/final paper/nonthesis option; final written/oral exam. For Ed.D.: 90 hours beyond the bachelor's, at least two semesters full-time residence; preliminary exam; dissertation; final written/oral exam. For Ph.D.: 60–90 hours beyond the bachelor's, at least two semesters in full-time residence; preliminary exam; dissertation; final written/oral exam; reading knowledge of foreign language required by some departments.

FIELDS OF STUDY.
Accountancy. M.Acc.
Aerospace Engineering. M.A.E., M.S., Ph.D.
Agricultural Economics. M.Ag., M.S., Ph.D.
Agricultural Engineering. M.S., Ph.D.
Agronomy and Soils. M.Ag., M.S., Ph.D.
Anatomy Physiology and Pharmacology. M.S., Ph.D.
Animal and Dairy Sciences. Includes behavior, biochemistry and molecular biology, breeding and genetics, growth biology, microbiology, muscle foods, nutrition, reproductive biology. M.Ag., M.S., Ph.D.
Biological Sciences. Includes animal, botany, cell biology, conservation biology, developmental biology, ecology, herpetology, ichthyology, microbiology, molecular biology, neurobiology, ornithology, parasitology, physiology, population genetics, stream biology, systematics evolution, wetland biology. M.S., Ph.D.
Biomedical Sciences. Includes anatomy and histology, animal genetic disease, animal parasitology, cardiovascular physiol-

ogy, cell and molecular pathobiology, cell and molecular physiology, endocrinology, hermatology, infectious disease, membrane biophysics, neurophysiology, oncology, pathobiology, pharmacology, reproduction, large animal surgery and medicine, toxicology.

Building Science. M.B.C.

Business. M.B.A., M.S.

Chemical Engineering. M.Ch.E., M.S., Ph.D.

Chemistry. M.S., Ph.D.

Civil Engineering. M.C.E., M.S., Ph.D.

Communication. M.A., M.Com.

Communication Disorders. M.C.D., M.S., Au.D.

Community Planning. M.C.P.

Computer Science and Software Engineering. M.C.W.E., M.S., Ph.D.

Consumer Affairs. M.S.

Counseling and Counseling Psychology. Includes community agency counseling, counselor education supervision, school counseling, school psychology, school psychometry. M.Ed., M.S., Ed.S., Ed.D., Ph.D.

Curriculum and Teaching. Includes agriscience, business, early childhood, elementary, music education (vocal and instrumental), secondary science (biology, chemistry, physics), secondary mathematics, English language arts, history, French, Spanish, reading, social science studies. M.Ed., M.S., Ed.S., Ph.D.

Discrete and Statistical Sciences. M.A.M., M.P.S., M.S., Ph.D.

Economics. M.S.

Educational Foundations, Leadership and Technology. Includes administration and supervision of curriculum, adult education, educational administration, educational psychology, higher education administration, library media. M.Ed., M.S., Ed.S., Ed.D., Ph.D.

Electrical and Computer Engineering. M.E.E., M.S., Ph.D.

English. M.A., Ph.D.

Entomology. M.Ag., M.S., Ph.D.

Finance. M.S.

Fisheries and Allied Aquacultures. M.Ag., M.S., Ph.D.

Forestry and Wildlife Sciences. Includes economics, forestry, wildlife sciences. M.F., M.S., Ph.D.

Geology. M.S.

Health and Human Performance. Includes exercise science, health promotion, physical education. M.Ed., M.S., Ed.S., Ed.D., Ph.D.

History. M.A., Ph.D.

Horticulture. M.Ag., M.S., Ph.D.

Human Development and Family Studies. M.S., Ph.D.

Industrial and Systems Engineering. M.I.S.E., M.S., Ph.D.

Industrial Design. M.I.D.

Integrated Textile and Apparel Science. Ph.D.

Large Animal Surgery and Medicine. M.S., Ph.D.

Management. Includes human resource, management information systems, management information technology and innovation, organizational analysis and change. M.M.I.S., M.S., Ph.D.

Marketing and Transportation. M.S.

Materials Engineering. M.Mtl.E., M.S., Ph.D.

Mathematics. M.A.M., M.S., Ph.D.

Mechanical Engineering. M.M.E., M.S., Ph.D.

Nutrition and Food Science. M.S., Ph.D.

Pathobiology. M.S., Ph.D.

Pharmacal Science. M.S., Ph.D.

Pharmaceutical Sciences. Includes medicinal chemistry, pharmaceutics, pharmacology. Ph.D.

Pharmacy Care System. M.S., Ph.D.

Physics. M.S., Ph.D.

Physiology and Pharmacology. M.S., interdepartmental Ph.D.

Plant Pathology. M.Ag., M.S., Ph.D.

Political Science. M.A.

Poultry Science. M.Ag., M.S., Ph.D.

Psychology. M.S., Ph.D.

Public Administration. M.P.A., Ph.D.

Radiology. M.S., Ph.D.

Rehabilitation and Special Education. Includes early childhood, special education, emotional conflict, learning disability, MR transition, rehabilitation.

Small Animal Surgery and Medicine. M.S., Ph.D.

Sociology. M.A., M.S.

Statistics. M.A.M., M.P.S., M.S., Ph.D.

Textile Science and Engineering. M.S.

Zoology. M.S., M.Z.S., Ph.D.

College of Veterinary Medicine (36949-5536)

Web site: www.vetmed.auburn.edu

College began as a department in 1892, became a college in 1907.

Annual tuition: full-time resident and nonresident contract $6500, nonresident $19,500. Total other expenses: $11,000.

Enrollment: first-year class 90, total full-time 360, postgraduate 60. Faculty: full-time 84, part-time 10. Degrees conferred: D.V.M., D.V.M.-M.S., D.V.M.-Ph.D. M.S., Ph.D. are offered through the Graduate School.

ADMISSION REQUIREMENTS. VMCAS report, two transcripts (prerequisite courses must be completed by June 1), letters of recommendation, GRE (October Test), narrative statement of purpose required in support of application. Interview by invitation only. Does not accept transfer applicants. Applicants must have completed at least three years of college study. Preference given to Kentucky and state residents. Apply to the Dean after August 1, but before October 1. Application fee $35. Phone: (334)844-2685; e-mail: admiss@vetmed.auburn.edu.

ADMISSION STANDARDS. Competitive. Accepts about 30% of annual resident applicants and only 3–5% of nonresident applicants. Kentucky quota 34, nonresident quota 10 acceptees, U.S. citizens only.

FINANCIAL AID. Scholarships, loans. Apply to Office of Student Financial Aid by March 15. Use FAFSA. About 20% of students receive aid other than loans.

DEGREE REQUIREMENTS. For D.V.M.: satisfactory completion of four-year program. For M.S. and Ph.D.: see Graduate School listing above.

FIELDS OF GRADUATE STUDY.

Anatomy.

Large Animal Surgery.

Pathobiology.

Pharmacology.

Physiology.

Radiology.

Small Animal Surgery.

AUBURN UNIVERSITY AT MONTGOMERY

Montgomery, Alabama 36124-4023

Web site: www.aum.edu

Founded 1969. Coed. State control. Semester system. Library: 675,000 volumes, 790,000 microforms, 5800 current periodicals, 50 PCs.

Tuition: resident per credit $120, nonresident per credit $360. On-campus housing available. Annual housing cost: $1830–$2060 (room only) for single student; $4120 for married students. Phone: (334)244-3572. Day-care facilities available.

Graduate Studies

Enrollment: full-time 264, part-time 538 (men 40%, women 60%). Faculty: full-time 116, part-time 9. Degrees conferred: M.B.A., M.P.A., M.Ed., M.P.S., M.S.J.P.S., M.P.G., Ed.S., M.L.A. (Master of Liberal Arts). Joint Ph.D. with Auburn main campus in Public Administration.

ADMISSION REQUIREMENTS. Official transcripts, GRE/MAT/GMAT required in support of application. Interview sometimes required. Accepts transfer applicants. Graduates of unaccredited institutions not considered. Apply to Director of Admissions at least three weeks prior to registration. Application fee: none. Phone: (334)244-3614; fax: (334)244-3762.

ADMISSION STANDARDS. Selective. Usual minimum average: 2.75 (A = 4).

FINANCIAL AID. Fellowships, assistantships, Federal W/S, loans. Approved for VA benefits. Apply to appropriate department for fellowships, assistantships; to Financial Aid for all other programs. No specified closing date. Phone: (334)244-3564. Use FAFSA.

DEGREE REQUIREMENTS. For M.B.A.: 46–49 credit hours program. For M.Ed.: 30 credit hour program. For M.L.A.: 30 credit hour program; thesis. For M.S.J.P.S.: 30–36 credit hour program; thesis/comprehensive exam option. For M.P.S.: 30 credit hour program; comprehensive exam. For M.S.P.: 50–52 credit hour program; practicium. For M.P.A.: 36 credit hour program; comprehensive exam. For Ed.S.: 30 credits program beyond the master's; comprehensive exam. For Ph.D.: 39 credit program beyond master's (M.P.A.); written and oral exam; dissertation; oral defense.

FIELDS OF STUDY.

SCHOOL OF BUSINESS:
Business Administration. M.B.A.

SCHOOL OF EDUCATION:
Art Education. M.Ed.
Counseling (N–12). Includes counseling and development, school counseling.
Early Childhood Education (P–3). M.Ed., Ed.S.
Educational Leadership. Includes nonschool, educational administrator (N–12). M.Ed.
Elementary Education. (K–6). M.Ed., Ed.S.
Physical Education. Includes exercise science, general physical education (N–12). M.Ed., Ed.S.
Reading Education. Includes reading teacher. M.Ed.
Secondary Education. Includes biology, history, language arts, mathematics, social studies. M.Ed.
Special Education. Includes early childhood special education (B–6), collaborative teacher (K–6), collaborative teacher (6–12). M.Ed., Ed.S.

SCHOOL OF LIBERAL ARTS:
Liberal Arts. M.L.A.

SCHOOL OF SCIENCES:
International Relations. M.I.R.
Justice and Public Safety. M.S.J.P.S.
Political Science. M.P.S.
Psychology. M.S.P.
Public Administration. M.P.A., Ph.D.

AUGUSTA STATE UNIVERSITY
Augusta, Georgia 30910-2200
Web site: www.aug.edu

Founded 1925. Public control. Coed. Semester system. Library: 275,100 volumes, 1866 current periodicals. About 180 computers on campus for student use.

Annual tuition: per credit resident $94, nonresident $376. No on-campus housing available. For off-campus housing information contact the Office of Student Affairs. Phone: (706)773-1411.

Graduate Studies

Graduate study since 1971. Enrollment: full-time 73, part-time 240. Faculty: full-time 59, part-time 1. Degrees conferred: M.Ed., M.B.A., M.P.A., M.S., Ed.S.

ADMISSION REQUIREMENTS. Transcripts, NTE/WCET/GRE/MAT (Education, Psychology), GMAT (Business Administration), Statement of Goals (Psychology) required in support of application. TOEFL required for international applicants. Accepts transfer applicants. Graduates of unaccredited institutions not considered. Apply to Admissions Office at least four weeks, prior to beginning of semester. Application fee $20. Phone: (706)737-1405; fax: (706)667-4355.

ADMISSION STANDARDS. Selective. Usual minimum average: 2.5 (A = 4).

FINANCIAL AID. Scholarships, research assistantships, partial tuition waivers, Federal W/S, loans. Approved for VA benefits. Apply to the Office of Financial Aid. No specified closing date. Phone: (706)737-1431; fax: (706)737-1777. Use FAFSA. About 3% of students receive aid other than loans from College and outside sources.

DEGREE REQUIREMENTS. For M.B.A.: 30–33 credit hour program. For M.Ed.: 36–48 credit hour program; candidacy. For M.P.A.: 30–33 credits; internship option; candidacy; thesis/capstone paper; oral comprehensive exam. For M.S.: two year program; candidacy; internship. Ed.S.: 30 credits beyond the master's.

FIELDS OF STUDY.
Business Administration. M.B.A.
Early Childhood Education. M.Ed., Ed.S.
Educational Leadership. M.Ed.
Health and Physical Education. M.Ed.
Middle Grades Education. M.Ed., Ed.S.
Psychology. GRE for admission. Fall admission only. M.S.
Public Administration. M.P.A.
School Counseling. M.Ed.
Seconary Education. Includes English, history, mathematics, social studies. M.Ed., Ed.S.
Special Education. Includes behavior disabilities, intellectual disorders, interrelated learning disabilities. M.Ed.

AUGUSTANA COLLEGE
Sioux Falls, South Dakota 57197
Web site: www.augie.edu

Founded 1860. Coed. Private control. Lutheran affiliation. 4-1-4 system. Library: 240,000 volumes, 1050 subscriptions. More than 350 computers on campus for student use.

Tuition: per credit hour $260. Limited on-campus housing available. Contact Director of Graduate Study. Has on-campus day-care facilities.

Graduate Division

Enrollment: part-time 59. College faculty teaching graduate students: full-time 26, part-time 2. Year-round program. Degree conferred: M.A.

ADMISSION REQUIREMENTS. Transcripts, two letters of recommendation required in support of college's application. TOEFL required for foreign applicants. Accepts transfer applicants. Apply to Dean of Graduate Study at least two weeks prior to registration. Application fee $50. Phone: (605)274-4043; fax: (605)274-4450; e-mail: graduate@inst.augie.edu.

ADMISSION STANDARDS. Selective. Usual minimum average: 3.0 (A = 4).

FINANCIAL AID. Limited to scholarships, Federal W/S, loans. Apply to office of Financial Aid: no specified closing date. Phone (605)336-5216. Use FAFSA.

DEGREE REQUIREMENTS. For M.A.: 32 credits minimum, at least 16 in residence; written English proficiency; written/oral comprehensive exam; a graduate paper. No language requirement.

FIELDS OF STUDY.
Bioethics.
Elementary Education.
Nursing. Includes community health nursing.
Secondary Education.
Special Education.
Youth Educateur.

AUSTIN PEAY STATE UNIVERSITY
Clarksville, Tennessee 37040-0001
Web site: www.apsu.edu

Founded 1927. CGS member. Coed. State control. Semester system. Library: 174,500 volumes, 1790 subscriptions. More than 400 computers on campus for student use.

Annual tuition: full-time resident $3593, nonresident $9921; per credit, resident $157, nonresident $400. On-campus housing available for both married and single graduate students. Average academic year housing costs: $4800 for married students, $1900–$3500 for single students. Apply by May 1. Contact Director of Housing for both on- and off-campus housing information. Phone: (931)221-7444. Day-care facilities available.

Graduate School

Graduate study since 1952. Enrollment: full-time 176, part-time 287. Faculty: full-time 58, part-time 21. Degrees conferred: M.A., M.S., M.A.Ed., M.M., Ed.S.

ADMISSION REQUIREMENTS. Two official transcripts, GRE required in support of School's application. Interview not required. TOEFL required of international students. Accepts transfer applicants. Graduates of unaccredited institutions not considered. Apply to Dean of Graduate School by July 1 (Fall), December 1 (Spring), May 15 (Summer). Application fee $25. Phone: (931)221-7414; fax: (931)221-7641.

ADMISSION STANDARDS. Relatively open. Usual minimum average: 2.5 (A = 4).

FINANCIAL AID. Annual awards from institutional funds: minority scholarships, assistantships, Federal W/S, loans. Approved for VA benefits. Apply by April 1 to Dean of Graduate School and appropriate chair for assistantships. Phone: (931)221-7907;

fax: (931)221-6305. Use FAFSA. About 20% of students receive aid from University and outside sources. Aid available for part-time students.

DEGREE REQUIREMENTS. For master's: 32–37 semester hours minimum, at least 24 in residence and one semester full-time attendance; research course; recital, performance, comprehensive exam for some programs; thesis or research paper, literacy paper, or field study report; final written/oral exam. For Ed.S.: 30 semester hours minimum beyond the master's; special project.

FIELDS OF STUDY.
Administration and Supervision. Ed.S.
Biology. M.S.
Communication Arts. Includes general, corporate. M.A.
Curriculum and Instruction. Includes instructional technology, leadership, mathematics. M.A.Ed.
Educational Leadership Studies. M.A.Ed.
Elementary Education. M.A.Ed., Ed.S.
English. M.A.
Guidance and Counseling. M.S., Ed.S.
Health and Human Performance. Includes exercise science, gerontology, health services, sport administration. M.S.
Music. Includes education, performance. M.M.
Psychology. Includes clinical, industrial/organizational, psychological science, school. M.A., Ed.S (School).
Reading. M.A.Ed.
Secondary Education. Ed.S.

AZUSA PACIFIC UNIVERSITY
Azusa, California 91702-7000
Web site: www.apu.edu

Founded 1899. Located 25 miles E of Los Angeles. CGS member. Coed. Private control. Library: 147,000 volumes, 1400 current periodicals, 10 PCs. More than 500 computers on campus for student use.

Tuition: per credit hour $380 minimum; some degree programs cost more. No on-campus housing for graduate students. Average monthly off-campus housing costs: $700.

Graduate Studies Division

Enrollment: full-time 1170, part-time 1874. College faculty teaching graduate students: full-time 206, part-time 135. Degrees conferred: M.A., M.Ed., M.M., M.S., M.A.M.F.T., M.A.H.O.D., M.A.O.M., M.Div., M.H.R.D., M.P.H., M.S., M.A.P.S., M.B.A., Ed.D., Psy.D.

ADMISSION REQUIREMENTS. Official transcripts, references required in support of application. Interviews may be requested by some departments. TOEFL required for international applicants. Accepts transfer applicants. Graduates of unaccredited institutions not considered. Apply to the Graduate Admissions Office; no specified closing date. Application fee $45 (domestic), $65 (international). Phone: (626)812-3016; fax: (626)815-3867.

ADMISSION STANDARDS. Selective. Usual minimum average for full admission: 3.0 (A = 4) ; 2.5–2.9 needed for provisional admission.

FINANCIAL AID. Fellowships, assistantships, grants, loans. Contact the Office of Student Financial Services for further information. Use FAFSA.

DEGREE REQUIREMENTS. For master's: 32–48 semester hours, at least 26–42 hours in residence; thesis/nonthesis option;

final written/oral exam, varies according to program. For Ed.D.: 60 semester hours minimum beyond the master's, at least one year in full-time residence; qualifying exam; dissertation; final oral exam. For Psy.D.: 89 credit program; practicum; dissertation; oral defense.

FIELDS OF STUDY.

Applied Computer Science and Technology. Includes client/server technology, computer information systems, end-user support, technical programming, telecommunications. M.S.

Business Administration. Includes strategic, international, general.

Christian Business and Professional Leaders. M.B.A.

Christian Education. Includes youth ministries. M.A.

College Student Affairs. M.A.Ed.

Curriculum and Instruction in Multicultural Contexts. M.A.Ed.

Divinity. M.Div.

Educational Leadership and Administration. Includes educational administration, higher education, teaching and learning. Ed.D.

Educational Technology. M.A.

Human and Organizational Development. M.A.H.O.M.

Human Resource Development. M.H.R.D.

Marital and Family Therapy. M.A.M.F.T.

Music. Includes education, performance (conducting, instrumental, piano, vocal). M.M.

Nonprofit Leadership and Theology. M.A.

Nursing. Includes family nurse practitioner, high-risk home health nursing, parent/child, parish nursing. M.S.

Organizational Management. M.A.O.M.

Pastoral Studies. Includes urban and intercultural ministries, church development. M.A.

Physical Education. M.Ed.

Pupil Personnel Services. M.A.

School Administration. M.A.Ed.

School Librarianship. M.A.Ed.

Social Science. Includes leadership studies. M.A.

Special Education. M.A.Ed.

Teaching. M.A.Ed.

TESOL. M.A., Certificate.

BABSON COLLEGE
Babson Park, Massachusetts 02157-0310
Web site: www.babson.edu

Founded 1919. Located 12 miles from Boston. Coed. Small independent college. Semester system. Library: 130,000 volumes, 1500 subscriptions. About 350 computers on campus for student use. Total enrollment on main campus 3400.

Tuition: per credit $819. On-campus housing for married and single students. Contact the Office of Campus Life for both on- and off-campus housing information. Phone: (781)239-4438. Apply by June 15.

F.W. Olin Graduate School of Business

Enrollment: full time 451, part-time 1195. Faculty: full-time 164, part-time 58. Degree conferred: M.B.A. (one-year program, two-year program, evening program).

ADMISSION REQUIREMENTS. Official transcripts, undergraduate degree, GMAT, resume, reference, essays, interview required in support of School's application. TOEFL and official English translation of all pertinent academic documents required of international applicants. Apply to M.B.A. Admissions Office by January 15 (Spring), March 1 (Fall). Rolling admissions process. Application fee $50. Phone: (800)488-4512; fax: (781)239-4194; e-mail: mbaadmission@babson.edu.

ADMISSION STANDARDS. Selective. Usual minimum average: 3.0 (A = 4). GMAT median score: 622. *U.S. News & World Report* ranks Babson in the top 5 of all business schools for part-time study.

FINANCIAL AID. Several forms of financial assistance for full-time M.B.A. students who are U.S. citizens or permanent residents. These awards include Babson Fellows, grants, graduate assistantships, scholarships, Federal W/S, loans. Apply to the Office of Financial Aid by April 15. Phone: (781)239-4219. Use FAFSA (College code: 002121).

DEGREE REQUIREMENTS. For M.B.A.: 45–60 credit hours, depending on previous degree, experience. Advanced standing may be granted for prior business course work. Program can be completed on a full- or part-time basis.

FIELD OF STUDY.
Business Administration.

BALL STATE UNIVERSITY
Muncie, Indiana 47306-1099
Web site: www.bsu.edu

Founded 1918. Located 55 miles NE of Indianapolis. CGS member. Coed. State control. Semester system. Library: 1.4 million volumes, 700,000 microforms, plus access to on-line data retrieval services. About 1500 computers on campus for student use.

Annual tuition: full-time resident $3188, nonresident $8448; fees for part-time students vary according to number of credits: on-campus 0–3 credits $478, off-campus $141 per credit. On-campus housing for 600 married students, about 2700 men, 4300 women. Average annual housing cost: $4800 for married students, $5400 (including board) for single student. Apply to Director of Housing. Phone: (765)285-1678. Day-care facilities available.

Graduate School

Graduate study since 1932. Enrollment: full-time 911, part-time 1101. Graduate faculty: full- and part-time 624. Degrees conferred: M.A., M.A. in Ed., M.S., M.P.A., M.Arch., M.L.A., M.U.R.P., M.B.A., M.M., Ed.S., D.A., Ed.D., Ph.D.

ADMISSION REQUIREMENTS. Transcripts required in support of application. For Ed.S. and doctoral Programs: GRE, letters of recommendation required. TOEFL required for foreign applicants. Accepts transfer applicants. Graduates of unaccredited colleges not considered. Apply to Graduate School's Office of Admissions at least one month prior to registration. Application fee $25 ($35 for international students). Phone (765)285-1286; e-mail: gradschool@bsu.edu.

ADMISSION STANDARDS. Selective. Usual minimum average: 2.8 (A = 4)

FINANCIAL AID. Annual awards from institutional funds: doctoral fellowships, master's graduate assistantships for teaching, research, or appropriate assignment, Federal W/S, loans. Apply to Dean of Graduate School by March 1. Phone: (765)285-5600; fax: (765)285-2173. Use FAFSA. About 10–15% of students receive aid other than loans from University and outside sources. No aid other than loans for part-time students.

DEGREE REQUIREMENTS. For master's: 30–55 semester hours minimum (counseling 48, clinical psychology 45, TESOL 32, historical preservation 55); thesis (required for M.S., except computer science, management, information and communication sciences), research paper, creative project or departmental designated research course included in most majors. For Ed.S.: 30 semester hours minimum beyond the master's, at least 24 in residence and one semester in full-time attendance; thesis included in 30 hours; final written/oral exams. For Ed.D., Ph.D.: 55–65 semester hours beyond the master's, at least 48 in residence and two consecutive semesters, in full-time attendance; internship (counseling psychology); dissertation included in 90 hours; preliminary, final written/oral exam. For D.A.: 90 credits beyond the bachelor's; teaching internship/externship; dissertation; oral exam.

FIELDS OF STUDY.
Accounting. M.S.
Actuarial Science. M.A.
Adult and Community Education. M.A., Ed.D.
Anthropology. M.A.
Applied Gerontology. M.A.
Architecture. M.Arch.
Art. Includes studio, art education, art history. M.A.
Audiology. M.A., Au.D.
Biology. M.A. M.S.
Business Administration. M.B.A.
Business Education. M.A.Ed.
Chemistry. M.A., M.S.
Clinical Psychology. M.A.
Cognitive and Social Processes. M.A.
Communication Studies. M.A.
Computer Science. M.S.
Counseling Psychology. Ph.D.
Curriculum. M.A.Ed., Ed.S.
Dietetics. M.S.
Educational Administration and Supervision. M.A.Ed., Ed.D.
Educational Psychology. M.A.
Elementary Education. M.A.Ed., Ed.D., Ph.D.
English. M.A., Ph.D.
Executive Development for Public Services. M.A.
Exercise Science. M.A., M.S.
Family and Consumer Sciences. M.A.
General Science. M.A.
Geography. M.S.
Geology. M.A., M.S.
Health Science. M.A., M.S.
History. M.A.
Historical Preservation. M.S.
Human Bioenergetics. Ph.D.
Industrial Vocational/Technology Education. M.A.
Information and Communication Sciences. M.S.
Journalism. M.A.
Junior High/Middle School Education. M.A.Ed.
Landscape Architecture. M.L.A. only.
Linguistics. M.A.
Management. M.S.
Mathematical Statistics. M.A.
Mathematics. M.A., M.S.
Mathematics Education. M.A.Ed.
Music. Includes conducting, history and musicology, literature, music education, performance, theory and composition. M.A., M.M., D.A.
Natural Resources and Environmental Management. M.A., M.S.
Nursing. M.S.
Physical Education. M.A., M.S.
Physics. M.A., M.A.Ed., M.S.
Physiology. M.A., M.S.
Political Science. M.A.
Public Administration. M.P.A. only.
Public Relations. M.A.
School Psychology. M.A., Ph.D.
School Superintendency. Ed.S.
Science Education. Ed.D.
Secondary Education. M.A.

Social Psychology. M.A.
Sociology. M.A.
Special Education. M.A., M.A.Ed., Ed.D.
Speech Pathology. M.A.
Teaching English to Speakers of Other Language (TESOL). M.A.
Technology Education. M.A.
Urban and Regional Planning. M.U.R.P. only.
Wellness Management. M.A., M.S.

UNIVERSITY OF BALTIMORE
Baltimore, Maryland 21201-5779
Web site: www.ubalt.edu

Founded 1925. Coed. Public. Semester system. Special facilities: Hoffberger Center for Professional Ethic, Institute for Publication Design, William Donald Schaefer Center for Public Policy Studies. Library: 389,000 volumes, 8000 subscriptions. Total University enrollment 4600.

Tuition: per credit hour, resident $306, doctoral $404, tax $487; nonresident $464, doctoral $694, tax $758. No on-campus housing available.

Graduate School

Enrollment: full-time 516, part-time 960. Faculty: full- and part-time 212. Degrees conferred: M.A., M.B.A., M.P.A., M.S., Certificate, D.C.D., Psy.D., D.P.A. (offered in Washington, D.C.).

ADMISSION REQUIREMENTS. Official transcripts, three letters of recommendation, GMAT (Business) required in support of School's application. TOEFL required for international applicants. Accepts transfer applicants. Graduates of unaccredited schools not considered. Apply to the Office of Graduate Admission by July 15 (Fall), November 15 (Spring). Application fee $30. Phone: (410)837-4777; fax: (410)837-4793.

ADMISSION STANDARDS. Selective for most departments. Usual minimum average: 3.0 (A = 4).

FINANCIAL AID. Fellowships, assistantships, scholarships, Federal W/S, loans. Approved for VA benefits. Apply by April 1 to Director of Financial Aid. Use FAFSA (School code: 002102). Aid available for part-time students.

DEGREE REQUIREMENTS. For M.A., M.P.A., M.S.: 30–42 credits minimum, at least 24 in residence; thesis/research paper/field experience; final written exam. For M.B.A.: 30 credits minimum, at least 24 in residence. For Certificate: at least 30 credits beyond master's. For D.C.D.: 48 credits beyond master's minimum; written/oral qualifying exam; satisfy competency requirement; major project. For Psy.D.: 42 credits beyond master's minimum; comprehensive exam; doctoral project; practicum. For D.P.A.: 42 credits beyond master's; qualifying exam; final project.

FIELDS OF STUDY.
Accounting. M.S.
Business Administration. M.B.A.
Business/Finance. M.S.
Business/Marketing and Venturing. M.S.
Criminal Justice. M.S.
Communications Design. D.C.D.
Health Systems Management. M.S.
Human Services Administration. M.S.
Interactional Design and Informational Architecture. M.S.
Legal and Ethical Studies. M.A.
Management Information Systems. M.S.
Negotiation and Conflict Management. M.S.
Psychology. Includes applied assessment and consulting. Psy.D.
Public Administration. M.P.A., D.P.A.

Publications Design. M.A.
Taxation. M.S.

School of Law (21201-5779)

Full-time day division established 1969. Semester system. Law library 316,850 volumes, 3530 subscriptions. Library has LEXIS, CARL, and WESTLAW.

Annual tuition: full-time resident $10,116, nonresident $17,552; part-time resident $8410, nonresident $13,810. On-campus housing only.

Enrollment: first-year class, day 184, evening 85. Day division 590, evening division 299. Faculty: full-time 35, part-time 70. Student to faculty ratio 18.7 to 1. Degrees conferred: J.D., J.D.-M.B.A., J.D.-M.P.A., J.D.-M.S. (Criminal Justice), LL.M. (Taxation), J.D.-Ph.D. (Policy Science).

ADMISSION REQUIREMENTS. LSDAS Law School report, transcripts, LSAT, at least three years of college work required in support of application. Interview not required. Accepts transfer applications. Graduates of unaccredited colleges not considered. Apply to Director of Admission of the School after September 1, before April 1. Admits Fall only. Application fee $35. Phone: (410)837-4459; fax: (410)837-4450; e-mail: lwadmiss@ubmail. ubalt.edu. For LL.M., Phone: (410)837-4200.

ADMISSION STANDARDS. Selective. Accepts 45% of total annual applicants. Gourman rating: 2.58. *U.S. News & World Report* ranking is in the fourth tier of all law schools.

FINANCIAL AID. Scholarships, assistantships, Federal W/S, loans. Apply to Office of Financial Aid by April 1; submit copies to Law School Admissions Office. Use FAFSA. About 10% of students receive some form of aid.

DEGREE REQUIREMENTS. For J.D.: satisfactory completion of three-year (day) or four-year (evening) program; 90 semester hours. Transfer credit individually considered. For LL.M.: at least 24 graduate hours beyond J.D. For other master's degrees, see Graduate School listing above.

BANK STREET COLLEGE OF EDUCATION

New York, New York 10025-1120
Web site: www.bankstreet.edu/

Founded 1916. Private control. Semester system. More than 50 computers on campus for student use. Special facilities: Early Childhood Four-College Consortium, Infancy Institute, Leadership Center, Midtown West School, The Principals Institute. Library: 124,000 volumes, 1794 subscriptions.

Tuition: per credit, $960. No on-campus housing. For off-campus housing information: contact Dean's Office. Phone: (212)875-4404.

Graduate Division

Graduate study since 1930. Enrollment: full-time 313, part-time 560. Faculty: full-time 78, part-time 78. Degrees conferred: M.S. in Ed., Ed.M. Dual degrees with Hunter and Columbia schools of Social Work, Parsons School of Design.

ADMISSION REQUIREMENTS. Transcripts, references, personal essay, interview required in support of application. TOEFL required for foreign applicants. Accepts transfer applicants. Apply to Director of Admissions prior to registration. Application fee $50. Phone: (212)875-4404; fax: (212)875-4678; e-mail: gradcourse@ bankstreet.edu.

ADMISSION STANDARDS. Selective. Usual minimum average: 3.0 (A = 4).

FINANCIAL AID. Scholarships, grants, internships, Federal W/S, loans. Apply to the Director of Financial Aid by March 1. Phone: (212)875-4408; fax: (212)875-4678. Use FAFSA. About 60% of students receive aid other than loans from College and outside sources.

DEGREE REQUIREMENTS. For M.S. in Ed.: 36–57 credit hours in graduate courses and seminars; 12 credit hours in supervised fieldwork; integrative master's study. For Ed.M.: 36 credits beyond the master's.

FIELDS OF STUDY.
Bilingual Education. Includes early childhood, early childhood special and general, childhood general, middle school general and special.
Child Life.
Childhood Education. Includes general education, special education, bilingual education, museum education, literacy and childhood general education.
Early Childhood. Includes general education, special education, bilingual education.
Educational Leadership. Includes early childhood, mathematical education, museum education, supervision and administration in the visual arts (with Parsons School of Design).
Literacy. Includes reading and literacy, teaching literacy, literacy and childhood general education.
Middle School Education (Grades 5–9). Includes general education, special education, bilingual education, museum education.
Museum Education. Includes childhood (1–6), middle school (5–9).
Special Education. Includes infant and parent development, early childhood, bilingual early childhood, middle school, bilingual middle school.

BARRY UNIVERSITY

Miami, Florida 33161-6695
Web site: www.barry.edu

Founded 1940. Coed. Private control. Roman Catholic. Semester system. Library: 233,938 volumes, 2880 subscriptions. More than 250 computers on campus for student use.

Tuition: per credit hour $565, Ph.D. $665. On-campus housing for single students only. Apply to Director, Residential Life. Phone (305)899-3875, or (800)756-6000, ext. 3875. Annual housing cost: $6340–$7380.

Graduate Programs

Enrollment: full-time 1249, part-time 1624. Faculty: full-time 128, part-time 86. Degrees conferred: M.A., M.S., M.S.E.C., M.S.N., M.S.W., M.B.A., or M.B.A.-M.S.N., Ed.S., Ph.D.

ADMISSION REQUIREMENTS. Transcripts, GRE/MAT/ MCAT/ GMAT, three letters of recommendation required in support of University's application. No admission test required for Social Work. TOEFL required for foreign applicants. Interview may be required. Accepts transfer applicants. Apply to Graduate Admissions Office by August 1 (Fall), December 1 (Spring), May 1 (Summer). Application fee $30. Phone: (800)695-2279, (305)899-3112; fax: (305)899-3149; e-mail: admissions@mail. barry.edu.

ADMISSION STANDARDS. Selective. Usual minimum average 3.0 (A = 4).

FINANCIAL AID. Limited to scholarships (M.S.W.), Federal W/S, loans. Approved for VA benefits. Apply to Director of Financial Aid by May 1. Phone: (305)899-3113; fax: (305)899-3104. Use FAFSA. Aid available for part-time students.

DEGREE REQUIREMENTS. For M.A., M.S., M.S.N., M.B.A.: 30–60 semester hours minimum; final comprehensive exam for some programs. For M.S.W.: 60 semester hours, at least 30 in residence; thesis optional. For Ph.D. in Education: 62 semester hours beyond master's; dissertation; final oral/written exam. For Ph.D. in Social Work: essentially the same as for Education except 45 semester hours.

FIELDS OF STUDY.

SCHOOL OF ADULT CONTINUING EDUCATION:
Information Technology. M.S.
Liberal Studies. M.A.

SCHOOL OF ARTS AND SCIENCE:
Clinical Psychology. M.S.
Communication. M.A.
Communication, Executive. M.S.
Communication, Organizational. M.S.
Ministry. D.Min.
Pastoral Ministry for Hispanics. M.A.
Pastoral Theology. M.A.
Photography. M.A., M.F.A.
Psychology. M.S.
Theology. M.A.

D. INEZ ANDREAS SCHOOL OF BUSINESS:
Business Administration. Includes concentrations in accounting, finance, health service administration, international business, management, management information systems, marketing.
E-Commerce. M.S.E.C.

ADRIAN DOMINICAN SCHOOL OF EDUCATION:
Counseling. M.S., Ed.S.
Counseling—Leadership and Education. Ph.D.
Curriculum and Instruction. Ed.S.
Educational Computing and Technology. M.S., Ed.S.
Educational Leadership. M.S., Ed.S., Ed.D.
Educational Technology—Leadership and Education. Ph.D.
Elementary Education. M.S.
Exceptional Student Education. M.S., Ed.S., Ph.D.
Guidance and Counseling. M.S., Ed.S.
Higher Education Administration—Leadership and Education. Ph.D.
Human Resources Development and Administration. Includes leadership of not-for-profit/religious organizations. M.S.
Marital, Couple and Family Counseling/Therapy. M.S., Ed.S.
Mental Health Counseling. M.S., Ed.S.
Montessori Early Childhood and Elementary Education. M.S., Ed.S.
PreK/Primary Education. M.S.
Reading. M.S., Ed.S.
Rehabilitation Counseling. M.S., Ed.S.

SCHOOL OF GRADUATE MEDICAL SCIENCES:
Anatomy. M.S.
Physician Assistant—Clinical Medical Science. M.C.M.Sc.
Podiatric Medicine and Surgery. D.P.M.

SCHOOL OF HUMAN PERFORMANCE AND LEISURE SCIENCES:
Movement Science. Includes athletic training, biomechanics, exercise science, sport and exercise psychology. M.S.
Sport Management. M.S., M.S.S.M.-M.B.A.

SCHOOL OF NATURAL AND HEALTH SCIENCES:
Anesthesiology. M.S.
Biology. M.S.

Biomedical Sciences. M.S.
Health Services Administration. M.S.
Occupational Therapy. M.S.

SCHOOL OF NURSING:
Nursing. M.S.N., M.S.N.-M.B.A.

SCHOOL OF SOCIAL WORK:
Social Work. M.S.W., Ph.D.

BERNARD M. BARUCH COLLEGE OF THE CITY UNIVERSITY OF NEW YORK
New York, New York 10010-5585
Web site: www.baruch.cuny.edu

Established 1919. Formerly a branch of City College, became independent unit in 1968. Municipal control. Semester system. Special facilities: The Center for the Study of Business and Government, The Coexistence Center, Lawrence N. Field Center for Entrepreneurship and Small Business, Bernard L. Schwartz Communication Institute, Jewish Resource Center, YIVO Institute for Jewish Research, Newman Real Estate Institute, Subotnick Financial Services Center, Weissman Center for International Business. Library: more than 410,000 volumes, 4167 subscriptions. More than 1500 computers on campus for student use.

Tuition: per credit, city resident $185, non-city resident $320. No on-campus housing.

Graduate Study

Graduate study since 1920. Enrollment: full-time 996, part-time 1621. College faculty: full-time 453, part-time about 390. Degrees conferred: M.B.A., M.P.A., M.S.Ed., M.S.Ed. in H.E.A., M.S. in Business, Ph.D., M.B.A.-J.D. (with New York Law or Brooklyn Law).

ADMISSION REQUIREMENTS. Transcripts, two letters of recommendation, essay, GMAT (M.B.A.), GRE (M.P.A.) required in support of application. TOEFL required for international applicants. Accepts transfer applicants. Apply to Office of Graduate Admissions by July 1 (Fall), December 1 (Spring). Application fee $40. Phone: (646)312-1300; fax: (646)312-1301. E-mail for Zichlin: zichlingradadmissions@baruch.cuny.edu; for Wiessman School of Arts and Science: wsas_ graduate_ studies@ baruch. cuny.edu; for Public Affairs: spa_admissions@baruch.cuny.edu.

ADMISSION STANDARDS. Very selective. Usual minimum average: 3.0 (A = 4). Average GMAT: 540.

FINANCIAL AID. Annual awards from institutional funds: scholarships, assistantships, fellowships, tuition waivers, Federal W/S, loans. Approved for VA benefits. Apply to Office of Financial Aid by May 15 (Fall), December 20 (Spring). Use FAFSA. Phone: (212)802-2240; fax: (212)802-2256. Aid available for part-time students.

DEGREE REQUIREMENTS. For M.B.A.: 54 semester hours minimum, depending on previous academic work. For M.P.A.: 42–45 semester hours minimum, depending on previous academic work; capstone seminar; internship. M.S.: 30–36 semester hours, including specialization courses; thesis/nonthesis option. For Ph.D.: 60 semester hours minimum, at least 38 in residence and two consecutive semesters in full-time residence, one may be required in some departments; written exam; oral/written exam; research methodology; dissertation; final exam.

FIELDS OF STUDY.
Accountancy.
Business Administration.

Business Computer Information Systems.
Business Education.
Business Journalism.
Computer Information Systems.
Corporate Communication.
Economics.
Educational Administration and Supervision.
Finance.
Finance and Investments.
Health Care Administration. Joint degree with Mount Sinai Graduate Program.
Higher Education Administration.
Industrial and Organizational Psychology.
International Business.
Management. Includes entrepreneurship and small business, operations management, organizational behavior—human resource.
Marketing. Includes advertising, international marketing, marketing management.
Operations Research.
Public Administration. Includes health care policy, nonprofit administration, policy analysis and evaluation, public management.
Statistics.
Taxation.

BAYLOR COLLEGE OF MEDICINE
Houston, Texas 77030-3498
Web site: www.bcm.tmc.edu

Founded 1903. Quarter system. Private control. Library: 270,650 volumes, 4500 subscriptions. Special facilities: DeBakey Heart Center, Huffington Center for Aging, Center for Medical Ethics. No on-campus housing available. Total average figure for other expenses $12,000. NIH ranking is 15th among all U.S. institutions with 490 awards/grants worth $221,611,903.

Graduate School of Biomedical Sciences

Annual Tuition: $6000.
Enrollment: full-time 399, postdoctoral Fellows 106. Degree conferred: Ph.D.

ADMISSION REQUIREMENTS. Official transcripts, letters of recommendation, GRE General/Subject Tests required in support of application. Interview required. Accepts transfer applicants. Graduates of unaccredited colleges not considered. Apply to Office of Admissions by April 30. Application fee $35.

ADMISSION STANDARDS. Selective.

FINANCIAL AID. Fellowships, teaching/research assistantships; apply to appropriate department chair after acceptance.

DEGREE REQUIREMENTS. For Ph.D.: 108 quarter hours minimum; preliminary exam; thesis; final oral exam.

FIELDS OF STUDY.
Audiology and Bioacoustics.
Biochemistry.
Biomedical Engineering (with Rice University).
Biophysics.
Cardiovascular Sciences.
Cell and Molecular Biology.
Developmental Biology.
Human Genetics.
Microbiology.
Molecular Physiology and Biophysics.
Molecular Virology.
Neuroscience.
Pharmacology.

Baylor College of Medicine

Special program: Medical Scientist Training Program.
Annual tuition: M.D. program, resident $6550, nonresident $19,650; student fees $1559.
Enrollment: M.D. program, first-year class 168 (EDP 5), total 790 (men 53%, women 47%). Faculty: full-time 1710, part-time 1778. Degrees conferred: M.D., M.D.-M.D.A. (Rice University), M.D.-Ph.D.

ADMISSION REQUIREMENTS. Official transcripts, MCAT required in support of application. Interview required of final candidates. Preference given to state residents. Accepts transfer applicants from both U.S. and foreign schools. Graduates of unaccredited colleges not considered. Does have EDP; apply between June 1 and August 1. Apply to Director of Admissions after June 1, before November 1. Application fee $35. Phone: (713)798-4842; fax: (713)798-5563.

ADMISSION STANDARDS. Competitive. Accepts about 15% of total annual applicants. M.D. mean GPA: 3.8 (A = 4), average MCAT: 34. *U.S. News & World Report* ranked Baylor 13th of U.S. Medical Schools and 27th for Primary Care. Approximately 65% are state residents.

FINANCIAL AID. For M.D. program: limited. Apply to Financial Aid Office after acceptance. About 90% of students receive aid other than loans from College.

DEGREE REQUIREMENTS. For M.D.: satisfactory completion of four-year program.

BAYLOR UNIVERSITY
Waco, Texas 76798
Web site: www.baylor.edu

Founded 1845. CGS member. Located 90 miles S of Dallas/ Fort Worth. Coed. Private control. Semester system. Special facilities: Glassock Energy Center, Institute of Environmental Studies, Institute for Famine Research and Alternative Agriculture, Van de Graaff accelerator laboratory. Library: 1,531,000 volumes, 9100 subscriptions. More than 1300 computers on campus for student use. Total University enrollment: 12,200.
Annual tuition: full-time $6390, per credit $355. On-campus housing available for graduate students. Average academic year housing costs: $4800 (including board) for single students, $3800 for married students. Contact Office of the Dean for Campus Life for both on- and off-campus housing. Phone: (254)710-3642, (254)710-1761.

Graduate School

Enrollment: full-time 920, part-time 353. Faculty: full-time 350, part-time 0. Degrees conferred: M.A., M.B.A., M.B.A.-M.I.M., M.C.G., M.E.S., M.F.A., M.H.A., M.M., M.S., M.S.G., M.S.Ed., M.S.E.C., M.S.S.P.A., M.T., M.P.P.A., M.P.T., M.I.J., Ed.S., Ed.D., Psy.D., Ph.D.

ADMISSION REQUIREMENTS. Official transcripts required in support of School's application. GRE required for many departments, GRE Subject Test for some departments, GMAT for business. Interview required for some departments. TOEFL (minimum score 550, 213 for computer-based version; 600, 250 for Business) required for international students. Accepts transfer students. Graduates of unaccredited institutions not considered. Apply to Office of Graduate School at least forty-five days prior to registration. Rolling admissions process. Application fee $25, $50 for Business. Phone: (254)710-6555; fax: (254)710-1173; e-mail: graduate_school@baylor.edu.

ADMISSION STANDARDS. Selective to very competitive. Usual minimum average: 2.75 (A = 4); minimum GRE combined score 1000.

FINANCIAL AID. Annual awards from institutional funds: fellowships, teaching assistantships, research assistantships, general duties assistantships, full and partial tuition waivers, Federal W/S, loans. Approved for VA benefits. Apply to appropriate department chair for fellowships, assistantships; to Director of Student Financial Aid for all other programs. No specified closing date. Phone: (254)710-2611. Use FAFSA. About 70% of students receive aid from School and outside sources.

DEGREE REQUIREMENTS. For M.A., M.M., M.S.: 30 credit hours minimum, at least 24 in residence; thesis/nonthesis option, comprehensive oral exam; reading knowledge of one foreign language for some programs. For M.S. in professional fields: 30 credit hours minimum, at least 24 in residence; thesis/nonthesis option; comprehensive exam. For M.B.A.: 36 credit hours minimum, at least 30 in residence. For Ed.S.: 30 credit hours minimum beyond master's. For Ph.D.: 78 credit hours minimum beyond the bachelor's, at least 48 in residence and two consecutive semesters in full-time attendance; reading knowledge of one foreign language; preliminary exam; dissertation; final oral exam. For Ed.D.: 60 credit hours minimum beyond the master's, at least two consecutive semesters in full-time residence; preliminary exam; dissertation; final oral exam. For Psy.D.: 107 credit hours minimum beyond the bachelor's, plus one year of internship; at least nine consecutive semesters of residence study; no foreign language or dissertation; comprehensive written and oral exam at end of third year to qualify for internship.

FIELDS OF STUDY.
Accountancy. M.Acc.
American Studies. M.A. only.
Anthropology. M.A. only.
Applied Sociology. Ph.D. only.
Biology. M.A., M.S., Ph.D.
Biomedical Studies. M.S., Ph.D.
Business Administration. GMAT for admission. Includes information systems management, international management. M.B.A., M.I.M., M.B.A.-M.I.M.
Chemistry. Includes biochemistry. M.S., Ph.D.
Christian Theology. M.C.T.
Church-State Studies. M.A., Ph.D.
Clinical Gerontology. M.C.G.
Clinical Psychology. M.S., Psy.D.
Communication Disorders. M.A., M.S.
Communication Studies. M.A. only.
Computer Science. M.S.
Earth Science. M.A.
Economics. Includes international. M.A., M.S.
Education. Includes administration, curriculum and instruction, educational psychology, health, human performance, recreation. M.S., M.A., Ed.S., Ph.D.
English. M.A., Ph.D.
Environmental Biology. M.S.
Environmental Chemistry. M.S.
Environmental Studies. M.S., M.E.S. only.
Fine Arts (Theater Arts). M.F.A.
Geology. M.S., Ph.D.
Gerontology. M.S.G.
Health Care Administration. M.H.A. only. For military personnel only. Offered in San Antonio.
Health, Human Performance, Recreation. M.S.
History. M.A. only.
Information Systems. M.S.
International Journalism. M.I.J. only.
International Management. M.I.M.
International Relations. M.A.
Limnology. M.S.L.

Mathematics. M.A., M.S. only.
Museum Studies. M.A.
Music. Includes church music, composition, conduction, education, history and literature, theory, performance, piano pedagogy, string pedagogy; qualifying exam. M.M. only.
Neuroscience. Ph.D. only.
Nursing. Includes family, patient care management, administration and management, neonatal.
Philosophy. M.A., Ph.D.
Physical Therapy. M.P.T. only. For military personnel only. Offered in San Antonio.
Physics. M.S., Ph.D.
Political Science. Includes international relations, public policy and administration. M.A., M.P.P.A.
Psychology. M.A., Psy.D., Ph.D. only.
Religion. M.A., Ph.D.
Social Work. M.S.W.
Sociology. M.A. only.
Spanish. M.A.
Statistics. M.A., Ph.D.
Taxation. M.T.
Theater Arts. M.A.

School of Law
Web site: law.baylor.edu

Founded 1857, the oldest law school in Texas. ABA approved since 1931. AALS member since 1932. Quarter system. Law library 188,500 volumes, 2456 subscriptions. Library has LEXIS, WESTLAW, DIALOG, OCLC.

Annual tuition: $15,521. On-campus housing available. Apply to Baylor Rental properties.

Enrollment: first-year class 63 (Fall), 77 (Spring); total full-time 379 (men 70%, women 30%), part-time 8. Faculty: full-time 22, part-time 38. Student to faculty ratio 20 to 1. Degrees conferred: J.D., J.D.-M.B.A., J.D.-M.Tax.

ADMISSION REQUIREMENTS. LSDAS Law School report, transcripts indicating at least 90 semester hours of college study. LSAT required in support of application. Interview not required. Accepts transfer applications. Graduates of unaccredited colleges not considered. Apply to Director of Admissions and Scholarship Coordinator by November 1 (Spring), February 1 (Summer), March 1 (Fall). Application fee $40. Phone: (254)710-1911; fax: (254)710-2316.

ADMISSION STANDARDS. Selective. Accepts 20–25% of total annual applicants. Gourman rating: 2.58. *U.S. News & World Report* ranking is in the second tier of all law schools.

FINANCIAL AID. Scholarships (one-third full tuition), Texas Tuition Equalization grants, Federal W/S, loans. About 80% of students receive aid other than loans from school funds. For all financial aid, apply by May 1 to the Director of Admissions and Scholarship Coordinator. Use FAFSA (School code: 003545).

DEGREE REQUIREMENTS. For J.D.: satisfactory completion of three-year program, at least 120 quarter hours minimum. Transfer credit individually considered. For other master's: see Graduate School listing above.

BEMIDJI STATE UNIVERSITY
Bemidji, Minnesota 56601
Web site: www.bemidjistate.edu

Founded 1919. Located 230 miles NW of Minneapolis. Coed. State control. Semester system. Library: 554,000 volumes, 1000 subscriptions. More than 400 computers on campus for student use. 721,000 microforms. Special facilities: Freshwater Aquatics Laboratory, Center for Environmental Studies, UNIVAC 1100/80, CDC CYBER 172.

Tuition: per credit, resident $107, nonresident $210. On-campus housing for 40 men, 32 women; none for married students. Average annual housing cost: $3880 (including board). Apply to Director of Housing by April 25. Phone: (218)755-3750. Day-care facilities available.

Graduate Studies

Enrollment: full-time 36, part-time 204 (men 30%, women 70%). Graduate faculty: full- and part-time 62. Degrees conferred: M.A., M.S.

ADMISSION REQUIREMENTS. Transcripts, GRE required in support of application. TOEFL required for foreign applicants. Interview not required. Accepts transfer applicants. Apply to Director of Graduate Studies prior to registration. Application fee $20. Phone: (218)755-3732; fax: (218)755-3788.

ADMISSION STANDARDS. Selective for some departments, relatively open for most. Usual minimum average: 2.5 (A = 4)

FINANCIAL AID. Annual awards from institutional funds: approximately teaching research assistantships, Federal W/S, loans. Apply to department chair; no specified closing date. Use FAFSA. Phone: (218)755-2034. Less than 10% of students receive aid other than loans from University and outside sources. No aid for part-time students.

DEGREE REQUIREMENTS. For M.A., M.S.: 30–32 credit hours minimum, at least 30 in residence; competency requirement; research paper or thesis; final oral exam.

FIELDS OF STUDY.
Biology. M.A.
Education. Includes elementary, curriculum and instruction, mathematics, music, special.
English. M.A., M.S.
Environmental Studies. M.S.
Industrial Technology. M.S.
Mathematics. M.S.
Physical Education. M.S.
Science. M.S.
Special Education. M.S.
Sports Studies. Includes physical education. M.S.
Teacher Education. M.S.

BENNINGTON COLLEGE
Bennington, Vermont 05201-9993
Web site: www.bennington.edu

Founded 1932. Located 40 miles E of Albany, New York. Coed. Private control. Semester system. Special facilities: Regional Center for Language and Culture, Visual and Performing Arts Center. Library: 121,000 volumes, 500 subscriptions. About 60 computers on campus for student use.

Annual tuition: $14,700. On-campus housing available. Average academic year housing costs: approximately $4800 (including board) for single student; $2900 for married students. Contact Director of Residential Life for both on- and off-campus housing information. Phone: (802)442-5401.

Graduate Programs

Enrollment: full-time 129, part-time 2. Faculty: full-time 41, part-time 11. Degree conferred: M.A.L.S., M.A.T., M.F.A.

ADMISSION REQUIREMENTS. Official transcript, references, interview/audition in support of application. Accepts transfer applicants. Apply to Assistant Director of Admission by February 1 (M.F.A.), March 1 (M.A.T.), July 1 (M.A.L.S.). Application fee $45. Phone: (800)833-6845 or (802)440-4312; fax: (802)440-4320; e-mail: admission@bennington.edu.

ADMISSION STANDARDS. Selective. Usual minimum average: 2.75 (A = 4).

FINANCIAL AID. Teaching assistantships, Federal W/S, loans. Apply to the appropriate department for assistantships; to Financial Aid office for all other programs. Apply by March 15. Use FAFSA.

DEGREE REQUIREMENTS. For master's: four semesters of study, master's project.

FIELDS OF STUDY.
Art.
Creative Writing.
Dance.
Drama.
Liberal Arts.
Literature.
Music.
Teaching a Second Language. Includes French, Spanish.
Visual Arts.
Writing.

BENTLEY COLLEGE
Waltham, Massachusetts 02154-4705
Web site: www.bentley.edu

Founded 1917. Located 9 miles W of Boston. Private control. Semester system. Special facilities: Center for Excellence in Teaching, Center for Business Ethics. New England Heritage Center, Center for Financial Analysis and Risk. Library: 208,000 volumes, 9300 subscriptions.

On-campus rooms and apartments available for both single and married students. Annual on-campus housing cost: single students $6120 (room only), $8155 (room and board); married students $11,160. Contact Graduate Housing Office for both on- and off-campus housing information; phone: (781)891-2348. Estimated annual budget for tuition, room and board and personal expenses: approximately $30,065. Total College enrollment approximately 6300.

McCallum Graduate School of Business

Established 1974. Semester system. Special programs: foreign exchange programs (Estonia, Japan, the Netherlands); internships. Annual tuition: full-time $24,000, part-time per three credit course $2330; evening full-time $18,640.

Enrollment: total full-time 350, part-time 1057 (men 53%, women 47%). Faculty: 227 full-time, 184 part-time. Degrees conferred: M.B.A. (full-time, part-time, day, evening), M.S.A., M.S.A.I.S. (Accounting Information Systems), M.S.C.F. (Corporate Finance), M.S.F.P. (Financial Planning), M.S.G.F.A. (Global Financial Analysis), M.S.H.F.I.D. (Human Factors in Information Design), M.S.I.A.M. (Information Age Marketing), M.S.I.T. (Information Technology), M.S.T. (Taxation).

ADMISSION REQUIREMENTS. Bachelor's degree from a recognized institution of higher education required. Submit an M.B.A. application (electronic application available), GMAT results (will accept GMAT test results from the last five years, latest acceptable date is August), two official transcripts from each undergraduate/graduate school attended, two letters of recommendation, personal statement, current résumé (prefers at least four years of work experience), and an application fee of $50 to the Admissions office. In addition, international students (whose native language is other than English) should submit a TOEFL report (minimum score 580), certified translations and evaluations of all official transcripts; recommendation should be in English or with certified translations and proof of sufficient financial resources for two years of academic study. Students are admitted Fall, Spring, and Summer. Both U.S. citizens and International applicants apply by June 1 (Fall), November 1 (Spring), March 1 (Summer). On-campus visits and interviews encouraged prior to the admissions committee reviewing completed application; interview required for Information Age Marketing. Admissions Committee will consider applicants with some academic course work deficiencies. Rolling admissions process, notification is made within three weeks of receipt of completed application and supporting documents. Admissions Office phone: (781)891-2108; fax: (781)891-2464; e-mail: gradadm@bentley.edu.

ADMISSION STANDARDS. For M.B.A.: number of applicants 1268; number accepted 918; number enrolled 490; median GMAT: 545; median GPA: 3.2 (A = 4).

FINANCIAL AID. Scholarships, International Grants, graduate and departmental assistantships, Federal Perkins loans, Stafford Subsidized and Unsubsidized loans, Federal W/S available. Financial aid is available for part-time study. Financial aid may be available for international students. Financial Aid applications and information are generally available at the on-campus visit/interview or after January 1; apply by May 1. Submit Graduate Assistantship application, résumé, two letters of reference directly to Graduate School of Business. Contact the College's Financial Aid Office for current need-based financial aid information. Phone: (781)891-3168. For most financial assistance and all Federal programs submit FAFSA (College code: 002124). Approximately 13% of students receive some form of financial assistance.

DEGREE REQUIREMENTS. For M.B.A.: 36–59 credit program (10–19 courses, up to 9 courses may be waived); Internship; degree program must be completed in seven years. For M.S. degrees: 30 credit program; internship option for some programs.

FIELDS OF STUDY.
Accounting. M.S.A.
Accounting Information System. M.S.A.I.S.
Business Administration. Includes concentrations in accountancy, business communication, business data analysis, business economics, business ethics, entrepreneurial studies, environmental management, finance, international business, management, management information systems, management of technology, marketing, operations management, taxation. M.B.A.
Corporate Finance. M.S.C.F.
Financial Planning. M.S.F.P.
Global Financial Analysis. M.S.G.F.A.
Human Factors in Information Design. M.S.H.F.I.D.
Information Age Marketing. M.S.I.A.M.
Information Technology. M.S.I.T.
Taxation. M.S.T.

BERRY COLLEGE
Mount Berry, Georgia 30149-0159
Web site: www.berry.edu

Founded 1902. Coed. Semester system. Library: 264,700 volumes, 1364 subscriptions. More than 100 computers on campus for student use.

Tuition: per credit $179, per 3 credit course $537. No on-campus housing available for graduate students. Contact Director of Residence Life for off-campus housing information.

Graduate Studies

Enrollment: full-time 28, part-time 125. Faculty: full-time 1, part-time 24. Degrees conferred: M.B.A., M.Ed.

ADMISSION REQUIREMENTS. Official transcript, bachelor's degree, two letters of reference, GMAT (Business) required in support of application. TOEFL required for international applicants. Accept transfer applicants. Graduates of unaccredited institutions not considered. Apply to Dean of Admissions at least thirty days prior to the beginning of semester. Rolling admission process. Application fee $25 (international applicants $30). Phone: (706)236-2215; fax: (706)236-2178.

ADMISSION STANDARDS. Selective. Usual minimum average: 3.0 (A = 4), with above average scores.

FINANCIAL AID. Assistantships, loans. Apply to Office of Financial Aid by April 1. Phone: (706)236-2276.

DEGREE REQUIREMENTS. For M.B.A.: 33 semester hours minimum; thesis not required. For M.Ed.: 33 semester hours minimum; thesis/nonthesis option.

FIELDS OF STUDY.
Business Administration.
Early Childhood Education.
Middle Grades Education.
Reading.
Secondary Education.

BLACK HILLS STATE UNIVERSITY
Spearfish, South Dakota 57799-9502
Web site: www.bhsu.edu

Founded 1883. Located 50 miles NW of Rapid City. Coed. State control. Semester system. Library: 230,000 volumes, 4481 subscriptions. More than 200 computers on campus for student use.

Tuition per credit, resident $92, nonresident $192. On-campus housing for married and single students. Annual housing cost: $1500 for single student. Apply to Housing Office by March 1. Phone: (605)642-6590. Day-care facilities available.

Graduate Division

Graduate study since 1959. Enrollment: full- and part-time 77, 200 in summer. Graduate faculty: full- and part-time 21. Degrees conferred: M.S.C.I., M.S.T.

ADMISSION REQUIREMENTS. Transcripts, GRE required in support of application. TOEFL required for International applicants. Interview not required. Accepts transfer applicants. Apply to Office of Admissions and Director of Graduate Studies six months prior to registration. Application fee $15; $100 for international applicants. Phone: (605)642-6270; fax: (605)642-6273.

ADMISSION STANDARDS. Selective. Usual minimum average: 2.75 (A = 4).

FINANCIAL AID. Limited to three research assistantships, partial tuition waivers, Federal W/S, loans. Apply to Director of Financial Aid; no specified closing date. Phone: (605)642-6254. Use FAFSA.

DEGREE REQUIREMENTS. For M.S.C.I.: 35 credit hours minimum, at least 22 in residence; thesis/final project; final oral exam. For M.S.T.: 32–35 credit hours minimum, at least 22 in residence; thesis/creative component; final oral exam.

FIELDS OF STUDY.
Curriculum and Instruction.
Tourism and Hospitality Management.
Note: Cooperative degrees in English and Speech. Students take 12 credits at BHSU and transfer to the receiving institution.

BLOOMSBURG UNIVERSITY OF PENNSYLVANIA
Bloomsburg, Pennsylvania 17815-1905
Web site: www.bloomu.edu

Founded 1839. Located 70 miles N of Harrisburg. CGS member. Coed. State control. Semester system. Special facilities: Institute for Comparative and International Management Studies, Institute for Interactive Technologies, Reading Clinic, Speech and Hearing Clinic. Library: 340,000 volumes, 2372 subscriptions. More than 700 computers on campus for student use.

Tuition: per hour, resident $230, nonresident $778. Limited on-campus housing for graduate students. Average academic year housing costs: $2854 (including board). Contact Office of Residence Life for both on- and off-campus housing information. Phone: (570)389-4088.

School of Graduate Studies
Web site: www.bloomu.edu/gradschool

Graduate study since 1960. Enrollment: full-time 210, part-time 351. College faculty teaching graduate students: full-time 203. Degrees conferred: M.A., M.B.A., M.Ed., M.S., M.S.N. Supervisory Certificates are also granted.

ADMISSION REQUIREMENTS. Transcripts, MAT, GRE, NTE, GMAT (Business Administration), interview required in support of School's application. TOEFL required for international applicants. Accepts transfer applicants. Graduates of unaccredited institutions not considered. Apply to Office of Graduate Studies and Research at least six weeks prior to registration. Application fee $30. Phone: (570)389-4015; fax: (570)389-3054.

ADMISSION STANDARDS. Relatively open. Usual minimum average 2.5 for admission, 3.0 for degree candidacy (A = 4).

FINANCIAL AID. Scholarships, research assistantships, teaching assistantships, Federal W/S, loans. Apply to Assistant Vice President Graduate Studies and Research at least one month prior to registration for assistantships; contact the Financial Aid Office for all other programs. Use FAFSA. Phone: (570)389-4498; fax: (570)389-4795. About 15% of students receive aid other than loans from College and outside sources. Aid available for part-time students.

DEGREE REQUIREMENTS. For M.A., M.Ed., M.S.: 30 credits minimum; thesis or research project; final oral/written exam. For M.S.N.: 39 credits minimum; thesis. For M.B.A.: 36 credits minimum.

FIELDS OF STUDY.
Accounting. M.A.C.
Art. Includes art studio, art history. M.A.
Audiology. M.S.
Biology. M.Ed.
Business Administration. M.B.A.

Business Education. M.Ed.
Curriculum and Instruction. M.Ed.
Early Childhood Education. M.Ed.
Education of the Deaf/Hard of Hearing. M.S.
Elementary Education. M.Ed.
Exercise Science and Adult Fitness. M.S.
Instructional Technology. M.S.
Nursing. M.S.N.
Reading. M.Ed.
Special Education. Includes mentally retarded, learning disabilities, behavioral disorders, and exceptional persons. M.S.
Speech Pathology. M.S.

BOISE STATE UNIVERSITY
Boise, Idaho 83725-0399
Web site: www.idbsu.edu

Established 1932. Coed. Public control. Semester system. Library: 505,000 volumes, 4800 subscriptions. More than 900 computers on campus for student use.

Annual tuition: resident $2578; nonresident $7924; per credit for both $108. There are 170 units available for full-time married students. Apply by August 1. Annual housing cost for single students: $4268. Monthly housing cost for married students: $450–$525. Phone: (208)385-3986.

Graduate College

Graduate study since 1969. Enrollment: full-time 306; part-time 942. Graduate faculty: full-time 265, part-time 99. Degrees conferred: M.A., M.B.A., M.H.S., M.S., M.M., M.P.A., M.S.W., Ed.D.

ADMISSION REQUIREMENTS. Transcripts, GMAT/GRE/MAT required in support of application. TOEFL required for foreign applicants. Accepts transfer applicants. Graduates of unaccredited institutions not considered. Apply to Graduate Admissions Office at least two months prior to registration. Application fee $20. Phone: (208)385-3903 or (208)385-4204; fax: (208)385-4061.

ADMISSION STANDARDS. Selective. Usual minimum average: 2.75 (3.0 last two years) (A = 4).

FINANCIAL AID. Graduate assistantships, Federal W/S, loans. Apply to Dean, Graduate College, phone: (208)385-3647, or Department Chair for assistantships; to Director of Financial Aid for W/S, loans; no specified closing date. Phone: (208)385-1644. Use FAFSA.

DEGREE REQUIREMENTS. For master's: 30 semester hours minimum, at least 21 in residence; thesis/project; final oral written exam. For M.S.F.: 30 semester hours, at least 24 in residence; thesis/project option. For M.S.W.: full-time two-year program. For Ed.D.: six semesters minimum beyond the bachelor's, at least two in residence; qualifying exam; dissertation; final oral exam.

FIELDS OF STUDY.
Accountancy. M.S.
Biology. M.A., M.S.
Business Administration. GMAT for admissions. M.B.A.
Civil Engineering. M.S.E.
Communication.
Computer Engineering. M.S.E.
Earth Science. M.S.
Education. Includes curriculum and instruction (Ed.D., GRE for admission), educational technology, early childhood, reading, special education, art, earth science, mathematics, school counseling. M.A., M.S.

Electrical Engineering. M.S.E.
English. GRE for admission. M.A.
Exercise and Sport Studies.
Geology. GRE for admission.
Geophysics. GRE for admission. M.S.
Health Science. GRE for admission. Includes addiction studies, environmental health, general health research, health policy, health promotion, leadership.
History. GRE for admission.
Instructional and Performance Technology. MAT for admission.
Management Information Systems. M.S.
Mechanical Engineering. M.S.E.
Interdisciplinary Studies.
Music. Includes education, pedagogy, performance. M.M.
Public Administration. GRE for admission.
Raptor Biology. GRE for admission. M.S.
Social Work. GRE for admission.
Technical Communication. M.F.A.

BOSTON COLLEGE

Chestnut Hill, Massachusetts 02167-9991
Web site: www.bc.edu

Founded 1863. CGS member. Located 6 miles from downtown Boston. Private control. Catholic affiliation. Semester system. Special facilities: Center for the Child, Family and Community Partnerships, Center for International Higher Education, Center for Corporate Community Relations, Center for East Europe, Russia and Asia, Center for Irish Management, Center for Educational Policy, Center for Work and Family, Institute for Medieval Philosophy and Theology, Institute for Scientific Research, Jesuit Institute, Lonergan Center, Management Center, Mathematics Institute, National Urban League Education Division, Small Business Development Center, Social Welfare Research Institute, Weston Observatory. Library: 2,000,000 volumes, 21,100 subscriptions. Total College enrollment: 4500.

Tuition: per hour $736. No on-campus housing for graduate students. Apply to Housing Office for off-campus housing information. Phone: (617)552-3075.

Graduate School of Arts and Sciences

Enrollment: full-time 322, part-time 678. Faculty: full- and part-time 350. Degrees conferred: M.A., M.S., M.A.T., M.S.T., C.A.G.S., Ph.D.

ADMISSION REQUIREMENTS. Transcripts, two letters of recommendation required in support of application. GRE General/Subject Tests, MAT required by some departments. Interview not required. TOEFL required for international applicants. Accepts transfer applicants. Apply to the Graduate Office by February 15, contact departments for Spring admissions deadlines. Application fee $50. Phone: (617)552-3265; fax: (617)552-3700.

ADMISSION STANDARDS. Selective for most departments, relatively open to very competitive for the others. Usual minimum average: 3.0 (A = 4).

FINANCIAL AID. Scholarships, teaching fellowships, assistantships, tuition waviers, Federal W/S, loans. Apply to the University Financial Aid Office by April 1. Phone: (617)552-4987. Use FAFSA. About 30% of students receive aid other than loans from School and outside sources. No aid for part-time students.

DEGREE REQUIREMENTS. For master's: 30 semester hours minimum, at least 24 in residence; language requirement varies by department; final oral/written exam. For C.A.G.S.: 30 credits

beyond the master's; final exam. For Ph.D.: 60 hours minimum beyond bachelor's, at least one year in full-time residence; comprehensive exam; dissertation; final oral exam.

FIELDS OF STUDY.
Biblical Studies. M.A.
Biology. M.S., M.S.T., Ph.D., M.S.-M.B.A., Ph.D.-M.B.A.
Chemistry. M.S., M.S.T., Ph.D.
Classics. M.A.
Economics. M.A., Ph.D.
English. M.A., M.A.T., Ph.D.
European National Studies. M.A.
French Literature and Culture. M.A., M.A.T., Ph.D., M.A.-M.B.A.
Geology. M.S., M.S.T., M.S.-M.B.A.
Geophysics. M.S., M.S.-M.B.A.
Greek. M.A.
Hispanic Literature and Culture. M.A., M.A.T., Ph.D., M.A.-M.B.A.
History. M.A., M.A.T.
Irish Studies. M.A.
Italian Literature and Culture. M.A., M.A.-M.B.A.
Latin. M.A., M.A.T.
Linguistics. M.A., M.A.-M.B.A.
Mathematics. M.A., M.S.T., M.A.-M.B.A.
Medieval Studies. M.A.
Medieval Studies/Romance Languages. Ph.D.
Pastoral Ministry. M.A., M.A.-M.S.W., M.A.-M.S.
Philosophy. M.A., Ph.D.
Physics. M.S., M.S.T., Ph.D.
Political Science. M.A., Ph.D., M.A.-M.B.A.
Psychology. Ph.D.
Religion and Education. Ph.D.
Romance Literature. Ph.D.
Russian. M.A., M.A.-M.B.A.
Slavic Studies. M.A., M.A.-M.B.A.
Sociology. M.A., Ph.D., M.A.-M.B.A., Ph.D.-M.B.A.
Theological Ethics. Ph.D.
Theology. M.A., Ph.D.

Lynch Graduate School of Education

Enrollment: full-time 442, part-time 574. Faculty: full-time 58, part-time 47. Degrees conferred: M.A., M.Ed., M.A.T., M.S.T., M.A.-J.D., M.A.-M.Ed. (Pastoral Ministry and Educational Administration), M.Ed.-J.D., M.A.-M.A. (Counseling and Pastoral Ministry), Ph.D.

ADMISSION REQUIREMENTS. Official transcripts, GRE for M.S.T. and Ph.D. candidates, GRE or MAT for all other programs, three letters of reference, statement of purpose, required in support of School's application. Résumé and writing sample required for all doctoral candidates. Interview is by invitation for Ph.D. TOEFL required for international applicants. Two applications required for all joint degree programs and observe deadlines for both schools. Apply to Office of Admissions by February 1, most programs. Exceptions are Higher Education, Counseling, Educational Psychology, January 1; Counseling Psychology, December 15. Application fee $50. Phone: (617)552-4214; fax: (617)552-0812; e-mail: gsoe@bc.edu

ADMISSION STANDARDS. Selective. Accepts about 50% of all applicants. *U.S. News & World Report* ranking was 21st in all Schools of Education.

FINANCIAL AID. Scholarships, fellowships, assistantships, Federal W/S, loans. Apply by March 1 to the School's Financial Aid Office for School-sponsored funds, to the College's Financial Aid Office for all Federal programs. Phone: (800)294-0294. Use FAFSA and College's FAF.

DEGREE REQUIREMENTS. For M.A. (Counseling Psychology): 60 credit hour program; practicum. For all other M.A.s: 30 credit hour programs. For M.Ed.: 30 credit hour program; comprehensive exam. For M.A.T., M.S.T.: 37–46 credit hours; practicum; comprehensive exam. For Ph.D.: 84 credit hour program; comprehensive exam; candidacy, dissertation; oral exam.

FIELDS OF STUDY.
Counseling Psychology/School Counseling. M.A., Ph.D.
Curriculum and Instruction. M.Ed., Ph.D.
Developmental and Educational Psychology/Early Childhood Specialist. M.A., Ph.D.
Early Childhood Education. M.Ed.
Educational Research, Measurement and Evaluation. M.Ed., Ph.D.
Educational Administration. M.Ed., Ph.D.
Elementary Teaching. M.Ed.
Higher Education. M.A., Ph.D.
Reading/Literacy Education. M.Ed.
Secondary Education. Includes biology, chemistry, English, French, geology (earth science), history, Latin & classical studies, mathematics, physics, Spanish. M.Ed.
Secondary Education—Arts. Includes English, French, history, Latin & classical studies, Spanish. M.A.T.
Secondary Education—Sciences. Includes biology, chemistry, geology, mathematics, physics. M.S.T.
Teacher of Students with Intensive/Severe Special Needs. M.Ed.
Teacher of Students with Moderate Special Needs. M.Ed.
Teacher of Students with Moderate Special Needs. (PreK–9). M.Ed.

Law School

Established 1929. Located at Newton (02459-1163). Semester system. ABA approved since 1932. AALS member. Law library 403,500 volumes, 6600 subscriptions. Library has LEXIS-NEXIS, WESTLAW, DIALOG, 25 Macintosh computers.

Annual tuition: full-time $25,854. No housing on-campus. Total average annual expenses: $12,960. Enrollment: first-year class 276; total full-time 800 (men 50%, women 50%). Faculty: full-time 48, part-time 26. Student to faculty ratio is 14 to 1. Degrees conferred: J.D., J.D.-M.B.A., J.D.-M.S.W.

ADMISSION REQUIREMENTS. LSDAS Law School report, transcripts, LSAT, recommendation, bachelor's degree required in support of application. Interview not required. Accepts transfer applicants. Graduates of unaccredited colleges not considered. Apply to the Director of Admissions; closing date March 1. Application fee $65. Phone: (617)552-4350; e-mail: bclawadm@bc.edu.

ADMISSION STANDARDS. Selective. Accepts 20–25% of total annual applicants. Gourman rating: 4.29. *U.S. News & World Report* ranking is 22nd of all law schools.

FINANCIAL AID. Scholarships, resident assistantships, Federal W/S, loans. About 75% receive aid other than loans from School funds. Apply by March 1 to the Boston College Office of Financial Aid. Use FAFSA.

DEGREE REQUIREMENTS. For J.D.: 85 credit hours minimum, at least the last four semesters in residence. For other master's degrees: see Graduate School listing above.
Note: Semester-abroad program (University of London) available.

Wallace E. Carroll School of Management
Web site: www.bc.edu

Graduate study since 1957. Semester system. Tuition: per course $1938.

Enrollment: full-time 369, part-time 623. Fac   57, part-time 10. Degrees conferred: M.B.A., M   M.B.A.-Ph.D. (Sociology, Finance, Organization

ADMISSION REQUIREMENTS. Transcripts,   ters of recommendation required in support of college's application. TOEFL, TSE, TWE required for foreign applicants. Interview recommended. Accepts transfer students. Graduates of unaccredited institutions not considered. Apply to the Director of Admissions by April 15 (Fall), December 1 (Spring). Application fee $45. Phone: (617)552-3920; fax: (617)552-8087.

ADMISSION STANDARDS. Selective. Usual minimum average: 3.1 (A = 4). Median GMAT: 600. *U.S. News & World Report* ranking: 39th for M.B.A.s, 17th for part-time M.B.A. programs.

FINANCIAL AID. Annual awards from School funds: academic scholarships, AHANA scholarships, and research assistantships, fellowships, tuition waivers, Federal W/S, loans. Apply to the Director of Financial Aid by March 1. Phone: (617)552-3320. Use FAFSA. About 25% of students receive aid other than loans from School and outside sources. Aid available for part-time students.

DEGREE REQUIREMENTS. For M.B.A.: 62 semester hours, 21 courses including 15 required courses in the common body of knowledge and 8 electives; consulting project. For M.S.A., M.S.F.: 30 semester hours, either a one-year full-time or 21-month part-time program. For Ph.D.: four-year full-time program; doctoral seminar in teaching; comprehensive exam, dissertation; oral defense.

FIELDS OF STUDY.
Accounting. M.S.A.
Business Administration. Concentrations in accounting, entrepreneurship, finance, international management, management, management consulting, management information systems, marketing, operations management, organization behavior/development, strategic management. M.B.A.
Finance. M.S.F., Ph.D.
Organizational Studies. Ph.D. only.
Note: International exchange program in France, Spain, Ireland, New Zealand.

Graduate School of Nursing

Enrollment: full-time 86, part-time 41. Faculty: full- and part-time 31. Degrees conferred: M.S., M.S.-M.A. (Pastoral Ministry), M.S.-M.B.A., Ph.D.

ADMISSION REQUIREMENTS. Official B.S.N. transcripts from an NLN accredited program, three letters of reference, goal statement, GRE required in support of School's application. In addition, RN license and one year experience as an RN required. Interview is by invitation for Ph.D. TOEFL required for international applicants. Apply to Office of Admissions by March 31. Application fee $50. Phone: (617)552-4250.

ADMISSION STANDARDS. Selective.

FINANCIAL AID. College-administered Federal W/S, loans. School-administered traineeships, scholarships, VA stipends, graduate assistantships, minority scholarships, and various grants on funds-available basis. Apply by March 1 to School's Financial Aid Office for School-sponsored funds, to the College's Financial Aid Office for all Federal programs. Phone: (800)294-0294. Use FAFSA and College's FAF.

DEGREE REQUIREMENTS. For M.S.: 30–33 semester hours; comprehensive exam; thesis. For Ph.D.: 46 semester hours bend master's; comprehensive exam; colloquium, dissertation; oral exam.

FIELDS OF STUDY.

Adult Health Nursing. Includes adult health clinical specialist, adult nurse practitioner.

Community Health Nursing. Includes family nurse practitioner, community nurse clinical specialist.

Maternal Child Health Nursing. Includes MCH clinical nurse specialist, pediatric nurse practitioner, women's health (OB/GYN) nurse practitioner.

Psychiatric Mental Health Nursing. Includes psychiatric and mental health clinical nurse specialist.

Graduate School of Social Work

Established 1936. Tuition: per credit $736. Enrollment: full-time 375, part-time 125. Faculty: full-time 22, part-time 27. Degrees conferred: M.S.W., Ph.D., M.S.W.-M.B.A., M.S.W.-J.D., M.S.W.-M.A. (Pastoral Counseling, Social Ministry).

ADMISSION REQUIREMENTS. Official transcripts, three letters of reference, GRE or MAT required in support of School's application. TOEFL required for international applicants. Interview not required. For Ph.D. candidates: M.S.W. degree, transcripts, essay, three references, MAT or GRE. Apply to Office of Admissions by March 1. Application fee $40. Phone: (617)552-4024; e-mail: swadmit@bc.edu.

ADMISSION STANDARDS. Multidimensional: MAT/GRE or UG content and GPA, related experience, references, and statement of purpose weighted.

FINANCIAL AID. College-administered Federal W/S, loans. School-administered work-study internships, VA stipends, Forensic grant, graduate assistantships, minority scholarships, and various grants on funds-available basis. Apply to School's Director of Financial Aid; no specified closing date. Phone: (617)552-4982. Use FAFSA.

DEGREE REQUIREMENTS. For M.S.W.: 81 semester hours, including field practicum; thesis. For Ph.D.: 14 courses beyond master's; qualifying exam; dissertation; oral exam.

FIELDS OF STUDY.

Clinical Social Work. M.S.W., Ph.D.

Community Organization.

Planning, Policy and Administration. Includes concentrations in child welfare, occupational social work, health and medical care, gerontology, forensic social work. M.S.W

Social Work. Ph.D.

BOSTON UNIVERSITY

Boston, Massachusetts 02215

Web site: www.bu.edu

Founded 1839. CGS member. Coed. Private control. Methodist affiliation. Semester system. Special facilities: Institute for Accounting Research and Education, Center for Advanced Biotechnology, African Studies Center, Center for Applied Research in Language, Asian Management Center, Center for Astrophysical Research, Center for BioDynamics, BioMolecular Engineering Research Center, Cancer Research Center, Institute for the Classical Tradition, Center for Communication and Deafness, Communication Research Center, Center for Computational Science, Center for Defense Journalism, International Center for East Asian Archaeology, Institute for Economic Development, Center for Einstein Studies, Center for Energy and Environmental Studies, Center for Enterprise Leadership, Center for Families, Communities, Schools and Children's Learning, Gerontology Center, Center for Human Genetics, Human Resources Policy Institute, Center for International Health, International History Institute, Center for Judaic Studies, Center for Law and Health Sciences, Center for Law and Technology, Institute for Literacy and Language, Center for Molecular Engineering, Design and Analysis, Morin Center for Banking and Financial Law, NeuroMuscular Research Center, Opera Institute, Center for Philosophy and History of Science, Institute for Philosophy and Religion, Photonics Center, Center for Polymer Studies, Institute for Religion and World Affairs, Center for Remote Sensing, Center for Space Physics, Institute for the Study of Conflict, Ideology and Policy, Institute for Study of Economic Culture, Institute for Television, Film and Radio Production, Theatre Institute, Center for Transportation Studies, United States Strategic Institute, Visual Arts Institute, Whitaker Cardiovascular Institute, Center on Work and Family. Library 2,000,000 volumes, 30,689 subscriptions. The NIH ranking for Boston University by awards was 39th, with 359 awards/grants; total dollars awarded $118,975,449. Total University enrollment approximately 30,000.

Annual tuition: full-time $24,700; per credit $720. Limited on-campus housing. Average annual housing cost: $8400 (includes board). Contact off-campus housing office. Phone (617)353-3523.

Graduate School of Arts and Sciences

Graduate study since 1874. Enrollment: full-time 1499, part-time 228. Arts and Science faculty: 600. Degrees conferred: M.A., Ph.D.

ADMISSION REQUIREMENTS. Official transcripts, two to three letters of recommendation required in support of application. GRE/Subject Tests for most departments, GMAT/MAT for some departments. TOEFL and statement of financial support required for foreign applicants. Interviews may be requested. Graduates of unaccredited institutions not considered. Apply to Office of Admissions by January 15 (Fall), October 15 (Spring). Application fee $60. Phone: (617)353-2693; fax: (617) 358-0540; e-mail: grartsci@bu.edu.

ADMISSION STANDARDS. Selective for most departments. Usual minimum average: 3.0 (A = 4).

FINANCIAL AID. Annual awards from institutional funds: research scholarships, graduate assistantships, fellowships, traineeships, Federal W/S, loans. Apply to Director of Financial Aid by March 1. Phone: (617)353-2697. Use FAFSA. About 65% of full-time students receive aid from School. Aid available for part-time students.

DEGREE REQUIREMENTS. For most M.A. programs: eight semester courses; thesis or final comprehensive exam; students who have not completed two years of undergraduate language study must make up deficiency. For most Ph.D. programs: eight semester courses beyond the master's; residency requirements of a minimum of two consecutive regular semesters of full-time study; qualifying exam; dissertation; candidacy; final oral exam; reading knowledge of one or more foreign languages.

FIELDS OF STUDY.

African-American Studies. M.A. only.

American and New England Studies. Ph.D. only.

Anthropology.

Applied Linguistics. Ph.D. only.

Archaeological Studies.

Art History.

Astronomy.

Bioinformatics.

Biology.

Biostatistics.

Cellular Biophysics.

Chemistry.

Classical Studies.

Cognitive and Neural Systems.

Computer Science.

Earth Sciences.

Economics.

Editorial Studies.

Energy and Environmental Studies. Includes Environmental Remote Sensing and Geographic Information. M.A. only.

English. Includes English and American literature, creative writing. M.A. only.

Geography.

History.

International Relations. Includes joint programs in international, relations and international communication, and international relations, and resource environmental management.

Mathematics.

Modern Foreign Languages and Literatures. Includes French, Hispanics.

Molecular Biology. Includes cell, biochemistry.

Music. Includes musicology; 12 semester courses for Ph.D.

Neuroscience.

Philosophy.

Physics.

Political Science.

Psychology. Includes clinical, community, developmental, experimental, social.

Religion and Theological Studies.

Sociology. Includes joint Ph.D. in Sociology/Social Work.

Statistics.

College of Communication

Graduate study since 1947. Annual tuition: $20,570. Graduate enrollment: full-time 284, part-time 82. Faculty: full-time 57, part-time 81. Degrees conferred: M.F.A., M.S., J.D.-M.S., M.B.A.-M.S.

ADMISSION REQUIREMENTS. Official transcripts, three letters of recommendation, MAT/GMAT/GRE/LSAT and program-related writing requirement required in support of College's application. Interview not required. TOEFL/ TSE/TWE required for international applicants. Transfer students not accepted. Graduates of unaccredited institutions not considered. Apply to Admissions Officer, preferably by February 15 (admits Fall only). Application fee $70 for paper application, $60 for on-line application. Phone: (617)353-3481; fax: (617)358-0399; e-mail: com@bu.edu.

ADMISSION STANDARDS. Very selective to competitive. Usual minimum average: 3.0 (A = 4).

FINANCIAL AID. Annual awards from institutional funds: scholarships, grants, tuition waivers, research assistantships, administrative assistantships, teaching assistantships, internships, Federal W/S, loans. Approved for VA benefits. Apply by April 30 to Graduate Financial Aid Coordinator. Phone: (617)353-4658. Use FAFSA. About 75% of students receive aid other than loans from School and outside sources. Aid available for part-time students.

DEGREE REQUIREMENTS, For M.S.: 32–48 credits minimum; thesis, creative project, analytical project or comprehensive exam. For M.F.A.: 64 credit program; thesis/project.

FIELDS OF STUDY.

Advertising. M.S.

Broadcast Journalism. M.S.

Business and Economics Journalism. M.S.

Film Production. M.F.A.

Film Studies. M.F.A.

Health Communication. M.S.

Journalism. Includes print, photo. M.S.

Mass Communication. Includes applied communication search, communications studies.

Public Relations. Includes public relations for the nonprofit sector, coporate. M.S.

Science Journalism. M.S.

Screenwriting. M.F.A.

Television Management. M.S.

DUAL DEGREE PROGRAMS:

J.D.-M.S. in Mass Communications.

M.B.A.-M.S. in Television Management.

College of Engineering

110 Cummington Street

Enrollment: full-time 311, part-time 59 (men 80%, women 20%). Faculty: full-time 87, part-time 16. Degrees conferred: M.S., M.S.-M.B.A., Ph.D.

ADMISSION REQUIREMENTS: Transcripts, GRE, two letters of recommendation, statement of personal and research goals required in support of application. TOEFL required for international applicants. Accepts transfer applicants. Graduates of unaccredited institutions not considered. Apply to Graduate Admission Office by April 1 (Fall), October 1 (Spring). Application fee $60. Phone: (617)353-9760; fax: (617)353-0259; e-mail: enggrad@bu.edu.

ADMISSION STANDARDS. Competitive for most departments, selective for the others. Usual minimum average: 2.75 (A = 4).

FINANCIAL AID. Annual awards from institutional funds: scholarships, fellowships, research assistantships, teaching assistantships, tuition waivers, Federal W/S, loans. Approved for VA benefits. Apply to Dean by January 15. Phone: (617)353-8970. Use FAFSA and University's FAF. More than 70% of students receive some form of financial aid.

DEGREE REQUIREMENTS. For M.S.: 32–36 semester hours minimum, at least 24 in residence; project, thesis, or laboratory course. For Ph.D.: a minimum of 32 credits beyond M.S. degree; qualifying exam; candidacy; dissertation; final oral exam.

FIELDS OF STUDY.

Aerospace Engineering.

Biomedical Engineering.

Computer Systems Engineering.

Electrical Engineering.

Engineering Sciences.

General Engineering.

Manufacturing Engineering.

Mechanical Engineering.

Systems Engineering. Interdepartmental Ph.D. Includes software engineering.

Note: Joint Program is with School of Management and Manufacturing Department. M.S.-M.B.A.; with the Medical School, Ph.D.–M.D.

College of Fine Arts

Annual tuition: $24,700. Graduate enrollment: full-time 330, part-time 3. Graduate faculty: full-time 68, part-time 34. Degrees conferred: M.F.A., Mus.M., Mus.A.D., Diploma.

ADMISSION REQUIREMENTS: Transcripts, two–three letters of recommendation required in support of College's application.

...tion, interview, or portfolio required depending upon major. GRE required for History and Literature of Music applicants. Curriculum vitae required for doctoral candidates. TOEFL and statement of financial support required for international applicants. Accepts transfer applicants. Applications should be filed by February 15 (for most programs) with the Office of Graduate Admissions of the College. Application fee $50. Phone: (617)353-3350; e-mail: arts@bu.edu. For audition information call (617)353-3341.

ADMISSION STANDARDS. Competitive for most departments. Usual minimum average of 3.0 (A = 4) in undergraduate studies.

FINANCIAL AID. More than 200 annual awards, including teaching fellowships, graduate assistantships, Director's Awards, Federal W/S, loans. Application for aid should be submitted with application for admission but before March 1. Use FAFSA (University code: 002130).

DEGREE REQUIREMENTS. For Mus.M. 32–36 credits minimum; recitals, thesis, or terminal project. For M.F.A.: 32–42 credits minimum; project. For Mus. A.D.: 48 credits minimum beyond the master's, at least two semesters in full-time residence; qualifying examinations; reading knowledge of French and German; dissertation/terminal project; final oral examination. For the Diploma/Certificate programs: usually it represents about two years of study beyond the master's degree.

FIELDS OF STUDY.

SCHOOL OF MUSIC:
Collaborative Piano. Mus.M., Mus.A.D.
Composition. Mus.M., Mus.A.D.
Conducting. Includes orchestral and choral. Mus.M., Mus.A.D.
History and Literature of Music. Mus.M.
Historical Performance. Mus.M, Mus.A.D.
Music Education. Mus.M., Mus.A.D.
Performance. Mus.M., Mus.A.D.
Theory. Mus.M.

SCHOOL OF THEATRE:
Design & Production. M.F.A.
Directing. M.F.A.
Theatre Education. M.F.A.

SCHOOL OF VISUAL ARTS:
Art Education. M.F.A.
Graphic Design. M.F.A.
Painting. M.F.A.
Sculpture. M.F.A.

Sargent College of Health and Rehabilitation Science

Annual tuition: $24,700. Graduate enrollment: full-time 466, part-time 55. Faculty: full-time 47, part-time 50. Degrees conferred: M.S., M.S.O.T., M.S.P.T., D.P.T., D.Sc.

ADMISSION REQUIREMENTS. Official transcripts, three letters of recommendation, MAT/GRE required in support of College's application (electronic application available). Interview required for doctoral candidates. TOEFL required for international applicants. Transfer students accepted. Graduates of unaccredited institutions not considered. Apply to Graduate Admissions Office for Communication Disorders February 1 (Fall), Health Sciences March 1, Occupational Therapy February 15, Physical Therapy January 5, Rehabilitation Counseling rolling admissions. Application fee $60. Phone: (617)353-2713; e-mail: sargrad@bu.edu.

ADMISSION STANDARDS. Selective to competitive. Usual minimum average 3.0 (A = 4).

FINANCIAL AID. Annual awards from institutional funds: scholarships, grants, research assistantships, teaching assistantships, traineeships, Federal W/S, loans. Approved for VA benefits. Apply by April 1 to Sargent College Financial Aid Office. Use FAFSA. Phone: (617)353-2714. Limited aid other than loans for part-time students.

DEGREE REQUIREMENTS. For M.S.: 32–64 credits minimum depending on program; thesis or comprehensive exam. For M.S.O.T.: two-year entry-level program; internship. For D.P.T.: 98 credit full-time program; preliminary exam; clinical experience; dissertation; final oral exam. For D.Sc.: 48 credit program beyond the master's degree; one year in full-time study (two consecutive semesters); qualifying tasks; dissertation; final oral exam.

FIELDS OF STUDY.
Audiology. M.S.
Applied Anatomy and Physiology. M.S., Ph.D.
Communication Disorders. M.S.
Dietetic Internship. M.S.
Movement and Rehabilitation Sciences. D.Sc.
Nutrition. M.S.
Occupational Therapy. M.S.O.T., M.S., D.Sc.
Physical Therapy. M.S.P.T., D.P.T.
Rehabilitation Counseling. M.S.
Speech-Language Pathology. M.S.
Therapeutic Studies. M.S.

Henry M. Goldman School of Dental Medicine

Founded 1963. D.M.D. program established 1972. Annual tuition $37,170. Total average cost for all other first-year expenses $24,000.

Enrollment: first-year class 117, total full-time 684 (men 55%, women 45%); full-time study only. Faculty: full-time 102, part-time 110. Degrees conferred: D.M.D., M.Sc., M.S., C.A.G.S., D.Sc.

ADMISSION REQUIREMENTS. AADSAS application, transcripts, DAT (no later than October), two letters of reference required in support of School's application. Interview by invitation only. Applicants must have completed at least three years of undergraduate study for D.M.D. Graduates of unaccredited colleges not considered. TOEFL required of international applicants. Does not have EDP. Apply to Admissions Committee after June 1 and before March 1 for all programs. Application fee $50. Phone: (617)638-4787, (617)638-4798.

ADMISSION STANDARDS. Competitive. Accepts 25% of total applicants. Usual minimum average: 3.21 (A = 4), mean DAT Academic: 19; PAT: 19. Approximately 10% are state residents. Gourman rating: 4.31; this places school in top 30 schools of dentistry.

FINANCIAL AID. Scholarships, grants, tuition waivers, APEX, DEAL, HEAL, loans. Apply by April 15 to the Dean for scholarships; to Office of Financial Management, Medical Center for all other programs. Phone: (617)638-5130; e-mail: OSFM@bu.edu. Use FAFSA. About 75% of students receive aid other than loans from School and outside sources.

DEGREE REQUIREMENTS. For D.M.D.: satisfactory completion of 4-year program; externship. For M.S., M.Sc.: 36 credits minimum in residence; final oral exam; research project. For C.A.G.S.: same as M.S., except no research project. For D.Sc.: 54 credits minimum, at least three years in residence; research project; final written/oral exam.

FIELDS OF STUDY.
Advanced Education in General Dentistry.
Dental Care Management. C.A.G.S. only.

Dental Public Health.
Endodontics.
Implantology.
Nutritional Science. D.Sc. only.
Operative Dentistry.
Oral and Maxillofacial Pathology.
Oral and Maxillofacial Surgery.
Oral Biology.
Orthodontics and Dentofacial Orthopedics.
Pediatric Dentistry.
Pedodontics.
Periodontology.
Prosthodontics.
Note: Ph.D. programs available through the Department of Medical and Dental Sciences, School of Medicine.

School of Education

Tuition: full-time $24,042; per credit $845; special late afternoon part-time tuition, per credit $423. Graduate enrollment: full-time 244, part-time 294 (men 30%, women 70%). Faculty: full-time 31, part-time 57. Degrees conferred: Ed.M., M.A.T., C.A.G.S., Ed.D.

ADMISSION REQUIREMENTS. Transcripts, MAT/GRE, three letters of recommendation required in support of School's application. Interview not required. TOEFL required for international applicants. Accepts transfer applicants. Graduates of unaccredited institutions not considered. Apply by February 15 (Fall), October 15 (Spring) to Office of Graduate Admissions. Rolling admissions process. Application fee $60. Phone: (617)353-4237; fax: (617)353-8937.

ADMISSION STANDARDS. Selective for most departments.

FINANCIAL AID. Scholarships, fellowships, teaching/research assistantships, partial tuition waivers, Federal W/S, loans. Approved for VA benefits. Apply by February 15 (Fall), October 15 (Spring) to Graduate School for fellowships, assistantships; to the Office of Graduate Financial Assistance for all other programs. Phone (617)353-4238. Use FAFSA. About 45% of full-time students receive aid from School and outside sources. No aid for part-time students.

DEGREE REQUIREMENTS. For Ed.M.: 32 credits minimum. For C.A.G.S.: 30 credits minimum beyond the master's, at least 24 in residence; final written/oral exam; no language requirement. For M.A.T.: twelve-month, 46 credit program. For Ed.D.: 60 credits minimum beyond the master's, at least 45 in residence and 24 in full-time attendance; preliminary exam; dissertation; no language requirement.

FIELDS OF STUDY.
Administration, Training, and Policy Studies.
Bilingual Education.
Counseling.
Counseling Psychology.
Curriculum and Instruction.
Early Childhood Education.
Educational Media and Technology.
Education of Deaf.
Elementary Education.
English and Language Arts Education.
English Education.
Health Education.
Higher Educational Administration.
Human Movement.
Human Resource Education.
International Educational Development.
Latin and Classical Humanities.
Leisure Education.

Mathematics Education.
Modern Foreign Language Education.
Policy, Planning, and Administration.
Policy, Planning, and Administration/Social Work.
Reading Education.
Science Education.
Social Studies Education.
Special Education.
Special Education/Social Work.
TESOL (Teaching English to Speakers of Other Languages).
Therapeutic Recreation.

School of Law

Founded 1872. ABA approved since 1925. AALS member. Semester system. Special facilities: Morin Co. for Banking Law Studies, Center for Law and Health, Center for Law and Technology. Library: 575,000 volumes, 6578 subscriptions. Library has LEXIS, NEXIS, WESTLAW, DIALOG.

Annual tuition: $25,034. On-campus housing available. Apply to Office of Housing. Total average annual expenses: $14,000. Enrollment: first-year class 312; total full-time 903 (men 47.3%, women 52.7%). Faculty: full-time 58, part-time 27; student to faculty ratio 12.2 to 1. Degrees conferred: J.D., J.D.-M.B.A. (Management, Health Care Management), J.D.-M.S. (Mass Communication), J.D.-M.A. (Historic Preservation, International Relations, Philosophy), J.D.-M.P.H. (Public Health), J.D.-M.S.W. (Social Work), LL.M. (Taxation, American Banking Law, International Banking Law), J.D.-LL.M.

ADMISSION REQUIREMENTS. LSDAS Law School report, transcripts, LSAT, letter of recommendation required in support of application. Interview not required, but visits encouraged. Accepts transfer applicants. In addition, international candidates submit TOEFL, unless the undergraduate degree was awarded by a U.S. institution. Graduates of unaccredited colleges not considered. Apply to the Office of Admissions after September 15, before March 1. Admits to Fall semester only. Application fee $60. Phone: (617)353-3100; fax: (617)353-0578; e-mail: bulawadm@bu.edu.

ADMISSION STANDARDS. Selective. Accepts 30–33% of total annual applicants. Gourman rating: 4.48. *U.S. News & World Report* ranking places the school of law among the top 25 of all law schools.

FINANCIAL AID. Partial tuition grants, MLK fellowships, scholarships, Federal W/S, loans. Apply by April 1 to the Assistant Dean. Use FAFSA. About 80% of students receive aid including loans from School funds.

DEGREE REQUIREMENTS. For J.D.: satisfactory completion of 3-year program; 84 semester units. For LL.M.: at least 24 credits beyond the J.D.; one year in full-time residence.
Note: Study abroad available at University of Buenos Aires (Argentina), Université Jean Moulin Lyon 3 (France), Université Panthéon-Assas (Paris II) (France), St. Catherine's College, University of Oxford (U.K.), Leiden University (The Netherlands), Tel Aviv University (Israel).

School of Management
Web site: management.bu.edu

Established 1913. Graduate study since 1974. Located on main campus. Library: 80,000 volumes, 350 subscriptions. Special program: Accelerated M.B.A. Special facilities: Asian Management Center, Center for Enterprise Leadership, Entrepreneurial Management, Human Resources Policy Institute, Institute for Accounting Research and Education, Leadership Institute. Annual tuition: full-time, M.B.A., M.S.I.S., D.B.A. $27,042; M.S.I.M. $37,000 (includes board, books, and fees).

Enrollment: full-time 544, part-time 578 (men 60%, women 40%). Faculty: full-time 106, part-time 72. Degrees conferred: M.B.A., A.M.B.A., E.M.B.A, M.S.I.M., M.S.I.S., M.B.A.-J.D., M.B.A.-M.S., M.B.A.-M.P.H., D.B.A.

ADMISSION REQUIREMENTS. Transcripts, two letters of recommendation, essays, résumé, GMAT required in support of School's application. Interview not required. TOEFL (minimum score 600) and Statement of Financial Support required for foreign applicants. Accepts transfer applicants. Graduates of unaccredited institutions not considered. Apply to Office of Admissions by April 1 (international applicants), May 1 (full-time, begins Fall semester only), July 15 (part-time), December 1 (January admissions), January 5 (D.B.A. admission). Application fee $60, $95 for doctoral candidates. Phone: (617)353-2670: fax: (617)353-7368; e-mail: mba@bu.edu, dba@bu.edu.

ADMISSION STANDARDS. Competitive. Usual minimum average: 3.0 (A = 4) median GMAT: 581.

FINANCIAL AID. Scholarships, merit scholarships, fellowships, assistantships, Federal W/S, loans. Apply to Financial Aid Office by March 15. Phone: (617)353-2670. Use FAFSA. Approximately 25% of students receive some form of aid.

DEGREE REQUIREMENTS. For A.M.B.A., E.M.B.A., M.B.A.: 64 semester hours maximum; advanced standing for previous academic background is possible; program must be completed in six years. For M.S.I.S.: one-year full-time (Summer and two semesters); field project. For M.S.I.M.: seventeen-month program. For D.B.A.: 14 courses minimum, at least eight in residence; curriculum paper; qualifying exam; teaching/applied research internships; dissertation.

FIELDS OF STUDY.
Accelerated M.B.A.
Executive M.B.A.
Health Care. M.B.A.
Information System. M.S.I.S.
International Management. M.B.A.
Investment Management. M.S.I.M.
Public and NonProfit Management. M.B.A.

D.B.A. CONCENTRATIONS:
Accounting.
Finance and Economics.
Information Systems.
Marketing.
Operations Management
Organizational Behavior.
Strategy and Policy.
Note: Dual degrees offered are M.B.A.-M.A. (Economics, International Relations, Medical Sciences), M.B.A.-M.S. (Television Administration, Management Information Sciences, Manufacturing Engineering), M.B.A.-J.D., M.B.A.-M.P.H.

Division of Graduate Medical Sciences

Annual tuition: $24,700.
Enrollment: full-time 50–60, first-year enrollment full-time (Fall) 10–15. Degrees conferred: Ph.D.

ADMISSION REQUIREMENTS. Official transcripts, letters of recommendation, GRE required in support of application (electronic application available). Interview required. Accepts transfer applicants. Graduates of unaccredited colleges not considered. Apply to Office of Admissions by March 30 (Fall), December 1 (Spring). Application fee $60. Phone: (617)638-5120; fax: (617)638-4842.

ADMISSION STANDARDS. Selective.

FINANCIAL AID. Fellowships, teaching/research assistantships; apply to appropriate department chair after acceptance. Apply by January 15 (Fall), October 15 (Spring). Use FAFSA.

DEGREE REQUIREMENTS. For Ph.D.: 8 semesters beyond master's; residency requirement of two consecutive semesters in full-time study; reading knowledge of at least one foreign language; qualifying exam; final oral exam.

FIELDS OF STUDY.
Anatomy
Behavior Neuroscience.
Biochemistry.
Biophysics.
Cell and Molecular Biology.
Clinical Investigation. M.A. only.
Human Genetics.
Immunology.
Medical Sciences. M.A. only.
Molecular Medicine.
Oral Biology.
Pathology.
Pharmacology.
Physiology.

School of Medicine

Established 1848. Located in Boston (02118). Acquired by Boston University in 1873. The Boston Medical Center is composed of the School of Medicine, School of Dental Medicine, School of Public Health, Center for Advancement in Health and Medicine, and the University Hospital. Library: 100,000 volumes. Annual tuition: $36,530. Off-campus housing only. Total average figure all other expenses: $13,500. Enrollment: first-year class 135 (3 EDP); total 629 (men 58%, women 42%). Degrees conferred: M.D., M.D-Ph.D., M.D.-M.P.H.

ADMISSION REQUIREMENTS. AMCAS, transcripts, MCAT (oldest score considered 2000), interview (by invitation), recommendations, and bachelor's degree from an approved college of arts and science required in support of application. Candidates of unusual ability sometimes accepted after three years in undergraduate school (90 semester hours required). Does have EDP. Accepts transfer candidates on a space available basis. Apply to School Office of Admissions after June 15, before October 1. Application fee $100. Phone: (617)638-4630.

ADMISSION STANDARDS. Very competitive. Accepts 10% total annual applicants. Approximately 20% are state residents. Gourman rating: 4.44. *U.S. News & World Report* ranking is in the top 39 U.S. medical schools; the NIH ranking for Boston University by awards was 39th, with 359 awards/grants; total dollars awarded $118,975,449.

FINANCIAL AID. Scholarships, loans available for accepted students. Apply to Financial Aid Office after acceptance. Approximately 40% receive aid other than loans from institutional funds.

DEGREE REQUIREMENTS. For M.D.: satisfactory completion of four-year program. For M.P.H., Ph.D.: see Graduate Schools listings.

School of Public Health

Annual tuition: $25,872, per credit $809. Graduate enrollment: full-time 282, part-time 319. Faculty: full-time 90, part-time 223. Degrees conferred: M.P.H., M.Sc., D.Sc., J.D.-M.P.H., M.A. (Medical Sciences)-M.P.H., M.B.A.-M.P.H., M.D.-M.P.H., M.S.W.-M.P.H.

ADMISSION REQUIREMENTS. All applicants should hold a baccalaureate degree. Official transcripts, three letters of recommendation, GRE required in support of College's application. GMAT/LSAT/MCAT can be submitted in lieu of GRE. Interview not required. TOEFL or IELTS required for international applicants. Transfer students not accepted. Graduates of unaccredited institutions not considered. Apply to the School's Office of Admissions. For M.P.H. and D.Sc. (Environmental Health Science) Fall applications completed by March 15 will be notified by April 15, those completed by April 15 will be notified by May 31. Spring applications completed by October 25 will be notified by November 25, applications completed after October 25 will be reviewed on a space available basis. For M.Sc., D.Sc. (Epidemiology) admits Fall only, apply by April 15. Application fee $60. Phone: (617)638-4640; fax: (717)638-5299; e-mail: sphadmis@bu.edu.

ADMISSION STANDARDS. Selective. Usual minimum average: 3.0 (A = 4).

FINANCIAL AID. Annual awards from institutional funds: Dean's scholarships, grants, traineeships, private loan programs, Federal W/S, loans. Approved for VA benefits. Apply by April 15 to Office of Student Financial Management. Phone: (617)638-5115; e-mail: osfmspj@bumc.bu.edu. Use FAFSA. 25% of students receive aid other than loans from School and outside sources. Aid available for part-time students.

DEGREE REQUIREMENTS. For M.P.H.: 48 credit program, at least 32 credits in residence. For Dr.P.H.: 40 credit program beyond master's degree; doctoral seminar; Field Practice placement; dissertation; final oral exam. For D.Sc.: 48 credit program beyond master's degree; one year of full-time study (two consecutive semesters); comprehensive; dissertation; final oral exam.

FIELDS OF STUDY.
Biostatistics. M.A, Ph.D. Both degrees are offered jointly with the Department of Mathematics, Graduate School of Arts and Science and with collaboration with the Division of Graduate Medical Sciences.
Epidemiology. M.Sc., D.Sc.
Environmental Health Sciences. D.Sc. only.
Public Health. Includes environmental health, epidemiology & biostatistics, health law, health services, international health, maternal and child health, social and behavior sciences. M.P.H., Dr.P.H.

School of Social Work

Annual tuition: $19,890, per credit on-campus $622, off-campus $440. On-campus housing available. Contact Housing Office. Phone: (617)353-3511. Day-care facilities available.

Enrollment: full-time 190, part-time 191. School faculty: full-time 26, part-time 93. Degree conferred: M.S.W., M.S.W.-J.D., M.S.W.-M.P.H., M.S.W.-M.T.S., M.S.W.-Ed.M., Ph.D. (Social Work and Sociology).

ADMISSION REQUIREMENTS. Transcripts, references, MAT/GRE, personal statement required in support of School's application. TOEFL required for international applicants. Interview not required. Accepts transfer applicants. Graduates of unaccredited colleges not considered. Apply to the School's Admissions Office by March 1. Application fee $50. Phone: (617)353-3765; fax: (617)353-5612; e-mail: busswad@bu.edu.

ADMISSION STANDARDS. Selective. Usual minimum GPA: 2.7. Average GPA: 3.2 (A = 4).

FINANCIAL AID. Annual awards from institutional funds: Scholarships, internships, grants, Federal W/S, loans. Apply to School's Financial Aid Office. Phone: (617)353-3765. Use FAFSA and School's application. About 50% of students receive aid other than loans from School and outside sources. Aid available for part-time students.

DEGREE REQUIREMENTS. For M.S.W.: 65 credit programs, advance standing may be awarded for candidates with a bachelor's degree in Social Work; field education. For Ph.D.: at least 48 credits beyond the master's; reading proficiency in one foreign language; qualifying exam; critical essay; dissertation; final oral exam.

FIELDS OF STUDY.
Social Work. Includes major in either Clinical Social Work practice with individuals, families, and groups, or Macro practice, which includes community organizing, management, and planning.

School of Theology

Graduate study since 1839. Coed. Semester system. Annual tuition: $10,800, per credit $340. Graduate enrollment: full-time 233, part-time 33. Faculty: full-time 21, part-time 14. On-campus housing available. Day care facilities available. Degrees conferred: M.Div., M.T.S., D.Min., S.T.M., M.S.M., Th.D. The A.M. and Ph.D. are offered through the Graduate School.

ADMISSION REQUIREMENTS. Official transcripts, four letters of recommendation required in support of application. GRE required for some degrees. TOEFL, TWE required for international applicants. Interview not required. Accepts transfer applicants. Apply to Director of Admissions by February 15 (Fall), October 15 (Spring). For A.M. or Ph.D., apply by November 1 (Fall), February 1 (Spring). Application fee $50. Phone: (617)353-3036; fax: (617)353-0140; e-mail: sthadmis@bu.edu.

ADMISSION STANDARDS. Very selective. Usual minimum average: 3.0 M.Div.; 3.3 D.Min; 3.3 Th.D. (A = 4).

FINANCIAL AID. Annual awards from institutional funds: fellowships, scholarships, research, teaching assistantships, Federal W/S, loans. Approved for VA benefits. Apply by July 15 to the Director of Financial Aid. Phone: (617)353-3053; fax: (617)353-3061. Use FAFSA. All D.Min. students and 50% of Ph.D. students receive aid other than loans from School; 80% of all students receive some form of financial aid. Aid available for part-time students.

DEGREE REQUIREMENTS. For M.Div.: 96 credits minimum, at least 32 in residence and two semesters in full-time attendance; functional competence in one Biblical language for Biblical Studies majors. For M.T.S.: 64 credits minimum, at least 32 in residence. For S.T.M.: 32 credits minimum beyond the M. Div., at least 24 in residence and two semesters in full-time attendance; final comprehensive exam or thesis. For M.S.M.: 60 credits minimum, at least 32 in residence and two semesters in full-time attendance; thesis or research project or composition or two recitals. For D.Min.: 40 credits minimum beyond the M.Div., at least two semesters in full-time residence. For Th.D.: 48 credits minimum; language and/or research competence; qualifying exam; dissertation; final oral exam.

FIELDS OF STUDY:
Biblical Studies.
Church History.
Church Ministries and Administration.
Ethics.
Liturgical Studies.
Missions and Evangelism.
Philosophical and Systematic Theology.
Psychology of Religion and Pastoral Counseling.
Religious Education.
Sacred Music.
Sociology of Religion and Social Ethics.

BOWIE STATE UNIVERSITY

Bowie, Maryland 20715-3318
Web site: www.bowiestate.edu

Established 1865. CGS member. Located 25 miles N of Washington, D.C. Coed. Public control. Semester system. Evening session only. Library: 180,000 volumes, 317,000 microforms, 1150 current periodicals.

Tuition: per credit, resident $144, nonresident $244. On-campus housing for single student only. Average academic year housing costs: $4455 (including board). Contact Housing Department for both on- and off-campus housing information. Phone (301)464-7135.

Division of Graduate Studies

Graduate study since 1970. Enrollment: full-time 304, part-time 1354. Faculty: full-time 31, part-time 43. Degrees conferred: M.A., M.B.A., M.P.A., M.S., M.Ed., Ed.D., M.M.I.S., M.S.N.

ADMISSION REQUIREMENTS. Official transcripts, three letters of recommendation required in support of application. Written essay required for Nursing. TOEFL required for international applicants. Accepts transfer applicants. Graduates of unaccredited institutions not considered. Apply to Graduate Office by June 29 (Fall), December 7 (Spring). Rolling admissions process. Application fee $30. Phone: (877)772-6943, (301)860-3422; e-mail: admissions@bowiestate.edu.

ADMISSION STANDARDS. Selective. Usual minimum average: 2.5 (A = 4).

FINANCIAL AID. Fellowships, assistantships, tuition waivers, Federal W/S, loans. Approved for VA benefits. Apply to Dean's Office for fellowships, assistantships; to Financial Aid Office for all other programs. No specified closing date. Phone: (301)464-6544. Use FAFSA.

DEGREE REQUIREMENTS. For most master's: 36–39 semester hours minimum; advancement to candidacy; seminar paper; comprehensive exam. For M.B.A.: 45 semester hours minimum. For M.S. in Nursing: 42–37 semester hours minimum; practicum; comprehensive exam; thesis. For Ed.D.: 60 credit program beyond the master's degree; qualifying exam; internship; dissertation; final order exam.

FIELDS OF STUDY.

SCHOOL OF ARTS AND SCIENCES:
Applied and Computational Mathematics. M.S.
Computer Science. M.S.
English. M.A.
Organizational Communications. M.A.

SCHOOL OF EDUCATION:
Educational Leadershp. Ed.D.
Elementary Education. M.Ed.
Guidance and Counseling. M.Ed.
Reading. M.Ed.
School Administration and Supervision. M.Ed.
Secondary Education. M.Ed.
Special Education. M.Ed.
Teaching. M.A.T.

SCHOOL OF PROFESSIONAL STUDIES:
Administrative Management. M.A.
Human Resources Development. M.A.
Business Administration. Includes concentrations in accounting, finance, management, marketing management. M.B.A.

Management Information Systems. M.M.I.S.
Nursing. M.S.N.
Public Administration. Includes concentrations in public administration, public policy & management, human resource management. M.P.A.

BOWLING GREEN STATE UNIVERSITY

Bowling Green, Ohio 43403-0180
Web site: www.bgsu.edu

Founded 1910. CGS member. Located 23 miles S of Toledo. Coed. State assisted. Semester system. Special facilities: Center for Archival Collections, Center for the Study of Popular Culture, Center for Photo Chemical Sciences, Center for Microscopy and Microanalysis, Institute for Great Lakes Research, Environmental Study Center, Laboratory of Marine Studies, Population and Society Research Center, Center for Governmental Research, Public Service Management Center, Institute for Psychological Research and Application, Social Philosophy and Policy Center. Library: 1,903,000 volumes, 1,772,000 microforms, 5427 current periodicals, 167 PCs in all libraries.

Tuition: per credit, resident $404, nonresident $720. On-campus housing available for graduate students. Average academic year housing costs: $3320–$4732; meal plans cost $2000–$3000. Contact Director of Student Housing and Residential Programs for both on- and off-campus housing information. Phone: (419)372-2011.

Graduate College

Enrollment: full-time 1550, part-time 934. University faculty: full-time 567, part-time 165. Degrees conferred: M.A., M.A.T., M.M., M.B.A., M.O.D., M.P.A., M.R.C., M.S., M.F.A., M.Ed., M.A.H.E., M.I.T., Specialist, Ed.S., Ph.D.

ADMISSION REQUIREMENTS. Two official transcripts, GRE/GMAT, three letters of recommendation to department required in support of College's application. TOEFL/MELAB required of international applicants. Accepts transfer students. Apply at least six months prior to semester of registration (Ph.D.), three months prior to semester of registration (Masters). Application fee $35. Phone: (419)372-2791; fax: (419)372-8569; e-mail: gradweb@bgnet.bgsu.edu.

ADMISSION STANDARDS. Competitive. Usual minimum average: 2.6 (A = 4).

FINANCIAL AID. Annual awards from institutional funds: Ph.D. fellowships, research assistantships, teaching assistantships, internships and externships, Federal W/S, loans. Approved for VA benefits. Admission process must be completed by January 15. Apply by February 15 to appropriate department chair for fellowships, assistantships; to Financial Aid Office for all other programs. Phone: (419)372-2651. Use FAFSA and submit as soon as possible after January 1. About 60% of students receive aid from Institution in the form of assistantships or fellowships.

DEGREE REQUIREMENTS. General requirements for master's: Plan I—30 hours minimum, minimum of 24 hours in residence thesis; final written/oral exam. Plan II—30 hours minimum, minimum of 24 hours in residence; final comprehensive exam. For M.A.: Plan I or II available. For M.Ed.: 30 hours minimum; thesis or written exam; 33 hours minimum; comprehensive exam. For M.A.T.: 35 hours minimum;; final written comprehensive. For M.M.: 34 hours minimum; option of thesis, recital and research document or composition. For M.B.A.: Phase I—for students with little or no previous work in business administration or economics; required work must be completed, but not to exceed the 30 hours of Phase II courses. For M.I.T.: 33 hours minimum; thesis or major project. For M.S.: 30 hours minimum; Plan I or Plan II available. For M.F.A.: in Art, 62 hours; thesis; exhibition; in Creative Writing, 40 hours minimum; thesis. For M.A.H.E.: 33 hours minimum; applied or research option. For M.O.D.: 33 hours minimum; thesis. For M.P.A.: 42 hours minimum; thesis; final written/oral exam. For M.R.C.; 48 hours minimum; thesis; final comprehensive exam. For Specialist: 30 hours minimum beyond the master's; comprehensive oral exam. For Ph.D.: 90 hours minimum beyond the bachelor's; proficiency in one foreign language, proficiency in computer research applications; preliminary exam; dissertation; final/oral written exam.

FIELDS OF STUDY.

Accountancy. M.Acc.
American Culture Studies. M.A., M.A.T., Ph.D.
Applied Biology. Specialist.
Applied Human Ecology. Includes human development, family studies, food and nutrition, textile and clothing. M.A.H.E.
Applied Philosophy. M.A., Ph.D.
Applied Statistics (Mathematics). M.S., Ph.D.
Applied Statistics and Operation Research. M.S.
Art. M.A., M.F.A.
Biological Sciences. M.A., Ph.D.
Business Administration. M.B.A.
Business Education. M.Ed.
Career and Technology Education. M.Ed.
Chemistry. M.S., M.A.T.
College Student Personnel. M.A., M.Ed.
Communication Disorders. M.S., Ph.D.
Communications Studies. M.A., Ph.D.
Computer Science. M.S.
Creative Writing. M.F.A.
Criminal Justice. M.S.C.J.
Curriculum and Instruction. Includes elementary, library and educational media, mathematics supervision, secondary, reading.
Economics. M.A.
Education. Includes elementary, secondary. M.Ed., Ph.D.
Educational Administration and Supervision. M.Ed., Ed.S., Ph.D.
Educational Teaching and Learning. M.Ed., Ed.S.
English. Includes creative, interpersonal, technical writing, teaching. M.A., Ph.D.
Family and Consumer Sciences. M.F.C.S.
French. M.A.
Geology. M.S., M.A.T.
German. M.A., M.A.T.
Guidance and Counseling. M.A., M.Ed.
History. M.A., M.A.T., Ph.D.
Human Movement, Sport, and Leisure Studies. M.Ed.
Industrial Technology. M.I.T.
Leadership Studies. Ed.D.
Mathematics and Statistics. Includes pure mathematics, mathematical statistics, scientific computation. M.A., M.A.T., Ph.D.
Mathematics Supervision. Ed.S.
Music. Includes performance, music education, instrumental specialist, music composition, music theory, music history. M.M.
Organizational Development. M.O.D.
Philosophy. M.A., Ph.D.
Photochemical Sciences. Ph.D.
Physics. Includes astrophysics, computational physics, theoretical physics, solid state, material science. M.A.T., M.S.
Political Science. M.A., M.A.T.
Popular Culture. M.A., Ph.D.
Psychology. Includes clinical, developmental, experimental, industrial, social. M.A., Ph.D.
Public Health. M.P.H. Joint degree composed of Medical College of Ohio, University of Toledo, and BGSU.
Public Administration. M.P.A.
Reading. M.Ed.
Rehabilitation Counseling. M.R.C.
School Psychology. M.Ed.
Sociology. M.A., Ph.D.
Spanish. M.A.
Special Education. Includes educable mentally retarded, trainable mentally retarded, learning/behavioral disorders. M.Ed.
Technology Management. Ph.D.
Theater. M.A., Ph.D.

BRADLEY UNIVERSITY

Peoria, Illinois 61625
Web site: www.bradley.edu

Founded 1897. CGS member. Located 163 miles SW of Chicago. Coed. Private control. Semester system. Special facilities: Center for Learning Resources (includes on-campus CCTV and satellite, teleproduction capacity, computer center), Caterpillar Global Communications Center, Materials Testing and Research Lab, Institute for Urban Affairs and Business Research. Library: 530,000 volumes, 1950 subscriptions. More than 2000 computers on campus for student use, 112 PCs in all libraries.

Annual tuition: per credit 1–7 hours $394, 7½–11½ hours $489; Master of Liberal Studies $209 per hour. No on-campus housing available. Average academic year housing costs: $700 per month. Contact Director of Housing for off-campus housing information. Phone: (309)677-3218.

Graduate School

Enrollment: full-time 183, part-time 652. Graduate faculty: full- and part-time 251. Degrees conferred: M.A.. M.S., M.F.A., M.B.A., M.M.E., M.M., M.S.C.E., M.S.E.E., M.S.I.E., M.S.M.E., M.L.S., M.S.N., M.N.S.

ADMISSION REQUIREMENTS. Two official transcripts, two references required in support of School's application. Interview, GRE required by some departments. GMAT for M.B.A. applicants, MAT or GRE for all Education and Nursing programs. Portfolio for Art program. TOEFL and evidence of financial resources required of international applicants. Accepts transfer applicants. Graduates of unaccredited institutions not considered. Apply to Dean of the Graduate School at least two months prior to registration. Rolling admission process. Application fee $40, $50 for international candidates. Phone: (309)677-2371; fax: (309)677-3343; e-mail: bugrad@bradley.edu.

ADMISSION STANDARDS. Selective. Usual minimum average: 2.5 (2.75 major areas) (A = 4). Nondegree students permitted.

FINANCIAL AID. Scholarships, fellowships, assistantships, full and partial tuition waivers, Federal W/S, loans. Approved for VA benefits. Apply by March 1 to Dean of the Graduate School for assistantships; to Financial Aid Office for all other programs. Phone: (309)677-3215. Use FAFSA. Aid available for part-time students.

DEGREE REQUIREMENTS. For master's: 30 semester hours minimum; thesis/nonthesis option; final comprehensive exam.

FIELDS OF STUDY.

FOSTER COLLEGE OF BUSINESS ADMINISTRATION:
Accounting. M.S.A.
Business Administration. M.B.A.
Executive Master of Business Administration. E.M.B.A.

SLANE COLLEGE OF COMMUNICATIONS AND FINE ARTS:
Art. Includes ceramics, painting, photography, printmaking, sculpture. M.A., M.F.A.

COLLEGE OF EDUCATION AND HEALTH SCIENCES:
Curriculum and Instruction. M.A.
Leadership in Educational Administration. M.A.
Human Development. M.A.
Human Service Administration. M.A.
Nurse Administered Anesthesia. M.S.N.
Nurse Administration. M.S.N.
Physical Therapy. M.P.T.

COLLEGE OF ENGINEERING AND TECHNOLOGY:
Civil Engineering. M.S.C.E.
Electrical Engineering. M.S.E.E.
Industrial Engineering. M.S.I.E.
Manufacturing Engineering. M.S.Mf.E.
Mechanical Engineering. M.S.M.E.z

COLLEGE OF LIBERAL ARTS AND SCIENCES:
Biology. M.S.
Chemistry. M.S.
Computer Information System. M.S.
Computer Science. M.S.
English. M.A.
Liberal Studies. M.L.S.

BRANDEIS UNIVERSITY
Waltham, Massachusetts 02254-9110
Web site: www.brandeis.edu

Founded 1948. CGS and AAU member. Located 8 miles NW of Boston. Coed. Private control. Semester system. Special facilities: research centers for biology, biochemistry, chemistry, mathematics, social sciences, physics; Judaic Center, American Civilization Center, Humanities Center, Rose Art Museum, music center, Rosenstiel Basic Medical Sciences Research Center, Center for Health Policy Analysis and Research, Levinson Policy Institute, Center for Employment and Income Studies, Center for Aging and Income Maintenance, theater arts center. Library: 1,100,000 volumes, 16,100 subscriptions. Total University enrollment: 4300.

Annual tuition: full-time $25,392, per course $3174. Some on-campus housing for graduate students. Housing costs: $500–$950 per month. Apply by June 15. Contact Housing Office for off-campus housing information. Phone: (781)736-3550.

Graduate School of Arts and Sciences

Graduate study since 1953. Enrollment: full- and part-time 1154 (men 53%, women 47%). Faculty: full-time 360, part-time 160. Degrees conferred: M.A., M.F.A., Ph.D.

ADMISSION REQUIREMENTS. Transcripts, statement of purpose, two letters of recommendation required in support of application (electronic application available). GRE, interview required for some departments. Writing samples, portfolio, or audition for theater and studio programs. GRE recommended for all departments. TOEFL (600 minimum score) required of all foreign applicants. Accepts transfer applicants. Graduates of unaccredited colleges not considered. Apply to the Associate Dean of the School by January 15, earliest deadline (Fall). Application fee $60, electronic fee $50. Phone: (781)736-3410; fax: (781) 736-3412; e-mail: gradschool@brandeis.edu.

ADMISSION STANDARDS. Very competitive. Usual minimum average: 3.0 (A = 4).

FINANCIAL AID. Scholarships, fellowships, assistantships for teaching/research, tuition waivers, Federal W/S, loans. Apply to the Associate Dean of the School by February 1. Phone: (781)736-3410. Use FAFSA. Aid available for part-time students.

DEGREE REQUIREMENTS. For M.A.: 24 semester hours minimum in residence; reading knowledge of one foreign language; thesis sometimes required; final written/oral exam. For M.F.A. in Music: 36 hours minimum in residence; reading knowledge of one or two foreign languages; moderate instrumental proficiency; general exams; composition for composers, thesis for music history or theory majors. For M.F.A. in Theater Arts: acting and dramatic writing; 48 semester hours in residence; thesis play for dramatic writing; design-technical, 54 semester hours in residence; thesis. For Ph.D.: 48 hours minimum beyond the bachelor's, at least one year in residence; reading knowledge of at least one foreign language for most departments; qualifying exams; dissertation; final oral exam.

FIELDS OF STUDY.
American History. M.A., Ph.D.
Anthropology. GRE for admission; apply by February 16. M.A., Ph.D.
Biochemistry. GRE, three letters of recommendation for admission. Apply by January 15, rolling admissions. M.S., Ph.D.
Biology. GRE, three letters of recommendation for admission. Rolling admission. M.S., Ph.D.
Biophysics and Structural Biology. GRE, three letters of recommendation for admission. Rolling admission. M.S., Ph.D.
Chemistry. GRE for admission. Apply by March 15. M.S., Ph.D.
Classical Studies. M.A.
Comparative History. For M.A.: writing sample for admission; apply by July 30. For Ph.D.: GRE, writing sample. Apply by February 1.
Computer Science. GRE, three letters of recommendation. Apply by March 1. M.A., Ph.D.
English and American Literature. GRE/Subject, writing sample. Apply by February 15. Ph.D.
Genetic Counseling. GRE, three letters of recommendation. Apply by February 15. M.S.
History of American Civilization. For M.A.: GRE, writing sample for admission. Apply by July 30.
International Economics and Finance. GRE or GMAT, three letters of recommendation for admission. Apply by March 1.
Jewish Communal Services. GRE or GMAT, interview, writing sample for admission. Apply by February 15. M.A.
Literary Studies. Writing sample for admission. Apply by March 15.
Mathematics. GRE/Subject. Apply by February 15. M.A., Ph.D.
Molecular and Cell Biology. Ph.D. only.
Music. For musicology, GRE and writing sample for admission; Composition, sample of work. Apply by January 31. M.A., M.F.A., Ph.D.
Near Eastern and Judaic Studies. GRE suggested. Apply by February 1. M.A., Ph.D.
Neuroscience. M.S., Ph.D.
Physics. GRE/Subject Test for admission. Apply by February 15. M.A., Ph.D.
Politics. GRE, writing sample, three letters of recommendation for admission. M.A., Ph.D.
Psychology and Cognitive Science. GRE/Subject Test for admission. For Ph.D.: apply by February 15; for M.S., apply by June 1. M.A., Ph.D.
Software Engineering. M.S.E.
Sociology. Writing sample for admission. Apply by February 15. M.A., Ph.D.
Theater Arts. For admission: designers, portfolio; actors, audition; writers, sample of work. M.F.A.
Women's Studies. Joint degree with anthropology, English, Near Eastern and Judaic studies, or sociology.

Graduate School of International Economics and Finance

Special program: a semester abroad at Partner Universities in twelve countries. Affiliated institutions are Copenhagen Business School (Denmark), Ecole Superieure des Sciences Economiques et Commerciales (France), Eramus University (The Netherlands), Escuela Superior de Administracion y Direccion de Empresas (Spain), Fundacao Getulio Vargas (Brazil), Instituto Tecnologico Autonomo de Mexico (Mexico), International University of Japan, Keio University (Japan), WHU Koblenz (Germany), Luigi Bocconi University (Italy), National University of Singapore, Tel Aviv University (Israel), Univeersiteit Maastricht (The Netherlands), University of Paris (France), Yonsei University (Korea).

Annual tuition: $27,345, per course $2465.

Graduate enrollment: full-time 167, part-time 29. Faculty: full-time 25, part-time 10. Degrees conferred: M.A.eif, M.B.A.i., M.S.F., Ph.D.

ADMISSION REQUIREMENTS. Official transcripts, three letters of recommendation, résumé, MAT or GRE required in support of College's application. Interview encouraged. TOEFL (minimum score 600, 250 on computer-based test) and official translations of all academic documents required for international applicants. Transfer students not accepted. Graduates of unaccredited institutions not considered. Apply to Admissions Office, preferably by February 1 (Fall). Application fee $50.

ADMISSION STANDARDS. Very selective. Usual minimum average: 3.3 (A = 4), GRE range: 510–660.

FINANCIAL AID. Scholarships, grants, assistantships, internships, Federal W/S, loans. Approved for VA benefits. Apply by March 1 to Financial Aid. Use FAFSA (School code: 002133). Phone: (781)736-2250.

DEGREE REQUIREMENTS. For M.A.eif: two-year, full-time program; knowledge of at least one foreign language; one semester at a Partner University. For M.B.A.i.: two-year program, 16 courses; basic knowledge of one foreign language other than English; semester of study at Partner University; capstone. For M.S.F.: 18–20 month program (full- or part-time), 10 courses; capstone. For Ph.D.: three- to four-year program; preliminary exam; two areas of specialization; research papers; thesis; final oral exam.

FIELDS OF STUDY.
Finance. M.S.F.
International Economics and Finance. M.A.eif.
International Finance. M.B.A.i.

The Heller School for Social Policy and Management
Web site: www.heller.brandeis.edu

Organized for training in social policy and health, and human services management, 1959. Semester system. Annual tuition master's: full-time $14,110, part-time evening $1485. For Ph.D.: $26,281 per year. On-campus housing available. Day-care facilities available.

Enrollment: full-time 125, part-time 54. Faculty: full-time 44, part-time 15. Degrees conferred: M.A., M.M., M.B.A. (Human Services), Ph.D.

ADMISSION REQUIREMENTS. Transcripts, successful academic and professional experience, writing sample, statement of purpose, two letters of recommendation, résumé, GMAT/GRE required in support of application. Interviews suggested. Apply no later than December 15 (Ph.D.), March 15 (Master's, Fall), November 1 (Master's, Spring), June 1 (Master's, part-time, Fall), priority given to early applicants. Application process on a rolling basis. Master's academic year starts in June. Application fee $50. Phone (781)736-3835; fax: (781)736-3881; e-mail: HellerAdmissions@brandeis.edu.

ADMISSION STANDARDS. Competitive. Usual minimum average: 3.0 (A = 4).

FINANCIAL AID. Scholarships, grants, fellowships, teaching assistantships, traineeships, tuition waivers, loans. Apply to Director of Financial Aid by February 15. Phone: (781)736-3820. Use FAFSA and CSSFA profile.

DEGREE REQUIREMENTS. For M.B.A, M.M.: (day) 17 semester courses; internship; (evening) program 17 semester courses; team consulting project. For M.A.: two-year program; one-year residence; practical training; fieldwork; project. For Ph.D.: 14–18 semester courses minimum; qualifying exam; dissertation; final oral exam.

FIELDS OF STUDY.
Health Care and Children, Youth and Family Services. M.M. only.
Social Policy. Ph.D.
Sustainable International Development. M.A.

UNIVERSITY OF BRIDGEPORT
Bridgeport, Connecticut 06601
Web site: www.bridgeport.edu

Founded 1927. CGS member. Located 60 miles NE of New York. Coed. Private control. Semester system. Special facilities: Bernhard Center for Arts and Humanities, Carlson Art Gallery, Connecticut Technology Institute, Center for Venture Management and Entrepreneurial Studies. Library: 310,000 volumes, 2117 subscriptions.

Tuition: per credit School of Education and Human Resources $365, School of Business $385, School of Engineering and Design $385. On-campus housing for single students, none for married students. Average academic year housing costs: $3780 ($7070 including board). Contact Office of Residential Life for both on- and off-campus housing information. Phone: (203)576-4461.

Graduate Studies

Enrollment: full-time 872, part-time 965. Faculty: full-time 92, part-time 232. Degrees conferred: M.S., M.B.A., Sixth Year Professional Diplomas, Ed.D.

ADMISSION REQUIREMENTS. Official transcripts, three letters of recommendation required in support of application (electronic application available). GRE/GMAT/MAT required by some departments. Supplemental application, personal statement, and/or an interview may be requested. TOEFL required for international applicants. Accepts transfer applicants. Apply to Office of Admissions at least 30 days (60 days for Business) prior to registration. Admits Fall, Spring, and Summer. Application fee $25, $35 for international applicants. Phone: (800)898-8278, (203)576-4552; fax: (203)576-4941. E-mail: admit@bridgeport.edu.

ADMISSION STANDARDS. Selective. Usual minimum average: 2.5 (A = 4).

FINANCIAL AID. Assistantships, endowed scholarships, internships, co-op, residence hall directors, Federal W/S, loans. Approved for VA benefits. For assistantship contact department, for all other aid apply to Financial Aid Office; no specified closing date. Phone: (203)576-4568. Use FAFSA.

DEGREE REQUIREMENTS. For master's: 30–33 credits minimum, at least 27 in residence; thesis/nonthesis options. For Sixth-Year Professional Certificate: 30 credits beyond master's, at least 24 in residence. For Ed.D.: at least two years in residence; qualifying exam; dissertation; final oral exam.

FIELDS OF STUDY.

NUTRITION INSTITUTE:
Human Nutrition.

SCHOOL OF BUSINESS:
Business Administration. Includes optional concentrations in accounting, computer applications and information systems, computer science, finance, global marketing, operations.

SCHOOL OF EDUCATION AND HUMAN RESOURCES:
Counseling. Includes human resource development, community, college student personnel services, school.
Education. Includes elementary, secondary.
Educational Leadership. Ed.D.
Human Resources.

SCHOOL OF ENGINEERING AND DESIGN:
Computer Engineering.
Computer Science.
Electrical Engineering.
Mechanical Engineering.
Technology Management.

BRIDGEWATER STATE COLLEGE
Bridgewater, Massachusetts 02325-0001
Web site: www.bridgew.edu

Founded 1840. CGS member. Located 35 miles S of Boston. Coed. State control. Semester system. Library: 280,000 volumes, 1600 subscriptions. Approximately 500 computers on campus for student use.

Tuition and fees: per hour, resident $135, nonresident $359. No on-campus housing available.

Office of Graduate and Continuing Education

Enrollment: approximately 1800 full- and part-time. Graduate faculty: approximately 140. Degrees conferred: M.A., M.A.T., M.Ed., M.P.A., M.S., M.S.M., C.A.G.S.

ADMISSION REQUIREMENTS. Official transcripts, three letters of reference, GRE required in support of College's application (GRE Subject Test for M.A. Only). Interview required for some programs. TOEFL required for international applicants. Accept transfer applicants. Apply to the Graduate Office by October 1 for November admission, December 1 for February admission, March 1 for May admission, June 1 for August admission. Application fee $25. Phone (508)531-1300; fax: (508)531-6162.

ADMISSION STANDARDS. Selective for most departments. Usual minimum average: 2.5 (A = 4).

FINANCIAL AID. Assistantships, scholarships, tuition waivers, grants, Federal W/S, loans. Apply by March 1 to Graduate School Dean for assistantships; to Financial Aid for all other programs. Phone: (508)531-1341. Use FAFSA.

DEGREE REQUIREMENTS. For M.A.: 30 semester hours minimum; research proficiency test; comprehensive exam; thesis. For M.A.T., M.S., M.S.M., M.Ed., M.P.A.: 30–36 semester hours minimum; thesis/nonthesis option; comprehensive exam. For

C.A.G.S.: 30 semester hours beyond the master's degree; special project.

FIELDS OF STUDY.
Accounting. M.S.M.
Biology. M.A.T.
Chemistry. M.A.T.
Computer Science. M.S.
Counseling. M.Ed., C.A.G.S.
Creative Arts. M.A.T.
Criminal Justice. M.S.
Earth Sciences. M.A.T.
Early Childhood Education. M.Ed.
Educational Leadership. M.Ed., C.A.G.S.
Elementary Education. M.Ed.
English. M.A., M.A.T.
Global Electronic Commerce. M.S.M.
Health Education. M.A.T.
Health Promotion. M.Ed.
History. M.A.T.
Instructional Technology. M.Ed.
Library Media Studies. M.Ed.
Marketing. M.S.M.
Mathematics. M.A.T.
Organizational Development. M.S.M.
Physical Education. M.A.T., M.S.
Physical Sciences. M.A.T.
Physics. M.A.T.
Psychology. M.A.
Public Administration. Includes financial and personnel administration, municipal development and management, public safety administration, nonprofit and human services administration. M.P.A.
Reading. M.Ed., C.A.G.S.
Social Studies. M.A.T.
Special Education. M.Ed.
Technology Management. M.S.M.

BRIGHAM YOUNG UNIVERSITY
Provo, Utah 84602-1001
Web site: www.byu.edu

Founded 1875. CGS member. Located 50 miles S of Salt Lake City. Coed. Private control; Church of Jesus Christ of Latter-day Saints. Trimester system. Library: 2,600,000 volumes, 16,200 subscriptions. Total University enrollment approximately 32,000.

Annual tuition and fees: full-time, LDS church members $3860, nonchurch members $5790; for Marriott School of Management, LDS church members $6140, nonchurch members $9120. On-campus housing for 1048 married students, 2210 for men, 2950 for women. Average annual housing cost: $6580 for single students (includes room and board). Apply to Assistant Director Housing Services. Phone: (801)378-2611. For off-campus housing information, contact Off-Campus Housing Manager. Phone: (801)422-1513.

Graduate Studies

Graduate study since 1918. Enrollment: full-time 1623, part-time 1393. Graduate faculty: full-time 1064, part-time 141. Degrees conferred: M.A., M.S., M.P.A., M.Acc., M.B.A., M.Ed., M.E.A., M.E.M., M.M., M.T.M., Ed.Spec. Cert., Ed.D., Ph.D., TESL Certificate.

ADMISSION REQUIREMENTS. Two transcripts, three letters of recommendation required in support of application. GRE/

GMAT/MAT required by some departments. TOEFL required of foreign applicants. Interview required by some departments. Accepts transfer applicants. Graduates of unaccredited colleges not considered. Usual deadline February 1 (Fall), June 30 (Winter), February 1 (Spring), March 15 (Summer). Apply to Office of Graduate Studies, B-356 ASB by published department deadlines. Application fee $30. Phone: (801)378-4091; fax: (801)378-5238; e-mail: gradstudies@byu.edu.

ADMISSION STANDARDS. Selective for most departments. Usual minimum average: 3.0 (A = 4).

FINANCIAL AID. Scholarships, internships, teaching/research assistantships, Federal W/S, loans. Apply by application deadline to department of specialization for scholarships and assistantships; to Office of Financial Aid for all other aid. Phone: (801)378-4104; fax: (801)378-4264. Use FAFSA.

DEGREE REQUIREMENTS. For master's: 30 semester hours minimum, at least 20 in residence for most programs; thesis/nonthesis option; final oral/written exam. For Certificate, Ed.Spec.Cert.: 30 semester hours beyond master's. For Ed.D.: three years minimum of full-time study or its equivalent beyond the bachelor's, two consecutive semesters in residence; qualifying exam; research project; final oral/written exam. For Ph.D.: ordinarily two years of full-time course work or research or its equivalent to be taken in residence; language/research tool; comprehensive exam; dissertation; final oral exam.

FIELDS OF STUDY.

COLLEGE OF BIOLOGY AND AGRICULTURAL SCIENCES:
Agronomy. M.S.
Animal Science. M.S.
Botany and Range Science. Includes biological science education, botany, range science, wildlife and range resources. M.S., Ph.D. (Botany)
Food Science. M.S.
Horticulture. M.S.
Microbiology. M.S., Ph.D.
Molecular Biology. M.S., Ph.D.
Nutrition. M.S.
Zoology. M.S., Ph.D.

COLLEGE OF ENGINEERING AND TECHNOLOGY:
Chemical Engineering. M.S., Ph.D.
Civil Engineering. M.S., Ph.D.
Electrical Engineering. M.S., Ph.D.
Engineering Technology. M.S.
Mechanical Engineering. M.S., Ph.D.
Technology Education. M.S.

COLLEGE OF FAMILY, HOME AND SOCIAL SCIENCES:
Anthropology. M.A.
Clinical Psychology. P.h.D.
Geography. M.A.
History. M.A.
Marriage and Family Therapy. M.S., Ph.D.
Marriage, Family, and Human Development. M.S., Ph.D.
Psychology. M.S., Ph.D.
Social Work. M.S.W.
Sociology. M.S., Ph.D.

COLLEGE OF FINE ARTS AND COMMUNICATIONS:
Mass Communication. M.A.
Music. Includes composition, conducting music education, musicology, pedagogy, performance. M.A., M.M.
Theater and Media Arts. M.A.

Visual Arts. Includes art education, art history, curatorial studies, studio art. M.A., M.F.A.

COLLEGE OF HUMANITIES:
Comparative Literature. M.A.
English. M.A.
French Studies. M.A.
German Literature. M.A.
Humanities. M.A.
Language Acquisition. Includes Arabic, Chinese, French, German, Japanese, Russian. M.A.
Linguistics. M.A.
Portuguese. M.A.
Spanish. M.A.
TESOL. M.A.

COLLEGE OF NURSING:
Nursing. Includes nursing administration, family nurse practitioner, pediatric nurse practitioner. M.S.

COLLEGE OF PHYSICAL AND MATHEMATICAL SCIENCES:
Biochemistry. M.S., Ph.D.
Chemistry. M.S., Ph.D.
Computer Science. M.S., Ph.D.
Geology. M.S.
Mathematics. Includes mathematics education. M.A., M.S., Ph.D.
Physics. M.S., Ph.D.
Physics and Astronomy. Ph.D.
Statistics. M.S.

COLLEGE OF HEALTH AND HUMAN PERFORMANCE:
Curriculum and Instruction in Physical Education. Ph.D.
Exercise Science. Ph.D.
Physical Education. M.S.
Public Health. M.P.H.
Youth and Family Recreation. M.S.

DAVID O. MCKAY SCHOOL OF EDUCATION:
Counseling Psychology. Ph.D.
Educational Leadership. M.Ed., Ph.D., Ed.D.
Instructional Psychology and Technology. M.S., Ph.D.
Reading. Ed.D.
School Counseling Psychology. M.S.
Special Education. M.S.
Speech-Language Pathology. M.S.
Teaching and Learning. M.A., M.Ed.

THE J. WILLARD AND ALICE S. MARRIOTT SCHOOL OF MANAGEMENT:
Accountancy. Includes professional accountancy, accounting information systems, tax. M.Acc.
Business Administration. M.B.A.
Information Systems Management. M.I.S.M.
Organizational Behavior. M.O.B.
Public Administration. M.P.A.

J. Reuben Clark Law School

Established 1971. ABA approved since 1974. AALS member. Semester system. Full-time study only. Exchange program with Central European University, Budapest, Hungary, and a clerkship with T. C. Beirne School of Law, University of Queensland, Australia. Law library 439,259 volumes, 5632 subscriptions. Library has LEXIS, NEXIS, RLIN, and WESTLAW.

Annual tuition: church members $6140, nonmembers $9210. On-campus housing available, contact University Housing Office. Total average cost of all other expenses: $11,300.

Enrollment: first-year class 160; total 487 (men 67%, women 33%). Faculty: full-time 26, part-time 31. Student to faculty ratio 19.2 to 1. Degrees conferred: J.D., J.D.-Ed.D., J.D.-M.B.A.,

J.D.-M.P.A., J.D.-M.Acc., J.D.-M.O.B., LL.M. (American and Comparative Legal Studies; for persons who have completed a basic legal education and received a degree in law in another country).

ADMISSION REQUIREMENTS. LSDAS Law School report, transcripts, LSAT, three recommendations, interview with a clergyman or bishop required in support of application. Accepts transfer applicants. Apply to Director of Admissions by February 15. Fall admission only. Application fee $50. Phone: (801)378-4277; fax: (801)378-5897.

ADMISSION STANDARDS. Selective. Accepts about 30–35% of total annual applicants. Gourman rating: 3.63. *U.S. News & World Report* ranking is in the top 37 of all law schools.

FINANCIAL AID. Scholarships, assistantships, Federal W/S, loans, church loans. Apply to Student Financial Aid Office; no specified closing date. Use FAFSA. About 49% of students receive some form of financial assistance.

DEGREE REQUIREMENTS. For J.D.: satisfactory completion of three-year program; 90 semester credits. For L.L.M.: at least 24 credits and two semesters in residence. For other master's degrees: see Graduate listing above.

BROOKLYN COLLEGE OF THE CITY UNIVERSITY OF NEW YORK

Brooklyn, New York 11210-2889
Web site: www.brooklyn.cuny.edu

Founded 1930. Coed. Municipal control. Semester system. Special facilities: Africana Research Institute, Applied Science Institute, Archaeological Research Institute, Computer Center, Dynamitron, Electronic Music Studio, Graduate Center for Worker Education, Center for Health Promotion, Center for Human Relations Training, Wolfe Institute for the Humanities, Infant Studies Center, Center for Italian-American Studies, Center for Puerto Rican Studies, Center for Nuclear Theory, Institute for Studies in American Music, Television Center, Speech and Hearing Clinic. Library: 1,300,000 volumes, 13,500 subscriptions. Approximately 600 computers on campus for student use.

Tuition: per semester, State residents $4350, non-State residents $7600; per credit, State resident $185, non-State $320. No on-campus housing available.

Division of Graduate Studies

Graduate study since 1935. Enrollment: full-time 329, part-time 2889. Faculty: full-time 187, part-time 140. Degrees conferred: M.A., M.F.A., M.S., M.S. in Ed., Advanced Certificate.

ADMISSION REQUIREMENTS. Official transcripts, two letters of reference required in support of application. GRE/Subject Tests, interview required by some departments. Accepts transfer applicants. Graduates of unaccredited colleges not considered. Apply to Office of Admissions by March 1 (Summer and Fall), November 1 (Spring), March 1 for selected teacher-education programs. Application fee $30. Phone: (718)951-5914; e-mail: adminqry@brooklyn.cuny.edu.

ADMISSION STANDARDS. Competitive. Usual minimum average: 2.75 overall, 3.0 in the major (A = 4).

FINANCIAL AID. Teaching/research fellowships, assistantships, lectureships, internships, tuition waivers, Federal W/S, loans. Approved for VA benefits. Apply by April 1 to appropriate department for fellowships and internships; to Office of Financial Aid for all other programs. Use FAFSA (college code: 002687) and City University's FAF.

DEGREE REQUIREMENTS. For all master's: 30 credits minimum, at least 24 in residence; thesis/nonthesis option; comprehensive exam. For liberal arts and science majors: thesis/written comprehensive exam; reading knowledge of one foreign language required in some programs. For Advanced Certificate: 30 credits beyond the master's degree; special project.

FIELDS OF STUDY.

Art. Portfolio required for admission. Includes drawing and painting, graphics, photography, sculpture. M.A., M.F.A.

Art History. Two languages for master's. M.A.

Audiology. Includes speech-language pathology. M.S.

Biology. One language for master's. M.A.

Chemistry. One language for master's. M.A.

Community Health. M.A.

Computer and Information Science. M.A.

Computer Science and Health Science. M.S.

Creative Writing. Includes fiction, playwriting, poetry. M.F.A.

Economics. M.A.

Education.

> *Elementary.* Special concentrations in early childhood, home economics, comparative and industrial education art, bilingual teaching, social science, mathematics, music, reading, science, teaching of Spanish-speaking children. M.S.Ed.

> *Secondary.* All junior and senior high-school subjects. M.S.Ed.

> *Special Education.* Education of children with retarded mental development/emotional handicaps/neuropsychological learning disabilities; bilingual special education; education of the speech and hearing handicapped; speech improvement. M.S.Ed.

> *Sixth-Year Certificate Program.* Includes administration and supervision, guidance and counseling, school psychologist, educational use of computers.

English. One language for master's. M.A.

Exercise Science and Rehabilitation. M.S.

French. M.A.

General Science. M.A.

Geology. M.A.

Guidance and Counseling. M.S.Ed.

Health and Nutrition Sciences. M.S.Ed.

History. M.A.

Information Systems. M.S.

Judaic Studies. M.A.

Liberal Studies. M.A.

Mathematics. M.A.

Music. One language for master's. Includes musicology, performance. M.A., M.M.

Nutrition. M.S.

Physical Education. Includes psychosocial aspects of physical activities, sports management. M.S.

Physics. M.A.

Political Economy. M.A.

Political Science. One language for master's. Includes urban policy and administration. M.A.

Psychology. Includes experimental, forensic, human relations, industrial and organizational. M.A.

School Psychologist. M.S.Ed.

Social Studies. M.A.

Sociology. M.A.

Spanish. M.A.

Speech. Includes public communication (M.A.); audiology, pathology, speech and hearing science (M.S.).

Theater. Includes criticism, history (M.A.); acting, design, technical production, directing, performing arts management (M.F.A.).

TV/Radio. Includes television production. M.F.A., M.S.

BROOKLYN LAW SCHOOL
250 Joralemon Street
Brooklyn, New York 11201-3798
Web site: www.brooklaw.edu

Established 1901. ABA approved since 1937. AALS member. Coed. A Private control. Semester system. Special facility: Center for the Study of International Law. Library: 492,162 volumes, 2789 subscriptions. Library has LEXIS, NEXIS, WESTLAW, DIALOG.

Annual tuition: full-time $25,335, part-time $19,040. Total average cost for all other expenses: $12,000–$15,000. Enrollment: first-year class full-time 280, part-time 185; total full and part-time 1499 (men 50%, women 50%). Faculty: full-time 57, part-time 62. Student to faculty ratio 19.6 to 1. No on-campus housing, but six Law School residence halls in close proximity to campus. Degrees conferred: J.D., combined J.D.-Master's program with Baruch College, Hunter College, Brooklyn College, and Pratt Institute.

ADMISSION REQUIREMENTS. LSDAS Law School report, transcripts, LSAT, bachelor's degree required in support of application. Interview not required. Graduates from unaccredited colleges not considered. Apply to the Office of Admissions after October 15, before April 1. Admits Fall only. Application fee $60. Phone: (718)780-7906; fax: (718)780-0395.

ADMISSION STANDARDS. Accepts 40–50% of total annual applicants. Gourman rating: 3.62. *U.S. News & World Report* ranking is in the second tier of all law schools.

FINANCIAL AID. Scholarships, fellowships, assistantships, Federal W/S, loans. Apply to the Financial Aid Office by March 15. Phone: (718)780-7915. Use FAFSA (School code: E00057). About 44% of full-time students receive aid other than loans from school.

DEGREE REQUIREMENTS. For J.D.: three-year program (full-time), four-year program (part-time), 84 semester hours minimum. For master's program: see other institutional listings.

BROWN UNIVERSITY
Providence, Rhode Island 02912
Web site: www.brown.edu

Founded in 1764. CGS and AAU member. Coed. Private control. Semester system. Special facilities: Biomedical Center, Computing Laboratory, East Asia Language and Area Center, Geology-Chemistry research centers, Graduate Center (dormitories and administrative offices), Haffenreffer Museum of Anthropology, herbarium, Hunter Psychological Laboratory, Institute of Life Sciences, Ladd Observatory, Lefschetz Center for Dynamic Systems, Population Studies and Training Center, Prince Engineering Laboratory, University Library (2,225,000 items), John Carter Brown Library (Americana, 40,000 volumes), Annmary Brown Memorial Library (Renaissance and Medieval culture). Library: 2,200,000 volumes. The NIH ranking for Brown University by awards was 103, with 131 awards/grants; total dollars awarded $36,764,143.

Annual tuition: full-time $27,856. On-campus housing available for single students, none for married students. Average annual housing cost: $4800 ($9000 including board). Apply to Housing Office, Box 1864. Phone: (401)863-2251.

Graduate School

Graduate study since 1887. Enrollment: full-time 1800, part-time 200. Faculty: full-time 500, part-time 30. Degrees conferred: A.M., Sc.M., M.A.T., M.M.Sc., Ph.D., M.D.-Ph.D.

ADMISSION REQUIREMENTS. Transcripts, three letters of recommendation required in support of application (electronic application accepted) and letter from the student stating plans for graduate study. GRE/Subject required for biochemistry, biology and medical science, comparative literature, computer science, English, French studies, Hispanic and Italian studies, mathematics, psychology. GRE for most other departments. TOEFL required of foreign applicants. Accepts transfer applicants. Graduates of unaccredited colleges not considered. Apply to Graduate School by January 2. Application fee $60. Phone: (401)863-2600.

ADMISSION STANDARDS. Competitive. Usual minimum average: 3.0 (A = 4).

FINANCIAL AID. Scholarships, fellowships, research assistantships, teaching assistantships, proctorships, grants, endowed awards, Federal W/S, loans. Apply to the Office of Financial Aid by January 15. Use FAFSA. About 75% of students receive aid other than loans from school and outside sources. No aid for part-time students.

DEGREE REQUIREMENTS. For master's: 8 semester courses minimum, additional courses required by some programs; thesis, special projects, special exams required by some departments. For Ph.D.: three years of full-time study or equivalent beyond master's, at least two semesters in residence; oral preliminary exam; final exam; dissertation.

FIELDS OF STUDY.
American Civilization. A.M., Ph.D.
Anthropology. A.M., Ph.D.
Applied Mathematics. Sc.M., Ph.D.
Biology and Medical Sciences. A.M., M.A.T., M.P.H. Sc.M., Ph.D., M.M.S., M.D.-Ph.D.
Biomedical Engineering. Sc.M.
Brain Science. Sc.M., Ph.D.
Chemistry. Sc.M., Ph.D.
Classics. A.M., Ph.D.
Cognitive and Linguistic Sciences. A.M. (Linguistics), Sc.M., Ph.D.
Computer Science. Sc.M., Ph.D.
Creative Writing. M.F.A.
Developmental Studies. A.M.
Economics. A.M., Ph.D.
Education. Includes secondary English, history/social studies, biology/science, elementary. M.A.T.
Egyptology. A.M., Ph.D.
Engineering. Includes electrical, computer, fluid, thermal and chemical process, material science, mechanics of solids and structures. Sc.M., Ph.D.
English. A.M., Ph.D.
Environmental Studies. A.M.
French Studies. A.M., Ph D
Geological Sciences. A.M., Sc.M., Ph.D.
German Studies. A.M., Ph.D.
Hispanic Studies. A.M., Ph.D.
History. A.M., Ph.D.
History of Art and Architecture. A.M., Ph.D.
History of Mathematics. A.M., Ph.D.
Mathematics. A.M., Sc.M., Ph.D.
Music. A.M., Ph.D.
Neuroscience. Ph.D.
Old World Archaeology and Art. A.M., Ph.D.
Philosophy. A.M., Ph.D.
Physics. Includes exerpimental, theoretical. Sc.M., Ph.D.
Political Science. A.M., Ph.D.
Portuguese and Brazilian Studies. A.M., Ph.D.
Psychology. A.M., Sc.M., Ph.D.
Religious Studies. Includes early Christianity, ancient Judaism, contemporary religious thought. A.M., Ph.D.

Slavic Languages. A.M., Ph.D.
Sociology. A.M., Ph.D.
Theater, Speech, and Dance. Includes history, performance studies, criticism, dramatic literature, acting, directing. M.F.A., A.M., Ph.D.

Medical School (02912-9706)

Four-year program in medicine leading to the M.D. was accredited in 1975. Majority of each class admitted into freshman 8 year program of the University. Special programs: Brown/Dartmouth medical program; M.D.-Ph.D.

Annual tuition: $24,984. Student fees $1548. On-campus housing available. Total average figure of other expenses: $8000.

Enrollment: first-year class 68; total 263 (men 50%, women 50%). Faculty: full-time 296, part-time 672. Degrees conferred: M.D., M.D.-M.M.Sc., M.D.-Ph.D. The M.M.Sc. and Ph.D. are offered through the Graduate School.

ADMISSION REQUIREMENTS. Entry into the first year of the Medical School is available to individuals to the M.D.-Ph.D. program; to students enrolled in postbaccalaureate premedical study at Brown University, Bryn Mawr College, or Columbia University; to students enrolled in the Early Identification Program at Providence College, Tougaloo College, Rhode Island College, and the University of Rhode Island; and to graduates of Brown University. MCAT or GRE (general and subject exams), transcripts, three letters of recommendation required in support of application. Accepts transfer applicants. Apply to Office of Admissions, Box G, after July 15, before March 1. Application fee $65. Phone: (401)863-2149; fax: (401)863-3801; e-mail: medschool_admissions@brown.edu.

ADMISSION STANDARDS. Competitive. Accepts about 20% of total annual applicants. Approximately 20% are state residents. Gourman rating: 4.14.

FINANCIAL AID. Scholarships, loans, awards. No qualified student will be denied admission solely because of financial disability. About 55% of students receive financial assistance. Apply to Dean; no specified closing date.

DEGREE REQUIREMENTS. For M.D.: satisfactory completion of eight-year program in Liberal Medical Education; at least two years in full-time residence for students admitted with advanced standing. For M.M.Sc., Ph.D.: see Graduate School listing above.

FIELDS OF GRADUATE STUDY.
Artificial Organs, Biomaterials and Cellular Technology.
Biostatistics and Health Services Research.
Cell Biology and Biochemistry.
Ecology and Evolutionary Biology.
Epidemiology.
Molecular Biology.
Molecular Pharmacology and Physiology.
Neuroscience.
Pathbiology.

BRYANT COLLEGE
Smithfield, Rhode Island 02917-1284
Web site: www.bryant.edu

Located 12 miles N of Providence. Coed. Private control. Semester system. Day and evening programs. Special facility: Center for International Business and Economic Development. Library: 127,000 volumes, 1500 subscriptions. Approximately 300 computers on campus for general student use.

Tuition: per credit $390. On-campus housing for single students. Average academic year housing costs: $5500 ($8500 including board); off-campus housing costs: $600 per month. Contact housing office for both on- and off-campus housing information. Phone: (401)232-6140.

Graduate School

Enrollment: full-time 55, part-time 380. Faculty: full-time 26, part-time 8. Degrees conferred: M.B.A., M.S.A., M.S.I.S., M.S.T.

ADMISSION REQUIREMENTS. Official transcripts, GMAT, statement of objectives, three letters of recommendation required in support of School's application. Accepts transfer applicants. Apply by August 1 (Fall), December 12 (Spring) to Director of Graduate Admissions. Rolling admissions process. Application fee $35. Phone: (401)232-6230; fax: (401)232-6494; e-mail: gradprog@bryant.edu.

ADMISSION STANDARDS. Selective. Usual minimum average: 2.5 (2.75 last two years) (A = 4).

FINANCIAL AID. Research assistantships, fellowships, tuition waivers, Federal W/S, loans. Approved for VA benefits. Apply by August 1 to Director of Financial Aid. Phone: (401)232-6020. Use FAFSA.

DEGREE REQUIREMENTS. For master's: 30–61 semester hours; no thesis or foreign language requirement.

FIELDS OF STUDY.
Accounting. M.S.A.
Business Administration. Concentration in accounting, computer information systems, e-strategy, finance, general business, management, marketing, operations management, taxation.
Information Systems. M.S.I.S.
Taxation. M.S.T.

BRYN MAWR COLLEGE
Bryn Mawr, Pennsylvania 19010-1097
Web site: www.brynmawr.edu

Founded 1885. Located 11 miles W of Philadelphia. CGS member. Coed on graduate level. Private control. Semester system. Special facility: Ella Riegel Museum of Classical Archaeology. Library: 932,400 volumes, 4000 subscriptions.

Annual tuition: full-time $22,260, per course $3770. Campus housing available at Glenmede Graduate Residence Center for men and women. Average annual housing cost: $8340 (including board). Contact Director of Graduate Housing for both on- and off-campus housing information. Phone: (610)526-7331.

Graduate School of Arts and Sciences
Web site: www.brynmawr.edu/gsas

Graduate study since 1885. Enrollment: full-time 76, part-time 127. College faculty: full-time 116, part-time 40. Degrees conferred: M.A., Ph.D.

ADMISSION REQUIREMENTS. Official transcripts, three letters of recommendation (including at least one from a professor in applicant's major field), GRE (Subject for Biology, Chemistry, Physics, Psychology, and Russian) required in support of School's application. TOEFL required for international applicants. Applicants for financial aid should apply by January 1 (Science programs), January 25 (Humanities), February 1 (Clinical Development), January 25 for foreign applicants, all others must be completed by June 30. Application fee $25. Phone: (610)526-5072; e-mail: gsas@brynmawr.edu.

ADMISSION STANDARDS. Competitive. Usual minimum average: 3.0 (A = 4).

FINANCIAL AID. Annual awards from institutional funds: scholarships, research fellowships, teaching assistantships, tuition awards, loans. Apply by January 2 (January 25 for foreign applicants) to the Dean of the School for fellowships, assistantships; to Financial Aid Office for all other programs. Phone: (610)526-5245. Aid available for part-time study.

DEGREE REQUIREMENTS. For M.A.: one year minimum in full-time residence; thesis; final oral/written exam. For Ph.D.: three years minimum, at least two in full-time residence; reading knowledge of foreign languages/computer languages/special techniques as required by individual departments; preliminary exam; dissertation; final oral exam.

FIELDS OF STUDY.
Biochemistry.
Biology.
Chemistry.
Classical and Near Eastern Archaeology.
Classical Studies.
Clinical, Developmental, and School Psychology. Apply by February 1; admits Fall only.
French. M.A. only.
Geology.
Greek.
History of Art.
Latin.
Mathematics.
Neural and Behavioral Sciences. Interdisciplinary.
Physics.
Russian.

Graduate School of Social Work and Social Research (19010-1697)

Web site: www.brynmawr.edu/socialwork

Tuition: per course $2380 (Master's), $3050 (Doctoral). Enrollment: full-time 146, part-time 77. Faculty: full-time 15, part-time 21. Degrees conferred: M.L.S.P., M.S.S., Ph.D.

ADMISSION REQUIREMENTS. Official transcripts, three letters of recommendation required in support of School's application. TOEFL required for international applications. Accepts transfer applicants. Graduates of unaccredited institutions not considered. Apply to Assistant Dean and Director of Admission. Applications must be completed by March 1. Rolling admissions process. Application fee $50. Phone: (610)520-2601; fax: (610)520-2655.

ADMISSION STANDARDS. Competitive. Usual minimum average: 2.75 (A = 4), 3.0 (Doctoral programs).

FINANCIAL AID. Annual awards from institutional fund; fellowships, grants, research assistantships, teaching assistantships, full and partial tuition waivers, Federal W/S, loans. Approved for VA benefits. Apply by March 1 to Assistant Dean for fellowships, assistantships; to Financial Aid Office for all other programs. Phone: (610)527-5403. Use FAFSA. Aid available for part-time students.

DEGREE REQUIREMENTS. For master's: 45–60 credits minimum, at least one year in full-time residence; field placement;

thesis/special project; final exam. For Ph.D.: three years minimum, at least two in full-time residence; advance practice internship; dissertation; final oral exam.

FIELDS OF STUDY.
Law and Social Policy. M.L.S.P.
Social Service. M.S.S.
Social Work. Ph.D.

BUCKNELL UNIVERSITY
Lewisburg, Pennsylvania 17837
Web site: www.bucknell.edu

Founded 1846. Located 155 miles NW of Philadelphia. Coed. Private control. Semester system. Library: 432,700 volumes, 2789 subscriptions. More than 350 computers on campus for general student use.

Tuition: per course $2710. Limited on-campus housing available for single students, none for married students. Average annual housing cost: $4925 (including board). Apply to Residential Life Director. Phone: (570)577-1195.

Graduate Studies

Enrollment: full-time 78, part-time 40, total 116 (men 30%, women 70%). University faculty teaching graduate students: full-time 16, part-time 0. Degrees conferred: M.A., M.S.

ADMISSION REQUIREMENTS. Transcripts, GRE/Subject Tests, GMAT (Business), two letters of recommendation required in support of application. TOEFL required for international applicants. Accepts transfer applicants. Graduates of unaccredited colleges not considered. Apply to Director of Graduate Studies by June 1 (Fall), December 1 (Spring), April 15 (Summer). Application fee $25. Phone: (570)577-1304; fax: (570)577-3760; e-mail: gradstds@bucknell.edu.

ADMISSION STANDARDS. Selective for most departments, very selective for some. Usual minimum average: 2.8 (A = 4).

FINANCIAL AID. Annual awards from institutional funds: scholarships, fellowships, assistantships, tuition waivers, Federal W/S, loans. Apply by March 1 to Graduate Office. Phone: (570)577-1304. Use FAFSA and University's FAF. About 50% of students receive aid other than loans from University and outside sources. Aid sometimes available for part-time students.

DEGREE REQUIREMENTS. For M.A., M.S.: 28 credit hours minimum, at least 22 in residence; thesis; final exam; reading knowledge of one foreign language required for M.A. (English).

FIELDS OF STUDY.
Animal Behavior.
Biology.
Chemical Engineering.
Chemistry.
Civil and Environmental Engineering.
Educational Research.
Electrical Engineering.
English.
Management.
Mathematics.
Mechanical Engineering.
Reading.
School Administration and Supervision.
School Psychology.

UNIVERSITY AT BUFFALO, STATE UNIVERSITY OF NEW YORK

Buffalo, New York 14260-1608

Web site: www.buffalo.edu

Founded 1846. CGS and AAU member. Coed. State control. Semester system. Special facilities: Canada-United States Trade Center, Center for Studies in American Culture, Center for Advanced Photonic and Electronic Materials, Center for Advanced Molecular Biology and Immunology, Center for Assistive Technology, Center for Comparative and Global Studies in Education, Center for Computational Research, Center for Critical Languages, Center for Curriculum Planning, Center for the Study of Psychoanalysis and Culture, National Center for Earthquake Engineering Research, National Center for Geographic Information and Analysis, Center for Electronic and Electro-optic Materials, Center for Applied Molecular Biology and Immunology, Center for Research in Special Environments, New York Center for Hazardous Waste Management, Center for Study of Aging, Baldy Center for Law and Social Policy, Center for Research on Urban Social Work Practice, Center for Behavioral and Social Aspects of Health, Center for Cognitive Sciences, Center for Research in Special Environments, Center for Hearing and Deafness, Center for Structural Biology, Research Center for Law and Jurisprudence, Center of Excellence for Document Analysis and Recognition, Comprehensive Oral Health Research Center, Research Institute on Addiction, Toxicology Research Center, Environment and Society Institute, Institute for Research and Education on Women and Gender, New York State Center for Engineering Design and Industrial Innovation. Library: 3,200,000 volumes, 26,000 subscriptions. The University's NIH ranking is 90th among all U.S. institutions with 174 awards/grants worth $45,494,103. Total University enrollment: 24,250.

Annual tuition: full-time, resident $5100, nonresident, $8416. Unlimited on-campus housing available for single graduate students. Average academic year housing costs: $4622–$5872 (including board); $8760 for married students. Contact Director of Residence Life for on-campus housing information, phone: (716)645-2171; for off-campus housing, phone: (716)829-2224. Day-care facilities available.

Graduate School

Graduate study since 1923. Enrollment: full-time 4805, part-time 3349. Graduate faculty: full- and part-time 1949. Degrees conferred: M.A., M.B.A., M.S., M.Arch., M.U.P., M.M., M.F.A., M.E., Ed.M., Ed.D., Ph.D., M.D., D.D.S., Pharm.D., D.N.S.

ADMISSION REQUIREMENTS. Transcripts required in support of application. On-line application available. GRE/MAT, letters of recommendation required by some departments. Interview not required. TOEFL (minimum score 550) required for foreign applicants. Accepts transfer applicants. Graduates of unaccredited institutions not considered. Contact individual program regarding deadlines for admission. Application fee $35. Phone: (716)645-2992; or (716)645-2000, ask for individual department chair.

ADMISSION STANDARDS. Relatively open to very competitive. Usual minimum average varies by department.

FINANCIAL AID. Annual awards from institutional funds: fellowships, teaching assistantships, graduate assistantships, research assistantships, grants, Federal W/S, loans. Approved for VA benefits. Apply to the appropriate department chair for fellowships, assistantships; to the Financial Aid Office for all other programs. Phone: (716)645-3724. Use FAFSA (School code: 002837). About 55% of full-time students receive aid other than loans from School and outside sources. Aid available for part-time students.

DEGREE REQUIREMENTS. For most master's: 30 semester hours minimum, at least 24 in residence; comprehensive exam; thesis/nonthesis option/special project; oral exam requirements vary by department. For Ph.D.: three years minimum, at least one year in full-time residence; preliminary exam; dissertation; final oral exam. Contact individual programs for other requirements.

FIELDS OF STUDY.

American Studies. M.A., Ph.D.

Anthropology. M.A., Ph.D.

Art. M.F.A. only.

Art History. M.A. only.

Biological Sciences. M.A., Ph.D.

Biomaterials. M.S.

Biometry. M.S. only.

Chemistry. M.A., Ph.D.

Classics. M.A., Ph.D.

Communication. M.A., Ph.D.

Communicative Disorders and Sciences. M.A., Ph.D.

Comparative Literature. M.A., Ph.D.

Economics. M.A., Ph.D.

English. M.A., Ph.D.

Geography. M.A., Ph.D.

Geology. M.A., Ph.D.

History. M.A., Ph.D.

Humanities. Interdisciplinary. M.A. only.

Linguistics. M.A., Ph.D.

Mathematics. M.A., Ph.D.

Medical Technology. M.S. only.

Modern Languages and Literature. Includes French, Spanish, German. M.A., Ph.D.

Music. Includes music history, music composition. M.A., M.M., Ph.D.

Natural Sciences. Interdisciplinary. M.S. only.

Nutrition. M.S. only.

Occupational Therapy. Includes hand rehabilitation. M.S. only.

Philosophy. M.A., Ph.D.

Physics. M.A., Ph.D.

Political Science. M.A., Ph.D.

Psychology. M.A., Ph.D.

Social Sciences. Interdisciplinary. M.A., Ph.D.

Sociology. Includes medical sociology. M.A., Ph.D.

Urban Planning. M.U.P. only.

Women's Studies. M.A.

School of Architecture and Planning

Web site: www.ap.buffalo.edu

Tuition: per credit, resident $213, nonresident $351. Enrollment full-time 189, part-time 55. Faculty: full-time 30, part-time 18. Degree conferred: M.U.P.

ADMISSION REQUIREMENTS. Official transcripts, three letters of recommendation, 500-word personal statement, résumé required in support of School's application. On-line application available. TOEFL (minimum score 550) and Financial Statement Form required for international applicants. Does not consider transfer applicants. Apply to Office of Academic Programs Administration in the School. Application fee $35 (on-line application), $50 fee for paper application. Phone: (716)829-2133, ext. 109; fax: (716)829-3256.

ADMISSION STANDARDS. Selective. Usual minimum average: 3.0 (A = 4).

FINANCIAL AID. Research/teaching assistantships, internships, traineeships, tuition waivers, Federal W/S, loans. Approved for VA benefits. Apply as early as possible to the Dean's Office for assistantships; to Financial Aid Office for all other programs. Phone: (716)645-2450. Use FAFSA. About 20% of full-time students receive some form of financial aid. Aid available for part-time students.

DEGREE REQUIREMENTS. For M.U.P.: 52 credit full-time, two-year program; planning practicum; thesis or professional planning project.

FIELDS OF STUDY.
Urban Planning.

School of Dental Medicine

Organized 1892. Joined SUNY system in 1962. Annual tuition: resident $10,840, nonresident $21,940. On-campus housing available. Average academic year housing cost: $8566. For housing, apply to SUNYAB, Housing Office. Phone: (716)636-2181. Total average cost for all other first-year expenses: $5500.

Enrollment: first-year class 86; total full-time 390 (men 65%, women 35%); postgraduates 40. Faculty: full-time 67, part-time 121. Degrees conferred: D.D.S., D.D.S.-M.S., D.D.S.-Ph.D.

ADMISSION REQUIREMENTS. AADSAS report, transcripts, DAT, three letters of recommendation required in support of School's application. Interviews by invitation only. Applicants must have completed at least three years of college, prefer four years of college. Accepts transfer students from U.S. and Canadian dental schools. Graduates of unaccredited colleges not considered. Apply to Admissions Office after July 1, before February 1. Application fee $50. Phone: (716)829-2839, or (716)829-2826.

ADMISSION STANDARDS. Selective. Usual minimum average: 2.8 (A = 4). Mean DAT: Academic 19.01, PAT 18.4; mean GPA: 3.34 (A = 4). Gourman rating: 4.58. Accepts 20–25% of total annual applicants. Approximately 85% are state residents.

FINANCIAL AID. Scholarships, fellowships, grants, loans. Apply to the Financial Aid Office by June 1. Phone: (716)829-2839. Use FAFSA (School code: 002837). About 90% of students receive some aid from School.

DEGREE REQUIREMENTS. For D.D.S.: satisfactory completion of forty-five-month program.

FIELDS OF GRADUATE STUDY.
Biomaterials.
Oral Biology.
Oral and Maxillofacial Surgery.
Oral Medicine.
Pediatric Dentistry.
Restorative Dentistry.

Graduate School of Education

Graduate study since 1931. Tuition: per credit, resident $213, nonresident $351. Graduate housing available. Apply to Office of Housing Services, 106 Spaulding Quad, Ellicott Housing. Phone: (716)645-2171. For off-campus housing, apply to Off-Campus Housing, 100 Allen. Phone: (716)829-2224.

Enrollment: full- and part-time 1100. Faculty: full-time 66, part-time 35. Degrees conferred: Ed.M., Ed.D. The M.A., M.S., and Ph.D. are offered through the Graduate School.

ADMISSION REQUIREMENTS. Transcripts, GRE/MAT, letters of reference required in support of all doctoral applications. Consult departments for additional requirements. TOEFL required for international applicants. Accepts transfer applicants. Graduates of unaccredited institutions not considered. Deadlines vary with department. Application fee $50. Phone: (716)645-2491.

ADMISSION STANDARDS. Competitive. Usual minimum average: 3.0 (A = 4).

FINANCIAL AID. Teaching assistantships, graduate assistantships, internships, Federal W/S, loans. Approved for VA benefits.

Apply to Director of Financial Aid; no specified closing date. Phone: (716)829-3724. Use FAFSA and TAP.

DEGREE REQUIREMENTS. For master's: 32 semester hours minimum; comprehensive exam. For Certificate: 30 credits beyond the master's. For Ed.D., Ph.D.: 72 semester hours minimum, at least two semesters in continuous full-time residence; preliminary exams; dissertation; final oral exam.

FIELDS OF STUDY.

DEPARTMENT OF COUNSELING, SCHOOL, AND EDUCATIONAL PSYCHOLOGY:
Counseling and School Psychology.
Counselor Education.
Educational Psychology.
Rehabilitation Counseling.
School Counseling.
School Psychology.

DEPARTMENT OF EDUCATIONAL LEADERSHIP AND POLICY:
Educational Administration.
Educational Leadership.
Foundations of Education.
Higher Educational Administration.
Sociology of Education.

DEPARTMENT OF LEARNING AND INSTRUCTION:
Bilingual Education.
Education. Includes bilingual education.
Elementary Education. Includes bilingual education, early childhood education (with emphasis in reading, language arts, mathematics, social studies, science).
English Education.
Foreign Language Education (grades 7–12). Includes French, German, Italian, Latin, Russian, Spanish.
Music Education.
Sciences Education. Includes bilingual education.
Special Education. Includes bilingual education.
TESOL.

School of Engineering and Applied Sciences
Web site: www.eng.buffalo.edu

Tuition: per credit, resident $213, nonresident $351. Enrollment full-time 421, part-time 391. Faculty: full-time 124, part-time 37. Degrees conferred: M.Eng., M.S., Ph.D.

ADMISSION REQUIREMENTS. Official transcripts, GRE required in support of School's application. On-line application available. TOEFL (minimum score 550) and Financial Statement Form required for international applicants. Will consider transfer applicants. Apply to Office of Academic Programs Administration in the School. Application fee $35 fee for on-line application, $50 fee for paper application. Phone: (716)829-2772, fax: (716)829-2495.

ADMISSION STANDARDS. Selective. Usual minimum average: 3.0 (A = 4).

FINANCIAL AID. Fellowships, research/teaching assistantships, grants, internships, tuition waivers, Federal W/S, loans. Approved for VA benefits. Apply as early as possible to the Dean's Office for assistantships; to Financial Aid Office for all other programs. Phone: (716)645-2450. Use FAFSA. About 40% of full-time students receive some form of financial aid. Aid available for part-time students.

DEGREE REQUIREMENTS. For Master's: 30 credit program, at least 24 credits in residence; comprehensive exam; admission to candidacy; thesis/nonthesis option/project. For Ph.D.: three-year program; qualifying exam; admission to candidacy; dissertation; final oral exam.

FIELDS OF STUDY.

Aerospace Engineering

Chemical Engineering

Civil Engineering. Includes computational engineering mechanics, geomechanics, geoenvironmental and foundation engineering.

Computer Science and Engineering.

Electrical Engineering. Includes communication and signal processing, energy systems, microlectronics, photonics and materials.

Engineering Management. Includes production management.

Environmental Engineering. Includes environmental engineering and science, water resources and environmental fluid mechanics.

Human Factors Engineering/Ergonomics.

Industrial Engineering.

Mechanical Engineering.

Operations Research.

Production Systems Engineering.

Structural Engineering. Includes construction engineering and management, structural and earthquake engineering.

School of Informatics

Annual tuition: resident $5100, nonresident $8416. Enrollment: full-time 132, part-time 202. Faculty: full-time 17, part-time 2. Degrees conferred: M.A., M.L.S., Ph.D.

ADMISSION REQUIREMENTS. Transcripts, bachelor's degree, GRE, computer skills required in support of School's application. TOEFL required for international applicants. Accepts transfer applicants. Graduates of unaccredited institutions not considered. Apply to School by September 15 (Spring), February 1 (Summer), April 1 (Fall). Application fee $35. Phone: (716)645-3162; fax: (716)645-3775.

ADMISSION STANDARDS. Selective. Usual minimum average: 3.0 (A = 4).

FINANCIAL AID. Annual awards from institutional funds: scholarships, fellowships, internships, Federal W/S, loans. Apply to Director of Financial Aid; no specified closing date. Phone: (716)645-2412. Use FAFSA.

DEGREE REQUIREMENTS. For M.A.: 36 credit program, at least 24 credits in residence; thesis. For M.L.S.: 36 credit hours minimum, at least 30 credits in residence. For Ph.D.: 72 credit program, at least 44 credits in residence; preliminary exam; dissertation; oral defense.

FIELDS OF STUDY.

Communications. Includes information and library science. M.A., Ph.D.

Informatics. M.A.

Library Studies. Includes music librarianship. M.L.S.

School of Law

Web site: www.law.buffalo.edu

Established 1887. Located on Amherst campus. ABA approved since 1936. AALS member. Semester system. Full-time, day study only. Special facilities: Baldy Center for Law and Social Policy, Buffalo Criminal Law Center, Buffalo Human Rights Center. Special programs: Government Law Program (Public Service), Public Service summer internships, externships in Public Interest. Law library: 536,316 volumes, 6717 subscriptions; has LEXIS, WESTLAW, RLIN, LRS, QUICKLAW (Canadian Database); is a Federal Government Depository.

Annual tuition: resident $9625, nonresident $15,175. On-campus housing available for both single and married students. Annual on-campus housing cost: $11,125. Housing deadline May 1. Contact University Residence Hall for on-campus information. Phone: (716)645-2171. Law students tend to live off-campus. For off-campus housing information contact the office of Off-campus Housing (a student-run organization); phone: (716)829-2224. Off-campus housing and personal expenses: approximately $9529.

Enrollment: first-year class 236, full-time 705 (men 53%, women 47%). Faculty: full-time 29, part-time 43. Student to faculty ratio 20.5 to 1. Degrees conferred: J.D., J.D.-M.A., J.D.-Ph.D.

ADMISSION REQUIREMENTS. LSDAS Law School report, bachelor's degree, transcript, LSAT, three recommendations required in support of application. Interview not required. Transfer applicants considered. Apply to Admissions Office after September 1, before March 15. Admits Fall only. Application fee $50. Phone: (716)645-2907.

ADMISSION STANDARDS. Selective. Accepts about 40–45% of total annual applicants. Mean LSAT: 154; mean GPA: 3.21 (A = 4). Gourman rating: 4.32. *U.S. News & World Report* ranking is in the second tier of all law schools.

FINANCIAL AID. TAP, SUSTA (New York State residents only), fellowships, assistantships, Federal W/S, loans. Apply to Financial Aid Office by March 1. Use FAFSA (School code: 002837). Approximately 55% of students receive some financial assistance.

DEGREE REQUIREMENTS. For J.D.: satisfactory completion of six-semester program, or five semesters plus two summer sessions; 82 credit hour program. For M.A., Ph.D. degrees: see Graduate School listing above.

School of Management

Web site: www.mgt.buffalo.edu

Established 1927. Tuition: per credit, resident $213, nonresident $351. Enrollment: full-time 507, part-time 200. Faculty: full-time 61, part-time 3. Degrees conferred: M.B.A., M.S., Ph.D.

ADMISSION REQUIREMENTS. Transcripts, GMAT required in support of School's application. On-line applications available. TOEFL required for international applicants. Does not consider transfer applicants. Apply to Office of Academic Programs Administration in the School. Application fee $50. Phone: (716)645-3204; fax: (716)645-2341.

ADMISSION STANDARDS. Selective. Usual minimum average: 3.2 (A = 4); GMAT 575 (M.B.A.), 645 (Ph.D.).

FINANCIAL AID. Fellowships, assistantships, internships, Federal W/S, loans. Approved for VA benefits. Apply as early as possible to the Dean's Office for assistantships but not later than February 15; to Financial Aid Office for all other programs. Phone: (716)829-3724; fax: (716)829-2022. Use FAFSA. About 41% of full-time students receive some form of financial aid.

DEGREE REQUIREMENTS. For M.B.A.: 60-hour program, 30 hours in residence. For M.S.: one-year, full-time program. For Ph.D.: formal requirements are primarily qualitative; qualifying exam; second-year research paper; admission to candidacy; dissertation; final oral exam.

FIELDS OF STUDY.

Accounting. M.S.

Business Administration. Includes accounting, corporate financial management, financial analysis, information systems and e-business, international management, management consulting, marketing management, supply chains and operations management. M.B.A. program (full-time).

Business Management. Includes accounting, financial managerial economics, management science and systems, marketing, organization and human resources. Ph.D. program.

International M.B.A.

Management Information Systems. M.S.

Supply Chains and Operations Management. M.S.

School of Medicine and Biomedical Sciences

Founded 1846. Located in Buffalo (14214-3013). Annual tuition: resident $13,945, nonresident $26,045; student fees $1105. Limited on-campus housing for single medical students only. Total average for all other expenses: $10,300.

Enrollment: first-year class 135 (EDP 5); total 654 (men 50%, women 50%). Faculty: full-time 184, part-time 241. Degrees conferred: M.D., M.D.-Ph.D. (Medical Scientist Training Program).

ADMISSION REQUIREMENTS. AMCAS report, transcripts, MCAT, letters of recommendation, interview required in support of application. Applicants must have completed at least three years of college study. Preference given to state residents. Has EDP; apply between June 1 and August 1. Accepts very few transfer applicants. Supplement application for MSTP. Apply to AMCAS after June 1, before November 1. Application fee $65. Phone: (716)829-3465.

ADMISSION STANDARDS. Competitive. Accepts about 7–8% of total annual applicants. Mean MCAT: 9.6; mean GPA: 3.63 (A = 4). Gourman rating: 4.36. Approximately 98% are state residents.

FINANCIAL AID. Scholarships, fellowships, assistantships, loans. Apply to Office of Financial Aid after acceptance, but prior to May 15. Use FAFSA (School code: 002837).

DEGREE REQUIREMENTS. For M.D.: satisfactory completion of four-year program; all students are encouraged to take the USMLE Step 1 and Step 2, but it is optional. For Ph.D. requirements refer to Graduate School listing above.

FIELDS OF GRADUATE STUDY.
Anatomy.
Biochemistry.
Biophysics.
Cell Biology.
Immunology.
Microbiology.
Molecular Biology.
Pathology.
Pharmacology.
Physiology.

School of Nursing

Tuition: per credit, resident $213 nonresident $351. Enrollment: full-time 83, part-time 102. Faculty: full-time 29, part-time 13. Degrees conferred: M.S., D.N.S.

ADMISSION REQUIREMENTS. Official transcripts, baccalaureate degree in nursing, three references required in support of School's application. GRE may be required for applicants with less than a 3.0 GPA (A = 4). On-line application available. TOEFL (minimum score 550) and Financial Statement Form required for international applicants. Will consider transfer applicants. D.N.S. applicants admitted Fall and Spring. Apply by May 1 (Fall), October 15 (Spring) to Office of Academic Programs Administration in the School. Application fee $35 for on-line ap-

plication, $50 for paper application. Phone: (716)829-3314, fax: (716)829-2021.

ADMISSION STANDARDS. Selective. Usual minimum average: 3.0 (A = 4.).

FINANCIAL AID. Fellowships, scholarships, research/ teaching assistantships, grants, tuition waivers, Federal W/S, loans. Approved for VA benefits. Apply as early as possible to the Dean's office for fellowships, scholarships, assistantships; to Financial Aid Office for all other programs. Phone: (716)645-2450. Use FAFSA (School code: 002837). About 25% of full-time students receive some form of financial aid. Aid available for part-time students.

DEGREE REQUIREMENTS. For master's: 42–53 credit program; comprehensive clinical training experience; admission to candidacy; research project. For D.N.S.: 48 credit program beyond master's; qualifying exam; admission to candidacy; dissertation; final oral exam.

FIELDS OF STUDY.
Acute Care Nurse Practitioner.
Adult Nurse Practitioner.
Family Nurse Practitioner.
Geriatric Nurse Practitioner.
Maternal and Women's Health Nurse Practitioner.
Nurse Anesthetist. 27-month, full-time program.
Pediatric Nurse Practitioner.

School of Pharmacy and Pharmaceutical Sciences

Established 1886. Annual tuition: full-time resident $5900, nonresident $10,350; per credit resident $246, nonresident $432. Graduate enrollment: full-time 234, part-time 23 (men 40%, women 60%). Faculty: full-time 27; part-time 20. Degrees conferred: M.S., Ph.D., Pharm.D.

ADMISSION REQUIREMENTS. Transcripts, GRE required in support of School's application. On-line application available. TOEFL (minimum score 550) required for international applicants. Accepts transfer applicants. Graduates of unaccredited institutions not considered. Apply to appropriate department at least 60 days prior to registration. Pharm.D. admits Fall only. Application fee $35. Phone: (716)645-2823; fax: (714)645-3688.

ADMISSION STANDARDS. Competitive. Usual minimum average: 3.0 (A = 4).

FINANCIAL AID. Fellowships, assistantships, tuition waivers, Federal W/S, loans. Apply by February 28 to appropriate department chair for assistantships; to Office of Financial Aid for all other programs. Use FAFSA.

DEGREE REQUIREMENTS. For M.S.: 30 semester hours minimum, at least 24 in residence; thesis, oral exam required by some departments. For Ph.D.: three years minimum, at least one year in full-time residence; preliminary exam; dissertation; final oral exam. For Pharm.D.: essentially the same as for Ph.D., except no foreign language requirement.

FIELDS OF STUDY.
Chemical and Pharmaceutical Sciences. Interdisciplinary.
Drug Discovery and Experimental Therapeutics. Interdisciplinary.
Pharmaceutical Sciences. Includes clinical research, drug formulation/delivery/development, drug metabolism/transport, drug analysis, experimental pharmacokinetics and pharmacodynamics, pharmacogenetics/pharmacogenomics, pharmacometrics. M.S.

Roswell Park Cancer Institute
Graduate Division (14263)
Web site: www.roswellpark.org

Founded 1898. The Institute's NIH ranking is 121st among all U.S. instiutions with 79 awards/grants worth $28,054,837.

Annual tuition: resident $5100, nonresident $8416.

Enrollment: full-time 180, part-time 90. Faculty: full-time 130. Degrees offered through the graduate school: M.A., M.S., Ph.D.

ADMISSION REQUIREMENTS. Transcripts, GRE, recommendations required in support of application. On-line application available. TOEFL required for foreign applicants. Apply by February 1. Application fee $35. Phone: (716)845-2339; fax: (716)845-8178; e-mail: gradapp@roswellpark.org.

ADMISSION STANDARDS. Usual minimum average: 3.0 (A = 4). TOEFL (minimum score 600) required.

FINANCIAL AID. Annual awards from insititutional funds: tuition scholarships, research fellowships, research assistantships, NIH stipends, Federal W/S, loans. Apply after acceptance to appropriate department. Use FAFSA. Phone: (716)831-3724. About 66% of students receive aid other than loans from Institute and outside sources.

DEGREE REQUIREMENTS. For M.A., M.S.: 30 semester hours minimum, at least 24 in residence; thesis, oral exam required by some departments. For Ph.D.: three years minimum, at least one year in full-time residence; preliminary exam; dissertation; final oral exam.

FIELDS OF STUDY.
Biochemistry.
Biometry. M.S. only.
Biophysics.
Cancer Therapeutic Development.
Cell and Tumor Biology.
Cellular-Molecular Biology.
Cellular Physiology.
Chemistry. Includes medicinal chemistry.
Experimental Pathology.
Genomics.
Microbiology/Immunology.
Molecular Pharmacology.
Pharmacology/Experimental Therapeutics.

School of Social Work

Established 1934. Annual tuition: resident $5100, nonresident $8416; per credit, resident $213, nonresident $351. On-campus housing available. Day care facilities available.

Enrollment: full-time 190, part-time 254. Faculty: full-time 18, part-time 2. Degrees conferred: M.S.W., Ph.D.

ADMISSION REQUIREMENTS. Transcripts, GRE, three letters of reference, personal statement required in support of School's application. On-line application available. TOEFL required for international applicants. Accepts transfer applicants and advanced-standing applicants. Graduates of unaccredited institutions not considered for advanced standing. Apply to Director of Admissions by April 1. Admits Fall only, for both full- and part-time programs. Application fee $50. Phone: (716)645-3381, ext. 246; fax: (716)645-3456.

ADMISSION STANDARDS. Selective. Usual minimum average: 3.0 (A = 4).

FINANCIAL AID. Scholarships, assistantships, tuition waivers, Federal W/S, loans. Apply by February 1. Phone: (716)829-3724. Use FAFSA. Aid available for part-time students.

DEGREE REQUIREMENTS. For M.S.W.: 60 credit hours minimum, for full-time at least two years in residence, for part-time one year in residence with advanced standing. For Ph.D.: a minimum of 47 credits beyond M.S.W.; pro-seminar; research internship; comprehensive exam; candidacy; dissertation; oral defense.

FIELDS OF STUDY.
Social Work. Includes alcohol and other drug problems, health, mental health and disability, children and youth, community, individualized. M.S.W.
Social Welfare. Ph.D.

BUTLER UNIVERSITY
Indianapolis, IN 46208-3485
Web site: www.butler.edu

Founded 1855. Coed. Private control. Semester system. Special facility: Holcomb Observatory and Planetarium. Library: 345,400 volumes, 2200 subscriptions. Approximately 250 computers on campus for student use.

Tuition: $240 per credit. On-campus housing available for graduate students. Average academic year housing costs: $6150 (including board). Contact Director of Residential Life for both on- and off-campus housing information. Phone: (317)283-9570.

Division of Graduate Studies

Graduate study since 1932. Enrollment: full-time 379, part-time 629. University faculty: full-time 68, part-time 43. Degrees conferred: M.A., M.S., M.M., M.B.A., Ed.S.

ADMISSION REQUIREMENTS. Two official transcripts, GRE/GMAT required in support of application (electronic application available). Interview not required. TOEFL (minimum score 550) required for international applicants. Accepts transfer applicants. Graduates of unaccredited institutions not considered. Apply to Office of Graduate Admissions by August 15. Application fee $25. Phone: (800)972-2882, (317)940-8100; fax: (317)940-8250.

ADMISSION STANDARDS. Selective. Usual minimum average: 2.75 (A = 4).

FINANCIAL AID. Scholarships, teaching fellowships, teaching assistantships, music awards, Federal W/S, loans. Apply to the Office of Graduate Studies for fellowships, assistantships; to Financial Aid Office for all other programs. No specified closing date. Phone: (800)972-2882. Use FAFSA.

DEGREE REQUIREMENTS. For master's; 30–36 hours for most programs; final written/oral exam for some majors; comprehensive exam. For Specialist: 30 credits beyond the master's; special project.

FIELDS OF STUDY.

COLLEGE OF BUSINESS ADMINISTRATION:
Business Administration. Up to 12 additional prerequisite hours for M.B.A., depending upon previous preparation; GMAT for admission. Concentrations in finance, leadership, marketing.

COLLEGE OF EDUCATION:
Educational Administration. M.S.Ed., Ed.S.

Effective Teaching. Includes elementary, institutional technology, middle level, secondary, reading, special. M.S.Ed.
School Counseling. M.S.

COLLEGE OF LIBERAL ARTS AND SCIENCES:
English. M.A.
History. M.A.

JORDAN COLLEGE OF FINE ARTS:
Composition.
Conducting.
Music Education.
Music History.
Performance.
Piano Pedagogy.
Theory.

COLLEGE OF PHARMACY:
Pharmacy. Pharm.D.

CALIFORNIA COLLEGE OF THE ARTS
San Francisco, California 94102-2247
Web site: www.cca.edu

Founded 1907. Graduate programs located in San Francisco; housing located at Oakland campus. Private control. Semester system. Special facilities: Graduate Center Gallery; MFA Student Gallery. Library: 57,000 volumes, 320 subscriptions. Total College enrollment: 1300.

Annual tuition: M.A. full-time $16,504, M.F.A. full-time $21,920; per credit $903. No on-campus housing. Off-campus room and board average $7272. For off-campus housing information, contact Student Services Office. Phone: (510)420-2000.

Graduate Division

Graduate study since 1956. Enrollment: full-time 130. Faculty: full- and part-time 39. Degrees conferred: M.A. M.F.A.

ADMISSION REQUIREMENTS. Transcripts, statement/personal essay, résumé, portfolio, slides/photographs of artwork required in support of College's application. TOEFL required of foreign applicants. Interview not required. Graduates of unaccredited colleges not considered. Apply to Office of Enrollment Services (San Francisco campus) by February 1 (Fall). Application fee $45, $50 for Internationals. Phone: (415)703-9523; fax: (415)703-9539.

ADMISSION STANDARDS. Selective. Admission based on talent.

FINANCIAL AID. Annual awards from institutional funds: scholarships, Federal W/S, loans. Apply to Director of Graduate Division by March 1 (Fall), October 1 (Spring). Phone: (415)703-9528. Use FAFSA and institutional FAF. About 63% of students receive aid other than loans from College and outside sources. No institutional aid for part-time students.

DEGREE REQUIREMENTS. For M.A.: 36 credit program; master's project. For M.F.A.: 60 units minimum, at least 48 in residence; thesis; final oral exam.

FIELDS OF STUDY.
Design. M.F.A.
Fine Arts. M.F.A.
Visual Criticism. M.A.
Writing. M.F.A.

CALIFORNIA INSTITUTE OF TECHNOLOGY
Pasadena, California 91125-0001
Web site: www.caltech.edu

Founded 1891. CGS and AAU member. Coed. Private control. Quarter system. Special facilities: well-equipped laboratories in fields of specialization, computing center (computing support services for IBM, DEC, Apple, Sun, NeXT; INTEL Touchstone Delta, Cray Y-MP), large telescopes at Big Bear Solar, Caltech Submillimeter (Mauna Kea, Hawaii) and Palomar Observatories, radio telescopes at Bishop and Palomar Observatories, seismological laboratory at Pasadena, Kerckhoff Marine Laboratory at Corona del Mar, Environmental Quality Laboratory, Kellog Radiation Laboratory, Graduate Aeronautics Laboratory, Jet Propulsion Lab at Pasadena. Library: 1,000,000 volumes, 3200 subscriptions.

Annual tuition: full-time $20,904. On- and off-campus housing available for single and married students. Average academic year housing costs: $5400–8500. Apply to Graduate Housing Office before May 1. Phone: (626)356-6178. Day-care facilities available.

Graduate Studies

Graduate study since 1916. Enrollment: full-time 1100 (men 80%, women 20%); no part-time study except in unusual cases. Institute faculty, research and teaching: full-time 339, part-time 56. Degrees conferred: M.S., Engineer, Ph.D.

ADMISSION REQUIREMENTS. Transcripts, three letters of recommendation required in support of application. GRE/Subject Tests required by some divisions, strongly recommended by all. Interview not required. TOEFL (minimum score 600, 250 on computer-based test) or IELTS (minimum score 7) required for international applicants, TSE and TWE strongly recommended. Graduates of unaccredited institutions not considered. Apply to Dean of Graduate Studies by January 15; applications received later considered as long as vacancies exist. Admits September only. Application fee, none. Phone: (626)395-6346; fax: (626)577-9246; e-mail: gradoffice@caltech.edu.

ADMISSION STANDARDS. Very competitive. Usual minimum average: 3.5 (A = 4).

FINANCIAL AID. Research fellowships, teaching assistantships, full and partial scholarships, loans. Most scholarships and fellowships have no teaching or research requirements. Apply to Graduate Office by January 15. Phone: (626)356-3811. Use FAFSA and University's FAF. Most students receive aid other than loans from Institute and outside sources.

DEGREE REQUIREMENTS. For M.S.: at least three terms in full-time residence; candidacy; thesis required by some divisions. For Engineer: at least six terms in full-time residence beyond the bachelor's; candidacy; thesis; final exam for some divisions. For Ph.D.: at least nine terms in full-time residence beyond the bachelor's; candidacy; foreign languages proficiency required by some programs; thesis; final oral exam.

FIELDS OF STUDY.

BIOLOGY DIVISION:
Biology. Ph.D.
Biochemistry. Ph.D.
Cell Biology. Ph.D.
Computation and Neural Systems (Interdisciplinary). Ph.D.
Developmental Biology. Ph.D.
Genetics. Ph.D.

Immunology. Ph.D.
Molecular Biophysics. Ph.D.
Neurosciencs. Ph.D.
Structural Biology. Ph.D.

CHEMISTRY AND CHEMICAL ENGINEERING DIVISION:
Chemistry. Ph.D.
Chemical Engineering. M.S., Ph.D.

ENGINEERING AND APPLIED SCIENCE DIVISION:
Aeronautics. M.S., Engr., Ph.D.
Applied and Computation Mathematics. M.S, Ph.D.
Applied Mechanics. M.S., Ph.D.
Applied Physics. M.S., Ph.D.
Bioengineering (Interdisciplinary). Ph.D. only.
Civil Engineering. M.S., Ph.D.
Computation and Neural Systems (Interdisciplinary). M.S., Ph.D.
Computer Science. M.S., Ph.D.
Control and Dynamical Systems. M.S., Ph.D.
Electrical Engineering. M.S., Ph.D.
Environmental Science and Engineering. M.S., Ph.D.
Materials Sciences. M.S., Ph.D.
Mechanical Engineering. M.S., Ph.D.

GEOLOGICAL AND PLANETARY SCIENCES DIVISION:
Geobiology. Ph.D.
Geochemistry. M.S., Ph.D.
Geology. M.S., Ph.D.
Geophysics. M.S., Ph.D.
Planetary Sciences. M.S., Ph.D.

PHYSICS, MATHEMATICS AND ASTRONOMY:
Astronomy. Ph.D.
Mathematics. Ph.D.
Physics. Ph.D.

CALIFORNIA INSTITUTE OF THE ARTS

Valencia, California 91355
Web site: www.calarts.edu

CalArts was established as a result of the merger of Los Angeles Conservatory of Music (founded in 1883) and the Chouinard Arts Institute (founded in 1921) and the generosity of Walt and Roy Disney and Lulu May Von Hagen and was incorporated in 1961. Private control. Semester system. Library: 98,000 volumes, 613 subscriptions. More than 80 computers on campus for general student use. Total Institute enrollment: 1200.

Annual tuition: full-time $22,190. On-campus housing available for single students only on a first-come, first-served basis. Average annual housing cost: $7000 (including board). For off-campus housing information, contact Student Services Office.

Graduate Studies

Enrollment: full-time 404. Institute faculty: full-time 136, part-time 122. Degree conferred: M.F.A.

ADMISSION REQUIREMENTS. Transcripts, portfolio, slides/photographs of artwork, three recent works (music composition), interview (directing), personal statement, three letters of recommendation required in support of College's application. TOEFL required of foreign applicants. Apply to Director of Admissions by January 15 (Fall, priority deadline), November 11 (Spring). Application fee $60. Phone: (661)253-7863; fax: (661)253-8352.

ADMISSION STANDARDS. Selective. Admission based on talent.

FINANCIAL AID. Annual awards from institutional funds: scholarships, grants, assistantships, Federal W/S, loans. Apply to Financial Aid Office by March 1. Use FAFSA.

DEGREE REQUIREMENTS. For M.F.A.: 60 units minimum, at least 48 in residence; final oral exam; projects.

FIELDS OF STUDY.

SCHOOL OF ARTS:
Art.
Graphic Design.
Photography.

SCHOOL OF CRITICAL STUDIES:
Writing.

SCHOOL OF FILM/VIDEO:
Film and Video.
Experimental Animation.
Character Animation.
Film Directing.

SCHOOL OF MUSIC:
Composition.
Composition New Media.
Music Technology.

SCHOOL OF THEATER:
Acting.
Design and Production.
Directing.
Performer/Composer. Includes African American, improvisational music.
Producing.
Writing for Performance.

CALIFORNIA LUTHERAN UNIVERSITY

Thousand Oaks, California 91360
Web site: www.clunet.edu

Founded in 1959. Coed. Located 50 miles NW of Los Angeles. Church sponsored—Lutheran. Library: 125,032 volumes, 586 subscriptions. About 150 computers on campus for student use.

Tuition: per credit, $425 M.B.A., $370 others. No on-campus housing available. For off-campus information contact Housing Office. Phone: (805)493-3220.

Graduate Studies

Graduate study since 1970. Enrollment: full-time 470, part-time 480. Faculty: full-time 26, part-time 89. Degrees conferred: M.A., M.Ed., M.S., M.B.A., M.B.A.F.P., M.P.P.A., Ed.D.

ADMISSION REQUIREMENTS. Transcripts, GRE/GMAT, three letters of recommendation, personal statement, interview required in support of application. TOEFL required for foreign applicants. Apply to Graduate Enrollment Services Office six weeks prior to registration. Application fee $50. Phone: (805)493-3127; fax: (805)493-3542.

ADMISSION STANDARDS. Selective. Usual minimum average 3.0 (A = 4).

FINANCIAL AID. Limited to scholarships, graduate assistantships, Lutheran Teacher awards, Federal W/S, loans. Apply to the Office of Financial Aid; no specified closing date. Phone: (805)493-3115; fax: (805)493-3114. Use FAFSA and Institutional FAF.

DEGREE REQUIREMENTS. For master's: 30–48 credits minimum; thesis/nonthesis option. For Ed.D: 60 credit program beyond master's degree; dissertation; final oral exam.

FIELDS OF STUDY.
Business Administration. Includes finance, information technology, management, management and organization behavior, marketing tracks. M.B.A.
Clinical Psychology. M.S.
Counseling and Guidance. M.S.
Counseling Psychology. M.F.T., M.S.
Curriculum and Instruction. Includes specializations in cross-cultural language and academic development, curriculum coordination, educational technology, elementary education, reading, subject areas. M.A.
Financial Planning. M.B.A.F.P.
Public Policy Administration. M.P.P.A.
Special Education. M.S.
Teacher Preparation. M.Ed.

CALIFORNIA POLYTECHNIC STATE UNIVERSITY

San Luis Obispo, California 93407
Web site: www.calpoly.edu

Founded 1901. Located 200 miles N of Los Angeles. Coed. Public control. Quarter system. Special facilities: Agricultural Safety Institute, Applied Research and Development facilities, Brock Center for Agricultural Communication, Center for Practical Politics, Coastal Resource Institute, Computer-Integrated Manufacturing Center, Dairy Products Technology Center, Design and Construction Institute, Electric Power Institute, Irrigation Training and Research Center, Small Business Institute. Library: 1,200,000 volumes, 2617 subscriptions. About 1900 computers on campus for general student use.

Tuition: residents $0, nonresident tuition and fees $9660 (three quarters). Fees: full-time (more than 6 units) $748 per quarter. No on-campus housing available. For off-campus housing, call (805)756-1226.

Research and Graduate Program

Enrollment: full-time 595, part-time 415. University faculty: full-time 344, part-time 291. Degrees conferred: M.A., M.S., M.B.A., M.C.R.P., M.S.I.T.S. teacher credential.

ADMISSION REQUIREMENTS. Transcripts required in support of application. GRE/GMAT required for some programs. TOEFL (minimum score 550), TWE (minimum score 4.5), and confidential financial certification required for foreign applicants. Accepts transfer applicants. Apply to Office of Admissions by July 1 (Fall), November 1 (Winter), March 1 (Spring), April 1 (Summer). Application fee $55. Phone: (805)756-2328; fax: (805)756-1725; e-mail: admprosp@polymail.calpoly.edu.

ADMISSION STANDARDS. Selective. Minimum average: 2.5 (A = 4).

FINANCIAL AID. Annual awards from institutional funds: graduate fellowships, equity fellowships, scholarships, Federal W/S, loans. Apply by March 1 to Financial Aid Office. Phone: (805)756-2927; fax: (805)756-7243. Use FAFSA.

DEGREE REQUIREMENTS. For master's: 45 quarter units minimum except for M.C.R.P. (72 units), English (48), Psychology (90), Business (48–96), at least 32 in residence; advancement to candidacy; thesis, project or culminating exam.

FIELDS OF STUDY.
Accounting. M.S.
Aeronautical Engineering. M.S.
Agriculture. Includes agribusiness, agricultural education, animal science, crop science, dairy products technology, engineering technology, environmental horticultural science, food science and nutrition, irrigation, soil science. M.S.
Architecture. M.S.
Biological Sciences. M.S.
Business Administration. M.B.A.
City and Regional Planning. M.C.R.P.
Civil and Environental Engineering. M.S.
Computer Science. M.S.
Credentials Programs. Include single subject, multiple subject, educational administration.
Education. Includes counseling and guidance, curriculum and instruction, education administration, literacy and reading, special education. M.A.
Electrical Engineering. Includes computer engineering, electronic. M.S.
Engineering. Includes biochemical, bioengineering, biomedical, industrial, materials, mechanical, water. M.S.
Engineering Management. M.B.A.-M.S.
English. M.A.
Forestry Sciences. M.S.
Industrial and Technical Studies. M.S.I.T.S.
Kinesiology. M.S.
Mathematics. M.S.
Mechanical Engineering. M.S.
Psychology. M.A.
Transportation Planning. M.C.R.P.-M.S.

CALIFORNIA STATE POLYTECHNIC UNIVERSITY

Pomona, California 91768-2557
Web site: www.csupomona.edu

Established 1938. Located 30 miles from Los Angeles. CGS member. Coed. Public control. Quarter system. Special facilities: W. K. Kellogg Arabian Horse Center, Center for Advanced Computer Technology, Institute for Cellular and Molecular Biology, Center for Regenerative Studies, Center for Community Affairs, Center for Geographic Information Research, Center for Entrepreneurship and Innovation, Center for Economic Education and Research, Equine Research Center, Institute for Ethics and Public Policy, Reproductive Physiology Center, Center for Science and Mathematics Education, Small Business Institute. Library 592,000 volumes, 5863 subscriptions. More than 1800 computers on campus for general student use.

Tuition per unit: resident $0, nonresident $188. Fees: $1855 per year. On-campus housing for single graduate students: $7113 (including board). Apply by May 1. Contact Director of Marketing for both on- and off-campus housing information. Phone: (909)869-3308.

Graduate School

Graduate study since 1968. Enrollment: full-time 528, part-time 526. Faculty: full- and part-time 750. Degrees conferred: M.A., M.S., M.Arch., M.B.A., M.L.A., M.S.E., M.S.E.E., M.S.B.A., M.U.R.P.

ADMISSION REQUIREMENTS. Transcripts, GRE/Subject Tests, GMAT (business) required in support of School's application. Interview required for Architecture, Urban and Regional Planning, and Landscape Architecture. TOEFL required of international applicants. Accepts transfer applicants. Graduates of unaccredited colleges not considered. Apply to Admissions Office by December 1 (Winter), March 1 (Spring), May 15 (Summer), August 1 (Fall). Application fee $55. Phone: (909)869-2991; fax: (909)869-4529.

ADMISSION STANDARDS. Selective. Usual minimum average: 3.0 (A = 4).

FINANCIAL AID. Graduate presidential fellowships, teaching assistantships, internships, Federal W/S, loans. Apply by March 1 to Dean's Office for fellowships, assistantships; to Financial Aid Office for all other programs. Phone: (909)869-3700; fax: (909)869-4757. Use FAFSA (University code: 001144)

DEGREE REQUIREMENTS. For master's: 45 units minimum, at least 32 units residence; reading knowledge of one foreign language may be required; thesis, project, or comprehensive examination, varies by program.

FIELDS OF STUDY.

COLLEGE OF AGRICULTURE:
Agricultural Nutrition and International Development. M.S.
Agricultural Sciences. M.S.
Animal Science. M.S.
Irrigation Science. M.S.
Nutrition and Food Science. M.S.
Plant Sciences. M.S.
Sports Nutrition. M.S.

COLLEGE OF BUSINESS:
Business Administration. M.B.A.
Business Administration. Includes entrepreneurship, creativity and innovation management, information systems auditing. M.S.

COLLEGE OF ENGINEERING:
Engineering. M.S.
Electrical Engineering. Includes computer systems, communication and microwave, control systems and robotics. M.S.

COLLEGE OF ENVIRONMENTAL DESIGN:
Architecture. M.Arch.
Landscape Architecture. M.L.A.
Urban and Regional Planning. M.U.R.P.

COLLEGE OF LETTERS, ARTS, AND SOCIAL SCIENCES:
Economics. Includes financial economics, environmental and natural resources economics, economic analysis, economic education. M.S.
English. Includes literature, rhetoric and composition, teaching English as a second language. M.A.
History. M.A.
Kinesiology. Includes sports nutrition. M.S.
Psychology. M.S.

COLLEGE OF SCIENCE:
Biological Sciences. M.S.
Chemistry. M.S.

Computer Science. M.S.
Mathematics. M.S.

COLLEGE OF EDUCATION AND INTEGRATIVE STUDIES:
Bilingual Crosscultural Education. M.A.Ed.
Curriculum and Instruction. M.A.Ed.
Educational Leadership. M.A.Ed.
Educational Multimedia. M.A.Ed.
Heritage Languages: Literacy & Leadership. M.A.Ed.
Special Education. M.A.Ed.

CALIFORNIA STATE UNIVERSITY, BAKERSFIELD

Bakersfield, California 93311-1022
Web site: www.csubak.edu

Established 1970. Located 125 miles N of Los Angeles. CGS member. Coed. Public control. Quarter system. Special facilities: Applied Research Center, Archaeological Information Center, Business Research and Education Center, California Well Sample Repository, Center for Research in Agriculture and Biology, Center for the Study of Classical Economics, Direct Marketing Institute, Center for International Studies, Center for Environmental Studies, Center for Living and Learning, Center for Mathematical and Statistical Studies, Center for Physiological Research, Kegley Institute of Ethics, Politics Research Center, Small Business Institute. Library: 354,000 volumes, 2260 subscriptions.

Tuition per unit: resident $0, nonresident $164 per quarter unit in addition to state university fee. Fees: 0–6 units $415; 6.1 or more units $625. On-campus housing for single and married students. Average academic year housing costs: $4430 (including board). Apply by August 1. Contact Director of Housing for both on- and off-campus housing information. Phone: (661)664-3014.

Division of Graduate Studies and Research

Web site: www.csubak.edu/on_campus.html

Enrollment: full-time 236, part-time 258. Faculty: full-time 165, part-time 100. Degrees conferred: M.A., M.S., M.B.A., M.H.A., M.P.A., M.S.W.

ADMISSION REQUIREMENTS. Transcripts, GRE/GMAT/MAT required in support of School's application. GRE Subject Test, letters of recommendation, interview required by some departments. TOEFL required for international applicants. Accepts transfer applicants. Graduates of unaccredited institutions not considered. Apply to Admissions Office at least two months prior to registration. Late admission will be considered. Application fee $55. Phone: (661)664-2231, fax: (661)664-3342.

ADMISSION STANDARDS. Selective. Usual minimum average: 2.75 (A = 4).

FINANCIAL AID. Scholarships, teaching assistantships, Graduate Equity Fellowships, Federal W/S, loans. Approved for VA benefits. Apply by March 1 to Dean, School of Graduate Studies for assistantships, fellowships; to Office of Financial Aid for all other programs. Phone: (661)664-2231. Use FAFSA. About 10% of students receive aid other than loans from College, 21% from all sources. Aid sometimes available for part-time students.

DEGREE REQUIREMENTS. For master's: 60–90 units minimum, at least 45 in residence; candidacy; final written/oral exam for most majors; reading knowledge of one foreign language for some majors; thesis/creative/research project.

FIELDS OF STUDY.
Anthropology. M.A.
Business Administration. GMAT for admission. M.B.A.
Counseling. M.S. only.
Counseling Psychology. M.A.
Early Childhood Education.
Educational Administration.
English. Includes creative writing; thesis or project for master's. M.A.
Geology. M.S.
Health Care Administration. M.H.A. only.
History. M.A.
Interdisciplinary Studies. M.A.
Nursing. Includes administration, child care, clinical, education, supervision. M.S.
Psychology. GRE Subject for admission; qualifying exam, thesis or project for master's. M.A.
Public Administration. M.P.A.
Pupil Personnel Services.
Reading.
Sociology. M.A.
Social Work. M.S.W.
Spanish. M.A.
Special Education.

CALIFORNIA STATE UNIVERSITY, CHICO

Chico, California 95929-0875
Web site: www.csuchico.edu

Founded 1887. Located 100 miles N of Sacramento. CGS member. Coed. State control. Semester system. Special facilities: Eagle Lake Biological Field Station, Instructional Media Center, Survey Research Center, Vertebrate Museum. Library: 1,365,000 volumes, 927,000 microforms, 13,000 subscriptions.

Tuition: per semester, resident $0, nonresident $246 for each semester unit in addition to state university fee. Fees: 0–6 units $438; 6.1 or more $753. On- campus housing for single students only. Average academic year housing costs: $4364 (including board); average off-campus housing costs: $225 per month. Contact Director Of University Housing and Food Service for both on- and off-campus housing information. Phone: (530)898-6328.

School of Graduate, International, and Sponsored Programs

Enrollment: full-time 628, part-time 321. University faculty: full-time 589, part-time 215. Degrees conferred: M.A., M.S., M.B.A., M.P.A., M.R.T.P., M.S.A., M.S.W.

ADMISSION REQUIREMENTS. Two official transcripts, GRE, two letters of recommendation required in support of application. GRE Subject/MAT/GMAT required for some departments. Interview not required. TOEFL required for international students. Accepts transfer applicants. Graduates of unaccredited institutions not considered. Apply to Graduate School by April 1 (Fall), October 15 (Spring), June 15 (Summer). Rolling admissions process. Application fee $55. Phone: (530)898-5396; fax: (530)898-6804.

ADMISSION STANDARDS. Selective. Usual minimum average: 2.5 in last 60 units. 3.0 in last 30 units (A = 4).

FINANCIAL AID. Annual awards from institutional funds: scholarships, equity fellowships, teaching assistantships, Federal W/S, loans. Approved for VA benefits. Apply by February 15 to the Dean's Office for fellowships, assistantships; to the Office of Financial Aid for all other programs. About 50% of students receive aid other than loans from College and outside sources.

DEGREE REQUIREMENTS. For most master's: 30 semester units minimum, at least 24 in residence; thesis/nonthesis option for most majors; final written/oral exam. For M.S.W.: 36–61 semester units depending on baccalaureate degree; thesis/special project/comprehensive exam.

FIELDS OF STUDY.
Accountancy. GMAT for admission.
Anthropology. Admits Fall only. Statement of purpose/intent for admission. Includes Museum Studies.
Art/Fine Arts. Portfolio for admission.
Biological Sciences. GRE for admission.
Botany. GRE for admission.
Business Administration. GMAT, three letters of recommendation, written statement of purpose for admission.
Communication Studies. Three letters of recommendation, one page personal statement for admission.
Computer Science.
Creative Writing. GRE, portfolio of original writings, critical paper, personal statement for admission. M.F.A.
Education. Includes curriculum & instruction, linguistically and culturally diverse learners, reading/language arts, special.
Electrical Engineering. GRE or MAT for admission. Includes computer engineering, electronic engineering.
English. GRE, writing sample for admission.
Environmental Science. GRE, statement of intent for admission.
Geography. GRE, written statement of interest for admission. Includes rural town planning.
Geosciencs. GRE, statement of interest for admission. Includes earth science, hydrology/hydrogeology.
History. GRE, statement of purpose, writing sample for admission.
Instructional Technology. GRE or MAT, three letters of recommendation, personal statement for admission.
Interdisciplinary Studies.
Music. Includes education, performance; GRE General, Subject Test, audition for admission.
Nursing. MAT for admission.
Nutritional Science. GRE, statement of purpose for admission. Includes nutrition education.
Physical Education. Written statement of purpose for admission.
Political Science. Written statement of purpose for admission.
Psychology. GRE/MAT, three letters of recommendation (on departmental form) for admission. Includes psychological science, applied psychology. M.A., M.S.
Public Administration. Includes health administration, local government management.
Recreation Administration. GRE, three letters of recommendation, statement of intent, résumé for admission.
Social Science. GRE, written statement of interest and goals.
Social Work. Three letters of recommendation (on departmental form), personal statement for admission.
Speech-Language Pathology and Audiology. MAT or GRE, three letters of recommendation, written statement of interest, résumé for admission. Admits Fall semester only, apply by March 1.
Teaching of International Languages.

CALIFORNIA STATE UNIVERSITY, DOMINGUEZ HILLS

Carson, California 90747-0001
Web site: www.csudh.edu

Founded 1965. Located in Los Angeles County. CGS member. Coed. Public control. Semester system. Special facilities: Center for Urban Research and Learning, Desert Studies Center, Social Systems Research Center, Southern California Ocean Studies Center; art gallery. Library: 440,000 volumes, 2300 subscriptions. Total university enrollment 12,500.

Tuition: full-time, resident $0, nonresidents $246 per unit plus fees. Fees: 0–6 units $459; 6.1 plus units $792. On-campus housing for married or graduate students. Apply by April 15. Average academic year housing costs: $5698 (room only) for single students; $7500 for married students. Average off-campus housing cost: $500–$900 per month. Contact Office of Dean of Student Affairs for both on- and off-campus housing information.

Division of Graduate Studies and Research

Graduate enrollment: full-time 1197, part-time 2620. University faculty teaching graduate students: full-time 292, part-time 243. Degrees conferred: M.A., M.S., M.B.A., M.H.S., M.P.A.

ADMISSION REQUIREMENTS. Two official transcripts required in support of application. Electronic application available. GRE may be required by some departments. TOEFL required for international applicants. Graduates of unaccredited institutions not considered. Accepts transfer applicants. Apply to Office of Admission and Records by June 1 (Fall), November 30 (Spring). Application fee $55. Phone: (310)243-3300.

ADMISSION STANDARDS. Selective. Usual minimum average: 2.5 overall, 2.75 in last two years (A = 4).

FINANCIAL AID. Scholarships, teaching/research assistantships, graduate equity fellowships, Federal W/S, loans. Apply to Financial Aid Office; no specified closing dates. Phone: (310)516-3647; e-mail: finaid@csudh.edu. Use FAFSA (University code: 001240). About 30% of students receive aid from University and outside sources. Aid sometimes available for part-time students.

DEGREE REQUIREMENTS. For master's: 30–48 semester hours minimum, at least 21 in residence; thesis/nonthesis option; final written/oral exam or project.

FIELDS OF STUDY.
Behavior Sciences. Includes gerontology, negotiation and conflict managment. M.A.
Biology. M.A.
Clinical Science. Includes cytotechnology, medical technology, nuclear medicine technology. M.S.
Business Administration. Includes general management, international. M.B.A.
Education. Includes technology-based, counseling, educational administration, multicultural, physical, teaching/curriculum. M.A.
English. Includes literature, rhetoric, and composition, TESL. M.A.
Health Sciences. Includes physician's assistant, professional studies. M.H.S.
Humanities. M.A.
Interdisciplinary Studies. M.A., M.S.
Marital and Family Therapy. M.S.
Nursing. Includes nurse educator, nurse administration, parent–child clinical nurse specialist, gerontology clinical nurse specialist, family nurse practitioner. M.S.
Quality Assurance. M.S.
Psychology. Includes clinical. M.A.
Public Administration. M.P.A.
Sociology. Includes general, research skills. M.A.
Special Education. Includes learning handicapped, severely handicapped. M.A.
Teaching Mathematics. M.A.

CALIFORNIA STATE UNIVERSITY, FRESNO

Fresno, California 93740-0051
Web site: www.csufresno.edu

Founded 1911. Located 185 miles SE of San Francisco. CGS member. Coed. Public control. Semester system. Special facilities: California Agricultural Technology Institute, Center for Agricultural Business, Center for Irrigation Technology, Center for Korean Studies, Central California Futures Institute, Computer Integrated Manufacturing Center, Digital Economy Center, Institute for Family Business, Moss Landing Marine Laboratory (shared by five state colleges), Small Business Development Center, University Business Center, Viticulture and Enology Research Center. Library: 977,100 volumes, 2500 subscriptions. More than 850 computers on campus for student use.

Tuition: full-time, resident $0, nonresident $246 per unit in addition to fees. Fees: 0–6 units $438; 7 or more units $753. On-campus housing for 555 men, 660 women; none for married students. Average annual housing cost: $5396 (including board). Off-campus moderately priced housing is also available. Apply by June 1 to Director of Housing. Phone: (559)278-2345.

Division of Graduate Studies

Graduate study since 1946. Enrollment: full-time 941, part-time 919. Faculty: full-time 429, part-time 133. Degrees conferred: M.A., M.S., M.B.A., M.F.A. M.S.W., M.P.A., M.P.T., M.P.H.

ADMISSION REQUIREMENTS. Transcripts, GRE required in support of University's application. Letters of recommendation, GMAT, interview required by some departments. TOEFL (minimum score 550) required for foreign applicants. Accepts transfer applicants. Apply to Admissions Office by March 1 (Fall), October 1 (Spring). Late admission will be considered. Application fee $55. Phone: (559)278-2448; fax: (559)278-4658.

ADMISSION STANDARDS. Selective. Usual minimum average: 2.75 (A = 4).

FINANCIAL AID. Scholarships, fellowships, teaching assistantships, traineeships, tuition waivers, Federal W/S, loans. Approved for VA benefits. Apply to Office of Financial Aid by March 1 for scholarships, to Department Chairperson for assistantships. Phone: (559)278-2183. Use FAFSA. About 20% of students receive aid other than loans from University. Aid sometimes available for part-time students.

DEGREE REQUIREMENTS. For master's: 30 units minimum, at least 21 in residence; GRE or GMAT for M.P.A., and M.B.A.; advancement to candidacy; final written/oral exam for most majors; reading knowledge of one foreign language for some majors; thesis/creative/research project.

FIELDS OF STUDY.
Agriculture. Includes agricultural chemistry, animal science, food science, nutrition.
Art. Includes art history, theory; thesis or project for master's. M.A.
Biology. Includes marine, microbiology. M.S.
Business Administration. M.B.A.
Chemistry. GRE Subject; thesis for master's. M.S.
Communication. M.A.
Communicative Disorders. Includes speech-language pathology, education of the deaf. M.A.
Computer Science. M.S.
Counseling. M.S.
Creative Writing. M.F.A.

Criminology. Includes law enforcement, corrections. M.S.

Education. Includes early childhood, elementary, secondary, curriculum and instruction, educational theory, administration, counselor, health, home economics, music, physical, reading, special. M.A.

Educational Leadership. Ed.D.

Engineering. M.A.

English. Includes creative writing; thesis or project for master's. M.A.

Family and Consumer Sciences. M.S.

Food and Nutritional Sciences. M.S.

Geology. M.S.

History. One language; GRE Subject, thesis for master's. M.A.

International Relations. Includes government; one language, GRE Subject, project for master's. M.A.

Industrial Technology. M.S.

Kinesiology. M.A.

Linguistics. Includes English as a second language. M.A.

Marine Science. M.S.

Mass Communication. M.A.

Mathematics. GRE Subject, thesis for master's. M.A.

Music. Includes performance, music education. M.A.

Nursing. Includes clinical, primary nurse practitioner. M.S.

Physical Therapy. M.P.T.

Physics. GRE Subject, thesis or project for master's. M.S.

Plant Science. M.S.

Psychology. GRE Subject, qualifying exam, thesis or project for master's. M.S.

Public Administration. M.P.A.

Public Health. M.P.H.

Rehabilitation Counseling. M.S.

Social Work. Admits Fall only; two years full-time, thesis for master's. M.S.W.

Spanish. M.A.

Special Education. M.A.

Special Major. M.A.

CALIFORNIA STATE UNIVERSITY, FULLERTON

Fullerton, California 92634-9480
Web site: www.fullerton.edu

Founded 1957. Located 35 miles SE of Los Angeles. CGS member. Coed. Public control. Semester system. Special facilities: Desert Studies Consortium, Center for Economic Education, Institute for Economics and Environmental Studies, Center for Governmental Studies, Center for International Business, Ruby Gerontology Center, Social Science Research Center, Twins Study Center. Library: 750,000 volumes, 2450 subscriptions. More than 1000 computers on campus for student use.

Tuition: resident $0; nonresident $246 per unit. Fees: 0–6 units $628; 7 or more units $943. On-campus housing available for single students only. Average annual housing cost: $3782 (including board). Contact the Housing Office for both on- and off-campus housing information. Phone: (714)773-2168.

Graduate Studies

Graduate study since 1960. Enrollment: full-time 457, part-time 2797 (men 39%, women 61%). College faculty; full-time 608, part-time 614. Degrees conferred: M.A., M.S., M.B.A., M.P.A., M.M., M.F.A., M.A.T.

ADMISSION REQUIREMENTS. Two official transcripts required with application. GRE required for some programs; GMAT for M.B.A., Accountancy, Taxation, Management Science. TOEFL required for international applicants. Accepts transfer applicants. Graduates of unaccredited institutions not considered. Apply to Office of Admissions and Records by July 1 (Fall), December 1 (Spring); earlier deadlines exist for some programs. Application fee $55. Phone: (714)773-2618.

FINANCIAL AID. Annual awards from institutional funds: equity fellowships, scholarships, assistantships, internships, grants, Federal W/S, loans. Approved for VA benefits. Apply by March 1 to appropriate department chair for assistantships; to Financial Aid Office for all other programs. Phone: (714)773-3125. Use FAFSA. Aid available for part-time students

DEGREE REQUIREMENTS. For master's: 30–51 units minimum, at least 21 in residence; advancement to candidacy; capstone, thesis, project, or comprehensive exam required for all programs.

FIELDS OF STUDY.

Accountancy. Project for M.S.

American Studies. Thesis or final exam for M.A.

Anthropology. Thesis or project for M.A.

Art. Includes studio and art history programs; thesis or project for M.A., M.F.A.

Biology. GRE General/Subject for admission; thesis for M.S.

Business Administration. Final exam or thesis for M.B.A.

Chemistry. Departmental exams for classified standing; thesis for M.S.

Civil Engineering. M.S.

Communications. GRE for admission; thesis or project for M.A.

Communicative Disorders. Thesis option; comprehensive exam required for M.A.

Comparative Literature. Thesis or final exam for M.A.

Computer Science. GRE for admission; project or thesis for M.S.

Counseling. Project required for M.S.

Economics. GRE for classified standing; thesis for M.A.

Education. Includes bilingual/bicultural education (Spanish/English), elementary curriculum/instruction, reading, special education, administration, TESOL; teaching experience required for classified standing; project/thesis/final exam as determined by concentration for M.S.

Engineering. Includes electrical, mechanical, civil, engineering mechanics systems, engineering science; thesis/project option; final exam for M.S.

English. Project option; final exam for M.A.

Environmental Studies. Thesis for M.S.

Foreign Languages. Includes French, German, Spanish; thesis option; final exam for M.A.

Geography. Project or thesis for M.A.

Geology. M.S.

Gerontology. M.S.

History. Thesis/project/final exam option for M.A.

Interdisciplinary Studies. M.A. only.

Kinesiology. Thesis or project; final exam for M.S.

Linguistics. Thesis option; final exam for M.A.

Management Science. Final exam for M.S.

Mathematics. Includes teaching. Final exam for M.A.

Music. Includes history and literature, performance, theory-composition, music education, proficiency exams for classified standing; thesis or project for M.M., M.A. Admits Fall only.

Physics. Final exam or thesis for M.S.

Political Science. Project, final exam for M.A.

Psychology. Includes clinical experimental. Admits Fall only. GRE/Subject Test for admission; thesis for M.A.; final exam for M.S.

Public Administration. GRE for classified standing; project/thesis/final exam option for M.P.A.

Radio, TV, and Film.

Science. Thesis or project for M.A.T.

Sociology. Thesis for M.A.

Speech Communication. Thesis option; final exam for M.A.

Taxation. Project for M.S.

Theater Arts. Includes acting, directing, technical theater and design. Thesis/project and final exam for M.A.; two projects for M.F.A. (technical theater and design, theater for children, acting). Admits Fall only.

CALIFORNIA STATE UNIVERSITY, HAYWARD

Hayward, California 94542-3000

Web site: www.csuhayward.edu

Founded 1957. Located in San Francisco Bay Area, 12 miles SE of Oakland. CGS member. Coed. State control. Quarter system. Special facilities: Institute of Mental Illness and Wellness Education, Microscope and Graphic Imaging Center, Moss Landing Marine Laboratory, C. F. Smith Museum of Anthropology. Library: 908,500 volumes, 2200 subscriptions. More than 700 computers on campus for general student use. Total enrollment: 12,800.

Tuition: resident $0, nonresident $164 per unit plus fees. Fees: 0–6 units $405; 7 or more units $615. On-campus apartments available. Apply by March 1. Annual housing cost: $2845. No on-campus housing for married students. Contact Director of Housing and Residential Life for off-campus housing information. Phone (510)885-7444. Day-care facilities available.

Graduate Study

Enrollment: full-time 1268, part-time 1854. College faculty teaching graduate students: approximately 368. Degrees conferred: M.A., M.B.A., M.P.A., M.S.

ADMISSION REQUIREMENTS. Transcripts required in support of application. GRE, GMAT, or MAT, required by some departments. TOEFL required of foreign students. Interview required by some departments. Accepts transfer applicants. Graduates of unaccredited institutions not considered. Apply by June 15 (Fall), October 15 (Winter), January 15 (Spring) to the Office of Admissions. Application fee $55. Phone: (510)885-3286; fax: (510)885-4795; e-mail: gradprograms@csuhayward.edu.

ADMISSION STANDARDS. Competitive. Minimum undergraduate GPA for postbaccalaureate status is 2.5 in last 90 quarter units (A = 4).

FINANCIAL AID. Scholarships, grants, fellowships, assistantships, internships, Federal W/S, loans. Apply to Director of Financial Aid by March 1. Phone: (510))885-3616. Use FAFSA and institution FAF. Aid available for part-time students. About 10% of students receive aid other than loans from University and outside sources.

DEGREE REQUIREMENTS. For master's: 45 quarter hours minimum, at least 32 in residence; thesis, project, or comprehensive exam; foreign language for several majors.

FIELDS OF STUDY.

Anthropology. Thesis and comprehensive exam.

Biological Science. Includes botany, zoology; thesis.

Business Administration. Thesis or comprehensive exam; ten options. M.B.A., M.S.

Chemistry. Thesis or comprehensive exam for M.S.

Computer Science. Thesis or comprehensive exam. M.S.

Counseling. Includes clinical and school; thesis, project, or comprehensive exam.

Economics. Thesis or comprehensive exam. M.A.

Education. Includes children's literature, ESL, environmental, mathematics, science, reading instruction, pupil personnel, curriculum, early childhood, special; thesis or project.

Educational Leadership. Thesis or project.

Educational Psychology.

English. One language for M.A.; comprehensive exam required; thesis optional.

Geography. Thesis or project for M.A.

Geology. Thesis. M.S.

Health Care Administration.

History. Thesis, project, or comprehensive exam; one language in most options.

Kinesiology.

Marine Science. Thesis. M.S.

Mathematics. Includes teaching, applied, pure math options for M.S.; comprehensive exam.

Multimedia. Interdisciplinary; project. M.A.

Music. Includes history-literature, education, performance, theory, composition; proficiency exams for admission; thesis/project; comprehensive exam.

Public Administration. Options in public policy development, public management, organizational change, health care administration; comprehensive exam.

Quantitative Business.

Sociology. Thesis/project; comprehensive exam.

Special Major. Self-designed M.A. or M.S., thesis/project; comprehensive exam.

Speech. Communication; thesis/project; comprehensive exam. M.A.

Speech Pathology and Audiology. Thesis optional; comprehensive exam. M.S.

Statistics. Comprehensive exam. M.S.

Taxation. Thesis for M.S. M.S.

Telecommunications Systems.

CALIFORNIA STATE UNIVERSITY, LONG BEACH

Long Beach, California 90840-0118

Web site: www.csulb.edu

Founded 1949. Located between Los Angeles and Orange County. CGS member. Coed. Public control. Semester system. Special facilities: Center for Asian Pacific American Studies, Center for Behavioral Research and Studies, Center for Collaboration in Education, Center for Commercial Deployment of Transportation Technology, Center for Criminal Justice Research and Training, Center for Educational Applications of Brain-Hemisphere Research, Center for Entrepreneurship, Center for European Studies, Center for First Amendment Studies, Center for Health Care Innovation, Center for Humanities, Center for Information Systems Technologies, Center for International Trade and Transportation, Center for Language Minority Education and Research, Molecular Ecology Institute, Center for the Preservation of Jazz, Center for Study of Southeast Asia, Center for Study of Judeo-Christian Origins, Center for Successful Aging. Library: 1,000,000 volumes, 5424 subscriptions. More than 2000 computers on campus for general student use.

Tuition: resident $0, nonresident $246 per unit plus fees. Fees: 0–6 units $438; 7 or more $753. On-campus housing for 725 men, 1075 women; none for married students. Average annual housing cost: $6850 (including board). Apply by April 1 to Director of Housing. Dance Center. Day-care facilities available.

Graduate Studies

Enrollment: full-time 1483, part-time 2327. University faculty: full- and part-time 773. Degrees conferred: M.A., M.S., M.F.A.,

M.P.A., Ph.D. (Engineering Mathematics with Claremont Graduate School).

ADMISSION REQUIREMENTS. Transcripts, GRE/GMAT required in support of University's application. Electronic application available. TOEFL required for foreign applicants. Accept transfer applicants. Graduates of unaccredited institutions not considered. Apply to Office of Admissions and Records by August 1 (Fall), December 1 (Spring). Application fee $55. Phone: (562)985-4128; fax: (562)985-1680.

ADMISSION STANDARDS. Very selective for some departments, relatively open for others. Minimum average: 2.5 in last 60 units attempted (A = 4).

FINANCIAL AID. Annual awards from institutional funds; scholarships, fellowships, grants, assistantships, Federal W/S, loans. Apply to the Office of Financial Aid between February 1 and March 1 for scholarships, loans, W/S; to appropriate department chair for assistantships. Phone: (562)985-4641. Use FAFSA. Aid available for part-time students.

DEGREE REQUIREMENTS. For master's: 30 units minimum, at least 24 in residence; reading knowledge of one foreign language for some major; candidacy exam; thesis/project or final written/oral exam. For Ph.D.: see degree requirements in Claremont Graduate School listing.

FIELDS OF STUDY.
Aerospace Engineering. M.S.
Anthropology. M.A.
Art. Includes studio, education, art history. M.A., M.F.A.
Asian Studies. M.A.
Biochemistry. M.S.
Biology. M.S.
Business Administration. M.B.A.
Chemical Engineering. M.S.
Chemistry. M.S.
Civil Engineering. M.S.
Communicative Disorders. M.A.
Computer Engineering. M.S.
Computer Sciences. M.S.
Criminal Justice. M.S.
Dance. M.F.A.
Design. M.A., M.F.A.
Economics. M.A.
Education. Includes administration, counseling, psychology (educational, school), and social and multicultural foundations, elementary, secondary.
Electrical Engineering. M.S.
Engineering. M.S.
English. Includes creative writing. M.A.
French. M.A.
Geography. M.A.
Geology. M.S.
German. M.A.
Health Care Administration. M.S.
Health Science. M.S., M.P.H.
History. M.A.
Interdisciplinary Studies. M.A., M.S.
Kinesiology and Physical Education. M.A.
Linguistics. M.A.
Mathematics. M.S.
Mechanical Engineering. M.S.
Microbiology. M.S.
Music. Includes applied, musicology, performance. M.A., M.M.
Nursing. M.S.
Nutritional Science. M.S.
Philosophy. M.A.
Physical Therapy. M.A.
Physics. M.S.

Political Science. M.A.
Psychology. Includes industrial, clinical. M.A.
Public Administration. M.P.A.
Recreation Administration. M.S.
Social Work. M.S.W.
Spanish. M.A.
Theater Arts. M.A., M.F.A.

CALIFORNIA STATE UNIVERSITY, LOS ANGELES

Los Angeles, California 90032-8350
Web site: www.calstatela.edu

Founded 1947. CGS member. Public control. Quarter system. Special facilities: Center for the Study of Business in Society, Chinese Studies Center, Center for Korean-American Studies, Center for Armament and Disarmament, Desert Studies Center. Library: 1,700,000 volumes, 2430 subscriptions. More than 1500 computers on campus for general student use.

Tuition: resident $0, nonresident $164 per quarter unit plus fees. Fees: 0–6 units $876; 6.1 or more units $1506. On-campus housing available. Total annual cost: $6200 (including board). For off-campus housing, contact Housing and Residence Life. Phone: (323)343-4800. Day-care facilities available.

Graduate Studies

Enrollment: full-time 1168, part-time 2529. Faculty: full-time 477, part-time 503. Degrees conferred: M.A., M.F.A., M.S., M.B.A., M.S.W., Ph.D. (Special Education) offered jointly with UCLA.

ADMISSION REQUIREMENTS. Two transcripts required in support of University's application. GRE and interview required by some departments. TOEFL required for international applicants. Accepts transfer applicants. Graduates of unaccredited institutions not considered. Apply by June 30 (Fall), October 1 (Winter), February 1 (Spring), April 1 (Summer) to Office of Admissions and Records. Application fee $55. Phone: (323)343-3891.

ADMISSION STANDARDS. Relatively open. Usual minimum average: 2.5 (A = 4).

FINANCIAL AID. Fellowships, assistantships, grants, internships, Federal W/S, loans. Approved for VA benefits. Apply by March 1 to Office of Student Financial Services. Phone: (323)343-3240. Use FAFSA. Aid available for part-time students.

DEGREE REQUIREMENTS. For master's: 45 quarter units minimum, at least 32 in residence; foreign language competency for some departments; thesis for some majors; advancement to candidacy; comprehensive; oral/written exam for some majors. For Ph.D.: 32 quarter units in residence; for additional Ph.D. requirements, see UCLA listing.

FIELDS OF STUDY.
Accountancy. M.S.
Anthropology. M.A.
Art. Includes education, history, design, studio. M.A., M.F.A.
Biochemistry. M.S.
Biology. M.S.
Business Administration. Includes accounting, business economics, business education, finance, health care management, information systems, international, management, marketing. M.B.A., M.S.
Chemistry. M.S.
Child Development. M.A., M.Ed.

Communication Studies. Includes speech, telecommunications and film. M.A.

Communicative Disorders. M.A.

Counseling. Includes school counseling and school psychology, rehabilitation counseling, community college counseling, applied behavior analysis.

Criminal Justice. M.S.

Criminalistics. M.S.

Economics. M.A.

Education. Includes early childhood, elementary, secondary, computer education, educational foundation, reading, special interests. M.A.

Educational Administration. M.A.

Engineering. Includes civil, electrical, mechanical. M.S.

English. Includes composition, literature, creative writing. M.A.

French. M.A.

Geography. M.A.

Geology. Offered jointly with California State University, Long Beach, California State University, Northridge. M.S.

Health Care Management. M.S.

Health Science. M.A.

History. M.A.

Industrial and Technical Studies. M.A.

Information Systems. M.S.

Kinesiology. M.A.

Latin-American Studies. M.A.

Mathematics. Includes applied and pure. M.S.

Mexican-American Studies. M.A.

Music. Includes music composition, commercial music, performance, musicology. M.A., M.Mus.

Music Education.

Nursing. Includes acute care nurse practitioner, administrator. M.S.

Nutritional Science. M.S.

Philosophy. M.A.

Physics. M.S.

Political Science. M.A.

Psychology. M.A., M.S.

Public Administration. M.S.

Social Work. M.S.W.

Sociology. M.A.

Spanish. M.A.

Special Education. Includes early childhood, gifted, mild/moderate disabilities, moderate/severe disabilities, multicultural/multilingual, resource specialist. M.A. Ph.D. offered jointly with UCLA.

Speech Communication. M.A.

TESOL. M.A.

Theater Arts. M.A.

CALIFORNIA STATE UNIVERSITY, NORTHRIDGE

Northridge, California 91330

Web site: www.csun.edu

Founded 1958. Located near Los Angeles. CGS member. Coed. Public control. Semester system. Special facilities: California African American Political Institute, Central American Studies, China Institute, Entertainment Industry Institute, Institute for the Advancement of Educational Studies and Programs, Institute for Business and Economics, Institute for Health and Human Development, Institute for Social and Behavioral Sciences, Center for Achievement for the Physically Disabled, Center for Cancer and Developmental Biology, Center for Earthquake Studies, Center for Ethics and Values, Center for Finance and Business Research, Center for Family Business Education and Research, Center for the Humanities, Center for

Mangement and Organizational Development, Center for Partnerships for Educational Reform, Center for Real Estate, Center for Research and Services, Center for Sex Research, Center for Southern California Studies, Center for Supramolecular Studies, Center for the Study of the San Fernando Valley Economy, Center for the Study of Biodiversity, Center for Study of Peoples of the Americas, Center for Small Business and Entrepreneurship, Center for the Visual and Performing Arts. Library: 1,200,000 volumes, 2754 subscriptions.

Tuition: full-time, resident $0; nonresident $246 per unit plus fees. Fees: 0–6 units $438; 7 or more units $753. On-campus housing for single students only. Average academic year housing costs: $5840 (including board). Contact Housing Office for both on- and off-campus housing information. Phone: (818)667-2160.

Graduate Studies

Enrollment: full-time 1226, part-time 1759. Faculty: full-time 829, part-time 632. Degrees conferred: M.A., M.B.A., M.P.A., M.P.H., M.S.

ADMISSION REQUIREMENTS. Two official transcripts, GRE/MAT/GMAT required in support of School's application. Departmental applications required for some programs. TOEFL required for international applicants. Interview required for some departments. Separate departmental applications required in some departments. Accepts transfer applicants. Apply to Admissions Office by August 1 (Fall), January 1 (Spring). Application fee $55. Phone: (818)677-2138; fax: (818)677-4691; e-mail: graduatestudies@csun.edu.

ADMISSION STANDARDS. Selective for most departments. Usual minimum average: 2.5 (A = 4).

FINANCIAL AID. Annual awards from institutional funds: scholarships, fellowships, assistantships, partial tuition waivers, internships, Federal W/S, loans. Approved for VA benefits. Apply by March 1 to the Office of Student Assistance. Phone: (818)677-2085. Use FAFSA. About 5% of students receive aid from University and outside sources. Aid available for part-time students.

DEGREE REQUIREMENTS. For master's: 30 units minimum, at least 21 in residence; thesis/project; comprehensive exam; reading knowledge of one foreign language for some departments. For M.B.A.: 33 units.

FIELDS OF STUDY.

Accounting. M.S.

Aerospace/Aeronautical Engineering. M.S.

Anthropology. M.A.

Applied Mechanics. M.S.

Art. Includes applied, 2-D, 3-D, history. Portfolio, creative project for M.A. M.A., M.F.A.

Automation Engineering. M.S.

Biology. GRE Subject for M.S. M.S.

Business Administration. GMAT required for admission. M.S., M.B.A.

Chemistry. M.S.

Computer Science. M.S.

Counselor. M.S. for M.F.C.C.

Education. Includes supervision and higher education; educational psychology, counseling and guidance; elementary education, secondary education, social, philosophical foundations, foundations of education. M.A.

Educational Administration. M.A.

Electrical Engineering. M.S.

Engineering Management. M.S.

English. M.A., M.F.A.

Environmental Occupational Health. M.S.

Family Consumer Sciences. M.S.

Genetic Counceling. M.S.

Geography. M.A.

Geology. M.S. offered cooperatively with CSU, Long Beach, and CSU, Los Angeles.

Health Science. Applications for health education option accepted Fall only; application by March 1. M.S.

History. One language required in area of concentration for M.A.

Interdisciplinary Studies. M.A., M.S.

Kinesiology. M.S.

Linguistics. One language required for M.A.

Mass Communication. Option I—news communication, Option II—radio-TV-film. M.A.

Materials Engineering. M.S.

Mathematics. M.S.

Mechanical Engineering. M.S.

Music. Includes theory, composition, performance, music education. Placement tests in theory and history for M.A. and M.M.

Physical Therapy. M.P.T.

Physics. Departmental proficiency exam.

Political Science. M.A.

Psychology. GRE subject for M.A.; Fall applications February 15 deadline; Spring applications November 1 deadline.

Public Administration. Departmental qualifing exam for M.P.A.

Public Health. M.P.H.

Recreation. Developmental qualifying exam for M.S.

Secondary Education. M.A.

Sociology. M.A.

Spanish. M.A.

Special Education. M.A.

Speech Communication. M.A.

Structural Engineering. M.S.

Taxation. M.S.

Theater Arts. Departmental qualifying exam for M.A.

CALIFORNIA STATE UNIVERSITY, SACRAMENTO

Sacramento, California 95819-6048

Web site: www.csus.edu

Founded 1947. CGS member. Coed. Public control. Semester system. Special facilities: California Center for Public Dispute Resolution, Center for California Studies, Real Estate and Land Use Institute. Library: 806,000 volumes, 4,000 subscriptions, more than 800 computers on-campus for general student use.

Tuition: resident $0, nonresident $246 per unit plus fees. Fees: 0–6 units $438; 7 or more units $753. On-campus housing for single students. Average academic year housing costs: $6250 (including board). Contact Office of Residence Hall Life for both on- and off-campus housing information.

Graduate Studies

Enrollment: full-time 2116, part-time 2188. Graduate faculty: full-time 399, part-time 222. Degrees conferred: M.A., M.S., M.S.B.A., M.B.A., M.P.P.A., M.S.W.

ADMISSION REQUIREMENTS. Two official transcripts required in support of application. GRE/GMAT required by some departments. Interview may be requested. TOEFL required for international applicants. Accepts transfer applicants. Graduates of unaccredited institutions not considered. Apply by April 15 (Fall), November 1 (Spring) to Office of Graduate Admissions.

Application fee $55. Phone: (916)278-6470; fax: (916)278-5669; e-mail: gradctr@csus.edu.

ADMISSION STANDARDS. Selective. Usual minimum average: 2.5 (A = 4).

FINANCIAL AID. Assistantships, internships, Federal W/S, loans. Apply by March 1 to the Dean for assistantships; to Financial Aid Office for all other programs. Use FAFSA. Aid available for part-time students.

DEGREE REQUIREMENTS. For most master's: 30 semester hours minimum, at least 21 in residence; thesis/nonthesis option for many majors; final written/oral exam for some majors. For M.B.A., M.P.A.: 30–57 hours, depending upon previous preparation. For M.S.W.: satisfactory completion of two-year program, at least one year in residence.

FIELDS OF STUDY.

Accounting. M.S.

Anthropology. M.A.

Art. Includes fine arts, art history. M.A.

Biological Sciences. M.A., M.S.

Business Administration. M.B.A.

Business Administration. Includes management information systems. M.S.B.A.

Chemistry. M.S.

Civil Engineering. M.S.

Communication Studies. M.A.

Computer Science. Includes software engineering, scientific and engineering applications, computer systems. M.S.

Counseling. Includes career counseling, generic counseling, school counseling, school psychology, marriage, family, and child counseling, rehabilitation counseling. M.S.

Criminal Justice. Includes forensic science. M.A.

Education. Includes behavioral sciences in education, art, bilingual/cross-cultural education, curriculum and instruction, early childhood education, educational administration, English language development, gifted/talented education, guidance, reading specialist, special education. M.A.

Electrical and Electronic Engineering. M.S.

English. Includes creative writing, teaching English to speakers of other languages. M.A.

Geology. M.S.

Government. M.A.

History. Includes public history. M.A.

International Affairs. M.A.

Kinesiology. Includes exercise physiology, sport performance, strength/conditioning.

Liberal Arts. M.A.

Marine Science. M.S.

Mathematics. M.A.

Mechanical Engineering. M.S.

Music. M.M.

Nursing. Includes family nurse practitioner. M.S.

Psychology. Includes counseling, industrial organizational. M.A.

Public History. Ph.D.

Public Policy and Administration. M.P.P.A.

Recreation Administration. M.S.

Social Work. Includes family and children's services, health care, mental health, social justice and corrections. M.S.W.

Sociology. M.A.

Software Engineering. M.S.

Spanish. M.A.

Special Major. M.A., M.S.

Speech Pathology and Audiology. Includes speech pathology, audiology. M.S.

TESOL. M.A.

Theater. M.A.

CALIFORNIA STATE UNIVERSITY, SAN BERNARDINO

San Bernardino, California 92407-2397
Web site: www.csusb.edu

Established 1965. Located 60 miles NE of Los Angeles. CGS member. Coed. Public control. Quarter system. Special facilities: Center for Equity in Education, Center for Global Management, Center for the Study of Hate and Extremism, Desert Research Center, Institute for Social and Public Policy Research, Water Resource Institute. Library: 550,000 volumes, 2350 subscriptions. More than 1000 computers on campus for student use.

Tuition: resident $0 per quarter; nonresident $164 per quarter unit plus fees. Fees: 0.1–6 units $292, 6.1 or more $502. On-campus housing for single students only. Average academic year housing costs including board $4506–$5390. Contact Housing Director for both on-and off-campus housing information. Day-care facilities available.

Graduate Studies

Graduate study since 1972. Enrollment: full-time 1396, part-time 860. Graduate faculty: full-time 100, part-time 21. Degrees conferred: M.A., M.S., M.B.A., M.P.A., M.S.W.

ADMISSION REQUIREMENTS. Transcripts GRE/GMAT required in support of application. TOEFL, TWE required for international applicants. Accepts transfer applicants. Graduates of unaccredited institutions not considered. Apply to the Office of Admissions by September 15 (Fall), December 15 (Winter), March 15 (Spring). Application fee $55. Phone: (909)880-5200.

ADMISSION STANDARDS. Selective. Usual minimum average: 2.5 in last 90 quarter/60 semester credits (A = 4).

FINANCIAL AID. Annual awards from institutional funds: scholarships, fellowships, assistantships, grants, Federal W/S, loans. Approved for VA benefits. Apply to Director of Financial Aid by July 1. Phone: (909)880-5200; fax: (909)880-7021. Use FAFSA. Aid available for part-time students.

DEGREE REQUIREMENTS. For master's: 45 quarter hours minimum, 36 in residence; thesis/nonthesis option; 3.0 GPA required.

FIELDS OF STUDY.
Art. M.A.
Biology. M.S.
Business Administration. Includes concentrations in accounting, corporate management, entrepreneurship, finance, information management, management of conflict, management and human resources, marketing management, operations management. M.B.A.
Communication Studies. M.A.
Computer Science. M.S.
Counseling and Guidance. M.S.
Education. Includes bilingual/cross-cultural career and technical, curriculum and instruction, environmental, health instructional technology, kinesiology, language literacy and culture, middle grades, reading, secondary (English, history, Spanish), special, TESOL.
Educational Administration. M.A.
English Composition. Includes ESL, literature. M.A.
Health Services Administration. M.S.
Interdisciplinary Studies. M.A.
Mathematics. M.A.
National Security Studies. M.A.
Nursing. M.S.

Psychology. Includes child development, general, industrial-organizational, lifespan. M.A., M.S.
Public Administration. M.P.A.
Rehabilitational Counseling. M.A.
Science. M.A.T.
Social Science. M.A.
Social Work. M.S.W.

CALIFORNIA STATE UNIVERSITY, SAN MARCOS

San Marcos, California 92096-0001
Web site: www.csusm.edu

Founded 1965. Located in San Diego County. Coed. Public control. Semester system. Library 148,000 volumes, 2136 subscriptions. More than 500 computers on campus for general student use.

Tuition: full-time, resident $0, nonresidents $282 per unit plus fees. Fees: 0–6 units $438, 7 or more $753. On-campus housing for married or graduate students. Average academic year housing costs: $2598 (room only) for single students; $3390 for married students. Contact Office of Dean of Student Affairs for both on-and off-campus housing information.

Graduate Studies

Graduate enrollment: full-time 164, part-time 289. University faculty teaching graduate students: full-time 92, part-time 18. Degrees conferred: M.A., M.S., M.B.A.

ADMISSION REQUIREMENTS. Two official transcripts, two letters of recommendation required in support of application. GRE and a departmental application may be required by some departments. Two essays, three recommendations, résumé, GMAT (or GRE) required for Business applicants. Interview required for Education applicants. TOEFL (minimum score 550, computer-based score 213), TWE required for international applicants. Accepts transfer applicants. Graduates of unaccredited institutions not considered. Apply to Office of Admission by April 15 (Fall), October 15 (Spring). Application fee $55. Phone: (760)750-4848; fax (760)750-3248.

ADMISSION STANDARDS. Selective. Usual minimum average: 2.5 overall, 2.75 in last two years (A = 4).

FINANCIAL AID. Scholarships, assistantships, graduate equity fellowships, traineeships, internships, Federal W/S, loans. Apply to Financial Aid Office; no specified closing dates. Use FAFSA. Aid available for part-time students.

DEGREE REQUIREMENTS. For master's: 30–36 semester hours minimum, at least 21 in residence; foreign langauge requirement for some programs; comprehensive thesis/nonthesis option or project; final written/oral exam.

FIELDS OF STUDY.

COLLEGE OF ARTS AND SCIENCES:
Biology. M.S.
Computer Sciences. M.S.
Literature and Writing Studies. M.A.
Mathematics. M.S.
Psychology. M.A.
Sociological Practice. M.A.
Spanish. M.A.

COLLEGE OF BUSINESS ADMINISTRATION:
Business Administration. M.B.A.

COLLEGE OF EDUCATION:
Biliteracy, Language and Culture. M.A.
Educational Administration. M.A.
Learning and Instruction. M.A.
*Science, Mathematics and Educational Technology for Diverse
    Populations.* M.A.
Special Education. M.A.

CALIFORNIA STATE UNIVERSITY, STANISLAUS

Turlock, California 95382
Web site: www.csustan.edu

Founded 1965. Located 13 miles S of Modesto. CGS member. Coed. Public control. 4-1-4 system. Special facilities: Moss Landing Marine Laboratories. Library: 338,700 volumes, 1980 subscriptions. More than 200 computers on campus for general student use.

Tuition: resident $0, nonresident $246 per unit plus fees. Fees: 0–6 units $552.50; 7 or more $867.50 On-campus housing for single graduate students only. Annual room and board cost: $7300. Apply to Director of Housing. Phone: (209)667-3675. Day-care facilities available.

Graduate Studies

Enrollment: full-and part-time 571. Faculty: full-time 262, part-time 70. Degrees conferred: M.A., M.S., M.B.A., M.P.A.

ADMISSION REQUIREMENTS. Two transcripts, GRE Subject Test (History, Education, Psychology, Marine Science, English), GRE (International Relations, Interdisciplinary Studies), GMAT (Business) required in support of University's application. Electronic application available. TOEFL required for foreign applicants. Accepts transfer applicants. Apply by May 30 (Fall), November 30 (Winter), January 30 (Spring) to Admissions and Records Office. Application fee $55. Phone: (209)667-3129; fax: (209)667-7025.

ADMISSION STANDARDS. Selective. Usual minimum average: 3.0 (A = 4).

FINANCIAL AID. Scholarships, fellowships, research assistantships, Federal W/S, loans. Approved VA benefits. Apply by March 1 to Office of Financial Aid. Phone: (209)667-3336. Use FAFSA and University's FAF. Aid available for part-time students.

DEGREE REQUIREMENTS. For master's: 30 units minimum, at least 24 in residence; thesis/project or final written/oral exam.

FIELDS OF STUDY.
Business Administration.
Criminal Justice.
Education. Includes administration and supervision, school counseling, curriculum and instruction (elementary, secondary, reading, special education), physical education.
English.
History.
Interdisciplinary Studies.
International Relations. (Concentration in M.A., History)
Marine Science.
Psychology.
Public Administration.
Social Work.

CALIFORNIA UNIVERSITY OF PENNSYLVANIA

California, Pennsylvania 15419-1394
Web site: www.cup.edu

Founded 1852. Located 35 miles S of Pittsburgh. CGS member. Coed. Public control. Semester system and two 5-week Summer terms. Library: 437,000 volumes, 880 subscriptions. More than 700 computers on campus for general student use. Total University enrollment: 5800.

Tuition: full-time, resident $4130, per credit $230; nonresident $7010, per credit $389. On-campus housing for single students only. Average academic year housing cost: $4662 (including board). Contact Director of Housing for both on- and off-campus housing information. Phone: (724)938-4439. Day-care facilities available.

School of Graduate Studies

Enrollment: full-time 325, part-time 569 (men 30%, women 70%). Faculty: full-time 11, part-time 93. Degrees conferred: M.A., M.A.T., M.S., M.Ed., M.S.W.

ADMISSION REQUIREMENTS. Transcripts, teacher certification for M.Ed. programs, MAT/GRE/GMAT, interview required for some programs in support of application. TOEFL, statement of financial support required for foreign applicants. Accepts transfer applicants. Graduates of unaccredited colleges not considered. Apply by August 23 (Fall), January 10 (Spring), April 27 (Summer). Application fee $25. Phone: (724)938-4187; fax: (724)938-5712; e-mail: gradschool@cup.edu.

ADMISSION STANDARDS. Selective. Usual minimum average: 2.50 (A = 4), some programs are higher.

FINANCIAL AID. Annual awards from institutional funds: assistantships, tuition waivers, internships, Federal W/S, loans. Apply to the Graduate Dean for assistantships; to Financial Aid Office for all other programs. No specified closing date. Phone: (724)938-4415. Use FAFSA. About 5% of students receive aid other than loans from College and outside sources.

DEGREE REQUIREMENTS. For master's: 30–36 credits minimum, 24 in residence; thesis/nonthesis option; final oral/written exam.

FIELDS OF STUDY.
Athletic Training. M.S. only.
Biology. M.Ed., M.S. only.
Business Administration. M.S.
Communication. M.A. only.
Communication Disorders. M.S.
Community and Agency Counseling. M.S.
Computer Science. M.Ed.
Counselor Education. Includes elementary, secondary guidance; M.Ed. only; business and industry counseling, M.S. only.
Early Childhood Education. M.Ed. only.
Earth Science. M.S. only.
Educational Administration. Includes elementary, secondary principal, superintendent's letter of eligibility.
Elementary Education. M.Ed. only.
English. M.A., M.Ed. only.
Geography and Regional Planning. M.A., M.Ed. only.
Mathematics. M.A.
Mathematics Education. M.Ed. only.
Mentally and Physically Handicapped. M.Ed.
Reading Specialist. M. Ed. only.
School Psychology. M.S. only.
Science Education. M.Ed., M.A.

Social Science. M.A.
Social Work. M.S.W.
Special Education. M.Ed.
Technology Education. M.Ed. only.

UNIVERSITY OF CALIFORNIA AT BERKELEY

Berkeley, California 94720
Web site: www.berkeley.edu

Founded 1868, Located 12 miles E of San Francisco. CGS and AAU member. Coed. Public control. Semester system. Special facilities: Lawrence Berkeley and Livermore National Laboratories, Bodega Marine Laboratory, Center for Pure and Applied Mathematics, Mathematical Sciences Research Institute, Space Sciences Laboratory, Virus Laboratory, Naval Biomedical Laboratory, International House, Low-Density Wind-Tunnel Facility; Laboratories for Electronics Research, Hydraulic Engineering, Sea Water Conversion, Structural and Sanitary Engineering; Institutes of Transportation, Traffic Engineering, Personality Assessment and Research, Business and Economic Research, Governmental Studies, Human Development, Human Learning, Industrial Relations, International Studies, Library Research, Marine Resources, Basic Research in Science, Urban and Rural Development; Operations Research Center, White Mountain Research Station, Lick Observatory; centers for study of Law and Society, Study of Higher Education, Research in Management Science, Survey Research; Chinese Studies, Japanese and Korean Studies, Latin American Studies, Planning Development and Research; computer facilities. NIH ranking is 51st among all U.S. institutions with 321 awards/grants worth $91,743,401. The 26 Berkeley campus libraries house more than 7,000,000 volumes, 3,000,000 microforms, plus online data retrieval services.

Annual fees/tuition: full-time, resident $4430, nonresident $15,752. Fifteen residence halls for graduate and upper division students. Rooms are double occupancy. 994 apartments for married and single students. Average annual housing cost for both on- and off-campus $16,222. Apply to Housing Services. Phone: (510)642-7781. For off-campus information, phone (510)643-6544.

Graduate Division

Graduate study since 1868. Enrollment: 8454 (men 4870, women 3584). Faculty: full-time 1790, part-time 0. Degrees conferred: M.A., M.S., M.A.T., M.Arch., M.B.A., M.C.P., M.Eng., M.F., M.J., M.F.A., LL.M., M.L.A., M.P.A., M.P.P., M.S.W., Ed.D., D.Eng., LL.M., J.S.D., Dr.P.H., Ph.D.

ADMISSION REQUIREMENTS. Transcripts, GRE/GMAT, three letters of recommendation (Form G) required in support of University's application. Interview normally not required. GRE Subject test for some departments. TOEFL (minimum score 570, 230 on computer-based test) or IELTS required for all non-English speaking applicants. Graduates of unaccredited colleges not considered. Request application materials directly from department. Deadline range: December 15–February 10 (Fall); September 1 (Spring). Many departments admit for the Fall only. Application fee $40. Phone: (510)642-7405; fax: (510)643-1524; e-mail: gradadm@uclink4.berkeley.edu.

ADMISSION STANDARDS. Very selective for most departments.

FINANCIAL AID. Fellowships, research assistantships, teaching assistantships, readers, Federal W/S, loans. Apply to appropriate department; no specified closing date. For Federal programs apply to Financial Aid Office. Phone: (510)642-0485. Use FAFSA.

DEGREE REQUIREMENTS. For M.A. and M.S.: Plan I–20 semester units minimum plus thesis, at least two semesters (one year) in residence. Plan II—24 semester units minimum without thesis, at least two semesters (one year) in residence, comprehensive exam. For other master's: the same requisites outlined above normally apply. For Ph.D.: normally at least two years minimum in residence beyond the bachelor's degree; reading knowledge of at least one foreign language required by most departments; qualifying exams; dissertation; final oral exam. For other doctorates: essentially the same minimum requisites as for Ph.D., except no foreign language requirement.

FIELDS OF STUDY.
African American Studies. Ph.D.
Agricultural and Environmental Chemistry. M.S., Ph.D.
Agricultural and Resource Economics and Policy. Ph.D. only
Ancient History and Mediterranean Archaeology.
Anthropology.
Applied Mathematics. Ph.D. only.
Applied Science and Technology.
Architecture. M.S., M.Arch., Ph.D.
Art. Studio; portfolio for admission; M.F.A. only.
Asian Studies. Emphasis on East Asia, Southeast Asia, South Asia, Northeast Asia studies for M.A.
Astrophysics. M.A., Ph.D.
Bioengineering (with UCSF). Ph.D. only.
Biophysics.
Biostatistics.
Buddhist Studies. Ph.D. only.
Business Administration. GMAT for admission; M.B.A. normally two-year program. M.B.A., M.S.
Chemical Engineering.
Chemistry.
City and Regional Planning. M.C.P., Ph.D.
Civil and Environmental Engineering.
Classical Archaeology.
Classics.
Comparative Biochemistry.
Comparative Literature.
Computer science.
Demography.
Design (Visual). M.A. only.
Dramatic Art. Ph.D. only.
Earth and Planetary Science.
East Asian Languages. Includes Chinese, Japanese.
Economics.
Education.
Electrical Engineering and Computer Science.
Endocrinology.
Energy and Resources.
English.
Environmental Health Sciences.
Environmental Planning. Ph.D. only.
Environmental Science Policy and Management.
Epidemiology.
Ethnic Studies.
Financial Engineering. M.F.E.
Folklore. M.A. only.
Forestry. M.F. only.
French.
Geography.
Geology.
Geophysics.
German.
Greek. M.A. only.
Health and Medical Sciences. Dual degree option; genetic counseling, M.S.; medical program (with UCSF), M.S., M.D.
Health Services and Policy Analysis. Ph.D. only.
Hispanic Languages and Literatures.
History.
History of Art. Ph.D. only.

Industrial Engineering and Operations Research.

Infectious Diseases and Immunity.

Information Management and Systems. M.I.M.S., Ph.D.

Integrative Biology.

Italian Studies. Ph.D. only.

Jewish Studies. Joint program with Graduate Theological Union. Ph.D. only.

Journalism. M.J. only.

Jurisprudence and Social Policy. Ph.D. only.

Landscape Architecture. M.L.A. only.

Latin. M.A. only.

Latin American Studies.

Law. LL.M., J.S.D.

Linguistics.

Logic and the Methodology of Science. Ph.D. only.

Materials Science and Engineering.

Mathematics.

Mechanical Engineering.

Medical Anthropology (with UCSF). Ph.D. only.

Microbiology.

Molecular and Cell Biology.

Music. Includes performance, musicology.

Near Eastern Religions. Joint program with Graduate Theological Union. Ph.D. only.

Near Eastern Studies.

Neuroscience. Ph.D. only.

Nuclear Engineering.

Nutrition.

Ocean Engineering.

Optometry. Certificate only. Must have O.D. degree.

Performance Studies.

Philosophy. Ph.D. only.

Physics.

Plant Biology.

Political Science.

Psychology.

Public Health. M.P.H., Dr.P.H.

Public Policy. M.P.P., Ph.D.

Range Management. M.S. only.

Rhetoric.

Romance Languages and Literatures. Includes French, Italian, Spanish; Ph.D. only.

Scandinavian Languages and Literatures. Includes Danish, Norwegian, Old Norse, Swedish.

Science and Mathematics Education. Ph.D. only.

Slavic Languages and Literatures. Includes Russian, Polish, Czech, Serbo-Croatian.

Social Welfare. M.S.W., Ph.D., M.S.W.-Ph.D.

Sociology.

South and Southeast Asian Studies. Includes Hindu-Urdu, Malay-Indonesian Sanscrit, South Asian Archaeology.

Special Education. Ph.D. only.

Statistics.

Urban Design. M.U.D.

Visual Science.

Wood Science and Technology.

Boalt Hall School of Law (94720-7200)

Web site: www.law.berkeley.edu

Established 1912. ABA approved since 1923. AALS member. Coed. Semester system. Law library: 821,500 volumes. Library has LEXIS, NEXIS, WESTLAW, INNOPAC, MELVYL; is a Federal Government Depository.

Annual tuition: resident $10,910, nonresident $21,614. On-campus housing available. Enrollment: first-year class 270; full-time 870 (men 52%, women 48%); to post-graduates 50. Faculty: full-time 45, part-time 54. Student to faculty ratio 15.9 to 1. Degrees conferred: J.D., J.D.-M.A.(Asian Studies, Economics, Journalism), J.D.-M.B.A., J.D.-M.P.H., J.D.-M.S.W., J.D.-M.C.P., J.D.-Ph.D. (Economics, Legal History), J.D.-M.A.L.O. (Fletcher

School of Law, Tufts University), J.D.-M.P.P. (J.F.K. School of Government, Harvard University), LL.M.

ADMISSION REQUIREMENTS. LSDAS Law School report, transcripts, LSAT (no later than December), personal statement, two references recommended in support of application. Applicants must have received the bachelor's prior to entrance. Accepts transfer applicants. Preference given to state residents. Graduates of unaccredited colleges not considered. Apply to Admissions Office after September, before February 1; early filing strongly recommended. Admission on full-time basis only; admits Fall only. Application fee $40. Phone: (510)642-2274; e-mail: admissions@law.berkeley.edu.

ADMISSION STANDARDS. Competitive. Median LSAT: 165; median GPA: 3.73 (A = 4). Accepts about 15% of total annual applicants. Gourman rating: 4.89. *U.S. News & World Report* ranking is in the top seven of all law schools.

FINANCIAL AID. Scholarships, fellowships, research assistantships, grants, Federal W/S, loans. All financial aid based on need. Apply to Office of Financial Aid by March 1. Use FAFSA. About 55% of students receive aid other than loans from institution and outside sources.

DEGREE REQUIREMENTS. For J.D.: six terms minimum, at least two terms in full-time residence; 81 units. For LL.M.: 24 units minimum in full-time residence; final research project. For other master's, Ph.D. programs: see Graduate School listing above or other institutional programs.

UNIVERSITY OF CALIFORNIA, DAVIS

Davis, California 95616

Web site: www.ucdavis.edu

Founded 1906. Located 15 miles W of Sacramento. CGS and AAU member. Coed. State control. Quarter system. Special facilities: Arboretum and Natural Reserve System, Agricultural Experiment Stations, Agricultural History Center, Agricultural Issues Center. Adult Fitness Laboratory, Bodega Marine Laboratory (off-campus), Botany Department Herbarium, California Regional Primate Research Center, Center for Consumer Research, Center for Image Processing and Integrated Computing Research (CIPICR), Computer Center, Crocker Nuclear Laboratory, Embryological Collection from Carnegie Institution, Facility for Advanced Instrumentation, Institute for Environment Health Research, Institute of Governmental Affairs, Humanities Institute, Institute of Marine Resources, Lawrence Livermore Laboratory, Nuclear Magnetic Resonance Facility, Plant Growth Laboratory, Serology Laboratory, Institute of Transportation Studies. NIH ranking is 56th among all U.S. institutions with 285 awards/grants worth $88,446,862. Library: 2,655,000 volumes, 3,315,000 microforms, 49,000 current periodicals. Total University enrollment: 24,000.

Annual fees/tuition: full-time, resident $4902, nonresident $16,224. On-campus housing for 476 married students, 180 single students. Average annual housing cost: $15,570 for married students, $15,684 (including board) for single students. Contact Housing Office for both on- and off-campus housing information. Phone: (530)752-2033. Day-care facilities available.

Graduate Studies

Graduate study since 1924. Enrollment: full- and part-time 4615, (men 50%, women 50%). University faculty teaching graduate students: full-time 1371, part-time 231. Degrees conferred: M.A., M.A.T., M.B.A., M.Ed., M.E., M.F.A., M.S., M.A.M., M.Admin., D.Engr., Ed.D., Ph.D.

ADMISSION REQUIREMENTS. Transcripts, three letters of recommendation required in support of application. Electronic application available. GRE/Subject Tests, GMAT required by most departments. TOEFL required for international applicants. Interview not required. Accepts transfer applicants. Graduates of unaccredited institutions not considered. Apply to the Office of Graduate Studies by April 1 (Fall). Rolling admission process. Application fee $40. Phone: (530)752-0655; fax: (530)752-6222.

ADMISSION STANDARDS. Selective. Usual minimum average: 3.0 (A = 4).

FINANCIAL AID. Annual awards from institutional funds: scholarships, research assistantships, teaching assistantships, nonresident tuition fellowships, Federal W/S, loans. Approved for VA benefits. Apply by January 15 to appropriate department for fellowships, assistantships; apply by March 1 to Graduate Financial Aid Office for all other programs. Phone: (530)752-2390. Use FAFSA. About 35–45% of students receive aid other than loans from University and outside sources.

DEGREE REQUIREMENTS. For master's: Plan I—30 units minimum in residence plus thesis, reading knowledge of one foreign language for some departments; Plan II—36 units minimum in residence, reading knowledge of one foreign language for some departments, final comprehensive exam. For Ph.D.: two years minimum in residence; dissertation; preliminary, final oral exams; reading knowledge of two foreign languages for some departments. For Ed.D., D.Eng.: essentially the same as for the Ph.D., except no foreign language requirement.

FIELDS OF STUDY.
Agricultural and Environmental Chemistry. M.S., Ph.D.
Agricultural and Resource Economics. M.S., Ph.D.
Agricultural Education. M.S.
Agronomy. M.S. only.
Animal Behavior. M.S., Ph.D.
Animal Science. M.S., M.A.M.
Anthropology. M.A., Ph.D.
Applied Mathematics. M.S., Ph.D.
Applied Science. M.S., Ph.D.
Art. Includes art only; portfolio for admission; M.F.A. only.
Art History. M.A. only.
Atmospheric Science. M.S., Ph.D.
Avian Sciences. M.S. only.
Biochemistry and Molecular Biology. M.S., Ph. D.
Biological Systems Engineering. M.S., Ph.D.
Biomedical Engineering. M.S., Ph.D.
Biophysics. M.S., Ph.D.
Biostatistics. M.S., Ph.D.
Cell and Developmental Biology. Ph.D.
Chemical Engineering. M.S., D.Engr., Ph.D.
Chemistry. M.S., Ph.D.
Child Development. M.S. only.
Civil and Environmental Engineering. M.S., D.Engr., Ph.D.
Community Development. M.S. only.
Comparative Literature. M.A., Ph.D.
Comparative Pathology. M.S., Ph.D.
Computer Science. M.S., Ph.D.
Cultural Studies. M.A., Ph.D.
Dramatic Art. Production; M.A.; M.F.A., Ph.D.
Ecology. M.S., Ph.D.
Economics. M.A., Ph.D.
Education. M.A., M.Ed., Ph.D.
Electrical and Computer Engineering. M.S., D.Engr., Ph.D.
English. M.A., Ph.D.
Entomology. M.S., Ph.D.
Epidemiology. M.S., Ph.D.
Exercise Science. M.S. only.
Food Science. M.S., Ph.D.
Forensic Science. M.S. only.

French. M.A., Ph.D.
Genetics. M.S., Ph.D.
Geography. M.A., Ph.D.
Geology. M.S., Ph.D.
German. M.A., Ph.D.
History. M.A., M.A.T., Ph.D.
Horticulture. M.S. only
Human Development. Ph.D. only.
Hydrologic Sciences. M.S., Ph.D.
Immunology. M.S., Ph.D.
International Agricultural Development. M.S. only.
International Commerical Law. M.A. only.
Linguistics. Interdepartmental; M.A. only.
Materials Science and Engineering. M.S., Ph.D.
Mathematics. M.A., M.A.T., Ph.D.
Mechanical and Aeronautical Engineering. M.Engr., M.S., D.Engr., Ph.D.
Medical Informatics. M.S. only.
Microbiology. M.S., Ph.D.
Music. Includes composition, musicology; M.A., M.A.T., Ph.D.
Native American Studies. M.A., Ph.D.
Neuroscience. Ph.D.
Nutrition. M.S., Ph.D.
Pharmacology and Toxicology. M.A., Ph.D.
Philosophy. M.A., Ph.D.
Physics. M.A., Ph.D.
Physiology. M.S., Ph.D.
Plant Biology. M.S., Ph.D.
Plant Pathology. M.S., Ph.D.
Plant Protection and Pest Management. M.S. only.
Political Science. M.A., Ph.D.
Population Biology. M.S., Ph.D.
Psychology. Ph.D.
Sociology. M.A., Ph.D.
Soil Science. M.S., Ph.D.
Spanish. M.A., Ph.D.
Statistics. M.S., Ph.D.
Textile Arts and Costume Design. M.S. only.
Textiles. M.S. only.
Transportation Technology and Policy. M.S., Ph.D.
Viticulture and Enology. M.S., Ph.D.

School of Law (King Hall) (95616-5201)

Opened 1965. ABA approved since 1968. AALS member. Coed. Library: 392,000 volumes; has LEXIS, NEXIS, WESTLAW, MELVYL; is both a Federal and State Depository.

Annual tuition: resident $11,179, nonresident $21,423. On-campus housing available. Apply well in advance of April 1 deadline. Total average annual additional expenses: $10,544.

Enrollment: first-year class 168; total full-time 500 (men 49%, women 51%); no part-time study. Faculty: full-time 36, part-time 6. Student to faculty ratio 12.9 to 1. Degrees conferred; J.D., J.D.-M.B.A. (Graduate School of Management).

ADMISSION REQUIREMENTS. LSDAS Law School report, transcripts indicating award of bachelor's degree, references, LSAT (no later than December) required in support of application. Interview not required. Accepts transfer applicants. Graduates of unaccredited colleges not considered. Apply to the Admissions Office of the School by February 1. Fall admission only. Application fee $40. Phone: (530)752-6477; e-mail: lawadmissions@ucdavis.edu.

ADMISSION STANDARDS. Selective. Accepts 30% of total annual applicants. Median LSAT: 162; median GPA: 3.4 (A = 4). Gourman rating: 4.43. *U.S. News & World Report* ranking in the top 32 of all law schools.

FINANCIAL AID. Fellowships, grants, Federal W/S, loans. Apply to Financial Aid office by March 1. Use FAFSA. About 80% of students receive aid other than loans from School.

DEGREE REQUIREMENTS For J.D.: 88 credit minimum; three years in full-time residence. For master's programs: see Graduate School listing above.

Graduate School of Management

Established 1981. Public control. Quarter system. Accredited program: M.B.A.

Annual tuition and fees: resident full-time $11,042, nonresident full-time $22,224.

Enrollment: total full-time 125, part-time 300 (men 56%, women 44%). Faculty: 24 full-time, 26 part-time; all have either a Ph.D. or D.B.A.

Degrees conferred: M.B.A. (Concentrations in Accounting, Agricultural Management, E-Commerce, Environmental and Natural Resource Management, Finance, Information Systems, International Management, Management Science, Marketing, Not-for-Profit Management, Technology Management; individually designed concentration), M.B.A. for Working Professionals, M.B.A.-J.D., M.B.A.-A.E. (Agricultural and Resource Economics), M.B.A.-M.E. (Engineering), M.B.A.-M.D.

ADMISSION REQUIREMENTS. All applicants should have a bachelor's degree from a recognized institution of higher education and a strong mathematics background. Submit a Graduate application, GMAT results (will accept GMAT test results from the last five years; latest acceptable date is March), official transcripts from each undergraduate/graduate school attended, three letters of recommendation, a writing sample, work history (prefers at least four years of work experience), and an application fee of $40 to the Office of Admission, Graduate School of Management. Electronic applications available. Beginning students are admitted Fall only. U.S. citizens apply by May 15 (Fall), international students apply by April 1 (Fall). In addition, international students (whose native language is other than English) should submmit a TOEFL (minimum score 600) report taken by March 1, certified translations and evaluations of all official transcripts; recommendation should be in English or with certified translations, and proof of sufficient financial resources for one year of academic study. For current information and/or modification in admission requirements the international applicant's contact telephone number is: (530)752-0864. On-campus visits are encouraged prior to the admissions committee reviewing completed applications. Joint degree applicants must apply to and be accepted to both schools/programs; contact the admissions office for current information and specific admissions requirements. Rolling admission process, notification is made as soon as possible after the receipt of completed application and all supporting documents, but no later than June 1. Admissions Office phone: (530)752-7366; fax: (530)752-2924.

ADMISSION STANDARDS. Selective. Mean GMAT 673; mean GPA 3.4 (A = 4). *U.S. News & World Report* ranked UC Davis in the top 40 of all U.S. business schools.

FINANCIAL AID. Special stipend for minorities, Graduate Opportunity Fellowships, State Grants, graduate assistantships, Federal W/S, loans. Financial aid is available for part-time study. Financial aid may be available for international students after the first year. Assistantships/fellowships may be available for joint degree candidates. Request scholarship, assistantship information from the Graduate School of Management. Apply by March 1 for all financial assistance. Contact the University's Financial Aid Office for current need-based financial aid information. Phone: (530)752-9246. For most financial assistance and all Federal programs submit FAFSA (School code: 001313); also submit Financial Aid Transcript, Federal Income Tax forms. Approximately 52% of students receive some form of financial assistance.

DEGREE REQUIREMENTS. For M.B.A.: 72 quarter hours for full-time program, including 33 elective hours; degree program must be completed in three years. For M.B.A.-Master's: generally a three- to four-year program. For M.B.A.-J.D.: four- to five-and-one-half-year program.

School of Medicine

Founded 1968. Coed. State control. Quarter System. First class entered 1968.

Annual tuition and fees: resident $10,465, nonresident $21,169. Average figure for all other expenses: $8200. Enrollment: first-year class 93; total full-time 400 (men 60%, women 40%). Faculty: full-time approximately 500, part-time/volunteers 1500. Degrees conferred: M.D., M.D.-Ph.D., M.D.-M.A., M.D.-M.S., M.D.-M.B.A., M.D.-M.P.H. (Berkeley).

ADMISSION REQUIREMENTS. AMCAS report, transcripts, MCAT required in support of application. Usually, bachelor's degree from an accredited U.S. or Canadian school required for admission. Preference given to state and WICHE residents. Interview required for all accepted candidates. Transfer applicants may be considered. Does not have EDP. Apply through AMCAS after June 15, before November 1. Application fee $40. Phone: (530)752-2717; e-mail: medadmisinfo@ucdavis.edu.

ADMISSION STANDARDS. Competitive. Median MCAT: 11.9; median GPA: 3.4 (A = 4). Accepts about 8% of total annual applicants.

FINANCIAL AID. Scholarships, fellowships, grants, loans. Apply to Financial Aid Office following admission. Phone: (530)752-6618; e-mail: medfinancialaid@ucdavis.edu. About 85% of students receive aid other than loans from institutional funds.

DEGREE REQUIREMENTS. For M.D.: satisfactory completion of four-year program. For M.A., M.S., M.B.A., M.P.H. (Berkeley), Ph.D., see graduate listing above.

School of Veterinary Medicine (95616-8731)

Established 1949. Annual fees/tuition: full-time, resident and WICHE contract students $11,072, nonresident $22,204. On-campus housing available. Total living expenses $10,500. Enrollment: first-year class 108; total full-time 721 (men 280, women 80). School faculty: full- and part-time 242. Degrees conferred: D.V.M., D.V.M.-M.P.V.M.

ADMISSION REQUIREMENTS. VMCAS report, transcripts, GRE in biology (October test), three letters of evaluation, personal statement, essay, Veterinary/Animal experience required in support of application. Electronic application available. Accepts transfer applicants if openings exist (priority to state and WICHE residents). Interviews by invitation only. Applicants must have completed at least three years of college study. Apply to the Admissions Office after July 1, before October 1. For transfer applicants after December 1, before May 1. Application fee $40. Phone: (530)752-1383.

ADMISSION STANDARDS. Competitive. Mean GRE scores: verbal 595, quantitative 700, analytical 724. Mean GPA: 3.45 (A = 4). Accepts 25% of total annual applicants. Accepts no more than two applicants from WICHE states.

FINANCIAL AID. Scholarships, fellowships, teaching assistantships, loans. Apply to UCD Financial Aid office. Use FAFSA. About 8% of students receive aid other than loans from School funds.

DEGREE REQUIREMENTS. For D.V.M.: satisfactory completion of four-year program. M.V.P.H. offered through the Graduate Division.

UNIVERSITY OF CALIFORNIA, HASTINGS COLLEGE OF THE LAW

San Francisco, California 94102-4978

Web site: www.uchastings.edu

Established 1878 as the University of California's first law school. ABA approved since 1937. AALS member. Coed. Is now the Law Department of the University of California. Semester system. Library: 638,000 volumes. Library has LEXIS, NEXIS, WESTLAW, DIALOG, INFOTRAC, DATATIMES, LEGITECH, FIRST SEARCH, EPIC.

Annual tuition: resident $11,232, nonresident $20,353. On-campus housing available for 480 students. Estimated housing cost: $16,936. Enrollment: first-year class 418; total 1262 (men 48%, women 52%). Faculty: full-time 48, part-time 81. Student to faculty ratio 20.5 to 1. Degrees conferred: J.D., J.D.-M.A. with Berkeley (Asian Studies, Business Administration, City and Regional Planning, Economics, History, Journalism, and Public Policy).

ADMISSION REQUIREMENTS. LSDAS Law School report, bachelor's degree, LSAT (no later than December), transcripts required in support of application. Personal statements and recommendations are considered. Graduates of unaccredited colleges not considered. Apply to Office of Admissions before February 1. Application fee $40. Phone: (415)565-4623; fax: (415)565-4863; e-mail: admiss@uchastings.edu.

ADMISSION STANDARDS. Selective. Median LSAT: 161; median GPA: 3.39 (A = 4). Gourman rating: 4.62. *U.S. News & World Report* ranking is in the top 40 of all law schools. Admits about 30% of total annual applications.

FINANCIAL AID. Scholarships, full and partial tuition waivers, Federal W/S, loans. Apply by February 1 to Office of Admissions. Use FAFSA and Student Financial Aid Supplement. About 80% of students receive some form of aid.

DEGREE REQUIREMENTS. For J.D.: satisfactory completion of three-year, 86 credit program.
Note: Exchange programs with Nihon University, Leiden University, University of British Columbia, Vermont Law School.

UNIVERSITY OF CALIFORNIA, IRVINE

Irvine, California 92697

Web site: www.uci.edu

Opened 1965. Located 40 miles S of Los Angeles. CGS and AAU member. Coed. Public control. Quarter system. Special facilities: Advanced Power and Energy Center, Beckman Laser Institute, Cancer Research Institute, Center for Arts Research in Education, Center for Asian Studies, Center for Community Health Research, Center for Decision Analysis, Center for Immunology, Center for Research in Educational Assessment and Measurement, Center for Research on Immigration, Population Dynamics and Public Policy, Center for Research on Latinos in a Global Society, Center for the Study of Democracy, Center for Virus Research, Critical Theory Institute, Developmental Biology Center, Epilepsy Research Center, Institute for Brain Aging and Dementia, Institute for Genomics and Bioinformatics, Institute of Geophysics and Planetary Physics, Institute for Mathematical Behavioral Sciences, Institute for Software Research, Institute of Transportation Studies, Newkirk Center for Science and Society, Reeve-Irvine Research Center, Urban Water Research Center. NIH ranking is 63rd among U.S. institutions with 270 awards/grants worth $79,025,536. Library: 2,400,000 volumes, 19,000 subscriptions.

Annual fees/tuition: full-time, resident $5293, nonresident $16,187. On-campus housing includes 862 one-, two-, and three-bedroom apartments for married and single graduate students; 203-unit complex for full-time graduate, medical, and postdoctoral students; residence hall for 60 single graduate students. Average annual housing cost: $6500 (excluding board). Apply to Housing Office. Phone: (949)824-6811. Day-care facilities available.

Office of Graduate Studies

Enrollment: approximately 3100. Faculty: full- and part-time 1624. Degrees conferred: M.A., M.S., M.B.A., M.F.A., M.A.T., M.U.R.P., Ed.D., Ph.D.

ADMISSION REQUIREMENTS. Transcripts, three letters of recommendation required in support of University's application. Electronic application available. GRE required for most majors. TOEFL required of foreign applicants. Interview not required. Accepts transfer applicants. Graduates of unaccredited institutions not considered. Apply to Office of Graduate Studies by January 15 (Fall), October 15 (Winter), January 15 (Spring). Application fee $40. Phone. (949)824-4611; fax: (949)824-2095.

ADMISSION STANDARDS. Very competitive to relatively open. Usual minimum average: 3.0 (A = 4)

FINANCIAL AID. Annual awards include fellowships, teaching and research assistantships, need-based grants, Federal W/S, loans. Approved for VA benefits. Apply by February 1 on Graduate Application form to appropriate academic unit. Apply to the Financial Aid Office for Federal programs. Phone: (949)824-6261. Use FAFSA. Most students receive aid other than loans from University and outside sources.

DEGREE REQUIREMENTS. For most master's: three quarters minimum, at least 80% of courses in residence; full-time attendance is normally expected, but part-time study is possible; thesis or final comprehensive exam. For M.F.A. (Creative Writing): six quarters minimum in residence; book-length thesis in recognized genre (poetry, short stories, plays, novel); final comprehensive exam. For Ph.D.: normally six quarters minimum in residence; one foreign language for some departments; qualifying exam and advancement to candidacy; dissertation; final oral exam. For Ed.D.: at least six quarters in residence; qualifying exam and advancement to candidacy; dissertation; final oral exam.

FIELDS OF STUDY.
Anthropology. M.A., Ph.D.
Chemical and Biochemical Engineering. M.S., Ph.D.
Chemistry. M.S., Ph.D.
Civil Engineering. M.S., Ph.D.
Classics. M.A., Ph.D.
Comparative Literature. M.A., Ph.D.
Criminology, Law, and Society. M.A., Ph.D.
Dance. M.F.A.
Drama. M.F.A.
Drama and Theatre. Ph.D.
Earth System Science. M.S., Ph.D.
East Asian Languages and Literatures. M.A., Ph.D.
Economics.
Education. Includes administrative services, bilingual/cross-cultural specialist, early childhood education specialist, multiple-subject instruction (elementary), pupil personnel service, single-subject instruction (secondary), special education (learning handicapped, physically handicapped, severely handicapped). State credential, M.A.T.
Educational Administration. Ed.D.
Electrical and Computer Engineering. M.S., Ph.D.
Engineering. M.S., Ph.D.

English. M.A., M.F.A., Ph.D.
Environmental Health Science and Policy. M.S., Ph.D.
Environmental Toxicology. M.S., Ph.D.
French. M.A., Ph.D.
Genetic Counseling. M.S.
German. M.A., Ph.D.
History. M.A., Ph.D.
Humanities. M.A., Ph.D.
Information and Computer Science. M.S., Ph.D.
Management. Ph.D.
Materials Science and Engineering. M.S., Ph.D.
Mathematics. M.S., Ph.D.
Mechanical and Aerospace Engineering. M.S., Ph.D.
Music. M.F.A.
Pharmacology and Toxicology. M.S., Ph.D.
Philosophy. M.A., Ph.D.
Physics. M.S., Ph.D.
Political Science. Ph.D.
Psychology. Ph.D.
Psychology and Social Behavior. Ph.D.
Social Ecology. Ph.D.
Social Science. M.A., Ph.D.
Sociology. M.A., Ph.D.
Spanish. M.A., M.A.T., Ph.D.
Studio Art. M.F.A.
Urban and Regional Planning. M.U.R.P., Ph.D.
Visual Studies. M.A., Ph.D.

College of Medicine (92697-4089)

Web site: www.com.uci.edu/admissions

Founded in 1896, merged with University of California at Irvine in 1965. State control. Quarter system.

Annual tuition/fee: resident $10,935, nonresident $21,639. Total average figure for all expenses $8158. Enrollment: first-year class 94; total 386 (men 60% women 40%), 120 graduate students. Faculty: full-time 450, part-time 1700. Degrees conferred: M.D., M.D.-M.B.A., M.D.-Ph.D.

ADMISSION REQUIREMENTS. AMCAS report, transcripts, letters of recommendation, MCAT required in support of U.C. application. Applicants must have completed at least three years of college study. Interview required for all final candidates. Preference given to California residents. Does not have EDP. Apply to the Director of Admissions after June 15, before November 1. Application fee $40. Phone (949)824-5388; fax: (949)824-2485.

ADMISSION STANDARDS: Competitive. Mean GPA: 3.6 (A = 4); mean MCAT: 10.3. Accepts about 3% of total annual applicants; 98% are state residents.

FINANCIAL AID. Scholarships, fellowships, grants, loans, summer research fellowships. Apply to the Office of Medical Student Financial Aid; no closing date. About 87% of students receive aid of some type. Phone: (949)824-6476.

DEGREE REQUIREMENTS. For M.D.: satisfactory completion of four-year program. For M.S., Ph.D.: see Graduate Division listing above for degree requirements.

FIELDS OF GRADUATE STUDY.
Anatomy.
Biochemistry.
Community and Environmental Toxicology.
Genetic Counseling. M.S. only.
Microbiology.
Molecular Genetics.
Neurobiology.
Pharmacology.
Physiology.

UNIVERSITY OF CALIFORNIA, LOS ANGELES

Los Angeles, California 90025-1301
Web site: www.ucla.edu

Founded 1919. CGS and AAU member. Coed. State control. Quarter system. Special facilities: Center for the Study of Comparative Folklore and Mythology, Center for Medieval and Renaissance Studies, Center for African Studies, Institute of Archaeology, Center for Latin American Studies, Gustave E. Von Grunebaum Center for Near Eastern Studies, Institute of Social Science Research, Dental Research Institute, Jules Stein Eye Institute, Mental Retardation Center, Brain Research Institute, Institute of American Cultures, Afro-American Studies Center, Asian American Studies Center, Chicano Studies Research Center, Institute of Geophysics and Planetary Physics, Institute of Industrial Relations, Laboratory of Biomedical and Environmental Sciences, Molecular Biology Institute, Institute of Medical Engineering, University Elementary School, Grunwald Center for the Graphic Arts, Frederick S. Wight Art Gallery, Mildred E. Mathias Botanical Gardens, Fernald School, Center for Plasma Physics and Fusion Technology, Dental Clinic, Cancer Research Center, Cardiovascular Research Laboratory, Reed Neurological Research Center, Committee on International and Comparative Studies, Neuropsychiatric Institute, Museum of Cultural History, UCLA Hospital and Clinics. NIH ranking is seventh among all U.S. institutions, with 800 awards/grants worth $273,487,582. Library: more than 7,500,000 volumes, 51,000 subscriptions. Total University enrollment: 32,900.

Annual fees/tuition: full-time, resident $4555, nonresident $15,444; for Nursing add $1800, for Theater add $2000; Educational Leadership $11,369, health professionals program $15,500. University maintains 1183 units for married graduate students five miles from campus, one residence hall on campus to house 334 single graduate students. Average academic year housing costs: $13,575 (including board) for single students; $12,000 for single students off-campus; $17,575–$19,375 for married students. Apply by May 15. Contact the Office of Residential Life for both on- (310-398-4692) and off-campus (310-390-1274) housing information. Day-care facilities available.

Graduate Division

Graduate study since 1933. Enrollment: full-time 7454 (men 50%, women 50%). Faculty: full-time 1526. Degrees conferred: M.A., M.S., M.B.A., M.A.T., M.Ed., M.Engr., M.F.A., M.P.H., M.S.W., M.Arch., M.L.S., M.M., M.N., Ed.D., C.Phil., D.M.A., D.N.Sc., Dr.P.H., D.Env., Engr.

ADMISSION REQUIREMENTS. Two transcripts, statement of purpose, required in support of application. Electronic application available. Additional application, supplementary information form, three letters of recommendation, GRE/GRE Subject/MAT required by some departments. Interview sometimes required. TOEFL (minimum score 560, 220 on computer-based test) or IELTS (overall band score of at least 7.0) required for international applicants. Accepts transfer applicants. Apply to Graduate Admissions/Student and Academic Affairs by December 15 (Fall), October 1 (Winter), December 31 (Spring). Application fee $40. Phone: (310)825-1711; fax: (310)206-4627.

ADMISSION STANDARDS. Selective for most departments, very competitive or competitive for the others.

FINANCIAL AID. Annual awards from institutional funds: fellowships and grants, research assistantships, teaching assistantships, Federal W/S, loans. Approved for VA benefits. Apply by March 1 to the appropriate department for assistantships, fellowships; to Financial Aid Office for all Federal programs. Use FAFSA and University's Supplemental FAF. Phone: (310)206-

0400. About 52% of students receive aid other than loans from University and outside sources.

DEGREE REQUIREMENTS. For M.A., M.S.: nine graduate courses, at least seven in residence and three in full-time attendance; advancement to candidacy; thesis or final written/oral exam; reading knowledge of one foreign language for some majors. For other master's: the same minimum requisites outlined normally apply. For Ph.D.: normally three years minimum in residence beyond the bachelor's; preliminary exam; reading knowledge of one or two foreign languages; written/oral qualifying exam; advancement to candidacy; dissertation; final oral exam. For other doctorates: essentially the same minimum requisites as for the Ph.D., except no foreign language requirement.

FIELDS OF STUDY.
Aerospace Engineering. GRE/Subject in engineering, mathematics or related area, departmental application for admissions; M.S., Ph.D.; admits Fall only; offered by School of Engineering and Applied Science.

African Area Studies. Interdepartmental. GRE, research paper for admission; one language (African) for M.A. M.A. only.

Afro-American Studies. Interdepartmental. GRE, writing sample for admission; one language for M.A. M.A. only; admits Fall only.

American Indian Studies. Interdepartmental. GRE recommended, not required. M.A. only; admits Fall only.

Anthropology. GRE for admission; one language for M.A., one language special proficiency for Ph.D.; admits Fall only.

Applied Linguistics. Interdepartmental. GRE for admission; two languages or one language special proficiency for Ph.D. Ph.D. only; admits Fall only.

Archaeology. Interdepartmental. GRE, three research papers for admission; one language for M.A., two languages for Ph.D. M.A., Ph.D. only; admits Fall only.

Architecture. Portfolio, GRE (Ph.D.) for admission; M.Arch. I and II, M.A., Ph.D.; urban design program; offered by Graduate School of Architecture and Urban Planning.

Art. Twenty slides due January 15 for admission. M.A., M.F.A.; admits Fall only; offered by School of the Arts.

Art History. GRE, thesis or three research papers for admission; two languages for M.A. and Ph.D.

Asian American Studies. Interdepartmental. Writing sample for admission; one language or research tool for M.A. M.A. only; admits Fall only.

Astronomy. GRE/Subject in physics for admission. M.S., Ph.D.; admits Fall only.

Atmospheric Sciences. GRE for admission. M.S., Ph.D.

Biochemistry and Molecular Biology. GRE/Subject in chemistry for admission. M.S., Ph.D.; admits Fall only; offered by Department of Chemistry and Biochemistry.

Biological Chemistry. GRE/Subject, three letters of recommendation for admission; admits Fall only. M.S., Ph.D.

Biomathematics. GRE/Subject for admission. M.S., Ph.D.

Biomedical Engineering. GRE/Subject, three letters of recommendation for admission; admits Fall and Spring. M.S., Ph.D.

Biomedical Physics. GRE for admission. M.S., Ph.D.; usually admits in Fall; offered by Department of Radiological Sciences.

Biostatistics. GRE for admission. M.S., Ph.D.; offered by School of Public Health.

Cellular and Molecular Pathology. GRE/Subject, three letters of recommendation for admission; admits Fall only. Ph.D. only.

Chemical Engineering. GRE/Subject in engineering, mathematics or related area, Departmental application for admission. M.S., Ph.D.; admits Fall only; offered by School of Engineering and Applied Science.

Chemistry. Apply by January 15; GRE/Subject for admission; one language for M.S. and Ph.D. M.S., Ph.D. only. Ph.D.; admits Fall only.

Civil and Environmental Engineering. GRE/Subject in engineering or mathematics or related area, departmental application for admission. M.S., Ph.D.; admits Fall only; offered by School of Engineering and Applied Science.

Classics. Apply by January 15; GRE, term paper for admission; one language for M.A., two languages for Ph.D., M.A., Ph.D.

Comparative Literature. Interdepartmental. Apply by January 15; GRE, writing sample for admission; two languages for M.A. and Ph.D. M.A., Ph.D.

Computer Science. Apply by January 15; GRE/Subject in mathematics or computer science for admission; M.S., Ph.D.; admits Fall only; offered by School of Engineering and Applied Science.

Culture and Performance. GRE, three letters of recommendation, writing sample, statement of purpose for admission; admits Fall only. M.A., Ph.D.

Dance. Audition, interview for admission. M.A., M.F.A.; admits Fall only; offered by School of the Arts.

Design Media. Twenty slides for admission, due January 15; admits Fall only. M.A., M.F.A.

East Asian Languages and Cultures. GRE, writing sample for admission; one year Japanese (Chinese majors) or one year Chinese (Japanese majors) for M.A., two languages for Ph.D. M.A., Ph.D.

East Asian Studies. GRE, three letters of recommendation for admission; admits Fall only. M.A. only.

Economics. GRE General for admission; one language for Ph.D. M.A., Ph.D.; admits Fall only.

Education. GRE, departmental application for admission; M.Ed., M.A., Ed.D., Ph.D.; Ph.D. in Special Education with CSULA, certificate (credential) program; admits Fall only for credential; offered by Graduate School of Education.

Educational Leadership. GRE, three letters of recommendation, essay, résumé, departmental application for admission; admits Fall only. Ed.D. only.

Electrical Engineering. GRE/Subject in engineering, mathematics or related area, departmental application for admission. M.S., Ph.D.; admits Fall only; offered by School of Engineering and Applied Science.

English. GRE General/Subject in literature for admission; one language for M.A., two languages for Ph.D. M.A., Ph.D.

Environmental Health Sciences. GRE for admission. M.S., Ph.D.; offered by School of Public Health.

Environmental Science and Engineering. Interdepartmental. GRE/Subject for admission. D. Env. only.

Epidemiology. GRE for admission. M.S., Ph.D; offered by School of Public Health.

Ethnomusicology. Biographical/purpose statement, sample work for admission; apply by December 30. M.A., Ph.D., offered by School of the Arts.

Film, Television, and Digital Media. GRE for admission. M.A., M.F.A., Ph.D.; offered by School of Theater, Film and Television.

Folklore and Mythology. Interdepartmental. GRE recommended; one language for M.A., two languages for Ph.D.

French and Francophone Studies. GRE, research paper or thesis for admission; one language for M.A., two languages for Ph.D. M.A., Ph.D.

Geochemistry. GRE/Subject for admission. M.S., Ph.D.; offered by Department of Earth and Space Sciences.

Geography. GRE for admission; research tool for M.A. and Ph.D. M.A., Ph.D.

Geology. GRE for admission; M.S., C.Phil., Ph.D.; offered by Department of Earth and Space Sciences.

Geophysics and Space Physics. GRE/Subject in physics for admission. M.S., Ph.D.; offered by Department of Earth and Space Sciences.

Germanic Languages. GRE, writing sample for admission; one language for Ph.D. Ph.D.; offered by Department of Germanic Languages.

Greek. GRE, term paper for admission; one language for M.A. M.A. only; offered by Department of Classics.

Health Services. GRE for admission. M.S., Ph.D.; offered by School of Public Health.

Hispanic Languages and Literatures. GRE, term paper for admission; two languages for Ph.D. Ph.D.; offered by the Department of Spanish and Portuguese.

History. GRE for admission; one language for M.A., two languages for Ph.D. M.A., Ph.D.; admits Fall only.

Human Genetics. GRE/Subject, three letters of recommendation, statement of purpose for admission; admits Fall only. M.S., Ph.D.

Indo-European Studies. Interdepartmental. Two languages for Ph.D. Ph.D.

Information Studies. GRE, three letters of recommendation, statement of purpose for admission; admits Fall only. M.L.I.S., Ph.D.

Islamic Studies. Interdepartmental. GRE for admission, recommended for international applicants; one language for M.A.; two languages for Ph.D.

Italian. GRE for admission, recommended for international applicants; one language for M.A., two languages for Ph.D. M.A., Ph.D.

Latin. GRE, term paper for admission, one language for M.A. M.A. only.

Latin American Studies. Interdepartmental. GRE for admission; two languages for M.A. M.A. only.

Linguistics. GRE, sample of work for admission; one language for M.A., two languages or one language special proficiency for Ph.D. M.A., Ph.D.; admits Fall only.

Management. GMAT (M.B.A.), GMAT or GRE (M.S., Ph.D.) for admission. M.B.A., M.S., Ph.D.; admits Fall only.

Manufacturing Engineering. GRE/Subject in engineering, mathematics or related area, departmental application for admission; M.S. only; admits Fall only; offered by School of Engineering and Applied Science.

Material Science and Engineering. GRE for admission. M.A., Ph.D.; admits Fall only; offered by School of Engineering and Applied Science.

Mathematics. GRE/Subject, departmental application for admission; two languages for Ph.D. M.A., M.A.T., Ph.D.; admits Fall only.

Mechanical and Aerospace Engineering. GRE/Subject in engineering, mathematics or related area, departmental application for admission. M.A., Ph.D.; admits Fall only; offered by the School of Engineering and Applied Science.

Microbiology and Immunology. GRE/Subject in biology for admission; apply by January 15. Ph.D. only; admits Fall only.

Microbiology and Molecular Genetics. GRE/Subject in biology or chemistry for admission. M.A., Ph.D.; admits Fall usually.

Molecular Biology. Interdepartmental. GRE for admission. Ph.D. only.

Molecular, Cell, and Development Biology. GRE, three letters of recommendation, personal statement for admission; admits Fall only. Ph.D. only.

Molecular, Cellular, and Integrative Physiology. GRE/Subject, three letters of recommendation, personal statement for admission; admits Fall only. Ph.D. only.

Molecular and Medical Pharmacology. GRE, personal statement for admission; admits Fall only. Ph.D. only.

Molecular Toxicology. GRE, departmental application, statement of purpose for admission. Ph.D. only.

Music. Departmental exam, sample work, biographical/purpose statement for admission; apply by December 30; one language for M.A. and M.F.A., two languages for Ph.D. M.A., M.F.A., M.M., D.M.A., Ph.D.; admits Fall only; offered by the School of Arts.

Musicology. Department exam, sample work, biographical/ purpose statement for admission; apply by December 30. M.A., Ph.D.

Near Eastern Languages and Cultures. GRE, recent term paper for admission; one language for M.A., two languages for Ph.D. M.A., Ph.D.

Neurobiology. GRE, three letters of recommendation for admission; admits Fall only. M.S., Ph.D.

Neuroscience. Interdepartmental. GRE for admission; apply by January 5. Ph.D. only; admits Fall only.

Nursing. GRE (D.N.Sc.), CGFNS exam for admission. M.N.-Ph.D.; admits Fall only.

Oral Biology. Apply by January 15. M.S., Ph.D.; offered by School of Dentistry.

Organismic Biology, Ecology, and Evolution. GRE/Subject, three letters of recommendation for admission; admits Fall only. M.A., Ph.D.

Pharmacology. GRE, personal statement for admission. Ph.D. only; admits Fall only.

Philosophy. GRE sample work, departmental application for admission; apply by January 10; one language for M.A., one language special proficiency for Ph.D. M.A., Ph.D.; admits Fall only.

Physics. GRE/Subject for admission. M.A.T., Ph.D.; admits Fall usually.

Physiological Science. GRE for admission. M.S., Ph.D.

Physiology. GRE/Subject for admission. M.S., Ph.D.; admits Fall only for Ph.D.

Political Science. GRE, sample work for admission; one language for Ph.D. (or substitute program). M.A., Ph.D.; admits Fall only.

Portuguese. GRE, personal statement, recent term paper for admission; one language for M.A. M.A. only.

Psychology. GRE/Subject, personal statement for admission. M.A., M.A.T., Ph.D.; admits Fall only to Ph.D.

Public Health. GRE for admission. M.P.H., M.S., Dr.P.H., Ph.D.; admits Fall only; offered by School of Public Health.

Public Policy. GRE, three letters of recommendation, departmental statement of purpose for admission; admits Fall only. M.P.P. only.

Romance Linguistics and Literature. Interdepartmental. GRE, writing sample, one language (M.A.), two languages (Ph.D.) for admission. M.A, Ph.D.

Scandinavian. One language for M.A. M.A., Ph.D.; offered by Department of Germanic Languages.

Slavic Languages and Literatures. GRE, personal statement for admission; one language for M.A., two languages for Ph.D. M.A., Ph.D.

Social Welfare. GRE, personal statement for admission. M.S.W., Ph.D.; admits Fall only.

Sociology. GRE, writing sample for admission; one language for Ph.D. M.A., Ph.D.; admits Fall only.

Spanish. GRE, personal statement, recent term paper for admission; one language for admission. M.A. only.

Special Education. GRE, three letters of recommendation, departmental application, statement of purpose; admits Fall only. Ph.D. only.

Statistics. GRE/Subject, three letters of recommendation, departmental application, statement of purpose; admits Fall only. M.S., Ph.D.

Teaching English as a Second Language. GRE, research paper for admission. M.A., Certificate only; admits Fall only.

Theater. GRE for admission; apply by December 1; one language for Ph.D. M.A., M.F.A., Ph.D.; admits Fall only.

Urban Planning. Departmental application for admission. M.A., Ph.D.; admits only; offered by Graduate School of Architecture and Urban Planning.

Women's Studies. GRE, three letters of recommendation, personal statement, departmental application, writing sample for admission; admits Fall only. M.A., Ph.D.

School of Dentistry (90095-1762)

Founded in 1960. Annual tuition fees: residents $9667, non-residents $19,911. Limited on-campus housing available. Total average cost for all other first-year expenses: $13,275. For housing information, phone: (310)825-4491.

Enrollment: first-year class 88, total 391 (men 60%, women 40%). Faculty: full-time 72, part-time 168. Degrees conferred: D.D.S., D.D.S.-M.S., D.D.S.-Ph.D. (Oral Biology).

ADMISSION REQUIREMENTS. AADSAS, transcripts, DAT, substantive letters of recommendation, comprehensive bibliography and personal statement required in support of application. Applicants must have completed at least three years of college study. Preference given to state and WICHE residents. Graduates of unaccredited colleges not considered. Apply to Office of Admissions or AADSAS after May 1, before January 1. Application fee $40. Phone: (310)794-7971.

ADMISSION STANDARDS. Competitive. Mean DAT: Academic 22; PAT 20; mean GPA: 3.5 (A = 4); science GPA: 3.51. Accepts about 20% of total annual applicants. Approximately 95% are state residents.

FINANCIAL AID. Limited number of scholarships, fellowships, loans, summer work study. Apply to Financial Aids Office by May 1. Phone: (310)825-6994. Use FAFSA. About 92% of students receive some aid from School.

DEGREE REQUIREMENTS. For D.D.S.: satisfactory completion of forty-five-month program. For D.D.S.-M.S.: Satisfactory completion of fifth-year program. For D.D.S.-Ph.D.: Satisfactory completion of six- to seven-year program; research project.

School of Law (90024-1445)
Web site: www.law.ucla.edu

Established 1947. ABA approved since 1950. AALS member. Semester system. Law library 570,000 volumes. Library has LEXIS, NEXIS, WESTLAW.
Annual fees: residents $11,110, nonresidents $21,354.
Enrollment: first-year class 304; full-time 947 (men 45%, women 55%); no part-time study. Faculty: full-time 53, part-time 14. Student to faculty ratio 14.6 to 1. Degrees conferred: J.D., LL.M. (Comparative Law), J.D.-M.A. (African American Studies, American Indian Studies, Urban planning); J.D.-M.B.A., J.D.-M.P.P., J.D.-M.S.W.

ADMISSION REQUIREMENTS. LSDAS Law School report, transcripts, LSAT (no later than December) required in support of application. Interview not required. Accepts transfer applicants. Graduates of unaccredited colleges not considered. Apply to Admissions and Records Office after October 1, before February 1, transfer applicants July 1. First-year students admitted Fall only. Application fee $40. Phone: (310)825-4041; e-mail: admissions@law.ucla.edu.

ADMISSION STANDARDS. Selective. Median LSAT: 163; median GPA: 3.65 (A = 4). Gourman rating: 4.75. *U.S. News & World Report* ranking is in the top 16 of all law schools. Accepts 15–20% of total annual applicants. About 25% of class are non-residents.

FINANCIAL AID. Scholarships, grants, Federal W/S, loans available. All financial aid, except for second- and third-year students, is administered by the campus-wide Office of Financial Aid. Apply by March 1. Use FAFSA. The Supplemental Financial Aid Application should be submitted to law school before February 1. About 50% of all students receive some form of financial aid.

DEGREE REQUIREMENTS. For J.D.: satisfactory completion of three-year program. For LL.M.: at least 24 credits beyond J.D.: one year in full-time residence. For M.A.: Course work divided in second and third year between both schools. M.A. awarded after fourth year in school of Architecture and upon acceptance of thesis. For M.B.A.: see Graduate School listing above.

John E. Anderson Graduate School of Management (Box 951481)
Web site: www.anderson.ucla.edu

Established 1935. Public control. Accredited programs: M.B.A.; recognized Ph.D. Quarter system. Special facilities: Center for Corporate Renewal, Center for Digital Media, Center for Healthcare Management, Center for International Business Education and Research, Center for Real Estate, Center for Operations and Technology Management, John M. Olin Center for Public Policy, Harold Price Center for Entrepreneurial Studies, Western Management Science Institute. Library: 147,000 volumes.
Annual tuition/fees: M.B.A. resident full-time $11,744; nonresident full-time $22,448. E.M.B.A. tuition: $31,000; F.E.M.B.A. tuition: $21,084. Ph.D. annual tuition/fee: resident $4503, nonresident $14,937. On-campus rooms and apartments available for both single and married students. Annual on-campus housing cost: $5600 (room and board). Contact Graduate Housing Office for both on- and off-campus housing information; phone: (310)825-4491. Estimated annual budget for tuition, room and board and personal expenses: residents approximately $31,000, nonresidents $39,500.
Enrollment: total full-time 640, part-time 534 (men 70%, women 30%). Faculty: 92 full-time, 50 part-time; 94% with Ph.D/D.B.A. Degrees conferred: M.B.A. (Concentrations in Accounting, Business Economics, Decision Science, Finance, Human Resource and Organizational Behavior, Information Systems, Marketing, Operations and Technology Management, Strategic and Organization), E.M.B.A. (weekends only, alternating Fridays, Saturdays), F.E.M.B.A., M.B.A.-J.D., M.B.A.-M.D., M.B.A.-M.A. (Latin American Studies, Urban Planning), M.B.A.-M.L.I.S. (Library and Information Science), M.B.A.-M.S. (Computer Science), M.B.A.-M.S.N. (Nursing), M.B.A.-M.U.P., M.S.M., Ph.D. in Management (concentrations in Accounting, Business Economics, Decision Sciences, Finance, Human Resources and Organizational Behavior, Information Systems, International Business and Comparative Management, Marketing, Operations and Technology, Strategy and Organization).

ADMISSION REQUIREMENTS. Students are required to have their own personal computer. Early applications are encouraged for both admission and financial aid consideration. U.S. citizens apply by April 1 (Fall), international students apply by February 28 (Fall). Submit an application, GMAT results (will accept GMAT test results from the last five years, if GMAT is retaken highest score is used), two offical transcripts from each undergraduate/graduate school attended, two letters of recommendation, Data Form, employment history (prefers at least four years of work experience), and an application fee of $125 to the Director of M.B.A. Admission. Applications can be downloaded from School's Web site. Accepts MBA Multi-App electronic application in lieu of institutional application. Admits Fall only. In addition, international students (whose native language is other than English) should submit a TOEFL (minimum score 600) report, two certified translations and evaluations of all official transcripts, recommendation should be in English or with certified translations, proof of health/immunization certificate, and proof of sufficent financial resources for one year of academic study. For current information and/or modification in admission requirements the international applicant's contact telephone number is: (310)825-6944. On-campus visits are strongly encouraged. Interviews are by invitation. Joint degree applicants must apply to and be accepted to both schools (LSAT required for Law, MCAT for Medicine), contact the admissions office for current information and specific admissions requirements. There are five decision rounds, notification is made on January 28, March 4, April 28, May 27, June 19. Admissions Office phone: (310)825-6944; fax: (310)825-8582; e-mail: mba.admissions@anderson.ucla.edu.

ADMISSION REQUIREMENTS FOR DOCTORAL CANDIDATES. Contact Ph.D. Program Office at (310)825-2824; e-mail: ms.phdadmissions@anderson.ucls.edu for application material and information. Beginning students are admitted Fall Only. Both U.S. citizens and international application apply by January 1 (Fall). Submit an application, a GMAT/GRE (will accept GMAT/GRE test results from the last five years), two official transcripts from each undergraduate/graduate school attended, two letters of recommendation, statement of purpose, and application fee of $40 to the Office of Graduate Admission. In addition, international students (whose native language is other than English) should submit a TOEFL (minimum score 600) report; two certified translations and evaluations of all offical transcripts, recommendation should be in English or with certified translations, proof of health/immunization certificate. International students' contact: (310)825-2824. Interviews strongly encouraged. Doctoral applicants must be accepted by both the Anderson School and the Graduate Division. Notifications are generally completed by mid-April.

ADMISSION STANDARDS. For M.B.A.: Very selective. Median GMAT 670; median GPA 3.5 (A = 4). Gourman rating: the M.B.A. program was rated in the top 8, the score was 4.87; the Ph.D. was rated in the top 10, the score was 4.85 (Scale: Very Strong 4.73–4.99), the E.M.B.A. program rated in the top 5, the score 4.85. *U.S. News & World Report* ranked Anderson in the top 7 for E.M.B.A. programs, and top 8 for M.B.A. programs of all U.S. business schools. *Business Week* listed Anderson in the top 12 American business schools.

FINANCIAL AID. For M.B.A.: Scholarships, merit scholarships, special stipends for minority students, state grants, merit-based fellowships, graduate assistantships, Federal Perkins loans, Stafford Subsidized and Unsubsidized loans, Federal W/S available. Apply by March 1. Financial aid is available for part-time study. Financial aid may be available for international students after first year. Assistantships/fellowships may be available for joint degree candidates. For assistantships, fellowships, scholarships the selection criteria places heavy reliance on GMAT and undergraduate GPA. Contact the University's Financial Aid Office for current need-based financial aid information; phone: (310)825-0629. For most financial assistance and all Federal programs, submit FAFSA to a federal processor (School code: #001315), also submit Financial Aid Transcript, Federal Income Tax forms. Approximately 65% of students receive some form of financial assistance.

For Ph.D.: fee waiver, nonresident fee waiver, Anderson School fellowships and stipends, research and teaching assistantships and UCLA graduate fellowships. For all need-based financial aid information, contact the university's Office of Financial Aid.

DEGREE REQUIREMENTS. For M.B.A.: 24 courses including 14 elective courses, two-year program; degree program must be completed in three years. For F.E.M.B.A.: 84 credits, a three-year program. For E.M.B.A.: 66 credit, twenty-three-month program. For M.S. (Decision Sciences): 9 courses; thesis. For M.B.A.-M.A. (Latin American Studies, Urban Planning): 129–144 quarter hours, three- to four-year program. For M.B.A.-J.D.: 185 quarter hours, four- to five-year program. M.B.A.-M.P.H.: 132 quarter hours, generally a three- to four-year program. For M.B.A.-M.L.I.S.: 124 quarter hours, three- to four-year program. For M.B.A.-M.S. (Computer Science): 96 quarter hours, two- to three-year program. For M.B.A.-M.S.N.: 96 quater hour program. For Ph.D.: three- to five-year program; specialization; research and

breadth requirement; oral qualifying exam; dissertation proposal and oral presentation; dissertation; final oral defense.

David Geffen School of Medicine (90095-7035)

Established 1951. State control. Quarter system. Annual tuition and fees: resident $10,173, nonresident $20,417. Total average for all other expenses $10,024. Enrollment: first-year class 121, full-time 575 (men 58%, women 42%). Faculty: full-time 250. Degrees conferred: M.D., M.D.-M.B.A., M.D.-M.P.H., Ph.D. Graduate study (Medical Scientist Training Program) in preclinical departments, degrees offered through UCLA Graduate Division and Graduate Departments at California Institute of Technology.

ADMISSION REQUIREMENTS. AMCAS report, transcripts, MCAT, letters of recommendation, interview required in support of application. Bachelor's is ordinarily required, but students who have completed three academic years may be admitted. Preference given to state residents. Accepts transfer applicants. Graduates of unaccredited colleges not considered. Does not have EDP. Apply to Office of Student Affairs Division of Admissions after June 1, before November 1, transfer applicants by January 1. Fall admission only. Screening fee $40. Phone: (310)825-6081.

ADMISSION STANDARDS. Very competitive. Mean science GPA: 3.64 (A = 4.0); mean nonscience GPA: 3.73. Accepts about 2% of total annual applicants. Gourman rating: 4.85. *U.S. News & World Report* ranking was 13th among all U.S. medical schools. Approximately 80% are state residents.

FINANCIAL AID. Scholarships, fellowships, research assistantships, loans. Apply after acceptance to Office of Student Affairs before March 1. Use FAFSA.

DEGREE REQUIREMENTS. For M.D.: 12 quarters minimum, at least the last 6 in residence. Candidates must be 21 years old. For M.S., Ph.D.: see Graduate Division listing above for degree requirements.

FIELDS OF GRADUATE STUDY.
Biochemistry and Molecular Biology.
Bioengineering, Nanosystems.
Bioinformatics.
Biomathematics.
Cell Biology.
Cell Physiology and Biophysics.
Developmental Biology.
Gene Expression.
Genetics.
Immunology.
Integrative and Regulatory Biology.
Microbiology and Virology.
Molecular Basis of Disease.
Molecular, Cellular, and Integrative Physiology.
Molecular Evolution.
Molecular Parasitology.
Molecular and Medical Pharmacology.
Neurobiology.
Structural Biology.
Tumor Cell Biology.

FIELDS OF GRADUATE STUDY AT CALTECH:
Applied Science.
Chemical Engineering.
Chemistry.
Engineering.

UNIVERSITY OF CALIFORNIA, RIVERSIDE

Riverside, California 92521-0102
Web site: www.ucr.edu

Founded 1954. Located 60 miles E of Los Angeles. CGS member. Coed. State control. Quarter system. Special facilities: California Museum of Photography, Centers for agricultural research, air pollution research, bibliographic studies, citrus research, dry lands research, geophysics and planetary physics, social and behavioral science research, extensive botanic gardens and natural area reserve system; entomological teaching and research collection, and academic computing center, laboratory for historic research. Library: 2,000,000 volumes, 19,000 subscriptions. More than 800 computers on campus for general student use.

Annual tuition/fees: resident $5001, nonresident $15,895; there is an additional charge of $5000 for M.B.A. program. University housing for 268 married students, 600 men, 600 women. Additionally, there are 316 University-owned apartments available for either married students without children or single students. Phone: (909)787-4307. For off-campus information: Phone (909)787-3770. Day-care facilities available.

Graduate Division

Established 1960. Enrollment: full-time 1394, part-time 45 (men 50%, women 50%). University faculty: full-time 470. Degrees conferred: M.A., M.S., M.B.A., Ph.D.

ADMISSION REQUIREMENTS. Two transcripts, GRE/Subject Test, GMAT, three letters of recommendation, statement of purpose required in support of University's application. Interview required for some departments. TOEFL (minimum score 550, 213 on computer-based test) required for foreign applicants. Graduates of unaccredited colleges not considered. Apply to Graduate Division by May 1 (Fall), September 1 (Winter), December 1 (Spring); international applicants apply by February 1 (Fall), July 1 (Winter), October 1 (Spring). Application fee $40. Phone: (909)787-3313; fax: (909)787-2238; for M.B.A. admissions, phone: (909)787-4551; e-mail: graduadmis@ucracl.usr.edu.

ADMISSION STANDARDS. Selective. Usual minimum average: 3.2 (A = 4).

FINANCIAL AID. Annual awards from institutional funds: scholarships, fellowships, teaching assistantships, research assistantships, tuition waivers, grants, Federal W/S, loans. Approved for VA benefits. GRE Test is required of all fellowship applicants. Apply to appropriate departments and Financial Aid Office by February 1. Phone: (909)787-3878. Use FAFSA. About 60% of students receive aid other than loans from University and outside sources. Aid available for part-time students.

DEGREE REQUIREMENTS. For M.A., M.Ed., M.S.: 36 quarter units minimum; thesis or comprehensive exam. For M.B.A.: 92 quarter units; capstone course; internship; thesis or case project. For Ph.D.: two years minimum beyond the bachelor's; written and qualifying exams; dissertation, final oral defense of dissertation.

FIELDS OF STUDY.

COLLEGE OF NATURAL AND AGRICULTURAL SCIENCES:
Applied Statistics. Ph.D.
Biochemistry and Molecular Biology. M.S., Ph.D.
Biology. M.S., Ph.D.
Botany. M.S., Ph.D.
Cell, Molecular, and Developmental Biology. M.S., Ph.D.
Chemistry. M.S., Ph.D.
Entomology. M.S., Ph.D.
Environmental Sciences. M.S., Ph.D.
Environmental Toxicology. M.S., Ph.D.
Genetics. M.S., Ph.D.
Geological Sciences. M.S., Ph.D.
Mathematics. M.A., M.S., Ph.D.
Microbiology. M.S., Ph.D.
Neuroscience. Ph.D.
Physics. M.A., M.S., Ph.D.
Plant Pathology. M.S., Ph.D.
Plant Science. M.S.
Soil and Water Sciences. M.S., Ph.D.
Statistics. M.S.

COLLEGE OF HUMANITIES, ARTS, AND SOCIAL SCIENCES:
Anthropology. M.A., M.S., Ph.D.
Art History. M.A.
Comparative Literature. M.A., Ph.D.
Dance. M.F.A.
Dance History and Theory. Ph.D.
Economics. M.A., Ph.D.
English. M.A., Ph.D.
History. M.A., Ph.D.
Music. M.A.
Philosophy. M.A., Ph.D.
Political Science. M.A., Ph.D.
Psychology. Ph.D.
Sociology. Ph.D.
Spanish. M.A., Ph.D.

DIVISION OF BIOMEDICAL SCIENCES:
Biomedical Sciences. Ph.D.

THE MARIAN AND ROSEMARY BOURNS COLLEGE OF ENGINEERING:
Computer Science. M.S., Ph.D.
Chemical and Environmental Engineering. M.S., Ph.D.
Electrical Engineering. M.S., Ph.D.
Mechanical Engineering. M.S., Ph.D.

A. GARRY ANDERSON GRADUATE SCHOOL OF MANAGEMENT:
Management. M.B.A.

SCHOOL OF EDUCATION:
Curriculum and Instruction. M.A., Ph.D.
Educational Administration. M.A., Ph.D.
Educational Psychology. Ph.D.
School Psychology. Ph.D.
Special Education. M.A., Ph.D.

UNIVERSITY OF CALIFORNIA, SAN DIEGO

La Jolla, California 92093-5003
Web site: www.ucsd.edu

Founded in 1964. CGS and AAU member. Coed. State control. Quarter system. Special facilities: California Space Institute, Cancer Center, Center for Astrophysics and Space Sciences, Center for Energy and Combustion Research, Center for Human Information Processing, Center for Iberian and Latin American Studies, Center for Magnetic Recording Research, Center for Research in Computing and the Arts, Center for Molecular Genetics, Center for Research in Language, Center for United States–Mexican Studies, Cray C90, Intel paragon supercomputer, Thinking Machine CM-Z, DEC Alpha Fany, Institute for Biomedical Engineering, Institute on Global Conflict and Cooperation, Institute for Geophysics and Planetary Physics, Institute for Neural Computation, Institute for Nonlinear Science, Institute for Pure and Applied Physical Sciences, Institute for Research on Aging, Intercampus Institute for Research and Particle Accelerators, Laboratory for Comparative Human Cognition, Laboratory for Mathematics and Statistics, Scripps Institution of Oceanography, International House, San

Diego Supercomputer Center. NIH ranking is 16th among all U.S. institutions, with 558 awards/grants worth $217,228,948. Library: 2,600,000 volumes, 25,000 subscriptions.

Annual tuition/fees: resident $4929, nonresident $15,822. On-campus housing for about 500 graduate students. Average annual housing cost: $10,000 (including board) for single students. Apply to Housing Office. Phone: (858)824-0850. For off-campus information call (858)534-3670. Limited day-care facilities available.

Graduate Studies and Research

Graduate study since 1965. Enrollment: full-time 2750, part-time 200. University faculty: 1100. Degrees conferred: M.A., M.S., M.F.A., M.P.I.A., C.Phil., Ph.D.

ADMISSION REQUIREMENTS. Transcripts, GRE (for all programs except M.F.A. programs and Leadership of Health Care Organizations), three letters of recommendation, statement of purpose required in support of University's application. Electronic application available. GRE Subject Test recommended for many degree programs. TOEFL required, TWE strongly recommended for foreign applicants. Interview not required. Accepts transfer applicants. Graduates of unaccredited institutions not considered. Apply to the prospective major department and Office of Graduate Admission; note program deadlines in Fields of Study below. Application fee $40. Phone: (858)534-1193; fax: (858)534-4722.

ADMISSION STANDARDS. Selective. Minimum average: 3.0 (A = 4).

FINANCIAL AID. Annual awards from institutional funds: fellowships, research assistantships/fellowships, teaching assistantships/fellowships, traineeships, Federal W/S, loans. Fellowship and assistantships applicants must take GRE no later than December. Apply to appropriate department and Financial Aid Office; no specified closing date. Phone: (858)534-4480. Use FAFSA. (University code 001317). About 80% of students receive aid from University and outside sources. Aid available for part-time students. Phone: (858)534-3807.

DEGREE REQUIREMENTS. For master's: requirements vary but normally include one year of course work; thesis or comprehensive exam; one year in residence. For Ph.D.: requirements vary but normally includes a minimum of two years beyond the master's; preliminary exam; dissertation; final oral exam.

FIELDS OF STUDY.
Aerospace Engineering. International applicants apply by January 31, U.S. citizens apply by May 31. M.S., Ph.D.
Anthropology. Apply by January 10. Ph.D.
Applied Mathematics. Appy by March 1. GRE Subject for admission. M.A. only.
Applied Mechanics. International applicants apply by January 31, U.S. citizens apply by May 31. M.S., Ph.D.
Applied Ocean Science. Apply by January 11. GRE for admission. M.S., Ph.D.
Applied Physics. Apply by January 11. GRE for admission. M.S., Ph.D.
Art History. Includes theory and criticism. Writing sample for admission. Ph.D.
Biochemistry. Apply by January 4. GRE Subject recommended for admissions. Ph.D.
Bioengineering. Apply by January 16. M.Eng., M.S., Ph.D.
Bioinformatics. Apply by January 18. Ph.D.
Biology. Apply by January 4. GRE Subject recommended for admission. Ph.D.
Biomedical Sciences. Apply January 7. Ph.D.
Biophysics. Apply by January 15. GRE Subject for admission. Ph.D.

Chemical Engineering. Apply by January 16. M.S., Ph.D.
Chemistry. Apply by January 18. GRE Subject for admission. Ph.D.
Cognitive Science. Apply by January 11.
Communication. Apply by January 18. Ph.D.
Communication Theory and Systems. Apply by January 11. GRE for admission. M.S., Ph.D.
Comparative Literature. Apply by January 16. M.A. only.
Computational Neurobiology. Apply by January 4. GRE Subject recommended for admission. Ph.D.
Computer Sciences. Apply by January 7. Statement of purpose, GRE Subject recommended for admission. M.S., Ph.D.
Computer Engineering. Apply by January 7. Statement of purpose required, GRE Subject recommended for admission. M.S., Ph.D.
Drama and Theatre. Apply by January 4. Audition and/or interview required for admission. GRE not for acting, design, directing, stage management. Ph.D.
Earth Sciences. Apply by January 6. Ph.D.
Economics. Apply by January 18. GRE Subject recommended for admission. Ph.D.
Economics and International Affairs. Apply by January 18. GRE Subject recommended for admission. Ph.D.
Education. Apply by February 1. CBEST for admission. M.Ed.
Electronic Circuits and Systems. Apply by January 11. GRE for admission. M.S., Ph.D.
Engineering. Apply by January 11. GRE for admission. M.Eng.
Engineering Physics. International applicants apply by January 31, U.S. citizens apply by May 31. M.S., Ph.D.
Ethnic Studies. Apply by January 15. Ph.D.
French Literature. Apply by January 16. M.A. only.
German Literature. Apply by January 16. M.A. only.
History. Apply by January 18. Writing sample for admission.
Intelligence Systems, Robotics, and Control. Apply by January 11. GRE required for admission. M.S., Ph.D.
Judaic Studies. Apply by January 18. M.A. only.
Latin American Studies. Apply by January 18. M.A. only.
Leadership of Health Care Organizations. Admits Fall, Winter, Spring. M.A.S.
Linguistics. Apply by January 18. Ph.D.
Literature. Apply by January 16. Ph.D.
Literature in English. Apply by January 16. M.A. only.
Marine Biology. Apply by January 6. GRE Subject for admission. Ph.D.
Materials Science. Admits Fall, Winter, Spring. M.S., Ph.D.
Mathematics. Apply by March 1. GRE Subject for admission. M.A., Ph.D.
Mechanical Engineering. International applicants apply by January 31, U.S. citizens apply by May 31. M.S., Ph.D.
Molecular Pathology. Apply January 15. GRE Subject for admission. Ph.D.
Music. Apply by January 12. M.A., Ph.D., D.M.A.
Neuroscience. Apply by December 17. GRE Subject for admission. Ph.D.
Oceanography. Apply by January 6. Ph.D.
Pacific International Affairs. Apply by February 15. Departmental application required, GMAT may be substituted for GRE for admission. M.P.I.A.
Philosophy. Apply by January 18. Writing sample for admission. Ph.D.
Photonics. Apply by January 11. GRE for admission. M.S., Ph.D.
Physics. Apply by January 15. GRE Subject for admission. M.S., Ph.D.
Political Science. Apply by January 5. Departmental application required for admission. Ph.D.
Political Science and International Affairs. Apply by January 5. Departmental application required for admission. Ph.D.
Psychology. Apply by January 5. Ph.D.
Signal and Image Processing. Apply by January 11. GRE for admission. M.S., Ph.D.
Sociology. Apply by January 2. Writing sample for admission. Ph.D.

Spanish Literature. Apply by January 16. M.A. only.

Statistics. Apply by February 15. GRE Subject for admission. M.S. only.

Structural Engineering. International applicants apply by January 31, U.S. citizens apply by May 31. M.S., Ph.D.

Teaching and Learning (Curriculum Design). Admits Summer only. Apply by February 15. M.A.

Teaching and Learning (Bilingual Education/ASL). Admits Summer only. Apply by February 1. CBEST for admission. M.A.

Theatre. Apply by January 4. Audition and/or interview, GRE (acting, design, directing or stage management) for admission. M.F.A.

Visual Arts. Apply by February 1. Portfolio for admission. M.F.A.

School of Medicine (92093-0621)

Opened 1968. State control. Quarter system. Annual tuition/fees: resident $10,570, nonresident $21,274. On-campus housing available. Total average figure all other expenses: $8000.

Enrollment: first-year class 122; total full-time 476 (men 56%, women 44%). Faculty: full-time 170, part-time 500. Degree conferred: M.D. M.D.-M.P.H. Graduate study (Medical Scientist Training Program) degrees offered through Graduate School.

ADMISSION REQUIREMENTS. AMCAS report, transcripts, MCAT, letters of recommendation, interview required in support of application. Applicants must have completed at least three years of college study. Interviews are by invitation. Graduates of unaccredited colleges not considered. Preference given to state and WICHE residents. Does not have EDP. Apply to Director of Admissions after June 1 and before November 1. Application fee $40. Phone: (858)534-3880; fax: (858)534-8282.

ADMISSION STANDARDS. Very selective. Mean science GPA 3.7 (A = 4). Accepts 5–8% of total annual applicants. Approximately 96% are state residents.

FINANCIAL AID. Scholarships, fellowships, grants, loans. About 90% of students receive aid other than loans from School funds. Apply to Financial Aids Officer as soon as possible after acceptance.

DEGREE REQUIREMENTS. For M.D.: satisfactory completion of four-year program. Senior thesis or equivalent required. For M.D.-Ph.D.: seven- to eight-year program.

FIELDS OF STUDY.
Biochemistry.
Bioengineering.
Biology.
Biomedical Sciences.
Biophysics.
Chemistry.
Epidemiology.
Molecular Pathology.
Neurosciences.
Physics.

UNIVERSITY OF CALIFORNIA, SAN FRANCISCO

San Francisco, California 94143
Web site: www.ucsf.edu

Founded 1864. CGS member. Coed. State control. Quarter system. Graduate study only. Special facilities: Cardiovascular Research Institute, Cancer Research Institute, Francis I. Proctor Foundation for Research in Ophthalmology, Hormone Research Laboratory, Institute for Health and Aging, Institute of Health Policy Studies, Laboratory of Radiobiology, Langley Porter Psychiatric Institute, Metabolic Research Unit, Reproductive Endocrinology Center, George Williams Hooper Foundation for Medical Research. NIH ranking is 4th among all U.S. institutions with 854 awards/grants worth $350,417,900. Library: 691,041 volumes, 160,000 microforms.

Tuition/fees: full-time, resident $4615, nonresident $15,509. On-campus housing for 165 married students. Average monthly housing cost: $1261 per month for single students; $2570 per month married students. Apply to Housing Officer. Phone: (415)476-2211.

Graduate Division

Established 1961. Enrollment: full-time 1047. Faculty: full-time 1200, part-time 30. Degrees conferred: M.S., M.A., M.P.T. (Physical Therapy), Ph.D.

ADMISSION REQUIREMENTS. Transcripts, GRE, letters of recommendation required in support of application. Electronic application available. Interview required by some programs. TOEFL (minimum score 550, 213 on computer-based test) required of all international applicants. Accepts transfer applicants. Graduates of unaccredited colleges not considered. Apply to graduate program by the deadline established by each department. Admits Fall only. Application fee $40. Phone: (415)476-2310.

ADMISSION STANDARDS. Very selective for most departments. Minimum average: 3.0 (A = 4).

FINANCIAL AID. Annual awards from institutional funds: fellowships, scholarships, traineeships, grants, teaching/research assistantships, Federal W/S, loans. Application for fellowships and assistantships should be filed with the application for admission, but prior to January 10. For all other aid apply to Office of Financial Aid: no specified closing date. Phone: (415)476-4181. Use FAFSA.

DEGREE REQUIREMENTS. For master's: Plan I—30 quarter units minimum; thesis; Plan II—36 quarter units minimum; advancement to candidacy; no thesis; final comprehensive exam. For Ph.D.: at least six quarters in full-time residence; foreign language requirement determined by department; advancement to candidacy; qualifying exams; dissertation; final oral exam.

FIELDS OF GRADUATE STUDY.
Biochemistry and Molecular Biology.
Bioengineering.
Biological and Medical Informatics.
Biomedical Sciences. Includes anatomy, endocrinology, immunology, microbiology, experimental pathology, physiology.
Biophysics.
Cell Biology.
Chemistry and Chemical Biology.
Genetics.
History of Health Sciences. One language for M.S.
Medical Anthropology.
Neurosciences.
Nursing. M.S., Ph.D.
Oral Biology. M.S., Ph.D.
Pharmaceutical Sciences and Pharmacogenomics.
Physical Therapy.
Sociology.

School of Dentistry (94143-0430)

Established 1881. Special program: International Dental Program for Foreign Trained Dentists. Annual tuition/fees: resident

$10,075, nonresident $21,207. Housing available. Average academic year housing costs: $11,200. Total average cost for all first-year expenses: $10,500. Contact Housing Office for both on- and off-campus housing information. Phone: (415)476-2231.

Enrollment: D.D.S. program, first-year class 82, total 317 (men 50%, women 50%). Graduate enrollment: 49. Faculty: full-time 105, part-time 35. Degree conferred: D.D.S., D.D.S.-M.S., D.D.S.-Ph.D. (DSTP program). The M.S. is offered through the Graduate Division.

ADMISSION REQUIREMENTS. AADSAS report, two official transcripts, DAT, three recommendations required in support of School's application. Supplemental application required by November 1. Interview sometimes requested by School. Applicants must have completed at least three years of college study. Preference given to state and WICHE residents. Does not accept transfer applicants. Does not have EDP. Apply after June 1, before January 1, to Dental Admissions Office, Room S-630. Application fee $40. Phone: (415)476-2737.

ADMISSION STANDARDS. Competitive. Mean GPA: 3.5 (A = 4); mean DAT academic average: 21.1; PAT: 20. Accepts about 25% of total annual applicants.

FINANCIAL AID. Scholarships, grant, Federal W/S, loans. Apply to Financial Aid Office after acceptance. Phone: (415)476-4181. About 52% of first-year students receive some aid from School.

DEGREE REQUIREMENTS. For D.D.S.: satisfactory completion of forty-eight-month program. For M.S., Ph.D.: see Graduate Division listing above.

FIELDS OF GRADUATE STUDY.
Bioengineering.
Bioinformatics.
Epidemiology.
Oral Biology.

School of Medicine

Established as Toland Medical College in 1864, affiliated with UCSF 1873. State Control. Quarter system. Annual tuition/fees: resident $10,340, nonresident $21,044. Total average cost for all other expenses: $15,000.

Enrollment: first-year class 141; total 580 (men 46%, women 54%). graduate 444. Faculty: full-time 1453, part-time 59, volunteers 3483. Degrees conferred: M.D., M.D.-M.S., M.D.-M.P.H., M.D.-Ph.D. Graduate study, Medical Scientist Training Program, joint M.S. program with University of California, Berkeley.

ADMISSION REQUIREMENTS. AMCAS report, transcripts, MCAT, three recommendations required in support of application. A second application is sent out after initial screening. Interview by invitation. Preference given to state and WICHE residents. Graduates of unaccredited colleges not considered. Does not have EDP. Apply to Admissions Office after June 15, before November 1. Application fee $40. Phone: (415)476-4044; e-mail: admissions@medsch.uscf.edu.

ADMISSION STANDARDS. Very competitive. Mean GPA: 3.72 (A = 4.0). Mean MCAT score (Biology): 11. Admits about 5% of total annual applications. Approximately 80% are state residents.

FINANCIAL AID. Limited scholarships, grants, loans (all need-based). Apply after acceptance to Financial Aid Office.

DEGREE REQUIREMENTS. For M.D.: satisfactory completion of four-year program. For M.D.-M.S.: satisfactory completion of five-year programs. For M.D.-Ph.D.: satisfactory completion of six- to seven-year program.

FIELDS OF STUDY.
Biophysics.
Cancer.
Cell Biology.
Chemical Biology.
Chemistry.
Developmental Biology.
Genetics.
Infection and Immunity.
Medical Anthropology.
Molecular Biology and Biochemistry.
Neurosciences.
Tissue and Organ Biology.

School of Nursing
Web site: nurseweb.ucsf.edu

Annual tuition/fees: $6818 resident; $17,950 nonresident.
Enrollment: 175 full-time, part-time 18. School's faculty: full-time 42, part-time 5. Degrees conferred: M.S.N., Ph.D.

ADMISSION REQUIREMENTS. Two transcripts, GRE (doctoral candidate), four letters of recommendation, evidence of licensure as a RN required in support of application. Personal interview is optional. Accepts graduates of accredited colleges only. TOEFL, TWE required for international applicants. Submit all documents by December 31 (doctoral candidates), February 28 (master's candidates) to both the School of Nursing and the Graduate division. Admits Fall only. Application fee $60. Phone (415)476-1435; fax: (415)476-9707.

ADMISSION STANDARDS. Selective. Usual minimum average: 3.0 (A = 4.0).

FINANCIAL AID. Scholarships, nonresident tuition scholarships, traineeships, nursing loans, Federal W/S, loans. Approved for VA benefits. Apply to the Financial Aid Office by February 1 for priority consideration. Phone: (415)476-4181. Use FAFSA for all Federal programs.

DEGREE REQUIREMENTS. For MSN: two-year, full-time 36 credit, six academic quarter program; area of specialization; comprehensive exam. For Ph.D.: four-year, full-time program; qualifying exam; two-year research residency; advancement to candidacy; dissertation; final oral exam.

FIELDS OF STUDY.
Acute Care Nursing.
Advanced Practice Perinatal Nursing.
Adult Nurse Practitioner. Includes integrated complementary healing focus, HIV-AIDS focus.
Cardiovascular Nursing. Includes nursing/genomics, clinical research associate.
Community-Based Care System. Includes clinical research management, community and cross-cultural health, administration.
Critical Care/Trauma Nursing.
Family Nurse Practitioner. Includes urban and rural option.
Gerontological Nursing. Includes nurse practitioner, nursing/genomics.
Health Policy Nursing.
Nurse Midwifery. Includes urban and rural options.
Occupational and Environmental Health. Includes clinical nurse specialist, adult nurse practitioner.
Oncology Nursing. Includes nursing/genomics, oncology/gerontological nurse practitioner.
Psychiatric/Mental Health Nursing. Includes child or adult clinical specialist, primary care.

School of Pharmacy

Tuition/fees: full-time resident $4885, nonresident $15,589. On-campus housing available for single and married students.

Average annual housing cost: $10,500. Apply to Housing office. Phone: (415)476-2231.

Enrollment: Full-time 117, part-time 0. Faculty: full-time 76, volunteers 700. Degrees conferred: M.S. Ph.D.

ADMISSION REQUIREMENTS. Transcripts, GRE, three letters of recommendation, statement of purpose, résumé/curriculum vitae required in support of School's application. TOEFL required for foreign applicants. Graduates of unaccredited institutions not considered. Apply to the Department of Pharmaceutical Chemistry by January 15. Admits Fall quarter only. Application fee $40. Phone: (415)476-2732.

ADMISSION STANDARDS. Competitive. Usual minimum average: 3.0 (A = 4).

FINANCIAL AID. Teaching assistantships, research assistantships, supplemental fellowships, tuition waivers, Federal W/S, loans. Apply to Department; no specified closing date. Use FAFSA. Most doctoral candidates receive funding at the standardized level of $15,200. No aid for M.S. students.

DEGREE REQUIREMENTS. For M.S.: 36 unit program; research project. For Ph.D.: curriculum is individualized to meet student's needs; at least two years in residence; oral qualifying exam; full-time dissertation research; one-year teaching experience as teaching assistant; proficiency in biostatistics for pharmaceutics pathway, and toxicology pathway; dissertation; final oral exam.

FIELDS OF GRADUATE STUDY.
Biological and Medical Informatics. M.S., Ph.D.
Biophysics. Ph.D.
Chemistry and Chemical Biology. Ph.D.
Medicinal Chemistry.
Pharmaceutical Sciences and Pharmacogenics. Ph.D.
Pharmaceutics.
Quantitative Biology. Ph.D.
Toxicology.

UNIVERSITY OF CALIFORNIA, SANTA BARBARA

Santa Barbara, California 93106
Web site: www.ucsb.edu

Founded 1891. Located 100 miles NW of Los Angeles. CGS and AAU member. Coed. State control. Quarter system. Special facilities: Federally Funded Research Centers: Center for Quantized Electronic Structures, Institute for Theoretical Physics, Materials Research Laboratory, National Center for Ecological Analysis & Synthesis, National Center for Geographic Information and Analysis, National Nanofabrication Users Network, Southern California Earthquake Center, Optoelectronics Technology Center; Other Federally Funded Research Centers: ARPA Center for Optical Communications, Center for Computational Modeling & Systems, Center for Non-Stoichiometric Semiconductors, High Performance Composites Center, Multidisciplinary Optical Switching Technology, Long-Term Ecological Research on the Antarctic Marine Ecosystem, Research Project on Forty Gigabit Per Second WDM Fiber Optic Components and Architecture for Telecommunication and Supercomputing, Robust Nonlinear Control of Stall and Flutter in Aeroengines; Organized Research Units: Center for Chicano Studies, Community and Organization Research Institute, Institute for Computational Earth Systems Science, Institute for Crustal Studies, Institute for Polymers and Organic Solids, Marine Science Institute, Neuroscience Research Institute, Quantum Institute; Multi-Campus Research Units: Linguistic Minority Research Institute, Institute for Nuclear Particle Astrophysics & Cosmology; Engineering Research Centers: Center for Computational Modeling & Systems, Center for

Control Engineering & Computation, Center for High-Speed Image Processing, Center for Information Processing Research, Center for Macro-Molecular Science & Engineering, Center for Risk Studies and Safety, Compound Semiconductor Research Center, Ocean Engineering Laboratory, other Research Groups: Center for Black Studies, Interdisciplinary Humanities Center, The Writings of Henry D. Thoreau, Five Natural Land and Water Reserves. Library: 2,200,000 volumes, 24,325 current periodicals.

Annual fees/tuition: full-time, resident $4921, nonresident $15,864. On-campus housing available, average academic year room and board cost: $7600–$11,500. Apply to Housing Office for University housing. Phone: (805)893-4501 (on-campus apartment living), (805)893-4371 (off-campus housing). Day-care facilities available.

Graduate Division

Web site: www.graddiv.uscb.edu

Graduate study since 1954. Enrollment: full-time 2600, part-time 102 (men 60%, women 40%). Faculty: full-time 650. Degrees conferred: M.A., M.Ed., M.E.S.M., M.S., M.F.A., M.M., Certificate Programs, D.M.A., Ph.D.

ADMISSION REQUIREMENTS. Transcripts, three letters of recommendation required in support of application. Electronic application available. GRE/MAT required for most departments. GRE required of all fellowship applicants. TOEFL required for foreign applicants. Interview not required. Graduates of unaccredited colleges not considered. Apply by May 1 (Fall), November 1 (Winter), February 1 (Spring), May 1 (Summer—earlier deadline for some majors and fellowships consideration, see Fields of Study below for early deadlines). Application fee $40. Phone: (805)893-2277; fax: (805)893-8259; e-mail: admissions@graddiv.uscb.edu.

ADMISSION STANDARDS. Selective for all departments. Usual minimum average: 3.0 (A = 4).

FINANCIAL AID. Annual awards from institutional funds: scholarships, teaching assistantships, research fellowships, nonresident waivers, Federal W/S, loans. Approved for VA benefits. Apply by mid-January to Graduate Division for scholarships, to appropriate department chair for assistantships and fellowships; apply by March 1 to Financial Aid Office for all other programs. Phone: (805)893-2432; e-mail: financial@graddiv.uscb.edu. Use FAFSA.

DEGREE REQUIREMENTS. For master's: Plan I—30 units minimum, at least 3 quarters in residence; thesis; final written exam; Plan II—36 units minimum, comprehensive exam; reading knowledge of one foreign language for some majors. For Ph.D.: two years (48–72 credits) minimum, at least 6 quarters in residence, including three consecutive quarters; qualifying exam; advancement to candidacy; dissertation or thesis; preliminary, final oral exams; reading knowledge of one or two foreign languages.

FIELDS OF STUDY.
Anthropology. Writing sample for admission. Apply by December 1. Includes Archaeology (M.A. only.) M.A., Ph.D.
Applied Mathematics. GRE Subject for admission. Apply by January 1. M.A., Ph.D.
Art History. Writing sample for admission. Apply by January 15. Ph.D.
Art Studio. Portfolio for admissions. Apply by January 1 for Financial support, April 1 for admission only. M.F.A.
Asian Studies. Apply by May 1. Includes East Asian Languages and Cultural Studies. M.A. only.
Biochemistry—Molecular Biology. GRE Subject recommended for admission. Apply by December 15. Includes bioengineering and biomaterials. Ph.D.
Chemical Engineering. Apply by January 31. Includes computational science and engineering. M.S., Ph.D.

Chemistry. Admits Fall, Winter, Spring. M.A., M.S., Ph.D.

Classics. Writing sample for admission. Includes ancient history, literature and theory. Admits Fall, Winter, Spring. M.A., Ph.D.

Communication. Includes human development, quantitative methods in the social sciences. Apply by January 15. Ph.D.

Comparative Literature. Writing sample for admission. Admits Fall, Winter, Spring. M.A., Ph.D.

Computer Science. Includes computational science and engineering. Apply by January 15 for financial support; by April 1 for admissions only. M.S., Ph.D.

Counseling, Clinical, School Psychology. GRE or MAT, writing sample, background questionnaire for admission. Apply by December 10. M.Ed., Ph.D.

Dramatic Art. Writing sample for admission. Includes European medieval studies. Apply by January 15 (Ph.D.), April 1 (M.A.). M.A., Ph.D.

Ecology, Evolution, and Marine Biology. Apply by December 15. M.A., Ph.D.

Economics. Includes business economics (M.A. only). Apply by December 15. M.A., Ph.D.

Education. Includes cultural perspectives, developmental studies, educational leadership, research methodology, special education, disabilities and risk studies, teaching and learning, administrative services. Apply by December 15 for financial support, May 1 for admission only. M.A., M.Ed., Credential Certificate, Ph.D.

Electrical and Computer Engineering. Includes computer engineering, communications, control and signal processing, electronic and photonics. Admits Fall (Ph.D. only), Winter, Spring. M.S., Ph.D.

English. GRE Subject, writing sample for admission. Includes European medieval studies, women's studies. M.A., Ph.D.

Environmental Science and Management. Admits December 15 for financial support, May 1 for admission only. M.E.S.M., Ph.D.

French. Writing sample, tape of spoken French for admission. Admits Fall, Winter, Spring. M.A., Ph.D.

Geography. Apply by January 15. M.A., Ph.D.

Geological Science. Includes geophysics (M.S.). Admits Fall, Winter, Spring. M.S., Ph.D.

Germanic Languages and Literatures. Writing sample, tape of spoken German and English, research paper in German or English for admission. Admits Fall, Winter, Spring. M.A., Ph.D.

Hispanic Languages and Literatures. Two writing samples for admission. Apply by January 5 (Fall) for financial support; admits Fall, Winter, Spring. M.A., Ph.D.

History. Two writing sample for admission. Includes public historical studies. Apply by December 15 for financial support, January 15 for admission only. Ph.D.

Latin American and Iberian Studies. Writing sample for admission. Apply Fall, Winter, Spring. M.A. only.

Linguistic. Copy of publications or professional papers. Apply by January 4. Ph.D.

Marine Science. Apply by December 15. M.S., Ph.D.

Materials. Admits Fall, Winter, Spring. M.S., Ph.D.

Mathematics. GRE Subject for admission. Apply January 1. M.A., Ph.D.

Mechanical Engineering. Apply by January 15 for financial support (Fall), May 1 for admission only. Admits Fall, Winter, Spring. M.S., Ph.D.

Media Arts and Technology. Includes multimedia engineering (M.S.), music and sound design (M.A.), visual and spatial arts (M.A.). Apply by January 15. M.A., M.S.

Molecular, Cellular and Developmental Biology. GRE Subject for admission. Apply by January 7. M.A., Ph.D.

Music. Writing sample, videotape, or audition for admission. Includes composition, ethnomusicology, musicology, theory (M.A., Ph.D.), conducting, keyboard, strings, voice (M.M., D.M.A), woodwinds/brass, piano accompanying (M.M.). M.A., M.M., D.M.A., Ph.D.

Philosophy. Writing sample for admission. Apply by December 15 for financial support, May 1 for admission. Admits Fall, Winter, Spring. Ph.D.

Physics. GRE Subject for admission. Apply by January 15. Ph.D.

Political Science. Writing sample for admission. Apply by January 1. M.A., Ph.D.

Portuguese. Two writing samples for admission. Apply by January 5 for financial support, April 15 for admission only. Admits Fall, Winter, Spring. M.A., Ph.D.

Psychology. GRE Subject suggested, GRE writing recommended for admission. Apply for December 15. M.A., Ph.D.

Religious Studies. Apply by December 15. M.A., Ph.D.

Sociology. Writing sample required, GRE Subject optional for admission. Apply by December 31. Ph.D.

Spanish. Two writing samples for admission. Apply by January 5 for financial support, April 15 for admission only (Fall). Admits Fall, Winter, Spring. M.A., Ph.D.

Spanish and Portuguese. Two writing samples for admission. Apply by January 5 for financial support, April 15 for admission only (Fall). Admits Fall, Winter, Spring.

Statistics and Applied Probability. Includes mathematical and empirical finance. Admits Fall, Winter, Spring. M.A., Ph.D.

Statistics and Applied Probability. Ph.D.

UNIVERSITY OF CALIFORNIA, SANTA CRUZ

Santa Cruz, California 95064

Web site: www.usc.edu

Opened 1965. Located in the redwoods of California's central coast, 75 miles S of San Francisco. CGS member. Coed. Public control. Quarter system. Special facilities: Syntax Research Center, Lick Observatory, forest ecology and marine environments, Center for Non-Linear Science, Santa Cruz Institute for Particle Physics, Tectonics Institute, Third World Teaching Resource Center. Library: more than 1,000,000 volumes, 600,000 microforms, 9100 current periodicals.

Annual tuition/fees: residents $5328, nonresidents $16,032. On-campus housing consists of 199 apartments for graduate men and women with priority given to married couples. Average academic year housing cost: $10,000 (includes board), $6600–$7600 for married students. Phone: (831)459-2394. For family student housing: phone: (831)459-2549.

Graduate Studies

Graduate study initiated in 1966. Enrollment: full- and part-time 1100. University faculty for graduate students: full-time 500. Degrees conferred: M.A., M.S., Professional Certificate, Ph.D.

ADMISSION REQUIREMENTS. Transcripts, GRE, three letters of recommendation, statement of purpose required in support of application. GRE/Subject recommended for most programs. TOEFL (minimum score 550, 220 for computer-based test) required for international applicants. Interview not required. Accepts transfer applicants. Graduate program deadlines vary: December 1–February 1. Fall admission only. Rolling admissions process. Application fee $40. Phone: (831)459-2301.

ADMISSION STANDARDS. Very selective or competitive for most departments. Usual minimum average: 3.0 (A = 4).

FINANCIAL AID. Annual awards from institutional funds: scholarships, teaching assistantships, research assistantships, grants, loans. Apply by February 1 to Graduate Office for assistantships; to the Financial Aid Office for all other programs. Phone: (831)459-2335. Use FAFSA (University code: 001321).

About 65% of students receive aid other than loans from University and outside sources.

DEGREE REQUIREMENTS. For master's: requirements vary, but normally include one year of course work; thesis/nonthesis option; final written exam. Some programs require reading knowledge of one foreign language. For Certificates: varies by program. For Ph.D.: requirements vary, but normally include two years of course work beyond the master's; preliminary exam; reading knowledge of one foreign language; dissertation; final written/oral exam.

FIELDS OF STUDY.
Anthropology. Ph.D. only.
Astronomy and Astrophysics. Ph.D. only.
Biology. M.A., Ph.D.
Chemistry and Biochemistry. M.S., Ph.D.
Computer Engineering. M.S., Ph.D.
Computer Sciences. M.S., Ph.D.
Earth Sciences. M.S., Ph.D.
Economics. Includes applied, international. M.S., Ph.D.
Education. M.A. only.
Environmental Studies. Ph.D. only
History. Ph.D. only.
History of Consciousness. Ph.D. only.
Linguistics. M.A., Ph.D.
Literature. M.A., Ph.D.
Marine Sciences. M.S. only.
Mathematics. M.A., Ph.D.
Music. M.A. only.
Ocean Sciences. Ph.D. only.
Philosophy. M.A., Ph.D.
Physics. M.S., Ph.D.
Psychology. Includes developmental, experimental, social. Ph.D. only.
Science Communication. Application deadline April 1. Certificate only.
Sociology. Ph.D. only.
Theater Arts. Application deadline March 1. Certificate only.

CALIFORNIA WESTERN SCHOOL OF LAW
225 Cedar Street
San Diego, California 92101-3046
Web site: www.cwsl.edu

Chartered in 1924. Located in downtown San Diego. ABA approved since 1962. AALS member since 1967. Private control. Trimester system. Library: 279,907 volumes. Library has LEXIS, NEXIS, WESTLAW, DIALOG. 12 PCs in library.

Annual tuition: $22,270. No on-campus housing available. Total average annual additional expenses: $13,976.

Enrollment: first-year class full-time 299, part-time 27; total full-time 735 (men 48%, women 52%). Faculty: full-time 28, part-time 27. Student to faculty ratio 20.9 to 1. Degree conferred: J.D., J.D.-M.B.A., J.D.-M.S.W., J.D.-Ph.D. (Political Science, History).

ADMISSION REQUIREMENTS. LSDAS Law School report, transcripts, LSAT, three recommendations, bachelor's degree required in support of application. Interview granted on request. Accepts transfer applicants from ABA accredited law schools only. Apply to Director of Admissions after September 1, before April 1 (Fall), November 1 (Spring). Application fee $45. Phone: (619)239-0391, (800)255-4252; fax: (619)615-1401; e-mail: admissions@cwsl.edu.

ADMISSION STANDARDS. Selective. Median LSAT: 151; median GPA: 3.08 (A = 4). Gourman rating: 3.05. *U.S. News &*

World Report ranking is in the fourth tier of all law schools. Accepts 45–50% of total annual applicants.

FINANCIAL AID. Scholarships, full and partial tuition grants, Federal W/S, loans. Apply to Director of Financial Aid after acceptance but before March 15. Use FAFSA. About 35% of students receive some aid from School.

DEGREE REQUIREMENTS. For J.D.: 89 semester hours minimum, at least forty-five hours and three semesters in residence. Optional two-year program is also available. For master's degrees: see San Diego State University's institutional listing. For Ph.D. degree: see University of California at San Diego listing.

CAMPBELL UNIVERSITY
Buies Creek, North Carolina 27506
Web site: www.campell.edu

Founded in 1887. Located 30 miles south of Raleigh. Coed. Private control. Southern Baptist. Semester system. Library: 196,000 volumes, 1700 subscriptions. More than 250 computers on campus for general student use.

Tuition: per semester hour $195 (Education), $290 (Business), $450 (M.S.C.R., M.S.P.S.). On-campus housing for single and married students. Annual housing cost: $3200. Apply by July 1 to Director of Housing. Phone: (910)893-1200, ext. 2226. Day-care facilities available.

Graduate Studies

Enrollment: full- and part-time 1286. Faculty: 99 full- and part-time. Degrees conferred: M.B.A., M.S., M.Ed., M.Div., M.A.C.E., M.S.C.R., M.S.P.S.

ADMISSION REQUIREMENTS. Transcripts, GRE/MAT, letters of recommendation required in support of University's application. GMAT required for business programs. TOEFL (minimum score 580) required for international applicants. Graduates of unaccredited colleges not considered. Apply to the Director of Graduate Admissions at least forty-five days prior to expected semester of entrance. Application fee $25. Phone: (910)893-1200, ext. 1318; fax: (910)893-9850.

ADMISSION STANDARDS. Relatively open. Usual minimum average: 2.5 (A = 4).

FINANCIAL AID. Scholarships, assistantships, internships, Federal W/S, loans. Apply to the Director of Financial Aid; no specified closing date. Phone: (800)334-4111, ext. 1310. Use FAFSA. Aid available for part-time students.

DEGREE REQUIREMENTS. For M.A., M.Ed., M.S.A.: 33–48 credits minimum, at least 24 in residence; thesis/research paper/field experience/final written exam. For M.S.C.R., M.S.P.S.: 46 credit program; research project. For M.B.A.: 33 credits minimum; comprehensive oral exam. For M.Div.: 90 semester hour, three-year, full-time program; supervised ministry. For M.A.C.E.: 60 semester hour, two-year, full-time program; concentration; supervised ministry.

FIELDS OF STUDY.

FUNDY-FETTERMAN SCHOOL OF BUSINESS:
Business Administration. M.B.A.

SCHOOL OF DIVINITY:
Christian Education. M.Div.
Christian Social Ministries. M.A.C.E.

Church Staff Ministries. M.A.C.E.
Counseling and Chaplaincy. M.Div.
Education and Music Ministries. M.A.C.E.
Lay and Marketplace Ministries. M.A.C.E.
Missions and Evangelism. M.Div.
Music and Worship. M.Div.
Pastoral Ministries. M.Div.

SCHOOL OF EDUCATION:
Administration. M.S.A.
Community Counseling. M.A.
Elementary Education. M.Ed.
Middle Grades Education. M.Ed.
Physical Education. M.Ed.
School Counseling. M.Ed.
Science Education. M.Ed.

SCHOOL OF PHARMACY:
Clinical Research. M.S.C.R.
Pharmaceutical Science. Includes concentrations in bioprocessing/biotechnology, industrial pharmacology, pharmaceutical analysis, pharmacology. M.S.P.S.

Norman Adrian Wiggins School of Law
Box 158

Established 1976. ABA approved since 1979. Private control. Semester system. Library: 196,000 volumes; has LEXIS, NEXIS, WESTLAW.
Annual tuition: resident $18,988. Enrollment: first-year class 120; total 304 (men 51%, women 49%). Faculty: full-time 16, part-time 8. Student to faculty ratio 15.8 to 1. Degree conferred: J.D., J.D.-M.B.A.

ADMISSION REQUIREMENTS. LSDAS Law School report, transcripts, bachelor's degree, LSAT, recommendations required in support of application. Interview by invitation. Graduates of unaccredited colleges not considered. Apply by March 31 (priority deadline) to Director of Admissions. Application fee $40. Phone: (910)893-1754; fax: (910)893-1780; e-mail: culaw@webster.campbell.edu.

ADMISSION STANDARDS. Selective. Median LSAT: 151; median GPA: 3.17 (A = 4). Gourman rating: 2.16. *U.S. News & World Report* rating is in the third tier of all law schools. Admits about 15% of total annual applications.

FINANCIAL AID. Full and partial scholarships, grants, assistantships, Federal W/S, loans. Apply by April 15 to Director of Admissions. Use FAFSA. About 20–30% of students receive some aid from School.

DEGREE REQUIREMENTS. For J.D.: satisfactory completion of 90 semester hour program. For M.B.A.: see Graduate Studies listing.

CANISIUS COLLEGE
Buffalo, New York 14208-1098
Web site: www.canisius.edu

Founded 1870. Coed. Private control. Roman Catholic Jesuit. Semester system. Library: 280,000 volumes, 502,300 microforms, 1150 current periodicals, 68 PCs in all libraries.
Tuition: per credit, Education $500, M.B.A. $621. On-campus housing for 100 graduate students. Average academic year housing costs: $7540 (including board). Contact Office of Residence Life for both on- and off-campus housing information. Phone: (716)888-2220.

Graduate Division

Graduate study since 1919. Enrollment: full-time 450, part-time 1000. Faculty teaching graduate students: full-time 40, part-time 100. Degrees conferred: M.S., M.B.A., M.B.A.P.A., M.S., M.S.O.C.D.

ADMISSION REQUIREMENTS. Two official transcripts, GRE, two letters of recommendation required in support of application. For Education program, two transcripts for admission. TOEFL required for international applicants. Accepts transfer applicants. Graduates of unaccredited institutions not considered. Apply to Director of Admissions by July 1 (Fall), November 1 (Spring), April 15 (Summer). Application fee $25. Phone: Education (800)950-2505 or (716)888-2545; fax: (716)888-3290; Business (800)543-7906.

ADMISSION STANDARDS. Selective. Usual minimum average: 2.5 (A = 4).

FINANCIAL AID. Scholarships assistantships, Federal W/S, loans. Apply to Office of Financial Aid; no specified closing date. Use FAFSA (College code: 002681). Phone: (716)888-2300.

DEGREE REQUIREMENTS. For M.B.A.: 48 credit program; internship. For M.B.A.P.A.: 61 credit program; capstone. For M.S. (Education): 33–45 credits for most majors; thesis/nonthesis options for all majors. For M.S. (Telecommunications): 37 credit program; capstone. For M.S.O.C.D.: 36 credit program; 15 credits are taken in School of Business.

FIELDS OF STUDY.

COLLEGE OF ARTS AND SCIENCES:
Organizational Communication and Development. M.S.O.C.D.

RICHARD J. WEHLE SCHOOL OF BUSINESS:
Business Administration. One-year, full-time. M.B.A.
Business Administration. Evening, part-time. M.B.A.
Professional Accounting. M.B.A.P.A.
Telecommunications. M.S.

SCHOOL OF EDUCATION AND HUMAN SERVICES:
College Student Personnel Administration.
Counseling Education. Includes agency counseling, rehabilitation counseling, school counseling, substance abuse counseling.
Deaf Education.
Educational Administration and Supervision.
Health and Human Performance.
Physical Education.
Reading Education.
Special Education.
Sport Administration.
Teacher Education (Elementary).
Teacher Education (Secondary).

CAPITAL UNIVERSITY
2199 E. Main Street
Columbus, Ohio 43209-2394
Web site: www.capital.edu

Founded 1830. Coed. Lutheran. Semester system. Library: 376,000 volumes, 90,000 microforms, 55 PC workstations; OHIONET.
Annual tuition: per credit hour, M.B.A. $340, Nursing $310, Music $295. Evening program only. No on-campus housing.

Graduate School of Administration

Enrollment: part-time 300 (men 150, women 150). Faculty: full-time 7, part-time 18. Degree conferred: M.B.A.

ADMISSION REQUIREMENTS. Transcripts, GMAT (minimum score 550), interview required in support of application. Accepts transfer applicants and graduates of accredited colleges. Applicants must have two years' work experience and be employed full-time. Preference given to Central Ohio residents. TOEFL (minimum score 550, 213 on computer-based test) required for international applicants. Apply to Director of Admissions; no specified closing date. Admits Fall and Spring. Application fee $25. Phone: (614)236-6162; fax: (614)236-6540.

ADMISSION STANDARDS. Selective. Usual minimum average. 3.0 (A = 4).

FINANCIAL AID. Federal W/S, loans only. Apply to Financial Aid Office; no specified closing date. Use FAFSA. Phone: (614)236-6511; e-mail: finaid@capital.edu.

DEGREE REQUIREMENTS. For M.B.A.: 40 credits in residence; research paper option.

Law School and Graduate Center (43215)

Established 1903 as Columbus College of Law, affiliated with Capital University in 1966. Located downtown in the Discovery district, adjacent to German Village. ABA approved since 1950. AALS member. Semester system. Special facilities: Center for Dispute Resolution, the Ethics Institute, Institute for Citizen Education, Institute for International Legal Education. Library: 252,100 volumes; has LEXIS, NEXIS, WESTLAW, INFOTRAC.

Annual tuition: full-time $16,352, part-time $11,680. Limited off-campus housing available. Total average annual additional expense: $11,681. Enrollment: first-year class 160 (day), 86 (evening); total 736 (men 53%, women 47%). Faculty: full-time 24, part-time 29. Student to faculty ratio 21.6 to 1. Degree conferred: J.D., J.D.-M.B.A., J.D.-M.S.(Nursing), J.D.-M.S.A. (Sports Administration with Ohio University), J.D.-LL.M. (Taxation), LL.M. (Taxation, Business and Taxation).

ADMISSION REQUIREMENTS. LSDAS Law School report, transcripts, LSAT, essay required in support of application. Interview by invitation only. Preference is given to state residents. Graduates of unaccredited colleges not considered. Apply to Director of Admissions by May 1. Application fee $35. Phone: (614)236-6500; fax: (614)236-6972; e-mail: admissions@law.capital.edu.

ADMISSION STANDARDS. Selective. Median LSAT: 149; median GPA: 3.11 (A = 4.0). Gourman rating: 2.78. *U.S. News & World Report* ranking is in the fourth tier of all law schools. Accepts about 50–60% of total annual applications. Approximately 45% of enrolled students are nonresidents.

FINANCIAL AID. Scholarships, research and teaching assistantships, Federal W/S, loans. Apply as early as possible after application has been filed to Director of Admissions before April 1. Use FAFSA. About 37% of students receive some aid from School.

DEGREE REQUIREMENTS. For J.D.: satisfactory completion of 86-semester hour program. For LL.M.: satisfactory completion of one-year program beyond J.D. For master's degree: see Graduate School listing above and Ohio University listings.

School of Nursing

Established in 1950, graduate study since 1994.

Enrollment: full-time 22, part-time 18. School's Faculty: full-time 11, part-time 5. Degree conferred: M.S.N., M.S.N.-M.B.A., M.S.N.-J.D.

ADMISSION REQUIREMENTS. Transcripts, writing sample, résumé, GRE, three professional references, interview required in support of application. Accepts transfer applicants and gradu-

ates of accredited colleges. Preference given to Central Ohio residents. TOEFL (minimum score 550) required for international applicants. Apply to Director of Admissions; no specified closing date. Admits Fall and Spring. Application fee $25. Phone: (614)236-6361; fax: (614)236-6157.

ADMISSION STANDARDS. Selective. Usual minimum average. 3.0 (A = 4).

FINANCIAL AID. Scholarships, Federal W/S, loans only. Apply to Financial Aid Office; no specified closing date. Phone: (614)236-6115. Use FAFSA.

DEGREE REQUIREMENTS. For M.S.N.: at least 36–42 credits in residence; thesis or project.

FIELDS OF STUDY.
Administration.
Family and Community Health Nursing.
Occupational Health Nursing.
Parish Nursing.
School Health Nursing.

CARDINAL STRITCH COLLEGE
Milwaukee, Wisconsin 53217-3985
Web site: www.stritch.edu

Chartered 1937. Coed. Private control. Roman Catholic. Semester system. Library: 773,000 volumes, 700 subscriptions. More than 250 computers on campus for general student use.

Tuition: per credit $415. On-campus single housing limited to a space-available basis; none for married students. Average academic year housing costs: $4800 (including board). Phone: (414)352-5400, ext. 347. Day-care facilities available.

Graduate Division

Graduate study since 1956. Enrollment: full- and part-time 1734. Graduate faculty: full-time 57, part-time 212. Degrees conferred: M.A., M.B.A., M.Ed, M.S.

ADMISSION REQUIREMENTS. Official transcripts, GMAT (Business), MAT (Education) required in support of application. TOEFL required for international applicants. Interview not required. Accepts transfer applicants. Graduates of unaccredited colleges not considered. Apply to Graduate Admission Office at least three weeks prior to registration. Application fee $25. Phone: (414)410-4040.

ADMISSION STANDARDS. Relatively open. Usual minimum average: 2.5 (A = 4).

FINANCIAL AID. Annual awards from College funds: assistantships, Federal W/S, loans. Approved for VA benefits. Apply by May 1 to Chair of the Graduate Committee for assistantships; to Financial Aid Office for all other programs. Phone: (800)347-8822, ext. 4048. Use FAFSA. About 5% of students receive aid other than loans from College and outside sources.

DEGREE REQUIREMENTS. For M.B.A.: 33–36 credits minimum, at least 24 in residence; thesis, research paper/field experience; final written exam. For M.A.: 35 credits minimum; practice/research option. For M.Ed., M.S.: 30–31 credits minimum; thesis/nonthesis option; comprehensive exam.

FIELDS OF STUDY.

COLLEGE OF ARTS AND SCIENCE:
Clinical Psychology. M.A.

History. M.A.
Religious Studies. M.A.
Visual Studies. M.A.

COLLEGE OF BUSINESS AND MANAGEMENT:
Business Administration. M.B.A.
Financial Services. M.S.
Health Care Executives. M.B.A.
Management. M.S.

COLLEGE OF EDUCATION:
Educational Computing. M.Ed.
Computer Science Education. M.S.
Educational Leadership. M.S.
Leadership for the Advancement of Learning and Service. M.Ed.
Professional Development. M.Ed.
Reading/Language Arts. M.A.
Reading/Learning Disability. M.A.
Special Education. M.A.
Teaching. M.A.

COLLEGE OF NURSING:
Nursing. M.S.

CARNEGIE MELLON UNIVERSITY

Pittsburgh, Pennsylvania 15213-3891
Web site: www.cmu.edu

Founded 1900. Coed. CGS and AAU member. Private control. Semester system. Special facilities: Center for the Materials of the Artist and Conservator, Center for Building Performance and Diagnostics, Center for Machine Translation, Center for the Management of Technology, Center for Molecular Genetics, Center for the Study of Public Policy, Communications Design Center, Engineering Design Center, Laboratory for Computational Linguistics, Mellon Institute, National Center for the Study of Writing, Robotics Institute, Software Engineering Institute, Statistical Center for Quality Improvement. Library: 961,500 volumes, 5700 subscriptions. Total University enrollment: 8000.

Annual tuition; full time $23,300, per credit $324. No on-campus housing available. Average annual housing cost: $11,760. For off-campus housing: phone (412)268-2139. Day-care facilities available.

Carnegie Institute of Technology
Graduate Engineering

Web site: www.cit.cmu.edu

Tuition: full-time $23,300, per credit $324. No on-campus housing available.

Enrollment: full-time 541, part-time 64. Faculty: full-time 190. Degrees conferred: M.S., M.Ch.E., M.E., Ph.D.

ADMISSION REQUIREMENTS. Transcripts, three letters of recommendation, GRE/Subject tests required in support of Institute's application. TOEFL required of foreign applicants. Interview not required. Accepts transfer applicants. Graduates of unaccredited institutions not considered. Apply to department of interest by February 1, January 15 for Electrical and Computer Engineering (Fall), October 15 (Spring). Application fee $35. Phone: (412)268-2482.

ADMISSION STANDARDS. Selective. Usual minimum average: 3.0 (A = 4). *U.S. News & World Report* ranked engineering program 10, computer engineering 10.

FINANCIAL AID. Teaching assistantships, fellowships, research assistantships/fellowships, tuition waivers, Federal W/S, loans. Approved for VA benefits. Apply by February 1 (preferably) to department of interest for scholarships, fellowships, and assistantships; to Financial Aid Office for Federal Funds, for priority consideration by February 1. Phone: (412)269-2478. Use FAFSA and CMU FAF.

DEGREE REQUIREMENTS. For M.S.: one-year, full-time study beyond bachelor's degree; comprehensive final oral/written exam; thesis for some departments. For M.E.: two-year, full-time study beyond bachelor's; comprehensive exam; project. For Ph.D.: three years minimum beyond the bachelor's degree, at least one in full-time residence; qualifying exam; dissertation; final oral public exam.

FIELDS OF STUDY.
Biomedical Engineering. Interdisciplinary.
Chemical Engineering. M.S., M.Ch.E., Ph.D.
Civil and Environmental Engineering. M.S., Ph.D.
Colloids, Polymer, and Surfaces. Interdisciplinary.
Electrical and Computer Engineering. M.S., Ph.D.
Engineering and Public Policy. Ph.D.
Information Networking. Interdisciplinary.
Materials Science and Engineering. M.E., Ph.D.
Mechanical Engineering. M.S., Ph.D.

College of Fine Arts Graduate Division

Web site: www.cmu.edu/cfa

Annual tuition: $26,380 (Architecture), $24,760 (School of Design), $25,000 (Drama). Enrollment: full-time 181, part-time 23. College faculty teaching graduate students: full-time 66, part-time 7. Degrees conferred: M.S., M.A.M., M.Des., M.F.A., M.M., M.M.M.Ed., Ph.D.

ADMISSION REQUIREMENTS. Transcripts, three letters of reference, statement of purpose, portfolio/audition required in support of application. Interview for most departments. TOEFL required for all students whose native language is not English. Accepts transfer applicants. Apply to the Department by February 1. Fall admission only. Application fee $50. Phone: (412)268-2349.

ADMISSION STANDARDS. Very competitive.

FINANCIAL AID. Annual awards from institutional funds: scholarships, fellowships and half-tuition fellowships, research assistantships, internships, tuition remission, Federal W/S, loans. Apply by April 1 to appropriate department chair for fellowships, assistantships; to Financial Aid Office for all other programs. Phone: (412)268-8186. Use FAFSA. About 50% of students receive aid other than loans from College and outside sources.

DEGREE REQUIREMENTS. For M.Arch: nine-month, full-time program; final project; thesis/nonthesis option; final written/oral exam. For M.F.A.: three-year, full-time program; M.F.A. project/thesis. For M.S., M.Des.: two-year, full-time programs. For M.M.: two-year, full-time program; recital. For M.M.M.Ed.: one-year, full-time program, candidacy; thesis/recital; comprehensive exam. For Ph.D.: two years minimum in residence; qualifying exam; dissertation; final oral exam.

FIELDS OF STUDY.

SCHOOL OF ARCHITECTURE:
Architecture. M.S.A.
Architecture Engineering Construction Management. M.S.A.E.C.M.
Design or Building Performance and Diagnostics. M.Sc., Ph.D.
Sustainable Design. M.S.

SCHOOL OF ART:
Art. M.F.A.

Arts Management. Joint degree with School of Public Policy and Management. M.A.M.

SCHOOL OF DESIGN:
Design Theory, Interaction Design, Typography and Information Design. M.Des.
Interactive Design, Communication Planning and Information Design. M.Des.
New Product Development. Ph.D.

SCHOOL OF DRAMA:
Directing. M.F.A.
Drama. M.F.A.
Dramatic Writing. M.F.A.
Production Design. Includes costumes, lighting, scenery. M.F.A.

SCHOOL OF MUSIC:
Composition. M.M.
Conducting. M.M.
Education. M.M.M.Ed.
Opera Theater. M.M.
Performance. M.M.

College of Humanities and Social Sciences

Enrollment: full-time 142 part-time 81. Faculty: full-time 180, part-time 37. Degrees conferred: M.A., M.S., Ph.D.

ADMISSION REQUIREMENTS. Transcripts, additional application form, three letters of recommendation, GRE required in support of College's application. TOEFL required for foreign applicants; TSE and TOEFL required for foreign applicants in psychology. Interview not required. Accepts transfer applicants. Apply to individual departmental chairs by April 15 (Fall) in History: February; in English: March 1; prior to registration for other sessions. Application fee: generally $35, but varies by department. Dean's Phone: (412)268-2830.

ADMISSION STANDARDS. Selective to very selective. Usual minimum average: 3.0 (A = 4).

FINANCIAL AID. Annual awards from institutional funds: scholarships, teaching fellowships, research fellowships, research assistantships, teaching assistantships, tuition waivers, Federal W/S, loans. Apply to the appropriate departmental chairman and to Financial Aid Office by March 15. Phone: (412)268-2068. Use FAFSA. About 100% of students receive aid other than loans from College and outside sources.

DEGREE REQUIREMENTS. For M.A., M.S.: two-year, full-time program; thesis. For Ph.D.: flexible individualized programs and varies by department.

FIELDS OF STUDY.
Economics. Provided by faculty of the Graduate School of Industrial Administration. Ph.D.
English. Includes rhetoric, literary and cultural studies, professional writing, creative writing. M.A., Ph.D.
History. Includes history and policy, social and cultural history. Ph.D.
Philosophy. Includes logic and computation (M.S.), logic, computation and logic (Ph.D.). M.A., M.S., Ph.D.
Psychology. Includes cognitive psychology, social psychology, developmental psychology, cognitive neuroscience.
Second Language Acquisition. Ph.D.
Social and Decision Sciences. Includes behavioral decision research, organizational behavior, organizational science, technological change and industrial evaluation, political psychology and economy.
Statistics. M.S., Ph.D.

Mellon College of Science

Annual tuition: $26,380 full-time, $293 per unit part-time.
Enrollment: full-time 192, part-time 6. Faculty full-time 196, part-time 3. Degrees conferred: M.S., Ph.D.

ADMISSION REQUIREMENTS. Transcripts, additional application form, three letters of recommendation, GRE required in support of departmental application. TOEFL (minimum score 600–620) required for all foreign applicants. Accepts transfer applicants. Apply to individual departmental chairs by April 15 (Fall master's programs), February 1 (Fall doctoral programs), January 15 (Fall mathematics programs). Application fee: $35. Dean's phone: (412)268-6400.

ADMISSION STANDARDS. Selective. Usual minimum average: 3.0 (A = 4).

FINANCIAL AID. Scholarships, fellowships, research/teaching assistantships, traineeships, tuition waiver, Federal W/S, loans. Apply to appropriate department chairman and to Financial Aid Office by April 15. Phone: (412)268-2086. Use FAFSA. 100% of students receive aid other than loans from College and outside sources.

DEGREE REQUIREMENTS. Determined by each department and varies by program.

FIELDS OF STUDY.
Chemistry. Includes organic, bioorganics and materials chemistry, bioorganic and organometallic chemistry, biophysical chemistry and spectroscopy, chemical physics, green and environmental chemistry, nuclear chemistry, polymer science, theoretical and computational chemistry.
Computational Biology.
Mathematics. Includes algorithms, combinatorics and optimization, computational finance, mathematical finance, mathematical sciences, pure and applied logic.
Physics. Includes astrophysics, biological physics, computational physics, experimental condensed matter physics, experimental high energy physics, experimental medium energy physics, quantun theory, theoretical condensed matter physics, theoretical high energy physics, theoretical nuclear/medium energy physics.
Note: Interdisciplinary programs available in Biomedical and Health Engineering, Colloids, Polymers and Surfaces, Merck Computational Biology and Computational Chemistry.

School of Computer Science
Web site: www.sc.cmu.edu

Department of Computer Science established in 1965, became School 1988.
Annual tuition: full-time $26,380, part-time $293 per unit.
Enrollment: 398 total (261 doctoral candidates, 137 master's candidates; men 85%, women 15%). Faculty: 197 full-time, 1 part-time. Degree conferred: Ph.D. School does not offer a master of Computer Science but does participate in many master's degrees jointly with related programs or disciplines of other CMU Schools/Colleges.

ADMISSION REQUIREMENTS. Transcripts, GRE, statement of purpose, résumé, three letters of recommendation required in support of application. GRE Subject recommended for most programs. TOEFL (minimum score 600–620) required for foreign applicants. Apply to School by January 5. Application fee $75. Dean's phone: (412)268-2592.

ADMISSION STANDARDS. Selective. Usual minimum average: 3.0 GPA (A = 4).

FINANCIAL AID. Scholarships, fellowships, research/teaching assistantships, grants, tuition waivers, Federal W/S, loans. Apply February 1 to appropriate departmental chair for fellowships, assistantships, by March 15 to Financial Aid Office for all need-based programs. Phone: (412)268-2086. Use FAFSA. About 100% of doctoral candidate's receive aid other than loans from School and outside sources.

DEGREE REQUIREMENTS. Determined by each department and varies by program.

FIELDS FOR DOCTORAL STUDY.
Computational and Statistical Learning.
Computer Science. Includes specializations in algorithms, combinatorics and optimization, neural basis of cognition, pure and applied logic.
Human-Computer Interaction.
Language and Information Technologies.
Robotics. Includes specialization in neural basis of cognition.
Software Engineering.

FIELDS FOR MASTER'S STUDY.
Computational Finance.
Computer-Assisted Language Learning.
Distance Education.
Electronic Commerce.
Entertainment Technology.
Human–Computer Interaction.
Information Networking.
Information Technology.
Knowledge Discovery and Data Mining.
Language Technology.
Robotics.
Software Engineering.

Graduate School of Industrial Administration

Web site: www.gsia.cmu.edu

Established 1949. Private control. Accredited programs: M.S.I.A.; recognized Ph.D. Located on main campus and in New York City; suburban environment. Six mini-semesters per year. Special programs: foreign exchange programs (Austria, France, Germany, Japan, United Kingdom), internships, cooperative program.

Annual M.S.I.A., Ph.D. tuition: full-time $29,750; for M.S.C.F. $37,500 Pittsburgh, $39,500 New York City. No on-campus housing available. Estimated annual budget for tuition, room and board and personal expenses: approximately $39,530.

Enrollment: total full-time 442, part-time 165 (men 80%, women 20%). Faculty: 90 full-time, 32 part-time; 95% with Ph.D./D.B.A. Degrees conferred: M.S.I.A. (Concentrations in Accounting, Decision Sciences, Economics, Entrepreneurship, Finance, Health Care Management, Human Resource Management, International Business/Management, Management, Management Information Systems, Marketing, Production and Operations Management and Information Management/Systems, Organizational Behavior, Quantitative Analysis, Real Estate, Strategic Planning), M.S.C.F. (Computational Finance), M.S.I.A.-J.D. (University of Pittsburgh), Ph.D.

ADMISSION REQUIREMENTS. All applicants should have a bachelor's degree from a recognized institution of higher education and a strong mathematics background. Early applications are encouraged for both admission and financial aid consideration. Does not accept transfer students. Submit an application, GMAT results (will accept GMAT test results from the last five years, latest acceptable date is January), official transcripts from each undergraduate/graduate school attended, three letters of evaluation, two essays, current résumé/work history, and a one-page cover letter highlighting objectives and qualifications (prefers at least four years of work experience), and an application fee of $40 ($30 for online application), M.S.C.F. $125 ($75

for online application) to the Director of Admissions. Will accept either the MBA Multi-App or Computer Edge electronic application in lieu of institutional application. In addition, international students (whose native language is other than English) should submit a TOEFL score, certified translations and evaluations of all official transcripts, recommendation should be in English or with certified translations, proof of health certificate, and proof of sufficient financial resources for two years of academic study. For current information and/or modification in admission requirements the international applicant's contact telephone number is (412)268-7055. Interviews are strongly encouraged either on campus, a field interview or a telephone interview prior to the admissions committee reviewing completed application. Application timetable: completed applications received by November 13 are notified by December 18, applications received by January 15, notification by February 19, applications received by March 12, notification by April 19, applications received by March 12, notification by April 19, applications receive after March 12 are notified on a rolling basis. Admits Fall only. Admissions Office phone: (800)850-GSIA; (412)268-2273; fax: (412)268-4209.

ADMISSION REQUIREMENTS FOR DOCTORAL CANDIDATES. Beginning students are admitted Fall Only. Contact the GSIA Doctoral Office at (412)268-2301 for application material and information. Submit the doctoral application, a GMAT/GRE (will accept GMAT/GRE test results from the last five years), official transcripts from each undergraduate/graduate school attended, three letters of evaluation, current résumé, statement of objectives and purpose, and application fee of $40 ($30 for online application) to the Doctoral Admission Office. In addition, international students (whose native language is other than English) should submit TOEFL scores; certified translations and evaluations of all official transcripts, recommendation should be in English or with certified translations, proof of health/immunization certificate. International students' contact: (412)268-7055. Interviews are strongly recommended. Notifications are generally completed by mid-April.

ADMISSION STANDARDS AND RANKINGS. Very selective. Median GMAT 647; median GPA 3.3 (A = 4.0). Gourman rating: the M.S.I.A. was rated in the top 20, the score was 4.78; the Ph.D. was rated in the top 20, the score was 4.76. *U.S. News & World Report* ranked GSIA in the top 15 of all U.S. business schools. *Business Week* listed GSIA in the top 20 of American business schools.

FINANCIAL AID. Scholarships, merit scholarship, special stipends programs for minorities, grants, fellowships, graduate assistantships, tuition waivers, internships, Federal Perkins loans, Stafford Subsidized and Unsubsidized loans, Federal W/S available. Financial aid is available for part-time study. Financial aid may be available for international students. Assistantships/fellowships may be available for joint degree candidates. Request scholarship, fellowship, assistantship information from the Graduate School. Contact the University's Financial Aid Office for current need-based financial aid information; phone: (412)368-7581. For most financial assistance and all Federal programs submit FAFSA by February 15 (School code: E00074), also submit a NEED ACCESS form, Financial Aid Transcript, Federal Income Tax forms. Approximately 80% of students receive some form of financial assistance.

DEGREE REQUIREMENTS. For M.S.I.A.: 204 units (3 units equal 1 semester hour of credit), two-year full-time program, three-year part-time program; degree program must be completed in thirty-six months. For M.S.C.F.: 144 units. For M.S.I.A.-J.D.: four-year program. For Ph.D.: four- to five-year program; a first and a second summer research papers; qualifying exam; dissertation proposal and oral presentation, dissertation; oral defense; degree programs must be completed within seven years; students who leave at the end of the second year may receive a M.S.I.A.

FIELDS OF STUDY.
Accounting. Ph.D.
Computational Finance. M.S.C.F.
Economics. Ph.D.
Finance. Ph.D.
Industrial Administration. M.S.I.A.
Manufacturing and Operating Systems. Ph.D.
Marketing. Ph.D.
Operations Research. Ph.D.
Organizational Behavior and Theory. Ph.D.
Note: The following joint Ph.D. programs are available: Algorithms, Combinatorics and Optimization (with Mathematics and Computer Science Department), Mathematical Finance (with the Mathematics Department), Management of Manufacturing and Automation (with the Robotics Institute).

H. John Heinz III School of Public Policy and Management
Web site: www.heinz.cmu.edu

Annual tuition: full-time $26,380, part-time $293 per unit.

Enrollment: total full-time 237, part-time 258 (men 45%, women 55%). Faculty: 48 full-time, 30 part-time. Degrees conferred: M.S.P.P.M., M.A.M., M.P.M., M.M.M., M.S.H.C.P.M., M.S.E.T.M., Ph.D.

ADMISSION REQUIREMENTS. All applicants should have a bachelor's degree from a recognized institution of higher education. Accepts transfer students. Submit an application, GMAT or GRE, official transcripts from each undergraduate/graduate school attended, three letters of recommendation, essays, current résumé and an application fee of $50 to the Director of Admission. Apply by February 1. Electronic application available. In addition, international students (whose native language is other than English) should submit a TOEFL score, certified translations and evaluations of all official transcripts, recommendations should be in English or with certified translations. Admits Fall only. Admissions Office phone: (800)877-3498; (415)268-2164; fax: (412)268-6718; e-mail: hnzadmitt@andrew.cmu.edu.

ADMISSIONS STANDARDS. Selective. Usual minimum average: 3.0 GPA (A = 4).

FINANCIAL AID. Scholarships, full and partial fellowships, graduate assistantships, tuition waivers, internships, Federal W/S, loans. Financial aid is available for part-time study. Financial aid may be available for international students. Request scholarship, fellowship, assistantship information from the Heinz School. Contact the University's Financial Aid Office for current need-based financial aid information; phone: (412)368-7581. For most financial assistance and all Federal programs submit FAFSA by February 15 (School code: E00074). Approximately 80% of master's candidates receive some form of financial assistance. All Ph.D. candidates receive a full-tuition scholarships as long as they are in good academic standing.

DEGREE REQUIREMENTS. For master's: individualized degrees and varies by program. For Ph.D.: four- to five-year program; two interdisciplinary research papers; qualifying exam; dissertation proposal and oral presentation; dissertation; final oral defense; degree programs must be completed within seven years.

FIELDS OF STUDY.
Art Management. Joint degree with the College of Fine Arts. M.A.M.
Educational Technology Management. M.S.E.T.M.
Health Care Policy and Management. M.S.H.C.P.M.
Medical Management. M.M.M.

Public Management. Includes specializations in management, organizational behavior, analytic techniques and communication skills. M.P.M.
Public Policy and Management. Includes concentrations in financial management and analysis, information systems, policy analysis, urban and regional economic development management. M.S.P.P.M.

CASE WESTERN RESERVE UNIVERSITY
Cleveland, Ohio 44106

University formed with merger in 1967 of Case Institute of Technology (founded 1880) and Western Reserve University (1826). CGS and AAU member. Coed. Private control. Semester system. Special facilities: Alzheimer Center, Center on Aging and Health, Center for Applied Polymer Research, Center for Automation and Intelligent Systems Research, Biology Field Station, Center for Biomedical Ethics, Cancer Research Center, Case Center for Adhesives, Sealants & Coatings, Case Center for Electrochemical Sciences, Center for Management Development and Research, Center for International Health, Mental Development Center, Institute of Pathology, Cleveland Hearing and Speech Center, Electronics Design Center, Genetics Center, Health Systems Management Center, Mandel Center for Nonprofit Organizations, Center for Urban Poverty and Social Change. Joint programs with Cleveland Museum of Art, Institute of Art, Institute of Music, Cleveland Playhouse. The University's NIH ranking was 20th among all U.S. institutions with 541 awards/grants worth $191,352,595. Library: 2,000,000 volumes, 8500 subscriptions. Total University enrollment: about 10,000.

Tuition: per credit $875. On-campus housing for single students only; 120 co-ed units. Average annual housing cost: $5200. Married students, contact University Off-Campus Housing Bureau. Phone: (216)368-3780. Day-care facilities available near campus.

School of Graduate Studies

Graduate study since 1926. Enrollment: full- and part-time 2090. University faculty teaching graduate students: full-time 1800, part-time 79. Degrees conferred; M.A., M.S., M.F.A., D.M.A., Ph.D.

ADMISSION REQUIREMENTS. Transcripts, three letters of recommendation required in support of application. GRE/MAT required for some departments. Interview generally not required. TOEFL (minimum score 550) required for international applicants. Accepts transfer applicants. Graduates of unaccredited institutions not considered. Apply to Office of Graduate Studies Admissions and appropriate department at least one month prior to registration. Application fee $25. Phone: (216)368-4390; fax: (216)368-4250.

ADMISSION STANDARDS. Very selective to very competitive. Usual minimum average: 3.0 (A = 4).

FINANCIAL AID. Fellowships, assistantships for teaching/research, partial tuition reimbursement, internships, Federal W/S, loans. Apply by March 1 (Fall), November 1 (Spring) to Office of Graduate Studies Admissions. Phone: (216)368-4530. Use FAFSA; program FAFs may be requested. About 45% of students receive aid other than loans from University and outside sources. Limited aid for part-time students.

DEGREE REQUIREMENTS. For M.A., M.S.: 27 semester hours minimum, at least 21 semester hours in residence; thesis/oral comprehensive exam (Plan A–thesis, Plan B–comprehensive exam). For M.F.A.: 60 semester hours minimum; thesis; oral and written exam. For D.M.A., Ph.D.: three years minimum beyond the bachelor's, at least one year in full-time residence; reading knowledge of one or two foreign languages and statistics for some departments; general/qualifying exam; advancement to candidacy dissertation; final oral defense.

FIELDS OF STUDY.
Accounting. Ph.D. only.
American Studies. GRE for admission.
Anatomy. GRE/Subject for admission. Ph.D. only.
Anesthesiology. GRE for admission. M.S. only.
Anthropology. GRE for admission.
Applied Mathematics.
Art Education. M.A. only.
Art History.
Art History and Museum Studies.
Astronomy. GRE for admission. Thesis required for M.S., two languages for Ph.D.
Biochemical Research. M.S. only.
Biochemistry. GRE for admissions.
Bioethics. GRE for admission. M.A. only.
Biology. Includes zoology; GRE/Subject for admission.
Biomedical Sciences (BSTP). Ph.D. only.
Biophysics and Bioengineering. Ph.D. only.
Cell Biology. Ph.D. only.
Cell Physiology. Ph.D. only.
Ceramics and Materials Sciences.
Chemistry. GRE/Subject for admission.
Clinical Psychology (Adult). Ph.D. only.
Clinical Psychology (Child). Ph.D. only.
Communication Sciences. Includes speech-language, pathology, and audiology. GRE for admission.
Comparative Literature. M.A. only.
Computer and Information Sciences.
Contemporary Dance. M.F.A.
Developmental Psychology. Ph.D. only.
Early Music Performance. M.A., D.M.A.
Economics. Ph.D. only.
Engineering. M.E. only.
Engineering. Includes aerospace, biomedical, chemical, civil, computer, electrical, fluid and thermal, mechanical, systems and control. GRE for admission. M.S., Ph.D.
English. GRE for admission.
Environmental Health Sciences. GRE for admission.
Epidemiology and Biostatistics. GRE for admission.
Experimental Psychology. Ph.D. only.
Genetics. GRE General/Subject for admission. Ph.D. only.
Genetic Counseling. M.S. only.
Geological Sciences. GRE/Subject for admission.
Health Systems Management. Ph.D. only.
History. Includes history of science and technology. GRE for admission.
Labor and Human Resource Policy. Ph.D.
Macromolecular Science.
Management. GMAT for admission, Ph.D. only.
Management Information and Decision. Ph.D. only.
Management Policy. Ph.D. only.
Marketing. Ph.D. only.
Materials Sciences and Engineering.
Mathematics. GRE/Subject for Admission.
Medical Anthropology.
Medical Scientist (MSTP). M.D.-Ph.D. only.
Mental Retardation Research. Ph.D. only.
Molecular Biology and Microbiology. GRE/Subject for admission. Ph.D. only.
Molecular Virology. GRE/Subject for admission. Ph.D. only.
Music. Include music history and research, Ph.D. in Musicology, D.M.A. in performance or composition.
Music Education. M.A., Ph.D.
Neurosciences. GRE/Subject for admission. Ph.D. only.
Nursing. GRE for admission. Ph.D. only.

Nutrition. Includes dietetic internship program.
Operations. GRE for admission. Ph.D. only.
Organizational Behavior. Ph.D. only.
Organization Development and Analysis. M.S. only.
Pathology. GRE for admission.
Pharmacology. GRE for admission. Ph.D. only.
Physics.
Physiology. M.S. only.
Physiology and Biophysics. GRE for admission. Ph.D. only.
Political Science. GRE for admission.
Psychology. GRE for admission.
Public Health. M.P.H.
Public Health Nutrition. M.S. only.
Social Welfare. M.S.W. required; MAT or GRE for admission. Ph.D. only.
Sociology. GRE/Subject for admission.
Statistics. GRE for admission.
Structural Biology. Ph.D. only.
Systems Physiology. Ph.D. only.
Theater Arts. Includes acting, contemporary dance. M.A., M.F.A. only.

Mandel School of Applied Social Sciences
Web site: www.msass.cwru.edu

Established 1916. Semester system. Tuition: per credit hour $875. Graduate study only. On-campus housing available for single students only. Apply to Director of Residence Life. Phone: (216)368-3780.

Enrollment: full-time 347, part-time 12. Faculty: full-time 35, part-time 40. Degrees conferred: M.S.S.A., Ph.D.

ADMISSION REQUIREMENTS. Transcripts, letters of reference required in support of School's application. GRE/MAT required for Ph.D. and applicants with G.P.A. below 2.7 (A = 4). Interview optional. TOEFL required of foreign students. Accepts transfer applicants. Graduates of unaccredited institutions not considered. Apply to Mandel School of Applied Social Sciences at least two months prior to registration. Fall admission only. Application fee $25 (not required of foreign students). Phone: (800)863-6772, ext. 2280; fax: (216)368-5065; e-mail: msassadmit@po.cwru.edu.

ADMISSION STANDARDS. Usual minimum average: 2.7 (A = 4). Personal suitability for human services and experience evaluated.

FINANCIAL AID. Annual awards from institutional fund: scholarships, MSASS grants, Federal W/S, loans. Apply to Admissions Office of the School by April 27. Phone: (216)368-22103; fax: (216)368-5065. Use FAFSA. About 60% of students receive aid other than loans from School and outside sources.

DEGREE REQUIREMENTS. For M.S.S.A. (Master of Science in Social Administration): 60 credits minimum. For Ph.D.: 54 credits minimum beyond the master's; general/qualifying exam; advancement to candidacy; dissertation; final oral exam.

FIELDS OF STUDY.
Aging Concentration.
Alcohol and Other Drug Abuse Concentration.
Children, Youth, and Families Concentration.
Community Development Concentration.
Health Concentration.
Management Concentration.
Mental Health Concentration.
Social Welfare. Ph.D.

School of Dentistry

Organized 1892. Located in the Health Science Center since 1969. Annual tuition: $28,030. On-campus housing available.

Average academic year housing costs: $10,770. Contact Director of Housing for more information. Phone (216)368-3780. Total average cost for all other first-year expenses $6271.

Enrollment: first-year class 70, total full-time 265 (men 70%, women 30%). Faculty: full-time 32, part-time 250. Degrees conferred: D.D.S., M.S.

ADMISSION REQUIREMENTS. AADSAS report, transcripts, DAT, letters of recommendation required in support of application. Interview by invitation only. Applicants must have completed at least two years of college study, prefer four years of college work. TOEFL required of international students. Accepts transfer applicants. Apply to Committee on Admissions after June 1, before February 1. Fall admission only. Application fee $45 (not required of foreign students). Phone: (216)368-2460.

ADMISSION STANDARDS. Competitive. Mean GPA: 3.34 (A = 4); mean DAT Academic: 18.46; PAT: 18.37. Accepts 15–18% of total annual applicants. Approximately 20% are state residents.

FINANCIAL AID. Scholarships, grants, tuition waivers, Federal W/S, loans. Students should not depend on aid from School for first semester of attendance. Apply by June 1 to Financial Aid Office. Phone: (216)368-3256. Use FAFSA. About 73% of students receive some aid from school and outside sources.

DEGREE REQUIREMENTS. For D.D.S.: satisfactory completion of 46-month program, at least 36 months in residence. For M.S.: see Graduate School listing above.

FIELDS OF GRADUATE STUDY.
Endodontics.
General Dentistry.
Oral Medicine.
Oral Surgery.
Orthodontics.
Pedodontics.
Periodontics.

School of Law
Web site: www.law.cwru.edu

Established 1892. ABA approved since 1923. AALS Charter member. Semester system. Special facilities: Center for Law, Technology and the Arts, International Law Center, Law-Medicine Center. Library: 372,468 volumes, 4917 subscriptions. Library has LEXIS and access to more than 700 databases. Annual tuition: $22,260, part-time $16,710; LL.M. $25,900. No on-campus housing available. Total average cost for off-campus housing: $11,180. Contact Director of Housing for off-campus information.

Enrollment: first-year 220, total full-time 620 (men 55%, women 45%). Faculty: full-time 34, part-time 39, student to faculty ratio 15.1 to 1. Degrees conferred: J.D., J.D.-M.B.A. (Management), J.D.-M.S.S.A. (Social Work), J.D.-M.A. (Bioethics, Legal History), J.D.-M.D., J.D-M.N.O. (Nonprofit Organizations), J.D.-M.P.H., LL.M. (Taxation), LL.M. (U.S. Legal Studies–only for persons who have completed basic legal education and received a university level law degree in another country).

ADMISSION REQUIREMENTS. LSDAS report, transcripts, LSAT (no later than December) required in support of application. Electronic application available. Interviews not required. Accepts transfer applicants on a space-available basis only. Graduates of unaccredited colleges not considered. Apply to Director of Admissions after July, before April 1. Fall admission only. Application fee $40. Phone: (216)368-3600; fax: (216)368-1042; e-mail: lawadmissions@po.cwru.edu.

ADMISSION STANDARDS. Competitive. Mean GPA 3.25 (A = 4), mean LSAT 144. Accepts 30% of total annual applica-

tions. Gourman rating 3.74; *U.S. News & World Report* ranking is in the second tier of all law schools.

FINANCIAL AID. Scholarships, grants, loans. Apply by May 1 to Director of Admissions. Use FAFSA (School code: E00082). School has a Loan Repayment Assistance program. About 37% of students receive aid other than School loans.

DEGREE REQUIREMENTS. For J.D.: satisfactory completion of three-year, 88 semester hour program. For LL.M. (Taxation): satisfactory completion of one-year, 24 credit program. For LL.M. (U.S. Legal Studies): satisfactory completion of 30 credit program, at least two semesters in residence, mentorship with a Cleveland law firm or corporation.

Weatherhand School of Management
Web site: www.weatherhead.cwru.edu

School established with the federation of the Division of Organizational Sciences and School of Business in 1967. Accredited programs: M.B.A., Accounting; recognized Ph.D. Semester system. Special programs: foreign exchange programs, Foreign Study at International Management Center, Budapest, Hungary.

Annual tuition: full-time $26,460, part-time $1102.50 per credit. On-campus rooms and apartments available for single students only. Estimated annual budget for tuition, room, board and personal expenses: approximately $35,500.

Enrollment: total full-time 536, part-time 671 (men 65%, women 35%). Faculty: 85 full-time, 20 part-time; 15% women; 97% with Ph.D./D.B.A. Degrees conferred: (full-time, part-time, day, evening) (Concentrations in Accounting, Economics, Entrepreneurship, Finance, Health Care Management, Human Resource Management, International Management, Management, Management Information Systems, Marketing, Nonprofit Management, Operations Management, Organizational Behavior/Development, Technology Management), E.M.B.A. (weekends only, alternating Fridays, Saturdays), M.S.M.I.S., M.N.O. (Nonprofit Organizations), M.B.A.-J.D., M.B.A.-M.D., M.B.A.-M.I.M. (with Thunderbird, the American Graduate School of International Management), M.B.A.-M.S., M.B.A.-M.S.M.S. (Management Science), M.B.A.-M.S.N. (Nursing), M. Acc., Ph. D. (Concentrations in Accountancy, Banking and Finance, Economics, Labor and Human Resource Policy, Management Information Systems, Management Policy, Marketing, Operations Research, Organizational Management), E.D.M. (Executive Doctorate in Management).

ADMISSION REQUIREMENTS. All applicants should have a bachelor's degree from a recognized institution of higher education, a strong mathematics background required. Beginning students are admitted Fall and Spring. U.S. citizens apply by February 1 (Fall), December 15 (Spring), international students apply by April (Fall). Submit an application, GMAT results, official transcripts from each undergraduate/graduate school attended, two letters of recommendation, essays, current employment résumé (prefers at least four years of work experience), and an application fee of $55 to the Director of Admission. In addition, international students (whose native language is other than English) should submit a TOEFL (minimum score 580) report, certified translations and evaluations of all official transcripts, recommendation should be in English or with certified translations. For current information and/or modification in admission requirements the international applicant's contact telephone number is: (216)368-2069. On-campus visits are encouraged; interviews are required for all full-time applicants prior to the admissions committee reviewing completed application. Joint degree applicants must apply to and be accepted to both schools/programs; contact the admissions office for current information and specific admissions requirements. Rolling admission process, notification is made within 6 weeks of receipt of completed application and supporting documents. Admissions Office phone:

M.B.A. (216)368-2030; fax: (216)368-5548; Accounting (216)368-2065.

ADMISSION REQUIREMENTS FOR DOCTORAL CANDI-DATES. Contact the Ph.D. Program coordinator for an application and current information. A master's degree in applicant's intended major required. Beginning students are admitted Fall only. U.S. citizens apply by February 1 (Fall), international students apply by January 1. Submit a Ph.D. application, a GMAT (will accept GMAT test results from the last five years), official transcripts from each undergraduate/graduate school attended, three letters of recommendation, essays, current résumé, statement of purpose, and application fee of $55 to the Director of Admissions. In addition, international students (whose native language is other than English) should submit a TOEFL (minimum score 600) report; certified translations and evaluations of all official transcripts, recommendation should be in English or with certified translations, proof of health/immunization certificate. International student contact: (216)368-2069. Interviews strongly encouraged prior to the admissions committee reviewing completed application. Notifications are generally completed by mid-April.

ADMISSION STANDARDS. Selective. Median GMAT: 603; median GPA: 3.2 (A = 4.0). Gourman rating: the MBA program was rated in the top 30, the score was 4.65; the Ph.D. program was rated in the top 30, the score was 4.65. *Business Week* listed School in the top 50 American business schools.

FINANCIAL AID. Scholarships, Enterprise Scholars, grants, fellowships, assistantships, Federal W/S, loans. Financial aid is available for part-time study. Assistantships/fellowships may be available for joint degree candidates. Apply by April 1. Request scholarship, fellowship, assistantship information from the School of Management. Contact the University's Financial Aid Office for current need-based financial aid information; phone: (216)368-2030. Submit FAFSA (School code: 003137), also submit Financial Aid Transcript, Federal Income Tax forms. Approximately 90% of current students receive some form of financial assistance.

DEGREE REQUIREMENTS. For M.B.A. (nonbusiness majors): 64 credit program including 18 elective credits, two-year program; degree program must be completed in six years. For M.B.A. (recent business majors): 48 credit program; degree program must be completed in six years. For E.M.B.A.: 45 credit two-year program. For M.Acc.: 36 credit program. For M.S.M.I.S., M.N.O.: 42 credit program. For M.B.A.-M.I.M.: 68–78 credit program. For M.B.A.-M.S.N.: 78–104 credit program. For M.B.A.-J.D.: 107 credit program; generally three-and-one-half- to five-year program. For Ph.D.: three- to five-year program; general exam; candidacy; teaching apprenticeship; dissertation proposal and oral defense; dissertation; oral defense.

School of Medicine (44106-4920)

Organized 1843. Library: 150,000 volumes, 3000 subscriptions. Annual tuition: $33,735. Total average figure for all other expenses $9,600.

Enrollment: first-year class 144 (EDP 10); full-time 571 (men 55%, women 45%). Faculty: full-time 350, part-time 700. Degrees conferred: M.D., M.D.-M.S., M.D.-Ph.D. (Medical Scientist Training program).

ADMISSION REQUIREMENTS. AMCAS report, transcripts, MCAT. Interviews at the discretion of Admissions Committee required in support of application. Applicants must have completed at least three years of college study. At least 50% are residents of Ohio. Accepts transfer applicants. Does have EDP; approximately 20–25 per year. Apply to AMCAS after June 1, before November 1. Application fee $75. Phone: (216)368-3450; fax: (216)368-6011.

ADMISSION STANDARDS. Very competitive. Median MCAT: 10.0; median GPA: 3.5 (A = 4). Gourman rating: 3.90. *U.S. News & World Report* ranking was 22 for all Schools of Medicine and 22 for Primary Care. Accepts about 5% of total annual applicants. Approximately 60% are state residents.

FINANCIAL AID. Scholarships, research fellowships, loans. Submit data for an analysis of need by NEED ACCESS to Office of the Dean of the School before May 1. About 30% of students receive aid other than loans from School, 75% from all sources.

DEGREE REQUIREMENTS. For M.D.: satisfactory completion of four-year program, at least three years in residence. Combined M.D./M.S., M.D./Ph.D. offered in most basic science departments. See Graduate School listing above.

FIELDS OF GRADUATE STUDY.
Anatomy. M.S. only.
Biochemistry.
Biomedical Engineering.
Biomedical Ethics. M.S. only.
Biophysics.
Cell Biology.
Genetics.
Immunology.
Microbiology.
Molecular Biology.
Neurosciences.
Pathology.
Pharmacology.
Physiology.

Frances Payne Bolton School of Nursing (44106-4804)
Web site: www.fpb.cwru.edu

Established 1898. Semester system.
Annual tuition: $22,500 full-time, per credit $938.
Graduate enrollment: full-time 261, part-time 220. Faculty: full-time 87, part-time 14. Degrees conferred: M.S.N., M.S.N.-M.A. (Bioethics, Anthropology), M.S.N.-M.B.A., N.D.

ADMISSION REQUIREMENTS. Transcripts, eligible for RN license in Ohio, three letters of reference, MAT or GRE for M.S.N., GRE for N.D., Ph.D. required in support of School's application. Interview strongly recommended; required for N.D. applicants. TOEFL required for international applicants. Accepts transfer applicants. Graduates of unaccredited institutions not considered. Apply to Assistant Dean by April 1 (Fall), December 1 (Spring), May 1 (Summer). Application fee $75. Phone: (216)368-2529; e-mail: admissions@fpb.cwru.edu.

ADMISSION STANDARDS. Selective. Usual minimum average: 3.0 (A = 4).

FINANCIAL AID. Scholarships, grants, fellowships, research assistantships, traineeships, teaching assistantships, partial tuition waivers, Federal W/S, loans. Approved for VA benefits. Apply when requesting admission but prior to June 30. Phone: (216)368-2183; e-mail: cfq@po.cwru.edu. Use FAFSA. About 85% of students receive financial assistance. Aid available for part-time students.

DEGREE REQUIREMENTS. For M.S.N.: 36 semester hours minimum; thesis or research project. For N.D.: completion of four levels of program; Licensure exam; thesis. For M.S.N.-M.A.: 45 credit hours, a minimum of 18 credits in each school. For M.S.N.-M.B.A.: 72 credits, a minimum of 30 credits in each school.

FIELDS OF STUDY.
Community Health Nursing.

Critical Care Nursing.
Geriatric Mental Health Nursing.
Gerontological Nursing.
Medical-Surgical Clinical Specialist. Includes critical care, oncology.
Nurse Anesthesia.
Nurse-Midwifery.
Nurse Practitioner. Includes acute care, adult, neonatal, pediatric, psychiatric mental health, women's health.
Nursing Administration.
Nursing Care of Childbearing Families.
Primary Health Nursing Care of Women.

THE CATHOLIC UNIVERSITY OF AMERICA

Washington, D.C. 20064
Web site: www.cua.edu

Founded 1887. CGS and AAU member. Coed. Private control. Semester system. University participates in Joint Graduate Consortium with American, Georgetown, George Washington, Howard Universities. Special facilities: Center for Advanced Training in Cell and Molecular Biology, Center for Global Standard Analysis, Latin American Center for Graduate Studies in Music, Life Cycle Institute; Center for the Study of Youth Development, Computer Center—VT320 terminals at various campus locations; fiber optics network; two VAX 4000 computers; laboratories for fluid mechanics, solid state, solid mechanics, acoustics, member Folger Institute of Renaissance and Eighteenth-Century Studies, Institute of Christian Oriental Research, Center for Service-Learning. Library: more than 1,500,000 volumes, 16,000 subscriptions. More than 1000 computers on campus for general student use. Total University enrollment: 5600.

Annual tuition: full-time $20,500, part-time $770 per credit. On-campus housing for single graduate students. Annual cost: $6208–7962 (including board). Contact Director of Housing for both on- and off-campus housing information. Phone: (202)319-5615; e-mail: housing@cua.edu/och.

School of Arts and Sciences

Graduate study since 1895. Enrollment: full-time 223, part-time 543. School faculty teaching graduate students: full-time 167, part-time 87. Degrees conferred: M.A., M.F.A., M.S., Ph.D.

ADMISSION REQUIREMENTS. Transcripts, GRE, two letters of recommendation required in support of application. GRE Subject/MAT/interviews required by some departments. TOEFL required of international applicants. Accepts transfer applicants. Apply to Office of Graduate Admissions at least two months prior to registration. Priority deadline is February 1. Application fee $55. Phone: (202)319-5057.

ADMISSION STANDARDS. Competitive for most departments, selective for others. Usual minimum average: 3.0 (A = 4).

FINANCIAL AID. Annual awards from institutional funds: scholarships, fellowships, teaching assistantships, research assistantships, Federal W/S, loans. Apply by February 1 to Committee on Fellowships and Scholarships, to appropriate department head for assistantships; to Office of Financial Aid for all other programs. Phone: (202)319-5185. Use FAFSA. About 50% of students receive aid other than loans from University and outside sources.

DEGREE REQUIREMENTS. For master's: 30–36 semester hours, 24 credits in residence; thesis/nonthesis/two research papers option; reading knowledge of one language for some majors; final comprehensive exam. For M.F.A.: same as above except no language and creative project instead of thesis. For Ph.D.: 53 credits minimum including the master's, at least 4 full-time semesters in residence; comprehensive exam; candidacy; reading knowledge of one foreign language; dissertation; final oral exam.

FIELDS OF STUDY.
Accounting. M.S.
Anthropology. Includes cultural and archaeological. M.A., Ph.D.
Biology. Includes cell and microbial, clinical laboratory science. M.S., Ph.D.
Chemistry. Includes chemical education. M.A.
Comparative Literature. M.A., Ph.D.
Drama. Includes theater history and criticism. M.A., M.F.A.
Early Christian Studies. M.A., Ph.D.
Economics. Includes financial, industrial organization/regulation of business, international, international political, public. M.A.
Education. Includes administration, curriculum, foundation and policy studies, Catholic leadership, counseling, ESL, learning and instruction, special (M.A.); administration and policy studies, clinical administration and policy studies, educational psychology (Ph.D.).
English Language and Literature. M.A., Ph.D.
Financial Management. M.A.
Greek and Latin. Includes classics. M.A.
History. M.A.
Human Resource Management. M.A.
Irish Studies. M.A.
Medieval and Byzantine Studies. M.A., Ph.D.
Modern Languages and Literature. Includes French, Italian, Spanish, romance languages and literature, romance philology (M.A.); French, Spanish, romance languages and literature (Ph.D.).
Physics. Includes astrophysics, condensed matter, material science, nuclear, statistical, vitreous state. M.S., Ph.D.
Politics. Includes American government, congressional studies, international affairs, international political economics, political theory, world politics (M.A.); American government, political theory, world politics (Ph.D.).
Psychology. Includes general, human factors (M.A.); applied-experimental, clinical, human development (Ph.D.).
Rhetoric Program. M.A., Ph.D.
Semitic and Egyptian Languages and Literature. M.A.

School of Engineering
Web site: www.ee.cua.edu

Graduate study since 1896. Semester system. Annual tuition: $20,220, per credit hour $770. On-campus housing available. For costs: See University listing above.

Enrollment: full-time 40, part-time 287 (men 90%, women 10%). School faculty: full-time 26, part-time 20. Degrees conferred: M.S.E., D.Arch., D.Eng., Ph.D.

ADMISSION REQUIREMENTS. Transcripts, two letters of recommendation required in support of School's application. GRE strongly recommended; required by some departments. TOEFL required of international applicants. Interview not required. Accepts transfer applicants. Graduates of unaccredited colleges not considered. Apply to Office of Graduate Admissions by August 1. Fall admission only. Application fee $30. Phone: (202)319-5097; fax: (202)319-4499.

ADMISSION STANDARDS. Selective. Usual minimum average: 2.5 (A = 4).

FINANCIAL AID. Annual awards from institutional funds: scholarships, teaching assistantships, research assistantships, Federal W/S, loans. Apply by March 1 to the Registrar for scholarships, to the Dean for assistantships, to Financial Aid Office for all other programs. Phone: (202)319-5185. Use FAFSA. About 50% of full-time students receive aid other than loans from

School and outside sources. No aid other than loans for part-time students.

DEGREE REQUIREMENTS. For master's: 30 semester hours minimum, at least 18 in residence; thesis/nonthesis option. For D.Eng., Ph.D.: 54 hours minimum beyond the bachelor's, at least four semesters in residence; qualifying exam; comprehensive exam; candidacy; dissertation; final written/oral exams.

FIELDS OF STUDY

Biomedical Engineering. Includes cell/tissue engineering, biomechanics, biosignal processing and medical imaging, home care technologies, rehabilitation engineering, telemedicine. M.B.E., M.S.E., D.Eng., Ph.D.

Civil Engineering. Includes environmental engineering and management, fluid and solid mechanics, geotechnical, management of construction, structures and structural mechanics, systems. M.C.E., D.Eng., Ph.D.

Engineering Management. M.S.E.

Electrical Engineering and Computer Science. Includes communication systems and networks, microwave, optics and materials, robotics and intelligent control, signal and image processing, software engineering, computer graphics. M.E.E., M.S.C.S., D.Eng, Ph.D.

Mechanical Engineering. Includes applied energy systems, biomechanics, controls and applied mechanics, dynamics, control and mechanics, environmental engineering, mechanical design and structural mechanics, thermal and fluid sciences (M.M.E., M.S.E.); controls and applied mechanics, thermal and fluid sciences (D.Eng., Ph.D.).

Columbus School of Law

Founded 1897. ABA approved since 1925. AALS member since 1921. Semester system. Special facilities: Institute for Communications Law, the Comparative and International Law Institute. Law library: 336,900 volumes; has LEXIS, NEXIS, WESTLAW, DIALOG.

Tuition: full-time $26,214 part-time $18,999. Total average cost for all other expenses: $13,592. Enrollment: first-year class 224 (day), 83 (night); total full-time 673, part-time 284 (men 50%, women 50%). Faculty: full-time 36, part-time 48. Student to faculty ratio 19.9 to 1. Degrees conferred: J.D., J.D.-M.A., J.D.-M.L.S., J.D.-M.S.W.

ADMISSION REQUIREMENTS. LSDAS Law School report, transcripts, two character references, LSAT (not later than December), bachelor's degree required in support of application. Interview not required. Accepts transfer applicants. Applicants from unaccredited institutions not considered. Apply to the Dean after October 1, before March 1; part-time, May 1. Admits first-year students Fall only. Application fee $55. Phone: (202)319-5151; e-mail: admissions@law.edu.

ADMISSION STANDARDS. Selective. Median LSAT: 154; median GPA: 3.08 (A = 4). Gourman rating: 3.89. *U.S. News & World Report* ranking is in the third tier of all law schools. Accepts 30% of total annual applicants.

FINANCIAL AID. Scholarships, grants, Federal W/S, loans. Apply to the Financial Aid Office by March 15. Phone: (202)319-5185. Use FAFSA. About 24% of full-time students receive aid other than loans from School.

DEGREE REQUIREMENTS. For J.D.: 84 semester hours in residence. Advanced standing from other law schools will be considered. Combined programs available in economics, accounting, history, management, philosophy, psychology, politics, social work, library science. For degree requirements: see Graduate School listing above.

School of Library and Information Science

Web site: slis.cua.edu

Annual tuition: full-time $21,050, per credit $810. On-campus housing available. See University listing above.

Enrollment: full-time 54, part-time 77. Graduate faculty: full-time 26, part-time 10. Degree conferred: M.S.L.S.

ADMISSION REQUIREMENTS. Transcripts, GRE, two letters of recommendation required in support of School's application. TOEFL (minimum score 550) required for international applicants. Interviews may be requested. Apply to Office of Graduate Admissions, attention SLIS Admissions at least forty-five days prior to beginning of semester. Application fee $55. Phone: (202)319-5057; fax (202)319-5199.

ADMISSION STANDARDS. Competitive. Usual minimum average: 3.0 (A = 4).

FINANCIAL AID. Scholarships (awarded for Fall admission only), research assistantships, teaching assistantships, Federal W/S, loans. Apply to Graduate Financial Aid Office by February 1. Phone: (202)319-5185. Use FAFSA. Aid is available for part-time study.

DEGREE REQUIREMENTS. For M.S.L.S.: 36 credit program, at least 30 credits in residence; computer competency.

FIELDS OF STUDY

Archives and Records Management.
Biomedical Information.
Book Arts.
Information Management.
Information Systems.
Law Librarianship.
Library and Information Services.
Music Librarianship.
School Library Media Services.
Services for Children and Young Adults.
Special Collections.

The Benjamin T. Rome School of Music

Web site: www.cua.edu

Graduate study since 1887. School established 1950. Annual tuition: fulltime $21,050, per credits $810. On-campus housing available. See University listing above.

Enrollment: full-time 74, part-time 107. Graduate faculty: full-time 16, part-time 100. Degrees conferred: M.A., M.M., M.L.M., Ph.D., D.M.A., M.A.-M.S.L.S.

ADMISSION REQUIREMENTS. Transcripts, two letters of recommendation required in support of School's application. Additional requirements vary by program (performance proficiency, recital, original composition, research paper). TOEFL required for international applicants. GRE and interview recommended for some programs. GRE required for University scholarship consideration. Apply to the Office of Graduate Admission at least forty-five days prior to beginning of semester. Application fee $55. Phone: (202)319-5057; fax: (202)319-5199.

ADMISSION STANDARDS. Competitive. Usual minimum average: 3.0 (A = 4).

FINANCIAL AID. Scholarships, research assistantships, teaching assistantships, performance awards, Federal W/S, loans. Apply to Dean and Financial Aid Office by February 1. Phone: (202)319-5185. Use FAFSA and University's FAF.

DEGREE REQUIREMENTS. For master's: 30–36 credits, at least one year in residence; language and thesis for M.A.; thesis optional for M.S.Mus.Ed.; performance for M.M. For D.M.A. (degree individualized): 54 credits beyond master's, at least two years in residence; comprehensive exam; candidacy; dissertation; composition/recital. For Ph.D.: 54 credits minimum, at least three years in residence; two foreign languages; comprehensive exam in both a major and minor field; candidacy; dissertation; written/oral exam.

FIELDS OF STUDY

Liturgical Music. M.L.M.

Music. Includes accompanying and chamber music (piano), composition, instrumental conducting, orchestral instruments (violin, viola, cello, string bass, solo woodwinds and bass instruments, percussion, harp, classical guitar), organ, harpsichord, piano, piano pedagogy, vocal pedagogy, vocal performance. M.M., D.M.A.

Music History. Ph.D.

Music Performance. Ph.D.

Music Theory, Ph.D.

Musicology. Includes history, theory. M.A.

Note: A concentration in Latin American Music is available in cooperation with the School's Latin American Center for Graduate Studies in Music.

School of Nursing

Graduate study since 1951. Semester system. Annual tuition: full-time $21,050, per credit $810.

Enrollment: full-time 60, part-time 72. School faculty: full-time 26, part-time 5. Degrees conferred: M.S.N., M.S.N.-M.A. (Health Services Management with George Washington University), Certificates.

ADMISSION REQUIREMENTS. Transcripts, a license to practice nursing in a state or jurisdiction of the U.S., three letters of recommendation, GRE required in support of School's application. TOEFL (minimum score 550) required for international applicants. Interview for some majors. Accepts transfer applicants. Graduates of unaccredited institutions not considered. Apply to School's Admissions Office by July 1 (Fall); November 1 (Spring), April 1 (Summer). Application fee $55. Phone: (202)319-6466; fax: (202)319-6485.

ADMISSION STANDARDS. Selective. Usual minimum average: 3.0 (A = 4).

FINANCIAL AID. Partial scholarships, internships, Federal traineeships, Federal W/S, loans. Apply to Dean and Financial Aid Office by April 1. Use FAFSA. Phone: (202)319-5307; fax: (202)319-5573.

DEGREE REQUIREMENTS. For M.S.N.: 30 semester hours; candidacy; thesis/nonthesis option; comprehensive exam. For M.S.N.-M.A.: 61 semester hours required. For certificates: varies by program, at least 18 semester hours.

FIELDS OF STUDY.

Administration of Nursing Service.

Adult Nurse Practitioner.

Advanced Practice Psychiatric–Mental Health Nursing.

Community/Public Health Nursing.

Education. Includes adult, higher.

Family Nurse Practitioner.

Geriatric Nurse Practitioner.

Pediatric Nurse Practitioner.

Psychiatric–Mental Health Nursing.

School Health Practitioner.

School of Philosophy

Founded 1895. Annual tuition: $20,050. Off-campus housing available. Annual housing cost: $5154, plus $3098 board. Apply to Office of Off-Campus Housing. Phone: (202)319-5680. Day-care facilities available.

Graduate enrollment: full-time 72, part-time 52. School faculty: full-time 12, part-time 2. Degrees conferred: M.A., Ph.L., Ph.D.

ADMISSION REQUIREMENTS. Transcripts, statement of intent, two recommendations, GRE required in support of School's application. TOEFL required for foreign applicants. Interview not required. Accepts transfer applicants. Apply to Office of Graduate Admission, at least one month in advance of registration day. Application fee $55. Phone: (202)319-5259.

ADMISSION STANDARDS. Very competitive. Usual minimum average: 3.0 (A = 4).

FINANCIAL AID. Scholarships, research fellowships, teaching assistantships, Federal W/S, loans. Apply by February 1 to the Dean for scholarships fellowships and assistantships, to the Financial Aid Office for all other programs. Phone: (202)319-5307; fax: (202)319-5573. Use FAFSA. About 50% of students receive aid other than loans from School and outside sources. Aid other than loans sometimes available for part-time students.

DEGREE REQUIREMENTS. For M.A., Ph.L.: 24 semester hours in full-time residence; transfer credit not accepted for M.A.; thesis and reading knowledge of one foreign language; final written/oral exam. For Ph.D.: 60 semester hours minimum beyond the bachelor's, at least 36 in residence; three Graduate Reading Program exams; preliminary exam; candidacy; reading knowledge of two foreign languages; dissertation, final oral exam.

FIELDS OF STUDY.

Ancient Philosophy.

Aquinas.

Husserl; Heidegger.

Logic and Epistemology.

Medieval Philosophy.

Metaphysics.

Modern Philosophy.

Moral Philosophy.

Phenomenology.

Philosophical Anthropology.

Philosophy of Science.

School of Religious Studies

Formal study since 1931. Annual tuition: full-time $14,612, per credit hour $563.

Enrollment: full-time 186, part-time 201. Faculty: full-time 48, part-time 15. Degrees conferred: M.Div., M.A., M.A.-Lit., M.R.E., D.Min., Ph.D., S.T.B., S.T.L., S.T.D.

ADMISSION REQUIREMENTS. Transcripts, bachelor's degree, two letters of recommendation, GRE/MAT required in support of application. Reading knowledge of Latin for some programs. TOEFL required for foreign applicants. Admission open to all qualified applicants. Apply by August 1 (Fall), December 1 (Spring) to the Office of Graduate Admissions. Application fee $55. Phone: (202)319-5057.

ADMISSION STANDARDS. Selective. Usual minimum average: 2.75 (A = 4).

FINANCIAL AID. Annual awards from institutional funds: scholarships, teaching assistantships, fellowships, Burses, Federal W/S, loans. Use FAFSA and institutional FAF. Apply to the Dean and Graduate Financial Aid Office by February 1. Phone: (202)319-5185.

DEGREE REQUIREMENTS. For M.Div: 90-credit program; demonstrated knowledge of Latin; three ministry seminars; supervised ministry. For D.Min.: 36 credits beyond M.Div., at least four semesters in full-time residence; two areas of specialization; D.Min. project; candidacy; dissertation; final oral exam. For S.T.B., S.T.L., S.T.D.: individualized programs, contact Dean for program specifics. For M.A., Ph.D.: requirements same as for School of Arts and Sciences, above.

FIELDS OF STUDY.
Adult Spiritual Formation.
Biblical Studies.
Canon Law.
Church History.
History of Religion.
Liturgical Studies.
Pastoral Care and Counseling.
Religion and Religious Education.
Theology. Includes systematic, moral, historical.

The National Catholic School of Social Service

Established 1918. Annual tuition: full-time $20,050, per credit $800. On-campus housing available. See University listing above.

Enrollment: full-time 180, part-time 190. Faculty: full-time 21, part-time 17. Degrees conferred: M.S.W. (full- and part-time study), Ph.D.

ADMISSION REQUIREMENTS. Transcripts, GRE or MAT, three letters of recommendation, personal statement, résumé required in support of School's application. TOEFL required for foreign applicants. Accepts advanced standing and M.S.W. transfer students. Interview sometimes required. Graduates of unaccredited institutions not considered. Apply to Office of Graduate Admissions by May 1. Fall admission only for M.S.W.; Ph.D. admits both Fall and Spring. Application fee $55. Phone: (202)319-5496; fax: (202)319-5093.

ADMISSION STANDARDS. Selective. Usual minimum average: 3.0 (A = 4).

FINANCIAL AID. Limited assistance available. Scholarships, fellowships, graduate assistantships (Ph.D.), loans. Approved for VA benefits. Apply by March 1 to Director of Admissions. Use FAFSA. About 35% of students receive aid other than loans.

DEGREE REQUIREMENTS. For M.S.W.: 60 credits and four semesters minimum, at least two semesters in full-time residence; thesis or major paper; two field placements. For Ph.D.: 45 credits beyond the master's minimum, at least four semesters in residence and two semesters in full-time attendance; qualifying exam; reading knowledge of one foreign language; written/oral comprehensive exams; dissertation; final oral exam.

FIELDS OF DOCTORAL STUDY.
Individual Educational Contract.
Theory and Research in Clinical Social Work.
Theory and Research in Policy and Administration in Social Work.

UNIVERSITY OF CENTRAL ARKANSAS
Conway, Arkansas 72035-0001
Web site: www.uca.edu

Founded 1907. CGS member. Located 30 miles NW of Little Rock. Coed. State control. semester system. Library: 414,700 volumes, 2500 subscriptions. More than 500 computers on campus for general student use.

Tuition: per hour, resident $148, nonresident $306. Limited on-campus housing graduate students. Annual housing cost $3250 (including board) for single students; $5460 (including board) for married students. Apply to Director of Housing. Phone: (501)450-3124.

Graduate School

Graduate study since 1955. Enrollment: full-time 388; part-time 499. College faculty teaching graduate students: full-time 216; part-time 11. Degrees conferred: M.A., M.S. in Ed., M.S., M.S.N., M.M.E., M.M., M.B.A., Ed.S.

ADMISSION REQUIREMENTS. Transcripts, GRE/MAT, three references required in support of application. TOEFL required for foreign applicants. Accept transfer applicants. Graduates of unaccredited institutions not considered. Apply to Office of Graduate Dean by February 15 (priority deadline for Summer and Fall), October 1 (priority deadline for Spring). Phone: (501)450-3124; fax: (501)450-5066.

ADMISSION STANDARDS. Selective. Usual minimum average: 2.7 (A = 4).

FINANCIAL AID. Annual awards from institutional funds: fellowships, grants, traineeships, assistantships, tuition waivers, Federal W/S, loans. Apply to Dean of Graduate School for assistantship information; February 15 (Fall), October 1 (Spring). Use FAFSA. Phone: (501)450-3140. About 10% of students receive aid other than loans from School and outside sources.

DEGREE REQUIREMENTS. For master's: 30 semester hours minimum (48 for counseling, 60 for counseling psychology, 60 for school psychology), at least 24 in residence; thesis/nonthesis options; final written and/or oral exam. For Ed.S.: 33 semester hours beyond master's; project.

FIELDS OF STUDY.
Applied Computing.
Art.
Biology.
Business Administration.
Business and Marketing Education.
College Student Personnel Services and Administration.
Community Development.
Community Service Counseling.
Chemistry.
Childhood Education.
Clinical Nurse Specialist.
Computer Science.
Counseling Psychology.
Early Childhood Education.
Educational Specialists.
Elementary Education.
Elementary Education (emphasis: Gifted).
Elementary School Psychology.
English.
Family and Consumer Sciences.
Foreign Language (Spanish).
Health Sciences.
Health Systems.
History.
International Business Administration.
Kinesiology and Physical Education.
Library Media and Information Technologies.
Mathematics Education.
Music. Includes performance, theory, choral conducting, instrumental conducting, music education.
Nurse Practitioner.
Occupational Therapy.
Physical Sciences.
Philosophy and Religion.
Physical Therapy.

Physics and Astronomy.
Political Science.
Public Health.
Reading.
School Leadership, Management, and Administration.
School Psychology.
Secondary School Counseling.
Sociology.
Special Education. Includes collaborative instructional specialist, ages 0–8; collaborative instructional specialist grades 4–12.
Speech-Language Pathology.

CENTRAL CONNECTICUT STATE UNIVERSITY

New Britain, Connecticut 06050-4010
Web site: www.ccsu.edu

Founded 1849. CGS member. Located 13 miles SW of Hartford. Coed. State control. Semester system. Library: 621,000 volumes, 2800 subscriptions. More than 250 computers on campus for general student use. Total University enrollment: 13,000.

Annual tuition/fees: resident $4462, nonresident $11,192. Limited on-campus housing. Average annual housing cost: $6728 per year. Apply by May 1. Contact the Director of Residence Life for on- and off-campus accommodations. Phone: (860)832-1660. Limited day-care facilities available.

School of Graduate Studies

Graduate study since 1954. Enrollment: full-time 529, part-time 1576. Graduate faculty: full-time 295, part-time 265. Degrees conferred: M.A., M.S., M.B.A., sixth-year certificate (Reading and Educational Leadership).

ADMISSION REQUIREMENTS. Transcripts, GMAT (International Business only) required in support of University's application. References, TOEFL, and proof of financial support required for international applicants. Apply to Assistant Director of Recruitment and Admission by June 1 (Fall), December 1 (Spring). at least one month prior to semester of entrance. Rolling admissions process. Application fee $40. Phone: (860)832-2350; fax: (860)832-2362.

ADMISSION STANDARDS. Moderately selective. Minimum average: 2.7 (A = 4).

FINANCIAL AID. Annual awards from institutional funds: scholarships, assistantships, internships, tuition waivers, Federal W/S, loans. Apply to Dean and Director of Financial Aid by March 15 (Fall), October 1 (Spring). Phone: (860)832-2200. Use FAFSA. Aid available for part-time students.

DEGREE REQUIREMENTS. For master's: 30–36 semester hours minimum, at least 21 in residence; thesis or final written exam or special project/capstone; no language requirement in most programs. For sixth-year program: 30 credits beyond master's, at least 21 in residence. Some programs requires capstone project.

FIELDS OF STUDY.
Art. Includes studio, education.
Biology. Includes general biology, environmental studies, nurse anesthesia, health sciences. M.A., M.S.
Business Education. M.S.
Chemistry. M.S.
Communication.
Computer Information Technology. M.S.
Counseling. Includes marriage/family therapy, rehabilitation, school guidance and student development in higher education. M.S.

Criminal Justice. M.S.
Earth Science. M.S.
Education. Includes business, early childhood, educational foundations, educational leadership and administration, educational media, elementary, modern languages, physical education, reading, science, special, technology education for regular or vocational environments. M.S.
English. M.A., M.S.
General Science. M.S.
Geography. M.S.
History. M.A., M.S.
Industrial and Technical Management. M.S.
Information Design. M.S.
International Business Administration. M.B.A.
International Studies. M.S.
Mathematics. Includes actuarial mathematics, computer science, operations research, statistics. M.A., M.S.
Media. M.S.
Modern Languages. Includes French, Spanish. M.A.
Music. M.S.
Organizational Communication. M.S.
Physics. M.S.
Psychology. Includes community and general options. M.A.
Social Science. M.S.
Spanish. M.S.
TESOL. M.S.
Technology Education. M.S.

UNIVERSITY OF CENTRAL FLORIDA

Box 160112
Orlando, Florida 32816-0112
Web site: www.ucf.edu

Founded 1963. CGS member. Located 15 miles from downtown. Coed. Public control. Semester system. Library: 1,200,000 volumes, 7400 subscriptions. More than 1200 computers on campus for student use. Total University enrollment: 33,000.

Annual tuition: residents $3659, nonresidents $12,749; per credit, resident $152, nonresident $531. On-campus housing available for single students only. Average academic year housing costs: $400 per month one-bedroom, $700 per month two-bedroom. Apply by March 1. Contact to Housing Office for both on- and off-campus housing.

Graduate Studies

Web site: www.graduate.ucf.edu

Enrollment: full-time 1899, part-time 3699. Graduate faculty: full- and part-time 794. Degrees conferred: M.A., M.S., M.Ed., M.S.A., M.B.A., M.A.A.E., M.P.H., M.S.T., M.S.W., M.C.E., M.S.E., M.S.I.E., M.S.M.E., M.S.Mfg.E., Ed.S., Ed.D., Ph.D.

ADMISSION REQUIREMENTS. Transcripts, GRE, GMAT (for business programs) required in support of application. Three letters of recommendation for most programs. TOEFL required for international students. Accepts transfer applicants. Graduates of unaccredited institutions not considered. Apply to the Office of Graduate Studies at least six months prior to the date of registration. Rolling admissions process. Application fee $20. Phone: (407)823-2766; fax: (407)823-3299; e-mail: graduate@mail.ucf.edu.

ADMISSION STANDARDS. Selective. Usual minimum average: 2.75 (A = 4).

FINANCIAL AID. Scholarships, fellowships, assistantships, internships, partial tuition waivers, Federal W/S, loans. Approved for VA benefits. Apply by March 1 to appropriate Dean's Office for fellowships, assistantships, to Financial Aid Office for all other programs. Use FAFSA. About 20% students receive aid from University and outside sources. Aid available for part-time students.

DEGREE REQUIREMENTS. For most master's: 30–48 semester hours minimum, at least one year in residence for most departments; however some departments require two or more years of full-time study; thesis/nonthesis option; reading knowledge of one foreign language for some departments; written/oral exam; completion of degree no later than five years from date of entrance. For M.B.A.: 39–51 credit program; core course must be completed in four consecutive years. For Ed.S.: 30 semester credits minimum beyond the master's degree; special project. For Ed.D.: 90 semester hours, at least three years minimum in residence; written comprehensive exam; dissertation; final oral exam; completion of all requirements no later than seven years from date of entrance. For Ph.D.: 60–67 semester hours minimum beyond the bachelor's, and three years of full-time study or equivalent in residence; written comprehensive exam; advancement to candidacy; internship for some programs; dissertation; final oral exam; completion of all requirements no later than seven years from date of entrance.

FIELDS OF STUDY.

COLLEGE OF ARTS AND SCIENCES:
Applied Sociology. Includes domestic violence. M.A.
Biology. M.S.
Biomolecular Sciences. Ph.D.
Clinical Psychology. M.S.
Communication. M.A.
Computer Sciences. M.S., Ph.D.
English. Includes creative writing, literature, technical writing. M.A.
History. Includes public history. M.A.
Industrial Chemistry. Includes forensic science. M.S.
Industrial/Organizational Psychology. M.S.
Liberal Studies. Includes Mayan studies. M.A.
Mathematics. Includes industrial mathematics. M.S., Ph.D.
Modeling and Simulation. M.S., Ph.D.
Physics. Includes optical physics. M.S., Ph.D.
Political Science. Includes environmental politics, political analysis, public policy. M.A.
Psychology. Includes applied experimental and human factors, clinical (M.A. track), industrial and organizational (M.S. track). Ph.D.
Spanish. M.A.
Statistical Computing. Includes actuarial science, data mining. M.S.
TESOL. M.A.
Texts and Technology. Ph.D.
Theatre. M.A., M.F.A. M.F.A. includes acting, design, musical theatre.

COLLEGE OF BUSINESS ADMINISTRATION:
Accounting. M.S.A., Ph.D.
Applied Economics. M.A.A.E.
Business Administration. M.B.A., E.M.B.A., Ph.D.
Finance. Ph.D.
Management. Includes human resources/change management. M.S.M., Ph.D.
Management Information Systems. M.S.M.I.S., Ph.D.
Marketing. Ph.D.
Sport Business Management. M.S.B.M.
Taxation. M.S.T.

COLLEGE OF EDUCATION:
Art Education. M.Ed.
Counselor Education. Includes mental health counseling, school counseling. M. Ed.
Curriculum and Instruction. M.Ed., Ed.S., Ed.D.
Early Childhood Education. M.Ed.
Educational Leadership. Includes student personnel administration in higher education. M.Ed., Ed.S., Ed.D.

Education. Includes counselor education, elementary education, exceptional education, instructional technology, mathematics. Ph.D.
Elementary Education. M.A., M.Ed.
English Language Arts Education. M.A.
Instructional Technology. Includes education media, educational technology, instructional systems. M.Ed.
Music Education. M.Ed.
Physical Education. Includes exercise physiology and wellness. M.Ed.
Reading Education. M.Ed.
School Psychology. Includes school counseling. Ed.S.
Science Education. Includes biology, chemistry, physics. M.Ed.
Secondary Education. M.Ed.
Social Science Education. M.Ed.
Vocational Education. M.Ed.

COLLEGE OF ENGINEERING:
Aerospace Engineering. Includes space system design and engineering, thermofluid aerodynamic system design and engineering. M.S.A.E.
Civil Engineering. Includes structural and geotechnical, transportation, water resources. M.S.C.E., M.S., Ph.D.
Computer Engineering. Includes computer architecture, digital systems, knowledge-based systems, software engineering. M.S.Cp.E., Ph.D.
Computer Science. M.S., Ph.D.
Electrical Engineering. Includes communication, controls/power, digital signal processing, electromagnetics, electronics/power electronics, electro-optics, solid state and microelectronics. M.S.E.E., Ph.D.
Engineering Management. M.S.
Environmental Engineering. M.S., M.S.Env.E., Ph.D.
Human Engineering/Ergonomics. M.S.
Industrial Engineering. M.S.I.E., Ph.D.
Interactive Simulation and Training. M.S.
Materials Science and Engineering. M.S.M.S.E., Ph.D.
Mechanical Engineering. Includes computer-aided, mechanical systems, miniature engineering, professional, thermofluids. M.S.M.E., Ph.D.
Modeling and Simulation. Ph.D.
Operations Research. M.S.
Quality Engineering. M.S.
Simulation Modeling and Analysis. M.S.
Structures and Foundation Engineering. M.S.
Transportation Systems Engineering. M.S.
Water Resources Engineering. M.S.

COLLEGE OF HEALTH AND PUBLIC AFFAIRS:
Biomolecular Sciences. Ph.D.
Communicative Disorders. M.A.
Criminal Justice. M.S.
Health Sciences. M.S.
Molecular Biology and Microbiology. M.S.
Nursing. Includes adult, clinical, family, pediatric nurse practitioner, leadership and management.
Physical Therapy. M.S.
Public Administration. M.P.A.
Public Affairs. Ph.D.
Social Work. M.S.W.

CENTRAL MICHIGAN UNIVERSITY
Mount Pleasant, Michigan 48859
Web site: www.cmich.edu

Founded 1892. CGS member. Located 70 miles N of Lansing. Coed. State control. Semester system. Special facilities: Beaver Island Neckercut Wood, Center for Computer Vision and Robotics, Center for Polymer Chemistry, Michigan Geographic Alliance. Library: 941,500 volumes, 4500 subscriptions. More than 1500 computers on campus for general student use. Total University enrollment 17,000.

Tuition: per credit, resident $163, nonresident $323. On-campus housing for married and single students. Annual cost for single students $8000–$9600 (including board), for married students $425–$500 per month (room only). Apply to Director of Housing. Phone: (989)774-3112. Day-care facilities available.

College of Graduate Studies

Graduate study since 1939. Enrollment: full-time 1013, part-time 1161 (men 45%, women 55%). Faculty: full- and part-time 707. Degrees conferred: M.A., M.S., M.B.A., M.F.A., M.M., M.S.A., Specialist, Psy.D., Au.D., Certificates.

ADMISSION REQUIREMENTS. Transcripts, GRE/GMAT (for some programs) required in support of College's application. TOEFL required for foreign applicants; TWE required for some programs. Interview required for some programs. Accepts transfer applicants. Graduates of unaccredited institutions not considered. Apply to Graduate Office by July 15 (Fall), December 1 (Spring). International applicants should apply at least six months prior to preferred time of enrollment. Application fee $30. Phone: (989)774-1059; fax: (989)774-1857; E-Mail:grad@cmich.edu.

ADMISSION STANDARDS. Selective. Usual minimum average: 2.5 (A = 4).

FINANCIAL AID. Annual awards from University funds: fellowships, research assistantships, teaching assistantships, internships, Federal W/S, loans. Apply by March 1 to Dean of College of Graduate Studies for fellowships, to appropriate department chair for assistantships, to Financial Aid Office for all other programs. Phone: (989)774-3674. Use FAFSA. About 30% of students receive aid other than loans from University. Aid available for part-time students.

DEGREE REQUIREMENTS. For most master's: 30–36 semester hours minimum; comprehensive exam for some programs; thesis/nonthesis option or two research papers. For M.S.P.T.: three-year full-time 110 credit program; thesis. For Specialist: 30 semester hours beyond the master's; thesis or field study; final oral exam. No language requirements. For Psy.D.: at least 60 credit hours beyond the master's; two years in full-time residence; qualifying exam; full-year internship; case study; final exam.

FIELDS OF STUDY.
Administration. Includes general, health services, human resources, international, leadership, organizational communication, public, recreation and parks, sport.
Art. M.A.
Audiology. Au.D.
Biology. Includes conservation biology. M.S.
Broadcast and Cinematic Arts. M.A.
Business Administration. Includes accounting, finance, management, marketing; GMAT for admission. M.B.A.
Business Education. M.B.E.
Chemistry. Includes teaching high school chemistry (M.A.), teaching college chemistry (M.A.). M.S.
Computer Science. M.S.
Counseling and Special Education. Includes school guidance personnel, professional counseling. M.A.
Economics. M.A.
Educational Administration. Includes general educational administration (M.A., Ed.S), community leadership (M.A.), school principalship (M.A.), educational leadership (Ed.D).
English Language and Literature. Includes composition and communication, creative writing, teaching English to speakers for other languages. M.A.
Fine Arts. M.F.A.

Geographic Information Sciences. M.S.
Health Promotion and Program Management. M.A.
History. M.A.
Human Development and Family Studies. M.A.
Humanities. M.A.
Industrial and Engineering Technology. Includes industrial education, industrial management and technology. M.A.
Information Systems. M.S.I.S.
Mathematics. M.A., M.A.T., Ph.D.
Music. Includes performance, music education supervision. M.M.
Nutrition and Dietetics. M.S.
Physical Education and Sport. Includes teaching, athletic administration, exercise science, coaching, sport administration. M.A.
Physical Therapy. M.S.
Physics. M.S.
Political Science. Includes public administration (M.P.A.), public management (M.P.A.), state and local government (M.P.A.). M.A.
Psychology. Includes applied experimental (Ph.D), clinical (Ph.D.), general (M.S.), experimental (M.S.), industrial/organizational (M.A., Ph.D.), school (Ph.D).
Recreation, Park, and Leisure Services Administration. Includes therapeutic recreation. M.A.
Sociology. Includes social & criminal justice. M.A.
Spanish. M.A.
Special Education. Includes counseling and special education. M.A.
Speech Communication and Dramatic Arts. Includes interpersonal public communication, oral interpretation, theatre. M.A.
Speech Language Pathology. M.A.
Teacher Education and Professional Development. Includes middle level, educational technology, elementary, classroom teaching, early childhood, reading in elementary school, secondary education, teaching in the senior high. M.A.

CENTRAL MISSOURI STATE UNIVERSITY
Warrensburg, Missouri 64093
Web site: www.cmsu.edu

Founded 1871. CGS member. Located 50 miles SE of Kansas City. Coed. State control. Semester system. Library 851,000 volumes, 3550 subscriptions. More than 1000 computers on campus for general student use.

Tuition per credit: resident $160, nonresident $318. On-campus housing for about 200 married students, 3000 men, 3000 women. Housing cost: $450–$600 per month for married students, $4500 per term (including board) for single students. Apply to Director of Residential Life. Phone: (660)543-4515.

Graduate Studies

Graduate study since 1947. Enrollment: full-time 209, part-time 1856. Graduate faculty: full-time 286, part-time 33. Degrees conferred: M.A., M.S., M.S.Ed. M.B.A., Ed.Specialist. Ph.D. (Technology awarded by Indiana State University; Educational Leadership awarded by University of Missouri–Columbia)

ADMISSION REQUIREMENTS. Transcripts, bachelor's degree required in support of University's application. Electronic application available. GRE/GMAT/MAT may be required by some departments. Accepts transfer applicants. Interview not required. Graduates from unaccredited institutions not considered. Application fee $25 ($50 for international applicants). Apply to Admissions Office by August 15 (Fall), January 5 (Spring), June 1 (Summer). Phone: (660)543-4328; e-mail: gradinfo@cmsu1.cmsu.edu.

ADMISSION STANDARDS. Relatively open. Usual minimum average 2.0 (A = 4).

FINANCIAL AID. Annual awards from institutional funds: scholarships, grants, fellowships, administrative assistantships, research assistantships, teaching assistantships, Federal W/S, loans. Apply by March 1 to chair of proposed major for assistantships, fellowships; to financial aid office for W/S, loans. Phone: (660)543-4040; fax: (660)543-8080. Use FAFSA. About 10% of students receive aid other than loans from College funds. Aid available for part-time students.

DEGREE REQUIREMENTS. For master's: 32 credits minimum; qualifying/comprehensive exam; some departments require thesis. For Ed.Specialist: 30 credits minimum beyond the master's; thesis or research project.

FIELDS OF STUDY.
Accountancy.
Administration. Includes elementary school princpalship, secondary school principalship, superintendancy.
Agriculture Technology.
Aviation Safety.
Biology.
Business Administration.
Business/Office Education.
Communication.
Communication Disorders.
Criminal Justice.
Curriculum and Instruction.
Economics.
Educational Technology.
English.
Guidance and Counseling.
Higher Education.
History.
Industrial Hygiene.
Industrial Management.
Industrial Technology.
Information Technology.
Learning Resources.
Library Information Technology.
Library Science and Information Services.
Mass Communication.
Mathematics.
Music.
Occupational Safety Management.
Physical Education, Exercise, and Sports Science.
Psychology.
Public Services.
Rural Family Nursing.
School Administration.
School Counseling.
Social Gerontology.
Social Studies.
Sociology.
Special Education.
Student Personnel Administration.
Teaching English as a Second Language.
Technology and Occupational Education.
Theater.
Note: Ed. Specialist available in most education-related programs.

UNIVERSITY OF CENTRAL OKLAHOMA

Edmond, Oklahoma 73034-5209
Web site: www.ucok.edu

Founded 1800. CGS member. Located 12 miles N of Oklahoma City. Coed. State control. Semester system. Library: 250,000 volumes, 3700 subscriptions.

Tuition: per hour, resident $88, nonresident $207. On-campus housing for 158 married students, 592 men, 716 women. Average annual housing cost: $2700 for married students, $2311 (including board) for single students. Apply by July 1 to Director of Housing for on-campus housing; to Vice President, Student Services for off-Campus housing information. Phone: (405)974-3368.

Dr. Joe C. Jackson College of Graduate Studies and Research

Graduate study since 1954. Enrollment: full-time 328, part-time 1428. Faculty: full-time 283, part-time 59. Degrees conferred: M.A., M.S., M.F.A., M.B.A., M.Ed., M.M.

ADMISSION REQUIREMENTS. Transcripts, GRE, GMAT (for business) required in support of College's application. Online application available. TOEFL required for international applicants. Interview not required. Accepts transfer applicants. Graduates of unaccredited colleges not considered. Apply to Dean of the Graduate College at least one month prior to registration. Application fee, $15. Phone: (405)974-3341; fax: (405)974-3830.

ADMISSION STANDARDS. Relatively open. Usual minimum average: 2.5 (2.5, last 60 hours) (A = 4).

FINANCIAL AID. Scholarships, grants, assistantships, internships, Federal W/S, loans. Apply by March 15 to appropriate department chair for assistantships. For W/S, loans apply by March 31 to Office of Student Financial Aid. Phone: (405)974-3336. Use FAFSA. Aid available for part-time students.

DEGREE REQUIREMENTS. For master's: 32–34 semester hours minimum, at least 24 in residence; comprehensive exam for some programs; thesis/nonthesis option/projects.

FIELDS OF STUDY.
Adult Education. Includes community service. M.Ed.
Applied Mathematical Sciences. Includes mathematics, computing, science, statistics, math/computing science teaching. M.S.
Biology. M.S.
Business Administration. M.B.A.
Criminal Justice. M.A.
Design–Interior Design. M.F.A.
Early Childhood Education. M.Ed.
Educational Administration. M.Ed.
Educational Guidance and Counseling. M.Ed.
Elementary Education. M.Ed.
English. Includes creative writing, contemporary literature, composition, TESL. M.A.
Forensic Sciences. Includes criminalistics, technical investigation. M.S.
General Education. M.Ed.
Gerontology. M.Ed.
History. Includes museum studies, social studies teaching. M.A.
Human Environmental Sciences. Includes family and child studies, nutrition-food management. M.S.
Industrial and Applied Physics. Includes teacher certificate in school psychometrist, school psychologist. M.S.
Instructional Media. Includes applied technology, library information. M.Ed.
Music. M.M.
Physics.
Political Science. Includes international relations, public affairs. M.A.
Professional Health Occupations. M.Ed.
Psychology. Includes general experimental, counseling, school counseling. M.A.
Reading. M.Ed.
Secondary Education. M.Ed

Special Education. Includes mild–moderate, severe–profound. M.S.

Speech/Language Pathology. M.S.

Wellness Management. Includes exercise science, health studies. M.S.

CENTRAL WASHINGTON UNIVERSITY

Ellensburg, Washington 98926-7510

Web site: www.cwu.edu

Founded 1890. CGS member. Located 36 miles N of Yakima and 100 miles E of Seattle. Coed. State control. Quarter system. Special facilities: educational television in conjunction with Ellensburg public schools, computer center, Geographic Information System Lab, Chimpanzee and Human Communication Institute. Library: 537,700 volumes, 1450 subscriptions. More than 700 computers on campus for general student use. Total University enrollment: 8000.

Annual tuition: full-time resident $4548, nonresident $13,248; per credits resident $151, nonresident $461. On-campus housing for married, single students. Average annual housing cost: $5031 (including board) for single students, $3195 for married students. Apply to Housing Office. Phone: (509)963-1831.

Graduate Studies and Research

Graduate study since 1947. Enrollment: full-time 218, part-time 159 (men 42%, women 58%). Graduate faculty: full- and part-time 330. Degrees conferred: M.A., M.Ed., M.S., M.A.T., M.M., M.F.A. M.P.A.

ADMISSION REQUIREMENTS. Transcripts, GRE (for some programs) required in support of University's application. TOEFL (minimum score 550, 213 on computer-based test) required for foreign applicants. Accepts transfer applicants. Apply to Office of Graduate Admissions by April 1 (Fall), October 1 (Winter), January 1 (Spring). Application fee $35. Phone: (509)963-3103; fax: (509)963-1799; e-mail: masters@cwu.edu.

ADMISSION STANDARDS. Relatively open. Required minimum average: 3.0 (A = 4).

FINANCIAL AID. Annual awards from College funds: graduate assistantships, minority fellowships, internships, Federal W/S, loans. Apply by March 1 to Dean of Graduate School. Use FAFSA. Phone: (509)963-1611. About 30% of students receive aid other than loans from College and outside sources.

DEGREE REQUIREMENTS. For M.A., M.Ed., M.S., M.A.T., M.M.: 45 credit hours minimum; thesis or project; advancement to candidacy: final oral/written exam. For M.F.A.: 90 credit hours minimum; at least three quarters in residence.

FIELDS OF STUDY.
Accountancy.
Administration.
Art.
Biological Sciences.
Business and Marketing Education.
Chemistry.
Counseling Psychology.
Educational Administration.
Engineering Technology.
English. Includes literature, TESL.
English Language Learning.
Experimental Psychology.
Family and Consumer Sciences.

Geology.
History.
Individualized Studies.
Master Teacher.
Mathematics.
Music.
Organization Development.
Physical Education, Health Education, and Leisure Studies.
Reading Specialist.
Resource Management.
School Counseling.
School Psychology.
Special Education.
Supervision and Curriculum.
Theater Production.

CHADRON STATE COLLEGE

Chadron, Nebraska 69337

Web site: www.csc.edu

Founded 1911. Located 300 miles NE of Denver, Colorado. Coed. State control. Semester system. Library: 280,000 volumes, 1200 subscriptions.

Tuition: per hour, resident $83, nonresident $165. On-campus housing for 62 married students, 800 single students. Annual housing cost (including board): $3508. Apply by June 1 to Director of Housing. Phone: (800)CHA-DRON. Day-care facilities available.

Graduate Program

Graduate study since 1955. Average enrollment per year: full-time 38, part-time 317. Graduate faculty: full-time 65, part-time 15. Degrees conferred: M.B.A., M.S. in Ed., M.A. in Ed., Specialist in Education.

ADMISSION REQUIREMENTS. Two transcripts, references, GRE or MAT required in support of College's application. TOEFL required for foreign applicants. Interview required for Specialist Degree only. Accepts transfer applicants. Graduates of unaccredited institutions not considered. Apply to Chair of the Graduate Council. Application fee $15. Phone: (800)CHA-DRON; fax: (308)432-4451.

ADMISSION STANDARDS. Selective. Usual minimum average: 2.75 (A = 4).

FINANCIAL AID. Scholarships, teaching assistantships, internships, Federal W/S, loans. Apply by June 1 to Financial Aid Officer for scholarships, Federal W/S, loans, to Chair of the Graduate Council for assistantships. Phone: (800)CHA-DRON. Use FAFSA. About 5% of students receive aid other than loans from College, 20% from all sources. Aid available for part-time students.

DEGREE REQUIREMENTS. For M.B.A., M.S., M.A. in Ed.: 36 credits minimum, at least 12 in residence; thesis/nonthesis option; final oral exam. For Specialist in Education Degree: 30 credits minimum, at least 15 in residence; thesis or field study option; final oral/written exams.

FIELDS OF STUDY.
Business Administration.
Education. Includes elementary, secondary teaching, administration; computer education, fine arts, language arts, mathematics, physical education, reading, science, social studies, guidance, supervision, reading.

CHAPMAN UNIVERSITY

Orange, California 92666-1011
Web site: www.chapman.edu

Founded 1861. Located 35 miles SE of Los Angeles. Coed. Private control. Disciples of Christ affiliation. Semester system. Special facilities: Center for Economic Research, Center for International Business. Library: 203,000 volumes, 2100 subscriptions. More than 250 computers on campus for general student use.

Tuition: per credit M.B.A. $635, M.P.T. $515, Education $420, all other programs $550. On-campus housing for married students, single graduate students. Average academic year housing costs: $6070–$9028 (including board) for single students; $634–$940 per month for married students. Contact Director of Residence Life for both on- and off-campus housing information. Phone: (714)997-6604.

Division of Graduate Studies

Enrollment: full- and part-time 2900. Faculty teaching graduate students: full- and part-time 313. Degrees conferred: M.A., M.B.A., M.F.A., M.H.A., M.P.T., M.S.

ADMISSION REQUIREMENTS. Official transcripts, GRE, two letters of recommendation required in support of application. GRE Subject/GMAT/MAT/NTE required for some programs. TOEFL or Institutionally administered TOEFL required for international applicants. Accepts transfer applicants. Graduates of unaccredited institutions not considered. Apply to Office of Graduate Admissions. Application fee $40. Phone: (888)CUAPPLY or (714)997-6786; fax: (714)997-6713.

ADMISSION STANDARDS. Competitive. Usual minimum average: 3.0 (A = 4).

FINANCIAL AID. Graduate assistantships, fellowships, internships, tuition awards, Federal W/S, loans. Approved for VA benefits. Apply by March 1 to Graduate Dean for fellowships, assistantships; to Financial Aid Office for all other programs. Phone: (714)997-6741. Use FAFSA (University code: 001167) and complete the Supplemental Application for Graduate Students.

DEGREE REQUIREMENTS. For master's: 33–60 credits at least 24 credits in residence; candidacy; thesis/nonthesis/project option; comprehensive exam; internship for most programs.

FIELDS OF STUDY.

SCHOOL OF BUSINESS AND ECONOMICS:
Business Administration. M.B.A., E.M.B.A.

SCHOOL OF COMMUNICATION ARTS:
Creative Writing. M.F.A.
English. Includes teaching literature and composition, literature. M.A.

SCHOOL OF EDUCATION:
Counseling and Pupil Personnel Services. M.A.
Education. Includes curriculum and instruction, reading. M.A.
Educational Leadership and Administration. M.A.
Educational Psychology and Pupil Personnel Services. M.A.
Elementary School Teaching. M.A. Teaching.
School Psychology. Ed.S.
Secondary School Teaching. M.A. Teaching.
Special Education. Includes mild/moderate, moderate/severe. M.A.

SCHOOL OF FILM AND TELEVISION:
Film and Television Production. Includes new media, production, producing, screenwriting. M.F.A.
Film Studies. M.A.

WILKINSON COLLEGE OF LETTERS AND SCIENCES:
Food Science and Nutrition. M.S.
Physical Therapy. D.P.T.
Psychology. Includes counseling, marriage, family, and therapy. M.A.

DEPARTMENT OF PROFESSIONAL STUDIES:
Career Counseling. M.A.
Criminal Justice. M.A.
Health Administration. M.H.A.
Human Resources. M.S.
Organizational Leadership. M.A.

CHICAGO STATE UNIVERSITY

Chicago, Illinois 60628
Web site: www.csu.edu

Founded 1867. Coed. State control. Semester system. Library: 323,000 volumes, 1500 subscriptions.

Annual tuition: full-time per hour, resident $164, nonresident $329. Limited on-campus housing available for single graduate students. Average academic year housing cost: $6500 (includes board). Contact Student Housing Director for on-campus housing information. Phone: (773)995-DORM. Day-care facilities available.

School of Graduate Studies

Graduate study since 1938. Enrollment: full-time 312, part-time 1540. Graduate faculty: full-time 133, part-time 87. Degrees conferred: M.A., M.S., M.S. in Ed.

ADMISSION REQUIREMENTS. Official transcripts required in support of School's application. On-line application available. Interview recommended by some departments. TOEFL, financial statement, certificate of sponsorship, two transcripts with credential evaluation required for international applicants. Accepts transfer applicants. Graduates of unaccredited institutions not considered. Apply to the Admissions and Records Office by March 15 (Fall), October 15 (Spring). Rolling admissions process. Students may enroll on a nondegree basis pending formal admission. Application fee $25. Phone: (773)995-2404; fax: (773) 995-3671.

ADMISSION STANDARDS. Selective. Usual minimum average: 2.75 (A = 4).

FINANCIAL AID. Scholarships, research fellowships, research/teaching assistantships, tuition waivers, Federal W/S, loans. Approved for VA benefits. Apply to the Director of Financial Aid; no specified closing date. Phone: (773)995-2304. Use FAFSA. Aid available for part-time students.

DEGREE REQUIREMENTS. For M.A., M.S.: 30–36 semester hours minimum, at least 21–27 in residence; thesis optional; final written/oral exam. For M.A. in Ed.: same as above, except·32 hours minimum.

FIELDS OF STUDY.
Bilingual Education. M.S.Ed.
Biological Science. M.S.
Corrections and Criminal Justice. M.S.
Counseling. M.A.
Criminal Justice. M.S.
Curriculum and Instruction. M.S.Ed.
Early Childhood Education. M.S.Ed.
Elementary Education. M.S.Ed.
English. M.A.

Geography. M.A.
History. M.A.
Library Science. M.A.
Mathematics. M.S.
Occupational Education. Includes business, industrial, industrial supervision. M.S.Ed.
Physical Education. M.S.Ed.
Social Work. M.S.W.
Special Education. Includes teaching of mentally retarded, learning disabled, emotionally disturbed, gifted. M.S.Ed.
Teaching of Reading. M.S.Ed.

THE UNIVERSITY OF CHICAGO
Chicago, Illinois 60637-1513
Web site: www.uchicago.edu

Founded 1890, CGS and AAU member. Coed. Private control. Quarter system. Special facilities: ASCI/Alliances Center for Astrophysical Thermonuclear Flashes, the Bell May Institute, Brain Research Imaging Center, the Cancer Research Center, the Center for Cosmological Physics, Center for East Asian Studies, Center for East European and Russian/Eurasian Studies, Center for Gender Studies, Center for International Studies, Center for Middle Eastern Studies, Center for School Improvement, Center for the Study of Race, Politics and Culture, the Computation Institute, Center for Computational Psychology, Cultural Policy Center, Enrico Fermi Institute, Film Studies Center, James Franck Institute, Franke Institute for the Humanities, Franklin McLean Memorial Research Institute, the Center for Health Administration Studies, Institute for Biophysical Dynamics, Institute for Mind and Biology, Center for Magnetic Resonance Imaging, Materials Research Science and Engineering Center, Oriental Institute, South Asia Language and Area Center. The University's NIH ranking is 32nd among all U.S. institutions with 360 awards/grants worth $131,240,668. Library: 5,710,000 volumes. Total University enrollment: 12,200.

On-campus housing available for graduate students. Approximately 1200 apartments and more than 500 single rooms are available. Additional housing planned to open in 2003. Average monthly housing cost: $557–$1142 for married, $426–$893 for single students. For specific Graduate Student Housing information, contact the Assignments Office, phone: (773) 753-2218. For International House information, contact the Housing Office, phone: (773)753-2270

Division of the Biological Sciences

Graduate study since 1892. Tuition: per course $3085.
Graduate enrollment: full- and part-time 333. Graduate faculty: full-time 476; no part-time faculty. Degrees conferred: S.M., Ph.D., M.D.-Ph.D.

ADMISSION REQUIREMENTS. Transcripts, GRE, three letters of recommendation required in support of application. TOEFL required for foreign applicants. Interview recommended. Accepts transfer applicants. Apply to Associate Dean for Graduate Affairs by December 28 (Fall quarter). Application fee $50, $55 for foreign applicants. Phone: (773)834-2105.

ADMISSION STANDARDS. Very selective for most departments, competitive to very competitive for the others. Usual minimum average 3.0 (A = 4).

FINANCIAL AID. Scholarships, research assistantships, fellowships, grants, traineeships, Federal W/S, loans. Apply to Associate Dean for Graduate Affairs; no specified closing date. Use FAFSA. 100% of students receive aid other than loans from University and outside sources.

DEGREE REQUIREMENTS. For S.M.: Individual degree granting units set requirements; thesis; final written/oral exam. For Ph.D.: six quarters in residence and completion of Research Residency; preliminary exam; teach twice in credit-approved positions; take the course Scientific Integrity and the Ethical Conduct of Research; dissertation; final written/oral exam. For M.D.: see School of Medicine listing below.

FIELDS OF STUDY.
Biochemistry and Molecular Biology.
Cancer Biology.
Computational Neuroscience.
Developmental Biology.
Ecology and Evolution.
Evolutionary Biology.
Genetics.
Health Studies.
Human Genetics.
Human Nutrition and Nutritional Biology.
Immunology.
Medical Physics (Radiology).
Microbiology.
Molecular Genetics and Cell Biology.
Neurobiology.
Ophthalmology and Visual Science.
Organismal Biology and Anatomy.
Pathology.
Pharmacology.
Physiology.
Virology.

Division of the Humanities

Graduate study since 1892.
Tuition: per course $1932. Graduate enrollment: full-time 1094, part-time 9 (478 men, 625 women). Division faculty: full-time 188, part-time 10. Degrees conferred: A.M., M.A.P.H., M.F.A., Ph.D.

ADMISSION REQUIREMENTS. Transcripts, GRE/Subject Test, three letters of recommendation, evidence of satisfactory training in one foreign language required in support of application. Writing sample required by some departments. TOEFL (minimum score 550) required for foreign applicants. Interview not required. Graduates of unaccredited institutions not considered. Apply to the Dean of Students, Division of the Humanities by January 5. Application fee $50, $55 for foreign applicants. Phone: (773)702-8512; fax: (773)702-9861.

ADMISSION STANDARDS. Competitive for most departments, very competitive for others. Usual minimum average: 3.5 (A = 4).

FINANCIAL AID. Scholarships, fellowships, tuition waivers, Federal W/S, loans. Apply by January 5 to the Dean of Students. Use FAFSA. About 70% of students receive aid other than loans from University and outside sources.

DEGREE REQUIREMENTS. For A.M., M.A.P.H.: 3 quarters minimum in residence; thesis/essay/similar project; final written/oral exam. For M.F.A.: 18 courses, final creative project and paper instead of thesis. For Ph.D.: 12 quarters minimum beyond the bachelor's, at least 3 quarters in residence; qualifying exam; reading knowledge of foreign languages set by individual departments; admission to candidacy; dissertation; final written/oral exam.

FIELDS OF STUDY.
Ancient Mediterranean World. Interdisciplinary. A.M. only.
Art. Includes history and theory; one language for A.M.; two languages for Ph.D.

Cinema and Media Studies. M.A.P.H.

Classical Languages and Literature. Greek, Latin, classical archaeology; reading knowledge of Greek, Latin, one other language for A.M., two other languages for Ph.D.

Comparative Literature. A.M., Ph.D.

Conceptual and Historical Studies of Science. A.M., Ph.D.

East Asian Languages and Civilizations. GRE for admission.

English Language and Literature. Includes creative writing program; GRE/Subject for admission; samples of work for admission to creative writing. A.M., Ph.D.

General Studies in the Humanities. A.M. only.

Germanic Studies. Includes German, Scandinavian; one language in addition to major for A.M.; specialization available in medieval studies.

History of Culture. Includes study of cultures of various geographic areas and historical periods. A.M., Ph.D.

Humanities. Master of Arts in Humanities program; M.A.P.H. only.

Jewish Studies. A.M. only.

Latin American Studies. A.M. only.

Linguistics. Includes Indo-European and Balkan studies. A.M., Ph.D.

Middle Eastern Studies. A.M. only.

Music. Includes composition, theory, history; term essay for admission; apply for fellowships before January 1; two languages (German required) for A.M.; 3 languages (German required) for Ph.D. in theory and history. A.M., Ph.D.

Near Eastern Languages and Civilizations. Includes Western Asia, Egypt, Judaic, Islam. A.M., Ph.D.

New Testament and Early Christian Literature. Competence in Greek for A.M., Greek and Hebrew for Ph.D.

Philosophy. A.M., Ph.D.

Romance Languages and Literatures. Includes French, Spanish, Italian; GRE for admission; one language in addition to major for A.M., two in addition to major for Ph.D.

Slavic Languages and Literatures. Includes Russian, Polish, Czech, and Slovak literatures, Slavic linguistics. A.M., Ph.D.

South Asian Languages and Civilization. Includes Bengali, Hindi, Sanskrit, Tamil, Urdu languages, literatures, and cultures; French and German in addition to major for A.M. and Ph.D.

Visual Arts. A.M., Ph.D.

Division of the Physical Sciences

Graduate study since 1892.

Tuition: full-time $21,420. Enrollment: full-time 533, part-time 60. Faculty: full-time 173, part-time 9. Degrees conferred: S.M., Ph.D.

ADMISSION REQUIREMENTS. Transcripts, GRE/Subject Test, three letters of recommendation required in support of application. TOEFL required for foreign applicants. Interview not required. Accepts transfer applicants. Apply to Department Chair before January 15 (priority date for Fall). Application fee $50, $55 for international applicants. Phone: (773)702-8789.

ADMISSION STANDARDS. Competitive. Usual minimum average: 3.0 (A = 4).

FINANCIAL AID. Scholarships, fellowships, assistantships, training grants, tuition waivers, Federal W/S, loans. Apply to department chair for scholarships, fellowships, assistantships, to Office of Financial Aid for federal programs; priority application date February 15. About 99% of students receive aid other than loans from University and outside sources. Aid available for part-time students.

DEGREE REQUIREMENTS. For S.M.: 9 courses and 3 quarters minimum in residence; full-time attendance normally expected. For Ph.D.: course requirements vary by department; candidacy qualifying exam sometimes required; two quarters of teaching; reading knowledge of foreign languages in some departments; dissertation; final dissertation defense.

FIELDS OF STUDY.

Applied Mathematics.

Astronomy and Astrophysics.

Chemistry. Ph.D. only.

Computer Sciences. Includes Conversion Master's Program.

Divisional Master's Program.

Financial Mathematics. Master's only.

Geophysical Sciences. Interdisciplinary.

Mathematics.

Physics.

Statistics. Includes biostatistics.

Division of Social Sciences.

Graduate study since 1992.

Tuition: per course $1932. Graduate enrollment: full- and part-time 1300. Division faculty: full-time 225. Degrees conferred: A.M., M.S.T., Ph.D.

ADMISSION REQUIREMENTS. Transcripts, three letters of recommendation, personal statement required in support of application. TOEFL required for international applicants. GRE General/Subject Tests and foreign language proficiency required for most departments. Interview not required. Accepts transfer applicants. Graduates of unaccredited institutions not considered. Application deadline for U.S. citizens and nationals is January 5, for international citizens January 1. Application fee $50, international applicants $55. Phone: (773)702-8415.

ADMISSION STANDARDS. Competitive for most departments, very competitive for others.

FINANCIAL AID. Scholarships, teaching assistantships, fellowships, tuition waivers, Federal W/S, loans. Apply by January 1 to Dean for fellowships, assistantships; to the University's Financial Aid Office for all other programs. Use FAFSA. About 70% of students receive aid from both Division and outside sources.

DEGREE REQUIREMENTS. For A.M.: 9 courses and 3 quarters minimum in residences, thesis or research paper, final comprehensive exam. For Ph.D.: 18 courses or 6 quarters in full-time residence; reading knowledge of at least one foreign language; preliminary oral exam; candidacy; internship for some departments; dissertations; final oral exam.

FIELDS OF STUDY.

Anthropology. GRE for admission. A.M. through divisional master's; joint Ph.D. in Anthropology and Linguistics available; social, cultural, and psychological anthropology, archaeology, linguistic anthropology, physical anthropology, and museology. Ph.D. only.

Divisional A.M. in Social Sciences. Interdepartmental. Concentrations in individual and society, urban studies, philosophy and history of the social sciences, communication, policy dimensions of social change, industrial relations, area and language studies, evaluation and survey research, economics and policy, individualized study; 9 courses and paper required for A.M.; admissions every quarter. A.M. only.

Economics. GRE for admission; A.M. through divisional master's; joint degree in law and economics; price theory, theory of income, employment, and price level, mathematical economic theory, monetary theory and banking, economic history, econometrics and statistics, history of economic thought, labor economics, agricultural economics, public finance, international economic relations, urban economics, industrial organization, economic development. Ph.D. only.

History. GRE for admission. High competence in reading either German or French required for admission; United States history, ancient history, medieval history, Byzantine history, Russian history, Renaissance and Reformation history, modern European history, British history, history of science and/or medicine, and the histories of the Chinese, Indian and Islamic civilizations. Ph.D. only.

Human Development. Includes life course development, mental health, personality and emotion, psychological anthropology, biosocial psychology, clinical psychology.

International Relations. GRE for admission. Interdepartmental: includes international politics, organization, economics; American foreign policy; international theory; economic development; strategic studies; international law and communism; and political geography. A.M. only.

Latin American and Caribbean Studies. Five-quarter A.M. program leads to competency in one of the Latin American or Caribbean languages in addition to studying history, culture, civilization, and current problems of the area. A.M. only.

Middle Eastern Studies. Five-quarter A.M. program leads to competency in one of the Middle Eastern languages in addition to studying history, culture, civilization, and current problems of the area. A.M. only.

Political Science. GRE for admission. Includes political theory; politics and parties; public administration and bureaucracy; international relations; public law and jurisprudence; comparative politics; and political sociology.

Psychology. Includes cognition and cognitive neuroscience, developmental psychology, language program, perception program, social psychology program; joint Ph.D. in Psychology–Linguistics.

Social Thought. GRE for admission. Interdepartmental; application deadline is January 1. Ph.D. only.

Sociology. GRE for admission. Includes community structure; demography; human ecology; deviance; economic and work institutions; family and socialization; formal organization; educational institutions; mathematical sociology; medical sociology; methodology; modernization; personality and social structure; political organization; race and ethnic relations; small groups; social change and social movements; social psychology; social stratification; and urban sociology.

Graduate School of Business

Established 1898. Private control. Accredited programs: M.B.A.; recognized Ph.D. Located on main campus and offers programs in downtown Chicago (M.B.A. part-time, evening and weekends; E.M.B.A.). Quarter system. Special Programs: International Business Exchange programs (in Australia, Austria, Belgium, Brazil, Chile, France, Germany, Hong Kong, Israel, Italy, Japan, Mexico, the Netherlands, People's Republic of China, Spain, South Africa, Sweden, Switzerland, United Kingdom); foreign Study in Barcelona, Singapore, Spain. Special facilities: Center for International Business Education and Research, Center for Decision Research, Center for Population Economics, Center for Research in Security Prices, Center for Statistics Research, Center for the Study of the Economy and the State.

Annual tuition: full-time $30,596, part-time $3250 per course. On-campus rooms and apartments available for both single and married students. Enrollment: total full-time 1016, part-time 1364 (men 75%, women 25%). Faculty: full-time 139, part-time 42; all have Ph.D./D.B.A. Degrees conferred: Campus M.B.A. (full-time, day), Evening M.B.A. (evening, weekends, located at Graduate School of Business's Gleacher Center), I.E.M.B.A. (International Executive M.B.A. in Barcelona, Spain), I.M.B.A. (International), M.B.A.-J.D., M.B.A.-M.D., M.B.A.-A.M. (Area Studies: East Asian, Latin American, Middle Eastern and South Asian; International Relations and Business; Social Services Administration and Business), M.B.A.-M.P.P., M.B.A.-S.M. (Physical Sciences and Business), Ph.D. (Dissertation areas in Behavior Science, Econometrics and Statistics Economics, Finance, Management Science, Marketing, Organizations and Markets, Production).

ADMISSION REQUIREMENTS. All applicants should have a bachelor's degree from a recognized institution of higher educa-

tion. Accepts MBA Multi-App and Computer Edge electronic applications in lieu of institutional application. Early applications are encouraged for both admission and financial aid consideration. Full-time students are admitted Summer, Fall only; part-time evening applicants may enter any quarter, part-time weekend applicants are admitted Fall only; International M.B.A. applicants begin Summer only. There are three deadlines for Fall and both U.S. citizens and international applicants should observe the following deadlines: November 15, January 1, March 15 (applicants who file after February are generally at a disadvantage); scholarship applicants should apply by January 1. Applicants to international M.B.A. should apply by January 15. Part-time applicants should apply at least six weeks in advance of quarter for which they are seeking admission. Submit an application, a GMAT result (will accept GMAT test results from the last five years, latest acceptable date is March), official transcripts from each undergraduate/graduate school attended, two letters of recommendation, personal statement, current résumé (prefers at least four years of work experience), and an application fee of $150 to the Director of Admissions. Phone: campus M.B.A. (773)702-7369; evening, weekend, phone: (773)464-8700. Applicants for I.M.B.A. whose native language is not English must submit a foreign language assessment. In addition, international students (whose native language is other than English) should submit a TOEFL (will not consider scores taken more than two years ago, minimum score 600), certified translations and evaluations of all official transcripts, recommendation should be in English or with certified translations and proof of sufficient financial resources for two years of academic study. In some cases full-time day applicants may be invited to an on-campus interview. Joint degree applicants must apply to and be accepted to both schools/programs, contact the admissions office for current information and specific admissions requirements.

ADMISSION REQUIREMENTS FOR DOCTORAL CANDIDATES. Contact the Office of Doctoral Programs for application material and current information. Applications may be downloaded from Web site. Beginning students are admitted Fall quarter only. Both U.S. citizens and international applicants apply by January 15. Submit an application, a GMAT/GRE (will accept GMAT/GRE test results from the last five years), two official transcripts from each undergraduate/graduate school attended, three letters of recommendation, essays, current resume, statement of purpose, and application fee of $150 to the Graduate School of Business. In addition, international students (whose native language is other than English and have completed at least two years of study in the U.S.) should submit TOEFL (minimum score 600), TSE scores, certified translations and evaluations of all official transcripts, recommendation should be in English or with certified translations. International student's contact: (773)702-7438. Interviews are strongly encouraged.

ADMISSION STANDARDS. Very selective. Median GMAT: 685; median GPA: 3.4 (A = 4). Gourman rating: the MBA was rated in the top five, the score was 4.90; the Ph.D. was rated in the top six, the score was 4.89. *U.S. News & World Report* ranked Graduate School in the top two for part-time M.B.A., top four for Accounting, top two in Finance, top six for E.M.B.A., top seven M.B.A. of all U.S. business schools. *Business Week* listed Graduate School in the top six American business schools.

FINANCIAL AID. Scholarships, minority stipend programs, corporate-sponsored fellowships, graduate assistantships, Federal W/S, loans available. Financial aid is available for part-time study. Financial aid may be available for international students. Assistantships/fellowships available for joint degree candidates. Apply by March 1 for most financial assistance, by January 1 for scholarships, fellowships, and assistantships. Request both need- and merit-based financial aid information from the Graduate School of Business; phone: (773)702-3694. For most financial assistance and all Federal programs submit FAFSA (School code: E00512). Approximately 65% of current students receive some form of financial assistance. For Ph.D. applicants the financial assistance is primarily merit-based. Full support is provided through tuition waivers or tuition waivers plus stipends for four years if all academic conditions are met. International applicants must be able to provide full financial support for the first year of doctoral study.

DEGREE REQUIREMENTS. For M.B.A. (both full- and part-time programs): 20 course program including 11 elective courses; a Leadership, Exploration and Development (LEAD) course for campus M.B.A.; two-year full-time program or two-and-one-half- to three-and-one-half-year program (part-time), degree program must be completed in five years. For M.B.A.-Master's: generally from three-and-one-half- to five-year programs. For M.B.A.-J.D.: four-and-one-half- to five-and-one-half-year program. For M.B.A.-M.D.: five-and-one-half- to seven-year program. For Ph.D.: 6–12 quarter program in residence depending on a student's prior degree; general exam; successfully complete both Breadth (4 courses) and Support (3 courses) courses; complete a curriculum paper; dissertation; oral defense.

M.B.A. AREAS OF CONCENTRATION.
Accounting.
Analytic Finance.
Econometrics and Statistics.
Economics.
Entrepreneurship.
Finance.
General Management.
Human Resource Management.
International Business.
Managerial and Organization Behavior.
Marketing Management.
Operations Management.
Strategic Management.

Divinity School

All study at the graduate level. Tuition: per course $1931. Enrollment: full-time 330. Faculty: full-time 30. Degrees conferred: A.M., A.M.R.S., Ph.D., M.Div.

ADMISSION REQUIREMENTS. Transcripts, four letters of recommendation, GRE, essay required in support of application. TOEFL required for foreign applicants. Interview not required. Apply to Dean of Students of the School, preferably by January 1 (A.M., A.M.R.S., and Ph.D. applicants), March 1 (M.Div.). Application fee $45, $50 international applicant. Phone: (773)702-8217; fax: (773)834-4581.

ADMISSION STANDARDS. Very competitive. Usual minimum average: 3.0 (A = 4).

FINANCIAL AID. Scholarships, fellowships, assistantships, field education/fieldwork stipends, Federal W/S, loans. Apply to Dean of Students of the School by January 1. Phone: (773)702-8217. Use FAFSA. About 90% of students receive aid other than loans from School.

DEGREE REQUIREMENTS. For A.M.: Two years of full-time residence; reading knowledge of French or German; three course sequence on the Modern Study of Religion. For A.M.R.S.: 1- to 2-year program in full-time residence; reading competency in one foreign language; oral exam. For Ph.D.: four years of full-time residence; reading knowledge of French and German; qualifying exams; research paper and oral exam; dissertation; oral defense. For M.Div.: three years of full-time residence beyond B.A. (27 courses); one Biblical language (either New Testament Greek or biblical Hebrew); M.Div. paper/essay.

FIELDS OF STUDY.
Biblical Studies.
Ethics.
History of Christianity.
History of Judaism.
History of Religions.
Philosophy of Religions.
Religion and Literature.
Psychology and Sociology of Religion.
Theology.
Note: Dual degrees available: M.Div.-A.M. (School of Social Science Administration), M.Div.-A.M. (Harris School of Public Policy), M.Div.-Ph.D. (Divinity School).

Law School

Opened 1902. ABA approved since 1923. AALS charter member. Quarter system. Special facilities: Center for Studies in Criminal Justice, Center for Constitutionalism and Eastern Europe. Law library 651,000 volumes, 8429 subscriptions. Library has LEXIS, NEXIS, WESTLAW, DIALOG. Annual tuition: $28,134. Total average cost for all other expenses: $15,677. Off-campus housing available (two blocks from School).

Enrollment: first-year 196, total full-time 583 (men 63%, women 37%); no part-time students. Postgraduates 5. Faculty: full-time 44, part-time 19. Student to faculty ratio 11 to 1. Degrees conferred: J.D., J.D.-A.M. (Economics, History, International Relations, Public Policy), J.D.-M.B.A., LL.M., J.S.D., M.C.L., D.C.L.

ADMISSION REQUIREMENTS. LSDAS Law School report, LSAT (not later than December), letters of recommendation required in support of application. Interview used in a number of cases; by invitation only. LSAT recommended but not required of graduate law applicants. Applicants must hold a bachelor's degree. Accepts about 10 transfer applicants annually. Graduates of unaccredited colleges not considered. Apply to Law School Admissions office after September 1 and preferably by January 1. Beginning students admitted Fall only. Application fee $60. Phone: (773)702-9484; fax: (773)702-0942.

ADMISSION STANDARDS. Very competitive. Mean GPA: 3.54 (A = 4); mean LSAT: 169. Gourman rating: 4.90. *U.S. News & World Report* ranking is in the top six of all law schools. Accepts 15–20% of total annual applicants.

FINANCIAL AID. Scholarships, tutorial and research fellowships. Apply to Admissions Office by April 1 for scholarships. No closing date for loans. Use FAFSA. About 95% of students receive aid other than loans from School.

DEGREE REQUIREMENTS. For J.D.: 9 full quarters and 140 credit hours minimum. For LL.M.: 3 consecutive quarters in full-time residence; final research paper. For J.S.D.: at least 3 consecutive quarters in full-time residence; dissertation; final oral exam. For M.C.L.: 3 consecutive quarters in full-time residence. For D.C.L.: at least 3 consecutive quarters in full-time residence; dissertation. The M.C.L. and D.C.L. programs available to law graduates primarily from foreign legal institutions.

Pretzker School of Medicine (60637-5416)

Established 1927. Annual tuition: $27,120. Total average figure for all other expenses $9500. Enrollment (M.D. program): first-year class 104 (2 EDP); total 400 (men 55%, women 45%). Faculty: same as for Division of the Biological Sciences. Degrees conferred: M.D., M.D.-Ph.D. (Medical Scientist Training program).

ADMISSION REQUIREMENTS. AMCAS report, transcripts, three letters of recommendation, MCAT, interview required in support of application. Applicants must have completed at least three years of college study. Has EDP (apply between June 15–August 1). Will consider transfers on a space available basis. Apply to University Director of Admissions after June 15, before October 15. Application fee $60. Phone: (773)702-1937; fax: (773)834-5412.

ADMISSION STANDARDS. Very competitive. Mean GPA: 3.61; mean MCAT scores: 10.1, 10.8, 10.8. Gourman rating: 4.88. *U.S. News & World Report* ranking is in the top 20 of all U.S. medical schools. Accepts 3% of total annual applicants. Approximately 45% are state residents.

FINANCIAL AID. Scholarships, tuition awards, loans. Apply by February 1 to Dean of Students of the School of Medicine. Use FAFSA (School code: G10141). About 82% of medical students receive aid other than loans from School.

DEGREE REQUIREMENTS. For M.D.: satisfactory completion of four-year program, or a three-year program for students who already have Ph.D. For Ph.D.: see Division of the Biological Sciences listing above.

FIELDS OF GRADUATE STUDY.
Biochemistry and Molecular Biology.
Cancer Biology.
Developmental Biology.
Genetics.
Human Genetics.
Immunology.
Microbiology.
Molecular Genetics and Cell Biology.
Neurosciences.
Pathology.
Pharmacology.
Physiology.
Virology.

The Irving B. Harris Graduate School of Public Policy

Established 1987.

Tuition: per course $1932. On-campus housing available. Enrollment: full-time 163, part-time none. Faculty: full-time 20, part-time none. Degrees conferred: A.M., M.P.P., S.M. (with the Division of the Physical Sciences), Ph.D.

ADMISSION REQUIREMENTS. Official transcripts, three letters of recommendation, GRE or GMAT required in support of School's application. TOEFL required for international applicants. Accepts transfer applicants. Graduates of unaccredited colleges may not be considered. Rolling admission process. Early application encouraged. Application fee $100. Phone: (773)702-8401; fax: (773)702-0926.

ADMISSION STANDARDS. Selective. Usual minimum average: 2.75 (A = 4), 3.0 in major field of undergraduate study.

FINANCIAL AID. Fellowships, assistantships, Federal W/S, loans. Apply by February 1 to appropriate department chair for fellowships, assistantships; to Office of Financial Aid for all other programs. Phone: (773)702-6062. Use FAFSA.

DEGREE REQUIREMENTS. For A.M.: 9 courses and 3 quarters minimum in residence; candidacy; thesis or essay, reading knowledge of one foreign language usually required; final written/oral exam. For M.P.P.: two-year full-time program; LEAD. For Ph.D.: 27 courses and 9 quarters minimum beyond the bachelor's, at least 3 quarters in residence; qualifying paper and exam; reading knowledge of at least one foreign language; dissertation; final oral defense. For S.M.: 18 course program; dissertation proposal and oral defense.

FIELDS OF STUDY.
Environmental Science and Policy. Joint degree. S.M.
Public Policy. Includes concentrations in education policy, environmental policy, child and family policy, health policy, international policy, public finance and regulation, public management, poverty and inequality. M.P.P., Ph.D.
Public Policy Studies. A.M. only.

School of Social Service Administration

Chartered 1908.

Tuition: per course $3419. Graduate enrollment: full-time 330, part-time 108. Faculty: full-time 33, part-time 40. Degrees conferred: A.M., Ph.D.

ADMISSION REQUIREMENTS. Transcripts required in support of School's application. TOEFL required for international applicants. Interview not required. Accepts transfer applicants. Graduates of unaccredited institutions not considered. Apply to the School by February 1 (priority date). Fall admission only. Rolling admission process. Application fee $60, $70 for international applicants. Phone: (773)702-1492; fax: (773)702-0874.

FINANCIAL AID. Annual awards from School funds: scholarships, teaching assistantships, fieldwork, Federal W/S, loans. Apply by April 15 to Dean's Office for assistantships; to Financial Office for all other programs. Phone: (773)702-1126. Use FAFSA. About 80% of students receive aid from School and outside sources. Aid available for part-time students.

DEGREE REQUIREMENTS. For A.M.: 18 courses, at least 3 quarters in full-time residence; field placement. For Ph.D.: minimum of 13 courses beyond the master's; evidence of research and statistics competency; qualifying exam; research project; dissertation; final oral exam.

FIELDS OF STUDY.
Clinical Practice. Includes social and psychological services to individuals, families, and groups. A.M.
Social Administration. Includes advocacy, community organizations, management, planning, policy development and implementation, evaluation. A.M., Ph.D.
Note: Joint degree programs available with Business School, Divinity School, and Harris Graduate School of Public Policy.

UNIVERSITY OF CINCINNATI
Cincinnati, Ohio 45221
Web site: www.uc.com

Founded 1819. CGS member. Coed. Public control. Quarter system. Cooperative graduate program in social work with Ohio State University. Special facilities: Biomedical Chemistry Research Center, Center for Computational Fluid Dynamics, Center for Cultural Resources, Center for Hazardous Waste Research, Center for Economic Education, Environmental Health Center, Center for Geographic Informational Systems and Spatial Analysis, Center for Neighborhood and Community Studies, Institute of Policy Research, Center for Women's Studies. The University's NIH ranking is 64th among all U.S. institutions with 229 awards/grants worth $76,506,873. Library: 2,600,000 volumes, 21,700 subscriptions. Total University enrollment: 34,000.

Tuition: full-time Cincinnati residents $2076, per quarter; nonresidents $4157 per quarter. On-campus housing for 656 single men or women. Average per month housing cost: $412–$600. Apply by July 1 to Housing Office. Phone: (513)556-0682; for off-campus information (513)566-7375.

Graduate School

Established 1906. Enrollment: full-time 3660, part-time 2276. Graduate faculty: full- and part-time 750. Degrees Conferred: M.A., M.S., M.Ed., M.A.T., M.B.A., M.C.P., M.Des., M.F.A., M.S.Arch., M.S.N., Ed.D., D.M.A., M.M., Pharm.D., Ph.D.

ADMISSION REQUIREMENTS. Transcripts, three letters of recommendation (two for engineering) required in support of application. Interview, GRE, GMAT, writing samples, portfolios, statement of purpose required by some departments. Accepts transfer applicants. TOEFL, TWE required for all international students; TSE optional. Graduates of unaccredited institutions not considered. Apply to appropriate Dean prior to registration. Foreign students apply to Foreign Students Office. Application fee $30. Phone: (513)556-4335; (513)556-0128.

ADMISSION STANDARDS. Selective. Usual minimum average: 2.75 (A = 4).

FINANCIAL AID. Scholarships, fellowships, research assistantships, teaching assistantships, internships, Federal W/S, loans. Graduate tuition reciprocity with surrounding counties in Ohio and Kentucky. Apply by February 15 to appropriate Dean for scholarships and fellowships, to appropriate department chair for assistantships, to the Office of Financial Aid for all other programs. Phone: (513)556-6982; fax: (513)556-9171; e-mail: financeaid@uc.edu. Use FAFSA. About 90% of full-time students receive aid other than loans from School and outside sources. No aid for part-time students.

DEGREE REQUIREMENTS. For master's: 45–90 quarter hours minimum, at least one year in residence for some departments; however some departments require two or more years of full-time study; thesis; reading knowledge of one foreign language for some departments; completion of degree no later than seven years from date of entrance; written/oral exam. For Ed.D.: three years minimum in residence; written comprehensive exam; dissertation. For Ph.D.: 135 quarter hours minimum and three years of full-time study or equivalent in residence; written comprehensive exam; advancement to candidacy; dissertation; final oral exam; completion of all requirements no later than nine years from date of entrance.

FIELDS OF STUDY.
Accounting. M.S.
Aerospace Engineering. M.S., Ph.D.
Anthropology. M.A.
Applied Economics. M.A.
Architecture. M.S. Arch., M.Arch.
Art Education. M.A.
Art History. M.A.
Biological Sciences. M.S., Ph.D.
Biomedical Engineering. M.S., Ph.D.
Blood Transfusion Medicine. M.S.
Business Administration. Ph.D.
Cell and Molecular Biology. Ph.D.
Chemical Engineering. M.S., Ph.D.
Chemistry. M.S., Ph.D.
Civil Engineering. M.S., Ph.D.
Classics. M.A., Ph.D.
Communication. M.A.
Communication Sciences and Disorders. M.A., Ph.D.
Community Counseling. M.A.
Community Planning. M.C.P.
Computer Engineering. M.S.
Computer Science. M.S.
Computer Science and Engineering. Ph.D.
Construction Management. M.B.A.
Counselor Education. Ed.D.
Criminal Justice. M.S., Ph.D.

Curriculum and Instruction. M.Ed., Ed.D.
Early Childhood Education. M.Ed.
E-Business. M.B.A.
Educational Administration. M.Ed., Ed.S.
Educational Foundations. M.Ed., Ed.D.
Electrical Engineering. M.S., Ph.D.
Elementary/Middle Education. M.Ed.
Economics. M.A., Ph.D.
Engineering Mechanics. M.S., Ph.D.
English and Comparative Literature. M.A., Ph.D.
Environmental Engineering. M.S., Ph.D.
Environmental Health. M.S., Ph.D.
Environmental Science. M.S., Ph.D.
Finance. M.B.A.
Fine Arts. M.F.A.
French. M.A., Ph.D.
Genetic Counseling. M.S.
Geography. M.A., Ph.D.
Geology. M.S., Ph.D.
Germanic Languages and Literature. M.A., Ph.D.
Health Physics. M.S.
Health Promotion and Education. M.Ed.
History. M.A., M.A.T., Ph.D.
Industrial Engineering. M.S., Ph.D.
Information Systems. M.B.A.
International Business. M.B.A.
Labor and Employment Relations. M.A.
Literacy. M.Ed., Ed.D.
Management. M.B.A.
Management of Advanced Technology and Innovation. M.B.A.
Marketing. M.B.A.
Materials Science. M.S., Ph.D.
Mathematics. M.S., M.A.T., Ph.D.
Mechanical Engineering. M.S., Ph.D.
Metallurgical Engineering. M.S., Ph.D.
Molecular and Cellular Pathophysiology. D.Sc.
Molecular and Cellular Physiology. Ph.D.
Molecular & Developmental Biology. M.S., Ph.D.
Molecular Genetics, Biochemistry, and Microbiology. M.S., Ph.D.
Molecular, Cellular, and Biochemical Pharmacology. M.S., Ph.D.
Nuclear and Radiological Engineering. M.S., Ph.D.
Nursing. Includes adult health, community health, critical care trauma, family nurse practitioner, neonatal, nurse anesthesia, nurse midwifery, nurse service administration, occupational health, pediatric nurse practitioner, perinatal health, psychiatric. M.S.N., Ph.D.
Nutrition. M.S.
Operations Management. M.B.A.
Pathobiology and Molecular Medicine. M.S., Ph.D.
Pharmaceutical Sciences. M.S., Ph.D.
Pharmacy Practice. Pharm.D.
Philosophy. M.A., Ph.D.
Physical Therapy. M.P.T.
Physics. M.S., Ph.D.
Political Science. M.A., Ph.D.
Psychology. Ph.D.
Quantitative Analysis. M.S.
Radiology—Radiological Sciences. Includes medical physics. M.S.
Regional Development Planning. Ph.D.
Real Estate. M.B.A.
School Counseling. M.Ed.
School Psychology. M.Ed., Ph.D.
Secondary Education. M.Ed.
Social Work. M.S.W.
Sociology. M.A., Ph.D.
Spanish. M.A., Ph.D.
Special Education. M.Ed., Ed.D.
Taxation. M.S.

Urban Educational Leadership. Ed.D.
Women Studies. M.A.

College of Law (45221-0040)

Established 1833. Fourth-oldest law school in U.S. ABA approved since 1923. AALS charter member. Coed. Semester system. Special facilities: the Center for Dispute Resolution, Urban Morgan Institute for Human Rights. Library 391,000 volumes, 2587 subscriptions; has LEXIS, NEXIS, WESTLAW, UCLIO, OHIOLINK, OCLC, DIALOG, EPIC, DATATIMES.

Annual tuition: full-time residents $8600, nonresidents $16,432. Limited on-campus housing available. Apply to University Office for Resident Living for both on- and off-campus housing. Total average cost for all other expenses: $10,907.

Enrollment: first-year class 140; full-time 392 (men 46%, women 54%). Faculty: full-time 24, part-time 19. Student to faculty ratio is 13.6 to 1. Degree conferred: J.D., J.D.-M.B.A., J.D.-M.C.P. (Community Planning), J.D.-M.A. (Women's Studies).

ADMISSION REQUIREMENTS. LSDAS Law School report, transcripts, bachelor's degree, two letters of recommendation, LSAT required in support of application. Interview not required. TOEFL required of international applicants. Accepts transfer applicants. Applicants from unaccredited colleges not considered. Apply to College after October 1, before April 1. Fall admission. Application fee $35. Phone: (513)556-6805; fax: (513)556-2391; e-mail: admissions@law.cu.edu.

ADMISSION STANDARDS. Selective. Mean GPA: 3.46; mean LSAT: 157. Gourman rating: 3.28. *U.S. News & World Report* ranking is in the second tier of U.S. law schools. Accepts 25% of total annual applicants.

FINANCIAL AID. Scholarships, fellowships, assistantships, Federal W/S, loans. Apply by March 1. Use FAFSA. About 60% of students receive aid other than loans from College.

DEGREE REQUIREMENTS. For J.D.: 90 semester hours minimum, at least one year in full-time residence; upper divisional writing course and professional responsibility course.

College of Medicine (45267-0552)

Established 1819. Annual tuition: residents $16,968, nonresidents $29,634. Total average figure for all other expenses $16,000.

Enrollment: first-year class 154; total full-time 637 (men 60%, women 40%). Faculty: full-time 400. Degrees conferred: M.D., M.D.-M.S., M.D.-Ph.D. (M.S.T.P., P.S.T.P.).

ADMISSION REQUIREMENTS. AMCAS, transcripts, letters of recommendation, MCAT secondary application required in support of application. Applicants must have completed at least three years of college study. Interview required of final candidates. Has EDP; apply between June 15 and August 1. Accepts transfer applicants. Graduates of unaccredited colleges not considered. Apply to Admissions Committee of the College after June 15, before November 15. Application fee $25. Phone: (513)558-7341; fax: (513)558-1165.

ADMISSION STANDARDS. Very competitive. Mean GPA: 3.45 (A = 4); mean MCAT scores 9.4, 9.9, 9.7. Gourman rating: 3.70. *U.S. News & World Report* ranking is in the top 44 of all medical schools. Accepts 5–10% of total annual applicants. Approximately 75% are state residents.

FINANCIAL AID. Scholarships, loans. Apply by May 1 to the Associate Dean. Phone: (513)558-6797. Use FAFSA. About 35% of students receive some aid from College.

DEGREE REQUIREMENTS. For M.D.: satisfactory completion of four-year program. For M.S., Ph.D.: see graduate school listing above.

FIELDS OF GRADUATE STUDY.
Cell and Molecular Biology.
Developmental Biology.
Environmental Health Sciences.
Molecular, Cellular, and Biochemical Pharmacology.
Molecular and Cellular Physiology.
Molecular Genetics, Biochemistry, and Microbiology.
Neuroscience.
Pathobiology and Molecular Medicine.

College-Conservatory of Music, Graduate Division

Graduate study since 1929, doctoral study since 1971. Coed. Quarter system.

Tuition; resident $1956 per quarter, nonresident $3917 per quarter; per credit, resident $228, nonresident $424.

Enrollment: full-time 400, part-time 175. Total college faculty: full-time 90, part-time 30. Degrees conferred: M.A., M.F.A., Artist Diploma, M.M., D.M.A., D.M.E., Ph.D.

ADMISSION REQUIREMENTS. Official transcripts, three letters of recommendation, audition/interview, GRE required in support of College's application. GMAT required for Art Administration. TOEFL (520 minimum score) and verification of available funding required for international applicants. Accepts transfer applicants. Apply to Assistant Dean for Admissions and Student Services by February 1 for priority consideration. Application fee $65. Phone: (513)556-5463, Fax: (513)556-1028.

ADMISSION STANDARDS. Selective on basis of demonstrated talent and academic background. Usual minimum average: 3.0 (A = 4).

FINANCIAL AID. Annual awards from institutional funds: scholarships, awards, prizes, teaching assistantships, Federal W/S, loans. Approved for VA benefits. Apply by February 15 to Assistant Dean for Admissions and Student Services. Phone: (513)556-6982; fax: (513)556-9171. Use FAFSA.

DEGREE REQUIREMENTS. For M.M.: 51–56 quarter hours minimum (theory 66 quarter hours, music history 65 quarter hours, orchestral conducting 68 quarter hours, accompanying 62 quarter hours, jazz studies 64 quarter hours, woodwinds 69 quarter hours); at least one year in residence; comprehensive review; recitals where appropriate; final oral exam; knowledge of one foreign language for some programs. For M.A.: 84 quarter hour program; research project; internship. For M.F.A.: 144–154 quarter hours, at least seven quarters in residence; thesis/thesis production/two professional internships. For D.M.A., D.M.E.: 90 quarter hours minimum beyond master's (135 quarter hours for D.M.E.); preliminary exam; final document; reading knowledge of one foreign language for D.M.A. For Ph.D.: 90 quarter hours, minimum beyond the master's; reading knowledge of two foreign languages; outside-of-field cognate; preliminary exam; dissertation; final oral exam.

FIELDS OF STUDY.
Accompanying. M.M.
Arts Administration. M.A.
Bassoon. M.M., D.M.A.
Choral Conducting. M.M., D.M.A.
Clarinet. M.M., D.M.A.
Classical Guitar. M.M.
Composition. M.M., D.M.A.
Conducting. Includes choral, orchestral, wind ensemble. M.M., D.M.A.
Directing. M.F.A.
Double Bass. M.M., D.M.A.
Euphonium. M.M.
Flute. M.M., D.M.A.
French Horn. M.M., D.M.A., A.D.
Harp. M.M.

Harpsichord. M.M., D.M.A., A.D.
Jazz Studies. M.M.
Music. Includes theory, musicology. Ph.D. only.
Music Education. M.M., D.M.E.
Music History. M.M.
Oboe. M.M., D.M.A.
Organ. M.M., D.M.A.
Percussion. M.M., D.M.A., A.D.
Piano. M.M., D.M.A., A.D.
Saxophone. M.M.
Theater Design and Production. Includes costume, makeup, sound, stage, stage lighting, stage management, technical production. M.F.A.
Theater Directing. M.F.A.
Theater Performance. M.F.A.
Theory. M.M., Ph.D.
Trombone. M.M., D.M.A.
Trumpet. M.M., D.M.A.
Tuba. M.M.
Viola. M.M., D.M.A.
Violin. M.M., D.M.A.
Violoncello. M.M., D.M.A.
Voice. M.M., D.M.A., A.D.
Woodwinds. M.M., D.M.A.

THE CITADEL

Charleston, South Carolina 29409
Web site: www.citadel.edu

Founded 1842. Located 100 miles S of Columbia. Coed on graduate level. State control. Semester system. Library: 197,000 volumes, 1300 subscriptions.

Tuition: per credit hour, resident $162, nonresident $323. No on-campus housing for graduate students.

College of Graduate and Professional Studies

Graduate study since 1968. Enrollment: full-time 143, part-time 527. Faculty teaching graduate students: full-time 47, part-time 17. Degrees conferred: M.A., M.A. Ed., M.A.T., M.B.A., M.Ed., Ed.S.

ADMISSION REQUIREMENTS. Transcripts, interview, MAT/ GRE/GMAT, two letters of recommendation required in support of application. TOEFL required for international applicants. Accepts transfer applicants. Graduates of unaccredited institutions not considered. Apply to Dean of Graduate Studies or Director of M.B.A. Program at least one month prior to registration. Application fee for Graduate Education and M.B.A. is $25. Phone: (843)953-5189; fax: (843)953-7630.

ADMISSION STANDARDS. Selective. Usual minimum average: 2.75 (A = 4).

FINANCIAL AID. Limited to graduate assistantships, Federal W/S, loans. Apply to Graduate Office for assistantship, to Financial Aid Office for all Federal programs; no specified closing date. Phone: (843)953-5187; fax: (843)953-6759. Use FAFSA.

DEGREE REQUIREMENTS. For M.A., M.A. Ed., M.A.T., M.Ed.: 39–45 semester hours minimum, at least 24 in residence; comprehensive exam; no language or thesis requirements. For M.B.A.: 30 semester hours minimum, at least 24 in residence; no language or thesis requirements; comprehensive exam. For Ed.S.: 39 semester hours beyond the master's.

FIELDS OF STUDY.
Biology. M.A.Ed.
Business Administration. M.B.A.

Clinical Counseling. M.A.
Computer Science. M.S.
Counselor Education. M.Ed.
Educational Leadership. Includes elementary, secondary (M.Ed.); superintendency, school psychology (Ed.S.).
English. M.A.
History. M.A.
Mathematics. M.A.Ed.
Physical Education. M.Ed.
Reading. M.Ed.
Secondary Education. Includes math, English, biology, social studies. M.A.T.
Social Sciences. M.A.Ed.
Special Education. Joint program with University of Charleston.

CITY COLLEGE OF THE CITY UNIVERSITY OF NEW YORK

New York, New York 10031-6977
Web site: www.ccny.cuny.edu

Founded 1847. Coed. Municipal control. Semester system. Special facilities: Benjamin Levich Institute, Center for Worker Education, Center for Analysis of Structures and Interfaces/ CASI, Center for Biomedical Engineering, Center for Teaching and Learning, Dominican Institute, Earthquake Engineering Center, International Center for Environmental Resources and Development, Institute for Municipal Waste Research, Institute for Research on the African Diaspora in the Americas and the Caribbean, Institute for Transportation Systems, Max E. & Filomen M. Greenberg Center for Legal Education and Urban Policy, Rifkind Center for the Humanities, Robinson Center for Graphic Arts and Communication Design, Sonic Arts Center. Library: 1,400,000 volumes; designated as a Federal depository in 1884.

Tuition: New York City and State residents $185 per credit, nonresidents $320. No on-campus housing.

College of Liberal Arts and Sciences— Graduate Division

Graduate study since 1944. Enrollment: full- and part-time 805. College faculty: full- and part-time 205. Degrees conferred: M.A., M.S., M.F.A., Ph.D. (offered through CUNY Graduate).

ADMISSION REQUIREMENTS. Transcripts, three letters of recommendation required in support of application. Some programs require writing samples, portfolios, or auditions. TOEFL or evidence of proficiency in English required of international students. Interview not required. Accepts transfer applicants. Apply to Office of Admissions, Room 100 by May 1 (Fall). December 1 (Spring). Application fee $40. Phone: (212)650-6980; fax: (212)650-6417.

ADMISSION STANDARDS. Relatively open for some departments, selective for others. Usual minimum average: 2.75 (A = 4).

FINANCIAL AID. Annual awards from institutional funds: scholarships, assistantships, full and partial tuition waivers, Federal W/S, loans. Apply by February 1 to University's Financial Aid Office for scholarships, fellowships, Federal funds; by March 1 to appropriate department chair for assistantships. Phone: (212)650-5819. Use FAFSA and CUNY's FAF. About 5–10% of students receive aid other than loans from University and outside sources. Aid available for part-time students.

DEGREE REQUIREMENTS. For master's: 30–48 credit hours minimum, at least two semesters in residence (24 credits); foreign language proficiency for some programs; thesis or comprehensive exam in many fields. For Ph.D.: two years minimum, at least one year in residence; preliminary exam; reading knowledge of one or two foreign languages; and proficiency in one research tool; dissertation; final oral exam.

FIELDS OF STUDY.
Anthropology. M.A.
Art. M.F.A.
Art History. M.A.
Biochemistry. M.A.
Biology. M.A.
Chemistry. M.A.
Creative Writing. M.A.
Earth and Environmental Science. Includes oceanography. M.A.
Economics. M.A.
English Literature—Language and Literacy. M.A.
History. M.A.
International Relations. M.A.
Mathematics. M.A.
Media Arts Production. M.F.A.
Music. M.A.
Physics. M.A.
Psychology. M.A.
Sociology. M.A.
Spanish. M.A.

School of Architecture, Urban Design and Landscape Architecture

Tuition: New York State resident $185 per credit, nonresident $320.

Enrollment: full-time 35, part-time 10. Faculty: full-time 12, part-time 10. Degrees conferred: M.Arch. I, M.Arch II, M.U.P.

ADMISSION REQUIREMENTS. Transcripts, three letters of reference, curriculum vitae, 500-word essay required in support of application. Interview not required, but encouraged. TOEFL required for international applicants. Apply to Admissions Office of the School by January 1. Application fee $40. Phone: (212)650-7118.

ADMISSION STANDARDS. Selective. Usual minimum average 2.75 (A = 4.0).

FINANCIAL AID. Scholarships, research/teaching assistantships, Federal W/S, loans. Apply to Dean for scholarships, assistantships, to Financial Aid Office for all other aid by May 1. Phone: (212)650-5819 or (212)650-6656. Use FAFSA.

DEGREE REQUIREMENTS. For M.Arch. I.: 108 credit full-time program; thesis. For M.Arch. II; 51 credit full-time program; thesis optional. For M.U.P.: 32 credit full-time program.

FIELDS OF STUDY.
Architecture.
Landscape Architecture
Urban Design.

School of Education—Graduate Division
Web site: www.ccny.cuny.edu

Graduate study since 1921. Semester system.
Tuition: per credit, New York State resident $185, nonresident and international $320. Enrollment: full- and part-time 687. Faculty: full-time 84, part-time 75. Degrees conferred: M.A., M.S., Advanced Certificate.

ADMISSION REQUIREMENTS. Transcripts, two letters of recommendation required in support of School's application. TOEFL required for international applicants. Interview required by some

departments. Accepts transfer applicants. Graduates of unaccredited institutions not considered. Apply to Graduate Admissions Office of the School by April 15 (Summer, Fall), November 15 (Spring). Application fee $40. Phone: (212)650-6296; fax: (212)650-6970.

ADMISSION STANDARDS. Selective. Usual minimum average: 2.5, 3.0 for Administration and Supervision, School Psychology (A = 4).

FINANCIAL AID. Graduate assistantships, research/teaching assistantships, Federal W/S, loans. Approved for VA benefits. Apply to Financial Aid Office. Phone: (212)650-6656. Use FAFSA and University's FAF. Aid available for part-time students.

DEGREE REQUIREMENTS. For M.A., M.S.: 30 credit hours minimum, at least 19 in residence; qualifying exam may be required based on GPA; thesis optional. For Advanced Certificate: 30 credit hours beyond master's.

FIELDS OF STUDY.
Administration and Supervision. A.C.
Art. Includes K–12. M.A.
Bilingual Childhood Education. M.S.Ed.
Bilingual Special Education. M.S.Ed.
Childhood Education. M.S.Ed.
Curriculum and Teaching in the Elementary School. M.S.Ed.
Developmental and Remedial Reading. M.S.Ed.
Early Childhood Education. M.S.Ed.
English. M.A., A.C.
Environmental Studies. Includes science and social studies.
Literacy. Includes Birth–6, 5–12. M.S.Ed.
Mathematics. M.A., A.C.
Reading. M.S.Ed.
Secondary Science Education. Includes biology, chemistry, Earth science, physic. M.A., A.C.
Social Studies. M.A., A.C.
Teaching Students with Disabilities in Childhood Education. M.S.Ed.
Teaching Students with Disabilities in Middle Childhood Education. M.S.Ed.
TESOL. M.S.

School of Engineering—Graduate Division

Tuition: New York State resident $185–$245 per credit, to a maximum of $2175 per semester; nonresident (including foreign students) $320–$425 per credit to a maximum of $3800 per semester.

Enrollment: full- and part-time 424 (men 84%, women 16%). Graduate faculty: full-time 72, part-time 24. Degrees conferred: M.E., M.S., Ph.D. (doctoral programs are administered by the Graduate School and University Center of CUNY).

ADMISSION REQUIREMENTS. Transcripts, letters of recommendation, GRE (for Ph.D.) required in support of application. Interview not required. TOEFL (500 minimum score) required for international applicants; GRE/Advanced test may also be required. Accepts transfer applicants. Apply to Admission Office of the School by May 15 (Fall), December 15 for Spring. Application fee $40. Phone: (212)650-6447, 642-2812 (Ph.D.).

ADMISSION STANDARDS. Selective. Usual minimum average 2.75 (A = 4).

FINANCIAL AID. For Ph.D. students only: Scholarships, fellowships, assistantships for teaching/research. Minority fellowships, Federal W/S, loans for both master's and Ph.D. candidates. Apply by May 1 to Dean for scholarship, fellowships, assistantships, to Financial Aid Office for all other aid. Use FAFSA. Aid sometimes available for part-time students.

DEGREE REQUIREMENTS. For M.E., M.S.: 30 credit hours minimum, at least 24 in residence; thesis/project/report/seminar. For Ph.D.: 60 credit hours minimum, at least 30 in residence; knowledge of tools of research; field of specialization; first and second exams; candidacy; dissertation; final oral exam.

FIELDS OF STUDY.

Biomedical Engineering. Interdepartmental and interdisciplinary. M.S., Ph.D.

Chemical Engineering. Includes solid processing, polymers and materials, systems engineering, process operations. M.E., Ph.D.

Civil Engineering. Includes structures, environmental engineering, water resources, transportation planning, traffic engineering, highway engineering, network analysis. M.E., Ph.D.

Computer Science. Includes networks and multimedia, database management, computer systems, computer-based modeling. Ph.D.

Computer Science Engineering. M.S.

Electrical Engineering. Includes computer engineering, systems engineering, telecommunications engineering, photonics engineering. M.E., Ph.D.

Mechanical Engineering. Includes mechanical systems and design, energy systems and design, biomedical engineering. M.E., Ph.D.

CLAREMONT GRADUATE SCHOOL

Claremont, California 91711

Web site: www.cgu.edu

Established 1925. CGS member. Located 35 miles E of Los Angeles. Coed. Private control. Semester system. Special facilities: Ancient Biblical Manuscript Center, Blaisdell Programs in World Religions and Cultures, California Institute of Public Affairs, Center for Process Studies, Claremont Information and Technology Institute, Claremont Institute for Economic Policy Studies, Claremont Research Institute of Applied Mathematical Sciences, Institute for Advanced Studies in Leadership, Institute for Antiquity and Christianity, Rancho Santa Ana Botanic Garden, Tomas Rivera Policy Institute, U.S./Japan Institute, Venture Finance Institute. Library: 3,400,000 volumes, 6000 subscriptions.

Annual tuition: full-time $21,580, per credit $913. Limited on-campus housing for married students, men, and women. Average annual living expenses: $15,309. Apply to Housing Office. Phone: (909)621-8036.

Graduate School

Enrollment: full-time 1152, part-time 812 (men 54%, women 46%), Faculty: full-time 85, part-time 85. Degrees conferred: M.A., M.B.A., M.F.A., M.S., D.C.M., M.Phil., Ph.D., D.M.A.

ADMISSIONS REQUIREMENTS. Transcripts, GRE/GMAT (not required for Art and Teacher Education), three letters of recommendation required in support of School's application. Electronic application available. TOEFL (550 minimum score), affidavit of financial support, certified English translation of all official transcripts required for foreign applicants. Accepts transfer applicants. Graduates of unaccredited institutions not considered. Apply to Office of Admissions by February 15 (priority consideration date), November 1 (Spring), April 1 (Summer). Rolling admissions process. Application fee $50. Phone: (909) 621-8069; fax: (909)607-7285; e-mail: admiss@cgu.edu.

STANDARDS. Very competitive for most programs. Usual minimum average: 3.0 (A = 4).

FINANCIAL AID. Fellowships, scholarships, assistantships, grants, tuition waivers, Federal W/S, loans. Apply to Office of Financial Aid by March 31 for fellowships, assistantships; for other aid April 16 (Fall), November 15 (Spring). Phone: (909)621-8337; fax: (909)607-7285; e-mail: finaid@cgu.edu. Use FAFSA and institution's FAF. Aid available for part-time students.

DEGREE REQUIREMENTS. For M.A., M.S.: 30 credits minimum, at least one semester of 12 credits for residence; thesis or critique; qualifying or final exam. For M.B.A., M.F.A.: 60 credits program; advancement to candidacy (M.F.A.). For Ph.D.: 3 years of full-time enrollment, or equivalent beyond the bachelor's (72 units); at least one year of full-time study for residence requirement; reading knowledge of two foreign languages or two optional research tools required; advancement to candidacy; oral/written qualifying exam; dissertation; final oral exam.

FIELDS OF STUDY.

Art. Portfolio, one introductory, one advanced art history course for M.F.A.; one-year full-time attendance required; undergraduate major in art, one semester of full-time study required for M.A. M.A., M.F.A.

Applied Women's Studies. M.A.

Botany. Emphasis on the systematics and evolution of higher plants and fungi; sub-fields including monographic and revisionary study of specific plant groups, cytotaxonomy, biochemical systematics, plant anatomy, comparative morphology, ecology, plant geography, physiology. M.S., Ph.D.

Cultural Studies. M.A. Ph.D.

Economics. Micro, Macro Theory and Econometrics emphasized; two languages or one language and mathematics for Ph.D. M.A., Ph.D.

Education. Includes administrative studies, curriculum, philosophy, instructional theory, language and learning, behavioral studies in human development, evaluation and research; study focusing on preschool and early childhood, elementary and secondary, higher education; elementary and secondary internship program and certification; administrative and professional credentials. M.A., Ph.D.

Engineering. M.E.

English. Includes English and American literature, literature and film; two foreign languages for Ph.D. M.A., M.Phil., Ph.D.

Financial Engineering. M.S.F.E.

History. Emphasizes United States, including Colonial period; Great Britain; Medieval Europe; Modern Europe; Latin America; new interdisciplinary Ph.D. program in European intellectual history. M.A., Ph.D.

Human Resource Design. M.S.

Information Science. M.I.S., M.S., Ph.D.

Management. Emphasis on practice of management. M.B.A., Executive M.B.A., Ph.D. in Management.

Mathematics. Includes applied mathematics, computer science and scientific computing, operations research, junior college teaching, M.A., M.S., Ph.D.

Music. Entrance audition required; one language required; major in music history, composition, performance and music education, music criticism, medieval studies, music librarianship, church music. M.A., Ph.D., D.M.A, D.C.M.

Philosophy. Concentration in Plato, Aristotle, Epistemology, Logic, Ethics, Phenomenology, philosophical topics; 2 foreign languages required. M.A., Ph.D.

Politics and Policy. Includes American government and politics, public law and criminal justice, political theory, public administration, methodology, comparative government and area studies, international relations, international political economy, foreign and defense policy, public policy, political philosophy, environmental and natural resources policy. M.A., Ph.D.

Psychology. Emphasis in social and environmental psychology, cognitive psychology, with sub-fields in attitudes and opinions, group processes, personality theory and research, environmental ecological psychology, human learning and memory, perception, attention and sensory psychology, problem-solving and conceptual behavior, language and thought. M.A., Ph.D.

Religion. Affiliated with institute for Antiquity and Christianity, The School of Theology at Claremont. German and French required, additional languages as necessary. Concentration in Old and New Testament, Church History, Philosophy of Religion and Theology, Women's Studies in Religion. M.A., Ph.D.

CLARION UNIVERSITY OF PENNSYLVANIA

Clarion, Pennsylvania 16214-1232
Web site: www.clarion.edu

Founded 1867. CGS member. Located 85 miles N of Pittsburgh. Coed. State control. Semester system. Library: 540,000 volumes, 12,198 subscriptions. Total University enrollment: 5600.

Tuition: per credit hour resident $230, nonresident $389. On-campus housing for 30 graduate men, 40 graduate women, none for married students. Average annual housing cost: $1776–$3644 (room only), $1008–$1474 (board). Apply to Student Affairs Housing Office. Phone: (814)226-2352.

College of Graduate Studies

Enrollment: full-time 174, part-time 204. Faculty: part-time 144. Degrees conferred: M.A., M.B.A., M.Ed., M.S., M.S. in L.S., M.S.N. (Joint program with Slippery Rock University of PA).

ADMISSION REQUIREMENTS. Transcripts, three current recommendations required in support of application. Interview recommended. TOEFL, proof of financial support required for foreign applicants. GRE required of graduates of unaccredited institutions and for Biology, English, Speech Pathology, and Nursing programs. GMAT required for Business program. Accepts transfer applicants. Apply to Dean of Graduate College by August 1 (Fall), December 1 (Spring), June 1 (Summer). Application fee $30. Phone: (814)393-2337; fax: (814)393-2722.

ADMISSION STANDARDS. Selective to relatively open. Usual minimum average: 2.75 (A = 4). S.P.A., Reading and Library Science require a minimum of 3.0.

FINANCIAL AID. Annual awards from institutional funds: graduate assistantships, loans. Apply to Graduate College by March 1. Phone: (814)226-2315.

DEGREE REQUIREMENTS. For master's: 30–45 semester hours minimum, 21–27 hours in residence (depending upon program); written comprehensive exam; qualifying papers for some programs; thesis optional in some programs.

FIELDS OF STUDY.
Biology. M.S.
Business Administration. Includes professional accountancy. M.B.A.
Communication Education, and Mass Media Technology. M.S.
Communication Science and Disorders. M.S.
Elementary Education. M.Ed.
English. M.A.
Library Science. M.S.
Mathematics. M.S.
Nursing. M.S.
Reading. M.Ed.
Rehabilitative Sciences. Includes developmentally disabled, gerontology, substance abuse. M.S.
Science Education. M.S.
Special Education. M.S.

CLARK ATLANTA UNIVERSITY

Atlanta, Georgia 30314-4385
Web site: www.cau.edu

Founded 1865. Name change 1988. CGS member. It is one of two historically black universities. Coed. Private control. Semester system. Special facilities: Biotechnology Research Center, Resource Center for Science and Engineering, Center for Computational Science, Center for Polymer and Material Research, Center for International Business, Institute for Community Development, Center on Aging, Criminal Justice Institute, Institute for International Affairs, Center for Afro-American Studies. Library: 800,000 items, 1300 subscriptions. Total University enrollment: 4464.

Tuition: per credit $489. On-campus housing for 400 graduate men and women; none for married students. Annual housing cost: $3900 (room only). Apply by June 1 to Director of Graduate Residential Complex. Phone: (404)880-8072.

Graduate Programs

Graduate study since 1929. Enrollment: full- and part-time 1333. Graduate faculty: full- and part-time 290. Degrees conferred: M.A., M.S., M.B.A., M.S.L.S., M.S.W., Specialist in Ed., Ph.D.

ADMISSION REQUIREMENTS. Transcripts, GRE/GMAT, three letters of recommendation required in support of application. TOEFL (minimum score 500) required for foreign applicants. Supplemental documents required for some degree programs. Interview not required. Graduates of unaccredited institutions not considered. Accepts transfer applicants. Admits September (Fall), January (Winter), June (Summer). Apply to Registrar at least one month prior to registration. Application fee $40 ($55 international applicants). Phone: (800)688-3228, (404)880-8765.

ADMISSION STANDARDS. Selective for most departments. Usual minimum average: 2.75 (A = 4).

FINANCIAL AID. Scholarships, grants, fellowships, assistantships, stipends, tuition waivers, Federal W/S, loans. Apply to the Office of Financial Aid by March 1 (Fall), November 1 (Spring). Phone: (404)653-8429. Use FAFSA (University code: 001559). About 20% of students receive aid other than loans from University and outside sources.

DEGREE REQUIREMENTS. For M.A., M.S.: 24–36 semester hours, at least 24 in residence; reading knowledge of one foreign language for some degree programs; thesis; final written/oral exam. For M.B.A.: 60 semester hours; no language requirement. For M.S.L.S.: same as for M.A., except thesis is optional. For M.S.W.: 53 semester hours minimum, at least 24 in full-time residence, including fieldwork experience; thesis; final exam. For M.A. in Ed.: 30–48 semester hours; final exam. For Specialist: 30 semester hours beyond the master's; research project; final oral exam. For Ph.D.: 72 semester hours minimum beyond the bachelor's, at least one year in full-time residence; qualifying exam; candidacy; reading knowledge of two foreign languages; dissertation; final written/oral exam.

FIELDS OF STUDY.

SCHOOL OF ARTS AND SCIENCES:
African Women's Studies. M.A.
African and African American Studies. M.A., D.A.
Biology. M.S., Ph.D.
Chemistry. M.S., Ph.D.
Computer and Information Sciences. M.S. only.
Criminal Justice Administration. M.A. only.
English. M.A. only.
Foreign Languages. M.A. only.
History. M.A. only.

Humanities. Includes African-American studies, English, history, romance languages. D.A.
International Affairs and Development. M.I.A.D., Ph.D.
Mathematics Sciences. M.S. only.
Physics. M.S. only.
Political Sciences. M.A., Ph.D.
Public Administration. M.P.A. only.
Systems Sciences. Includes computer and information sciences, engineering, mathematics, physics. Ph.D.

SCHOOL OF BUSINESS ADMINISTRATION:
Decision Sciences & Information Systems. M.B.A.
Economics. M.A.
Finance. M.B.A.
Marketing. M.B.A.

SCHOOL OF EDUCATION:
Counseling and Human Development. M.A., Ed.S., Ph.D.
Curriculum and Instruction. M.A., Ed.S.
Educational Leadership. M.A., Ed.S., Ed.D.
Exceptional Education and Psychological Services. M.A., Ed.S., Ph.D.

SCHOOL OF LIBRARY AND INFORMATION STUDIES:
Academic Library Administration. M.S.L.S., S.L.S
Public Library Administration. M.S.L.S., S.L.S.
School Library Administration. M.S.L.S., S.L.S.
Special Library Administration. M.S.L.S., S.L.S.

SCHOOL OF SOCIAL WORK:
Social Work Planning & Administration and Social Sciences. Ph.D.
Clinical Social Work. M.S.W.
Social Work and Public Health. M.S.W.-M.P.H.

CLARK UNIVERSITY
Worcester, Massachusetts 01610-1477
Web site: www.clarku.edu

Founded 1887. Located 40 miles W of Boston. CGS member. Coed. Private control. Semester system. Special facilities: American Language and Culture Institute, Computer Career Institute, George Perkins Marsh Institute, Jacob Hiatt Center for Urban Education, Heinz Werner Institute for Development Analysis, Institute for Economic Studies, Arthur M. Sackler Science Center, Teachers Center for Global Studies. Library: 500,000 volumes, 4600 subscriptions.

Annual tuition: full-time $25,000, part-time $3200 per course. No on-campus housing. Apply to Off-campus Housing Office for housing information. Phone: (508)793-7453.

Graduate School

Graduate study since 1887. Enrollment; full- and part-time 656 (men 48%, women 52%). Faculty: full-time 176, part-time 20. Degrees conferred: M.A., M.A. in Ed., M.B.A., M.H.A., Ph.D.

ADMISSION REQUIREMENTS. Transcripts, three letters of recommendation required in support of University's application. TOEFL required for foreign applicants. Some departments require, the others recommend GRE Subject Tests/GMAT. Interview usually not required. Accepts transfer applicants. Apply to chair of proposed major department by February 15 (Fall), January 15 (Spring). Application fee $40. Phone: (508)793-7676; fax: (508)793-8834.

ADMISSION STANDARDS. Competitive for most departments. Usual minimum average: 2.75 (A = 4).

FINANCIAL AID. Annual awards from institutional funds: scholarships, teaching assistantships, full and partial tuition remission, grants, tuition waivers, Federal W/S, loans. Apply to chair of proposed major department by February 15. Use FAFSA and institutional FAF. About 60% of students receive aid other than loans from University and outside sources. Aid available for part-time students.

DEGREE REQUIREMENTS. For M.A., M.B.A., M.H.A.: 30 semester hours minimum, at least 24 in full-time residence; reading knowledge of one foreign language for some programs; thesis; final oral exam. For M.A. in Ed.: same as above, except thesis may be replaced by six additional hours or by election of double seminar. For Ph.D.: 48 semester hours minimum beyond the bachelor's, at least 24 in full-time residence; reading knowledge of foreign language is set by department; preliminary written/oral exam; dissertation; final oral exam.

FIELDS OF STUDY.
Biology. GRE Subject for admission; M.A. usually requires three or four semesters.
Biomedical Sciences.
Business Administration. Includes accounting, finance, global business, health care, information technology, management, marketing. M.B.A.
Chemistry. Includes inorganic, organic, physical.
Community Development.
Economics.
Education. Includes elementary, secondary, counseling, one- or two-year M.A. program, interview usually required for admission.
English. M.A.
Environmental Science and Policy. M.A.
Finance. M.S.F.
Geography. GRE for admission; full-time only.
History.
International Development, Community, and Environment.
Liberal Studies.
Mathematics. Two languages for Ph.D.
Physics.
Psychology. GRE Subject, interview for admission; admits Fall only; full-time only.
Women's Studies.

CLARKE COLLEGE
Dubuque, Iowa 52001-3198
Web site: www.clarke.edu

Founded 1843. Located 185 miles W of Chicago. Graduate coed. Private control. Roman Catholic. Semester system. Library: 97,000 volumes, 7600 microforms, 550 current periodicals.

Tuition: per semester credit $415. On-campus housing available for single students. Average academic year housing costs: $5700 (including board). Contact Office of Residential Life for both on- and off-campus housing information. Phone: (563)588-6313.

Graduate Studies

Graduate study since 1964. Enrollment: full-time 38, part-time 137. College faculty teaching graduate students: full-time 15, part-time 9. Degrees conferred: M.A., M.S.M., M.S.N., M.P.T.

ADMISSION REQUIREMENTS. Official transcripts, three letters of recommendation, eligibility for School Certification, GRE or MAT (Nursing) required in support of application. TOEFL required for international applicants. Accepts transfer applicants. Apply to Coordinator of Graduate Studies at least one month prior to registration. Application fee $25. Phone: (563)588-8183; fax (563)588-6789; e-mail: graduate@clarke.edu.

ADMISSION STANDARDS. Selective. Usual minimum average: 2.5 (A = 4).

FINANCIAL AID. None other than loans and area Professional Development Grants. Phone (563)599-6327; e-mail: financial aid@clarke.edu. Use FAFSA.

DEGREE REQUIREMENTS. For M.A.: 36 semester credits minimum, at least 30 in residence; degree candidacy; thesis/non-thesis option/comprehensive exam/special project. For M.S.M.: 36 credit program. For M.S.N.: 33–36 credit program; clinical experience. For M.P.T.: three-year full-time program; four clinical internships; summative evaluation.

FIELDS OF STUDY.
Elementary Reading. M.A.
Elementary School Administration. M.A.
Management. Includes finance, general management, information management and technology, operations management. M.S.M.
Nursing. Includes nurse educator, family nurse practitioner, administration of nursing systems. M.S.N.
Physical Therapy. M.P.T.
Technology in Education. M.A.

CLARKSON UNIVERSITY

Potsdam, New York 13699
Web site: www.clarkson.edu

Founded 1896. CGS member. Located 150 miles NE of Syracuse. Coed. Private control. Semester system. Special facilities: Center for Advanced Materials Processing, New York State Center for Advanced Technology, Center for the Environment, Clarkson Space Grant Program (with Cornell University), Institute for Nonlinear Studies, Institute for Statistical Physics, computer center. Library: 235,800 volumes, 845 subscriptions.

Annual tuition: per credit hour $742. Very limited on-campus housing. Average annual off-campus housing cost: $5500–$7200 (includes room and board). Apply to Residence Life Office. Phone: (315)268-6442.

Graduate Division

Enrollment: full-time 315, part-time 23. College teaching faculty: full-time 158, part-time 21. Degrees conferred: M.E., M.S., M.B.A., M.P.T., Ph.D.

ADMISSION REQUIREMENTS. Transcripts, GRE, three references required in support of University's application. GMAT required for business programs. TOEFL (minimum score 550, 213 on computer-based test) required for foreign applicants. Interview not required. Accepts transfer applicants. Apply to Dean of Graduate School, preferably by March 15 (Fall), prior to registration for other terms. M.P.T. admits Spring only. Application fee $25; $35 for application sent from outside the U.S. Phone: (315)268-6442; fax: (315)268-7994. Engineering (315)268-7929, fax: (315)268-3841; Science (315)268-3802, fax: (315)268-6670; M.P.T. (315)268-3786, fax: (315)208-1539.

ADMISSION STANDARDS. Selective in some departments, competitive in others. Usual minimum average: 3.0 (A = 4).

FINANCIAL AID. Annual awards from institutional funds: fellowships, scholarships, teaching assistantships, research assistantships, graduate assistantships, industrial fellowships, tuition waivers, Federal W/S, loans. Apply to the Dean of the Graduate School by March 1. Use FAFSA. About 80% of students receive aid other than loans from University and outside sources.

DEGREE REQUIREMENTS. For M.S., M.E.: 30 credit hours minimum, at least 20 in residence; qualifying exam; thesis (6–10 credit hours); nonthesis option in some departments. For M.B.A.: 32 credit hours beyond foundation requirements. For M.P.T.: Seven semester full-time program; three clinical experiences. For Ph.D.: 90 credit hours minimum beyond the bachelor's, at least two years in residence; language/research tool may be required; comprehensive exam (physics); dissertation; comprehensive exam; final oral exam.

FIELDS OF STUDY.

SCHOOL OF ENGINEERING:
Chemical Engineering.
Civil and Environmental Engineering. Includes cold region engineering, environmental and water resources engineering, hydraulics and water resources engineering, infrastructure engineering, structural engineering and solid mechanics, geotechnical engineering, transportation engineering.
Electrical and Computer Engineering. Includes motion control and robotics engineering, power engineering.
Mechanical and Aeronautical Engineering.

SCHOOL OF SCIENCE:
Basic Science.
Chemistry.
Mathematics and Computer Science.
Physics. Includes primary theoretical research and primary experimental research areas.

SCHOOL OF BUSINESS:
Business Administration.
Management Systems.

CENTER FOR HEALTH SCIENCES:
Physical Therapy.

CLEMSON UNIVERSITY

Clemson, South Carolina 29634
Web site: www.clemson.edu

Founded 1889. CGS member. Located 25 miles SW of Greenville. Coed. Land grant, state assisted. Semester system. Special facilities: Archbold Tropical Research Center (Dominica), Belle W. Baruch Forest Science Institute, Center for Advanced Engineering Fibers, Center for Advanced Manufacturing, Center for Computer Communication, Center for Engineering Ceramic Manufacturing, Center for International Trade, Center for Semiconductor Device Reliability Research, Division of Computing and Information Technology, Electron Microscope, Institute of Wildlife and Environment Toxicology, Lee Hall Art Gallery, Daniel Center (Genoa, Italy), Nursing and Wellness Center, Recreation, Travel and Tourism Center, South Carolina Energy Research and Development Center, South Carolina Water Resources Research Institute, Strom Thurman Institute of Government and Public Policy. Library: 1,637,000 volumes, 5978 subscriptions. More than 1000 computers for general student use.

Annual tuition: resident full-time $4710; per credit $260; nonresident $11,289, per credit $466. On-campus housing for 100 married students, 200 graduate men, 200 graduate women. Average annual housing cost: $1510–$2200 (room only) for single students; $1960–$2380 (apartment rent only) for married students. Apply to Housing Office. Phone: (803)656-2295.

Graduate Division

Enrollment: full-time 1747, part-time 1051 (men 50%, women 50%). University faculty teaching graduate students: full-time 912, part-time 93. Degrees conferred: M.A., M.S., M.B.A., M.Ed., M.Ag.Ed., M.Arch., M.C.R.P., M.C.S.M., M.E.Com., M.F.A., M.E.R., M.P.Acc., M.H.R.D., M.P.R.T.M., M.of.Ed., M.N.S., M.Engr., M.Ag., Ed.S., Ed.D., Ph.D.

ADMISSION REQUIREMENTS. Transcripts required in support of University's application. Electronic application available. GRE required for M.A,, M.S., Ed.D., Ph.D, GMAT required for M.B.A., M.P.Acc. and M.S. in Industrial Management, MAT for some programs in the College of Health, Education, and Human Development. TOEFL required for non-English-speaking international applicants. Interview not required. Graduates of unaccredited institutions not considered. Accepts transfer applicants. Apply to Graduate School Office by July 1 (Fall); for international applicants all application materials must arrive by April 15 (Fall), September 15 (Spring). Application fee $40. Phone: (803)656-3195; fax: (803)656-5344.

ADMISSION STANDARDS. Very competitive for some departments, competitive or selective for the others. Usual minimum average: 2.75 (A = 4).

FINANCIAL AID. Annual awards from institutional funds: scholarships, grants, fellowships, traineeships, teaching assistantships, research assistantships, internships, Federal W/S, loans. Apply by April 1 to appropriate Department for fellowships, assistantships, to Office of Student Aid for need based programs. Aid may be available for international students. Use FAFSA. About 90% of full-time students receive aid other than loans from University and outside sources. Aid available for part-time students.

DEGREE REQUIREMENTS. For professional master's: 30 credit hours minimum; final oral/written exam. For M.A., M.S.: 30 hours may include 6 in research; knowledge of one foreign language for some programs; thesis/nonthesis option. For Ed.S.: 30 credit program beyond master's. For Ed.D., Ph. D.: 3 years minimum beyond the bachelor's, at least 2 consecutive semesters in residence; preliminary/qualifying exam for some programs; comprehensive written/oral exam; reading knowledge of foreign language required for some departments; admission to candidacy; dissertation; final oral defense of dissertation.

FIELDS OF STUDY.

COLLEGE OF AGRICULTURAL, FORESTRY, AND LIFE SCIENCES:
Agricultural and Applied Economics. M.S.
Agricultural Education. M.Ag.Ed.
Animal and Food Industries. M.S.
Animal Physiology. M.S., Ph.D.
Applied Economics. M.S., Ph.D.
Aquaculture, Fish, and Wildlife Biology. M.S., Ph.D.
Biosystems Engineering. M.Engr., M.S., Ph.D.
Biochemistry. M.S., Ph.D.
Botany. M.S.
Environmental Toxicology. M.S., Ph.D.
Food Technology. Ph.D. only.
Forest Resources. M.F.R., M.S., Ph.D.
Genetics. M.S., Ph.D.
Microbiology. M.S., Ph.D.
Packaging Science. M.S.
Plant and Environmental Sciences. M.S., Ph.D.
Zoology. M.S., Ph.D.

COLLEGE OF ARCHITECTURE, ARTS, AND HUMANITIES:
Architecture. M.Arch., M.S.
City and Regional Planning. M.C.R.P.
Construction Science and Management. M.C.S.M.
English. M.A.
History. M.A.
Professional Communication. M.A.
Visual Studies. M.F.A.

COLLEGE OF BUSINESS AND BEHAVIORAL SCIENCE:
Accounting. M.P.Acc.
Applied Economics. Ph.D.
Applied Psychology. M.S.
Applied Sociology. M.S.
Business Administration. M.B.A.
Economics. M.A.
Electronic Commerce. M.E.Com.
Graphic Communication. M.S.
Industrial Management. M.S., Ph.D.
Industrial/Organizational Psychology. Ph.D.
Management Science. Ph.D.
Public Administration. M.P.A.

COLLEGE OF ENGINEERING AND SCIENCE:
Biosystems Engineering. M.Engr., M.S., Ph.D.
Bioengineering. M.S., Ph.D.
Ceramic and Materials Engineering. M.S., Ph.D.
Chemistry. M.S., Ph.D.
Chemical Engineering. M.S., Ph.D.
Civil Engineering. M.Engr., M.S., Ph.D.
Computer Engineering. M.S., Ph.D.
Computer Science. M.S., Ph.D.
Electrical Engineering. M.Engr., M.S., Ph.D.
Environmental Engineering and Science. M.Engr., M.S., Ph.D.
Hydrogeology. M.S.
Industrial Engineering. M.S., Ph.D.
Materials Science and Engineering. M.S., Ph.D.
Mathematical Sciences. M.S., Ph.D.
Mechanical Engineering. M.Engr., M.S., Ph.D.
Management Science. Ph.D.
Physics. M.S., Ph.D.
Textile, Fiber, and Polymer Science. M.S., Ph.D.

COLLEGE OF HEALTH, EDUCATION, AND HUMAN DEVELOPMENT:
Administration and Supervision. M.Ed., Ed.S.
Counseling and Guidance Services. M.Ed.
Career and Technology Education. M.C.T.E.
Curriculum and Instruction. Ph.D.
Educational Leadership. Ph.D.
Elementary Education. M.Ed.
Health Administration. M.H.A.
Human Resource Development. M.H.R.D.
Nursing. M.S.
Parks, Recreation, and Tourism Management. M.P.R.T.M.
Reading. M.Ed.
Secondary Education. Includes English, history, mathematics, natural science. M.Ed.
Special Education. M. Ed.
Vocational/Technical Education. Ed.D.

INTERDISCIPLINARY PROGRAMS:
Fine Arts in Computing. M.F.A.C.
Policy Studies. Ph.D.

CLEVELAND STATE UNIVERSITY
Cleveland, Ohio 44115-2440
Web site: www.csuohio.edu

Formerly private, Fenn College became state university in 1965. CGS member. Coed. Semester system. Special facilities: Advanced Manufacturing Center, Biomedical and Health Institute, Center for Economic Development, Center for Environmental Science, Technology, and Policy, Center for Housing Research and Policy, Center for Public Management, Center for Nonprofit Practice and Policy, Center for Public Management, Center for Sacred Landmarks, Cleveland Health Institute, Great Lakes Environmental Center, Labor-Management Relations Center, Cleveland Center for Mass Spectrometry, Ohio Center for the Advancement of Women in Public Service, Center for the Study of Real Estate Brokerage and Markets, Real Estate Research Center, Unger Croatia Center for Local Government Leaders, the Urban Center, Urban Child Research Center. Library: 900,000 volumes, 6500 subscriptions. More than 600 computers on campus for general student use. University enrollment: 16,000.

Tuition: per quarter hour, resident $228, nonresident $451. Limited on-campus housing. Average academic housing costs: $5236 (three quarters). Contact Residence Life Office for both on- and off-campus housing information. Phone: (216)697-7330.

College of Graduate Studies

Enrollment: full-time 945, Part-time 2571. Faculty: full- and part-time 500. Degrees conferred: M.A., M.Ed., M.S., M.B.A., M.M., M.C.I.S., M.L.R.H.R., M.P.A., M.S.U.S., M.S.W., M.U.P.D.D., Ed.S., D.B.A., D. Engr., Ph.D.

ADMISSION REQUIREMENTS. Transcripts, two letters of recommendation required in support of College's application. GRE for arts, sciences, and engineering applicants; GMAT for business applicants; MAT for education applicants. TOEFL/IELTS/MELAB and proof of financial support required for international applicants. Accepts transfer applicants. Apply to College of Graduate Studies at least six weeks prior to registration. Some programs have early deadline. International applicants apply by June 1 (Fall), November 1 (Spring), March 15 (Summer). Application fee: $30. Phone: (216)687-5599.

ADMISSION STANDARDS. Selective for most majors. Usual minimum average: 2.75 (A = 4)

FINANCIAL AID. Tuition grants, graduate assistantships, Federal W/S, loans. Approved for VA benefits. Apply by May 15 to appropriate department chair for assistantships; to Financial Aid for all other programs. Use FAFSA. Phone: (216)687-3764.

DEGREE REQUIREMENTS. For master's: 32 semester hours minimum, at least 24 in residence; thesis (for up to 6 credits) or final comprehensive exam. No language requirement. For D.B.A.: 60 semester hours beyond master's; oral/written qualifying exam; dissertation; final oral exam. For Ph.D.: 60–75 semester hours beyond the master's; oral/written qualifying exam; dissertation; final oral exam.

FIELDS OF STUDY.
Accountancy and Financial Information Systems.
Applied Communication Theory and Methodology.
Biology. M.S., Ph.D.
Business Administration. M.B.A., D.B.A.
Chemical Engineering.
Chemistry. Includes analytical, inorganic, organic, physical, M.S., Ph.D.
Civil Engineering.
Clinical and Analytical Chemistry. Ph.D. only.
Computer and Information Systems.
Counseling. Ed.S. only.
Economics.
Education. Includes counselor, curriculum and institution, educational administration, early childhood, exercise science, multiple handicapped, health, physical, reading, secondary, special, sports management. M.Ed., Ph.D.

Educational Administration. Ed.S.
Electrical and Computer Engineering.
Engineering. Dr. Engr. only.
Engineering Mechanics.
English.
Environmental Engineering.
Environmental Science.
Environmental Studies.
Health Science.
History. Includes art history.
Industrial and Manufacturing Engineering.
Labor Relations and Human Resources.
Mathematics. Includes applied. M.A., M.S.
Mechanical Engineering.
Music.
Philosophy.
Physics.
Psychology. Includes clinical counseling, experimental.
Public Administration.
Public Affairs. Ph.D. only.
Public Health.
Pupil Personnel Administration. Ed.S. only.
School Psychology. Ed.S. only.
Social Work.
Sociology.
Spanish.
Speech Pathology.
Urban Education. Ph.D. only.
Urban Planning.
Urban Studies. M.A., Ph.D.

Cleveland-Marshall College of Law

Cleveland Law School established 1887. John Marshall Law School established 1916. Merged into University 1969. Semester system. Library: 463,100 volumes, 3871 subscriptions; has LEXIS, NEXIS, WESTLAW.

Tuition: full-time day resident $8313, day nonresident $16,470; part-time resident $6395, nonresident $12,670. Enrollment: first-year class, full-time 173, part-time 105. Total full- and part-time 789 (men 50%, women 50%). Faculty: full-time 35, part-time 19. Student to faculty ratio 16.2 to 1. Degrees conferred: J.D., J.D.-M.A.E.S., J.D.-M.B.A., J.D.-M.P.A., J.D.-M.U.P.D.D.

ADMISSION REQUIREMENTS. LSDAS Law School report, transcripts, bachelor's degree, LSAT (no later than December), two letters of recommendation, writing sample required in support of application. Applicants must have completed at least four years of college study. Apply to the Assistant Dean after September 1, before April 1. Application fee $35. Phone: (216)687-2304; fax: (216)687-6881.

ADMISSION STANDARDS. Selective. Mean GPA: 3.17; mean LSAT: 150. Gourman rating: 2.80. *U.S. News & World Report* ranking is in the fourth tier of U.S. law schools. Accepts 25% of total annual applicants. Approximately 20–25% of enrolled students are nonresidents.

FINANCIAL AID. Scholarships, grants, loans. Apply to the Dean by April 1; use FAFSA (College code: 003032). About 55% of students receive aid other than loans from College funds. Aid available for part-time students.

DEGREE REQUIREMENTS. For J.D.: Three academic years minimum (day), or four years minimum (evening), at least one year or equivalent in residence; 87 semester hours. For LL.M.: 20 credits for graduates of American law schools, 24 credits for graduates of foreign law schools. one year minimum in residence; final essay.

COLGATE UNIVERSITY
Hamilton, New York 13346-1386

Founded 1819. Located 38 miles SE of Syracuse. Coed. Private control. Semester system. Library: 634,800 volumes, 2300 subscriptions. More than 500 computers on campus for general student use.

Tuition: per course $2840. No on-campus housing available. For off-campus housing, contact Director of Residential Life. Phone: (315)824-7367.

Graduate Studies

Enrollment: full-time 16, part-time 8. Faculty: 10 full-time. Degrees conferred: M.A., M.A.T.

ADMISSION REQUIREMENTS. Transcripts, GRE, writing sample, three letters of recommendation, personal statement required in support of application. Interview required by most departments. Accepts transfer applicants. Graduates of unaccredited institutions not considered. Apply by March 15 to Director of Graduate Studies. Application fee $50. Phone: (315)824-7220; fax: (315)228-7831.

ADMISSION STANDARDS. Competitive. Usual minimum average: 3.0 (A = 4).

FINANCIAL AID. Scholarships, Federal W/S, loans. Apply by April 1 to Director of Financial Aid. Phone: (315)824-7431. Use FAFSA. About 90% of students receive aid from University and outside sources. Aid sometimes available for part-time students.

DEGREE REQUIREMENTS. For M.A. in an academic subject, M.A.T.: 7 graduate courses minimum, for counseling 9–10 courses; thesis; final oral exam.

FIELDS OF STUDY.
Academic Subject. Includes English, geology, history, philosophy, psychology, religion, sociology and anthropology.
English.
Mathematics.
Natural Science. Includes biology, chemistry, earth science, physics.
Social Studies.

COLORADO SCHOOL OF MINES
Golden, Colorado 80401-1887
Web site: www.mines.edu

Founded 1874. CGS member. Located 10 miles W of Denver. Coed. State control. Semester system. Special facilities: Colorado Advanced Materials Institute, Advanced Steel Processing and Products Center, Center for Ground Water Research, Center for Research on Hydrates and Other Solids, Center for Wave Phenomena, Center for Waste Management, Center for Directional Drilling, Energy and Mineral Field Institute, Excavation Engineering and Earth Mechanics Institute, Kroll Institute for Extractive Metallurgy, Center for Welding and Joining Research, Colorado Center for Advanced Ceramics. Library 144,900 volumes, 1800 subscriptions.

Annual tuition: full-time, resident $5246, nonresident $16,576; part-time, per credit, resident $261, nonresident $875. On-campus housing for married students and for single graduate students. Average annual housing cost: $5400 for single students; $530–$600 per month for married students. Apply to Director of Student Housing. Phone: (303)273-3351.

Graduate School

Enrollment: full-time 543 (men 70%, women 30%), part-time 163. Faculty: full-time 189, part-time 34. Degrees conferred: M.Eng., M.S., Ph.D., Professional Engr.

ADMISSION REQUIREMENTS. Two transcripts, three letters of recommendations, GRE, GRE Subject Test in some departments required in support of School's application. Electronic application available. TOEFL (minimum score 550) required for foreign applicants. Interview not required. Accepts transfer applicants. Graduates of unaccredited colleges not considered. Apply to Graduate Office preferably by December 1 (Fall), August 1 (Spring). Rolling admissions process. Application fee $45, $55 for international applicants. Phone: (800)245-1064 (toll-free in state), (800)446-9488 (toll-free outside state), (303)273-3348; fax: (303)384-2253; e-mail: grad-school@mines.edu.

ADMISSION STANDARDS. Very selective. Usual minimum average: 3.0 (A = 4).

FINANCIAL AID. Annual awards from institutional funds: scholarships, fellowships, research assistantships, teaching assistantships, internships, Federal W/S, loans. Apply by February 1 (Fall), August 1 (Spring) to the Financial Aid Office. Use FAFSA. About 75% of students receive aid other than loans from School and outside sources. No aid for part-time students.

DEGREE REQUIREMENTS. For M.Eng., M.S.: 24 semester hours minimum plus 12 hours of research, at least 14 in residence; qualifying exam; thesis; final oral exam. For M.S. (nonthesis): at least 36 credits. For Ph.D.: 72 hours minimum beyond the bachelor's, at least 30 in residence and two semesters in full-time attendance; minor field requirement; preliminary exam; foreign language is a department option; comprehensive exams; dissertation; final written/oral exam.

FIELDS OF STUDY.
Applied Chemistry.
Applied Physics.
Chemical and Petroleum Refining Engineering.
Chemistry. Includes geochemistry.
Engineering and Technology Management.
Engineering Geology.
Engineering Systems.
Environmental Sciences and Engineering.
Geochemistry.
Geological Engineering.
Geology.
Geophysical Engineering.
Geophysics.
Hydrogeology.
Materials Science.
Mathematics and Computer Science.
Metallurgical and Materials Engineering.
Mineral Economics.
Mineral/Petroleum Exploration and Development.
Mining Engineering.
Petroleum Engineering.
Physics.

COLORADO STATE UNIVERSITY
Fort Collins, Colorado 80523-0015
Web site: www.colostate.edu

Founded 1879. CGS member. Located 65 miles N of Denver. Coed. Public control. Semester system. Special facilities: Archaeomagnetic Laboratory, Engineering Research Center, Electron Microscope, Radiological Health Lab, National Seed Storage Lab, Colorado Water Resource Center, Rocky Mountain Forest and Range Experimental Station. Library: 1,600,000 volumes, 21,208 subscriptions. The University's NIH ranking is 116th among all U.S. institutions with 113 awards/grants worth $29,640,191.

Annual tuition: full-time, resident $3630, nonresident $12,162, part-time, per credit, resident $169.90, nonresident $691. On-campus housing for 700 married students, 200 graduate men or women. Average academic year housing costs: $5670 single, $7500 married. Apply to Office of Housing and Food Service for both on- (970-491-6511) and off-campus (970-491-2248) housing information. Day-care facilities available.

Graduate School

Web site: www.colostate.edu/depts/grad

Graduate study since 1893. Enrollment: full-time 1826, part-time 1682. University faculty: full-time 993. Degrees conferred: M.A., M.Ag., M.A.T., M.B.A., M.Ed., M.F., M.F.A., M.M., M.S., M.S.W., Ph.D.

ADMISSION REQUIREMENTS. Two official transcripts, GRE, GMAT, three letters of recommendation required in support of School's application. Interview not required. TOEFL required for international applicants. Accepts transfer applicants. Graduates of unaccredited institutions not considered. Apply to proposed major department and Graduate School by February 15 (Fall), August 1 (Spring), November 15 (Summer); some departments may have earlier deadlines. Application fee $30. Phone: (970)491-6817; fax: (970)491-2194; e-mail: gschool@grad.colostate.edu.

ADMISSION STANDARDS. Very competitive for some departments, competitive or selective for the others. Usual minimum average: 3.0 (A = 4).

FINANCIAL AID. Annual awards from institutional funds: scholarships, teaching assistantships, research assistantships, traineeships, fellowships, tuition waivers, Federal W/S, loans. Apply by February 1 to appropriate department for fellowships, internships, assistantship; to Student Financial Services for all other aid. Phone: (970)491-6321. Use FAFSA (University code: 001350) and University's FAF. About 55% of students receive aid other than loans from University and outside sources. Aid available for part-time students.

DEGREE REQUIREMENTS. For most master's: 30–36 credits minimum, at least 24 in residence; thesis required for many majors, optional for others; reading knowledge of one foreign language for some majors; final written/oral exam. For M.M.: 33 credits minimum; thesis may be required. For M.S.W.: 40–63 credits minimum; thesis optional. For M.F.A.: 48–60 credits minimum, at least three years of full-time study; M.F.A. thesis; final written/oral exam. For Ph.D.: 72 credits minimum beyond the bachelor's, at least 32 in residence or thesis; preliminary exam; dissertation or thesis; final written/oral exam.

FIELDS OF STUDY.
Agricultural and Resource Economics. M.S., Ph.D.
Agricultural Engineering. M.S., Ph.D.
Agricultural Sciences. M.Ag.
Agronomy. M.S., Ph.D.
Anatomy. M.S., Ph.D.
Animal Sciences. M.S., Ph.D.
Anthropology. M.A.
Art. M.F.A.
Atmospheric Science. M.S., Ph.D.
Biochemistry. M.S., Ph.D.
Bioresource and Agricultural Engineering. M.S., Ph.D.
Botany. M.S., Ph.D.
Business Administration. M.B.A., M.S.

Cell and Molecular Biology. M.S., Ph.D.
Chemical Engineering. M.S., Ph.D.
Chemistry. M.S., Ph.D.
Civil Engineering. M.S., Ph.D.
Clinical Sciences. M.S., Ph.D.
Computer Science. M.S., Ph.D.
Creative Writing. M.F.A.
Design and Merchandising. M.A., M.S.
Earth Resources. M.S., Ph.D.
Ecology. M.S., Ph.D.
Economics. M.A., Ph.D.
Education and Human Resources Studies. M.Ed., Ph.D.
Electrical Engineering. M.E.E., M.S., Ph.D.
English. M.A.
Entomology. M.S., Ph.D.
Environmental Health. M.S., Ph.D.
Fishery and Wildlife Biology. M.S., Ph.D.
Food Science and Nutrition. M.S., Ph.D.
Foreign Languages and Literatures. M.A.
Forest Sciences. M.F., M.S., Ph.D.
Geology. M.S.
Health and Exercise Science. M.S.
History. M.A.
Horticulture. M.S., Ph.D.
Human Development and Family Studies. M.S.
Manufacturing Technology and Construction Management. M.S.
Mathematics. M.S., Ph.D.
Mechanical Engineering. M.S., Ph.D.
Microbiology. M.S., Ph.D.
Music. M.M.
Occupational Therapy. M.S.
Pathology. M.S., Ph.D.
Philosophy. M.A.
Physics. M.S., Ph.D.
Physiology. M.S., Ph.D.
Plant Pathology and Weed Science. M.S., Ph.D.
Political Science. M.A., Ph.D.
Psychology. M.S., Ph.D.
Radiological Health Sciences. M.S., Ph.D.
Rangeland Ecosystems Science. M.S., Ph.D.
Recreation Resources. M.S., Ph.D.
Social Work. M.S.W.
Sociology. M.A., Ph.D.
Soil and Crop Sciences. M.S., Ph.D.
Speech Communication. M.A.
Statistics. M.S., Ph.D.
Student Affairs in Higher Education. M.S.
Technical Communication. M.S.
Watershed Sciences. M.S.
Zoology. M.S., Ph.D.

College of Veterinary Medicine and Biomedical Sciences

Web site: www.cvmbs.colostate.edu

Annual tuition for the professional school: WICHE and state resident $9228, nonresident $31,828. Living expenses approximately $8000. Enrollment: first-year class 134; total full-time 701. Faculty: full-time 155. Degrees conferred: D.V.M., D.V.M.-M.S., D.V.M.-Ph.D.

ADMISSION REQUIREMENTS. VMCAS report, transcripts, GRE, three letters of recommendation, essay, animal/veterinary experience required in support of application. Electronic application available. Will consider international applicants. Interview by invitation only. Applicants must have completed at least three years of college study. State residents and WICHE residents given preference. Accepts transfer applicants if opening exists. Has EAP, applicants must have at least 68 credits, G.P.A. 3.8, GRE combined score of 1750. Apply to the Office of the Dean of the College after August before October 1. Transfer applicants apply by May 1. Application deadlines for M.S. and Ph.D.: January 1 (Fall), October 1 (Spring). Application fee $40. Phone: (970)491-7052; fax: (970)491-2250.

ADMISSION STANDARDS. Selective. Mean GPA: 3.60 (A = 4.0); mean GRE: verbal 511, quantitative 612, analytical 640. Accepts 33% of total annual applicants. Nonresident quota 15–20%. Approximately 50% are state residents.

FINANCIAL AID. Scholarships, assistantships, fellowships, traineeships, tuition waivers, Federal W/S, loans. Apply to the Office of Financial Aid following admission.

DEGREE REQUIREMENTS. For D.V.M.: Satisfactory completion of four-year program. For M.S. Plan A—30 credit program, thesis/comprehensive exam, Plan B—40 credit program, professional paper/departmental report; internship. For Ph.D.: 72 credit program beyond the bachelor's, written and oral preliminary exam; dissertation; final oral exam.

FIELDS OF GRADUATE STUDY.
Anatomy.
Cellular and Molecular Radiobiology.
Critical Care/Emergency Medicine.
Environmental Toxicology.
Epidemiology.
Equine Medicine.
Equine Reproduction.
Experimental Radiation Oncology.
Food Animal Medicine.
Health Physics/Radiation Protection.
Industrial Hygiene.
Interdisciplinary Programs. Includes cell and molecular biology, molecular, cellular and integrative neurosciences, anthropod-borne and infectious diseases, mycobacteria research, integrated livestock management.
Large and Small Animal Surgery.
Microbiology.
Neurobiology.
Pathology.
Radioecology.
Reproductive Biology.
Small Animal Medicine.
Veterinary Neurology.
Veterinary Oncology.
Veterinary Ophthalmology.
Veterinary Radiology.

UNIVERSITY OF COLORADO, BOULDER

Boulder, Colorado 80309
Web site: www.colorado.edu

Founded 1876. CGS and AAU member. Located 28 miles NW of Denver. Public control. Semester system. Special facilities: Center for Advanced Decision Support for Water and Environmental Systems, Center for Advanced Manufacturing and Packaging of Microwave, Optical, and Digital Electronics, Center for Applied Mathematics, Center for Asian Studies, Center for Astrophysics and Space Astronomy, Center for Computer Research in the Humanities, Center for Geography Education, Center for Integrated Plasma Studies, Center for Limnology, Center for Physical Activity, Disease Prevention, and Aging, Center for Separations using Thin Film, Center for Space and Geosciences Policy, Center for Study of Ethnicity and Race in America, Center for Values and Social Policy, Center for the Study of the Native Languages of the Plains and Southwest, Colorado Center for Astrodynamics Research, Colorado Center for Chaos and Complexity,

Cooperative Institute for Research in Environmental Sciences, Ferro-Electric Liquid Crystal Materials Research Science and Engineering Center, Institute for Behavioral Genetics, Institute of Arctic and Alpine Research, Institute of Behavioral Science, the Institute of Cognitive Science, Natural Hazards Center. The University's NIH ranking is 112th among all U.S. institutions with 130 awards/grants totaling $31,189,202. Library: 2,700,000 volumes, 14,700 subscriptions. More than 1700 computers on campus for student use. Total University enrollment: 25,100.

Annual tuition: full-time, resident $3084, nonresident $13,698. Limited on-campus housing available. Annual average housing cost: $8650. Off-campus Housing Office. Phone: (303)492-7053. Family Housing Office: Phone: (303)492-6384. Day-care facilities available.

Graduate School

Graduate study since 1892. Enrollment: full-time 2764, part-time 923. University faculty: approx. 1000. Degrees conferred: M.A., M.S., M.F.A., M.E., M.Mus., M.Mus.Ed., M.B.S., D.Mus.A., Ph.D.

ADMISSION REQUIREMENTS. Two transcripts, four letters of reference required in support of School's application. GRE/GMAT, three letters of recommendation required for many departments. Contact Departments for the supplemental materials required. TOEFL required for international applicants. Interview not required. Accepts transfer applicants. Graduates of unaccredited colleges not considered. Apply to office of the major department at least 120 days before term admission is sought. Application fee $50, $60 for international. Phone: (303)492-6301.

ADMISSION STANDARDS. Selective to competitive. Usual minimum average: 2.75 (A = 4), 3.0 in some departments.

FINANCIAL AID. Annual awards from institutional funds: scholarships, fellowships, teaching/research assistantships, traineeships, Federal W/S, loans. Number of awards varies. Apply by January 15 through appropriate department, to the Financial Aid Office for all Federal programs. Phone: (303)492-5091; e-mail: finaid@colorado.edu. Use FAFSA (University code: 001370). Aid sometimes available for part-time students.

DEGREE REQUIREMENTS. For most master's: 24 semester hours minimum with thesis or 30 semester hours minimum without thesis, at least two semesters in residence; qualifying exam; up to 9 semester hours in transfer; final written/oral exam. For M.F.A.: 48 hours minimum; written, creative thesis. For M. Mus.: same as for the master's, except final creative or performance project. Some departments require foreign languages for master's. For Ph.D., D.Mus.A.: 30 hours minimum beyond the master's, at least 6 semesters in residence; preliminary exam; final written/oral exam; dissertation. Some departments require foreign language for Ph.D.

FIELDS OF STUDY.

COLLEGE OF ARTS AND SCIENCES:
Anthropology. M.A., Ph.D.
Applied Mathematics. M.S., Ph.D.
Astrophysical and Planetary Sciences. M.S., Ph.D.
Atmospheric and Ocean Sciences. M.S., Ph.D.
Biology. Includes environmental, population and organismic, molecular, cellular and developmental. M.A., Ph.D.
Chemistry and Biochemistry. M.S., Ph.D.
Chemical Physics. Ph.D.
Classics. M.A., Ph.D.
Cognitive Science. Ph.D.
Communication. M.S., Ph.D.
Comparative Literature. M.A., Ph.D.

Dance. M.F.A.
East Asian Languages and Civilizations. M.A.
Economics. M.A., Ph.D.
English. M.A., Ph.D.
Environmental Studies. M.S., Ph.D.
Fine Arts. M.A., M.F.A.
French. M.A., Ph.D.
Geography. M.A., Ph.D.
Geological Sciences. M.S., Ph.D.
Geophysics. Ph.D.
German and Slavic Languages and Literature. M.A.
History. M.A., Ph.D.
Kinesiology. M.S., Ph.D.
Linguistics. M.A., Ph.D.
Mathematics. M.A., Ph.D.
Museum and Field Studies. M.S.
Neuroscience. Ph.D.
Philosophy. M.A., Ph.D.
Physics. M.A., Ph.D.
Political Science. M.A., Ph.D.
Psychology. M.A., Ph.D.
Religious Studies. M.A.
Sociology. M.A., Ph.D.
Spanish. M.A., Ph.D.
Speech, Language, and Hearing Sciences. M.A., Ph.D.
Theatre. M.A., Ph.D.

COLLEGE OF ENGINEERING:
Aerospace Engineering Sciences. M.S., Ph.D.
Chemical Engineering. M.S., Ph.D.
Civil, Environmental, and Architectural Engineering. M.S., Ph.D.
Computer Science. M.S., Ph.D.
Electrical and Computer Engineering. M.S., Ph.D.
Engineering Management. M.E.
Mechanical Engineering. M.S., Ph.D.
Telecommunications. Interdisciplinary. M.S.

SCHOOL OF EDUCATION:
Educational Psychological Studies. M.A., Ph.D.
Instruction and Curriculum. M.A., Ph.D.
Research and Evaluation Methodology. Ph.D.
Social, Multicultural, and Bilingual Foundations. M.A., Ph.D.

SCHOOL OF JOURNALISM:
Journalism. M.A., Ph.D.

SCHOOL OF MUSIC:
Music. M.Mus., Ph.D.
Music Education. M.Mus.Ed.
Musical Arts. D.M.A.

Graduate School of Business Administration

Graduate study since 1965. Accredited programs: M.B.A.; recognized Ph.D. Semester system. Special facilities: Burridge Center for Financial Analysis, Center for Sustainable Tourism, Deming Center for Entrepreneurship, Real Estate Center. Library: 69,000 volumes, 1200 subscriptions.

Annual tuition: resident M.B.A. full-time $3710, M.S. $3548, part-time $588 per semester; nonresident M.B.A. full-time $14,670, M.S. $14,400, part-time $2400 per semester.

Enrollment: total full-time 293, part-time 10 (men 70%, women 30%). Faculty: 176 full-time, 10 part-time; 97% with Ph.D./D.B.A. Degrees conferred: M.B.A. (FT, PT, days), M.S.Acct., M.S.Actx., M.B.A.-J.D., M.B.A.-M.S. (Telecommunications), Ph.D.

ADMISSION REQUIREMENTS. All applicants should have a bachelor's degree from a recognized institution of higher education, a strong mathematics background, a 3.0 GPA (A = 4), and a GMAT score of 550. Submit two official transcripts from each

undergraduate/graduate school attended, GMAT, three letters of recommendation, essay, résumé (prefers at least four years of work experience), and an application fee of $40 ($60 international applicants) to the Director of Graduate Student Services. In addition, international students (whose native language is other than English) should submit a TOEFL (minimum score 550) report, certified translations and evaluations of all official transcripts, recommendation should be in English or with certified translations, and proof of sufficient financial resources for two years of academic study. On-campus visits and interviews are required. Beginning students are admitted Fall only. U.S. citizens apply by December 15 round-one deadline, February 15 round-two deadline, May 1 late deadline (Fall), international students apply by December 1 round-one deadline, February 1 round-two deadline. Joint degree applicants must apply to and be accepted to both schools/programs, contact the admissions office for current information and specific admissions requirements. Rolling admissions process, notification is made two weeks after receipt of completed application and supporting documents. Admissions Office phone: (303)492-7831; fax: (303)492-1727; e-mail: busgrad@colorado.edu.

ADMISSION REQUIREMENTS FOR DOCTORAL CANDIDATES. Contact the Application Request Service at (303)492-7662 for applications and current information. Beginning students are admitted Fall Only. Both U.S. citizens and international applicants apply by January 1 (Fall). Submit an application, a GMAT (will accept GMAT test results from the last five years), two official transcripts from each undergraduate/graduate school attended, four letters of recommendation, résumé, statement of purpose, and application fee of $40 ($60 international applicants) to the Graduate Admission Office. In addition, international student (whose native language is other than English) should submit TOEFL (minimum score 590) report, certified translations and evaluations of all official transcripts, recommendation should be in English or with certified translations, proof of health/immunization certificate. International students' contact: (303)492-7536. Interviews encouraged. Notification is made by mid-April.

ADMISSION STANDARDS. Competitive. Mean GMAT: 647; mean GPA: 3.11 (A = 4). Gourman rating: the MBA program was not rated; the Ph.D. program was rated in the top 45, the score was 4.30.

FINANCIAL AID. Minority scholarships, grants, fellowships, graduate assistantships, Federal W/S, loans. Financial aid is available for part-time study. Financial aid may be available for international students. Assistantships/fellowships may be available in the second year for joint degree candidates. Request scholarship, fellowship, assistantship information from the Graduate School of Business. Contact the University's Financial Aid Office for current need-based financial aid information. Phone: (303)492-5091. Submit FAFSA (School code: 001370), also submit Financial Aid Transcript, Federal Income Tax forms. Approximately 75% of students receive some form of financial assistance.

DEGREE REQUIREMENTS. For M.B.A.: 51-credit program including 27 elective credits, two-year program; degree program must be completed in five years. For M.S.Acct., M.S.Actx.: 32-credit program. For M.B.A.-M.S. (Telecommunications): 60-credit program, a two-and-one-half- to five-year program. For M.B.A.-J.D.: 141 credit program, four-and-one-half- to six-year program. For Ph.D.: 60 credit, three- to five-year program; comprehensive (written, oral, or both) exam; teaching experience; research internship; dissertation proposal and oral defense, dissertation; oral defense.

FIELDS OF STUDY.
Accounting. M.S.Acct., M.S.Actx., Ph.D.
Business Strategy. Ph.D.

Entrepreneurship. Ph.D.
Finance. M.B.A., Ph.D.
Information Systems. Ph.D.
Marketing. M.B.A., Ph.D.
Operations Research. Ph.D.
Organizational Management. M.B.A., Ph.D.
Self-Designed Option. M.B.A. only.
Technology and Innovation Management. M.B.A. only.

School of Law (80309-0403)

Organized 1892. ABA approved since 1923. AALS member. Semester System. Special facilities: Natural Resources Law Center, Indian Law Clinic, National Wildlife Federation's Natural Resources Litigation Clinic. Library: 397,000 volumes, 4230 subscriptions; has LEXIS, NEXIS, WESTLAW, LEGISLATE.

Annual tuition: resident $6069, nonresident $18,549. On-campus housing available for single and married students. Apply to University Housing Office. Total average cost for all other expenses: $13,026.

Enrollment: first-year class 167, full-time 480 (men 47%, women 53%); no part-time study. Faculty: full-time 32, part-time 12. Student to faculty ratio 12.5 to 1 Degrees conferred: J.D., J.D.-M.B.A., J.D.-M.I.A. J.D.-M.P.A.

ADMISSION REQUIREMENTS. LSDAS Law School report, two transcripts, LSAT, recommendations required in support of application. Applicants must have received bachelor's prior to admission. Accepts 5–10 transfer applicants each year. Graduates of unaccredited colleges not considered. Apply to School by February 15. Entering students admitted Fall only. Application fee $55. Phone: (303)492-7203; fax: (303)492-2542.

ADMISSION STANDARDS. Selective. Mean GPA: 3.52 (A = 4); mean LSAT: 160. Gourman rating: 3.50. *U.S. News & World Report* ranking is in the top 40 of all law schools. Accepts 30% of total annual applicants.

FINANCIAL AID. Scholarships, grants-in-aid, Federal W/S, loans; research assistantships for advanced students only. For best aid packages apply by January 1. Financial Aid deadline, March 1. Use FAFSA (School code: 001370). About 62% of students receive aid other than loans from School. Priority given to state residents.

DEGREE REQUIREMENTS. For J.D.: 6 semesters minimum; 89 semester hours; advanced standing for work completed at other approved law schools. For M.B.A., M.I.A., M.P.A.: see Graduate School listing above.

UNIVERSITY OF COLORADO, COLORADO SPRINGS
Colorado Springs, Colorado 80918
Web site: www.uccs.edu

Established 1965. Public control. Semester system. Library: 380,900 volumes, 2171 subscriptions. More than 600 computers on campus for student use. Total University enrollment: 6500.

Annual tuition: resident $2385, per credit $150; nonresident $8156, per credit $505. On-campus housing for single students only. Average on-campus housing costs: $5524 (including board). Day-care facilities available.

Graduate School

Enrollment: full-time 869, part-time 651. Faculty: full-time 197, part-time 38. Degrees conferred: M.A., M.B.A., M.B.S., M.C.J., M.E., M.P.A., M.S., M.S.N., Ph.D.

ADMISSION REQUIREMENTS. Two transcripts, three letters of recommendation, statement of purpose required in support of Part I and Part II of School's application. GRE, GMAT (minimum score 400), writing sample required for some departments. On-line application available. TOEFL required for international applicants. Accepts transfer applicants. Graduates of unaccredited colleges not considered. Apply to the appropriate program office at least 60 days prior to the beginning of anticipated semester of entrance. Application fee $60, $75 for international applicants. General information phone number: (719)262-3417; fax: (719)262-3037.

ADMISSION STANDARDS Selective. Usual minimum average: 2.75 (A = 4), 3.0 in some programs.

FINANCIAL AID. Annual awards from institutional funds: scholarships, fellowships, teaching/research assistantships, grants, Federal W/S, loans. Apply by March 1 through appropriate program for fellowships, assistantships, to the Office of Student Aid for all other programs. Phone: (800)990-UCCS; e-mail: finaidse@uccs.edu. Use FAFSA. Aid available for part-time students.

DEGREE REQUIREMENTS. For master's: Plan I—30 semester credit program, at least two semesters in residence; comprehensive exam; admission to candidacy; thesis, Plan II (nonthesis option)—30 semester credit program, at least two semesters in residence; comprehensive exam; admission to candidacy; final written/oral exam or special project/report. For Ph.D.: 75 credit hour program, at least three semesters in residence;. foreign language proficiency; preliminary exam; specialty exam; comprehensive exam; admission to candidacy; dissertation proposal; dissertation; public defense.

FIELDS OF STUDY
Applied Geography M.A.
Applied Mathematics. M.S.
Basic Science. M.B.S.
Business Administration. M.B.A.
Communication M.A.
Computer Science. M.S., Ph.D.
Counseling and Human Services. M.A.
Criminal Justice. M.C.J.
Curriculum and Instruction. M.A.
Educational Leadership and Innovation. Ph.D.
Electrical Engineering. M.S., Ph.D.
Engineering. M.E.
English. M.A.
History. M.A.
Mechanical and Aerospace Engineering. M.S.
Mechanical Engineering. M.S.
Nursing. M.S.N.
Psychology. M.A.
Public Administration. M.P.A.
Public Affairs. Ph.D.
Sociology. M.A.
Software Systems Engineering. M.E.
Special Education. M.A.

UNIVERSITY OF COLORADO, DENVER
Denver, Colorado 80202
Web site: www.cudenver.edu

CGS member. Public control. Semester system. Library: 555,794 volumes, 4346 subscriptions. More than 600 computers on campus for student use. Total University enrollment: approximately 12,000.

Tuition: per credit, resident $189 Architecture, $222 Business, $196 Education, $209 Engineering and Public Affairs, $176 Liberal Arts; per credit nonresident $739 Architecture, Education,

Engineering, Public Affairs, $651 Business, $694 Liberal Arts. No on-campus housing available. Day-care facilities available.

Graduate Programs

Enrollment: full-time 1340, part-time 2667. Faculty: full- and part-time approximately 350. Degrees conferred: M.A., M.Arch., M.B.A., M.B.S., M.C.J., M.Eng., M.H., M.L.A., M.P.A., M.S., M.S.I.B., M.S.S., M.U.D., M.U.R.P., Ed.S., Ph.D.

ADMISSION REQUIREMENTS. Two transcripts, three letters of reference, statement of purpose required in support of School's application. GRE, GMAT (minimum score 400), interview, portfolios, writing sample required for some departments. TOEFL (minimum score range 500–575 depending on program) required for international applicants. Accepts transfer applicants. Graduates of unaccredited colleges not considered. Apply to office of the major department at least 120 days before term admission is sought. Application fee $50, $60 for international. General information phone number: (303)556-2704.

ADMISSION STANDARDS. Selective to competitive. Usual minimum average GPA: 2.75 (A = 4), 3.0 in some schools.

FINANCIAL AID. Annual awards from institutional funds: scholarships, fellowships, teaching/research assistantships, Federal W/S, loans. Number of awards varies. Apply by February 1 through appropriate department for fellowships, assistantships, to Office of Student Aid for all other programs. Use FAFSA. Aid available for part-time students.

DEGREE REQUIREMENTS. For most master's: 24 semester hours minimum with thesis or 30 semester hours minimum without thesis, at least 2 semesters in residence; comprehensive (written or oral or both) exam; up to 9 semester hours in transfer; admission to candidacy; final written/oral exam; project/report. For Ph.D.: 30–46 hours minimum beyond the master's, at least 3 semesters in residence; foreign language proficiency; preliminary review/annual review; comprehensive exam; final written/oral exam; admission to candidacy; dissertation; public defense/dissertation colloquium.

FIELDS OF STUDY.

COLLEGE OF ARCHITECTURE AND PLANNING:
Architecture. M.Arch.
Design and Planning. Ph.D.
Landscape Architecture. M.L.A.
Urban and Regional Planning. M.U.R.P.
Urban Design. M.U.D.

GRADUATE SCHOOL OF BUSINESS ADMINISTRATION:
Accounting. M.S.
Business Administration. M.B.A., E.M.B.A.
Finance. M.S.
Health Administration. M.S.
Information Systems. M.S.
International Business. M.S.I.B.
Management and Organization. M.S.
Marketing. M.S.

SCHOOL OF EDUCATION:
Administrative Leadership and Policy Studies. M.A., Ed.S., Ph.D.
Counseling Psychology and Counselor Education. M.A.
Curriculum and Instruction. M.A.
Early Childhood Education. M.A.
Educational Psychology. Ed.S.
Information and Learning Technologies. M.A.

School Psychology. Ed.S.
Special Education. M.A.

COLLEGE OF ENGINEERING:
Civil Engineering. M.S., Ph.D.
Computer Science and Engineering. M.S.
Electrical Engineering. M.S.
Engineering. M.Eng.
Mechanical Engineering. M.S.

COLLEGE OF ARTS AND SCIENCES:
Anthropology. M.A.
Applied Mathematics. M.S., Ph.D.
Basic Science. M.B.S.
Biology. M.A.
Chemistry. M.S.
Communication. M.A.
Economics. M.A.
English. M.A.
Environmental Studies. M.S.
Health and Behavioral Science. Ph.D.
History. M.A.
Humanities. M.H.
Political Science. M.A.
Psychology. M.A.
Social Science. M.S.S.
Sociology. M.A.
Technical Communication. M.S.

GRADUATE SCHOOL OF PUBLIC AFFAIRS:
Criminal Justice. M.C.J.
Public Administration. M.P.A., E.M.P.A.
Public Affairs. Ph.D.

UNIVERSITY OF COLORADO HEALTH SCIENCES CENTER

Denver, Colorado 80262
Web site: www.uchsc.edu

Established 1965. CGS member. Coed Public control. Quarter system. Special facilities: Alcohol Research Center, Barbara Davis Center for Childhood Diabetes, Center for Computational Biology, Center for Aging and Division of Geriatrics, Center of Excellence in Molecular Biology, Center for Health Services and Policy Research, Center for Human Caring and Caring Science, Center for Human Nutrition, Center for Nursing Research, Center for Pharmaceutical Biotechnology, Center for Schizophrenia Research, Clinical Investigation Center, Colorado Emergency Medicine Research Center, Colorado Prevention Center, Colorado Sickle Cell Treatment and Research Center, Denver Institute for Psychoanalysis, Eleanor Roosevelt Institute for Cancer Research, Hepatobiliary Research Center, John F. Kennedy Center for Developmental Disabilities, Mental Retardation Research Center, National Center for American Indian and Alaska Native Mental Health Research, National Resource Center for Health and Safety in Child Care, Native Elder Health Care Resource Center, Pediatric General Clinical Research Center, Rocky Mountain Center for Sensor Technology, University of Colorado Cardiovascular Institute, Webb-Waring Institute for Cancer, Aging and Antioxidant Research. Library: 250,000 volumes, 1750 subscriptions. The Center's NIH ranking is 30th among all U.S. institutions with 432 awards/grants worth $145,095,518. Total Center enrollment 2400.

No on-campus housing available. Average annual off-campus housing costs: $11,000–$13,000. Contact Student Assistance Office for off-campus housing information. Phone: (303)315-7620.

Graduate School

Annual tuition: residents $8900 (Child Health Associate program); per credit $60 (Clinical and Basic Science programs), $170 (Genetic Counseling, Public Health), $117 (Physical Therapy), nonresident $21,700 (Child Health Associate program); per credit $292 (Clinical and Basic Science programs), $391 (Genetic Counseling, Public Health), $433 (Physical Therapy),

Enrollment: full-time 1410, part-time 362, Faculty: full- and part-time 600. Degrees conferred M.S., M.S.P.H., Ph.D.

ADMISSION REQUIREMENTS. Two official transcripts, GRE, three letters of recommendation required in support of Part I and Part II of School's application. TOEFL (minimum score 550) required for all international applicants. Apply by January 31 to the Graduate School. Application fee $50. Phone: (303)315-7929; fax: (303)315-6932.

ADMISSION STANDARDS. Selective for most programs, very selective for some programs. Usual minimum average GPA: 3.0 (master's programs), 3.2 (doctoral programs) (A = 4).

FINANCIAL AID. Fellowships, traineeships, research/teaching assistantships, grants, Federal W/S, loans. Apply to Student Financial Aid Office by March 15. Use FAFSA. Aid available for part-time students.

DEGREE REQUIREMENTS. For master's: 45 quarter credit hour programs; comprehensive exam; admission to candidacy; thesis/nonthesis option. For Ph.D.: 90 quarter credit hour program, preliminary exam; foreign language proficiency; comprehensive exam; admission to candidacy; dissertation; oral defense.

FIELDS OF STUDY.
Biochemistry and Molecular Genetics. Ph.D.
Bioinformatics. Ph.D.
Biomedical Sciences. Ph.D.
Biometrics. M.S., Ph.D.
Biomolecular Structure. Ph.D.
Cell and Developmental Biology. Ph.D.
Child Health Associate/Physician Assistant Program. M.S.
Clinical Science. Ph.D.
Epidemiology. Ph.D.
Experimental Pathology. Ph.D.
Genetic Counseling. M.S.
Human Medical Genetics. Ph.D.
Immunology. Ph.D.
Microbiology. Ph.D.
Molecular Biology. Ph.D.
Neuroscience. Ph.D.
Nursing. M.S., Ph.D.
Pharmaceutical Sciences. Ph.D.
Pharmacology. Ph.D.
Physical Therapy. M.S.
Physiology and Biophysics. Ph.D.
Public Health. M.S.P.H.
Toxicology. Ph.D.

School of Dentistry (80262)

Established 1967. Located at University Health Science Center. Annual tuition: resident $7555, nonresident $26,947. Off-campus housing only. Average academic year housing costs: $13,000. Average first-year academic costs: $11,000.

Enrollment: first-year class 38; total 140 (men 70%, women 30%). Degree conferred: D.D.S.

ADMISSION REQUIREMENTS. AADSAS, official transcripts, DAT (no later than October), two letters of recommendation required in support of School's application. Applicant must have completed at least three years of study; prefer four years of study. Interview by invitation. Accepts transfer applicants. Preference given to state residents and WICHE participating states. Graduates of unaccredited colleges not considered. Apply after June 1, before January 1 to Admission Committee, Room C-284. Application fee $50. Phone: (303)315-7259.

ADMISSION STANDARDS. Competitive. Mean DAT Academic: 18.78, PAT: 17.68; mean GPA: 3.57 (A = 4). Gourman rating: 4.10. Admits about 15–20% of total annual applications. Approximately 65% are state residents.

FINANCIAL AID. Scholarships, grants, tuition waivers, loans. Apply to Director, Student Financial Aid Office of Medical Center after acceptance. Phone: (303)315-8364. Use FAFSA (School code: 004508). About 92% of students receive some aid from School and outside sources. Reduced tuition for residents who will upon graduation practice in underserved areas of Colorado.

DEGREE REQUIREMENTS. For D.D.S: satisfactory completion of forty-five-month program.

School of Medicine

Opened 1883. Located at the University Health Sciences Center. Medical library: 161,000 volumes, 2100 subscriptions.

Annual tuition: resident $11,966, nonresident $59,597, student fees $1529. No on-campus housing available. Contact Student Assistance Office for off-campus housing. Phone: (303)315-7620. Total average figure for all other expenses: $13,000.

Enrollment: first-year class 127, total 525 (men 59%, women 41%). Faculty: full-time 1200, part-time volunteers 2000. Degree conferred: M.D., M.D.-Ph.D (M.S.T.P.). The M.S. and Ph.D. (Medical) are offered through the Graduate School.

ADMISSION REQUIREMENTS. AMCAS report, transcripts, MCAT, letters of recommendation requires in support of application. Interviews for final selections. Applicants must have completed 120 semester hours of college study. Accepts transfer applicants into the sophomore year only. Preference given to residents of Colorado, Wyoming, and Montana. Apply to Office of Admissions and Records of School after June 1, before November 1. Application fee $70. Phone: (303)315-7361; fax: (303)315-1614.

ADMISSION STANDARDS. Competitive. Mean MCAT: 10; mean GPA: 3.6 (A = 4). Accepts 15% of total annual applicants. Approximately 85% are state residents.

FINANCIAL AID. Scholarships, grants, loans. Apply by May 31 to the Associate Dean. Phone: (303)315-8364. About 50% of students receive aid other than loans from School.

DEGREE REQUIREMENTS. For M.D.: satisfactory completion of four-year program. For M.S., Ph.D: see Graduate School listing above.

FIELDS OF GRADUATE STUDY.
Biochemistry.
Biophysics.
Cell Biology.
Developmental Biology.
Genetics.
Immunology.
Microbiology.
Molecular Biology.
Neurosciences.
Pharmacology.
Physiology.

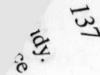
...UNIVERSITY

...ork 10027

...umbia.edu

...r. CGS and AAU member. Coed. Private control, ...system. Special facilities: Institute of Nutrition Sci-...es, Lamont Geological Observatory, Russian Institute, East Asian Institute, Institute on Western Europe, Middle East Institute, Institute on East Central Europe, Institute of African Studies, Institute of Latin American and Iberian Studies, Nevis Synchrocyclotron Laboratory, Armstrong Field Laboratories for Microwave Research, Cooperative Industrial Reactor Laboratories, Institute of Administrative Research, Institute of Field Studies, Institute of Psychological Research, Horace Mann-Lincoln Institute of School Experimentation, Institute of Research and Service in Nursing Education, Institute of Language Arts, Curriculum Service Center, Evaluation and Measurement Service Center, Institute of Higher Education, Institute of Educational Technology, Institute of Philosophy and Politics of Education, Institute of the Education of the Handicapped, Nevis Biological Station, Columbia Radiation Laboratory. University libraries have more than 4,000,000 volumes, 3,388,000 microforms. Total University enrollment: 22,892.

On-campus housing for married students, 611 graduate men, 391 graduate women. Average annual housing cost: $9000–$11,000 for married students, $8282 for single students. Apply to Livingston Hall (on-campus housing for single and married students), to Housing Office for off-campus housing information. Phone: (212)854-3923.

Graduate School of Arts and Sciences

Graduate study since 1880. Annual tuition: full-time $27,528. Enrollment: full- and part-time 3590. Faculty: full- and part-time 700. Degrees conferred: M.A., Liberal Studies M.A. (Interdisciplinary), M.Phil., Ph.D.

ADMISSION REQUIREMENTS. Transcripts, GRE, three letters of recommendation required in support of School's application. GRE Subject Test recommended for all applicants. TOEFL (minimum score 600, 250 on computer-based test) required for international applicants from non-English-speaking countries. Interview not required. Accepts transfer applicants. Graduates of unaccredited institutions not considered. Apply to Graduate School of Arts and Sciences Office of Admissions by January 3 (for priority consideration for both admissions and Financial Aid), April 30 for regular consideration (Fall). Application fee $65. Phone: (212)854-3808; fax: (212)854-2863.

ADMISSION STANDARDS. Very competitive for some departments, competitive or very selective for the others. Usual minimum average 3.0 (A = 4).

FINANCIAL AID. Annual awards from institutional funds: scholarships, fellowships, teaching assistantships, research assistantships, Federal W/S, loans. Apply by the first Monday in January (for priority consideration) to Office of Student Affairs for scholarships and fellowships. Phone: (212)854-3808. Use FAFSA. About 90% of students receive aid other than loans from University and outside sources. Aid usually not available for part-time students.

DEGREE REQUIREMENTS. For M.A.: Two semesters minimum in full-time residence; reading knowledge of one foreign language for some departments; essay required by many departments. For Liberal Studies M.A.: 36 credit program; final paper. For M.Phil.: essentially the same as Ph.D., except no dissertation requirement. For Ph.D.: six semesters minimum beyond the master's in full-time residence; reading knowledge of two foreign languages; qualifying exam; dissertation; final oral exam.

FIELDS OF STUDY.

African-American Studies. M.A.

American Studies. Liberal Studies M.A.

Anthropology. Includes interdisciplinary programs in applied anthropology (Ph.D. only), ecology, medical anthropology. M.A., Ph.D.

Architecture (History and Theory). Ph.D.

Art History and Archaeology. M.A., Ph.D.

Biological Sciences. Ph.D.

Biotechnology. M.A.

Chemistry. Ph.D.

Classics. M.A., Ph.D.

Classical Studies. M.A.

Conservation Biology. M.A.

Dental Sciences. M.A.

Earth and Environmental Sciences. Ph.D.

Earth and Environmental Sciences Journalism. M.A.-M.S.

East Asian Languages and Cultures. M.A., Ph.D.

East Asian Regional Studies. M.A.

East Asian Studies. Liberal Studies M.A.

Ecology and Evolutionary Biology. Ph.D.

Economics. Ph.D.

English and Comparative Literature. M.A.

French. M.A.

French Cultural Studies (in Paris). M.A.

Germanic Languages. M.A., Ph.D.

History. Ph.D.

Human Rights. Liberal Studies M.A.

Islamic Studies. Liberal Studies M.A.

Italian. M.A., Ph.D.

Japanese Pedagogy. M.A.

Jewish Studies. Liberal Studies M.A.

Mathematics. M.A., Ph.D.

Mathematics of Finance. M.A.

Medieval Studies. Liberal Studies M.A.

Middle East and Asian Languages and Culture. Ph.D.

Middle Eastern Languages and Cultures. Includes Akkadian, Caucasian, Iranian, Tarkic. M.A.

Modern European Studies. Liberal Studies M.A.

Museum Anthropology. M.A.

Music. Ph.D.

Philosophy. M.A., Ph.D.

Philosophical Foundations for Physics. M.A.

Physics. Ph.D.

Political Science. M.A., Ph.D.

Psychology. Ph.D.

Quantitative Methods in the Social Sciences. M.A.

Religion. Ph.D.

Religion—Journalism. M.A.-M.S.

Russian Translation. M.A.

Slavic Culture. M.A.

Slavic Languages and Literature. M.A., Ph.D.

Sociology. M.A., Ph.D.

South Asian Studies. Liberal Studies M.A.

Spanish and Portuguese. M.A., Ph.D.

Statistics. M.A., Ph.D.

Theatre. Ph.D.

Urban Planning. Ph.D.

School of the Arts

Web site: www.columbia.edu/cu/arts

Established 1965. Special facility: LeRoy Neiman Center for Print Studies, Oscar Hammerstein Center for Theatre Studies, Fritz Reiner Center for Contemporary Music, Computer Music Center, Digital Media Center. Annual tuition: full-time $27,910, per credit $900. Enrollment: full-time 740. Faculty: full-time 44, part-time 156. Degrees conferred: M.F.A., D.M.A.

ADMISSION REQUIREMENTS. Transcripts, three letters of recommendation, statement of intent, portfolio or samples of work, audition/interview (depending upon major), at least three years of relevant professional experience required in support of application. Electronic application available. TOEFL required for international applicants. Accepts transfer applicants. Apply to Office of the Dean for Admission and Financial Aid. Application deadlines vary, depending on field of study. Fall and Spring admissions, except in Painting and Sculpture (Fall only). Application fee $90. Phone: (212)854-2134; e-mail: admission_arts@columbia.edu.

ADMISSION STANDARDS. Competitive or very competitive. Usual minimum average: 3.25 (A = 4).

FINANCIAL AID. Scholarships, tuition waivers, research assistantships, teaching assistantships, Federal W/S, loans. Apply by February 7. Phone: (212)854-2875. Use FAFSA. About 80% of students receive aid other than loans from School and outside sources.

DEGREE REQUIREMENTS. For M.F.A.: 60 credit program, four semesters in full-time residence; program by advisement; knowledge of at least one foreign language; final project or thesis project. For D.M.A.: usually six semesters beyond the bachelor's or 30 credits beyond the M.F.A., at least four semesters in residence; final project/dissertation.

FIELDS OF STUDY.
Acting.
Digital Media.
Dramaturgy/Script Analysis.
Fiction.
Film Production.
Film Screenwriting.
Nonfiction.
Painting.
Photography.
Poetry.
Printmaking.
Sculpture.
Theatre Directing.
Theatre Management.
Theatre Playwriting.
Visual Arts.
Writing.
Note: Joint J.D.-M.F.A. program in Entertainment Law.

Graduate School of Business
Web site: www.gsb.columbia.edu

Established 1916. Accredited programs: M.B.A.; recognized Ph.D. Semester system. Special Programs: foreign exchange programs (Australia, Austria, Belgium, Brazil, Finland, Germany, Hong Kong, Israel, Italy, the Netherlands, the Philippines, Republic of Singapore, Spain, Sweden, Switzerland, United Kingdom), foreign study, global studies. Special facilities: Center for Chinese Business Studies, Center for Human Resource Management, Center for Japanese Economy and Business, Center for Research in the Marketing Financial Services, Center for Global Consumers, Brands and Communication, Columbia Institute for Tele-Information, Institute for Marketing Studies, Center for the Studies of Futures Marketing, Center for International Business Education, Deming Center for Quality, Productivity, and Competitiveness. Library: 360,000 volumes, 3000 subscriptions.

Annual tuition: full-time $30,334.

Enrollment: new students 485 (Fall), 184 (Spring); total full- and part-time 1642 (men 65%, women 35%). Faculty: 108 full-time, 85 part-time; 99% with Ph.D./D.B.A. Degrees conferred: M.B.A. (FT, PT, day, evening), E.M.B.A. (Company Sponsored), M.B.A.-J.D., M.B.A.-M.I.A. (International Affairs), M.B.A.-M.P.H. (Public Health), M.B.A.-M.S. (Engineering and Applied Science, Journalism, Nursing, Social Work, Urban Planning),

M.B.A.-Ed.D. (Educational Administration and Higher Education with Teachers College), Ph.D.

ADMISSION REQUIREMENTS. A bachelor's degree from a recognized institution of higher education and a strong mathematics background are required for consideration. Submit an application, GMAT results (will accept GMAT test results from the last five years, latest acceptable date is April 15), official transcripts from each undergraduate/graduate school attended, two letters of recommendation, résumé (prefers at least four years of work experience), and an application fee of $180 to the Office of Admission and Financial Aid. Online application available. Beginning students are admitted Fall and Spring. U.S. citizens apply by April 20 (Fall), October 1 (Spring); international applicants apply by March 1 (Fall), October 1 (Spring). In addition, international students (whose native language is other than English) should submit a TOEFL (minimum score 610) report, certified translations and evaluations of all official transcripts, recommendation should be in English or with certified translations, proof of health/immunization certificate, and proof of sufficient financial resources for one year of academic study. On-campus visits are encouraged. Interviews are by invitation of the Admissions Committee. Joint degree applicants must apply to and be accepted to both schools/programs, contact the admissions office for current information and specific admissions requirements. Rolling admissions process, notification is made within 8–10 weeks of receipt of completed application and supporting documents. Admissions Office phone: (212)854-1961; fax: (212)662-6754.

ADMISSION REQUIREMENTS FOR DOCTORAL CANDIDATES. All applicants should have a bachelor's degree from a recognized institution of higher education, master's degree is optional. Strong mathematics background required. Contact the Ph.D. Programs, Graduate School of Business at (212)854-2836 for application material and information. Beginning students are admitted Fall only. Both U.S. citizens and international applicants apply by February 1 (Fall). Submit an application, a GMAT/GRE (will accept GMAT/GRE test results from the last five years, scores must arrive at admissions office prior to February 1), GRE including writing assessment required for Finance and Economics, official transcripts from each undergraduate/graduate schools attended, two letters of recommendation, 500-word essay, résumé, Statistical Information Sheet, and application fee of $60 to the Office of Admission and Financial Aid. Online application encouraged. In addition, international students (whose native language is other than English) should submit a TOEFL (minimum score 610) report; certified translations and evaluations of all official transcripts, recommendation should be in English or with certified translations, proof of health/immunization certificate. Interviews are not required, but can be arranged. Phone: (212)854-2836. Notification is made by mid-April.

ADMISSION STANDARDS. Competitive. Mean GMAT: 660; mean GPA: 3.45 (A = 4). Gourman rating: the M.B.A. was rated in the top six, the score was 4.89; the E.M.B.A. was rated in the top three, the score 4.87; the Ph.D. was rated in the top five, the score was 4.90. *U.S. News & World Report* ranked Columbia in the top three (M.B.A.), top five (E.M.B.A.) of all U.S. business schools. *Business Week* listed Columbia in the top six of American business schools.

FINANCIAL AID. Need-based scholarships, international fellowships, minority fellowships, graduate assistantships, State Grants, Federal W/S, loans. Financial aid is available for part-time study. Financial aid may be available for international students. Assistantships/fellowships may be available for joint degree candidates. Request scholarship, fellowship, assistantship information as well as current need-based financial aid information from the School of Business. Phone: (212)854-4057.

For most financial assistance and all Federal programs submit FAFSA (School code: E00116), also submit Financial Aid Transcript, Federal Income Tax forms. Approximately 65% of current students receive some form of financial assistance. Financial Aid for doctoral students: fellowships, assistantships, tuition exemptions, dissertation research support, loans. Apply for Financial Aid at the same time as admissions by submitting the Financial Assistance Application.

DEGREE REQUIREMENTS. For M.B.A.: 21-course program including 10 elective courses, two-year program; degree program must be completed in five years. For E.M.B.A.: 60 credit program. For M.B.A.-M.S.: 75–90 credit programs (Computer Science 75 credits, Industrial Engineering 75 credits, Journalism 78 credits, Mining Engineering 75 credits, Nursing 75 credits, Operations Research 75 credits, Social Work 90 credits, Urban Planning 90 credits). For M.B.A.-M.I.A.: 90 credit program. For M.B.A.-M.P.H.: 80 credit program. For M.B.A.-Ed.D.: 90 credit program. For M.B.A.-J.D.: 118 credit program, four- to five-year program. For Ph.D.: 20 course minimum, three- to five-year program; comprehensive exam; field exam; oral major field exam; at least two teaching assignments; dissertation proposal and oral defense; dissertation; oral defense.

FIELDS OF STUDY.
Accounting. M.B.A., Ph.D.
Business Economics.
Construction Management.
Decision, Risk Operations. Ph.D.
Finance.
Finance and Economics. Ph.D.
Human Resource Management.
International Business.
Management. Ph.D.
Management of Information Communications and Media.
Management of Organizations.
Management Science.
Marketing. M.B.A., Ph.D.
Operations Management.
Public and Nonprofit Management.
Real Estate.

School of Dental and Oral Surgery

Established 1852. Semester system. Annual tuition: full-time $31,056. Off-campus housing only. Average academic year housing costs: $13,000. Total average cost for all first-year expenses: $5700.

Enrollment: D.D.S. program, first-year class 72 (men 65%, women 35%) full-time 280, none part-time; postgraduate program, full-time 48, part-time 4. Faculty: full-time 39, part-time 4. Degrees conferred: D.D.S., D.D.S.-M.P.H., D.D.S.-M.S. (Health Care Management), D.D.S.-M.A. (Education).

ADMISSION REQUIREMENTS. AADSAS, official transcripts, three letters of recommendation, DAT required in support of School's application. Interview by invitation only. Applicants must have completed at least three years of college study. Graduates of unaccredited institutions not considered. Does not have EDP. Apply to Director of Student Affairs of the School after July 1, before February 15. Application fee $60. Phone: (212)305-3478.

ADMISSION STANDARDS. Very competitive. Mean DAT: academic 21, PAT 20; mean GPA: 3.30 (A = 4). Gourman rating: 4.09 (among the top five dental schools). Accepts about 20% of total annual applicants. Approximately 20% are state residents.

FINANCIAL AID. Scholarships, grants, tuition waivers, loans. Apply to Director of Student Affairs of the School. Phone: (212)305-4100. Use FAFSA (School code: E00119). No specified closing date. About 95% of students receive aid other than loans from School and outside sources.

DEGREE REQUIREMENTS. For D.D.S.: satisfactory completion of forty-five-month program.

Fu Foundation School of Engineering and Applied Science—Graduate Division

Special facilities: Center for Advanced Technology in Computers and Information Systems, Center for Telecommunications Research, Microelectronics Sciences Laboratories, Schapiro Center for Engineering and Physical Science Research.

Annual tuition: full-time $27,528, per credit $917. On-campus housing available. See housing information above. Enrollment: full-time 548, part-time 311. Faculty: full-time 148, part-time 20. Degrees conferred: M.S., Eng., Sc.D., Ph.D., Prof. Engr., M.B.A.-M.S.

ADMISSION REQUIREMENTS. Official transcripts, GRE, two letters of recommendation required in support of School's application. Electronic application available. GRE Subject required for Computer Science. TOEFL required for international applicants. Accept transfer applicants. Graduates of unaccredited institutions not considered. Apply to Office of Graduate Student Services by January 1 (Fall, for both admission and financial aid), February 15 (Fall, M.S. only and professional degree), October 1 (Spring). Application fee $60, $45 if you apply on-line. Phone: (212)854-6438.

ADMISSION STANDARDS. Very selective. Usual minimum average: 3.0 (A = 4). *U.S. News & World Report* ranking is in the top 26 of all U.S. schools.

FINANCIAL AID. Annual awards from institutional funds: scholarships, fellowships, research assistantships, teaching assistantships, Federal W/S, loans. Approved for VA benefits. Apply by January 15 (Fall) to Office of Graduate Student Services of the School for scholarships, fellowships, assistantships; to the Office of Financial Aid for all other programs. Phone: (212) 854-3442; e-mail: engradfinaid@columbia.edu. Use FAFSA. Aid available for international applicants.

DEGREE REQUIREMENTS. For master's: 30 semester hours of approved graduate courses beyond the bachelor's; thesis at discretion of department or division program. For Eng., Sc.D.: 30 semester hours of approved graduate courses beyond the master's, or 60 residence units beyond the bachelor's; foreign language proficiency at discretion of department/division; departmental qualifying exam; thesis and research required; final exam; degree completion within seven years. For Ph.D.: see Graduate School of Arts and Sciences listing above.

FIELDS OF STUDY.
Applied Chemistry.
Applied Mathematics.
Applied Physics.
Bioengineering.
Biomechanics.
Biomedical Imaging.
Cellular Engineering.
Chemical Engineering.
Civil Engineering.
Computer Engineering.
Computer Science.
Design Engineering.
Earth Resources Engineering.
Electrical Engineering. Includes multimedia networking, telecommunications engineering, new media engineering, lightwave (photonics) engineering, wireless and mobile communications, microelectronic circuits, microelectronic devices.
Engineering Mechanics. Includes continuum mechanics, vibration, random processes and reliability, fluid mechanics, computational mechanics.

Environmental Control Engineering.
Genomics Science and Technology.
Industrial Engineering. Includes engineering and management systems, production and operations management, industrial regulations studies, manufacturing, financial engineering.
Manufacturing Engineering.
Materials Science and Engineering.
Medical Physics.
Optical Physics.
Pharmaceutical Engineering.
Plasma Physics.
Process Engineering.
Solid-State Physics.
Solid-State Science and Engineering.

School of International and Public Affairs and the Regional Institutes

Established 1946. Graduate study only. Annual tuition: full-time $28,724, per credit $1226.

Enrollment: full- and part-time 650. Faculty: full-time 134. Degrees conferred: M.I.A., M.P.A., E.M.P.A.

ADMISSION REQUIREMENTS. Transcripts, personal statement, CV or résumé, GRE, three letters of recommendation required in support of School's application. Interviews are encouraged. TOEFL (minimum score 600, 250 on computer-based test) required for international applicants. Graduates of unaccredited institutions not considered. Apply to Office of University Admission, Low Memorial Library, by March 15 (Fall), October 15 (Spring). Application fee $75. Phone: (212)854-4737.

ADMISSION STANDARDS. Competitive. Usual minimum average: 3.0 (A = 4). Accepts about 35% of annual applicants.

FINANCIAL AID. Annual awards from institutional funds: fellowships, grants, assistantships, Federal W/S, career-related internships, loans. Apply by January 5 for fellowships, assistantships to Director of Admissions of the School. Phone: (212)854-6216. Use FAFSA (School code: 00128). About 35% of students receive aid other than loans from School. Financial assistance is available for international students.

DEGREE REQUIREMENTS. For M.I.A., M.P.A.: 54 credits minimum, full-time four-semester program, at least 30 in residence; functional or regional concentration for M.I.A.; proficiency in one foreign language (M.I.A.); internships; thesis.

PROGRAMS OF STUDY.
Humanitarian Affairs.
International Conflict Resolution.
UN Studies.

M.I.A. FUNCTIONAL CONCENTRATIONS:
Economic and Political Development.
Environmental Policy Studies.
Human Rights.
International Energy Management.
International Finance and Business.
International Media and Communications.
International Security Policy.
Science and Technology Policy.

M.P.A. CONCENTRATIONS:
Advanced Policy Analysis Techniques.
Education Policy
Environmental Policy.
Gender and Public Policy.
Individually Designed Concentration.
International Affairs Policy.

International Energy Management and Policy.
Law and Public Policy.
Science and Technology Policy.
Social Services and Welfare Policy.
Urban Policy.

REGIONAL INSTITUTES:
African Studies.
East Asian.
East Central Europe.
Latin American Studies.
Middle East.
Southern Asian.
Study of Europe.

Graduate School of Journalism

Established 1912. Annual tuition: $30,929, per credit $1015. Graduate study only. Enrollment: full-time 180, part-time 15. Faculty: full-time 19, part-time 78. Degree conferred: M.S.

ADMISSION REQUIREMENTS. Official transcripts, up to three letters of recommendation, two essays, résumé, writing test required in support of School's application. On-line application available. TOEFL (minimum score 600, 270 on computer-based test) required for international applicants. Transfer applicants not considered. Graduates of unaccredited institutions not considered. Apply to Office of Journalism Admissions by December 15 (Fall, full-time), May 1 (Fall, part-time), November 1 (Spring, part-time). Application fee $75. Phone: (212)854-3828; e-mail: admissions@jrn.columbia.edu.

ADMISSION STANDARDS. Competitive. Decisions based on professional promise, academic excellence, and writing test.

FINANCIAL AID. Annual awards from institutional funds: fellowships, grants, scholarships, loans, on- and off-campus employment. Apply to Office of Journalism Admissions. Phone: (212)854-3829. Use FAFSA (School code: E00122). Aid available for international students through the School's International Division (ID). About 80% of students receive aid from School and outside sources.

DEGREE REQUIREMENTS. For M.S.: 30–34 credits minimum; master's project (major paper or tape of publishable or broadcast quality).

FIELD OF STUDY.
Journalism. Include news-editorial in all print and broadcast aspects of professional journalism.
Note: Ph.D. is offered by the Graduate School of Arts and Sciences in the following areas: Journalism and Public Life, Social Impacts of Media, Economics and Regulation of Communications, Information and Technological Systems.

School of Law

Established 1858. ABA approved since 1923. AALS member. Semester system. Special facilities: Kernochan Center for Law and the Arts, Center for Law and Philosophy, Center for Law and Economic Studies, Center for the Study of Law and Culture, Center for Public Interest Law, Human Rights Institute, Center for Chinese Legal Studies, Center for Japanese Legal Studies, Center for Korean Legal Studies, European Legal Studies Center. Law library: 1,003,032 volumes, 7341 subscriptions; a Federal Government Depository.

Annual tuition: full-time $29,376. Total average for all other expenses: $15,245. Enrollment: first-year class 367; total full-time 1129 (men 52%, women 48%). Faculty: full-time 72, part-time 49. Student to faculty ratio 12.9 to 1. Degrees conferred: J.D., LL.M., J.S.D.

ADMISSION REQUIREMENTS. For J.D. program: LSDAS report, transcripts, LSAT required in support of application. In addition, international students must submit TOEFL (not older than two years), TSE, TWE. Interview not required. Accepts transfer applicants. Apply to Law Admissions Office after September 1, before February 15. Application fee $65. Phone: (212)854-2670. For graduate program: transcripts, written statement, résumé required in support of application. Apply to Office of Graduate Legal Studies of the School by December 15. Fall admission only. Accepts full-time students only. Application fee $75. Phone: (212)854-2670.

ADMISSION STANDARDS. Competitive. Mean LSAT: 169; mean GPA: 3.62 (A = 4). Accepts about 15% of total annual applicants. Gourman rating: 4.87. *U.S. News & World Report* ranking is in the top 4 of all law schools.

FINANCIAL AID. For J.D. program: scholarships, fellowships, assistantships, Federal W/S, apply for financial aid at time of application for admission, but before March 1. Use FAFSA (School code: E00488). For graduate program: apply for fellowships by March 1 to Office of Graduate Legal Studies of the School. About 35% of students receive aid other than loans from School.

DEGREE REQUIREMENTS. For J.D.: satisfactory completion of three-year program; 83 credits. For LL.M.: 24 credits minimum, at least one year in residence; up to six credits may be taken in other Columbia University Graduate Schools. For J.S.D.: at least one year in residence; publishable dissertation; oral exam.

FIELDS OF GRADUATE STUDY.
Civil Procedure.
Commercial Law.
Constitutional Law.
Corporation Securities Law.
Criminal Law.
Government Service.
Human Rights Law.
International Law.
Labor Law.
Legal History.
Legal Philosophy.
Property.
Taxation.
Note: School has joint degree programs with the Graduate Schools of the Arts, Arts and Sciences, Business, Journalism, International Affairs, Social Work; programs in Public Affairs, Urban Planning, with Princeton University's Woodrow Wilson School of Public and International Affairs.

School of Nursing

Founded 1892, graduate study since 1956. Semester system. Special facilities: Center for AIDS Research, Center for Health Policy, World Health Organization Center for the International Nursing Development in Advanced Practice, Center for Evidence-Based Practice in the Underserved.

Tuition: per credit $798 master's, per credit $2110 D.N.Sc.

Enrollment: full- and part-time 382. Faculty: full-time 46, part-time 26. Degrees conferred; M.S., D.N.Sc.

ADMISSION REQUIREMENTS. Official transcripts, personal statement, three letters of recommendation, GRE, MAT or another appropriate objective test, copy of nursing license required in support of School's application. Interview sometimes required. TOEFL required for international applicants. Graduates of unaccredited institutions not considered. Apply to Office of Student Services of the School at least three months prior to preferred date of enrollment. Admits Fall, Spring, and Summer.

Application fee $70, $100 for D.N.Sc. applicants. Phone: (212)305-5756; e-mail: nursing@columbia.edu.

ADMISSION STANDARDS. Competitive. Usual minimum average: 3.0 (A = 4).

FINANCIAL AID. Scholarships, grants, assistantships, Federal W/S, Federal Nursing loans, loans. Apply by March 1 to Student Service Office. Phone: (212) 305-8147; fax: (212)305-6937. Use FAFSA (School code: E00124). About 50% of students receive aid from all sources. Aid sometimes available for part-time students.

DEGREE REQUIREMENTS. For M.S.: see credit requirements in Fields of Study below, at least one year in full-time residence. For D.N.Sc.: 45–75 credit program (depending on preparation), at least one semester in full-time residence; comprehensive written and oral exam; research and speciality practicum experience; dissertation proposal defense, dissertation; final exam.

FIELDS OF SPECIALIZATION.
Acute Care Nursing Practitioner. 47-credit M.S. program.
Adult Nurse Practitioner. 46-credit M.S. program.
Advanced Clinical Management. 45-credit M.S. program.
Family Nurse Practitioner. 46–48-credit M.S. program.
Geriatric Nurse Practitioner. 49-credit M.S. Program.
Informatics. 45-credit M.S. program.
Neonatal Nurse Practitioner. 46-credit M.S. program.
Nurse Anesthesia. 59-credit M.S. program.
Nurse Midwifery. 49-credit M.S. program.
Oncology Nurse Practitioner. 54–56 credit M.S. program.
Pediatric Nurse Practitioner. 46-credit M.S. program.
Psychiatric Mental Health Nurse Practitioner. 46-credit M.S. program.
Women's Health Nurse Practitioner. 48–52-credit M.S. program.

College of Physicians and Surgeons

Established 1767. The first school to award an M.D. in the American colonies. Library: 450,000 volumes, 4000 subscriptions.

Annual tuition: $32,454. Housing available. Total average figure for all other expenses: $15,000. Enrollment: first-year class 150; total 600 (men 60%, women 40%). College faculty: full-time 800, part-time 900. Degrees conferred: M.D., M.D.-M.B.A., M.D.-J.D., M.D.-M.S., M.D.-M.P.H., M.D.-Ph.D. The M.S. and Ph.D. are offered through the Graduate School. Graduate study, Medical Scientist Training Program.

ADMISSION REQUIREMENTS. Transcripts, MCAT, recommendations required in support of application. Interview may be required. Applicants must have completed at least three years of college study. Does not have EDP. Apply to Office of the Dean of the College after June 15, before October 15. Application fee $85. Phone: (212)305-3595; fax: (212)305-3601.

ADMISSION STANDARDS. Very competitive. Mean MCAT: 11.44; mean GPA: 3.65 (A = 4). Gourman rating: 4.86. *U.S. News & World Report* ranking is in the top seven of all U.S. medical schools. Accepts 8% of total annual applicants. Approximately 15% are state residents.

FINANCIAL AID. Scholarships, grants, assistantships, fellowships, Federal and institutional loans. Apply after acceptance. Phone: (212)305-4100. Use FAFSA (College code: E00117). About 68% of students receive some aid from institutional funds.

DEGREE REQUIREMENTS. For M.D.: satisfactory completion of four-year program. For M.B.A., J.D., M.S., M.P.H., Ph.D.: see Graduate School listing above.

FIELDS OF GRADUATE AND POSTGRADUATE STUDY.
Anatomy and Cell Biology.
Biochemistry and Molecular Biophysics.
Genetics and Development.
Health Professionals. M.S.
Integrated Program.
Medical Informatics.
Microbiology.
Neurobiology and Behavior.
Nutrition. M.S., Ph.D.
Occupational Therapy. M.O.T.
Pathology.
Pharmacology, Physiology, and Cellular Biophysics.
Physical Therapy. M.P.T.

Joseph L. Mailman School of Public Health

Graduate study since 1921. Semester system. Special facilities: Center for Applied Public Health, Columbia Center for Children's Environmental Health, Center for Community Health and Education, Center for Environmental Health in Northern Manhattan, Harlem Health Promotion Center, Harlem Lung Center, Center for the History and Ethics of Public Health, Center for Infectious Disease Epidemiology Research, Center for Lesbian, Gay, Bisexual, and Transgender Health, National Center for Children in Poverty, Center for Psychosocial Study of Health and Illness, Center for Public Health Preparedness, Statistical Analysis Center for Clinical Trials, Center for Violence Research and Prevention.

Tuition: per credit $860.

Enrollment: full- and part-time 740 (men 30%, women 70%). Faculty: full-time 86, part-time 206. Degrees conferred: M.P.H., Executive M.P.H., M.S., Dr.P.H. The Ph.D. is administered by the Graduate School of Arts and Sciences.

ADMISSION REQUIREMENTS. Official transcripts, GRE or another appropriate objective test, personal statement, three letters of reference required in support of School's application. Interview sometimes required. M.P.H. or equivalent master's, internship required for Dr.P.H. applicants. TOEFL required for international applicants. Accepts transfer applicants. Graduates of unaccredited institutions not considered. Apply to Office of Admissions of the School before February 15 (Fall), October 1 (Spring), February 1 (Summer). Application fee $60. Phone: (212) 305-3927, Fax: (212)305-6450.

ADMISSION STANDARDS. Competitive. Usual minimum average 3.0 (A = 4).

FINANCIAL AID. Assistantships, traineeships, Federal W/S, loans. Apply to Financial Aid Office; no specified closing date. Phone: (212)305-4113; fax: (212)305-6450. Use FAFSA. About 50% of students receive aid from all sources.

DEGREE REQUIREMENTS. For M.P.H.: 45 credits minimum, at least one year in full-time residence; practicum; master's essay or culminating experience. For M.S.: 30-credit program, at least one year in residence; master's essay. For Dr.P.H.: two-year, 40-credit minimum program, at least one year in residence; qualifying exam; dissertation; final oral exam. For Ph.D.: see Graduate School listing above.

FIELDS OF STUDY.
Aging and Public Health. M.P.H.
Biostatistic Clinical Research Methods. M.S.
Biostatistics Patient Oriented Research. M.S.
Biostatistic Theory and Methods. M.S.
Executive Program in Health Services Management. M.P.H.
Forced Migration and Health. M.P.H.
General Biostatistics. M.P.H., Dr.Ph.H., Ph.D.

General Environmental Health. M.P.H., Dr.P.H., Ph.D.
General Epidemiology. M.P.H., M.S., Dr.P.H., Ph.D.
General Public Health. M.P.H.
General Social Services. M.P.H., Dr.P.H., Ph.D.
Health Effectiveness and Outcomes Research. M.P.H.
Health Management. M.P.H.
Health Policy. M.P.H.
Health Prevention/Disease Prevention. M.P.H.
History and Ethics of Public Health and Medicine. M.P.H., Ph.D.
Medical/Health Physics. M.P.H., Dr.P.H., Ph.D.
Reproductive, Adolescent, and Child Health. M.P.H.
Toxicology. M.P.H., Dr.P.H., Ph.D.
Note: Dual degree programs are available with the Medical School, Dental School, Nursing School, Business, International Affairs, Public Administration, Social Work, and Urban Planning.

School of Social Work

Annual tuition: Full-time $23,948. On-campus housing available. See Housing listing above. Enrollment: full-time 595, part-time 139 (men 15%, women 85%). Faculty: full-time 44, part-time 53. Degrees conferred: M.S.S.W., D.S.W.

ADMISSION REQUIREMENTS. Official transcripts, three letters of reference, personal statement required in support of School's application. Electronic application available. Interviews sometimes requested by School. TOEFL (minimum score 575), TWE, TSE required for international applicants. Accepts transfer applicants. Especially interested in minority group applicants. Apply to Office of Admissions by March 15 (Fall) for full-time; November 1 (Spring). Application fee $50. Phone: (212)954-2856; fax: (212)854-2975.

ADMISSION STANDARDS. Selective. Usual minimum average: 3.0 (A = 4).

FINANCIAL AID. Annual awards from institutional funds: scholarships, merit scholarships, teaching assistantships, internships, Federal W/S, loans. Apply by June 15 (Fall) to Office of Admissions. Use FAFSA. About 90% of students receive aid from School and outside sources.

DEGREE REQUIREMENTS. For M.S.S.W: 60 credits full-time, two-year or 17-month (accelerated) minimum. For D.S.W: 30 credits minimum beyond the master's, at least two consecutive terms in full-time residence; qualifying paper; comprehensive exam; dissertation; dissertation defense.

FIELDS OF STUDY.
Aging.
Advanced Practice. D.S.W.
Contemporary Social Problems.
Family, Youth, and Children's Services.
Health, Mental Health, and Disabilities.
International Social Welfare and Services to Immigrants and Refugees.
Social Policy, Planning, and Administration. D.S.W.
Social Policy, Planning, and Policy Analysis. D.S.W.
World of Work.
Note: Joint degree programs with Jewish Theological Seminary of America, Bank Street College of Education.

Teachers College
Web site: www.tc.columbia.edu

Founded 1887. Graduate study only. Affiliated with the University since 1898 and is designated the Graduate Faculty of Education. Semester system. Special facilities: Center for Health Promotion, Center for Infants and Parents, Institute for

Urban and Minority Education, Institute of Higher Education, Institute of Philosophy and Politics of Education, Institute for Learning Technologies, Institute for Education and Economy, International Center for Cooperation and Conflict Resolution, Center for the Study and Education of the Gifted, Institute of International Education, Center for Community Colleges, Center for Nursing Leadership Development, National Center for Restructuring Education, Schools and Teaching, Institute of Research and Service in Nursing Education. Milbank Library houses the largest American collection on education, psychology, and health services. Library: 603,500 volumes, 2267 subscriptions.

Annual tuition: $18,120.

Enrollment: full-time 965, part-time 3980 (men 30%, women 70%). Faculty: full-time 134, part-time 227. Degrees conferred: M.A., M.S., Ed.M., Sixth-Year Professional Diploma, Ed.D., Ph.D.

ADMISSION REQUIREMENTS. Official transcripts, personal statement, two letters of recommendation required in support of application. Interview, GRE/MAT required by some departments. TOEFL required for international applicants. Accepts transfer applicants. Graduates of unaccredited institutions not considered. Apply to Teachers College Admissions Office by February 1 (Fall, for some programs and scholarships), July 1 (Fall), December 15 (Spring), April 15 (Summer). Application fee $50. Phone: (212)678-3710; fax: (212)678-4171.

ADMISSION STANDARDS. Competitive for most departments, very competitive for the others. Usual minimum average: 3.0 (A = 4).

FINANCIAL AID. Annual awards from institutional funds: scholarships, teaching fellowships, research assistantships, grants, Tuition Assistance Awards, Federal W/S, loans. Apply by December 15 (Fall, all Ph.D., Psychology), January 1 (Fall, all Ed.D. programs), January 15 (Fall, all master's programs), November 1 (Spring) to appropriate department chair for assistantships, scholarships, fellowships; to Director of Student Aid of the College for all other programs. Phone: (212)678-3714; fax: (212)678-4089. Use FAFSA (College code: G03979). About 25% of students receive aid other than loans from College and outside sources.

DEGREE REQUIREMENTS. For M.A., M.S.: 30 credits minimum, at least one year in residence; thesis or essay. For Ed.M.: 60 credits minimum, at least 30 in residence. For Ed.D.: 90 credits minimum beyond the bachelor's, at least 45 in residence; certification exam; dissertation; final oral/written exam. For Sixth-Year Diploma: 60 semester hours beyond bachelor's; research project. For Ph.D.: 75 credits minimum beyond the bachelor's, at least 45 in residence; certification exam; Proficiency in foreign languages for some programs; dissertation; final oral/written exam.

FIELDS OF STUDY.
Administration of Special Education.
Adult Education and Organizational Learning.
Adult Learning and Leadership.
Anthropology and Education.
Applied Anthropology.
Applied Linguistics.
Applied Physiology.
Applied Physiology and Nutrition.
Applied Statistics.
Art and Art Education.
Arts Administration.
Audiology.
Bilingual/Bicultural Education.

Blindness and Visual Impairment.
Clinical Psychology.
Cognitive Studies in Education.
College Teaching of Biological Science.
College Teaching of Earth Science.
College Teaching of Physical Science.
Communication and Education.
Communication, Computing, and Technology in Education.
Community Nutrition Education.
Comparative and International Education.
Computing and Education.
Conflict Resolution.
Counseling Psychology.
Curriculum and Teaching.
Curriculum and Teaching in Physical Education.
Deaf or Hard of Hearing.
Developmental Psychology.
Early Childhood Special Education.
Economics and Education.
Education Leadership. Includes private school leadership.
Education of Teacher of Science.
Educational Policy.
Elementary School Science Education.
Elementary/Childhood Education—Preservice.
Gifted Education.
Guidance and Habilitation.
Healthcare Human Resources.
Higher Education.
History and Education.
Humanities.
Instructional Practice.
Instructional Technology and Media.
Interdisciplinary Studies in Education.
International Educational Development.
Law and Educational Institutions.
Learning Disabilities.
Measurement and Evaluation.
Mental Retardation.
Motor Learning and Control.
Movement Sciences and Education.
Music and Music Education.
Neurosciences and Education.
Nurse Executive.
Nursing Education.
Nutrition.
Nutrition and Public Health.
Nutrition Education.
Organizational Psychology.
Physical Disabilities.
Physical Education.
Politics and Education.
Psychological Counseling.
Psychology in Education.
Reading Specialist.
Religion and Education.
Research in Special Education.
Science Education.
Secondary School Science Education.
Social Studies.
Social-Organizational Psychology.
Sociology and Education.
Special Education.
Speech and Language Pathology.
Speech-Language Pathology and Audiology.
Supervision of Science Education.
Supervision of Special Education.
Teaching of American Sign Language as a Foreign Language.
Teaching of English.
Teaching of English and English Education.
Teaching of Spanish.

COLUMBUS STATE UNIVERSITY

Columbus, Georgia 31907-5645
Web site: www.colstate.edu

Founded in 1963. Public control. Coed. Semester system. Library 250,000 volumes, 1400 subscriptions.

Annual tuition: full-time resident $2320, nonresident $9280; per credit, resident $97, nonresident $387. Limited on-campus housing for single students only. Average academic year housing costs: $4570–$6720 (includes a limited board plan). Contact Office of Residential Life for both on- and off-campus housing information. Phone: (706)568-2026.

Graduate Studies

Graduate program since 1973. Enrollment: full-time 188, part-time 511 (men 45%, women 55%). Faculty: full-time 102, part-time 7. Degrees Conferred: M.B.A., M.Ed., M.M., M.S., Ed.S.

ADMISSION REQUIREMENTS. Transcripts, GRE/MAT/GMAT required in support of application. Audition required for M.M. TOEFL/MTELP (minimum TOEFL 550, MTELP 75) required for international applicants. Accepts transfer applicants. Graduates of unaccredited institutions not considered. Apply to Admissions Office before July 1 (Fall), December 1 (Spring). Application fee $25. Phone: (706)568-2279; fax: (706)568-2462.

ADMISSION STANDARDS. Selective. Usual minimum average: 2.75 (A = 4).

FINANCIAL AID. Scholarships, graduate assistantships, internships, grants, tuition waivers, Federal W/S, loans. Approved for VA benefits. Apply to Director of Financial Aid before May 1. Phone: (706)568-2036, fax: (706)568-2230; e-mail: financial_aid@colstate.edu. Use FAFSA. About 10% of students receive aid other than loans from University and outside sources.

DEGREE REQUIREMENTS. For M.Ed., M.M., M.P.A.: 36–37 credit hours minimum, at least 30 in residence. For M.B.A.: 30–55 credit hours minimum, depending upon previous preparation; at least 30 hours in residence. For M.S..: 36 credit hours minimum, at least 30 in residence. For Ed.S.: at least 30 hours beyond master's.

FIELDS OF STUDY.
Administration. M.Ed., Ed.S.
Applied Computer Science. M.S.
Art Education. M.Ed.
Business Administration. M.B.A.
Community Counseling. M.S.
Early Childhood Education. M.Ed.
Environmental Science. M.S.
General Government Administration. M.P.A.
Health and Physical Education. M.Ed.
Health Services Administration. M.P.A.
Information Technology Management. M.S.
Instructional Technology. M.S.
Justice Administration. M.P.A.
Middle Grades Education. M.Ed., Ed.S.
Music Education. Includes general music, conducting (choral and instrumental). M.M.
School Counseling. M.Ed., Ed.S.
Secondary Education. Includes biology, English language arts, history, mathematics. M.Ed., Ed.S.
Special Education. Includes behavioral disorders, learning disabilities, mental retardation. M.Ed.

CONCORDIA UNIVERSITY

Seward, Nebraska 68434-1599
Web site: www.cune.edu

Founded 1894. Located 20 miles NW of Lincoln. Coed. Private control. Lutheran-Missouri Synod. Semester system. Library: 165,000 volumes.

Tuition: per credit hour $115. On-campus housing for 200 graduate men, 200 graduate women, 30 married students. Housing cost: (2½-week session) $120. Apply to Student Life Office for on-campus information. Phone: (402)643-7411, for off-campus information (402)643-7239.

College of Graduate Studies

Enrollment: full-time 36, part-time 197. College faculty: full-time 40, part-time 8. Degrees conferred: M.Ed., M.S., M.P.Ed., D.C.E.SP.

ADMISSION REQUIREMENTS. Transcripts, three letters of recommendations, MAT required in support of College's application. TOEFL required for international applicants. Interview not required. Accepts transfer applicants. Graduates of unaccredited institutions not considered. Apply to Director of Admissions by June 1 (Summer), August 1 (Fall). Application fee 15. Phone: (800)535-5494 or (402)643-4073; admiss@seward.cune.edu.

ADMISSION STANDARDS. Selective. Usual minimum average: 3.0 (last two years) (A = 4).

FINANCIAL AID. Scholarships, Federal W/S, loans. Apply to Financial Aid Officer by April 15. Phone: (402)643-7270; fax: (402)643-4073. Use FAFSA and College's FAF.

DEGREE REQUIREMENTS. For master's: 36 credit hours minimum, at least 24 residence; thesis option; final written/oral exam.

FIELDS OF STUDY.
Christian Education. D.C.E.SP.
Family Life Ministry.
Parish Education.
Teacher Education. Includes early childhood, classroom teacher, administration, reading.

CONCORDIA UNIVERSITY

River Forest, Illinois 60305-1499
Web site: www.curf.edu

Founded 1864. CGS member. Located 10 miles W of Chicago. Coed. Private control. Lutheran-Missouri Synod. Semester system. Library: 165,000 volumes, 470 subscriptions.

Tuition: per hour $460. On-campus housing available. Annual housing cost: $5400 (includes board). Apply to Director of Housing for on- and off-campus housing information. Phone: (708)209-3006. Day-care facilities available.

School of Graduate Studies

Graduate study since 1957. Enrollment: full- and part-time 620. College faculty: full-time 48, part-time 30. Degrees conferred: M.A., M.A.T., M.C.M., C.A.S., Ed.D.

ADMISSION REQUIREMENTS. Transcripts, recommendations, GRE required in support of University's application. TOEFL and proof of financial support required for international applicants. Interview not required. Accepts transfer applicants.

Graduates of unaccredited institutions not considered. Apply to Office of Graduate Admission; no specified closing dates. Rolling admissions process. Application fee, none. Phone: (708)209-4093; fax: (708)209-3454.

ADMISSION STANDARDS. Selective. Usual minimum average 2.85 (A = 4).

FINANCIAL AID. Annual awards from institutional funds: scholarships, assistantships, tuition waivers, Federal W/S, loans. Apply by April 1 to Dean of Graduate Studies. Use FAFSA. About 45% of students receive aid other than loans from School and outside sources. Aid sometimes available for part-time students.

DEGREE REQUIREMENTS. For M.A., M.A.T.: 33–37 hours minimum, at least 24 in residence; candidacy; capstone experience (written/oral exam, thesis, independent research project). For M.C.M.: 36 credit program. For C.A.S.: at least 30 credits beyond master's. For Ed.D.: 60–63 credit program, at least 30 in residence; fieldwork component, admission to candidacy; dissertation; final oral exam.

FIELDS OF STUDY.
Church Music. M.C.M.
Curriculum and Instruction. M.A.
Early Childhood Education. M.A., M.A.T., Ed.D.
Educational Leadership. Ed.D.
Elementary Education. M.A.T.
Gerontology. M.A.
Human Services. M.A.
Human Services—Administration. M.A.
Human Services—Exercise Science. M.A.
Professional Counseling. M.A.
Psychology. M.A.
Reading Education. M.A.
Religion. M.A.
School Leadership. M.A.
School Counseling. M.A.
Secondary Education. M.A.T.
Superintendent. C.A.S.
Urban Teaching. M.A.

CONNECTICUT COLLEGE
New London, Connecticut 06320-4196
Web site: www.conncoll.edu

Founded 1911. Located 40 miles W of Providence, R.I. Coed. Private control. Semester system. Day-care facilities available. Library: 460,000 volumes, 1700 subscriptions.

Tuition per course: $1115. No on-campus housing for graduate students. Contact Office of Continuing Education. Phone: (860)439-2060.

Graduate Studies

Enrollment: full-time 20, part-time 61. College faculty: full-time 143, part-time 9. Degrees conferred: M.A., M.A.T.

ADMISSION REQUIREMENTS. Official transcripts, personal statement or essay, three references required in support of application. GRE for some programs. TOEFL (minimum score 600) required for international applicants. Accepts transfer applicants. Graduates of unaccredited colleges not considered. Apply to Graduate Studies Program by February 1 (Fall) for Psychology; for other programs March 15 (Fall), October 15 (Spring). Rolling admissions process. Application fee $55. Phone: (860)439-2062; fax: (860)439-5416 (most programs); (860)439-2760 (Education); (860)439-2330 (Psychology).

ADMISSION STANDARDS. Competitive. Usual minimum average: 3.0 (A = 4).

FINANCIAL AID. Limited to five teaching assistantships, Federal W/S, loans. Apply to Office of Financial Aid; no specified closing date. Phone: (860)439-2216; e-mail: finaid@conncoll.edu. Use FAFSA (College code: 001379) and Connecticut College FAF.

DEGREE REQUIREMENTS. For M.A.: 9–12 semester courses minimum (32 credits), at least 5 courses in residence. Thesis usually required and counted as 2-semester course; final comprehensive exam when thesis is not required; reading knowledge of one foreign language for some majors. For M.A.T.: 8 or 9 semester courses minimum, at least 5 courses in residence.

FIELDS OF STUDY.
Botany. M.A.
Chemistry. M.A.
Music. Includes performance. M.A.
Psychology. GRE Subject for admission. Includes clinical, behavior medicine/health, social/personality, neuroscience/psychobiology. M.A.
Secondary Education. Includes English, history-social studies, French, German, Spanish, Italian, Japanese, Russian, mathematics, biology, chemistry, earth science, general science, physics. M.A.T.
Zoology.

UNIVERSITY OF CONNECTICUT
Box U-6-A
Storrs, Connecticut 06269
Web site: www.uconn.edu

Founded 1881. Located 30 miles E of Hartford. The Schools of Law and Social Work are located in West Hartford; the Schools of Dental Medicine and Medicine are located at the University's Health Center in Farmington. Part-time evening M.B.A. programs offered at off-campus centers in Hartford and Stamford. Coed, State control. Semester system. Special facilities: Institute of Materials Science, Marine Science Institute, Institute of Water Resources, Institute of Social Inquiry. The University's NIH ranking is 83rd among all U.S. institutions with 201 awards/grants worth $51,901,931. Library: 2,444,000 volumes, 2,465,000 items in microform, 131 PC workstations in all libraries. Total University enrollment: 23,500.

Annual tuition/fees: maximum per semester, resident $6836, New England Region $9682, nonresident $15,928; per credit resident $316, New England Region $474, nonresident $821. On-campus housing limited. Average annual housing cost: $5700, board charges $3064. Apply to Division of Housing and Food Services, Housing Services Officer. Phone: (860)486-2926.

Graduate School

Graduate study since 1920. Enrollment: full-time 3332, part-time 2381 (men 50%, women 50%). University faculty: full-time 1150, part-time 48. Degrees conferred: M.A., M.S., M.B.A., M.M., M.P.A., M.F.A., M.P.H., M.Dent.Sc., M.S.W., D.M.A., Ph.D.

ADMISSION REQUIREMENTS. Transcripts, two or three letters of recommendation, personal letter required in support of School's application. GRE/MAT required by some departments, recommended for all. Audition required for music programs. TOEFL (minimum score 550) required for international students. Interview required by some departments. Accepts transfer applicants. Graduates of unaccredited institutions not considered. Apply to the Graduate Admissions Office by June 1 (Fall),

November 1 (Spring); international applicants by April 1 (Fall), October 1 (Spring). Apply directly to professional schools, Application fee $40, international applicants $45. Phone: (860)486-3617.

ADMISSION STANDARDS. Selective for most departments. Usual minimum average: 3.0 (last 2 years) (A = 4).

FINANCIAL AID. Annual awards from institutional funds: scholarships, fellowships, research assistantships, Federal W/S, loans. Apply by February 15 to appropriate department head on forms available from Office of Student Financial Aid Services; phone: (860)486-2819. Use FAFSA and institutional FAF. About 50% of students at Storrs receive aid other than loans from University and outside sources. Aid sometimes available for part-time and international students.

DEGREE REQUIREMENTS. For M.A., M.S.: 15 credits minimum plus thesis or 24 credits minimum without thesis; final (written, oral, or both) exam. For M.B.A.: 57 credits, which may be reduced depending upon previous registration, at least 24 credits in residence; final written/oral exam. For M.S.W.: 60 credits minimum, at least one year in full-time residence; final paper and group project; final written/oral exam. For M.F.A.: two years full-time study minimum; final project. For D.M.A.: two years full-time study beyond master's, at least 43 credits; general exam; foreign language proficiency; dissertation proposal; candidacy; recital; dissertation; final oral exam. For Ph.D.: three years minimum beyond the bachelor's, at least one year in full-time residence; general exam.; reading knowledge of one foreign language or 6 credits of advanced work in a related or supporting area; candidacy; dissertation; oral defense.

FIELDS OF STUDY.
Accounting. M.S.
Adult Learning. Ph.D. only.
Agricultural and Resource Economics. M.S., Ph.D.
Allied Health. M.S.
Animal Science. Includes physiology of reproduction. M.S., Ph.D.
Anthropology. Includes social science and health care (Ph.D. only). M.A., Ph.D.
Art. M.F.A.
Biochemistry. M.S., Ph.D.
Biological Engineering. Interdisciplinary. M.S., Ph.D.
Biophysics. M.S., Ph.D.
Biotechnology. M.S. only.
Botany. Includes morphology, natural products chemistry, paleobotany, phycology, plant cell and molecular biology, plant physiology, plant systematics.
Business Administration. Full-time M.B.A. program at Storrs includes finance, health care management, information technology, interactive marketing, management consulting; part-time evening M.B.A. programs at Hartford and Stamford include accounting, finance, general, health care management, international business, management; Ph.D. programs include accounting, finance, management, marketing, operations and information management. GMAT for admission; September admission only; apply by March 15. M.B.A., Ph.D.
Cell Biology. Includes cytology, development biology, plant cell and molecular biology, plant physiology.
Chemical Engineering. M.S., Ph.D.
Chemistry. M.S., Ph.D.
Civil Engineering. Includes applied mechanics, environmental engineering, fluid dynamics, geotechnical engineering, structural engineering, transportation and urban engineering. M.A., Ph.D.
Communication Science. Includes communication, communication process and marketing communication (Ph.D. only), speech, language, and hearing. M.A., Ph.D.

Comparative Literary and Cultural Studies. Interdisciplinary. M.A., Ph.D.
Computer Science and Engineering. M.S., Ph.D.
Curriculum and Instruction. Includes bilingual and bicultural education, elementary, secondary. Ph.D. only.
Dramatic Arts. Includes acting, design, directing, performance/production, puppetry, technical direction, theater history and criticism. M.A., M.F.A.
Ecology. Includes ecology and biological control, plant ecology. M.S., Ph.D.
Economics. M.A., Ph.D.
Education. M.A.
Educational Administration. Ph.D. only.
Educational Leadership. Ed.D. only
Educational Psychology. Includes cognition/instruction, counseling psychology, evaluation and measurement, gifted and talented education, school psychology. Ph.D. only.
Educational Studies. Includes history and philosophy of education, social foundations of education. Ph.D. only.
Educational Technology. Ph.D.
Electrical Engineering. Includes control and communication systems, electromagnetics and physical electronics, fluid dynamics. M.S., Ph.D.
Engineering. Includes civil and environmental, chemical, computer science and engineering, electrical and systems, mechanical, metallurgy, and materials. M. Eng.
English. Includes American studies (interdisciplinary). GRE Subject for admission; apply by May 1 (Fall), December 1 (Spring). M.A., Ph.D.
Entomology. Includes morphology and physiology, systematics. M.S., Ph.D.
Environmental Engineering. Interdisciplinary. M.S., Ph.D.
French. M.A., Ph.D.
Genetics. M.S., Ph.D.
Geography. M.A., Ph.D.
Geological Sciences. Includes geology, geophysics. M.S., Ph.D.
German. M.A., Ph.D.
History. Includes American studies (interdisciplinary), Latin American, medieval European, modern European, United States. M.A., Ph.D.
Human Development and Family Relations. M.A., Ph.D.
International Studies. Includes African studies, European studies, Italian history and culture, Latin American studies. M.A. only.
Instructional Media and Technology. Ph.D. only.
International Studies. M.A. only.
Italian. M.A., Ph.D.
Judaic Studies. Interdisciplinary. M.A.
Kinesiology. Includes exercise science, social science of sport and leisure. Ph.D.
Linguistics. M.A., Ph.D.
Materials Science. Includes alloy science, biomaterials, corrosion science, crystal science, dental materials, metallurgy, polymer science. Interdisciplinary. M.S., Ph.D.
Mathematics. Includes actuarial science. M.S., Ph.D.
Mechanical Engineering. Includes applied mechanics, design, dynamics and control, energy and thermal science, fluid dynamics, manufacturing. M.S., Ph.D.
Medieval Studies. Interdisciplinary. M.A., Ph.D.
Metallurgy and Material Engineering. M.S., Ph.D.
Microbiology. M.S., Ph.D.
Music. Audition during first semester of enrollment. Includes conducting, historical musicology, music education, music theory and history, performance, theory. M.Mus., M.A., D.M.A., Ph.D.
Natural Resources: Land, Water, and Air. M.S., Ph.D.
Nursing. M.S., Ph.D.
Nutritional Science. M.S., Ph.D.
Oceanography. M.S., Ph.D.
Pathobiology. D.V.M. for admission to comparative pathology major. Includes bacteriology, pathology, virology. M.S., Ph.D.

Pharmaceutical Sciences. Includes medicinal and natural products chemistry, neurosciences, pharmaceutics, pharmacology and toxicology. M.S., Ph.D.

Philosophy. M.A., Ph.D.

Physics. M.S., Ph.D.

Physiology and Neurobiology. Includes comparative physiology, endocrinology, neurobiology, neurosciences. M.S., Ph.D.

Plant Science. Includes agronomy, horticulture, landscape, plant breeding, plant environment, soil science. M.S., Ph.D.

Political Science. Includes American studies (interdisciplinary), survey research. M.A., Ph.D.

Polymer Science. M.S., Ph.D.

Psychology. GRE General/Subject, MAT for admission. Includes behavioral neuroscience, clinical, cognition/instruction, development, ecological psychology, general experimental, industrial/organizational, language, neurosciences, social. M.A., Ph.D.

Public Administration. M.P.A. only.

Public Health. M.P.H. only.

Social work. Interviews required; offered in Hartford. M.S.W., Ph.D.

Sociology. Includes social science and health care, survey research. M.A., Ph.D.

Spanish. M.A., Ph.D.

Special Education. Ph.D. only.

Survey Research. M.A. only.

Statistics. Includes industrial statistics. M.S., Ph.D.

Zoology. Includes biological/anthropology, parasitology, systematics and evolution. M.S., Ph.D.

School of Law

Web site: www.law.uconn.edu

Founded in 1921. ABA approved since 1933. AALS member. Semester system. Located in Hartford (06105-2213). Special facilities: Connecticut Urban Legal Initiative, Center for Children's Advocacy, Insurance Law Center. Special programs: student/faculty exchange programs with University of Exeter (United Kingdom), University of Puerto Rico, the University of International Business and Economics (People's Republic of China), Trinity College (Dublin, Ireland), Aix-en-Provence (France). Library: 482,700 volumes, 5512 subscriptions; has LEXIS, NEXIS, WESTLAW.

Annual tuition and fees: full-time, resident $11,394, nonresidents $23,538; part-time resident $7962, nonresident $16,422; per credit, resident $360, nonresident NEHEC $540, other nonresident $692. No on-campus housing available. Contact School for off-campus accommodations. Total average cost for all other expenses: $9450.

Enrollment: first-year class day 120, evening 62; full-time 576 (men 53%, women 47%), part-time 220. Faculty: full-time 38, part-time 36. Student to faculty ratio 11.2 to 1. Degrees conferred: J.D., J.D.-M.B.A., J.D.-M.P.A., J.D.-M.S.W., J.D.-M.L.S. (with Southern Connecticut State University), J.D.-M.A. (with Trinity College), LL.M.

ADMISSION REQUIREMENTS. LSDAS Law School report, bachelor's degree, transcript, LSAT, two letters of recommendation required in support of application. Interview not required. Accepts transfer applicants. Graduates of unaccredited colleges not considered. Apply to the Dean of Admissions after October 1, before March 15. Application fee: day or evening $30; day and evening $45. Phone: (860)570-5100; fax: (860)570-5153.

ADMISSION STANDARDS. Selective. Mean LSAT: 159; mean GPA: 3.23 (A = 4.0). Gourman rating: 3.38. *U.S. News & World Report* ranking is in the top 43 of all law schools. Accepts 20% of total day applicants; 25% of total evening applicants.

FINANCIAL AID. Scholarships, tuition remission, grants, loans. About 44% of students receive aid other than loans from School

funds. Apply by March 15. Use FAFSA (School code: E00387) and school forms. Aid available for part-time students.

DEGREE REQUIREMENTS. For J.D.: 84 semester hours minimum; advanced standing for work completed at other law school individually considered. For LL.M.: 24–30 credits beyond the J.D; at least 2 semesters in residence.

UNIVERSITY OF CONNECTICUT HEALTH CENTER

Farmington, Connecticut 06030-3906

Coed. State control. Semester system. No on-campus housing available.

Graduate School

Annual tuition: full-time $5272, nonresident $13,696; per credit, resident $293, nonresident $761. Enrollment: full-time 100, part-time 40. Total enrollment: 400. Faculty: full-time 20, part-time 141. Degrees conferred: M.P.H., M.D.S., Ph.D., M.D.-Ph.D., D.M.D.-Ph.D., M.D.-M.P.H., M.D.S.-Ph.D.

ADMISSION REQUIREMENTS. Official transcripts, three letters of recommendation, GRE required in support of College's application. TOEFL required for international applicants. Interviews may be arranged. Accepts transfer applicants. Graduates of unaccredited institutions not considered. Combined degree candidates must be accepted by both schools. Apply to Office of Graduate Admissions by January 1, March 1 (M.P.H.). Rolling admissions process. Application fee $40, $45 for international applicants. Phone: (860)679-4306.

ADMISSION STANDARDS. Competitive. Usual minimum average: 3.0 (A = 4).

FINANCIAL AID. Fellowships, research assistantships, teaching assistantships, tuition waivers, Federal W/S, loans. Approved for VA benefits. Apply by April 1 to the office of the Graduate School for fellowships, assistantships; to the Financial Aid Office at Storrs for all other programs. Use FAFSA. Aid available for part-time students.

DEGREE REQUIREMENTS. For M.D.S.: 30 credit hours, at least 24 in residence; thesis/nonthesis option. For M.P.H.: 36 credit hours minimum, at least 30 in residence; thesis. For Ph.D.: 60 credit hours minimum beyond the bachelor's, 30 credit hours in full-time residency; qualifying exam; dissertation defense.

FIELDS OF STUDY.

Cell Biology. Ph.D.

Dental Science. M.D.S.

Developmental Biology. Ph.D.

Genetics, Molecular Biiology, and Biochemistry. Ph.D.

Immunology. Ph.D.

Molecular and Cellular Pharmacology. Ph.D.

Neuroscience. Ph.D.

Pharmacology. Ph.D.

Public Health. M.P.H.

Skeletal, Craniofacial, and Oral Biology. Ph.D.

School of Dental Medicine

Located in Farmington (06030). First class entered September 1968. Public control. Semester system. Annual tuition/fees: resident $8385, New England resident $12,580, others $21,490. No on-campus housing. Average off-campus academic year housing costs: $15,125. Total average academic cost for all other first-year expenses excluding instruments: $5665.

Enrollment: first-year class 40; total 163 (men 65%, women 35%); postgraduates 67. School faculty: full-time 18, part-time none. Degrees conferred: B.S.-D.M.D. (with University of Connecticut, Spellman College, Morehouse College), D.M.D., D.M.D.-Ph.D., D.M.D.-M.P.H., D.M.D.-M.D.

ADMISSION REQUIREMENTS. AADSAS, transcripts, DAT (not later than October), three letters of recommendation required in support of School's application. Applicants must have completed at least three years of college study. Preference given to state residents. Accepts transfer students. Has EDP for state and New England residents only. Apply to the Associate Dean, Student Affair, after June 1, before February 1. Application fee $60. Phone: (860)679-3748; fax: (860)679-1899.

ADMISSION STANDARDS. Competitive. Mean DAT: academic 19.3, PAT 18; mean GPA: 3.43 (A = 4). Gourman rating: 4.33. Accepts 15% of total annual applicants. Approximately 35% are state residents.

FINANCIAL AID. Scholarships, grants, tuition waivers, DEAL, HEAL, loans. Apply by April 1 to Office Financial Aid Office. Phone: (860)679-3873. Use FAFSA (School code: G11215) and institutional application. About 80% of students receive some aid from School funds.

DEGREE REQUIREMENTS. For D.M.D.: satisfactory completion of four-year program. For D.M.D.-Ph.D.: a minimum of three additional years.

School of Medicine
Web site: www.uchc.edu

Located at the Health Center (06030-1905). First class entered September 1968. Public control. Library: 160,000 volumes. Annual tuition/fees: resident $10,040, nonresident $22,840; student fees $4260. For off-campus housing, apply to Student Affairs Office. Total average figure for all other expenses: $9100.
Enrollment: first-year class 76 (EDP 8); full-time 328 (men 50%, women 50%). School faculty: full-time 203, part-time 90. Degrees conferred: M.D., M.D.-Ph.D.

ADMISSION REQUIREMENTS. AMCAS report, transcripts, MCAT, recommendations required in support of application. Accepts transfer applicants. Preference given to state residents. Has EDP; apply between June 1 and August 1. Apply to Admissions Office after June 1, before December 15. Application fee $75. Phone: (860)679-4713; fax: (860)679-1282.

ADMISSION STANDARDS. Competitive. Mean MCAT: 10.0; mean GPA: 3.55 (A = 4). Gourman rating: 3.88. *U.S. News & World Report* ranking is in top 35 schools in primary care education. Accepts about 10% of annual applicants. Approximately 86% are state residents.

FINANCIAL AID. Scholarships, Federal W/S, loans. Information regarding financial aid applications provided following admission from Director of Financial Aid. Use FAFSA (School code: G09867). About 80% of students receive some aid from School funds.

DEGREE REQUIREMENTS. For M.D.: satisfactory completion of four-year program. For Ph.D., see Graduate School listing above.

FIELDS OF GRADUATE STUDY.
Cell Biology.
Developmental Biology.
Genetics, Molecular Biology, and Biochemistry.
Immunology.
Neurosciences.
Pharmacology.

CONVERSE COLLEGE
Spartanburg, South Carolina 29301-0006
Web site: www.converse.edu

Established 1889. Located 70 miles SW of Charlotte, North Carolina. Coed on graduate level. Private independent. Semester system. Library: 139,360 volumes, 1467 subscriptions. More than 75 computers available for general student use.
Tuition: per credit hour $225. No on-campus housing for graduate students.

Graduate Division

Enrollment: full-time 169, part-time 590. College faculty: full-time 76, part-time 11. Degrees conferred: M.M., M.Ed., Ed.S.

ADMISSION REQUIREMENTS. Official transcripts, GRE/NTE, research paper required in support of application. Audition/composition required for some programs. Accepts transfer applicants. Apply to the Director of the Graduate Education by May 1 (Fall), January 30 (Spring). Phone: (864)596-9021 (Music); (864)596-9082 (Education). Rolling admissions process. Application fee $35.

ADMISSION STANDARDS. Selective. Usual minimum average: 2.75 (A = 4).

FINANCIAL AID. Annual awards from institutional funds: assistantships, grants, Federal W/S, loans. Approved for VA benefits. Apply to Graduate Office or appropriate programs for assistantships, grants; to Director of Financial Aid for all other need-based programs. Phone: (864)596-9019. Use FAFSA.

DEGREE REQUIREMENTS. For M.Ed.: 36 semester hours minimum, at least two summer sessions in residence. For M.M.: 30 semester hours minimum, at least two semesters in residence; thesis/final project, or performance in music. For Ed.S.: 36 semester hours minimum, at least two summer sessions in residence.

FIELDS OF STUDY.
Administration. Ed.S.
Curriculum and Instruction. Ed.S.
Elementary Education. M.Ed.
Gifted Education. M.Ed.
Leadership. M.Ed.
Music. Includes vocal/instrumental performance, music education, musicology, piano pedagogy, music theory, composition, vocal; two languages for M.M. in musicology. M.M.
Secondary Education. M.Ed.
Special Education. M.Ed.

CORNELL UNIVERSITY
Ithaca, New York 14850
Web site: www.cornell.edu

Founded 1865. Located 220 miles NW of New York City. CGS and AAU member. Coed. Private control. Some graduate divisions are statutory colleges of the State University of New York. Semester system. Special facilities: Africana Studies and Research Center; American Indian Program; American Studies; Center for Applied Mathematics; Full-Year Asian Language Concentration (FALCON); Laboratory of Atomic and Solid State Physics; James A. Baker Institute for Animal Health; Biophysics Program; Boyce Thompson Institute for Plant Research; Bronfenbrenner Life Course Center; Community and Rural Development Institute; Institute for Comparative and Environmental Toxicology; Program of Computer Graphics; Institute for the Study of Continents; Cornell Institute for Social and Economics Research; Cornell International Institute for Food, Agriculture and Development; East Asia Program; Mario Einaudi Center for International Studies; Center for the Environment; Program on Ethics and Public Life; Institute for European Studies; Exchange Scholar Program; International Network for Graduate Student Exchange; Family Life Development Center; Farming Alternatives Programs; Center for High-Energy Synchrotron Studies; Society for the Humanities; Program in International Nutrition; Latin American Studies Program; Latino Studies Program; Center for Manufacturing Enterprise; Materials Science Center; National Nanofabriction Facility (NNF); New York State Agricultural Experiment Stations; Floyd R. Newman Laboratory of Nuclear Studies; Northeast Regional Climate Center; Peace Studies Program; Laboratory of Plasma Studies; Center for Radiophysics and Space Research; Renaissance Studies; Rural Development; South Asia Program; Southeast Asia Program; Center for Statistics; Center for Theory and Simulation in Science and Engineering; Ward Laboratory of Nuclear Engineering; Library: over 6,300,000 volumes, 61,900 subscriptions.

Annual tuition, for endowed divisions $27,270; for state-supported divisions (Colleges of Agriculture and Life Sciences, Human Ecology, and School of Industrial and Labor Relations), $15,200; Veterinary Medicine, $15,600. On-campus housing for 411 married students and 262 single students. Average annual cost: single students $3825–$5425; per month cost for married students $595–$775. Inquire at Campus Life Office. Phone: (607)255-5368; e-mail: gpsh@cornell.edu.

Graduate School

Web site: www.gradschool.cornell.edu

Enrollment: full-time 4036 (men 60%, women 40%). University faculty teaching graduate students: full-time 1600. Degrees conferred: M.A., M.S., M.Arch., M.L.A., M.A.T., M.F.A., M.F.S., M.H.A., M.I.L.R., M.M.H., M.P.A., M.P.S., M.R.P., M.S.T., M.Eng., LL.M., D.M.A., Ph.D., J.S.D.

ADMISSION REQUIREMENTS. Transcripts, two or three letters of recommendation (depending on the field), statement of purpose required in support of School's application. GRE required by most fields, GMAT for Hotel Administration. TOEFL (minimum score 550, 213 on computer-based test) required for international applicants unless he or she (1) has received a degree from a college or a university in a country where the native language is English or (2) has studied for two or more years in an undergraduate or graduate program in a country where the native language is English. Accepts transfer students. Graduate of unaccredited institutions not considered. Apply to the Graduate School by January 10 for Fall admission (some fields have later deadlines). Application fee $65. Phone: (607)255-4884.

ADMISSION STANDARDS. Very competitive to very selective. Usual minimum average: 3.0 (A = 4).

FINANCIAL AID. Annual awards from institutional funds: merit-based fellowships, fellowships, teaching assistantships, research assistantships, graduate assistantships, Federal W/S, loans. Apply by January 10 for Fellowships, assistantships; most programs use this deadline date, some are later. Apply to Financial Aid Office for all federal programs. Phone: (607)255-5820; e-mail: gfao@cornell.edu. Use FAFSA. About 75% of students receive primary support from University and outside sources; 97% of all doctoral students receive primary support from Cornell or outside sources.

DEGREE REQUIREMENTS. For master's: 2 semester minimum in full-time residence; for research master's degrees, thesis and final oral/written exam; for professional master's degrees, usual course requirements, no thesis. Additional requirements may vary by field. For doctorate: 6 semester minimum in full-time residence; admission to candidacy examination; dissertation; final oral exam. Additional requirements vary by field.

FIELDS OF STUDY.

Aerospace Engineering. M.Eng., M.S., Ph.D.

Africana Studies. M.P.S.

Agricultural and Biological Engineering. M.Eng., M.P.S. (Agr.), M.S., Ph.D.

Agricultural Economics. M.P.S. (Agr.), M.S., Ph.D.

Animal Breeding. M.S., Ph.D.

Animal Science. M.P.S. (Agr.), M.S., Ph.D.

Anthropology. M.A., Ph.D.

Applied Mathematics. Ph.D.

Archaeology. M.A.

Architecture. M.S., M.A., M.Arch., Ph.D.

Art. M.F.A.

Asian Religion. M.A.

Asian Studies. M.A.

Astronomy and Space Sciences. M.S., Ph.D.

Atmospheric Science. M.S., Ph.D.

Biochemistry, Molecular, and Cell Biology. Ph.D.

Biomedical Engineering. Ph.D.

Biometry. M.S., Ph.D.

Biophysics. Ph.D.

Chemical Engineering. M.Eng., M.S., Ph.D.

Chemistry and Chemical Biology. M.S., Ph.D.

City and Regional Planning. M.A., M.R.P., Ph.D.

Civil and Environmental Engineering. M.Eng., M.S., Ph.D.

Classics. M.A., Ph.D.

Communication. M.A.

Community and Rural Development. M.A., M.R.P., Ph.D.

Comparative Literature. Ph.D.

Computer Science. M.Eng., Ph.D.

Design and Environmental Analysis. M.A., M.P.S. (Hu.Ec.), M.S.

Developmental Sociology. M.P.S. (Agr.), M.S., Ph.D.

East Asian Literature. M.A., Ph.D.

Ecology and Evolutionary Biology. M.S., Ph.D.

Economics. Ph.D.

Education. M.A.T., M.P.S. (Agr.), M.S., Ph.D.

Electrical and Computer Engineering. M.Eng., M.S., Ph.D.

English Language and Literature. M.A., M.F.A., Ph.D.

Entomology. M.S., Ph.D.

Environmental Toxicology. M.S., Ph.D.

Food Science and Technology. M.E.S., M.P.S. (Agr.), M.S., Ph.D.

Genetics and Development. Ph.D.

Geological Sciences. M.Eng., M.S., Ph.D.

Germanic Studies. M.A., Ph.D.

Government. Ph.D.

History. M.A., Ph.D.

History of Art and Archaeology. Ph.D.

Horticulture. M.P.S. (Agr.), M.S., Ph.D.

Hotel Administration. M.P.S. (H.Ad.), M.H.A., M.S., Ph.D.

Human Development. M.A., Ph.D.

Immunology. M.S., Ph.D.

Industrial and Labor Relations. M.I.L.R., M.P.S. (I.L.P), M.S., Ph.D.

International Agriculture and Rural Development. M.P.S. (Agr.).

International Development. M.P.S. (I.P.).

Landscape Architecture. M.L.A.

Law. LL.M., J.S.D.

Linguistics. M.A., Ph.D.

Management. Ph.D.

Materials Science and Engineering. M.Eng., M.S., Ph.D.

Mathematics. Ph.D.

Mechanical Engineering. M.Eng., M.S., Ph.D.

Medieval Studies. Ph.D.

Microbiology. Ph.D.

Music. M.A., M.F.A., D.M.A., Ph.D.

Natural Resources. M.P.S. (Agr.)., M.S., Ph.D.

Near Eastern Studies. M.A., Ph.D.

Neurobiology and Behavior. Ph.D.

Nuclear Science and Engineering. M.Eng., M.S., Ph.D.

Nutrition. M.P.S. (Hu.Ec.), M.S., Ph.D.

Operations Research. M.Eng., Ph.D.
Pharmacology. M.S., Ph.D.
Philosophy. M.A., Ph.D.
Physics. M.S., Ph.D.
Physiology. M.S., Ph.D.
Plant Biology. Ph.D.
Plant Breeding. M.P.S. (Agr.), M.S., Ph.D.
Plant Pathology. M.P.S. (Agr.), M.S., Ph.D.
Plant Protection. M.P.S. (Agr.)
Psychology. Ph.D.
Public Affairs. M.P.A.
Real Estate. M.P.S.
Romance Studies. M.A., Ph.D.
Science and Technology Studies. M.A., Ph.D.
Slavic Studies. M.A., Ph.D.
Sociology. M.A., Ph.D.
Soil and Crop Sciences. M.P.S. (Agr.), M.S., Ph.D.
Statistics. M.S., Ph.D.
System Engineering. M.S., Ph.D.
Textiles. M.A., M.P.S. (Hu.Ec.), M.S., Ph.D.
Theatre Arts. M.A., Ph.D.
Theoretical and Applied Mechanics. M.Eng., M.S., Ph.D.
Veterinary Medicine. M.S., Ph.D.
Zoology. M.S., Ph.D.

College of Human Ecology

Special facilities: Bronfenbrenner Life Course Center, Community and Rural Development Institute, Cornell Applied Gerontology Research Institute, Cornell Employment and Family Careers Institute, Cornell Institute for Research on Children, Family Life Development Center. The Division of Nutrition was established in 1974 and is a union of the Graduate School and the Department of Food and Nutrition in the College of Human Ecology and the College of Agriculture and Life Science.

Tuition: $15,200. Enrollment: full-time 200. Faculty: full-time 102, part-time 0. Degrees conferred: M.A., M.N.S., M.S., M.P.S.; Ph.D. offered in conjunction with Graduate School.

ADMISSION REQUIREMENTS. Transcripts, GRE (except for interior design) required in support of College's application. Portfolio required for Interior Design. TOEFL (minimum score 550) required of all international applicants. Interview not usually required. Accepts transfer applicants. Graduates of unaccredited colleges not considered. Apply to Cornell Graduate School by January 10 (for fellowship consideration), May 1 (Fall). Application fee $65. Phone: (607) 255-2138.

ADMISSION STANDARDS. Very competitive in some departments, selective to competitive in others. Usual minimum average: 3.0 (A = 4).

FINANCIAL AID. Annual awards from institutional funds: teaching/research assistantships, fellowships, traineeships, tuition waiver, Federal W/S, loans. Applications received by January 10 will receive consideration for all financial aid; final deadline February 15. Use FAFSA. About 80% of students receive aid other than loans from College and outside sources.

DEGREE REQUIREMENTS. For master's: 2 residence units minimum; thesis; final exam. For M.P.S., M.N.S.: 30 credits beyond master's. For Ph.D.: 6 residence units minimum; qualifying exam; dissertation; final exam.

FIELDS OF STUDY.
Apparel Design.
Community Nutrition.
Developmental Psychology.
Facility Planning and Management.
Fiber Science.
Foods.

Human Development.
Human Factors/Ergonomics.
Human Ecology.
Human–Environment Relations.
Human Nutrition.
Interior Design.
International Nutrition.
Life Course Development.
Molecular and Human Nutrition
Nutrition Intervention and Policies.
Nutritional Sciences.
Policy Analysis and Management. Includes consumer policy, evaluation, family/social welfare policy, health management and policy.
Polymer Sciences.
Textile Science.
Textile, Economics, and Marketing.

Weill Medical College of Cornell University

Web site: www.med.cornell.edu

Established 1898. Name changed from Cornell University Medical School in 1998. Located on the Upper East side of New York City (10021) Library: 1,322,000 volumes, 1830 subscriptions. Affiliated hospitals for clinical instruction: Memorial Sloan-Kettering Cancer Center, the Hospital for Special Surgery, the New York Hospital Medical Center of Queens, the New York Methodist Hospital, the New York Community Hospital of Brooklyn, St. Barnabas Hospital, the Burke Rehabilitation Center in White Plains, United Hospital Medical Center in Port Chester, Cayuga Medical Center in Ithaca.

Annual tuition: $27,650; fees $555. Medical College residences are available for both single and married students. All housing is subsidized by the College. Housing and personal expenses per year: approximately $12,000.

Enrollment: first-year class 101(EDP 2); total full-time 412 (men 46%, women 54%). Faculty: full-time/part-time 1500. Degree conferred: M.D., M.D.-Ph.D., M.S.T.P. (in conjunction with Rockefeller University and Memorial Sloan-Kettering Cancer Center).

ADMISSION REQUIREMENTS. AMCAS report, transcripts, letters of recommendation, interview required in support of application. MCAT recommended. Has EDP; apply between June 1 and August 1. Apply to Chair of the Admissions Committee after June 1, before October 15. Application fee $75. Phone: (212)746-1067. Phone for M.D.-Ph.D. program: (212)746-6023.

ADMISSION STANDARDS. Very competitive. Mean MCAT: 10.2; mean GPA: 3.69 (A = 4). Gourman rating: 4.84. *U.S. News & World Report* ranking is in the top 11 of all U.S. medical schools. Accepts 2% of total annual applicants. Approximately 40% are state residents.

FINANCIAL AID. Grants, loans. Apply upon notification of acceptance to Committee on Financial Aid of the College. No closing date. About 80% receive aid other than loans from School funds.

DEGREE REQUIREMENTS. For M.D.: satisfactory completion of four-year program.

FIELDS OF GRADUATE STUDY.
Biochemistry and Structural Biology.
Cell Biology and Genetics.
Clinical Epidemiology and Health Services Research.
Immunology.
Molecular Biology.
Neurosciences.
Pharmacology.
Physiology and Biophysics.

New York State College of Veterinary Medicine
Web site: www.vet.cornell.edu

Professional graduate study since 1894. Coed. State supported. Special facilities: On-campus Teaching Hospital, Regional Veterinary Laboratories for Poultry Disease Diagnosis, New York State Mastitis Control Program Laboratories, James A. Baker Institute for Animal Health, Equine Research Park. Library 70,000 volumes.

Annual tuition: resident $15,400, nonresident $21,100 and Contract nonresidents $15,400. Living expenses $15,000. Enrollment: first-year class 80; full-time 320 (women 60%, men 40%). Faculty: full-time 125, part-time 3. Degrees conferred: D.V.M., D.V.M.-Ph.D.

ADMISSION REQUIREMENTS. VMCAS report, transcripts, prerequisite course work: English composition, 6 credits; Biology (with laboratory), 6 credits; Inorganic Chemistry (with laboratory), 6 credits; Organic Chemistry (with laboratory), 6 credits; Biochemistry, 4 credits; Physics (with laboratory), 6 credits; GRE (test older than five years will not be considered), experience with animals and the veterinary profession, essay, three recommendations (one from an academic advisor), required in support of application. At least three years of undergraduate college study leading to a bachelor's degree. Interview by invitation. Preference given to state or contract state residents. Accepts transfers only if vacancies exist. Apply to the Office of Admissions beginning August 15 for an application, deadline of October 1. For transfer April 1. Fall admission only. Application fee $60. Phone: (607)253-3720.

ADMISSION STANDARDS. Selective. Minimum GPA: 3.0 (A = 4); media GPA: 3.6. Minimum GRE score: 1200, median score: 1350. There are 60 places reserved for state residents. Accepts 16% of total annual applicants.

FINANCIAL AID. Loans, grants, scholarships, fellowships, assistantships. Apply to College Financial Aid Office. Use FAFSA. Apply by March 15.

DEGREE REQUIREMENTS. Satisfactory completion of four-year D.V.M. program. For Ph.D.: see Graduate School listing.

New York State School of Industrial and Labor Relations
Web site: www.ilr.cornell.edu

Graduate study since 1945. Annual tuition: $13,910. On-campus housing for married, single students. Average academic year housing costs: $10,000. Contact Housing Office. Phone: (607)255-5511.

Graduate enrollment: first-year class 30–40, full-time 150 (men 50%, women 50%). Faculty: full-time 50. Degrees conferred: M.I.L.R., M.P.S., M.S., Ph.D.

ADMISSION REQUIREMENTS. Official transcripts, three letters of recommendation, GRE/GMAT (if degree is from English-speaking institution) required in support of School's application. Interview not required. TOEFL required for international applicants. Graduates of unaccredited institutions not considered. Apply to Graduate School by February 15 (Fall), November 15 (Spring). Application fee $65. Phone: (607)225-2227; fax: (607)255-7774.

ADMISSION STANDARDS. Competitive. Usual minimum average: 3.0 (A = 4). Accepts 25% of total applicants.

FINANCIAL AID. Annual awards from institutional funds: scholarships, fellowships, research assistantships, teaching assistantships, loans. Approved for VA benefits. Apply by January 15 (Fall), November 1 (Spring), to Graduate department for fellow-

ships, assistantships; to Director of Financial Aid for all other programs. Phone: (607)255-4884, Fax: (607)255-1816. Use FAFSA. About 70% of students receive aid other than loans from University/School and outside sources.

DEGREE REQUIREMENTS. For M.I.L.R.: 13 courses (48 credit hours), one year minimum in full-time residence; qualifying exam; admission to candidacy. For M.P.S.: 30 credits, minimum; one year minimum in full-time residence. For M.S.: one year minimum in full-time residence; thesis; final oral/written exam. For Ph.D.: four semesters minimum in full-time residence; thesis; qualifying and candidacy exams; final exam.

FIELDS OF STUDY.
Collective Bargaining, Labor Law and Labor History.
Human Resource Studies.
Industrial Labor Relations. M.I.L.R. only.
International and Comparative Labor Relations.
Labor Economics.
Organizational Behavior.
Social Statistics.
Note: A special one-year (9 course) M.I.L.R. program is available for applicants with either M.B.A. or J.D.

School of Law (14853-4901)
Web site: www.law.cornell.edu

Established 1888. ABA approved since 1923. AALS member. Semester system. Special program: Summer Institute at University of Paris I. Library: 632,900 volumes, 6399 subscriptions; is a Federal Government Depository. Library has LEXIS, NEXIS, WESTLAW, DIALOG.

Annual tuition: $27,350. Total average cost for all other expenses: $12,450 single, $17,000 married. On-campus housing available.

Enrollment: first-year class 184, total full-time 552 (men 51%, women 49%). School faculty: full-time 37, part-time 10. Student to faculty ratio 13 to 1. Degrees conferred: J.D., J.D.-M.A., J.D.-Maitrise en Droit, J.D.-M.B.A., J.D.-M.P.A., J.D.-M.I.L.R., J.D.-Ph.D., J.D.-LL.M. (International and Comparative Law), LL.M., J.S.D.

ADMISSION REQUIREMENTS. LSDAS Law School report, bachelor's degree, transcripts, LSAT (not later than December) required in support of application. Accepts transfer applicants from other law schools. Graduates of unaccredited colleges not considered. Apply to Director of Admissions of the School after September 1 and before February 1. Application fee $65. Phone: (607)255-5141; e-mail: lawadmit@law.mail.cornell.edu.

ADMISSION STANDARDS. Selective. Mean LSAT: 164; mean GPA: 3.47 (A = 4). Gourman rating: 4.79. *U.S. News & World Report* ranking in top 13 of all law schools. Accepts 10–12% of total annual applicants.

FINANCIAL AID. Scholarships, grants-in-aid, fellowships, assistantships, Federal W/S, loans. About 50% of students receive aid other than loans from School. Apply to Director of Admissions of the School by March 15. Use FAFSA (School code: 002711). Has a Public Interest Low-Income Protection Plan.

DEGREE REQUIREMENTS. For J.D.: satisfactory completion of three-year program. For LL.M.: 2 semesters beyond J.D.; oral exam. For J.S.D.: 4 semesters beyond J.D.; thesis; final exam.

Johnson Graduate School of Management
Web site: www.johnson.cornell.edu

Established 1946. Private control. Accredited programs: M.B.A.; recognized Ph.D. Semester system. Special programs:

twelve-month M.B.A. program for individuals with an advanced scientific or technological degree; foreign exchange programs (in Australia, Belgium, China, France, Italy, the Netherlands, Norway, Spain, Sweden, Switzerland, Venezuela, Thailand, United Kingdom). Library: 140,000 volumes, 1900 subscriptions.

Annual tuition: full-time $23,460. Enrollment: total full-time 619 (men 75%, women 25%). Faculty: M.B.A. 37 full-time, 10 part-time; 96% with Ph.D./D.B.A. Degrees conferred: M.B.A. (FT day only), M.B.A.-M.A. (Asian Studies), M.B.A.-M.E. (Engineering), M.B.A.-J.D., M.B.A.-M.I.L.R. (Industrial and Labor Management), Ph.D.

ADMISSION REQUIREMENTS. All applicants should have a bachelor's degree from a recognized institution of higher education and a strong mathematics background. Submit an application, a GMAT, two official transcripts from each undergraduate/graduate school attended, two evaluations, two essays, résumé (prefers at least four years of work experience), and an application fee of $90 ($120 international applicants) to the Director of Admission. In addition, international students (whose native language is other than English) should submit a TOEFL (minimum score 600) report, certified translations and evaluations of all official transcripts, recommendation should be in English or with certified translations, proof of health/immunization certificate, and proof of sufficient financial resources for two years of academic study. On-campus visits and interviews are encouraged. Beginning students are admitted Fall only. U.S. citizens apply by December 1 (first read period), January 15 (second read period), March 1 (third read period), April 15 (fourth read period), international students apply by March 1 (Fall). Joint degree applicants must apply to and be accepted to both schools/programs, contact the admissions office for current information and specific admissions requirements. Decisions are mailed by January 31 (first read), March 15 (second read), May 15 (third read), June 15 (fourth read). Admissions Office phone: (607)254-2082; fax: (607)254-8886; e-mail: mba@johnson.cornell.edu.

ADMISSION REQUIREMENTS FOR DOCTORAL CANDIDATES. Contact either the Graduate School at (607)255-4884 or the Doctoral Programs Office, Johnson Graduate School, at (800) 847-2082, for application material and information. Beginning students are admitted Fall Only. Both U.S. citizens and international applicants apply by January 15 (Fall). Submit a Graduate School application, a GMAT or GRE (will accept GMAT or GRE test results from the last five years), official transcripts from each undergraduate/graduate schools attended, two letters of recommendation, résumé, statement of purpose, and application fee of $75 to the Graduate School. In addition, international students (whose native language is other than English and have not studied at least one year in the U.S.) should submit TOEFL (minimum score 600), certified translations and evaluations of all official transcripts, recommendation should be in English or with certified translations, proof of health/immunization certificate. Interviews may be requested by doctoral committee. Notification is generally made by early April. E-mail contact: phd@johnson.cornell.edu.

ADMISSION STANDARDS. For M.B.A.: median GMAT: 634; median GPA: 3.3 (A = 4). Gourman rating: the M.B.A. was rated in the top 15, the score was 4.81; the Ph.D. was rated in the top 15, the score was 4.80. *U.S. News & World Report* ranked the Johnson School in the top 16 of all U.S. business schools. *Business Week* listed Johnson School in the top 20 of all American business schools. For the Ph.D.: median GMAT: 700; acceptance rate is approximately 5%.

FINANCIAL AID. Scholarships, merit-based scholarships (for both U.S. and international applicants), minority scholarships, Park Fellowships (U.S. students only), graduate, research, teaching assistantships, State Grants, Federal W/S, loans. Financial assistance is available for international students. Assistantships/

fellowships may be available for joint degree candidates. Apply by March 1, deadline for Park Fellowships is January 15. Request scholarship, fellowship, assistantship information from the Johnson School. For most financial assistance and all Federal programs submit FAFSA (School code: 002711), also submit Financial Aid Transcript, Federal Income Tax forms. Approximately 65% of current students receive some form of financial assistance. For Ph.D.: The Johnson School offers both fellowships and assistantships, which cover tuition, fees, and include a stipend.

DEGREE REQUIREMENTS. For M.B.A.: 60-credit program including 37 elective credits and a strategy course; two-year program; a twelve-month M.P.A. option available. For M.B.A.-M.A.: six- to seven-semester program. For M.B.A.-M.I.L.R., M.Eng.: five-semester program. For M.B.A.-J.D.: four- to five-year program. For Ph.D.: three- to four-year program, at least six semesters in full-time residence; qualifying written and oral exam; admission to candidacy; research paper; dissertation; oral defense.

DOCTORAL FIELDS OF STUDY.
Accounting.
Behavioral Sciences.
Finance.
Management Information Systems.
Managerial Economics.
Marketing.
Organizational Behavior.
Production and Operations Management.
Quantitative Analysis for Administration.

CRANBROOK ACADEMY OF ART
Box 801
Bloomfield Hills, Michigan 48303-0801
Web site: www.cranbrook.edu/art

Founded 1932. Located 20 miles from Detroit. Coed. Private control. Semester system. Special facility: semiprivate studios in most. Library: 27,000 volumes, 4 PC workstations.

Annual tuition: full-time $17,900. Limited on-campus housing for 95 students; none for married students. Average annual housing cost: $5000 for single students. Estimated cost for 9 months: meals $3200, supplies $2700, personal expenses $1600, transportation $1400. Apply to the Dean of Admission for housing information. Phone: (248)645-3300.

Graduate Program

Enrollment: full-time 140 (men 70, women 70); no part-time students. Academy faculty: full-time 9, part-time 0. Degrees conferred: M.F.A., M.Arch.

ADMISSION REQUIREMENTS. Transcripts, references, statement of purpose, portfolio required in support of application. Electronic application available. TOEFL required for foreign applicants. Interview not required. Accepts transfer applicants, but two years' residence still required for degree. Apply to Dean of Admission by February 1 (Fall), November 1 (Spring). Application fee $50. Phone: (248)645-3300, (248)646-0046; e-mail: caaadmission@cranbrook.edu.

ADMISSION STANDARDS. Competitive.

FINANCIAL AID. Scholarships, grants, assistantships, Federal W/S, loans. Apply by February 1 to the Registrar. Phone: (248)645-3303. Use FAFSA (Academy code: G02248). Assistantships reserved for second-year students. About 70% of students receive aid from the Academy.

DEGREE REQUIREMENTS. For M.F.A., M.Arch.: 60 semester hours minimum in full-time residence; thesis including photographic record of work.

FIELDS OF STUDY.
Architecture.
Ceramics.
Design. Includes 2-D, 3-D.
Fiber.
Metalsmithing.
Painting.
Photography.
Print/Media.
Sculpture.

THE CREIGHTON UNIVERSITY
Omaha, Nebraska 68178-0150
Web site: www.creighton.edu

Founded 1878. CGS member. Coed. Private control, Roman Catholic affiliation. Semester system. Library: 481,800 volumes, 1666 subscriptions. Total University enrollment: 6200.

Tuition: per credit $507. On-campus housing for both married and single students. Average annual housing cost: $10,350. Apply to Housing Office. Phone: (402)280-3016.

Graduate School

Enrollment: full-time 181, part-time 304. Faculty; full- and part-time 251. Degrees conferred: M.A., M.B.A., M.S., M.C.S., M.C.S.M., Ph.D.

ADMISSION REQUIREMENTS. Transcripts, GRE/GMAT, three letters of reference required in support of School's application. TOEFL required for international applicants. Interview varies by department. Apply to Graduate School Office by July 15 (Fall), December 15 (Spring), May 15 (Summer). Application fee $40. Phone: (402)280-2870; fax: (402)280-5762; e-mail: gradsch@creighton.edu.

ADMISSION STANDARDS. Selective. Usual minimum average: 3.0 (A = 4).

FINANCIAL AID. Scholarships, research assistantships, teaching assistantships, tuition waivers, grants, Federal W/S, loans. Apply by March 15 to Dean of the Graduate School. Phone: (402)280-2731; e-mail: gpfinaid@creighton.edu. Use FAFSA. About 15% of students receive aid other than loans from University and outside sources. Aid available for part-time students.

DEGREE REQUIREMENTS. For most master's: 30–38 credit hours minimum; thesis; reading knowledge of one foreign language; comprehensive oral/written exam; or 33 credit hours minimum; written comprehensive exam. For M.B.A.: 33 credit hours minimum. For Ph.D.: 90 credits beyond the bachelor's, one year in full-time study; two foreign languages or one language and alternative tool for some departments; comprehensive exam; dissertation.

FIELDS OF STUDY.
Atmospheric Sciences.
Biomedical Sciences.
Business Administration. GMAT for admission: M.B.A. only.
Christian Spirituality.
Clinical Anatomy.
Computer Science.
Counseling.

Electronic Commerce.
Elementary School Administration.
English.
Health Services Administration.
Information Technology.
International Relations.
Liberal Studies.
Mathematics/Computer Science.
Medical Microbiology. 2 years minimum in full-time residence for M.S.
Ministry.
Nursing.
Pharmaceutical Sciences.
Pharmacology.
Physics.
Secondary School Administration.
Theology.

School of Dentistry

Founded 1905. Annual tuition: $27,316. Some housing for single students only. Average academic year housing costs: $9900. Contact Student Personnel Office for housing information. Phone: (402)280-3016. Total average cost for all other first-year expenses: $6200.

Enrollment: first-year class 84 (men 58, women 26). Total enrollment 316 (men 70%; women 30%). Faculty: full-time 51, part-time 78. Degree conferred: D.D.S.

ADMISSION REQUIREMENTS. AADSAS, official transcripts, three letters of recommendation, DAT required in support of application. Applicants must have completed at least three years of college study; prefer four years of study. Interview not required. Graduates of unaccredited colleges not considered. Preference given to educational compact states of Idaho, New Mexico, Nevada, North Dakota, Utah, and Wyoming. Apply to Director of Admissions after July 15, before April 1. Application fee $35. Phone: (402)280-2695, (800)544-5072.

ADMISSION STANDARDS. Competitive. Median DAT: Academic 18.5, PAT 19.2; median GPA: 3.35 (A = 4). Gourman rating: 4.53. Accepts about 15–20% of total annual applicants. Approximately 15% are state residents.

FINANCIAL AID. Scholarships, grants, tuition waivers, loans. Apply by June 1 to the Director of Financial Aid. Phone: (402)280-2731, (800)282-5835. Use FAFSA. About 94% of students receive some aid from School.

DEGREE REQUIREMENTS. For D.D.S.: satisfactory completion of four-year program.

School of Law
Web site: culaw.creighton.edu

Organized 1904. ABA approved since 1924. AALS member since 1907. Semester system. Law library: 265,000 volumes, 4300 subscriptions; has LEXIS, NEXIS, WESTLAW.

Annual tuition: full-time $19,432, part-time $11,760. On-campus housing available. Total average annual additional expenses: $11,270.

Enrollment: first-year class 175, total full-time 456 (men 54%, women 46%). Faculty: full-time 23, part-time 28. Student to faculty ratio 16.1 to 1. Degrees conferred: J.D., J.D.-M.B.A. J.D.-M.S. (E-Commerce).

ADMISSION REQUIREMENTS. LSDAS Law School report, transcripts, LSAT, bachelor's degree required in support of application. Two letters of recommendation suggested. Accepts transfer applicants. Graduates of unaccredited colleges not considered. Apply to University Admissions Office after August 31, before May 1. Application fee $45. Phone: (402)280-2872; fax: (402) 280-3161.

ADMISSION STANDARDS. Selective. Mean LSAT: 151; mean GPA: 3.14 (A = 4). Gourman rating: 3.09. *U.S. News & World Report* ranking is in the third tier of all law schools. Accepts 50% of total annual applicants.

FINANCIAL AID. Scholarships, fellowships, assistantship, partial tuition waiver, Federal W/S, loans. Apply by July 1 to Dean of the School. Phone: (402)280-2761. Use FAFSA (School code: 002542). About 43% of students receive aid other than loans from School.

DEGREE REQUIREMENTS. For J.D.: 94 hours minimum, at least final two semesters in residence.

School of Medicine

Established 1892. Clinical instruction at St. Joseph Hospital, Children's Memorial, Veteran's Administration, Alegent Health System Hospital. Annual tuition: $33,520; student fees $770. On-campus housing available. Total average figure for all other expenses: $9000. Enrollment: first-year class 115 (15 EDP); total full-time 522 (men 60%, women 40%), postgraduates 128. Faculty: full-time 289, part-time 210. Degrees conferred: M.D., M.D.-M.S., M.D.-Ph.D.

ADMISSION REQUIREMENTS. AMCAS report, transcripts, MCAT, interview required in support of application. Applicants must have completed at least three years of college study. Preference given to residents of midwestern states. Has EDP; apply between June 15 and August 1. For regular admission apply between June 15 and December 1. Application fee $75. Phone: (402)280-2799; fax: (402)280-1241.

ADMISSION STANDARDS. Competitive. Median MCAT: 9.2; median GPA: 3.74 (A = 4). Gourman rating: 3.86. Accepts 2% of total annual applicants. Approximately 9% are state residents.

FINANCIAL AID. Scholarships, grants, fellowships, assistantships, loans. Apply to Office of the Dean, preferably before January 15. About 87% of students receive some aid from School.

DEGREE REQUIREMENTS. For M.D.: satisfactory completion of four-year program. For M.S., Ph.D.: see Graduate School listing above.

FIELDS OF GRADUATE STUDY.
Anatomy.
Biochemistry.
Microbiology.
Pharmacology.
Physiology.

UNIVERSITY OF DALLAS
Irving, Texas 75062-4799
Web site: www.udallas.edu

Founded 1956. Coed. Located 8 miles from downtown Dallas and 25 miles from Forth Worth. Private control. Roman Catholic. Semester for Braniff Graduate School. Trimester for Graduate School of Management. Library: 300,000 volumes, 800 subscriptions. Total University enrollment: 2000.

Tuition: per credit $423 (LA), $444 (GSM). On-campus housing is limited. Average annual off-campus housing cost: $600–$700 per month, plus board. Apply by April 1 to Director of Housing. Phone: (972)721-5113.

Graduate Divisions

Enrollment: full-time 400, part-time 1500. Graduate faculty: full-time 58, part-time 85. Degrees conferred: M.A., M.B.A., M.F.A., M. Pol., M.R.E., M.Eng., M.H., M.Mgt., M.Th., M.T.S., Ph.D.

ADMISSION REQUIREMENTS. Transcripts, letter of intent, two letters of recommendation, résumé, portfolio for art programs required in support of University's applications. GMAT required for Business. TOEFL required for foreign applicants. GRE Subject Test recommended. Accepts transfer applicants. Graduates of unaccredited institutions not considered. Apply to Graduate Office by February 1 (doctoral programs), February 15–June 15 (master's programs). Application fee $50. Phone: (972)721-5106; e-mail: graduate@acad.udallas.edu. Graduate School of Management: (972)714-5174; fax: (972)721-4009.

ADMISSION STANDARDS. Selective. Usual minimum average: 3.0 (A = 4).

FINANCIAL AID. Scholarships, assistantships, Federal W/S, loans. Apply by August 5 to Graduate Dean. For all need-based programs apply to the Financial Aid Office. Phone: (972)721-5384. Use FAFSA.

DEGREE REQUIREMENTS. For master's: 30 semester hours, minimum, at least 24 in residence and 12 in full-time attendance; language requirement for some programs; thesis; final oral exam. For M.B.A.: 37–49 credit hours and attendance at 10 lectures in GSM's Ethics & Management Lecture series. For M. Mgt.: 25 credit hours (8 courses and attendance at 10 lectures in GSM's Ethics & Management Lecture series). Ph.D.: 84 Semester hours, at least 40 in full-time residence; qualifying exam; dissertation; final written/oral exam.

FIELDS OF STUDY.

BRANIFF GRADUATE SCHOOL OF LIBERAL ARTS:
American Studies.
Art. M.A., M.F.A.
Education.
English. M.A., M.Eng.
Fine Arts. M.A.
Humanities. M.A.
Literature. M.A., Ph.D.
Pastoral Ministries.
Philosophy. M.A., Ph.D.
Politics. M.A., M. Pol.
Psychology. M.A.
Theology. M.A., M.S.T., M.R.E., M.Th.

GRADUATE SCHOOL OF MANAGEMENT:
Business Management.
Corporate Finance.
eBusiness.
Engineering Management.
Entrepeneurship.
Financial Services.
Global Business.
Health Services Management.
Human Resource Management.
Information Assurance.
Information Technology.
International Accounting.
Marketing.
Not-for-Profit Management.
Sport and Entertainment Management.
Supply Chain Management and Market Logistics.
Telecommunications Management.

DARTMOUTH COLLEGE

Hanover, New Hampshire 03755-3526
Web site: www.dartmouth.edu

Founded 1769. CGS member. Located 135 miles NW of Boston. Coed. Private control. Year-round operation. Special facilities: Fairchild Science Center, Gilman Biomedical Center, Murdough Center. The College's NIH ranking is 79th among all U.S. institutions with 159 awards/grants worth $56,882,834. Library: more than 2,400,000 volumes, 20,679 subscriptions. More than 12,000 network ports on campus. Total College enrollment: 5300.

On-campus housing for 136 married students, a few available rooms for single students. Average housing cost: $16,600 for married students, $11,000 for single students. Apply to Director of Rental Housing. Phone: (603)646-2170.

School of Arts and Sciences

Graduate study since 1960. Tuition per year: $27,600. Enrollment: full-time 479 (men 265, women 214), part-time 34. Faculty teaching graduate students: full-time 202. Degrees conferred: A.M., M.S., M.A.L.S., Ph.D.

ADMISSION REQUIREMENTS. Transcripts, three letters of recommendation, GRE required in support of School's application. TOEFL required of foreign students. Interview not required. Accepts transfer applicants. Graduates of unaccredited institutions not considered. Apply by February 1 to department of study. Application fee, varies by field of study. General information number: Phone: (603)646-2107; fax: (603)646-3488.

ADMISSION STANDARDS. Competitive for most departments, very competitive for others. Usual minimum average: 3.0 (A = 4).

FINANCIAL AID. Annual awards from institutional funds: tuition scholarships, fellowships, research assistantships, grants, Federal W/S, loans. Apply to Financial Aid Office by February 15. Phone: (603)646-2451. Use FAFSA. All applicants for graduate program simultaneously considered for financial aid and all financial resources available at College. Most Ph.D. students received financial assistance from College funds.

DEGREE REQUIREMENTS. Vary by department, but generally for A.M., M.S.: eight courses minimum, at least three terms in residence; thesis; final oral exam. For M.A.L.S.: two to three summers in residence. For Ph.D.: eight courses minimum, at least six terms in residence; language requirement established by department; qualifying exam; dissertation; final oral exam.

FIELDS OF STUDY.
Biochemistry. M.S.
Biology. M.S.
Chemistry. M.S.
Comparative Literature. A.M.
Computer Science. M.S.
Earth Sciences. M.S.
Electro-Acoustic Music. A.M.
Engineering Sciences. M.S.
Evaluative Clinical Sciences. M.S.
Genetics. M.S.
Immunology and Microbiology. M.S.
Liberal Studies. M.A.L.S.
Mathematics. M.S.
Molecular and Cell Biology. Cross-disciplinary program with Medical School and Thayer. M.S.
Pharmacology and Toxicology. M.S.
Physics and Astronomy. M.S.
Physiology. M.S.
Psychological and Brain Sciences. M.S.

Amos Tuck School of Business Administration

Web site: www.tuck.dartmouth.edu

Established 1900, the oldest graduate school of business in world. Private control. Accredited programs: M.B.A. Trimester system. Library: 115,000 volumes, 3000 subscriptions. Special Programs: foreign exchange programs (France, Germany, Japan, Spain, United Kingdom), internships. Special facilities: Center for Asia and the Emerging Economics.

Annual tuition: full-time $30,250. On-campus rooms available during first year.

Enrollment: total full-time 397 (men 268, women 129). Faculty: 44 full-time, 22 part-time, all have Ph.D./D.B.A. Degrees conferred: M.B.A. (full-time only), M.B.A.-M.D., M.B.A.-M.A.L.D. (Law and Diplomacy with Fletcher School at Tufts University), M.B.A.-M.E.

ADMISSION REQUIREMENTS. All applicants should have a bachelor's degree from a recognized institution of higher education and a strong mathematics background. Students are required to have their own personal computer. Submit an application, a GMAT (will accept GMAT test results from the last five years, latest acceptable date is March), two official transcripts from each undergraduate/graduate school attended, two letters of recommendation, three or four essays, résumé (prefers at least four years of work experience), and an application fee of $150 to the Office of Admission. In addition, international students (whose native language is other than English) should submit a TOEFL (may be waived under special conditions, contact Admissions Officer for current information), certified translations and evaluations of all official transcripts, recommendation should be in English or with certified translations, proof of health/immunization certificate, and proof of sufficient financial resources for two years of academic study. On-campus interviews are strongly recommended; appointment phone: (603)646-3162. Beginning students are admitted Fall only. U.S. citizens have four deadlines: December 5, January 20, February 24, April 24, international students apply by April 10 (Fall). Joint degree applicants must apply to and be accepted to both schools/programs, contact the admissions office for current information and specific admissions requirements. Notification is made within 4–6 weeks of application deadlines if application is complete and all supporting documents have been received. Admissions Office phone: (603)646-3162; fax: (603)646-1441; e-mail: tuck.admissions@dartmouth.edu.

ADMISSION STANDARDS. Very selective. Median GMAT: 670; median GPA: 3.4 (A = 4). Gourman rating: 4.79. *U.S. News & World Report* ranked Tuck School in the top nine of all U.S. business schools. *Business Week* listed Tuck in the top ten of all American business schools.

FINANCIAL AID. Scholarships, minority scholarships, fellowships, low-interest Tuck Loans, Federal W/S, loans. Financial aid may be available for international students. Assistantships/fellowships may be available for joint degree candidates. Request scholarship, assistantship as well as need-based information from the School of Business. Apply by March 1. For most financial assistance and all Federal programs submit FAFSA (School code: 002573), also submit Financial Aid Transcript, Federal Income Tax forms. Approximately 70% of students receive some form of financial assistance.

DEGREE REQUIREMENTS. For M.B.A.: 26-course program including 12 elective courses all in second year, two-year program. For M.B.A.-Masters: generally a three- to four-year program, For M.B.A.-M.D.: five- to six-year program.

Thayer School of Engineering—Graduate Division

Web site: www.dartmouth.edu/thayer

Established 1871. Tuition: $26,400 for three terms. Enrollment: full-time 133 (men 98, women 35). Faculty: full-time 32, part-time 8, Degrees conferred: B.E., M.E.M., M.E.M.-M.B.A., M.S., Ph.D., M.D.-Ph.D.

ADMISSION REQUIREMENTS. Transcripts, two letters of reference, GRE required in support of School's application. Joint degree applicants must be accepted by both programs. TOEFL required for foreign applicants. Graduates of unaccredited institutions not considered. Apply to Graduate Admission by January 1. Application fee $40, $50 for application originating out of the U.S. Phone: (603)646-2606; fax: (603)646-3856; e-mail: engg .admissions@dartmouth.edu.

ADMISSION STANDARDS. Competitive. Usual minimum average 3.0 (A = 4).

FINANCIAL AID. Fellowships and teaching assistantships are available from institutional funds; research assistantships are available from contract research. Such support normally covers tuition plus a monthly stipend. Approved for VA benefits. Apply to Director of Financial Aid by January 15. Phone: (603)646-3844; fax: (603)646-3856. Use FAFSA.

DEGREE REQUIREMENTS. For B.E.: 9 courses, proficiency in design, analytical and experimental work, and economic analysis of engineering problems. For M.E.M.: nonthesis option requires 13–18 courses with distribution in engineering, design and manufacturing, and management; internship. For M.S.: 6–10 courses minimum, at least three consecutive terms in residence; thesis; oral defense. For Ph.D.: two-year minimum in residence; candidacy; oral exam; thesis.

FIELDS OF STUDY.
Biomedical Engineering.
Biotechnology/Biochemical Engineering.
Electrical and Computer Engineering.
Engineering Management.
Environmental Engineering.
Materials Science and Engineering.
Mechanical Engineering.

Medical School

Web site: www.dartmouth.edu/dms

Founded 1797. The fourth oldest medical school in U.S. Clinical instruction Brattleboro Retreat (VT), Family Medical Institute (ME), Hartford Hospital (CT), Tuba City Indian Health Service Hospital (AZ), Mary Hitchcock Memorial Hospital (NH). Annual tuition: $28,655; student fees $1700. Total average figure for all other expenses: $8500. Enrollment: first-year class 81, total 401 (men 56%, women 44%). Faculty: full-time 410, part-time 354. 20 Rhode Island residents admitted each year to Brown-Dartmouth program. Faculty: full- and part-time 900. Degrees conferred: M.D., M.D.-M.B.A., M.D.-Ph.D.

ADMISSION REQUIREMENTS. AMCAS report, transcripts indicating completion of three years of college work, letters of recommendation, MCAT, interview required in support of application. Does not have EDP. Transfer applicants, graduates of unaccredited colleges not considered. Preference given to residents of New Hampshire and Rhode Island. Apply to Admissions Office of the School after June 15, before November 1. Application fee $75. Phone: (603)650-1505; fax: (603)650-1560.

ADMISSION STANDARDS. Very competitive. Median MCAT: 10.0; median GPA: 3.50 (A = 4). Gourman rating: 4.22. *U.S. News & World Report* ranking is in the top 34 of all U.S. medical schools. Accepts about 3% of total annual applicants. Approximately 13% are state residents.

FINANCIAL AID. Scholarships, part-time jobs, loans. Apply to Office of Financial Aid of the School after acceptance. Use FAFSA, the Needs Access form, and MS financial aid application. About 75% of students receive some aid from School.

DEGREE REQUIREMENTS. For M.D.: completion of four-year program.

FIELDS OF GRADUATE STUDY.
Biochemistry.
Biomedical Engineering.
Genetics.
Immunology.
Microbiology.
Molecular and Cell Biology. Cross-disciplinary program with Arts & Sciences and Thayer.
Pharmacology/Toxicology.
Physiology.

UNIVERSITY OF DAYTON

Dayton, Ohio 45469-1620
Web site: www.udayton.edu

Founded 1850. CGS member. Coed. Private control. Roman Catholic affiliation. Trimester system. Library: about 1,150,463 volumes, 4196 subscriptions. Total University enrollment: 9500.

No on-campus housing for graduate students. Contact Residents Services for off-campus information. Phone: (937)229-3317. Day-care facilities available.

Graduate School

Tuition, per credit: College of Arts & Science and Engineering $453, M.B.A. $481, doctoral programs $494. University fee $25.

Enrollment: full-time 1272, part-time 1905. Graduate faculty: full-time 159, part-time 65. Degrees conferred: M.A., M.B.A., M.C.L.T., M.C.S., M.P.A., M.S., M.S.Ed., M.S.T., Ed.S., Ph.D., D.E., J.D.-M.B.A.

ADMISSION REQUIREMENTS. Transcripts, three letters of recommendation, GMAT for M.B.A., GRE/MAT for Psychology, Biology, and Clinical Psychology required in support of School's application. On-line application available. TOEFL or evidence of proficiency in English required of international students. Accepts transfer applicants. Graduates of unaccredited colleges not considered. Apply to the Graduate School by August 1 (Fall), December 1 (Spring), April 1 (Third Term). Application fee $30. Phone: (937)229-2343; fax: (937)229-4545.

ADMISSION STANDARDS. Varies for each program, usually 3.0 in areas desired for graduate study (A = 4).

FINANCIAL AID. Fellowships, scholarships, teaching/research assistantships, traineeships, Federal W/S, loans. Apply by March 1 for assistantships, for all other programs apply to Graduate School at time of application. Use FAFSA. Aid available for part-time students.

DEGREE REQUIREMENTS. For master's: 30–36 semester hours minimum (includes 6 in research if thesis required), at least 24 in residence; thesis/comprehensive oral/written exam/internship or project required by some departments. For Ed.S.: at least 30 semester hours beyond the master's. For Ph.D.: 60 semester hours minimum, at least two years in residence; preliminary exam; qualifying exam; candidacy exam; dissertation; research tool. For D.E.: essentially the same as for the Ph.D., except one-year internship.

FIELDS OF STUDY.

COLLEGE OF ARTS AND SCIENCES:
American Studies.
Applied Mathematics.
Biology.
Chemistry.
Clinical Psychology.
Communication.
Computer Science.
English.
History.
Mathematics.
Pastoral Ministries.
Philosophy.
Political Science.
Psychology. Includes clinical, experimental, general, human factors.
Public Administration.
Theological Studies.

SCHOOL OF BUSINESS ADMINISTRATION:
Business Administration. Includes accounting, finance, international business, MIS, marketing, operations management. M.B.A.

SCHOOL OF EDUCATION:
Educational Leadership. Ph.D. only.
Educational Specialist in Educational Leadership.
Elementary Education. Usual subject areas.
Physical Education.
School Administration.
School Counseling.
School Psychology.
Secondary Education. Usual subject areas.
Student Services in Higher Education.

SCHOOL OF ENGINEERING:
Aerospace Engineering.
Chemical Engineering.
Civil Engineering.
Electrical Engineering.
Electro-Optics.
Engineering.
Engineering Management.
Engineering Mechanics.
Materials Engineering.
Mechanical Engineering.

School of Law (45469-1320)

Reopened 1974. ABA approved since 1975. AALS member. Semester system. Library 277,000 volumes, 4516 subscriptions.

Annual tuition: $20,886. Limited on-campus housing available. Total average annual additional expenses: $8800.

Enrollment: first-year class 167; total 449 (men 57%, women 43%). Faculty: full-time 19, part-time 18. Student to faculty ratio 19.7 to 1. Degree conferred: J.D., J.D.-M.B.A., J.D.-M.S. (Educ. Admin.).

ADMISSION REQUIREMENTS. LSDAS Law School report, bachelor's degree, transcripts, LSAT, recommendations required in support of application. Accepts transfers from other ABA approved School. Graduates of unaccredited colleges not considered. Apply to Admissions Office by May 1. Application fee $50. Phone: (937)229-3555; fax: (937)229-4194.

ADMISSION STANDARDS. Selective. Mean LSAT: 151; mean GPA: 3.07 (A = 4). Gourman rating: 2.62. *U.S. News & World Report* ranking is in the fourth tier of all law schools. Accepts about 40–45% of total annual applications.

FINANCIAL AID. Full and partial scholarships, grants, Federal W/S, loans. Apply by March 1 to Financial Aid Office. Use FAFSA. About 60% of students receive some aid from School.

DEGREE REQUIREMENTS. For J.D.: Satisfactory completion of three-year program. For master's degrees: see Graduate School listing above.

UNIVERSITY OF DELAWARE
Newark, Delaware 19716-1501
Web site: www.udel.edu

Established 1743, degree granting since 1834. CGS member. Located 15 miles SW of Wilmington. Coed. State-related. Semester system. Special facilities: Institute of Applied Mathematics, Center for the Study of Catalysts, Center for the Study of Composite Materials, University Computing Center, Agricultural Experiment Station, Bartol Research Institute, Institute for Energy Conversion, Science Teaching Center, Mathematics, Teaching Center, Mt. Cuba Astronomical Observatory, Marine Biology Field Station; cooperative program in American Studies and related fields with the Henry Francis du Pont Winterthur Museum and in American technological, business and Labor History with the Hagley Museum. Library: 2,400,000 volumes, 12,600 subscriptions.

Annual tuition: full-time, resident $4310, nonresident $13,260; per credits, resident $251, nonresident $737; for M.B.A./ E.M.B.A. resident $316, nonresident $596. On-campus housing for both married and single students. Average academic year housing costs: $6120 (including board) single students; $6360 for married students. Contact Office of Housing and Residence Life for both on- and off-campus housing information. Phone: (302)831-6573.

Graduate Studies

Graduate study since 1900. Enrollment: full-time 2146, part-time 806. University faculty teaching graduate students: full-time 998, part-time 20. Degrees conferred: M.A., M.S., M.B.A., M.Ed., M.C.E., M.E.E., M.M.S., M.M.E., M.A.S., M.P.A., M.C., M.F.A., M.M., M.P.T., M.M.P., M.I., M.S.N., Ph.D., Ed.D.

ADMISSION REQUIREMENTS. Transcripts, GRE, GMAT (Business), three letters of recommendation required in support of application. TOEFL required of international applicants. Accepts transfer applicants. Graduates of unaccredited institutions not considered. Apply to the Office of Graduate Studies before July 1 (Fall), December 1 (Spring), April 1 (Summer). Application fee $50. Phone: (302)831-2129; fax: (302)831-8745.

ADMISSION STANDARDS. Selective to very competitive.

FINANCIAL AID. Annual awards from institutional funds: scholarships, University fellowships, teaching assistantships, research assistantships, traineeships, Federal W/S, loans. Approved for VA benefits. Apply by March 1 to appropriate department chair in each Graduate College for assistantships, fellowships; to the Financial Aid Office for all other programs. Phone: (302)931-9761. Use FAFSA. About 70% of students receive aid from University.

DEGREE REQUIREMENTS. For master's: 30–48 semester hours minimum; proficiency in one language for some departments thesis/nonthesis option/special project. For Ph.D.: three years minimum beyond the bachelor's, at least one year in continuous residence; language proficiency for some programs; oral/written qualifying exam; dissertation; final oral exam.

FIELDS OF STUDY.

COLLEGE OF AGRICULTURE AND NATURAL RESOURCES:
Agricultural and Resource Economics.
Agricultural and Technology Education.
Animal Science. Ph.D.

Animal Science and Food Science. M.S.
Applied Ecology.
Entomology.
Food Science. M.S. only.
Operations Research.
Plant Biology. Includes plant molecular biology, plant breeding, plant tissue culture, horticulture, crop science, plant anatomy, plant physiology. M.S., Ph.D.
Plant Biology and Biotechnology.
Soil Science. Includes soil chemistry, soil fertility and management, soil physics, soil microbiology and biochemistry, soil biochemistry, environmental microbiology, soil and water quality. M.S., Ph.D.
Statistics.

COLLEGE OF ARTS AND SCIENCE:
Art. M.A., M.F.A. only.
Art Conservation. Ph.D.
Art History.
Biomechanics and Movement Science. Interdisciplinary.
Biological Sciences. Interdepartmental; includes marine biology, morphology, ichthyology, botany, zoology, microbiology; one language for master's. M.S., Ph.D.
Chemistry and Biochemistry. M.A., M.S., Ph.D.
Climatology. Ph.D. only.
Communication.
Computer and Information Science. M.S., Ph.D.
Early American Culture. Two-year program; M.A. only.
English. One language; general qualifying exam for M.A.
Foreign Languages and Literatures. Includes French, German, Spanish. M.A.
Foreign Languages and Pedagogy.
Geography and Climatology. M.A., M.S.
Geology. M.S., Ph.D.
History. M.A., Ph.D.
Liberal Studies. M.A.
Linguistics. M.A., Ph.D.
Mathematical Sciences. M.A., M.S., Ph.D.
Music. Includes performance, teaching. M.M. only.
Physical Therapy. M.P.T.
Physics and Astronomy. Oral exam for M.S.
Political Science and International Relations. M.A. only.
Psychology. Includes clinical, cognitive, social, neuroscience. Ph.D. only.
Sociology and Criminology. M.A., Ph.D.
Theatre. Includes acting, stage management, technical production. M.F.A. only.

COLLEGE OF BUSINESS AND ECONOMICS:
Accounting. M.S. only.
Business Administration. GMAT for admission. M.B.A. only.
Economics. M.A., M.S., Ph.D.
Economics-Business Administration. M.A.-M.B.A.
Management Information Systems. M.S.

COLLEGE OF EDUCATION:
Cognition, Development, and Instruction. M.A., Ph.D.
College Counseling. M.Ed.
Curriculum and Instruction. M.Ed., Ph.D.
Educational Leadership. M.Ed., Ed.D.
Educational Policy. M.A., Ph.D.
ESL/Bilingualism. M.A.
Exceptional Children and Youth. Includes elementary, special, secondary, special education technology, severe disabilities, educational diagnosis. M.Ed.
Exceptionality. Ph.D.
Instruction. M.I.
Measurement, Statistics, and Evaluation. M.A., Ph.D.
School Counseling. M.A., M.Ed.
School Psychology. M.A.
Secondary Education. M.Ed.

COLLEGE OF ENGINEERING:
Biomechanics and Movement Science. Interdisciplinary.
Chemical Engineering. M.CH.E., Ph.D.
Civil and Environmental Engineering. M.C.E., Ph.D.
Electrical and Computer Engineering. M.E.E., Ph.D.
Materials Science and Engineering. M.M.S.E., Ph.D.
Mechanical Engineering. M.M.E., Ph.D.
Ocean Engineering. M.S., Ph.D.

COLLEGE OF HEALTH AND NURSING:
Biomechanics and Movement Science. Interdisciplinary.
Health and Exercise Science.
Health Promotion.
Health Services Administration.
Nursing.
Nutrition and Dietetics.

COLLEGE OF HUMAN SERVICES, EDUCATION, AND PUBLIC POLICY:
Education. See College of Education above.
Hotel, Restaurant, and Institutional Management. M.S.
Individual and Family Studies. M.S., Ph.D.
Urban Affairs and Public Policy. See School of Urban affairs and Public Policy below.

COLLEGE OF MARINE STUDIES:
Marine Policy. M.M.P. only.
Marine Studies. M.A., M.S., Ph.D.
Oceanography. Ph.D. only.

SCHOOL OF URBAN AFFAIRS AND PUBLIC POLICY:
Environmental and Energy Policy. M.E.E.P., Ph.D.
Public Administration. M.P.A.
Urban Affairs and Public Policy. M.A., Ph.D.

DELTA STATE UNIVERSITY

Cleveland, Mississippi 38733-0001
Web site: www.deltast.edu

Founded 1924. Located 100 miles S of Memphis, Tennessee. Coed. State control. Semester system. Library: 208,855 volumes, 1337 subscriptions.

Annual tuition: resident $3696; nonresident $6412; per credit resident $156, nonresident $412. On- and off-campus housing available. Annual on-campus housing cost: $2990. Phone: (662) 846-4151. Day-care facilities available.

Graduate Studies

Graduate study since 1964. Enrollment: full-time 170, part-time 279. Faculty: full-time 42, part-time 33. Degrees conferred: M.B.A., M.C.A., M.Ed., M.S., M.M.E., M.S.N., M.P.A., M.S.C.J., Ed.S., Ed.D.

ADMISSION REQUIREMENTS. Two transcripts, GRE/GMAT/MAT required in support of application. TOEFL required for international applicants. Graduates of unaccredited colleges not considered. Accepts transfer applicants. Apply to Coordinator of Admissions at least thirty days prior to registration. Application fee: none. Phone: (662)846-4018; fax: (662)846-4683.

ADMISSION STANDARDS. Selective. Usual minimum average: 2.5 (A = 4).

FINANCIAL AID. Scholarships, grants, graduate assistantships, Federal W/S, loans. Apply to the Office of Student Financial Assistance: no specified closing date. Phone: (662)846-4670. Use FAFSA and institutional FAF. About 80% of students receive aid from all sources.

DEGREE REQUIREMENTS. For master's: 33 semester hours minimum, at least 27 in residence and one semester in full-time attendance; thesis optional; final oral/written exam. For Ed.S.: 30 semester hours beyond the master's; paper, final oral/written exam. For Ed.D.: 90 semester hours beyond the bachelor's degree; dissertation and residency requirement.

FIELDS OF STUDY.
Biological Science. M.S.
Business Administration. M.B.A.
Commercial Aviation. M.C.A.
Community Development. M.C.D.
Counseling. M.Ed.
Criminal Justice. M.C.J.
Educational Administration and Supervision. Ed.S.
Elementary Education. M.Ed., Ed.S.
English Education. M.Ed.
Health, Physical Education, and Recreation. M.Ed.
History Education. M.Ed.
Mathematical Education. M.Ed.
Music Education. M.M.
Natural Science. M.S.
Nursing. M.S.N.
Physical Science. M.S.
Professional Studies. Ed.D.
Social Science Education. M.Ed.
Special Education. M.Ed.

UNIVERSITY OF DENVER
Denver, Colorado 80208
Web site: www.du.edu

Founded 1864. CGS member. Coed. Private. Quarter system. Special Facilities: Humanities Institute, Echo Lake Lab, Mount Evans Observatory, Denver Research Institute, Child Study Center, Center of Marital Studies, Center for Policy and Contemporary Issues. Library: 2,900,00 volumes, 5788 subscriptions; a U.S. government document depository. Total University enrollment: 8700.

Tuition: per credit $596. On-campus housing for single and married students. Housing cost: One bedroom $5724 (9-month academic year); meal plan available: $1965 (9-month academic year). Two-bedroom units and suites available; monthly costs $650–$725. Contact Graduate Housing Office. Phone: (303)871-2246, fax: (303)871-4064.

Division of Arts and Humanities

Enrollment: full- and part-time graduate students: 386 (men 45%, women 55%). Faculty: full-time 112. Degrees Conferred: M.A., M.M., M.F.A., Ph.D.

ADMISSION REQUIREMENTS. Two transcripts, GRE (Subject Test for some programs) required in support of application. Contact department for additional requirements. TOEFL required for international students. TSE required for some programs. TSE is required for all international graduate teaching assistants. The TWE required by Communications. Application fee: $40. Phone: Graduate Admissions (303)871-3119, or request application materials directly from Web site: www.du.edu.

ADMISSION STANDARDS. Selective to competitive for most departments. Usual minimum average: 2.75 (A = 4).

FINANCIAL AID: Annual awards from institutional funds: scholarships, fellowships, minority student fellowships, teaching assistantships, grants, Federal W/S, loans. Apply by March 1 to departments for scholarships and assistantships, to Financial Aid Office for all other programs. Phone: (303)871-2681. Use FAFSA.

DEGREE REQUIREMENTS. For M.A., M.M.: 45–75 quarter hours; qualifying exam; reading knowledge of one foreign language for some departments; comprehensive exam; thesis required by many departments, optional in others, final oral/written exam required by some programs. For M.F.A.: 90 quarter hours, at least two years in residence; qualifying exam, advancement to candidacy, thesis, oral exam; gallery exhibition. For Ph.D.: 135 quarter hours minimum beyond bachelor's degree or 90 quarter hours beyond master's; at least six quarters in residence, including two consecutive quarters of full-time attendance; reading knowledge of two foreign languages or advanced proficiency in one language; preliminary exam; advancement to candidacy; dissertation; final oral exam.

FIELDS OF STUDY.
Anthropology. M.A.
Art History. Includes museum studies. M.A.
Composition (Music). M.M.
Conducting (Music). M.M.
Economics. M.A.
English. Includes literary studies, creative writing. M.A., Ph.D.
French. M.A.
German. M.A.
History. M.A.
Human Communication Studies. M.A., Ph.D.
Judaic Studies. M.A., M.A.-M.S.W.
Mass Communications and Journalism Studies. M.A.
Music History and Literature. M.A.
Music Theory. M.A.
Philosophy. M.A.
Piano Pedagogy. M.M.
Piano Performance. M.M.
Public Policy. M.P.P.
Psychology. Includes child, clinical, experimental, developmental. Ph.D.
Public Relations. M.S.
Religious Studies. M.A. (Joint Ph.D. program with Iliff School of Theology.)
Russian. M.A.
Sociology. M.A.
Spanish. M.A.
Studio Art. M.F.A.
Suzuki Pedagogy. M.M.
Note: University offers Flexible Dual Degrees; students design their own programs.

Division of Natural Sciences, Mathematics and Engineering

Enrollment: full- and part-time graduate students: 386 (men 45%, women 55%). Faculty: full-time 112. Degrees Conferred: M.A., M.S., Ph.D.

ADMISSION REQUIREMENTS. Two transcripts, GRE (Subject Test for some programs) required in support of application. Contact department for additional requirements. TOEFL required for international students. TSE required for some programs. TSE is required for all international graduate teaching assistants. Application fee: $40. Phone: Graduate Admissions (303)871-3119, or request application materials directly from Web site: www.du.edu.

ADMISSION STANDARDS. Selective to competitive for most departments. Usual minimum average: 2.75 (A = 4).

FINANCIAL AID. Annual awards from institutional funds: scholarships, fellowships, minority student fellowships, teaching assistantships, grants, Federal W/S, loans. Apply by March 1 to departments for scholarships and assistantships, to Financial Aid Office for all other programs. Phone: (303)871-2681. Use FAFSA.

DEGREE REQUIREMENTS. For M.A., M.S., M.S.M.: 45–75 quarter hours; qualifying exam; reading knowledge of one foreign language for some departments; comprehensive exam; thesis required by many departments, optional in others, final oral/written exam required by some programs. For Ph.D.: 135 quarter hours minimum beyond bachelor's degree or 90 quarter hours beyond master's; at least six quarters in residence, including two consecutive quarters of full-time attendance; reading knowledge of two foreign languages or advanced proficiency in one language; preliminary exam; advancement to candidacy; dissertation; final oral exam.

FIELDS OF STUDY.
Biological Sciences. M.A., Ph.D.
Chemistry and Biochemistry. M.A., M.S., Ph.D.
Computer Science. M.S.
Electrical Engineering. M.S.
Electrical Engineering and Computer Science. M.S.
Engineering and Computer Science. M.S.
Geography. Includes geographic information science (M.S.). M.A., M.S., Ph.D.
Management and Engineering. M.S.M.
Mathematics and Computer Science. Ph.D.
Mechanical Engineering. M.S.
Natural Science. M.S., Ph.D.

Daniels College of Business—Graduate Studies
Web site: www.dcb.du.edu

Established 1908. Private control. Accredited programs: M.B.A. (accredited since 1923), Accounting. Quarter system. Special Programs: foreign exchange program in Denmark. Special facilities: Center for Management and Development.

Annual tuition: full-time $21,885 (three quarters), part-time $14,733.

Enrollment: total full-time 260, part-time 356 (men 62%, woman 38%). Faculty: 60 full-time, 15 part-time; 90% with Ph.D./D.B.A. Degrees conferred: M.B.A. (full-time, part-time, day, evening) (General Business Concepts), E.M.B.A. (weekends only), M.Acc., M.I.M. (International Management), M.S.F. (Finance) M.S.M. (Management), M.S.R.T.M. (Resort and Tourism Management), M.T. (Taxation), M.B.A.-J.D., M.I.M.-J.D.

ADMISSION REQUIREMENTS. All applicants should have a bachelor's degree from a recognized institution of higher education and a strong mathematics background. Submit application, GMAT (will accept GMAT test results from the last five years, latest acceptable date is March; will accept GRE), official transcripts from each undergraduate/graduate school attended, two letters of recommendation, essays, résumé, and work history (prefers at least four years of work experience), and an application fee of $50 to the College's Office of Admission. In addition, international students (whose native language is other than English) should submit a TOEFL (minimum score 550) report, certified translations and evaluations of all official transcripts, recommendation should be in English or with certified translations, proof of health/immunization certificate, and proof of sufficient financial resources for nine months of academic study. On-campus visits are encouraged. Admissions Committee will consider applicants with some academic course work deficiencies. Joint degree applicants must apply to and be accepted by both schools, contact the admissions office for current information and specific admissions requirements. Beginning students are admitted Fall, Spring only. U.S. citizens apply by March 1 (Fall), January 1 (Spring), international students apply by March 1 (Fall only). Rolling admissions process. Admissions Office phone: (303) 871-3416; fax: (303) 871-4466; e-mail: dcb@du.edu.

ADMISSION STANDARDS. Competitive for most programs. For M.B.A.: median GMAT: 563; median GPA: 3.2 (A = 4).

FINANCIAL AID. Scholarships, Colorado Resident Grants, international assistantships, research and teaching assistantships, Federal W/S, loans. Financial aid is available for part-time study. Financial assistance is available for international students. Assistantships/fellowships may be available for joint degree candidates. Apply by March 1 for scholarship, fellowship, assistantship from the Daniels College of Business. Contact the University's Financial Aid Office for current need-based financial aid information; phone: (303)871-3416. For most financial assistance and all Federal programs submit FAFSA (School code: 001371), also submit Financial Aid Transcript, Federal Income Tax forms. Approximately 50% of current students receive some form of financial assistance.

DEGREE REQUIREMENTS. For M.B.A., M.I.M.: 72 quarter hours including 16 elective hours, one- to two-year program; degree program must be completed in five years. For E.M.B.A.: 70 quarter hour eighteen-month program. For M.Acc., 56 quarter hour program. For M.S.F.: 64 quarter hour program. For M.R.C.M.: 64 quarter hour program. M.S.T.: 60 quarter hour program. For M.T., LL.M.: 45 quarter hour program. For M.B.A.-Masters: generally a two- to five-year program. For M.B.A., M.I.M.-J.D.: four- to five-and-one-half-year program.

FIELDS OF STUDY.
Accountancy. M.Acc.
Business Administration. M.B.A.
Finance. M.S.F.
Information Technology. Includes business information technology, electronic commerce. M.S.M.
InternationalManagement. Joint degree with the Graduate School of International Studies. M.I.M.
Management. Includes education, healthcare systems, public health, sport and entertainment. M.S.M.
Management and Cable/Telecommunication. Joint degree with the School of Communications. M.S.M.
Management and Engineering. Joint degree with the department of Engineering. M.S.M.
Real Estate and Construction Management. M.R.C.M.
Resort and Tourism Management. M.S.T.
Taxation. Interdisciplinary degree with the College of Law. M.Tax., LL.M.

College of Education

Enrollment: full-time 77, part-time 151. Faculty teaching graduate students: full-time 22, part-time 2. Degrees conferred: M.A., Ph.D.

ADMISSION REQUIREMENTS. Transcripts, letters of recommendation required in support of application. On-line application available. TOEFL required for international applicants. Accepts transfer applicants. Graduates of unaccredited colleges not considered. Apply to Office of Admission by January 1 (priority date). Rolling admissions process. Application fee $45. Phone: (303)871-2509, Fax: (303)871-4566.

ADMISSION STANDARDS. Competitive. Usual minimum average 2.75 (A = 4).

FINANCIAL AID. Annual awards from institutional funds: Scholarships, fellowships, research assistantships, teaching assistantships, Federal W/S, loans. Apply by March 1 to the Financial Aid Office. Phone: (303)871-2681. Use FAFSA. About 30% of students receive aid other than loans from University and outside sources. Aid available for part-time students.

DEGREE REQUIREMENTS. For M.A.: 45 quarter hours minimum, at least 35 in residence; thesis or extra credit required for some departments; final written/oral exam. For Ph.D.: 135 quarter hours minimum beyond the bachelor's degree, at least 90 quarter hours in full-time study; qualifying exam; comprehensive exam; advancement to candidacy; research tool; dissertation; final oral exam.

FIELDS OF STUDY.
Child and Family Studies. M.A., Ph.D.
Counseling Psychology. Ph.D.
Counseling Research. M.A.
Curriculum Leadership. M.A., Ph.D.
Educational Leadership and Policy Studies. M.A., Ph.D.
Educational Psychology. M.A., Ph.D.
Guidance and Counseling. M.A.
Higher Education and Adult Studies. M.A., Ph.D.
International Studies. M.A.
Library and Information Sciences. M.L.I.S.
Management and Education. M.S.M. with concentration in Education.
Mental Health Counseling. M.A.
Quantitative Research Methods. M.A., Ph.D.
School Psychology. Ed.S., Ph.D.

College of Law (80220)
Web site: www.law.du.edu

Established 1892. ABA approved since 1975. AALS member. Located in downtown Denver. Semester system. Special facilities: Earth Justice Clinic, National Center for Preventive Law, Rocky Mountain Mineral Law Foundation, Rocky Mountain Land Use Institute. Library: 340,000 volumes, 4783 subscriptions; has LEXIS, NEXIS, WESTLAW, DIALOG, INFOTRAC.

Annual Tuition: full-time $20,640, part-time $15,480, Total average annual additional expenses: $12,569.

Enrollment: first-year class, full-time 336, part-time 116; total enrollment 860 (men 56%, women 44%). Faculty: full-time 49, part-time 66. Student to faculty ratio 18 to 1. Degrees conferred: J.D., LL.M., M.S.L.A., M.T., J.D.-M.B.A., J.D.-M.I.M., J.D.-M.A. (History, Psychology, Sociology), J.D.-M.S.W.

ADMISSION REQUIREMENTS. LSDAS Law School report, bachelor's degree, transcripts, LSAT, written statement required in support of application. Interview discouraged. Accepts transfer applicants. Graduates of unaccredited colleges not considered. Apply to Admissions Committee after November 1, before May 1 (flexible). Admits Fall only. Application fee $45. Phone: (303)871-6135; e-mail: admissions@mail.law.du.edu.

ADMISSION STANDARDS. Competitive. Mean LSAT: 153; mean GPA: 2.96 (A = 4.0). Gourman rating: 3.85.; *U.S. News & World Report* ranking is in the 2nd tier of all U.S. law schools. Accepts 30–35% of total annual applicants.

FINANCIAL AID. Scholarships, fellowships, Federal W/S, loans, internships, externships. Apply by February 15 to Scholarship Committee Use FAFSA. About 26% of students receive aid other than loans from College.

DEGREE REQUIREMENTS. For J.D.: satisfactory completion of three-year program. For dual degrees in History, International Studies, International Management, Mineral Economics, Psychology, Social Work, Sociology: the J.D. is reduced by 10 credits; the other degree is reduced by 9–12 quarter hours. For LL.M., M.S.L.A., M.T.: satisfactory completion of two-semester program.

Graduate School of International Studies

Graduate study since 1929. Annual tuition: full-time $21,456, per credit $596. Graduate housing available. Enrollment: full- and part-time 300 (men 45%, women 55%). Faculty teaching graduate students: full-time 17, part-time 6. Degrees conferred: M.A., M.I.M., M.P.P., M.A.–M.S.W., M.A.–J.D., Ph.D.

ADMISSION REQUIREMENTS. Transcripts, 3 letters of recommendation, GRE (GMAT or LSAT may be substituted), statement of purpose required in support of the school's application. TOEFL (minimum score 550) required for international applicants. Accepts transfer applicants. Graduates of unaccredited institutions not considered. Apply to the Office of Admission by January 15 (priority date). Application fee $50, $45 for international applicants. Phone: (303)871-2544; fax: (303)871-2456; e-mail: gsisadm@du.edu.

ADMISSION STANDARDS. Competitive. Mean GPA: 3.3 (A = 4.0). Mean GRE: 500–530 (Verbal), 570–590 (Quant.), 590–610 (Analytical). Usual minimum average: 3.0 (A = 4).

FINANCIAL AID. Annual awards from institutional funds: fellowships (includes Foreign Language and Area Studies Fellowships), graduate research/teaching assistantships, grants, Federal W/S, loans. Apply to department chair by February 15 for all non-Federal programs; to Student Financial Services for all Federal programs. Phone: (303)871-2681. Use FAFSA (School code: 001371) and Departmental FAF.

DEGREE REQUIREMENTS. For M.A.: 90 quarter hour program (must include the core, one field, one concentration, and two methodology courses); thesis; foreign language proficiency. For M.P.P.: 90 quarter hour program (must include the core, one policy analysis area, one policy issue area, and a participant-observer experience). For Ph.D.: 135 quarter hour beyond bachelor's, at least three consecutive quarters in residence; most programs include the core, two fields, one concentration, three methodology courses; research tool; advancement to candidacy; one foreign language proficiency; written/oral comprehensive exam; dissertation.

FIELDS OF STUDY.
Global Finance, Trade, and Economic Integration. M.A.
Intercultural Communication. Joint degree with School of Communication. M.A.
International Administration. M.A.
International Business Transactions. M.A.
International Development. M.A.
International Management. Joint degree with Daniels College of Business. M.I.M.
International Studies. M.A., Ph.D.
International Technology Analysis and Management. M.A.
Policy Analysis. M.A.
Technology and International Public Policy. M.A.

Graduate School of Professional Psychology

Graduate study since 1976. Tuition: per credit $596. Enrollment: full- and part-time 137 (men 25%, women 75%). Faculty teaching graduate students; full-time 4, part-time 31. Degree conferred: Psy.D.

ADMISSION REQUIREMENTS. Transcripts, GRE Subject Test, four letters of recommendation required in support of School's application. TOEFL, TSE required for international applicants. Accepts transfer applicants. Graduates of unaccredited colleges not considered. Apply to Office of Admission by January 1. Application fee $45. Phone: (303)871-3873; fax: (303)871-4220.

ADMISSION STANDARDS. Competitive. Usual minimum average 3.0 (A = 4). Mean GRE: 550; mean GPA: 3.5 (A = 4).

FINANCIAL AID. Annual awards from institutional funds: fellowship, research/teaching assistantships, Federal W/S loans. Apply by March 1 to the Financial Aid Office. Phone: (303)871-2681. Use FAFSA. About 20% of students receive aid other than loans from University and outside. Aid available for part-time students.

DEGREE REQUIREMENTS. For M.A.: 72 quarter hours, two years in full-time residency; supervised field placement; competency exam/thesis. For Psy.D.: 135 quarter hours minimum beyond the bachelor's degree, at least two years minimum in full-time study; clinical experience; advancement to candidacy; research tool; practicum; twelve-month clinical psychology internship; doctoral paper.

FIELD OF STUDY.
Clinical Psychology. Psy.D.
Forensic Psychology. M.A.

Graduate School of Social Work

Tuition: per credit $596. Enrollment: full- and part-time 313 (men 15%, women 85%). Faculty teaching graduate students: full-time 21, part-time 0. Degrees conferred: M.S.W., Ph.D.

ADMISSION REQUIREMENTS. Official transcripts, three letters of recommendation required in support of School's application. A personal interview may be requested by School. TOEFL, TSE required for international applicants. Accepts transfer applicants. Graduates of unaccredited colleges not considered. Apply to Office of Admissions by May 31. Rolling admission process. Application fee $50. Phone: (303)871-2841; fax: (303)871-2845.

ADMISSION STANDARDS. Competitive. Usual minimum average: 2.75 (A = 4).

FINANCIAL AID. Annual awards from institutional funds: fellowships, scholarships, teaching/research assistantship, Federal W/S, loans. Apply by February 1 to the Financial Aid Office. Phone: (303)871-2841. Use FAFSA. About 10% of students receive aid from School and outside sources. Aid available for part-time students.

DEGREE REQUIREMENTS. For M.S.W.: 90 quarter hours minimum, at least three quarters in full-time study; advancement to candidacy; six quarters of field practicum. For Ph.D.: 135 quarter hours minimum beyond the bachelor's degree, at least 75 quarter hours in full-time study; preliminary exam; advancement to candidacy; research tool; dissertation; final oral exam.

FIELDS OF STUDY.
Advanced Clinical Practice. Includes social work with individuals, couples, families, small groups.
Advanced Community Practice. Includes social work in organizations and communities in the policy arena.

DEPAUL UNIVERSITY
Chicago, Illinois 60604-2287
Web site: www.depaul.edu

Founded 1898. CGS member. The largest Catholic University in the country. Coed. Private control. Roman Catholic affiliation. Quarter system. Graduate study at Loop, Lincoln Park, O'Hare, and Oakbrook campuses. Special facilities: Institute for Applied Artificial Intelligence, Chicago Area Studies Center, Center for Church/State Studies, DePaul Performance Center, Hispanic Research Center, Center for the Studies of Values, Institute for Business Ethics, Kellstadt Center for Marketing Analysis and Planning, Learning Disabilities Center, Mental Health Clinic, Blackstone Theatre, Psychological Testing Center. Library: 1,200,000 volumes, 14,500 subscriptions. Total University enrollment: 19,000.

Tuition: per credit $362. No on-campus housing available. Average academic year off-campus housing costs: $7000–$10,500.

Graduate Study

Enrollment: full-time 4397, part-time 3715. Faculty teaching graduate students: full-time 598, part-time 952. Degrees conferred: M.A., M.S., M.M., M.F.A., M.B.A., M.Ed., M.S.A., M.S.T., M.Acc., M.S.-M.I.S., Ph.D.

ADMISSION REQUIREMENTS. Official transcripts, written statement of purpose required in support of application. Letters of recommendation, GRE/GMAT interview required for some departments. TOEFL required for international applicants. Accepts transfer applicants. Graduates of unaccredited colleges not considered. Apply to appropriate Graduate College/School at least one month prior to registration. For some programs there are earlier deadlines. Rolling admission process. Application fee $25, $40 (Psychology). Phone: Business (312)362-8810; Liberal Arts and Sciences (312)362-5367; Computer Science (312)362-8381; Education (773)325-7323; Music (773)325-7444; School for New Learning (312)362-8512; Theater School (773)325-7999.

ADMISSION STANDARDS. Selective to competitive for most departments. Usual minimum average 2.75 (A = 4).

FINANCIAL AID. Annual awards from institutional funds: scholarships, research assistantships, teaching assistantships, tuition waivers, Federal W/S, loans. Approved for VA benefits. Apply by May 1 to head of appropriate department for scholarships, assistantships; to Financial Aid Office for all other programs. Phone: (312)362-8526. Use FAFSA and institutional FAF. About 20% of students receive aid other than loans from University and outside sources. Aid available for part-time students.

DEGREE REQUIREMENTS. For master's: 44–60 quarter hours minimum, at least three quarters in residence for full-time students, five quarters in residence for part-time student; reading knowledge of one or two foreign languages for some department; thesis required by many departments, optional in others; final oral/written exam required by some programs. For Ph.D.: 90 quarter hours minimum, at least six quarters in residence; comprehensive exam; advance to candidacy; dissertation; final oral exam.

FIELDS OF STUDY.

COLLEGE OF LIBERAL ARTS AND SCIENCES:
Biological Sciences.
Chemistry.
Communications.
Economics.
English.
Health Law and Policy.
History.
Interdisciplinary Studies.
International Studies.
Liberal Studies.
Mathematical Sciences.
Mathematics Education.
Nursing.
Philosophy. M.A., Ph.D.
Physics.
Public Services.
Public Service Management.
Psychology. Includes clinical, experimental, general, industrial, school. GRE/Subject for admission; additional departmental application for admission. M.A., Ph.D.
Sociology.
Writing.

CHARLES H. KELLSTADT GRADUATE SCHOOL OF BUSINESS:
Accountancy. M.Acc., M.S.
Business Economics. M.B.A. evening.

E-Business. M.B.A. evening.

Entrepreneurship. M.B.A. evening.

Enterprise Resource Plan. M.B.A. evening.

Finance. M.S.F., M.B.A. evening.

Financial Management and Control. M.B.A. evening.

Human Resource Management. M.B.A. evening.

International Business. M.B.A. evening.

International Markets and Finance. Full-time day program. M.B.A./I.M.F.

Management Accounting. M.B.A. evening.

Management of Information Systems. M.S.M.I.S., M.B.A. evening.

Marketing Analysis. M.S.M.A.

Marketing Management. M.B.A. evening.

Operations Management. M.B.A. evening.

Taxation. M.S.T. only.

SCHOOL OF COMPUTER SCIENCE TELECOMMUNICATION AND INFORMATION SYSTEMS:

Computer Science. Includes artificial intelligence, data analysis, data communication, database systems, systems foundations, computer graphics, computer vision.

Distributed Systems.

E-Commerce Technology.

Human–Computer Interaction.

Information Systems. Includes computer supported collaborative work, data warehousing, e-commerce, IT project management, networking, systems development.

Management of Information Systems.

Software Engineering. Includes project management, software development, software systems.

Telecommunication Systems. Includes computer science, standard telecommunication.

SCHOOL OF EDUCATION:

Bilingual/Bicultural Education.

Curriculum Studies. Includes middle school mathematics program. Ed.D.

Educational Leadership. Ed.D.

Human Development and Learning.

Human Services and Counseling.

Language, Literacy, and Special Instruction. Includes reading and learning disabilities.

Social and Cultural Foundations in Education. Includes early childhood education, elementary education, secondary education.

SCHOOL OF MUSIC:

Composition.

Jazz Studies.

Music Education.

Performance.

SCHOOL FOR NEW LEARNING:

Customized Adult Master's Program. M.A.

THEATRE SCHOOL:

Acting.

Directing.

College of Law

Founded 1912. ABA approved since 1925. AALS member. Semester system. Located at Loop Campus. Special facilities: Center for Church/State Studies, Center for Intellectual Property Law, Center for Law and Science, Center for Justice in Capital Cases, Health Law Institute, International Human Rights Law Institute. Library: 353,352 volumes, 5005 subscriptions; has LEXIS, NEXIS, WESTLAW, DIALOG, ILLINET; 95 PCs.

Tuition: day $21,815, evening $14,815. On-campus housing limited. Contact Director of Housing. Total average annual additional expenses: $12,441.

Enrollment: first-year class 226 day, 68 evening; total full- and part-time 1076 (men 48%, women 52%); L.L.M. enrollment 70. Faculty: full-time 34, part-time 44. Student to faculty ratio 23.7 to 1. Degrees conferred: J.D., J.D.-M.B.A., J.D.-M.S. (Public Service Management), LL.M. (Taxation, Health Law).

ADMISSION REQUIREMENTS. LSDAS Law School report, bachelor's degree, transcripts, LSAT required in support of application. Letters of recommendation helpful. Accepts transfer applications. Graduates of unaccredited colleges not considered. Apply to Director of Admissions after September 1, before April 1. Application fee $40. Phone: (312)362-6831, outside Illinois (800)428-7453; fax: (312)362-5280.

ADMISSION STANDARDS. Selective. Mean LSAT: 153; mean GPA: 3.26 (A = 4). Gourman rating: 3.85. *U.S. News & World Report* ranking is in the third tier of all U.S. law schools. Accepts 40–45% of total applicants.

FINANCIAL AID. Scholarships, Federal W/S, loans. Apply to Office of Financial Aid by March 1. Use FAFSA. Aid available for part-time students. Approximately 45% of students receive aid other than loans from the College.

DEGREE REQUIREMENTS. For J.D.: 86 semester hours, 6 semesters (day) or 8 semesters (evening) in residence; acceleration possible through attendance at two summer sessions; "C" average required. For LL.M.: at 24 credits beyond J.D.

DES MOINES UNIVERSITY OF HEALTH SCIENCES

3200 Grand Avenue

Des Moines, Iowa 50312-4198

Web site: www.dmu.edu

Gained University status in 1980. Private control. Graduate study only. Special facilities: the University operates five clinics; an on-campus Medical Center opened in 1987. Library: 28,000 volumes, 1400 subscriptions. Total University enrollment: 1325.

College of Osteopathic Medicine and Surgery

Established 1898 as the Dr. S.S. Still College of Osteopathic Medicine. Second oldest and second largest osteopathic school in U.S. Affiliated with Des Moines General Hospital and twelve other hospitals throughout the East and Midwest.

Annual tuition: $24,900. No on-campus housing available. Contact Off-campus Housing office for information; phone: (515)271-1504. Off-campus housing and personal expenses: approximately $18,580.

Enrollment: first-year class 200; total full-time 797 (men 70%, women 30%). Faculty: full-time 59. Degree conferred: D.O., D.O.-M.P.H., D.O.-M.H.A.

ADMISSION REQUIREMENTS. Preference given to State residents, U.S. citizens and permanent residents only. Bachelor's degree from an accredited institution required. All applicants have bachelor's degree awarded prior to enrollment. Apply through AACOMAS (file after June 1, before February 1), submit MCAT (will accept test results from last two years: one year is recommended), official transcripts for each school attended (should show at least 90 semester credits/135 quarter credits), service processing fee. After a review of the AACOMAS application and supporting documents a decision is made concerning which candidates should receive supplemental materials. The supplementary application, an application fee of $50, a statement of purpose, and three recommendations (one from a premed adviser and two from science faculty members) should be returned to Office of Admission by April

3. Interviews are by invitation only and generally for final selection. Accepts transfer applicants on a space available basis. First-year students admitted Fall only. Rolling admissions process, notification starts in January and is finished when class is filled. School does maintain an alternate list. Phone: (515)271-1450, (800)240-2767, ext. 1450; fax: (515)271-1578.

ADMISSION STANDARDS. Selective. Usual minimum average: GPA 3.0 (A = 4). Mean MCAT: 8; mean GPA: 3.44 (A = 4).

FINANCIAL AID. Scholarships, merit scholarships, minority scholarships, Grants-in-Aid, institutional loans, NOF, HEAL, alternative loan programs, NIH stipends; Federal Perkins loans, Stafford Subsidized and Unsubsidized loans, Service Obligation Scholarships programs, Military and National Health Service programs are available. Financial Aid applications and information are given out at the on-campus by invitation interview. Contact the Financial Aid Office for current information. Use FAFSA (School code: 015616), also submit Financial Aid Transcript, Federal Income Tax forms. Approximately 85% of students receive some form of financial assistance.

DEGREE REQUIREMENTS. For D.O.: satisfactory completion of four-year program.

UNIVERSITY OF DETROIT MERCY
Detroit, Michigan 48219-0900
Web site: www.udmercy.edu

Founded 1877. In 1990 the University of Detroit and Mercy College consolidated to form a new university. Private control. Roman Catholic affiliation. Coed. Semester system. The Colleges of Business Administration, Engineering and Sciences, and Liberal Arts are at the McNichols Campus; the Colleges of Health Services, and Education and Human Services, and Housing are at Outer Drive Campus. Special facilities: Center for the Study of Development and Aging, Manufacturing Institute, Institute for Business and Community Services, Kellstadt Consumer Research Center, Polymer Institute, Center for Excellence in Environmental Engineering and Science. Library: 645,000 volumes, 777,000 microforms, 5500 current periodicals. Total University enrollment: 6000.

Tuition: full-time $12,760 (Physician Assistant), $10,890 (Engineering), $10,620 all other programs; per credit $425–$450. On-campus housing for 200 single students, 30 married student accommodations. Annual room and board costs: $6750. Apply to Director of Residential Life for on-campus housing, to Director of Students Activities for off-campus housing information. Phone: (313)993-1230.

Graduate Studies

Graduate study since 1885. Enrollment: full-time 1279, part-time 1591 (men 55%, women 45%). Graduate faculty: full-time 165, part-time 32. Degrees conferred: M.A., M.S., M.B.A., S.Sec., M.A.T.M., M.P.A., M.Engr.Mgt., M.A.C.S., Ed.S., M.E., M.C.S., Ph.D., D.E.

ADMISSION REQUIREMENTS. Official transcripts, GRE/GMAT required in support of application. Proof of English proficiency required for international applicants. Interview not required. Accepts transfer applicants. Graduates of unaccredited institutions not considered. Apply to Graduate Office of the College or School listed below at least six weeks prior to registration. Application fee $25, $35 for international applicants. Phone: (313)993-1245; E-mail: admission@udmercy.edu.

ADMISSION STANDARDS. Selective to competitive. Usual minimum average: 3.0 (A = 4).

FINANCIAL AID. Annual awards from institutional funds: scholarships, teaching fellowships, graduate assistantships, residence assistantships, coaching assistantship, internships, Federal W/S, loans. Approved for VA benefits. Apply by April 1 to appropriate department chair for fellowships, assistantships; to Scholarships and Financial Aid Office for all other programs. Phone: (313)993-3350. Use FAFSA (University code: 002323).

DEGREE REQUIREMENTS. For master's: 30–36 semester hours minimum (counseling master's: 48–54 credit program), at least 18 in residence; six hours for thesis when required or elected; final written/oral exam in some programs. For Ed.S.: 30 semester hours minimum beyond master's. For D.E.: two-year minimum beyond master's (total of 51 hours including dissertation), usually at least 30 hours in full-time residence, must be in residence in the trimester in which the final qualifying exam is taken; dissertation; oral exam. For Ph.D.: about 60–65 hours beyond the master's, at least 30 in full-time residence; language proficiency for some departments; preliminary exam; dissertation; final oral exam.

FIELDS OF STUDY.

COLLEGE OF BUSINESS ADMINISTRATION:
Business Administration. 36 hours minimum for M.B.A.
Information Systems, Computer, and Software Management. M.S.
Product Development. M.P.D.

COLLEGE OF ENGINEERING AND SCIENCE:
Chemistry. M.S.
Civil Engineering. M.E., D.E.
Computer and Information Systems/Software Management. M.S.
Computer Science. M.A.
Electrical and Computer Engineering. M.E., D.E.
Engineering Management. M.E.M.
Mechanical Engineering. M.E., D.E.
Teaching of Mathematics. M.A.

COLLEGE OF HEALTH PROFESSIONS:
Health Services Administration. M.S.
Physician Assistant. M.S.

COLLEGE OF LIBERAL ARTS AND EDUCATION:
Clinical Psychology. M.A., Ph.D.
Counseling. M.A.
Criminal Justice Studies. M.A.
Educational Administration (Early Childhood). M.A.
Educational Research (Early Childhood). M. A.
Emotionally Impaired (Early Childhood). M.A.
History. M.A.
Industrial/Organizational Psychology. M.A.
Learning Disabilities (Early Childhood). M.A.
Liberal Studies. Interdepartmental. M.A.
Political Science. M.A.
Psychology. M.A.
School Psychology. M.A., Ph.D.
Security Administration. M.S.

SCHOOL OF ARCHITECTURE:
Architecture. M. Arch.

MCAULEY SCHOOL OF NURSING:
Nurse Anesthesia. M.S.N.
Family Nurse Practitioner. M.S.N.
Health Systems Management. M.S.N.

School of Dentistry (48219-0900)

Established 1932. School relocated in 1997 to a facility in NW Detroit. Private control. Annual tuition: $27,400. Contact Office of Student Affairs for housing information. Phone: (313)446-1825. Total average cost for all other first-year expenses: $14,850.

Enrollment: first-year class 73; total 274 (men 40%, women

60%); postgraduates 7. Faculty: full-time 52; part-time 120. Degree conferred: D.D.S.

ADMISSION REQUIREMENTS. AADSAS, official transcripts, DAT (October date preferred), three letters of recommendation required in support of School's application. Interview may be requested by applicant. Applicants must have completed at least three years of college study. Accepts transfer applicants. Preference given to state residents. Apply to Director of Admissions after June 1, before March 1 Fall admission only. Application fee $50. Phone: (313)494-6659; fax: (313)494-6659; e-mail: dental@udmercy.edu.

ADMISSION STANDARDS. Competitive. Median DAT: Academic 18.0, PAT 17.0; median GPA: 3.31 (A = 4.0). Gourman rating: 4.23. Accepts about 20–25% of total annual applicants. Approximately 95% are state residents.

FINANCIAL AID. Scholarships, grants, tuition waivers, DEAL, HEAL, loans. Apply after acceptance to the University Financial Aid office. Use FAFSA, (School code: E00635). Phone: (313)993-1405. About 76% of Michigan students receive some aid from School and outside sources.

DEGREE REQUIREMENTS. For D.D.S.: satisfactory completion of forty-five-month program.

School of Law (48226)

Established 1912. ABA approved since 1933. AALS member. Semester system. Special facility: Intellectual Property Law Institute. Law library: 317,366 volumes, 3549 subscriptions; has NEXIS, WESTLAW. Tuition: full-time $19,400, part-time $14,240. Limited on-campus housing for single and married students available. Total average annual additional expense: $12,065.

Enrollment: first-year class full-time 74, part-time 52; total full- and part-time 356 (men 45%, women 55%). Faculty: full-time 12, part-time 23. Student to faculty ratio 20.6 to 1. Degrees conferred: J.D. (special J.D. for Canadian lawyers), J.D.-M.B.A.

ADMISSION REQUIREMENTS. LSDAS Law School report, bachelor's degree, transcripts, two letters of recommendation, LSAT, required in support of application. Interview not required. Accepts transfer applicants. Apply to Director of Admissions after September 1, before April 15. Fall admissions only. Application fee $50. Phone: (313)596-0264; e-mail: admlawao@udmercy.edu.

ADMISSION STANDARDS. Selective. Mean LSAT: 147; mean GPA: 3.13 (A = 4.0). Gourman rating: 3.46. *U.S. News & World Report* ranking is in the fourth tier of all U.S. law school. Accepts about 40% of total annual applicants.

FINANCIAL AID. Scholarships, grants, Federal W/S, loans. Apply to Director of Financial Aid before April 1 (flexible). Use FAFSA. About 18% of students receive aid other than loans from institutional funds.

DEGREE REQUIREMENTS. For J.D.: 86 hours required. For J.D.-M.B.A.: 108–111 hours required, 72 hours of law, 36–39 boom of M.B.A.
Note: Study-abroad programs available.

UNIVERSITY OF THE DISTRICT OF COLUMBIA
Washington, D.C. 20008-1175
Web site: www.udc.edu

Founded in 1976 by the merger of District of Columbia Teachers College, Federal City College, and Washington Technical Institute. Located in NW Washington. Coed. Public control. Semester system. Library: 500,000 volumes, 1500 subscriptions.

The University's other Graduate Colleges/Schools: School of Arts and Science, College of Professional Studies.

The David A. Clarke School of Law
4200 Connecticut Avenue, NW
Washington, D.C. 20008
Web site: www.law.udc.edu

Established 1986. Merged with University in 1996, name changed in 1998. Located on main campus. ABA approved since 1998. AALS member. Semester system. Full-time, day study only. Law library: 184,000 volumes, 2450 current subscriptions; has LEXIS, WESTLAW, DIALOG, CALI.

Annual tuition: resident $7135, nonresident $14,135. No on-campus housing available. Contact Law School's Orientation Committee for off-campus information. Off-campus housing and personal expenses; approximately $20,865.

Enrollment: first-year class 40; total full-time 141 (men 39%, women 61%); no part-time students.

Faculty: full-time 13, part-time 13; student to faculty ratio 9 to 1. Degree conferred: J.D.

ADMISSION REQUIREMENTS. LSDAS Law School report, LSAT (not later than December test date, if more than one LSAT, highest is used), bachelor's degree from an accredited institution, personal statement, two recommendations, transcripts (must show all schools attended and at least three years of study) required in support of application. Applicants must have received bachelor's degree prior to enrollment. Accepts transfer applicants. Interview not required but may be requested by School. In addition, international applicants whose native language is not English must submit TOEFL (not older than two years). Apply to Office of Admission after September 30, before April 1. First-year students admitted Fall only. The rolling admissions process is finished when the class is filled. Application fee $35. Phone: (202)274-7341; fax: (202)274-5583.

ADMISSION STANDARDS, Selective. Mean LSAT: 145; mean GPA: 2.83 (A = 4). Accepts about 90% of total annual applicants. Gourman rating: 2.10; *U.S. News & World Report* ranking is in the fourth tier of all law schools.

FINANCIAL AID. Need-based scholarships, merit scholarships, fellowships, private and institutional loans, Federal loans and Federal W/S available. Apply as soon as possible after January 1, but before May 1 deadline. Phone: (202)274-7337. For all Federal programs submit FAFSA (School code: B08083), also submit Financial Aid Transcript, Federal Income Tax forms. Approximately 91% of students receive some form of financial assistance.

DEGREE REQUIREMENTS. For J.D.: 85 (61 required) credits with a GPA of at least 2.0 (A = 4), plus completion of upper divisional writing course; three-year program. No accelerated J.D. program; limited number of summer courses available.

DOMINICAN UNIVERSITY
River Forest, Illinois 60305-1099
Web site: www.dom.edu

Founded 1901. Located 10 miles W of the Chicago Loop. Coed. Private control. Roman Catholic. Semester system. Library: 280,475 volumes, 4000 subscriptions.

Tuition: per three-credit course $1650. On-campus housing available for single students only. Annual housing cost: $5360 (including board). Apply to Housing Office. Phone: (708)524-6237. Day-care facilities available.

Graduate School of Business

Enrollment: full-time 62, part-time 198. Faculty: full-time 12, part-time 22. Degrees conferred: M.B.A., M.S.A., M.B.A.-M.L.I.S., M.S./C.I.S., M.S./M.I.S., M.S.O.M., M.B.A.-J.D. (with John Marshall Law School).

ADMISSION REQUIREMENTS. Transcripts, three letters of recommendation, GMAT required in support of School's application. On-line application available. TOEFL required for international applicants. Accepts transfer applicants. Apply to School at least one month prior to registration. Application fee $25. Phone: (708)524-6807; fax: (708)522-6939.

ADMISSION STANDARDS. Selective. Usual minimum average: 2.5 (A = 4).

FINANCIAL AID. Scholarships, assistantships, tuition waivers, Federal W/S, loans. Approved for VA benefits. Apply by April 15 to Dean for scholarships, assistantships; to the Director of Financial Aid for all other programs. Phone: (708)524-6809. Use FAFSA. Aid available for part-time students.

DEGREE REQUIREMENTS. For master's: 30–51 semester hours minimum, at least 24 in residence; practicum (for some programs); computer proficiency for M.B.A.

FIELDS OF STUDY.
Accounting. M.S.A.
Business Administration. Concentrations in accounting, entrepreneurship, finance, general management, health care administration, human resource management, international business administration, management information systems, marketing.
Computer Information Systems. M.S./C.I.S.
Knowledge Management. M.S.
Management Information Systems. M.S./M.I.S.
Organizational Management. M.S.O.M.

Graduate School of Education

Tuition: per credit $420. On-campus housing available.
Enrollment: full-time 14, part-time 284. Faculty: full-time 10, part-time 19. Degrees conferred: M.A.E.A., M.A.Ed., M.S.Ed., M.S.Sp.Ed., M.A.T.

ADMISSION REQUIREMENTS. Transcripts, three letters of recommendation, required in support of School's application. TOEFL required for international applicants. Accepts transfer applicants. Apply to School by August 15 (Fall), January 10 (Spring). Rolling admissions process. Application fee $25. Phone: (708)524-6921; fax (708)524-6665.

ADMISSION STANDARDS, Selective. Usual minimum average: 3.0 (A = 4).

FINANCIAL AID. Fellowships, assistantships, internships, grants. Federal W/S, loans. Approved for VA benefits. Apply by August 15 to Dean for fellowships, assistantships; to the Director of Financial Aid for all other programs. Phone: (708)524-6809. Use FAFSA. Aid available for part-time students.

DEGREE REQUIREMENTS. For master's: 32–40 semester hours minimum, at least 24 in residence; thesis/nonthesis option.

FIELDS OF STUDY.
Education. M.A.Ed., M.S.Ed.
Education Administration. M.A.E.A.
Special Education. M.S.Sp.Ed.
Teaching. M.A.T.

Graduate School of Library and Information Science

Graduate study since 1949. Tuition: per 3-credit course $1635. Enrollment full-time 87, part-time 259 (men 22%, women 78%). Faculty: full-time 10, part-time 33. Degrees conferred: M.L.I.S., several Certificates of Special Studies.

ADMISSION REQUIREMENTS. Transcripts of all postsecondary study, two letters of recommendation required in support of School's application. GRE required for some applicants. TOEFL required for international applications. Accepts transfer applicants. Graduates of unaccredited institutions not considered. Apply to the Graduate School at least one month prior to registration. Application fee $25. Phone: (708)524-6844.

ADMISSION STANDARDS. Selective. Usual minimum average: 3.0 (A = 4).

FINANCIAL AID. Annual awards from institutional funds: scholarships, assistantships, internships, tuition waivers, Federal W/S, loans. Approved for VA benefits. Apply to Director of Financial Aid by April 15. Phone: (708)524-6845. Use FAFSA. Aid available for part-time students.

DEGREE REQUIREMENTS. For M.L.I.S.: 36 semester hours minimum; thesis. Degree must be completed within 5 years or 6 summers.

FIELDS OF STUDY.
Library Information Science. Includes library media specialist.
Management Information System. Combined program with School of Business.
Note: Collaborative programs with College of St. Catherine in St. Paul, MN. Requires courses at Dominican University as well as at CSC.

DOMINICAN UNIVERSITY OF CALIFORNIA
San Rafael, California 94901-8008
Web site: www.dominican.edu

Founded 1890. Coed. Private control, Roman Catholic. Semester system. Library: 103,000 volumes, 369 subscriptions.
Annual tuition: full-time $14,040, part-time $585 per credit. On-campus housing for single students only. Average academic year housing cost: $8625 (including board); off-campus housing costs: $1100 per month. Contact the Dean of Student Services. Phone: (415)485-3277.

Graduate Division

Graduate study since 1950. Enrollment: full-time 127, part-time 210. Faculty: full-time 25, part-time 47. Degrees conferred: M.A., M.B.A., M.S.

ADMISSION REQUIREMENTS. Official transcripts, three letters of recommendation, interview required in support of application. TOEFL required for international applicants. Accepts transfer applicants. Graduates of unaccredited institutions not considered. Apply to chair of appropriate department. Admissions deadlines vary by departments. Applications processed on a rolling basis. Application fee $40. Phone: (415)257-1336; fax: (415)485-3293.

ADMISSION STANDARDS. Selective. Usual minimum average: 2.75 (A = 4).

FINANCIAL AID. Annual awards from institutional funds: scholarships, fellowships, grants, assistantships, Federal W/S, loans. Approved for VA benefits. Apply by March 2 to Financial Aid Office. Phone: (415)485-3204; fax: (415)485-3205. Use FAFSA. About 20% of students receive aid other than loans from College and outside sources. Aid available for part-time students.

DEGREE REQUIREMENTS. For master's: 30–43 units depending on degree, at least 24 in residence; reading knowledge of one foreign language for some programs; thesis for M.S. in Education; thesis option for M.A. Humanities; final comprehensive exam or internship.

FIELDS OF STUDY.
Clinical Nurse Specialist. M.S.
Counseling Psychology.
Curriculum and Instruction. M.S.
Global Strategic Management. M.B.A.
Humanities. Includes history, literature, art history, religion, philosophy. M.A.
Integrated Health Practices. M.S.
Strategic Leadership. M.B.A.

DRAKE UNIVERSITY
Des Moines, Iowa 50311-4516
Web site: www.drake.edu

Founded 1881. Coed. Private control. Semester system. Special facilities: Agricultural Law Center, Center for Hypertension Research, Health Issues Research Center, Information System Research Center, Insurance Research and Professional Development Center, Center for the Study of Urban Problems, Library 500,000 volumes, 2100 subscriptions. Total University enrollment: 6000.

Annual tuition: full time $17,230; per credit $260–$340. On-campus housing available for both single and married students. Average academic year housing costs: $315–350 per month; off-campus $400–$650 per month. Apply by August 1, housing is based on first-come, first-served basis. Contact Housing Office for both on- and off-campus housing information. Phone: (515)271-2196.

Graduate Programs

Graduate study since 1881. Enrollment full- and part-time 1582. Faculty: full-time 252, part-time 41. Degrees conferred: M.A., M.S., M.S.T., M.A.T., M.S. in Education, M.S.N., Ed.S., Ed.D., Doctor of Pharmacy. Joint programs: M.B.A.-J.D., M.P.A.-J.D., M.A.(Mass Communication)-J.D., M.B.A.-Pharmacy.

ADMISSION REQUIREMENTS. Official transcripts, GRE or MAT required in support of application. On-line application available. GMAT is required for M.B.A. degree program. Interview usually not required. TOEFL required for international applicants. Accepts transfer applicants. Graduates of unaccredited institutions not considered. Apply to the Office of Graduate Admissions at least six weeks prior to registration; Doctoral applicants apply by February 1. Application fee $30. Phone: (515)271-3181 or toll-free (800)44-DRAKE; fax: (515)271-2831; e-mail: gradadmit@acad.drake.edu

ADMISSION STANDARDS. Competitive for some departments, selective for the others. Usual minimum average: 2.5 (3.0 last two years in major) (A = 4).

FINANCIAL AID. Assistantships, fellowships, Federal W/S, loans. Approved for VA benefits. Apply by March 1 to appropriate department chair for assistantships, fellowships; to Office of Student Financial Planning for all other aid. Priority deadline March 1. Phone: (515)271-2905. Use FAFSA. Aid available for part-time students.

DEGREE REQUIREMENTS. For master's: 30–36 semester hours minimum, at least two-thirds of the course work in residence; 3–8 hours are given for graduate project, usually a thesis, field report, or creative project; final written/oral exam. For Ed.S.: 30 hours minimum beyond the master's. For Ed.D.: 60 hours minimum beyond master's, at least 2 semesters in residence; written/oral exam; dissertation; internship experience.

FIELDS OF STUDY.

COLLEGE OF BUSINESS AND PUBLIC ADMINISTRATION:
Accounting. M.Acc.
Business Administration. M.B.A.
Public Administration. M.P.A.

COLLEGE OF EDUCATION:
American History. M.A.T.
Art. M.A.T.
Biology. M.A.T.
Chemistry. M.A.T.
Community and Agency Counseling. M.S.Ed.
Counselor Education. Includes rehabilitation administration, rehabilitation counseling, rehabilitation placement. M.S.
Early Childhood Education. M.S. Ed.
Earth Science. M.A.T.
Educational Leadership. Includes elementary and secondary. M.S.Ed., Ed.S., Ed.D.
Effective Teaching, Learning, and Leadership. M.S.Ed.
Elementary Education. M.S.T.
English. M.A.T.
Foreign Language. M.A.T.
General Business. M.A.T.
Journalism. M.A.T.
Mathematics. M.A.T.
Physical Science. M.A.T.
Physics. M.A.T.
Rhetoric and Communication Studies/Theater. M.A.T.
School Counseling. Includes elementary, secondary. M.S.Ed.
Sociology. M.A.T.
Special Education. M.S.Ed
World History. M.A.T.

COLLEGE OF PHARMACY AND HEALTH SCIENCES:
Pharmacy. D. Pharm.

Law School
Web site: www.law.drake.edu

Founded 1865. ABA approved since 1923. AALS charter member. Private control. Semester system. Special facilities: Constitutional Law Center, Agricultural Law Center, Center for Legislative Practice. Special program at the University of Nantes, France. Library: 292,100 volumes, 3159 subscriptions.

Annual tuition: full-time $18,230, part-time $12,200. Limited on-campus housing available. Total average annual additional expense: $11,200.

Enrollment: first-year class 156, total full-time 387 (men 50%, women 50%). Faculty: full-time 20, part-time 11. Student to faculty ratio is 16.0 to 1. Degrees conferred: J.D., J.D.-M.B.A., J.D.-M.P.A., J.D.-M.A. (Mass Communication, Political Science—Iowa State University), J.D.-M.S. (Economics—Iowa State University), J.D.-M.S.W. (University of Iowa).

ADMISSION REQUIREMENTS. LSDAS Law School report, bachelor's degree, transcripts, letters of recommendation, LSAT, writing sample required in support of application. Interview not required. Accepts transfer applicants. Graduates of unaccredited colleges not considered. Apply to Admissions Director after September 1, before April 1 (Fall admission). Fall and Summer admission (Conditional Admission programs only), Application fee

$40. Phone: (800)44-DRAKE, ext. 2782, (515)271-2782; e-mail: lawadmit@drake.edu.

ADMISSION STANDARDS. Selective. Mean LSAT: 152; mean GPA: 3.27 (A = 4). Gourman rating: 3.35. *U.S. News & World Report* ranking is in the third tier of all U.S. law schools. Accepts 70% of total annual applicants.

FINANCIAL AID. Scholarships, merit awards, fellowships, Federal W/S, loans. Apply by March 1 to Director, Financial Aid Office. Use FAFSA (School code: 001860). About 46% of students receive aid other than loans from School funds.

DEGREE REQUIREMENTS. For J.D.: 90 hours minimum, at least three semesters in residence.

DREW UNIVERSITY
Madison, New Jersey 07940-1493
Web site: www.drew.edu

Founded 1867. CGS member. Located 25 miles W of New York City. Coed. Private control. Semester system. Special facilities: Center for Holocaust Studies, United Methodist Archive and History Center. Library: about 500,00 volumes, 800 subscriptions; depository for both Federal government and New Jersey documents. Total University enrollment: 2400.

Annual tuition: full-time $23,238; per credit $688, reduced rates for senior citizens. Limited on-campus housing for single and married students. Average academic year housing cost: $4000–$10,000 (including board). Apply by July 1 to University Housing Office. Phone: (973)408-3037. Day-care facilities available.

Caspersen School of Graduate Studies

Graduate study 1912. Enrollment: full-time 282, part-time 270 (men 46%, women 54%). Graduate faculty: full- and part-time 117. Degrees conferred: M.A., C.M.H., M.M.H., M.Litt., Ph.D.

ADMISSION REQUIREMENTS. Transcripts, GRE (for U.S. and Canadian citizens), three letters of reference, writing sample required in support of School's application. TOEFL, TWE required for international applicants. Interview encouraged. Accepts transfer applicants. Graduates of Unaccredited Institutions not considered. Apply to Office of Graduate Admissions by February 1 (M.A., Ph.D. candidates). For Spring application deadline contact Admissions Office. Application fee $35. Phone: (973)408-3110; fax: (973)408-3242; e-mail: gradm@drew.edu.

ADMISSION STANDARDS. Selective. Usual minimum average: 3.3 (A = 4).

FINANCIAL AID. Scholarships, fellowships, merit awards, Federal W/S, loans. Apply to the Financial Aid Office by February 15. Phone: (973)408-3112; fax: (973)408-3188. Use FAFSA. About 70% of students receive aid other than loans from University and outside sources. Aid available for part-time students.

DEGREE REQUIREMENTS. For master's: one year minimum in residence; reading knowledge of French or German or substitute; thesis. For Ph.D.: three years in full-time residence beyond the bachelor's; reading knowledge of French and German or substitute for one; final comprehensive; dissertation.

FIELDS OF STUDY.
Arts and Letters. Interdisciplinary. M.Litt., D. Litt.
Biblical Studies and Early Christianity. M.A., Ph.D.
English Literature. Includes British and American. M.A., Ph.D.

Liturgical Studies. M.A., Ph.D.
Medical Humanities. C.M.H., M.M.H., D.M.H.
Modern History and Literature. M.A., Ph.D.
Religion and Society. Includes Christian social ethics; sociology and anthropology of religion; psychology and religion. M.A., Ph.D.
Theological and Religious Studies. Includes philosophic, theology, historical, theology and church history, theological studies, Methodist and Wesley studies, American religious studies, contemporary theology. M.A., Ph.D.
Wesleyan and Methodist Studies. M.A., Ph.D.
Women's Studies. M.A., Ph.D.

DREXEL UNIVERSITY
Philadelphia, Pennsylvania 19104-2875
Web site: www.drexel.edu

Founded 1891. CGS member. Coed. Private control. Quarter system. Special facilities: Art Museum, Center for Applied Neurogerontology, Image Processing Center, Bioelectrode Research Laboratory, Center for Multidisciplinary Study and Research, Biomedical Engineering and Science Institute, Environmental Studies Institute, Survey Research Center. Library: 450,000 volumes, 7000 subscriptions. More than 6500 computers on campus for student use. Total University enrollment: 13,000.

No on-campus housing available. For off-campus information contact Dean of Students Office. Average academic year expenses: $13,500. Phone: (215)895-3507.

College of Arts and Sciences

Tuition: per credit $667 (sciences), $583 (humanities). Enrollment: full-time 67, part-time 241 (men 54%, women 46%). College faculty: full-time 58, part-time 89. Degrees conferred: M.S., Ph.D.

ADMISSION REQUIREMENTS. Transcripts, at least two letters of recommendation required in support of application. On-line application available. GRE General/Subject Test suggested for some departments. TOEFL (score must be two years old or less) required for international applicants. Accepts transfer applicants. Graduates of unaccredited institutions not considered. Apply to University Office of Admissions, Box P by August 20 (Fall), November 2 (Winter), March 1 (Spring), May 31 (Summer); International students June 20 (Fall), September 25 (Winter), January 3 (Spring), March 31 (Summer). Application fee $35. Phone: (215)895-6700; fax: (215)895-5939; e-mail: enroll@drexel.edu.

ADMISSIONS STANDARDS. Selective for most departments. Usual minimum average: 3.0 (A = 4) for last two years, 2.75 (A = 4) may be admitted on a probationary basis, departmental approval required.

FINANCIAL AID. Annual awards from institutional funds, research assistantships, teaching assistantships, research fellowships, tuition waivers, Federal W/S, loans. USE FAFSA. Phone: (215)895-1021. Apply to appropriate department chair by February 1. About 50% of full-time students receive aid from University and outside sources. Aid available for part-time students.

DEGREE REQUIREMENTS. For M.S.: 45 quarter credits minimum, at least 30 in residence; comprehensive exam. For Ph.D.: three-year minimum beyond the bachelor's, at least one year in full-time residence; preliminary exam; advancement to candidacy; dissertation; final oral exam.

FIELDS OF STUDY.
Bioscience and Biotechnology. M.S., Ph.D.
Chemistry. M.S., Ph.D.
Clinical Psychology. Ph.D.

Computer Science. M.S. only.
Education. M.S.
Food Science and Nutrition. M.S., Ph.D.
Human Nutrition. M.S. only.
Mathematics. Ph.D.
Neuropsychology. M.S. only.
Physics and Atmospheric Science. M.S., Ph.D.
Publication Management. M.S.
Science of Instruction. M.S. only.
Technical and Science Communication. M.S.

Bennett S. Lebow College of Business
Web site: www.lebow.drexel.edu

Private control. Accredited programs: M.B.A., Accounting; recognized Ph.D. Quarter system.

Tuition: $583 per credit. Estimated annual budget for room and board and personal expenses: approximately $12,500.

Enrollment: total full-time 294, part-time 483 (men 65%, women 35%). Faculty: 85 full-time, 23 part-time; 85% with Ph.D./D.B.A. Degrees conferred: M.B.A. (full-time, part-time, day, evening), M.S.Acc., M.S.D.S. (Decision Sciences), M.S.F. (Finance), M.S.M. (Marketing), M.S.T. (Taxation), Ph.D.

ADMISSION REQUIREMENTS. All applicants should have a bachelor's degree from a recognized institution of higher education, a strong mathematics background and a 3.0 (A = 4) GPA. Submit Application, GMAT (will accept GMAT test results from the last five years, latest acceptable date is June), two official transcripts from each undergraduate/graduate school attended, two letters of recommendation, essays, résumé (prefers at least four years of work experience), and an application fee of $35 to the Graduate Admissions Office of the College of Business. In addition, international students (whose native language is other than English) should submit TOEFL (scores not older than two years, minimum score 570), certified translations and evaluations of all official transcripts, recommendation should be in English or with certified translations, proof of health/immunization certificate, and proof of sufficient financial resources for two years of academic study. Beginning students are admitted Fall, Winter, Spring, Summer. U.S. citizens apply by August 1 (Fall), December 1 (Winter), March 1 (Spring), May 1 (Summer), international students apply by June 15 (Fall), September 20 (Winter), January 1 (Spring), June 1 (Summer). On-campus visits are encouraged. Admissions Office phone: (215) 895-6700; e-mail: enroll@drexel.edu.

ADMISSION REQUIREMENTS FOR DOCTORAL CANDIDATES. University has adopted an alternate year approach to doctoral study and will admit doctoral candidates in odd-number years only. Contact Doctoral Programs in Business for application material and information; phone: (215)895-2131; fax: (215) 895-1745. For serious consideration an applicant should have at least a 3.0 (A = 4) UGPA and a 3.3 (A = 4) Graduate GPA. Beginning students are admitted Fall Only. Both U.S. citizens and international applicants should apply by February 1 (Fall). Submit application, GMAT/GRE (will accept GMAT/GRE test results from the last five years), official transcripts from each undergraduate/graduate schools attended, two letters of recommendation, personal statement, résumé, statement of purpose, and application fee of $35 to the Office of Graduate Admission. In addition, international students (whose native language is other than English) should submit a TOEFL (score not older than two years, minimum score 600) report; certified translations and evaluations of all official transcripts, recommendation should be in English or with certified translations, proof of health/immunization certificate. Graduate Admissions Office phone: (215)895-6704; Doctoral Programs office phone: (215)895-1745.

ADMISSION STANDARDS. Selective. Mean GMAT: 535; mean GPA: 3.4 (A = 4). Accepts about 37% of total annual applicant pool.

FINANCIAL AID. State grants, fellowships, graduate assistantships, Federal W/S, loans. Request fellowship and assistantships information from the College of Business. Financial Aid applications should be completed by March 1. Contact the University's Financial Aid Office for current need-based financial aid information; phone: (215)895-2537. For most financial assistance and all Federal programs submit FAFSA (College code: 003256), also submit Financial Aid Transcript, Federal Income Tax forms. Approximately 20% of students receive some form of financial assistance. Aid available for part-time study.

DEGREE REQUIREMENTS. For M.B.A.: 84 quarter hour program including 12 elective hours, two-year program; degree program must be completed in seven years. For M.S.Acc., M.S.F., M.S.D.S., M.S.M., M.S.T.: 48 quarter hour program. For Ph.D.: 57 quarter hours beyond masters, at least three consecutive terms in full-time study, generally a three- to five-year program; comprehensive exam in major and minor field; written and oral candidacy exam, Core exams, Specialization exams; dissertation proposal and oral defense; dissertation; oral defense.

FIELDS OF STUDY.
Accounting. M.S.Acc., Ph.D.
Business Administration. Ph.D.
Decision Sciences. M.S.D.S., Ph.D.
Economics. M.B.A., Ph.D.
Finance. M.S.F., Ph.D.
Legal Studies. M.B.A.
Management. M.B.A.
Marketing. M.S.M., Ph.D.
Organizational Sciences. Ph.D.
Quantitative Methods. M.S.
Statistics. Ph.D.
Strategic Management. Ph.D.
Taxation. M.S.T.

College of Engineering

Tuition: per credit $667. Enrollment: full-time 300, part-time 644 (men 80%, women 20%). Faculty: full-time 100, part-time 20. Degrees conferred: M.S., Ph.D.

ADMISSION REQUIREMENTS. Transcripts, two letters of recommendation required in support of College's application. GRE strongly recommended for applicants requesting assistantships. TOEFL (scores must be two years old or less) required for international applicants. Accepts transfer applicants. Graduates of unaccredited institutions not considered. Apply to University Office of Admissions by August 20 (Fall), November 2 (Winter), March 1 (Spring), May 30 (Summer); international students June 20 (Fall), September 25 (Winter), January 3 (Spring), March 31 (Summer). Application fee $35. Phone: (215)895-6700; fax: (215)895-5939; e-mail: enroll@drexel.edu.

ADMISSION STANDARDS. Selective for most departments. Usual minimum average: 3.0 (A = 4) for last two years; 2.75 may be admitted on a probationary basis; departmental approval required.

FINANCIAL AID. Annual awards from institutional funds: research assistantships, teaching assistantships, fellowships, tuition waivers, Federal W/S, loans. Approved for VA benefits. Apply by February 1 to appropriate department chair for fellowships, assistantship; to Financial Aid Office for all other programs. Phone: (215)895-2964. About 50% of full-time students receive aid from University and outside sources. Aid available for part-time students.

DEGREE REQUIREMENTS. For M.S.: 45 credit hours minimum, at least 30 in residence; comprehensive exam. For Ph.D.:

90 credits, three-year minimum beyond the bachelor's, at least one year in residence (requirement varies by Department); qualifying exam; candidacy; dissertation; final oral exam.

FIELDS OF STUDY.
Biochemical Engineering.
Biomedical Engineering and Sciences. Multidisciplinary.
Chemical Engineering.
Civil Engineering.
Computer Engineering.
Electrical Engineering.
Engineering Geology. M.S. only.
Engineering Management. M.S. only.
Materials Engineering.
Mechanical Engineering.
Software Engineering.
Telecommunications Engineering.

College of Information Science and Technology

Founded 1892. Tuition: per credit $515. Enrollment: full-time 81, part-time 480. Faculty: full-time 27, part-time 25. Degrees conferred: M.S., M.S.I.S., Ph.D.

ADMISSION REQUIREMENTS. Official transcripts, GRE required in support of College's application. TOEFL (scores must be two years old or less) required for international applicants. Interview not required. Accepts transfer applicants. Graduates of unaccredited institutions not considered. Apply to Office of Graduate Admissions of the College at least one month prior to registration. Application fee $35. Phone: (215)895-6700; fax: (215)895-5939; e-mail: enroll@drexel.edu.

ADMISSION STANDARDS. Competitive. Usual minimum average: 3.0 (A = 4).

FINANCIAL AID. Annual awards from institutional funds: scholarships, research/teaching assistantships, Federal W/S, loans. Apply by February 1 to Office of the Dean for assistantships; to Financial Aid Office for all other programs. Phone: (215)895-2474. Use FAFSA. About 20% of students receive aid other than loans from School and outside sources. Aid available for part-time students.

DEGREE REQUIREMENTS. For M.S., M.S.I.S.; 60 quarter hours minimum, at least 30 in residence. For Ph.D.: one year, full-time residence; approved plan of study; dissertation; final oral exam.

FIELDS OF STUDY.
Information Studies. Ph.D. only.
Information Systems. M.S.I.S. only.
Library and Information Science. M.S. only.

College of Media Arts and Design

Graduate study since 1952. Tuition: per credit $583. Enrollment: full-time 72, part-time 90. Graduate faculty: full-time 35, part-time 90. Degrees conferred: M.S., M.Arch.

ADMISSION REQUIREMENTS. Transcripts, two letters of recommendation required in support of application. TOEFL (scores must be no more than two years old) required for international applicants. Interview recommended. Accepts transfer applicants and a limited number of nonmatriculants. Graduates of unaccredited institutions not considered. Apply to Dean of Graduate Admissions. Application fee $25. Phone: (215)895-6700; fax: (215)895-5939.

ADMISSION STANDARDS. Very selective. Usual minimum average: 3.0 (A = 4).

FINANCIAL AID. Research assistantships, teaching assistantships, Federal W/S, loans. graduate assistantships for second-year students. Apply by February 1 to Office of the Dean for assistantships; to Financial Aid Office for all other programs; no specified closing date. Phone: (215)895-2474. Use FAFSA.

DEGREE REQUIREMENTS. For M.S.: 45 quarter credits minimum, at least 30 in residence; major comprehensive project. For M.Arch.: 48 credits, two- to three-year evening program.

FIELDS OF STUDY.
Architecture. M.Arch.
Arts Administration. M.S.
Fashion Design.
Interior Design.

School of Biomedical Engineering, Science, and Health Systems

Founded 1961 as the Biomedical Engineering Institute. Tuition: per credit $667. Enrollment: full-time 21, part-time 52 (men 70%, women 30%). Faculty: full-time 17, part-time 45. Degrees conferred; M.S., Ph.D.

ADMISSION REQUIREMENTS. Transcripts, two letters of recommendation required in support of School's application. GRE required for applicants requesting assistantships. TOEFL (minimum score 550) required for international applicants. Accepts transfer applicants. Graduates of unaccredited institutions not considered. Apply to University Office of Admissions by August 15 (Fall), November 15 (Winter), February 15 (Spring), May 15 (Summer); international students June 15 (Fall), September 15 (Winter), December 15 (Spring), March 15 (Summer). Application fee $35. Phone: (215) 895-6700, fax (215) 895-5939; e-mail: enroll@drexel.edu.

ADMISSION STANDARDS. Selective for most departments. Usual minimum average: 3.0 (A = 4) for last two years; applicants with 2.75 may be admitted on a nonmatriculated basis; departmental approval required.

FINANCIAL AID. Annual awards from institutional funds: research assistantships, teaching assistantships, fellowships, tuition waivers, Federal W/S, loans. Career Integrated Education is available. Approved for VA benefits. Apply by February 28 to appropriate department chair for fellowships, assistantship; to Financial Aid Office for all other programs. Phone: (215) 895-2964. Use FAFSA. About 50% of full-time students receive aid from University and outside sources. Aid available for part-time students.

DEGREE REQUIREMENTS. For M.S.: 45 credit hours minimum, at least 30 in residence; comprehensive exam. For Ph.D.: 90 credit minimum, three-year program beyond the bachelor's, at least one year in full-time residence (requirement varies by Department); qualifying exam; candidacy exam; dissertation; oral defense.

FIELDS OF STUDY
Biochemical Engineering. Includes biomedical/imaging, biomechanics and biomaterials, clinical and rehabilitative engineering, human factors and performance engineering, neuroengineering. M.S., Ph.D.
Biomedical Science. Includes biostatictics, genome science, systems biology. M.S., Ph.D.
Health Care Management, Technology, and Information Systems. Nonthesis program.

School of Environmental Science Engineering and Policy

Formed in 1963 as the Environmental Studies Institute. Tuition: per credit $667 Enrollment: full- and part-time 100 (men

50%, women 50%). Faculty: full-time 12, part-time 7. Degrees conferred: M.S.E.E., M.S.E.S., M.S.E.P., Ph.D.

ADMISSION REQUIREMENTS. Transcripts, engineering or science degree, two letters of recommendation required in support of School's application. GRE required for applicants requesting assistantships. TOEFL (minimum score 550) required for international applicants. Accepts transfer applicants. Graduates of unaccredited institutions not considered. Apply to University Office of Admissions by August 15 (Fall), November 15 (Winter), February 15 (Spring), May 15 (Summer); international students June 15 (Fall), September 15 (Winter), December 15 (Spring), March 15 (Summer). Application fee $35. Phone: (215)895-6700; fax (215)895-5939; e-mail: enroll@drexel.edu.

ADMISSION STANDARDS. Selective. Usual minimum average: 3.0 (A = 4) for last two years; applicants with a 2.75 may be admitted on a nonmatriculated basis; departmental approval required.

FINANCIAL AID. Annual awards from institutional funds: research assistantships, teaching assistantships, fellowships, tuition waivers, Federal W/S, loans. Career Integrated Education is available. Approved for VA benefits. Apply by February 28 to appropriate department chair for fellowships, assistantship; to Financial Aid Office for all other programs. Phone: (215)895-2964. Use FAFSA. About 50% of full-time students receive aid from University and outside sources. Aid available for part-time students.

DEGREE REQUIREMENTS. For M.S.: 45–48 credit hours minimum, at least 30 in residence; thesis/nonthesis option. For Ph.D.: 90 credit minimum, three-year program beyond the bachelor's, at least one year in full-time residence (requirement varies by department); qualifying exam; candidacy exam; dissertation; oral defense.

FIELDS OF STUDY
Environmental Engineering. Includes air pollution, hazardous and solid waste, subsurface contaminant hydrology, water resources, water and wastewater treatment. M.S.E.E.
Environmental Policy. M.S.E.P.
Environmental Science. Includes air pollution, ecology, environmental assessment, environmental biotechnology, environmental chemistry, environmental health, hazardous and solid waste, subsurface contaminant hydrology, water and wastewater treatment, water resources. M.S.E.S.

DREXEL UNIVERSITY HEALTH SCIENCES

Established 2002. Located at the Hahneman Center City campus. On-campus housing available. Housing costs $500–$800 per month.

College of Nursing and Health Professions
Web site: cnhp.drexel.edu

Established 2002. Tuition: $20,200, Nursing $18,675.
Enrollment full- and part-time 1425. Faculty: full- and part-time more than 450. Degrees conferred M.F.T., M.H.S., M.S., M.S.N., D.P.T., Ph.D., J.D.-Ph.D. (Psychology).

ADMISSION REQUIREMENTS. Official transcripts, three letters of recommendation required in support of application. GRE/ MAT, interview, essays, résumés required for some programs. On-line application available. TOEFL (minimum score 550) required for international applicants. Accepts transfer applicants in some programs. Admits Fall only. Apply to the Office of Enrollment Services by December 1 (Physician Assistant entry-level),

December 15 (D.P.T. entry-level), January 15 (Clinical Psychology—Ph.D.), February 1 (Couple and Family Therapy), February 15 (Clinical Psychology—M.A., M.S., J.D.-Ph.D.), March 15 (Rehabilitation Sciences), April 1 (Family Therapy), June 1 (Art Therapy, Dance Therapy), July 1 (Music Therapy), 16–24 months in advance of January start date (M.S.N. in Anesthesia). Phone: (800)2-DREXEL, ext. 6333.

ADMISSION STANDARDS. Selective. Usual minimum average: 2.75 (A = 4).

FINANCIAL AID. Scholarships, fellowships, research/teaching assistantships, internships, traineeships, grants. Federal W/S, loans. Apply to Office of University Student Financial Affairs by January 1 for assistantships, fellowships; March 1 for all other programs. Phone: (215)762-7739; fax (215)762-4261. Use FAFSA (School code: 003271). About 40% of students receive some financial assistance from school; about 95% of doctoral students receive aid from School.

DEGREE REQUIREMENTS For M.F.T., M.S.: usually a two-year full-time program; supervised practica/internships. For M.H.S.: 119 semester hour, 27-month program; graduate project. For M.S.N.: 39–48 credit program, practicum/clinical practicum. For M.S.N. in Anesthesia program: 27-month, 66-credit full-time program; clinical practicum. For D.P.T. three-year full-time, 8 academic semester program; research project.

FIELDS OF STUDY.
Advanced Physician Assistant Studies. M.H.S.
Art Therapy. M.S.
Couple and Family Therapy. Ph.D.
Dance/Movement Therapy. M.S.
Emergency and Public Safety. M.S.
Entry-Level Physician Assistant Studies. M.H.S.
Family Therapy. M.F.T.
Hand and Upper Quarter Rehabilitation. M.H.S.
Music Therapy. MS.
Nurse Anesthesia. M.S.N.
Nurse Education. M.S.N.
Nursing. Includes M.S.N. in public health nursing, M.S.N. in clinical trials research, M.S.N. in nurse practitioner, M.S.N. completion—women's health. M.S.N.
Physical Therapy (Entry-Level Doctoral Program). D.P.T.
Physical Therapy (Post-Professional Doctoral Program). D.P.T.

College of Medicine
Web site: www.drexel.edu/med

Medical College of Pennsylvania founded 1850, Hanemann University School of Medicine founded 1948; merged with Drexel University and name was changed 2002. Coed. Private control. Semester system.
Annual tuition: $30,305, student fees $910. Total average cost for all other expenses: approximately $13,500. Enrollment first-year class 250 (EDP 15), total full-time 850 (men 60%, women 40%). Faculty: full-time, part-time and volunteers: approximately 4000. Degrees conferred: M.D., M.D.-M.B.A., M.D.-M.P.H., M.D.-Ph.D.

ADMISSION REQUIREMENTS. AMCAS report, transcripts, MCAT required in support of application. Supplemental application will be sent 4–6 weeks after applying to AMCAS. Interviews are by invitation. Will consider transfer applicants on a space-available basis. Has EDP: apply between June 1 and August 1. The combined degree programs require acceptance to both the College of Medicine and the respective University program. Apply to AMCAS by December 1; to M.D.-Ph.D. by November 15. Application fee $75. Phone: (215)762-8288.

ADMISSION STANDARDS. Very selective. Accepts about 5% of total applicants. Approximately 50% are state residents. Mean MCAT: 9.6; mean GPA: 3.44 (A = 4). Gourman rating: 3.39.

FINANCIAL AID Merit scholarships, fellowships, Federal W/S, loans. Apply to the Office of Student Financial Affairs after acceptance, before May 31. Phone: (215)991-8210. Use PHEAA and FAFSA. About 85% of students receive aid from School.

DEGREE REQUIREMENTS. For M.D.: satisfactory completion of four-year program. Accelerated M.D. available. All students must pass USMLE Step 1 prior to entering third year and must pass USMLE Step 2 prior to awarding of M.D.

FIELDS OF GRADUATE STUDY.
Biochemistry.
Microbiology and Immunology.
Molecular and Cell Biology and Genetics.
Molecular Pathobiology.
Neurosciences.
Pharmacology and Physiology.
Radiation Sciences.

Biomedical Graduate Studies

Annual tuition $13,000, per credit $802; Certificate programs $10,000–$17,876. Enrollment in degree programs: full-time 75, part-time 90, total 245. Faculty: 75, part-time 25. Degrees conferred: M.S., Ph.D., M.D.-Ph.D, Certificates.

ADMISSION REQUIREMENTS. Official transcripts, GRE, three letters of recommendation, personal statement of research interest required in support of application. VCAT can be used in lieu of GRE for Certificate programs; MCAT can be used in lieu of GRE. On-line application available. Interviews required for some programs. TOEFL required for international applicants. Accepts transfer applicants. Graduates of unaccredited institutions not considered. Apply by November 15 (M.D.-Ph.D.), July 1–July 15 (Certificate programs) to Office of Enrollment Services. Phone: (866)-6BIOMED. Application fee $50.

ADMISSIONS STANDARDS. Selective. Usual minimum average 3.0 (A = 4).

FINANCIAL AID. Scholarships, stipends, research/teaching assistantships, Federal W/S, loans. Apply to the Biomedical Graduate Studies Office for scholarships, assistantships, to the Office of Student Financial Services for all other programs. Phone: (215)762-7739. Use FAFSA. About 70% of students receive some form of financial assistance.

DEGREE REQUIREMENTS. For M.S.: 39–48 credit programs, comprehensive exam, thesis/nonthesis option. For Ph.D.: 60 semester hours program; preliminary exam after one year; qualifying exam; dissertation; final oral defense. For Certificates: generally two semesters in full-time study.

FIELDS OF STUDY.
Biological Sciences. Certificate.
Biochemistry. Ph.D.
Laboratory Animal Science. Certificate.
Medical Sciences. M.S., Certificate
Microbiology and Immunology. M.S., Ph.D
Molecular and Cell Biology and Genetics. M.S., Ph.D
Molecular Pathobiology, Ph.D.
Pharmacology and Physiology. Ph.D.
Radiation Studies. M.S., Ph.D.
Veterinary Medical Sciences. Certificate.

School of Public Health

Established 1996. Semester system. Annual tuition: $20,470, Enrollment: full- and part-time 75 (men 25%, women 75%). Fac-

ulty: full- and part-time 21. Degrees conferred, M.P.H., M.D.-M.P.H.

ADMISSION REQUIREMENTS. Official transcripts, three letters of recommendation, interview required in support of application. Will accept GRE, MCAT, LSAT, GMAT. On-line application available. TOEFL (minimum score 550) required for international applicants. Admits Fall only. Apply by August 1 to the Office of Enrollment Management. Phone: (215)762-8785. Application fee $35.

ADMISSION STANDARDS. Selective. Usual minimum average: 2.75 (A = 4).

FINANCIAL AID. Scholarships, assistantships, traineeships, Federal W/S, loans. Apply by April 1 to the office of University Student Financial Affairs. Phone: (215)762-7739; fax: (215)762-4261. Use FAFSA (School code: 003271).

DEGREE REQUIREMENTS. For M.P.H.: satisfactory completion of 52-credit, four- to twelve-week interdisciplinary blocks; community-based master's project. For M.D.-M.P.H.: five-year program; the third year is spent in full-time study in the School of Public Health.

FIELDS OF STUDY.
Biostatistics.
Community Health and Prevention.
Environmental and Occupation Health.
Epidemiology.
Health Management and Policy.

DRURY UNIVERSITY
Springfield, Missouri 65802-3791
Web site: www.drury.edu

Founded 1873. Located 180 miles SE of Kansas City. Coed. Private control, United Church of Christ Congregational Church. Semester system. Library: 244,000 volumes, 800 subscriptions.

Tuition; M.B.A., per semester hour $210; M.Ed., per semester hour $204. On-campus housing for single students only. Average annual housing cost: single student $4000 (including board), married students $3500 (room only). During Summer terms (two 5-week terms): single person $295 per term. Apply to Dean of Students. Phone: (417)873-7215.

Graduate Program

Enrollment: 300, most are part-time. College faculty teaching graduate students: full-time 25, part-time 20. Degrees conferred: M.B.A., M.Ed.

ADMISSION REQUIREMENTS: Transcripts, MAT or GMAT (depending on major) required in support of application. On-line application available. TOEFL required for international applicants. Accepts transfer applicants. Graduates of unaccredited institutions not considered. Apply to Director of appropriate program well in advance of registration. Application fee $20. Phone: (417)873-7271; fax: (417)873-7269.

ADMISSION STANDARDS. Selective. Usual minimum average: 2.75 (A = 4).

FINANCIAL AID. Fellowships, teaching assistantships, Federal W/S, loans. Apply by May 15 to Director of appropriate program for fellowships, assistantships; to Financial Aid Office for federal programs. Phone: (417)873-7312. Use FAFSA.

DEGREE REQUIREMENTS. For M.Ed.: 36 semester hours for degree. For M.B.A.: 31 semester hours required, 25 in residence plus 24 hours of undergraduate prerequisite courses.

FIELDS OF STUDY.

Business Administration. Includes joint program with Thunderbird, the American Graduate School of International Management. M.B.A.

Communication. M.A.

Criminal Justice. M.S.C.J.

Criminology. M.A.C.

Education. Includes elementary, English, social science, science, middle school, gifted education. M.Ed.

UNIVERSITY OF DUBUQUE
Dubuque, Iowa 52001-5050
Web site: www.dbq.edu

Founded 1852. Located 185 miles W of Chicago. Coed. Private control. Affiliated with the Presbyterian Church (U.S.A.). Semester system. Library: 165,000 volumes, 700 subscriptions.

Tuition: per semester credit $355. On-campus housing available for single students, but limited for married students. Average academic year housing costs: single students $5300 (including board). Contact the Director of Housing for both on- and off-campus housing information. Phone: (563)589-3583.

Graduate Studies

Graduate study since 1964. Enrollment: full-time 192, part-time 120. College faculty teaching graduate students: full-time 21, part-time 12. Degrees conferred: M.A., M.A.R., M.B.A., M.Div., D.Min. (pastoral leadership, congregational revitalization).

ADMISSION REQUIREMENTS. Transcripts, two letters of recommendation, eligibility for School Certification (Education), GRE/MAT/GMAT required in support of application. TOEFL (minimum score 550) required for international applicants. Accepts transfer applicants. Apply to Graduate Studies at least one month prior to registration. Application fee $25. Phone: (563)589-3200, (800)722-5583.

ADMISSION STANDARDS. Selective. Usual minimum average: 2.5 (A = 4).

FINANCIAL AID. Limited to Federal W/S, loans, and area Professional Development Grants. Apply by May 1 to the Office of Financial Aid. Phone: (563)589-3170; e-mail: finaid@duq.edu. Use FAFSA.

DEGREE REQUIREMENTS. For masters's: 36–45 semester hours minimum, at least 30 in residence; thesis/nonthesis option. For M.Div.: three-year program of full-time study. For M.A.R.: two-year program of full-time study. For D.Min.: three- to five-year part-time weekend and summer program for full-time clerical workers.

FIELDS OF STUDY.

Business Administration M.B.A.

Communication. Includes information technology communication, leadership and management communication, strategic and corporate communication. M.A.C.

Divinity. M.Div., D.Min.

Religion. Includes specializations in biblical studies, history and theology, pastoral theology and counseling, rural ministry, spiritual foundation. M.A.R.

DUKE UNIVERSITY
Durham, North Carolina 27708-0065
Web site: www.duke.edu

Founded 1838. CGS and AAU member. Private control. Semester system. Special facilities: Animal Behavior Station, Asian-Pacific Institute, Botanical and Zoological Laboratories, Canadian Studies program, Center for Demographic Studies, Center for Documentary Studies, Center on East-West Trade Investments and Communications, Center for Emerging Cardiovascular Technologies, Center for Health Policy Research and Education, Center for International Development Research, Center for International Studies, Center for Mathematics and Computation in Life Sciences and Medicine, Center for the Study of Aging and Human Development, Center for Tropical Conservation, Center for Research on Women, Duke Forest with 7700 acres, Marine Laboratory, Morphometrics Laboratory, Oak Ridges National Laboratory, Organization for Tropical Studies, Phytotron, Primate Facilities, Program in Integrative Biology, Program in Latin-American Studies, Program in Political Economy, Program in Russian and East European Studies. The University's NIH ranking is 13th among all U.S. institutions with 610 awards/grants worth $232,179,874. Library: 5,000,000 volumes, 31,941 subscriptions. Total University enrollment: 13,060.

Annual tuition: full-time $22,230 (Ph.D. students); per unit $790 (master's students). On-campus apartments: 206 available for single students. Average cost per academic year of an on-campus single room $5150, board $4150. Contact Office of Housing Administration for both on- and off-campus housing information. Phone: (919)684-4304.

Graduate School

Enrollment: full-time 2185, part-time 100. Faculty: full-time 800, part-time 267. Degrees conferred: A.M., M.S., M.A.T., Ph.D.

ADMISSION REQUIREMENTS. Two copies of official transcript from each college, university, or seminary attended, three letters of recommendation, GRE required in support of School's application. On-line application available. GRE Subject Test required for some programs. International applicants must submit a TOEFL (minimum score 550, 213 on computer-based test) report and a financial statement. Accepts transfer applicants. Graduates of unaccredited colleges not considered. Apply to the Dean of the Graduate School by December 31 (Fall), November 1 (Spring). For Summer Session apply to the Dean of the Graduate School and to the Director of the Summer Session by April 15 (Summer Session I), May 15 (Summer Session II). Application fee $75. Phone: (919)684-3913; E-mail: grad-admission@duke.edu.

ADMISSION STANDARDS. Competitive for most departments, very competitive for the other. Usual minimum average: 3.0 (A = 4).

FINANCIAL AID. Annual awards: Scholarships, fellowships, teaching assistantships, traineeships, research assistantships, Federal W/S, loans. Apply to the Dean of the Graduate School for fellowships, assistantships. The application form for admission is also the application for financial aid, and should be completed by December 31. Use FAFSA. About 80% of full-time students receive aid other than loans from University and outside sources.

DEGREE REQUIREMENTS. For A.M., M.S., M.A.T.: 30 credits minimum; thesis; final oral exam; nonthesis option in some departments. For Ph.D.: 60 credits minimum beyond the bachelor's, at least one year full-time in residence; language requirements vary by department; preliminary exam; dissertation; final oral exam.

FIELDS OF STUDY.

Art History. A.M., Ph.D.
Biochemical Engineering. M.S., Ph.D.
Biochemistry. Ph.D. only.
Biological Anthropology and Anatomy. Ph.D.
Biology. Ph.D.
Biomedical Engineering. Ph.D.
Botany. Ph.D.
Business Administration. Ph.D.
Cell Biology. Ph.D.
Chemistry. Ph.D.
Civil and Environmental Engineering. M.S., Ph.D.
Classical Studies. Ph.D.
Computer Science. Ph.D.
Cultural Anthropology. Ph.D.
East Asian Studies. A.M.
Earth and Ocean Sciences (Geology). M.S., Ph.D.
Ecology. Ph.D.
Economics. A.M., Ph.D.
Electrical and Computer Engineering. M.S., Ph.D.
English. Ph.D.
Environmental Engineering. A.M., M.S., Ph.D.
Genetics. Ph.D.
Germanic Studies. Ph.D.
History. Ph.D.
Humanities Program. A.M.
Immunology. Ph.D.
International Development Policy. A.M.
Liberal Studies. A.M.
Literature. Ph.D.
Mathematics. Ph.D.
Mechanical Engineering and Materials Science. M.S., Ph.D.
Microbiology. Ph.D.
Molecular Cancer Biology.
Music. A.M., Ph.D.
Neurobiology. Ph.D.
Pathology. Ph.D.
Pharmacology. Ph.D.
Philosophy. Ph.D.
Physics. Ph.D.
Political Science. A.M., Ph.D.
Psychology. Includes experimental, social and health science. Ph.D. only.
Public Policy Studies. A.M. only.
Religion. Ph.D.
Romance Studies. Ph.D.
Slavic Languages and Literatures. Ph.D.
Sociology. A.M., Ph.D.
Statistics and Decision Sciences. Ph.D.

Fuqua School of Business

Web site: www.fuqua.duke.edu

Established 1969. Accredited programs: M.B.A.; recognized Ph.D. Semester/term system. Library: 22,000 volumes, 1200 subscriptions. Special programs: foreign exchange programs (Australia, Belgium, Costa Rica, Denmark, France, Italy, the Netherlands, Norway, South Africa, Spain, Sweden, Switzerland, Thailand, United Kingdom). Special facilities: Management Communication Center, R. David Thomas Executive Conference Center, Thomas F. Keller Center for M.B.A. Education.

Annual tuition: M.B.A. full-time $29,600, M.B.A.—Cross-Continent $71,000, W.E.M.B.A. $14,040 per semester/term, G.E.M.B.A. $95,000 (total program includes laptop, printer, tuition, books, room and board).

Enrollment: total full-time 676 (men 60%, women 40%). Faculty: 64 full-time, 25 part-time; 75% with Ph.D./D.B.A. Degrees conferred: M.B.A., G.E.M.B.A. (Global Executive), W.E.M.B.A. (Weekend Executive), M.B.A.-J.D., M.B.A.-M.D., M.B.A.-M.F. (Forestry), M.B.A.-M.E.M. (Environmental Management), M.B.A.-M.P.P. (Public Policy), M.B.A.-M.S. (Engineering, Nursing), Ph.D.

ADMISSION REQUIREMENTS. All applicants should have a bachelor's degree from a recognized institution of higher education and a strong mathematics background. Students are required to have their own personal computer. Will accept institutional on-line application. Submit application, GMAT (will accept GMAT test results from the last five years, latest acceptable date is January), official transcripts from each undergraduate/graduate school attended, three letters of recommendation, two essays, résumé (prefers at least four years of work experience), and an application fee of $150 to the Admission Office. In addition, international students (whose native language is other than English) should submit a TOEFL (minimum score 600) report, certified translations and evaluations of all official transcripts, recommendation should be in English or with certified translations, proof of health/immunization certificate, and proof of sufficient financial resources for two years of academic study. On-campus interviews are strongly recommended prior to the admissions committee reviewing completed application. To arrange an interview call: (919)660-7704. Joint degree applicants must apply to and be accepted to both schools/programs, contact the admissions office for current information and specific admissions requirements. Beginning students are admitted Fall only. Both U.S. citizens and international applicants apply by April 1 (Fall, final deadline). Applications received and interview completed by November 15 will be notified by December 18; applications received and interview completed by December 18 will be notified by January 29; applications received and interview completed by February 6 will be notified by April 7; applications received and interview completed by March 19 will be notified by April 23; applications received and interview completed by April 16 will be notified by May 21. Admissions Office phone: (919)660-7805; G.E.M.B.A. and W.E.M.B.A. phone: (919)660-7804; e-mail: fuqua-wemba@mail.duke.edu.

ADMISSION REQUIREMENTS FOR DOCTORAL CANDIDATES. Contact Ph.D. Programs at (919)660-7862 for application material and information. Beginning students are admitted Fall Only. Both U.S. citizens and international applicants apply by February 1. Submit Graduate School application (on-line preferred), a GMAT/GRE (will accept GMAT/GRE test results from the last five years), official transcripts from each undergraduate/graduate school attended, three letters of recommendation, résumé, statement of purpose, and application fee of $75 to the Graduate School's Director of Admission, 127 Allen Building. In addition, international students (whose native language is other than English) should submit a TOEFL (minimum score 600) report; certified translations and evaluations of all official transcripts, recommendation should be in English or with certified translations, proof of health/immunization certificate. International student's contact: (919)660-7807. Interviews encouraged. Notification is generally completed by mid-April. Graduate School phone: (919)684-3913.

ADMISSION STANDARDS. For M.B.A.: median GMAT: 663; median GPA: 3.5 (A = 4). Gourman rating: the MBA was rated in the top 15, the score was 4.82; the E.M.B.A. was rated in the top 11, the score was 4.62. For Ph.D: average GPA range; 3.5–3.7; average GMAT range: 520–795. Gourman rated Ph.D. in the top 20, the score was 4.75. *U. S. News & World Report* ranked Fuqua (M.B.A.) in the top 10 of all U.S. business schools. *Business Week* listed Fuqua in the top 11 of all American business schools.

FINANCIAL AID. Scholarships, merit scholarship, school funded minority scholarships, full tuition grants, fellowship, graduate assistantships, Federal W/S, loans. Financial aid is available for part-time study and aid may be available for international students. Assistantships/fellowships may be available for joint degree candidates. Financial Aid applications and information are generally available at the on-campus visit/interview or after January 1; apply by February 1. Request scholarship, fellowship, assistantship information from the Fuqua School of Business. Contact the University's Financial Aid Office for current need-based financial aid information; phone: (919)660-7934; fax: (919)681-6243. Use FAFSA (School code: E00160), also submit Financial Aid Transcript, Federal Income Tax forms. Approximately 65% of current students receive some form of financial assistance.

DEGREE REQUIREMENTS. For M.B.A.: at least 79 units including 39 elective term credits, two-year program; degree program must be completed in two years. For M.B.A. Cross-Continent: 20-month program. For G.E.M.B.A.: 19-month program. For W.E.M.B.A.: 20-month program. For M.B.A.-Master's: generally a two-and-one-half- to three-and-one-half-year programs. For M.B.A.-J.D.: four-and-one-half- to five-and-one-half-year program. For M.B.A.-M.D.: five-and-one-half- to six-and-one-half-year program. For Ph.D.: four- to five-year program; comprehensive exam; candidacy, dissertation proposal and oral defense; dissertation; oral defense.

FIELDS OF DOCTORAL STUDY (Through the Graduate School).
Accounting.
Decision Sciences.
Finance.
Management.
Marketing.
Operations Management.

Divinity School

Founded 1926. Annual tuition: full-time $11,250; per course $1125. Enrollment: full-time 243, part-time 69. Faculty: full-time 32, part-time 73. Degrees conferred: M.Div., M.C.M., M.T.S., Th.M.

ADMISSION REQUIREMENTS. Transcripts, five letters of recommendations, required in support of School's application. TOEFL, TSE required for international applicants. Interview not required. Accepts transfer applicants. Apply to Director of Admissions by April 1 (Fall), February 1 (Fall M.T.S.), December 1 (January). Application fee $25. Phone: (919)660-3436; fax: (919)660-3535; e-mail: divinity.info@duke.edu.

ADMISSION STANDARDS. Selective. Usual minimum average: 2.7 (A = 4); for M.T.S.: 3.0; for Th.M.: 3.25.

FINANCIAL AID. Tuition grants, field education grants, scholarships, Federal W/S, loans. Apply to Financial Aid Office by May 1. Phone: (919)660-3442; fax: (919)660-3473. Use FAFSA. No aid for nondegree candidates.

DEGREE REQUIREMENTS. For M.Div.: 24 course units plus 2 field education credits. For M.C.M.: 16 course units plus 1 field education credit. For M.T.S.: 16 course units with a 2.5 GPA average. For Th.M.: 8 course units with a B average.

Nicholas School of the Environmental

P.O. Box 90330
Web site: www.env.duke.edu

Graduate study since 1938. School moved into a new Research Center (Levine Science Research Center) in 1994. Annual tuition: $21,300; per credit $890. Graduate enrollment: full-time 218, part-time 2 (men 48%, women 52%). Faculty: full-time 60 (includes Durham at Marine Laboratory), part-time 12. Degrees conferred: M.F., M.E.M., M.S., A.M., Ph.D. through the Graduate School.

ADMISSION REQUIREMENTS. Transcripts, three letters of recommendation, GRE General Test required in support of School's application. TOEFL required for international applicants. Interview not required. Graduates of unaccredited institutions not considered. Apply to Office of Enrollment Services by December 31 for M.S., A.M., Ph.D.; February 15 for M.F., M.E.M. Application fee $75. Phone: (919)613-8070; fax: (919)684-8741; e-mail: envadm@duke.edu.

ADMISSION STANDARDS. Average of all accepted applicants: 3.4 (A = 4), 650 score on each section of GRE.

FINANCIAL AID. Scholarships, fellowships, assistantship, Federal W/S, loans. Apply by February 1 to Office of Enrollment Services. Phone: (919)613-8070. Use FAFSA.

DEGREE REQUIREMENTS. For M.F., M.E.M.: 48 semester credits (with a possible exception for professionals in the field), at least four semesters in residence; master's project. For A.M., M.S., Ph.D.: see Graduate School listing above.

FIELDS OF STUDY.
Coastal Environmental Management. M.E.M.
Environmental Law. M.F./M.E.M.-J.D., A.M.-J.D.
Environmental Management and Business. M.F./M.E.M.-M.B.A.
Environmental Management and Public Policy. M.F./M.E.M.-M.P.P.
Environmental Toxicology, Chemistry and Risk Assessment. M.E.M.
Forest Resource Management. M.E.M., M.F.
Ocean Sciences. M.S., Ph.D.
Resource Ecology. M.E.M., M.F.
Resource Economics and Policy. M.E.M.
Water and Air Resources. M.E.M.

School of Law (Box 90393)
Web site: www.law.duke.edu

Founded 1904. ABA approved since 1931. AALS member. Semester system. Special facilities: Private Adjudication Center, Center on Law, Ethics, and National Security. Law library: 550,000 volumes, 6658 subscriptions. Annual tuition: $28,147. Total average cost for all other expenses: $12,580. On-campus housing available.

Enrollment: first-year class 200. Total full-time 648 (men 50%, women 50%). Faculty: full-time 33, part-time 30. Student to faculty ratio 16.1 to 1. Degrees conferred: J.D., J.D.-LL.M. (International and Comparative Law), LL.M., S.J.D., M.L.S.

ADMISSION REQUIREMENTS. LSDAS Law School report, bachelor's degree, transcripts, LSAT (no later than December), two recommendations required in support of application. Interview not required. Transfer applicants considered. Graduates of unaccredited colleges not considered. Applications should be completed by January 1. Fall admission only. Application fee $65. Phone: (919)613-7200; fax: (919)613-7257.

ADMISSION STANDARDS. Selective. Mean LSAT: 164; mean GPA: 3.54 (A = 4). Gourman rating: 4.85. *U.S. News & World Report* ranking is in top 12 of all law schools. Accepts about 20–25% of total annual applicants.

FINANCIAL AID. Scholarships, Federal W/S, loans. Submit financial aid application with admission application. Use FAFSA. About 30% of students receive aid other than loans from School, 50% from all sources. A loan forgiveness plan is available.

DEGREE REQUIREMENTS. For J.D.: 84 semester hours minimum, at least four semesters in residence. For LL.M., S.J.D., M.L.S.: programs arranged on an individual basis. School offers joint master's programs in Business Administration, Divinity,

Economics, English, Environmental Management, Mechanical Engineering, Policy Science, Medicine and Health Administration, Public Policy, Ph.D. in Political Science. Additional summer prior to beginning the law program is generally required for joint degree programs.

School of Medicine (27710)

Web site: www.dukemed.duke.edu

Established 1930. Located at Durham. Library 239,000 volumes. Annual tuition: $28,566; student fees $3377. Total average figure for all other expenses $9000.

Enrollment: first-year class 104; total full-time 434 (men 55%, women 45%). Faculty: full-time 551, part-time 1. Degrees conferred: M.D., M.D.-J.D., M.D.-M.A., M.D.-Ph.D. [Medical Scientist Training Program], M.D.-M.P.H., M.D.-M.P.P., M.D.-M.B.A.

ADMISSION REQUIREMENTS. AMCAS report, transcripts, MCAT, interview required in support of application. Applicants must have completed at least three years of college study. Interviews are by invitation only. Graduates of unaccredited colleges not considered. Special consideration given to North Carolina residents. Does not have EDP. Apply to Committee on Admissions after June 1, before November 1. Application fee $75. Phone: (877)684-2985; fax: (919)684-8893.

ADMISSION STANDARDS. Very competitive. Mean MCAT: 11.3; median GPA: 3.60 (A = 4). Gourman rating: 4.78. *U.S. News & World Report* ranking is in the top five of all U.S. medical schools. Accepts about 4% of total annual applicants. Approximately 10% are state residents.

FINANCIAL AID. Scholarships, loans, summer research fellowships. Apply to Coordinator, Financial Aid after acceptance, before April 1. Use FAFSA. About 80% of students receive some aid from School.

DEGREE REQUIREMENTS. For M.D.: satisfactory completion of four-year program. For all joint degree programs: there is usually an additional year needed to complete both degrees.

FIELDS OF GRADUATE STUDY.
Anatomy.
Biochemistry.
Biomedical Engineering.
Cell Biology.
Genetics.
Immunology.
Medical History.
Microbiology.
Molecular Biology.
Neurosciences.
Pathology.
Pharmacology.
Physiology.

School of Nursing

Web site: www.nursing.duke.edu

Founded 1931. Tuition: per credit $646. Graduate enrollment: full-time 77, part-time 85. Faculty: full-time 20, part-time 6. Degree conferred: M.S.

ADMISSION REQUIREMENTS. Two transcripts, three letters of recommendation, GRE or MAT, personal interview, licensure or eligibility for licensure in North Carolina required in support of School's application. TOEFL required for international applicants. Graduates of unaccredited institutions not considered. Apply to Office of Admission by March 1 (Fall), October 1 (Spring).

Application fee $65, Phone: (877)415-3853; fax: (919)684-4278.

ADMISSION STANDARDS. Usual minimum average: 3.0 (A = 4).

FINANCIAL AID. Merit scholarships, Federal W/S, loans. Apply by March 1 (Fall), October 1 (Spring) to the Office of Financial Aid. Phone: (919)613-8070. Use FAFSA (School code: E00162).

DEGREE REQUIREMENTS. For M.N.: 39–52 credit program; research option (thesis, research project, or a course in research utilization); capstone residency course.

FIELDS OF STUDY.
Clinical Nurse Specialist.
Clinical Research Management.
Health and Nursing Ministries.
Health Systems Administration.
Leadership in Community-Based Long-Term Care.
Nurse Practitioner.
Nurse Anesthesia.
Nursing Education.
Nursing Informatics.

DUQUESNE UNIVERSITY
Pittsburgh, Pennsylvania 15282-0001
Web site: www.duq.edu

Founded 1878. CGS member. Coed. Private control. Roman Catholic affiliation. Semester system. Library: 648,000 volumes, 3400 subscriptions. Total University enrollment: 9500. Tuition: per credit $588. On-campus housing for single students only. Average annual housing cost: $5418 (including board). Contact Housing Director for both on- and off-campus housing information. Phone: (412)396-5028 or (412)396-6660.

McAnulty Graduate School of Liberal Arts

Enrollment: full-time 436, part-time 328. Faculty: full-time 117, part-time 60. Degrees conferred: M.A., M.L.S., M.S., Ph.D.

ADMISSION REQUIREMENTS. Official transcripts, GRE/MAT, three letters of recommendation required in support of School's application. TOEFL required for international applicants. Interview required by some departments. Accepts transfer applicants. Graduates of unaccredited institutions not considered. Apply to Office of Graduate School by May 1 (Fall), January 1 (Spring). Application fee $40. Phone: (412)396-6400; fax: (412)396-5265.

ADMISSION STANDARDS. Selective to very competitive. Usual minimum average: 3.0 (A = 4).

FINANCIAL AID. Annual awards from institutional funds: scholarships, research assistantships, teaching assistantships, Federal W/S, loans. Apply by May 1 to Dean of School for assistantships, scholarships; to Financial Aid Office for all other programs. Phone: (412)396-6607. Use FAFSA. About 25% of students receive aid other than loans from School and outside sources.

DEGREE REQUIREMENTS. For master's: 24 credit hours minimum, at least one year in residence; reading knowledge of one foreign language in some departments; thesis; comprehensive exam; or 30 credit hours minimum, at least one year in residence; reading knowledge of one foreign language in some departments; comprehensive exam. For Ph.D.: 56 credits hours minimum, at least one year in residence; preliminary exam; reading knowledge of two foreign languages or one language and one language equivalency; dissertation; final oral/written exam.

FIELDS OF STUDY.
Archival, Museum, and Editing Studies. M.A.
Church Administration and Canon Law. M.A.
Computational Mathematics. M.A.
Conflict Resolution. M.A.
Corporate Communications. M.A.
English. M.A., Ph.D.
Health-Care Ethics. M.A., Ph.D.
History. M.A.
Liberal Studies. M.L.S.
Multimedia Technology. M.A.
Pastoral Ministry. M.A.
Philosophy. M.A., Ph.D.
Psychology. Essay, two letters of recommendation for admission; 30 hours minimum; thesis for M.A.; 48 hours minimum beyond the master's for Ph.D. Admits Fall semester only.
Rhetoric and Philosophy of Communication. M.A., Ph.D.
Social and Public Policy. M.A.
Theology. M.A., Ph.D.

John F. Donahue Graduate School of Business
Web site: www.bus.duq.edu

Established 1958. Private control. Accredited programs: M.B.A., Accounting. Semester system. Special Programs: Foreign Study (U.S./China M.B.A.). Special facilities: Small Business Development Center.

Tuition: $588 per credit. On-campus rooms and apartments available for single students only.

Enrollment: total full-time 134, part-time 538 (men 60%, women 40%). Faculty: 46 full-time, 12 part-time; 87% with Ph.D./D.B.A. Degrees conferred: M.B.A. (FT, PT, day, evening), M.S.I.S.M. (Information Systems Management), M.B.A.-J.D., M.B.A.-M.L.S. (Liberal Studies), M.B.A.-M.Pharm. (Pharmacy), M.B.A.-M.S. (Environmental Sciences, Health Management Systems, Industrial Pharmacy, Informational Systems, Nursing), M.S.T. (Taxation).

ADMISSION REQUIREMENTS. All applicants should have a bachelor's degree from a recognized institution of higher education, a strong mathematics background, and a 3.0 (A = 4) GPA. Submit application, GMAT (will accept test results from the last five years, latest acceptable date is June), official transcripts from each undergraduate/graduate school attended, three letters of recommendation, one comprehensive essays, résumé (prefers at least four years of work experience), and an application fee of $40 to the Office of Graduate Admission. In addition, international students (whose native language is other than English) should submit a TOEFL (minimum score 550) report, TSE (recommended) score, certified translations and evaluations of all official transcripts, recommendation should be in English or with certified translations, proof of health/immunization certificate, and proof of sufficient financial resources to complete the academic program. Beginning students are admitted Fall and Spring. Both U.S. citizens and international applicants apply by June 1 (Fall), November 1 (Spring). On-campus interviews may be requested by the Admissions Committee. Admissions Committee will consider applicants with some academic course work deficiencies. Joint degree applicants must apply to and be accepted to both schools/programs, contact the admissions office for current information and specific admissions requirements. Rolling admissions process, notification is made within 4-6 weeks of receipt of completed application and supporting documents. Admissions Office phone: (412)396-6276; fax: (412)396-5304.

ADMISSION STANDARDS. Selective. For M.B.A.: median GMAT: 510; median GPA: 3.0 (A = 4).

FINANCIAL AID. Scholarships, research assistantships, Federal W/S, loans. Financial aid is available for part-time study. Assistantships/fellowships may be available for joint degree candidates. Request assistantship information from the Graduate School of Business; phone: (412)396-6976. Contact the University's Financial Aid Office for current need-based financial aid information; phone: (412)396-6607. Apply by March 1 for most financial assistance and all Federal programs; use FAFSA (School code: 003258), also submit Financial Aid Transcript, Federal Income Tax forms. Approximately 5% of students receive some form of financial assistance.

DEGREE REQUIREMENTS. For M.B.A.: 56-credit program including 21 elective credits, two-year program; research project; degree program must be completed in six years. For U.S./China M.B.A.: one year at Duquesne, one year at Northern Jiatong University, P.R.C. For M.S.T.: 30-credit program. For M.B.A.-M.S.I.S.M.: 80-credit program. For M.B.A.-M.L.S.: 68 credit program. For M.B.A.-M.S. 64–75-credit programs. For M.B.A.-M.Pharm.: 75-credit program. For M.B.A.-J.D.: 126-credit four-and-one-half- to six-year program.

FIELDS OF STUDY.
Accounting.
Business Ethics.
Economics.
Entrepreneurship.
Finance.
Human Resource Management.
International Management.
Management.
Management Information Systems.
Marketing.
Real Estate.
Taxation.

School of Education—Graduate Division

School established 1929. Enrollment: full- and part-time 888. Graduate faculty: full-time 48, part-time 50. Degrees conferred: M.S.Ed., C.A.G.S., Ed.D.

ADMISSION REQUIREMENTS. Official transcripts required in support of School's application. MAT, three letters of recommendation, interviews sometimes required. TOEFL required for international applicants. Accepts transfer applicants. Graduates of unaccredited institutions not considered. Apply to the School by August 1 (Fall), January 1 (Spring), June 1 (Summer). Application fee $40. Phone: (412)396-6091; fax: (412)396-5585.

ADMISSION STANDARDS. Selective. Usual minimum average: 2.50 (A = 4).

FINANCIAL AID. Assistantships, tuition waivers, Federal W/S, loans. Approved for VA benefits. Apply to Dean's Office for assistantships; to Financial Aid Office for all other programs. No specified closing date. Phone: (412)396-6607; fax: (412)396-5284. Use FAFSA and institution's FAF. Aid available for part-time students.

DEGREE REQUIREMENTS. For master's: 30 credit hours minimum, at least 24 in residence; comprehensive exam in some programs; thesis option. For C.A.G.S.: 30 credit hour minimum beyond master's. For Ed.D.: 60 credit hours minimum beyond the master's; qualifying exam; candidacy; dissertation; final oral exam.

FIELDS OF STUDY.
Counselor Education.
Early Childhood Education.

Educational Studies. Interdisciplinary Doctoral Program for Educational Leaders (IDPEL).
Elementary Education.
Instructional Leadership.
Instructional Technology.
Reading and Language Arts.
Religious Education/CCO.
School Administration. Includes elementary and secondary.
School Psychology.
School Supervision.
Secondary Education.
Secondary Mathematics.
Special Education. Includes mentally/physically handicapped.

Rangos School of Health Science

Enrollment: full- and part-time 888. Faculty: full-time 48, part-time 50. Degrees conferred: M.H.M.S., M.O.T., M.P.T., M.S., Ph.D., D.P.T.

ADMISSION REQUIREMENTS. Official transcripts, GRE, three letters of recommendation, curriculum vitae, evidence of computer literacy, statement of personal goals required in support of School's application. GRE or GMAT for Health Management Systems. 250 hours experience at two separate clinical site required for Physical Therapy program. TOEFL required for international applicants. Accepts transfer applicants. Graduates of unaccredited institutions not considered. Apply to the School by May 1 (Fall). Application fee $40. Phone: (412)396-6091; fax: (412)396-5585.

ADMISSION STANDARDS. Selective. Usual minimum average: 3.0 (A = 4).

FINANCIAL AID. Assistantships, tuition waivers, Federal W/S, loans. Approved for VA benefits. Apply by May 31 to appropriate department for assistantships; to Financial Office for all other programs. Phone: (412)396-6607; fax (412)396-5284. Use FAFSA. Aid available for part-time students.

DEGREE REQUIREMENT, For M.S.H.S., M.S.: 36 credit hour minimum, at least 30 credits in residence; comprehensive exam. For M.O.T.: two-year 78–82 credit program; fieldwork experience, For M.P.T.: three-year 114-credit full-time program; clinical experience. For M.S.P.: two-year program; practicum. For M.P.T.: three-year 111-credit full-time program; 8-week clinical experience. For Ph.D.: 60 credit hour minimum, at least one-year of full-time residence; qualifying exam; thesis proposal and defense; candidacy; dissertation; final oral exam.

FIELDS OF STUDY.
Health Management System. M.H.M.S.
Occupational Therapy. M.O.T.
Physical Therapy. M.P.T., D.P.T.
Rehabilitation Science. M.S., Ph.D.
Speech-Language Pathology. M.S.P.

School of Law

Web site: www.duq.edu/law

Established 1911. ABA approved since 1960. AALS member. Semester system. Special programs: ABA-approved summer program at the European Union at University College, Dublin. Law library: 254,600 volumes, 3383 subscriptions; has LEXIS, WESTLAW.

Annual tuition: $17,791, evening $13,824. On-campus housing available. Total average annual additional expense: $9228.

Enrollment: first-year class day 128, evening 79; total full- and part-time 656 (men 54%, women 46%). Faculty: full-time 18, part-time 26. Student to faculty ratio 25.4 to 1. Degrees conferred: J.D., J.D.-M.B.A., J.D.-M.Div., J.D.-M.S. (Environmental Science and Management), J.D.-M.S.T. (Taxation).

ADMISSION REQUIREMENTS. LSDAS Law School report, bachelor's degree, transcripts, LSAT, two letters of recommendation required in support of application. Interview sometimes required. Transfer applicants considered. Apply to Office of Admissions after September 1, before April 1 (Day), May 1 (evening). Fall admission only. Application fee $50. Phone: (412)396-6296.

ADMISSION STANDARDS. Competitive. Mean LSAT: 150; mean GPA: 3.26 (A = 4). Gourman rating: 3.32. *U.S. News & World Report* ranking is in the third tier of all law schools. Accepts 40% of total annual applicants. About 30% of entering class are nonresidents.

FINANCIAL AID. Scholarships, grants-in-aid, Federal W/S, loan. Apply to University's Financial Aid Office by May 1. Use FAFSA or PHEAA. About 17% (full-time 28%, part-time 5%) of students receive aid other than loans from School funds.

DEGREE REQUIREMENTS. For J.D.: satisfactory completion of three-year (day), or four-year (evening) program; 86 credit hours minimum.

Bayer School of Natural and Environmental Sciences

Tuition: per credit $570. Enrollment: full-and part-time 800. Graduate faculty: full-time 48, part-time 50. Degrees conferred: M.S., Ph.D.

ADMISSION REQUIREMENTS. Official transcripts, GRE, two or three letters of recommendation, personal interview required in support of School's application. On-line application available. GRE subject required for several programs. TOEFL (TSE required for assistantship consideration) required for international applicants. Accepts transfer applicants. Graduates of unaccredited institutions not considered. International applicants apply to School by February 15 (Fall), October 1 (Spring). Domestic students recommended dates April 1 (Fall), November 1 (Spring); contact appropriate department for final application deadlines. Application fee $40. Phone (412)396-6091; fax: (412)396-5585.

ADMISSIONS STANDARDS. Selective. Usual minimum average: 2.8 (A = 4).

FINANCIAL AID. Assistantships, tuition waivers, Federal W/S, loans. Approved for VA benefits. Apply by May 31 to appropriate departments for assistantships; to Financial Aid Office for all other programs. Phone: (412)396-6607; fax: (412)396-5274. Use FAFSA. Aid available for part-time students.

DEGREE REQUIREMENTS. For M.S. Plan A (thesis): 32–42 credit hours minimum, at least 24–36 in residence; thesis. For M.S. Plan B (nonthesis): 32–42 credit hours minimum, at least 24–36 in residence; comprehensive exam. For Ph.D.: 46–56 credit hours beyond the bachelor's; comprehensive exam, candidacy, dissertation; final defense.

FIELDS OF STUDY.
Biological Sciences.
Chemistry and Biochemistry.
Environmental Science and Management.
Health and Safety Management.

EAST CAROLINA UNIVERSITY
Greenville, North Carolina 27834-4353
Web site: www.ecu.edu

Founded 1907. CGS member. Located 80 miles E of Raleigh. State control. Semester system. Special facilities: Center on Aging, Center for Coastal and Marine Resources, Mental Health Training Institute, East Carolina Development Institute. Library: 1,112,000 volumes, 6000 subscriptions. Total University enrollment: 18,000.

Annual tuition: full-time resident $2300, nonresident $11,162. On-campus housing for single students. Average academic year housing costs: $4870 (including board) for single students. Contact the Housing office for both on- and off-campus housing information. Phone: (919)328-6012.

Graduate School

Graduate study since 1929. Enrollment: full-time 1518, part-time 1276. Graduate faculty: full-time 526, part-time 4. Degrees conferred: M.A., M.A.Ed., M.B.A., M.S.A., M.P.A., M.S.E.H., M.F.A., M.M., M.S., M.Physics, Ed.S., C.A.S., Ph.D. (Medical Sciences), Ed.D. (Educational Leadership).

ADMISSION REQUIREMENTS. Two official transcripts, GRE/ GMAT (Business) required in support of School's application. MAT/GRE Subject Tests, interviews, letters of reference sometimes required. TOEFL required for international applicants. Accepts transfer applicants. Graduates of unaccredited institutions not considered. Apply to Graduate School June 1 (Fall), October 15 (Spring); some programs have earlier deadlines. Rolling admission process. Application fee $45. Phone: (919)329-6012; fax: (919)328-6071; e-mail: gradschool@mail.ecu.edu.

ADMISSION STANDARDS. Selective for most departments. Usual minimum average: 2.5 (3.0 in major or senior year) (A = 4).

FINANCIAL AID. Annual awards from institutional funds: assistantships, fellowships, Federal W/S, loans. Approved for VA benefits. Apply by April 15 to appropriate department chair for assistantships, fellowships; to Financial Aid Office for all other programs. Use FAFSA. Phone: (919)328-6610. About 20% of students receive aid other than loans from University and outside sources.

DEGREE REQUIREMENTS. For M.A., M.S., M.F.A.: 30 semester hours minimum; reading knowledge of one foreign language or other research skill; thesis for most programs; final oral/ written exam. For M.A. in Ed., M.B.A., M.M., M.S.H.E., M.Physics: same as for M.A., except no thesis or language requirement. For C.A.S., Ed.S.: 30 credits minimum beyond the master's; comprehensive exam. For Ed.D.: 60 semester hours beyond the master's, at least one year in full-time residency; internships, candidacy exam; dissertation. For Ph.D.: 58 semester hours, one calendar year of full-time study; candidacy exam; dissertation; final oral exam.

FIELDS OF STUDY.
Accounting. M.S.A.
Adult Education. M.A.Ed.
Anatomy and Cell Biology. Ph.D.
Anthropology. M.A.
Art. Includes art education. M.A., M.F.A., M.A.Ed.
Biochemistry. Ph.D.
Bioenergetics. Ph.D.
Biological Sciences. Ph.D.
Biology. Includes molecular/biotechnology. M.S.
Business Administration. M.B.A.
Chemistry. M.S.
Child Development and Family Relations. M.S.

Coastal Resource Management. Ph.D.
Communication Sciences and Disorders. Ph.D.
Computer Science. M.S.
Counselor Education. M.S., Ed.S.
Criminal Justice. M.S.
Economics. M.S.
Educational Leadership—Educational Administration and Supervision. Ed.S.
Educational Leadership—Higher Education. Ph.D.
Educational Leadership—K–12. Ph.D.
Educational Leadership—Supervision and School Administration. M.A.Ed., M.S.A.
Elementary Education. M.A.Ed.
English. M.A., M.A.Ed.
Environmental Health. M.S.E.H.
Exercise and Sport Science. M.A., M.A.Ed.
Geography. M.A.
Geology. M.S.
Health Education. M.A., M.A.Ed.
History. Includes maritime history. M.A., M.A.Ed.
Industrial Technology. M.S.I.T.
Instructional Technology Education. M.A.Ed., M.S.
Instructional Technology Specialist—Computers. M.A.Ed., M.S.
International Studies. M.A.I.S.
Library Science. M.L.S., C.A.S.
Maritime Studies. M.A.
Marriage and Family Therapy. M.F.T.
Mathematics. M.A., M.A.Ed.
Microbiology and Immunology. Ph.D.
Middle Grades Education. M.A.Ed.
Music. Includes theory/composition, education, therapy, performance. M.M.
Nursing. M.S.N., Ph.D.
Nutrition and Dietetics. M.S.
Occupational Safety. M.S.
Occupational Therapy. M.S., M.S.O.T.
Pharmacology. Ph.D.
Physical Therapy. M.P.T.
Physical Education. M.A., M.A.Ed.
Physics. M.S., Ph.D.
Physiology. Ph.D.
Psychology. Includes clinical, general and theoretic, school. M.A., C.A.S.
Public Administration. M.P.A.
Reading Education. M.A.Ed.
Recreation and Leisure Facilities and Service Administration. M.S.
Recreational Therapy Administration. M.S.
Rehabilitation Studies. Includes rehabilitation counseling, substance abuse and clinical counseling, vocational evaluation. M.S.
Science Education. M.A., M.A.Ed.
Social Work. M.S.W.
Sociology. M.A.
Special Education. Includes learning disabilities, low incidence disabilities, mental retardation. M.S.
Speech-Language Pathology and Audiology. M.S.
Technology Management (Consortium Program). Ph.D.
Vocational Education. M.S.

Brody School of Medicine (27858-4354)
Web site: www.med.ecu.edu

Four-year program established 1977. Library: 138,000 volumes, 1800 subscriptions. Annual tuition: resident $2951, nonresident $23,618; student fees $1113. Average expense for all other costs: $5641. Enrollment: first-year class 72 (EDP 9); total 316 (men 49%, women 51%). Faculty: full-time 88, part-time 2. Degrees conferred: M.D., M.D.-Ph.D.

ADMISSION REQUIREMENTS. AMCAS report, transcripts, MCAT, recommendations required in support of application. Interview by invitation only. Preference given to state residents. Graduates of unaccredited colleges not considered. Has EDP for North Carolina residents only; apply between June 15 and August 1. Apply to Office of Admissions after June 15, before November 15. Application fee $50. Phone: (252)816-2202.

ADMISSION STANDARDS. Selective. Median MCAT: 8.5; median GPA: 3.5 (A = 4). Gourman rating: 3.14. Admits about 40% of total annual applications; 100% are state residents.

FINANCIAL AID. Scholarships, fellowships, assistantships, loans. Apply after acceptance to Financial Aid Office. About 65% of student receive some financial assistance.

DEGREE REQUIREMENTS. For M.D.: satisfactory completion of four-year program.

FIELDS OF GRADUATE STUDY.
Anatomy.
Biochemistry.
Cell Biology.
Immunology.
Microbiology.
Pathology.
Pharmacology.
Physiology.

EAST CENTRAL UNIVERSITY
Ada, Oklahoma 74820-6999
Web site: www.ecok.edu

Established 1909. CGS member. Located 90 miles SE of Oklahoma City. Coed. state control. Semester system. Special facilities: Center for Oklahoma Studies. Library 221,000 volumes, 793,000 microforms, 12 PC workstations.

Tuition: per semester hour resident $75, nonresident $205. On-campus housing for 95 married students, 418 single men, 558 single women. Academic year housing cost: $3200. Apply to Director of Housing. Phone: married housing information (580)332-8000, ext. 226; single housing information (580)332-8000, ext. 208. Day-care facilities available.

School of Graduate Studies

Enrollment: full-time 50, part-time 550 (academic year), about 575 (Summer). College faculty teaching graduate students: full-time 50, part-time 10. Degrees conferred: M.Ed., M.S. in Psychological Services, M.S. in Human Resources.

ADMISSION REQUIREMENTS. Transcripts, GRE/MAT required in support of application. Departmental writing exam for Education. TOEFL required for foreign applicants. Accepts transfer applicants. Apply to Graduate School at least 30 days prior to registration. Phone: (580)332-8000, ext. 709.

ADMISSION STANDARDS. Selective. Usual minimum average: 2.5 (M.Ed. M.S.H.R.), 3.0 (M.S.P.S.) (A = 4).

FINANCIAL AID. Awards from institutional funds: scholarships, assistantships, Federal W/S, loans; no specified closing date. Phone: (580)322-8000, ext. 242. Use FAFSA.

DEGREE REQUIREMENTS. For M.Ed.: 32 semester hours minimum, at least 24 in residence; thesis optional. For M.S.P.S.: 36 semester hours minimum; thesis optional. For M.S.H.R.: 36 semester hours minimum; rehabilitation counselor option 51 semester hours.

FIELDS OF STUDY.
Elementary Education.

Elementary School Principal.
Human Resources Administration.
Human Resources Counseling.
Human Resources Criminal Justice.
Human Resources Rehabilitation Counseling.
Library Media.
Psychological Services.
Reading Specialist.
School Counselor.
Secondary Education. Includes technology, sports administration.
Secondary School Principal.
Special Education (LD).
Vocational Evaluation and Work Adjustment.

EAST STROUDSBURG UNIVERSITY OF PENNSYLVANIA
East Stroudsburg, Pennsylvania 18301
Web site: www.esu.edu

Founded 1893. Located 75 miles W of New York City. Coed. State control. Semester system. Library: 411,000 volumes, 1800 subscriptions. Total University enrollment: 5500.

Tuition: full-time resident $4138, nonresident $7008. Limited on-campus housing for graduate students. Average academic year cost: $4864. On-campus housing in Summer only for single students. Average Summer cost: $100 per week (including board). Apply to director of Housing. Phone: (570)422-3461.

Graduate Studies

Enrollment: full-time 225, part-time 800 (men 30%, women 70%). Faculty: full-time 111, part-time 10. Degrees conferred: M.A., M.S., M.Ed., M P.H.

ADMISSION REQUIREMENTS. Two official transcripts required in support of School's application. GRE required for some programs. TOEFL required for international applicants. Interview required by some departments. Accepts transfer applicants. Apply to Dean of Graduate Studies at least six weeks prior to registration. Admits to Fall and Spring semesters. Application fee $15. Phone: (570)424-3536; fax: (570)422-3506.

ADMISSION STANDARDS. Selective. Usual minimum average: 2.5, 3.0 major field (A = 4).

FINANCIAL AID. Annual awards from institutional funds: graduate assistantships, tuition waivers, Federal W/S, loans. Apply to the Graduate School by March 1. Phone: (570)422-3340. Use FAFSA and University's FAF. About 95% of full-time students receive aid other than loans from College and outside sources. Aid available for part-time students, sometimes available for international students.

DEGREE REQUIREMENTS. For M.A.: 30 credit hours minimum, at least 24 in residence; thesis. For M.Ed. or M.S.: 30 credits minimum, at least 24 in residence, plus thesis; or 34 credits, at least 28 in residence, and research project; written comprehensive exam; final oral exam. For M.P.H.: 48 credit hours, at least 32 credits in residence; thesis.

FIELDS OF STUDY.
Biological Science. M.Ed.
Biology. M.S.
Cardiac Rehabilitation and Exercise Science. M.S.
Community Health Education. M.P.H.
Computer Science. M.S.
Elementary Education. M.Ed.

General Science. M.S., M.Ed.
Health and Physical Education. M.Ed.
Health Education. M.S.
History. M.A., M.Ed.
Physical Education. M.S.
Political Science. M.A., M.Ed.
Reading. For Reading Specialist, 36 credit hours. M.Ed.
Secondary Education. M.Ed.
Special Education. M.Ed.
Speech Language Pathology. M.S.

EAST TENNESSEE STATE UNIVERSITY

Johnson City, Tennessee 37614-0054
Web site: www.etsu.edu

Founded 1911. CGS member. Located 100 miles E of Knoxville. Coed. State control. Semester system. Library: 594,000 volumes, 3400 subscriptions. Total University enrollment: 12,000.

Graduate tuition fees: per semester hour, resident $194, nonresident $243. On-campus housing available for both single and married students. Average academic year cost: single $3818 (including board), married $4948 (including board). Apply to Director of Housing. Phone: (423)929-4446. Day-care facilities available.

School of Graduate Studies

Enrollment: full-time 1034, part-time 856. University faculty: full-time 463, part-time 54. Degrees conferred: M.A., M.A.L.S., M.B.A., M.S., M.S.N., M.S.E.H., M.F.A., M.A.T., M.P.M., M.P.H., M.P.T., Ed.S., Ed.D., Ph.D.

ADMISSION REQUIREMENTS. Transcripts, personal essay required in support of School's application. GRE/GMAT, letters of recommendation required in some departments. Interview sometimes required. TOEFL required for international applicants. Accepts transfer applicants. Graduates of unaccredited institutions not considered. Apply to Dean, School of Graduate Studies by August 1 (Fall), December 1 (Winter), March 1 (Spring), May 1 (Summer). International applicants should apply at least 12 weeks prior to expected date of enrollment. Application fee $25, $35 for international applicants. Phone: (423)929-4221; fax: (423)929-5624; e-mail: gradsch@etsu.edu.

ADMISSION STANDARDS. Selective. Usual minimum average: 2.5 (A = 4).

FINANCIAL AID. Annual awards from institutional funds: scholarships, fellowships, graduate assistantships, research assistantships, grants, Federal W/S, loans. Approved for VA benefits. Apply by May 1 to appropriate department chair. Use FAFSA and University's FAF. About 50% of students receive aid other than loans from School and outside sources. Aid available for part-time students.

DEGREE REQUIREMENTS. For all master's: 30 semester hours minimum; thesis, final oral/written exam; or 36 semester hours minimum, final oral exam. For Ed. S.: 30 semester hours beyond the master's; dissertation. For Ed.D.: 90 semester hours minimum, at least one year in full-time study; preliminary exam; qualifying exam; final exam; dissertation. For Ph.D.: 60 semester hours beyond the master's; preliminary and qualifying exam; language/computer option; final exam; dissertation.

FIELDS OF STUDY.
Accounting. M.Acc.
Art. Includes education, history, studio (M.F.A.). M.A., M.F.A
Biology. Includes microbiology. M.S.

Biomedical Sciences. Includes anatomy, biochemistry, microbiology, pharmacology, physiology. M.S.
Business Administration. M.BA.
Chemistry. M.S.
Clinical Nutrition. M.S.
Communication. M.A.
Communicative Disorders. Includes audiology, speech-language pathology. M.S.
Computer and Information Sciences. Includes computer science, information systems science, software engineering. M.S.
Counseling. Includes community agency, marriage and family therapy, elementary, secondary. M. A.
Criminal Justice and Criminology. M.A.
Early Childhood Education. M.A., M.Ed.
Educational Leadership. M.Ed.
Educational Media and Educational Technology. Includes educational communications, school library media. M.Ed.
Elementary Education. M.Ed.
English. M.A.
Environmental Health. M.S.E.H.
History. M.A.
Liberal Studies. M.A.L.S.
Mathematical Sciences. M.S.
Music. M.Mu.Ed.
Nursing. M.S.N.
Physical Education. Includes exercise physiology, fitness leadership, sports management, sports sciences. M.S., M.Ed.
Physical Therapy. M.P.T.
Psychology. Includes clinical, general. M.A.
Public Health. Includes administration, community health. M.P.H.
Public Management. Includes administration, urban and regional economic development, municipal service management, city planning, urban and regional planning. M.P.M.
Reading. Includes education, reading and storytelling. M.A., M.Ed.
Secondary Education. Includes classroom technology. M.Ed.
Sociology. Includes applied, general. M.A.
Special Education. Includes early childhood, advanced practitioner. M.Ed.
Technology. Includes engineering technology, industrial arts/technology education, digital media. M.S.

James H. Quillen College of Medicine (37614-1708)

Established 1978. Annual tuition: resident $13,082; nonresident $26,666. Total average cost of all other expenses: $10,000. Enrollment: first-year class 60 (EDP 6); total 264 (men 47%, women 53%). Faculty: full-time 135; part-time, 47; volunteers 425. Degrees conferred: M.D., M.D.-Ph.D.

ADMISSION REQUIREMENTS. AMCAS report, transcripts, MCAT, recommendations required in support of application. Interview by invitation. Preference given to state residents and veterans of U.S. military service. Graduates of unaccredited colleges not considered. Has EDP; apply between June 15 and August 1. Apply to Admissions Office/Registrar after June 15, before December 1. Application fee, $50. Phone. (423)439-4753; fax: (423)439-8206.

ADMISSION STANDARDS. Competitive. Mean MCAT: 9.5; mean GPA: 3.5 (A = 4). Gourman rating: 3.14. Admits about 10% of total annual applications; 100% are state residents.

FINANCIAL AID. Scholarships, fellowships, tuition waivers, grants, loans. Apply after acceptance to Financial Aid Office. Use FAFSA.

DEGREE REQUIREMENTS. For M.D.: satisfactory completion of four-year program.

FIELDS OF GRADUATE STUDY.
Anatomy.

Biochemistry.
Biophysics.
Cell Biology.
Immunology.
Microbiology.
Pathology.
Pharmacology.
Physiology.

EASTERN CONNECTICUT STATE UNIVERSITY

Willimantic, Connecticut 06226-2295

Web site: www.csu.ctstateu.edu

Founded 1889. Located 30 miles E of Hartford. Coed. State control. Semester system.

Tuition: per hour $165. No on-campus housing for married or single graduate students. Apply to Student Affairs office for off-campus housing information. Phone: (860)465-5369.

School of Education and Graduate Division

Enrollment: full-time 20, part-time 165. College faculty teaching graduate courses: full-time 16, part-time 4. Degree conferred: M.S.

ADMISSION REQUIREMENTS. Transcripts, two recommendations required in support of application. TOEFL required for international applicants. Accepts transfer applicants. Apply to appropriate department. No specified closing date. Admits Fall, Spring. Application fee $20. Phone: (860)465-5192; fax: (860)465-4543.

ADMISSION STANDARDS. Selective. Usual minimum average: 2.7 (A = 4).

FINANCIAL AID, Annual awards from institutional funds: assistantships, grants, Federal W/S, loans. Apply to appropriate department by March 15. Phone: (860)456-5205. Use FAFSA and institutional FAF.

DEGREE REQUIREMENTS. For M.S.: 36 semester hours minimum, at least 21 in residence; thesis or comprehensive exam.

FIELDS OF STUDY.
Accounting. Includes financial reporting, international operations, taxation, accountancy for nonprofit/governmental units.
Education. Includes early childhood, educational technology, elementary, language arts, reading, science.
Organizational Management. Includes individual behavior, group dynamics, organizational processes and structure.

EASTERN ILLINOIS UNIVERSITY

Charleston, Illinois 61920-3099

Web site: www.eiu.edu

Founded 1895. CGS member. Located 180 miles S of Chicago. Coed. State control. Semester system. Library: 950,000 volumes, 3100 subscriptions. Total University enrollment: 10,600.

Annual tuition/fees: full-time, resident $3820, nonresident $8860; per credit resident $154, nonresident $364. On-campus housing for 100 married students, 600 graduate men, 600 graduate women. Average academic year housing costs: $1680 for married students, $1488 for single graduate students. Contact Director, University Housing for both on- and off-campus housing information. Phone: (217)581-3923.

Graduate Studies

Enrollment: full- and part-time 1500. University faculty teaching graduate students: full-time 362, part-time 25. Degrees conferred: M.A., M.A.M., M.A.P.S., M.S., M.S.C., M.S.C.D.S., M.S.N.S., M.S. in Ed., M.B.A., Ed.S., S.S.P.

ADMISSION REQUIREMENTS. Transcripts, GRE, MAT, GMAT may be required in support of application. Interview not required. TOEFL (minimum score 550) required for international applicants. Accepts transfer applicants. Graduates of unaccredited institutions not considered. Apply to Graduate School's Admissions Office at least ten days prior to registration. Application fee $25. Phone: (217)581-2220, Fax: (217)581-6020.

ADMISSION STANDARDS. Relatively open. Usual minimum average: 2.75 (A = 4); higher in some programs.

FINANCIAL AID. Annual awards from institutional funds: tuition waiver scholarships, research assistantships, teaching assistantships, residence hall assistantships, Federal W/S, loans. Approved for VA benefits. Apply by February 15 to appropriate department for assistantships; to the Financial Aid Office for all need-based programs. Phone: (217)581-3713. Use FAFSA. About 25% of students receive aid other than loans from University and outside sources. Scholarships for international students available.

DEGREE REQUIREMENTS. For master's: 30–32 semester hours; final oral/written exam. For Ed.S., S.S.P.: 64 semester hours minimum beyond the bachelor's; final oral/written exam/special project.

FIELDS OF STUDY.

COLLEGE OF ARTS AND HUMANITIES:
Art. M.A.
English. M.A.
History. Includes historical administration. M.A.
Music. M.A.
Speech Communication. M.A.

LUMPKIN COLLEGE OF BUSINESS AND APPLIED SCIENCES:
Business Administration. Includes accountancy. M.B.A.
Family and Consumer Sciences. Includes dietetics. M.S.
Gerontology. M.A.
Technology. M.S.

COLLEGE OF EDUCATION AND PROFESSIONAL STUDIES:
College Student Affairs. M.S.
Counseling. M.S.
Educational Administration. M.S.Ed., Ed.S.
Physical Education. M.S.
Special Education. M.S.Ed.

COLLEGE OF SCIENCES:
Chemistry. M.S.C.
Communication Disorders and Sciences. M.S.C.D.S.
Economics. M.A.
Mathematics. Includes education. M.A.M.
Natural Sciences (for Teachers of Science). Includes biological sciences, chemistry, earth science, physics. M.S.N.S.
Political Science. Includes American government and politics, comparative and international relations, and public administration and public policy. M.A.P.S.
Psychology. Includes clinical, school. M.A.C.P., S.S.P.

EASTERN KENTUCKY UNIVERSITY

Richmond, Kentucky 40475-3101
Web site: www.eku.edu

Founded 1906. CGS member. Located 26 miles SE of Lexington. Coed. State control. Semester system. Library: about 811,000 volumes, 1,151,000 microforms, 4000 current periodicals. Special facilities: Hummel Planetarium, Lilley Cornett Woods, Oral History Center, Spenser Morton Preserves.

Annual tuition: full-time, resident $3168, nonresident $8766; per hour, resident $176, nonresident $487. On-campus housing for married students: 292 units, single on-campus housing available for about 3000 men, 4000 women. Average academic year housing costs: $778–$1241 per semester for single students, about $928 per semester for married students. Contact Director of Housing for both on- and off-campus housing information. Phone: (859)622-1575.

Graduate School

Graduate study since 1935. Enrollment: full-time 446, part-time 1521 (men 439, women 1082). Graduate faculty: full-time 350, part-time 10. Degrees conferred: M.A., M.A.C., M.A.Ed., M.S., M.B.A., M.I.O.P., M.P.A., M.M., M.S.N., Ed.S., joint doctoral programs available.

ADMISSION REQUIREMENTS. Official transcripts, statement of personal and professional objectives, GRE/GMAT (Business) required in support of application. On-line application available. Interview required for some programs. TOEFL required for international applicants. Accepts transfer applicants. Graduates of unaccredited institutions not considered. Apply to Graduate Office at least two weeks prior to registration. Foreign students must be clearly admitted at least 60 days prior to the beginning of the semester of attendance. Application fee, none. Phone: (859)622-1742; e-mail: graduate@eku.edu.

ADMISSION STANDARDS. Selective. Usual minimum average: 2.5 (A = 4).

FINANCIAL AID. Annual awards from institutional funds: scholarships, fellowships, teaching/research assistantships, Federal W/S, loans. Approved for VA benefits. Apply by March 1 to Graduate Office for assistantships; to Financial Aid Office for all other programs. Use FAFSA and University's FAF. About 50% of full-time students receive aid other than loans from University and outside sources. Aid available for part-time students.

DEGREE REQUIREMENTS. For most master's: 24 semester hours plus thesis, or 30 semester hours without thesis; final oral/comprehensive exam. For M.A.Ed.: same as for M.A., except candidates are required to hold the teaching certificate. For Ed.S.: 30–39 semester hours beyond the master's; special project.

FIELDS OF STUDY.
Administration and Supervision. Ed.S., joint Ed.D. with University of Kentucky.
Applied Computing—Software Engineering. M.S.
Applied Computing—Business Computing. M.S.
Applied Computing—Industrial Computing. M.S.
Biology. Includes ecology. M.S. Joint Ph.D. with University of Kentucky.
Business Administration. M.B.A.
Business Computing. M.A.C.
Chemistry. M.S.
Clinical Psychology. M.S.
Communication Disorders. M.A.Ed.
Community Nutrition. M.S.

Criminal Justice. Includes corrections and juvenile justice studies, police administration. M.S.
Educational Psychology. Joint Ed.D. with University of Kentucky.
Educational Policies, Studies, and Evaluation. Joint Ed.D. with University of Kentucky.
Elementary Education. Includes early elementary, middle grades, reading. M.A.Ed.
English. M.A., M.A.Ed.
Geology. M.S. Joint Ph.D. with the University of Kentucky.
Health, Physical Education, and Recreation. Joint Ed.D. with University of Kentucky.
History. M.A., M.A.Ed.
Human Services—Student Personnel Services. M.A.
Human Services—Community Agencies. M.A.
Industrial Computing. M.A.C.
Industrial Education. Includes occupational training/development, technology, vocational administration. M.S.
Industrial Organizational Psychology. M.I.O.P., M.S.
Instructional Leadership. M.A.Ed. Joint Ed.D. with the University of Kentucky.
Library Science. Includes K–12. M.A.Ed.
Loss Prevention and Safety. M.S.
Manufacturing Technology. M.S.
Mathematical Sciences. Includes computer science, statistics. M.S.
Mental Health Counseling. M.A.
Music. Includes choral/instrumental conducting, general, performance, theory/composition. M.M.
Nursing. Includes rural health family nurse practitioner, rural community health care nursing. M.S.N.
Occupational Training/Development. M.A.Ed.
Occupational Therapy. M.S.
Physical Education. Includes exercise/sport science, exercise/wellness, sports administration. M.S.
Political Science. M.A., M.A.Ed.
Psychology. Includes clinical, education, school. Psy.S. Joint Ph.D. with University of Kentucky.
Public Administration. Includes community development, community health administration. M.P.A.
Public Health. Includes chemical abuse, community health, environmental health science, wellness. M.P.H., M.S.
School Counseling. M.A.Ed.
Secondary Education. Includes agriculture, allied health (nonteaching), art, biology, business, English, family and consumer sciences, mathematics, music, physical education, physical science, social studies (geography, history), technology. M.A.Ed.
Software Engineering. M.A.C.
Special Education. Includes deaf and hard of hearing, early childhood, early childhood (nonteaching), LBD, moderate and severe. M.A.Ed. Joint Ed.D. with the University of Kentucky (LBD, TMH, hearing impaired).
Student Personnel Services. Ed.S.
Vocational Education. Joint Ed.D. with University of Kentucky.

EASTERN MICHIGAN UNIVERSITY

Ypsilanti, Michigan 48197
Web site: www.emich.edu

Founded 1849. CGS member. Located 30 miles W of Detroit. Coed. State control. Semester system. Library: 951,062 volumes, 6240 subscriptions.

Tuition: per hour, resident $246, nonresident $500. On-campus housing for married students, graduate men and women. Average academic year housing cost: $5597 per academic year (including board) for single students. Apply to Director of Auxiliary Services. Phone: (734)487-0445.

Graduate School

Graduate study since 1953. Enrollment: full-time 1291, part-time 4081 (men 40%, women 60%). University faculty: full- and part-time 687. Degrees conferred: M.A., M.S., M.S.A. M.B.A., M.L.S., M.O.T., M.P.A., M.B.E., M.F.A., M.S.E.S., M.S.N., M.S.W., Sp.A., C.A.S., Ed.D.

ADMISSION REQUIREMENTS. Transcripts, GRE/MAT/GMAT, letters of recommendation required in support of School's application. Interview not required. TOEFL required for international applicants. Accepts transfer applicants. Graduates of unaccredited institutions not considered. Apply to Graduate School Office at least 60 days before registration; priority deadlines May 15 (Fall), November 1 (Spring). Application fee $30. Phone: (734)487-3400; fax: (734)487-1484; e-mail: graduate.admission@emich.edu.

ADMISSION STANDARDS. Selective. Usual minimum average: 2.75 (A = 4).

FINANCIAL AID. Annual awards from institutional funds: fellowships, assistantships, tuition waivers, Federal W/S, loans. Apply to appropriate department head; no specified closing date. Apply by March 15 (Spring), February 15 (Fall) to Financial Aid Officer for federal funds. Phone: (734)487-0455. Use FAFSA. Aid sometimes available for part-time students.

DEGREE REQUIREMENTS. For master's: 30 semester hours minimum (maximum varies by department), at least 6 in residence; thesis/nonthesis option; research paper may be included; final written/oral exam may be required. For Sp.A., C.A.S.: normally 32 hours beyond the master's, at least 16 in residence. For Ed.D.: 28 hours beyond University's specialist degree; all in residence; major project; written/oral exam.

FIELDS OF STUDY.

COLLEGE OF ARTS AND SCIENCES:
Applied Statistics. M.A.
Applied Economics. M.A.
Art Education. M.A.
Arts Administration. M.A.
Biology. Includes general biology, community college teaching, molecular/cellular, physiology. M.S.
Chemistry. M.S.
Children's Literature. M.A.
Clinical Behavior Psychology. M.S.
Clinical Psychology. M.S., Ph.D.
Communication. M.A.
Computer Science. Includes artificial intelligence. M.S.
Creative Writing. M.A.
Criminology and Criminal Justice. M.A.
Drama/Theatre for the Young. M.A., M.F.A.
Economics. M.A.
Economics/Health Economics. M.A.
Economics/International Economics and Development. M.A.
English Linguistics. M.A.
Foreign Language—French. M.A.
Foreign Language—German. M.A.
Foreign Language—Spanish. M.A.
General Science. M.S.
Geographic Information Systems. M.S.
Geographic Information System and Remote Sensing. M.S.
Geographic Information Systems—Planning. M.S.
Geography. M.S.
Heritage Interpretation and Tourism. M.S.
Historic Preservation. M.S.
Historic Preservation Administration. M.S.
Historic Preservation Planning. M.S.

History. M.A.
Literature. M.A.
Math–Computer Science. M.A.
Math Education. M.A.
Mathematics. M.A.
Music. Includes choral music, education, theory/literature, performance, pedagogy. M.A.
Physics. M.S.
Physics/Physics Education. M.S.
Psychology. M.S.
Public Administration. M.P.A.
School Psychology. M.A.
Social Science. M.A.
Social Science and American Culture. M.L.S.
Sociology. M.A.
Sociology—Family Specialty. M.A.
Spanish Bilingual/Bicultural. M.A.
Teaching English to Speakers of Other Languages. M.A.
Theatre Arts. M.A.
Trade and Development. M.A.
Urban and Regional Planning. M.S.
Women's Studies. M.A.
Written Communication. M.A.

COLLEGE OF BUSINESS:
Accounting. M.S.
Accounting Information Systems. M.S.
Business Administration. Includes accounting/financial and operational controls, accounting/taxation, management information systems, finance, international business, management/human resource, marketing, organizational development, strategic quality. M.B.A.
Human Resource and Organizational Development. M.S.
Information Systems. M.S.

COLLEGE OF EDUCATION:
Adapted Physical Education. M.S.
College Student Personnel. M.A.
Community Counseling. M.A.
Curriculum and Instruction. M.A.
Development and Personality. M.A.
Early Childhood Education. M.A.
Educational Media and Technology. M.A.
Educational Psychology Research and Evaluation. M.A.
Elementary Education. M.A.
Leadership. M.A., Ed.D.
Middle School Education. M.A.
Physical Education—Pedagogy. M.S.
Reading. M.A.
School Psychology. M.A.
Secondary Education. M.A.
Special Education. Includes emotionally impaired, hearing impaired, learning disabilities, mentally impaired, visually impaired, speech and language impaired, physically and otherwise health impaired. M.A.
Sports Medicine—Biomechanics. M.S.
Sports Medicine—Corporate/Adult Fitness. M.S.
Sports Medicine—Exercise Physiology. M.S.
Teaching for Diversity. M.A.

COLLEGE OF HEALTH AND HUMAN SERVICES:
Apparel, Textiles, and Merchandising. M.S.
Hotel and Restaurant Management. M.S.
Human Nutrition. M.S.
Interior Design. M.S.
Mental Health and Chemical Dependency. M.S.W.
Nursing. M.S.N.
Occupational Therapy. M.O.T., M.S.

Services to the Aging. M.S.W.

COLLEGE OF TECHNOLOGY:
Business Education. M.B.E.
Information Security. M.L.S.
Industrial Technology. Includes CAD/CAM, construction, quality. M.S.
Interdisciplinary Technology. M.L.S.
Polymer Technology. M.S.
Technology Education. M.S.

EASTERN NEW MEXICO UNIVERSITY
Portales, New Mexico 88130
Web site: www.enmu.edu

Founded 1927. CGS member. Coed. State control. Branches located in Roswell, Ruidoso. Semester system. Library: 500,000 volumes, 8795 subscriptions. Total University enrollment: 3500.

Annual tuition: full-time, resident $2166, nonresident $7100; per credit, resident $90, nonresident $285. On-campus housing for 181 married students, 540 graduate men, 918 graduate women. Average academic year housing costs: $1700–$2500 for single students; $260–$300 per month for married students. Contact Director of Housing for both on- and off-campus housing information. Phone: (505)562-2631. Day-care facilities available.

Graduate School

Enrollment: full-time 23, part-time 320. University faculty: full-time 89, part-time 13. Degrees conferred: M.A., M.B.A., M.Ed., M.M., M.S., M.S.Ed.

ADMISSION REQUIREMENTS. One official transcript, GRE/GMAT (business) required in support of School's application. On-line application available. Interview not required. TOEFL required for international applicants. Accepts transfer applicants. Graduates of unaccredited institutions not considered. Apply to Dean of Graduate School at least 30 days prior to registration. Application fee $10. Phone: (505)562-2147; fax: (505)562-2168.

ADMISSION STANDARDS. Relatively open. Usual minimum average: 3.0 (regular), 2.5 (provisional) (A = 4).

FINANCIAL AID. Annual awards from institutional funds; research assistantships, teaching assistantships, fellowships for minorities, women and handicapped, tuition waivers, Federal W/S, loans. Approved for VA benefits. Apply by March 1 to appropriate department chair for assistantships; to the Financial Aid Office for all other programs. Use FAFSA and University's FAF. Phone: (505)562-2147. About 85% of students receive aid from University and outside sources. No aid for part-time students.

DEGREE REQUIREMENTS. For master's: 30 credit hours minimum, at least 24 in residence; thesis; final oral exam; or 32 credit hours minimum, at least 16 in residence; final oral written exam.

FIELDS OF STUDY.
Anthropology. M.A.
Bilingual Education. M.Ed.
Biology. Includes botany, microbiology, cell and molecular biology, zoology. M.S.
Business Administration. M.B.A.

Chemistry. One language for M.S. Includes chemical physics, geochemistry.
Communication. Includes mass communication, speech communication. M.A.
Communicative Disorders. Includes speech-language pathology. M.S.
Counseling. M.A.
Counseling and Guidance. M.Ed.
Educational Administration. M.Ed.
Elementary Education. M.Ed.
English. M.A.
English as a Second Language. M.Ed.
Mathematics. M.A.
Music. M.M.
Physical Education. Includes sports administration, sports science. M.S.
Psychology. M.A.
Reading Education. M.Ed.
School Guidance. M.Ed.
Special Education. M.S.E.

EASTERN OREGON UNIVERSITY
La Grande, Oregon 97850-2899
Web site: www.eou.edu

Founded 1929. Located 265 miles E of Portland. Coed. State control. Quarter system. Library: 329,000 volumes, 1000 subscriptions.

Annual tuition: per credit, resident $125, nonresident $225. On-campus housing for married and single students. Average academic year housing costs: $5450 (including board) for single students. Contact Director of Residence Life for both on- and off-campus housing information. Phone: (541)962-3553.

Graduate Studies

Established 1952. Enrollment: full-time 66, part-time 118. Faculty: full-time 0, part-time 20. Degrees conferred: M.S., M.T.E. for Interns, M.T.E. for Practitioners.

ADMISSION REQUIREMENTS. Transcripts, two letters of reference, CBEST/TSPC required in support of application. TOEFL required for international applicants. Accepts transfer applicants. Apply to Office of Admission well in advance of registration. Application fee $50. Phone: (541)962-3772; fax: (541)962-3701.

ADMISSION STANDARDS. Relatively open. Usual minimum average: 2.5 (A = 4).

FINANCIAL AID. Scholarships, tuition waivers, Federal W/S, loans. Approved for VA benefits. Apply to Financial Aid Office with admission application. Phone: (541)962-3393. Use FAFSA.

DEGREE REQUIREMENTS. For master's: 53 quarter hours minimum, at least 30 in residence; qualifying exam; written/oral comprehensive exam. M.T.E. Intern, during academic year; M.T.E. Practitioner, primarily summers.

FIELDS OF STUDY.
Elementary Education—Fifth Year.
Reading.
Secondary Education—Fifth Year.
Special Education.
Teacher Education. Includes early childhood, elementary, middle school, secondary.

EASTERN VIRGINIA MEDICAL SCHOOL OF THE MEDICAL COLLEGE OF HAMPTON ROADS

Norfolk, Virginia 23507-2000
Web site: www.evms.edu

Established 1973. Special facilities: Jones Institute for Reproductive Medicine, Center for Pediatric Research, Strelitz Diabetes Institute, Glennan Center for Geriatics and Gerontology. Library: 86,000 volumes, 1800 subscriptions. Annual tuition: resident $16,000, nonresident $29,500. Graduate tuition: full-time $18,500, student fees $1819. Total average figure for all other expenses $9100. No on-campus housing available, call for information on off-campus housing. Phone: (757)446-5812.

Enrollment: first-year class 105 (5 EDP); total 416 (men 54%, women 46%). Faculty: full-time 299, part-time and volunteers 900. Degrees conferred: M.D., M.D.-Ph.D., M.D.-Psy.D., M.P.A., M.S.

ADMISSION REQUIREMENTS. AMCAS report, transcripts, MCAT, two letters of recommendation, interview required in support of application. Preference given to residents of Tidewater area. Transfer applicants and graduates of unaccredited colleges not considered. Has EDP; apply between June 15 and August 1. Apply to Chair of Admissions Committee after June 15, before November 15. Application fee $85. Phone: (757)446-5812; fax: (757)446-5896.

ADMISSION STANDARDS. Selective. Mean MCAT: 10; mean GPA: 3.41 (A = 4). Gourman rating: 3.12. Accepts about 89% of total annual applicants. Approximately 62% are state residents.

FINANCIAL AID. Scholarships, loans available. Apply to Financial Aid Office after acceptance, before March 15. Phone: (757)446-5813. Use FAFSA. About 90% of students receive financial assistance.

DEGREE REQUIREMENTS. For M.D.: satisfactory completion of four-year program. For M.S.: 30 credit program with a thesis and nonthesis track. For M.P.A. 60 credit, two-year full-time program; nine clinical experiences.

FIELDS OF GRADUATE STUDY.
Biomedical Sciences. Includes biological chemistry, cell biology and molecular pathogenesis, clinical chemistry, pure and applied biomedical sciences, systems biology and biophysics. M.S., Ph.D. (with Old Dominion University).
Physical Assistant. M.P.A.
Public Health. Includes epidemiology, health management/policy. M.P.H. (with Old Dominion University).
Psychology. Psy.D. (with the College of William and Mary).

EASTERN WASHINGTON UNIVERSITY

Cheney, Washington 99004-2431
Web site: www.ewu.edu

Founded 1882. CGS member. Located 16 miles SW of Spokane. Coed. State control. Quarter system. Library: 1,000,000 volumes, 6240 subscriptions.

Tuition: part-time resident $144 per credit, nonresident $428 per credit. On-campus housing for 143 married students, 1749 single students. Average academic year housing cost: $2364 married students, $4828 (including board) for single students. Apply to Director of Residential Life. Day-care facilities available.

Graduate School

Graduate study since 1947. Enrollment: full-time 589, part-time 440. College faculty teaching graduate students: full-time 230, part-time 16. Degrees conferred: M.A., M.S., M.Ed., M.B.A., M.F.A., M.N., M.P.A., M.P.T., M.S.W., M.U.R.P.

ADMISSION REQUIREMENTS. Transcripts, letters of recommendation required in support of application. GRE, interview for some programs, GMAT for business. TOEFL required for international applicants. Accepts transfer applicants. Apply to Graduate Program Office at least one month prior to beginning of quarter. Application fee $35. Phone: (509)359-6297; fax: (509)359-6044; e-mail: gradprogram@mail.ewu.edu.

ADMISSION STANDARDS. Selective. Minimum average: 3.0 (A = 4) in the last three years.

FINANCIAL AID. Annual awards from institutional funds: Scholarships, assistantships, Federal W/S, loans. Apply by February 1 to appropriate department for assistantships, to Financial Aid Office for federal programs. Phone: (509)359-2314. Use FAFSA. Aid available for part-time students. About 45% of students receive aid from University and outside sources.

DEGREE REQUIREMENTS. For M.A., M.S.: 45 quarter hours minimum, at least 34 credits in residence; final comprehensive exam; thesis, reading knowledge of one foreign language sometimes required. For M.Ed., M.B.A.: 49 quarter hours minimum, at least 36 credits in residence; final comprehensive exam; thesis or research paper. For M.P.A.: 60 quarter hours minimum, at least 45 in residence; final comprehensive exam; thesis or research paper. For M.P.T.: 127 quarter hours minimum, at least 100 credits in residence: final comprehensive exam. For M.S.W.: 84 quarter hours minimum, 63 in residence; final comprehensive exam; thesis or research paper. For M.F.A., M.U.R.P.: 72 quarter hours minimum, 54 in residence; thesis (M.F.A.); final comprehensive exam. For M.N.: 59 quarter hours minimum, 44 in residence; thesis; final comprehensive exam.

FIELDS OF STUDY.
Adult Education. M.Ed.
Applied Psychology. M.S.
Biology. M.S.
Biology-Medical Technology Option.
Business Administration. M.B.A.
College Instruction. M.A., M.S.
Communication. M.S.
Communications Disorders. M.S.
Computer Science. M.S.
Creative Writing. M.F.A.
Curriculum and Instruction. M.Ed.
Early Childhood Education. M.Ed.
Educational Leadership. M.Ed.
Elementary Teaching. M.Ed.
English. Includes English in the public school, literature, rhetoric and composition, teaching English as a second language, technical and professional writing. M.A.
Foundations of Education. M.Ed.
French. M.Ed.
History. M.A.
Instructional Media and Technology. M.Ed.
Interdisciplinary. M.A., M.S.
Literacy Specialist Studies. M.Ed.
Mathematics. M.Ed., M.S.
Music. Includes composition, music education, performance. M.A.
Nursing. M.N.
Physical Education. M.S.
Physical Therapy. M.P.T.

Psychology. Includes clinical, developmental, experimental, mental health counseling, school counseling. M.S.
Public Administration. M.P.A.
School Library Media Administration. M.Ed.
Science Education. M.Ed.
Social Science Education. M.Ed.
Social Work. M.S.W.
Special Education. M.Ed.
Supervising (Clinic) Teaching. M.Ed.
Urban and Regional Planning. M.U.R.P.
Vocational Administration.

EDINBORO UNIVERSITY OF PENNSYLVANIA
Edinboro, Pennsylvania 16444
Web site: www.edinboro.edu

Founded 1857. Located 20 miles S of Erie. State control. Semester system. Library: 468,900 volumes, 1829 subscriptions.

Tuition: per credit, resident $230, nonresident $389. On-campus housing available for single and married graduate students. Average academic year housing costs: $4104 (including board) for single students; $4500 for married students. Off-campus housing cost; $500 per month. Contact Housing Office for both on- and off-campus housing information. Phone: (814)732-2818. Day-care facilities available.

Graduate Studies

Graduate study since 1957. Enrollment: full-time 292, part-time 360. College faculty teaching graduate students: full-time 83. Degrees conferred: M.Ed., M.A., M.S., M.F.A., M.I.T., M.S.N., M.S.W.

ADMISSION REQUIREMENTS. Transcripts, interview required in support of application. On-line application available. MAT/GRE required for some departments. TOEFL required for international applicants. Accepts transfer applicants. Graduates of unaccredited institutions not considered. Apply to Coordinator of Graduate Studies Admissions at least one month prior to registration. Rolling admission process. Application fee $25. Phone: (814)732-2856; fax: (814)732-2611.

ADMISSION STANDARDS. Relatively open. Usual minimum average: 2.5 (A = 4).

FINANCIAL AID. Annual awards from institutional funds: Scholarships, assistantships, Federal W/S, loans. Apply by May 1 to Financial Aid Office. Phone: (814)732-2821. Use FAFSA and institutional FAF for graduate assistantship. Aid available for part-time students.

DEGREE REQUIREMENTS. For M.A., M.S., M.Ed., M.I.T.: 30 semester hours minimum, at least 21 in residence; thesis/nonthesis option. For M.F.A., M.S.W.: 60 semester hours, at least 45 in residence. For M.S.N.: 42 semester hours, at least 30 in residence.

FIELDS OF STUDY.
Art. M.A.
Biology. M.S.
Ceramics. M.F.A.
Clinical Psychology. M.A.
Communication Studies. M.A.
Community Counseling. M.A.
Educational Psychology. M.Ed.
Elementary Education. M.Ed.
Elementary School Administration. M.Ed.
Information Technology. M.I.T.

Jewelry/Metalsmithing. M.F.A.
Middle and Secondary Education. M.Ed.
Nurse Practitioner. M.S.N.
Painting. M.F.A.
Printmaking. M.F.A.
Reading. M.Ed.
Rehabilitation Counseling. M.A.
School Guidance. M.A.
Sculpture. M.F.A.
Secondary School Administration. M.Ed.
Social Science. M.A.
Social Work. M.S.W.
Special Education. M.Ed.
Speech-Language Pathology. M.A.
Student Personnel Services. M.A.
Studio Art. Includes ceramics, painting, printmaking, sculpture. M.F.A.

ELMIRA COLLEGE
Elmira, New York 14901
Web site: www.elmira.edu

Founded 1855. Located 54 miles SW of Binghamton, New York. Coed. Private control. 12-12-6-6 term. Special facility: off-campus graduate centers at Oswego, Bath, Corning, Ithaca, Rome, Watkins Glen, N.Y.; multimedia learning center, Center for Mark Twain Studies at Quarry Farms. Library: 389,000 volumes, 1755 subscriptions. Total College enrollment: 1200.

Graduate tuition: per credit $820. Limited on-campus housing available for single students only. Annual housing cost: $7850 (including board). Apply to Coordinator of Housing.

Graduate Studies

Enrollment: about 618 (evening and summer sessions only). College faculty teaching graduate students: about 25. Degrees conferred: M.S.Ed.

ADMISSION REQUIREMENTS. Transcripts required in support of College's application. On-line application available. Accepts transfer applicants. Apply to Dean of Continuing Education and Graduate Studies at least two weeks prior to registration. Phone: (607)735-1825; fax: (607)735-1758; e-mail: graduate@elmira.edu.

ADMISSION STANDARDS. Relatively open. Usual minimum average 2.5 (A = 4).

FINANCIAL AID. Limited to Federal W/S, loans. Approved for VA benefits. Apply to Financial Aid Office at time of application. Use FAFSA.

DEGREE REQUIREMENTS. For master's: 36 semester hours, at least 30 on campus; research experience required.

FIELDS OF STUDY.
Adult Education.
Childhood Education (Grades 1–6).
General Education.
Literacy (Birth–12).

EMERSON COLLEGE
Boston, Massachusetts 02116-4624
Web site: www.emerson.edu

Founded 1880. CGS member. Located in downtown Boston. Coed. Private control. Semester system. Special facilities: one television and two radio stations, speech clinic, theater facilities, Center for Acquired Communication Disorders, Early Childhood Communication Center, Robbins Speech, Language, and Hearing Center. Library: 193,000 volumes, 7400 subscriptions.

Annual tuition: per credit $610. No on-campus housing available for graduate students. Average academic year housing costs: $7782 (including board). Off-campus housing costs: $600–$800 per month shared living accommodations. Contact Office of Housing for both on- and off-campus housing information. Phone: (617)824-7863.

Graduate Division

Enrollment: full-time 730, part-time 202. Faculty: full-time 109, part-time 55. Degrees conferred: M.A., M.F.A., M.S.

ADMISSION REQUIREMENTS. Official transcripts, three letters of recommendation, GRE/GMAT, portfolio or writing sample required in support of application. Interview required by some departments. TOEFL required for international applicants. Accepts transfer applicants. Graduates of unaccredited institutions not considered. Apply to Director of Graduate Admission by July 15 (Fall, priority deadline March 1), December 15 (Spring, priority deadline November 1). Application fee $45, $75 for international students. Phone: (617)824-8610; fax: (617)824-8614; e-mail: gradapp@emerson.edu.

ADMISSION STANDARDS. Selective. Usual minimum average: 3.0 (A = 4), 2.7 for provisional admission.

FINANCIAL AID. Annual awards from institutional funds: fellowships, assistantships, scholarships, Federal W/S, loans. Approved for VA benefits. Apply by March 1 to the appropriate department for assistantships; to Office of Financial Aid for all other programs. Phone: (617)578-8655. Use FAFSA. Aid available for part-time students.

DEGREE REQUIREMENTS. For M.A.: 36–40 credits: thesis/nonthesis program; final written/oral exam. For M.S.: 51 credits. For M.F.A.: 52 credits; thesis/nonthesis program; final written/oral exam.

FIELDS OF STUDY.
Communication Sciences and Disorders. Includes speech-language pathology. M.S.
Creative Writing. M.F.A.
Global Marketing Communication and Advertising. M.A.
Health Communication. M.A.
Integrated Marketing Communications. M.A.
Journalism. Includes broadcast, print, multimedia. M.A.
Management and Organizational Communication. M.A.
Marketing Communication. M.A.
Media Arts. Includes audio, video, new media. M.F.A.
Political Communication. M.A.
Publishing and Writing. Includes book, electronic, magazine. M.A.
Theater Education. Includes theater and community. M.A.
Writing and Publishing. M.A.

EMORY UNIVERSITY
Atlanta, Georgia 30322-1100
Web site: www.emory.edu

Founded 1836. Located in a suburban area 6 miles NE of downtown Atlanta. CGS and AAU member. Private control. Methodist affiliation. Semester system. Special facilities: Carter Center of Emory University, Center for Public Health Practice, Emerson Center for Scientific Computation, Emory Fertility

Center, Institute for Women's Studies, Institute for African Studies, National Institute of Church Finance and Administration, Nutrition and Health Science Center, Vascular Surgery Center, Institute of the Liberal Arts, Yerkes Regional Primate Research Center, Michael C. Carlos Museum, Winship Cancer Center, Center for Research in Social Change. Library: 2,300,000 volumes, 24,600 subscriptions. The University's NIH ranking is 27th among all U.S. institutions with 511 awards/grants worth $154,430,330. Total University enrollment: 11,500.

Annual tuition: full-time $23,770, per credit $990. On-campus graduate housing: approximately 272 units. Average academic year housing cost: $8000. Apply to Graduate and Family Housing Office. Phone: (404)727-8830.

Graduate School of Arts and Sciences

Graduate study since 1919. Enrollment: full- and part-time 1362 (579 men, 783 women). Faculty: 325. Degrees conferred: M.A., M.S., M.A.T., M.Ed., M.M., M.S.M., Ph.D.

ADMISSION REQUIREMENTS. Two copies of transcripts, three letters of recommendation, GRE required in support of School's application. International applicants whose native language is not English must demonstrate proficiency in English as specified by the individual department. Accepts transfer applicants. Graduates of unaccredited institutions not considered. Apply to Graduate School at least one month prior to registration. (To be considered for Financial Aid in the Fall, apply by January 20; some departments have earlier deadlines.) Application fee $50. Phone: (404)727-0184; fax: (404)727-4990.

ADMISSION STANDARDS. Competitive to selective for most departments. Usual minimum average: 3.0 in major (A = 4).

FINANCIAL AID. Annual awards from institutional funds: tuition scholarships, graduate assistantships, teaching assistants, nonservice fellowships, tuition waivers, Federal W/S, loans. Apply by January 20 to the Financial Aid Office. Phone: (404)727-1141. Use FAFSA. About 60% of students receive aid. These awards available on a competitive basis. Aid available for part-time students.

DEGREE REQUIREMENTS. For M.A., M.S.: 24 semester hours minimum, two semesters in residence; thesis, final oral/written exam. For M.A.T., M.Ed., M.M., M.S.M.: 40 semester hours minimum, three semesters in residence; no thesis or language requirement. For Ph.D.: 48 semester hours beyond the master's; comprehensive exam; reading knowledge of one or more foreign languages in some departments; dissertation; final oral exam.

FIELDS OF STUDY.
Anthropology. Ph.D. only.
Art History. M.A., Ph.D.
Biological and Biomedical Sciences. Includes biochemistry and molecular biology, cell and developmental biology, genetic and molecular biology, immunology and molecular pathogenesis, microbiology and molecular genetics, neuroscience, nutrition and health sciences, population biology, ecology, and evolution, physiological and pharmacological sciences. Ph.D. only.
Biomedical Engineering. Ph.D.
Biostatistics. M.S., Ph.D.
Chemistry. M.S., Ph.D.
Comparative Literature. Ph.D. only.
Economics. Ph.D. only.
Educational Studies. M.A., M.A.T., M.Ed., D.A.S.T., Ph.D.
English. M.A., Ph.D.
Epidemiology. M.S., Ph.D.
Film Studies. M.A. only.
French. Ph.D. only.

History. Ph.D. only.

Jewish Studies. M.A. only.

Liberal Arts, Graduate Institute of the. Includes American and African-American culture, history, and theory. Ph.D.

Mathematics. M.S.

Mathematics and Computer Science. M.S., Ph.D.

Music. Includes choral conducting, organ performance, sacred music. M.M., M.S.M.

Nursing. Ph.D.

Philosophy. Ph.D. only.

Physical, Materials, and Computational Sciences. Ph.D.

Physics. Ph.D. only.

Political Science. Ph.D. only.

Psychology. Includes clinical, cognitive and developmental, psychobiology. Ph.D. only.

Religion. Includes Hebrew Bible, New Testament, historical, theological, ethics and society, West and South Asian religion. Ph.D. only.

Sacred Music. M.A.

Sociology. Ph.D.

Spanish. Ph.D.

Women's Studies. Ph.D. only.

Roberto C. Goizueta Business School

Web site: www.emory.edu/bus

Established 1954. Public control. Accredited programs: M.B.A., E.M.B.A. offered in Buckhead and in downtown Atlanta; suburban environment. Semester system. Special Programs: accelerated M.B.A. program; foreign exchange programs (in Austria, Chile, Costa Rica, Finland, France, Germany, Hungary, Italy, Korea, Mexico, People's Republic of China, Republic of Singapore, Russia, Spain, United Kingdom, Venezuela); internships; Scholar Partnership Program with Spelman College. Special facilities: Center for Leadership and Career Studies, Center for Relationship Marketing.

Annual tuition: full-time $23,600. Enrollment: total full-time 462, part-time 190 (men 60%, women 40%). Faculty 72 full-time, 8 part-time; 99% with Ph.D./D.B.A. Degrees conferred: M.B.A. (full-time, part-time, day, evening), E.M.B.A. (weekends only, alternating Fridays, Saturdays), M.B.A.-J.D., M.B.A.-M.Div., M.B.A.-M.N., M.B.A.-M.P.H.

ADMISSION REQUIREMENTS. All applicants should have a bachelor's degree from a recognized institution of higher education and a strong mathematics background. Students are required to have their own personal computer. Submit application, GMAT (will accept GMAT test results from the last five years, latest acceptable date is March), official transcripts from each undergraduate/graduate school attended, three letters of recommendation, four essays, résumé (prefers at least four years of work experience), and an application fee of $70 to the Office of Admission and Student Services. Accept MBA Multi-App electronic application in lieu of institutional application. In addition, international students (whose native language is other than English) should submit a TOEFL (minimum score 600) report, certified translations and evaluations of all official transcripts; recommendation should be in English or with certified translations, proof of health/immunization certificate, and proof of sufficient financial resources for two years of academic study. Beginning students are admitted Fall only. U.S. citizens apply by April 1 (Fall), international students apply by February 15 (Fall). On-campus interviews are strongly encouraged. Joint degree applicants must apply to and be accepted to both schools, contact the Admissions Office for current information and specific admissions requirements. Completed applications received by December 31 will be notified by January 31, after December 31 a rolling admissions process is used, notification is made within 4–6 weeks of receipt of completed application and supporting documents, Admissions Office phone: (404)727-6311; fax: (404)727-4612; e-mail: admissions@bus.emory.edu.

ADMISSION STANDARDS. Highly selective. Median GMAT: 626; median GPA: 3.2 (A = 4). Gourman rating: the MBA was rated in the top 48, the score was 4.24. *U.S. News & World Report* ranking is in the top 25 of all U.S. business schools. *Business Week* listed Business School in the top 50 American business schools.

FINANCIAL AID. Scholarships, Dean's Scholar Awards, minority scholarships, grants, Woodruff Fellowships, teaching assistantships, Dietz Loan Fund, Federal W/S, loans. Financial aid is available for part-time study. Financial aid may be available for international students. Assistantships may be available for joint degree candidates. Financial Aid applications and information are generally available at the on-campus visit/interview or after January 1; apply by March 1. Request scholarship, fellowship, assistantship information from the Business School; phone: (404)727-6039. Contact the University's Financial Aid Office for current need-based financial aid information. Phone: (404)727-1141. Use FAFSA (School code: 001564), also submit Financial Aid Transcript, Federal Income Tax forms. Approximately 45% of students receive some form of financial assistance.

DEGREE REQUIREMENTS. For M.B.A.: 63 credit program including 27 elective credits, two-year program; degree program must be completed in 9 semesters. For E.M.B.A.: sixteen-month program; International Business Colloquium (ten days abroad). For M.B.A.-M.N.: 6-semester program. For M.B.A.-M.Div.: Four-year program. For M.B.A.-M.P.H: 5-semester program. For M.B.A.-J.D.: four-year program.

M.B.A. AREAS OF CONCENTRATION:

Accounting.

Decision and Information Analysis.

Economics.

Finance.

Human Resource Management.

International Business.

Management.

Management Information Systems.

Marketing.

Operations Management.

Organizational and Management.

Quantitative Analysis.

Strategic Management.

The School of Law

Founded 1916. ABA approved since 1923. AALS member. Semester system. Law library: 368,153 volumes, 5555 subscriptions. Library has LEXIS, NEXIS, WESTLAW, DOBIS.

Annual tuition $25,296. Limited on-campus housing available. Total average cost for all other expenses: $10,980.

Enrollment: first-year class 222; total full-time 636 (men 47%, women 53%); postgraduates 112. Faculty: full-time 27, part-time 38. Student to faculty ratio 19.6 to 1. Degrees conferred: J.D., J.D.-M.B.A., J.D.-M.P.H., J.D.-M.Div., J.D.-M.T.S., LL.M. (Taxation, Litigation).

ADMISSION REQUIREMENTS. LSDAS report, transcripts, letters of recommendation, LSAT (not later than December), bachelor's degree required in support of application. Interview not required, but visits are encouraged. Accepts transfer applicants. Apply to Director of Admissions after September 1, before March 1. Beginning students admitted Fall only. Application fee $50. Phone: (404)727-6802; fax: (404)727-2477; e-mail: lawinfo@law.emory.edu.

ADMISSION STANDARDS Selective. Mean LSAT: 161; mean GPA: 3.43 (A = 4). Gourman rating: 3.90. *U.S. News & World Report* ranking is in the top 22 of all law schools. Accepts about 25–30% of total annual applicants.

FINANCIAL AID Scholarships, fellowships (advanced students only), assistantships, Federal W/S, loans. Apply to Director of Admissions by April 1. Use FAFSA. About 29% of students receive aid other than loans from School funds.

DEGREE REQUIREMENTS, For J.D.: 88 semester hours minimum. For LL.M.: 24 semesters beyond the J.D.; one-year minimum in residence. For the master's degrees: see Graduate School listing above.

School of Medicine (30322-4510)

Founded as Atlanta Medical College in 1854. Library 107,000 volumes.

Annual tuition: $29,548; student fees $700. On-campus housing for married students only. Apply to University Housing Office. Total average figure for all other expenses $7590.

Enrollment: first-year class 112; total full-time 796 (men 53%, women 47%); postgraduates 650; fellows 95. Faculty: approximately 1200 full- and part-time, volunteers. Degree conferred: M.D.; M.M.Sc., M.D.-M.P.H. are offered through Division of Allied Health Professions. The combined degree programs, M.S. and Ph.D. (Medical Scientist Training Program) are offered through the Graduate School of Arts and Sciences.

ADMISSION REQUIREMENTS. AMCAS report, transcripts, letters of reference, MCAT (preferably in Spring), supplemental application, interview required in support of application. Interview by invitation only. Applicants must have completed at least three years of college study. Accepts transfer applicants. Does not have EDP. Apply to Office of the Dean, School of Medicine, after June 15, before October 15. Application fee $70. Phone: (404)727-5660; fax: (404)727-5456; e-mail: medschadmiss@medadm.emory.edu.

ADMISSION STANDARDS. Very competitive. Mean MCAT: 10.0; mean GPA: 3.73 (A = 4). Gourman rating: 4.31. *U.S. News & World Report* ranking is in the top 20 of all U.S. medical schools. Accepts 3% of total annual applicants. Approximately 40% are state residents.

FINANCIAL AID. Scholarships (merit and minority), fellowships, assistantships, NIH stipends, Federal W/S, loans. Apply to Financial Aid Office. Phone: (800)727-6039. Use FAFSA (school code: 001564). About 71% of students receive aid other than loans from School funds.

DEGREE REQUIREMENTS. For M.D.: satisfactory completion of four-year program. For M.P.H. see Division of Allied Health Professions listing below. For M.S., Ph.D., see Graduate School of Arts and Sciences listing above.

FIELDS OF GRADUATE STUDY.
Biochemistry.
Biomedical Engineering.
Biophysics.
Cell Biology.
Genetics.
Immunology.
Microbiology.
Molecular Biology.
Neurosciences.
Pharmacology.
Physiology.

Nell Hodgson Woodruff School of Nursing

Web site: www.nursing.emory.edu

Annual tuition: $16,450, per credit $678. Enrollment: full-time 74, part-time 41. School faculty: full-time 34, part-time 21. Degrees conferred: M.S.N., M.S.N.-M.P.H., M.S.N.-M.B.A.

ADMISSION REQUIREMENTS. Transcripts, B.S.N., MAT or GRE, one year experience in a clinical area required in support of School's application. On-line application available. TOEFL required for international applicants. Accepts transfer applicants. Graduates of unaccredited institutions not considered. Apply by February 15 (Fall), November 1 (Spring) to Office of Student Affairs. Application fee $50. Phone: (404)727-7980 or (800)222-3879; fax: (404)727-8509; e-mail: admit@nursing.emory.edu.

ADMISSION STANDARDS. Selective. Usual minimum overall average: 3.0; average for nursing courses: 3.3 (A = 4).

FINANCIAL AID. Scholarships, fellowships, assistantships, Federal W/S, loans. Approved for VA benefits. Apply by February 15 to the Programs Director for scholarships, fellowships, assistantships; to the Financial Aid Office for all other programs. Phone: (404)727-6039. Use FAFSA and CSS Profile. Aid available for part-time students.

DEGREE REQUIREMENTS. For M.S.N.: 48 semester hours minimum, all in residence; thesis option.

FIELDS OF STUDY.
Adult Critical Care.
Adult Medical Surgical Nurse Practitioner.
Adult Nurse Practitioner.
Adult Immunology Oncology.
Family Nurse Midwife.
Family Nurse Practitioner.
Gerontological Nurse Practioner.
International Health. M.S.N.-M.P.H.
Leadership in Healthcare.
Nursing Administration.
Pediatric Nurse Practitioner.
Women's Health Care Nurse.

Rollins School of Public Health

Web site: www.sph.emory.edu

Semester system. Annual tuition: $15,960, per credit $508. On-campus housing available. Apply to University Housing Office. Phone: (404)727-5481; fax: (404)727-3996.

Enrollment: full-time 465, part-time 297 (men 29%, women 71%). Faculty: full-time 108, part-time 233. Degrees conferred: M.P.H., M.S.P.H., M.B.A.-M.P.H., M.D.-M.P.H., M.S.N.-M.P.H., J.D.-M.P.H.

ADMISSION REQUIREMENTS. Transcript, GRE, bachelor's degree required in support of School's application. TOEFL (minimum score 550) required for foreign applicants. Graduates of unaccredited institutions not considered. Apply to School by March 15. Application fee $50. Phone: (404)727-5481; fax: (404)727-3996; e-mail: admit@sph.emory.edu.

ADMISSION STANDARDS. Selective. Usual minimum average: 3.0 (A = 4).

FINANCIAL AID. Scholarships, grants, fellowships, teaching assistantships, Federal W/S, loans. Apply by February 15 to the Financial Aid Office and to Program Director. Phone: (404)727-3958. Use FAFSA.

DEGREE REQUIREMENTS. For M.P.H., M.S.P.H.: 42–48 semester hours minimum, at least two in residence; comprehensive written exam or thesis. For Ph.D.: for degree requirements, please consult Graduate School of Arts and Sciences listing above.

FIELDS OF STUDY.
Biostatistics. Ph.D.
Epidemiology. Ph.D.
Nutrition and Health Sciences. Ph.D.

Public Health. M.P.H., M.S.P.H.
Public Health Informatics. M.S.P.H.

EMPORIA STATE UNIVERSITY

Emporia, Kansas 66801-5087
Web site: www.emporia.edu

Founded 1863. CGS member. Located 55 miles SW of Topeka. Coed. State control. Semester system. Special facilities: Ross Natural History Reservation, Butcher Laboratory School, Charles Coughlen Tall Grass Preserve, Reading Woods. Library: 733,000 volumes, 1405 subscriptions. Total University enrollment: 4850.

Tuition: per semester, full-time resident $1316, nonresident $3369, per credit resident $119, nonresident $290. On-campus housing for 93 married students, unlimited for single students. Average academic year housing cost: $1890 for married students, $1860–$3702 for single students. Apply to Residential Life and Housing Coordinator. Phone: (620)343-5264, (620)341-5909. Day-care facilities available.

Graduate Division

Enrollment: full-time 305, part-time 559. College faculty teaching graduate students: full-time 204, part-time 79. Degrees conferred: M.A., M.A.T., M.B.A., M.M., M.L.S., M.S., Ed.S., Ph.D.

ADMISSION REQUIREMENTS. Transcript, letters of recommendation required in support of University's application. On-line application available. GRE/GMAT/MAT required by some departments. TOEFL required for international applicants. Interview required for library science major. Accepts transfer applicants. Graduates of unaccredited institutions not considered. Apply to Graduate Office at least 30 days before the first day of enrollment period. Application fee $20, $30 (Ph.D.). Phone: (620)341-5909.

ADMISSION STANDARDS. Relatively open. Usual minimum average: 2.5 (A = 4) in last 60 credits.

FINANCIAL AID. Annual awards from institutional funds: fellowships, research assistantships, teaching assistantships, graduate aides, special graduate assistantships, grants, Federal W/S, loans. Approved for VA benefits. Apply to Graduate Office by March 15. Phone: (620)343-5457. Use FAFSA. About 30% of students receive aid other than loans from University and outside sources. Aid available for part-time students.

DEGREE REQUIREMENTS. For M.A., M.B.A., M.M., M.S.: 30 semester hours with thesis, or 32–38 hours without thesis, at least 22 in residence and one semester in full-time attendance; final written/oral exams. For M.A.T.: 36 semester hours minimum, at least 22 in residence and one semester in full-time attendance; thesis/nonthesis option; final written/oral exam. For M.L.S.: 42 specified hours; thesis/nonthesis option; final written/oral exam. For Ed.S.: 22 hours minimum in residence beyond the master's, thesis included, at least one semester in full-time attendance; GRE for candidacy; final written/oral exam. For Ph.D.: 60 semester hours beyond master's minimum, at least 42 in full-time residence; advancement to candidacy; research tool; comprehensive exam; dissertation; final oral exam.

FIELDS OF STUDY.
Accounting. M.B.A.
Art Therapy. M.S.
Biology. M.S.
Business Administration. M.B.A.
Business Education.
Education. Includes art, early childhood, education of the gifted, elementary, reading, secondary, counselor education, rehabilitation counseling, curriculum and instruction. M.S.
Educational Administration. M.S.

English. M.A.
Health, Physical Education and Recreation. M.S.
History. Includes American and world. M.A.
Library and Information Management. M.L.S., Ph.D.
Mathematics. M.S.
Mental Health Counseling. M.S.
Music. Includes music education, performance; recital for performance majors. M.M.
Physical Science. Includes chemistry, earth science, physics. M.S.
Psychology. Includes clinical, organizational, school psychology. M.S., Ed.S.
Rehabilitation Counseling. M.S.
School Counseling. M.S.
Social Science. M.A.T.
Special Education. M.S.

FAIRFIELD UNIVERSITY

Fairfield, Connecticut 06430-5195
Web site: www.fairfield.edu

Founded 1942. Located 50 miles NE of New York City. Coed on graduate level. Private control. Roman Catholic. Semester system. Library: 293,100 volumes, 1790 subscriptions. Total University enrollment 5100.

No on-campus housing available for graduate students.

Graduate School of Education and Allied Professions

Graduate study since 1950. Tuition: per credit hour $390. Enrollment: full-time 99, part-time 402. University faculty teaching graduate students: full-time 19, part-time 28. Degrees conferred: M.A., C.A.S.

ADMISSION REQUIREMENTS. Transcripts, two letters of recommendation, PRAXIS I CBT or waiver required in support of School's application. TOEFL required for international applicants. Graduates of unaccredited institutions not considered. Apply to Graduate School Office; no specified closing date except for MMTP and Counselor Education program. Rolling admission process. Application fee $50. Phone: (203)254-4000, ext. 2414; fax: (203)254-4241.

ADMISSION STANDARDS. Relatively open. Usual minimum average: 2.67 (A = 4).

FINANCIAL AID. Annual awards from institutional funds: scholarships, fellowships, tuition waivers, grants, graduate assistantships, Federal W/S, loans. Apply to Dean by May 1 (Fall) December 15 (Spring). Phone: (203)254-4125. Use FAFSA and University's FAF. Loans available for part-time students.

DEGREE REQUIREMENTS. For M.A.: 33–54 credits; comprehensive examination or thesis. For C.A.S.: 30 credits minimum beyond the master's, at least 24 in residence. No thesis or language requirement.

FIELDS OF STUDY.
Applied Psychology. Includes human services, foundations of advanced psychology, industrial/organizational/personal. M.A.
Community Counseling. M.A., C.A.S.
Computers in Education. M.A., C.A.S.
Curriculum and Instruction. Includes curriculum and teaching, elementary education, secondary education. M.A., C.A.S.
Educational Technology. M.A., C.A.S.
Marriage and Family Therapy. M.A.
School Counseling. M.A., C.A.S.
School Psychology. M.A., C.A.S.

Special Education. M.A., C.A.S.
TESOL Foreign Languages and Bilingual/Multicultural Education. M.A., C.A.S.

Charles F. Dolan School of Business

Graduate study since 1978. Accredited program: M.B.A. Tuition: per credit $510. Enrollment: full-time 43, part-time 161. University faculty teaching graduate students: full-time 39, part-time 3. Degrees conferred: E.M.B.A., M.B.A., M.B.A.P.A. (Public Accounting), M.S.F.

ADMISSION REQUIREMENTS. Transcripts, statement of self-evaluation, two references, GMAT required in support of School's application. On-line application available. For M.B.A.P.A. a Statement of Certification is required. In addition, a sponsorship by a public accounting firm required for practicum. TOEFL (minimum score 550) required for international applicants. Graduates of unaccredited institutions not considered. Apply to School Office by May 1. Rolling admissions process. Application fee $55. Phone: (203)254-4000, ext. 2662.

ADMISSION STANDARDS. Admission formula: 200 × GPA + GMAT must equal 1100 or better.

FINANCIAL AID. Annual awards from institutional funds: grants, assistantships, Federal W/S, loans. Approved for VA benefits. Apply to Dean by May 1 (Fall), December 15 (Spring). Phone: (203)254-4000. Use FAFSA (School code: 001385) and University's FAF. Loans available for part-time students.

DEGREE REQUIREMENTS. For M.B.A.: 62 credits, at least 35 in residence. For M.B.A.P.A.: 12–15 month program (includes 150 hour criterion to sit for Uniform CPA Exam); practicum. For M.S.F.: 30 credits program, at least 24 in residence.

FIELDS OF STUDY.
Business Administration. Includes concentrations in accounting, e-business, finance, health care management, human resource management, information systems and operations, international business, marketing, taxation. M.B.A.
Finance. M.S.F.
Public Accounting. Includes concentrations in finance, information systems and operations management, taxation. M.B.A.P.A.

FAIRLEIGH DICKINSON UNIVERSITY
College at Florham
Madison, New Jersey 07940-1099
Web site: www.fdu.edu

Established 1942. Private control. Coed. Semester system. Special facilities: Contemporary Center for Advanced Psychoanalytic Studies, Corporate Communication Institute, Florham Center for University Women's Issues, Institute for Global Commerce, Center for Global Teaching and Learning, Center for Human Resource Management Studies, New York/New Jersey Economic Research Center, Public Administrations Institute, Regional Center for College Students with Learning Disabilities, Rothman Institute of Entrepreneurial Studies, Center for Service Professionals. Library: 182,000 volumes, 1259 subscriptions. Daycare facilities available. Total University enrollment: 10,000.

Tuition: $597 per graduate credit. Contact Office of Student Life for off-campus housing. Phone: (973)443-8570.

Graduate Studies

Enrollment: full- and part-time 1500. Faculty: full-time 62, part-time 84. Degrees conferred: M.A., M.A.T., M.B.A., M.P.A., M.S., M.S.T.

ADMISSION REQUIREMENTS. Official transcripts required in support of application. Three letters of recommendation, GRE/GMAT/MAT/PRAXIS required for some programs. TOEFL required for international applicants. Accepts transfer applicants. Graduates of unaccredited institutions may not be considered. Rolling admissions process. Early application encouraged. Application fee $35. Phone: (973)442-8905.

ADMISSION STANDARDS. Selective. Usual minimum average: 2.5, 3.0 in major field of undergraduate study (A = 4).

FINANCIAL AID. Limited to fellowships, loans. Approved for VA benefits. Apply to appropriate department chair for fellowships; to Office of Financial Aid for loans. Phone: (973)443-8700. Use FAFSA.

DEGREE REQUIREMENTS. For master's: 32–60 semester credits minimum, at least 26 in residence; final written exam: thesis/nonthesis option; other requirements vary by department.

FIELDS OF STUDY.

MAXWELL BECTON COLLEGE OF ARTS AND SCIENCES:
Addictions Counseling. M.A.
Applied Social and Community Psychology. M.A.
Biology. M.S.
Chemistry. M.S.
Clinical/Counseling Psychology. M.A.
Computer Science. M.S.
Corporate and Organizational Communications. M.A.
Creative Writing. M.F.A.
English Language and Literature. M.A.T.
General Experimental Psychology. M.A.
Industrial/Organizational Psychology. M.A.
Mathematics. M.S.
Physical Science. M.A.T.
Teaching. Includes elementary education, English as a second language, English language and literacy, secondary education, social studies education, world languages. M.A.T.

SAMUEL J. SILBERMAN COLLEGE OF BUSINESS ADMINISTRATION:
Accounting.
Accounting (for Non-Accountants).
Administrative Science.
Corporate and Organizational Communication.
Entrepreneurial Studies.
Finance.
Hospitality Management Studies.
Human Resource Management.
International Business.
Management. Includes corporate and organizational communication, corporate communication.
Marketing.
Pharmaceutical-Chemical Studies.
Public Administration. M.P.A.
Taxation. M.S.T.

FAIRLEIGH DICKINSON UNIVERSITY
Metropolitan Campus
Teaneck, New Jersey 07666-1914
Web site: www.fdu.edu

Established 1942. Private control. Coed. Semester system. Library: 435,700 volumes, 15,000 subscriptions.

Tuition: per credit $597. No on-campus housing available. Contact the Office of Student Life for off-campus housing information. Phone: (201)692-2231.

Graduate Studies

Enrollment: full-time 593, part-time 1150. Faculty: full-time 148, part-time 67. Degrees conferred: M.A., M.A.T., M.B.A., M.S., M.P.A., M.S., M.S.E.E., M.S.N., M.S.T., Ph.D. (Clinical Psychology).

ADMISSION REQUIREMENTS. Transcripts, three letters of recommendation, GRE/GMAT/MAT/PRAXIS required in support of applications. TOEFL required for international applicants. Accepts transfer applicants. Graduates of unaccredited institutions may not be considered. Rolling admissions process. Early application encouraged. Application fee $40. Phone: (201)692-2551.

ADMISSION STANDARDS. Selective. Usual minimum average: 2.5 (A = 4), 3.0 in major field of undergraduate study.

FINANCIAL AID. Scholarships, research fellowships, teaching fellowships, M.P.A., M.A.T. paid internships, loans. Approved for VA benefits. Apply to appropriate department chair for fellowships; to Office of Financial Aid for all other programs. Phone: (201)692-2362. Use FAFSA.

DEGREE REQUIREMENTS. For master's: 32–60 semester credits minimum, at least 26 in residence; final written exam; thesis/nonthesis option; other requirements vary by department. For Ph.D.: 60 semester credits beyond the master's; qualifying exam; internship; dissertation; final exam.

FIELDS OF STUDY.

UNIVERSITY COLLEGE:
Biological Sciences. M.A.T.
Biology. M.S.
Clinical Psychology. M.A., Ph.D.
Computer Engineering. M.S.
Computer Science. M.S.
Educational Leadership. M.A.
Electrical Engineering. M.S.E.E.
Electronic Commerce. M.S.
English and Comparative Literature. M.A.
General-Theoretical Psychology. M.A.
History. M.A.
International Studies. M.A.
Learning Disabilities. M.A.
Management Information Systems. M.S.
Medical Technology. M.S.
Multilingual Education. M.A.
Nursing. M.S.N.
Physical Sciences. M.A.T.
Physics. Includes photonics. M.S.
Political Science. M.A.
Science. Includes science education, elementary science, cosmetic science. M.A.
School Psychology. M.A., Psy.D.
System Science. Includes environmental studies. M.S.
Teaching. Includes elementary education, English as a second language, secondary education. M.A.T.

SAMUEL J. SILBERMAN COLLEGE OF BUSINESS ADMINISTRATION:
Accounting.
Accounting (for Non-Accountants).
Administrative Science.
Economics.
Entrepreneurial Studies.
Finance.
Financial Economics. M.A.
Global Management.
Hospitality Management Studies.

Health Systems Management. E.M.B.A.
Human Resource Management.
International Business.
Management. Includes corporate communication, health systems management, information systems.
Marketing.
Pharmaceutical-Chemical Studies.
Public Administration. M.P.A.
Taxation. M.S.T.

HERMAN M. FINCH UNIVERSITY OF HEALTH SCIENCES/THE CHICAGO MEDICAL SCHOOL

3333 Green Bay Road
North Chicago, Illinois 60064-3095
Web site: www.finchcms.edu

Founded in 1912. University established in 1968, with Chicago Medical School as core component of three allied units. CGS member. Private control. Quarter system. Special facilities: Electron microscope facility, Protein Sequence Laboratory, Special Pathogen-Free Swine Facility, Computer Center, and Medical Library. Library: 94,000 volumes, 1063 subscriptions. Total University enrollment: 1400.

Off-campus housing available. Average living expenses: $1200 per month. Contact Office of Student Affairs.

School of Graduate and Postdoctoral Studies

Graduate study since 1968. Tuition: per credit $403.
Enrollment: full- and part-time 313. Faculty: full- and part-time 92. Degrees conferred: M.S., Ph.D.

ADMISSION REQUIREMENTS. Completed application, transcripts, three letters of recommendation, GRE required in support of School's application. Interview recommended. TOEFL, TWE, financial statement required for international applicants. Graduates of unaccredited institutions not considered. Early application advised for applicants seeking fellowships. All applications must be completed by June 1. Apply to the Office of Graduate Admissions. Application fee $30. Phone: (847)578-3209.

ADMISSION STANDARDS. Competitive for most departments. Usual minimum average: 3.0 (A = 4).

FINANCIAL AID. Fellowships, research assistantships, research grants, tuition waivers, loans. Approved for VA benefits. Apply to chairman of department for fellowships and assistantships; to the Office of Financial Aid for loans. Phone: (847)578-3217. Use FAFSA. Almost all students in basic medical science doctoral programs who are in good standing receive some sort of financial aid through University fellowships, research grants, and/or other sources.

DEGREE REQUIREMENTS. For M.S. (research master's): minimum of 30 units of course work and 15 units of research; minimum of one year of full-time residence; thesis; final oral exam. For Ph.D.: minimum of 60 units of course work and 75 units of research credit; minimum of two years of full-time residence; preliminary exam; thesis; final oral exam.

FIELDS OF STUDY.
Applied Physiology M.S.
Biochemistry and Molecular Biology. M.S., Ph.D.
Cell Biology and Anatomy. M.S., Ph.D.

Cellular and Molecular Pharmacology. M.S., Ph.D.
Clinical Immunology. M.S.
Clinical Psychology. M.S., Ph.D
Medical Imaging Sciences. M.S.
Medical Radiation Physics. M.S., Ph.D.
Microbiology and Immunology. M.S., Ph.D.
Molecular and Cellular Sciences. Ph.D.
Neuroscience. M.S., Ph.D.
Pathology. M.S., Ph.D.
Physiology and Biophysics. M.S., Ph.D.

Chicago Medical School

Founded 1912. Annual tuition: $35,673. Total average cost for all other expenses: $9900. Enrollment: first-year class 193 (EDP 3); total full-time 737 (men 60%, women 40%). School faculty: full-time 191, part-time 430. Degrees conferred: M.D., M.D.-Ph.D.

ADMISSION REQUIREMENTS. AMCAS report, transcripts, references, MCAT, interview required in support of application. On-line application available. Applicants must have completed at least four years of college study. Has EDP; apply between June 1 and August 1. Apply to Office of Admissions after June 15, before November 15 (firm). Application fee $90. Phone: (847)578-3206; fax: (847)578-3284.

ADMISSION STANDARDS. Very competitive. Mean MCAT: 9.0; mean GPA: 3.41 (A = 4). Gourman rating: 3.31. Accepts 3% of total annual applications. Approximately 30% are state residents.

FINANCIAL AID. Scholarships, loans. Apply to Associate Dean (Student Affairs); no specified closing date. Use FAFSA. About 75% of students receive aid other than loans from School funds.

DEGREE REQUIREMENTS. For M.D.: satisfactory completion of three-, four-, or five-year program; pass Step 1 and Step 2 of the USMLE. For M.D.-M.S.: satisfactory completion of five-year program. For M.D.-Ph.D.: satisfactory completion of program.

FIELDS OF GRADUATE STUDY.
Biochemistry and Molecular Biology.
Cell Biology and Anatomy.
Cellular and Molecular Pharmacology.
Clinical Psychology.
Medical Radiation Physics.
Microbiology and Immunology.
Molecular and Cellular Sciences.
Neuroscience.
Pathology.
Physiology and Biophysics.

FISK UNIVERSITY

Nashville, Tennessee 37208-3051
Web site: www.fisk.edu

Established 1867. Coed. Private control. Semester system. Library: 260,000 volumes, 5600 microforms, 350 current periodicals.
Annual tuition: full-time $8740; per credit $364. On-campus housing for single and married students. Average academic year housing cost: $5030 (including board) for single students; $4000 for married students. Contact Dean of Students for both on- and off-campus housing information. Phone: (615)329-8557.

Graduate Programs

Graduate study since 1889. Enrollment: about 37. Faculty: full- and part-time: 18. Degree conferred: M.A.

ADMISSION REQUIREMENTS. Transcripts, letters of recommendation required in support of application. GRE recommended for most programs. TOEFL required for international applicants. Accepts transfer applicants. Apply to Office of Admissions at least one month prior to date of registration. Rolling admission process. Application fee $25. Phone: (615)329-8668; fax: (615)329-8774.

ADMISSION STANDARDS. Selective. Usual minimum average: 2.5 (A = 4).

FINANCIAL AID. Fellowships, assistantships, loans. Apply to appropriate Department for fellowships, assistantships; to Office of Financial Aid for all other programs. No specified closing date. Use FAFSA. Phone: (615)329-8737.

DEGREE REQUIREMENTS. For M.A.: 30 semester hours minimum full-time; thesis; final written/oral exam.

FIELDS OF STUDY.
Biology.
Chemistry. Reading knowledge of one foreign language for M.A.
Clinical Psychology. GRE for admission.
Physics.
Psychology. GRE for admission.

FITCHBURG STATE COLLEGE

160 Pearl Street
Fitchburg, Massachusetts 01420-2697
Web site: www.fsc.edu

Founded 1894. CGS member. Located 26 miles N of Worcester. Coed. State control. Semester system. Library: 229,505 volumes, 1799 subscriptions.
Tuition: per hour, resident $150, nonresident $150. Limited on-campus housing available. Average academic year housing costs: $4680 (including board). Contact Office of Residence Life for both on- and off-campus housing information. Phone: (978)665-3219. Day care facilities available.

Division of Graduate and Continuing Education

Enrollment: full-time 150, part-time 591. Graduate faculty: part-time 150. Degrees conferred: M.A.T., M.B.A., M.Ed. M.S., C.A.G.S.

ADMISSION REQUIREMENTS. Transcripts, GRE/MAT/GMAT required in support of application. TOEFL required for international applicants. Accepts transfer applicants. Graduates of unaccredited institutions not considered. Apply to Director of Admission at least one month prior to entrance. Rolling admissions process. Application fee $10, $40 for international applicants. Phone: (978)655-3144; fax: (978)655-4540; e-mail: admissions@fsc.edu.

ADMISSION STANDARDS. Selective. Usual minimum average: 2.8 (A = 4). Minimum GMAT score 400, MAT 50th percentile.

FINANCIAL AID. Scholarships, research and graduate assistantships, loans. Apply to the Graduate Office by September 15 (Fall), January 15 (Spring) for scholarships; by May 15 (Fall) for assistantships; to Financial Aid Office for all other programs. Phone: (978)665-3185. Use FAFSA.

DEGREE REQUIREMENTS. For master's: 33–36 semester hours minimum, at least 30 in residence; no language requirement; thesis/nonthesis option. For C.A.G.S.: 30 semester hours beyond the master's; special project/final exam.

FIELDS OF STUDY.
Arts Education. M.Ed.
Biology. M.A., M.A.T.
Business Administration and Management. M.B.A.
Communication and Media Management. M.S.
Computer Science. M.S.
Consultation and Peer Leadership. C.A.G.S.
Counseling. Includes psychological, school. M.S.
Criminal Justice. M.S.
Earth Science. M.A., M.A.T.
Early Childhood Education. M.Ed.
Educational Leadership and Management. C.A.G.S.
Educational Staff Development. C.A.G.S.
Elementary Education. M.Ed.
English. M.A., M.A.T.
History. M.A., M.A.T.
Interdisciplinary Studies. C.A.G.S.
Mathematics. M.A., M.A.T.
Middle School Education. M.Ed.
Nursing. M.S.
Occupational Education. M.Ed.
Science Education. M.Ed.
Secondary Education. M.Ed.
Special Education. M.Ed.
Teacher Leadership. C.A.G.S.
Technology Education. M.Ed.

FLORIDA AGRICULTURAL AND MECHANICAL UNIVERSITY

Tallahassee, Florida 32307
Web site: www.famu.edu

Founded 1887. CGS member. Coed. State control. Semester system. Special facilities: Community Development and Research Center, Environmental Technology Transfer Center, Center for Water Quality, Small Business Development Center, Viticulture and Small Farm Development Center, Environmental Sciences Institute, Cooperative Institute for Internal Policy Research and Education, Institute for Building Sciences, Institute on Urban Policy and Commerce. Library: 466,000 volumes, 2200 subscriptions.

Tuition: full-time resident $1969, nonresident $6855; per hour, resident $164, nonresident $571. On-campus housing for 85 married students. Average per semester housing cost: $1171–$1868 per single occupancy. Apply to Business Manager for on-campus housing; to Dean of Men or Dean of Women for off-campus housing information. Phone: (850)599-3992.

School of Graduate Studies

Graduate study since 1945. Enrollment: full-time 800, part-time 1,591. Graduate faculty: full-time 200, part-time 20. Degrees conferred: M.Arch., M.S., M.Ed., M.B.A., M.A.S.S., M.L.A., M.P.T., M.P.H., M.S.S.C.P., M.S.W., Pharm.D., Ph.D.

ADMISSION REQUIREMENTS. Transcripts, GRE/GMAT required in support of School's application. On-line application available. TOEFL (minimum score 550) required for international applicants. Interview not required. Accepts transfer applicants. Graduates of unaccredited colleges not considered. Apply by July 22 (Fall), April 2 (Summer), November 30 (Spring). Application fee $20. Phone: (850)599-3796.

ADMISSION STANDARDS. Selective. Usual minimum average: 2.5 (A = 4). For Business the admission formula is 200 × GPA + GMAT must be 1000 or above.

FINANCIAL AID. Scholarships, fellowships, Federal W/S, loans. Apply to Graduate Dean at least thirty days prior to registration for fellowships and scholarships; to Financial Aid Office for Federal programs. Phone: (850)599-3730. Use FAFSA (University code: 001480). About 20% of students receive aid other than loans from School and outside sources. No aid other than loans for part-time students.

DEGREE REQUIREMENTS. For master's: 36 hours minimum including thesis, at least 30 in residence; final written/oral exam. For Pharm. D.: series of clinical clerkships, covering approximately 2000 hours; written comprehensive exam; clinical research project. For Ph.D.: 90 semester hours minimum beyond bachelor's; one foreign language or research tool; qualifying exam; dissertation; final oral exam.

FIELDS OF STUDY.

COLLEGE OF ARTS AND SCIENCES:
African American History. M.A.S.S.
Biology. M.S.
Chemistry. M.S.
Computer Software Engineering. M.S.
Criminal Justice. M.A.S.S.
Economics. M.A.S.S.
Engineering. Includes real-time systems, computer science, software development. M.S.
History. M.A.S.S.
Physics. M.S., Ph.D.
Political Sciences. M.A.S.S.
Psychology. Includes community, (M.S.), school (M.S.). M.A.S.S. M.S.
Public Administration. M.A.S.S.
Public Management. M.A.S.S.
Sociology. M.A.S.S.
Social Work. M.A.S.S., M.S.W.

COLLEGE OF EDUCATION:
Adult Education. M.Ed., M.S.
Business Education. M.Ed., M.S.
Counselor Education. M.Ed., M.S.
Educational Leadership. M.Ed., M.S., Ph.D.
Elementary Education. M.Ed., M.S.
Physical Education. Includes sport and leisure management. M.Ed., M.S.
Secondary Education. Includes biology, chemistry, English, history, mathematics, physics. M.Ed., M.S.
Vocational Education. M.Ed., M.S.

COLLEGE OF PHARMACY AND PHARMACEUTICAL SCIENCES:
Pharmaceutical Sciences. Includes medicinal chemistry (M.S., Ph.D.), pharmacology and toxicology (M.S., Ph.D.), environmental toxicology (M.S., Ph.D.), pharmacoeconomics (M.S.), pharmacoepidemiology (M.S.), pharmaceutics (M.S., Ph.D.).

COLLEGE OF ENGINEERING SCIENCES, TECHNOLOGY, AND AGRICULTURE:
Agricultural Sciences. Include agribusiness, animal science, engineering tech, international program, entomology, biotechnology, plant science. M.S.
Entomology. Includes aquatic entomology, biological control. Ph.D. in cooperation with the University of Florida.

COLLEGE OF ENGINEERING:
Chemical Engineering. M.S., Ph.D.
Civil Engineering. M.S., Ph.D.
Industrial Engineering. Includes engineering management. M.S., Ph.D.
Mechanical Engineering. M.S., Ph.D.

ENVIRONMENTAL SCIENCES INSTITUTE:
Environmental Science. Includes environmental restoration and waste management, marine and estuarine science, environmental policy and management, environmental biotechnology, radiation protection. M.S.
Environmental Science. Includes aquatic and terrestrial ecology, environmental chemistry, biomolecular science, environmental policy and management. Ph.D.

SCHOOL OF ALLIED HEALTH SCIENCES:
Health Care Administration. M.S.
Physical Therapy. M.P.T.

SCHOOL OF ARCHITECTURE:
Architecture. M.Arch, M.S.
Landscape Architecture. M.L.A.

SCHOOL OF BUSINESS:
Business Administration. M.B.A.

SCHOOL OF JOURNALISM, MEDIA, AND GRAPHIC ARTS:
Journalism, Media, and Graphic Arts. M.S.
Professional Development Track. Includes broadcast journalism, copy editing, newspaper journalism.

SCHOOL OF NURSING:
Nursing. Includes adult/gerontology nursing. M.S.

FLORIDA ATLANTIC UNIVERSITY

P.O. Box 3091
Boca Raton, Florida 33431-0991
Web site: www.fau.edu

Opened 1964. CGS member. Main campus located midway between Ft. Lauderdale and West Palm Beach just off I-95, other campus in Broward County. Coed. State control. Semester system. Library: 725,800 volumes, 4300 subscriptions. Total University enrollment: 23,200.

Tuition: per semester hour, resident $186, nonresident $678. On-campus housing for graduate single men and women; none for married students. Annual housing cost: $7993 (including board). Apply to Director of Housing. Phone: (561)267-2880; e-mail: housing@fau.edu.

Graduate Studies

Enrollment: degree-seeking students full-time 1038, part-time 1581. University faculty teaching graduate students: full-time 600. Degrees conferred: M.Ed., M.S., M.A., M.Acc., M.A.T., M.F.A., M.J.P.M., M.N.M., M.S.T., M.P.A., M.B.A., M.B.S., M.Tax., M.U.R.P., M.S.W., Ed.S., M.S.N., Ed.D., Ph.D., D.N.S.

ADMISSION REQUIREMENTS. Transcripts, letters of recommendation, GRE Subject Tests/GMAT required in support of application. On-line application available. TOEFL required for foreign applicants. Accepts transfer applicants. Graduates from unaccredited institutions not considered. Apply to Director of Admissions at least ninety days prior to registration. Application fee $20. Phone: (561)267-3624; e-mail: gradadm@fau.edu.

ADMISSION STANDARDS. Selective. Usual minimum average: 3.0 (A = 4), and combined score of 1000 on GRE, 450 GMAT.

FINANCIAL AID. Scholarships, assistantships, fellowships, teaching/research assistantships, nonresident tuition waivers, Federal W/S, loans. Apply to appropriate department chair for assistantship, fellowships; to Office of Student Financial Aid for all other programs. No specified closing date. Phone: (561)267-3530. Use FAFSA.

DEGREE REQUIREMENTS. For master's: 30–40 semester hours minimum, thesis/nonthesis option. For Ed.D.: 90 semester hours minimum beyond the bachelor's degree; essentially the same as for the Ph.D., except no language requirement. For Ph.D.: 40–80 semester hours minimum beyond master's; one foreign language or research tool; qualifying exam; admission to candidacy; dissertation; final oral exam.

FIELDS OF STUDY.
Accounting.
Anthropology.
Art.
Biological Sciences.
Business Administration.
Chemistry.
Communication.
Comparative Literature.
Comparative Studies.
Complex Systems and Brain Sciences.
Computer Arts.
Computer Engineering.
Computer Science.
Counselor Education. Includes mental health, rehabilitation, school.
Curriculum and Instruction.
Economics.
Educational Leadership.
Electrical Engineering.
Elementary Education.
English.
Environmental M.B.A.
Environmental Science.
Exceptional Student Education.
Exercise Science and Wellness Education.
French.
Geography.
Geology.
German.
Graphic Design.
History.
International Business.
Justice Policy and Management.
Languages and Linguistics.
Liberal Studies.
Manufacturing Systems Engineering.
Mathematics.
Mechanical Engineering.
Music.
Non-Profit Management.
Nursing.
Ocean Engineering.
Physics.
Political Science.
Psychology.
Public Administration.
Reading.
Social Foundations. Includes educational psychology, educational research, education technology, multicultural education.
Social Work.
Sociology.
Spanish.
Speech-Language Pathology.
Taxation.
Teacher Education.
Theatre.
Urban and Regional Planning.
Women's Studies.

FLORIDA INSTITUTE OF TECHNOLOGY

Melbourne, Florida 32901-6975
Web site: www.fit.edu

Founded 1958. Located within an hour's drive of Kennedy Space Center and Disney World. CGS member. Coed. Private control. Semester system. Special facilities: Vero Beach Marine Research Center, Center of Electronics Manufacturability, Center for Energy Alternatives, Claude Pepper Institute for Aging and Therapeutic Research, Infectious Diseases Laboratory. Library: 210,000 volumes, 5325 subscriptions.

Tuition: per credit $650. Limited on-campus housing for married and single graduate students. Average academic year housing cost: $5590 (includes board). Apply to Assistant Dean of Students. Phone: (321)674-8080.

Graduate School

Enrollment: full-time 399, part-time 1763. Faculty teaching graduate students: full-time 116, part-time 176. Degrees conferred: M.B.A., M.S., Ed.S., Psy.D., Ph.D.

ADMISSION REQUIREMENTS. Transcripts required in support of School's application. On-line application available. GRE/GMAT required for some majors. TOEFL required for international applicants. Accepts transfer students. Graduates of unaccredited institutions not considered. Apply to Graduate Admissions office; no specified closing date. Rolling admission process. Application fee $40, for international applicants $50. Phone: (321)674-8027 or (800)944-4348; fax: (321)674-9468.

ADMISSION STANDARDS. Usual master's level minimum average: 3.0 (A = 4).

FINANCIAL AID. Annual awards from institutional funds: fellowships, research/teaching assistantships, tuition waivers, Federal W/S, loans. Apply to Graduate School Admissions Office by March 1; February 15 for assistantships. Phone: (321)674-8070. Use FAFSA. About 80% of students receive aid other than loans from institute and outside sources. Aid available for part-time students.

DEGREE REQUIREMENTS. For master's: 32–48 credits minimum, at least 24–36 credits in residence; thesis option; final written/oral exam in some programs. For Ph.D.: 60 credits minimum, at least 32 credits, in full-time study; preliminary exam; advancement to candidacy; one foreign language or research tool; dissertation; final oral exam. For Psy.D.: essentially the same as Ph.D., except no foreign language requirement; special project may be substituted for dissertation.

FIELDS OF STUDY.
Aeronautics. Includes airport development, management, aviation safety.
Aerospace Engineering.
Applied Behavior Analysis.
Applied Mathematics.
Aviation Human Factors.
Biological Sciences.
Business Administration.
Chemical Engineering.
Chemistry.
Civil Engineering.
Clinical Psychology.
Coastal Resource Management.
Communication.
Computer Education.
Computer Engineering.
Computer Information Systems.
Computer Science.
Contract and Acquisition Management.
Electrical Engineering.
Engineering Psychology.
Environmental Engineering.
Environmental Resources Management.
Industrial/Organizational Psychology.
Interdisciplinary Science.
Management of Technology.
Mechanical Engineering.
Meteorology.
Ocean Engineering.
Oceanography. Includes bio-environmental, chemical, geological, physical-environments.
Operations Research.
Personnel Psychology.
Physics.
Science Education.
Software Engineering.
Space Sciences.

FLORIDA STATE UNIVERSITY

Tallahassee, Florida 32306
Web site: www.fsu.edu

Founded 1857. CGS member. Coed. State control. Semester system. Special facilities: The National High Magnetic Field Laboratory, The Center for Materials Research and Technology (MARTECH), 9 Mev Super FN tandem Van de Graaff accelerator, Florida State University Marine Laboratory, Center for Music Research, Antarctic Research Facility, Two Supercomputers: The Cray Y-MP and a Connection Machine, FSU Proton-Induced X-Ray Emission (PIXE) Laboratory, Supercomputer Computations Research Institute (SCRI), Institute of Science and Public Affairs, Institute for Social Research, Geophysical Fluid Dynamics Institute, Institute of Molecular Biophysics, Creative Writing Program, Educational Research Center for Child Development, Center for Information Systems Research, Beaches and Shores Resource Center. Library: 2,300,000 volumes, 15,450 subscriptions. Total University enrollment: 30,500.

Tuition: per credit, resident $153, nonresident $532. Capacity for on-campus housing for graduate students is 791. Average academic year housing costs: $12,220 for married students, $8220 (includes board) for single students. Contact Office of Resident Student Development for both on- (850)644-0089 and off-campus (850)644-2860 housing information.

Graduate School

Enrollment: full-time 3454, part-time 2161. Graduate faculty: full-time 966, part-time 136. Degrees conferred: M.A., M.S., M.Acc., M.B.A., M.M., M.M.Ed., M.S.N., M.S.P., M.S.W., Adv.M., Ed.Sp., Ad.M.L.S., M.F.A., M.P.A., Ed.D., D.Mus., Ph.D.

ADMISSION REQUIREMENTS. Two transcripts, GRE/GMAT required in support of School's application. On-line application available. TOEFL (minimum score 550) required for international applicants. Interview, GRE Subject Test, auditions, personal interviews, departmental applications, letters of recommendation required for some departments. Accepts transfer applicants. Graduates of unaccredited institutions not considered. Apply to Office of Admissions by July 16 (Fall), November 25 (Spring), April 2 (Summer). Application fee $20. Phone: (850)644-3420; fax: (850)644-0197.

ADMISSION STANDARDS. Competitive or very selective for some departments, selective for most. Usual minimum average: 3.0 (A = 4); GRE total: 1000.

FINANCIAL AID. Annual awards from institutional funds that meet the minimum University requirements for tuition waivers: graduate fellowships, research and service assistantships, assistantships with instructional responsibility, assistantships assisting faculty with instruction, scholarships, Federal W/S, loans. Approved for VA benefits. Apply by March 1 to appropriate department chair for fellowships, assistantships; to University's Office of Financial Aid for all other programs. Phone: (850)644-5871; fax: (850)644-6404. Use FAFSA. About 45% of students receive aid other than loans from University and outside sources. Aid available for part-time students.

DEGREE REQUIREMENTS. For M.A., M.S.: 30 semester hours minimum including thesis or 32 hours minimum without thesis, reading knowledge of one language for M.A. sometimes required for M.S.; final written/oral exams required by some departments. For M.Acc.: 33 hours minimum. For M.B.A., M.P.A.: 39 hours minimum. For M.M., M.M.Ed., M.P.: 30 hours minimum, including thesis, recital, or composition, or 36 hours minimum without thesis. For M.S.W.: 4 semesters (Fall and Spring consecutively), 60 hours minimum; 36 hours on-campus instruction, 24 hours field instruction. For M.F.A.: 75 hours minimum in Creative Art; 60 hours minimum in Theater; includes creative project and final exhibition; final written/oral exams sometimes required. For Ph.D.: at least 24 hours during any one-year period after completion of 30 hours or master's degree, additional hours may be required by departments; a minimum of 24 hours of dissertation credit; preliminary exam; dissertation; final oral exam. For D.Mus.: 80 hours minimum beyond the bachelor's; diagnostic exam; five recitals: two public, one studio, two chamber works; one performance with a large ensemble for performance majors; for theory/composition majors, 70 hours minimum beyond the bachelor's, diagnostic exam, public performance of original chamber works, dissertation (which must be a major work for composition majors); final written/oral exams.

FIELDS OF STUDY.

COLLEGE OF ARTS AND SCIENCES:
American Studies.
Anthropology.
Biological Sciences. Includes microbiology, botany, ecology, genetics, physiology, zoology, marine, molecular. Thesis, one language for M.A., M.S.; GRE Subject for admission.
Chemistry.
Classics. Includes Latin, Greek. One language in addition to major for M.A., M.A. only.
Computer Science.
English.
Geological Sciences. Thesis for master's.
Geophysical Fluid Dynamics. Ph.D. only.
History. GRE Subject for admission; thesis for M.A.
Humanities.
Mathematics.
Meteorology.
Modern Languages. Includes French, German, Russian, Slavic, Spanish. GRE Subject for admission.
Molecular Biophysics. Ph.D. only.
Neuroscience.
Oceanography. Includes physical, biological, geological.
Philosophy. Thesis; one language for M.A.
Physics.
Psychology. Three recommendations, GRE Subject for admission; thesis for M.A.
Religion. One or more languages for M.A., Ph.D.
Statistics.

COLLEGE OF BUSINESS:
Accounting.
Business Administration.
Finance.
Hospitality.
Information and Management Sciences.
Management.
Marketing.
Risk Management and Insurance.

COLLEGE OF COMMUNICATION:
Communication.
Communication Disorders.

SCHOOL OF CRIMINOLOGY AND CRIMINAL JUSTICE:
Criminology.

COLLEGE OF EDUCATION:
Adult Education.
Comprehensive Vocational Education.
Counseling and Human Systems. Master's only.
Counseling Psychology and Human Systems. Ed.D. only.
Curriculum and Instruction.
Early Childhood Education.
Educational Leadership and Policy Standards.
Educational Psychology.
Educational Research.
Educational Theory and Practice.
Elementary Education.
Emotional Disturbances and Learning Disabled. Master's only.
English Education.
Evaluation and Measurement.
Foundations of Education.
Health Education.
Higher Education.
Human Services and Studies.
International and Intercultural Development.
Leisure Services and Studies. Master's only.
Mathematics Education.
Mental Retardation. Master's only.
Multilingual and Multicultural Education.
Physical Education.
Psychological Services.
Reading Education.
Recreation and Leisure Services Administration.
Rehabilitation Services.
Science Education.
Social Studies Education.
Special Education.

COLLEGE OF ENGINEERING:
Chemical Engineering.
Civil Engineering.
Electrical Engineering.
Industrial Engineering.
Mechanical Engineering.

SCHOOL OF MOTION PICTURE, TELEVISION, AND RECORDING ARTS:
Narrative, Dramatic Film Productions.

SCHOOL OF MUSIC:
Arts Administration.
Brass.
Composition.
Conducting. Includes choral, orchestral.
Ethnomusicology.
Harpsichord.
Harp.
Historical Musicology.
Jazz Studies.
Music Education. Includes music therapy.
Music Theory.
Multiple Winds.
Opera. Includes coaching, directing, performance.
Organ.

Percussion.
Piano. Includes accompanying, pedagogy.
Strings. Includes guitar.
Voice.
Woodwinds.

SCHOOL OF NURSING:
Adult Nurse Practitioner.
Nurse Case Manager.
Nurse Educator.

COLLEGE OF SOCIAL SCIENCES:
Aging Studies.
Asian Studies.
Demography. Master's only.
Economics.
Geography.
Health Policy Research.
International Affairs.
Political Science.
Public Administration and Policy.
Russian and East European Studies.
Social Science. Interdisciplinary.
Sociology.
Urban and Regional Planning.

SCHOOL OF SOCIAL WORK:
Social Work. Includes clinical social work, social policy, and administration.

SCHOOL OF THEATRE:
Acting.
Costume Design.
Directing.
Lighting Design.
Scenic Design.
Technical Production.
Theatre Management.
Theatre Studies.

SCHOOL OF VISUAL ARTS AND DANCE:
Art Education.
Art History.
Art Therapy.
Arts Administration.
Dance. Master's only.
Interior Design. Master's only.
Studio Art.

COLLEGE OF HUMAN SCIENCES:
Family and Child Sciences.
Marriage and the Family.
Nutrition, Food, and Movement Science.
Textile and Consumer Sciences.

SCHOOL OF INFORMATION STUDIES:
Information Architecture.
Information Needs of Youth.
Information Policy and Management.
Information Technology.
Knowledge Management.

College of Law (32306-1034)

Established 1965. ABA approved since 1968. AALS member. Semester system. Special facilities: Children's Advocacy Center, Florida Dispute Resolution Center. Library 360,000 volumes; has LEXIS, NEXIS, WESTLAW, OCLC. Annual tuition, full-time resident $4952, nonresident $16,393. On-campus housing available. Total average annual additional expenses: $13,978. Apply to Director of Housing.

Enrollment: first-year class 245; total full-time 727 (men 54%, women 46%). Faculty: full-time 29, part-time 12. Student to faculty ratio 20.9 to 1. Degrees conferred: J.D., J.D.-M.B.A., J.D.-M.A., J.D.-M.P.A., J.D.-M.S.

ADMISSION REQUIREMENTS. LSDAS Law School report, bachelor's degree, transcripts, LSAT, personal statement, letters of recommendation required in support of application. Accepts transfer applicants. Graduates of unaccredited colleges not considered. Apply to Office of Admissions after September 1, before February 15. Admits first-year students, Fall only; transfers Fall and Summer. Application fee $20, Phone: (850)644-3787; fax: (850)644-7284.

ADMISSION STANDARDS. Selective. Mean LSAT: 155; mean GPA: 3.31 (A = 4). Gourman rating: 3.42. *U.S. News & World Report* ranking is in the second tier of all U.S. law schools. Accepts about 35–40% of total applicants.

FINANCIAL AID. Scholarships, fellowships, Federal W/S, loans. Apply to University Office of Financial Aid by March 1. Use FAFSA. About 24% of students receive aid other than loans from College and outside sources.

DEGREE REQUIREMENTS. For J.D.: satisfactory completion of three-year program; 88 semester hours. J.D.-M.B.A. offered with School of Business, J.D.-M.A./M.S. with the departments of Economics, International Affairs, Public Affairs, Urban and Regional Planning, Graduate School of Arts and Science. The J.D.-M.P.A. with the School of Criminology and Criminal Justice.

UNIVERSITY OF FLORIDA

Gainesville, Florida 32611-8140
Web site: www.ufl.edu

Founded 1953. CGS and AAU member. Located 75 miles SW of Jacksonville. Coed. State control. Semester system. Sponsoring University of Oak Ridge associated universities. Special facilities: Agricultural Research Center, Cancer Center, Florida Engineering and Experiment Station, Center for Applied Optimization, Center for Applied Thermodynamics and Corrosion, Center for Aquatic Sciences, Engineering Research Center for Particle Science and Technology, Clinical Research Center, Center for Gerontological Studies, Human Development Center, Center for Information Research, Center for Intelligent Machines and Robotics, Center for International Studies, Center for Latin American Studies, Center for Research on Human Prosthesis, Florida Museum of Natural History, Florida Water Resources Research Center. The University's NIH ranking is 58th among all U.S. institutions with 305 awards/grants worth $85,650,494. Library: more than 5,000,000 volumes, 28,100 subscriptions. Total University enrollment: 45,000.

Annual tuition: resident, per credit hour $152, nonresident $530. On-campus housing for 980 married students, graduate men, women. Annual housing cost: $2400–$5400. On-campus one-bedroom apartments rent for about $475 per month. Apply to Division of On-Campus Housing; to Division of Off-Campus Housing for information. Phone: (352)392-2161.

Graduate School

Graduate study since 1906. Enrollment: full-time 6420 (men 55%, women 45%), part-time 1646 (men 50%, women 50%). University faculty: full- and part-time 2500. Degrees conferred: M.A., M.S., M.A.T., M.S.T., M.Ag., M.Arch., M.Acc., M.A.E., M.H.S.E., M.S.H.S.E., M.A.M.C., M.A.M.R.D., M.A.U.R.P., M.ER.C., M.S.R.S., M.H.S., M.Nsg., M.S.B.C., M.S.Nsg.,

M.S.P., M.Stat., M.S.Stat., M.B.C., M.E., M.Ed., M.B.A., M.F.A., Ed.S., Engr., M.S.A.S., M.C.E., M.S.E.S.S., M.E.S.S., M.L.A., M.M., LL.M., D.Aud., Ed.D., Ph.D.

ADMISSION REQUIREMENTS. Two transcripts, letters of recommendation, GRE/GMAT/LSAT required in support of School's application. On-line application available. GRE Subject Test recommended. Interview required by some departments. TOEFL (minimum score 550) required for international applicants. Accepts transfer applicants. Graduates of unaccredited institutions not considered. Apply to Director of Admissions by June 9 (Fall), November 1 (Spring), March 1 (Summer). Anthropology, Architecture, Business Administration, Clinical Health Psychology, Counseling Education, Counseling Psychology, History Programs have earlier deadline dates. Application fee $20. Phone: (352)392-1365; fax: (352)392-3987.

ADMISSION STANDARDS. Very selective for most departments. Usual minimum G.P.A.: 3.0 (A = 4).

FINANCIAL AID. Annual awards from institutional funds: fellowships, research fellowships, assistantships, Federal W/S, loans. Approved for VA benefits. Apply by February 15 to appropriate department chair for fellowships, assistantships; to Office of Student Aid for all other aid. Use FAFSA. Phone: (352)392-1275. About 44% of students receive aid other than loans from University and outside sources. Aid available for part-time students.

DEGREE REQUIREMENTS. For master's: 30 credits minimum, thesis, final written/oral exam; 32 minimum nonthesis option, written comprehensive exam; reading knowledge of one foreign language required for many majors. Exceptions to the above include: LL.M. in Tax: 24 credits; M.Acc.: 34 credits; M.Ag.: 32 credits; M.Arch.: 52 credits; M.A.M.R.D.: 32 credits; M.A.T.: 36 credits; M.A.U.R.P.: 52 credits; M.B.A.: 48 credits; M.B.C.: 33 credits; M.Ed.: 36 credits; M.E.S.S.: 34 credits; M.F.A.: 60 credits for art and theater; 48 credits for English; M.F.R.C.: 32 credits; M.H.S.: 36 credits for occupational therapy, 43 credits for rehabilitation counseling; M.H.S.E.: 36 credits; M.L.A.: 48 credits; M.M.: 32 credits; M.S.R.S.: 34 credits; M.Nsg. and M.S.Nsg.: 48 credits; M.S.T.: 36 credits; M.Stat.: 36 credits; Engr.: 30 credits beyond the master's; Ed.S.: 36 credits beyond the master's. For Ph.D. and Ed.D.: 90 credits beyond the bachelor's, 30 credits in one calendar year, qualifying written and oral exam, dissertation, final written/oral exam.

FIELDS OF STUDY.

COLLEGE OF AGRICULTURE AND LIFE SCIENCE:
Agricultural and Biological Engineering.
Agricultural Education and Communication.
Agronomy.
Animal Science.
Botany.
Entomology and Nematology.
Environmental Horticulture.
Family, Youth, and Community Science.
Fisheries and Aquatic Sciences.
Food and Resource Economics.
Food Science and Human Nutrition.
Forest Resources and Conservation.
Horticultural Science. Includes fruit crops, vegetable crops.
Microbiology and Cell Science.
Plant Molecular and Cellular Biology.
Plant Pathology.
Soil and Water Science.
Statistics.
Wildlife Ecology and Conservation.

COLLEGE OF DESIGN, CONSTRUCTION, AND PLANNING:
Architecture.
Architectural Studies.
Building Construction and International Construction.
Interior Design.
Landscape Architecture.
Urban and Regional Planning.

COLLEGE OF LIBERAL ARTS AND SCIENCES:
Anthropology.
Astronomy.
Botany.
Chemistry.
Classics.
Communication Sciences and Disorders.
English.
Geography.
Geological Sciences.
German.
History.
Latin.
Latin American Studies.
Linguistics.
Mathematics.
Philosophy.
Physics.
Political Science.
Political Science–International Relations.
Psychology.
Religion.
Romance Languages and Literatures—French.
Romance Languages and Literatures—Spanish.
Sociology.
Statistics.
Zoology.

COLLEGE OF BUSINESS:
Accounting.
Business Administration. Includes decision and information sciences, finance and insurance, management, marketing, real estate.
Economics.

COLLEGE OF EDUCATION:
Curriculum and Instruction.
Educational Leadership.
Educational Psychology.
Educational Technology.
Elementary Education.
English Education.
English to Speakers of Other Languages (ESOL).
Foreign Language Education.
Marriage and Family Counseling.
Mathematics Education.
Mental Health Counseling.
Reading Education.
Research and Evaluation Methodology.
School Counseling and Guidance.
School Psychology.
Science Education.
Social Studies Education.
Special Education.
Speech Pathology.

COLLEGE OF ENGINEERING:
Aerospace Engineering.
Agricultural and Biological Engineering.
Biomedical Engineering.
Chemical Engineering.
Civil Engineering. Includes geomatics.
Coastal Engineering.
Computer and Information and Engineering.
Electrical and Computer Engineering.
Engineering Mechanics.

Engineering Science.
Environmental Engineering Sciences.
Industrial and Systems Engineering.
Materials Science and Engineering.
Mechanical Engineering.
Nuclear and Radiological Engineering.

COLLEGE OF DENTISTRY:
Endodontic.
Orthodontics.
Periodontics.
Prosthodontics.

COLLEGE OF FINE ARTS:
Art.
Art Education.
Art History.
Digital Arts and Sciences.
Museum Studies.
Music.
Music Education.
Studio Art.
Theater.

COLLEGE OF HEALTH PROFESSIONS:
Audiology.
Clinical Psychology.
General Health Psychology.
Health Services Administration. Includes health service research.
   E.M.H.A.
Occupational Therapy.
Physical Therapy.
Rehabilitation Counseling.
Rehabilitation Sciences.

COLLEGE OF JOURNALISM AND COMMUNICATIONS:
Advertising.
International Communication.
Journalism—Print.
Mass Communication.
News and Documentary.
Public Relations.
Science-Health Communication.
Telecommunication.

COLLEGE OF LAW:
Comparative Law.
Taxation.

COLLEGE OF MEDICINE:
Biochemistry and Molecular Biology.
Medical Sciences. Includes anatomical sciences, molecular genetics and microbiology, neuroscience, oral biology, pathology, pharmacology, physiology.

COLLEGE OF NURSING:
Nursing.

COLLEGE OF PHARMACY:
Medicinal Chemistry.
Pharmaceutics.
Pharmacodynamics.
Pharmacy Health Care Administration.
Physician's Assistant.

COLLEGE OF HEALTH AND HUMAN PERFORMANCE:
Exercise and Sport Sciences.
Health and Human Performance.
Health Science Education.
Public Health.
Recreation, Parks, and Tourism.

COLLEGE OF VETERINARY MEDICINE:
Large Animal Clinical Sciences.
Pathobiology.
Physiological Sciences/VM.
Small Animal Clinical Sciences.

INTERDISCIPLINARY PROGRAMS:
Animal Molecular and Cellular Biology.
Hydrologic Sciences.
Jewish Studies.
Mammalian Genetics.
Toxicology.
Women's/Gender Studies.
Note: The Graduate Catalog, Graduate Coordinators for each program are listed on the University's home page noted above.

College of Dentistry (32610-0445)
Web site: www.dental.ufl.edu

Established 1972. Annual tuition: resident $11,736, nonresident $29,010. On-campus housing available. Average academic year housing costs: $10,165. Contact Housing Office for both on- and off-campus housing information. Phone: (352)392-2161. Total average academic cost for all other first-year expenses: $10,753.

Enrollment: first-year class 80, total 279 (men 65%, women 35%). Faculty: full-time 98, part-time 34. Degree conferred: D.M.D.

ADMISSION REQUIREMENTS. AADSAS report, official transcripts, DAT (not later than October), three letters of recommendation, at least three years of college required in support of application. TOEFL required for international applicants. Accepts transfer applicants. Interview by invitation only. Preference given to state residents. Graduates of unaccredited colleges not considered. Apply after June 1, before October 15 to Director of Admissions. Application fee $20. Phone: (352)392-4866; fax: (352)846-0311.

ADMISSION STANDARDS. Selective. Mean DAT: Academic 18.97, PAT 18.43; mean GPA: 3.48 (A = 4). Gourman rating: 4.08. Accepts about 50% of total annual applicants. Approximately 99% are state residents.

FINANCIAL AID. Scholarships, grants, loans. Apply to Office of Dental Admissions after acceptance; no specified closing date. Phone: (352)846-1384. Use FAFSA (College code: 001535). Approximately 89% of class receives some financial assistance from College.

DEGREE REQUIREMENTS. For D.M.D.: satisfactory completion of 11-semester program.
Note: College has B.S./D.M.D. program with the following colleges/universities: University of Florida, University of South Florida, Florida International University, University of North Florida, University of South Florida, Florida A&M University, Edward Waters College, Bethune-Cookman College, Florida Memorial College.

Fredric G. Levin College of Law (P.O. Box 117622)
Web site: www.law.ufl.edu

Founded 1909. ABA approved since 1925. AALS member since 1920. Semester system. Law library: 584,564 volumes, 7838 subscriptions; has LEXIS, WESTLAW, DIALOG, PLATO.

Tuition: resident $4790, nonresidents $15,820. Total average annual additional expense: $10,340. Enrollment: first-year class 213 (Fall), 209 (Spring), total full-time 1145 (men 50%, women 50%); no part-time study. Faculty full-time 51, part-time 22. Student to faculty ratio 18.7 to 1. Degrees conferred: J.D., J.D.-M.B.A., J.D.-M.A. (Accounting, Political Science, Sociology, Urban and Regional Planning), J.D.-Ph.D. (History), LL.M. (Tax),

LL.M. (for persons who have completed a basic legal education and received a university degree in law in another country).

ADMISSION REQUIREMENTS. LSDAS Law School report, transcript showing bachelor's degree completion, LSAT (no later than December) required in support of application. Interview not required. Accepts transfer applicants. Graduates of unaccredited colleges not considered. Apply to Assistant Dean for Admission and Financial Aid by February 1 (Fall), May 15 (Spring). Application fee $20. Phone: (352)392-2087; fax: (352)392-3087; e-mail: admissions@law.ufl.edu.

ADMISSION STANDARDS. Selective. Mean LSAT: 156 (Fall), 155 (Spring); mean GPA: 3.45 (Fall), 3.35 (Spring). Gourman rating: 3.78. *U.S. News & World Report* ranking is in the top 45 of all U.S. law schools.

FINANCIAL AID. Limited scholarship, loans available; most funds directed toward loans. Use FAFSA and College's Financial Aid form. Applications should be completed no later than March 1. About 15% of students receive aid other than loans.

DEGREE REQUIREMENTS. For J.D.: 88 hours minimum; transfer credit from other law school considered. For LL.M.: 24–30 credits of study beyond J.D.

College of Medicine (32610-0216)
Web site: www.med.ufl.edu

Established 1956. Annual tuition: full-time, resident $10,931, nonresident $30,885. Total cost for all other expenses: $10,300.

Enrollment: first-year class 97; total full-time 500 (men 55%, women 45%); postgraduate 446. Faculty: full-time 799, part-time 185. Degrees conferred: B.S.-M.D. (junior honors program and bachelor's completion program with FSU and FAMU). M.D., M.D.-J.D., M.D.-M.S., M.D.-Ph.D. Medical Scientist Training Program. The M.S. and Ph.D. are offered through the Graduate School.

ADMISSION REQUIREMENTS. AMCAS report, transcripts, MCAT, recommendations, interview required in support of application. Florida residents given preference. Graduates of unaccredited colleges not considered. Bachelor's normally required for admission. Does not have EDP. Apply to Chairman, Medical Selection Committee after June 15, before December 1 (flexible). Admits Fall only. Application fee: none. Phone: (352)392-4569; fax: (352)392-1307.

ADMISSION STANDARDS. Competitive. Mean MCAT: total 29.81; mean GPA: 3.66 (A = 4). Gourman rating: 3.80. *U.S. News & World Report* ranking is in the top 45 of all U.S. medical schools. Accepts 10% of total annual applicants. Approximately 98% are state residents.

FINANCIAL AID. Scholarships, summer fellowships, assistantships, NIH stipends, loans. Apply to Office for Student Financial Aid after acceptance and prior to June 1. Phone: (352)392-9800. Use FAFSA (School code: 001535). About 55% of students receive aid other than loans from College.

DEGREE REQUIREMENTS. For B.S.-M.D.: satisfactory completion of either a six-year or seven-year program. For M.D.: satisfactory completion of four-year program. Advanced standing for work completed in another school will be considered. For M.S., Ph.D.: see Graduate School listing above.

FIELDS OF GRADUATE STUDY.
Anatomy and Cell Biology.
Biochemistry and Molecular Biology.
Molecular Genetics and Microbiology.

Genetics. Interdisciplinary
Immunology and Microbiology. Interdisciplinary.
Molecular Cell Biology. Interdisciplinary.
Neuroscience. Interdisciplinary.
Oral Biology.
Pathology, Immunology, and Laboratory Medicine.
Pharmacology and Therapeutics.
Physiology and Functional Genomics. Interdisciplinary.

College of Veterinary Medicine (32610-0125)

Annual tuition: full-time resident $8631, nonresident $22,846. Total other expenses: $10,300.

Enrollment: first-year class 79, total full-time 365, postgraduate 60. Faculty: full-time 88, part-time 10. Degree conferred: D.V.M. The M.S. and Ph.D. are offered through the Graduate School.

ADMISSION REQUIREMENTS. VMCAS report, two transcripts, animal/veterinary experience, GRE, essay, three letters of recommendation (one from an academic adviser) required in support of application. Interview by invitation only. Transfer applicants for second-year class rarely considered. Applicants must have completed at least three years of college study. Preference given to state residents. Apply to the Dean after July 1, before October 1. Application fee $20. Phone: (352)392-4700, ext. 5300; fax: (352)392-8351.

ADMISSION STANDARDS. Competitive. Minimum GPA: 2.75 (A = 4). Mean GRE total: 1197; mean Science GPA: 3.58 (A = 4). Accepts about 30% of annual applicants. Not more than 15% of class can be nonresidents.

FINANCIAL AID. Scholarships, fellowships, assistantships, loans. Apply to Office of Financial Aid by February 15. Use FAFSA. About 20% of students receive aid other than loans.

DEGREE REQUIREMENTS, For D.V.M.: satisfactory completion of 9-semester program. For M.S. and Ph.D.: see Graduate School listing above.

FORDHAM UNIVERSITY
Rose Hill Campus
Bronx, New York 10458
Web site: www.fordham.edu

Founded in 1841. CGS member. Coed. Independent institution in the Jesuit tradition. Semester system. Library: 1,700,000 volumes, 13,000 subscriptions. Total University enrollment: 14,000.

Tuition: per credit $625. Limited on-campus housing for single graduate students only. Annual housing cost: $5400; shared rental units $400–$600 per month. Apply to Director of Residential Life. Phone: (718)817-3080.

Graduate School of Arts and Sciences

Established in 1916. Enrollment: full-time 300, part-time 715. Graduate faculty: full-time 220, part-time 20. Degrees conferred: M.A., M.S., Ph.D.

ADMISSION REQUIREMENTS. Transcripts, two letters of recommendation, GRE required in support of School's application. MAT required in Psychology. Evidence of Proficiency in English or TOEFL required of all international applicants. Interview not required. Accepts transfer applicants. Graduates of unaccredited institutions not considered. Apply to Office of Graduate Admission by April 1 (Summer), May 1 (Fall), December 1 (Spring). Psychology applications must be completed by January 15. Application fee $55. Phone: (718)817-4416; fax: (718)817-3566.

ADMISSION STANDARDS. Very competitive for some departments, competitive or selective for others. Usual minimum average: 3.0 (A = 4).

FINANCIAL AID. Awards from institutional funds: scholarships, teaching fellowships, research assistantships, Federal W/S, loans. Apply to Office of Graduate Admissions by January 30 for most departments. Phone: (718)817-3800. No aid for part-time students.

DEGREE REQUIREMENTS. For master's: 30–36 credits minimum, up to six transfer credits accepted; thesis optional in some departments; comprehensive exam required; reading knowledge of one foreign language or demonstrated computer/research skill required. For Ph.D.: 60–72 credits minimum; at least two years in residence; reading knowledge of two foreign languages or one computer/research skill and one language; comprehensive exam; dissertation required; final oral exam.

FIELDS OF STUDY.
Biological Sciences. M.S., Ph.D.
Classical Languages and Literatures. M.A., Ph.D.
Communication. M.A.
Computer Science. M.S.
Economics. M.A., Ph.D.
English Language and Literature. M.A., Ph.D.
History. M.A., Ph.D.
Humanities and Sciences. M.A.; interdisciplinary.
International Political Economy and Development. M.A.; interdisciplinary.
Medieval Studies Program. M.A., Ph.D.; interdisciplinary.
Philosophy. M.A., Ph.D.
Political Science. M.A., Ph.D. only.
Psychology. M.A., Ph.D.
Sociology. M.A., Ph.D.
Theology. M.A., Ph.D.

Graduate School of Business Administration

113 West 60th Street
New York, New York 10023
Web site: www.bnet.fordham.edu

Established 1969. Private control, Accredited programs: M.B.A., Accounting. Located on Manhattan campus near Lincoln Center, courses also offered in Tarrytown; urban environment. Semester system. Special programs: foreign exchange programs (in Belgium, Finland, France, Spain).

Annual tuition: full-time $24,280, part-time $12,310. Enrollment: total full-time 517, part-time 1108 (men 60%, women 40%). Faculty: 91 full-time, 94 part-time; 96% with Ph.D./ D.B.A. Degrees conferred: M.B.A. (full-time, part-time, day, evening, weekends), M.B.A. in Accounting and Taxation, M.B.A. in Professional Accounting, M.B.A. in Quality Management, G.P.M.B.A. (Global Professional), T.M.B.A. (Transnational), M.B.A.-J.D., M.S.T. (Taxation).

ADMISSION REQUIREMENTS. All applicants should have a bachelor's degree from a recognized institution of higher education and a strong mathematics background. Submit application, GMAT (will accept GMAT test results from the last five years, latest acceptable date is March), official transcripts from each undergraduate/graduate school attended, two letters of recommendation, two personal statements, résumé (prefers at least four years of work experience), and an application fee of $65 to the Office of Admission and Financial Aid. In addition, international students (whose native language is other than English) should submit a TOEFL report (minimum score 600), certified translations and evaluations of all official transcripts; recommendation should be in English or with certified translations, proof of health/immunization certificate, and proof of sufficient financial

resources for two years of academic study. Beginning students are admitted Fall, Winter, Spring. U.S. citizens apply by June 1 (Fall), November 1 (Winter), March 1 (Spring), international students apply by May 1 (Fall), October 1 (Winter), February 1 (Summer). Interviews are encouraged. Admissions Committee will consider applicants with some academic course work deficiencies. Joint degree applicants must apply to and be accepted to both schools/programs; contact the Admissions Office for current information and specific admissions requirements. Rolling admissions process; notification is made within 4–6 weeks of receipt of completed application and supporting documents. Admissions Office phone: (212)636-6200; fax: (212)636-7076; e-mail: admissionsgb@school.fordham.edu.

ADMISSION STANDARDS. Selective. Median GMAT: full-time 580, part-time 570; median GPA: 3.15 (A = 4). *U.S. News & World Report* ranked Fordham in the top 15 of all U.S. business schools for part-time M.B.A. programs.

FINANCIAL AID. Scholarships, merit scholarships, minority fellowships, fellowships/graduate assistantships, Federal W/S, loans. Financial aid is available for part-time study. Assistantships/fellowships may be available for joint degree candidates. Request scholarship, fellowship, assistantship information from the Graduate School of Business. Contact the Assistant Dean, Admissions and Financial Aid for current need-based financial aid information. Phone: (212)636-6200. Apply by April 1. Use FAFSA (School code: 002722), also submit Financial Aid Transcript, Federal Income Tax forms.

DEGREE REQUIREMENTS. For M.B.A.: 60 credit program including 36 elective credits, two-year program; degree program must be completed in six years. For G.P.M.B.A., T.M.B.A.: 69 credit programs. For M.S.T.: 54 credit program. For M.B.A. in Accounting and Taxation: 90 credit program. For Deming Scholars M.B.A. in Quality Management: eighteen-month program. For M.B.A.-J.D.: four-and-one-half- to five-and-one-half-year program.

FIELDS OF CONCENTRATION FOR M.B.A.:
Accounting.
Finance.
Information Systems.
Management.
Marketing.

Graduate School of Education

Located at Lincoln Center Campus, New York City (10023). Special facilities: Early Childhood Center, Center for Non-Public Education, Center for Technology in Education, Intensive Teacher Institute in Bilingual Education.

Tuition: per credit $595. On-campus housing available. Average academic year housing cost: $5800–6900. Contact University's Residential Life Office for both on- and off-campus housing information. Phone: (212)579-2327.

Enrollment: full-time 201, part-time 1096. Graduate faculty: full-time 41, part-time 100. Degrees conferred: M.S.Ed., M.A.T., Advance Certificate, Ed.D., Ph.D.,

ADMISSION REQUIREMENTS. Official transcripts required in support of School's application. GRE required for Ed.D. and Ph.D. applicants. Evidence of proficiency in English required of international students. Accepts transfer applicants. Graduates of unaccredited institutions not considered. Apply to Office of Admissions by May 15 (Fall), October 15 (Spring), March 15 (Summer). Rolling admissions process. Application fee $65. Phone: (212)636-6400; fax: (212)636-7826.

ADMISSION STANDARDS. Selective. Usual minimum average: 2.75 (A = 4).

FINANCIAL AID. Annual awards from institutional funds: scholarships, fellowships, assistantships, Federal W/S, loans. Approved for VA benefits. Apply by February 1 to Dean's Office for assistantships; to the Financial Aid Office for all other programs. Phone: (212)636-6700. Use FAFSA. About 20% of students receive aid other than loans from School and outside sources. Aid available for part-time students.

DEGREE REQUIREMENTS. For master's: 30–36 credits minimum; thesis/nonthesis option; comprehensive exam. For Professional Diploma: 30 credits beyond the master's; comprehensive exam. For Ph.D.: 39–57 credits minimum beyond the master's; matriculation exam; reading knowledge of one foreign language or proficiency in a computer language and statistics; written comprehensive exam; dissertation; final oral exam. For Ed.D.: 66 credits minimum beyond the master's; requirements essentially the same as Ph.D. except no foreign language requirement.

FIELDS OF STUDY.
Administration and Supervision.
Administration and Supervision—Catholic Educational Leadership.
Administration and Supervision—Executive Leadership Program. Ed.D. only.
Adult Education. Includes adult literacy, continuing and higher educational administration, human relations skills, human resource development, resource enhancement and leadership, TESOL, technology learning, workforce development.
Bilingual Special Education.
Bilingual Teacher Education.
Church and Non-Public School Leadership. Ph.D. only.
Counseling Psychology. Fall admission only. Ph.D. only.
Curriculum and Teaching. Includes elementary and secondary.
Early Childhood Education.
Early Childhood Special Education.
Educational Psychology. Includes psychology of bilingual students, preschool psychology, bilingual school psychology.
Elementary Education.
Human Resource Education.
Leadership for Learning Organization. Ph.D. only.
Reading and Literacy.
School District Administration.
School Psychology. Includes urban bilingual.
Secondary Education.
Special Education.
Teaching. Includes English 7–12, social studies 7–12, biology 7–12.
Teaching English as a Second Language.

School of Law
Web site: www.law.fordham.edu

Founded 1905. ABA approved since 1936. AALS member since 1936. Semester system. Full- and part-time study. Located at Lincoln Center Campus, New York City (10023). Special facilities: Center on European Community Law and International Antitrust, Brendan Moore Advocacy Center, Crowley Institute for International Human Rights, Stein Institute on Law and Ethics. Law library: 560,800 volumes, 6212 subscriptions; has LEXIS, NEXIS, WESTLAW, DIALOG; 36 PCs. Limited on-campus housing.

Annual tuition: $26,429 (Day Division), $19,850 (Evening Division). Estimated living expenses: $18,155.

Enrollment: first-year class 343 (day), 120 (evening); total 1453 (men 51%, women 49%). Faculty: full-time 61, part-time 108. Student to faculty ratio 18.3 to 1. Degrees conferred: J.D., J.D.-M.B.A., LL.M. (International Business; Banking, Corporate, and Finance Law).

ADMISSION REQUIREMENTS. LSDAS Law School report, bachelor's degree, transcripts, LSAT required in support of application. Interview not required. Accepts transfer applicants.

Graduates of unaccredited colleges not considered. Apply to Office of Admissions of School after September 1, before March 1. Application fee $60. Phone: (212)636-6810; e-mail: Lawadmissions@law.fordham.edu.

ADMISSION STANDARDS. Selective. Mean LSAT: full-time 163, part-time 158; mean GPA: full-time 3.49 (A = 4), part-time 3.26 (A = 4). Gourman rating: 4.47. *U.S. News & World Report* ranking is in the top 32 of all U.S. law schools. Accepts about 20% of total annual applicants.

FINANCIAL AID. Scholarships, grants, loans. Apply by May 15 to Financial Aid Office of School. Use FAFSA (School code: 002722). About 10% of students receive aid other than loans from School. Aid sometimes available for part-time students. A Public Service loan forgiveness program available.

DEGREE REQUIREMENTS. For J.D.: three-year program for day students; four-year program for evening students; 83 credits minimum. For LL.M.: 2 semesters beyond J.D.

Graduate School of Social Service

Established 1916. Located at Lincoln Center Campus. Special facility: Langenfeld Research and Demonstration Center. Tuition: per credit $449. On-campus housing for single students only. Enrollment: full-time 300, part-time 450. Faculty: full-time 35, part-time 6. Degrees conferred: M.S.W., Ph.D.

ADMISSION REQUIREMENTS. Transcripts, three letters of recommendation, autobiographical statement, interview required in support of School's application. On-line application available. GRE required for Ph.D. program. TOEFL required for international applicants. Accepts transfer applicants. Graduates of unaccredited institutions not considered. Apply to Office of Admissions by June 1 (Fall), December 1 (Spring). Full-time students admitted Fall only. Application fee $40. Phone: (212)636-6668; fax: (212)636-6613.

ADMISSION STANDARDS. Competitive. Usual minimum average: 3.0 (A = 4).

FINANCIAL AID. Scholarships, fellowships, assistantships, grants, loans. Approved for VA benefits. Apply to Financial Aid Office by April 1. Phone: (212)636-6700. Use FAFSA. About 5% of students receive aid other than loans from School, 98% from all sources. Aid available for part-time students.

DEGREE REQUIREMENTS. For M.S.W.: 60 credits minimum, at least one year in full-time residence; two-semester internship; thesis optional. For Ph.D.: 48 credits minimum beyond M.S.W., at least two semesters in residence; oral and written exam; dissertation; final oral/written exam.

FORT HAYS STATE UNIVERSITY
Hays, Kansas 67601
Web site: www.fhsu.edu

Founded 1902. CGS member. Located 300 miles W of Kansas City. Coed. State control. Semester system. Library: 500,000 volumes, 3400 subscriptions.

Tuition: per credit, resident $108, nonresident $291. On-campus housing for 92 married students, unlimited for single graduate students. Annual academic year average cost: $4300 (including board). Apply to Housing Director. Phone: (785)628-4245.

Graduate School

Graduate study since 1929. Enrollment: full-time 154, part-time 495; about 1500 students during Summer session. Faculty:

full-time 126, part-time 26. Degrees conferred: M.A., M.S., M.A.T., M.B.A., M.S.N., M.F.A., Ed.S.

ADMISSION REQUIREMENTS. Official transcripts, personal statement, three letters of recommendation, GRE Subject Tests (Psychology, Counseling, Speech Language, and Pathology), MAT (Administration, Education, Nursing, Specialist in Educ. Ed.S.), GMAT (M.B.A.) required in support of School's application. On-line application available. Interview not required. Accepts transfer applicants. Graduates of unaccredited institutions not considered. Apply to Dean of Graduate School; no specified closing dates. Application fee $25. Phone: (785)628-4234.

ADMISSION STANDARDS. Selective for most departments. Usual minimum average. 2.5 (A = 4). Some departments require 3.0 G.P.A. minimum.

FINANCIAL AID. Annual awards from institutional funds: scholarships, grants, teaching assistantships, research assistantships, administrative assistantships, Federal W/S, loans. Apply to Dean of Graduate School for scholarships, assistantships; for all other aid apply to the Office of Financial Aid; no specified closing date. Phone: (785)628-4408; fax: (785)628-4014. Use FAFSA. Aid available for part-time students.

DEGREE REQUIREMENTS. For M.A., M.F.A., M.S.: 30 semester hours minimum; thesis or research paper for most majors; final written exam; final oral exam for thesis writers. For Ed.S.: 30 semester hours minimum beyond the master's; field study or research project; final written/oral exams.

FIELDS OF STUDY.
Art. M.F.A.
Biology.
Business.
Communication.
Counseling.
Elementary Education.
English.
Geology.
Health, Physical Education, and Recreation.
Instructional Technology.
Liberal Studies.
Mathematics.
Nursing.
Psychology.
School Psychology.
Secondary Education.
Special Education.

FORT VALLEY STATE UNIVERSITY
Fort Valley, Georgia 31030-3262

Founded 1895. Located 25 miles from Macon, Georgia. Coed. State control. Semester system. Library: 190,000 volumes, 880 subscriptions. Total University enrollment: 2561.

Tuition: per hour, resident $97, nonresident $387. On-campus housing for single students only. Average academic year housing cost: $3716 (including board); off-campus room and board charges: $800 per month. Contact Dean of Students for both on- and off-campus housing information. Phone: (478)825-6293. Day-care facilities available.

Graduate Division

Graduate study since 1957. Enrollment: full- and part-time 349. Faculty: full-time 7, part-time 15. Degree conferred: M.S.

ADMISSION REQUIREMENTS. Official transcripts, MAT or GRE required in support of application. On-line application

available. TOEFL required for international applicants. Accepts transfer applicants. Apply to Admissions Office in month prior to beginning of registration. Application fee: none. Phone: (478) 825-6307.

ADMISSION STANDARDS. Selective. Usual minimum average: 2.5 (A = 4).

FINANCIAL AID. Annual awards from institutional funds: assistantships, Federal W/S, loans. Apply to Graduate Dean; no specified closing date. Phone: (478)825-6351. Use FAFSA and institutional form. Aid available for part-time students.

DEGREE REQUIREMENTS. For M.S.: 30 semester hours minimum, at least 24 in residence: thesis/nonthesis option; written exam/oral exam.

FIELDS OF STUDY.
Agricultural Education.
Animal Science. Includes animal nutrition, reproductive biology, animal products technology.
Art Education.
Bilingual and Bicultural Education.
Business Education.
Computer Education.
Counseling.
Dairy Science.
Drug, Alcohol, Substance Abuse Counseling.
Early Childhood Education.
Elementary Education.
English Education.
Environmental Education.
Foreign Languages Education.
Home Economics Education.
Industrial Arts.
Industrial Education.
Marriage and Family Counseling.
Mathematics Education.
Mental Health Counseling.
Music Education.
Poultry Science.
Reading Education.
Rehabilitation Counseling.
Science Education.
Secondary Education.
Social Science Education.
Teaching English as a Second Language.
Urban Education.
Vocational and Technical Education.

FRAMINGHAM STATE COLLEGE
Framingham, Massachusetts 01701-9101
Web site: www.framingham.edu

Founded 1839. Located 20 miles W of Boston. Coed. State control. Semester system. Library: 198,250 volumes, 1123 subscriptions.

Tuition: per course resident $550, nonresident $1848. Limited on-campus housing available for single students only. Contact Housing Office for both on- and off-campus housing information. Phone: (508)626-4636.

Office of Graduate Studies

Graduate study since 1961. Enrollment: full-time 52, part-time 815 (men 40%, women 60%). Graduate faculty: full-time 24, part-time 39. Degrees conferred: M.A., M.A.A., M.S., M.Ed.

ADMISSION REQUIREMENTS. Two transcripts, two letters of recommendation, MAT required in support of application. Interview not required. Accepts transfer applicants. Graduates of unaccredited colleges not considered. Apply to Office of Graduate Studies by April 1 (Fall), October 1 (Spring). Application fee $25. Phone: (508)626-4550.

ADMISSION STANDARDS. Selective. Usual minimum average: 3.0 (A = 4).

FINANCIAL AID. Limited to loans. Apply to Financial Aid Office by March 1. Use FAFSA. Phone: (508)626-4534. About 5% of students receive aid other than loans from College and outside sources.

DEGREE REQUIREMENTS. For master's: ten courses or seminars minimum; final oral exam; no thesis or language requirement.

FIELDS OF STUDY.
Art.
Biology.
Business Administration.
Counseling Psychology. Includes alcohol, substance abuse, community, families.
Criminal Justice. In cooperation with Westfield State College.
Curriculum and Administration.
Educational Leadership.
Elementary Education. Includes mathematics, reading and language arts. M.Ed. only.
English.
Food and Nutrition. Includes dietetics, food science, nutrition science, human nutrition. M.S. only.
Health Care Administration.
History.
Home Economics.
Human Resources Administration.
Human Services Administration.
Literacy and Language.
Mathematics.
Museum Administration.
Public Administration.
Reading and Language Arts. Part-time only.
Secondary Education. Includes biology, English, history, home economics, mathematics. M.Ed. only.
Spanish.
Special Education.
Teaching English as a Second Language.

FRANKLIN PIERCE LAW CENTER
Concord, New Hampshire 03301
Web site: www.fplc.edu

Established 1973. ABA approved since 1974. AALS member. Semester system. Special facilities: Germeshauser Center for the Law of Innovation and Entrepeneurship, Institute for Health, Law, and Ethics, the Patent, Trademark, and Copyright Research Foundation. Library: 187,000 volumes; has LEXIS, NEXIS, WESTLAW, DIALOG; 22 personal computers.

Annual tuition: resident $18,525. Total average annual additional expense: $12,840.

Enrollment: first-year class 134; total 381 (men 64%, women 36%). Faculty: full-time 16, part-time 32. Student to faculty ratio 19.6 to 1. Degree conferred: J.D., J.D.-M.E.L. (Education Law), J.D.-M.I.P. (Intellectual Property).

ADMISSION REQUIREMENTS. LSDAS Law School report, bachelor's degree, transcripts, LSAT, recommendations, personal statement, résumé required in support of application. Accepts transfer applicants. TOEFL required of foreign students. Apply to Admissions Office by May 1 (flexible), rolling admissions process. Application fee $55. Phone: (603)228-9217; fax: (603)228-4661; e-mail: admission@fplc.edu.

ADMISSION STANDARDS. Selective. Mean LSAT: 149; mean GPA: 3.0 (A = 4). Gourman rating: 2.60. *U.S. News & World Report* ranking is in the third tier of all law schools. Accepts about 45% of total annual applicants.

FINANCIAL AID. Scholarships, Federal W/S, loans. Apply to Financial Aid office by April 15. Phone: (603)228-1514. Use FAFSA (FPLC code: G20979) and FPLC Financial Aid Application. About 57% of students receive some aid from School.

DEGREE REQUIREMENTS. For J.D.: satisfactory completion of three-year program. For J.D.-M.I.P., J.D.-M.E.L.: satisfactory completion of three- or four-year program.

FROSTBURG STATE UNIVERSITY
Frostburg, Maryland 21532
Web site: www.frostburg.edu

Founded 1898. Located 110 miles S of Pittsburgh and 150 miles from both Baltimore and Washington, D.C. Coed. State control. Semester system. Library: 510,000 volumes, 3353 subscriptions.

Tuition: per credit resident $180, nonresident $208. On-campus housing for limited number of graduate students, none for married students. Average academic year housing cost: $5266 (board included). Apply to Director of Residence Life. Phone: (301)687-4121. Day-care facilities available.

Graduate Study

Enrollment: full-time 188, part-time 675. University faculty: full- and part-time 90. Degrees conferred: M.A., M.A.T., M.E., M.Ed., M.S., M.B.A.

ADMISSION REQUIREMENTS. Transcripts required in support of application. On-line application available. TOEFL required for international applicants. Accepts transfer applicants. Apply to Office of Graduate Admissions at least sixty days prior to registration. Application fee $30. Phone: (301)687-7053; fax: (301)687-4597; e-mail: gradservices@frostburg.edu.

ADMISSION STANDARDS. Relatively open. Minimum average: 2.5 (A = 4).

FINANCIAL AID. Scholarships, grants, graduate assistantships, Federal W/S, loans. Apply by April 1 to Director of Financial Aid. Phone: (301)689-4301; fax: (301)687-4937. Use FAFSA.

DEGREE REQUIREMENTS. For M.A., M.Ed., M.A.T.: 33 semester hours minimum. For M.S., M.E.: 36–42 semester hours. For M.B.A.: 45 semester hours.

FIELDS OF STUDY.
Administration and Supervision. M.Ed.
Applied Ecology and Conservation Biology. M.S.
Applied Computer Science. M.S.
Biology. M.Ed.
Business Administration. M.B.A.
Counseling Psychology. M.S.
Curriculum and Instruction. M.Ed.
Elementary Administration. M.Ed.
Elementary Education. M.A.T.

Engineering. M.E.
Guidance and Counseling. M.Ed.
Health and Physical Education. M.Ed.
Human Performance. M.S.
Interdisciplinary. M.Ed.
Modern Humanities. M.A.; Summer only.
Park and Recreation Resource Management. M.S.
Reading. M.Ed.
School Counseling. M.Ed.
Science Education. M.Ed.
Secondary Administration. M.Ed.
Secondary Education. M.Ed.
Special Education. M.Ed.
Wildlife/Fisheries Biology. M.S.

FURMAN UNIVERSITY
Greenville, South Carolina 29613
Web site: www.furman.edu

Founded in 1826. Coed. Private control. Three-term system. Library: 445,900 volumes, 3347 subscriptions.
Tuition: per credit, $205. No on-campus housing available.

Graduate Studies

Enrollment: full-time 360, part-time 155. University faculty teaching graduate students: full-time 40, part-time 10. Degrees conferred: M.A. in Ed.

ADMISSION REQUIREMENTS. Transcripts, bachelor's degree, twelve hours in undergraduate education for Ed. majors required in support of application. Accepts transfer students. Graduates of unaccredited institutions not considered. Application fee $30. Phone: (864)294-2213.

ADMISSION STANDARDS. Usual minimum average: 3.0 (A = 4).

FINANCIAL AID. None available at this time.

DEGREE REQUIREMENTS. For M.A. in Ed.: 30–42 credit program; submit score on Praxis II subject test; master's seminar or comprehensive exam.

FIELDS OF STUDY.
Early Childhood Education.
Elementary Education.
Reading.
School Leadership.
Special Education. Includes learning disabilities, emotional/behavioral disorders.

GALLAUDET UNIVERSITY
Washington, D.C. 20002-3625

Founded 1864. CGS member. Coed. Private control. Semester system. Special facilities: Center for Auditory and Speech Sciences, Center for Global Education, Center for ASL Literacy, Gallaudet Research Institute, Genetic Counseling Center, Fendall Demonstration School, Model Secondary School for the Deaf, Center for Assessment and Demographic Studies, Center for Studies in Education and Human Development. Library: 220,000 volumes, 372,000 microforms, 1700 current periodicals, 5 PCs.
Tuition: $4635 per semester, per credit $515. On-campus housing for single students only. Average housing cost: $3820 (including board) per semester. Contact Director of Housing for both on- and off-campus housing information. Phone: (202)651-5255.

Graduate School

Enrollment: full-time 258 (men 45, women 213), part-time 114. Graduate faculty: full-time 55, part-time 20. Degrees conferred: M.A., M.S., M.S.W., Au.D., Ph.D.

ADMISSION REQUIREMENTS. Official transcripts, three letters of recommendation, GRE or MAT required in support of application. Accepts transfer applicants. Apply by February 15 to Director of Admissions. Application fee $50. Phone: (202)651-5253; fax: (202)651-5744; E-mail: adm_bennetti@gallua.gallaudet.edu.

ADMISSION STANDARDS. Competitive. Usual minimum average: 3.0 (A = 4).

FINANCIAL AID. Scholarships, partial tuition waiver, assistantships, grants-in-aid, Federal W/S, loans. Apply by April 1 to Director of Financial Aid. Use FAFSA and submit FAT. About 60% of students receive aid other than loans from College and outside sources. Limited aid for part-time students.

DEGREE REQUIREMENTS. For master's: 30–42 hours minimum full-time study; sign language proficiency for some programs; final oral/written exam. For Au.D.: 114–116 credit four-year program; internship; clinical practicum; research project. For Ph.D.: two years minimum beyond the master's, two consecutive semesters in residence; comprehensive exam; sign language proficiency for some programs; internship; dissertation; final written exam.

FIELDS OF STUDY.
Administration. M.S.
Audiology. Au.D.
Clinical Psychology. Ph.D.
Deaf Education. Ph.D.
Deaf Studies. M.A.
Developmental Psychology. M.A.
Family-Centered Early Education. M.A.Ed.
Interpretation. M.A.
Leisure Services Administration. M.S.
Linguistics. M.A., Ph.D.
Mental Health Counseling. M.A.
School Counseling and Guidance. M.A.
School Psychology. M.A., Psy.S.
Social Work. M.S.W.
Special Education Administration. Ph.D.
Speech/Language Pathology. M.S.

GANNON UNIVERSITY
Erie, Pennsylvania 16541
Web site: www.gannon.edu

Founded 1925. Private control. Roman Catholic. Semester system. Library: 300,000 volumes, 1850 subscriptions.
Tuition: per semester credit, Counseling Psychology $610, Nursing and other programs $320; Physical Therapy per semester $8670. Limited on-campus housing for single graduate students. Contact Director of Student Living. Phone: (814)871-7660.

School of Graduate Studies

Enrollment full-time 149, part-time 388. College faculty teaching graduate students full-time 94, part-time 91. Degrees conferred: M.A., M.S., M.Ed., M.B.A., M.P.A., M.S.N., M.P.T., M.S.N.-M.B.A.

ADMISSION REQUIREMENTS. Transcripts, GRE Subject Tests or GMAT, three letters of recommendation required in support of School's application. Interviews required for some programs. Vita/résumé required for Ph.D. TOEFL required for international applicants. Accepts transfer applicants. Graduates of unaccredited institutions not considered. Apply to Center for Adult Learning well in advance of registration; by March 1 for Ph.D. program. Application fee $25 for most programs; $50 fee for Ph.D. program. Phone: (814)871-7474; fax: (814)871-5827.

ADMISSION STANDARDS. Relatively open. Usual minimum average 2.75 (A = 4); 3.25 for Ph.D. program.

FINANCIAL AID. Scholarship, grants, teaching assistantships, administrative assistantships, Federal W/S, loans. Apply to Director of Financial Aid by March 1 (Fall), November 1 (Spring). Use FAFSA. Phone: (814)871-7337; fax: (814)871-5803.

DEGREE REQUIREMENTS. For M.A., M.S.: 30–48 credit hours; statistics or reading knowledge of one foreign language; thesis/nonthesis option/research project; comprehensive exam. For M.B.A.: 30–48 credit hours minimum, at least 36 in residence; research thesis. For M.P.A.: 36 credit hour program; internship; comprehensive exam. For M.Ed.: 30 credit hours minimum, at least 24 in residence; research essay or project; comprehensive exam. For M.P.T.: 63 credit hours; research thesis; plus clinical practicum. For M.S.N.: 42–48 credit hours; clinical practicum; research thesis. For Ph.D.: 3- to 4-year full-time program; 2000 hours internship; dissertation; final oral exam.

FIELDS OF STUDY.
Business Administration. Concentrations in accounting, entrepreneurship, finance, health service management, human resource management, marketing, public administration, risk management.
Community Counseling.
Counseling Psychology.
Early Childhood Intervention.
Education. Includes curriculum and instruction, educational computing technology, natural sciences and environmental sciences, reading.
Electrical Engineering.
Embedded Software Engineering.
Engineering Management.
English.
Environmental Studies.
Mechanical Engineering.
Natural Environmental Science.
Nursing. Includes anesthesia, case management, family nurse practitioner, medical/surgical, nurse administration.
Pastoral Studies. Includes pastoral ministry, religious education.
Physical Therapy.
Public Administration. Includes administrative studies, organizational leadership.

GEORGE MASON UNIVERSITY
Fairfax, Virginia 22030-4444
Web site: www.gmu.edu

Established 1957. Coed. Public. Semester system. Special facilities: Pyramid 90x, CDC CYBER 180/830, DEC/VAX 8500 and 8920, Center for Applied Research and Development in Education, Center for Conflict Analysis and Resolution, Center for Constitutional Rights, Federal Theatre Archives, Institute for Information Technology, Center for Innovative Technology, Center for Market Process, Photographic Archives, Performing Arts Archives, Institute for Computational Sciences and Informatics, Center for Artificial Intelligence, Center for Robotics and Control, Center for Public Choice, Center for Software Engineering. Library: 947,288 volumes, 18,820 subscriptions. Total University enrollment: 23,408.

Tuition: per credit resident $191, nonresident $529. On-campus housing for both single and married students. Average academic year housing cost: $5400 (including board) for single students, $6240 for married students. Contact Director of Housing for both on- and off-campus housing information. Phone: (703)993-2720. Day-care facilities available.

Graduate School

Graduate study since 1972. Enrollment: full-time 1822, part-time 4936 (men 45%, women 55%). Faculty: full-time 720, part-time 504. Degrees M.A., M.A.I.S., M.B.A., M.Ed., M.F.A., M.P.A., M.S., M.S.N., Certificate, D.A.Ed., Ph.D.

ADMISSION REQUIREMENTS. Two official transcripts, three letters of recommendation required in support of School's applications. On-line application encouraged. GRE Subject Tests/GMAT/MAT, interview required by some departments. TOEFL (minimum score 575) required of international applicants. Apply to Graduate School's Admissions Office MSN 3A4 by May 1 for most departments. Rolling admissions process. Application fee $30. Phone: (703)933-2423; fax: (703)993-8714.

ADMISSION STANDARDS. Competitive for many departments, selective for others. Usual minimum average: 2.5 (A = 4) for master's, 3.0 for doctoral studies.

FINANCIAL AID. Scholarships and tuition waivers (limited), fellowships, assistantships, career-related internships, Federal W/S, loans. Apply by April 1 to the Dean, Graduate School for fellowships, assistantships, scholarships, and tuition waivers; to Director of Financial Aid for all other programs. Phone: (703)933-2353. Use FAFSA. Aid available for part-time students.

DEGREE REQUIREMENTS. For master's: 24 semester hours minimum plus thesis; reading knowledge of one foreign language for some programs; final exam/final project for some programs. For D.A.Ed.: 72 credits minimum beyond the bachelor's, at least 32 in residence; written preliminary exam; three comprehensive written exams, dissertation, final oral exam. For Ph.D.: a minimum of 72 semester hours beyond the bachelor's (or 50 beyond the master's); completion of foreign language requirements (if applicable); preliminary exam, dissertation; final written/oral exam.

FIELDS OF STUDY.
Administration of Justice. M.P.A.
Art and Visual Technology. M.A., M.F.A.
Bioinformatics. M.S.
Biology. M.S.
Biosciences. Ph.D.
Biotechnology. M.S.
Business Administration. M.B.A.
Chemistry. M.S.
Civil, Environmental, and Infrastructure Engineering. M.S.
Communication. M.A.
Community College Education. D.A.
Computational Sciences and Informatics. Ph.D.
Computer Engineering. M.S.
Computer Science. M.S.
Conflict Analysis and Resolution. M.S., Ph.D.
Counseling and Development. Includes school, nonschool. M.Ed.
Creative Writing. M.F.A.
Cultural Studies. Ph.D.
Curriculum and Instruction. Includes early, middle secondary, bilingual/multicultural, instructional applications of microcomputers, reading, teaching of English as a second language. M.Ed.
Dance. M.F.A.
E-Commerce. M.S.
Economics. M.A., Ph.D.

Education. Ph.D.
Educational Leadership. M.Ed.
Electrical Engineering. M.S.
English. M.A.
Environmental Science and Public Policy. Ph.D.
Enterprise Engineering and Policy. M.S.
Exercise, Fitness, and Health Promotion. M.S.
Foreign Languages. M.A.
Forensic Biosciences. M.S.
French Foreign Language. M.A.
Geography and Cartographic Sciences. M.S.
Health Systems Management. M.S.
History. M.A., Ph.D.
Information Systems. M.S.
Information Technology. Ph.D.
Interdisciplinary Studies. Includes tracks in archaeology, gerontology, video-based production, regional economic development and technology. M.A.I.S.
International Commerce and Policy. M.A.
International Transaction. M.A.
Liberal Studies. M.A.L.S.
Linguistics. M.A.
Mathematics. M.S.
Music. M.A.
Nursing. M.S., Ph.D.
Operations Research. M.S.
Peace Operations. M.A., M.S.
Physics, Applied and Engineering. M.S.
Political Sciences. M.A.I.S.
Professional Writing, Editing, English. M.A.
Psychology. Includes clinical, school. M.A., Ph.D.
Public Administration. M.P.A.
Public Policy. M.P.P., Ph.D.
Recreation Resources Management. M.A.I.S.
Social and Organizational Learning. M.A., M.S.
Social Work. M.S.W.
Sociology. M.A.
Software Systems Engineering. M.S.
Spanish Foreign Language. M.A.
Special Education. M.Ed.
Statistical Science. M.S.
System Engineering. M.S.
Teaching of Writing and Literature, English. M.A.
Technology Management. M.S.
Telecommunication. M.A.
Transportation Policy Operations and Logistics. M.A., M.S.
Video-Based Production. M.A.I.S.
Visual information Technology. M.S.

School of Law (22201-4498)

Affiliated in 1979. ABA approved since 1980. AALS member. Semester system. Located at the Metro Campus, Arlington. Special facility: National Center for Technology and Law. Library: 300,000 volumes; has LEXIS, NEXIS, WESTLAW, LEGAL-TRAK.

Annual tuition: resident $7280, per credit $260; nonresident $17,920, per credit $882. Limited on-campus housing available. Total average annual additional expense: $9000.

Enrollment: first-year class, full-time 110, part-time 104; total 694 (men 58%, women 42%). Faculty: full-time 31, part-time 57. Studenty to faculty ratio 15.5 to 1. Degree conferred: J.D.

ADMISSION REQUIREMENTS. LSDAS Law School report, bachelor's degree, transcripts, LSAT, writing sample, personal statement, letters of recommendation required in support of application. Preference given to state residents. Graduates of unaccredited colleges not considered. Apply to Admissions Office by March 15. Application fee $35. Phone: (703)993-8010; fax: (703)993-8260.

ADMISSION STANDARDS. Competitive. Mean LSAT: full-time 159, part-time 156; mean GPA: full-time 3.32, part-time 3.17 (A = 4). Gourman rating: 2.73. *U.S. News & World Report* ranking is in the top 47 of all U.S. law schools. Admits about 25% of total annual applications.

FINANCIAL AID. Limited to fellowships, Federal W/S, loans. Apply to Admissions Office by March 1. Phone: (703)993-2353. Use FAFSA (School code: 003749) and institutional Financial Aid Application. Aid available for part-time students.

DEGREE REQUIREMENTS. For J.D.: satisfactory completion of three-year program.

THE GEORGE WASHINGTON UNIVERSITY
Washington, D.C. 20052
Web site: www.gwu.edu

Founded 1821. Located in downtown Washington. CGS member. Coed. Private control. Semester system. Member of consortium of Universities of the Washington Metropolitan Area. Special facilities: Biostatistics Center, The Burdetsky Labor-Management Institute, Center for the Advanced Study of Human Paleobiology, Center for International Health, Center for International Science and Technology Policy, Center for Nuclear Studies, Center for the Study of Combustion and the Environment, Center for Social and Organizational Learning, Center for Structural Dynamics Research, Center for Washington Area Studies, Center for the Advancement of Small Business, Cyberspace Policy Institute, Educational Resources Information Center, Institute for Artificial Intelligence, Institute on Crime, Justice, and Corrections, Institute for Ethnographic Research, Institute for European, Russian, Eurasian Studies, Institute for History in the Media, Institute for Management Science and Engineering, Institute for Materials Science, Institute for Reliability and Risk Analysis, Institute for the Study of Fatigue Fracture and Structural Reliability, Institute for Urban Development Research, Institute for the Environment, Institute for Medical Imaging and Image Analysis, Institute for Technology and Strategic Research, Institute of Brazilian Business and Public Management Issues, International Water Resource Institute, International Rule of Law Center, Joint Institute for Advancement of Flight Sciences, The Sigur Center for Asian Studies, Space Policy Institute. Library: 1,800,000 volumes, 14,729 subscriptions. The University's NIH ranking is 77th among U.S. institutions with 67 awards/grants worth $57,576,036. Total University enrollment: 19,000.

Tuition: per semester hour $760. Limited on-campus housing for graduate students based on a first-come, first-served basis. Contact the Office of Residential and off-Campus Housing for both on- and off-campus housing information. Phone (202)994-6688.

Columbian School of Arts and Sciences

Graduate study since 1886. Enrollment: full-time about 915, part-time 1110. Graduate faculty: full-time 236, part-time 78. Degrees conferred: M.A., M.F.A., M.F.S., M.S.F.S., M.S., Psy.D., Ph.D.

ADMISSION REQUIREMENTS. Transcripts, GRE, statement of purpose, letters of reference required in support of School's application. On-line application available. TOEFL (minumum score 550) required for international applicants; TWE recommended, TSE required for international applicants applying for graduate assistantships. GRE subject test, writing samples, portfolio required by some departments. Accepts transfer applicants. Apply to Office of Graduate Admissions by April 1 (Fall), October 1 (Spring), March 1 (Summer). Earlier submission required by some programs. Application fee $55. Phone: (202)994-6211; fax: (202)994-6213; e-mail: asgrad@gwu.edu.

ADMISSION STANDARDS. Very selective for most departments, competitive or selective for the others. Usual minimum average: 3.0 (A = 4).

FINANCIAL AID. Annual award from institutional funds: fellowships, assistantships, Federal W/S, loans. Apply by February 1 to Office of Student Financial Assistance (January 15 for students in clinical psychology). Phone: (202)994-6210. Use FAFSA. About 20% of students receive aid from School and outside sources. Aid available for part-time students.

DEGREE REQUIREMENTS. For master's: 30–36 semester hours; thesis/nonthesis option; comprehensive exam. For Ph.D.: 72 semester hours beyond the bachelor's; general exam for candidacy; dissertation; final oral exam.

FIELDS OF STUDY.
Administrative Science. M.A. only.
American Literature.
American Religious History. Ph.D. only.
American Studies.
Anthropology. M.A. only.
Applied Mathematics.
Art. Includes ceramics, design, interior design, printmaking, painting, photography, sculpture, visual communications. M.F.A. only.
Art History.
Art Therapy. M.A. only.
Biochemistry.
Biological Sciences. Includes biology, botany, zoology.
Biostatistics.
Chemical Toxicology. M.S. only.
Chemistry.
Computer Fraud Investigation.
Criminal Justice. M.A. only.
Economics.
English Literature.
Environmental and Resource Policy. M.A. only.
Epidemiology.
Forensic Sciences. M.F.S., M.S.F.S. only.
Genetics.
Geobiology.
Geochemistry. M.S. only.
Geography. M.A. only.
Geology.
Geoscience.
History.
History of Religion.
Hominid Paleobiology.
Human Sciences. Ph.D. only.
Immunology. Ph.D. only.
Industrial and Engineering Statistics. M.S only.
Legislative Affairs. M.A. only.
Mathematics.
Media and Public Affairs.
Microbiology.
Molecular and Cellular Oncology. Ph.D. only.
Museum Studies. M.A. only.
Neuroscience. Ph.D. only.
Pharmacology.
Philosophy and Social Policy. M.A. only.
Physics.
Political Management.
Political Science.
Professional Psychology. Psy.D. only.
Psychology. Includes clinical, cognitive, neuropsychobiology, industrial/organizational/applied social. Ph.D., Psy.D. (Clinical).
Public Policy. Ph.D. only.

Radiological Sciences. Ph.D. only.
Security Management.
Sociology. M.A. only.
Speech-Language Pathology and Audiology. M.A. only.
Statistics.
Telecommunications. M.A. only.
Theater. Includes a concentration in acting, scenic design. M.F.A. only.
Women's Studies. M.A. only.

School of Business and Public Management
710 21st Street, N.W.
Washington, D.C. 20052
Web site: www.sbpm.gwu.edu

Established 1928. School began as Department of Comparative Jurisprudence and Diplomacy in 1898, became a School of Government in 1928, in 1960 name changed to Government, Business and International Affairs, current name adopted in 1990. Private control, Accredited programs: M.B.A. (first M.B.A. awarded in 1954), Accounting; recognized Ph.D. Courses also offered in Loudon County and Alexandria, Virginia. Semester system. Special facilities: Center for Excellence in Municipal Management, Center for Law Practice Strategy and Management, Center for Latin American Issues, Center for Real Estate and Urban Analysis, European Union Research Center, Institute for Global Management and Research, International Institute of Tourism Studies. Special Programs: accelerated MBA program; foreign exchange programs (in Chile, Denmark, France, Germany, Hungary, Portugal, Republic of Korea, Spain, Sweden, Thailand).

Tuition: $743 per credit. Enrollment: total full-time 834, part-time 1208 (men 60%, women 40%). Faculty: 106 full-time, 44 part-time; 88% with Ph.D./D.B.A. Degrees conferred: M.B.A. (full-time, part-time, day, evening, weekends), M.B.A.I.B. (International Business), E.M.B.A. (weekends only), M.B.A.-M.A. (International Affairs with Elliot School) M.B.A.-J.D., M.Accy., M.P.A., M.P.P. (Public Policy), M.S.A.M. (Acquisition Management), M.S.F., M.S.I.S.T. (Information Systems Technology), M.S.P.M. (Project Management), M.T.A. (Tourism Administration), M.Tax., Ph.D.

ADMISSION REQUIREMENTS. All applicants should have a bachelor's degree from a recognized institution of higher education and a strong mathematics background. Students are required to have their own personal computer. Early applications are encouraged for both admission and financial aid consideration. Submit application for Graduate Study, GMAT (will accept GMAT test results from the last five years, latest acceptable date is March; GRE for M.S.F., M.T.A.), official transcripts from each undergraduate/graduate school attended, three letters of recommendation, statement of purpose, résumé (prefers at least four years of work experience), and an application fee of $55 to the Office of Graduate Enrollment Support Services. An interactive application is also available. In addition, international students (whose native language is other than English) should submit a TOEFL report (minimum score 550), TWE (strongly recommended), certified translations and evaluations of all official transcripts; recommendation should be in English or with certified translations, proof of health/immunization certificate, and proof of sufficient financial resources for two years of academic study. Beginning students are admitted Fall and Winter. Both U.S. citizens and international applicants apply by April 1 (Fall), October 1 (Winter). Accepts transfer applicants. On-campus visits and interviews are encouraged prior to the admissions committee reviewing completed application. Joint degree applicants must apply to and be accepted to both schools; contact the Office of Enrollment Support Services for current information and specific admissions requirements. Rolling admissions process, notification is made within 4–6 weeks of receipt of completed application and supporting documents. Admissions Office phone for M.B.A.: (202)994-6584; fax: (202)994-6382; for E.M.B.A.: (202)729-8282.

ADMISSION REQUIREMENTS FOR DOCTORAL CANDIDATES. Contact the Office of Graduate Enrollment Support Services at (202)994-3900 for application material and information. Beginning students are admitted Fall Only. Both U.S. citizens and international applicants apply by February 1 (Fall). Submit application for Graduate Study, a GMAT/GRE (will accept GMAT/GRE test results from the last five years), two official transcripts from each undergraduate/ graduate schools attended, three applicant evaluation forms, letter of intent, résumé, statement of purpose, and application fee of $55 to the Doctoral Programs Office. In addition, international students (whose native language is other than English) should submit a TOEFL report (minimum score 600), TSE and TWE (strongly recommended), certified (notarized) translations and evaluations of all official, transcripts, recommendation should be in English or with certified translations, proof of health/immunization certificate. Interviews strongly recommended with the lead professor from primary field prior to the admissions committee reviewing completed application. Notification is made within four to six weeks of receipt of completed application and all supporting documents. Doctoral Programs Office phone: (202)994-6298; fax (202)994-6382.

ADMISSION STANDARDS. Selective. For M.B.A.: median GMAT: full-time 601, part-time 542; median GPA: full-time 3.32, part-time 3.02 (A = 4) Gourman rating: the M.B.A. program rated in the top 36, the score was 4.50; the Ph.D. program rated in the top 35, the score was 4.49.

FINANCIAL AID. Presidential Merit Fellowships, minority scholarships, graduate fellowships, graduate and teaching assistantships, Federal W/S, loans. Financial aid is available for part-time students. Financial aid may be available for international students. Assistantships/fellowships may be available for joint degree candidates. Financial Aid applications and information are generally available at the on-campus visit/interview or after January 1; apply by April 1. Request scholarship, fellowship, assistantship information from the School of Business. Contact the University's Director of Student Assistance for current need-based financial aid information. Phone: (202)994-6620. Use FAFSA (School code: 001444), also submit Financial Aid Transcript, Federal Income Tax forms. Approximately 20% of students receive some form of financial assistance.

DEGREE REQUIREMENTS. For M.B.A., M.B.A.I.B.: 60 credit program including 15 elective credits, two-year program; degree program must be completed in five years. For M.Accy., M.Tax.; 35–40 credit program. For M.F.S.: 48–69 credit program. For M.S.I.S.T.: 30–33 credit program. For M.S.A.M., M.S.P.M.: 30–36 credit program. For M.T.A.: 36 credit program. For M.B.A.-Master's: 72 credit program, generally a three- to four-year program. For M.B.A.-J.D.: 108 credit program, generally a four- to five-year program. For Ph.D.: three- to five-year program; comprehensive evaluation covering both primary and supporting field; dissertation proposal and oral defense, dissertation; oral defense; degree program must be completed in seven years.

FIELDS OF STUDY.
Accountancy. M.Accy.
Acquisition Management. M.S.A.M.
Business Administration. M.B.A. Concentrations include accountancy, environmental policy and management, finance and investments, health services administration, human resource management, information systems management, international business, logistic, operations and materials management, management decision making, management for science, technology and innovation, marketing, organizational behavior and

development, real estate and urban development, small business and entrepreneurship, strategic management and public policy, tourism and hospitality management.
Business Administration. Ph.D. Concentrations include accountancy, business administration (includes finance, international business, marketing, strategic management and public policy), management and technology (includes human resource management, information and decision systems, logistics, technology and project management, organization behavior), public administration.
Finance. M.S.F.
Information Systems Technology. M.S.I.S.T.
International Business. M.B.A.I.B.
Project Management. M.S.P.M.
Public Administration. M.P.A.
Public Policy. M.P.P.
Tourism Administration. M.T.A.
Taxation. M.Tax.

Graduate School of Education and Human Development

Tuition: per hour $725. Graduate enrollment: full-time 410, part-time 889. School faculty: full-time 65, part-time 56. Degrees conferred: M.A. in Ed., M.Ed., Ed.S., Ed.D.

ADMISSION REQUIREMENTS. Transcripts, GRE/MAT, two letters of recommendation (out-of-area applicants), statement of purpose, interview required in support of School's application. TOEFL (minimum score 550, 213 on computer-based test) required for international applicants. Accepts transfer applicants. Graduates of unaccredited institutions not considered. Apply to Dean of the School by January 15 (Fall), October 1 (Spring), February 1 (Summer Session). Application fee $55. Phone: (202)994-6160; fax: (202)994-7207.

ADMISSION STANDARDS. Selective. Usual minimum average 2.75 (A = 4); 2.3 to 2.74 for provisional admission.

FINANCIAL AID. Fellowships, assistantships are available at Ed.D. level, tuition waivers, Federal W/S, loans. Apply to Office of Student Financial Services by February 15. Phone: (202)994-6620. Use FAFSA. Some employment opportunities are available at the University. Information is available through the Personnel Office. Aid available for part-time students.

DEGREE REQUIREMENTS. For M.A. in Ed., M.Ed.: 24 semester hours minimum in residence; thesis optional for 6 semester hours; comprehensive exam for some programs; additional courses in lieu of comprehensive in some programs. For Ed.S.: 30 semester hours minimum beyond the master's, at least 21 in residence; comprehensive exams; final oral. For Ed.D.: usually about 75 to 90 semester hours beyond the bachelor's, about 60 semester hours in residence and at least one semester in full-time attendance; preliminary exams; dissertation; final oral exam.

FIELDS OF STUDY.
Community Counseling.
Counseling.
Curriculum and Instruction.
Early Childhood Special Education.
Education Policy Studies.
Educational Administration and Policy Studies.
Educational Leadership and Administration.
Educational Technology Leadership.
Elementary Education.
Higher Education Administration.
Human Resource Development.
Individualized Program.
Infant Special Education.
International Education.
Museum Education.

Rehabilitation Counseling.
School Counseling.
Secondary Education.
Special Education. Includes adolescents with emotional and behavioral disabilities.

School of Engineering and Applied Science
Web site: www.seas.gwu.edu

Tuition: per credit hour $725. Graduate enrollment: full-time 416, part-time 1103. Graduate faculty: full-time 70, part-time 97. Degrees conferred: M.S., M.E.M., professional degrees of Engineer and Applied Scientist; D.Sc.

ADMISSION REQUIREMENTS. Transcripts required in support of School's application. GRE Subject Tests recommended; GRE required for Financial Aid applicants. Interview not required, but desirable for doctoral applicants. TOEFL or IELTS, financial certificate required for international applicants. Accepts transfer applicants. Graduates of unaccredited institutions not considered. Apply to Manager of Engineering Admissions by February 1 (Fall), October 1 (Spring), February 1 (1st Summer Session), April 1 (2nd Summer Session). Application fee $60. Phone: (202)994-6158; fax: (202)994-4522; e-mail: admis@seas.gwu.edu.

ADMISSION STANDARDS. Selective. Usual minimum average: 3.0 (A = 4).

FINANCIAL AID. Annual awards from institutional funds: research/teaching assistantships, fellowships, tuition waivers, Federal W/S, loans. Approved for VA benefits. Apply to the Office of Student Financial Services by March 1 (Summer and Fall), September 1 (Spring). Phone: (202)994-6620; fax: (202)994-7221. Use FAFSA. Aid available for part-time students.

DEGREE REQUIREMENTS: For M.S. (Electrical Engineering and Computer Science): 30 credit hours including thesis; M.S. (Civil, Mechanical, and Environmental and Operations Research): 33 credit hours including thesis; M.S., M.E.M. (Engineering Management): 36 semester hours including thesis. For the Professional Engineering degree: 30 semester hours beyond the master's. For D.Sc.: 30 hours minimum beyond the master's; 54 credit hours beyond the baccalaureate; qualifying exam; dissertation; final oral exam.

FIELDS OF STUDY.
Civil and Environmental Engineering. Includes engineering mechanics, environmental engineering, geotechnical engineering, structural engineering, water resources engineering.
Computer Science. Includes algorithms and theory, artificial intelligence and computer vision, computer and communications security, computer engineering and architecture, graphics and multimedia, industrial engineering, parallel and distributed computing, software engineering and systems.
Electrical and Computer Engineering. Includes biomedical engineering, communications, controls, systems, and signal processing, electrical power and engineering management, electrophysics and fiber optics, energy conversion, power, and transmission, industrial engineering, microelectronics and VLSI systems.
Engineering Management and Systems Engineering. Includes domain-specific engineering management; economics, finance, and cost engineering; engineering management principles, practices, and methods; industrial engineering; information and process engineering; systems engineering; and quantitative analysis.
Mechanical and Aerospace Engineering. Includes aerospace engineering, design of mechanical engineering systems, fluid mechanics, thermal sciences and energy, industrial engineering, solid mechanics and materials science, transportation safety engineering.

The Elliott School of International Affairs
Established 1898. Name change in 1988. Special facilities: Center for International Science and Technology, Institute for European, Russian, and Eurasian Studies, Sigur Center for Asian Studies, Space Policy Institute.
Tuition: per credit $811.
Enrollment: full-time 338, part-time 139. School faculty: full-time 50, part-time 21. Degrees conferred: M.A., M.I.S., M.I.P.P., M.A.-M.B.A., M.A.-J.D., M.A.-M.P.H. The Ph.D. is offered through the Graduate School of Arts and Sciences.

ADMISSION REQUIREMENTS. Transcripts, GRE, three letters of recommendation, foreign language proficiency, work experience, personal statement required in support of School's application. TOEFL (minimum score 600) required for international applicants. TWE is recommended for international applicants. Graduates of unaccredited institutions not considered. Admits Fall only. Apply to Graduate Admissions Office by February 1. International, graduate fellowship, and assistantship applicants apply by January 15. Application fee $55. Phone: (202)994-7050; fax: (202)994-9537; e-mail: esiagrad@gwu.edu.

ADMISSION STANDARDS. Very selective. Usual minimum average: 3.0 (A = 4).

FINANCIAL AID. Fellowships, assistantships, tuition waivers, off-campus employment, Federal W/S, loans. Apply to the Office of Student Financial Services by January 15. Phone: (202)994-6620; fax: (202)994-0906. Use FAFSA. Aid available for part-time students.

DEGREE REQUIREMENTS. For M.A.: two options (except in Security Policy studies): 30 semester hours minimum in residence including thesis, or 36 semester hours of course work; reading knowledge of one foreign language or specified level of statistics; final comprehensive exam(s). For M.I.S.: 28 credit minimum; proficiency in a modern foreign language; capstone. For M.I.P.P.: 27 hour program; core seminar; skills-based workshops.

FIELDS OF STUDY.
Asian Studies. M.A.
European Studies. M.A.
European and Eurasian Studies. M.A.
International Affairs. M.A.
International Development Studies. M.A.
International Policy and Practice. M.I.P.P.
International Studies. Includes conflict and conflict resolution, international security studies, international economic affairs, international affairs and development, international public health, technology and international affairs, international law and organizations, U.S. foreign policy. M.I.S.
International Trade and Investment Policy. M.A.
Latin American Studies. M.A.
Russian and East European Studies. M.A.
Science, Technology, and Public Policy. M.A.
Security Policy Studies. M.A.

Law School
Web site: www.law.gwu.edu

Established 1865. ABA approved since 1923. AALS member. Semester system. Law library: 542,674 volumes, 5660 subscriptions; has LEXIS, NEXIS, WESTLAW, DIALOG, ALADIN.
Annual costs: $26,860, part-time $18,910. On- and off-campus housing available. Contact University Housing Office. Total annual average additional expense: $14,510.
Enrollment: first-year class 372 day, 84 evening; full-time 1256, part-time 238 (men 54%, women 46%); postgraduates

275. Faculty: full-time 64, part-time 109. Student to faculty ratio 18.4 to 1. Degrees conferred: J.D., J.D.-M.A., J.D.-M.B.A., J.D.-M.P.A., J.D.-M.H.S.A., LL.M., (Environmental Law, Intellectual Property Law, International and Comparative Law, Government Procurement Law, Litigation and Dispute Resolution) LL.M.-M.P.H., S.J.D.

ADMISSION REQUIREMENTS. LSDAS Law School report, bachelor's degree, transcripts, LSAT (no later than December), three letters of recommendation required in support of application. Interview not required. Accepts very limited number of transfer applicants. Graduates of unaccredited colleges not considered. Apply to Office of the Dean after October 1, before March 1. Beginning students admitted Fall only. Application fee $65. Phone: (202)739-0648; fax: (202)739-0624.

ADMISSION STANDARDS. Selective. Mean LSAT: full-time 161, part-time 159; mean GPA: full-time 3.42, part-time 3.25. Gourman rating: 4.39. *U.S. News & World Report* ranking is in the top 25 of all law schools. Accepts 20–25% of total annual applicants.

FINANCIAL AID. Scholarships, teaching fellowships (for LL.M. candidates), assistantships, Federal W/S, loans. Apply to Office of Financial Aid by March 1. Use FAFSA. About 35% of students receive aid other than loans from Law Center.

DEGREE REQUIREMENTS. For J.D.: 84 (32 required) credits with a GPA of at least 2.0 (A = 4), plus completion of upper divisional writing course; three-year program, four-year program. Accelerated J.D. with one summer of course work. For J.D.-Master's: a maximum of 6 credits can be applied to J.D. For LL.M.: 24 credits; a GPA of 2.67 (A = 4) required; thesis; one calendar year full-time, two calendar years part-time. For LL.M. (foreign law school graduates): one full year in residence; a GPA of 2.33 (A = 4) required; thesis/nonthesis option. For S.J.D.: two semesters minimum in residence beyond the master's; dissertation; oral defense.

School of Medicine and Health Sciences (20037)

First class in 1825. Annual tuition: $34,800, student fees $1540. Total average figure for all other expenses $10,200. Enrollment: first-year class 150 (2 EDP), full-time 789, part-time 43 (men 55%, women 45%). Faculty: full-time 696, part-time and volunteers 1902. Degrees conferred: M.D., M.D.-M.P.H. The M.S. and Ph.D. are offered through the Graduate School and the School of Engineering.

ADMISSION REQUIREMENTS. AMCAS report and supplemental application, transcripts, MCAT, interview required in support of application. Applicants must have completed at least three years of college study. Has EDP; apply between June 15 and August 1. Accepts transfer applicants. First-year students apply AMCAS after June 15, before December 1. Advanced standing students apply to Admissions Office by December 1. Application fee $80. Phone: (202)994-3506; e-mail: medadmit@gwu.edu.

ADMISSION STANDARDS. Very competitive. Mean GPA: 3.55; mean MCAT: 10.0. Gourman rating: 4.35. Accepts 10% of total annual applicants. Approximately 1% are district residents.

FINANCIAL AID. Scholarships, minority scholarships, grants, NIH stipend, Federal W/S, loans. About 78% of students receive aid other than loans from School. Apply to the Director of Financial Aid after acceptance but by April 15. Use FAFSA (School code: E00197).

DEGREE REQUIREMENTS. For M.D.: satisfactory completion of four-year program. For M.S., M.P.H., Ph.D.: see the Graduate listings above.

FIELDS OF GRADUATE STUDY.
Biochemistry.
Cell Biology.
Genetics.
Genomics and Bioinformatics. M.S. only.
Immunology.
Microbiology.
Molecular and Cellular Oncology.
Neurosciences.
Pharmacology.

GEORGETOWN COLLEGE
Georgetown, Kentucky 40324-1696

Founded 1829. Located 12 miles N of Lexington. Coed. Private control. Baptist. Semester system. Special facility: Center for Leadership and Ethics. Library: 130,000 volumes, 120,000 microforms, 8 PCs.

Tuition: per hour $200. No on-campus housing for graduate students.

Graduate Studies

Enrollment: full- and part-time 342. Faculty: full-time 4, part-time 10. Degree conferred: M.A. in Ed.

ADMISSION REQUIREMENTS. Transcripts, letters of recommendation required in support of School's application. GRE is strongly recommended. Interview sometimes required. Accepts transfer applicants. Graduates of unaccredited colleges not considered. Apply to Office of Graduate Study at least 30 days prior to start of semester. Application fee: none. Phone: (502)863-8009; fax: (502)868-8888.

ADMISSION STANDARDS. Relatively open. Minimum average: 2.7 (A = 4).

FINANCIAL AID. Limited to Federal W/S, loans. Approved for VA benefits. Apply to Director of Financial Aid; no specified closing date. Phone: (800)788-9985. Use FAFSA.

DEGREE REQUIREMENTS. For M.A. in Ed.: 30 semester hours minimum, at least 24 in residence; final comprehensive exam.

FIELD OF STUDY.
Education. Includes early elementary, elementary, secondary, middle school.

GEORGETOWN UNIVERSITY
Washington, D.C. 20057
Web site: www.georgetown.edu

Founded 1789. Coed. Private control. Roman Catholic, Jesuit affiliated. Semester system. Special facilities: Center for Contemporary Arab Studies, computation center, Joseph and Rose Kennedy Institute of Ethics, Lombardi Cancer Research Center, Center for Child Development, Center for German and European Studies, Center for Latin American Studies, Center for Muslim-Christian Understanding: History and International Affairs, Institute for the Study of Diplomacy. Participates in the Consortium of Universities of the Washington Metropolitan Area, includes the American, Catholic, Gallaudet, George Mason, George Washington, and Howard Universities, the University of the District of Columbia, the University of Maryland College Park, Mt. Vernon and Trinity Colleges. The University's NIH ranking is 72nd among all U.S. institutions with 193 awards/grants worth $63,749,675. Library: 2,071,000 volumes, 12,800 subscriptions. Total University enrollment: 12,600.

Annual tuition: full-time $23,832; per credit $993. No on-campus housing available for graduate students. Contact Director of Campus Housing for off-campus housing information. Phone: (202)687-4560.

Graduate School of Arts and Sciences

Graduate study since 1820. Enrollment: full-time 2089, part-time 786. Graduate faculty: full-time 1320, part-time 406. Degrees conferred: M.A., M.S., M.A.T., M.B.A., M.P.P., Ph.D.

ADMISSION REQUIREMENTS. Official transcripts, three letters of reference, statement of purpose required in support of School's application. On-line application available. GRE/MAT required by some departments. TOEFL (minimum score 550, some departments require higher scores) required for international applicants. Interview not required. Accepts transfer applicants. Graduates of unaccredited institutions not considered. Apply by February 1 (Fall), November 1 (Spring) to the Graduate School's Admission Office. Application fee $65 for students with an undergraduate degree from a U.S. institution, $70 for students with an undergraduate degree from a non-U.S. institution. On-line application fee $55. Phone: (202)687-5568; fax: (202) 687-6802; e-mail: gradmail@georgetown.edu.

ADMISSION STANDARDS. Competitive for most departments. Minimum average: 3.0 (A = 4).

FINANCIAL AID. Annual awards from institutional funds: scholarships, fellowships, assistantships, Federal W/S, loans. Approved for VA benefits. Aid available for international students. Apply by February 1 to the Graduate School Office for scholarships; to Financial Aid Office for all other programs. Phone: (202)687-4547; fax: (202)687-6542. Use FAFSA and graduate student supplement. About 50% of full-time students receive aid other than loans from School and outside sources.

DEGREE REQUIREMENTS. For master's: 24 semester hour minimum, at least 18 in residence; foreign language requirement varies by department; thesis; final written/oral exam; or 30 hour minimum without thesis in some departments. For Ph.D.: 50 hours minimum beyond the bachelor's, at least 45 in residence; preliminary exam; language requirement varies by department; thesis; final written/oral exam.

FIELDS OF STUDY.
Arab Studies. GRE for admission. M.A. only.
Arabic Language, Literature, and Linguistics. M.S., M.S.-Ph.D., Ph.D.
Biochemistry and Molecular Biology. GRE Subject in biology, biochemistry, or chemistry for admission. Ph.D. only.
Biology. GRE Subject for admission. M.S., Ph.D.
Cell Biology. GRE for admission. Ph.D. only.
Chemistry and Biochemistry. GRE for admission. M.S., M.S.-Ph.D., Ph.D.
Communication, Culture, and Technology. GRE for admission. M.A. only.
Demography. GRE for admission. M.A. only.
Economics. GRE for admission. Ph.D. only.
English. GRE for admission. M.A. only.
Eurasian, Russian, and East European Studies. M.A. only.
Foreign Service. GRE for admission. M.S. only.
German. M.S., M.S.-Ph.D., Ph.D.
German and European Studies. GRE for admission. M.A. only.
Government. GRE for admission. M.A., Ph.D.
Health Physics. M.S. only.
History. GRE for admission. Ph.D. only.
Latin American Studies. GRE for admission. M.A. only.

Liberal Studies. M.A. only.
Linguistics. M.A.T., M.S., Ph.D.
Microbiology and Immunology. GRE for admiss
Neuroscience. GRE for admission. Ph.D. only.
Pharmacology. GRE for admission. Ph.D. only
Philosophy. GRE for admission. M.A., Ph.D.
Physics. Includes industrial leadership in physics. Ph.D.
Physiology and Biophysics. GRE or MCAT for admission. M.S., Ph.D.
Psychology. GRE Subject for admission. Ph.D. only.
Public Policy. GRE for admission. M.P.P. only.
Security Studies. GRE or MAT for admission. M.A. only.
Spanish. M.S., M.S.-Ph.D., Ph.D.
Tumor Biology. M.S., Ph.D.

McDonough School of Business
Web site: www.msb.georgetown.edu

Established 1981. Private control. Accredited programs: M.B.A. Semester system. Special programs: foreign exchange programs (in Australia, Belgium, Czech Republic, Germany, Hong Kong, Japan, Sweden, United Kingdom). Special facilities: Center for International Business, Center for Business-Government Relations, The Connelly Program in Business Ethics, Global Entrepreneurship Program.

Annual tuition: full-time $28,440. Enrollment: total full-time 509 (men 70%, women 30%). Faculty: 66 full-time, 28 part-time; 94% with Ph.D./D.B.A. Degrees conferred: M.B.A., I.E.M.B.A. (International Executive), M.B.A.-J.D., M.B.A.-M.D., M.B.A.-M.P.P. (Public Policy), M.B.A.-M.S.F.S. (Foreign Service).

ADMISSION REQUIREMENTS. All applicants should have a bachelor's degree from a recognized institution of higher education and a strong mathematics background. Beginning students are admitted Fall only. Submit graduate application, GMAT (will accept GMAT test results from the last five years, latest acceptable date is March; GRE may be required for some joint degree programs), official transcripts from each undergraduate/graduate school attended, two letters of recommendation, three essays, résumé (prefers at least four years of work experience), and an application fee of $65 to the office of Graduate Admission. In addition, international students (whose native language is other than English) should submit a TOEFL report (minimum score 600), certified translations and evaluations of all official transcripts; recommendation should be in English or with certified translations, proof of health/immunization certificate, and proof of sufficient financial resources for two years of academic study. U.S. citizens apply by April 1 (Fall; February 1 for joint degree candidates), international students apply by February 1 (Fall). Transfer applicants are rarely considered. On-campus visits and interviews are required for all applicants prior to the admissions committee reviewing completed application. Joint degree applicants must apply to and be accepted to both schools; contact the admissions offices for current information and specific admissions requirements. Rolling admissions process, notification is made within 6–8 weeks of receipt of completed application and supporting documents. Graduate Business Program office phone: (202)687-4200.

ADMISSION STANDARDS. Selective. Median GMAT: 662; median GPA: 3.35 (A = 4). *U.S. News & World Report* ranked Georgetown in the top 30 of all U.S. business schools. *Business Week* listed Georgetown in the top 50 of American business schools.

FINANCIAL AID. Partial and full tuition scholarships, merit scholarships for international students, M.B.A. Scholars Program, minority scholarships, graduate assistantships, Federal W/S, loans. Financial aid is available for international students. Assistantships/fellowships may be available for joint degree candidates. Financial Aid applications and information are generally available at the on-campus visit/interview or after January 1;

by April 1. Request scholarship, fellowship, assistantship ormation from the School of Business. Contact the University's Office of Student Financial Services for current need-based financial aid information. Phone: (202)687-4547. Use FAFSA not later than February 15 (School code: 001445), also submit Financial Aid Transcript, Federal Income Tax forms. Approximately 40% of current students receive some form of financial assistance.

DEGREE REQUIREMENTS. For M.B.A.; 60 credit program including 21 elective credits, two-year program; degree program must be completed in three years. For I.E.M.B.A.: 60 credit program. For M.B.A.-J.D.: 122 credit program, four-and-one-half-to five-year program. For M.B.A.-M.D.: generally a five- to six-year program. For M.B.A.-M.P.P.: 87 credit program. For M.B.A.-M.S.F.S.: 90 credit program.

Law Center (20001)

Founded 1902. ABA approved since 1924. AALS member. Semester system. Law library: 995,306 volumes, 12,420 subscriptions; has LEXIS, NEXIS, WESTLAW, DIALOG.

Annual tuition: $26,860; per credit $950. No on-campus housing available. For off-campus housing contact Student Life Office. Phone: (202)661-9292. Total average cost for all other expenses: $15,140.

Enrollment: first-year class 593; day 461, evening 132; total full-time 1524 (men 50%, women 50%); total part-time 430; postgraduates 320. Faculty: full-time 97, part-time 97. Student to faculty ratio 15.5 to 1. Degrees conferred: J.D., LL.M., S.J.D., M.L.T.

ADMISSION REQUIREMENTS. LSDAS Law School report, bachelor's degree, transcripts, three references, LSAT required in support of application. Interview not required. Graduates of unaccredited colleges not considered. Part-time study available. Apply to Law Center Director of Admissions after September 1, before February 1 (Day), March 1 (Evening). First-year students admitted Fall only. For LL.M. candidates: apply by March 1 (Early Action applicants apply by January 1, international applicants by February 1). For S.J.D.: apply by February 1. Application fee $65. Phone: (202)662-9010; fax: (202)662-9439; e-mail: admis@law.georgetown.edu.

ADMISSION STANDARDS. Selective. Mean LSAT: full-time 167, part-time 162; mean GPA: full-time 3.57, part-time 3.55 (A = 4). Gourman rating: 4.69. *U.S. News & World Report* ranking is in top of 14 of all U.S. law schools. Accepts 20% of total annual applicants.

FINANCIAL AID. Scholarships including Public Interest Law Scholars Program, Federal W/S, loans. Apply to the Office of Financial Aid by March 1. Use FAFSA (School code: G21075). and institutional FAF. About 20% of students receive aid other than loans from Center. No University aid for part-time students except for students with extreme need.

DEGREE REQUIREMENTS. For J.D.: 83 semester hours required minimum, at least two in residence. For LL.M.: 24 credits beyond the J.D.; one year in residence, two research papers. For M.L.T.: same as LL.M., except at least 20 credits must be in tax courses. For S.J.D.: two years of residence, first year in full-time attendance; publishable thesis.

FIELDS OF GRADUATE STUDY.
Common Law Studies.
International and Comparative Law.
International Legal Studies. For international students only.
Securities and Financial Regulation.
Taxation.

Note: Combined degree programs offered in conjunction with the School of Business, the School of Foreign Service, and the Johns Hopkins School of Public Health.

School of Medicine

Opened 1851. Medical library 100,000 volumes. Annual tuition: $30,838. Total average figure for all other expenses $12,500.

Enrollment: M.D. program, first-year class 170; total 677 (men 52%, women 48%); graduate program, full-time 72. Faculty: full-time 626, part-time 2000. Degrees conferred: M.D., M.D.-M.B.A. M.D.-Ph.D. The M.S. and Ph.D. are offered in cooperation with the Graduate School of Arts and Sciences.

ADMISSION REQUIREMENTS. AMCAS report, transcripts, two references, MCAT (Spring test date) required in support of application. Interview by invitation only. Accepts transfer applicants. Apply to Office of Admissions after June 1, before November 1 (credentials by February 15). Admits Fall only. Application fee $100. Phone: (202)687-1154; fax: (202)687-3079.

ADMISSION STANDARDS. Very competitive. Mean science GPA: 3.59 (A = 4); mean MCAT: 10.0. Gourman rating: 4.38. Accepts 5% of total annual applicants. Approximately 3% are district residents.

FINANCIAL AID. Limited scholarships, loans, work-study. Apply, after acceptance, to Office of Student Financial Planning. Phone: (202)687-1693. Use FAFSA (School code: E00518). About 95–98% of students receive aid from School and outside sources.

DEGREE REQUIREMENTS. For M.D.: satisfactory completion of four-year program. For M.S., Ph.D.: see Graduate School listing above.

FIELDS OF GRADUATE STUDY.
Biochemistry and Molecular Biology.
Biomedical Sciences.
Cellular Biology.
Microbiology and Immunology.
Neurosciences.
Pharmacology.
Physiology.
Radiation Medicine.
Tumor Biology.
Note: Special program for fourth-year students to travel in Third World countries to gain practical experience.

GEORGIA COLLEGE AND STATE UNIVERSITY
Milledgeville, Georgia 31061
Web site: www.gcsu.edu

Founded 1889. Located 100 miles SE of Atlanta. State control. Semester system. Library: 170,000 volumes, 1037 subscriptions.

Annual tuition and fees: resident $3132, nonresident $12,528; part-time $131, nonresident $522. Limited on-campus housing available. Average annual housing cost: $4502 (including board); apartment living; $382–450 per month. Apply to Associate Director of Residence Life. Phone: (478)445-5160.

Graduate School

Graduate study since 1958. Graduate study available at Macon, Warner Robins, and Dublin campuses. Enrollment: full-time

687, part-time 409. Faculty: full-time 109, part-time 50. Degrees conferred: M.A., M.Accy., M.A.T., M.S., M.Ed., M.B.A., M.I.S., M.P.A., M.S.A., M.S.L.S., M.S.N., Ed.S., M.S.N.-M.B.A.

ADMISSION REQUIREMENTS. Transcripts, GRE/GMAT/MAT required in support of School's application. TOEFL required for foreign applicants. T-5 Georgia Certification or equivalent for Specialist. Interview may be requested. Accepts transfer applicants. Graduates of unaccredited institutions not considered. Apply to Office of Enrollment Services at least one month prior to quarter of entrance. Application fee $10. Phone: (478) 445-6289 or (800)342-0471.

ADMISSION STANDARDS. Relatively open. M.B.A. admission formula: GMAT + 200 × UGPA = 1050.

FINANCIAL AID. Annual awards from institutional funds: academic scholarships, assistantships, unlimited internships, Federal W/S, loans. Approved for VA benefits. Apply to Dean of Graduate School; no specified closing date. Use FAFSA and institutional FAF. Phone: (478)445-2063.

DEGREE REQUIREMENTS. For M.A., M.Accy., M.A.T., M.S., M.S.A., M.Ed.: 30–36 semester hours, at least 24 in residence; admission to candidacy; knowledge of one foreign language required by some departments; thesis/nonthesis option. For M.B.A., M.M.I.S., M.P.A.: 30–60 semester hour program. For Ed.S.: minimum of 27 semester hours beyond master's.

FIELDS OF STUDY.

COLLEGE OF ARTS AND SCIENCE.
Biology. M.S.
Creative Writing. M.F.A.
Criminal Justice. M.S.C.J.
English. M.A.
History. Includes archival management, U.S. and Europe. M.A.
Logistics Management. M.S.A.
Psychology. M.S.
Public Administration. M.P.A.
Public Affairs. M.P.A.

SCHOOL OF BUSINESS:
Accountancy. M.Accy.
Business Administration. M.B.A.
Management Information Systems. M.M.I.S.

SCHOOL OF EDUCATION:
Education (grades P–12). Includes art, French, health, Spanish.
Instructional Technology—Distance and Alternative Education. M.Ed.
Instructional Technology—Library Media. M.Ed.
Instructional Technology—Professional Educator. M.Ed.
Instructional Technology—Technology Coordinator. M.Ed.
Secondary Education (Grades 7–12). Includes biology, broad field science, business education, chemistry, English, history, mathematics, physics, political science. M.A.T.
Secondary Education. Includes English, mathematics, natural sciences, social sciences, foreign languages. M.Ed.

SCHOOL OF HEALTH SCIENCES:
Family Health. Includes adult nursing. M.S.N.
Family Nurse Practitioner. M.S.N.
Health and Physical Education. Includes health and physical education, health education, outdoor education and administration. M.Ed., Ed.S.
Music Therapy. M.M.T.
Nurse Administration. Includes health informatics, nursing service. M.S.N.

GEORGIA INSTITUTE OF TECHNOLOGY
Atlanta, Georgia 30332-0001
Web site: www.gatech.edu

Founded in 1885. Coed. State control. Semester system. Special facilities: Georgia Tech Research Institute and more than 40 interdisciplinary research centers on campus, including Microelectronics Research Center, Manufacturing Research Center, Bioengineering Research Center, Multimedia Technology Laboratory, video-based master's programs; various mainframe and microcomputing environments; graduate cooperative program; research affiliations Oak Ridge National Labs, Emory University Medical Center, Skidaway Institute of Oceanography. Library: more than 2,100,000 volumes, 23,639 subscriptions.

Tuition: per semester full-time resident $2234, nonresident $8956; per credit, resident $60, nonresident $245. On-campus housing for 300 married students. Average academic year housing cost: single students $1063 per semester on-campus, off-campus $1100 per semester; married students from $514 per month for one-bedroom apartments. Apply to Director, Housing Office. Phone: (404)894-2470.

Graduate Studies and Research

Graduate study since 1922. Enrollment: full-time 2730, part-time 833. Graduate faculty: full-time 595, part-time 12. Degrees conferred: M.S., Ph.D.

ADMISSION REQUIREMENTS. Transcripts, GRE, three letters of recommendation required in support of application. GRE Subject Tests or GMAT for most programs. Additional materials required by some departments. TOEFL (minimum score 550) required for international applicants. Interview not required. Accepts transfer applicants. Graduates of unaccredited colleges not considered. Apply directly to individual Schools or Graduate Academic and Enrollment Services no later than June 1 (Fall), February 1 recommended for financial aid and international applicants, November 1 (Spring), March 1 (Summer); some programs have later deadlines. Application fee $50. Phone: (404)894-4612.

ADMISSION STANDARDS. Selective. Usual minimum average: 3.0 (A = 4).

FINANCIAL AID. Annual awards from institutional and sponsored funds: fellowships, teaching assistantships, research assistantships, out-of-state tuition waivers, Federal W/S, loans. Apply to appropriate School Directors; no specified closing dates. Phone: (404)894-4160. Use FAFSA for Federal W/S, loans. About 60% of students receive aid other than loans from Institute and outside sources.

DEGREE REQUIREMENTS. For master's: 33 semester hours minimum; candidacy; reading knowledge of one foreign language for some departments; thesis/nonthesis option for some departments. For M.S.M.: two-year, full-time program. For Ph.D.: normally 50 semester hours minimum beyond the bachelor's, at least three semesters in residence; qualifying exam; reading knowledge of one foreign language for some departments; dissertation; final oral/written exams.

FIELDS OF STUDY.
Aerospace Engineering.
Algorithms, Combinatorics, and Optimization. Multidisciplinary Ph.D.
Architecture. GRE for admission to some programs. Portfolio, one year of experience in an architectural firm for admission.
Biology.
Bioengineering. Multidisciplinary.

Bioinformatics. Multidisciplinary.
Biomedical Engineering.
Building Construction and Facility Management.
Chemical Engineering.
Chemistry and Biochemistry. GRE/Subject for admission.
City Planning.
Civil Engineering. GRE for Financial Aid. Includes engineering science and mechanics, environmental engineering.
Computer Science. GRE/Subject for admission.
Earth and Atmospheric Sciences.
Economics.
Electrical and Computer Engineering.
History of Technology. GRE for admission.
Human-Computer Interaction. Multidisciplinary.
Industrial and System Engineering. Includes health systems, operations research, international logistics.
Information Design and Technology.
Information Security. GRE for admission.
International Affairs.
Management. GMAT for admission. Includes accounting, finance, information technology management, international business, marketing, operations management, organizational behavior, strategic management.
Management of Technology.
Mathematics. GRE/Subject for admission.
Mechanical Engineering. Includes nuclear and radiological engineering, health physics.
Physics.
Polymers. Multidisciplinary.
Psychology. GRE/Subject for admission.
Public Policy.
Quantitative and Computational Finance. Multdisciplinary.
Statistics. Multidisciplinary.
Textiles and Fiber Engineering. Includes textiles, textiles and fiber chemistry, textile engineering.

MEDICAL COLLEGE OF GEORGIA

Augusta, Georgia 30912-1003
Web site: www.mcg.edu

Chartered 1828. School of Graduate Studies awarded its first degree in 1953. Public control. Quarter system. Special facilities: Alzheimer's Disease Center, Center for Biotechnology and Genomic Medicine, Center for Clinical Investigation, Center for Disaster Medicine, Center for Health Care Improvement, Center for Nursing Research, Center for the Study of Occupational Therapy Education, Center for the Study of Physical Therapy Education, Comprehensive Sickle Cell Center, Dental Research Center, Neuroscience Center, Telemedicine Center, Vascular Biology Center, Institute of Molecular Medicine and Genetics, Institute for the Prevention of Human Disease and Accidents. The Medical College's NIH ranking was 137th with 87 awards/grants worth $23,789,000. Library: 176,000 volumes, 1672 subscriptions. Total College enrollment: 2061.

Annual tuition: graduate program, full-time resident $3006, nonresident $12,024; per hour, resident $62, nonresident $214. On-campus housing for 108 graduate men, 195 graduate women, 64 married students. Average annual housing cost: $6000–$8000. Apply to Director of Housing. Phone: (706)721-3471. Day-care facilities available.

School of Graduate Studies

Enrollment: full-time 280, part-time 92 (men 35%, women 65%). Faculty: full-time 176. Degrees conferred: M.S., M.S.N., M.H.E., Ph.D.

ADMISSION REQUIREMENTS. Transcripts, three letters of recommendation, GRE Subject Tests required in support of

School's application. Interview required for some departments. TOEFL required of all international applicants. Accepts transfer applicants. Apply to the Dean of School of Graduate Studies: deadlines vary by program. Application fee: none. Phone: (706)721-2725; fax: (706)721-7279.

ADMISSION STANDARDS. Competitive for most departments. Usual minimum average: 3.0 (A = 4).

FINANCIAL AID. Fellowships, NIH stipends, assistantships, traineeships, Federal W/S, loans. Apply by April 1 to Financial Aid Office. Phone: (706)721-4901. Use FAFSA (College code: 001579). About 85% of students receive aid other than loans from College and outside sources. Aid available for part-time students.

DEGREE REQUIREMENTS. For M.S., M.S.N., M.H.E.; 45 quarter hours minimum, at least 36 in full-time residence; reading knowledge of one foreign language; comprehensive exam; thesis, final oral exam. For M.S. in Medical Illustration: same as above, except graphics project may be submitted in lieu of thesis, and language not required. For Ph.D.: 90 hours and three full years minimum beyond the bachelor's, at least three consecutive quarters or equivalent in full-time residence; preliminary exams; dissertation; final oral exam.

FIELDS OF STUDY.
Adult Nursing. M.S.N. only.
Biochemistry. M.S., Ph.D.
Cellular Biology and Anatomy. M.S., Ph.D.
Community Health Nursing. M.S.N. only.
Diagnostic Medical Sonography. M.S. only.
Endocrinology. M.S., Ph.D.
Health Education. M.S., M.H.E.
Medical Illustration. GRE for admission; apply by March 1. Fall admission only; M.S. only.
Mental Health-Psychiatric Nursing. M.S.N. only.
Molecular Medicine.
Nuclear Medicine Technology. M.S. only.
Nurse Anesthetist. M.N. only.
Nurse Practitioner. Includes adult/family, pediatric, neonatal. M.N. only.
Nursing. Ph.D.
Occupational Therapy. M.S., M.H.E.
Oral Biology. M.S., Ph.D.
Parent-Child Nursing. M.S.N. only.
Pharmacology. M.S., Ph.D.
Physical Therapy. M.S., M.H.E.
Physician Assistant. M.S. only.
Physiology. M.S., Ph.D.
Radiation Therapy Technology. M.S. only.
Radiography. M.S. only.
Respiratory Therapy. M.S. only.
Vascular Biology. Ph.D.

School of Dentistry (30912)

First class entered 1969. Semester system. Tuition: residents $8628, nonresidents $33,252. On-campus housing available. Contact Director of Housing for housing information. Phone: (706)721-3471. Total average academic costs for all other first-year expenses: $5637.

Enrollment: first-year class 56 (men 55%, women 45%), total 194; postgraduates 15. Faculty: full-time 89, part-time 32. Degrees conferred: D.M.D., D.M.D.-M.S. (Oral Biology), D.M.D.-Ph.D. (Oral Biology).

ADMISSION REQUIREMENTS. Official transcripts, DAT (not later than October), three letters of reference, a pre-dental adviser's recommendation required in support of School's application. Preference given to state residents. Applicants must have completed at least three years of college study. Interviews by invitation only. Apply to Associate Director of Student Affairs after July 1, before November 1. Application fee: none. Phone: (706)721-3587; fax: (706)721-6276.

ADMISSION STANDARDS. Competitive. Median DAT: Academic 17, PAT 17; median GPA: 3.26 (A = 4). Gourman rating: 4.14. Accepts 75% of total annual applicants. 100% are state residents.

FINANCIAL AID. Scholarships, loans, grants, Federal loans. Apply between January 1 and March 1 to Director of Financial Aid. Phone: (706)721-4901. Use FAFSA (School code: 001579). About 86% of students receive aid other than loans from School.

DEGREE REQUIREMENTS. For D.M.D.: satisfactory completion of 45-month program.

School of Medicine (30912-4760)

Founded 1828. Eleventh oldest medical school in the U.S. Semester system.

Tuition: residents $7340, nonresidents $29,358. Total average figure for all other expenses: $10,880. Enrollment: first-year class 180 (EDP 55); total 711 (men 70%, women 30%). Faculty: full-time 438, part-time 54. Degrees conferred: M.D., M.D.-Ph.D.

ADMISSION REQUIREMENTS. AMCAS report, transcripts, references, MCAT, interview required in support of application. Applicants must have completed at least three years of college study. Preference given to Georgia residents. Has EDP, state residents only. Apply between June 15 and August 1. Apply to Associate Dean for Admissions after June 15, before November 1. Application fee $30. Phone: (706)721-3186; fax: (706)721-0959.

ADMISSION STANDARDS. Selective. Mean MCAT: 9.7; mean GPA: 3.63 (A = 4). Accepts 40% of annual applicants. Approximately 96% are state residents.

FINANCIAL AID. Scholarships, fellowships, tuition waivers, loans. Apply to Office of Student Financial Aid; no closing date. Use FAFSA (School code: 001579). Less than 85% of students receive aid other than loans from School.

DEGREE REQUIREMENTS. For M.D.: satisfactory completion of four-year program, at least one year in residence.

FIELDS OF GRADUATE STUDY.
Biochemistry and Molecular Biology.
Cell Signaling.
Cellular Biology and Anatomy.
Developmental Biology.
Developmental Neurobiology.
Gene Regulation.
Molecular Immunology.
Molecular Medicine.
Pharmacology and Toxicology.
Physiology and Endocrinology.
Vascular Biology.

GEORGIA SOUTHERN UNIVERSITY
Statesboro, Georgia 30460-8133
Web site: www.gasou.edu

Founded 1906. Located 50 miles E of Savannah. CGS member. Coed. State control. Semester system. Library: 463,000 volumes, 3511 subscriptions. Total University enrollment: 14,200.

Annual tuition: resident $2320, nonresident $9280; per credit,

resident $97, nonresident $387. On-campus housing for 1370 men, 1818 women. Average academic year housing cost: $4154. Apply to Director of Housing. Phone: (912)681-5406.

College of Graduate Studies

Enrollment: full- and part-time 1305 (men 35%, women 65%). University faculty teaching graduate students: full-time 240, part-time 28. Degrees conferred: M.A., M.S., M.B.A., M.F.A., M.H.S.A., M.P.H., M.S.N., M.S.S.M., M.P.A., M.Ed., Ed.S., M.R.A., M.T., Ed.D.

ADMISSION REQUIREMENTS. Two transcripts, GRE (M.A., M.S., M.P.A., M.R.A., M.S.N., M.T., Ed.D.), GMAT (M.B.A.), MAT (M.Ed., Ed.S., M.S.N.) required in support of School's application. On-line application available. TOEFL (minimum score 550), certified transcripts and diplomas, financial statement required for international applicants. Interview not required. Accepts transfer applicants. Graduates from unaccredited institutions not considered. Apply to Graduate School by July 1 (Fall), November 15 (Spring), earlier deadlines for international applicants. Application fee: none. Phone: (912)681-5384; fax: (912)681-0740; e-mail: gradschool@gasou.edu.

ADMISSION STANDARDS. Selective. Usual minimum average: 2.5 (A = 4).

FINANCIAL AID. Annual awards from institutional funds: scholarships, teaching assistantships, research assistantships, Federal W/S, loans. Apply by April 1 to chair of appropriate division for assistantships; to Financial Aid Office for all other programs. Phone: (912)681-5413. Use FAFSA. About 20% of students receive aid other than loans from College and outside sources. Aid available for both international and part-time students.

DEGREE REQUIREMENT. For M.A., M.S.: 30 semester hours minimum; thesis. For M.Ed., M.R.A.: 45 hours minimum, final comprehensive exam. For Ed.S.: 30 hours minimum; final comprehensive exam. For M.B.A.: 36 hours minimum. For M.P.A.: 45 hours minimum; internship; capstone course; final oral exam. For M.T.: 45 hours minimum; thesis; final oral exam. For M.F.A.: 60 hours; thesis. For M.H.S.A.: 37–39 semester hours; managerial residency or thesis. For M.P.H.: 45 semester hour program; practicum or thesis. For M.S.N.: 45 hours minimum; thesis or project; final exam. Minimum residence requirement for a master's degree is one academic year or three summer sessions. For Ed.D.: 75 hours beyond the master's; comprehensive/qualifying exam; advancement to degree candidacy; dissertation; final oral defense.

FIELDS OF STUDY.
Accounting. M.Acc.
Adult and Vocational Education. M.Ed.
Art. M.F.A., M.Ed.
Art Education. M.Ed., Ed.S.
Biology. M.S.
Business. M.B.A.
Business Education. M.Ed.
Counseling. Ed.S.
Counselor Education. M.Ed., Ed.S.
Curriculum Studies. Ed.D.
Early Childhood Education. M.Ed., Ed.S.
Educational Administration. M.Ed., Ed.D.
Educational Leadership. M.Ed.
English. M.A.
English Education. M.Ed., Ed.S.
French. M.Ed.
Health and Physical Education. M.Ed., Ed.S.
Health Services Administration. M.H.S.A.
Higher Education. M.Ed.
History. M.A.

Instructional Technology. M.Ed., Ed.S.
Kinesiology. M.S.
Mathematics. M.S.
Mathematics Education. M.Ed., Ed.S.
Middle Grades Education. M.Ed., Ed.S.
Music. M.M.
Music Education. M.Ed., Ed.S.
Nursing. Includes family nurse practitioner, women's health nurse practitioner, rural community health nurse specialist. M.S.N.
Political Science. M.A.
Psychology. M.S.
Public Administration. M.P.A.
Public Health. M.P.H.
Reading Specialist. M.Ed., Ed.S.
Recreation Administration. M.S.R.A.
School Administration and Supervision. M.Ed., Ed.S.
School Psychology. M.Ed., Ed.S.
Science Education. M.Ed., Ed.S.
Social Science Education. M.Ed., Ed.S.
Sociology. M.A.
Spanish. M.Ed.
Special Education. M.Ed., Ed.S.
Sport Management. M.S.S.M.
Technology. M.T.
Technology Education. M.Ed., M.S.T., Ed.S.

GEORGIA STATE UNIVERSITY

Atlanta, Georgia 30303-3083
Web site: www.gsu.edu

Founded 1913. CGS member. Coed. State control. Semester system. Special facilities: Center for Biotechnology and Drug Design, Center for Brain Sciences and Health, Center for Creative Writing, Center for Ethics, Center for Environmental Research, Center for Ethics and Public Affairs, Center for Health Policy, Center for High Angular Resolution Astronomy, Center for Integrative Neurosciences and Health, Center for International Media Research and Training, Center for Latin American Studies, Center for Learning Disorders, Center for Learning and Teaching, Center for Neural Communication and Computation, Center for Professional Communication, Center for Sports Medicine, Gerontology Center, Language Research Center. Library: 1,572,000 volumes, 12,053 subscriptions. Total University enrollment: 24,300.

Tuition: per credit, resident $125, nonresident $417. No on-campus housing. Contact Dean of Students for off-campus housing information.

Division of Graduate Studies—
College of Arts and Sciences

Enrollment: full- and part-time 1387. Faculty: full-time 380, part-time 38. Degrees conferred: M A., M.A.Ed., M.H.P., M.S., M.A.T., M.F.A., M.Mu., Certificate, Ph.D.

ADMISSION REQUIREMENTS. Transcripts, GRE required in support of College's application. Some programs require letters of recommendation, portfolio, audition, résumé, interview, writing sample, or list of references. TOEFL required for international applicants. Accepts transfer applicants. Graduates of unaccredited institutions not considered. Apply by August 1 (Fall), December 1 (Spring), June 1 (Summer)—some programs have earlier deadlines—to the Office of Graduate Admissions. Application fee $25. Phone: (404)651-2469; fax: (404)651-4811.

ADMISSION STANDARDS. Competitive. Usual minimum average: 3.0 (A = 4).

FINANCIAL AID. Annual awards from institutional funds: fellowships, scholarships, minority scholarships, graduate assistantships, tuition waivers, Federal W/S, loans. Approved for VA benefits. Apply to head of proposed major department prior to registration; to Office of Financial Aid for all other programs. Phone: (404)651-2227; fax: (404)651-1519. Use FAFSA.

DEGREE REQUIREMENTS. For M.A., M.S.: 30–33 semester hours minimum, at least 24 hours in residence; thesis/nonthesis option; reading knowledge of one foreign language for some departments; research tool may be substituted in some departments; general exam; thesis. For Certificates: 30 semester hours minimum beyond the master's. For M.A.T.: 36 semester hours minimum; final written/oral exam. For M.F.A.: 60 semester hours minimum; final written/oral exam. For M.M.: 35–36 semester hour program; general written/oral exam. For Ph.D.: four semester in residence, at least two consecutive semsters in full-time attendance; ordinarily, reading knowledge of one or two foreign languages; research skill may be substituted for one or two languages in some departments; general exam; admission to candidacy; dissertation; final exam.

FIELDS OF STUDY.
Anthropology. Includes health policy and planning, urban policy and planning, community development, ethnicity, ethnomedicine, health behavior, urban development, social impact assessment. M.A.
Applied Linguistics. M.A., Ph.D.
Art. Includes ceramics, drawing, interior design, jewelry design and metalsmithing, painting, photography, printmaking, sculpture, textiles. M.A., M.F.A.
Art Education. M.A.E.
Art History. M.A.
Astronomy. Includes astronomy, astrophysics. Ph.D.
Biological Sciences. Ph.D.
Biology. Includes microbiology, molecular genetics, neurobiology and behavior, physiology. M.S.
Chemistry. Includes analytical, biochemical, inorganic, organic, physical chemistry. M.S., Ph.D.
Communication. Includes print journalism, public relations, broadcast journalism, film and video, speech. M.A., Ph.D.
Computer Science. M.S., Ph.D.
Creative Writing. M.F.A.
English. Includes American and British literature, creative writing, rhetoric and composition. M.A., Ph.D.
Geography. Includes metropolitan area studies, cartography, physical geography/environmental studies. M.A.
Geology. Includes geochemistry, environmental geology, hydrogeology. M.S.
Geochemistry. Ph.D.
German. M.A.
Heritage Preservation. Includes archaeology, planning, architectural history, historical research, urban history. M.H.P.
History. Includes United States, European, Asian, Latin American, African, and Middle-Eastern history. M.A., Ph.D.
Mathematics. Includes statistics. M.A., M.A.T., M.S.
Music. Includes music education, guitar, performance, music theory, choral conducting, instrumental conducting, composition, jazz studies, piano pedagogy, sacred music. M.M.
Philosophy. Includes applied ethics, history of philosophy, Wittgenstein, religious studies. M.A.
Physics. Includes atomic physics, biophysics, molecular physics, nuclear physics, condensed matter physics. M.S., Ph.D.
Political Science. Includes electoral politics, international relations. M.A., Ph.D.
Psychology. Includes clinical psychology, community psychology, neuropsychology and behavioral neurosciences, psychological foundations. M.A., Ph.D.
Sociology. Includes family, life course, social inequality, conflict. M.A.

Spanish. M.A., Ph.D.
Women's Studies. M.A.

J. Mack Robinson College of Business
Web site: www.cba.gsu.edu

Established 1958. Accredited programs: M.B.A., Accounting. Courses offered at University's North Metro Center. Semester system. Special programs: foreign study (in Amsterdam, Frankfurt, London). Special facilities: Center for Business and Industrial Marketing, Center for Digital Commerce, Center for Mature Consumer Studies, Center for Risk Management and Insurance Research, Decision Sciences Institute, Economic Forecasting Center, Institute for Small Business, Institute of Health Administration, Institute of International Business, W. T. Beebe Institute of Personnel and Employment Relations.

Tuition: full-time resident $4382, nonresident $15,482; part-time resident $155 per credit, nonresident $620 per credit. Enrollment: total full-time 648, part-time 1647 (men 65%, women 35%). Faculty: 165 full-time, 22 part-time; 98% with Ph.D./D.B.A.

Degrees conferred: M.B.A. (full-time, part-time, day, evening), E.M.B.A., F.M.B.A. (Flexible), M.A.S. (Actuarial Science), M.S., M.S.H.A. (Health Administration), M.S.R.E. (Real Estate), M.P.A. (Professional Accounting), M.Tx. (Taxation), M.B.A.-J.D., M.B.A.-M.S.H.A. (Health Administration), Ph.D.

ADMISSION REQUIREMENTS. All applicants should have a bachelor's degree from a recognized institution of higher education and a strong mathematics background. Early applications are encouraged for both admission and financial aid consideration. Submit application, GMAT (will accept GMAT test results from the last five years, latest acceptable date is March), official transcripts from each undergraduate/graduate school attended, three letters of recommendation, résumé (prefers at least four years of work experience), and an application fee of $25 to the Office of Academic Assistance and Master's Admission. In addition, international students (whose native language is other than English) should submit a TOEFL report (minimum score 550), certified translations and evaluations of all official transcripts; recommendation should be in English or with certified translations, proof of health/immunization certificate, and proof of sufficient financial resources to complete entire academic program. Beginning students are admitted into all semesters. Both U.S. citizens and international applicants apply by June 1 (Fall), October 15 (Spring), March 1 (Summer). On-campus visits are required. Interviews are required for E.M.B.A. applicants prior to the admissions committee reviewing completed application. Joint degree applicants must apply to and be accepted to both colleges; contact the admissions office for current information and specific admissions requirements. Rolling admissions process; notification is made within six to eight weeks of receipt of completed application and supporting documents. Admissions office phone: (404)651-1913; fax: (404)651-0219; E.M.B.A.: (404)651-3760.

ADMISSION REQUIREMENTS FOR DOCTORAL CANDIDATES. Contact the Director of Doctoral Programs, College of Business for application material and information. Beginning students are admitted Fall Only. Both U.S. citizens and international applicants apply by March 1 (Fall). Submit the Doctoral Program Application for Admission, a GMAT (will accept GMAT test results from the last five years), two official transcripts from each undergraduate/graduate schools attended, three letters of recommendation, résumé, statement of purpose, and application fee of $25 to the Doctoral Program Office. In addition, international students (whose native language is other than English) should submit a TOEFL report (minimum score 600); certified translations and evaluations of all official transcripts, recommendation should be in English or with certified translations, proof of health/immunization certificate. Interviews are by invitation and are generally requested prior to the admissions

committee reviewing completed application. Notification is made by mid-April.

ADMISSION STANDARDS. For M.B.A.: median GMAT: full-time 580, part-time 570; median GPA: 3.06 (A = 4). *U.S. News & World Report* ranked College of Business in the top five of all U.S. business schools for part-time M.B.A. programs. For Ph.D.: mean GMAT: 660; mean GPA: 3.3 (A = 4).

FINANCIAL AID. Scholarships, merit scholarship, Regent's Opportunity Scholarships, grants, nonresident fee waivers, graduate assistantships, Federal W/S, loans. Financial aid is available for part-time study. Assistantships may be available for joint degree candidates. Financial aid applications and information are generally available at the on-campus visit or after January 1; apply by May 1. Request scholarship and assistantship information from the College of Business; phone: (404)651-1913. For assistantships and scholarships the selection criteria places heavy reliance on GMAT and undergraduate GPA. Contact the University's Financial Aid Office for current need-based financial aid information; phone: (404)651-2227. Use FAFSA (School code: 001574), also submit Financial Aid Transcript, Federal Income Tax forms. Approximately 20% of students receive some form of financial assistance.

DEGREE REQUIREMENTS. For M.B.A.: 39–60 credit, 13–20 course program including four elective courses, two-year program. For E.M.B.A.: 45 credit, eighteen-month program. For M.A.S., M.P.A., M.S.: 30 credit programs. For M.I.B.: 33 credit program; foreign-language proficiency. For M.S.H.A., M.S.R.E.: 36 credit program. M.Tx.: 33 credit program. For M.B.A.-M.S.H.A.: two-and-one-half-year program. For M.B.A.-J.D.: three-and-one-half- to five-year program. For Ph.D.: three- to five-year full-time program; comprehensive exam in major field and related area; dissertation proposal and oral defense, dissertation; oral defense; degree must be completed within seven years.

FIELDS OF STUDY.
Accountancy. Ph.D.
Actuarial Science. M.A.S.
Business Administration. Concentrations in accounting, actuarial science, decision sciences, economics, electronic commerce, finance, general business, health administration, hospitality administration, human resource management, information systems, international business, management, marketing, personal financial planning, personnel and employment relations, real estate, risk management and insurance. M.B.A.
Business Economics. M.S.
Computer Information Systems. M.S., Ph.D.
Decision Sciences. M.S.
Finance. M.S., Ph.D.
Health Administration. Includes finance, human resource management, information systems, management, marketing, risk management and insurance. M.S.H.A.
Human Resource Management. M.S.
International Business. M.I.B.
Management. M.S., Ph.D.
Marketing. M.S., Ph.D.
Personal Financial Planning. M.S.
Professional Accountancy. Includes accounting systems, financial accounting and reporting, management accounting. M.P.A.
Real Estate. M.S.R.E., Ph.D.
Risk Management and Insurance. M.S., Ph.D.
Strategic Management. Ph.D.
Taxation. M.Tx.

College of Education

Special facilities: Center for Sports Medicine, Science, and Technology, Center for the Study of Adult Literacy, Center for Urban Educational Excellence, Instructional Technology Center.

Tuition: per credit resident $125, nonresident $417. Enrollment: full-time 601, part-time 897. College faculty: full-time 97, part-time 61. Degrees conferred: M.Ed., M.L.M., M.S., Ed.S., Ph.D.

ADMISSION REQUIREMENTS. Two official transcripts, two letters of recommendation, goals statement, GRE/MAT/GSTEP (Georgia State Test of English Proficiency) required in support of College's application. TOEFL, GSTEP required for international applicants. Interviews may be required. Accepts transfer applicants. Apply for master's 90 days prior to registration. For Ph.D., application deadlines vary by major; usually accepted once or twice yearly. Rolling admissions process. Application fee $25. Phone: (404)651-2540.

ADMISSION STANDARDS. Usual minimum average master's: 2.5 GPA, GRE 800, MAT 44; Specialist: 3.25 GPA, GRE 900, MAT 48; Ph.D.: varies by degree.

FINANCIAL AID. Fellowships, research assistantships, teaching assistantships, tuition waivers, Federal W/S, loans. Approved for VA benefits. Apply to chairman of appropriate department for fellowships, assistantships; to Director of Financial Aid for all other programs. No specified closing date. Phone: (404)651-2227. Use FAFSA. About 20% of students receive aid from University and outside sources. Aid available for part-time students.

DEGREE REQUIREMENTS. For M.Ed., M.L.M., M.S.: 36–45 semester hours minimum, at least 27 in residence; comprehensive exam; project, thesis, capstone. For Ed.S.: 30 semester hour program, at least 27 in residence; comprehensive exam; final written/oral exams/projects. For Ph.D.: 54 semester hour program, at least 36 in residence; comprehensive exam; candidacy; dissertation; oral defense.

FIELDS OF STUDY.
Behavior/Learning Disabilities. M.Ed.
Communication Disorders. M.Ed.
Counseling. Ph.D.
Counseling Psychology. Ph.D.
Early Childhood Education. M.Ed., Ed.S., Ph.D.
Education of Students with Exceptionalities. Ph.D
Educational Leadership. M.Ed., Ed.S.
Educational Policy Studies. Ph.D.
Educational Psychology. M.S., Ph.D
Educational Research. M.S.
English Education. M.Ed.
Exercise Science. M.S.
Health and Physical Education. M.Ed.
Instructional Technology. M.S., Ph.D.
Library Media Technology. M.L.M.
Mathematics Education. M.Ed.
Middle Childhood Education. M.Ed.
Multiple and Severe Disabilities. M.Ed.
Professional Counseling. M.S., Ed.S.
Reading, Language, and Literacy Education. M.Ed.
Rehabilitation Counseling. M.S., Ed.S.
School Counseling. M.Ed., Ed.S.
School Psychology. M.Ed., Ed.S., Ph.D.
Science Education. M.Ed.
Social Foundations of Education. M.S.
Social Studies Education. M.Ed.
Special Education. Ed.S.
Sports Administration. M.S.
Sport Science. Ph.D.
Teaching and Learning. Ed.S., Ph.D.

College of Health and Human Sciences

Tuition: full-time resident $4030, nonresident $17,074; per credit resident $140, nonresident $558. Enrollment: full-time 229, part-time 151. Faculty: full-time 78, part-time 15. Degrees conferred: M.P.T., M.S., Ph.D.

ADMISSION REQUIREMENTS. Transcripts, GRE, Certification of Immunization required in support of College's application. Some programs require letters of recommendation, statement of professional goals. TOEFL required for international applicants. Accepts transfer applicants. Graduates of unaccredited institutions not considered. Apply to the Office of Graduate Admissions; application deadlines vary by department. Application fee $25. Phone: (404)651-3030.

ADMISSION STANDARDS. Competitive. Usual minimum average: 3.0 (A = 4).

FINANCIAL AID. Annual awards from institutional funds: scholarships, minority fellowships, fellowships, research assistantships, teaching assistantships, traineeships, Federal W/S, loans. Approved for VA benefits. Apply to head of proposed major department for fellowships, assistantships; to Office of Financial Aid for all other programs. Phone: (404)651-2227; fax (404)651-1519. Use FAFSA.

DEGREE REQUIREMENTS. For M.S.: 36–51 semester hours minimum, thesis/nonthesis option; practicum for nursing. For M.P.T.: 107 semester hours minimum; internships. For M.S.W.: 60 semester hours program. For Ph.D.: 51–60 credit program, a minimum of two consecutive semesters in full-time residence; comprehensive exam; candidacy; dissertation; final exam.

FIELDS OF STUDY.
Allied Health Professions. Includes nutrition, physical therapy, respiratory care. M.S.
Criminal Justice. M.S.
Nursing. M.S., Ph.D.
Physical Therapy. M.P.T.
Social Work. M.S.W.

College of Law (30302-4049)

Web site: www.law.gsu.edu

Established 1982. ABA approved since 1984. AALS member. Semester system. Library: 280,778 volumes, 3550 subscriptions; has LEXIS, NEXIS, WESTLAW.

Tuition: full-time resident $4240, nonresident $14,800; part-time resident $3954, nonresident $13,634. No on-campus housing available. Off-campus housing costs range from $375–$500 per month. Total average annual additional expense: $13,280.

Enrollment: first-year class, full-time 149, part-time 52; total 603 (men 47%, women 53%). Faculty: full-time 33, part-time 4. Student to faculty ratio 13.6 to 1. Degrees conferred: J.D., J.D.-M.B.A.

ADMISSION REQUIREMENTS. LSDAS Law School report, bachelor's degree, transcripts, LSAT, letters of recommendation, personal statement required in support of application. Accepts transfer applicants. Preference given to state residents. Apply to Admissions Office by March 15. Application fee $30. Phone: (404)651-2048; fax: (404)651-1244.

ADMISSION STANDARDS. Selective. Mean LSAT: full-time 156, part-time 155; mean GPA: full-time 3.2, part-time 3.13 (A = 4). Gourman rating: 2.12. *U.S. News & World Report* ranking is in the second tier of all U.S. law schools. Accepts about 20–25% of total annual applicants.

FINANCIAL AID. Scholarships, tuition waiver, research assistantships, grants, Federal W/S, loans. Apply by April 1 to Office of Financial Aid. Use FAFSA. About 25% of students receive some aid from School.

DEGREE REQUIREMENTS. For J.D.: satisfactory completion of 135 quarter hours program. For M.B.A.: see Graduate School listing above.

Andrew Young School of Policy Studies

Established 1996. Semester system. Special facilities: Applied Research Center, Environmental Policy Center, the GSU Economic Forecasting Center, Georgia Health Policy Center.

Tuition: full-time resident $4030, nonresident $17,074; per credit resident $140, nonresident $558. Enrollment: full-time 117, part-time 148. Faculty; full-time 48, part-time 10. Degrees conferred: M.A., M.P.A., M.S.H.R.D., M.S.U.P.S., J.D.-M.P.A., Ph.D.

ADMISSION REQUIREMENTS. Two transcripts, GRE or GMAT, Certification of Immunization required in support of School's application; doctoral application required for Ph.D. applicants. Some programs require letters of recommendation, goal statement, résumé, interview. TOEFL required for international applicants. Accepts transfer applicants. Graduates of unaccredited institutions not considered. Apply to the Office of Academic Assistance; self-managed application process. Master's deadlines: July 1 (Fall), November 1 (Spring), April 12 (Summer); Doctoral deadlines: admits Fall only, Economics March 15, Public Policy February 1. Application fee of $25 for master's and Ph.D. in Economics, for Public Policy $50. Telephone: (404)651-3504; fax: (404)651-3536.

ADMISSION STANDARDS. Competitive. Usual minimum average: 3.0 (A = 4).

FINANCIAL AID. Scholarships, fellowships, research assistantships, teaching assistantships, tuition waivers, Federal W/S, loans. Approved for VA benefits. Apply to head of proposed major department for fellowships, assistantships; to Office of Financial Aid for all other programs. Phone: (404)651-2227; fax (404)651-1519. Use FAFSA. Aid available for part-time students.

DEGREE REQUIREMENTS. For M.A.: 36 credit hour program, at least 30 hours in residence; reading knowledge of one foreign language; research tool may be substituted in some programs; thesis/nonthesis option; written/oral exam. For M.P.A.: 39 semester hours minimum; internship or practicum. For M.S.: 36 credit, two-year full-time program; internship or practicum or thesis. For Ph.D.: 66 credit, full-time program; written qualifying exam; dissertation proposal, defense; dissertation; final oral exam.

FIELDS OF STUDY.
Economics. M.A., Ph.D.
Human Resource Development. M.S.H.R.D.
Public Administration. M.P.A.
Public Policy. Ph.D.
Urban Policy Studies. M.S.U.P.S.

UNIVERSITY OF GEORGIA
Athens, Georgia 30602-7402
Web site: www.uga.edu

Founded 1785. Located 70 miles E of Atlanta. The oldest state university in U.S. CGS member. Coed. State control. Semester system. Sponsoring university of the Oak Ridge Associated Universities. Special facilities: Institute of Behavioral Research, Biomedical and Health Sciences Institute, Center for Tropical and Emerging Diseases, Complex Carbohydrate Research Center, Institute of Ecology, Institute of Higher Education, Marine Institute on Sapelo Island, Poultry Disease Research Center, Institute of Remote Sensing and Mapping, Skidaway Institute of Oceanography, Social Science Research Institute, Organization of Tropical Studies. The University's NIH ranking is 119th among

all U.S. institutions with 89 awards/grants worth $28,331,908. Library: 3,800,000 volumes, 54,000 subscriptions. Total University enrollment: 30,100.

Tuition: per credit $153, nonresident $626; Social Work per credit resident $140, nonresident $600. On-campus housing for 545 married students, unlimited for single students. Average housing costs: $3500–$4500 (including board) for single students. Contact University Housing Office for both on- and off-campus housing information. Phone: (706)542-1421.

Graduate School

Graduate study since 1868. Enrollment: full-time 3714, part-time 1859. Graduate faculty: full-time 1495, part-time none. Degrees conferred: M.A., M.Acc., M.A.E., M.Ag.Ext., M.A.Ed., M.AM., M.A.M.S., M.A.T., M.B.A., M.C.S.S., M.Ed., M.F.A., M.F.C.S., M.F.R., M.F.T., M.H.P., M.L.A., M.I.T., LL.M., M.M.C., M.M., M.M.Ed., M.P.A., M.P.P.P.M., M.S., M.S.W., Ed.S., D.M.A., D.P.A., Ed.D., Ph.D.

ADMISSION REQUIREMENTS. Two official transcripts, two copies of GRE/GMAT/MAT required in support of School's application (sent directly to Office of Graduate Admission); three letters of recommendation, goal statements, and any other materials are sent to the department or program. TOEFL required for international applicants. Interview not required. Accepts transfer applicants, Graduates of unaccredited institutions not considered. For international applicants apply to Graduate Admissions Office June 15 (Fall), October 15 (Spring), February 15 (Summer); for domestic applicants apply July 1 (Fall), November 15 (Spring), April 1 (Summer); for assistantships apply by January 1; some departments have earlier deadlines, contact department directly. Application fee $30. Phone: (706)542-1739; fax: (706)542-9480; e-mail: gradadm@uga.edu.

ADMISSION STANDARDS. Selective for most departments. Usual minimum average: 3.0 (A = 4).

FINANCIAL AID. Annual awards from institutional funds: fellowships, scholarships, graduate assistantships, Federal W/S, loans. Approved for VA benefits. Apply by January 1 to Graduate School Office for assistantships; by February 15 to Financial Aid Office for all other programs. Phone: (706)542-6147. Use FAFSA. Aid available for part-time students.

DEGREE REQUIREMENTS. For M.A., M.S., M.Ed.: 28–36 credit hours minimum, at least 24–30 in residence; thesis; reading knowledge of one foreign language for some majors; final oral exam. For M.Acc.: 30 semester hour program. For M.B.A.: 60 credit, full-time program, additional hours may be required depending upon previous preparation. For M.A.Ed.: 30–36 credit hours minimum, at least 24–30 in residence; final written/oral exam. For M.A.E.: 30–36 credit hours minimum depending upon program, at least 24–30 in residence; final written/oral exam. For M.F.A.: 60 semester hours minimum; creative project, depending upon major; final written/oral exam. For M.F.R.: 33 credit program. For M.F.C.S.: 36–55 credit program; internship; project. For M.L.A.: 60 credit hours minimum; thesis; final written/oral exam. For M.M.C.: 30–33 credit program; thesis/nonthesis. For M.S.W.: 60 credit, two-year, full-time program, including instruction and fieldwork; problems course or thesis; practicum. For M.Ag.Ext.: 30 credit hours minimum; written problem. For M.A.M.S.: 33 credit hours minimum; 12 technical reports. For M.A.T.: 33 credit hours minimum in subject area; 15 hours minimum in education; comprehensive exam. For M.A.M.: 30–36 credit program; thesis/research project/practice base paper; oral exam. For M.H.P.: 54–61 credit, two-year program; internship; thesis. For M.I.T.: 32 credit program; technology project. For LL.M.: 27 semester hours; thesis; oral exam. For M.M.: 30–36 credit hours minimum and final project. For M.M.Ed.: 30–36 credit hour minimum. For M.P.P.P.M.: 33 credit hour minimum; two internships; final written and oral exams. For Ed.S.: 33 semester hours beyond master's; student portfolio; final oral exam. For Ph.D.: three years beyond the bachelor's, at least two consecutive semesters in residence; comprehensive written/oral exam; candidacy; research skills requirements; dissertation; final oral exam. For Ed.D., D.M.A., D.P.A.: essentially the same as for the Ph.D.

FIELDS OF STUDY.

COLLEGE OF AGRICULTURAL AND ENVIRONMENTAL SCIENCES:
Agricultural Economics. M.A.E., M.S., Ph.D.
Agricultural Engineering. M.S.
Agricultural Extension. M.A.Ext.
Agronomy. M.S., Ph.D.
Animal Nutrition. Ph.D.
Animal Science. M.S.
Animal and Dairy Science. Ph.D.
Biological and Agricultural Engineering. M.S., Ph.D.
Crop and Soil Science. M.C.S.S.
Dairy Science. M.S.
Entomology. M.S., Ph.D.
Environmental Economics. M.S.
Environmental Health. M.S.
Food Science. M.S., Ph.D.
Food Technology. M.F.T.
Horticulture. M.S., Ph.D.
Plant Pathology. M.S., Ph.D.
Plant Protection and Pest Management. Includes agronomy, entomology, horticulture, plant pathology, (M.P.P.P.M.), poultry science (M.S., Ph.D.).

FRANKLIN COLLEGE OF ARTS AND SCIENCE:
Anthropology. M.A., Ph.D.
Applied Mathematical Sciences. Includes computer science, mathematics, statistics. M.A.M.S.
Art. M.F.A., Ph.D.
Artificial Intelligence. M.S.
Biochemistry and Molecular Biology. M.S., Ph.D.
Cellular Biology. M.S., Ph.D.
Chemistry. M.S., Ph.D.
Classical Languages. M.A.
Comparative Literature. M.A., Ph.D.
Computer Science. M.S., Ph.D.
Conservation Ecology and Sustainable Development. M.S.
Drama. M.F.A., Ph.D.
Ecology. M.S., Ph.D.
English. M.A., M.A.T., Ph.D.
French. M.A., M.A.T.
Genetics. M.S., Ph.D.
Geography. M.A., M.S., Ph.D.
Geology. M.S., Ph.D.
German. M.A., M.A.T.
Greek. M.A.
History. M.A., Ph.D.
Latin. M.A.
Linguistics. M.A., Ph.D.
Marine Sciences. M.S., Ph.D.
Mathematics. M.A., Ph.D.
Microbiology. M.S., Ph.D.
Music. M.A., M.M., D.M.A., Ph.D.
Nonprofit Organizations. M.A.
Philosophy. M.A., Ph.D.
Physics. M.S., Ph.D.
Plant Biology. M.S., Ph.D.
Political Science. M.A., Ph.D.
Psychology. Ph.D.
Public Administration. M.P.A., D.P.A.
Religion. M.A.
Romance Languages. M.A., M.A.T., Ph.D.

Sociology. M.A., Ph.D.
Spanish. M.A., M.A.T.
Speech Communication. M.A., Ph.D.
Statistics. M.S., Ph.D.

TERRY COLLEGE OF BUSINESS:
Accounting. Includes audit and systems track, taxation track. M.Acc.
Business Administration. M.A., M.B.A., Ph.D.
Economics. M.A., Ph.D.
Marketing Research. M.M.R.

COLLEGE OF EDUCATION:
Adult Education. M.A., M.Ed., Ed.S., Ed.D., Ph.D.
Agricultural Education. M.Ed.
Art Education. M.A.Ed., Ed.S., Ed.D.
Business Education. M.Ed.
College Student Affairs Administration. M.A., M.Ed.
Communication Sciences and Disorder. M.A., M.Ed., Ed.S., Ph.D.
Counseling and Pupil Personnel Services. Ph.D.
Counseling Psychology. Ph.D.
Early Childhood Education. M.Ed., Ed.S., Ph.D.
Education of Gifted. Ed.D.,
Educational Psychology. M.A., M.Ed., Ed.S., Ed.D., Ph.D.
Elementary Education. Ph.D.
English Education. M.A., M.Ed., Ed.S.
Exercise Science. M.A., M.Ed., Ed.D., Ph.D.
Family and Consumer Sciences Education. M.Ed.
Guidance and Counseling. M.A., M.Ed., Ed.S.
Health Promotion and Behavior. M.A., M.Ed., Ph.D.
Higher Education. Ed.D., Ph.D.
Instructional Technology. M.Ed., Ed.S., Ed.D., Ph.D.
Language Education. Ph.D.
Marketing Education. M.Ed.
Mathematics Education. M.A., M.Ed., Ed.S., Ed.D., Ph.D.
Middle School Education. M.Ed., Ed.S., Ph.D.
Music Education. M.M.Ed., Ed.S., Ed.D., Ph.D.
Occupational Studies. M.Ed., Ed.S., Ed.D., Ph.D.
Physical Education and Sport Studies. M.A., M.Ed., Ed.S., Ed.D., Ph.D.
Reading Education. M.A., M.Ed., Ed.S., Ed.D., Ph.D.
Recreation and Leisure Studies. M.A., M.Ed., Ph.D.
School Psychology. Ed.S.
Science Education. M.A., M.Ed., Ed.S., Ed.D., Ph.D.
Social Foundations of Education. Ph.D.
Social Science Education. M.A., M.Ed., Ed.S., Ed.D., Ph.D.
Special Education. M.A., M.Ed., Ed.S., Ed.D., Ph.D.
Teaching Additional Languages. M.A., M.Ed., Ed.S.
Technological Studies. M.Ed.

SCHOOL OF ENVIRONMENTAL DESIGN:
Historic Preservation. M.H.P.
Landscape Architecture. M.L.A.

SCHOOL OF FOREST RESOURCES:
Forest Resources. M.F.R., M.S., Ph.D.

COLLEGE OF FAMILY AND CONSUMER SCIENCES:
Child and Family Development. M.F.C.S., M.S., Ph.D.
Foods and Nutrition. M.F.C.S., M.S., Ph.D.
Housing and Consumer Economics. M.S., Ph.D.
Textiles, Merchandising, and Interiors. M.S.
Textile Sciences. Ph.D.

COLLEGE OF JOURNALISM AND MASS COMMUNICATION:
Journalism and Mass Communications. M.A. Mass *Communication.* M.M.C., Ph.D.

SCHOOL OF LAW:
Law. LL.M.

COLLEGE OF PHARMACY:
Pharmaceutical and Biomedical Sciences. M.S., Ph.D.
Clinical and Administrative Sciences. M.S., Ph.D.

SCHOOL OF SOCIAL WORK:
Social Work. M.S.W., Ph.D.

COLLEGE OF VETERINARY MEDICINE:
Anatomy. M.S.
Avian Medicine. M.A.M.
Medical Microbiology. M.S., Ph.D.
Pharmacology. M.S., Ph.D.
Physiology. M.S., Ph.D.
Veterinary Parasitology. M.S., Ph.D.
Veterinary Pathology. M.S., Ph.D.

INTERDISCIPLINARY PROGRAMS:
Internet Technology. M.I.T.
Toxicology. Includes clinical and administrative pharmacy, ecology, entomology, environmental health, foods and nutrition, forest resources, medical microbiology, pathology, pharmaceutical and biomedical sciences, physiology and pharmacology, poultry science. M.S., Ph.D.

School of Law (30602-6012)
Web site: www.lawsch.uga.edu

Established 1859. ABA approved since 1930. AALS member. Semester system. Special facility: The Dean Rusk Center for International and Comparative Law. Law library: 481,100 volumes, 7097 subscriptions; has LEXIS, NEXIS, WESTLAW, INFOTRAC, INNOPAC.

Annual tuition: resident $5042, nonresident $17,858. On- and off-campus housing available. Total average annual additional cost: $9888.

Enrollment: first-year class 201; full-time 628 (men 52%, women 48%). Faculty: full-time 31, part-time 9. Student to faculty ratio 16.9 to 1. Degrees conferred: J.D., LL.M., J.D.-M.B.A., J.D.-M.H.P. (Historic Preservation); J.D.-M.S.W., J.D.-M.P.A., J.D.-M.Ed. (Sports Studies).

ADMISSION REQUIREMENTS. LSDAS Law School report, bachelor's degree, transcripts, LSAT (not later than December), three references required in support of application. Some priority given state residents after January. Interview not required. Four-year undergraduate degree required. May accept transfer applicants. Apply to the Director of Admissions prior to March 1. First-year students admitted Fall only. Application fee $30. Phone: (706)542-7060; fax: (706)542-5556.

ADMISSION STANDARDS. Competitive. Mean LSAT: 160; mean GPA: 3.52 (A = 4). Gourman rating: 3.87. *U.S. News & World Report* ranking is in the top 32 of all U.S. law schools. Accepts 20–25% of total annual applicants.

FINANCIAL AID. Scholarships, tuition Equalization scholarships, grants, Federal W/S, loans. Apply by January 31 to Office of Admissions for scholarships, grants; apply to the Office of Financial Aid for all other programs, deadline July 31. Phone: (706)542-6147. Use FAFSA (School code: 001598) and School FAF. About 43% of students receive aid from School.

DEGREE REQUIREMENTS. For J.D.: 88 semester hours minimum, at least 30 semester hours in full-time residence. For LL.M.: at least 24 semester hours beyond the J.D.; 2 semesters of graduate study in residence; final thesis.

Note. There are formal exchange agreements with Southhampton University (Great Britain), and the University of Brussels (Belgium).

College of Veterinary Medicine
Web site: www.vet.uga.edu

Professional and graduate study since 1930. Tuition: resident and contract nonresidents $6834, nonresident $19,109. Living expenses approximately: $8000–9000. Enrollment: first-year class 80; total full-time 406 (men 60%, women 40%); graduate program, full-time 100. Faculty: full-time 77. Degrees conferred: D.V.M. The M.S. and Ph.D. are offered through the Graduate School.

ADMISSION REQUIREMENTS. Professional program: transcripts, GRE General/GRE Subject Test in Biology, animal experience, three recommendations (one from an academic adviser), essay required in support of application. At least three years of undergraduate study prior to entrance. Interview by invitation. Admission limited to residents of Georgia, Delaware, South Carolina, West Virginia, and U.S. citizens. Apply to Dean after July 15, before October 1. Admits Fall only. Graduate program: transcripts, GRE, recommendations required in support of application. Apply to individual department at least thirty days prior to beginning of quarter of entry. Application fee $30. Phone: (706)542-5728; fax: (706)542-8254.

ADMISSION STANDARDS. Selective. Accepts 35% of total annual applicants. Usual minimum GPA: 3.0 (A = 4); minimum GRE total: 1200.

FINANCIAL AID. Scholarships, fellowships, assistantships, partial fee waivers, Federal W/S, loans. Apply to Office of Student Aid at least two months prior to entrance; for graduate program, apply to appropriate department; no specified closing date. Use FAFSA. About 60% of students receive aid other than loans from School.

DEGREE REQUIREMENTS. For D.V.M.: Four years in residence. For M.S., Ph.D., see Graduate School listing.

FIELDS OF GRADUATE STUDY.
Anatomy.
Avian Medicine.
Medical Microbiology.
Pathology.
Pharmacology.
Physiology.
Veterinary Parasitology.
Veterinary Pathology.

GODDARD COLLEGE
Plainfield, Vermont 05667
Web site: www.goddard.edu

Founded 1938, began offering graduate study leading to the M.A. in 1940. Located 200 miles NW of Boston. Coed. Semester system. Library: 70,000 volumes, 300 active periodicals, on-line databases (DIALOG).

Tuition/fees: per semester $4922 (M.A.), $4922 (Psychology and Counseling), $5017 (M.F.A.). On-campus housing available. Annual academic year housing cost: $4520 (room and board).

Graduate Program

Enrollment: full- and part-time 220. Combined faculty: full-time 44, part-time 47. Degrees conferred: M.A., M.F.A.

ADMISSION REQUIREMENTS. Self-initiated study plan, transcripts, interview, three letters of recommendation, personal statement, preliminary bibliography required in support of application. On-line application available. Accepts transfer applicants. Apply to Director of Admissions; no specified closing date. Rolling admissions process. Application fee $40. Phone: (800)468-4888; e-mail: admissions@goddard.edu.

ADMISSION STANDARDS. Selective. Usual minimum average: 2.75 (A = 4).

FINANCIAL AID. Graduate/teaching assistantships, Federal W/S, loans. Apply to Financial Aid Office; no specified closing date. Use FAFSA and CSS Profile. About 50% of students receive aid other than loans from both College and outside sources.

DEGREE REQUIREMENTS. For M.A., M.F.A.: satisfactory completion of individually planned program supervised by a study supervisor and a second reader drawn from the Goddard faculty as a whole.

FIELDS OF STUDY.
Creative Writing.
Health Arts and Science.
Individualized Studies. M.A.
Interdisciplinary Arts. M.F.A.
Psychology Counseling.
School Guidance.
Teacher Education.
Transformative Language Arts.

GOLDEN GATE UNIVERSITY

San Francisco, California 94105-2968
Web site: www.ggu.edu

Founded 1853. Coed. Private control. Trimester system. Library: 126,500 volumes, 3335 subscriptions. Total University enrollment: 6360.

Tuition: per 3-unit course $1656, except Taxation $1824. No on-campus housing available. Contact Student Affairs Office for off-campus housing information. Phone: (415)442-7294.

Graduate Programs

Graduate study since 1950. Enrollment: full-time 1297, part-time 2714 (men 50%, women 50%). Graduate faculty: full-time 97, part-time 290. Degrees conferred: M.A., M.Ac., M.B.A., M.P.A., M.S., D.B.A., D.P.A. (C.P.A. exam preparation program also available).

ADMISSION REQUIREMENTS. Transcripts required in support of application. On-line application available. GMAT required for M.B.A. applicants. Personal statement optional. TOEFL required for international applicants. Interview not required. Accepts transfer applicants. Graduates of unaccredited institutions not considered. Apply to the Office of Enrollment Services at least one month prior to registration. Rolling admissions process. Application fee $55, doctoral $75, $90 for international applicants. Phone: (415)442-7800; fax: (415)442-7807; e-mail: info@ggu.edu.

ADMISSION STANDARDS. Selective. Usual minimum average: 2.5 for M.P.A., M.B.A., M.S.; 3.0 for M.Ac. and M.S.T.; 3.0 in graduate work for D.B.A., D.P.A. (A = 4).

FINANCIAL AID. Annual awards from institutional funds: one hundred scholarships, Federal W/S, loans. Approved for VA benefits. Apply to Director of Financial Aid; no specified closing date. Use FAFSA, Student loan application. Phone: (415)442-7270; fax: (415)442-7807. Aid available for part-time students.

DEGREE REQUIREMENTS. For M.A.: 30 units minimum; thesis; foreign language required by some departments. For M.Ac.: 30-unit program. For M.B.A.: 36 units minimum plus 12 units in general business or undergraduate units if not completed before entrance; thesis optional for 3 units. For M.S.: 30 units minimum, plus 6 general business units if not completed before entrance. For M.P.A.: 39 units minimum plus 9 undergraduate units if act completed before entrance. No language or thesis requirement for master's degrees; limited number of transfer credits considered. For D.B.A., D.P.A.: 56 units in graduate core requirements beyond master's; qualifying exam; dissertation; final oral/written exam.

FIELDS OF STUDY.
Accountancy. M.Ac.
Applied Psychology. Includes counseling, industrial/organizational. M.A.
Business Administration. Includes accounting, computer information systems, e-business, finance, human resource management, international business, management, marketing, operations and supply chain management, telecommunications management. M.B.A., D.B.A.
Computer Information Systems. M.S.
Database Development and Administration. M.S.
Digital Security. M.S.
E-Business Systems and Technologies. M.S.
Finance. M.S.
Financial Planning. M.S.
Human Resources Management. M.S.
Integrated Marketing Communication. Includes public relations. M.S.
Management of Technology. M.S.M.O.T.
Marketing. M.S.
Psychology. Includes marriage, family, and child counseling. M.A.
Software Engineering. M.S.
Taxation. M.S.
Technology Management. M.S.
Telecommunications Management. M.S.
Web Design and Development. M.S.

School of Law

Established 1901. ABA approved since 1956. AALS member. Semester system. Law library: 236,628 volumes, 3357 subscriptions; has LEXIS, WESTLAW, CALI.

Annual tuition: $22,048, part-time $15,280. On-campus housing available. Total average annual additional expense: $13,500.

Enrollment: first-year class full-time 140, part-time 60; total 536 (men 38%, women 62%). Faculty: full-time 26, part-time 58. Student to faculty ratio 15.7 to 1. Degrees conferred: J.D., J.D.-M.B.A., J.D.-M.A. (International Relations), J.D.-Ph.D. (Clinical Psychology), LL.M. (Environmental Law, Taxation, International Legal Studies).

ADMISSION REQUIREMENTS. LSDAS Law School report, bachelor's degree, transcripts, LSAT, personal statement, letters of recommendation required in support of application. Interview not required. Accepts transfer applicants. Graduates of unaccredited colleges not considered. Apply to Admissions Office by April 15 (Fall), November 15 (Spring). Application fee $40. Phone: (415)442-6630; fax: (415)442-6631.

ADMISSION STANDARDS. Selective. Mean LSAT: full- and part-time 148; mean GPA: full-time 3.11, part-time 3.02 (A = 4). Gourman rating: 3.43. *U.S. News & World Report* ranking is in the fourth tier of all U.S. law schools. Accepts 50–55% of total annual applicants.

FINANCIAL AID. Scholarships, fellowships, assistantships, full and partial tuition waivers, Federal W/S, loans. Apply to Financial Aid Officer by April 15. Use FAFSA.

DEGREE REQUIREMENTS. For J.D.: 86 semester hours minimum. For LL.M.: at least 24 semester hours beyond the J.D.

Note: School has exchange program with Chulalongkorn University (Thailand).

GONZAGA UNIVERSITY
Spokane, Washington 99258-0001
Web site: www.gonzaga.edu

Founded 1887. Coed. Private control. Jesuit, Roman Catholic. Semester system. Library: 550,000 volumes, 1470 subscriptions. Total University enrollment: 3900.

Annual tuition: full-time $8370; per credit $465. Limited on-campus housing for single graduate students; none for married students. Average annual housing cost: $6300 (double room including board). Contact Residence Life Office for both on- and off-campus housing information. Phone: (509)328-4220, ext. 4103.

Graduate School

Enrollment: full-time 1146, part-time 426. Faculty teaching graduate students: full-time 92, part-time 52. Degrees conferred: M.A., M.Acc, M.B.A., M.B.A.-J.D., M.A.P., M.A.A., M.A.C.E., M.Anthes.Ed., M.Ed., M.E.S., M.P.E., M.T.A., M.I.T., M.A.O.L., M.S.N., M.E.L., Ph.D.

ADMISSION REQUIREMENTS. Two official transcripts, statement of purpose or letter of intent, résumé or vita required in support of School's application. GRE/MAT/GMAT, recommendation/reference letters and interview required by some departments. TOEFL required for international applicants. Accepts transfer applicants. Graduates of unaccredited institutions not considered. Rolling admissions process. Application $40. Phone: (509)328-4220, ext. 3546; fax: (509)324-5399.

ADMISSION STANDARDS. Selective. Usual minimum average: 3.0 G.P.A.; 3.5 G.P.A. for doctoral applicants (A = 4).

FINANCIAL AID. Fellowships, teaching assistantships, tuition waivers, Federal W/S, loans. Approved for VA benefits. Apply by March 1 to appropriate department chair for fellowships, assistantships; to Financial Aid Office for all other programs. Phone: (509)328-4220, ext. 3182. Use FAFSA. Aid sometimes available for part-time students.

DEGREE REQUIREMENTS. For master's: 30–34 semester hours minimum, at least 24 in residence; thesis required for some programs; final oral/written exam; one research skill; reading knowledge of one foreign language for programs in arts. For Ph.D.: 60 credits minimum beyond the bachelor's, at least 45 in residence; qualifying exam; proficiency in one foreign language; dissertation; final oral exam.

FIELDS OF STUDY.
Accounting. M.Acc. only.
Administration and Curriculum. M.A.A.
Anesthesia Education. Admits Spring only; apply by December 1. M.Anesth.Ed.
Business Administration. M.B.A., M.B.A.-J.D.
Computer Education. M.A.C.E.
Counseling Psychology. Admits fall only; apply by March 1. M.A.P.
Curriculum and Instruction.
Educational Administration. M.A.
English. M.A., M.E.L.
Initial Teaching. M.I.T.

Leadership Studies. Ph.D.
Nursing. Admits Fall and Spring; apply by April 1 (Fall), November 1 (Spring). M.S.N.
Organizational Leadership. M.A.O.L.
Special Education. M.E.S., M.Ed.
Spirituality. M.A.
Sport and Athletic Administration. M.A.
Teaching. M.Ed., M.T.A.

School of Law (Box 3528)
Web site: www.law.gonzaga.edu

Established 1912. ABA approved since 1951. AALS member. Semester system. Full-time study only. Special facility: Center for Law and Justice. Law library: 257,667 volumes; has LEXIS, NEXIS, WESTLAW, DIALOG, CARL.

Annual tuition: $19,830. Evening program available. No on-campus housing available. Total average annual additional expense: $8275.

Enrollment: first-year class 167; total 472 (men 52%, women 48%). Faculty: full-time 18, part-time 22. Student to faculty ratio 21.4 to 1. Degrees conferred: J.D., J.D.,-M.B.A., J.D.-M.Acc.

ADMISSION REQUIREMENTS. LSDAS Law School report, bachelor's degree, transcripts, LSAT required in support of application. Interview not required. Accepts transfer applicants. Graduates of unaccredited colleges not considered. Apply to Dean by April 1. Admits Fall only. Application fee $40. Phone: (800)793-1710 (Continental U.S.), (509)323-3713; fax (509)323-3697.

ADMISSION STANDARDS. Selective. Mean LSAT: 150; mean GPA: 3.12 (A = 4). Gourman rating: 3.48. *U.S. News & World Report* ranking is in the third tier of all U.S. law schools. Accepts 50–55% of total annual applicants.

FINANCIAL AID. Scholarships, full and partial tuition waivers, fellowships, assistantships, Federal W/S, loans. Apply to Law School Financial Aid Office by February 1. Use FAFSA. Approximately 50% of students receive some form of aid from School.

DEGREE REQUIREMENTS. For J.D.: 90 semester hours minimum, at least one year in residence.

GOUCHER COLLEGE
Baltimore, Maryland 21204-2794
Web site: www.goucher.edu

Private control. Coed. Semester system. Library: 295,593 volumes, 1138 subscriptions.

Tuition: per credit Education $270; M.A., M.F.A. $515. No housing for graduate students.

Graduate Program

Enrollment: full-time 225, part-time 553. Graduate faculty: full-time 16, part-time 70. Degrees conferred: M.A., M.F.A., M.Ed., M.A.T.

ADMISSION REQUIREMENTS. Transcripts, two letters of recommendation, bachelor's required in support of application. TOEFL required for international applicants. Accepts transfer students. Apply to the Office of Graduate and Professional Studies; no specified closing date. Rolling admissions process. Application fee $50. Phone: (410)337-6044; fax: (410)337-6354.

FINANCIAL AID. Limited to grants, loans. Approved for VA benefits. Apply to the Office of Financial Aid. Phone: (410)337-6500. Use FAFSA and institutional FAF.

DEGREE REQUIREMENTS. For M.A., M.Ed.: 35 semester credits; action research project; thesis; internship. For M.A.T.: 36 credits; year-long student teaching internships. For M.F.A.: 36 credit program; three summer residencies; critical paper; internship.

FIELDS OF STUDY.
Arts Administration. M.A.A.A.
Creative Nonfiction. M.F.A.
Education. Includes urban and diverse learners, middle school, the at-risk student, school mediation, school improvement leadership, athletic program leadership/administration. M.Ed.
Historic Preservation. M.A.
Teaching. M.A.T.

GOVERNORS STATE UNIVERSITY

University Park, Illinois 60466
Web site: www.govst.edu

Established 1969. Located 30 miles S of Chicago. Coed. Trimester system. Library: 246,000 volumes, 2700 subscriptions.

Tuition: resident, per hour $105, or $1250 full-time, per term (12 hours or more); nonresident, per hour $315 or $3780 per term (12 hours or more). No on-campus housing available. Day-care facilities available.

Graduate Studies

Enrollment: full-time 207, part-time 2865 (men 25%, women 75%). Faculty: full-time 150, part-time 160. Degrees conferred: M.A., M.S., M.B.A., M.P.A., M.P.T., M.H.S., M.H.A., M.O.T., M.S.N., M.S.W.

ADMISSION REQUIREMENTS. Official transcripts, bachelor's degree required in support of application. TOEFL (minimum score 550) required for international applicants. Accepts transfer applicants. Graduates of unaccredited colleges not considered. Apply by July 15 (Fall), November 1 (Spring) to Office of Admissions. Applications and credentials required approximately two months prior to registration. Rolling admissions process. Application fee: none. Phone: (708)534-4492; fax: (708)534-1640.

ADMISSION STANDARDS. Relatively open for some departments, selective for others. Usual minimum average: 2.5 (A = 4).

FINANCIAL AID. Annual awards from institutional funds: scholarships, research assistantships, teaching assistantships, tuition waivers, Federal W/S, loans. Approved for VA benefits. Apply by May 1 to Director of Financial Aid; no specified closing date. Phone: (708)534-5000. Use FAFSA. About 44% of students receive aid from University and outside sources. Aid available for part-time students.

DEGREE REQUIREMENTS. For master's: at least 32–48 credit hours in graduate-level courses; candidacy; thesis/nonthesis option; at least 2 credit hours are designated as master's final project or practicum/internship.

FIELDS OF STUDY.
Accounting. M.S.
Addiction Studies. M.H.S.
Analytical Chemistry. M.S.
Art. M.A.
Business Administration. M.B.A.
Communication Disorders. M.H.S.
Communication and Training. M.A.
Computer Science. M.S.
Counseling. Includes community, marriage and family, school. M.A.
Early Childhood Education. M.A.

Education. M.A.
Educational Administration. M.A.
English. M.A.
Environmental Biology. M.S.
Health Administration. M.H.A.
Mangement Information Systems. M.S.
Multicategorical Special Education. M.A.
Nursing. M.S.N.
Occupational Therapy. M.O.T.
Physical Therapy. M.P.T.
Political Studies and Justice Studies. M.A.
Psychology. Includes school. M.A.
Public Administration. M.P.A.
Reading. M.A.
Social Work. M.S.W.

HAMLINE UNIVERSITY

St. Paul, Minnesota 55104-1284
Web site: www.hamline.edu

Founded 1854. Coed. Private control. United Methodist Church. Hamline is the oldest institution of higher learning in the state of Minnesota. Special facility: Center for Excellence in Urban Teaching. Library: 445,902 volumes, 3800 subscriptions. Total University enrollment: 4,100.

Tuition: per course $1270. On-campus housing for single students only. Average academic year housing cost: $2152 (room only). Contact Office of Residential Life for both on- and off-campus housing information. Phone: (651)523-2061.

Graduate Studies

Enrollment: full-time 120, part-time 643. Faculty; full- and part-time 159. Degrees conferred: M.A., M.A.Ed., M.A.T., M.A.P.A., Certificate.

ADMISSION REQUIREMENTS. Official transcripts, three letters of recommendation required in support of School's application. TOEFL (minimum score 550, higher scores required by some departments) required for international applicants. Accepts transfer applicants. Apply by July 1 (Fall), November 1 (Spring) to Graduate Studies Office. Rolling admissions process. Application fee $30. Phone: (651)523-2900; fax: (651)523-2458.

ADMISSION STANDARDS. Selective. Usual minimum average: 2.9 (A = 4).

FINANCIAL AID. Limited to Federal W/S, loans. Approved for VA benefits. Apply by March 1 to the Office of Financial Aid. Phone: (651)523-3000. Use FAFSA (University code: 002354). Aid sometimes available for part-time students.

DEGREE REQUIREMENTS. For M.A.L.A.: 38–40 semester credits; final project/capstone. For M.A.Ed., M.A.T.: 30 credit programs; capstone (thesis). For M.A. in ESL: 41–48 semester credit program; capstone (thesis). For M.A.M., M.A.N.M.: 12 courses; 4 professional development series seminars; internship; capstone project (thesis). For M.A.P.A.: 8 required core courses; independent problem analysis; 4 noncredit one-day public management seminars; final capstone course. For M.F.A.: 10 courses; capstone (thesis). For D.P.A.: 48 semester credits beyond the master's; final comprehensive exam; dissertation; oral defense.

FIELDS OF STUDY.

GRADUATE LIBERAL STUDIES:
Liberal Studies. M.A.L.A.
Writing. M.F.A.

GRADUATE SCHOOL OF EDUCATION:
Education. M.A.Ed.
ESL. M.A. in ESL.
Teaching. M.A.T.

GRADUATE SCHOOL OF PUBLIC ADMINISTRATION:
International/Comparative/InterGovernmental Relations. D.P.A.
Management. M.A.M.
Nonprofit Management. M.A.N.M.
Public Administration. Includes administering local government, managing state and local government, public dispute resolution, law and government. M.A.P.A.
Public Management. D.P.A.
Public Policy. D.P.A.

School of Law

Established 1972. ABA approved since 1975. AALS member. Semester system. Special programs: study abroad in Bergen, Norway; Hebrew University, Israel; University of Modena, Italy; Central European University, Budapest, Hungary. Library: 254,595 volumes, 2710 subscriptions; has LEXIS, NEXIS, WESTLAW, DIALOG.

Annual tuition: full-time $18,240, part-time $13,156. On-campus housing available. Housing cost: $8000–$11,000. Apply to Director of University Housing for off-campus housing.

Enrollment: first-year class full-time 174, part-time 13; total 535 (men 44%, women 56%). Faculty: full-time 22, part-time 39. Student to faculty ratio 19.7 to 1. Degrees conferred: J.D., J.D.-M.A.P.A., J.D.-M.B.A. and J.D.-A.M.B.A. (Accounting) (offered with University of St. Thomas).

ADMISSION REQUIREMENTS. LSDAS Law School report, bachelor's degree, transcripts, LSAT, recommendations required in support of application. Preference given to state residents. Graduates of unaccredited colleges not considered. Apply to Admissions Office by March 31. Phone: (651)641-2461. Application fee $40.

ADMISSION STANDARDS. Selective. Mean LSAT: full-time 152, part-time 149; mean GPA: full-time 3.28, part-time 3.06 (A = 4). Gourman rating: 2.76. *U.S. News & World Report* ranking is in the fourth tier of all U.S. law schools. Admits about 55–60% of total annual applicants.

FINANCIAL AID. Scholarships, Federal W/S, loans. Apply by April 15. Use FAFSA (School code: 002354). About 95% of students receive some aid from School. Public Law forgiveness program available.

DEGREE REQUIREMENTS. For J.D.: satisfactory completion of 88-semester-hour program.

HAMPTON UNIVERSITY

Hampton, Virginia 23668
Web site: www.hampton.edu

Founded 1868. Located SE of Richmond. Coed. CGS member. Private control. Semester system. Special facilities: Marine Science Center for Coastal and Environmental Studies, Center for Non-linear Analysis, Nuclear/High Energy Physics Research Center of Excellence, Research Center for Optical Physics, National Center for Minority Special Education Research, Hampton University Museum. Library: 400,000 volumes. Total University enrollment: 5800.

Annual tuition: full-time $9966; per credit $245. Limited on-campus housing for single students. Average academic year off-campus housing cost: $4800 excluding board. Contact Office of Auxiliary Enterprises for off-campus housing information. Phone: (757)727-5210.

Graduate College

Graduate study since 1928. Enrollment: full- and part-time 415. Graduate faculty: full-time 90, part-time 11. Degrees conferred: M.A., M.S., M.B.A., M.T., D.P.T., Ph.D.

ADMISSION REQUIREMENTS. Transcripts, GRE/GMAT required in support of College's application. TOEFL required for international applicants. Accepts transfer applicants. Apply to Dean of Graduate College at least six weeks prior to registration. Application fee $15. Phone: (757)727-5454 or (757)727-5496; fax: (757)727-5084; e-mail: hugrad@hamptonu.edu.

ADMISSION STANDARDS. Competitive. Usual minimum average: 2.8 (A = 4).

FINANCIAL AID. Fellowships, traineeships, assistantships, Federal W/S, loans. Approved for VA benefits. Apply by May 1 to Dean of Graduate College for fellowships, assistantships; to the Office of Financial Aid for all other programs. Phone: (757)727-5332. Use FAFSA.

DEGREE REQUIREMENTS. For M.A., M.T.: 30–32 hours, at least 24 hours in residence; thesis/special project/comprehensive exam. For M.S.: 32–45 hours; thesis/nonthesis option/comprehensive exam. For M.B.A.: 36–60 semester hours. For Ph.D., D.P.T.: 72 semester hours; qualifying exam; dissertation; final oral exam.

FIELDS OF STUDY.
Applied Mathematics. M.S.
Biology. M.A., M.S.
Business Administration. M.B.A.
Chemistry. M.S.
Communicative Sciences and Disorders. M.A.
Computer Science. M.S.
Counseling. Includes college student development, community agency counseling. M.A.
Early Childhood Education. M.T.
Elementary Education. M.A.
Middle School. M.T.
Museum Studies. M.A.
Nursing. Includes education, administration, practitioner, community health, community mental health/psychiatric, advanced adult nursing. M.S., Ph.D.
Physical Therapy. D.P.T.
Physics. M.S., Ph.D.
Secondary Education. M.T.
Special Education. Includes emotionally disturbed/reeducation specialist, learning disabilities. M.A.

HARDIN-SIMMONS UNIVERSITY

Abilene, Texas 79698-0001
Web site: www.hsutx.edu

Founded 1891. Coed. Private control, Baptist. Semester system. Library: 413,000 volumes, 4000 subscriptions. Total University enrollment: 2300.

Tuition: per credit $340. On-campus housing for 55 married students, 59 graduate men, 67 graduate women. Average academic year housing cost: $3663 (including board). Apply to Director of Housing. Phone: (915)670-1329.

Graduate Studies

Graduate study since 1926. Enrollment: full-time 159, part-time 191. University faculty: full-time 80, part-time 13. Degrees conferred: M.A., M.B.A., M.Ed., M.M., M.Div.

ADMISSION REQUIREMENTS. Transcript, GRE/GMAT, essay or writing sample, résumé, letters of recommendation required in support of School's application. On-line application available. TOEFL, English translation of foreign documentation, certificate of financial support required for international applicants. Accepts transfer applicants. Graduates of unaccredited institutions not considered. Apply to Dean of the Graduate School at least two weeks prior to registration. Application fee $25. Phone: (915)670-1298; fax: (915)670-1564; e-mail: gradoff@hsutx.edu.

ADMISSION STANDARDS. Selective for most departments. Usual minimum average: 3.0 (A = 4)

FINANCIAL AID. Annual awards from institutional funds: scholarships, fellowships, graduate assistantships, tuition waivers, Federal W/S, loans. Approved for VA benefits. Apply at least one month prior to registration to Dean of the Graduate School. Phone: (915)670-1331. About 10% of students receive aid other than loans from University and outside sources. Aid sometimes available to part-time students.

DEGREE REQUIREMENTS. For M.A.: 30–36 credit hours minimum, at least 24 in residence; thesis; comprehensive oral exam. For M.Ed.: 36 credit hours minimum, at least 24 in residence; comprehensive oral exam. For M.M.: by advisement. For M.B.A.: 36 credit hours; oral/written exam. For M.Div.: 72 credit hour, full-time program.

FIELDS OF STUDY.
Business Administration. M.B.A.
Counseling and Human Development. M.Ed.
English. M.A.
Environmental Management. M.S.
Family Ministry. M.A. (60 credit hour program).
Family Psychology. M.A. (54 credit hour program).
Gifted and Talented Education. M.Ed.
History. M.A.
Ministry. Includes pastoral ministry, educational ministry, family ministry, spiritual care ministry, missions and cross-cultural ministry. M.Div.
Music. Includes church music, music education, performance, theory and composition. M.M.
Nursing. M.S.
Physical Education. M.Ed.
Physical Therapy. M.P.T.
Reading Specialist Education. M.Ed.
Religion. M.A.
Sports and Recreation Management. M.Ed.

HARDING UNIVERSITY

Searcy, Arkansas 72143-0001
Web site: www.harding.edu

Founded 1924. Located 50 miles N of Little Rock. Coed. Private control. Church of Christ. Semester system. Library: 407,000 volumes, 1350 subscriptions.

Tuition: per credit $273. On-campus housing for 99 married students. Average academic year housing cost: $4336 for single students. Per month $225–$350 for married students. Apply to Director of Housing. Phone: (501)270-4256.

Graduate Program

Enrollment: full-time 71, part-time 362. University faculty: full-time 3, part-time 30. Degrees conferred: M.Ed., M.S.E.

ADMISSION REQUIREMENTS. Two transcripts, letter of recommendation required in support of application. GRE, GMAT, or MAT required for business. TOEFL required for international applicants. Accepts transfer applicants. Apply to Director of Grad-

uate Studies at least two months prior to registration. Application fee $25. Phone: (501)279-4242; fax: (501)279-4685.

ADMISSION STANDARDS. Selective. Usual minimum average: 2.5 (A = 4).

FINANCIAL AID. Annual awards from institutional funds: academic scholarships, fellowships, Federal W/S, loans. Approved for VA benefits. Apply to Director of Graduate Program; no specified closing date. Phone: (501)279-4315. About 25% of students receive aid other than loans from University and outside sources. Aid sometimes available for part-time students.

DEGREE REQUIREMENTS. For M.A.T., M.Ed., M.S.E.: 35 semester hours minimum, at least 29 in residence; final written exam; thesis/nonthesis option (thesis may replace 3–6 hours of course work); comprehensive exam. For M.B.A.: 12–15 month, 36–48 credit hour program. For M.S.N.: 39 credit program.

FIELDS OF STUDY.
Business Administration. Includes controllership and financial management, leadership and organizational management, health care management. M.B.A.
Elementary Education.
Nursing. Includes managed care for high-risk populations and community health, international nursing. M.S.N.

UNIVERSITY OF HARTFORD

West Hartford, Connecticut 06117-1599
Web site: www.hartford.edu

Established 1957. CGS member. Private control. Semester system. Library: 522,640 volumes, 3131 subscriptions.

Tuition: Arts and Sciences, per credit $300, Business and Public Administration, per credit hour $450, Engineering per credit hour $405, Education, Nursing, and Health, per credit hour $290–450, Hartt School of Music, per credit hour $290–$576. On-campus housing for graduate students. Monthly room charge: $500–$700 for single students, $500–$650 for married students. Phone: (860)768-7793.

Graduate Studies

Graduate enrollment: full-time 528, part-time 747. Faculty: full-time 130, part-time 83. Degrees conferred: M.A., M.A.T., M.Ed., M.Mus., M.M.Ed., M.B.A., M.P.A., M.S.O.B., M.S.T., M.S.I., M.S., M.S.P.A., M.F.A., Certificate, C.A.G.S. Specialist diploma, Sixth-year Certificate.

ADMISSION REQUIREMENTS. Transcripts, GRE/GMAT/MAT required in support of application. Letters of recommendation, auditions required for some programs. TOEFL required for international applicants. Accepts transfer applicants. Graduates of unaccredited institutions not considered. Apply to Admissions Office by July 1 (Fall), November 15 (Spring). Application fee $35, $50 for international applicants. Phone: (860)768-4371; fax (860)768-5160.

ADMISSION STANDARDS. Selective for most departments. Usual minimum average: 3.0 (A = 4).

FINANCIAL AID. Annual awards from institutional funds: teaching assistantships, research fellowships, internships, Federal W/S, loans. Apply to Dean of appropriate school for assistantships, fellowships by May 1; to the Office of Financial Aid for all other programs: no specified closing date. Phone: (860)768-4296. Use FAFSA and institutional FAF. Very few students receive aid other than loans from University. Aid available for part-time students.

DEGREE REQUIREMENTS. For most master's: 30–45 semester hours minimum, at least two semesters in residence; thesis/nonthesis option. For M.B.A.: 51 semester hours maximum, at least two semesters in residence. For C.A.G.S., Specialist, Certificate: 30 credit hours minimum beyond the master's; research paper; comprehensive exam.

FIELDS OF STUDY.

BARNEY SCHOOL OF BUSINESS:
Accounting. M.S.A.T.
Business Administration. M.B.A.
Business Administration for Health Care Professionals. E.M.B.A.-H.C.P.
Taxation. M.S.A.T.

COLLEGE OF ARTS AND SCIENCES:
Biology. M.S.
Clinical Psychology. Psy.D.
Clinical Psychology Practices. M.A.
Communication. M.A.
General Experimental Psychology. M.A.
School Psychology. M.S.

COLLEGE OF EDUCATION, NURSING, AND HEALTH PROFESSIONS:
Counseling. M.Ed., M.S.
Early Childhood Education. M.Ed.
Educational Computing and Technology. M.Ed.
Educational Leadership. C.A.G.S., Ed.D.
Elementary Education. M.Ed.
Guidance and Counseling. M.Ed., M.S.
Nursing. Includes community and public health nursing, nursing education, nursing management. M.S.N.
Physical Therapy. M.S.P.T.

HARTT SCHOOL OF MUSIC:
Choral Conducting.
Composition.
Guitar.
Instrumental Conducting.
Kodaly Training.
Liturgical Music.
Music Education.
Music History.
Music Theory.
Opera.
Performance. Includes voice, instrument, instrument Suzuki pedagogy.
Piano.
Piano Accompanying.
Piano Pedagogy.
Theory.
Voice.

HARVARD UNIVERSITY
Cambridge, Massachusetts 02138
Web site: www.harvard.edu

Founded 1636. Located adjacent to Boston. Coed. CGS and AAU member. Private control. Semester system. Special facilities: Astronomical and Blue Hill meteorological observatories; Peabody Museum of Archaeology and Ethnology; several art museums; Harvard Forest, geological laboratories; seismograph station; research centers/institutes in International Affairs and Russian, Middle Eastern, East Asian Studies, Jewish Studies, World Religions, Japanese Studies, International Development, Afro-American Studies, Urban Studies, American Political Studies; rare book and manuscript collection; biological, chemical, psychological, and social relations laboratories; biological museums, Herbaria, computer center; engineering and physics laboratories. The University's NIH ranking is eighth among all U.S. institutions with 649 awards/grants worth $243,710,837. Library: more than 13,400,00 volumes, 97,568 subscriptions. Total University enrollment: 18,310.

On-campus housing for about 350 single graduate students from Graduate School of Arts and Sciences. Approximately 1400 apartment units for which graduate students are eligible. Annual housing cost: $3640–$5840 (room only); apartments $838–$2568 per month. Contact Harvard Real Estate, Inc., Housing Office, 7 Holyoke Street, for both on- and off-campus housing. Phone: (617)495-5060. Day-care facilities available.

Graduate School of Arts and Sciences
Web site: www.gsas.harvard.edu

Graduate study since 1872. Annual tuition: full-time $24,854. Enrollment: 3000 (men 57%, women 43%). Faculty teaching graduate students: 800. Degrees conferred: A.M., S.M., M.F.S., M.E., Ph.D.

ADMISSION REQUIREMENTS. Transcripts, three letters of recommendation, personal statement required in support of College's application. Many departments require GRE. Interview not required. Transfer credit for work done elsewhere considered only for Ph.D. Admits Fall only. Apply by January 2 Natural Sciences, December 14 Social Sciences and Humanities, to the Office of Admissions and Financial Aid. Application fee $70. Phone: (617)495-5315; e-mail: admiss@fas.harvard.edu.

ADMISSION STANDARDS. Very competitive for most departments.

FINANCIAL AID. Annual awards from institutional funds: scholarships, fellowships, research assistantships, teaching assistantships, Federal W/S, loans. File for financial aid with application for admission. Phone: (617)495-5396. FAFSA and institutional FAF. About 85% of students receive aid and/or loans from School and outside sources.

DEGREE REQUIREMENTS. For A.M.: two terms minimum in full-time residence; reading knowledge of one foreign language for most majors; thesis normally not required; final written/oral exam. For S.M., M.E., M.S.F.: two terms minimum in full-time residence; final written/oral exam; no language or thesis requirement. For Ph.D.: minimum of two years in full-time residence and sixteen half courses minimum beyond the bachelor's; general or qualifying exam; reading knowledge of two foreign languages for most majors; thesis; final written/oral exam.

FIELDS OF STUDY.
African American History.
Anthropology. Includes archaeology, biological anthropology, social anthropology. Ph.D. only.
Applied Mathematics.
Applied Physics.
Architecture. Ph.D.
Astronomy. Ph.D.
Biochemistry. Ph.D.
Biological Sciences in Dental Medicine. Includes oral biology, molecular, supramolecular, cellular, and supracellular processes.
Biological Sciences in Public Health. Includes cancer cell biology, environmental health, immunology and infectious diseases, nutrition.
Biology. Includes cellular and developmental biology, organismic and evolutionary biology. Ph.D.
Biomedical Engineering.

Biophysics. Includes structural molecular biology, cell and membrane biophysics, molecular genetics, physical biochemistry, mathematical biophysics. Ph.D.

Business Economics. Ph.D.

Cellular Biology.

Celtic Languages and Literatures. Irish, Welsh; A.M., Ph.D.

Chemical Physics. Ph.D.

Chemistry. Includes chemistry, inorganic chemistry, biological chemistry, physical chemistry. Ph.D.

Classics. Includes classical philology, classical philosophy, classical archaeology, Byzantine Greek, medieval Latin. Ph.D.

Comparative Literature. Ph.D.

Computer Science.

Earth and Planetary Sciences. Ph.D.

East Asian Languages and Civilizations. Includes Chinese, Japanese, Korean, Mongolian. Ph.D.

Economics. Ph.D.

Electrical Engineering.

English and American Literature and Language. Includes English literature to 1500, English literature 1660–1825, English literature 1800–present, American literature. Ph.D.

Environmental Engineering.

Fine Arts.

Forest Science. M.F.S.

Germanic Languages and Literatures. Ph.D.

Government. Includes political thought and its history, American government, law and administration, comparative government, international relations, quantitative methods for political science. Ph.D.

Health Policy.

History. Includes ancient history, medieval history, early modern European history, American history, African history, East Asian history, English history, Latin American history, Russian history. Ph.D.

History and East Asian Languages. Ph.D.

History and Middle Eastern Studies. Ph.D.

History of American Civilization. Ph.D.

History of Art and Architecture. Includes ancient art, medieval art, Renaissance art, Baroque art, 17th- and 18th-century art, modern art, Islamic art, Oriental art. Ph.D.

History of Science Department. Ph.D.

Information Technology and Management.

Inner Asian and Altaic Studies. Ph.D.

Landscape Architecture. Ph.D.

Linguistics. Includes linguistic theory, descriptive linguistics, historical linguistics, linguistics anthropology, psycholinguistics, sociolinguistics, comparative philology. Ph.D.

Mathematics. Ph.D.

Medical Sciences. Includes biological and biomedical sciences (biological chemistry and molecular pharmacology, cell biology, genetics, microbiology and molecular genetics, pathology), immunology, neuroscience, virology. Ph.D.

Mechanical Engineering.

Middle Eastern Studies. Includes regional studies, Middle East anthropology and Middle Eastern studies, economics and Middle Eastern studies, history and Middle Eastern studies, fine arts and Middle Eastern studies. Ph.D.

Molecular Biology. Ph.D.

Music. Includes musicology, composition. Ph.D.

Near Eastern Languages and Civilizations. Includes Akkadian and Sumerian, Arabic, Armenian, Biblical history and Northwest Semitic philology, Indo-Muslim culture, Iranian, Persian, post-Biblical Jewish history and literature, Syro-Palestinian archaeology, Turkology. Ph.D.

Organismic and Evolutionary Biology. Ph.D.

Organizational Behavior. Ph.D.

Philosophy. Ph.D.

Physics. Includes theoretical physics, experimental physics. Ph.D.

Political Economy and Government. Open only to holders of Harvard M.P.A.; write to Kennedy School for instructions; Ph.D.

Psychology. Includes experimental psychology, personality and developmental studies, social psychology. Ph.D.

Public Policy. Open only to holders of Harvard M.P.P.; write to Kennedy School for instructions; Ph.D.

Regional Studies. China, Japan, Korea, Mongolia, Vietnam. A.M.

Regional Studies—Middle East. See Middle Eastern Studies.

Regional Studies—Soviet Union Committee. A.M.

Religion. Ph.D.

Romance Languages and Literatures. Includes French, Italian, Portuguese, Spanish; A.M., Ph.D.

Sanskrit and Indian or Tibetan and Himalayan Studies. A.M., Ph.D.

Slavic Languages and Literatures. Ph.D.

Social Policy.

Sociology. Ph.D.

Statistics. A.M., Ph.D.

Urban Planning. Ph.D.

Graduate School of Business Administration
Soldiers Field
Web site: www.hbs.edu

Established 1908. Private control. Accredited programs: M.B.A.; recognized D.B.A. (initiated in the 1920s). Term system. Baker Library (largest business library in the world): 2,5000,000 volumes, 6500 subscriptions.

Annual tuition: full-time $31,800. Enrollment: September cohort 560 students, January cohort 330 students; total full-time 1900 (men 75%, women 25%). D.B.A.: full-time 100 students. Faculty: full-time 194; all have Ph.D./D.B.A. Degrees conferred: M.B.A., M.B.A.-J.D., D.B.A. (offered through the Graduate School of Arts and Sciences).

ADMISSION REQUIREMENTS. All applicants should have a bachelor's degree from a recognized institution of higher education and a strong mathematics background. Does not consider transfer applicants. Submit application, GMAT (will accept GMAT test results from the last five years, latest acceptable date is March), official transcripts from each undergraduate/graduate school attended, three letters of recommendation, seven or eight essays, résumé (prefers at least five years of work experience), and an application fee of $190 to the M.B.A. Admission Office. In addition, international students (whose native language is other than English) should submit a TOEFL score, TWE (strongly encouraged), certified translations and evaluations of all official transcripts; recommendation should be in English or with certified translations, proof of health/ immunization certificate, and proof of sufficient financial resources for two years of academic study. Both U.S. citizens and international applicants apply by March 1. On-campus visits are encouraged. Interviews are by invitation only. Joint degree applicants must apply to and be accepted to both schools; contact the admissions office for current information and specific admissions requirements. Application materials received by November 10 will have notifications sent by January 15; application materials received by January 6 will have notifications sent by March 30; application materials received by March 1 will have notifications sent by May 15. Admissions Office phone: (617)495-6127; fax: (617)495-9272; e-mail: admissions@hbs.edu.

ADMISSION REQUIREMENTS FOR DOCTORAL CANDIDATES. Contact either the Graduate School of Arts and Sciences at (617)495-5315 or Graduate School of Business at (617)495-6127 for application material and information. The D.B.A. application materials can be downloaded at: www.hbs.edu/doctoral. Beginning students are admitted to begin study in July only. Both U.S. citizens and international applicants apply by December 30. Submit Graduate School application, GMAT/GRE (will accept GMAT/GRE test results from the last five years), official transcripts from each undergraduate/graduate school attended, three letters of recommendation, four or five essays, résumé, statement of purpose, and application fee of $75 to the Office of Doctoral Programs, Cotting

House. In addition, international students (whose native language is other than English) should submit a TOEFL score, both TSE and TWE are encouraged, certified translations and evaluations of all official transcripts; recommendation should be in English or with certified translations, proof of health/immunization certificate. Interviews are encouraged. Notification is made by mid-March. Doctoral Programs phone: (617)495-6101.

ADMISSION STANDARDS. Very selective. Median GMAT: 702; median GPA: 3.5 (A = 4). Gourman rating: MBA was rated number one, the score was 4.94; the D.B.A. was rated number one, the score was 4.94. *U.S. News & World Report* ranked the Business School in the top two of all U.S. business schools. *Business Week* listed the Business School in the top five of all American business schools.

FINANCIAL AID. Scholarships, merit scholarships, minority scholarships, grants, fellowships, research assistantships, teaching assistantships, international loans, Federal W/S, loans. Financial assistance available for international students. Assistantships/fellowships may be available for joint degree candidates. Financial Aid applications and information are generally available at the on-campus visit/interview or after January 1; apply by March 1. Request scholarship, fellowship, assistantship and need-based information from the School's Office of Financial Aid Services. Phone: (617)495-6640, fax: (617)496-3955. Use FAFSA (School code: 002155), also submit the School's FAF, a Financial Aid Transcript, Federal Income Tax forms. Approximately 70% of students receive some form of financial assistance. Merit fellowships covering 12 months of study are available for D.B.A. applicants.

DEGREE REQUIREMENTS. For M.B.A.: a four-term full-time program. For M.B.A.-J.-D.: four-and-one-half- to five-year program. For D.B.A.: four- to five-year program; teaching experience required; general exam in business; qualifying exam in field of specialization; thesis; oral defense.

FIELDS OF DOCTORAL SPECIALIZATION.
Accounting and Control.
Management Information Systems.
Marketing, Policy, and Management.
Technology and Operations Management.

School of Dental Medicine

Established 1867. Located in Boston (02115). Medical-dental library: 412,000 volumes. Annual tuition: $28,070. Total average academic costs for all other first-year expenses: $1728. Limited on-campus housing for single students only. Average academic year housing cost: $11,905. For off-campus housing, contact Assistant Dean for Student Affairs.

Enrollment: first-year class 35 (men 60%, women 40%); postgraduates 65. No part-time students. Faculty: full-time 14, part-time 123. Degrees conferred: D.M.D., D.M.D.-M.P.H., D.M.D.-M.P.P., D.M.D.-S.M. D.M.D.-Sc.D., D.M.D.-M.D.

ADMISSION REQUIREMENTS. AADSAS, official transcripts, high school and college faculty evaluations, DAT required in support of School's application. Interview by invitation only. Students with three years of undergraduate preparation are considered, but normally four years of college are expected. Accepts transfer applicants from other dental and medical schools. Graduates of unaccredited colleges not considered. Apply to Assistant Dean after June 1, before January 1. Application fee $50. Phone: (617)432-1443.

ADMISSION STANDARDS. Competitive. Mean DAT: Academic 21.6, PAT 21.3; mean GPA: 3.60 (A = 4). Gourman rating: 4.93. Usual minimum average: 2.8 (A = 4). Accepts 15–20% of total annual applicants. Approximately 20% are state residents.

FINANCIAL AID. Scholarships, fellowships, grants, tuition waivers, DEAL, HEAL, loans. Apply by July 1 to Office of Fi-

nancial Aid. Phone: (617)432-1527. Use FAFSA (School code: E00508) and CSS profile. About 66% of students receive aid other than loans from School.

DEGREE REQUIREMENTS. For D.M.D.: 53 months minimum, normally at least two years in full-time residence; transfer students occasionally permitted to enter in fourth year. For M.P.H., M.P.P., S.M., Sc.D.: see Graduate Schools listings above.

FIELDS OF STUDY.
Endodontics.
Maxillofacial Surgery.
Oral Biology.
Oral Pathology.
Oral Surgery.
Orthodontics.
Pediatric Dentistry.
Periodontology.
Prosthetic Dentistry.

Graduate School of Design

Annual tuition: full-time $26,330; doctoral students $41,180.
Enrollment: full-time 525 (men 50%, women 50%). Faculty: full-time 32, part-time 66. Degrees conferred: M.Arch., M.L.A., M.Des.S., M.Arch. in Urban Design, M.L.A. in Urban Design, M.U.P., D. Des.

ADMISSION REQUIREMENTS. Transcripts, three letters of recommendation, résumé and essay, portfolio, GRE required in support of School's application. Supplemental forms are required by some programs. TOEFL required for international applicants. Interview not required. Apply to Graduate School of Design by December 1. Fall admission only. Application fee $65. Phone: (617)495-5453; fax: (617)495-8949.

ADMISSION STANDARDS. Very selective.

FINANCIAL AID. Scholarships, grants, Federal W/S, loans (master's candidates); grants, fellowships, teaching/research assistantships (doctoral candidates). Apply by February 15 to the Dean's Office or appropriate department chair. Use FAFSA (School code: E00212) and institutional FAF. No aid for special (nondegree) students.

DEGREE REQUIREMENTS. For M.Arch.: (first professional degree): three and a half years minimum in residence; terminal project. For M.Des.S.: one-year full-time program. For M.U.P.: two years minimum in residence. For M.Arch. (second professional degree): B.Arch. required for admission; one and a half years minimum in residence; terminal project. For M.L.A.: normally three years in residence; terminal project. For D.Des.: a minimum of 32 units of course work; thesis proposal; general exam; thesis. For Ph.D.: see GSAS listing above for degree requirements.

FIELDS OF STUDY.
Architecture.
Design Studies.
Landscape Architecture.
Urban Design and Planning.
Note: Distance learning option in the area of Digital Media and Production Environments, Mangement of Design and Construction.

Divinity School

Theology study since 1636. Annual tuition: full-time M.T.S., M.Div. $17,220, Th.D. $24,630.
Enrollment: full-time 507, part-time 78 (men 45%, women 55%). Faculty: full-time 37, part-time 39. Degrees conferred:

M.Div., M.T.S., Th.M., Th.D. The Ph.D. is offered through the Graduate School of Arts and Sciences.

ADMISSION REQUIREMENTS. Official transcripts, three letters of recommendation, personal statement required in support of School's application. GRE optional except for Th.D. applicants. Interview not required. Accepts transfer applicants. Apply by February 1 (Fall), December 1 (Spring), December 31 (Th.D.), March 15 (Th.M.) to Dean of Admissions of School. Rolling admissions process. Application fee $50. Phone: (617) 495-5796; fax: (617)495-0345.

ADMISSION STANDARDS. Selective. Usual minimum average: 3.0 (A = 4).

FINANCIAL AID. Annual awards from institutional funds: scholarships, grants, teaching fellowships (for advanced students only), Federal W/S, loans. Apply to Dean of Admission by January 10 for Th.M., Th.D.; by February 15 for M.Div. Use FAFSA (School code: E00210) and institutional supplementary form. Phone: (617)495-5772. About 81% of students receive aid in the form of grants and/or loans. Aid rarely available for part-time students or Th.M. students.

DEGREE REQUIREMENTS. For M.Div.: 24 half-courses minimum, at least two years in full-time residence; distribution and arts of ministry requirements, senior thesis; reading knowledge of Hebrew, Greek, Latin, German, French, or Spanish. For M.T.S.: 16 half-courses minimum, two years in full-time residence; distribution requirements; reading knowledge of one language of theological scholarship. For Th.M.: 8 half-courses minimum in residence; reading knowledge of two of Hebrew, Greek, Latin, German, French, or Spanish; one major or two smaller research papers; final oral exam. For Th.D.: two years minimum beyond the M.Div. in full-time residence; seven-year limit for degree; knowledge of one classical and two modern languages indicated for M.Div., Th.M.; general exam; dissertation; final oral exam.

Graduate School of Education

Established 1920. Tuition: per semester $12,572. Limited on-campus housing available. Contact Director of Student Affairs for on- and off-campus information. Phone: (617)495-8035. Day care facilities available.

Enrollment: full-time 872, part-time 223 (men 25%, women 75%). Faculty: full-time 38, part-time 58. Degrees conferred: Ed.M., C.A.S., Ed.D.

ADMISSION REQUIREMENTS. Transcripts, GRE or MAT, three academic/professional references, statement of purpose required in support of School's application. Interview not required. TOEFL (minimum score 600, 250 on computer-based test), TWE (minimum 5) required for international applicants. Graduates of unaccredited institutions and transfer applicants not considered. Doctoral applicants apply to the Office of Admissions by January 2; January 10 for all others. Admits Fall only. Application fee $65. Phone: (617)495-3414; fax: (617)496-3577; e-mail: gseadmissions@harvard.edu.

ADMISSION STANDARDS. Competitive to very selective.

FINANCIAL AID. Scholarships, fellowships, research assistantships, teaching assistantships, grants, Federal W/S, loans. Approved for VA benefits. Apply by January 15 to the Office of Financial Aid. Phone: (617)495-3416; fax: (617)495-0840; Fellowship office phone: (617)496-2805. Use FAFSA (School code: E00213), institutional FAF, CSS profile (doctoral candidates). Students enrolled half-time or more in the Ed.D., Ed.M., and C.A.S. programs are eligible to receive financial aid.

DEGREE REQUIREMENTS. For Ed.M.: One year or equivalent in residence; no transfer of credit permitted; no language, thesis, or comprehensive exam requirement; ordinarily, requirements must be met through full-time study during the academic year. For C.A.S.: one year or equivalent in residence beyond the master's; full-time study during academic year ordinarily required, but exceptions are considered; no language or thesis requirement. For Ed.D.: two years or equivalent beyond the bachelor's, at least two semesters in full-time attendance; written qualifying paper; thesis; final oral exam; no language requirement.

FIELDS OF STUDY.
Administration Planning and Social Policy. Includes communities and schools, elementary and secondary education, higher education, international education, research, urban superintendency. Ed.D., C.A.S., Ed.M.
Arts in Education. Ed.M., C.A.S.
Higher Education. Ed.M.
Human Development and Psychology. Includes language and literacy. Ed.D., C.A.S.
Individualized Program. Includes self-designed, administration, planning and social policy, human development and psychology, learning and teaching, international education, gender studies, mind, brain and education. Ed.M.
International Education. Ed.M.
Language and Literacy. Ed.M., C.A.S.
Learning and Teaching. Includes learning and knowing, learning in a sociohistorical context. Ed.D., C.A.S., Ed.M.
Risk and Prevention. Ed.M., C.A.S.
School Leadership. Ed.M., C.A.S.
Teacher Certification Programs. Includes teaching and curriculum, midcareer math and science. Ed.M., C.A.S.
Technology Education. Ed.M., C.A.S.

John Fitzgerald Kennedy School of Government
Web site: www.ksg.harvard.edu

Established 1936 as the Graduate School of Public Administration, changed in 1978 to current name. Special facilities: Belfer Center for Science and International Affairs, Carr Center for Human Rights Policy, Center for Business and Government, Center for International Development at Harvard University, Center for Public Leadership, the Hauser Center for Nonprofit Organizations, the Institute of Politics, Joan Shorenstein Center on the Press, Politics, and Public Policy.

Annual tuition: full-time $26,488.

Enrollment: full-time about 547; no part-time. Faculty: full-time 70. Degrees conferred: M.P.A., M.P.P., M.P.P.-M.U.P., Ph.D.

ADMISSION REQUIREMENTS. Transcripts, three letters of reference, GRE or GMAT, responses to essay questions required in support of School's application. On-line application available. Seven years of administrative public-interest work required for Mid-Career M.P.A. TOEFL, TWE, TSE required for foreign applicants. Interview not required. Graduates of unaccredited colleges normally not considered. Apply to Admissions Office by January 4 for M.P.P. and Ph.D.; Mid-Career M.P.A. has rolling admissions from January 15 through May 14. Admits Fall only. Application fee $80. Phone: (617)495-1155; e-mail: ksg-admissions@harvard.edu.

ADMISSION STANDARDS. Competitive.

FINANCIAL AID. Scholarships, grants, assistantships, fellowships, Federal W/S, loans. Apply to Office of Financial Aid by February 1 for M.P.P. and April 16 for Mid-Career M.P.A. Phone: (617)495-1152. Use FAFSA and CSS profile.

DEGREE REQUIREMENTS. For M.P.P.: two years of full-time study; 18 units of academic credit, 10 in required courses. For the M.P.A.: two years of full-time study; 8 semester-length courses. For Ph.D.: 16 half-course minimum; advancement to candidacy; oral defense of research paper; dissertation; written and oral defense.

FIELDS OF STUDY.

Health Policy.

Political Economy and Government.

Public Administration. Includes international development, mid-career program.

Public Policy. Includes urban planning.

Social Policy.

Note: Students choose courses from Kennedy School of Government, as well as from other Harvard graduate and professional schools, the Fletcher School of Law and Diplomacy at Tufts University, and MIT.

Law School

Web site: www.law.harvard.edu

Established 1817. The oldest law school in the U.S. Located with most of the other units of the University in Cambridge. ABA approved since 1923. AALS member. Semester system. Full-time, day study only. Law library: 2,039,634 volumes; 15,336 subscriptions; has LEXIS, NEXIS, WESTLAW, DIALOG, OCLC, RLIN, Vu/Text, among others; is a Federal Government Depository. Special programs: Criminal Justice Institute, the East Asian Legal Studies Program, the Islamic Legal Studies Program, the Human Rights Program, the Program on International Financial Systems, the European Law Research Center, the Program in Law and Economics, the Program on the Legal Profession, the Program on Negotiation.

Annual tuition: $26,745. Total average cost for all other expenses: $14,050.

Enrollment: first-year class 556. Total full-time J.D. students 1653 (men 55%, women 45%), LL.M. and S.J.D. students 160. Faculty: full-time 76, part-time 17. Student to faculty ratio 19.7 to 1. Degrees conferred: J.D., LL.M., S.J.D.

ADMISSION REQUIREMENTS. LSDAS Law School report, bachelor's degree, transcripts, references, LSAT, personal statement required in support of application. Interview not required. Accepts transfer applicants. Graduates of unaccredited colleges not considered. Apply to Admissions Office of School after September 15, before February 1. Admits Fall only. Application fee $70 (J.D. applicants only). Phone: (617)495-3109.

ADMISSION STANDARDS. Competitive. Mean LSAT: 169; mean GPA: 3.84 (A = 4). Gourman rating: 4.93. *U.S. News & World Report* ranking is in the top three of all U.S. law schools. Accepts about 10–12% of total annual applicants.

FINANCIAL AID. Scholarships, fellowships, assistantships, Federal W/S, loans. Apply by March 1 to Financial Aid Office (entering J.D. students), by February 1 to Chair of Division of Graduate Studies (postbaccalaureate students). Phone: (617)495-4606. Use FAFSA. All students receive aid who demonstrate need according to a combination of Federal and institutional guidelines. A Low-Income Protection Plan is available.

DEGREE REQUIREMENTS. For J.D.: three years minimum in residence; advanced standing for study completed in other law schools considered in exceptional cases; final written paper. For LL.M.: at least 24 credits beyond the J.D.; one year in full-time residence; final written essay or thesis. For S.J.D.: one year minimum in full-time residence; dissertation; final oral exam.

Medical School

Web site: www.hms.harvard.edu

Established 1782. Located in Boston (02115-6092). Library: 608,900 volumes.

Annual tuition: $29,000, student fees $1897. Total average figure for all other expenses: $9055. Limited housing available. Enrollment: first-year class 165; total 688 (men 47%, women 53%). Faculty: full- and part-time 3000. Degrees conferred: M.D., M.D.-M.P.H., M.D.-M.P.P., M.D.-Ph.D. (Medical Scientist Training Program in cooperation with Massachusetts Institute of Technology.)

ADMISSION REQUIREMENTS. Transcripts, MCAT, recommendations, essay required in support of application. Interview by invitation. Applicants must have completed at least two years of college study, but four recommended. Does not have EDP. Apply after June 1, before October 15 to Director of Admissions. Application fee $75. Phone: (617)432-1550; fax: (617)432-3307.

ADMISSION STANDARDS. Competitive. Mean MCAT: VR 10.5, PS 11.9, BS 11.7; mean GPA: 3.8 (A = 4). Gourman rating: 4.93. *U.S. News & World Report* ranking is number one among all U.S. medical schools. Accepts about 7% of total annual applicants. Approximately 9% are state residents.

FINANCIAL AID. All Financial Aid is based on documented need. Grants, institutional loans, HEAL, alternative loan programs, NIH stipends, Federal Perkins Loans, Stafford Subsidized and Unsubsidized Loans, Service Commitment Scholarship programs are available. Assistantships/fellowships may be available for joint degree candidates. Contact the Financial Aid Office for current information. Phone: (617)432-1575; fax: (617)432-4308; e-mail: hmsfao@warren.med.harvard.edu. For most financial assistance and all Federal programs use FAFSA (School code: E00472), also submit Financial Aid Transcript, Federal Income Tax forms, CSS Profile. Approximately 70% of students receive some form of financial assistance.

DEGREE REQUIREMENTS. For M.D.: satisfactory completion of four-year program. For M.P.H., M.P.P., Ph.D.: see Graduate School listing above.

FIELDS OF GRADUATE STUDY.

Biochemistry.

Biomedical Engineering.

Biophysics.

Cell Biology.

Genetics.

Immunology.

Microbiology.

Molecular Biology.

Neurosciences.

Pathology.

Pharmacology.

Public Administration.

Public Health.

School of Public Health

Founded 1922. Special facilities: Center for Biostatistics in AIDS Research, Center for Health Communication, Center for Quality of Care Research and Education, Center for Risk Analysis, Francois-Xavier Bagnoud Center for Health and Human Rights, Harvard AIDS Institute, Harvard Center for Populations and Development Studies, Harvard Center for Society and Health, Harvard Injury Control Research Center, John B. Little Center for Radiation Sciences and Environmental Health, Kresge Center for Environmental Health.

Annual tuition: full-time $26,300, half-time $13,150, per credit $660. Oncampus housing available. Enrollment: full-time 526, part-time 156 (men 45%, women 55%). Faculty: full-time 155, part-time 115. Degrees conferred; S.M., M.P.H., M.O.H., S.D., D.P.H.

ADMISSION REQUIREMENTS. Official transcripts, three letters of reference, GRE (requests to substitute MCAT/DAT/GMAT/LSAT are normally approved) required in support of School's application. On-line application available. TOEFL (minimum score 560) required for international applicants. Graduates of unaccredited institutions not considered. Apply by December 15 (priority deadline) to Office of Admissions. Admits Fall only. Application fee $60. Phone: (617)432-1031.

ADMISSION STANDARDS. Competitive. Usual minimum average: 2.75 (A = 4).

FINANCIAL AID. Fellowships, research/teaching assistantships, tuition grants, Federal W/S, loans. Apply by March 15 to Director of Financial Aid. Use FAFSA. Phone: (617)432-1867. Aid rarely available for part-time or foreign students.

DEGREE REQUIREMENTS. For M.P.H.: 40 credit units minimum, two semesters in residence; applicants ordinarily must be graduates of schools of medicine, dental medicine, veterinary health, law, or hold a doctorate in field related to public health. For S.M.: 40 units minimum in residence for students with prior doctoral (and some master's) degree or 80 units minimum in residence for students with relevant bachelor's degrees. For M.O.H.: 40 units minimum in residence; applicants must hold M.D. For S.D.: two years in residence; applicants must hold bachelor's or master's degree depending on department; qualifying exam; thesis; final oral exam. For D.P.H.: essentially the same as the S.D.; applicants must be graduates of schools of medicine, dental medicine, or veterinary medicine, or hold another doctorate in field related to public health; applicants must also hold M.P.H.

FIELDS OF STUDY.
Biological Sciences.
Biostatistics.
Cancer Cell Biology
Environmental Epidemiology.
Environmental Health.
Environmental Science and Engineering.
Epidemiology.
Health and Social Behavior. Includes health and social policy, planned social change, social determinants of health.
Health Policy and Management.
Immunology and Infectious Diseases. Includes immunology and molecular biology of parasitic and other infections, infectious disease epidemiology and tropical public health, vector biology, ecology, control, virology.
Maternal and Child Health.
Molecular Genetics.
Occupational Health.
Physiology.
Population and International Health. Includes doctoral concentrations in international health epidemiology and ecology, international health policy and economics, population and reproductive health, bio- and public health mathematics.
Population Genetics.
Public Health. Includes clinical effectiveness, family and community health, health care management, international health, law and public health, occupational and environmental health, quantitative methods.
Radiation Biology.
Toxicology.

HAWAII PACIFIC UNIVERSITY
Honolulu, Hawaii 98623-2785
Web site: www.hpu.edu

Coed. Private control. Semester system. Library: 159,000 volumes, 1700 subscriptions. Total University enrollment: 8000.

Annual tuition: full-time $9840; per credit $410. On-campus housing for single graduate students; none for married students.

Average academic year housing cost: $17,980 (including board). Contact Director of Residence Life for both on- and off-campus housing information. Phone: (808)233-3184.

Graduate Studies

Enrollment: full-time 672, part-time 568. University faculty teaching graduate students: full-time 47, part-time 38. Degrees conferred: M.A.G.L., M.A.O.C., M.A.Com., M.A.T.E.S.L., M.A.D.M.S., M.B.A., M.A. in H.R.M., M.S.I S., M.S.N.

ADMISSION REQUIREMENTS. Official transcripts, GMAT, two letters of recommendation required in support of application. On-line application available. TOEFL required for international applicants. Accepts transfer applicants. Graduates of unaccredited institutions not considered. Apply to the Graduate Admissions Coordinator at least one month prior to registration. Rolling admissions process. Application $50. Phone: (808)544-0279; fax: (808)544-0280; e-mail: gradservctr@hpu.edu.

ADMISSION STANDARDS. Selective. Usual minimum average: 3.0 (A = 4).

FINANCIAL AID. Assistantships, Federal W/S, loans. Approved for VA benefits. Apply after January 1 to Financial Aid Office; no specified closing date. Use FAFSA. Aid sometimes available for part-time students.

DEGREE REQUIREMENTS. For master's: 36–45 semester hours minimum, at least 30 in residence; thesis/nonthesis option.

FIELDS OF STUDY.
Accounting.
Business Administration.
Communication.
Diplomacy and Military Studies.
Global Leadership.
Human Resource Management. M.A. in H.R.M.
Information Systems. M.S.I.S.
Nursing.
Organization Change.
TESL.

UNIVERSITY OF HAWAII AT MANOA
Honolulu, Hawaii 96822
Web site: www.uhm.hawaii.edu

Founded 1907. CGS member. Coed. State control. Semester system. Special facilities: Institute for Astronomy; Computing Center; English Language Institute; Environmental Center; Foreign Languages Laboratories; Hawaii Agricultural Experiment Station; Hawaii Cooperative Fisheries Unit; Hawaii Institute of Geophysics; Hawaii Institute of Marine Biology; Industrial Relations Center; Institute for Astronomy; Instructional Resources Service Center; Laboratory of Sensory Sciences; JKK Look Laboratory of Oceanographic Engineering; Harold L. Lyon Arboretum; Pacific and Asian Linguistics Institute; Pacific Biomedical Research Center; Population Genetics Laboratory; Social Science Research Institute; Social Welfare Development and Research Center; Speech and Hearing Clinic; Survey Research Office; University of Hawaii Press; Waikiki Aquarium; Water Resources Research Center. The University's NIH ranking is 106th among U.S. institutions with 51 awards/grants worth $32,943,239. Library: 3,100,000 volumes, 26,767 subscriptions. Total University enrollment: 19,000.

Annual tuition: full-time resident $4320, nonresident $10,392; per credit resident $180, nonresident $433. On-campus housing for about 1300 single students, with preference given to Hawaii residents. No on-campus housing facilities for married students. Average academic year housing cost: $4486 (including board) for single students, $8100 (including board) for married students. Contact Student Housing Office for both on- and off-campus housing information. Phone: (808)956-8177.

Graduate Division

Enrollment: full-time 2470 (men 45%, women 55%), part-time 1658 (men 40%, women 60%). University faculty: full-time 1320, part-time 192. Degrees conferred: M.Arch., M.A., M.Acc., M.B.A., M.Ed., M.Ed.T., M.F.A., M.L.S., M.M., M.Mus., M.P.A., M.P.H., M.P.S., M.S., M.S.W., M.U.R.P., Ed.D., Dr.P.H., Ph.D.

ADMISSION REQUIREMENTS. Official transcripts required in support of application. MAT required for some departments; GMAT required by College of Business Administration. GRE required by some fields of study, recommended in others. Two to three letters of recommendation required by some departments. Interview not required. TOEFL (minimum score for most programs 560) required for international applicants. Accepts transfer applicants. Graduates of unaccredited colleges not considered. Apply to Admissions Office, Graduate Division for most programs before January 15 internationals; February 1, U.S. citizens and permanent residents (Fall); August 1 (Spring) internationals; September 1 (Spring) U.S. citizens and permanent residents. Application fee $25, $50 for international applicants. Phone: (808)956-8950; fax: (808)956-4261.

ADMISSION STANDARDS Selective. Usual minimum average: 3.0 (A = 4); usual minimum GMAT: 500.

FINANCIAL AID. Scholarships; fellowships, assistantships for teaching/research, Federal W/S, loans. Approved for VA benefits. Apply to Dean of Graduate Division for scholarships, fellowships; for East-West Center scholarships, write to East-West Center; to appropriate department chair by February 1 for assistantships; to Financial Aid Office for all other programs. Use FAFSA. About 32% of students receive aid other than loans from University, about 50% from all sources. Aid available for part-time students.

DEGREE REQUIREMENTS. For master's (M.A., M.Ed., M.S.) Plan A: 30 credit hours minimum, at least half of credits in residence; general exam (optional), candidacy; thesis; final written/oral exam. For master's (M.A., M.Ed., M.S.) Plan B: 30 credit minimum, at least 24 credits in residence; general exam (optional); culminating experience; final written/oral or both. For master's (M.A., M.Ed., M.S.) Plan C: preliminary conference to establish plan of study/degree plan; general oral/written exam; final written and oral exam. For M.F.A.: 60 credits program minimum depending on field of study offered under Plan A and B; performance/major project/major exhibition. For M.B.A.: 54 credits, thesis/nonthesis option. For M.L.S.: 36 credit hours minimum, thesis/nonthesis program. For M.S.W.: 52 credit hours minimum; final group project or thesis. For M.M.: 28 credit hours minimum plus thesis/composition, or 30 credit hours; performance; final oral exam. For M.P.H.: 30 credit hours minimum; nonthesis program; qualifying exam; final oral exam. For M.Arch., M.U.R.P.: 36 credit hours minimum; thesis. For Ph.D.: 3 semesters minimum in full-time residence beyond the master's; no specific credit requirements; reading knowledge of one foreign language is an optional requirement determined by each field of study; qualifying exam (optional); advancement to candidacy; comprehensive exam; dissertation; final written/oral exam.

FIELDS OF STUDY.
Accounting. GMAT for admission.

American Studies. GRE for admission.
Animal Sciences. GRE/Subject for admission. M.S.
Anthropology. GRE for admission; admits Fall only.
Architecture, ETS Architectural School Test, samples of work, documented evidence of 600 hours of supervised architecture work experience required for admission. M.Arch. only.
Art. M.A. in Asian, Pacific art history; M.F.A. (thesis program only) for creative studio work. M.A., M.F.A. only.
Asian Studies. GRE for admission; interdepartmental program. M.A. only.
Astronomy. GRE/Subject for admission. M.S., Ph.D.
Bioengineering. GRE for admission. M.S., Ph.D.
Biophysics. GRE for admission. M.S., Ph.D.
Biostatistics and Epidemiology. GRE for admission. Ph.D.
Botany. GRE for admission; one language for Ph.D.; fields include plant physiology. M.S., Ph.D.
Business Administration. GMAT for admission. M.B.A. only.
Cell and Molecular Biology. GRE for admission. M.S., Ph.D.
Chemistry. GRE/Subject for admission of international applicants, recommended for domestic applicants; one language for Ph.D. M.S., Ph.D.
Chinese. GRE for admission. M.A., Ph.D.
Civil Engineering. GRE for admission. M.S., Ph.D.
Classics. M.A.
Communication. M.A.
Communication and Information Sciences. GRE or GMAT for admission. Ph.D.
Computer Science. GRE/Subject for admission. Ph.D.
Counselor and Guidance. GRE for admission. M.Ed.
Curriculum Studies. M.Ed.
Dance. M.A., M.F.A.
Early Childhood Education. M.Ed.
Education. GRE writing assessment for admission. Ph.D.
Economics. GRE for admission. M.A., Ph.D.
Educational Administration. Course work or professional experience in education required for admission. Fall admission only. M.Ed.
Educational Foundations. M.Ed.
Educational Psychology. GRE for admission; proficiency in computer language for Ph.D.; Fall admission only. Ph.D.
Educational Technology. GRE for admission. M.Ed.
Electrical Engineering. GRE recommended for admission to M.S., required for Ph.D. program.
English. GRE/Subject for admission. M.A., Ph.D.
English as a Second Language. GRE for all native English speakers. M.A.
Entomology. GRE/Subject for admission. One language for Ph.D. M.S., Ph.D.
Food Science and Technology. GRE for admission. M.S.
French. M.A.
Geography. GRE for admission; one language for Ph.D. M.A., Ph.D.
Geology and Geophysics. GRE for admission; one language for Ph.D. M.S., Ph.D.
German. M.A.
History. GRE for admission; one language for M.A.; two languages for Ph.D.
Human Resource Management. GMAT for admission. M.H.R.M.
Information and Computer Sciences. GRE for admission, Subject recommended, knowledge of programming language required for admission. M.S.
International Management. GMAT for admission. Ph.D.
Japanese. GRE required for admission. M.A., Ph.D.
Kinesiology and Leisure Science. M.S.
Korean. GRE for admission. M.A., Ph.D.
Library Studies and Information Studies. GRE for admission. M.L.I.S.
Linguistics. GRE for admission; one language for M.A.; two languages for Ph.D.

Mathematics. GRE/Subject for admission; two languages for Ph.D. M.A., Ph.D.

Mechanical Engineering. GRE for admission. M.S., Ph.D.

Meteorology. GRE recommended for M.S., for Ph.D.; one language for Ph.D. M.S., Ph.D.

Microbiology. GRE for admission; one language for Ph.D. M.S., Ph.D.

Molecular Biosciences and Engineering. GRE for admission. M.S., Ph.D.

Music. GRE recommended for M.A., M.M., required for Ph.D.; thesis program only for M.A. in dance ethnology, ethnomusicology, musicology, music education, theory; nonthesis program for M.A. in performance only; M.Mus. in composition and performance; one language for M.A. thesis program; M.A., M.Mus. only.

Natural Resources and Environmental Management. GRE recommended for M.S., required for Ph.D. M.S., Ph.D.

Nursing. Bachelor's degree in nursing, licensure in Hawaii for practice of nursing, GRE for admission; areas of specialization for M.S.: mental health–maternal–child nursing, medical-surgical nursing. M.S.

Nutritional Sciences. GRE recommended for admission; M.S. only.

Ocean and Resources Engineering. GRE for admission; one language for Ph.D.

Oceanography. GRE for admission; one language, digital computing for Ph.D.

Pacific Islands Studies. GRE for admission; one language for M.A.; M.A.

Philosophy. GRE recommended for native English speakers. Includes Western, Asian, Comparative; two Western languages for Ph.D.

Physics. GRE/Subject for admission. M.S., Ph.D.

Physiology. GRE or MCAT for admission. M.S., Ph.D.

Plant Pathology. GRE for admission. M.S., Ph.D.

Political Science. GRE for admission.

Psychology. GRE for admission; admits Fall only.

Public Administration. M.P.A. only.

Public Health. GRE for admission; admits Fall only. M.P.H., M.S.

Religion (Asian). M.A.

Russian. M.A.

Second Language Acquisition. GRE for admission. Ph.D.

Social Welfare. GRE recommended for admission. Ph.D.

Social Work. M.S.W.

Sociology. GRE for admission. M.A., Ph.D.

Spanish. M.A.

Special Education. GRE for admission. M.Ed.

Speech. GRE required for admission.

Speech Pathology and Audiology. GRE required for admission. M.S.

Theatre. GRE for admission. Includes history, theory and criticism, fine arts. M.A., M.F.A., Ph.D.

Tropical Medicine. GRE/Subject for admission. M.S., Ph.D.

Tropical Plants and Soil Science. GRE recommended for M.S., required for Ph.D. M.S., Ph.D.

Travel Industry Management. GRE or GMAT for admission. M.S.

Urban and Regional Planning. GRE for admission. M.U.R.P.

Zoology. GRE/Subject for admission; one language for Ph.D. M.S., Ph.D.

William S. Richardson School of Law (96822)

Established 1973. ABA approved since 1974. AALS member since 1989. Semester system. Special programs: Environmental/Ocean Law, Pacific-Asian Legal Studies; exchange program with Hiroshima, Japan Law Faculty. Law library: 283,578 volumes, 3332 subscriptions; has LEXIS, NEXIS, WESTLAW, INNOPAC.

Annual tuition: resident $10,200, nonresident $16,472. On-campus housing available for both single and married students. Estimated living expenses: $9646.

Enrollment: first-year class 74; total 229 (men 45%, women 55%). Faculty: full-time 17, part-time 13. Student to faculty ratio 11.2 to 1. Degrees conferred: J.D., J.D.-M.A. (Asian Studies), J.D.-M.B.A., J.D.-M.U.R.P.

ADMISSION REQUIREMENTS. LSDAS Law School report, bachelor's degree, transcripts, LSAT, recommendations required in support of application. Accepts transfer applicants on a space available basis only. Graduates of unaccredited institutions are not considered. Preference given to state residents; up to 30% of class can be nonresidents. Apply to Office of Admissions by March 1. Application fee $45. Phone: (808)956-3000; fax: (808)956-3813.

ADMISSION STANDARDS. Selective. Mean LSAT: 157; mean GPA: 3.31 (A = 4). Gourman rating: 2.66. *U.S. News & World Report* ranking is in the second tier of all U.S. law schools. Admits about 25–30% of total annual applicants.

FINANCIAL AID. Scholarships, Federal W/S, loans. Apply by March 1 to Director of Financial Aid. Use FAFSA. About 90% of students receive some aid from School.

DEGREE REQUIREMENTS. For J.D.: satisfactory completion of 89 credit hours of study.

John A. Burns School of Medicine
Web site: hawaiimed.hawaii.edu

First class entered September 1967. Located on Manoa Campus. Annual tuition: resident $14,208, nonresident $27,912. Total average figure for all other expenses: $9000. Enrollment: first-year class 62 (2 EDP), total 265 (men, 46%, women 54%); postgraduates 105. Faculty: full-time 153, part-time 101. Degrees conferred: M.D., M.D.-M.S., M.D.-Ph.D.

ADMISSION REQUIREMENTS. AMCAS report, MCAT, three years of college, recommendations, and the completion of at least 90 credits are required. Interview by invitation. An evaluation of what the potential student might contribute to the health profession in the Pacific is an integral part of the selection process. Has EDP; apply between June 1 and August 1. Apply through AMCAS after June 1, before December 1. AMCAS application fee $50. Phone: (808)956-8300; fax: (808)956-9547.

ADMISSION STANDARDS. Competitive. Median MCAT: 10; median GPA: 3.46 (A = 4). Gourman rating: 3.25. Accepts about 25% of total annual applicants. Approximately 95% of all students have ties to the State of Hawaii.

FINANCIAL AID. Scholarships, NIH stipends, loan fund. Apply after acceptance to University of Hawaii Financial Aids Office. Use FAFSA (School code: 001610). About 80% of students receive some aid from School and outside sources.

DEGREE REQUIREMENTS. For M.D.: satisfactory completion of four-year program and passing USMLE Step 2.

FIELDS OF GRADUATE STUDY.
Anatomy.
Biochemistry.
Biophysics.
Genetics.
Immunology.
Microbiology.
Molecular Biology.
Neuroscience.
Pharmacology.

Physiology.
Reproductive Biology.
Tropical Medicine.

UNIVERSITY OF HEALTH SCIENCES

Kansas City, Missouri 64124-2395
Web site: www.uhs.edu

College of Osteopathic Medicine

Founded 1916, relocated to current location in 1921. One of the oldest osteopathic colleges. Coed. Private control. Library: 93,700 volumes, 262 subscriptions; has MEDLINE, CANCER-LINE, BIOETHIC, HEALTH, TOXLINE, DIALOG, OCLC. No on-campus housing available. Average academic year housing cost: $550 per month. Contact the Admissions Office for off-campus housing information.

Annual tuition: $29,440. Enrollment: first-year class 225, total 869 (men 74%, women 26%). Faculty: full-time 43, part-time 155. Degree conferred: D.O. D.O.-M.B.A. (Rockhurst University).

ADMISSION REQUIREMENTS. AACOMAS report, bachelor's degree preferred, transcripts, MCAT, letters of recommendation from premed advisory committee, evaluation from a physician (preferably a D.O.) required in support of College's application. Interview by invitation only. Graduates of unaccredited college not considered. Apply by February 1. Admits first-year students Fall only. Application fee: $50. Phone: (800)234-4UHS, (816)283-2339; fax: (816)283-2484.

ADMISSION STANDARDS. Selective. Median MCAT: 8.5; median GPA: 3.37 (A = 4). Accepts approximately 15% of annual applicants. Usual minimum average: 2.75.

FINANCIAL AID. Scholarships, grants, HEAL, loans. Apply after acceptance to Office of Financial Aid. Phone: (816)283-2000. Use FAFSA (University code: G24524).

DEGREE REQUIREMENT. For D.O.: satisfactory completion of four-year program.

HEBREW COLLEGE

Brookline, Massachusetts 02146-9616
Web site: www.hebrewcollege.edu

Founded 1921. Located adjacent to Boston. Coed. Private control. Semester system. Library: 110,000 volumes, 275 subscriptions.

Tuition: $525 per credit. No on-campus housing. For off-campus information: Phone: (617)279-4944.

Graduate Studies

Graduate study since 1951. Enrollment: full-time 20, part-time 40. Graduate faculty: full-time 6, part-time 14. Degrees conferred: M.A. Judaic Studies, M.J.Ed.

ADMISSION REQUIREMENTS. Transcripts, GRE, three letters of reference, essay, bachelor's degree required in support of department's application. Interview recommended for admission. TOEFL required for international applicants. Apply by April 15 (Fall), November 30 (Spring) to the Admissions and Recruitment Assistant. Application fee $25. Phone: (617)278-4948; fax: (617)264-9264; e-mail: admissions@hebrewcollege.edu.

FINANCIAL AID. Internal scholarships, fellowships, loans available. Approved for VA benefits. Apply by April 15 to the Office of Financial Aid. Aid available for part-time students. Phone: (617)278-4944.

DEGREE REQUIREMENTS. For MA: 39 credit hours minimum, thesis. For M.J.Ed.: 45 credit hours minimum; program normally requires two and a half to three years of study.

FIELDS OF STUDY.
Jewish Education. Includes day school education, Jewish family education, early childhood Jewish education, special education in Jewish settings, school administration, youth leadership.
Jewish Studies.

HENDERSON STATE UNIVERSITY

Arkadelphia, Arkansas 71999-0001
Web site: www.hsu.edu

Founded 1890. Located 75 miles SW of Little Rock. Coed. State control. Semester system. Library: 274,639 volumes, 1500 subscriptions.

Tuition: per semester hour, resident $162, nonresident $324. On-campus housing for 600 men, 600 women, 27 married students. Average academic year housing cost: $2500 (room and board) for single students. $275 per month for married students. Apply to Dean, Residence Life. Phone: (870)230-5083.

Graduate Studies

Graduate study since 1954. Enrollment: full-time 51, part-time 316. Faculty teaching graduate students: full-time 55, part-time 9. Degrees conferred: M.A.T., M.L.A., M.S.E., M.S., M B.A.

ADMISSION REQUIREMENTS. Transcripts, GRE/GMAT/ MAT required in support of application. TOEFL required for foreign applicants. Accepts transfer applicants. Graduates of unaccredited institutions not considered. Apply to Dean by May 1 (Fall), December 1 (Spring). Application fee none for domestic applicants, $30 for international applicants. Phone: (870)230-5126; fax: (870)230-5479.

ADMISSION STANDARDS. Selective. Usual minimum average: 2.7 (A = 4).

FINANCIAL AID. Annual awards from institutional funds: scholarships, teaching/research assistantships, Federal W/S, loans. Approved for VA benefits. Apply to Dean of Graduate School; no specified closing date. Phone: (870)230-5094; fax: (870)230-5000. Use FAFSA. Aid available for part-time students.

DEGREE REQUIREMENTS. For master's: 30–48 semester hours minimum, at least 24–42 in residence; candidacy; thesis optional for M.S.E.

FIELDS OF STUDY.
Business Administration. M.B.A.
Community Counseling. M.S.
Counselor Education. Includes elementary, secondary. M.S.E.
Curriculum and Instruction. Includes ESL, middle school, physical education, P–4 education, reading. M.S.E.
Educational Leadership. M.S.E.
English. M.S.E.
Liberal Arts. M.L.A.

Mathematics. M.S.E.
Social Studies. M.S.E.
Special Education. Includes mild disabilities, early childhood. M.S.E.
Sports Administration. M.S.
Teaching. M.A.T.

HOFSTRA UNIVERSITY

Hempstead, New York 11550-1090
Web site: www.hofstra.edu

Founded 1935. Located 25 miles E of New York City. CGS member. Coed. Private control. Semester system. Library: more than 1,600,000 volumes, 7000 subscriptions. Total University enrollment: 13,200.

Tuition: per credit $495. On-campus housing for both single and married students. Average academic year housing cost: $7240 (including board). Contact Specialty Housing Coordinator. Phone: (516)463-6936. Day care facilities available.

Graduate Division

Graduate study since 1951. Enrollment: full-time 528, part-time 2616. Faculty teaching graduate students: full-time 174, part-time 143. Degrees conferred: M.A., M.S., M.B.A., M.P.S., J.D.-M.B.A., C.A.S., Professional Diploma, Ed.D., Psy.D., Ph.D.

ADMISSION REQUIREMENTS. Transcripts, GRE/MAT/GMAT required in support of Divisional application. TOEFL (minimum score 550) required for international applicants. Interview, recommendations required by some departments. Accepts transfer applicants. Graduates of unaccredited institutions not considered. Apply to Admissions Office at least sixty days prior to registration. Application fee $40, $75 for international applicants. Phone: (516)560-7660, fax: (516)560-7600.

ADMISSION STANDARDS. Competitive to very competitive. Usual minimum average: 3.0 (A = 4).

FINANCIAL AID. Scholarships, fellowships, teaching assistantships, tuition waivers, Federal W/S, loans. Approved for VA benefits. Apply to appropriate department chairman for scholarships or assistantships; to the Financial Aid Office of all other programs. Phone: (516)463-6680; fax: (516)463-4936. Use FAFSA. Aid available for part-time students.

DEGREE REQUIREMENTS. For M.A.: 30–36 semester hours minimum, at least 24 in residence; master's essay; one language or knowledge of statistics for many majors; oral/written comprehensive exam; thesis/nonthesis option. For M.S.: 30–37 semester hours minimum, at least 24 in residence; comprehensive exam or alternative; thesis/nonthesis option. For M.B.A.: 36 hours minimum, at least 24 in residence; thesis/nonthesis option; comprehensive exam. For C.A.S., Professional Diploma: 30 hours beyond the master's. For Ed.D.: 90 semester hours minimum; preliminary exam, research project; final oral exam. For Ph.D.: 93 semester hours minimum, at least one year in full-time residence; preliminary exam; reading knowledge of one foreign language; dissertation; final oral exam.

FIELDS OF STUDY.

HOFSTRA COLLEGE OF LIBERAL ARTS AND SCIENCES:
Applied Linguistics. M.A.
Applied Mathematics. M.S.
Audiology. M.A.
Bilingualism. M.A.

Biology. M.A., M.S.
Clinical and School Psychology. Ph.D.
Clinical/School Psychology. Psy.D.
Computer Science. M.A., M.S.
English. M.A.
English and Creative Writing. M.A.
Human Cytogenetics. M.A.
Humanities. M.A.
Industrial/Organizational Psychology. M.A.
Mathematics. M.A.
School-Community Psychology. Psy.D.
Speech-Language Pathology. M.A.

NEW COLLEGE:
Interdisciplinary Studies. M.A.

FRANK G. ZARB SCHOOL OF BUSINESS:
Accounting. M.S.
Accounting and Taxation. M.S.
Accounting Information Systems. M.S.
Business Administration. M.B.A., E.M.B.A.
Computer Information Systems. M.S.
Finance. M.S.
Human Resource Management. M.S.
Marketing Research. M.S.
Taxation. M.S.

SCHOOL OF COMMUNICATION:
Speech Communication and Rhetorical Studies. M.A.

SCHOOL OF EDUCATION AND ALLIED HUMAN SERVICES:
Bilingual Elementary Education. M.S.Ed.
Bilingual Secondary Education. M.S.Ed.
Counseling. M.S., M.S.Ed.
Creative Arts Therapy. M.A.
Early Childhood Education (PreK–6). M.S.
Early Childhood Special Education. M.S.Ed.
Educational Administration. Ed.D.
Educational Administration and Policy Studies. M.S., M.S.Ed.
Elementary Education (PreK–6). M.S.
Foundations of Education. M.S., M.S.Ed.
Gerontology. M.S.
Health Administration. M.A.
Health Education. M.S.Ed.
Marriage and Family Therapy. M.A.
Physical Education. M.S.
Program Evaluation. M.S., M.S.Ed.
Reading. M.S.
Reading and Special Education. M.S.Ed.
Reading, Language, and Cognition. Ed.D., Ph.D.
Reading, Language, and Cognition—Bilingual/Bicultural. Ed.D., Ph.D.
Rehabilitation Counseling. M.S., M.S.Ed.
Secondary Education. M.S.
Special Education. M.S., M.S.Ed.
Special Education and Art Therapy. M.S.Ed.
Teaching English as a Second Language. M.S.

School of Law

Web site: www.hostra.edu/law

Established 1970. ABA approved since 1971. AALS member. Semester system. Full-time, day study only. Special facility: Center for Children, Families, and the Law. Special programs: summer study abroad at the University of Nice, France. Law library: 505,936 volumes, 5895 subscriptions; has LEXIS, NEXIS, WESTLAW, DIALOG.

Annual tuition: full-time $25,752, part-time $18,276; LL.M. full-time $25,936, part-time $16,389. Law students tend to live off-campus. Off-campus housing and personal expenses: approximately $12,700.

Enrollment: first-year class 274; total enrollment 802 (men 55%, women 45%). Faculty: full-time 32, part-time 18. Student to faculty ratio 20.7 to 1. Degrees conferred: J.D., J.D.-M.B.A., LL.M. (American Legal Studies, International Law)

ADMISSION REQUIREMENTS. LSDAS Law School report, bachelor's degree, transcripts, LSAT required in support of application. Graduates of unaccredited colleges not considered. Apply to Admissions Office after October 1, before April 15. Admits Fall only. Application fee $60. Phone: (516)463-5916; fax: (516)463-6264.

ADMISSION STANDARDS. Selective. Mean LSAT: full-time 155, part-time 152; mean GPA: full-time 3.35, part-time 3.15 (A = 4). Gourman rating: 4.20. *U.S. News & World Report* ranking is in the third tier of all U.S. law schools. Accepts about 20% of total annual applicants.

FINANCIAL AID. Scholarships, grants, full and partial tuition waivers, assistantships, Federal W/S, loans. Apply to University Financial Aid Office by June 1. Use FAFSA (School code: 002732). About 56% of students receive aid other than loans from School and outside sources.

DEGREE REQUIREMENTS. For J D.: satisfactory completion of three-year (87 credit hours) program. For J.D.-M.B.A.: 105–108 credit program; thesis/nonthesis option. For LL.M.: 24 credit hour, full-time, two-semester program; a part-time four-semester program is also available.

HOLLINS UNIVERSITY
Roanoke, Virginia 24020-1688
Web site: www.hollins.edu

Established 1842. Located 6 miles N of Roanoke. Coed at graduate level. Private control. Semester system. Library: 220,000 volumes, 6380 subscriptions.

Annual tuition: full-time $17,470, per credit varies by program. No on-campus housing for graduate students.

Graduate Programs

Enrollment: full-time 116, part-time 157 (men 20%, women 80%). Graduate faculty: full-time 46, part-time 27. Degrees conferred: M.A., M.A.L.S., M.A.T., C.A.S.

ADMISSION REQUIREMENTS. Transcripts, GRE Subject Tests required in support of School's application. On-line application avaiable. Interview not required. TOEFL required for international applicants. Transfer applicants, graduates of unaccredited colleges not considered. Apply to Office of Admissions by March 15, one month prior to registration for other sessions. Application fee $35. Phone: (540)362-6575; fax: (540)362-6288.

ADMISSION STANDARDS. Competitive. Usual minimum average: 3.0 (A = 4)

FINANCIAL AID. Scholarships, fellowships, grants, research fellowships, work stipends, Federal W/S, loans. Approved for VA benefits. Apply by April 15 to Chair of Graduate Council for scholarships, grants, fellowships; apply by July 15 to Financial Aid Office for all other programs. Phone: (540)362-6332; fax: (540)362-6093. Use FAFSA and Institutional FAF. All M.A. graduate students receive aid from College. About 50% of students receive aid other than loans from College and outside sources. Aid available for part-time students.

DEGREE REQUIREMENTS. For M.A., M.A.L.S., M.A.T.: 30 semester hours minimum; final oral/written exam; thesis/final document. For C.A.S.: 30 semester hours minimum beyond master's; special project.

FIELDS OF STUDY.
Children's Literature. Primarily a summer program. Four to five summer sessions for completion of degree requirements.
Classroom Technology Integration.
Creative Writing.
English. One language for M.A.
Liberal Studies. Interdisciplinary. M.A.L.S.
Psychology.
Social Science.
Screenwriting and Film Studies.
Teaching. At least three years of teaching experience required for admissions. M.A.T.

HOLY NAMES COLLEGE
Oakland, California 94619-1699
Web site: www.hnc.edu

Founded 1868. Private control. Roman Catholic. Semester system. Library: 111,062 volumes, 376 subscriptions.

Tuition: per credit $445. On-campus housing for single students only. Average academic year room and board cost: $6400. Apply to Director of Residents for off-campus housing information. Phone: (510)436-1292.

Graduate Programs

Graduate study since 1956. Enrollment: full-time 125, part-time 219 (men 10%, women 90%). College faculty teaching graduate students: full-time 23, part-time 33. Degrees conferred: M.A., M.S., M.M. in Mus. Ed., M.Ed., M.B.A.

ADMISSION REQUIREMENTS. Two transcripts, two letters of recommendation required in support of Divisional application. TOEFL required for international applicants. Interview and NTE required for Education, Clinical Psychology, Pastoral Counseling. Graduates of unaccredited colleges not considered. Apply to Graduate Admission Office at least six to eight weeks prior to registration. Application fee $35. Phone: (510)436-1317; fax: (510)436-1325.

ADMISSION STANDARDS. Selective. Minimum average: 2.6 cumulative, 3.0 in major (A = 4).

FINANCIAL AID. Annual awards from institutional funds: Scholarships, Kodaly grants, Federal W/S, loans. Apply to Director of Financial Aid by March 2. Phone: (510)436-1327. Use FAFSA. About 40% of students receive financial aid. Aid available for part-time students.

DEGREE REQUIREMENTS. For master's: 30–36 semester hours; thesis, project or final comprehensive exam, recital.

FIELDS OF STUDY.
Business Administration.
Counseling Psychology.
Culture and Spirituality.
Education.
English.
Music. Includes performance, piano pedagogy, music education with Kodaly emphasis; preliminary qualifying exam.
Nursing.
Pastoral Counseling.

HOOD COLLEGE

Frederick, Maryland 21701-8587
Web site: www.hood.edu

College founded 1895. Located 45 miles from Washington, D.C. CGS member. Private. Semester system. Library: 200,000 volumes, 6300 subscriptions.

Tuition: per credit hour $310. No on-campus housing available.

Graduate School

Enrollment: full-time 52, part-time 803 (men 40%, women 60%). Faculty: full- and part-time 90. Degrees conferred: M.A., M.B.A., M.S.

ADMISSION REQUIREMENTS. Transcripts, two letters of recommendation, statement of goals required in support of application. GMAT required for Business applicants. TOEFL required for international applicants. Interview recommended. Accepts transfer applicants. Graduates of unaccredited colleges not considered. Apply to Graduate Enrollment Manager. Application fee $30. Phone: (301)696-3600; fax: (301)696-3597; e-mail: hoodgrad@hood.edu.

ADMISSION STANDARDS. Selective. Usual minimum average: 2.5 (A = 4).

FINANCIAL AID. Scholarships, internships, tuition waivers, Federal W/S, loans. Phone: (301)696-3411. Use FAFSA (College code: 002076). Aid available for part-time students.

DEGREE REQUIREMENTS. For M.A., M.S.: 30–39 credit hours minimum; thesis required in some programs; comprehensive written exam. For M.B.A.: 36 credit hours minimum.

FIELDS OF STUDY.
Biomedical Sciences. Includes biotechnology/molecular biology, microbiology/immunology/virology, regulatory compliance. M.S.B.S.
Business Administration. Includes accounting, finance, human resource management, information systems, marketing, public management. M.B.A.
Computer and Information Sciences. Includes computer science, information technology. M.S.C.I.S.
Curriculum and Instruction. Includes early childhood education, elementary education, elementary school science and mathematics, reading specialist, secondary education, special education. M.S.C.I.
Educational Leadership. M.S.E.L.
Environmental Biology. M.S.E.B.
Human Science. Includes psychology. M.A.H.S.
Humanities. Includes general/experimental psychology, gerontology, helping relationships. M.A.H.
Management of Information Technology. M.S.M.I.T.
Thanatology. M.A.

UNIVERSITY OF HOUSTON

Houston, Texas 77004
Web site: www.uh.edu

Founded 1934. CGS member. Coed. State control. Semester system. Special facilities: Blaffer Gallery, Center for Critical Cultural Studies, Institute for Molecular Design, Institute for Public History, Center for Public Policy, Southwest Center for International Business, Space Vacuum Epitaxy Center, Center for Study of Issues Management, Texas Center for Superconductivity, Institute for Texas German Studies. Library: 2,100,000 volumes, 15,203 subscriptions; is a depository for U.S. and Texas government documents.

Annual tuition: full-time resident $1440, nonresident $5274; per credit, resident $80, nonresident (U.S. citizen) $293. On-campus housing for 2600 single students; for 200 married students. Average academic year housing cost: $5475 (including board) for single students; $8856 (including board) for married students. Contact Director of Housing for both on- and off-campus housing information. Phone: (800)247-7184. Day-care facilities available.

Graduate Division

Graduate study since 1939. Enrollment: full-time 4609, part-time 4158. Graduate faculty: full-time 588, part-time 337. Degrees conferred: M.A., M.S., M.S.A., M.B.A., M.Ed., M.M., M.Arch., M.S.Accy., M.S.A., M.S.Ch.E., M.Ch.E., M.S.C.E., M.C.E., M.S.E.E., M.E.E., M.H.M., M.S.I.E., M.I.E., M.S.M.E., M.M.E., M.F.A., M.S.Phar., M.S.O.T., Ed.D., Ph.D., D.M.A., O.D.

ADMISSION REQUIREMENTS. Two official transcripts, GRE/GMAT/MAT required in support of application. Interview required for some departments. Departmental applications in some cases. TOEFL required for international applicants. Accepts transfer applicants. Graduates of unaccredited colleges not considered. Apply to Director of Admissions; deadlines vary by Schools. Rolling admissions process. International applicants should apply to International Student Office by May 1. Application fees vary by Schools. Phone: (713)743-1010; fax: (713)743-9653; e-mail: admissions@uh.edu.

ADMISSION STANDARDS. Very competitive for some departments, selective for others. Usual minimum average: 3.0 for most departments, 2.6 for conditional admission to most departments (A = 4).

FINANCIAL AID. Annual awards from institutional funds: fellowships, assistantships, Federal W/S, loans. Approved for VA benefits. Apply by March 1 to appropriate department chair for assistantships, fellowships; to the Financial Aid Office for all other programs. About 20% of students receive aid from University and outside sources. Aid available for part-time students.

DEGREE REQUIREMENTS. For M.A., M.S.: 30 semester hours minimum, at least 24 in residence; qualifying exam; thesis, final exam; or 36 hours minimum, at least 27 in residence; qualifying exam; final comprehensive exam. For M.B.A.: 48 semester hours minimum, at least 27 in residence. For M.Ed.: 36 semester hours minimum, at least 27 in residence; comprehensive written exam; or 30 semester hours minimum, at least 24 in residence; written comprehensive exam; thesis; final oral exam. For M.M.: 30 semester hours minimum, at least 24 in residence; thesis; final oral exam. For M.S.O.T.: 30–36 semester hours; thesis. For M.F.A.: 60 semester hours; one year in residence; written and oral comprehensive exam. For M.S.W.: 63 semester hours. For Ed.D.: 66 semester hours minimum beyond the master's, at least 30 in residence and 24 consecutive hours in full-time attendance; qualifying exam; dissertation; final written/oral exams. For D.M.A.: 60 semester hours minimum beyond master's; four public performances, written and oral comprehensive exams; research document. For Ph.D.: two to four years beyond the master's, at least one year in full-time residence; reading knowledge of one or two foreign languages; comprehensive exam; dissertation; final oral exams.

FIELDS OF STUDY.

GERALD D. HINES COLLEGE OF ARCHITECTURE:
Architecture.

C. T. BAUER COLLEGE OF BUSINESS:
Accountancy. M.S.
Administration. M.S.
Business Administration. M.B.A.
Finance. M.S., Ph.D.
Management. Ph.D.
Management Information Systems. Ph.D.
Marketing. Ph.D.
Operations Research. Ph.D.
Statistics. Ph.D.
Taxation. Ph.D.

COLLEGE OF EDUCATION:
Allied Health Education and Administration.
Art Education.
Bilingual Education.
Counseling.
Counseling Psychology.
Curriculum and Instruction.
Early Childhood Education.
Educational Administration and Supervision.
Educational Psychology.
Educational Psychology and Individual Differences.
Elementary Education.
Exercise Science.
Gifted and Talented Education.
Health Education.
Historical, Social, and Cultural Education.
Higher Education.
Instructional Technology.
Kinesiology.
Mathematics Education.
Physical Education.
Reading and Language Arts.
Science Education.
Second Language Education.
Secondary Education.
Social Studies Education.
Special Education.

CULLEN COLLEGE OF ENGINEERING:
Aerospace Engineering.
Biomedical Engineering.
Chemical Engineering.
Civil Engineering.
Computer and Systems Engineering.
Electrical Engineering.
Environmental Engineering.
Industrial Engineering.
Materials Engineering.
Mechanical Engineering.
Petroleum Engineering.

CONRAD HILTON COLLEGE OF HOTEL AND RESTAURANT
MANAGEMENT:
Hospitality Management.

COLLEGE OF LIBERAL ARTS AND SOCIAL SCIENCES:
Accompanying.
Anthropology.
Applied Music.
Art. Includes interior design, graphic communication, painting, photography, sculpture.
Ceramics.
Communication.
Communication Disorders.
Composition.
Conducting.
Creative Writing.
Economics.

English.
French.
German.
History.
Literature and Creative Writing.
Mass Media Studies.
Music Education.
Music Literature.
Music Performance and Pedagogy.
Music Theory.
Organizational and Interpersonal Studies.
Philosophy.
Political Science.
Psychology.
Public Administration.
Sociology.
Spanish.
Speech Communication.
Theatre.

COLLEGE OF NATURAL SCIENCE AND MATHEMATICS:
Applied Mathematics.
Biochemical Sciences.
Biochemistry.
Biology. Includes evolutionary.
Chemistry. Includes analytical, biological, inorganic, organic, physical, theoretical.
Computer Science.
Geology.
Geophysics.
Mathematics.
Physics.

COLLEGE OF OPTOMETRY:
Optometry.
Physiological Optics.

COLLEGE OF PHARMACY:
Hospital Pharmacy and Pharmacy Administration.
Pharmaceutics.
Pharmacology.

GRADUATE SCHOOL OF SOCIAL WORK:
Social Work.

COLLEGE OF TECHNOLOGY:
Construction Management Technology.
Industrial Technology.
Manufacturing Systems Technology.
Microcomputer Systems Technology.
Occupational Technology. Includes industrial distribution.

Law Center (77204-6390)

Web site: www.law.uh.edu

Established 1974 as a College of Law. Located in metropolitan Houston. ABA approved since 1950. AALS member. Semester system. Full-time, part-time study. Law library: 501,862 volumes, 3850 subscriptions; has LEXIS, NEXIS, WESTLAW, DIALOG; is a Federal government Depository. Special facilities: Health Law and Policy Institute, Institute for Higher Education Law and Governance, International Law Institute, Trial Advocacy Institute. Special programs: Mexican Legal Studies Program.

Annual tuition: full-time resident $6690, nonresident $11,730. Limited on-campus housing available. Estimated living expenses $10,058.

Enrollment: first-year class 290 (241 day, 49 evening); total full- and part-time 938 (men 53%, women 47%); LL.M. total 120. Faculty: full-time 44, part-time 46. Student to faculty ratio 16.6 to 1. Degrees conferred: J.D., J.D.-M.B.A., J.D.-M.P.H.

(University of Texas, School of Public Health), J.D.-M.A. (History, Rice University), LL.M. (Energy, Environmental, and Natural Resources Law, Health Law, International Economic Law, Intellectual Property Law, Tax), LL.M. (Comparative Law for persons who have completed a basic legal education and received a university degree in law in another country).

ADMISSION REQUIREMENTS. LSDAS Law School report, bachelor's degree, transcripts, LSAT (not later than December) required in support of application. Interview not required. Accepts transfer applicants. Graduates of unaccredited colleges not considered. Apply to College after September 1, before February 15. Part-time students begin studies in summer only. Application fee $50. Phone: (713)743-1070.

ADMISSION STANDARDS. Selective. Mean LSAT: full-time 159, part-time 159; mean GPA: full-time 3.28, part-time 3.24 (A = 4). Gourman rating: 3.85. *U.S. News & World Report* ranking is in the second tier of all U.S. law schools. Accepts about 20–25% of total annual applicants.

FINANCIAL AID. Scholarships, teaching assistantships, Federal W/S, loans. Apply after acceptance, by April 1 to Financial Aid Office. Use FAFSA. About 40% of students receive aid other than loans from College. Aid available for part-time students.

DEGREE REQUIREMENTS. For J.D.: 88 semester credits minimum, at least 44 in residence. For LL.M.: 24 semester credits, 18 in residence (concentrations in Energy, Environmental, and Natural Resources Law; Health Law; Intellectual Property Law; International Law; Taxation Law).

UNIVERSITY OF HOUSTON, CLEAR LAKE

Houston, Texas 77058-1098
Web site: www.cl.uh.edu

Founded 1974. Located between Houston and Galveston, adjacent to NASA's Johnson Space Center. CGS member. Coed. State control. Semester system. Library: 405,797 volumes, 2200 subscriptions. Total University enrollment: 7500.

Tuition: per credit resident $120, nonresident $262. No on-campus housing available. Day-care facilities available.

Graduate Studies

Graduate study since 1974. Enrollment: full-time 1075, part-time 2554. Graduate faculty: full- and part-time 234. Degrees conferred: M.A., M.S., M.B.A., M.H.A., M.B.A.-M.H.A.

ADMISSION REQUIREMENTS. Two official transcripts, GRE/GMAT/MAT required in support of application. Interview required for some departments. Departmental applications in some cases. TOEFL (minimum score 550) required for international applicants. Accepts transfer applicants. Graduates of unaccredited colleges not considered. Apply to Office of Enrollment Services by August 1 (Fall), December 1 (Spring), May 1 (Summer); international applicants apply by June 1 (Fall), October 1 (Spring), March 1 (Summer). Some programs have earlier deadlines. Rolling admissions process. Application fees $35, $70 for international applicants. Admissions Office phone: (281)263-2517; fax: (281)283-2530.

ADMISSION STANDARDS. Selective for most programs. Usual minimum average: 2.75 (A = 4) for most departments.

FINANCIAL AID. Annual awards from institutional funds: scholarships, assistantships, Federal W/S, loans. Approved for

VA benefits. Apply by March 1 to appropriate department chair for assistantships; to the Financial Aid Office for all other programs. Use FAFSA. About 20% of students receive aid from University and outside sources. Aid available for part-time students.

DEGREE REQUIREMENTS. For M.A., M.S.: 30 semester hours minimum, at least 24 in residence; qualifying exam; thesis, final exam; or 36 hours minimum, at least 27 in residence; qualifying exam; final comprehensive exam. For M.B.A., M.H.A.: 36 semester hours minimum, at least 27 in residence.

FIELDS OF STUDY.

SCHOOL OF BUSINESS AND PUBLIC ADMINISTRATION:
Accounting. M.S.
Business Administration. Includes environmental management, international business, human resource management, management information systems, management of technology, studies of the future. M.B.A.
Environmental Management. M.S.
Finance. Includes health care administration. M.S.
Healthcare Administration. M.H.A.
Human Resource Management. M.A.
Management Information Systems. M.S.

SCHOOL OF EDUCATION:
Counseling. M.S.
Curriculum and Instruction. M.S.
Early Childhood Education. M.S.
Educational Management. M.S.
Instructional Technology. M.S.
Learning Resources. M.S.
Multicultural Studies in Education. M.S.
Reading. M.S.
School Library and Information Science. M.S.

SCHOOL OF HUMAN SCIENCES AND HUMANITIES:
Behavior Sciences. M.A.
Cross-Cultural Studies. M.A.
Family Therapy. M.A.
Fitness and Human Performance. M.A.
General Clinical Psychology. M.A.
History. M.A.
Humanities. M.A.
Literature. M.A.
Psychology. M.A.
School Psychology. M.A.
Sociology. M.A.
Studies of the Future. M.S.

COLLEGE OF NATURAL AND APPLIED SCIENCES:
Biochemical Sciences. M.S.
Chemistry. M.S.
Computer Engineering. M.S.
Computer Science. M.S.
Computer Information Systems. M.S.
Environmental Science. M.S.
Mathematical Science. M.S.
Physical Sciences. M.S.
Software Engineering. M.S.
Statistics. M.S.

HOWARD UNIVERSITY

Washington, D.C. 20059-0002
Web site: www.howard.edu

Founded 1867. CGS member. Private control. Howard participates in Joint Graduate Consortium with George Washington, Georgetown, and Catholic universities, the University of the District of Columbia, and three Associate Members (Gallaudet, Mount Vernon, and Trinity colleges). Founders Library for graduate students ranks among top 100 in the United States and Canada. Special facilities: Computer Center, Laser Chemistry Laboratory, Solid-State Electronics Laboratory, Center for Hypertension Control, 5 specialized research institutes, Cancer Research Center, Center for Sickle Cell Disease, modern 500-bed teaching hospital, 5-million-watt public educational television station (WHMM, Channel 32), 24-thousand-watt commercial radio station (WHUF-FM, 96.3 MHz), and the Moorland-Spingarn Research Center, which houses the world's most comprehensive collection of materials on Africa and persons of African descent. The University's NIH ranking is 138th among all U.S. institutions with 41 awards/grants worth $23,621,955. Library: 1,729,875 volumes, 1,453,000 microforms.

Annual tuition: full-time $11,590; part-time, per credit hour, $622. On-campus housing usually unavailable. Off-campus academic year cost: $12,700 (including board). Contact Supervisor of Off-Campus Housing. Phone: (202)806-5749.

Graduate School

Graduate study since 1919. Enrollment: full- and part-time 1200. Graduate faculty: full- and part-time 360. Degrees conferred: M.A., M.S., M.Eng., M.S.C.S., Ph.D.

ADMISSION REQUIREMENTS. Transcripts, GRE, three letters of recommendation, statement of intent required in support of School's application. On-line application available. TOEFL required for all international applicants. Interview not required. Transfer applicants accepted. Graduates from unaccredited institutions not considered. Apply to the Office of Student Relations and Enrollment Management by February 1 (Fall), October 1 (Spring), March 15 (Summer). Application fee $45. Phone: (202)806-7469/6800; fax: (202)806-4664; e-mail: hugsadmission@howard.edu.

ADMISSION STANDARDS. Selective. Usual minimum average: 3.0 (A = 4).

FINANCIAL AID. Scholarships, graduate assistantships, fellowships, teaching assistantships, traineeships, Federal W/S, loans. Apply by April 1 (Fall), February 1 (Clinical Psychology), November 1 (Spring), March 15 (Summer) to appropriate department for assistantships; to Financial Aid Office for scholarships and other financial aid programs. Use FAFSA. About 43% of students receive aid other than loans from University and outside sources. No aid for part-time students.

DEGREE REQUIREMENTS. For master's: 30 semester hours minimum, at least two semesters in residence; qualifying exam; admission to candidacy; thesis/nonthesis option; reading knowledge of one foreign language in some departments; demonstrated proficiency in expository writing; final/oral exam. For Ph.D.: 72 semester hours minimum beyond the bachelor's degree, at least four semesters in full-time residence (two of which are consecutive); reading knowledge of two foreign languages in some departments; qualifying exam; admission to candidacy; dissertation; final written/oral (defense) exam.

FIELDS OF STUDY.

African Studies. Includes development studies and public policy. M.A., Ph.D.

Anatomy. Includes cell biology, developmental biology, neuroanatomy & neurophysiology, gross anatomy/paleontology. M.S., Ph.D.

Art. Includes art history. M.A.

Atmospheric Science. Ph.D.

Biochemistry. Includes enzymology, metabolism, molecular biology, biochemical nutrition, clinical biochemistry. M.S., Ph.D.

Biology. Includes cell and molecular biology, ecological, environmental and systematic biology. M.S., Ph.D.

Chemical Engineering. M.S.

Chemistry. Includes analytical, biochemistry, inorganic, laser, organic, physical, theoretical. M.S., Ph.D.

Civil Engineering. Includes environmental and water resources engineering, structural and engineering mechanics, transportation systems engineering, geotechnical engineering. M.S.

Communication and Culture. M.A., Ph.D.

Communication Science and Disorders. Includes speech pathology, audiology (M.S. only). M.S., Ph.D.

Economics. Includes development economics, urban economics, monetary/fiscal economics, human resource economics. M.A., Ph.D.

Education. Includes counseling, school psychology, educational psychology, educational administration and policy, curriculum and instruction, human development. M.A., M.S. Ph.D.

Electrical Engineering. Includes antennas and microwaves, solid state electronics, control engineering and power systems, communications and signal processing (M.Eng.); communications and signal processing, applied microelectronics and solid state electronics, control engineering and power systems (Ph.D.). M.Eng., Ph.D.

English. Includes African American literature, American literature, Caribbean literature, British literature, literary criticism. M.A., Ph.D.

Genetics and Human Genetics. Includes biochemical and molecular genetics, cytogenetics, immogenetics, clinical genetics–genetic counseling. M.S., Ph.D.

History. Includes United States history, Africa, African diaspora, Latin American and the Caribbean, modern Europe (M.A. only). M.A., Ph.D.

Material Science and Engineering. Ph.D.

Mathematics. M.S., Ph.D.

Mechanical Engineering. Includes aerospace, applied mechanics, fluid and thermal sciences, CAD/CAM and robotics. M.Eng., Ph.D.

Microbiology. Includes immunology, molecular and cellular microbiology, microbial genetics, microbial physiology, pathogenic bacteriology, medical mycology, medical parasitology, virology. Ph.D.

Modern Languages and Literatures. Includes French, Spanish, Afro-Hispanic. M.A.

Nutritional Sciences. M.S., Ph.D.

Pharmacology. Includes cardiovascular, neurobehavioral, toxicology, biochemical, clinical. M.S., Ph.D.

Philosophy. Includes history of philosophy, philosophy of science, political, African, epistemology metaphysics. M.A.

Physical Education and Recreation. Includes exercise physiology, recreation and leisure studies, health education. M.S.

Physics and Astronomy. Includes astronomy/astrophysics, atomic/molecular physics, biophysics, condensed matter physics, magnetic/optical properties, laser/optical spectroscopy, theoretical physics, M.S., Ph.D.

Physiology and Biophysics. Includes neurophysiology, endocrinology and cellular physiology, cardiovascular physiology, pulmonary physiology, membrane biophysics, renal physiology. Ph.D.

Political Science. Includes American government and politics, public administration and public policy, comparative government, international relations, political theory, black politics and political economy. M.A., Ph.D.

Psychology. Includes clinical, developmental, experimental personality, social. M.S., Ph.D.

Social Work. Ph.D.

Sociology and Anthropology. Includes demography, medical sociology, sociology of aging, social control and deviance, social psychology, urbanization and developmental, race and ethnic relations. M.A., Ph.D.

Systems and Computer Sciences. Includes programming and languages, software engineering, graphics, artificial intelligence, fault-tolerant computing, systems design and analysis. M.C.S.

College of Dentistry

600 W Street, N.W. 20059

Organized 1881. Library: 85,000 volumes. Annual tuition: $14,085. No on-campus housing available. Off-campus housing cost: $13,675. Total average cost for all other first-year expenses: $5426.

Enrollment: first-year class 80 (men 55%, women 45%); total full-time 462, postgraduates 25. Faculty: 140. Degrees conferred: B.S.-D.D.S. (with Howard University's College of Liberal Arts), D.D.S.

ADMISSION REQUIREMENTS. AADSAS, transcripts, three letters of recommendation, DAT required in support of College's application. Applicants must have completed at least two years of college study. Apply to Dean after July 1, before March 1. Application fee $45. Phone: (202)806-0400.

ADMISSION STANDARDS. Competitive. Mean DAT: Academic 16, PAT 15; mean GPA: 2.98 (A = 4). Gourman rating: 4.04. Usual minimum average: 2.3 in sciences. Accepts about 20–25% of total annual applicants. Approximately 90% are District residents.

FINANCIAL AID. Limited scholarships, loans. Apply to Financial Aid Committee by July 1. Approximately 83% of needy students receive some aid from Institution. Phone: (202)806-0375. Use FAFSA (College code: 001448).

DEGREE REQUIREMENTS. For D.D.S.: satisfactory completion of 42-month program.

FIELDS OF POSTGRADUATE STUDY.
Oral and Maxillofacial Surgery. Certificate only.
Orthodontics. Certificate only.
Pediatric Dentistry. Certificate only.

College of Medicine

Web site: www.med.howard.edu

Organized 1868. Annual tuition: $18,070. Total average figure for all other expenses: $10,349. Very limited housing available. Contact Dean, Resident Life.

Enrollment: first-year class 106; total 415 (men 51%, women 49%). Faculty: full-time 240, part-time 350. Degrees conferred: M.D., M.D.-M.S., M.D.-Ph.D. The M.S. and Ph.D. are offered through the Graduate School.

ADMISSION REQUIREMENTS. AMCAS report, transcripts, letters of recommendation, MCAT required in support of application. Interview by invitation. Applicants must have completed at least three years of college study. Accepts transfer applicants. Does not have EDP. Apply to AMCAS after June 1, before December 15. Application fee $45. Phone: (202)806-6270; fax: (202)806-7934.

ADMISSION STANDARDS. Very competitive. Median MCAT: 8.0; median GPA: 3.10 (A = 4). Gourman rating: 3.30. Accepts 5% of total annual applicants. Approximately 5% are District residents.

FINANCIAL AID. Scholarships, fellowships, assistantships, HEAL, loans. Apply to Office of the Dean before May 1. Use FAFSA (College code: 001448). About 85% of students receive some aid.

DEGREE REQUIREMENTS. For M.D.: satisfactory completion of four-year program, at least the final two years in residence; passing of Step 2 USMLE. For M.S., Ph.D.: see Graduate School listing above.

FIELDS OF GRADUATE STUDY.
Anatomy.
Biochemistry.
Biology.
Chemistry.
Human Genetics.
Microbiology.
Pharmacology.
Physiology.

School of Law (20008)

Web site: www.law.howard.edu

Organized 1868. ABA approved since 1931. AALS member. Semester system. Law library: 281,366 volumes, 1707 subscriptions; has LEXIS, NEXIS, WESTLAW, CALI, OCLC, LEGALTRAC.

Annual tuition: $13,685. Total average annual additional expense: $15,959.

Enrollment: first-year class 140, total 390 (men 41%, women 59%). Faculty: full-time 20, part-time 16. Student to faculty ratio 16.2 to 1. Degrees conferred: J.D., J.D.-M.B.A., LL.M. (for foreign law graduates).

ADMISSION REQUIREMENTS. LSDAS Law School report, bachelor's degree, LSAT (GMAT for J.D.-M.B.A. program), transcripts, two letters of recommendation required in support of application. Applicants must have completed at least four years of college study. Accepts transfer applicants. Graduates of unaccredited colleges not considered. Apply to University Office of Admissions after September 1, before March 31. Application fee $60. Phone: (202)806-8008.

ADMISSION STANDARDS. Selective. Mean LSAT: 152; mean GPA: 2.97 (A = 4). Gourman rating: 2.87. *U.S. News & World Report* ranking is in the third tier of all U.S. law school. Accepts 30–35% of total annual applicants.

FINANCIAL AID. Scholarships, grants, Federal W/S, loans. Apply before March 1 to Chairman, Financial Aid Committee. Use FAFSA. About 50% of students receive aid other than loans from School.

DEGREE REQUIREMENTS. For J.D.: satisfactory completion of three-year program, 88 semester hours minimum. For LL.M.: at least 24 credit hours beyond J.D.; thesis.

School of Social Work

Organized 1945. Semester system. Tuition: full-time $11,590. Limited on-campus housing available. Contact Dean of Residence Life. Phone: (202)806-6131.

Enrollment: full- and part-time 358. Faculty: full-time 24, part-time 18. Degrees conferred: M.S.W., Ph.D.

ADMISSION REQUIREMENTS. Transcripts, three letters of recommendation required in support of School's application. On-line application available. TOEFL required for international applicants. Accepts transfer applicants. Apply to School by October 1 (Spring), February 1 (Fall). Application fee $45. Phone: (202)806-6450; fax: (202)387-4309.

ADMISSION STANDARDS. Selective. Usual minimum average: 2.5 (A = 4).

FINANCIAL AID. Very limited scholarships, fellowships, and graduate assistantships, federal grants. Apply to Financial Aid Office; no specified closing date. Use FAFSA. Phone: (202)806-2800.

DEGREE REQUIREMENTS. For M.S.W.: satisfactory completion of 60-hour program, at least 30 hours in residence. For Ph.D.: satisfactory completion of 48 semester credit hours beyond the master's; qualifying exam; comprehensive exam; dissertation; oral defense.

FIELDS OF PRACTICE.
Criminal Justice.
Displaced Persons.
Family and Child Welfare.
Mental Health.
Social Gerontology.
Social Work in Health Care Settings.

HUMBOLDT STATE UNIVERSITY

Arcata, California 95521-8299
Web site: www.humboldt.edu

Founded 1913. Located 300 miles N of San Francisco. CGS member. Coed. State control. Semester system. Special facilities: Arts Center, Marine Biological and Oceanography Station, Natural History Museum, Center for Indian Community Development, Center for the Resolution of Environmental Disputes, Lamphere Dunes, Schatz Tree Farm Experimental Forest, fish hatchery. Library: 900,000 volumes, 3169 subscriptions.

Tuition/fees: resident 0.–6.0 units $438, 7 or more units $753, nonresident $246 per semester unit. On-campus housing for graduate students. Average academic year housing cost: $6092 (including board) for single students. Apply to Director of Housing. Phone: (707)826-3451.

Graduate Studies

Enrollment: full- and part-time 480. Faculty teaching graduate students: 313. Degrees conferred: M.A., M.S., M.B.A., M.F.A.

ADMISSION REQUIREMENTS. Transcripts required in support of application. On-line application available. GRE Subject Tests for some departments; letters of recommendation for some departments. TOEFL required for international applicants. Interview not required. Accepts transfer applicants. Graduates of unaccredited institutions not considered. Call for application deadlines for individual programs. Application fee $55. Phone: (707)826-4402.

ADMISSION STANDARDS. Selective for most departments. Usual minimum average: 2.5 for last 60 credits (A = 4).

FINANCIAL AID. Annual awards from institutional funds: scholarships, research fellowships, teaching assistantships, research assistantships, Federal W/S, loans. Apply by March 1 to appropriate department or division chair for fellowships and assistantships; to Financial Aid Office for all other programs. Phone: (707)826-4321. Use FAFSA. About 25% of students receive aid other than loans from College and outside sources. Aid available for part-time students.

DEGREE REQUIREMENTS. For M.A., M.S., M.B.A.: 30 semester units minimum, at least 21 in residence; thesis/nonthesis option. For M.F.A.: 60 semester units, at least 42 in residence; creative project.

FIELDS OF STUDY.
Biology. M.A.
Business Administration. M.B.A.
Education. M.A.
English. Includes literature, teaching, or writing. M.A.

Environment and Community. M.A.
Environmental Systems. Includes environmental resource engineering, international development technology, math modeling. M.S.
Kinesiology. M.S.
Natural Resources. Includes fisheries, forestry, planning and interpretation, rangeland resources and wildland soils, wastewater utilization, watershed, wildlife. M.S.
Psychology. Includes academic research, counseling, school psychology. M.A.
Social Science. M.A.
Sociology. M.A.
Theatre Arts. M.F.A., M.A.

HUNTER COLLEGE OF THE CITY UNIVERSITY OF NEW YORK

New York, New York 10021-5085
Web site: www.hunter.cuny.edu

Founded 1870. Coed. Municipal control. Semester system. Special facilities: Brookdale Center on Aging, Center for AIDS, Drugs and Community Health, Center for Biomolecular Structure and Function, Center for Communication Disorders, Center for Occupational and Environmental Health, Center for Puerto Rican Studies, Urban Research Center. University libraries: 750,000 volumes, 2300 subscriptions. Total College enrollment: 20,000.

Annual tuition: resident $4350, per credit $185; nonresident $7600, per credit $320. No on-campus housing. Contact Graduate Housing Office for off-campus housing information. Phone: (212)481-4310.

Graduate School

Enrollment: full- and part-time 4500 (men 30%, women 70%). Graduate faculty: full-time 674, part-time 547. Degrees conferred: M.A., M.S., M.U.P., M.S.W., M.F.A., M.S.Ed., M.P.H., Advanced Certificate. The Ph.D. is offered through the University's Graduate Center.

ADMISSION REQUIREMENTS. Official transcripts, three letters of recommendation, GRE (Arts and Sciences areas) required in support of School's application. Interview required for some departments. TOEFL required for international applicants; TWE for some programs. Accepts transfer applicants. Graduates of unaccredited colleges not considered. Apply to Office of Graduate Admissions by March 1 (Fall), November 1 (Spring). Application fee $35. Phone: (212)772-4490; e-mail: admissions@hunter.cuny.edu

ADMISSION STANDARDS. Competitive for most departments, very competitive or selective for others. Usual minimum average: 2.75 (A = 4).

FINANCIAL AID. Scholarships, fellowships, assistantships for teaching/research, tuition waivers, traineeships, grants, Federal W/S, loans. Approved for VA benefits. Apply by April 1 to Office of Graduate Fellowships and Scholarships; to Office of the Dean of Humanities, Sciences, and Mathematics, or Social Sciences for assistantships; to the Office of Financial Aid for all other programs. Phone: (212)772-4820. Closing dates subject to change; consult Financial Aid Office for specific dates. Use FAFSA and CUNY FAF. No aid for part-time students.

DEGREE REQUIREMENTS. For master's: 30–45 semester hours minimum; reading knowledge of one foreign language normally required; thesis/nonthesis option; final comprehensive written exam for most departments.

FIELDS OF STUDY.
Administration and Supervision. Advanced certificate.
Anthropology. M.A.
Art. Includes history, studio, education. M.A., M.F.A.
Biochemistry. M.A.
Biological Sciences. M.A.
Communication Sciences. Includes speech pathology, audiology, speech, and hearing sciences. M.S.
Communications. M.A.
Creative Writing. M.F.A.
Dance, Drama, Music Therapy.
Economics. M.A.
Education. Includes elementary, reading, bilingual, gifted, foreign languages, health, secondary, guidance and counseling, reading, rehabilitation counseling, science, social sciences, special, speech and hearing, TESL (M.S.Ed.); secondary Education; biology (7–12), chemistry (7–12), physics (7–12) (M.A.).
English Literature. M.A.
Environmental and Occupational Health Science. M.S.
French. M.A.
Geography. M.A.
History. M.A.
Italian. M.A.
Mathematics. M.A.
Music. Includes composition, ethnomusicology, history, performance. M.A.
Nursing. Includes adult nurse practitioner, medical-surgical, psychiatric, administration, maternity–child health, gerontological practitioner, pediatric nurse practitioner, public and community health nursing. M.S.
Physical Therapy. M.P.T.
Physics. M.A.
Psychology. Includes clinical, developmental, experimental. M.A.
Public Health. Includes community health education, public health nutrition. M.P.H.
Social Research. M.S.
Social Work. M.S.W.
Spanish. M.A.
Theater. M.A.
Urban Affairs. M.A.
Urban Planning. M.U.P.

IDAHO STATE UNIVERSITY

Pocatello, Idaho 83209
Web site: www.isu.edu

Founded 1901. Located 165 miles N of Salt Lake City. CGS member. Coed. State control. Semester system. Library: 406,000 volumes, 1,355,000 microforms, 30 PCs in all libraries.

Annual tuition/fees: full-time, resident $4318, nonresident $10,558; per credit resident $189, nonresident $279. On-campus housing for 150 married and 1200 single students. Average academic year housing cost: $2730–$5000 for married students; $2850–$3140 (including board) for single students. Apply to Housing Office. Phone: (208)282-2120.

Graduate School

Enrollment: full-time 622, part-time 1401 (men 40%, women 60%). Graduate faculty: full-time 219, part-time 0. Degrees conferred: M.A., M.S., M.Ed., M.H.E., M.P.A.S., M.P.E., M.F.A., M.Coun., M.O.T., M.P.T., M.T.D., Ed.S., D.A., M.N.S., Ph.D., Ed.D., D.P.T.

ADMISSION REQUIREMENTS. Two transcripts, GRE/GMAT/MAT required in support of School's application. TOEFL (minimum score 550) required for international applicants. Interview not required. Accepts transfer applicants. Graduates from unaccredited institutions not considered. Apply to Office of Registrar and Admissions by July 1 (Fall), December 1 (Spring), May 1 (Summer). Some programs have earlier deadlines. Application fee $35. Phone: (208)282-2475; fax: (208)282-4529.

ADMISSION STANDARDS. Relatively open for most departments. Usual minimum average: 2.75 (A = 4), 35th percentile on at least one GRE subscore.

FINANCIAL AID. Annual awards from institutional funds: scholarships, teaching and research assistantships, fellowships, Federal W/S, loans. Approved for VA benefits. Apply by March 1 to appropriate department chair for fellowships and assistantships; to Financial Aid Office for all other programs. Use FAFSA. Phone: (208)282-2756, fax: (208)282-4231. About 60% of students receive aid other than loans from University and outside sources. Aid available for part-time students.

DEGREE REQUIREMENTS. For master's: 30–36 semester hours minimum, at least 22 in residence; reading knowledge of a foreign language for some departments; thesis/nonthesis options; final written/oral exam. For M.B.A.: 45 credit program; final oral exam. For M.Ed.: 33 credit program; thesis/field project/case study; final exam. For M.O.T.: 88 credit, 8 semester, full-time program; 4 clinical affiliations; professional project; practicum. For M.P.A.S. 72 credit full-time program; capstone experience. For M.T.D.: 30 credit program; thesis or practicum and research project. For M.Coun.: 48–64 credit program; practicum; internships. For M.P.H.: 47–50 credit program; internships; thesis or project. For Ed.S.: 30 semester hours beyond master's; project. For D.A.: 48 credits minimum beyond master's, at least 30 in residence; comprehensive exam; 2 supervised teaching internships; foreign language proficiency; professional project; final oral exam. For Ed. D.: 64 semester credits, at least 30 in residence; final program of study; comprehensive exam; dissertation; oral defense. For D.P.T.: 98 credit, three-year full-time program; 5 clinical affiliations; practicum; professional project. For Ph.D.: 72 credits minimum beyond bachelor's, at least 30 in residence; reading knowledge of a foreign language for some departments; qualifying exam; admission to candidacy; comprehensive exam; internships for some programs; dissertation; final oral exam.

FIELDS OF STUDY.

COLLEGE OF ARTS AND SCIENCES:
Anthropology. Thesis for M.A., M.S.
Art. One-person show for M.F.A.
Biology. Includes botany, zoology. M.S., M.N.S., D.A., Ph.D.
Chemistry. Combine B.S.-M.S. with entry at junior level.
Clinical Psychology. M.S., Ph.D.
English. Thesis for M.A., D.A.
General Experimental Psychology. M.S.
Geosciences. Includes environmental. M.S., M.N.S.
Mathematics. M.S., M.N.S., D.A.
Microbiology. M.S., Ph.D.
Physics. Includes health physics. M.S., M.N.S.
Political Science. M.A., M.P.A., D.A.
Sociology. Thesis for M.A.
Speech Communication. Includes organizational communication. M.A.
Theatre. M.A.

COLLEGE OF BUSINESS:
Business Administration. M.B.A.

COLLEGE OF EDUCATION:
Athletic Administration. M.P.E.
Child and Family Studies. M.Ed.
Curriculum Leadership. M.Ed.
Human Exceptionality. Includes special education. M.Ed.

Instructional Technology. M.Ed.
Literacy. M.Ed.
School Psychology. Ed.S.

COLLEGE OF ENGINEERING:
Engineering and Applied Science. Ph.D.
Engineering Structures and Mechanics. M.S.
Environmental Engineering. M.S.
Hazardous Waste Management. M.S.
Measurement and Control Engineering. M.S.
Nuclear Science and Engineering. M.S.

KASISKA COLLEGE OF HEALTH PROFESSIONS:
Audiology. M.S.
Counseling. Ed.S., Ph.D.
Counselor Education. Ph.D.
Deaf Education. M.S.
Health Education. M.H.E.
Health and Nutrition Sciences. M.H.E., M.P.H.
Marriage and Family Counseling. M.Coun.
Mental Health Counseling. M.Coun.
Nursing. M.S.
Occupational Therapy. M.O.T.
Physical Therapy. M.P.T.
Speech-Language Pathology. M.S.
Physician Assistant Studies. M.P.A.S.
School Counseling. M.Coun.
Student Affairs and College Counseling. M.Coun.

COLLEGE OF PHARMACY:
Pharmacy. Includes pharmaceutical chemistry, pharmacology, pharmaceutics, pharmacy administration. M.S.
Pharmaceutical Sciences. Includes biopharmaceutics, biopharmaceutical analysis, pharmacokinetics, pharmacology, pharmacy administration. Ph.D.

COLLEGE OF TECHNOLOGY:
Human Resource Training and Development. Includes technical program management, training management. M.T.D.

INTERDISCIPLINARY PROGRAMS:
Natural Science. M.N.S.
Waste Management and Environmental Science. M.S.

UNIVERSITY OF IDAHO
Moscow, Idaho 83844
Web site: www.uidaho.edu

Founded 1889. Located 85 miles SE of Spokane, Wash. CGS member. Coed. State control. Semester system. Special facilities: Cooperative Fishery Research Unit, Cooperative Park Studies Unit, Cooperative Wildlife Research Unit, Microelectronics Research Center, Institute for Molecular and Agricultural Genetic Engineering, Laboratory of Anthropology, Remote Sensing Research Unit, Graduate Center at Idaho Nuclear Engineering Laboratory, cooperative graduate course program and library usage exchange with Washington State University, Computer Center, Agricultural Experiment Station, Center for Business Development and Research, Bureau of Education Research and Service, Bureau of Mines and Geology, Bureau of Public Affairs Research, Engineering Experiment Station, Forest, Wildlife and Range Experiment Station, Materials Testing Laboratory, U.S. Forest Service, Intermountain Forest Sciences Laboratory, Water Resources Research Institute. Library: 1,400,000 volumes, 14,230 subscriptions.

Annual tuition fee: full-time, resident $3044, nonresident $9764; part-time per credit, resident $108, nonresident $198. On-campus housing for 276 married students, 1700 men, 1040 women. Housing cost: $7200 per year for married students, $6550 per year (including board) for single students. Apply to Director of Housing. Phone: (208)885-7961. Day care facilities available.

College of Graduate Studies

Graduate study since 1896. Enrollment: full-time 888, part-time 1240. University faculty: full-time 599, part-time 10. Degrees conferred: M.A., M.S., M.Arch., M.F.A., M.M., M.Ed., M.N.S., M.A.T., M.Acct., M.Engr., M.P.A., Ed.D., Ed.S., Ph.D.

ADMISSION REQUIREMENTS. Transcript required in support of College's application. GRE required by some departments. TOEFL required for international applicants. Interview not required. Accepts transfer applicants. Graduates of unaccredited colleges not considered. Apply to Admissions Officer by August 1 (Fall), December 15 (Spring). International application deadline: June 1 (Fall), December 1 (Spring). Application fee $35, $45 for international applicants. Phone: (208)885-6243; fax: (208)885-6198; e-mail: uigrad@uidaho.edu.

ADMISSION STANDARDS. Selective for most departments. Usual minimum average: 2.8 (A = 4). Some departments require higher GPA.

FINANCIAL AID. Annual awards from institutional funds: scholarships, research fellowships, teaching assistantships, research assistantships, tuition waivers, Federal W/S, loans. Apply by February 15 to appropriate department head for fellowships, assistantships; to Financial Aid Office for all other aid. Phone: (208)885-6312. Use FAFSA and institutional FAF. About 50% of students receive aid other than loans from University and outside sources. Aid available for part-time students.

DEGREE REQUIREMENTS. For M.A., M.S., M.Arch., M.F.A.: 30 credits minimum, at least 18 in residence; thesis; final oral exam. For M.Acct.: 30 credit program; internship; written comprehensive exam or thesis. For M.N.S.: 30 credits minimum, at least 22 in residence; final written exam. For M.M.: 30 credits minimum, at least 22 in residence; thesis, composition, or recital; final written exam. For M.B.A.: 30 credits; calculus and computer proficiency. For M.P.A.: 30 credits minimum, at least 18 in residence; comprehensive exam. For M.Engr.: 30 credits minimum; final document. For Ed.S.: 30 credits beyond the master's. For Ph.D.: 78 credits minimum beyond the bachelor's; at least one year in residence; preliminary exam; reading knowledge of one foreign language required by some departments; dissertation; final written/oral exam. For Ed.D.: essentially the same as for the Ph.D., except no language requirement.

FIELDS OF STUDY.
Accountancy. M.Acct.
Adult Education. M.S., M.Ed., Ed.S.
Agricultural Economics. M.S.
Agricultural Education. M.S.
Animal Physiology. M.S., Ph.D.
Animal Sciences. M.S.
Anthropology. M.A.
Architecture. M.Arch., M.A.
Art. M.A.T., M.F.A.
Biological and Agricultural Engineering. M.S., M.Engr., Ph.D.
Biological Sciences. M.N.S.
Botany. M.S., Ph.D.
Business Education. M.Ed.
Chemical Engineering. M.S., M.Engr., Ph.D.
Chemistry. M.S., M.A.T., Ph.D.
Civil Engineering. M.S., M.Engr., Ph.D.
Computer Engineering. M.S., M.Engr.
Computer Science. M.S., Ph.D.
Counseling and Human Services. M.S., M.Ed., Ed.S.

Creative Writing. M.F.A.
Curriculum and Instruction. M.S., M.Ed.
Earth Science. M.A.T.
Economics. M.S.
Education. Includes elementary, secondary, special education; business, administration, guidance and counseling, distributive. Ed.S., Ed.D., Ph.D.
Educational Leadership. M.S., Ed.S.
Educational Technology. M.Ed.
Electrical Engineering. M.S., M.Engr., Ph.D.
Elementary Education. M.S., M.Ed.
Engineering Management. M.Engr.
English. M.A., M.A.T.
Entomology. M.S., Ph.D.
Environmental Engineering. M.S., M.Engr.
Environmental Science. M.S.
Family and Consumer Sciences. M.S.
Fishery Resources. M.S.
Food Sciences. M.S.
Forest Products. M.S.
Forest Resources. M.S.
French. M.A.T.
Geography. M.S., M.A.T., Ph.D.
Geological Engineering. M.S.
Geology. M.S., Ph.D.
Geophysics. M.S.
German. M.A.T.
History. M.A., M.A.T., Ph.D.
Hydrology. M.S.
Industrial Technology Education. M.S., M.Ed.
Interdisciplinary Studies. M.A., M.S.
Landscape Architecture. M.S.
Mathematics. M.S., M.A.T., Ph.D.
Mechanical Engineering. M.S., M.Engr., Ph.D.
Metallurgical Engineering. M.S.
Metallurgy. M.S.
Microbiology, Molecular and Biochemistry. M.S., Ph.D.
Mining Engineering. M.S.
Mining Engineering–Metallurgy. Ph.D.
Music. Includes performance, history and literature, composition, applied; M.A., M.M.
Natural Resources. M.N.R., Ph.D.
Nuclear Engineering. M.S., M.Engr., Ph.D. (Idaho Falls only).
Physical Education. M.S., M.Ed.
Physics. M.S., M.A.T., Ph.D.
Plant Sciences. M.S., Ph.D.
Political Science. M.S., Ph.D.
Psychology. M.S.
Public Administration. M.P.A.
Rangeland Ecology. M.S.
Recreation. M.S.
Resource Recreation and Tourism. M.S.
School Psychology. Ed.S.
Secondary Education. M.S., M.Ed.
Soil Science. M.S., Ph.D.
Spanish. M.A.T.
Special Education. M.S., M.Ed., Ed.S.
Statistics. M.S.
Systems Engineering. M.Engr.
Teaching English as a Second Language. M.A.
Technology Education. M.Ed., M.S., Ed.S.
Theater Arts. M.F.A.
Veterinary Science. M.S.
Wildlife Resources. M.S.
Zoology. M.S., Ph.D.

College of Law

Established 1909. ABA approved since 1925. AALS member since 1925. Semester system. Library: 184,051 volumes, 3628 subscriptions; has LEXIS, NEXIS, WESTLAW, DIALOG.

Annual tuition: resident, no tuition charge, but mandatory fees $4416 per year, nonresident $10,416. On-campus housing available. Estimated living expenses: $14,820.

Enrollment: first-year class 112; total full-time 291 (men 68%, women 32%). Faculty: full-time 15, part-time 5. Student to faculty ratio 16.7 to 1. Degrees conferred: J.D., J.D.-M.B.A., J.D.-M.S. (Environmental Science).

ADMISSION REQUIREMENTS. LSDAS Law School report, bachelor's degree, transcripts, LSAT required in support of application. Interview not required. Preference given to state residents. Graduates of unaccredited colleges not considered. Apply to Admissions Officer after September 1, before February 1. Admits to Fall only. Application fee $40. Phone: (208)885-6423; fax: (208)885-5709.

ADMISSION STANDARDS. Selective. Mean LSAT: 152; mean GPA: 3.28 (A = 4). Gourman rating: 2.71. *U.S. News & World Report* ranking is in the third tier of all U.S. law schools. Accepts 50–55% of total annual applicants. Approximately 30% of first-year class are nonresidents.

FINANCIAL AID. Scholarships, assistantships, Federal W/S, loans. Apply by February 15 to Financial Aid Office. Phone: (208)885-6312. Use FAFSA (College code: 001626). About 24% of students receive aid other than loans from institutional funds.

DEGREE REQUIREMENTS. For J.D.: satisfactory completion of three-year program; 88 semester hours.

ILLINOIS INSTITUTE OF TECHNOLOGY

Chicago, Illinois 60616
Web site: www.iit.edu

Formed in 1940 by merger of Armour Institute and Lewis Institute. CGS member. Coed. Private control. Semester system with quarter courses. Special facilities: Center for the Study of Ethics and the Professions, National Center for Food Safety and Technology, Hazardous Waste Management Center, Center for Research on Industrial Strategy and Policy, Centers for Biotechnology, Energy Technology, Fluid Dynamics, Industrial Waste Elimination, Railroad Engineering. Library: 500,000 volumes, 177,000 microforms, 750 current periodicals. Total Institute enrollment: 6000.

Annual tuition: full-time $16,350; per credit $590. On-campus housing for 360 married graduate students, 132 graduate men, 45 graduate women. Average academic year housing cost: $7296 for married students, $5532 (including board) for single students. Contact Director of Housing for both on- and off-campus housing information. Phone: (312)567-5075.

Graduate College
Web site: www.grad.iitu.edu

Enrollment: full-time 1055, part-time 1416. Institute faculty: full-time 202, part-time 114. Degrees conferred: M.S., M.Arch., M.B.A., M.Ch.E., M.C.E., M.C.R.P., M.Met.E., M.M.E., M.P.A., Ph.D.

ADMISSION REQUIREMENTS. Transcripts, two letters of recommendation required in support of application. GRE/Subject Tests required in chemistry, psychology, electrical engineering. TOEFL required for international applicants. Interview not required. Accepts transfer applicants. Graduates of unaccredited institutions not considered. Apply to appropriate department by June 1 (Fall), November 1 (Spring). Deadlines for Architecture and Psychology are earlier. Rolling admissions process. Application fee $30. Phone: (312)567-3024; e-mail: gradstu@iit.edu.

ADMISSION STANDARDS. Very selective for most departments. Usual minimum average: 3.0 (A = 4).

FINANCIAL AID. Annual awards from institutional funds: scholarships, fellowships, teaching assistantships, research assistantships, internships, full or partial tuition waivers, Federal W/S, loans. Approved for VA benefits. Apply by March 1 to appropriate department chair for scholarships, fellowships, assistantships; to Director of Financial Aid for all other programs. Use FAFSA and institutional FAF. Phone: (312)567-3303. About 50% of students receive aid other than loans from Institute and outside sources. No aid for part-time students.

DEGREE REQUIREMENTS. For master's: 32–36 semester hours minimum; comprehensive exam; project; includes 6–8 hours for thesis (when required); final written/oral exam. For Ph.D.: usually 84–96 semester hours beyond the bachelor's, two semesters in full-time residence; foreign language proficiency for some programs; qualifying exam; comprehensive exam; dissertation; final oral exam.

FIELDS OF STUDY.
Applied Mathematics. M.S., Ph.D.
Architecture. Admits Fall only. M.Arch., Ph.D.
Architectural Engineering. M.S.
Biology. Includes biochemistry, microbiology, physiology. M.S., Ph.D.
Biomedical Engineering. Includes neural engineering, medical imagery, cell and tissue engineering. Ph.D.
Business Administration. GMAT for admission. Includes e-business, entrepreneurship, environmental management, financial management, information management, international business, management science, marketing, operations management, organization and management, quality management, strategic management. M.B.A.
Chemical Engineering. M.S., Ph.D.
Chemistry. One foreign language for Ph.D., M.S., M.C.E., Ph.D.
City and Regional Planning. Admits Fall only. M.C.R.P. only.
Civil Engineering. M.S., Ph.D.
Computer Engineering. M.S.Cp.E
Computer Science. M.S., M.C.S., Ph.D.
Construction Engineering and Management. M.S., Ph.D.
Design. Includes photography, product design, visual design. M.S., M.Des., Ph.D.
Electrical and Computer Engineering. M.E.C.E.
Electrical Engineering. M.S.E.E., Ph.D.
Electrical Markets. M.E.M.
Environmental Engineering. M.S., Ph.D.
Environmental Management. M.S.E.M.
Finance. M.S.F.
Food Processing Engineering. M.S.
Food Safety and Technology. M.F.S.
Geoenvironmental Engineering. M.S., Ph.D.
Geotechnical Engineering. M.S., Ph.D.
Information Architecture. M.S.
Management Science. Ph.D.
Manufacturing Engineering. M.M.E., M.S.M.E.
Manufacturing Technology and Operations. M.M.T.O.
Marketing Communication. M.S.M.C.
Materials Engineering. M.M.E.
Mathematics Education. M.S., M.S.E., M.M.E., Ph.D.
Mechanical and Aerospace Engineering. M.S., Ph.D.
Metallurgical Engineering. M.M.E.
Molecular Biochemistry and Biophysics. M.S., Ph.D.
Personnel and Human Resources Development. M.S.P.H.R.D.
Physics. M.S., Ph.D.
Psychology. Doctoral specializations: clinical, industrial/organizational, rehabilitation. M.S., Ph.D.

Public Administration. Includes specialization in public works. M.P.A.
Public Works. Includes infrastructure engineering and management. M.S.
Rehabilitation Counseling. M.S.R.C.
Science Education. M.S.S.E., Ph.D.
Structural Engineering. M.S., Ph.D.
Technical Communication and Information Design. M.S.
Telecommunications and Software Engineering. M.T.S.E.
Transportation Engineering. M.S., Ph.D.

Chicago-Kent College of Law (60661-36912)
Web site: www.kentlaw.com

Established 1887. In the late 1800s the Chicago College of Law and Kent College of Law merged to form Chicago-Kent College of Law. In 1969 Chicago-Kent College of Law became an integral part of IIT, in 1992 Chicago-Kent moved to its new quarters in downtown Chicago on Adams Street. ABA approved since 1951. AALS member. Semester system. Full-time, part-time study. Law library: 564,412 volumes, 9068 subscriptions; has LEXIS, NEXIS, WESTLAW, DIALOG, EPIC; is a Federal Government Depository. Special facilities: Global Law and Policy Institute, Institute for Science, Law, and Technology, Institute for Law and the Workplace, Chicago-Kent Institute for the Law and the Humanities, Center for Law and Computers. Special programs: Environmental and Energy Law, Intellectual Property Law, Labor and Employment Law.

Annual tuition: full-time $22, 950, part-time $16, 865; LL.M. $16, 865. Total average annual additional expense: $12,631.

Enrollment: first-year class full-time 314, part-time 210; total enrollment 1041 (men 49%, women 51%). Faculty: full-time 46, part-time 45. Student to faculty ratio 16.8 to 1. Degrees conferred: J.D., J.D.-M.B.A., J.D.-M.P.A., J.D.-LL.M. (Financial Services Law, Taxation), J.D.-M.P.H. (with the University of Illinois at Chicago), J.D.-M.S. (Financial Markets and Trading, Environmental Management), LL.M. (Tax and Financial Services), LL.M. (International and Comparative Law for persons who have completed a basic legal education and received a university degree in law in another country).

ADMISSION REQUIREMENTS. LSDAS Law School report, bachelor's degree, transcripts, LSAT, two letters of recommendation required in support of application. Minority and disadvantaged applicants encouraged to apply. Transfer applicants accepted from ABA-approved law schools only. Apply by March 1, rolling admissions process. Application fee $45. Phone: (312)906-5020; fax: (312)906-5274.

ADMISSION STANDARDS. Selective. Mean LSAT: full-time 155, part-time 153; mean GPA: full-time 3.23, part-time 3.14 (A = 4). Gourman rating: 3.83. *U.S. News & World Report* ranking is in the second tier of all U.S. law schools. Accepts 40–45% of total annual applicants.

FINANCIAL AID. Scholarships, grants, Federal W/S, loans. Apply to Financial Aid Office after acceptance, before April 15. Use FAFSA (College code: 001691) and institutional FAF. About 46% of students receive aid other than loans from the College and outside sources.

DEGREE REQUIREMENTS. For J.D.: 84 credits with a GPA of at least 2.0 (A = 4), plus completion of upper divisional writing course; three-year program, four-year program. Accelerated J.D. with one summer of course work. For J.D.-M.B.A.: up to course reduction: four-year program full-time, five-and-one-half-year program part-time. For J.D.-M.P.A.: up to 7 course reduction; four-year program full-time, five-and-one-half-year program part-time. For J.D.-M.S. (Financial Marketing): up to 7 course reduction; four-year program full-time, five-and-one-half-year program part-time. For J.D.-M.S. (Environmental Management): up to 9 course reduction; four-year program full-time, five-and-one-half-year program part-time. For J.D.-LL.M.: up to 6 credits may be used toward J.D.; one additional semester for LL.M. (full-time study). For LL.M. (Tax): 24 credits; a GPA of 2.5 (A = 4) required. For LL.M. (Financial Services): 24 credits; a GPA of 3.0 (A = 4) required; publishable paper. For LL.M. (International and Comparative Law): individually designed degree depending upon previous law degree and legal experience; one full year in residence.

ILLINOIS STATE UNIVERSITY

Normal, Illinois 61761-2000
Web site: www.ilstu.edu

Founded 1857. Located 130 miles S of Chicago. CGS member. Coed. State control. Semester system. Library: 1,900,000 volumes, 8915 subscriptions. Total University enrollment: 20,000.

Annual tuition/fees: full-time, resident $3840 (12 hours each semester), Fall, Spring semester, nonresident $7030; per credit resident $160, nonresident $286. On-campus housing for 292 married students, 125 single men, and 125 single women. Average academic year cost: $4936 for single. Apply to Office of Residential Life. Phone: (309)438-8611 or (800)366-4675. Day care facilities available.

Graduate School

Graduate study since 1943. Enrollment: full-time 983, part-time 1330. University faculty: full- and part-time 517. Degrees conferred: M.A., M.S., M.S. in Ed., M.M.Ed., M.F.A., M.B.A., M.P.A., M.S.N., S.S.P., Ed.D., Ph.D.

ADMISSION REQUIREMENTS. Two transcripts required in support of School's application. Applicants to degree programs must submit scores of GRE for some departments. Applicants to the Departments of Psychology and Sociology and Anthropology must submit scores on the GRE Subject Test in their field of study. Applicants for Business should submit the GMAT. Doctoral applicants must submit three letters of recommendation. TOEFL required for international applicants. Interview sometimes required. Accepts transfer applicants. Graduates of unaccredited institutions not considered. Apply to Office of Admissions at least three weeks (master's) or two months (doctoral programs) prior to registration. Application fee: none. Phone: (309)438-2181; fax: (309)438-3932; e-mail: ugradadm@ilstu.edu.

ADMISSION STANDARDS. Selective. Usual minimum average: 2.6 (A = 4).

FINANCIAL AID. Annual awards from institutional funds: scholarships, grants, fellowships, assistantships, teaching assistantships, internships, traineeships, tuition waivers, Federal W/S, loans. Approved for VA benefits. Apply by April 1 to Graduate Office for fellowships, to head of proposed major department for assistantships; to Financial Aid Office for all other programs. Phone: (309)438-2231; fax: (309)438-3755. Use FAFSA. About 60% of students receive aid other than loans from University and outside sources. No aid for students-at-large or part-time students with less than 5 hours in a degree-seeking program. Departmental tuition waivers are available to part-time students (in-state) on a limited basis.

DEGREE REQUIREMENTS. For master's: 32 semester hours minimum, at least 24 in residence and one semester in full-time attendance for selected majors; optional thesis for 4–6 hours, final oral exam; without thesis, final written exam; reading knowledge of one foreign language (for M.A.). For S.S.P.: 30 semester hours minimum. For Ed.D., Ph.D.: approximately 60 semester hours minimum beyond the master's; research project; final written/oral exam. Knowledge of two foreign languages for Ph.D., or approved substitute; approved alternate research tool for Ed.D. Residency requirements vary.

FIELDS OF STUDY.

COLLEGE OF APPLIED SCIENCE AND TECHNOLOGY:
Agribusiness. M.S.
Applied Computer Science. M.S.
Criminal Justice Sciences. M.A., M.S.
Environmental Health and Safety. M.S.
Family and Consumer Sciences. M.A., M.S.
Health, Physical and Recreation Education. M.S.
Industrial Technology. M.S.

COLLEGE OF ARTS AND SCIENCES:
Biological Sciences. M.S., Ph.D.
Chemistry. M.S.
Communication. M.A., M.S.
Economics. M.A., M.S.
English. M.A., M.S., Ph.D.
Foreign Languages. M.A.
Geohydrology. M.S.
History. M.A., M.S.,
Mathematics. M.A., M.S.
Mathematics Education. Ph.D.
Political Science. M.A., M.S.
Psychology. M.A., M.S.
School Psychology. S.S.P., Ph.D.
Sociology. M.A., M.S.
Speech Pathology and Audiology. M.A., M.S.
Writing. M.A., M.S.

COLLEGE OF BUSINESS:
Accounting. M.S., M.P.A.
Business Administration. Includes finance and law; management, quantitative methods, marketing. M.B.A.

COLLEGE OF EDUCATION:
Counselor Education. M.S., M.S. in Ed.
Curriculum and Instruction. M.S. in Ed., Ed.D.
Educational Administration. M.S., M.S. in Ed., Ed.D., Ph.D.
Reading. M.S. in Ed.
Special Education. M.S. in Ed., Ed.D.

COLLEGE OF FINE ARTS:
Art. M.A., M.S., M.F.A.
Arts Technology. M.S.
Music. M.M., M.M.Ed.
Theater. M.A., M.S., M.F.A.

COLLEGE OF NURSING:
Nursing. M.S.N.

UNIVERSITY OF ILLINOIS AT CHICAGO

Chicago, Illinois 60680
Web site: www.uic.edu

Created in 1992 by combining the resources and facilities of the two University of Illinois campuses in Chicago: the 20-year-old Chicago Circle and the Medical Center in existence for more than 100 years. CGS member. Coed. Public control. Semester system. Special facilities: Anatomy Museum, Institute for Humanities, Pathology Museum, Research and Educational Hospitals, Neuropsychiatric Institute, Molecular Biology Research Facility, Biologic Resource Laboratory, Electron Microscope Facility, Energy Resources Center, Engineering Research Facility, Environmental Stress Facility, Center for Urban Transportation, Center for Women's Studies, Institute for the Study of Developmental Disabilities, Survey Research Laboratory. The University's NIH ranking is 46th among all U.S. institutions with 337 awards/grants worth $99,719,484. Total University enrollment: 24,500. Library: 2,100,000 volumes, 20,800 subscriptions.

On-campus housing for single students only. Apply to Director of Housing for on-campus information to the Housing Listing Office, 704 CCC, 503 S. Halsted, Chicago, Illinois 60607-7014. Phone: (312)413-5418. Day-care facilities available.

Graduate College

Annual tuition/fees: full-time resident $7156; nonresident $15,138; M.A.S., M.B.A. tuition/fees full-time resident $12,156, nonresident $20,638; nursing tuition/fees full-time resident $10,156, nonresident $18,128.

Enrollment: full-time 2986, part-time 2480. Faculty: full- and part-time 1300. Degrees conferred: M.A., M.Arch., M.A.T., M.B.A., M.Ed., M.F.A., M.P.A., M.S., M.S.T., M.S.W., M.H.P.E., M.A.M.S., D.A., Ph.D.

ADMISSION REQUIREMENTS. Transcripts, three letters of recommendation, GRE/GMAT required in support of College's application. TOEFL required for international applicants. Accepts transfer applicants. Graduates of unaccredited colleges not considered. Apply to Office of Admissions by May 15 (Fall), November 1 (Spring), March 15 (Summer); international applicants March 15 (Fall), July 15 (Spring), December 15 (Summer). Some programs have earlier deadlines. Application fee $40, $50 for international applicants. Phone: (312)413-2550; email: gradcoll@ uic.edu.

ADMISSION STANDARDS. Competitive for most departments, selective for others. Usual minimum average: 2.75 (A = 4).

FINANCIAL AID. Scholarships, research assistantships, teaching assistantships, traineeships, tuition waivers, Federal W/S, loans. Approved for VA benefits. Special support programs exist for minority students. Apply by March 1 to appropriate departments for assistantships, scholarships; to Director of Financial Aid for all other programs. Use FAFSA and institutional FAF. Phone: (312)996-3126; fax: (312)996-3385.

DEGREE REQUIREMENTS. For most master's: 32 semester hours minimum; thesis/nonthesis option; language required for some departments. For M.Ed.: same as most master's programs except no thesis. For M.F.A.: 64 semester hours minimum in residence; written report required for majors in design, painting and printmaking, sculpture, art history; reading knowledge of one foreign language for art history majors. For M.P.A.: 54 semester hours minimum; no thesis. For M.S.W.: 60 semester hours minimum, three semesters in residence; field work experience. For M.H.P.E.: 32 semester hours minimum; thesis; final oral exam. For M.A.M.S.: 45–47 semester hours minimum. For D.A., Ph.D.: 96 semesters hours minimum beyond the bachelor's, at least three consecutive semesters in residence; preliminary exam; dissertation; final oral exam.

FIELDS OF STUDY.
Accounting. M.S.
Anatomy and Cell Biology. M.S., Ph.D.
Anthropology. M.A., Ph.D.
Architecture. M.Arch.
Art History. M.A., Ph.D.
Art Therapy. M.A.
Associated Medical Sciences. M.S., M.A.M.S.
Biochemistry and Biophysics. M.S., Ph.D.
Bioengineering. M.S., Ph.D.
Biological Chemistry. M.S., Ph.D.
Biological Sciences. Includes cell, developmental, evolutionary, microbiology, molecular, neurobiology, radiation. M.S., D.A., Ph.D.
Biomedical Engineering. Ph.D.
Biomedical Visualization. M.A., M.S.
Business Administration. M.B.A., Ph.D.
Chemical Engineering. M.S., Ph.D.
Chemistry. M.S., Ph.D.
Civil Engineering. M.S., Ph.D.
Communication. M.A.
Computer Science. M.S., Ph.D.
Criminalistics. M.S.
Criminal Justice. M.A.
Curriculum and Instruction. Ph.D.
Disability and Human Development. M.S.
Disability Studies. Ph.D.
Earth and Environmental Sciences. M.S.
Economics. Includes urban, quantitative, information and decision science. M.A., Ph.D.
Electrical Engineering and Computer Science. M.S., Ph.D.
Electronic Visualization. M.F.A.
Engineering. M.Engr.
English. M.A.
Environmental and Urban Geography. M.A.
Film/Animation/Video. M.F.A.
Finance.
French. M.A.
Forensic Science. M.S.
Genetics. Ph.D.
Geological Sciences. M.S.
Geotechnical Engineering and Geosciences. Ph.D.
German. M.A., Ph.D.
Graphic Design. M.F.A.
Health Informatics. M.S.
Health Professions Education. M.H.P.E.
Hispanic Studies. M.A., Ph.D.
History. M.A., M.A.T., Ph.D.
Human Nutrition. M.S., Ph.D.
Industrial Engineering. M.S.
Industrial Design. M.F.A.
Industrial Engineering and Operations Research. Ph.D.
Instructional Leadership. M.Ed.
Kinesiology. M.S., Ph.D.
Leadership and Administration. M.Ed.
Linguistics. M.A.
Management Information Systems. M.S., Ph.D.
Marketing. Ph.D.
Materials Engineering. M.S., Ph.D.
Mathematics. Includes applied. M.A., M.S., M.S.T., D.A., Ph.D.
Mathematics and Information Sciences for Industry. M.S.
Mechanical Engineering. M.S., Ph.D.
Medical Laboratory Sciences. M.S.
Medicinal Chemistry. M.S., Ph.D.
Microbiology and Immunology. M.S., Ph.D.
Molecular Biology. M.S., Ph.D.
Molecular Genetics. M.S., Ph.D.
Nursing. Includes maternity, adult health, administration, medical-surgical, pediatric, psychiatric, public health. M.S., Ph.D.
Occupation Therapy. M.S.
Oral Science. M.S.
Pathology. M.S., Ph.D.
Pharmacognosy. M.S., Ph.D.
Pharmacology. M.S., Ph.D.
Pharmacy. M.S., Ph.D.
Philosophy. M.A., Ph.D.
Photography. M.F.A.
Physical Therapy. M.S.
Physics. M.S., Ph.D.
Physiology and Biophysics. M.S., Ph.D.
Policy Studies in Urban Education. Ph.D.
Political Science. M.A., Ph.D.

Psychology. M.A., Ph.D.
Public Administration. M.P.A., Ph.D.
Public Health. M.P.H., Dr.P.H.
Public Health Sciences. M.S., Ph.D.
Public Policy Analysis. Ph.D.
Slavic Languages and Literature. Ph.D.
Slavic Studies. M.A.
Social Work. M.S.W., Ph.D.
Sociology. M.A., Ph.D.
Special Education. M.Ed., Ph.D.
Studio Arts. M.F.A.
Surgery. M.D. for admission. M.S.
Urban Planning and Policy. M.U.P.P.
Theatre. M.F.A.

College of Dentistry (60612-7211)

Founded 1898, became part of University of Illinois in 1913. Special program: Urban Health Program. Annual tuition: resident $10,902 nonresident $31,354. On-campus housing for single students only. Average academic year housing cost: $15,202. Total average cost for all other first-year expenses: $8200.

Enrollment: first-year class 65; total full-time 333 (men 50%, women 50%). Faculty: full-time 72, part-time 171. Degrees conferred: D.D.S., D.D.S.-M.S., D.D.S.-Ph.D.

ADMISSION REQUIREMENTS. AADSAS report, transcripts, DAT, recommendations required in support of application. Interview often required. Applicants must have completed at least two years of college study, preferably three years of study. Apply to Office of Admissions and Records after June 1, before February 1. Application fee $40. Phone: (312)996-2873.

ADMISSION STANDARDS. Selective. Mean DAT: Academic 18.7, PAT 18; mean GPA: 3.27 (A = 4). Gourman rating: 4.72. Usual minimum average: 2.75. Accepts 60% of total annual applicants. Approximately 85% are state residents.

FINANCIAL AID. Scholarships, research scholarships, grants-in-aid, DEAL, HEAL, loans. Apply to Office of Student Financial and Services of Health Science Center; no specified closing date. Phone: (312)996-5563/4940. Use FAFSA (College code: 001776). About 68% of students receive some aid from College.

DEGREE REQUIREMENTS. For D.D.S.: satisfactory completion of forty-five-month program. The D.D.S.-M.S. program can normally be completed during four-year period.

FIELDS OF GRADUATE STUDY.
Endodontics.
General Dentistry.
Oral Pathology.
Oral Surgery.
Orthodontics.
Pediatric Dentistry.
Periodontics.

College of Medicine (60612-7302)

Founded 1881. College of Medicine has campuses at Urbana-Champaign, Peoria, Rockford. There are two separate curriculum tracks within the College of Medicine. Students assigned to the Chicago campus will pursue their full four-year program of medical education under the supervision of the faculty at that site. Students assigned for their first year of instruction to the Urbana-Champaign campus either will remain assigned to the site for the last three years or will transfer to Peoria or Rockford for the remaining years of the program

Annual tuition: resident $17,644, nonresident $41,420 Total average figure for all other expenses $12,500.

Enrollment: first-year class 317 (approximately 75–80 students enter UIC), total full-time 1451 (men 66%, women 34%). Faculty and volunteers: about 4000 at all four campuses. On-campus housing for 132 single students; none for married students. Average annual housing cost: $6500 for single students. Contact Housing Office, Medical Center. Phone: (312)413-5418. Degrees conferred: M.D., M.D.-M.S., M.D.-Ph.D.

ADMISSION REQUIREMENTS. AMCAS report, transcripts, letters of recommendation, MCAT required in support of application. Interview may be requested. Preference given to state students. Applicants must have completed bachelor's or equivalent. Has EDP for state residents only; apply between June 1 and August 1. Apply to Office of Admissions and Records after June 1, before December 15. Application fee $40. Phone: (312)996-5635; fax: (312)996-6693.

ADMISSION STANDARDS. Competitive. Mean MCAT: 9.7; mean GPA: 3.48 (A = 4). Gourman rating: 4.41. Accepts 10–15% of total annual applicants. Approximately 90% are state residents.

FINANCIAL AID. Scholarships, awards, HEAL, NIH stipends, loans. About 17% of students receive aid other than loans from College funds. Apply to Office of Student Affairs by July 1. Phone: (312)413-0127. Use FAFSA (College code: 001776).

DEGREE REQUIREMENTS. For M.D.: satisfactory completion of four-year program. For M.S., Ph.D. requirements refer to Graduate College listing above.

FIELDS OF GRADUATE STUDY.
Anatomy and Cell Biology.
Biochemistry.
Biomedical Engineering.
Biophysics.
Genetics.
Health Professions Education.
Immunology.
Microbiology.
Molecular Biology.
Molecular Genetics.
Pathology.
Pharmacology.
Physiology.

UNIVERSITY OF ILLINOIS AT SPRINGFIELD

Springfield, Illinois 62794-9243
Web site: www.uis.edu

Established 1969 as Sangamon State University, became part of University of Illinois in 1995. Located 100 miles NE of St. Louis. CGS member. Coed. State control. Semester system. Library: 512,000 volumes, 2200 subscriptions. Total University enrollment: 4288.

Tuition: resident per credit $112, nonresident $336. On-campus housing for both single and married students. Average academic year housing cost: $1350–$5000 for single students; $3850 for married students. Apply to Housing Office. Day-care facilities available.

Graduate Studies

Enrollment: full-time 317, part time 1507. Faculty: full-time 164, part-time 79. Degrees conferred: M.A., M.S., M.B.A., M.P.A., M.P.H., D.P.A.

ADMISSION REQUIREMENTS. Transcript required in support of College's application. GRE/MAT/GMAT/recommendations/interview/writing exam required by some departments. TOEFL required for international applicants. Accepts transfer applicants. Graduates of unaccredited institutions not considered. Apply to Office of Enrollment Services at least three months in advance of registration, international applicants at least six months in advance of registration. Application fee: none. Phone: (800)252-8533, (217)206-6626; fax: (217)206-6720.

ADMISSION STANDARDS. Competitive for most departments. Usual minimum average: 2.5 (A = 4); 3.25 for D.P.A.

FINANCIAL AID. Annual awards from institutional funds: scholarships, fellowships, teaching assistantships, research assistantships, internships, grants, tuition waivers, Federal W/S, loans. Approved for VA benefits. Apply by June 1 to appropriate department head for fellowships, assistantships; for other aid programs apply to Office of Financial Assistance. Use FAFSA. About 20% of students receive aid other than loans from University and outside sources. Aid available for part-time students.

DEGREE REQUIREMENTS. For M.A.: 36 credit program; thesis/project/exam. For M.B.A.: 51–60 credit program depending on previous degree. For M.P.A.: 40–48 credit program; no thesis. For M.P.H.: 48 credit program; internships; comprehensive exam. For M.S.: 36 credit program: thesis/project. For D.P.A.: 66 credit program beyond master's, 20 credit concentration; qualifying exam; admission to candidacy, dissertation; oral defense.

FIELDS OF STUDY
Accountancy.
Biology.
Business Administration.
Communication.
Computer Science.
Educational Leadership.
English.
Environmental Studies.
History.
Human Development Counseling.
Human Services.
Individual Option.
Legal Studies.
Management Information Systems.
Political Science. Includes practical politics, international affairs.
Public Administration. Includes concentrations in community arts management, criminal justice (M.P.A.); nonprofit management, state government (D.P.A.). M.P.A., D.P.A.
Public Affairs Reporting.
Public Health.

UNIVERSITY OF ILLINOIS AT URBANA-CHAMPAIGN
Urbana-Champaign, Illinois 61820
Web site: www.uiuc.edu

Founded 1967. Located 125 miles S of Chicago. CGS and AAU member. Coed. State control. Semester system. Special facilities: Beckman Institution for Advanced Science and Technology, Biotechnology Center, Center for Advanced Construction Technology, Center for African Studies, Center for Latin American and Caribbean Studies, Center for Russian and East European Studies, Center for Complex System Research, Center for Cement Composite Materials, Center for Composite Materials Research, Center for Compound Semiconductor Microelectronics, Center for East Asian and Pacific Studies, Center for South and West Asian Studies, Center for the Study of Reading, National Center for Supercomputing Applications, Illinois Electron Paramagnetic Research Center, Institute for Environmental Studies, Krannert Art Museum, World Heritage Museum. The University's NIH ranking is 93rd among all U.S. institutions with 183 awards/grants worth $43,016,668. Library (third-largest university library): 9,500,000 volumes, 90,000 subscriptions. Total University enrollment: 36,100.

Annual tuition fees: full-time, resident $7156, nonresident $15,138. On-campus housing: 750 married student apartments; 1000 graduate dormitory rooms (mixed sex). Average academic year housing cost: $4000–$5500 (plus utilities) for married students, $5844 (including board) for single students. Apply to Division of Housing. Phone: (217)333-5656 (on-campus information), (217)333-1420 (off-campus information).

Graduate College

Graduate study since 1867. Enrollment: full-time 8109, part-time 135. Graduate teaching faculty: full- and part-time 1900. Degrees conferred: A.M., M.S., M.A.S., M.Arch., M.F.A., M.B.A., Ed.M., M.L.A., LL.M., M.C.S., M.M., M.Ext.Ed., M.S.B.A., M.S.W., M.U.P., A.C.Ed., C.A.S., Ed.D., D.M.A., Ph.D.

ADMISSION REQUIREMENTS. Transcript required in support of College's application. GRE/MAT/GMAT/recommendations/interview required by some departments. TOEFL required for international applicants. Accepts transfer applicants. Graduates of unaccredited institutions not considered. Apply to Office of Admissions and Records at least three months in advance of registration, international applicants at least six months in advance of registration. Application fee $40 domestic students, $50 international students. Phone: (217)333-0302.

ADMISSION STANDARDS. Competitive for most departments. Usual minimum average: 3.0 (A = 4).

FINANCIAL AID. Annual awards from institutional funds: academic tuition scholarships, fellowships, administrative assistantships, teaching assistantships, research assistantships, grants, traineeships, tuition waivers, Federal W/S, loans. Approved for VA benefits. Apply by February 15 to appropriate department head for fellowships, assistantships; for other aid programs apply to Office of Financial Aid. Phone: (217)333-0100. Use FAFSA. About 65% of students receive aid other than loans from University and outside sources. Aid available on a limited basis for part-time students.

DEGREE REQUIREMENTS. One unit = 4 semester hours. For most master's: 8 units minimum, at least 4 units in residence; thesis/nonthesis option; language required for some departments. For M.A.S., Ed.M.: same as for most master's, except no thesis requirement. For M.M.: same as for most master's, except reading knowledge of one foreign language for musicology majors. For M.F.A.: 16 units minimum in residence; written report required for majors in design, painting and printmaking, sculpture, art history; no thesis for A.M. in Art Education; reading knowledge of one foreign language for art history majors. For M.B.A.: 18 units minimum; no thesis. For LL.M.: 8 units minimum, at least 2 for research; thesis. For M.S.W.: 16 months in residence and field work. For M.U.P.: normally 2 years in residence; thesis. For A.C.Ed.: 8 units beyond the master's, at least 4 in residence. For Ph.D.: 24 units minimum beyond the bachelor's, at least 16 in residence; departmental qualifying exam; preliminary exam; teaching experience; dissertation; final oral exam. For Ed.D.: essentially the same as for the Ph.D. For D.M.A.: essentially the same as for the Ph.D., except special performance or composition projects in addition to dissertation.

FIELDS OF STUDY.
Accounting.
Advertising. M.S. only.

Aeronautical and Astronautical Engineering.

African Studies.

Agricultural and Consumer Economics.

Agricultural Education. M.S.

Agricultural Engineering.

American Civilization.

Animal Biology.

Animal Sciences.

Anthropology.

Architecture. Portfolio for admission. M.Arch. only.

Arms Control, Disarment, and International Security.

Art and Design. Includes applied, creative, art education, art history, graphic design; portfolio for admission to creative majors; Ed.D. in art education; Ph.D. in art history.

Astronomy. Includes astrophysics.

Atmospheric Sciences.

Biochemistry.

Bioengeering.

Biology. Interdepartmental.

Biophysics and Computational Biology.

Business Administration.

Cell and Structural Biology.

Ceramic Engineering.

Chemical Engineering.

Chemical Physics.

Chemistry. Includes biophysical chemistry.

Civil and Environmental Engineering.

Classics. Includes Latin, Greek, classics; Ph.D. in classical philology only.

Communications. Ph.D.

Community Health.

Comparative Literature. Interdepartmental.

Computer Science and Engineering.

Computer Science.

Crop Sciences.

Dance. Performance; M.F.A. only.

East Asian Languages and Culture.

Ecology.

Economics. GRE for admission; thesis optional for A.M., M.S.

Education. Includes elementary, secondary teaching; administration and supervision, adult curriculum, exceptional children, bilingual education, educational psychology, early childhood teaching, reading research, guidance and counseling, rehabilitation counseling, educational policy studies, history and philosophy, measurement and evaluation, research methods, school psychology; vocational and technical education; all subject fields; thesis for A.M., M.S.

Electrical and Computer Engineering.

English. One language for A.M.; thesis optional.

English as International Language. A.M. only.

Entomology. Thesis required for M.S.

Finance. Eight units with thesis or ten units without thesis for master's.

Food Science and Human Nutrition.

French.

General Engineering. M.S. only.

Genetics. Interdepartmental; Ph.D. only.

Geography.

Geology.

Germanic Languages and Literatures. Thesis, one language in addition to German for A.M.; two additional languages for Ph.D.

Government and Policy Affairs.

History. One language for A.M.

Human and Community Development. M.S. or A.M. only; thesis optional.

Journalism. Thesis or special project for M.S.; M.S. only.

Kinesiology. GRE, MAT for admission; thesis for M.S.

Labor and Industrial Relations. Eight units with thesis, 10 units without thesis for M.S.

Landscape Architecture. Twelve units for M.L.A.; M.L.A. only.

Latin American and Caribbean Studies.

Law. J.D. admission.

Leisure Studies.

Library and Information Science. GRE for admission; 10 units required for M.S.

Linguistics. One language, final essay for A.M.

Materials Science and Engineering.

Mathematics. Includes applied, statistics.

Mechanical and Industrial Engineering.

Microbiology.

Molecular and Integrative Physiology.

Music. Includes performance, musicology, music education, composition; qualifying exam for admission, including performance when appropriate; one language for M.M. in musicology.

Natural Resources and Environmental Science.

Neuroscience.

Nuclear, Plasma, and Radiological Engineering.

Nutritional Science.

Philosophy. GRE for admission; essay for A.M.

Physics.

Plant Biology.

Political Science. Thesis or research paper for A.M.

Psychology. GRE for admission; thesis for A.M.

Romance Linguistics.

Russian and East European Studies.

Second Language Acquistion and Teacher Education.

Slavic Languages and Literatures.

Social Work.

Sociology. GRE for admission.

Spanish, Italian, and Portuguese. A.M., Ph.D. in all three languages.

Speech and Hearing Science. Includes education of the deaf.

Speech Communication. GRE for admission; thesis for A.M.

Statistics.

Theater.

Theoretical and Applied Mechanics.

Urban and Regional Planning. Thesis or master's project required; 12–13½ units for M.U.P.; Ph.D. in regional planning.

Veterinary Medical Science. Includes veterinary biosciences, clinical medicine, pathology, and hygiene; D.V.M. or appropriate B.S. for admission.

Women's Studies.

Writing Studies.

College of Law

Established 1897. ABA approved since 1923. AALS member. Semester system. Law library: 709,673 volumes, 8435 subscriptions; has LEXIS, NEXIS, WESTLAW.

Annual tuition: resident $10,286, nonresident $22,280. Total average annual additional expense: $10,742.

Enrollment: first-year class 220; total full-time 638 (men 60%, women 40%); postgraduates 25; no part-time study. Faculty: full-time 34, part-time 28. Student to faculty ratio 15.6 to 1. Degrees conferred: J.D., J.D.-M.D., J.D.-M.Acc., J.D.-M.B.A., J.D.-M.A. (Labor and Industrial Relations, Urban Planning), J.D.-M.Ed., J.D.-Ed.D., J.D.-M.S. (Journalism, Chemistry, Natural Resources, and Environmental Sciences). The LL.M., J.S.D. are offered through the Graduate College.

ADMISSION REQUIREMENTS. LSDAS Law School report, bachelor's degree, transcripts, LSAT required in support of application. Interview not required. Accepts transfer applicants. Apply to Admission Office of the College by March 15 (preference given to applications received by January 15). Admits first-year students Fall only. Application fee $40. Phone: (217)244-6415.

ADMISSION STANDARDS. Selective. Mean LSAT: 161; mean GPA: 3.4 (A = 4). Gourman rating: 4.33. *U.S. News & World Report* ranking is in the top 25 of all U.S. law schools. Accepts 30–35% of total annual applicants.

FINANCIAL AID. Scholarships, fellowships, assistantships, full and partial tuition waiver, loans. Apply to Financial Aid Office, preferably by March 15. Use FAFSA. Graduate students apply through Graduate College and use University FAF. About 50% of students receive aid other than loans from College.

DEGREE REQUIREMENTS. For J.D.: 90 hours minimum, at least 6 semesters in full-time residence. Transfer credit from other law schools individually considered. For LL.M.: at least 2 semesters beyond J.D. For J.S.D.: first professional degree required; 16 courses, individually arranged. Refer to Graduate College listings for joint degree requirements.

College of Veterinary Medicine

Established 1944. Annual tuition: resident $10,090, nonresident $24,822. Total average cost for other expenses: $7842.

Enrollment: first-year class 104; total full-time 480 (men 35%, women 65%); no part-time students; graduate students 100. Faculty: full-time more than 100. Degrees conferred: D.V.M., D.V.M.-Ph.D., D.V.M.-J.D. The Ph.D. is offered through the Graduate College.

ADMISSION REQUIREMENTS. VMCAS report, transcripts, GRE, essay, animal/veterinary experience, three recommendations (one from an academic adviser) required in support of application. Interview by invitation only. Applicants must have completed at least two years of college study. Preference given to residents and to nonresidents from states that do not have veterinary schools. Apply to Assistant Dean after August 15 but before October 1 for nonresidents, by December 15 for residents. Fall admission only. Application fee $40, $50 for international applicants. Phone: (217)333-1192; e-mail: admissions@cvm.uiuc.edu.

ADMISSION STANDARDS. Selective. Mean GPA for an interview: 3.67 (A = 4). Accepts 45% of total annual applicants. 20–30% nonresidents are offered admission each year.

FINANCIAL AID. Scholarships, research fellowships, teaching/research assistantships, full and partial tuition waivers, loans. Apply to University Office of Student Financial Aid by January 15. Use FAFSA.

DEGREE REQUIREMENTS. For D.V.M.: 153 semester hours in full-time residence. For M.S., Ph.D.: see Graduate College listing above.

FIELDS OF GRADUATE STUDY.
Veterinary Biosciences. Includes physiology, pharmacology, toxicology.
Veterinary Clinical Sciences.
Veterinary Pathobiology.

UNIVERSITY OF THE INCARNATE WORD
San Antonio, Texas 78209
Web site: www.iwtx.edu

Founded 1881. Coed. Private control—Catholic. Semester system. Library: 235,000 volumes, 3436 subscriptions.

Tuition: per credit $445. On-campus housing for graduate men and women. Annual academic year housing cost: $4870 (including board). Apply to Director of Campus Life. Phone: (210)829-6034.

School of Graduate Studies and Research

Graduate study since 1950. Enrollment: full-time 133, part-time 566. School faculty: full-time 52, part-time 24. Degrees conferred: M.A., M.S., M.B.A., M.S.N., M.Ed.

ADMISSION REQUIREMENTS. Transcripts, GRE/MAT/GMAT required in support of application. Interview required for some disciplines. TOEFL required for foreign applicants. Accepts transfer applicants. Graduates of unaccredited colleges usually not considered. Apply to Admissions Office at least six weeks prior to registration. Application fee $20. Phone: (210)829-6005; fax: (210)829-3921.

ADMISSION STANDARDS. Selective. Usual minimum average: 2.5 (3.0 in major) (A = 4).

FINANCIAL AID. Annual awards from institutional funds: fellowships, research assistantships, administrative assistantships, internships, traineeships, Federal W/S, loans. Approved for VA benefits. Apply to the Financial Aid office; no specified closing date. Phone: (210)829-6008. Use FAFSA and institutional FAF. Aid available for part-time students.

DEGREE REQUIREMENTS. For M.A., M.Ed., M.S., M.S.N.: 36 credit hours minimum, at least 24 in residence; thesis/nonthesis option. For M.B.A.: 48 credit hours minimum, at least 36 in residence (specific undergraduate prerequisites required).

FIELDS OF STUDY.
Administration. Includes sports management, international administration, organizational development.
Biology.
Business Administration. Joint M.B.A.-M.S.N. program.
Communication Arts.
Education. Includes reading, special, educational diagnostician, deaf education, curriculum, teaching, instructional technology, international education, organizational learning, physical education, early childhood, adult.
English.
Mathematics.
Multidisciplinary Sciences.
Multidisciplinary Studies.
Nursing. Joint M.S.N.-M.B.A. program.
Nutrition.
Religious Studies.
Social Gerontology.
Sports Management.

INDIANA STATE UNIVERSITY
Terre Haute, Indiana 47809-1401
Web site: www.indstate.edu

Founded 1865. Located 170 miles S of Chicago. CGS member. Coed. State control. Semester system. Special facilities: Biotech Center, Center for Governmental Studies, Hearing Disorder Center, Porter School Psychology Center, Special Education Center, Speech Pathology Center, Technology Services Center, Turman Art Gallery, Center for Urban-Regional Studies. Library: 1,000,000 volumes, 5000 subscriptions.

Tuition: per credit, resident $154, nonresident $351. On-campus housing for 393 married students, limited number of graduate men, women. Average academic year housing cost: $340–$550 per month for married students, $4603 for single students. Apply to Director, University Housing. Phone: (812)237-7697. Daycare facilities available.

School of Graduate Studies

Graduate study since 1927. Enrollment: full-time 692 (men 353, women 339); part-time 948. University faculty teaching graduate students: full-time 343, part-time 12. Degrees conferred: M.A., M.M., M.M.E., M.S., M.B.A., M.P.A., M.F.A., Ed.S., Ph.D., Psy.D.

ADMISSION REQUIREMENTS. Transcript required in support of School's application. Interview required for all Ph.D. applicants. GRE required for some M.A. departments, all Ed.S., doctoral applicants, five letters of recommendation for doctoral applicants. GMAT required for M.B.A. candidates. TOEFL (minimum score 550) required for international applicants. Accepts transfer applicants. Graduates of unaccredited colleges considered. Apply to Dean, School of Graduate Studies one month prior to registration. Application fee $35. Phone: (812)237-3111; fax: (812)237-8060; e-mail: gradsch@amber.indstate.edu.

ADMISSION STANDARDS. Selective. Usual minimum average: 2.5 (A = 4).

FINANCIAL AID. Annual awards from institutional funds: scholarships, research fellowships, assistantships, Federal W/S, loans. Apply by March 1 to appropriate department chair for fellowships, assistantships; to Office of Student Financial Aid for all other programs. Phone: (812)237-2215. Use FAFSA. About 50% of full-time students receive aid other than loans from University and outside sources.

DEGREE REQUIREMENTS. For M.A., M.M., M.M.E., M.S., M.B.A., M.P.A., M.F.A.: 32 semester hours minimum; reading knowledge of one foreign language for some departments; GMAT for M.B.A. candidacy; final oral exam with thesis. For Ed.S.: 30 semester hours minimum beyond the master's, at least 20 in residence and one semester in full-time attendance; research project; final oral exam. For Ph.D., Psy.D.: 83–90 semester hours minimum beyond the bachelor's, at least 30 in residence and two consecutive semesters in full-time attendance; preliminary exam; reading knowledge of two foreign languages or one language and statistics or computer science; dissertation final oral exam.

FIELDS OF STUDY.
Art. Includes history, graphic design. M.A., M.F.A.
Athletic Training.
Business Administration.
Clinical Psychology. Admits Fall only.
Communication.
Communication Disorders. Includes speech-language pathology.
Counseling Psychology.
Career Technology Education.
Curriculum and Instruction.
Early Childhood Education.
Educational Technology.
Electronics and Computer Technology.
Elementary Education.
Elementary School Administration and Supervision.
English.
Family and Consumer Sciences.
Fine Arts.
Geography. Includes economic, physical.
Geology.
Guidance and Psychological Services.
Health and Safety.
History.
Human Resource Development.
Industrial Technology.
Language, Literature, and Linguistics.
Life Sciences. Includes microbiology, systematics, ecology, physiology.
Literacy.
Marriage and Family Therapy
Mathematics.
Music.
Nursing.
Physical Education.
Political Science.
Psychology.

Public Administration.
Recreation and Sports Management.
School Counselor.
Social Psychology.
Secondary Administration and Supervision.
Sociology.
Special Education.
Student Affairs Administration.
Technology Education.
Vocational-Technical Education.

INDIANA UNIVERSITY
Bloomington, Indiana 47405
Web site: www.indiana.edu

Founded 1820. Main campus in Bloomington; Medical Center campus and Law School in Indianapolis. CGS and AAU member. Coed. State control. Semester system. Special facilities: Center for American Studies, Bowen Research Center, CDC CYBER 170/855, Dec VAX-11/780, Geological Field Station in Montana, observatory, biological research station, participant in CIC Traveling Scholar Program with other Big Ten universities, Cyclotron facility, East Asian Languages and Cultures Center, Russian and East European Institute, Fine Arts Museum, Center for Health and Safety Studies, Hilltop and Garden Center, Center for the Study of Law in Action, Indiana Business Research Center, Indiana Museum (anthropology, archaeology, history), Lilly rare book library, Kinsey Sex Institute, Glen Black Archaeological Laboratory, Archives of Traditional Music, Folklore Institute, Nuclear Magnetic Resonance Laboratory, Institute of Psychiatric Research, Institute for Social Research, Semiotics Institute, Transportation Research Center. The University's NIH ranking is 44th among all U.S. institutions with 352 awards/grants worth $107,419,547. Library: 6,000,000 volumes, 40,000 subscriptions. Total University enrollment: 36,200.

Tuition: per unit, resident $196, nonresident $572; Business resident $373, nonresident $747; M.B.A. flat fee resident $5600; nonresident $11,204. On-campus housing for 1467 married students, 850 graduate men, 850 graduate women. Average academic year housing cost: $2600–$4696, for married students $541–$676 per month. Apply to University Halls of Residence. Phone: (812)855-5601. Day-care facilities available.

Graduate School
Web site: www.indiana.edu/~grdschl/index.html

Graduate study since 1881. Enrollment: full-time 3200, part-time 800 (men 65%, women 35%). Graduate faculty: full-time 1887. Degrees conferred: M.A., M.S., M.A.T., M.F.A., M.H.A., D.B.A., Ph.D., LL.M.

ADMISSION REQUIREMENTS. Two transcripts, three reference letters required in support of School's application. GRE or other entrance exams may be required for most programs. Interview not required. Accepts transfer applicants. Graduates of unaccredited institutions not considered. Apply to Office of Graduate School by January 15 (Fall), August 15 (Spring), January 1 (Summer). Application fee $35, $50 for international applicants. Phone: (812)855-0661; fax: (812)855-4266.

ADMISSION STANDARDS. Varies, from relatively open to very competitive. Usual minimum average: 3.0 (A = 4).

FINANCIAL AID. Scholarships; research assistantships, graduate assistantships, faculty assistants, associate instructors, counselors, grants, Federal W/S, loans. Apply by February 1 to proposed major department for fellowships, assistantships; to Financial Aid Office for all other programs. Phone: (812)855-0321. Use

FAFSA. About 50% of students receive aid other than loans from University and outside sources. Aid sometimes available for part-time students.

DEGREE REQUIREMENTS. For M.A., M.S.: 30 hours minimum, at least one semester or two summer sessions in full-time attendance; thesis for up to 6 hours' credit; reading knowledge of one foreign language for some programs; final written or oral exam may be required. For M.A.T., M.H.A.: 36 hours minimum, at least 24 in residence and one semester in full-time attendance. For M.F.A.: 60 hours minimum in residence, at least one semester in full-time attendance; final creative project in chosen studio area. For LL.M.: 30 hours minimum in residence; thesis; final oral exam sometimes required. For Ph.D., D.B.A.: 90 hours minimum beyond the bachelor's, at least 60 in residence and two consecutive semesters in full-time attendance; proficiency in depth in one foreign language, reading knowledge in two foreign languages, or reading proficiency in one language and research skill may be required; qualifying exam; dissertation for up to 30 hours' credit; final oral exam.

FIELDS OF STUDY.
American Studies. Ph.D. is combined with related major field.
Anthropology. Thesis or exam required for M.A.
Apparel Merchandising and Interior Design. M.S. only.
Applied Mathematics.
Arabic.
Archaeology.
Arts Administration. M.A. only.
Astronomy. Thesis ordinarily required for M.A.
Astrophysics. Ph.D. only.
Biochemistry. Interdepartmental; programs at Bloomington and Indianapolis campuses; thesis for M.S.; Ph.D.
Biology. M.A.T.; genetics, Ph.D.; microbiology, M.A., Ph.D.; molecular and cellular biology, Ph.D.; plant sciences, M.A., Ph.D.; zoology, M.A., Ph.D.; ecology and evolutionary biology, M.A., Ph.D.
Business. Ph.D. only.
Central Eurasian Studies. M.A., Ph.D.
Ceramics.
Chemical Physics. Ph.D. only.
Chemistry. Thesis for M.S., M.A.T., Ph.D.
Classical Studies. Includes Greek, Latin; thesis for M.A., M.A.T.; GRE for admission to Ph.D.
Clinical Psychology. GRE for admission.
Cognitive Science. Ph.D. is combined with related major field.
Communication and Culture. M.A, M.A.T., Ph.D.
Comparative Literature. Proficiency in one, fluency in one foreign language; thesis for M.A., M.A.T.; fluency in two, proficiency in three foreign languages for Ph.D.
Computer Science. M.S., Ph.D.
Creative Writing.
Criminal Justice.
Dentistry. Program at Indianapolis campus; apply to Secretary of Dental Graduate Program; thesis for Ph.D.
East Asian Languages and Cultures. Includes Chinese, Japanese, East Asian Studies (M.A. only); one East Asian language for admission; thesis, two languages for M.A.; two languages for Ph.D.
Economics. GRE Subject for admission. M.A., M.A.T., Ph.D.
Education. M.A., Ph.D. through Graduate School; M.S. in Ed., Ed.S., Ed.D. through Graduate School of Education.
English. Includes creative writing major for M.A.; one language for M.A., M.A.T.; two languages for admission to Ph.D. in English language.
Environmental Risk Analysis.
Environmental Science. Ph.D. only.
Evolution and Ecology.
Fine Arts. Includes studio, art history; one language for M.A. in art history, portfolio for admission to M.F.A., M.A.T.; Ph.D. in art history only.
Folklore. Thesis optional; one language for M.A., Ph.D.

French and Italian. GRE for admission; three languages for Ph.D.; French M.A., M.A.T., Ph.D.; Italian M.A., Ph.D.
General Science. M.A.T. only.
Genetics. Interdepartmental; Ph.D.
Geography. M.A., M.A.T., Ph.D.
Geological Sciences. Includes biogeochemistry, environmental geosciences and hydrogeology, geobiology, geochemistry, geophysics. M.S., Ph.D.
Geology. M.S.
Germanic Studies. M.A., M.A.T., Ph.D.
Health, Physical Education, Recreation. Ph.D. only; others through School of HPER.
History. GRE, one language for admission. M.A., M.A.T., Ph.D.
History and Philosophy of Science. M.A., Ph.D.
Hungarian Studies. Certificate only.
Information Sciences. Ph.D. only.
Journalism. Thesis or project for M.A., M.A.T., Ph.D.
Latin American Caribbean Studies. One language for M.A.
Law. LL.M., Ph.D.
Library and Information Science. M.L.S. offered by School of Library and Information Sciences, Ph.D. by Graduate School.
Linguistics. One language; thesis optional for M.A. Includes applied, general. M.A., Ph.D.
Mass Communication. Interdepartmental; GRE for admission. Ph.D. only.
Mathematical Physics. Interdepartmental. Ph.D. only.
Mathematics. M.A., M.A.T., Ph.D.
Medical Sciences (Bloomington). Includes anatomy, M.A., Ph.D.; pathology, M.S., Ph.D.; physiology, M.A., Ph.D.; pharmacology, M.S., Ph.D.; (Indianapolis) anatomy, M.S., Ph.D.; medical biophysics, M.S., Ph.D.; medical genetics, M.S., Ph.D.; medical neurobiology, M.S., Ph.D.; microbiology and immunology, M.S., Ph.D.; pharmacology, M.S., Ph.D.; physiology, M.S., Ph.D.; toxicology, M.S., Ph.D.
Medical Sciences Combined Degree Program (Bloomington and Indianapolis). M.S. or Ph.D., and M.D.
Music. Includes Composition, M.A.; musicology, theory, education, M.A., M.A.T. (music education only), Ph.D. offered by Graduate School; for M.M., M.S.Mus., M.M.Ed., D.Mus.Ed., D.Mus., admission is through School of Music; entrance exams required; thesis for M.A.; several years' experience for admission to M.A.T.
Near Eastern Languages and Cultures. Includes Arabic, Hebrew; for Ph.D.: thesis, one language in addition to Arabic, Hebrew.
Neural Sciences. Ph.D.
Pathology. M.S., Ph.D.
Pharmacology. M.S., Ph.D.
Philosophy. GRE for admission; thesis, one language for M.A., Ph.D.
Physics. M.S., M.A.T., Ph.D.
Physiological Optics. Thesis for M.S., Ph.D.
Physiology. M.A., Ph.D.
Political Science. M.A., M.A.T., Ph.D.
Psychology. Thesis for M.A., Ph.D.
Public Affairs. Ph.D.
Public Policy. Ph.D.
Religious Studies. M.A., Ph.D.
Russian and East European. M.A.
Slavic Languages and Literatures. Includes Russian major for M.A., M.A.T., Russian literature or Slavic linguistics for Ph.D., one language in addition to Russian for M.A., two languages in addition to Russian for Ph.D. in Russian literature; comprehensive knowledge of one Slavic language, reading knowledge of French, German, and one other Slavic language for Ph.D. in Slavic linguistics.
Social Studies. M.A.T.
Sociology. Special project for M.A., Ph.D.
Spanish and Portuguese. Includes Spanish major for M.A., M.A.T.; Hispanic literature or Spanish linguistics for Ph.D.; some knowledge of Latin plus two other languages in addition to Spanish for Ph.D.

Speech and Hearing Sciences. Includes speech pathology and audiology; thesis for M.S.; thesis may be creative in nature; M.A.T., Ph.D.

Telecommunication. Thesis for M.A., M.S., Ph.D.

Theater and Drama. M.A., M.A.T., M.F.A., Ph.D.

Vision Sciences. M.S., Ph.D.

Western European Studies. Thesis, comprehensive knowledge of one language, reading knowledge of one other. M.A.

Kelley School of Business

Web site: www.bus.indiana.edu

Established 1936. Public control. Accredited programs: M.B.A., Accounting; recognized Ph.D. Full-time study at Bloomington; part-time study at Indianapolis, Fort Wayne. Semester system. Special facilities: Center for Education and Research in Retailing, Johnson Center for Entrepreneurship and Innovation, Center for International Business Education and Research, Center for Real Estate Studies, Center for Sales Studies and Market Research, Indiana Business Research Center, Indiana Center for Econometric Model Research, Institute for Urban Transportation, Leadership Research Institute, Special Programs: global exchange programs (in Australia, France, Norway, Spain, Switzerland, United Kingdom), international internships (in Germany, Slovenia), summer internships (Germany, France, and People's Republic of China). Library: 160,000 volumes, 1000 subscriptions.

Annual tuition: resident full-time M.B.A. flat fee $5600, nonresident full-time $11,204; other business programs per credit resident $373, nonresident $747. on-campus rooms and apartments available for both single and married students.

Enrollment: total full-time 589 (men 75%, women 25%). Faculty: 109 full-time, 20 part-time; 88% with Ph.D./D.B.A. Degrees conferred: M.B.A., M.B.A.-J.D., M.B.A.-M.A. (East Asian Studies, Russian and East European Studies, West European Studies), M.P.A. (Professional Accountancy), Ph.D. (offered through the Graduate School).

ADMISSION REQUIREMENTS. All applicants should have a bachelor's degree from a recognized institution of higher education. Students are required to have their own personal computer. Beginning M.B.A. and M.P.A. students are admitted Fall only. Submit application, GMAT (will accept GMAT test results from the last five years, latest acceptable date is January), official transcripts from each undergraduate/graduate school attended, two letters of recommendation, three essays, personal statement, résumé (prefers at least four years of work experience), and an application fee of $50 ($65 international applicants) to the Admission Office, School of Business. Accepts MBA Multi-App electronic application in lieu of institutional application. U.S. citizens apply by December 1 (Fall early admission), March 1 (Fall regular admission), international students apply by February 1 (Fall). In addition, international students (whose native language is other than English) should submit a TOEFL report (minimum score 580), certified translations and evaluations of all official transcripts; recommendation should be in English or with certified translations, and proof of sufficient financial resources for two years of academic study. On-campus visits and interviews are strongly urged prior to the admissions committee reviewing completed application. Joint degree applicants must apply to and be accepted to both schools/programs, contact the admissions office for current information and specific admissions requirements. M.B.A. program phone: (812) 855-8006; Accounting graduate program: (812) 855-7200; e-mail: acctgrad@indiana.edu.

ADMISSION REQUIREMENTS FOR DOCTORAL CANDIDATES. Contact Kelley School of Business for application material and information. Beginning students are admitted Fall only. U.S. citizens apply by February 1 (Fall), international students apply by December 15. Submit application, GMAT/GRE (will accept GMAT/GRE test results from the last five years), two official transcripts from each undergraduate/graduate school attended, three letters of recommendation, four or five essays, current résumé, statement of purpose, and application fee of $40 to the Chairperson of the Doctoral Programs, Graduate School of Business. In addition, international students (whose native language is other than English) should submit a TOEFL report (minimum score 600); certified translations and evaluations of all official transcripts; recommendation should be in English or with certified translations, proof of health/immunization certificate. Interviews are strongly encouraged prior to the admissions committee reviewing completed application. Notification is made by mid-April.

ADMISSION STANDARDS. Very competitive for M.B.A., Ph.D. Median GMAT: 630; median GPA: 3.2 (A = 4). Gourman rating: 4.84; E.M.B.A. 4.83; Ph.D. 4.87. *U.S. News & World Report* ranked Kelley in the top 21 of all U.S. business schools. *Business Week* listed Kelley in the top 15 of all American business schools.

FINANCIAL AID. Scholarships, tuition waivers, merit scholarship, fellowships, research and teaching assistantships, Federal W/S, loans. Financial aid may be available for international students. Assistantships/fellowships may be available for joint degree candidates. Financial Aid applications and information generally available at the on-campus visit/interview; apply by March 1. Request all financial aid information from the School of Business. Phone: (812)855-8006. Use FAFSA (School code: 001809), also submit an institutional FAF, a Financial Aid Transcript, Federal Income Tax forms. Approximately 35% of current students receive some form of financial assistance. For Doctoral students there are fee scholarships, teaching appointments, research appointments, and fellowships. For Doctoral Financial Aid information call (812)855-3476.

DEGREE REQUIREMENTS. For M.B.A.: 54 credit program including 18 elective credits, two-year program; degree must be completed within seven years. For M.P.A.: 30 credit program. For M.B.A.-M.A.: 64 credit, generally a two-and-one-half- to seven-year program. For M.B.A.-J.D.: 118 credit, generally four- to seven-year program. For Ph.D.: four- to five-year program; comprehensive exam; candidacy; teaching development component; dissertation proposal and oral defense, dissertation; oral defense.

FIELDS OF STUDY.

Accounting. M.P.A.

M.B.A. Program. Includes concentrations in accounting, entrepreneurship, finance, human resource management, individually designed major, information systems, international business, management, marketing, production/operations management.

M.B.A. in Accounting.

Information Systems. M.S.

Kelley Direct On-Line M.B.A.

Ph.D. Program. Includes majors in accounting; business economics and public policy, decision sciences, finance, management information systems, marketing, operations management, organizational behavior and human resource management, strategic management and organization theory.

School of Education—Graduate Studies

Web site: www.education.indiana.edu

Graduate degrees since 1930. Semester system. Special facilities: Center for Adolescent and Family Studies, Center for Human Growth, Center for Postsecondary Planning and Research, Center for Research on Learning and Technology, Indiana Center for Evaluation, Indiana Education Policy Center, Institute for Child Study, Social Studies Development Center. Tuition: per credit resident $196, nonresident $572. Enrollment: full-time 1013, part-time 186. Graduate faculty: full-time 105, part-time

41. Degrees conferred: M.S. in Ed., Ed.S., Ed.D. The M.A. and Ph.D. are awarded by the Graduate School.

ADMISSION REQUIREMENTS. Transcripts, GRE, two letters of recommendation, goal statement required in support of School's application. On-line application available. Interview may be required. TOEFL (minimum score 550) required for international applicants. Accepts transfer applicants. Graduates of unaccredited institutions not considered. Apply to Office of Graduate Studies by June 1 (Fall), November 1 (Spring), March 1 (Summer). Earlier deadlines for Counseling, Educational Psychology, School Psychology, Student Affairs Administration. Deadlines for international applicants December 15 (Summer, Fall), September 15 (Spring). Application fee $45. Phone: (812)856-8504; fax: (812)856-8505.

ADMISSION STANDARDS. Selective for most departments. Usual minimum average: 3.0 (A = 4) (master's applicants), average GRE combined score 1300; 3.30 (doctoral applicants), average GRE combined score 1500.

FINANCIAL AID. Annual awards from institutional funds: grants, fellowships, research assistantships, teaching assistantships, internships, other assistantships, Federal W/S, loans. Apply by February 15 to Director of Financial Aid. Phone: (812)855-FAST. Use FAFSA, FAC sheet. About 15% of students receive aid other than loans from both School and outside sources.

DEGREE REQUIREMENTS. For M.S. in Ed.: 36 semester hours minimum without thesis, at least 27 in residence, 15 credits at the campus awarding the degree; some programs require more than 36. For Ed.S.: 65 hours minimum beyond the bachelor's, at least 35 in residence at the Bloomington or Indianapolis campus; 9 credits in full-time attendance in either one semester, or summer. For Ed.D., Ph.D.: 90 hours minimum beyond the bachelor's or 60 credits with a master's degree, at least two consecutive semesters in residence; qualifying written/oral exams; thesis for up to 15 hours; final oral exam.

FIELDS OF STUDY.
Art Education. M.S., Ph.D.
Counseling and Counselor Education. Includes school, agency. 48 credit master's. M.S., Ed.S.
Counseling Psychology. Ph.D.
Curriculum and Instruction. Ed.D., Ph.D.
Educational Leadership. Includes elementary, secondary. M.S., Ed.S., Ed.D.
Educational Psychology. M.S., Ph.D.
Elementary Education. Includes early childhood. M.S., Ed.S., Ph.D.
Higher Education. M.S., Ed.D., Ph.D.
History, Philosophy, and Policy Studies. M.S., Ph.D.
International and Comparative Education. M.S.
Instructional Systems Technology. M.S., Ed.S., Ed.D., Ph.D.
Language Education. Includes English, foreign language, reading. M.S., Ed.S., Ed.D., Ph.D.
School Psychology. Ed.S., Ph.D.
Secondary Education. Includes mathematics, science. M.S., Ed.S.
Social Studies. M.S., Ed.S.
Special Education. M.S., Ed.S., Ed.D., Ph.D.
Student Affairs Administration. M.S.

School of Health, Physical Education, and Recreation—Graduate Division

In operation since 1946. Tuition: per credit, resident $140, nonresident $408. Enrollment: full- and part-time 330. Faculty teaching graduate students: full-time 50, part-time 12. Degrees conferred: M.S., M.P.H., Director, Ph.D.

ADMISSION REQUIREMENTS. Transcripts, GRE, letters of recommendation required in support of School's application. TOEFL required for international applicants. Interview usually not required. Accepts transfer applicants. Apply by February 1 to Associate Dean for Academic Services for priority consideration. Application fee $45. Phone: (812)855-1561; fax: (812)855-4983.

ADMISSION STANDARDS. Selective. Usual minimum average: for M.S. 2.8; for doctoral degree 3.0 (A = 4).

FINANCIAL AID. Annual awards from institutional funds: fellowships, assistantships, grants, student academic appointments, Federal W/S, loans. Apply to Dean for academic appointments; to Financial Aid Office for all other programs. Use FAFSA. Phone: (812)855-0321.

DEGREE REQUIREMENTS. For M.S.: 35 semester hours minimum, at least 25–30 in residence; 45 credits for exercise physiology. For M.P.H.: 40 credit hours minimum, at least 25–30 in residence. For Director's degree: 65 hours minimum beyond the bachelor's, at least 35 in residence; final project; one year of professional experience; final written exam. For Ph.D. human performance: 90 hours beyond the bachelor's, at least 60 hours in residence; qualifying exams; dissertation; language/statistics option; final oral exam.

FIELDS OF STUDY.
Applied Health Science. Includes public health, human development and family studies, nutrition science, safety management, school and college health education, health promotion. M.P.H.
Kinesiology. Includes adapted physical education, applied sport science, athletic administration/sport management, exercise physiology, exercise science, clinical exercise physiology, social science of sport. M.S.
Recreation and Park Administration. Includes park and recreation management, outdoor recreation management, recreational sports administration, therapeutic recreation.

School of Informatics
Web site: www.informatics.indiana.edu

Established 1999. Special facilities: Center for Genomics and Bioinformatics, Informatics Research Institute. Semester system.
Tuition: per credit resident $180, nonresident $525. Enrollment: full- and part-time 50. Faculty: full- and part-time 15. Degree conferred: M.S.

ADMISSION REQUIREMENTS. Transcripts, GRE, three letters of reference, personal statement or sample of creative work required in support of School's application. GRE required for applicants with less than 3.0 GPA. TOEFL (minimum score 600) required for international applicants. Will consider transfer applicants. Graduates of unaccredited colleges not considered. Admits Fall only. Apply to School by January 15 for admissions and financial aid, April 1 admissions only. Application fee $45, $55 international applicants. Phone: (812)856-5754; fax: (812)856-7464.

ADMISSION STANDARDS. Selective. Usual minimum average: 3.0 (A = 4).

FINANCIAL AID. Annual awards from institutional funds: scholarships, fellowships, assistantships, grants, fee reduction assistance for nonresidents also available, Federal W/S, loans. Approved for VA benefits. Apply by January 15 to School for scholarships, fellowships, assistantships; to Office of Scholarships and Financial Aid for all other programs. Phone: (812)855-0321. Use FAFSA and institutional FAF. About 20% of students receive aid from University and outside sources.

DEGREE REQUIREMENTS. For M.S.: 36 credit interdisciplinary program; 30 credit interdisciplinary program for Media Arts and Science.

FIELDS OF STUDY.
Bioinformatics.
Chemical Informatics.
Health Informatics.
Human–Computer Interaction.
Medial Arts and Science.

School of Law

Web site: www.law.indiana.edu

Established 1842. Located on main campus. ABA approved since 1923. AALS member. Semester system. Full-time, day study only. Special programs: Center for the Study of Law and Society; summer study abroad in London, England; foreign exchange program with the Universite Pantheon-Assas (Paris II) Law School, Paris, France and ESADE Law School in Barcelona, Spain. Law library: 658,373 volumes, 8283 subscriptions; has LEXIS, NEXIS, WESTLAW, DIALOG, LEGISLATE.

Annual tuition: resident $7708, nonresident $19,283. Total average additional expenses: $12,415.

Enrollment: first-year class 212; total full-time 619 (men 61%, women 39%). Faculty: full-time 43, part-time 5. Student to faculty ratio 15.1 to 1. Degrees conferred: J.D., J.D.-M.B.A., J.D.-M.P.A., J.D.-M.S.E.S. (Environmental Sciences), J.D.-M.L.S., LL.M., M.C.L. (only for persons who have completed a basic legal education and received a university degree in law in another country), J.S.D.

ADMISSION REQUIREMENTS. LSDAS Law School report, bachelor's degree, transcripts, LSAT, recommendations required in support of application. Graduates of unaccredited colleges not considered. Apply to Admissions Office; no specified closing date. Priority given to applications received before March 1, rolling admissions process. Application fee $35. Phone: (812)855-4765; fax: (812)855-0555; e-mail: lawadmis@indiana.edu.

ADMISSION STANDARDS. Selective. Mean LSAT: 158; mean GPA: 3.3 (A = 4). Gourman rating: 4.41. *U.S. News & World Report* ranking is the top 39 of all U.S. law schools. Admits about 25–30% of total annual applications.

FINANCIAL AID. Scholarships, fellowships, assistantships, Federal W/S, loans. Apply by March 1 to Admissions Office for fellowships, to Office of Scholarships and Financial Aid for loans; no specified closing date. Use FAFSA (School code: 001809). About 57% of students receive some aid from School.

DEGREE REQUIREMENTS. For J.D.: satisfactory completion of an eighty-six-credit-hour program; accelerated twenty-seven-month program is also available. For LL.M., M.C.L.: at least 24 credits minimum beyond J.D. For S.J.D.: at least one year of full-time residence; dissertation of publishable quality; oral defense.

School of Library and Information Science

Web site: www.slis.lib.indiana.edu

Organized library and information science study since 1930. Semester system. Special facilities: Center for Applied Semiotics, Center for Social Informatics.

Tuition: per credit, resident $208, nonresident $605. On-campus housing available. Enrollment: full-time 170, part-time 479 (men 30%, women 70%). Faculty: full-time 22. Degrees conferred: M.L.S., M.I.S., Sp.L.I.S. The Ph.D. is offered by the Graduate School.

ADMISSION REQUIREMENTS. Transcripts, letters of reference, professional goals statement required in support of School's application. On-line application available. GRE required for applicants with less than 3.0 GPA. TOEFL required for international applicants. Interview may be required. Accepts transfer applicants. Graduates of unaccredited colleges not considered. Apply to Office of School by June 15 (Fall), November 15 (Spring), March 15 (Summer). Application fee $35. Phone: (812)855-2018; fax: (812)855-6166; e-mail: slis@indiana.edu.

ADMISSION STANDARDS. Selective. Usual minimum average: 3.0 (A = 4).

FINANCIAL AID. Annual awards from institutional funds: merit scholarships, fellowships, graduate assistantships, fee reduction assistance for nonresidents also available, Federal W/S, loans. Approved for VA benefits. Apply by January 15 (Fall), October 1 (Spring) to appropriate department for scholarships, fellowships, assistantships; to Office of Scholarships and Financial Aid for all other programs. Phone: (812)855-7787. Use FAFSA and institutional FAF. About 10% of students receive aid from University and outside sources. Aid available for part-time students; part-time work opportunities in the library generally available.

DEGREE REQUIREMENTS. For M.L.S.: 36 hours minimum; computer-based information tool. For M.I.S.: 42 hours minimum; computer-based information tool. For Sp.L.I.S.: 30 hours minimum beyond the master's; computer-based information tool. For Ph.D.: see Graduate School listing above.

FIELDS OF STUDY.
Information Science. Includes information architecture and design, human–computer interaction and communication, strategic information management and leadership, information retrieval systems design. Entire program available in Bloomington and Indiana University–Purdue University Indianapolis. M.I.S.
Library Science. Entire program available in Bloomington, Indiana University–Purdue University Indianapolis, Indiana University South Bend. Courses offered in the Fall, Spring, and during two Summer Sessions. M.L.S.

School of Music

Organized music study since 1910. Semester system. Music library: 380,000 volumes. On-campus housing available.

Tuition: per credit, resident $180, nonresident $525. Graduate enrollment: full-time 730. School faculty: full-time 120, part-time 25. Degrees conferred: M.M., M.M.Ed., M.S., D.Mus.Ed., D.Mus. The M.A., M.A.T., and Ph.D. are offered through the Graduate School.

ADMISSION REQUIREMENTS. Transcripts, references required in support of application. GRE Music Subject Test strongly recommended for all applicants. GRE required for applicants in Music Education, Music Theory, and Musicology. TOEFL required for international applicants. Audition and/or interview required for most degree and diploma programs. Entrance exams at time of first registration. Accepts transfer applicants. Apply to Director of Admissions by June 15 (Fall), December 1 (Spring), May 1 (Summer). Audition dates: January 11–12, February 1–2, March 1–2. Application fee $35. Phone: (812)855-7998; fax: (812)855-6086; e-mail: musicadm @indiana.edu.

ADMISSION STANDARDS. Selective. Usual minimum average: 3.0 (A = 4).

FINANCIAL AID. Annual awards from institutional funds: research assistantships, teaching assistantships, fellowships, full and partial tuition waivers. Apply to Dean by March 15. Phone: (812)855-3278. Use FAFSA and institutional FAF. About 35% of students receive aid other than loans from School and outside sources.

DEGREE REQUIREMENTS. For master's: 30–35 semester hours minimum, at least 30 in residence and one year or four summer sessions in full-time attendance; reading knowledge of one or more foreign languages for some majors; thesis required for some majors, optional for others; comprehensive exam. For D.M.E., D.M.: 90 semester hours minimum beyond the bachelor's, at least 30 hours and two consecutive semesters in full-time residence; reading knowledge of one to three foreign languages/ research techniques, depending upon program; qualifying exam; recitals or other public performance for most majors; dissertation or project (document, essay, lecture/recital, or composition); final oral exam. For M.A., M.A.T., Ph.D.: see Graduate School listing above.

FIELDS OF STUDY.
Arts Administration. M.A.
Ballet. M.S.
Composition. Sample compositions for admission. M.M., D.M.
Computer Music Composition. M.M.
Conducting. Includes choral, instrumental, wind. M.M., D.M.
Early Music. M.M., D.M.
Jazz Studies. M.M.
Music Education. M.A.T., M.M.E., D.M.E., Ph.D.
Music Literature and Pedagogy. D.M.
Music Theatre Scenic Techniques. M.S.
Music Theory. M.A., M.M., Ph.D.
Musicology. M.A., Ph.D.
Organ and Church Music. M.M., D.M.
Performance. Includes most instruments and voice. M.M., D.M.
Stage Direction for Opera. M.S.

INDIANA UNIVERSITY–PURDUE UNIVERSITY INDIANAPOLIS

Indianapolis, Indiana 46202-5143
Web site: www.iupui.edu

Founded 1908. Main campuses in Bloomington and West Lafayette; Medical Center campus and Law School in Indianapolis. Coed. State control. Semester system. Library: 500,000 volumes, 3,442,000 microforms. Total University enrollment: 27,600. Limited on-campus housing available. Day-care facilities available.

Indiana University Graduate School

Graduate study since 1908. Tuition: per unit, resident $196, nonresident $572. Enrollment: full-time 3200, part-time 800 (men 65%, women 35%). Graduate faculty: full-time 1397, part-time 887. Degrees conferred: M.A., M.S., M.A.T., M.H.A., Ph.D.

ADMISSION REQUIREMENTS. Two transcripts, three letters of reference required in support of School's application. GRE or other entrance exams may be required. Interview not required. Accepts transfer applicants. Graduates of unaccredited institutions not considered. Apply to Office of Graduate School by January 15 (Fall), August 15 (Spring), January 1 (Summer). Application fee $35, $50 for international applicants. Phone: (812)855-8853, fax (812)855-4266.

ADMISSION STANDARDS. Varies, from relatively open to very competitive. Usual minimum average: 3.0 (A = 4).

FINANCIAL AID. Scholarships, research assistantships, graduate assistantships, faculty assistants, associate instructors, counselors. Apply by February 1 to proposed major department for fellowships, assistantships; to Financial Aid Office for all other programs. Use FAFSA. About 50% of students receive aid other

than loans from University and outside sources. Aid sometimes available to part-time students.

DEGREE REQUIREMENTS. For M.A., M.S.: 30 hours minimum, at least 1 semester or 2 summer sessions in full-time attendance; thesis for up to 6 hours' credit; reading knowledge of one foreign language for some programs; final written or oral exam may be required. For M.A.T., M.H.A.: 36 hours minimum, at least 24 in residence and 1 semester in full-time attendance. For Ph.D.: 90 hour minimum beyond the bachelor's, at least 60 in residence and 2 consecutive semesters in full-time attendance; proficiency in one foreign language, reading knowledge in two foreign languages, or reading proficiency in one language and research skill may be required; qualifying exam; dissertation for up to 30 hours' credit; final oral exam.

FIELDS OF STUDY.
Anatomy and Cell Biology.
Biochemistry and Molecular Biology.
Biotechnology (Training Program).
Cancer Biology (Training Program).
Cellular and Integrative Physiology.
Diabetes (Training Program).
Dental Science.
Economics.
English.
Geographic Information Science.
Geology.
History.
Medical Biophysics.
Medical and Molecular Genetics.
Medical Neurobiology.
Microbiology and Immunology.
Musculoskeletal (Training Program).
Museum Studies.
Nursing.
Nutrition and Dietetics.
Pathology and Laboratory Medicine.
Pharmacology and Toxicology.
Philanthropic Studies.
Social Work
Sociology.
Spanish.
Teaching English as a Second Language.
Therapeutic Outcomes Research.
Theatre and Drama. M.A., M.A.T., M.F.A., Ph.D.
Western European Studies. Thesis, comprehensive knowledge of one foreign language, reading knowledge of one other. M.A. only.
Zoology.

Kelley School of Business

Semester systems. Accredited programs: M.B.A., Professional Accounting.
Tuition: M.B.A.: per credit resident $330, nonresident $630; Accounting: per credit resident $187.50, nonresident $375.
Enrollment: Total full- and part-time 650. Faculty: full- and part-time 85. Degrees conferred: M.B.A., M.P.A., M.B.A.-J.D., M.B.A.-M.H.A., M.B.A.-M.D.

ADMISSION REQUIREMENTS. All applicants should have a bachelor's degree from a recognized institution of higher education. Will consider transfer applicants. Submit application, GMAT (will accept GMAT results from the last five years, latest acceptable date is January), official transcripts from each undergraduate/graduate school attended, two recommendations, three essays, personal statement, résumé and an application fee of $50, $65 for international applicants to the Admissions Office, Kelley School of Business. Phone: M.B.A. (317)274-4895; fax: (317)274-2483; Accounting: (317)278-3885. For M.P.A.: there are nine prerequisite courses that need to be completed prior to entrance into the program. For M.B.A.: U.S. citizens apply by April 1 (Fall), November 1 (Spring). For M.P.A.: apply at least two weeks prior to the beginning of semester of preferred entrance. International applicants should apply by February 1 (Fall). In addition, international students (whose native language is other than English) should submit a TOEFL report (minimum score 580), certified translations and evaluations of all official transcripts; recommendation should be in English or with certified translation, and proof of sufficient financial resources for two years of academic study. Dual degree applicants must apply to and be accepted by both schools/programs. Contact the admission office for current information and specific admissions requirements.

ADMISSION STANDARDS. Competitive. For M.B.A.: mean GMAT: 600; mean GPA: 3.0 (A = 4).

FINANCIAL AID. Scholarships, partial tuition waivers, Federal W/S, loans. Request all financial aid information from the School of Business. Phone: (317)278-FAST. Use FAFSA. Also submit an institutional FAF, Financial Aid Transcript, Federal Income Tax forms.

DEGREE REQUIREMENTS. For M.B.A.: 54 credit program including 18 elective credits, at least 45 credits in residence; degree must be complete within 7 years. For M.P.A.: 30 credit program with a bachelor's degree in business or accounting.

FIELDS OF STUDY.
Accounting. Includes specializations in advisory services and consulting, auditing and financial reporting, information systems management, taxation. M.P.A.
Business Administration. Includes concentration in finance, general administration.

School of Dentistry

Established 1879, became part of state system in 1925. Located at Indianapolis campus (46202). Medical Center housing for 99 married students. Average academic year housing cost: $15,324. Contact Housing Office for both on- and off-campus housing information. Phone: (317)274-5159.

Annual tuition: resident $13,166, nonresident $28,196. Total average cost for all other first-year expenses: $8500.

Enrollment: first-year class 99; total 475 (men 65%, women 35%), postgraduates 91. Faculty: full-time 112, part-time 113. Degrees conferred: D.D.S., M.S.D. The M.S. and Ph.D. are offered through the Graduate School.

ADMISSION REQUIREMENTS. AADSAS report, transcripts, DAT (no later than October), three letters of recommendation required in support of School's application. Applicants must have completed at least three years of college study, prefer four years of study. Interview by invitation only. Preference given to Indiana residents. Accepts transfer applicants from foreign schools at the second-year level on a space available basis. Graduates of unaccredited institutions not considered. Apply to Director of Admissions after June 1, before January 1. Application fee $35, $55 for international applicants. Phone: (317)274-8173.

ADMISSION STANDARDS. Selective. Mean DAT: Academic 17.7, PAT 17; mean GPA: 3.24 (A = 4). Gourman rating 4.43. Accepts 20–25% of total annual applicants. Approximately 85% are state residents.

FINANCIAL AID. Scholarships, fellowships, DEAL, HEAL, loans. Apply to the Loan and Scholarship Committee after acceptance, before February 15. Phone: (317)274-4162. Use FAFSA (School code: 001813). About 85% of students receive aid from School.

DEGREE REQUIREMENTS. For D.D.S.: satisfactory completion of four-year program. For M.S.D.: 30 hours minimum in residence; thesis; final written/oral exam. For M.S., Ph.D.: see Graduate School listing above.

FIELDS OF GRADUATE STUDY.
Endodontics.
Operative Dentistry.
Orthodontics.
Pediatric Dentistry.
Periodontics.
Preventive Dentistry.
Prosthodontics.

School of Education
Web site: education.iupui.edu

Semester systems. Tuition: per credit resident $190.50, nonresident $375.

Enrollment: Total full- and part-time 600. Faculty: full- and part-time 80. Degrees conferred: M.S. in Education.

ADMISSION REQUIREMENTS. Official transcripts from each undergraduate/graduate school attended, GRE, two letters of recommendation, personal statement required in support of School's application. On-line application available. Interview may be requested. TOEFL (minimum score 550) required for international applicants. Accepts transfer applications. Graduates of unaccredited institutions not considered. Apply to School of Education by May 1 (Fall), November 1 (Spring), March 1 (Summer). Application fee $35. Phone: (317)274-6801; fax: (317) 274-6864.

ADMISSION STANDARDS. Selective for most programs. Usual minimum average: 2.75 (A = 4); minimum GRE: combined score: 1300.

FINANCIAL AID. Limited to partial tuition waivers, Federal W/S, loans. Request all financial aid information from the School of Education. No specified closing date. Use FAFSA. Aid available for part-time students.

DEGREE REQUIREMENTS. For M.S.: 36 semester hours minimum without thesis, at least 27 in residence, 15 credits on the campus awarding the degree.

FIELDS OF STUDY.
Educational Leadership. Includes elementary, secondary. M.S.
Educational Psychology. M.S.
Elementary Education. Includes early childhood education, educational technology. M.S.
Higher Education/Student Affairs. A Bloomington program with some classes at IUPUI. M.S.
School Counseling/Counselor Education. M.S.
Secondary Education. Includes education technology. M.S.
Special Education. Includes exceptional needs. M.S.

School of Informatics
Web site: informatics.iupui.edu

Program established 2001. Semester systems. Tuition: per credit resident $180, nonresident $525.

Enrollment: Total full- and part-time 5. Faculty: full- and part-time 20. Degree conferred: M.S.

ADMISSION REQUIREMENTS. Official transcripts from each undergraduate/graduate school attended, three letters of recommendation, statement of purpose, résumé required in support of School's application. Sample of creative work required for News

Media. GRE required for applicants with less than 3.0 GPA (A = 4). On-line application available. TOEFL (minimum score 600) required for international applicants. Accepts transfer applications. Graduates of unaccredited institutions not considered. Admits Fall only. Apply to School of Informatics by March 1. Application fee $45, $55 for international applicants, Phone (317)278-7666; e-mail: info@informatics.iupui.edu..

ADMISSION STANDARDS. Selective. Usual minimum average: 3.0 (A = 4).

FINANCIAL AID. Limited to grants, Federal W/S, loans. Apply by March 1 (priority deadline) to the Office of Student Financial Aid Services. Phone: (317)274-4162. Use FAFSA. Aid available for part-time students.

DEGREE REQUIREMENTS. For M.S.: 36 credit interdisciplinary program.

FIELDS OF STUDY.
Bioinformatics.
Chemical Informatics.
Health Informatics.
Human–Computer Interaction.
News Media.

School of Law—Indianapolis
Web site: www.iulaw.indy.indiana.edu

Established 1894. Located near downtown. ABA approved since 1936. AALS member. Semester system. Full-time, part-time study. Law library: 523,370 volumes, 7200 subscriptions; has LEXIS, NEXIS, WESTLAW, DIALOG, OCLC; is a U.S. Government Depository for United Nations. Special facility: Center for Law and Health. Special programs: summer study abroad in Renmin (People's) University of China, People's Republic of China and at the Universite of Lille, France.
Annual tuition: full-time resident $7220, nonresident $17,094; part-time resident $5246, nonresident $12,298. Limited on-campus housing available. Estimated living expenses $12,423.
Enrollment: first-year class 185, part-time 79; total full- and part-time 852 (men 52%, women 48%). Faculty: full-time 24, part-time 11. Student to faculty ratio 26.4 to 1. Degrees conferred: J.D., J.D.-M.B.A., J.D.-M.H.A., J.D.-M.P.A., J.D.-M.P.H.

ADMISSION REQUIREMENTS. LSDAS Law School report, bachelor's degree, transcripts, LSAT, personal statement, letters of recommendation required in support of application. Interview not required. Transfer applicants accepted. Applicants must have completed 90 credits prescribed by ABA. Graduates of unaccredited colleges not considered. Apply after September 1, before March 1 to Admissions Office. Beginning part-time students admitted May or August only. Application fee $35. Phone: (317)274-2459.

ADMISSION STANDARDS. Selective. Mean LSAT: full-time 154, part-time 154; mean GPA: full-time 3.32, part-time 3.21 (A = 4). Gourman rating: 3.15. *U.S. News & World Report* ranking is in the second tier of all U.S. law schools. Accepts 50% of total annual applicants.

FINANCIAL AID. Scholarships, fellowships, assistantships, partial tuition waivers, Federal W/S, loans. Apply to Office of Student Financial Aid by March 1. Use FAFSA (School code: 001813). About 16% of students receive aid other than loans from School.

DEGREE REQUIREMENTS. For J.D.: 90 semester hours and 6 semesters in full-time residence or 8 semesters in part-time residence. For master's degree: see Graduate School listing above.

School of Library and Information Science
Web site: www.slis.iupui.edu

Semester system. Tuition: per credit resident $190.50, nonresident $555.90.
Enrollment: total full-time 100, part-time 175. Faculty: full- and part-time 12. Degrees conferred: M.L.S., M.L.S.-M.A. (History), M.L.S. M.P.A., M.L.S.-L.T.M (Library Technology Management).

ADMISSION REQUIREMENTS. Official transcripts from each undergraduate/graduate school attended, three recommendations, personal goals statement required in support of School's application. GRE required for applicants with less than 3.0 GPA (A = 4). All applicants must demonstrate they are computer, network, and information literate. On-line application available. TOEFL (minimum score 600) required for international applicants. Accepts transfer applications. Graduates of unaccredited institutions not considered. Dual degree applicants must apply to and be accepted to both Schools/programs, Apply to School of Library and Information Science by July 15. Application fee $45, $55 for international applicants. Phone: (886)758-6254 (toll free); (317)278-2375.

ADMISSION STANDARDS. Selective. Usual minimum average: 3.0 (A = 4).

FINANCIAL AID. Scholarships, tuition waivers, Federal W/S, loans. Apply by March 1 (priority deadline) to the Office of Student Financial Aid Services. Phone: (317)274-4162. Use FAFSA. Aid available for part-time students, part-time work opportunities in the library generally available.

DEGREE REQUIREMENTS, For M.L.S.: 36 credit hours minimum, computer-based, information tool. For M.L.S.-L.T.M: 45 credit hour program, internship. For M.L.S.-M.A.: 50 credit hour program (30 credits taken for M.L.S., 20 credits taken for M.A.). For M.L.S.-M.P.A.: 66 credit hour program (30 credits taken for M.L.S., 36 credits taken for M.P.A.).

FIELDS OF STUDY.
Library Science. Includes library technology management. M.L.S.

School of Medicine (46202-5113)
Web site: www.medicine.iu.edu

Founded 1903. In 1971 became the hub of statewide medical education system. After admission, students select which center they will attend. Centers located at Indianapolis, Bloomington, Gary, South Bend, Fort Wayne, Muncie, Terre Haute, Lafayette, Evansville. Special program for disadvantaged and underrepresented minorities. Library: 202,200 volumes, 1849 subscriptions.
Annual tuition: resident $15,300, nonresident $33,238. Total average figure for all other expenses $10,000–$12,000. Medical Center housing for 175 married students, 160 men, 130 women.
Enrollment: first-year class 280 (20 EDP) (men 60%, women 40%); total 1060. Faculty: full-time 550, part-time 200. Degrees conferred: M.D., M.D.-M.S., M.D.-Ph.D. The M.S. and Ph.D. are offered through the Graduate School at either Bloomington or Indianapolis.

ADMISSION REQUIREMENTS. AMCAS report, transcripts, letters of recommendation, MCAT required in support of application. Interview by invitation. Applicants must have completed at least three years of college study. Does have EDP; apply between June 1 and August 1. Preference given to Indiana residents. Accepts transfer applicants. Apply to School Admissions Office after June 1, before December 15. Application fee $35. Phone: (317)274-3772; fax: (317)278-0211.

ADMISSION STANDARDS. Selective. Median MCAT: 9.7; median GPA: 3.69 (A = 4). Gourman rating: 4.43. *U.S. News & World Report* raking is in the top 47 of all U.S. medical schools, 43rd in primary care provider. Accepts 25% of total annual applicants. Approximately 90% are state residents.

FINANCIAL AID. Scholarships, fellowships, assistantships, HEAL, grants, full and partial fee waivers, loans. Apply to Student Financial Services Office. Phone: (317)274-8568. Use FAFSA (School code: 001813). About 75% of students receive aid other than loans from School.

DEGREE REQUIREMENTS. For M.D.: satisfactory completion of four-year program. For M.S. and Ph.D.: see Graduate School listing above.

FIELDS OF GRADUATE STUDY.
Anatomy.
Biochemistry.
Biophysics.
Genetics.
Immunology.
Microbiology.
Molecular Biology.
Neurosciences.
Pathology.
Pharmacology.
Physiology.

PROGRAMS WITH PURDUE UNIVERSITY AT LAFAYETTE:
Engineering.
Medicinal Chemistry.
Molecular Biology.
Neurosciences.

School of Nursing

Established 1945. Located at Indianapolis campus (46202). Tuition: per credit resident $157, nonresident $454.

Graduate enrollment: full-time 92, part-time 421. Faculty full-time 47, part-time 1. Degrees conferred: M.S.N., M.S.N.-M.P.M., D.N.S., Ph.D.

ADMISSION REQUIREMENTS. Official transcripts, three letters of reference, résumé or vita, interview, current Indiana R.N. license required in support of School's application. GRE required for all applicants without a B.S.N. and for Ph.D. applicants. On-line application available. TOEFL (minimum score 550) required for international applicants. Accepts transfer applicants. Graduates of unaccredited institutions not considered. Apply to Graduate Recorder, School of Nursing by April 1 (Fall), October 1 (Spring). Deadline for Ph.D. applicants is January 1. Rolling admissions process. Application fee $45, $55 for international applicants. Phone: (317)274-0003; fax: (317)274-2996.

ADMISSION STANDARDS. Selective. Usual minimum average: 2.8 (A = 4).

FINANCIAL AID. Scholarships, fellowships, research assistantships, teaching assistantships, traineeships, Federal W/S, loans. Apply by May 1 to School of Nursing for fellowships, assistantships, to Traineeships Program for traineeships; to Director of Scholarships and Financial Aid IUPUI for scholarships and all other programs. Use FAFSA. Phone: (317)274-4162. Aid available for part-time students.

DEGREE REQUIREMENTS. For M.S.N.: 36–42 hours minimum, at least 20 in residence; final document. For D.N.S.: Three years minimum beyond the master's, at least one year in full-time residence; qualifying exam; comprehensive exam; dissertation; final oral exam. For Ph.D.: see Graduate School listing above.

FIELDS OF STUDY.
Adult Care Nurse Practitioner.
Adult Nurse Practitioner.
Adult Health Clinical Nurse Specialist.
Adult Psychiatric/Mental Health Clinical Nurse Specialist.
Child/Adolescent Psychiatric Clinical Nurse Specialist.
Community Health Clinical Nurse Specialist.
Family Nurse Practitioner.
Neonatal Nurse Practitioner.
Nursing Administration.
Pediatric Clinical Nurse Specialist.
Pediatric Nurse Practitioner.
Women's Health Nurse Practitioner.

School of Social Work

Main campus for School of Social Work is located in Indianapolis. M.S.W. programs since 1911. Semester system.

Tuition: per credit resident $190.20, nonresident $548.45. M.S.W. enrollment: full- and part-time 240. School faculty: full- and part-time 48. Degrees conferred: M.S.W., Ph.D. (offered through the Graduate School).

ADMISSION REQUIREMENT. Official transcript, three letters of recommendation, writing sample required in support of IUPUI and School's application. On-line application available. TOEFL and international application required of international application. Call (317)274-7294 for current information. Accepts transfer applicants. Graduates of unaccredited degree programs will not be considered. Submit IUPUI application first and then send the School of Social Work's paper application to the School's Admissions Coordinator by February 1 (Fall priority deadline), June 1 (deadline for part-time evening and part-time Saturday programs). Application fee $45. Phone: (317)274-6727.

ADMISSION STANDARDS. Selective. Usual minimum average: 3.0 (A = 4).

FINANCIAL AID. Fellowships, research assistantships, tuition grants, Federal W/S, loans, Apply by March 1 to the School of Social Work for fellowships, assistantships, tuition grants; to the Office of Students Financial Aid Services for all other assistance. Phone: (317)274-4162. Use FAFSA.

DEGREE REQUIREMENTS. For M.S.W.: 60 credit program, at least 48 credits in residence; field practicum.

FIELDS OF STUDY.
Social Work. Includes concentrations in child welfare, health, families and school, mental health and addictions, social work leadership. M.S.W.

Purdue University School of Engineering and Technology

Semester system. Tuition: per credit resident $203, nonresident $580.50. Enrollment: full- and part-time 350 (men 50%, women 50%). Faculty: full- and part-time 132. Degrees conferred: M.S., M.S.Bm.E., M.S.E., M.S.E.C.E., M.S.M.E., Ph.D.

ADMISSION REQUIREMENTS. Two official transcripts, GRE, three letters of recommendation, statement of purpose required in support of School's application. On-line application available. TOEFL and Financial Information Form with an official letter or statement from bank verifying there are the required funds for at least two years of academic study required for international applicants. Accepts transfer applicants. Graduates of unaccredited institutions not considered. Apply to appropriate major department at least one semester in advance, but not later that May 1 (Fall), September 1 (Spring). Application fee $45, $55 for international applicants. Phone: (317)278-4961; fax: (317)278-2032.

ADMISSION STANDARDS. Selective for most departments, Usual minimum average: 3.0 (A = 4).

FINANCIAL AID. Scholarships, research/teaching assistantships, Federal W/S, loans. Apply by March 15 to department for scholarships, assistantships; to Office of Student Financial Aid Services for all other aid. Phone: (317)274-4162. Use FAFSA. Aid available for part-time students.

DEGREE REQUIREMENTS. For master's: 30 credit hour programs, at least two semesters in residence; thesis/nonthesis option; final written/oral exam. For Ph.D.: 60 credit program beyond bachelor's degree; qualifying exam; preliminary exam; reading knowledge of one foreign language for some programs, dissertation; final oral defense.

FIELD OF STUDY.
Biomedical Engineering. Ph.D. degree program is jointly administered with University in West Lafayette. M.S.Bm.E., Ph.D.
Electrical and Computer Engineering. M.S., M.S.E., M.S.E.C.E.
Interdisciplinary Engineering. M.S., M.S.E.
Mechanical Engineering. M.S., M.S.M.E.

Purdue University School of Science
Web site: www.science.iupui.edu

Semester system. Special facilities: Center for Earth and Environmental Science, Center for Regenerative Biology and Medicine.
Tuition: per credit resident $203, nonresident $580.50. Enrollment: full- and part-time 247 (men 41%, women 59%). Faculty: full- and part-time 132. Degrees conferred: M.S., Ph.D.

ADMISSION REQUIREMENTS. Two official transcripts, GRE, three letters of recommendation, statement of purpose required in support of School's application. On-line application available. TOEFL and Financial Information Form with an official letter or statement from bank verifying there are the required funds for at least two years of academic study are required for international applicants. Accepts transfer applicants. Graduates of unaccredited institutions not considered. Apply to appropriate major department at least one semester in advance, but not later that May 1 (Fall), September 1 (Spring). Application fee $45, $55 for international applicants.

ADMISSION STANDARDS. Selective for most departments. Usual minimum average: 3.0 (A = 4).

FINANCIAL AID. Scholarships, research/teaching assistantships, Federal W/S, loans. Apply by March 15 to department for scholarships, assistantships; to Office of Student Financial Aid Services for all other aid. Phone: (317)274-4162. Use FAFSA. Aid available for part-time students.

DEGREE REQUIREMENTS. For M.S.: 30 credit hour programs, at least two semesters in residence, thesis/nonthesis option; final written/oral exam. For Ph.D.: 60 credit program beyond bachelor's degree; qualifying exam; preliminary exam; reading knowledge of one foreign language for some programs; dissertation; final oral defense.

FIELD OF STUDY,
Biology. M.S., Ph.D.
Chemistry. M.S., Ph.D.
Clinical Rehabilitation. Ph.D.
Computer and Information Science. M.S., Ph.D.
Geology. Degree awarded by Indiana University. M.S.
Industrial/Organizational Psychology. M.S.
Mathematical Sciences. Includes math and statistics. M.S., Ph.D.
Physics. M.S., Ph.D.
Psychobiology of Addictions. Ph.D.

INDIANA UNIVERSITY OF PENNSYLVANIA
Indiana, Pennsylvania 15705-1081
Web site: www.iup.edu

Founded 1875. Located 60 miles NE of Pittsburgh. CGS member. Coed. State control. Semester system. Library: 775,000 volumes, 3600 subscriptions; designated Federal Depository. Total University enrollment: 13,400.
Annual tuition: full-time resident $4138, nonresident $7008; per credit, resident $230, nonresident $389. Limited on-campus housing available. Average academic year housing cost: $1822–$4060 (including board). Contact Housing and Residence Life Office for on- and off-campus housing information. Phone: (724)357-2696. Day-care facilities available.

Graduate School and Research

Graduate study since 1957. Enrollment: full-time 853, part-time 822. University faculty teaching graduate students: full- and part-time 366. Degrees conferred: M.A., M.S., M.B.A., M.Ed., M.F.A. Ed.D., Psy.D., Ph.D.

ADMISSION REQUIREMENTS. Transcripts, letters of recommendation, GRE/GMAT required in support of application. Interview required by some departments. TOEFL required for international applicants. Accepts transfer applicants. Graduates of unaccredited institutions not considered. Apply to the Graduate Office by July 1 (Fall), November 1 (Spring), April 1 (Summer). Application fee $20. Phone: (724)357-2222; fax (724)357-4862; e-mail: graduate_admissions@grove.iup.edu.

ADMISSION STANDARDS. Selective. Usual minimum average: 2.75 (A = 4).

FINANCIAL AID. Annual awards from institutional funds: scholarships (based on merit and need), research fellowships, teaching assistantships, internships, tuition waivers, Federal W/S, loans. Approved for VA benefits. Apply by March 15 to Assistant Dean of Graduate School for assistantships, fellowships; to Director of Financial Aid for all other programs. Phone: (724)357-2218. Use FAFSA. About 30% of students receive aid other than loans from University. Aid available for part-time students.

DEGREE REQUIREMENTS. For master's: 30–36 credit hours minimum for most, at least 24 in residence; thesis/nonthesis option. For Ed.D., Ph.D., Psy.D.: minimum of 60 credits beyond the bachelor's degree; qualifying exam; dissertation; final oral exam.

FIELDS OF STUDY.
Administration.
Adult/Community Education.
Applied Mathematics.
Art.
Art Education.
Biology.
Business Administration.
Business Workplace Development.
Chemistry.
Clinical Psychology.
Counseling Services. Includes certifications in elementary school counselor, secondary school counselor, and supervisor of guidance services.
Criminology.
Curriculum and Instruction.
Early Childhood Education.
Educational Psychology.
Education of Exceptional Persons.
Elementary School Mathematics.
Elementary School Counseling.

English. Includes English education, literature, teaching English to speakers of other languages.
Fine Arts.
Food and Nutrition.
Geography.
History.
Industrial and Labor Relations.
Leadership Studies. Includes educational, human services.
Literacy.
Mathematics.
Middle School Mathematics.
Music.
Nursing.
Physics.
Political Science.
Professional Growth.
Psychology.
Public Affairs.
Safety Science.
School Psychology.
Secondary School Counseling.
Sociology.
Speech-Language Pathology.
Sports Sciences.
Student Affairs in Higher Education.

UNIVERSITY OF INDIANAPOLIS
Indianapolis, Indiana 46227-3697
Web site: www.uindy.edu

Founded 1902. Private control, United Methodist. Semester system. Library, 153,000 volumes, 1200 subscriptions.

Tuition: $496 per credit. No on-campus housing for graduate students. Estimated annual housing costs $5000–$5490.

Graduate Programs

Graduate enrollment: full-time 313, part-time 591. Faculty teaching graduate students: full-time 19, part-time 42. Degrees conferred: M.A., M.B.A., M.Acc., M.S., M.H.S., M.S.N., D.H.S., D.P.T., O.T.D., Psy.D.

ADMISSION REQUIREMENTS. Transcripts, GRE/GMAT/ PRAXIS, statement of purpose, three letters of recommendation, interview required in support of Graduate application. On-line application available. TOEFL (minimum score 550) required for international applicants. Accepts transfer applicants. Apply to the individual program offices. Rolling admissions process. Application fee $50. Phone: (800)232-8634.

ADMISSION STANDARDS. Relatively open for some programs, selective for others. Usual minimum average: 2.75 (A = 4).

FINANCIAL AID. Fellowships, assistantships, Federal W/S, loans. Approved for VA benefits. Apply to Financial Aid Office; no specified closing date. Phone: (317)788-3217. Use FAFSA (University code: 00184).

DEGREE REQUIREMENTS. For M.A.: 32 semester hours and thesis, or 36 semester hours, without thesis, at least 24 in residence. For M.Acc.: 30 semester hours. For M.S., M.H.S.: 36 semester hours. For M.B.A.: 42 semester hours minimum. For M.S.N.: 40 semester hour program. For D.H.S.: 90 credit programs beyond the bachelor's; critical inquiry; clinical practice. For D.P.T.: 37 credit program beyond the master's. For O.T.D.: 72 credit program beyond bachelor's; plan of study; project; clinical practice; residency. For Psy.D.: 108 semester hour program:

final-year internship. All master's degrees must be completed within five years.

FIELDS OF STUDY.
Accounting.
Applied Sociology.
Art.
Business Administration. Includes finance, technology management, organizational leadership.
Clinical Psychology. Psy.D. only.
Curriculum and Instruction.
English.
Family Nurse Practitioner. M.S.N. only.
History and Political Sciences.
Human Biology.
International Relations.
Mental Health Counseling.
Occupational Therapy. Includes administrative, neuroscience, orthopedic tracks at doctoral level. M.S., O.T.D.
Physical Therapy. M.S., M.H.S., D.H.S., D.P.T.
Psychology.
Teaching.

COLLEGE OF INSURANCE
New York, New York 10007-2165
Web site: www.tci.edu

Founded 1962. Private control (sponsored by more than 350 companies in the insurance and financial services industry). Semester system. Library: 99,000 volumes, 520 subscriptions.

Tuition: full-time $14,964. On-campus housing for single graduate students. Average academic year housing cost: $9414. Contact Housing Office for both on- and off-campus housing information. Phone: (212)815-9292.

Graduate Program

Enrollment: evening only; full- and part-time 83 (men 75%, women 25%). College faculty: full-time 10, part-time 25. Degree conferred: M.B.A.

ADMISSION REQUIREMENTS. Official transcripts, GMAT required in support of College's application. TOEFL (minimum score 550) required for international applicants. Accepts transfer applicants. Apply to Office of Admissions by May 1 (Fall), October 1 (Spring). Application fee $30. Phone: (212)815-9232; fax: (212)964-3381; e-mail: admissions@tci.edu.

ADMISSION STANDARDS. Selective. Usual minimum average: 3.0 (A = 4), plus 500 GMAT.

FINANCIAL AID. Annual awards from institutional funds: graduate assistantships, research assistantships, internships, Federal W/S, loans. Approved for VA benefits. Apply by May 15 to Director of Financial Aid. Phone: (212)815-9221; fax: (212)964-3381. Use FAFSA. Aid available for part-time students.

DEGREE REQUIREMENTS. For M.B.A.: completion of 51-credit program with at least a 3.0 (A = 4); 27 credits in core curriculum, 9 credits in major, 15 credits of electives.

FIELDS OF STUDY.
Actuarial Science.
Financial Management.
Financial Management of Risk.
Insurance.
Risk Management.

INTER AMERICAN UNIVERSITY OF PUERTO RICO

San German, Puerto Rico 00683-5008
Web site: www.sg.inter.edu

College-level study since 1921. Coed. Private control. Semester system. Main campuses at San German and San Juan. Regional colleges at Aguadilla, Arecibo, Barranquitas, Fajardo, Guayama, and Ponce. Library: 162,544 volumes, 1750 subscriptions.

Tuition: per graduate credit hour $165. On-campus housing available only at San German campus for single students. Average academic year housing cost: $2400 (including board). Contact Dean of Students Office for both on- and off-campus housing information. Phone: (787)264-1912, ext. 215.

Graduate Study

Offered at San German campus and San Juan campus. Enrollment: full-time 324, part-time 563. Graduate faculty: full-time 39, part-time 40. Degrees conferred: M.A., M.A.Ed., M.B.A., M.L.S., M.S., M.S.Ed.

ADMISSION REQUIREMENTS. Official transcripts, two letters of recommendations, PAEG or GRE required in support of application. Accepts transfer applicants. Apply by May 1 (Fall), November 15 (Spring), April 1 (Summer) to the Admissions Director. Rolling admissions process. Application fee $25. Phone: (787)892-4300, ext. 7358; fax: (787)892-6350.

ADMISSION STANDARDS. Selective. Usual minimum average: 3.0 (last 60 credits) or 2.75–2.99 (last 60 credits plus GRE) for full standing (A = 4).

FINANCIAL AID. Limited to assistantships, loans. Apply to appropriate department chair well in advance of registration. Use FAFSA and University's FAF. Phone: (787)264-1912. Aid available for part-time students.

DEGREE REQUIREMENTS. For master's: 36–45 credit hours minimum, at least 30 credits in residence; thesis/nonthesis option; comprehensive exam for some programs.

FIELDS OF STUDY.
Administration of Higher Education.
Art.
Business Administration. Includes accounting, finance, human resources, industrial relations, marketing.
Curriculum and Instruction.
Educational Administration.
English.
Environmental Sciences.
Library Science.
Physical Education.
Psychology. 51 credits for M.A.
Science Education.
Special Education.
TESOL.

School of Law (P.O. Box 70351)

Established 1961. ABA approved since 1969. AALS member. Semester system. Located in San Juan (00936). Library: 162,000 volumes, 1658 subscriptions; has LEXIS, NEXIS, DIALOG, DOBIS/LUVEN, MICRO JURIS.

Tuition: resident $10,958, part-time resident $8859. No on-campus housing available. Total average annual additional expense: $8900.

Enrollment: first-year class, full-time 118, part-time 109; total full- and part-time 701 (men 48%, women 52%). Faculty: full-

time 23, part-time 28. Student to faculty ratio 21 to 1. Degree conferred: J.D.

ADMISSION REQUIREMENTS. Transcripts, bachelor's degree, LSAT, PAEG, three letters of recommendation, personal interview required in support of application. Interview by invitation. Proficiency in Spanish required, non-Spanish speakers must take PAEG (minimum score 575). Graduates of unaccredited colleges not considered. Apply by March 31. Application fee $63. Phone: (809)751-1912, ext. 2012, 2013.

ADMISSION STANDARDS. Selective. Mean LSAT: full-time 140, part-time 140; mean GPA: full-time 3.17, part-time 3.16 (A = 4). *U.S. News & World Report* ranking is in the fourth tier of all U.S. law schools. Admits approximately 25–30% of total annual applicants.

FINANCIAL AID. Scholarships, grants, Federal W/S, loans, and a deferred payment plan available. Apply to Financial Aid Office by March 31. Use FAFSA (School code: 017202). About 10% of students receive some aid from School.

DEGREE REQUIREMENTS. For J.D.: satisfactory completion of three-year (full-time), four-year (part-time) program, 92 credits hours.

IONA COLLEGE

New Rochelle, New York 10801
Web site: www.iona.edu

Founded 1940. Located 16 miles NE of New York City. Coed. Private control. Roman Catholic. Semester and trimester systems. Library: 313,000 volumes, 1400 subscriptions. Total University enrollment: 5000.

Tuition: per credit $515. No on-campus housing available. Apply to Housing Office for off-campus housing information. Phone: (914)633-2336.

Graduate Study

Graduate enrollment: full- and part-time 1400. Faculty teaching graduate students: full-time 66, part-time 40. Degrees conferred: M.A., M.S., M.S. in Ed., M.S.T., M.B.A.

ADMISSION REQUIREMENTS. Transcripts, three letters of recommendation required in support of application. On-line application available. GMAT required in business. GRE and interview required for some programs. TOEFL required for international applicants. Accepts transfer applicants. Apply to Graduate School of Arts and Science for Education and Arts and Sciences, or Hagan School of Business for Business and Management; no specified closing date. Admit to Fall, Spring, Summer trimesters. Application fee $35, $50 for M.B.A. Phone: (800)231-IONA, (914)633-2502 (Arts & Science), (914)633-2288 (Business).

ADMISSION STANDARDS. Selective. Usual minimum average: 2.75 (A = 4).

FINANCIAL AID. Scholarships, graduate assistantships, tuition waivers, loans. Approved for VA benefits. Apply to the Office of Financial Aid: no specified closing date. Use FAFSA. Phone: (914)633-2497.

DEGREE REQUIREMENTS. For master's: 30–61 credit hours minimum, at least 24 in residence; written/oral comprehensive exam in some programs.

FIELDS OF STUDY.

Business Administration. Includes financial management, human resources management, information and decision technology management, management, marketing.

Computer Science.

Criminal Justice.

Economics.

Educational Administration.

Educational Technology.

Elementary Education. Includes specialization in science.

English.

Family Counseling.

Health Services Administration.

History.

Journalism. Includes on-line, print.

Marketing.

Mass Communication. Includes organizational, public relations.

Multicultural Education.

Pastoral Counseling.

Psychology.

Secondary Education. Includes biology, business education, English, mathematics, Spanish, social studies.

Spanish.

Telecommunications.

IOWA STATE UNIVERSITY OF SCIENCE AND TECHNOLOGY

Ames, Iowa 50011-2010

Web site: www.iastate.edu

Founded 1858. Located 40 miles N of Des Moines. CGS and AAU member. Coed. State control. Semester system. Special facilities: Ames Laboratory, National Soil Tilth Laboratory, National Animal Disease Center, Institute for Physical Research and Technology, Iowa Agriculture and Home Economics Experiment Station, Leopold Center for Sustainable Agriculture, Center for Agricultural and Rural Development, Center for Nondestructive Evaluation, Industrial Relations Center, Center for Transportation Research and Education, Veterinary Medical Research Institute, the Institute for Social and Behavioral Research, Utilization Center for Agricultural Products, Plant Sciences Institutes, Center for Immunity Enhancement in Domestic Animals, Computation Center, Center for Designing Foods to Improve Nutrition, Iowa Energy Center. Library: 2,500,000 volumes, 21,239 subscriptions. Total University enrollment: 26,845.

Annual tuition: resident $3902, nonresident $10,898. Unlimited on-campus housing for married and single students. Housing costs range from $259 per month (double occupancy) to monthly apartment rates of $424–447. Apply to Director of Residential Life. Phone: (515)294-2900.

Graduate College

Graduate study since 1868, first graduate degree conferred in 1877. Enrollment: full- and part-time 4,223. Graduate faculty: full-time 1300. Degrees conferred: M.A., M.S., M.Acc., M.Agr., M.Arch., M.B.A., M.C.R.P., M.Ed., M.Eng., M.F.A., M.F.C.S., M.L.A., M.P.A., M.S.M. specialist, Ph.D.

ADMISSION REQUIREMENTS. Transcripts, letters of reference required in support of College's application. On-line application available. GRE required for most departments. Interview not required. Accepts transfer applicants. TOEFL (minimum score 173 on computer-based test) required for international applicants. Graduates of unaccredited colleges not considered. Apply to Graduate College Office at least two months prior to beginning of term (some departments have earlier deadlines); international applicants should apply between nine and twelve months before entering term. Application fee $20, $50 for international applicants. Phone: (800)262-3810; e-mail: grad_admissions@iastate.edu.

ADMISSION STANDARDS. Very competitive for most departments, competitive for some. Usual minimum average: 2.75 (A = 4).

FINANCIAL AID. Scholarships, fellowships, teaching/research assistantships, grants, Federal W/S, loans; deferred payment plan. Approved for VA benefits. Apply to head of proposed major department for scholarships, fellowships, assistantships, preferably by March 15; to Financial Aid Office for all other programs. Use FAFSA and institutional FAF. About 50% of students receive aid other than loans from University and outside sources. Aid available for part-time students.

DEGREE REQUIREMENTS. For master's: 30 credits minimum, at least 22 credits in residence; reading knowledge of one foreign language for some majors; thesis for most majors; final oral exam. For M.Arch.: 30 credits minimum beyond Bachelor's of Architecture degree; 60 credit program beyond B.A., B.S. degree; up to 100 credit program for students with other degrees. For M.Acc.: 32 credit program; creative project. For M.Agr.: 32 credit nonthesis program. For M.B.A.: 48 credits minimum (a combination of integrated core modules and advanced electives). For M.C.R.P.: 48 credit program; thesis/nonthesis option. For M.Ed.: 30–40 credit program; creative project or field-based activity. For M.F.C.S.: 36 credit program; 2 nonthesis options. For M.F.A.: 60–61 credit program; thesis-exhibition or thesis. For M.L.A.: 36 credit program; thesis or creative project. For M.P.A.: 37 credit program; internship or thesis. For M.S.M.: 36 credit program; creative project. For Ph.D.: 72 credits minimum with 36 credits under supervision of Student's Program of Study Committee; at least 24 credits must be earned during 2 consecutive semesters or a continuous period of 2 semesters in a summer term; preliminary exam; dissertation; final oral exam.

FIELDS OF STUDY.

Accounting. M.Acc. only.

Aerospace Engineering.

Agricultural Economics.

Agricultural Education.

Agricultural Engineering.

Agricultural History and Rural Studies. Ph.D. only.

Agricultural Meteorology.

Agronomy. M.S. only.

Analytical Chemistry.

Animal Breeding and Genetics.

Animal Ecology.

Animal Nutrition.

Animal Physiology.

Animal Science.

Anthropology. M.A. only.

Applied Mathematics.

Applied Physics.

Architectural Studies. M.S. only.

Architecture.

Art and Design. M.A. only.

Astrophysics.

Biochemistry.

Bioinformatics and Computational Biology.

Biomedical Engineering.

Biophysics.

Botany.

Business. M.S. only.

Business Administration. M.B.A. only.

Chemical Engineering.

Chemistry.

Civil Engineering.

Community and Regional Planning. M.C.R.P. only.

Computer Engineering.
Computer Science.
Condensed Matter Physics.
Crop Production and Physiology.
Earth Science.
Ecology and Evolutionary Biology.
Economics.
Education. Includes curriculum and instructional, educational leaderships and policy studies.
Electrical Engineering.
Engineering Mechanics.
English. M.A. only.
Entomology.
Exercise and Sport Science. M.S. only.
Family and Consumer Science Education.
Family and Consumer Sciences. M.F.C.S. only.
Fisheries Biology.
Food Science and Technology.
Forestry.
Genetics.
Geology.
Graphic Design. M.F.A. only.
Health and Human Performance. Ph.D. only.
High Energy Physics.
History. M.A. only.
History of Technology and Science.
Horticulture.
Hotel, Restaurant, and Institutional Management.
Human Development and Family Studies.
Immunobiology.
Industrial Education and Technology.
Industrial Engineering.
Industrial Relations. M.S. only.
Information Assurance. M.S. only.
Inorganic Chemistry.
Integrated Visual Arts. M.F.A. only
Interdisciplinary Graduate Studies. M.A., M.S. only.
Interior Design. M.F.A. only.
Journalism and Mass Communication. M.S. only.
Landscape Architecture. M.L.A. only.
Material Science and Engineering.
Mathematics.
Meat Science.
Mechanical Engineering.
Meteorology.
Microbiology.
Molecular, Cellular, and Developmental Biology.
Neuroscience.
Nuclear Physics.
Nutrition.
Operations Research. M.S. only.
Organic Chemistry.
Physical Chemistry.
Physics.
Physiology.
Plant Breeding.
Plant Pathology.
Plant Physiology.
Political Science. M.A. only.
Professional Agriculture. M.Ag. only.
Psychology.
Public Administration. M.P.A. only.
Rhetoric and Professional Communication. Ph.D. only.
Rural Sociology.
School Mathematics. M.S.M.
Sociology.
Soil Science.
Statistics.
Sustainable Agriculture.
Systems Engineering. M.Eng. only.
Textiles and Clothing.
Toxicology.
Transportation. M.S. only
Veterinary Anatomy.
Veterinary Clinical Sciences.
Veterinary Microbiology.
Veterinary Pathology.
Veterinary Preventive Medicine. M.S. only.
Water Resources.
Wildlife Biology.
Zoology.
Note: There are only six approved dual degree programs: M.Arch.-M.B.A., M.Arch.-M.C.R.P., M.C.R.P.-M.B.A., M.L.A.-M.C.R.P., M.P.A.-M.C.R.P., M.S. (Statistics)-M.B.A.

College of Veterinary Medicine (50011)

Established 1879. Annual tuition: resident and contract students $6630, nonresident $18,074. Total average cost for all other expenses: $17,280. On-campus housing available.

Enrollment: first-year class 100, total full-time 462 (men 45%, women 55%). Faculty: full-time 119, part-time 22. Degree conferred: D.V.M. The M.S. and Ph.D. are offered through the Graduate College.

ADMISSION REQUIREMENTS. VMCAS report, transcripts, GRE, three letters of recommendation (from an academic adviser veterinarian) required in support of application. Applicants must have completed at least three years of college study. Early Decision Option available. Accepts transfer applicants on space available basis only. Preference given to state, New Jersey, North Dakota, and South Dakota residents. Apply to University Director of Admissions and Records before October 1. Fall admission only. Application fee $20. Phone: (515)294-1242, toll-free outside Iowa (800)262-3810.

ADMISSION STANDARDS. Competitive. Mean GPA: 3.57 (A = 4). Accepts about 30% of total applicants. Accepts approximately 25 nonresidents (at large) applicants.

FINANCIAL AID. Scholarships, fellowships, teaching assistantships, Federal W/S, loans. Apply by March 1 to Student Financial Aid Office, to appropriate department head for fellowships and assistantships. About 50% of students receive aid other than loans from College funds.

DEGREE REQUIREMENTS. For D.V.M.: satisfactory completion of four-year program. For M.S., Ph.D.: see Graduate College listing above.

FIELDS OF GRADUATE STUDY.
Biomedical Sciences. Includes physiology, pharmacology, veterinary anatomy. M.S., Ph.D.
Veterinary Clinical Sciences. Includes surgery, swine production medicine, theriogenology, veterinary medicine, veterinary diagnostic and production animal medicine. M.S.
Veterinary Microbiology and Preventive Medicine. Includes swine production medicine, veterinary microbiology, veterinary preventive medicine. M.S., Ph.D.
Veterinary Pathology. Includes cellular and molecular pathology, veterinary clinical pathology, veterinary parasitology, veterinary toxicology. M.S., Ph.D.

THE UNIVERSITY OF IOWA
Iowa City, Iowa 52242
Web site: www.uiowa.edu

Founded 1847. Located 250 miles SW of Chicago. CGS and AAU member. Coed. State control. Semester system. Special facilities: Computer-assisted Image Analysis Facility, Electron Microscopy Facility, High Field Nuclear Magnetic Facility, High Resolution Mass Spectrometry Facility, Institute of Hydraulic Research, Laser Science Research Facility, Large Scale Fermentation Facility, Museum of Art, Museum of Natural History, Public Policy Center, Social Science Institute. The University's NIH ranking is 29th among all U.S. institutions with 428 awards/grants worth $148,697,690. Library: 4,000,000 volumes, 44,500 subscriptions.

On-campus housing for 749 married students, 5356 single students. Average academic year housing cost: $5760 for married students, $5555 (including board) for single students. Apply to Family Housing Office. Phone: (319)335-9199 or Housing Assignment Office (319)335-3009; for off-campus housing, the University Housing Clearinghouse (319)335-3055.

Graduate College

Graduate study since 1900. Academic year tuition: resident $3692, nonresident $13,334. Enrollment: full-time 2570, part-time 1914. University faculty teaching graduate students: full-time 1618, part-time 96. Degrees conferred: M.A., M.S., M.Ac., M.F.A., M.A.T., M.H.A., M.P.A., M.P.H., M.P.T., M.S.W., M.S.N., Ed.S., D.M.A., Ph.D.

ADMISSION REQUIREMENTS. Transcripts, three letters of recommendation required in support of College's application. Interview, GRE Subject Tests, GMAT required by some departments. TOEFL required for international applicants. Accepts transfer applicants. Graduates of unaccredited institutions not considered. Apply to University Director of Admissions by July 15 (Fall), December 1 (Spring), April 15 (Summer). Application fee $20. Phone: (319)335-1525; fax: (319)335-1535; e-mail: admissions@uiowa.edu.

ADMISSION STANDARDS. Very selective or competitive for most departments. Usual minimum average: 2.5 (A = 4).

FINANCIAL AID. Annual awards from institutional funds: scholarships, fellowships, teaching assistantships, research assistantships, internships, Federal W/S, loans. Approved for VA benefits. Apply by February 1 to appropriate department for scholarships, fellowships, assistantships: to Director of Financial Aid for all other programs. Use FAFSA and institutional FAF. Phone: (319)335-1450; fax: (319)335-3060. Approximately 50% of students receive aid other than loans from College and outside sources. Aid available for part-time students.

DEGREE REQUIREMENTS. For M.A., M.S., M.Ac.: 30–48 semester hours minimum with or without thesis, at least 24 in residence; comprehensive/final oral exam; candidacy; no language for most majors. For M.F.A.: ordinarily two years of full-time residence, but requirement may be reduced to a minimum of one year at discretion of department head; thesis/creative project. For M.A.T.: 38 hours minimum, at least 24 in residence; final written/oral exam. For M.P.H.: 39–48 semester hour program; practicum; final written report and oral presentation. For M.H.A.: 60 semester hour full-time program; internship. For M.S.W.: 36–60 hours required, at least 24 in residence; final written/oral exam. For M.P.T.: 67 hours minimum, four semesters of full-time residence plus internship; written/oral exam. For M.P.A.: 92 hours minimum, at least 24 in residence; final project/comprehensive exam. For M.S.N.: 40–52 hours required, at least 24 in residence; thesis/nonthesis option; final written/oral exam. For Ed.S.: ordinarily two years, at least one year in residence and 1 semester in full-time attendance; final written/oral exam. For Ph.D.: 72 hours minimum, at least 18 in full-time residence; preliminary written/oral exam; candidacy; dissertation; knowledge of foreign languages or knowledge of special research tools, as determined by department; final oral exam. For D.M.A.: same as for the Ph.D., except qualifying recital and doctoral essay instead of dissertation.

FIELDS OF STUDY.

Accounting. M.Ac.

Afro-American World Studies. M.A.

American Studies. M.A., Ph.D.

Anatomy and Cell Biology. M.S., Ph.D.

Anthropology. M.A.

Applied Mathematical and Computational Sciences. Ph.D.

Art. M.A., M.F.A.

Art History. M.A., Ph.D.

Asian Civilizations. M.A.

Astronomy. M.S.

Biochemistry. M.S., Ph.D.

Biological Sciences. Includes developmental, ecology, evolutionary, genetics, molecular and cell biology, neurobiology, plant science. M.S., Ph.D.

Biomedical Engineering. M.S., Ph.D.

Biosciences. Ph.D.

Business Administration. Includes accounting, finance, management and organizations, management sciences, marketing. M.A., M.B.A., Ph.D.

Chemical and Biochemical Engineering. M.S., Ph.D.

Chemistry. M.S., Ph.D.

Civil and Environmental Engineering. M.S., Ph.D.

Classics. No thesis for M.A. M.A., Ph.D.

Communication Studies. M.A., Ph.D.

Comparative Literature. M.A., Ph.D.

Comparative Literature/Translation. M.F.A.

Computer Science. M.C.S., M.S., Ph.D.

Dance. M.F.A.

Dental Public Health. M.S.

Economics. M.A., Ph.D.

Education—Counseling, Rehabilitation, and Student Development. Includes counselor education (Ph.D.), rehabilitation counseling (M.A., Ph.D.), school counseling, (M.A.), student development (M.A., Ph.D.), substance abuse counseling (M.A.), student affairs administration and research (Ph.D.).

Education—Curriculum and Instruction. Includes early childhood education (M.A.), elementary education (M.A., M.S., Ph.D.), secondary education (M.A., M.A.T., Ph.D.), special education (M.A., Ph.D.).

Education—Educational Policy and Leadership Studies. Includes educational administration (M.A., Ed.S., Ph.D.), higher education (M.A., Ed.S., Ph.D.), social foundations of education (M.A., Ph.D.).

Education—Psychological and Quantitative Foundations. Includes counseling psychology (Ph.D.), educational measurement and statistics (M.A., Ph.D.), educational psychology (M.A., Ph.D.), instructional design and technology (M.A., Ed.S., Ph.D.), school psychology (Ph.D.).

Electrical and Computer Engineering. M.S., Ph.D.

English. Includes literary studies (M.A., Ph.D.), nonfiction writing (M.F.A.) creative writing (M.F.A.). M.A., M.F.A., Ph.D.

Exercise Science. M.S., Ph.D.

Film and Video Production. M.F.A.

Film Studies. M.A., Ph.D.

Free Radical and Radiation Biology. M.S., Ph.D.

French. M.A., Ph.D.

Genetics. Ph.D.

Geography. M.A., Ph.D.

Geoscience. M.S., Ph.D.

German. M.A., Ph.D.

Greek. M.A.

Health and Sport Studies. M.A., Ph.D.

History. M.A., Ph.D.

Immunology. Ph.D.

Industrial Engineering. M.S., Ph.D.

Journalism. M.A.

Latin. M.A.

Law. LL.M.

Leisure Studies. M.A.

Library and Information Science. M.A.

Linguistics. M.A., Ph.D.
Mass Communications. Ph.D.
Mathematics. M.S., Ph.D.
Mechanical Engineering. M.S., Ph.D.
Microbiology. M.S., Ph.D.
Molecular Biology. Ph.D.
Music. M.A., M.F.A., D.M.A., Ph.D.
Neuroscience. Ph.D.
Nursing. M.S.N., Ph.D.
Operative Dentistry. M.S.
Oral and Maxillofacial Surgery. M.S.
Oral Science. M.S., Ph.D.
Orthodontics. M.S.
Pathology. M.S.
Pharmacology. M.S., Ph.D.
Pharmacy. M.S., Ph.D.
Philosophy. M.A., Ph.D.
Physical Therapy. M.A., M.P.T., Ph.D.
Physician Assistant Studies. M.P.A.
Physics. M.S., Ph.D.
Physiology and Biophysics. M.S., Ph.D.
Political Science. M.A., Ph.D.
Psychology. M.A., Ph.D.
Public Health. Includes biostatistics (M.S., Ph.D.), epidemiology (M.S., Ph.D.), health management and policy (M.H.A., Ph.D.), occupational and environmental health (M.S., Ph.D.), public health (M.P.H.).
Religion. M.A., Ph.D.
Russian. M.A.
Science Education. M.S., Ph.D.
Second Language Acquisition. Ph.D.
Social Studies. M.A.
Social Work. M.S.W., Ph.D.
Sociology. M.A., Ph.D.
Spanish. M.A., Ph.D.
Speech and Hearing Science. Ph.D.
Speech Pathology and Audiology. M.A.
Statistics. Includes actuarial science (M.S.). M.S., Ph.D.
Stomatology. M.S.
Theatre Arts. M.F.A.
Third World Development Support. M.A.
Translational Biomedicine. M.S., Ph.D.
Urban and Regional Planning. M.A., M.S.
Women's Studies. Ph.D.

College of Dentistry

Established 1882. Located at Health Science Campus. Special facilities: Dows Institute of Dental Research, Center for Clinical Studies, Center for Oral and Maxillofacial Implants, Oral Health Research Clinical Core Center, Research Center on Oral Health in Aging, Specialized Caries Research Center. Special programs: summer programs for underrepresented minorities. Postgraduate specialties: Dental Public Health, Endodontics, General Dentistry, Operative Dentistry, Oral and Maxillofacial Pathology, Oral and Maxillofacial Surgery, Oral Science, Orthodontics, Pediatric Dentistry, Prosthodontics, Radiology and Medicine. Library: 18,000 volumes, 283 subscriptions.

Annual tuition: resident $9670, nonresident $23,630. Limited on-campus housing available. Married students contact Family Housing Office for housing information; phone: (319)335-9199. For off-campus housing information contact the Housing Clearinghouse, phone: (319)335-3055. Total average annual cost for all other first-year expenses: approximately $10,273.

Enrollment: first-year class 76; total full-time 372 (men 60%, women 40%); postgraduates 60. Faculty: full-time 81, part-time 78. Degrees conferred: D.D.S., M.S., Ph.D., D.S.T.P. (NIH-funded program).

ADMISSION REQUIREMENTS. AADSAS report, transcripts, DAT (not later than October), three letters of recommendation,

interview required in support of application. Preference given to Iowa and Arkansas residents. Applicants must have completed at least three years of college study. Apply to Associate Dean for Academic Affairs after June 1, before November 1. Application fee $30. Phone: (319)335-7157; fax: (319)335-7155.

ADMISSION STANDARDS. Competitive. Usual minimum average: 3.0 (A = 4). Mean DAT: Academic 19, PAT 18; mean GPA: 3.49 (A = 4). Gourman rating: 4.38. Accepts about 25–30% of total annual applicants. Approximately 60% are state residents.

FINANCIAL AID. Scholarships, dental research and teaching awards, federal programs, loans. Apply by November 30 to University Office of Student Aid. Phone: (319)335-1450. Use FAFSA (College code: 001892). About 100% of students receive aid from College.

DEGREE REQUIREMENTS. For D.D.S.: satisfactory completion of forty-five-month program. For M.S.: thirty-hour minimum in residence, final exam. For Ph.D.: see Graduate College listing above.

FIELDS OF GRADUATE STUDY.
Dental Public Health.
Endodontics.
General Dentistry.
Operative Dentistry.
Oral and Maxillofacial Pathology.
Oral and Maxillofacial Surgery.
Oral Science.
Orthodontics.
Pediatric Dentistry.
Pedodontics.
Periodontics.
Prosthodontics.
Radiology.

College of Law

Founded 1865. Oldest law school school west of the Mississippi. ABA approved since 1923. AALS member. Semester system. Law library: 961,377 volumes, 8663 subscriptions; has LEXIS, NEXIS, WESTLAW, ILP.

Annual tuition: residents $7824, nonresidents $19,040. Total cost for all other expenses: $9920.

Enrollment: first-year class 233 (Fall), 45 (Summer) full- and part-time total 653 (men 54%, women 46%). Faculty: full-time 45, part-time 5. Student to faculty ratio 12.2 to 1. Degrees conferred: J.D., J.D.-M.A., LL.M. (International and Comparative Law).

ADMISSION REQUIREMENTS. LSDAS Law School report, bachelor's degree, transcripts, LSAT required in support of application. Interview not required. Accepts transfer applicants. Preference given to state residents. Graduates of unaccredited colleges not considered. Apply to Director of Admissions after September 1, before March 1. Fall and Summer admission only. Application fee $30, foreign application fee $40. Phone: (800)553-IOWA; phone: (319)335-9095; fax: (319)335-9019; e-mail: law-admissions@uiowa.edu.

ADMISSION STANDARDS. Selective. Mean LSAT: 159; mean GPA: 3.94 (A = 4). Gourman rating: 4.50. *U.S. News & World Report* ranking is in the top 18 of all U.S. law schools. Accepts less than 30–35% of total annual applicants. Limited to no more than 30% nonresidents.

FINANCIAL AID. Scholarships, fellowships, assistantships, full and partial tuition waivers, Federal W/S, loans. Apply by January 1 to Associate Director of Admission. Phone: (319)335-9142. Use FAFSA (College code: 001892). About 85% of students receive some aid from College.

DEGREE REQUIREMENTS. For J.D.: 90 credit hours minimum, at least two years in residence. For LL.M.: at least 24 credits minimum beyond the J.D.

College of Medicine (52242-1101)
Web site: www.medadmin.uiowa.edu

Established 1850. Located at Health Science Campus. Special facilities: Center for Macular Degeneration, Center for Health Effects of Environmental Contamination, Center for the Study of the Brain and Language, Cooperative Human Linkage Center, Iowa Cystic Fibrosis Center, Iowa Geriatric Education Center, Iowa Specialized center for Pulmonary Research, Schizophrenia Research Center, Specialized Center for Occupational and Immunological Lung Disease. Library: 260,521 volumes, 2583 subscriptions.

Annual tuition: resident $14,504, nonresident $32,972. On-campus rooms and apartments available for both single and married students. Annual housing cost: $275–$700 per month. Married students contact Family Housing Office for housing information, phone: (319)335-9199. For off-campus housing information contact the Housing Clearinghouse, phone: (319)335-3055. Off-campus housing and personal expenses: approximately $10,273.

Enrollment: first-year class 142; total 650 (men 56%, women 44%). Faculty: full- and part-time 677. Degrees conferred: M.D., M.D.-Ph.D. (Medical Scientist Training Program). The M.A., M.S., and Ph.D. are offered through the Graduate College.

ADMISSION REQUIREMENTS. AMCAS report, transcripts, letters of evaluation, MCAT required in support of application. Interviews may be requested. Preference given to Iowa residents. Has EDP; apply between June 1 and August 1. Accepts transfer applicants. Applicants must have completed at least three years of college study. Graduates of unaccredited colleges not considered. Apply after June 1, before November 1. Application fee $30. Phone: (319)335-8052; fax: (319)335-8049; e-mail: medical-admissions@uiowa.edu.

ADMISSION STANDARDS. Selective. Gourman rating: 4.40. *U.S. News & World Report* ranking in the top 30 of all U.S. medical schools, and in the top 10 primary care. Accepts 15% of total annual applicants. Approximately 88% are state residents.

FINANCIAL AID. Scholarships, summer fellowships, grants, tuition waivers, loans. Apply to Associate Dean by June 1. Use FAFSA (College code: 001892). Approximately 95% of students receive aid from College and outside sources.

DEGREE REQUIREMENTS. For M.D.: satisfactory completion of four-year program. For M.A., M.S., Ph.D., see Graduate College listing above. For M.D.-Ph.D.: generally a seven-year program.

FIELDS OF GRADUATE STUDY.
Anatomy and Cell Biology. Includes biology of differentiation and transformation, developmental and vascular cell biology, neurobiology, molecular medicine, and gene therapy.
Biochemistry.
Biophysics.
Biosciences.
Genetics.
Immunology.
Microbiology.
Molecular Biology.
Neurosciences.
Pathology.
Pharmacology.
Physiology.

ITHACA COLLEGE
Ithaca, New York 14850-7142
Web site: www.ithaca.edu

Founded 1892. Located 50 miles SW of Syracuse. CGS member. Coed. Private control. Semester system. Library: 335,000 volumes, 238,600 microforms, 2500 subscriptions.

Tuition: per credit $629. No on-campus housing for graduate students. Contact Room Assignments Coordinator of Residential Life for off-campus housing information.

Division of Graduate Studies

Enrollment: full-time 228, part-time 20. Faculty: full- and part-time 109. Degrees conferred: M.S., M.M.

ADMISSION REQUIREMENTS. Official transcripts, two letters of recommendation (four letters if applying for an assistantship), GRE scores (for Speech Pathology, Audiology, and Exercise and Sport Science applicants) required in support of application. Auditions required for Music applicants. TOEFL required for international applicants. Accepts transfer applicants. Graduates of unaccredited institutions not considered. Apply to Dean of Graduate Studies by March 1 (Fall), December 1 (Spring). Application fee $40. Phone: (607)274-3527; fax: (607)274-1263; e-mail: gradstudies@ithaca.edu.

ADMISSION STANDARDS. Selective. Usual minimum average: 3.0. (A = 4).

FINANCIAL AID. Annual awards from institutional funds: teaching assistantships, internships, grants, Federal W/S, loans. Approved for VA benefits. Apply with admission application but not later than March 1 to Dean of Graduate Studies for assistantships; to Financial Aid Office for all other programs. Phone: (607)274-3131; fax: (607)274-1895. Use FAFSA. About 40% of students receive aid other than loans from College. No aid for part-time students.

DEGREE REQUIREMENTS. For M.S.: 30–39 credits minimum; thesis; 36–39 credit hours nonthesis; final oral/written exam. For M.M.: 30 credits minimum; recital; final oral/written exam.

FIELDS OF STUDY.
Business Administration.
Communication.
Exercise and Sports Sciences.
Music. Includes composition, conducting, music education, theory, string, woodwinds, brass.
Occupational Therapy.
Physcial Education.
Speech-Language, Pathology and Audiology.
Teaching Students with Speech and Language Disabilities.

JACKSON STATE UNIVERSITY
Jackson, Mississippi 39217-0195
Web site: www.jsums.edu

Founded 1877. CGS member. Coed. State control. Semester system. Library: 400,000 volumes, 2706 subscriptions.

Tuition: per semester hour $155, or $1394 per semester. Out-of-state students pay an additional fee of $1813 per semester. On-campus housing. Average academic year housing cost: $2112 for single students. Contact the Director of Residential Life for both on- and off-campus information. Phone: (601)968-2326.

Graduate School

Enrollment: full- and part-time about 1349. University faculty teaching graduate students: full-time 200, part-time 0. Degrees conferred: M.A., M.S., M.M.Ed., M.S.Ed., M.S.T., M.A.T., M.B.A., M.Bus.Ed., M.P.A., M.P.P.A., Ed.S., Ed.D., Ph.D.

ADMISSION REQUIREMENTS. Transcripts, GRE/GMAT, three letters of recommendation required in support of application. TOEFL required for international students. Accepts transfer applicants. Apply to Office of Admissions before March 15 (Summer), March 1 (Fall), October 1 (Spring). Application fee $20, $50 for nonresidents. Phone: (601)979-2455; fax: (601)979-4325.

ADMISSION STANDARDS. Relatively open. Usual minimum average: 2.5 (A = 4).

FINANCIAL AID. Scholarships, assistantships, tuition waivers, Federal W/S, loans. Approved for VA benefits. Apply to department of interest before March 1 (Summer), May 1 (Fall), November 1 (Spring) for scholarships, assistantships; to the Office of Aid for all other programs. Phone: (601)979-2227. Use FAFSA.

DEGREE REQUIREMENTS. For master's: 30 semester hours, 36 hours without thesis or project; thesis or project option, written comprehensive exam/final oral exam. For Ed.S.: 30 semester hours beyond the master's. For M.S.W.: 60 semester hours beyond the bachelor's degree. For Ed.D.: 60–66 semester hours. For Ph.D.: 60 semester hours; comprehension exam; dissertation; final oral exam.

FIELDS OF STUDY.
Accounting. M.P.A.
Biology. M.S.T., M.S.
Business Administration. M.B.A., Ph.D.
Business Education. M.B.Ed.
Chemistry. M.S., Ph.D.
Clinical Psychology. Ph.D.
Communicative Disorders. M.S.
Computer Science. M.S.
Criminology and Justice Services. M.A.
Early Childhood. M.S.Ed., Ed.D.
Educational Administration. Ph.D.
Educational Administration and Supervision. M.S.Ed., Ed.S.
Elementary Education. M.S.Ed., Ed.S.
English. M.A.T., M.A.
Environmental Science. M.S., Ph.D.
Guidance and Counseling. M.S.Ed., M.S., Ed.S.
Hazardous Materials Management. M.S.
Health, Physical Education, and Recreation. M.S.Ed.
History. M.A.
Industrial Arts Education. M.S.Ed.
Mass Communication. M.S.
Mathematics. M.S.T., M.S.
Mathematics Eduation. M.S.Ed.
Music Education. M.M.Ed.
Political Science. M.A.
Public Administration. Ph.D.
Public Health. M.P.H.
Public Policy and Administration. M.P.P.A.
Reading. M.S.Ed., Ed.S.
Rehabilitation Services. M.S.
Science Education. M.S.Ed., Ed.S.
Secondary Education. M.S.
Social Work. M.S.W., Ph.D.
Sociology. M.A.
Special Education. M.S.
Systems Management. M.S.S.M.

Technology Education. M.S.Ed.
Urban and Regional Planning. M.S., Ph.D.

JACKSONVILLE STATE UNIVERSITY
Jacksonville, Alabama 36265-1602
Web site: www.jsu.edu

Founded 1883. Located 76 miles NE of Birmingham. Coed. Public control. Semester system. Library: 420,583 volumes, 4790 subscriptions.

Annual tuition: resident, full-time $2940, nonresident $5880; per credit hour, resident $147, nonresident $294. On-campus housing for all graduate men and women who apply; none for married students. Average academic year housing cost: $2200–4400 (including board). Apply to Director of University Housing. Phone: (256)782-5122.

College of Graduate Studies

Graduate study since 1957. Enrollment: full-time 277, part-time 912 (men 20%, women 80%). Faculty teaching graduate students: full-time 157. Degrees conferred: M.S. in Ed., M.S., M.B.A., M.A., M.M., M.M.Ed., M.P.A.

ADMISSION REQUIREMENTS. Transcripts, GRE Subject Tests/GMAT/MAT required in support of College's application. Interview not required. TOEFL required for international applicants. Accepts transfer applicants. Apply to College of Graduate Studies; no specified closing date. Application fee $20. Phone: (256)782-5329; fax: (256)782-5321; e-mail: graduate@jsu.edu.

ADMISSION STANDARDS. Unconditional admissions; 450 x UGPA + GRE = 2000 or more; or 15 x UGPA + MAT = 60 or more; or 200 x UGPA + GMAT = 950 or more.

FINANCIAL AID. Limited to research assistantships, teaching assistantships, Federal W/S, loans. Approved for VA benefits. Apply by April 1 to Financial Aid Office. Phone: (256)782-5006. Use FAFSA. Aid available for part-time students.

DEGREE REQUIREMENTS. For M.A., M.M.Ed., M.M., M.P.A., M.S., M.S. in Ed.: Plan I, 24–36 semester hours plus thesis. For M.B.A.: Plan II, 30–42 semester hours without thesis. Under both plans, final oral/comprehensive exam.

FIELDS OF STUDY.
Biology.
Business Administration. Includes accounting.
Community Agency Counseling.
Computer Systems and Software Design.
Counselor Education.
Criminal Justice.
Early Childhood Education.
Early Childhood Special Education.
Educational Administration.
Elementary Education.
Emergency Managment.
English.
English Language Arts.
Environmental Science Management.
General Science.
General Studies.
History.
Library Media.
Mathematics.
Music.
Music Education.

Nursing.
Physical Education.
Political Science.
Psychology.
Public Administration.
Reading Specialist.
School Counseling.
Secondary Education. Eight subject areas.
Social Science.
Special Education.

JACKSONVILLE UNIVERSITY
Jacksonville, Florida 32211-3394
Web site: www.ju.edu

Founded 1934. Coed. Private control. Semester system. Library: 294,000 volumes, 900 subscriptions; library is an offical depository for both U.S. and Florida government documents.

Tuition: per hour $300; for M.B.A. $380; for Nursing $310. No on-campus housing for married students. Annual housing cost: $5500 (including board). Contact Dean of Students Office for both on- and off-campus housing information. Phone: (904)745-3950.

Graduate Program

Enrollment: full-time 130, part-time 208. Graduate faculty: full-time 60, part-time 20. Degrees conferred: M.A.T., M.B.A., M.S.N.

ADMISSION REQUIREMENTS. Transcripts, GRE/MAT, three letters of recommendation (two for M.B.A.), GMAT (M.B.A.), Florida nursing license (Nursing) required in support of application. On-line application available. Interview required for most departments. TOEFL (minimum score 550), TSE, TWE required for international applicants. Accepts transfer applicants. Apply to Director of M.A.T. or M.B.A. program at least 30 days prior to registration. Application fee $25, $50 for Business. Phone: Education (904)745-7132; Business (904)745-7459; Nursing (904)745-7286.

ADMISSION STANDARDS. Selective. Usual minimum average: 3.0 (A = 4).

FINANCIAL AID. Scholarships, assistantships, Federal W/S, loans. Approved for VA benefits. Apply by March 15 to the Office of Financial Aid. Phone: (904)745-7060. Use FAFSA.

DEGREE REQUIREMENTS. For M.A.T.: 36 semester hours, at least 30 in residence; six semester hours of internship or three years of teaching; final written exam. For M.B.A.: 30 semester hours, which must be completed within five years of completion of first graduate course. For M.S.N.: 32 semester hours; concentration; practicum.

FIELDS OF STUDY.
Art Education.
Business Administration.
Computing Science.
Educational Leadership.
Educational Technology.
Elementary Education.
English Education.
Foreign Languages.
Guidance Counseling.
Health Care Administration.
International Business.
Management.
Management/Marketing.
Marketing.

Mathematics Education.
Music Education.
Nursing. Includes nursing education, nursing administration.
Reading Education.
Social Sciences.

JAMES MADISON UNIVERSITY
Harrisonburg, Virginia 22807
Web site: www.jmu.edu

Established 1908. Located approximately 2½ hours from Washington, D.C. CGS member. Coed. Public control. Semester system. Special facilities: Center for Economics Education, Center for Entrepreneurship, Human Development Center, Speech and Hearing Center. Library: 1,300,000 volumes, 3367 subscriptions. Total University enrollment: 15,000.

Tuition: per credit, resident $143, nonresident $465. Limited on-campus housing for graduate students.

Graduate School

Graduate study since 1954. Enrollment: full-time 418, part-time 1315 (men 40%, women 60%). University faculty: full-time 156, part-time 30. Degrees conferred: M.A., M.S., M.S.Ed., M.B.A., M.A.T., M.Ed., M.M., M.P.A., M.F.A., Ed.S., Psy.D.

ADMISSION REQUIREMENTS. Transcripts, GRE Subject Tests (for some majors), GMAT for M.B.A. required in support of School's application. On-line application available. TOEFL required for international applicants. Interview required by some departments. Accepts transfer applicants. Graduates of unaccredited institutions not considered. Apply to Office of Dean at least 60 days prior to registration. Application fee $55. Phone: (540)568-6131; fax: (540)568-6266.

ADMISSION STANDARDS. Selective. Usual minimum average: 2.5 (A = 4).

FINANCIAL AID. Annual awards from institutional funds: scholarships, teaching assistantships, research assistantships, internships, service assistantships, Federal W/S, loans. Approved for VA benefits. Apply by March 1 to Dean of Graduate School. Phone: (540)568-7820; fax: (540)568-7994. Use FAFSA and University's FAF. About 30% of students receive aid other than loans from both College and outside sources.

DEGREE REQUIREMENTS. For master's: 30 semester credits minimum; thesis optional for many departments; final written/oral exam. For Ed.S.: 30 semester credits minimum; thesis optional for many departments, final written/oral exam. For Psy.D.: 60 semester credits minimum beyond master's degree; qualifying exam; advancement to candidacy; internship; special project; final written/oral exam.

FIELDS OF STUDY.
Accounting. M.S.
Art. M.F.A., M.A.
Biology. M.S.
Business Administration. Includes concentrations in health services administration, information security. M.B.A.
Community Counseling. Ed.S., Psy.D.
Computer Science. M.S.
Early Childhood Education. M.Ed.
English. M.A., M.A.T.
Fine Arts. Includes ceramics, drawing and painting, jewelry and metalwork, papermaking, photography, printmaking, sculpture. M.F.A.
Health Education. M.S.Ed.

Health Science. M.S.
Hearing Disorders. M.Ed.
History. M.A., M.A.T.
Human Resource Development. M.S.Ed.
Integrated Science and Technology. M.S.
Kinesiology. M.S.
Middle Education. M.Ed.
Music. Includes conducting, music education, performance, theory and composition. M.M.
Psychology. M.A.
Public Administration. Includes nonprofit organizations. M.P.A.
Reading Education. M.Ed.
School Administration. M.Ed.
School and Counseling Psychology. M. A., Psy.D.
School Counseling. M.Ed.
School Library Media Services. M.Ed.
School Psychology. M.Ed., Ed.S., Psy.D.
Secondary Education. M.Ed.
Special Education. M.Ed.
Speech Pathology. M.S.
Technical/Scientific Communication. M.A., M.S.

JERSEY CITY UNIVERSITY
Jersey City, New Jersey 07305-1957
Web site: www.njcu.edu

Founded 1927. Name changed 1998. Coed. Public control. Semester system. Special facilities: ADA Technology Center, Center for the Advancement of Teaching and Learning, Peter W. Rodino Jr. Institute of Criminal Justice. Library: 250,000 volumes, 500,000 microforms, 1550 current periodicals.

Tuition: per credit, resident $254, nonresident $446. No on-campus housing for graduate students. Contact Director of Student Services for off-campus housing information. Phone: (201)200-2338. Day-care facilities available.

Graduate Studies

Graduate study since 1960. Enrollment: full-time 49, part-time 1275. Graduate faculty: full-time 87, part-time 22. Degrees conferred: M.A., M.F.A., M.S., Professional Diploma.

ADMISSION REQUIREMENTS. Official transcripts, two letters of recommendation, interview, GRE/MAT required in support of application. TOEFL required for all international applicants. Accepts transfer applicants. Graduates of unaccredited institutions not considered. Apply to Director of Graduate Studies by August 1 (Fall), December 1 (Spring), May 1 (Summer). Application fee: none. Phone: (877)NJCUGRAD.

ADMISSION STANDARDS. Selective. Usual minimum average: 2.75 (A = 4).

FINANCIAL AID. Assistantships, Federal W/S, loans. Approved for VA benefits. Apply by June 1 to Office of Graduate Studies. Use FAFSA and institutional FAF. About 4% of students receive aid from all sources. Aid sometimes available to part-time students.

DEGREE REQUIREMENTS. For M.A., M.S.: 32 credit hours minimum, at least 24 in residence; thesis or final document; practicum or comprehensive exam. For M.F.A.: 60 credit hours minimum, at least 45 in residence; special project. For M.S. in Health, Criminal Justice, Nursing: 36–42 credit programs; residency; thesis/project. For Professional Diploma: 33 credits minimum beyond the master's.

FIELDS OF STUDY.
Accounting. M.S.
Counseling. M.S.
Criminal Justice. M.S.
Early Childhood Education. Includes a leadership track. M.A.
Early Childhood Education (Birth–8). M.A.
Educational Psychology. M.A.
Elementary Reading. M.A.
Health Sciences. Includes health administration, school health education. M.S.
Mathematics Education. M.A.
Music Education. M.A.
Nursing. Includes holistic nursing, urban health. M.S.
Reading Specialist. M.A.
Secondary Reading. M.A.
School Psychology. Professional Diploma.
Special Education. Includes mental retardation, behavioral disorders, pervasive development disorders, physical and multiple disabilities. M.A.
Studio Art. Includes fine arts, design and crafts, communication design. M.A.
Urban Education. Includes administration and supervision, basic and urban studies, bilingual and bicultural, ESL. M.A.

JOHN CARROLL UNIVERSITY
Cleveland, Ohio 44118-4581
Web site: www.jcu.edu

Founded 1986. CGS member. Coed. Private control. Roman Catholic. Semester system. Library: 620,000 volumes, 2198 subscriptions.

Tuition: per credit $550, M.B.A. $676. No separate on-campus housing for graduate students. Apply to Dean of Students Office for off-campus housing. Phone: (216)397-4401.

Graduate School

Enrollment: full-time 187, part-time 606. Graduate faculty: full-time 133, part-time 56. Degrees conferred: M.A., M.S., M.B.A., M.Ed.

ADMISSION REQUIREMENTS. Transcripts required in support of application. GRE Subject Tests/MAT recommended; M.A.T. required for Community Counseling program. TOEFL required of international students. Accepts transfer applicants. Deadline to Admissions Office, 30 days prior to registration. Application fee $25, $35 for international applicants. Phone: (216)397-4284; fax: (216)397-3009.

ADMISSION STANDARDS. Selective. Usual minimum average: 2.5. Some programs require 3.0 (A = 4).

FINANCIAL AID. Scholarships, teaching and research assistantships, tuition waivers, Federal W/S, loans. Apply by March 1 to Dean, Graduate School. Phone: (216)397-4248. Use FAFSA. About 30% of students receive aid other than loans from School. Aid available for part-time students.

DEGREE REQUIREMENTS. For M.A., M.S., M.Ed.: 30–33 semester hours, at least 24 in residence; reading knowledge of one foreign language for M.A. in some departments; thesis/research essay; oral/written comprehensive exam. For M.A. (Community Counseling): 60 credit full-time program; clinical experience; practicum; internship. For M.B.A.: 60 semester hours.

FIELDS OF STUDY.
Biology. GRE Subject in Biology for admission.
Business. GMAT for admission.
Chemistry.

Communications Management.

Community Counseling.

Education. Includes school counseling, school psychology, administration, professional teacher, instructional technology, reading, educational psychology.

English. GRE for admission to degree programs.

History.

Humanities.

Mathematics.

Physics.

Religious Studies. MAT or GRE for admission.

JOHN JAY COLLEGE OF CRIMINAL JUSTICE

New York, New York 10019-1093
Web site: www.jjay.edu

Established 1965. A unit of the City University of New York. Coed. Municipal control. Semester system. Special facilities: Center for Study of Law and Society in China, Center on Violence and Human Survival, Fire Science Institute, Institute on Alcohol and Substance Abuse. Library: 310,000 volumes, 1325 subscriptions.

Tuition: per credit, resident $185, nonresident $320. No on-campus housing. Apply to Dean of Students for off-campus housing information. Phone: (212)237-8737.

Graduate Division

Program intended for students seeking careers in public services, for personnel in various criminal justice agencies. Enrollment: full-time 235, part-time 814. Faculty: full-time 45, part-time 14. Degrees conferred: M.A., M.S., M.P.A.

ADMISSION REQUIREMENTS. Transcripts, GRE, three letters of recommendation, essay required in support of College's application. On-line application available. TOEFL required for all international applicants. Accepts transfer applicants. Apply to Graduate Office of Admissions by June 30 (Fall), December 15 (Spring). Application fee $40. Phone: (212)JOHNJAY; fax: (212)237-8777. For Ph.D.: apply to CUNY Graduate Center. Phone: (212)817-7470.

ADMISSION STANDARDS. Selective. Usual minimum average: 3.0 in major area of concentration (A = 4).

FINANCIAL AID. Limited to Federal W/S, loans. Approved for VA benefits. Apply to Director of Financial Aid for all programs. Phone: (212)237-8151. Use CUNY's FAFSA. About 80% of students receive aid other than loans from College and outside sources. Aid available for part-time students.

DEGREE REQUIREMENTS. For master's: credit hours vary from 36–42 credit hours, depending on the selected major. For Ph.D.: three- to four-year, 45–60 credit program; three comprehensive exams; dissertation; final oral defense.

FIELDS OF STUDY.

Criminal Justice. Includes specializations in criminology and deviance, forensic psychology, law and philosophy, public policy and organizational behavior (Ph.D. only). M.A.

Forensic Psychology. M.A., Ph.D. interdisciplinary.

Forensic Science. M.S.

Protection Management. M.S.

Public Administration. M.P.A.

THE JOHN MARSHALL LAW SCHOOL

315 South Plymouth Court
Chicago, Illinois 60604-3968
Web site: www.jmls.edu

Established 1899. Located in the heart of Chicago's legal and financial district. ABA approved since 1951. AALS member. Semester system. Full-time, part-time study. Special programs: summer study abroad in Ireland, Czech Republic, Lithuania, China. Law library: 361,778 volumes, 5290 subscriptions; has LEXIS, NEXIS, WESTLAW, CALI.

Annual tuition: full-time $21,100, part-time $15,100; per semester credit $750. No on-campus housing available. All law students off-campus. Contact the Admissions Office for off-campus information. Off-campus housing and personal expenses: approximately $13,410. Additional costs: books approximately $700.

Enrollment: first-year class 281, part-time 119; total full- and part-time 1159 (men 52%, women 48%), postgraduates 125. Faculty: full-time 48, part-time 119. Student to faculty ratio 17.9 to 1. Degrees conferred: J.D., J.D.-M.B.A. (Dominican University), J.D.-M.P.A. (Roosevelt University), J.D.-M.A. (Political Science, Roosevelt University), LL.M. (Comparative Legal Studies), LL.M. (General, for persons who have completed a basic legal education and received a university degree in law in another country).

ADMISSION REQUIREMENTS. LSDAS Law School report, bachelor's degree, transcripts, LSAT, letters of recommendation required in support of application. Accepts transfer applicants. Apply after October 1, before March 1 (Fall), October 1 (Spring) to Director of Admissions, Application fee $50. Phone: (312)987-1406; outside Chicago (800)537-4280.

ADMISSION STANDARDS. Selective. Mean LSAT: full-time 150, part-time 149; mean GPA: full-time 2.94, part-time 3.04 (A = 4). Gourman rating: 3.08. *U.S. News & World Report* ranking is in the fourth tier of all law schools. Accepts 35–40% of total annual applicants.

FINANCIAL AID. Scholarships, grants, loans. Apply by June 1 (Fall), November 1 (Spring) to Financial Aid Office. Use FAFSA (School code: G01698) and JMLS financial aid form.

DEGREE REQUIREMENTS. For J.D.: satisfactory completion of 90 semester hour program. For master's degree: see Dominican University, Roosevelt University listing for requirements. For LL.M.: at least 24 credits minimum beyond J.D.

THE JOHNS HOPKINS UNIVERSITY

Baltimore, Maryland 21218
Web site: www.jhu.edu

Founded 1876. CGS and AAU member. Coed. Private control. Semester system. Special facilities: Center for Astrophysical Sciences, Applied Physics Laboratory, Bologna Center (Italy), Carnegie Institute, Center for Social Organization of Schools, Center for Non-Destructive Testing, Geology Field Station, Homewood Computing Center, McCollum-Pratt Institute, Nanjing Center (PRC), Oceanographic Research Vessels, Space Telescope Science Institute, Villa Spelman (Italy). The University's ranking is first among all U.S. institutions with 1171 awards/grants worth $457,361,528. Library: more than 3,400,000 volumes, 23,000 subscriptions.

Annual tuition: full-time $27,390. On-campus housing for married students, single men and women. Average academic year housing cost: $7000–$10,000 for married students; $7000 for single students. Apply to Director of Housing. Phone: (410)516-7960.

Zanvyl Krieger School of Arts and Science

Enrollment: full-time 982, part-time 6 (men 60%, women 40%). Graduate faculty: full-time 268, part-time 10. Degrees conferred: M.A., Ph.D.

ADMISSION REQUIREMENTS. Two transcripts, two to three letters of recommendation required in support of School's application. On-line application available. GRE Subject Tests strongly recommended. Samples of work required by some programs. TOEFL required for international applicants. Accepts transfer applicants. Graduates of unaccredited institutions not considered. Admission requirements vary by department and applicants should first contact the individual department to obtain pertinent formation. Submit applications as directed, but not later than January 1. Application fee $55. Dean's Phone: (410)516-8174; e-mail: grad_adm@jhu.edu.

ADMISSION STANDARDS. Very competitive.

FINANCIAL AID. Scholarships, fellowships, research assistantships, teaching assistantships, full and partial tuition waivers, Federal W/S, loans. Apply January 15 (for priority consideration) to appropriate department chair for fellowships, assistantships, scholarships; to Office of Student Financial Services for all other programs. Phone: (410)516-8028. Use FAFSA.

DEGREE REQUIREMENTS. For M.A.: One year minimum in full-time residence; reading knowledge of one foreign language optional by department; thesis or comprehensive exam for some departments. For Ph.D.: generally three years minimum beyond the bachelor's; at least one year in full-time residence; reading knowledge of one foreign language optional by department; preliminary oral exam; dissertation; final oral/written exam.

FIELDS OF STUDY.
Anatomy. Ph.D. only.
Anthropology. Ph.D. only.
Art. Includes art history, architecture.
Biochemistry. Ph.D. only. The D.Sc., D.P.H. are offered by School of Hygiene and Public Health.
Biology. Includes chemical biology, developmental biology, genetic biology. Ph.D. only.
Biomedical Engineering. Ph.D. and postdoctoral study only.
Biophysics. Ph.D. only.
Biostatistics. Two years minimum of full-time residence for Ph.D.
Cell Biology.
Chemistry. Generally Ph.D. only.
Classics. Knowledge of Greek and Latin in addition to French, Italian, or German for M.A.; German and French or Italian for admission to Ph.D.
Cognitive Science. Ph.D. only.
Earth and Planetary Sciences. Includes petrology and geochemistry.
Economics. Ph.D. only.
English. Ph.D. only.
German. Oral/written exam for M.A.; qualifying exam for Ph.D.
History. Includes American studies, medieval history.
History of Art.
History of Science, Medicine, and Technology. Offered by School of Medicine; comprehensive written exam, oral qualifying exam for Ph.D. Ph.D. only.
Mathematical Science.
Mathematics.
Medical and Biological Illustration. Offered by School of Medicine; M.A. only.
Microbiology. Offered by School of Medicine.
Near Eastern Studies. Ph.D. only.
Pharmacology and Experimental Therapeutics. Offered by School of Medicine.

Philosophy. Apply to department chair; two years minimum in full-time residence. Ph.D. only.
Physics and Astronomy. Ph.D. only.
Physiological Chemistry. Offered by School of Medicine; Ph.D. only.
Physiology. Offered by School of Medicine; Ph.D. only.
Political Science. Includes public law and jurisprudence, public administration; oral/written exam for M.A.
Psychological and Brain Science.
Public Policy.
Psychology. Comprehensive exam for M.A.
Romance Languages and Literature. Includes French, Italian, Spanish.
Sociology. Includes sociology and public health; Ph.D. only.
Writing. Interdepartmental; M.A. only.

G.W.C. Whiting School of Engineering

Annual tuition: full-time $27,390.
Enrollment: full-time 457, part-time 44. Faculty: full-time 112, part-time 78. Degrees conferred: M.A., M.M.S.E., M.S., M.S.E., Ph.D.

ADMISSION REQUIREMENTS. Official transcripts, GRE, three letters of reference required in support of School's application. TOEFL required for international applicants. Interview not required. Accepts transfer applicants. Graduates of unaccredited institutions not considered. Apply to the Office of Admission by January 15. Application fee $55. Phone: (410)516-8174.

ADMISSION STANDARDS. Selective. Usual minimum average: 3.0 (A = 4).

FINANCIAL AID. Sixty-six fellowships, 207 research assistantships, 90 teaching assistantships, tuition waivers, Federal W/S, loans. Approved for VA benefits. Apply by January 15 (for priority consideration) to Office of Students Financial Services. Phone: (410)516-8028. Use FAFSA.

DEGREE REQUIREMENTS. For master's: One year minimum in full-time residence; thesis or comprehensive exam for some departments. For Ph.D.: generally three years minimum beyond the bachelor's, at least one year in full-time residence; preliminary exam; dissertation; Graduate Board oral exam.

FIELDS OF STUDY.
Biomedical Engineering. M.S.E., Ph.D.
Chemical Engineering. M.S., Ph.D.
Civil Engineering. M.S., Ph.D.
Computer Science. M.S., Ph.D.
Electrical and Computer Engineering. M.S., Ph.D.
Geography and Environmental Engineering. M.S., Ph.D.
Materials Science. M.S., Ph.D.
Mathematical Science. M.S., Ph.D.
Mechanical Engineering. M.S., Ph.D.

Paul H. Nitze School of Advanced International Studies (22036)

Established 1943. Located in Washington, D.C. Special facilities: Washington Center of Foreign Policy Research, Center for Canadian Studies, Foreign Policy Institute, Center for International Business and Policy, Center for Strategic Education, Center for Transatlantic Relations, Reischauer Center for East Asia Studies. Special programs: European Center in Bologna, Italy; Center in Nanjing, People's Republic of China. Library: 100,000 volumes.

Annual tuition: full-time $24,000. Graduate enrollment: full-time 488, part-time 25. School faculty: full-time 43, part-time 113. No on-campus housing available. Average academic year costs for off-campus housing: $9000. Degrees conferred: M.A., M.I.P.P., Ph.D.

ADMISSION REQUIREMENTS. Official transcripts, three letters of recommendation required in support of School's application. GRE, interview recommended. TOEFL required for international applicants. Graduates of unaccredited colleges not considered. Candidates should have at least nine years of experience. Apply to Director of Admissions by January 15, February 15 (Ph.D.) (Fall), November 1 (Spring). Rolling admissions process. Application fee $75. Phone: (202)663-5700; fax: (202)663-7788; e-mail: admissions.sais@jhu.edu. Ph.D. phone: (202)663-5709.

ADMISSION STANDARDS. Competitive. Usual minimum average: 3.5 (A = 4).

FINANCIAL AID. Annual awards from institutional funds: fellowships, research/teaching assistantships, internships, grants, Federal W/S, loans. Apply by February 1 to Office of Admissions. Phone: (202)663-5706. Use FAFSA (School code: E00474). About 50% of students receive aid from School and outside sources. Aid available for part-time students.

DEGREE REQUIREMENTS. For M.A.: two-year, full-time program; two core exams; speaking and reading knowledge of one modern foreign language; final oral exam. For M.I.P.P.: one-year program (midcareer); completion of eight courses within the nine-month period. For Ph.D.: three years minimum beyond the bachelor's; reading knowledge of two foreign languages; comprehensive exam; International Economics competence; dissertation prospectus and defense; dissertation; final oral exam.

FIELDS OF STUDY.
Area Programs. Includes African, American Foreign Policy, Asian, Canadian, European, Latin American, Middle Eastern, Russian and Eurasian Studies.
International Economics.
International Development.
International Public Policy.
International Relations. Includes general international relations, global theory and history, international law, conflict management, strategic studies, energy, environment, science and technology.

PH.D. PROGRAMS ARE OFFERED IN THE FOLLOWING AREAS:
African Studies.
Asian Studies.
Conflict Management.
Energy, Environmental, Science, and Technology.
European Studies.
Global Theory and History.
International Law.
International Relations.
Russian and Eurasian Studies.
Strategic Studies.
Western Hemisphere Program.
Note: Joint programs are available. M.A.-M.B.A. with Wharton School at the University of Pennsylvania or from the European Institute of Business Administration (INSEAD), Fontainebleau, France; M.A.-J.D. with Stanford Law School; M.A.-M.H.S. with Bloomberg School of Public Health.

School of Medicine (21205-2196)

Founded 1893. Library: 300,000 volumes. Annual tuition: $28,100; student fees $2656. Total average figure for all other expenses: $12,000. On-campus housing available.

Enrollment: first-year class 120 (EDP 3); total full-time 716 (men 55%, women 45%). Faculty: full-time 1100, part-time 1200. Degrees conferred: M.D., M.D.-M.P.H., M.D.-M.S.E. (Biomedical Engineering), M.D.-Ph.D. (Medical Scientist Training Program).

ADMISSION REQUIREMENTS. Transcripts, MCAT, letters of recommendation, interview required in support of application. Has EDP; apply between June 1 and August 15. Applicants must have completed at least two years of college study. Apply to Committee on Admission after June 1, before October 15. Application fee $75. Phone: (410)955-3182; Web site: www.infonet.welch.jhu.edu.

ADMISSION STANDARDS. Competitive. Median GPA: 3.8. Gourman rating: 4.92. *U.S. News & World Report* ranking is 2nd of all U.S. medical schools and 11th in primary care. Accepts 7% of total annual applicants. Approximately 7% are state residents.

FINANCIAL AID. Scholarships, summer fellowship, loans. MSTP funded by NIH. Apply to Committee on Admission; no specified closing date. About 85% of students receive some aid from School funds.

DEGREE REQUIREMENTS. For M.D.: satisfactory completion of four-year program for those who enter with bachelor's; satisfactory completion of five- or six-year program for those who enter with less than four years of undergraduate study. For M.P.H., Ph.D.: see Graduate School listing above.

FIELDS OF GRADUATE STUDY.
Biochemistry and Molecular Biology.
Biological Chemistry.
Biomedical Engineering.
Biophysics.
Cell Biology and Anatomy.
Cellular and Molecular Medicine.
Epidemiology.
History of Medicine.
Human Genetics.
Microbiology and Immunology.
Neurosciences.
Pathobiology.
Pharmacology.
Physiology.
Public Health.

The Peabody Institute of the Johns Hopkins University (21202)

Web site: www.peabody.jhu.edu

Founded 1857. Coed. Private control. Semester system. Music library: 70,000 volumes; audio visual library: 13,510 discs.

Annual tuition: full-time $24,750; diploma programs $18,580. On-campus housing available. Apply to Director of Admissions. Graduate enrollment: full-time 286, part-time 32. Institute faculty: full-time 69, part-time 58. Degrees conferred: M.M., D.M.A., Graduate Performance Diploma, Artist Diploma.

ADMISSION REQUIREMENTS. Official transcripts, entrance audition and entrance exams in music history, theory, and ear training required in support of application. TOEFL required for international applicants. Apply to Director of Admissions by December 15. Application fee $55. Phone: (800)368-2521, (410)659-8110; fax: (410)659-8102.

ADMISSION STANDARDS. Selective.

FINANCIAL AID. Scholarships, assistantships, grants, Federal W/S, loans. Apply by March 1 to Director of Admissions. Phone: (410)659-8100, ext. 3023. Use FAFSA and institutional FAF. Approximately 40% of students receive aid other than loans from Institute; 77% from all sources.

DEGREE REQUIREMENTS. For M.M.: 32 semester hours minimum; recital. For D.M.A.: 90 hours beyond the bachelor's, at least one year in full-time residence; preliminary exam; final written/oral exam; final dissertation or lecture-recital document for all majors; six public recitals; reading knowledge of languages required. For diploma programs: one to two years of full-time study; recital.

FIELD OF STUDY.
Music. Performance, conducting, theory, composition, electronic and computer music, music history, music criticism, and music education.

Bloomberg School of Public Health

Established 1916. Semester system. Special facilities: Bill and Melinda Gates Institute for Population and Reproduction, Bioethics Institute, Biostatistics Center, Center for Human Nutrition, Center for a Livable Future, Center for Law and the Public's Health, Education and Research Center in Occupational Safety and Health, Hopkins Population Center, Institute for Vaccine Safety, Johns Hopkins Center in Urban Environmental Health, Johns Hopkins Malaria Research Institute, Mid-Atlantic Health Leadership Institute, Primary Care Policy Center for Underserved Populations.

Annual tuition: full-time $33,805 (M.P.H.), per credit $564. All other programs full-time $27,045, per credit $564. Graduate enrollment: full-time 941, part-time 531 (men 39%, women 61%). School faculty: full-time 429, part-time 593. Degrees conferred: M.P.H., Sc.M., M.H.S., Dr.P.H., Sc.D., Ph.D., M.D.-M.P.H., M.S.W.-M.P.H., M.S.N.-M.P.H., J.D.-M.P.H., M.A.-M.P.H.

ADMISSION REQUIREMENTS. Official transcripts, GRE (MCAT, GMAT, LSAT can be substituted for GRE for M.P.H.), three letters of reference, résumé or curriculum vitae, supplemental form (M.P.H. applicants) required in support of School's application. On-line appliation available. TOEFL or evidence of proficiency in English required of international students. Interview not required. Accepts transfer applicants. Apply to Admissions Office of School by February 1 for all full-time programs, two terms in advance for part-time programs. Rolling admissions process from October 1 to February 1. Application fee $75, $45 for on-line applicants. Phone: (410)955-3543; fax: (410)955-0464.

ADMISSION STANDARDS. Selective for most departments. *U.S. News & World Report* ranking is first of all U.S. public health schools. Usual minimum average: 3.0 (A = 4).

FINANCIAL AID. Scholarships, fellowships, research assistantships, teaching assistantships, Federal W/S, loans, and federal training grants are offered. Approved for VA benefits. Apply to appropriate departmental chairperson or Master of Public Health Office for scholarships and traineeships support; the Office of Student Financial Services for all other aid. Phone: (410)955-5332; fax: (410)955-0464. Use FAFSA (School code: E00234). Approximately 70% of students receive either school scholarships, loans, or FWS; 19% receive federal training grants; and 50% receive other aid.

DEGREE REQUIREMENTS. For full-time M.P.H.: Eleven months, 64–95 credits minimum in residence and satisfactory completion of approved schedule of studies. For part-time M.P.H.: 64–95 credit units within three years. For Sc.M.: Two years minimum, one in residence; thesis; written exam. For M.H.S.: 64 credit program, one to two academic years in residence; thesis and field studies vary by department. For Dr.P.H.: Three years minimum beyond the bachelor's, one year minimum in residence. For Dr.P.H. students who do not already have the M.P.H., the first eleven months of study is for M.P.H. degree; preliminary oral exam; comprehensive written exam; thesis; oral defense of thesis. For Sc.D.: Two years minimum in residence; preliminary oral exam; comprehensive written exam; thesis; oral defense of thesis. For Ph.D.: One year minimum in residence; comprehen-

sive written exam; two to three oral exams; thesis; oral defense of thesis. For the doctoral degrees, some departments may require reading knowledge of one foreign language.

FIELDS OF STUDY.
Biochemistry and Molecular Biology.
Biostatistics.
Clinical Investigation.
Environmental Health Sciences. Includes toxicological sciences, physiology, environmental chemistry and biology, radiation health sciences, environmental health engineering, occupational health.
Epidemiology.
Health Policy and Management. Includes behavioral sciences and health education, health finance and management, health policy, public health.
International Health. Includes disease control, vaccine sciences, human nutrition, health systems.
Internet-Based M.P.H.
Maternal and Child Health.
Mental Hygiene.
Molecular Microbiology and Immunology.
Population and Family Health Sciences.

THE JUILLIARD SCHOOL
New York, New York 10023-6588
Web site: www.juilliard.edu

Founded 1905. Located at Lincoln Center. Coed. Private control. Semester system. Library: 80,793 volumes, 220 subscriptions.

Annual tuition: full-time $17,400. On-campus housing for 350 students. Annual academic year housing cost: $7000. Apply to Office of Students Affairs for on- and off-campus housing information. Phone: (212)799-5000, ext. 7400 (on-campus), ext. 200 (off-campus).

Graduate Study

Graduate study since 1924. Enrollment: full-time 256; part-time 34 (women 50%, men 50%). Faculty: full-time 115, part-time 131. Degrees conferred: M.M., D.M.A. Graduate Diploma, Artist's Diploma.

ADMISSION REQUIREMENTS. Transcripts, recommendations, interview, performance audition entrance exam required in support of School's application. TOEFL (minimum score 570), TWE required for international applicants. Apply to Admissions Office by December 1. Fall admission only. Application and entrance exam fees $100. Phone: (212)799-5000, ext. 223; fax: (212)769-6420.

ADMISSION STANDARDS. Very competitive.

FINANCIAL AID. Scholarships, teaching fellowships, assistantships, Federal W/S, loans. Approved for VA benefits. Apply by March 1 to Financial Aid Office. Phone: (212)799-5000. Use FAFSA and institutional FAF.

DEGREE REQUIREMENTS. For M.M.: 54 semester hours minimum, at least two years in full-time residency; graduation performance; final exam. For D.M.A.: 98 semester hours minimum beyond the bachelor's, at least 60 in full-time residence; preliminary exam; reading knowledge of one foreign language; final project/recital/document, depending upon major; final oral exam.

FIELDS OF STUDY.
Collaborative Piano.
Composition.

Conducting (Orchestral).
Guitar. M.M. only.
Harpsichord.
Jazz Studies.
Orchestral Instruments.
Opera Studies.
Organ.
Performance Piano.
Playwriting.
String Quartet Studies.
Voice.
Theater Directing.

KANSAS STATE UNIVERSITY

Manhattan, Kansas 66506
Web site: www.ksu.edu

Founded 1863. Located 55 miles from Topeka. CGS member. Coed. State control. Semester system. Special facilities: nuclear reactor, Flight Research Laboratory, Higuch Biosciences Center, 12 MEV Van de Graaff accelerator, observatory, fish hatchery, botanical garden, Kansas Geological Survey, Konza Prairie Research Area, Natural Science Museum, Wheat Genetics Resource Center, Institute for Environmental Research, Food and Feed Grain Institute, computer center, environmental laboratory, Cereal Technology Laboratory, engineering and agriculture experiment stations. Library: 1,500,000 volumes, 9400 subscriptions.

Tuition: per credit hour resident $126, nonresident $391. On-campus housing for 625 married students, 400 graduate men, 200 graduate women. Average academic year housing cost: $3890 for married students, $4090 (including board) for single students. Apply to Director of Housing. Phone: (785)532-6453 (on-campus), (785)532-2097 (off-campus). Day-care facilities available.

Graduate School

Graduate study since 1868. Enrollment: full- and part-time 3277. University faculty: full-time 1006, part-time 97. Degrees conferred: M.A., M.S., M.Acc., M.B.A., M.F.A., M.M., M.Arch., M.P.A., M.R.P., M.L.A., Ed.D., Ph.D.

ADMISSION REQUIREMENTS. Two transcripts, GRE required in support of School's application. GMAT required for M.B.A., M.Acc. TOEFL (minimum score 550) required for international applicants. Interview sometimes required. Accepts transfer applicants. Graduates of unaccredited institutions not considered. Apply to head of the department concerned at least two months prior to registration; May 1 (Fall), October 1 (Spring) for international applicants. Application fee: none, $25 for international applicants. Phone: (785)532-7927; fax: (785)532-2983.

ADMISSION STANDARDS. Selective for most departments. Usual minimum average: 2.75 (A = 4).

FINANCIAL AID. Annual awards from institutional funds: scholarships, fellowships, teaching assistantships, internships, grants, research assistantships, Federal W/S, loans. Apply by March 1 to Dean of Graduate School for assistantships; to the Financial Aid Office for all other programs. Phone: (785)532-6420; fax: (785)532-7628. Use FAFSA. About 65% of students receive aid other than loans from University and outside sources. Aid available for part-time students.

DEGREE REQUIREMENTS. For most master's: 30 semester hours minimum including thesis, at least one academic year in full-time residence; transfer credit from other graduate schools

individually considered; final oral exam. For M.R.C.P.: 48 hours minimum, at least one academic year in full-time residence. For M.F.A.; 60 hours minimum. For Ph.D.: 90 semester hours minimum beyond the bachelor's, at least one year in full-time residence; preliminary exam; language requirements vary; dissertation; final written/oral exam. For Ed.D.: essentially the same as Ph.D. except no language requirement.

FIELDS OF STUDY.
Accounting. M.Acc.
Agribusiness. M.A.B.
Agricultural Economics. M.S.
Agricultural Engineering. Ph.D.
Agronomy. M.S., Ph.D.
Anatomy and Physiology. M.S., Ph.D.
Animal Science. Includes animal breeding and genetics. M.S., Ph.D.
Architectural Engineering. M.S.
Architecture. M.Arch.
Art. M.F.A.
Biochemistry. M.S., Ph.D.
Biological and Agricultural Engineering. M.S.
Biology. M.S., Ph.D.
Business Administration. M.B.A.
Chemical Engineering. M.S., Ph.D.
Civil Engineering. M.S., Ph.D.
Clinical Sciences. Includes agricultural practice, anesthesiology, equine medicine and surgery, exotic and wildlife medicine, ophthalmology, radiology, small animal medicine, small animal surgery and theriogenology. M.S.
Computer and Information Science. M.S., Ph.D.
Economics. M.A., Ph.D.
Education. Includes adult, elementary, secondary, administration, school counseling, student counseling and personnel services, special; three recommendations for admission; GRE for continuance in program.
Electrical and Computer Engineering. M.S., Ph.D.
Engineering Management. M.E.M.
English. Creative writing major for M.A.; GRE for continuance in program.
Entomology. M.S., Ph.D.
Family Studies and Human Services. M.S.
Food Service, Hospitality Management, and Administrative Dietetics. M.S., Ph.D.
Genetics. M.S., Ph.D.
Geography. M.A., Ph.D.
Geology. M.S., Ph.D.
Grain Science. M.S., Ph.D.
History. Two languages for Ph.D. M.A., Ph.D.
Horticulture. Includes ornamental, floriculture, turfgrass, vegetable crops, fruit crops, horticultural therapy, stress physiology, molecular biology, tissue culture, plant growth regulators. M.S., Ph.D.
Human Ecology. Ph.D.
Human Nutrition. M.S., Ph.D.
Industrial Engineering. M.S.I.E.
Journalism and Mass Communication. M.S.
Kinesiology. M.S.
Landscape Architecture. M.L.A.
Mass Communication. M.S.
Mathematics. M.S., Ph.D.
Mechanical Engineering. M.S., Ph.D.
Microbiology. M.S., Ph.D.
Modern Languages. Includes French, German, Spanish; one language in addition to major.
Music. Includes applied, music education, music literature; recital for master's. M.M.
Nuclear Engineering. M.S., Ph.D.
Operations Research. M.S.O.R.
Pathobiology. M.S., Ph.D.

Physics. M.S., Ph.D.
Plant Pathology. M.S.
Political Science. M.A.
Psychology. M.S., Ph.D.
Public Administration. M.P.A.
Regional and Community Planning. Interdepartmental. M.R.C.P.
Sociology. M.A., Ph.D.
Software Engineering. M.S.E.
Speech. Includes rhetoric/communication, theater. M.A.
Statistics. M.S., Ph.D.
Veterinary Laboratory Medicine. M.S.
Veterinary Pathology. M.S., Ph.D.

College of Veterinary Medicine

Founded 1905. Annual tuition: resident and contract state resident $6880; nonresident $23,680. Total average costs for all other expenses: $7500. On-campus housing available.

Enrollment: first-year class 100; total 404 (men 45%, women 55%); postgraduates 65. Faculty: full-time 68, part-time 16. Degree conferred: D.V.M. The M.S. and Ph.D. are offered through the Graduate School.

ADMISSION REQUIREMENTS. VMCAS report, transcripts showing completion of seventy hours of preprofessional college work, GRE, animal/veterinary experience, essay, three names and addresses for potential recommendations (one from an academic adviser) required in support of application. Interview by invitation only. Accepts transfer applicants, on a space-available basis. Preference given to state, contract, and U.S. residents. Apply to Assistant Dean after September 1, prior to October 1. Application fee $20. Phone: (785)532-5660.

ADMISSION STANDARDS. Selective. Usual minimum average: 2.8 (A = 4.). Mean GPA: 3.43. Accepts 40% of total annual applicants. Approximately 15–20% of class from nonresident (at-large) applicants.

FINANCIAL AID. Scholarships, assistantships, Federal W/S, loans. Apply by March 1 to Dean after acceptance.

DEGREE REQUIREMENTS. For D.V.M.: 152 semester hours and four years in residence. For M.S. and Ph.D.: see Graduate School listing above.

FIELDS OF GRADUATE STUDY.
Anatomy and Physiology.
Clinical Sciences. Includes agricultural practice, anesthesiology, equine medicine and surgery, exotic and wildlife medicine, ophthalmology, radiology, small animal medicine, small animal surgery, theriogenology. M.S.
Veterinary Laboratory Medicine. M.S.
Veterinary Pathology. M.S., Ph.D.

UNIVERSITY OF KANSAS
Lawrence, Kansas 66045
Web site: www.ku.edu

Founded 1866. Main campus is 40 miles W of Kansas City. College of Health Sciences and Hospital located at Kansas City. CGS and AAU member. State control. Semester system. Special facilities: Museum—anthropology, art, invertebrate paleontology, natural history, entomological; Herbarium, computer facilities, Kansas Geological Survey, Higuchi Biosciences Center, Bureau of Child Research, Flight Research Laboratory, Infant Research Laboratory, Retardation Research Center, Gerontology Center, Institute for Social and Environmental Studies, Institute for Economic and Business Research, Transportation Research Group, Space Technology Center, Biological Anthropology Laboratory, Enzyme Laboratory, Chemical Biology Laboratory, Nuclear Reactor Center, field facilities, Water Resources Institute, Paleontological Institute, Tertiary Oil Recovery Project, mineral resources research, animal care units, health and safety research, center for research, children's rehabilitation unit, cancer center program, drug design program. The University's NIH ranking is 81st among all U.S. institutions with 175 awards/grants worth $54,126,942. Library: 4,400,000 volumes, 32,700 subscriptions. Total University enrollment: 27,400.

Annual tuition: full-time, resident $2534, nonresident $7412; per credit hour, resident $118, nonresident $322. On-campus housing for 300 married students. Average academic year housing cost: $3544–$4524 (including board) for single students, $2500 for married students. Contact Director of Student Housing for both on- and off-campus housing information. Phone: (785)864-7224. Day-care facilities available.

Graduate School

Organized 1894. Enrollment: full-time 2723, part-time 2623. Graduate faculty: full-time 1021, part-time 95. Degrees conferred: M.A., M.S., M.B.A., M.S.Ed., M.F.A., M.M., M.E., M.M.Ed., M.M.E., M.H.D., M.F.A., M.U.P., M.Arch., Ed.S., D.M.A., D.E., Ed.D., Ph.D.

ADMISSION REQUIREMENTS. Two official transcripts required in support of School's application. GRE/MAT, letters of recommendation required by some departments. Interview not required. TOEFL required for international applicants. Accepts transfer applicants. Graduates of unaccredited institutions not considered. Apply to Graduate Advisor of proposed major department by July 1 (Fall), December 1 (Spring), May 1 (Summer); some departments have earlier deadlines. Application fee varies by department $10–$40, $40–$55 for international applicants. Phone: (785)864-4141; fax: (785)864-4555.

ADMISSION STANDARDS. Competitive for most departments, very competitive for others. Usual minimum average: 3.0 (A = 4).

FINANCIAL AID. Annual awards from institutional funds: scholarships, fellowships, teaching assistantships, research assistantships, tuition waivers, internships, grants, Federal W/S, loans. Approved for VA benefits. Apply by February 1 (earlier for some departments) to appropriate department chair for fellowships, assistantships; to Financial Aid Office for all other programs. Phone: (785)864-4700, (785)864-5469. Use FAFSA. About 50% of students receive aid other than loans from University and outside sources. Aid available for part-time students.

DEGREE REQUIREMENTS. For master's: 30 credit hours minimum, at least 24 in residence; research component; thesis/nonthesis options for some departments; final general exam. For M.Arch.: 60 credit hours; project/thesis; final general exam. For M.B.A.: 60 credit hours; final exam. For M.E., M.M.E.: 36 credit hours; project; internships; final general exam. For M.F.A.: 48–60 credit hours; thesis/exhibition; final general exam. For M.H.D.: 36 credit hours; practicum experience; thesis option; final general exam. For M.M.: 30 credit hours; thesis/recital/project; final general exam. For M.M.Ed.: 30 credit hours; thesis; final general exam. For M.P.A.: 30 credit hours; internship; project; final general exam. For M.U.P.: 50 credit hours; thesis/nonthesis option; final general exam. For Ed.S.: 60 credit hours beyond bachelor's; special project. For Ed.D., D.E., D.M.A.: some variations but all basically the same as for the Ph.D. For

Ph.D.: three years beyond the baccalaureate; at least one year in full-time residence; foreign language or other research skills; comprehensive oral exam; candidacy; dissertation; final oral exam.

FIELDS OF STUDY.

SCHOOL OF ARCHITECTURE AND URBAN DESIGN:
Architectural Engineering. M.S.
Architecture. M.Arch.
Urban Planning. M.U.P.

SCHOOL OF BUSINESS:
Accounting and Information Systems.
Business.
Business Administration. M.B.A. only.

COLLEGE OF LIBERAL ARTS AND SCIENCES:
American Studies.
Anthropology.
Biology. Includes cell, physiology.
Chemistry.
Child Clinical Psychology.
Communication Studies.
East Asian Languages and Cultures. M.A. only.
Ecology and Evolutionary Biology.
Economics.
English.
Entomology.
French.
Geography.
Geology.
Germanic Languages and Literature.
Gerontology.
Historical Administration and Museum Studies.
History.
History of Art.
Human Development and Family Life.
Indigenous Nation Studies. M.A.
International Studies. M.A.
Latin American Studies. M.A.
Linguistics.
Mathematics.
Molecular Biosciences.
Philosophy.
Physics.
Political Science.
Psychology.
Public Administration.
Religious Studies. M.A. only.
Slavic Languages and Literature.
Sociology.
Spanish.
Speech-Language-Hearing.
Theater and Film.

SCHOOL OF EDUCATION:
Counseling Psychology..
Curriculum and Instruction.
Educational Policy and Leadership.
Educational Psychology and Research.
Foundations of Education.
Health, Sport, and Exercise Sciences.
Higher Education Foundations.
School Psychology.
Special Education.

SCHOOL OF ENGINEERING:
Aerospace Engineering.
Chemical and Petroleum Engineering.
Chemical Engineering. M.S.

Civil Engineering.
Computer Engineering. M.S.
Construction Engineering. M.S.
Electrical Engineering.
Engineering Management. M.S. only.
Environmental Engineering.
Mechanical Engineering.
Petroleum Engineering.
Water Resources Engineering. M.S.

SCHOOL OF FINE ARTS:
Art. M.F.A. only.
Design. Includes interior, textiles. M.F.A. only.
Music. Includes composition, conducting, performance, musicology, theory.
Music Education.
Music Therapy.
Scenography.
Visual Arts Education.

SCHOOL OF JOURNALISM AND MASS COMMUNICATION:
Journalism. M.S.

SCHOOL OF PHARMACY:
Medicinal Chemistry.
Neuroscience. Ph.D.
Pharmacy Practice. M.S.
Pharmaceutical Chemistry.
Pharmacology.
Toxicology.

SCHOOL OF SOCIAL WORK:
Social Work. M.S.W., Ph.D.

School of Law

Web site: www.law.ku.edu

Founded 1891. ABA approved since 1923. AALS charter member. Semester system. Law library: 353,132 volumes, 4520 subscriptions; has LEXIS, NEXIS, WESTLAW, DIALOG.

Annual tuition: full-time resident $7182, nonresident $14,866. On-campus housing available for both single and married students. Total average cost for all other expenses: $10,994.

Enrollment: first-year class 150; full-time 492 (men 56%, women 44%); no part-time students. Faculty: full-time 27, part-time 6. Student to faculty ratio 15.1 to 1. Degrees conferred: J.D., J.D.-M.B.A., J.D.-M.P.A., J.D.-M.A. (Economics, Philosophy), J.D.-M.S. (Health Services Administration, Urban Planning).

ADMISSION REQUIREMENTS. LSDAS Law School report, bachelor's degree, transcripts, LSAT required in support of application. Interview not required. Accepts transfer applicants. Preference given to state residents. Graduates of unaccredited colleges not considered. Apply to Director of Law Admission before March 15 for both Summer and Fall admission. Admits Summer and Fall only. Application fee $40. Phone: (785)864-4378; fax: (785)864-5054.

ADMISSION STANDARDS. Selective. Mean LSAT: 155; mean GPA: 3.36 (A = 4). Gourman rating: 3.71. *U.S. News & World Report* ranking is in the second tier of all U.S. law schools. Accepts about 40–45% of total annual applicants. Approximately 82% of class are state residents.

FINANCIAL AID. Scholarships, assistantships, Federal W/S, loans. Apply to Office of Student Financial Aid by March 1. Use FAFSA. About 10% of students receive aid from School.

DEGREE REQUIREMENTS, For J.D.: 90 hours minimum, at least 30 in full-time residence. For master's degree: see Graduate School listings above.

UNIVERSITY OF KANSAS MEDICAL CENTER
Kansas City, Kansas 66103
Web site: www.kumc.edu

Medical study since 1905. Includes Allied Health, Nursing, Medical School, Graduate School (administered by University's Graduate School). Special facilities: Cancer Center, Center for Aging, Radiation Therapy Center, Center on Environmental and Occupational Law. Library: 179,130 volumes, 1500 subscriptions.

Graduate Programs

Tuition: per credit, resident $113, nonresident $357.75. Enrollment: full-time 271, part-time 380. Faculty: full-time 235, part-time 40. Degrees conferred: M.A., M.N., M.P.H., M.S., M.S.O.T., M.S.P.T., Ph.D., P.T.-Ph.D.

ADMISSION REQUIREMENTS. Official transcripts, three letters of recommendation, GRE required in support of application. TOEFL required for international applicants. Accepts transfer applicants. Graduates of unaccredited insti tutions not considered. Apply by July 1 (Fall), December 1 (Spring). Rolling admissions process. Application fee: none. Phone: (913)588-1238.

ADMISSION STANDARDS. Competitive. Usual minimum average: 3.0 (A = 4).

FINANCIAL AID. Scholarships, fellowships, assistantships, Federal W/S, loans. Approved for VA benefits. Apply by May 1 to appropriate department for assistantships, fellowships; to Financial Aid Office for all other programs. Phone: (913)588-5170. Use FAFSA. Aid available for part-time students.

DEGREE REQUIREMENTS. For M.S., M.A., M.N., M.P.H., M.S.O.T., M.S.P.T., Ph.D.: see University of Kansas Graduate School listing above.

FIELDS OF STUDY.

SCHOOL OF ALLIED HEALTH:
Hearing and Speech. M.A., Ph.D
Dietetics and Nutrition. M.S.
Nurse Anesthesia Education. M.S.
Occupational Therapy Education. M.O.T., M.S.O.T.
Physical Therapy and Rehabilitation Sciences. M.S., Ph.D.
Rehabilitation Science. Ph.D., P.T.-Ph.D.
Speech-Language Pathology. M.S., Ph.D.
Therapeutic Science. Ph.D.

SCHOOL OF GRADUATE STUDIES:
Anatomy and Cell Biology. M.A., Ph.D.
Biochemistry and Molecular Biology. M.S., Ph.D.
Health Policy and Management. M.H.S.A.
Microbiology, Molecular Genetics, and Immunology. M.S., Ph.D.
Molecular and Integrative Physiology. Ph.D.
Pathology. M.A., Ph.D.
Pharmacology, Toxicology, and Therapeutics. M.S., Ph.D.
Public Health. M.P.H.

SCHOOL OF NURSING:
Nursing Specialist. M.S.
Nurse Researcher. Ph.D.

School of Medicine

Founded 1899. Located in Kansas City (66160-7301). Annual tuition: resident $10,600, nonresident $24,812. Total average figure for all other expenses $13,162. Enrollment: first-year class 175 (EDP 35); total full-time 700 (men 65%, women 35%). Faculty: full-time 317, part-time 98. Degrees conferred: M.D., M.D.-Ph.D. Library: 170,000 volumes.

ADMISSION REQUIREMENTS. AMCAS, transcripts, recommendation from premedical adviser, MCAT required in support of application. Interview by invitation. Has EDP; apply between June 1 and August 1. Accepts transfer applicants. Bachelor's degree required for admission. Preference given to Kansas residents. Apply to Office of Student Admissions and Records after June 1, before October 15. Application fee: nonresidents $40. Phone: (913)588-5245; fax: (913)588-5259.

ADMISSION STANDARDS. Competitive. Mean MCAT: 9.1; mean GPA: 3.65 (A = 4). Gourman rating: 3.87. Accepts 12% of total annual applicants. Approximately 92% are state residents.

FINANCIAL AID. Scholarships, assistantships, fellowships, loans. Apply by March 30 to Office of Student Financial Aid. Phone: (913)588-5170. About 75% of students receive aid from School.

DEGREE REQUIREMENTS. Satisfactory completion of four-year program. Advanced standing for medical study completed elsewhere considered on individual basis. For Ph.D.: see Graduate School listing above.

FIELDS OF GRADUATE STUDY.
Anatomy and Cell biology. M.A., Ph.D.
Biochemistry and Molecular Biology. M.S., Ph.D.
Biomedical Sciences. Interdisciplinary.
Health Policy and Management. M.H.S.A.
Microbiology, Molecular Genetics, and Immunology. M.S., Ph.D.
Molecular and Integrative Physiology. Ph.D.
Pathology and Laboratory Medicine. M.A., Ph.D.
Pharmacology, Toxicology, and Therapeutics. M.S., Ph.D.
Public Health. M.P.H.

KEAN UNIVERSITY
Union, New Jersey 07083
Web site: www.kean.edu

Founded 1855. Located 15 miles W of New York City. CGS member. Coed. State control. Semester system. Library: 271,000 volumes, 1350 subscriptions. Total University enrollment: 12,000.
Annual tuition: full-time, resident $6780, nonresident $9106; per hour, resident $283, nonresident $347. No on-campus housing available for graduate students.

Nathan Weiss College of Graduate Studies

Graduate study since 1954. Enrollment: full-time 152, part-time 1092. Faculty: full-time 280, part-time 40. Degrees conferred: M.A., M.P.A., M.S., M.S.N., M.A.L.S., Professional Diploma in School Psychology, Marriage and Family Therapy.

ADMISSION REQUIREMENTS. Official transcripts, recommendations, GRE/MAT/GMAT/PRAXIS required in support of School's application. Interview is usually required. TOEFL required for international applicants. Accepts transfer applicants. Graduates of unaccredited institutions not considered. Apply to Office of Graduate Admissions, T-106 by June 15 (Fall), November 1 (Spring). All documents including test scores must be received by deadline in order for application to be reviewed. Application fee $35. Phone: (908)527-2665.

ADMISSION STANDARDS. Selective for most departments. Usual minimum average: 2.75 (A = 4).

FINANCIAL AID. Annual awards from institutional funds: assistantships; scholarships, tuition waivers, Federal W/S, loans. Approved for VA benefits. Apply to Office of Financial Aid; no specified closing date. Phone: (908)572-2050. About 50% of full-time students receive aid other than loans from both College and outside sources. Aid sometimes available for part-time students.

DEGREE REQUIREMENTS. For master's: 33 credits minimum; comprehensive exam; thesis/nonthesis option. For Professional Diploma: 30 credits minimum beyond master's.

FIELDS OF STUDY.
Accounting. M.S.
Behavioral Sciences. M.A.
Biotechnology. M.S.
Communication Sciences.
Computing. M.S.
Counselor Education. M.A.
Early Childhood Education. M.A.
Educational Administration. M.A.
Educational Media. M.A.
Educational Psychology. M.A.
Fine Arts. M.A.
Graphic Communication Technology Management. M.S.
Instruction and Curriculum. M.A.
Liberal Studies. M.A.
Management Information Systems. M.S.
Mathematics. M.S.
Mathematics Education. M.A.
Nursing. M.S.N.
Occupational Therapy. M.S.
Public Administration. M.P.A.
Reading. M.A.
School Psychology. Professional Diploma.
Social Work. M.S.W.
Special Education. M.A.
Speech Pathology. M.A.
Statistics. M.S.

KEENE STATE COLLEGE
Keene, New Hampshire 03435-1701
Web site: www.keene.edu

Founded 1909. Located 90 miles NW of Boston. Coed. Semester system. State control. Library: 195,000 volumes, 950 subscriptions.

Tuition: per credit hour, resident $190, nonresident $425. On-campus housing for single and married students. Annual housing cost: $5068 (including board) single students, $7000 married students. Apply to Director of Residential Life. Phone: (603)358-2339. Day-care facilities available.

Graduate Studies

Graduate study since 1947. Enrollment: full-time 29, part-time 74. Faculty: full-time 21, part-time 15. Degree conferred: M.Ed.

ADMISSION REQUIREMENTS. Transcripts, three letters of recommendation, essay required in support of application. TOEFL required for international applicants. Accepts transfer applicants. Graduates of unaccredited institutions not considered. Apply by June 15 (Fall), October 15 (Spring) to the Assistant Director of Admissions. Application fee $25 resident, $35 nonresident. Phone: (603)358-2276; fax: (603)358-2767; e-mail: admissions@keene.edu.

ADMISSION STANDARDS. Selective. Usual minimum average: 2.90 (A = 4).

FINANCIAL AID. Scholarships, assistantships, Federal W/S, loans. Apply to Office of Student Financial Management; no specified closing date. Phone: (603)358-2280. Use FAFSA. Aid available for part-time students.

DEGREE REQUIREMENTS. For master's: 36–39 credit hours minimum.

FIELDS OF STUDY.
Curriculum and Instruction.
Educational Administration.
Educational Leadership.
School Counselor.
Special Education.

KENT STATE UNIVERSITY
Kent, Ohio 44242-0001
Web site: www.kent.edu

Founded 1910. Located 35 miles SE of Cleveland. CGS member. Coed. State control. Semester system. Special facilities: Applied Psychology Center, Center for Aquatic Ecology, Center for Educational Leadership Services, Center for Executive Education and Development, Center for Health Promotion Through Education, Center for International and Comparative Programs, Center for International and Intercultural Education, Center for Literature and Psychoanalysis, Lyman L. Lemnitzer Center for NATO and European Studies, Center for Nuclear Research, Center for Nursing Research, Center for Public Administration and Public Policy, Center for the Study of World Musics, Institute for Applied Linguistics, Institute for Bibliography and Editing, Glen H. Brown Liquid Crystal Institute, Institute for Computational Mathematics, Water Resource Research Institute. Library: 1,800,000 volumes, 14,895 subscriptions.

Annual tuition: resident $5622, nonresident $10,798; per credit, resident $306, nonresident $542. On-campus housing for 250 single students, 259 married students. Average academic year housing cost: $5500 for married students, $5024 (including board) for single students. Contact Director of Residence Services for both on- and off-campus housing information. Phone: (330)672-7000.

Division of Research and Graduate Schools

Graduate study since 1935. Enrollment: full-time 1992, part-time 2352. University faculty teaching graduate students: full-time 765. Degrees conferred: M.Arch., M.A., M.A.T., M.B.A., M.Ed., M.F.A., M.L.S., M.M., M.P.A., M.S., M.S.Acct., M.S.N., Ed. Specialist, Ph.D. Graduate work is administered by the Division of Research and Graduate Studies.

ADMISSION REQUIREMENTS. Official transcripts, three letters of recommendation required in support of application. Online application available. GRE/GMAT required for some programs. TOEFL required for all international applicants. Interview not required. Accepts transfer applicants. Graduates of unaccredited institutions not considered. Apply to appropriate Graduate School at least six weeks prior to registration. Application fee $30. Phone: (330)672-2661.

ADMISSION STANDARDS. Very selective for most departments, competitive for others. Usual minimum average: 2.75 (A = 4).

FINANCIAL AID. Annual awards from institutional funds: fellowships, research/teaching assistantships, internships, tuition waivers, Federal W/S, loans. Approved for VA benefits. Apply by March 1 to appropriate department chair for fellowships, assistantships; to the Financial Aid Office for all other programs. Phone: (330)672-2972. Use FAFSA. About 25% of full-time students receive aid other than loans from School and outside sources.

DEGREE REQUIREMENTS. For M.A.: 32 semester hours minimum; thesis in most departments; final exam in some. For M.S.: 32 semester hours; thesis. M.S.Acct.: 33 semester hours beyond the bachelor's in accounting or 64 semester hours beyond other bachelor's; internship. For M.A.T.: 44–45 credit program, at least 39 in residence; internship. For M.Ed.: 32 semester hours minimum; one year teaching experience required in most programs. For M.F.A.: 60 semester hours; studio thesis; qualifying exam. For M.M.: 32 semester hours; recital; essay. For M.L.S.: 36 semester hours; thesis or research paper. For M.S.N.: 36–40 semester hours. For M.P.A.: 45 semester hours; thesis/nonthesis option. For M.Arch.: 32 semester hours minimum. For Ed.S.: 60 semester hours beyond the bachelor's or 30 semester hours beyond the master's; comprehensive exam; final oral exam. For Ph.D.: 60 semester hours beyond the bachelor's minimum, at least two years in residence; qualifying exam; one foreign language for some programs; dissertation; final oral exam.

FIELDS OF STUDY.

COLLEGE OF ARTS AND SCIENCE:
Anthropology.
Analytical Chemistry.
Chemical Physics.
Chemistry.
Clinical Psychology.
Computer Science.
English.
Geography.
Geology.
History.
Justice Studies.
Liberal Studies.
Mathematical Sciences.
Modern and Classical Language Studies.
Philosophy.
Physics.
Political Science.
Psychology.
Sociology.

COLLEGE OF FINE AND PROFESSIONAL ARTS:
Architecture and Environmental Design.
Art.
Exercise, Leisure, and Sport.
Family and Consumer Studies.
Music.
Public Health.
Theatre and Dance.

COLLEGE OF COMMUNICATION AND INFORMATION:
Communication Studies.
Information Architecture and Knowledge Management.
Journalism and Mass Communication.
Library and Information Science.
Visual Communication Design.

COLLEGE OF NURSING:
Adult Primary Care Nurse Practitioner.
Gerontology. Interdisciplinary.
Nursing of the Adult.
Nursing and Health Care Management.
Parent-Child Nursing.
Pediatric Nurse Practitioner.
Psychiatric Mental Health Nursing.
Women's Health Nurse Practitioner.

GRADUATE SCHOOL OF MANAGEMENT:
Accounting.
Business Administration. Includes finance, human resources management, information systems, international business, marketing.
Economics.
Financial Engineering.
Marketing.

SCHOOL OF BIOMEDICAL SCIENCES:
Biological Anthropology.
Cellular and Molecular Biology.
Neuroscience.
Pharmacology.
Physiology.
Note: Programs offered in cooperation with Northeastern Ohio Universities College of Medicine.

SCHOOL OF EDUCATION:
Adolescence/Young Adult.
Community Counseling.
Computer Technology.
Counseling and Human Development Services.
Cultural Foundations.
Curriculum and Instruction.
Deaf Education.
Early Childhood Education.
Early Childhood Intervention Specialist.
Educational Administration. Includes K–12 leadership, higher educational administration and student personnel.
Educational Interpreter.
Educational Psychology.
Elementary Education.
Evaluation and Measurement.
Gifted Education.
Health Education and Promotion.
Instructional Technology.
Library/Media.
Math Specialist.
Middle Childhood Education.
Mild/Moderate Intervention Specialist.
Moderate/Intensive Intervention Specialist.
Reading.
Reading and Language Arts.
Rehabilitation Counseling.
School Counseling.
School Psychology.
Secondary Education.
Transition to Work.

SCHOOL OF TECHNOLOGY:
Technology.

UNIVERSITY OF KENTUCKY
Lexington, Kentucky 40506-0032
Web site: www.uky.edu

Founded 1865. CGS member. Coed. State control. Semester system. Sponsoring university of Oak Ridge Institute of Nuclear Studies in Tennessee. Special facilities: Appalachian Center, Center for the Arts, Center for Business and Economic Research, Maxwell H. Gluck Equine Research Center, Gaines Center for the Humanities, Lucille Parker Mackey Cancer Research Center, Multidisciplinary Center on Gerontology, Institute for Mining/Minerals Research, Sanders-Brown Center for Aging, Survey Research Center, Kentucky Transportation Center, Water Resources Institute. The University's NIH ranking is 73rd among all U.S. institutions with 250 awards/grants worth $63,717,492. Library: more than 2,900,000 volumes, 29,580 subscriptions. Total University enrollment: 29,400.

Annual tuition: full-time, resident $4346.50, nonresident $11,564; per credit, resident $227, nonresident $628; M.B.A. full-time, resident $4652, nonresident $11,888; per credit, resident $244, nonresident $646. On-campus housing is available for both single and married students. Room rates: $403–$545 per month. For housing information, call (859)257-1866. Day-care facilities available.

Graduate School

Graduate study since 1870. Enrollment: full-time 2392, part-time 2611. Graduate faculty: full- and part-time 875. Degrees conferred: M.A., M.S., M.S.Acc., M.S.Agr.E., M.S.Ch.E., M.S.C.E., M.S.C.N., M.S.Ed., M.S.E., M.S.E.M., M.S.F.S., M.S.M.E., M.S.R.M.P., M.S.N., M.S.O.R., M.S.R.H., M.S.B.E., M.S.P.H., M.B.A., M.A.T., M.M., M.P.A., M.S.D., M.S.L.S., M.F.A., M.S.W., Ed.S., D.M.A., D.B.A., Ed.D., Ph.D.

ADMISSION REQUIREMENTS. Two official transcripts from each school attended, GRE/GMAT required in support of School's application. TOEFL (minimum score 550) required for international applicants. Interview not required. Accepts transfer applicants. Graduates of unaccredited institutions not considered. Apply to Graduate Admissions Office by July 15 (Fall), November 1 (Spring), April 1 (Summer). Many programs have earlier deadlines; see Fields of Study below. Application fee $30, $35 for international applicants. Phone: (859)257-4613; fax: (859) 323-1928; e-mail: gradapp@uky.edu.

ADMISSION STANDARDS. Relatively open for some departments, selective to very selective for others. Minimum average: 3.0 (A = 4).

FINANCIAL AID. Annual awards from institutional funds: academic scholarships, research/teaching assistantships, fellowships, Federal W/S, loans. Apply by March 1 to Graduate Dean for fellowships, to appropriate department chair for assistantships; to Financial Aid Office for all other programs. Phone: (859)257-3172. Use FAFSA.

DEGREE REQUIREMENTS. For M.A., M.A.T., and all M.S. programs: 30–36 credit hours minimum with or without thesis; final written/oral exam; reading knowledge of one language for some majors. For M.B.A., M.P.A.: same as for M.A. except comprehensive exam instead of thesis. For M.M.: same as M.A., except recital for applied music major, composition for composition major, in lieu of thesis; thesis optional for music education or theory majors. For M.F.A.: 48 credits minimum, at least 40 in residence. For M.S.W.: 60 credits minimum, at least one and a half years in residence; thesis. For Ed.S.: 30 credit hours minimum beyond the master's, research problem and written report included; final written/oral exam. For Ph.D.: three years minimum beyond the bachelor's, at least two semesters in full-time residence; qualifying exam; reading knowledge of one or two foreign languages; dissertation; final written/oral exam. For Ed.D., D.B.A.: same as for Ph.D., except at least 72 credit hours minimum beyond the bachelor's; no foreign language requirement.

FIELDS OF STUDY.

COLLEGE OF AGRICULTURE:
Agricultural Economics.
Animal Sciences.
Crop Science
Entomology.
Forestry.
Plant and Soil Science.
Plant Pathology.
Plant Physiology.
Soil Science.
Veterinary Science. Apply by May 16 (Fall).

COLLEGE OF ARCHITECTURE:
Historic Preservation. Apply by July 15 (Fall).

COLLEGE OF ALLIED HEALTH PROFESSIONS:
Clinical Nutrition.
Communication Disorders.
Physical Therapy.
Radiation Sciences.

COLLEGE OF ARTS AND SCIENCES:
Anthropology. Apply by February 15 (Fall).
Applied Mathematics.
Biology.
Chemistry.
Classical Languages. Apply by February 15 (for financial aid consideration).
English. Apply by January 15 (Fall).
French Language and Literature.
Geography.
Geology.
German.
History. Apply by March 1 (Fall for financial aid consideration).
Mathematics.
Philosophy. Apply by April 1 (Fall for financial aid consideration).
Physics and Astronomy.
Political Science.
Psychology—Clinical. Apply by January 15 (Fall).
Psychology—Experimental. Apply by February 1 (Fall).
Sociology. Apply by January 15 (Fall).
Spanish and Italian.
Statistics.

COLLEGE OF BUSINESS AND ECONOMICS:
Accounting.
Business Administration. Apply by March 15 (Fall for financial aid consideration).
Economics.

COLLEGE OF COMMUNICATIONS AND INFORMATION STUDIES:
Communication. Apply by February 1 (Fall), October 1 (Summer)
Library Science. Apply by July 15 (Fall, April 1 for financial aid consideration), November 1 (Spring), March 1 (Summer).

COLLEGE OF EDUCATION:
Administration and Supervision. Apply by July 15 (Fall), December 1 (Spring).
Counseling Psychology.
Curriculum and Instruction.
Early Childhood Education.
Educational and Counseling Psychology. Apply by March 1 (master's degrees), January 15 (doctoral degrees).
Educational Policy Studies and Evaluation. Apply by March 1 (Fall), October 15 (Spring).
Elementary Education.
Exercise Science.
Higher Education.
Instructional System Design.
Kinesiology and Health Promotion.
Middle School Education.
Reading.
Rehabilitation Counseling.
School Psychology.
Secondary Education. Includes English, mathematics, science, social science.
Social and Philosophical Studies in Education.
Special Education.

COLLEGE OF ENGINEERING:
Biosystems and Agricultural Engineering.
Chemical Engineering.

Civil Engineering.
Computer Science.
Electrical Engineering.
Engineering Mechanics.
Manufacturing Systems Engineering.
Materials Science and Engineering.
Mechanical Engineering.
Mining Engineering.

COLLEGE OF FINE ARTS:
Art Education.
Art History. Apply by June 1 (Fall).
Art Studio.
Composition.
Music. Apply by April 1 (Fall for financial aid consideration).
Music Education.
Music Theory.
Musicology.
Performance.
Theatre Arts.

COLLEGE OF HEALTH SCIENCES:
Clinical Sciences.
Communication Disorders.
Physical Therapy.
Physician Assistant Studies.
Radiation Science.
Rehabilitation Sciences. Apply by July 1 (Fall), December 1 (Spring).

COLLEGE OF HUMAN ENVIRONMENTAL SCIENCE:
Family Studies. Apply by January 15 (Fall), August 1 (Spring).
Hospitality and Dietetic Administration.
Interior Design, Merchandising, and Textiles.
Vocational Education.

COLLEGE OF DENTISTRY:
Dentistry.

COLLEGE OF MEDICINE:
Anatomy and Neurobiology.
Medical Sciences.
Microbiology,
Molecular and Biomedical Pharmacology.
Molecular and Cellular Biochemistry.
Physiology.
Public Health.

COLLEGE OF NURSING:
Nursing. Doctoral candidates: apply by February 15 (Fall), September 15 (Spring); master's candidates: apply by March 1 (Fall), November 1 (Spring).

COLLEGE OF PHARMACY:
Pharmaceutical Science.

COLLEGE OF SOCIAL WORK:
Social Work. Apply by February 1 (Fall).

GRADUATE SCHOOL (INTERDISCIPLINARY, INTERDEPARTMENTAL PROGRAMS):
Biomedical Engineering.
Diplomacy and International Commerce. Apply by February 1 (Fall).
Gerontology.
Health Administration.
Nutritional Sciences. For assistantships apply by March 1 (Fall), October 1 (Spring).
Public Administration.
Toxicology.

College of Dentistry (40536-0297)

First classes 1962. Medical Center library: 100,000 volumes. Annual tuition: resident $9500, nonresident $22,700. On-campus housing available. Contact Housing Office. Phone: (859)257-3721. Total average cost for all other first-year expenses: $6744.

Enrollment: first-year class 53, total 202 (men 60%, women 40%); postgraduates 45. Faculty: full-time 66, part-time 42. Degrees conferred: B.S.-D.M.D. (with the University's College of Arts and Sciences), D.M.D.

ADMISSION REQUIREMENTS. AADSAS report, transcripts, DAT (not later than October), three letters of recommendation, interview required in support of application. Accepts transfer applicants. Graduates of unaccredited institutions are not considered. Preference given to state residents. Apply to Admissions Office after June 1, before February 1. Application fee: $25. Phone: (859)233-6071.

ADMISSION STANDARDS. Selective. Mean DAT: Academic 17.4, PAT 16.8; mean GPA: 3.5 (A = 4). Gourman rating: 4.07. Usual minimum average: 3.0 (A = 4). Accepts 80% of state residents, 1% of nonresidents. Approximately 90% are state residents.

FINANCIAL AID. Limited number of scholarships, loans. Apply to Financial Aid Office after acceptance. Phone: (859)323-6071. Use FAFSA. About 92% of students receive some aid from College and outside sources.

DEGREE REQUIREMENTS. For D.M.D.: satisfactory completion of forty-month program.

FIELDS OF GRADUATE STUDY.
General Practice Residency.
Oral and Maxillofacial Surgery.
Orofacial Pain.
Orthodontics.
Pediatric Dentistry.
Periodontics.

College of Law (40506-0054)

Established 1908. ABA approved since 1925. AALS member since 1912. Semester system. Special facility: The Mineral Law Center. Law library: 425,154 volumes, 3795 subscriptions; has LEXIS, NEXIS, WESTLAW, DIALOG.

Annual tuition: resident $6226, nonresident $15,800. Limited on-campus housing available. Total average annual additional expense: $10,414.

Enrollment: first-year class 134; total full-time 379 (men 56%, women 44%); no part-time study. Law faculty: full-time 21, part-time 12. Student to faculty ratio 15.6 to 1. Degrees conferred: J.D., J.D.-M.B.A., J.D.-M.P.A.

ADMISSION REQUIREMENTS. LSDAS Law School report, bachelor's degree, transcripts, LSAT (not later than February), letters of recommendations required in support of application. Interview not required. Accepts transfer applicants. Graduates of unaccredited colleges not considered. Approximately 85% of students are state residents. Apply to Associate Dean for Admissions by March 1. Admits Fall only. Application fee $35. Phone: (859)257-1678; (859)257-7938 for catalogs only.

ADMISSION STANDARDS. Selective. Mean LSAT: 158; mean GPA: 3.46 (A = 4). Gourman rating: 3.26. *U.S. News & World Report* ranking is in the top 50 of all U.S. law schools. Accepts about 30–35% of total annual applicants.

FINANCIAL AID. Scholarships, full and partial tuition waivers, grants, Federal W/S, loans. Apply to University's Student Financial Aid Office by April 1. Phone: (859)257-3172. Use FAFSA (College code: 001989). About 42% of students receive aid other than loans from both College and outside sources.

DEGREE REQUIREMENTS. For J.D.: 90 semester hours minimum. Note: transfer credit from other ABA-accredited law schools considered.

College of Medicine (40536-0298)

First class admitted 1960. Medical Center library: 100,000 volumes. Annual tuition: resident $11,089, nonresident $25,803; student fees $522. Total average figure for all other expenses: $14,000. On-campus housing for both married and single students available.

Enrollment: first-year class 95 (EDP 30); total full-time 489 (men 68%, women 32%); postgraduates 12. Faculty: full-time 45, part-time 64. Degrees conferred: M.D., M.D.-M.S., M.D.-Ph.D. The M.S. and Ph.D. are offered through the Graduate School.

ADMISSION REQUIREMENTS. AMCAS report, transcripts, MCAT, interview required in support of application. Accepts transfer applicants. Has EDP; apply between June 1 and August 1. Preference given to state residents. Apply to Office of Admissions after June 1, before November 1. Application fee $30. Phone: (859)233-6161; fax: (859)323-2076.

ADMISSION STANDARDS. Selective. Mean MCAT: 9.5; mean GPA: 3.66 (A = 4). Gourman rating: 3.65. *U.S. News & World Report* ranking is in the top 43 of all U.S. law schools. Accepts about 15% of total annual applicants. Approximately 85% are state residents.

FINANCIAL AID. Rural Kentucky Medical Scholarship Fund, summer fellowships, assistantships, loans. Apply to Office of Student Services after acceptance. Phone: (859)323-6271. Use FAFSA. About 85% of students receive aid from College and outside sources.

DEGREE REQUIREMENTS. For M.D.: satisfactory completion of four-year program. For M.S., Ph.D.: see Graduate School listing above.

FIELDS OF GRADUATE STUDY.
Anatomy and Neurobiology.
Medical Science.
Microbiology.
Molecular and Biomedical Pharmacology.
Molecular and Cellular Biochemistry.
Physiology.
Public Health.

KIRKSVILLE COLLEGE OF OSTEOPATHIC MEDICINE

Kirksville, Missouri 63501-1497
Web site: www.kcom.edu

Established 1892 by Andrew Taylor Still, the founder of Osteopathic Medicine, as the first school of Osteopathic Medicine in the U.S. The College is located next to the Kirksville Osteopathic Medical Center and Diagnostic and Treatment Center. Private control. Special facility: Rea Cancer Treatment Center. The Southwest Center for Osteopathic Medical Education and Health Sciences of Kirksville College of Osteopathic Medicine is located on the campus of Grand Canyon University in Phoenix, Arizona. Library: 87,000 volumes, 906 subscriptions.

Limited on-campus rooms and apartments available for both single and married students. Annual on-campus housing cost: single students $4140 (room only), married students $4620. Con-

tact Office of Student Affairs for both on- and off-campus housing information. Phone: (660)626-2236. Medical students tend to live off-campus. Off-campus housing and personal expenses: approximately $15,000.

Annual tuition: $24,950; fees $1000. Enrollment: first-year class 156; total full-time 616 (men 70%, women 30%). Faculty: full-time 11, part-time/volunteers 60.

Degrees conferred: D.O., M.P.H., M.G.H., M.H.A., M.S.

ADMISSION REQUIREMENTS. AACOMAS report, supplemental school application, bachelor's degree preferred, transcripts, MCAT, two letters of recommendation from premed advisory committee. Interview by invitation only. Graduates of unaccredited college not considered. Apply by February 1. Admits first-year students Fall only. Application fee: $50. Phone: (660)626-2237; fax: (660)626-2969; e-mail: admissions@kcom.edu.

ADMISSION STANDARDS. Selective. Median MCAT: 9.1; median GPA: 3.4 (A = 4). Accepts approximately 15% of annual applicants. Usual minimum average: 2.5 (A = 4).

FINANCIAL AID. Institutional scholarships, National Health Services Corps Scholarships, loans including HEAL. Special loan programs for minorities and rural students. Apply by May 1 to Students Affairs Office. Phone: (660)626-2529. Use FAFSA (College code: G02477).

DEGREE REQUIREMENT. For D.O.: satisfactory completion of four-year program. All students must take the National Board of Osteopathic Medical Examination Level I and II prior to the awarding of D.O.

KUTZTOWN UNIVERSITY OF PENNSYLVANIA

Kutztown, Pennsylvania 19530
Web site: www.kutztown.edu

Founded 1866. Located 15 miles NE of Reading. CGS member. Coed. State control. Semester system. Library: 492,117 hardcover volumes, 1308 subscriptions. Total University enrollment: 7200.

Tuition: per credit, resident $297, nonresident $478. On-campus housing generally not available to graduate students. For information contact Director of Off-Campus Housing: (610) 683-4022.

College of Graduate Studies

Graduate study since 1959. Enrollment: full-time 176, part-time 834. Faculty: full-time 54, part-time 12. Degrees conferred: M.A., M.S., M.Ed., M.L.S., M.P.A., M.B.A.

ADMISSION REQUIREMENTS. One transcript from all postsecondary institutions attended, three letters of recommendation, interview, GRE/GMAT required in support of College's application. TOEFL, TSE required for international applicants. Résumé and statement of goals are needed when applying for M.B.A. Accepts transfer applicants. Graduates of unaccredited institutions not considered. Apply to Graduate Office by February 1 (Fall), July 1 (Spring). Application fee $35. Phone: (610)683-4200; fax: (610)683-1393.

ADMISSION STANDARDS. Selective. Usual minimum average: 2.5 plus test scores (A = 4).

FINANCIAL AID. Assistantships, grants, tuition waivers, Federal W/S, loans. Approved for VA benefits. Apply to Director of Financial Aid. Phone: (610)683-4077. Use FAFSA. Less than 5% of students receive aid other than loans from University.

DEGREE REQUIREMENTS. For master's: 30–57 credit hours minimum, at least 24 in residence (for most programs); thesis/nonthesis option; final written/oral exam.

FIELDS OF STUDY.
Art Education. M.Ed.
Business Administration. M.B.A.
Computer and Information Science. M.S.
Counseling Psychology. M.A.
Counselor Education. Includes elementary, secondary, student affairs in higher education. M.Ed.
Elementary Education. M.Ed.
English. M.A.
Library Science. M.L.S.
Mathematics. M.A.
Public Administration. M.P.A.
Reading. M.Ed.
Secondary Education. Includes biology, curriculum and instruction, English, mathematics, social studies. M.Ed.
Telecommunications. M.S.

LAGRANGE COLLEGE
LaGrange, Georgia 30240-2999
Web site: www.lgc.edu

Founded 1831. Coed. Private. Methodist. Quarter system. Library: 135,000 volumes, 3200 subscriptions.

Annual tuition: full-time $7950, part-time, per credit $475. No on-campus housing available for graduate students. Average academic year off-campus housing cost: $4846 (including board). Contact Dean of Students for off-campus information. Phone: (706)880-2911.

Graduate Program

Enrollment: full-time 25, part-time 16. Faculty: full- and part-time 13. Degrees conferred: M.Ed., M.B.A.

ADMISSION REQUIREMENTS. Transcripts, GRE/MAT/GMAT, 3 references, interview required in support of application. On-line application available. TOEFL required for international applicants. Accepts transfer applicants. Apply to Director of Admissions by August 1 (Fall), December 31 (Spring). Application fee $20, $25 for international students. Phone: (706)880-8253; fax: (706)880-8010.

ADMISSION STANDARDS. Selective. Usual minimum average: 2.5, 3.0 (A = 4) for last 90 quarter hours, 60 semester hours.

FINANCIAL AID. Assistantships, internships, Federal W/S, loans. Approved for VA benefits. Apply to the Financial Aid Office; no specified closing date. Phone: (706)812-7241. Use FAFSA and Institutional FAF.

DEGREE REQUIREMENTS. For M.Ed.: 60 quarter hours minimum; candidacy; final exam. For M.B.A.: 65–90 quarter hours minimum; comprehensive exam.

FIELDS OF STUDY.
Business Administration.
Curriculum and Instruction.
Teaching. Includes music, art, secondary education.

THE LAKE ERIE COLLEGE OF OSTEOPATHIC MEDICINE
Erie, Pennsylvania 16509
Web site: www.lecom.edu

Founded 1992. Special facility: Cappabianca Research Center. Library: 7400 volumes, 124 subscriptions.

Annual tuition: in state $22,720, out of state $23,720. No on-campus housing available. Contact Admissions Office for both on- and off-campus housing information. Off-campus housing and personal expenses: approximately $13,000–16,000.

Enrollment: first-year class 192; total full-time 576 (men 60%, women 40%). Faculty: full-time 49, part-time/volunteers 133. Degree conferred: D.O.

ADMISSION REQUIREMENTS. Preference given to state residents, U.S. citizens, and permanent residents only. Bachelor's degree from an accredited institution required. 100% of applicants have bachelor's degree awarded prior to enrollment. Apply through AACOMAS (file after June 1, before December 1), submit MCAT (will accept test results from last three years), official transcripts for each school attended (should show at least 90 semester credits/135 quarter credits), service processing fee. After review of AACOMAS application and supporting documents decision is made concerning which candidates should receive supplemental materials. The LECOM supplemental application, an application fee of $50, a personal statement, and a premed committee letter and two additional recommendations, one from a D.O. and one general recommendation, should be returned to Office of Admission as soon as possible, but not later than February 1. Interviews are by invitation only and generally for final selection. First-year students admitted Fall only. Rolling admissions process, notification starts in December and is finished when class is filled. Applicant's response to offer and $1500 deposit due within two weeks of receipt of acceptance letter. School does maintain an alternate list. Phone: (814)866-6641; fax: (814)866-8123; e-mail: admissions@lecom.edu.

ADMISSION STANDARDS. For serious consideration an applicant should have at least a 2.75 GPA (A = 4). Median MCAT: 7.9; median GPA: 3.3.

FINANCIAL AID. Scholarships, merit scholarships, minority scholarships, Grants-in-Aid, institutional loans, NOF, HEAL, alternative loan programs, Military and National Health Service program, and Federal loan are available. Financial Aid applications and information are generally available at the on-campus by-invitation interview. Contact the Admissions Office for current information. Phone: (814)866-6441. For most programs use FAFSA (School code: G30908), for all Federal programs, also submit Financial Aid Transcript, Federal Income Tax forms.

DEGREE REQUIREMENTS. For D.O.: satisfactory completion of 4-year program. All students must pass the National Board of Osteopathic Medical Examination Level I and II prior to the awarding of D.O.

LAMAR UNIVERSITY
Beaumont, Texas 77705
Web site: www.lamar.edu

Founded 1923. CGS member. Coed. State control. Semester system. Special facilities: Dishman Art Gallery, Center for Criminal Justice, Gulf Coast Hazardous Substance Research Center, Center for Public Policy Studies, Space Exploration Center. Library: 628,000 volumes, 2900 subscriptions. Total University enrollment: 8600.

Tuition: per credit resident $148, nonresident $296, part-time tuition varies according to credit hours. On-campus housing for married, single students. Average annual housing cost: $6000 for married students, $3900 (including board) for single students. Apply to Residence Life Office. Phone: (409)880-2314.

College of Graduate Studies

Graduate study since 1962. Enrollment: full-time 396, part-time 442. Graduate faculty: full-time 184, part-time 20. Degrees conferred: M.A., M.B.A., M.Ed., M.S., M.E.S., M.E., M.E.M., M.Mu., M.Mu.Ed., M.P.A., D.E., Ed.D.

ADMISSION REQUIREMENTS. Transcripts, GRE/GMAT required in support of College's application. Interview not required. TOEFL required for international applicants. Accepts transfer applicants. Graduates of unaccredited colleges not considered. Apply to Dean of College of Graduate Studies at least 4 weeks prior to registration. International students apply 90 days prior to registration. Application fee $25, $50 for international applicants. Phone: (409)880-8356 or (800)443-5638; fax: (409)880-8414; e-mail: gradadmissions@hal.lamar.edu.

ADMISSION STANDARDS. Selective. Usual minimum average: 2.5 (A = 4).

FINANCIAL AID. Annual awards from institutional funds: scholarships, research fellowships, research/teaching fellowships, tuition waivers, grants, Federal W/S, loans. Approved for VA benefits. Apply by April 1 to Dean of College of Graduate Studies for scholarships, fellowships, assistantships; to the Financial Aid Office for all other programs. Phone: (409)880-8450. Use FAFSA. About 15% of students receive aid. Aid available for part-time students.

DEGREE REQUIREMENTS. For M.A., M.E.S., M.Mu.: 30 credit boom minimum, at least 24 in residence; thesis; final oral exam; reading knowledge of one foreign language required for M.A. only. For M.S., M.B.A., M.E., M.E.M., M.P.A., M.Ed.: 30 credit hours minimum, at least 24 in residence; thesis; final oral exam, or 36 credit hours minimum and final written exam in lieu of thesis. For D.E.: 30 credit hours minimum beyond master's; thesis; final oral exam. For Ed.D.: at least 60 credit hours beyond master's; qualifying exam; dissertation; final written/oral exam.

FIELDS OF STUDY.
Applied Criminology. M.S.
Audiology. M.S.
Biology. M.S.
Business Administration. M.B.A.
Chemical Engineering. M.E., M.E.S.
Chemistry. M.S.
Civil Engineering. M.E., M.E.S.
Community and Counseling Psychology. M.S.
Computer Science. M.S.
Counseling and Development. M.Ed.
Deaf Studies and Habilitation. M.S.
Education Administration. M.Ed.
Electrical Engineering. M.E., M.E.S.
Elementary Education. M.Ed.
Engineering Management. M.E.M.
English. M.A.
Environmental Engineering. M.S., M.E.S.
Family and Consumer Science. M.S.
History. M.A.
Industrial and Organizational Psychology. M.S.
Industrial Engineering. M.E., M.E.S.
Kinesiology. M.Ed.
Mathematics. M.S.
Mechanical Engineering. M.E., M.E.S.
Music. M.Mu.

Music Education. M.Mu.Ed.
Nursing Administration. M.S.
Public Administration. M.P.A.
Secondary Education. M.Ed.
Special Education. M.Ed.
Speech-Language Pathology. M.S.
Supervision. M.Ed.
Theater. M.S.
Visual Arts. Includes art history. M.A.

UNIVERSITY OF LA VERNE
La Verne, California 91750-4443
Web site: www.ulaverne.edu

Founded 1891. Located 30 miles E of Los Angeles. Coed. Independent. Semester system. Library: 250,000 volumes, 3600 subscriptions.

Tuition: per hour $395–$525 (master's), $540–$700 (doctorate). No on-campus housing available.

Graduate Program

Enrollment: full-time 961, part-time 1400. Graduate faculty: full-time 54, part-time 147. Degrees conferred: M.Ed., M.S., M.A., M.H.A., M.P.A., M.B.A., Ed.D., D.P.A.

ADMISSION REQUIREMENTS. Transcripts, three letters of reference required in support of application. On-line application available. GRE/GMAT/MAT for some programs. Accepts transfer applicants. TOEFL required for international applicants. Graduates of unaccredited institutions not considered. Apply to Graduate Studies Office; specified closing date. Application fee $40 (master's), $75 (doctorate). Phone: (909)593-3511, ext. 4504; fax: (909)392-2761.

ADMISSION STANDARDS. Selective. Usual minimum average: 2.5–3.0 for master's programs, 3.0 for doctoral (A = 4).

FINANCIAL AID. Annual awards from institutional funds: departmental scholarships, assistantships, grants, internships, Federal W/S, loans. Apply by May 1 to Financial Aid Office. Phone: (909)543-3511, ext. 4135. Use FAFSA. No aid for part-time students carrying less than half a full-time program.

DEGREE REQUIREMENTS. For master's: 32–50 semester hours minimum (6–12 credits may be transferred into program); thesis or graduate seminar. For Ed.D.: 54 semester hours beyond master's. For D.P.A.: 54 semester hours beyond master's. For Psy.D.: five-year full-time program; clinical practica; internship; dissertation; oral defense.

FIELDS OF STUDY.
Business Administration. M.B.A.
Business Organizational Mangement. M.S.
Child Development.
Child Life.
Counseling.
Educational Management. M.Ed.
Gerontology.
Health Administration.
Leadership and Management.
Learning Handicapped.
Marriage, Family, and Child Counseling.
Organizational Leadership. Ed.D.
Psychology. Psy.D.
Public Administration. M.P.A., D.P.A.
Reading.
School Counseling.
Special Education.

LEHIGH UNIVERSITY
Bethlehem, Pennsylvania 18015-3174
Web site: www.lehigh.edu

Founded 1865. Located 60 miles N of Philadelphia. CGS member. Coed. Private control. Semester system. Special facilities: Research centers in Chemical Process Modeling and Control, Design and Manufacture Innovation, Economic Education, Innovation Management Studies, International Studies, Molecular Bioscience and Biotechnology, Polymer Science and Engineering Social Research, Energy Research, Advanced Technology for Large Structural Systems, Environmental Studies, Jewish Studies, Study of Private Enterprise, Materials Research, Business Communications, Solid State Studies, Small Business Development, Technology Studies, Surface Studies; Research institutes in Emulsion Polymers, Fracture and Solid Mechanics, Metal Forming, Study of the High-Rise Habitat, Thermo-Fluid Engineering and Science, 18th-Century Studies, Studies of Commodities, Health Science, Biomedical Engineering and Mathematical Biology. Library: 1,200,000 volumes, 6271 subscriptions. Total University enrollment: 6500.

Tuition: per credit College of Arts and Sciences $920, College of Business $610, College of Education $480, College of Engineering $920. Limited on-campus housing for both married and single students. Average monthly housing cost: $395–$535 for single graduate students, $7500 for married students. Apply to Residential Operations Office. Phone: (610)758-3500.

Graduate Studies

Graduate study since 1866. Enrollment: full-time 575, part-time 1212. University faculty: full-time 391, part-time 77. Degrees conferred: M.A., M.B.A., M.Ed., M.Eng., M.S., Ed.D., D.A., Ph.D.

ADMISSION REQUIREMENTS. Transcripts, GRE/GMAT/MAT, two letters of recommendation required in support of application. On-line application available. International students must submit evidence of competence in English or TOEFL. Interview not required. Accepts transfer applicants. Graduates of unaccredited colleges not considered. Apply to appropriate colleges by July 15 (Fall), December 1 (Spring). Application fee $50. Graduate Studies phone: (610)758-4500; fax: (610)758-4244.

ADMISSION STANDARDS. Competitive for some departments, very selective for others. Minimum average: 2.75 (A = 4).

FINANCIAL AID. Annual awards from institutional funds: scholarships, research assistantships, teaching fellowships, internships, tuition waivers, Federal W/S, loans. Approved for VA benefits. Apply by January 15 to appropriate department chair for scholarships, fellowships, assistantships; to the Financial Aid Office for all other programs. Use either FAFSA. Phone: (610)758-3181. About 75% of students receive aid from University and outside sources.

DEGREE REQUIREMENTS. For master's: 30 credit hours minimum, at least 24 in residence; thesis/research report/comprehensive exam. For Ph.D.: 42–48 credits, three years minimum beyond the bachelor's, at least one year in residence; reading knowledge of foreign languages varies with department; qualifying exam; comprehensive exam; dissertation; final oral exam. For Ed.D.: same as for Ph.D., except no language requirement. For D.A.: same as for Ph.D., except college teaching internship, appropriate project instead of dissertation.

FIELDS OF STUDY.

COLLEGE OF ARTS AND SCIENCES:
American Studies. Interdisciplinary. M.A.
Biological Sciences. Includes biochemistry, integrative biology, molecular biology. M.S., Ph.D.
Chemistry. Includes clinical chemistry, pharmaceutical chemistry. M.S., Ph.D., D.A.
Earth and Environmental Sciences. M.S., Ph.D.
English. M.A., Ph.D.
History. M.A., Ph.D.
Mathematics. Includes applied mathematics, statistics. M.S., Ph.D.
Physics. M.S., Ph.D.
Political Science. M.A.
Polymer Science and Engineering. Interdisciplinary. M.S., Ph.D.
Psychology. M.S., Ph.D.
Sociology and Anthropology. M.A.

COLLEGE OF BUSINESS AND ECONOMICS:
Accounting and Information Analysis. M.S.
Business Administration. M.B.A.
Business and Economics. Ph.D.
Economics. M.S.

COLLEGE OF EDUCATION:
Counseling Psychology. Includes counseling and human services, school counseling. M.Ed., Ph.D.
Education Leadership. M.Ed., Ed.D.
Educational Technology. M.Ed., M.S.
School Psychology. Ph.D.

P.C. ROSSIN COLLEGE OF ENGINEERING AND APPLIED SCIENCE:
Applied Mathematics. M.S., Ph.D.
Chemical Engineering. M.Eng., M.S., Ph.D.
Civil and Environmental Engineering. M.Eng., M.S., Ph.D.
Computer Engineering. M.S., Ph.D.
Electrical Engineering. M.Eng., M.S., Ph.D.
Engineering and Applied Science. M.Eng., M.S., Ph.D.
Industrial Engineering. M.Eng., M.S., Ph.D.
Information and Systems Engineering. M.Eng., M.S., Ph.D.
Management Science. M.S.
Manufacturing Systems Engineering. M.Eng., M.S., Ph.D.
Material Science and Engineering. M.Eng., Ph.D.
Mechanical Engineering. M.Eng., M.S., Ph.D.
Mechanics. M.Eng., M.S., Ph.D.
Photonics. M.S.
Quality Engineering. M.S.

HERBERT H. LEHMAN COLLEGE OF THE CITY UNIVERSITY OF NEW YORK
Bronx, New York 10468-1589
Web site: www.lehman.cuny.edu

Founded in 1932 as branch of Hunter College, became independent unit of City University in 1968. Coed. Municipal control. Semester system. Library: 541,944 volumes, 1350 subscriptions. Day-care facilities available.

Tuition: per credit, state resident $185, nonresident $320. No on-campus housing available.

Graduate Division

Enrollment: full-time 83, part-time 1624. Faculty: full-time 110, part-time 36. Degrees conferred: M.A., M.A.T., M.S., M.S.Ed., M.F.A.

ADMISSION REQUIREMENTS. Transcripts, letters of recommendation, TOEFL required for all international applicants. Accepts transfer applicants. Graduates of unaccredited institutions not considered. Apply to Office of Admissions by April 1 (Fall), November 1 (Spring). Application fee $40. Phone: (718)960-8856; fax: (718)960-8172.

ADMISSION STANDARDS. Competitive. Usual minimum average: 3.0 (A = 4).

FINANCIAL AID. Teaching assistantships, tuition waivers, graduate TAP, loans. Apply to Student Financial Aid Office by May 15. Phone: (718)960-8545. Use FAFSA and University's FAF. Aid available for part-time students.

DEGREE REQUIREMENTS. For master's: 30 credit hours minimum; thesis and/or comprehensive exams for most majors.

FIELDS OF STUDY.

DIVISION OF ARTS AND HUMANITIES:
Applied Music.
Art. M.A., M.F.A.
English. Includes literature, composition.
History.
Music Teaching (Kindergarten–12).
Secondary School Teachers of Spanish.
Speech-Language Pathology.

DIVISION OF EDUCATION:
Adolescent Childhood Education.
Business and Technology Education. 33–36 credit program
Childhood Education (Grades 1–6). 39 credit program.
Childhood Education—Special Education.
Counselor Education. 48 credit program.
Early Childhood Education (Birth–Grade 2). 42–48 credit program.
Early Childhood Special Education.
English Education.
Literacy Studies—Early Childhood Education. 36 credit program.
Literacy Studies—Middle and Adolescent Education. 36 credit program.
Mathematics Education (Grades 7–12).
Science Education (Grades 7–12).
Social Studies Education. (Grades 7–12).
TESOL.

DIVISION OF NATURAL AND SOCIAL SCIENCES:
Accounting. M.S.
Biology. M.A.
Computer Science. M.S.
Health Education and Promotion. M.A.
Health Teacher (K–12). M.S.Ed.
Mathematics.
Mathematics Education for Secondary Teacher of Mathematics.
Nursing. Includes advanced nursing, adult health, nursing of older adults, parent–child, pediatric nurse practitioner. M.S. 43 credit program.
Nutrition.
Recreation Education. M.S.Ed.
Secondary School Teachers of Biology and General Science. M.A.

LEWIS AND CLARK COLLEGE
Portland, Oregon 97219-7879
Web site: www.lclark.edu

Founded 1867. Coed. Private control. Presbyterian. Semester system. Library: 270,000 volumes, 1900 subscriptions. Total University enrollment: 2900.

Tuition: $525 per semester hour. No on-campus housing available.

Graduate School of Education

Enrollment: full- and part-time 576. Faculty teaching graduate students: full-time 35, part-time 63. Degrees conferred: M.A., M.S., M.A.T., M.Ed.

ADMISSION REQUIREMENTS. Official transcripts, résumé or vita, personal statement, GRE required in support of School's application. TOEFL required for international applicants. Accepts transfer applicants. Graduates of unaccredited institutions not considered. Apply to the program chairman at least 2 weeks prior to registration for part-time applicants. Applicants in some programs admitted quarterly. Teacher Education applicants apply by January 15. Rolling admissions process. Application fee $50. Phone: (503)768-7700.

ADMISSION STANDARDS. Selective. Usual minimum average: 3.0 (A = 4).

FINANCIAL AID. Limited to Federal W/S, loans. Apply by March 1 to Office of Student Financial Services. Phone: (503)768-7090. Use FAFSA.

DEGREE REQUIREMENTS. For master's: 10–15 courses minimum, at least 8–12 in residence; thesis/nonthesis option.

FIELDS OF STUDY.
Counseling Psychology. Includes addictions. M.A., M.S.
Educational Administration.
School Psychology. M.S.
Special Education. Includes deaf and hard-of-hearing.
Teacher Education. Includes early childhood/elementary, middle level/high school, music.

Northwestern School of Law

Established 1884; affiliated with Lewis and Clark in 1965 and initiated a day division. ABA approved since 1970. AALS member. Semester system. Library: 455,210 volumes, 4956 subscriptions; has LEXIS, NEXIS, WESTLAW, DIALOG, CALI, FIRSTSEARCH, QLSYSTEMS. No on-campus housing.

Annual tuition: $21,290 (day), $15,970 (evening). Total average annual additional expense: $11,665.

Enrollment: first-year class, day 194, evening 39; total 679 (men 52%, women 48%). Faculty: full-time 35, part-time 23. Student to faculty ratio 19.8 to 1. Degrees conferred: J.D., LL.M. (Environmental and Natural Resources Law).

ADMISSION REQUIREMENTS. LSDAS Law School report, bachelor's degree, transcripts, LSAT, short essay, letters of recommendation required in support of application. Accepts transfer applicants. Personal visit encouraged. Graduates of unaccredited colleges not considered. Apply to Assistant Dean for Admissions by March 15. Admits Fall only. Application fee $50. Phone: (503)768-6600; fax: (503)768-6671.

ADMISSION STANDARDS. Selective. Mean LSAT: full-time 158, part-time 155; mean GPA: full-time 3.35, part-time 3.20 (A = 4). Gourman rating: 3.01. *U.S. News & World Report* ranking is in the second tier of all U.S. law schools. Accepts about 40–45% of total annual applicants.

FINANCIAL AID. Scholarships, grants, fellowships, full and partial tuition waivers, Federal W/S, loans. Apply to Financial Aids Office by March 1. Use FAFSA (School code: 003197). Approximately 33% of all students receive some form of financial assistance.

DEGREE REQUIREMENTS. For J.D.: satisfactory completion of three-year (day), four-year (evening) program; 86 credit hours.

LINCOLN UNIVERSITY
Jefferson City, Missouri 65102
Web site: www.lincolnu.edu

Founded 1866. Located 125 miles W of St. Louis. Coed. State control. Semester system. Library: 151,595 volumes, 761 subscriptions.

Tuition: per hour, resident $136, nonresident $272. On-campus housing for single students available. Housing cost per semester: $2717 (includes board). Apply to Director of Residential Life. Phone: (573)681-5478.

Graduate Studies

Enrollment: full-time 22, part-time 135 (men 20%, women 80%). University faculty teaching graduate students: full-time 2, part-time 39. Degrees conferred: M.A., M.Ed., M.B.A.

ADMISSION REQUIREMENTS. Transcripts, three letters of recommendation required in support of application. GRE/MAT required for M.A., M.Ed.; GMAT required for M.B.A. TOEFL required for international applicants. Accepts transfer applicants. Apply to Office of Graduate Studies and Continuing Education by July 1 (Fall), November 30 (Spring). Application fee $17. Phone: (573)681-5074; fax: (573)681-5078; e-mail: gradschool@lincolnu.edu.

FINANCIAL AID. Limited to Federal W/S, loans. Approved for VA benefits. Use FAFSA. Phone: (573)681-6156; fax: (573)681-5566. Aid for part-time students carrying at least six credits.

DEGREE REQUIREMENTS. For M.A.: 33 semester hours minimum; thesis/nonthesis option. For M.Ed.: 36 semester hours minimum. For M.B.A.: 36 semester hours minimum.

FIELDS OF STUDY.
Business Administration. Includes accounting, management. M.B.A.
Elementary Education. M.Ed.
Guidance and Counseling. M.Ed.
History. M.A.
School Administration and Supervision. M.Ed.
Secondary Education. M.Ed.
Sociology. M.A.
Sociology/Criminal Justice. M.A.
Special Education. M.Ed.

LOMA LINDA UNIVERSITY
Loma Linda, California 92350
Web site: www.llu.edu

Founded in 1905. CGS member. Located in the San Bernardino Redlands area about 5 miles from each city. Coed. Quarter system. Loma Linda University offers programs in graduate professional education through the Graduate School. The programs utilize resources in the Schools of Allied Health Professions, Dentistry, Medicine, Nursing, and Public Health. The University is operated by the Seventh-Day Adventist Church with approximately 40% of its student body belonging to other religious faiths. Library: 322,657 volumes, 1394 subscriptions.

Tuition: per unit $350, graduate dental programs full-time $17,000–$40,000. On-campus housing for 100 graduate men, 32–64 graduate women, none for married students. Average academic year cost: $5450–$6250. Apply to Dean of Students. Phone: (909)824-4510. Day-care facilities available.

Graduate School

Opened 1954. Enrollment: full-time 392, part-time 178. University faculty: full-time 36, part-time 58. Degrees conferred: M.A., M.S., M.S.W., M.P.H., Psy.D., Dr.P.H., Ph.D., Ph.D.-M.P.H., Psy.D.-M.P.H., Psy.D.-Dr.P.H.

ADMISSION REQUIREMENTS. Two transcripts, letters of reference, GRE/Subject Tests required in support of School's application. TOEFL required for foreign applicants. Interview not required for most programs. Accepts transfer applicants. Apply to Dean of Graduate School by August 1. Most department prefer Fall entrance. Application fee $50. Phone: (909)824-4528; fax: (909)824-4859.

ADMISSION STANDARDS. Very selective for some departments, selective for others. Usual minimum average: 3.0 (A = 4).

FINANCIAL AID. Annual awards from institutional funds: scholarships, fellowships, stipends, teaching assistantships, grants, full and partial tuition waiver, Federal W/S, loans. Approved for VA benefits. Apply by March 1 to appropriate department chair for scholarships, fellowships, assistantships; to Financial Aid Office for all other programs. Use FAFSA and institutional FAF. Phone: (909)824-4509, (800)422-4558. Aid available for part-time students.

DEGREE REQUIREMENTS. For master's: 48 quarter units minimum, at least 12 in residence; advancement to candidacy; thesis/nonthesis option; final written/oral exams. For Ph.D.: 72 quarter units, three years minimum beyond the bachelor's, at least two years in residence and 30 units in full-time attendance; some require reading knowledge of two foreign languages; dissertation; final oral exam. For Psy.D.: essentially the same as Ph.D., except no foreign language; internship; special research project.

FIELDS OF STUDY.
Anatomy.
Biochemistry.
Biology. M.S., Ph.D.
Dentistry. Includes implant dentistry, oral surgery, periodontics. Apply by October 1; D.D.S. or D.M.D. for admission. M.S. only.
Family Life Education.
Family Studies. M.A. only.
Geology. M.S., Ph.D.
Marriage and Family Therapy. M.S. only.
Microbiology.
Paleontology. M.S., Ph.D.
Pharmacology.
Physiology.
Psychology. Includes clinical, experimental. Psy.D., Ph.D.
Social Policy and Social Research. Ph.D.
Social Work. M.S.W.
Speech Language Pathology. M.S. only.

School of Allied Health Professions

Established 1966. Quarter system. Tuition: per credit $420. Enrollment: full-time 224, part-time 56. University faculty: full-time 96, part-time 38. Degrees conferred: M.H.I.S., M.O.T., M.P.A., M.P.T., D.P.T.

ADMISSION REQUIREMENTS. Two transcripts, three letters of reference, GRE, statement of professional goals, résumé required in support of School's application. TOEFL (minimum score 550) required for foreign applicants. Preference given to SDA applicants. Accepts transfer applicants. Apply to Director of Admissions by August 1; M.P.A. applicants use CASPA (an on-line service) by March 1; M.P.A. admits Fall only. Application fee $50. Phone: (909)824-4599; fax (909)824-4291; e-mail: admissions@sahp.llu.edu.

ADMISSION STANDARDS. Selective for most programs. Usual minimum GPA: 3.0 (A = 4); 3.2 for D.P.T.

FINANCIAL AID. Annual awards from institutional funds: scholarships, fellowships, teaching assistantships, grants, internships, tuition waivers, Federal W/S, loans. Approved for VA benefits. Apply by March 1 to appropriate department chair for scholarships, fellowships, assistantships; by March 15 to Financial Aid Office for all other programs. Phone: (909)824-4509 or (800) 422-4558; e-mail: finaid@univ.llu.edu. Use FAFSA (School code: 001218) and institutional FAF. Aid sometimes available for part-time students.

DEGREE REQUIREMENTS. For M.H.I.S.: 54 quarter units, 15-month full-time program; internship. For M.O.T.: 144 quarter unit full-time program; practicum. For M.O.T. (Post-Professional): 45 quarter unit full-time program; practicum. For M.P.T.: two-and-one-half-year full-time program; practicum. For D.P.T.: 189 quarter hour full-time program; clinical experience.

FIELDS OF STUDY.
Health Information Systems. M.H.I.S.
Occupational Therapy. M.O.T., M.O.T. (Post-Professional).
Physical Therapy. M.P.T., D.P.T.
Physician Assistant. M.P.A.

School of Dentistry

Founded 1953. Quarter system. Annual tuition: $26,751. On-campus housing for single graduate students only. Apply to Dean, Student Services. Phone: (909)558-4510. Total average cost for all other first-year expenses: $6860.

Enrollment: first-year class 87; total 450 (men 65%, women 35%). School faculty: full-time 84, part-time 189. Degrees conferred: D.D.S., D.D.S.-M.P.H., D.D.S.-M.S., D.D.S.-Ph.D. The M.S., Ph.D. is offered through the Graduate School.

ADMISSION REQUIREMENTS. AADSAS report, Loma Linda supplemental form, official transcripts, three letters of recommendation, DAT (preference given to October test takers), dexterity test required in support of School's application. Interview by invitation only. Applicants must have completed at least three years of college study, preferably four years of study. Preference given to Seventh-Day Adventist Church members. Graduates of unaccredited institutions not considered. Apply to AADSAS after June 1, before December 1. Application fee $60. Phone: (909)558-4621, (800)422-4558.

ADMISSION STANDARDS. Competitive. Mean DAT: Academic 19.9, PAT 19.5; mean GPA: 3.21 (A = 4). Accepts about 20% of total annual applicants. Approximately 80% are state residents.

FINANCIAL AID. Scholarships, loans. Apply to Financial Aid Office after acceptance, before May 1. Phone: (909)558-4509. Use FAFSA (School code: 001218). About 73% receive aid from School.

DEGREE REQUIREMENTS. For D.D.S.: satisfactory completion of 45-month program. For D.D.S.-M.P.H.: usually requires two additional quarters. For M.S., Ph.D.: see Graduate School listing above.

FIELDS OF GRADUATE STUDY.
Oral and Maxillofacial Surgery.
Oral Implantology.
Orthodontics.
Pediatric Dentistry.
Periodontics.

School of Medicine

Organized 1909. Annual tuition: $28,015; student fees: $1235. Total average figure for all other expenses: $10,200. Enrollment: first-year class 159 (EDP 10); total 663 (men 53%, women 47%). Faculty: full-time 675, part-time 100. Degrees conferred: M.D., M.D.-M.S., M.D.-Ph.D. The M.S., Ph.D. is offered through the Graduate School.

ADMISSION REQUIREMENTS. AMCAS report, transcripts, recommendations, MCAT, supplementary form, required in support of application. Interview by invitation. Has EDP: apply between June 1 and August 1. Applicants must have completed at least three years of college study. Some preference to members of Seventh-Day Adventist Church. Apply to Dean of Admissions after June 1, before November 1. Application fee $75. Phone: (909)558-4467; fax: (909)558-0359.

ADMISSION STANDARDS. Very competitive. Mean MCAT: 9.6; mean GPA: 3.67 (A = 4). Gourman rating: 4.29. Accepts 8% of total annual applicants. Approximately 60% are state residents.

FINANCIAL AID. Scholarships, grants, HEAL, loans. Apply to Director of Student Finance. Phone: (909)558-4509. Use FAFSA (School code: 001218).

DEGREE REQUIREMENTS. For M.D.: satisfactory completion of four-year program. For M.S.-Ph.D.: see Graduate School listing above.

FIELDS OF GRADUATE STUDY.
Anatomy.
Biochemistry.
Genetics.
Immunology.
Microbiology.
Molecular Biology.
Neuroscience.
Pharmacology.
Physiology.

School of Public Health

Established 1967. Quarter system. Special facilities: Center for Health and Development, Center for Health Promotion, Center for Health Research. Enrollment: full-time 266, part-time 124. University faculty: full-time 65, part-time 6. Degrees conferred: M.H.A., M.P.H., Dr.P.H.

ADMISSION REQUIREMENTS. Two transcripts, three letters of reference, GRE (GRE or MCAT for Dr.P.H.), statement of professional goals required in support of School's application. TOEFL (minimum score 550) required for foreign applicants. Interview required for Dr.P.H. Accepts transfer applicants. Apply to Director of Admissions by August 1. Application fee $100. Phone: (909)824-4694; fax (909)824-8087.

ADMISSION STANDARDS. Selective for most programs. Usual minimum GPA: 3.0 (A = 4); 3.2 for Dr.P.H.

FINANCIAL AID. Annual awards from institutional funds: scholarships, fellowships, research assistantships, teaching assistantships, grants, internships, tuition waiver, Federal W/S, loans. Approved for VA benefits. Apply by May 5 to appropriate department chair for scholarships, fellowships, assistantships; to Financial Aid Office for all other programs. Phone: (909)824-4509 or (800)422-4558; e-mail: finaid@univ.llu.edu. Use FAFSA (School code: 001218) and institutional FAF. Aid available for part-time students.

DEGREE REQUIREMENTS. For M.P.H., M.H.A.: 52–54 quarter units minimum; practicum. For Dr.P.H.: 2-year full-time program; comprehensive exam; dissertation; final oral exam.

FIELDS OF STUDY.
Biostatistics.
Community Wellness. 54 unit program.
Environmental and Occupational Health.
Environmental Epidemiology.

Epidemiology.
Health Administration. M.H.A., M.P.H.
Health Education.
Health Promotion.
International Health. Collaborative program with the U.S. Peace Corps. M.P.H.-M.I.P.
Maternal and Child Health.
Nutrition in Health Promotion.
Public Health Nutrition.

LONG ISLAND UNIVERSITY, BROOKLYN CAMPUS

Brooklyn, New York 11201
Web site: www.liu.edu

Founded 1926. Coed. Private control. Semester system. Library: 400,000 volumes, 6500 subscriptions. Total Campus enrollment: 11,100.

Tuition: per credit, $572. Rooms and apartments available for single and married students. Average academic year housing cost: single student $6090 (including board), married $6000 (room only). Apply to Director of Housing. Phone: (718)488-1046.

Enrollment: full-time 694, part-time 1098. Faculty: full-time 143, part-time 148. Degrees conferred: M.A., M.S., M.B.A., M.S.Acc., M.P.A., M.S.Ed., Pharm.D., Ph.D.

Graduate Programs

ADMISSION REQUIREMENTS. Transcripts, GRE/GMAT, two letters of recommendation required in support of application. TOEFL (minimum score 500), affidavit of financial support required for international applicants. Interview not required. Accepts transfer applicants. Graduates of unaccredited institutions not considered. Apply to Graduate Admissions Office at least 1 month prior to beginning of semester. Application fee $30. Phone: (718)403-1011; fax: (718)797-2399.

ADMISSION STANDARDS. Competitive to relatively open. Usual minimum average 2.75 (A = 4).

FINANCIAL AID. Scholarships, teaching fellowships, research assistantships, administrative assistantships, teaching assistantships, Federal W/S, loans. Approved for VA benefits. Apply by May 1 (Fall), November 1 (Spring), March 1 (Summer) to appropriate department chair for scholarships, fellowships, assistantships; to Graduate Admissions Office for all other programs. Use FAFSA and institutional FAF. Phone: (718)488-1037; fax: (718)488-3343.

DEGREE REQUIREMENTS. For M.A., M.S., M.S.Ed.: 30–36 semester hours minimum, at least 24 in residence; thesis for many departments; final oral/written exam. For M.B.A., M.P.A.: 36 credits beyond core; thesis/nonthesis option; comprehensive exam. For Ph.D.: by advisement.

FIELDS OF STUDY.
Accounting. M.S.Acc., M.B.A.
Adapted Physical Education. M.S.
Adult Neurologic Rehabilitation. M.S.
Advanced Athletic Training and Sport. M.S.
Athletic Training and Sports Sciences. M.A.
Banking Financial Services. M.B.A.
Biology. Includes microbiology, molecular-cellular, medical microbiology. M.S.
Business Administration. M.B.A.
Certified Public Accounting. M.B.A.

Chemistry. M.S.
Clinical Psychology. Ph.D.
Coaching and Conditioning. M.S.
Community Health. M.S.
Computer Science. M.S.
Counseling and Development. M.S., M.S.Ed.
Economics. M.A.
English. Includes English literature, professional and creative writing, teaching of writing. M.A.
Exercise Physiology. M.S.
Finance. M.B.A.
Health Administration. M.P.A.
Health Science. Includes athletic training and sports sciences, exercise physiology, physical therapy, adapted physical education, therapeutic recreation. M.S.
History. M.A.
Human Resource Management. M.S.
International Business. M.B.A.
Management. M.B.A.
Management Information System. M.B.A.
Marketing. M.B.A.
Musculoskeletal Physical Therapy. M.S.
Pediatric Physical Therapy. M.S.
Physical Therapy. M.S.
Political Science. M.A.
Psychology. M.A.
Quantitative Analysis. M.B.A.
Social Science. M.S.
Sociology. M.A.
Speech-Language Pathology. M.S.
Taxation. M.S., M.B.A.
Urban Studies. M.A.

LONG ISLAND UNIVERSITY, C.W. POST CAMPUS

Brookville, New York 11548-1300
Web site: www.cwpost.liu.edu

Established 1954. Coed. Private control. Semester system. Special facilities: Hillwood Art Museum, Center for Aging, Tilles Center for Performing Arts, Accounting and Tax Research Library, Center for Economic Research, Center for Business Research. Library: 1,297,800 volumes, 11,446 subscriptions.

Tuition: per credit $572. Rooms and apartments available for single and married students. Average academic year housing cost: $4021 (room only), $7010 (including board). Contact Director of Housing for both on- and off-campus housing information. Phone: (516)299-2326.

Graduate Division

Graduate study since 1954. Enrollment: full-time 933, part-time 1537. Faculty: full-time 470. Degrees conferred: M.A., M.S., M.B.A., M.S.Ed., M.F.A., M.P.A., C.A.S., Ph.D., Psy.D.

ADMISSION REQUIREMENTS. Official transcripts, GRE/GMAT, 2 letters of recommendation required in support of applications. Department interview may be required. All requirements vary by department. TOEFL or ASPECT program required for international applicants. Accepts transfer applicants. Graduates of unaccredited institutions not considered. Apply to Graduate Admissions Office at least 1 month prior to beginning of semester. Application fee $30. Phone: (516)299-2719; fax: (516)299-2137; e-mail: enroll@cwpost.liu.edu.

ADMISSION STANDARDS. Selective to relatively open. Usual minimum average: 2.5 (A = 4).

FINANCIAL AID. Scholarships, research/teaching assistantships, fellowships, internships, Federal W/S, loans. Approved for VA benefits. Apply by May 15 (Fall), October 1 (Spring), April 1 (Summer) to appropriate department chair for fellowships, assistantships; to Graduate Admissions Office for scholarships; to Financial Aid Office for all other programs. Phone: (516)299-2338. Use FAFSA, TAP for New York State residents. Aid available for part-time students.

DEGREE REQUIREMENTS. For M.A., M.S., 30–36 semester hours minimum, at least 24 in residence; thesis/nonthesis option for many departments; final oral/written exam. For M.B.A., M.P.A.: 48 credits beyond core; thesis/nonthesis option; comprehensive exam. For M.F.A.: 60 credits minimum beyond bachelor's, at least 45 in residence; project.

FIELDS OF STUDY.

COLLEGE OF ARTS AND SCIENCES:
Applied Mathematics.
Biology.
Clinical Psychology. Psy.D. only.
Computer Science Education.
English.
Environmental Studies.
History.
Information Systems.
Interdisciplinary Studies.
Management Engineering.
Math for Secondary School Teachers.
Political Science.
Psychology.
Spanish.

COLLEGE OF MANAGEMENT:
Accounting.
Criminal Justice. Includes security administration.
Finance.
Fraud Examination. Certificate.
Health-Care Administration.
International Business.
Logistics and Supply Chain Management.
Management.
Management Information Systems.
Marketing.
Public Administration.
Strategic Management—Accounting.
Taxation.

SCHOOL OF EDUCATION:
Art Education (K–12).
Bilingual Education. Includes elementary, secondary.
Biology Education.
College Student Development Counseling.
Computers in Education.
Earth Science Education.
Elementary Education (N–6).
English Education.
Mathematics Education.
Mental Health Counseling.
Middle School Education.
Music Education (K–12).
Reading Teacher.
School Administration and Supervisor.
School Business Administration.
School Counseling.
School District Administration.
Social Studies Education.
Spanish Education.
Speech-Language Pathology.
Teacher of Gifted and Talented.

Teacher of Special Education.
Teaching English to Speakers of Other Languages.

SCHOOL OF HEALTH PROFESSIONS:
Advanced Practice Nursing.
Biological Science. Includes hematology, immunology, medical chemistry, medical microbiology.
Cardiac Perfusion.
Clinical Laboratory Management.
Dietetics.
Family Nurse Practitioner Studies.
Medical Biology.
Nutrition.

SCHOOL OF VISUAL AND PERFORMING ARTS:
Art.
Art Education.
Clinical Art Therapy.
Fine Art and Design.
Interactive Media Arts.
Music.
Theater.

Palmer School of Library and Information Science

Tuition: per credit, $405.
Enrollment: full-time 67, part-time 352. Faculty: full-time 17, part-time 15. Degrees conferred: M.S.L.S., Certificate (Archives and Records Management).

ADMISSION REQUIREMENTS. Official transcripts, GRE/MAT, statement of career objectives, three letters of recommendation, interview required in support of School's application. TOEFL required for international applicants. Accepts transfer applicants. Graduates of unaccredited institutions not considered. Apply by May 15 (Fall), October 15 (Spring), to Graduate Admission. Rolling admissions process. Application fee $30. Phone: (516)299-2866; fax: (516)626-4168; e-mail: palmer@cwpost.liu.edu.

ADMISSION STANDARDS. Selective. Usual minimum average: 3.0 (A = 4).

FINANCIAL AID. Scholarships, fellowships, assistantships, Federal W/S, loans, tuition reductions for students with a 3.5 or higher undergraduate average. Apply to Dean's Office for fellowships, assistantships; to Office of Financial Aid for all other programs. No specified closing date. Use FAFSA. Phone: (516)299-2338.

DEGREE REQUIREMENTS. For master's: 36 semester hours minimum, at least 12 in residence; thesis/nonthesis option. For Certificate: 15–30 semester hours beyond master's; special project.

FIELDS OF STUDY.
Archives.
Information Studies.
Library and Information Science.
Library Sciences.
Records Management.

LONGWOOD UNIVERSITY
Farmville, Virginia 23909-1800
Web site: www.longwood.edu

Founded 1839. Located 65 miles W of Richmond. Coed. State control. Semester system. Library: 241,641 volumes, 2500 subscriptions.

Tuition: per credit, resident $189, nonresident $402. Limited housing for graduate students in Fall and Spring semesters. Contact Director of Housing for on- and off-campus information. Phone: (804)395-2080.

Graduate Studies

Graduate study since 1954. Enrollment: full- and part-time 477. College faculty: full-time 40, part-time 20. Degrees conferred: M.A., M.S.

ADMISSION REQUIREMENTS. Transcripts, 2 letters of recommendation, essay required in support of application. TOEFL required for international applicants. Accepts transfer applicants. Graduates of unaccredited colleges not considered. Apply by May 1 (Fall), October 15 (Spring) to the Director of Graduate Studies. Application fee $25. Phone: (804)395-2707; e-mail: graduate@longwood.lwc.edu.

ADMISSION STANDARDS. Selective. Usual minimum average: 2.5 (A = 4).

FINANCIAL AID. Assistantships, Federal W/S, loans. Apply to the appropriate department for assistantships; to the Office of Financial Aid for loans. No specified closing date. Use FAFSA.

DEGREE REQUIREMENTS. For M.A.: 30 credit hours minimum, at least 24 in residence; thesis; oral defense. For M.S.: 30–36 credit hours minimum, at least 24 in residence; thesis/nonthesis option; comprehensive exam for nonthesis option.

FIELDS OF STUDY.
Administration and Supervision.
Community and College Counseling.
Curriculum and Instruction Specialist—English.
Curriculum and Instruction Specialist—Mild disabilities.
Curriculum and Instruction Specialist—Modern Languages.
Curriculum and Instruction Specialist—Physical Education.
Curriculum and Instruction Specialist—Speech and Theatre.
Elementary Curriculum and Instruction Specialist.
English. Includes literature, English education, writing.
Environmental Studies.
Guidance and Counseling.
Liberal Studies/Special Education. Five-year program.
Reading Specialist.
School Librarian/Media Specialist.
Sociology. M.S.
Supervision.

LORAS COLLEGE
Dubuque, Iowa 52004-0178
Web site: www.loras.edu

Founded 1839. Coed. Private control. Roman Catholic. Semester system. Special facilities: Bioethics Resource Center, Center for Business and Research, Center for Dubuque Area History, Center for Environmental Research. Library: 340,000 volumes, 963 subscriptions.

Tuition: per credit hour $375. On-campus housing for graduate students during summer only; none for married students. Average summer housing cost: $600 for six-week summer session. Contact Office of Student Life for housing information. Phone: (563)588-7137.

Graduate Division

All courses offered through Tri College Department of Education. Graduate enrollment: full-time 13, part-time 86. Faculty teaching graduate students: full-time 22, part-time 5. Degree conferred: M.A.

ADMISSION REQUIREMENTS. Official transcripts, GRE/MAT, 2 letters of recommendation required in support of application. Interview required by some departments. TOEFL required for international applicants. Accepts transfer applicants. Apply to Office of Admissions at least 6 weeks prior to registration. Application fee $25. Phone: (563)588-7236; fax: (563)588-7964.

ADMISSION STANDARDS. Selective. Usual minimum average: 3.0 (A = 4).

FINANCIAL AID. Limited to loans. Phone: (563)588-7339. Use FAFSA.

DEGREE REQUIREMENTS. For M.A.: 30–39 semester hours minimum, at least 24 in residence; admission to candidacy; comprehensive exam (varies by department); reading knowledge of one foreign language; thesis/nonthesis option. For M.M.: 34 semester credits; admission to candidacy; capstone experience; internship.

FIELDS OF STUDY.
Applied Psychology.
Effective Teaching.
Elementary School Administration.
English.
History.
Multidisciplinary Studies.
Pastoral Studies. M.M.
Physical Education.
Religious Studies. M.A., M.M.
Secondary Education.
Special Education.
Theology.

LOUISIANA STATE UNIVERSITY AND AGRICULTURAL AND MECHANICAL COLLEGE
Baton Rouge, Louisiana 70803

Established 1860. CGS member. Coed. State control. Semester system. Member institution of Organization for Tropical Studies. Special facilities: Coastal Studies Institute, System Network Computer Center, Center for French and Francophone Studies, Center for Life Course and Population Studies, Southern Regional Climate Center, Louisiana Office of State Climatology, The U.S. Civil War Center, Eric Voegelin Institute for American Renaissance Studies, Public Management Program, Louisiana Real Estate Research Institute, Louisiana Education Policy Research Center, Center for Scientific and Mathematical Literacy, Hazardous Waste Research Center, Louisiana Transportation Research Center, Louisiana Water Resource Research Institute, Institute for Recyclable Materials, Remote Sensing and Image Processing Laboratory, Center for Coastal Energy and Environmental Resources, Basin Research Institute, Center for Energy Studies, Coastal Ecology Institute, Coastal Fisheries Institute, Mining and Mineral Resources Research Institute, Wetland Biogeochemistry Institute, National Ports and Waterways Institute, Office of Sea Grant Development, Louisiana Space Consortium, Museum of Art, Vascular Plant Herbarium, Mycological Herbarium, Rural Life Museum, LSU Agricultural Center, Pennington Biomedical Research Center, Museum of Natural Science, Nuclear Science Center, Center for Advanced Microstructures and Devices, T. Henry Williams Center for Oral History. Founding member of the Council of Sponsoring Institutions of Oak Ridge Associated Universities. Library: 2,700,000 volumes, 22,000 subscriptions.

Annual tuition: full-time resident $3488, nonresident $9788. On-campus housing for 578 married students, unlimited for graduate men and women. Average academic year housing cost: $2500 for married students, $4270 (including board) for single students. Apply to Director of Housing. Phone: (225)578-8663.

Graduate School

Graduate study since 1868. Enrollment: full-time 2897, part-time 1347. Faculty teaching graduate students: full-time 1100, part-time 27. Degrees conferred: M.A., M.B.A., M.Ed., M.L.A., M.M.Ed., M.M., M.N.S., M.A.H., M.F.A., M.Ap.Stat., M.E., M.P.A., M.S.W., Ed.S., D.M.A., D.V.M., M.M.E., M.L.I.S., C.L.I.S., Ph.D.

ADMISSION REQUIREMENTS. Transcripts, GRE/GMAT required in support of School's application. On-line application available. TOEFL (minimum score 550), financial statement required for international applicants. TSE required of international students seeking financial aid. Interview not required. Accepts transfer applicants. Graduates of unaccredited institutions not considered. Apply to the Office of Graduate Admissions by May 15 (Fall), October 15 (Spring), May 15 (Summer). Application fee $25. Phone: (225)578-2311.

ADMISSION STANDARDS. Selective for most departments, very selective for others. Usual minimum average: 3.0 (A = 4).

FINANCIAL AID. Annual awards from institutional funds: scholarships, research assistantships/teaching assistantships, fellowships, internships, grants, Federal W/S, loans. Approved for VA benefits. Apply to appropriate department chair for scholarships, fellowships, assistantships; to Office of Financial Aid for all other programs. No specified closing date; priority date for Fall: January 25. Phone: (225)388-3103; fax: (225)578-6300. Use FAFSA. About 60% of students receive aid other than loans from University and outside sources. Aid sometimes available for part-time students.

DEGREE REQUIREMENTS. For master's: 30 semester hours minimum, at least 24 in residence; thesis; final oral/written exam; or 36 semester hours minimum, at least 30 in residence; final oral/written exam in some departments; reading knowledge of one foreign language for some departments. For Ph.D.: 60 semester hours minimum beyond the master's, at least one year in continuous residence; oral/written qualifying exam in some departments; oral/written general exam; dissertation; final oral exam.

FIELDS OF STUDY.
Accounting.
Agribusiness.
Agricultural Economics.
Agronomy.
Animal Science.
Architecture.
Art (School of). Includes art education, art history, photography, studio art.
Biological and Agricultural Engineering.
Biological Sciences. Includes biochemistry, genetics, microbiology, plant biology, zoology.
Business Administration.
Chemical Engineering.
Chemistry.
Civil and Environmental Engineering.
Communication Sciences and Disorders.
Communication Studies.
Comparative Biomedical Science.
Comparative Literature.
Computer Science. Includes systems science.
Curriculum and Instruction.
Dairy Science.
Economics.

Educational Leadership, Research, and Counseling.
Electrical and Computer Engineering.
Engineering Sciences.
English.
Entomology.
Environmental Studies.
Experimental Statistics.
Finance.
Food Science.
French Studies.
Genetics.
Geography and Anthropology.
Geology and Geophysics.
History.
Horticulture.
Human Ecology.
Industrial and Manufacturing Systems Engineering.
Information Systems and Decision Science.
Kinesiology.
Landscape Architecture (School of).
Liberal Arts.
Library and Information Science (School of).
Linguistics.
Management.
Marketing.
Mass Communication.
Mathematics.
Mechanical Engineering.
Microbiology.
Music (School of).
Natural Sciences.
Oceanography.
Petroleum Engineering.
Philosophy and Religious Studies.
Physics and Astronomy.
Plant Pathology and Crop Physiology.
Plant Physiology.
Political Science.
Psychology. Includes clinical, developmental, industrial and organizational, school.
Public Administration.
Renewable Natural Resources.
Social Work (School of).
Sociology.
Spanish.
Theater.

Paul M. Hebert Law Center
Web site: www.law.lsu.edu

Established 1906 as LSU Law School, renamed in 1979. ABA approved since 1926. AALS member. Semester system. Full-time, day study only. Special facility: Center of Civil Law Studies, Louisiana Judicial College. Special programs: summer study abroad in France at University of Aix-Marseille III Law School. Law library: 582,384 volumes, 2602 subscriptions; has LEXIS, NEXIS, WESTLAW, DIALOG; is both a State and Federal Government Depository.

Annual tuition: resident $7164, nonresident $13,005. Off-campus housing and personal expenses: approximately $10,550.

Enrollment: first-year class 233; total full-time 650 (men 56%, women 44%); no part-time students. Faculty: full-time 25, part-time 18. Student to faculty ratio 21.7 to 1. Degrees conferred: J.D., J.D.-M.B.A., J.D.-M.P.A., LL.M., M.C.L. (only for persons who have completed a basic legal education and received a university degree in law in another country).

ADMISSION REQUIREMENTS. For J.D. program: LSDAS Law School report, bachelor's degree, transcripts, LSAT (not later than December) required in support of application. Preference given to state residents. Accepts transfer applicants. Graduates from unaccredited institutions not considered. Apply to Admissions Office after November 1, before February 1. Admits Fall only. Application fee $25. For Graduate Program: transcripts required in support of application, TOEFL required for foreign applicants. Apply to Office of Admissions. Phone: (225)578-8646; fax: (225)578-8647; e-mail: admissions@law.lsu.edu.

ADMISSION STANDARDS. Selective. Mean LSAT: 151; mean GPA: 3.32 (A = 4). Gourman rating: 3.39. *U.S. News & World Report* ranking is in the third tier of all U.S. law schools. Accepts 45–50% of total annual applicants. Highly selective for LL.M., M.C.L.

FINANCIAL AID. Limited scholarships, loans. Apply to LSU Office of Financial Aid by April 1. Use FAFSA (School code: 002010). Approximately 20% of students receive some form of financial assistance.

DEGREE REQUIREMENTS. For J.D.: 87 semester hours minimum, at least 29 in residence. For LL.M., M.C.L.: 24 semester hours minimum, at least two semesters in residence; thesis.

School of Social Work

Graduate study since 1937. Semester system. Annual tuition: resident $2654, nonresident $5954.

Enrollment: full-time 153, part-time 45. School faculty: full-time 14, part-time 10. Degrees conferred: M.S.W., Ph.D.

ADMISSION REQUIREMENTS. Transcripts, GRE, three letters of recommendation required in support of School's application. TOEFL (minimum score 550), financial statement required for international applicants. Interview may be required. Accepts transfer applicants. Graduates of unaccredited institutions not considered. Apply to Office of Student Services by February 1. Application fee $25. Phone: (225)578-1234.

ADMISSION STANDARDS. Selective. Usual minimum average: 3.0 (A = 4). GRE combined score (analytic section not included): 1000.

FINANCIAL AID. Child Welfare Stipends, Corrections Stipends, scholarships, teaching assistantships, research assistantships, internships, minority student tuition waivers, Federal W/S, loans. Approved for VA benefits. Apply by March 1 to Office of Admissions. Phone: (225)578-3103; fax: (225)578-6300. Use FAFSA. About 30% of students receive aid from School and outside sources. Aid available for part-time students.

DEGREE REQUIREMENTS. For M.S.W.: 60-hour program, including internship. Advanced standing awarded to qualified B.S.W. degree holders. For Ph.D.: 48 semester hours beyond the master's; at least two semesters in residence; general exam; practicum; dissertation; final defense.

School of Veterinary Medicine
Web site: www.vetmed.lsu.edu

Annual tuition: resident and contract state resident $6734; nonresident $19,484. Total average cost for all other expenses: $6800. On-campus housing available.

Enrollment: first-year class 80; total 326 (men 40%, women 60%); postgraduates 65. Faculty: full-time 72, part-time 4. Degrees conferred: D.V.M., D.V.M.-M.S., D.V.M.-Ph.D. The M.S. and Ph.D. are offered through the Graduate School.

ADMISSION REQUIREMENTS. VMCAS report, transcripts showing completion of sixty-six hours of preprofessional college work, MCAT or GRE recommendations, animal/veterinary experience, essay required in support of application. Interview always required. Accepts transfer applicants. Preference given to state and contract residents. Apply to Assistant Dean after September 1, prior to October 1. Application fee $50. Phone: (225)578-9537; fax: (225)578-9546.

ADMISSION STANDARDS. Selective. Mean GPA: 3.55; mean GRE: combined score 1121. Accepts 40% of total annual applicants. Accepts nine from Arkansas, fifteen from outside state.

FINANCIAL AID. Fellowships, assistantships, full tuition waivers, Federal W/S, loans. Apply to Office of Financial Aid after acceptance.

DEGREE REQUIREMENTS. For D.V.M.: 152 semester hours and four years in residence. For M.S. and Ph.D.: see Graduate School listing above.

FIELDS OF GRADUATE STUDY.
Anatomy and Cell Biology.
Comparative Biomedical Science.
Microbiology and Parasitology.
Pathobiological Science.
Pathology.
Veterinary Clinical Sciences.

LOUISIANA STATE UNIVERSITY HEALTH SCIENCES CENTER
New Orleans, Louisiana 70112-2223
Web site: www.lsuhsc.edu

The Health Sciences Center was established as a separate unit in 1965 and includes six professional schools in both New Orleans and Shreveport. CGS member. Public control. Semester system. Special facilities: Pennington Biomedical Research Center, Cardiovascular Center, Center for Arthritis and Rheumatology, Center for Molecular and Human Genetics, Ernest N. Morial Asthma, Allergy, and Respiratory Disease Center, LSU Eye Center, Feist-Weiller Cancer Center, Neuroscience Center, Stanley S. Scott Cancer Center. The University's NIH ranking is 156th among U.S. institutions with 75 awards/grants worth $17,334,863. Library: 389,000 volumes, 3500 subscriptions. Total enrollment at University's Health Sciences Centers: 2965.

Annual tuition: full-time, resident $2522, nonresident $5022. On-campus housing available for both single and married students. Average academic year housing cost: $6000-$9000 (including board); off-campus housing $350 per month. Contact Director of Housing for both on- and off-campus housing information. Phone: (504)568-6260.

School of Graduate Studies

Graduate study since 1967. Enrollment: full-time 83, part-time 21. Faculty teaching graduate students: full-time 138, part-time 29. Degrees conferred: M.S., Ph.D.

ADMISSION REQUIREMENTS. Two official transcripts, two letters of recommendation, GRE required in support of School's application. TOEFL required of international applicants. Interview not required. Accepts transfer applicants. Apply to the Office of Graduate Studies; no specified closing date. Rolling admissions process. Application fee $30. Phone: (504)568-2211; fax: (504)568-5588; e-mail: gradschool@lsuhsc.edu.

ADMISSION STANDARDS. Selective. Usual minimum average: 2.75 (A = 4).

FINANCIAL AID. Fellowships, research assistantships, teaching assistantships, tuition waivers, stipends, Federal W/S, loans. Apply to appropriate department chair for assistantships, fellowships; to Office of Financial Aid for all other programs. Phone: (504)568-4820. Priority deadlines: April 15 (Fall), November 15 (Spring), April 15 (Summer). Use FAFSA and institutional FAF. About 20% of students receive aid other than loans from University and outside sources. Aid sometimes available for part-time students.

DEGREE REQUIREMENTS. For M.S.: 30–36 semester hours minimum, at least 24–36 in residence; thesis/nonthesis option; final written/oral exam for some programs. For Ph.D.: 42 semester hours minimum beyond the master's degree, at least two years in full-time residence; qualifying exam; foreign language proficiency for some programs; dissertation; final oral exam.

FIELDS OF STUDY.
Biochemistry and Molecular Biology.
Biostatistics.
Cell Biology and Anatomy.
Genetics.
Microbiology, Immunology, and Parasitology.
Neuroscience. Ph.D. only.
Oral Biology.
Pathology.
Pharmacology and Experimental Therapeutics. Ph.D. only.
Physiology.

School of Dentistry

Established 1968. Annual tuition: resident $7458, nonresident $19,832. No on-campus housing available. Average off-campus housing cost: $11,800. Total average cost for all other expenses: $6500.

Enrollment: first-year class 57, total 226 (men 65%, women 35%). Faculty: full-time 73, part-time 63. Degree conferred: D.D.S.

ADMISSION REQUIREMENTS. Transcripts, DAT, interview, recommendations, at least three years of college required in support of School's application. Preference given to residents of Louisiana and Arkansas. Graduates of unaccredited colleges not considered. Apply to Assistant Dean of Admissions after September 1, before February 28. Application fee $50. Phone: (504)619-8579.

ADMISSION STANDARDS. Selective. Mean DAT: Academic 18.5, PAT 18; mean GPA: 3.41 (A = 4). Gourman rating: 4.21. Accepts about 60% of total annual applicants. Approximately 84% are state residents.

FINANCIAL AID. Limited. Scholarships, loans. Apply to Medical Center's Office of Financial Aid after acceptance. Phone: (504)619-8556. About 80% of students receive aid from School and outside sources.

DEGREE REQUIREMENTS. For D.D.S.: satisfactory completion of four-year program.

School of Medicine (70112-1393)

Established 1931. Annual tuition: resident $8856, nonresident $23,004. Enrollment: first-year class 165 (EDP 10), total 703 (men 60%, women 40%). Faculty: full-time 679, part-time 115. Degrees conferred: M.D., M.D.-Ph.D.

ADMISSION REQUIREMENTS. AMCAS report, transcripts, MCAT required in support of application. Interview by invitation only. Has EDP; apply June 1–August 1. Applicants must have completed at least three years of college study. Accepts state residents only. Accepts transfer applicants. Apply after June 1, before November 15 to Admissions Office. Application fee $50. Phone: (504)568-6262; fax: (504)568-7701.

ADMISSION STANDARDS. Competitive. Mean MCAT: 9.2; mean GPA: 3.6 (A = 4). Gourman rating: 3.68. Accepts 35% of total annual applicants. 100% are state residents.

FINANCIAL AID. Scholarships, merit scholarships, minority scholarships, Grants-in-Aid, State and institutional loans, HEAL, alternative loan programs, NIH stipends, Federal Perkins loans, Stafford Subsidized and Unsubsidized Loans, Service Commitment Scholarship programs are available. Stipends/tuition waivers may be available for Combined Degree candidates. Financial Aid applications and information are given out at the on-campus by-invitation interview. For merit scholarships, the selection criteria places heavy reliance on MCAT and undergraduate GPA. Contact the Student Financial Aid Office for current information. Phone: (504) 568-4820. For most financial assistance and all Federal programs submit FAFSA to a Federal processor (School code: 002014), also submit Financial Aid Transcript, Federal Income Tax forms.

DEGREE REQUIREMENTS. For M.D.: satisfactory completion of four-year program; passing Step 2 of the USMLE prior to graduation.

FIELDS OF GRADUATE STUDY.
Biochemistry and Molecular Biology.
Biostatics.
Cell Biology and Anatomy.
Genetics.
Immunology.
Microbiology, Immunology, and Parasitology.
Neurosciences.
Pathology.
Pharmacology.
Physiology.

School of Medicine in Shreveport
Web site: www.lib-sh.lsumc.edu

Established 1966. Located in Shreveport (71130-3932). Library: 98,000 volumes, 1300 subscriptions.

Annual tuition: resident $8581, nonresident $22,729. Total average cost for all other expenses: $13,940. On-campus housing available.

Enrollment: first-year class 100 (EDP 5); total 387 (men 55%, women 45%). Faculty: full-time 25, part-time 9. Degrees conferred: M.D., M.D.-Ph.D.

ADMISSION REQUIREMENTS. AMCAS reports, transcripts, MCAT, recommendations, interview required in support of application. Has EDP; apply June 1–August 1. Applicants must have completed at least three years of college. Accepts transfer applicants. Graduates of unaccredited colleges are considered. Accepts state residents only. Apply to Admission Committee after June 1, before November 15. Application fee $50. Phone: (318)675-5190; fax: (318)675-5244.

ADMISSION STANDARDS. Selective. Mean GPA: 3.6 (A = 4). Gourman rating: 3.63. Accepts about 20% of total annual applicants. Approximately 100% are state residents.

FINANCIAL AID. Scholarships, long-term loans. Apply to Office of Student Affairs after acceptance, before March 31. About 80% of students received are from school and outside sources.

DEGREE REQUIREMENTS. For M.D.: satisfactory completion of four-year program.

FIELDS OF GRADUATE STUDY.
Anatomy.
Biochemistry.
Cell Biology.

Immunology.
Microbiology.
Pharmacology.
Physiology.

School of Nursing—Graduate Program
Web site: www.lsumc.edu

Graduate study since 1972. Semester system. Annual tuition: resident $2522, nonresident $5022. On-campus housing available. Enrollment: full-time 73, part-time 135. Faculty: full-time 11, part-time 5. Degrees conferred: M.N., D.N.S.

ADMISSION REQUIREMENTS. Transcripts, Louisiana license or current license to practice in any state, GRE/MAT, three letters of recommendation required in support of School's application. TOEFL (minimum score 550) required for foreign applicants. Accepts transfer applicants. Graduates of unaccredited institutions not considered. Apply to Graduate Program by March 15. Application fee $50. Phone: (504)568-4141.

ADMISSION STANDARDS. Selective. Usual minimum average: 3.0 (A = 4); minimum GRE: combined 1500, MAT 50.

FINANCIAL AID. Limited to three graduate assistantships, fifteen grants, Federal W/S, loans. Approved for VA benefits. Apply to the Graduate Program for assistantships, grants; to the Financial Aid Office for all other programs. Phone: (504)568-4820; fax: (504)568-5545. Use FAFSA and institutional FAF.

DEGREE REQUIREMENTS. For M.N.: 38–46 credits minimum, at least three semesters of full-time study; up to 12 credits may be transferred; clinical practice; thesis optional. For D.N.S.: 48 credits minimum, four semesters of full-time study; up to 15 credits may be transferred; candidacy; comprehensive exam; dissertation; oral defense.

FIELDS OF STUDY.
Adult Health and Nursing.
Clinical Nurse Specialist.
Neonatal/Nurse Practitioner.
Nurse Anesthetist.
Nursing Administration.
Parent–Child Health Nursing.
Primary Care/Nurse Practitioner.

LOUISIANA STATE UNIVERSITY IN SHREVEPORT
Shreveport, Louisiana 71115
Web site: www.lsus.edu

Founded 1967. Coed. State control. Semester system. Special facilities: Life Science Museum, Pioneer Heritage Center, Social Science Research and Analysis Unit. Library: 279,821 volumes, 1150 subscriptions. Total University enrollment: 4400.

Tuition/fees: per credit, resident $185, nonresident $410. Limited on-campus housing. Contact Director, University Court Apartments for housing information. Phone: (318)797-8588.

Graduate Studies
Graduate study since 1978. Enrollment: full-time 127, part-time 559. Faculty teaching graduate students: full-time 84, part-time 29. Degrees conferred: M.L.S., M.B.A., M.Ed., M.S.T.

ADMISSION REQUIREMENTS. Transcripts, letters of recomendation, GRE/GMAT required in support of application. TOEFL (minimum score 550) and financial affidavit required of interna-

tional applicants. Interview not required. Accepts transfer applicants. Apply to the Office of Admissions at least 30 days prior to anticipated registration date. Application fee $10, $20 for international applicants. Phone: (318)797-5061; fax: (318)797-5286.

ADMISSION STANDARDS. Selective. Usual minimum average: 3.0 (A = 4).

FINANCIAL AID. Graduate assistantships, Federal W/S, loans. Approved for VA benefits. Apply to appropriate department chair for assistantships; to Office of Financial Aid for all other programs. No specified closing date. Phone: (318)797-5363; fax: (318)797-5180. Use FAFSA and institutional FAF. About 10% of students receive aid other than loans from University and outside sources. Aid sometimes available for part-time students.

DEGREE REQUIREMENTS. For master's: 30–48 semester hours minimum, at least 24–36 in residence; thesis/nonthesis option/final project; final written/oral exam for some programs. For M.B.A.: 54 credit program, at least 30 credits in residence.

FIELDS OF STUDY.
Biochemistry and Molecular Biology. Offered cooperatively with LSU Health Center. M.S.
Business Administration. Includes accounting, finance, health care management, international business, marketing, real estate. M.B.A.
Cellular Biology and Anatomy. Offered cooperatively with LSU Health Center. M.S.
Counseling Psychology. M.S.
Education. Includes elementary, secondary, administration. M.Ed.
English. Offered cooperatively with LSU A&M, Louisiana Tech. M.A.
Environmental Science. Offered cooperatively with LSU A&M. M.S.
History. Offered cooperatively with Louisiana Tech. M.A.
Human Services Administration. M.S.
Liberal Arts. M.L.A.
Microbiology and Immunology. Offered cooperatively with LSU Health Center. M.S.
Pharmacology and Therapeutics. Offered cooperatively with LSU Health Center. M.S.
Physiology and Biophysics. Offered cooperatively with LSU Health Center. M.S.
School Psychology. S.Sp.
System Technology. Interdisciplinary. M.S.S.T.

LOUISIANA TECH UNIVERSITY
Ruston, Louisiana 71272
Web site: www.latech.edu

Founded 1894. Located 72 miles E of Shreveport. Coed. State control. Quarter system. Special facilities: Center for Applied Physics Studies, Center for Biomedical Engineering and Rehabilitation Science, Center for Entrepreneurship and Information Technology, Center for Numerical Simulation and Modeling, Fitness Institute of Technology, Institute for Micromanufacturing, Trenchless Tech Center, Water Resource Center, Center for Robotics and Automated Manufacturing, Rehabilitation Engineering Research and Development Training Center, Small Business Institute. Library: more than 981,000 volumes, 6700 subscriptions.

Annual tuition: resident $2769, nonresident $8769, per credit resident (1–3) $269, nonresident (1–3) $269. On-campus housing for 42 married students, 2052 men, 1860 women. Average academic year housing cost: for 3 quarters $3330–$4060 (including board) for single students. Apply to Director of Housing by July 15. Phone: (318)257-4917.

Graduate School

Authorized 1958. Enrollment: full-time 862, part-time 711. Faculty: full- and part-time 270. Degrees conferred: M.A., M.S., M.B.A., M.P.A., M.F.A., Specialist, D.B.A., Ph.D., D.Engr., Ed.D.

ADMISSION REQUIREMENTS. Transcripts, GRE/GMAT required in support of School's application. Three letters of recommendation, résumé for some programs. TOEFL (minimum score 550), financial affidavit required for foreign applicants. Interview not required. Accepts transfer applicants. Graduates of unaccredited institutions not considered. Apply to Admissions Office at least one month prior to registration. Application fee $20. Phone: (318)257-2924; fax: (318)257-4487.

ADMISSION STANDARDS. Selective. Usual minimum average: 3.0 (A = 4).

FINANCIAL AID. Scholarships, teaching fellowships, research fellowships, Federal W/S, loans. Approved for VA benefits. Apply at least five months prior to registration to department concerned for scholarships, fellowships; to Financial Aid Office for all other programs. Phone: (318)257-2641. Use FAFSA and institutional FAF. About 20% of students receive aid other than loans from University and outside sources. Aid sometimes available for part-time students.

DEGREE REQUIREMENTS. For master's: 30 semester hours minimum without thesis or creative project or including thesis or creative project, at least 24 in residence; final written/oral exam; reading knowledge of one foreign language for some majors. For D.B.A., Ph.D.: 60 credits minimum beyond the bachelor's, at least 24 in residence; qualifying exam; language requirement for some majors; dissertation; final oral exam.

FIELDS OF STUDY.
Accounting. M.P.A.
Applied Computational Analysis and Modeling. M.S.
Art. Includes graphic design, interior design (Architecture), photography, studio. M.F.A.
Biology. M.S.
Biomedical Engineering. M.S., Ph.D.
Business Administration. Includes accounting, economics, finance, general business, management, marketing, quantitative analysis (M.B.A.); accounting, finance, management, marketing, quantitative analysis (D.B.A.).
Chemistry. One foreign language, thesis for M.S.
Computational Analysis and Modeling. Interdisciplinary. Ph.D.
Computer Science. M.S.
Counseling and Guidance. Includes general, school. M.A.
Counseling Psychology. Ph.D.
Curriculum and Instruction. Includes adult, early childhood, instructional technology, educational leadership, middle grades, reading, subject areas (M.S.). M.S., Ed.D.
Education. Includes art, business, elementary, English, foreign language, health and physical, mathematics, music, science, social studies, special, speech, vocational agricultural. M.Ed.
Educational Leadership. Ed.D.
Educational Psychology. Includes educational diagnostician, research, gifted/talented, mild moderate, orientation and mobility. M.A.
English. One foreign language; thesis or six additional credits for M.A.
Engineering. Interdisciplinary. Includes chemical, civil, electrical, industrial, mechanical (M.S.). M.S., Ph.D.
Engineering Management. Interdisciplinary. M.S.
Family and Consumer Sciences. Includes early childhood administration, early childhood education, family and child development, family and consumer science education, human ecology. M.S.

Health and Physical Education. Includes adapted physical education, exercise science, sports science. M.S.
History. M.A.
Industrial/Organizational Psychology. M.A.
Manufacturing System Engineering. Interdisciplinary. M.S.
Mathematics. M.S.
Nutrition and Dietetics. Includes clinical dietetics, community dietetics. M.S.
Physics. M.S.
Reading. M.S.
Special Education. M.S.
Speech. Includes speech communication, theater. M.A.
Speech—Language Pathology and Audiology. M.S.
Statistics. M.S.

UNIVERSITY OF LOUISIANA AT LAFAYETTE

Lafayette, Louisiana 70504
Web site: www.louisiana.edu

Founded 1900. Located 110 miles W of New Orleans. CGS member. Coed. State control. Semester system. Special facilities: Center for Louisiana Studies, Acadiana Research Laboratory, Center for Crustacean Research, New Iberia Research Center, Center for Advanced Computer Studies, Center for Socioeconomic Education. Library: 425,000 volumes, 5000 subscriptions.

Annual tuition: full-time, resident $2275, nonresident $9227; per credit, resident $70, nonresident $368. On-campus housing for 150 married students, 1397 men, 1168 women. Average academic year housing costs: single $2726 (including board); married $3500. Contact Director of Housing for both on- and off-campus housing information. Phone: (337)482-6471.

Graduate School

Graduate study since 1956. Enrollment: full-time 756, part-time 460. Faculty: full- and part-time 329. Degrees conferred: M.A., M.S., M.Ed., M.E., M.M., M.B.A., M.M.Ed., Ph.D.

ADMISSION REQUIREMENTS. Two official transcripts, GRE required in support of School's application. TOEFL required for international applicants. Interview not required. Accepts transfer applicants. Graduates of unaccredited institutions not considered. Apply to Dean (P.O. Box 44610) two months prior to registration. Application fee $20 (American), $30 (international). Phone: (337)482-6965; fax: (337)482-6195.

ADMISSION STANDARDS. Selective. Usual minimum average: 2.75 (A = 4).

FINANCIAL AID. Fellowships, research assistantships, teaching assistantships, internships, tuition waivers, Federal W/S, loans. Approved for VA benefits. Apply to Dean of Graduate School by May 1. Use FAFSA. Aid available for part-time students.

DEGREE REQUIREMENTS. For master's: 30 semester hours minimum, at least 24 in residence; final written/oral exam; reading knowledge of one foreign language in some majors; thesis required for most majors. For M.B.A.: 56 semester hours minimum, at least 30 in residence; computer proficiency. For Ph.D.: 50–60 semester hours beyond the master's, one year in full-time residence; proficiency in one language and research tool; general exam; dissertation; final oral exam.

FIELDS OF STUDY.
Applied Language and Speech Sciences. Ph.D.
Architecture.
Biology. Ph.D.

Business Administration. Includes health care administration.
Cognitive Science. Ph.D.
Communication.
Computer Engineering. Ph.D.
Computer Science. Ph.D.
Education. Includes administration and supervision, curriculum and instruction, education of the gifted, guidance and counseling.
Engineering. Includes chemical, civil, mechanical.
Engineering Management.
English. Includes American literature, British literature, creative writing, folklore studies, linguistics, rhetoric (Ph.D). M.A., Ph.D.
Francophone Studies. Ph.D.
French.
Geology.
History.
Human Resources.
Mathematics. Ph.D.
Music.
Nurse Practitioner.
Nursing.
Physics.
Psychology.
Rehabilitation Counselor Education.
Speech Pathology and Audiology.
Telecommunications.

UNIVERSITY OF LOUISIANA AT MONROE

Monroe, Louisiana 71209-0600
Web site: www.ulm.edu

Founded 1931. Located 100 miles E of Shreveport. Coed. State control. Semester system. Special facilities: Cancer Research Center, Louisiana Drug and Poison Information Center, Small Business Development Center, Center for Educational Research and Services, Herbarium, Human Performance Laboratory, Marriage and Family Counseling Center, Institute of Gerontology, Pharmaceutics Research and Technical Service center, Speech and Hearing center, Institute of Toxicology. Library: 539,000 volumes, 502,000 microforms, 2900 current periodicals.

Annual tuition: full-time, resident $2486, nonresident $8444; per credit, resident and nonresident $128. On-campus housing for single students only. Average academic year housing costs: $3800 (including board) for single students. Contact Director of University Housing for both on- and off-campus housing information. Phone: (318)342-5240. Day-care facilities available.

Graduate Studies and Research

Established 1961. Enrollment: full-time 562, part-time 417. Graduate faculty: full-time 222, part-time 36. Degrees conferred: M.A., M.S., M.B.A., M.M., M.M.Ed., Ed.S., Ed.D., Ph.D.

ADMISSION REQUIREMENTS. Official transcripts, GRE or GMAT required in support of application. TOEFL required for international applicants. Interview not required. Accepts transfer applicants. Graduates of unaccredited institutions not considered. Apply to Registrar at least 60 days prior to date of enrollment. Application fee $15, $25 for non-U.S. citizens. Phone: (318)342-1036; fax: (318)342-1042.

ADMISSION STANDARDS. Selective. Usual minimum average: 2.75 (A = 4).

FINANCIAL AID. Annual awards from institutional funds: teaching assistantships, research assistantships, laboratory, nonteaching, Federal W/S, loans. Approved for VA benefits. Apply to Dean of Graduate Studies for assistantships; to Financial Aid for

all other programs. No specified closing date. Phone: (318)342-3539. Use FAFSA. About 15% of students receive aid other than loans from University. Aid available for part-time students.

DEGREE REQUIREMENTS. For M.A., M.S., M.M.: 30 semester hours minimum, at least 20 in residence; field study/thesis/nonthesis option or final project (Pharmacy only); comprehensive written/oral exam. For M.B.A.: 33 hours minimum, at least 27 in residence. For M.Ed.: same as for M.A., except thesis is optional. For M.M.Ed.: same as for M.A., except recital for three hours or thesis for six may be elected. For Ed.S.: 60 semester hours minimum beyond the bachelor's, at least two semesters in residence; final written/oral exam. For Ph.D. (Pharmacy only): 60 semester hours minimum beyond the bachelor's, at least two semesters in residence; qualifying exam; reading knowledge of at least one foreign language; dissertation; final oral exam.

FIELDS OF STUDY.

COLLEGE OF ALLIED HEALTH AND REHABILITATION PROFESSIONS:
Communicative Disorders.

COLLEGE OF BUSINESS ADMINISTRATION:
Business Administration.

COLLEGE OF EDUCATION AND HUMAN DEVELOPMENT:
Education Leadership. Includes counseling, curriculum and instruction, marriage and family therapy, teacher education.
Exercise Science.
Psychology.

COLLEGE OF LIBERAL ARTS:
Communications.
Criminal Justice.
English.
Gerontology.
History.
Music.

COLLEGE OF PURE AND APPLIED SCIENCES:
Biology.
Chemistry.
Geosciences.

UNIVERSITY OF LOUISVILLE

Louisville, Kentucky 40292-0001
Web site: www.louisville.edu

Founded 1798. Joined state university system in 1970. CGS member. Coed. State control. Semester system. Special facilities: sponsoring university of Oak Ridge Institute of Nuclear Studies in Tennessee, Applied Microcirculation Center, Cancer Center, Center for the Humanities, Institute for the Environment and Sustainable Development, Center for Leadership Studies, Performance Research Laboratory, Water Resources Laboratory, Archaeology Survey, Computer Science Center, Center for Urban and Economic Research, Urban Studies Institute. The University's NIH ranking is 123rd among all U.S. institutions with 106 awards/grants worth $21,574,124. Library: 1,300,000 volumes, 13,000 subscriptions. Total University enrollment: 21,200.

Annual tuition: resident $3767, nonresident $10,704; per credit hour, resident $149.50, nonresident $425. On-campus housing for 110 married students, 46 graduate women, 82 graduate men. Average academic year housing cost: $2100–3150 (room only) for single students; $456–626 per month for married students. Contact Director of Residential Life for both on- and off-campus housing information. Phone: (502)852-6636. Day-care facilities available.

Graduate School

Graduate study since 1907. Enrollment: full-time 1500, part-time 2500. Graduate faculty: full-time 549, part-time 302. Degrees conferred: M.A., M.Ac., M.A.T., M.Ed., M.S., M.Eng., M.M., M.B.A., M.F.A., M.S.N., M.P.A., Ed.S., Ed.D., Ph.D.

ADMISSION REQUIREMENTS. Official transcripts, two letters of recommendation, GRE/MAT required in support of application. GRE Subject required for some departments. GMAT for business. TOEFL required of international applicants. Accepts transfer applicants. Graduates of unaccredited institutions not considered. Apply to Office of Research and Graduate Programs at least three months prior to date of entrance. Application fee: none. Phone: (502)588-6525; e-mail: graduate@louisville.edu.

ADMISSION STANDARDS. Relatively open for most departments. Usual minimum average: 2.75 (A = 4).

FINANCIAL AID. Annual awards from institutional funds: scholarships, assistantships, research assistantships, fellowships in doctoral programs, tuition remission, Federal W/S, loans. Approved for VA benefits. Apply to appropriate department for assistantships, fellowships; to Office of Financial Aid for all other programs. No specified closing date. Phone: (502)588-5511. Use FAFSA. About 50% of students receive aid other than loans from School and outside sources.

DEGREE REQUIREMENTS. For most master's: 30 semester hours minimum, at least 24 in residence; qualifying exam; thesis for 6 hours required in most departments; final written/oral exam. For M.M.: same as above, except final recital for applied music majors, composition for composition majors in lieu of thesis. For M.F.A. (Theater): 72 hours minimum. For M.S.S.W. (one year advanced-standing program): 42 semesters hours minimum in full-time residence; supervised fieldwork experience. For M.S.S.W. (two-year regular program): 60 semester hours minimum, at least 45 in residence; supervised fieldwork experience. For Ed.S.: 30 hours minimum beyond the master's. For Ph.D., Ed.D.: three years minimum beyond the bachelor's, at least two years in residence and one year in full-time attendance; reading knowledge of two foreign languages or one language and computer science required by some departments; preliminary exam; dissertation; final oral exam.

FIELDS OF STUDY.
Accounting. M.Ac.
Anatomical Sciences and Neurobiology. M.S., Ph.D.
Art Education. M.A.T.
Art History. Ph.D.
Art Therapy. M.A.
Audiology. Ph.D.
Biochemistry and Molecular Biology. M.S., Ph.D.
Biology. M.S.
Biostatistics—Decision Science. Ph.D.
Business and Economics. Includes communications, electronic commerce, entrepreneurship, health care administration, international business. M.B.A.
Chemical Engineering. M.Eng., M.S., Ph.D.
Chemistry. M.S., Ph.D.
Civil Engineering. M.Eng., M.S.
Clinical Psychology. Ph.D.
Communicative Disorders. M.S.
Computer Engineering and Computer Science. M.Eng.
Computer Science. M.S.
Computer Science and Engineering. Ph.D.
Counseling and Personnel Services. Includes community counseling, counseling psychology, elementary school, secondary school, college student personnel services. M.Ed.
Early Childhood Education. M.Ed.
Early Elementary Education. M.A.T., M.Ed.
Education. M. Ed., M.A., Ed.S., Ed.D.

Educational Administration. Includes principalship, superintendent, supervision (Ed.S.). M.Ed., Ed.S.
Electrical Engineering. M.Eng., M.S.
Engineering. Includes chemical, civil, electrical, mechanical, computer science, M.S. only; chemical engineering, industrial engineering, computer science and engineering, Ph.D. only.
English. Includes M.A. in creative writing; Ph.D. in Rhetoric and Composition.
Environmental Biology. Ph.D.
Epidemiology. M.S.
Exercise Physiology. M.S.
Experimental Psychology. Ph.D.
Expressive Therapies. M.A.
Fine Arts. Includes art history, critical and curatorial studies, studio. For creative, art history; one foreign language for M.A. in art history; studio project and paper instead of thesis for M.A. in creative art. M.A., M.A.T.
French. M.A.
Health Promotion. M.S.
Higher Education. Includes sports administration. M.A.
History. M.A., M.A.T. only.
Humanities. Includes civic leadership, linguistics. M.A.
Human Resource Education. M.Ed.
Industrial Engineering. M.Eng., M.S.
Instructional Technology. M.Ed.
Justice Administration.
Mathematics. M.A.
Mechanical Engineering. M.S.
Microbiology and Immunology. M.S., Ph.D.
Middle School Education. M.A.T., M.Ed.
Modern Languages. M.A.T. in French, German, Spanish; M.A. in French, German. M.A., M.A.T.
Music (Performance). Includes instrumental conducting, choral conducting, jazz, piano pedagogy. M.M.
Music Education. M.A.T., M.M.E.
Music History and Literature. M.M.
Music Theory and Composition. M.M.
Nursing. M.S.N.
Oral Biology. D.D.S. or equivalent for admission. M.S.
Pharmacology and Toxicology. M.S., Ph.D.
Physical Education. M.A.T., M.Ed.
Physics. M.S.
Physiology and Biophysics. M.S., Ph.D.
Political Science. M.A.
Psychology. M.A., Ph.D.
Public Administration. Includes labor–public management relations, public policy and administration, urban development and environment. M.P.A.
Public Health. M.S.
Reading Education. M.Ed.
Secondary Education. M.A.T., M.Ed.
Social Work. M.S.S.W.
Sociology. Includes pan-African studies, communication, urban geography. M.A., M.A.T.
Spanish. M.A.
Special Education. Includes learning and behavior disorders, learning disabilities, mental retardation, moderate and severe disabilities, severe behavior disorders, visual impairment. M.Ed.
Sport Administration. M.S.
Theatre Arts. Includes African American theatre. M.A., M.F.A.
Urban and Public Affairs. Ph.D. only.
Urban Education. Ed.D.
Urban Planning. Includes land use and environmental planning, administration of planning organizations, spatial analysis for planning. M.U.P.
Visual Sciences. Ph.D.

School of Dentistry (49292-0001)

Organized 1886. State supported. Semester system. Annual tuition: resident $9458, nonresident $23,437. Medical-dental housing for married and single students. Average academic year housing cost: $9000. Total average cost for all other first-year expenses: $2150.

Enrollment: first-year class 80, total 200 (men 65%, women 35%). School faculty: full-time 71, part-time 65. Degree conferred: D.M.D. The M.S. (Oral Biology) is offered through the Graduate School.

ADMISSION REQUIREMENTS. AADSAS report, official transcripts, recommendations, DAT (October date preferred) required in support of School's application. Interview often required. Applicants must have completed at least three, preferably four, years of college study. Ninety percent of class must be residents. Accepts transfer applicants. Apply to Committee on Admissions between June 1 and February 1. Application fee, none for residents, nonresident $25. Phone: (502)852-5081, (800)334-8635, ext. 5081.

ADMISSION STANDARDS. Competitive. Mean DAT: Academic 17.3, PAT 17.1; mean GPA: 3.32 (A = 4). Gourman rating: 4.32. Usual minimum average: 2.75 (A = 4). Accepts about 20% of total annual applicants. Approximately 90% are state residents.

FINANCIAL AID. Scholarships, tuition waivers, loans. Apply to Student Affairs Office after acceptance. Phone: (502)852-5075. About 91% of students receive some aid from School.

DEGREE REQUIREMENTS. For D.M.D.: satisfactory completion of forty-five-month program. For M.S., see Graduate School listing above.

FIELDS OF POSTDOCTORAL STUDY,
Advanced Education in General Dentistry.
Advanced Education Program in Orthodontics.
Graduate Endodontics.
Graduate Periodontics.
Graduate Prosthodontics.
Oral Biology. M.S.
Oral and Maxillofacial Surgery Residency.

Louis D. Brandeis School of Law (40292)

Established 1846. ABA approved since 1931. AALS member. Semester system. Special facilities: Center for Environmental Policy, Center for Women and Families. Special program: Samuel L Greenbaum Public Service Program. Law Library: 358,620 volumes, 5300 subscriptions; has LEXIS, WESTLAW, OCLC.

Annual tuition: full-time resident $6275, nonresident $16,348; part-time resident $5281, nonresident $13,681. Total average annual additional expense: $10,210. Limited on-campus housing available; moderate cost housing available near campus.

Enrollment: first-year class 81 (day), 40 (evening); total approximately 370 (men 50%, women 50%). Faculty: full-time 22, part-time 9. Student to faculty ratio 12.8 to 1. Degrees conferred: J.D., J.D.-M.B.A., J.D.-M.Div. (with Louisville Presbyterian Theological Seminary), J.D.-M.S.S.W.

ADMISSION REQUIREMENTS. LSDAS Law School report, bachelor's degree, transcripts, LSAT (not later than December) required in support of application. Interview not required. Accepts transfer applicants. Graduates of unaccredited colleges not considered. Preference given to state residents. Apply to Law School Admissions Office after October 1, before March 1. Fall admission only. Application fee $40. Phone: (502)852-6364.

ADMISSION STANDARDS. Selective. Mean LSAT: full-time 157, part-time 153; mean GPA: full-time 3.31, part-time 3.42 (A = 4). Gourman rating: 3.29. *U.S. News & World Report* ranking is in the second tier of all U.S. law schools. Accepts 30–35% of total annual applicants.

FINANCIAL AID. Scholarships, assistantships, loans. For scholarships, apply to Associate Dean by April 15. Use FAFSA. Students

seeking financial aid should contact University's Student Financial Aid Office. Approximately 50% of all students receive financial assistance from the School.

DEGREE REQUIREMENTS. For J.D.: 90 semester hours minimum, at least the last 28 in residence.
Note: School has an exchange program with law schools in England, Finland, France, Germany, Japan, Australia, People's Republic of China, South Africa.

School of Medicine (40292-3866)

Founded 1833 as Louisville Medical Institute; affiliated with University in 1984.

Annual tuition: resident $12,424, nonresident $31,046. Medical-dental housing for married and single students. Total average figure for all other expenses: $10,500.

Enrollment: first-year class 141 (EDP 13); total 500 (men 53%, women 47%). Faculty: full-time 458; part-time 55. Degrees conferred: M.D., M.D.-M.B.A., M.D.-M.S., M.D.-Ph.D. The M.B.A., M.S. and Ph.D. are offered through the Graduate School.

ADMISSION REQUIREMENTS. AMCAS report, transcripts, recommendations, MCAT required in support of application. Interview by invitation only. Applicants must have completed at least three years of college study. Preference given to four-year college graduates and state residents. Accepts transfer applicants. Has EDP; apply between June 1 and August 1. Apply to Director of Admissions after June 1, before November 1. Application fee $15. Phone: (502)582-5193.

ADMISSION STANDARDS. Competitive. Mean MCAT: 9.1; mean GPA: 3.6 (A = 4). Gourman rating: 4.26. Accepts about 15% of total annual applicants. Approximately 90% are state residents.

FINANCIAL AID. Scholarships, summer research scholarships, HEAL, loans. 85% of students receive some financial aid. Apply to Office of Student Affairs by June 1. Phone: (502)852-5187. Use FAFSA (School code: 001999).

DEGREE REQUIREMENTS. For M.D.: satisfactory completion of four-year program; all students must take Step 2 of USMLE prior to graduation. For M.S., Ph.D.: see Graduate School listing above.

FIELDS OF GRADUATE STUDY.
Anatomical Sciences and Neurobiology.
Biochemistry and Molecular Biology.
Clinical Research, Epidemiology, and Statistical Training. Multidisciplinary.
Microbiology and Immunology.
Pharmacology and Toxicology.
Physiology and Biophysics.
Structural Biology. Multidisciplinary.

LOYOLA COLLEGE IN MARYLAND
Baltimore, Maryland 21210-2699
Web site: www.loyola.edu

Founded 1852. Coed. Private control. Roman Catholic. Semester system. Library: 380,000 volumes, 2100 subscriptions.

Tuition: per credit $244. No on-campus housing for graduate students. Contact Dean of Students for off-campus housing information.

Graduate Division

Graduate study since 1949. Enrollment: full-time 625, part-time 1972. Graduate faculty: full-time 65, part-time 97. Degrees conferred: M.A., M.Ed., M.S., M.M.S., M.B.A., M.I.B., M.S.F., M.M.S., M.E.S., Psy.D.

ADMISSION REQUIREMENTS. Official transcripts in support of application. GMAT required for M.B.A., M.S.E, and M.P.A. Two letters of recommendation required for M.E.S., three letters for M.A. or M.S. in psychology. Accepts transfer applicants. Graduates of unaccredited institutions not considered. Apply to Graduate Admissions Office by May 15 (Summer), August 15 (Fall), December 15 (Spring). Application fee $50. Phone: (410)617-5020, ext. 2407; fax: (410)617-2002.

ADMISSION STANDARDS. Selective. Usual minimum average: 3.0 (A = 4).

FINANCIAL AID. Internships, graduate assistantships, Federal W/S, loans. Approved for VA benefits. Apply to appropriate department for assistantships; to Financial Aid Office for all other programs. Use FAFSA. Less than 1% of students receive aid other than loans from College and outside sources.

DEGREE REQUIREMENTS. For master's: 30–36 semester hours minimum, at least 24 in residence; thesis for M.A., no language requirement.

FIELDS OF STUDY.
Administration and Supervision. M.A.
Business Administration. Includes accounting, business economics, e-business, finance, general business, health care management, international business, management, management information systems, marketing. M.B.A.
Computer and Engineering Science. M.S.
Curriculum and Instruction. M.A.
Educational Technology. M.A.
Modern Studies. M.A.
Montessori Education. M.A.
Pastoral Counseling. M.A.
Psychology. Includes clinical, counseling. M.A., M.S., Psy.D.
Reading. M.A.
School Counseling. M.A.
Special Education. M.A.
Speech-Language Pathology. M.A.

LOYOLA MARYMOUNT UNIVERSITY
Los Angeles, California 90045-8350
Web site: www.lmu.edu

Founded 1911. CGS member. Coed. Private control. Roman Catholic. Library: 487,232 volumes, 2900 subscriptions.

Tuition: per unit $575; for Communication Arts and Marriage and Family Therapy per credit $600, for MBA per credit $710. No on-campus housing available for graduate students. Average academic year off-campus housing cost: $450–$900 per month. Contact Student Housing Office for housing information. Phone: (213)338-2963.

Graduate Division

Graduate Study since 1948. Enrollment: full-time 770, part-time 334. Graduate faculty: full-time 154, part-time 243. Degrees conferred: M.A., M.A.T., M.B.A., M.F.A., M.Ed., M.S., M.S.E.

ADMISSION REQUIREMENTS. Two official transcripts, letters of recommendation, GRE, GMAT (for M.B.A. applicants) required in support of applications. On-line application available. Two letters of recommendation required for Counseling Psychology. TOEFL (minimum score 550 for Engineering and Education, 600 for all others) and translation of all foreign credentials required for international applicants. Accepts transfer applicants. Graduates of unaccredited institutions not considered. Apply to Graduate Admissions Office. Application fee $35. Phone: (310)338-2721; fax: (310)338-6086.

ADMISSION STANDARDS. Competitive. Usual minimum average: 3.0 (A = 4).

FINANCIAL AID. Scholarships, grants, internships, assistantships, Federal W/S, loans. Apply by July 1 (Fall), December 1 (Spring) to appropriate department chair for assistantships; to Office of Financial Aid for all other programs. Use FAFSA. Phone: (310)338-2753. About 10% of students receive some aid other than loans from University and outside sources. Aid available for part-time students.

DEGREE REQUIREMENTS. For most master's: 10 courses minimum, at least 8 in residence; thesis/nonthesis option or final written/oral exam. For M.B.A.: 10–18 courses depending on previous degree; project. For M.F.A.: 18 courses, at least 15 in residence; final project.

FIELDS OF STUDY.

COLLEGE OF LIBERAL ARTS:
English. Includes creative writing, literature.
Pastoral Studies.
Philosophy.
Theology.

COLLEGE OF BUSINESS ADMINISTRATION:
Business Administration. Includes entrepreneurial organization, financial decision systems, human resource management, international business systems, management and organizational behavior, marketing management. M.B.A.

COLLEGE OF SCIENCE AND ENGINEERING:
Civil Engineering.
Computer Science.
Electrical Engineering.
Engineering and Production Management.
Environmental Science.
Mechanical Engineering.

COLLEGE OF COMMUNICATION AND FINE ARTS:
Film Production.
Screenwriting.
Television Production.

SCHOOL OF EDUCATION:
Administration.
Bilingual/Bicultural Education.
Catholic School Administration.
Child and Adolescent Literacy.
Counseling.
Educational Psychology.
Elementary Education.
General Education.
Literacy and Language Arts.
School Counseling.
School Psychology.
Secondary Education.
Special Education.
Teaching. Includes biology, English, history, mathematics, social studies.
TESL. Includes multicultural education.

DEPARTMENT OF MARITAL AND FAMILY THERAPY:
Marital and Family Therapy.

Loyola Law School (90015-3980)
Web site: www.lls.edu

Established 1920. ABA approved since 1935. AALS member. Semester system. Special facilities: Center for Conflict Resolution, Western Law Center for Disability Rights, Center for Ethical Lawyering. Law library: 493,238 volumes, 7116 subscriptions. Library has LEXIS, NEXIS, WESTLAW, DIALOG, CALI.

Annual tuition: $23,884 (day), $16,036 (evening). No on-campus housing available. Estimated housing cost: $15,579.

Enrollment: first-year class 345 (day), 96 (evening); total full-time 1364 (men 50%, women 50%). Faculty: full-time 57, part-time 33. Student to faculty ratio 18.9 to 1. Degrees conferred: J.D., J.D.-M.B.A., LL.M. (Tax).

ADMISSION REQUIREMENTS. LSDAS Law School report, bachelor's degree, transcripts, LSAT (no later than December), letters of recommendation required in support of application. Interview not required. Accepts transfer applicants. Graduates of unaccredited colleges not considered. Apply to Office of Admissions by February 1 (Fall, day), April 17 (Fall, evening). Evaluation fee $50. Phone: (213)736-1180; fax: (213)736-6523; e-mail: admissions@lls.edu.

ADMISSION STANDARDS. Selective. Mean LSAT: full-time 158, part-time 155; mean GPA: full-time 3.30, part-time 3.23 (A = 4). Gourman rating: 4.34. *U.S. News & World Report* ranking is in the second tier of all U.S. law schools. Accepts about 30–35% of total annual applicants.

FINANCIAL AID. Scholarships, full and partial tuition waivers, assistantships, Federal W/S, loans. Apply to Financial Aid Office after acceptance. Preference given to applications received by March 2. Phone: (213)736-1140. Use FAFSA (School code: 001234). Fellowships available only to advanced students. About 30% of full-time students receive some aid from School. Aid sometimes available for part-time students.

DEGREE REQUIREMENTS. For J.D.: 87 semester units minimum; completion of three-year program (day), four-year program (evening). For LL.M.: 24 credit program.
Note: Summer programs in Central America, People's Republic of China, Italy.

LOYOLA UNIVERSITY NEW ORLEANS
New Orleans, Louisiana 70118-6195
Web site: www.loyno.edu

Established 1912. Coed. Private control. Roman Catholic. Semester system. Special facilities: Center for Environmental Communications, Center for the Study of Catholics in the South, Economics Institute, Gillis Long Poverty Law Center, Institute for Politics, Institute for the Study of Catholic Culture and Tradition, International Business Center, Shawn M. Donnelley Center for Nonprofit Communications, Twomey Center for Peace Through Justice, Women's Resource Center. Library: 437,000 volumes, 5111 subscriptions.

Tuition: per credit $275 (Math Teaching, Religious Studies, Loyola Institute for Ministry, Education); $429 (Communication, Education Counseling, Music, Nursing). On-campus housing for 24 graduate men, 24 graduate women; none for married students. Average academic year housing costs: $6366 (including board). Apply to Director of Residential Life. Phone: (504)865-3736. Day-care facilities available.

Graduate School
Graduate study since 1912. Enrollment: full-time 658, part-time 946. Faculty: full-time 164, part-time 70. Degrees conferred: M.A., M.B.A., M.M., M.M.E., M.M.T., M.S., M.S.N., M.C.J., M.S.T., M.R.E., M.P.S., J.D.-M.A., J.D.-M.B.A., J.D.-M.C.M.

ADMISSION REQUIREMENTS. Application, transcripts, statement of intent, résumé, letters of recommendation, GMAT (Business), GRE (Criminal Justice, Mass Communications, Nursing), MAT (Education) required in support of School's application. TOEFL required for international applicants. An interview is required for education programs, recommended for other programs. Accepts transfer applicants. Application deadlines: Nursing, April 15 (Fall); Mass Communications, July 1 (Fall), November 1 (Spring); Education, August 1 (Fall), December 1 (Spring), May 1 (Summer); other programs August 1 (Fall), December 1 (Spring), and May 1 (Summer). Application fee $20. Phone: (504)865-3240 or (800)4-LOYOLA; fax: (504)865-3383; e-mail: admit@loyno.edu.

ADMISSION STANDARDS. Selective for most departments. Usual minimum average: 3.0 (A = 4).

FINANCIAL AID. Scholarships, assistantships, tuition waivers, Federal W/S, loans. Apply by May 1 to Financial Aid Office. Phone: (504)865-3231. Use FAFSA. Aid available for part-time students.

DEGREE REQUIREMENTS. For master's: 30–36 semester hours minimum, at least 24 in residence; candidacy; comprehensive exam; thesis/capstone/practicum; final written/oral exam for some departments. For M.S.N.: 45 credit program; comprehensive exam; research project; practicum.

FIELDS OF STUDY.
Counseling.
Criminal Justice.
Elementary Education.
Mass Communications.
Mathematics and Computer Science. M.S.T.
Music (Performance).
Music Education.
Music Therapy.
Nursing. Includes family nurse practitioner. M.S.N.
Pastoral Studies. M.P.S.
Reading.
Religious Education. M.R.E.
Religious Studies. M.A.
Secondary Education.

Joseph A. Butts, S.J. College of Business Administration
Web site: www.cba.loyno.edu

College founded in 1947, Graduate School established 1961. Private control. Accredited programs: M.B.A. Semester system. Special programs: foreign exchange programs in Belgium, France, and Spain.

Tuition: per credit M.B.A. $501, M.Q.M. $584.

Enrollment: total full-time 27, part-time 97 (men 70%, women 30%). Faculty: full-time 34, part-time 10; all have Ph.D./D.B.A. Degrees conferred: M.B.A. (full-time, part-time, evenings and weekends), M.Q.M. (Quality Management), M.B.A.-J.D.

ADMISSION REQUIREMENTS. All applicants should have a bachelor's degree from a recognized institution of higher education; a strong mathematics background and a 3.0 (A = 4) GPA. Admission is based on a formula, which is 200 × UGPA plus GMAT. Submit application, GMAT (will accept GMAT test results from the last five years, latest acceptable date is March), official transcripts from each undergraduate/graduate school attended, two letters of recommendation, MBA statement, résumé (prefers at least four years of work experience), and an application fee of $20 to the Office of Graduate Business Programs. On-line application available. In addition, international students (whose native language is other than English) should submit a TOEFL (minimum score 580, 600 for M.Q.M.) report, certified translations and evaluations of all official transcripts, recommendation should be in English or with certified translations, proof of health/ immunization certificate, and proof of sufficient financial resources for two years of academic study. U.S. citizens apply by June 15 (Fall), November 25 (Spring), March 15 (Summer), international students apply by June (Fall). Rolling admissions process. On-campus visits are encouraged. Admissions Committee will consider applicants with some academic course work deficiencies, Joint degree applicants must apply to and be accepted to both schools, contact the admissions office for current information and specific admissions requirements. Notification is made within two weeks of receipt of completed application and supporting documents.

ADMISSION STANDARDS. Selective. Median GMAT: 489; median GPA: 3.0 (A = 4).

FINANCIAL AID. Research assistantships, internships, Federal W/S, loans. Financial aid available for part-time students. Assistantships may be available for joint degree candidates. Apply by May 1. Request assistantship information from the Coordinator, Graduate Business Programs. Contact the University's Financial Aid Office for current need-based financial aid information. Phone: (504)865-3231. Use FAFSA (School code: 002016), also submit Financial Aid Transcript, Federal Income Tax forms. Approximately 24% of students receive some form of financial assistance.

DEGREE REQUIREMENTS. For M.B.A.: 33–56 credit program including 18 elective credits, one- to two-year program; capstone course; degree program must be completed in seven years. For M.Q.M.: 36 credit program. For M.B.A.-J.D.: 105 credit program; four- to five-year program.

FIELDS OF STUDY.
Accounting.
Finance.
International Business.
Management.
Quality Management.

School of Law

Established 1914. ABA approved since 1931. AALS member since 1934. Semester system. Special facility: Public Law Center. Law library: 235,000 volumes, 3375 subscriptions; has LEXIS, NEXIS, WESTLAW, DIALOG.

Annual tuition: full-time $20,712 (day), $13,922 (evening). Limited on-campus housing. Total average annual additional expense: $9675.

Enrollment: first-year class, full-time 220, evening 72; total full- and part-time 702 (men 47%, women 53%). Faculty: full-time 28, part-time 22. Student to faculty ratio 19.1 to 1. Degrees conferred: J.D., J.D.-M.A. (Communications, Religious Studies). J.D.-M.B.A.

ADMISSION REQUIREMENTS. LSDAS Law School report, bachelor's degree, transcripts, LSAT required in support of application. Interview not required. Graduates of unaccredited colleges not considered. Accepts transfer applicants. Apply to Director of Admissions after September 1, before April 1 for priority consideration. Rolling admissions process. For part-time study, apply by June 1. Admits beginning students Fall only. Application fee $40. Phone: (504)861-5575; fax: (504)801-5772; e-mail: ladmit@loyno.edu.

ADMISSION STANDARDS. Competitive. Mean LSAT: full-time 150, part-time: 151; mean GPA: full-time 3.15, part-time 2.94 (A = 4). Gourman rating: 2.50. *U.S. News & World Report* ranking is in the third tier of all U.S. law schools. Accepts about 45–50% of total annual applicants.

FINANCIAL AID. Scholarships, assistantships, full and partial tuition waivers, Federal W/S, loans. Apply to Office of Financial Aid by May 1. Use FAFSA (School code: 002016). About 38% of full-time students receive financial assistance from School. Aid available for part-time study.

DEGREE REQUIREMENTS. For J.D.: 90 credit hours minimum, at least one year in residence. For M.B.A. and M.A.: see Graduate School listing above.
Note: Summer study programs in Mexico, Japan, and Eastern Europe available.

LOYOLA UNIVERSITY CHICAGO
Chicago, Illinois 60626
Web site: www.luc.edu

Established 1870. CGS member. Coed. Private control. Roman Catholic—Jesuit. Semester system. Special facilities: Martin D'Arcy Museum of Art, Ann Ida Gannon, R.V.M., Center for Women, Rome Center for Liberal Arts. The University's NIH ranking is 125th among all U.S. institutions with 112 awards/grants worth $27,245,407. Library: 1,700,000 volumes, 7800 subscriptions. Total University enrollment: 14,000.

Limited on-campus housing available. Contact Dean, Residence Life for off-campus information. Phone: (773)508-3300. Day-care facilities available.

Graduate School

Graduate study since 1918. Tuition: per credit $578. Enrollment: full-time 1091, part-time 675. Faculty teaching graduate students: full-time 543. Degrees conferred: M.A., M.S., M.B.A., M.Div., M.Ed., M.J., M.P.S., M.R.E., M.S.I.R., M.S.O.D., M.S.N., Ed.D., Ph.D., M.D.-Ph.D., M.D.-M.S., J.D.-M.A.

ADMISSION REQUIREMENTS. Transcripts required in support of School's application. On-line application available. GRE/Subject tests for some departments. Interview required in some departments. TOEFL required for international applicants. Accepts transfer applicants. Graduates of unaccredited institutions not considered. Apply to Dean of Graduate School at least eight weeks prior to registration. Application fee $35. Phone: (773) 508-3396; fax: (773)508-2460.

ADMISSION STANDARDS. Competitive. Usual minimum average: 3.0 (A = 4).

FINANCIAL AID. Annual awards from institutional funds: fellowships, assistantships, internships, Federal W/S, loans. Approved for VA benefits. Apply by March 1 to Dean of School for assistantships, fellowships; to Graduate Financial Assistance for all other programs. Phone: (773)508-3155. Use FAFSA (School code: 001710) and institutional FAF. About 35% of students receive aid other than loans from School and outside sources. Aid available for part-time students.

DEGREE REQUIREMENTS. For master's: generally 30 semester hours minimum; research tool requirement for some departments; final oral/written exam. For Ed.D., Ph.D.: 60 semester hours minimum beyond the bachelor's, at least two semesters in residence; research tool requirement in most departments; preliminary exam; dissertation; final oral exam.

FIELDS OF STUDY.
Administration and Supervision.
Biochemistry.
Chemistry.
Chicago Studies.
Child Development.
Clinical Psychology.
Community Counseling.
Computer Science.
Criminal Justice.
Curriculum and Instruction.
Developmental Psychology.
Educational and School Psychology.
Educational Leadership and Policy Studies.
Greek.
Higher Education.
History.
Human Resources.
Industrial Relations.
Latin.
Mathematical Sciences.
Microbiology.
Molecular Biology.
Neuroscience.
Nursing.
Organizational Development.
Pastoral Counseling.
Pastoral Studies.
Pharmacology.
Philosophy.
Physiology.
Political Science.
Religious Education.
Research Methodology and Human Development.
Social Psychology.
Social Work.
Sociology.
Spanish.
Theology.
Women's Studies.

Graduate School of Business
Web site: www.gsb.luc.edu

Graduate School established 1966. Private control. Accredited program: M.B.A. (offered at downtown campus, in Wilmette and Rome, Italy. Quarter, integrated system). Special programs: foreign study programs in Greece, Italy, Republic of Korea, Thailand. Special facilities: Center for Family Business, Center for Financial and Policy Studies, Center for Futures, Center for Values in Business.

Tuition: $2331 per course. Enrollment: total full-time 192, part-time 550 (men 58%, women 42%). Faculty: full-time 69, part-time 38; 97% with Ph.D./D.B.A. Degrees conferred: M.B.A. (full-time, part-time, evenings and weekends), M.S.A. (Accounting), M.S.I.S.M. (Information Systems Management), M.S.I.M.C. (Integrated Marketing Communication), M.B.A.-J.D., M.B.A.-M.S.N.

ADMISSION REQUIREMENTS. All applicants should have a bachelor's degree from a recognized institution of higher education, a strong mathematics background, a 2.5 (A = 4) GPA, and a GMAT score of 450. Admission is based on a formula, which is $200 \times$ UGPA plus GMAT. Submit application, GMAT results (will accept GMAT test results from the last five years, latest acceptable date is July), official transcripts from each undergraduate/graduate school attended, three letters of recommendation, résumé (prefers at least four years of work experience), and an application fee of $50 to the Committee on Admission, Graduate School of Business. In addition, international students (whose native language is other than English) should submit a TOEFL report (minimum score 550), certified translations and evalua-

tions of all official transcripts, recommendation should be in English or with certified translations, proof of health/immunization certificate, and proof of sufficient financial resources for two years of academic study. U.S. citizens apply by July 31 (Fall), October 1 (Winter), December 31 (Spring), April 1 (Summer), international students apply by June 1 (Fall), August 1 (Winter), November 1 (Spring), February 1 (Summer). On-campus visits are encouraged. Joint degree applicants must apply to and be accepted to both schools; contact the Admissions Office for current information and specific admissions requirements. Rolling admissions process, notification is made within two weeks of receipt of completed application and supporting documents.

ADMISSION STANDARDS. Selective. Usual minimum GPA: 2.5 (A = 4). Median GMAT: 530; median GPA: 3.05 (A = 4).

FINANCIAL AID. Graduate Business Scholars Program (partial tuition reduction), grants, graduate assistantships, internships, Federal W/S, loans. Financial aid is available for part-time study. Assistantships may be available for joint degree candidates. Request scholarship and assistantship information from the Graduate School of Business. Contact the University's Office of Student Financial Assistance for current need-based financial aid information. Phone: (312)915-6636. Apply by April 1 (Fall). Use FAFSA (School code: 001710), also submit Financial Aid Transcript, Federal Income Tax forms. Approximately 30% of students receive some form of financial assistance.

DEGREE REQUIREMENTS. For M.B.A.: 18 course program including 8 elective courses, two-year program; degree program must be completed in five years. For M.S.A., M.S.I.S.M., M.S.I.M.C.: 45 quarter hour programs. For M.B.A.-M.S.N.: 69–81 quarter hour programs. For M.B.A.-J.D.: 128–140 quarter hours, four- to five-year program.

FIELDS OF STUDY.
Accounting.
Economics.
Finance.
Health Care Administration.
Information Systems Management.
Integrated Marketing Communication.
Management.
Marketing.
Production Management.
Science and Information Systems.

School of Education

Semester system. Tuition: per credit $540. Enrollment: full-time 441, part-time 647. Faculty teaching graduate students: full-time 37, part-time 32. Degrees conferred: M.A., M.Ed., Ed.S., Ed.D., Ph.D.

ADMISSION REQUIREMENTS. Transcripts, GRE or MAT, personal statement, three letters of reference required in support of application. Résumé and writing sample required for some programs. Passing scores on State of Illinois Basic Skills and Subject Matter test required for Elementary and Secondary Education programs. On-line application available. TOEFL (minimum score 550) required for international applicants. Transfer applicants considered. Apply to the Admission Coordinator by July 1 (Fall), November 1 (Spring), April 1 (Summer); some programs have earlier deadlines, "Self-Managed" application process in effect. Application fee $35. Phone: (847)853-3323; fax: (847)853-3375; e-mail: schleduc@luc.edu.

FINANCIAL AID. Annual awards from institutional funds: fellowships, research assistantships, teaching assistantships, internships, Federal W/S, loans. Apply by April 1 to program directors for fellowships, assistantships; to University's Financial Aid Office for all other programs. Phone: (773)508-3155. About 25% of students receive aid other than loans from School and outside sources. Aid available for part-time students.

DEGREE REQUIREMENTS. For M.Ed.: 10 course, 30 credit program, all in residence; comprehensive exam. For Ed.S.: 22 courses or 66 credits beyond bachelor's (transfer credit accepted); comprehensive exam or culminating portfolio project; internships. For Ed.D.: 60 semester credits beyond bachelor's minimum; comprehensive exams in depth area and two collateral areas; doctoral candidacy; dissertation; oral defense. M.A., Ph.D. are offered through the Graduate School. Consult the Graduate School listing above.

FIELDS OF STUDY.
Administration and Supervision. M.A., M.Ed., Ed.D.
Community Counseling. Ph.D.
Cultural and Educational Policy Studies. Includes comparative international education, history of education, philosophy of education, sociology education. M.A., M.Ed., Ph.D.
Curriculum and Instruction. Includes classroom assessment, elementary, school improvement, secondary, technology. M.A., M.Ed., Ed.D.
Educational Policy. Ed.D.
Education Psychology. M.A., M.Ed., Ph.D.
Higher Education. M.Ed., Ed.D., Ph.D.
Instructional Leadership. M.Ed.
Research Methodology. M.A., M.Ed. Ph.D.
School Counseling. M.A., M.Ed.
School Psychology. Ed.S., Ph.D.
Special Education. M.A., M.Ed.

School of Law
Web site: www.luc.edu/law

Established 1908. Located on the Water Tower Campus about 1 mile N of downtown. ABA approved since 1925. AALS member since 1924. Semester system. Full-time, part-time study. Special facilities: Institute for Consumer Antitrust Studies, Civitas Childlaw Center, Institute for Health Law, Corporate Law Center, Center for Public Service, National Institute for Trial Advocacy. Special program: summer study abroad in Rome at University's campus, Nottingham-Trent University, England, McGill University Center for Medicine, Ethics, and Law, Montreal, Canada. Law library: 345,035 volumes, 3688 subscriptions; has LEXIS, NEXIS, WESTLAW.

Annual tuition: full-time $23,920, part-time $18,006; M.J. (evening) per credit $670, LL.M. (evening) per credit $807. Law students tend to live off-campus. Off-campus housing and personal expenses: approximately $12,500.

Enrollment: first-year class full-time 178, part-time 53; total full-time 553, part-time 179 (men 40%, women 60%). Faculty: full-time 28, part-time 66. Student to faculty ratio 19.1 to 1. Degrees conferred: J.D., J.D.-M.B.A., J.D.-H.S.I.R., J.D.-M.A. (Political Science), J.D.-M.S.W., LL.M. (Health Law, full- and part-time), M.J. (Child Law, Health Law, evenings), S.J.D. (Health Law and Policy), D.H.L.P. (Health Law and Policy).

ADMISSION REQUIREMENTS. LSDAS Law School report, bachelor's degree, transcripts, LSAT required in support of application. Interview sometimes required. Accepts transfer applicants. Apply to Director of Admission after September 1, before April 1. Fall admission only for beginning students. Application fee $50. Phone: (312)915-7170, (800)545-5744; e-mail: law-admissions@luc.edu.

ADMISSION STANDARDS. Selective. Mean LSAT: full-time 159, part-time 154; mean GPA: full-time 3.34, part-time 3.13 (A = 4). Gourman rating: 3.49. *U.S. News & World Report* rating is in the second tier of all U.S. law schools. Accepts 35–40% of total annual applicants.

FINANCIAL AID. Scholarships, partial tuition waivers, Federal W/S, loans. Apply to Financial Aid Office March 1. Use FAFSA. About 56% of students receive aid other than loans from School.

DEGREE REQUIREMENTS. For J.D.: 86 (46 required) credits with a GPA of at least 2.0 (A = 4), plus completion of upper divisional writing course; a course in philosophical and historical perspective of Law; three-year program, four-year program. Accelerated J.D. with summer course work of up to a maximum of 9 credits. For J.D.-master's: individually designed programs, usually a four-year program (full-time) rather than five years if taken consecutively. For M.J. (Child Law, begins in June): 27 credits; 3 credit thesis; two-year program. For M.J. (Health Law, begins in June): 23 credits of required course work (includes thesis), 7 credits of electives; optional externship. For LL.M. (Child Law): 21 credits; thesis; a GPA of 2.5 (A = 4). For LL.M. (Health Law): 24 credits; a GPA of 2.5 (A = 4); thesis of publishable quality. For D.Law, S.J.D.: two-year full-time programs, thesis in first year, dissertation in second year; presentation of dissertation to Law School Community, Health Law community, where appropriate the Medical community.

Stritch School of Medicine (60153)

Established 1920. Located in Maywood, Illinois. Annual tuition: $31,155. Limited on-campus housing available. Apply to Director of Student Personnel Services for off-campus housing. Total average figure for all other expenses: $16,500.

Enrollment: first-year class 130; total 516 (men 54%, women 46%); postgraduate 93. Faculty: full-time 638, part-time 790. Degrees conferred: M.D., M.D.-M.S., M.D.-Ph.D.

ADMISSION REQUIREMENTS. AMCAS report, transcripts, MCAT required in support of application. Interview by invitation only. Applicants must have completed at least 3 years of college study. Does not have EDP. Preference given to residents of Illinois and the Midwest. Apply to Committee on Admissions of School after June 1, before November 15. Application fee $60. Phone: (708)216-3229.

ADMISSION STANDARDS. Very competitive. Mean MCAT: 9.8; mean GPA: 3.62 (A = 4). Gourman rating: 4.25. Accepts 5% of total annual applicants. Approximately 50% are state residents.

FINANCIAL AID. Scholarships, grants, loans. Apply to Director of Financial Aid as soon as possible after acceptance. Use FAFSA (School code: 001710). About 90% of students receive aid from School and outside sources.

DEGREE REQUIREMENTS. For M.D.: satisfactory completion of three-year program; take USMLE Step 2 prior to graduation. For M.S., Ph.D.: see Graduate listing above.

FIELDS OF GRADUATE STUDY.
Anatomy.
Biochemistry.
Cell Biology.
Genetics.
Immunology.
Microbiology.
Molecular Biology.
Neurosciences.
Pathology.
Pharmacology.
Physiology.

School of Social Work

Semester system. Annual tuition: full-time $10,250. Limited on-campus housing for single students only. Apply to Dean, Residence Life (60626). Phone: (312)508-3300.

Enrollment: full-time 212, part-time 250. Graduate faculty: full-time 22, part-time 23. Degrees conferred: M.S.W., D.S.W.

ADMISSION REQUIREMENTS. Transcripts, letters of recommendation, personal statement required in support of School's application. TOEFL required for international applicants. Accepts transfer applicants. Graduates of unaccredited institutions not considered. Apply to School by July 15. Application fee $50. Phone: (312)915-7005; fax: (312)915-7645; e-mail: socialwork@luc.edu.

ADMISSION STANDARDS. Selective. Usual minimum average: 3.0 (A = 4) plus knowledge of the values of the field and experience in working with people.

FINANCIAL AID. Annual awards from institutional funds: scholarships, research fellowships, internships, tuition waiver, loans. Apply by March 1 to School. Use FAFSA and institutional FAF. About 37% of students receive aid other than loans from School and outside sources. Aid available to part-time students.

DEGREE REQUIREMENTS. For M.S.W.: 55 semester hours minimum; internships. For D.S.W.: 60 semester hours minimum; comprehensive exam; dissertation; final oral exam.
Note: Program emphasis is on the Clinical Practice of Social Work.

LYNCHBURG COLLEGE
Lynchburg, Virginia 24501-3199
Web site: www.lynchburg.edu

Founded 1903. Located 120 miles W of Richmond. Coed. Private control. Semester system. Special facilities: Center for Advanced Engineering, Belle Boone Beard Gerontology Center, Earl Childhood Special Education Technical Assistance Center, Center for Economics Education. Library: 218,000 volumes.

Tuition: per credit $300, depending on program. On-campus housing for single students only. Average academic year housing cost: $4245. Contact Office of Residential Living for both on- and off-campus housing. Phone: (434)544-8320.

Graduate Studies

Graduate study since 1964. Enrollment: full-time 88, part-time 413. Faculty teaching graduate students: full-time 48, part-time 20. Degrees conferred: M.Ad., M.B.A., M.Ed.

ADMISSION REQUIREMENTS. Official transcripts, three letters of recommendation, personal essay, GRE, GMAT (Business) required in support of application. TOEFL required for international applicants. Interview not required. Accepts transfer students. Graduates of unaccredited institutions not considered. Apply to Director of Graduate Studies by May 1 (Summer), July 31 (Fall), November 30 (Spring). Application fee $30. Phone: (434)544-8238 (Education), (434)544-8256 (Business).

ADMISSION STANDARDS. Selective. Usual minimum average: 3.0 (A = 4).

FINANCIAL AID. Scholarships, assistantships, grants, Federal W/S, loans. Apply by March 1 to the Office of Financial Aid. Phone: (434)544-8228. Use FAFSA (College code: 003720).

DEGREE REQUIREMENTS. For M.Ed.: 36–39 semester hours minimum, at least 30 in residence; optional final project/capstone. For M.B.A.: 33 semester hours.

FIELDS OF STUDY.
Agency Counseling.
Business Administration. M.B.A.

Community Counseling. 48 credit program.
Educational Leadership. Includes administration/supervision, instructional leadership. M.Ed.
English Education.
School Counseling. 48 credit program.
Special Education. Includes early childhood, mental retardation, learning disabilities, emotional/behavioral disorders. 39 credit program.

UNIVERSITY OF MAINE
Orono, Maine 04469-5782
Web site: www.umaine.edu

Founded 1865. Located 8 miles N of Bangor. CGS member. Coed. State control. Semester system. School of Law in Portland (04102). Special facilities: Center for Marine Studies, Canadian American Center, Migratory Fish Research Institute, Margaret Chase Smith Center for Public Policy, Institute for Quaternary Studies, College of Forest Resources, computer facilities, Darling Center for Research, Teaching, and Service (marine laboratory at Walpole). Library: 921,000 volumes, 17,000 subscriptions.

Tuition: per credit, resident $203, nonresident $576. Housing for 40 married students, 100 single students. Average housing cost: per semester $5360 (including board) single students, $3500 married students (room only). Apply to Housing Office, Hilltop Complex. Phone: (207)581-4580.

Graduate School

Graduate study since 1881. Enrollment: total full-time 900, part-time 1100. Graduate faculty: full- and part-time 600. Degrees conferred: M.A., M.S., M.Ed., M.A.T., M.B.A., M.Eng., M.M., M.P.A., M.P.S., M.S.W., M.W.C., C.A.S., Ph.D., Ed.D.

ADMISSION REQUIREMENTS. Transcripts, three letters of reference, GRE required in support of School's application. GRE Subject Test, interview required for some programs. GMAT required for M.B.A. TOEFL required for international applicants. Accepts transfer applicants. Application and all credentials required six weeks prior to registration. Apply to the Graduate School; no specified closing date. Application fee $50. Phone: (207)581-3218; fax: (207)581-3232; e-mail: graduate@maine.edu.

ADMISSION STANDARDS. Selective for some departments, competitive or relatively open for others. Usual minimum average: 2.75 (A = 4).

FINANCIAL AID. Annual awards from institutional funds: scholarships, fellowships, teaching assistantships, research assistantships, traineeships, Federal W/S, loans. Apply by January 15 to department chair for scholarships, assistantships, and fellowships; to Financial Aid Office for all other programs. Use FAFSA. Phone: (207)581-1324; fax: (207)581-3085. About 45% of students receive aid other than loans from School and outside sources. No aid for part-time students.

DEGREE REQUIREMENTS. For M.A., M.S.: 30 semester hours minimum; thesis; final oral exam; nonthesis option in some programs. For M.Ed.: 33 hours minimum. For M.B.A.: 30 hours minimum; additional course work required for those with little or no undergraduate work in business. For M.A.T.: 33 hours minimum. For M.Eng., M.P.S., M.M.: essentially same as M.A., except thesis not required. For M.P.A.: 36 hours minimum. For M.S.W.: 60 hours total; advanced standing for B.S.W. For C.A.S.: 30 hours minimum. For Ed.D., Ph.D.: two consecutive academic years beyond the bachelor's or one year beyond the master's; comprehensive exam; dissertation; final exam. Foreign language requirements in some fields of study. Language requirements vary by department.

FIELDS OF STUDY.
Accounting. M.Acc.
Agricultural and Resource Economics. M.S., M.P.S. only.
Animal Veterinary and Aquatic Sciences. M.S., M.P.S.
Biochemistry. M.S., M.P.S.
Biochemistry and Molecular Biology. Ph.D.
Biological Sciences. Ph.D.
Bioresource Engineering. M.S.
Botany and Plant Pathology. M.S. only.
Business Administration. M.B.A. only.
Chemical Engineering. M.E., M.S., Ph.D.
Chemistry. M.S., Ph.D.
Civil Engineering. M.E., M.S., Ph.D.
Clinical Psychology. Ph.D.
Communication. M.A.
Communication Sciences and Disorders. M.A.
Community Development. M.S., M.P.S. only.
Computer Engineering. M.S.
Computer Science. M.S., Ph.D.
Counselor Education. M.A., M.S.
Ecology and Environmental Science. Ph.D.
Economics. M.A. only.
Education. M.A., M.S., Ed.D.
Educational Leadership. Ph.D.
Electrical Engineering. M.E., M.S. only.
Elementary Education. M.A., M.S.
English. M.A. only.
Entomology. M.S. only.
Financial Economics. M.A.
Food and Nutrition Sciences. Ph.D.
Food Science and Human Nutrition. M.S. only.
Forest Resources. Ph.D. only.
Forestry. M.S. only.
French. M.A., M.A.T.
Geological Sciences. M.A., Ph.D.
German. M.A.T.
Higher Education. M.A., Ph.D.
History. M.A., Ph.D.
Horticulture. M.S.
Human Development. M.S.
Individualized Program. Ph.D. only.
Kinesiology and Physical Education. M.A., Ph.D.
Liberal Studies. M.A. only.
Literacy Education. M.A.
Manufacturing Management. M.M.M. only.
Marine Biology. Ph.D.
Marine Bio-Resources. M.S., Ph.D.
Marine Policy. M.A.
Mathematics. M.A. only.
Mechanical Engineering. M.S., M.E.
Microbiology. M.S., Ph.D.
Music. M.M.
Nursing. M.S.
Oceanography. M.S., Ph.D.
Physics. M.S., Ph.D.
Plant Science. Ph.D.
Plant, Soil, and Environmental Sciences. M.S.
Psychology. M.A., Ph.D.
Public Administration. M.P.A.
Quaternary Studies. M.S.
Resource Economics and Policy. Ph.D.
Resource Utilization. M.S.
Science Education. M.A.T.
Secondary Education. M.A., M.S.
Social Studies Education. M.A.T.
Social Work. M.S.W.
Spatial Information Sciences and Engineering. M.S., Ph.D.
Special Education. M.A., M.S.
Speech Communication. M.A. only.
Surveying Engineering. M.S. only.
Theater. M.A.

Wildlife Conservation. M.S., M.W.C.
Wildlife Ecology. Ph.D.
Zoology. M.S., Ph.D.

School of Law

Reestablished 1961. Located on the University of Southern Maine Campus in Portland (04102). ABA approved since 1962. AALS member. Semester system. Special facilities: Marine Law Institute, Technology Law Center. Library: 325,199 volumes, 3721 subscriptions; has LEXIS, NEXIS, WESTLAW.

Annual tuition: full-time resident $10,516, nonresident $18,316. Total average annual additional expense: $8670.

Enrollment: first-year class 80; full-time 243 (men 54%, women 46%); no part-time or evening study. Faculty: full-time 12, part-time 9. Student to faculty ratio 16.7 to 1. Degrees conferred: J.D., J.D.-M.A. (Public Policy and Management).

ADMISSION REQUIREMENTS. LSDAS Law School report, bachelor's degree, transcripts, LSAT, letter of recommendation required in support of application. Accepts transfer applicants. Graduates of unaccredited colleges not considered. Apply to Registrar of School after September 1, before February 15. Transfer applications due June 1. Fall admission only. Application fee: $25. Phone: (207)780-4341.

ADMISSION STANDARDS. Selective. Mean LSAT: 154; mean GPA: 3.18 (A = 4). Gourman rating: 2.54. *U.S. News & World Report* ranking is in the third tier of all U.S. law schools. Accepts 40–45% of total annual applicants.

FINANCIAL AID. Full and partial tuition waivers, Federal W/S, loans. Apply to Financial Aid Office by February 1. Approximately 37% receive aid other than loans from School and outside sources. Phone: (207)581-1324. Use FAFSA (School code: 009762). New England students may qualify for a special rate under the NEBHE Compact. NEBHE is in-state tuition plus 50%.

DEGREE REQUIREMENTS. For J.D.: satisfactory completion of 89 credit hour program; 80 hours of pro bono legal services during the three years of study. For M.A.: see Graduate School listing under the University of Southern Maine.

MANHATTAN COLLEGE
Bronx, New York 10471
Web site: www.manhattan.edu

Founded 1853. Private control. Library: 236,266 volumes, 1590 subscriptions. Total College enrollment: 3024.

Tuition: per semester hour $395 (Education), $430 (Business), $510 (Engineering). Limited on-campus housing available for single graduate students. Average academic year housing cost: $7350; $550 per month for off-campus housing. Apply to Director of Residence Life for both on- and off-campus housing information. Phone: (718)862-7200.

Graduate Division

Enrollment: full-time 76, part-time 363. College faculty: full-time 171, part-time 83. Degrees conferred: M.A., M.S.Ed., M.B.A., M.E., M.S.

ADMISSION REQUIREMENTS. Transcripts, GRE/GMAT required in support of application. TOEFL (minimum score 550) required for international applicants. Accepts transfer applicants. Graduates of unaccredited institutions not considered. Apply to Dean of Admissions before May 2 (Fall—Business, Engineering, Biotechnology), August 10 (Fall—all other programs), January 7

(Spring). For full-time Engineering program apply by February 1. Application fee $50. Phone: (718)862-7200; fax: (718)863-8019; e-mail: admit@manhattan.edu.

ADMISSION STANDARDS. Competitive. Usual minimum average; 3.0 (A = 4).

FINANCIAL AID. Scholarships, assistantships, research fellowships, grants, Federal W/S, loans. Apply by February 1 to appropriate departmental chair for scholarships, assistantships, fellowships; to Director of Financial Aid for all other programs; no specified closing date for these programs. Phone: (718)862-7100. Use FAFSA.

DEGREE REQUIREMENTS. For master's: 30–42 credits minimum, at least 24 in residence; thesis/nonthesis option/major research paper/project; internship practicum for some programs. For M.B.A.; 39 credits minimum; master's project.

FIELDS OF STUDY.
Alcohol/Substance Abuse Counseling. M.S.
Biotechnology. Interdisciplinary. M.S.
Business Administration. Includes accounting, finance, international business, management, management information systems. Part-time only. M.B.A.
Chemical Engineering. M.S.
Civil Engineering. M.S.
Computer Engineering. M.S.
Counseling. M.A.
Electrical Engineering. M.S.
Environmental Engineering. M.E.E., M.S.
Mechanical Engineering. M.S.
Reading. M.A.
School Administrators and Supervisors. M.S.Ed.
Special Education. Includes adaptive physical education. M.S.Ed.

MANHATTAN SCHOOL OF MUSIC
120 Claremont Avenue
New York, New York 10027-4698
Web site: www.msmnyc.edu

Founded 1918. Coed. Private control. Semester system. Special facilities: 1000-seat auditorium, 3 recital halls, 2 electronic music studios, 1 recording studio. Library: 80,000 volumes, 20,000 recordings.

Annual tuition: full-time $21,000. On-campus housing for single students only. Average academic year housing costs: $10,000. Contact Director of Campus and Residential Life. Phone: (212)749-2802, ext. 462.

Graduate Division

Enrollment: full-time 391, part-time 75. Faculty: full-time 25, part-time 225. Degrees conferred: M.M., D.M.A., Diploma.

ADMISSION REQUIREMENTS. Official transcripts, interview, three letters of recommendation, school entrance exam, audition required in support of application. On-line unified application available. TOEFL required for international applicants. Accepts transfer applicants. Apply to Office of Admission at least one month prior to one of the four separately scheduled audition dates, but no later than December 1. Application fee $85. Phone: (212)749-2802, ext. 510; fax (212)749-5471.

ADMISSION STANDARDS. Very competitive for some departments, competitive for others. Talent basis for admission.

FINANCIAL AID. Scholarships, tuition waivers, fellowships, teaching assistantships, Federal W/S, loans. Apply four weeks prior to the scheduled audition date. Phone: (212)749-2802. Use FAFSA. About 50% of students receive aid from School and outside sources.

DEGREE REQUIREMENTS. For M.M.: 56–64 semester credits minimum, at least 54 in residence; recital. For D.M.A.: 54 semester credits minimum, at least 54 in residence; proficiency in one foreign language (French, German, or Italian); thesis; two recitals; oral exam; comprehension exam.

FIELDS OF STUDY.
Accompanying. M.M.
Classical Performance. Includes orchestral instruments, voice, piano, guitar. M.M.
Composition. M.M., D.M.A.
Guitar. D.M.A.
Jazz/Commercial Music. M.M.
Orchestral Instruments. D.M.A.
Orchestral Performance. M.M.
Organ. D.M.A.
Piano. D.M.A.
Voice. D.M.A.

MANHATTANVILLE COLLEGE
2900 Purchase Street
Purchase, New York 10577-2132
Web site: www.mville.edu

Founded 1841. Located 25 miles NE of midtown New York City and 5 miles from Greenwich, Connecticut. Coed. Private control. Nondenominational. Semester system. Library: 273,000 volumes, 912 subscriptions.

Tuition: per credit $530. On-campus housing for men, women. Average academic year housing cost: $4850 (including board), $620 for summer. For housing information, phone: (914)323-5217.

Graduate Program

Enrollment: full-time 144, part-time 717. Graduate faculty: full-time 38, part-time 20. Degrees conferred: M.A.T., M.P.S., M.A.L.S., M.S.

ADMISSION REQUIREMENTS. Transcripts, two letters of recommendation required in support of application. On-line application available. TOEFL required for international applicants. Accepts transfer applicants. Graduates of unaccredited institutions not considered. For Education, contact School of Education (914)323-5214; Graduate and Professional Studies (914)694-3425; no specified application closing date. Application fee $40.

ADMISSION STANDARDS. Competitive. Usual minimum average: 2.75 (A = 4).

FINANCIAL AID. Fellowships, assistantships, tuition reduction program for recently unemployed, Federal W/S, loans. Apply by April 15 to Committee on Financial Aid. Phone: (914)323-5357. Use FAFSA. About 20% of students receive aid from College and outside sources.

DEGREE REQUIREMENTS. For master's: 30–39 credit hours minimum; final written/oral exam/project; internships for some programs.

FIELDS OF STUDY.
Elementary and Special Education. M.A.T.
Leadership and Strategic Management. M.S.
Liberal Studies. M.A.L.S.

Management Communication. M.S.
Organizational Management and Human Resource Development. M.S.
Secondary and Special Education. M.A.T.
Writing. M.A.

MANSFIELD UNIVERSITY OF PENNSYLVANIA

Mansfield, Pennsylvania 16933
Web site: www.mansfield.edu

Founded 1857. Located in north-central Pennsylvania. Coed. State control. Semester system. Library: 238,181 volumes, 3110 subscriptions.

Tuition: per credit, resident $230, nonresident $389. On-campus housing for single graduate students; none for married students. Annual academic year housing cost: $4198 including board. Apply to Director of Residence Life for off-campus housing information. Phone: (570)662-4933.

Graduate Division

Graduate study since 1966. Enrollment: full-time 63, part-time 160. Faculty: full-time 1, part-time 35. Degrees conferred: M.Ed., M.A., M.S., M.M.

ADMISSION REQUIREMENTS. Transcript required in support of Division's application. GRE/MAT for Psychology only. Audition required for music students. TOEFL required for international applicants. Accepts transfer applicants. Apply to Associate Provost at least 2 weeks prior to registration. Application fee $25. Phone: (570)662-4807; fax: (570)662-4115.

ADMISSION STANDARDS. Selective. Usual minimum average: 2.5 (A = 4).

FINANCIAL AID. Annual awards from institutional funds: internships, assistantships, Federal W/S, loans. Approved for VA benefits. Apply to Associate Provost prior to entrance. Phone: (570)662-4129; fax: (570)662-4112. Use FAFSA. About 70% of students receive aid other than loans from University and outside sources. Aid available for part-time students.

DEGREE REQUIREMENTS. For master's: 30–40 credit hour minimum; thesis/nonthesis option; final oral/written exam.

FIELDS OF STUDY.
Art Education. Includes art studio, art history. M.Ed.
Community Psychology. M.A.
Early Childhood Education. M.Ed.
Education. M.S.
Elementary Education. M.Ed.
Music. M.M.
Reading. Specialist Certificate only.
School Library and Information Technologies. M.S.
Secondary Education. M.Ed.
Special Education. M.Ed.

MARQUETTE UNIVERSITY

Milwaukee, Wisconsin 53233
Web site: www.marquette.edu

Founded 1881. CGS member. Coed. Private control. Roman Catholic. Semester system. Special facilities: Center for Biological and Biomedical Research, Bradley Institute for Democracy and Public Values, Center for Applied Economic Analysis, Center for Energy Studies, Center for Ethnic Studies, Center for Highway and Traffic Engineering, Center for Industrial Processes and Productivity, Center for Intelligent Systems, Center for Mass Media Research, Center for Sensor Technology, Hartman Family Literacy Center, Institute of the Catholic Media, Center for Citizenship Public Policy, Institute for Family Studies, Material Science and Technology Center, Parenting Center, Center for Psychological Services, Rapid Prototyping Center, Signal Processing Research Center. Library: 900,000 volumes, 9225 subscriptions.

Tuition: per credit $565, $858 for M.B.A. program, $575 for M.S. Programs in Dentistry, $420 Education. On-campus housing, 260 units for graduate students. Average monthly cost: $335–$700 (apartments and single rooms). Apply to Office of Residence Life. Phone: (414)288-7208. For off-campus housing information: (414)288-7281.

Graduate School

Established 1922. Enrollment: full-time 869, part-time 1403. Faculty: full-time 482, part-time 113. Degrees conferred: M.A., M.S.A.E., M.A.T., M.B.A., M.Ed., M.S., M.S.N., M.S.E.M., M.S.H.R., M.S.A., Ed.D., Ph.D.

ADMISSION REQUIREMENTS. Transcripts required in support of School's application. GRE/MAT/ GMAT, three letters of recommendation and interviews required in many programs. Evidence of proficiency in English or TOEFL required of international students. Accepts transfer applicants. Apply to Graduate School at least six weeks prior to registration. Application fee $40. Phone: (414)288-7137; fax: (414)288-1902; e-mail: mugs@ marquette.edu.

ADMISSION STANDARDS. Competitive for most departments, very competitive or selective for others. Usual minimum average: 3.0 (A = 4).

FINANCIAL AID. Annual awards available from institutional funds: research assistantships, teaching assistantships, fellowships and scholarships, Federal W/S, loans. Approved for VA benefits. Apply by February 15 to Graduate School for fellowships, assistantships, scholarships; to Financial Aid Office for all other programs. Phone: (414)288-7390; fax: (414)288-1718. Use FAFSA. About 35% of graduate students receive some form of financial assistance from School. Aid available for part-time students.

DEGREE REQUIREMENTS. For M.A., M.S., M.A.T.: 30 semester hours minimum, at least 24 in residence; thesis; comprehensive oral/written exam; or 30 semester hours minimum; master's essay; comprehensive oral/written exam; written exam in some departments. For M.B.A.: 33 semester hours minimum. For M.Ed.: 30 semester hours minimum; comprehensive oral/written exam. For Ph.D.: 60 semester hours minimum beyond the bachelor's; two semesters in full-time residence within an eighteen-month period carrying at least nine credits; qualifying exam; dissertation; final oral exam. For Ed.D.: 60 semester hours minimum beyond the bachelor's, at least one year in full-time residence; qualifying exam; dissertation; dissertation defense.

FIELDS OF STUDY.
Accounting.
Advertising.
Biology. Three letters of recommendation for admission.
Biomedical Engineering. GRE for admission.
Broadcast and Electronic Communication.
Business Administration. GMAT for admission. M.B.A. only.
Chemistry. Ph.D.
Civil Engineering. Ph.D.
Clinical Psychology. Ph.D.
Communication Studies.
Computing.
Counseling. Ph.D.

Dentistry. M.S. only.

Dispute Resolution.

Economics. GRE or GMAT for admission. M.S.A.E. only.

Educational Policy and Leadership. Ed.D.

Educational Psychology. Ph.D.

Electrical and Computer Engineering. Ph.D.

Engineering Management. GRE or GMAT for admission. M.S.E.M. only.

English. GRE for admission. Ph.D.

Foreign Languages and Literature (Spanish).

Health Care Technologies Management.

History. GRE for admission.

Human Resources. GRE or GMAT for admission. M.S.H.R. only.

International Affairs. GRE for admission. M.A. only.

Journalism.

Mass Communication.

Material Science.

Materials Science and Engineering. Ph.D.

Mathematics, Statistics, and Computer Science. Ph.D.

Mechanical and Industrial Engineering. Includes materials science.

Medieval Studies. GRE for admission. M.A. only.

Nursing. GRE for admission. M.S.N. only.

Philosophy. GRE for admission. Ph.D.

Political Science. GRE for admission.M.A. only.

Psychology. GRE/Subject, MAT for admission; 36 hours for M.S.

Public Service. GRE for admission. M.A.P.S. only.

Religious Studies. Ph.D.

Speech-Language Pathology. GRE for admission. M.S.

Theology. GRE for admission. Ph.D.

School of Dentistry

Established 1894. Semester system. Annual tuition: residents $20,570, nonresidents $32,240. No on-campus housing available. Average academic year housing cost: $10,300. For off-campus housing, apply to Office of Student Affairs. Phone: (414)288-7208. Total average cost for all other first-year expenses: $6896.

Enrollment: first-year class 75; total full-time 260 (men 65%, women 35%). Faculty: full-time 46, part-time and volunteers 245. Degrees conferred: D.D.S., M.S., D.D.S.-M.S.

ADMISSION REQUIREMENTS. AADSAS report, transcripts, three letters of recommendation, DAT required in support of School's application. Interview by invitation only. Applicants must have completed at least three years of college study. Preference given to Wisconsin, North and South Dakota residents. Apply to Director of Admissions after June 1, before March 1. Application fee $35. Phone: (414)288-3532 or (800)445-5385; fax: (414)288-3586.

ADMISSION STANDARDS. Selective. Mean DAT: Academic 17.2, PAT 16.9; mean GPA: 3.39 (A = 4). Gourman rating: 4.48. Accepts 10–15% of total annual applicants. Approximately 20% are state residents.

FINANCIAL AID. Scholarships, awards, DEAL, HEAL, assistantships, loans. Apply by April 1 to University Office of Financial Aid. Phone: (414)288-7390. Use FAFSA (School code: 003863).

DEGREE REQUIREMENTS. For D.D.S.: satisfactory completion of forty-five-month program. For M.S.: satisfactory completion of one-year program.

FIELDS OF GRADUATE STUDY.

Dental Biomaterials.

Emergency Treatment.

Endodontics.

General Dentistry.

Oral Medicine.

Oral Surgery.

Orthodontics.

Pediatric Dentistry.

Pedodontics.

Periodontics.

Prosthodontics.

Law School

Established 1892. ABA approved since 1925. AALS member. Semester system. Law library: 281,000 volumes; 3435 subscriptions; has LEXIS, NEXIS, WESTLAW, DIALOG, LEGALTRAC, CALI, WISCAT, OCLC.

Annual tuition: full-time $21,550, part-time $17,900. No on-campus housing available. Off-campus housing available; contact Office of Residential Life. Phone: (414)288-7208. Total average annual additional expense: $13,100.

Enrollment: first-year class full-time 161, part-time 34; total 616 (men 55%, women 45%). Faculty: full-time 23, part-time 30. Student to faculty ratio 20.2 to 1. Degrees conferred: J.D., J.D.-M.B.A., J.D.-M.A. (Political Science, International Affairs).

ADMISSION REQUIREMENTS. LSDAS Law School report, bachelor's degree, transcripts, LSAT required in support of application. Interview not required. Accepts transfer applicants. Graduates of unaccredited colleges not considered. Apply to Registrar after September 1, before April 1. Fall admission only. Application fee $40. Phone: (414)299-6767; fax: (414)228-0676.

ADMISSION STANDARDS. Selective. Mean LSAT: 155; mean GPA: 3.22 (A = 4). Gourman rating: 4.31. *U.S. News & World Report* ranking is in the third tier of all U.S. Law schools. Accepts 45–50% of total annual applicants.

FINANCIAL AID. Scholarships, Federal W/S, loans. Apply to the Office of Financial Aid by March 1. Phone: (414)288-7390. Use FAFSA. About 37% (full-time), 18% (part-time) of students receive aid other than loans from School.

DEGREE REQUIREMENTS. For J.D.: satisfactory completion of 90 semester-hour program. For master's degree: see Graduate School listing above.

MARSHALL UNIVERSITY

Huntington, West Virginia 25755-2100

Web site: www.marshall.edu

Founded 1837. CGS member. Coed. State control. Semester system. Special facilities: WMUL-FM, WPBY-TV, Robert C. Byrd Institute for Advanced Flexible Manufacturing Systems, Research and Economic Development Center. Library: 1,400,000 volumes, 13,405 subscriptions. Library is repository for General Chuck Yeager memorabilia and Blake Collection of antebellum American literary materials. Total University enrollment: 16,000.

Annual tuition and fees; full-time area resident $2396, state resident $5008, nonresident $7070; per credit area resident $133, state resident $278, nonresident $426. On-campus housing for 84 married students, 1050 graduate men, 1050 graduate women. Average academic year housing cost: approximately $4500–$5600 for married students, $4850 for single students (including board). Apply to Director of Student Housing. Phone: (304)696-3171; (304)696-2564 (off-campus housing information).

Graduate College

Graduate study since 1938. Graduate College established 1948. Enrollment: full-time 920, part-time 1917. Graduate faculty: full-time 200, part-time 20. Degrees conferred: M.A., M.B.A., M.S., M.A.J., M.A.T., M.S.N., Ph.D.

ADMISSION REQUIREMENTS. Transcript, GRE, MAT, GMAT (for M.B.A.) required in support of School's application. On-line application available. TOEFL required of international students. Interview required by some departments. Accepts transfer applicants. Graduates of unaccredited institutions not considered. Apply to Admissions Office at least one month prior to registration. Some departments have earlier deadlines. Application fee residents $10, nonresidents $25. Phone: (800)642-3499 or (304)746-2500, ext. 1907; fax: (304)746-1902.

ADMISSION STANDARDS. Vary by department. Usual minimum average: 2.75 (A = 4).

FINANCIAL AID. Scholarships, fellowships, grants, academic tuition waivers, research assistantships, teaching assistantships, administrative assistantships, internships, tuition waivers, Federal W/S, loans. Approved for VA benefits. Apply to Director of Financial Aid; no specified closing date. Phone: (304)696-3162; fax: (304)696-3242. Use FAFSA and institutional FAF. Aid available for part-time students.

DEGREE REQUIREMENTS. For master's: 32 credit hours minimum including thesis or 36 credit hours minimum without thesis; final written/oral exam. For Ph.D.: at least 60 credits beyond the master's; reading knowledge of one foreign language for some departments; qualifying exam; dissertation; final oral exam.

FIELDS OF STUDY.

COLLEGE OF BUSINESS:
Business Administration. Includes accounting, finance management, marketing economics. M.B.A.
Health Care Administration. M.S.
Industrial Relations. M.S.

COLLEGE OF EDUCATION:
Adult and Technical Education. Includes business, career, cooperative, marketing, vocational-technical. M.A., M.S.
Counseling. Includes elementary, secondary school, higher education, agency counseling. M.A.
Educational Administration. Includes elementary and secondary principal studies, higher education, supervision, school superintendent studies. M.A., Ed.D.
Family and Consumer Science. Includes food and nutrition, home management, consumer economics, teacher education. M.A.
Health and Physical Education. Includes athletic training, adult physical fitness, cardiac rehabilitation. M.S.
School Psychology. Ed.S.
Teacher Education. Includes early childhood, elementary, middle childhood, secondary, reading, special (behavioral disorders, gifted, learning disabilities, mentally impaired, physical handicapped). M.A.
Teaching. M.A.T.

COLLEGE OF FINE ARTS:
Art. Includes art education, art history, ceramics, drawing, graphics, painting, sculpture. M.A.
Music. Includes instrumental, vocal, church, performance, history, literature, theory, composition, music supervisor, teacher education. M.A.

COLLEGE OF LIBERAL ARTS:
Communication Studies. Includes speech communication. M.A.
Criminal Justice. Includes correction, law enforcement. M.S.
English. Includes American and English literature and language. M.A.
Geography. Includes cultural geography, conservation cartography. M.A., M.S.

History. Includes American, European, Asian. M.A.
Humanities. M.A.
Political Science. Includes American national and state government, comparative government, international government, public administration, theory. M.A.
Psychology. Includes general-theoretical, clinical, school. M.S.
Sociology and Anthropology. Includes general, community development, industrial relations, sociology of the Appalachian region, medical anthropology. M.A.

COLLEGE OF SCIENCE:
Biological Sciences. Includes aquatic ecology, biological science education, evolutionary biology and systematics, plant cell chemistry, plant and animal toxonomy, environmental biology. M.A., M.S.
Chemistry. Includes organic, physical, analytical chemistry. M.S.
Mathematics. Includes algebra, topology, analysis, teacher education. M.A.
Physical Science and Physics. Includes interdisciplinary program in physical science, teacher education. M.S.

COLLEGE OF INFORMATION TECHNOLOGY AND ENGINEERING:
Engineering. Includes chemical, engineering management, environmental engineering. M.S.
Environmental Science. M.S.
Safety Technology. Includes ergonomics, industrial hygiene, occupational safety and health, safety management, mine safety. M.S.

SCHOOL OF MEDICINE:
Biological Sciences. Includes anatomy, biochemistry, microbiology, pharmacology, physiology. M.S., Ph.D.

COLLEGE OF NURSING AND HEALTH PROFESSIONALS:
Communication Disorders. Includes speech pathology and audiology. M.A.
Nursing. Includes family nurse practitioner studies. M.S.N.

COLLEGE OF JOURNALISM AND MASS COMMUNICATION.
Journalism. Includes news-editorial writing, public relations, broadcast-TV journalism, advertising, teacher education.

Joan C. Edwards School of Medicine (25704)
Web site: www.musom.marshall.edu

Established 1972. Annual tuition: resident $10,080, nonresident $26,010. Total average figure for all other expenses: $9200. Enrollment: first-year class 48; total full-time 277 (men 60%, women 40%). Faculty: full-time 155, part-time 17. Degree conferred: M.D.

ADMISSION REQUIREMENTS. AMCAS report, transcripts, MCAT, recommendations required in support of application. Interview by invitation only. Preference given to state residents. Apply to Admissions Office after June 1, before November 15. Application fee resident $40, nonresident $80. Phone: (304)691-1738; (800)544-8514; fax: (304)691-1744.

ADMISSION STANDARDS. Competitive. Mean MCAT: 9.0; mean GPA: 3.5 (A = 4). Gourman rating: 3.13. Admits about 15% of total annual applicants. Approximately 88% are state residents.

FINANCIAL AID. Scholarships, tuition waiver, HEAL, loans. Apply after acceptance to University's Office of Financial Assistance. Phone: (304)696-3162. Use FAFSA (School code: G06869). Approximately 90% of students receive some financial assistance.

DEGREE REQUIREMENTS. For M.D.: satisfactory completion of four-year program; all students must pass USMLE Step 2 prior to awarding M.D.

MARYGROVE COLLEGE

Detroit, Michigan 48221-2599
Web site: www.marygrove.edu

Founded 1910. Moved to Detroit in 1927. Coed. Private control. Roman Catholic. Semester system. Library: 187,000 volumes, 16,000 microforms.

Tuition: per credit $361. On-campus housing available for single students only. Annual academic year housing cost: $5600–$6800. Apply to Residence Director.

Graduate Division

Enrollment: full- and part-time 250. College faculty: full-time 9, part-time 18. Degrees conferred: M.A., M.Ed., M.A.T.

ADMISSION REQUIREMENTS. Transcripts, career plan, interview required in support of application. Teacher certification required for some programs. TOEFL (minimum score 500) required for international applicants. Accepts transfer applicants. Apply to Graduate Admissions Office; no specified closing dates. Application fee $25. Phone: (313)927-1509.

ADMISSION STANDARDS. Selective. Usual minimum average: 3.0 (A = 4).

FINANCIAL AID. Scholarships, tuition grants, Federal W/S, loans. Approved for VA benefits. Apply by March 1 to Financial Aid Office. Phone: (313)927-1246. Use FAFSA.

DEGREE REQUIREMENTS. For M.Ed., M.A.T.: 30 semester hours minimum, at least 24 in residence; no language or thesis requirement. For M.A. (Pastoral Ministry): 36 semester hours minimum, internship; final project. For M.A. (Administration): 36 semester hours minimum.

FIELDS OF STUDY.
Adult Learning. M.Ed.
Art of Teaching. M.A.T. only.
Educational Leadership. M.A.
Human Resource Management. M.A.
Pastoral Ministry. M.A.
Reading. M.Ed.

MARYLAND INSTITUTE COLLEGE OF ART

Baltimore, Maryland 21217
Web site: www.mica.edu

Founded 1826. Coed. Private control. Semester system. Library: 80,000 volumes, 305 subscriptions.

Annual tuition: full-time $19,800, per credit $825. Limited on-campus housing. Annual academic year housing cost: $6540. Apply to Housing and Residence Life Office for on- and off-campus housing information. Phone: (410)225-2398.

Graduate Studies

Enrollment: full-time 146, part-time 2. Faculty: full-time 9, part-time 7. Degree conferred: M.F.A.

ADMISSION REQUIREMENTS. Transcripts, three letters of recommendation, portfolio required in support of application. TOEFL required for international applicants. Apply by March 1 (Fall), October 1 (Spring) for painting, ceramics, sculpture, printmaking, and photography. Fall admission for all majors except art education. Application $50. Phone: (410)225-2255; fax: (410)225-2408; e-mail: graduate@mica.edu.

ADMISSION STANDARDS. Competitive for most departments, relatively open for others. Usual minimum average: 2.75 (A = 4).

FINANCIAL AID. Scholarships, grants, teaching assistantships, internships, loans. Apply to Dean, Graduate Studies, before March 1. Phone: (410)225-2285; fax: (410)669-9206. Use FAFSA. About 65% of students receive aid other than loans from College. No aid for part-time students.

DEGREE REQUIREMENTS. For M.F.A.: 60 semester hours minimum, at least 54 in full-time residence; thesis/creative project; no language requirement.

FIELDS OF STUDY.
Art Education. Portfolio required for admission to all programs.
Digital Arts.
Graphic Design.
M.F.A. for Art Educators. Four summers in residence.
Mixed Media.
Painting. Private studios for full-time students.
Photography and Digital Imaging. Private studios for full-time students.
Sculpture. Private studios for full-time students; large shop and foundry.

UNIVERSITY OF MARYLAND

College Park, Maryland 20742-5121
Web site: www.umd.edu

Established 1856. CGS and AAU member. College Park campus located 10 miles N of Washington, D.C.; Schools of Medicine, Dentistry, Nursing, Pharmacy, Social Work, and Law are located in Baltimore. Coed. State control. Semester system. Special facilities: Center for Aging, Automation Research Center, Institute for Criminal Justice and Criminology, Center for Estuarine and Environmental Sciences, Center for Language, Institute for Philosophy and Public Policy, Institute for Physical Science and Technology, Center for Renaissance and Baroque Studies, Survey Research Center, electron microscope, linear accelerator, wind tunnel, marine laboratory, research farms, laboratory-equipped vessels for water research, Transportation Studies Center. The University's NIH ranking is 181st among all U.S. institutions with 68 awards/grants worth $13,941,400. Library: more than 2,900,000 volumes, 32,290 subscriptions.

Tuition: per hour, resident $278, nonresident $430. On-campus housing for 476 married students, limited number of single graduate students. Average academic year housing cost: $525–$700 per month. Contact Office of Residential Life. Phone: (301)314-2100, (301)314-5274 (off-campus housing information).

Graduate School

Established 1919. Enrollment: full-time 4919, part-time 3585 (men 50%, women 50%). Graduate faculty: full-time more than 2690, part-time 914. Degrees conferred: M.A., M.S., M.Ed., M.F.A., M.L.S., M.M., M.B.A., M.C.P., M.A.A., M.Arch., M.Eng., A.G.S., Ed.D., D.M.A., Ph.D.

ADMISSION REQUIREMENTS. Transcripts, GRE/MAT/GMAT, three letters of recommendation required in support of School's application. On-line application available. GRE Subject Test for many programs. TOEFL, TWE required for international applicants. Interview usually not required. Accepts transfer applicants. Graduates of unaccredited institutions not considered. Apply to Director of Graduate Admission and Records by March 1 (Fall), October 1 (Spring), May 1 (Summer); international February 1 (Fall), June 1 (Spring). Application fee $50, $70 international applicants. Phone: (301)405-4198; fax: (301)314-9305; e-mail: grschool@deans.umd.edu.

ADMISSION STANDARDS. Selective for most departments. Usual minimum average: 3.0 (A = 4).

FINANCIAL AID. Annual awards from institutional funds: grants, scholarships, teaching/research/administrative assistantships, research fellowships, internships, tuition waivers, Federal W/S, loans. Approved for VA benefits. Apply by February 1 to appropriate department for scholarships, assistantships, fellowships; to Financial Aid Office for all other programs. Phone: (301)314-8313; fax: (301)314-9587. Use FAFSA and FATS. About 31% of students receive aid other than loans from School and outside sources. Aid available for part-time students.

DEGREE REQUIREMENTS. For most master's: 30–39 semester hours minimum, at least 24 in residence: thesis/nonthesis option; final oral exam. For M.L.S.: 36 hours minimum. For A.G.S.: 30 semester hours beyond the master's. For Ph.D.: three years minimum beyond the bachelor's, at least one in residence; qualifying exam; oral comprehensive exam; dissertation; final oral exam. For D.M.A.: essentially the same as for the Ph.D., except reading knowledge of one language required; composition/final recital.

FIELDS OF STUDY.

Aerospace Engineering. M.S., M.E., Ph.D.
Agricultural and Resource Economics. M.S., Ph.D.
Agronomy. M.S., Ph.D.
American Studies. M.A., Ph.D.
Animal Sciences. M.S., Ph.D.
Anthropology. M.A.A.
Applied Mathematics and Scientific Computation. M.S., Ph.D.
Architecture. M.Arch.
Art. Includes studio. M.F.A.
Art History and Archaeology. M.A., Ph.D.
Astronomy. M.S., Ph.D.
Behavior, Ecology, Evolution, and Systematics. M.S., Ph.D.
Biochemistry. M.S., Ph.D.
Bioengineering. M.S., Ph.D.
Biological Resource Engineering. M.S., Ph.D.
Biology. M.S., Ph.D.
Business and Management. GMAT for admission. M.S., M.B.A., M.S., Ph.D.
Cell Biology and Molecular Genetics. M.S., Ph.D.
Chemical Engineering. M.S., M.E., Ph.D.
Chemical Physics. Interdepartmental. M.S., Ph.D.
Chemistry. M.S., Ph.D.
Civil Engineering. M.E., Ph.D.
Classics. M.A.
Clinical Audiology. Au.D., Ph.D.
Communication. M.A., Ph.D.
Comparative Literature. M.A., Ph.D.
Computer Science. M.S., Ph.D.
Counseling and Personnel Services. M.Ed., M.A., Ph.D., A.G.S.
Creative Writing. M.F.A.
Criminal Justice and Criminology. M.A., Ph.D.
Curriculum and Instruction. Includes elementary and secondary. M.Ed., M.A., Ed.D., Ph.D., A.G.S.
Dance. M.F.A.
Economics. M.A., Ph.D.
Education Policy and Leadership. M.A., M.Ed., Ed.D., Ph.D., A.G.S.
Electrical Engineering. M.S., M.E., Ph.D.
English Language and Literature. M.A., Ph.D.
Entomology. M.S., Ph.D.
Family Studies. M.S., Ph.D.
Fire Protection Engineering. M.S., M.E.
Food Science. M.S., Ph.D.
French Language and Literature. M.A., Ph.D.
Geography. M.A., Ph.D.
Geography/Library and Information Systems. M.A., M.L.S.
Geology. M.S., Ph.D.
Germanic Language and Literature. M.A., Ph.D.

Government and Politics. M.A., Ph.D.
Hearing and Speech Science. M.A., Ph.D.
Historical Preservation. M.H.P.
History. M.A., Ph.D.
History/Library and Information. M.A., M.L.S.
Human Development. M.Ed., M.A., Ed.D., Ph.D., A.G.S.
Journalism. M.A., Ph.D.
Kinesiology. M.A., Ph.D.
Library and Information Services. M.L.S., Ph.D.
Life Science. M.L.S.
Linguistics. M.A., Ph.D.
Marine-Estuarine-Environmental Sciences. M.S., Ph.D.
Material Sciences and Engineering. M.S., M.E., Ph.D.
Mathematical Statistics. M.A., Ph.D.
Mathematics. M.A., Ph.D.
Measurement, Statistics, and Evaluation. M.A., Ph.D.
Mechanical Engineering. M.S., M.E., Ph.D.
Meteorology. M.S., Ph.D.
Molecular and Cell Biology. Ph.D.
Music. M.M., M.A., M.Ed., D.M.A., Ph.D., Ed.D.
Natural Resources Sciences. M.S., Ph.D.
Neuroscience and Cognitive Science. M.S., Ph.D.
Nuclear Engineering. M.S., M.E., Ph.D.
Nutrition. M.S., Ph.D.
Philosophy. M.A., Ph.D.
Physics. M.S., Ph.D.
Psychology. M.A., M.S., Ph.D.
Public Affairs. Includes policy studies, public management. M.P.M., M.P.P.
Public and Community Health. M.P.H., Ph.D.
Reliability Engineering. M.S., M.E., Ph.D.
Russian Language and Linguistics. M.A.
Second Language Acquistion and Application. M.A.
Sociology. M.A., Ph.D.
Spanish Language and Literature. M.A., Ph.D.
Special Education. M.Ed., M.A., Ed.D., Ph.D.
Survey Methodology. M.S., Ph.D.
Sustainable Development and Conservation Biology. M.S.
Systems Engineering. M.S., M.E.
Telecommunications. M.S.
Theatre. M.A., M.F.A., Ph.D.
Urban and Regional Planning and Design. Ph.D.
Urban Studies and Planning. M.C.P.
Veterinary Medical Science. M.S., Ph.D., D.V.M.
Women's Studies. M.A., Ph.D.

UNIVERSITY OF MARYLAND AT BALTIMORE

Baltimore, Maryland 21201-1627
Web site: www.umaryland.edu

Founded 1807. CGS member. Coed. Semester system. Special facilities: Aquatic Pathology Center, Cancer Center, Clinical Stroke Research Center, Biotechnology Research Center, Center for Health Policy Research, Center for Human Virology, Center for Drugs and Public Policy, Center for Vaccine Development. Library: 410,000 volumes, 2609 subscriptions. Total University enrollment: 5800.

Tuition: per credit, resident $274, nonresident $489. On-campus housing available for graduate men and women. Annual academic year average cost: $3500 (room only). Apply to Office of Residential Life. Phone: (410)706-7766.

Graduate School

Web site: www.graduate.umaryland.edu

Enrollment: full-time 351, part-time 773. Faculty: full-time 146, part-time 4. Degrees conferred: M.S., Ph.D.

ADMISSION REQUIREMENTS. Transcripts, GRE, three letters of recommendation required in support of School's application. On-line application available. TOEFL required of international applicants. Accepts transfer applicants. Graduates of unaccredited colleges not considered. Apply to Graduate Admission and Records Office; no specified closing date. Application fee $50. Phone: (410)706-7131; fax: (410)706-3473; e-mail: gradinfo@ graduate.umaryland.edu.

ADMISSION STANDARDS. Selective in some departments, competitive in others. Usual minimum average: 3.0 (A = 4).

FINANCIAL AID. Annual awards from institutional funds: fellowships, teaching assistantships, research assistantships, internships, grants, traineeships, tuition waivers, Federal W/S, loans. Approved for VA benefits. Use FAFSA. Phone: (410)455-7347; fax: (410)706-0824. About 30% of students receive aid other than loans from both University and outside sources. Aid available for part-time students.

DEGREE REQUIREMENTS. For M.S.: 30 semester hours minimum; thesis/nonthesis option; final exam. For Ph.D.: three years of full-time study, at least one year in residence; preliminary exam; dissertation; final exam.

FIELDS OF STUDY.
Anatomy and Neurobiology.
Applied and Professional Ethics.
Biochemistry.
Dental Hygiene.
Epidemiology.
Gerontology. Ph.D. only.
Human Genetics.
Marine-Environmental-Estuarine Studies.
Medical and Research Technology.
Microbiology and Immunology.
Molecular and Cell Biology.
Neuroscience and Cognitive Science.
Nursing.
Oral and Craniofacial Biological Science. Includes cellular and molecular biology, infectious disease, neuroscience.
Oral Biology.
Oral Pathology.
Pathology. Includes forensic toxicology, medical pathology.
Pharmaceutical Health Service Research.
Pharmaceutical Sciences.
Pharmacology and Experimental Therapeutics.
Physical and Rehabilitative Science.
Physiology.
Preventive Medicine.
Social Work. Ph.D. only.
Toxicology.

Baltimore College of Dental Surgery

Founded 1840; the first dental school in U.S. Located in Baltimore (21201). Annual tuition: resident $10,998, nonresident $23,596. Average academic year housing cost: $13,000. Total average cost for all other first-year expenses: $5200.

Enrollment: first-year class 98; total 387 (men 60%, women 40%). Faculty: full-time 117, part-time 98. Degrees conferred: B.S.-D.D.S., D.D.S., M.D.-Ph.D. The Ph.D. (Physiology) is awarded through the Graduate School.

ADMISSION REQUIREMENTS. AADSAS report, transcripts, DAT (not later than October), three letters of recommendation required in support of application. Interviews by invitation only. Applicants must have completed at least three but preferably four years of study in an accredited college of arts and sciences. Transfer applicants accepted. Preference given to state residents. Ap-

ply after June 1, before January 1 to the Office of Admissions of the Dental School. Application fee $60. Phone: (410)706-7472.

ADMISSION STANDARDS. Competitive. Mean DAT: Academic 18.9, PAT 17.6; mean GPA: 3.32 (A = 4). Gourman rating: 4.17. Usual minimum average: 3.0 (A = 4). Accepts about 25% of annual applicants. Approximately 65% are state residents.

FINANCIAL AID. Scholarships, work-study; Federal, state, and private loans. Apply to Office of Student Financial Aid, University of Maryland at Baltimore; priority consideration given applications received by February 15. Phone: (410)706-7347. Use FAFSA (School code: 002104). About 85% of students receive some aid from the School.

DEGREE REQUIREMENTS. For B.S.-D.D.S.: satisfactory completion of seven-year program. For D.D.S.: satisfactory completion of forty-five-month program. For Ph.D.: see Graduate School listing above.

School of Law

Founded 1816. Located in downtown Baltimore in the business and legal district. ABA approved since 1930. AALS member. Semester system. Law library: 382,192 volumes, 4052 subscriptions; has LEXIS, WESTLAW, DIALOG, CARL, UNCOVER, OCLC.

Annual tuition: full-time resident $10,908, nonresident $19,594; part-time resident $8220, nonresident $14,732. No on-campus housing is available. Estimated living expenses: $17,400.

Enrollment: full-time first-year class 188, part-time 62; total full- and part-time 842 (men 46%, women 54%). Faculty: full-time 47, part-time 42. Student to faculty ratio 13.4 to 1. Degrees conferred: J.D., J.D.-Master's (Business Administration, Criminal Justice, Marine and Environmental Sciences, Policy Sciences, Public Management, Social Work).

ADMISSION REQUIREMENTS. LSDAS Law School report, bachelor's degree, transcript, LSAT (no later than February) required in support of application. Interview not required. Accepts transfer applicants. Graduates of unaccredited colleges not considered. Apply to Director of Admissions after September 1, before March 1 (priority deadline). Fall admission only for beginning students. Application fee $60. Phone: (410)706-3492; fax: (410)706-4045.

ADMISSION STANDARDS. Selective. Mean LSAT: full-time 155, part-time 153; mean GPA: full-time 3.35, part-time 3.15 (A = 4). Gourman rating: 3.77. *U.S. News & World Report* ranking is in the second tier of all U.S. law schools. Accepts 30–35% of total annual applicants.

FINANCIAL AID. Scholarships, grants, loans. Apply by March 15 to Financial Aid Office. Use FAFSA (School code: 002104). About 38% of students receive aid other than loans from School. Aid available for part-time students.

DEGREE REQUIREMENTS. For J.D.: satisfactory completion of three-year program, at least one year in residence; 85 semester-hours program. For J.D.-Masters: see Graduate School listing above.

School of Medicine

Chartered 1808. Located in Baltimore (21201). Annual tuition: resident $13,594, nonresident $26,701; student fees $2040. Total average figure for all other expenses: $8500. Enrollment: first-year 150 (EDP 10), total 411 (men 50%, women 50%). Faculty: full- and part-time 426. Degrees conferred: M.D.,

M.D. Ph.D. The M.S. and Ph.D. are awarded by the Graduate School.

ADMISSION REQUIREMENTS. AMCAS report, transcripts, MCAT, letters of recommendation required in support of application. Interview by invitation only. Applicants must have completed at least three years of college study. Preference given to Maryland residents. Accepts transfer applicants in second and third years only. Graduates of unaccredited colleges not considered. Has EDP for Maryland residents only; apply between June 1 and August 1. Apply to Director of Admissions after June 1, before November 1. Application fee $50. Phone: (410)706-7478.

ADMISSION STANDARDS. Competitive. Mean MCAT: 10; mean GPA: 3.68 (A = 4). Gourman rating: 3.79. *U.S. News & World Report* is in the top 39 (research) and top 34 (primary care) of all U.S. medical schools. Accepts 8% of total annual applicants. Approximately 82% are state residents.

FINANCIAL AID. Scholarships, Summer fellowships, HEAL, NIH stipends, loans. Use FAFSA (School code: 002104). About 70% of students receive some aid from School. Apply by June 1 to Office of Financial Aid.

DEGREE REQUIREMENTS. For M.D.: satisfactory completion of four-year program, at least one year in residence. For M.S., Ph.D.: see Graduate School listing above.

FIELDS OF GRADUATE STUDY.
Anatomy.
Biochemistry.
Biomedical Engineering.
Cell Biology.
Epidemiology.
Genetics.
Immunology.
Microbiology.
Molecular Biology.
Neurosciences.
Pathology.
Pharmacology.
Physiology.
Preventive Medicine.

UNIVERSITY OF MARYLAND, BALTIMORE COUNTY
Baltimore, Maryland 21228-5398
Web site: www.umbc.edu

Founded 1807. CGS member. Coed. Semester system. Special facilities: Bioimaging Center, Center for Educational Research and Development, Bradley Center for Employment and Training, Center for Fluorescience Spectrocopy, Molecular Graphic Center, Institute for Policy Analysis and Research, Sargent and Eunice Shriver Center, Structural Biochemistry Center. Library: 650,000 volumes, 4508 subscriptions.

Tuition: per credit, resident $231, nonresident $416. On-campus housing for single students only. Average academic year housing cost: $4546 (including board). Contact Office of Residential Life for both on- and off-campus housing information.

Graduate School
Web site: www.umbc.edu/umgsb

Enrollment: full-time 765, part-time 893. Faculty: full-time 400, part-time 17. Degrees conferred: M.A., M.F.A., M.P.S., M.S., Ph.D.

ADMISSION REQUIREMENTS. Transcripts, GRE, three letters of recommendation required in support of School's application. TOEFL required of international applicants. Accepts transfer applicants. Graduates of unaccredited colleges not considered. Apply to Director, Graduate Admissions and Records Office; no specified closing date. Application fee $45. Phone: (410)455-2199; fax: (410)455-1130.

ADMISSION STANDARDS. Selective in some departments, competitive in others. Usual minimum average: 3.0 (A = 4).

FINANCIAL AID. Annual awards from institutional funds: fellowships, teaching assistantships, research assistantships, internships, grants, traineeships, Federal W/S, loans. Approved for VA benefits. Apply by April 1 to the Dean's Office for fellowships, assistantships; to the Financial Aid Office for all other programs. Use FAFSA. About 30% of students receive aid other than loans from both University and outside sources. Aid available for part-time students.

DEGREE REQUIREMENTS. For master's: 30–39 semester hours minimum; thesis/nonthesis option; final exam. For M.F.A.: 60 semester hours minimum, all in full-time residence or equivalent; special final project. For Ph.D.: three years of full-time study, at least one year in residence; preliminary exam; dissertation; final exam.

FIELDS OF STUDY.
Applied and Professional Ethics.
Applied Developmental Psychology.
Applied Mathematics.
Applied Molecular Biology.
Applied Physics.
Biochemistry.
Biological Sciences.
Chemical and Biochemical Engineering.
Chemistry.
Computer Science.
Economic Policy Analysis.
Education.
Electrical Engineering.
Emergency Health Services.
Engineering Management.
Historical Studies.
Imaging and Digital Arts.
Information Systems.
Instructional Systems Development.
Intercultural Communication.
Language, Literacy, and Culture. Includes French, German, Spanish.
Marine-Estuarine-Environmental Sciences.
Mechanical Engineering.
Molecular Biology.
Neuroscience and Cognitive Sciences.
Operations Analysis.
Physics.
Policy Sciences.
Psychology. Includes human services psychology.
Sociology. Includes applied.
Statistics.

MARYVILLE UNIVERSITY OF SAINT LOUIS
St. Louis, Missouri 63141-7299
Web site: www.maryville.edu

Founded 1872. Coed. Semester system. Library: 149,483 volumes, 3700 subscriptions.

Annual tuition: $12,880; per credit $386. On-campus housing semi-private and private accommodations. Annual academic year housing cost: $4750 (includes board). Apply to Director of Residential Life. Phone: (314)529-9505.

Graduate Studies

Graduate study for Education since 1982, for Business since 1990. Enrollment: full-time 90, part-time 392 (men 25%, women 75%). Faculty: full-time 56, part-time 36. Degrees conferred: M.A., M.B.A.

ADMISSION REQUIREMENTS. Transcripts required in support of application. For Business: GMAT, personal letter explaining qualifications for graduate study. For Education: three letters of recommendation, essay. TOEFL required for international applicants. Accepts transfer applicants. Graduates of unaccredited institutions not considered. Apply to Admission Office of appropriate school; no specified closing date. Application fee $20. School of Education phone: (314)529-9542; fax: (314)519-9921; e-mail: teachered@maryville.edu; School of Business phone: (314)529-9382; fax: (314)529-9975; e-mail: business@maryville.edu; School of Health Professions phone: (314)529-9625; fax: (314)529-9139; e-mail: hlthprofessions@maryville.edu.

FINANCIAL AID. Professional educator scholarships, corporate reimbursement, Federal W/S, loans. Approved for VA benefits. Apply to Financial Aid Office; no specified closing date. Use FAFSA. Phone: (314)576-9360; fax: (314)542-9085; e-mail: fin_aid@maryville.edu.

DEGREE REQUIREMENTS. For master's: 30 credits minimum; thesis/nonthesis option. M.B.A.: 36 credits.

FIELDS OF STUDY.
Business Administration. M.B.A.
Early Childhood. M.A.Ed.
Early Childhood and Leadership. M.A.Ed.
Education/Education Leadership. M.A.
Elementary Education. M.A.Ed.
Environmental Education. M.A.Ed.
Health Administration. M.H.A.
Middle School Education. M.A.Ed.
Nursing. Includes adult nurse practitioner, gerontological clinical nurse specialist. M.S.N.
Occupational Therapy. M.O.T.
Physical Therapy. M.P.T.
Rehabilitation Counseling. M.A.
Secondary Education. M.A.Ed.

MARYWOOD UNIVERSITY
Scranton, Pennsylvania 18509-1598
Web site: www.marywood.edu

Founded 1915. Located approximately 100 miles W of New York City and 100 miles N of Philadelphia. Coed. Private control. Roman Catholic. Semester system. Library: 202,000 volumes, 221,000 microforms, 1100 subscriptions. Total University enrollment: 3000.

Tuition: per credit $524; $535 for M.F.A; doctoral programs $560. On-campus housing for single students only. Average academic year housing cost: $4650–$7310 (including board). Contact Office of Student Affairs for on- and off-campus housing information. Phone: (570)348-6236.

Graduate School of Arts and Sciences

Graduate study since 1922. Enrollment: full-time 181, part-time 466 (men 25%, women 75%). Graduate faculty: full-time 80, part-time 63. Degrees conferred: M.A., M.S., M.P.A., M.B.A., M.F.A., M.P.A.-M.S.W., C.A.G.S., Ph.D.

ADMISSION REQUIREMENTS. Transcripts, two letters of recommendation, GRE or MAT, GMAT (Business) required in support of School's application. On-line application available. TOEFL required for international applicants. Accepts transfer applicants. Graduates of unaccredited institutions not considered. Apply by July 1 (Fall), December 1 (Spring), April 15 (Summer). Application fee $20. Phone: (570)340-6002; fax: (570)961-4745; e-mail: gsas_adm@ac.marywood.edu.

ADMISSION STANDARDS. Selective. Usual minimum average: 3.0 (A = 4).

FINANCIAL AID. Annual awards from institutional funds: scholarships, assistantships, internships, tuition waivers, loans. Apply by February 15 to Dean of Graduate School of Arts and Sciences for scholarships, assistantships; to Financial Aid Office for loans. Phone: (570)348-6225. Use FAFSA. About 55% of students receive aid other than loans from College and outside sources. Aid available for part-time students.

DEGREE REQUIREMENTS. For master's: 30–60 credits; thesis/professional contribution; comprehensive exams. For C.A.G.S.: 30 credits beyond the master's; special project. For Ph.D.: 60 credits beyond the master's minimum, at least one year in full-time residence; qualifying exam; dissertation; final oral exam.

FIELDS OF STUDY.
Art. Includes two-dimensional, three-dimensional. M.F.A.
Art Education. M.A.
Art Therapy. M.A.
Business Administration. M.B.A.
Business and Managerial Science. M.S.
Church Music. M.A.
Communication Arts. M.A.
Communication Sciences and Disorders. M.S.
Counseling. Includes addictions, agency, pastoral. M.A.
Counseling. Includes elementary, secondary. M.S.
Criminal Justice. M.P.A.
Dietetics. M.S.
Early Childhood Intervention. M.S.
Education. Includes school leadership, early childhood, elementary, instructional technology, reading. M.S.
Finance and Investments. M.B.A.
Fine Arts. M.F.A.
Foods and Nutrition. Includes nutrition, sports nutrition, critical care/nutritional support, food systems management, gerontology. M.S.
Gerontology. M.P.A.
Health Services Administration. M.B.A., M.P.A.
Human Development. Interdisciplinary. M.A., Ph.D.
Industrial Management. M.B.A.
Information Systems Technology. M.B.A.
Instructional Leadership. M.A.
Instructional Technology. M.S.
International Business. M.B.A.
Management Information Systems. M.S.
Management of Nonprofit Organizations. M.P.A.
Music. M.A.
Music Education. M.A.
Musicology. M.A.
Nursing. M.S.
Psychology. Includes clinical services, general/theoretical, school/child. M.A.

Public Administration. M.P.A.
Reading. M.S.
School Leadership. M.S.
Special Education. M.S.
Speech-Language Pathology. M.S.
Studio Art. M.A.
Teaching. M.A.
Theological Studies. M.A.

School of Social Work

Established 1968. Coed. Annual tuition: per credit hour $524 main campus, $540 Lehigh Valley campus.

Enrollment: full-time 194, part-time 100. Faculty: full-time 14, part-time 29. Degree conferred: M.S.W.

ADMISSION REQUIREMENTS. Transcripts, three letters of reference, personal statement required in support of School's application. TOEFL required for international applicants. Interview may be required. Accepts transfer applicants. Apply to Coordinator of Admissions by May 15 (Fall), October 15 (Spring). Application fee $20. Phone: (570)348-6282; fax: (570)348-4742.

ADMISSION STANDARDS. Selective. Usual minimum average: 3.0 (A = 4).

FINANCIAL AID. Scholarships, research/administrative assistantships, internships, tuition waivers, loans. Apply to Coordinator of Financial Aid Office by May 1. Phone: (570)348-6225. Use FAFSA and institutional FAF. Aid available for part-time students.

DEGREE REQUIREMENTS. For M.S.W.: 60 credit hours minimum including fieldwork. Advanced standing for graduates of accredited undergraduate social work programs.

FIELDS OF STUDY.
Administration.
Gerontology.
Interpersonal Intervention.

MASSACHUSETTS COLLEGE OF ART

Boston, Massachusetts 02115-3393
Web site: massart.edu

Founded 1873. Coed. State control. Semester system. Library: 231,586 volumes, 757 subscriptions.

Tuition: per credit $245. No on-campus housing available for graduate students. Contact Housing Office for off-campus housing information. Phone: (617)879-7750.

Graduate Program

Enrollment: full-time 73, part-time 28. Faculty: full-time 13, part-time 13. Degrees conferred: M.S., M.S.A.E., M.F.A.

ADMISSION REQUIREMENTS. Transcripts, bachelor's degree, three letters of recommendation, statement of purpose, portfolio required in support of application. TOEFL required for international applicants. Accepts transfer applicants. Apply to Admissions Office by February 1. Application fee $50. Phone: (617)879-7225; fax: (617)879-7250.

ADMISSION STANDARDS. Competitive. Portfolio/talent-based selection process.

FINANCIAL AID. Annual awards from institutional funds: administrative assistantships, teaching assistantships, technical as-

sistantships, internships, Federal W/S, loans. Apply by May 1 to the Financial Aid Office. Phone: (617)879-7850. Use FAFSA (College code: 002180). Aid available for part-time students.

DEGREE REQUIREMENTS. For M.S., M.S.A.E.: 36 semester hours. For M.F.A.: 60 semester hours.

FIELDS OF STUDY.
Art Education. M.S.A.E.
Fine Arts. Includes painting, printmaking, sculpture, design, fibers, glass, metalsmithing, photography, film/video, studio for interrelated media. M.F.A.

MASSACHUSETTS COLLEGE OF PHARMACY AND ALLIED HEALTH SCIENCES

Boston, Massachusetts 02115-5896
Web site: www.mcp.edu

Founded 1823. Coed. Private control. Special facilities: Samuel M. Best Research Laboratory, Pfeiffer Pharmaceutics Laboratory. Library: 75,000 volumes, 790 subscriptions.

Tuition: per hour $580. Housing on nearby campus. Annual academic year housing cost: approximately $9000.

Graduate Study

Enrollment: full-time 33, part-time 61. Graduate faculty: full-time 18, part-time 3. Degrees conferred: M.S., Ph.D.

ADMISSION REQUIREMENTS. Transcripts, GRE, three letters of recommendation required in support of application. TOEFL, TSE required for international applicants. Interview not required. Accepts transfer applicants. Graduates of unaccredited colleges not considered. Apply by February 1 for September admission. Admits normally to Fall only. Application fee $60. Phone: (617)732-2986; fax: (617)732-2801; e-mail: admission@mcp.edu.

ADMISSION STANDARDS. Selective. Usual minimum average: 3.0 (A = 4).

FINANCIAL AID. Annual awards from institutional funds: teaching fellowships, research assistantships, tuition waivers, Federal W/S, loans. Approved for VA benefits. Apply to appropriate department by February 1 for assistantships, fellowships; to Financial Aid Office for all other programs. Phone: (617)732-2861; fax: (617)732-2801. Use FAFSA. About 25% of students receive aid other than loans from the College, 30% from other sources. No aid for part-time students.

DEGREE REQUIREMENTS. For M.S.: 30 semester hours minimum, normally in full-time residence; thesis; final oral exam. For Ph.D.: 50 semester hours minimum beyond bachelor's, normally in full-time residence; one language or research skill; preliminary exam; dissertation; final written/oral exam.

FIELDS OF STUDY.
Analytical Chemistry. M.S., Ph.D.
Drug Regulatory Affairs and Health Policy. M.S.
Medicinal Chemistry. M.S., Ph.D.
Organic Chemistry. M.S., Ph.D.
Pharmaceutics/Industrial Pharmacy. M.S., Ph.D.
Pharmacology. M.S., Ph.D.
Physician Assistant Studies. M.S.

MASSACHUSETTS INSTITUTE OF TECHNOLOGY

Cambridge, Massachusetts 02139
Web site: www.mit.edu

Founded 1861. Located adjacent to Boston. CGS and AAU member. Coed. Private control. 4-1-4 system. Special facilities: Biotechnology Process Engineering Center, Center for Cognitive Science, Center for Environmental Health Sciences, Center for Global Change Science, Center for Information Systems Research, Center for International Studies, Center for Materials Science and Engineering, Materials Processing Center, Center for Space Research, Center for Transportation, Computation Center, Joint Center for Urban Studies with Harvard University, Laboratory for Nuclear Science, Haystack Observatory, Lincoln Laboratory for Research and Development in Advanced Electronics, media laboratory, Leaders for Manufacturing, National Magnet Laboratory, Operations Research Center, Research Laboratory of Electronics, nuclear reactor, Whitehead Institute for Biomedical Research, MIT-Japan Science and Technology, spectroscopy laboratory. Library: 2,395,000 volumes, 2,041,000 microforms, 310 PCs.

Annual tuition: full-time $28,030. On-campus housing for 40 married students, 800 graduate men and women. Average monthly housing cost: $2200–$2500 for married students, $1650 for single students. Apply to Manager of Ashdown House (single students) or to Campus Housing Office (married students). Phone: (617)253-5148; apply to Off-Campus Housing Service for off-campus housing information. Phone: (617)253-4449.

Graduate School

Graduate study since 1886. Enrollment: full-time 5691 (men 75%, women 25%). Faculty: full-time 933, part-time 14. Degrees conferred: M.Arch., M.B.A., S.M., M.Eng., Engineer, Sc.D., M.Arch.A.S., M.C.P., Ph.D.

ADMISSION REQUIREMENTS. Transcripts, three references, statement of purpose required in support of School's application. On-line application available. GRE required by some departments, recommended for the others. Interview not required. TOEFL required of international students. Accepts transfer applicants. Graduates of unaccredited institutions not considered. Contact individual Departments for most current information. Apply to your Department of choice by December 15 (Fall or Summer), September 15 (Spring). Later applications are considered if vacancies still exist. Application fee $55. Phone: (617)253-2917; fax: (617)253-8304; e-mail: mitgrad@mit.edu.

ADMISSION STANDARDS. Competitive. Usual minimum average: 3.5 (A = 4).

FINANCIAL AID. Annual awards from institutional funds: scholarships, fellowships, teaching assistantships, research assistantships, traineeships, Federal W/S, loans. Apply by January 15 to Director of Admissions for scholarships or traineeships, loans; to appropriate department chair for assistantships. Phone: (617) 253-4971; fax: (617)258-8301. Use FAFSA and institutional FAF. About 80% of students receive aid other than loans from School and outside sources. No aid for part-time students. Aid may be available for international students after the first year of full-time study.

DEGREE REQUIREMENTS. For S.M.: 66 subject units minimum, at least one term in residence; thesis. For M.Eng.: 90 subject units minimum, at least one term in residence; thesis. For M.C.P.: 126 subject units; at least two terms in residence; thesis. For M.Arch.: 164 subject units minimum, at least 96 in residence; thesis. For Engineering: 162 units minimum beyond the bachelor's, at least one year in residence; thesis. For Sc.D., Ph.D.: three years minimum beyond the bachelor's, at least four terms full-time in residence; general written exam in two fields; language requirements vary with department; dissertation; final oral exam.

FIELDS OF STUDY.

SCHOOL OF ARCHITECTURE AND PLANNING:
Architectural Studies. S.M., Arch.S.
Architecture. M.Arch., M.Arch.A.S.; no doctorate.
Building Technology. S.M.B.T.
Media Arts and Sciences. S.M.
Media Technology. S.M.
Urban Studies and Planning. S.M., M.C.P., Ph.D.
Visual Studies. S.M.Vis.S.

SCHOOL OF ENGINEERING:
Aeronautics and Astronautics.
Chemical Engineering.
Civil and Environmental Engineering.
Electrical Engineering and Computer Science.
Materials Science and Engineering.
Mechanical Engineering.
Nuclear Engineering.
Ocean Engineering.

SCHOOL OF HUMANITIES AND SOCIAL SCIENCE:
Comparative Media Studies.
Economics.
Linguistics.
Philosophy.
Political Science.
Science, Technology, and Society.

SCHOOL OF SCIENCE:
Biology.
Brain and Cognitive Sciences.
Chemistry.
Earth, Atmospheric, and Planetary Sciences.
Mathematics.
Physics.

WHITAKER COLLEGE:
Health Sciences and Technology.
Toxicology.

Sloan School of Management

Web site: mitsloan.mit.edu

Established 1925. Private control. Accredited programs: M.B.A. Semester system. Special programs: foreign exchange programs in Spain, United Kingdom. Special facilities: Center for Computational Research in Economics and Management Science, Center for Coordination Science, Center for Energy and Environmental Policy Research, Center for Information Systems Research, Center for Innovation in Product Development, Finance Research Center, International Center for Research on the Management of Technology, the MIT Entrepreneurship Center, Operations Research Center.

Annual tuition: full-time $32,270. Estimated annual budget for tuition, room and board, and personal expenses: $41,200. Enrollment: total full-time 714 (men 70%, women 30%). Faculty: 91 full-time, 5 part-time; all have Ph.D./D.B.A. Degrees conferred: M.B.A. (full-time only) (concentrations in Entrepreneurship, Finance, Management, Management Information Systems, Management Science, Marketing, Operations Management, Strategic Management), M.S. (majors in Management, Management Information Systems, Management Science, Operations Management, Strategic Management), Ph.D. (concentrations in Accounting and Control, Financial Economics, Dynamics, Industrial Relations/Human Resources, Information Technologies, Management of Technological Innovation, Marketing, Operations Management/Systems, Organization Studies, Strategy and International Management).

ADMISSION REQUIREMENTS. All applicants should have a bachelor's degree from a recognized institution of higher education, a strong mathematics background, a 3.0 (A = 4) GPA, and a GMAT score of 600. Students are required to have their own personal computer. Early applications are encouraged for both admission and financial aid consideration. Submit application, GMAT results (will accept GMAT test results from the last five years, latest acceptable date is January), official transcripts from each undergraduate/graduate school attended, two letters of recommendation, two essays, résumé (prefers at least four years of work experience), and an application fee of $175 ($200 for international applicants) to the Director of Master's Admission. Beginning students are admitted Fall only. Both U.S. citizens and international applicants apply by January 15 (Fall). In addition, international students (whose native language is other than English) should submit a TOEFL report (minimum score 600), certified translations and evaluations of all official transcripts, recommendation should be in English or with certified translations, proof of health/immunization certificate, and proof of sufficient financial resources for two years of academic study. On-campus interviews are by invitation. Notification is made by mid-March. Admissions Office phone: (617)253-3730; fax: (617)253-6405.

ADMISSION REQUIREMENTS FOR DOCTORAL CANDIDATES. Contact Sloan Doctoral Programs at (617)253-7188 for application material and information. Beginning students are admitted Fall only. Both U.S. citizens and international applicants apply by January 15 (Fall). Submit application, GMAT/GRE (General only; will accept GMAT/GRE test results from the last five years), official transcripts from each undergraduate/graduate schools attended, three letters of recommendation, written description of background, interests, and career expectations, résumé, statement of purpose, and application fee of $75 to Sloan Doctoral Programs Office. In addition, international students (whose native language is other than English) should submit a TOEFL report (minimum score 600), certified translations and evaluations of all official transcripts, recommendation should be in English or with certified translations, proof of health/immunization certificate. International students' contact: (617)253-3795. Interviews by invitation. Notification is made by mid-March.

ADMISSION STANDARDS. For M.B.A.: median GMAT: 650; median GPA: 3.5 (A = 4). For Ph.D.: number of applications 400–500; number enrolled 15–20. Gourman rating: the M.B.A. was rated in the top five the score was 4.91; the Ph.D. was rated in the top five, the score was 4.91. *U.S. News & World Report* ranked Sloan School in the top four of all U.S. business schools. *Business Week* listed Sloan School in the top ten of all U.S. business schools.

FINANCIAL AID. Fellowships, research and teaching assistantships, Federal W/S, loans. Financial aid may be available for international students. Financial Aid applications and information are generally available at the on-campus interview or included in application materials; apply by January 15. Request fellowship and assistantship information from the Sloan School. Contact the University's Financial Aid Office for current need-based financial aid information; phone: (617)258-5775. Use FAFSA (School code: 002103), also submit Financial Aid Transcript, Federal Income Tax forms. Approximately 60% of students receive some form of financial assistance.

DEGREE REQUIREMENTS. For M.B.A., M.S.: 18–24 month programs. For M.Acc., M.P.A., M.S.T.: 32 credit program. For M.B.A.-master's: generally a three-and-one-half- to five-year program. For M.B.A.-J.D.: four-and-one-half- to five-year program. For Ph.D.: three- to five-year program; general exam in major and minor field; dissertation proposal and oral defense, dissertation; oral defense.

UNIVERSITY OF MASSACHUSETTS AMHERST

Amherst, Massachusetts 01003-0001
Web site: www.umass.edu

Founded 1863. Located 90 miles W of Boston. Amherst campus is primary graduate school location. CGS member. State control. Semester system. Special facilities: University Computing Center, Donahue Institute for Government Services, Institute for Advanced Studies in the Humanities, Polymer Research Institute, Labor Relations and Research Center, Environmental Institute, Water Resources Center, Hampshire Inter-Library Center, Marine Station, Suburban Experiment Station, University of Massachusetts Abroad, Center for Instructional Resources and Improvement, Office of Research Services, University Press, Center for Business and Economic Research, Polymer Research Institute. Five-College (Amherst, Hampshire, Mount Holyoke, Smith, University of Massachusetts) cooperative undergraduate and graduate programs. The University's NIH ranking is 199th among all U.S. institutions with 65 awards/grants worth $12,078,414. Library: 4,700,000 volumes, 15,300 subscriptions. Total University enrollment: 23,800.

Annual tuition: full-time, resident $2640, nonresident $9940; per hour, resident $110, nonresident $414. Mandatory fees: full-time resident $2056, nonresident $2509. On-campus housing for 300 graduate single students; 345 married students. Average academic year housing cost: $5259 (including board) for single students; $7000–$9000 for married students. Apply to Housing Office. Phone: (413)545-2100. Day-care facilities available.

Graduate School

Web site: www.umass.edu/gradschool

Graduate study since 1876. Enrollment: full-time 2013, part-time 2319. University faculty: full-and part-time 1161. Degrees conferred: M.A., M.S., M.S.E.C.E., M.R.P., M.A.T., Ch.E., M.S.C.E., M.S.Envr.E., M.S.I.E.O.R., M.S.M.E., M.P.A., M.P.H., M.Ed., M.B.A., M.F.A., M.L.A., M.M., C.A.G.S., Ed.D., Ph.D., Five-College Ph.D.

ADMISSION REQUIREMENTS. Transcripts, two recommendations, GRE or GMAT, proof of residency form required in support of School's application. Interview not required. TOEFL required for international applicants. Graduates of unaccredited institutions not considered. Apply to Graduate Admissions Office by March 1 (Fall and Summer), October 1 (Spring). Some programs may have earlier deadline. Application fee $40. Phone: (413)545-0721; fax: (413)577-0010; e-mail: gradinfo@ resgs.umass.edu.

ADMISSION STANDARDS. Very selective for most departments. Usual minimum average: 3.0 (A = 4).

FINANCIAL AID. Annual awards from institutional funds: fellowships, internships, teaching assistantships, research assistantships, grants, tuition waivers, NSF and NIH traineeships, Federal W/S, loans. Apply to Financial Aid Office; no specified closing date. Phone: (413)545-0801. Use FAFSA. About 50% of students receive aid other than loans from University and outside sources.

DEGREE REQUIREMENTS. For most master's: 30 credits; thesis; final general exam. For M.A.T.: 39–45 credits. For M.Ed.: 33 credits. For M.B.A.: 55 credits. For M.F.A.: 60 credits; final M.F.A. creative project (English, Art, Theater). For M.R.P., M.L.A.: 46 credits; internships; research project; thesis optional. For M.M.: 33 credits; one original composition in lieu of thesis for composition majors. For C.A.G.S.: 30 credits beyond master's. For Ph.D., Ed.D.: course work as specified by program, at least two consecutive semesters in full-time residence; comprehensive exam; foreign language requirement varies by program; dissertation; final oral exam. The Statute of Limitations (maximum time allowed in which to earn the degree) is six years for the doctorate, four years for the M.F.A., and three years for all other master's degree programs; a part-time student may apply for an additional year in which to complete a program.

FIELDS OF STUDY.
Accounting.
Afro-American Studies.
Animal Science.
Anthropology.
Applied Mathematics.
Art.
Art History.
Astronomy.
Biochemistry.
Biology.
Chemical Engineering.
Chemistry.
Chinese.
Civil Engineering.
Classics.
Communication.
Communication Disorders.
Comparative Literature.
Computer Science.
Economics.
Education.
Electrical and Computer Engineering.
Engineering Management.
English.
Entomology.
Environmental Engineering.
Exercise Science.
Food Science.
Forestry.
French and Francophone Studies.
Geography.
Geology.
Geosciences.
Germanic Language and Literatures.
Hispanic Literature and Linguistics.
History.
Hotel, Restaurant, and Travel Administration.
Industrial Engineering and Operations Research.
Italian Studies.
Japanese.
Labor Studies.
Landscape Architecture.
Latin and Classical Humanities.
Linguistics.
Management.
Manufacturing Engineering.
Mathematics.
Mechanical Engineering.
Microbiology.
Molecular and Cellular Biology.
Music.
Neuroscience and Behavior.
Nursing.
Nutrition.
Organismic and Evolutionary Biology.
Philosophy.
Physics.
Plant and Soil Sciences.
Plant Biology.
Plant Pathology.
Political Science.
Polymer Science and Engineering.
Psychology.

Public Administration.
Public Health.
Regional Planning.
Resource Economics.
School Psychology.
Sociology.
Sport Studies.
Theater.
Wildlife and Fisheries Conservation.

Medical School

Established 1962. Located in Worcester (01655-0115). Annual tuition: resident $8352, nonresident not applicable; student fees $2010. Total average cost for all other expenses: $15,300. Very limited housing available.

Enrollment: first-year class 100 (EDP 10); total 407 (men 50%, women 50%). Faculty: approximately 689 full- and part-time. Degrees conferred: M.D., M.D.-Ph.D.

ADMISSION REQUIREMENTS. Transcripts, MCAT, recommendations, interview required in support of application. Non-Massachusetts residents, graduates of unaccredited colleges not considered. Has EDP; apply between June 1 and August 1. Apply after June 1, before November 1. Application fee $75. Phone: (508)856-2323.

ADMISSION STANDARDS. Selective. Median MCAT: 10; median GPA: 3.50 (A = 4). Gourman rating: 3.24. *U.S. News & World Report* ranked the Medical School in the top 5 schools of all U.S. medical schools for primary care.

FINANCIAL AID. Scholarships, minority scholarships, grants, institutional loans, HEAL, alternative loan programs, learning contracts, tuition waivers, loans, Service Commitment Scholarships to the Commonwealth in primary care are available. Tuition waivers/stipends may be available for M.D.-Ph.D. degree candidates. Financial Aid applications and information are given out at the on-campus by-invitation interview or sent with the letter of acceptance. Contact the Financial Aid Office for current information. Phone: (508)856-2265. Use FAFSA (School code: G09756), also submit Financial Aid Transcript, Federal Income Tax forms; use CSS Profile for all campus-based funds. Approximately 75% of students receive some form of financial assistance.

DEGREE REQUIREMENTS. For M.D.: satisfactory completion of four-year program. For M.D.-Ph.D.: generally a six- to seven-year program.

FIELDS OF GRADUATE STUDY.
Biochemistry and Molecular Biology.
Biomedical Sciences.
Cell Biology.
Cellular and Molecular Physiology.
Immunology and Virology.
Molecular Biology.
Molecular Genetics and Microbiology.
Neurosciences.
Pharmacology and Molecular Toxicology.

UNIVERSITY OF MASSACHUSETTS BOSTON
Boston, Massachusetts 02125-3393
Web site: www.umb.edu

Founded 1964. CGS member. Coed. State control. Semester system. Special facilities: Center for the Advancement of Teaching in the Sciences, Asian-American Institute, Gerontology Institute, Gaston Institute for Latino Affairs, Institute for Learning and Teaching, McCormack Institute of Public Affairs, Center for Survey Research, Joiner Center for the Study of War and Social Consequences, Trotter Institute for the Study of Black Culture, Urban Harbors Institute. Library: 572,000 volumes, 2772 subscriptions. Total University enrollment: 13,500.

Tuition: per credit, resident $108, nonresident $407. No on- or off-campus housing available (commuter institution). Day-care facilities available.

Graduate Studies and Research

Enrollment: full-time 770, part-time 1739 (men 35%, women 65%). University faculty: full-time 488, part-time 71. Degrees conferred: M.A., M.S., M.Ed., M.B.A., C.A.G.S., Ph.D., Ed.D., Graduate Certificate.

ADMISSION REQUIREMENTS. Transcripts, GRE/MAT/GMAT required in support of application. TOEFL required for international applicants. Accepts transfer applicants. Graduates of unaccredited institutions not considered. Apply to Office of Graduate Admissions and Records. Application deadlines vary by program; priority deadlines March 1 (Fall), November 1 (Spring); for international applicants apply by May 1 (Fall), October 1 (Spring). Application fee $25 (residents), $40 (nonresidents). Phone: (617)287-6400; fax: (617)287-6264.

ADMISSION STANDARDS. Selective. Usual minimum average: 2.75 (A = 4).

FINANCIAL AID. Academic scholarships, grants, research assistantships, administrative assistantships, teaching assistantships, internships, tuition waivers, Federal W/S, loans. Approved for VA benefits. Apply by March 1 to Director of Financial Aid. Phone: (617)287-6300; fax: (617)287-6323. Use FAFSA and institutional FAF. Aid available for part-time students.

DEGREE REQUIREMENTS. For master's: 30 credits minimum; thesis and general exam for some departments. For Ph.D.: 60 credits beyond the master's minimum; two semesters in full-time residence; qualifying exam; one foreign language required for some departments; dissertation; final oral exam. For Ed.D.: essentially the same as Ph.D. except no foreign language requirement.

FIELDS OF STUDY.
Adapting the Curriculum. M.Ed.
American Studies. M.A.
Applied Linguistics. M.S.
Applied Physics. M.S.
Applied Sociology. M.A.
Bilingual Education. M.A.
Biology. M.S.
Biomedical Engineering and Biotechnology. M.S.
Biotechnology and Biomedical Science. M.S.
Business Administration. M.B.A.
Chemistry. M.S.
Clinical Psychology. Ph.D.
Computer Science. M.S., Ph.D.
Counseling. M.Ed., C.A.G.S.
Critical and Creative Thinking. M.A., Graduate Certificate.
Database Technology. M.S.
Dispute Resolution. M.A., Graduate Certificate.
Education/Higher Educational Administration. Ed.D.
Education/Leadership in Urban Schools. Ed.D.
Educational Administration. M.Ed., C.A.G.S.
English. M.A.
Environmental Sciences. M.S., Ph.D.
Environmental Sciences—Environmental Biology. M.S., Ph.D.
Environmental Sciences—Environmental, Coastal, and Ocean Sciences. M.S., Ph.D.

Environmental Sciences—Green Chemistry. M.S., Ph.D.
Forensic Services. M.S.
Gerontology. Ph.D.
History. M.A.
History/Archival Methods. M.A.
History/Historical Archaeology. M.A.
Human Services. M.S.
Instructional Design. M.Ed.
Instructional Technology. M.Ed.
International Relations. M.A.
Marine Sciences and Technology. M.S.
Nursing. M.S., Ph.D.
Nursing/Business Administration. M.S.
Orientation and Mobility. M.S.
Public Affairs. M.S.
Public Policy. Ph.D.
School Psychology. M.Ed., C.A.G.S.
Special Education. M.Ed.
Women in Politics and Public Policy. M.A.

UNIVERSITY OF MASSACHUSETTS DARTMOUTH

North Dartmouth, Massachusetts 02747-2300
Web site: www.umassd.edu

Founded 1895. Located 50 miles S of Boston. Coed. State control. Semester system. Special facilities: Center for Marine Science and Technology (CMAST), Northeast Regional Aquaculture Center; research affiliations with Brookhaven National Lab (physics), Marine Biological Lab (marine sciences), and Woods Hole Oceanographic Institute (marine sciences); 2 Digital VAX 6610 mainframe computers; 150 IBM and Macintosh personal computers in cluster labs. Library: 334,000 volumes, 2925 subscriptions.

Annual tuition/fees: full-time (9 credits each semester) resident $6740, nonresident $18,426. Limited on-campus housing for graduate students. Average academic year housing cost: $3391. Contact Office of Residential Life for both on- and off-campus housing information. Phone: (508)999-8140.

Graduate School

Enrollment: full-time 227, part-time 321, Graduate faculty: full-time 250, part-time 78. Degrees conferred: M.A., M.S., M.F.A., M.B.A., M.A.E.

ADMISSION REQUIREMENTS. Official transcripts, three letters of recommendation required in support of School's application. GRE Subject Test/GMAT/MAT required by some programs. Interview not required. TOEFL required for international applicants. Accepts transfer applicants. Graduates of unaccredited institutions not considered. Apply to Graduate Admissions Office by April 20 (September), November 20 (January); international applicants apply by February 20 (September), September 15 (January). Application fee resident $20, nonresident $40. Phone: (508)999-8026; fax: (508)999-8183; e-mail: graduate@umass.edu.

ADMISSION STANDARDS. Selective. Usual minimum average: 2.75 (A = 4).

FINANCIAL AID. Research fellowships, teaching assistantships, internships, tuition waivers, Federal W/S, loans. Approved for VA benefits. Apply by March 1 to Dean, Graduate School for fellowships, assistantships; to Financial Aid Office for all other programs. Phone: (508)999-9632. Use FAFSA and University's FAF. About 20% of students receive aid other than loans from University. Aid available for part-time study.

DEGREE REQUIREMENTS. For master's: 30 credits minimum, at least 24 in residence; comprehensive exam; thesis/nonthesis option.

FIELDS OF STUDY.

Art Education.

Artisanry. Includes ceramics, jewelry/metals, textile/fiber arts, wood and furniture design.

Biology/Marine Biology.

Business Administration.

Chemistry. Joint Ph.D. program with University of Massachusetts, Amherst and Lowell.

Computer Science.

Design. Portfolio for admission.

Electrical and computer Engineering.

Elementary Education.

Fine Arts. Includes studios in drawing, painting, printmaking, sculpture.

Graphic Design.

Marine Sciences and Technology. University-of-Massachusetts-wide joint Ph.D.

Mechanical Engineering.

Middle Education.

Nursing.

Physics.

Professional Writing.

Psychology.

Secondary Education. Includes business, English, foreign literature and languages (French, Portuguese, Spanish), history, mathematics, social studies.

Textile Chemistry.

Textile Technology.

Visual Design. Includes studios in graphic design, electronic imaging, illustration, multimedia, photography, typography.

UNIVERSITY OF MASSACHUSETTS LOWELL

Lowell, Massachusetts 01854-2881

Web site: www.uml.edu

Founded 1897. Located 25 miles N of Boston. CGS member. State control. Semester system. Special facilities: Center for the Arts, Center for Criminal Justice, Center for Family and Community Studies, Center for Field Service, Center for Health Promotion, Center for Lowell History, Pinaski Energy Center, Institute for Plastics Innovation, Center for Productivity Enhancement, Toxic Use Reduction Center, Tsongas Industrial History Center. Library: 549,000 volumes, 7855 subscriptions. Total University enrollment: 12,200.

Tuition/fees: per credit resident $277.50, nonresident $622.29. On-campus housing available. Average academic year housing cost: $5464 (including board). Contact Housing Officer for on- and off-campus housing information. Phone: (508)934-2107.

The Graduate School

Founded 1935. Enrollment: full-time 613, part-time 1840 (men 55%, women 45%). Faculty: full-time 450, part-time 50. Degrees conferred: M.S., M.Ed., M.B.A., M.M.S., M.S.Eng., M.A., C.A.G.S., M.M., Ph.D., D.Sc., D.Eng., D.Ed., Certificate.

ADMISSION REQUIREMENTS. Transcripts, three references, GRE/GMAT/MAT required in support of School's application. On-line application available. TOEFL required for international applicants. Interview not required. Accepts transfer applicants. Graduates of unaccredited institutions not considered. Apply to Graduate School Office by May 1 (Fall), October 1 (Spring). Application fee $20, $35 for international applicants. Phone: (800)656-GRAD or (978)934-2380; fax: (978)934-3010; e-mail: graduate_school@uml.edu.

ADMISSION STANDARDS. Selective. Usual minimum average: 2.75 (A = 4).

FINANCIAL AID. Annual awards from institutional funds: scholarships, research assistantships, teaching assistantships, fellowships, Federal W/S, loans. Approved for VA benefits. Apply by April 1 to appropriate department chair for assistantships; to Financial Aid Office for all other programs. Use FAFSA. Phone: (508)934-4220. About 10% of students receive aid other than loans from University and outside sources. Aid available for part-time students.

DEGREE REQUIREMENTS. For master's: 30 credit hours minimum including thesis, at least one year in residence; final written/oral exam. For C.A.G.S.: 30 credits beyond the master's; project for some programs. For Certificates: twelve credits minimum; all credits applicable to master's degree. For Ph.D.: two to three years minimum in residence beyond the master's, depending upon previous preparation; preliminary exam; qualifying exam; dissertation; final oral exam. For D.Sc., D.Eng.: requirements are essentially the same as for Ph.D.

FIELDS OF STUDY.

Biological Sciences. Includes biotechnology.

Biomedical Engineering and Biotechnology.

Business Administration.

Chemical Engineering.

Chemistry. Includes biochemistry, environmental studies.

Civil Engineering. Includes geotechnical, structural, transportation, environmental, and geoenvironmental.

Clinical Laboratory Sciences.

Community and Social Psychology.

Computer Engineering.

Computer Science. Includes computational mathematics, mathematical science.

Criminal Justice.

Curriculum and Instruction. Includes ESL.

Economic and Social Development of Regions.

Educational Administration.

Electrical Engineering. Includes opto-electronics.

Energy Engineering. Includes solar, nuclear.

Environmental Studies. Includes atmospheric sciences.

Language Arts and Literacy.

Leadership in Schooling.

Mathematics. Includes applied, mathematics for teachers, scientific computing, statistic and operators research.

Mathematics and Science Education.

Mechanical Engineering.

Music Education.

Music Performance.

Nursing. Includes gerontological, family health, adult psychiatric/mental health, health promotion.

Physical Therapy.

Physics. Includes applied mechanics, energy engineering, optical sciences.

Plastics Engineering. Includes coatings and adhesives, fiber/composites.

Polymer Science. Includes polymer science/plastics engineering.

Radiological Sciences and Protection.

Reading and Language.

Work Environment. Includes industrial hygiene, occupational ergonomics, epidemiology, work environment policy, cleaner production and pollution prevention.

MAYO CLINIC AND MAYO FOUNDATION
Rochester, Minnesota 55901
Web site: www.mayo.edu

Founded 1863. There are three sites: Rochester, Minnesota; Jacksonville Florida; Scottsdale, Arizona. Private control. One of the world's largest group practices. Special facilities: Cancer Center, Mass Spectrometry Resource Laboratory, Analytical Nuclear Magnetic Resonance Resource Laboratory, Electron Microscopy Resource Laboratory, Molecular Biology Resource Laboratory, Biomedical Imaging Resource Laboratory. The Mayo Clinic's NIH ranking is 41st among all U.S. institutions with 332 awards/grants worth $115,729,246. The Mayo Medical center is a member of Council of Teaching Hospitals. *U.S. News & World Report*'s Hospital/Medical Center national rankings for all hospitals placed the Mayo Clinic in the top 20 of all U.S. hospitals. Library: 353,000 volumes, 4300 subscriptions.

Mayo Medical School
Web site: www.mayo.edu/mms

Established 1972. Graduate programs affiliated with the University since 1914.

Annual tuition: $20,500, Mayo scholarships and Minnesota state funds reduces this cost for residents of Arizona, Florida, and Minnesota to $4925 and for nonresidents to $9850. Only off-campus housing available. Contact Admissions Office for off-campus housing information. Off-campus housing and personal expenses: approximately $7820 (single students).

Enrollment: first-year class 42 (EDP 1, M.D.-Ph.D. 6); total full-time 165 (men 38%, women 62%). Faculty: full- and part-time/volunteers 1000. Degrees conferred: M.D., M.D.-Ph.D.

ADMISSION REQUIREMENTS. AMCAS report, transcripts, MCAT, bachelor's degree, interview, recommendations required in support of application. Preference given to residents of Arizona, Florida, and Minnesota. Graduates of unaccredited colleges not considered. Has EDP; apply between June 1 and August 1. Apply to Director of Admissions after June 1, before November 1. Application fee $60. Phone: (507)284-3671; fax: (507)284-2634.

ADMISSION STANDARDS. Very competitive. Mean MCAT: 10; mean GPA: 3.78 (A = 4). Gourman rating: 3.84. *U.S. News & World Report* ranking is 15th of all U.S. medical schools. Accepts 4% of total annual applicants. Approximately 12% are state residents.

FINANCIAL AID. Full-tutition scholarships, merit scholarships, NIH stipends, loans. Apply to Office of Student Affairs after appointment but not later than May 1. Phone: (507)284-4839. There are special merit scholarships for residents of Arizona, Florida, and Minnesota. Use FAFSA.

DEGREE REQUIREMENTS. For M.D.: satisfactory completion of four-year program. For M.S.: one year beyond M.D.; knowledge of one foreign language; thesis/nonthesis option. For Ph.D.: at least two years beyond M.D.; knowledge of two foreign languages; one language/research tool; preliminary oral/written exam thesis; final oral exam.

FIELDS OF GRADUATE STUDY.
Biochemistry.
Biomedical Engineering.
Cell Biology and Genetics.
Immunology.
Molecular Biology.
Molecular Neurosciences.
Molecular Pharmacology and Experimental Therapeutics.
Oral and Maxillofacial Surgery. D.D.S. required for admission.
Physiology.
Tumor Biology.

MCDANIEL COLLEGE
Westminster, Maryland 21157-4390
Web site: www.mcdaniel.edu

Founded 1867. Located 32 miles NW of Baltimore. Coed. Private control. Semester system. Library: 200,000 volumes, 750 subscriptions.

Tuition: per credit $240. Limited on-campus housing available during academic year and Summer session for single students only. Average academic year housing costs: $5465. Contact Housing Office for both on- and off-campus housing information. Phone: (410)857-2240.

Graduate Studies

Enrollment: full-time 76; part-time 1102 (men 30%, women 70%). Graduate faculty: full-time 25, part-time 60. Degrees conferred: M.S., M.L.A.

ADMISSION REQUIREMENTS. Official transcripts, three letters of reference, interview; GRE or MAT required in support of application. TOEFL required for international applicants. Accepts transfer applicants. Apply to Dean of Graduate Admissions. Application fee $40. Phone: (410)857-2500; fax: (410)857-2515.

ADMISSION STANDARDS. Selective. Usual minimum average: 2.75 (A = 4).

FINANCIAL AID. Graduate assistantships available in housing, education department, physical education department, grants, loans. Approved for VA benefits. Apply to the Office of Graduate and Professional Studies; no specified closing date. Phone: (410)857-2235; fax: (410)386-4608. Use FAFSA. About 5% of students receive aid other than loans from both College and outside sources.

DEGREE REQUIREMENTS. For master's: 30-33 hours; thesis/nonthesis option; comprehensive exam.

FIELDS OF STUDY.
Counselor Education.
Curriculum and Instruction.
Deaf Education. Includes the teaching of sign language, the teaching of interpreting.
Educational Administration.
Exercise Science and Physical Education.
Human Resource Development.
Human Services Management.
Liberal Arts.
Reading.
School Library Media.
Secondary Education.
Special Education.

MCNEESE STATE UNIVERSITY
Lake Charles, Louisiana 70609-2495
Web site: www.mcneese.edu

Founded 1938. Located 130 miles W of Baton Rouge. Coed. State control. Semester system. Library: 249,000 volumes, 483,000 microforms.

Annual tuition, depending upon credit load: $2200 resident, nonresident $8300; 0–3 credits, resident $436, nonresident $824. On-campus housing for 116 married students, 1177 men, 425 women. Average annual housing cost: $4500 married students, $2500 (including board) for single students. Apply to Office of Student Housing for housing information. Phone: (337)475-5606.

School of Graduate Studies

Enrollment: full-time 203, part-time 955. Graduate faculty: full-time 130, part-time 20. Degrees conferred: M.A., M.S., M.F.A., M.Eng., M.B.A., M.Ed., M.M., Ed.S.

ADMISSION REQUIREMENTS. Transcripts, GRE/GMAT required in support of School's application. TOEFL (minimum score 550) and affidavit of support required for international applicants. Interview not required. Accepts transfer applicants. Graduates of unaccredited colleges not considered. Apply to Office of Registrar at least thirty days prior to registration; May 1 (Fall), October 1 (Spring). Application fee $20, international students $40. Phone: (337)475-5147.

ADMISSION STANDARDS. Selective. Usual minimum score of 1100 (150 × UGPA + GRE) required for consideration.

FINANCIAL AID. Scholarships, research assistantships, teaching assistantships, Federal W/S, loans. Apply by May 1 to appropriate department head for scholarships, assistantships; to Office of Financial Aid for all other programs. Use FAFSA (University code: 002017) and University's FAF. Phone: (337)475-5065. About 3% of students receive aid other than loans from University and outside sources. Aid available for part-time students.

DEGREE REQUIREMENTS. For master's: 30 semester hours minimum, at least 24 in residence; thesis required (for 6 hours) for M.A., M.S., optional for other master's; reading knowledge of one foreign language for some majors; final oral exam for all majors; final written exam for some majors. For Ed.S.: 30 semester hours minimum beyond the master's in residence; three years' teaching experience.

FIELDS OF STUDY.

COLLEGE OF BUSINESS:
Business Administration.

BURTON COLLEGE OF EDUCATION:
Administration and Supervision. Includes principalship, supervision of instruction.
Early Childhood Education.
Educational Technology. Includes computer, instructional technology.
Elementary Education.
Health and Human Performance. Includes exercise science, health education. health promotion.
Psychology. Includes counseling, general-experimental, school psychology.
School Counseling.
Secondary Education. Includes business, English, mathematics, science, social studies, speech.
Special Education. Includes curriculum/materials, early childhood, educational diagnostician.

COLLEGE OF ENGINEERING AND TECHNOLOGY:
Chemical Engineering.
Civil Engineering.
Electrical Engineering.
Engineering Management.
Mechanical Engineering.

COLLEGE OF LIBERAL ARTS:
Creative Writing.
English.
Music Education.

COLLEGE OF NURSING:
Nursing. Includes clinical nurse specialist, nurse practitioner.
Nursing Administration.
Nursing Education.

COLLEGE OF SCIENCE:
Environment and Chemical Sciences. Includes environmental science.
Environmental and Chemical Sciences. Includes chemistry, chemistry education, environmental science education.
Mathematical Sciences. Includes computer science, mathematics, statistics.

UNIVERSITY OF MEDICINE AND DENTISTRY OF NEW JERSEY
Newark, New Jersey 07103-2400
Web site: www.umdnj.edu

Established 1970, became a free-standing University in 1981. Coed. State control. Quarter system. Special facilities: Center for Advanced Biotechnology and Medicine, Environmental and Occupational Health Science Center, New Jersey Cancer Institute, New Jersey Eye Institute. The University's NIH ranking is 55th among all U.S. institutions with 267 awards/grants worth $89,189,368. Library: 205,000 volumes, 2900 subscriptions. Total University enrollment: 4500.

Graduate School of Biomedical Science

Established in 1956 as part of the former Seton Hall College of Medicine and Dentistry and became a separate School of the State's Health Sciences University in 1969. Branch campuses located in Newark, Piscataway, and Stratford.

Annual tuition: resident full-time $5097, nonresident $7984; resident per credit $270, nonresident $407. Enrollment: full-time 729, part-time 29. Degrees conferred: M.S., Ph.D.

ADMISSIONS REQUIREMENTS. Official transcripts, GRE or MAT, statement of purpose, three letters of recommendation required in support of application. TOEFL required for all international applicants. Apply to the specific campus and program by February 1 (Fall), October 1 (Spring). Phone: (973)972-4511 (Newark); (732)235-5016 (Piscataway); (609)566-6037 (Stratford). Application fee $40.

ADMISSIONS STANDARDS. Selective. Usual minimum GPA 3.0 (A = 4).

FINANCIAL AID. Fellowships, research assistantships, teaching assistantships, traineeships, tuition waivers, Federal W/S, loans. Apply by May 1 to appropriate campus Financial Aid Office. Use FAFSA (School code: 013645).

DEGREE REQUIREMENTS. For M.S.: two-year full-time programs; thesis/nonthesis option. For Ph.D.: two- to three-year full-time program; qualifying exam; dissertation; final oral defense.

FIELDS OF STUDY.

NEWARK CAMPUS:
Biochemistry and Molecular Biology.
Biomedical Sciences.

Cell Biology and Molecular Medicine.
Experimental Pathology.
Microbiology and Molecular Genetics.
Neurosciences.
Pharmacology and Physiology.

PISCATAWAY CAMPUS:
Biochemistry and Molecular Biology.
Biomedical Engineering.
Cellular and Molecular Pharmacology.
Environmental Science/Exposure Assessment.
Molecular Genetics and Microbiology.
Physiology and Neurobiology.

STRATFORD CAMPUS:
Cell and Molecular Biology. Ph.D. only.
Molecular Biology. M.S.

New Jersey Dental School

Established 1956. Located in Newark. Annual tuition: resident $16,694, nonresident $26,134. Total average cost for all other first-year expenses: $6000. On-campus housing available. Contact housing office for both on- and off-campus information. Phone: (973)972-5362. Estimated average annual living expenses: $10,215.

Enrollment: first-year class 75; total 323 (men 55%, women 45%); postgraduates 23. Faculty: full-time 70, part-time 81. Degrees conferred: D.M.D., D.M.D.-Ph.D., Certificates.

ADMISSION REQUIREMENTS. AADSAS report, transcripts, 3 letters of recommendation, DAT required in support of application. Interview by invitation only. Preference given to state residents. Applicants must have completed at least 3 but preferably 4 years of college study; most applicants have bachelor's degree. Apply to AADSAS after June 1, before February 1. Application fee $75. Phone: (973)972-5362.

ADMISSION STANDARDS. Competitive. Mean DAT: Academic 18.87, PAT 17.36; mean GPA: 3.34 (A = 4). Gourman rating: 4.11. Accepts 20–25% of total annual applicants. Approximately 93% are state residents.

FINANCIAL AID. Scholarships, fellowships. Apply after acceptance to Office of Financial Aid. Phone: (973)972-4376. Use FAFSA. About 91% of students receive aid from School.

DEGREE REQUIREMENTS. For D.M.D.: satisfactory completion of four-year program.

FIELDS OF GRADUATE STUDY.
Anatomy.
Biochemistry and Molecular Biology.
Cell Biology and Injury Science.
Laboratory Medicine and Pathology.
Microbiology and Molecular Genetics.
Neurosciences.
Pharmacology and Toxicology.
Physiology.

CERTIFICATE PROGRAMS.
Endodontics.
Oral and Maxillofacial Surgery.
Orthodontics.
Pediatric Dentistry.
Periodontics.
Prosthodontics.

New Jersey Medical School
Web site: www.umdnj.edu

Located in Newark (07103). Annual tuition: resident $17,362, nonresident $27,169; student fees $2002. Total average figure for all other expenses: $11,000.

Enrollment: first-year class 170 (EDP 7); total 705 (men 56%, women 44%); postgraduates 318. School faculty: full-time 608. Degrees conferred: M.D., B.A./B.S.-M.D., M.D.-J.D., M.D.-M.P.H., M.D.-M.B.A., M.D.-Ph.D.

ADMISSION REQUIREMENTS. AMCAS report, transcripts, MCAT required in support of application. Applicants must have completed at least three years of college study. Preference given to New Jersey residents. Interviews by invitation only. Has EDP; apply between June 1 and August 1. Apply to Director of Admissions after June 1, before December 1. Application fee $75. Phone: (973)972-4631; fax: (973)972-7986; e-mail: njmsadmiss@ umdnj.edu.

ADMISSION STANDARDS. Competitive. Median MCAT: 9.8; median GPA: 3.44 (A = 4). Gourman rating: 3.43. Accepts 10% of total annual applications. Approximately 90% are state residents.

FINANCIAL AID. Academic Excellence Scholarships, minority scholarships, Grants-in-Aid, institutional loans, HEAL, alternative loan programs, NIH stipends, loans. Service Commitment Scholarship programs are available. The UMDNJ Financial Aid applications and information are available at the on-campus, by-invitation interview. All students are considered for all aid they are eligible for. Assistantships/fellowships may be available for Dual Degree candidates. Contact the Financial Aid Office for current information. Phone: (973)972-4376. Use FAFSA (School code: 013465), also submit Financial Aid Transcript, Federal Income Tax forms. Approximately 70% of students receive some form of financial assistance.

DEGREE REQUIREMENTS. For M.D.: satisfactory completion of four-year program. All students must pass USMLE Step 1 prior to entering third year; all students must pass USMLE Step 2 prior to awarding of M.D.

FIELDS OF GRADUATE STUDY.
Anatomy.
Biochemistry.
Cell Biology.
Microbiology and Molecular Genetics.
Neurosciences.
Oral Biology.
Pathology.
Pharmacology.
Physiology.

Robert Wood Johnson Medical School
Web site: www.rwjms.umdnj.edu

Established 1966; formerly known as Rutgers Medical School. Located at Piscataway (08854-5635) and a division at Camden. Annual tuition: resident $17,362, nonresident $27,169, student fees $1952. Total average figure for all other expenses: $11,000.

Enrollment: first-year class 142 (EDP 5); total 598 (men 54%, women 46%). Faculty: full- and part-time 636. Degrees conferred: M.D., M.D.-M.P.H., M.D.-Ph.D., M.D.-J.D. (Rutgers Law School or Seton Hall Law School), M.D.-M.S. (Seton Hall Law School), M.D.-M.S. (Medical Informatics with N.J. Institute of Technology), M.D.-M.B.A. (Rutgers School of Management).

ADMISSION REQUIREMENTS. AMCAS report, transcripts, MCAT required in support of application. Interview by invitation only. Applicants should have completed four years of college study. Preference given to state residents. Has EDP; apply between June 1 and August 1. Apply to Committee on Admissions of School after June 1, before December 15 (Fall). Application fee $75. Phone: (732)235-4576; fax: (732)235-5078.

ADMISSION STANDARDS. Competitive. Mean MCAT: 9.6; mean GPA: 3.62 (A = 4). Gourman rating: 3.26. Accepts 10–12% of total annual applicants. Approximately 90% are state residents.

FINANCIAL AID. Scholarships, minority scholarships, Grants-in-Aid, institutional loans, HEAL, alternative loan programs, Federal Perkins Loans, Stafford Subsidized and Unsubsidized Loans. Service Commitment Scholarship programs are available. Assistantships/fellowships may be available for Dual Degree candidates. UMDNJ Financial Aid applications and information are given out at the on-campus by-invitation interview. Most aid is based on demonstrated need. Contact the University's Financial Aid Office for current information. Phone: (973)972-7030. Use FAFSA (School code: 013645), also submit Financial Aid Transcript, Federal Income Tax forms, statement of educational purpose and default/refund statement. Approximately 80% of students receive some form of financial assistance.

DEGREE REQUIREMENTS. For M.D.: satisfactory completion of four-year program. All students must pass USMLE Step 1 prior to entering third year; all students must pass USMLE Step 2 prior to awarding of M.D.

FIELDS OF GRADUATE STUDY.
Biochemistry.
Biomedical Engineering.
Cell Biology.
Genetics.
Immunology.
Microbiology.
Molecular Biology.
Pathology.
Pharmacology.
Physiology.

School of Osteopathic Medicine
Web site: www.som.umdnj.edu

Founded 1976. Located in Stratford (08084-1504). No on-campus housing available.

Annual tuition: resident $16,694, nonresident $26,124. Enrollment: first-year class 75, total 302 (men 56%, women 44%), 90% state residents. Faculty: full-time 107, part-time 18. Degrees conferred: D.O., D.O.-PhD., D.O.-J.D., D.O.-M.P.A., D.O.-M.P.H.

ADMISSION REQUIREMENTS. Bachelor's degree from an accredited institution required. Apply through AACOMAS (file after June 1, before February 1), submit MCAT (will accept test results from last three years), official transcripts for each school attended (should show at least 90 semester credits/135 quarter credits), service processing fee. Preference given to state residents. After a review of the AACOMAS application and supporting documents a decision is made concerning which candidates should receive supplemental materials. The supplemental application, an application fee of $75, a personal statement, and three recommendations (one from a D.O.) should be returned to Office of Admission as soon as possible. Joint Degree applicants must apply to and be accepted to both Schools, contact the admissions office for current information and specific admissions requirements. Interviews are by invitation only and generally for final selection. In addition, international applicants must submit foreign transcripts to the World Education Service for translation and evaluation. TOEFL may be required of those applicants whose native language is other than English. First-year students admitted Fall only. Rolling admissions process, notification starts in January and is finished when class is filled. Applicants response to offer due within two weeks of receipt of acceptance letter. Phone: (856)566-7050; fax: (856)566-6895.

ADMISSION STANDARDS. Selective. Mean MCAT: 8.4; mean GPA: 3.46 (A = 4). Accepts approximately 15% of annual applications. Usual minimum average: 3.0 (A = 4).

FINANCIAL AID. Scholarships, merit scholarship, MLK scholarships, grants, institutional loans, NOF, HEAL, alternative loan programs, NIH stipends, Federal Perkins Loans, Stafford Subsidized and Unsubsidized Loans. Service Obligation Scholarship programs, Military and National Health Service programs are available. Financial Aid applications and information are generally available at the by-invitation interview; however, all accepted students are sent applications and information. All accepted applicants are considered for merit scholarships. Contact the Financial Aid Office for current information. Phone: (856)566-6008. Use FAFSA (School code: 013465), also submit Financial Aid Transcript, Federal Income Tax forms. Approximately 80% of students receive some form of financial assistance.

DEGREE REQUIREMENTS. For D.O.: satisfactory completion of four-year program. All students must pass the National Board of Osteopathic Medical Examination Level I and II prior to the awarding of D.O.

MEHARRY MEDICAL COLLEGE
Nashville, Tennessee 37208-9989
Web site: www.mmc.edu

Founded 1876. CGS member. Coed. Private control. Semester system. The College's NIH ranking is 152nd among all U.S. institutions with 43 awards/grants worth $18,534,017. Library: 98,000 volumes, 1100 subscriptions. Total College enrollment: 900.

On-campus housing for single students only. Average academic year housing cost: $6500 (including board).

School of Graduate Studies

Established 1938. Annual tuition: $9400; M.S.P.H. $6500. Enrollment: full-time 151, part-time 11. Faculty: full-time 9. Degrees conferred: M.S.P.H., Ph.D.

ADMISSION REQUIREMENTS. Official transcripts, GRE, two letters of recommendation, statement summarizing research interests and career plans required in support of School's application. TOEFL required for international applicants. Accepts transfer applicants. Graduates of unaccredited institutions not considered. Apply to Director of Admissions and Records by June 1. Application fee $45. Phone: (615)327-6533; fax: (615)321-2933.

ADMISSION STANDARDS. Competitive. Usual minimum average: 3.0 (A = 4).

FINANCIAL AID. Annual awards from institutional funds: fellowships, scholarships, assistantships, internships, Federal W/S, loans. Apply to Financial Aid Office by April 1. Phone: (615)327-6826. Use FAFSA.

DEGREE REQUIREMENTS. For M.S.P.H.: 60 credits minimum; thesis and extensive fieldwork. For Ph.D.: 40 credits minimum beyond the bachelor's, at least 30 in residence; qualifying exam; dissertation; final oral exam.

FIELDS OF STUDY.
Biochemistry.

Biomedical Sciences.
Cell Biology.
Community Health Sciences. M.S.P.H.
Microbiology.
Molecular Biology.
Neurosciences.
Pharmacology.
Physiology.

School of Dentistry

Organized 1886. Annual tuition: $21,824. Housing for 158 married students, 100 single graduate students. Average academic year housing cost: $15,595. Apply to Director of Housing Services. Total average cost for all other first-year expenses: $2719.

Enrollment: first-year class 51; total 203 (men 35%, women 65%). School faculty: full-time 62, part-time 39. Degrees conferred: D.D.S., B.S.-D.D.S. (Fisk University).

ADMISSION REQUIREMENTS. AADSAS report, transcripts, three letters of recommendation, DAT, supplemental application required in support of School's application. Applicants must have completed at least three years of college study. Interview not required. Preference given to SREB member states. Accepts transfer applicants from U.S. and Canadian dental schools. Apply to Office of Admissions and Records after June 1 and before March 1. Application fee $45. Phone: (615)327-6223.

ADMISSION STANDARDS. Selective. Mean DAT: Academic 15.6, PAT 14.8; mean GPA: 2.82 (A = 4). Gourman rating: 4.3. Accepts 15–20% of total annual applicants. Approximately 10% are state residents.

FINANCIAL AID. Scholarships, grants, loans. Apply to Director of Financial Aid after acceptance. Phone: (615)327-8626. Use FAFSA. About 98% of students receive some aid from School funds.

DEGREE REQUIREMENTS. For D.D.S.: satisfactory completion of forty-four-month program.

School of Medicine

Founded 1876 as Medical Department of Central Tennessee College; became independent in 1915. Annual tuition: $23,208; student fees $3911. Total average cost for all other expenses: $10,000.

Enrollment: first-year class 80 (EDP 0); total 322 (men 44%, women 56%). Degrees conferred: M.D., M.D.-M.S., M.D.-Ph.D.

ADMISSION REQUIREMENTS. AMCAS, transcripts, MCAT, interview required in support of application. Applicants must have completed at least three years of college study. Accepts transfer applicants. Has EDP; apply between June 1 and August 1. Apply to Director of Admissions after June 1, before December 15. Application fee $60. Phone: (615)327-6223; fax: (615)327-6228.

ADMISSION STANDARDS. Selective. Mean MCAT: 7.6; mean GPA: 3.0 (A = 4). Gourman rating: 3.77. Accepts about 10% of total applicants. Approximately 25% are state residents.

FINANCIAL AID. Scholarships, Grants-in-Aid, institutional loans, HEAL, alternative loan programs, Federal Perkins Loans, Stafford Subsidized and Unsubsidized Loans. Service Commitment Scholarship programs are available. Assistantships/fellowships may be available for Combined Degree candidates. Financial Aid applications and information are given out at the on-campus by-invitation interview. Contact the Financial Aid Office for current information. Phone: (615)327-6826. Use FAFSA (School code: G03506), also submit Financial Aid Transcript, Federal Income Tax forms. Approximately 85% of students receive some form of financial assistance.

DEGREE REQUIREMENTS. For M.D.: satisfactory completion of four- or five-year program. All students must pass USMLE Step 1 prior to entering third year; all students must pass USMLE Step 2 prior to awarding of M.D. For M.D.-M.S.: generally a four-and-one-half- to five-and-one-half-year program. For M.D.-Ph.D.: generally a seven-year program.

FIELDS OF GRADUATE STUDY.
Biochemistry.
Cell Biology.
Microbiology.
Molecular Biology.
Neurosciences.
Pharmacology.
Physiology.

THE UNIVERSITY OF MEMPHIS
Memphis, Tennessee 38152
Web site: www.memphis.edu

Established in 1912, name changed from Memphis State University in 1994. CGS member. Coed. State control. Semester system. Special facilities: Center for Applied Psychological Research, Center for Earthquake Research and Information, Center for Research Initiatives and Strategies for the Communicatively Impaired, Center for Research in Educational Policy, the Institute of Egyptian Art and Archaeology. Library: more than 1,000,000 volumes, 10,000 subscriptions. Total University enrollment: 20,000.

Annual tuition: resident $4407, nonresident $10,568. On-campus housing for single students and families. Apply to Director of Residence Life. Phone: (901)678-2295. Day-care facilities available.

Graduate School

Graduate study since 1951. Enrollment: full-time 2236, part-time 2637 (men 45%, women 55%). Faculty: full-time 524, part-time 75. Degrees conferred: M.A., M.A.T., M.B.A., M.H.A., M.S., M.F.A., M.P.A., M.C.R.P., D.M.A., M.Mu., Ed.S., Ed.D., Ph.D.

ADMISSION REQUIREMENTS: Transcripts, GRE/GMAT/MAT required in support of School's application. On-line application available. For additional requirements contact individual program chair. TOEFL required of international students. Accepts transfer applicants. Graduates of unaccredited colleges not considered. Graduate School application deadlines: August 1 (Fall), December 1 (Spring), May 1 (Summer). Some programs may have earlier deadlines. Apply to both Graduate Admissions and to the appropriate Department. Application fee $25, $50 for international applicants. Phone: (901)678-2911; fax: (901)678-3003; e-mail: gradsch@memphis.edu.

ADMISSION STANDARDS. Selective for most departments, very selective for some departments. Usual minimum average: 2.75 (A = 4).

FINANCIAL AID. Fellowships, research assistantships, administrative assistantships, teaching assistantships, grants, internships, Federal W/S, loans. Apply to individual chairs for assistantships; to Financial Aid Office for all other programs.

Phone: (901)678-4825; fax: (901)678-3590. Use FAFSA (University code: 003509). Aid available for part-time students.

DEGREE REQUIREMENTS. For master's: 30 semester hours minimum; thesis; final oral/written exam; or 36 semester hours minimum; no thesis; final oral/written exam for most departments. For M.F.A.: 60 semester hour program; comprehensive exam; thesis/exhibition. For Doctorates: 72 credits, three years, at least one year in full-time residence; reading knowledge of one foreign language or statistics/research tool or both; comprehensive exam; admission to candidacy; dissertation; final oral exam. Contact program chair for additional degree requirements.

FIELDS OF STUDY.

Accounting. Includes accounting systems, taxation. M.S.

Anthropology. Includes medical, public archaeology, urban. M.A.

Art. Includes ceramics, graphic design, interior design, painting, printmaking/photography, sculpture. M.F.A.

Art History. Includes Egyptian art and archeology. M.A.

Audiology. Au.D.

Biology. Includes microbiology, molecular cell sciences. M.S., Ph.D.

Biomedical Engineering. Ph.D.

Business Administration. Includes accounting, economics, finance, insurance and real estate, international business, law, management, management information systems, management science and operations, marketing. M.B.A., M.S., Ph.D.

Chemistry. Includes analytical, computational, inorganic, physical. M.S., Ph.D.

City and Regional Planning. M.C.R.P.

Civil Engineering. Includes environmental, foundation, structural, transportation, water resources. M.S.

Clinical Nutrition. M.S.

Communication. Includes film and video production. M.A.

Communication Arts. Ph.D.

Consumer Science and Education. M.S.

Counseling and Personnel Services. Includes community agency, rehabilitation, school, student personnel services. M.S., Ed.D.

Counseling Psychology. Ph.D.

Creative Writing. M.F.A.

Criminal Justice. M.A.

Earth Sciences. Ph.D.

Economics. M.A.

Education. Ed.S.

Educational Psychology and Research. M.S., Ph.D.

Electrical Engineering. Includes automatic control systems, communication and propagation systems, electro-optical systems, engineering computer systems. M.S.

Electronic Commerce. M.S.

Engineering. Includes civil, electrical, mechanical. Ph.D.

Engineering Technology. Includes architectural, electronics, manufacturing. M.S.

English. Includes applied linguistics, ESL, language and linguistics, literature, writing (creative and professional). M.A.

Geography. M.A., M.S.

Geological Sciences. Includes geology, geophysics. M.S.

Health Administration. M.H.A. only.

Higher and Adult Education. Ed.D.

History. Includes ancient Egyptian. M.A., Ph.D.

Human Movement Science. Includes exercise and sport sciences, health promotion, sport and leisure commerce. M.S.

Industrial and Systems Engineering. M.S.

Instruction and Curriculum Leadership. Includes early childhood, elementary, secondary, special. M.A.T., M.S., Ed.D.

Journalism. Includes journal administration. M.A.

Leadership and Policy Studies. Includes leadership, school administration and supervision (M.S.), community education, educational leadership, policy studies (Ed.D.). M.S., Ed.D.

Liberal Studies. M.A.L.S.

Mathematics. Includes applied, applied statistics, bioinformatics, computer science, statistics. M.S., Ph.D.

Mechanical Engineering. Includes design and mechanical systems, energy systems, mechanical systems, power systems. M.S.

Music. Includes composition, jazz and studio, music education, music history, pedagogy, performance, Orff-Schulwerk, sacred (M.Mu.), composition, music education, performance, sacred (D.M.A.), musicology (Ph.D.). M.Mu., D.M.A., Ph.D.

Philosophy. M.A., Ph.D.

Physics. M.S.

Political Science. M.A.

Psychology. Includes general (M.S.), clinical, experimental, school (Ph.D). M.S., Ph.D.

Public Administration. Includes general, health services administration, human resources administration, nonprofit administration, urban management and planning. M.P.A.

Romance Languages. Includes French, Spanish. M.A.

School Psychology. M.A.

Sociology. M.A.

Theatre. M.F.A.

Cecil C. Humphreys School of Law (38152)

Web site: www.law.memphis.edu

Founded 1962. ABA approved since 1965. AALS member. Semester system. Law library: 279,886 volumes, 2513 subscriptions; has LEXIS, NEXIS, WESTLAW, DIALOG.

Annual tuition: full-time, resident $5617, nonresident $14,997; part-time resident $4869, nonresident $12,879. On-campus housing available; expenses: $12,187 (includes room and board). Apply to Director of Residence Life.

Enrollment: first-year class full-time 148, part-time 14; total 431 (men 53%, women 47%). Faculty: full-time 19, part-time 23. Student to faculty ratio 18.4 to 1. Degrees conferred: J.D., J.D.-M.B.A.

ADMISSION REQUIREMENTS. LSDAS Law School report, bachelor's degree, transcripts, LSAT required in support of application. Interview not required. Accepts transfer applicants. Graduates of unaccredited colleges not considered. Apply by February 15. Fall admission only. Application fee $25. Phone: (901)678-5403; fax: (901)678-5210.

ADMISSION STANDARDS. Mean LSAT: full-time 153, part-time 147; mean GPA: full-time 3.25, part-time 3.13 (A = 4). Gourman rating: 2.63. *U.S. News & World Report* ranking is in the third tier of all U.S. law schools. Selective. Accepts 40–45% of total annual applicants.

FINANCIAL AID. Scholarships, assistantships, Federal W/S, loans. Apply to Financial Aid Office by April 1. About 28% of students receive aid other than loans from School. Use FAFSA (School code: 003509).

DEGREE REQUIREMENTS. For J.D.: satisfactory completion of three-year program; 90 credit-hour program.

MERCER UNIVERSITY

Macon, Georgia 31207-0001

Web site: www.mercer.edu

Founded 1833. Located 92 miles S of Atlanta. Private control. Baptist. Semester system. Library: 439,100 volumes, 9500 subscriptions. Total University enrollment 5000.

Tuition: per credit hour $300, Business $454. On-campus housing for 70 married students, 650 men, 510 women. Average academic year housing cost: $4500–$6000 for married students,

$5800 (includes full board) for single students. Phone: (478)301-2687.

Graduate Studies

Enrollment: full-time 46, part-time 207. University faculty teaching graduate students: full-time 57, part-time 13. Degrees conferred: M.Ed., M.B.A., M.S.E., M.S., M.S.M., M.F.S., S.Ed.

ADMISSION REQUIREMENTS. Transcripts, letters of reference, GRE/NTE/MAT/GMAT tests required in support of application. On-line application available. TOEFL required for international applicants. Interview not required. Accepts transfer applicants. Graduates of unaccredited institutions sometimes considered. Apply to Director of Graduate Programs; no specified closing dates. Application fee: none. Phone: (478)301-2700; fax: (478)301-2828; e-mail: admissions@mercer.edu.

ADMISSION STANDARDS. Selective for most departments. Usual minimum average: 3.0 (A = 4); GRE score: 35th percentile.

FINANCIAL AID. Supervising teacher scholarships, internships, Federal W/S, loans (academic year). Approved for VA benefits. Apply to the Financial Aid Office; no specified closing date. Phone: (478)301-2670. Use FAFSA. Aid available for part-time students.

DEGREE REQUIREMENTS. For M.Ed., M.B.A.: 36 semester hours minimum. For M.S.E., M.S.: 33 semester hours minimum; thesis. For M.S.M., M.F.S.: 45 semester hours minimum. For S.Ed.: 30 semester hours minimum; special project.

FIELDS OF STUDY.

MACON CAMPUS

SCHOOL OF EDUCATION:
Broad-Field Science Education (7–12).
Early Childhood Education (P–5).
English Education (7–12).
Mathematics Education (7–12).
Middle Grades Education (4–8).
Reading (P–12).
Social Science Education (7–12).

SCHOOL OF ENGINEERING:
Electrical Engineering.
Engineering Management.
Mechanical Engineering.
Software Engineering.
Software Systems.
Technical Communication Management.
Technical Management.

STETSON SCHOOL OF BUSINESS AND ECONOMICS:
Business Administration. M.B.A.

CECIL B. DAY CAMPUS (ATLANTA)

SCHOOL OF EDUCATION:
Early Childhood Education (P–5).
Middle Grades Education (4–8).
Reading (P–12).

SCHOOL OF ENGINEERING:
Electrical Engineering.
Engineering Management.
Mechanical Engineering.
Software Engineering.
Software Systems.
Technical Communication Management.
Technical Management.

STETSON SCHOOL OF BUSINESS AND ECONOMICS:
Business Administration.
Executive Business Administration.
Health Care Management.

Walter F. George School of Law

Web site: www.law.mercer.edu

Established 1873. Oldest private law school in U.S. ABA approved since 1925. AALS member since 1923. Semester system. Law library: 298,000 volumes, 3360 subscriptions; has LEXIS, NEXIS, WESTLAW, DIALOG.

Annual tuition: full-time $17,490. No on-campus housing available.

Enrollment: first-year class 173; total full-time 430 (men 51%, women 49%); no part-time students. Faculty: full-time 20, part-time 30. Student to faculty ratio 17.9 to 1. Degrees conferred: J.D., J.D.-M.B.A.

ADMISSION REQUIREMENTS. LSDAS Law School report, bachelor's degree, transcripts, LSAT, three letters of recommendation required in support of application. Interviews are encouraged. Accepts transfer applicants. Graduate of unaccredited colleges not considered. Apply to Director of Admissions after September 1, before March 15. Beginning students admitted Fall only. Application fee $45. Phone: (478)301-2605; fax: (478)301-2989.

ADMISSION STANDARDS. Selective. Mean LSAT: 153; mean GPA: 3.11 (A = 4). Gourman rating: 2.94. *U.S. News & World Report* ranking is in the third tier of all U.S. law schools. Accepts 45–50% of total annual applicants.

FINANCIAL AID. Scholarships, Federal W/S, loans. Apply by January 15 (Scholarships), May 1 (flexible) to Director of Admissions. Use FAFSA (School code: E00561). About 32% of students receive aid other than loans from School.

DEGREE REQUIREMENTS. For J.D.: satisfactory completion of three-year program; 90 credit-hour program. For M.B.A.: see Graduate School listing above.

School of Medicine

Web site: medicine.mercer.edu

Established 1982. Annual tuition: resident $23,620. Enrollment: first-year class 56 (EDP 15); total 175 (men 55%, women 45%). Faculty: full-time 186, part-time 81. Degree conferred: M.D.

ADMISSION REQUIREMENTS. AMCAS report, transcripts, MCAT, two letters of recommendation or one premedical committee evaluation, personal history, Certificate of Georgia residency required in support of application. Interview by invitation only. Accepts only state residents. Has EDP; apply between June 1 and August 1. Graduates of unaccredited colleges not considered. Apply to Office of Admissions and Student Affairs after June 1, before November 1. Application fee $40. Phone: (478)301-2524.

ADMISSION STANDARDS. Competitive. Mean MCAT: 8.4; mean GPA: 3.33 (A = 4). Gourman rating: 3.05. Admits about 30% of total annual applicants. 100% are state residents.

FINANCIAL AID. Scholarships, loans. Apply after acceptance to Office of Admissions and Student Affairs. Use FAFSA (School code: E00560). About 90% of students receive some aid from School.

DEGREE REQUIREMENTS. For M.D.: satisfactory completion of four-year program. All students must pass USMLE Step 1 prior to entering third year; all students must pass USMLE Step 2 prior to awarding of M.D.

MIAMI UNIVERSITY
Oxford, Ohio 45056
Web site: www.muohio.edu

Founded 1809. Located 35 miles NW of Cincinnati. CGS member. Coed. State control. Semester system. Special facilities: academic centers located in Hamilton, Middletown; Bachelor Wildlife Reserve, Willard Sherman Turrell Herbarium, Ecology Research Center, Institute of Environmental Sciences, Scripps Gerontology Center. Library: 1,800,000 volumes, 12,200 subscriptions. Total University enrollment: 16,000.

Annual tuition: full-time, resident $5802, nonresident $12,842. Limited on-campus housing available. Annual academic year housing cost: $6200. Apply to Office of Student Housing for housing information. Phone: (513)529-5000. Day-care facilities available.

Graduate School

Graduate study since 1826, became Graduate School 1947. Enrollment: full-time 996, part-time 231. Faculty teaching graduate students: full- and part-time 623. Degrees conferred: M.A., M.A.T., M.B.A., M.Ed., M.F.A., M.M., M.S., M.Arch., M.Env.Sci., M.G.S., M.S. in Stats., M.T.S.C., M.Acc., Specialist, Ph.D.

ADMISSION REQUIREMENTS. Two transcripts, GRE/MAT/GMAT required in support of School's application. On-line application available. Proof of proficiency in English or TOEFL required of international applicants. Accepts transfer applicants. Graduates of unaccredited institutions not considered. Apply to School at least one month prior to registration. Financial Aid applicants apply by March 1 (Fall). Application fee $35. Phone: (513)529-4126; fax: (513)529-4127.

ADMISSION STANDARDS. Selective for all departments. Minimum average: 2.75 (A = 4).

FINANCIAL AID. Annual awards from institutional funds: scholarships, grants, tuition waivers, research assistantships, administrative assistantships, teaching assistantships, fellowships, internships, Federal W/S, loans. Apply by March 1 to Dean of Graduate School. Phone: (513)529-8734. Use FAFSA. About 75% of full-time students receive aid other than loans from both School and outside sources. Aid available for part-time students.

DEGREE REQUIREMENTS. For M.A.: 30 credit hours minimum, at least 15 in residence; preliminary oral/written exam; thesis; final oral/written exam. For M.A.T.: 30 credit hours minimum, at least 15 in residence; thesis; preliminary oral/written exam; final oral/written exam. For M.B.A.: 76 credit hours minimum, all in residence; oral/written comprehensive exam. For M.Env.Set.: 36 credit hours minimum; written comprehensive exam; thesis. For M.Ed.: 30 credit hours minimum; field study; preliminary oral/written exam; comprehensive oral/written exam. For M.F.A., M.Arch.: 60 credit hours minimum; preliminary oral/written exam; thesis; final project; final oral/written exam. For M.M.: 33 credit hours generally required. For M.S., M.S. in Stats.: 30 hours minimum, at least 15 in residence; preliminary oral/written exam; final oral/written exam. For M.T.S.C.: 32 credit hours minimum, at least 16 in residence; thesis or internship; qualifying exam; final oral/written exam. For M.Acc.: 33 credit hours minimum, at least 17 in residence; oral/written comprehensive exam. For M.G.S., Specialist: 30 credits beyond the master's, at least 24 in residence. For Ph.D.: 60 credit hours beyond the master's, at least 48 in residence; language requirement determined by department; oral/written comprehensive exam; dissertation; final exam.

FIELDS OF STUDY.
Accountancy. GMAT for admission. Master's only.

Architecture. Master's only.
Art. Master's only.
Art Education. Master's only.
Biological Sciences. Master's only.
Botany. M.A., M.S., M.A.T., Ph.D.
Business Administration. GMAT for admission. Master's only.
Chemistry. M.S., Ph.D.
College Student Personnel.
Economics. Master's only.
Education. Includes adolescent, educational administration, student personnel services, curriculum and leadership, elementary, secondary, reading, sport studies, exercise and health studies, educational psychology. Ph.D./Ed.D. in administration and curriculum only.
English. M.A., M.A.T., M.T.S.C., Ph.D.
Environmental Sciences. MAT for admission. Master's only.
Exercise and Health Studies.
Family and Child Studies.
Finance. GMAT for admission. Master's only.
French. Master's only.
Geography. Master's only.
Geology. M.A., M.S., Ph.D.
Gerontological Studies. Master's only.
History. Master's only.
Management. GMAT for admission. Master's only.
Management Information Systems. Master's only.
Marketing. GMAT for admission. Master's only.
Mass Communication. Master's only.
Mathematics. Master's only.
Microbiology. M.A., M.S., Ph.D.
Molecular Biology.
Music. Includes music education, performance. Master's only.
Paper Science and Engineering. Master's only.
Philosophy. Master's only.
Physics. Master's only.
Political Science. M.A., M.A.T., Ph.D.
Psychology. GRE for admission. Ph.D. only.
Religion. Master's only.
School Psychology. Nine-month internship for M.S. M.S., Ed.S.
Spanish. Master's only.
Special Education. Master's only.
Speech Communication. Master's only.
Speech Pathology and Audiology. Master's only.
Sport Studies.
Statistics. Master's only.
System Analysis. Master's only.
Theater. Master's only.
Women's Studies.
Zoology. M.A., M.S., M.A.T., Ph.D.

UNIVERSITY OF MIAMI
Coral Gables, Florida 33124
Web site: www.miami.edu

Founded 1925. Located 12 miles SW of Miami. CGS member. Coed. Private control. Semester system. Special facilities: Lowe Art Museum, Bascome Palmer Eye Institute, Comprehensive Cancer Center for Florida, Rosenstiel School of Marine and Atmospheric Sciences, Graduate School International Studies, Mailman Center for Child Development, the Ungar Computing Center; Organization for Tropical Studies, Inc., sponsoring university of the Oak Ridge Associated Universities in Oak Ridge, Tennessee, special environmental-ecology field stations, Long Pine Key, Fairchild Tropical Gardens. The University's NIH ranking is 58th among all U.S. institutions with 305 awards/grants worth $85,650,494. Library: 2,030,000 volumes, 17,155 subscriptions. Total University enrollment: 13,500.

Tuition: per credit $960. On-campus housing for married and single students. Average academic year housing cost: $6935. Apply to Director, Residence Halls. Phone: (305)284-4505.

Graduate School

Organized 1941. Enrollment: full-time 2577, part-time 669. Graduate faculty: full- and part-time 750. Degrees conferred: M.A., M.S., M.B.A., M.S.Ed., M.Arch., M.M., M.F.A., M.P.Acc., M.S.Tax., M.P.H., M.S.P.H., M.P.A., M.P.T., M.S.P.T., M.S.N., M.S.B.E., M.S.I.E., M.S.C.E., M.S.M.E., M.S.E.C.F., M.S.O.E., Spec.M., Ed.S., Ed.D., Ph.D., D.M.A., D.A.

ADMISSION REQUIREMENTS. Transcripts, letters of recommendation, GRE Subject Tests required in support of School's application. On-line applications available. GMAT for M.B.A. TOEFL required for international applicants. Interview required for some programs. Graduates of unaccredited institutions not considered. Apply to individual program directors. Admissions by February 1 (Fall). Application fee $50. Phone: (305)284-4154; fax: (305)284-5441; e-mail: graduateschool@miami.edu.

ADMISSION STANDARDS. Selective for most departments, very competitive for others. Usual minimum average: 3.0 (A = 4).

FINANCIAL AID. Annual awards from institutional funds: scholarships, fellowships, research assistantships, teaching assistantships, internships, Federal W/S, loans. Approved for VA benefits. Apply by February 1 to individual program directors for scholarships, assistantships, fellowships; to Financial Aid Office for all other programs. Phone: (305)284-5212; fax: (305)284-4082. Use FAFSA. About 50% of students receive aid other than loans from University and outside sources. Aid available for part-time students.

DEGREE REQUIREMENTS. For M.A., M.S.: 30 semester credits minimum, at least 24 in residence; reading knowledge of one foreign language for many departments; thesis/comprehensive exam; up to 6 credits for thesis if required. For M.B.A.: 39 credits minimum, at least 30 in residence; additional study may be required, depending upon previous preparation. For M.S.Ed.: 30–60 credits, depending on department, at least 30 in residence. For M.M.: 30 credits minimum, at least 24 in residence; thesis for up to 6 credits for majors in music education or theory-composition; recital for three credits for applied music major; final oral exam in defense of thesis for music education majors. For M.F.A.: 36–60 credits, depending on department. For D.M.A.: 90 credits beyond the bachelor's, essentially the same as for the Ph.D., except a creative effort/performance and doctoral essay instead of dissertation. For D.A.: essentially the same as for the Ph.D., except a college teaching internship and scholarly investigation replace the dissertation. For Ph.D.: 60 credits minimum beyond the bachelor's, at least 24 in residence and two consecutive semesters in full-time attendance; qualifying exam; dissertation for at least 12 credits; final oral exam; final written exam sometimes required. For Ed.D.: 85 credits minimum beyond the bachelor's, at least 30 in residence and two consecutive semesters in full-time attendance; preliminary exam; written comprehensive exam; proficiency in four research tools, which may include language, statistics, or similar methods; research project; final oral exam.

FIELDS OF STUDY.

COLLEGE OF ARTS AND SCIENCES:
Art. Includes art history (M.A.), painting, sculpture, weaving, graphic design, printmaking, art studio. M.F.A.
Biology.
Chemistry.
Computer Science.
English and Creative Writing.
Foreign Languages. Includes French, German, Portuguese, Russian, Spanish; three languages for M.A.
History.
International Studies.
Liberal Studies.
Mathematics.
Philosophy.
Physics.
Psychology.
Sociology.
Statistics.

SCHOOL OF BUSINESS ADMINISTRATION:
Accounting.
Business Administration.
Computer Information System.
Economics.
Management Science.
Public Administration.

SCHOOL OF EDUCATION AND ALLIED PROFESSIONS:
Childhood Special Education
Counseling Psychology.
Elementary Education.
Emotional Handicaps/Learning Disabilities.
Enrollment Management.
Exercise Physiology.
Marriage and Family Therapy.
Mental Health Counseling.
Pre-Kindergarten/Primary Education.
Reading.
Reading/Learning Disabilities.
Research and Evaluation.
Research/Exercise Physiology.
Research in Education and Behavioral Sciences.
Specialist in Education.
Sport Medicine.
Sports Administration.
Sports Health/Athletic Training.
TESOL.
Teaching English as a Foreign Language.

COLLEGE OF ENGINEERING:
Architectural Engineering.
Biomedical Engineering.
Civil Engineering.
Electrical Engineering.
Environmental Engineering.
Industrial Engineering.
Mechanical Engineering.

ROSENSTILL SCHOOL OF MARINE AND ATMOSPHERIC SCIENCES:
Applied Marine Physics.
Marine Affairs and Policy.
Marine and Atmospheric Chemistry.
Marine Biology and Fisheries.
Marine Geology and Geophysics.
Meteorology and Physical Oceanography.
Joint Degree. Programs with Engineering and Law Schools available.

SCHOOL OF MEDICINE—LIFE SCIENCES:
Biochemistry and Molecular Biology.
Cellular and Molecular Biology.
Epidemiology and Public Health.
Microbiology and Immunology.
Molecular and Cellular Pharmacology.
Molecular Cell and Development Biology.

Neuroscience.
Pharmacology.
Physiology and Biophysics.
Physical Therapy.
Radiological Science.

SCHOOL OF MUSIC:
Accompanying and Chamber Music.
Composition.
Conducting. Includes instrumental, choral.
Electronic Music.
Jazz Composition.
Jazz Performance.
Keyboard Performance and Pedagogy.
Media Writing and Production.
Music Business and Entertainment Industries.
Music Education.
Music Engineering Technology.
Musicology.
Music Performance.
Music Theory.
Music Therapy.
Studio Jazz Writing.

SCHOOL OF NURSING:
Adult Health.
Transcultural Nursing.

SCHOOL OF ARCHITECTURE:
Architecture.

School of Law
Web site: www.law.miami.edu

Established 1926. ABA approved since 1941. AALS member. Semester system. Full-time (day), part-time (evening) study. Special facility: Center for Ethics and Public Service. Special program: summer study abroad at University College, London, England. Law library: 533,178 volumes, 6923 subscriptions; has LEXIS, NEXIS, WESTLAW, DIALOG, CCH.

Annual tuition: full-time $24,168, part-time $17,870. On-campus housing available for both single and married students. Contact Department of Residence Halls. Phone: (305)284-4505. Law students tend to live off-campus. Contact office of Student Recruitment for off-campus information. Off-campus housing and personal expenses: approximately $16,330.

Enrollment: first-year class 340 full-time, 51 part-time; total 1079 (men 53%, women 47%). Faculty: full-time 42, part-time 103. Student to faculty ratio 20.5 to 1. Degrees conferred: J.D., J.D.-M.B.A., J.D.-M.P.H., J.D.-M.Marine Affairs. LL.M. (Taxation, Estate Planning, Real Property Development), LL.M. (Inter-American Law, International Law, Ocean and Coastal Law), LL.M. (Comparative Law; for persons who have completed a basic legal education and received a university degree in law in another country).

ADMISSION REQUIREMENTS. LSDAS Law School report, bachelor's degree, transcripts, LSAT, three letters of recommendation, personal statement required in support of application. Interview not required. Accepts transfer applicants. Graduates of unaccredited colleges not considered. Admits Fall only. Apply to Director of Law Admissions after September 1, before July 1. Application fee $50. Phone: (305)284-2523; fax: (305) 284-3084.

ADMISSION STANDARDS. Selective. Mean LSAT: full-time 154, part-time 150; mean GPA: full-time 3.34, part-time 3.09 (A = 4). Gourman rating: 3.35. *U.S. News & World Report* ranking is in the second tier of all U.S. law schools. Accepts 45–50% of total annual applicants.

FINANCIAL AID. Scholarships, Federal W/S, loans. Apply to Financial Aid Office by March 1 (Fall), July 1 (Spring). Use FAFSA (School code: E00532). About 30% of students receive aid other than loans from School funds.

DEGREE REQUIREMENTS. For J.D.: 88 credits minimum, at least the last 28 credits and 36 weeks in residence. For LL.M.: at least 24 credits minimum beyond the J.D. and 36 weeks in resident; thesis.

School of Medicine (33101)
Web site: www.med.miami.edu

Established 1952. Located next to Jackson Memorial Hospital in the Civic Center area of Miami. Block curriculum system. Special facilities: Applebaum Magnetic Resonance Imaging Center, Bascombe Palmer Eye Institute/Anne Bates Leach Eye Hospital, Sylvester Comprehensive Cancer Center, Ryder Trauma Center, Diabetes Research Institute, Mailman Center for Child Development. Affiliated hospitals: Jackson Memorial Hospital, Veterans Affairs Medical Center. Special Programs: Summer programs for underrepresented minorities. Library: 180,000 volumes, 2100 subscriptions.

Annual tuition: resident $27,223, nonresident $35,670; fees $578. No on-campus housing available. Contact Admissions Office for off-campus housing information. Off-campus housing and personal expenses: approximately $13,840.

Enrollment: first-year class 145 (EDP 10); total full-time 578 (men 50%, women 50%). Faculty: full-time 1077, part-time 60. Degrees conferred: M.D., B.S.-M.D., M.D.-M.S., M.D.-Ph.D. The M.S. and Ph.D. are offered through the Graduate School.

ADMISSION REQUIREMENTS. AMCAS, transcripts, undergraduate faculty evaluation, two personal references, MCAT (preferably in Spring) required in support of application. Interview by invitation only. Applicants must have completed at least three years of college study. Preference given to Florida residents. Accepts transfer applicants. Apply to Office of Admissions after June 1, before December 15. Application fee $55. Phone: (305)547-6791; fax: (305)547-6548. For M.D.-Ph.D. program GRE required. Application fee $50.

ADMISSION STANDARDS. Selective. Mean MCAT: 9.3; mean GPA: 3.66 (A = 4). Gourman rating: 3.78. *U.S. News & World Report* ranking is in the top 50 of all U.S. medical schools. Accepts 20% of total annual applicants. Approximately 90% are state residents.

FINANCIAL AID. Limited. Scholarships, loans. Apply to Office of Financial Aid after acceptance, before April 1. Phone: (305)547-6211. Use FAFSA. About 80% of students receive aid from School and outside sources.

DEGREE REQUIREMENTS. For B.S.-M.D.: satisfactory completion of seven-year program. For M.D.: satisfactory completion of four-year program. For Ph.D. to M.D.: satisfactory completion of two-year M.D. program. For M.S., Ph.D.: see Graduate School listing above.

FIELDS OF GRADUATE STUDY.
Anatomy.
Biochemistry.
Biophysics.
Cell Biology.
Immunology.
Microbiology.
Molecular Biology.
Neurosciences.
Pharmacology.
Physiology.

MICHIGAN STATE UNIVERSITY

East Lansing, Michigan 48824-1020

Web site: www.msu.edu

Founded 1855. Located 80 miles NW of Detroit. CGS and AAU member. Coed. State control. Semester system. Special facilities: Abrams Planetarium, African Studies Center, Agricultural Experiment Station, Alumni Memorial Chapel, Animal Health Diagnostic Laboratory, Asian Studies Center, Bioelectromagnetics Laboratory, Biological Research Center, Breslin Student Events Center, Carcinogenesis Laboratory, Career Information Center, Center for Advanced Study of International Development, Center for Electron Optics, Center for Environmental Toxicology, Center for International Programs, Center for International Transportation Exchange, Center for Remote Sensing, Center for Urban Affairs, Clinical Center (outpatient facility), Cooperative Extension Service, Counseling Center, English Language Center, Fairchild Theater, Forest Akers Golf Courses, Genetics Clinic, Hematology Oncology Clinic, Hidden Lake Gardens, Institute for Research on Teaching, Institute for Water Research, Institute of Agricultural Technology, Institute of International Agriculture, Institute of Nutrition, Institute of Public Utilities, IPTV (3 TV stations, TV teaching auditorium, closed-circuit TV), Jenison Gymnasium and Fieldhouse, Journalism/Law Institute, Kellogg Center (hotel/restaurant), Kellogg Center for Continuing Education, Kresge Art Center and Museum, Laboratory Animal Care Service, Language Laboratory, Latin American Studies Center, Learning Resources Center, Livestock Pavilion, Living-Learning (dorm-classroom) Centers, MSU/DOE Plant Research Laboratory, MSU Laboratory Preschool, MSU Union, Munn Ice Arena, National Superconducting Cyclotron, Olin Health Center, Pesticide Research Center, Psychological Clinic, Service-Learning Center (volunteers), Social Science Research Bureau, Spartan Nursery School, Spartan Stadium, Speech and Hearing Clinic, University Auditorium, University Center for International Rehabilitation, University Museum, university radio stations (AM/FM), Veterinary Clinical Center, Wharton Center for Performing Arts (Festival Stage and Great Hall), W. J. Beal Botanical Garden and Campus Plant Collection, and W. K. Kellogg Biological Station. Graduate study available through many of seven off-campus extensions centers. The University's NIH ranking is 126th among all U.S. institutions with 117 awards/grants worth $26,868,016. Library: approximately 4,000,000 volumes, 27,324 subscriptions. Total University enrollment: 41,500.

Annual tuition (academic year): full-time, resident $5034, nonresident $10,182; per credit, resident $203, nonresident $412. On-campus housing: Owen Graduate Center (476 graduate men and 396 graduate women at $3532 per academic year with minimum board included) and 2175 apartments available to undergraduate and graduate single and married students (1160 one-bedroom apartments, each available to 1-2 students at average monthly cost of $340 per apartment, and 1025 one- and two-bedroom family apartments at average monthly cost of $365 per apartment). Apply to University Housing Office or University Apartments for on-campus housing or to Off-Campus Housing Office. Phone: (517)355-7457. Day-care facilities available.

Graduate School

Graduate study since 1863. Enrollment: full-time 4383, part-time 3274. University faculty teaching students: full- and part-time 1977. Degrees conferred: M.A., M.A.T., M.B.A., M.F.A., M.L.R.H.R., M.Mus., M.P.A., M.S., M.S.N., M.S.W., M.U.R.P., Ed.S., D.M.A., Ed.D., Ph.D.

ADMISSION REQUIREMENTS. Transcripts, three letters of recommendation required in support of School's application. On-line application available. TOEFL (minimum score 580; some programs have higher minimums) required for international applicants. GRE/GMAT/MAT required by some departments. Interview usually not required. Accepts transfer applicants. Graduates of unaccredited institutions not considered. Apply to Office of Admissions and Scholarships at least forty-five days prior to registration. Application fee $30, $40 for international applicants. Phone: (517)355-8332; fax: (517)353-1674; e-mail: admis@msu.edu.

ADMISSION STANDARDS. Selective or very selective for most departments, competitive for others. Usual minimum average: 3.0 (A = 4).

FINANCIAL AID. Annual awards from institutional funds: grants/scholarships, fellowships, teaching assistantships, research assistantships, internships, tuition waivers, Federal W/S, loans. Approved for VA benefits. Apply by February 1 to appropriate department chair for assistantships, fellowships; to Financial Aid Office for all other programs. Phone: (517)353-5940; fax: (517)432-1155. Use FAFSA. About 57% of students receive aid other than loans from School and outside sources. Aid available for part-time students.

DEGREE REQUIREMENTS. For M.A., M.F.A., M.L.R.H.R., M.Mus., M.P.A., M.S.: 30–33 credits minimum, at least 6 in residence; thesis/nonthesis options; oral exam required with thesis option; final written and/or oral certifying exam may be required with nonthesis option; no language requirements for most majors. For M.S.N.: 37 credits minimum, at least 6 in residence; thesis/nonthesis option; final written and/or oral certifying exam (oral exam when thesis is offered). For M.B.A.: 37 credits minimum, at least 27 in residence. For M.U.P.: 48 credits minimum, at least 24 in residence. For M.S.W.: 57 credits minimum, at least 29 in residence (Social Work Plan I), and 61 credits minimum, at least 6 in residence (Social Work Plan II). For M.A.T.: 30 credits minimum, at least 9 in residence; completion of requirements for the secondary provisional certificate; thesis usually not required. For Ed.S.: normally two years beyond bachelor's; 30 credits minimum beyond the master's, at least 22 in residence; competence in statistics or a reading knowledge of a foreign language may be required. For Ph.D.: normally at least three years beyond the bachelor's, at least 12 credits or one year in residence; qualifying exam for some departments; written and/or oral comprehensive exams; language requirements vary by department; thesis; final oral exam. For D.M.A., Ed.D.: essentially the same as for the Ph.D. For D.O.: completion of eleven-term professional program, including 6 semesters of clerkships; endorsement of the Committee on Student Evaluation; an affirmative vote from College faculty. For D.V.M.: completion of 12 semesters professional program (minimum of 163 credits), including three terms (minimum of 60 credits) of clerkships. For M.D.: completion of three-phase professional program (normally extending from 10 to 13 semesters), including clinical clerkships in community hospitals; preclinical comprehensive exams (NBME Exams, Parts I and II).

FIELDS OF STUDY.

COLLEGE OF AGRICULTURE AND NATURAL RESOURCES:

Agricultural and Extension Education. GRE or MAT for admission. M.S., Ph.D.

Agricultural Economics. GRE for admission. M.S., Ph.D.

Agricultural Engineering. Thesis required for M.S., Ph.D.

Agricultural Technology and Systems Management. Thesis required for M.S. M.S., Ph.D.

Animal Science. M.S., Ph.D.

Biosystems Engineering. M.S., Ph.D.

Building Construction Management. Thesis required for M.S. M.S. only.

Crop and Soil Sciences. M.S., Ph.D.

Ecology and Evolutionary Biology. Includes crop and soil sciences, fisheries and wildlife, forestry, horticulture. M.S., Ph.D.

Environmental Toxicology. Includes animal science, crop and soil sciences, fisheries and wildlife, food science, resource development. M.S., Ph.D.

Evolutionary Biology and Behavior. Ph.D.

Fisheries and Wildlife. GRE Subject (biology) for admission. M.S., Ph.D.

Food Science. Includes food science and foods, human nutrition and institution administration; GRE for admission. M.S., Ph.D.

Forestry. M.S., Ph.D.

Horticulture. M.S., Ph.D.

Packaging. GRE for admission. M.S., Ph.D.

Park, Recreation, and Tourism Resources. GRE for admission. M.S., Ph.D.

Plant Breeding and Genetics. Includes crop and soil sciences, forestry, horticulture or botany, plant pathology. Thesis required for M.S., Ph.D.

Resource Development. GRE for admission. M.S., Ph.D.

Resource Economics. Includes agricultural economics, fisheries and wildlife, forestry, park, recreation, and tourism resources, resource development. M.S., Ph.D.

Urban Studies. Includes forestry, park, recreation, and tourism resources, resource development. M.S., Ph.D.

Note: Oral final exam required for all M.S. degrees.

COLLEGE OF ARTS AND LETTERS:

Adult Language Learning. M.A.

African American and African Studies. M.A.

American Studies. M.A., Ph.D.

Applied Music. Language requirement for admission to Applied Voice program; audition or tape for admission to D.M.A. or Ph.D. programs; public recital and final written and/or oral exam required for M.Mus.; four recitals and document required for D.M.A. M.Mus., D.M.A.

Comparative Literature. GRE for admission; qualifying exam for M.A.; M.A. only.

Critical Studies in the Teaching of English. For teachers in middle schools, junior-high schools, secondary schools, two-year college teaching. GRE Subject (English), writing sample, two years of college-level foreign language for admissions. M.A., Ph.D.

English. GRE Subject (English literature or a cognate area) for admission; GPA of 3.5 in English courses for admission to M.A. program; two years of college-level foreign language for admission; predissertation exam required for Ph.D.; M.A., Ph.D.

English: Teaching of English to Speakers of Other Languages. GRE Subject (English literature or a cognate area) and overall GPA of 3.25 for admission. M.A., Ph.D.

French. GRE Subject (French) and department proficiency exam in French for admission. M.A., Ph.D.

French Language and Literature. GRE Subject (French) and qualifying exam for admission; reading proficiency in two languages other than major language required. Ph.D. only.

French Secondary School Teaching. GRE Subject (French) and department proficiency exam in French for admission. M.A., Ph.D.

German Studies. Oral and written exams, nonthesis option for M.A. M.A., Ph.D.

Health and Humanities. M.A.

Hispanic Cultural Studies. Ph.D.

Hispanic Literature. M.A.

History. Includes urban studies. GPA of 3.5 in history courses, GRE Subject (history) and term paper for admission; oral exam and competence in one foreign language required for M.A.; competence in two foreign languages and written and oral comprehensive required for Ph.D. M.A., Ph.D.

History of Art. GRE for admission. Two years college-level French, German, Italian, and minimum of 18 credits in History of Art upper-level courses or the equivalent for admission. M.A. only.

History—Secondary School Teaching. One year secondary school teaching experience and overall GPA of 3.0 for admission. M.A. only.

History—Urban Studies. M.A.

Linguistics. Two years of a college-level foreign language for admission; major linguistic research paper and qualifying exam required for admission to Ph.D. program; written exam required for M.A.; nonthesis option; demonstrated ability in two foreign languages required for Ph.D. M.A, Ph.D.

Literature in English. Includes literary studies, creative writing.

Music Composition. Two original compositions for admission to M.M., Ph.D.; original composition and final written and/or oral exam required for M.Mus., Ph.D. M.Mus., and Ph.D.

Music Conducting. M.M., D.M.A.

Music Education. GRE or MAT and orientation exam for admission to Ph.D. program; final written exam; oral exam required for M.Mus.; dissertation, written and/or oral exam for Ph.D. M.Mus., Ph.D.

Musicology. Reading knowledge of one foreign language for admission; thesis/dissertation, final written and/or oral exam required. M.A. only.

Music Performance. M.M., D.M.A.

Music Theory. Writing or sample composition for admission to M.Mus., Ph.D.; thesis and final written and/or oral exam required for M.Mus.; dissertation, written exams, oral exam for Ph.D. M.Mus., Ph.D.

Music Therapy. Thesis and final written and/or oral exam required. M.Mus. only.

Piano Pedagogy. M.M.

Philosophy. Sample of philosophic writing for admission; GRE optional. Public demonstration of philosophic competence required for M.A. with nonthesis option; reading knowledge of one foreign language, written comprehensive exam for Ph.D. M.A., Ph.D.

Romance Language and Literature. Ph.D.

Russian. Oral and written exams and reading knowledge of another foreign language required. M.A. only.

Spanish. GRE Subject (Spanish) and department proficiency exam in Spanish for admission. M.A. only.

Spanish Language and Literature. GRE Subject (Spanish) and qualifying exam for admission; reading proficiency in two languages other than major language required. Ph.D. only.

Spanish: Secondary School Teaching. GRE Subject (Spanish) for admission. M.A. only.

Studio Art. Includes ceramics, graphic design, painting, printmaking, sculpture. 10–15 color slides and/or other media (CDs, video) of creative work, and B.F.A. for admission to M.F.A. program; qualifying and terminal reviews required for M.F.A. M.A. and M.F.A. only.

TESOL. GRE Subject (English) for admission. M.A., Ph.D.

Theater. Audition required for admission to M.F.A., program; written and oral exams required for M.A. nonthesis option. M.A., M.F.A. (production design, acting).

Note: GRE and personal statement required for admission for most programs.

ELI BROAD GRADUATE SCHOOL OF MANAGEMENT:

Accounting. Ph.D.

Accounting and Business Process. M.S.

Business Administration. M.B.A., Ph.D.

Business Information Systems. M.B.A.

Business Management in Manufacturing. M.S.

Corporate Accounting. M.B.A.

Economics. Includes econometrics, development, history, international labor. GRE for admission to Ph.D. program; written comprehensive required for M.A. M.A., Ph.D.

Entrepreneurship.

Finance. M.B.A., Ph.D.

Financial Administration. M.B.A. only.

Foodservice Management. M.S.

Hospitality Business. M.B.A.

Human Resource Management. M.B.A.

Industrial Organization and Public Policy. M.A., Ph.D.

Integrative Management. M.B.A.

International Business. M.B.A.

Logistics. M.S.

Management Policy and Strategy. Ph.D. only.

Management Science. M.B.A.

Manufacturing and Engineering Management. M.S.

Manufacturing and Innovation. M.S.

Marketing. M.S., Ph.D.

Materials and Logistics Management—Operations Management. M.B.A. only.

Materials and Logistics Management—Purchasing Management. M.B.A. only.

Materials and Logistics Management—Transportation/Physical Distribution Management. M.B.A. only.

Operations and Sourcing Management. Ph.D.

Operations Research Management. Comprehensive oral exam on course work required. M.S. only.

Organizational Behavior: Human Resource Management. Ph.D. only.

Personnel—Human Relations. M.B.A. only.

Production and Operations Management. Ph.D. only.

Professional Accounting. Minimum overall GPA of 3.25 and personal statement for admission. M.B.A. only.

Strategic Management. Ph.D.

Supply Chain Management. M.S.

Transportation Distribution. M.B.A. and Ph.D. only.

Note: GMAT required for admission to M.B.A. program; oral and written comprehensive exams required for D.B.A. and Ph.D. programs.

COLLEGE OF COMMUNICATION ARTS AND SCIENCES:

Advertising. Minimum third- or fourth-year undergraduate GPA of 3.25 for admission. M.A. only.

Audiology and Speech Sciences. 43 credit master's. M.A., Ph.D.

Audiology and Speech Sciences—Urban Studies. Interdepartmental. Ph.D.

Communication. M.A., Ph.D.

Communication Arts and Sciences—Mass Media. Ph.D. only.

Communication—Urban Studies. Interdepartmental. 33 credit master's. M.A. only.

Health Communication. 33 credit master's. M.A.

Journalism. GRE, autobiography, and personal statement for admission. M.A. only.

Mass Media. Ph.D.

Public Relations. Minimum third- or fourth-year undergraduate GPA of 3.25 for admission. M.A. only.

Telecommunication. Minimum third- or fourth-year undergraduate GPA of 3.25 for admission. 40 credit master's. Includes information and telecommunication management, digital media arts and technology, information policy and society. M.A. only.

Telecommunication—Urban Studies. Interdepartmental. Includes multichannel/broadcast management (37 credit master's), information technologies and services management (40 credit master's), social effects of media (34 credit master's), media arts (31 credit master's). M.A.

Note: Written and oral exams required for nonthesis option.

COLLEGE OF EDUCATION:

Counseling. Interview and one-year counseling experience for admission to Ed.S. program; internship (21 credits) required for M.A. in rehabilitation counseling; one major and two minor field exams, prepracticum, three terms of practicum, and one-year internship required for Ed.D. and Ph.D.

Counseling Psychology. Ph.D.

Curriculum and Teaching. M.A. only.

Curriculum, Teaching and Educational Policy. Ed.S., Ph.D.

Education. M.A.

Educational Policy. Ph.D.

Higher, Adult, and Lifelong Education. M.A., Ph.D.

K–12 Educational Administration. Personal statement for admission; interview and short, written essay exam for admission to Ed.S., Ed.D., and Ph.D. programs.

Kinesiology. M.S., Ph.D.

Kinesiology—Urban Studies. Interdepartmental. M.S.

Learning Technology and Culture. Ph.D.

Literary Instruction. M.A.

Measurement and Quantitative Methods. M.A., Ph.D.

Rehabilitation Counseling. M.A.

Rehabilitation Counselor Education. Ph.D.

School Psychology. Ed.S., Ph.D.

Special Education. Elementary or secondary teaching credential, eligibility for additional endorsement as a teacher of severely or mildly impaired learner, and one full year of successful teaching experience for admission to M.A. program; interview and samples of both scholarly and spontaneous writing required for admission to Ed.D. and Ph.D. programs; internship (1 term) required for Ed.S.

Student Affairs Administration. M.A.

Teaching and Learning with Technology. M.A.

Note: GRE required for Ed.S., Ed.D., and Ph.D. admission; M.A., M.A.T. (joint with College of Natural Science); Ed.S., Ed.D., and Ph.D.

COLLEGE OF ENGINEERING:

Chemical Engineering.

Civil Engineering.

Civil Engineering: Urban Studies. M.S. only.

Computer Science.

Electrical Engineering.

Environmental Engineering.

Environmental Engineering—Urban Studies. M.S. only.

Materials Science and Engineering.

Mechanical Engineering.

Mechanics.

Note: GRE required for all international applicants, GRE strongly recommended for domestic applicants; certifying exam or thesis defense for M.S. degrees; qualifying exams for all Ph.D. degrees.

COLLEGE OF HUMAN ECOLOGY:

Apparel and Textiles. M.A. only.

Child Development. M.A. only.

Community Services. M.S. only.

Family and Child Ecology. GRE for admission. Ph.D. only.

Family Studies. M.A. only.

Human Environment—Design and Management. M.A. only.

Human Nutrition. GRE for admission. M.S., Ph.D.

Human Nutrition—Environmental Toxicology. Ph.D.

Interior Design and Facilities Management. M.A. only.

Marriage and Family Therapy. M.A. only.

Merchandising Management. M.S. only.

Note: Oral or written comprehensive exam required for master's nonthesis option.

COLLEGE OF HUMAN MEDICINE:

Biochemistry. GRE Subject or MCAT (M.D.-Ph.D.) for admission.

Cell and Molecular Biology. GRE Subject for admission.

Epidemiology. M.S., Ph.D.

Genetics. GRE Subject for admission.

Microbiology. GRE Subject (biology) and personal statement for admission; participation in lab teaching, predissertation oral exam, and publishable manuscript required for Ph.D. M.S., Ph.D.

Microbiology and Molecular Genetics. Ph.D.

Molecular Biology. M.S., Ph.D.

Neuroscience. GRE Subject for admission.

Pharmacology. GRE for admission to Ph.D. program.

Surgery. M.S.

Toxicology. M.S., Ph.D.

Note: Thesis/oral exam required for master's degrees; see separate listings below.

COLLEGE OF NATURAL SCIENCE:

Analytical Chemistry.

Applied Mathematics.

Biochemistry. GRE Subject for admission.

Biological Science. Interdepartmental. Teacher's certificate, or candidacy for, required for admission to M.A.T. program; reading knowledge of one foreign language and one term's residency at a recognized biological station required for M.S. M.S., M.A.T. only.

Biotechnology. Interdepartmental.

Botany and Plant Pathology. Certifying exam required for M.S.

Cell and Molecular Biology. Interdepartmental. GRE for admission.

Chemical Physics. GRE for admission.

Chemistry. Orientation exam required for admission; teacher's certificate, or candidacy for certificate, required for admission to M.A.T. program; qualifying exam required for M.S. and M.A.T. degrees and for admission to Ph.D. program; reading knowledge of German, Russian, or French and preoral exam required for Ph.D. M.S., M.A.T., and Ph.D.

Clinical Laboratory Science.

Computational Mathematics.

Earth Science. Interdepartmental. Teacher's certificate, or candidacy for certificate, required for admission. M.A.T. only.

Ecology and Evolutionary Biology. Interdepartmental.

Entomology. GRE for admission; appropriate master's degree with thesis required for admission to Ph.D. program; final oral exam required for M.S.; qualification exam and written and oral comprehensive required for Ph.D.

Entomology: Urban Studies. Admission and degree requirements same as for Entomology.

Environmental Geoscience.

Environmental Toxicology. Interdepartmental.

General Science. Interdepartmental. Teacher's certificate, or candidacy for certificate, required for admission; M.A.T. only.

Genetics. Interdepartmental. Ph.D. only.

Geology. GRE for admission. M.S., M.A.T., Ph.D.

Inorganic Chemistry.

Mathematics. Reading knowledge of two foreign languages required for Ph.D. M.A., M.S., M.A.T., Ph.D.

Mathematics Education.

Microbiology. GRE Subject (biology) and personal statement for admission; final oral exam required. M.S. only.

Nuclear Chemistry. M.S., Ph.D.

Operations Research Statistics. M.S. only.

Pathology. Ph.D. only.

Physical Science. Interdepartmental. Certifying exam required for M.S. M.S., M.A.T. only.

Physics. Qualifying exam required for M.S. and Ph.D.; one term of half-time teaching required for Ph.D. M.S., M.A.T., Ph.D.

Physiology. GRE for admission; thesis/oral exam required for M.S.; qualifying exam required for Ph.D.

Statistics. Qualifying exam and reading ability in French, German, or Russian required for Ph.D. M.A., M.S., Ph.D.

Theoretical Chemistry. Ph.D. only.

Zoology. GRE for admission. M.S., M.A.T., Ph.D.

Note: Requirements for secondary provisional certificate must be met for M.A.T.

COLLEGE OF NURSING:

Nursing. Includes adult, family and gerontological nursing. GRE (within the last five years), personal interview, statistics course, B.S.N. from accredited nursing program with GPA of 3.0 for years three and four; one-year work experience as R.N. during previous five years or the equivalent, current licensure to practice nursing in the U.S., and eligibility for Michigan licensure required for admission; 42 credit program. M.S.N. only.

COLLEGE OF OSTEOPATHIC MEDICINE:

Biochemistry. GRE/Subject for admission.

Microbiology. GRE/Subject (Biology) and personal statement for M.S., plus lab teaching, predissertation oral exam, publishable manuscript for Ph.D. M.S. Ph.D.

Microbiology and Molecular Genetics. Ph.D.

Molecular Biology. M.S., Ph.D.

Neuroscience. Interdepartmental. GRE for admission. Ph.D. only.

Pathology. Thesis/oral exam, publishable manuscript for M.S., Ph.D. M.S., Ph.D.

Pharmacology. GRE for admission to Ph.D.

Physiology. GRE for admission; thesis/oral exam required for M.S.; qualifying exam required for Ph.D.

Toxicology. M.S., Ph.D.

Note: Final oral exam required for M.S. Also see separate listing below.

COLLEGE OF SOCIAL SCIENCE:

Anthropology. Thesis/oral exam required for M.A. (can substitute qualifying exam or doctoral comprehensive exam if directly admitted to doctoral program without M.A.). Includes professional applications in anthropology. M.A., Ph.D.

Criminal Justice. GRE or MAT (social science professional scale) and minimum overall undergraduate GPA of 3.2 for admission; policy paper and oral exam required for nonthesis option. M.S., Ph.D.

Criminal Justice—Urban Studies. Interdepartmental. M.S.

Economics. Includes history of economic thought, advanced economic theory, econometrics, labor economics, industrial organization, advanced macro and monetary economics, public economics, international economics, economic development. M.A., Ph.D.

Environmental Design. M.A.

Forensic Sciences. M.S.

Geographic Information Science. M.A., M.S., Ph.D.

Geography. GRE and a minimum GPA of 3.4 in all geography courses and all junior-senior courses for admissions to M.A. or M.S. programs; minimum GPA of 3.6 for admission to Ph.D. M.A., M.S., Ph.D.

Geography—Urban Studies. GRE and a minimum GPA of 3.4. Interdepartmental. M.A. only.

Infant Studies. Interdepartmental. M.A.

Labor Relations and Human Resources. Includes collective bargaining and employment relations, and employment and training programs options; GRE for admission. M.L.R.H.R. only.

Labor Relations and Human Resources—Urban Studies. Interdepartmental.

Political Science. GRE and 3.2 GPA for admission. M.A., Ph.D.

Political Science—Urban Studies. GRE and 3.2 GPA for admission. Interdepartmental. M.A., Ph.D.

Psychology. GRE/Subject (Psychology) for admission to M.A., Ph.D.; thesis/oral exam required for M.A. M.A., Ph.D.

Psychology—Urban Studies. GRE/Subject (Psychology) for admission. M.A., Ph.D.

Public Administration. GRE for admission. M.P.A. only.

Public Administration—Urban Studies. Interdepartmental. M.P.A.

Social Science—Criminal Justice. GRE for admission. Ph.D. only.

Social Science—Global Application. M.A.

Social Science—Industrial Relations and Human Resources. GRE for admission. Ph.D. only.

Social Science—Social Work. GRE for admission. Ph.D. only.

Social Science—Urban and Regional Planning. GRE for admission. Ph.D. only.

Social Work. Includes administration and program evaluation and interpersonal intervention; MSWI (two-year) and MSWII (one-

344 Michigan State University

year) program options; bachelor's in social work from CSEW-accredited program and full-time student status required for admission to MSWII program. M.S.W., Ph.D.

Social Work—Urban Studies. Includes administration and program evaluation and interpersonal intervention; no thesis option. Includes clinical social work—urban studies, organizational and community practice—urban studies. M.S.W. only.

Sociology. GRE for admission; master's thesis or original research paper for admission to Ph.D. program.

Sociology—Urban Studies. GRE for admission; master's thesis or original research paper for admission to Ph.D. program; thesis/oral exam required for M.A.

Urban and Regional Planning. M.U.R.P. only.

Urban and Regional Planning—Urban Studies. Interdepartmental. M.U.R.P.

COLLEGE OF VETERINARY MEDICINE:

Anatomy. GRE for admission; thesis/oral exam or publishable manuscript required for M.S.; publishable manuscript required for Ph.D.

Environmental Toxicology. Multidepartmental program, granting a Ph.D. only, anatomy (GRE for admission), microbiology (GRE/Subject (Biology) for admission), pathology, pharmacology (GRE for admission), physiology (GRE/Subject for admission).

Food Safety. Inter-College program. M.S., Ph.D.

Large Animal Clinical Sciences. M.S., Ph.D.

Microbiology. GRE/Subject (Biology) and personal statement for admission; final oral exam required. M.S., Ph.D.

Pathology. Thesis/oral exam and publishable manuscript required for M.S.; publishable manuscript required for Ph.D.

Pharmacology and Toxicology. GRE for admission to Ph.D. program.

Physiology. GRE/Subject for admission; thesis/oral exam required for M.S.; qualifying exam required for Ph.D.

Small Animal Clinical Sciences. M.S. only.

Note: Also see separate listing below.

College of Human Medicine (48824-1317)

First class entered 1964. Tuition (three semesters): resident $16,419, nonresident $36,219. Student fees $1,028. On-campus housing available. Total average figure for all other expenses: $16,000.

Enrollment: first-year class 96; total 454 (men 50%, women 50%). Faculty: full-and part-time approximately 2700. Degrees conferred: B.A., M.S.-M.D., M.D., M.D.-Ph.D. The M.S. and Ph.D. are available through the Graduate School.

ADMISSION REQUIREMENTS. AMCAS report, transcripts, letters of recommendation, MCAT, autobiographical statement required in support of application. Interview by invitation only. Has EDP; apply between June 1 and August 1. Applicants must have completed at least three years of college study. Preference given to state residents. Apply to Office of Admissions after June 1, before November 15. Application fee $55. Phone: (517)353-9620; fax: (517)432-0021; e-mail: MDadmissions@msu.edu.

ADMISSION STANDARDS. Competitive. Mean MCAT: 9.1; mean GPA: 3.53 (A = 4). Gourman rating: 3.77. *U.S. News & World Report* ranking is 17th of all U.S. medical schools for primary care. Accepts 15–20% of total annual applicants. Approximately 80% are state residents.

FINANCIAL AID. Scholarships, minority scholarships, Grants-in-Aid, institutional loans, HEAL, alternative loan programs, NIH stipends, Federal Perkins Loans, Stafford Subsidized and Unsubsidized Loans, Service Commitment Scholarship programs are available. All Financial Aid is based on proven need. Assistantships/fellowships may be available for M.D.-Advanced Graduate Degree candidates. Financial Aid applications and information are available at the on-campus, by-invitation interview. For scholarships, the selection criteria places heavy reliance on MCAT and undergraduate GPA. Contact the MSU Health Professions Financial Aid Office for current information. Phone: (517)353-5188. Apply for aid as soon as possible. For most financial assistance and all Federal programs submit FAFSA to a Federal processor (School code: 002290), also submit Financial Aid Transcript, Federal Income Tax forms. Approximately 75% of students receive some form of financial assistance.

DEGREE REQUIREMENTS. For B.A./B.S.-M.D.: an eight-year program. For M.D.: satisfactory completion of four-year program. All students must pass USMLE Step 1 prior to entering third year; all students must pass USMLE Step 2 prior to awarding of M.D. For M.D.-M.S.: generally a four-and-one-half- to five-and-one-half-year program. For M.D.-Ph.D.: generally a seven-year program.

FIELDS OF GRADUATE STUDY.

Anatomy.
Cellular and Molecular.
Ecology and Evolutionary Biology.
Epidemiology.
Genetics.
Health Ethics and Humanities.
Microbiology.
Neurosciences.
Pathology.
Pharmacology and Toxicology.
Physiology.

College of Osteopathic Medicine

Web site: www.com.msu.edu

College opened in 1971. Located on main campus. Semester system. The College's ranking by NIH awards/grants was third among Osteopathic Schools with 14 awards/grants worth $2,284,099.

Annual tuition: resident $16,911, nonresident $36,006. On-campus rooms and apartments available for both single and married students. Contact Housing Office for both on- and off-campus housing information. Phone: (517)353-7457. Off-campus housing and personal expenses: approximately $19,170.

Enrollment: first-year class 125; total full-time 518 (men 52%, women 48%). Degrees conferred: D.O., D.O.-M.H.H. (Health and Humanities), D.O.-M.P.H., D.O.-Ph.D., M.S.T.P.

ADMISSION REQUIREMENTS FOR FIRST-YEAR APPLICANTS. Preference given to state residents, U.S. citizens, and permanent residents only. Has EDP for state residents only. EDP applicants must apply through AMCAS (official transcripts sent by mid-May) between June 1 and August 1. Early applications are encouraged. Submit secondary/supplemental application, a personal statement, two recommendations to Office of Admission within two weeks of receipt of application. Interviews are by invitation only and generally for final selection. Notification normally begins October 1. All other applicants apply through AACOMAS (file after June 1, before December 1), submit MCAT (will accept test results from last three years), official transcripts for each school attended (should show at least 90 semester credits/135 quarter credits) and service processing fee. After a review of the AACOMAS application and supporting documents a decision is made concerning which candidates should receive supplemental materials. The supplemental application, an application fee of $60, a personal statement, and three recommendations (one from a D.O.) should be returned to Office of Admission as soon as possible. Phone: (517)353-7740. International applicants are subject to Michigan State University's requirements for international students. Contact the Office of International Students and Scholars, 103 Center for International Programs, MSU, East

Lansing, Michigan 48824 for current information and specific requirements. Interviews are by invitation only and generally for final selection. Applicants to joint degree programs and M.S.T.P. must be accepted by both the College and the Graduate School. Request applications from both schools and mark M.S.T.P. clearly on both forms. First-year students admitted Fall only. Rolling admissions process; notification starts in October and is finished when class is filled.

ADMISSION STANDARDS. Competitive. Median MCAT: 8.4; median GPA: 3.0. Approximately 80% of students are state residents.

FINANCIAL AID. Scholarships, minority scholarships, grants, institutional loans, NOF, HEAL, alternative loan programs, NIH stipends; Service Obligation Scholarship programs, Military and National Health Service programs are available; private loans. All aid is based on documented need. Assistantships/fellowships may be available for joint degree and M.S.T.P. applicants. Financial Aid applications and information are sent out periodically during the year. Contact the MSU Health Professions Financial Aid Office for current information. Phone: (517)353-5188. Use FAFSA for all Federal programs (School code: 002290), also submit Financial Aid Transcript, Federal Income Tax forms. Approximately 80% of students receive some form of financial assistance.

DEGREE REQUIREMENTS. For D.O.: satisfactory completion of Units I, II, and III. For D.O.-M.H.H., D.O.-M.P.H.: generally a five- to six-year program. For M.D.-Ph.D.: generally a seven-year program.

FIELDS OF GRADUATE STUDY.
Anatomy.
Biochemistry.
Microbiology.
Neuroscience. Interdisciplinary.
Pathology.
Pharmacology and Toxicology.
Physiology.

College of Veterinary Medicine (48824-1316)
Web site: www.cum.msu.edu

Annual tuition: resident $11,490, nonresident $23,694. Total average cost for all other expenses: $12,000.

Enrollment: first-year class 100; total full-time 469 (men 50%, women 50%); no part-time students. Faculty: full-time 180. Degree conferred: D.V.M. The M.S. and Ph.D. are offered through the Graduate School.

ADMISSION REQUIREMENTS. VMCAS report, completion of required preveterinary courses, transcripts, MCAT or GRE, interview, autobiography, three recommendations required in support of application. TOEFL required if English is not the applicant's primary language. Has EDP; apply after August 1, before October 15. Preference given to Michigan residents. Graduates of unaccredited colleges not considered. All application materials must be received by the Office of Admissions and Scholarships by October 1. Application fee $65. Phone: (517)355-9793; fax: (517)432-2391.

ADMISSION STANDARDS. Selective. Mean MCAT: 7.94; mean GPA: 3.61 (A = 4). *U.S. News & World Report* ranking is eighth of all U.S. veterinary schools. Accepts 35–40% of total annual applicants. Accepts 5% of nonresident applicants.

FINANCIAL AID. Fellowships, research assistantships, Federal W/S, loans. Apply to Office of Admissions and Scholarships. Use FAFSA.

DEGREE REQUIREMENTS. For D.V.M.: satisfactory completion of three-year, year-round, professional curriculum. For M.S., Ph.D.: see Graduate School listing above.

FIELDS OF GRADUATE STUDY.
Anatomy.
Environmental Toxicology.
Large-Animal Clinical Sciences.
Microbiology.
Pathology.
Pharmacology.
Physiology.
Small-Animal Clinical Sciences.

MICHIGAN STATE UNIVERSITY— DETROIT COLLEGE OF LAW
316 Law College Building
East Lansing, Michigan 48824-1300
Web site: www.dcl.edu

Established 1891. Located at Michigan State University. Private control. ABA approved since 1941. AALS member. Semester system. Full-time, part-time. Special facilities: Center for Canadian–U.S. Law. Special programs: summer study abroad at University of Ottawa, Canada, and Babes/Bolyai University, Cluj, Romania. Law library: 237,432 volumes, 3460 subscriptions; has LEXIS, NEXIS, WESTLAW, INFOTRAC, MERIT.

Annual tuition: full-time $17,024, part-time $12,160. On-campus housing available for both single and married students at Michigan State University. Contact University's Housing Office for both on- and off-campus housing information. Phone: (800)678-4679, (517)355-7460. Off-campus housing and personal expenses: approximately $7236. Additional costs: books approximately $700.

Enrollment: first-year class 176, part-time 60; total full- and part-time 704 (men 62%, women 38%). Faculty: full-time 26, part-time 33. Student to faculty ratio 20.8 to 1. Degrees conferred: J.D., J.D.-M.B.A.

ADMISSION REQUIREMENTS. LSDAS Law School report, LSAT (not later that December test date; if more than one LSAT, highest is used), bachelor's degree from an accredited institution, résumé, personal statement, interview, two recommendations, transcripts (must show all schools attended and at least three years of study) required in support of application. Applicants must have received bachelor's degree prior to enrollment. Interview not required but may be requested by School. In addition, international applicants for whom English is not their native language must submit TOEFL (not older than two years). Apply to Director of Admission after September 30, before April 15. First-year students admitted Fall only. Rolling admissions process, notification starts in November and is finished by late May. Application fee $50. Phone: (517)432-6800; fax: (517)432-0098; e-mail: law@msu.edu.

ADMISSION STANDARDS. Selective. Mean LSAT: full- and part-time 152; mean GPA: full-time 3.13, part-time 2.96 (A = 4). Gourman rating: 3.22. *U.S. New & World Report* ranking is in the fourth tier of all U.S. law schools.

FINANCIAL AID. Scholarships, minority scholarships, Grants-in-Aid, institutional loans; Federal loans and Federal W/S offered through University's Financial Aid Office. Assistantships may be available for upper divisional Joint Degree candidates. Apply to Office of Financial Aid after January 1 and before April 15. Phone: (517)965-0672. For all other programs use FAFSA (College code: G02254). Approximately 11% full-time, 9% part-time of first-year class receive scholarships/Grants-in-Aid. Approximately 85% of students receive some form of financial assistance.

DEGREE REQUIREMENTS. For J.D.: 85 (60 required) credits with a GPA of at least a 2.0 (A = 4), plus completion of upper divisional writing course; three-year program, four-year program. Accelerated J.D. with one summer of course work. For J.D.-M.B.A.: up to 6 M.B.A. credits can be used for the J.D., up to 9 J.D. credits can be used for the M.B.A.

MICHIGAN TECHNOLOGICAL UNIVERSITY

Houghton, Michigan 49931-1295
Web site: www.mtu.edu

Founded 1885. Located 400 miles N of Chicago. CGS member. Coed. State control. Semester system. Special facilities: A. E. Seaman Mineralogical Museum, National Center for Clean Industrial and Treatment Technologies, Center for Advanced Manufacturing and Material Processing, Environmental Engineering Center, Keweenaw Research Center, Center for Clean Manufacturing and Research, Ford Forestry Center, Remote Sensing Institute, Institute of Wood Research, Institute of Materials Processing, Regional Groundwater Education in Michigan Center. Library: 992,197 volumes, 10,500 subscriptions. Total University enrollment: 6300.

Annual tuition: full-time, resident $4876, nonresident $9752. On-campus housing for 352 married units, 110 single units. Average academic year housing cost: $4917 (including board) for single students; $3186 for married students. Contact Director of Housing for both on- and off-campus housing information. Phone: (906)487-2682.

Graduate School

Enrollment: full-time 542, part-time 128. University faculty: full-time 303, part-time 16. Degrees conferred: M.S., Ph.D.

ADMISSION REQUIREMENTS. Official transcripts, GRE, GMAT required in support of School's application. TOEFL required for international applicants. Interview not required. Accepts transfer applicants. Graduates of unaccredited institutions not considered. Apply to Graduate School Office at least six weeks prior to the desired semester of registration. Application fee $30, $35 for international applicants. Phone: (906)487-2327; fax: (906)487-2245; e-mail: gradadm@mtu.edu.

ADMISSION STANDARDS. Selective. Usual minimum average: 2.7 (A = 4).

FINANCIAL AID. Fellowships, research assistantships, teaching assistantships, internships, grants, Federal W/S, loans. Approved for VA benefits. Apply February 1 to Dean, Graduate School for fellowships, assistantships; to Financial Aid Office for all other programs. Phone: (906)487-2622. Use FAFSA. About 71% of students receive aid other than loans from University and outside sources. Aid available for part-time students.

DEGREE REQUIREMENTS. For M.S.: 30 credits minimum, at least 24 in residence; 6 credits may be assigned to thesis; final oral exam. For Ph.D.: total number of credits variable, at least four semesters in residence; preliminary written/oral exam; foreign language proficiency recommended by some departments; dissertation; final oral exam.

FIELDS OF STUDY.
Applied Science Education. M.S.
Biological Sciences. M.S., Ph.D.
Chemical Engineering. M.S., Ph.D.
Chemistry. M.S., Ph.D.
Civil Engineering. M.S., Ph.D.
Computational Science. Interdepartmental. Ph.D. only.
Computer Science. M.S. only.
Electrical Engineering. M.S., Ph.D.
Engineering Mechanics. M.S. only.
Environmental Engineering. Interdepartmental. Ph.D. only.
Environmental Engineering Science. M.S.
Environmental Policy. M.S.
Forest Molecular Genetics and Biotechnology. Ph.D.
Forest Science. Ph.D. only.
Forestry. M.S. only.
Geological Engineering. M.S., Ph.D.
Geology. M.S., Ph.D.
Geophysics. M.S. only.
Industrial Archaeology. M.S. only.
Mathematics. M.S., Ph.D.
Mechanical Engineering. M.S.
Mechanical Engineering/Engineering Mechanics. Ph.D. only.
Mineral Economics. M.S. only.
Mining Engineering. M.S., Ph.D.
Physics. M.S., Ph.D.
Rhetoric and Technical Communication. M.S., Ph.D.

THE UNIVERSITY OF MICHIGAN

Ann Arbor, Michigan 48109
Web site: www.umich.edu

Founded 1817. Located 40 miles W of Detroit. CGS and AAU member. Coed. State control. Trimester system. Special facilities: computer center; four astronomical laboratories; experimental school; nuclear reactor; statistical research laboratory; installations for handling radioisotopes and high-intensity radiation sources; centers for ancient and modern studies, Afro-American and African studies, Chinese studies, Near Eastern and North African studies, Russian and East European studies, South and Southeast Asian studies, Western European studies, research on economic development, human growth and development, research on learning and teaching; institutes for environmental quality, labor and industrial relations, mental health research, public policy, science and technology, social research. The University's NIH ranking is sixth among all U.S. institutions with 823 grants with $302,311,405. Library: 6,000,000 volumes, 3,470,000 microforms. Total University enrollment: 36,600.

Annual tuition: full-time (9 or more credits), resident $11,876 (some programs may have additional charges), nonresident $24,452. On-campus housing for 2100 married students, 750 graduate men, 750 graduate women. Average academic year housing cost: $7124–$8000 for married students, $3666–$5801 for 8 months (including board) for single students. Apply to Housing Office. Phone: (734)763-2084.

Horace H. Rackham School of Graduate Studies

Graduate study since 1849. Enrollment: 5943 (men 55%, women 45%). Graduate faculty: full-time 3349. Degrees conferred: A.M., M.S., M.F.A., M.I.L.S., M.L.Arch., M.L.S., M.P.A., M.P.P., M.S.Pharm., M.U.P., M.S.E., Engineer, Ed.S., Ed.D., A.Mus.D., Ph.D.

ADMISSION REQUIREMENTS. Transcripts, letters of reference required in support of School's application. GRE either required or strongly recommended for most departments. TOEFL or MELAB required of international students. Interview not required. Accepts transfer applicants. Graduates of unaccredited institutions not considered. Apply by January 15. Application fee $55. Phone: (734)764-8129.

ADMISSION STANDARDS. Selective to competitive for most departments. Usual minimum average: 3.0 (A = 4).

FINANCIAL AID. Annual awards from institutional funds: fellowships, assistantships, internships, traineeships, tuition waivers, Federal W/S, loans. Approved for VA benefits. Apply by February 1 to Fellowships, Assistantships Office; to Financial Aid Office for all other programs. Use FAFSA and University's FAF. 1040 IRS form must be submitted. Phone: (734)763-6600; fax: (734)647-3081. About 75% of students receive aid other than loans from University and outside sources. Aid available for part-time students.

DEGREE REQUIREMENTS. For master's: 30–36 hours minimum, at least 18 in residence; thesis, final written/oral exam for most majors; reading knowledge of one foreign language for some majors. For M.S.E.: 30 hours minimum, at least 24 in residence. For Engineering: 30 hours minimum beyond the bachelor's, at least 24 in residence. For Ed.S.: 54 hours minimum beyond the bachelor's, at least 48 in residence; final research report. For Ph.D.: six terms of study/research minimum beyond the bachelor's, at least two terms of not less than eight hours each in residence; no specific hour requirement except 60 hours minimum for education; language requirements vary by major; qualifying exam; preliminary exam; candidacy; dissertation; final oral exam. For Ed.D.: 72 hours minimum beyond the bachelor's, at least two terms in residence; preliminary exam; dissertation; final oral exam. For A.Mus.D.: essentially the same as for the Ph.D.

FIELDS OF STUDY.
Aerospace Engineering. GRE for admission. M.S., Ph.D.
Aerospace Science. M.S., Ph.D.
American Culture. GRE for admission; interdepartmental. A.M., Ph.D.
Anthropology. GRE for admission. Ph.D.
Anthropology and History. GRE for admission; interdepartmental. Ph.D.
Applied Physics. GRE for admissions. Ph.D.
Architecture. M.S., Ph.D.
Archives and Records Management. M.S.I.
Art and Design. Includes photography, art education; portfolio for admission. M.A., M.F.A.
Asian Languages and Culture. GRE for admission; includes Chinese language and literature, Japanese language and literature, Buddhist studies; one language for M.A. candidacy, plus two years study in Far Eastern language.
Asian Studies. GRE for admission; interdepartmental; includes China, Japan, South and Southeast Asia. A.M.
Astronomy and Astrophysics. GRE/Subject for admission. Ph.D.
Atmospheric and Space Sciences. GRE recommended. M.S., Ph.D.
Bioinformatics. M.S., Ph.D.
Biological Chemistry. GRE for admission. Ph.D.
Biology. GRE for admission. M.S., Ph.D.
Biomedical Engineering. GRE for admission; interdepartmental.
Biophysics. Interdepartmental. Ph.D.
Biostatistics. GRE for admission. M.S., Ph.D.
Business Administration. M.B.A., M.A.S., M.H.A. granted by School of Business Administration. Ph.D.
Cell and Development Biology. Ph.D.
Cellular and Molecular Biology. GRE for admission; interdepartmental. Ph.D.
Chemical Engineering. GRE for admission. M.S.E., Ph.D.
Chemistry. GRE for admission. Ph.D.
Civil Engineering. Includes civil, construction engineering and management, environmental engineering. GRE for admission. M.S.E., Ph.D.
Classical Art and Archaeology. GRE for admission; interdepartmental. Ph.D.
Classical Studies. GRE for admission. A.M. in Greek and Latin; Ph.D. in Classical Studies.

Clinical Research Design and Statistical Analysis. M.S.
Communication Studies. GRE for admission. Includes radio, TV, film, journalism.
Comparative Literature. Interdepartmental; one language for admission; substantial knowledge of two languages, some facility in another for Ph.D.
Computer Science and Engineering. M.S., M.S.E., Ph.D.
Creative Writing. M.F.A.
Dentistry. D.D.S. for admission, except in biomaterials (M.S., Ph.D.), dental hygiene (M.S.), endondontics (M.S.), oral health sciences (Ph.D.), Orthodontics (M.S.), pediatrics dentistry (M.S.), periodontics (M.S.), Prosthodonics (M.S.), restorative dentistry (M.S.).
Ecology and Evolutionary Biology. M.S., Ph.D.
Economics. Includes applied (A.M.). GRE/Subject for admission. Ph.D.
Education. GRE for admission. Includes educational studies, higher and postsecondary education. A.M., M.S., Ph.D.
Education and Psychology. GRE for admission; interdepartmental. Ph.D.
Electrical Engineering. GRE for admission. M.S., M.S.E., Ph.D.
Electrical Engineering—Systems. M.S., M.S.E., Ph.D.
English and Education. GRE for admission; interdepartmental. Ph.D.
English and Women's Studies. Ph.D.
English Language and Literature. GRE, writing sample for admission. Ph.D.
Environmental Health Science. M.S., Ph.D.
Epidemiologic Science. GRE for admission. Normally admits to Ph.D. only.
Financial Engineering. M.S.E.
Genetic Counseling. M.S.
Geology. GRE for admission. M.S., Ph.D.
Geoscience and Remote Sensing. Ph.D.
Germanic Languages and Literatures. GRE for admission. A.M., Ph.D.
Health Behavior and Health Education. GRE for admission. Ph.D.
Health Services Organization and Policy. Ph.D.
History. GRE for admission. Ph.D.
History and Women's Studies. Ph.D.
History of Art. GRE for admission. One language for A.M. Ph.D.
Human Computer Interaction. M.S.I.
Human Genetics. GRE for admission. M.S., Ph.D.
Information. M.S.I.
Information Economics, Management, and Policy. M.S.I.
Immunology. Ph.D.
Industrial and Operations Engineering. GRE for admission. M.S., M.S.E., Ph.D.
Industrial Health. M.S., Ph.D.
Information and Library Studies. M.I.L.S., Ph.D.
Journalism. A.M.
Judaic Studies. A.M.
Kinesiology. A.M., M.S., Ph.D.
Landscape Architecture. M.L.Arch., Ph.D.
Library and Information Services. M.S.I.
Linguistic and Slavic Languages and Literatures. Ph.D.
Linguistics. GRE for admission. Ph.D.
Linguistics and Germanic Language and Literatures. Ph.D.
Linguistics and Romance Languages and Literatures. Ph.D.
Macromolecular Science and Engineering. GRE for admission. Interdepartmental. M.S., Ph.D.
Materials Science and Engineering. GRE for admission. M.S.E., Ph.D.
Mathematics. GRE for admission. Includes applied and interdisciplinary. A.M., M.S., Ph.D.
Mechanical Engineering. M.S.E., Ph.D.
Medical and Biological Illustration. M.F.A. only.
Medical Scientist Training Program. M.D.-Ph.D. program.
Medicinal Chemistry. GRE for admission. Interdepartmental. Ph.D.

Microbiology and Immunology. GRE for admission. Ph.D.

Mineralogy. M.S., Ph.D.

Modern Middle Eastern and North African Studies. GRE for admission; interdepartmental. A.M.

Molecular, Cellular, and Developmental Biology. M.S., Ph.D.

Music. Includes composition (A.Mus.D., A.M.), composition and music theory (Ph.D.), conducting (band, choral, orchestral, A.Mus.D.), dance (M.F.A.), music education (Ph.D.), music theory (A.M., Ph.D.), musicology—ethnomusicology (A.M., Ph.D.); musicology—history (A.M., Ph.D.), performance (all instruments and voice, A.Mus.D.), piano accompanying and chamber music (A.Mus.D.), piano pedagogy and performance (A.Mus.D.).

Natural Resources and Environment. GRE for admission. M.S., Ph.D.

Naval Architecture and Marine Engineering. GRE for admission. M.S., M.S.E., Ph.D.

Near Eastern Studies. GRE for admission. A.M., Ph.D.

Neuroscience. GRE for admission; interdepartmental. Ph.D.

Nuclear Engineer. M.S., M.S.E.

Nuclear Engineering. Ph.D.

Nuclear Science. M.S., Ph.D.

Nursing. GRE for admission. Includes community health nursing (M.S.), gerontological nursing (M.S.), medical-surgical nursing (M.S.), nursing (Ph.D.), nurse health services administration (M.S.), nursing business and health systems (M.S.), parent–child nursing (M.S.), psychiatric–mental health nursing (M.S.). M.S., Ph.D.

Nutritional Science. M.S.

Oceanography—Marine Geology and Geochemistry. M.S., Ph.D.

Oceanography—Physical. M.S., Ph.D.

Pathology. Ph.D.

Pharmaceutical Chemistry. GRE for admission. Ph.D.

Pharmaceutical Sciences. GRE for admission. Ph.D.

Pharmacology. GRE for admission. Ph.D.

Philosophy. GRE, writing sample for admission. A.M., Ph.D.

Physics. GRE for admission. M.S., Ph.D.

Physiology. GRE for admission. Ph.D.

Political Science. GRE for admission. Ph.D.

Psychology. GRE for admission; admits to Ph.D. only, additional departmental application required for admission. Ph.D.

Psychology and Women's Studies. Ph.D.

Public Administration. GRE for admission. M.P.A.

Public Policy Studies. GRE for admission; interdepartmental. Includes public policy (M.P.P.), public policy and economics (Ph.D.), public policy and political science (Ph.D.), public policy and sociology (Ph.D). M.P.P., Ph.D.

Romance Languages and Literature. Includes French, Italian, Spanish. GRE for admission. A.M., Ph.D.

Russian and East European Studies. GRE for admission; interdepartmental. A.M.

Scientific Computing. Ph.D.

Slavic Languages and Literatures. GRE for admission. A.M., Ph.D.

Social and Administrative Sciences. Ph.D.

Social Work and Social Science. Includes social work and anthropology, social work and economics, social work and political science, social work and psychology, social work and sociology. Ph.D. only.

Sociology. GRE/Subject for admission. Ph.D.

Space and Planetary Physics. Ph.D.

Statistics. GRE for admission. Includes applied statistics (A.M. only). A.M., Ph.D.

Survey Methodology. M.S., Ph.D.

Teaching Arabic as a Foreign Language. A.M.

Theatre. Includes theatre practice (Ph.D.), design (M.F.A.). M.F.A., Ph.D.

Toxicology. M.S., Ph.D.

Urban Planning. GRE for admission. M.U.P. only.

Urban, Technological, and Environmental Planning. GRE for admission. Ph.D.

University of Michigan Business School

Web site: www.bus.umich.edu

Established 1924. Public control. Accredited programs: M.B.A., Accounting; recognized Ph.D. Courses offered in Dearborn. Semester (both seven- and fourteen-week courses) system. Special programs: foreign exchange programs in Australia, Austria, Costa Rica, Denmark, Finland, France, Germany, Italy, the Netherlands, Republic of Singapore, Spain, Sweden, United Kingdom; there are domestic (Washington Campus Program) and international internships, overseas business residencies. Special facilities: Center for International Business Education, Frederick A. and Barbara M. Erb Environmental Management Institute, Mitsui Life Financial Research Center, National Quality Research Center, Paton Center for Research in Accounting, Tauber Manufacturing Institute, William Davidson Institute. Library: 144,000 volumes, 3,100 subscriptions.

Annual tuition: resident full-time $27,130, part-time $1618 per credit; nonresident full-time $32,130, part-time $1618 per credit.

Enrollment: total full-time 837, part-time 1059 (men 60%, women 40%). Faculty: full-time 121, part-time 57; 98% with Ph.D./D.B.A. Degrees conferred: M.B.A. (full-time, part-time, day, evening), M.B.A.-M.Arch., M.B.A.-M.A. (Chinese Studies, Japanese Studies, Middle Eastern and North African Studies, Russian and East European Studies, South and Southeast Asian Studies), M.B.A.-M.H.S.A. (Health Service Administration), M.B.A.-J.D., M.B.A.-M.P.P. (Public Policy), M.B.A.-M.M. (Music), M.B.A.-M.M.E. (Manufacturing Engineering), M.B.A.-M.S. (Construction Engineering, Engineering, Industrial and Operations Engineering, Natural Resources and Environment, Nursing Administration), M.B.A.-M.S.W. (Social Work), Ph.D.

ADMISSION REQUIREMENTS. All applicants must have a bachelor's degree from a recognized institution of higher education. Students are required to have their own personal computer. Application can be downloaded from Web site, Adobe Acrobat Reader required. Accepts MBA Multi-App application in lieu of institutional application. Early applications are encouraged for both admission and financial aid consideration. Beginning full-time students are admitted Fall only, part-time admitted both Fall and Spring. For full-time Decision I applicants apply by December 1; Decision II deadline January 15; Decision III deadline March 1; international applicants are encouraged to apply for either Decision I or II. Part-time applicants apply by May 1 (Fall), October 1 (Spring). Submit an MBA/Graduate School application, a GMAT results (will accept GMAT test results from the last five years, latest acceptable date is January (full-time), March (part-time)), official transcripts from each undergraduate/graduate school attended, two letters of recommendation, four essays, résumé (prefers at least four years of work experience), and an application fee of $125 to the Office of Admission. In addition, international students (whose native language is other than English) should submit a TOEFL report (minimum score 600), TSE, TWE (recommended), certified translations and evaluations of all official transcripts, recommendation should be in English or with certified translations and proof of sufficient financial resources for two years of academic study. Interviews are strongly recommended prior to the admissions committee reviewing completed application. Joint degree applicants must apply to and be accepted to both schools/programs, contact the Admissions Office for current information and specific admissions requirements. Notification for Decision I applicants is made on February 1; Decision II applicants are notified March 15; Decision III applicants are notified May 1. Part-time Fall applicants are notified on July 1 and Spring applicants are notified December 1. Admissions Office phone: (734)763-5796; e-mail: umbusmba@umich.edu, ummbaeve @umich.edu (part-time applicants).

ADMISSION REQUIREMENTS FOR DOCTORAL CANDI-DATES. Contact Ph.D. Office at (734)764-2343 for application material and information. Beginning students are admitted Fall Only. Both U.S. citizens and international applicants apply by January 15. U.S. citizens and permanent residents mail the following items to Rackham Graduate School: application form—Rackham copy, application fee of $55. Mail the following items to the Business School Doctoral Studies Office: application form—Department copy, official GRE or GMAT test scores from ETS, official transcripts from each college or university in sealed envelopes, three letters of recommendation, and statement of purpose. International applicants mail the following items to Rackham Graduate School: application form—Rackham copy, application fee of $55, one set of official transcripts from each college or university in sealed envelopes. Mail the following items to the Business School Doctoral Studies Office: application form—department copy, Official TOEFL and GRE or GMAT test scores from ETS, one set of official transcripts from each college or university in sealed envelopes, three letters of recommendation, and statement of purpose. Interviews strongly encouraged. Notification is made by mid-March. E-mail: umbusphd@umich.edu.

ADMISSION STANDARDS. Very selective. Mean GMAT: 645; mean GPA: 3.3 (A = 4). Gourman rating: the MBA program was rated in the top 11, the score was 4.84; the Ph.D. program was rated in the top 20, the score was 4.77. *U.S. News & World Report* ranked the Business School in the top 13 of all U.S. business schools and rated the part-time MBA program in the top 5. *Business Week* listed Business School in the top 2 of all American business schools.

FINANCIAL AID. Business School scholarships, fellowships, Dean's Fellowships, graduate assistantships, Federal Perkins Loans, Stafford Subsidized and Unsubsidized Loans, Federal W/S available; Loan Repayment Assistance Program for students entering the nonprofit or public sectors. Aid is available for part-time study. Aid for international students is limited to scholarships only. Assistantships/fellowships may be available for joint degree candidates. Financial Aid applications and information are generally available at the on-campus interview or included with admissions application; apply by March 1 (Fall), by September 30 (Spring). Request scholarship, fellowship, assistantship, and need-based information from the Business School. Phone: (734)764-5139. For most financial assistance and all Federal programs submit FAFSA (School code: 002325), also submit Financial Aid Transcript, Federal Income Tax forms. Approximately 50% of students receive some form of financial assistance.

DEGREE REQUIREMENTS. For M.B.A.: 60 credit program including 29 elective credits (of which 10 credits may be taken at any graduate school at University of Michigan), two-year program; degree program must be completed in six years. For M.B.A.-M.Arch.: 90 credit program. For M.B.A.-M.A., M.M., M.S.: 65–81 credits, two-and-one-half- to four-year programs. For M.B.A.-M.H.S.A.: 90 credit program. For M.B.A.-M.P.P.: 90 credit program. For M.B.A.-M.S.W.: 84 credit program. For M.B.A.-J.D.: four-and-one-half- to five-year program. For Ph.D.: at least three years in full-time residency; preliminary written exam; dissertation proposal and oral defense; dissertation; oral defense; offered through the Rackham Graduate School.

M.B.A. CONCENTRATIONS.
Accounting.
Business Administration.
Business Economics and Policy.
Computer and Information Systems.
Corporate Strategy.
Entrepreneurial Track.
Finance.

International Business.
Law, History, and Communication.
Marketing.
Operations Management.
Organizational Behavior and Human Resource Management.
Statistics and Management Science.

PH.D. CONCENTRATIONS.
Accounting.
Corporate Strategy.
Finance.
Individualized Program.
International Business.
Marketing.
Operations Management.
Organizational Behavior and Human Resource Management.

School of Dentistry (48109-1078)

Originated 1875. Annual tuition: resident $16,960, nonresident $29,946. On-campus housing available. Average academic year cost: $12,930. Housing Office phone: (734)763-3164. Total average cost for all other first-year expenses: $2500.

Enrollment: first-year class 103; full-time 450 (men 48%, women 52%). Degrees conferred: D.D.S., D.D.S.-M.P.H., M.S. (Biomaterials, Dental Hygiene), D.D.S.-Ph.D. (Oral Health Sciences). The M.S., M.P.H., and Ph.D. are offered through the School of Graduate Studies.

ADMISSION REQUIREMENTS. AADSAS, transcripts, three letters of recommendation, DAT (not later than October) required in support of School's application. Interview often required. Applicants must have completed at least two but preferably three years of college study. Preference given to state residents. Accepts transfer applicants from U.S. and Canadian dental schools. Apply to AADSAS after June 1, before February 1. Application fee $50. Phone: (734)763-3313.

ADMISSION STANDARDS. Selective. Mean DAT: Academic 19.23, PAT 18.27; mean GPA: 3.38 (A = 4). Usual minimum average: 2.75 (A = 4). Accepts 20–25% of total annual applicants. Approximately 80% are state residents.

FINANCIAL AID. Scholarships, minority scholarships, research stipends, grants, institutional loans, State Loan Programs, DEAL, HEAL, alternative loan programs; Federal Perkins Loans, Stafford Subsidized and Unsubsidized Loans, Military Service Commitment Scholarship programs are available. Assistantships/fellowships may be available for Combined Degree candidates. Institutional Financial Aid applications and information are generally available at the on-campus by-invitation interview and applications are sent to all accepted applicants. Contact the Office of Student Affairs and Financial Aid for current information. Phone: (734)763-3313. All awards are made through the University's Office of Financial Aid. For most financial assistance and all need-based programs use FAFSA (School code: 002325), also submit Financial Aid Transcript, Federal Income Tax forms, and use of Federal Funds Certification. Approximately 82% of students receive some form of financial assistance.

DEGREE REQUIREMENTS. For D.D.S.: satisfactory completion of four-year program. For D.D.S.-M.P.H.: generally a five-year program. For D.D.S.-M.S.: generally a four-and-one-half- to five-and-one-half-year program, thesis/nonthesis option; research project. For D.D.S.-Ph.D.: generally a six- to seven-year program; candidacy; dissertation; oral defense; final exam.

FIELDS OF GRADUATE STUDY.
Dental Hygiene. Undergraduate degree in dental hygiene required for admission. M.S. only.

Dental Materials. M.S., Ph.D.

Dental Public Health. M.P.H., Ph.D.

Endodontics. M.S. only.

Oral Diagnosis. M.S. only.

Oral Health Sciences. Ph.D.

Oral Pathology. M.S. only.

Oral Surgery. Three years of full-time study; M.S. only.

Orthodontics. M.S. only.

Pedodontics. M.S. only.

Periodontics. M.S. only.

Prosthodontics. Includes crown and bridge prosthodontics, occlusion, operative dentistry. M.S. only.

Note: All programs require thesis.

School of Law (48109-1215)

Web site: www.law.umich.edu

Opened 1869 and is one oldest in the U.S. ABA approved since 1923. AALS member. Semester system. Full-time, day study only. Special programs: summer "Start Program," externships, internships. Law library: 862,197 volumes, 8719 subscriptions; has LEXIS, NEXIS, WESTLAW, LEXCALIBUR; is a Federal Government Depository.

Annual tuition: resident $20,986, nonresident $26,596. On-campus housing available for both single and married students. Contact Housing Office at (734)763-1316 or Lawyers Club at (734)764-1116 for both on- and off-campus housing information. Law students tend to live off-campus. For family housing contact Officer of University Housing. Phone: (734)763-3164. Off-campus housing and personal expenses: approximately $12,495.

Enrollment: first-year class 367; total full-time 1101 (men 58%, women 42%). Faculty: full-time 70, part-time 17. Student to faculty ratio 14.9 to 1. Degrees conferred: J.D., J.D.-M.B.A., J.D.-M.H.S.A., J.D.-M.A. (Modern Middle Eastern and North African Studies, Russian and East European Studies, Law and Philosophy, History), J.D.-M.S. (Natural Resources), J.D.-M.P.P. (Public Policy), J.D.-Ph.D. (Economics), LL.M., M.C.L. (only for persons who have completed a basic legal education and received a university degree in law in another country), LL.M.-S.J.D.

ADMISSION REQUIREMENTS. LSDAS Law School report, bachelor's degree, transcripts, LSAT, letters of recommendation required in support of application. TOEFL required of international students. Interview not required. Accepts transfer applicants. Graduates of unaccredited colleges not considered. Apply to Director of Admissions after September 1, before February 15. Application fee $70. Phone: (734)764-0537.

ADMISSION REQUIREMENTS. For LL.M., M.C.L., LL.M.-S.J.D. Applicants must have an accredited B.S., B.S. degree or its equivalent and LL.B. or J.D. from accredited Law School; achieved High Honors (Order of the Coif or equivalent academic distinction); letters of recommendation from Law School faculty, official transcripts should include an explanation of grading and rank-in-class, résumé, personal statement, a statement of purpose including academic interest and ability to benefit from graduate study are required in support of International and Graduate Application. In addition, international applicants from non-English-speaking countries are required to take TOEFL (usual minimum 600) or MELAB before December 1 (one calendar year before year for which admission is sought). Admits Fall only. Apply by January 1 to Office of International and Graduate Programs. Phone: (734)764-0535; fax: (734)936-1973; e-mail: law.grad.Admissions@umich.edu. Notification of decision is generally made in March. The LL.M., M.C.L. class is 30–35, the LL.M.-S.J.D. class is no more than 15.

ADMISSION STANDARDS. Competitive. Mean LSAT: 166; mean GPA: 3.53 (A = 4). Gourman rating: 4.92. *U.S. News &*

World Report ranking is in the top seven of all U.S. law schools. Accepts about 30% of total annual applicants. Approximately 25% of entering class are nonresidents.

FINANCIAL AID. Scholarships, grants, fellowships (overseas travel fellowships for legal studies abroad), assistantships, Federal W/S, loans. Apply for financial aid by February 1. Use FAFSA (School code: E00506). Apply to Director of Advanced Studies for fellowships for advanced degrees. About 30% of students receive aid from School. Most state residents with need are aided. Has a Debt Management Program.

DEGREE REQUIREMENTS. For J.D.: 83 (31 required) credits with a GPA of at least a 2.0 (A = 4), plus completion of upper divisional writing course; four-year program. For J.D.-master's: individually designed programs, generally completed in three and a half to four years rather than four and a half to five years if each degree were taken consecutively. For LL.M.: 24 credits at least two semester in full-time residence; a 3.0 (A = 4) GPA required. For M.C.L. (International): 20 credits; at least two semesters in full-time residence; one course in U.S. Constitutional Law; research paper; GPA of 2.3 (A = 4) required. For LL.M.-S.J.D.: completion of a LL.M. of 24 credits taken in two semesters; research paper, thesis project; a GPA of 3.0 (A = 4); admission to candidacy; thesis; oral exam; completion of program within five years.

Medical School (48109-0611)

Web site: www.med.umich.edu/medschool

Established 1850. Located at Medical Center. Special facilities: Comprehensive Cancer Center, Geriatrics Center, Historical Center for the Health Sciences, Howard Hughes Medical Institute at University of Michigan, Kresge Hearing Research Institute, Mental Health Research Institute, Michigan Human Genome Center, Michigan Transplant Center, Multipurpose Arthritis and Musculoskeletal Disease Center, Center for Organogensis. Special programs: summer programs for underrepresented minorities, for information contact Director. Phone (734)763-1296. Library: 200,000 volumes, 3000 subscriptions.

Annual tuition: resident $18,538, nonresident $28,898; fees $793. Limited on-campus housing available. Contact Office of University Housing for both on- and off-campus housing information. Phone: (734) 763-3164. Medical students tend to live off-campus. Off-campus housing and personal expenses: approximately $15,000.

Enrollment: first-year class 170, M.D.-Ph.D. approximately 8 each year; total full-time 653 (men 60%, women 40%). Faculty: full-time 750, over 1000 part-time and volunteers. Degrees conferred: M.D., B.A./B.S.-M.D. (Inteflex Program), M.D.-M.P.H., M.D.-M.S., M.D.-Ph.D., M.S.T.P. The M.S. and Ph.D. are offered through the School of Graduate Studies.

ADMISSION REQUIREMENTS. AMCAS report, transcripts, references, MCAT, interview required in support of application. Applicants must have completed at least 90 semester hours of university work. Does not have EDP. Accepts transfer applicants. Apply after June 1, before November 15. Application fee $60, after initial screening procedure. Phone: (734)764-6317; fax: (734)763-0453.

ADMISSION STANDARDS. Competitive. Median MCAT: 11.3; median GPA: 3.6 (A = 4). Gourman rating: 4.91. *U.S. News & World Report* ranking is in the top eight of all U.S. medical schools. Accepts 8% of total annual applicants. Approximately 75% are state residents.

FINANCIAL AID. Scholarships, minority scholarships, Grants-in-Aid, institutional loans, HEAL, alternative loan programs, NIH stipends; Federal Perkins Loans, Stafford Subsidized and

Unsubsidized Loans, Service Commitment Scholarship programs are available. Students selected for M.S.T.P. receive full tuition, health insurance, and $15,000 stipend. Assistantships/fellowships may be available for Joint Degree candidates. Financial Aid applications and information are given out at the on-campus by-invitation interview. Contact the Financial Aid office for current information. Phone: (734)763-4147; e-mail: medfinaid@ umich.edu. For most financial assistance and all Federal programs use FAFSA (School code: E00398), also submit Financial Aid Transcript, Federal Income Tax forms. Approximately 85% of students receive some form of financial assistance.

DEGREE REQUIREMENTS. For B.A./B.S.-M.D.: an eight-year program. For M.D.: satisfactory completion of four-year program. All students must pass USMLE Step 1 prior to entering third year; all students must pass USMLE Step 2 prior to awarding of M.D. For M.D.-M.B.A., M.D.-M.P.H.: generally a five-year program. For M.D.-M.S.: generally a four-and-one-half- to five-and-one-half-year program. For M.D.-Ph.D.: generally a seven- to eight-year program.

FIELDS OF GRADUATE STUDY.
Anatomy and Cell Biology.
Bioengineering.
Biological Chemistry.
Biology.
Biophysics.
Biostatistics.
Cellular and Molecular Biology.
Chemistry.
Epidemiology.
Genetic Counseling. M.S.
Human Genetics.
Medicinal Chemistry.
Microbiology and Immunology.
Molecular Biology.
Neurosciences.
Pathology.
Pharmacology.
Physiology.

School of Music
Web site: www.music.umich.edu

Organized 1880.
Annual tuition: resident $11,876, nonresident $24,452; per credit, resident $770, nonresident $1464.
Enrollment: full-time 286, part-time 25 (men 55%, women 45%). Faculty: full-time 84, part-time 34. Degrees conferred: M.M., Specialist in Music. The A.M., A.Mus.D., D.M.A., Ph.D. are offered through the School of Graduate Studies

ADMISSION REQUIREMENTS. Varies by department, but generally one official transcript, audition, or tape (for M.M., D.M.A.), GRE (for some majors) required in support of School's application. MELAB required for international applicants. Accepts transfer applicants. Apply to Associate Dean by February 15 (Fall), November 15 (Winter); February 1 for Composition, Music History, and Conducting. Application fee $55. Phone: (734)764-0593; fax: (734)763-5097; e-mail: music.admissions@umich.edu.

ADMISSION STANDARDS. Selective for most programs, very selective for others. Usual minimum average: 3.0 (A = 4).

FINANCIAL AID. Annual awards from institutional funds: scholarships, teaching assistantships, internships, Federal W/S, loans. Approved for VA benefits. Apply February 15 to Associate Dean for scholarships, assistantships; to Financial Aid Office for all other programs. Phone: (734)763-6600; fax: (734)747-3081. Use FAFSA. About 40% of students receive aid other than loans from School and outside sources. No aid available for part-time students.

DEGREE REQUIREMENTS. For M.M.: 30–36 semester hours minimum; placement exam in theory; thesis, composition, final exam, or public recital, depending upon major. For Specialist in Music: 30 credit programs; 16 hour concentration. For other degree requirements, consult the Associate Dean, or see the School of Graduate Studies listing above.

FIELDS OF STUDY.
Arts Administration. Joint M.M.-M.B.A. program.
Chamber Music. Includes bassoon, cello, clarinet, double bass, euphonium, flute, horn, oboe, saxophone, trombone, trumpet, tuba, viola, violin. M.M.
Church Music. M.M., Spec.M.
Composition. M.M.
Conducting. Includes band/wind ensemble, choral, orchestral. M.M.
Early Keyboard Instruments. M.M.
Ethnomusicology. Spec.M.
Improvisation. M.M.
Keyboard Instruments. M.M.
Music Education. M.M., Spec.M.
Performance. All instruments and voice. M.M., Spec.M.
Piano Accompanying and Chamber Music. M.M., Spec.M.
Piano Accompanying and Performance. M.M.
Piano Pedagogy and Performance. M.M.
Wind Instruments. M.M.

School of Public Health
Web site: www.sph.umich.edu

Established 1941.
Annual tuition: resident $11,876, nonresident $24,452.
Enrollment: full- and part-time 762. Faculty; full-time 109. Degrees conferred: M.P.H., M.H.S.A., Dr.P.H., M.H.S.A.-M.B.A., M.H.S.A.-M.N.A., M.H.S.A.-M.P.P., M.P.H.-M.P.P., M.H.S.A.-M.S.I.O.E., M.H.S.A.-J.D., M.P.H.-J.D., M.P.H.-M.D., M.P.H.-D.O. The M.S. and Ph.D. are offered through the School of Graduate Studies.

ADMISSION REQUIREMENTS. Transcript, three letters of recommendation, GRE required in support of School's application. Interview required for M.P.H. only. TOEFL required for international applicants. Joint degree applicants must apply to and be accepted by both degree programs/departments/schools. Apply to Office of Student Affairs. School-wide application deadline is March 1. Application fee $55. Phone: (734)764-5425; fax: (734)763-5455.

ADMISSION STANDARDS. Very selective for most programs, selective for others. Usual minimum average: 3.0 (A = 4).

FINANCIAL AID. Fellowships, teaching assistantships, internships, grants, Federal W/S, loans. Approved for VA benefits. Apply to the Office of Student Affairs and to the University of Michigan Office of Financial Aid. Phone: (734)763-0931. Use FAFSA.

DEGREE REQUIREMENTS. For M.P.H.: 60 credit hours; field experience. For M.H.S.A.: 60 credit hours; field experience. For Dr.P.H.: two years minimum beyond master's; preliminary exam; dissertation; final oral exam. Joint degree programs generally reduce the time needed to complete both degrees by half a year or more if the degrees had been taken separately. For M.S., Ph.D. see Horace H. Rackham School of Graduate Studies listing above.

FIELDS OF STUDY.
Biostatistics.
Dental Public Health.
Environmental Health Sciences.

General Epidemiology.
Hazardous Substance Academic Training.
Health Behavior and Health Education.
Health Management and Policy.
Health Services Administration.
Hospital and Molecular Epidemiology.
Human Nutrition.
Industrial Hygiene.
International Health.
Occupational and Environmental Epidemiology.
Occupational and Environmental Medicine.
Public Health.
Toxicology.

School of Social Work (48109-1285)

Established 1921. Semester system. Annual tuition: resident $12,706, nonresident $23,546.

Enrollment: full-time 570, part-time 23. School faculty: full-time 43, part-time 8. Degrees conferred: M.S.W., M.S.W.-Ph.D. (Anthropology, Economics, Political Science, Psychology, Sociology). The Ph.D. is offered through the Horace H. Rackham School of Graduate Studies.

ADMISSION REQUIREMENTS. Transcripts, letters of reference, supplementary statement dealing with applicant's career objectives and personal qualifications, interviews required in support of School's application. TOEFL or MELAB TSE (recommended) required for international applicants. Apply to M.S.W. program director by March 1 (Fall), Ph.D. application January 2 (Fall). Application fee $50. Phone: (734)764-3309.

ADMISSION STANDARDS. Selective. Usual minimum average: 3.0 (A = 4).

FINANCIAL AID. Grants, scholarships, fellowships, traineeships, Federal W/S, loans. Apply at the same time as admission to program to University's Office of Financial Aid. Phone: (734)763-6600. Use FAFSA (School code: 002325).

DEGREE REQUIREMENTS. For M.S.W.: 60 credit hours; full-time program; research papers. For Ph.D.: see Horace H. Rackham School of Graduate Studies listing above.

SPECIALIZATIONS AND CERTIFICATIONS.
Jewish Communal Service and Judaic Studies. Certificate.
Social Work in Public School.
Social Work in the Workplace.
Specialization in Aging. Certificate.

MIDDLEBURY COLLEGE
Middlebury, Vermont 05753-6002
Web site: www.middlebury.edu

Founded 1800. Located 35 miles S of Burlington. Coed. Private control. 4-1-4 system. Special facilities: Music Library, Performing Arts Center, Museum of Art. Library: 580,000 volumes, 2496 subscriptions.

Tuition: summer study (includes room and board) on campus $3090, academic year abroad at Language Schools (Florence, Italy; Madrid, Spain; Mainz, Germany; Paris, France) $35,900 (comprehensive fee covers Fall, Winter, Spring).

Graduate Study

Graduate study since 1915. Enrollment: full- and part-time 800. Faculty: full-time 100. Degrees conferred: M.A., D.M.L.

The M.A. and D.M.L. may be earned either during a series of summers in Vermont, or by combining summer study in Vermont with an academic year at one of College's five schools abroad.

ADMISSION REQUIREMENTS. For M.A.: transcripts, proficiency in the language equivalent to an undergraduate major required in support of College's application. For D.M.L.: transcripts, equivalent of an M.A. in the primary language. Apply to Language School Office of the primary language of interest. Rolling admissions process. Application fee $50. Phone: (802)388-3711, ext. 5552; fax: (802)388-1253.

FINANCIAL AID. Awards from institutional funds: scholarships, grants, Federal W/S, loans. Approved for VA benefits. Apply to Office of Financial Aid as soon as possible after January 1. Use FAFSA. Phone: (802)388-3711, ext. 5158.

DEGREE REQUIREMENTS. For M.A. in foreign languages: 12 course units. Transfer credits limited to 3 approved course units. For M.S.: 9 courses, at least 6 in residence; laboratory teaching. For D.M.L.: 12 units beyond the M.A.; teaching experience; residence in country of primary language; proficiency in one other language in addition to primary language; dissertation; final written/oral exams.

FIELDS OF STUDY.
Biology. M.S.

ACADEMIC YEAR LANGUAGE PROGRAMS (M.A., D.M.L.):
French.
German.
Italian.
Russian.
Spanish.

MIDDLE TENNESSEE STATE UNIVERSITY
Murfreesboro, Tennessee 37132
Web site: www.mtsu.edu

Founded 1911. Located 30 miles SE of Nashville. CGS member. Coed. State control. Semester system. Library: 1,000,000 volumes, 3600 subscriptions.

Annual tuition: full-time, resident $2984, nonresident $8612; per hour, resident $156, nonresident $400. Annual academic year housing cost for single students: $2400–$4715 (excluding board). Contact Housing Office for both on- and off-campus housing information. Phone: (615)898-2971. Day-care facilities available.

College of Graduate Studies

Enrollment: full-time 227, part-time 1477. Faculty teaching graduate students: full-time 350, part-time 38. Degrees conferred: M.A., M.A.T., M.B.A., M.B.E., M.C.J., M.Ed., M.S., M.S.T., M.V.T.E., Ed.S., D.A.

ADMISSION REQUIREMENTS. Transcripts, three letters of reference, MAT/GRE/GMAT in support of School's application. On-line application available. TOEFL required for international applicants. Accepts transfer applicants. Graduates of unaccredited institutions not considered. Apply to Dean of Graduate School, by August 1. Application fee $25. Phone: (615)898-2840; fax: (615)904-8020.

ADMISSION STANDARDS. Selective. Usual minimum average: 3.0 (A = 4).

FINANCIAL AID. Fellowships, research assistantships, administrative assistantships, teaching assistantships, internships, tuition waivers, Federal W/S, loans. Approved for VA benefits. Contact the Office of Financial Aid; no specified closing date. Phone: (615)898-2830. Use FAFSA and University's FAF. Aid available for part-time students.

DEGREE REQUIREMENTS. For M.A., M.S.: 30 semester hours minimum; admission to candidacy; reading knowledge of one foreign language or approved research tool; thesis (three semester hours minimum). For M.A.T., M.S.T., M.V.T.E.: 30 semester hours minimum; teaching certification; admission to candidacy; comprehensive exam. For M.Ed.: 33 semester hours; admission to candidacy; comprehensive exam. For M.B.A.: 36 semester hours; admission to candidacy; comprehensive exam. For M.B.E.: 32 semester hours; admission to candidacy; comprehensive exam. For M.C.J.: 36 semester hours; admission to candidacy; comprehensive exam. For Ed.S.: 30 semester hours; admission to candidacy; comprehensive exam. For D.A.: 48 semester hours beyond master's; qualifying exam; admission to candidacy; 3 hours externship, 3 hours internship; dissertation (6 semester hours minimum); defense of dissertation.

FIELDS OF STUDY.
Accounting/Information Systems. M.S.
Administration and Supervision. Includes K–12 public school, higher education. M.Ed., Ed.S.
Aerospace Education. M.Ed.
Aviation Administration. Includes airline/airport management, aviation assist management. M.S.
Biology. M.S., M.S.T.
Business Administration. M.B.A.
Business Education. Includes marketing education, office management. M.B.E.
Chemistry. M.S., D.A.
Computer Science. M.S.
Criminal Justice Administration. M.C.J.
Curriculum and Instruction. Includes ESL, early childhood, elementary. M.Ed., Ed.S.
Economics. Includes industrial relations, financial economics. M.A., D.A.
English. M.A., D.A.
Exercise Science and Health Promotion. M.S.
Foreign Language. Includes French, German, Spanish. M.A.T.
Health, Physical Education, Recreation, and Safety. Includes health, physical education (M.S., Ph.D.), recreation, sport management. M.S., Ph.D.
History. Includes public history, historic preservation. M.A., D.A.
Human Sciences. Includes nutrition and food science, child development and family studies. M.S.
Industrial Studies. Includes engineering technology, occupational health and safety. M.S.
Mass Communications. M.S.
Mathematics. Includes general mathematics, industrial mathematics, research preparation (M.S.); middle grades mathematics, secondary mathematics (M.S.T.). M.S., M.S.T.
Music. M.A.
Psychology. Includes clinical, experimental, industrial/organizational, quantitative, school psychology. M.A.
Reading. M.Ed.
School Counseling. M.Ed.
Sociology. M.A.
Special Education. Includes mildly/moderately disabled, preschool disabled, severe/profoundly disabled, vision disabilities. M.Ed.
Vocational-Technical Education. Includes agriculture, business distributive education, home economics, industrial studies. M.V.T.E.

MIDWESTERN STATE UNIVERSITY
Wichita Falls, Texas 76308-2096
Web site: www.mwsu.edu

Founded 1922. Coed. State control. Semester system. Library: 366,350 volumes, 1100 subscriptions.

Annual tuition: full-time, resident $3062, nonresident $9602; per credit, resident $38, nonresident $181. On-campus housing for single students. Average academic year housing cost: $4278 (including board). Apply to Director of Housing. Phone: (940)397-4217.

Graduate School

Graduate study since 1952. Enrollment: full-time 132, part-time 526 (men 45%, women 55%). Graduate faculty: full-time 58, part-time 12. Degrees conferred: M.A., M.S., M.Ed., M.S.K., M.B.A.

ADMISSION REQUIREMENTS. One official transcript from each institution attended, GRE or GMAT required in support of School's application. On-line application available. TOEFL required for international applicants. Accepts transfer applicants. Graduates of unaccredited institution. Admission deadlines: August 7 (Fall), December 15 (Spring), May 15 (Summer I), June 15 (Summer II). International applications must be received 5 months prior to registration. Application fee $10, $50 for international applicants. Phone: (940)397-4321; fax: (940)397-4672; e-mail: admissions@mwsu.edu.

ADMISSION STANDARDS. Varies with program. Usual minimum average: 3.0 (A = 4). Must meet index GRE/GMAT + (200 times the GPA on last 60 hours of undergraduate work.)

FINANCIAL AID. Annual awards from institutional funds: scholarships, research assistantships, teaching assistantships, internships, Federal W/S, loans. Approved for VA benefits. Apply by March 1 to Division Director of major field. Phone: (940)397-4214. Use FAFSA. Aid sometimes available for part-time students.

DEGREE REQUIREMENTS. For M.A.: 30 semester hours minimum, at least 24 in residence; reading knowledge of one foreign language; thesis; final comprehensive exam. For M.Ed., M.B.A., M.S., M.S.K.: 36 hours minimum, at least 30 in residence; final comprehensive exam; substantial research paper.

FIELDS OF STUDY.
Business Administration.
Counseling.
Curriculum and Instruction.
Educational Leadership.
Elementary Education.
English.
Family Nurse Practitioner.
History.
Human Rescource Development.
Kinesiology.
Liberal Arts.
Nurse Educator.
Nurse Practitioner.
Political Science.
Psychology.
Public Administration.
Radiologic Education.
Radiologic Sciences.
Reading.
School Counseling.
Special Education.

MIDWESTERN UNIVERSITY
Downers Grove, Illinois 60515-1235
Web site: www.midwestern.edu

Founded 1900. Located 25 miles W of Chicago. Coed. Private control. Graduate study only. Semester system. Library: 84,000 volumes, 1450 current subscriptions; has MEDLINE, CANCERLINE, BIOETHIC, HEALTH, TOXLINE, DIALOG, OCLC. The University's NIH ranking was fifth among Schools of Osteopathic Medicine with two awards/grants worth $257,992. Total University enrollment: 2700.

Limited on-campus housing available. Annual on-campus housing cost: single students $2244 (room only), married students $4863. Contact Housing Director for both on- and off-campus housing information. Phone: (630)971-6400. Medical students tend to live off-campus. Off-campus housing and personal expenses: approximately $6354.

The University's Graduate Colleges include Chicago College of Osteopathic Medicine, College of Allied Health Professions; at the Arizona campus, the Arizona College of Osteopathic Medicine.

Downers Grove Campus
Chicago College of Osteopathic Medicine

Established 1900 as the College of Osteopathic Medicine and Surgery, merged and created Littlejohn College and Hospital, name changed to Chicago College in 1970. Semester system. Affiliated hospitals: Chicago Osteopathic Hospital and Medical Center, Olympia Fields Osteopathic Hospital and Medical Center.

Annual tuition: resident $22,816, nonresident $27,711. Enrollment: first-year class 160; total full-time 639 (men 60%, women 40%) Faculty: full-time 141, part-time 244. Degrees conferred: D.O., D.O.-Ph.D.

ADMISSION REQUIREMENTS. Preference given to state residents, U.S. citizens and permanent residents only. Bachelor's degree from an accredited institution required. Apply through AACOMAS (file after June 1, before December 1), submit MCAT (will accept test results from last three years), official transcripts for each school attended (should show at least 90 semester credits/135 quarter credits), service processing fee. After a review of the AACOMAS application and supporting documents a decision is made concerning which candidates should receive supplemental materials. Supplemental applications are sent to all students with a 2.75 (A = 4) science GPA. The supplemental application, an application fee of $50, a personal statement, and three recommendations (one from a D.O.) should be returned to Office of Admission as soon as possible, no later than early January. Interviews are by invitation only and generally for final selection. First-year students admitted Fall only. Rolling admissions process, notification starts in October and is finished when class is filled. Phone: (630)969-4400; fax: (630)971-6086; e-mail: admiss@midwestern.edu.

ADMISSION STANDARDS. Selective. Usual minimum average: 2.75. Median MCAT: 8.7; median GPA: 3.5 (A = 4). Accepts approximately 5% of total annual applicants.

FINANCIAL AID. Scholarships, institutional loans, NOF, HEAL, alternative loan programs, Federal Perkins Loans, Stafford Subsidized and Unsubsidized Loans, Service Obligation Scholarship programs, Military and National Health Service programs are available. Financial Aid applications and information are available at the on-campus, by-invitation interview. Contact the Financial Aid Office for current information. Use FAFSA (School code: 001657), also submit Financial Aid Transcript, Federal Income Tax forms. Approximately 87% of students receive some form of financial assistance.

DEGREE REQUIREMENTS. For D.O.: satisfactory completion of 4-year (45-month) program. All students must pass the National Board of Osteopathic Medical Examination Level I to advance to the third year. All students must take the National Board of Osteopathic Medical Examination Level II prior to the awarding of D.O.

College of Health Sciences

Founded 1992. Annual tuition: resident $22,816, nonresident $27,711. Enrollment: total full- and part-time 258. Faculty: full-time 22, part-time 61. Degrees conferred: M.B.S., M.M.S., M.O.T., M.P.T.

ADMISSION REQUIREMENTS. Official transcripts, GRE or MCAT or PCAT, two letters of recommendation required in support of application. On-line application available. Apply to the Office of Admissions by May 15. Application fee $50. First-year students admitted Fall only. Rolling admissions process. Phone: (800)458-6253; fax: (630)971-6086; e-mail: admissil@midwestern.edu.

ADMISSION STANDARDS. Selective. Usual minimum average: 2.75 (A = 4).

FINANCIAL AID. Scholarships, grants, assistantships, Federal W/S, loans. Contact the Office of Financial Services for current information. Apply by April 1. Phone: (630)515-6101. Use FAFSA (School code: 001657). Approximately 90% of students receive some type of financial assistance.

DEGREE REQUIREMENTS. For M.B.S.: 72 quarter hour, full-time program; research project; thesis. For M.M.S.: 27-month full-time program. For M.O.T.: 27-month, full-time program; field placement. For M.P.T.: 30-month, full-time program.

FIELDS OF STUDY.
Biological Sciences. M.B.S.
Occupational Therapy. M.O.T.
Physical Therapy. M.P.T.
Physician Assistant Studies. M.M.S.

Glendale Campus
Arizona College of Osteopathic Medicine
19555 North 59th Avenue
Glendale, Arizona 85308
Web site: www.acom.edu or www.midwestern edu

Established 1995. Located 15 miles NW of Phoenix, the newest school of osteopathic medicine. Semester system.

Annual tuition: $26,700. Limited on-campus housing available. Contact Manager of Residence Life for both on- and off-campus housing information. Phone: (602)572-3848. Medical students tend to live off-campus. Off-campus housing and personal expenses: approximately $12,251.

Enrollment: first-year class 135, total 460 (men 68%, women 32%). Degree conferred: D.O.

ADMISSION REQUIREMENTS. Bachelor's degree from an accredited institution required. 100% of applicants have bachelor's degree awarded prior to enrollment. Apply through AACOMAS (file after June 1, before December 1), submit MCAT (will accept test results from last three years), official transcripts for each school attended (should show at least 90 semester credits/135 quarter credits), service processing fee. After a review of the AACOMAS application and supporting documents a decision is made concerning which candidates should receive supplemental materials. The supplemental application, an application fee of $50, a personal statement, and two recommendations (one from a D.O.) should be returned to Office of Admission as soon as possible. In addition, international applicants must submit foreign transcripts to the World Education Service for translation and evaluation. TOEFL may be required of those applicants whose native language is other than English. Interviews are by invitation only and generally for final selection. First-year students admitted Fall only. Rolling admissions process, notification starts in October and is finished when class is filled. School does maintain an alternate list. Phone: (888)247-9277; e-mail: admissaz@ arizona.midwestern.edu.

ADMISSION REQUIREMENTS FOR TRANSFER APPLICANTS. Accepts transfers from other accredited U.S. osteopathic medical schools. Admission limited to space available. Contact the Office of Admissions for current information and specific requirements.

ADMISSION STANDARDS. Selective. Usual minimum GPA: 2.75 (A = 4). Median MCAT: 11.0; median GPA: 3.3.

FINANCIAL AID. Scholarships, institutional loans, NOF, HEAL, alternative loan programs, Federal Perkins Loans, Stafford Subsidized and Unsubsidized Loans, Service Obligation Scholarship programs, Military and National Health Service programs are available. Financial Aid applications and information are available from either the Arizona campus or from Downers Grove. Contact the Financial Aid Office for current information. Phone Glendale: (602) 572-3321, Downers Grove: (630)515-6035. Use FAFSA (School code: 001657), also submit Financial Aid Transcript, Federal Income Tax forms. Approximately 87% of students receive some form of financial assistance.

DEGREE REQUIREMENTS. For D.O.: satisfactory completion of four-year (45-month) program. All students must pass the National Board of Osteopathic Medical Examination Level I and all must take level II prior to the awarding of D.O.

MILLERSVILLE UNIVERSITY OF PENNSYLVANIA

Millersville, Pennsylvania 17551-0302
Web site: www.millersville.edu

Founded 1855. Located 3 miles SW of Lancaster. CGS member. Coed. Semester system. State control. Library: 496,100 volumes, 2500 subscriptions. Total University enrollment: 7500.

Tuition: per credit, resident $230, nonresident $389. On-campus housing for single graduate students. Housing cost: $4900 (including board). Apply to Office of Resident Life. Phone: (717)872-3162.

Graduate School

Graduate study since 1959. Enrollment: full-time 138, part-time 562. Faculty: full-time 205, part-time 67. Degrees conferred: M.Ed., M.S., M.A.

ADMISSION REQUIREMENTS. Transcripts, statement of academic and professional goals, three recommendations, GRE/ GMAT or MAT required in support of application. TOEFL required for international applicants. Accepts transfer applicants. Graduates of unaccredited institutions not considered. Apply to Graduate Office by March 1 (Summer, Fall), October 1 (Spring). Rolling admissions process. Application fee $30. Phone: (717)872-3030; fax: (717)871-2022; e-mail: gradstu@millersville.edu.

ADMISSION STANDARDS. Selective for most departments, Usual minimum average: 2.75 (A = 4).

FINANCIAL AID. Annual awards from institutional funds: assistantships, internships, Federal W/S, loans. Approved for VA benefits. Apply by March 15 to Dean, Graduate School for assistantships; to Financial Aid Office for all other aid. Use FAFSA. Phone: (717)872-3026. About 20% of students receive aid other than loans from College and outside sources. Loans available for part-time students.

DEGREE REQUIREMENTS. For M.Ed.: 30 credit hours minimum, 36 credit hours without research papers; qualifying exam; research paper. For M.A., M.S.: 30 credit hours minimum; qualifying exam; thesis/nonthesis option by program.

FIELDS OF STUDY.
Art.
Biology.
Business Administration.
Early Childhood Education.
Educational Leadership.
Education Supervision. Post-master's program only.
Elementary Education.
English.
Foreign Language. Includes French, German, Latin, Spanish.
History.
Mathematics.
Psychology.
Reading and Language Arts.
Reading Supervision. Post-master's program only.
School Psychology.
Special Education.
Sports Management.
Technology Education.

MILLS COLLEGE

Oakland, California 94613-1000
Web site: www.mills.edu

Founded 1852. Located 12 miles E of San Francisco. Coed on graduate level. Private control. Semester system. Library: 193,000 volumes, 2000 subscriptions. Total College enrollment: 1065.

Annual tuition: full-time $12,700; per course $2810. On-campus housing for single graduate students. Average academic year cost: $7964 (including board). Contact Director of Residence Life. Phone: (510)430-2130. Day-care facilities available.

Graduate Programs

Enrollment: full-time 324, part-time 55. College faculty teaching graduate students: full-time 67, part-time 72. Degrees conferred: M.A., M.A.L.A., M.F.A.

ADMISSION REQUIREMENTS. Two transcripts, GRE, three letters of recommendations required in support of application. Samples of creative work required for art, music, and writing majors. Interview required for some programs. TOEFL required for international applicants. Apply to Director of Graduate Study by February 1 (Fall), November 1 (Spring). Application fee $50. Phone: (510)430-3309; fax: (510)430-2159; e-mail: grad-studies@ mills.edu.

ADMISSION STANDARDS. Very selective. Usual minimum average: 3.2 (A = 4).

FINANCIAL AID. Limited annual awards from institutional funds: academic scholarships, teaching assistantships, special scholarships, music lesson scholarships, internships, grants, Federal W/S, loans. Apply to Director of Graduate Study by February 1 for scholarships, assistantships; to Financial Aid Office for all other programs. Use FAFSA and FAF of CSS. Phone: (510)430-2134. About 46% of students receive some form of financial aid, including loans. Aid available for part-time students.

DEGREE REQUIREMENTS. For M.F.A., M.A., M.A.L.A.: 10–12 semester course credits minimum, two years in residence; petition for candidacy; thesis or final project; final written/oral exam. Thesis is credited as a two-semester course.

FIELDS OF STUDY.
Art. Includes ceramics, intermedia, electronic, painting, sculpture, photography. M.F.A. only, admits Fall term only.
Computational Science. Interdisciplinary.
Creative Writing. Includes fiction, nonfiction, poetry. M.F.A. only.
Dance. Includes choreography, performance. M.A., M.F.A.
Education. Includes child development, early childhood, elementary, secondary, child life in hospitals. M.A., teaching credentials.
Educational Leadership.
English. Includes American literature. M.A.
Interdisciplinary Computer Science. M.A.
Liberal Studies. M.A. (part-time evening program).
Management. B.A.-M.B.A.
Music. Composition (M.A.), performance and literature (M.F.A.), electronic music and recording media (M.F.A.). M.A., M.F.A.

MILWAUKEE SCHOOL OF ENGINEERING
Milwaukee, Wisconsin 53201-3109
Web site: www.msoe.edu

Founded 1903. Coed. Private control. Quarter system. Graduate study available on part-time evening basis only. Special facilities: Applied Industrial Research Institute, Applied Technology Center, Biomedical Research Center, Center for Biomolecular Modeling, Fluid Power Institute, Photonics and Applied Optics Center, High Impact Materials and Structures Center. Library: 60,000 volumes, 750 subscriptions.

Tuition: per credit $462. Limited on-campus housing as most students are part-time evening. Contact Housing Office for information. Phone: (414)277-7400.

Graduate School

Enrollment: part-time only, about 400. Faculty teaching graduate students: 30. Degrees conferred: M.S.E., M.S.E.E., M.S.E.M., M.S.Ev., M.S.M.I., M.S.S.T., M.S.P.

ADMISSION REQUIREMENTS. Transcripts, GRE/GMAT, two letters of recommendation, interview required in support of School's application. On-line application available. TOEFL (minimum score 550) required for international applicants. Accepts transfer applicants. Apply to Graduate School by July 1. Application fee $30. Phone: (414)277-6763 or (800)332-6763; fax: (414)277-7475.

ADMISSION STANDARDS. Selective. Usual minimum average: 2.8 (A = 4).

FINANCIAL AID. Limited to three research assistantships, loans. Use FAFSA.

DEGREE REQUIREMENTS. For master's: 50–54 quarter hours minimum, at least 41–45 quarter hours in residence; thesis/oral presentation/special projects.

FIELDS OF STUDY.
Engineering. M.S.E.
Engineering Management. M.S.E.M.
Environmental Engineering. M.S.EV.
Medical Informatics. M.S.M.I.
Perfusion. M.S.P.
Structural Engineering. M.S.S.T.

MINNESOTA STATE UNIVERSITY, MANKATO
Mankato, Minnesota 56002-8400
Web site: www.mnsu.edu

Founded 1867. Located 80 miles SW of Minneapolis–St. Paul. CGS member. Coed. State control. Semester system. Special facilities: Biotechnology Research Center, Andreas and Standeford Astronomy Observatories, Performing Arts Center, Trafton Science Center, Water Resource Center, Urban Studies Institute, Conkling Art Gallery. Library: 1,100,000 volumes, 4300 subscriptions.

Tuition: per credit hour, resident $199, nonresident $298.50 (out-of-state students from Wisconsin, North Dakota, South Dakota, Manitoba may be eligible for reciprocity or an out-of-state tuition scholarship). On-campus housing available for single students only. Average academic year housing cost: $3676 (including board). Contact the Office of Residential Life for both on- and off-campus housing information. Phone: (507)389-1011. Day-care facilities available.

College of Graduate Studies

Graduate degrees authorized in 1953. Enrollment: full-time 677, part-time 1002. Graduate faculty: full- and part-time 405. Degrees conferred: M.A., M.B.A., M.S., M.A.T., M.F.A., M.M., Specialist.

ADMISSION REQUIREMENTS. Two official transcripts required in support of application. GRE/Subject/MAT/ GMAT required for some majors. TOEFL (minimum score 500) and Financial Statement Form required for international applicants. Accepts transfer applicants. Graduates of unaccredited institutions not considered. Apply to Graduate Studies Office by August 15 (Fall), December 1 (Spring); for international applicants May 22 (Fall), October 9 (Spring). Applicants for Graduate assistantships apply by February 3 for the Fall. Application fee $20. Phone: (800)772-0544 or (507)389-2321; fax: (507)389-5974; e-mail: grad@mnsu.edu.

ADMISSION STANDARDS. Selective for most departments, relatively open for others. Usual minimum average: 2.75 (A = 4).

FINANCIAL AID. Annual awards from institutional funds: fellowships, assistantships, tuition waivers, internships, Federal W/S, loans. Approved for VA benefits. Apply by March 1 to the Dean for assistantships; to Financial Aid Office for all other programs. Use FAFSA. Phone: (507)389-1185. About 50% of full-time students receive aid other than loans from College and outside sources. Aid available for part-time students.

DEGREE REQUIREMENTS. For M.A.: 30 credit hours with thesis, or 34 credit hours plus research paper; final written/oral exams. For M.S.: same as for M.A., no language requirement. For M.B.A.: 30 credit program hours; research paper. For M.A.T.: similar to M.A., but includes teaching internships. For Specialist: 30 credit program beyond master's. For M.F.A.: 60 credit hour program; special project.

FIELDS OF STUDY.

COLLEGE OF ALLIED HEALTH AND NURSING:
Communication Disorders. M.S.
Family Consumer Science. M.S.
Health Science. M.S.
Human Performance. M.A., M.S.
Nursing. M.S.N.
Rehabilitation Counseling. M.S.

COLLEGE OF ARTS AND HUMANITIES:
Art. Includes studio (M.A.). M.A., M.S.

English. Includes literature (M.A.), TESL (M.A.), technical communication (M.A.), creative writing (M.F.A.). M.A., M.F.A.
French. M.A.
Music. M.M.
Spanish. M.S.
Speech Communication. M.A., M.S.
Theatre and Dance. M.A., M.F.A.

COLLEGE OF EDUCATION:
Counseling and Student Personnel. M.S.
Educational Technology. M.S.
Elementary Education. M.S.
Experiential Education. M.S.
Gifted Education and Talent Development. M.S.
Library Media Education. M.S.
Special Education. M.S.
Teaching. Includes secondary education in art, earth science, English, English/TESL, family consumer science, French, general science, life science, mathematics, music, physical education, school health, social studies, Spanish, speech, speech/theatre, theatre arts. M.A.T.
Teaching and Learning. Includes middle and secondary education, curriculum and instruction, environmental education. M.S.

COLLEGE OF SCIENCE, ENGINEERING, AND TECHNOLOGY:
Biology. M.S.
Chemistry. M.A., M.S.
Computer Science. M.S.
Electrical Engineering. M.S.
Environmental Science. M.S.
Manufacturing Engineering Technology. M.S.
Mathematics. M.A.
Mechanical Engineering. M.A.
Physics. M.S.
Science Education. M.S.

COLLEGE OF SOCIAL AND BEHAVIORAL SCIENCES:
Anthropology. M.S.
Geography. M.S.
Gerontology. M.S.
History. M.A., M.S.
Political Science. M.A.
Psychology. Includes clinical, industrial/organizational. M.A.
Public Administration. M.A.P.A.
Sociology. Includes corrections (M.S.), human services planning and administration (M.S.). M.A., M.S.
Urban and Regional Studies. Includes urban planning. M.A.
Women's Studies. M.S.

MINNESOTA STATE UNIVERSITY, MOORHEAD

Moorhead, Minnesota 56563
Web site: www.mnstate.edu

Founded 1887. Located 260 miles NW of Minneapolis. Coed. State control. Semester system. Library: 367,000 volumes, 1539 subscriptions.

Tuition: per credit hour Minnesota residents $185.14, North Dakota residents with reciprocity $185.14, South Dakota and Manitoba residents with reciprocity $185.14, Wisconsin residents with reciprocity $204.15; nonresidents $347.08. No on-campus housing available. Contact Housing Office for off-campus housing information. Phone: (218)236-2118.

Graduate Studies

Graduate study since 1952. Enrollment: full-time 90 (men 39%, women 61%); part-time 284. Graduate faculty: full-time 55, part-time 28. Degrees conferred: M.A., M.S., M.B.A., M.F.A., M.L.A., Specialist.

ADMISSION REQUIREMENTS. Transcripts required in support of application. On-line application available. GRE/GMAT/MAT may be required by some programs. Immunization record required for all applicants. TOEFL required for international applicants. Interview required for some programs. Accepts transfer applicants. Apply to Graduate Admissions Office by May 1 (Fall semester), September 1 (Spring semester). International students accepted Fall semester only. Application fee $20, $35 for international applicants. Phone: (218)236-2344; fax: (218)236-2168.

ADMISSION STANDARDS. Selective. Usual minimum average: 2.75 or 3.25 (A = 4) in last 30 semester hours of graded course work.

FINANCIAL AID. Annual awards from institutional funds: graduate assistantships, internships, Federal W/S, loans. Approved for VA benefits. Apply by July 15 to Dean of Academic Services for assistantships; to Financial Aid Office for all other programs. Use FAFSA and institutional FAF. About 20% of students receive aid from all sources. Aid available for part-time students.

DEGREE REQUIREMENTS. For master's Plan A: 30 credit minimum; written comprehensive exam; thesis; final oral exam. For master's Plan B: 32 credit minimum; written comprehensive exam; project paper; oral exam. For M.F.A.: 42 credit minimum; thesis; oral discourse. For M.L.A.: 32 credit minimum; thesis; oral exam. For M.S.N.: Plan A & B; written comprehensive exam; thesis or classroom-based research project; oral exam. For Specialist: 30 semester hours minimum beyond master's.

FIELDS OF STUDY.
Counseling and Student Affairs. Includes community counseling, student affairs, school counseling. Plan B: 48 credit, full-time program. M.S.
Creative Writing. M.F.A.
Curriculum and Instruction. Plan B: 32 credit program. M.S.
Educational Administration. Plan A: 33–47 credit program.
Liberal Studies. M.L.A.
Music. Plan A and B. M.A.
Music Education. Plan A and B. M.S.
Nursing. Includes clinical nurse specialist in adult health, family nurse practitioner, nurse educator, parish nurse specialist, transcultural nurse specialist. M.S.N.
Public Human Service and Health Administration. Plan B: 35 credit program. M.S.
Reading. Plan A and B: 33 credit program. M.S.
School Psychology. Plan A. M.S.
Special Education. Includes developmental disabilities, early childhood special education, emotional/behavioral disorders, learning disabilities, physical and health disabilities. Plan A and B. M.S.
Speech/Language Pathology. Plan A and B: 48 credit program; clinical practica. M.S.

UNIVERSITY OF MINNESOTA, TWIN CITIES

Minneapolis, Minnesota 55455-0213
Web site: www.umn.edu

Established 1851. Coed. State control. CGS and AAU member. Semester system. Member of Committee on Institutional Cooperation with other Big Ten universities and the University of Chicago. Graduate study also offered at the Duluth campus. Special facilities: Bell Museum of Natural History, Dairy Foods Research Center, Rural Health Research Center, MIS Research

Center, Avian Research Center, Limnological Research Center, Center for Advanced Research in Language Acquisition, Water Resource Center, Center for Infectious Disease Research and Policy, Center for Insurance Research, Agricultural Research Center, Immigration Health Research Center, Center for Violence Prevention and Control. The University's NIH ranking is 19th among all U.S. institutions with 557 awards/grants worth $192,081,653. Library: more than 6,000,000 volumes, 45,000 subscriptions. Total University enrollment: 37,000.

Annual tuition: full-time resident $6800, nonresident $13,358; per credit resident $566, nonresident $1113; some programs have higher tuition costs, contact University for current charges. On-campus housing for married students, single men and women. Average academic year housing costs: $325–395 per month for married students; $2800 per semester (including board) for single students. Apply to the Housing office. Phone: (612)624-2994. Day-care facilities available.

Graduate School

Graduate study since 1879. Enrollment: full- and part-time 7694 (men 50%, women 50%). Faculty: full- and part-time 2700. Degrees conferred: M.A., M.Ed., M.S., M.Arch., M.B.A., M.F.A., M.E., M.F., M.P.P., M.P.A., M.U.R.P., M.S.W., Ed.D., Ph.D., and many other designated degrees.

ADMISSION REQUIREMENTS. Transcripts required in support of School's application. GRE Subject Tests, MAT, GMAT required for some departments. TOEFL required for international applicants. Accepts transfer applicants. Graduates of unaccredited institutions not considered. Apply to Graduate School by June 15 (Fall), October 15 (Spring), March 15 (Summer). Application fee $40, $50 for international applicants. Phone: (612)625-3014.

ADMISSION STANDARDS. Acceptance ratios vary among degree programs; admission based on competition generated by spaces available and applications received.

FINANCIAL AID. Individual departments award and administer graduate assistantships. Limited number of fellowships; program nomination is required for consideration. Apply to individual department.

DEGREE REQUIREMENTS. For M.A., M.S. Plan A: 30 credit program; thesis; final written/oral exam. For M.A., M.S. Plan B: 32 credit program; three lengthy papers; final written exam. For M.F.A.: three-year program; thesis. For M.P.P., M.U.R.P.: 45–48 credit programs. For M.S.: 40 credit, two-year program; capstone project. For Ph.D.: 60 credit, full-time program; minor field of study; reading knowledge of two foreign languages or one language/research tool/collateral field in some departments; comprehensive oral and written exam; thesis; final oral. For Ed.D.: 84 credit, full-time program beyond bachelor's; a minor field of study; supervised internship/clinical experience/fieldwork; preliminary written/oral exam; thesis/project; final oral exam.

FIELDS OF STUDY.
Aerospace Engineering.
Agricultural and Applied Economics.
American Studies.
Animal Sciences.
Anthropology.
Applied Plant Sciences.
Architecture.
Art.
Art History.
Astrophysics.
Biochemistry, Molecular Biology, and Biophysics.
Biological Science.
Biomedical Engineering.

Biophysical Sciences and Medical Physics.
Biostatistics.
Biosystems and Agricultural Engineering.
Business Administration.
Business and Marketing Education.
Business Taxation.
Cellular and Integrative Physiology.
Chemical Engineering.
Chemical Physics.
Chemistry.
Child Psychology.
Chinese.
Civil Engineering.
Classical and Near Eastern Studies.
Clinical Laboratory Science.
Clinical Research.
Communication Disorders.
Communication Studies.
Comparative Literature.
Comparative Studies in Discourse and Society.
Computer and Information Sciences.
Computer Engineering,
Conservation Biology.
Control Science and Dynamical Systems.
Creative Writing.
Design, Housing, and Apparel.
East Asian Studies.
Ecology, Evolution, and Behavior.
Economics.
Education. Includes curriculum and instruction, educational policy and administration, recreation, park and leisure studies, work, community and family education.
Educational Administration.
Educational Psychology. Includes counseling and student personnel psychology, psychological foundations of education, school psychology, special education.
Electrical Engineering.
English.
English as a Second Language.
Entomology.
Environmental Health.
Epidemiology.
Experimental Surgery.
Family Social Science.
Feminist Studies.
Fisheries and Aquatic Biology.
Food Science.
French.
Geographic Information Science.
Geography.
Geological Engineering.
Geology.
Geophysics.
German Studies.
Health Informatics.
Health Services Research, Policy, and Administration.
Hispanic and Luso-Brazilian Literatures and Linguistics.
Hispanic Linguistics.
Hispanic Literature.
History.
History of Medicine and Biological Sciences.
History of Science and Technology.
Human Resources and Industrial Relations.
Industrial Engineering.
Infrastructure Systems Engineering.
Japanese.
Journalism.
Kinesiology.
Landscape Architecture.
Liberal Studies.
Linguistics.

Luso-Brazilian Literature.
Management of Technology.
Manufacturing Systems Engineering.
Mass Communication.
Materials Science and Engineering.
Mathematics.
Mechanical Engineering.
Mechanics.
Medicinal Chemistry.
Microbial Engineering.
Microbiology, Immunology, and Cancer Biology.
Molecular, Cellular, Developmental Biology and Genetics.
Molecular Veterinary Biosciences.
Music.
Music Education.
Musicology.
Natural Resources Science and Management.
Neuroscience.
Nursing.
Nutrition.
Occupational Therapy.
Oral Biology.
Otolaryngology.
Pharmaceutics.
Pharmacology.
Philosophy.
Physical Therapy.
Physics.
Plant Biological Sciences.
Plant Pathology.
Political Science.
Psychology.
Public Affairs.
Public Policy.
Radiology.
Rhetoric and Scientific and Technical Communication.
Russian Area Studies.
Science and Environmental Technology Policy.
Scientific and Technical Communication.
Scientific Computation.
Social, Administrative, and Clinical Pharmacy.
Social Work.
Sociology.
Software Engineering.
Soil Science.
South Asian Languages.
Spanish.
Statistics.
Surgery.
Theatre Arts. Includes directing, design.
Toxicology.
Urban and Regional Planning.
Veterinary Medicine.
Water Resources Science.
Wildlife Conservation.

School of Dentistry

Founded 1888. Located at the University's Health Sciences Center. Quarter system. Special facilities: Dental Research Institute, Minnesota Dental Research Center for Biomaterials and Biomechanics, Minnesota Oral Health Clinical Research Center. Special Programs: externships; Summer Research Fellowships; foreign exchange in Denmark, Norway, Germany, and Peru. Postgraduate specialties: Basic Medical Sciences (Ph.D.), Endodontics (M.S.), Oral Biology (Ph.D.), Oral Health Services for older Adults (M.S.), Oral Pathology, Oral and Maxillofacial Surgery (Certificate), Orthodontics (M.S.), Pediatric Dentistry (M.S.), Periodontics (M.S.), Prosthodontics (M.S.), TMJ and Orofacial Pain (M.S.).

Annual tuition: resident $13,125, nonresident $22,153. On-campus housing available. Average academic year housing cost: $12,567. Contact Housing Office at (612)624-2994. Total average cost for all other first-year expenses: $5000.

Enrollment: first-year class 86, total 300 (men 65%, women 35%); postgraduates: about 800. Degrees conferred: D.D.S., B.A.-D.D.S., D.D.S.-M.S., D.D.S.-Ph.D. The M.S. and Ph.D. are offered through the Graduate School.

ADMISSION REQUIREMENTS. AADSAS, transcripts, three letters of recommendations, DAT (not later than October) required in support of School's application. TOEFL, TWE required for nonnative speakers of English. Applicants must have completed at least three years of college study. Has early admission program. Interview by invitation only. Accepts transfer applicants from U.S. and Canadian dental schools. Preference given to residents of Minnesota, nearby states, and Manitoba. Apply to the Office of Enrollment Management after June 1, before January 1. Application fee $55. Phone: (612)625-7149.

ADMISSION STANDARDS. Selective. Mean DAT: Academic 18.82, PAT 18.24; mean GPA: 3.52 (A = 4). Gourman rating: 4.76. Usual minimum average: 2.5 (A = 4). Accepts 25–30% of total annual applicants. Approximately 60% are state residents.

FINANCIAL AID. Scholarships, summer research fellowships, loans. Apply to University Student Financial Aid Office after acceptance; no specified closing date. Phone: (612)626-1665. Use FAFSA. Approximately 90% of students demonstrating need receive financial assistance.

DEGREE REQUIREMENTS. For B.D.: satisfactory completion of three-year undergraduate program and one year at School. For D.D.S.: satisfactory completion of forty-five-month program. For M.S., Ph.D.: requirements vary with department; see Graduate School listing above.

FIELDS OF GRADUATE STUDY.
Basic Medical Sciences. Ph.D.
Endodontics. M.S.
Oral and Maxillofacial Surgery. Certificate only.
Oral Biology. Ph.D.
Oral Health Services for Older Adults. M.S.
Oral Microbiology.
Oral Pathology.
Orthodontics. M.S.
Pediatric Dentistry. M.S.
Periodontics. M.S.
Prosthodontics. M.S.
TMJ and Orofacial Pain. M.S.

Law School
Web site: www.law.umn.edu

Established 1888. ABA approved since 1923. AALS member. Semester system. Law library: 905,588 volumes, 10,252 subscriptions; has LEXIS, NEXIS, WESTLAW, LUMINA. Special facility: Center for Computer Assisted Legal Invention.

Annual tuition: full-time, resident $10,536, nonresident $17,384. Limited on-campus housing available. Total average annual additional expense: $10,044.

Enrollment: first-year class 241; total full-time 692 (men 51%, women 49%); no part-time students. Faculty: full-time 38, part-time 59. Student to faculty ratio 15.1 to 1. Degrees conferred: J.D., J.D.-M.B.A., J.D.-M.P.A., LL.M. (only for persons who have completed a basic legal education and received a University degree in law in another country).

ADMISSION REQUIREMENTS. LSDAS Law School report, bachelor's degree, transcripts, LSAT, personal statement, letters of recommendation required in support of application. Interview not required. Occasionally accepts transfer applicants. Graduates of unaccredited colleges not considered. Apply to the Director of Admission after October 1, before March 1. Application fee $40. Phone: (612)625-3487; fax: (612)626-1874.

ADMISSION STANDARDS. Selective. Mean LSAT: 162; mean GPA: 3.58 (A = 4). Gourman rating: 4.64. *U.S. News & World Report* ranking is in the top 18 of all U.S. law schools. Accepts 25–30% of total annual applicants.

FINANCIAL AID. Scholarships, full and partial tuition waivers, Federal W/S, loans. Apply to the University's Office of Financial Aid by March 1. Use FAFSA (School code: 003969). About 58% of students receive some aid from School.

DEGREE REQUIREMENTS. For J.D.: satisfactory completion of three-year program; 88 credit hours. For LL.M.: at least 24 credit hours beyond the J.D.; one year in full-time residence. *Note:* Summer study available at Université Jean Moulin, Lyon (France), and Uppsala University Law School (Sweden). Joint degree programs exist with Hubert H. Humphrey Institute of Public Affairs and Curtis L. Carlson School of Management.

Medical School (55455-0310)

Web site: www.med.umn.edu

Founded 1888. Annual tuition: resident $21,615, nonresident $40,156. On-campus housing available. Apply to Admissions Office, Medical School. Total average figure for all other expenses: $7500.

Enrollment: first-year class 165 (EDP 15), total 813 (men 53%, women 47%). Faculty: full-time 919, part-time 1642. Degrees conferred: M.D., M.D.-M.B.A., M.D.-M.S., M.D.-Ph.D. Medical Scientist Training Program. The M.S. and Ph.D. are offered through the Graduate School.

ADMISSION REQUIREMENTS. AMCAS report, transcripts, letters of evaluation, MCAT required in support of application. Applicants must have completed bachelor's degree. Preference given to residents of Minnesota. Interview by invitation only. Accepts transfer students from University of Minnesota-Duluth. Has EDP; apply between June 1 and August 1. Apply to AMCAS after June 1, before November 15. Application fee $75. Phone: (612)624-7977; fax: (612)624-4200; e-mail: meded@umn.edu.

ADMISSION STANDARDS. Selective. Mean MCAT: 9.9; mean GPA: 3.63 (A = 4). Gourman rating: 4.71. *U.S. News & World Report* ranking is in the top 36 of all U.S. medical schools. Accepts 16% of total annual applicants. Approximately 90% are state residents.

FINANCIAL AID. Scholarships, merit scholarship, minority scholarships, Grants-in-Aid, institutional loans, HEAL, alternative loan programs, NIH stipends; Federal Perkins Loans, Stafford Subsidized and Unsubsidized Loans, Service Commitment Scholarship programs are available. All M.D.-Ph.D. students are accepted into fully funded positions which include stipends, tuition waivers, fees, and health insurance. Financial Aid applications and information are generally available at the on-campus, by-invitation interview. Contact the Financial Aid Office for current information. Phone: (612)625-4998. Use FAFSA (School code: E00477), also submit Financial Aid Transcript, Federal Income Tax forms, ACT-FFS needs analysis form. Approximately 90% of students receive some form of financial assistance.

DEGREE REQUIREMENTS. For M.D.: satisfactory completion of four-year program. All students must pass USMLE Step 1 prior to entering third year; all students must pass USMLE Step 2 prior to awarding of M.D. For M.D.-Ph.D.: generally a seven-year program.

FIELDS OF GRADUATE STUDY.
Biochemistry.
Biomedical Engineering.
Biophysics.
Cell Biology.
Genetics.
Immunology.
Microbiology.
Molecular Biology.
Neurosciences.
Pharmacology.
Physiology.

College of Veterinary Medicine

Web site: www.cvm.umn.edu

Established in 1947. Located in St. Paul (55108). Annual tuition: resident and nonresident contract $10,302, nonresident $20,572. Off-campus housing only. Annual living expenses: $3500–$5500.

Enrollment: first-year class 80; full-time 300 (men 50%, women 50%); postgraduates 80. Faculty: full-time 80, part-time 10. Degrees conferred: D.V.M., D.V.M.-Ph.D.

ADMISSION REQUIREMENTS. VMCAS report, transcripts, GRE General, animal/veterinary knowledge required in support of application. On-line application available. Interview not required. Preference given to state residents, then to residents of North Dakota, South Dakota, Manitoba. Applicants must have completed at least three years of college study (by Spring prior to entrance) with a specific area distribution. Accepts a limited number of transfer applicants. Apply to the Office of Student Affairs and Admissions after August 1, before October 1. Admits Fall only. Preference given to state and contract residents. Application fee $50. Phone: (612)624-4747.

ADMISSION STANDARDS. Selective. Mean GRE: 1880 (three test total); mean GPA: 3.56 (A = 4). Accepts about 40% of total annual applicants. Accepts not more than 20% of nonresident applicants.

FINANCIAL AID. Awards, scholarships, fellowships, assistantships, internships, Federal W/S, loans. Apply to University Office of Student Financial Aid by March 1. Use FAFSA. Most students receive loans or have part-time employment.

DEGREE REQUIREMENTS. For D.V.M.: satisfactory completion of four-year program. For M.S., Ph.D.: see Graduate School listing above.

FIELD OF GRADUATE STUDY.
Molecular Veterinary Biosciences. Includes molecular mechanisms of disease, comparative biomedical sciences.
Note: M.P.H. in Veterinary Public Health offered through the School of Public Health.

UNIVERSITY OF MINNESOTA, DULUTH

Duluth, Minnesota 55812-2596
Web site: www.d.umn.edu

Founded in 1895. State control. Semester system. Special facilities: Alworth Institute for International Studies, Large Lakes Observatory, Marshall Performing Arts Center, Natural Resource Research Institute, Small Business Development Center, Tweed Museum of Art. Library: 614,367 volumes, 4500 subscriptions. Total campus enrollment: 9000.

Annual tuition: resident $6800, nonresident $13,358; per

credit, resident $566.80, nonresident $1,113.29; MBA resident/nonresident $539.70. On-campus housing for single graduate men and women; none for married students. Average academic year housing cost: $6125 (including board) for single students. Phone: (218)726-9119.

Graduate School

Graduate study since 1957. Enrollment: full-time 247, part-time 110. Faculty teaching graduate students: full- and part-time 283. Degrees conferred: M.A., M.S., M.B.A., M.L.S., M.M., M.S.W.

ADMISSION REQUIREMENTS. Two transcripts required in support of School's application. GRE/GMAT/MAT required for some departments. TOEFL required for international applicants. Accepts transfer students. Apply to Associate Dean of Graduate School at least eight weeks prior to registration. Application fee $50, $55 for international applicants. Phone: (218)726-7523; fax: (218)726-6970; e-mail: grad@umn.edu.

ADMISSION STANDARDS. Selective. Usual minimum average: 3.0 (A = 4).

FINANCIAL AID. Annual awards from institutional funds: fellowships, teaching assistantships, research assistantships, tuition remission for TA, RA, and fellowship recipients, internships, grants, Federal W/S, loans. Approved for VA benefits. Apply to director of each program for fellowships, assistantships; to director of Financial Aid for loans. No specified closing date. Use FAFSA. About 60% of students receive aid other than loans from University and outside sources.

DEGREE REQUIREMENTS. For master's Plan A: 44 credit minimum, thesis, final written/oral exam. Plan B: 30 credit minimum without thesis; reading knowledge of one foreign language; two major projects; comprehensive final written and oral exam.

FIELDS OF STUDY.
Applied and Computational Mathematics. M.S. (Plans A and B).
Art. Includes graphic design, M.F.A. (Plan B).
Biology. Includes botany, zoology, environmental, cellular, physiological. M.S. (Plans A and B).
Business Administration. M.B.A. (Plan B).
Chemistry. Includes analytical, inorganic, physical, organic. M.S. (Plans A and B).
Communication Sciences and Disorders. M.A. (Plan B).
Computer Science. M.S. (Plans A and B).
Educational Psychology. M.A. (Plan B).
Engineering Management. M.S.E.M. (Plan B).
English. Includes teaching of English. M.A. (Plan B).
Geological Sciences. M.S. (Plan A and B).
Liberal Studies. M.L.S. (Plan B).
Music. Includes music education, performance. M.M. (Plan B).
Physics. M.S. (Plan A and B).
Social Work. M.S.W. (Plan B).
Toxicology. M.S. (Plans A and B); Ph. D. (offered jointly with Twin Cities Campus).
Water Resources Science. M.S. (Plan A and B); Ph.D. (offered jointly with Twin Cities Campus).

School of Medicine Duluth (55812)

Web site: penguin.d.umn.edu

Established 1972. Annual tuition: resident $21,615, nonresident $40,156. Total average cost for all other expenses: $7500.

Enrollment: first-year class 59 (EDP 6); total 111 (men 65%, women 35%); postgraduates 24. Faculty: full-time 40, part-time and volunteers 250. Degree conferred: none, two-year transfer program.

ADMISSION REQUIREMENTS. AMCAS report, transcripts, MCAT, recommendations, screening questionnaire required in support of application. Interview by invitation only. Preference given to state residents and residents of North Dakota, South Dakota, Iowa, and northern Wisconsin. Has EDP; apply between June 1 and August 1. Graduates of unaccredited colleges not considered. Apply to Associate Dean after June 1, before November 15 (firm). Application fee $75. Phone: (218)726-8511; fax: (218)726-6235; e-mail: medadmis@d.umn.edu.

ADMISSION STANDARDS. Selective. Mean MCAT: 9.1; mean GPA: 3.66 (A = 4). Accepts about 10% of total annual applicants. Approximately 95% are state residents.

FINANCIAL AID. Scholarships, loans. Apply to University Financial Aid Program following admission. Phone: (218)726-8786. Use FAFSA (School code: E00477). About 93% of students eligible for aid receive assistance.

DEGREE REQUIREMENTS. Satisfactory completion of two-year program. All students transfer to University of Minnesota Medical School in Minneapolis to complete studies for M.D.

MINOT STATE UNIVERSITY
Minot, North Dakota 58702-0002
Web site: www.minotstateu.edu

Founded 1913. Coed. State control. Semester system. Library: 299,000 volumes, 1400 subscriptions.

Annual tuition: resident $2805, nonresident $6719. Limited on-campus housing available. Average academic year housing cost: $1140–$1980 (room only), $1696–$1992 (board only). Contact Housing Office for both on- and off-campus housing information. Phone: (701)858-3360.

Graduate School

Enrollment: full- and part-time 267. University faculty teaching graduate students: full- and part-time 100. Degrees conferred: M.S., M.M.E., M.A.T.

ADMISSION REQUIREMENTS. Official transcripts from all colleges/universities attended, GRE/GMAT, three letters of recommendation, autobiography required in support of School's application. On-line application available. TOEFL required for international applicants. Apply to the Dean of the Graduate School at least four weeks prior to registration. Application fee $25. Phone: (701)858-3250; fax: (701)858-4286.

ADMISSION STANDARDS. Selective. Usual minimum average: 3.00 (A = 4).

FINANCIAL AID. Annual awards from institutional funds: scholarships, Federal W/S, loans. Approved for VA benefits. Apply to Financial Aid Office by April 15, February 15 for scholarship consideration. Phone: (701)858-3375; fax: (701)858-4310. Use FAFSA (School code: 002994).

DEGREE REQUIREMENTS. For master's: 30–36 semester hours minimum; thesis option/written comprehensive exam; oral exam.

FIELDS OF STUDY.
Communication Disorders.
Criminal Justice.
Education.
Management. M.S.
Mathematics. M.A.T.
Music. M.M.E.
School Psychology.
Science. M.A.T.

Special Education—Early Childhood.
Special Education—Education of the Deaf.
Special Education—Learning Disabilities.
Special Education—Severely Multihandicapped.

MISSISSIPPI COLLEGE
Clinton, Mississippi 39058
Web site: www.mc.edu

Founded 1826. Located 5 miles W of Jackson. Coed. Private control. Semester system. Library: 276,245 volumes, 5300 subscriptions. Total College enrollment: 3000.

Tuition: per hour $349. On-campus housing for single students only. Average academic year housing cost: $3540–$5080 (including board); off-campus housing cost: $500–$700 per month. Contact the Dean of Students Office for both on- and off-campus housing information. Phone: (601)925-3248.

Graduate School

Graduate study since 1950. Enrollment: full-time 87, part-time 417. College faculty: full-time 67, part-time 12. Degrees conferred: M.A., M.Ed., M.B.A., M.F.A., M.M., M.C.C., M.C.P., M.C.S., M.H.S., M.S., M.S.S., Ed.Sp.

ADMISSION REQUIREMENTS. Two transcripts, two photographs, GRE/NTE/GMAT required in support of application. GRE Subject for some programs. Interview required for most departments. TOEFL required for foreign applicants. Accepts transfer applicants. Graduates of unaccredited colleges not considered. Apply to Graduate Office by August 20 (Fall), May 15 (Summer). Rolling admissions process. Application fee $25, $75 for international applicants. Phone: (601)925-3260; fax: (601)925-3889; e-mail: graduate@mc.edu.

ADMISSION STANDARDS. Relatively open. Usual minimum average: 2.75 (A = 4).

FINANCIAL AID. Annual awards from institutional funds: teaching assistantships, internships, tuition waivers, loans. Apply by April 1 to appropriate department chair; to Financial Aid Office for all other programs. Use FAFSA. About 20% of students receive aid other than loans from College and outside sources. Aid sometimes available for part-time students.

DEGREE REQUIREMENTS. For master's: 30–36 semester hours minimum, at least 24–36 in residence; thesis or final project; reading knowledge of one foreign language for M.A.; internship for M.Ed.; final oral/written comprehensive exam. For M.F.A.: 60 credit program; project.

FIELDS OF STUDY.
Accounting. M.B.A.
Administration of Justice. M.S.S.
Applied Communication. M.S.C.
Art. M.A.
Art Education. M.Ed.
Biological Sciences. M.S.C.
Biology Education. M.Ed.
Business Administration. M.B.A.
Business Education. M.Ed.
Chemistry. M.C.S., M.S.
Combined Sciences. M.C.S.
Community Psychology. M.Ed.
Computer Science. M.S.
Computer Science Education. M.Ed.
Counseling. Ed.Sp.
Educational Leadership. M.Ed., Ed.Sp.
Elementary Education. M.Ed.

English. M.A.
Health Services Administration. M.H.S.A.
History. M.A., M.Ed., M.S.S.
Marriage and Family Therapy. M.S.
Mass Communication. M.S.
Mathematics. M.C.S., M.S.
Mathematics Education. M.Ed.
Mental/Behavioral Health. M.S.C.
Music. Includes applied, education, performance, accompanying. M.M.
Political Science. M.S.S.
Public Relations and Corporate Communication. M.S.C.
School Administration. M.Ed.
School Counseling. M.Ed.
Science Education. M.Ed.
Secondary Education. Includes art, biological sciences, business education, computer science, English, mathematics, social sciences (history), teaching arts (elementary/secondary). M.Ed.
Social Sciences. M.S.S.
Sociology. Includes general. M.S.S.
Visual Arts. M.F.A.

School of Law (39201-1391)
Web site: www.law.mc.edu

Established 1975. ABA approved since 1980. AALS member. Semester system. Library: 303,200 volumes, 3546 subscriptions.

Annual tuition: full-time $14,354. No on-campus housing available. Total average annual additional expenses: $15,110.

Enrollment: first-year class, full-time 216; total 379 (men 57%, women 43%). Faculty: full-time 14, part-time 15. Student to faculty ratio 22.6 to 1. Degree conferred: J.D.

ADMISSION REQUIREMENTS. LSDAS Law School report, bachelor's degree, transcripts, LSAT (not later than March), recommendations required in support of application. Graduates of unaccredited colleges not considered. Apply to Office of Admissions by May 1. Application fee $40. Phone: (601)925-7150; fax: (601)925-7185.

ADMISSION STANDARDS. Selective. Mean LSAT: 147; mean GPA: 2.98 (A = 4). Gourman rating: 2.14. U.S. News & World Report ranking is in the fourth tier of all U.S. law schools. Accepts about 45–50% of total annual applications.

FINANCIAL AID. Full and partial scholarships, Federal W/S, loans. Apply to Office of Financial Aid by May 1. Phone: (601)925-3254. Use FAFSA (School code: E00479). About 22% of students receive some aid from School.

DEGREE REQUIREMENTS. For J.D.: satisfactory completion of three-year (full-time), four-year (extended division) program; 88 credit hours.

MISSISSIPPI STATE UNIVERSITY
Mississippi State, Mississippi 39762
Web site: www.msstate.edu

Founded 1878. Located 130 miles NE of Jackson. CGS member. Coed. State control. Semester system. Special facilities: Institute for Humanities, Cobb Institute for Archaeology, Center for Robotics, Automation, and Artificial Intelligence, electron microscope, Mississippi Energy Research Center, Mississippi State Chemical Laboratory, Radiological Safety Office, Water Resource Research Institute, Center for International Security and Strategic Studies, Mississippi Alcohol Safety Education Program, John C. Stennis Institute of Government, Social Science Research Center, Gulf Coast Research Laboratory at Ocean

Springs. Library: 1,600,000 volumes, 15,500 subscriptions. Total University enrollment: 15,200.

Annual tuition: full-time, resident $3117, nonresident $7065; per credit, resident $173, nonresident $393. On-campus housing for 268 married students. Average academic year housing cost: $3000 for married students, $2100 (room only) for single students. Contact Housing Director. Phone: (662)325-3557. Daycare facilities available.

Graduate Studies

Graduate study since 1893. Enrollment: full-time 1748, part-time 1506 (men 55%, women 45%). University faculty: full-time 934, part-time 122. Degrees conferred: M.A., M.S., M.Ag., M.A.B.M., M.B.A., M.F.A., M.P.P.A., M.Prof.Acc., M.Tax., Ed.S., Ed.D., Ph.D.

ADMISSION REQUIREMENTS. Official transcripts, GRE, GMAT, three letters of recommendation required in support of School's application. Interview not required. TOEFL required of international students. Accepts transfer applicants. Apply to Office of Admissions at least twenty days prior to registration. Application fee $25. Phone: (662)325-2224; fax: (662)325-7360; e-mail: admit@admission.msstate.edu.

ADMISSION STANDARDS. Selective for some departments, relatively open for others. Usual minimum average: 2.5 for master's, 3.0–3.5 for Ed.S., Ed.D., Ph.D. (A = 4).

FINANCIAL AID. Annual awards from institutional funds: scholarships, grants, teaching assistantships, research assistantships, Federal W/S, loans. Approved for VA benefits. Apply by March 1 to Dean of the Graduate School for assistantships; to Financial Aid Office for all other programs. Use FAFSA and institutional FAF. Phone: (662)325-2450; fax: (662)325-0702. About 40% of students receive aid other than loans from University and outside sources. Aid sometimes available for part-time students.

DEGREE REQUIREMENTS. For M.A., M.S.: 30 semester hours minimum, at least 24 in residence; reading knowledge of one foreign language for majors in English, physical and biological sciences; final oral exam. For M.Ag.: same as for M.A., except thesis is optional; no language requirement; final written/oral exam. For M.B.A., M.Prof.Acc.: 30 semester hours minimum, at least 24 in residence; no thesis or language requirement; final written/oral exam. For Ed.S.: 30 semester hours beyond the master's, at least 24 in residence; special problem or thesis included; final written/oral exam. For Ph.D.: three years beyond the bachelor's, at least one year in full-time residence, preliminary exam; foreign language proficiency for some programs; qualifying exam; dissertation; final oral exam. For Ed.D.: essentially the same as for the Ph.D., except no language requirement.

FIELDS OF STUDY.
Accounting.
Aerospace Engineering.
Agribusiness Management. M.Agri.Bus.Mgt. only.
Agricultural and Extension Education.
Agricultural Economics.
Agricultural Pest Management. M.Ag. only.
Agronomy.
Animal Physiology. Interdepartmental. Ph.D. only.
Applied Anthropology.
Applied Economics. Ph.D. only.
Architecture.
Biochemistry.
Biological Engineering.
Biological Sciences.
Biomedical Engineering.
Business Administration.
Business Education.

Chemical Engineering. M.S. only.
Chemistry. Includes analytical, inorganic, organic, physical. Placement exam; one language for M.S.
Civil Engineering.
Cognitive Science. Ph.D. only.
Community College Leadership. Ph.D. only.
Computational Engineering.
Computer Engineering.
Computer Science.
Counselor Education.
Economics.
Education.
Educational Psychology.
Electrical Engineering.
Electronic Visualization. M.F.A. only.
Elementary Education.
Engineering.
Engineering Mechanics.
Engineering Physics.
English. One language for M.A.; M.A. only.
Entomology.
Environmental Toxicology. Ph.D. only.
Food Science and Technology.
Foreign Languages. French, German, Spanish; M.A. only.
Forest Products.
Forest Resources. Includes forest products, forestry, and wildlife and fisheries science. Ph.D. only.
Forestry. M.F., M.S. only.
General Engineering.
Genetics. Interdepartmental; one language for M.S.
Geosciences.
History.
Horticulture.
Industrial Engineering. M.S. only.
Information Systems.
Instructional Technology.
Landscape Architecture. M.L.A. only.
Mathematics. Includes applied mathematics. One language for M.S.
Mechanical Engineering.
Molecular Biology.
Nutrition.
Physical Education.
Physics. One language for M.S.
Plant Pathology.
Political Science. Master's only.
Poultry Science.
Project Management.
Psychology. Master's only.
Public Administration.
Public Policy and Administration. M.P.P.A. only.
School Administration.
School Psychology. Ed.SP.
Secondary Education.
Sociology.
Special Education. Master's, Ed.S. only.
Statistics.
Taxation. Master's only.
Technology.
Veterinary Medical Science.
Weed Science.
Wildlife Ecology.
Workforce Education Leadership.

College of Veterinary Medicine (P.O. Box 9825)
Web site: www.cvm.msstate.edu

Annual tuition: resident $6000, nonresident $20,740. Total average costs for all other expenses: $6000. On-campus housing available.

Enrollment: first-year class 50; total 216 (men 47%, women 53%); postgraduate, 65. Faculty: full-time 62, part-time 11. Degrees offered: D.V.M., D.V.M.-M.S., D.V.M.-Ph.D. The M.S. and Ph.D. are offered through the Graduate School.

ADMISSION REQUIREMENTS. VMCAS report, transcripts showing completion of sixty-five hours of preprofessional college work, VCAT or GRE, recommendations, animal/veterinary experience, essay required in support of application. Interview by invitation only. Accepts transfer applicants on a space-available basis. Preference given to state residents. Apply to Assistant Dean after August 1, prior to October 1. Application fee $25. Phone: (662)325-1129.

ADMISSION STANDARDS. Selective. Usual minimum GPA: 2.8; mean GPA: 3.59 (A = 4). Accepts 40% of total annual applicants. Approximately 20% are nonresidents.

FINANCIAL AID. Fellowships, research assistantships, Federal W/S, loans. Apply by April 1 to Dean. Use FAFSA.

DEGREE REQUIREMENTS. For D.V.M.: 152 semester hours and four years in residence. For M.S. and Ph.D.: see Graduate School listing above.

FIELDS OF GRADUATE STUDY.
Environmental Toxicology. Ph.D.
Veterinary Medical Science. M.S., Ph.D.

MISSISSIPPI UNIVERSITY FOR WOMEN

Columbus, Mississippi 39701-9998
Web site: www.muw.edu

Founded 1884. State control. Semester system. Library: 426,500 volumes, 1629 subscriptions.

Annual tuition: resident $3398, nonresident $7965. On-campus housing for 250 graduate students. Average academic year housing cost: $3500 (including meals). Apply to Graduate Housing Office for both on- and off-campus housing. Phone: (662)329-7142. Day-care facilities available.

Graduate Studies

Enrollment: full-time 21, part-time 110. College faculty teaching graduate students: full-time 5, part-time 3. Degrees conferred: M.Ed., M.S., M.S.N.

ADMISSION REQUIREMENTS. Official transcripts, letters of recommendation, GRE required in support of School's application. TOEFL and Graduate English Proficiency required of international applicants. Accepts transfer applicants. Apply to the Dean of the Graduate School by April 1. Application fee: none. Phone: (662)329-7110; fax: (662)329-8515.

ADMISSION STANDARDS. Selective. Usual minimum average: 2.75; 3.0 in area of study (A = 4).

FINANCIAL AID. Annual awards from institutional funds: fellowships, federal traineeships (when available), in-state scholarships, Federal W/S, loans. Apply by April 1 to Dean of the Graduate School. Phone: (662)329-7142. About 80% of students receive aid other than loans from College and outside sources.

DEGREE REQUIREMENTS. For master's: 30–36 semester hour minimum, at least 30 in residence; written/oral final exam; thesis/nonthesis option; language optional with department/student.

FIELDS OF STUDY.
Gifted Studies. M.Ed.
Health Education. M.S.
Instructional Management. M.Ed.
Nursing. Includes family, gerontological practitioner.
Speech/Language Pathology. M.S.
*Teaching.*M.A.

THE UNIVERSITY OF MISSISSIPPI

University, Mississippi 38677
Web site: www.olemiss.edu

Founded 1848. Located 76 miles SE of Memphis, Tenn. CGS member. Coed. State control. Semester system. New Science Center complex. Special facilities: Center for Computational Hydroscience and Engineering, Center for the Study of Southern Culture, Mary Buie Museum, National Center for Physical Acoustics, Research Institute for Pharmaceutical Sciences. The University's NIH ranking is 178th among all U.S. institutions with 49 awards/grants worth $14,262,673. Library: 951,259 volumes, 8495 subscriptions. Total University enrollment: 10,100.

Annual tuition: full-time, resident $3926, nonresident $8826; per credit, resident $217.50, nonresident $490.25. On-campus housing for both single and married students. Average academic year housing cost: $2420 (room only) for single students; $2800 for married students. Contact Director of Housing for both on- and off-campus housing. Phone: (662)915-7328.

Graduate School

Graduate study since 1870. Enrollment: full-time 1093, part-time 457. Graduate faculty: full- and part-time 400. Degrees conferred: M.A., M.S., M.B.A., M.Ed., M.F.A., M.M., M.Acc., M.S.S., M.Tax., D.A., Ed.Sp., Ed.D., Ph.D.

ADMISSION REQUIREMENTS. Official transcripts, three letters of recommendation, GRE, GMAT (Business), NTE (Education) required in support of School's application. Interview usually not required. TOEFL required for international applicants. Accepts transfer applicants. Graduates of unaccredited institutions not considered. Apply by April 1 to the Registrar's Office. Rolling admissions process. Application fee: none, $25 for international applicants. Phone: (662)915-7474; fax: (662)915-7577.

ADMISSION STANDARDS. Selective. Usual minimum average: 3.0, 2.75 for last 60 credits (A = 4).

FINANCIAL AID. Scholarships, fellowships, special minority fellowships, teaching/research assistantships, internships, Federal W/S, loans. Approved for VA benefits. Apply by March 1 to Graduate School for Honors Fellowships and Minority Fellowships; to appropriate department for assistantships; to Office of Financial Aid for all other programs. Phone: (662)915-7175. Use FAFSA. About 55% of students receive aid other than loans from University and outside sources. Aid available to part-time students.

DEGREE REQUIREMENTS. For M.A., M.S., M.S.S., M.Acc., M.Tax.: 30 semester hours minimum, at least 24 in residence; thesis included for six hours; reading knowledge of one foreign language for some majors; final oral exam. For M.B.A.: one year minimum in residence; specific number of hours depends upon previous preparation. For M.Ed.: 30 hours minimum, at least 24 in residence; final oral exam. For M.F.A.: 60 hours minimum, at least two years in residence; creative project included for six hours; final exhibition and final oral exam may be required. For M.M.: 30 hours minimum, at least 24 in residence; recital, composition, or thesis; final oral exam. For Ed.Sp.: 30 hours beyond the master's; special project; final oral exam. For D.A., Ed.D.: 60

hours of course work beyond the master's degree; one year of continuous full-time attendance; internship; doctoral essay; comprehensive exam. For Ph.D.: three years minimum beyond the bachelor's, at least two years in residence, and one year of continuous full-time attendance; preliminary exam; written, oral comprehensive exam; dissertation; final oral exam.

FIELDS OF STUDY.

Accountancy. GMAT for admission. M.Acc., Ph.D.

Anthropology. M.A.

Art. Includes art education. M.A., M.F.A. only.

Art History. M.A.

Biological Sciences. M.S., Ph.D.

Business Administration. GMAT required for admission. M.B.A., Ph.D.

Chemistry. M.S., Ph.D., D.A.

Classics. Greek, Latin, classical archaeology; one language in addition to major. M.A. only.

Communicative Disorders. Includes audiology, speech pathology. M.S., Sp.Ed.

Computational Engineering Science. M.S., Ph.D.

Counselor Education. M.Ed., Ed.Sp., Ph.D.

Curriculum and Instruction. M.A., M.Ed., Ed.Sp.

Economics. M.A., Ph.D.

Education. Includes curriculum and instruction, educational leadership (K–12), educational psychology. M.A., M.Ed., Ed.Sp., Ph.D.

Elementary Education. Ed.D.

Engineering. Includes civil, environmental engineering, computer science, geology and geological engineering, mechanical engineering, chemical engineering, electrical engineering. M.S., Ph.D.

English. M.A., Ph.D.

Exercise Science. M.S., Ph.D.

Fine Arts. Includes art, creative writing, theatre. M.F.A.

French. M.A.

Geology. M.S.

German. M.A.

Health Promotion. M.S.

Higher Education and Student Personnel. M.A.

History. One language for M.A., Ph.D.

Journalism. M.A. only.

Leisure Management. M.A. only.

Mathematics. M.A., M.S., Ph.D.

Music. Includes applied, composition, performance, theory, opera production, music education. M.M., D.A.

Parks and Recreation Management. M.A.

Pharmaceutical Sciences. Includes pharmacology, medicinal chemistry, pharmaceutics, pharmacognosy, pharmacy administration. M.S., Ph.D.

Philosophy. M.A. only.

Physics. One language for M.A., M.S., Ph.D.

Political Science. M.A., Ph.D.

Psychology. M.A., Ph.D.

Social Science. M.S.

Sociology. One language or research tool for M.A. M.A., M.S.S. only.

Southern Studies. M.A. only.

Spanish. M.A.

Taxation. M.T.

Theater Arts. M.A., M.F.A. only.

School of Law

Established 1854 as a Department of Law; fourth-oldest state-supported law school in U.S. Semester system. Law library: 306,215 volumes, 2648 subscriptions; has LEXIS, NEXIS, WESTLAW, DIALOG. Special facilities: National Center for Justice and the Rule of Law, National Remote Sensing and Space Law Center. Annual tuition: resident $4681, nonresident $9454. On-campus housing available. Total average annual expense: $10,828.

Enrollment: full-time, J.D. program, first-year class 179, total full-time 472 (men 63%, women 37%); graduate program 25. School faculty: full-time 19, part-time 9. Student to faculty ratio 20.7 to 1. Degrees conferred: J.D., J.D.-M.B.A., M.M.L.S., LL.M., M.C.L., J.S.D.

ADMISSION REQUIREMENTS. For J.D.: LSDAS Law School report, bachelor's degree, transcripts, LSAT, five letters of recommendation required in support of application. Accepts a limited number of transfer applicants. Apply to Law School Director of Admissions by March 1 (nonresidents for Summer, Fall), April 1 (residents for Summer). Fall or Summer admission only. Preference given to state residents. Application fee $25. Phone: (662)915-9610; fax: (662)915-1289. For graduate degrees: transcripts required in support of application. Applicants should have graduated in upper half of law school class. Apply to Chair of the Graduate Program at least twenty days prior to registration.

ADMISSION STANDARDS. Selective. Mean LSAT: 154; mean GPA: 3.49 (A = 4). Gourman rating: 3.25. *U.S. News & World Report* ranking is in the second tier of all U.S. law schools. Accepts 20–25% of total applicants.

FINANCIAL AID. Scholarships, fellowships, assistantships, Federal W/S, loans. Apply to University Financial Aid Officer for loans, to Scholarship Coordinator for all others by March 1; to Chair of Graduate Programs by March 1. Use FAFSA (School code: 002440). About 50% of students receive aid other than loans from School.

DEGREE REQUIREMENTS. For J.D.: satisfactory completion of ninety credit-hour program. For M.C.L., LL.M., M.M.L.S.: 24 hours minimum beyond the J.D.; thesis included for 6 hours. M.C.L. is designed for graduates of international law schools. For J.S.D.: 24 hours minimum beyond the LL.M.; thesis. For M.B.A.: see Graduate School listing above.

Note: Summer program at Dowling College, Cambridge (England), available.

UNIVERSITY OF MISSISSIPPI MEDICAL CENTER

Jackson, Mississippi 39216-4505
Web site: www.umsmed.edu

Includes Schools of Medicine, Nursing, Health-Related Professions, Dentistry, and University Hospital. Library: 100,000 volumes. Limited on-campus housing. Contact Housing Office for both on- and off-campus housing information. Phone: (601)984-1491. Estimated living expenses: $9500.

School of Dentistry

Established 1973. State control. Quarter system.

Annual tuition: resident $5481, nonresident $11,841. No on-campus housing available. Average academic year housing cost: $8832. Total average cost for all other first-year expenses: $3457.

Enrollment: first-year class 30; total 118 (men 70%, women 30%). Faculty: full-time 42, part-time 41. Degree conferred: D.M.D.

ADMISSION REQUIREMENTS. Transcripts, DAT, three letters of recommendation required in support of School's application. Interview by invitation only. Applicants must have completed at least three years of college study. Strong preference given to state residents. Accepts transfer applicants. Apply to Office of Student Services and Records after July 1, before December 1. Application fee: resident $25, nonresident $50. Phone: (601)984-6009.

ADMISSION STANDARDS. Selective. Mean DAT: Academic 18.07, PAT 17.97; mean GPA: 3.56 (A = 4). Accepts about 80% of total annual applicants. About 100% are state residents.

FINANCIAL AID. Scholarships, grants, tuition waivers, loans. Apply to Financial Aid Office; no specified closing date. Preference given to applications received before April 15. Phone: (601)984-1117. Use FAFSA. About 93% of students receive aid from School and outside sources.

DEGREE REQUIREMENTS. For D.M.D.: satisfactory completion of forty-five-month program; advanced standing for work completed at other dental schools considered.

School of Medicine

Founded 1903, became four-year school in 1955.
Annual tuition: resident $6938, nonresident $13,298.
Enrollment: M.D. program, first-year class 100 (EDP 10); total 386 (men 70%, women 30%); graduate program, total full-time 150 (men 85%, women 15%); part-time 102. Faculty: full-time 374; part-time 1069. Degrees conferred: M.D., M.D.-M.S., M.D.-Ph.D.

ADMISSION REQUIREMENTS. For M.D. program: AMCAS report, transcripts, MCAT, recommendations required in support of application. Interview by invitation only. Applicants must have completed at least three years of college study. Preference given to state residents only. Has EDP; apply between June 1 and August 1. For graduate program: transcripts, five references, GRE/Subject Tests required in support of application. Interview required for most departments. Accepts transfer applicants for M.D. and graduate program. Graduates of unaccredited colleges not considered. Apply to Registrar after June 1, before October 1 (M.D.). Application fee: none. Phone: (601)984-5010; fax: (601)984-5008.

ADMISSION STANDARDS. Selective for M.D., selective for most graduate programs. Mean MCAT: 9.4; mean GPA: 3.69 (A = 4). Gourman rating: 3.39. Accepts 30% of total annual applicants for M.D. About 100% are state residents.

FINANCIAL AID. Scholarships and loans available to medical students; research fellowships and teaching/research assistantships for graduate programs. Apply to Division of Student Services and Records for scholarships and loans, to appropriate department chair for fellowships and assistantships; no specified closing date, April 15 suggested. Use FAFSA (School code: 004688).

DEGREE REQUIREMENTS. For M.D.: satisfactory completion of four-year program; advanced standing for work completed at other medical schools considered. For M.S., Ph.D.: see graduate degree program at the University of Mississippi.

FIELDS OF GRADUATE STUDY.
Biochemistry.
Microbiology.
Nutrition.
Pathology.
Pharmacology.
Physiology.
Preventive Medicine.

School of Nursing

Graduate program began in 1970. Tuition: full-time resident $3926, nonresident $8826; per credit, resident $217.50, nonresident $490.25. On-campus housing available for single and married students. Average academic year cost: $2500–$2800 (room only). Contact Housing Office for married student information. Phone: (601)984-1490.

Enrollment: full-time 59, part-time 81. Faculty with graduate appointment: full-time 23, part-time 5. Degree conferred: M.S.N.

ADMISSION REQUIREMENTS. Transcript, B.S.N., GRE, license (R.N.), at least one year of nursing experience, one page biography, three letters of recommendation required in support of School's application. On-line application available. Accepts transfer applicants. Applicants accepted for admission each semester. Apply to Registrar by December 15 (priority date). Application fee $10. Phone: (601)984-6211; fax: (601)984-5957.

ADMISSION STANDARDS. Selective. Usual minimum average: 2.75 cumulative; 3.0 for nursing courses (A = 4). Combined GRE: 900.

FINANCIAL AID. Grants, Federal Nurse Traineeships, loans. Approved for VA benefits. Apply to Director of Student Financial Aid; no specified closing date. Preferred date April 1. Phone: (601)984-1117; fax: (601)984-1099. Use FAFSA. Aid available for part-time students.

DEGREE REQUIREMENTS. For M.S.N.: 46–50 credits minimum; accepts up to 9 hours in transfer; thesis or non-thesis option.

FIELDS OF STUDY.
Adult Acute Care Clinician/Practitioner.
Adult/Family Clinician/Practitioner.
Neonatal Nurse Clinician.
Nurse Educator.
Nurse Executive.
Note: A R.N.-B.S.N.-M.S.N. program is available for qualified students.

UNIVERSITY OF MISSOURI— COLUMBIA

Columbia, Missouri 65211
Web site: www.missouri.edu

Founded 1839. Located 120 miles W of St. Louis. CGS and AAU member. Coed. State control. Semester system. Special facilities: Center for Aging, Agricultural Experiment Station Research Farms, Business and Public Administration Research Center, Capsule Pipeline Research Center, Dalton Center for Cardiovascular Research, Financial Research Institute, Freedom of Information Center, Geographic Resource Center, Nuclear Magnetic Resonance Center, Power Electronics Research Center, Research Reactor Center, Center for Research in Social Behavior, Space Sciences Center, Water Resources Research Center; Museums of Anthropology Art and Archaeology, Entomology, Geological Sciences; herbarium; extensive acreage for research in soils, field crops, horticulture; art collections. The University's NIH ranking is 89th among all U.S. institutions with 192 awards/grants worth $45,619,041. Library: 2,680,304 volumes, 20,524 subscriptions. Total University enrollment: 22,300.

Tuition: full-time resident $4466, nonresident $13,267. On-campus housing for 352 married students, 2100 single men, 2880 single women. Average academic year housing cost: $3620 (double room, including board). Apartments per month $315–$355 (one-bedroom), $365–$435 (two-bedroom); meal plans $1650–2470. Apply to Residential Life Office. Phone: (573)882-7275.

Graduate School

Graduate study since 1846. Enrollment: full-time 1813, part-time 1651. Faculty: full-time 1179, part-time 35. Degrees conferred: M.A., M.S., M.Acc., M.P.A., M.H.A., M.H.S., M.A.P.E., M.S.W., M.S.P.H., M.B.A., M.S.T., M.F.A., M.Ed., M.M., Ed.Sp., Ed.D., Ph.D.

ADMISSION REQUIREMENTS. Transcripts required in support of School's application. GRE/GMAT/MAT, recommendations required by some departments. Interview not required. TOEFL required for international applicants. Accepts transfer students. Graduates of unaccredited institutions not considered. Apply to Director of Admissions by July 1 (Fall), December 1 (Winter), May 1 (Summer). Two-part application process; 1 application for Graduate School, second part for departments. Some departmental application deadlines may be earlier. Application fee $25, $50 for international applicants. Phone: (573)882-9576.

ADMISSION STANDARDS. Very selective for most departments, selective to very competitive for others. Usual minimum average: 3.0 (A = 4).

FINANCIAL AID. Annual awards from institutional funds: academic scholarships/fellowships, teaching assistantships, research assistantships, internships, traineeships, tuition waivers, Federal W/S, loans. Approved for VA benefits. Apply by January 1 to appropriate department chair for assistantships; to Financial Aid Office for all other programs. Phone: (573)882-7506. Use FAFSA (School code: 002516). Aid available for part-time study.

DEGREE REQUIREMENTS. For master's: 30 hours minimum; thesis required for many majors; final written/oral exam. For Ed.Sp.: 30 hours minimum beyond the master's; final written/ oral exam. For Ph.D.: 72 credits beyond the bachelor's (all in residence), at least 18 semester hours within an 18-month period; language requirements vary by department; comprehensive exam; dissertation; final oral exam. For Ed.D.: 82 hours minimum beyond the bachelor's (all in residence), at least 18 semester hours within an 18-month period; knowledge of statistics; matriculation exam; no language requirement; dissertation; final oral exam.

FIELDS OF STUDY.

COLLEGE OF AGRICULTURE, FOOD, AND NATURAL RESOURCES:
Agricultural Economics.
Agronomy.
Animal Sciences.
Biochemistry.
Entomology.
Fisheries and Wildlife.
Food Science.
Forestry.
Horticulture.
Park, Recreation, and Tourism. M.S. only.
Plant Pathology.
Rural Sociology.
Soil and Atmospheric Sciences.

COLLEGE OF ARTS AND SCIENCE:
Anthropology.
Applied Mathematics. M.S. only.
Art History and Archaeology.
Biological Sciences.
Chemistry.
Classical Studies.
Communication. Includes speech pathology-audiology (interdepartmental).
Economics.
English.
French.
Geography. M.A. only.
Geological Sciences.
History. M.A. only.
Mathematics.
Philosophy.
Physics.
Political Science.
Psychological Sciences. Includes clinical psychology, cognition and neurosience psychology, development psychology, quantitative psychology, social psychology.

Religious Studies. M.A. only.
Russian. M.A. only.
Sociology.
Spanish.
Statistics.

SCHOOL OF FINE ARTS:
Art. M.F.A. only.
Music.
Theatre.

COLLEGE OF BUSINESS:
Accountancy. M.Acc., Ph.D.
Business. Ph.D. only.
Business Administration.
Finance.
Management. Includes organizational sciences.
Marketing.

COLLEGE OF EDUCATION:
Curriculum and Instruction. Includes art education, early childhood education, elementary education, English education, foreign language education, learning and instruction, mathematics education, music education, reading education, science education, social studies education.
Educational Leadership and Policy Analysis. Includes administration and supervision of special education, continuing education teaching, educational administration, educational leadership, educational policy studies, elementary school administration and supervision, general school administration, higher education, higher and continuing education, junior college education, learning and instruction.
Education and Counseling Psychology. Includes counseling psychology, school psychology.
Information Science and Learning Technologies. Includes education technology, instructional theory and practice, learning and instruction, library science.
Practical Arts and Vocational Education. Includes agriculture education, business and office education, family and consumer, industrial education, learning and instruction, marketing education, sciences education, technology teaching, vocational-technical education.
Special Education. Includes administration and supervision of special education, behavior disorders, curriculum development for exceptional students, early childhood special education, learning disabilities, mental retardation.

COLLEGE OF ENGINEERING:
Biological Engineering.
Chemical Engineering.
Civil and Environmental Engineering.
Computer Engineering. M.S. only.
Computer Engineering and Computer Science. Ph.D. only.
Computer Science. M.S. only.
Electrical Engineering.
Industrial and Manufacturing Systems Engineering.
Mechanical and Aerospace Engineering.
Nuclear Engineering.

GRADUATE SCHOOL (INTERDIVISIONAL):
Genetics Program. Ph.D. only
Neuroscience.
Research Resource.

HARRY S. TRUMAN SCHOOL OF PUBLIC AFFAIRS:
Public Administration.

COLLEGE OF HUMAN ENVIRONMENTAL SCIENCES:
Consumer and Family Economics. M.S. only.
Environmental Design.
Exercise Physiology.

Human Development and Family Studies. M.A., M.S. only.
Human Environmental Sciences. Ph.D. only.
Human Nutrition, Foods, and Food Systems Management. M.S. only.
Social Work. M.S.W., Ph.D.
Textile and Apparel Management. M.A., M.S. only.

SCHOOL OF JOURNALISM:
Journalism. Includes advertising, broadcast news, design, editing, environmental reporting, international, magazine, media management, new media, news media and society, photo journalism, public policy, reporting/writing.

SCHOOL OF LAW:
Dispute Resolution. LL.M.

SCHOOL OF MEDICINE:
Biochemistry.
Health Administration. M.H.A. only.
Health Informatics. M.S. only.
Microbiology—Medicine.
Pathology. M.S. only.
Pharmacology.
Physiology.
Public Health. M.S. only.

SCHOOL OF HEALTH PROFESSIONS:
Communication Science and Disorders. M.H.S.
Nursing.
Physical Therapy. M.P.T.
Speech-Language Pathology. Interdepartmental.

COLLEGE OF VETERINARY MEDICINE:
Biomedical Sciences. M.S. only.
Laboratory Animal Medicine.
Pathobiology Area Program. Ph.D. only.
Physiology Area Program. Ph.D. only.
Veterinary Biomedical Sciences.
Veterinary Clinical Sciences.
Veterinary Pathobiology.

School of Law
Web site: www.law.missouri.edu

Established 1872. ABA approved since 1923. AALS charter member. Semester system. Special facility: Center for the Study of Dispute Resolution. Law library: 303,756 volumes, 3138 subscriptions; has LEXIS, WESTLAW, INFOTRAC, LUMIN/OCLC.

Annual tuition/fee: resident $9420, nonresident $18,229. Total average annual additional expense: $12,580.

Enrollment: first-year class 197; total full-time 538 (men 55%, women 45%). Faculty: full-time 27, part-time 8. Student to faculty ratio 16.7 to 1. Degrees conferred: J.D., J.D.-M.B.A., J.D.-M.P.A., J.D.-M.A. (Educational Leadership and Policy, Human Development and Family Studies).

ADMISSION REQUIREMENTS. LSDAS Law School report, bachelor's degree, transcripts, LSAT required in support of application. Interview not required. Accepts transfer applicants. Graduates of unaccredited colleges not considered. Apply to Admissions Office, preferably by March 1. Students accepted for Fall only. Application fee $40. Phone: (573)882-6042; fax: (573)882-9625.

ADMISSION STANDARDS. Selective. Mean LSAT: 154; mean GPA: 3.31 (A = 4). Gourman rating: 3.79. *U.S. News & World Report* ranking is in the second tier of all U.S. law schools. Accepts about 45% of total annual applicants.

FINANCIAL AID. Scholarships, assistantships, Federal W/S, loans. Apply to School of Law Scholarship Committee by March 1.

Use FAFSA (School code: 002516). About 38% of students receive aid other than loans from School.

DEGREE REQUIREMENTS. For J.D.: 89 hours minimum, at least two years in residence.
Note: One-semester study abroad program in London, England, available for second- and third-year students.

School of Medicine (65212)

Founded 1872 as a two-year school, expanded to four years in 1956. Annual tuition: resident $15,458, nonresident $31,082. On-campus housing available. Apply to Housing Office. Total average figure for all other expenses: $8550.

Enrollment: first-year class 96 (EDP 3), full-time 582 (men 50%, women 50%); postgraduates 317. Medical faculty: 309; part-time 36. Degrees conferred: M.D., M.D.-M.S., M.D.-Ph.D. The M.S. and Ph.D. are offered through the Graduate School.

ADMISSION REQUIREMENTS. AMCAS report, transcripts, letters of recommendation, MCAT required in support of application. Applicants must have completed at least three years of college study. Interview by invitation only. Has EDP; apply between June 1 and August 1. Preference given to Missouri residents. Accepts transfer applicants. Apply to Assistant Dean after June 1, before November 1. Application fee $50. Phone: (573)882-9219; fax: (573)884-2988.

ADMISSION STANDARDS. Competitive. Mean MCAT: 9.8; mean GPA: 3.59 (A = 4). Gourman rating: 4.19. *U.S. News & World Report* rank for primary care is in the top 11 of all U.S. medical schools. Accepts about 25% of total annual applicants. Approximately 95% are state residents.

FINANCIAL AID. Scholarships, loans. Apply to Financial Aid Office. Phone: (573)882-2923. Use FAFSA (School code: 002516). About 85% of students receive some aid from School.

DEGREE REQUIREMENTS. For M.D.: satisfactory completion of four-year program and passing Step 2 of USMLE for graduation. For M.S., Ph.D.: see Graduate School listing above.

FIELDS OF GRADUATE STUDY.
Biochemistry.
Biomedical Engineering.
Genetics.
Immunology.
Microbiology.
Pathology.
Pharmacology.
Physiology.

College of Veterinary Medicine

Established 1949. Annual tuition: resident $10,570, nonresident $20,550. On-campus housing available; estimated living expenses: $18,112.

Enrollment: first-year class 64; full-time 260 (men 45%, women 55%); no part-time students. Faculty: full-time 178, part-time 19. Degree conferred: D.V.M. The M.S. and Ph.D. are offered through the Graduate School.

ADMISSION REQUIREMENTS. Transcripts, VCAT (must be received by February 1), two recommendations, animal/veterinary experience, essay, interview required in support of application. For combined programs, a bachelor's degree is required. Accepts transfer applicants on a space-available basis. Will consider American students with two years in foreign college of veterinary medicine. Graduates of unaccredited colleges not considered. Applicants must have completed at least two years of preprofessional college study. Preference given to state residents. Apply to Dean, School of

Veterinary Medicine after September 1, before November 1. Fall admission only. Application fee $50. Phone: (573)882-3554.

ADMISSION STANDARDS. Selective. Usual minimum GPA: 2.5 (A = 4); mean GPA: 3.57. Accepts 30% of total annual applications. Can enroll eight nonresident applicants.

FINANCIAL AID. Scholarships, fellowships, assistantships, internships, tuition waivers, Federal W/S, loans, grants. Apply to Director of Student Aids; no specified closing date. Use FAFSA.

DEGREE REQUIREMENTS. For D.V.M.: satisfactory completion of four-year program. For M.S., Ph.D.: see Graduate School listing above.

FIELDS OF GRADUATE STUDY.
Biological Sciences. Ph.D. only
Laboratory Animal Medicine. Includes animal resource management, diseases and pathology of laboratory animals.
Pathobiology.
Veterinary Biomedical Sciences. Includes anatomy, endocrinology, molecular biology, pharmacology, physiology, reproductive biology.
Veterinary Clinical Sciences. Includes anesthesiology, comparative cardiology, medicine, neurology, ophthalmology, radiology, surgery, theriogenology.
Veterinary Pathobiology. Includes anatomic pathology, clinical pathology, epidemiology, immunology, microbiology, molecular biology, parasitology, pathobiology, toxicology.

UNIVERSITY OF MISSOURI— KANSAS CITY

Kansas City, Missouri 64110-2499
Web site: www.umkc.edu

Founded 1929. Coed. State control. CGS member. Semester system. Special facilities: Institute for Study in American Music, Electronic Music Laboratory, Center for Underground Space Studies, Drug Information Center, Biopharmacokinetics Laboratory, Hormone Research Laboratory, Family Study Center, Center for the Study of Metropolitan Problems in Education, Center for Labor Studies, Institute for Human Development. Library: 942,000 volumes, 1,773,000 microforms, 6800 subscriptions. Total University enrollment: 12,697.

Tuition and fees: per credit hour, resident $179.10, nonresident $538.70 plus prorated tuition 7–10 hours. On-campus housing for single students only. Average academic year housing cost: $4866 (including board). Contact University Housing Office for both on- and off-campus housing information. Phone: (816)235-2800.

Graduate Studies

Graduate study since 1939. Enrollment: full- and part-time 4606. University faculty teaching graduate students: full-time 489, part-time 233. Degrees conferred: M.A., M.S., M.A. in Ed., M.Ed., M.B.A., M.P.A., LL.M., M.M., M.M.Ed., Ed.S., D.M.A., Ph.D.

ADMISSION REQUIREMENTS. Two official transcripts, GRE/GMAT required in support of application. Interview not required. TOEFL required of international applicants whose first language is not English. Accepts transfer applicants. Graduates of unaccredited institutions not considered. Apply to the Admissions Office by February 1 (Summer and Fall), September 1 (Winter). Application fee: none. Phone: (816)235-1111; fax: (816)235-5544.

ADMISSION STANDARDS. Selective for some departments, competitive for most departments. Usual minimum average: 3.0; probationary status: 2.75 (A = 4).

FINANCIAL AID. Chancellor nonresident awards, scholarships, teaching assistantships, internships, full and partial fee waiver, Federal W/S, loans. Apply by March 1 to appropriate department chair for assistantships, scholarships; to the Financial Aid Office for all other programs. Use FAFSA. About 10% of students receive aid other than loans from University. No aid for part-time students.

DEGREE REQUIREMENTS. For M.A., M.S.: 30 semester hours minimum, at least 24 in residence; reading knowledge of one foreign language for some departments; qualifying exam for many departments; thesis/nonthesis option; final master's competency written/oral exam. For M.A. in Ed., M.Ed.: 30 semester hours minimum, at least 24 in residence; thesis not required. For M.B.A.: 36 hours minimum or 43 hours minimum, depending upon previous education, at least 30 or 37 hours in residence; thesis sometimes required for 6 hours. For M.P.A.: 36 hours minimum, at least 30 in residence; thesis optional for 6 hours. For LL.M.: 24 hours minimum beyond the J.D.; thesis for 8 hours. For M.M.: 30 semester hours minimum, at least 24 in residence, qualifying exam sometimes required; thesis/recital/research project; final oral/written exam. For M.M.Ed.: 30 semester hours minimum, at least 24 in residence; thesis for 4–6 hours; final written/oral exam. For Ed.S.: 60 hours minimum beyond the bachelor's, at least 20 in residence and one semester in full-time attendance; field project; final oral exam; offered in counseling and guidance, educational administration, and reading. For Ph.D.: usually 90 hours minimum beyond the bachelor's, at least 45 hours in residence and two consecutive semesters, one summer session in full-time attendance; qualifying exam; reading knowledge of two foreign languages or one language and one other acceptable research tool; comprehensive exam; dissertation; final oral exam. For D.M.A., Ed.D.: essentially the same as for the Ph.D., except composition/recitals may replace thesis in appropriate fields.

FIELDS OF STUDY.
Accounting. M.S. only.
Administration of Justice. M.A. only.
Art. Includes art history, graphic design, photography. Portfolio and interview required. M.A. only.
Biochemistry.
Biology. M.A., M.S. only.
Business Administration. GMAT for admission. M.B.A. only.
Cell Biology and Biophysics. Ph.D.
Cellular and Molecular Biology.
Chemistry. Includes analytical, inorganic, organic, physical. M.S., Ph.D.
Communication Studies. M.A.
Computer Networking. Ph.D.
Computer Science. M.S.
Counseling and Guidance. M.A.
Counseling Psychology.
Criminal Justice.
Curriculum and Instruction.
Dental Hygiene Education. B.S. in dental hygiene for admission. M.S. only.
Dentistry. Includes anatomy, biochemistry, microbiology, oral histology and embryology, oral medicine and diagnosis, oral radiology, periodontics, restorative dentistry, oral surgery, orthodontics, pedodontics, prosthodontics, oral pathology; D.D.S. for admission. M.S. only.
Economics. GRE for admission. M.A., Ph.D.
Education. Includes elementary and secondary curriculum and instruction, administration and community leadership, adult foundations and philosophy of education. M.A., Ed.S.; Ph.D. in curriculum and instruction, administration and community leadership, counseling, and guidance.
Engineering. Includes civil, electrical, industrial, mechanical; degrees awarded by University of Missouri—Columbia. M.S., Ph.D.
English Language and Literature. One language for M.A. M.A., Ph.D.

Geosciences.

Health Psychology.

History. M.A., Ph.D.

Liberal Studies.

Mathematics. M.S., Ph.D.

Microbiology. Interdivisional. M.S. only.

Molecular Biology and Biochemistry. Ph.D.

Music. Includes applied music, theory, composition, conducting, performance, sacred music, music education; GRE Subject, audition for admission. M.M., Ph.D.

Nursing. Includes child-care nursing.

Oral Biology. M.S., Ph.D.

Pharmaceutical Sciences. M.S., Ph.D.

Pharmacology. Ph.D.

Philosophy. Ph.D.

Physics. M.S., Ph.D.

Policy Studies in Education. Ph.D.

Political Science. GRE for admission. M.A., Ph.D.

Psychology. M.A., Ph.D.

Public Administration. GRE for admission. M.P.A. only.

Public Affairs and Administration. Ph.D.

Reading. M.Ed.

Religious Studies.

Romance Languages and Literature. M.A. only.

Social Sciences.

Social Work.

Sociology. M.A., Ph.D.

Software Architecture.

Special Education. M.Ed.

Studio Art.

Taxation.

Telecommunications. Ph.D.

Theater. Includes acting, directing, design and technology. Production thesis or new play may replace thesis. M.A. only.

Urban Affairs.

Urban Environmental Geology. M.S. only.

Urban Studies. M.S., Ph.D.

School of Dentistry

Founded 1881. In 1963 Dental School joined University of Missouri. Annual tuition: resident $13,754, nonresident $27,664. No on-campus housing available. Average academic year housing cost: $11,640. Contact Housing Office for off-campus housing information. Phone: (816)235-1428. Total average cost for all other first-year expenses: $7100.

Enrollment: first-year class 86; total 314 (men 60%, women 40%). Faculty: full-time 70, part-time 65. Degree conferred: D.D.S. The M.S. (Oral Biology) is offered through the School of Graduate Studies.

ADMISSION REQUIREMENTS. AADSAS report, official transcripts, DAT (no later than October), three letters of recommendation required in support of School's application. Interviews of students under serious consideration are required. Applicants must have completed at least two years of college study. Accepts transfer applicants. Preference given to residents of Missouri, Arkansas, Kansas, New Mexico. Apply to Office of Student Affairs after June 1, before January 1. Application fee $25. Phone: (816)235-2080 (local), (800)776-8652.

ADMISSION STANDARDS. Selective. Mean DAT: Academic 17.8, PAT 17.7; mean GPA: 3.41 (A = 4). Gourman rating: 4.27. Accepts 20–25% of total annual applicants. Approximately 50% are state residents.

FINANCIAL AID. Limited scholarships, grants, loans. Apply to Student Financial Aid Office. Phone: (816)235-1154. Use FAFSA (School code: G24821).

DEGREE REQUIREMENTS. For D.D.S.: satisfactory completion of forty-month program. For M.S.: see School of Graduate Studies listing above.

FIELDS OF GRADUATE STUDY AND ADVANCED EDUCATION.

Diagnostics Sciences.

General Dentistry.

Oral and Maxillofacial Surgery.

Oral Biology.

Orthodontics and Dentofacial Orthopedics.

Pediatric Dentistry.

Periodontics.

Prosthodontics.

School of Law

Web site: www.law.umkc.edu

Founded 1895. ABA approved since 1923. AALS member. Semester system. Law library: 285,149 volumes, 1805 subscriptions; has LEXIS, NEXIS, WESTLAW, DIALOG.

Annual tuition, fees: full-time resident $9446, nonresident $18,256; part-time resident $6806, nonresident $13,098. No on-campus housing available. Total average annual additional expense: $13,210.

Enrollment: first-year class 175; total enrollment 457 (men 51%, women 49%). LL.M. candidates 70. Faculty: full-time 22, part-time 17. Student to faculty ratio 17.3 to 1. Degrees conferred: J.D., J.D.-M.B.A., J.D.-LL.M. (Taxation), LL.M. (Taxation and Urban Affairs).

ADMISSION REQUIREMENTS. LSDAS Law School report, bachelor's degree, transcripts, LSAT required in support of application. Interview not required. Accepts transfer applicants. Preference given to state residents. Graduates of unaccredited institutions not considered. Apply to Office of the Associate Dean; no closing date. Fall admission only for beginning law students. Application fee $25. Phone: (816)235-1644; fax (816)235-5276.

ADMISSION STANDARDS. Selective. Mean LSAT: full-time 153, part-time 155; mean GPA: full-time 3.25, part-time 3.36 (A = 4). Gourman rating: 3.37. *U.S. News & World Report* ranking is in the third tier of all U.S. law schools. Accepts about 50% of total applicants.

FINANCIAL AID. Scholarships, loans. Apply by March 1 to Office of the Dean for scholarships, to University's Financial Aid Office for loans. Use FAFSA (School code: 002518) and UMKC FAF. About 33% of students receive some form of financial assistance from the school.

DEGREE REQUIREMENTS. For J.D.: 90 credit hours minimum, at least the last year in residence. For LL.M.: at least 24 credit hours beyond the J.D., at least one year in residence. For M.B.A.: see Graduate School listing above.

School of Medicine (64108)

Established 1969. Six-year baccalaureate, medical program only. Annual tuition: resident $22,752, nonresident $46,099. Limited on-campus housing available for married and single students. Total average figure for all other expenses: $13,000.

Enrollment: first-year class 111; total 347 (men 45%, women 55%). Faculty: full-time 543, part-time 824. Degree conferred: B.A.-M.D. (six calendar year program).

ADMISSION REQUIREMENTS. Transcripts, ACT, three letters of recommendation, screening interview required in support of application. Preference given to state residents. Accepts a limited number of upper division applicants between the program's second and third years. MCAT required for transfer applicants. Graduates of unaccredited colleges not considered. Apply to Director of Admissions and Registrar after August 1, before December 15. Application fee: resident $25, nonresident $50. Phone: (816)235-1870; fax: (816)235-5277.

ADMISSION STANDARDS. Selective. Accepts about 40% of total annual applicants. Approximately 85% are state residents.

FINANCIAL AID. Scholarships, CWSP, loans. Apply to University's Financial Aid Office by March 15. Use FAFSA (School code: 002518).

DEGREE REQUIREMENTS. For M.D.: satisfactory completion of six-year program; all students must pass USMLE Step 2 prior to awarding of M.D.

UNIVERSITY OF MISSOURI—ROLLA

Rolla, Missouri 65401-0249
Web site: www.umr.edu

Founded 1871. Located 100 miles SW of St. Louis. Coed. State control. Semester system. Special facilities: nuclear reactor, Graduate Center for Materials Research, Graduate Center for Cloud Physics Research, Rock Mechanics and Explosives Research Center, Institute for River Studies, fully equipped mine for research and study. Library: 440,000 volumes, 1495 subscriptions.

Annual tuition and fees: full-time, resident $4298, nonresident $12,929; per credit, resident $179, nonresident $539. On-campus housing for 50 married students, 1340 single students. Average academic year housing cost: $3500 (including board) for single students; $4895 per for married students. Off-campus housing cost: $380–$500 per month. Contact Housing office for on- and off-campus housing information. Phone: (573)341-4218.

Graduate School

Enrollment: full-time 621, part-time 232. University faculty: full-time 238, part-time 52. Degrees conferred: M.S., M.S.T., Ph.D., D.E.

ADMISSION REQUIREMENTS. Official transcripts required in support of School's application. Interview not required. GRE and TOEFL required of international students. Accepts transfer applicants. Graduates of unaccredited institutions not considered. Apply to the Admission Office by July 1 (Fall), December 1 (Spring), May 1 (Summer). Rolling admissions process. Application fee $20, $50 for international applicants. Phone: (573)341-4315; fax: (573)341-4062.

ADMISSION STANDARDS. Competitive for most departments. Usual minimum average: 2.75 (A = 4).

FINANCIAL AID. Academic scholarships, fellowships, teaching and research assistantships, internships, tuition waivers, Federal W/S, loans. Approved for VA benefits. Apply to chair of proposed major department for fellowships, assistantships; to Financial Aid Office for all other programs. No specified closing date. Phone: (573)341-4282. Use FAFSA. About 35% of students receive aid. Aid available for part-time students.

DEGREE REQUIREMENTS. For M.S.: 30 semester hours with thesis, 33 without thesis; final oral exam. For M.S.T.: 36 semester hours minimum, at least 24 in residence; final written exam; no thesis. For Ph.D., D.E.: about 90 semester hours beyond the bachelor's, at least two semesters in full-time residence; proficiency in foreign language for Ph.D.; dissertation; final oral exam.

FIELDS OF STUDY.
Aerospace Engineering.
Applied and Environmental Biology.
Applied Mathematics. M.S. only.
Ceramic Engineering.
Chemical Engineering.
Chemistry.
Civil Engineering.
Computer Engineering.
Computer Science.
Electrical Engineering.
Engineering Management.
Engineering Mechanics.
Environmental Engineering. M.S. only.
Geological Engineering.
Geology and Geophysics.
Information Science and Technology. M.S. only.
Manufacturing Engineering. M.S. only.
Mathematics. Ph.D. only.
Mechanical Engineering.
Metallurgical Engineering.
Mining Engineering.
Nuclear Engineering.
Petroleum Engineering.
Physics.
Systems Engineering. M.S. only.

UNIVERSITY OF MISSOURI— ST. LOUIS

St. Louis, Missouri 63121-4499
Web site: www.umsl.edu/

Founded 1963. CGS member. Coed. State control. Semester system. Special facilities: Art Gallery 210, Center for Business and Industrial Studies, Center for Humanities, Center for International Studies, Center for Molecular Electronics, Center for Neurodynamics, International Center for Tropical Ecology, Joint Center for East Asian Studies (in cooperation with Washington University), Public Policy Research Center, Center for Science and Technology, St. Louis Historical Research Center. Library: 1,100,000 volumes, 3807 subscriptions. Total University enrollment: 13,200.

Tuition: per credit hour, resident $173, nonresident $539. On-campus housing available for single graduate students only. Apartments located approximately three blocks from campus. Average academic year housing cost: $5400 (including board). Day-care facilities available.

Graduate School

Graduate study since 1968. Enrollment: full-time 443, part-time 1910 (men 35%, women 65%). Faculty: full-time 401. Degrees conferred: M.A., M.S., M.B.A., M.M.E., M.Ed., M.P.P.A., M.Acc., Ed.D., Ph.D.

ADMISSION REQUIREMENTS. Transcripts, GRE/GMAT required in support of School's application. On-line application available. TOEFL required of all foreign students. Accepts transfer applicants. Graduates of unaccredited colleges not considered. Apply to Director of Admissions by July 1 (Fall), December 1 (Spring), May 1 (Summer); Clinical Psychology, doctoral programs, M.F.A. programs have earlier deadlines. Application fee $25, $40 for international applicants. Phone: (314)516-5458; fax: (314)516-6759; e-mail: gradadm@umsl.edu.

ADMISSION STANDARDS. Selective. Usual minimum average: 2.75 (A = 4).

FINANCIAL AID. Annual awards from institutional funds: scholarships, teaching assistantships, research assistantships, graduate-school-funded dissertation fellowships, summer research fellowships, internships, Federal W/S, loans. Approved for VA benefits. Apply by July 1 to department chair for fellowships, assistantships; to Financial Aid Office for all other programs. Phone: (314)516-5526; fax: (314)516-5310. Use FAFSA. Aid available for part-time students.

DEGREE REQUIREMENTS. For master's: 30 credits minimum, at least 21 credits in residence; thesis required by some departments; final written/oral exam. For Ph.D.: at least three academic years of full-time study or equivalent, at least two years in residence; two consecutive semesters full-time; qualifying exam; reading knowledge of two foreign languages or one language and one research skill; dissertation; final exam.

FIELDS OF STUDY.
Accounting.
Applied Mathematics.
Biology. M.S., Ph.D.
Business Administration. GMAT for admission; 39–60 credits. M.B.A., M.S., M.Acc.
Chemistry. M.S., Ph.D.
Communications.
Computer Science.
Counseling.
Criminology and Criminal Justice. M.A., Ph.D.
Economics. M.A. only.
Education. Includes counseling, educational administration, elementary education, secondary education, special education, learning-instructional processes, and behavioral developmental processes. M.Ed., Ed.D.
English. M.A. only.
Gerontology. M.A. only.
History. M.A. only.
Management Information Systems.
Mathematics. M.A.
Museum Studies.
Music Education. M.M.E. only.
Nursing. M.S., Ph.D.
Philosophy.
Physiological Optics. M.S., Ph.D.
Political Science. Includes urban and regional politics, American politics, political process and behavior, international public administration, M.A.; politics, comparative politics, Ph.D.
Psychology. M.A., Ph.D.
Public Policy Administration. Includes policy analysis, public administration, management, accounting and economics.
Social Work.
Sociology. M.A. only.
Special Education.

MONMOUTH UNIVERSITY
West Long Branch, New Jersey 07764-1898
Web site: www.monmouth.edu

Founded in 1933. Located 50 miles S of New York City, 75 miles NE of Philadelphia. Private control. Semester system. Library: 248,000 volumes, 1300 subscriptions. Total University enrollment: 5635.

Tuition: per credit hour $523. Limited on-campus housing for graduate students but available for international students. Annual academic year housing cost: $4500–$5500. For off-campus housing contact Office of Student Services. Phone: (732)571-3465.

Graduate School

Graduate study since 1967. Enrollment: full-time 355, part-time 1087. Degrees conferred: M.B.A., M.A., M.A.L.A., M.S., M.A.T., M.S.Ed.

ADMISSION REQUIREMENTS. Transcripts, two letters of recommendation, GRE, GMAT Test (for M.B.A.) required in sup-

port of application. TOEFL required for foreign applicants. Accepts transfer applicants. Graduates of unaccredited institutions not considered. Apply to Director of Adult and Graduate Admissions by August 15 (Fall), December 15 (Spring). Rolling admissions process. Application fee $35. Phone: (732)571-3452; fax: (732)263-5123; e-mail: gradadm@ monmouth.edu.

ADMISSION STANDARDS. Selective. Usual minimum average: 2.5 overall, 3.0 in major. For M.B.A. program only: GPA x 200 + GMAT = 1000.

FINANCIAL AID. Research assistantships, internships, tuition waivers, Federal W/S, loans. Apply by March 1 to Financial Aid Office. Phone: (732)571-3463; fax: (732)571-3629. Use FAFSA. Aid available for part-time students.

DEGREE REQUIREMENTS. For M.B.A.: 30–60 semester hours depending upon previous preparation. For M.S. Computer Science: 33 semester hours. For M.S. Software Engineering: 36 semester hours depending upon previous preparation. For M.S. Electronic Engineering: 30 semester hours. For M.A.L.A., M.A. (History): 36 semester hours. For M.A.T. with certification, M.A.T. Advanced, M.S.Ed. Student Personnel Services: 36 semester hours. For M.S.N.: 40 semester hours. For the M.A. Psychological Counseling: 30 semester hours. For the M.A. Criminal Justice: 36 semester hours.

FIELDS OF STUDY.
Business Administration. Includes health care management. M.B.A.
Computer Science. M.S.
Corporate and Public Communications.
Criminal Justice. M.A.
Education. Includes elementary, secondary, supervision, principal, school administrator, school business administrator, special education, student personnel services, reading. M.S.Ed.
Electronic Engineering. M.S.
History. M.A.
Liberal Arts. M.A.L.A.
Nursing. M.S.N.
Psychological Counseling. M.A.
Reading Specialist Studies.
Social Work. M.S.W.
Software Engineering. M.S.
Special Education.

MONTANA STATE UNIVERSITY
Billings, Montana 59101-0298
Web site: www.msubillings.edu

Founded 1927. Coed. State control. Semester system. Special facilities: Montana Center for Disabilities, Native American Cultural Institute, Red Mountain Biological Field Station. Library: 200,000 volumes, 1550 subscriptions.

Annual tuition: resident $4364.80, nonresident $11,947.60. On-campus housing for graduate men, women; none for married students. Average academic year housing cost: $3000–$7000. Apply to Director of Resident Life for both on-campus housing and off-campus information. Phone: (408)657-2333.

Graduate Studies

Established 1954. Enrollment: full-time 72, part-time 325. University faculty teaching graduate students: full-time 72. Degrees conferred: M.Ed., M.S.Psyc., M.S.P.R., M.S.R.M.H.C., M.S.S.E., M.S.R.C., M.S.I.P.C., M.S.S.M.

ADMISSION REQUIREMENTS. Transcripts, GRE/MAT required in support of application. On-line application available.

TOEFL and certified statement of support required for international applicants. Accepts transfer applicants. Graduates of unaccredited institutions not considered. Apply to Office of Graduate Studies at least six weeks prior to registration. Application fee $40. Phone: (406)657-2338; fax: (406)657-2299.

ADMISSION STANDARDS. Selective for most departments. Usual minimum average: 3.0 (A = 4).

FINANCIAL AID. Annual awards from institutional funds: scholarships, grants, graduate assistantships, Federal W/S, loans. Approximately thirty resident fee waivers and five nonresident fee waivers available. Approved for VA benefits. Apply to Director of Graduate Studies for scholarships, assistantships; to Office of Financial Aid for all other programs. Phone: (406)657-2188; fax: (406)657-2302. Use FAFSA. About 30% of students receive aid other than loans from both University funds and outside sources.

DEGREE REQUIREMENTS. For M.Ed., M.S.: 36–45 semester hours minimum, at least 30 in residence; thesis/nonthesis options. For M.S.R.C.: 60 semester hours.

FIELDS OF STUDY.

COLLEGE OF ARTS AND SCIENCE:
Psychology. M.S. Psyc.
Public Relation. M.S.P.R.

COLLEGE OF BUSINESS:
Information Processing and Communication. M.S.I.P.C.

COLLEGE OF EDUCATION AND HUMAN SERVICES:
Curriculum and Instruction (K–8). M.Ed.
Early Childhood. M.Ed.
Educational Technology. M.Ed.
Interdisciplinary Studies. M.Ed.
Reading. M.Ed.
Rehabilitation and Mental Health Counseling. M.S.R.M.H.C.
School Counseling (K–12). M.Ed.
Special Education. M.S.S.E.
Sport Management. M.S.S.M.

MONTANA STATE UNIVERSITY
Bozeman, Montana 59717
Web site: www.montana.edu

Founded 1893. Located 90 miles N of Yellowstone Park. CGS member. Coed. State control. Semester system. Special facilities: Animal Research Center, Engineering Research Center, Local Government Center, Marsh Laboratory, Water Center. Library: 569,000 volumes, 1,300,000 microforms, 40 PCs.

Annual tuition: full-time, resident $3533, nonresident $9530. On-campus housing for 704 married students, 50 single students. Average academic year housing cost: $3915 (including board) for single students; $4365 for married students. Apply to Housing Office. Phone: (406)994-2661.

College of Graduate Studies

Graduate study since 1898. Enrollment: full-time 475; part-time 463. Graduate faculty: 425, part-time 20. Degrees conferred: M.A., M.Ed., M.N., M.S., Ed.D., Ph.D.

ADMISSION REQUIREMENTS. Transcripts, GRE, three letters of recommendation required in support of College's application. On-line application available. Interview may be required by some departments. TOEFL and GRE required for international applicants. Apply to appropriate department by July 15 (Fall), December 1 (Spring), April 1 (Summer). Some departments have earlier deadlines. Late applicants considered as nondegree students. Rolling admissions process. Application fee $50. Phone: (406)994-4145; fax: (406)994-4733; e-mail: gradstudy@montana.edu.

ADMISSION STANDARDS. Selective. Usual minimum average: 3.0 (A = 4).

FINANCIAL AID. Annual awards from institutional funds: scholarships, fellowships, teaching assistantships, research assistantships, internships, grants, Federal W/S, loans. Approved for VA benefits. Apply prior to registration to appropriate department chair for fellowships, assistantships; to Financial Aid Office for all other programs. Phone: (406)994-2845; fax: (406)994-6962. Use FAFSA. About 70% of students receive aid from College and outside sources. Aid available for part-time students.

DEGREE REQUIREMENTS. For master's Plan A: 30 credit program; one foreign language for some programs; thesis. For master's Plan B: 30 credit program; professional paper or project. For Ed.D.: 44 credits beyond the master's, at least 30 credits in residence; qualifying exam may be required; reading knowledge of one foreign language required by some departments; written/oral comprehensive exam; thesis; final written/oral exam. For Ph.D.: normally three years minimum beyond the bachelor's, at least 48 credits in residence; qualifying exam may be required; language requirements vary by department; oral/written comprehensive exam; dissertation; final written/oral exam.

FIELDS OF STUDY.
Agricultural Education. M.S. only.
Animal and Range Science. M.S. only.
Architecture. M.Arch.
Art. Portfolio required for admission; M.F.A. only.
Biochemistry.
Cell Biology and Neurosciences.
Chemical Engineering. M.S. only.
Chemistry.
Civil Engineering. M.S. only.
Computer Science.
Construction Engineering and Management. M.C.E.M.
Earth Sciences. GRE Subject for admission. Includes geography, geology, meteorology. M.S. only.
Economics. Includes applied. M.S. only.
Education. Includes adult and higher, curriculum and instruction, education administration. M.Ed., Ed.S., Ed.D.
Electrical Engineering. M.S. only.
Engineering. Includes applied mechanics (Ph.D.), chemical and computer (Ph.D.), environmental (Ph.D.), industrial and management (M.S.).
English. M.A. only.
Entomology. M.S. only.
Environmental Engineering. M.S. only.
Fish and Wildlife Biology. Ph.D. only.
Fish and Wildlife Management. M.S. only.
Health and Human Development. Includes family and consumer science (M.S.), family financial planning (M.S.), food and nutrition (M.S.), health, exercise and wellness (M.S.), school counseling (M.Ed.).
History. M.A. only.
Land Rehabilitation. Includes animal and range science, biology, civil engineering, earth sciences, resources and environmental science. M.S. only.
Land Resource and Environmental Science.
Mathematics.
Mathematics Education. M.S. only.
Mechanical Engineering. M.S. only.
Microbiology.
Native American Studies. M.A. only.

Nursing. Includes family nurse practitioner. M.N. only.
Physics.
Plant Pathology.
Professional Accountancy. M.P.Ac. only.
Project Engineering and Management. M.P.E.M. only.
Psychology. Includes applied. M.S. only.
Public Administration. M.P.A. only.
Science Education. M.S. only.
Science and Natural History Filmmaking. M.F.A. only.
Statistics.
Veterinary Molecular Biology.

MONTANA TECH OF THE UNIVERSITY OF MONTANA
Butte, Montana 59701-8997
Web site: www.mtech.edu

Founded in 1900. Located 300 miles E of Spokane, Washington, and 400 miles N of Salt Lake City. Coed. State control. Semester system. Special facilities: Mineral Research Center for Advanced Mining Processing, Montana Bureau of Mines and Geology. Library: 108,000 volumes, 950 subscriptions. Total Campus enrollment: 2000.

Annual tuition: full-time, resident $3368, nonresident $10,327. On-campus housing limited. Housing for married students both on- and off-campus. Average academic year housing cost: $3500 double (includes board) for single students; $2800 for married students (60 apartments on campus). Apply to Director, Resident Life. Phone: (406)496-4425. Day-care facilities available.

Graduate School

Graduate study since 1929. Enrollment: full-time 72, part-time 18. Faculty teaching graduate students: full-time 36, part-time 6. Degree conferred: M.S.

ADMISSION REQUIREMENTS. Transcripts, GRE Subject Tests, three references required in support of application. Interview not required. TOEFL required for international applicants. Accepts transfer applicants. Apply to Administrator of Graduate School before March 31. Application fee $30 (for U.S./Canada), $90 for international applicants. Phone: (406)496-4304; fax: (406)496-4334.

ADMISSION STANDARDS. Very competitive. Usual minimum average: 3.0 (A = 4).

FINANCIAL AID. Annual awards from institutional funds: fellowships, teaching assistantships, research assistantships, fee waivers, Federal W/S, loans. Approved for VA benefits. Apply by April 1 to Administrator, Graduate School. Phone: (406)496-4212; fax: (406)496-4133. Use FAFSA and institutional FAF. Aid available for part-time students.

DEGREE REQUIREMENTS. For M.S.(thesis required): 30 semester hours. For M.S. (nonthesis): 36 semester hours.

FIELDS OF STUDY.
Environmental Engineering.
General Engineering.
Geoscience. Includes geochemistry, hydrogeology, hydrogeological engineering, geology, geological engineering, geophysical engineering.
Industrial Hygiene.
Metallurgical/Mineral Processing Engineering.
Mining Engineering.
Petroleum Engineering.

Project Engineering and Management. Joint program with Montana State University.
Technical Communications. In affiliation with University of Montana.

UNIVERSITY OF MONTANA
Missoula, Montana 59812
Web site: www.umt.edu

Established 1893. Coed. State control. Semester system. Special facilities: University Biological Station, Wood Chemistry Laboratories, Animal Behavior Laboratory, Bureau of Business and Economic Research, Computer Center, Lubrecht Forestry Camp, Montana Forest and Conservation Experiment Station, Performing Arts and Radio/TV Center, Institute for Social Science Research, Bureau of Government Research, Wildlife Research Unit, Division of Educational Research and Services, Bureau of Press and Broadcasting, Stella Duncan Memorial Institute for Respiratory Disease Research Center, Mansfield Center of Ethics and Asian Affairs. Library: 700,000 volumes, 6248 subscriptions. Total University enrollment: 11,700.

Tuition: per credit resident $177, nonresident $240. On-campus housing for 394 married students, limited number for single graduate students. Average per month housing cost: $338–$508 for married students; academic year housing cost for single students: $2136–$3284. Apply to Family Housing Office. Phone: (406)549-0134 (married students); to Off-Campus Housing Clearinghouse. Phone: (406)243-4636 (off-campus housing information).

Graduate School

Enrollment: full-time 678, part-time 549 (men 50%, women 50%). Faculty: full-time 380, part-time 109. Degrees conferred: M.A., M.Acc., M.A.S., M.A.T., M.B.A., M.Ed., M.F., M.S.T., M.M.Ed., M.I.S., M.F.A., M.M., M.P.A., M.S., Ed.S., Ed.D., Ph.D.

ADMISSION REQUIREMENTS. One official transcript, GRE, three letters of recommendation required in support of School's application. On-line application available. GMAT required for business. Interview not required. TOEFL required for international applicants. Accepts transfer applicants. Graduates of unaccredited institutions not considered. Apply to department concerned at least two months prior to registration. Some departments have earlier deadlines. Application fee $45. Phone: (406)243-2572; fax: (406)243-4593.

ADMISSION STANDARDS. Very competitive for some departments, competitive or selective for others. Usual minimum average: 3.0 (A = 4).

FINANCIAL AID. Annual awards from institutional funds: scholarships, research assistantships, teaching assistantships, internship, grants, Federal W/S, loans. Approved for VA benefits. Apply by March 1 to department for assistantships; to Financial Aid Office for all other programs. Phone: (406)243-5373. Use FAFSA. About 40% of students receive aid other than loans from School and outside sources. Aid sometimes available for part-time students.

DEGREE REQUIREMENTS. For master's: 30 semester credits minimum, at least 12 in residence; final oral/written exam; thesis/final project; reading knowledge of one foreign language required by some departments. For Ed.D.: 90 semester credits minimum, at least 30 in residence; comprehensive exam; dissertation; final oral exam. For Ph.D.: three years minimum beyond the bachelor's, at least three semesters in residence; language requirement varies with department; comprehensive exam; dissertation; final oral exam.

FIELDS OF STUDY.

Accounting. M.Acc.

Anthropology. Includes cultural heritage, linguistics. M.A.

Art. Includes art (M.A.), integrated arts and education (M.A.), art history (M.F.A.), ceramics (M.F.A.), painting and drawing (M.F.A.), photography (M.F.A.), printmaking (M.F.A.), sculpture (M.F.A.). Portfolio for admission to M.F.A. program. M.A., M.F.A.

Biochemistry. M.S.

Biochemistry-Microbiology. Includes microbial ecology. Ph.D. only.

Biological Sciences. M.S.T.

Business Administration. M.B.A.

Chemistry. Includes analytical/environmental, inorganic, organic, physical, teaching. M.S., M.S.T.C., Ph.D.

Communication Studies. M.A.

Computer Science. M.S.

Counselor Education. Includes school counseling (M.A.). M.A., M.Ed., Ed.S.

Creative Writing. Includes fiction, nonfiction, poetry. M.F.A.

Curriculum and Instruction. Includes curriculum studies, elementary education, library media services, literacy education, secondary education. M.Ed., Ed.D.

Drama. Includes acting, design technology, directing, drama (M.A.). M.A., M.F.A.

Economics. M.A.

Ecosystem Management. M.E.M.

Educational Leadership. M.Ed., Ed.S., Ed.D.

English. Includes literature. M.A.

Environmental Studies. M.S.

Fish and Wildlife Biology. Ph.D.

Foreign Languages. Includes French, German, Spanish. M.A.

Forestry. M.S., Ph.D.

Geography. Includes cartography and GIS, rural town and regional planning. M.A.

Geology. M.S., Ph.D.

Health and Human Performance. Includes exercise science, health promotion. M.S.

History. M.A.

Interdisciplinary Studies. Includes individualized interdisciplinary studies (Ph.D.). M.I.S., Ph.D.

Journalism. Includes photojournalism, print, radio and TV. M.A.

Linguistics. Includes applied, general. M.A.

Mathematics. Includes mathematics education, college teaching and general practitioner (Ph.D.), traditional (Ph.D.). M.A., Ph.D.

Medial Arts. M.F.A.

Microbiology. Includes microbial ecology. M.S.

Music. Includes music history and literature (M.A.), composition/technology, music education, performance. M.A., M.M.

Organismal Biology and Ecology. M.S., Ph.D.

Pharmacology/Pharmaceutical Sciences. Ph.D.

Pharmacy. M.S.

Philosophy. Includes teaching ethics. M.A.

Physical Therapy. M.S.

Political Science. M.A.

Psychology. Includes animal behavior, clinical, developmental. M.A., Ph.D.

Public Administration. M.P.A.

Recreation Management. M.S.

Resource Conservation. M.S.

School Psychology. M.A., Ed.S.

Social Work. M.S.W.

Sociology. Includes criminology, rural environmental change. M.A.

Technical Communications. M.S.

Toxicology. Ph.D.

Wildlife Biology. M.S.

School of Law

Established 1911. ABA approved since 1923. AALS member since 1914. Semester system. Law library: 125,000 volumes, 1946 subscriptions; has LEXIS, WESTLAW.

Annual tuition: full-time, resident $6842, nonresident $12,624. On-campus housing available. Total average annual additional expense: $7750.

Enrollment: first-year class 93; total full-time 251 (men 58%, women 42%). Faculty: full-time 11, part-time 15. Student to faculty ratio 11 to 1. Degrees conferred: J.D., J.D.-M.B.A., J.D.-M.S. (Environmental Studies), J.D.-M.P.A.

ADMISSION REQUIREMENTS. LSDAS Law School report, bachelor's degree, transcripts, LSAT (not later than February) required in support of application. Interview not required. Preference given to state residents. Graduates of unaccredited colleges not considered. Apply to Dean of the Law School after September 1, before March 1. Fall admission only. Application fee $60. Phone: (406)243-4311.

ADMISSION STANDARDS. Selective. Mean LSAT: 153; mean GPA: 3.12 (A = 4). Gourman rating: 2.84. *U.S. News & World Report* ranking is in the third tier of all U.S. law schools. Accepts 55% of total annual applicants.

FINANCIAL AID. Limited to loans; research assistantships for third-year students only. Apply by March 1 to Financial Aid Office. Phone: (406)243-5373. Use FAFSA (School code: 00256) and Montana FAF. About 40% of students receive aid other than loans from School.

DEGREE REQUIREMENTS. For J.D.: satisfactory completion of three-year program; 90 credit-hour program.

MONTCLAIR STATE UNIVERSITY
Upper Montclair, New Jersey 07043-1624
Web site: www.montclair.edu

Founded 1908. Located 15 miles W of New York City. CGS member. Coed. State control. Semester system. Special facilities: Center for Adult Learning, Center for Archaeological Studies, Center for Child Advocacy, Center for Community-Based Learning, Center for Pedagogy, Center for Economic Research on Africa, DuMont TV Center, International Trade Counseling Center, Preparatory Center for the Arts, Institute for the Advancement of Philosophy for Children, Institute for the Humanities, Institute for Community Studies. Library: 455,185 volumes, 2233 subscriptions. Total University enrollment: 13,000.

Tuition: per credit: resident $237, nonresident $325. Limited on-campus housing for graduate students. Contact Office of Residence Life for both on- and off-campus housing information. Phone: (973)655-5188. Day-care facilities available.

Graduate School

Graduate study since 1932. Enrollment: full-time 497, part-time 1652. College faculty: full- and part-time 395. Degrees conferred: M.A., M.B.A., M.A.T., M.Ed., M.S., Ed.D.

ADMISSION REQUIREMENTS. Official transcripts, GRE/GMAT/MAT/NTE, interview required in support of application. On-line application available. Portfolios, auditions required for some programs. TOEFL required for international applicants. Accepts transfer applicants. Graduates of unaccredited institutions not considered. To be considered for matriculation, applications and credentials need to be received by the Graduate Office before April 1 (Summer and Fall), November 1 (Spring). Some programs have earlier deadlines. Application fee $40. Phone: (800)331-9207, (973)655-5147; e-mail: gradstudies@montclair.edu.

ADMISSION STANDARDS. Admission decisions based on combination of GPA and standardized test score. Usual minimum average: 2.75 (A = 4).

FINANCIAL AID. Annual awards from institutional funds: scholarships, graduate assistantships, Federal W/S, loans. Apply by March 1 to the Office of Graduate Studies for assistantships; to Office of Financial Aid for all other programs. Phone: (973)655-4461. Use FAFSA. Aid available for part-time students.

DEGREE REQUIREMENTS. For M.A., M.S.: 32 semester hours minimum, at least 30 in residence; additional hours may be required depending on undergraduate major; thesis/special project/comprehensive exam. For M.A.T.: 45 semester hours minimum, at least 30 in residence. For M.B.A.: 45–60 semester hours depending on undergraduate major, at least 30 in residence. For Ed.D.: 60 credit program; dissertation seminar; dissertation; final defense.

FIELDS OF STUDY.
Accounting. M.B.A.
Administration and Supervision. Includes educator, trainer. M.A.
Anthropology. M.A.
Biology. M.S.
Business Administration. M.B.A.
Business Education. Includes distributive. M.A.
Chemistry. M.S.
Communication Sciences and Disorders. Includes audiology, early childhood special education, learning disabilities, speech/language pathology. M.A.
Computer Science. Includes applied mathematics, applied statistics. M.S.
Counseling. Includes human services. M.A.
Education. M.Ed. only.
Educational Psychology. M.A.
English. M.A.
Environmental Studies. Includes education, health, management, science. M.A.
Fine Arts. Includes art history, studio. M.A., M.F.A.
French. M.A.
Geoscience. M.S.
Health Education. M.A.
Home Ecology. Includes family life education, family relations/child development, education, home management/consumer economics. M.A.
Legal Studies. M.A.
Linguistics. M.A.
Mathematics. Includes computer science, education, pure and applied mathematics, statistics. M.S.
Music. Includes education, performance, theory/composition. M.A.
Pedagogy. Includes mathematics education, philosophy for children. Ed.D. only.
Physical Education. Includes coaching and sports administration, exercise science, teaching and administration of physical education. M.A.
Psychology. Includes clinical for Spanish-English bilinguals, industrial and organizational, school. M.A.
Reading. M.A.
Social Sciences. Includes anthropology, economics, geography, history, urban studies. M.A.
Sociology. M.A.
Spanish. M.A.
Special Education. M.Ed.
Speech and Theatre. Includes communication arts. M.A.
Statistics. M.S.
Teaching. M.A.T.

MONTEREY INSTITUTE OF INTERNATIONAL STUDIES
Monterey, California 93940-2691
Web site: www.miis.edu

Founded 1955. Located 124 miles S of San Francisco. Coed. Private control. Semester system. Library: 82,000 volumes, 500 subscriptions.

Annual tuition: full-time $21,100. No on-campus housing available for graduate students. Average academic year housing and food expense: $8,325.

Graduate Programs

Enrollment: full-time 548, part-time 63. Institute's faculty: full-time 70, part-time 25. Degrees conferred: M.A., M.A.C.D., M.A.C.I., M.A.I.E.P., M.A.I.P.S., M.A.T., M.A.TESOL, M.A.T.F.L., M.A.T.I., M.B.A., M.P.A.

ADMISSION REQUIREMENTS. Transcripts, two letters of recommendation, statement of purpose, résumé required in support of application. All students must be able to work at the third-year university level in the proposed language of study. GRE for native English speakers for M.A. Translation and Interpretation applicants. GMAT required for M.B.A. applicants. TOEFL (minimum score 550) required for international applicants. Campus visits/interviews recommended. Apply to the Admission Office by June 1. M.B.A. admitted in August, January, and June. Application fee $50. Phone: (831)647-4123; fax (831)647-6405; e-mail: admit@miis.edu.

ADMISSION STANDARDS. Selective. Usual minimum average: 3.0 (A = 4).

FINANCIAL AID. Annual awards from institutional funds: scholarships, grants, assistantships, internships, Federal W/S, loans. Approved for VA benefits. Apply by March 15 to Financial Aid Office. Phone: (831) 647-4119; fax: (831)647-4199. Use FAFSA. About 65% of full-time students receive aid other than loans from Institute and outside sources.

DEGREE REQUIREMENTS. For M.A.I.P.S., M.A.I.E.P., M.P.A., M.A.C.D.: 60 credit, two-year, full-time programs; capstone project/master's project. For M.A.TESOL, M.A.T.F.L.: 48 credit programs. For M.A.T., M.A.T.I., M.A.C.I.: 60 credit, four-semester, full-time programs; comprehensive professional exam; research project/translation thesis. For M.B.A.: two-year full-time program (also have 12-month program for advanced entry candidates, a summer language program and master's international in cooperation with the Peace Corps).

FIELDS OF STUDY.

FISCHER GRADUATE SCHOOL OF INTERNATIONAL BUSINESS:
Business Administration. Specializations in entrepreneurial management, international trade management, international marketing, international finance and economics, international human resources management, regional business environments, global business management, international environmental management, nonprofit and public management. M.B.A.

GRADUATE SCHOOL OF INTERNATIONAL POLICY STUDIES:
Commercial Diplomacy. M.A.C.D.
International Environmental Policy. M.A.I.E.P.
International Policy Studies. M.A.I.P.S.
Public Administration in International Management. M.P.A.

GRADUATE SCHOOL OF LANGUAGE AND EDUCATIONAL LINGUISTICS:
Teaching English to Speakers of Other Languages. M.A.TESOL.
Teaching Foreign Language. M.A.T.F.L.

GRADUATE SCHOOL OF TRANSLATION AND INTERPRETATION:
Conference Interpretation. M.A.C.I.
Translation. M.A.T.
Translation and Interpretation. M.A.T.I.
Note: Study available in the following languages: Chinese, English, French, German, Japanese, Korean, Russian, Spanish.

UNIVERSITY OF MONTEVALLO

Montevallo, Alabama 35115

Web site: www.montevallo.edu

Founded 1896. Located 32 miles from Birmingham. Coed. State control. Semester system. Library: 248,000 volumes, 868 subscriptions.

Tuition: per credit hour resident $145, nonresident $290. On-campus housing in Summer for 200 men, 200 women; none for married students. Annual academic year housing cost: $2318–$4224; board cost $860–$1320. Single students apply to Director of Housing and Residence Life. Phone: (205)665-6235. Married students make own arrangements for off-campus housing.

Graduate Studies

Graduate study since 1955. Enrollment: full-time 124, part-time 295. University faculty teaching graduate students: full- and part-time 97. Degrees conferred: M.A., M.S., M.Ed., M.M.

ADMISSION REQUIREMENTS. Transcripts, GRE/MAT required in support of application. Interview not required. TOEFL (minimum score 550) required for international applicants. Accepts transfer applicants. Graduates of unaccredited colleges not considered. Apply to Office of Graduate Studies two to three months prior to registration. Application fee $25. Phone: (205)665-6350; fax: (205)665-6353.

ADMISSION STANDARDS. Relatively open. Usual minimum average: 2.5, 2.75 last 60 credits (A = 4).

FINANCIAL AID. Limited to Federal W/S, loans. Approved for VA benefits. Apply to Office of Financial Aid; no specified closing date. Phone: (205)665-6050. Use FAFSA.

DEGREE REQUIREMENTS. For master's: 30 semester hours minimum; comprehensive exam; thesis/nonthesis option. For Ed.S.: 30 semester hours beyond master's; comprehensive exam.

FIELDS OF STUDY.
Counseling. M.Ed.
Early Childhood Education. M.Ed.
Educational Administration. M.Ed.
Educational Leadership. Ed.S.
Elementary Education. M.Ed.
English. M.A.
Music. Includes composition, music education, performance, theory-composition. M.M.
Preschool to 12th Grade Education (P–12). M.Ed.
Secondary Education (6–12). M.Ed.
Speech Pathology and Audiology. M.S.
Teacher Leader. Ed.S.

MOREHEAD STATE UNIVERSITY

Morehead, Kentucky 40351

Web site: www.moreheadstate.edu

Founded 1922. Located 65 miles E of Lexington. CGS member. Semester system. Library: 400,000 volumes, 1300 subscriptions.

Annual tuition: full-time, resident $3168, nonresident $8494. On-campus housing for married and single students. Average academic year housing cost: $2100–$2320 for single students; $3300 for married students. Contact Director of Housing for both on- and off-campus housing information. Phone: (606)783-2060.

Graduate Programs

Enrollment: full- and part-time 1701. Faculty: full-time 139, part-time 24. Degrees conferred: M.A., M.B.A., M.S., M.M., M.A.Ed., M.S.W., Ed.S., Ed.D. (cooperative program with University of Kentucky), Ph.D. (cooperative program with University of Kentucky).

ADMISSION REQUIREMENTS. Official transcripts, GRE required in support of application. On-line application available. TOEFL required for international applicants. Accepts transfer applicants. Graduates of unaccredited colleges not considered. Apply to Graduate Admissions Office at least two months prior to registration. Rolling admissions process. Application fee: none. Phone: (606)783-2039; fax: (606)783-5061.

ADMISSION STANDARDS. Selective. Usual minimum average: 2.5 (A = 4).

FINANCIAL AID. Annual awards from institutional funds: research/teaching assistantships, internships, Federal W/S, loans. Approved for VA benefits. Apply by April 1 to Dean of Graduate and Extended Campus Programs for assistantships; to Financial Aid Office for all other programs. Phone: (606)783-2039. Use FAFSA and University's FAF. About 15% of students receive aid from University. No aid available for part-time students.

DEGREE REQUIREMENTS. For master's: 33–45 semester hours minimum, at least 27–36 in residence; thesis/nonthesis optional; final written/oral exams. For Ed.S.: 30 semester hours beyond the master's. For Ph.D.: 60 credits minimum, at least one year in full-time residence; qualifying exam; proficiency in one foreign language for some programs; dissertation; final oral exam.

FIELDS OF STUDY.
Adult and Higher Education. M.A., Ed.S.
Art. Includes art education, studio art. M.A.
Biology. M.S.
Business Administration. M.B.A.
Career and Technical Education. Includes agriculture, human sciences, industrial education. M.S.
Communications. Includes advertising/public relations, electronic media, journalism, speech, theatre. M.A.
Curriculum and Instruction. Ed.S.
Education. Includes elementary (P–5), elementary (5–9), elementary guidance, international educator, secondary (8–12), secondary guidance, special education. M.A.Ed.
Educational Policy Studies and Evaluation. Cooperative doctoral program with University of Kentucky.
Educational Psychology.
English. M.A.
Guidance and Counseling. Ed.S.
Health, Physical Education, and Recreation. Includes athletic training, exercise physiology, health and physical education, sports and recreation administration. M.A.
Industrial Technology. M.S.
Instructional Leadership. Ed.S.
Instruction and Administration. Cooperative doctoral program with University of Kentucky.
Kinesiology and Health Promotion. Cooperative doctoral program with University of Kentucky.
Music. Includes music education, performance.
Psychology. Includes general-experimental, clinical, counseling.
School Administration. M.A.
Social Work. M.S.W. Cooperative program with University of Kentucky.
Sociology. Includes criminology, general, social gerontology. M.A.
Special Education and Rehabilitation Counseling. Cooperative doctoral program with the University of Kentucky.

MOREHOUSE SCHOOL OF MEDICINE
Atlanta, Georgia 30310-1495
Web site: www.msm.edu

Established 1978. Primary mission is to provide physicians for medically underserved rural and inner-city areas. Library: 90,170 volumes, 791 subscriptions.

Annual tuition and fees: $20,160; student fees $2660. There is no medical school housing. Total average cost for all other expenses: $9502. Enrollment: first-year class 42 (EDP 1), total 145 (men 45%, women 55%). Faculty: full-time 90; part-time and volunteers 130. Degrees conferred: M.D., M.D.-M.P.H. (with Clark Atlanta University), M.D.-Ph.D. (Biomedical Sciences).

ADMISSION REQUIREMENTS. AMCAS report, transcripts, MCAT, three letters of recommendation, biographical questionnaire, personal statement required in support of application. Has EDP; apply between June 1 and August 1. Interview by invitation. Preference given to state residents. Apply to Office of Admissions and Student Affairs after June 1, before December 1. Application fee $50. Phone: (404)752-1650; fax: (404)752-1512.

ADMISSION STANDARDS. Competitive. Mean MCAT: 7.0. Gourman rating: 3.06. Admits about 10% of total annual applications. Approximately 70% are state residents.

FINANCIAL AID. Scholarships, limited merit scholarships, minority scholarships, Grants-in-Aid, institutional loans, HEAL, alternative loan programs, Federal Perkins Loans, Stafford Subsidized and Unsubsidized Loans, Service Commitment Scholarship programs are available. All Financial Aid is based on documented need. For merit scholarships, the selection criteria places heavy reliance on MCAT and undergraduate GPA. Contact the Office of Student Fiscal Affairs for current information. Phone: (404)752-1656. For most financial assistance and all Federal programs use FAFSA (School code: G24821), also submit Financial Aid Transcript, Federal Income Tax forms. Approximately 94% of students receive some form of financial assistance.

DEGREE REQUIREMENTS. For M.D.: satisfactory completion of four-year program. All students must pass USMLE Step 1 prior to entering third year; all students must pass USMLE Step 2 prior to awarding of M.D.

MORGAN STATE UNIVERSITY
Baltimore, Maryland 21239
Web site: www.morgan.edu

Founded 1867. CGS member. Coed. State control. Semester system. Library: 652,000 volumes, 2526 subscriptions.

Tuition: per credit, resident $193, nonresident $364. No on-campus housing for graduate students during academic year, some housing during Summer session. Annual academic year housing cost: $3950 (including board). Apply to Director, Residence Life. Phone: (443)885-3217.

School of Graduate Studies

Graduate study since 1964. Enrollment: full-time 282, part-time 302. Graduate faculty: full-time 70, part-time 10. Degrees conferred: M.A., M.S., M.B.A., M.Arch., M.L.A., M.C.R.P., M.E., M.P.H., D.E., Ed.D., Ph.D.

ADMISSION REQUIREMENTS. Transcripts, GRE/GMAT/MAT required in support of School's application. Interview not required. TOEFL required for international applicants. Accepts transfer applicants. Apply to Graduate School by August 1 (Fall), December 1 (Spring), June 1 (Summer). Application fee, none. Phone: (443)885-3185; fax: (443)885-3837.

ADMISSION STANDARDS. Selective. Usual minimum average: 3.0 (unconditional), 2.5 (conditional) (A = 4).

FINANCIAL AID. Annual awards from institutional funds: scholarships, fellowships, teaching assistantships, minority fellowships, internships, grants, Federal W/S, loans. Approved for VA benefits. Phone: (443)885-3170; fax: (443)885-3852. Use FAFSA and University's FAF. Aid available for part-time students.

DEGREE REQUIREMENTS. For M.A., M.S.: 30–42 semester hours, depending upon major, at least 25–36 hours in residence; thesis/final written/oral exam. For M.B.A.: 30–51 hours depending upon academic background. For M.C.R.P.: 51 semester hours. For M.Arch.: 30–90 semester hours, depending on academic background. For M.L.A.: 90 semester hours, depending on academic background. For D.E., Ed.D.: 60 semester hours minimum beyond the master's. For Ph.D.: 60 semester hours minimum beyond the master's, qualifying exam; one foreign language and research tool for some programs, dissertation; final oral exam.

FIELDS OF STUDY.
African American Studies. M.A.
Architecture. M.Arch.
Bio-Environmental Sciences. Ph.D. only.
Bioinformatics. M.A.
Biology. M.S.
Business Administration. Includes accounting, finance, international, management, marketing. M.B.A., Ph.D.
Chemistry. M.S.
City and Regional Planning. M.C.R.P.
Community College Leadership. Ed.D.
Economics. M.A.
Educational Administration and Supervision. M.S.
Elementary Education. M.S.
Engineering. M.E., D.E.
English. M.A., Ph.D.
Health Education Administration. Ph.D. only.
History. Ph.D.
International Studies. M.A.
Landscape Architecture. M.L.A.
Mathematics. M.A.
Mathematics Education. Ed.D.
Music. Includes choral and instrumental conducting, musicology, theory, performance. M.A.
Public Health. M.P.H., Dr.P.H.
Physics. M.S.
Science. M.S.
Science Education. Ed.D.
Sociology. M.S.
Teaching. M.A.T.
Telecommunication Management. M.S.
Transportation Studies. M.S.
Urban Education Leadership. Ed.D. only.

MORNINGSIDE COLLEGE
Sioux City, Iowa 51106-1751
Web site: www.morningside.edu

Founded 1894. Coed. Private control. Methodist affiliation. Semester system. Library: 168,000 volumes, 650 subscriptions.

Tuition: per credit $280, per credit $180 for educators. On-campus housing for graduate men, women; some for married students. Average academic year expenses: $4714. Contact Director of Housing for on- and off-campus information. Phone: (712)274-5104.

Graduate Program

Summer study with evening program during academic year. Enrollment: part-time only, 300 (men 10%, women 90%). College faculty teaching graduate students: full-time 18, part-time 3. Degree conferred: M.A.T.

ADMISSION REQUIREMENTS. Transcripts, writing sample, MAT required in support of application. On-line application available. TOEFL required for international applicants. Accepts transfer applicants. Apply to Director of Graduate Study at least one month prior to registration. Application fee: $25. Phone: (712)274-5375.

ADMISSION STANDARDS. Relatively open. Minimum average: 2.7 (A = 4).

FINANCIAL AID. Rebates for qualified students, Federal W/S, loans. Apply to Director of Graduate Studies; no specified closing date. Phone: (712)274-5159. Use FAFSA. More than 90% of students receive financial assistance.

DEGREE REQUIREMENTS. For M.A.T.: 31–32 semester hours minimum; final written comprehensive exam; three final research papers.

FIELDS OF STUDY.
Behavior Disorders.
Elementary Education.
Learning Disabilities.
Mental Disabilities (Mild–Moderate).
Multicategorical Disabilities (Mild).
Technology-Based Learning.

MOUNT ST. MARY'S COLLEGE

Los Angeles, California 90049-1599
Web site: www.msmc.la.edu

Founded 1925. Coed. Private control. Roman Catholic. Semester system. Special facility: Center for Cultural Fluency. Library: 140,000 volumes, 800 subscriptions. Total College enrollment: 2000.
Tuition: per credit $458. No on-campus housing.

Graduate School

Graduate study since 1931. Enrollment: full- and part-time 270 (men 35%, women 65%). Graduate faculty: full-time 16, part-time 23. Degrees conferred: M.A., M.S.

ADMISSION REQUIREMENTS. Transcripts, MAT, letters of recommendation required in support of application. TOEFL required of foreign students. Accepts transfer applicants. Apply to Director of Admissions at least six weeks prior to registration (earlier deadline for Physical Therapy program). Application fee $50. Phone: (213)477-2800.

ADMISSION STANDARDS. Relatively open. Usual minimum average: 2.5 (A = 4).

FINANCIAL AID. Limited to loans. Tuition discount available for employees of the Archdiocese of Los Angeles and Orange Counties. Approved for VA benefits. Apply to Financial Aid Office; no specified closing date. Phone: (213)477-2800. Use FAFSA.

DEGREE REQUIREMENTS. For master's: 30 units minimum, at least 24 in residence; final written/oral exams; final project or thesis. For master's (no project/thesis): 39 unit program; oral integration interview.

FIELDS OF STUDY.
Administrative Services.
Counseling Psychology. Includes human services and marriage, family, and child counseling.

Elementary Education.
Individually Designed Program.
Nursing Education.
Physical Therapy.
Religious Studies. Includes certificate progra gious studies, Hispanic pastoral ministry, seling, youth and young adult ministry.
Secondary Education.
Special Education. Includes mild/moderate disabilities.

MOUNT SINAI SCHOOL OF MEDICINE
New York, New York 10029

Mount Sinai Medical Center
One Gustave L. Levy Place
New York, New York 10029

Established 1852. Public Control. Mount Sinai Hospital is a member of Council of Teaching Hospitals. Special facilities: Division of Environment and Occupational Medicine, Clinical Genetics Center, Gerald A. Ruttenberg Cancer Center, General Clinical Research Center, Institute for Gene Therapy and Molecular Medicine, Center for Jewish Genetic Diseases, Institute for Medicare Practice, Fishberg Research Center for Neurobiology of Aging, Recanati/Miller Transplantation Institute, Wiener Cardiovascular Institute, Lucy Moses Cardiothoracic Center. The School's NIH ranking is 36th among all U.S. institutions with 362 awards/grants worth $121,964,497. Library: 154,000 volumes, 2500 subscriptions.

Graduate School of Biological Sciences
(P.O. Box 1022)
Web site: www.mssm.edu/gradschool

Graduate study since 1965. Enrollment: full- and part-time 217. Faculty: full- and part-time 200. Degrees conferred: M.Sc., Ph.D.

ADMISSION REQUIREMENTS. Official transcripts, GRE, three letters of recommendation required in support of School's application. Interviews by invitation. TOEFL or evidence of proficiency in English required for international students. Accepts transfer applicants. Graduates of unaccredited institutions not considered. Admits Fall only. Apply by February 15 (Fall), January 15 (for priority consideration) to Graduate School (P.O. Box 1022). Rolling admissions process. Application fee $50. Phone: (212)241-0651; fax (212)241-6546; e-mail: grads@mssm.edu.

ADMISSION STANDARDS. Competitive for most departments, selective for all others. Usual minimum average: 3.0 (A = 4).

FINANCIAL AID. Traineeships, fellowships, assistantships, loans. Apply by February 1 to Dean for assistantships, fellowships; to Financial Aid Office for all other programs. Phone: (212)241-5245. Use FAFSA.

DEGREE REQUIREMENTS. For M.Sc.: two-year part-time program; field practicum: thesis/project. For Ph.D.: three-year full-time program; qualifying exam; selection of preceptor's laboratory; thesis proposal; dissertation: dissertation defense.

FIELDS OF STUDY.
Biological Services. Includes biomathematical sciences, biophysics, structural biology and biomathematics, genetics and genomic science, microbiology, molecular, cellular, and environmental pathology, neuroscience, pharmacology, physiology and biophysics. Ph.D.
Community Medicine. M.Sc.

...c Counseling. M.Sc. (both a physician and nonphysician ...ogram).

Mount Sinai School of Medicine (10029-6574)
Web site: www.mssm.edu

Established 1968. Officially affiliated with New York University. Special programs: an Early Acceptance program with Amherst College, Brandeis University, Princeton University, Wesleyan University, Williams College, Cooper Union; a seven-year Biomedical Education program with City College of City University of New York; prematriculation summer sessions.

Annual tuition: $25,250; fees $1575. On-campus rooms and apartments available for both single and married students. Annual on-campus housing cost: $11,500. Contact Office of Student Affairs for both on- and off-campus housing information. Medical students tend to live off-campus. Off-campus housing and personal expenses: approximately $12,500.

Enrollment: first-year class 120 (EDP 5); total full-time 455 (men 47%, women 53%). Faculty: full-time 1000, part-time 250. Degrees conferred: M.D., M.D.-Ph.D., M.S.T.P. (Medical Scientist Training Program).

ADMISSION REQUIREMENTS. AMCAS report, transcripts, MCAT, references, interview required in support of application. On-line application available. Has EDP; apply between June 1 and August 1. Accepts transfer applicants. Applicants must have completed at least three years of college study. Apply to Office for Admissions after June 1, before November 1. Application fee $100. Phone: (212)241-6696; fax: (212)369-6013.

ADMISSION STANDARDS. Very competitive. Mean MCAT: 10.76; mean GPA: 3.67 (A = 4). Gourman rating: 3.89. *U.S. News & World Report* ranking is in the top 22 of all U.S. medical schools. Accepts about 5% of total applicants. Approximately 40% are state residents.

FINANCIAL AID. Scholarships, loans. Apply to Financial Aid Officer after acceptance. Phone: (212)241-6696. MSTP funded by NIH. Use FAFSA (School code: G07026). About 65% of students receive aid other than loans from School; over 80% receive some form of financial assistance.

DEGREE REQUIREMENTS. For M.D.: satisfactory completion of four-year program.

FIELDS OF GRADUATE STUDY.
Anatomy.
Biochemistry.
Biophysics.
Cell Biology.
Community Medicine.
Genetics.
Immunology.
Microbiology.
Molecular Biology.
Neuroscience.
Pathology.
Pharmacology.
Physiology.

MURRAY STATE UNIVERSITY
Murray, Kentucky 42071-0009
Web site: www.murraystate.edu

Founded 1922. Located 110 miles W of Nashville, Tennessee. CGS member. Coed. State control. Semester system. Library: 831,000 volumes, 3000 subscriptions.

Annual tuition: full-time, resident $2674, nonresident $7446; per credit, resident $156, nonresident $418. On-campus housing for 144 married students, 1383 men, 1449 women. Average annual housing cost: $4170 for married students, $1940 for single students. Contact Housing Office for on- and off-campus information. Phone: (270)762-2310.

Graduate Studies

Graduate study since 1936. Enrollment: full-time 439, part-time 1225. University faculty: full- and part-time 319. Degrees conferred: M.A., M.S., M.B.A., M.A.Ed., M.S.N., M.M.E., M.A.T., M.P.A., Ed.S.

ADMISSION REQUIREMENTS. Transcripts, GRE Subject Tests/GMAT required in support of School's application. TOEFL (minimum score 500) required for international applicants. Interview required by some departments. Accepts transfer applicants. Graduates of unaccredited colleges not considered. Apply to Graduate Office at least one month prior to registration. Application fee $20. Phone: (270)762-3895; fax: (270)762-3799.

ADMISSION STANDARDS. Relatively open. Usual minimum average: 2.75 (A = 4).

FINANCIAL AID. Annual awards from institutional funds: scholarships, teaching fellowships, research assistantships, internships, Federal W/S, loans. Apply by April 1 to chair of proposed major department for fellowships and assistantships; to Financial Aid Office for all other programs. Phone: (270)762-2546. Use FAFSA. About 10% of students receive aid other than loans from University and outside sources. Aid available for part-time students.

DEGREE REQUIREMENTS. For master's: 30–45 semester hours, at least 18–33 in residence; final written/oral exams; reading knowledge of one foreign language for some degrees, majors; thesis usually required for M.A., M.S. For Ed.S.: 30 semester hours minimum beyond master's.

FIELDS OF STUDY.
Agriculture.
Biology. One language for M.S. Joint doctoral program with the University of Louisville.
Business Administration. GMAT for admission.
Chemistry.
Clinical Psychology.
Economics.
Education. Includes elementary, middle school, secondary, educational administration and supervision, guidance and counseling, special education, reading and writing. M.A.Ed.: 27 hours with thesis, 33 without. Joint doctoral program with University of Kentucky.
English.
Fine Arts. Includes music education.
General Psychology.
Geography.
Geosciences.
Health, Physical Education, and Recreation.
History. One language for M.A.
Human Services.
Industrial Education.
Management of Technology.
Mass Communications. Includes advertising, journalism, public relations, radio-TV.
Mathematics.
Music Education.
Nursing.
Occupational Safety and Health.
Organizational Communication.
Physics.

Public Administration.
Recreation and Leisure Services.
Speech Language Pathology.
Teaching English to Speakers of Other Languages (TESOL).
Telecommunication Systems Management.
Vocational and Technical Education.
Water Science.

NATIONAL-LOUIS UNIVERSITY
Evanston, Illinois 60201-1796
Web site: www.nl.edu

Founded 1866 as National College of Education. Name changed in 1992. Regional campuses located in Atlanta, Chicago area, McLean/Washington, Milwaukee/Beloit, Orlando, Tampa, Heidleberg, Nowy Sacz. Coed. Private control. Semester system. Library: 180,000 volumes, 1200 subscriptions.

Tuition: per credit, Education $484, Management and Business $558. On-campus housing for limited number of men, women; none for married students. Average annual housing expense $1920–$2862. Apply to Director of Housing. Phone: (847)475-1100.

Graduate Programs

Graduate study since 1951. Enrollment: full-time 1490, part-time 3283. Graduate faculty: full-time 125, part-time 456. Degrees conferred: M.Ed., M.A.T., M.S.Ed., Ed.S., Ed.D.

ADMISSION REQUIREMENTS. Transcripts, three letters of recommendation, MAT required in support of School's application. GRE for Ed.S. and doctoral program. TOEFL, financial affidavits required for international applicants. Accepts transfer applicants. Graduates of unaccredited institutions not considered. Apply to Director of Admission by April 15 (Fall), October 15 (Spring). Rolling admissions process. Application fee $40. Phone: (847)465-0575, ext. 5571.

ADMISSION STANDARDS. Selective. Usual minimum average: 3.0 (A = 4).

FINANCIAL AID. Annual awards from institutional funds: scholarships, fellowships, Federal W/S, loans. Apply to Office of Financial Assistance; no specified closing date. Use FAFSA. Phone: (847)465-0575, ext. 5770. Aid sometimes available for part-time students.

DEGREE REQUIREMENTS. For master's: 32–38 credits minimum; internship option; thesis/nonthesis option. No language requirement. For Ed.S.: at least 30 credits beyond master's. For Ed.D.: 63 credits minimum; qualifying exam; dissertation; final oral exam.

FIELDS OF STUDY.

COLLEGE OF ARTS AND SCIENCES:
Adult Education.

COLLEGE OF MANAGEMENT AND BUSINESS:
Business Administration.
Electronic Commerce.
Health Services Administration.
Human Resources Management.
Managerial Leadership.

NATIONAL COLLEGE OF EDUCATION:
Administration and Supervision.
Behavior Disorders.

Curriculum and Instruction.
Curriculum and Social Inquiry.
Development Studies.
Early Childhood Education.
Educational Leadership.
Educational Psychology. Includes human learning and development, school psychology.
Elementary Education.
Human Services.
Language Minority Education.
Mathematics Education.
Middle Level Education.
Psychology.
Reading and Language.
Reading Specialist.
School Nurse.
Science Education.
Special Education.
Technology in Education.
Written Communication.

NATIONAL UNIVERSITY
San Diego, California 92108-4107
Web site: www.nu.edu

Chartered 1971. Fourteen branch campuses—San Diego, Vista, La Jolla, Costa Mesa, San Bernadino, Bakersfield, Redding, Orange, Twenty-Nine Palms, Irvine, Riverside, Los Angeles, Sacramento, San Jose, Fresno, Stockton. CGS member. Coed. Private control. One-course-per-month format, quarter system. Library: 195,783 volumes, 3700 subscriptions.

Tuition: $960 per 4.5 quarter-hour course. No on-campus housing available.

Graduate Studies

Graduate study since 1975. Enrollment: full-time 7739, part-time 3992. Graduate faculty: full-time 100, part-time 560. Degrees conferred: M.A., M.B.A., M.F.S., M.P.A., M.S.

ADMISSION REQUIREMENTS. Official transcripts, three letters of recommendation required in support of application. TOEFL required for international applicants. Accepts transfer applicants. Graduates of unaccredited institutions not considered. Apply to Admission Office: no specified closing date. Rolling admissions process. Application fee $60, $100 for international applicants. Phone: (800) NAT-UNIV, (858)642-8180; fax: (858)642-8710; e-mail: advisor@nu.edu.

ADMISSION STANDARDS. Relatively open. Usual minimum average: 2.5 (A = 4).

FINANCIAL AID. Annual awards from institutional funds: scholarships, grants, Federal W/S, loans. Approved for VA benefits. Apply to Office of Financial Assistance; no specified closing date. Use FAFSA. Aid available for part-time students.

DEGREE REQUIREMENTS. For master's: 45–60 credits minimum, at least 35 in residence; thesis/nonthesis option; no foreign language requirement.

FIELDS OF STUDY.

SCHOOL OF ARTS AND SCIENCES:
Counseling Psychology. M.A.
Film Arts Studies. M.F.A.
English. M.A.
Human Behavior. M.A.

Instructional Technology. M.S.
Nursing. M.S.

SCHOOL OF BUSINESS AND TECHNOLOGY:
Business Administration. Includes accountancy, e-commerce, environmental management, financial management, health care management, human resource management, international management, marketing, public administration, technology management. M.B.A.
Electronic Commerce. M.S.
Forensic Sciences. M.F.S.
Health Care Administration. M.H.C.A.
Human Resource Management. M.A.
Management. M.A.
Public Administration. M.P.A.
Software Engineering. M.S.
Technology Management. M.S.
Telecommunication Systems Management. M.S.

SCHOOL OF EDUCATION AND HUMAN SERVICES:
Cross-Cultural Teaching. M.Ed.
Educational Administration. M.S.
Educational Counseling. M.A.
Educational Technology. M.S.
School Psychology. M.S.
Special Education. M.S.

NAVAL POSTGRADUATE SCHOOL

Monterey, California 93943-5100
Web site: www.nps.navy.mil

Organized 1909. Located 125 miles S of San Francisco. Enrollment limited to military officers and sponsored civilian federal employees and selected international officers. CGS member. Federal control. Quarter system. Library: 500,000 volumes, 1200 subscriptions.

Annual tuition: fully funded. On-campus housing for single and married students. Average academic year housing cost: $9200. Day care facilities available.

Enrollment: full-time 1439, 253 international. Faculty: full-time 348; part-time 34. Degrees conferred: M.A., M.S., Engr., D.Eng., Ph.D.

ADMISSION REQUIREMENTS. Official transcripts, recommendations required in support of application. Interview not required. TOEFL, TWE required for international applicants. Officers on active duty with all branches of the armed services eligible for enrollment. Apply to branch personnel division; no specified closing dates. Phone: (831)656-3059; fax: (831)656-2891.

ADMISSION STANDARDS. Competitive. Usual minimum average: 2.5 (A = 4).

DEGREE REQUIREMENTS. For M.A., M.S.: 45 quarter hours minimum in full-time residence; thesis; no language requirement. For M.B.A.: 44 credit hour program. For Engineering: 45 quarter hours beyond the master's; special project. For Ph.D.: 72 credits; three years minimum beyond the bachelor's, at least two years in full-time residence; qualifying exam; reading knowledge of one foreign language; advancement to candidacy; dissertation; final oral exam. D.Eng.: essentially the same as Ph.D., except no foreign language requirement.

FIELDS OF STUDY.

GRADUATE SCHOOL OF BUSINESS AND PUBLIC POLICY:
Business Administration. Includes concentrations in acquisition and contract management, financial management, human resource management, information technology management, logistics and transportation management, systems acquisition management. Defense focused M.B.A.
Contract Management.
International Resource Planning and Management.
Leadership Education and Development.
Management. Interdisciplinary.
Program Management.

GRADUATE SCHOOL OF ENGINEERING AND APPLIED SCIENCE:
Aeronautical Engineering.
Aeronautical Engineering Avionics.
Applied Mathematics.
Applied Physics.
Combat Systems Sciences and Technology.
Electrical and Computer Engineering.
Engineering Acoustics. Interdisciplinary.
Engineering Science.
Materials Science and Engineering.
Mathematics.
Mechanical Engineer.
Mechanical Engineering.
Meteorology.
Oceanography.
Space Systems Engineering.
Systems Engineering.

SCHOOL OF INTERNATIONAL GRADUATE STUDIES:
International Security and Civil–Military Relations. M.A.
Regional Studies. Includes Middle East, South Asia, Far East, Southeast Asia and the Pacific, Western European, the former Soviet states, Eastern Europe and Western Hemisphere.
Security Studies. Includes civil-military security building in post-conflict environments, defense decision-making and planning, homeland security. M.A.

GRADUATE SCHOOL OF OPERATIONS AND INFORMATION SCIENCES:
Computer Science.
Electronic Warfare.
Information Systems and Operation.
Information Systems Technology.
Information Warfare
Intelligence Information Management.
Operational Logistics.
Operations Analysis.
Software Engineering.
Space Systems Operations.
Special Operations.

UNIVERSITY OF NEBRASKA AT KEARNEY

Kearney, Nebraska 68849-0001
Web site: www.unk.edu

Founded 1903. Located 125 miles W of Lincoln. CGS member. Coed. State control. Semester system. Special facilities: Center for Economic Education, Center for Rural Research, Museum of Nebraska Art, Nebraska Business Development Center, Nebraska State Arboretum, Safety Center. Library: 320,915 volumes, 1650 subscriptions.

Tuition: per credit hour, resident $93, nonresident $175. Limited on-campus housing available for single graduate students, about 100 apartments for married students. Housing cost: $1350 per semester for single students; $1800 per semester for married students. Contact Director of Residence Life for on- and off-campus housing information. Phone: (308)865-8519.

College of Graduate Study

Graduate study since 1956. Enrollment: full-time 140, part-time 445. Graduate faculty: full-time 90, part-time 50. Degrees conferred: M.S. in Ed., M.A. in Ed., M.B.A., Specialist.

ADMISSION REQUIREMENTS. Transcripts, GRE/GMAT required in support of College's application. TOEFL required for foreign applicants. Interview not required. Accepts transfer applicants. Graduates of unaccredited institutions not considered. Apply to Dean of Graduate School prior to registration. Application fee $35. Phone: (308)865-8838; fax: (308)865-8837.

ADMISSION STANDARDS. Selective. Usual minimum average: 2.75 (A = 4); GRE: minimum 750–950.

FINANCIAL AID. Annual awards from institutional funds: academic scholarships, nonresident tuition scholarships, grants, teaching/research assistantships, internships, Federal W/S, loans. Approved for VA benefits. Apply to Dean of Graduate Studies for scholarships, assistantships; to Financial Aid Office for all other programs. Apply by March 1. Phone: (308)865-8520; fax: (308) 865-8096. Use FAFSA. About 5% of students receive aid from College and outside sources. Aid sometimes available for part-time students.

DEGREE REQUIREMENTS. For M.A. and M.S. in Ed.: 36 credit hours minimum, at least 27 in residence; optional thesis included; comprehensive written exam. For M.B.A.: 36 credit hours; final exam. For Specialist: 30 credits beyond the master's.

FIELDS OF STUDY.
Art Education.
Biology.
Business Administration.
Communication Disorders.
Community Counseling.
Counseling and School Psychology.
Curriculum and Instruction.
Educational Administration.
Elementary/Early Childhood Education.
English.
Exercise Science.
Foreign Languages. Includes French, German, Spanish.
History.
Instructional Technology.
Modern Languages.
Music Education.
Physical Education.
School Counseling.
School Principalship.
School Psychology. Specialist only.
Science Teaching.
Teaching the Secondary School. Usual subject fields.

UNIVERSITY OF NEBRASKA AT LINCOLN
P.O. Box 880434
Lincoln, Nebraska 68588-0434
Web site: www.unl.edu

Founded 1869. CGS and AAU member. Coed. State control. Semester system. Special facilities: Barkley Memorial Center, G.W. Beadle Center for Genetics and Biomaterial Research, Bureau of Sociological Research, Government Research Institute, Lied Center for Performing Arts, Midwestern Center for Mass Spectrometry, Nebraska State Museum of Natural History, Sheldon Art Gallery. Library: 2,200,000 volumes, 20,000 subscriptions. Total University enrollment: 24,300.

Annual tuition: full-time, resident $2190, nonresident $4840; per credit hour, resident $99, nonresident $245. On-campus housing for single graduate students. Apartment housing for 70 married students. Average monthly housing cost: $300-$375 for married students. Average academic year housing cost for single students:

$3990. Contact Office of University Housing for both on- and off-campus housing information. Phone: (402)472-3561.

Graduate College
Web site: www.unl.edu/gradstud

Graduate study since 1886. Graduate enrollment: full-time 1775, part-time 1292. Graduate faculty: full-time 860, part-time 43. Degrees conferred: M.A., M.S., M.Arch., M.Ed., M.A.T., M.Sc.T., M.F.A., M.B.A., M.L.S., M.P.A., M.M., M.P.E., M.C.R.P., M.S.T., Ed.S., Ed.D., D.M.A., Ph.D.

ADMISSION REQUIREMENTS. Two transcripts required in support of College's application. On-line application available. GRE/ Subject Tests/MAT required by some programs. GMAT required for business programs. TOEFL required for international applicants. Interview not required. Accepts transfer applicants. Graduates of unaccredited institutions not considered. Apply to Graduate Office by March 1 (Fall), September 1 (Spring), February 1 (Summer). Admission fee $35. Phone: (800)742-8800, (402)472-2875; fax: (402)472-0589; e-mail: grad_admissions@unl.edu.

ADMISSION STANDARDS. Competitive for most departments, very competitive or selective for others. Usual minimum average: 2.5 for master's, 3.0 for doctoral candidates (A = 4).

FINANCIAL AID. Fellowships, teaching and research assistantships, internships, Federal W/S, loans. Approved for VA benefits. Apply by February 15 to Office of Graduate Studies for information regarding fellowships, to appropriate department chair for assistantships; to Office of Financial Aid for all other programs. Phone: (402)472-2030. Use FAFSA. About 33% of students receive aid other than loans from College. Aid available for part-time students.

DEGREE REQUIREMENTS. For M.A., M.S., M.S.T., M.Sc.T.: 30 semester credits minimum, at least 12 in residence; thesis; final oral/written exams; or 36 credits minimum, at least 18 in residence; final oral/written exam in some departments. For M.Ed., M.A.T., M.P.E.: 30 semester hours minimum, at least 12 in residence; qualifying exam; thesis; final oral/written comprehensive exam; or nonthesis option, 36 semester hours minimum, at least 18 in residence. For M.F.A., M.Arch., M.C.R.P.: 60 semester hours minimum; final project; final exam. For M.B.A., M.P.A.: 48 hours minimum, at least 18 in residence. For Ed.S.: 64 hours beyond bachelor's. For Ed.D., Ph.D., D.M.A.: three full years minimum; 90 semester hours; reading knowledge of one foreign language, plus reading knowledge of second language or comprehensive knowledge of one foreign language or proficiency in research techniques or evidence of knowledge of a collateral field; residency, 27 hours graduate work within a consecutive 18-month period or less; comprehensive exam; dissertation; final oral exam.

FIELDS OF STUDY.

COLLEGE OF AGRICULTURAL SCIENCES AND NATURAL RESOURCES:
Agricultural Economics.
Agriculture. M.Ag. only.
Agronomy.
Animal Science.
Biochemistry.
Biometry. M.S. only.
Entomology.
Food Science and Technology.
Horticulture. Includes horticulture and forestry.
Leadership Education. M.S. only.
Mechanized Systems Management. M.S. only.
Natural Resource Sciences. M.S. only.
Nutrition.
Veterinary and Biomedical Science.

COLLEGE OF ARTS AND SCIENCES:
Anthropology. M.A. only
Biological Sciences.
Chemistry.
Classics. M.A. only.
Communication Studies.
Computer Science.
English.
Geography.
Geosciences.
History.
Mathematics and Statistics. M.A., M.S., M.A.T.
Modern Languages and Literatures.
Philosophy.
Physics and Astronomy.
Political Science.
Psychology.
Sociology.

COLLEGE OF ARCHITECTURE:
Architecture. M.Arch., M.S.
Community and Regional Planning. M.C.R.P.

COLLEGE OF BUSINESS ADMINISTRATION:
Accountancy. M.P.A.
Actuarial Science. M.S.
Business. Includes agribusiness (M.B.A.), finance (M.A.), management (M.A.), marketing (M.A.). M.A., M.B.A., Ph.D.
Economics.

COLLEGE OF ENGINEERING AND TECHNOLOGY:
Agricultural and Biological Systems. M.S.
Architectural Engineering. M.A.E.
Chemical Engineering. M.S.
Civil Engineering. M.S.
Electrical Engineering. M.S.
Engineering. Unified doctoral program. Ph.D.
Engineering Mechanics. M.S.
Environmental Engineering. M.S.
Industrial and Management Systems. M.S.
Manufacturing Systems. M.S.
Master of Engineering. Includes construction, engineering management, software engineering. M.Eng.
Mechanical Engineering. M.S.
Telecommunications Engineering. M.S.

COLLEGE OF HUMAN RESOURCES AND FAMILY SCIENCES:
Family and Consumer Sciences. M.S.
Human Resources and Family Sciences. M.S., interdepartmental Ph.D.
Nutritional Science and Dietetics. M.S.
Textile, Clothing, and Design. M.A., M.S.

COLLEGE OF JOURNALISM:
Journalism. M.A.

COLLEGE OF LAW:
Legal Studies. M.L.S.

HIXON-LIED COLLEGE OF FINE AND PERFORMING ARTS:
Art. M.F.A.
Music. M.M., D.M.A.
Theater Arts. M.F.A.

TEACHERS COLLEGE:
Administration, Curriculum, and Instruction. Ed.D., Ph.D.
Community and Human Resources. Ed.D., Ph.D.
Curriculum and Instruction. M.A., M.Ed.
Educational Administration. M.A., M.Ed., Ed.D.
Educational Psychology. M.A., Ed.D.
Health and Human Performance. M.Ed., M.S.

Psychological and Cultural Studies. Ed.D., Ph.D.
Special Education. M.A., M.Ed.
Special Education and Communication Disorders. Ed.S.
Speech-Language Pathology and Audiology. M.S.

College of Dentistry (68583-0740)

Founded 1899. Affiliated with University in 1917, became part of the University's Medical Center in 1976, but is located in Lincoln.

Annual tuition: full-time, resident $11,200, nonresident $25,940. On-campus housing available. Average academic year housing cost: $14,400. Contact Housing Office for both on- and off-campus housing information. Phone: (402)472-3561. Total average cost for all other first-year expenses: $3250.

Enrollment: first-year class 45 (men 65%, women 35%); total D.D.S. enrollment: 160; postgraduates 50. College faculty: full-time 79, part-time 54. Degrees conferred: D.D.S. M.S., Ph.D.

ADMISSION REQUIREMENTS. AADSAS report, transcripts, DAT (no later than October) required in support of application. TOEFL (minimum score 575) and Certification of Financial Support required of international students whose first language is not English. Interview not required. At least three years of college preferred. Preference given to Nebraska residents and residents of North Dakota and Wyoming. Apply to Admissions Committee after July 1, before February 1. Phone: (402)472-1363. Application fee $25.

ADMISSION STANDARDS. Selective. Mean DAT: Academic 17.8, PAT 17.5; mean GPA: 3.68. Gourman rating: 4.16. Accepts 20-25% of total annual applicants. Approximately 65% are state residents.

FINANCIAL AID. Scholarships, merit scholarships, minority scholarships, Grants-in-Aid, institutional loans, State Loan Programs, DEAL, HEAL, alternative loan programs, Federal Perkins Loans, Stafford Subsidized and Unsubsidized Loans, Military Service Commitment Scholarship programs are available. Institutional Financial Aid applications and information are generally available at the on-campus by-invitation interview. Contact the Financial Aid Office at Medical Center for current information. Phone: (402)559-4199. For most financial assistance and all need-based programs use FAFSA (School code: 006895); also submit Financial Aid Transcript, Federal Income Tax forms, and Use of Federal Funds Certification. Approximately 95% of students receive some form of financial assistance. Average award: resident $20,312, nonresident $32,667.

DEGREE REQUIREMENTS. For D.D.S.: satisfactory completion of forty-four-month program.; three summer sessions required. For graduate degrees, see Graduate College listing above.

FIELDS OF GRADUATE STUDY.
Endodontics.
General Dentistry.
Oral Biology.
Orthodontics.
Pediatric Dentistry.
Periodontics.
Prosthodontics.

College of Law (P.O. Box 830902)
Web site: www.unl.edu/lawcoll

Established 1891. ABA approved since 1923. AALS charter member. Semester system. Full-time, day study only. Law library: 360,800 volumes, 2779 subscriptions; has LEXIS, NEXIS, WESTLAW, DIALOG.

Annual tuition: resident $4993, nonresident $10,243. On-campus housing available for both single and married students. Contact

Housing Office for both on- and off-campus housing information. Phone: (402)472-3561. Law students tend to live off-campus. Off-campus housing and personal expenses: approximately $9564.

Enrollment: first-year class 121; total full-time 373 (men 57%, women 43%); no part-time students. Faculty: full-time 24, part-time 15. Student to faculty ratio 13.3 to 1. Degrees conferred: J.D., J.D.-M.A. (Economics, Political Sciences, Psychology), J.D.-M.B.A., J.D.-M.P.Acc., J.D.-Ph.D. (Psychology, Educational Administration).

ADMISSION REQUIREMENTS. LSDAS Law School report, bachelor's degree, transcripts, LSAT, letters of recommendation required in support of application. Interview not required. Transfer applicants and graduates of unaccredited colleges not considered. Apply to Dean of College after September 1, before March 1 for preferred consideration. First-year students admitted September only. Application fee $25. Phone: (402)472-2161; fax: (402)472-5185; e-mail: lawadm@unl.edu.

ADMISSION STANDARDS. Selective. Mean LSAT: 155; mean GPA: 3.48 (A = 4). Gourman rating: 3.23. *U.S. News & World Report* ranking is in the second tier of all U.S. law schools. Accepts about 45–50% of total annual applicants.

FINANCIAL AID. Scholarships, fellowships, assistantships, Federal W/S, loans. Apply to the University Financial Aid Office by May 1. Phone: (402)472-2030. Use FAFSA (College code: 002565) and College's need-based grant application. Approximately 48% of first-year class receives some form of financial assistance.

DEGREE REQUIREMENTS. For J.D.: satisfactory completion of three-year program, last two semesters required in residence; 96 credit-hour program. For J.D.-master's and doctoral programs: see Graduate school listing above.

UNIVERSITY OF NEBRASKA AT OMAHA

Omaha, Nebraska 68101
Web site: www.unomaha.edu

Founded 1908. CGS member. Coed. State control. Semester system. Special facilities: Center for Afghanistan Studies, Aviation Institute, Center for Faculty Development, Center for International Telecommunications Management, Center for Urban Education, Small Business Development Center. Library: 750,000 volumes, 3200 subscriptions. Total University enrollment: 15,000.

Tuition: per credit hour, resident $105, nonresident $252. No on-campus housing. For off-campus housing, contact Office of Student Housing. Day-care facilities available.

Graduate College

Graduate study since 1931. Enrollment: full-time 578, part-time 1609. Faculty teaching graduate students: full-time 272, part-time 15. Degrees conferred: M.A., M.S., M.B.A., M.M., M.P.A., M.S.W., Ed.S., Ph.D.

ADMISSION REQUIREMENTS. Transcripts, GRE/MAT/GMAT required in support of College's application. On-line application available. Evidence of English proficiency or TOEFL required of international students. Accepts transfer applicants. Graduates of unaccredited institutions not considered. Apply to Director of Admissions by May 1 (Fall), October 1 (Spring), May 1 (Summer). Application fee $35. Phone: (402)554-2341; fax: (402)554-3143; e-mail: graduate@unomaha.edu.

ADMISSION STANDARDS. Selective for most departments. Usual minimum average: 3.0 (A = 4).

FINANCIAL AID. Annual awards from institutional funds: fellowships, graduate assistantships, internships, tuition waivers, Federal W/S, loans. Approved for VA benefits. Apply by March 31 to appropriate department chair for assistantships; to Financial Aid Office for all other programs. Phone: (402)554-2327. Use FAFSA. Aid sometimes available to part-time students.

DEGREE REQUIREMENTS. For M.A.: 30 semester hours minimum, at least 24 in residence; thesis included; final written/oral exam. For M.B.A., M.S., M.M., M.P.A., M.S.W.: 36 semester hours minimum, at least 30 in residence; final written/oral exam. For Ed.S.: one year minimum beyond the master's, at least one semester and one summer in full-time residence; field project; final oral exam. For Ph.D.: three years minimum, 90 semester hours, 27 hours graduate work within a consecutive 18-month period or less; reading knowledge of one foreign language, plus reading knowledge of one foreign language or proficiency in research techniques or evidence of knowledge of a collateral field; comprehensive exam; dissertation; final oral exam.

FIELDS OF STUDY.
Accounting.
Biology.
Business Administration.
Communication.
Computer Science.
Counseling.
Criminal Justice.
Economics.
Educational Administration and Supervision.
English.
Geography.
Gerontology.
Health, Physical Education, and Recreation.
History.
Management Information Systems.
Mathematics.
Music.
Political Science.
Psychology. Includes educational, school industrial, organizational.
Public Administration.
Social Work.
Sociology.
Special Education and Communication Disorders.
Teacher Education.
Theatre.
Urban Studies.

UNIVERSITY OF NEBRASKA MEDICAL CENTER

600 South 42nd Street
Omaha, Nebraska 68198-0001
Web site: www.unmc.edu

Public Control. Nebraska Health System is a member of Council of Teaching Hospitals. Schools located at Medical Center are the College of Dentistry, College of Medicine, College of Nursing, College of Pharmacy, Graduate College, School of Allied Health. Special facilities; Geriatric Center, Eppley Cancer Research Institute, C. Louis Meyer Children's Rehabilitation Center. The Medical Center's NIH ranking was 97th with 72 awards/grants worth $15,712,930. Library: 247,434 volumes, 1741 subscriptions.

Graduate College

Web site: www.unmc.edu/grad.html

Tuition: per semester-hour credit, resident $134, Nursing $145; nonresident $345, Nursing $388. On- and off-campus housing is available. Phone: (402)559-5201.

Enrollment: full-time 176, part-time 210. Graduate faculty: 350. Degrees conferred: M.P.H., M.S., Ph.D.

ADMISSION REQUIREMENTS. Transcripts, GRE required in support of College's application. TOEFL (minimum score 550) required for foreign applicants. Accepts transfer applicants. Graduates of unaccredited colleges not considered. Deadlines for applications vary by program. Application fee $40. Phone: (402)559-6448; fax: (402)559-9671.

ADMISSION STANDARDS. Selective. Usual minimum average: 3.0 for M.S. and Ph.D. (A = 4).

FINANCIAL AID. Scholarships, fellowships, assistantships for teaching and research, internships, traineeships, tuition waivers, loans. Approved for VA benefits. Phone: (402)559-4199; fax: (402)559-9671. Use FAFSA. About 50% of students receive aid other than loans from all sources. Aid available for part-time students.

DEGREE REQUIREMENTS. For master's: six didactic courses; seminars; admission to candidacy; thesis/final document; final oral/written exam. For Ph.D.: three years minimum; reading knowledge of foreign language(s)/research tool may be required; admission to candidacy; dissertation; final oral/written exam.

FIELDS OF STUDY.
Biochemistry and Molecular Biology.
Cell Biology and Anatomy.
Dentistry. Interdepartmental. M.S. only.
Medical Sciences. Interdepartmental.
Nursing.
Pathology and Microbiology.
Pharmaceutical Sciences.
Physiology.
Public Health. M.P.H.
Toxicology.

College of Medicine

Web site: www.unmc.edu/uncom

Established 1880. Located in Omaha since 1913. Annual tuition: resident $15,700, nonresident $31,355. Total average figure for all other expenses: $13,500.

Enrollment: first-year class 120 (20 EDP), total 496 (men 53%, women 47%); resident training 285. College faculty: full-time 395, part-time and volunteers 1100. Degree conferred: M.D., M.D.-M.S., M.D.-Ph.D.

ADMISSION REQUIREMENTS. AMCAS report, transcripts, MCAT, screening interview required in support of application. Applicants must have completed at least three years of college study but degree recommended. Has EDP. Apply between June 1 and August 1. Preference given to state residents. Apply to Office of Dean of College after June 1, before November 1. Application fee $25. Phone: (402)559-2259; fax: (402)559-6804.

ADMISSION STANDARDS. Selective. Mean MCAT: 9.5; mean GPA: 3.67 (A = 4). Gourman rating 3.66. *U.S. News & World Report* ranking for primary care medical school is 39th among all U.S. medical schools.

FINANCIAL AID. Scholarships, some merit scholarships, Grants-in-Aid, institutional loans, HEAL, alternative loan programs, Primary Care Loan Program, Federal Perkins Loans, Stafford Subsidized and Unsubsidized Loans, Service Commitment Scholarship programs are available. Assistantships/fellowships may be available for Combined Degree candidates. Financial Aid applications and information are sent out with the letter of acceptance and are due back within 30 days of date of acceptance. Contact the Financial Aid Office for current information. Phone: (404)

559-4199. Use FAFSA (School code: 006895); also submit Financial Aid Transcript, Federal Income Tax forms. Approximately 60% of students receive some form of financial assistance.

DEGREE REQUIREMENTS. For M.D.: satisfactory completion of four-year program. All students must pass USMLE Step 1 prior to entering third year; taking USMLE Step 2 is optional. For M.D.-M.S.: generally a four-and-one-half- to five-and-one-half-year program. For M.D.-Ph.D.: generally a seven-year program.

FIELDS OF GRADUATE STUDY.
Biochemistry.
Cell Biology and Anatomy.
Genetics.
Immunology.
Medical Sciences.
Molecular Biology.
Pharmaceutical Sciences.
Pharmacology.
Physiology.

UNIVERSITY OF NEVADA, LAS VEGAS
Las Vegas, Nevada 89154-9900
Web site: www.unlu.edu

Founded 1957. CGS member. Coed. State control. Semester system. Special facilities: Desert Biology Research Center, Education Equity Resource Center, Center for Energy Research, Harry Reid Center, Information Science Research Center, Center for In-Service Training and Educational Research, International Gaming Institute, Limnological Research Center, Nevada Small Business Development Center, Arnold Shaw Popular Music Research Center, Center for Public Data Research, Supercomputing Center for Energy and the Environment, Center for the Study of Public Policy, Sports Injury Research Center, Transportation Research Center, Center for Volcanic and Tectronic Studies. Library: 1,200,000 volumes, 12,000 subscriptions. Total University enrollment: 20,000.

Tuition: per credit, resident $103.50, nonresident $103.50 plus $160.50 per credit (1–6), $103 per credit (7 or more), plus $7215 per semester. Summer registration fees assessed at $84 per hour. Limited on-campus housing. Room and board: $3300–$3800 per semester. Contact the Office of Student Personnel Services for both on- and off-campus information. Phone: (702)895-3489.

Graduate College

Enrollment: full-time 1019, part-time 1551. Faculty: full-time 500, part-time 200. Degrees conferred: M.A., M.S., M.Ed., M.Arch., M.B.A., Ed.S., M.M., M.F.A., M.P.A., Ed.D., Ph.D.

ADMISSION REQUIREMENTS. Transcripts, two letters of recommendation; appropriate undergraduate background required in support of College's application. Individual departments may impose special requirements such as GRE, GMAT, MAT. Interview not normally required. TOEFL (minimum score 550) required for international applicants. Transfer applicants considered. Graduates of unaccredited institutions not considered. Apply to Dean, Graduate College; deadlines vary by department for U.S. applicants; May 1 (Fall), October 1 (Spring) for international applicants. Application fee $40, $55 for international applicants. Phone: (702)895-4391; fax: (702)895-4180.

ADMISSION STANDARDS. Selective. Usual minimum average: 2.75; 3.0 for last two years (A = 4).

FINANCIAL AID. Fellowships, partial scholarships, assistantships, internships, tuition waivers, Federal W/S, loans. Approved for VA benefits. Apply to Graduate Dean by March 1 for fellowships, scholarships, assistantships; to Financial Aid Office for all other programs. Phone: (702)895-3424. Use FAFSA and institutional FAF. Aid available for part-time students.

DEGREE REQUIREMENTS. Minimum of 30 hours. Varies with department and degree. Final examination required in all programs except M.B.A. Thesis required in most programs. For Ph.D., Ed.D.: 72 semester credits (Ph.D.), 90 credits (Ed.D.) beyond the bachelor's degree; seven-year time limit; at least two successive semesters in full-time residence; qualifying exam; comprehensive exam; dissertation; final oral exam.

FIELDS OF STUDY.

COLLEGE OF BUSINESS:
Accountancy. M.S.
Business Administration. M.B.A., E.M.B.A.
Economics. M.A.

COLLEGE OF EDUCATION:
Curriculum and Instruction. Includes educational computing and technology, elementary education, English language arts education, library science, mathematics education, middle level education, multicultural education (K–12), postsecondary teaching English as a second language, reading and language arts, secondary education, TESOL. M.Ed., M.S.
Educational Leadership. Includes higher education administration, educational leadership (K–12), executive educational leadership (K–12, Ed.D.), higher education administration (Ph.D.). M.Ed., M.S., Ed.S., Ed.D., Ph.D.
Educational Psychology. Includes school counseling. M.Ed., M.S.
Health Promotion. M.Ed. only.
Learning and Technology. Ph.D. only.
Physical Education. M.Ed. only.
Special Education. Includes generalist–mild disabilities, severe mental retardation, severe emotional disturbance, early childhood special education, gifted and talented, special education administration, school psychology, general special education in higher education (Ph.D). M.Ed., M.S., Ed.S., Ed.D., Ph.D.
Teacher Education. Ph.D. only.

COLLEGE OF ENGINEERING:
Civil and Environmental Engineering. M.S.E., Ph.D.
Computer Science. M.S., Ph.D.
Construction Management. M.S.C.M.
Electrical Engineering. M.S., Ph.D.
Mechanical Engineering. M.S., Ph.D.
Transportation. M.S.T.

COLLEGE OF FINE ARTS:
Architecture. M.Arch.
Art. Includes ceramics, drawing, painting, photography, printmaking, sculpture. M.F.A.
Music. Includes applied music, composition, music education. M.M., D.M.A.
Screenwriting. M.F.A.
Theatre Arts. Includes design technology, music theatre performance, playwriting. M.A., M.F.A.

COLLEGE OF HEALTH SCIENCES:
Health Physics. M.S. only.
*Kinesioiogy.*M.S.
Nursing. Includes family nurse practitioner, pediatric nurse practitioner, geriatric nurse practitioner. M.S.N.
Physical Therapy. M.S.

WILLIAM F. HARRAH COLLEGE OF HOTEL ADMINISTRATION:
Hospitality Administration. Includes executive hotel administration. M.H.A., Ph.D.

Hotel Administration. Includes food service administration, hotel management, tourism and convention administration. M.S.
Sport and Leisure Service Management. M.S.

COLLEGE OF LIBERAL ARTS:
Anthropology.
Creative Writing. M.F.A. only.
English.
Ethics and Policy Studies. M.A. only.
Foreign Languages. Includes French, Spanish. M.A. only.
History.
Political Science. M.S. only.
Psychology. Includes clinical, experimental.

COLLEGE OF SCIENCES:
Biological Sciences.
Biochemistry. M.S. only.
Chemistry. Includes analytical, biological, organic. M.S. only.
Exercise Physiology. M.S. only.
Geoscience. Includes economic geology, environmental geology, geochemistry, geochronology, geographic information systems, geomorphology, hydrogeology, igneous and metamorphic petrology, invertebrate paleontology, palynology, quaternary geology, sedimentology, soil studies, stratigraphy, structural geology, surficial process, tectonics, volcanology.
Mathematical Sciences. Includes applied mathematics, applied statistics, pure mathematics. M.S. only.
Physics. Includes astronomy.
Science. M.A.S. only.
Water Resources Management. M.S. only.

GREENSPUN COLLEGE OF URBAN AFFAIRS:
Communication Studies. M.A. only.
Counseling. Includes community, marriage and family. M.S. only.
Criminal Justice. M.A. only.
Environmental Science. Includes environmental policy, environmental chemistry.
Public Administration. M.P.A. only.
Social Work. M.S.W. only.

William S. Boyd School of Law (P.O. Box 451003)
Web site: www.law.unlv.edu

Established 1998. Public control. ABA approved since 2000. Semester system. Full-time, part-time. Law library: 185,220 volumes, 1201 subscriptions; has LEXIS, NEXIS, WESTLAW, DIALOG, OCLC, CALI.

Annual tuition: resident full-time $7274, part-time $5242; nonresident full-time $14,274, part-time $12,242. Limited on-campus housing available. Contact Admissions Office for both on- and off-campus information. Off-campus housing and personal expenses: approximately $8750–$9570.

Enrollment: first-year class 90, part-time 50; total full-time 245, part-time 155 (men 52%, women 48%). Faculty: full-time 17, part-time 3. Student to faculty ratio 17 to 1. Degree conferred: J.D.

ADMISSION REQUIREMENTS. LSDAS Law School report, LSAT (not later than February test date; if more than one LSAT, repeated scores are used if higher), bachelor's degree from an accredited institution, personal statement, two recommendations, transcripts (must show all schools attended and at least three years of study) required in support of application. Applicants must have received bachelor's degree prior to enrollment. Interview not required but may be requested by School. In addition, international applicants whose native language is not English must submit TOEFL (not older than two years), degree must be certified as equivalent to an American baccalaureate, certified transcripts must be sent directly to School. Apply to Office of Admission after September 15, before April 1 (priority deadline). First-year students admitted Fall only. Rolling admissions process, notification starts in November and is finished by late April. Application fee $40. Phone: (702)865-3671; e-mail: request@ law.unlv.edu.

ADMISSION STANDARDS. Selective. Mean LSAT: full-time 151, part-time 152; Mean GPA: full-time 3.21, part-time 3.10 (A = 4).

FINANCIAL AID. Scholarships, merit scholarships, Grants-in-Aid, private and institutional loans, Federal loans, Federal W/S available. For all other programs apply after January 1, before February 1 to Financial Aid Office. Use FAFSA, also submit Financial Aid Transcript, Federal Income Tax forms. Approximately 42% of students receive some form of financial assistance. Average scholarships grant: $2000 (full-time), $2250 (part-time).

DEGREE REQUIREMENTS. For J.D.: three-year full-time program; four-year part-time program.

UNIVERSITY OF NEVADA, RENO
Reno, Nevada 89557-0035
Web site: www.unr.edu

Founded 1864. Coed. State control. Semester system. Special facilities: Center for Advanced Study, Agricultural Experiment Station; Biological Science Center, Bureaus of Business, Economics, and Government Research; Desert Research Institute; Engineering Research and Development Center, Energy and Environmental Engineering Center, Fleischmann Atmospherium-Planetarium; nuclear reactor; Nevada Mining Analytical Laboratory; Mackay Mineral Resource Research Institute; Nevada Bureau of Mines; Reno Metallurgy Research Center, Water Resource Center. The University's NIH ranking is 190th among all U.S. institutions with 47 awards/grants worth $13,233,006. Library: 861,000 volumes, 7200 subscriptions. Total University enrollment: 12,000.

Tuition: per credit, resident $103.50, nonresident $103.50 plus $160.50 per credit (1–6), $103 per credit (7 or more), plus $7215 per semester. On-campus housing for both single and married students. Average academic year housing cost: $7440–$10,125. Contact Housing Services Office for both on- and off-campus housing information. Phone: (775)784-6107.

Graduate School

Semester enrollment: full-time 1105, part-time 855. University faculty teaching graduate students: full-time 485, part-time 32. Degrees conferred: M.A., M.Acc., M.S., M.Ed., M.B.A., M.J.S., M.M., M.S.W., Ph.D., Ed.D.

ADMISSION REQUIREMENTS. Two official transcripts from each college or institution attended, GRE/Subject Tests, GMAT (for M.B.A.) required in support of School's application. On-line application available. Written statement of purpose, biography, writing sample, letters of recommendation required by some programs. TOEFL, financial statement, and medical history and exam for international applicants. Accepts transfer applicants. Graduates of unaccredited institutions not considered. Apply to Office of Admissions and Records three weeks prior to registration. Many departments have earlier deadlines. Application fee $40. Phone: (775)784-6869; fax: (775)784-6064; e-mail: gradadmissions@ unr.edu.

ADMISSION STANDARDS. Selective, for most departments. Usual minimum average: 2.75 for master's; 3.0 for doctoral programs (A = 4).

FINANCIAL AID. Annual awards from institutional funds: 20 scholarships, 214 teaching assistantships, 517 research assistant-ships, 30 internships, Federal W/S, loans. Apply to Chair of Scholarships, Committee for Scholarships; to Dean of College for internships and fellowships; to department concerned for assistantships; to Financial Aid Office for all other programs. Use FAFSA. Phone: (775)784-4666. About 50% of full-time students receive aid other than loans from School and outside sources.

DEGREE REQUIREMENTS. For M.A., M.S., M.Acc., M.B.A., M.M.: 30–33 semester credits minimum, at least 21 in residence; thesis/nonthesis option; reading knowledge of one foreign language required by some departments; final oral/written exam. For M.Ed., M.S.W.: 32 credits minimum, at least 24 in residence; two years' educational experience; final paper or comprehensive exam; final oral/written exam; six-year time limit. For Ph.D., 72 semester credits; comprehensive exam; dissertation; final oral defense. For Ed.D.: 90 semester credits minimum beyond the bachelor's; eight-year time limit; at least two successive semesters in full-time residence; qualifying exam; comprehensive exam; dissertation; final oral exam.

FIELDS OF STUDY.
Accountancy. M.Acc. only.
Animal Science. M.S. only.
Anthropology.
Atmospheric Sciences.
Basque Studies. Ph.D. only.
Biochemistry.
Biology. M.S. only.
Biomedical Engineering.
Business Administration. M.B.A. only.
Cell and Molecular Biology. Ph.D.
Cellular and Molecular Pharmacology and Physiology. Ph.D. only.
Chemical Engineering.
Chemical Physics. Ph.D. only.
Chemistry.
Civil Engineering.
Computer Science. M.S. only.
Counseling and Educational Psychology.
Curriculum and Instruction. Ed.D., Ph.D.
Ecology, Evolution, and Conservation Biology. Ph.D. only.
Economics. M.A., M.S. only.
Educational Leadership.
Electrical Engineering.
Elementary Education. M.A., Ed.D., M.S. only.
English.
Environmental and Natural Resource Science. M.S. only.
Environmental Science and Health.
Foreign Languages and Literatures. Includes French, German, Spanish. M.A. only.
Geochemistry.
Geo-Engineering. Ph.D. only.
Geography. M.S. only.
Geological Engineering. M.S. only.
Geology and Related Earth Sciences.
Geophysics. Ph.D. only.
Health Ecology. M.S. only.
History.
Human Development and Family Studies. M.S. only.
Hydrogeology.
Hydrology.
Journalism. M.A. only.
Judicial Studies. For sitting judges only. M.J.S.
Land Use Planning. M.S. only.
Mathematics. M.S. only.
Mechanical Engineering.
Metallurgical Engineering.
Mining Engineering. M.S. only.
Music. M.A., M.M. only.
Nursing. M.S. only.
Nutrition. M.S. only.
Philosophy. M.A. only.

Physics.
Political Science.
Psychology. Includes behavior analysis, clinical, experimental.
Public Administration and Policy. M.P.A. only.
Public Health. M.P.H.
Resource and Applied Economics. M.S. only.
Secondary Education. M.A., M.Ed., M.S. only.
Social Psychology. Ph.D. only.
Social Work. M.S.W. only.
Sociology. M.A. only.
Special Education. M.A., M.Ed., M.S. only.
Speech Communication. M.A. only.
Speech Pathology. Ph.D. only.
Speech Pathology and Audiology. M.S. only.
Teaching of English as a Second Language. M.A. only.
Teaching of Mathematics. M.A.T.M. only.

School of Medicine (89557)

Established 1969. Annual tuition: resident $8417, nonresident $24,669, student fees $2239. Limited on-campus housing. Total average figure for all other expenses: $8100. Enrollment: first-year class 52 (EDP 2), full-time 200 (men 63%, women 37%). Faculty: full-time 30, part-time none. Degrees conferred: M.D., M.D.-Ph.D.

ADMISSION REQUIREMENTS. AMCAS report, transcripts, MCAT, three letters of evaluation required in support of application. Interview by invitation only. Graduates of unaccredited colleges not considered. Preference given to residents of Nevada and residents of Alaska, Idaho, Montana, and Wyoming. Will consider transfer applicants. Has EDP; apply between June 1 and October 1. Apply to Admissions Office after June 1, before November 1. Application fee $45. Phone: (775)784-6063; fax: (775)784-6096.

ADMISSION STANDARDS. Selective. Mean MCAT: 8.9; mean GPA: 3.6 (A = 4). Accepts 20–25% of total annual applicants. Approximately 80% are state residents.

FINANCIAL AID. Scholarships, loans. Apply to Director of Student Affairs; no specified closing date. Phone: (775)784-6063. Use FAFSA (School code: 002568). About 80% of students receive some aid from School and outside sources.

DEGREE REQUIREMENTS. For M.D: satisfactory completion of four-year program; all students must pass USMLE Step 2 prior to awarding of M.D. Third and fourth years are spent in Reno, Las Vegas, and rural Nevada. For Ph.D.: see Graduate School listing above.

FIELDS OF GRADUATE STUDY.
Biochemistry.
Cell and Molecular Biology.
Pathology.
Pharmacology.
Physiology.

NEW ENGLAND CONSERVATORY OF MUSIC

Boston, Massachusetts 02115-5000
Web site: www.newenglandconservatory.edu

Founded 1867. Coed. Private control. Semester system. Library: 75,600 volumes, 255 subscriptions.

Annual tuition: full-time $21,550. On-campus housing available for single students. Average academic year housing cost: $8900 (including board).

Graduate Program

Enrollment: full-time 339, part-time 37. Faculty: full-time 81, part-time 123. Degrees conferred: M.M., Graduate Diploma, Artist Diploma, D.M.A.

ADMISSION REQUIREMENTS. Transcripts, bachelor's, three letters of recommendation, audition required in support of application. Interview required by some departments. TOEFL required for international applicants. Apply by January 15 (Fall), November 1 (Spring) to the Dean of Admissions and Financial Aid. Application fee $100. Phone: (617)585-1106; fax: (617)585-1115.

ADMISSION STANDARDS. Selective. Usual minimum average: 3.0 (A = 4).

FINANCIAL AID. Scholarships, teaching fellowships, teaching assistantships, tuition waivers, Federal W/S, loans. Apply to the Financial Aid Office; no specified closing date. Phone: (617)585-1110. Use FAFSA (School code: 002194) and institutional FAF. Approximately 60% of students receive aid other than loans from School. Aid sometimes available for part-time students.

DEGREE REQUIREMENTS. For master's: 32 credits. For diplomas: at least 30 credits beyond the master's; music history exam, music theory exam, language exam (for vocal pedagogy and vocal performance); public performance; special project for some programs. For D.M.A.: 60 semester hours beyond the master's degree, at least 30 credits in full-time residence; reading knowledge of one foreign language/research technique, depending on program; qualifying exam; three recitals or other public performance for most programs; dissertation or final document; final oral exam.

FIELDS OF STUDY.
Bassoon.
Choral Conducting.
Clarinet.
Collaborative Piano.
Composition.
Contemporary Improvisation.
Double Bass.
Euphonium.
Flute.
Guitar.
Harp.
Historical Performance.
Horn.
Jazz Studies. Includes performance and composition.
Music Education. Concentration in supervision.
Musicology.
Oboe.
Opera.
Orchestral Conducting.
Organ.
Percussion.
Piano.
Saxophone.
Theoretical Studies.
Trombone.
Trumpet.
Tuba.
Viola.
Violin.
Violoncello.
Vocal Pedagogy.
Voice Performance.
Wind Ensemble Conducting.

NEW ENGLAND SCHOOL OF LAW

154 Stuart Street
Boston, Massachusetts 02116
Web site: www.nesl.edu

Established 1908 as Portia Law School; it was the first law school in the nation exclusively for women. Name changed 1969. ABA approved since 1969. AALS member. Semester system. Full-time (day), part-time (evening), part-time (flexible to accommodate child-care responsibilities). Special facilities: Center for International Law and Policy. Special program: foreign study in London, Galway, Malta, New Zealand, the Netherlands. Law library: 309,423 volumes, 3104 subscriptions; has LEXIS, NEXIS, WESTLAW, DIALOG, OCLC, CALI.

Annual tuition: full-time $17,500, part-time $13,160. No on-campus housing available. Law students live off-campus. Contact Admissions Office for off-campus information. Off-campus housing and personal expenses: approximately $13,750.

Enrollment: first-year class 239, part-time 105; total full- and part-time 981 (men 43%, women 57%). Faculty: full-time 30, part-time 46. Student to faculty ratio 23.8 to 1. Degree conferred: J.D.

ADMISSION REQUIREMENTS. LSDAS Law School report, bachelor's degree, transcripts, LSAT, two letters of recommendation required in support of application. Accepts transfer applicants. Graduates of unaccredited colleges not considered. Apply to Director of Admissions by June 1. Application fee $50. Phone: (617)422-7210; fax: (617)422-7200.

ADMISSION STANDARDS. Selective. Mean LSAT: full-time 148, part-time 147; mean GPA: full-time 2.99, part-time 2.83 (A = 4). Gourman rating: 3.07. *U.S. News & World Report* ranking is in the fourth tier of all U.S. law schools. Accepts about 30–35% of total annual applicants.

FINANCIAL AID. Minority and disadvantaged scholarships, grants, Federal W/S, loans. Apply to Office of Financial Aid by April 15. Use FAFSA (School code: G08916) and NESL financial aid application. Approximately 42% of students receive some form of financial assistance.

DEGREE REQUIREMENTS. For J.D.: satisfactory completion of 84 credit-hour program.

UNIVERSITY OF NEW ENGLAND

11 Hills Beach Road
Biddeford, Maine 04005-9526
Web site: www.une.edu

The University's charter dates back to 1831; however, the University was formed in 1978. A 20-minute drive from Portland. University has a suburban campus in Portland. Private control. Semester system. Special facilities: Harold Alfond Center for Health Sciences, Center for Human Services. Library: 86,000 volumes, 1280 subscriptions; has CANCERLINE, BIOETHIC, HEALTH, TOXLINE, DIALOG, OCLC. Total University enrollment: 2500.

The University's graduate programs include College of Osteopathic Medicine, the College of Professional and Continuing Studies.

College of Osteopathic Medicine

College established 1970 as St. Francis College of Osteopathic Medicine, merged with University in 1978. Affiliated with 20 community hospitals and medical centers. The College's NIH ranking was sixth among osteopathic schools with one award/grant received worth $181,323.

Annual tuition: $27,690. Limited on-campus housing available. Annual on-campus housing cost: single students $4150 (room only), married students $5250. Contact Graduate Housing Office for both on- and off-campus housing information. Medical students tend to live off-campus. Phone: (207)283-0171, ext. 2272. Off-campus housing and personal expenses: approximately $9500.

Enrollment: first-year class 117; total full-time 453 (men 52%, women 48%) Faculty: full-time 14, part-time 18. Degree conferred: D.O.

ADMISSION REQUIREMENTS. Preference given to students who will practice in New England; U.S. citizens and permanent residents only. For serious consideration an applicant should have a 2.75 (A = 4) GPA or above. Bachelor's degree from an accredited institution required. Apply through AACOMAS (file after June 1, before January 1), submit MCAT (will accept test results from last two years; MCAT should be taken no later than September of the year prior to the year of anticipated enrollment), official transcripts from each school attended (should show at least 90 semester credits/135 quarter credit), service processing fee. After a review of the AACOMAS application and supporting documents a decision is made concerning which candidates should receive supplemental materials. The supplemental application, an application fee of $55, a personal statement, and three recommendations (at least two from science faculty; one from a D.O. is highly recommended) should be returned to Office of Admission as soon as possible. In addition, international applicants must submit foreign transcripts to the World Education Service for translation and evaluation. TOEFL may be required of those applicants whose native language is other than English. Interviews are by invitation only and generally for final selection. First-year students admitted Fall only. Rolling admissions process, notification starts in October and is finished when class is filled. Phone: (800)477-4UNE, (207)283-0171 ext. 218; fax: (207)283-3249.

ADMISSION STANDARDS. Selective. Accepts approximately 5% of total annual applicants. Median MCAT: 8.3; median GPA: 3.4 (A = 4).

FINANCIAL AID. Scholarships, minority scholarships, grants, institutional loans, Maine Osteopathic Loan Fund, NOF, HEAL, alternative loan programs, Federal Perkins Loans, Stafford Subsidized and Unsubsidized Loans, Service Obligation Scholarship programs, Military and National Health Service programs are available. Financial Aid applications and information are generally available at the on-campus, by-invitation interview. Apply by April 15. Contact the Office of Financial Aid for current information. Phone: (207)283-0171. Use FAFSA (School code: 002050); also submit Financial Aid Transcript, Federal Income Tax forms. Approximately 80% of students receive some form of financial assistance.

DEGREE REQUIREMENTS. For D.O.: satisfactory completion of four-year program.

UNIVERSITY OF NEW HAMPSHIRE

Durham, New Hampshire 03824-3547
Web site: www.unh.edu

Founded in 1866. Located 60 miles N of Boston. CGS member. Coed. State control. Semester system. Special facilities: Agricultural Experiment Station, Center for Business and Economics Research, Family Research Center, Center for Humanities, Institute on Disabilities, Environmental Research Group, Manchester Manufacturing Management Center, New Hampshire Small Business Development Center, Institute for Policy and Social Science Research, Institute for the Study of Earth,

Oceans and Space, Center for Venture Research, Water Resources Research Center. Library: more than 1,000,000 volumes, 6500 subscriptions. Total University enrollment: 10,500.

Annual tuition: full-time resident $9105, nonresident $15,140; part-time, resident $337 per credit, nonresident $618. On-campus housing available for married students (154 units) and single students (180 rooms). Average academic year housing cost: $7500. For on-campus housing, apply to Residential Life, Pettee House. Phone: (603)862-2120; for off-campus housing, contact Commuter Transfer Center. Phone: (603)862-3612.

Graduate School

Graduate study since 1928. Enrollment: full-time 914, part-time 1164. Graduate faculty: 602. Degrees conferred: M.A., M.A.L.A., M.S., M.A.T., M.S.W., M.S.T., M.A.O.E., M.B.A., M.Ed., M.H.A., M.P.A., C.A.G.S., Ph.D.

ADMISSION REQUIREMENTS. Transcripts, three letters of recommendation required in support of School's application. On-line application available. GRE required by some departments; GMAT required for M.B.A. applicants. TOEFL required for international applicants. International applicants admitted Fall only. Apply to Dean of the Graduate School by April 1 (Fall), December 1 (Spring), April 1 (Summer), by February 15 to ensure financial aid consideration (earlier applications encouraged). Application fee $50. Phone: (603)862-3000; fax: (603)862-0275; e-mail: grad.school@unh.edu.

ADMISSION STANDARDS. Selective to competitive. Usual minimum average: 2.75 (A = 4).

FINANCIAL AID. Annual awards from institutional funds: academic scholarships, tuition scholarships, teaching assistantships, internships, tuition waivers, Federal W/S, loans. Approved for VA benefits. Apply by February 1 to Graduate School for scholarships, assistantships; to Financial Aid Office for all other programs. Phone: (603)862-3600. Use FAFSA. Financial aid available for part-time students.

DEGREE REQUIREMENTS. For master's: 30 credits minimum; thesis/nonthesis option in some departments. For C.A.G.S.: 32–40 credits beyond master's. For Ph.D.: three years beyond bachelor's, at least one year in residence; written exam; language required in some programs.

FIELDS OF STUDY.
Accounting. M.S.
Adult and Occupational Education. M.A.O.E.
Animal and Nutritional Sciences. M.S., Ph.D.
Animal Science. M.S.
Biochemistry. M.S., Ph.D.
Biology. M.S.
Business Administration. M.B.A.
Chemical Engineering. M.S.
Chemistry. M.S., M.S.T., Ph.D.
Civil Engineering. M.S.
Communication Science and Disorders. M.S.
Computer Science. M.S., Ph.D.
Counseling. M.A., M.Ed.
Earth Sciences. Includes geology, oceanography. M.S., Ph.D.
Economics. M.A., Ph.D.
Education. Includes administration/supervision, elementary, secondary, early childhood, reading, reading/writing instruction, special. M.A., M.A.T., C.A.G.S., M.Ed., Ph.D.
Electrical and Computer Engineering. M.S.
Engineering. Ph.D.
English. Includes literature, language and linguistics, and writing. M.A., M.S.T., Ph.D.
Environmental Education. M.A.
Family Studies. Includes marriage and family therapy. M.S.

Genetics. M.S., Ph.D.
History. M.A., Ph.D.
Hydrology. M.S.
Kinesiology. M.S.
Liberal Studies. M.A.L.S.
Literacy and Schooling. Ph.D.
Materials Science. M.S.
Mathematics. Includes applied mathematics, statistics. M.S., M.S.T. (Summer only), Ph.D.
Mechanical Engineering. M.S.
Microbiology. M.S., Ph.D.
Music. M.A., M.S.
Natural Resource. Includes environmental conservation, forestry, soil science, water resources, wildlife. M.S., Ph.D.
Nursing. M.S., Ph.D.
Nutritional Science. M.S.
Ocean Engineering. M.S.
Ocean Mapping. M.S.
Ocean Systems Design. Ph.D.
Occupational Therapy. M.S.
Painting. M.F.A.
Physical Education. M.S.
Physics. M.S., Ph.D.
Plant Biology. M.S., Ph.D.
Political Science. M.A.
Psychology. Ph.D.
Public Administration. M.P.A.
Resource Administration and Management. M.S.
Resource Economics. M.S.
Sociology. M.A., Ph.D.
Social Work. M.S.W.
Spanish. M.A.
Zoology. M.S., Ph.D.

UNIVERSITY OF NEW HAVEN
West Haven, Connecticut 06516-1916
Web site: www.newhaven.edu

Established 1920. CGS member. Coed. Trimester system. Private control. Library: 300,000 volumes.

Tuition: per credit $420. Limited on-campus housing available. Contact the Residential Services office for on- and off-campus housing information. Phone: (203)932-7176.

Graduate School

Graduate study since 1969. Enrollment: full- and part-time 1900 (men 40%, women 60%). Faculty: full-time 250, part-time 150. Degrees conferred: M.A., M.S., M.B.A., M.P.A., M.S.I.E., Sc.D., M.B.A.-M.S.I.E., M.B.A.-M.P.A.

ADMISSION REQUIREMENTS. Transcripts, two letters of recommendation required in support of School's application. GRE required for M.S.-Forensic Science, GMAT for business. TOEFL and certified financial support form required of all international applicants. Accepts transfer applicants. Graduates of unaccredited colleges not considered. Apply to Graduate School by June 15 (Fall), October 1 (Winter), January 15 (Spring). Application fee $50. Phone: (800)DIAL-UNH, ext. 7133, (203)932-7133; fax: (203)932-7137.

ADMISSION STANDARDS. Competitive. Usual minimum average: 2.75 (A = 4).

FINANCIAL AID. Annual awards from institutional funds: thirty-five fellowships, twenty-seven administrative assistantships, eighteen research assistantships, nineteen teaching assistantships,

Federal W/S, loans. Approved for VA benefits. Apply by April 15 to Dean for fellowships, assistantships; to Director of Financial Aid for all other programs. Phone: (203)932-7315. Use FAFSA. About 12% of students receive aid other than loans from University and outside sources. Aid sometimes available for part-time students.

DEGREE REQUIREMENTS. For M.A., M.S.: 36–48 credit hours minimum, depending on program; 30 credits in residence; thesis/nonthesis option. For M.P.A.: 42 credit hours minimum, 30 credits in residence; internship; special project. For M.B.A.: 57 credit hours minimum, at least 30 in residence; thesis/nonthesis option. For Sc.D.: 30 credits beyond the master's minimum; dissertation; final oral exam.

FIELDS OF STUDY.
Accounting.
Aviation Science.
Business Administration. Includes options in accounting, finance, international business, technology management, marketing, health care administration, human resources, public relations, sports management.
Cellular and Molecular Biology.
Community Psychology.
Computer and Informational Science.
Criminal Justice.
Education.
Electrical Engineering.
Environmental Engineering.
Environmental Science.
Executive Engineering Management.
Executive M.B.A.
Finance and Financial Services.
Fire Science.
Forensic Science.
Health Care Administration.
Hospitality and Tourism.
Human Nutrition.
Industrial Engineering.
Industrial Hygiene.
Industrial/Organizational Psychology.
Industrial Relations.
Management Systems. Sc.D. only.
Mechanical Engineering.
Occupational Safety and Health Management.
Operations Research.
Public Administration.
Taxation.
Tourism and Hospitality Management.

COLLEGE OF NEW JERSEY

P.O. Box 7718
Ewing, New Jersey 08628
Web site: www.tcnj.edu

Established 1855. CGS member. Coed. State control. Semester system. Library: 560,000 volumes, 1400 subscriptions.

Tuition: per credit, resident $360, nonresident $488. No on-campus housing available. Contact Off-campus Housing Office for off-campus information. Phone: (609)771-2466. Day-care facilities available.

Graduate Division

Graduate study since 1947. Enrollment: full-time 97, part-time 599 (men 25%, women 75%). Graduate faculty: full-time 41, part-time 12. Degrees conferred: M.A., M.S., M.Ed., M.A.T., M.S.N., Ed.S.

ADMISSION REQUIREMENTS. Transcripts, GRE or MAT, letters of recommendation required in support of application. TOEFL required for international applicants. Accepts transfer applicants. Graduates of unaccredited institutions are not considered. Apply to the Office of Graduate Admission by April 15 (Fall), October 15 (Spring). Application fee $50. Phone: (609)771-2300; fax: (609)637-5105; e-mail: graduate@tcnj.edu.

ADMISSION STANDARDS. Selective. Usual minimum average: 2.75 (A = 4).

FINANCIAL AID. Graduate assistantships, internships, Federal W/S, loans. Apply by May 1 to Dean of Graduate Study for assistantships, Financial Aid Office for all other programs. Phone: (609)771-2211. Use FAFSA. About 2-5% of students receive aid other than loans from College and outside sources. Aid available for part-time students.

DEGREE REQUIREMENTS. For master's: 30 credits minimum; final written exam. For M.A.T.: 40–56 credits; final written exam. For M.S.N.: 36 credits; final written exam.

FIELDS OF STUDY.
Audiology.
Counselor Education.
Developmental Reading.
Education.
Educational Technology.
Elementary Education.
English.
ESL.
Health Education.
Music. Includes applied, composition, conducting, education.
Nursing.
Physical Education.
Secondary Education.
Special Education. Includes teaching developmentally handicapped, learning disabilities; Ed.S. only.
Speech. Includes speech correction, pathology.
Speech Pathology.

NEW JERSEY INSTITUTE OF TECHNOLOGY

Newark, New Jersey 07102-1982
Web site: www.njit.edu

Founded 1881. CGS member. Coed. State control. Semester system. Special facilities: Biomedical Engineering Center for Manufacturing Systems, Hazardous Substance Management Research Center, Center for Transportation Studies and Research. Library: 204,471 volumes, 1100 subscriptions. Total Institute enrollment: 8862.

Annual tuition: full-time resident $8066, nonresident $11,334. Limited on-campus housing available. Average academic year housing cost: $4500–$6500. Contact the Office of Residence Life for both on- and off-campus housing information. Phone: (973)596-3041. Day-care facilities available.

Graduate Studies

Enrollment: full-time 1220, part-time 1963. Faculty: full-time 404, part-time 223. Degrees conferred: M.Arch., M.F.S., M.S., Ph.D.

ADMISSION REQUIREMENTS. Two official transcripts, GRE, three letters of recommendation required in support of application. On-line application available. TOEFL required for international applicants. Interview not required. Accepts transfer applicants. Graduates of unaccredited institutions not considered. Apply to Office of University Admissions by June 1 (Fall), October 15 (Spring); Architecture applicants apply by April 1 (fall), October 15 (Spring). Application fee $50. Phone: (973)596-3300; fax: (973)596-3461; e-mail: admissions@njit.edu.

ADMISSION STANDARDS. Selective for most departments. Usual minimum average: master's, GPA of at least 2.5; doctoral, GPA of at least 3.5.

FINANCIAL AID. More than 400 annual awards from institutional funds: teaching/research assistantships, tuition remission, Federal W/S, loans. Approved for VA benefits. Apply by March 15 to appropriate department chair for assistantships; to Financial Aid Office for all other programs. Phone: (973)-596-3479. Use FAFSA. About 50% of full-time students receive aid other than loans from College and outside sources.

DEGREE REQUIREMENTS. For master's: 30 credit hours minimum; thesis/project. For Ph.D.: 60 credit hours minimum beyond the master's degree, at least one year in residence; qualifying exam; thesis/research design; final oral exam.

FIELDS OF STUDY.
Applied Chemistry. M.S.
Applied Mathematics. M.S.
Applied Physics. M.S., Ph.D.
Applied Statistics. M.S.
Architecture. M.Arch.
Architectural Studies. M.S.
Biology. M.S., Ph.D.
Biomedical Engineering. M.S.
Biomedical Informatics. M.S., Ph.D.
Business Administration in Management of Technology. M.S.
Chemical Engineering. M.S., Ph.D.
Chemistry. Ph.D.
Civil Engineering. M.S., Ph.D.
Computer and Information Science. Ph.D. only.
Computer Engineering. M.S., Ph.D.
Computer Science. M.S., Ph.D.
Electrical Engineering. M.S., Ph.D.
Engineering Management. M.S.
Engineering Science. M.S.
Environmental Engineering. M.S., Ph.D.
Environmental Policy Studies. M.S.
Environmental Science. M.S., Ph.D.
Industrial Engineering. M.S., Ph.D.
Information Systems. M.S.
Infrastructure Planning. M.S.
Internet Engineering. M.S.
Management. M.S., Ph.D. (cooperatively with Rutgers—Newark).
Manufacturing Systems Engineering. M.S.
Materials Science and Engineering. M.S., Ph.D.
Mathematical Sciences. Ph.D. only.
Mechanical Engineering. M.S., Ph.D.
Occupational Safety and Health Engineering. M.S.
Occupational Safety and Industrial Hygiene. M.S.
Professional and Technical Communication. M.S., Ph.D.
Public Health. M.S.
Telecommunication. M.S.
Transportation. M.S., Ph.D.
Urban Systems. Ph.D. only.

NEW MEXICO HIGHLANDS UNIVERSITY
Las Vegas, NM 87701
Web site: www.nmhu.edu

Founded 1893. CGS member. Located 60 miles E of Santa Fe. Coed. State control. Semester system. Library: 551,276 volumes, 4700 subscriptions. Total University enrollment: 3000.

Annual tuition: full-time resident $2130, nonresident $9,000; per credit, resident $89, nonresident $360. On-campus housing for 64 married and 154 single graduate students. Average academic year housing cost: $5600 for married students; $2599 for single students. Apply to Coordinator of Housing. Phone: (505)454-3197. Day-care facilities available.

Graduate Studies

Enrollment: full-time 278; part-time 314. University faculty teaching graduate students: full-time 112, part-time 15. Degrees conferred: M.A., M.S., M.B.A., M.S.W.

ADMISSION REQUIREMENTS: Transcripts required in support of Divisional application. TOEFL required for international applicants. Interview required for some programs. Accepts transfer applicants. Graduates of unaccredited institutions not considered. Apply to Graduate Division, Office of the Vice President for Academic Affairs at least 30 days prior to registration. Application fees: Social Work, $50; all others $15. Phone: (505)454-3220 (Social Work); (505)454-3266; fax: (505)454-3558; e-mail: portega@merlin.nmhu.edu.

ADMISSION STANDARDS: Selective for some disciplines, relatively open for others. Usual minimum average: 3.0 in major field (A = 4).

FINANCIAL AID: Awards from institutional funds: academic scholarships, fellowships, assistantships, stipends, internships, tuition waivers, Federal W/S, loans. Approved for VA benefits. Apply by March 1 to Office of Vice President for assistantships; to Financial Aid Office for all other programs. Use FAFSA. Phone: (505)454-3318; fax: (505)454-3398. About 45% of students receive aid from University and outside sources. Aid sometimes available for part-time students.

DEGREE REQUIREMENTS: For master's: 34 credits minimum; thesis/nonthesis option; case/field study; comprehensive exam.

FIELDS OF STUDY.

COLLEGE OF ARTS AND SCIENCES:
Applied Chemistry. M.S.
English. Includes literature, language, rhetoric and composition, creative writing. M.A.
Life Science. Includes biology, environmental science and management. M.S. only.
Media Arts and Computer Science. Includes cognitive science, computer graphics, design studies, digital audio and video production, multimedia systems, networking technology. M.A., M.S.
Public Affairs. Includes administration, applied sociology, historical and cross-cultural perspective, political and governmental process. M.A.
Southwest Studies. Includes anthropology, Hispanic language and literature, history/political science. M.A.
Psychology. Includes general, clinical. M.S.

SCHOOL OF BUSINESS:
Business Administration. Includes electronic commerce, general management, government and not-for-profit management, international business, management information systems. M.B.A.

SCHOOL OF EDUCATION:

Counseling and Guidance. Includes school counseling, professional counseling, rehabilitation counseling. M.A.

Curriculum and Instruction. Includes English, math, history, bilingual education. M.A.

Educational Administration. M.A.

Human Performance and Sport. Includes sport administration, teacher education. M.A.

Special Education. M.A.

SCHOOL OF SOCIAL WORK:

Social Work. Includes clinical social work practice, community and administration practice, direct practice. M.S.W.

NEW MEXICO INSTITUTE OF MINING AND TECHNOLOGY

Saceur, New Mexico 87801
Web site: www.nmt.edu

Founded 1889. Located 75 miles S of Albuquerque. State control. Special facilities: Center for Explosive Technology Research, Geophysical Research Center, Joint Observatory for Cometary Research, Waldo Experimental Mine, Petroleum Recovery Research Center, New Mexico Bureau of Mines and Mineral Resources, Langmuir Laboratory for Atmospheric Physics, Sullivan Center of In-Situ Mining Research, Very Large Array radio telescope, Very Large Baseline Array. Cooperative research opportunities with Sandia National Laboratories. Library: 137,000 volumes, 766 subscriptions. Total Institute enrollment: 1340.

Tuition: per credit, resident $101, nonresident $413. On-campus housing for 36 married students, 10 graduate dorms for men, 10 graduate dorms for women. Average academic year housing cost: $4950 for married students, $4414 (including board) for single students. Apply to Office of Auxiliary Services. Phone: (505)835-5900. Day-care facilities available.

Graduate Studies

Graduate study since 1946. Enrollment; full-time 230, part-time 58 (men 80%, women 20%). Institute faculty: full-time 29, part-time 7. Degrees conferred: M.S., Ph.D.

ADMISSION REQUIREMENTS. Transcripts, GRE/Subject Test, three letters of reference required in support of application. TOEFL required for international applicants. Interview not required. Accepts transfer applicants. Graduates of unaccredited institutions not considered. Apply to Dean of Graduate Studies by March 15 (Fall). Application fee $16. Phone: (505)835-5513 or (800)428-8324; fax: (505)835-5476; e-mail: graduate@nmt.edu.

ADMISSION STANDARDS. Selective for most departments. Usual minimum average: 3.0 (A = 4).

FINANCIAL AID. Annual awards from institutional funds: teaching fellowships, research fellowships, HEW fellowships, Federal W/S, loans. Approved for VA benefits. Apply by March 15 to Dean of Graduate Studies for fellowships, assistantships; to Financial Aid Office for all other programs. Use FAFSA. Phone: (505)835-5300. About 70% of students receive aid from Institute and outside sources.

DEGREE REQUIREMENTS. For M.S.: 30 credit hours minimum, at least 24 in residence; thesis/nonthesis option; final oral exam; faculty review. For Ph.D.: three years minimum beyond the bachelor's, at least two in residence; reading knowledge of one foreign language; dissertation; preliminary exam/faculty review; oral defense.

FIELDS OF STUDY.

Biology. M.S., Ph.D.
Chemistry. M.S., Ph.D.
Computer Science. M.S., Ph.D.
Engineering Mechanics. M.S.
Environmental Engineering. M.S.
Geological Engineer. M.S.
Geochemistry. M.S., Ph.D.
Geology. M.S., Ph.D.
Geophysics. M.S., Ph.D.
Hydrology. M.S., Ph.D.
Materials Engineer. M.S., Ph.D.
Mathematics. M.S.
Mining Engineering. M.S., Ph.D.
Petroleum Engineering. M.S., Ph.D.
Physics. M.S., Ph.D.
Teaching. Includes mathematics, science. M.S.

NEW MEXICO STATE UNIVERSITY

Las Cruces, New Mexico 88003-8001
Web site: www.nmsu.edu

Established 1899. Located 40 miles N of El Paso, Texas. CGS member. Coed. State control. Semester system. Special facilities: Agricultural Experiment Station, Arts and Sciences Research Center, Astrophysical Research Consortium, Border Research Institute, Center for Business Research and Services, Center for Educational Development, Center for Latin American Studies, Computer Center, Computing Research Laboratory, Consortium for International Development, Cooperative Extension Service, Educational Research Center, Engineering Research Center, Branson Hall Library and New Library, New Mexico Department of Agriculture, New Mexico Regional Primate Research Laboratory, New Mexico Water Resources Research Institute, Physical Science Laboratory, Plant Genetic Engineering Laboratory, Southwest Technology Development Institute, United States Department of Agriculture (Cotton Genetics, Ars-Jornada Experimental Range, Southwest Cotton Ginning Research Laboratory, Economics Research), University Statistics Center, cooperative program with White Sand Missile Range. Library: 1,254,000 volumes, 11,700 suscriptions. Total University enrollment: 22,300.

Annual tuition: full-time, resident $3234, nonresident $10,278; per credit, resident $134.75; nonresident $134.75 (1–6 credits), $428.25 (7–11 credits). On-campus housing for married students, single men and women. Average academic year housing cost: $3892 for single students (including board), $330 per month for married students. Contact the Director of Housing for on- and off-campus housing information. Phone: (505)646-3203. Day-care facilities available.

Graduate School

Web site: www.nmsu.edu/~gradcolg

Graduate study since 1895. Enrollment: full-time 1251, part-time 932. University faculty teaching graduate students: full- and part-time 566. Degrees conferred: M.A., M.B.A., M.Acc., M.Ag., M.A.G., M.C.J., M.F.A., M.A.T., M.S., M.M., M.S.N., M.P.H., M.P.A., M.S.W., Ed.S., Ed.D., Ph.D.

ADMISSION REQUIREMENTS. Two transcripts, letters of recommendation, letter of intent required in support of School's application. On-line application available. Interview, GRE/Subject Tests/GMAT/MAT required by some departments. TOEFL required for international applicants. Accepts transfer applicants. Graduates of unaccredited colleges not considered. Apply to Dean of Graduate School by July 1 (Fall), November 1 (Spring),

April 1 (Summer). Application fee $15, $35 for international applicants. Phone: (505)646-5746; fax: (505)646-7721.

ADMISSION STANDARDS. Selective for most departments. Usual minimum average: 3.0 (A = 4).

FINANCIAL AID. Annual awards from institutional funds: minority assistantships, minority/women fellowships, teaching/research assistantships, internships, traineeships, grants, Federal W/S, loans. Approved for VA benefits. Apply by March 15 to appropriate department chairman for assistantships, fellowships; to Financial Aid Office for all other programs. Phone: (505)646-4205; fax: (505) 646-7381. Use FAFSA. Aid available for part-time students.

DEGREE REQUIREMENTS. For master's: 30–36 semester hours minimum, at least 24 in residence; reading knowledge of one foreign language for some departments; thesis/nonthesis option; final oral/written exam. For Doctorate: three years minimum beyond the bachelor's, at least one year in residence: language requirements and psychometric tools vary by department; preliminary exam; dissertation; final oral/written exam.

FIELDS OF STUDY.
Accounting.
Agricultural Economics.
Agricultural Engineering.
Agricultural Extension and Education.
Agronomy and Horticulture.
Animal and Range Science.
Anthropology.
Art.
Astronomy.
Biochemistry.
Biology.
Business Administration.
Chemical Engineering.
Chemistry.
Civil Engineering.
Communication Studies.
Computer Science.
Counseling and Educational Psychology.
Criminal Justice.
Curriculum and Instruction.
Economics.
Educational Management and Development.
Electrical Engineering.
English.
Entomology.
Environmental Engineering.
Experimental Statistics.
Family and Consumer Science.
Fishery and Wildlife Sciences.
Geography.
Geological Engineering.
Geology.
Government.
Health Science.
History.
Industrial Engineering.
Interdisciplinary.
Mathematical Sciences.
Mechanical Engineering.
Molecular Biology.
Music.
Nursing.
Physics.
Plant Pathology.
Psychology.
Social Work.
Sociology.

Spanish.
Special Education/Communication Disorders.

THE UNIVERSITY OF NEW MEXICO
Albuquerque, New Mexico 87131-2039
Web site: www.unm.edu

Founded 1889. CGS member. State control. Semester system. Coed. Special facilities: Bureau of Engineering Research, Bureau of Business and Economic Research, Center for Southwest Research, Office of Contract Archeology, Maxwell Museum of Anthropology, Museum of Southwestern Biology, New Mexico Engineering Research Center, Technology Application Center; Centers for Advanced Studies, Alcohol and Substance Abuse, Design and Assistance, Economic Development, Communications, Health Sciences, High Performance Computing and Education and Research, High Technology Materials Integrative Studies, Microelectronics Research, MicroEngineering Ceramics, Radioactive Waste Management; Institutes for Applied Research Services, Astrophysics, Environmental Education, Latin American Institute, Meteoritics, Modern Optics, New Mexico Engineering Research Institute, Organizational Communication, Plastics, Public Policy, Social Research, Space and Nuclear Power Studies, Southwest Hispanic Research, Manufacturing Engineering and Development; UNM Business Link, Latin American Institute, Tamarind Institute. Library system: 2.3 million volumes, 17,000 subscriptions. Total University enrollment: 25,000. Off-Campus Graduate Centers: Los Alamos, Santa Fe, and Taos.

Tuition and fees: per credit hour, resident $128.50; nonresident $128.50 (up to 6 credits), $345 (7 or more). Housing available for single and married graduate students; 200 apartments for married students. Annual academic year housing cost: $5699 (including board). Contact Housing Reservations for both on- and off-campus housing information. Phone: (505)277-2606.

Graduate Studies

Graduate study since 1916. Enrollment: full-time 2287, part-time 1569. Faculty: full- and part-time 1237. Degrees conferred: M.A., M.S., M.B.A., M.F.A., M.P.A., M.P.H., M.Mu., M.Arch., M.C.R.P., M.E.M.E., M.W.R.A., E.M.B.A., Ed.D., Ph.D.

ADMISSION REQUIREMENTS. Transcripts required in support of application. On-line application available; Self-Managed Application Process. GRE/Subject Tests/GMAT recommended or required by some departments. TOEFL required for international students. Interview generally not required. Accepts transfer applicants. Graduates of unaccredited institutions not considered. U.S. applicants apply to Graduate Studies by published departmental deadline dates. Application fee $40. Phone: (505)277-2711; fax: (505)277-7405. International applicants apply to International Admissions, Student Services Center. Phone: (505)277-3136.

ADMISSION STANDARDS. Selective for most departments. Usual minimum average: 3.0 (A = 4).

FINANCIAL AID. Annual awards from institutional funds: scholarships, research fellowships, research assistantships, teaching assistantships, internships, grants, tuition waivers, Federal W/S, loans. Apply by March 1 to the appropriate departmental chair for fellowships, assistantships; to Student Financial Aid Office for all other programs. Application dates vary by department. Use FAFSA. Phone: (505)277-2041. About 33% of students receive aid through loans from School and outside sources. Aid available for part-time students.

DEGREE REQUIREMENTS: For master's: thesis/nonthesis options offered by many departments, others designate one of the two plans. PLAN I: minimum of 24 semester hours of course work, thesis; final oral/written exam. PLAN II: minimum of 32 semester hours of course work, no thesis; final oral/written exam. Some programs require demonstration of competence in one or more foreign languages. For Ph.D., Ed.D., M.F.A.: minimum of 48 semester hours of course work beyond the bachelor's degree; at least 18 semester hours exclusive of dissertation credit must be earned in courses numbered 500 or above at UNM (some programs require more course work). Ph.D. requires at least three years of intensive study and research beyond the bachelor's degree.

FIELDS OF STUDY.
American Studies. M.A., Ph.D.
Anthropology. M.A., M.S., Ph.D.
Architecture. M.Arch.
Art. Includes art history. M.A., Ph.D.
Art Education. M.A.
Biology. M.S., Ph.D.
Biomedical Sciences. M.S., Ph.D.
Buddhist Philosophy. MA.
Business and Administrative Services. Ph.D.
Chemistry. M.S., Ph.D.
Communication. M.A., Ph.D.
Communicative Disorders. M.S.
Community and Regional Planning. M.C.R.P.
Comparative Literature. M.A.
Computer Science. Ph.D.
Counseling. Ph.D.
Dramatic Writing. M.F.A.
Earth and Planetary Sciences. M.S., Ph.D.
Economics. M.A., Ph.D.
Education. Includes administration and supervision, art, counseling, educational administration, educational linguistics, educational thought and sociocultural studies, elementary, family studies, foundations of education, health, physical education and recreation, multicultural teacher and childhood, nutrition, psychological foundations, secondary, special, training and learning technologies. M.A., M.S., Ed.D.
Educational Leadership. Ph.D.
Educational Linguistics. Ph.D.
Educational Psychology. Ph.D.
Educational Thought and Sociocultural Studies. Ph.D.
Elementary Education. Ph.D.
Engineering. Includes chemical, civil, computer science, electrical and computer, engineering, manufacturing, mechanical, nuclear. M.S., Ph.D.
English. M.A., Ph.D.
Family Studies. Ph.D,
Foundations of Education. Ph.D.
French. M.A.
Geography. M.A.
German Studies. M.A.
Hazardous Waste Engineering. M.S.
Health Education. M.A., M.S.
Health, Physical Education, and Recreation. Ph.D.
History. M.A., Ph.D.
Latin American Studies. M.A., Ph.D.
Linguistics. M.A., Ph.D.
Management. M.B.A., E.M.B.A.
Mathematics. M.A., Ph.D.
Multicultural Teacher and Childhood Education. Ph.D.
Music. M.Mu.
Nursing. M.S.
Nutrition. M.S.
Occupational Therapy. M.O.T.
Optical Sciences. Includes physics. Ph.D.
Organizational Learning and Instructional Technologies. Ph.D.
Pharmaceutical Sciences. Includes hospital pharmacy, pharmacy administration.

Philosophy. M.A., Ph.D.
Philosophy of Literature. M.A.
Philosophy of Science. M.A.
Physical Therapy. M.P.T.
Physics. M.S., Ph.D.
Political Science. M.A., Ph.D.
Portuguese. M.A.
Psychology. M.S., Ph.D.
Public Administration. M.P.A.
Public Health. M.P.H.
Radiopharmacy. M.S.
Recreation. M.S.
Romance Languages. Ph.D.
Secondary Education. Ph.D.
Sociology. M.A., Ph.D.
Spanish. M.A.
Spanish and Portuguese. Ph.D.
Special Education. Ph.D.
Speech and Hearing Sciences. M.S.
Statistics. Ph.D.
Studio Art. M.F.A.
Theatre and Dance. M.A.
Toxicology. Ph.D.
Water Resources Administration. M.W.R.A.

School of Law
Web site: www.lawschool.unm.edu

Founded in 1947. ABA approved since 1948. AALS member. Semester system. Special facilities: American Indian Law Center, the Institute of Public Law, the Natural Resource Center, International Transboundary Center, Center for Environmental Law, Center for Wildlife Law. Law library: 399,579 volumes, 3287 subscriptions; has LEXIS, NEXIS, WESTLAW, DIALOG, Q/L.

Annual tuition: resident $5040, nonresident $16,872. Total average annual additional expense: $11,148.

Enrollment: first-year class 107, total full-time 334 (men 40%, women 60%). Faculty: full-time 25, part-time 16. Student to faculty ratio 11.4 to 1. Degrees conferred: J.D., J.D.-M.A. (Latin American Studies), J.D.-M.B.A., J.D.-M.P.A.

ADMISSION REQUIREMENTS. LSDAS Law School report, bachelor's degree, two transcripts, LSAT (no later than December), personal statement, letters of recommendation required in support of application. Interview not required. Accepts transfer applicants. Graduates of unaccredited institutions not considered. Preference given to state residents. Apply to School of Law after September 1, before February 15. Admits beginning students Fall only. Application fee $40. Phone: (505)277-0572.

ADMISSION STANDARDS. Selective. Mean LSAT: 154; mean GPA: 3.13 (A = 4). Gourman rating: 2.85. *U.S. News & World Report* ranking is in the second tier of all U.S. law schools. Accepts 30–35% of total annual applicants.

FINANCIAL AID. Scholarships; grants for Native Americans; loans. Apply to Financial Aid Office, School of Law, by March 1. Use FAFSA (School code: 002663) and UNM supplemental application. About 20% of students receive aid other than loans from School.

DEGREE REQUIREMENTS. For J.D.: 86 semester hours program, at least two years in full-time residence.

School of Medicine

Medical study since 1964. Library: 100,000 volumes. Annual tuition: resident $9015, nonresident $25,843. Student fees: $1333. Total average figure for all other expenses: $10,200.

Enrollment: first-year class 75 (EDP 25); total 301 (men 35%, women 65%). Faculty: full-time 408, part-time 117. Degrees conferred: M.D., M.D.-Ph.D.

ADMISSION REQUIREMENTS. AMCAS report, transcripts, MCAT required in support of application. Interview by invitation only. Applicants must have completed at least three years of college study. Preference given to New Mexico and WICHE residents. Accepts transfer applicants. Has EDP; apply between June 1 and August 1. Graduates of unaccredited colleges not considered. Apply to Director of Admissions after June 1, before November 15. Application fee $50. Phone: (505)272-4766; fax: (505)272-8239.

ADMISSION STANDARDS. Selective. Mean MCAT: 9.34; mean GPA: 3.51 (A = 4). Gourman rating: 3.29. *U.S. News & World Report* ranking is fourth of all U.S. medical schools in primary care programs. Accepts 25% of total annual applicants. Approximately 90% are state residents.

FINANCIAL AID. Scholarships, loans (short-term, and no-interest). Apply after acceptance to Office of Student Affairs Graduate Committee. Use FAFSA (School code: G24593). About 10% of students receive aid other than loans from School and outside sources.

DEGREE REQUIREMENTS. For M.D.: satisfactory completion of four-year program; all students must take USMLE Step 2 prior to awarding of M.D.

FIELDS OF GRADUATE STUDY.
Anatomy.
Biochemistry.
Biomedical Engineering.
Biophysics.
Cell Biology.
Genetics.
Immunology.
Microbiology.
Molecular Biology.
Neurosciences.
Pathology.
Pharmacology.
Physiology.

UNIVERSITY OF NEW ORLEANS
New Orleans, Louisiana 70148
Web site: www.uno.edu

Opened 1958. Formerly Louisiana State University at New Orleans. CGS member. Coed. State control. Semester system. Special facilities: Center for Energy Resource Management, Energy and Environmental Materials Research Institute, Environmental Social Science Research Institute, Gulf Coast Region Maritime Technology Center, Center for the Industrial Application of Electric Power and Instrumentation, Small Business Development Center, Urban Waste Management and Research Center, Computer Research Center. Library: 864,400 volumes, 3900 subscriptions. Total University enrollment: 17,000.

Annual tuition: resident $2876, nonresident $9920. On-campus housing for 360 graduate men, 252 graduate women; 120 apartments for married students. Annual cost: single student $3600–$4650; married $390–$450 per month. Contact Director, Auxiliary Enterprises for both on- and off-campus housing information. Phone: (504)286-6590.

Graduate School

Enrollment: full-time 1299, part-time 2659. University faculty teaching graduate students: full- and part-time 440. Degrees con-

ferred: M.A., M.A.E.T., M.A.S.T., M.S., M.B.A., M.F.A., M.Ed., M.E.D., M.U.R.P., Ph.D., Ed.D.

ADMISSION REQUIREMENTS. Official transcripts required in support of application. GRE Subject Tests required by many departments; GMAT for M.B.A., M.S. in accounting majors. Interview for some departments. TOEFL (TSE recommended) required for international applicants. Accepts transfer applicants. Graduates of unaccredited institutions not considered. Apply to Dean of Graduate School by July 1 (Fall), November 15 (Spring), May 1 (Summer). Application fee $20. Phone: (504)280-6836; fax: (504)280-6298.

ADMISSION STANDARDS. Very selective for some departments. Usual minimum average: 2.5 (A = 4).

FINANCIAL AID. Annual awards from institutional funds: fellowships, teaching assistantships, research assistantships, internships, grants, Federal W/S, loans. Approved for VA benefits. Apply by April 15 to the appropriate department chairman for assistantships; to Financial Aid Office for all other programs. Phone: (504)286-6689. Use FAFSA (University code: 002015). About 30% of students receive aid other than loans from University and outside sources. Aid sometimes available for part-time students.

DEGREE REQUIREMENTS. For master's: 30–48 credits, at least 24 in residence; thesis for most majors; reading knowledge of one foreign language in some programs; final written/oral exam. For Ph.D., Ed.D.: 60 credits minimum beyond the bachelor's, normally at least one year in residence; reading knowledge of one or two foreign languages; qualifying exam; general exam; dissertation; final oral exam.

FIELDS OF STUDY.
Accounting. Tax option available. M.S. only.
Art. Includes fine arts, graphic design, photography. M.A., M.F.A.
Arts Administration. M.A.
Biological Sciences. M.S. only.
Biopsychology.
Business Administration. Additional study may be required for students lacking previous preparation in the field. M.B.A. only.
Chemistry.
Civil Engineering.
Computer Science.
Communication.
Conservation Biology.
Counselor Education.
Creative Writing.
Curriculum and Instruction.
Drama and Communications. M.A., M.F.A.
Economics. M.A., Ph.D.
Educational Administration.
Electrical Engineering.
Engineering and Applied Science.
Engineering Management.
English. M.A. only.
English Teaching. M.A.E.T. only
Financial Economics.
Fine Arts.
Geology and Geophysics.
Geography. M.A. only.
Health Care Management.
History. M.A. only.
History Teaching.
Human Performance and Health.
Mathematics. M.S. only.
Mechanical Engineering.
Music. M.M. only.
Naval Architecture and Marine Engineering.
Physics. Includes applied. M.S. only.

Political Science. M.A., Ph.D.
Psychology. M.S., Ph.D.
Public Administration. M.P.A. only.
Romance Languages. Options in French and Spanish; M.A. only.
Science Teaching. M.A.S.T only.
Sociology. M.A. only.
Special Education.
Taxation.
Urban and Regional Planning. M.U.R.P.
Urban Studies. M.S. only.

COLLEGE OF NEW ROCHELLE

New Rochelle, New York 10805-2339
Web site: www.cnr.edu

Founded 1904. Composed of 4 schools. Located 16 miles NE of New York City. CGS member. Coed. Private control. Semester system. Library: 220,000 volumes, 1440 subscriptions.

Tuition: per credit $390. On-campus housing available for single students only. Average academic year housing cost: $3125 plus $450 declining food balance (5 months), $5650 plus a $900 declining food balance (9 months). Contact Director Residence for both on- and off-campus housing information. Phone: (914)654-5365.

Graduate School

Established 1969. Enrollment: full-time 118, part-time 829. Faculty: full-time 19, part-time 66. Degrees conferred: M.A., M.S.Ed., M.S.

ADMISSION REQUIREMENTS. Transcripts, three references, personal interview required in support of School's application. TOEFL required for international applicants. Accepts transfer applicants. Graduates of unaccredited colleges not considered. Apply by August 2 (Fall), December 1 (Spring) to the Office of the Dean. Rolling admissions process. Application fee $35. Phone: (914)654-5334; fax: (914)654-5593.

ADMISSION STANDARDS. Selective. Usual minimum average: 2.7, 3.0 in major field (A = 4).

FINANCIAL AID. Scholarships, research assistantships, staff assistantships, internships, tuition waivers, grants, Federal W/S, loans. Apply to the Office of the Dean for assistantships; to the Financial Aid Office for all other programs. No specified closing date. Phone: (914)654-5224. Use FAFSA and College's FAF.

DEGREE REQUIREMENTS. For master's: 33-45 credits minimum (depending on program), at least 28-35 in residence.

FIELDS OF STUDY.
Art Therapy. M.S.
Career Development. M.S.
Communication Studies. M.S.
Community/School Psychology. M.S.
Early Childhood Education. M.S.Ed.
Education of the Gifted. M.S.Ed.
Elementary/Early Childhood Education. M.S.Ed.
Gerontology. M.S.
Guidance and Counseling. M.S.
Literacy Education. M.S.Ed.
Multilingual/Multicultural Education. M.S.Ed.
School Administration and Supervision. M.S.Ed.
Special Education. M.S.Ed.
Speech-Language Pathology. M.S.Ed.

Studio Arts. M.
TESL. M.S.Ed.
Therapeutic Education. M.S.Ed.

THE NEW SCHOOL UNIVERSITY

New York, New York 10011-8603
Web site: www.newschool.edu

Founded 1919. Coed. Private control. Semester system. Special facilities: Center for Economic Policy Analysis, Center for Studies of Social Change, Community Development Research Center, Center for the Study of Politics, Theory, and Policy, Environmental Simulation Center, European Union Center of New York, International Center for Migration, Ethnicity, and Citizenship, Transregional Center for Democratic Studies. Library: 4,063,000 volumes, 2000 subscriptions. Total University enrollment: 7000.

Tuition: full-time per credit $1086. Off-campus housing for graduate students. Average academic year housing costs: $9083 (including board). Contact Director of Housing for both on- and off-campus housing information. Phone: (212)229-5459.

Graduate Faculty of Political and Social Science

Founded 1933.

Tuition: per credit: $1086. Enrollment: full-time 797, part-time 226. Graduate faculty: full-time 74, part-time 55. Degrees conferred: M.A., M.S.Sc. Ph.D., D.S.Sc.

ADMISSION REQUIREMENTS. Transcripts, letters of reference, GRE required in support of application. TOEFL required for international applicants. Interview not required. Accepts transfer applicants. Graduates of unaccredited institutions not considered. Apply to Director of Admissions by August 1 (Fall), December 1 (Spring), May 1 (Summer). Rolling admissions process. Application fee $30. Phone: (800)523-5411; fax: (212)229-7102; e-mail: gfadmit@newschool.edu.

ADMISSION STANDARDS. Selective for most departments. Usual minimum average: 3.0 (A = 4).

FINANCIAL AID. One hundred fifty scholarships, 55 teaching/research assistantships, Federal W/S, loans. Approved for VA benefits. Apply by January 15 to the department chair for scholarships and assistantships; to the Office of Financial Aid for all other aid. Phone: (212)741-5714. Use FAFSA. About 30% of students receive aid other than loans from School, 50% from all sources. Loans available for part-time study.

DEGREE REQUIREMENTS. For M.A.: 30-36 credits, thesis/nonthesis option; other requirements vary by department. For Ph.D.: 60 credits minimum beyond the bachelor's, at least 30 credits in full-time residence; written qualifying exam; oral comprehensive exam; reading knowledge of one foreign language, computer/statistics substitute possible; dissertation; final oral defense. For D.S.Sc.: 92 credits minimum beyond the bachelor's; other requirements essentially the same as for Ph.D.

FIELDS OF STUDY.
Anthropology.
Economics.
Global Political Economy and Finance.
Historical Studies. Interdisciplinary. M.A.
Liberal Studies. Interdisciplinary. M.A.
Philosophy.
Political Science.
Psychoanalytic Studies. Interdisciplinary. M.A.

Psychology.
Sociology.

Robert J. Milano Graduate School of Management and Urban Policy

Graduate study since 1975. Semester system. Tuition: per credit $794. Enrollment: full-time 154, part-time 451. Graduate faculty: full-time 24, part-time 79. Degrees conferred: M.S., Adv.C.

ADMISSION REQUIREMENTS. Transcripts, letters of reference required in support of School's application. GMAT considered if available. TOEFL required for international applicants. Accepts transfer students. Graduates of unaccredited institutions not considered. Apply to Admission Office by August 1 (Fall), December 1 (Spring), May 1 (Summer). Application fee $30. Phone: (212)229-5462; fax: (212)229-8935.

ADMISSION STANDARDS. Selective for most departments. Usual minimum average: 3.0 (A = 4).

FINANCIAL AID. Academic scholarships, grants, fellowships, research assistantships, administrative assistantships, teaching assistantships, tuition waivers, Federal W/S, loans. Approved for VA benefits. Apply by March 1 to department chair for scholarships, fellowships, assistantships; to the Office of Financial Aid for all other programs. Phone: (212)229-5462; fax: (212)229-8935. Use FAFSA and CSS/FA Profile. Aid available for part-time students.

DEGREE REQUIREMENTS. For M.S.: 42 credits minimum; internship (strongly encouraged); thesis/nonthesis option. For Adv.C.: 18 credits minimum beyond master's. For Ph.D.: 60 credit minimum beyond bachelor's, at least 30 credits in residence; qualifying exam; comprehensive exam; dissertation; oral defense.

FIELDS OF STUDY.
Health Services Management and Policy.
Human Resources Management.
Nonprofit Management.
Public and Urban Policy. Ph.D. only.
Urban Policy Analysis and Management.

The New School

The University's founding division. Semester system. Annual tuition: full-time $11,550; per credit $550. Enrollment: full-time 307, part-time 221. Graduate faculty: full-time 15, part-time 60. Degrees conferred: M.A., M.S., M.F.A., M.S.T.

ADMISSION REQUIREMENTS. Transcripts, letters of reference required in support of School's application. GMAT considered if available. TOEFL required for international applicants. Accepts transfer students. Graduates of unaccredited institutions not considered. Apply to Admission Office by August 1 (Fall), December 1 (Spring), May 1 (Summer). Application fee $30. Phone: (212)229-5613.

ADMISSION STANDARDS. Selective for most departments. Usual minimum average: 3. 0 (A = 4).

FINANCIAL AID. Scholarships, fellowships, research assistantships, teaching assistantships, internships, grants, Federal W/S, loans. Approved for VA benefits. Apply by March 1 to department chair for scholarships, fellowships, assistantships; to the Office of Financial Aid for all other programs. Use FAFSA. Aid available for part-time students.

DEGREE REQUIREMENTS. For master's: 42 credits minimum; internship (strongly encouraged); thesis/nonthesis option.

FIELDS OF STUDY.
Creative Writing. M.F.A.
International Affairs. M.A., M.S.
Media Studies. M.A.
Teacher Education. M.S.T.

Parsons School of Design
Web site: www.parsons.edu

Annual tuition: $24,500; per credits $866. Enrollment: full-time 285; part-time 96. Faculty: full-time 15, part-time 30. Degrees conferred: M.A., M.Arch., M.F.A.

ADMISSION REQUIREMENTS. Transcripts, three letters of recommendation, resume, statement of intent, portfolio of 15–20 pieces of work required in support of School's application. Interview sometimes required. TOEFL required for international applicants. Apply to Admissions Committee by March 1. Application fee $40. Phone: (800)252-0852 or (212)229-8910; fax: (212)229-8975.

ADMISSION STANDARDS. Selective. Admission based on portfolio review.

FINANCIAL AID. Annual awards from institutional funds: scholarships, fellowships, assistantships, internships, tuition waivers, Federal W/S, loans. Apply by April 1 to Financial Aid Office; no specified closing date. Phone: (212)229-8930; fax: (212)229-8975. Use FAFSA, institutional FAF, and CSS profile. About 20% of students receive aid other than loans from School and outside sources.

DEGREE REQUIREMENTS. For M.A.: 32 credits minimum, at least 24 in residence; thesis option. For M.Arch.: 30–36 credits minimum, at least 24 in residence; master's project. For M.F.A.: 48 credits minimum, at least 40 in residence; departmental requirements determined by portfolio review; final essay; applied project, gallery exhibition.

FIELDS OF STUDY.
Architecture.
Design and Technology.
History of Decorative Arts.
Lighting Design.
Painting.
Sculpture.

THE CITY UNIVERSITY OF NEW YORK
The Graduate School and University Center
365 Fifth Avenue
New York, New York 10016
Web site: www.gc.cuny.edu

Established 1961. Public control. Semester system. Special facilities: Center for Advanced Study in Education, Center for Jewish Studies, Center for Research in Cognition and Affect, Center for Research in Speech and Hearing Sciences, Center for Social Research, Center for Urban and Policy Studies, Center for the Study of Women and Sex Roles. Library: 272,000 volumes, 31,000 subscriptions.

Tuition: per semester full-time (up to 45 credits) resident $2175, nonresident $3800; per semester full-time (from 45 credits to completion of course work) resident $360, nonresident $3025; per semester full-time (from completion of course work to completion of degree) resident $540, nonresident $1080. On-campus housing available. Contact the Office of Residence Life for current information. Phone: (212)817-7480.

Graduate Studies

Enrollment: full-time 3586, part-time 478 (men 45%, women 55%). Faculty: full- and part-time 1600. Degrees conferred: M.A., D.M.A., D.S.W., Ph.D.

ADMISSION REQUIREMENTS. Official transcripts, GRE, GMAT (Business Ph.D. program only), two faculty recommendations required in support of application. TOEFL required for international applicants. Accepts transfer applicants. Apply to Admissions Office by March 1 for most programs (Fall), November 15 (Spring). Application fee $40. Phone: (212)642-2812.

ADMISSION STANDARDS. Selective. Usual minimum average: 3.0 (A = 4).

FINANCIAL AID. Fellowships (service and nonservice), grants, assistantships, traineeships, Federal W/S, loans. Apply to the Office of Financial Aid by February 1. Phone: (212)642-2811. Use CUNY Student Aid form.

DEGREE REQUIREMENTS. For M.A.: 30 credits minimum, at least 24 in residence; final comprehensive exam; thesis. For D.S.W.: 30 credits minimum beyond the master's, at least two terms in residence; preliminary exam; dissertation; final oral/written exam. For D.M.A., Ph.D.: 60 credits minimum, at least 30 in residence and two consecutive semesters in full-time residence; preliminary exam; candidacy exam; dissertation; final defense of dissertation.

FIELDS OF STUDY.
Anthropology. Admits Fall only. Apply by January 8.
Art History.
Biochemistry.
Biology. Apply by February 1.
Biomedical Sciences. At Mount Sinai Graduate School of Biological Sciences.
Business. Admits Fall only.
Chemistry.
Classics.
Comparative Literature.
Computer Science. Admits Fall only.
Criminal Justice. Admits Fall only. Apply by January 15.
Earth and Environmental Sciences.
Economics.
Educational Psychology. Admits Fall only. Apply by February 15.
Engineering.
English. Admits Fall only. Apply by January 15.
French. Apply by February 1.
Germanic Languages and Literature.
Hispanic and Luso-Brazilian Literature. Apply by January 15.
History.
Liberal Studies.
Linguistics. Admits Fall only. Apply by January 15.
Mathematics.
Music. Admits Fall only. Apply by January 1.
Philosophy.
Physics.
Political Science.
Psychology. Admits Fall only. Apply by March 1, January 1 for clinical and neuropsychology, February 1 for social-personality, March 15 for learning processes.
School Psychology. Apply by February 15.
Social Welfare. Admits Fall only. D.S.W. only.
Sociology. Admits Fall only.
Speech and Hearing Sciences.
Theater. Admits Fall only.
Urban Education. Admits Fall only. Apply by February 15.

NEW YORK INSTITUTE OF TECHNOLOGY
Old Westbury, New York 11568-8000
Web site: www.nyit.edu

Main campus located 35 miles E of New York City; other branches are located in NYC and Islip, Long Island, New York. CGS member. Coed. Private control. Semester system. Special facilities: Center for Labor and Industrial Relations, Management Information Systems Center, Science and Technology Research Center, Video Center. Library: 213,600 volumes, 2900 subscriptions.

Tuition: per credit $525. On-campus housing available. Average academic year housing cost: $6640 (including board) for single students; $3680 for married students. Off-campus housing cost: $700–$900 per month. Contact Office of Residential Life for both on- and off-campus housing information. Phone: (516)348-3340.

Graduate Division

Enrollment: full-time 759, part-time 1829. University faculty teaching graduate students: full-time 215, part-time 145. Degrees conferred: M.A., M.B.A., M.P.S., M.S.

ADMISSION REQUIREMENTS. Transcripts, GMAT (Business) required in support of application. On-line application available. GRE required by some programs. TOEFL required for international applicants. Interview not required. Accepts transfer applicants. Graduates of unaccredited institutions not considered. Apply to Graduate Admissions Office at least one month prior to registration. Rolling admissions process. Application fee $50. Phone: (516)686-7925; fax: (516)686-7613.

ADMISSION STANDARDS. Selective. Usual minimum average: 2.85 (A = 4).

FINANCIAL AID. Scholarships, fellowships, assistantships, grants, tuition waivers, Federal W/S, loans. Apply to appropriate dean for assistantships; to Financial Aid Office for all other programs. No specified closing date. Use FAFSA. Aid available for part-time students.

DEGREE REQUIREMENTS. For master's: 33–45 credit hours minimum; at least 30 credit hours in residence; thesis/nonthesis option; final oral exam for some programs.

FIELDS OF STUDY.

SCHOOL OF ALLIED HEALTH AND LIFE SCIENCES:
Clinical Nutrition. M.S.
Human Relations. M.P.S.
Occupational Therapy. M.S.
Physical Therapy. M.S.

SCHOOL OF ARCHITECTURE AND DESIGN:
Urban and Regional Design. M.Arch.

SCHOOL OF ARTS, SCIENCES, AND COMMUNICATION:
Communication Arts. Includes advertising, corporate communication, design graphics, electronic cinematography, intercultural communication, mass communication, media management, writing for media, journalism, painting, public relations, studio art. M.A.

SCHOOL OF EDUCATION:
Counseling. Includes mental health. M.S.
Elementary Education. M.S.
Instructional Technology. M.S.

SCHOOL OF ENGINEERING AND TECHNOLOGY:
Computer Science. M.S.
Electrical Engineering and Computer Engineering. M.S.

Energy Management. M.S.

Environmental Technology. Includes pollution prevention, regulatory compliance, waste management. M.S.

SCHOOL OF MANAGEMENT:

Business Administration. Includes accounting, finance, general management, international business, management of information systems, marketing, personnel and industrial relations. M.B.A.

Human Resources Management and Labor Relations. M.S.

New York College of Osteopathic Medicine

Web site: www.nyit.edu/nycom

Coed. Private control. Library: 60,000 volumes, has MEDLINE, BIOETHIC, HEALTH, TOXLINE, DIALOG, OCLC.

Annual tuition: $25,000. No on-campus housing available. Enrollment: first-year class 260, total 1008 (men 65%, women 35%). Faculty: full-time, 40. Degree conferred: D.O., D.O.-M.S. (Clinical Nutrition), D.O.-M.B.A.

ADMISSION REQUIREMENTS. AACOMAS report, bachelor's degree, official transcripts, MCAT (no later than September), three letters of recommendation, one from premed advisory committee, evaluation from a physician (preferably a D.O.), supplemental form required in support of application. Interview by invitation only. Graduates of unaccredited colleges not considered. Apply by February 1 to the Director of Admissions. Admits first-year students Fall only. Application fee: $60. Phone: (516)686-3747; fax: (516)686-3831.

ADMISSION STANDARDS. Selective. Usual minimum average: 2.75 (A = 4). Mean MCAT: 7.3; mean GPA: 3.2 (A = 4). Accepts approximately 15% of annual applicants.

FINANCIAL AID. Scholarships, fellowships, grants, tuition waivers, loans. Apply by April 1 to the Financial Aid Office. Phone: (516)686-7960. Use FAFSA (College code: 002782).

DEGREE REQUIREMENT. For D.O.: satisfactory completion of four-year program.

NEW YORK LAW SCHOOL

57 Worth Street
New York, New York 10013-2960
Web site: www.nyls.edu

Established 1891. Located in lower Manhattan in TriBeCa. ABA approved since 1954. AALS member. Semester system. Full-time, part-time study. Special facilities: Communications Media Center, Center for New York City Law, Center for International Law. Special programs: Law School exchange with Vermont Law School; externships and judicial internships. Law library: 475,188 volumes, 5329 subscriptions; has LEXIS, NEXIS, WESTLAW, LEGALTRAC, OCLC, RLIN.

Annual tuition: full-time $24,687, part-time $18,514. No on-campus housing available. Law students live off-campus. Contact New York Law School Housing office for off-campus information. Phone: (212)431-2166. Off-campus housing and personal expenses: approximately $11,645.

Enrollment: first-year class, full-time 340, part-time 122; total 1347 (men 48%, women 52%). School faculty: full-time 45, part-time 66. Student to faculty to ratio 22.6 to 1. Degrees conferred: J.D., J.D.-M.B.A., J.D.-M.P.A. (with Baruch College of CUNY).

ADMISSION REQUIREMENTS. LSDAS Law School report, bachelor's degree, transcripts, LSAT required in support of application. Applicants must have completed four years of college.

Accepts transfer applicants. Graduates of unac[credited institu]tions not considered. Apply to Admissions Offi[ce after Octo]ber 1, before April 1. Admits full-time stud[ents Fall and] Spring. Application fee $50. Phone: (212)431-2[...].

ADMISSION STANDARDS. Selective. Mea[n LSAT: full-time] 151, part-time 149; mean GPA: full-time 3.10, part-time 2.90 (A = 4). Accepts approximately 10–15% of total annual applicants.

FINANCIAL AID. Scholarships, grants, Federal W/S, loans. Apply to Office of Financial Aid, preferably by April 15. Use FAFSA (School code: G02783). About 31% of students receive aid other than loans from School.

DEGREE REQUIREMENTS. For J.D.: satisfactory completion of three-year day program or four-year evening program; 86 credit hour program. For M.B.A., M.P.A.: see appropriate Graduate School listing in Baruch College, CUNY.

NEW YORK MEDICAL COLLEGE

Valhalla, New York 10595
Web site: www.nymc.edu

Established 1960. Located about 25 miles N of New York City. CGS member. Special facilities: Brander Cancer Research Institute, Cardiovascular Research Institute, Center for Lyme Disease, Center for Pediatric Hypotension, Center for Primary Care Education and Research, Institute for Genetic Analysis of Common Diseases, Institute for Bioethics at New York Medical College, Institute for International Health, Institute for Trauma Emergency Care, Westchester Institute for Human Development. The College's NIH ranking is 149th among all U.S. institutions with 54 awards/grants worth $19,456,256. Library: 148,000 volumes, 1200 subscriptions.

Annual tuition: graduate program, per credit $360. On-campus housing available. Average academic year housing cost: $12,000 for married students, $10,000 for single students; off-campus cost: $600–$1000 per month. Contact Housing Office for both on- and off-campus housing information. Phone: (914)993-4532.

Graduate School of Basic Medical Sciences

Established 1963. Tuition: per credit $470. Enrollment: full-time 200, part-time 54. Faculty: full- and part-time 83. Degrees conferred: M.S., Ph.D.

ADMISSION REQUIREMENTS. Official transcripts, GRE, two letters of recommendation required in support of School's application. GRE Subject required for some programs. TOEFL, or evidence of proficiency in English required of international applicants. Accepts transfer applicants. Apply to Dean of the School by July 1 (Fall), December 1 (Spring). Application $35, $60 for international applicants. Phone: (914)594-4110; fax: (914)594-4944.

ADMISSION STANDARDS. Competitive. Usual minimum average: 3.3 (A = 4).

FINANCIAL AID. Scholarships, fellowships, assistantships, internships, grants, loans. Apply to Dean of the School; no specified closing date. Phone: (914)594-4521. Use FAFSA. Aid available for part-time students.

DEGREE REQUIREMENTS. For M.S.: 30–36 credits minimum, at least 24–30 credits in residence; qualifying exam; thesis. For Ph.D.: 60 credits minimum beyond the bachelor's; at least two years in full-time residence; reading knowledge of one foreign language or research tool; qualifying exam; dissertation; final oral exam.

DS OF STUDY.
ic Medical Sciences. Interdisciplinary.
Biochemistry and Molecular Biology.
Cell Biology and Anatomy.
Experimental Pathology.
Microbiology and Immunology.
Molecular Biology.
Pharmacology.
Physiology.

Medical College

Established 1860. Located in Valhalla (10595).

Annual tuition: $31,320; student fees $700. Total cost of all other expenses: $12,389. Enrollment: first-year class 186 (EDP 2); total 781 (men 52%, women 48%). Faculty: full-time 1000, part-time and volunteers 1800. Degrees conferred: M.D., M.D.-Ph.D.

ADMISSION REQUIREMENTS. AMCAS report, transcripts, MCAT, screening interview, recommendations required in support of application. Supplemental on-line application may be requested. Applicants must possess bachelor's degree. Has EDP; apply between June 1 and August 1. Apply to Admissions Office after June 1, before December 15. Application fee $100. Phone: (914)594-4507; fax: (914)594-4976.

ADMISSION STANDARDS. Very competitive. Mean MCAT: 10; mean GPA: 3.4 (A = 4). Gourman rating: 3.50. Accepts 3% of total annual applicants. Approximately 23% are state residents.

FINANCIAL AID. Scholarships, loans. Apply to Director of Financial Aid; no specified closing date. Phone: (914)594-4491. Use FAFSA. About 85% of students receive some aid from College.

DEGREE REQUIREMENTS. For M.D.: satisfactory completion of four-year program.

School of Public Health

Founded 1981. Courses offered in Suffern, New York, and Danbury, Connecticut. Enrollment: full- and part-time 600. Faculty: full-time 10, part-time 50. Degrees conferred: M.S., M.P.H.

ADMISSION REQUIREMENTS. Official transcripts, GRE, personal statement, two letters of recommendation required in support of School's application. Separate applications for Physical Therapy and Speech-Language Pathology. TOEFL (minimum score 600) or evidence of proficiency in English required for international students. Accepts transfer applicants. Graduates of unaccredited institutions not considered. Apply by August 1 (Fall), December 1 (Spring) to Office of Admissions. Rolling admissions process. Application fee $35, $60 for international applicants. Phone: (914)594-4510.

ADMISSION STANDARDS. Competitive for some departments, selective for all others. Usual minimum average: 3.0 (A = 4).

FINANCIAL AID. Traineeships, assistantships, loans. Apply by June 15 to Dean for assistantships, to Office of Student Financial Planning for all other programs. Phone: (914)594-4491. Use FAFSA.

DEGREE REQUIREMENTS. For M.S., M.P.H.: 36–45 credit program, one and a half years minimum, at least 24–30 credits in residence; thesis and defense/research report/qualifying exam.

FIELDS OF STUDY.
Behavioral Sciences and Health Promotion. M.P.H.
Biostatistics. M.P.H., M.S.

Clinical Research Administration. M.S.
Developmental Disabilities. M.P.H.
Emergency Medical Services. M.S., M.P.H.
Environmental and Occupational Health Services. M.S., M.P.H.
Epidemiology. M.S., M.P.H.
Gerontology. M.P.H.
Health Informatics. M.P.H.
Health Policy and Management. M.S., M.P.H.
International Health. M.S., M.P.H.
Maternal and Child Health. M.P.H.
Physical Therapy. M.S.
Public Health. M.P.H.
Speech-Language Pathology. Two-year, 66 credit program. M.S.

STATE UNIVERSITY OF NEW YORK AT BINGHAMTON

Binghamton, New York 13902-6000
Web site: www.binghamton.edu

Founded 1950. CGS member. Coed. State control. Special facilities: Center for Cognitive and Psycholinguistic Sciences, Center for Developmental Psychobiology, Center for Global Cultural Studies, Integrated Electronic Engineering Center, Center for Leadership Studies, Center for Medieval and Early Renaissance Studies, Center for Research in Translation, Center for Women's Studies, Institute for Research on Multicultural and International Labor. Library: 1,700,000 volumes, 9100 subscriptions.

Annual tuition: residents $5100, nonresidents $8416; per credit, residents $213, nonresidents $351. On-campus housing available in a new graduate apartment complex consisting of three- and four-person apartments each with living room, dining area, kitchen, and bathroom. Annual academic year housing cost: $3710 for a single, $5990 for family apartment. Apply to Coordinator, Graduate Community. Phone: (607)777-2904. Day-care facilities available.

Graduate School

Graduate study since 1961. Enrollment: full-time 1335, part-time 1380. University faculty teaching graduate students: full-time 467, part-time 196. Degrees conferred: M.A., M.S., M.A.T., M.Eng., M.M., M.S.Ed., M.S.T., M.B.A., M.P.A., Certificate, Ed.D., Ph.D.

ADMISSION REQUIREMENTS. Transcripts, GRE, two letters of recommendation required in support of School's application. On-line application available. GMAT required for School of Management. GRE Subject required by some departments. Interview is not required. TOEFL required for international applicants. Accepts transfer applicants. Graduates of unaccredited institutions not considered. Apply to Graduate School Admissions Office at least one month prior to registration. Application fee $50. Phone: (607)777-2151.

ADMISSION STANDARDS. Competitive. Usual minimum average: 3.0 (A = 4).

FINANCIAL AID. Annual awards from institutional funds: tuition scholarships, teaching assistantships, research assistantships, fellowships, internships, tuition waivers, Federal W/S, loans. Approved for VA benefits. Apply by February 15 to appropriate Academic Program Directors for assistantships, fellowships, internships; to Director of Student Financial Aid for all other programs. Phone: (607)777-2428. Use FAFSA. About 64%

of students receive aid other than loans from University and outside sources. Aid available for part-time students.

DEGREE REQUIREMENTS. For master's: 30 credit hours minimum, at least 24 in residence; thesis and nonthesis options; final oral/written exam; most departments require reading knowledge of one foreign language. For Ph.D.: 60 credit hours, at least 24 in full-time residence; knowledge of at least one foreign language; dissertation; final written/oral exam.

FIELDS OF STUDY.
Advanced Technology. Includes computer science, electrical engineering, mechanical engineering, industrial engineering, systems science, computer science. M.S., Ph.D.
Applied Science. M.S.
Art History. M.A., Ph.D.
Biological Sciences. M.A., M.A.T., M.S.T., M.S.Ed., Ph.D.
Chemistry. M.A., M.S., Ph.D.
Comparative Literature. M.A., Ph.D.
Computer Science. M.S., M.Eng., Ph.D.
Creative Writing. Certificate, M.A.
Economics. M.A., Ph.D.
Education. Includes early childhood elementary, reading, secondary, special. M.S.Ed.
Educational Theory and Practice. Ed.D.
Electrical Engineering. M.S., M.Eng., Ph.D.
English. M.A., M.A.T., M.S.T., M.S.Ed., Ph.D.
Environmental Policy and Resource Management.
Family Nurse Practitioner. Certificate only.
French. M.A.
Geography. M.A.
Geological Sciences. Includes earth science. M.A., M.A.T., M.S.T., M.S.Ed., Ph.D.
Geophysics.
History. M.A., Ph.D.
Industrial Engineering. M.S., M.Eng.
Interdepartmental Publishing. Certificate only.
Italian. M.A.
Latin American and Caribbean Area Studies. Certificate only.
Management. M.B.A., M.S., Ph.D.
Mathematical Sciences. M.A., Ph.D.
Mechanical Engineering. M.S., M.Eng., Ph.D.
Medieval and Early Renaissance Studies. Certificate only.
Modern Drama and Theater. Certificate only.
Music. M.A., M.M.
Nursing. M.S. Includes family nurse practitioner, Certificate; gerontological nurse practitioner, Certificate; community health/primary care nurse practitioner, Certificate.
Philosophy. M.A., Ph.D.
Physics. M.A., M.A.T., M.S., M.S.T., M.S.Ed.
Political Science. M.A., Ph.D.
Professional Accounting. M.S.
Psychology. Includes general experimental psychology, clinical psychology, and psychobiology. M.A., Ph.D.
Public Administration. M.A.
Reading and Language Arts. Certificate of Advanced Study.
Romance Languages and Literatures. Includes French (M.A., M.A.T., M.S.T.), Italian (M.A.), Spanish (M.A., M.A.T., M.S.T.).
Social Sciences. M.A., M.A.T., M.S.T., M.S.Ed.
Sociology. M.A., Ph.D.
Southwest Asian (Middle East) and North African (Maghreb) Studies. Certificate only.
Spanish. M.A.
Systems Science. Includes manufacturing systems. M.S., Ph.D.
Theater. M.A., M.F.A.
Women's History.

OTHER PROGRAMS:
M.B.A. Management with M.A. History. M.B.A.-M.A.
M.B.A. with Specialization in Arts Administration. M.B.A.

STATE UNIVERSITY OF NEW YORK COLLEGE AT BROCKPORT
Brockport, New York 14420-2997
Web site: www.brockport.edu

Founded 1841. Located 18 miles W of Rochester. Coed. State control. Semester system. Special facilities: Center for Applied Aquatic Science and Aquaculture, Center for Philosophic Exchange, Child and Adolescent Stress Management Institute, Congress on Research in Dance, Monroe County Historian's office. Library: more than 551,000 volumes, 1485 subscriptions. Total College enrollment: 8500.

Annual tuition: full-time, resident $5100, nonresident $8416; per credit, resident $231, nonresident $351. On-campus housing for single graduate students. Average academic year housing cost: $6200. Contact Director of Residential Life for on- and off-campus housing information. Phone: (716)395-2122.

Graduate Studies

Graduate study since 1948. Enrollment: full-time 266, part-time 940. Faculty teaching graduate students: full- and part-time 222. Degrees conferred: M.A., M.F.A., M.S., M.S.Ed., M.P.A., M.S.S.W. (in collaboration with Nazareth College of Rochester), C.A.S.

ADMISSION REQUIREMENTS. Transcripts, three letters of recommendation required in support of application. GRE required for some programs. Portfolio in lieu of GRE for M.F.A. TOEFL required for international applicants. Accepts transfer applicants. Apply to the Office of Graduate Admission; closing date varies by program. Application fee $50. Phone: (716)395-5465; fax: (716)395-2515; e-mail: gradadmit@brockport.edu.

ADMISSION STANDARDS. Selective. Usual minimum average: 3.0 (A = 4).

FINANCIAL AID. Annual awards from institutional funds: full and partial scholarships, fellowships, research assistantships, teaching assistantships, minority fellowships, Federal W/S, loans. Approved for VA benefits. Apply by April 15 to academic department for fellowships, assistantships; to Financial Aid Office for all other programs. Phone: (800)295-9150, (716)395-2501; fax: (716)395-5445. Use FAFSA.

DEGREE REQUIREMENTS. For master's: 30 credits minimum. For C.A.S., M.F.A.: 60 credits minimum beyond the bachelor's.

FIELDS OF STUDY.
Biological Sciences. Includes botany, zoology. M.S.
Communication. M.A.
Computational Science. M.S.
Counselor Education. M.S.Ed., C.A.S.
Dance. M.F.A.
Educational Administration. Includes school administration, school business administration. M.S.Ed., C.A.S.
Educational and Human Development. Includes bilingual, elementary, reading teacher, secondary (English, mathematics, science, social studies).
English.
Family Nurse Practitoner and Studies. M.S.
Health Education. M.S.Ed.
History.
Liberal Studies.
Mathematics.
Physical Education.
Psychology.
Public Administration.

Recreation and Leisure Studies. M.S.
Social Work. M.S.S.W.
Special Physical Education.
Visual Studies. Includes book arts, computer imaging, photography, video.

STATE UNIVERSITY OF NEW YORK COLLEGE AT BUFFALO

Buffalo, New York 14222-1095
Web site: www.buffalostate.edu

Established 1871. CGS member. Coed. State control. Semester system. Special facilities: Burchfield Center, Center for Development of Human Services, Great Lakes Center for Environmental Research and Education, Prevention Resources Center, Center for Study in Creativity. Library: 359,433 volumes, 3000 subscriptions.

Annual tuition: full-time, resident $5100, nonresident $8416; per semester hour, resident $213, nonresident $351. On-campus housing for men and women; none for married students. Average annual housing cost: $4820 (including board). Apply to Director of Residential Life. Phone: (716)878-6806. Day-care facilities available.

Graduate Studies and Research

Established 1945. Enrollment: full-time 382, part-time 1631. College faculty teaching graduate students: full-time 185, part-time 31. Degrees conferred: M.A., M.S., M.S.Ed., M.P.S., C.A.S.

ADMISSION REQUIREMENTS. Transcripts required in support of application. TOEFL required for international applicants. Accepts transfer applicants. Apply to Office of Graduate Studies by May 1 (Fall), October 1 (Spring), March 1 (Summer). Application fee $50. Phone: (716)878-5601; e-mail:gradoffc@buffalostate.edu.

ADMISSION STANDARDS. Relatively open. Usual minimum average: 2.75 for M.A.; 2.5 for M.S., M.S.Ed. for last two years (A = 4).

FINANCIAL AID. Research assistantships, fellowships, minority fellowships, internships, tuition waivers, Federal W/S, loans. Approved for VA benefits. Apply by March 1 to individual graduate departments for fellowships, assistantships; to Office of Financial Aid for all other programs. Phone: (716)878-4901. Use FAFSA. About 50% of students receive aid other than loans from outside agencies. Aid available for part-time students.

DEGREE REQUIREMENTS. For master's: 30 semester hours minimum, at least 24 in residence; comprehensive exam/thesis for M.A. For C.A.S.: 30 semester hours beyond master's, at least 27 in residence.

FIELDS OF STUDY.
Adult Education.
Applied Economics.
Art Conservation.
Art Education (K–12).
Biology.
Biology Education (7–12).
Business and Distributive Education.
Business and Marketing Education.
Career and Technical Education.
Chemistry.
Chemistry Education (7–12).
Childhood and Early Childhood Curriculum and Instruction.
Childhood Education (Grades 1–6).

Creative Studies.
Criminal Justice.
Early Childhood Education (Birth–Grade 2).
Earth Science Education (7–12).
Educational Computing.
Educational Leadership and Facilitation.
Elementary Education (Pre-K–6).
English.
English Education (7–12).
History. Includes museum studies.
Industrial Technology.
Literary Specialist (5–12).
Mathematical Education (7–12).
Multidisciplinary Studies. Includes environmental research and education, human services administration, public relations management.
Museum Studies.
Physics Education (7–12).
Social Studies Education (7–12).
Spanish Education (7–12).
Speech-Language Pathology.
Student Personnel Administration.
Teaching Bilingual Exceptional Individuals. Includes adolescence, childhood, early childhood.
Technology Education.

STATE UNIVERSITY OF NEW YORK COLLEGE AT CORTLAND

Cortland, New York 13045
Web site: www.cortland.edu

Founded 1868. Located 35 miles S of Syracuse. Coed. State control. Semester system. Library: 396,200 volumes, 2744 subscriptions. Annual tuition: resident, full-time $5100, nonresident $8416, per credit $213; nonresident $351. No on-campus housing for graduate students. Apply to Office of Student Housing for off-campus housing information.

Graduate Studies

Graduate study since 1947. Enrollment: full- and part-time 1350. Faculty: full- and part-time 62. Degrees conferred: M.A., M.S., M.S.E., M.A.T., M.S.T., C.A.B., C.A.S.

ADMISSION REQUIREMENTS. Transcripts required in support of application. GRE/MAT required by some departments. TOEFL required for international applicants. Interview not required. Accepts transfer applicants. Graduates of unaccredited institutions not considered. Apply to Office of Graduate Admissions by August 1 (Fall), January 1 (Spring), May 1 (Summer). Application fee $50. Phone: (607)753-4711; fax: (607)753-5999.

ADMISSION STANDARDS. Selective. Usual minimum average: 3.0 (A = 4).

FINANCIAL AID. Annual awards from institutional funds: teaching fellowships, internships, tuition waivers, Federal W/S, loans. Approved for VA benefits. Apply to Director of Financial Aid by March 15. Phone: (607)753-4717; fax: (607)753-5999. Use FAFSA and TAP application.

DEGREE REQUIREMENTS. For master's: 30 semester hours minimum, at least 24 in residence; admission to candidacy; written comprehensive exam/thesis/special project. For C.A.S., C.A.B.: 30 semester hours beyond the master's.

FIELDS OF STUDY.

Adolescence Education (7–12). Includes biology, chemistry, earth science, English, mathematics, physics, physics and mathematics, social studies. M.A.T.

Childhood Education (1–6). Includes math and science, social studies, technology. M.S. Ed., M.S.T.

Elementary and Early Secondary English. M.S.Ed.

Elementary and Early Secondary Science. M.S.Ed.

Elementary and Early Secondary Social Studies. M.S.Ed.

Elementary Education. Includes curriculum and instruction, foundations of education, mathematics, reading teacher, science. M.S.Ed.

English. M.A.

Health Education (K–12). M.S.Ed., M.S.T.

History. M.A.

Physical Education (K–12). M.S.Ed.

Reading Teacher (K–12). M.S.Ed.

Recreation. Includes environmental and outdoor education, management of leisure services, therapeutic recreation. M.S.

Recreation Education. Includes environmental and outdoor education, management of leisure services, therapeutic recreation. M.S.Ed.

Second Language Education. Includes English as second language, French, Spanish. M.S.Ed.

Secondary Education (7–12). Includes biology, chemistry, earth science, English, French, mathematics, physics, physics and mathematics, social studies. M.A.T., M.S.Ed.

Teaching Students with Disabilities. Includes severe and multiple disabilities. M.S.Ed.

STATE UNIVERSITY OF NEW YORK COLLEGE AT FREDONIA

Fredonia, New York 14063

Web site: www.fredonia.edu

Established 1948. Located 45 miles from Buffalo. Coed. State control. Semester system. Library: 396,000 volumes, 2270 subscriptions.

Annual tuition: full-time, resident $5100, nonresident $8416; per credit, resident $213, nonresident $351. On-campus housing for single students only. Annual academic year housing cost: $3270; $5600 (including board). Contact Director of Housing for off-campus housing information. Phone: (716)673-3341.

Graduate Studies

Graduate study since 1956. Enrollment: full-time 85, part-time 263 (men 20%, women 80%). Graduate faculty: full-time 35, part-time 12. Degrees conferred: M.A., M.S., M.S. in Ed., M.M., C.A.S.

ADMISSION REQUIREMENTS. Transcripts, two letters of recommendation required in support of application. On-line application available. TOEFL required for international applicants. Interview sometimes required. Accepts transfer applicants. Apply to Graduate Admissions, Fenner House, by August 5 (Fall), December 1 (Spring), April 20 (Summer). Application fee $50. Phone: (716)673-3251; fax: (716)673-3249.

ADMISSION STANDARDS. Relatively open for most departments. Usual minimum average: 2.5 (A = 4).

FINANCIAL AID. Annual awards from institutional funds: graduate assistantships, various research assistantships, tuition waivers; free tuition for disadvantaged students, internships, tuition waivers, Federal W/S, loans. Approved for VA benefits. Apply by March 15 to appropriate department chair for fellowships and assistantships; to Financial Aid Office for all other programs. Phone: (716)673-3253. Use FAFSA. About 12% of students receive aid

other than loans from College and outside sources. Aid available for part-time students.

DEGREE REQUIREMENTS. For master's: 30 credits minimum, at least 15 in residence; thesis/final oral/written exam for some departments. For C.A.S.: 30 hours beyond the master's; internship; research paper.

FIELDS OF STUDY.

Biology.

Chemistry.

Education. Includes elementary, secondary teaching; most subject fields; speech pathology and audiology; reading.

Educational Administration.

English.

Interdisciplinary Studies.

Mathematics.

Music. Includes music education, performance, theory/composition.

Speech Pathology and Audiology.

STATE UNIVERSITY OF NEW YORK COLLEGE AT GENESEO

Geneseo, New York 14454-1401

Web site: www.geneseo.edu

Founded 1871. Located 30 miles S of Rochester. Coed. State control. Semester system. Library: 502,500 volumes, 2200 subscriptions. Total College enrollment: 5000.

Annual tuition: full-time resident $5100, nonresident $8416; per credit, resident $213, nonresident $351. No on-campus housing available. Day care facilities available.

Graduate Studies

Graduate study since 1952. Enrollment: full-time 42, part-time 187. Graduate faculty: full-time 38, part-time 20. Degrees conferred: M.A., M.S.Ed.

ADMISSION REQUIREMENTS. Transcripts, two letters of recommendation, interview, GRE required in support of application. TOEFL required for international applicants. Accepts transfer applicants. Apply to Graduate Studies by June 1 (Fall), October 1 (Spring), May 1 (Summer). Application fee $35. Phone: (585)245-5546; fax: (585)245-5005; e-mail: tag@geneseo.edu.

ADMISSION STANDARDS. Selective. Usual minimum average: 2.75 (A = 4).

FINANCIAL AID. Annual awards from institutional funds: fellowships, teaching assistantships, internships, Federal W/S, loans. Apply by April 1 to appropriate department chair for assistantships; to Financial Aid Office for all other programs. Phone: (585)245-5731. Use FAFSA and TAP application. About 65% of students receive aid from College and outside sources. Aid available for part-time students.

DEGREE REQUIREMENTS. For master's: 33–42 credit hours minimum; final written/oral exam or thesis.

FIELDS OF STUDY.

Biology.

Education of the Hearing Impaired. (Presently not admitting to program.)

Elementary Education.

Reading Teacher.

Secondary Education.

Special Education.

Speech Pathology.

STATE UNIVERSITY OF NEW YORK AT NEW PALTZ

New Paltz, New York 12561-2449
Web site: www.newpaltz.edu

Founded 1885. Located 80 miles N of New York City. Coed. State control. Semester system. Library: 524,000 volumes, 4900 subscriptions.

Tuition: full-time, resident $5100, nonresident $8416; per credit, resident $213, nonresident $351. On-campus housing for single students; none for married students. Average annual housing cost: $3200, $5368 (including board). Apply to Director of Residence Life. Phone: (845)257-4444. Day-care facilities available.

Graduate Division

Graduate study since 1947. Enrollment: full-time 349, part-time 1310. Faculty teaching graduate students: full-time 116, part-time 90. Degrees conferred: M.S., M.S.Ed., M.S.T., M.A.T., M.A., M.F.A., M.P.S., C.A.S.

ADMISSION REQUIREMENTS. Transcripts, GRE/MAT/ GMAT required in support of application. Provisional or permanent teaching certificate for M.S. in Ed. TOEFL required for international applicants. Interview not required. Accepts transfer applicants. Graduates of unaccredited colleges not considered. Apply to Director of Graduate Admissions at least one month prior to registration. Application fee $50. Phone: (845)257-3470.

ADMISSION STANDARDS. Selective. Usual minimum average: 3.0 (A = 4).

FINANCIAL AID. Annual awards from institutional funds: minority student scholarships, teaching assistantships, internships, tuition waivers, Federal W/S, loans. Approved for VA benefits. Apply one month prior to registration to Division chair for scholarships, assistantships; to Director of Financial Aid for all other programs. Phone: (845)257-3250. Use FAFSA. About 4% of students receive aid other than loans from School. No aid for part-time students.

DEGREE REQUIREMENTS. For master's: 30–36 semester hours minimum, at least 24 in residence; final comprehensive exam. For C.A.S.: 30 hours minimum beyond the master's.

FIELDS OF STUDY.
Art Education. M.S. Ed.
Art Studio. Includes ceramics, metal, painting, printmaking, sculpture. M.A.
Biology. M.A., M.A.T.
Business Administration. M.B.A.
Ceramics. M.F.A.
Chemistry. M.S.Ed., M.A.T.
Communication Disorders. M.S., M.S.Ed.
Computer Sciences. M.S.
Early Childhood. M.S.Ed.
Earth Science. M.A., M.A.T.
Educational Administration. M.S.Ed.
Elementary Education. M.S.Ed., M.S.T.
Electrical Engineering. M.S.
English. M.A., M.A.T.
English as a Second Language. M.A.
French. M.A.T.
Geology. M.A.
Humanistic/Multicultural Education. M.P.S. only
Mathematics. M.A., M.A.T.
Metal. M.F.A.
Nursing. M.S.

Painting. M.F.A.
Physics. M.S.Ed., M.A.T.
Printmaking. M.F.A.
Psychology. M.A.
Reading (K–12). M.S.Ed.
Sculpture. M.F.A.
Second Language Education. M.S.Ed.
Secondary Education. Includes biology, chemistry, earth science (geology), English, French, mathematics, social studies (economics, geography, history, interdisciplinary, political science), Spanish. M.S.Ed.
Social Studies. M.A.T.
Sociology. M.A.
Spanish. M.A.T.
Special Education. M.S. Ed.

STATE UNIVERSITY OF NEW YORK COLLEGE AT ONEONTA

Oneonta, New York 13820
Web site: www.oneonta.edu

Founded 1889. Located 200 miles NW of New York City. CGS member. Coed. State control. Semester system. Library: 546,700 volumes, 2200 subscriptions.

Annual tuition: full-time, resident $6000, nonresident $10,416. Limited dormitory housing for single students. No housing for married students. Average academic year housing cost: $3276. Contact Housing Office for both on- and off-campus housing information. Phone: (607)436-3725. Day-care facilities available.

Graduate Studies

Established 1948. Enrollment: full-time 36, part-time 163. College faculty teaching graduate students: full- and part-time 144. Degrees conferred: M.A., M.S., M.S.Ed., C.A.S.

ADMISSION REQUIREMENTS. Transcripts, GRE required in support of application. TOEFL required for international applicants. Accepts transfer applicants. Graduates of unaccredited institutions not considered. Apply to Graduate Office by March 15 (Summer and Fall), October 1 (Spring). Application fee $50. Phone: (800)786-9123, or (607)436-3084.

ADMISSION STANDARDS. Selective. Usual minimum average: 2.8 (A = 4).

FINANCIAL AID. Annual awards from institutional funds: fellowships, teaching assistantships, Federal W/S, loans. Apply to Financial Aid Office by April 15. Use FAFSA and TAP application. Financial aid largely in form of federal and state loan programs.

DEGREE REQUIREMENTS. For M.A., M.S.: 30–48 semester hours minimum, at least 24 in residence; reading knowledge of one foreign language sometimes required for M.A.; thesis sometimes required; written/oral comprehensive exam. For C.A.S.: 27 semester hours beyond master's; thesis required for some programs.

FIELDS OF STUDY.
Biology.
Business Economics. M.S.
Earth Science.
Education. Includes elementary (N–6), secondary (usual subject fields, K–12), counselor education.

History Museum Studies. Forty hours for M.A.; program located at Cooperstown Graduate Center.
Reading Teacher (N–12).

STATE UNIVERSITY OF NEW YORK AT OSWEGO
Oswego, New York 13126
Web site: www.oswego.edu

Founded 1861. Located 35 miles NW of Syracuse. CGS member. Coed. State control. Semester system. Library: 453,400 volumes, 1802 subscriptions.

Annual tuition: full-time, resident $5100, nonresident $8416; per credit, resident $213, nonresident $351. On-campus dormitory housing available. Average academic year housing cost: $3450, $6070 (including board). Contact Director of Housing for both on- and off-campus housing information. Phone: (315)341-2246. Day care facilities available.

Division of Graduate Studies and Research

Graduate study since 1948. Enrollment: full-time 268, part-time 577. Faculty: full-time 75, part-time 31. Degrees conferred: M.A., M.S., M.S. Ed., C.A.S., M.S.-C.A.S.

ADMISSION REQUIREMENTS. Transcripts, letters of recommendation, GRE Subject Test, GMAT required in support of application. Interview required by some departments. TOEFL required for international applicants. Accepts transfer applicants. Graduates of unaccredited colleges not considered. Apply to Office of Graduate Studies at least one month prior to registration. Application fee $50. Phone: (315)341-3152; fax: (315)341-3577.

ADMISSION STANDARDS. Selective. Usual minimum average: 3.0 (A = 4).

FINANCIAL AID. Annual awards from institutional funds: scholarships, teaching assistantships, research fellowships, internships, tuition waivers, Federal W/S, loans. Approved for VA benefits. Apply by November 15 (Spring), April 1 (Fall) to Graduate Office for scholarships, fellowships, assistantships; to Financial Aid Office for all other programs. Phone: (315)341-2248. Use FAFSA and TAP application. About 20% of students receive aid other than loans from College and outside sources.

DEGREE REQUIREMENTS. For master's: 30–36 credit hours minimum; thesis required for some programs. For C.A.S.: 60 credit hours minimum; thesis required for some programs.

FIELDS OF STUDY.
Accounting.
Art.
Art Education.
Business Administration.
Chemistry.
Chemistry Education.
Educational Administration.
Elementary Education.
English.
History.
Human Services/Counseling.
Reading Education.
School Psychology.
Secondary Education. Includes English, mathematics, science, social science.
Special Education.
Technology Education.
Vocational Teacher Preparation.

STATE UNIVERSITY OF NEW YORK AT PLATTSBURGH
Plattsburgh, New York 12901
Web site: www.plattsburgh.edu

Organized 1889. Located 60 miles S of Montreal, Canada, 160 miles N of Albany, New York. Coed. State control. Semester system. Library: 300,000 volumes, 122,000 microforms, 30 PCs.

Annual tuition: full-time, resident $5100, nonresident $8416; per credit, resident $213, nonresident $351. On-campus housing for single students only. Annual academic year housing cost: $2620-$3340. Contact the Office of Campus Life/Housing for housing information. Phone: (518)564-3824.

Graduate Studies

Graduate study since 1950. Enrollment: full-time 205, part-time 523. Faculty: full-time 49, part-time 7. Degrees conferred: M.A., M.S., C.A.S.

ADMISSION REQUIREMENTS. Transcripts, statement of purpose, three letters of reference, GRE/MAT/GMAT required in support of application. Interview required for some departments. TOEFL (minimum score 550) required for international applicants. Accepts transfer applicants. Apply to Admissions Office by March 1 (Fall) School Psychology, Counselor Education, Speech-Language Pathology; May 15 (Fall) Education, Liberal Studies; October 15 (Spring) Liberal Studies, Education, Counselor Education; February 15 (Summer) Counselor Education, Speech-Language Pathology. Application fee $50. Phone: (518)564-4723; fax: (518)564- 4722; e-mail: graduate@plattsburgh.edu.

ADMISSION STANDARDS. Selective. Usual minimum average: 2.5 (A = 4).

FINANCIAL AID. Annual awards from institutional funds: assistantships. Federal W/S, loans. Approved for VA benefits. Apply to Office of Financial Aid; no specified closing date. Phone: (518)564-2072; fax: (518)564-4079. Use FAFSA and TAP application. About 1% of students receive aid other than loans from College, 27% from all sources.

DEGREE REQUIREMENTS. For M.A., M.S.: 30 credits minimum, at least 18 in residence. For C.A.S.: 60 credits.

FIELDS OF STUDY.
Administration and Leadership.
Biology (7–12).
Chemistry (7–12).
Community Counseling.
Curriculum and Instruction.
Elementary and Early Secondary Education.
Elementary Education (PreK–6). Includes English, general science, mathematics, social studies.
English (7–12).
English Language and Literature.
Historical Studies.
Natural Sciences.
Reading Teacher.
School Counselor.
School Psychologist.
Secondary Education. Includes biology, chemistry, earth science, English, French, mathematics, physics, social studies, Spanish.
Social Studies (7–12).
Special Education.
Speech-Language Pathology.
Student Affairs Practice in Higher Education.

STATE UNIVERSITY OF NEW YORK COLLEGE AT POTSDAM

Potsdam, New York 13676
Web site: www.potsdam.edu

Founded 1816. Located 120 miles NW of Albany. Coed. State control. Semester system. Library: 325,000 volumes, 1300 subscriptions.

Annual tuition: full-time, resident $5100, nonresident $8416; per credit, resident $213, nonresident $351. On-campus housing available for graduate students. Annual housing cost: $3520, $6100 (including board). Apply to Director of Residence Life. Phone: (315)267-2350. On-campus day-care facilities available.

Graduate Studies

Enrollment: full-time 287, part-time 282. College faculty teaching graduate students: full-time 48. Degrees conferred: M.A, M.S.Ed., M.M., M.S.T.

ADMISSION REQUIREMENTS. Transcripts, NYSTCE required in support of application. TOEFL required for international applicants. Accepts transfer applicants. Graduates of unaccredited institutions not considered. Apply to Admissions Office by April 1 (Summer and Fall), October 15 (Spring) for M.S. Ed., M.S.T.; no specified closing date for M.A., M.M. Application fee $50. Phone: (315)267-2180; fax: (315)267-4802.

ADMISSION STANDARDS. Usual minimum average: 2.75 (A = 4) final 60 semester credits of undergraduate studies.

FINANCIAL AID. Scholarships, graduate assistantships, minority graduate fellowships, Federal W/S, loans. Approved for VA benefits. Apply to the Financial Aid Office; no specified closing date. Phone: (315)267-2162. Use FAFSA. Aid available for part-time students.

DEGREE REQUIREMENTS. For master's: 30–33 credits minimum, 24 in residence. For M.S.T.: 42 credits minimum.

FIELDS OF STUDY.

SCHOOL OF ARTS AND SCIENCES:
English. M.A.
Mathematics. M.A.

SCHOOL OF EDUCATION:
Elementary Education. M.S.Ed., M.S.T.
General Professional Education. M.S.Ed.
Instruction Technology. M.S.Ed.
Media Management. M.S.Ed.
Reading. M.S.Ed.
Secondary Education. Includes biology, chemistry, English, earth science, mathematics, physics, social studies. M.S.Ed., M.S.T.
Special Education. M.S.Ed.

CRANE SCHOOL OF MUSIC:
Composition. M.M.
Music Education. M.M.
Music History and Literature. M.M.
Music Theory. M.M.
Performance. M.M.

STATE UNIVERSITY OF NEW YORK COLLEGE OF ENVIRONMENTAL SCIENCE AND FORESTRY AT SYRACUSE

Syracuse, New York 13210-2779
Web site: www.esf.edu

Coed. State control. Semester system. Special facilities: Archer and Anna Huntington Wildlife Forest, Adirondack Ecological Center, Cranberry Lake Biological Station, Empire State Paper Research Institute, Heiberg Memorial Forest, Wanakena Campus, Institute of Environmental Program Affairs, State University Polymer Research Center, U.S. Forest Service Cooperative Research Unit. Library: 130,300 volumes, 2000 subscriptions.

Annual tuition (9 months): resident $5100, nonresident $8416; per credit, resident $213, nonresident $351. On-campus housing available for married and single students. Housing cost: married students $500–$640 per month, single $4170, $8310 (including board). Phone: (315)443-2567. Day-care facilities available.

Graduate Studies

Graduate study since 1913. Enrollment: full-time 272, part-time 203. College faculty: full- and part-time 121. Degrees conferred: M.L.A., M.P.S., M.S., Ph.D.

ADMISSION REQUIREMENTS. Transcripts, GRE, bachelor's degree, three letters of reference, statement of educational objectives required in support of application. GRE Subject test for some programs. Interview desirable. TOEFL required of international students. Accepts transfer applicants. Apply to Office of Instruction and Graduate Studies by April 15 (Fall), November 15 (Spring). Application fee $50. Phone: (315)470-6599; fax: (315)470-6978; E-mail: esfgrad@esfedu.

ADMISSION STANDARDS. Very selective for most departments. Usual minimum average: 3.0 (A = 4).

FINANCIAL AID. Annual awards from institutional funds: teaching assistantships, research assistantships, fellowships, internships, Federal W/S, loans. Apply to Financial Aid Office; no specific closing date. Phone: (315)470-6670. Use FAFSA. About 70% of students receive aid other than loans from outside sources.

DEGREE REQUIREMENTS. For M.S. and M.L.A.: 30–37 semester hours minimum; thesis; project; oral exam. For M.P.S.: 30–39 semester hours minimum; internship or course work and comprehensive exam or terminal experience depending on area of study. For Ph.D.: 60 credit, three-year program beyond the bachelor's; written/oral candidacy exam; advancement to dissertation; oral exam. Additional requirements upon decision of student's program director.

FIELDS OF STUDY.
Environmental and Forest Biology. Includes ecology, entomology, environmental physiology, fish and wildlife biology and management, forest pathology and mycology, plant science and biotechnology, and chemical ecology. M.P.S.
Environmental and Forest Chemistry. Includes forest chemistry, biochemistry, environmental chemistry, organic chemistry of natural products, and polymer chemistry.
Environmental and Resource Engineering. Includes forest engineering, paper science engineering, and wood products engineering. M.P.S.
Environmental Science. Includes environmental land planning, environmental policy and democratic processes, environmental modeling and risk analysis, and water resources management. M.P.S.

Forest Resources Management. Includes forest management, recreation and tourism, policy and administration, forest economics, quantitative methods, silvics, silviculture, forest soil science, tree improvement, international forestry, urban forestry, watershed management/hydrology, and forest information management.

Landscape Architecture. Includes course work in social/behavioral studies, natural/physical applied science, design process, methods and management. M.L.A.

STATE UNIVERSITY OF NEW YORK DOWNSTATE MEDICAL CENTER AT BROOKLYN

Brooklyn, New York 11203-2098
Web site: www.downstate.edu

Founded 1860; merged with State University of New York in 1950. Name changed 1986. Coed. State control. Semester system. The Center's NIH ranking is 139th among all U.S. institutions with 60 awards/grants worth $23,510,464. Medical library: 357,200 volumes, 2104 subscriptions. Total Center enrollment: 1064.

College of Graduate Studies

Annual tuition: resident $5420, nonresident $10,970. Enrollment: full-time 88, part-time 1 (men 66%, women 33%). Faculty: full-time 115, part-time none. Degrees conferred: M.S., Ph.D.

ADMISSIONS REQUIREMENTS. Transcripts, three letters of recommendation, GRE required in support of application. TOEFL, TSE required for international applicants. Interview may be arranged. Accepts transfer applicants. Apply to Office Graduate Studies by July 1. Application fee $35. Phone: (718)270-2738; fax: (718)270-3378.

ADMISSION STANDARDS. Competitive. Usual minimum average: 3.0 (A = 4).

FINANCIAL AID. Fellowships, research assistantships, teaching assistantships, internships, full and partial tuition waivers, Federal W/S, loans. Apply to Office of Financial Aid, no specified closing date. Use FAFSA.

DEGREE REQUIREMENTS. For M.S.: 30 credit hours; no residency required; thesis defense. For Ph.D.: 90 credit hours beyond bachelor's, 24 credit hours in full-time residency; qualifying exam; dissertation defense.

FIELDS OF STUDY.
Anatomy.
Biochemistry.
Biophysics.
Cell Biology.
Immunology.
Microbiology.
Neurosciences.
Pharmacology.
Physiology.

College of Medicine

Founded 1860. Annual tuition: resident $12,840, nonresident $24,940; student fees $1393. Enrollment: first-year class 185 (EDP 20), total 769 (men 51%, women 49%). Faculty: full- and part-time and volunteers approximately 2500. Degrees conferred: B.A.-M.D. (with Brooklyn College), M.D., M.D.-Ph.D.

ADMISSION REQUIREMENTS. AMCAS report, transcripts, letters of recommendation, MCAT required in support of application. Has EDP; apply between June 1 and August 1. Interviews by invitation only. Applicants must have completed at least three years of college study. Preference given to state residents. Apply to Office of Admissions after June 1, before December 15. Application fee $65. Phone: (718)270-2446; fax: (718)270-7592.

ADMISSION STANDARDS. Competitive. Mean MCAT: 9.6; median GPA: 3.57 (A = 4). Gourman rating: 3.71. Accepts 8% of total annual applicants. Approximately 90% are state residents.

FINANCIAL AID. Scholarships, fellowships, grants, loans, work-study. Financial aid application materials are sent to all selected applicants. Use FAFSA (School code: 002839) and institutional application. About 85% of students receive some aid from College.

DEGREE REQUIREMENTS. For M.D.: satisfactory completion of four-year program. All students must pass USMLE Step 1 prior to entering third year.

STATE UNIVERSITY OF NEW YORK INSTITUTE OF TECHNOLOGY AT UTICA/ROME

Utica, New York 13504-3050
Web site: www.sunyit.edu

Founded 1966. Coed. State control. Upper Division institution. Semester system. Library: 193,600 volumes, 1090 subscriptions. Total Institute enrollment: 2660.

Annual tuition: full-time resident $5779, nonresident $9095; per credit resident $233, nonresident $731. On-campus housing available for graduate students. Annual housing cost: $4080, $6430 (including board). Apply to Director of Residence Life.

Graduate Studies (P.O. Box 3050)

Enrollment: full-time 86, part-time 384. College faculty teaching graduate students: full-time 54, part-time 7. Degrees conferred: M.S., M.S.A.T.

ADMISSION REQUIREMENTS. Transcripts, GRE/MAT required in support of application. TOEFL (minimum score 550) required for international applicants. Accepts transfer applicants. Graduates of unaccredited institutions not considered. Apply to Director of Admission by June 15 (Fall), November 15 (Spring). Application fee $50. Phone: (315)792-7500, fax (315)792-7837; e-mail: admission@sunyit.edu.

ADMISSION STANDARDS. Usual minimum average: 2.75 (A = 4) final 60 semester credits of undergraduate studies.

FINANCIAL AID. Assistantships, graduate minority fellowships, tuition waivers, Federal W/S, loans. Approved for VA benefits. Apply to the Financial Aid Office; no specified closing date. Use FAFSA. Aid available for part-time students.

DEGREE REQUIREMENTS. For master's: 30–36 credits minimum, 24 in residence; professional project.

FIELDS OF STUDY.

SCHOOL OF ARTS AND SCIENCES:
Applied Sociology.
Information Design and Technology.

SCHOOL OF INFORMATION SYSTEMS AND ENGINEERING TECHNOLOGY:

Advanced Technology. Interdisciplinary. M.S.A.T.
Computer and Information Science.
Telecommunications.

SCHOOL OF MANAGEMENT:

Accountancy. Includes corporate accounting, government accounting, not-for-profit accounting.
Business Management. Includes health services management, human resources management, research/MIS.
Finance.
Health Services Administration.
Management Accounting.
Marketing.

STATE UNIVERSITY OF NEW YORK UPSTATE MEDICAL UNIVERSITY AT SYRACUSE

Syracuse, New York 13210-2334

Founded 1834; merged with State University of New York in 1950. Name changed in 1986. Name changed to Upstate Medical University in 1999. CGS member. Coed. State control. Semester system. The University's NIH ranking is 192nd among all U.S. institutions with 52 awards/grants worth $12,710,110. Library: 132,500 volumes, 1800 subscriptions. Total University enrollment: 950.

On-campus housing available for both single and married students. Annual academic year housing cost: $4200 for single students, $4800 for married students.

College of Graduate Studies

Annual tuition: resident $5100, nonresident $8416. Enrollment: full-time 92, part time 5 (men 48%, women 52%). Center faculty: 80. Degrees conferred: M.S., Ph.D., M.D.-Ph.D.

ADMISSION REQUIREMENTS. Transcripts, three letters of recommendation, GRE required in support of College's application. TOEFL, TSE required for international applicants. Interviews may be arranged. Accepts transfer applicants. Graduates of unaccredited institutions not considered. Apply to Office of Graduate Studies by February 1. Application fee $40. Phone: (315)464-4538; fax: (315)464-4544; e-mail: gradstud@mail.upstate.edu.

ADMISSION STANDARDS. Competitive. Usual minimum average: 3.0 (A = 4).

FINANCIAL AID. Predoctoral fellowships, graduate/research assistantships, tuition waivers, Federal W/S, loans. Approved for VA benefits. Contact Office of the Dean for information. Use FAFSA.

DEGREE REQUIREMENTS. For M.S.: 30 credit hours; no residency required; thesis defense. For Ph.D.: 90 credit hours, 24 credit hours in full-time residency; qualifying exam; dissertation defense. For M.D. requirements refer to College of Medicine listing below.

FIELDS OF STUDY.
Anatomy and Cell Biology.
Biochemistry and Molecular Biology.
Cell Biology and Developmental Biology.
Cell Biology and Molecular Biology.
Microbiology and Immunology.
Neuroscience.
Pharmacology.
Physiology.

College of Medicine

Annual tuition; resident $12,840, nonresident $25,940; student fees $740. Total average cost for all other expenses: $7500. On-campus housing for 235 married students, 90 men, 90 women. Apply to Director of Housing. Phone: (315)464-6498.

Enrollment: first-year class 156 (EDP 5); total 633 (men 55%, women 45%). Faculty: about 600. Degrees conferred: M.D., M.D.-Ph.D., M.S.T.P. (Medical Scientist Training Program).

ADMISSION REQUIREMENTS. AMCAS report, transcripts, MCAT, recommendations required in support of application. Interview by invitation only. Applicants must have completed at least three years of college study. Preference given to state residents. Has EDP; apply between June 1 and August 1. Apply to Admissions Committee after June 1, before November 1 (firm). Application fee $100. Phone: (315)464-4570; fax: (315)464-8867.

ADMISSION STANDARDS. Competitive. Mean MCAT: 9.0; mean GPA: 3.54 (A = 4). Gourman rating: 3.69. Accepts 10% of total annual applicants. Approximately 90% are state residents.

FINANCIAL AID. Scholarships, grants, tuition waivers, loans. Apply to Office of Admissions and Student Affairs by May 1. Phone: (315)464-4329. Use FAFSA (College code: 002840) and ACT needs analysis. About 35% of students receive aid other than loans from College.

DEGREE REQUIREMENTS. For M.D.: satisfactory completion of four-year program. All students must pass USMLE Step 1 and take Step 2.

NEW YORK UNIVERSITY

New York, New York 10276-0907
Web site: www.nyu.edu

Founded 1831. CGS and AAU member. Coed. Private control. Semester system. Special facilities: Center for Latin American and Caribbean Studies, Institute for Developmental Studies, Maison Française, Courant Institute of Mathematical Sciences, National Academy of Television Arts and Sciences Archives, Institute of French Studies, Institute of Physical Medicine and Rehabilitation, Grey Art Gallery, Institute of Fine Arts, Murray and Leonie Guggenheim Foundation, Institute for Dental Research, C. J. Devine Institute of Finance, C.V. Starr Center for Applied Economics, Hargop Kevorkian Center for Near Eastern Studies, Institute of Retail Management, Institute of Planning and Housing, Institute of Labor Relations, Institute of Environmental Medicine, Henry W. and Albert A. Berg Institute for Experimental Physiology, Surgery, and Pathology, Institute of Judicial Administration, Institute of International Law, Copyright Publications Center, Onassis Center for Hellenic Studies. The University's NIH ranking is 40th among all U.S. institutions with 371 awards/grants worth $117,362,281. University libraries: 4,500,000 volumes, 32,700 subscriptions. Total University enrollment: 50,000.

Limited on-campus housing for married students, 602 graduate men and women. Housing cost: $600–$850 per month for married students, $10,250–$13,600 per academic year for single students. Apply to Office of Director of Housing. Phone: (212)998-4600.

Graduate School of Arts and Sciences

Graduate study since 1886. Tuition: per credit $855. Enrollment: full-time 2367, part-time 1589. School faculty: full-time 597, part-time 393. Degrees conferred: M.A., M.Phil., M.S., Ph.D.

ADMISSION REQUIREMENTS. Transcripts, three letters of recommendation required in support of School's application. Interview, GRE, TSE required for some departments. TOEFL required for international applicants. Accepts transfer applicants. Graduates of unaccredited institutions not considered. Apply to Office of Graduate Enrollment Services by January 4 (priority deadline). International applicants apply to International Student Center by November 1. Application fee $60. Phone: (212)998-8050; fax: (212)995-4557; e-mail: gsas.admission@nyu.edu.

ADMISSION STANDARDS. Selective to very competitive. Usual minimum average: 3.3 (A = 4).

FINANCIAL AID. Annual awards from institutional funds: scholarships, grants, fellowships, teaching/research/administrative assistantships, tuition waivers, Federal W/S, loans. Multi-year fellowships available for Ph.D. students. Approved for VA benefits. Apply by January 4 to Fellowship Office for scholarships, internships, and fellowships; to appropriate department head for assistantships; to Financial Aid Office for Federal W/S, loans. Phone: (212)998-4486. Use FAFSA. About 30% of students receive aid other than loans from School.

DEGREE REQUIREMENTS. For M.A., M.S., M.Phil.: 32 credits minimum, at least 24 in residence; reading knowledge of one foreign language; thesis for most departments; final written exam for some departments. For Ph.D.: 72 credits minimum beyond the bachelor's, at least 32 in residence; reading knowledge of two foreign languages for most departments; qualifying exam; dissertation; final oral exam.

FIELDS OF STUDY.
Africana Studies.
American Studies.
Anthropology. Research papers, oral exam for M.A.
Basic Medical Sciences. Includes anatomy, biochemistry, biophysics, microbiology, pathology, pharmacology, physiology; combined M.D.-Ph.D. programs available.
Biology. Includes training program in basic cancer research, cell and molecular, developmental, environmental, evolutionary, physiology, neurobiology, population biology; preliminary oral exam for Ph.D.
Biomaterials Science.
Biomedical Science.
Chemistry.
Cinema Studies.
Classics. Includes Greek, Latin, Byzantine, and Hellenic studies.
Comparative Literature. Three languages for Ph.D.
Computer Science.
Creative Writing.
Economics.
English. Essay required for M.A. in lieu of thesis.
Environmental Health Sciences.
Ergonomics and Biomechanics.
European Studies. M.A. only.
Fine Arts. Includes history of art, archaeology, conservation, anatorial studies; creative art major offered by School of Education; French and German for M.A.; for Ph.D. in Far Eastern art and archaeology, competence in Chinese/Japanese for Ph.D. in Near Eastern art and archaeology, reading knowledge of Arabic and Persian, or Akkadian/Sumerian; written comprehensive exam for M.A.; final oral/written exam for Ph.D.
French Studies.
Germanic Languages and Literatures.
Hebrew and Judaic Studies.
History.
Humanities and Social Thought.
Italian.
Journalism. M.A. only.
Latin American and Caribbean Studies. M.A. only.

Law and Society.
Linguistics.
Mathematics. Thesis/nonthesis options for M.S.
Middle Eastern Studies.
Museum Studies. Certificate program only.
Music. Includes musicology, theory, composition.
Near Eastern Studies. M.A. only.
Neural Science. Ph.D. only.
Performance Studies.
Philosophy. M.A. only.
Physics.
Poetics and Theory.
Politics. Includes international relations; regional study programs are available.
Psychology. Includes chemical, developmental, individual and organizational, social.
Religious Studies. M.A. only.
Russian and Slavic Studies. Includes Russian; written comprehensive exam for M.A. in Russian; qualifying exam for Ph.D. in Slavic philology and linguistics.
Sociology.
Spanish and Portuguese Languages and Literatures.

Tisch School of the Arts—Graduate Division
721 Broadway, 7th Floor, 10003-6807

Graduate study since 1968. Semester system.
Annual tuition: full-time $27,564. On-campus housing available. Average academic year housing cost: $10,500.
Enrollment: full-time 793, part-time 49. School faculty teaching graduate students: full-time 76. Degrees conferred: M.F.A., M.P.S. The M.A., Ph.D. awarded through the Graduate School of Arts and Sciences.

ADMISSION REQUIREMENTS. Transcripts, two or three letters of recommendation, interview/audition or portfolio required in support of School's application. Deadlines vary. Please consult Office of Graduate Admissions at (212)998-1918. Application fee $50. Admits Fall only. Apply to Director of Graduate Admission, 721 Broadway, 7th Floor, New York, NY 10003-6807. Phone: (212)998-1918; fax: (212)995-4060; e-mail: tisch.gradadmissions@nyu.edu.

ADMISSION STANDARDS. Competitive. Evidence of professional promise.

FINANCIAL AID. Annual awards from institutional funds: fellowships, graduate teaching assistantships, funded awards, internships, grants, tuition waivers, Federal W/S, loans. Apply by February 1 to Financial Aid Office. Phone: (212)998-1900; fax: (212)995-4060. Use FAFSA and Tisch FAF.

DEGREE REQUIREMENTS. For M.F.A.: Design, 108 credits; Dance, 72 credits; Acting, 108 credits; Dramatic Writing, 70 credits; Film, 108 credits; Musical Theater, 72 credits. For M.P.S.: Interactive Telecommunications, 60 credits. For M.A., Ph.D., see Graduate School of Arts and Sciences listing above.

FIELDS OF STUDY.
Cinema Studies. M.A., Ph.D.
Dramatic Writing. Includes writing for film, theater, television.
Film and Television. Includes film production-direction, cinematography, animation degree program by advisement.
Interactive Telecommunications. Focus on application of new media and telecommunications technologies.
Performance Studies. M.A., Ph.D.
Theater. Includes acting, dance, design, musical.

Leonard N. Stern School of Business Administration, Graduate Division
Web site: www.stern.nyu.edu

Graduate study since 1916. Semester system. Located at 44 West 4th Street, New York, NY 10012-1126. Tuition: per credit $1130. Enrollment: full-time 1210, part-time 1937. Faculty: full-time 215, part-time 109. Degrees conferred: M.S. (Accounting), M.B.A., Ph.D.

ADMISSION REQUIREMENTS. Transcripts, letters of recommendation, GMAT, personal essay, résumé required in support of application. Interview by invitation only. TOEFL (minimum score 600) required for international applicants. Graduates of unaccredited colleges not considered. Apply to Admissions Office of the School by February 1 (Ph.D. only), March 15 (Fall), May 15 (part-time only Fall), September 15 domestic (part-time only Spring). Application fee $100, international students $75. Phone: (212)998-0600; fax: (212)995-4231.

ADMISSION STANDARDS. Very selective. Mean undergraduate average: 3.32 (A = 4); mean GMAT: 646. Gourman rating: M.B.A. 4.80; Ph.D. 4.82. *U.S. News & World Report* ranking is in the top 13 of all U.S. business schools. *Business Week* ranked Stern in the top 15 of all U.S. business schools.

FINANCIAL AID. Annual awards from institutional funds; scholarships, research fellowships, graduate assistantships, internships, tuition waivers, Federal W/S, loans. Approved for VA benefits. Apply by January 15 to the Office of Financial Aid. Use FAFSA (School code: 002785). About 40% of students receive aid other than loans from School and outside sources. Loans available for part-time students.

DEGREE REQUIREMENTS. For M.B.A.: 60 credits (20 courses) plus comprehensive business project; calculus, computer economics and business writing proficiencies. For M.S. in Accounting: 60 credits. For Ph.D.: 72 credits.

FIELDS OF STUDY.
Accounting.
Business Administration.
Economics.
Finance.
Information Systems.
International Business. Multidisciplinary program.
Management.
Marketing.
Operations Management.
Statistics and Operations Research.

College of Dentistry—David B. Kriser Dental Center
Web site: www.nyu.edu/dental.nyu

Founded 1865. Located 345 East 24th St, New York 10010.
Annual tuition: $38,516. On-campus housing for married students, men, women. Average academic year housing cost: $19,000. Apply to Office of the Manager, Hall of Residence, New York University Medical Center. Total average cost for all other first-year expenses: $5000.
Enrollment: D.D.S. program: first-year class 228 (men 50%, women 50%); total 618; postgraduates 80. Faculty: full-time 135, part-time 455. Degrees conferred: A.B.-D.D.S., D.D.S., D.D.S.-M.S. (Management), D.D.S.-M.B.A., Advanced Education Programs.

ADMISSION REQUIREMENTS. For D.D.S. program: AAD-SAS, transcripts, three letters of recommendation, DAT required in support of College's application. Interviews by invitation only. Applicants must have completed at least three years of college study. TOEFL required for international applicants. Accepts transfer applicants from U.S. and Canadian dental Schools. International transfer applicants accepted into a three-year program only. Apply to Director of Admissions after July 15, before June 1. Fall admission only. Application fee $35. Phone: (212)998-9818; fax: (212)995-4240. For Certificate programs: official transcripts, two letters of recommendation, D.D.S. or D.M.D., interview required in support of College's application. Apply to Director of Advanced Education of School by March 31. Fall admission only.

ADMISSION STANDARDS. Selective. Usual minimum average: 3.0 (A = 4). Mean DAT: Academic 17.54, PAT 16.23; mean GPA: 3.28 (A = 4). Gourman rating: 4.64. Accepts 25–30% of total annual applicants. Approximately 65% are state residents.

FINANCIAL AID. Scholarships, grants, loans. Apply by March 1 to Dental Center Financial Aid Office after acceptance. Phone: (212)998-9825. Use FAFSA (College code: 002785). About 100% of students receive some aid from College and outside sources.

DEGREE REQUIREMENTS. For A.B.-D.D.S.: satisfactory completion of seven-year program. For D.D.S.: satisfactory completion of forty-five-month program. For Advanced Education Programs: varies by program.

FIELDS OF GRADUATE STUDY.
Biomaterial Science. M.S.
Clinical Research. M.S.
Endodontics. A.E.P.
Implant Dentistry. A.E.P.
Oral and Maxillofacial Surgery. A.E.P.
Oral Biology. M.S.
Orthodontics. A.E.P.
Pediatric Dentistry. A.E.P.
Periodontics. A.E.P.
Prosthodontics. A.E.P.

The Steinhardt School of Education— Graduate Division
Web site: www.education.nyu.edu

Graduate study since 1980. Semester system. Special facilities: Center for Research and Community Service, Center for Nursing Research, Center for the Study of American Culture and Education, Center for Urban Community College Leadership, Metropolitan Center for Urban Education, New York University Institute for Education and Social Policy, Reading Recovery Teacher Leader Training Center.
Tuition: per credit $834. Enrollment: full-time 1728, part-time 2425. School faculty: full-time 234, part-time 536. Degrees conferred: M.A., M.S., M.P.H., Sixth-Year Certificate, D.A., Ed.D., Psy.D., Ph.D.

ADMISSION REQUIREMENTS. Transcripts required in support of application. GRE required for all doctoral applicants. TOEFL (minimum score 550) required for all non-native speakers of English. Interview required for some graduate applicants. Apply to School of Education, Graduate Admissions, by March 1 for master's and February 1 for doctoral programs (Fall), and December 1 for master's only (Spring). Application fee $40, international students $60. Phone: (212)998-5030; fax: (212)995-4328.

ADMISSION STANDARDS. Selective to very selective (varies by program).

FINANCIAL AID. Annual awards from institutional funds: fellowships, teaching and research assistantships, graduate assistantships, internships, tuition waivers, Federal W/S, loans. Approved for VA benefits. Apply by March 1 for Fall term and by November 1 for Spring term to Office of Graduate Admissions. Phone: (212)998-4444. Use FAFSA, and New York State residents use TAP application. About 44% of full-time students receive aid other than loans from University and outside sources. Aid available for part-time students.

DEGREE REQUIREMENTS. For M.A.: 34 credits minimum without thesis, at least 24 in residence; or 30 credits minimum plus thesis, at least 24 in residence. For Sixth-Year Certificate: 30 credits minimum beyond a 34-credit master's degree, at least 24 credits in residence. For Ph.D., Ed.D., Psy.D., D.A.: 30 credit basic core, plus department requirements, at least 54 credits in residence beyond bachelor's, at least 30 credits in residence beyond master's; departmental candidacy exam; final oral exam; tool requirement for research; research proposal; dissertation; one or two semesters in full-time residence for some departments.

FIELDS OF STUDY.
Art Education.
Art Therapy.
Arts and Humanities Education.
Bilingual Education.
Business Education.
Counseling and Guidance.
Counseling Psychology.
Dance Education.
Deafness Rehabilitation.
Drama Therapy.
Educational Administration.
Educational Communication and Technology.
Educational Psychology.
Educational Theatre.
English Education.
Environmental Conservation Education.
Food Studies and Food Management.
Foreign Language Education.
Graphic Communications Management and Technology.
Health Education.
Higher Education Administration.
History of Education.
International Education.
Media Ecology—Studies in Communication.
Music Business.
Music Education.
Music Performance and Composition.
Music Technology.
Music Therapy.
Nursing.
Nursing Science—Research and Theory Development. Ph.D.
Nutrition and Dietetics.
Occupational Therapy.
Performing Arts Administration.
Philosophy of Education.
Physical Therapy.
Psychology Development.
Public Health Nutrition.
Rehabilitation Counseling.
School Psychology.
Science Education.
Social Studies Education.
Sociology of Education.
Special Education.
Speech and Interpersonal Communication.
Speech-Language Pathology.
Studio Art.
Teaching and Learning.
TESOL
Visual Arts Administration.
Visual Culture.

School of Law
Web site: www.law.nyu.edu

Established 1835. Located at the Washington Square campus. ABA approved since 1930. AALS member. Semester system. Full-time, day study only. Special facilities: Center for International Studies, Center for Research in Crime and Justice, Public Interest Center, Institute for Judicial Administration. Special programs: Global Law Program, Arthur Garfield Hays Civil Liberties Program, Program for Study of Law Philosophy and Social Theory, Program on Philanthropy and the Law. Law library: 1,023,016 volumes, 6987 subscriptions; has LEXIS, NEXIS, WESTLAW, DIALOG; is a Federal Government Depository.

Annual tuition: $30,024; LL.M. and J.S.D $16,225, per credit $1504. On-campus housing available for both single and married students. Law School has more than 400 on-campus accommodations. Annual on-campus housing cost: $19,025. Contact Law School Residence Hall for both on- and off-campus housing information. Many law students live in off-campus housing. Off-campus housing and personal expenses: approximately $18,555.

Enrollment: first-year class 426; total full-time 1368 (men 50%, women 50%). Faculty: full-time 91, part-time 56. Student to faculty ratio 12.5 to 1. Degrees conferred: J.D., J.D.-M.B.A., J.D.-M.P.A. (Princeton University or NYU), J.D.-M.U.P., J.D.-M.S.W., J.D.-LL.M., LL.M. (Corporate Law, International Legal Studies, International Tax Program for Foreign Students, Taxation, Trade Regulations), LL.M.C.J. (only for persons who have completed a basic legal education and received a university degree in law in another country), J.S.D.

ADMISSION REQUIREMENTS. For J.D.: LSDAS Law School report, bachelor's degree, transcripts, LSAT, three letters of recommendation required in support of application. Interview not required or encouraged. Evidence of proficiency in English required for international applicants. Accepts transfer applicants. Apply to Committee on Admissions of the School by February 1 (Fall), October 15 (Spring). Accepts full-time students only. Application fee $65. Phone: (212)998-6060; fax: (212)995-4527. For graduate program: transcripts in support of application. English language proficiency evaluation by American Language Institute at NYU for international applicants. Apply to Graduate Office of School by August 10 (Fall), December 10 (Spring), May 10 (Summer).

ADMISSION STANDARDS. Very competitive for J.D. Mean LSAT: 169; mean GPA: 3.68 (A = 4). Gourman rating: 4.76. *U.S. News & World Report* ranking is in the top five of all U.S. law schools. Accepts 15–20% of total annual applications. For graduate programs: accepts 65% of total annual applicants.

FINANCIAL AID. For J.D.: scholarships, Federal W/S, loans. Apply to Committee on Admissions by April 15. About 50% of students receive aid other than loans from School. For graduate program: fellowships, assistantships; apply to Financial Aid Office of the School by May 1. Use FAFSA (School code: 002785). About 25% of students receive aid other than loans from School. Public service loan forgiveness plan available.

DEGREE REQUIREMENTS. For J.D.: 82 semester hours minimum, six semesters in full-time residence. For LL.M.: at least 24 credit hours beyond the J.D. minimum, at least 16 in residence. For LL.M.C.J.: at least one year in full-time residence; essay; for foreign lawyers other than those trained in Common Law countries. For J.S.D.: an NYU LL.M. required; 36 credit hours minimum, at least one year in full-time residence; advancement to candidacy; oral exam; dissertation. Refer to other Graduate School listings for joint degree requirements.

FIELDS OF GRADUATE STUDY.
Comparative Jurisprudence. Open only to lawyers whose training is in civil law.

Corporation Law
General Studies.
International Legal Studies.
International Taxation.
Labor and Employment Law.
Public Service Law.
Taxation.
Trade Regulation.
Note: Joint degree program in public affairs with Woodrow Wilson School, Princeton University, also available.

School of Medicine (P.O. Box 1924)

Web site: www.med.nyu

Organized 1841. Located 550 First Avenue, New York 10016. Annual tuition: $24,620, student fees $4700. On-campus housing for married students, men and women. Apply to Housing Department, New York University Medical Center. Total average figure for all other expenses: $12,000.

Enrollment: first-year class 160 (men 54%, women 46%); total 595. Faculty: full-time 663, part-time 105. Degrees conferred: M.D., M.D.-Ph.D. (Medical Scientist Training Program).

ADMISSION REQUIREMENTS. Transcripts, two letters of recommendation, MCAT, screening interview required in support of application. Interview for serious candidates only. Applicants must have completed at least three years of college study. TOEFL required for foreign applicants. Does not have EDP. Accepts transfer applicants. Graduates of unaccredited colleges not considered. Apply to Office of Admissions of School after August 15, before November 15. Foreign students apply to International Student Center. Fall admission only. Application fee $75. Phone: (212)263-5290; fax: (212)725-2140.

ADMISSION STANDARDS. Competitive. Mean MCAT: 11.0; mean GPA: 3.7 (A = 4). Gourman rating: 4.62. *U.S. News & World Report* ranking is in the top 26 of all U.S. medical schools. Accepts about 10–12% of total annual applicants. Approximately 55% are state residents.

FINANCIAL AID. Scholarships, research fellowships, assistantships, Federal W/S, loans, MSTP funded by NIH. Apply to Office of the Associate Dean; no specified closing date. Phone: (212)263-5286. Use FAFSA (School code: G24543). About 48% of students receive aid other than loans from School.

DEGREE REQUIREMENTS. For M.D.: satisfactory completion of four-year program, at least two years in residence. For M.D.-Ph.D.: consult Director, Institute of Graduate Biomedical Sciences.

FIELDS OF GRADUATE STUDY.
Biochemistry.
Biophysics.
Cell Biology.
Genetics.
Microbiology.
Molecular Biology.
Neurosciences.
Pathology.
Pharmacology.
Physiology.

Robert F. Wagner Graduate School of Public Service

Web site: www.wagner.nyu.edu

Established 1938. Semester system. Tuition: per credit $627. Enrollment: full-time 321, part-time 523 (men 318, women 526).

Faculty: full-time 27, part-time 40. Degrees conferred: M.S., M.P.A., M.U.P., Ph.D., Advanced Professional Certificates.

ADMISSION REQUIREMENTS. Transcripts required in support of application. GRE required for doctoral students. Interview not required. TOEFL, TWE required for international applicants. Accepts transfer applicants. Graduates of unaccredited institutions not considered. Apply to Office of Admissions of School by July 15 (Fall), January 1 (Spring). Application fee $50, $70 for international applicants. Phone: (212)998-7414; fax: (212)995-4164.

ADMISSION STANDARDS. Selective. Usual minimum average: 3.0 (A = 4); 3.3–3.5 for doctoral applicants.

FINANCIAL AID. Annual awards from institutional funds: scholarships, fellowships, research assistantships, internships, tuition waivers, Federal W/S, loans. Approved for VA benefits. Apply by February 15 to Office of Admissions. Phone: (212)998-4486. Use FAFSA. About 40% of students receive aid other than loans from School and outside sources. Aid available for part-time students.

DEGREE REQUIREMENTS. For M.P.A., M.U.P.: 60 credits minimum, at least 32 in residence; capstone project. For Ph.D.: 72 credits minimum beyond the bachelor's, at least 32 in residence; written preliminary exam; three comprehensive written exams; foreign language or advanced statistics; dissertation; final oral exam. For Adv. Prof. Cert.: 20 credits minimum beyond the master's, at least 15 in residence.

FIELDS OF STUDY.
Health Policy and Management.
Infrastructure Management.
Management.
Management/International.
Public and Nonprofit Management and Policy.
Urban Planning.

Shirley M. Ehrenkranz School of Social Work

Established in 1960. Semester system. Annual tuition: per credit $646. Enrollment: full-time 589, part-time 394. Faculty: full-time 46, part-time 128. Degrees conferred: M.S.W., Ph.D.

ADMISSION REQUIREMENTS. Transcripts, personal essay required in support of School's application. Interview may be required. TOEFL required for international applicants. Accepts limited number of transfer applicants. Graduates of unaccredited colleges not considered. Apply to Director of Admissions of School by July 1 (Fall), November 1 (Spring). Fall admission for full-time program. Rolling admissions process. Application fee $50. Phone: (212)998-5910; fax: (212)995-4171.

ADMISSION STANDARDS. Competitive. Usual minimum average: 3.0 (A = 4).

FINANCIAL AID. Assistantships, internships, tuition remission program, grants, tuition waivers, Federal W/S, loans. Apply by March 1 to the Director of Admissions. Use FAFSA, and New York State residents use TAP application. About 85% of students receive aid other than loans from School and outside sources. Only loans available for part-time students.

DEGREE REQUIREMENTS. For M.S.W.: 65 credits minimum, at least one year in full-time residence. For Ph.D.: 60 credits beyond the master's.

FIELD OF STUDY.
Clinical Social Work.

NIAGARA UNIVERSITY

Niagara University, New York 14109

Web site: www.niagara.edu

Founded 1856, located 25 miles NW of Buffalo. Coed. Private control. Roman Catholic. Semester system. Library: exceeds 313,895 volumes, 4500 subscriptions.

Tuition: per credit Elementary and Secondary Education $435, other Education programs $400, M.B.A. $530, Criminal Justice $435. Limited on-campus housing. Annual academic year housing cost: $6660. Apply to Director of University Housing. Phone: (716)285-8568.

Graduate Studies

Enrollment: full-time 249, part-time 298 (men 35%, women 65%). University faculty: full-time 27, part-time 24. Degrees conferred: M.S., M.B.A., M.S.Ed.; Professional Diploma in Educational Administration, School Counseling.

ADMISSION REQUIREMENTS. Transcripts, two letters of recommendation, GRE/GMAT scores, personal statement, interview required in support of application. TOEFL required for international applicants. Accepts transfer applicants. Graduates of unaccredited institutions not considered. Apply to Director of Graduate Recruitment at least one month prior to registration. Phone: (716)286-8719; fax: (716)286-8710. Application fee $30.

ADMISSION STANDARDS. Selective. Usual minimum average: 3.0 (A = 4).

FINANCIAL AID. Scholarships, fellowships, research assistantship, Federal W/S, loans. Apply by March 1 to Financial Aid Office; no specified closing date. Phone: (716)286-8686. Use FAFSA. About 40% of students receive aid other than loans from University and outside sources. Aid available for part-time students.

DEGREE REQUIREMENTS. For M.S.: 33–36 semester hours minimum; thesis/oral exam; comprehensive exam. For M.S. Ed.: 36 semester hours; comprehensive exam. For M.B.A.: 48 semester hours. For Professional Diplomas: 30 hours beyond the master's.

FIELDS OF STUDY.

GRADUATE DIVISION OF ARTS AND SCIENCES:
Criminal Justice. M.S.

GRADUATE DIVISION OF BUSINESS:
Business Administration. Includes accounting, human resource management, international business, strategic management. M.B.A. only.

GRADUATE DIVISION OF EDUCATION:
Educational Administration and Supervision.
Foundations and Teaching.
Mental Health Counseling.
School Counselor.
Teacher Education.

UNIVERSITY OF NORTH ALABAMA

Florence, Alabama 35632-0001

Web site: www.una.edu

Founded 1830. Located 120 miles N of Birmingham. Coed. State control. Semester system. Library: 343,000 volumes, 1792 subscriptions.

Tuition: per credit, resident $112, nonresident $224. On-campus housing for 50 married students, unlimited for single graduate men and women. Average annual housing cost: $4034–$4310 (including board) for single students; $5000 for married students. Contact Office of Student Affairs for both on- and off-campus housing information. Phone: (256)765-4280.

Graduate Division

Enrollment: full-time 103, part-time 478. University faculty teaching graduate students: full- and part-time 49. Degrees conferred: M.A., M.A.Ed., M.B.A., M.S.

ADMISSION REQUIREMENTS. Transcripts, GRE Subject Tests or MAT/GMAT required in support of application. On-line application available. TOEFL required for international applicants. Interview not required. Accepts transfer applicants. Apply to Director of Admissions at least one month prior to registration. Application fee $25. Phone: (256)765-4221; fax: (256)765-4329.

ADMISSION STANDARDS. Selective. Usual minimum average: 2.75 unconditional, 2.0 conditional (A = 4).

FINANCIAL AID. Limited to Federal W/S, loans. Apply to Financial Aid Office; no specified closing date. Phone: (256)765-4278. Use FAFSA.

DEGREE REQUIREMENTS. For master's: 33 credit hours minimum; at least 24 credit hours in residence; thesis/nonthesis option; final oral exam.

FIELDS OF STUDY.

COLLEGE OF ARTS AND SCIENCE:
Criminal Justice. M.S.
English. M.A.

COLLEGE OF BUSINESS:
Business Administration. M.B.A.

COLLEGE OF EDUCATION:
Counseling (P–12). M.A.Ed.
Educational Administration. Ed. S.
Elementary Education (K–6). M.A.Ed.
Health Education (P–12). M.A.Ed.
Health, Physical Education, and Recreation. M.A.
Instrumental Music (P–12). M.A.Ed.
Non-School Counseling. M.A.
Non-School Based Teaching. M.A.
Physical Education (P–12). M.A.Ed.
Secondary Education (6–12). Includes biology, business and office education, chemistry, English/language arts, general science, geography, history, mathematics, mathematics/computer science, physics, political science, social science. M.A.Ed.
Special Education Collaborative. Includes K–6 grades, 6–12 grades, K–12 grades. M.A.Ed.
Vocal/Chorus Music (P–12). M.A.Ed.

NORTH CAROLINA AGRICULTURAL AND TECHNICAL STATE UNIVERSITY

Greensboro, North Carolina 27411

Web site: www.ncat.edu

Founded 1891. CGS member. Coed. State control. Semester system. Special facilities: Center for Advanced Materials and Smart Structures, Center of Aerospace Research, Center for Autonomous Control Engineering, Center for Composite Materials Research, Center for Electronics Manufacturing, Center for Energy Research and Technology, Center for Environmental Remediation and Pollution Prevention, Institute for Human–Machine Studies, International Trade Center, Transportation Institute, Waste Management Institute. Library 483,700 volumes, 4500 subscriptions.

Annual tuition: full-time resident $2306, nonresident $9576 On-campus housing for single students only Average academic year cost: $4470 (including board). Contact Dean of Students for both on- and off-campus housing information, Phone: (336)334-7920. Day-care facilities available.

School of Graduate Studies

Graduate study since 1939. Enrollment: full-time 385, part-time 513. Faculty: full-time 360, part-time 102. Degrees conferred: M.A., M.S., M.S.E., M.S.A.E., M.S.M.E., M.S.I.T., Ph.D.

ADMISSION REQUIREMENTS. Two official transcripts, GRE required in support of School's application. TOEFL required for international applicants. Interview not required. Accepts transfer applicants. Graduates of unaccredited institutions not considered. Apply to Graduate Office by June 1 (Fall), December 1 (Spring). Rolling admissions process. Application fee $35. Phone: (336)334-7920; fax: (336)334-7282.

ADMISSION STANDARDS. Selective. Usual minimum average: 2.5 (A = 4).

FINANCIAL AID. Fellowships, research assistantships, teaching assistantships, internships, Federal W/S, loans. Approved for VA benefits. Apply to Dean of Graduate School for fellowships, assistantships; to Financial Aid Office for all other programs. No specified closing date. Use FAFSA. About 10% of students receive aid other than loans from School. Aid available for part-time students.

DEGREE REQUIREMENTS. For master's: 30–36 semester hours minimum, at least 22 in residence; a reading knowledge of one foreign language required by some programs; qualifying exam; thesis/nonthesis option; comprehensive oral/written exam. For Ph.D.: minimum of 36 semester hours beyond the master's; qualifying exam; reading knowledge of one foreign language required by some programs; preliminary oral exam; admission to candidacy; dissertation; final oral exam.

FIELDS OF STUDY
Adult Education. M.S.
Agricultural and Biosystems Engineering. M.S.
Agricultural Education. M.S.
Agricultural Economics. M.S.
Animal Health Science. M.S.
Applied Mathematics. M.S.
Applied Physics. M.S.
Architectural Engineering. M.S.
Biology. M.S.
Chemical Education. M.A.
Chemical Engineering. M.S.Ch.E.
Chemistry. M.S.
Civil Engineering. M.S.
Computer Science. M.S.
Counselor Education. M.S.
Elementary Education. M.A.Ed
Electrical Engineering. M.S., Ph.D.
English and African American Literature. M.A.
English Education. M.S.
Food and Nutrition. M.S.
Health and Physical Education. M.S.
History Education. M.S.
Human Resource. Includes business and industry, community/ agency. M.S.
Industrial Engineering. M.S., Ph.D.

Industrial Technology. Includes manufacturing systems, electronic and computer technology, graphic communication systems, construction management, occupational safety and health. M.S.I.T.
Instructional Technology. M.S.
Management Information Systems. M.S.
Mathematics Secondary Education. M.S.
Mechanical Engineering. M.S.M.E., Ph.D
Plant and Soil Science. M.S.
Professional Physics. M.S.
Social Work. Joint programs with University of North Carolina, Greensboro. M.S.W.
Technology Education. M.S.
Transportation and Logistics. M.S.M.
Vocational-Industrial Education. M.S.

NORTH CAROLINA CENTRAL UNIVERSITY
Durham, North Carolina 27707-3129
Web site: www.nccu.edu

Founded 1910. CGS member. Coed. State control. Semester system. Library: 614,000 volumes, 860,000 microforms, 4500 current periodicals, 30 PCs.

Annual tuition: full-time, resident $1754, nonresident $8902. On-campus housing for single students only. Average academic year housing cost: $3837 (including board). Contact Director of Residence Operations for both on- and off-campus for housing information. Phone: (919)560-6517. Day-care facilities available.

Graduate Program

Enrollment: full-time 253, part-time 560. Faculty: full-time 194, part-time 77. Degrees conferred: M.A., M.S., M.Ed., M.B.A., M.I.S., M.L.S., M.P.A.

ADMISSION REQUIREMENTS. Official transcripts, three letters of reference required in support of application. TOEFL (minimum score 500) required for international applicants. Interview not required. Accepts transfer applicants. Graduates of unaccredited institutions not considered. Apply to the Admissions Office at least one month prior to registration. Application fee $30. Phone: (919)560-6230.

ADMISSION STANDARDS. Selective. Usual minimum average: 2.5, 3.0 in undergraduate major (A = 4).

FINANCIAL AID. Assistantships, teaching/research fellowships, internships, grants, Federal W/S, loans. Approved for VA benefits. Apply by May 1 to the Vice Chancellor's Office for assistantships, fellowships; to the Financial Aid Office for all other programs. Phone: (919)560-6202. Use FAFSA and University's FAF. About 25% of students receive aid other than loans from College and outside sources. Aid available for part-time students.

DEGREE REQUIREMENTS. For master's: 30–42 semester hours minimum with at least three summers in full-time attendance; thesis/nonthesis option or research project; reading knowledge of one foreign language or other research tool for some programs; final oral/written exam.

FIELDS OF STUDY.

COLLEGE OF ARTS AND SCIENCES:
Biology. M.S.
Chemistry M.S.
Criminal Justice. M.S.

Earth Science. M.S.
English. M.A.
History. M.A.
Human Sciences. M.S.
Mathematics. M.S.
Physical Education and Recreation. M.S.
Psychology M.A.
Public Administration. M.S.

SCHOOL OF BUSINESS:
Business Administration. M.B.A.

SCHOOL OF EDUCATION:
Agency Counseling. M.A.
Behaviorally-Emotionally Handicapped. M.Ed.
Career Counseling and Placement. M.A.
Communication Disorders. M.Ed.
Education Technology. M.A.
Elementary Education (K–6). M.Ed.
Mentally Handicapped. M.Ed.
Middle Grade Education (6–9). M.Ed.
School Counseling. M.A.
Sociology. M.A.
Speech and Hearing. M.Ed.
Visual Impairment. M.Ed.

SCHOOL OF LIBRARY AND INFORMATION SCIENCE:
Academic Librarian. M.L.S.
Archives and Records Manager. M.L.S.
Information Science. Includes project management, information network management, information counseling, database management, institutional research. M.I.S.
Law Librarian. M.L.S.
Public Librarian. M.L.S.
School Media Coordinator. M.L.S.
Special Librarian M.L.S.

School of Law

Established 1939. ABA approved since 1950. AALS member. Semester system. Law library: 297,518 volumes, 3974 subscriptions; has LEXIS, NEXIS, WESTLAW, DIALOG. On-campus housing available for single students only. Apply to Director of Housing. Phone: (919)560-6227.

Annual tuition: resident $2330, nonresident $11,434. Total average annual additional expense: $10,205.

Enrollment: first-year class, 89 (day), 26 (evening); full-time 239, part-time 115 (men 43%, women 57%). Faculty: full-time 11, part-time 12. Student to faculty ratio 23.1 to 1. Degrees conferred: J.D., J.D.-M.L.S. (Law Librarianship).

ADMISSION REQUIREMENTS. LSDAS Law School report, bachelor's degree, transcript, two letters of recommendation, LSAT required in support of application. Interview not required. Accepts transfer applicants. Graduates of unaccredited colleges not considered. Apply to Office of Admissions after September 1, before April 15. Application fee $30. Phone: (919)560-5243.

ADMISSIONS STANDARDS. Selective. Mean LSAT: full-time 147, part-time 154; mean GPA: full-time 3.15, part-time 3.27 (A = 4). Gourman rating: 2.17. *U.S. News & World Report* ranking is in the fourth tier of all U.S. law schools. Accepts about 15% of total annual applicants.

FINANCIAL AID. Scholarships, assistantships, Federal W/S, loans. Apply to Director of Student Financial Aid by February 1. Use FAFSA (School code: 002950). About 29% of students receive aid other than loans from School. Aid sometimes available for part-time students.

DEGREE REQUIREMENTS. For J.D.: satisfactory completion of three-year program; 88 semester hour program.

NORTH CAROLINA STATE UNIVERSITY AT RALEIGH
Raleigh, North Carolina 27695
Web site: www.ncsu.edu

Established 1987. CGS member. Coed. State control. Semester system. Special facilities: Center for Electric Power Research, Center for Sound and Vibration, Electron Microscope Facilities, Highlands Biological Station, Reproductive Physiology Research Laboratory, Phytotron, Triangle Universities Nuclear Laboratory, Mars Mission Research Center, Nuclear Reactor Program Facilities, Pesticide Residue Research Laboratory, Precision Engineering Center, Southeastern Plant Environment Laboratories, Sea Grant College Program, Triangle Universities Computation Center, Institute of Statistics, member Institution Research Program at Oak Ridge, Water Resources Research Institute. The University's NIH ranking is 205th among all U.S. institutions with 57 awards/grants worth $11,459,725. Library: 2,398,000 volumes, 18,500 subscriptions.

Annual tuition/fees: full-time, resident $3496, nonresident $13,806; part-time, graduated scale depending upon number of credits. On-campus housing for 300 married students, 4000 men, 1500 women. Average academic year housing cost: $425–$510 per month for married student housing; $3200 for single students. Off-campus housing cost: $650 per month. Contact Director of Student Housing for both on- and off-campus housing information. Phone: (919)515-2440.

Graduate School

Graduate study since 1993. Enrollment: full-time 3336, part-time 1756. University faculty: full-time 1800. Degrees conferred: M.S., M.A., Master of a Designated Field, Ed.D., Ph.D.

ADMISSION REQUIREMENTS. Official transcripts, GRE/MAT/GMAT required in support of School's application. GRE Subject Test recommended for some programs. On-line application available. TOEFL (minimum score 550) required for international applicants. Interview not required. Accepts transfer applicants. Graduates of unaccredited institutions not considered. Apply to Graduate Admissions Office by March 1 (Fall), July 15 (Spring). Application fee $55, $65 international applicants. Phone: (919) 737-2871.

ADMISSION STANDARDS. Selective. Usual minimum average: 3.0 (A = 4).

FINANCIAL AID. Annual awards from institutional funds: scholarships, fellowships, research assistantships, teaching assistantships, traineeships, Federal W/S, loans. Approved for VA benefits. Apply by March 1 to appropriate department chair for fellowships, assistantships; to Financial Aid Office for all other programs. Phone: (919)737-2421. Use FAFSA and University's FAF. About 50% of students receive aid other than loans from School and outside sources.

DEGREE REQUIREMENTS. For master's: 33–48 credits minimum, at least one academic year in residence; thesis/nonthesis option; final oral/written exam. For professional degrees: 30–36 credits, at least one academic year in residence; project paper required by some departments; final oral exam. For Ph.D.: 6 semesters beyond the bachelor's, at least two semesters in full-time residence; reading knowledge of at least one foreign language required by some departments; dissertation; oral/written qualifying exam; final oral exam. For Ed.D.: essentially the same as Ph.D., except no language requirement.

FIELDS OF STUDY.
Accounting.
Adult and Community College Education.

Aerospace Engineering.
Agency Counseling.
Agricultural and Resource Economics.
Agricultural Education.
Animal Science.
Architecture.
Biochemistry.
Bioinformatics.
Biological and Agricultural Engineering.
Botany.
Business Administration.
Chemical Engineering.
Chemistry.
Civil Engineering.
Communication.
Comparative Biomedical Sciences.
Computer Engineering.
Computer Networking.
Computer Science.
Counselor Education.
Curriculum and Instruction. Includes elementary, English, reading, social studies.
Design.
Economics.
Educational Administration and Supervision.
Educational Research and Policy Analysis.
Electrical Engineering.
English.
Entomology.
Extension Education.
Fiber and Polymer Science.
Fisheries and Wildlife Sciences.
Food Science.
Forestry.
Functional Genomics.
Genetics.
Graphic Design.
Health Occupations Teacher Education.
Higher Education Administration.
History.
Horticultural Science.
Immunology.
Industrial Design.
Industrial Engineering.
Instructional Technology—Computers.
Integrated Manufacturing Systems Engineering.
International Affairs.
Landscape Architecture.
Liberal Studies.
Marine, Earth, and Atmospheric Sciences.
Materials Science and Engineering.
Mathematics. Includes applied.
Mathematics Education.
Mechanical Engineering.
Microbiology.
Middle School Education.
Natural Resources.
Nuclear Engineering.
Nutrition.
Occupational Education.
Operations Research.
Parks, Recreation, and Tourism Management.
Physics.
Physiology.
Plant Pathology.
Poultry Science.
Psychology.
Public Administration.
Public History.
School Administration.

Science Education.
Sociology.
Soil Science.
Special Education. Includes behavior disorders, learning disabilities, mental retardation.
Specialized Veterinary Medicine.
Statistics.
Technical Communication.
Technical Education.
Textile and Apparel Technology Management.
Textile Chemistry.
Textile Materials Science.
Textile Technology Management.
Toxicology.
Training Development.
Wood and Paper Science.
Zoology.

College of Veterinary Medicine (27606)

Established 1981. Annual tuition: resident $6501, nonresident $26,500. Total average cost for all other expenses: $9000.

Enrollment: first-year class 76; total full-time 288 (men 65%, women 35%); postgraduates 40. Faculty: full-time 120. Degrees conferred: D.V.M., D.V.M.-Ph.D. The M.S. and Ph.D. are offered through the Graduate School.

ADMISSION REQUIREMENTS. VMCAS report, transcripts, GRE, recommendations, personal essay, animal/veterinary experience, interview required in support of application. Preference given to state and South Carolina residents. Graduates of unaccredited colleges not considered. Considers transfer applicants on a space-available basis. Apply to the College after July 31. Application packets must be completed and returned by October 1. Application fee $45. Phone: (919)829-6262; fax: (919)829-4222.

ADMISSION STANDARDS. Selective. Accepts 30–35% of qualified applicants. Approximately twelve are nonresident (at large) applicants.

FINANCIAL AID. Scholarships, fellowships, assistantships, Federal W/S, loans available. Apply to the Financial Aid Office after acceptance. No specified closing date. Use FAFSA.

DEGREE REQUIREMENTS. For D.V.M., satisfactory completion of four-year program. For Ph.D., see Graduate School listing above.

FIELDS OF GRADUATE STUDY.
Comparative Biomedical Sciences.
Immunology.
Physiology.
Specialized Veterinary Medicine.

THE UNIVERSITY OF NORTH CAROLINA AT CHAPEL HILL
Chapel Hill, North Carolina 27599
Web site: www.unc.edu

Chartered 1789; first state university in U.S. Located 28 miles NW of Raleigh. CGS and AAU member. Coed. State control. Semester system. Special facilities: Biological Sciences Research Center, Cancer Research Center, Center for Urban and Regional Studies, Center for Alcohol, Institute for Research in Social Science, Institute for Environmental Studies, Child Development Institute, Institute of Statistics, Institute of Marine Science, Institute of Government, Institute of Latin American Studies, Research Laboratories of Anthropology, Member of the Research Triangle Institute of North Carolina. The University's NIH ranking is 12th among all U.S. institutions with 647 awards/grants worth $236,803,562. Library: 4,900,000 volumes, 44,000 subscriptions. Total University enrollment: 24,000.

Annual tuition: full-time, resident $3538, nonresident $12,112. On-campus housing for 306 married students, 325 men, 325 women. Average academic year housing cost: $350–$400 per month (housing only) for married students, $1255–$1825 per semester for single students. Contact the Director of Housing for both on- and off-campus housing information. Phone: (919)966-5661. Day-care facilities available.

Graduate School

Web site: www.gradschool.unc.edu

Graduate study since 1853. Enrollment: full-time 3322 (men 35%, women 65%), part-time 2187. Graduate faculty: 1200. Degrees conferred: M.A., M.B.A., M.M., M.Ed., M.P.H., M.R.P., M.S., M.S.L.S., M.S.S.E., M.S.P.H., M.S.W., M.P.A., M.F.A., M.A.T., Ed.D., D.P.H., Ph.D.

ADMISSION REQUIREMENTS. Two transcripts, three letters of reference, GRE Subject Tests/GMAT required in support of School's application. Interview required by some departments. TOEFL required for international applicants. Accepts transfer applicants. Graduates of unaccredited institutions not considered. Apply to Office of the Dean by January 1 (Fall), October 15 (Spring). Application fee $60. Phone: (919)966-1538; fax: (919)966-4010.

ADMISSION STANDARDS. Selective to competitive. Usual minimum average: 3.0 (A = 4).

FINANCIAL AID. Annual awards from institutional funds: scholarships, fellowships, traineeships, teaching/research assistantships, tuition waivers, Federal W/S, loans. Approved for VA benefits. Apply by January 31 to the Graduate School. Phone: (919)962-8396; fax: (919)962-2716. Use FAFSA. About 57% of students receive aid other than loans from University and outside sources. Aid sometimes available for part-time students.

DEGREE REQUIREMENTS. For M.A., M.S.: 30 semester hours minimum, at least two semesters in residence; reading knowledge of one foreign language or approved options in some departments; thesis or acceptable option; written/oral comprehensive exam. For M.B.A.: two years minimum. For M.Ed.: 30 semester hours minimum; written comprehensive exam. For M.A.T., M.P.H., M.S.P.H., M.S.S.E.: 30 semester hours minimum, at least two semesters in residence; final written/oral exam. For M.F.A.: 40 semester hours minimum, at least two semesters in residence; oral exam. For M.S.L.S.: 48 semester hours minimum, at least two semesters in residence; final written exam. For M.P.A.: 45 semester hours minimum, at least two semesters in residence; oral exam. For M.S.W.: 53 semester hours minimum, at least two semesters in residence; final written/oral exam. For Ph.D.: four semesters minimum in residence, at least two semesters in continuous attendance; reading knowledge of two foreign languages or approved options in some departments; doctoral oral exam; written exam; dissertation; final oral exam. For D.P.H., Ed.D.: requirements essentially the same as for the Ph.D., except no language requirement.

FIELDS OF STUDY.
Anthropology.
Art. Includes creative art, art history; Ph.D. in art history only.
Audiology.
Biochemistry and Biophysics.
Biology.
Biomedical Engineering.
Business Administration. GMAT for admission to M.B.A.

Cell and Molecular Physiology.
Cell Biology and Anatomy.
Chemistry.
City and Regional Planning. Two years for M.R.P.
Classics.
Communication Studies.
Comparative Literature. Latin for Ph.D.
Computer Science.
Dramatic Art. M.F.A.
Ecology.
Economics.
Education. M.A.T., M.A. in college teaching; internship, comprehensive written exam for M.A.; includes administration and supervision, adult education, curriculum and instruction, educational media, elementary, higher education, educational psychology, educational leadership, counseling, school psychology, reading and language arts, physical education, social foundations of education, special education.
English. Latin for Ph.D.
Environmental Sciences and Engineering.
Epidemiology.
Folklore. M.A. only.
Genetics and Molecular Biology. Interdepartmental.
Geography.
Geology.
German Languages. French for M.A., Ph.D.
Health Behavior and Health Education.
Health Policy and Administration.
History.
Human Movement Science.
Information and Library Science. Thirty-six hours for M.S.L.S., Ph.D.
Journalism. M.A. only; interdepartmental program, mass communications research for Ph.D.
Linguistics.
Marine Sciences.
Materials Sciences.
Maternal and Child Health.
Mathematics. Written qualifying exam for M.S.; apply by February 11 (Fall).
Microbiology and Immunology.
Music. Original composition for M.S.; other requirements as for M.A.
Neurobiology. Ph.D. only.
Nursing.
Nutrition.
Occupational Sciences. M.S. only.
Operations Research.
Oral Biology.
Pathology.
Pharmacology.
Pharmacy.
Philosophy.
Physical Education, Exercise, and Sport Science. M.A. only.
Physical Therapy. M.S. only.
Physics and Astronomy.
Physiology.
Political Science. Includes public administration; M.P.A. only; 40 hours, internship, comprehensive written exam, final oral exam.
Psychology. GRE, MAT for admission.
Public Administration.
Public Health. Includes environmental sciences and engineering, biostatistics, epidemiology, maternal and child health, health behavior and health education, public health nursing, nutrition, health policy and administration.
Public Policy Analysis. Ph.D. only.
Radio, Television, and Motion Pictures. M.A.
Recreation and Leisure Studies.
Rehabilitation Psychology and Counseling. M.S. only.

Religious Studies.
Romance Languages. Includes Spanish; Latin, German for Ph.D.
Russian/East European Studies.
Slavic Languages and Literature.
Social Work. GRE, MAT for admission; four semesters, one Summer term in residence for M.S.W.; M.S.W., Ph.D.
Sociology.
Speech Communications. M.A. only.
Speech and Hearing Science. M.S. only.
Statistics.
Studio Art.
Toxicology.

Oral and Maxillofacial Surgery. Fall admission only; two years and one summer session for M.S.
Oral Biology.
Oral Radiology.
Orthodontics. Nineteen months including two summer sessions for M.S.
Pedodontics. Two years and two summer sessions for M.S.
Pediatric Dentistry.
Periodontics. Summer session admission only; two years and two summer sessions for M.S.
Prosthodontics. Fall admission only; two years and one summer session for M.S.

School of Dentistry (27599-7450)

Established 1950. Special facility: Dental Research Center. Annual tuition: D.D.S., resident, first and second year $5710; nonresident, first and second year $31,986. Total average cost for all other first-year expenses: $6519.

Enrollment: D.D.S., first-year class 75; total 386 (men 65%, women 35%); graduate study 45. Faculty: full-time 80, part-time 15. Degrees conferred: D.D.S., M.S., D.D.S.-Ph.D., D.D.S.-M.P.H.

ADMISSION REQUIREMENTS. For D.D.S.: AADSAS report, official transcripts, DAT (April test in Junior year preferred) required in support of School's application. UNC Supplementary Application also required. Applicants must have completed at least three years of college study, prefer four years of study. TOEFL required for international applicants. Preference given to state residents. Interview by invitation only. Accepts transfer students. Apply to Office of Admission, School of Dentistry after June 1, before November 1. Application fee $60. Phone: (919)966-4451. For graduate study: official transcripts, GRE required in support of School's application. Graduates of unaccredited colleges not considered.

ADMISSION STANDARDS. Selective. Usual minimum average: 3.0 (A = 4). Mean DAT: Academic 19.4, PAT 17.9; mean GPA: 3.5 (A = 4). Gourman rating: 4.42. Accepts 25–30% of total applicants. Approximately 80% are state residents.

FINANCIAL AID. Board of Governors Scholarships (for minority and disadvantaged students), Dental Scholars Program, merit scholarships, North Carolina School of Dentistry Minority Grants, institutional loans, North Carolina Loan Programs, DEAL, HEAL, alternative loan programs; Federal Perkins Loans, Stafford Subsidized and Unsubsidized Loans, Military Service Commitment Scholarships programs are available. All Financial Aid is based on documented need. Fellowships may be available for Joint Degree candidates. Institutional Financial Aid applications and information are available after January 1. Apply for Financial Aid by March 1 (priority deadline). Contact the University's Office of Scholarships and Student Aid for current information. Phone: (919)962-8936. Use FAFSA (School code: 002974), also submit Financial Aid Transcript, Federal Income Tax forms, and Use of Federal Funds Certification. Approximately 85% of students receive some form of financial assistance. Graduate study: fellowships, assistantships, loans. Apply after acceptance to Office of Admissions, School of Dentistry. About 76% of graduate students receive aid from School and outside sources.

DEGREE REQUIREMENTS. For D.D.S.: satisfactory completion of four-year program. For M.S.: 45–60 credits; thesis; final oral exam. Refer to other Graduate School listings above for joint degree requirements.

FIELDS OF GRADUATE STUDY.
Dentistry. Language not required for M.S. M.S., Certificate only. (See School of Dentistry Listing.)
Endodontics.
Operative Dentistry.

School of Law (27599-3380)

Web site: www.law.unc.edu

Opened 1845. ABA approved since 1923. AALS member since 1920. Semester system. Law library: 427,298 volumes, 6342 subscriptions; has LEXIS, NEXIS, WESTLAW.

Annual tuition: resident $5031, nonresident $17,131. Total average annual additional expense: $11,614.

Enrollment: first-year class 324; total 780 (men 50%, women 50%). Faculty: full-time 38, part-time 16. Student to faculty ratio 17.5 to 1. Degrees conferred: J.D., J.D.-M.B.A., J.D.-M.P.A., J.D.-M.R.P.

ADMISSION REQUIREMENTS. LSDAS Law School report, bachelor's degree, transcripts, LSAT (not later than December) required in support of application. Accepts transfer applicants. Graduates of unaccredited institutions not considered. Preference is given to state residents. Apply to Admissions Office after September 1, before January 15. Application fee $60. Phone: (919)962-5106.

ADMISSION STANDARDS. Competitive. Mean LSAT: 160; mean GPA: 3.60 (A = 4). Gourman rating: 4.46. *U.S. News & World Report* ranking is 31st among all U.S. law schools. Accepts about 15–20% of total annual applicants.

FINANCIAL AID. Chancellor's scholarships, merit scholarships, minority presence scholarships, Grants-in-Aid, institutional loans; Federal loans and Federal W/S offered through University's Financial Aid Office. Assistantships may be available for upper-divisional Joint Degree candidates. All accepted students are automatically considered for both merit- and need-based scholarships (selection criteria places heavy reliance on LSAT and Undergraduate GPA). For all other programs apply after January 1, before March 1 to University's Office of Scholarship and Student Aid. Phone: (919)962-8396. Use FAFSA (School code: 002974). Also submit Financial Aid Transcript, Federal Income Tax forms. Approximately 20% of first-year class received scholarships/Grants-in-Aid. Approximately 50% of students receive some form of financial assistance.

DEGREE REQUIREMENTS. For J. D.: satisfactory completion of three-year program; 86 credit hour program. For master's degrees, see Graduate School listing above.

School of Medicine (27599-7000)

Web site: www.med.unc.edu

Established 1879. Medical library: 263,000 volumes. Annual tuition: resident $6095, nonresident $29,098, student fees $942. Total average figure for all other expenses: $8900.

Enrollment: first-year class 160, total 656 (EDP 7) (men 59%, women 41%). Faculty: full-time 290, part-time 335. Degrees conferred: M.D., M.D.-Ph.D., M.D.-M.P.H.

ADMISSION REQUIREMENTS. AMCAS report, transcripts, two letters of recommendation, MCAT, supplementary application, interview required in support of application. Applicants must have completed at least three years of college study. Preference given to state residents. Has EDP; apply between June 1 and August 1. Accepts transfer applicants. Graduates of unaccredited colleges not considered. Apply to Office of the Dean after June 1, before November 15. Application fee $65. Phone: (919)962-8331; fax: (919)966-9930.

ADMISSION STANDARDS. Competitive. Mean MCAT: 10.4; mean GPA: 3.64 (A = 4). Gourman rating: 4.64. *U.S. News & World Report* ranking is 22 among all U.S. medical schools. Accepts 8–10% of total annual applicants. Approximately 90% are state residents.

FINANCIAL AID. Scholarships, loans. Apply after acceptance to Chair, Student Aid Committee. Phone: (919)962-6118. Use FAFSA (School code: 002974). About 80% of students receive aid other than loans from School.

DEGREE REQUIREMENTS. For M.D.: satisfactory completion of four-year program. Passing USMLE Step 1 is required to enter third year, and passing USMLE Step 2 is required for graduation. Refer to other Graduate School listings above for joint degree requirements.

FIELDS OF GRADUATE STUDY.
Anatomy.
Biochemistry.
Biomedical Engineering.
Biophysics.
Biostatistics.
Cell Biology.
Epidemiology.
Genetics.
Immunology.
Microbiology.
Molecular Biology.
Neurosciences.
Pathology.
Pharmacology.
Physiology.
Public Health.
Toxicology.

THE UNIVERSITY OF NORTH CAROLINA AT CHARLOTTE
Charlotte, North Carolina 28223
Web site: www.uncc.edu

Established 1965. CGS member. Coed. State control. Semester system. Special facilities: Cameron Applied Research Center, Small Business and Technology Development Center, Urban Institute. Library: 874,800 volumes, 5000 subscriptions.

Annual tuition: full-time, resident $1880, nonresident $9820; per credit, graduated scale for resident, nonresident students. Limited on-campus housing for graduate men and women, none for married students. Average academic year housing cost: $4879 (including board). Contact the Director of Residence Life for both on- and off-campus housing information. Phone: (704)687-2585.

Graduate School

Enrollment: full-time 738, part-time 1334. University faculty: full-time 484, part-time 148. Degrees conferred: M.A., M.A.L.S., M.B.A., M.Ed., M.S.A., M.S.E., M.S.C.E., M.S.E.E., M.S.M.E., M.L.S., M.S.N., M.P.A., C.A.S., Ph.D.

ADMISSION REQUIREMENTS. Two transcripts, GRE, three letters of recommendation, statement of purpose required in support of School's application. MAT/GMAT required by some departments. Interview/auditions/portfolio required by some departments. On-line application available. TOEFL required for international applicants. Accepts transfer applicants. Apply to the Assistant Dean for Graduate Admissions at least sixty days prior to date of desired registration; many programs have early deadlines. Application fee $35. Phone: (704)687-3366; fax: (704) 687-3279.

ADMISSION STANDARDS. Competitive. Usual minimum average: 2.75 (A = 4).

FINANCIAL AID. Annual awards from institutional funds: fellowships, teaching assistantships, research assistantships, internships, traineeships, Federal W/S, loans. Approved for VA benefits. Apply by April 1 to appropriate department chair for fellowships, assistantships; to Office of Financial Aid for all other programs. Use FAFSA. About 40% of students receive aid from School and outside sources. Aid available for part-time students.

DEGREE REQUIREMENTS. For master's: 30–32 semester hours minimum; thesis; written/oral candidacy exam; reading knowledge of one foreign language for many departments. For M.Arch.: 42 credit, full-time program; thesis. For M.Ed.: 32 semester hours minimum; final written exam. For M.L.S.: 36 semester hours minimum; written/oral exam. For M.B.A., M.P.A.: 42 semester hours minimum; written exam. For M.S.N.: 49–55 semester hours minimum; internship, practicum; thesis; written/oral exam. For C.A.S.: 30 semester hours beyond the master's. For Ph.D.: six full semesters minimum beyond the bachelor's, at least two consecutive semesters or equivalent in full-time residence; reading knowledge of one or more foreign languages or equivalent in some departments; preliminary exam; dissertation; final oral exam.

FIELDS OF STUDY.
Accountancy.
Adult Health Nursing.
Applied Mathematics. M.S., Ph.D.
Architecture.
Biology.
Business Administration. Includes business finance, economics, electronic business, financial institutions/commercial banking, information and technology management, management, marketing, self-structured (health care, human resources, international business).
Chemistry.
Child and Family Studies—Early Childhood.
Civil Engineering.
Communication Studies.
Community Health Nursing.
Computer Science.
Counseling.
Counselor Education. Includes community, school.
Criminal Justice.
Curriculum and Supervision.
Earth Sciences.
Economics.
Educational Leadership.
Elementary Education (K–6).
Electrical Engineering. Includes computer engineering, microelectronics, optoelectronics.
Engineering Management.
English.
English Education.
Family Nurse Practitioner.
Geography. Includes community planning.
Gerontology.
Health Administration.
Health Promotion.

History.
Information Technology.
Instructional Systems Technology.
Liberal Studies.
Library Science. M.L.S. with the University of North Carolina at Greensboro.
Mathematics.
Mathematics Education.
Mechanical Engineering. Includes computer-integrated manufacturing, materials engineering, precision engineering.
Mental Health Nursing.
Middle Grades and Secondary Education.
Nurse Anesthesia.
Physics. Includes applied.
Psychology. Includes clinical/community, industrial/organizational.
Public Policy.
Reading Education.
School Administration.
Social Work.
Sociology.
Spanish.
Special Education.
Teacher Education.
Teaching English as a Second Language.

THE UNIVERSITY OF NORTH CAROLINA AT GREENSBORO

Greensboro, North Carolina 27412-5001
Web site: www.uncg.edu

Established 1891. CGS member. Coed. State control. Semester system. Special facilities: Three College Observatory, Center for Applied Research, Center for Critical Inquiry into the Liberal Arts, Center for Educational Research and Evaluation, Center for Social Research, Center for Social Welfare, Center for Applied Research, Weatherspoon Art Gallery. Library: 914,000 volumes, 5300 subscriptions. Total University enrollment: 13,000.

Annual tuition: full-time, resident $1995, nonresident $10,403; per credit, graduated scale for resident, nonresident students. Limited on-campus housing for graduate men and women, none for married students. Average academic year housing cost: $4860 (including board, medical services fee). Contact the Director of Residence Life for both on- and off-campus housing information. Phone: (336)334-5636.

Graduate School

First graduate degree conferred in 1922. Enrollment: full-time 994, part-time 1716. University faculty: full-time 487, part-time 38. Degrees conferred: M.A., M.B.A., M.Ed., M.F.A., M.M., M.S., M.A.L.S., M.I.L.S., M.S.A., M.S.N., M.P.A., Ed.S., Ph.D., Ed.D., D.M.A.

ADMISSION REQUIREMENTS. Transcripts, GRE required in support of School's application. MAT/NTE/GMAT required by some departments. Interview/auditions/portfolio required by some departments. TOEFL required for international applicants. Accepts transfer applicants. Apply to Graduate School (P.O. Box 26176) at least sixty days prior to date of desired registration; many programs have early deadlines. Application fee $35. Phone: (336)334-4881; (336)334-4424.

ADMISSION STANDARDS. Competitive. Usual minimum average: 2.75 (A = 4).

FINANCIAL AID. Annual awards from institutional funds: fellowships, academic scholarships, Minority Presence Grants, teaching assistantships, research assistantships, administrative assistant-ships, internships, Federal W/S, loans. Approved for VA benefits. Apply by March 1 to appropriate department chair for assistantships; to Office of Financial Aid for all other programs. Phone: (336)334-5702; fax: (336)334-3010. Use FAFSA. About 90% of students receive aid other than loans from School and outside sources. Aid not available to part-time students.

DEGREE REQUIREMENTS. For M.A., M.S.: 30 semester hours minimum; thesis; written/oral exam; reading knowledge of one foreign language for many departments. For M.Ed.: 32 semester hours minimum; final written exam. For M.F.A.: 60 semester hours minimum (except for creative writing, 36 semester hours); final written/oral exam; thesis/final project. For M.M.: 30 semester hours minimum; recital. For M.A.L.S., M.I.L.S.: 36 semester hours minimum; written/oral exam. For M.P.A.: 36 semester hours minimum; written exam. For M.S.N.: 36 semester hours minimum; thesis; written/oral exam. For Ed.S.: 30 semester hours beyond the master's. For Ph.D., Ed.D.: six full semesters minimum beyond the bachelor's, at least two consecutive semesters or equivalent in full-time residence; reading knowledge of one or more foreign languages or equivalent in some departments; preliminary exam; dissertation; final oral exam. For D.M.A.: requirements essentially the same as for Ph.D. except a final project/recital/performance required.

FIELDS OF STUDY.
Accounting.
Art. Includes fine arts, interior design, studio, art education.
Biology.
Business Administration.
Business Education.
Chemistry.
Communication Studies.
Computer Science.
Counseling and Development.
Counselor Education.
Creative Writing.
Curriculum and Teaching.
Dance.
Drama. Includes film/video, acting, directing, design, theater for youth.
Economics.
Educational Leadership.
Educational Research, Measurement, and Evaluation.
Educational Supervision.
Elementary Education.
English.
Exercise and Sport Science.
French.
Genetic Counseling.
Geography.
Gereontology.
Higher Education.
History.
Housing and Interior Design.
Human Development and Family Studies.
Information Systems and Operations Management.
Latin.
Liberal Studies.
Library and Information Studies.
Mathematics.
Music. Includes composition, conducting, education, performance, theory.
Nutrition and Food Service Systems.
Nursing. Includes nurse anesthesia, administration, gerontological.
Parks and Recreation Management. Includes therapeutic recreation.
Physics.
Political Science.
Psychology. Includes clinical.
Public Affairs.

Public Health.
School Administration.
Secondary Education. Includes the usual majors.
Social Work.
Sociology.
Spanish.
Special Education.
Speech Pathology and Audiology.
Studio Art.
Textile Products Design and Marketing.

THE UNIVERSITY OF NORTH CAROLINA AT WILMINGTON
Wilmington, North Carolina 28401-3201
Web site: www.uncwil.edu

Established 1975. CGS member. Coed. State control. Semester system. Special facility: Center for Marine Science Research. Library: 852,000 volumes, 4300 subscriptions.

Annual tuition: full-time, resident $3146, nonresident $12,433; M.B.A. full-time resident $3626, nonresident $12,932; per credit, graduated scale for resident, nonresident students. Limited on-campus housing for graduate men and women, none for married students. Average academic year housing cost: $4862 (including board). Contact the Housing Office for both on- and off-campus housing information. Phone: (910)395-3241.

Graduate School

Enrollment: full-time 213, part-time 414. University faculty: full-time 127, part-time 12. Degrees conferred: M.A., M.A.T., M.B.A., M.Ed., M.F.A.

ADMISSION REQUIREMENTS. Transcripts, GRE, three letters of recommendation, a statement of purpose required in support of School's application. MAT/NTE/GMAT required by some departments. Interview required by some departments. TOEFL required for international applicants. Accepts transfer applicants. Apply to the Assistant Dean for Graduate Admissions at least 60 days prior to date of desired registration; some programs have early deadlines. Rolling admissions process. Application fee $45. Phone: (910)350-3311.

ADMISSION STANDARDS. Competitive. Usual minimum average: 2.75 (A = 4).

FINANCIAL AID. Annual awards from institutional funds: scholarships, fellowships, teaching assistantships, research assistantships, administrative assistantships, internships, Federal W/S, loans. Approved for VA benefits. Apply by March 15 to appropriate department chair for fellowships, assistantships; to Office of Financial Aid for all other programs. Phone: (910)962-3177. Use FAFSA. About 20% of students receive aid from School and outside sources. Aid available for part-time students.

DEGREE REQUIREMENTS. For M.A: 30 semester hours minimum; thesis; written/oral exam; reading knowledge of one foreign language for some departments. For M.Ed.: 32 semester hours minimum; final written exam. For M.B.A.: 36 semester hours minimum; written exam. For M.F.A.: 48 credit program; thesis; M.F.A. exam.

FIELDS OF STUDY.

COLLEGE OF ARTS AND SCIENCES:
Biology.
Chemistry.
Creative Writing.
English.
Geology.
History.
Liberal Studies.
Mathematics.
Marine Biology.
Marine Science.
Psychology.
Public Administration.

CAMERON SCHOOL OF BUSINESS:
Accountancy.
Business Administration.

WATSON SCHOOL OF EDUCATION:
Curriculum Instruction/Supervision.
Elementary Education.
Instructional Technology.
Language and Literacy.
Middle Grades Education.
School Administration.
Special Education.
Teaching.

SCHOOL OF NURSING:
Nursing.

NORTH DAKOTA STATE UNIVERSITY
Fargo, North Dakota 58105-5790
Web site: www.ndsu.edu

Founded 1890. CGS member. Coed. State control. Semester system. Special facilities Agricultural Experiment Station, the Center for Main Group Chemistry, the Center for Cooperatives, Computer Systems Institute, Natural Resources and Economic Development Institute, North Dakota Census Data Center, North Dakota Institute for Regional Studies, Center for Agriculture Policy and Trade Studies, Upper Great Plains Transportation Institute, Radiation Research Laboratory, Water Resources Institute. Library: 498,000 volumes, 3834 subscriptions. Total University enrollment: 9700.

Tuition: per credit resident $117.25, $134 for Minnesota residents, $175.88 for residents of Saskatchewan, Manitoba, South Dakota, and Montana, $313.04 for all other nonresidents. On-campus housing for 305 married students, limited for single students. Average academic year housing cost: for single students $3600 with seven day meals, $5520–$6380 for married students. Contact the Director of Housing for both on- and off-campus housing information. Phone: (701)231-7557. Day-care facilities available.

Graduate School

Graduate study since 1895. Enrollment: full-time 629, part-time 364. Faculty: full-time 400, part-time 26. Degrees conferred: M.A., M.S., M.Ed., M.B.A., Ed.S., Ph.D.

ADMISSION REQUIREMENTS. Official transcript, three letters of reference, personal statement required in support of School's application. GRE or MAT or GMAT required by some departments. TOEFL required for foreign applicants. Interview not required. Accepts transfer applicants. Graduates of unaccredited institutions not considered. Apply to Graduate School Admission Office at least one month prior to registration; some departments have earlier deadlines. Application fee $25. Phone: (701)231-7033; fax: (701)231-6524.

ADMISSION STANDARDS. Very selective for most departments. Usual minimum average: 3.0 (A = 4).

FINANCIAL AID. Annual awards from institutional funds: scholarships, teaching assistantships, research assistantships, tuition waivers, Federal W/S, loans. Approved for VA benefits. Apply by March 15 to Graduate Dean for scholarships, to appropriate department chair for assistantships; to Financial Aid Office for all other programs. Phone: (701)231-7533. Use FAFSA. About 35% of students receive aid other than loans from University and outside sources. Aid available for part-time students.

DEGREE REQUIREMENTS. For all master's: 30 semester hours minimum, at least 20 in residence; thesis/nonthesis option; final oral exam. For M.Ed.: two seminar papers. For M.B.A.: 30 semester hours minimum. For Ed.S.: 30 semester hours beyond the master's, at least 24 in residence. For Ph.D.: normally three years beyond the bachelor's; comprehensive exam; dissertation; final written/oral exam.

FIELDS OF STUDY.
Agribusiness and Applied Economics. M.S. only.
Agricultural and Biosystems Engineering.
Agricultural Education. M.S. only.
Animal and Range Sciences.
Biochemistry.
Biology.
Botany.
Business Administration.
Cell and Molecular Biology.
Cereal Science.
Chemistry.
Child Development and Family Science.
Civil Engineering.
Computer Science.
Communication.
Conservation and Environmental Sciences.
Counseling and Guidance.
Criminal Justice.
Educational Administration.
Electrical Engineering.
Emergency Management.
English.
Entomology.
Environmental Engineering.
Family and Consumer Sciences Education.
Food Safety.
Genomics.
Health, Nutrition, and Exercise Sciences.
History.
Horticulture.
Human Development.
Industrial Engineering and Management.
Manufacturing Engineering.
Mass Communication.
Mathematics.
Mechanical Engineering.
Microbiology.
Molecular Pathogenesis.
Music.
Musical Arts.
Natural Resources and Management.
Nursing.
Pharmaceutical Sciences.
Physics.
Plant Pathology.
Plant Sciences.
Polymers and Coatings Science.
Psychology.
Secondary Education.
Social Science.
Software Engineering.
Soil Science.
Speech Communication.
Statistics.
Zoology.

UNIVERSITY OF NORTH DAKOTA
Grand Forks, North Dakota 58201
Web site: www.und.edu

Established 1883. CGS member. Located 300 miles NW of Minneapolis. Coed. State control. Semester system. Special facilities: Center for Aerospace Studies, Ireland Cancer Research Laboratory, Energy and Environmental Research Center, biological field stations. Library: 658,000 volumes, 10,400 subscriptions.

Tuition: per credit resident $164, nonresident $359. On-campus housing for 892 married students, 3100 single students. Average academic year housing cost: single students $3938 (including board); married students $4500. Contact the Director of Housing for both on- and off-campus housing information. Phone: (701)777-4251. Day-care facilities available.

Graduate School

Graduate study since 1883. Enrollment: full-time 650, part-time 572. University faculty: full-time 396, part-time 18. Degrees conferred: M.A., M.S., M.Ed., M.B.A., M.P.A., M.F.A., M.Engr., Specialist, Ed.D., D.A., Ph.D.

ADMISSION REQUIREMENTS. Transcripts, GRE/MAT/GMAT/NTE, letters of recommendation required in support of School's application. Interview not required. TOEFL required for international applicants. Accepts transfer applicants. Graduates of unaccredited institutions not considered. Apply to Graduate School at least one month prior to registration; some programs have earlier deadlines. Application fee $30. Phone: (701)777-2945; fax: (701)777-3619.

ADMISSION STANDARDS. Selective for most departments. Usual minimum average: 3.0 (A = 4).

FINANCIAL AID. Annual awards from institutional funds: scholarships, fellowships, teaching assistantships, research assistantships, internships, tuition waivers, Federal W/S, loans. Approved for VA benefits. Apply by March 15 to Dean of Graduate School for fellowships, assistantships; to Financial Aid Office for all other programs. Phone: (701)777-3121. Use FAFSA. Aid available for part-time students.

DEGREE REQUIREMENTS. For master's: 30–32 credits minimum; thesis and nonthesis programs; comprehensive exam; final oral/written exam. For M.F.A.: 60 credit program with at least two semesters in residence; advancement to candidacy; comprehensive evaluation; professional exhibition; final evaluation. For Ed.D.: 96 credits minimum beyond the bachelor's, at least two consecutive semesters in full-time residence; preliminary exam; dissertation for 10 credits; final oral exam. For D.A.: 90 semester hours, two years in residence; comprehensive exam; research project/oral exam. For Ph.D.: 90 credits minimum beyond the bachelor's, at least two consecutive semesters in full-time residence; competence in scholarly tools as specified by department; preliminary exam; advancement to candidacy; dissertation; final oral exam.

FIELDS OF STUDY.
Anatomy and Cell Biology.
Atmospheric Sciences.
Aviation.

Biochemistry and Molecular Biology.
Biology.
Business Administration.
Career and Technical Education.
Chemical Engineering.
Chemistry.
Civil Engineering.
Clinical Laboratory Science.
Communication.
Communication Sciences and Disorders.
Computer Science.
Counseling.
Counseling Psychology.
Criminal Justice.
Early Childhood Education.
Educational Leadership.
Education—General Studies.
Electrical Engineering.
Elementary Education.
Energy Engineering.
English.
Geography.
Geology.
History.
Industrial Technology.
Instructional Design and Technology.
Kinesiology.
Linguistics.
Mathematics.
Mechanical Engineering.
Microbiology and Immunology.
Music.
Nursing.
Occupational Therapy.
Pharmacology, Physiology, and Therapeutics.
Physical Therapy.
Physician Assistant.
Physics.
Psychology.
Public Administration.
Reading Education.
Social Work.
Sociology.
Space Studies.
Special Education.
Speech-Language Pathology.
Teaching and Learning.
Theatre Arts.
Visual Arts.

School of Law (P.O. Box 9003)

Established 1899. ABA approved since 1923. AALS member since 1910. Semester system. Special facilities: Agricultural Law Center, Center for American Indian Legal Program and Resources. Law library: 250,000 volumes; has LEXIS, WEST-LAW.

Annual tuition: full-time, resident $4508, nonresident $9558. Estimated living expenses: $12,300.

Enrollment: first-year class 74; total full-time 194 (men 54%, women 46%). Faculty: full-time 10, part-time 3. Student to faculty ratio 16.2 to 1. Degree conferred: J.D.

ADMISSION REQUIREMENTS. LSDAS Law School report, bachelor's degree, transcripts, LSAT required in support of application. Interview not encouraged. Accepts transfer applicants. Preference given to state residents. Graduates of unaccredited colleges not considered. Admits beginning students in Fall only. Apply to Office of the Dean after August 15, before April 1. Application fee $35. Phone: (701)777-2104; fax: (701)777-2217.

ADMISSION STANDARDS. Selective. Mean LSAT: 152; mean GPA: 3.18 (A = 4). Gourman rating: 2.35. *U.S. News & World Report* ranking is in the third tier of all U.S. law schools. Accepts 50–60% of total annual applicants.

FINANCIAL AID. Scholarships, full and partial tuition waivers, Federal W/S, loans. Apply to Dean of the School for scholarships by April 15; for loans apply to the University's Financial Aid Office. Use FAFSA (School code: 003005). About 56% of students receive aid other than loans from School. No aid available for part-time students.

DEGREE REQUIREMENTS. For J.D.: 90 credits minimum, at least one year in residence. Up to 30 transfer credits of advance standing may be accepted from another accredited school.
Note: An exchange program at the University of Oslo in Norway is available.

School of Medicine and Health Sciences

Established 1905. Library: 75,000 volumes. Annual tuition: resident $13,371; nonresident $34,307, student fees $833. Total average figure for all other expenses: $9250.

Enrollment: first-year class 57, total 226 (men 52%, women 48%). School faculty: full-time 163, part-time 91. Degrees conferred: M.D., M.D.-Ph.D.

ADMISSION REQUIREMENTS. Transcripts, letters of recommendation. MCAT, interview required in support of application. Has special program for Native Americans wishing to enter medicine (INMED). Special consideration for residents of Minnesota and WICHE states. Does not have EDP. Apply to Secretary of Admissions of School after July 1, before November 1. Application fee $50. Phone: (701)777-4221; fax: (701)777-4942.

ADMISSION STANDARDS. Selective. Mean MCAT: 8.9; mean GPA: 3.56 (A = 4). Gourman rating: 3.17. Accepts 60% of total annual applicants. Approximately 67% are state residents.

FINANCIAL AID. Scholarships, merit scholarships, minority scholarships, Grants-in-Aid, institutional loans, HEAL, alternative loan programs, Federal Perkins Loans, Stafford Subsidized and Unsubsidized Loans, Service Commitment Scholarship programs are available. Assistantships/fellowships may be available for Dual Degree candidates. Immediately after acceptance, Financial Aid applications and information are sent to students. All Financial Aid is based on demonstrated need. Contact the Financial Aid Office for current information. Phone: (701)777-2849; fax: (701)777-4942. Use FAFSA (School code: 003005); also submit Financial Aid Transcript, Federal Income Tax forms. Approximately 85% of students receive some form of financial assistance.

DEGREE REQUIREMENTS. For M.D.: successful completion of four-year program. For Ph.D.: see Graduate School listing above.

FIELDS OF GRADUATE STUDY.
Anatomy.
Biochemistry.
Clinical Laboratory Science.
Microbiology.
Pharmacology.
Physiology.

UNIVERSITY OF NORTH FLORIDA

Jacksonville, Florida 32224-2645

Web site: www.unf.edu

Authorized by Florida Legislature in 1965 and opened in 1972. Coed. Public control. Semester system. Special facilities: Center for Membrane Physics, Florida Institute of Education, Center for Local Government, Small Business Development Center. Library: more than 704,000 volumes, 3000 subscriptions.

Tuition: per semester hour, resident $125, nonresident $485. On-campus housing for 100 married students and unlimited housing for single students. Annual academic year housing costs: $2820–$4990. Contact the Director of Residential Life for both on- and off-campus housing information. Phone: (904)620-2636. On-campus day-care facilities available.

Graduate Studies

Enrollment: full-time 441, part-time 1154 (men 40%, women 60%). University faculty: full-time 279, part-time 20. Degrees conferred: M.A., M.P.A., M.S., M.B.A., M.Ed., M.H.A., M.H.R.M., M.Acc.

ADMISSION REQUIREMENTS. Transcripts, bachelor's degree, GRE/GMAT required in support of application. On-line application available. TOEFL (minimum score 550) required for international applicants. Accepts transfer applicants. Graduates of unaccredited institutions not considered. Apply at least eight weeks prior to registration for the desired term. Application fee $20. Phone: (904)620-2524.

ADMISSION STANDARDS. Selective. Usual minimum average: 3.0 (A = 4), a composite score of 1000 or more on GRE (College of Education and Human Services), a score of 500 or more on GMAT (College of Business Administration).

FINANCIAL AID. Annual awards from institutional funds: scholarships, research/teaching assistantships, tuition waivers, Federal W/S, loans. Approved for VA benefits. Apply by April 1 to Financial Aid Office. Phone: (904)620-2604; fax: (904)620-2703. Use FAFSA and University's FAF. Aid available for part-time students.

DEGREE REQUIREMENTS. For M.A.: 30–39 credit program; thesis/nonthesis option. For M.S.: 36 credit program; thesis or comprehensive exam. For M.A. in Mathematical Sciences: 30 semester hours. For M.P.A.: 36 credit hours for those with significant government experience or 39 credit hours for those who do not have background. For M.S. Criminal Justice: 37 credit hours. For M.A. in Counseling: 40 semester hours. For M.B.A.: Part I—a foundation for regular graduate study; Part II—36 semester hours. For M.Acc.: 36 semester hours. For M.H.R.M.: 36 credit hours. For M.Ed.: 36–39 hours selected from component cores. For M.S. in Allied Health Services: 36 semester hours.

FIELDS OF STUDY.

COLLEGE OF ARTS AND SCIENCES:
Applied Sociology.
Counseling Psychology.
Criminal Justice.
English.
General Psychology.
History.
Mathematics and Statistics.
Public Administration.

COLLEGE OF BUSINESS ADMINISTRATION:
Accountancy.
Business Administration.
Human Resource Management.

COLLEGE OF COMPUTING SCIENCES AND ENGINEERING:
Computer and Information Sciences.

COLLEGE OF EDUCATION AND HUMAN SERVICES:
Counselor Education. Includes mental health counseling, school guidance.
Educational Leadership. Includes instructional leadership, school principal.
Elementary Education. Includes reading (K–6).
Secondary Education. Includes adult learning, English education (6–12), reading education (6–12).
Special Education. Includes disability services, emotionally handicapped, learning disabilities, mentally handicapped, hearing impaired, varying exceptionalities.

COLLEGE OF HEALTH:
Community Health.
Geriatric Management.
Health Administration.
Health Promotion/Health Education.
Nursing.
Nutrition.
Rehabilitation Counseling.
Physical Therapy.

UNIVERSITY OF NORTH TEXAS

Denton, Texas 76203-5449

Web site: www.unt.edu

Founded 1890. Located 35 miles NW of Dallas. CGS member. Coed. State control. Semester system. Special facilities: Institute for Studies in Addiction, Institute for Applied Sciences, Institute of Criminal Justice, Center for Economic Education, Center for Environmental Economic Studies and Research, Center for Inter-American Studies and Research, Center for Network Neuroscience, Center for Organometallic Research and Education, Center for Public Service, Center for Remote Sensing and Land-Use Analysis, University Center for Texas Studies. Library: 1,800,000 volumes, 12,243 subscriptions. Total University enrollment: 26,500.

Tuition: per credit, resident $160, nonresident $293. On-campus housing for 50 married students, unlimited for single students. Average academic year housing costs: $4800 (including board) for single students; $3200 for married students. Contact Director of Housing for both on- and off-campus housing information. Phone: (940)565-2605.

Robert B. Toulouse School of Graduate Studies (Box 305459)

Graduate study since 1935. Enrollment: full-time 1783, part-time 2693. Graduate faculty: full-time 623, part-time 200. Degrees conferred: M.A., M.S., M.B.A., M.F.A., M.J., M.P.A., M.Ed., M.L.S., M.M., M.M.Ed., Ed.D., D.M.A., Ph.D., D.F.A.

ADMISSION REQUIREMENTS. Official transcripts, GRE/MAT/GMAT (for business) required in support of School's application. TOEFL required for international applicants. Interview not required. Accepts transfer applicants. Graduates of unaccredited institutions not considered. Apply to Dean of Graduate School at least six weeks prior to registration, some departments have earlier deadlines. Application fee: $25 (U.S. students), $50 (international students). Phone: (940)565-2383; fax: (940)565-2141.

ADMISSION STANDARDS. Selective. Usual minimum average: 2.80, 3.0 on last 60 hours of undergraduate study (A = 4).

FINANCIAL AID. Annual awards from institutional funds: scholarships, teaching fellowships, research assistantships, Federal W/S, loans. Approved for VA benefits. Apply by March 1 to appropriate department chair for fellowships and assistantships; to Financial Aid Office for all other programs. Phone: (940)565-2016. Use FAFSA. About 25–30% of students receive aid other than loans from University and outside sources. Aid generally not available for part-time students.

DEGREE REQUIREMENTS. For M.A., M.S.: 30–36 credit hours minimum, depending upon program and degree; comprehensive oral/written exam; reading knowledge of one foreign language for some departments; for 30-hour M.A. program, thesis or research problem. For M.B.A.: 36 credit hours minimum; final oral/written exam. For M.Ed., M.L.S., M.P.A.: 36 credit hours minimum; final oral/written exam. For M.M.: 32 credit hours; thesis; reading knowledge of one foreign language; final oral/written exam. For M.F.A.: 60 credit hours minimum; final oral/written exam. For M.M.Ed.: 36 credit hours minimum; final written/oral exam. For D.M.A., Ph.D., D.F.A.: normally 60 credit hours or three years in residence beyond the bachelor's and at least two consecutive semesters in full-time attendance; reading knowledge of one or two foreign languages or completion of tool subject; qualifying exam; dissertation; final written/oral exam. For Ed.D.: 60 credit hours beyond the master's, at least two consecutive semesters in full-time residence; qualifying exam; dissertation; final oral exam.

FIELDS OF STUDY.

COLLEGE OF ARTS AND SCIENCES:
Applied Geography.
Audiology.
Biochemistry.
Biological Sciences.
Chemistry.
Clinical Psychology.
Communication Studies.
Computer Sciences.
Counseling Psychology.
Dance and Theater Arts.
Economics.
Engineering Technology.
English.
Environmental Science.
Experimental Psychology.
Foreign Languages and Literature.
French.
Health Psychology and Behavioral Medicine.
History.
Industrial Psychology.
Journalism.
Labor and Industrial Relations.
Materials Science.
Mathematics.
Molecular Biology.
Philosophy.
Physics.
Political Science.
Radio, Television, and Film.
Psychology.
Spanish.
Speech and Hearing Sciences.
Theater Arts.

COLLEGE OF BUSINESS ADMINISTRATION:
Accounting.
Administrative Management.
Business Computer Information Systems.

Finance.
Human Resource Management.
Insurance.
Management Science.
Marketing.
Operations Management Science.
Real Estate Analysis.

COLLEGE OF EDUCATION AND HUMAN SERVICES:
Applied Technology and Development.
Computer Education and Cognitive Systems.
Counseling.
Curriculum and Instruction.
Development, Family Studies, and Early Childhood Education.
Early Childhood Education.
Educational Administration.
Educational Computing.
Educational Research.
Elementary Education.
Health Promotion.
Higher Education.
Human Development and Family Studies.
Kinesiology.
Reading Education.
Recreation and Leisure Studies.
Secondary Education.
Special Education.
Supervision.

COLLEGE OF MUSIC:
Jazz Studies.
Music.
Music Education.
Music Composition.
Music Theory.
Musicology.
Performance.

SCHOOL OF COMMUNITY SERVICE:
Administration of Aging Organizations.
Administration of Long-Term Care and Retirement Facilities.
Applied Economics.
Applied Gerontology.
Behavior Analysis.
Criminal Justice.
Public Administration.
Rehabilitation Services.
Sociology.

SCHOOL OF MERCHANDISING AND HOSPITALITY MANAGEMENT:
Hotel Management.
Merchandising.

SCHOOL OF LIBRARY AND INFORMATION SCIENCE:
Information Science.
Library and Information Science.

SCHOOL OF VISUAL ARTS:
Art Education.
Art History.
Ceramics.
Communication Design.
Drawing and Painting.
Fashion Design.
Fibers.
Interior Design.
Metalsmithing and Jewelry.
Photography.
Printmaking.
Sculpture.

Texas College of Osteopathic Medicine

Web site: www.hsc.unt.edu

Founded 1970. Coed. State control. Semester system. Library; 38,000 volumes, 520 current periodicals, has MEDLINE, CANCERLINE, BIOETHIC, HEALTH, PALINET, TOXLINE, DIALOG, OCLC.

Annual tuition: resident $6550, nonresident $19,650. Total of all other first year expenses $19,511. Enrollment: first-year class 115, total 455 (men 65%, women 35%). Faculty: full-time 150, part-time 300. Degrees conferred: D.O., D.O.-Ph.D. (Biological Sciences), D.O.-M.P.H. (Public Health).

ADMISSION REQUIREMENTS. AACOMAS report, bachelor's degree preferred, official transcripts, MCAT (no later than the Spring of junior year), three recommendations (one from premed advisory committee, one evaluation from a physician, preferably a D.O.), supplemental form required in support of application. Has EDP (apply September 1). Interview by invitation only. Graduates of unaccredited colleges not considered. Preference given to state residents. Apply by November 1 to the Office of Medical Student Admissions. Admits first year students Fall only. Application fee $50. Phone: (800)735-TCOM, (817)735-2204; fax: (817)735-2225.

ADMISSION STANDARDS. Selective. Mean MCAT: 9.0; mean GPA: 3.45 (A = 4). Usual minimum average: 3.0 (A = 4). Accepts approximately 25% of total annual applicants. About 90% are state residents.

FINANCIAL AID. Scholarships, fellowships, assistantships, grants, loans. Apply by May 1 to the Financial Aid Office. Use FAFSA (College code: 003954) and institutional FAF. Approximately 80% of students receive some form of financial assistance.

DEGREE REQUIREMENTS. For D.O.: satisfactory completion of four-year program. For M.P.H., Ph.D: see Graduate Studies listing above.

NORTHEASTERN ILLINOIS UNIVERSITY

Chicago, Illinois 60625-4699

Web site: www.neiu.edu

Founded 1896, this campus 1961. CGS member. Coed. State control. Trimester system. Special facilities: Mazon Creek Paleontological Collection, Center for Exercise Science and Cardiovascular Research, Center for Inner Cities Studies. Library: 498,000 volumes, 3451 subscriptions.

Tuition: per credit, resident $117, nonresident $323. No on-campus housing. Day-care facilities available.

Graduate College

Graduate study since 1961. Enrollment: full-time 238, part-time 1354. Graduate faculty: full-time 257, part-time 164. Degrees conferred M.A., M.B.A., M.Ed., M.S.

ADMISSION REQUIREMENTS. Official transcripts required in support of College's application. TOEFL (minimum score 500) required for international applicants. Interview not required. Accepts transfer applicants. Graduates of unaccredited institutions not considered. Apply to Graduate Office by April 1 (Fall), August 15 (Spring). Application fee, none. Phone: (773)442-6003; fax: (773)442-6020.

ADMISSION STANDARDS. Competitive. Usual minimum average: 2.75 (A = 4).

FINANCIAL AID. Annual awards from institutional funds: research assistantships, teaching assistantships, internships, tuition waivers, Federal W/S, loans. Apply to appropriate department chair for assistantships; to Financial Aid Office for all other programs. No specified closing date. Use FAFSA. About 5–10% of students receive aid other than loans from College and outside sources. Aid available for part-time students.

DEGREE REQUIREMENTS. For master's: 30–48 hours minimum, at least 24–42 in residence; thesis or final paper for most majors; final written/oral exam.

FIELDS OF STUDY.

COLLEGE OF ARTS AND SCIENCES:
Biology.
Chemistry.
Computer Science.
Earth Science.
English. Includes literature, composition/writing.
Geography and Environmental Studies.
Gerontology.
History.
Linguistics.
Mathematics. Includes applied mathematics, secondary education.
Mathematics for Elementary School Teachers.
Music.
Political Science.
Speech.

COLLEGE OF BUSINESS AND MANAGEMENT:
Accounting.
Business Administration. Includes accounting, finance, marketing, management, international management, interdisciplinary.

COLLEGE OF EDUCATION:
Counseling. Includes community counseling, school counseling.
Educational Leadership. Includes higher education leadership, chief school business official, school leadership.
Exercise Science and Cardiac Rehabilitation.
Family Counseling.
Gifted Education.
Human Resource Development.
Inner City Studies.
Instruction. Includes bilingual/bicultural (elementary education), language arts (elementary education, secondary education).
Reading.
Special Education. Includes educating children with behavior disorders, educating individuals with mental retardation, early childhood special education, teaching children with learning disabilities.
Teaching. Includes bilingual/bicultural (elementary education), language arts.

NORTHEASTERN OHIO UNIVERSITIES

Rootstown, Ohio 44272-0095

Web site: www.neoucom.edu

College of Medicine (P.O. Box 95)

Established 1973 as a medical school consortium. Public control. Coed. Library: 105,500 volumes, 1036 subscriptions.

Annual tuition: resident $13,806, nonresident $27,612, student fees $588. Total average cost for all other expenses: $6825.

Enrollment: first-year class, B.S.-M.D. 105, M.D. 25 (EDP 5); total 405 (men 59%, women 41%). Faculty: full- and part-time 1700. Degrees conferred: B.S.-M.D., M.D.

ADMISSION REQUIREMENTS. AMCAS report, transcripts, MCAT, recommendations required in support of application. Interview by invitation only. Preference given to state residents. For B.S.-M.D.: preference given to applicants from Kent State, University of Akron, Youngstown State University. Has EDP; apply between June 1 and August 1. Graduates of unaccredited colleges not considered. For M.D.: apply to Office of Student Affairs after June 1, before November 1. Application fee $30. Phone: (800)686-2511 (in Ohio); (330)325-2511 (outside Ohio); e-mail: admissions@neoucom.edu.

ADMISSION STANDARDS. Very competitive. Mean MCAT: 8.8; mean GPA: 3.62 (A = 4). Gourman rating: 3.15. For M.D. program: admits about 3% of total annual applicants. Approximately 100% are state residents.

FINANCIAL AID. Scholarships, loans. Apply after acceptance to Fellowships and Awards Committee. Use FAFSA (College code: G24544). About 75% of students receive some aid from School.

DEGREE REQUIREMENTS. For B.S.-M.D.: satisfactory completion of six-year program. For M.D.: satisfactory completion of four-year program. All students required to pass Step 1 and Step 2 of the USMLE.

NORTHEASTERN STATE UNIVERSITY

Tahlequah, Oklahoma 74464-7099
Web site: www.nsuok.edu

Founded 1846. Located 75 miles SE of Tulsa. Coed. State control. Semester system. Library: 379,100 volumes, 3442 subscriptions.

Tuition: per credit, resident $83, nonresident $192 plus fees. On-campus housing for 140 married students, 800 men, 800 women. Cost varies with type of accommodation; approximate costs: $2960–$4328 per year. Contact Director of Housing for both on- and off-campus housing information. Phone: (918)456-5511, ext. 4700.

Graduate College

Graduate study since 1954. Enrollment: full- and part-time 983. College faculty teaching graduate students: full-time 82, part-time 42. Degrees conferred: M.A., M.B.A., M.Ed., M.S.

ADMISSION REQUIREMENTS. Official transcripts, three letters of reference, GRE/MAT/GMAT required in support of College's application. TOEFL required for international applicants. Interview not required. Accepts transfer applicants. Graduates of unaccredited institutions not considered. Apply to Office of Graduate Dean by June 1 (Fall), December 1 (Spring), May 1 (Summer). Application fee: none. Phone: (918)456-5511, ext. 2093; fax: (918)458-2061.

ADMISSION STANDARDS. Relatively open. Usual minimum average: 2.5 overall (A = 4), 2.75 (for last 60 hours).

FINANCIAL AID. Annual awards from institutional funds: scholarships, research assistantships, teaching assistantships, internships, grants, Federal W/S, loans. Approved for VA benefits. Apply by March 1 to Dean of Graduate College for assistantships; to Financial Aid Office for all other programs. Phone: (918)456-5511. Use FAFSA.

DEGREE REQUIREMENTS. For master's: 32–36 semester hours minimum, at least 24 hours including the last 8 in residence.

FIELDS OF STUDY.
Accounting and Financial Analysis. M.S.
American Studies. M.A.
Business Administration. M.B.A.
College Teaching. M.S.
Communication. M.A.
Counseling Psychology. M.S.
Criminal Justice. M.S.
Curriculum and Instruction. M.Ed.
Early Childhood Education. M.Ed.
Elementary Education. M.Ed.
English. M.A.
Industrial Management. M.S.
Library Media and Information Technology. M.S.
Optometry. O.D.
Reading. M.Ed.
School Administration. M.Ed.
School Counseling. M.Ed.
Special Education.
Teaching. M.Ed.

NORTHEASTERN UNIVERSITY

Boston, Massachusetts 02115-5096
Web site: www.neu.edu

Founded 1898. CGS member. Coed. Private control. Quarter system. Special facilities: Center for Advanced Microgravity, Center for Applied Social Research, Barnett Institute of Chemical Analysis and Materials Science, Burdnick Center for the Study of Conflict and Violence, Center for Biotechnology Engineering, Center for Comparative Democracy, Center for Criminal Justice Policy Research, Cultural and Arts Policy Research Institute, Center for Digital Signal Processing, Domestic Violence Institute, Center for Electromagnetic Research, Electron Microscopy Center, Center for European Economic Studies, Center for Labor Market Studies, Marine Science Center, Center for the Study of Sports in Society, Center for Innovation in Urban Education, Institute on Writing and Teaching, World History Center. Library: 893,500 volumes, 8590 subscriptions. Total University enrollment: 17,880.

Tuition varies with program; see school listing below. On-campus housing for single students only. Housing costs per quarter: $1715–$1925. Apply to Director of Residential Life for both on- and off-campus housing information. Phone: (617)373-4872.

Graduate School of Arts and Sciences

Tuition: per quarter hour $480. Enrollment: full-time 493, part-time 184. School faculty: full-time 234, part-time 25. Degrees conferred: M.A., M.A.T., M.S., M.P.A., M.S.H.S., M.S.E.P.P., M.J.N.M.M., M.T.P.W., C.A.G.S., Ph.D.

ADMISSION REQUIREMENTS. Official transcripts, two or three letters of recommendation required in support of School's application. GRE, GRE Subject Tests required for many departments. On-line application available. TOEFL and certification of finances required from international applicants. Accepts transfer applicants. Graduates of unaccredited institutions not considered. Apply by March 15 (in many cases) to the Graduate School of Arts and Sciences. Application fee $50. Phone: (617)373-3982; fax: (617)373-2942; e-mail: a&sgradinfo@casdn.neu.edu.

ADMISSION STANDARDS. Selective for most departments. Usual minimum average: 2.75 (A = 4).

FINANCIAL AID. Annual awards from institutional funds: research fellowships, teaching assistantships, Northeastern tuition assistantships, minority fellowships and MLK scholarships, tuition waivers, Federal W/S, loans. Approved for VA benefits. Apply by March 15 to Graduate School for assistantships, fellowships; to the Financial Aid Office for all other programs. Phone: (617) 373-3982. Use FAFSA. Aid available for part-time students.

DEGREE REQUIREMENTS. For master's: 40 quarter hours minimum, at least 29 in residence; thesis/final comprehensive exam/language required for most departments. For Ph.D.: normally 40 quarter hours beyond the master's, at least one year in residence; qualifying exam; final written/oral exams; reading knowledge of one or two foreign languages; dissertation; final oral exam. For C.A.G.S.: 45 quarter hours beyond the master's degree; comprehensive exam.

FIELDS OF STUDY.
American Government and Politics.
Bioinformatics.
Biology. GRE Subject, three references for admission; M.S. in biology, research, or literature, thesis required; M.S. in health science, thesis optional; M.S. full- or part-time; two languages for Ph.D. or research tool.
Chemistry. Includes analytical, clinical, organic, inorganic, physical; two references for admission, M.S. full- and part-time; one language for Ph.D.
Economics. Includes economic policy and planning; two references for admission, comprehensive exam for M.A., M.S.E.P.P.; thesis optional for M.A., M.S.E.P.P.
English. Includes linguistics, literature, writing. Three references for admission; one language for M.A., thesis optional, Master of Technical and Professional Writing, C.A.G.S. in humanistic literary study also offered.
History. GRE Subject, two references for admission; one language and comprehensive exam for M.A., thesis optional; includes historical agencies and administration.
Journalism. Includes news media management, technical and professional writing, technical writing, writing; GRE, two references for admission. M.A., M.J.N.M.M.; comprehensive exam for both degrees.
Law, Policy, and Society. M.S., Ph.D.; interdisciplinary programs; one language for Ph.D.
Mathematics. Includes applied and pure mathematics; three references for admission, one language for Ph.D.
Operations Research. Offered jointly with the School of Engineering.
Physics. GRE recommended, two references for admission. M.S. full- and part-time.
Political Science. Includes comparative government, international relations. Three references for admission; comprehensive exam for M.A., thesis optional. M.P.A. full- and part-time study.
Psychology. GRE Subject, MAT for Ph.D.; three references for admission; includes applied behavior analysis, experimental; thesis required for M.A.
Public Administration. Includes development, public policy, personnel administration, policy and planning, public financing, health administration.
Sociology-Anthropology. GRE, three references for admission; thesis optional for M.A.; comprehensive, dissertation, research tool for Ph.D.; full- and part-time study.
Technical and Professional Writing.

Graduate School of Professional Accounting

Graduate study since 1965. Quarter system. Fifteen-month cooperative program includes three-month internship where student is able to earn $8000–$10,000.

Total tuition: $24,675. On-campus housing available. Contact University's Housing Office. Phone: (617)373-5877.

Enrollment: full-time 35, part-time 91. School faculty: full-time 15, part-time 1. Degree conferred: M.S.T.

ADMISSION REQUIREMENTS. Transcripts, three letters of reference, interview, GMAT or LSAT required in support of School's application. On-line application available. TOEFL required for international applicants. Applicants cannot be undergraduate accounting majors. Apply to Director of School, preferably before March 1. Classes start in June. Application fee $50. Phone: (617)373-3244; fax: (617)373-8890; E-mail: GSPA@neu.edu.

ADMISSION STANDARDS. Very selective. Usual minimum average: 3.2 (A = 4).

FINANCIAL AID. Annual awards from institutional funds: scholarships, research assistantships, teaching assistantships, internships, Federal W/S, loans. Approved for VA benefits. Apply by March 1 to Director of School. Use FAFSA and institutional FAF. About 75% of students receive aid other than loans from School and outside sources. Aid available for part-time students.

DEGREE REQUIREMENTS. For M.S.T.: 42 quarter hours; 6 required, seven electives; successful completion of internship.

FIELDS OF STUDY.
Accounting.
Taxation.

Graduate School of Business Administration

Special facilities: DEC VAX 8650 computer, 300 IBM PCs.
Tuition: per quarter hour $550.
Enrollment: full-time 337, part-time 494. Faculty: full-time 94, part-time 46. On-campus housing available. Degrees conferred: M.B.A., E.M.B.A., M.S.F.

ADMISSION REQUIREMENTS. Official transcripts, GMAT, references required in support of School's application. On-line application available. TOEFL required for international applicants. Accepts transfer applicants. Graduates of unaccredited institutions not considered. Apply by May 1 to the Director of Admission. Rolling admissions process. Application fee $50. Phone: (617)373-5992; fax: (617)373-8564.

ADMISSION STANDARDS. Selective. Usual minimum average: 3.2 (A = 4); average GMAT 540.

FINANCIAL AID. Annual awards from institutional funds: fellowships, teaching assistantships, research assistantships, internships, Federal W/S, loans. Approved for VA benefits. Apply by March 1 to appropriate department chair for fellowships, assistantships; to the Director of Financial Aid for all other programs. Phone: (617)373-3190. Use FAFSA. About 25% of students receive aid other than loans from School and outside sources. Aid available for part-time students.

DEGREE REQUIREMENTS. For master's: 84–90 credits minimum, at least 54 in residence.

FIELD OF STUDY.
Business Administration. Includes finance, marketing, production, human relations, quantitative methods, economics, management, management systems, international business.

Graduate School of Computer Science
Web site: www.ccs.neu.edu

Graduate study since 1988. Tuition: $510 per quarter hour. On-campus housing available. Contact University's Housing Office for both on- and off-campus housing information. Phone: (617)373-5877.

Enrollment: full-time 115, part-time 50. Faculty: full-time 18, part-time 3. Degrees conferred: M.S., Ph.D.

ADMISSION REQUIREMENTS. Transcripts, three letters of recommendation, GRE required in support of School's application. TOEFL required for international applicants. Accepts transfer applicants. Graduates of unaccredited institutions not considered. Apply to Graduate School Office by August 15 (Winter), November 1 (Spring). Application fee $50. Phone: (617)373-2462; fax: (617)373-5121.

ADMISSION STANDARDS. Selective. Usual minimum average: 3.0 (A = 4).

FINANCIAL AID. Annual awards from institutional funds: fellowship, research assistantships, teaching assistantships, internships, Federal W/S, loans. Approved for VA benefits. Apply by February 15 to Graduate School Office for fellowships, assistantships; to Financial Aid Office for all other programs. Phone: (617)373-3190; fax: (617)373-8735. Use FAFSA.

DEGREE REQUIREMENTS. For M.S.: 48 quarter hours minimum, including required courses and concentration area. For Ph.D.: normally 60 quarter hours beyond master's, at least one year in residence; qualifying exam, reading knowledge of one foreign language; dissertation; final oral exam.

FIELD OF STUDY.
Computer Science. Includes artificial intelligence, communications and networks, databases, distributed systems, programming languages, operating systems, theory.
Information Resources Management.

Graduate School of Criminal Justice

Graduate study since 1974. Quarter system. Tuition: $480 per quarter hour.
Enrollment: full-time 49, part-time 20. Faculty: full-time 14, part-time 5. Degree conferred: M.S.

ADMISSION REQUIREMENTS. Official transcripts, three letters of recommendation from academic and professional sources, GRE or LSAT, essay expressing academic and personal objectives required in support of School's application. On-line application available. TOEFL required for international applicants. Accepts transfer applicants. Apply by June 1, full-time (admits Fall only); June 1, part-time (Fall), November 1 (Winter), February 1 (Spring). Application fee $40. Phone: (617)373-3327; fax: (617)373-8723.

ADMISSION STANDARDS. Selective. Usual minimum average: 3.0 (A = 4), but lower considered for provisional admission.

FINANCIAL AID. Annual awards from institutional funds: research assistantships, teaching assistantships, Federal W/S, loans. Approved for VA benefits. Apply by March 31 to the Graduate School for assistantships; to Financial Aid Office for all other programs. Phone: (617)372-3190; fax: (617)373-8735. Use FAFSA and institutional FAF. Aid available for part-time students.

DEGREE REQUIREMENTS. For master's: 42 quarter hours minimum; comprehensive exam; thesis optional. Full-time students may complete program in one year.

FIELD OF STUDY.
Criminal Justice.

Graduate School of Engineering
Web site: www.neu.edu/gradschool/engineering.html

Tuition: $415 per quarter hour. Enrollment: full-time 483, part-time 468. Faculty: full-time 79, part-time 21. Degrees conferred: M.S., M.S.C.E., M.S.C.S.E., M.S.E.E., M.S.E.M., M.S.I.E., M.S.I.S., M.S.M.E., M.S.O.R., Ph.D., E.Engr., I.Engr., M.Engr.

ADMISSION REQUIREMENTS. Transcripts, GRE, two letters of recommendation required in support of School's application. For Ph.D.: statement of purposes required. TOEFL required for international applicants. Accepts transfer applicants. Graduates of unaccredited colleges not considered. Apply to Graduate School Admissions Office by April 15. Rolling admissions process. Application fee $50. Phone: (617)373-2711; fax: (617)373-2501; e-mail: grad-eng@coe.neu.edu.

ADMISSION STANDARDS. Selective. Usual minimum average: 2.8 (A = 4).

FINANCIAL AID. Annual awards from institutional funds: fellowships, teaching assistantships, research assistantships, internships, tuition waivers, Federal W/S, loans. Approved for VA benefits. Apply by February 15 to appropriate department chair for fellowships, assistantships; to Financial Aid Office for all other programs. Phone: (617)373-3190. Use FAFSA. About 35% of students receive aid other than loans from School and outside sources. Aid available for part-time students.

DEGREE REQUIREMENTS. For master's: 40–48 quarter hours minimum, at least 28 in residence; thesis in most programs, or project, written report, and final exam. For Ph.D.: full-time program credit, requirements vary; reading knowledge of one foreign language for some programs; qualifying exam; final written/oral exam; thesis; final oral exam.

FIELDS OF STUDY.
Chemical Engineering. Apply by April 15 for Ph.D.; one language for Ph.D. M.S., M.S.C.E., Ph.D.
Civil Engineering. Includes construction, environmental, geotechnical/geoenvironmental, public works engineering management, transportation; thesis option for M.S.; apply by April 15 for Ph.D. M.S., M.S.C.E., Ph.D.
Computer Engineering. Ph.D.
Computer Systems Engineering. Includes CAD/CAM, engineering software design, robotics. M.S.C.S.E.
Electrical Engineering. Includes communications and signal processing, computer, control systems and signal processing, electromagnetics, plasma and optics, electronic circuits and semiconductor devices, power systems; thesis option for M.S.; apply by April 15 for Ph.D.; one language for Ph.D. M.S., M.S.E.E., Ph.D., E.Engr.
Engineering Management. Includes computer and information systems, manufacturing, operations research, quality control and reliability analysis; thesis for M.S.E.M.; M.S.E.M.
Industrial Engineering. Includes computer and information systems, manufacturing, operations research, quality control and reliability analysis; thesis for M.S., M.S.I.E.; apply by April 15 for Ph.D. M.S., M.S.I.E., Ph.D., I.Engr.
Information Systems. Thesis for M.S.I.S.; M.S.I.S.
Interdisciplinary Engineering. Ph.D. only.
Mechanical Engineering. Includes materials science and engineering, mechanics and design, thermofluids; thesis normally required for M.S.; apply by April 15 for Ph.D.; one language for Ph.D. M.S., M.S.M.E., Ph.D., M.Engr.
Operations Management. M.S.O.R. only.
Telecommuncation Systems Management. M.S.

Bouve College of Health Sciences
Web site: www.neu.edu/gradschool/bouve.html

Tuition: per quarter credit $480. Enrollment: full-time 598, part-time 286. Faculty: full-time 54. Degrees conferred: M.S., C.A.G.S., M.H.P., Ph.D., Pharm.D.

ADMISSION REQUIREMENTS. Official transcripts, references, essay, test (vary by program and degree), required in support of School's application. TOEFL (miminum score 600) required of those applicants whose native language is not English. Accepts transfer applicants. The application deadline for the Pharm.D. program is February 1; Ph.D. program deadline is April 15. All application materials for master's program must be submitted to the Director of Graduate Admissions at least one month prior to registration. Application fee $50. Phone: (617)373-2708; fax: (617)373-4701.

ADMISSION STANDARDS. Selective for most departments. Usual minimum average: 3.0 (A = 4).

FINANCIAL AID. Scholarships, fellowships, assistantships, a limited number of minority fellowships and Martin Luther King, Jr. Scholarships, internships, tuition waivers, Federal W/S, loans. Approved for VA benefits. Need-based financial aid is available only to American citizens or permanent residents of the United States. Apply by March 1 to appropriate department for assistantships, fellowships; to Office of Financial Aid for all other programs. Phone: (617)373-5899. Use FAFSA. Aid available for part-time students.

DEGREE REQUIREMENTS. For M.S.: 45–76 quarter hours minimum; comprehensive exam. For C.A.G.S.: one year beyond the master's; qualifying exam; comprehensive exam. For Pharm.D.: 76 quarter hours beyond the master's; qualifying exam; comprehensive exam; dissertation; final oral exam. For Ph.D.: normally 60 quarter hours beyond master's, at least one year in residence; qualifying exam; dissertation; final oral exam.

FIELDS OF STUDY.
Applied Behavior Analysis. M.S.
Audiology. M.S.
Clinical Exercise Physiology. M.S.
College Student Development and Counseling. M.S.
Counseling Psychology. M.S.
Intensive Special Needs. M.S.Ed.
Perfusion Technology. MS.
Physician Assistant Studies. M.S.
Rehabilitation Counseling. M.S.
School Counseling. M.S.
School and Counseling Psychology. Ph.D.
School Psychology. Ph.D.
Special Needs. M.S.Ed.
Speech-Language Pathology. M.S.

School of Law (P.O. Box 728)

Established 1968. ABA approved since 1969. AALS member. Quarter systems. Based on cooperative plan of legal education. Special facilities: Urban Law and Public Policy Institute, Center for Artificial Intelligence and Law. Law library: 243,751 volumes, 3264 subscriptions; has LEXIS, NEXIS, WESTLAW, DIALOG.

Annual tuition: $24,586. No on-campus housing available. Total average annual additional expense: $13,440.

Enrollment: first-year class 193; total full-time 612 (men 43%, women 57%). Faculty: full-time 26, part-time 17. Student to faculty ratio 19.9 to 1. Degrees conferred: J.D., J.D.-M.S. (Accounting), J.D.-M.B.A.

ADMISSION REQUIREMENTS. LSDAS Law School report, bachelor's degree, transcripts, LSAT required in support of application. Interviews are recommended. Accepts transfer applicants. Graduates of unaccredited colleges not considered. Apply to Director of Admissions by March 1. Admits first-year students Fall only. Begin study in August. Application fee $65. Phone: (617)373-2395; fax: (617)373-8793.

ADMISSION STANDARDS. Selective. Mean LSAT: 156; mean GPA: 3.23 (A = 4). Gourman rating 3.10. *U.S. News & World Report* ranking is in the third tier of all U.S. law schools. Accepts about 25% of total annual applicants.

FINANCIAL AID. Full and partial tuition waivers, fellowships, assistantships, Federal W/S, loans. Apply to Director of Financial Aid by March 1. Use FAFSA (School code: 002199). About 60% of students receive aid other than loans from School and outside sources.

DEGREE REQUIREMENTS. For J.D.: satisfactory completion of two-year, nine-month continuous co-op program. Cooperative legal education program integral part of J.D. For M.B.A.: see Graduate School listing above.

NORTHERN ARIZONA UNIVERSITY
P.O. Box 4125
Flagstaff, Arizona 86011-4125
Web site: www.nau.edu

Founded 1899. CGS member. Coed. State control. Semester system. Special facilities: Arizona Center for Research in Vocational Education, Arizona Earthquake Center, Bilby Research Center, Center for Colorado Plateau Studies, Center for Excellence in Education, Institute for Human Development, Center for Ecological Research, Center for Quaternary Studies. Library: 523,800 volumes, 6253 subscriptions.

Annual tuition: full-time resident $2346, nonresident $11,124; per credit, $129, nonresident $501. On-campus housing with attractive options available for single students. Annual academic year housing costs: $4500 (including board), $3450 for married students. On-campus family housing limited (one-year waiting list). Phone: (520)523-3978.

Graduate School

Enrollment: full-time 1367, part-time 3154. University faculty: full-time 533, part-time 337. Degrees conferred: M.A., M.A.T., M.Ed., M.B.A., M.M., M.P.A., M.P.T., M.V.E., M.S., M.S.N., Ph.D., Ed.D.

ADMISSION REQUIREMENTS: Transcripts, GRE/GMAT/MAT required in support of application. On-line application available. TOEFL required for international applicants. Accepts transfer applicants. Graduates of unaccredited institutions not considered. Apply to Director of Admissions by March 1. Application fee $45. Phone: (520)523-4348; fax: (520)523-8950.

ADMISSION STANDARDS. Selective. Usual minimum average: 2.9 (A = 4).

FINANCIAL AID. Annual awards from institutional funds: academic scholarships, fellowships, research assistantships, teaching assistantships, internships, tuition waivers, Federal W/S, loans. Approved for VA benefits. Apply by March 1 to department chair for assistantships; to Financial Aid Office for all other programs. Phone: (520)523-4951. Use FAFSA. Loans and part-time work available.

DEGREE REQUIREMENTS. For master's: Thesis Plan—32 hours including thesis or practicum; Comprehensive Examination Plan—33 hours plus written comprehensive exam; Extended Coursework Plan—36–45 hours, 8–10 hours of transfer credit may be accepted. For Ed.D.: 90 semester hours beyond bachelor's; residence requirement; dissertation; final oral exam. For Ph.D.: 75 semester hours, two semesters in full-time study; foreign language; dissertation; final oral exam.

FIELDS OF STUDY.
Anthropology.
Applied Linguistics.
Bilingual and Multicultural Education.

Biology.
Business Administration.
Career and Technical Education.
Chemistry.
Counseling.
Criminal Justice.
Curriculum and Instruction.
Early Childhood Education.
Earth Science.
Educational Leadership.
Educational Psychology.
Educational Technology.
Elementary Education.
Engineering.
English.
Environmental Sciences and Policy.
Exercise and Health Sciences.
Forestry.
Forest Science.
Geography. Includes rural.
Geology
History.
Liberal Studies.
Management.
Mathematics.
Music.
Nursing.
Physical Science.
Physical Therapy.
Physics. Includes applied.
Political Science.
Psychology.
Public Administration.
Quaternary Sciences.
School Psychology.

UNIVERSITY OF NORTHERN COLORADO

Greeley, Colorado 80639
Web site: www.unco.edu

Founded 1889. Located 50 miles N of Denver. CGS member. Coed. State control. Semester system. Special facilities: Center for Educational Technology, Mathematics and Science Teaching Center, Laboratory School (K-12). Library: 771,900 volumes, 3219 subscriptions.

Annual tuition: full-time resident $2451, nonresident $9961. On-campus housing for 94 married students, 20 graduate men, 20 graduate women. Average academic year housing costs: $2586–$2786 (room only) for single students; $550 per month for married students; off-campus housing $400–$800 per month. Contact Director of Residence Life for both on- and off-campus housing information. Phone: (970)351-2721.

Graduate School

Graduate study since 1913. Enrollment: full-time 1079, part-time 318 (men 35%, women 65%). Graduate faculty: full-time 242, part-time 27. Degrees conferred: M.A., M.S., M.P.H., Ed.S., D.A., Ed.D., Psy.D., Ph.D.

ADMISSION REQUIREMENTS. Two transcripts, GRE, three letters of reference (Ed.S., D.A., Psy.D. applicants) required in support of School's application. TOEFL required for international applicants. Accepts transfer applicants. Graduates of unaccredited institutions not considered. Apply to Dean of Graduate School, preferably at least sixty days prior to registration. Application fee $35, $50 for international applicants. Phone: (800)776-GRAD, or (970)351-1806; fax: (970)351-2371.

ADMISSION STANDARDS. Selective. Usual minimum average 2.7, 3.0 for doctoral applicants (A = 4).

FINANCIAL AID. Annual awards from institutional funds: fellowships, teaching/graduate assistantships with stipend and partial/full tuition waiver, internships, Federal W/S, loans. Approved for VA benefits. Apply by March 1 to appropriate department chair for fellowships, assistantships; to Financial Aid Office for all other programs. Phone: (970)351-2502. Use FAFSA. About 30% of students receive aid other than loans from University and outside sources. Aid available for part-time students.

DEGREE REQUIREMENTS. For M.A., M.S.: 30 semester hours minimum; thesis or creative project/internship; comprehensive exams or capstone project. For Ed.S.: 30 semester hours beyond the master's; practicum report; final written exam. For Ph.D., Ed.D., D.A., Psy.D.: 64 semester hours minimum beyond the master's, at least 18 hours residence and two semesters in full-time attendance; dissertation; final written/oral exam. Ph.D. students must also demonstrate competency in using two research tools (foreign language, applied statistics, mathematical statistics, or computer languages/application).

FIELDS OF STUDY.

COLLEGE OF ARTS AND SCIENCE:
Biological Sciences.
Biological Education.
Chemical Education.
Chemistry. Includes education, research.
Communication. Includes human communication.
Earth Sciences.
Educational Mathematics.
English.
Foreign Languages. Includes Spanish teaching.
History.
Mathematics. Includes liberal arts, teaching.
Psychology. Includes general psychology, human neuropsychology.
Social Science. Includes clinical sociology.

COLLEGE OF EDUCATION:
Applied Statistics and Research Methods.
Community Counseling. Includes marriage and family therapy.
Counseling Psychology.
Counselor Education and Supervision.
Educational Leadership.
Educational Media.
Educational Psychology.
Educational Technology.
Elementary Education. Includes early childhood education, middle school, primary education.
Higher Education and Student Affairs Leadership.
Interdisciplinary Degree Program. Includes teacher education.
Reading.
School Counseling.
School Psychology.
Special Education. Includes early childhood special education, moderate needs, profound needs, severe needs (affective, cognitive, communication, hearing, vision), teaching the gifted and talented.

COLLEGE OF HEALTH AND HUMAN SCIENCES:
Communication Disorders. Includes audiology, speech-language pathology.
Gerontology. Includes direct service, general studies, management/administration.
Human Rehabilitation.
Nursing. Includes education, family nursing practitioner.
Physical Education. Includes kinesiology, outdoor education, pedagogy, sport administration.

Public Health. Includes community health education.
Rehabilitation Counseling. Includes vocational evaluation.

COLLEGE OF PERFORMING AND VISUAL ARTS:
Music. Includes choral conducting, instrumental performance, music education, music history and literature, music theory and composition, performance and pedagogy, vocal performance, wind/orchestra conducting.
Visual Arts.

NORTHERN ILLINOIS UNIVERSITY
De Kalb, Illinois 60115-2864
Web site: www.niu.edu

Founded 1895. Located 65 miles W of Chicago. CGS member. Coed. State control. Semester system. Special facilities: Center for Black Studies, Center for Biochemical and Biophysics Studies, Center for Governmental Studies, Plant Molecular Biology Center, Regional History Center, Social Science Research Center, Center for Southeast Asian Studies, Center for Burma Studies. Library: 1,600,000 volumes, 17,000 subscriptions. Total University enrollment: 23,440.

Tuition: per credit, resident $130, nonresident $260. On-campus housing for 80 married students, 3400 single men, 3200 single women. Average academic year housing costs: $4168–$6610 (including board) for single students; $4000 for married students. Contact the Office of Housing Services for information on both on- and off-campus housing. Phone: (815)753-1525.

Graduate School
Web site: www.niu.edu/grad

Graduate study since 1951. Enrollment: full-time 1495, part-time 2780. Graduate faculty: full-time 693, part-time 50. Degrees conferred: M.A., M.S., M.B.A., M.A.S., M.M., M.S.Ed., M.F.A., M.P.A., M.P.H., Ed.S., Performer's Certificate, Ed.D., Ph.D.

ADMISSION REQUIREMENTS. Transcripts, two letters of recommendation for master's (three for doctorate) required in support of School's application. GRE/GMAT/MAT may be required for some programs. TOEFL required for applicants whose native language is not English; TSE for international applicants applying for teaching assistantships and M.A. program in Communication Studies. GRE Subject Test required by Department of Biological Sciences. Interview typically not required. Accepts transfer applicants. Graduates of unaccredited institutions not considered. Apply to Graduate School by June 1 (Fall), November 1 (Spring), April 1 (Summer); international applicant deadlines May 1 (Fall), October 1 (Spring). Application fee: $30. Phone: (815)753-0395; fax: (815)753-6366; e-mail: gradsch@niu.edu.

ADMISSION STANDARDS. Selective. Usual minimum average: 2.75 (A = 4).

FINANCIAL AID. Annual awards from institutional funds: academic scholarships, fellowships, assistantships, internships, tuition waivers, Federal W/S, loans. Approved for VA benefits. Apply to specific department for fellowships, assistantships; to Office of Financial Aid for all other programs. No specified closing date. Phone: (815)753-1395; fax: (815)753-9475. Use FAFSA and institutional FAF. Aid available for part-time students.

DEGREE REQUIREMENTS. For most M.A.s, M.M., M.P.A., M.P.H., M.M., M.S., M.S.Ed.: 30 semester hours minimum; final comprehensive exam in most programs; some departments require thesis; some require a reading knowledge of one foreign language. For M.B.A., M.A.S.: 30 semester hours plus 0–18 hours of deficiencies; no thesis required. For M.F.A.: 60 semester hours beyond the bachelor's degree; qualifying exam; final written/oral exam; final individual show or project. For Ed.S.: 30 semester hours minimum beyond the master's; final written/oral exam. For Performer's Certificate: 24 semester hours; two public recitals. For Ed.D., Ph.D.: about 90 semester hours beyond the bachelor's degree; qualifying exam in some programs; candidacy exam; final oral exams; proficiency in foreign language/research tool for Ph.D.; dissertation.

FIELDS OF STUDY.
Accountancy. GMAT for admission. M.A.S.
Adult-Continuing Education. Thesis optional for M.S.Ed. M.S.Ed., Ed.D.
Anthropology. Thesis optional. M.A.
Applied Family and Child Studies. Includes marriage and family therapy.
Applied Probability and Statistics. Thesis optional. M.S.
Art. Includes studio, art history, art education, art therapy; studio art M.A., M.F.A; one language, thesis for art history M.A., M.F.A.
Biochemistry and Biophysics. Interdepartmental.
Biological Sciences. Includes human anatomical sciences; GRE Subject Test in Biology for admission; thesis optional for M.S. M.S. Ph.D.
Business Administration. GMAT for admission; M.B.A.; joint M.B.A.-J.D.
Chemistry. Thesis required for M.S. M.S., Ph.D.
Communication Studies. Thesis optional. M.A.
Communicative Disorders. Includes speech language pathology, audiology, deafness rehabilitation counseling; thesis optional. M.A.
Computer Science. No thesis. M.S. only.
Counseling. Thesis optional for M.S.Ed. M.S.Ed., Ed.S., Ed.D.
Curriculum and Instruction. Includes outdoor teacher education, secondary education. Thesis optional for M.S.Ed. M.S.Ed., Ed.S., Ed.D.
Curriculum and Supervision. Thesis optional for M.S.Ed. M.S.Ed., Ed.S., Ed.D.
Early Childhood Education. Thesis optional. M.S.Ed.
Economics. Thesis optional for M.A. M.A., Ph.D.
Educational Administration. Thesis optional for M.S.Ed. M.S.Ed., Ed.S., Ed.D.
Educational Psychology. Thesis optional for M.S.Ed. M.S.Ed., Ed.D.
Electrical Engineering. Thesis required; M.S.
Elementary Education. Thesis optional; M.S. Ed.
English. Thesis optional for M.A. M.A., Ph.D.
Family and Child Studies. See Human and Family Resources.
Finance. GMAT for admission; thesis optional. M.S.
Foreign Languages and Literatures. Includes French, Spanish; thesis optional. M.A.
Foundation of Education. Thesis optional. M.S. Ed.
Geography. Thesis optional. M.S.
Geology. Thesis optional for M.S. M.S., Ph.D.
Gerontology. Interdepartmental program.
Higher Education. Interdepartmental.
History. Thesis optional for M.A. M.A., Ph.D.
Human and Family Resources. Includes applied family and child studies; home economics, resources, and services; marriage and family therapy; nutrition and dietetics; thesis optional. M.S.
Industrial Engineering. Thesis required. M.S.
Industrial Management. Thesis optional. M.S.
Instructional Technology. Thesis optional for M.S.Ed. M.S.Ed., Ed.D.
Law. Joint M.B.A.-J.D.
Management. See Business Administration.
Management Information Systems. M.S.
Marketing. See Business Administration.

Marriage and Family Therapy. See Human and Family Resources.

Mathematical Sciences. Includes applied, computational, pure mathematics, mathematics education; thesis optional for M.S. M.S., Ph.D.

Mechanical Engineering. Thesis required. M.S.

Music. Includes music education, theory and composition, history and literature, performance and pedagogy; individualized major, thesis or recital required. M.M., Performer's Certificate.

Nursing. Thesis optional. M.S.

Nutrition and Dietetics.

Philosophy. Thesis optional. M.A.

Physical Education. Includes adapted, exercise physiology/fitness leadership; thesis optional. M.S.Ed.

Physical Therapy. M.S.

Physics. Thesis optional. M.S.

Political Science. Includes public administration (M.P.A.); no thesis for M.P.A.; thesis optional for M.A. M.A., M.P.A., Ph.D.

Psychology. Thesis optional for M.A. M.A., Ph.D.

Public Administration. Includes comparative and development, fiscal, human services administration, urban management; no thesis. M.P.A. only.

Public Health. Thesis optional. M.P.H. only.

Reading. Thesis optional for M.S.Ed. M.S.Ed., Ed.D.

School Business Management. Thesis optional. M.S.Ed.

Secondary Education. Thesis optional. M.S.Ed., Ed.S., Ed.D.

Sociology. Includes criminology; thesis optional. M.A.

Southeast Asian Studies. Interdepartmental.

Special Education. Thesis optional. M.S.Ed. only.

Speech Communication. For M.A. see Communication Studies.

Sports Management.

Statistics. Thesis optional. M.S. only.

Taxation.

Theater Arts. Includes acting, design, technology; thesis optional. M.A., M.F.A.

Women's Studies. Interdepartmental.

College of Law (60115-2890)

Established 1975. Located in downtown DeKalb. ABA approved since 1978. AALS member. Semester system. Library: 216,863 volumes, 3305 subscriptions; has LEXIS, WESTLAW, LIS.

Annual tuition: resident $7496, nonresident $13,580. On-campus housing available. Total average annual additional expenses: $9986.

Enrollment: first-year class full-time 100, part-time 11; total 297 (men 56%, women 44%). Faculty: full-time 16, part-time 15. Student to faculty ratio 15.2 to 1. Degrees conferred: J.D., J.D.-M.B.A.

ADMISSION REQUIREMENTS. LSDAS Law School report, bachelor's degree, transcripts, recommendation, LSAT required in support of application. Preference given to state residents. Graduates of unaccredited institutions not considered. Apply by May 15. Rolling admissions process. Application fee $40. Phone: (815)753-9485; fax: (815)753-4501.

ADMISSION STANDARDS. Selective. Mean LSAT: full-time 153, part-time 153; mean GPA: full-time 3.19, part-time 3.21 (A = 4). Gourman rating: 2.43. *U.S. News & World Report* ranking is in the third tier of all U.S. law schools. Admits about 30–35% of total annual applications.

FINANCIAL AID. Scholarships, grants, assistantships, loans. Apply by March 1 to Financial Aid Office. Use FAFSA (School code: 001737). About 90% of students receive some aid from School.

DEGREE REQUIREMENTS. For J.D.: satisfactory completion of three-year program. For M.B.A.: see Graduate School listing above.

Note: Summer study abroad at University of Bordeaux-Montesquieu, Agen, France.

UNIVERSITY OF NORTHERN IOWA
Cedar Falls, Iowa 50614
Web site: www.uni.edu

Founded 1876. Located 96 miles NE of Des Moines. CGS member. Coed. State control. Semester system. Special facilities: Iowa Teachers Conservation Camp, Iowa Lakeside Laboratory, Institute for Environmental Education. Library: 735,000 volumes, 6781 subscriptions.

Annual tuition: full-time resident $3452, nonresident $8508; per hour resident $192, nonresident $402. On-campus housing for 365 married graduate students, limited for single graduate students. Average academic year housing costs: $4161 (including board) for single students; $3400 for married student apartments. Apply to Director of Housing for both on- and off-campus housing information. Phone: (319)273-2333.

The Graduate College

Graduate study since 1951. Enrollment: full-time 525, part-time 684 (men 35%, women 65%). Graduate faculty: full- and part-time 536. Degrees conferred: M.A., M.Acc., M.A.Ed., M.M., M.B.A., M.P.P., M.S., Ed.S., D.I.T., Ed.D.

ADMISSION REQUIREMENTS. Official transcripts required in support of College's application. GRE/GMAT required for some programs. Interview not required. TOEFL required for international applicants. Accepts transfer applicants. Apply to Registrar by August 10 (Fall), January 15 (Spring). Rolling admissions process. Application fee $20, $50 for international applicants. Phone: (319)273-2748; fax: (319)273-2243.

FINANCIAL AID. Annual awards from institutional funds: scholarships, fellowships, assistantships, internships, tuition waivers, Federal W/S, loans. Approved for VA benefits. Apply by March 1 to major department for fellowships, assistantships; to Financial Aid Office for all other aid. Phone: (319)273-2700. Use FAFSA. About 40% of students receive aid other than loans from College and outside sources. Aid available for part-time students.

DEGREE REQUIREMENTS. For master's: 30 or 32 semester hours minimum; qualifying exam; thesis/nonthesis option; final written exam for nonthesis plan. For Ed.S.: 30 hours minimum beyond the master's, at least 20 in residence and one semester or two Summer sessions in full-time attendance; final written exam often required; final oral exam. For Ed.D.: 60 semester hours minimum beyond the master's, at least 45 in residence; GRE required prior to starting dissertation; dissertation; final oral exam. For D.I.T.: 64 semester hours minimum beyond the master's, at least 52 in residence; GRE required prior to starting dissertation; dissertation; final oral exam.

FIELDS OF STUDY.
Accounting. M.Acc.
Art. Includes studio, education; final creative project optional. M.A.
Audiology. M.A.
Biology. M.A., M.S.
Business Administration. M.B.A.
Chemistry. M.A., M.S.
Communication Studies. M.A.
Computer Science. M.S.
Computer Science Education. M.A.
Counseling. Ed.D.

Curriculum and Instruction. Includes education of the gifted, education technology, elementary education, literacy education, middle level education. M.A.Ed., Ed.D.

Early Childhood Education. M.A.Ed.

Educational Leadership. Ed.D.

Educational Psychology. Includes professional development for teachers. M.A.Ed.

English. M.A.

Environmental Science/Technology and Health. M.S.

French. M.A.

Geography. M.A.

German. M.A.

Health Education. M.A.

History. M.A.

Industrial Technology. D.I.T.

Leisure, Youth, and Human Services. M.A.

Mathematics. M.A.

Mathematics for Middle Grades (4–8). M.A.

Mental Health Counseling. M.A.

Music. M.A., M.M.

Performance and Training Technology. M.A.

Physical Education. M.A.

Physics Education. M.A.

Political Science. M.A.

Postsecondary Education. Includes student affairs. M.A.Ed.

Principalship. M.A.Ed.

Psychology. M.A.

Public Policy. M.P.P.

School Counseling. M.A.Ed.

School Library Media Studies. M.A.

School Psychology. Ed.S.

Science Education. M.A.

Science Education for Elementary Schools (K–6). M.A.

Social Work. M.S.W.

Sociology. M.A.

Spanish. M.A.

Special Education. Includes career/vocational programming and transition, consultant, M.A.Ed.

Speech-Language Pathology. M.A.

TESOL. M.A.

Technology. M.A.

Theatre. M.A.

Two Languages. Includes French/German, Spanish/French, German/Spanish. M.A.

Women's Studies. M.A.

SALMON P. CHASE COLLEGE OF LAW OF NORTHERN KENTUCKY UNIVERSITY

Highland Heights, Kentucky 41099

Web site: www.nku.edu/~chase

Established 1893. ABA approved since 1954. AALS member. Special facility: Ohio Valley Environmental and Natural Resources Law Institute. State control. Semester system. Law library: 246,832 volumes, 1899 subscriptions; has LEXIS, NEXIS, WESTLAW, DIALOG.

Annual tuition: full-time resident $7098, nonresident $15,066; part-time resident $5166, nonresident $11,142. On-campus housing available. Total average annual additional expense: $3600–$10,800.

Enrollment: first-year class, full-time 97, part-time 55; total 372 (men 55%, women 45%). Faculty: full-time 20, part-time 32. Student to faculty ratio 13.1 to 1. Degrees conferred: J.D., J.D.-M.B.A.

ADMISSION REQUIREMENTS. LSDAS Law School report, bachelor's degree, transcripts, LSAT required in support of applica-

tion. Transfer applicants accepted. Preference given to state residents. Graduates of unaccredited colleges not considered. Apply to the Office of Admissions, after October 1, before March 1. Rolling admissions process. Application fee $30. Phone: (606)572-6476.

ADMISSION STANDARDS. Selective. Mean LSAT: full-time 150, part-time 151; mean GPA: full-time 3.25, part-time 3.29 (A = 4). Gourman rating: 2.24. *U.S. News & World Report* ranking is in the fourth tier of all U.S. law schools. Accepts about 25–30% of total annual applicants.

FINANCIAL AID. Scholarships, tuition waivers, Federal W/S, loans. Apply to Financial Aid Office of University by March 1. Use FAFSA (College code: 009275). Approximately 30% of all students receive some form of financial assistance.

DEGREE REQUIREMENTS. For J.D.: satisfactory completion of three-year (full-time) or four-year (part-time) program; 90 credit hour program.

NORTHERN MICHIGAN UNIVERSITY

Marquette, Michigan 49855-5301

Web site: www.nmu.edu

Founded 1899. Located 300 miles N of Milwaukee. Coed. State control. Semester system. Library: 511,000 volumes, 2200 subscriptions.

Tuition: per semester hour resident $198, nonresident $310. On-campus housing for 3200 students, 200 apartments for married students. Average academic year housing costs: $5630 (room and board) for single students; $2202 for married students. Contact Director of Housing for both on- and off-campus housing information. Phone: (906)227-2622.

College of Graduate Studies

Graduate study since 1960. Enrollment: full-time 120, part-time 254. University faculty: full-time 98, part-time 7. Degrees conferred: M.A., M.A.Ed., M.M.E., M.P.A., M.S.

ADMISSION REQUIREMENTS. Official transcripts required in support of School's application. On-line application available. GRE/GMAT/MAT required for some programs. TOEFL required for international applicants. Suggest international students allow one year to complete all application procedures. Accepts transfer applicants. Apply to Dean of Graduate Studies by July 1 (Fall), November 15 (Spring), March 15 (Summer). Rolling admissions process. Application fee: $25. Phone: (906)227-2300; e-mail: gdcoll@nmu.edu.

ADMISSION STANDARDS. Selective. Usual minimum average: 2.5 (A = 4). May be higher for some departments.

FINANCIAL AID. Scholarships, graduate assistantships, grants, tuition waivers, Federal W/S, loans. Approved for VA benefits. Apply by March 1 to Director of Financial Aid. Phone: (906)227-2327. Use FAFSA.

DEGREE REQUIREMENTS. For master's: 32 semester hours minimum, at least 28 in residence and one semester or one Summer session in full-time residence; thesis/nonthesis option/special project.

FIELDS OF STUDY.

Administrative Service. Includes community planning, general administration, public administration.

Biochemistry.

Biology.

Chemistry.

Communication Disorders.

Creative Writing.

Criminal Justice.

Educational Administration.

Elementary Education.

English. Includes writing, pedagogy.

Enhanced Mathematics/Science Education.

Exercise Science.

Individualized Studies. M.I.S.

Instructional Leadership.

Mathematics Education.

Nursing. Includes advanced practice nursing, nursing administration.

Public Administration. Includes general administration, health care administration, personnel and labor relations, state and local administration, community planning, financial administration, criminal justice.

School Counseling.

Science Education.

Secondary Education. Includes nine major disciplines.

Special Education.

Training and Development.

NORTHERN STATE UNIVERSITY

Aberdeen, South Dakota 57401-7198

Web site: www.northern.edu

Founded 1801. Located 288 miles W of Minneapolis. Coed. State control. Semester system. Library: 187,000 volumes, 1000 subscriptions.

Annual tuition: per hour resident $97, nonresident $279. On-campus housing for 411 graduate men and 582 graduate women; none for married students. Annual academic year housing costs: $2600–$3185. Apply to Director of Student Housing. Phone: (605)626-3007.

Graduate Study

Graduate study since 1956. Enrollment: full-time 22, part-time 68; Summer, full-time 200. College faculty teaching graduate students: full- and part-time 80. Degree conferred: M.S. in Ed.

ADMISSION REQUIREMENTS. Transcripts required in support of application. GRE required for some programs. TOEFL required for international applicants. Accepts transfer applicants. Apply to Director of Graduate Studies at least one month prior to registration. Application fee $15. Phone: (605)626-2558; fax: (605)626-3022.

ADMISSION STANDARDS. Selective. Usual minimum average: 2.75 (A = 4).

FINANCIAL AID. Annual awards from institutional funds: graduate assistantships, internships, Federal W/S, loans. Approved for VA benefits. Apply by March 1 to Director of Graduate Studies for assistantships; to Financial Aid Office for all other programs. Phone: (605)622-2640; fax: (605)626-3022. Use FAFSA. Aid available for part-time students.

DEGREE REQUIREMENTS. For master's: 24 semester hours minimum plus 6-hour thesis, or 27 semester hours and a 3-hour project paper, or 32 semester hours; admission to candidacy; final oral exam. Guidance and Counseling: 48-hour program.

FIELDS OF STUDY.

E-Learning.

E-Learning Design and Instruction.

E-Learning Technology and Administration.

Guidance and Counseling. Includes agency, school.

Leadership and Administration. Includes elementary principalship, secondary principalship.

Teaching and Learning. Includes education studies, elementary classroom teaching, health, physical education and coaching, language and literacy, secondary classroom teaching, special education.

NORTHWEST MISSOURI STATE UNIVERSITY

Maryville, Missouri 64468-6001

Web site: www.nwmissouri.edu

Founded 1905. Located 95 miles N of Kansas City. Coed. State control. Trimester system. Special facilities: Alternative Crop Center, Biomass Applied Research Center, Institute for Quality Productivity, Poultry Compost Research Center. Library: 335,000 volumes, 1469 subscriptions.

Tuition: per credit hour resident $138, nonresident $232. On-campus housing available for graduate students. Annual academic year housing costs; $2170 (excluding board). Apply to Housing Office. Phone: (660)562-1363.

Graduate School

Enrollment: full-time 133; part-time 741 (men 35%, women 65%). Faculty teaching graduate students: full- and part-time 165. Degrees conferred: M.A., M.S., M.S. in Ed., M.B.A., Ed.S.

ADMISSION REQUIREMENTS. Transcripts, GRE required in support of School's application. GMAT for M.B.A. applicants. On-line application available. TOEFL required for international applicants. Accepts transfer applicants. Graduates of unaccredited institutions not considered. Apply to Dean of Graduate School by July 1 (Fall), December 1 (Spring), March 1 (Summer). Application fee: none, $50 for international students. Phone: (660)562-1145.

ADMISSION STANDARDS. Relatively open. Usual minimum average: 2.5 (A = 4).

FINANCIAL AID. Annual awards from institutional funds: assistantships, teaching assistantships, Federal W/S, loans. Approved for VA benefits. Apply by March 1 to Dean of the Graduate School for assistantships; to Director of Financial Aid for all other programs. Phone: (660)562-1363. Use FAFSA. About 10% of students receive aid other than loans from University and outside sources.

DEGREE REQUIREMENTS. For master's: 32 semester hours minimum, at least 24 in residence; admission to candidacy; thesis optional; final comprehensive exam; no language requirement. For Ed.S.: 32 credits beyond the master's, at least 24 in residence.

FIELDS OF STUDY.

Agriculture. M.S.

Biology. M.S.

Business Administration. Includes accounting, agriculture economics, management information systems. M.B.A.

Counseling Psychology. M.S.

Educational Leadership. Includes elementary, secondary. M.S.Ed.
English. Includes speech. M.A., M.A.Ed.
Elementary Principalship. Ed.S.
Guidance and Counseling. M.A.Ed.
Health and Physical Education. M.A.Ed.
History. M.A.
Learning Disabilities. Includes elementary, elementary/secondary, secondary. M.A.Ed.
Mentally Handicapped. Includes elementary, elementary/secondary, secondary. M.A.Ed.
Reading. M.A.Ed.
School Computer Studies. M.S.
Secondary Principalship. Ed.S.
Science Education. M.A. Ed.
Superintendency. Ed.S.
Teaching. Includes agriculture, early childhood, elementary, English, history, instructional technology, mathematics, middle school, music, secondary. M.A.Ed.

NORTHWESTERN OKLAHOMA STATE UNIVERSITY

Alva, Oklahoma 73717-2799
Web site: www.nwalva.edu

Founded 1897. Located 150 miles NW of Oklahoma City. Coed. State control. Library: 225,000 volumes, 1411 subscriptions.

Tuition: per credit, resident $78, nonresident $187. On-campus housing available for graduate students. Average academic year housing costs: $1876 (including board). Apply to Housing Director. Phone: (580)327-8418.

Graduate School

Graduate study since 1954. Enrollment: full-time 37, part-time 153. College faculty: full-time 50, part-time 1. Degrees conferred: M.Ed., M.B.S.

ADMISSION REQUIREMENTS. Transcripts, GRE or MAT required in support of School's application. Interview not required. Accepts transfer applicants. Apply to Dean of Graduate School; no specified closing dates. Application fee $15. Phone: (580) 327-8410.

ADMISSION STANDARDS. Selective. Usual minimum average: 2.75 overall or 3.0 in last 60 hours (A = 4).

FINANCIAL AID. Limited to Oklahoma tuition grants, fellowships, Federal W/S, loans. Apply by May 1 to Director of Financial Aid. Phone: (580)327-8542. Use FAFSA. Aid available for part-time students.

DEGREE REQUIREMENTS. For M.Ed.: 32–34 credit hours minimum, optional paper; final written/oral exam. For M.B.S.: 45 credits minimum; National Counselor Examination.

FIELDS OF STUDY.
Behavioral Science. M.B.S.
Elementary Education.
Elementary School Principal.
Guidance and Counseling (K–12).
Library Media Specialist.
Reading Specialist.
School Counselor.
School Psychometrist.

Secondary Education.
Secondary School Principal.

NORTHWESTERN STATE UNIVERSITY OF LOUISIANA

Natchitoches, Louisiana 71497
Web site: www.nsula.edu

Founded 1884. Located 75 miles SW of Shreveport. CGS member. Coed. State control. Semester system. Special facilities: Northwest Louisiana Lignite Institute, Southern Studies Institute, Williamson Museum. Library: 330,145 volumes, 1749 subscriptions.

Annual tuition: full-time resident $2612, nonresident $5874. On-campus housing for 40 married students, 1000 men, 1240 women. Average academic year housing costs: $245–$275 per month for married students, $3800 (including board) for single students. Apply to Director of Housing. Phone: (318)357-6703. On-campus day-care facilities available.

Graduate Studies and Research

Graduate work since 1954. Enrollment: full-time 253, part-time 765. Graduate faculty: full-time 55, part-time 12. Degrees conferred: M.A., M.Ed., M.S., M.M., M.M.Ed., M.S.N., Ed.S.

ADMISSION REQUIREMENTS. Transcripts, GRE required in support of application. GMAT required for Business. Interview not required. TOEFL required of international students. Accepts transfer applicants. Apply to Dean of Graduate School 30 days prior to registration. Application fee $5, foreign students $15. Phone: (318)357-5851; fax: (318)357-5019.

ADMISSION STANDARDS. Selective. Usual minimum average: 2.5 (A = 4).

FINANCIAL AID. Annual awards from institutional funds: fellowships, teaching assistantships, service assistantships, research assistantships, internships, Federal W/S, loans. Approved for VA benefits. Apply by July 15 to appropriate department head for assistantships; to Financial Aid Office for all other programs. Use FAFSA. About 75% of full-time and 30% of all students receive aid other than loans from School and outside sources. Aid available for part-time students.

DEGREE REQUIREMENTS. For master's: 30 semester hours minimum including thesis, at least 24 in residence; admission to candidacy; comprehensive final written exam. For M.A. in Ed., M.S. in Ed., M.M.Ed., M.Ed.: same as above, except student may elect 33 semester hour program and special research report instead of thesis. For Ed.S.: 60 hours minimum beyond the bachelor's degree; one semester or two consecutive summers of full-time residence; thesis.

FIELDS OF STUDY.
Art.
Clinical Psychology.
Education. Includes elementary, early childhood, secondary, reading, administration, business, English, distributive, health, home economics, mathematics, reading, guidance, student personnel services, media, library.
Educational Leadership and Instruction.
English.
Health and Physical Education.
History.
Music. Includes applied, education, composition, theory.
Nursing.
Psychology.

NORTHWESTERN UNIVERSITY
Evanston, Illinois 60208
Web site: www.northwestern.edu

Founded 1851. Located 12 miles N of Chicago. CGS and AAU member. Coed. Private control. Quarter system. Special facilities: Basic Industry Research Laboratory, Biomedical Engineering laboratory, Center for Experimental Animal Resources, Materials Science Research Center, Center for Mathematical Studies in Economics and Management, Center for Urban Affairs and Policy, Vogelback Computing Center, Van de Graaff accelerator, cooperative arrangement with Argonne National Laboratory, Gas Dynamics Laboratory, Transportation Center. On the Chicago campus are the Medical School, School of Law, Dental School, Kellogg Graduate School of Management. The University's NIH ranking is 43rd among all U.S. institutions with 378 awards/grants worth $111,298,824. Library: 4,100,000 volumes, 37,767 subscriptions (both campuses). Total University enrollment: 17,900.

Annual tuition: full-time $23,301, per course $2764. On-campus housing for limited number of graduate students. Average academic year housing costs: $7750 for married students, $5000 for single students. Apply to Director of Graduate Housing. Phone: (847)491-5127.

Graduate School

Graduate study since 1893. Enrollment: full-time 2288, part-time 100. Faculty: full- and part-time 1952. Degrees conferred: M.A., M.E.M., M.S., M.F.A., Ph.D.

ADMISSION REQUIREMENTS. Transcripts, two letters of recommendation required in support of School's application. TOEFL required for international applicants. GRE required for financial aid applicants, recommended for admission; GRE or GMAT required for management. Interview required for some departments. Accepts transfer applicants, but no advanced standing toward master's degree. Apply to Admissions Office of the Graduate School at least four weeks prior to registration, by January 15 for financial aid consideration. Application fee $50, international students $55. Phone: (847)491-8532; fax: (847) 491-5070.

ADMISSION STANDARDS. Selective for most departments, very competitive for some.

FINANCIAL AID. Traineeships, research assistantships, teaching assistantships, fellowships, internships, Federal W/S, loans. Apply by January 15 to Office of the Graduate School for scholarships, to appropriate chairperson for assistantships; to Financial Aid Office for all other programs. Phone: (847)491-7264. Use FAFSA. About 60% of students receive aid other than loans from University and outside sources. No aid available for part-time students.

DEGREE REQUIREMENTS. For master's: equivalent of three quarters of full-time study; thesis required by many departments; no language requirement; final written/oral exam. For Ph.D.: equivalent of nine quarters of full-time study with at least three consecutive quarters in full-time study with at least three consecutive quarters in full-time attendance; admission to candidacy; qualifying exam; dissertation; final oral exam.

FIELDS OF STUDY.

WEINBERG COLLEGE OF ARTS AND SCIENCES:
Anthropology.
Art History.
Art Theory and Practice.
Biological Sciences Program. Interdepartmental.
Chemistry.
Classics.
Comparative Literary Studies.
Economics.
English.
French and Italian.
Geological Sciences.
German Literature and Critical Thought.
History.
Linguistics.
Mathematics.
Neurobiology and Physiology.
Philosophy.
Physics and Astronomy.
Political Science.
Religion.
Slavic Language and Literature.
Sociology.
Statistics.

SCHOOL OF COMMUNICATION:
Communication Sciences and Disorders. Includes audiology and hearing sciences, learning disabilities, speech and language pathology.
Communication Studies.
Performance Studies.
Radio/Television/Film.
Theatre.

SCHOOL OF EDUCATION:
Human Development and Social Policy.
Learning Sciences.

MCCORMICK SCHOOL OF ENGINEERING AND APPLIED SCIENCE:
Applied Mathematics.
Biomedical Engineering.
Chemical Engineering.
Civil Engineering.
Computer Science.
Electrical and Computer Engineering.
Industrial and Management Sciences.
Materials Science and Engineering.
Mechanical Engineering.
Theoretical and Applied Mechanics.

KELLOGG SCHOOL OF MANAGEMENT:
Accounting Information and Management.
Finance.
Management and Organizations.
Managerial Economics and Strategy.
Marketing.

SCHOOL OF MUSIC:
Music Cognition.
Music Education.
Musicology.
Music Technology.
Music Theory.

INTERDISCIPLINARY DEGREE PROGRAMS:
Counseling Psychology.
Liberal Studies.
Literature.
Management and Organization and Sociology.
Mathematical Methods/Social Sciences.
Medical Scientist Training Program.
Public Health.

Medill School of Journalism

Evanston campus. Annual tuition: $23,478 (M.S.J.), $8280 (M.S.M.C.). Graduate enrollment: full-time 260 (men 45%, women 55%). School faculty: full-time 45, part-time 29. Degrees conferred: M.S.J., M.S.M.C.

ADMISSION REQUIREMENTS. Transcripts, GRE/GMAT/ LSAT, three letters of recommendation, résumé, 500-word autobiography, 500-word report on a news event or marketing campaign, news writing test clip of any published material (editorial candidates) required in support of School's application. TOEFL (minimum score 650) required for international applicants. Interview required for domestic M.S.M.C. applicants. Graduates of unaccredited colleges not considered. Apply to Office of Graduate Admissions by December 1 (M.S.M.C.-Summer). Application fee $50. Phone: (847)491-5228; fax: (847)491-2052.

ADMISSION STANDARDS. Competitive. Usual minimum average: 3.0 (A = 4).

FINANCIAL AID. Scholarships, fellowships, grants, Federal W/S, loans. Approved for VA benefits. Apply by February 1 to Office of Graduate Admissions. Phone: (847)491-5228; fax: (847)467-2319. Use FAFSA (School code: E00513) and Medill's FAF. About 80% of students receive aid other than loans from School and outside sources.

DEGREE REQUIREMENTS. For M.S.J.: a twelve-unit, twelve-month program. For M.S.M.C.: fifteen-month, full-time program, includes a summer residency.

FIELDS OF STUDY.
Broadcast Journalism.
Magazine Publishing.
New Media.
Reporting and Writing. Includes business and economics reporting specialization.

School of Law (P.O. Box 11064)

Founded 1859. Located in downtown Chicago. The national headquarters for ABA and AALS are located in the Northwestern University Law School complex. ABA approved since 1923. AALS member. Semester system. Full-time, day study only. Special facilities: Center for International Human Rights, Children and Family Justice Center, Center on Wrongful Convictions, Center for Urban Affairs and Research. Law library: 670,184 volumes, 8388 subscriptions; has LEXIS, NEXIS, WESTLAW, DIALOG, CCH Access.

Annual tuition: $28,488. On-campus housing available for both single and married students. Annual on-campus living expenses: $16,152. Contact Admission Office for both on- and off-campus housing information. Law students tend to live off-campus.

Enrollment: first-year class 210; total full-time 656 (men 50%, women 50%); no part-time study. Faculty: full-time 37, part-time 36; student to faculty ratio 14.8 to 1. Degrees conferred: J.D., J.D.-M.M., J.D.-Ph.D., two-year J.D. (for persons who have completed a basic legal education and received a university degree in law in another country.)

ADMISSION REQUIREMENTS. LSDAS Law School report, bachelor's degree, transcripts, LSAT (not later than December), two recommendations, personal statement required in support of application. Graduates of unaccredited colleges not considered. Apply after October 1, before February 15. Candidates for LL.M. and J.S.D. must submit two additional recommendations, but not the LSAT. Apply to Law School Office of Admissions preferably no later than February 1. Admits first-year students Fall only. Application fee $80 ($90 after February 1). Phone: (312)503-8465; fax: (312)503-0178.

ADMISSION STANDARDS. Competitive. Mean LSAT: 166; mean GPA: 3.52 (A = 4). Gourman rating: 4.73. *U.S. News &*

World Report ranking is 11 among all U.S. law schools. Accepts 20% of total annual applicants.

FINANCIAL AID. Need-based scholarships, minority scholarships, Grants-in-Aid, private and institutional loans, Federal loans, Federal W/S. Assistantships may be available for upper-divisional joint degree candidates. All accepted students who show need are automatically considered for scholarships (selection criteria places heavy reliance on LSAT and undergraduate GPA). Apply by March 15. For all other programs, apply to the Office of Financial Aid. Phone: (312)503-8722. Use FAFSA (School code: E00293); also submit Financial Aid Transcript, Federal Income Tax forms, and use Access Disk. Approximately 38% of first-year students receive scholarships/Grants-in-Aid. Approximately 70% of students receive some form of financial assistance. For LL.M.: fellowships in the form of grants, Graduate-Professional Alternative Loans (GPAL) available. Apply on LL.M. Admissions application form and complete LL.M. Financial Aid Form. Apply by March 15. If eligible for Federal programs, submit FAFSA. No employment opportunities are available.

DEGREE REQUIREMENTS. For J.D.: satisfactory completion of 86 semester hour program. For LL.M.: at least 24 credits beyond the J.D.; one year in full-time residence; thesis; final written/oral exam. For J.S.D.: at least one year in residence beyond the J.D., but more time normally required; thesis; final written/ oral exam. Refer to Graduate School listings above for joint degree requirements.

J. L. Kellogg Graduate School of Management
Web site: www.kellogg.northwestern.edu

Quarter system. Annual tuition: $30,255. Full-time program located on Evanston campus, part-time (evening) program on Chicago campus. On-campus housing for single, married students. Contact Assistant Director of Student Affairs for housing information. Phone: (708)491-3300.

Enrollment: full-time 1201, part-time 1300. Faculty: full- and part-time 183. Degrees conferred: M.B.A., M.M. Manufacturing (combined program with School of Engineering). The Ph.D. is offered through the Graduate School.

ADMISSION REQUIREMENTS. Transcripts, GMAT (GRE required for doctoral applicants), interview, letters of reference required in support of School's application. TOEFL (minimum score 600) required of international applicants. Transfer applicants not accepted. Apply to Office of Admissions by March 30 for M.B.A.; by February 1 for Ph.D. Admission June or September quarters only. Application fee $100. Phone: (847)491-3308; fax: (847)491-4960.

ADMISSION STANDARDS. Very selective. No minimum G.P.A. or GMAT required. Mean LSAT: 700; mean GPA: 3.45. Gourman rating: 4.88 (M.B.A. and Ph.D.). *U.S. News & World Report* ranking is in the top five of all business schools.

FINANCIAL AID. Annual awards are from government, institutional, and corporate funds, including minority fellowships, grants, scholarships, internships, loans. Apply by February 1 to Office of Admission. Phone: (847)491-3308. Use FAFSA (School code: E00302). Ph.D. students should apply by January 15; there are approximately 40 research assistantships. About 60% of students receive aid. Aid available for part-time students.

DEGREE REQUIREMENTS. For M.B.A., M.M.M.: six quarters in residence, beginning in September, for candidates other than graduates of accredited business schools. For Ph.D.: see Graduate School listing above.

FIELDS OF STUDY.
Accounting and Information Systems.
Analytical Consulting.
Analytical Finance.
Biotechnology.
Business in Its Social Environment.
Decision Sciences.
Entrepreneurship and Innovation.
Finance.
Health Industry Management.
Human Resources Management.
International Business and Markets.
Management and Strategy.
Managerial Economics.
Marketing.
Media Management.
Operations Management.
Public and Nonprofit Management.
Real Estate.
Technology Industry Management.
Transportation and Logistics Management.

The Feinberg Medical School

Founded 1859. Chicago campus (60611). Medical library: 250,000 volumes. Annual tuition: $32,805, student fees $165. Total average figure for all other expenses $9500.

Enrollment: first-year class 170 (men 54%, women 46%), total 678. Faculty: more than 2200 full- and part-time. Degrees conferred: B.A.-M.D., B.S. (Engineering)-M.D., M.D., M.D.-M.B.A., M.D.-Ph.D., (Medical Scientist Training Program) M.P.H., M.D.-M.P.H. The M.B.A. (Kellogg Graduate School of Management) and Ph.D. are offered through the Graduate School.

ADMISSION REQUIREMENTS. AMCAS report, transcripts, two letters of recommendation, MCAT required in support of application. At least three years of premedical work required for admission. Does not have EDP. Interview required for all applicants under serious consideration. Accepts transfer applicants. Apply to Office of Admissions after June 15, before October 15. Application fee (after screening) $50. Phone: (312) 503-8206.

ADMISSION STANDARDS. Very competitive. Mean MCAT: 10.1, mean GPA: 3.7 (A = 4). *U.S. News & World Report* ranked School 22nd among all U.S. medical schools. Accepts 3% of total annual applicants. Approximately 30% are state residents.

FINANCIAL AID. Scholarships, fellowships, loans. Apply to Financial Aid Committee after acceptance. Use FAFSA (School code: E00295). MSTP funded by NIH. About 60% of students receive some aid from School.

DEGREE REQUIREMENTS. For B.A., B.S.-M.D.: satisfactory completion of seven-year program. For M.D.: satisfactory completion of four-year program. For M.B.A.: see J. L. Kellogg Graduate School of Management listing above. For M.P.H.: one year beyond M.D., in certain cases it can be accomplished during four-year M.D. program; see Graduate School listing above. For Ph.D.: see the Graduate School listing above.

FIELDS OF GRADUATE STUDY.
Anatomy.
Biochemistry.
Biomedical Engineering.
Biophysics.
Cell Biology.
Genetics.
Immunology.
Management.
Microbiology.

Molecular Biology.
Neuroscience.
Pathology.
Pharmacology.
Physiology.
Public Health.

School of Music

Established 1895. Annual tuition: full-time $18,100, per course $1509. On-campus housing is available for graduate students. Enrollment: full-time 236, part-time 6. School of Music faculty: 60 full-time, 53 part-time. Degrees conferred: M.M., D.M. The Ph.D. is offered through the Graduate School.

ADMISSION REQUIREMENTS. Transcripts and two recommendations required in support of School's application. On-line application available. GRE required for Ph.D. applicants only. TOEFL required for international applicants. Accepts transfer applicants. For M.M.: audition or recording for performance majors, scores for composition majors, research papers for theory majors, music history and literature majors, essays for music education majors. For D.M.: theory and music history exams; interview and audition for performance majors; scores and tape recording of compositions for composition majors. Transfer credits for M.M. not accepted. Limited transfer credit for D.M. from an accredited college accepted. Apply to Office of Music Admission and Financial Aid. Apply by January 15 (Fall), April 15 (Summer, M.M. Music Education). Early filing is given preference. Application fee $40. Phone: (847)491-3141; fax: (847)491-5260.

ADMISSION STANDARDS. Highly selective. Minimum usual average 3.0 (A = 4).

FINANCIAL AID. Annual awards from institutional funds: grants, fellowships, graduate assistantships, internships, tuition waivers, stipends, Federal W/S, loans. Approved for VA benefits. Financial Aid application sent out after admissions application is received. Apply by January 15 for D.M., February 15 for M.M. to Office of Admissions and Financial Aid. Phone: (847)491-3141. Use FAFSA and institutional FAF. About 80% of students receive aid other than loans from School of Music and outside sources. No aid is offered part-time students.

DEGREE REQUIREMENTS. For M.M.: 12 units minimum in residence; recital for performance and conducting majors; large composition for composition majors; comprehensive exams for music theory, music history, and music education majors; optional thesis or project for music education majors. For D.M.: 18 units minimum in residence, at least 9 units in full-time attendance; recitals-projects, lecture-recitals, or document, depending on major; reading knowledge of one or two foreign languages, depending on major; qualifying exam; final oral exam.

FIELDS OF STUDY:
Choral Conducting. M.M.
Collaborative Arts and Piano Performance. D.M.
Jazz Pedagogy. M.M.
Music Composition. M.M.
Music Education. M.M., Ph.D.
Musicology. M.M.
Music Technology. M.M.
Music Theory. M.M.
Performance. Includes jazz, voice, winds, percussion, strings, piano, organ. M.M., D.M.
Orchestral Conducting. M.M.
Piano Pedagogy. M.M., D.M.
String Pedagogy. M.M.
Wind/Band Conducting. M.M.

NOTRE DAME DE NAMUR UNIVERSITY

Belmont, California 94002-1997
Web site: www.ndnu.edu

Established 1851. Located 25 miles S of San Francisco. CGS member. Coed. Private control. Roman Catholic affiliation. 4-4-4 system. Library: 115,000 volumes, 726 subscriptions.

Tuition: per credit $550. On-campus housing available. Annual cost: $7620–$10,972. Contact Director of Housing for both on- and off-campus housing information. Phone: (650)508-3513.

Graduate School

Graduate study since 1972. Enrollment: full-time 224, part-time 462 (men 30%, women 70%). College faculty: full-time 19, part-time 103. Degrees conferred: M.A., M.M., M.Ed., M.B.A., M.P.A., M.A.-A.T., M.A.-C.P., M.S.S.M., M.A.-Geron.

ADMISSION REQUIREMENTS. Official transcripts, GMAT (business), two letters of recommendation required in support of application. On-line application available. GRE required for some programs. Interview required for some programs. TOEFL (minimum score 550) and a statement of financial and family support required for international applicants. Accepts transfer applicants. Graduates of unaccredited colleges not considered. Apply to Graduate Office at least one month prior to date of registration. Rolling admissions process. Application fee $50. Phone: (800)263-0545; fax: (650)508-3662.

ADMISSION STANDARDS. Selective. Usual minimum average: 2.5 (A = 4).

FINANCIAL AID. Scholarships, teaching assistantships, Federal W/S, loans. Apply to Director of Financial Aid. Scholarship deadlines: July 15 (Fall), December 1 (Spring). Phone: (650) 508-3509. Use FAFSA.

DEGREE REQUIREMENTS. For master's: 30–39 credits minimum, at least 24–33 in residence; advancement to candidacy; thesis/nonthesis option.

FIELDS OF STUDY.
Art Therapy. M.A.
Business Administration. M.B.A.
Counseling Psychology. M.A.
Education. M.Ed.
Educational Technology Administration. M.S.
Electronic Business Management. M.S.
English. M.A.
Gerontology. M.A.
Management. M.S.
Marital and Family Therapy. M.A.
Music. Includes pedagogy, performance. M.M.
Public Administration. M.P.A.
Special Education. M.A.
Systems Management. M.S.S.M.
Teaching. M.A.

UNIVERSITY OF NOTRE DAME

Notre Dame, Indiana 46556-5602
Web site: www.nd.edu

Founded 1842. Located 80 miles SE of Chicago. CGS member. Coed on graduate level. Private control. Roman Catholic affiliation. Semester system. Special facilities: Center for Applied Mathematics, Center for Bioengineering and Pollution Control, Computing Center with IBM 3033 system with peripheral equipment, Center for Catalysis and Reaction Engineering, Center for Environmental Science and Technology, Center for Molecularly Engineering Materials, Center for Nano Science and Technology, Center for the Philosophy of Religion, Center for Tropical Disease and Training, Center for Zebrafish Research, Cushwa Center for the Study of American Catholicism, Center for the Study of Contemporary Society, Hessert Center for Aerospace Research, Institute for Latino Studies, Institute for Pastoral Liturgy, Joan B. Kroc Institute of International Peace Studies, Helen Kellogg Institute for International Studies, Keough Institute for Irish Studies, LOBUND Laboratory (germfree life equipment), Radiation Laboratory, The Library of the Medieval Institute, Center for the Study of Man in Contemporary Society, Nanovic Institute for European Studies, Reilly Center for Sciences, Technology and Values, Walther Cancer Research Center. Library 2,600,000 volumes, 18,416 subscriptions. Total University enrollment: 10,563.

Annual tuition: full-time $24,220, per credit $1346. On-campus housing for 132 married students and 253 single students. Average academic year housing cost: $352–$472 (per month) for married students, $3899 (including board) for single students. Apply to Director of Student Residences. Phone: (219)631-5878. Daycare facilities available.

Graduate School

Organized 1918. Enrollment: full-time 1404, part-time 53. University faculty: full- and part-time 615. Degrees conferred: M.A., M.B.A., M.S., M.Div., M.F.A., M.M., M.Arch., M.M.S., Ph.D.

ADMISSION REQUIREMENTS. Transcripts, three letters of recommendation, GRE Subject Tests required in support of School's application. On-line application available. TOEFL required for international applicants. Interview not required. Accepts transfer applicants. Graduates of unaccredited institutions not considered. Apply to Director of Graduate Admissions, preferably by February 1 (Fall), November 1 (Spring). New students normally begin Fall only. Application fee $50. Phone: (219)631-7706; fax: (219)631-4183; e-mail: gradsch@nd.edu.

ADMISSION STANDARDS. Selective for most departments. Usual minimum average: 3.0 in area of concentration (A = 4).

FINANCIAL AID. Annual awards from institutional funds: scholarships, teaching assistantships, research assistantships, fellowships, internships, grants, Federal W/S, loans. Apply to Director of Graduate Admissions by February 1. Phone: (219) 631-6436. Use FAFSA. About 90% of students receive aid other than loans from University and outside sources. Aid available for part-time students.

DEGREE REQUIREMENTS. Degree programs are all determined by departmental advisement. The following are illustrative degree programs. For M.A., M.S.: Plan I—30 semester hours minimum; thesis (6 semester boom), admission to candidacy; final written/oral exam. Plan II—30 semester hours minimum; admission to candidacy; no thesis or language requirement; normally a terminal degree. For M.A. (Art): 32 semester hours minimum; final portfolio and essay. For M.B.A.: 60 semester hours minimum in residence. For M.F.A.: 60 semester boom minimum; final portfolio; studio thesis. For M.M.: 36 semester hours minimum; final music project. For M.M.S.: 38 semester hours minimum and knowledge of Latin required for entrance. For M.Div.: 72 semester hours. For Ph.D.: 72 semester hours, at least four consecutive semesters in full-time residence; foreign language requirements determined by department; candidacy exam; dissertation; defense of dissertation.

FIELDS OF STUDY.

Aerospace—Mechanical Engineering.
American Studies. Interdepartmental; master's only.
Applied Mathematics.
Architecture. M.Arch. only.
Art. Includes art history (M.A.), studio, design. M.F.A.
Biochemistry and Biophysics. Interdisciplinary.
Bioengineering.
Biological Sciences.
Chemical Engineering.
Chemical Physics. Interdisciplinary.
Chemistry.
Civil Engineering.
Computer Science and Engineering.
Creative Writing.
Early Christian Studies.
Economics.
Education.
Electrical Engineering.
English.
Environmental Engineering.
Geological Sciences.
German Language and Literature. Master's only.
Government and International Studies.
History.
History and Philosophy of Science.
Literature. Interdisciplinary.
Mathematics.
Medieval Studies.
Molecular Biosciences.
Music. Master's only.
Peace Studies. Master's only.
Philosophy.
Physics.
Psychology
Romance Languages and Literature. Master's only.
Sociology.
Theological Studies.
Theology.

Mendoza College of Business

P.O. Box 399
Web site: www.nd.edu/~cba

Graduate Business School established 1967. Private control. Accredited programs: M.B.A. Institution draws from a national and international population. Located on main campus; suburban environment. Semester system. Special facility: Research Center in Banking and Finance. Special programs: accelerated M.B.A. program for students with an undergraduate degree in business; foreign exchange programs in London, England, Santiago, Chile, Monterrey, Mexico; international internships.

Annual tuition: $24,969. On-campus rooms and apartments available for both single and married students. Enrollment: full-time 490, part-time 9 (men 70%, women 30%). Faculty: full-time 78, part-time 12. Degrees conferred: M.B.A., E.M.B.A. (weekends only), M.S.A. (Administration), M.S.Acct., M.B.A.-J.D.

ADMISSION REQUIREMENTS. All applicants should have a bachelor's degree from a recognized institution of higher education and a strong mathematics background. Contact College of Business for application material and information; phone: M.B.A. (219)631-8671; E.M.B.A. (800)631-3622; Accountancy (219)631-9732. Early applications are encouraged for both admission and financial aid consideration. Beginning students are admitted Fall and Summer. Both U.S. citizens and international applicants should apply by April 15 (Fall, two-year program), March 1 (Summer, one-year program). Submit an application, GMAT (will accept GMAT test results from the last five years; latest acceptable date is June), official transcripts, two letters of recommendation, four essays, résumé (prefers at least four years of work experience), and an application fee of $75 to the Office of Admission. In addition, international students (whose native language is other than English) should submit a TOEFL report (minimum score 600), certified translations and evaluations of all official transcripts, recommendation should be in English or with certified translations, proof of health/immunization certificate, and proof of sufficient financial resources for two years of academic study. Interviews are strongly encouraged prior to the admissions committee reviewing completed applications. Joint degree applicants must apply to and be accepted to both schools; contact the Admissions Office for current information and specific admissions requirements. Rolling admissions process.

ADMISSION STANDARDS. Selective. Median GMAT: 611, median GPA: 3.16 (A = 4). Gourman rating: 4.37. *U.S. News & World Report* ranked the College of Business in the top 24 of all U.S. business schools. *Business Week* listed the College of Business in the top 50 of all American business schools.

FINANCIAL AID. Scholarships, merit fellowships, minority stipend program, grants, M.B.A. fellowship, graduate assistantships, Federal Perkins Loans, Stafford Subsidized and Unsubsidized Loans, Federal W/S available. Financial aid is available for part-time study and may be available for international students. Assistantships/fellowships may be available for joint degree candidates. Financial aid applications and information are generally available at the on-campus visit/interview and is included with the admissions application; apply by March 1. Request scholarship, fellowship, assistantship, and all need-based information from the College of Business. Phone: (219)631-8488. For assistantships, fellowships, scholarships the selection criteria places heavy reliance on GMAT and undergraduate GPA. Use FAFSA (School code: 001840); also submit Financial Aid Transcript, Federal Income Tax forms. Approximately 70% of students receive some form of financial assistance.

DEGREE REQUIREMENTS. For M.B.A.: 44–63 credit program including 24 elective credits, one- or two-year program; degree program must be completed in five years. For E.M.B.A.: 48 credit program. For M.S.A.: 42 credit intensive Summer program; some electives can be completed through a distance learning option. For M.S.Acct.: 30–36 credit program. For M.B.A.-J.D.: 123 credit, four-and-one-half- to five-and-one-half-year program.

FIELDS OF STUDY.
Accountancy. M.S.Acct.
Administration. M.S.A.

M.B.A. FIELDS OF ELECTIVE CONCENTRATIONS.
Accountancy.
Business Consulting. Includes strategy focus.
E-MBA. Includes e-commerce, e-consulting, e-entrepreneurship.
Entrepreneurship.
Finance. Includes banking, corporate finance, investments.
General Management.
Human Resource Management.
International Business.
Manufacturing Management.
Marketing. Includes consumer marketing, business-to-business marketing, market and customer measurement and analysis.

Law School (46556-0959)

Web site: www.law.nd.edu

Established 1869. ABA approved since 1925. AALS member. Semester system. Special facilities: Center for Civil and Human Rights, Thomas J. White Center on Law and Government.

Library: 519,477 volumes, 5707 subscriptions; has LEXIS, NEXIS, VU/TEXT, DIALOG, WESTLAW.

Annual tuition: $23,922. On-campus housing available. Apply to University Housing Office. Total average annual additional expenses: $9000.

Enrollment: first-year class 184, total full-time 553 (men 58%, women 42%). Faculty: full-time 25, part-time 21. Student to faculty ratio 17.0 to 1. Degrees conferred: J.D., J.D.-M.B.A., LL.M. (Comparative and International Law), J.S.D.

ADMISSION REQUIREMENTS. LSDAS Law School report, bachelor's degree, transcripts, LSAT required in support of application. Interview usually not required. Accepts transfer applicants. Apply to the Director of Admission for the School after September 1, before March 1. Application fee $55. Phone: (219)631-6626; fax: (219)631-3980.

ADMISSION STANDARDS. Selective. Mean LSAT: 161, mean GPA: 3.42 (A = 4). Gourman rating: 4.68. *U.S. News & World Report* ranking is the top 24 of all U.S. law schools. Accepts 20% of total annual applicants.

FINANCIAL AID. Scholarships, fellowships, resident assistantships, Federal W/S, loans. Apply to the Financial Aid Office by April 1. Use FAFSA (School code: 001840). About 60% of students receive aid other than loans from School.

DEGREE REQUIREMENTS. For J.D.: satisfactory completion of three-year program. For LL.M., J.S.D.: at least 24 credit hours beyond the J.D.; thesis; for J.S.D. one year in full-time study and a final written/oral exam. For M.B.A., see Graduate School listing above.

Note: Academic year and summer program in London for J.D. candidates.

NOVA SOUTHEASTERN UNIVERSITY
Fort Lauderdale, Florida 33314-7721
Web site: www.nova.edu

Chartered 1964. Merged with Southeastern University of Health Sciences in 1994. Offers degree programs throughout United States and four foreign countries. CGS member. Coed. Private control. Special facilities: Family Center for Child Development, Institute for Marine and Coastal Studies, Institute for Social Services to Families, Center for Youth Policy. Library: 362,600 volumes, 8821 subscriptions.

Tuition: per credit $325–$600, varies by program. On-campus housing for married and single graduate students. Average academic year housing costs: $7200 (including board), $4400–$6200 for married students. Contact Director of Residential Life for both on- and off-campus housing information. Phone: (305) 475-7052.

Graduate Programs

Enrollment: full-time 2854, part-time 5610. Faculty: full-time 290, part-time 569. Degrees conferred: M.S., M.B.A., M.P.A., M.Acc., M.A., M.I.B.A., M.O.T., M.P.T., M.P.H., D.I.B.A., Sc.D., Psy.D., D.S., D.A., D.P.A., D.O.T., Ed.S., Ed.D., Ph.D., D.B.A., D.I.B.A.

ADMISSION REQUIREMENTS. Official transcripts, letters of recommendation required in support of application. On-line application available. GRE Subject Tests, GMAT required for some programs. Accepts transfer applicants. Graduates of unaccredited institutions not considered. Apply to Office of Admissions for the program of interest, or the Registrar's Office. Closing date varies with the program; rolling admissions for most programs. Application fee $40. Phone: (800)541-6682.

ADMISSION STANDARDS. Selective. Usual minimum average: 3.0 (A = 4).

FINANCIAL AID. Scholarships, research fellowships, research assistantships, Federal W/S, loans. Approved for VA benefits. Apply to appropriate department for fellowships/assistantships; to Financial Aid Office for all other programs. Phone: (800)806-3680. Use FAFSA (University code: 001509). About 20% of students receive aid other than loans from both University and outside sources.

DEGREE REQUIREMENTS. For master's: generally 36–45 hours minimum, varies with program; thesis/nonthesis option. For Ed.S.: 36 hours beyond the master's. For doctorate: satisfactory completion of core instructional sequence, areas of specialization and research experiences; dissertation; final exam. Residence requirements: varies with program; Ph.D. and other doctoral programs typically require three to four years and 90 credits beyond baccalaureate.

FIELDS OF STUDY.

SCHOOL OF COMPUTER AND INFORMATION SCIENCES:
Computer Information Systems. M.S., Ph.D.
Computer Science. M.S., Ph.D.
Computing Technology in Education. M.S., Ed.D., Ph.D.
Information Science. Ph.D.
Information Systems. Ph.D.
Management Information Systems. M.S.

H. WAYNE HUIZENGA GRADUATE SCHOOL OF BUSINESS
AND ENTREPRENEURSHIP:
Accounting. M.Acc.
Business Administration. M.B.A., D.B.A.
Health Service Administration. M.B.A., M.S.
Human Resource Management. M.S.
International Business Administration. M.I.B.A., D.I.B.A.
Public Administration. M.P.A., D.P.A.
Taxation. M.S.

FISCHLER GRADUATE SCHOOL OF EDUCATION
AND HUMAN SERVICES:
Audiology. Au.D.
Child and Youth Studies. Ed.D.
Education. M.S.
Educational Leadership. Ed.D.
Higher Education. Ed.D.
Human Services. M.S.
Instructional Technology and Distance Education. M.S., Ed.D.
Organizational Leadership. Ed.D.
Speech-Language Pathology. M.S., SLP.D.
Teaching and Learning. M.A.

GRADUATE SCHOOL OF HUMANITIES AND SOCIAL SCIENCES:
Conflict Analysis and Resolution. M.S., Ph.D.
Family Therapy. M.S., Ph.D.
Marriage and Family Therapy. D.M.F.T.

HEALTH PROFESSIONS DIVISION:
Biomedical Sciences. M.B.S.
Clinical Vision Research. M.S.
Health Sciences. D.H.Sc.
Medical Science. M.M.S.
Occupational Therapy. M.O.T., D.O.T.
Optometry. O.D.
Pharmacy. Pharm.D.
Physical Therapy. M.P.T., Ph.D.
Public Health. M.P.H.

OCEANOGRAPHIC CENTER:
Coastal Zone Management. M.S.
Marine Biology. M.S.
Marine Environmental Sciences. M.S.
Oceanography/Marine Biology. Ph.D.

CENTER FOR PSYCHOLOGICAL STUDIES:
Clinical Psychology. Ph.D., Psy.D.
Mental Health Counseling. M.S.
Psychopharmacology. M.S.
School Guidance and Counseling. M.S.
School Psychology. Psy.S.

CROSS-CENTER PROGRAM:
Criminal Justice. M.S.

College of Dental Medicine

Established 1996. Located on main campus. Basic science courses are taught by both the College's and Medical Sciences' faculty. Postgraduate specialties: Endodontics, Orthodontics, Pediatric Dentistry, Periodontics.

Annual tuition: resident $27,550, nonresident $27,990. No on-campus housing available at this time. Contact Office of Residential Life for both on- and off-campus housing information. Phone: (954)262-7052. Off-campus housing, food, transportation, and personal expenses: approximately $14,200. Estimated additional first-year expense: $8300. Enrollment: first-year class 95; total full-time 300 (men 55%, women 45%). Faculty: full-time 16, part-time/volunteers 25. Degree conferred: D.M.D.

ADMISSION REQUIREMENTS. Preference given to state residents, U.S. citizens, and permanent residents only. The Junior College transfer credit is limited to 60 credits. For serious consideration, applicants should have at least a 2.5 GPA (A = 4). Will consider applicants with only three years of undergraduate preparation; prefer applicants who will have a bachelor's degree prior to enrollment. Apply through AADSAS (file after June 1, before April 1), send official transcripts (should show at least 90 semester credits/135 quarter credits), service processing fee; at the same time submit official DAT scores directly to the Office of Admission. TOEFL may be required of applicants whose native language is other than English. Submit the following materials only after being contacted by an Admissions Officer: an application fee of $75, a secondary/supplemental application, official transcripts, predental committee evaluation or two recommendations from science professors and one from a humanities professor to Office of Admission within two weeks of receipt of supplemental materials. Interviews are by invitation only and generally for final selection. First-year students admitted Fall only. Rolling admissions process; notification starts in December and is finished when class is filled, but generally no later than June 1. School does maintain an alternate/waiting list. Phone: (954)262-1101, (800)356-0026; fax: (954)916-2282.

ADMISSION STANDARDS. The College's first year was 1997; median DAT: Academic 18, PAT 18; median GPA: 3.31 (A = 4).

FINANCIAL AID. Limited number of scholarships, grants, institutional loans, State Loan Programs, DEAL, HEAL, alternative loan programs, loans, Military Service Commitment Scholarship programs. Institutional Financial Aid applications and information are generally available at the on-campus, by-invitation interview. Contact the Financial Aid Office for current information. Phone: (954)262-1114. Use FAFSA (School code: 001509); also submit Financial Aid Transcript, Federal Income Tax forms, and Federal Funds Certification.

DEGREE REQUIREMENTS. For D.M.D.: satisfactory completion of four-year program.

Shepard Broad Law Center (33315)

Web site: www.nsulaw.nova.edu

Established 1974. ABA approved since 1975. AALS member. Semester system. Special facilities: Disability Law Institute, Center for the Study of Youth Policy. Library: 322,700 volumes, 5537 subscriptions; has LEXIS, NEXIS, WESTLAW, DIALOG, CALI.

Annual tuition: full-time $20,370, part-time $15,280. On-campus housing available. Total average annual additional expense: $15,500.

Enrollment: first-year class full-time 245, part-time 73; total full- and part-time 968 (men 60%, women 40%). Faculty: full-time 46, part-time 62. Student to faculty ratio 16.2 to 1. Degrees conferred: J.D., J.D.-M.B.A., J.D.-M.S. (Psychology), J.D.-M.U.R.P.

ADMISSION REQUIREMENTS. LSDAS Law School report, bachelor's degree, transcripts, LSAT, personal statement required in support of application. Accepts transfer students. Apply to Office of Admissions by March 1. Rolling admissions process. Application fee $50. Phone: (954)451-6117; fax: (954)262-3844.

ADMISSION STANDARDS. Selective. Mean LSAT: full- and part-time 147; mean GPA: full-time 2.93, part-time 2.95 (A = 4). Gourman rating: 2.55. *U.S. News & World Report* ranking is in the fourth tier of all U.S. law schools. Admits about 30–35% of total annual applicants.

FINANCIAL AID. Scholarships, grants, partial tuition waivers, assistantships, Federal W/S, loans. Apply to the Financial Aid Office by March1. Use FAFSA (School code: 001509). About 13% of students receive some aid from School.

DEGREE REQUIREMENTS. For J.D.: satisfactory completion of 87 credit hour program. For master's degrees: see Graduate School listing above.

College of Osteopathic Medicine

Founded 1979. Coed. Private control. Semester system. Library: 35,000 volumes, 480 current periodicals, has MEDLINE, CANCERLINE, BIOETHIC, HEALTH, TOXLINE, DIALOG, OCLC.

Annual tuition: in-state $20,525, out-of-state $25,497. Enrollment: first-year class 180, total 711 (men 70%, women 30%). Faculty: full-time 45, part-time 145. Degree conferred: D.O.

ADMISSION REQUIREMENTS. AACOMAS report, bachelor's degree, official transcripts, MCAT (no later than the Spring of junior year), three recommendations (one from premed advisory committee, one evaluation from a physician, preferably a D.O.), supplemental form required in support of application. Interview by invitation only. Graduates of unaccredited colleges not considered. Preference given to state residents. Apply by January 15, to AACOMAS, March 1 (for supplemental materials) to the Director of Admissions. Rolling admissions process. Admits first year students Fall only. Application fee $50. Phone: (800)356-0026, ext. 1101, or (954)262-1101.

ADMISSION STANDARDS. Selective. Usual minimum average: 2.75 (A = 4). Mean MCAT: 8.7; mean GPA: 3.4 (A = 4). Accepts approximately 15% of total annual applicants.

FINANCIAL AID. Scholarships, fellowships, Federal W/S, loans. Apply by April 1 to the Financial Aid Office. Use FAFSA (College code: 001509) and institutional FAF. Approximately 75% of students receive some form of financial assistance.

DEGREE REQUIREMENT. For D.O.: satisfactory completion of four-year program. All students must take and pass the

National Board of Osteopathic Medical Examination Parts I and II prior to the awarding of D.O.

OAKLAND UNIVERSITY
Rochester, Michigan 48309-4401
Web site: www.oakland.edu

Founded 1957. Located 25 miles N of Detroit. CGS member. Coed. State control. Trimester system. Special facilities: Eye Research Institute, Biochemistry and Biotechnology Institute, Center for Robotics and Advanced Automation, Cumulative Trauma Research Institute, Michigan Center for Automotive Research, Public Affairs Research Laboratory, Meadow Brook Health Enhancement Institute. Library: 688,000 volumes, 2600 subscriptions. Total University enrollment: 15,200.

Tuition: per credit resident $227, nonresident $489. On-campus housing for graduate men and women, 48 units for married students. Average academic year housing costs: $4800 (including board) for single students; $5200 for married students. Contact Director, Residence Halls for both on- and off-campus housing information. Phone: (248)370-3570.

Graduate Studies

Enrollment: full-time 862, part-time 2371 (men 40%, women 60%). University faculty: full- and part-time 426. Degrees conferred: M.A., M.Ed., M.S., M.A.T., M.M., M.P.A., M.P.T., M.B.A., M.S.N., Ed.S., Ph.D.

ADMISSION REQUIREMENTS. Official transcripts, two recommendations required in support of application. GRE/GMAT required for some programs. Interview not required. On-line application available. TOEFL and GRE required for international applicants. Accepts transfer applicants. Apply to Office of Admission by July 15 (Fall), November 20 (Winter), March 15 (Spring), May 15 (Summer). Application fee $30. Phone: (248)370-3167; fax: (248)370-4114; e-mail: gradmail@oakland.edu.

ADMISSION STANDARDS. Selective for some departments, competitive for others. Usual minimum average: 3.0 (A = 4).

FINANCIAL AID. Annual awards from institutional funds: fellowships, teaching assistantships, research assistantships, internships, full tuition waivers, Federal W/S, loans. Apply to appropriate department chairman by March 15. Use FAFSA and University's FAF. Phone: (248)370-3370. About 10% of students receive aid other than loans from University and outside sources. Aid available for part-time students.

DEGREE REQUIREMENTS. For master's: 36–45 semester hours minimum, at least 30 in residence; candidacy; thesis/nonthesis option. For Ed.S.: 30 semester hours beyond master's. For Ph.D.: 60 credits beyond the bachelor's minimum, at least one year in full-time residence; proficiency in at least one foreign language for some programs; qualifying exam; dissertation; final oral exam.

FIELDS OF STUDY.
Accounting. M.S.
Applied Mathematical Sciences. Ph.D.
Applied Statitics. M.S.
Biological Sciences. M.S., Ph.D.
Biology. M.S.
Biomedical Sciences. Includes health and environmental chemistry, medical physics. Ph.D.
Business Administration. M.B.A.
Cellular Biology. M.S., Ph.D.
Chemistry. M.S., Ph.D.
Computer Education. M.Ed.

Computer Science and Engineering. M.S.
Counseling. M.A.
Curriculum, Instruction, and Leadership. M.Ed.
Early Childhood Education. M.Ed.
Educational Administration. Ed.S.
Electrical and Computer Engineering. M.S.
Engineering Management. M.S.
English. M.A.
Exercise Science. M.S.
History. M.A.
Industrial Applied Mathematics. M.S.
Linguistics. M.A.
Mathematics. M.S., M.A.
Mechanical Engineering. M.S.
Music. M.M.
Nursing. M.S.N.
Physical Therapy. M.P.T.
Physics. M.S., Ph.D.
Public Administration. M.P.A.
Reading. Ph.D.
Reading and Language Arts. M.A.T.
School Administration. Ed.S.
Software Engineering. M.S.
Special Education. M.Ed.
Systems Engineering. M.S., Ph.D.
Training and Development. M.S.

OCCIDENTAL COLLEGE
Los Angeles, California 90041-3314
Web site: www.oxy.edu

Founded 1887. Coed. Private control. Semester system. Library: 500,000 volumes, 1100 subscriptions.

Annual tuition: full-time $23,510; part-time, per unit $980. No on-campus housing for graduate students. Contact Residence Life Office for off-campus housing information. Phone: (323)259-2531.

Graduate Study

Enrollment: full-time 17 (men 3, women 14). College faculty: full-time 134, part-time 50. Degrees conferred: M.A., M.A.T.

ADMISSION REQUIREMENTS. Official transcripts, three recommendations, GRE required in support of application. GRE Subject Test required for some majors. TOEFL and GRE required for international applicants. Interview not required. Does not accept transfer applicants. Graduates of unaccredited institutions not considered. Apply to Graduate Office by March 1 (Fall), October 1 (Spring), March 1 (Summer). Application fee $50. Phone: (323)259-2921.

ADMISSION STANDARDS. Selective. Usual minimum average: 3.0 (A = 4), minimum TOEFL score 625.

FINANCIAL AID. Limited to scholarships, Federal W/S, loans. Apply by March 1 to Financial Aid Office. Use FAFSA and institutional FAF. Phone: (323)259-2548. About 90% of students receive aid other than loans from College and outside sources. Aid sometimes available for part-time students.

DEGREE REQUIREMENTS. For M.A., M.A.T.: a minimum of 6 courses (30 units) including thesis, internships, or creative project, final written/oral exam.

FIELDS OF STUDY.
Biology. Thesis for M.A.; M.A. only.
Elementary Education. M.A.T. only.
Secondary Education. M.A.T. only.

OGLETHORPE UNIVERSITY
Atlanta, Georgia 30319-4484
Web site: www.oglethorpe.edu

Founded 1835. Coed. Private control. Semester system. Library: 150,000 volumes, 752 current periodicals, 12 PCs.

Tuition: $795 per course. On-campus housing for single students only. Average academic year housing costs: $6360 (including board). Contact Housing office for both on- and off-campus housing information. Phone: (404)261-1441.

Graduate Study

Graduate study since 1971. Enrollment: full- and part-time 59 (men 5%, women 95%). Faculty: full-time 4, part-time 5. Degree conferred: M.A.T., M.B.A.

ADMISSION REQUIREMENTS. Transcripts, GRE/GMAT, Praxis I (for MAT), essay, résumé, three recommendations required in support of application. On-line application available. TOEFL required for international applicants. Accepts transfer applicants. Graduates of unaccredited colleges not considered. Apply to Director of Graduate Studies by mid-April (Summer), 15 days prior to other semesters. Rolling admissions process. Application fee $30. Phone: (404)364-8307.

ADMISSION STANDARDS. Selective. Usual minimum average: 2.8 (A = 4).

FINANCIAL AID. Limited to loans.

DEGREE REQUIREMENTS. For M.A.T.: 36 semester hours minimum, at least 30 in residence; comprehensive final exam. For M.B.A.: 40 credit program; practicum.

FIELDS OF STUDY.
Business Administration. Includes entrepreneurship, strategy and finance, international trade and economic history, marketing, accounting.
Elementary Education. Concentrations in early childhood (K–4), or middle grades (4–8).

OHIO NORTHERN UNIVERSITY
Ada, Ohio 45810-1599
Web site: www.onu.edu

Founded 1885. Located 85 miles SE of Toledo. Private control. Methodist affiliation. Semester system. Special facilities: Pharmacy Law Institute. Total University enrollment: 2900.

Claude W. Pettit College of Law

Established 1884. ABA approved since 1948. AALS member. Law library: 287,500 volumes, 3014 subscriptions; has LEXIS, NEXIS, WESTLAW.

Annual tuition: $19,040. On-campus housing available. Total average annual additional expense: $9890.

Enrollment: first-year class 111; total 287 (men 59%, women 41%); no part-time students. College faculty: full-time 15, part-time 10. Student to faculty ratio 15.9 to 1. Degree conferred: J.D.

ADMISSION REQUIREMENTS. LSDAS Law School report, bachelor's degree, transcripts, four character references, LSAT required in support of application. Interview not required. Accepts transfer applicants. Graduates of unaccredited colleges not considered. Apply to Director of Admissions, preference given to applications received by March 15. Rolling admissions process.

Admits first-year students in Fall only. Application fee $40. Phone: (419)772-2211.

ADMISSION STANDARDS. Selective. Mean LSAT: 148; mean GPA: 3.01 (A = 4). Gourman rating: 2.67. *U.S. News & World Report* ranking is in the fourth tier of all U.S. law schools. Accepts 55–60% of total annual applicants.

FINANCIAL AID. Scholarships, need-based grants, assistantships, Federal W/S, loans. Apply to Financial Aid Office by June 1. Phone: (419)882-2272. Use FAFSA (College code: 003089). About 15% of students receive aid other than loans from College.

DEGREE REQUIREMENTS. For J.D.: satisfactory completion of required 87 semester hour program.
Note: Exchange program with the University of Iceland.

THE OHIO STATE UNIVERSITY
Columbus, Ohio 43210-1270
Web site: www.osu.edu

Established 1870. CGS and AAU member. Coed. State control. Quarter system. Special facilities: Advanced Computing Center for the Arts and Design, Center for Advanced Study in Telecommunication, Atmospheric Sciences Program, Ohio State Biochemistry Program, Laboratory for Artificial Intelligence Research, Biomedical Engineering Center, Biostatistics Program, Byrd Polar Research Center, Campus Chemical Instrument Center, Chemical Physics Program, Center for Cognitive Science, Criminal Justice Research Center, Electroscience Laboratory, Engineering Research Center for Net Shape Manufacturing, Environmental Biology Program, Center for Human Resource Research, International Area Studies, Center for Lake Erie Area Research, Center for Mapping, Center for Materials Research, Center for Medieval and Renaissance Studies, Mershon Center for Research and Education in National Security and Public Policy, Molecular, Cellular, and Developmental Biology Program, National Regulatory Research Institute, OSU Comprehensive Cancer Center, OSU Nisonger Center for Mental Retardation and Developmental Disabilities, Ohio Supercomputer Center, Physiological Optics Program, Slavic and East European Studies Program, Comprehensive Program in Vocational Education, Water Resources Center. The University's NIH ranking is 53rd among all U.S. institutions with 280 awards/grants worth $89,403,532. Library: 5,400,000 volumes, 42,700 subscriptions. Total University enrollment: 54,500.

Annual tuition: full-time resident $6307, nonresident $16,377. On-campus housing for 396 married students, 890 single students. Average annual housing cost: $4866 (including board) for single students. Apply to the Office of Contracts and Assignments. Phone: (614)292-8266.

Graduate School

Graduate study since 1878. Enrollment; full-time 6837, part-time 2316. Graduate faculty: 2877. Degrees conferred: M.Appl.Stat., M.Arch., M.A., M.B.A., M.C.R.P., M.Ed., M.F.A., M.H.A., M.L.H.R., M.Land.Arch., M.Mus., M.P.A., M.P.H., M.S., M.S.W., D.M.A., Ph.D., Cert.Sp'l., Edu'l.Adm., Cert.Sp'l. (Latin American Studies), Cert.Sp'l. (Russian Area Studies), Cert.Sp'l. (Medieval and Renaissance Studies).

ADMISSION REQUIREMENTS. Transcripts, three letters of recommendation, autobiography required in support of School's application. Additional items may be required by individual departments. GRE Subject Tests for most departments. GMAT required for some departments. Interview required by some departments. Evidence of proficiency in English required of international applicants, either TOEFL or MELAB. Accepts transfer applicants. Graduates of unaccredited institutions not considered. Apply to Admissions Office by August 15 (Autumn), December 1 (Winter), March 1 (Spring), May 15 (Summer); prior to February 1 if a fellowship applicant. Earlier dates established for international applicants. Application fee $30; international applicants $40. Phone: (614)292-9444; fax: (614)292-3895; e-mail: admissions@osu.edu.

ADMISSION STANDARDS. Very competitive for some departments, competitive for the others. Minimum average required (unless otherwise specified by individual graduate program): 2.7 (A = 4).

FINANCIAL AID. Annual awards from institutional funds: fellowships, research associateships, administrative associateships, teaching associateships, internships, Federal W/S, loans. Apply before February 1 (prior to the intended academic year of enrollment) to Admissions Office for fellowships; by April 1 to appropriate department chair for associateships; to Office of Financial Aid for all other programs. Phone: (614)292-0300; fax: (614) 292-9264. Use FAFSA. About 47% of students receive aid other than loans from institution and outside sources. Aid available to part-time students.

DEGREE REQUIREMENTS. For master's: 45 quarter hours minimum, at least 36 in residence; either a thesis and an oral and/or written exam or a four-hour written comprehensive exam which may include an oral portion. For Ph.D.: 135 quarter hours minimum beyond the bachelor's degree, a minimum of 90 credits in residence; a minimum of three out of four consecutive quarters in full-time study; foreign language requirement for some departments; general comprehensive exam; candidacy exam; dissertation; final oral exam. For D.M.A.: essentially the same as for Ph.D., except a D.M.A. document and performance for some areas.

FIELDS OF STUDY.

Accounting and Management Information Systems. GMAT and additional requirements for admission; contact department for additional materials. M.A., Ph.D.

Aeronautical and Astronautical Engineering. GRE required for admission, additional department materials required; contact department. Admits primarily for Autumn quarter, apply by January 15. M.S., Ph.D.

African American and African Studies.

Agricultural, Environmental, and Developmental Economics. GRE or GMAT required for admission, GRE required for fellowship applicants.

Agricultural Engineering. GRE Subject Test strongly recommended. Fifty-hour M.S., if nonthesis.

Agronomy. GRE required for admission. M.S., Ph.D.

Allied Medical Professions. GRE required for all applicants whose GPA is below 3.5. Health professions certification, registration, or licensure required. M.S. only.

Anatomy. GRE Subject Test in Biology required for admission. M.S., Ph.D.

Animal Science. GRE required for admission. Thesis for M.S. M.S., Ph.D.

Anthropology. GRE required for admission. Prefer Autumn quarter applicants.

Architecture. Admits Autumn quarter only. Applicants for three-year plus (90 hour) program admitted Summer quarter. GRE, portfolio required for admission. Thesis (45 hour program)/nonthesis (50 hours).

Art. Admits Autumn quarter only. Application completed by January 20. For additional admission requirements contact department. 90-hour program; public exhibition of studio work, thesis.

Art Education. Apply by April 5 (Autumn), January 5 (Summer). GRE for fellowship applicants and Art Administration. For additional admissions requirements contact department. 60- or 70-hour master's; thesis.

Arts Policy and Administration.

Astronomy. Admits Summer and Autumn quarters only; apply by January 15. GRE Subject Test in Physics for admission. Thesis required. M.S., Pd.D.

Atmospheric Sciences. Autumn quarter preferred. Apply by February 1 for associateships. GRE required for admission; thesis required for M.S. M.S., Ph.D.

Biochemistry Program (OSBP). Autumn quarter applications strongly recommended; apply by February 1. GRE required for admission. Thesis for M.S. M.S., Ph.D.

Biomedical Engineering. GRE required for admission; thesis required for M.S. Statement of purpose, title and abstract of master's thesis for Ph.D.; M.S., Ph.D.

Biophysics. GRE recommended for all applicants, required if GPA is below 3.0. M.S., Ph.D.

Biostatistics. GRE required for admission; Summer quarter applications strongly recommended; January 15 deadline for fellowship consideration. Ph.D. only.

Business Administration. Admits Autumn quarter only. GMAT for admission, except for organizational behavior, GRE may be substituted; 104-hour full-time M.B.A. program. M.B.A. applicants apply by March 1, February 1 for Financial Aid; Ph.D. applicants apply by February 1. M.B.A., Ph.D.

Chemical Engineering. GRE recommended for all applicants and required of graduates of foreign universities, holders of nonengineering degrees and applicants whose GPA is below 3.0; thesis required for M.S. M.S., Ph.D.

Chemical Physics. Summer and Fall quarters preferred. GRE Subject Test in Physics or Chemistry required of graduates of foreign universities and highly recommended for all other applicants, particularly if GPA is below 3.0. M.S., Ph.D.

Chemistry. Admits Summer (international applicants preferred) and Autumn (domestic applicants preferred). Apply by February 1. GRE Subject Test in Chemistry required. M.S., Ph.D.

City and Regional Planning. GRE for master's applicants with GPA below 3.0 and all Ph.D.s and fellowship applicants. 90 hours for M.C.R.P. M.C.R.P., Ph.D.

Civil Engineering. No Summer quarter admission. GRE required of all applicants with undergraduate GPA below 2.7 and of applicants with graduate GPA below 3.0, of nonengineering majors, of fellowship applicants and of engineering graduates from non-ABET-accredited or non-CAB-accredited institutions. GPA of 3.6 of fellowships. M.S., Ph.D.

Classics. GRE required for admission. Apply January 29 for teaching associateships, 60 hours for M.A., M.A., Ph.D.

Communication. Admits Autumn quarter only. Apply by May 15, by March 1 for associateships consideration. GRE required for admission. Contact department for additional requirements. 50 hours for M.A. M.A., Ph.D.

Comparative Studies. Apply by April 1 (Summer and Autumn quarter), January 1 (for financial aid consideration), November 1 (Winter), January 15 (Spring). GRE required for admission. 50 hours for M.A. M.A. only.

Computer and Information Science. Admits Autumn quarter only. GRE Subject Test required for admission. M.S., Ph.D.

Dance. Admits Autumn quarter only. Qualifying audition required for admission. 90 hours for M.F.A./ M.A., M.F.A.

Dentistry. Admits Summer quarter only. Apply by October 1. GRE; D.D.S. or D.M.D. required for admission, except those wanting dental materials or oral biology. Thesis required. M.S. only.

East Asian Languages and Literature. No Summer quarter admission; prefer Autumn quarter. Apply by February 15, prefer earlier submission. GRE for financial aid consideration and if GPA is less than 3.0. 65 hours for M.A. M.A., Ph.D.

Economics. Admits Autumn quarter only. Apply by February 15 for priority financial aid consideration. GRE required for admission; Subject Test in Economics recommended. M.A., Ph.D.

Education. No Summer quarter admission. GRE/MAT required for most programs. Includes educational policy and leadership; educational services and research; educational studies: humanities, science, technological and vocational; educational theory and practice. Contact the School of Education for specific program listing for requirements and contact information. M.Ed., M.A., Ph.D., Certificate of Specialist in Education Administration.

Electrical Engineering. GRE required of M.S. applicants and if GPA is less than 3.0, and of all graduates of foreign universities. Ph.D. applicants should submit thesis or thesis abstract (in English) and letter of recommendation from thesis adviser. 50 hours required for nonthesis M.S. M.S. Ph.D.

English. Admits Autumn quarter only. Apply by January 15. GRE, sample of critical writing required of M.A., Ph.D. applicants; subject test recommended. 50 hours for M.A. 65 hours for M.F.A. M.A., M.F.A., Ph.D.

Entomology. GRE Subject Test in Biology, curriculum vitae required for admission. M.S., Ph.D.

Environmental Science. Admits Autumn quarter only. Apply by May 1 (preferably by March 1), February 15 for financial aid consideration. GRE required for admission. Contact department for additional application materials. M.S., Ph.D.

Evaluation, Ecology, and Organismal Biology.

Family Resource and Human Development. Admits Autumn quarter only. Apply by February 1. GRE required for admission. 50-hour nonthesis option for M.S. M.S., Ph.D.

Family Resource Management. GRE required for admission. M.S., Ph.D.

Food, Agricultural, and Biological Engineering.

Food Science and Nutrition. GRE required for admission. 50 hours required for nonthesis M.S. M.S., Ph.D.

French and Italian. Admits Autumn quarter only. Apply by February 15 for associateships consideration. GRE required for all applicants with degrees from American universities. Scholarly paper required for Ph.D. applicants. M.A., Ph.D.

Geodetic Science and Surveying. Autumn quarter preferred; Summer quarter if prerequisites required. Mathematics through differential and integral calculus required for admission; one course in linear algebra and knowledge of computer programs recommended. M.S., Ph.D.

Geography. Autumn quarter admission preferred. GRE required for admission. Statement of purpose for Ph.D. applicants; contact department for details. M.A., Ph.D.

Geological Sciences. GRE Subject Test in Geology or allied science in undergraduate area of study required for admission; thesis required for M.S. M.S., Ph.D.

German Languages and Literature. Autumn quarter strongly recommended. Apply by January 15 for priority consideration. GRE required for admission. M.A., Ph.D.

Greek and Latin.

Health Services Management and Policy. Admits Autumn quarter only. Apply by March 15 for priority consideration. GRE/GMAT required for admission. Contact department for additional admission materials. 84 hours for M.H.A. M.H.A. only.

History. Admits Summer and Autumn quarter only. Apply by January 10. GRE required for all U.S. citizens. Sample of written work required. M.A., Ph.D.

History of Art. Admits Summer and Autumn quarters only. Apply by January 15 for associateship or fellowship consideration. GRE, writing sample required for admission. 50-hour nonthesis option for M.A. M.A., Ph.D.

Horticulture and Crop Science. GRE required for admission. M.S., Ph.D.

Human and Community Resource Development. Includes family relations and human development, family resource management, home economics education, human nutrition and food management, and textiles and clothing. Contact School of Human Ecology for specific admission requirements. M.S., Ph.D.

Human Nutrition and Food Management. GRE required for admission. M.S., Ph.D.

Industrial and System Engineering. Admits Autumn quarter only. Apply by March 1; February 1 for financial aid consideration. GRE required for admission. M.S., Ph.D.

Industrial, Interior, and Visual Communication Design. Admits Autumn only. Apply by April 15. Portfolio of recent academic or professional visual work required. Contact department for additional admission requirements. 60-hour nonthesis option for M.A. M.A. only.

Journalism and Communication. Admits Autumn and Winter quarters only. Apply by June 1 (Autumn), October 1 (Winter). GRE required for admission. 50-hour nonthesis option for M.A. M.A. only.

Labor and Human Resources. Admits Ph.D. applicants to Autumn quarter only; apply by February 1. Apply for M.L.H.R. by July 1 (Autumn), October 1 (Winter), February 1 (Spring), April 1 (Summer). GRE/GMAT required for admission. 50 hour nonthesis option for M.L.H.R. M.L.H.R., Ph.D.

Landscape Architecture. Prefer applicants for Autumn quarter. Apply by March 31. Applicants with landscape architecture or allied field may apply for Winter or Spring quarter. GRE, portfolio, statement of intent required for admission. Contact department for additional admission requirements. M.Land, Arch. only.

Linguistics. Admits Autumn quarter only. Apply by December 15. GRE required for admission. M.A., Ph.D.

Materials Science and Engineering. GRE required for graduates of foreign universities and of holders of nonengineering degrees. M.S., Ph.D.

Mathematics. Prefer applicants for Summer quarter. GRE Subject Test in mathematics required for admission. Contact department for additional admission requirements. 51 hours for M.A.; writing project. 50-hour nonthesis M.S. M.A., M.S., Ph.D.

Mechanical Engineering. Apply by July 1 (Autumn), November 1 (Winter), February 1 (Spring), May 1 (Summer); January 1 for associateship consideration. GRE required for M.S. applicants with below 3.3 GPA. M.S. applicants who hold nonengineering baccalaureate or degrees from a foreign university; all doctoral applicants with GPA below 3.7, applicants with a master's degree from a foreign university, and fellowships applicants. M.S., Ph.D.

Medical Microbiology and Immunology. Autumn quarter applications strongly recommended. Apply by March 1 for priority consideration; by February 1 for associateships, fellowships. GRE required for admission; Subject Test in Biology recommended. M.S., Ph.D.

Microbiology. Autumn quarter application strongly recommended. Apply by February 1. GRE required for admission. Subject Test in Biology or Biochemistry recommended. 60-hour nonthesis M.S. option. M.S., Ph.D.

Molecular, Cellular, and Developmental Biology. Prefer Autumn quarter applicants. GRE/Subject Test (Biology, Chemistry, or Biochemistry, Cell and Molecular Biology preferred) required for admission. Thesis required for M.S. M.S., Ph.D.

Molecular Genetics. Includes genetics. GRE Subject Test (Biology or Biochemistry, Cell and Molecular Biology) required for admission. Thesis required for M.S. M.S., Ph.D.

Music. GRE required for M.A., Ph.D. applicants in music education, music history and music theory; and for M.Mus. D.M.A. in music composition. Contact department for additional requirements. 50-hour nonthesis M.A. option. 45 hours for M.Mus., plus tape-recorded recital. M.A., M.Mus., D.M.A., Ph.D.

Natural Resources. Apply by February 15. GRE required for admission. 55-hour nonthesis M.S. option. M.S. only.

Near Eastern Languages and Literature. GRE recommended. M.A. only.

Neuroscience. GRE/Subject Test (Biology, Psychology, Biochemistry, Cell and Molecular Biology) required for admission. Contact department for statement of purpose guidelines. Ph.D. only.

Nuclear Engineering. GRE required for admission. 50-hour non-thesis M.S. option, plus written task report. M.S., Ph.D.

Nursing. Admits M.S. May 1 (Autumn), November 1 (Winter), February 1 (Spring). Admits Ph.D. January 15 (Autumn only). GRE required for admission. Applicants must hold or be eligible for licensure as an RN in Ohio. Contact department for additional admission requirements. 52-hour nonthesis M.S. option. M.S., Ph.D.

Oral Biology. Admits Autumn quarter only. GRE required for admission. Ph.D. only

Pathology. GRE Subject (Biology, Cell, and Molecular Biology required for admission. Contact department for additional admission requirements. Thesis required M.S. M.S., Ph.D.

Pharmacology. Admits Autumn quarter only. GRE Subject (Biology or Chemistry, Cell and Molecular) required for admission. MCAT scores in lieu of GRE for M.D.-Ph.D. applicants. M.S., Ph.D.

Pharmacy. Includes pharmaceutical administration (admits Autumn quarter only, GRE or GMAT for applicants with GPA below 3.0), pharmacology (GRE for admission), pharmaceutical chemistry (GRE for admission), medicinal chemistry and Pharmacognosy (GRE for admission). M.S., Ph.D.

Philosophy. Autumn quarter strongly recommended. Apply by February 1 for priority consideration. GRE, sample of work required for admission. M.A., Ph.D.

Physical Therapy.

Physics. Admits Summer and Autumn quarters; Summer preferred. GRE Subject Test in Physics required for admission. 50 hour nonthesis M.S. option. M.S., Ph.D.

Plant Biology. Apply by March 15 for associateship consideration. GRE Subject Test in Biology required for admission. TOEFL, TSE required for applicants whose native language is not English. 55-hour nonthesis M.S. option. M.S., Ph.D.

Plant Pathology. GRE required for admission. M.S., Ph.D.

Political Science. Admits Autumn quarter only. Apply by March 1; January 1 for fellowships consideration. GRE required for admission. M.A., Ph.D.

Psychology. Admits Autumn quarter only. Apply by February 1; January 1 for fellowship consideration. GRE Subject Test in Psychology required for admission. Contact department for additional admission requirements. Thesis required for M.A. M.A., Ph.D.

Public Health.

Public Policy and Management. Autumn quarter applicants preferred. GRE/GMAT (all M.P.A. applicants), GRE/GMAT (M.A. applicants with GPA below 2.7), GRE (for all Ph.D. applicants) required for admission. 50 hours for M.A., 74 hours for M.P.A. M.A., M.P.A., Ph.D.

Rural Sociology.

Slavic and East European Languages and Literature. Autumn quarter applicants preferred. GRE required for admission. M.A., Ph.D.

Slavic and East European Studies. GRE recommend for admission. 50 hour M.A. M.A. only.

Social Work. Admits M.S.W. Autumn and Summer quarters; Ph.D. Autumn quarter only (apply by April 1). Contact programs for additional admission requirements. 90 hours for M.S.W.; 60 hours for M.S.W. for applicants with advance standing available. M.S.W., Ph.D.

Sociology. Admits Autumn quarter only. Apply by March 1 for associateship consideration. GRE required for admission. Contact department for additional admissions requirements. Thesis required for M.A. M.A., Ph.D.

Soil Science.

Spanish and Portuguese. Autumn Quarter application strongly recommended. Apply by March 1 for associateship consideration. GRE (for all graduates from U.S. and Canadian Universities), TSE (for all applicants required to take TOEFL/MELAB; minimum score 230 for teaching associateships), tape recordings (for all nonnative Spanish speakers); telephone interview, scholarly paper required for Ph.D. applicants. M.A., Ph.D.

Speech and Hearing Science. Admits M.A. Autumn quarter only; Ph.D. all quarters. Apply by January 15 for financial aid consideration. GRE required for admission. 57-hour nonthesis M.A. option. M.A., Ph.D.

Statistics. Summer quarter strongly recommended. Apply by January 15 for fellowship consideration. GRE required for admission. 50 hours for M.Appl.Stat. M.Appl.Stat., M.S., Ph.D.

Textiles and Clothing. Admits Autumn quarter only. Apply by February 1. GRE required for admission. Contact program for statement of purpose guidelines. 50-hour nonthesis M.S. option. M.S., Ph.D.

Theater. Admits mainly Autumn and Winter quarters for M.A., Ph.D. programs. Apply by January 1 (fellowship consideration), February 15 (associateships); April 15 (M.F.A. acting and design associateships). Acting program accepting for Autumn 1996, 1997. GRE required for M.A., Ph.D. applicants; audition for M.F.A.(acting), portfolio (design). Thesis required for M.A.; M.F.A. in design. 99 hours for M.F.A. M.A., M.F.A., Ph.D.

Veterinary Biosciences. D.V.M. or equivalent required. GRE required for applicants with GPA below 3.0 (unless they have a completed master's degree at time of evaluation) and of all graduates of foreign universities. Thesis required for M.S. M.S., Ph.D.

Veterinary Clinical Sciences. D.V.M. or equivalent required. Most applicants admitted through AAVC's Residency MATCH Program. Contact program for admission procedures. GRE required of all graduates of foreign universities and to theriogenology and equine exercise physiology. Thesis required for M.S. M.S., Ph.D.

Veterinary Preventive Medicine. D.V.M. or equivalent required. GRE required of all graduates of non-AVMA-accredited veterinary colleges. Thesis required for M.S. M.S., Ph.D.

Vision Science.

Welding Engineering. GRE Subject Test in Engineering required for applicants with GPA below 2.7. M.S., Ph.D.

Women's Studies. Admits Autumn quarter only. Apply by January 15. GPA of 3.0 and at least four women's studies courses required for admission. Duplicate copies of all application materials must be sent to program. M.A. only.

College of Dentistry

Organized 1890. Joined Ohio State University in 1914. Annual tuition: resident $11,784, nonresident $31,494. On-campus housing available. Average academic year housing costs: $7848. Contact the Housing Office. Phone: (614)292-8266. Total average cost for all other first-year expenses: $2700.

Enrollment: first-year class 100, total 380 (men 65%, women 35%); postgraduates 65. Faculty: full-time 91, part-time 134. Degrees conferred: D.D.S.-B.A./B.S. (Ohio State University undergraduates only), D.D.S., D.D.S.-M.S. The M.S. is offered through the Graduate School.

ADMISSION REQUIREMENTS. AADSAS, transcripts, DAT (not later than October) required in support of application. Interview by invitation only. Accepts transfer applicants. Applicants must have completed at least two years of college study. Preference given to state residents. Apply to Director of Admissions after June 1, before December 1. Application fee $30. Phone: (614)292-3361; fax: (614)292-0813.

ADMISSION STANDARDS. Selective. Mean DAT: Academic 19, PAT 18.6; mean GPA: 3.54 (A = 4). Gourman rating: 4.77. Accepts 20–25% of total annual applicants. Approximately 85% are state residents.

FINANCIAL AID. Scholarships, grants, loans. Apply to University's Financial Aid Office after acceptance, before July 1. Phone: (614)292-7768. Use FAFSA. About 91% of students receive some aid from College-controlled and outside sources.

DEGREE REQUIREMENTS. For D.D.S.-B.A./B.S.: satisfactory completion of seven-year program. For D.D.S.: satisfactory completion of forty-five-month program. For M.S., see Graduate School listing above.

FIELDS OF GRADUATE STUDY.
Dental Anesthesiology.
Dental Materials Science.
Endodontics.
General Practice Residency.
Oral and Maxillofacial Pathology.
Oral and Maxillofacial Surgery.
Oral Biology.
Orthodontics.
Pediatric Dentistry.
Periodontology.
Prosthodontics.

College of Law

Founded 1891. ABA approved since 1923. AALS member. Semester system. Special facility: Comprehensive National Resources Center. Law library: 691,723 volumes, 8374 subscriptions; has LEXIS, NEXIS, WESTLAW, DIALOG.

Annual tuition: full-time resident $9984, nonresident $20,342. On-campus housing available for married and single students. Total average annual additional expense: $10,954.

Enrollment: first-year class 220, total full-time 655 (men 53%, women 47%). Faculty: full-time 40, part-time 27. Student to faculty ratio 13.6 to 1. Degrees conferred: J.D., J.D.-M.B.A., J.D.-M.H.A., J.D.-M.P.A.

ADMISSION REQUIREMENTS. LSDAS Law School report, bachelor's degree, transcripts, writing sample, letters of recommendation, résumé, LSAT (not later than February) required in support of application. Interview required for final selection. Accepts transfer applicants. Graduates of unaccredited institutions not considered. Apply to Director of Admissions after October, before March 15. Admits first-year students Fall only. Application fee $30. Phone: (614)292-8810; fax: (614)292-1492; e-mail: lawadmit@osu.edu.

ADMISSION STANDARDS. Selective. Mean LSAT: 157; mean GPA: 3.54 (A = 4). Gourman rating: 4.38. *U.S. News & World Report* ranking is in the top 37 of all U.S. law schools. Accepts 20% of total annual applicants.

FINANCIAL AID. Scholarships, grants, Federal W/S, loans. Apply to the Financial Aid Office by March 1. Use FAFSA (College code: 003090). About 64% of students receive aid other than loans from College.

DEGREE REQUIREMENTS. For J.D.: 88 semester hours minimum, three years in residence.
Note: Has summer programs with Oxford University (Great Britain).

College of Medicine and Public Health (43210-1238)
Web site: medicine.osu.edu

Established 1914. Library: 155,00 volumes, 2600 subscriptions. Annual tuition: resident $13,848, nonresident $35,853; student fees $708. Total average figure for all other expenses: $7500.

Enrollment: M.D. program, first-year class 210 (EDP 15); total 890 (men 63%, women 37%). Faculty: full- and part-time 1700. Degrees conferred: M.D., M.H.A., M.P.H., M.S., M.D.-M.B.A., M.D.-M.H.A., M.D.-M.P.H.

ADMISSION REQUIREMENTS. For M.D. program: AMCAS report, transcripts, letters of recommendation, bachelor's degree, MCAT, interview required in support of application. Has EDP;

apply between June 1 and August 1. Accepts transfer applicants. Preference given to Ohio residents. Apply to AMCAS after June 1, before November 1. Application fee $25. Phone: (614)292-7137; fax: (614)247-7959.

ADMISSION STANDARDS. Selective. Mean MCAT: 10; mean GPA: 3.61 (A = 4). Gourman rating: 4.37. Accepts 6–8% of total applicants. Approximately 80% are state residents.

FINANCIAL AID. Scholarships, assistantships, loans. About 35% of students receive aid other than loans from College. Apply to the Office of Financial Aid. Use FAFSA.

DEGREE REQUIREMENTS. For M.D.: satisfactory completion of four-year program. All students must pass USMLE Step 1 prior to entering third year; all students must pass USMLE Step 2 prior to awarding of M.D. For M.S.: 45–50 credit hour program, all requirements must be completed in five years. For M.P.H.: 60 credit program; practicum.

FIELDS OF GRADUATE STUDY.
Allied Medical Professions. M.S. only.
Anatomy.
Biometrics.
Epidemiology.
Health Behavior and Health Promotion.
Health Services Management and Policy.
Integrated Biomedical Science Graduate program. A College-wide program.
Physical Therapy.

College of Veterinary Medicine

Established 1885. Third oldest veterinary college. Annual tuition: resident and contract nonresident $11,076, nonresident $31,440. On-campus housing available. Annual living expenses: single $9826; married $12,826.

Enrollment: first-year class 135; total full-time 590 (men 50%, women 50%); postgraduates 54. Faculty: full-time 110, part-time 11. Degrees conferred: D.V.M., D.V.M.-M.S., D.V.M.-Ph.D. The M.S. and Ph.D. are offered through the Graduate School.

ADMISSION REQUIREMENTS. Transcripts, VCAT or GRE or MCAT, two recommendations, animal/veterinary experience, required in support of application. Interview by invitation only. Preference given to state and contract state residents. Applicants must have completed at least 101 quarter hours of college study. Accepts transfer applicants on a space-available basis. Apply to Chairperson, Admissions Committee, by October 1. Application fee $30. Phone: (614)292-8831; fax: (614)262-6989.

ADMISSION STANDARDS. Selective. Minimum GPA: 2.8 (A = 4). Accepts 30–40% of total annual applicants. Fifteen to thirty spaces available for nonresidents.

FINANCIAL AID. Scholarships, grants, fellowships, assistantships, Federal W/S, loans. Apply to Financial Aid Officer of the College after acceptance, before March 15. About 50% of students receive aid other than loans from College. Aid available to part-time students.

DEGREE REQUIREMENTS. For D.V.M.: satisfactory completion of four-year program. For M.S., Ph.D.: successful completion of first year of veterinary curriculum required for consideration; see Graduate School listing above.

FIELDS OF GRADUATE STUDY.
Anatomy.
Cellular and Molecular Biology.
Epidemiology.
Food Safety.

Health Economics.
Health Management of Food-Producing Animals.
Infectious Disease Control.
Laboratory Animal Medicine.
Microbiology and Immunology.
Parasitology.
Pathology.
Physiology/Pharmacology.
Public Health.
Toxicology.

OHIO UNIVERSITY

Athens, Ohio 45701
Web site: www.ohiou.edu

Chartered 1804. Located 76 miles SE of Columbus. CGS member. Coed. State control. Quarter system. Library: 2,800,000 volumes, 20,800 subscriptions.

Annual tuition: full-time, resident $4802, nonresident $10,521; per credit resident, $203, nonresident, $435. Limited on-campus housing for married and single graduate students. Average annual housing cost: $7600 (12 months, room only) for married students; $8368 (12 months) for single students. Phone: (740)593-4090.

Graduate College

Graduate study since 1950. Enrollment: full-time 2081, part-time 619 (men 55%, women 45%). University faculty: full-time 718, part-time 99. Degrees conferred: M.A., M.S., M.S.S., M.M., M.B.A., M.Ed., M.F.A., M.H.S.A., M.P.A., M.P.T., M.S.A., Ph.D.

ADMISSION REQUIREMENTS. Transcripts required in support of School's application. GRE Subject Tests, MAT, GMAT, interview required for some departments. On-line application available. TOEFL required for international applicants; TSE required by some departments. Accepts transfer applicants. Graduates of unaccredited institutions not considered. Apply to Office of Graduate Student Services at least six weeks prior to registration; international application at least six months prior to registration. Application fee $30. Phone: (740)593-2800; fax: (740)593-4625.

ADMISSION STANDARDS. Relatively open for many departments, competitive or very competitive for the others. Usual minimum GPA: 2.75 (A = 4).

FINANCIAL AID. Scholarships, research assistantships, teaching assistantships, internships, grants, tuition waivers, Federal W/S, loans. Approved for VA benefits. Apply to the individual departmental Graduate Committee chairman for scholarships, assistantships; to the Financial Aid Office for all other programs. Phone: (740)593-4141; fax: (740)593-4140. Use FAFSA. About 50% of students receive aid other than loans from College and outside sources.

DEGREE REQUIREMENTS. For master's: 45-60 quarter hours minimum; thesis; final oral exam; nonthesis option in some departments. For M.B.A.: 90 quarter hours minimum. For Ph.D.: 9 quarters minimum beyond the bachelor's, at least 3 quarters in full-time residence; comprehensive exam; scholarly disciplines are determined by department; dissertation; final oral exam.

FIELDS OF STUDY.

COLLEGE OF ARTS AND SCIENCES:
Anthropology.
Biological Sciences. Includes cell biology and physiology, ecology and evolutionary biology, exercise physiology and muscle biology, microbiology, neurobiology.

Chemistry. Includes analytical, biological, inorganic, organic, physical.
Economics. M.A. only.
English Language and Literature.
Environmental Plant Biology. Includes biochemistry, cell biology, ecology, ethnobotany, evolution, molecular biology, plant morphology, mycology, paleobotany, plant physiology, plant systematics.
Environmental Studies. M.S. only.
Foreign Languages and Literature. Includes French, Spanish. M.A. only.
Geography. M.S. only.
Geological Sciences. Includes geology, hydrogeology, environmental geography, environmental geochemistry, geophysics. M.S. only.
History.
Linguistics. Includes general linguistics, teaching English as a second or foreign language. M.A.
Mathematics. Includes applied, computer science, mathematics for secondary school teachers, pure (M.S.); algebra, analysis, topology, applied (Ph.D.).
Philosophy. M.A. only.
Physics.
Political Science. Includes public administration.
Psychology. Includes clinical, experimental, industrial/organizational psychology.
Social Work. M.S.W. only.
Social Sciences. M.S.S. only.
Sociology. M.A. only.

COLLEGE OF BUSINESS:
Accounting. M.S.A.
Business. M.B.A.

COLLEGE OF COMMUNICATION:
Interpersonal Communication. Includes organization communication, rhetorical and communication theory.
Journalism. M.S. only.
Mass Communication. Interschool program. Ph.D.
Telecommunication. Includes international communication, management, policy/regulation, media studies. M.A.
Visual Communication. Includes photography. M.A. only.

COLLEGE OF EDUCATION:
College Student Personnel. M.Ed.
Counselor Education.
Cultural Studies in Education. M.Ed.
Curriculum and Instruction. Ph.D.
Educational Administration.
Education Research and Evaluation.
Elementary Education. M.Ed.
Higher Education.
Math Education. M.Ed.
Middle Child Education.
Reading Education. M.Ed.
Secondary Education. M.Ed.
Social Studies. Ph.D.
Special Education.
Supervision. Ph.D.
Teaching the Talented and Gifted. M.Ed.
Technology in Education.

RUSS COLLEGE OF ENGINEERING AND TECHNOLOGY:
Chemical Engineering. Includes atmospheric chemistry, coal conversion and utilization, corrosion and multiphase flow, polymerization reaction engineering, control and dynamics, biochemical engineering, semiconductor materials, separation processes.
Civil Engineering. Includes geotechnical, environmental, structure, solid mechanics, water resources, transportation.

Electrical Engineering and Computer Science. Includes avionic, applied and theoretical computer science, communications, controls, information theory, solid-state electronics, energy conversion, power electronics, power systems, electromagnetics, signal processing, computer vision, robotics, electronic, opto-electronics.

Industrial and Manufacturing Systems Engineering. Includes human factors engineering and ergonomics, manufacturing systems, manufacturing information systems, quality systems. M.S. only.

Integrated Engineering. Includes materials processing, geotechnical and environmental, intelligent systems. Ph.D. only.

Mechanical Engineering. Includes mechanical systems, CAD/CAM, manufacturing, thermofluid sciences. M.S. only.

COLLEGE OF FINE ARTS:

Art. Includes ceramics, painting, photography, printmaking, sculpture, art history, art history/studio (M.F.A.); art education, photography (M.A.).

Comparative Arts. Ph.D.

Film.

Music. Includes composition, history and literature, music education, music therapy, performance, theory. M.M. only.

Theater. Includes theater history and critics, (M.A.); acting, directing, playwriting, production design and technology (M.F.A.); theater (M.A.).

COLLEGE OF HEALTH AND HUMAN SERVICES:

Health Sciences. Includes health administration. M.B.A. only.

Hearing and Speech Sciences. Includes audiology, speech-language pathology.

Human and Consumer Sciences. Includes early childhood education, family studies, international and community nutrition, nutrition science. M.S.H.C.S.

Physical Therapy. M.P.T. only.

Recreation and Sport Sciences. Includes athletic administration, athletic training, physical education pedagogy, recreation studies, sport industry, sport physiology and adult fitness (M.S.P.E.); exercise physiology (M.S.P.Ex.); sports administration/facility management (M.S.A.).

CENTER FOR INTERNATIONAL STUDIES:

International Affairs. Includes African studies, communication and development studies, development studies, Latin American studies, Southeast Asian studies. M.A. only.

College of Osteopathic Medicine

Founded 1975. Coed. Public control. Library: 70,000 volumes, has MEDLINE, CANCERLINE, BIOETHIC, HEALTH, TOXLINE, DIALOG, OCLC.

Annual tuition: resident $14,274, nonresident $20,052. Enrollment: first-year class 100, total 410 (men 55%, women 45%). Faculty: full-time 80, part-time/volunteers 400. Degrees conferred: D.O., D.O.-M.B.A., D.O.-M.H.A., D.O.-M.A., D.O.-M.S., D.O.-Ph.D.

ADMISSION REQUIREMENTS. AACOMAS report, bachelor's degree preferred, official transcripts, MCAT (no later than September), three letters of recommendation, one from premed advisory committee, evaluation from a physician (preferably a D.O.), supplemental form required (before March 1) in support of application. Interview by invitation only. Graduates of unaccredited colleges not considered. Preference given to state residents. Apply by January 1 to the Director of Admissions. Admits first year students Fall only. Application fee: $25. Phone: (800)345-1560, or (740)593-4313; fax: (740)593-0761.

ADMISSION STANDARDS. Selective. Mean MCAT: 8.2; mean GPA: 3.4 (A = 4). Usual minimum average: 3.0 (A = 4). Accepts approximately 35% of annual applications. 80% of class are state residents.

FINANCIAL AID. Scholarships, fellowships, Federal W/S, loans. Apply by February 15 to the Financial Aid Office. Use FAFSA (College code: E00306) and institutional FAF. About 80% of students receive aid from College and outside sources.

DEGREE REQUIREMENT. For D.O.: satisfactory completion of four-year program; all students must pass the National Board of Osteopathic Medical Examination Part I and Part II. For Ph.D., see Graduate College listing above.

MEDICAL COLLEGE OF OHIO AT TOLEDO
Toledo, Ohio 43614
Web site: www.mco.edu

School of Medicine

Established 1968. CGS member.

Annual tuition: resident $13,566, nonresident $29,640. On-campus housing available. Total average figure for all other expenses: $9500.

Enrollment: first-year class 140 (EDP 10) total 537 (men 60%, women 40%). Faculty: full-time 400, part-time/volunteers 1100. Degrees conferred: M.D., M.D.-M.S., M.D.-Ph.D.

ADMISSION REQUIREMENTS. AMCAS report, transcripts, MCAT, recommendations required in support of application. Interviews by invitation only. Preference given to state residents. Has EDP; apply between June 1 and November 1. Graduates of unaccredited colleges not considered. Apply to Director of Admissions after June 1, before November 1. Application fee $30. Phone: (419)381-4229; fax: (419)381-4005.

ADMISSION STANDARDS. Selective. Mean MCAT: 9.4; mean GPA: 3.51 (A = 4). Gourman rating: 3.32. Accepts about 6–8% of total annual applicants. Approximately 78% are state residents.

FINANCIAL AID. Need-based scholarships, merit scholarships, minority scholarships, Grants-in-Aid, institutional loans, HEAL, alternative loan programs, NIH stipends, Federal Perkins Loans, Stafford Subsidized and Unsubsidized Loans, Service Commitment Scholarship programs are available. Assistantships/fellowships may be available for Dual Degree candidates. All accepted students receive Financial Aid applications in early February. Contact the Financial Aid Office for current information. Phone: (419)383-3436. Use FAFSA to a Federal processor (Title IV School code: G07737); also submit Financial Aid Transcript, Federal Income Tax forms. Approximately 75% of students receive some form of financial assistance.

DEGREE REQUIREMENTS. For M.D.: satisfactory completion of four-year program. Students required to pass Step 1 of USMLE and Step 2 for graduation. For M.S.: 32 semester hours minimum; thesis or comprehensive exam. For Ph.D.: at least 90 credits beyond bachelor's. Foreign language required by some departments; comprehensive exam; dissertation; final oral exam.

FIELDS OF GRADUATE STUDY.

Anatomy.
Biochemistry.
Microbiology.
Molecular Biology.
Neurosciences.
Pathology.
Pharmacology.
Physiology.

OKLAHOMA CITY UNIVERSITY

Oklahoma City, Oklahoma 73106-1402
Web site: www.okcu.edu

Founded 1904. Coed. Private control. Methodist affiliation. Semester system. Library: 280,400 volumes, 5600 subscriptions.

On-campus housing for married and single graduate students. Average academic year housing costs: $5200 for married students, $4650 (including board) for single students. Contact Dean of Students Office for both on- and off-campus housing information. Phone: (405)744-9164.

Petree College of Arts and Science

Tuition: per credit $460. Enrollment: full-time 268, part-time 121. Faculty: full-time 40, part-time 34. Degrees conferred: M.A., M.Ed., M.L.A., M.C.J.A.

ADMISSION REQUIREMENTS. Official transcripts, two letters of recommendation required in support of College's application. Interview sometimes required. TOEFL required for international applicants. Accepts transfer applicants. Graduates of unaccredited institutions not considered. Apply by August 25 (Fall), January 15 (Spring) to Office of Graduate Admissions. Rolling admissions process. Application fee $35, $70 for international applicants. Phone: (405)521-5351 or (800)633-7242, ext. 4; fax: (405)521-5356; e-mail: gadmissions@okcu.edu.

ADMISSION STANDARDS. Selective for some programs, very selective for others. Usual minimum average: 3.0 (A = 4).

FINANCIAL AID. Fellowships, internships, full and partial tuition waivers, Federal W/S, loans. Approved for VA benefits. Apply by August 1 to the Dean's Office for fellowships; to Financial Aid Office for all other programs. Use FAFSA. Phone: (800)633-7242, ext. 5211. About 35% of students receive aid from University and outside sources. Aid available to part-time students.

DEGREE REQUIREMENTS. For master's: 36–45 semester hours minimum, at least 27 in residence; thesis/nonthesis option.

FIELDS OF STUDY.
Computer Science. M.S.
Criminal Justice Administration. M.C.J.A.
Early Childhood Education. M.Ed.
Elementary Education. M.Ed.
Gifted and Talented Education. M.Ed.
Liberal Arts. M.L.A.
Performing Arts. M.A.
Science Education. Includes biology, chemistry, physics. M.Ed.
Secondary Education. Includes art, business, health, physical education and recreation, mathematics, music, social studies, language arts. M.Ed.
TESOL. M.A.

Meinders School of Business

Web site: www.okcu.edu/business

Graduate study since 1904. Semester system. Tuition: per credit $500. Enrollment: full-time 723, part-time 335. Graduate faculty: full-time 34, part-time 24. Degrees conferred: M.B.A., M.S.A.

ADMISSION REQUIREMENTS. Transcripts, GMAT required in support of School's application. TOEFL required for international applicants. Interview not required. Accepts transfer applicants. Apply to Director of M.B.A. Program by August 25

(Fall), January 15 (Spring). Application fee $35, $70 for international applicants. Phone: (800)683-7242, ext. 4; fax: (405)521-5356.

ADMISSION STANDARDS. Relatively open. Usual minimum average: 2.75 (A = 4).

FINANCIAL AID. Scholarships, fellowships, tuition waivers, Federal W/S, loans. Approved for VA benefits. Apply by August 1 to Financial Aid Office. Phone: (405)521-5211; fax: (405)521-5466. Use FAFSA (School code: 003166). Aid available for part-time students.

DEGREE REQUIREMENTS. For M.S. Accounting: 30 semester hours, 24 in residence. For M.B.A.: 36 semester hours minimum, at least 24 in residence; comprehensive written exam.

FIELDS OF STUDY.
Accounting. M.S A. only.
Arts Management.
Business Administration.
Finance.
Health Administration.
Information Technology.
International Business.
International Marketing.
International Marketing Communications.
Marketing.
Note: M.B.A./J.D. available.

School of Law

Opened 1952. ABA approved since 1969. AALS member. Semester system. Special facility: Native American Legal Resource Center. Law library: 222,400 volumes; has LEXIS, NEXIS, WESTLAW, OCLC.

Annual tuition: full-time $17,130, part-time $11,500. Limited on-campus housing available. Total average annual additional expense: $12,540.

Enrollment: first-year class 139 (day), 40 (evening); total full- and part-time 493 (men 59%, women 41%). Faculty: full-time 21, part-time 12. Student to faculty ratio 17.8 to 1. Degrees conferred, J.D., J.D.-M.B.A., J.D.-M.Div.

ADMISSION REQUIREMENTS. LSDAS Law School report, bachelor's degree, transcripts, LSAT, recommendation required in support of application. Accepts limited transfer applicants. Graduates of unaccredited colleges not considered. Apply by August 1 to the School. Beginning students Fall admission only. Application fee $35. Phone: (800)663-7242, ext. 5354, (405)521-5354.

ADMISSION STANDARDS. Selective. Mean LSAT: full-time 145, part-time 147; mean GPA: full-time 2.98, part-time 2.94 (A = 4). Gourman rating: 2.69. *U.S. News & World Report* ranking is in the fourth tier of all U.S. law schools. Accepts 50–55% of total annual applicants.

FINANCIAL AID. Scholarships, tuition remission, fellowships, assistantships, Federal W/S, loans. Apply to the Director of Financial Aid by March 1. Use FAFSA (School code: 003166). About 16% of students receive aid other than loans from School.

DEGREE REQUIREMENTS. For J.D.: day students may complete the J.D. degree in 24 months by year-round attendance, evening students in 33 months by year-round attendance; 90 hour semester program.

OKLAHOMA STATE UNIVERSITY

Stillwater, Oklahoma 74078-1019

Web site: www.okstate.edu

Founded 1890. Located in north-central Oklahoma approximately one hour from Tulsa and Oklahoma City. CGS member. Special facilities: Twenty-First Century Center for Agriculture and Renewable Natural Resources, University Center for Water Research, Center for Applications of Remote Sensing, Center for Global Studies, Center for Laser and Photonics Research, Center for Local Government and Technology, Center for Poets and Writers, Center for Science Literacy, Center for Sensors and Sensor Technologies, Educational Technology Center, Ethics Center, Multicultural Development and Assessment Center, Institute for Energy Analysis, Center for International Trade and Development, Oklahoma Center for the Advancement of Science and Technology, Oklahoma Food and Agricultural Products Research and Technology Center, Oklahoma Industrial Assessment Center, Virgin Prairie and Woodland Study and Research Site, Wes Watkins Center for International Trade Development. Library: 2,100,000 volumes, 35,600 subscriptions. Total University enrollment: 19,500.

Tuition: per credit hour resident $102, nonresident $290. On-campus housing available for graduate students. Average academic year housing costs: $4785 (including board) for single students; $6138 for married student housing. Contact the Graduate Student Housing Office for both on- and off-campus housing information. Phone: (405)744-9164.

Graduate College

Graduate study since 1905. Enrollment: full-time 1791, part-time 2212. Faculty: full-and part-time 941. Degrees conferred: M.A., M.Ag., M.M.S.E., M.S., M.Arch., M.Arch.Eng., M. Eng., M.B.A., Ed.S., Ed.D., Ph.D.

ADMISSION REQUIREMENTS. Two official transcripts required in support of College's application. GRE/MAT/GMAT required for some programs. On-line application available. TOEFL required of international applicants. Accepts transfer applicants. Graduates of unaccredited institutions not considered. Apply to Graduate College at least thirty days prior to the semester of expected enrollment; international students five months prior to enrollment. Application fee $25. Phone: (405)744-6368; fax: (405)744-0355.

ADMISSIONS STANDARDS. Competitive for most departments, selective for the others. Usual minimum average: 2.75 (A = 4).

FINANCIAL AID. Scholarships, research assistantships, teaching assistantships, internships, tuition waivers, social justice waiver, Federal W/S, loans. Approved for VA benefits. Apply directly to the academic department or unit in which the student desires the appointment for assistantships. Contact individual department for date. Apply by March 1 to the Office of Financial Aid for all other programs. Phone: (405)744-6604. Use FAFSA. Approximately 35% of students receive aid from both College and outside agencies. Aid available for part-time students.

DEGREE REQUIREMENTS. For master's: Plan I—30 credit hours including 6 hours for thesis, 21 hours in residence; thesis. Plan II—32 credit hours including 2 credit hours for special report, 23 credit hours in residence; special report. Plan III—32 credit hours, 23 credit hours in residence; creative component/project. For Ed.S.: 60 credit hours beyond the bachelor's degree; one year or equivalent in residency; qualifying exam; thesis with final exam. For Ed.D.: 90 hours beyond the bachelor's degree; 75% of course work at 5000 and 6000 level; 10-hour thesis; maintain B average; qualifying exams; thesis defense. For Ph.D.: 60 hours minimum beyond the bachelor's degree or 30 hours minimum beyond the master's degree; one year in residence; one or two foreign languages for some departments; qualifying exam; dissertation (minimum 15 credit hours); final oral exam.

FIELDS OF STUDY.

COLLEGE OF AGRICULTURAL SCIENCE AND NATURAL RESOURCES:
Agricultural Economics.
Agricultural Education.
Animal Breeding and Reproduction. Ph.D. only
Animal Nutrition. Ph.D. only.
Animal Sciences.
Biochemistry and Molecular.
Biosystems and Agricultural Engineering.
Biotechnology. Ph.D only.
Breeding and Genes. Ph.D. only.
Entomology.
Environmental Science.
Food Science.
Forest Resources.
Horticulture.
Physiology. Ph.D. only.
Plant Pathology. M.Ag. only.
Plant and Soil Sciences.
Production and Management. Ph.D. only.
Range Science. Ph.D. only.
Soil Science. Ph.D. only.
Weed Science. Ph.D. only.

COLLEGE OF ARTS AND SCIENCES:
Applied Music. M.M. only.
Botany. M.S. only.
Chemistry.
Clinical Psychology.
Communication Sciences and Disorders. M.S. only.
Computer Science.
Conducting. M.M. only.
Creative Writing.
Environmental Sciences.
Experimental Psychology.
Film.
Fire and Emergency Management. M.S. only.
Geography. M.S. only.
Geology. M.S. only.
History.
Literature.
Mass Communications. M.S. only.
Mathematics.
Microbiology, Cell, and Molecular Biology.
Philosophy. M.A. only.
Physics.
Plant Science. Ph.D. only.
Political Science. M.A. only.
Sociology.
Statistics.
Teaching English as a Second Language.
Technical Writing.
Theater. M.A. only.
Wildlife and Fisheries Ecology.
Zoology.

COLLEGE OF BUSINESS ADMINISTRATION:
Accounting.
Accounting Information Systems. M.S. only.
Business Administration. M.B.A. only.
Economics.
Finance. Ph.D. only.
Management. Ph.D. only.
Management Information Systems. M.S. only.
Marketing. Ph.D. only.

Quantitative Financial Management. M.S. only.
Telecommunications Management. M.S. only.

COLLEGE OF EDUCATION:
Adult and Continuing Education.
Applied Behavioral Studies. Ed.D. only.
Applied Exercise Science. M.S. only.
Aviation and Space Education. Ed D. only.
College Interdisciplinary. Ed.D. only.
Community Counseling. M.S. only.
Counseling Psychology. Ph.D.
Curriculum and Leadership Studies. M.S. only.
Curriculum and Social Foundation. Ph.D. only.
Educational Administration.
Educational Evaluation. M.S. only.
Educational Leadership in Higher Education. M.S. only.
Educational Leadership in School Administration. M.S. only.
Educational Psychology.
Elementary/Middle/Secondary Education/K–12 Education. M.S. only.
Elementary School Counseling. M.S. only.
Environmental Sciences.
Gifted and Talented. M.S. only.
Health and Human Performance. Ph.D. only.
Health Promotion. M.S. only.
Higher Education. Ed.D.
Human Resource Development.
Leisure. Ph.D. only.
Leisure Services Management. M.S. only.
Occupational Education Studies.
Physical Education. M.S. only.
Professional Education Studies. Ph.D. only.
Reading and Literacy. M.S. only.
Research and Evaluation. Ph.D. only.
School Psychology.
Special Education. Ph.D. only.
Secondary School Counseling. M.S. only.
Student Personnel Administration. Ph.D. only.
Student Personnel Service. M.S. only.
Therapeutic Recreation. M.S. only.

COLLEGE OF ENGINEERING, ARCHITECTURE, AND TECHNOLOGY:
Architectural Engineering. M.A.E. only.
Architecture. M.Arch.
Biosystems and Agricultural Engineering.
Chemical Engineering.
Civil Engineering.
Control Systems Engineering.
Electrical Engineering.
Engineering and Technology Management. M.S. only.
Environmental Engineering.
Environmental Sciences.
General Engineering. M.Eng. only.
Industrial Engineering and Management.
Manufacturing Systems Engineering. M.Eng. only.
Mechanical Engineering.

GRADUATE COLLEGE:
Aviation and Space Science. M.S. only.
Environmental Sciences.
Gerontology. M.S. only.
Health Care Administration. M.S. only.
Interdisciplinary Science. M.S. only.
Photonics.
Telecommunication Management. M.S. only.
Veterinary and Biomedical Science.

COLLEGE OF HUMAN ENVIRONMENTAL SCIENCES:
Design, Housing, and Merchandising.
Family Financial Planning. M.S. only.

Family Relations and Child Development. Ph.D. only.
Hospitality Administration.
Human Development and Family Sciences.
International Studies. M.S. only.
Nonprofit Services Administration. M.S. only.
Nutrition. M.S. only.
Nutritional Sciences.

College of Veterinary Medicine (74078-2003)

Annual tuition: resident $7300, nonresident $19,200. Total average cost for all other annual expenses: $7000.

Enrollment: first-year class 74; total full-time 323 (men 50%, women 50%); postgraduates 40. Faculty: full- and part-time 158. Degrees conferred: D.V.M., D.V.M.-M.S. The M.S. and Ph.D. are offered through the Graduate College.

ADMISSION REQUIREMENTS. VMCAS, transcripts, GRE/Subject Biology, recommendations, personal essay, animal/veterinary experience required in support of application. Interview by invitation only. Preference given to state residents. Accepts transfer applicants on a space-available basis only. Graduates of unaccredited colleges not considered. Apply to the College after July 1, before October 1. Application fee $15. Phone: (405)744-6653; fax: (405)744-0356.

ADMISSION STANDARDS. Selective. Usual minimum GPA: 2.80; mean GPA: 3.49 (A = 4). Accepts 33–50% of qualified applicants. Accepts up to fourteen nonresidents.

FINANCIAL AID. Scholarships, fellowships, assistantships, partial tuition waivers, Federal W/S, loans available. Apply to Office of Financial Aid by March 1.

DEGREE REQUIREMENTS. For D.V.M.: satisfactory completion of four-year program. For M.S., Ph.D., see Graduate College listing above.

FIELDS OF GRADUATE STUDY.
Cell and Molecular Bioscience. Includes molecular reproduction and development, molecular immunology, molecular virology, signal transduction.
Infectious Diseases. Includes virology, microbiology, parasitology, epidemiology.
Pathobiology. Includes disease in organism, tissues, and cell.
Physiological Sciences. Includes physiology, morphology, pharmacology, toxicology.
Veterinary Clinical Sciences. Includes biophotonics, clinical orthopedics, exercise physiology, oncology.

OKLAHOMA STATE UNIVERSITY

Tulsa, Oklahoma 74107-1898
Web site: osu.com.okstate.edu

College of Osteopathic Medicine

Founded 1972. Coed. Public control. Semester system. Library: 54,700 volumes, 515 subscriptions; has MEDLINE, CANCERLINE, BIOETHIC, HEALTH, TOXLINE, DIALOG, OCLC.

Annual tuition: resident $10,208, nonresident $24,900. No on-campus housing available. Enrollment: first-year class 88, total 350 (men 65%, women 35%). Faculty: full-time 80, part-time 400. Degree conferred: D.O.

ADMISSION REQUIREMENTS. AACOMAS report, bachelor's degree preferred, official transcripts, MCAT (no later than Spring of year prior to application) from premed advisory committee, evaluation from a physician (preferably a D.O.), supplemental form required in support of application. Interview by invitation only. Graduates of unaccredited college not considered. Preference given to state residents. Apply by January 15 to the assistant Dean of Students. Admits first year students Fall only. Rolling admissions process. Application fee $25. Phone: (800)677-1972 or (918)528-1972; fax: (918)561-8412.

ADMISSION STANDARDS. Selective. Accepts about 5% of total annual applications. Usual minimum average: 3.0 (A = 4), mean GPA: 3.42.

FINANCIAL AID. Scholarships, grants, partial tuition waivers, Federal W/S, loans. Apply by June 1 to the Financial Aid Office. Use FAFSA and institutional FAF.

DEGREE REQUIREMENT. For D.O.: satisfactory completion of four-year program.

UNIVERSITY OF OKLAHOMA
Norman, Oklahoma 73019-4076
Web site: www.ou.edu

Founded 1890. Located 18 miles S of Oklahoma City. CGS member. Coed. State control. Special facilities: Center for the Investigation of Mesoscale Meteorological Systems; permanent biological station on Lake Texoma; earth sciences observatory at Leonard; geological field camp at Canon City, Colo.; aquatic biology and fisheries research center in Noble; virgin prairie and woodland plots for study and research; Sarkey's Energy Center; Surfactant Institute; Rock Mechanics Institute; Ground Water Institute; cooperative program with Oak Ridge Institute of Nuclear Studies. The University's NIH ranking is 108th among all U.S. institutions with 101 awards/grants worth $31,976,104. Library: more than 3,700,000 volumes, 15,800 subscriptions; features the Western History Collection, Degolyer Collection in the History of Science and Technology and the Bass Business History Collection. Total University enrollment: 21,400.

Tuition: per credit resident $98, nonresident $286. On-campus housing for 922 married students, 100 men, list women. Average annual housing cost: $4500–$6500 for married students, $6262 (including board) for single students. Apply to Director of the Office of Housing. Phone: (405)325-2511. Day-care facilities available.

Graduate College

Graduate study since 1899. Enrollment: full-time 2336, part-time 3232. Graduate faculty: full-time 784. Degrees conferred: M.Ac., M.A., M.Arch., M.A. in Art, M.A. in L.Sci., M.P.A., M.B.A., M.Ed., M.Ed. in HPER., M.Env.Sci., M.F.A. in Art, M.F.A. in Dance, M.F.A. in Design, M.F.A. in Drama, M.H.R., M.L.S., M.Land.Arch., M.L.Sc., M.Mus., M.Mus.Ed., M.Nat.Sci., M.P.H., M.R.C.P., M.S., M.S. in Const.Set., M.S. in Metr., M.Soc.Sci., M.Soc.Work, D.Mus.Arts, Ed.D., Ph.D., Dr.P.H., D.P.A.

ADMISSION REQUIREMENTS. Transcripts required in support of College's application. GRE/GMAT/MAT/interview for some departments. TOEFL required for international applicants. Accepts transfer applicants. Graduates of unaccredited institutions not considered. Apply to Office of Admissions and Records by June 1 (Fall), November 1 (Spring), April 1 (Summer); international applicants April 1 (Fall), September 1 (Spring), February 1 (Summer). Application fee $25, $50 for international applicants. Phone: (405)325-3811; fax: (405)325-6029; e-mail: cs@ou.edu.

ADMISSION STANDARDS. Selective for most departments, very selective for others. Usual minimum average: 3.0 (A = 4).

FINANCIAL AID. Annual awards from institutional funds: fee waiver scholarships, fellowships, teaching assistantships, research assistantships, internships, tuition waivers, Federal W/S, loans. Approved for VA benefits. Apply by March 31 to Graduate College and appropriate department chair for scholarships, assistantships; to Financial Aid Office for all other programs. Phone: (405)325-4521; fax: (405)325-7608. Use FAFSA. About 30% of students receive aid other than loans from College and outside sources. Aid sometimes available for part-time students.

DEGREE REQUIREMENTS. For most master's: 30 semester hours minimum, at least 22 in residence; thesis; comprehensive oral/written exam sometimes required; 32 semester hours minimum, at least 24 in residence; comprehensive oral/written exam for some departments. For M.Ac.: 33 hours minimum; comprehensive oral/written exam. For M.B.A.: 36 hours minimum; comprehensive written exam. For M.R.C.P.: 54 hours minimum, final project. For M.S.W.: 60 hours minimum; fieldwork; thesis/final project. For M.L.A.: 62 hours minimum; research project. For M.F.A.: 60 hours minimum; final project/exhibition. For Ph.D.: 3 years minimum and at least 90 semester hours beyond the bachelor's degree, at least 2 semesters in residence; general oral/written exam, dissertation; final oral exam. For Ed.D.: evidence of proficiency in statistics/methods of research or reading knowledge of one foreign language; other requirements essentially the same as the Ph.D. For D.P.A., D.Mus.Arts, essentially the same as for the Ph.D.

FIELDS OF STUDY.

NORMAN CAMPUS:
Accounting. M.Ac., M.A.
Adult and Higher Education. M.Ed., Ph.D.
Aerospace Engineering. M.S., Ph.D.
Anthropology. M.A., Ph.D.
Architecture. M.Arch. only.
Architectural Urban Studies. M.Arch. only.
Art. Portfolio for admission; master's only.
Biochemistry.
Biomedical Library Sciences.
Botany. M.S., Ph.D.
Business Administration. M.B.A., Ph.D.
Chemical Engineering. M.S., Ph.D.
Chemistry. M.S., Ph.D.
Chemistry and Biochemistry. M.S.
Choral Conducting. M.M., M.M.Ed., D.M.A.
Civil Engineering. M.S., Ph.D.
Communication. Ph.D.
Community Counseling. M.Ed.
Computer Science. M.S., Ph.D.
Construction Administration. M.S.C.A.
Counseling Psychology. Ph.D.
Dance. M.F.A. only.
Design. M.F.A.
Drama. M.A., M.F.A. only.
Economics. M.A., Ph.D.
Educational Administration, Curriculum, and Supervision. M.Ed., Ph.D.
Electrical Engineering. M.S., Ph.D.
Engineering. M.S., Ph.D.
Engineering Physics. M.S., Ph.D.
English. M.A., Ph.D.
Environmental Science. M.Env.Sc., Ph.D.
Fisheries Biology. M.S. only.
French. M.A., Ph.D.
Geography. M.A., Ph.D.
Geological Engineering. M.S., Ph.D.

Geology. M.S., Ph.D.
Geophysics. M.S. only.
German. M.A.
Health Administration. M.H.A.
Health and Sport Sciences. M.S., Ph.D.
History. M.A., Ph.D.
History, Philosophy, and Social Foundations of Education. M.Ed., Ph.D.
History of Science. M.A., Ph.D.
Human Relations. M.H.R. only.
Industrial Engineering. M.S., Ph.D.
Instructional Leadership and Academic Curriculum. M.Ed., Ph.D.
Instructional Psychology and Technology. M.Ed., Ph.D.
Instrumental Conducting. M.M., M.M.Ed., D.M.A.
International Relations. M.A. in Intl. Rel.
Journalism and Mass Communication. M.A. only.
Landscape Architecture. M.L.A. only.
Liberal Studies. M.L.S. only.
Library and Information Science. M.L.I.S. only.
Management Information Systems. M.I.S.
Mathematics. M.A., M.S., Ph.D.
Mechanical Engineering. M.S., Ph.D.
Meteorology. M.S. in Metr., Ph.D.
Microbiology. M.S., Ph.D.
Modern Languages. Includes French, German, Spanish; M.A. only in German.
Music Composition. M.M., D.M.A.
Music Education. Ph.D.
Music History. M.M.
Music Theory. M.M.
Natural Gas. M.S.
Natural Science. Emphasis on earth science, botany, physical science. M.N.S. only.
Organ. M.M., D.M.A.
Petroleum Engineering. M.S., Ph.D.
Philosophy. M.A., Ph.D.
Physics. M.S., Ph.D.
Piano. M.M., D.M.A.
Political Science. M.A., Ph.D.
Professional Meteorology. M.S. in Prof. Metr.
Psychology. M.S., Ph.D.
Public Administration. M.P.A.
Public Health. M.P.H.
Regional and City Planning. M.R.C.P. only.
Social Science. M.Soc.Sci. only.
Social Work. M.S.W. only.
Sociology. M.A., Ph.D.
Spanish. M.A., Ph.D.
Special Education. M.Ed., Ph.D.
Telecomputing.
Voice. M.M., D.M.A.
Wind, Percussion, String Instruments. M.M., M.M.Ed., D.M.A.
Zoology. M.S., Ph.D.

HEALTH SCIENCES CENTER:
Allied Health Sciences. Ph.D.
Biochemistry and Molecular Biology. Ph.D.
Biological Psychology. M.S., Ph.D.
Biostatistics and Epidemiology. M.S., Ph.D,
Cell Biology. M.S., Ph.D.
Communication Sciences and Disorders. M.S., Ph.D.
Health Administration and Policy. M.S., Ph.D.
Health Promotion Sciences. M.S., Ph.D.
Microbiology and Immunology. M.S., Ph.D.
Neuroscience. M.S., Ph.D.
Nursing. M.S.
Nutritional Sciences. M.S.
Occupational and Environmental Health. M.S., Ph.D.
Orthodontics. M.S.
Periodontics. M.S.

Pathology. Ph.D.
Pharmaceutical Sciences. M.S., Ph.D.
Physiology. M.S., Ph.D.
Radiological Sciences. M.S., Ph.D.
Rehabilitation Sciences. M.S.

College of Law (73019)

Web site: www.law.ou.edu

Organized 1909. Semester system. Special facility: American Indian Law and Policy Center. Library: 326,726 volumes, 4517 subscriptions; has LEXIS, WESTLAW, OLIN.

Annual tuition: full-time resident $5560, nonresident $13,775. On-campus housing available. Total average annual additional expense: $12,138.

Enrollment: first-year class 160; total 518 (men 56%, women 44%). Faculty: full-time 29, part-time 20. Student to faculty ratio 14.9 to 1. Degrees conferred: J.D., J.D.-M.B.A., J.D.-M.P.A., J.D.-M.S. (Health Administration, Environmental Management, Occupational Health).

ADMISSION REQUIREMENTS. LSDAS Law School report, bachelor's degree, transcripts, LSAT required in support of application. Accepts transfer applicants. Graduates of unaccredited colleges not considered. Apply to the Admissions Office by March 15. Application fee $50 (nonresident only). Phone: (405)325-4726.

ADMISSION STANDARDS. Selective. Mean LSAT: 155; mean GPA: 3.43 (A = 4). Gourman rating: 3.41. *U.S. News & World Report* ranking is in the second tier of all U.S. law schools. Accepts 30–35% of total annual applicants.

FINANCIAL AID. Scholarships, full and partial tuition waivers, fellowships, assistantships, Federal W/S, loans. Apply to the Office of Financial Aid, preferably by March 1. Use FAFSA (College code: 003184). About 56% of students receive aid other than loans from College.

DEGREE REQUIREMENTS. For J.D.: 90 credit minimum, at least final year in residence. For master's degrees, see Graduate College listing above.
Note: Summer study abroad at Oxford University (Great Britain) available.

UNIVERSITY OF OKLAHOMA HEALTH SCIENCES CENTER

Oklahoma City, Oklahoma 73190
Web site: www.uohsc.edu

CGS member. Coed. State control. Semester system. Special facilities: Alcohol Research Center, Child Study Center, John W. Keys Speech and Hearing Center, Oklahoma Center for Neurosciences, Toxicology Center. Library: 268,000 volumes, 2600 subscriptions; has MEDLINE, HEALTHLINE. No on-campus housing available.

Graduate College

Tuition: per credit, resident $74, nonresident $234. Enrollment: full- and part-time 713 (men 20%, women 80%). Faculty: full-time 320, part-time 141. Degrees conferred: M.P.H., M.S., Dr.P.H., Ph.D., M.D.-Ph.D. (Biomedical Sciences), M.P.H.-M.B.A. (with Oklahoma State University).

ADMISSION REQUIREMENTS. Official transcripts, three letters of recommendation required in support of College's application. GRE required by some programs. TOEFL (minimum score

550), TWE required for international applicants. Interviews may be arranged. Accepts transfer applicants. Graduates of unaccredited institutions not considered. Apply to Office of Graduate Admissions (P.O. Box 26901) by April 1. Rolling admissions process. Application fee $25. Phone: (405)271-2359; fax: (405)271-2480; e-mail: admissions@ouhsc.edu.

ADMISSION STANDARDS. Competitive. Usual minimum average: 3.0 (A = 4).

FINANCIAL AID. Fellowships, research assistantships, teaching assistantships, tuition waivers, Federal W/S, loans. Approved for VA benefits. Apply by April 1 to the Office of the Dean for fellowships, assistantships; to the Financial Aid Office for all other programs. Use FAFSA. Aid available for part-time students.

DEGREE REQUIREMENTS. For M.S.: 30 credit hours; no residency required; thesis defense. For M.P.H.: 36 credit hours minimum, at least 30 in residence; thesis. Dr.P.H.: at least one and up to three years in full-time residence, depending upon previous preparation and experience; qualifying exam; dissertation; final oral exam. For Ph.D.: 60 credit hours minimum beyond the bachelor's, 30 credit hours in full-time residency; qualifying exam; dissertation defense. For M.D. requirements refer to College of Medicine listing below.

FIELDS OF STUDY.
Allied Health Sciences. M.S., Ph.D.
Biochemistry and Molecular Biology. Ph.D.
Biological Psychology. M.S., Ph.D.
Biostatistics and Epidemiology. M.P.H., M.S., Ph.D., Dr. P.H.
Cell Biology. Ph.D.
Communication Sciences and Disorders. M.S., Ph.D.
Health Administration and Policy. M.P.H., M.H.A.
Health Promotion Sciences. M.S., M.P.H., Dr.P.H.
Microbiology and Immunology. Ph.D.
Neuroscience. Ph.D.
Nursing. M.S.
Nutritional Sciences. M.S.
Occupational and Environmental Health. M.P.H., M.S., Dr.P.H., Ph.D.
Orthodontics. M.S.
Pathology. Ph.D.
Periodontics. M.S.
Pharmaceutical Sciences. M.S., Ph.D.
Physiology. M.S., Ph.D.
Radiological Sciences. M.S., Ph.D.
Rehabilitation Sciences. M.S.

School of Dentistry (P.O. Box 26901)

Established 1972. Located in Oklahoma City (73190). Special facility: Native American Center of Excellence. Annual tuition: resident $7592, nonresident $19,764. No on-campus housing available. Average academic year off-campus housing costs: $13,200. Contact Office for off-campus housing information. Phone: (405)325-2511. Total average cost for all other expenses: $7500.
Enrollment: first-year class 54; total 195 (men 55%, women 45%). Faculty: full-time 62, part-time 75. Degrees conferred: D.D.S., M.S.

ADMISSION REQUIREMENTS. AADSAS, official transcripts, three letters of recommendation, DAT (no later than October) required in support of School's application. Applicants must have completed at least two years of college study. Interviews by invitation only. Preference given to state residents. Apply to Office of Admissions after July 1, before September 1 (nonresident), before December 1 (resident). Application fee $15. Phone: (405)271-3530.

ADMISSION STANDARDS. Selective. Mean DAT: Academic 17.4, PAT 17.2; mean GPA: 3.44 (A = 4). Gourman rating: 4.09. Accepts about 30–35% of total annual applicants. Approximately 80% are state residents.

FINANCIAL AID. Limited to scholarships, tuition waivers, grants, loans. Apply to Director, University Office of Financial Aid after acceptance and before March 1. Phone: (405)271-2118. Use FAFSA (College code: 005889). About 81% of students receive some aid from School and outside sources.

DEGREE REQUIREMENTS. For D.D.S.: satisfactory completion of forty-five-month program. For M.S.: satisfactory completion of one-year program.

FIELDS OF GRADUATE STUDY.
Oral and Maxillofacial Surgery.
Orthodontics.
Periodontics.
Prosthetic Dentistry.

School of Medicine (P.O. Box 26901)
Web site: www.medicine.ouhsc.edu

Established 1900. Located in Oklahoma City (73190). Annual tuition: resident $10,698, nonresident $26,439; student fees $582. Total average figure for all other expenses: $8000.
Enrollment: first-year class 150 (10 EDP); total 650 (men 51%, women 49%). Faculty: full-time 150, part-time 250. Degree conferred: M.D., M.D.-Ph.D. The M.S. and Ph.D. are offered through the Graduate College.

ADMISSION REQUIREMENTS. AMCAS report, transcripts, letters of recommendation, MCAT required in support of application. Interview by invitation only. Applicants must have completed at least three years of college study. Preference given to state residents. Does have EDP; apply after June 1, before August 1. Apply to Assistant Dean for Admissions after June 1, before October 15. Application fee $50. Phone: (405)271-2331; fax: (405)271-3032.

ADMISSION STANDARDS. Selective. Mean MCAT: 9.36; mean GPA: 3.66 (A = 4). Gourman rating: 3.48. Accepts about 30% of total applicants. Approximately 90% are state residents.

FINANCIAL AID. Scholarships, fee waivers, loans. Apply to Director of Financial Aids; no specified closing dates. Use FAFSA (School code: 005889). About 94% of students receive some financial assistance.

DEGREE REQUIREMENTS. For M.D.: satisfactory completion of four-year program; all students must take USMLE Step 1 and Step 2 prior to graduation. For M.S., Ph.D.: see Graduate College listing above.

FIELDS OF GRADUATE STUDY.
Anatomical Sciences.
Biochemistry.
Biophysics.
Cell Biology.
Immunology.
Microbiology.
Molecular Biology.
Neurosciences.
Pathology.
Pharmacology.
Physiology.

OLD DOMINION UNIVERSITY

Norfolk, Virginia 23529
Web site: www.odu.edu

Established 1930. CGS member. Coed. State control. Semester system. Special facilities: Center for Coastal Physical Oceanography, Center for Regional and Global Study, Social Science Research Center. Library: 585,396 volumes, 7985 subscriptions.

Tuition: per credit, resident $197, nonresident $521. On-campus housing for 750 graduate men, 750 graduate women; none for married students. More housing available on competitive basis with undergraduate students. Average annual housing cost; $5232 (including board). Apply to Housing Office. Phone: (757)683-3843.

School of Graduate Studies

Enrollment: full-time 1306, part-time 2100. Faculty teaching graduate students: full-time 607, part-time 200. Degrees conferred: M.A., M.S., M.B.A., M.E., M.S.Ed., M.S.N., M.U.S., M.P.A., M.P.H., M.P.T., M.E.M., M.F.A., M.Tx., C.A.S., Psy.D., Ph.D., D.B.A.

ADMISSION REQUIREMENTS. Transcripts, three references (depending on program) required in support of School's application. GRE/GMAT required for certain programs. TOEFL required for international applicants. Accepts transfer applicants. Graduates of unaccredited institutions not considered. Apply to appropriate graduate program director at least two months prior to registration. Application fee $30. Phone: (757)683-3685; fax: (757)683-3255; e-mail: admit@odu.edu.

ADMISSION STANDARDS. Selective. Usual minimum average: regular status 2.5, 3.0 for major (A = 4).

FINANCIAL AID. Scholarships, assistantships, grants-in-aid, internships, tuition waivers, Federal W/S, loans. Approved for VA benefits. Apply by February 15 to appropriate graduate program director for fellowships, assistantships; to Financial Aid Office for all other programs. Use FAFSA and institutional FAF. Phone: (757)683-3638; fax: (757)683-5920.

DEGREE REQUIREMENTS. For master's: 30–33 semester hours minimum, at least 24 in residence; thesis/nonthesis option; final oral/written exam. For C.A.S.: 30 semester hours beyond the master's. For Ph.D.: up to 48 semester hours beyond the master's; preliminary exam; language requirement; research tool; dissertation; final oral defense.

FIELDS OF STUDY.

COLLEGE OF ARTS AND LETTERS:
Applied Linguistics. M.A.
Applied Sociology. M.A.
Creative Writing. M.F.A.
English. M.A.
History. M.A.
Humanities. M.A.
International Studies. M.A., Ph.D.
Visual Studies. M.A., M.F.A.

COLLEGE OF BUSINESS AND PUBLIC ADMINISTRATION:
Accounting. M.S.
Business Administration. M.B.A., Ph.D.
E-Commerce Systems. M.S.
Economics. M.A.
Public Administration. M.P.A.
Taxation. M.Tx.
Urban Services. Includes urban management. Multidisciplinary. Ph.D.
Urban Studies. M.U.S.

COLLEGE OF EDUCATION:
Counseling. M.S.Ed., Ed.S.
Early Childhood Education. M.S.Ed.
Educational Leadership. M.S.Ed., Ed.S.
Elementary/Middle Education. M.S.Ed.
Higher Education. Includes community college (Ph.D.). M.S.Ed., Ed.S., Ph.D.
Occupational and Technical Studies. M.S.
Physical Education. Includes athletic training. M.S.Ed.
Reading Education. M.S.Ed.
Secondary Education. M.S.Ed.
Special Education. M.S.Ed.
Urban Services. Includes urban education. Multidisciplinary. Ph.D.

COLLEGE OF ENGINEERING AND TECHNOLOGY:
Aerospace Engineering. M.E., M.S., Ph.D.
Civil Engineering. M.E., M.S., Ph.D.
Computer Engineering. M.E., M.S.
Electrical Engineering. M.E., M.S.
Electrical and Computer Engineering. Ph.D.
Engineering Management. M.S., M.E.M., Ph.D.
Engineering Mechanics. M.E., M.S., Ph.D.
Environmental Engineering. M.E., M.S., Ph.D.
Global Engineering. M.E.
Materials Science and Engineering. M.E., M.S.
Mechanical Engineering. M.E., M.S., Ph.D.
Modeling and Simulation. M.E., M.S., Ph.D.
Operations Research and Systems Analysis. M.E.

COLLEGE OF HEALTH SCIENCES:
Community Health. M.S.
Dental Hygiene. M.S.
Nursing. M.S.N.
Physical Therapy. M.P.T.
Public Health. M.P.H.
Urban Services. Includes health services. Multidisciplinary. Ph.D.

COLLEGE OF SCIENCES:
Biology. M.S.
Biomedical Sciences. Ph.D.
Chemistry. M.S.
Clinical Psychology. Psy.D.
Computer Science. M.S., Ph.D.
Computational and Applied Mathematics. M.S., Ph.D.
Ecology Sciences. Ph.D.
Geology. M.S.
Industrial/Organizational Psychology. Ph.D.
Oceanography. M.S., Ph.D.
Physics. M.S., Ph.D.
Psychology. M.S.
Statistics. M.S., Ph.D.

OLIVET NAZARENE UNIVERSITY

Bourbonnais, Illinois 60901-0592
Web site: www.olivet.edu

Founded 1907. Located 50 miles S of Chicago. Coed. Semester system. Private control. Church of the Nazarene affiliation. Library: 155,000 volumes, 1500 subscriptions. Total University enrollment: 3300.

Annual tuition: full-time $6700, per credit $230. Limited on-campus housing for graduate students. Contact the Admissions Office for housing information. Phone: (815)939-5203.

School of Graduate and Adult Studies

Graduate study since 1961. Enrollment: full-time 273, part-time 32. Graduate faculty: full-time 48, part-time 119. Degrees conferred: M.A., M.A.E., M.A.T., M.B.A., M.C.M., M.A.P.C., M.P.C.

ADMISSION REQUIREMENTS. Official transcripts, three references, interview, photograph required in support of application. GRE required for some programs. TOEFL required for international applicants. Accepts transfer applicants. Apply by July 1 (Fall), December 1 (Spring), May 1 (Summer). Phone: (815)939-5291; fax: (815)935-4991; e-mail: gradadmissions@olivet.edu.

ADMISSION STANDARDS. Selective. Usual minimum average: 2.5 (A = 4).

FINANCIAL AID. Thirty-seven grants, three teaching assistantships, Federal W/S, loans. Approved for VA benefits. Apply by March 1 to Office of Financial Aid. Phone: (815)939-5249; fax: (815)935-4990. Use FAFSA and institutional FAF.

DEGREE REQUIREMENTS. For M.A., M.A.E., M.C.M., M.P.C.: 30–39 semester hours minimum; thesis or scholarly option of 2–4 credits. For M.B.A., M.A.T.: 36 semester hours minimum; project.

FIELDS OF STUDY.
Business Administration. M.B.A.
Church Management. M.C.M.
Education. Includes elementary, English, reading, science, social studies. M.A.E.
Nursing. M.S.N.
Pastoral Counseling. M.P.C.
Professional Counseling. M.A.P.C.
Religion. M.A.R.
Teaching. Includes elementary and secondary. M.A.T.

ORAL ROBERTS UNIVERSITY

Tulsa, Oklahoma 74171-0001
Web site: www.oru.edu

Founded 1965. Coed. Private control. Semester system. Library: 210,625 volumes, 5613 subscriptions.

Limited on-campus housing available. Rooms/apartments for both single and married students. Average academic year on- and off-campus housing costs: $5076–$7200. Apply to Director, Residential Life. Phone: (918)495-7700.

Graduate School of Business

Graduate study since 1978. Tuition: per credit $245. Enrollment: full-time 27, part-time 40. Faculty: full-time 6, part-time 3. Degrees conferred: M.B.A., M.M.

ADMISSION REQUIREMENTS. Transcripts, letters of recommendation, GMAT (minimum score 500) required in support of School's application. TOEFL required (minimum score 600) for international applicants. Accepts transfer students. Apply by July 1 (Fall), December 1 (Spring). Application fee $35. Phone: (918)495-6236; fax: (918)495-7965.

ADMISSION STANDARDS. Selective. Usual minimum average: 3.0 (A = 4).

FINANCIAL AID. Scholarships, grants, assistantships, fellowships, career-related internships, Federal W/S, loans. Approved for VA benefits. Apply by March 15 to Director of University Financial Aid. Use FAFSA. Phone: (918)495-7035; fax: (918)395-6803. About 30% of students receive aid other than loans from University and outside sources.

DEGREE REQUIREMENTS. For M.B.A.: 36–42 credits minimum; final exam. For M.M.: 35 credit hour program.

FIELDS OF STUDY.
Accounting. M.B.A.
Business Administration. M.B.A.
Finance. M.B.A.
Human Resource Management. M.M.
International Business. M.B.A.
Management. M.B.A.
Marketing. M.B.A.
Non-Profit Management. M.M.

Graduate School of Education

Graduate study since 1965. Tuition: per credit $425. Enrollment: full-time 39, part-time 272. Faculty: full-time 7, part-time 7. Degree conferred: M.A.Ed.

ADMISSION REQUIREMENTS. Transcripts, letters of recommendation, GRE/MAT required in support of School's application. TOEFL (minimum score 500) required for international applicants. Accepts transfer students. Apply by July 1 (Fall), December 1 (Spring). Application fee $35. Phone: (800)643-7976, (918)495-6058; fax: (918)495-7965.

ADMISSION STANDARDS. Selective. Usual minimum average: 2.5 (A = 4).

FINANCIAL AID. Scholarships, grants, assistantships, internships, Federal W/S, loans. Approved for VA benefits. Apply by June 15 to Director of University Financial Aid. Phone: (918)495-6510; fax: (918)395-6803. Use FAFSA. About 30% of students receive aid other than loans from University and outside sources. Aid available for part-time students.

DEGREE REQUIREMENTS. For M.A.Ed.: 30–36 credit hours depending upon program; thesis optional.

FIELDS OF STUDY.
Christian School Administration. Includes elementary/secondary/postsecondary.
Christian School Teaching. Includes public school certification.
Curriculum and Instruction.
Early Childhood Education.
Public School Administration.
School Administration.
TESOL.

Graduate School of Theology and Missions

Graduate study since 1965. Tuition: per credit $180. Enrollment: full-time 264, part-time 156. Faculty: full-time 16, part-time 15. Degrees conferred: M.A., M.Div., D.Min.

ADMISSION REQUIREMENTS. Transcripts, letters of recommendation, photograph, GRE/MAT/GMAT required in support of School's application. TOEFL (minimum score 550) required for international applicants. Accepts transfer students. Apply by July 1 (Fall), December 1 (Spring). Application fee $35. Phone: (800)643-7976, (918)495-6127; fax: (918)495-7965.

ADMISSION STANDARDS. Selective. Usual minimum average: 2.5 (A = 4).

FINANCIAL AID. Scholarships, assistantships, grants, Federal W/S, loans. Approved for VA benefits. Apply by June 1 to Director of University Financial Aid. Phone: (918)495-6510; fax: (918)395-6803. Use FAFSA. About 30% of students receive aid other than loans from University and outside sources.

DEGREE REQUIREMENTS. For M.A.: 51–57 credit hours depending upon program; thesis/nonthesis option. For M.Div.: 88 credits minimum in full-time residence; final comprehensive exam or research paper. For D.Min.: 36 credits minimum beyond M.Div., at least two semesters in full-time residence; thesis.

FIELDS OF STUDY.
Advanced Languages.
Biblical Literature.
Charismatic/Pentecostal Studies.
Christian Counseling.
Christian Education.
Divinity.
Marriage and Family Therapy.
Ministry and Missions.
Practical Theology.
Sacred Music.
Substance Abuse.
Theological Historical Studies.

OREGON HEALTH AND SCIENCES UNIVERSITY

Portland, Oregon 97201-3098
Web site: www.ohsu.edu

Founded in 1867. Located on top of Marquam Hill, a short distance from downtown. In 1974 the University of Oregon's Schools of Dentistry, Medicine, and Nursing were unified at the University of Oregon Health Sciences Center in Portland; in 1981 it was renamed the Oregon Health Sciences University and it became an Independent Non-Profit Public Corporation. It is an upper-level/graduate institution. In 2001 it merged with Oregon Graduate Institute of Science and Technology and the name was changed to Oregon Health and Sciences University. Special facilities: Center for Human Computer Communication, Center for Ethics in Health Care, Center for Information Technology, General Clinical Research Center, Heart Research Center, Cancer Institute, Oregon Hearing Research Center, Oregon Health Policy Institute, Oregon Institute on Disability and Development, Vaccine and Gene Therapy Institute, Vollum Institute for Advanced Biomedical Research, Oregon Regional Primate Research Center, Center for Research on Occupational and Environmental Toxicology, Biomedical Information Communication Center, Center for the Application of Advanced Materials Science and Engineering Concepts, Center for Coastal and Land-Margin Research, Center for Groundwater Research, Center for Molecular Cardiology, Center for Semiconductor Research, Center for Spoken Language Understanding, Data-Intensive Systems Center, Change Research Center, Pacific Software Research Center. University Hospital is a member of the Council of Teaching Hospitals. The University's NIH ranking is 34th among all U.S. institutions with 413 awards/grants worth $129,751,737. Library: 200,000 volumes, 2615 subscriptions. Total University enrollment: 1757.

On-campus housing available. Contact Student Housing Office for current information. Phone (503)494-7747. Annual housing cost: $19,278.

OGI School of Science and Technology

Graduate study only. Coed. Quarter system.

Tuition: per credit $561; Software Engineering $495. Enrollment: full-time 319, part-time 261. Faculty: full-time 63, part-time 40. Degrees conferred: M.S., Ph.D.

ADMISSION REQUIREMENTS. Transcripts, GRE, three letters of recommendation required in support of Institute's application. TOEFL (minimum score 550) required for international applicants. Accepts transfer applicants. Graduates of unaccredited institutions not considered. Apply to the Department of Graduate Education at least two months prior to the date of registration. Rolling admissions process. Application fee $65. Phone: (503)748-1121.

ADMISSION STANDARDS. Selective for most departments, competitive for the others. Usual minimum average: 3.0 (A = 4).

FINANCIAL AID. Fellowships, scholarships, assistantships, Federal W/S, loans. Apply to the appropriate department chair for fellowships, assistantships; to Financial Aid Office for all other programs. Phone: (503)494-7800. Use FAFSA. About 65% of students receive aid from Institute and outside sources.

DEGREE REQUIREMENTS. For M.S.: 45 credit hours minimum, at least 30 credits in residence; thesis/nonthesis option; final written/oral exam. For Ph.D.: three years minimum beyond the bachelor's degree; residency requirement; qualifying exam; candidacy; dissertation; final exam.

FIELDS OF STUDY.
Biochemistry and Molecular Biology. M.S., Ph.D.
Computational Finance. M.S.
Computer Science and Engineering. M.S., Ph.D.
Electrical and Computer Engineering. M.S., Ph.D.
Environmental Science and Engineering. M.S., Ph.D.
Management in Science and Technology. M.S.
Software Engineering. Oregon M.S.E.

School of Dentistry (97201-3097)

Founded 1900. Joined state system in 1945. Quarter system. Annual tuition: resident $10,146, nonresident $21,030. Total average cost for all other expenses: $9700. Enrollment: first-year class 70; total 296 (men 75%, women 25%). Faculty: full-time 72, part-time 91. Degrees conferred: D.M.D., M.S., Certificates.

ADMISSION REQUIREMENTS. Priority given to state residents and WICHE residents, U.S. citizens and permanent residents only. The Junior College transfer credit limit is 60/90 credits. Applicants must have completed at least one year at a four-year institution prior to enrollment. Will consider applicants with only three years of undergraduate preparation, prefer applicants who will have a bachelor's degree prior to enrollment. Around 68 out of 70 enrolled students have bachelor's degree awarded prior to enrollment. Apply through AADSAS (file after July 1, before November 1), submit official transcripts for each school attended (should show at least 90 semester credits/135 quarter credits), service processing fee; at the same time as you send in AADSAS materials submit Official DAT scores (taken no later than October of the year prior to the year of anticipated enrollment) directly to the Office of Admission and Student Affairs. TOEFL may be required of an applicant whose native language is other than English. Submit the following materials only after being contacted by an Admissions Officer: an application fee of $40, a supplemental application, official transcripts, predental committee evaluation or three recommendations from science professors to the Office of Admission and Student Affairs. Interviews are by invitation only and generally for final selection. Joint Degree applicants must apply to and be accepted to both Schools, contact the Office of Admissions and Student Affairs for current information and specific requirements. First-year students admitted Fall only. Rolling admissions process, notification starts December 1 and is finished when class is filled. School does maintain an alternate list. Phone: (503)494-5274; fax: (503)494-6244; e-mail: cromleyn@ohsu.edu.

ADMISSION STANDARDS. Selective. Accepts 30–35% of total annual applicants. Approximately 60% are state and WICHE residents.

FINANCIAL AID. Grants, scholarships, loans. Apply to Financial Aid Office by March 1; Financial Aid interview required. Phone: (503)494-7800; fax: (503)494-4629. Use FAFSA (School code: 003223). About 97% of students receive some aid from School and outside sources.

DEGREE REQUIREMENTS. For D.M.D.: satisfactory completion of forty-five-month program. Students take Part I of the National Board Exam after their sophomore year and Part II in December of their senior year. For M.S.: 45 quarter hours minimum, at least three quarters in residence; thesis; final oral exam.

FIELDS OF GRADUATE STUDY.
Endodontics.
Oral and Maxillofacial Surgery.
Orthodontics.
Periodontics.

School of Medicine

Established 1887. Annual tuition: M.D. program, resident $15,888, nonresident $33,483, student fees $3033. On-campus housing available. Phone: (503)494-7747. Total average figure for all other expenses: $13,000.

Enrollment: M.D. program, first-year class 102; total full-time 393 (men 60%, women 40%); graduate programs 117. Faculty: full-time 350, part-time 50. Degrees conferred: M.D., M.D.-Ph.D., M.S., Ph.D.

ADMISSION REQUIREMENTS. For M.D. program: AMCAS report, transcripts, letters of recommendation, MCAT, interview required in support of application. Applicants must have completed at least three years of college study. Preference given to Oregon residents, ethnic minorities, and residents of WICHE states without medical schools. Does not have EDP. Apply to Office of Admissions after June 1, before October 15. Application fee $75. Phone: (503)494-2998; fax: (503)494-3400. For graduate study: transcripts, letters of recommendation, GRE Subject Tests required in support of application. Interview sometimes required. Accepts transfer applicants. Graduates of unaccredited colleges not considered. Apply to Director of Admissions at least three months prior to date of expected entrance.

ADMISSION STANDARDS. For M.D. program: selective. Mean MCAT: 10.0; mean GPA: 3.6 (A = 4). Gourman rating: 3.83. *U.S. News & World Report* ranking is in the top 21 of all primary care programs among U.S. medical schools. Accepts 5–10% of total annual applicants. Approximately 85% are state residents. For graduate study: very competitive for some departments, competitive for the others.

FINANCIAL AID. For M.D. program: scholarships, loans. Apply to Financial Aid Office; no specified closing date. For graduate study: research fellowships, assistantships. Apply to appropriate department chair; no specified closing date. About 80% of students receive some aid from School.

DEGREE REQUIREMENTS. For M.D.: satisfactory completion of four-year program. For M.S.: 45 credit hours minimum, at least three terms in residence; thesis; final oral exam. For Ph.D.: 135 credit hours minimum, at least six terms in residence; reading knowledge of one foreign language; written qualifying exam; thesis; final oral exam.

FIELDS OF GRADUATE STUDY.
Behavioral Neuroscience.
Biochemistry and Molecular Biology.
Cell and Developmental Biology.
Integrative Biomedical Sciences.
Molecular Microbiology and Immunology Neuroscience.
Molecular and Medical Genetics.
Neurosciences.
Physiology and Pharmacology.

OREGON STATE UNIVERSITY
Corvallis, Oregon 97331
Web site: www.orst.edu

Founded 1868. Located 85 miles S of Portland. CGS member. Coed. State control. Quarter system. Special facilities: Agricultural Experiment Station, Center for Advanced Materials Research, Center for Gene Research and Biotechnology, Center for Analysis of Environmental Change, Computer Center, Cooperative Center for Marine Resources Studies, Engineering Experiment Station, Environmental Health Sciences Center, Environmental Remote Sensing Laboratory, Forest Research Laboratory, Center for Humanities, Integrated Plant Protection Center, Mark O. Hatfield Marine Science Center, Nuclear Science and Engineering Institute, Nutrition Research Institute, Radiation Center, Sea Grant College Program, Survey Research Center, Transportation Research Institute, Water Resources Research Institute, the Western Rural Development Center. Library: 1,225,000 volumes, 12,254 subscriptions.

Annual tuition: full-time resident $6,891, nonresident $11,703; per credit resident $219, nonresident $398. On-campus housing includes dormitories, cooperative living groups, apartments for married students, and miscellaneous rental properties owned by the University. Average annual (12 month) housing costs: $5963 (including board). Apply to Director of Housing and Dining Services. Phone: (541)737-4771.

Graduate School
Web site: www.oregonstate.edu/dept/grad_school

Graduate study since 1876. Enrollment: full-time 2036, part-time 452 (men 50%, women 50%). Graduate faculty: full- and part-time 1800. Degrees conferred: M.A., M.Agr., M.A.I.S., M.A.T., M.B.A., Ed.M., M.Eng., M.F., M.Oc.E., M.P.H., M.P.P., M.S., Ed.D., Ph.D.

ADMISSION REQUIREMENTS. Transcripts, letters of recommendation, statement indicating special fields of interest required in support of School's application. GRE/GMAT/NTE required by some departments. TOEFL and certification of financial support required for international applicants. Accepts transfer applicants. Graduates of unaccredited institutions not considered. Apply by February 1 to Office of Admission and Orientation. Some departments may establish earlier deadlines. Application fee $50. Phone: (541)737-4411; fax: (541)737-2482.

ADMISSION STANDARDS. Selective. Usual minimum average: 3.0 (A = 4) on the last 90 graded quarter hours of undergraduate work.

FINANCIAL AID. Annual awards from institutional funds: teaching assistantships, research assistantships, internships, Federal W/S, loans. Approved for VA benefits. Apply to appropriate department chair for assistantships; to Financial Aid Office for all other programs. Phone: (541)737-2241; fax: (541)737-2400. Use FAFSA. Aid available for part-time students.

DEGREE REQUIREMENTS. For master's: 45 credit hours minimum, at least 30 in residence; thesis/nonthesis option; final exam for some programs. For Ph.D.: three years minimum beyond the bachelor's; residency requirement; preliminary exam; thesis; final exam. For Ed.D.: two years teaching experience; other requirements essentially the same as for the Ph.D.

FIELDS OF STUDY.
Adult Education. Ed.M.
Agricultural and Resource Economics. M.S., Ph.D.
Agricultural Education. M.S.
Agriculture. M.Agr.
Animal Science. M.S., Ph.D.

Apparel, Interiors, and Merchandising. M.A., M.S., Ph.D.
Applied Anthropology. M.A.
Applied Physics. M.S.
Atmospheric Sciences. M.A., M.S., Ph.D.
Biochemistry and Biophysics. M.A., M.S., Ph.D.
Bioresource Engineering. M.S., Ph.D.
Botany and Plant Pathology. M.A., M.S., Ph.D.
Business Administration. M.B.A.
Chemical Engineering. M.S., Ph.D.
Chemistry. M.A., M.S., Ph.D.
Civil Engineering. M.S., Ph.D.
College Student Services Administration. Ed.M., M.S.
Comparative Veterinary Medicine. Ph.D.
Computer Science. M.A., M.S., Ph.D.
Counseling. M.S., Ph.D.
Creative Writing. M.F.A.
Crop Science. M.S., Ph.D.
Economics. M.A., M.S., Ph.D.
Education. Ed.M., M.S., Ed.D., Ph.D.
Electrical and Computer Engineering. M.S., Ph.D.
English. M.A.
Entomology. M.A., M.S., Ph.D.
Environmental Health Management. M.S.
Fisheries Sciences. M.S., Ph.D.
Food Science and Technology. M.S., Ph.D.
Forest Engineering. M.F., M.S., Ph.D.
Forest Products. M.F.
Forest Resources. M.F., M.S., Ph.D.
Forest Science. M.F., M.S., Ph.D.
Genetics. M.A., M.S., Ph.D.
Geography. M.A., M.S., Ph.D.
Geology. M.A., M.S., Ph.D.
Geophysics. M.A., M.S., Ph.D.
Health Education. M.S.
Health and Safety Administration. M.S.
History of Science. M.A., M.S., Ph.D.
Home Economics. M.S.
Horticulture. M.S., Ph.D.
Human Development and Family Studies. M.S., Ph.D.
Human Performance. M.S., Ph.D.
Industrial Engineering. M.S., Ph.D.
Interdisciplinary Studies. M.A.I.S.
Manufacturing Engineering. M.Eng.
Marine Resource Management. M.A., M.S.
Materials Science. M.S.
Mathematics. M.A., M.S., Ph.D.
Mathematics Education. M.A., M.S., Ph.D.
Mechanical Engineering. M.S., Ph.D.
Microbiology. M.A., M.S., Ph.D.
Molecular and Cellular Biology. Ph.D.
Movement Studies in Disability. M.S.
Nuclear Engineering. M.S., Ph.D.
Nutrition and Food Management. M.S., Ph.D.
Ocean Engineering. M.Oc.E.
Oceanography. M.A., M.S., Ph.D.
Operations Research. M.A., M.S.
Pharmacy. M.S., Ph.D.
Physics. M.A., M.S., Ph.D.
Plant Physiology. M.S., Ph.D.
Poultry Science. M.S., Ph.D.
Public Health. M.P.H., M.S., Ph.D.
Public Policy. M.P.P.
Radiation Health Physics. M.A., Ph.D.
Rangeland Resources. M.S., Ph.D.
Science Education. M.A., M.S., Ph.D.
Scientific and Technical Communication. M.A., M.S.
Software Engineering. M.S.E.
Soil Science. M.S., Ph.D.
Statistics. M.A., M.S., Ph.D.
Teaching. M.A.T.

Toxicology. M.S., Ph.D.
Veterinary Science. M.S.
Wildlife Science. M.S., Ph.D.
Wood Science. M.S., Ph.D.
Zoology. M.A., M.S., Ph.D.

College of Veterinary Medicine (97331-4801)
Web site: www.vet.orst.edu

Established 1949. Annual tuition: resident and contract nonresidents $10,860, nonresident $21,159. On-campus housing available; estimated living expenses: $8500.

Enrollment: first-year class 36; full-time 120 (men 60%, women 40%); no part-time students. Faculty: full-time 36, part-time 2. Degree conferred: D.V.M. The M.S. and Ph.D. are offered through the Graduate School.

ADMISSION REQUIREMENTS. VMCAS report, transcripts, GRE, two recommendations, animal/veterinary experience, essay required in support of application. Interview by invitation only. Accepts transfer applicants on a space-available basis only. Graduates of unaccredited colleges not considered. Applicants must have completed at least two years of preprofessional college study. Preference given to state and Western Regional Compact state residents. Apply to Dean, College of Veterinary Medicine after July 1, before November 1. Fall admission only. Application fee $40. Phone: (503)737-2098; fax: (503)737-4245.

ADMISSION STANDARDS. Selective. Mean GPA: 3.54 (A = 4). Accepts 10% of total annual applications. Accepts up to a maximum of 8 nonresident applicants.

FINANCIAL AID. Scholarships, fellowships, assistantships, Federal W/S, loans, grants. Apply by February 1 to Director of Student Aids. Use FAFSA.

DEGREE REQUIREMENTS. For D.V.M.: satisfactory completion of four-year program. For Compact state residents: first year at OSU, second and third years at Washington State University, fourth year back at OSU. For M.S., Ph.D.: see Graduate School listing above.

FIELDS OF GRADUATE STUDY.
Veterinary Sciences. Includes anatomy, clinical sciences, immunology, microbiology, pathology, physiology, toxicology. M.S.
Comparative Veterinary Medicine. Includes in basic sciences—anatomy, biochemistry, histology, immunology, molecular biology; in biological fields—microbiology, nutrition. pathology, toxicology. Ph.D.

UNIVERSITY OF OREGON
Eugene, Oregon 97403-1217
Web site: www.uoregon.edu

Established 1871. CGS and AAU member. Coed. State control. Quarter system. Special facilities: Institute for Chemical Physics, Humanities Center, Institute for Molecular Biology, Institute for Neuroscience, Institute of Theoretical Science, Computing Center, Advanced Science and Technology Institute, Bureau of Government Research, Institute on Violence and Destructive Behavior, Center for the Study of Women in Society, Oregon Institute of Marine Biology, Solar Energy Center. The University's NIH ranking is 150th among all U.S. institutions with 71 awards/grants worth $19,343,025. Library: 2,600,000 volumes, 18,500 subscriptions. Total University enrollment: 17,100.

Tuition: full-time, per term resident $2650, nonresident $4423. On-campus housing for married students and single students. Average academic year housing costs: $495–$1200 (per month) for married students off-campus; $6,255 (including board) for single students on-campus. Contact Housing Office for both on- and off-campus housing information. Phone: (541)346-4277.

Graduate School

Organized 1900. Enrollment: full- and part-time 3750. Faculty: full-time 539, part-time 55. Degrees conferred: M.A., M.Arch., M.B.A., M.Ed., M.F.A., M.Mus., M.S., M.U.P., Ed.D., D.M.A., Ph.D.

ADMISSION REQUIREMENTS. Two different sets of materials must be submitted to the University. Official transcripts, $50 application fee, and the graduate application should be sent to the Office of Admissions. Official transcripts, letters of recommendation, GRE/MAT (if required), and the graduate application should be sent directly to the major department. On-line application available. TOEFL (minimum score 500), TSE (required for assistantship applicants), and the International Students Financial Statement are required for international applicants. Accepts transfer applicants. Graduates of unaccredited institutions not considered. Apply to appropriate department or school at least one month prior to registration. Most departments admit Fall only. Rolling admissions process. Application fee $50. Phone: (541)346-5129.

ADMISSION STANDARDS. Selective. Usual minimum average: 3.0 (A = 4).

FINANCIAL AID. Annual awards from institutional funds: research/teaching assistantships, full tuition waiver, Federal W/S, loans. Approved for VA benefits. Apply by February 1 to appropriate department for fellowships, assistantships; to the Office of Student Financial Aid for all other programs. Phone: (541)346-3221. Use FAFSA. About 30% of students receive aid other than loans from School. Aid available for part-time students.

DEGREE REQUIREMENTS. For most master's: 45 quarter hours minimum, at least 39 in residence; reading knowledge of one foreign language for M.A.; qualifying exam/final exam/ thesis required for some departments. For M.F.A.: two years minimum, at least one year in full-time residence; final project; oral/written final exam. For M.Arch., M.L.A., M.U.P.: 45 quarter hours minimum, at least 39 in residence; thesis/final project. For Ph.D.: three years minimum beyond the bachelor's, at least one year in residence; qualifying exam; advancement to candidacy; oral/written comprehensive exam; thesis; oral/written final exam. For Ed.D.: essentially the same as for the Ph.D., except no specified language requirement.

FIELDS OF STUDY.

SCHOOL OF ARCHITECTURE AND ALLIED ARTS:
Architecture. M.Arch. only.
Art. M.F.A. only.
Art History.
Arts Management.
Ceramics. M.F.A.
Community and Regional Planning. M.C.R.P. only.
Fibers. M.F.A.
Historic Preservation. M.S. only.
Interior Architecture. M.I.Arch.
Landscape Architecture. Includes planning, public policy, and management. M.L.A. only.
Metalsmithing and Jewelry. M.F.A.
Multimedia Design. M.F.A.
Painting. M.F.A.
Photography. M.F.A.
Printmaking. M.F.A.
Public Policy and Management. M.A., M.S.

Sculpture. M.F.A.
Visual Design. M.F.A.

COLLEGE OF ARTS AND SCIENCES:
Anthropology. Includes archaeology, cultural, linguistics, physical.
Applied Physics. M.S. only.
Asian Studies. Interdisciplinary. Includes China, Japan, Southeast Asia. M.A., M.S.
Biology. Includes cell, developmental, ecology, genetics, marine, microbiology, molecular, neuroscience.
Chemistry. Includes biochemistry, cell biology, chemical physics, materials science, organic, physical, theoretical.
Classics. Includes classics, Greek, Latin. M.A. only.
Comparative Literature. Interdisciplinary.
Computer Science and Information Science.
Creative Writing. M.A. only.
East Asian Languages and Literatures.
Economics. Includes advanced macroeconomics, applied econometrics, economic growth and development, industrial organization, international, labor, public finance, urban-regional.
English. Includes American literature, creative writing, English literature.
Environmental Studies. M.A., M.S.
Environmental Sciences, Studies, and Policy. Ph.D. only.
Exercise and Movement Science. Includes biomechanics, motor control, physiology of exercise, social psychology of sport, sport medicine.
French. M.A. only.
Geography. Includes biogeography, cultural, physical, quaternary geography.
Geological Sciences. Includes mineral deposits, mineralogy-petrology-geochemistry, stratigraphy-sedimentary petrology, paleontology, structural geology-geophysics, volcanology.
Germanic Languages and Literature.
History. Includes ancient, Britain and its empire, East Asia and Southeast Asia, German-speaking world, Latin American, medieval, early modern and modern Europe, Soviet Union, United States.
International Studies. Interdisciplinary. M.A. only.
Italian. M.A. only.
Linguistics. Includes applied, general. M.S., Ph.D.
Mathematics. Includes algebra, analysis, combinatorics, differential and algebraic geometry, geometry, mathematical physics, numerical analysis, probability, statistics, topology.
Philosophy.
Physics. Includes astronomy, astrophysics, cosmology; atomic and molecular; optical; biophysics; condensed-matter; elementary-particle; fluid and superfluid mechanics; nuclear.
Political Science. Includes American government, classical and contemporary political theory, comparative politics, international relations, public policy, research methodology.
Psychology. Includes clinical, cognitive, developmental, physiological-neuroscience, social and personality.
Romance Languages. Includes French, Italian, Spanish language and literature.
Russian and East European Studies. M.A.
Sociology. Includes sex and gender; labor, organization, and political; environment; social psychology; language and culture; theory.
Software Engineering. M.S.
Spanish. M.A.
Theater Arts.

CHARLES H. LUNDQUIST COLLEGE OF BUSINESS:
Accounting.
Decision Sciences. Includes business statistics, production, operations management.
Finance.
Management. Includes corporate strategy and policy (Ph.D.), general business (M.B.A.), human resources management (Ph.D.), organizational studies (Ph.D.).
Marketing.

COLLEGE OF EDUCATION:

Communication Disorders and Sciences.

Counseling. Family, and Human Services. Includes community and other agency settings, early intervention, employment and vocational, individual and family.

Counseling Psychology. Ph.D. only.

Early Intervention.

Educational Leadership.

School Psychology.

Special Education. Includes developmental disabilities, handicapped learner, rehabilitation (Ph.D.).

GRADUATE SCHOOL:

Applied Information Management. M.S.

Folklore. M.A.

Individualized Program. M.A.

SCHOOL OF JOURNALISM AND COMMUNICATION:

Communication and Society. Ph.D. only.

Journalism. Includes advertising, electronic media, magazine, news-editorial, public relations. M.A., M.S. only.

SCHOOL OF MUSIC:

Conducting. M.Mus.

Dance. M.A.

Intermedia Music Technology. M.Mus.

Jazz Studies. M.Mus.

Music Composition.

Music Education.

Music History.

Music Performance.

Music Theory.

Piano Pedagogy.

School of Law (97403-1221)

Web site: www.law.uoregon.edu

Established 1884. Located in Eugene. Semester system. ABA approved since 1923. AALS member. Law library: 371,630 volumes, 3112 subscriptions; has LEXIS, NEXIS, WESTLAW; 21 computer workstations. Summer study available.

Annual tuition: resident $11,204, nonresident $15,536. On-campus housing available. Total average annual additional expense: $8342.

Enrollment: first-year class 181; total full-time 497 (men 54%, women 46%). Faculty: full-time 19, part-time 10. Student to faculty ratio 21.7 to 1. Degrees conferred: J.D., J.D.-M.B.A., J.D.-M.S. (Environmental Studies).

ADMISSION REQUIREMENTS. LSDAS law school report, bachelor's degree, transcripts, LSAT required in support of application. Written recommendations and personal statements encouraged. Accepts transfer applicants. Graduates of unaccredited institutions not considered. Apply to Admissions Office after September 1, before February 15. Fall admission only. Application fee $50. Phone: (541)346-3846.

ADMISSION STANDARDS. Selective. Mean LSAT: 155; mean GPA: 3.43 (A = 4). Gourman rating: 3.67. *U.S. News & World Report* ranking is in the second tier of all U.S. law schools. Accepts 25–30% of total annual applicants.

FINANCIAL AID. Scholarships, partial tuition waivers, Federal W/S, loans, grants for second- and third-year students. Apply to Office of Financial Aid by March 1. Phone: (541)346-3221. Use FAFSA (School code: 003223). About 40% of students receive aid other than loans from School.

DEGREE REQUIREMENTS. For J.D.: satisfactory completion of three-year program. For M.B.A., M.S.: see Graduate School listing above.

OTIS COLLEGE OF ART AND DESIGN

Los Angeles, California 90045

Web site: www.otis.edu

Founded 1918. Coed. Private control. Semester system. Library: 27,000 volumes, 154 subscriptions.

Annual tuition: full-time $19,894; per credit $663. On-campus housing for single students only. Annual academic year housing costs: $2700 (double occupancy). Contact Office of Student Affairs for both on- and off-campus housing information. Phone: (310)665-6960.

Graduate Study

Enrollment: full-time 24, part-time 4. Faculty: full-time 3, part-time 21. Degree conferred: M.F.A.

ADMISSION REQUIREMENTS. Transcripts, three letters of recommendation, portfolio of fifteen to twenty pieces of work (can be photographs or color slides) required in support of application. Interview sometimes required. TOEFL (minimum score 600) required for international applicants. Accepts transfer applicants. Apply to Admissions Committee by March 25. Application fee $50. Phone: (310)665-6820; fax: (310)665-6805.

ADMISSION STANDARDS. Selective. Admission based on talent.

FINANCIAL AID. Annual awards from institutional funds: scholarships, teaching assistantships, grants, Federal W/S, loans. Approved for VA benefits. Apply to Financial Aid Office; no specified closing date. Phone: (310)665-6880. Use FAFSA and institutional FAF. About 60% of students receive aid other than loans from College and outside sources.

DEGREE REQUIREMENTS. For M.F.A.: at least four semesters in full-time residence; departmental requirements determined by portfolio review; final essay; applied project; gallery exhibition.

FIELDS OF STUDY.

Ceramics.

Drawing.

Painting.

Photography.

Printmaking.

Sculpture.

Writing.

OUR LADY OF THE LAKE UNIVERSITY

San Antonio, Texas 78207-4666

Web site: www.ollusa.edu

Founded 1985. Coed. Independent. Roman Catholic. Semester system, except Weekend College's M.B.A. is on trimester system. Library: 166,000 volumes, 3000 subscriptions.

Tuition: full-time $9840; per credit hour $410. On-campus housing available for single and married students. Average academic year housing costs: $4468. Apply to Office of Campus Activities and Services. Phone: (210)434-6711.

College of Art and Sciences

Graduate study since 1911. Enrollment: full-time 2 and part-time 30. Graduate faculty: full-time 5, part-time 3. Degrees conferred: M.A., Psy.D.

ADMISSION REQUIREMENTS. Transcripts, GRE required in support of application. On-line application available. TOEFL required for foreign applicants. Accepts transfer applicants. Apply to Director of Admissions by August 15 (Fall), December 15 (Spring), May 5 (Summer). Application fee $15. Phone: (210)434-6711, ext. 314; fax: (210)434-2314; e-mail: gradadm@lake.ollusa.edu.

ADMISSION STANDARDS. Selective. Usual minimum average: 2.5, or 3.0 (A = 4) in last 60 undergraduate credits.

FINANCIAL AID. Scholarships, assistantships, internships, tuition waivers, Federal W/S, loans. Approved for VA benefits. Apply by April 15 to the Office of Financial Aid. Phone: (210) 434-6711.Use FAFSA.

DEGREE REQUIREMENTS. For M.A.: 30–36 credits minimum; thesis/nonthesis. For Psy.D.: 54 credits in residence beyond master's degree, at least 30 credits in residence; candidacy; clinical case study; final oral exam.

FIELDS OF STUDY.
English Communication Arts.
English Education.
English Language and Literature.
Note: Cooperative programs with University of the Incarnate Word and St. Mary's University.

School of Business and Public Administration

Graduate study since 1978. Coed. Trimester system. A weekend instructional format.

Tuition: per credit $410. Enrollment: full-time 65, part-time 488. Graduate faculty: full-time 12, part-time 17. Degree conferred: M.B.A.

ADMISSION REQUIREMENTS. Transcripts, GRE/MAT/ GMAT, two letters of recommendation, detailed résumé required in support of School's application. TOEFL required for international applicants. Accepts transfer applicants. Graduates of unaccredited institutions not considered. Apply to Director of Admission by at least one week prior to Weekend College orientation for the trimester of registration. Application fee $25. Phone: (210)434-6711; fax: (210)434-0821.

ADMISSION STANDARDS. Selective. Usual minimum average: 2.5, or 3.0 (A = 4) in last 60 undergraduate credits.

FINANCIAL AID. Grants, loans. Approved for VA benefits. Apply by April 15 to the Office of Financial Aid. Phone: (210)434-6711. Use FAFSA.

DEGREE REQUIREMENTS. For M.B.A.: 36 credits minimum; advancement to candidacy; thesis/professional project option in lieu of six semester hours of electives.

FIELDS OF STUDY.
Business Administration. Includes finance, international business, management.
Electronic Commerce Management.
Health Care Management.

School of Education and Clinical Studies

Graduate study since 1950. Tuition: per credit $314; doctoral tuition per credit $357.

Enrollment: full-time 161, part-time 321 (men 25%, women 75%). Graduate faculty: full-time 32, part-time 21. Degrees conferred: M.A., M.Ed., M.S., Psy.D.

ADMISSION REQUIREMENTS. Transcripts, GRE/MAT, two letters of recommendation required in support of School's application. On-line application available. TOEFL required for foreign applicants. Accepts transfer applicants. Apply to School of Education by August 6 (Fall), January 4 (Spring), May 5 (Summer); some programs have earlier deadlines. Application fee $15. Phone: (210)434-6711; fax: (210)434-2314.

ADMISSION STANDARDS. Selective. Usual minimum average: 2.5, or 3.0 (A = 4) in last 60 undergraduate credits.

FINANCIAL AID. Fellowships, assistantships for teaching/research, internships, grants, Federal W/S, loans. Approved for VA benefits. Apply by April 15 to the Office of Financial Aid. Phone: (210)434-6711, ext. 314. Use FAFSA.

DEGREE REQUIREMENTS. For M.A.: 36 credits minimum, at least 24 in residence; final oral/written exam. For M.Ed.: 36 credits minimum, at least 30 in residence; final written exam. For M.S. (Psychology): 60 credits minimum; comprehensive exam. For Psy.D.: 119 credits beyond the bachelor's degree, two consecutive 9-hour semesters in residence; dissertation; written/oral exam.

FIELDS OF STUDY.
Curriculum and Instruction. Includes bilingual/bicultural, early childhood, education technology, English as a second language, integrated science teaching, master reading teacher, master technology teacher—online, reading specialist. M.Ed.
Early Elementary Education. Includes bilingual, early childhood, generic special education, professional studies. M.Ed.
Intermediate Education. Includes generic special education, math/science education, professional studies. M.Ed.
Learning Resources Specialist. M.Ed.
Principal. M.Ed.
Secondary Education. Includes generic special education, math/science education, professional studies. M.Ed.
School Counseling. M.Ed.
Special Education. Includes early childhood, generic special education, educational diagnostician, severely emotionally disturbed autistic, severe to profound handicapped. M.A.

Worden School of Social Services

Graduate study since 1942. Coed. Semester system.
Enrollment: full-time 93, part-time 47. Graduate faculty: full-time 12, part-time 3. Degree conferred: M.S.W.

ADMISSION REQUIREMENTS. Transcripts, GRE/MAT, three letters of recommendation required in support of School's application. TOEFL required for international applicants. Interview may be required. Accepts transfer applicants. Graduates of unaccredited institutions not considered. Apply to Director of Admission by April 2 (Fall), November 1 (Spring). Application fee $15. Phone: (210)434-7111, ext. 231; fax: (210)434-2314.

ADMISSION STANDARDS. Selective. Usual minimum average: 2.5, or 3.0 (A = 4) in last 60 undergraduate credits.

FINANCIAL AID. Assistantships, internships, tuition waivers, Federal W/S, loans. Approved for VA benefits. Apply by April 15 to the Office of Financial Aid. Phone: (210)434-6711, ext. 319. Use FAFSA.

DEGREE REQUIREMENTS. For M.S.W.: 58 credits minimum, at least one year in residence; field practicum; final oral/written exam.
Note: A 36 credit hour program is available for eligible undergraduates with a B.S.W. from a CSWE accredited program.

PACE UNIVERSITY
New York, New York 10038
Web site: www.pace.edu

Founded 1906. Westchester campuses at Pleasantville/Briarcliff and White Plains. CGS member. Not all programs available at all campuses. Private control. Semester system. Special facilities: Center for Applied Research, Center for International Business, Center for Nursing Research and Clinical Practice. Library: 825,000 volumes, 2637 subscriptions. Total University enrollment: 14,100.

Tuition: per credit $600. On-campus housing for single students at all campuses. Average academic year housing costs: $5070.

Lubin School of Business Graduate Programs

Graduate study since 1906. Enrollment: full-time 415, part-time 748 (men 55%, women 45%). Graduate faculty: full-time 87, part-time 42. Degrees conferred: M.S., M.B.A., Advanced Professional Certificate, D.P.S.

ADMISSION REQUIREMENTS. Transcript, GMAT required in support of School's application. TOEFL required for international applicants. Interview may be required. Accepts transfer applicants. Graduates of unaccredited colleges not considered. Apply to Graduate Admissions Office by July 31 (Fall), November 30 (Spring); for D.P.S.: July 1 (Fall), November 1 (Spring). Application fee $60. Phone: (212)346-1531; fax: (212)346-1585; e-mail: gradnyc@pace.edu.

ADMISSION STANDARDS. Selective. Usual minimum average: 3.0 (A = 4).

FINANCIAL AID. Scholarships, research/administrative assistantships, internships, tuition waivers, Federal W/S, loans. Approved for VA benefits. Apply to Graduate Admissions Office by May 15 (Summer and Fall), December 15 (Spring). Phone: (212)346-1300. Use FAFSA. About 65% of students receive aid from University and outside sources. Aid available to part-time students.

DEGREE REQUIREMENTS. For M.B.A.: 36 credits minimum, at least 33 in residence. For M.S.: 36 credit hours minimum, at least 30 in residence. For D.P.S.: 57 credits beyond the master's; written/oral exam; dissertation. For A.P.C.: 18 credits minimum.

FIELDS OF STUDY.
Accounting. M.B.A., M.S.
Banking and Finance. M.B.A.
Business Economics. M.B.A., M.S.
Economics. M.S.
Financial Economics. M.B.A.
Financial Management. M.B.A.
Information Systems. M.B.A.
International Business. M.B.A.
Investment Management. M.S.
Management. M.B.A., M.S.
Management Science. M.B.A.
Managerial Accounting. M.B.A.
Marketing. M.B.A.
Operations Planning and Analysis. M.B.A., M.S.
Taxation. M.B.A., M.S.
Note: Special degree programs include J.D./M.B.A., International Exchange Programs; M.S. Accounting/Internship Program; Dual concentration M.B.A.

Dyson College of Arts and Science

Graduate study since 1906. Tuition: per credit $545. Enrollment: full-time 119, part-time 52. Graduate faculty: full-time 26, part-time 56. Degrees conferred: M.S., M.S.Ed., M.P.A., Psy.D.

ADMISSION REQUIREMENTS. Transcript, GRE/MAT required in support of College's application. TOEFL required for international applicants. Interview may be required. Accepts transfer applicants. Graduates of unaccredited colleges not considered. Apply to Graduate Admissions Office by August 15 (Fall), December 15 (Spring), March 15 (May term), May 1 (Summer). Rolling admissions process. Application fee $60. Phone: (212)346-1652; fax: (212)346-1585; e-mail: gradnyc@pace.edu.

ADMISSION STANDARDS. Selective. Usual minimum average: 3.0 (A = 4).

FINANCIAL AID. Scholarships, research assistantships, teaching assistantships, internships, tuition waivers, Federal W/S, loans. Approved for VA benefits. Apply to Financial Aid Office at 1 Pace Plaza by May 15 (Summer and Fall), December 15 (Spring). Phone: (212)346-1300. Use FAFSA. About 25% of students receive aid from University and outside sources. Aid available for part-time students.

DEGREE REQUIREMENTS. For M.P.A.: 36 credits minimum, at least 33 in residence. For M.S.: 36 credit hours minimum, at least 30 in residence. For Psy.D.: 57 credits beyond the master's; qualifying exam; internship; written/oral exam; special research project.

FIELDS OF STUDY.
Bilingual School Psychology. M.S.Ed.
Counseling. M.S.
Environmental Science. M.S.
Government Management. M.P.A.
Health Care Administration. M.P.A.
Psychology. M.A.
Public Administration. Includes management of government, health care, nonprofit organization. M.P.A.
Publishing. M.S.
School-Clinical Child Psychology. Psy.D.
School Psychology. M.S.Ed.

School of Computer Science and Information Systems

Located in White Plains (10606). Special facilities: Center for Advanced Media, Center for the Advancement of Formal Method Education.

Annual tuition: $17,000 for first two years, $16,000 for third year. Enrollment: full-time 54, part-time 227. Graduate faculty: full-time 16, part-time 49. Degrees conferred: M.S., D.P.S. (part-time program).

ADMISSION REQUIREMENTS. Transcript, GRE, personal statement, two letters of recommendation, interview, supplemental information required in support of College's application. On-line application available. TOEFL required for international applicants. Interview may be required. Accepts transfer applicants. Graduate of unaccredited colleges not considered. Apply to Graduate Admissions Office by June 1 (Fall), December 15 (Spring); for D.P.S. applicants May 1 (Fall). Rolling admissions process. Application fee $65. Phone: (914)422-4191; for D.P.S. (914)422-4447.

ADMISSION STANDARDS. Selective. Usual minimum average: 3.0 (A = 4).

FINANCIAL AID. Research assistantships, tuition waivers, Federal W/S, loans. Approved for VA benefits. Apply to Graduate Admissions Office by March 15 (Summer and Fall), December 15 (Spring). Phone: (914)422-4050. Use FAFSA (School code: 002727). About 25% of students receive aid from University and outside sources. Aid available for part-time students.

DEGREE REQUIREMENTS. For M.S.: 36 credits minimum, at least 33 in residence; thesis. For D.P.S.: three- to four-year, 48 credit program; qualifying exam; written/oral exam; dissertation; final oral defense.

FIELDS OF STUDY.
Computer Science. M.S.
Computing. D.P.S.
Information Systems. M.S.
Internet Technology for E-Commerce. M.S.
Telecommunication. M.S.

School of Education

Special facilities: Center for Urban Education, Center for Literacy, Center for Economic Education, Center for Care Studies.

Tuition: per credit $525. Enrollment: full-time 35, part-time 130. Graduate faculty: full-time 18, part-time 25. Degrees conferred: M.S.Ed., M.S.T.

ADMISSION REQUIREMENTS. Transcript, personal statement, two letters of recommendation required in support of College's application. On-line application available. TOEFL required for international applicants. Interview may be required. Accepts transfer applicants. Graduates of unaccredited colleges not considered. Apply to Graduate Admissions Office by August 1 (Fall), December 15 (Spring). Rolling admissions process. Application fee $60. Phone: (212)346-1531.

ADMISSION STANDARDS. Selective. Usual minimum average: 3.0 (A = 4).

FINANCIAL AID. Research assistantships, internships, tuition waivers, Federal W/S, loans. Approved for VA benefits. Apply to Graduate Admissions Office by March 15 (Summer and Fall), December 15 (Spring). Phone: (914)422-4050. Use FAFSA (School code: 002791). About 25% of students receive aid from University and outside sources. Aid available for part-time students.

DEGREE REQUIREMENTS. For M.S.: 36 credit program, at least 30 in residence.

FIELDS OF STUDY.
Curriculum and Instruction. Includes computer and education, reading, special education. M.S.Ed.
Educational Administration and Supervision. M.S.Ed.
Teachers. Includes nursery–grade 6, grades 7–12. M.S.T.

School of Law
Web site: www.law.pace.edu

Established 1976. Located in White Plains (10603), Westchester County's seat. ABA approved since 1978. AALS member. Semester system. Full-time, part-time study. Special facilities: Women's Justice Center, Land Use Law Center, Social Justice Center, Pace Institute for International Law. Law library: 343,610 volumes, 3836 subscriptions; has LEXIS, NEXIS, WESTLAW, DIALOG, OCLC, VUTEXT, EPIC, RLIN; is a Federal Government Depository.

Annual tuition: full-time $24,100, part-time $18,100. On-campus housing available for single students. Annual on-campus housing cost: single room $6360, double room $5160. Contact Law School's Residence Halls for on-campus housing information. Law students can live off-campus. Contact Admissions Office for off-campus information. Off-campus housing and personal expenses: approximately $13,850.

Enrollment: first-year class full-time 129, part-time 98; total full- and part-time 738 (men 45%, women 55%) Faculty: full-time 30, part-time 30. Student to faculty ratio 17.5 to 1. Degrees conferred: J.D., J.D.-M.B.A., J.D.-M.P.A., LL.M. (Environmental Law), S.J.D. (Environmental Law).

ADMISSION REQUIREMENTS. For J.D.: LSDAS Law School report, LSAT (not later that February test date; if more than one LSAT, highest is used), bachelor's degree from an accredited institution, personal statement, two appraisals (recommendations), official transcripts (must show all schools attended and at least three years of study) required in support of application. Applicants must have received bachelor's degree prior to enrollment. Interview not required but may be requested by School. In addition, international applicants whose native language is not English must submit a TOEFL report (minimum score 600). Accepts transfer applicants. Graduates of unaccredited institutions not considered. Apply to Office of Admission after September 30, before February 1; February 1 for scholarships consideration. First-year students admitted Fall only. Rolling admissions process. Notification starts in January and is finished by late April. Application fee $55. Phone: (914)422-4210; fax: (914)422-4010; e-mail: admissions@law.pace.edu. For LL.M., S.J.D.: Applicants must hold a final degree in law (J.D., LL.B) approved by the section of Legal Education of ABA. Submit all official transcripts, at least two professional recommendations, résumé, personal statement to the Office of Admission before March 1. Admits Fall only. Application fee $55. S.J.D. applicants must apply to and be accepted for LL.M.; completion of LL.M. program required before advancement to candidacy.

ADMISSION STANDARDS. Selective. Mean LSAT: full-time 152, part-time 151; mean GPA: 3.19 (A = 4). Gourman rating: 2.40. *U.S. News & World Report* ranking is in the third tier of all U.S. law schools. Admits about 30% of total annual applicants.

FINANCIAL AID. Scholarships, merit scholarships, minority scholarships, Grants-in-Aid, institutional loans; Federal loans and Federal W/S offered through University's Financial Aid Office. Assistantships may be available for upper-divisional Joint Degree candidates. Apply to Admissions Office by February 1. For all other programs apply before April 30. Phone: (914)422-4050. Use FAFSA (School code: 002727)), TAP application (New York State residents only), also submit Financial Aid Transcript, Federal Income Tax forms. Approximately 32% of students receive some form of financial assistance.

DEGREE REQUIREMENTS. For J.D.: 90 (40 required) credits with a GPA of at least 2.0. (A = 4), plus completion of upper divisional writing course; three-year program, four-year part-time program. Accelerated J.D. with summer course work. For J.D.-master's: a four-year program rather than a five-year program if both degrees are taken consecutively. For LL.M. (Environmental Law): 24 credits; one year full-time, two years part-time; major research paper. For S.J.D.: completion of LL.M., advancement to candidacy; one year in full-time residence; thesis of publishable quality; oral defense.
Note: School has summer program in conjunction with the University of London (Great Britain).

Lienhard School of Nursing

Tuition: per credit $525. Enrollment: full-time 12, part-time 47. Graduate faculty: full-time 10, part-time 17. Degree conferred: M.S.N.

ADMISSION REQUIREMENTS. Transcript, GRE, personal statement, two letters of recommendation required in support of School's application. On-line application available. TOEFL required for international applicants. Interview may be required. Accepts transfer applicants. Graduates of unaccredited colleges not considered. Apply to Graduate Admissions Office by July 31 (Fall), November 30 (Spring). Rolling admissions process. Application fee $60. Phone: (212)346-1531.

ADMISSION STANDARDS. Selective. Usual minimum average: 3.0 (A = 4).

FINANCIAL AID. Research assistantships, internships, tuition waivers, Federal W/S, loans. Approved for VA benefits. Apply to Graduate Admissions Office by March 15 (Summer and Fall), December 15 (Spring). Phone: (914)422-4050. Use FAFSA (School code: 002791). About 25% of students receive aid from University and outside sources. Aid available to part-time students.

DEGREE REQUIREMENTS. For M.S.N.: 42 credit program.

FIELDS OF CONCENTRATION.
Case Management.
Family Nurse Practitioner.
Nursing Informatics.
Psychiatric Nursing.

PACIFIC LUTHERAN UNIVERSITY
Tacoma, Washington 98447
Web site: www.plu.edu

Founded 1890. Coed. Private control. Lutheran affiliation. 4-1-4 calendar system. Library: 365,021 volumes, 2186 subscriptions. Total University enrollment: 3500.

Tuition: $554 per credit hour. On-campus housing for 27 married students; single students accommodated in dormitories. Average academic year housing cost: $5300 (including board) for single students. Contact Assistant Director for Residential Life for both on- and off-campus housing information. Phone: (253)535-7200.

Division of Graduate Studies

Enrollment: full-time 136, part-time 84. Faculty: full-time 38, part-time 4. Degrees conferred: M.A., M.A. in Ed., M.A. in Social Sci., M.B.A., M.S. in Nursing.

ADMISSION REQUIREMENTS. Transcripts, two references, statement of goals, MAT or GRE (Education) required in support of application. GMAT for admission to M.B.A. program. TOEFL required for international applicants. Interview required for M.A.S.S. (Marriage and Family Therapy) and M.A.E. Accepts transfer applicants. Apply to Office of Admissions at least one month prior to registration. Rolling admissions process. Application fee $35. Phone: (800)274-6758, (253)535-7151; fax: (253)536-5136; E-mail: admission@plu.edu.

ADMISSION STANDARDS. Selective for most departments. Usual minimum average: 2.75 (A = 4).

FINANCIAL AID. Annual awards from institutional funds: summer scholarships, fellowships, research assistantships, internships, Federal W/S, loans. Approved for VA benefits. Apply to Dean of Graduate Studies by March 1. Use FAFSA. Phone: (253)535-7161. Aid available for part-time students.

DEGREE REQUIREMENTS. For master's: 32 semester hours minimum, at least 24 in residence; thesis or research paper; final oral/written exam.

FIELDS OF STUDY.
Business Administration. Includes technology, innovative management. M.B.A.
Education. Includes concentrations in educational administration, classroom teaching, literacy education, special education; teaching experience required. M.A.
Nursing. Includes care and outcomes manager, nurse practitioner studies. M.S.N.
Social Sciences. Includes concentrations in marriage and family therapy.

PACIFIC UNION COLLEGE
Angwin, California 94508
Web site: www.pac.edu

Founded 1882. Located 76 miles NE of San Francisco. Coed. Quarter system. Private control. Seventh-day Adventist. Library: 240,000 volumes, 930 subscriptions.

Annual tuition: full-time $14,985; per credit $433. Limited on-campus housing for married and single students. Single students need permission to live off-campus. Average academic year housing costs: $4530 (including board) for single students. Apply to the Office of Enrollment Services. Phone: (800)862-7080.

Graduate Division

Graduate study since 1933. Enrollment: full- and part-time 9. College faculty: 128; graduate faculty full-time 4, part-time none. Degree conferred: M.A.

ADMISSION REQUIREMENTS. Official transcripts, GRE, written essay, two letters of recommendation, MSAT (as required), CBEST, interview required in support of application. All applicants must possess a teaching credential. Accepts transfer applicants. Graduates of unaccredited colleges considered on an individual basis. Apply by May 1 to Office of Enrollment Services. Application fee $30. Phone: (800)862-7080; (707)965-6643; fax: (707)965-6645.

ADMISSION STANDARDS. Selective. Usual minimum average: 3.0 (overall), 3.0 (U.G. major), 3.0 (Education courses) (A = 4).

FINANCIAL AID. Assistantships, grants, Federal W/S, loans. Apply to Student Financial Services; no specified closing date. Use FAFSA. Phone: (800)862-7080; fax: (707)965-6400.

DEGREE REQUIREMENTS. For master's: 45 quarter hours minimum including graduate project, at least 33 hours in residence; final oral exam. Teacher training emphasis.

FIELD OF STUDY.
Education. Includes a reading emphasis.

PACIFIC UNIVERSITY
Forest Grove, Oregon 97116-1797
Web site: www.pacificu.edu

Founded 1842. Located 23 miles W of Portland. Coed. Private control. United Church of Christ. Semester system. Special facilities: Malheur Field Station, Blodget Arboretum. Library: 225,000 volumes, 1052 subscriptions.

Annual tuition: Education full-time $16,410; per credit $375; Occupational Therapy full-time $17,330, per credit $580; Optometry full-time $22,366, per credit $715; Physical Therapy full-time $18,140, per credit $580; Physician Assistant Studies full-time $18,450, per credit $580; Professional Psychology full-time $17,550, per credit $500. On-campus housing for graduate men and women; none for married students. Average academic year housing costs: $5300 (including board) for single students. Contact Dean of Students Office for both on- and off-campus housing information. Phone: (503)357-6151, ext. 2200.

Graduate Division

Enrollment: full-time 847; part-time 145. University faculty teaching graduate students: full-time 76, part-time 74. Degrees conferred: M.S., M.A. in Ed., M.A.T., M.S.P.T., M.S.T.

ADMISSION REQUIREMENTS. Official transcripts, three letters of recommendation, brief essay required in support of application.

TOEFL required for international applicants. Accepts transfer applicants. Apply by March 15 (Fall), October 15 (Spring) to Director of Admissions for Professions programs, School of Education (rolling admissions process), February 15 (Fall) for School of Physical Therapy, December 15 (Fall) for School of Professional Psychology. Application fee $40. Phone: (503)359-2900; fax: (503)359-2975.

ADMISSION STANDARDS. Selective or relatively open. Usual minimum average: 2.75 (A = 4).

FINANCIAL AID. Annual awards from institutional funds: research/teaching assistantships, internships, grants, Federal W/S, loans. Approved for VA benefits. Apply by May 1 to Director of the Professional Programs for assistantships; to Financial Aid Office for all other programs. Use FAFSA. About 35% of students receive aid other than loans from University and outside sources. Aid available for part-time students.

DEGREE REQUIREMENTS. For master's: 30 semester hours minimum, at least 21 in residence; GRE for candidacy; thesis/final project. For Psy.D.: 45 semester hours beyond the master's, at least two years in residence or equivalent; qualifying exam; internship; research paper; final exam.

FIELDS OF STUDY.
Education. Includes early childhood, elementary, middle school, high school.
Occupational Therapy.
Optometry.
Physical Therapy.
Physician Assistant.
Professional Psychology.

UNIVERSITY OF THE PACIFIC
Stockton, California 95211-0197
Web site: www.uop.edu

Founded 1851. Located 90 miles E of San Francisco. CGS member. Coed. Private control. Semester system. Library: 689,733 volumes, 3747 subscriptions. Total University enrollment: 5850.

Annual tuition: full-time $22,655. On-campus housing available. Average academic year housing costs: $7198–$9357 (including board). Apply to Director of Housing. Phone: (209)946-2331.

Graduate School

Enrollment: full-time 834, part-time 249. University faculty: full-time 144, part-time 3. Degrees conferred: M.A., M.S., M.Ed., M.A.T., Mus.M., Ed.D., D.A., Ph.D.

ADMISSION REQUIREMENTS. Transcripts, references, GRE Subject Tests required in support of School's application. TOEFL score of 550 required for international applicants. Accepts transfer applicants. Apply to Dean of Graduate School by March 1 (Summer, Fall), October 15 (Spring). Application fee $50. Phone: (209)946-2261; fax: (209)946-2858; e-mail: gradschool@uop.edu.

ADMISSION STANDARDS. Selective. Usual minimum average: 3.0 (A = 4).

FINANCIAL AID. Annual awards from institutional funds: scholarships, fellowships, grants, teaching assistantships, Federal W/S, loans. Approved for VA benefits. Apply by March 1 to the Dean for assistantships; to Financial Aid Office for all other programs. Use FAFSA. Phone: (209)946-2421. About 20% of students receive aid other than loans from University and outside sources. Aid available for part-time students.

DEGREE REQUIREMENTS. For master's: 28–32 units minimum, at least 24 in residence; thesis/nonthesis option; final oral exam. For Ph.D.: 45 units beyond master's; preliminary written/oral exam, reading knowledge of 2 foreign languages; dissertation; final oral exam. For Ed.D.: 65 units minimum beyond the bachelor's, at least 36 in residence and 2 semesters in full-time attendance; preliminary written/oral exam; foreign language usually not required; dissertation; final oral exam.

FIELDS OF STUDY.
Biological Sciences. Includes microbiology, botany, zoology; M.S. only.
Business Administration. M.B.A.
Communication. M.A.
Education. Includes curriculum and instruction, educational administration, educational/school psychology.
Intercultural Relations. M.A.
Music (Pacific Conservatory of Music). Includes applied music, theory and composition, music education. M.A., Mus.M. only.
Music Therapy. M.A.
Pharmaceutical and Medical Chemistry. Includes chemistry, pharmacy practice, physiology and pharmacology.
Physical Therapy. M.S. only.
Psychology. M.A. only.
Speech-Lanquage, Pathology. M.S.
Sports Sciences. M.A.

School of Dentistry

Established 1896. Quarter system. Located in San Francisco, 2155 Webster Street (94115).

Annual tuition: $35,025. Off-campus housing only. Average academic year housing costs: $13,000. Contact Off-campus Housing Office. Phone: (415)929-6491. Total average cost for all other first year expenses: $12,500.

Enrollment: first-year class 139; total 400 (men 60%, women 40%); postgraduates 12. School faculty: full-time 50, part-time 75. Degrees conferred: B.A.-D.D.S., D.D.S., M.S. (Orthodontics).

ADMISSION REQUIREMENTS. AADSAS report, official transcripts, DAT (no later than November) required in support of School's application. TOEFL, TSE, TWE required for international applicants whose native language is not English. Interview by invitation only. Applicants must have completed at least three years of college study. Preference given to Asia Pacific Islanders and state residents. Apply to Office Admission after June 1, before February 1. Application fee $75. Phone: (415)929-6491.

ADMISSION STANDARDS. Selective. Mean DAT: Academic 19.9, PAT 19.5; mean GPA: 3.21 (A = 4). Gourman rating: 4.30. Accepts 30% of total annual applicants. Approximately 90% are Asia Pacific Islanders and state residents.

FINANCIAL AID. Scholarships, grants, loans. Apply to Office of Financial Aid after acceptance. Phone: (415)929-6452. Use FAFSA (School code: O13292). About 85% of students receive aid from School and outside sources.

DEGREE REQUIREMENTS. For D.D.S.: satisfactory completion of thirty-six-month, twelve-quarter program.

McGeorge School of Law
Web site: www.mcgeorge.edu

Founded 1924, amalgamated with the University in 1966. Located at Sacramento (95817). ABA approved since 1969. AALS member. Semester system. Law library: 444,822 volumes, 4312 subscriptions; has LEXIS, NEXIS, WESTLAW, DIALOG. Day and evening programs. Annual tuition: day $22,994, evening $15,298. On-campus housing available. Apply to the Housing

Office. Early applications advised. Total average annual additional expense: $14,100.

Enrollment: first-year class day 270, evening 67; total full- and part-time 921 (men 50%, women 50%). Faculty: full-time 31, part-time 32. Student to faculty ratio 21.6 to 1. Degrees conferred: J.D., J.D.-M.B.A., J.D.-M.P.P.A., LL.M. (Taxation, Business and Taxation, Transnational Business Practice).

ADMISSION REQUIREMENTS. LSDAS Law School report, bachelor's degree, transcripts, LSAT, three letters of recommendation required in support of application. Applicants must have completed at least three years of college study. Interview not required. Accepts transfer applicants. Apply by May 15 to Admissions Committee; early applications encouraged. Application fee $40. Phone: (916)739-7105.

ADMISSION STANDARDS. Selective. Mean LSAT: full-time 152, part-time 151; mean GPA: full-time 2.95, part-time 2.95 (A = 4). Gourman rating: 4.28. *U.S. News & World Report* ranking is in the third tier of all U.S. law schools. Accepts about 40–45% of total annual applicants.

FINANCIAL AID. Scholarships, Federal W/S, loans. Apply to Financial Aid Office by April 1. Use FAFSA (School code: G03592) and institutional financial aid form. About 53% of students receive aid other than loans from School and outside sources.

DEGREE REQUIREMENTS. For J.D.: 88 credit hour program, at least 84 in residence. For LL.M.: at least 24 credit hours beyond the J.D.; one year in residence; thesis.

PENNSYLVANIA COLLEGE OF OPTOMETRY

Elkins Park, Pennsylvania 19027-1598
Web site: www.pco.edu

Founded 1919. Coed. Private control. Quarter systems. Special facilities: Feinbloom Vision Rehabilitation Center, Lynch Pediatric Center, the Eye Institute. Library: 21,000 volumes, 280 subscriptions.

Tuition: per credit $281. On-campus housing available. For off-campus housing information contact the Office of Student Affairs. Phone: (800)824-6262.

Enrollment: O.D.: full-time 593, M.S./M.Ed. part-time 33. College faculty: full-time 49, part-time 21. Degrees conferred: O.D., M.S., M.Ed.

ADMISSION REQUIREMENTS. O.D. program: transcripts, OAT, essay, letters of recommendation required in support of College's application. Graduates of unaccredited institutions not considered. Apply to the Office of Admissions by March 31 for priority consideration. Rolling admissions process. For M.S./M.Ed.: O.D. required for admission. Apply by May 20 for priority consideration. Application fee $50. Phone: (800)824-6242, (215)780-1280; fax: (215)276-6081.

ADMISSION STANDARDS. Competitive.

FINANCIAL AID. Scholarships, Federal W/S, loans. Some surrounding states have contractual arrangements with College. Contact Admissions Office for pertinent information. For other aid apply by May 1 to Office of Admissions. Use FAFSA. About 55% of students receive aid other than loans from College and outside sources.

DEGREE REQUIREMENTS. For O.D.: four years beyond minimum three years of pre-optometry college study; final written

exam; passage of National Board of Examiners in Optometry part 1 and part 2. For M.S., M.Ed.: 51 quarter hour program; field practice; internship.

FIELDS OF GRADUATE STUDY.
Audiology.
Clinical Optometry. M.S.
Education of Children and Youth with Visual and Multiple Impairments. M.Ed.
Orientation and Mobility. M.S.
Rehabilitation Teaching. M.S.
Vision Impairment. M.S.

PENNSYLVANIA STATE UNIVERSITY

University Park, Pennsylvania 16802
Web site: www.psu.edu

Founded 1855. Located 90 miles NW of Harrisburg. CGS and AAU member. Coed. State control. Semester system. Special facilities: Agricultural Experiment Station, Agricultural and Home Economics Extension Services, Computation Center, Nuclear Reactor, Psychology Clinic, Reading Center, Institute of Public Administration, Ionosphere Research Laboratory, Materials Research Laboratory, Earth and Mineral Sciences Experiment Station, Applied Research Laboratory, Petroleum Refining Laboratory. Graduate work is offered in the Milton S. Hershey Medical Center in Hershey, Penn State Great Valley Center in Malvern near Philadelphia, Penn State Harrisburg, and the Penn State Erie; cooperative program with the Jefferson Medical College of Philadelphia. Library: 4,300,000 volumes, 39,879 subscriptions.

Annual tuition: full-time resident $7484, nonresident $14,980; per credit resident $316, nonresident $624. On-campus housing available for graduate students. Annual academic year housing costs: $4800–$7200 (including board) for single students, $4020 for one- and two-bedroom apartments. Apply to Assignment Office for Campus Residences, 101 Shields Building. Phone: (814)865-7501.

Graduate School

Web site: www.gradsch.psu.edu

Graduate study since 1862. Enrollment: full-time 4249, part-time 1914. Graduate faculty: 2600. Degrees conferred: M.A., M.S., M.Agr., M.B.A., M.C.P., M.Ed., M.Eng., M.E.P.C., M.F.A., M.F.R., M.H.A., M.J., M.H.R.I.M., M.L.A., M.P.A., M.Mgt., M.Mus., D.Ed., Ph.D.

ADMISSION REQUIREMENTS. Two transcripts, GRE/GMAT/MAT (varies by department) required in support of School's application. TOEFL required for international applicants. Accepts transfer applicants. Apply to Office of Graduate Admissions; completed forms must be received at least one month prior to registration. Application fee $45. Phone: (814)865-1795; fax: (814)863-4627; e-mail: gadm@psu.edu.

ADMISSION STANDARDS. Usual minimum average: 3.0 (A = 4).

FINANCIAL AID. Annual awards from institutional funds: fellowships, research/teaching assistantships, tuition waivers, traineeships, Federal W/S, loans. Approved for VA benefits. Apply to departments for assistantships, fellowships; to the Office of Student Aid for all other aid. Phone: (814)865-6301. Use FAFSA. About 65% of students receive aid other than loans from School and outside sources.

DEGREE REQUIREMENTS. For M.A., M.S.: 30 credits minimum, at least 20 in residence; thesis for most M.S. and M.A.

candidates. For M.Agr.: 30 credits minimum, at least 20 in residence; final paper/report of internship training. For M.B.A.: 48 credits minimum; project paper. For M.C.P.: 36 credits minimum, at least 20 in residence. For M.Ed.: 30 credits minimum, at least 20 in residence. For M.Eng.: 30 credits minimum; final document. For M.E.P.C.: 30 credits minimum, at least 20 in residence; thesis/paper. For M.F.A.: 48 credits minimum; professional project plus monograph. For M.H.A.: 51 credits minimum; professional paper. For M.H.R.I.M.: 36 credits minimum; professional paper. For M.J.: 30 credits minimum. For M.L.A.: 44 credits minimum, at least 34 in residence; individual project. For M.Mgt.: 33 credits minimum. For M.P.A.: 45 credits minimum; professional paper. For M.Mus.: 36 credits minimum, at least 30 in residence; paper. For M.F.R.: 30 credits minimum. For Ph.D.: two consecutive semesters minimum in residence; candidacy exam; language requirement varies by department; comprehensive oral/written exam; final oral exam; thesis. For D.Ed.: minimum six semesters full-time or equivalent; 30 credits in residence; comprehensive exam; final oral exam; thesis.

FIELDS OF STUDY.

Acoustics.
Adult Education.
Aerospace Engineering.
Agricultural Economics.
Agricultural and Extension Education.
Agronomy.
American Studies.
Anatomy.
Animal Science.
Anthropology.
Applied Psychology.
Architectural Engineering.
Architecture.
Art.
Art Education.
Art History.
Astronomy and Astrophysics.
Biobehavioral Health.
Biochemistry and Molecular Biology.
Biochemistry, Microbiology, and Molecular Biology.
Bioengineering.
Biology.
Biotechnology.
Business Administration.
Cell and Molecular Biology.
Chemical Engineering.
Chemistry.
Civil Engineering.
Communication Disorders.
Community Psychology and Social Change.
Community and Economic Development.
Comparative and International Education.
Comparative Literature.
Composition/Theory.
Computer Science and Engineering.
Conducting.
Counseling Psychology.
Counselor Education.
Crime, Law, and Justice.
Curriculum and Instruction.
Demography.
Earth Sciences.
Ecology.
Economics.
Educational Administration.
Educational Psychology.
Educational Theory and Policy.
Electrical Engineering.
Engineering Mechanics.
Engineering Science.

Engineering Science and Mechanics.
English.
Entomology.
Environmental Engineering.
Environmental Pollution Control.
Food Science.
Forest Resources.
French.
Fuel Science.
Genetics.
Geoenvironmental Engineering.
Geography.
Geosciences.
German.
Health Administration.
Health Education.
Health Evaluation Sciences.
Health Policy and Administration.
Higher Education.
History.
Horticulture.
Hotel, Restaurant, and Institutional Management.
Human Development and Family Studies.
Humanities.
Industrial Engineering.
Industrial Relations and Human Resources.
Information Science.
Information Sciences and Technology.
Information Systems.
Instructional Systems.
Integrative Biosciences.
Kinesiology.
Laboratory Animal Medicine.
Landscape Architecture.
Leisure Studies.
Manufacturing Engineering.
Manufacturing Systems Engineering.
Mass Communications.
Materials.
Materials Science and Engineering.
Mathematics.
Mechanical Engineering.
Media Studies.
Meteorology.
Microbiology and Immunology.
Mineral Economics.
Mineral Engineering Management.
Mineral Processing.
Mining Engineering.
Music and Music Education.
Music Theory and History.
Neuroscience.
Nuclear Engineering.
Nursing.
Nutrition.
Operations Research.
Pathobiology.
Performance.
Petroleum and Natural Gas Engineering.
Pharmacology.
Philosophy.
Physics.
Physiology.
Piano Pedagogy and Performance.
Plant Pathology.
Plant Physiology.
Political Science.
Psychology.
Public Administration.
Quality and Manufacturing Management.
Rural Sociology.

Russian and Comparative Literature.
School Psychology.
Sociology.
Software Engineering.
Soil Science.
Spanish.
Special Education.
Speech Communication.
Statistics.
Systems Engineering.
Teaching and Curriculum.
Teaching English as a Second Language.
Telecommunications Studies.
Theater Arts.
Training and Development.
Voice Performance and Pedagogy.
Wildlife and Fisheries Science.
Workforce Education and Development.
Youth and Family Education.

Dickinson School of Law

Carlisle, Pennsylvania 17013-2899
Web site: www.dsl.psu.edu

Established 1834. Effective July 1, 1997, Dickinson affiliated with Pennsylvania State University and will be known as Dickinson School of Law of the Pennsylvania State University. ABA approved since 1931. AALS member. Semester system. Full-time, day study only. Special facility: Agricultural Law Research and Education Center. Special programs: ABA-approved summer study abroad at the University of Florence, Italy, and in the cities of Brussels, Strasbourg, Vienna; externships. Law library: 440,387 volumes, 4665 subscriptions; has LEXIS, WESTLAW; is a depository for U.S. government documents.

Annual tuition: $17,440. On-campus housing available for single students only. Annual on-campus housing cost: single students $3000 (room only), $5680 (room and board). Housing deadline May 15. Law students generally live off-campus. Contact Administrative Services Office for both on- and off-campus housing information. Phone: (717)240-5000. Off-campus housing and personal expenses: approximately $12,975.

Enrollment: first-year class 180; total full-time 515 (men 57%, women 43%); no part-time students. Faculty: full-time 24, part-time 35. Student to faculty ratio 18.5 to 1. Degrees conferred: J.D., J.D.-M.B.A., J.D.-M.P.A. (Penn State at Harrisburg), J.D.-M.S.I.S. J.D.-M.Eng. (Environmental Pollution Control), J.D.-M.E.P.C. (Environmental Pollution Control), J.D.-M.S.E.P.C. (Environmental Pollution Control), LL.M. (only for persons who have completed a basic legal education and received a university degree in law in another country).

ADMISSION REQUIREMENTS. LSDAS Law School report, bachelor's degree, transcripts, two letters of recommendation. LSAT required in support of application. Interview not required. Accepts transfer applications. Graduates of unaccredited colleges not considered. Apply to Office of Admissions preferably after September 1, before March 1, before June 15 (transfers). Fall admission only. Application fee $50. Phone (800)840-1122; fax: (717)241-3503.

ADMISSION STANDARDS. Selective. Mean LSAT: 154; mean GPA: 3.30 (A = 4). Gourman rating: 3.27. *U.S. News & World Report* ranking is in the third tier of all U.S. law schools. Accepts about 30–40% of total annual applicants.

FINANCIAL AID. Scholarships, grants Federal W/S, loans. Apply to Chair, Scholarship Committee by February 15. Phone:

(717)241-3524. Use FAFSA (School code: G03254). About 37% of students receive aid other than loans from School.

DEGREE REQUIREMENTS. For J.D.: satisfactory completion of 88 semester hours minimum, summer session abroad available. For LL.M.: at least 24 credits beyond J.D.; thesis.

PENNSYLVANIA STATE UNIVERSITY AT HARRISBURG—THE CAPITAL COLLEGE

Middletown, Pennsylvania 17057-4898
Web site: www.hbg.psu.edu

Established 1966. Public. Coed. Semester system. Library: 246,143 volumes, 2447 subscriptions. Total University enrollment: 3500.

Annual tuition: resident $7314, nonresident $13,348; per credit resident $309, nonresident $557; M.B.A. resident $358, nonresident $680. On-campus housing for single and 20 married students. Annual academic year housing costs: $2800–$5100 single students, $4300 for married students.

Enrollment: full- and part-time 1147. Faculty: full-time 83, part-time 5. Degrees conferred: M.A., M.B.A., M.E.P.C., M.Ed., M.E.E., M.Eng., M.H.A., M.P.A., M.S., M.S.I.S., Ph.D., Ed.D., M.Com.Psy.

Graduate Center

ADMISSION REQUIREMENTS. Transcripts, recommendations required in support of College's application. GRE/GMAT/MAT required for some programs. TOEFL (minimum score 550) required for international applicants. Accepts transfer applicants. Apply to Office of Enrollment Services. Application fee $45. Phone: (717)948-6250.

ADMISSION STANDARDS. Selective. Usual minimum average: 2.5 (A = 4).

FINANCIAL AID. Scholarships, fellowships, research assistantships, grants, Federal W/S, loans. Approved for VA benefits. Apply to Financial Aid Office; no specified closing date. Use FAFSA. Phone: (717)654-7728. About 1% of students receive aid other than loans from both College and outside sources.

DEGREE REQUIREMENTS. For master's: 30 credits minimum; research paper. For Doctorate: 90 credits minimum; qualifying exam; dissertation; final oral exam.

FIELDS OF STUDY.
Adult Education.
American Studies.
Applied Psychology.
Business Administration.
Community Psychology and Social Change.
Computer Science.
Electrical Engineering.
Engineering Science.
Environmental Pollution Control.
Health Administration.
Health Education.
Humanities.
Information Systems.
Public Administration.
Teaching and Curriculum.
Training and Development.

PENNSYLVANIA STATE UNIVERSITY MILTON S. HERSHEY MEDICAL CENTER

500 University Drive
Hershey, Pennsylvania 17033
Web site: www.hmc.psu.edu

Founded 1966. Located about 8 miles from Harrisburg. Public control. The Medical Center is a member of the Council of Teaching Hospitals. Special facilities: Penn State Center for Sports Medicine, University Hospital.

College of Medicine

P.O. Box 850
Hershey, Pennsylvania 17033-0650
Web site: www.hmc.psu.edu/med

Established 1967. Located at the Medical Center. Special Program: overseas study program for selected fourth-year students. Library: 135,000 volumes, 1800 subscriptions.

Annual tuition: resident $21,936, nonresident $30,496. On-campus rooms and apartments available for both single and married students. Annual on-campus housing cost: single students $3,217 (room only), married students $5593. Contact Office of Admissions for both on- and off-campus housing information. Some medical students live off-campus. Off-campus housing and personal expenses: approximately $10,985.

Enrollment: first-year class 125; total full-time 480 (men 50%, women 50%) . Faculty: full-time 485, part-time 40. Degrees conferred: M.D., M.D.-Ph.D.

ADMISSION REQUIREMENTS. Preference given to State residents, U.S. citizens, and permanent residents only. Bachelor's degree from an accredited institution required. All applicants must have bachelor's degree awarded prior to enrollment. Has EDP; applicants must apply through AMCAS (official transcripts sent by mid-May) between June 1 and August 1. Early applications are encouraged. Submit secondary/supplemental application, personal statement, two recommendations to Office of Admissions within two weeks of receipt of application. Notification normally begins October 1. Apply through AMCAS (file after June 1, before November 15), submit MCAT (will accept MCAT test results from 1995), official transcripts for each school attended (should show at least 90 semester credits/135 quarter credits; submit transcripts by mid-May to AMCAS), service processing fee. Submit an application fee of $55, a supplemental application, a personal statement, pre-professional committee evaluation, and two recommendations from science faculty to Office of Admissions within two to three weeks of the receipt of supplemental materials, but no later than January 15. Interviews are by invitation only and generally for final selection. M.D.-Ph.D. degree applicants must apply to and be accepted to both Schools; contact Office of Admissions for current information and specific admissions requirements. First-year students admitted Fall only. Rolling admissions process; notification starts October 15 and is finished when class is filled. School does maintain an alternate list. Phone: (717)531-8755; e-mail: studentadmissions@hmc.psu.edu.

ADMISSION STANDARDS. Competitive. Mean MCAT: 10; mean GPA: 3.62 (A = 4). Gourman rating: 3.67. Accepts 5–6% of state residents, less than 1% of nonresident applicants. Approximately 40% are state residents.

FINANCIAL AID. Scholarships, merit scholarships, minority scholarships, Grants-in-Aid, institutional loans, HEAL, alternative loan programs, NIH stipends; Federal Perkins Loans, Stafford Subsidized and Unsubsidized Loans, Service Commitment Schol-arship programs are available. Assistantships/f available for dual degree candidates. Financi and information are generally available at the tation interview. For scholarships assistance, t places heavy reliance on MCAT and underg gested deadline February 15. Contact the O fairs for current information. Phone: (717)531-4103. Use FAFSA (School code: G06813); also submit Financial Aid Transcript, Federal Income Tax forms. Approximately 85% of students receive some form of financial assistance; 60% receive funds from College sources.

DEGREE REQUIREMENTS. For M.D.: satisfactory completion of four-year program; research project. All students must pass USMLE Step 1 prior to entering third year; all students must pass USMLE Step 2 prior to awarding of M.D. For M.D.-Ph.D.: generally a seven-year program.

FIELDS OF GRADUATE STUDY.
Biochemistry and Molecular Biology.
Bioengineering.
Cell and Molecular Biology.
Genetics.
Integrative Bioscience.
Microbiology and Immunology.
Neurosciences.
Pharmacology.
Physiology.

UNIVERSITY OF PENNSYLVANIA

Philadelphia, Pennsylvania 19104
Web site: www.upenn.edu

Founded 1740 by Benjamin Franklin. CGS and AAU member. Coed. Private control. Semester system. Special facilities: University Museum, Institute for Environmental Studies, Ackoff Center for Advancement of Systems Approaches, Center for Bioinformatics, Center for Health, Achievement, Neighborhood, Growth and Ethnic Studies (CHANGE), Center for Human Modeling and Simulation, Center for Science and Engineering of Nanoscale Systems, Institute for Medicine and Engineering, Institute for Research in Cognitive Science, International Literacy Institute, National Center on Fathers and Families, National Institute on Adult Literacy, Institute of Neurological Sciences, Lauder Institute, Population Studies Center, Leonard Doves Institute of Health Economics, Center for the Study of Aging, Early American Studies Center, Center for Urban Ethnography, Wistar Institute of Anatomy and Biology. The University's NIH ranking is second among all U.S. institutions with 1093 awards/grants worth $376,031,622. Library: 4,900,000 volumes, 35,543 subscriptions. Total University enrollment: 20,400.

Average academic year housing costs: $14,270 for single students. Apply to Director of Residential Living for on-campus housing, to office of Off-Campus Living for off-campus housing. Phone: on-campus information, (215)989-3676, off-campus information (215)898-8500.

School of Arts and Sciences—Graduate Division

Annual tuition: $25,750, per course $3260.
Enrollment: full-time 1688, part-time 366. Faculty: 1022. Degrees conferred: A.M., M.S., Ph.D., postdoctoral study in most departments.

ADMISSION REQUIREMENTS. Transcripts, letters of recommendation, GRE required in support of School's application. GRE Subject Tests for fellowships. On-line application available. Evidence of proficiency in English, TOEFL/TSE required for in-

onal applicants. Accepts transfer applicants. Graduates of
credited institutions not considered. Apply by January 1 (for
lowships), July 15 (Fall), December 1 (Spring), May 1 (First
Summer Session), June 1 (Second Summer Session). Application
fee $65. Phone: (215)898-5720; fax: (215)898-0821.

ADMISSION STANDARDS. Very selective. Usual minimum
average: 3.0 (A = 4).

FINANCIAL AID. Annual awards from institutional funds:
grants, fellowships, assistantships for teaching/research, traineeships, tuition waivers, loans. Approved for VA benefits. Apply by
January 15 for fellowships. GRE required of all financial aid
applicants. Use FAFSA. Phone: (215)898-1988; fax: (215)898-
5428. About 60% of students receive aid other than loans from
School. Aid available for part-time students.

DEGREE REQUIREMENTS. For A.M., M.S.: 8 units minimum
in residence; thesis/final project; oral/written exam. For Ph.D.:
20 units minimum, at least 12 in residence; reading knowledge of
two foreign languages for most departments; preliminary exam;
dissertation; final oral/written exam.

FIELDS OF STUDY.
Ancient History. Ph.D. only.
Anthropology.
Art and Archaeology of the Mediterranean World. Ph.D. only.
Asian and Middle Eastern Studies.
Bioethics. M.B.E.
Biology. Ph.D. only.
Chemistry. Ph.D. only.
Classical Studies. Ph.D. only.
Comparative Literature and Literary Theory. Ph.D. only.
Criminology. Ph.D. only.
Demography.
Earth and Environment Science.
Economics. Ph.D. only.
English.
Environmental Studies. M.E.S.
Folklore and Folklife.
Germanic Languages and Literatures.
Government. M.G.A.
History.
History and Sociology of Science.
History of Art.
International Studies. A.M., M.B.A.
Liberal Studies. M.L.A. only.
Linguistics.
Mathematics.
Music. Ph.D. only.
Organizational Dynamics. M.S., M.Phil.
Philosophy. Ph.D. only.
Physics and Astronomy.
Political Science.
Psychology. Ph.D. only.
Religious Studies. Ph.D. only.
Romance Languages. Ph.D.
Russian Language and Literature. Ph.D. only.
Sociology. Ph.D. only.
South Asia Regional Studies.

Annenberg School for Communication

Founded 1959. Annual tuition: full-time $25,750. Enrollment:
full-time 94, part-time 5. Faculty: full- and part-time 27. Degrees
conferred: M.A.C., Ph.D.

ADMISSION REQUIREMENTS. Transcripts, three letters of
recommendation, GRE required in support of application. On-
line application available. TOEFL required for international applicants. Transfer applicants not accepted. Apply to School by

January 2 (Fall). Application fee $65. Phone: (215)898-7041;
fax: (215)898-2024.

ADMISSION STANDARDS. Competitive. Usual minimum average: 3.0 (A = 4).

FINANCIAL AID. Scholarships, fellowships, assistantships, Federal W/S, loans. Approved for VA benefits. Apply at date of application for admission, but before January 1. Phone: (215)
898-2046. Use FAFSA. About 80% of students receive aid other
than loans from School and outside sources.

DEGREE REQUIREMENTS. For M.A.C.: 12 courses minimum; thesis. For Ph.D.: 20 courses minimum; preliminary exam;
dissertation.

FIELD OF STUDY.
Communication.

School of Dental Medicine (19104-6003)

Established 1878 as the Thomas W. Evans Museum and Dental Institute. Name changed in 1964. Special facility: Center for
Oral Health Research. Special programs: foreign exchange program at 17 different international locations; research fellowships;
externships; Program for Advanced Standing Students (PASS).
Postgraduate specialties: Endodontics, General Dentistry, Dental
Public Health, Oral and Maxillofacial Pathology, Oral and Maxillofacial Surgery, Orthodontics, Pediatric Dentistry, Periodontics, Prosthodontics. Library: 53,000 volumes, 435 subscriptions.

Annual tuition: $37,394; equipment and supplies $6350. On-
campus rooms and apartments available for both single and married students. Contact Graduate Housing Office for both on- and
off-campus housing information. Phone: (215)898-8271. Dental
students tend to live off-campus. Off-campus housing, food, transportation and personal expenses: approximately $13,432 annually.

Enrollment: first-year class 92 (men 50%, women 50%); total
full-time 355. Faculty: full-time/part-time/volunteers 260. Degrees conferred: D.M.D., B.S.-D.M.D. (with College of Arts and
Sciences of the University of Pennsylvania, Lehigh University,
Muhlenberg College, Rensselaer Polytechnic Institute, Villanova
University), D.M.D.-M.B.A., M.S. (Oral Biology), D.D.S.-Ph.D.
(no formal program but is available with special arrangements).

ADMISSION REQUIREMENTS. AADSAS, official transcript
indicating completion of at least six semesters or their equivalent
of college work, three letters of recommendation, DAT (April
test of junior year preferred) required in support of School's application. Interviews by invitation only. Accepts transfer applicants
from U.S. schools only. Graduates of unaccredited institutions
not considered. Apply to Director of Admissions after June 1, before January 15. Application fee $50. Phone: (215)898-8943.

ADMISSION STANDARDS. Competitive. Mean DAT: Academic 19.1, PAT 17.4; mean GPA: 3.41 (A = 4). Gourman rating:
4.88. Usual minimum average: 3.0 (A = 4). Accepts 15–20% of
total annual applicants.

FINANCIAL AID. Scholarships, research fellowships, grants,
loans. Apply after acceptance to Director of Student Affairs. Phone:
(215)898-4550. Use FAFSA (School code: 009737). About 82% of
students receive some aid from School and outside sources.

DEGREE REQUIREMENTS. For D.M.D.: satisfactory completion of four-year program. For M.S.: see School of Education
listing above. For M.S., Ph.D.: see Graduate School of Arts and
Sciences listing above.

Graduate School of Education

Graduate study since 1930. Annual tuition: $26,895, per course
unit $3407.

Enrollment: full-time 551, part-time 299. Faculty: full- and part-time 84. Degrees conferred: M.S.Ed., Ed.D., Ph.D.

ADMISSION REQUIREMENTS. All undergraduate and graduate transcripts, three letters of recommendation, GRE Subject Test/MAT required in support of School's application. On-line application available. Evidence of proficiency in English required of international applicants. Interview not required. Accepts transfer applicants. Graduates of unaccredited institutions not considered. Apply to Graduate School of Education by July 15 (Fall), December 1 (Spring), May 1 (Summer). Application fee $65. Phone: (215)898-6455; fax: (215)573-2166; e-mail: admissions@gse.upenn.edu.

ADMISSION STANDARDS. Competitive. Usual minimum average: 3.0 (A = 4).

FINANCIAL AID. Scholarships, fellowships, research assistants, teaching assistantships, tuition waivers, Federal W/S, loans. Approved for VA benefits. Apply by February 1 to the appropriate department for fellowships, assistantships; to Financial Aid Office for all other programs. Use FAFSA and institutional FAF. Phone: (215)898-1501; fax: (215)573-2166. About 80% of students receive aid other than loans from School and outside sources. Aid available for part-time students.

DEGREE REQUIREMENTS. For M.S.: 10 units minimum; specialization exam; comprehensive exam. For Ph.D.: 20 units minimum, at least 12 in residence; qualifying exam; written major exam; written comprehensive exam; thesis; final oral exam. For Ed.D.: essentially the same as for the Ph.D.

FIELDS OF STUDY.
Education, Culture, and Society. M.S.Ed., Ph.D.
Educational Leadership. M.S.Ed., Ed.D.
Educational Linguistics. Ph.D.
Educational Policy. M.S.Ed., Ph.D.
Higher Education Management. M.S.Ed., Ed.D., Ph.D.
Intercultural Communication. M.S.Ed.
Interdisciplinary Studies in Human Development. M.S.Ed., Ph.D.
Policy Research and Educational Measurement. M.S.Ed.
Policy Research, Evaluation, and Measurement. M.Phil., Ph.D.
Psychological Services. Includes school counseling. M.S.Ed.
Reading, Writing, and Literacy. M.S.Ed., Ed.D., Ph.D.
Statistics, Measurement, and Research Technology. M.S.
Teaching, Learning, and Curriculum. M.S.Ed., Ed.D., Ph.D.
Teacher Education. M.S.Ed.
TESOL. M.S.Ed.

School of Engineering and Applied Science— Graduate

Web site: www.seas.upenn.edu

Established 1852. Annual tuition: full-time $27,362.
Enrollment: full- and part-time 833. Graduate faculty: full- and part-time 190. Degrees conferred: M.S.E., Ph.D.

ADMISSION REQUIREMENTS. Transcripts, GRE, two letters of recommendation required in support of School's application. On-line application available. TOEFL score of 600 required for international applicants. Accepts transfer applicants. Graduates of unaccredited institutions not considered. Apply to Graduate Admission Office by July 1 (Fall), November 1 (Spring). Application fee $65. Phone: (215)898-8241; fax: (215)573-5577.

ADMISSION STANDARDS. Competitive. Usual minimum average: 3.0 (A = 4).

FINANCIAL AID. Fellowships, teaching assistantships, research assistantships, Federal W/S, loans. Approved for VA benefits. Apply by February 1 to Office of Student Financial Services. Phone: (215)898-1988. Use FAFSA and institutional FAF.

DEGREE REQUIREMENTS. For M.S.E.: 10 course units; thesis optional for some departments. For Ph.D.: 20 course units; dissertation; preliminary exam; final oral/written exam.

FIELDS OF STUDY.
Bioengineering.
Biotechnology. Interdisciplinary. M.B. only.
Chemical Engineering.
Computer and Information Science.
Computer and Information Technology. M.C.I.T. only.
Electrical Engineering.
Materials Science and Engineering.
Mechanical Engineering and Applied Mechanics.
Systems Engineering.
Technology Management. E.M.T.M. only.
Telecommunications.
Telecommunications and Networking. Interdisciplinary. T.C.O.M. only.

Graduate School of Fine Arts

Annual tuition: full-time $27,362.
Enrollment: full-time 512, part-time 26. School faculty: full- and part-time 126. Degrees conferred: M.Arch., M.C.P., M.L.A., M.F.A., M.C.P., M.S., Ph.D.

ADMISSION REQUIREMENTS. Official transcripts, personal statement, three letters of recommendation, portfolio required in support of application. On-line application available. TOEFL required for international applicants. Interview not required. Transfer applicants considered. Graduates of unaccredited institutions not considered. Apply to appropriate department chair by March 1 (February 1 for Architecture). Fall admission only. Application fee $65. Admissions Coordinator's phone: (215)898-6520; fax: (215)573-3927.

ADMISSION STANDARDS. Competitive for most departments. Usual minimum average: 3.0 (A = 4).

FINANCIAL AID. Fellowships, research assistantships, teaching assistantships, full and partial tuition waivers, grants, internships, Federal W/S, loans. Approved for VA benefits. Apply by January 1 to Graduate School of Fine Arts for fellowships, assistantships; for Financial Aid Office for all other programs. Use FAFSA. About 75% of students receive aid other than loans from School and outside sources.

DEGREE REQUIREMENTS. For M.S.: one year in full-time residence; thesis/nonthesis option; final exam. For M.Arch.: two to four years, depending upon previous education; thesis. For M.C.P.: four terms minimum of full-time study; one summer of office practice; thesis. For M.L.A.: generally two-year program, including one summer semester; thesis. For M.F.A.: two to three years, depending upon previous education. For Ph.D.: three to four years, depending upon previous education; at least two years in residence; reading knowledge of two foreign languages or one language and research tool; preliminary exam; dissertation; final oral/written exam.

FIELDS OF STUDY.
Architecture. M.Arch., M.S., Ph.D.
City and Regional Planning. A.M., M.C.P., Ph.D.
Fine Arts. Includes painting and sculpture. M.F.A.
Historic Preservation. M.S.
Landscape Architecture. M.L.A.

Law School
Web site: www.law.upenn.edu

Established 1852. ABA approved since 1923. AALS member. Semester system. Law library: 714,820 volumes; 7398 subscriptions; has LEXIS, NEXIS, WESTLAW, DIALOG, BRS, VU/TEXT.

Annual fees/tuition: $28,360. On-campus housing for 166 single students. Apply to Office of Graduate Housing. Total average annual additional expense: $12,840.

Enrollment: first-year class 251; total 765 (men 53%, women 47%); postgraduates 25; no part-time students. Faculty: full-time 44, part-time 38. Student to faculty ratio 14.5 to 1. Degrees conferred: J.D., J.D.-M.A. (Economics, Middle Eastern Studies, Public Policy Analysis), J.D.-M.B.A., J.D.-M.C.P., J.D.-M.S.W., J.D.-Ph.D., LL.M., LL.C.M., S.J.D.

ADMISSION REQUIREMENTS. For J.D. program: LSDAS Law School report, bachelor's degree, transcripts, two letters of recommendation, LSAT required in support of application. TOEFL required of international students. Interview not required. Accepts transfer applicants. Graduates of unaccredited institutions not considered. Apply to Assistant Dean for Admissions and Student Aid after August 30, before March 1. Fall admission only. Application fee $70. Phone: (215)898-7400; fax: (215)572-2025.

ADMISSION REQUIREMENTS. For LL.M., LL.C.M., S.J.D.: all applicants must have J.D. or LL.B (or the equivalent) from a U.S. ABA/AALS-approved Law School. If applicants are from outside the U.S., the Law School/Faculty must be approved by organization/government agency of comparable standing. Official transcripts, two recommendations, résumé, personal statement, writing sample required in support of Graduate Application. Admits Fall only (new class enrollment is normally 40–50 each Fall). Apply by March 1 to Graduate Admissions Office. Application fee $65. Phone: (215)898-9606. For S.J.D.: this degree is normally open only to those candidates who have spent at least one academic year in residence at the Law School, have earned an LL.M., and have a fully developed scholarly project before admission. Normally admits 6–7 candidates each year.

ADMISSION STANDARDS. Selective. Mean LSAT: 164; mean GPA: 3.55 (A = 4). Gourman rating: 4.83. *U.S. News & World Report* ranking is in the top seven of all U.S. law schools. Accepts 20–25% of total annual applicants.

FINANCIAL AID. For J.D. program: scholarships, Federal W/S, loans. Apply to Dean of Admissions and Student Aid by March 1. Use FAFSA (School code: 003378) and institutional financial aid application. For graduate program: apply to the Assistant Dean, Graduate Studies and Research before February 1. About 75% of J.D. students receive some aid from School. A loan forgiveness program for those who work in the public sector is available.

DEGREE REQUIREMENTS. For J.D.: satisfactory completion of three-year program. For LL.M., LL.C.M.: at least 24 credits minimum beyond the J.D.; one year in full-time residence. For S.J.D.: one year minimum in full-time residence; dissertation of publishable quality; oral defense. For M.A., M.B.A., M.C.P., Ph.D.: see Graduate School listing above.

School of Medicine (19104-6056)
Web site: www.med.upenn.edu

Established 1765; the first in U.S. Annual tuition: $31,940; student fees $1860. Limited on-campus housing. Apply to Residence Office. Total annual average figure for all other expenses: $14,100.

Enrollment: first-year class 145; total 650 (men 55%, women 45%). Faculty: full-time 1876, part-time 1000. Degrees conferred: M.D., M.D.-Ph.D. (Medical Scientist Training Program).

ADMISSION REQUIREMENTS. AMCAS report, transcripts, two letters of recommendation (one from premed advisor), MCAT required in support of application. Bachelor's required

for matriculation. Has EDP; apply after June 1, before August 1. Interview by invitation only. Accepts transfer applicants. Apply to Director of Admissions of School after June 1, before November 1 (Fall). Application fee $65. Phone: (215)898-8001; fax: (215)573-6645.

ADMISSION STANDARDS. Very competitive. Mean MCAT: 11.5; mean GPA: 3.78 (A = 4). Gourman rating: 4.91. *U.S. News & World Report* ranking is in the top four of all U.S. medical schools. Accepts 3–5% of total annual applicants. Approximately 30% are state residents.

FINANCIAL AID. Scholarships, loans. Apply to Director of Admissions after admission. MSTP-funded by NIH. Use FAFSA. About 75% of students receive some aid from School.

DEGREE REQUIREMENTS. For M.D.: satisfactory completion of four-year program. For Ph.D.: see Graduate School listing above.

FIELDS OF GRADUATE STUDY.
Biochemistry and Molecular Biology.
Bioengineering.
Cell and Molecular Biology.
Epidemiology and Biostatistics.
Genomics and Computational Biology.
Immunology.
Neurosciences.
Parasitology.
Pharmacological Sciences.

School of Nursing—Graduate Division
Web site: www.upenn.edu/nursing

Graduate study since 1961. Annual tuition: full-time $24,908. Enrollment: full-time 165; part-time 204. Faculty: full- and part-time 189. Degrees conferred: M.S.N., M.S.N.-M.B.A., Ph.D., Ph.D.-M.B. (Bioethics), Ph.D.-M.B.A.

ADMISSION REQUIREMENTS. Transcripts, three letters of reference, essay, interview, GRE required in support of School's application. GMAT required for M.S.N.-M.B.A. applicants. Online application available. TOEFL required for international applicants. Accepts transfer applicants. Graduates of unaccredited institutions not considered. For master's: apply at least two months prior to start of semester. Apply to the Office of Enrollment Management. Application fee $65. Phone: (215)898-3301; fax: (215)898-8439.

ADMISSION STANDARDS. Usual minimum average for M.S.N. applicants: 3.0 (A = 4). Usual minimum average for doctoral applicants: 3.2 (A = 4) at the master's level.

FINANCIAL AID. Fellowships, teaching/research assistantships, Federal W/S, loans. Approved for VA benefits. Apply by January 1 to School for fellowships, assistantships; to the Office of Student Financial Services for all other programs. Phone: (215)898-8191. Use FAFSA and institutional FAF. Aid available for part-time students.

DEGREE REQUIREMENTS. For M.S.N.: 12 course units minimum; 16 course units for Nurse-Midwifery, Nursing Administration, Family Nurse Practitioner, and Occupational Health Nursing programs. For Ph.D.: 13 required courses; maximum seven calendar years allowed beyond master's, one year or more of full-time study recommended; qualifying exam; preliminary exam; dissertation; related field final oral exam.

FIELDS OF STUDY.
Adult Acute Care Nurse Practitioner.
Adult Health Nurse Practitioner.

Adult Home Care.
Adult Oncology Nurse Practitioner.
Clinical Nurse Specialist.
Family Health Nurse Practitioner.
Gerontological Nurse Practitioner.
Health Leadership.
Neonatal Nurse Practitioner.
Occupational and Environmental Health.
Nurse—Midwifery.
Nursing and Health Care Administration. In cooperation with the Wharton School. M.S.N.-M.B.A., Ph.D.-M.B.A.
Pediatric Acute/Chronic Care Nurse Practitioner.
Pediatric Critical Care Nurse Practitioner.
Pediatric Nurse Practitioner.
Pediatric Oncology Nurse Practitioner.
Psychiatric Mental Health Nursing.
Women's Health Care Nurse Practitioner.

School of Social Work

Established 1909. Annual tuition: $24,950. Enrollment: full-time 194, part-time 106. Faculty: full-time 19, part-time 33. Degrees conferred: M.S.W, Ph.D., M.S.W.-M.B.A., M.S.W.-M.S.Ed., M.S.W.-M.C.P., M.S.W.-J.D.

ADMISSION REQUIREMENTS. Official transcript, three references required in support of School's application. On-line application available. Interview may be required. Accepts transfer applicants. Graduates of unaccredited institutions not considered. Apply to Office of Admissions before March 31. Application fee $65. Phone: (215)898-5521; fax: (215)573-2099.

ADMISSION STANDARDS. Selective. Usual minimum average: 3.0 (A = 4).

FINANCIAL AID. Fellowships, research assistantships, teaching assistantships, grants, internships, Federal W/S, loans. Apply by April 15 to the Dean's Office for fellowships, assistantships; to the Financial Aid Office for all other programs. Use FAFSA. Fifty percent of students receive aid from University and outside sources. Aid available for part-time students.

DEGREE REQUIREMENTS. For M.S.W.: 65 credits minimum, at least one year in full-time residence; thesis. For Ph.D.: one year minimum beyond M.S.W.; qualifying exam; field practice; dissertation; final oral exam.

School of Veterinary Medicine (19104-6044)
Web site: www.vet.upenn.edu

Established 1884. Annual tuition: full-time, resident and nonresident contract students $24,220, nonresident $28,800. On-campus housing available. Apply to Graduate Housing. Total annual average cost for all other expenses: $10,000–$12,000.

Enrollment: first-year class 119 (men 40%, women 60%); full-time 433 (men 40%, women 60%); no part-time students. Faculty: full-time 230, part-time 5. Degrees conferred: V.M.D., V.M.D.-M.B.A., V.M.D.-Ph.D. (Veterinary Medical Scientist Training Program).

ADMISSION REQUIREMENTS. VMCAS report, transcript, completion of 90 credits or three years of college study with prescribed courses, animal/veterinary experience, three recommendations, GRE General required in support of application. Interview by invitation only. Graduates of unaccredited colleges not considered. Transfers accepted on a space-available basis. Apply to Admissions Office after July 1, before October 1. Application fee $50. Phone: (215)898-5434, (215)898-5435.

ADMISSION STANDARDS. Selective. Mean GRE: 575; mean GPA: 3.5 (A = 4). Accepts 18–20% of total annual applicants. Accepts 45 to 50 nonresidents, including international applicants.

FINANCIAL AID. Scholarships, fellowships, internships, Federal W/S, loans available. VMSTP funded by NIH. Apply after acceptance to Associate Dean for Student Affairs. Use FAFSA. About 50% of students receive aid other than loans from all sources.

DEGREE REQUIREMENTS. For V.M.D.: satisfactory completion of four-year program. For M.B.A., Ph.D.: see Graduate School listings above.

FIELDS OF GRADUATE STUDY.
Comparative Medical Sciences. Ph.D.
Molecular Genetics. Includes molecular mechanisms, therapy of genetic diseases. Ph.D.

The Wharton School
Web site: www.wharton.upenn.edu

Established 1881. Accredited programs: M.B.A., Accounting; recognized Ph.D. Semester and quarter system: first year is quarter system; second year is semester system. Special programs: four week pre-term program; foreign exchange programs in Australia, Brazil, France, Italy, Japan, the Netherlands, the Philippines, Spain, Sweden, United Kingdom, Wharton Global Immersion Program, Wharton/Johns Hopkins School of Advanced International Studies. Special facility: Joseph H. Lauder Institute of Management and International Studies. Library: 200,000 volumes, 3500 subscriptions.

Annual tuition: full-time $34,946. Enrollment: total full-time 1871 (men 70%, women 30%). Faculty: full-time 215, part-time 41; all have Ph.D./D.B.A. Degrees conferred: M.B.A., W.E.M.B.A., M.S. (Accounting, for Wharton undergraduates only), M.B.A.-J.D., M.B.A.-M.A. (International Relations, Communications), M.B.A.-M.D., M.B.A.-D.M.D., M.B.A.-D.V.M., M.B.A.-M.S.E. (Engineering), M.B.A.-M.S.N., M.B.A.-M.S.W., M.B.A.-Ph.D. (Nursing, Medical Sciences at Wharton), Ph.D.

ADMISSION REQUIREMENTS. All applicants should have a bachelor's degree from a recognized institution of higher education and a strong mathematics background. Students are required to have their own personal computer. Contact Wharton for application material and information; phone: M.B.A. (215)898-6183, W.E.M.B.A. (215)898-1776. Early applications are encouraged for both admission and financial aid consideration. Beginning students are admitted Fall only. Both U.S. citizens and international applicants apply by April 10 (Fall). Submit application, GMAT results (will accept GMAT test results from the last five years, latest acceptable date is March), official transcripts from each undergraduate/graduate school attended, three letters of recommendation, four essays, résumé (prefers at least four years of work experience), and an application fee of $160 to the Director of MBA Admission. On-line application available. In addition, international students (whose native language is other than English) should submit a TOEFL score, certified translations and evaluations of all official transcripts; recommendation should be in English or with certified translations and proof of sufficient financial resources for two years of academic study. On-campus interviews are strongly encouraged prior to the admissions committee reviewing completed application. Dual Degree applicants must apply to and be accepted to both schools/programs. Contact the Admissions Office for current information and specific admissions requirements. Phone: (215) 898-8183. Rolling admissions process; notification is made within 8–10 weeks of receipt of completed application and supporting documents.

ADMISSION REQUIREMENTS. Contact Doctoral Programs at (215)898-4877 for application material and information. Beginning students are admitted Fall Only. Both U.S. citizens and international applicants apply by February 1 (Fall). Submit two-part application form, GMAT (will accept GMAT test results from the last five years), official transcripts from each undergraduate/graduate school attended, three letters of recommendation, résumé, statement of purpose, and application fee of $65 to the University of Pennsylvania Office of Graduate Admission. In addition, international students (whose native language is other than English) should submit TOEFL, TSE, and TWE scores; certified translations and evaluations of all official transcripts; recommendation should be in English or with certified translations. International students' contact: (215)898-5000. All accepted students are invited for interviews. Notification is made on or near April 1.

ADMISSION STANDARDS. Very selective. Usual minimum average: M.B.A. 3.0, Ph.D. 3.3 (A = 4). Mean M.B.A. GMAT: 700; median M.B.A. GPA: 3.5 (A = 4). Gourman rating: MBA 4.93; E.M.B.A. 4.90. *U.S. News & World Report* ranked Wharton's M.B.A. program in the top three of all U.S. business schools. *Business Week* listed Wharton as number one among all U.S. business schools. For Ph.D.: approximately 600–800 applications; 30–40 will enroll. Gourman rating: 4.93.

FINANCIAL AID. Scholarships, international scholarships, minority scholarships, grants, fellowships, graduate assistantships, Federal Perkins Loans, Stafford Subsidized and Unsubsidized Loans, Federal W/S available. Some financial assistance is available for international students. Assistantships/fellowships may be available for joint degree candidates. Financial Aid applications and information are included with admission materials; apply by March 1. Request scholarship, fellowship, assistantship, and need-based information from Wharton. Use FAFSA (School code: 003378); also submit an institutional FAF, a Financial Aid Transcript, Federal Income Tax forms. Approximately 65% of students receive some form of financial assistance.

DEGREE REQUIREMENTS. For M.B.A.: 19 course, two-year program; degree program must be completed in two years. For W.E.M.B.A.: two-year program. For M.B.A.-Masters: generally a three-and-one-half- to five-year program. For M.B.A.-J.D.: four-and-one-half- to five-year program. For M.B.A.-D.M.D., M.D., D.V.D.: generally a five- to six-year program. For Ph.D.: three- to five-year program, 20 course units; teacher development program; preliminary exam; candidacy; dissertation proposal; dissertation; oral defense.

M.B.A. MAJORS.
Accounting. Includes financial accounting, management information and control.
Business and Public Policy. Includes international policy, public finance, public/nonprofit management, regulation (business and government relations), urban economic development.
Environmental and Risk Management.
Finance. Includes banking and financial institutions, corporate finance, international finance, investment management, real estate and urban public finance.
Health Care Management.
Insurance and Risk Management. Includes actuarial science, insurance and risk management.
Management. Includes entrepreneurial management, human resource and organizational management, multinational management, strategic management.
Managing Electronic Commerce.
Marketing. Includes marketing management, market research.
Marketing and Operations Management.
Operations and Information Management. Includes information (strategy, systems, and economics).
Real Estate.
Technological Innovation.

DOCTORAL PROGRAMS.
Accounting.
Business and Public Policy.
Finance.
Health Care Systems.

Insurance and Risk Management.
Management.
Marketing.
Operations and Information Management.
Real Estate.
Statistics.

PEPPERDINE UNIVERSITY
Culver City, California 90230-7615
Web site: www.pepperdine.edu

Founded 1937. Coed. Private control. Church of Christ. Trimester system. Library: 110,000 volumes, 875 subscriptions.

Tuition: per unit, varies from $785. No on-campus housing available.

Graduate Programs

Enrollment: full- and part-time 3375. Faculty: full-time 136, part-time 135. Degrees conferred: M.A., M.S., M.S.O.D., M.S.T.M., M.B.A., M.I.B., Ed.D., Psy.D.

ADMISSION REQUIREMENTS. Official transcripts, GRE/GMAT/MAT, recommendations required in support of application. TOEFL and evidence of financial support required for international applicants. Interview may be required. Accepts transfer applicants. Graduates of unaccredited institutions not considered. Apply to the Director of Admission for appropriate School. Application fee $55. Phone: (310)456-4392.

ADMISSION STANDARDS. Selective. Usual minimum average: 2.5 (A = 4).

FINANCIAL AID. Scholarships, research assistantships, teaching assistantships, internships, Federal W/S, loans. Approved for VA benefits. Apply by July 1 to appropriate department chair for assistantships; to Financial Aid Office for all other programs. Phone: (310)506-4301. Use FAFSA (University code: 001264). Aid available for part-time students.

DEGREE REQUIREMENTS. For master's: 30 semester units minimum, at least 24 in residence; thesis/nonthesis option. For M.B.A.: 48 units, at least 40 in residence. For Ed.D., Psy.D.: GRE Subject Tests for candidacy; thesis or research project; final written/oral exam.

FIELDS OF STUDY.

GRADUATE SCHOOL OF EDUCATION AND PSYCHOLOGY:
Administration.
Clinical Psychology.
Education.
Educational Leadership.
Educational Technology.
General Psychology.
Organizational Change.
Organizational Leadership.
Psychology.

GRAZIADO SCHOOL OF BUSINESS AND MANAGEMENT:
Business Administration.
Executive Business Administration.
International Business.
Organizational Development.
Technology Management.

SCHOOL OF PUBLIC POLICY:
American Politics.
Economics.

International Relations.
Political Science.
Regional and Local Policy.
Social Science.

PEPPERDINE UNIVERSITY
Pacific Coast Highway, Malibu, California 90263-0001
Web site: www.pepperdine.edu

Founded 1937. CGS member. Coed. Private control—Church of Christ. Trimester system. Has centers in Culver City, Long Beach, Orange County, San Fernando Valley, and Ventura; international centers in Argentina, England, Germany, and Italy. Special facilities: Ira Sherman Center for Ethical Awareness, Center for Educational Leadership, National School Safety Center, Institute for the Study of Asian Culture. Library: 640,972 volumes, 3880 subscriptions.

Tuition: per unit, varies from $786. On-campus housing available for single students only. Average academic year housing costs: $5700–$13,000. Contact the Office of Residential Life for both on- and off-campus housing information. Phone: (310)456-4104.

Graduate Programs

Enrollment: full-time 11, part-time 109. Faculty: full-time 34, part-time 5. Degrees conferred: M.A., M.S., M.Div.

ADMISSION REQUIREMENTS. Transcripts, GRE, three recommendations required in support of College's application. TOEFL required for international applicants. Interview may be required. Accepts transfer applicants. Graduates of unaccredited institutions not considered. Apply by May 1 (Fall), September 1 (Spring) to Admissions Office. Rolling admissions process. Application fee $55. Phone: (310)456-4392.

ADMISSION STANDARDS. Selective. Minimum average: 2.5 (A = 4).

FINANCIAL AID. Scholarships, fellowships, research assistantships, teaching assistantships, grants, Federal W/S, loans. Approved for VA benefits. Apply by February 15 to Dean's Office for assistantships; to Financial Aid Office for all other programs. Phone: (310)456-4301. Use FAFSA. Aid available for part-time students.

DEGREE REQUIREMENTS. For master's: 30 semester units minimum and at least 24 in residence; thesis/nonthesis option; comprehensive exam.

FIELDS OF STUDY.

SEAVER COLLEGE:
American Studies.
Communications.
History.
Psychology.
Public Policy.
Religion.

GRADUATE SCHOOL OF EDUCATION:
Administration.
Clinical Psychology.
Education.
Educational Leadership.
Educational Technology. Ed.D. only.
General Psychology.
Organizational Change.
Organizational Leadership.
Psychology.

GRAZIADO SCHOOL OF BUSINESS AND MANAGEMENT:
Business Administration.
Organizational Development.

School of Law
Web site: www.pepperdine.edu

Formerly Orange University College of Law. Affiliated 1969. Located in Malibu (90263). ABA approved since 1972. AALS member. Semester system. Special facilities: Center for Entrepreneurship and Technology, Institute for Dispute Resolution. Library: 338,157 volumes, 3603 subscriptions; LEXIS, NEXIS, WESTLAW, DIALOG.

Annual tuition: $24,870. University housing available near campus. Total average annual additional expense: $16,078.

Enrollment: first-year class 214; total full-time 637 (men 54%, women 46%). Faculty: full-time 27, part-time 34. Student to faculty ratio 18.3 to 1. Degrees conferred: J.D., J.D.-M.B.A., M.D.R. (Dispute Resolution), J.D.-M.D.R.

ADMISSION REQUIREMENTS. LSDAS Law School report, bachelor's degree, transcripts, LSAT, two letters of reference required in support of application. Accepts transfer applicants. Graduates of unaccredited colleges not considered. Apply to Admissions Office by March 1. Application fee $50. Phone: (310)456-4631; fax: (310)506-7668.

ADMISSION STANDARDS. Selective. Mean LSAT: 156; mean GPA: 3.31 (A = 4). Gourman rating: 3.68. *U.S. News & World Report* ranking is in the third tier of all U.S. law schools. Accepts about 45–50% of total annual applicants.

FINANCIAL AID. Scholarships, assistantships, Federal W/S, loans. Apply to Director of Financial Aid by April 1. Use FAFSA. About 85% of students receive some aid from School.

DEGREE REQUIREMENTS. For J. D.: satisfactory completion of three-year program; 88 credit hour program. For M.D.R.: 32 units; thesis/project or externship.
Note: Study abroad program in London (Great Britain) available each Fall term for second- and third-year students.

PHILADELPHIA COLLEGE OF OSTEOPATHIC MEDICINE
Philadelphia, Pennsylvania 19118-1694
Web site: www.pcom.edu

Founded 1899. Largest of the 15 Osteopathic Schools. Coed. Private control. Semester system. Library: 71,000 volumes, 785 subscriptions; has MEDLINE, CANCERLINE, BIOETHIC, HEALTH, PALINET, TOXLINE, DIALOG, OCLC.

Annual tuition: $25,696. No on-campus housing available.

Enrollment: first-year class 250; total 995 (men 63%, women 37%). Faculty: full-time 64, part-time 862. Degrees conferred: D.O., M.Sc., D.O.-M.B.A. (Saint Joseph's University), D.O.-M.P.H. (Temple University).

ADMISSION REQUIREMENTS. AACOMAS report (deadline February 1), bachelor's degree, official transcripts, MCAT, three recommendations (one from premed advisory committee, one evaluation from a physician, preferably a D.O.), supplemental form required in support of application. Interview by invitation only. Graduates of unaccredited colleges not considered. Preference given to state residents. Apply by March 1 (supplemental deadline) to the Assistant Dean for Admissions and Enrollment. Admits first year students Fall only. Rolling admissions process. Application fee: $50 for nonresidents. Phone: (800)999-6998; e-mail: admissions@pcom.edu.

ADMISSION STANDARDS. Selective. Usual minimum average: 2.75 (A = 4), mean GPA: 3.1. Accepts approximately 15% of total annual applicants.

FINANCIAL AID. Scholarships, minority scholarships, fellowships, assistantships, grants, Federal W/S, loans. Apply by April 1 to the Financial Aid Office. Phone: (215)871-6170. Use FAFSA (College code: 015979) and institutional FAF. About 90% of students receive some form of financial assistance.

DEGREE REQUIREMENT. For D.O.: satisfactory completion of four-year program; all students must pass the National Board of Osteopathic Medical Exam Part I and take Part II. For M.S.: 36 credit program; comprehensive exam; thesis for some programs.

FIELDS OF GRADUATE STUDY.
Biomedical Science.
Forensic Medicine.
Medical Research.
Organizational Development and Leadership.
Physician Assistant Studies.
Psychology.

UNIVERSITY OF PHOENIX
Phoenix, Arizona 85072-2069
Web site: www.phoenix.edu

Chartered 1976. Classes offered at 116 campuses and Learning Centers. University offers programs in Arizona (Phoenix, Tucson), California (Fountain Valley, Pleasanton, Sacramento, San Diego), Colorado (Lone Tree, Colorado Springs), Commonwealth of Puerto Rico (Guaynabo), Florida (Orlando, Tampa), Hawaii (Honolulu), Louisiana, Maryland (Columbia), Michigan (Grand Rapids, Troy), Missouri (St. Louis), Nevada (Las Vegas), New Mexico (Albuquerque), Ohio (Independence), Oklahoma (Oklahoma City, Tulsa), Oregon (Portland), or Pennsylvania (Philadelphia, Pittsburgh), Texas (Houston, Dallas/Fort Worth), Utah (Salt Lake City), Washington (Seattle), British Columbia (Vancouver). Not all programs are offered at all locations. Coed. Private proprietary (Apollo Group) control. One-course-per-month format, six weeks in duration. Special facilities: Center for Distance Learning, Center for Higher Education and Economic Development. Library: 27,000,000 volumes, 1,366,000 microforms, 2500 current subscriptions, several thousand PCs at all campuses and Learning Centers. Total University enrollment: 125,364; 80,000 on campuses, 48,000 using on-line instruction or distance learning.

Tuition: varies by campus. No on-campus housing available.

Graduate Programs

Graduate study since 1975. Enrollment: full- and part-time approximately 25,000. Graduate faculty: full-time 30, part-time 1100. Degrees conferred: M.A.Ed., M.A.O.M., M.B.A., M.C., M.S.N., M.S.C.I.S.

ADMISSION REQUIREMENTS. Official transcripts required in support of application. TOEFL required for international applicants. Accepts transfer applicants. Graduates of unaccredited institutions not considered. Apply to appropriate Admission Office at least one month prior to date of registration. Rolling admissions process. Phone: (800)MY-SUCCESS. Application fee $85. Contact Web site for appropriate Admissions Office number.

ADMISSION STANDARDS. Relatively open. Usual minimum average: 2.5 (A = 4).

FINANCIAL AID. Annual awards from institutional funds: Federal W/S, loans. Most sites are approved for VA benefits. Apply

to Office of Financial Assistance at each site; no specified closing date. Use FAFSA. Aid available for part-time students.

DEGREE REQUIREMENTS. For master's: 36–51 credits minimum, at least 30–45 in residence; thesis/nonthesis option; no foreign language requirement; final exams/internships in some programs.

FIELDS OF STUDY.
Business Administration. Includes e-business, global management, health care management, technology management. M.B.A.
Computer information Systems. M.S.C.I.S
Counseling. Includes community counseling, marriage, family, and child counseling. M.C.
Education. Includes administration and supervision, adult education and distance learning, curriculum and instruction, curriculum and technology, educational counseling, special education/ cross-categorical, teacher education. M.A.Ed.
Nursing. Includes family nurse practitioner, women's health nurse practitioner. M.S.N., M.S.N.-M.B.A. (Health Care Management).
Organizational Management. M.A.O.M.
Note: The above fields of study were obtained by visiting ten campuses on-line. Consult the campus closest to you to obtain current and complete information.

PITTSBURG STATE UNIVERSITY
Pittsburg, Kansas 66762-5880
Web site: www.pittstate.edu

Founded 1903. Located 125 miles S of Kansas City. CGS member. Coed. State control. Semester system. Library: 350,000 volumes, 1368 subscriptions. Total University enrollment: 6750.

Annual tuition: resident $2932, nonresident $4896; per credit, resident $124, nonresident $315. On-campus housing for 47 married students, 630 men, 700 women. Average academic year housing costs: $3890 (room only). Apply to Director of Residence Life. Phone: (316)235-4245.

Graduate School

Graduate study since 1929. Enrollment: full-time 331, part-time 865. College faculty teaching graduate students: 268. Degrees conferred: M.A., M.S., M.B.A., M.M., M.S.N., Ed.S.

ADMISSION REQUIREMENTS. Official transcripts, recommendations required in support of application. GRE/GMAT required by several departments. TOEFL (minimum score 520–550 depending on department) required for international applicants. Accepts transfer applicants. Apply by July 15 (Fall), December 5 (Spring), April 30 (Summer) to the Office of Graduate Studies and Research. Rolling admissions process. Application fee: none, international applicants $40. Phone: (316)235-4220; fax: (316)235-4219.

ADMISSION STANDARDS. Selective. Usual minimum average: 2.5 (A = 4).

FINANCIAL AID. Annual awards from institutional funds: teaching assistantships, research assistantships, internships, fee waivers, Federal W/S, loans. Approved for VA benefits. Apply to Graduate Office for assistantships; to Financial Aid Office for all other programs. Phone: (316)235-7000. Use FAFSA. About 60% of students receive aid other than loans from College and outside sources.

DEGREE REQUIREMENTS. For master's: 30–36 semester hours minimum; admission to candidacy; comprehensive exam; research problem, seminar; or thesis/nonthesis option. For Ed.S.: 30 semester hours minimum beyond the master's; thesis problem; comprehensive exam; admission to candidacy.

FIELDS OF STUDY.
Art. Includes art education, studio arts.
Biology.
Business Administration. Includes accounting.
Chemistry.
Communications.
Community College and Higher Education.
Counseling. Includes community agency, counseling (Ed.S.), elementary school, secondary school, vocational.
Educational Leadership.
Educational Technology.
Engineering Technology.
English.
General School Administration. Ed.S. only.
History.
Human Resource Development.
Industrial Education. Ed.S. only.
Justice Studies and Justice Administration.
Mathematics.
Music. Includes choral conducting, performance (harpsichord, organ, piano, winds, strings, percussion, voice), vocal music.
Nursing. Includes nurse practitioner.
Physical Education.
Physics.
Psychology. Includes clinical.
Reading. Includes classroom teacher, reading specialist.
School Administration.
School Psychology. Ed.S. only.
Social Science. Includes sociology.
Special Education Teaching.
Teaching. Includes early childhood, elementary, ESOL, secondary.
Technical Teacher Education.
Technology. Includes printing management.
Technology Education.
Note: Cooperative Ph.D. and Ed.D. programs available from University of Kansas, Kansas State University, University of Arkansas.

UNIVERSITY OF PITTSBURGH
Pittsburgh, Pennsylvania 15261
Web site: www.pitt.edu

Chartered 1787. CGS and AAU member. Coed. State related. Trimester system. Regional campuses in Titusville, Bradford, Greensburg, Johnstown. Special facilities: Applied Research Center, Center for Biotechnology and Bioengineering, Cleft-Palate-Craniofacial Center, Frick Fine Arts Building, Center for International Studies, Learning Research and Development Center, Mid-Atlantic Technology Application Center, Center for Neuroscience, Center for Philosophy of Science, Pittsburgh Cancer Institute, Center for Social and Urban Research, Surface Science Center. The University's NIH ranking is ninth among all U.S. institutions with 724 awards/grants worth $264,561,026. Library: 3,600,000 volumes, 22,058 subscriptions. Total University enrollment: 26,100.

Annual tuition: varies by school. No on-campus housing. For off-campus housing, contact Graduate Housing Office. Phone: (412)624-7115.

College and Faculty of Arts and Sciences

Former Divisions of Humanities, Natural Sciences, and Social Sciences combined into Faculty of Arts and Sciences. Annual tuition: full-time resident $10,726, nonresident $21,312; per credit

resident $438, nonresident $876. Graduate enrollment: full-time 1255, part-time 147 (men 55%, women 45%). Faculty teaching graduate students: full-time 534, part-time 189. Degrees conferred: M.A., M.F.A., M.S., Ph.D.

ADMISSION REQUIREMENTS. Transcripts required in support of application. GRE required for some departments. On-line application available. TOEFL required for international applicants. Accepts transfer applicants. Graduates of unaccredited institutions not considered. Apply to chair of proposed graduate department by August 1 (Fall), December 1 (Winter), April 1 (Spring), June 1 (Summer). Earlier deadlines may be applicable for some programs. Application fee $40, $50 for international applicants. Phone: (412)624-6094; fax: (412)624-6855.

ADMISSION STANDARDS. Selective for most departments, competitive for others. Usual minimum average: 3.0 (A = 4).

FINANCIAL AID. Annual awards from institutional funds: scholarships, fellowships, research assistantships, teaching assistantships, internships, Mellon fellowships, full and partial tuition waivers, Federal W/S, loans. Approved for VA benefits. Apply by April 1 to departmental chairperson for fellowships, assistantships; to the Financial Aid Office for all other programs. Use FAFSA and institutional FAF. About 60% of full-time students receive aid other than loans from University and outside sources.

DEGREE REQUIREMENTS. For master's: 9 courses minimum; comprehensive exam; thesis/nonthesis. For Ph.D.: 72 credit minimum or 24 courses minimum beyond the bachelor's; preliminary, comprehensive exams; dissertation; final oral exam; additional requirements may be determined by each department.

FIELDS OF STUDY.
Anthropology.
Applied Mathematic.
Applied Statistics.
Art History.
Astronomy.
Bioethics. M.A. only.
Biological Sciences. Includes molecular, cellular and developmental biology, molecular biophysics, ecology and evolution.
Chemistry.
Classics. Includes Greek history and literature, Latin literature.
Computer Science. Includes information science.
East Asian Studies. M.A. only.
Economics.
English. Includes composition, cultural and critical studies, writing.
French.
Geology and Planetary Sciences. Includes environmental science, GIS/remote sensing, paleontology.
Germanic Languages and Literatures.
Hispanic Languages and Literatures. Includes Portuguese, Spanish.
History.
History and Philosophy of Science.
History of Art and Architecture. Includes fine arts.
Intelligent Systems Studies.
Italian. M.A. only.
Linguistics.
Mathematics.
Music.
Neuroscience.
Philosophy.
Physics.
Political Science.
Psychology. Includes clinical, cognitive, developmental, health, social, individualized.
Religion. Ph.D. only.
Religious Studies. M.A. only.
Slavic Languages and Literatures.

Sociology.

Statistics.

Theatre Arts. Includes dramatic arts, speech, theatre and performance studies.

The Joseph M. Katz Graduate School of Business
Web site: www.katz.pitt.edu

Established 1960. Special facilities: Center for Economic Development, Small Business Development Center, Center for International Business, Strategic Management Institute, Program in Corporate Culture, Business, Society, and Government Research Institute, and Center for Research on Contracts and the Structure of Enterprise.

Annual tuition: resident $25,370, nonresident $38,202.

Enrollment: full-time 355, part-time 554. Faculty: full-time 70, part-time 23. Degrees conferred: M.B.A., E.M.B.A., M.S. in MOIS, M.H.A., M.B.A.-J.D., Ph.D., M.I.B., M.B.A.-M.S.N., M.B.A.-M.P.I.A.

ADMISSION REQUIREMENTS. Baccalaureate or higher degree; introductory calculus; GMAT required in support of School's application. On-line application available. TOEFL (minimum score 600) required for international applicants. Accepts transfer applicants. Graduates of unaccredited institutions not considered. Apply prior to May 1 (Fall), November 1 (Spring) to the Admission Office. Full-time M.B.A. applicants admitted Fall only. Part-time applicants admitted Fall, Spring, Summer terms. Application fee $50. Phone: (412)648-1700; fax: (412)648-1552.

ADMISSION STANDARDS. Very selective. Mean GMAT: 621; mean GPA: 3.20 (A = 4). Gourman rating: M.B.A. 4.82, Ph.D. 4.83. Usual minimum average: 3.1 (A = 4), usual GMAT range 550–650.

FINANCIAL AID. Annual awards from institutional funds: scholarships, tuition fellowships, research assistantships, teaching assistantships, grants, Federal W/S, loans. Approved for VA benefits. Apply to Dean's Office for fellowships, assistantships; to Financial Aid Office for all other programs. Submit FAFSA (School code: 008815) and completed institutional application with GMAT scores by March 15. Phone: (412)624-PITT. No scholarship aid is available for part-time students or international students in M.B.A. program. Approximately 70% of M.B.A. students and 90% of doctoral students receive some form of financial assistance.

DEGREE REQUIREMENTS. For master's: 39–51 credit hours depending on previous degree and experience; thesis/nonthesis option; final comprehensive exam for some programs. For Ph.D.: 72 credit hours; comprehensive exam in major and minor fields; dissertation; final oral exam.

FIELDS OF STUDY.

Accounting.

Business Environments.

Finance.

Health Administration.

Human Behavior in Organizations.

Human Resource Management.

International Business Management.

International Executive M.B.A. Program located in either the Czech Republic (Prague) or Brazil (São Paulo).

Management Information Systems.

Managerial Economics.

Marketing

Operations Research.

Organizational Behavior.

Strategic Planning and Policy.

School of Dental Medicine (15261-1945)

Founded 1896.

Annual tuition: resident $20,900, nonresident $30,420. Limited on-campus housing available. Average academic year housing costs: $13,200. Contact Assistant Director of Housing. Phone: (412)648-8422. Total average cost for all other first-year expenses: $7500.

Enrollment: D.M.D. program: first-year class 71 (men 70%, women 30%). Faculty: full-time 49, part-time 50. Degrees conferred: D.M.D., M.D.S., M.S., Ph.D.

ADMISSIONS REQUIREMENTS. For D.M.D. program: AADSAS report, official high school and college transcripts, three letters of recommendation, essay, DAT (April test in junior year preferred) required in support of School's application. Interview by invitation only. Applicants must have completed at least three years of college study. Preference given to state residents. Apply to Office of Admissions after August 1, before December 1. Application fee $35. Phone: (412)648-8437; fax: (412)648-8219. For graduate program: official transcripts, three letters of recommendation required in support of School's application. Apply to Director, Graduate Education by December 1. Phone: (412)648-8500.

ADMISSION STANDARDS. For D.M.D. program: Selective. Mean DAT: Academic 18.04, PAT 17.4; mean GPA: 3.51 (A = 4). Gourman rating: 4.55. Accepts about 40% of total annual applicants. Approximately 90% are state residents. For graduate program: competitive for most departments, very competitive, selective for others.

FINANCIAL AID. D.M.D. programs: scholarships, grants, loans. Apply to University Office of Financial Aid after acceptance. Approximately 89% of all D.M.D. students receive some form of financial assistance. For Graduate students: fellowships, assistantships, loans. Apply April 1 to Financial Aid Office. Phone: (412)648-8422. Use FAFSA (School code: 024824).

DEGREE REQUIREMENTS. For D.M.D.: satisfactory completion of four-year program. For Master's degrees: see program listing below. For Ph.D.: 60 credit hours minimum; preliminary exam; dissertation; final oral exam.

FIELDS OF GRADUATE STUDY.

Anesthesiology.

Endodontics. Twenty-four months minimum; thesis. M.D.S. and/or certification.

General Dentistry. Twenty-four months minimum. M.S. only.

Maxillofacial Prosthodontics. Twenty-four months minimum. M.D.S. and/or certification.

Oral Diagnosis. Twenty-four months minimum; thesis. M.S. only.

Oral and Maxillofacial Surgery. Hospital certification.

Orthodontics. Apply by December 1; Summer admission; minimum thirty-six months. M.D.S. and/or certification,

Pediatric Dentistry. Twenty-four months minimum; thesis. M.D.S. and/or certification.

Pedodontics. Twenty-four months minimum.

Periodontics. Twenty-four months minimum. M.D.S. and/or certification.

School of Education
Web site: www.pitt.edu/education.html

Graduate study since 1910. Semester system.

Annual tuition: full-time resident $10,726, nonresident $21,312, per credit resident $438, nonresident $876.

Enrollment: full-time 490, part-time 714. Faculty: full-time 80, part-time 10. Degrees conferred: M.A., M.Ed., M.A.T., M.S., Ed.D., Ph.D.

ADMISSION REQUIREMENTS. Official transcripts, GRE required in support of School's application. Interview/MAT required by some departments. TOEFL required for international applicants. Accepts transfer applicants. Graduates of unaccredited institutions not considered. Apply to the Office of Student Personnel Services, School of Education, by February 1 (Fall), November 15 (Spring). Application fee $40, international applicants $50. Phone (412)648-2230; fax: (412)648-1899.

ADMISSION STANDARDS. Selective for master's, usual minimum average 3.0; 3.3 (A = 4) for doctorate.

FINANCIAL AID. Five scholarships, teaching assistantships, research assistantships, internships, traineeships, tuition waivers, Federal W/S, loans. Approved for VA benefits. Apply by April 15 to department chair for fellowships, assistantships; to Office of Financial Aid for all other programs. Phone: (412)624-PITT. Use FAFSA and institutional FAF. Aid available for part-time students.

DEGREE REQUIREMENTS: For master's: 36 credit hours minimum; comprehensive exam. For Ed.D., Ph.D.: 90 credit hour minimum beyond bachelor's degree, at least 60 credits in residence; comprehensive written exam; dissertation; final oral exam.

FIELDS OF STUDY
Administrative and Policy Studies. Includes developmental education, educational administration, foundations of education, higher education administration, international and development education, school administration, social and comparative analysis in education.
Health, Physical, and Recreation Education. Includes exercise physiology, health promotion education.
Instruction and Learning. Includes communication education, early childhood, elementary, English education, foreign language education, humanities education, instructional design and technology, mathematic education, science education, social studies education, special education, teacher development.
Psychology in Education. Includes child development and child care, counseling psychology, research methodology.

School of Engineering

Annual tuition: resident $12,314, nonresident $24,470; per credit resident $589, nonresident $1162.

Enrollment; full-time 286, part-time 225. Faculty: full-time 94, part-time 20. Degrees conferred: M.S., M.S.B.Eng., M.S.C.E., M.S.Ch.E., M.S.E.E., M.S.E.R., M.S.I.E., M.S.M.E., M.S.Met.E., M.S.Mf.S.E., M.S.M.S.E., M.S.P.E., Ph.D.

ADMISSION REQUIREMENTS. Official transcript, GRE required in support of School's application. GRE Subject Test required for some programs. Interview not required. On-line application available. TOEFL required for international applicants. Accepts transfer applicants. Graduates of unaccredited institutions not considered. Apply to appropriate department chair by August 1 (Fall), December 1 (Spring), April 1 (Summer). Rolling admissions process. Application fee $40, international applicants $50. Phone: (412)624-9800; fax: (412)624-9808.

ADMISSION STANDARDS. Selective. Usual minimum average: 3.0 (A = 4) from ABET-accredited undergraduate institution. Applicants with lower averages considered on limited and exceptional basis.

FINANCIAL AID. Fellowships, teaching assistantships, research assistantships, grants, Federal W/S, loans. Approved for VA benefits. Apply by February 1 to appropriate department chair for assistantships, fellowships; to Financial Aid Office for all other programs. Phone: (412) 624-7488. Use FAFSA.

DEGREE REQUIREMENTS. For master's: 30 credit hours minimum; comprehensive exam; thesis/nonthesis option; final exam. For Ph.D.: 72 credit hours minimum, at least two consecutive

terms in residence; qualifying exam; comprehensive exam; dissertation; final oral exam.

FIELDS OF STUDY.
Bioengineering. M.S.B.Eng., Ph.D.
Chemical Engineering. M.S.Ch.E., Ph.D.
Civil Engineering. M.S.C.E., Ph.D.
Electrical Engineering. M.S.E.E., Ph.D.
Industrial Engineering. M.S.I.E., Ph.D.
Materials Science and Engineering. M.S.M.E., Ph.D.
Mechanical Engineering. M.S.M.E., Ph.D.
Metallurgical Engineering. M.S.Met.E., Ph.D.
Petroleum Engineering. M.S.P.E.

School of Health and Rehabilitation Sciences
4019 Forbes Tower (15260)

Annual tuition: full-time resident $12,578, nonresident $25,010; per credit, resident $517, nonresident $1029.

Enrollment: full-time 206, part-time 121. Faculty: full- and part-time 63. Degrees conferred: M.S., M.P.T., Ph.D.

ADMISSION REQUIREMENTS. Official transcripts, three recommendations required in support of School's application. GRE required for M.P.T., Ph.D. applicants. TOEFL required for international applicants. Accepts transfer applicants. Application deadlines: M.S. June 1 (Fall), November 15 (Spring); M.P.T. January 31; Ph.D. April 1 (Fall), September 1 (Spring). Application fee $30, international applicants $40, M.P.T. application fee $50. Phone: (412)674-1258; fax: (412)647-1255.

FINANCIAL AID. Scholarships, teaching fellowships, teaching assistantships, internships, grants, Federal W/S, loans. Approved for VA benefits. Apply to departmental chair for fellowships, assistantships; to Financial Aid Office for all other programs. Use FAFSA and institutional FAF. Phone: (412) 624-7488; fax (412) 648-8815. Financial assistance also available for selected minority students. About 50% of students receive aid other than loans from School and outside sources.

DEGREE REQUIREMENTS. For M.S., M.P.T.: 8-course minimum; comprehensive exam; thesis/nonthesis option. For Ph.D.: 90 credit hours minimum beyond the bachelor's degree, at least 60 credits in residence; qualifying exam; candidacy; dissertation; final oral exam.

FIELDS OF STUDY.
Audiology.
Communication Science and Disorders.
Health and Rehabilitation Sciences.
Occupational Therapy.
Physical Therapy.
Rehabilitation Sciences. Ph.D.

School of Information Science
Web site: www.lis.pitt.edu

Established 1962.
Annual tuition: full-time resident $11,280, nonresident $22,412; per credit resident $463, nonresident $927.
Enrollment: full-time 239, part-time 341. Faculty: full-time 32, part-time 12. Degrees conferred: M.L.S., M.S.I.S., M.S.T., C.A.S., Ph.D.

ADMISSION REQUIREMENTS. Official transcripts, GRE, letters of recommendation required in support of School's application. TOEFL required for international applicants. Accepts transfer applicants. Graduates of unaccredited institutions not considered. Apply to School at least two months prior to registration. Application fee $30, international applicants $40. Phone: (412)624-5230; fax: (412)624-5231.

FINANCIAL AID. Annual awards from institutional funds: Twenty-five fellowships, three assistantships, Federal W/S, loans. Approved for VA benefits. Apply to the School for fellowships, assistantships; to the Office of Financial Aid for all other programs. Phone: (412) 624-7488; fax: (412)648-8815. Use FAFSA and institutional FAF. Financial assistance also available for selected minority students.

DEGREE REQUIREMENTS. M.L.S., M.S.I.S.,: 36 credit hours minimum, at least 30 in residence. For M.S.T.: 48 credit hours minimum, at least 36 in residence. For Ph.D. in L.S.: 54 credit hours minimum beyond the Master's; preliminary exam; comprehensive exam; proficiency in language determined by Committee on Doctoral Studies; dissertation. For Ph.D. in I.S.: 60 credit hours minimum beyond the Master's; 6 credits in linguistics; preliminary exam; comprehensive exam; 18 dissertation credits. For Certificate: 24 credit hours minimum beyond the master's.

FIELDS OF STUDY.
Information Science.
Library and Information Science.
Telecommunications.

School of Law (15260)

Founded 1895. ABA approved since 1923. AALS charter member. Semester system. Special facility: Center for International Legal Education. Library: 369,870 volumes, 4760 subscriptions; has LEXIS, NEXIS, WESTLAW.

Annual tuition: resident $13,586, nonresident $20,910. On-campus housing available. Total average annual additional expense: $11,810.

Enrollment: first-year class 267, full-time 712 (men 53%, women 47%). Faculty: full-time 38, part-time 36. Student to faculty ratio 15.6 to 1. Degrees conferred: J.D., J.D.-M.A., J.D.-M.B.A., J.D.-M.P.A., J.D.-M.P.I.A., J.D.-M.P.H., J.D.-M.S. (Carnegie Mellon's Schools of Industrial Management and Urban and Public Affairs), J.D.-M.S.I.A., J.D.-M.U.R.P., LL.M. (for persons who have completed a basic legal education and received a university degree in law in another country).

ADMISSION REQUIREMENTS. LSDAS Law School report, bachelor's degree, transcripts, LSAT required in support of application. Accepts transfer applicants. Graduates of unaccredited institutions not considered. Apply to Director of Admissions after September 1, before March 1. Dual degree applicants must apply to and be accepted to both Schools/programs. Application fee $50. Phone: (412)649-1412.

ADMISSION STANDARDS. Selective. Mean LSAT: 155; mean GPA: 3.21 (A = 4). Gourman rating: 3.75. *U.S. News & World Report* ranking is in the second tier of all U.S. law schools. Accepts about 45–50% of total annual applicants.

FINANCIAL AID. Scholarships, fellowships, assistantships, Federal W/S, loans. Apply to the Financial Aid Office by March 1. Phone: (412)648-1415. Use FAFSA (School code: 008815) and institutional financial aid form. Approximately 43% of all students receive some form of financial assistance.

DEGREE REQUIREMENTS. For J.D.: three years minimum, at least the final year in full-time residence; 88 credit hour program. For LL.M.: at least 24 credit hours minimum beyond J.D.; final project.
Note: School has a faculty exchange program with the University of Augsburg (Germany).

School of Medicine (15261)

Established 1883.
Annual tuition: resident $24,100, nonresident $32,542, student fees $523. Total average figure for all other expenses: $12,200.

Enrollment: first-year class 147 (EDP 2); total 665 (men 51%, women 49%). Faculty: about 1350. Degrees conferred: M.D., M.D.-M.A. (Ethics), M.S., M.D.-M.S., M.D.-M.P.H. M.D.-Ph.D. (Medical Scientist Training Program in Cooperation with Carnegie-Mellon University.)

ADMISSION REQUIREMENTS. AMCAS report, transcripts, letters of recommendation, preprofessional committee evaluation, MCAT, interview required in support of application. Has EDP; apply between June 1 and August 1. Apply to Office of the Associate Dean of the School after June 1, before December 1 (firm). Dual degree applicants must apply to and be accepted to both Schools/programs. Application fee $60. Phone: (412)648-9891; fax: (412)648-8768. M.D.-Ph.D.: (412)648-2324.

ADMISSION STANDARDS. For M.D. program: competitive. Mean MCAT: 10.5; mean GPA: 3.68 (A = 4). Gourman rating: 4.30. *U.S. News & World Report* ranking is in the top 17 of all U.S. medical schools. Accepts about 3–5% of total annual applicants. Approximately 65% are state residents.

FINANCIAL AID. Scholarships, loans, research fellowships. MSTP funded by NIH. Apply after acceptance to Financial Aid Committee. Use FAFSA (School code: E00516).

DEGREE REQUIREMENTS. For M.D.: satisfactory completion of four-year program; all students must pass USMLE Step 1 prior to entering third year; all students must pass USMLE Step 2 prior to awarding of M.D. For M.S.: 32 credit hours minimum; final project/thesis.

FIELDS OF GRADUATE STUDY.
Biochemistry and Molecular Biology.
Biomedical Engineering.
Biophysics.
Cell Biology.
Cellular and Molecular Pathology.
Immunology.
Molecular Virology and Microbiology.
Neurosciences.
Pharmacology.

School of Nursing—Graduate Division

Annual tuition: full-time resident $10,726, nonresident $21,312; per credit resident $438, nonresident $876.
Enrollment: full-time 92, part-time 166. Faculty: full-time 68, part-time 24. Degrees conferred: M.S.N., Ph.D.

ADMISSION REQUIREMENTS. Transcripts, GRE required in support of School's application. Interview may be required. TOEFL required for international applicants. Accepts transfer applicants. Graduates of unaccredited colleges not considered. Apply to the School by February 1 (Fall), September 15 (Spring). Application fee $40, international applicants $50.

ADMISSION STANDARDS. Competitive. Usual minimum average: 3.0 (A = 4).

FINANCIAL AID. Scholarships, fellowships, research assistantships, teaching assistantships, internships, Federal W/S, loans. Approved for VA benefits. Apply by March 1 to Assistant Dean of the School for assistantships; to Financial Aid Office for all other programs. Phone: (412)624-6302. Use FAFSA and School's FAF. About 45% of students receive aid other than loans. Aid available for part-time students.

DEGREE REQUIREMENTS. For M.S.N.: 42 credits minimum. For Ph.D.: 42 credits minimum beyond the master's; comprehensive exam; dissertation; final oral defense.

FIELDS OF STUDY.
Clinical Nurse Specialist. M.S.N.
Nurse Anesthesia. M.S.N.
Nurse Practitioner. M.S.N.
Nurse Specialty Roles. M.S.N.
Nursing. Ph.D.

School of Pharmacy—Graduate Studies (15261)

Founded 1878. Coed. Semester system.
Tuition: per credit resident $517, nonresident $646; Pharm.D. per credit resident $580, nonresident $782.
Enrollment: full-time 357, part-time 5. Faculty full-time 72, part-time 3. Degrees conferred: Pharm.D., M.S., Ph.D.

ADMISSION REQUIREMENTS. Transcripts, GRE, personal statement outlining goals, letters of reference required in support of School's application. TOEFL, TSE, TWE required for international applicants. Interview not required, but may be requested. Accepts transfer applicants. Apply to Director of Graduate Programs by March 1 (Fall). Admits Fall only. Application fee $40, international students $50. Phone: (412)648-8579; fax: (412)648-1086.

ADMISSION STANDARDS. Very selective. Usual minimum average: 3.0 (A = 4).

FINANCIAL AID. Scholarships, teaching assistantships, internships, Federal W/S, loans. Apply by March 1 to Director of Graduate Programs for scholarships, assistantships; to the Financial Aid Office for all other programs. Phone: (412)648-7488. Use FAFSA and institutional FAF. Nearly 100% of students receive aid from School or outside sources.

DEGREE REQUIREMENTS. For M.S.: at least 24 credits, but usually 30 credits of approved graduate study; comprehensive written exam; thesis; final oral exam. For Pharm.D: six-year "lock step" program with two years of preprofessional study; experiential learning sequence. For Ph.D.: at least 72 credits; thesis; preliminary exam; dissertation; final oral exam.

FIELDS OF STUDY.
Pharmaceutical Sciences.
Pharmacy.

Graduate School of Public and International Affairs

Web site: www.pitt.edu/~gspia

Graduate study since 1957. Semester system.
Annual Tuition: full-time resident $10,726, nonresident $21,312, per credit resident $438, nonresident $876.
Enrollment: full-time 286, part-time 120 (men 48%, women 52%). Faculty: full-time 27, part-time 17. Degrees conferred: M.I.D., M.P.A., M.P.I.A., M.P.P.M., Ph.D.

ADMISSION REQUIREMENTS. Transcripts, essay, letters of reference required in support of School's application. GRE and a major paper required of doctoral applicants, recommended for master's applicants. On-line application available. Evidence of proficiency in English required of international students. Interview not required. Accepts transfer applicants. Graduates of unaccredited institutions not considered. Apply to Office of Admissions by March 1 (Fall), October 1 (Spring). Rolling admissions process. Application fee $40, international applicants $50. Phone: (412) 648-7643; fax (412)648-7641.

ADMISSION STANDARDS. Selective. Usual minimum average: 3.0 (A = 4).

FINANCIAL AID. Scholarships, minority scholarships, fellowships, research fellowships, teaching assistantships, internships, Federal W/S, loans. Apply by February 1 to Admissions Office of School for scholarships, fellowships, assistantships; to the Financial Aid Office for all other programs. Phone: (412)648-7647; fax: (412)648-2605. Use FAFSA and institutional FAF. About 41% of students receive aid other than loans from School.

DEGREE REQUIREMENTS. For master's: 48 hours minimum in residence; policy seminar, and internship. For Ph.D.: 78 credit hours minimum, at least four terms in residence; proficiency in advanced research and quantitative analysis; preliminary exam; comprehensive exam; dissertation; final oral exam.

FIELDS OF STUDY.
Development Planning and Environmental Sustainability. M.I.D.
Global Political Economy. M.P.I.A.
Nongovernmental Organizations and Civil Society. M.I.D.
Policy Research and Analysis. M.P.A.
Public and International Affairs. Ph.D.
Public and Nonprofit Management. M.P.A.
Public Policy and Management. M.P.P.M.
Security and Intelligence Studies. M.P.I.A.
Urban and Regional Affairs. M.P.A.

Graduate School of Public Health

Established 1948.
Annual tuition: resident $12,578, nonresident $25,010; per credit resident $517 nonresident $1029. No on-campus housing available.
Enrollment: full-time 250, part-time 248 (men 45%, women 55%). Faculty: full-time 110, part-time 7. Degrees conferred: M.P.H., M.H.A., M.S., M.H.P.E., D.P.H., Ph.D.

ADMISSION REQUIREMENTS. Transcripts, two letters of recommendation, GRE, GMAT (Health Administration) required in support of application. TOEFL, statement of financial responsibility required of all international applicants. Interview not required for most programs. Accepts transfer applicants. Graduates of unaccredited colleges not considered. Apply to Admissions Office of the School; deadlines vary by program. Fall and Winter admission for most programs. Application fee $50; international fee $60. Phone (412)624-5200; fax (412)624-3755.

ADMISSION STANDARDS. Competitive. Usual minimum average: 3.0 (A = 4).

FINANCIAL AID. Annual awards from institutional funds vary from year to year; scholarships, research assistantships, teaching assistantships, internships, postdoctoral positions, Federal W/S, loans. Approved for VA benefits. Apply to appropriate department chairman for scholarships, assistantships, internships, postdoctoral positions; to the Financial Aid Office for all other programs. Phone: (412)624-3002. Use FAFSA and institutional FAF. About 50% of Students receive aid other than loans from School and outside sources. Limited aid for part-time students.

DEGREE REQUIREMENTS. For master's program by advisement: thesis/final document; final oral/written exam. For doctoral programs by advisement: knowledge of one computer language; preliminary exam; comprehensive exam; dissertation; final oral exam.

FIELDS OF STUDY.
Behavioral and Community Health Sciences.
Biostatistics.
Environmental and Occupational Health.
Environmental Health Risk Assessment.
Epidemiology.
Genetic Counseling.
Health Administration.
Health Promotion and Education. M.H.P.E.
Human Genetics.

Infectious Diseases and Microbiology.
Multidisciplinary Public Health.
Radiation Health.
Note: Joint programs with Joseph M. Katz School of Business, the School of Social Work, and the School of Education.

School of Social Work—Graduate Division

Graduate study since 1942. Semester system.

Annual tuition: full-time resident $10,726, nonresident $21,312; per credit resident $438, nonresident $876.

Enrollment: full-time 339, part-time 235. Faculty: full-time 16, part-time 45. Degrees conferred: M.S.W., Ph.D.

ADMISSION REQUIREMENTS. Transcripts required in support of School's application. Interview may be required. TOEFL required for international applicants. Accepts transfer applicants. Graduates of unaccredited colleges not considered. Apply to the School by March 31. Fall admission only. Application fee $40, $50 for international applicants. Phone: (412)624-6346; fax: (412)624-6323.

ADMISSION STANDARDS. Competitive. Usual minimum average: 3.0 (A = 4).

FINANCIAL AID. Scholarships, traineeships, research assistantships, teaching assistantships, internships, tuition waivers, Federal W/S, loans. Approved for VA benefits. Apply by June 1 to Assistant Dean of Admissions of the School for assistantships; to Financial Aid Office for all other programs. Phone: (412)624-6302. Use FAFSA and School's FAF. About 45% of students receive aid other than loans. No aid for part-time students.

DEGREE REQUIREMENTS. For M.S.W.: 58 credits minimum, including 18 credits field practicum. For Ph.D.: 42 credits minimum beyond the Master's; comprehensive exam; dissertation; final oral defense.

FIELDS OF STUDY.
Family and Marital Therapy.
Gerontology.
Social Work.

PLYMOUTH STATE COLLEGE
Plymouth, New Hampshire 03264
Web site: www.plymouth.edu

Founded 1871. Located 125 miles N of Boston. Coed. State control. Semester system. Library: 315,000 volumes, 1065 subscriptions.

Tuition: per credit resident $247, nonresident $272. On-campus housing available for married and single students. Average annual housing cost: $5400 (room and board). Apply to Office of Residential Life. Phone: (603)535-2260.

Graduate Division

Graduate study since 1948. Enrollment: full-time 60, part-time 183 (men 25%, women 75%). College faculty teaching graduate students: full-time 23, part-time 5.

ADMISSION REQUIREMENTS. Transcripts, GRE/MAT/GMAT, recommendations required in support of application On-line application available. TOEFL required for international applicants. Accepts transfer applicants. Apply to Director of Graduate Studies at least 60 days prior to the semester of preferred registration. Application fee $40, international applicants $50. Phone: (603)535-2636; fax: (603)535-2572.

ADMISSION STANDARDS. Minimum average: 2.75 (A = 4).

FINANCIAL AID, Scholarships, assistantships, internships, Federal W/S, loans. Apply to the Office of Graduate Studies; no specified closing date. Use FAFSA. Aid available for part-time students.

DEGREE REQUIREMENTS. For M.B.A.: 36 credit program, research project option. For M.Ed: 33–42 credit programs; thesis/nonthesis option.

FIELDS OF STUDY.
Athletic Training.
Business Administration. M.B.A.
Computer Education.
Counseling.
English Education.
Environmental Science.
Health Education.
Heritage Studies.
Integrated Arts.
Reading and Writing Specialist.
Special Education.

POINT LOMA NAZARENE UNIVERSITY
San Diego, California 92106-2899
Web site: www.ptloma.edu

Founded 1902 in Los Angeles, California; located in Pasadena, California, 1910–1973. Formerly Pasadena College. Coed. Private control. Church of the Nazarene. Semester system. Library: 151,000 volumes, 637 subscriptions.

Tuition: per unit $450. On-campus housing for a limited number of single graduate students. Average annual housing cost: $5990 (including board) for single students. Apply to Associate Dean for Residential Life. Phone: (619)221-2482.

Graduate Studies

Enrollment: full-time 280, part-time 149. College faculty teaching graduate students: full-time 10, part-time 40. Degrees conferred: M.A., M.Min., Ed.S.

ADMISSION REQUIREMENTS. Transcripts, personal essay, three recommendations, MAT or GRE General/Subject Tests/GMAT required in support of application. On-line application available. TOEFL (minimum score 550) required of international applicants. Accepts transfer applicants. Apply to Director of Admissions by May 15 (priority Fall consideration), November 1 (Spring). Rolling admissions process. Application fee $30. Phone: (619)849-2639; fax: (619)849-7018; e-mail: gradinfo@ptloma.edu.

ADMISSION STANDARDS. Selective. Usual minimum average: 2.5 (A = 4).

FINANCIAL AID. Limited to Federal W/S, loans. Apply to the Office of Financial Aid; no specified closing date. Phone: (619)221-2296. Use FAFSA.

DEGREE REQUIREMENTS. For M.A., M.Min.: 36 credit program without thesis, or 32 including thesis; reading knowledge of Greek for M.A. in Religion. For Ed.S.: 32 credit hour program beyond the master's; internship; written comprehensive exam.

FIELDS OF STUDY.
Business Administation.
Education. Includes counseling and guidance, educational leadership, teaching, learning, and technology.
Nursing.
Religion. Includes biblical studies, theology.

POLYTECHNIC UNIVERSITY

6 Metrotech Center
Brooklyn, New York 11201-2990
Web site: www.poly.edu

Founded 1854 as Polytechnic Institute of Brooklyn, became Polytechnic University in 1973. Polytechnic is the second oldest private institution of science and engineering in the United States. CGS member. Coed. Private control. Semester system. Three campuses: Brooklyn, Long Island, Westchester. The Brooklyn Center is the focus of an exciting new environment with the arrival of Metrotech, a joint University-industry development. Four major industrial companies now share a common campus with Polytechnic University, with the university as its core. Specialized facilities: Center for Advanced Technology in Telecommunications, Aerospace Research Laboratories, Center for Applied Large-Scale Computing, Center for Digital Systems, Center for Transportation Research, Dibner Library/Center for Advanced Technology in Communications, Microwave Research Institute, Philosophy and Technology Center, Polymer Research Institute, Institute for Imaging Sciences, and the Weber Research Institute. Library: 200,000 volumes, 613 subscriptions.

Tuition: per unit $810. On-campus housing for 150 students. Average academic year housing costs: $5250 (including board). Apply to Dean of Student Life. Phone: (718)260-3800.

Graduate Studies

Graduate study since 1902. Enrollment: full- and part-time 927 (men 85%, women 15%). Faculty: full-time 176, part-time 134. Degrees conferred: M.S., Engineer, Ph.D.

ADMISSION REQUIREMENTS. Transcripts, two letters of recommendation required in support of application. TOEFL required for international applicants. Accepts transfer applicants. Graduates of unaccredited colleges not considered. Apply to Office of Admissions by August 1 (Fall), November 1 (Spring), May 1 (Summer). Application fee $45. Phone: (800) POLY-TECH, (718)260-3200; fax: (718)260-3446.

ADMISSION STANDARDS. Competitive. Usual minimum average: 2.75 (A = 4).

FINANCIAL AID. Annual awards from institutional funds: teaching assistantships, teaching fellowships, research fellowships, stipends, Federal W/S, loans. Apply by March 1 to Office of Financial Aid or major department. Phone: (718)260-3300. Use FAFSA. Aid available for part-time students.

DEGREE REQUIREMENTS. For M.S.: 36 semester units minimum, at least 27 in residence; thesis/project optional. For Engineer: 36 semester units beyond the M.S., at least 27 in residence; thesis/project, required; final oral exam. For Ph.D.: three years minimum, at least one year in residence; reading knowledge of one foreign language, two foreign languages required by some departments; qualifying oral/written exam; dissertation; final oral defense.

FIELDS OF STUDY.
Biomedical Engineering. M.S.
Chemical Engineering. Includes polymer science. M.S., Ph.D.
Chemistry. M.S.
Civil Engineering. M.S., Ph.D.
Computer Engineering. M.S.
Computer Science. M.S., Ph.D.
Construction Management. M.S.
Electrical Engineering. M.E., Ph.D.
Electrophysics. M.S., Ph.D.
Environment-Behavior Studies. M.S.
Environment Engineering. M.S., Ph.D.
Environmental Science. M.S.
Financial Engineering. M.S.
History of Science. M.S.
Industrial Engineering. M.S.
Informatics in Chemistry and Biology. M.S.
Information Systems Engineering. M.S.
Management. M.S., Ph.D.
Management of Technology. M.S.
Manufacturing Engineering. M.S.
Materials Chemistry. Ph.D.
Materials Science. M.S.
Mathematics. M.S., Ph.D.
Mechanical Engineering. M.S., Ph.D.
Organizational Behavior. M.S.
Polymer Science and Engineering. M.S.
System Engineering. M.S.
Technical and Professional Communication. M.S.
Transportation Management. M.S.
Transportation Planning and Engineering. M.S., Ph.D.
Urban Systems Engineering and Management. M.S., Ph.D.
Wireless Innovation. M.S.

PONCE SCHOOL OF MEDICINE

P.O. Box 7004
Ponce, Puerto Rico 00732-7004

Formerly Catholic University of Puerto Rico School of Medicine, reorganized 1980. Annual tuition: resident $17,835, nonresident $26,597, student fees, $2340. Enrollment: first-year class 60 (EDP 3); total 240 (men 55%, women 45%). Degree conferred: M.D.

ADMISSION REQUIREMENTS. AMCAS report, transcripts, MCAT, recommendations required in support of application. Interview by invitation. Has EDP (for Puerto Rican students only); apply between June 1 and August 1. Fluency in Spanish required. Preference given to residents of Puerto Rico. Apply to Admissions Office after June 1, before December 15. Application fee $50. Phone: (787)840-2575; fax: (787)842-0461.

ADMISSION STANDARDS. Competitive. Admits about 20% of total annual applicants. Approximately 75% are residents.

FINANCIAL AID. Scholarships, grants, loans. Apply after acceptance to Student Financial Aid Office. Phone: (787)840-2511. Use FAFSA (School code: 024824). About 86% of students receive some aid from School.

DEGREE REQUIREMENTS. For M.D.: satisfactory completion of four-year program. All students must pass USMLE Step 1 before being promoted to the third year.

PONTIFICAL CATHOLIC UNIVERSITY OF PUERTO RICO

Ponce, Puerto Rico 00731-6382
Web site: www.pucpr.edu

Founded 1949. Located 140 miles S of San Juan. Coed. Private control. Semester system. Library: 286,800 volumes, 3700 subscriptions.

The University's other Graduate Colleges/Schools: College of Arts and Humanities, College of Business Administration, College of Education, College of Sciences. Total University enrollment at main campus: 11,800.

School of Law

Las Americas Avenue, Suite 543
Ponce, Puerto Rico 00731-6382

Established 1961. Located on main campus. ABA approved since 1967. AALS member. Semester system. Full-time, part-time study. Law library: 193,714 volumes, 2400 subscriptions; has LEXIS, NEXIS, WESTLAW, DIALOG; is a Federal Government and United Nations Depository.

Annual tuition: full-time $10,159, part-time $7247. On-campus housing available for single students only. Annual on-campus housing cost: single students $6327 (including board). Housing deadline July 15. Contact Housing Office for both on- and off-campus housing information. Phone: (787)841-2000, ext. 232. Law students generally prefer to live off-campus. Off-campus housing and personal expenses: approximately $9900.

Enrollment: first-year class full-time 116, part-time 63; total full- and part-time 524 (men 48%, women 52%). Faculty: full-time 22, part-time 18. Student to faculty ratio 17.5 to 1. Degrees conferred: J.D., J.D.-M.B.A.

ADMISSION REQUIREMENTS. LSDAS Law School report, LSAT (not later than February test date; if more than one LSAT, highest is used), PAEG, bachelor's degree from an accredited institution, personal statement, personal interview, two recommendations; transcripts (must show all schools attended and at least three years of study) required in support of application. Applicants must have received bachelor's degree prior to enrollment. Joint Degree applicants must apply to and be accepted to both Schools. Apply to Office of Admission after November 1, before April 15. First-year students admitted Fall only. Rolling admissions process. Application fee $75. Phone: (787)841-2200, ext. 1839 or 1837.

ADMISSION STANDARDS. Selective. Mean LSAT: full-time 136, part-time 134; mean GPA: full-time 3.28, part-time 3.11 (A = 4). Gourman rating: 2.28. *U.S. News & World Report* ranking is in the fourth tier of all law schools. Accepts 68% of total annual applicants. Most enrolled students are from Puerto Rico.

FINANCIAL AID. Scholarships, merit scholarships, Grants-in-Aid, private and institutional loans; Federal W/S, loans offered through University's Financial Aid Office. For scholarships apply to Admissions Office after January 1, before April 1. For all other programs apply to University's Office of Financial Aid. Use FAFSA (School code: 003936), also submit Financial Aid Transcript, Federal Income Tax forms. Approximately 50% of students receive some form of financial assistance. Aid available for part-time students.

DEGREE REQUIREMENTS. For J.D.: 94 (82 required) credits with a GPA of at least 2.0 (A = 4), plus completion of upper-divisional writing course; three-year program, four-year part-time program. For J.D.-M.B.A.: a four-year program rather than a five-year program if both degrees are taken consecutively.

PORTLAND STATE UNIVERSITY

Portland, Oregon 97270-0751
Web site: www.pdx.edu

Established 1946. CGS member. Coed. State control. Quarter system. Library: more than 1,800,000 volumes, 10,230 subscriptions.

Annual tuition: resident $5700, nonresident $9795. Limited on- and off-campus housing for married and graduate students. Annual academic year housing costs: $4050 single students, $6150 for married students. Apply through College Housing Northwest, 1802 SW 10th Ave. (97201). Phone: (800)547-8887, ext. 4333, (503)725-4333.

Graduate Studies

Enrollment: full-time 1636, part-time 1560. University faculty: full-time 590; part-time 171. Degrees conferred: M.A., M.E., M.I.M., M.S., M.Ed., M.P.A., M.P.H., M.T., M.U.S., M.U.R.P., M.A.T., M.S.T., M.B.A., M.F.A., M.S.W., Ed.D., Ph.D.

ADMISSION REQUIREMENTS. Two official transcripts required in support of application. GRE required for most programs, GMAT required for M.B.A., M.I.M., M.T. TOEFL required for international applicants. Accepts transfer applicants. Apply to Office of Graduate Admissions by March 1. Application fee $50. Phone: (503)725-3511; fax: (503)725-4882.

ADMISSION STANDARDS. Relatively open or selective. Usual minimum average: 2.75, or 3.0 for last two years (A = 4).

FINANCIAL AID. Annual awards from institutional funds: academic scholarships, fellowships, research assistantships, teaching assistantships, internships, Federal W/S, loans. Approved for VA benefits. Apply to Graduate Office; no specified closing dates. Phone: (503)725-3461; fax: (503)725-5965. Use FAFSA and institutional FAF. About 18% of students receive aid other than loans from University and outside sources. Aid available for part-time students.

DEGREE REQUIREMENTS. For master's: 45–90 quarter hours depending on degree program, at least 30 in residence; thesis/final exam varies by department. Reading knowledge of one foreign language for M.A., M.A.T. For Ed.D., Ph.D.: three years beyond the bachelor's, at least three consecutive terms in full-time residence; competency in at least one foreign language (Ph.D. only); comprehensive written/oral exam; dissertation; final oral exam.

FIELDS OF STUDY.

COLLEGE OF LIBERAL ARTS AND SCIENCES:
Anthropology. M.A.
Biology. M.A., M.S.
Chemistry. M.A., M.S.
Economics. M.A., M.S.
English. M.A., M.A.T.
Foreign Language. M.A., M.A.T.
General Social Sciences. M.A.T., M.S.T.
Geography. M.A., M.S.
Geology. M.A., M.S.
History. M.A.
Mathematics. M.A., M.S., M.A.T., M.S.T.
Physics. M.A., M.S.
Science. M.A., M.S.T.
Sociology. M.A., M.S.
Speech and Hearing Sciences. M.A., M.S.
Speech Communication. M.A., M.S.
TESOL. M.A.

COLLEGE OF ENGINEERING AND COMPUTER SCIENCE:
Civil Engineering.
Civil Engineering Management.
Computer Science.
Electrical and Computer Engineering.
Engineering Management. Includes project management, technology management.
Mechanical Engineering.
Software Engineering.
Systems Engineering.
Systems Science.

COLLEGE OF URBAN AND PUBLIC AFFAIRS:
Administration of Justice. M.S.
Community Health Education. M.P.H., M.S.
Health Promotion. M.P.H.
Mindbody Health. M.A., M.S.
Physical Activity/Exercise. M.A., M.S.
Political Science. M.A.
Public Administration. M.P.A.
Public Administration and Policy. Ph.D.
Urban and Regional Planning. M.S.

GRADUATE SCHOOL OF EDUCATION:
Counselor Education. Includes community counseling, couples, marriage and family counseling, rehabilitation counseling, school counseling.
Curriculum and Instruction.
Educational Policy, Foundations, and Administrative Studies. Includes educational leadership, postsecondary, adult and continuing education.
Special Education.

GRADUATE SCHOOL OF SOCIAL WORK:
Social Work. M.S.W.
Social Work and Social Research. Ph.D.

SCHOOL OF FINE AND PERFORMING ARTS:
Art. Includes painting, sculpture. M.F.A.
Music. Includes conducting, performance, teacher. M.A.T., M.S.T., M.M.P., M.M.C.
Theater Arts. Includes theater education. M.S.

SCHOOL OF BUSINESS ADMINISTRATION
Business Administration.
Financial Analysis.
International Management.
Systems Science.

UNIVERSITY OF PORTLAND
Portland, Oregon 97203-5798
Web site: www.up.edu

Founded 1901. Coed. Private control. Semester system. Library: 310,000 volumes, 1446 subscriptions.

Tuition: per credit $645. Limited on-campus housing for graduate students during academic year. Average academic year housing costs: $6212 (including board). Apply to Dean of Students for both on- and off-campus information. Phone: (503)943-7205.

Graduate School

Graduate study since 1936. Enrollment: full-time 144, part-time 248 (men 48%, women 52%). Graduate faculty: full-time 84, part-time 11. Degrees conferred: M.A., M.Ed., M.F.A., M.M., M.M.Ed., M.B.A., M.A.T., M.S.M.E., M.S.E.E., M.S.C.E., M.S.N.

ADMISSION REQUIREMENTS. Transcripts, three letters of recommendation, GRE/GMAT/MAT/NTE required in support of School's application. On-line application available. TOEFL required for international applicants. Accepts transfer applicants. Apply to Dean of Graduate School at least one month prior to registration. Application fee $40. Phone: (503)943-7107; fax: (503)943-7178; e-mail: gradschl@up.edu.

ADMISSION STANDARDS. Competitive for some departments, selective for others. Usual minimum average: 3.0 (A = 4).

FINANCIAL AID. Internships, Federal W/S, loans. Approved for VA benefits. Apply by March 15 to the Office of Financial Aid. Phone: (503)283-7311. Use FAFSA.

DEGREE REQUIREMENTS. For master's: 30 semester hours minimum, at least 21 in residence; comprehensive exam; thesis or final research project required for M.A.; final oral/written exam.

FIELDS OF STUDY.
Business Administration. M.B.A.
Communication Studies. M.A., M.S.
Drama. M.F.A.
Education. 36 hours minimum for M.Ed., M.A.T., M.A.
Engineering. Includes civil, electrical, mechanical. M.S.M.E., M.S.E.E., M.S.C.E.
History and Government. M.A.
Music. Includes theory, performance, education. M.A., M.M.Ed.
Nursing. M.S.N.
Theology. M.A.

PRAIRIE VIEW A&M UNIVERSITY
Prairie View, Texas 77446-0188
Web site: www.pvamu.edu

Founded 1876. Located 45 miles NW of Houston. Coed. State control. Semester system. A unit of the Texas A&M University system. Special facilities: Cooperative Agricultural Research Center, Particle Detector Research Center, Center for Social and Economic Research. Library: 284,000 volumes, 1300 subscriptions.

Tuition: per credit, resident $48, nonresident $262. On-campus housing for single students only. Average academic year housing costs: $5287 (including board). Average off-campus housing costs: $375–$500 per month. Contact the Housing Office for both on- and off-campus housing information.

Graduate School

Founded 1938. Enrollment: full-time 408, part-time 664. Faculty: full-time 75, part-time 18. Degrees conferred: M.A., M.C.D., M.Ed., M.S., M.S.Ag., M.S.Eng., M.S.N., M.B.A.

ADMISSION REQUIREMENTS. Official transcripts, three letters of recommendation, GRE/GMAT (Business) required in support of application. TOEFL required for international applicants. Accepts transfer applicants. Graduates of unaccredited institutions not considered. Apply by June 1 (Fall), October 1 (Spring) to Dean of Graduate School. Rolling admissions process. Application fee $25, $50 for international applicants. Phone: (936)857-2315; fax: (936)857-4127.

ADMISSION STANDARDS. Relatively open. Usual minimum average: 2.75 (A = 4).

FINANCIAL AID. Fellowships, teaching assistantships, research assistantships, tuition waivers, Federal W/S, loans. Apply by April 1 to the Dean of the Graduate School for assistantships; to Financial Aid Office for all other programs. Use FAFSA. About 65% receive aid from School and outside sources. Aid available for part-time students.

DEGREE REQUIREMENTS. For master's: 30–36 semester hours minimum (depending upon program), at least 20 hours in residence; thesis usually required for M.A., M.S.

FIELDS OF STUDY.

COLLEGE OF AGRICULTURE AND HUMAN SCIENCES:
Agriculture. Includes agricultural economics, animal science, soil science. M.S.Ag.
Human Sciences. Includes marriage and family studies, family and consumer studies, interdisciplinary studies in human sciences. M.S.

COLLEGE OF ARTS AND SCIENCES:
Biology. Includes environmental toxicology. M.S.
Chemistry. M.S.
English. M.A.
Mathematics. M.S.
Sociology. M.A.

COLLEGE OF BUSINESS:
Business Administration. M.B.A.

COLLEGE OF EDUCATION:
Counseling. Includes counselor education. M.A., M.S.Ed.
Curricula and Instruction. Includes agriculture education, educational media and technology, elementary education (early childhood), home economics education, industrial education, mathematics education, reading education, science education (biology, chemistry). M.A. Ed., M.Ed., M.S.Ed.
Educational Administration. M.Ed., M.S.Ed.
Health and Physical Education. M.Ed., M.S.Ed.
Special Education. M.Ed., M.S.Ed.

COLLEGE OF ENGINEERING:
Chemical Engineering. M.S.
Civil Engineering. M.S.
Computer Science. M.S.
Electrical Engineering. M.S.
Mechanical Engineering. M.S.

COLLEGE OF NURSING:
Family Nurse Practitioner. M.S.N.

SCHOOL OF ARCHITECTURE:
Architecture. M.Arch.
Community Development. M.C.D.

SCHOOL OF JUVENILE JUSTICE AND PSYCHOLOGY:
Juvenile Justice. M.S., Ph.D.
Juvenile Forensic Psychology. M.S.

PRATT INSTITUTE

Brooklyn, New York 11205-3899
Web site: www.pratt.edu

Founded 1887. Coed. Private control. Semester system. Special facilities: Center for Community and Environmental Development, Printmaking/Fine Arts Center, Schaffler Art Gallery. Library: 220,000 volumes, 540 subscriptions. 100,000 pictures and prints.

Annual tuition: full-time $18,000; per credit $750. On-campus housing for married and single students. Average academic year housing costs: $4666 for married students, $7266 (including board) for single students. Contact Residential Life Office for both on- and off-campus housing information. Phone: (718)636-3669.

Graduate Programs

Graduate study since 1950. Enrollment: full-time 715, part-time 562. Faculty: full- and part-time 134. Degrees conferred: M.Arch., M.Arch.I, M.S., M.S.C.R.P., M.I.D., M.S.U.E.S.M., M.S.U.D., M.F.A., M.L.S.

ADMISSION REQUIREMENTS. Official transcripts, three letters of reference required in support of application. Interview often required. GRE Subject Tests recommended. Portfolio required for Art, Design, and Architecture Departments. TOEFL recommended for international applicants. Accepts transfer applicants. Graduates of unaccredited institutions not considered. Apply to Graduate Admissions Office by February 1 (Fall), October 1 (Spring). Rolling admissions process. Application fee

$40, $90 for international applicants. Phone: (718)636-3669; fax: (718)636-3670.

ADMISSION STANDARDS. Very competitive for some departments, very selective for most. Usual minimum average: 2.5 (A = 4).

FINANCIAL AID. Scholarships, fellowships, assistantships, internships, Federal W/S, loans. Approved for VA benefits. Apply by February 1 to Director of Graduate Program of the appropriate program for fellowships, assistantships; to Financial Aid Office for all other programs. Use FAFSA. About 20–25% of students receive aid from Institute and outside sources. Aid available for part-time students.

DEGREE REQUIREMENTS. For M.Arch.: 36 credits minimum, at least 22 in residence. For M.S.: 36–50 credits minimum, at least 24 in residence. For M.I.D.: 34 credits minimum, at least 26 in residence. For M.L.S.: 36 credits minimum, at least 30 in residence. For M.F.A.: 48 credits minimum, at least 40 in residence. For M.S.C.R.P., M.S.U.E.S.M., M.S.U.D.; 62 credits minimum, at least 45 in full-time residence; special project.

FIELDS OF STUDY.

SCHOOL OF ARCHITECTURE:
Architecture. M.Arch., M.Arch. I
City and Regional Planning. M.S.
Environmental Planning. M.S.
Facilities Management. M.S.
Planning and Law. M.S.
Urban Design. M.S.

SCHOOL OF ART AND DESIGN:
Art and Design Education. M.S.
Art Therapy. M.P.S.
Art Therapy and Creativity Development. M.P.S.
Arts and Cultural Management. M.P.S.
Communications Design. M.S.
Computer Graphics and Interactive Media. Includes 2-D, 3-D, experimental media. M.F.A.
Dance/Movement Therapy. M.S.
Design Management. M.P.S.
Drawing. M.F.A.
Graphic Design and Packaging. M.F.A.
Industrial Design. Includes products, furniture, transportation, exhibition, and tabletop. M.I.D.
Interior Design. M.S.
Jewelry. M.F.A.
Packaging Design. M.S.
Painting. M.F.A.
Photography. M.F.A.
Printmaking. M.F.A.
Sculpture. M.F.A.
Theory, Criticism, and History of Art. M.S.

SCHOOL OF INFORMATION AND LIBRARY SCIENCE:
Library and Information Science. M.S.

PRINCETON UNIVERSITY

Princeton, New Jersey 08544-1019
Web site: www.princeton.edu

Founded 1746. Located 50 miles SW of New York City. CGS and AAU member. Private control. Semester system. Special facilities: cooperative with the Institute for Advanced Study, Center for Human Values, Geophysical Fluid Dynamics Lab of NOAA, Plasma Physics Fusion Research Laboratory; affiliation with Princeton Theological Seminary, Office for Survey Research and Statistical Studies, Princeton Materials Institute, Textile Research Institute, Center for Studies in Twentieth-Century American Statecraft and Public Policy, Center of International Studies. Library: 4,000,000 volumes, 1,500,000 microforms.

Annual tuition: full-time $27,830. On-campus housing for more than 400 married students, 570 single students. Average academic year housing costs: $1296 per month plus $525 for each child for married students, $1029 per month plus partial board for single students. Apply to Assistant Director for Graduate Housing. Phone: (609)258-3720.

Graduate School

Established 1869. Enrollment: full-time 1769 (men 63%, women 37%); no part-time students. Faculty: full-time 693, part-time 69. Degrees conferred: M.A., M.Eng., M.F.A., M.P.A., M.P.P., M.S., M.Arch., M.S.E., Ph.D.

ADMISSION REQUIREMENTS. Transcripts, three letters of recommendation, GRE Test required in support of School's application. GRE Subject Test strongly recommended or required according to department. On-line application available. TOEFL required of international applicants. Apply by the first Wednesday in January. Admits full-time students only. Fall admission only. Application fee $55, $60 for international students. Phone: (609)258-3034; fax: (609)258-6180.

ADMISSION STANDARDS. Very competitive for some departments, competitive for the others.

FINANCIAL AID. Annual awards from institutional funds: fellowships, teaching/research assistantships, Federal W/S, loans. Apply by first Wednesday in January to Graduate School Office for fellowships, assistantships; to Financial Aid Office for all other programs. Phone: (609)258-3028; fax: (609)258-6180. Use FAFSA and University's FAF. About 95% of students receive aid other than loans from School and outside sources.

DEGREE REQUIREMENTS. For master's: one year minimum in full-time residence; general exam (one year minimum full-time before sitting for general exam); thesis for M.S. and for M.A. in Near Eastern Studies; M.A. generally regarded as incidental degree. For Ph.D.: one year minimum in full-time residence; oral/written general exam; dissertation; final public oral exam.

FIELDS OF STUDY.
African Studies. Interdepartmental.
Afro-American Studies. Interdepartmental program in combination with an established discipline.
Anthropology. Ph.D. in cultural anthropology; competence in one foreign language, usually French.
Applied and Computational Mathematics. Interdepartmental in combination with science and engineering departments.
Architecture. One- and two-year M.Arch. program; design project and oral exam for M.Arch.
Art and Archaeology. Includes joint program in classical archaeology; two languages for Ph.D.
Astrophysical Sciences. Includes astronomy, astrophysics, plasma physics.
Atmospheric and Oceanic Sciences.
Biology and Neuroscience.
Chemical Engineering. M.Eng., M.S.E., Ph.D.
Chemistry. Includes cooperative program in physics and chemical physics; Ph.D. applicants given preference for admission; one language appropriate to study of chemistry for Ph.D.; M.S. available for local and regional firms (part-time).
Chinese Art and Archaeology. Interdepartmental; proficiency in classical and modern Chinese; also French or German for Ph.D.
Civil and Environmental Engineering. M.Eng., M.S.E., Ph.D.
Classical Archaeology. Interdepartmental; proficiency in Greek, Latin, French, and German for Ph.D.

Classics. Competence in Greek and Latin plus French and German for Ph.D.
Comparative Literature. Competence in two foreign languages plus Greek or Latin for Ph.D.
Computer Science. M.Eng., Ph.D.
Demography. Admission to Ph.D. program granted to students in economics, sociology, statistics; language requirement of that department must be fulfilled.
East Asian Studies. High degree of competence in Chinese or Japanese plus one European language for Ph.D.
Ecology and Evolutionary Biology.
Economics. Strong mathematical/statistical background recommended.
Economics and Demography.
Electrical Engineering. M.Eng., Ph.D.
English. Reading knowledge of Latin or Greek and reading knowledge of German and French.
French and Italian.
Geosciences.
Germanic Languages and Literatures. Two languages in addition to German for Ph.D.
History. Reading knowledge of at least one language; more may be required depending on area of study.
History of Science. French and German required for students of history of science; French or German for students of philosophy of science; Latin/Greek for medieval or ancient periods.
History and Theory of Architecture.
History and Theory of Engineering and Building Technology.
History and Theory of Landscape.
History and Theory of Urbanism.
Latin American Studies. Interdepartmental program.
Material Science. Interdepartmental.
Mathematical Physics.
Mathematics. Reading knowledge of mathematical texts in German or Russian for Ph.D.
Mechanical and Aerospace Engineering. M.Eng., M.S.E., Ph.D.
Molecular Biology.
Music. Includes music history, theory, composition; reading knowledge of at least one of the following—German, French, or Italian for Ph.D.
Near Eastern Studies.
Operations Research and Financial Engineering. M.Eng., M.S.E., Ph.D.
Philosophy. Reading knowledge of French or German for Ph.D.
Physics. Includes mathematical, chemical, plasma.
Plasma Science and Technology.
Political Philosophy. Interdepartmental.
Politics.
Psychology.
Psychology and Neuroscience.
Public Affairs. Two-year M.P.A.
Public Affairs and Demography.
Public Policy. M.P.P.
Religion. Two languages in addition to competence in biblical, classical, Oriental languages as required in field of specialization.
Slavic Languages and Literature.
Sociology. One language and knowledge of general sociological theory, statistical theory and procedure, competence in research methodology including computer application for Ph.D.
Spanish and Portuguese Language and Culture.
Statistics and Operations Research.
Transportation. Interdepartmental.
Water Resources. Interdepartmental.

Woodrow Wilson School of Public and International Affairs (08544-1013)

Web site: www.wws.princeton.edu

Established 1930. Graduate enrollment: full-time, M.P.A. 130, Ph.D. 25. Faculty: full-time 53, adjunct 20. Degrees conferred:

M.P.A., M.P.P., M.P.A.-J.D. (with Columbia University, NYU, Stanford University), M.P.A.-U.R.P., Ph.D., Certificate.

ADMISSION REQUIREMENTS. Transcripts, three letters of reference, public policy essay, personal statement, GRE required in support of School's application. TOEFL required for international applicants. Accepts transfer applicants. Graduates of unaccredited institutions not considered. Apply to Office of Graduate Admissions by January 8. Fall admission only. Application fee $55, $60 if mailed outside the United States, Canada, and Mexico. Phone: (609)258-4836; fax: (609)258-2095; e-mail: wwsadmit@princeton.edu.

ADMISSION STANDARDS. Very competitive. Usual minimum average: 3.6 (A = 4).

FINANCIAL AID. Academic scholarships, research fellowships, teaching fellowships, research assistantships, internships, Federal W/S, loans. Approved for VA benefits. Apply in early January to Graduate School for scholarships, fellowships, assistantships; to Financial Aid Office for all other programs. Phone: (609)258-3037. Use FAFSA and University's FAF. About 92% of M.P.A.s and 100% of Ph.D.s receive aid from School and outside sources.

DEGREE REQUIREMENTS. For M.P.A., M.P.P.: two-year program, one year in residence; two qualifying examinations. For M.P.A.-J.D.: three semesters in residence. For M.P.A.-U.R.P.: four semesters in residence. For Ph.D.: at least ten courses; reading knowledge of one foreign language; general exam; dissertation; final oral exam.

FIELDS OF STUDY.
Demography. Certificate.
Development Studies.
Domestic Policy.
Economics and Public Policy.
International Relations.
Public Affairs. Ph.D. only.
Science Technology and Environmental Policy. Certificate.
Urban Affairs and Domestic Policies.
Urban and Regional Policy and Planning.

PROVIDENCE COLLEGE
Providence, Rhode Island 02918
Web site: www.providence.edu

Founded 1917. Private control. Roman Catholic affiliation. Semester system. Library: 296,000 volumes, 27,800 microforms, 5 PCs.

Tuition: per credit $286. Limited on-campus housing available. Usual housing cost: $4120–$6330; board cost: $1800–$4000. Contact Director of Life for both on- and off-campus housing information. Phone: (401)865-2392.

Graduate Studies

Graduate study since 1965. Enrollment: full-time 45, part-time 880 (men 240, women 640). Faculty teaching graduate students: full-time 36, part-time 43. Degrees conferred: M.A., M.A.T. (Math), M.B.A., M.Ed.

ADMISSION REQUIREMENTS. Transcripts, two letters of recommendation, GMAT/MAT required in support of School's application. Interview required for some programs. TOEFL required for foreign applicants. Accepts transfer applicants. Apply to Office of Admissions; no specified closing date. Application fee $50. Phone: (401)865-2247; fax: (401)865-2057.

ADMISSION STANDARDS. Selective. Usual minimum average: 3.0 (A = 4).

FINANCIAL AID. Annual awards from institutional funds: scholarships, grants, assistantships, Federal W/S, loans. Approved for VA benefits. Apply by March 15 to appropriate department chair for assistantships; to Financial Aid Office for all other programs. Phone: (401)865-2286. Use FAFSA. About 10% of students receive aid other than loans from School and outside sources.

DEGREE REQUIREMENTS. For M.A. (History), M.S.: 30 credit hours minimum; reading knowledge of one foreign language; comprehensive exam; thesis/final document. For M.B.A., M.Ed.: 36 credit hours; comprehensive exam.

FIELDS OF STUDY.
Biblical Studies. M.A.
Business Administration.
Education.
History.
Literacy.
Mathematics. M.A.T. only.
Religious Studies.

UNIVERSITY OF PUERTO RICO, MAYAGUEZ
Mayaguez, Puerto Rico 00681-9020
Web site: www.uprm.edu

Established in 1911. CGS member. Public control. Coed. Semester system. Formerly the College of Agriculture and Mechanic Arts. Special facilities: Center for Applied Social Research, Center for Computing Research and Development, Center for Energy and Environmental Research, Civil Infrastructure Research Center, Engineering Research Center, Mechatronics Center, Puerto Rico Commercial Aquaculture Research and Development Center, Puerto Rico and U.S. Virgin Island Climatology Center, Agricultural Experimental Station, Tropical Center for Earth and Space Studies, Water Resource Research Institute. Library: 849,000 volumes, 12,000 subscriptions.

Tuition: U.S. citizens, residents of Puerto Rico, $75 per credit; U.S. nonresidents of Puerto Rico $75 per credit plus additional amount equivalent to what a Puerto Rican student would pay in the public university in the applicant's state of origin. Foreign students: $3500 per year. There are also applicable regular or special fees. Limited on-campus housing available. Average off-campus housing costs: $600–$850 per month. Contact Office of Residential Life for on- and off-campus housing information. Phone: (787)834-0589.

Graduate Studies

Graduate study since 1957. Graduate enrollment: full-time 675, part-time 50. Graduate faculty: 400. Degrees conferred: M.A., M.B.A., M.S., M.E., Ph.D.

ADMISSION REQUIREMENTS. Bachelor's degree, transcript, three letters of recommendation, working knowledge of Spanish and English required in support of application. GRE/GMAT required for some programs. Interview required for some departments. Apply to the Director, Office of Graduate Studies by February 15 (Fall), September 15 (Winter). Application fee $27. Phone: (787)265-3809; fax: (787)831-1115.

ADMISSION STANDARDS. Selective. Usual minimum average: 2.5 (A = 4).

FINANCIAL AID. Annual awards from institutional funds: scholarships, research assistantships, teaching assistantships, grants,

Federal W/S, loans. Approved for VA benefits. Apply to Director of Financial Aid; no specified closing date. Phone: (787)832-4040; fax: (787)265-1920. Use FAFSA and institutional FAF. Approximately 72% of all students receive some form of financial aid.

DEGREE REQUIREMENTS. Master's: 36 credits minimum, at least 24 in residence; candidacy; thesis; final oral exam. For Ph.D.: 72 credits beyond the bachelor's minimum; at least 30 credits in residence; comprehensive exam; candidacy; dissertation; final exam.

FIELDS OF STUDY.

COLLEGE OF AGRICULTURAL SCIENCES:
Agricultural Economics.
Agricultural Education.
Agronomy and Soils.
Crop Protection.
Food Science and Technology.
Horticulture.
Soils.

COLLEGE OF ARTS AND SCIENCES:
Biology.
Chemistry.
English.
Geology.
Hispanic Studies.
Marine Sciences. Includes biological oceanography, chemical oceanography, geological oceanography, physical oceanography.
Mathematics.
Physics.
Pure Mathematics.

COLLEGE OF ENGINEERING:
Chemical Engineering.
Civil Engineering and Surveying.
Electrical and Computer Engineering.
Industrial Engineering.
Mechanical Engineering.

INTERDISCIPLINARY PROGRAMS:
Computer and Information Sciences and Engineering. Ph.D.
Food Science and Technology. Ph.D.

UNIVERSITY OF PUERTO RICO
Rio Piedras, Puerto Rico 00931-3303
Web site: www.rrp.upr.edu

Founded 1903. Located 8 miles S of San Juan. CGS member. Coed. Public control. Semester system. Special facilities: Center for Studies of American Arts, Center for Archaeological Research, Caribbean Studies Institute, Institute of Cooperativism, Economic Research Center, Center for Historical Research, Natural Science Academic Computer Center, Resource Center for Scientific Engineering, Social Science Research Center. Library: 4,091,000 volumes, 5599 subscriptions. Total University enrollment: 21,000.

Annual tuition: full-time $2202; per credit $75. Limited on-campus housing for single graduate students. Average academic year housing costs: $1800 (room only). Contact Dean of Students Office for both on- and off-campus housing information. Phone: (787)764-0000, ext. 5651.

Graduate Division

Graduate study since 1927. Enrollment: full-time 1400, part-time 1600. Graduate faculty: full-time 195, part-time 146. Degrees conferred: M.A., M.S., M.B.A., M.L.S., M.Ed., M.P., M.P.A., M.S.W., M.Arch., M.C.R., Ed.D., Ph.D.

ADMISSION REQUIREMENTS. Two official transcripts required in support of application. GRE, interview required for some departments. Accepts transfer applicants. Apply February 15 to Office of Admissions of appropriate College/School. Earlier application deadline for some departments. Application fee $17. Phone: Education (787)764-0000, ext. 4368; Humanities (787)764-0000, ext. 3600; Social Sciences (787)767-2040; Natural Science (787)763-5101; Business (787)764-0000, ext. 4142; Librarianship, (787)764-0000, ext. 5827; Planning (787)764-0000, ext. 3449; Architecture (787)764-0000, ext. 3449; Communication (787)764-0000, ext. 5043.

ADMISSION STANDARDS. Competitive. Usual minimum average: 3.0 (A = 4).

FINANCIAL AID. Scholarships, fellowships, assistantships, partial tuition waivers, Federal W/S, loans. Apply by May 31 to appropriate department chair for fellowships, assistantships; to Financial Aid Office for all other programs. Phone: (787)764-0000, ext. 3148. Use FAFSA and University's FAF. About 60% of students receive aid from University and outside sources.

DEGREE REQUIREMENTS. For master's: one year minimum in residence; thesis/nonthesis; final oral exam; final written exam. For Ph.D.: 30 semester hours minimum beyond the master's, at least two semesters in full-time attendance; reading knowledge of two foreign languages for most programs; qualifying written exam; dissertation; final oral exam. For Ed.D.: essentially the same as Ph.D., except no language requirement.

FIELDS OF STUDY.

1COLLEGE OF EDUCATION:
Biology Education. M.Ed.
Chemistry Education. M.Ed.
Child Education. M.Ed.
Curriculum and Teaching. Ed.D.
Educational Research and Evaluation. M.Ed.
English Education. M.Ed.
Guidance and Counseling. M.Ed., Ed.D.
History Education. M.Ed.
Mathematics Education. M.Ed.
Physics Education. M.Ed.
School Administration and Supervision. M.Ed., Ed.D.
Secondary Education. M.Ed.
Spanish Education. M.Ed.
Special Education. M.Ed.
TESL. M.Ed.

COLLEGE OF HUMANITIES:
Comparative Literature. M.A.
English. M.A.
Hispanic Studies. M.A., Ph.D.
History. M.A., Ph.D.
Humanities. M.A., Ph.D.
Linguistics. M.A.
Philosophy. M.A. only.
Translation. M.A.

COLLEGE OF SOCIAL SCIENCES:
Economics. M.A. only.
Psychology. M.A., Ph.D.
Public Administration. M.P.A.
Rehabilitation Counseling. M.C.R.
Social Sciences. M.A., Ph.D.
Social Work. M.S.W.
Sociology. M.A.

FACULTY OF NATURAL SCIENCES:
Applied Physics. M.S.
Biology. M.S., Ph.D.
Chemistry. M.S., Ph.D.
Mathematics. M.A. only.
Natural Sciences. M.S., Ph.D.
Physics. M.S. only.
Physics—Chemical. Ph.D. only.

GRADUATE SCHOOL OF BUSINESS ADMINISTRATION:
Business Administration. M.B.A.

GRADUATE SCHOOL OF LIBRARIANSHIP:
Librarianship and Information Services. M.L.S.

GRADUATE SCHOOL OF PLANNING:
Planning. M.P.

SCHOOL OF ARCHITECTURE:
Architecture. M.Arch.

SCHOOL OF PUBLIC COMMUNICATION:
Public Communication. M.A.

School of Dentistry

Established 1956. Located in San Juan (00936-5067). Annual tuition: resident $5180, nonresident varies. Limited on-campus housing available for single students only. Average academic year housing costs: $6000. Contact Dean of Students Office for both on- and off-campus housing information. Total average cost for all other first-year expenses: $7900.

Enrollment: D.M.D. programs, first-year class 46 (men 30%, women 70%); graduate program, full-time 16 (men 15, women 1). Faculty: full-time 66, part-time 31. Degrees conferred: D.M.D., M.S.

ADMISSION REQUIREMENTS. For D.M.D. program: AAD-SAS, official transcripts, three letters of recommendation, DAT (no later than October), proficiency in Spanish required in support of application. Preference given to Puerto Rican students. Interview by invitation only. Applicants must have completed at least three years of college study. Accepts transfer applicants. Apply to Director of Admissions after June 30, before December 15. Application fee $15. Phone: (787)758-2525, ext. 1113. For graduate programs: official transcripts, two letters of recommendation, interview required in support of School's application. Accepts transfer applicants. Enrollment limited to residents. Apply to Chair of Graduate Committee by December 15. Application fee $15.

ADMISSION STANDARDS. For D.M.D. program: Mean DAT: Academic 16, PAT 16; mean GPA: 3.55. Gourman rating: 4.03. Accepts 65% of total annual applicants; 100% are residents of Puerto Rico. For graduate program: competitive. Usual minimum GPA: 3.0 (A = 4).

FINANCIAL AID. For D.M.D. program: scholarships, grants, loans for Puerto Rican resident students only; apply to the University's Dean of Students Office; no specified closing date. About 75% of students receive aid from School and outside sources. For graduate program: fellowships for hospital residency. All graduate students receive aid during residency.

DEGREE REQUIREMENTS. For D.M.D.: satisfactory completion of 46-month program. For M.S. (oral surgery): 36 months minimum, at least 2 semesters in hospital residency; thesis; final written exam. For M.S.: 24 months minimum, hospital residency; thesis; final written exam.

FIELDS OF GRADUATE STUDY.
General Practice.
Oral and Maxillofacial Surgery.

Orthodontics.
Pediatric Dentistry.
Prosthodontics.

School of Law (P.O. Box 23349)
San Juan, Puerto Rico 00931-3349

Established 1913. Located in metropolitan San Juan. ABA approved since 1945. AALS member. Semester system. Full-time, part-time study. Exchange program with the University of Arizona, the University of Connecticut; summer study abroad at University of Barcelona. Law library: 290,300 volumes, 4250 subscriptions; has LEXIS, NEXIS, WESTLAW, DIALOG, COMPU-CLERK, CUMPULEQ, LEGALTRAC, INFOTRAC; is a selective depository for U.S. Government Documents and European Document Center.

Annual tuition: full-time $2395, residents and American citizens; nonresident, non-American citizens $3595. Annual on-campus living expenses: single $9975. Housing deadline June 15. Contact Housing Office for both on- and off-campus housing information. Phone: (787)764-0000, ext. 5651. Law students tend to live off-campus. Off-campus housing and personal expenses: approximately $10,040.

Enrollment: first-year class full-time 111, part-time 41; total 517 (men 47%, women 53%) Faculty: full-time 23, part-time 21. Student to faculty ratio 16.4 to 1. Degrees conferred: J.D., J.D.-M.B.A., J.D.-M.P.P. (University of Minnesota), LL.M. (For Latin American Lawyers), J.D.-Lic. en Derecho (University of Barcelona).

ADMISSION REQUIREMENTS. LSDAS Law School report, bachelor's degree, two transcripts, LSAT, PAEG required in support of application. Interview not required. Accepts transfer applicants. Graduates of unaccredited colleges not considered. Apply to Office of Admission after September 1, before February 15. Fall admission only. Application fee $15. Phone: (787)764-1655.

ADMISSION STANDARDS. Selective. Mean LSAT: full-time 149, part-time 146; mean GPA: full-time 3.56, part-time 3.55 (A = 4). Gourman rating: 2.32. *U.S. News & World Report* ranking is in the fourth tier of all U.S. law schools. Accepts 20–25% of total annual applicants.

FINANCIAL AID. Scholarships, grants, tuition waivers, assistantships, loans. Apply to the University's Office of Financial Aid in San Juan after acceptance, before May 1. Use FAFSA (School code: 007108). About 10% of students receive aid other than loans from outside sources.

DEGREE REQUIREMENTS. For J.D.: 92 credits minimum, at least 60 in residence, three-year (day) or four-year (evening) program; 92 credit hour program. For LL.M.: 24 credit program.

Medical Sciences Campus—
Division of Graduate Studies
Web site: www.rcm.upr.edu

Established 1960. Located in San Juan (00936-5067). Public control. Special facilities: Caribbean Primate Research Center, Center for Environmental and Toxicological Studies, Center for Informatics and Technology, Center for Sports, Health, and Exercise Sciences, Puerto Rican Cancer Center, Center for the Study of Sexually Transmitted Disease, Center for Energy and Environmental Research, Clinical Research Center. The University's NIH ranking is 109th among all U.S. institutions with 48 awards/grants worth $31,479,311. Library: 42,092 volumes, 1132 subscriptions.

Tuition: per credit $75. Enrollment: full-time 509 (men 70%, women 30%). Faculty: full-time 41, part-time 3. Degrees conferred: M.S., M.S.N., M.P.H., Ph.D.

ADMISSION REQUIREMENTS. Transcripts, GRE Subject Tests, interview, two recommendations, proficiency in English and Spanish required in support of application. On-line application available. Accepts transfer applicants. Apply by February 15 (Fall), by November 1 (Spring) to Director of Graduate Studies. Phone: (787)753-2962.

ADMISSION STANDARDS. Selective for most departments. Usual minimum average: 2.75 (A = 4).

FINANCIAL AID. Annual awards from institutional funds: scholarships, assistantships, fellowships, loans. Apply to appropriate department chairman for fellowships, assistantships. Use FAFSA. About 30% of students receive aid other than loans from university and outside sources.

DEGREE REQUIREMENTS. For M.S., M.P.H.: 30–36 credit hours minimum, at least 24 in residence; reading knowledge of one foreign language; thesis/nonthesis; final oral exam. For M.S.N.: 48 credit program; research project. For Ph.D.: 60 credit hours minimum beyond the bachelor's, at least 40 in residence; qualifying exam; reading knowledge of two foreign languages; comprehensive exam; dissertation; final oral exam.

FIELDS OF STUDY.
Anatomy.
Biochemistry.
Biology.
Clinical Nurse Specialist.
Environmental Health.
Epidemiology.
Health Services Administration.
Microbiology.
Nursing Anesthesia.
Nursing Services Administration.
Occupational Health.
Pharmacy.
Pharmacology.
Physiology.
Public Health.
Speech Pathology.
Teaching of Nursing in Higher Education.

School of Medicine
P.O. Box 365067

Established 1949. Located in San Juan (00936-5067). Library: 100,000 volumes. Annual tuition: $5000. Tuition varies for nonresident students according to program; approximately $10,500. Total average figure for all other annual expenses: $6500.

Enrollment: first-year class 115, total 419 (men 39%, women 61%); Faculty: about 400, full- and part-time. Degrees conferred: M.D., M.S., Ph.D.

ADMISSION REQUIREMENTS. For M.D. program: transcripts, letters of recommendation, fluency in English and Spanish, MCAT required in support of application. Does not have EDP. Interview by invitation only. Applicants must have completed at least three years of college study. Accepts limited number of nonresidents. Apply to Office of Dean after June 1, before December 1. Application fee $15. Phone: (787)758-2525, ext. 1810; fax: (787)282-7117.

ADMISSION STANDARDS. Selective. Mean MCAT: 7.0; mean GPA: 3.69 (A = 4). Gourman rating: 4.03. Accepts 25–30% of total annual applicants. Approximately 100% are residents.

FINANCIAL AID. Scholarships for resident students only. Apply by April 30 to Financial Aid Office. Use FAFSA (School code: 003945). About 50% of students receive some aid from School.

DEGREE REQUIREMENTS. For M.D.: satisfactory completion of four-year program. For M.S., Ph.D.: see Graduate Division listing above.

FIELDS OF GRADUATE STUDY.
Anatomy.
Biochemistry.
Biology.
Microbiology and Medical Zoology.
Pharmacology and Toxicology.
Physiology.

UNIVERSITY OF PUGET SOUND
Tacoma, Washington 98416-0005
Web site: www.ups.edu

Founded 1888. Coed. Private control. Methodist affiliation. Semester system. Library: 363,000 volumes, 4510 subscriptions.
Tuition: per unit $3000 (for M.A.T., M.O.T., M.P.T.), $1950 (for M.Ed.). No on-campus housing available for graduate students.

Graduate Studies

Enrollment: full-time 155, part-time 49. University faculty: full-time 27, part-time 22. Degrees conferred: M.A.T., M.Ed., M.O.T., M.P.T.

ADMISSION REQUIREMENTS. Official transcripts, three letters of recommendation, GRE/MAT required in support of application. Interview required for Education. On-line application available. Proficiency in English or TOEFL required of international students. Accepts transfer applicants. Graduates of unaccredited institutions not considered. Apply to Office of Admissions one month prior to registration. Application deadline for M.O.T. and M.P.T. is February 1. Rolling admissions process. Application fee $40. Phone: (253)879-3211; e-mail: admission@ups.edu.

ADMISSION STANDARDS. Selective for all departments. Usual minimum average: 3.0 (A = 4). 50th percentile or higher on tests.

FINANCIAL AID. Scholarships, fellowships, research assistantships, teaching assistantships, Federal W/S, loans. Approved for VA benefits. Apply by March 1 to appropriate school for assistantships; to Financial Aid Office for all other programs. Phone: (253)879-3214. Use FAFSA (University code: 003797). About 25% of students receive aid from both University and outside sources. Aid available for part-time students.

DEGREE REQUIREMENTS. For master's: 8 units (32 semester hours) minimum, at least 6 units in residence; oral/written comprehensive exam; thesis/nonthesis option for some degrees.

FIELDS OF STUDY.
Counseling. Includes agency, pastoral. M.Ed.
Education Administration. M.Ed.
Education. M.A.T.
Occupational Therapy. M.O.T.
Physical Therapy. M.P.T.

PURDUE UNIVERSITY
West Lafayette, Indiana 47907-1968
Web site: www.purdue.edu

Founded 1869. Located 65 miles NW of Indianapolis. CGS and AAU member. Coed. State control. Semester system. Special facilities: Agricultural Experiment Station, Animal Science Research

Center, Center for Applied Ethology and Human/Animal Interaction, Center for Applied Mathematics, Center for Artistic Endeavors, Center for Asian Studies, Hellenbrand Biomedical Engineering Center, Center for Classical Studies, Center for Comparative Literature, Engineering Research Center for Intelligent Manufacturing Systems, Engineering Experiment Station, Center for Film Studies, Gifted Education Resource Center, Center for Humanistic Studies, Jet Propulsion Center, Center for Leadership Studies, Center for Medieval Studies, Center for AIDS Research, Center for Intelligent Manufacturing Systems, Marriage and Family Center, Center for Paralysis Research, Center for Plant Environmental Stress Physiology, Policy Center for Life Long Learning, Retail Institute, Center for Research on the Aging, Center for Rural Development, Social Research Center, Center for Technology Transfer and Pollution Prevention, University Research Park. The University's NIH ranking is 114th among all U.S. institutions with 116 awards/grants with $30,177,662. Library: 2,107,000 volumes, 18,635 subscriptions.

Annual tuition: full-time resident $3772, nonresident $12,804; per hour resident $135, nonresident $422. On-campus housing for 1300 married students, 800 graduate men and women. Average annual housing cost: $5800 for married students, $3800 for single students. Apply to Director's Office, Young Graduate House, Purdue University, for graduate housing; Director, Married Student Housing, Nimitz Drive, Purdue University, for married student housing; for off-campus housing, apply to Off-Campus Housing Services, Hovde Hall, Office of the Dean of Students. Phone: (765)494-7045.

Graduate School

Enrollment: full-time 4173, part-time 1475. Graduate faculty: full- and part-time 1741. Degrees conferred: M.A., M.Agr., M.F.A., M.A.T., M.S., full- and part-time M.S.A.A.E., M.S.Ag.E., M.S.C.E., M.S.Ch.E., M.S.Ed., M.S.E.E., M.S.F., M.S.I.A., M.S.I.E., M.S.Met.E., M.S.N.E., Ed.S., Ph.D.

ADMISSION REQUIREMENTS. Official transcripts, three letters of reference required in support of School's application. GRE/MAT/GMAT required by many departments. TOEFL required for international applicants. Accepts transfer applicants. Graduates of unaccredited institutions not considered. Apply to department of major interest one semester in advance and not later than May 1 (Fall), September 1 (Spring), March 1 (Summer). Application fee $30. Phone for general information: (765)494-2600; fax: (765)494-0136; e-mail: gradinfo@purdue.edu.

ADMISSION STANDARDS. Selective for most departments, very selective for the others. Usual minimum average: 3.0 (A = 4).

FINANCIAL AID. Annual awards from institutional funds: scholarships, fellowships (including minority fellowships), teaching assistantships, research fellowships, administrative assistantships, full and partial tuition waivers, grants, Federal W/S, loans. Approved for VA benefits. Apply by February 1 to appropriate department for fellowships, assistantships; to Financial Aid Office for all other programs. Use FAFSA. About 60% of full-time students receive aid from University and outside sources. Aid available for part-time students.

DEGREE REQUIREMENTS. For master's: usually about 33 hours, at least two semesters in residence; thesis/nonthesis option: final written/oral exams for most majors; reading knowledge of one foreign language for some majors. For Ph.D.: usually 50–60 hours minimum beyond the bachelor's, at least one year in residence; qualifying exam for most majors; preliminary exam; reading knowledge of one foreign language for most majors; thesis; final written/oral exam.

FIELDS OF STUDY.
Accounting. M.S., Ph.D.
Aeronautics and Astronautics. M.S., M.S.A.A.E., M.S.E., Ph.D.
Agricultural and Biological Engineering. M.S., M.S.Ag.E., M.S.E., Ph.D.

Agricultural Economics. M.S., Ph.D.
Agronomy. M.S., Ph.D.
American Studies. M.A., Ph.D.
Animal Sciences. M.S., Ph.D.
Anthropology. M.S., Ph.D.
Art and Design. M.A.
Audiology and Speech Sciences. M.S., Ph.D.
Basic Medical Sciences. M.S., Ph.D.
Biochemistry. Interdisciplinary program. M.S., Ph.D.
Biochemistry and Molecular Biology. M.S., Ph.D.
Biomedical Engineering and Bioengineering. Interdisciplinary.
Botany and Plant Pathology. M.S., Ph.D.
Cell and Developmental Biology. Ph.D.
Chemical Engineering. M.S., M.S.Ch.E., M.S.E., Ph.D.
Chemistry. Includes analytical, geochemistry, inorganic, organic, physical.
Child Development and Family Studies. M.S.Ed., M.S., Ph.D.
Civil Engineering. M.S., M.S.C.E., M.S.E., Ph.D.
Communication. M.A., M.S., Ph.D.
Comparative Literature. Interdisciplinary. M.A., Ph.D.
Computer Sciences. M.S., Ph.D.
Consumer Sciences and Retailing. M.S., Ph.D.
Counseling and Development. M.S., M.S.Ed., Ph.D., Ed.S.
Creative Arts. M.A. or M.F.A. only.
Curriculum and Instruction. M.S.Ed., Ph.D.
Developmental Biology. M.S.
Earth and Atmospheric Sciences. M.S., Ph.D.
Ecology, Evolutionary, and Population Biology. M.S., Ph.D.
Economics. Ph.D.
Educational Studies. M.S.Ed., Ph.D.
Electrical and Computer Engineering. M.S., M.S.E., M.S.E.E., Ph.D.
Elementary Education. M.A.T., M.S.Ed., Ph.D.
English.
Entomology. M.S., Ph.D.
Food and Agricultural Business. M.S., Ph.D.
Food Science. M.S., Ph.D.
Foods and Nutrition. M.S.
Foreign Language and Literature. M.A., Ph.D.
Forestry and Natural Resources. M.S., M.S.F., Ph.D.
Genetics. M.S., Ph.D.
Geographic Information System and Remote Sensing. Interdisciplinary.
Gerontology. M.S., Ph.D.
Health and Kinesiology. M.S.
Health Sciences. M.S., Ph.D.
History. M.A., Ph.D.
Horticulture. M.Agr., M.A., Ph.D.
Hospitality and Tourism Management. M.S.
Immunology. M.S., Ph.D.
Industrial Engineering. M.S.I.E., Ph.D.
Industrial and Physical Pharmacy. Ph.D.
International Management. M.S.
Linguistics. M.A., Ph.D.
Management Information Systems. M.S., Ph.D.
Management. M.S., Ph.D.
Materials Engineering. M.S., M.S.E., Ph.D.
Mathematics. M.S., Ph.D.
Mechanical Engineering. M.S., M.S.M.E., Ph.D.
Medicinal Chemistry and Molecular Pharmacology. M.S.
Medicinal Chemistry and Pharmacognosy. Ph.D.
Microbiology. Ph.D.
Mineral Resources. Interdisciplinary.
Neuroscience. Ph.D.
Nuclear Engineering. M.S., M.S.N.E., Ph.D.
Organizational Behavior and Human Resource Management. M.S., Ph.D.
Pharmacology and Toxicology. M.S., Ph.D.
Pharmacy Practice. M.S.
Philosophy. M.A., Ph.D.
Physics. M.S., Ph.D.

Physiology. M.S., Ph.D.
Plant Biology. Interdisciplinary. M.S., Ph.D.
Political Science. M.A., Ph.D.
Psychological Sciences. M.S., Ph.D.
Sociology. M.S., Ph.D.
Statistics. M.S.
Technology. M.S.
Theater. M.A., M.F.A.
Veterinary Clinical Sciences. M.S., Ph.D.
Veterinary Pathology. M.S., Ph.D.
Visual and Performing Arts. Includes art, design, theater. M.A., M.F.A.

Graduate Study at Other Campuses

Purdue University maintains a system-wide graduate school under which some courses and/or programs are offered at the regional campuses located at Hammond and Westville, as well as at the Indiana University–Purdue University campuses at Fort Wayne and Indianapolis.

School of Veterinary Medicine (47907-1240)

Established 1957. Tuition/fees: resident $8908, nonresident $21,480. Total living expenses: $5800.

Enrollment: first-year class 70, total 327 (men 40%, women 60%). School faculty: 82. Degrees conferred: D.V.M., D.V.M.-M.S., D.V.M.-Ph.D.

ADMISSION REQUIREMENTS. VMCAS report, two transcripts, GRE, animal/veterinary experience, essay required in support of application. Interview by invitation only. Applicants must have completed at least two years of college study. Accepts transfer applicants on a space-available basis only. Preference given first to Indiana residents, second to residents of states without veterinary schools. Apply to Student Services Office after July 1 and before October 1. Fall admission only. Application fee: none. Phone: (765)494-7893; e-mail: admissions@vet.purdue.edu.

ADMISSION STANDARDS. Selective. Usual minimum GPA: 3.0; mean GPA: 3.56 (A = 4). Accepts about 12–15% of total annual applicants. Approximately 20 nonresident applicants are accepted.

FINANCIAL AID. Scholarships, assistantships, fellowships, full and partial tuition waivers, Federal W/S, grants. Apply to Office of Financial Aid by March 1. Use FAFSA.

DEGREE REQUIREMENTS. For D.V.M.: satisfactory completion of four-year program, at least three years in residence. For Ph.D., see Graduate School listing above.

FIELDS OF GRADUATE STUDY.
Animal Behavior. M.S.
Biomedical Engineering. M.S., Ph.D.
Bone and Articulation. M.S., Ph.D.
Cancer Biology. M.S., Ph.D.
Cancer Biology and Therapeutics. M.S.
Cellular Biology and Physiology. M.S., Ph.D.
Developmental Biology. M.S., Ph.D.
Environmental Toxicology. M.S., Ph.D.
Epidemiology of Infectious or Metabolic Diseases. M.S., Ph.D.
Equine Medicine and Surgery. M.S.
Fatty Acids and Immune Function. M.S., Ph.D.
Herd Health. M.S.
Information Technology in Veterinary Medicine. M.S., Ph.D.
Innovative Educational Strategies. M.S., Ph.D.
Microbiology of Infectious Disease. M.S., Ph.D.
Molecular Biology. M.S., Ph.D.
Molecular Pathogenesis of Pulmonary Carcinogenesis. M.S., Ph.D.
Molecular Pathogenesis of Viral and Bacterial Infections. M.S., Ph.D.

Molecular Virology. M.S., Ph.D.
Mucosal Immunity. M.S., Ph.D.
Neurosciences. M.S., Ph.D.
Parasitology. M.S., Ph.D.
Pathology and Pathogenesis of Disease of Animals (Birds and Fish). M.S., Ph.D.
Reproductive Endocrinology. M.S., Ph.D.
Reproductive Toxicology. M.S., Ph.D.
Theriogenology. M.S.
Tissue Engineering. M.S., Ph.D.

PURDUE UNIVERSITY CALUMET
Hammond, Indiana 46323-2094
Web site: www.calumet.purdue.edu

Established 1948. Coed. State control. Semester system. Library: 205,000 volumes, 1300 subscriptions.

Tuition: per credit hour, resident $135, nonresident $422. No on-campus housing for graduate students. Day-care facilities available.

Graduate School

Enrollment: full-time 96, part-time 907. Faculty: full-time 140, part-time 16. Degrees conferred: M.A., M S., M.S.E.

ADMISSION REQUIREMENTS. Two transcripts, three letters of recommendation required in support of application. GRE/GMAT/MAT required by some departments. On-line application available. TOEFL required for international applicants. Accepts transfer applicants. Apply to the Office of Graduate Study; no specified closing date. Application fee $55. Phone: (219)989-2257; e-mail: grad@calumet.purdue.edu.

ADMISSION STANDARDS. Selective. Usual minimum average: 3.0 (A = 4).

FINANCIAL AID. Research fellowships, teaching assistantships, Federal W/S, loans. Apply to appropriate departments for fellowships, assistantships; to Financial Aid Office for all other programs. Phone: (219)989-2660. Use FAFSA.

DEGREE REQUIREMENTS. For master's: 33–48 semester hours; knowledge of one foreign language required by some departments; candidacy; final oral/written exam.

FIELDS OF STUDY.
Behavior Sciences. M.S.
Biological Sciences. M.S.
Communications. M.A.
Education. M.S.
Engineering. M.S.E.
English. M.A.
History. M.A.
Management. GMAT for admission; 48 credits for M.S. M.B.A., M.S.
Mathematics. M.S.
Nursing. M.S.

QUEENS COLLEGE OF THE CITY UNIVERSITY OF NEW YORK
Flushing, New York 11367-1597
Web site: www.cqc.edu

Established 1937. CGS member. Coed. New York State control. Semester system. Library: 753,000 volumes, 3800 subscriptions.

Tuition: full-time, state resident $4350, per credit $185; nonresident $7600, per credit $320. No housing available. Day-care facilities available.

Division of Graduate Studies

Graduate study since 1950. Enrollment: full- and part-time 4100 (men 30%, women 70%). Faculty: full-time 637, part-time 476. Degrees conferred: M.A., M.A.S.S., M.L.S., M.F.A., M.S.Ed., M.A.L.S., Professional Diploma.

ADMISSION REQUIREMENTS. Transcripts required in support of application. GRE and GRE Subject Test, interview required for some departments. TOEFL required for international applicants. Accepts transfer applicants. Graduates of unaccredited institutions not considered. Apply to Office of Graduate Admissions by April 1 (Fall; some programs have earlier deadline), November 1 (Spring; not all programs admit in Spring). Application fee $40. Phone: (718)997-5200.

ADMISSION STANDARDS. Selective or very selective. Usual minimum average: 2.75, 3.0 for major (A = 4).

FINANCIAL AID. Fellowships, assistantships, tuition waivers, Federal W/S, loans. Approved for VA benefits. Apply by April 1 to appropriate department chair for fellowships, assistantships; to Financial Aid Office for all other programs. Use FAFSA and University's FAF. Phone: (718)977-5100. Aid available for part-time students.

DEGREE REQUIREMENTS. For master's: generally 30 semester hours; thesis and comprehensive exam required for some degrees. For Post-Baccalaureate Certificate (teacher certification): 30 credits beyond the bachelor's degree. For Advanced Certificate: 30 semester hours beyond the master's.

FIELDS OF STUDY.
Accounting. M.S.Ed.
Applied Linguistics. M.A.
Art History. M.A., M.F.A.
Bilingual Elementary Education. M.S.Ed.
Biology. M.A.
Biochemistry. M.A.
Chemistry. M.A.
Computer Science. M.A.
Counselor Education. M.S.Ed.
Elementary Education. M.S.Ed.
English. M.A.
French. M.A.
Fine Arts. M.F.A.
Geology. M.A.
History. M.A.
Italian. M.A.
Liberal Studies. M.A.L.S.
Library Science. Includes specializations in school or public, academic and special; M.L.S.; Advanced Certificate in Librarianship.
Mathematics. M.A.
Media Studies. M.A.
Music. M.A.
Music Performance. M.A.
Nutrition and Exercise Sciences. M.A.
Physics. M.A.
Psychology. M.A.
Reading. M.S.Ed.
School Psychology. M.S.Ed.
Secondary Education. Includes art, English, French, general science (biology, chemistry, earth science, physics), home economics, Italian, mathematics, music, physical education, social studies, Spanish. M.S.Ed.
Social Sciences. M.A.S.S.
Sociology. M.A.
Spanish. M.A.

Special Education. M.S.Ed.
Speech Pathology. M.A.
Studio Arts. M.F.A.
TESOL. M.S.Ed.
Urban Affairs. M.A.

City University of New York School of Law at Queens College

Flushing, New York 11367-1358
Web site: www.law.cuny.edu

Established 1983. Located on the Queens College campus in Flushing. ABA approved since 1985. AALS member. Semester system. Public control. Full-time, day study only. Law library: 261,755 volumes, 2871 subscriptions; has LEXIS, NEXIS, WESTLAW, DIALOG.

Annual tuition: resident $3225, nonresident $4840. No on-campus housing available. Law students tend to live off-campus. Contact Admissions Office for off-campus information. Off-campus housing and personal expenses: approximately $10,588. Enrollment: first-year class 148; total full-time 383 (men 40%, women 60%); no part-time students. Faculty: full-time 26, part-time 17. Student to faculty ratio 12.2 to 1. Degree conferred: J.D.

ADMISSION REQUIREMENTS. LSDAS Law School report, LSAT (not later than February test date; if more than one LSAT, highest is used), bachelor's degree from an accredited institution, personal statement, two recommendations, transcripts (must show all schools attended and at least three years of study) required in support of application. Applicants must have received bachelor's degree prior to enrollment. Accepts transfer applicants. Interview not required but may be requested by School. In addition, international applicants whose native language is not English must submit TOEFL (not older than two years). Apply to Office of Admission after October 1, before March 14. First-year students admitted Fall only. Rolling admissions process. Application fee $40. Phone: (718)575-4210.

ADMISSION STANDARDS. Selective. Mean LSAT: 149, mean GPA: 3.07 (A = 4). Gourman rating 2.10. *U.S. News & World Report* ranking is in the fourth tier of all law schools. Accepts 20–25% of total applicants.

FINANCIAL AID. Scholarships, Grants-in-Aid, private and institutional loans, Federal W/S, loans. For scholarships apply to Admissions Office after January 1, before May 1; use CUNY's Financial Aid Form, also submit Financial Aid Transcript, Federal Income Tax forms. Approximately 59% of first-year class received scholarships/Grants-in-Aid. Approximately 80% of students receive some form of financial aid.

DEGREE REQUIREMENTS. For J.D.: 92 (70 required) credits with a GPA of at least 2.0 (A = 4), plus completion of upper-divisional writing course; three-year program.

QUINNIPIAC UNIVERSITY

Hamden, Connecticut 96518-1940
Web site: www.quinnipiac.edu

Founded 1929. Located 20 miles S of Hartford. Coed. Semester system. Library: 285,000 volumes, 4400 subscriptions.

Tuition: per credit $430; annual tuition costs: Physician Assistant $37,000, Pathologist $32,000, M.A.T. $18,000, M.B.A. $18,000. On-campus housing available for single students only. Average academic year housing costs: $6500 (including board); off-campus housing costs: $500–$700 per month. Contact Housing Office for both on- and off-campus housing information. Phone: (203)582-8666.

Graduate Programs

Graduate study since 1965. Enrollment: full-time 450, part-time 450. Graduate faculty: full-time 76, part-time 34. Degrees conferred: M.A.T., M.B.A., M.H.A., M.H.S., M.S.P.T.

ADMISSION REQUIREMENTS. Official transcripts required in support of application. Interviews required for some programs. TOEFL required for international applicants. Accepts transfer applicants. Graduates of unaccredited institutions not considered. Apply to Director of Graduate Admissions at least one month prior to date of registration; for Physician Assistant program apply by December 1, Pathologist program apply by January 15. Rolling admissions process. Application fee $40. Phone: (203)582-8672, (203)582-5238; e-mail: graduate@quinnipiac.edu.

ADMISSION STANDARDS. Selective. Usual minimum average: 2.75 (A = 4).

FINANCIAL AID. Annual awards from institutional funds: assistantships, Federal W/S, loans. Approved for VA benefits. Apply to Office of Financial Assistance; no specified closing date. Use FAFSA. Aid available for part-time students.

DEGREE REQUIREMENTS. For master's: 32–60 credits minimum, at least 26–54 in residence; thesis/nonthesis option; no foreign language requirement; final exams/internships in some programs.

FIELDS OF STUDY.
Biomedical Sciences.
Business Administration.
E-Media.
Forensic Nursing.
Health Administration.
Journalism.
Medical Laboratory Sciences.
Molecular and Cell Biology.
Nurse Practitioner Studies.
Pathologist Assistant Studies.
Physical Therapy.
Physician Assistant Studies.
Teaching.

School of Law

Web site: www.law.quinnipiac.edu

Founded in 1979 as part of the University of Bridgeport, name changed in 1995 and School moved to Hamden, Connecticut. ABA approved since 1992. AALS member. Special program: Pre-Admission Summer Program. Law library: 354,167 volumes, 2794 subscriptions; has LEXIS, WESTLAW, DIALOG.

Annual tuition: full-time $23,465, part-time $17,865. On-campus housing available; room and board: approximately $13,909.

Enrollment: first-year class full-time 186, part-time 94, total enrollment 747 (men 52%, women 48%). Faculty: full-time 33, part-time 28. Student to faculty ratio 16.5 to 1. Degrees conferred: J.D., J.D.-M.B.A., J.D.-M.H.A., LL.M. (Taxation, Taxation and Business).

ADMISSION REQUIREMENTS. LSDAS Law School report, LSAT, transcripts, references required in support of application. Graduates of unaccredited colleges not considered. Apply to the Office of Admissions. Admissions on a rolling basis, early applicants given special consideration. Application fee $40. Phone: (203)582-3400; fax: (203)582-3339.

ADMISSION STANDARDS. Selective. Mean LSAT: full-time 147, part-time 149; mean GPA: full-time 2.90, part-time 2.93 (A = 4). Gourman rating: 2.02. *U.S. News & World Report* ranking is in the fourth tier of all U.S. law schools. Accepts about 40–45% of total annual applicants.

FINANCIAL AID. Scholarships, Federal W/S, loans. Apply to Financial Aid Office by May 1. Use FAFSA (School code: E00545) and Quinnipiac Financial Aid Application. About 42% of students receive some aid from school.

DEGREE REQUIREMENTS. For J.D.: 86 semester hour program, minimum of two years in residence. For LL.M.: at least 24 credits beyond J.D.

RADFORD UNIVERSITY
Radford, Virginia 24142
Web site: www.radford.edu

Founded 1913. Located 40 miles SW of Roanoke. CGS member. Coed. State control. Semester system. Special facilities: Center for Brain Research and Informational Sciences, Curriculum Materials Center, Economics Research Center, Geography Research Center, Institute for Engineering Geosciences. Library: 527,789 volumes, 3200 subscriptions. Total University enrollment: 8800.

Annual tuition: resident $3810, nonresident $7620; per credit hour resident $167, nonresident $323. On-campus housing for single students only. Annual academic year housing costs: $5300 for single students, $7000 for married students living off-campus. Contact Director of Residential Life for off-campus housing information. Phone: (540)831-5375. Day-care facilities available.

Graduate College

Enrollment: full-time 444, part-time 520. Graduate faculty: full-time 196, part-time 11. Degrees conferred: M.A., M.B.A., M.F.A., M.S., M.S.W., Ed.S.

ADMISSION REQUIREMENTS. Transcripts, two letters of recommendation, GRE/GMAT/ MAT/NTE required in support of College's application. On-line application available. TOEFL required for international applicants. Accepts transfer applicants. Graduates of unaccredited institutions not considered. Apply to Graduate Studies Admissions (Box 6905) by February 1 (Fall), October 1 (Spring), April 1 (Summer). Application fee $25. Phone: (540)831-5431; fax: (540)831-6061.

ADMISSION STANDARDS. Relatively open. Usual minimum average: 2.75, for candidacy 3.0 (A = 4).

FINANCIAL AID. Fellowships, research assistantships, teaching assistantships, internships, grants, Federal W/S, loans. Approved for VA benefits. Apply by February 1 to Graduate Office for assistantships; to Financial Aid Office for all other programs. Phone: (540)831-5408. Use FAFSA. About 50% of full-time Graduate students receive aid other than loans from University and outside sources.

DEGREE REQUIREMENTS. For master's: 30–49 semester hours minimum; thesis/nonthesis; NTE, GRE, or MAT required for admission to candidacy; GMAT required for admission to candidacy for business majors in the nonteaching option. For M.F.A.: 60 credit program. For M.S.W.: 61 credit program. For Ed.S.: 30 semester hours beyond master's.

FIELDS OF STUDY.
Art.
Art Education.
Business Administration.

Communication Sciences and Disorders. Includes audiology, speech, language pathology.
Computational Sciences.
Corporate and Professional Communication.
Counselor Education.
Criminal Justice.
Curriculum and Instruction.
Education. Includes elementary, secondary, leadership.
Educational Leadership.
Educational Media.
Engineering Geosciences.
English.
International Economics.
Leisure Services.
Music.
Music Therapy.
Nursing.
Physical Education.
Psychology. Includes clinical, counseling, experimental, industrial/organizational.
Reading.
School Psychology. Ed.S.
Science Education.
Social Work.
Special Education. Includes emotional/behavioral disorders, specific learning disabilities, mental retardation and severe disabilities.

UNIVERSITY OF REDLANDS

Redlands, California 92373-0999
Web site: www.redlands.edu

Founded 1907. Located 60 miles E of Los Angeles. Coed. Private control. Modified semester system. Library: 200,000 volumes, 1200 subscriptions. Total University enrollment: 2000.

Tuition: per credit $463. Limited on-campus housing for graduate students. Contact Director of Housing for both on- and off-campus housing information. Phone: (909)793-2121.

Graduate Studies

Enrollment: full-time 40, part-time 200. Faculty: full-time 12, part-time 100. Degrees conferred: M.A., M.M., M.S., M.B.A.

ADMISSION REQUIREMENTS. Official transcripts, three letters of recommendation, statement of intent, résumé usually required in support of application, GRE/GMAT required for some programs. On-line application available. TOEFL (minimum score 550) required for international applicants. Accepts transfer applicants. Apply to appropriate department, preferably by March 31. Some programs have earlier deadlines. Application fee $40. Phone: (909)793-2121, ext. 2200.

ADMISSION STANDARDS. Selective. Usual minimum average: 2.5 or 3.0, depending on program (A = 4).

FINANCIAL AID. Assistantships, internships, Federal W/S, loans. Approved for VA benefits. Apply to Director of Financial Aid. Phone: (909)-793-2121. Use FAFSA.

DEGREE REQUIREMENTS. For master's: 36–48 units minimum; thesis/nonthesis option; final oral/written exam.

FIELDS OF STUDY.
Administrative Services. M.A.
Adult Education. M.A.
Business Administration. M.B.A.
Communicative Disorders. Includes clinical rehabilitative services. M.S.

Composition. M.S.
Curriculum and Instruction. M.A.
Educational Administration. M.A.
Geographic Information Systems. Includes geographic information systems and management. M.S.
Interactive Telecommunications. M.S.
Music. M.M.
Performance and Woodwind Doubling. M.M.
Pupil Personnel Services. M.A.
School Counseling. M.A.

REED COLLEGE

Portland, Oregon 97202-8199
Web site: www.reed.edu

Founded 1911. Coed. Private control. Semester system. Library: 470,000 volumes, 1858 subscriptions.

Tuition: $2480 per unit. No housing available for graduate students. Contact the Office of Residential Life for off-campus housing. Phone: (503)777-7536.

Graduate Division

Enrollment: 19 part-time. Faculty: full-time 2 (rotated each semester). Degree conferred: M.A.L.S.

ADMISSION REQUIREMENTS. Transcripts, two letters of recommendation, interview required in support of application. M.A.L.S. applicants must complete two Reed courses before formal candidacy. TOEFL required for international applicants. Accepts transfer applicants. Apply to Graduate Studies Office. Application fee $20. Phone: (503)777-7511; fax: (503)777-7581; e-mail: admissions@reed.edu.

ADMISSION STANDARDS. Very selective.

FINANCIAL AID. Scholarships, Federal W/S, loans. Approved for VA benefits. Apply to Financial Aid Office; no specified closing date. Phone: (503)777-7223. Use FAFSA (College code: 003217).

DEGREE REQUIREMENTS. For M.A.L.S.: 39 units; admission to candidacy; final oral exam; degree paper or final project.

FIELD OF STUDY.
Liberal Studies. Interdisciplinary degree. No major within degree.

REGENT UNIVERSITY

Virginia Beach, VA 23464-9800
Web site: www.regent.edu

Founded 1977. Has branch campus located in Northern Virginia. Coed. Private control. Christian Broadcasting Network affiliation. Primarily graduate studies. Offers both campus-based classroom programs and on-line courses via Regent Worldwide Campus; some degree programs are offered only on-line and some are offered in a combination of both. Special facilities: Center for Applied Domestic and International Studies, Center for Career Advancement and Training, Center for Grassroots Politics, Center for Latin American Leadership, Institute for Christ-Centered Counseling. Library: 600,000 volumes, 1400 subscriptions. Total University enrollment: 2400.

Tuition: varies by school, see listings below. No on-campus housing available. Off-campus housing within a mile of campus. Annual average housing costs: $300–$370 per month single students; $565–$695 per month married students. Contact Regent Village, phone: (757)226-4890; fax: (757)226-4896.

Graduate School of Business

Annual tuition: $24,912 M.B.A., $25,884 E.M.B.A.; per credit $350 M.A. in Management. Enrollment: full-time 75, part-time 182. Faculty: full-time 9, part-time 6. Degrees conferred: M.B.A., E.M.B.A., P.M.B.A., M.A. in Management.

ADMISSION REQUIREMENTS, Transcripts, GMAT, Community Life Form, personal goals statement, two letters of recommendation required in support of application. On-line application available. TOEFL (minimum score 577), TWE, and official translations of transcript required for international applicants. Apply by April 1 (Fall priority date), October 15 (Spring priority date) to the Central Enrollment Management Office. Phone: (800)477-3642; fax: (757)226-4369: e-mail: admissions@regent.edu. Application fee $40.

ADMISSION STANDARDS. Selective. Usual minimum academic average: 2.75 (A = 4).

FINANCIAL AID. Scholarships, research assistantships, internships, grants, loans. Apply to the Central Financial Aid Office by August 1. Phone: (757)226-4125; fax: (757)266-4118. Use FAFSA.

DEGREE REQUIREMENTS. For M. A. in Management: 16- to 20-month, 33 credit program; culminating experience. For M.B.A.: 16- to 20-month, 48–54 full-time credit program. For P.M.B.A.: 24- to 48-month, 48 credit program (combines classroom attendance and distance education). For E.M.B.A.: 36 credit program.

FIELDS OF STUDY.
Business Administration. Includes specialization in e-business, entrepreneurship, finance and accounting, human resource management, international business, marketing, not-for-profit management, organizational change and development. M.B.A., P.M.B.A., E.M.B.A.
Management. Includes specialization in e-business, entrepreneurship, finance and accounting, human resource management, international business, marketing, not-for-profit management, organizational change and development. M.A. in Management.

School of Communication and the Arts

Tuition: per credit $800. Enrollment: full-time 148, part-time 130. Faculty: full-time 18, part-time 8, Degrees conferred: M.A., M.F.A., Ph.D

ADMISSION REQUIREMENTS. For master's candidates: transcripts, GRE or MAT, Community Life Form, personal goals statement, two letters of recommendation required in support of application. For Ph.D. candidates: master's in communication preferred, transcripts, GRE, Community Life Form, three letters of recommendation, writing sample, interview required in support of application. For distance candidates: submit résumé/vitae, computer literacy survey. On-line application available. TOEFL (minimum score 550) and official translations of transcript required for international applicant. Apply by February 15 (doctoral candidates), April 1 (Fall), October 15 (Spring) to the Central Enrollment Management Office. Application fee $40. Phone: (800)477-5504; fax: (757)226-4394: e-mail admissions@regent.edu.

ADMISSION STANDARDS. Selective. Usual minimum academic average: 2.75 (A = 4).

FINANCIAL AID, Scholarships, research assistantships, internships, grants, loans. Apply to the Central Financial Aid office by March 15 (priority deadline), April 1 (for scholarships). Phone: (757)226-4125; fax: (757)226-4118. Use FAFSA.

DEGREE REQUIREMENTS. For M.A., M.F.A.: 38 credit program; thesis/portfolio. For M.A., M.F.A.: 39 credit program; internship; comprehensive written/oral exam. For Ph.D.: at least two years in full-time residency; qualifying exam; dissertation proposal defense; dissertation; oral defense.

FIELDS OF STUDY.
Communication. Includes communication studies, cinema/T.V., design and technical theater, performance studies, script and screenwriting, theater. M.A., Ph.D.
Digital Animation. M.A.
Journalism. Includes news journalism, professional writing/magazine, journalism, public relation. M.A.
Script and Screenwriting. M.F.A.

School of Education

Tuition: per credit $379 (master's), $488 (doctoral studies). Enrollment: full-time 139, part-time 313, Faculty: full-time 13, part-time 34. Degrees conferred: M.Ed., Ed.D.

ADMISSION REQUIREMENTS. Transcripts, GRE, Community Life Form, writing sample, two letters of recommendation, interview required in support of application. On-line application available. TOEFL (minimum score 550) and official translations of transcript required for international applicant. Apply by February 15 (doctoral candidates), April 1 (Fall), October 15 (Spring) to the Central Enrollment Management Office. Application fee $40. Phone: (800)477-5504, (757)226-4498; fax: (757)226-4394: e-mail: admissions@regent.edu.

ADMISSION STANDARDS. Selective. Usual minimum academic average: 2.75 (A = 4).

FINANCIAL AID. Scholarships, tuition remission, internships, grants, loans. Apply to the Central Financial Aid Office by March 15 (priority deadline), April 1 (for scholarships). Use FAFSA.

DEGREE REQUIREMENTS. For M.Ed.: 33–45 credit programs; internship; professional project. For Ed.D.: 60 credit, 3- to 4-year full-time program; one cognate area of specialization; candidacy; comprehensive exam; culminating experience.

FIELDS OF STUDY.
Christian School. M.Ed.
Cross-Categorical Special Education. M.Ed.
Education. Includes K–12 school leadership, higher education administration, staff development/adult education, educational psychology, special education, distance education. Ed.D.
Educational Leadership. M.Ed.
Individualized Degree Plan. M.Ed.
Master Teacher Program. M.Ed.
TESOL. M.Ed.

Robertson School of Government

Tuition: per credit $450. Enrollment: full-time 60, part-time 44. Faculty: full-time 8, part-time 6. Degrees conferred: M.P.A., M.P.M., M.P.P.

ADMISSION REQUIREMENTS, Transcripts, Community Life Form, three letters of recommendation, public policy writing sample, personal essay, résumé, interview required in support of application. On-line application available. TOEFL (minimum score 550) and official translations of transcript required for international applicant. Apply by April 1 (Fall), October 15 (Spring) to the Central Enrollment Management Office. Application fee $40. Phone: (800)477-5504; fax: (757)226-4394: e-mail: admissions@regent.edu.

ADMISSION STANDARDS. Selective. Usual minimum academic average: 2.75 (A = 4).

FINANCIAL AID. Scholarships, research assistantships, internships, grants, loans, Apply to the Central Financial Aid office by March 15 (priority deadline), April 1 (for scholarships). Phone: (757)226-4125; fax: (757)226-4118. Use FAFSA.

DEGREE REQUIREMENTS. For M.P.A.: 39 credit, two-year full-time program; internship; administrative project. For M.P.M.: 39 credit, two-year full-time program. For M.P.P.: 36 credit, two-year full-time program; culminating experience.

FIELDS OF STUDY.
Government. M.A.
Political Management. Includes campaign management. M.P.M.
Public Administration. Includes leadership studies. M.P.A.
Public Policy. Includes domestic policy analysis, economic policy analysis, political philosophy, strategic leadership. M.P.P.

School of Law

Web site: www.regent.edu/acad/schlaw

Established 1986 as the successor to O. W. Coburn School of Law at Oral Roberts University. Located on main campus. ABA approved since 1989. AALS member. Private control. Semester system. Law library: 354,000 volumes, 4515 subscriptions; has LEXIS, NEXIS, WESTLAW, DIALOG, INFOTRAC, LEGAL-TRAC.

Annual tuition: full-time $16,504, part-time $13,414. Law students live off-campus. Contact Admissions Office for off-campus information. Off-campus housing and personal expenses: approximately $11,350.

Enrollment: first-year class 130, part-time 39; total 475 (men 52%, women 48%). Faculty: full-time 19, part-time 13. Student to faculty ratio 19.3 to 1. Degrees conferred: J.D., J.D.-M.B.A., J.D.-M.A. (Communications, Public Policy), LL.M. (only offered on-line), M.I.T. (only offered on-line).

ADMISSION REQUIREMENTS. LSDAS Law School report, LSAT (not later that February test date; if more than one LSAT, average is used), bachelor's degree from an accredited institution, personal statement, two recommendations, transcripts (must show all schools attended and at least three years of study) required in support of application. Applicants must have received bachelor's degree prior to enrollment. Interview not required but may be requested by School. In addition, international applicants whose native language is not English must submit TOEFL (not older that two years). Joint degree applications must apply to and be accepted to both Schools. Apply to Office of Admission after September 30, before June 1. First-year students admitted Fall only. Rolling admissions process. Application fee $40. Phone: (757)226-4584; fax: (757)226-4139; e-Mail: lawschool@regent.edu.

ADMISSION REQUIREMENTS FOR TRANSFER APPLICANTS. Accepts transfers from other ABA-accredited schools. Admission limited to space available. At least one year of enrollment, Dean's letter indicating the applicant is in good standing, prefer applicants in the upper half of first-year class, LSAT, LSDAS, personal statement regarding reason for transfer, current law school transcript required in support of School's application. Apply to Admission Office by June 15. Admission decision made by mid-July. Application fee $40. Will consider visiting students.

ADMISSION STANDARDS. Selective. Mean LSAT: full-time 149, part-time 146; mean GPA: full-time 3.15, part-time 2.90 (A = 4). *U.S. News & World Report* ranking is in the fourth tier of all U.S. law schools. Accepts 20–25% of total annual application.

FINANCIAL AID. Scholarships, merit scholarships, minority scholarships, private and institutional loans; Federal loans and Federal W/S offered through University's Financial Aid Office. Apply to University's Central Financial Aid Office after January 1, before June 1. Use FAFSA (School code: 030913), also submit

Financial Aid Transcript, Federal Income Tax forms. Approximately 90% of students receive some form of financial assistance.

DEGREE REQUIREMENTS. For J.D.: 90 (66 required) credits with a GPA of at least 2.0 (A = 4), plus completion of upper-divisional writing course; 3-year program. For LL.M., M.I.T.: 24 credit on-line programs. For J.D.-Master's: three-and-one-half- or four-year program rather than a four- or five-year program if both degrees are taken consecutively.

FIELDS OF GRADUATE STUDY.
International Taxation. LL.M., M.I.T.

School of Leadership Studies

Tuition: per credit $445 (master's), $595 (doctoral). Enrollment: full-time 180, part-time 93, Faculty: full-time 20, part-time 7. Degrees conferred: M.O.L., D.S.L., Ph.D.

ADMISSION REQUIREMENTS. Transcripts, GRE/MAT/GMAT, Community Life Form, two letters of recommendation, personal goals statement, résumé or curriculum vitae required in support of application. Three years of relevant professional experience, a master's degree, and a writing sample required for doctoral applicants. On-line application available. TOEFL (minimum score 575) and official translations of transcript required for international applicants. Apply by February 15 (doctoral applicants), April 1 (Fall), October 15 (Spring) to the Central Enrollment Management Office. Application fee $30. Phone: (800)477-5504, (757)226-4609; fax: (757)226-4394: e-mail admissions@regent.edu.

ADMISSION STANDARDS. Selective. Usual minimum academic average: 2.75 (A = 4).

FINANCIAL AID. Scholarships, research assistantships, internships, grants, loans. Apply to the Central Financial Aid office by March 15 (priority deadline), April 1 (for scholarships). Phone: (757)226-4125; fax: (757)226-4118. Use FAFSA.

DEGREE REQUIREMENTS. For M.O.L.: 33 credit program; culminating experience. For D.S.L.:. 60 credits (beyond the master's) four-year full-time program; candidacy; three residencies; culminating integrative paper; D.S.L. project. For Ph.D.: 60 credit (beyond the master's) three-year minimum full-time program; comprehensive exam; admission to candidacy; dissertation, oral defense.

FIELDS OF STUDY.
Organizational Leadership. Includes church and ministry leadership, computer-mediated communication, corporate communication leadership, leadership in business, interdisciplinary studies, leadership in education, leadership in government. M.O.L., Ph.D.
Strategic Leadership. D.S.L.

School of Psychology and Counseling

Tuition: per credit $400 (master's), $500 (doctoral Studies). Enrollment: full-time 153, part-time 63. Faculty: full-time 11, part-time 11. Degrees conferred: M.A., Psy.D., Ph.D.

ADMISSION REQUIREMENTS. For master's candidates: transcripts, GRE or MAT, Community Life Form, two letters of recommendation required in support of application. For doctoral candidates: transcripts, GRE, writing sample, Community Life Form, three letters of recommendation, interview required in support of application. A video, 10-page writing sample, personal goals statement required for Ph.D. applicants. On-line application available. TOEFL (minimum score 550) and official translations of transcript required for international applicants. Apply by February 15 (doctoral candidates), April 1 (Fall), October 15 (Spring) to the Central Enrollment Management Office. Application fee $40, $50 for doctoral applicant. Phone: (800)477-5504, (757)226-4498; fax: (757)226-4394: e-mail: admissions@regent.edu.

ADMISSION STANDARDS. Selective. Usual minimum academic average: 2.75 for M.A., 3.0 UGPA, 3.2 (A = 4) in graduate studies for doctoral candidates.

FINANCIAL AID. Scholarships, tuition remission, internships, grants, loans. Apply to the Central Financial Aid Office by March 15 (priority deadline), April 1 (for scholarships). Use FAFSA.

DEGREE REQUIREMENTS. For M.A.: 51 credit full-time program; practicum; internship. For Psy.D.: 123 credit, four- to five-year full-time program; clinical internships; dissertation, oral defense. For Ph.D.: 60 credit three- to four-year full-time program, yearlong internship; dissertation proposal defense; dissertation; oral defense.

FIELDS OF STUDY.
Clinical Psychology. Psy.D.
Counseling. Includes community, school guidance. M.A.
Counselor Education and Supervision. Ph.D.
Human Services Counseling. M.A.

RENSSELAER POLYTECHNIC INSTITUTE
Troy, New York 12180-3590
Web site: www.rpi.edu

Founded 1824. Located 10 miles N of Albany. CGS member. Coed. Private control. Special facilities: Rensselaer Design Research Center, Center for Composite Materials and Structure, Lighting Research Institute, Center for Infrastructure and Transportation Studies, Clean Room, Materials Research Center, Fresh Water Institute, G. M. Low Center for Industrial Innovation, Geo technical Centrifuge Research Center, Center for Manufacturing Productivity, Center for Integrated Electronics, Scientific Computation Center, Center for Science and Technology Policy. University-affiliated Technology Park. Library: 420,0000 volumes, 10,200 subscriptions. Total University enrollment: 7000.

Tuition: per credit $700. On-campus housing for 265 married students, unlimited housing for graduate men and women. Average academic year housing costs: $7859 for single students, per month $592–$720 for married students. Apply to Residence Life and Student Dining. Phone: (518)276-6284. Day-care facilities available.

Graduate School

Graduate study since 1826. Enrollment: full-time 1500, part-time 996. Graduate faculty: full- and part-time 370. Degrees conferred: M.Eng., M.S., M.B.A., M.F.A., M.Arch., M.Arch.I, D.Eng., Ph.D.

ADMISSION REQUIREMENTS. Two transcripts, two letters of reference in support of School's application. GRE Subject Test required for some programs, recommended for others; GMAT required for M.B.A. TOEFL required for international applicants. Interview not required. Accepts transfer applicants. Graduates of unaccredited institutions not considered. Apply by January 15 to Dean of Enrollment Management. Application fee $45. Phone: (518)276-6216; fax: (518)276-4072; e-mail: admissions@rpi.edu.

ADMISSION STANDARDS. Competitive to very selective. Usual minimum average: 3.0 (A = 4).

FINANCIAL AID. Scholarships, fellowships, teaching assistantships, tuition waivers, Federal W/S, loans. Approved for VA benefits. Apply by February 1 to Department Chair for scholarship, fellowships, assistantships; to Office of Financial Aid for all other programs. Use FAFSA. About 65% of students receive aid other than loans from Institute and outside sources. Aid available for part-time students.

DEGREE REQUIREMENTS. For master's: 30 credit hours minimum, except M.Arch., which is three-and-one-half years of study beyond master's, and M.B.A. in School of Management, which requires 60 credits; M.S. in Lighting requires 48; M.S. in Environmental Management and Policy requires 45 credits, at least 24 in residence; thesis required by some departments. For Ph.D., D.Eng.: 90 credit hours minimum beyond the bachelor's, at least 45 in residence; candidacy exam; thesis; final oral exam.

FIELDS OF STUDY.

SCHOOL OF ARCHITECTURE:
Architecture. M.Arch., M.Arch.I, M.S.
Building Sciences. M.S.
Informatics. M.S.
Lighting. M.S.

SCHOOL OF ENGINEERING:
Aeronautical Engineering.
Biomedical Engineering.
Chemical Engineering.
Civil Engineering.
Computer and Systems Engineering.
Decision Sciences and Engineering Systems.
Electrical Engineering.
Electric Power.
Engineering Physics.
Industrial and Management Engineering.
Manufacturing Systems.
Materials Engineering.
Mechanical Engineering.
Nuclear Engineering.
Operations Research and Statistics.
Transportation.

SCHOOL OF HUMANITIES AND SOCIAL SCIENCES:
Communication and Rhetoric.
Economics.
Ecological Economics, Values, and Technology.
Science and Technology.

SCHOOL OF MANAGEMENT:
Business Administration. M.B.A., M.S., Ph.D.

SCHOOL OF SCIENCE:
Biology.
Chemistry.
Computer Science.
Geology.
Mathematics.
Physics.

Rensselaer at Hartford
Hartford, Connecticut 06120-2991
Web site: www.hgc.edu

Established 1955. Located in Hartford, Groton, and Waterbury Connecticut. Coed. Library: 30,000 volumes, 535 subscriptions.

Tuition: per credit $650. No on-campus housing. Enrollment: part-time 1800 (men 68%, women 32%). Faculty: full-time 37, part-time 53. Degrees conferred: M.S., M.B.A. Certificate Programs.

ADMISSION REQUIREMENTS. Transcripts, GMAT/GRE, two letters of recommendation required in support of Center's application. Accepts transfer applicants. Graduates of unaccredited institutions not considered. Apply to Director of Admissions at least 30 days prior to the start of term. Application fee $35. Phone: (860)548-2420; fax: (860)548-7823; e-mail: mstr@hgc.edu.

ADMISSION STANDARDS. Selective. Usual minimum average: 3.0 (A = 4).

FINANCIAL AID. Grants, scholarships, research assistantships, tuition waivers, loans. Approved for VA benefits. Apply to Office of Student Affairs; no specified closing date. Use FAFSA. Aid available for part-time students.

DEGREE REQUIREMENTS. For M.S.: 30–39 credit hours minimum, at least 24 in residence; thesis/nonthesis option. For M.B.A.: 46 credit hours minimum. For certificates: minimum of four courses.

FIELDS OF STUDY.
Business Administration. M.B.A.
Computer and Systems Engineering. M.S.
Computer Science. Includes graduate certificates in bioinformatics, computer network communication, database systems, graphical user interface, information systems, software engineering. M.S.
Electrical Engineering. M.S.
Engineering. Includes graduate certificates in high-temperature materials for propulsion and power generation, pollution and waste prevention in manufacturing, quality and reliability engineering, systems modeling and analysis. M.S.
Engineering Science. M.S.
Information Technology. M.S.
Management. M.S.
Mechanical Engineering. M.S.

RHODE ISLAND COLLEGE
Providence, Rhode Island 02908-1924
Web site: www.ric.edu

Founded 1854. CGS member. Coed. State control. Semester system. Library: 540,000 volumes, 1766 subscriptions. Total College enrollment: 9000.

Annual tuition: full-time resident $3024, nonresident $6030; per credit, resident $168, nonresident $335. Limited on-campus housing for graduate students. Average academic year costs: $5715 (including board). Contact the Director of Housing for both on- and off-campus housing information. Phone: (401) 456-8240. Day-care facilities available.

Graduate Studies

Graduate study since 1924. Enrollment: full-time 285, part-time 1510. College faculty teaching graduate students: full-time 80, part-time 12. Degrees conferred: M.A., M.Ed., M.F.A., M.A.T., M.M.Ed., M.P.A., M.S.W., C.A.G.S., M.S.

ADMISSION REQUIREMENTS. Transcripts, three letters of recommendation required in support of School's application. GRE/MAT required by some programs. TOEFL required for foreign applicants. Accepts transfer applicants. Graduates of unaccredited institutions not considered. Apply to Graduate Office by April 1 (Fall), November 1 (Spring), February 1 (M.S.W. deadline). Application fee $25. Phone: (401)456-8700; fax: (401)456-8117.

ADMISSION STANDARDS. Selective for most departments. Usual minimum average: 3.0 (A = 4).

FINANCIAL AID. Fellowships, research and teaching assistantships, internships, tuition waivers, Federal W/S, loans. Approved for VA benefits. Apply by April 1 to Dean of Graduate Studies for assistantships; to Office of Financial Aid for all other programs. Phone: (401)456-8700. Use FAFSA. About 30% of students receive aid other than loans from College and outside sources. Aid available for part-time students.

DEGREE REQUIREMENTS. For master's: 30 credit hours minimum; final written comprehensive exam. For M.A. (Agency Counseling): 45 credit program. For M.A.T.: 35–45 credit programs. For M.Ed.: 36 credit program. For M.S.W.: 61 credits minimum, at least 30 in residence; individual or group thesis. For C.A.G.S.: 30 credit hours minimum beyond the master's.

FIELDS OF STUDY.
Accounting. M.P.A.
Agency Counseling. Includes alcohol and substance abuse.
Art.
Art Education.
Bilingual/Bicultural Education.
Biology.
Counselor Education.
Educational Administration. Includes elementary, secondary.
Educational Psychology.
Elementary Education. Includes early childhood education.
English.
French.
General Science.
Health Education.
History.
Industrial Technology.
Mathematics.
Media Studies.
Music.
Physical Science.
Psychology.
Reading.
Secondary Education.
Secondary School Administration.
Social Work. Includes clinical practice, organizing policy and administration.
Spanish.
Special Education. Includes behavior disorders, learning disabilities, preschool disabilities, secondary special needs, severe and profound disabilities.
Teaching English as a Second Language (TESL).
Technology Education.
Theatre.

RHODE ISLAND SCHOOL OF DESIGN
Providence, Rhode Island 02903-2784
Web site: www.risd.edu

Founded 1877. Coed. Private control. Semester system. Special facility: Museum of Art. Library: 115,000 volumes, 423 subscriptions. Total School enrollment: 2000.

Annual tuition and fees: full-time $24,300. On-campus housing available for single graduate students. Average academic year housing costs: $7038 (including board). Off-campus housing per month: $425. Contact Housing and Residence Life for on- and off-campus housing information. Phone: (401)454-6650.

Graduate Studies

Enrollment: full-time 330 (men 45%, women 55%). Faculty: full-time 51, part-time 10. Degrees conferred: M.A.Art.Ed., M.Arch., M.A.T., M.F.A., M.I.D., M.L.A.

ADMISSION REQUIREMENTS. Transcripts, full portfolio required in support of application. TOEFL required for international applicants. Interview not required, but recommended. Accepts transfer applicants. Apply to Division of Graduate Studies by February 1. Fall admission only. Application fee $45. Phone: (401)454-6300; fax: (401)454-6309; e-mail: admissions@ risd.edu.

ADMISSION STANDARDS. Competitive. Admission based on talent.

FINANCIAL AID. Grants, scholarships, assistantships, fellowships, internships, grants, Federal W/S, loans. Approved for VA benefits. Apply by February 15 to Graduate Studies Committee. Phone: (401)454-6635; fax: (401)454-6412. Use FAFSA and CSS Profile. About 30% of students receive aid from School and outside sources.

DEGREE REQUIREMENTS. For M.I.D., M.F.A., M.L.A.: 66 semester credits minimum, two years in residence; thesis. For M.A.T.: 34–37 semester credits minimum; thesis. For M.A.Art.Ed.: 33–39 semester credits minimum; thesis. M.Arch.: 111 credits, three years in residence.

FIELDS OF STUDY.
Apparel Design.
Architecture.
Art Education.
Ceramics.
Digital Media.
Film/Animation/Video.
Furniture Design.
Glass.
Graphic Design.
Illustration.
Industrial Design.
Interior Architecture.
Jewelry and Metalsmithing.
Landscape Architecture.
Painting.
Photography.
Printing.
Sculpture.
Textile Design.
Visual Arts.

UNIVERSITY OF RHODE ISLAND

Kingston, Rhode Island 02681
Web site: www.uri.edu

Founded 1888. Located 30 miles S of Providence. CGS member. Coed. State control. Semester system. Special facilities: Biotechnology Center, Research Center in Business, Child Development Center, Center for Energy Studies, Institute of Human Sciences and Services, Labor Research Center, International Center for Marine Resource Development, Marriage and Family Center, Center for Ocean Management, Robotics Research Center. Library: 955,000 volumes, 7966 subscriptions.

Annual tuition: full-time, resident $3636, nonresident $10,390. On-campus housing for single and married students. Average academic year housing costs: $6384 (including board) for single students; $8328 for married students. Contact Residential Life Office for both on- and off-campus housing information. Phone: (401)874-2935. Day-care facilities available.

Graduate School

Enrollment: full-time 1296, part-time 2642. Faculty: full-time 659, part-time 10. Degrees conferred: M.A., M.S., M.O., M.P.A., M.C.P., E.M.B.A., M.B.A., M.L.I.S., M.M.A., M.M., Ph.D.

ADMISSION REQUIREMENTS. Two official transcripts, three letters of recommendation required in support of School's application. GRE or MAT required for most departments, GRE Subject Test for some departments, GMAT for business programs. Interview required in some programs. TOEFL required of international students. Accepts transfer applicants. Graduates of unaccredited colleges not considered. Apply to Dean of Graduate School by April 15 (Fall), November 15 (Spring). Earlier dates in some programs. Application fee $35. Phone: (401)874-2262; fax: (401)874-5491.

ADMISSION STANDARDS. Very competitive to selective. Usual minimum average: 2.75 (A = 4).

FINANCIAL AID. Scholarships, fellowships, diversity fellowships, teaching/research assistantships, tuition waivers, Federal W/S, loans. Approved for VA benefits. Apply by February 15 to Dean for scholarships and fellowships; to appropriate departments for assistantships; to Financial Aid Office for all other programs. Phone: (401)874-2314. Use FAFSA. Aid available for part-time students.

DEGREE REQUIREMENTS. For master's: 30 credits minimum, at least 24 in residence; thesis with oral defense (6 credits) for most departments, or nonthesis with major paper; comprehensive exam. For Ph.D.: 72 credits minimum beyond the bachelor's, at least 24 in full-time residence or two consecutive semesters in full-time attendance; preliminary exam; proficiency in research tool/foreign language required in some programs; dissertation; final oral exam.

FIELDS OF STUDY.
Accounting. M.S.
Adult Education. M.A.
Applied Mathematics. Ph.D.
Applied Pharmaceutical Sciences. M.S., Ph.D.
Applied Probability. Ph.D.
Audiology. M.S.
Biochemistry. M.S.
Biological Sciences. M.S., Ph.D.
Business Administration. M.B.A., Ph.D.
Chemical Engineering. M.S., Ph.D.
Chemistry. M.S., Ph.D.
Civil and Environmental Engineering. M.S., Ph.D.
Clinical Laboratory Science. M.S.
Clinical Psychology. Ph.D.
College Student Personnel. M.S.
Communication Studies. M.A.
Community Planning. M.C.P.
Computer Science. M.S., Ph.D.
Economics. M.A.
Education. Ph.D.
Electrical Engineering. M.S., Ph.D.
Elementary Education. M.A., M.S.
English. M.A., Ph.D.
Entomology. M.S., Ph.D.
Environmental and Natural Resources Economics. M.S., Ph.D.
Experimental Psychology. Ph.D.
Finance. M.B.A.
Fisheries, Animal, and Veterinary Science. M.S., Ph.D.
Food Science and Nutrition. Ph.D.
French. M.A.
Geosciences. M.S., Ph.D.
History. M.A.
Human Development and Family Studies. M.S.
Industrial and Manufacturing Engineering. Ph.D.
International Business. M.B.A.
International Sports Management. M.B.A.
Labor and Industrial Relations. M.S.
Library and Information Studies. M.L.I.S. only.
Management. M.B.A.
Manufacturing Engineering. M.S.

Marine Affairs. M.A., M.M.A., Ph.D.
Marketing. M.B.A.
Marriage and Family Therapy. M.S.
Mathematics. M.S., Ph.D.
Mechanical Engineering and Applied Mechanics. M.S., Ph.D.
Medicinal Chemistry. M.S., Ph.D.
Microbiology. M.S., Ph.D.
Music. M.M.
Natural Resources Science. M.S., Ph.D.
Nursing. Includes nursing service administration, teaching of nursing. M.S., Ph.D.
Nutrition and Food Sciences. M.S.
Ocean Engineering. M.S., Ph.D.
Oceanography. M.O., M.S., Ph.D.
Operations Research. Ph.D.
Pharmaceutics. M.S.
Pharmacognosy. M.S., Ph.D.
Pharmacology and Toxicology. M.S., Ph.D.
Pharmacy Administration. M.S.
Physical Education. M.S.
Physical Therapy. M.S.
Physics. M.S., Ph.D.
Political Science. M.A.
Public Administration. M.P.A.
Reading Education. M.A.
School Psychology. M.S., Ph.D.
Secondary Education. M.A.
Spanish. M.A.
Speech-Language Pathology. M.S.
Statistics. M.S., Ph.D.
Textiles, Fashion Merchandising, and Design. M.S.

RICE UNIVERSITY
Houston, Texas 77005-1892
Web site: www.rice.edu

Founded 1912. CGS and AAU member. Coed. Private control. Semester system. Special facilities: James A. Baker III Institute for Public Policy, Center for Applied Psychological Systems, Center for Biological and Environmental Nanotechnology, Center for Chemical Processing Technology, Center for Computational Geophysics, Center for High Performance Software Research, Center for the History of Leadership Institutions, Center for Medical Ethics and Health Policy, Center for Multimedia Communication, Center for Nanoscale Science and Technology, Center for the Study of Cultures, Center for the Study of Environment and Society, Center for the Study of Institutions and Values, Center for the Study of Languages, Center for Sustainability in the Built Environment, Center for Technology in Teaching and Learning, Center for Urbanism, Center on the Management of Information Technology, Computer and Information Technology Institute, Environmental and Energy Systems Institute, Goethe Center for Central European Studies, Hazardous Substances Research Center/South and Southwest, Institute of Biosciences and Bioengineering, National Center for Ground Water Research, W. M. Keck Center for Computational Biology, Rice Center for Organizational Effectiveness Studies, Rice Quantum Institute, Texas Center for Crystallography. Library: 2,000,000 volumes, 14,000 subscriptions.

Annual tuition: full-time $16,700, part-time per credit $930. On-campus housing available for graduate students. Average housing costs: $380–$665 for single students, $485–$665 (room only) for married students. Contact the Housing Office for both on- and off-campus information. Phone: (713)348-1096.

Graduate Division

Enrollment: full-time, 1587 (men 65%, women 35%); part-time 56. University faculty: full-time 434, part-time 150. Degrees conferred: M.A., M.B.A., M.M., M.Arch., M.S., M.Stat., D.Arch., D.M.A., Ph.D.

ADMISSION REQUIREMENTS. Transcripts, three letters of recommendation, GRE or GMAT required in support of application. On-line application available. TOEFL required for foreign applicants. Interview not required. Accepts transfer applicants. Graduates of unaccredited institutions not considered. Apply to Dean by February 1. Most students enter Fall semester. Application fee $25. Phone: (713)348-4002.

ADMISSION STANDARDS. Competitive. Usual minimum average: 3.0 (A = 4).

FINANCIAL AID. Scholarships, fellowships, research assistantships, teaching assistantships, internships, tuition waivers, Federal W/S, loans. Approved for VA benefits. Apply by February 1 to appropriate department chair for fellowships, assistantships; to Financial Aid Office for all other programs. Phone: (713)348-4958. Use FAFSA. About 90% of all thesis students receive aid other than loans from University and outside sources. No aid for part-time students.

DEGREE REQUIREMENTS. For master's: 30 semester hours minimum, at least 24 in residence; qualifying exam; final oral exam; thesis/nonthesis option. For M.M.: 43–57 semester hours, at least 36 in residence. For M.B.A.: a minimum of two years in residence. For Ph.D., D.Arch.: 90 credit program, normally three or more years beyond the bachelor's degree, at least two years in full-time residence; qualifying exam; candidacy; final oral exam; thesis.

FIELDS OF STUDY.

SCHOOL OF ARCHITECTURE:
Architecture. M.Arch., D. Arch.
Urban Design. M.Arch.

GEORGE R. BROWN SCHOOL OF ENGINEERING:
Bioengineering. M.S., Ph.D.
Chemical Engineering. M.Ch.E., M.S., Ph.D.
Civil and Environmental Engineering. M.C.E., M.E.E., M.E.S., M.S., Ph.D.
Computational and Applied Mathematics. M.C.A.M., M.C.S.E., M.A., Ph.D.
Computer Science. M.C.S., M.S., Ph.D.
Electrical and Computer Engineering. M.E.E., M.S. Ph.D.
Mechanical Engineering and Materials Sciences. M.M.E., M.M.S., M.S., Ph.D.
Statistics. M.Stat., M.A., Ph.D.

SCHOOL OF HUMANITIES:
English. M.A., Ph.D.
French Studies. M.A., Ph.D.
Hispanic and Classical Studies. M.A.
History. M.A., Ph.D.
Linguistics. Ph.D.
Philosophy. M.A., Ph.D.
Religious Studies. M.A., Ph.D.

JESSE H. JONES GRADUATE SCHOOL OF MANAGEMENT:
Business Administration. Includes informal concentrations in accounting, entrepreneurship, finance, general management, international business, information technology, marketing, operations management, organizational behavior and human resource management, health-care management, strategic management and planning. M.B.A., M.B.A. for Executives.

SHEPHERD SCHOOL OF MUSIC:
Composition. M.Mus.
Choral and Instrumental Conducting. M.Mus.

Historical Musicology. M.Mus.
Music Theory. M.Mus.
Performance. M.Mus.

WIESS SCHOOL OF NATURAL SCIENCES:
Biochemistry and Cell Biology. M.A., Ph.D.
Chemistry. M.A., Ph.D.
Ecology and Evolutionary Biology. M.A., Ph.D.
Earth Science. M.A., Ph.D.
Mathematics. M.A., Ph.D.
Physics and Astronomy. M.A., M.S., Ph.D.

SCHOOL OF SOCIAL SCIENCES:
Anthropology. M.A., Ph.D.
Economics. M.A., Ph.D.
Political Science. M.A., Ph.D.
Psychology. M.A., Ph.D.

INTERDEPARTMENTAL PROGRAMS:
Applied Physics. Master's, Ph.D.
Computational Science and Engineering. Master's, Ph.D.
Environmental Analysis and decision Making. Master's.
Material Science and Engineering. Master's, Ph.D.
Nanoscale Physics. Master's.
Systems Theory. Master's, Ph.D.

COOPERATIVE PROGRAMS:
Biomedical Ethics. With University of Texas Health Science Center at Houston. M.A. Ph.D.
Computational Biology. With Baylor College of Medicine and University of Houston. Ph.D.

UNIVERSITY OF RICHMOND

Richmond, Virginia 23173
Web site: www.richmond.edu

Founded 1830. Private control. Baptist affiliation. Semester system. Library: 716,677 volumes, 3579 subscriptions. Total University enrollment: 4700.

Annual tuition: full-time $22,360, per credit $400 for first course, then $1010 for additional credits. No on-campus housing available.

Arts and Sciences Graduate School

Graduate study since 1921. Enrollment: full-time 45, part-time 60. Faculty: full-time 105, part-time 8. Degrees conferred: M.A., M.L.A., M.S.

ADMISSION REQUIREMENTS. Transcripts, three letters of recommendation, statement of purpose, GRE/GMAT required in support of School's application. TOEFL (minimum score 550) required of international students. Interview not required. Transfer applicants considered. Graduates of unaccredited institutions not considered. Apply to Graduate School by March 15 (Fall). Application fee $30. Phone: (804)289-8417; fax: (804)289-8818.

ADMISSION STANDARDS. Selective for most departments. Usual minimum average: 3.0 (A = 4).

FINANCIAL AID. Tuition remission program for full-time students; special tuition rates for part-time students. Fellowships, academic scholarships, teaching and research assistantships, Federal W/S, loans. Approved for VA benefits. Apply by March 15 to Dean of Graduate School for assistantships, scholarships; to the Office of Financial Aid for all other programs. Phone: (804)289-8438. Use FAFSA. About 60% of full-time students receive aid other than loans from University and outside sources.

DEGREE REQUIREMENTS. For M.A., M.S.: 27–36 semester hours; thesis/nonthesis; comprehensive exam. For M.L.A.: 30 hours minimum; thesis/nonthesis option.

FIELDS OF STUDY.
Biology.
English.
History.
Liberal Arts. Cross-disciplinary.
Psychology.

The E. Claiborne Robins School of Business— Graduate Division

Annual tuition: $22,360. Enrollment: full-time 10, part-time 262. Faculty: full-time 39, part-time 10. Degree conferred: M.B.A.

ADMISSION REQUIREMENTS. Transcripts, three letters of recommendation, statement of purpose, GMAT required in support of School's application. TOEFL required of international students. Interview not required. Transfer applicants considered. Graduates of unaccredited institutions not considered. Apply to Graduate Division by May 1 (Fall), November 1 (Spring). Roll ing admissions process. Application fee $25. Phone: (804)289-8553; fax: (804)287-6544.

ADMISSION STANDARDS. Selective. Mean GMAT: 617; mean GPA: 3.0 (A = 4). Usual minimum average: 2.75 (A = 4).

FINANCIAL AID. Assistantships, loans. Approved for VA benefits. Apply to Financial Aid Office; no specified closing date. Use FAFSA (School code: 003744). Phone: (804)289-8438. About 60% of full-time students receive aid other than loans from University and outside sources. Aid available for part-time students.

DEGREE REQUIREMENTS. For M.B.A.: 30–51 semester hours minimum; degree program must be completed in 5 years.

FIELD OF STUDY.
Business Administration.

T. C. Williams School of Law

Established 1870. ABA approved since 1928. AALS member. Semester system. Special facility: Alternative Dispute Resolution Center. Law library: 294,542 volumes, 4265 subscriptions; has LEXIS, NEXIS, WESTLAW, DIALOG, VU/TEXT.

Annual tuition: $20,740. Limited on-campus housing for single students. Total average annual additional expense: $11,690.

Enrollment: first-year class 161; total full-time 461 (men 52%, women 48%). School faculty: full-time 24, part-time 45. Student to faculty ratio 16 to 1. Degrees conferred: J.D., J.D.-M.B.A., J.D.-M.H.A., J.D.-M.S.W., J.D.-M.U.S.P.

ADMISSION REQUIREMENTS. LSDAS Law School report, bachelor's degree, transcripts, LSAT required in support of application. Personal interviews optional. Accepts transfer applicants. Graduates of unaccredited institutions not considered. Apply to School after September 1, before January 15. Admits beginning students Fall only. Application fee $35. Phone: (804) 289-8189.

ADMISSION STANDARDS. Selective. Mean LSAT: 158; mean GPA: 3.11 (A = 4). *U.S. News & World Report* ranking is in the fourth tier of all U.S. law schools. Accepts 20–25% of total annual applicants.

FINANCIAL AID. Scholarships, assistantships, Federal W/S, loans. Apply to Financial Aid Office by February 25. Phone: (804)289-3438. Use FAFSA (School code: 030913). About 50% of students receive aid other than loans from School.

DEGREE REQUIREMENTS. For J.D.: satisfactory completion of three-year program; 86 semester hours minimum. For master's degrees, see Graduate School listing above.

Note: Summer programs in Cambridge (Great Britain), and an exchange program with the University of Paris.

RIDER UNIVERSITY
Trenton, New Jersey 08648-3001
Web site: www.rider.edu

Founded 1865. Coed. Private control. Semester system. Library: 394,000 volumes, 2763 subscriptions.

Tuition: per credit, $470. On-campus housing for single students available. Average housing costs: $3648, $6908 (including board). Contact Graduate Housing Office for both on- and off-campus housing information. Phone: (609)896-5102.

Graduate Studies

Enrollment: full-time 209, part-time 887. Faculty: full-time 75, part-time 63. Degrees conferred: M.A., M.Acc., M.B.A., M.M.

ADMISSION REQUIREMENTS. Official Transcript, two professional recommendations required in support of application. GMAT and Audition required for some programs. On-line application available. TOEFL required for international applicants. Accepts transfer applicants. Graduates of unaccredited institutions not considered. Apply to Director of Graduate Services at least one month prior to registration. Rolling admissions process. Application fee $35. Phone: (609)896-5036; fax: (609)896-5261.

ADMISSION STANDARDS. Selective. Usual minimum average: 2.5 (A = 4).

FINANCIAL AID. Fellowships, research assistantships, teaching assistantships, internships, Federal W/S, loans. Approved for VA benefits. Apply by April 1 to the Director of Financial Aid. Phone: (609)896-5360. Use FAFSA.

DEGREE REQUIREMENTS. For M.A., M.Acc.: 33–36 credit hours minimum, depending on program; thesis/nonthesis option. For M.B.A.: 30–57 credit hours, depending on previous degree and number of foundation courses waived. For M.M.: 30–36 credit hours minimum; thesis/nonthesis option/recital. For Ed.S.: 30 credit program; special project.

FIELDS OF STUDY.

COLLEGE OF BUSINESS ADMINISTRATION:
Accountancy. M.Acc.
Business Administration. M.B.A.

SCHOOL OF GRADUATE EDUCATION AND HUMAN SERVICES:
Counseling Services. M.A., Ed.S.
Curriculum, Instruction, and Supervision. M.A.
Education Administration. M.A.
Human Services Administration. M.A.
Reading Language Arts. M.A.
School Psychology. Ed.S.
Special Education. M.A.

WESTMINSTER CHOIR COLLEGE OF RIDER UNIVERSITY:
Choral Conducting. M.M.
Composition. M.M.
Music Education. M.M., M.M.Ed.
Organ Performance. M.M.
Piano Accompanying and Coaching. M.M.

Sacred Music. M.M.
Voice Pedagogy and Performance. M.M.

RIVIER COLLEGE
Nashua, New Hampshire 03060-5086
Web site: www.rivier.edu

Founded 1933. Located NW of Boston. Coed. Private control—Roman Catholic. Semester system. Library: 150,000 volumes, 1800 subscriptions.

Tuition: per credit $360; Nursing $563. No on-campus housing for graduate students.

School of Graduate Studies

Enrollment: full-time 125, part-time 478 (men 40%, women 60%). Graduate faculty: full-time 28, part-time 43. Degrees conferred: M.A., M.B.A., M.A.T., M.Ed., M.S., C.A.G.S.

ADMISSION REQUIREMENTS. Transcripts, three letters of recommendation, personal statement required in support of School's application. On-line application available. MAT required for education applicants. TOEFL required for international applicants. Accepts transfer applicants. Apply to Office of Graduate Admission by August 1 (Fall), November 30 (Spring). Application fee $25. Phone: (603)897-8219; fax: (603)897-8810; e-mail: gadmissions@rivier.edu

ADMISSION STANDARDS. Selective. Usual minimum average: 2.75 (A = 4).

FINANCIAL AID. Limited to assistantships, Federal W/S, loans. Approve for VA benefits. Phone: (603)897-8510. Use FAFSA. Aid available for part-time students.

DEGREE REQUIREMENTS. For M.A., M.S., M. Ed.: 30 semester hours minimum including thesis, or 33 hours without thesis; final written exam. For M.B.A.: 36–45 semester hours. For C.A.G.S.: 30 credit program beyond master's.

FIELDS OF STUDY.
Business Administration. Includes accounting, marketing, quality management. M.B.A.
Clinical Mental Health Counseling. M.Ed.
Computer Information System. M.S.
Computer Science. M.S.
Counselor Education. M.Ed.
Curriculum and Instruction. M.Ed.
Early Childhood Education. M.Ed.
Educational Administration. M.Ed.
Elementary Education. M.Ed.
Elementary Education and General Special Education. M.Ed.
Elementary Education and Learning Disabilities. M.Ed.
Educational Studies. M.Ed.
Emotional and Behavior Disabilities. M.Ed.
English. M.A.T.
Health Care Administration. M.B.A.
Human Resource Management. M.S.
Learning Disabilities. M.Ed.
Learning Disabilities and Reading. M.Ed.
Mathematics Education. M.A.T.
Nursing. Includes family nursing, nurse education, psychiatric mental health nursing. M.S.
Reading. M.Ed.
Secondary Education. M.Ed.
Social Studies. M.A.T.
Spanish. M.A.T.
Writing and Literature. M.A., M.A.T.

ROBERT MORRIS COLLEGE

Moon Township, Pennsylvania 15108-1189
Web site: www.robert-morris.edu

Founded 1921. A second campus is located in downtown Pittsburgh. Coed. Private control. Semester system. Library: 212,000 volumes, 853 subscriptions. Total College enrollment: 4500.

Tuition: per credit $370; Instructional Leadership and Business Education $336; Taxation $387; D.Sc. a flat fee of $15,000. Limited on-campus housing available. Annual average housing cost: $3720, $6320 (including board). Contact Housing Office for both on- and off-campus housing information. Phone: (412)262-8408.

Graduate Studies

Enrollment: 846 part-time. Faculty: full-time 25, part-time 28. Degrees conferred: M.B.A., M.S., D.Sc.

ADMISSION REQUIREMENTS. Official transcript, two professional recommendations required in support of application. On-line application available. GMAT strongly recommended. Interview required for M.S. in Communication and Information Systems and D.Sc. Accepts transfer applicants. Apply to Office of Graduate Admission at least two months prior to registration. Application fee $25. Phone: (800)762-0097; fax (412)299-2425.

ADMISSION STANDARDS. Selective. Usual minimum average: 2.5 (A = 4)

FINANCIAL AID. Limited to assistantships, loans. Apply to the Financial Aid Office; no specified closing date. Use FAFSA. Aid available for part-time students.

DEGREE REQUIREMENTS. For M.S.; 33–36 credit hours minimum, depending on program. For M.B.A.: 30–57 credit hours, depending on previous degree and number of foundation courses waived. For D.Sc.: 60 credit program; doctoral candidacy; field project.

FIELDS OF STUDY.
Accounting. M.S.
Business Administration. M.B.A.
Business Education. M.S.
Computer and Information Systems. M.B.A., M.S.
Finance. M.S.
Information Systems and Communication. D.Sc.
Information Systems Management. M.S.
Instructional Leadership. M.S.
Internet Information Systems. M.S.
Management. M.S.
Marketing. M.S.
Sport Management. M.S.
Taxation. M.S.

ROCHESTER INSTITUTE OF TECHNOLOGY

Rochester, New York 14623-5604
Web site: www.rit.edu

Founded 1829. CGS member. Coed. Private control. Quarter system. Special facilities: Chester F. Carlson Center for Imagining Science, Center for Excellence in Mathematics, Science, and Technology, Center for Integrated Manufacturing Studies. Library: 354,000 volumes, 4300 subscriptions. Total Institute enrollment: 14,750.

Annual tuition: full-time $20,928; part-time $587 per quarter hour. On-campus housing for married students on space-available basis. Annual housing costs: $6996 (including board). Apply to Center for Residence Life for on- and off-campus housing information. Phone: (716)475-8815 (on-campus), (716)475-2575 (off-campus).

Graduate Studies

Graduate study since 1959. Enrollment: full-time 846, part-time 1159. Institute faculty: full-time 500, part-time varies by quarter. Degrees conferred: M.B.A., M.E., M.F.A., M.S., M.S.T., Ph.D.

ADMISSION REQUIREMENTS. Transcripts, personal statement, letters of recommendation required in support of application. On-line application available. GMAT required for M.B.A.; GRE, MAT for some programs. Slide portfolio for some programs. Evidence of proficiency in English (TOEFL or Michigan Test of English administered at RIT) required of international students. Interview required for some departments. Accepts transfer applicants. Apply to Office of Graduate Enrollment Services by March 1; some programs have earlier deadlines. Application fee $50. Phone: (716)475-7284; fax: (716)475-7464; e-mail: gradinfo@rit.edu.

ADMISSION STANDARDS. Selective. Usual minimum average varies by department.

FINANCIAL AID. Annual awards from institutional funds: scholarships, research and teaching assistantships, tuition waivers, Federal W/S, loans. Approved for VA benefits. For scholarships, apply at time of admission to appropriate department head and to Dean of Graduate Studies (but not later that March 15); to Financial Aid Office for all other programs. Phone: (716)475-2186. Use FAFSA. Loans are also available under New York State's Supplemental Higher Education Loan Financing Program. Aid available for part-time students.

DEGREE REQUIREMENTS. For M.S.: 45–72 quarter hours minimum. For M.F.A.: 85–90 quarter hours minimum. For M.S.T.: 48 quarter hours minimum. For M.B.A.: 76 quarter hours minimum. For M.E.: 48 quarter hours minimum. Thesis required for some programs. Ph.D.: as determined by committee review.

FIELDS OF STUDY.
Accounting. M.B.A.
Applied Statistics. M.S.
Art Education. M.S.T. only.
Business Administration. M.B.A.
Career and Human Resource Development. M.S.
Ceramics and Ceramic Sculpture. M.F.A., M.S.T.
Chemistry. M.S.
Clinical Chemistry. M.S.
Communication and Media Technologies. M.S.
Computer Graphics Design. M.F.A.
Computer Integrated Manufacturing. M.S.
Computer Engineering. M.S.
Computer Science. M.S.
Computer Science and Information Technology. M.S.
Electrical Engineering. M.S.
Engineering Management. M.S.
Environmental Health and Safety Management. M.S.
Finance. M.S.
Fine Studio Arts. M.F.A.
Glass and Glass Sculpture. M.F.A.
Graphic Arts Publishing. M.S.
Graphic Art Systems. M.S.
Graphic Design. M.F.A.
Hospitality Tourism Management. M.S.
Human Resource Development. M.S.
Imagining Arts/Computer Animation and Film. M.F.A.
Imaging Arts/Photography. M.F.A.

Industrial Design. M.F.
Industrial Engineering. M.E.
Information Technology. M.S.
International Business. M.B.A.
Instructional Technology. M.S.
Manufacturing Management and Leadership. M.S.
Materials Science and Engineering. M.S.
Mechanical Engineering. M.S.
Medical Illustration. M.F.A.
Microelectronics Manufacturing Engineering. M.E.
Packaging Science. M.S.
Photography. M.F.A.
Printing Technology. M.S.
Product Development. M.S.
Public Policy. M.S.
School Psychology. M.S.
Secondary Education of Students Who Are Deaf and Hard of Hearing. M.S.
Service Management. M.S.
Software Development and Management. M.S.
Systems Engineering. M.E.

UNIVERSITY OF ROCHESTER
Rochester, New York 14627-0250
Web site: www.rochester.edu

The University of Rochester, established in 1850, is independent and coeducational, and operates on a semester system. CGS and AAU member. Three of the University's 6 schools and colleges are on the River Campus. The School of Medicine and Dentistry and the School of Nursing are within a 5-minute walk, and the Eastman School of Music is 2 miles away. Special facilities include a large biology-chemistry-mathematics complex, a nuclear structure research laboratory with a 24-MeV tandem Van Degraaff accelerator, the Mees Observatory (at the highest location in the eastern United States), an atomic energy ERDA project (radiation biology and biophysics), a well-staffed computing center, campus-wide access to the Internet, and several hundred microcomputers linked to the campus network, the Managerial Economics Research Center, Center for Environmental Health Sciences, the New York State Center for Optical Technology, Center for Photoinduced Charge Transfer, Center for Superconductive Circuits, the Center for Visual Science, the Laboratory for Laser Energetics, Center for Research in Government Policy and Business. The University's NIH ranking is 37th among all U.S. institutions with 394 awards/grants worth $121,953,760. Library: 3,000,000 volumes, 11,254 subscriptions. Total University enrollment: 9000.

Tuition: per credit $795, Simon School $1010; Eastman School of Music $820. On-campus housing available; contact Housing Coordinator. Phone: (716)275-5521.

Graduate Studies

Graduate study since 1851. Enrollment: full-time 2300, part-time 700. Graduate faculty: full-time 1000, part-time 200. Degrees conferred: M.A., M.S., M.B.A., M.H.P., M.M., M.A.T., Ed.D., D.M.A., Ph.D.

ADMISSION REQUIREMENTS. Transcripts, three letters of recommendation required in support of application. GRE Subject Tests, GMAT recommended. TOEFL required for international applicants. Accepts transfer applicants. Graduates of unaccredited institutions not considered. Apply by February 1 to department offering specific degree program. Application fee $25 (Simon School $75). Phone: (716)275-2121 (general information number).

ADMISSION STANDARDS. Competitive. Usual minimum average: 3.0 (A = 4).

FINANCIAL AID. Most Ph.D. candidates receive grants, assistantships, or fellowships. For M.A., M.S., M.M., D.M.A., M.B.A. candidates: scholarships, fellowships, tuition waivers, Federal W/S, loans. Approved for VA benefits. To be eligible for aid, new students must apply by February 1. Phone: (585)275-3226. Use FAFSA. Phone appropriate department for information regarding assistantships, fellowships.

DEGREE REQUIREMENTS. For M.A., M.A.T.: 30 semester hours minimum, at least 20 in residence; thesis; final oral exam; for nonthesis option, master's essay for some departments; comprehensive exam. For M.B.A.: 64–67 semester hours minimum, at least 48 semester hours in residence; comprehensive exam; thesis not required. For M.S.: 36–39 credit programs. For Ed.D.: 90 semester hours minimum beyond the bachelor's, comprehensive exam; dissertation; final oral exam. For Ph.D.: 90 semester hours beyond the bachelor's degree or 60 semester hours minimum beyond the master's, at least two consecutive semesters in full-time residence; competence in foreign languages required by some departments; written/oral qualifying exam; dissertation; final oral exam. For D.M.A.: 60 semester hours minimum beyond the master's, at least one year in full-time residence; demonstrated proficiency in performance; oral/written exam; qualifying exam; dissertation; final oral exam. For joint M.D.-Ph.D.: same requirements for both programs individually, although course work and research may overlap.

FIELDS OF STUDY.

COLLEGE OF ARTS AND SCIENCES:
Applied Mathematics. M.S.
Biology. M.S., Ph.D.
Brain and Cognitive Sciences. M.A., Ph.D.
Chemistry. M.S., Ph.D.
Clinical Psychology. Ph.D.
Computer Science. M.S., Ph.D.
Developmental Psychology. Ph.D. (Through the Department of Clinical and Social Psychology.)
Developmental Psychology. Ph.D. (Through the Department of Brain and Cognitive Sciences.)
Economics. M.A., Ph.D.
English. M.A., Ph.D.
Geological Sciences. M.S., Ph.D.
History. M.A., Ph.D.
Mathematics. M.A., Ph.D.
Mathematics—Statistics. M.A.
Philosophy. M.A., Ph.D.
Physics. M.A., M.S., Ph.D.
Physics and Astronomy. Ph.D.
Political Science. M.A., Ph.D.
Public Policy Analysis. M.S.
Social-Personality Psychology. Ph.D.
Statistics. M.A., Ph.D.
Visual and Cultural Studies. M.A., Ph.D.

SCHOOL OF ENGINEERING AND APPLIED SCIENCES:
Biomedical Engineering. M.S., Ph.D.
Chemical Engineering. M.S., Ph.D.
Electrical Engineering. M.S., Ph.D.
Materials Science. M.S., Ph.D.
Mechanical Engineering. M.S., Ph.D.
Optics. M.S., Ph.D.

EASTMAN SCHOOL OF MUSIC:
Conducting. D.M.A.
Conducting (Choral). M.M.
Jazz Studies and Contemporary Media. M.M.
Music Composition. M.A,, M.M., D.M.A., Ph.D.
Music Education. M.A., M.M., D.M.A., Ph.D.
Music Theory. M.A., Ph.D.
Musicology. M.A., Ph.D.

Pedagogy of Music Theory. M.A.
Performance and Literature. M.M., D.M.A.
Piano Accompanying and Chamber Music. M.M., D.M.A.

MARGARET WARNER GRADUATE SCHOOL OF EDUCATION
AND HUMAN DEVELOPMENT:

Counseling and Counselor Education. Ed.D.
Counseling and Human Development. Includes school and community counselors. M.S., Ph.D.
Educational Leadership. Includes school administration, higher education. M.S., Ph.D.
Elementary Teacher Education. M.S.
Secondary Education. Includes biology, chemistry, earth science, English, French, German, mathematics, physics, social studies, Spanish. M.S.
Secondary Education. Includes biology, chemistry, earth science, English, French, German, mathematics, physics, social studies, Spanish. M.A.T. (Offered jointly with the College.)
Teaching and Curriculum. Includes elementary, secondary, TESOL. M.S., Ph.D.

SCHOOL OF MEDICINE AND DENTISTRY:

Biochemistry. M.S., Ph.D.
Biophysics. M.S., Ph.D.
Dental Sciences. M.S.
Epidemiology. Ph.D.
Genetics. M.S., Ph.D.
Health Services Research and Policy. Ph.D.
Marriage and Family Therapy. M.S.
Medical Statistics. M.S.
Medicine. M.D.
Microbiology. M.S.
Microbiology and Immunology. Ph.D.
Neuroscience. M.S., Ph.D.
Pathology. M.S., Ph.D.
Pharmacology. M.S., Ph.D.
Physiology. M.S., Ph.D.
Public Health. M.P.H.
Statistics. M.A., Ph.D.
Toxicology. M.S., Ph.D.

SCHOOL OF NURSING:

Nursing. M.S., Ph.D., M.S.-Ph.D.

WILLIAM E. SIMON GRADUATE SCHOOL
OF BUSINESS ADMINISTRATION:

Business Administration. Includes specializations in accounting and information systems, business and public policy, competitive and organizational strategy, computers and information systems, corporate accounting, electronic commerce, entrepreneurship, finance, health sciences management, international management, marketing, operations management—manufacturing, operations management—service, public accounting. M.B.A., Ph.D.
Finance. M.S.
Information Management. M.S.
Manufacturing Management. M.S.
Service Management. M.S.
Technology Transfer and Commercialization. M.S.

School of Medicine and Dentistry (14642)

Web site: www.urmc.rochester.edu

Founded 1920. Annual tuition: $21,500; student fees $1310. On-campus housing available for married, single students. Apply to the Housing Coordinator, Medical Center. Total average figure for all other expenses: $6964.

Enrollment: first-year class 100; total full-time 703 (men 41%, women 59%); postgraduates 370. Faculty: full-time 800, part-time 72. Degrees conferred: M.D., M.D.-M.B.A., M.D.-M.P.H., M.D.-Ph.D. (Medical Scientist Training Program), M.S., Ph.D. Graduate study only in dentistry; no D.D.S.

ADMISSION REQUIREMENTS. For M.D.: transcripts, letters of recommendation, personal statement, MCAT, required in support of application. Applicants must have completed at least three years of college study. Interview by invitation only. Does not have EDP. Does not accept transfer or foreign applicants. Apply to Director of Admission (Medical Center Box 601A) after June 1, before October 15. Application fee $60. Phone: (585)275-4539; fax: (585)756-5479.

ADMISSION STANDARDS. For M.D.: very competitive. Mean MCAT: 10.1; mean GPA: 3.62 (A = 4). Gourman rating: 4.68. *U.S. News & World Report* ranking is 28th among all U.S. medical schools. Accepts 5% of total annual applicants. Approximately 35% are state residents.

FINANCIAL AID. For M.D.: scholarships, loans. Apply to Financial Aid Office. Phone: (585)275-4523. MSTP funded by NIH. Use FAFSA (School code: G24601). About 80% of students receive some aid from School.

DEGREE REQUIREMENTS. For M.D.: satisfactory completion of four-year program. For M.S., Ph.D., see Graduate Studies above.

FIELDS OF GRADUATE STUDY.

Biochemistry. M.S., Ph.D.
Biophysics. M.S., Ph.D.
Dental Sciences. M.S.
Epidemiology. Ph.D.
Genetics. M.S., Ph.D.
Health Services Research and Policy. Ph.D.
Marriage and Family Therapy. M.S.
Medical Statistics. M.S.
Medicine. M.D.
Microbiology. M.S.
Microbiology and Immunology. Ph.D.
Neuroscience. M.S., Ph.D.
Pathology. M.S., Ph.D.
Pharmacology. M.S., Ph.D.
Physiology. M.S., Ph.D.
Public Health. M.P.H.
Statistics. M.A., Ph.D.
Toxicology. M.S., Ph.D.

THE ROCKEFELLER UNIVERSITY
New York, New York 10021-6399
Web site: www.rockefeller.edu

Founded 1901. CGS member. Coed. Private control. Graduate study only. Special facilities: Center for Biochemistry, Structural Biology, and Chemistry, Bio-Imaging Resource Center, Chemical Biology Spectroscopy Resource Center, DNA Sequencing Resource Center, Flow Cytometry Resource Center, Gene Array Resource Center, High-Throughput Screening Resource Center, Center for Human Genetics, Laboratory Animal Research Center, Media and Glassware Resource Center, Media Resource Center, Protein Resource Center, Research Center for Ecology and Ethology, Center for Research on Alzheimer's Disease, Center for Studies in Physics and Biology. Library: 184,000 volumes, 390 subscriptions.

No tuition charge. On-campus housing for married and single students. Average academic year housing costs: $5500–$7000. Contact the Office of the Dean for all housing information.

Graduate Programs

Established 1954. Enrollment: full-time 225, part-time 179. Faculty: full-time 175. Degree conferred: Ph.D.

ADMISSION REQUIREMENTS. Transcripts, at least three letters of recommendation, letter from applicant, interview required in support of application. On-line application available. GRE and GRE Subject Test strongly recommended. TOEFL recommended for international applicants. Applications should be completed by January 1, October 16 for M.D.-Ph.D. applicants. Address inquiries to Office of the Dean. Application fee $65. Phone: (212)327-8086; fax: (212)327-8505; e-mail: phd@mail.rockefeller.edu.

ADMISSION STANDARDS. Very competitive.

FINANCIAL AID. All students receive a stipend and tuition remission.

DEGREE REQUIREMENTS. For Ph.D.: Five years of research and study generally required; dissertation; final oral exam.

FIELDS OF STUDY.
Biochemistry.
Bioinformatics and Computational Biology.
Biophysics.
Cell Biology.
Chemical Biology.
Chemistry.
Genetics.
Information in Biology.
Molecular Biology.
Neuroscience.
Physics and Biology.
Structural and Chemical Biology.

ROCKFORD COLLEGE
Rockford, Illinois 61108-2393
Web site: www.rockford.edu

Founded 1847. Located on new campus 90 miles NW of Chicago. Coed. Private control. Semester system. Library: 165,000 volumes, 7400 microforms.

Annual tuition: full-time $18,320, per credit $600. On-campus housing for graduate students; no married student housing. Average academic year housing costs: $5900. Contact the Dean, Student Services for housing information. Phone: (815)226-4045.

Graduate Study

Graduate study since 1950. Enrollment: full-time 51, part-time 300. Faculty: full-time 15, part-time 27. Courses offered evenings and Summer. College does not seek full-time or nonlocal students, although such applicants are considered. Degrees conferred: M.A.T., M.B.A.

ADMISSION REQUIREMENTS. Transcripts, GRE/GMAT for M.B.A., three letters of recommendation required in support of application. TOEFL required for international applicants. Interview sometimes required. Accepts transfer applicants. Apply to Office of Graduate Studies prior to registration. Application fee $35. Phone: (815)226-4013; fax: (815)226-4119.

ADMISSION STANDARDS. Selective. Usual minimum average: 3.0 (A = 4).

FINANCIAL AID. Grants, loans. Approved for VA benefits. Apply to Office of Graduate Studies; no specified closing date. Phone: (815)226-3383; fax: (815)226-4119. Use FAFSA.

DEGREE REQUIREMENTS. For M.A.T.: 32–36 semester hours minimum, at least 24 in residence; candidacy; no language requirement; thesis required for some programs. For M.B.A.: 36 semester hours minimum; prerequisite courses or competency test, in economics, accounting, finance, statistics, mathematics; ten required courses and two electives required.

FIELDS OF STUDY.
Art.
Economics and Business.
Elementary Education.
English.
Learning Disabilities.
Mathematics.
Reading.
Secondary Education.
Social Studies.

ROGER WILLIAMS UNIVERSITY
Bristol, Rhode Island 02809
Web site: www.rwu.edu

Founded 1967. Located on a peninsula 20 miles from Providence. Coed. Private control. Semester system. Library: 168,460 volumes, 1225 subscriptions. Total University enrollment: 1500.

Ralph R. Papitto School of Law
Web site: www.rwu.edu/law

Established 1992. Located on main campus. ABA approved since 1995. Semester system. Full-time, part-time study. Special facilities: Marine Affair Institute, Feinstein Institute. Law library: 251,766 volumes, 3718 subscriptions; has LEXIS, NEXIS, WESTLAW, DIALOG.

Annual tuition: full-time $21,200, part-time $16,265. On-campus housing available for both single and married students. Contact the University's Housing Office for both on- and off-campus housing information. Law students tend to live off-campus. Off-campus housing and personal expenses: approximately $15,670.

Enrollment: first-year class full-time 103, part-time 81; total 365 (men 50%, women 50%). Faculty: full-time 18, part-time 16. Student to faculty ratio 14.8 to 1. Degrees conferred: J.D. joint degree programs with the University of Rhode Island: J.D.-M.C.P., J.D.-M.M.A., J.D.-M.S. (Labor Relations, Human Resources).

ADMISSION REQUIREMENTS. LSDAS Law School report, LSAT (not later that February test date; if more than one LSAT, highest is used), bachelor's degree from an accredited institution, personal statement, résumé, transcripts (must show all schools attended and at least three years of study) required in support of application. Applicants must have received bachelor's degree prior to enrollment. Interview and recommendations not required. Accepts transfer candidates. Apply to Office of Admission after September 30, before May 15 (priority deadline). First-year students admitted Fall only. Rolling admissions process; notification starts in January and is finished when class is filled. Application fee $60. Phone: (800)633-2727, (401)254-4555; fax: (401)254-4516.

ADMISSION STANDARDS. Selective. Mean LSAT: full-time 149, part-time 148; mean GPA: full-time 3.06, part-time 3.01 (A = 4). *U.S. News & World Report* ranking is in the fourth tier of all U.S. law schools.

FINANCIAL AID. Scholarships, merit scholarships, minority scholarships, Grants-in-Aid, institutional loans; Federal loans and Federal W/S offered through University's Financial Aid Office. For scholarships apply to Admissions Office after January 1 before May 15; use School's Financial Aid Form. For all other programs apply to the University's Office of Financial Aid. Phone: (401)254-4656. Use FAFSA (School code: 003410), also submit Financial Aid Transcript, Federal Income Tax forms. Approximately 5% (full-time), 2–6% (part-time) of 1st year class received scholarships/Grants-in-Aid. Approximately 77% of students receive some form of financial assistance. Average scholarships grant $3000 for both full- and part-time.

DEGREE REQUIREMENTS. For J.D.: 90 (54 required) credits with a GPA of at least 2.0 (A = 4), plus completion of upper-divisional writing course; three-year program, four-year part-time program. For J.D.-M.C.P., J.D.-M.M.A., J.D.-M.S.: four-year programs rather than five-year programs if both degrees are taken consecutively.

ROLLINS COLLEGE
Winter Park, Florida 32789-4499
Web site: www.rollins.edu

Established 1885. Located adjacent to Orlando. Coed. Private control. Semester system. Library: 263,000 volumes, 37,400 microforms. No on-campus housing available for graduate students. Annual average housing costs: $12,000. Contact the Office of Residential Life for off-campus housing information. Phone: (800)866-2405, (407)646-2405.

Roy E. Crummer Graduate School of Business
Web site: www.crummer.rollins.edu

Graduate study since 1957. Annual tuition: $22,430, per credit $710. Enrollment: full-time 231, part-time 150; Executive M.B.A. 45. Faculty: full-time 19, part-time 4. Degree conferred: A.M.B.A. (applicants must have at least three years of significant work experience), E.A.M.B.A. (for applicants with little or no work experience), P.M.B.A., E.M.B.A.

ADMISSION REQUIREMENTS. Transcripts, GMAT, personal interview required in support of School's application. TOEFL (minimum score 550) required for international applicants. Apply by April 1 (Fall), December 1 (Spring). Rolling admissions process. Late applications considered on a space available basis. Application fee for A.M.B.A., E.A.M.B.A., P.M.B.A., E.M.B.A. $50. Phone: (800)866-2405, (407)646-2405; fax: (407)646-1550.

ADMISSION STANDARDS. Selective. Mean LSAT: full-time 569, part-time 537; full- and part-time mean GPA: 3.23 (A = 4). Usual minimum average: 3.2 (A = 4).

FINANCIAL AID. Scholarships, fellowships, administrative assistantships, grants, Federal W/S, loans. Apply by March 1 to the Office of Student Financial Planning. Phone: (407)646-2395. Use FAFSA (School code: 001515) and institutional FAF. About 50% of students receive aid other than loans from College and outside sources.

DEGREE REQUIREMENTS. For A.M.B.A.: eleven-month accelerated program. For E.A.M.B.A.: two-year program. For P.M.B.A.: thirty-two-month program. For E.M.B.A.: twenty-month program.

FIELD OF STUDY.
Business Administration. Includes accounting, finance, marketing, management, operation.

Hamilton Holt School—Graduate Division

Tuition: per credit Counseling $299, Human Resources $290, Corporate Communications $368.75, Teaching $226, Liberal Studies $192.50. Enrollment: full-time 43, part-time 298. Faculty: full-time 31, part-time 11. Degrees conferred: M.A., M.A.T., M.H.R., M.L.S.

ADMISSION REQUIREMENTS. Transcripts, GRE required in support of School's application. TOEFL required for interna-

tional applicants. Accepts transfer applicants. Graduates of unaccredited institutions not considered. Apply to Coordinator of Records and Registration; no specified closing date. Rolling admissions process. Late applications considered on a space available basis. Application fee $50. Phone: (407)646-2232; fax: (407)646-1551.

ADMISSION STANDARDS. Selective. Usual minimum average: 2.75 (A = 4).

FINANCIAL AID. Scholarships, fellowships, assistantships, loans. Approved for VA benefits. Apply by March 15 to the Dean for scholarships, fellowships, assistantships; to Financial Aid Office for loans. Phone: (407)646-2395. Use FAFSA (College code: 001515) and institutional FAF. About 35% of students receive aid other than loans from College and outside sources. Aid available for part-time students.

DEGREE REQUIREMENTS. For master's: 30–36 credit hour program; thesis/nonthesis option.

FIELDS OF STUDY.
Corporate Communication and Technology.
Elementary Education.
Human Resources.
Liberal Studies.
Mental Health Counseling.
School Counseling.
Secondary Education. Includes English, mathematics, music.

ROOSEVELT UNIVERSITY
Chicago, Illinois 60605-1394
Web site: www.roosevelt.edu

Founded 1945. Coed. Private control. Semester system. Branch campus at Schaumburg, IL (60173). Library: 225,000 volumes, 1200 subscriptions.
Tuition: per hour $505. Limit on-campus housing for single students only. Annual housing costs: $4500–$6500. Apply to Office of Residence Life for housing information. Phone: (312)341-2004.

Graduate Division

Enrollment: full-time 550, part-time 2000. Faculty: full-time 89, part-time 76. Degrees conferred: M.A., M.B.A., M.M., M.P.A., M.S., M.S.J., M.G.S.

ADMISSION REQUIREMENTS. Transcripts required in support of application. GMAT required for Business. Accepts transfer applicants. Apply to Coordinator of Graduate Admissions by August 1 (Fall), December 1 (Spring); international students apply three months prior to the intended semester. Application fee $25, $35 for international applicants. Phone: (312)341-3515; fax: (312)341-4316. Schaumberg Admission Office phone: (847)619-8600.

ADMISSION STANDARDS. Selective. Usual minimum average: 2.7–3.0 (A = 4) depending on program.

FINANCIAL AID. Scholarships, teaching assistantships, grants, tuition waivers, Federal W/S, loans. Approved for VA benefits. Apply by February 15 to Graduate Admissions for scholarships; to appropriate department chair for assistantships; to Financial Aid Office for all other programs. Phone: (312)341-3565. Use FAFSA. Limited merit awards available for part-time students.

DEGREE REQUIREMENTS. For master's: 30–60 semester hours of graduate work; thesis/nonthesis option; final written/oral exam; research paper.

FIELDS OF STUDY.

Accounting.

Biotechnology and Chemical Science.

Business Administration. M.B.A.

Chemistry.

Clinical Psychology. Psy.D. only.

Computer Science.

Economics.

Education. Includes administration and supervision, counseling and human services, early childhood, elementary, reading, secondary, teacher leadership.

Educational Leadership and Organizational Change. Ed.D. only.

English.

General Studies. Interdepartmental.

History.

Hospitality and Tourism Management.

Human Resource Management.

Information Systems.

Integrated Marketing Communications.

International Business. M.S.I.B.

Journalism. M.S.J.

Mathematical Sciences.

Music. Includes performance, theory, composition, music history, music education, theater.

Political Science.

Psychology.

Public Administration.

Sociology. Includes gerontology.

Spanish.

Telecommunications.

Training and Development.

Women's Studies.

ROSE-HULMAN INSTITUTE OF TECHNOLOGY

Terre Haute, Indiana 47803-3920

Web site: www.rose-hulman.edu

Founded 1874. Coed. Private control. Quarter system. Special facilities: digital computers, high-flux neutron generator, observatory, Center of Applied Optics, Center of Technology Assessment. Library: more than 150,000 volumes, 589 subscriptions.

Annual tuition: full-time $20,559, per credit $579. On-campus housing for 700 students; none for graduate students. Average academic year housing costs: $3000, $5751 (including board). Apply to Dean of Students. Phone: (812)877-8257.

Graduate Studies

Graduate study since 1894. Enrollment: full-time 58, part-time 86. Institute faculty: full-time 77, part-time 2. Degree conferred: M.S.

ADMISSION REQUIREMENTS. Transcripts, GRE, three references required in support of application. Interview desirable. TOEFL (minimum score 580) and GRE required for international applicants. Accepts transfer applicants. Apply to Dean for Research and Graduate Studies; no specified closing dates, though preference is given to those applying by February 1. Application fee: none. Phone: (800)248-7448; fax: (812)877-8941.

ADMISSION STANDARDS. Selective. Usual minimum average: 3.0 (A = 4).

FINANCIAL AID. Annual awards from institutional funds: international fellowships, graduate assistantships, research assistantships, grants, tuition waivers, Federal W/S, loans. Apply by April 1 to Dean of Research and Graduate Studies for fellowships, assistantships; to Financial Aid Office for all other programs. Phone: (812)877-8403. Use FAFSA. About 60–80% of students receive aid other than loans from Institute and outside sources.

DEGREE REQUIREMENTS. For M.S.: 51 quarter hours minimum; thesis; final oral exam; no language requirement.

FIELDS OF STUDY.

Applied Optics.

Biomedical Engineering.

Chemical Engineering.

Civil Engineering.

Electrical Engineering.

Engineering Management.

Environmental Engineering.

Mechanical Engineering.

ROWAN UNIVERSITY

Glassboro, New Jersey 08028-1701

Web site: www.rowan.edu

Founded 1923. Name changed in 1992, granted university status in 1997. Located 35 miles SE of Philadelphia. CGS member. Coed. State Control. Semester system. Library: 350,000 volumes, 2000 subscriptions; is a U.S. government depository. Total University enrollment: 10,000.

Annual tuition: full-time resident $7315, nonresident $11,227; per credit resident $311, nonresident $474. No on- or off-campus housing available.

Graduate School

Graduate study since 1950. Enrollment: full-time 155, part-time 570. Graduate faculty: full-time 84, part-time 20. Degrees conferred: M.A., M.B.A., M.S. in Teaching.

ADMISSION REQUIREMENTS. Transcripts, letters of recommendation, GRE/GMAT/MAT/NTE required in support of application. Personal interview required for some programs. TOEFL required for international applicants. Interview required by some departments. Accepts transfer applicants. Apply to Graduate Admissions Office prior to registration. Application fee $30. Phone: (856)256-4050; fax (856)256-4436.

ADMISSION STANDARDS. Selective. Usual minimum average: 2.8 for last 60 credits (A = 4).

FINANCIAL AID. Annual awards from institutional funds: graduate and residence assistantships (non-teaching), internships, tuition waivers, Federal W/S, loans. Apply to Graduate Office. Phone: (856)256-4250. Use FAFSA. About 10% of students receive aid from University. Aid available for part-time students.

DEGREE REQUIREMENTS. For master's: 32–48 credit hours minimum; thesis or final project; written comprehensive exam.

FIELDS OF STUDY.

COLLEGE OF BUSINESS:

Accounting. M.S.

Business Administration. M.B.A.

COLLEGE OF COMMUNICATION:

Public Relations. M.A.

Writing. M.A.

COLLEGE OF EDUCATION:

Educational Leadership. Ed.D.

Educational Services. Ed.S. only.

Educational Technology.
Elementary School Teaching.
Environmental Education and Conservation.
Higher Education.
Learning Disabilities.
Reading Education.
School Administration. Includes elementary, secondary.
School and Public Librarianship.
School Business Administration.
School Psychology.
Special Education.
Student Personnel Services.
Subject Matter Teaching. Includes art, biological science, chemistry/physics, mathematics, music education.
Supervision and Curriculum.
Teaching. Includes elementary, secondary, special. M.S.T.

COLLEGE OF ENGINEERING:
Chemical Engineering.
Civil and Environmental Engineering.
Electrical Engineering.
Engineering. Mechanical Engineering.

COLLEGE OF LIBERAL ARTS AND SCIENCES:
Applied Psychology. M.A.
Mathematics. M.A.

COLLEGE OF FINE AND PERFORMING ARTS:
Music. M.M.
Theatre. M.A.

RUSH UNIVERSITY
Chicago, Illinois 60612-3832
Web site: www.rushu.rush.edu

Private control. Special facilities: Computer Research Institute, Comparative Research Center, Electron Microscope. The University's NIH ranking is 96th among all U.S. institutions with 84 awards/grants worth $39,789,122. Library: 596,600 volumes, 2147 subscriptions. Total University enrollment at main campus: 1477.

On-campus rooms and apartments available for both single and married students. Annual on-campus housing cost: single students $4500 (room only), married students $8500. Contact Admissions Office for both on- and off-campus housing information. Medical students tend to live off-campus. Off-campus housing and personal expenses: approximately $15,400.

Rush Medical College

Established 1837, closed in 1942. Reopened in 1971 and merged with Presbyterian-St. Luke's Medical Center. Located on the University's campus. Semester system; traditional four-year curriculum. Affiliated hospitals: Holy Family Medical Center, Illinois Masonic Medical, Lake Forest Hospital, Oak Park Hospital, Riverside Medical Center, Rush-Copley Medical, Rush North Shore Medical Center, Westlake Community Hospital, Johnston R. Bowman Health Center for the Elderly. Special programs: Primary Care Preceptorships. Library: 97,000 volumes, 2050 subscriptions.

Annual tuition: $29,616; fees $1314. Enrollment: first-year class 120 (EDP 10); total full-time 489 (men 53%, women 47%). Degrees conferred: M.D., M.D.-M.S., M.D.-Ph.D.

ADMISSION REQUIREMENTS. AMCAS report, transcripts, MCAT, three recommendations (one from premedical committee) required in support of application. Interview by invitation only. Preference given to state residents. Will consider transfer applicants on a space-available basis. Has EDP; apply between June 1 and August 1. Apply through AMCAS after June 1, before November 15. Application fee $65. Phone: (312)942-6913; fax: (312)942-2333; e-mail: rmc_admissions@rush.edu.

ADMISSION STANDARDS. Competitive. Mean MCAT: 9.0; mean GPA: 3.51 (A = 4). Gourman rating: 3.36. Accepts about 3–5% of total annual applicants. Approximately 85% are state residents.

FINANCIAL AID. Scholarships, assistantships, loans, grants. Apply to Financial Aid Office after acceptance; before May 1. Phone: (312)942-6256. Use FAFSA (College code: 009800). About 80% of students receive some aid from College.

DEGREE REQUIREMENTS. For M.D.: satisfactory completion of four-year curricular plan; all students must pass USMLE Step 1 prior to entering third year and must take USMLE Step 2 prior to awarding of M.D. For M.D.-Ph.D.: generally a seven-year program.

FIELDS OF GRADUATE STUDY.
Anatomical Sciences.
Biochemistry.
Immunology.
Medical Physics.
Microbiology.
Neurosciences.
Pharmacology.
Physiology.

RUTGERS, THE STATE UNIVERSITY OF NEW JERSEY, CAMDEN
Camden, New Jersey 08102-1401
Web site: camden-www.rutgers.edu

Established 1950. Coed. State control. Semester system. Library: 300,000 volumes, 1300 subscriptions. Campus enrollment: 5000.

Annual tuition: full-time resident $7116, nonresident $10,434; per credit resident $293, nonresident $433. On-campus housing available. Average academic year housing costs: $4508 for single students, $7697 for married students. Contact the Housing Office for both on- and off-campus housing information. Phone: (856)225-6471.

Graduate School

Established 1981. Enrollment: total full-time 45, part-time 250. Faculty: full-time 82, part-time 18. Degrees conferred: M.A., M.S., M.P.A., M.P.T.

ADMISSION REQUIREMENTS. Transcripts, GRE/GMAT required in support of School's application. On-line application available. TOEFL required for international applicants. Accepts transfer applicants. Graduates of unaccredited institutions not considered. Apply to Director of Graduate Admissions by July 1 (Fall), December 1 (Spring); for P.T. program, December 15 (Fall admission only). Application fee $50. Phone: (856)225-6056; fax: (856)225-6498.

ADMISSION STANDARDS. Competitive. Usual minimum average: 2.5 (A = 4).

FINANCIAL AID. Annual awards from institutional funds: fellowships, teaching assistantships, research assistantships, internships, grants, Federal W/S, loans. Approved for VA benefits. Apply by March 15 to Dean for assistantships; to Director of Financial Aid for all other programs. Phone: (609)225-6149. Use FAFSA.

DEGREE REQUIREMENTS. Essentially the same as those for main campus.

FIELDS OF STUDY.
Biology.
Chemistry.
English.
History.
Liberal Studies.
Mathematics.
Nursing.
Physical Therapy.
Public Policy and Administration.
Social Work.

School of Business

Web site: camden-www.rutgers.edu

Established 1988. Public control. Accredited programs: M.B.A. Courses offered in Atlantic City. Semester system.

Annual tuition: full-time resident $8408, nonresident $12,600; part-time per credit resident $348, nonresident $520. Enrollment: total full-time 13, part-time 169 (men 75%, women 25%). Faculty: full-time 32, part-time 4; all have Ph.D./D.B.A. Degrees conferred: M.B.A., M.B.A.-J.D.

ADMISSION REQUIREMENTS. All applicants should have a bachelor's degree from a recognized institution of higher education; a strong mathematics background; a 2.5 GPA (A = 4); and a GMAT score of 500. Admission is based on the formula 200 × UGPA + GMAT. Beginning students are admitted Fall and Spring. U.S. citizens apply by August 1 (Fall), December 1 (Spring), April 1 (Summer); international students apply by December 12 (Fall only). Submit an application, GMAT results (will accept GMAT test results from the last five years, latest acceptable date is June), official transcripts from each undergraduate/graduate school attended, three letters of recommendation, personal statement, résumé (prefers at least four years of work experience), and an application fee of $50 to the Office of Graduate and Undergraduate Admission. Accepts transfer candidates. In addition, international students (whose native language is other than English) should submit a TOEFL report (minimum score 550), certified translations and evaluations of all official transcripts, recommendation should be in English or with certified translations, proof of health/immunization certificate, and proof of sufficient financial resources for one year of academic study. On-campus visits are encouraged. Joint degree applicants must apply to and be accepted to both schools, contact the admissions office for current information and specific admissions requirements. Rolling admissions process; notification is made within two weeks of receipt of completed application and supporting documents.

ADMISSION STANDARDS. Selective. Mean GMAT: 566; mean GPA: 3.2 (A = 4).

FINANCIAL AID. Graduate and Professional Scholar awards, New Jersey State Grants, research assistantships, Federal Perkins Loans, Federal W/S, loans. Assistantships may be available for joint degree candidates. Financial Aid applications and information are generally included with the admissions materials; apply by April 1. Request assistantship information from the School of Business. Contact the University's Financial Aid Office for current need-based financial aid information. Phone: (609)225-2074. Use FAFSA (School code: 004741), also submit Financial Aid Transcript, Federal Income Tax forms. Approximately 5% of students receive some form of financial assistance. Aid available for part-time students.

DEGREE REQUIREMENTS. For M.B.A.: 36–60 credit program including 24 elective credits, one- to two-year program; degree program must be completed in six years. For M.B.A.-J.D.: 108–120 credit, four- to five-year program.

M.B.A. FIELDS OF CONCENTRATION.
Accounting.
Finance.
Health Care Management.
Human Resource Management.
International Business Management.
Management.
Management Information Systems.
Marketing.

School of Law (08102-3650)

Web site: www.camlaw.rutgers.edu

Established 1926. ABA approved since 1951. AALS member. Semester system. Law library: 413,548 volumes, 3213 subscriptions; has LEXIS, NEXIS, WESTLAW.

Annual tuition: residents $11,835, nonresidents $16,793; part-time resident $9321; nonresident $13,497. No on-campus housing. Total average annual additional expense: $10,000–$12,500.

Enrollment: first year class, 175 (day), 50 (evening); total full- and part-time 762 (men 52%, women 48%). Faculty: full-time 32, part-time 35. Student to faculty ratio 18.3 to 1. Degrees conferred: J.D., J.D.-M.A. (Political Science), J.D.-M.B.A., J.D.-M.C.R.P., J. D.-M.P.A.

ADMISSION REQUIREMENTS. LSDAS Law School report, bachelor's degree, transcripts, letters of recommendation, LSAT required in support of application. On-line application available. Interview sometimes required. Accepts transfer applicants. Graduates of unaccredited colleges not considered. Apply to Admissions Office by April 1. Application fee $50. Admits Fall only. Phone: (856)225-6102; fax: (856)225-6537.

ADMISSION STANDARDS. Selective. Mean LSAT: full-time 158, part-time 156; mean GPA: full-time 3.18, part-time 3.20 (A = 4). Gourman rating: 3.69. *U.S. News & World Report* ranking is in the second tier of all U.S. law schools. Accepts 40–45% of total annual applicants.

FINANCIAL AID. Scholarships, fellowships, Federal W/S, loans, legal employment. Apply to Director of Financial Aid by March 15. Use FAFSA (School code: 004741) and Institutional financial aid application. About 30% of students receive some aid from School.

DEGREE REQUIREMENTS. For J.D.: 84 credits minimum, at least final two terms in residence. Evening program: nine semesters plus one summer session. For master's degrees: see Graduate School listing, main campus, below.

RUTGERS UNIVERSITY

New Brunswick, New Jersey 08901
Web site: www.rutgers.edu

Established 1766. Located 33 miles SW of New York City. CGS and AAU member. Coed. State control. Semester system. Special facilities: Center for Advanced Biotechnology and Medicine, Center for Advanced Food Technology, Center for Agriculture, Center for Alcohol Studies, American Affordable Housing Institute, Center for American Women in Politics, Art Museum, Institute for Biostatistics, Center for Ceramic Research, Center of Cognitive Sciences, Center for Computer Aids for Industrial Productivity, Center for Discrete Mathematics and Theoretical Computer Science, Controlled Drug-Delivery Research Center, Institute for Criminological Research, Center for the Critical

Analysis of Contemporary Culture, Eagleton Institute of Politics, Environmental and Occupational Health Sciences Institute, Fiber Optics Materials Research, Institute for Health, Health Care Policy and Aging Research, Center for Historical Analysis, Center for International Conflict Resolution and Peace Studies, Institute of Marine and Coastal Sciences, Center for Materials Synthesis, Center for Operations Research, Laboratory for Surface Modification, Center for Urban Policy Research, Waksman Institute of Microbiology, Wireless Information Network Laboratory, Institute for Research on Women. Library: 5,267,000 volumes, 28,760 subscriptions. Total University enrollment: 28,070.

Annual tuition: full-time residents $7116, nonresidents $10,434; per credit residents $293, nonresidents $433. On-campus housing for 380 married students, 703 single students. Average academic year housing costs: $4182–$6992 for single students; per month $525–$750 for family housing. Contact Graduate and Family Housing Office for both on- and off-campus information. Phone: (732)445-2215.

The Graduate School

Graduate study since 1876. Enrollment: full-time 2050, part-time 1537 (men 52%, women 48%). Graduate faculty: full- and part-time 1842. Degrees conferred: M.A., M.A.T., M.C.R.P., M.S., M.S.T., M.Phil., Dr.P.H., Ph.D.

ADMISSION REQUIREMENTS. Transcripts, GRE, two or three letters of recommendation required in support of School's application. GRE Subject Test required for many programs. TOEFL required for international applicants. Interview not required. Accepts transfer applicants. Graduates of unaccredited colleges not considered. Apply to Admissions Office by July 1 (Fall), December 1 (Spring), March 1 (Summer). Applicants seeking financial support should apply by February 1 for the Fall term. Application fee $50. Phone: (732)932-7711; fax: (732)932-8231.

ADMISSION STANDARDS. Very competitive or selective.

FINANCIAL AID. Academic scholarships, fellowships, teaching assistantships, graduate assistantships, internships, grants, tuition waivers, Federal W/S, loans. Approved for VA benefits. Apply by February 1 to appropriate department Chair for assistantships, fellowships; to Admissions Office for all other programs. Phone: (732)932-7755; fax: (732)932-7385. Use FAFSA and institutional FAF. About 80% of students receive aid other than loans from School and outside sources. Aid available for part-time students.

DEGREE REQUIREMENTS. For master's: 30 credit hours minimum; thesis required by some departments; final oral/written comprehensive exam. For Ph.D.: 3 years minimum beyond the bachelor's, at least one year in full-time residence required by some programs; reading knowledge of one or two foreign languages required by some programs; qualifying exam; thesis; final oral exam.

FIELDS OF STUDY.
Agricultural Economics. M.S.
Animal Sciences. M.S., Ph.D.
Anthropology. M.A., Ph.D.
Art History. M.A., Ph.D.
Biochemistry. M.S., Ph.D.
Biomedical Engineering. M.S., Ph.D.
Bioresource Engineering. M.S.
Cell and Developmental Biology. M.S., Ph.D.
Ceramic and Materials Science Engineering. M.S., Ph.D.
Chemical and Biochemical Engineering. M.S., Ph.D.
Chemistry. M.S., M.S.T., Ph.D.
Civil and Environmental Engineering. M.S., Ph.D.
Classics. M.A., M.A.T., Ph.D.

Communication, Information and Library Studies. Ph.D.
Comparative Literature. Ph.D.
Computer Science. M.S., Ph.D.
Ecology and Evolution. M.S., Ph.D.
Economics. M.A., Ph.D.
Electrical and Computer Engineering. M.S., Ph.D.
English. Ph.D.
Entomology. M.S., Ph.D.
Environmental Sciences. M.S., Ph.D.
Food Science. M.S., Ph.D.
French. M.A., M.A.T., Ph.D.
Geography. M.A., M.S., Ph.D.
Geological Sciences. M.S., Ph.D.
German. M.A., Ph.D.
History. Ph.D.
Industrial and System Engineering. M.S., Ph.D.
Industrial Relations and Human Resources. Ph.D.
Italian. M.A., M.A.T., Ph.D.
Linguistics. Ph.D.
Mathematics. M.S., Ph.D.
Mechanical and Aerospace Engineering. M.S., Ph.D.
Mechanics. M.S., Ph.D.
Medicinal Chemistry. M.S., Ph.D.
Microbiology and Molecular Genetics. M.S., Ph.D.
Music. M.A., Ph.D.
Nutritional Sciences. M.S., Ph.D.
Oceanography. M.S., Ph.D.
Operations Research. Ph.D.
Pharmaceutical Science. M.S., Ph.D.
Pharmacology—Cellular and Molecular. Ph.D.
Philosophy. Ph.D.
Physics and Astronomy. M.S., M.S.T., Ph.D.
Physiology and Neurobiology. Ph.D.
Plant Biology. M.S., Ph.D.
Political Science. Ph.D.
Psychology. Ph.D.
Public Health. Ph.D. (Offered jointly with and administered by UMDNJ-SPH.)
Social Work. Ph.D.
Sociology. M.A., Ph.D.
Spanish. M.A., M.A.T., Ph.D.
Statistics. M.S., Ph.D.
Toxicology. M.S., Ph.D.
Urban Planning and Policy Development. Ph.D.
Women's and Gender Studies. M.A.

Mason Gross School of the Arts
Web site: www.masongross.rutgers.edu

Graduate study since 1998. Semester system.
Enrollment: full-time 182, part-time 59. Faculty: full-time 70, part-time 69. Degrees conferred: M.F.A., M.M., D.M.A., A.D.

ADMISSION REQUIREMENTS. Transcripts, three letters of recommendation, graduate audition questionnaire form (Music Program), personal statement required in support of School's application. TOEFL (minimum score 550) required for international applicants. Accepts transfer applicants. Graduates of unaccredited institutions not considered. Apply to Graduate Admissions Office by March 1 (Fall). Application fee $50. Phone: (732)932-7711; fax (732)932-8231.

ADMISSION STANDARDS. Selective. Usual minimum average: 2.75 (A = 4.).

FINANCIAL AID. Scholarships, fellowships, assistantships, teaching assistantships, internships, Federal W/S, loans. Approved for VA benefits. Apply to program chair for scholarships, fellowships, assistantships; to Office of Financial Aid; no specified closing date. Phone: (732)932-7755; fax: (732)932-7385. Use FAFSA and institutional FAF. About 20% of students reutgers University

e aid from School and outside sources. Aid available for part-
ame students.

DEGREE REQUIREMENTS. For M.F.A.: 75 credit, three-year
full-time program; internship (playwriting); special showcase/
thesis production/thesis play. For M.M.: 36 credit, two-year full-
time program; one solo recital; comprehensive exam. For
D.M.A.: three-year full-time residency; reading knowledge of either German, French, or Italian; comprehensive exam; two solo
recitals; two lecture recitals; one chamber music program; final
written/oral comprehensive exam.

FIELDS OF STUDY.
Dance. M.F.A.
Music. Includes music education, jazz studies. M.M., D.M.A.
Theater Arts. Includes acting, design, directing, playwriting.
  M.F.A.
Visual Arts. M.F.A.

Rutgers Business School
Web site: www.business.rutgers.edu

Established 1965. Private control. Accredited programs: M.B.A.
and Accounting. Located on Newark and New Brunswick campuses, courses offered at Princeton and Morristown. Trimester
system. Special Programs: Foreign Exchange programs in France,
Italy, the Netherlands, United Kingdom, Republic of Singapore;
E.M.B.A., offered entirely in Singapore; foreign study (joint
E.M.B.A. with Dalian University of Technology in People's Republic of China). Special facilities: Center for Entrepreneurial
Management, Center for Information Management, Integration
and Connectivity, Center for International Business Education
and Research, Center for Research in Regulated Industries, New
Jersey Center for Research in Financial Services, New Jersey
Small Business Development Center, Rutgers Accounting Re-
search Center, Technology Management Research Center.

Annual tuition: full-time resident $8408, nonresident $12,538;
part-time per credit resident $348, nonresident $520. On-campus
rooms and apartments available for single students only.

Enrollment: total full-time 394, part-time 1132 (men 65%,
women 35%) Faculty: full-time 136, part-time 60; 98% with
Ph.D./D.B.A. Degrees conferred: M.B.A., M.B.A. in Profes-
sional Accounting, E.M.B.A., M.Accy., M.B.A.-J.D., M.B.A.-
M.D., M.B.A.-M.P.H., M.B.A.-M.S. (Biomedical Sciences),
M.Q.F., Ph.D. in Management (in cooperation with New Jersey
Institute of Technology), Ph.D.

ADMISSION REQUIREMENTS. Transcripts, two letters of recommendation, two essays, GMAT required in support of
School's application. TOEFL required for international applicants. Accepts transfer applicants. Graduates of unaccredited
institutions not considered. For M.B.A.: apply to Admissions
Office, 190 New Street, Newark, NJ 07102. Most full-time programs admit Fall and Spring, except M.B.A. in Management (admits Fall only) M.B.A. in Professional Accounting (admits
Spring only). Most part-time programs admit Spring and Fall,
except M.S.-M.B.A. (admits Fall only). Apply by May 1 (Summer), June 1 (Fall), November 1 (Spring). For Ph.D., apply to
Admissions Office, Graduate School-Newark, 249 University
Avenue, Newark, NJ 07102. Application fee $50. M.B.A. phone:
(973)353-1234; Ph.D. phone: (973)353-5371.

ADMISSION STANDARDS. Competitive. Usual minimum average: 3.0, mean GPA: 3.27 (A = 4); mean GMAT: 580; work experience: full-time students three years, part-time students five
years.

FINANCIAL AID. Annual awards from institutional funds:
scholarships, fellowships, teaching assistantships (Ph.D. only),
internships, tuition waivers, Federal W/S, loans. Apply by March 1
to Dean for scholarships, fellowships, assistantships; to Admis-

sions Office for all other programs. Phone: (973)353-1234. Use
FAFSA (School code: 002631). About 25% of students receive
aid other than loans from School. No aid for part-time students.

DEGREE REQUIREMENTS. For M.B.A.: 60–61 credits, at
least 49 in residence. For M.B.A. in Professional Accounting: 63
credits. For M.Accy.: 30 credits. For Ph.D.: 72 credits, at least 65
in residence; qualifying exam; dissertation; final oral exam.

FIELDS OF STUDY.
Accounting. Ph.D.
Accounting Information Systems. Ph.D.
Computer Information Systems. Ph.D.
Finance. Ph.D.
Governmental Accounting. M.Accy.
Individualized Major. Ph.D.
Information Technology. Ph.D.
International Business. Ph.D.
Management. M.B.A. Concentrations include applied statistics,
  arts management, e-commerce, economics, entrepreneurship,
  finance, human resources management, information technol-
  ogy, international business, management of innovation and
  technology, marketing, pharmaceutical management, strategic
  management, supply chain management.
Management Science. Ph.D.
Organization Management. Ph.D.
Professional Accounting. M.B.A.
Quantitative Finance. M.Q.F.
Taxation. M.Accy.

School of Communication, Information and Library Studies

Graduate study since 1953. Semester system.
Enrollment: full-time 107, part-time 218 (men 20%, women
80%). Faculty: full-time 39, part-time 14. Degrees conferred:
M.L.I.S., M.C.I.S., Ph.D.

ADMISSION REQUIREMENTS. Transcripts, GRE, three letters of reference, personal statement required in support of
School's application. On-line application available. TOEFL required of international students. Interview not required. Accepts
transfer applicants. Graduates of unaccredited institutions not
considered. Apply to Director of Admissions by May 1 (Fall),
November (Spring). Application fee $50. Phone: (732)932-7711;
fax: (732)932-8231.

ADMISSION STANDARDS. Selective. Usual minimum average: 3.0 (A = 4).

FINANCIAL AID. Scholarships, fellowships, teaching assistantships, internships, tuition waivers, Federal W/S, loans. Approved
for VA benefits. Apply as part of admission application. Phone:
(732)932-7755; fax: (732)932-7385. Use FAFSA and institutional FAF. About 5% of students receive aid other than loans
from School and outside sources. Aid available for part-time
students.

DEGREE REQUIREMENTS. For M.L.I.S.: 36 credit hours. For
M.C.I.S.: 36 credit hours, at least 30 in residence. For Ph.D.: essentially the same requirements as for the Graduate School.

FIELDS OF STUDY.
Communication and Information Studies. M.C.I.S.
Communication, Information, and Library Studies. Ph.D.
Library and Information Science. M.L.I.S.

Graduate School of Education

Graduate study since 1924. Semester system.
Enrollment: full-time 262, part-time 546. Faculty: full-time
53, part-time 30. Degrees conferred: Ed.M., Ed.S., Ed.D.

ADMISSION REQUIREMENTS. Transcripts, GRE, three letters of recommendation required in support of School's application. On-line application available. TOEFL required for international applicants. Accepts transfer applicants. Graduates of unaccredited institutions not considered. Apply to Graduate Admissions Office by March 1 (Fall), November 1 (Spring); Counseling Psychology by January 15. Application fee $50. Phone: (732)932-7496; fax: (732)932-8206.

ADMISSION STANDARDS. Selective. Usual minimum average: master's 3.0 (A = 4) and GRE 1000, doctorate 3.5 and GRE 1100.

FINANCIAL AID. Academic scholarships, grants, fellowships, research assistantships, teaching assistantships, internships, Federal W/S, loans. Approved for VA benefits. Apply by March 1 to appropriate department chair for scholarships, fellowships, assistantships; to Office of Financial Aid for all others. Phone: (732)932-7755; fax: (732)932-7385. Use FAFSA and institutional FAF. About 20% of students receive aid from School and outside sources. Aid available for part-time students.

DEGREE REQUIREMENTS. For Ed.M.: 30 credit hours minimum; comprehensive written exam/thesis for some departments. For Ed.S.: 64 credit hours minimum beyond the bachelor's, at least 24 in residence; qualifying exam. For Ed.D.: 72 credit hours minimum beyond the bachelor's, at least 42 at Rutgers; qualifying exam; dissertation; final oral exam.

FIELDS OF STUDY.
Administration and Supervision. Includes elementary, general, higher, secondary, urban. M.Ed.
Counseling Psychology. M.Ed.
Educational Administration and Supervision. Ed.S., Ed.D.
Early Childhood/Elementary Education. M.Ed., Ed.S., Ed.D.
Educational Statistics and Measurement. M.Ed.
English/Language Arts. M.Ed.
Language Education. M.Ed., Ed.S., Ed.D.
Learning/Cognition and Development. M.Ed.
Literacy Education. Ed.S., Ed.D.
Mathematics Education. M.Ed., Ed.S., Ed.D.
Reading. M.Ed.
Science Education. M.Ed.
School Business Administration. M.Ed.
Social and Philosophical Foundations. Ed.S., Ed.D.
Special Education. M.Ed., Ed.S., Ed.D.

Edward J. Bloustein School of Planning and Public Policy

Graduate study since 1965. Semester system.
Enrollment: full- and part-time 432 (men 45%, women 55%). Faculty: full-time 45, part-time 35. Degrees conferred: M.C.R.P., M.C.R.S., M.P.A.P., M.P.P., M.P.A.P.-J.D., M.P.A.P.-M.B.A., M.C.R.P.-J.D., M.C.R.P.-M.S. (Agricultural Economics), M.C.R.S.-M.B.A.

ADMISSION REQUIREMENTS. Transcripts, GRE, three letters of recommendation, personal statement or essay required in support of School's application. TOEFL required for international applicants. Accepts transfer applicants. Graduates of unaccredited institutions not considered. Apply to the Office of Graduate and Professional Admissions by February 15 (Fall); for Urban Planning June 1 (Fall), November 1 (Spring); Public Policy admits Fall only, apply by February 15. International applicants apply by April 1 (Fall), November 1 (Spring). Application fee $50. Phone: (732)932-7711; fax: (732)932-8231.

ADMISSION STANDARDS. Selective. Usual minimum average: master's 3.0 (A = 4).

FINANCIAL AID. Diversity scholarships, graduate awards, fellowships, graduate assistantships, teaching assistantships, traineeships, Federal W/S, loans. Approved for VA benefits. Apply to program chair for scholarships, fellowships, awards, assistantships; to Office of Financial Aid for all other programs. Financial Aid applications due for Urban Planning by February 1 Fall), November 1 (Spring); for Public Policy by February 15 (Fall). Phone: (732)932-7057; fax: (732)932-7385. Use FAFSA and institutional FAF. Aid available for part-time students.

DEGREE REQUIREMENTS. For M.C.R.S.: 30 credit hours minimum; comprehensive written exam. For M.C.R.S.: 48 credit full-time program. For M.P.A.P., M.P.P.: two-year full-time program.

FIELDS OF STUDY.
City and Regional Studies. Includes international development planning. M.C.R.S.
Public Affairs and Politics. M.P.A.P.
Public Policy. M.P.P.
Urban Planning and Policy Development. Ph.D. awarded through the Graduate School.
Note: Programs in Public Health are offered jointly with the Graduate School, New Brunswick, and the University of Medicine and Dentistry of New Jersey.

School of Social Work

Graduate study since 1955. Located at Camden, Newark, and New Brunswick.
Enrollment: full-time 308, part-time 410. Faculty: full-time 49, part-time 31. Degrees conferred: M.S.W., Ph.D.: (offered through Graduate School).

ADMISSION REQUIREMENTS. Transcripts, personal statement, three letters of recommendation required in support of School's application. On-line application available. GRE required for doctoral applicants. TOEFL required for international applicants. Accepts transfer applicants. Graduates of unaccredited institutions not considered. Apply to Office of Graduate Admissions by May 1 (Fall); March 1 (advanced standing accelerated program), November 1 (Spring). Application fee $35. Phone: (732)932-7711; fax: (732)932-8231.

ADMISSION STANDARDS. Selective. Usual minimum average: 3.0 (A = 4).

FINANCIAL AID. Fellowships, research assistantships, field placement, stipends, Federal W/S, loans. Approved for VA benefits. Apply to University Financial Aid Office by March 1. Phone: (732)932-7057; fax: (732)932-7385. Use FAFSA and institutional FAF. About 46% of students receive aid other than loans from School and outside sources.

DEGREE REQUIREMENTS. For M.S.W.: 60 credit hours minimum, at least 36 in residence; research project. For Ph.D.: see Graduate School listing above.

FIELDS OF STUDY.
Administration, Policy, and Planning.
Children and Families.
Direct Practice.
Health, Mental Health, and Aging.

School of Law—Newark Campus (07102-3094)

Established 1908. ABA approved since 1941. AALS member. Semester system. Library: 488,100 volumes, 3500 subscriptions; has LEXIS, NEXIS, WESTLAW, DIALOG.
Annual tuition: resident $11,129, nonresident $16,087; part-time resident $7282, nonresident $10,623. No on-campus

housing available. Total average annual additional expense: $14,000– $16,000.

Enrollment: first-year class 178 (day), 51 (evening); total 713 (men 50%, women 50%). Faculty: full-time 25, part-time 26. Student to faculty ratio 21.7 to 1. Degrees conferred: J.D., J.D.-M.A. (Criminal Justice, Political Science), J.D.-M.C.R.P., J.D.-Ph.D.

ADMISSION REQUIREMENTS. LSDAS Law School report, bachelor's degree, transcripts, LSAT required in support of application. Interview not required. Accepts transfer applicants. Graduates of unaccredited institutions not considered. Minority Student Program available. Apply to Director of Admissions of School by March 1. Application fee $50. Fall admission only. Phone: (973)353-5557; fax: (973) 353-3459.

ADMISSION STANDARDS. Selective. Mean LSAT: full-time 155, part-time 154; mean GPA: full-time 3.2, part-time 3.16 (A = 4). Gourman rating: 3.73. *U.S. News & World Report* ranking is in the second tier of all U.S. law schools. Accepts 20–25% of total annual applicants.

FINANCIAL AID. Scholarships, fellowships, Federal W/S, loans. Apply to the University's Financial Aid Office by March 1. Use FAFSA (School code: 002631) and institutional FAF. About 20% of students receive aid other than loans from School.

DEGREE REQUIREMENTS. For J.D.: satisfactory completion of three-year program; 84 credits hours minimum.

Note: Semester study abroad program with the University of Leiden, Netherlands.

THE SAGE COLLEGES

Troy, New York 12180-4115
Web site: www.sage.edu

Founded 1916. Located 10 miles E of Albany; has two campuses, one in Troy and one in Albany. Coed on graduate level. Private control. Semester system. Library: 379,736 volumes, 1070 subscriptions. Library fully automated.

Tuition: per credit: $400. Limited on-campus housing. Average annual costs: $6164 (including board). Contact the Director of Residence Life for both on- and off-campus housing information. Phone: (518)270-2008.

Sage Graduate School

Graduate study since 1949. Enrollment: full- and part-time 1015. Faculty: full-time 37, part-time 32. Degrees conferred: M.A., M.S., M.B.A., M.S.Ed.

ADMISSION REQUIREMENTS. Transcripts, two recommendations, résumé, career essay required in support of School's application. GRE/GMAT required for some programs. TOEFL required for international applicants. Accepts transfer applicants. Graduates of unaccredited institutions not considered. Apply to Dean, Sage Graduate School; no specified closing date. Rolling admissions process. Application fee $40. Phone: (518)244-6878; fax: (518)244-6880; e-mail: sgsadm@sage.edu.

ADMISSION STANDARDS. Selective. Usual minimum average: 2.75 (A = 4).

FINANCIAL AID. Grants, teaching assistantships, federal traineeships, Federal W/S, loans. Approved for VA benefits. Apply by March 1 to Sage Graduate School for assistantships; to Financial Aid Office for all other programs. Phone: (518)270-2341.Use FAFSA.

DEGREE REQUIREMENTS. For master's: 31–54 credits; thesis/nonthesis option; seminar/comprehensive exam.

FIELDS OF STUDY.
Art Therapy.
Business Administration. Includes finance, management, human resources. M.B.A.
Child Care and Children's Services.
Chemical Dependence.
Chemical Dependence Administration.
Community Counseling.
Community Health Education.
Community Psychology.
Counseling.
Elementary Education. Includes reading, special education. M.S.Ed.
Forensic Psychology.
General Psychology.
Health Education. Includes community health education, school health education. M.S.
Health Services Administration. Includes administration, health education. M.S.
Nursing. Includes adult health, community health nursing, gerontological, nurse practitioner studies, medical-surgical nursing, nurse practitioner studies, psychiatric-mental health nursing. M.S., M.S.-M.B.A.
Nutrition. M.S.
Occupational Therapy. M.S.
Physical Therapy.
Public Administration. Includes communications, human services administration, public management. M.S.
Reading/Special Education. M.S.Ed.
School Health Education. M.S.
Secondary Education. Includes usual academic subjects. M.S.Ed.
Special Education.

SAGINAW VALLEY STATE UNIVERSITY

University Center, Michigan 48710
Web site: www.svsu.edu

Founded 1963. Located 8 miles from Saginaw. State control. Coed. Early semester system. Library: 358,000 volumes, 2000 subscriptions. Total University enrollment: 8300.

Tuition: per credit hour, resident $174, nonresident $342. Limited on-campus housing available for single students only. Average housing costs: $5015 (including board). Contact Director of Housing for both on- and off-campus housing information. Phone: (517)790-4255. Day-care facilities available.

Graduate Program

Enrollment: full-time 75, part-time 1488. Faculty: full- and part-time 91. Degrees conferred: M.A., M.A.T., M.B.A., M.Ed.

ADMISSION REQUIREMENTS. Transcripts, GRE/GMAT, letters of recommendation, interview required in support of application. Michigan Teaching Certificate required for M.A.T., M.Ed. TOEFL required for international applicants. Accepts transfer applicants. Graduates of unaccredited institutions not considered. Apply to Director of Admissions; no specified closing date. Rolling admissions process. Application fee $25. Phone: (517)249-1696; fax: (517) 790-0180; e-mail: gradadm@svsu.edu.

ADMISSION STANDARDS. Selective. Usual minimum average: 3.0 (A = 4).

FINANCIAL AID. Fellowships, assistantships, Federal W/S, loans. Approved for VA benefits. Apply by April 1 to the Office of Financial Aid. Phone: (517)790-4103; fax: (517)790-0180. Use FAFSA. Aid available for part-time students.

DEGREE REQUIREMENTS. For M.A., M.A.T., M.Ed.: 33–39 hours; thesis/nonthesis option/project. For M.B.A.: 36–48 credit hours minimum depending upon previous preparation, 24 in residence.

FIELDS OF STUDY.
Business Administration. M.B.A.
Chief Business Official. M.Ed.
Communication and Multimedia. M.A.
Directorship of Athletics. Ed.S.
Directorship of Curriculum. Ed.S.
Directorship of Early Childhood Programs. Ed.S.
Early Childhood Education. M.A.T.
Educational Leadership. M.Ed.
Elementary Classroom Teaching. M.A.T.
Leadership and Public Administration. M.A.
Middle School Classroom Teaching. M.A.T.
Nursing. M.S.N.
Principalship. M.Ed., Ed.S.
Reading Education. M.A.T.
Secondary Classroom Teaching. M.A.T.
Special Education. M.A.T.
Superintendency. M.Ed.
Superintendency and Central Office Personnel. Ed.S.
Technological Processes. M.S.

ST. BONAVENTURE UNIVERSITY

Bonaventure, New York 14778-2284
Web site: www.sbu.edu

Established 1859. Located 70 miles SE of Buffalo. CGS member. Coed. Private control. Roman Catholic. Semester system. Library: 372,090 volumes, 1621 subscriptions.

Tuition: per credit $490. On-campus housing for single students only. Average academic year housing costs: $3670 (including board). Contact Coordinator of Residence Living for both on- and off-campus housing information. Phone: (716)375-2512.

School of Graduate Studies

Enrollment: full-time 276, part-time 322 (men 45%, women 55%). Faculty: full-time 65, part-time 28. Degrees conferred: M.A., M.A.T., M.S., M.S.Ed., M.B.A.

ADMISSION REQUIREMENTS. Official transcripts, two letters of recommendation, GRE/GMAT required in support of School's application. On-line application available. GRE Subject Test, interview required by some departments. TOEFL required for international applicants. Accepts transfer applicants. Graduates of unaccredited institutions not considered. Apply to Graduate School at least thirty days prior to registration. Rolling admission process. Application fee $35. Phone: (716)375-2021; fax: (716)375-7834; e-mail: gradsch@sbu.edu.

ADMISSION STANDARDS. Selective for many departments. Usual minimum average: 2.5 (A = 4).

FINANCIAL AID. Research assistantships, teaching assistantships, internships, tuition waivers, Federal W/S, loans. Approved for VA benefits. Apply by April 1 to School of Graduate Studies for assistantships; to Financial Aid Office for all other programs. Use FAFSA. Phone: (716)375-2528. About 10% of students receive aid from School and outside sources. Aid available for part-time students.

DEGREE REQUIREMENTS. For master's: 30 semester hours minimum, at least 24 in residence; thesis/nonthesis option; final

oral exam for some departments; reading knowledge of one foreign language for some departments; written/oral comprehensive exam.

FIELDS OF STUDY.

SCHOOL OF ARTS AND SCIENCES:
English. M.A.
Theology. M.A.

SCHOOL OF BUSINESS:
Business Administration. Includes accounting/finance, general business, international business, management/marketing. M.B.A.
Professional Leadership. M.S.

SCHOOL OF EDUCATION:
Adolescent Literacy. M.S.Ed.
Childhood Literacy. M.S.Ed.
Counseling Education. Includes agency, school. M.S., M.S.Ed.
Educational Leadership. M.S., M.S.Ed.
Health Education. M.S.Ed.

SCHOOL OF FRANCISCAN STUDIES:
Franciscan Studies. M.A.

SCHOOL OF JOURNALISM AND MASS COMMUNICATION:
Integrated Marketing Communication. M.A.

ST. CLOUD STATE UNIVERSITY

St. Cloud, Minnesota 56301-4498
Web site: www.stcloudstate.edu

Founded 1869. Located 62 miles NW of Minneapolis on Interstate 94. CGS member. Coed. State control. Semester system. Library: 775,000 volumes, 8300 subscriptions.

Tuition: per credit resident $149, nonresident $225. On-campus housing for single students only. Average academic year housing costs: $3500 (including board). Apply to Director of Housing. Phone: (320)255-2166.

School of Graduate Studies

Graduate study since 1953. Enrollment: full-time 410, part-time 546. Graduate faculty: full-time 338, part-time 67. Degrees conferred: M.A., M.M., M.S., M.B.A., Specialist program.

ADMISSION REQUIREMENTS. Two transcripts, GRE required in support of application. GMAT required for Business applicants. TOEFL required of international applicants. Interview required for Applied Psychology. Apply to Graduate Studies Office; no specified closing dates. Application fee $15. Phone: (320)255-2113; fax: (320)654-5371.

ADMISSION STANDARDS. Selective for most departments. Usual minimum average: 2.75 (A = 4).

FINANCIAL AID. Scholarships, full/part-time assistantships, Federal W/S, loans. Apply by March 1 to appropriate department Chair for scholarships, assistantships; to Financial Aid Office for all other programs. Phone: (320)255-2047; fax: (320)654-5424. Use FAFSA and University's FAF. Aid sometimes available for part-time students.

DEGREE REQUIREMENTS. For master's: Plan A—36–39 credits, at least 30 in residence; thesis or creative work; final written/oral exam. Plan B—32–36 credits minimum, at least 30 in residence; final comprehensive exam; no thesis; starred paper required by some departments. For Specialist program: 30 credits beyond master's; field study.

FIELDS OF STUDY.
Applied Behavioral Analysis.
Applied Economics.
Art.
Biological Sciences. Includes cell and molecular, ecology and natural resources.
Business Administration. GMAT for admission.
Child and Family Studies. Includes early childhood special education, early education, family studies.
Communication Disorders.
Community Education.
Computer Science.
Counseling. Includes college student development, community, rehabilitation, school.
Criminal Justice.
Curriculum and Instruction. Includes elementary, middle school/ junior high, senior high, reading.
Educational Administration. M.S., Specialist.
English. Includes TESL. M.A., M.S.
Exercise Science.
Geography. Includes geographic information science, tourism planning and development.
Gerontology.
History. Includes public history.
Human Resource Development/Training.
Industrial/Organizational Psychology.
Information Media.
Information Technologies.
Mass Communications.
Mathematics.
Mechanical Engineering.
Music Conducting. M.M.
Music Education. M.M.
Music—Piano Pedagogy. M.M.
Physical Education.
Public and Nonprofit Institutions.
Public Safety Executive Leadership.
Social Responsibility.
Special Education.
Sports Management.

ST. EDWARD'S UNIVERSITY
Austin, Texas 78704-6489
Web site: www.stedwards.edu

Founded in 1885. Coed. Independent. Trimester system. Evening sessions. Library: 145,000 volumes, 2100 subscriptions.
Tuition: per credit $402. On-campus housing available for 40–60 single students. Annual academic year costs: $5000 (including board). Phone: (512)448-8400.

Graduate Program

Graduate study since 1970. Enrollment: full-time 121, part-time 572. Faculty: full-time 7, part-time 38. Degrees conferred: M.B.A., M.A.C., M.A.H.S., M.L.A., M.S.C.I.S., M.S.O.L.E.

ADMISSION REQUIREMENTS. Transcripts, GRE/GMAT required in support of application. On-line application available. TOEFL required for international applicants. Accepts transfer applicants. Graduates of unaccredited institutions not considered. Apply by August 1 (Fall), December 1 (Spring) to Graduate admissions office. Application fee $30, international applicants $50. Phone: (512)428-1061; fax: (512)428-1032.

ADMISSION STANDARDS. Selective. Usual minimum average: 2.75 (A = 4).

FINANCIAL AID. Scholarships, loans. Approved for VA benefits. Apply by March 1 to Financial Aid Office. Phone: (512)448-8520. Use FAFSA. Aid available for part-time students.

DEGREE REQUIREMENTS. For M.B.A.: 36–60 semester hours. For M.A.H.S.: 36 semester hours. For M.L.A.: 33 credit program. For M.A.C.: 54 credit program; practicum; comprehensive exam. For M.S.C.I.S.: 36 credit program. For M.S.O.L.E.: 36 credit program; leadership capstone.

FIELDS OF STUDY.
Business Administration. Includes concentrations in accounting, business management, e-commerce, global business, human resource management, management information systems, marketing, nonprofit and association management, operations management (service and promotion), sports management. M.B.A.
Computer Information Sciences. M.S.C.I.S.
Counseling. M.A.C.
Human Services. Includes administration, conflict resolution, human resource management, sports management. M.A.H.S.
Liberal Arts. M.L.A.
Organizational Leadership and Ethics. M.S.O.L.E.

UNIVERSITY OF ST. FRANCIS
2701 Spring Street
Fort Wayne, Indiana 46808-3994
Web site: www.sf.edu

Founded 1890. Coed. Private Control. Roman Catholic. Semester system. Library: 88,000 volumes, 580 subscriptions.
Tuition: per hour $470. On-campus housing for 46 men, 170 women; none for married students. Average academic year housing costs: $5000–$5500 (including board). Contact Director of Residence Life for both on- and off-campus housing information. Phone: (260)434-7411.

Graduate School

Graduate study since 1961. Enrollment: full-time 33, part-time 153. Graduate faculty: full-time 20, part-time 5. Degrees conferred: M.A.F.A., M.B.A., M.S., M.S.Ed., M.S.N.

ADMISSION REQUIREMENTS. Transcripts, interview required in support of School's application. GMAT required for business; MAT required for Nursing and Education. Accepts transfer applicants. Apply to Dean of Graduate Studies two months prior to registration. Application fee $20. Phone: (260) 434-3279; fax: (260)434-7601.

ADMISSION STANDARDS. Relatively open. Usual minimum average: 2.5 (A = 4).

FINANCIAL AID. Scholarships, assistantships, internships, Federal W/S, loans. Approved for VA benefits. Apply to Dean of Graduate Studies for assistantships; to Director of Financial Aid for all other programs. No specified closing date. Phone: (260) 434-3283; fax: (260)434-3183. Use FAFSA. Aid available for part-time students.

DEGREE REQUIREMENTS. Varies according to program.

FIELDS OF STUDY.
Business Administration. M.B.A., M.S.
Exceptional Needs. M.S.Ed.
Family Nurse Practitioner. M.S.N.
Fine Arts. M.A.
Mental Health Counseling. M.S.
Nursing in Health Systems. M.S.N.

Physician Assistant Studies. M.S.
Psychology. M.S.
School Counseling. M.S.Ed.

ST. FRANCIS UNIVERSITY
Loretto, Pennsylvania 15940-0600
Web site: www.sfcpa.edu

Founded 1847. Located 90 miles E of Pittsburgh. Private control. Roman Catholic. Semester system. Library: 188,800 volumes, 975 subscriptions.

Tuition: per credit $473. Limited on-campus housing for single students. Average academic year housing cost: $6500 (including board). Contact the Office of Residence Life for on- and off-campus housing information. Phone: (814)472-3029.

Graduate Program

Graduate study since 1961. Enrollment: full-time 175, part-time 402. Graduate faculty: full-time 31, part-time 35. Degrees conferred: M.A., M.B.A., M.H.R.M., M.M.S., M.O.T., M.P.T., M.P.A.S.

ADMISSION REQUIREMENTS. Transcripts, essay, letters of reference required in support of School's application. TOEFL required for international applicants. Accepts transfer applicants. Graduates of unaccredited institutions not considered. Apply to Director of Graduate School by August 1 (Fall), one month prior to registration for other sessions. Rolling admissions process. Application fee $30. Phone: (814)472-3085; fax: (814)472-3365.

ADMISSION STANDARDS. Selective. Usual minimum average: 2.5 (A = 4).

FINANCIAL AID. Annual awards from institutional funds: scholarships, fellowship, research assistantship, loans. Approved for VA benefits. Apply by March 31 to individual programs for scholarships, fellowships, assistantships; to Financial Aid Office for loans. Phone: (814)472-3010; fax: (814)472-3335. Use FAFSA. About 3–5% of students receive aid other than loans from School and outside sources. Aid available for part-time students.

DEGREE REQUIREMENTS. For master's: 30 credit hours minimum, research project. For M.B.A.: 48 credit programs.

FIELDS OF STUDY.
Business Administration. Includes accounting, finance, health care administration, human resource management, labor relations, marketing. M.B.A.
Educational Leadership. M.Ed.
Human Resources Management. M.A., M.H.R.M.
Industrial Relations. M.A.
Medical Science. M.M.S.
Occupational Therapy. M.O.T.
Physical Therapy. M.P.T.
Physician Assistant Science. M.P.A.S.

ST. JOHN'S COLLEGE
Annapolis, Maryland 21404-2800
Web site: www.sjca.edu

Founded in 1696. Located 30 miles from Washington, D.C. Coed. Private control. Library: 92,806 volumes, 114 subscriptions.
Annual tuition: $9980; per credit hour $555. No on-campus housing available. Average off-campus housing cost: $750 per month.

Graduate Institute

Graduate study since 1977. Enrollment: full-time 62, part-time 6. Faculty taken from regular full-time faculty of 60 who teach in both undergraduate and graduate programs. Degree conferred: M.A.L.A.

ADMISSION REQUIREMENTS. Transcripts, essay required in support of Institute's application. TOEFL required for international applicants. Accepts transfer applicants. Graduates of unaccredited institutions considered. Application fee: none. Phone: (410)626-2541; fax: (410)626-2880; e-mail: giadm@sjca.edu.

ADMISSION STANDARDS. Selective. Usual minimum average: 3.0 (A = 4). Essay given more weight than GPA.

FINANCIAL AID. Scholarships, Federal W/S, loans. Apply to Director of Financial Aid; no specified closing date. Use FAFSA.

DEGREE REQUIREMENTS. For M.A.L.A., M.A.E.C.: 36 credit hours minimum; thesis or special project.

FIELDS OF STUDY.
Liberal Arts. Includes history, literature, mathematics and natural science, philosophy and theology, politics and society.
Western Classics.

ST. JOHN'S COLLEGE
Santa Fe, New Mexico 87501-4599
Web site: www.sjcsf.edu

Founded in 1964. Located 65 miles from Albuquerque, N.M. Coed. Private control. Library: 60,000 volumes, 135 subscriptions.
Annual tuition: $9980; per credit hour $555. On-campus housing available. Average academic year housing costs: $3900 (including board); 8-week summer session $1900 (including board).

Graduate Institute

Graduate study since 1967. Summer session and academic year evening program. Enrollment: full-time 170. Approximately 60 full-time faculty are taken from regular faculty who teach in both undergraduate and graduate programs. Degree conferred: M.A.L.A., M.A.E.C.

ADMISSION REQUIREMENTS. Transcripts, essay required in support of Institute's application. TOEFL required for international applicants. Accepts transfer applicants. Graduates of unaccredited institutions considered. Application fee: none. Phone: (505)984-6083; fax: (505)984-6003; e-mail: giadmiss@mail.sjcsf.edu.

ADMISSION STANDARDS. Selective. Usual minimum average: 3.0 (A = 4.0). Essay given more weight than GPA.

FINANCIAL AID. Scholarships, loans. Apply by May 1 to Director of Financial Aid. Phone: (505)984-6058. Use FAFSA. Approximately 30–35% of all graduate students receive some form of aid.

DEGREE REQUIREMENTS. For M.A.L.A., M.A.E.C.: 36 credit hours minimum; thesis or special project.

FIELDS OF STUDY.
Eastern Classics. Proficiency in Sanskrit or Classical Chinese required for degree. M.A.E.C.
Liberal Arts. Includes literature, mathematics and natural science, philosophy and theology, politics and society.

ST. JOHN'S UNIVERSITY

Collegeville, Minnesota 56321
Web site: www.csbsju.edu

Founded 1857. Located 80 miles NW of Minneapolis. Coed on the graduate level. Private control. Roman Catholic. Semester system. Library: 600,000 volumes, 4200 subscriptions.

Tuition: per credit Summer $190, Fall and Spring $525. On-campus housing for graduate students. Average academic year housing cost: $2800. Apply to Director of Admissions. Phone: (320)363-2102.

Graduate School of Theology

Open to clerical, religious, and lay students. Enrollment: summer full-time 65, part-time 152; academic year, full-time 76, part-time 64. Graduate faculty: full-time 6, part-time 16. Degrees conferred: M.A., M.Div.

ADMISSION REQUIREMENTS. Transcripts, letters of recommendation required in support of application. On-line application available. TOEFL required for international applicant. MAT or GRE required during first semester. Interview not required. Accepts transfer applicants. Apply to Director of Admissions; no specified closing date. Application fee $25. Phone: (320)363-2102; fax: (320)363-3145.

ADMISSION STANDARDS. Selective. Usual minimum average: 3.0 (A = 4.0).

FINANCIAL AID. Scholarships, fellowships, assistantships, grants, Federal W/S, loans. Apply to Director of Admissions; no specified closing date. Phone: (320)363-2102. Use FAFSA. About of 90% of full-time students receive aid other than loans from University and outside sources. Some aid for part-time students.

DEGREE REQUIREMENTS. For M.A. (Theology; Liturgical Studies): 30 credit minimum; reading knowledge of one foreign language; final comprehensive exam. For M.A. (Liturgical Music; Pastoral Ministry), M.Div.: 30 credits minimum; final comprehensive exam.

FIELDS OF STUDY.
Divinity. M.Div.
Liturgical Music. M.A.
Liturgical Studies. M.A.
Pastoral Ministry. M.A.
Theology. Includes Scripture, systematic, church history, liturgy, monastic studies, spirituality. M.A.

ST. JOHN'S UNIVERSITY

Queens Campus
Jamaica, New York 11439
Staten Island Campus
Staten Island, New York 10301
Web site: www.stjohns.edu

Founded 1870. CGS member. Coed. Private control. Roman Catholic. Semester system. Library: 2,400,000 volumes, 6000 subscriptions. Total University enrollment: 17,400.

Tuition: per credit varies between $605 and $760 depending upon program. No on-campus housing for graduate or married students. Contact Dean of Students for off-campus housing information. Phone: (718)990-6161, ext. 6573.

College of Liberal Arts and Sciences

Queens campus only. Enrollment: full-time 286, part-time 499 (men 25%, women 75%). Faculty: full-time 161, part-time 111.

Degrees conferred: M.A., M.L.S., M.S., M.Div., M.Phil., M.A.-M.L.S., M.L.S.-M.S., D.A., Ph.D.

ADMISSION REQUIREMENTS. Transcripts, two letters of recommendation required in support of School's application. GRE required for Ph.D. programs, GRE/interview for some departments. TOEFL required for international applicants. Graduates of unaccredited institutions not considered. Accepts transfer applicants. Apply to Office of Dean of Admissions at least three months prior to registration. Application fee $40. Phone: (718)990-2000; fax: (718) 990-2096; e-mail: admissions@stjohns.edu.

ADMISSION STANDARDS. Selective. Usual minimum average: 3.0 for master's, 3.5 (in major) for doctorates (A = 4).

FINANCIAL AID. Annual awards from institutional funds: scholarships, doctoral fellowships, graduate assistantships, research assistantships, Federal W/S, loans. Apply by March 1 to the Office of the Dean for fellowships, assistantships; to the Financial Aid Office for all other programs. Phone: (718)990-6161. Use FAFSA. About 19% of students receive aid other than loans from School. Aid available for part-time students.

DEGREE REQUIREMENTS. For master's programs: varies between 30 and 60 semester hours, at least one year in residence; research tool for some departments; written/oral comprehensive exam; thesis/nonthesis option. For M.Div.: 99 semester hours required. For program: 45 semester hours minimum beyond the master's; two-year minimum residence; foreign language/research tool required; written comprehensive exam; research essay. For Ph.D.(Biology): minimum of 60 credits beyond the B.S. degree, or 32 hours beyond the master's, at least two years in residence; foreign language/research tool required; written comprehensive exam; dissertation; oral exam. For Ph.D. (Clinical Psychology): 90 semester hours beyond the bachelor's; full-time residency; one-year internship; written/oral comprehensive exam; dissertation; oral exam.

FIELDS OF STUDY.
Biology. M S., Ph.D.
Chemistry. M.S.
Chinese. M.A.
Clinical Psychology. Ph.D.
East Asian Studies. M.A.
English. M.A., D.A.
General-Experimental Psychology. M.A.
Government and Politics. M.A.
History. M.A.
Library Science. M.L.S.
Mathematics. M.A.
Ministerial Studies. M.Div.
Modern World History. D.A.
School Psychology. M.S., Psy.D.
Sociology. M.A.
Spanish. M.A.
Speech-Language Pathology and Audiology. M.A.
Theology. M.A.

The Peter J. Tobin College of Business

Graduate division established 1959. Tuition: per credit $630. Enrollment: full-time 167, part-time 638. Graduate faculty: full-time 90, part-time 36. Degrees conferred: M.B.A., M.S., Advanced Professional Certificate.

ADMISSION REQUIREMENTS. Official transcripts, GMAT, two letters of recommendation, written statement of objectives required in support of School's application. TOEFL required for international applicants. Interview not required. Accepts transfer applicants. Graduates of unaccredited institutions not considered. Apply to Office of Dean of Admission and Registrar at least three months prior to registration. Application fee $40. Phone: (718)990-2000; fax: (718)990-2096.

ADMISSION STANDARDS. Selective. Usual minimum average: 3.0 (A = 4).

FINANCIAL AID. Scholarships, research assistantships, tuition awards, stipends, Federal W/S, loans. Approved for VA benefits. Apply by March 1 to the Financial Aid Office. Phone: (718)990-6403; fax: (718)969-4773. Use FAFSA, TAP. Aid available for part-time students.

DEGREE REQUIREMENTS. For M.B.A.: 36 credits minimum; thesis optional. For M.S.: 33 credit program. For A.P.C.: 18 credits beyond the M.B.A.

FIELDS OF STUDY.
Accounting. M.S.
Business Administration. Includes specializations in accounting, computer information systems, decision science, economics, executive management, finance, international business, international finance, financial services, marketing, marketing management, risk management, systems for managers, taxation. M.B.A.
Forecasting and Planning. M.S.
Note: The School's center of study in Rome, Italy, has concentrations in international finance and marketing.

School of Education and Human Services

Tuition: $605. Enrollment: full-time 115, part-time 1033. Faculty: full-time 41, part-time 70. Degrees conferred: M.S. Professional Diploma, Ed.D., Ph.D.

ADMISSION REQUIREMENTS. Transcripts, GRE required in support of School's application. TOEFL required for international applicants. Accepts transfer applicants. Apply to Office of Dean, at least three months prior to registration. Rolling admissions process. Application fee $40. Phone: (718)990-2000; fax: (718)990-2096.

ADMISSION STANDARDS. Very competitive for some departments, selective in others. Usual minimum average: 3.0 (A = 4).

FINANCIAL AID. Annual awards from institutional funds: scholarships, fellowships, assistantships, internships, Federal W/S, loans. Approved for VA benefits. Apply by March 1 to department chair for scholarships, fellowships, assistantships; to Financial Aid Office for all other programs. Phone: (718)990-6403; fax: (718)990-4773. Use FAFSA. Aid available for part-time students.

DEGREE REQUIREMENTS. For M.S.: 33 semester hours minimum, at least 27 in residence; comprehensive written exam. For Professional Diploma: 60 semester hours minimum beyond the bachelor's. For Ph.D.: 90 semester hours minimum beyond the bachelor's; reading knowledge of one foreign language or statistics; written comprehensive exam; dissertation; final oral exam. For Ed.D.: 90 semester hours minimum beyond the bachelor's; written comprehensive exam; dissertation; final oral exam.

FIELDS OF STUDY.
Administration and Supervision.
Adolescent Education.
Childhood Education.
Counselor Education.
Curriculum and Teaching. Includes elementary, early childhood education.
Early Childhood Education.
Elementary Education.
Instructional Leadership.
Multilingual/Multicultural Education.
Reading.
Rehabilitation Counseling.
School Counseling.
Secondary Education. Includes most subject fields.
Special Education.
Student Development Practice in Higher Education.
TESOL.

School of Law

Established 1925. Located at Jamaica (Queens) campus (11439). ABA approved since 1937. AALS member. Semester system. Law library: 452,000 volumes, 5477 subscriptions; has LEXIS, NEXIS, WESTLAW, DIALOG.

Annual tuition: $23,800 (day), $17,850 (evening). No on-campus housing available. Total average annual additional expense: $13,190.

Enrollment: first-year class, day 244, evening 50; total full- and part-time 923 (men 55%, women 45%). Faculty: full-time 38, part-time 24. Student to faculty ratio 19.1 to 1. Degrees conferred: J.D., J.D.-M.A. (Government and Politics), J.D.-M.B.A.

ADMISSION REQUIREMENTS. LSDAS Law School report, bachelor's degree, transcripts, LSAT required in support of application. Accepts transfer applicants. Graduates of unaccredited institutions not considered. Apply to Director of Admissions by April 1 (Fall), October 1 (Spring). Application fee $60. Phone: (718)990-6600.

ADMISSION STANDARDS. Selective. Mean LSAT: full-time 157, part-time 154; mean GPA: full-time 3.25, part-time 3.19 (A = 4). Gourman rating: 3.64. *U.S. News & World Report* ranking is in the second tier of all U.S. law schools. Accepts about 30–35% of total annual applicants.

FINANCIAL AID. Scholarships, assistantships, Federal W/S, loans. Apply to University's Financial Aid Office by March 1. Use FAFSA (School code: 002823) and institutional financial aid form. Aid available for part-time students.

DEGREE REQUIREMENTS. For J.D.: 84 semester hours minimum, at least 30 in residence.

College of Pharmacy and Allied Health Professions

Graduate study since 1929.

Tuition: per credit $630. No on-campus housing available. Contact Student Life Office for off-campus housing information. Phone: (718)990-6783.

Enrollment: full-time 99, part-time 120 (men 55%, women 45%). Faculty: full-time 52, part-time 12. Degrees conferred: M.S., Ph.D., Pharm.D.

ADMISSION REQUIREMENTS. Transcripts, GRE, two letters of recommendation required in support of application. TOEFL required for foreign applicants. Interview required for Pharm.D. only. Accepts transfer applicants. Graduates of unaccredited institutions not considered. Apply to Office of Graduate Admissions at least one month prior to registration. Application fee $40. Phone: (718)990-2000; fax: (718)990-2096.

ADMISSION STANDARDS. Selective. Usual minimum average: 3.0 (A = 4).

FINANCIAL AID. Annual awards from institutional funds: doctoral fellowships, graduate assistantships, internships, Federal W/S, loans. Approved for VA benefits. Apply by March 1 to Dean of Graduate Division of College for fellowships, assistantships; to Financial Aid Office for all other programs. Phone: (718)990-6403; fax: (718)969-4773. Use FAFSA. About 30% of students receive aid other than loans from College and outside sources. Aid available for part-time students.

DEGREE REQUIREMENTS. For Pharm.D.: 66 semester hours minimum; comprehensive oral/written exam; thesis. For M.S.: 30–33 semester hours minimum; comprehensive oral/written exam; thesis. For Ph.D.: 36 semester hours beyond the master's, exclusive of dissertation research; dissertation; comprehensive written/oral exam.

FIELDS OF STUDY.
Medical Technology.
Pharmaceutical Sciences.
Pharmacy.
Pharmacy Administration.
Toxicology.

ST. JOSEPH COLLEGE

West Hartford, Connecticut 06117-2700
Web site: www.sjc.edu

Founded 1932. Located 3 miles W of Hartford. Coed on graduate level. Private control. Roman Catholic affiliation. Semester system. Special facilities: Athletic Center, Gengras Center for Exceptional Children, Marriage and Family Center, School for Young Children. Library: 164,283 volumes, 600 subscriptions.

Annual tuition: per credit $510. On-campus housing for graduate students available. Annual cost: $8200–$10,460 (including board). Apply to Director, Residential Life. Phone: (860)232-4571, ext. 214.

Graduate School

Graduate study since 1959. Enrollment: full-time 61, part-time 391 (men 10%, women 90%). College faculty: full-time 36, part-time 28. Degrees conferred: M.A., M.S., M.A.M.F.T., six year certificate.

ADMISSION REQUIREMENTS. Transcripts, two references, interview, GRE or MAT required in support of application. TOEFL required for international applicants. Accepts transfer applicants. Apply to Graduate Office; no specified closing date. Application fee $25. Phone: (860)231-5261; fax: (860)231-8396.

ADMISSION STANDARDS. Selective. Usual minimum average: 3.0 (A = 4).

FINANCIAL AID. Scholarships, assistantships, internships, tuition waivers, loans. Approved for VA benefits. Apply by July 15 to Director of Financial Aid. Phone: (860)231-5223. Use FAFSA (College code: 001409) and institutional FAF. Aid available for part-time students.

DEGREE REQUIREMENTS. For M.A.: 30 semester hours minimum; thesis optional, may supply 6 credits; final comprehensive evaluation. For S.Y.C.: 32 credits minimum beyond the master's.

FIELDS OF STUDY.
Biology.
Chemistry.
Counseling.
Early Childhood Special Education.
Education.
Marriage and Family Therapy.
Nursing. Includes psychiatric/mental health, family health.
Special Education.

ST. JOSEPH'S UNIVERSITY

Philadelphia, Pennsylvania 19131-9977
Web site: www.sju.edu

Founded 1851. Coed. Private control. Roman Catholic (Jesuit). Semester system. Library: 350,000 volumes, 1850 subscriptions. Total University enrollment: 7000.

Tuition: per credit $530–$570; M.B.A. $610. No on-campus housing for graduate and married students. Average annual housing cost: $5500. Apply to Residence Life Office for off-campus housing. Phone: (610)660-1063.

Graduate Program

Enrollment: full-time 368, part-time 2076. Graduate faculty: full- and part-time 89. Degrees conferred: M.S., M.B.A.

ADMISSION REQUIREMENTS. Transcripts, three letters of recommendation, résumé required in support of application. On-line application available. GRE required for some programs. GMAT for M.B.A. programs. TOEFL required for international applicants. Accepts transfer applicants. Graduates of unaccredited colleges not considered. Apply to appropriate School at least two months prior to registration. Application fee $35. Phone: (610)660-1289 (Art & Science), (610)660-1690 (Business).

ADMISSION STANDARDS. Selective. Usual minimum average: 3.0 (A = 4).

FINANCIAL AID. Annual awards from institutional funds: scholarships, assistantships, tuition waivers, Federal W/S, loans. Apply by February 15 to Chairman, Chemistry Department, for teaching assistantships; to Director, Computer Science Graduate Program, for teaching assistantships: to Chairman, Criminal Justice, for research assistantships; to Chairman, Education Department, for assistantships; to Director of M.B.A. Program, for assistantships. Phone: (610)660-1760. Use FAFSA. About 5–10% of students receive aid other than loans from University. Aid available for part-time students.

DEGREE REQUIREMENTS. For M.S. Biology: 36 credits minimum. For M.S. Chemistry: 31 credits minimum. For M.S. Computer Sciences: 31 credits minimum. For M.S. Criminal Justice: 30 credits. For M.S. Education or Health Education: 36 credits. For M.S. Health Administration: 36 credits. For M.S. Gerontological Services: 36 credits. For M.S. Public Safety: 33 credits minimum. For M.S. Training and Development: 36 credits. For M.B.A.: 33 credits minimum.

FIELDS OF STUDY.
Biology.
Business Administration. Includes accounting, management, food marketing, finance, health administration, information systems, international business, law and court administration, marketing, medical management.
Chemistry.
Chemistry Education.
Computer Science. Includes information systems management.
Criminal Justice. Includes administration, probation, parole and corrections, criminology.
Education. Includes business, chemistry, computer science, educational leadership, elementary, health, mathematics, reading, secondary.
Gerontological Services. Includes gerontological counseling, human services administration.
Health Administration.
Health Education. Includes employee assistance, nutritional marketing.
Nurse Anesthesia.

Psychology. Includes biopsychology, health psychology, and so-cial psychology.
Training and Organizational Development.

ST. LAWRENCE UNIVERSITY
Canton, New York 13617-1455

Founded 1856. Located 130 miles N of Syracuse, 80 miles S of Ottawa. Coed. Private control. Library: 509,348 volumes, 2000 subscriptions.

Annual tuition: per credit $515. On-campus housing available for single students. The annual average cost: $3900, $6900 (in-cluding board).

Graduate Division

Enrollment: full-time 20, part-time 80. Faculty: full-time 6, part-time 21. Degrees conferred: M.A., M.Ed., C.A.S.

ADMISSION REQUIREMENTS. Transcripts, three letters of recommendation, GRE required in support of application. TOEFL required for international applicants. Interview recommended. Ac-cepts transfer applicants. Graduates of unaccredited institutions not considered. Apply to Chair, Education Department; no spec-ified closing date. Application fee $30. Phone: (315)229-5872; fax: (315)229-7423.

ADMISSION STANDARDS. Selective. Usual minimum aver-age 2.75 (A = 4).

FINANCIAL AID. Resident hall counseling/assistantships, teach-ing fellowships, internships, Federal W/S, loans. Approved for VA benefits. Phone: (315)379-5265. Use FAFSA. Apply to Di-rector of Student Services. Aid available for part-time students.

DEGREE REQUIREMENTS. For master's: 36–39 semester hours minimum; 6 transfer hours allowed; internship. For C.A.S.: 30 semester hours minimum beyond master's.

FIELDS OF STUDY.
Counseling and Development. Includes school counseling. M.Ed. or 60-hour program leading to Certificate of Advanced Standing (C.A.S.).
Educational Administration. M.Ed. or 60-hour program leading to Certificate of Advanced Standing (C.A.S.).
General Studies. 33 credit M.Ed.

SAINT LOUIS UNIVERSITY
St. Louis, Missouri 63103-2097
Web site: www.slu.edu

Founded 1818. CGS member. Coed. Private control. Roman Catholic affiliation. Semester system. Special facilities: Center for Applied Behavior Science, Center for Irish Law, Institute for Mol-ecular Virology, Seismographic Stations Network, Center for Pub-lic Policy, Center for Jewish Law, Center for Medieval and Renaissance Studies, Yalem Computing Center, Reis Biological Station, Doisy Hall of Medical Research, Vatican Film Library. The University's NIH ranking is 129th among all U.S. institutions with 95 awards/grants worth $26,527,983. Library: 1,500,000 vol-umes, 14,700 subscriptions. Total University enrollment: 11,300.

Tuition: per credit $630. On-campus housing for 400 single students. Average academic year housing costs: $7300 (including board) for single students. Contact the Director of Residence Life for both on- and off-campus housing information. Phone: (314)977-2797.

Graduate School

Graduate study since 1832. Enrollment: full-time 680, part-time 1161 (men 35%, women 65%). Graduate faculty: full-time 512, part-time 98. Degrees conferred: M.A., M.A.U.A., M.S., M.S. in Dent., M.S. in Diet., M.S.S. in N.R., M.H.A., M.P.A., M.A.P.A., M.P.H., M.S.D., M.S.N., M.Pr.Gph., M.Pr.Met., M.U.P.R.E.D., Ed.S., Ed.D., Ph.D., Certificates.

ADMISSION REQUIREMENTS. Transcripts, GRE, three refer-ences, autobiographical sketch, goals statement required in sup-port of School's application. GMAT required for Business. TOEFL required for international applicants. Accepts transfer applicants. Apply to Dean of Graduate School at least two months prior to registration. Application fee $50. Phone: (314) 977-2240; fax: (314)977-3943.

ADMISSION STANDARDS. Relatively open to very competi-tive. Usual minimum average 3.0 in last 60 credits for master's (A = 4).

FINANCIAL AID. Annual awards from institutional funds: fel-lowships, teaching assistantships, research assistantships, spe-cialized assistantships, traineeships, tuition waivers, Federal W/S, loans. Approved for VA benefits. Apply preferably by Feb-ruary 1 to Dean of the Graduate School for fellowships, assis-tantships; to Office of Scholarships and Financial Aid by April 1 for all other programs. Phone: (314)977-2350. Use FAFSA. About 65% of all students receive aid other than loans from University and outside sources.

DEGREE REQUIREMENTS. For master's: 30 semester hours minimum including 6 hours of thesis for research degree; re-search tool (foreign language, computer literacy, statistics); final oral exam. For Ed.S.: 30 semester hours minimum beyond mas-ter's. For Ed.D.: about 75 hours beyond bachelor's degree; re-search-methods sequences; preliminary exam; culminatory project. For Ph.D.: about 48–60 hours, plus 12 hours research, beyond the bachelor's degree, minimum one year in full-time residence, preliminary written and oral exams; research tool; dis-sertation.

FIELDS OF STUDY.
Aerospace Engineering. M.S. only.
American Studies.
Anatomy.
Biochemistry. Ph.D. only.
Biology.
Business Administration. GMAT for admission. Includes ac-counting, economics, international business, management and decision sciences, marketing, personnel and industrial rela-tions.
Chemistry. M.S. only.
Communication. M.A. only.
Communication Sciences and Disorders. M.A. only.
Community Health. M.P.H. only.
Counseling and Family Therapy. M.A., Ph.D.
Dietetics. M.S. only.
Economics.
Educational Leadership. M.A., Ed.S., Ed.D., Ph.D.
Educational Studies. M.A., M.A.T., Ph.D.
Endodontics. M.S. only.
English.
French. M.A. only.
Geology. M.S. only.
Geophysics.
Health Administration. M.H.A.
Health-Care Ethics. Ph.D.
Health Services Research. Ph.D. only.
Historical Theology.
History.

Mathematics.
Meteorology.
Microbiology. Ph.D. only.
Neurobiology. Ph.D. only.
Nursing.
Nutrition and Dietetics. M.S. only.
Orthodontics. M.S. only.
Pathology. Ph.D.
Pharmacological and Physiological Sciences. Ph.D.
Philosophy.
Psychology.
Public Administration. M.A.P.A.
Public Policy Analysis. Ph.D.
Spanish. M.A. only.
Theology. M.A. only.
Urban Affairs. M.A.U.A. only.
Urban Planning and Real Estate Development. M.U.P.R.E.D.

John Cook School of Business

Established 1910. Private control. Accredited programs: M.B.A.; recognized Ph.D. Semester system. Special programs: foreign exchange programs in Hong Kong, Spain, Sweden. Special facilities: Emerson Electric Center for Business Ethics, Institute for International Business, Jefferson Smurfit Center for Entrepreneurial Studies, Small Business Development Center.

Annual tuition: full-time $24,360, part-time $695 per credit.

Enrollment: total full-time 169, part-time 183 (men 65%, women 35%). Faculty: full-time 61, part-time 23; 97% with Ph.D./D.B.A. Degrees conferred: M.B.A. (full-time, part-time, day, evening, weekends), E.M.I.B. (Executive Masters in International Business), M.I.B. (International Business), M.M.I.S. (Information Systems), M.M.S. (Management Sciences), M. P.A. (Professional Accounting), M.S.F. (Finance), M.B.A.-J.D., M.B.A.-M.D.S. (Decision Sciences), M.B.A.-M.H.A. (Health Administration), M.B.A.-M. S.N.A. (Nursing Administration), Ph.D.

ADMISSION REQUIREMENTS. All applicants should have a bachelor's degree from a recognized institution of higher education and a strong mathematics background (competency in calculus). Admission is based on the formula: $200 \times$ UGPA + GMAT. Early applications are encouraged for both admission and financial aid consideration. Beginning students are admitted Fall, Spring, and Summer. U.S. citizens apply by July 1 (Fall), December 1 (Spring), April 15 (Summer), international students apply by January 15 (Fall), June 1 (Spring), November 15 (Summer). Submit an application, GMAT (will accept GMAT test results from the last five years, latest acceptable date is June), official transcripts from each undergraduate/graduate school attended, two letters of recommendation, statement of intent, résumé (prefers at least four years of work experience), and an application fee of $40 to the Office of Admission. On-line application available. In addition, international students (whose native language is other than English) should submit a TOEFL (minimum score 550) or the Michigan Language Test (minimum score 4.5); certified translations and evaluations of all official transcripts; recommendations should be in English or with certified translations; proof of health/immunization certificate; and proof of sufficient financial resources for two years of academic study. On-campus visits are encouraged. Joint degree applicants must apply to and be accepted to both schools/programs. Contact the admissions office for current information and specific admissions requirements. Rolling admissions process; notification is made within four weeks of receipt of completed application and supporting documents.

ADMISSION REQUIREMENTS FOR DOCTORAL CANDIDATES. Contact either the Graduate School at (314)977-2240 or the Director of Graduate and Professional Programs, School of Business, at (314)977-3801 for application material and information. A preliminary application may be required for Ph.D. in Business. Beginning students are admitted Fall only. Both U.S. citizens and international applicants apply by February 15 (Fall). Submit a Graduate School application, GMAT/GRE (will accept GMAT/GRE test results from the last five years), official transcripts from each undergraduate/graduate school attended, three letters of recommendation, biographical sketch, résumé, statement of purpose, and application fee of $40 to the Dean, Graduate School. In addition, international students (whose native language is other than English) should submit TOEFL (minimum score 600); certified translations and evaluations of all official transcripts; recommendations should be in English or with certified translations; proof of health/immunization certificate. International students' contact: (314)977-2318. Interviews are strongly encouraged prior to admissions committee reviewing completed application. Notification is generally made by mid-April.

ADMISSION STANDARDS. Selective. Mean GMAT: full-time 577, part-time 554; mean GPA: 3.19 (A = 4).

FINANCIAL AID. Fellowships, research and teaching assistantships, Federal Perkins Loans, Stafford Subsidized and Unsubsidized Loans, Federal W/S available. Financial aid is available for part-time study. Assistantships/fellowships may be available for Joint Degree candidates. Financial Aid applications and information are included in admissions materials; apply by June 1. Request fellowship and assistantship information from the School of Business. Contact the University's Financial Aid Office for need-based financial aid information. Phone: (314)977-2350. Use FAFSA (School code: 002506), also submit Financial Aid Transcript, Federal Income Tax forms. Approximately 40% of students receive some form of financial aid.

DEGREE REQUIREMENTS. For M.B.A.: 39–57 credit program including 12 elective credits, one- to two-year program; degree program must be completed in five years. For E.M.I.B.: 36 credit program. For M.D.S.: 30–48 credit program. For M.I.B.: 35 credit program. For M.M.S., M.S.F.: 30–48 credit programs. For M.P.A.: 30–63 credit program. For M.B.A.-J.D.: 130 credit, four-and-one-half- to five-year program. For M.B.A.-M.H.A.: 91 credit program. For M.B.A.-M.S.N.A.: 73 credit program. For Ph.D.: 54 credits beyond master's, three- to five-year program, at least three years in full-time residence; comprehensive exam in area of study; dissertation proposal and oral defense; dissertation; oral defense.

M.B.A. AND PH.D. CONCENTRATIONS.
Accounting. M.B.A.
Business Administration. Ph.D.
Decision Sciences. M.B.A.
Economics. M.B.A., Ph.D.
Finance. M.B.A.
Management. M.B.A.
Management Information Systems. M.B.A.
Marketing. M.B.A.

School of Law
Web site: www.law.slu.edu

Established 1842. ABA approved since 1924. AALS member. Semester system. Full-time, part-time study. Special facilities: Center for Health Law Studies, Center for International and Comparative Law, Wefel Center for Employment Law. Special programs: Summer Institute; faculty exchange programs with Sichuan University in the People's Republic of China, Ruhr University in Bochum, Germany, University of Warsaw, Poland. Law library: 487,300 volumes, 6253 subscriptions; has LEXIS, NEXIS, WESTLAW, DIALOG; is a Federal Government Depository.

Annual tuition: full-time $21,540, part-time $15,990. On-campus housing available for both single and married students.

Contact Office of Housing for both on- and off-campus housing information. Phone: (314)977-2797. Law students generally live off-campus. Off-campus housing and personal expenses: approximately $12,000.

Enrollment: first-year class full-time 189, part-time 64; total full- and part-time 767 (men 52%, women 48%). Faculty: full-time 32, part-time 21. Student to faculty ratio 18.2 to 1.

Degrees conferred: J.D., J.D.-M.B.A., J.D.-M.H.A., J.D.-M.A. (Public Affairs, Urban Affairs), J.D.-M.S.W., LL.M. (Health Law, Employment Law), LL.M. (American Law for Foreign Lawyers who have completed a basic legal education and received a university degree in law in another country).

ADMISSION REQUIREMENTS. LSDAS Law School report, transcripts, LSAT (not later than December), letters of recommendation required in support of application. Interview not required. Accepts transfer applicants. Graduates of unaccredited colleges not considered. Apply to Director of Admissions by March 1. Admits first-year students. Fall only. Application fee $55. Phone: (314)977-2800; fax: (314)977-1464; e-mail: admissions@law.slu.edu.

ADMISSION REQUIREMENTS. For LL.M. (Health Law, Employment Law): Applicants must have a J.D. from an ABA/AALS-accredited/approved Law School. Official transcripts from undergraduate, graduate, and law schools, résumé/curriculum vitae, two letters of recommendation, personal statement including interest and career goals required in support of application. Approximately five students accepted each year. For LL.M. (Foreign Lawyers): Applicants must have a degree in law from a foreign university. Certified translations and evaluations of all foreign academic credentials, TOEFL (for those whose native language is not English, minimum score 575), two letters of recommendation, personal statement including your interests and career goals, résumé/curriculum vitae required in support of application. All LL.M. programs admit Fall only. Apply by May 1 to School of Law—Graduate Programs. Phone: (314)977-3067.

ADMISSION STANDARDS. Selective. Mean LSAT: full-time 154, part-time 151; mean GPA: full-time 3.3, part-time 3.03 (A = 4). Gourman rating: 3.65 *U.S. News & World Report* ranking is in the third tier of all U.S. law schools. Accepts 35–40% of total annual applicants.

FINANCIAL AID. Scholarships, full and partial tuition waivers, fellowships, Federal W/S, loans. Apply to the Financial Aid Office by March 1. Phone: (314)977-3437. Use FAFSA (School code: 002506). About 50% of students receive aid other than loans from School.

DEGREE REQUIREMENTS. For J.D.: 88 (36 required) credits with a GPA of at least 2.0 (A = 4), plus completion of upper-divisional writing course; three-year program, four-year part-time program. Accelerated J.D. with summer course work. For J.D.-master's: four-year programs rather than five-year programs if both degrees are taken consecutively. For LL.M. (Health Law, Employment Law): 24 credits completed over two years, full- and part-time study; thesis of publishable quality; oral defense. For LL.M. (Foreign Lawyers): 24 credits; at least two semesters in residence; thesis of publishable quality; oral defense.

School of Medicine

Established 1836. Present school acquired in 1903. Semester system. Special facilities: Firmin Desloge Hospital, Bordley Pavilion, David P. Wohl Memorial Mental Health Institute, Cardinal Glennon Children's Hospital. SLU Anheuser-Busch Eye Institute, Institute of Molecular Virology. Special program: summer programs for underrepresented minorities. Library: 113,000 volumes, 1765 subscriptions.

Annual tuition: $33,300; student fees $1284. Limited housing available. Contact Director of Housing for current information. Total average costs for all other expenses: $13,000.

Enrollment: first-year class 150 (EDP 8), total 578 (men 52%, women 48%). Faculty: full-time 584, part-time 800. Degrees conferred: M.D., M.D.-Ph.D., M.D.-M.P.H.

ADMISSION REQUIREMENTS. AMCAS report, transcripts, recommendations, MCAT, interview required in support of application. Has EDP; apply between June 1 and August 1. Apply to Committee on Admissions after June 1, before December 15. Admits Fall only. Applicants planning to begin medical studies after only three years of college work considered. Application fee $100. Phone: (314)577-8205; fax: (314)577-8214.

ADMISSION STANDARDS. Very competitive. Mean MCAT: 10.2; mean GPA: 3.66 (A = 4). Gourman rating: 4.24. Accepts 5–8% of total annual applicants. Approximately 32% are state residents.

FINANCIAL AID. Scholarships, loans. Apply by May 1 to Office of Student Financial Planning. Use FAFSA (School code: 002506). About 87% of students receive aid other than loans from School.

DEGREE REQUIREMENTS. For M.D.: satisfactory completion of four-year program. All students must pass USMLE Step 1 prior to entering third year and Step 2 prior to awarding of M.D.

FIELDS OF GRADUATE STUDY.
Anatomy and Neuroanatomy-Neuroscience.
Biochemistry.
Cell and Molecular Biology.
Molecular Micobiology and Immunology.
Neurobiology.
Pathology.
Pharmacological Sciences.
Physiological Sciences.

School of Social Service

Graduate study since 1930. Semester system. Tuition: per hour $630.

Graduate enrollment: full-time 148, part-time 146. Faculty: full-time 20, part-time 22. Degrees conferred: M.S.W., M.S.W.-M.P.H., M.S.W.-M.A. (Pastoral Studies).

ADMISSION REQUIREMENTS. Transcripts, interview, three letters of reference, personal statement, interview required in support of School's application. GRE or MAT strongly recommended. TOEFL required for international applicants. Accepts transfer applicants. Apply to Director of Admission by April 1 (Fall), October 1 (Spring). Application fee $40. Phone: (314)977-2752; fax: (314)977-2931.

ADMISSION STANDARDS. Selective. Usual minimum average: 3.0 (A=4).

FINACIAL AID. Annual awards for institutional funds: scholarships, fellowships, research assistantships, internships, Federal W/S, loans. Approved for VA benefits. Apply by March 1 to Director of Admissions. Phone: (314)977-2350. Use FAFSA. About 50% of students receive aid other than loans from School and other sources. Aid available for part-time students.

DEGREE REQUIREMENTS. For M.S.W.: 57 semester hours minimum; practicum.

FIELD OF STUDY.
Social Work. Includes concentration in community, family, health.

SAINT MARY'S UNIVERSITY OF MINNESOTA

Winona, Minnesota 55987-1399
Web site: www.smumn.edu

Founded 1912. Private control. Roman Catholic affiliation. Semester system. Tuition: per credit $315 (M.A.I.), $260 (Pastoral Ministries). No on-campus housing available.

Graduate Programs

Enrollment: full-time 347, part-time 2088. Faculty: full-time 43, part-time 312. Degrees conferred: M.A., M.A.I., M.S.

ADMISSION REQUIREMENTS. Official transcripts, personal statement, three letters of recommendation, résumé required in support of application. Additional requirements vary by program. TOEFL (minimum score 550) required for international applicants. Accepts transfer applicants. Graduates of unaccredited institutions not considered. Apply to the Graduate Office at least one month prior to registration. Rolling admissions process. Application fee $25. Phone: (507)457-7500; fax: (507)457-1752.

ADMISSION STANDARDS. Selective for most programs. Usual minimum average: 2.75 (A = 4).

FINANCIAL AID. Limited to scholarships, assistantships, loans. Apply to the Financial Aid Office; no specified closing date. Phone: (800)635-5987. Use FAFSA.

DEGREE REQUIREMENTS. For master's: 41–48 semester hours depending on program; thesis/nonthesis option; final oral colloquia presentation for most programs. For M.S.: 3–4 semester individually designed programs.

FIELDS OF STUDY.
Counseling and Psychological Services.
Developmental Disabilities.
Educational Administration.
Human Development.
Instruction. M.A.I. only.
International Business.
Nurse Anesthesia.
Pastoral Ministries. 36 credit master's. M.A.
Philanthropy and Development.
Resource Analysis. Includes concentrations in business administration, criminal justice, natural resources, public administration/local government.

ST. MARY'S UNIVERSITY

San Antonio, Texas 78228-8572
Web site: www.stmarytx.edu

Founded 1852. Coed. Private control. Semester system. Library: 525,000 volumes, 1500 subscriptions. Total University enrollment: 4100.

Tuition: per credit $481. On-campus housing available for single students only. Average academic year housing costs: $2524–$3550 (room only). Contact Housing office for both on- and off-campus housing information. Phone: (210)436-3534.

Graduate School

Graduate study since 1936. Enrollment: full- and part-time 1200. Graduate faculty: full-time 50, part-time 25. Degrees conferred: M.A., M.B.A., M.J.A., M.P.A., M.S., Ph.D.

ADMISSION REQUIREMENTS. Transcripts, two letters of recommendation, GRE/GMAT required in support of School's application. TOEFL required for international applicants. Interview not required. Accepts transfer applicants. Apply to Graduate School by August 1 (Fall), two weeks prior to registration for other semesters. Application fee $35. Phone: (210)436-3101; fax: (210)431-2220.

ADMISSION STANDARDS. Selective. Usual minimum average: 3.0 (A = 4).

FINANCIAL AID. Assistantships, Federal W/S, loans. Approved for VA benefits. Apply by March 1 to Dean of the Graduate School for assistantships; to Financial Aid Office for all other programs. Use FAFSA. About 5–10% of students receive aid other than loans from university.

DEGREE REQUIREMENTS. For master's: 30–36 semester hours minimum, at least 24 in residence, thesis; 30–36 hours, nonthesis option for all departments; reading knowledge of 1 foreign language for some departments; final oral/written exam. For Ph.D.: 78 semester hours beyond master's; reading knowledge of one foreign language; comprehensive exam; dissertation; final oral exam.

FIELDS OF STUDY.
Accounting.
Business Administration. GMAT for admission.
Catholic School Leadership.
Communication Studies.
Computer Information Systems.
Computer Science.
Counselor Education.
Economics.
Educational Leadership.
Electrical Engineering.
Engineering Systems Management.
English Literature and Language.
History.
Industrial Engineering.
International Relations.
Marriage and Family Therapy. 48 credit master's program.
Mathematics.
Pastoral Ministry.
Political Science.
Psychology. 42 credit program.
Public Administration.
Reading.
Software Engineering.
Theology.

School of Law (78228-8601)

Web site: www.stmarylaw.edu

Established 1927. ABA approved since 1948. AALS member. Semester system. Full-time, day study only. Special facilities: Center for Legal and Social Justice, Center for Conciliation and Arbitration, Center for International Legal Studies, Institute for World Legal Problems in Innsbruck, Austria, Institute for International Human Rights in Guatemala. Special programs: Judicial Internships. Law library: 338,904 volumes, 3474 subscriptions; has LEXIS, NEXIS, WESTLAW, DIALOG.

Annual tuition: $19,019. On-campus housing available for single students only. Contact Housing Office for both on- and off-campus housing information. Telephone: (210)436-3534. Law students tend to live off-campus. Off-campus housing and personal expenses: approximately $13,000.

Enrollment: first-year class 239; total full-time 736 (men 52%, women 48%). Faculty: full-time 33, part-time 43. Student to faculty ratio 18.6 to 1. Degrees conferred: J.D., J.D.-M.B.A., J.D.-

M.P.A., J.D.-E.C., J.D.-I.R., J.D.-M.Theo., J.D.-M.C.I.S., LL.M. (International and Comparative Law for U.S.-trained attorneys), LL.M. (American Legal Studies for persons who have completed a basic legal education and received a university degree in law in another country).

ADMISSION REQUIREMENTS. LSDAS Law School report, bachelor's degree, transcripts, LSAT, recommendations required in support of application. Graduates of unaccredited colleges not considered. Apply to Chairperson, Faculty Admissions Committee by March 1. Application fee $45. Phone: (210)436-3523; fax: (210)431-4202.

ADMISSION STANDARDS. Selective. Mean LSAT: 149; mean GPA: 2.98 (A = 4). Gourman rating: 2.52. *U.S. News & World Report* ranking is in the fourth tier of all U.S. law schools. Admits about 30–35% of total annual applications.

FINANCIAL AID. Scholarships, assistantships, Federal W/S, loans. Apply to Director of Financial Aid by April 1. Use FAFSA (School code: 003623). About 23% of students receive some aid from School.

DEGREE REQUIREMENTS. For J.D.: 90 (46 required) credits with a GPA of at least 2.0 (A = 4), plus completion of upper-divisional writing course; three-year program. Accelerated J.D. with summer course work. For J.D.-Master's: four-year programs rather than five-year programs if both degrees are taken consecutively. For LL.M. (International and Comparative Law): 24 credits, at least two semesters in full-time residence; thesis of publishable quality. For LL.M. (American Legal Studies): 24 credits; at least two semesters in residence in full-time residence; three required courses in U.S. legal system; thesis of publishable quality.

ST. MICHAEL'S COLLEGE
Colchester, Vermont 05439
Web site: www.smcvt.edu

Founded 1904. Located near Burlington. Private control. Roman Catholic affiliation. Semester system. Library: 176,000 volumes, 1200 subscriptions. Total College enrollment: 1900.

Tuition: per credit $345. Limited on-campus housing available for single students only. Average academic year housing costs: $4510 (room only). Contact assistant Dean of Students for both on- and off-campus housing information. Phone: (802)654-2566. Day-care facilities available.

Graduate Programs

Graduate study since 1926. Enrollment: full-time 142, part-time 741. Faculty: full-time 9, part-time 137. Degrees conferred: M.A., M.Ed., M.S.A.

ADMISSION REQUIREMENTS. Transcripts, two letters of recommendation, personal essay, GRE required in support of School's application. TOEFL (minimum score 550) required for international applicants. Interview recommended for some programs. Accepts transfer applicants. Apply to Dean at least one month prior to registration. Application fee $35. Phone: (802)654-2100; fax: (802)654-2664; e-mail: gradprograms@smcvt.edu.

ADMISSION STANDARDS. Selective. Usual minimum average: 2.8 (A = 4).

FINANCIAL AID. Three assistantships, grants, Vermont loans and scholarships, Federal W/S, loans. Apply by March 15 to Di-

rector of Financial Aid. Phone: (802)654-3243; fax: (802)654-2591. Use FAFSA (College code: 003694) and institutional FAF.

DEGREE REQUIREMENTS. For master's: 36–42 semester hours.

FIELDS OF STUDY.
Administration and Management. M.S.A. only.
Clinical Psychology. Sixty semester hours. M.A.
Education.
Teaching English as a Second/Foreign Language.
Theology and Pastoral Ministry.

THE COLLEGE OF SAINT ROSE
Albany, New York 12203-1419
Web site: www.strose.edu

Founded 1920. CGS member. Coed. Private control. Semester system. Library: 200,987 volumes, 975 subscriptions. Total College enrollment: 4231.

Tuition: per credit $383. Limited housing for graduate students. Average monthly housing costs: $350–$550. Contact the Director of Residence Life for both on- and off-campus housing information. Phone: (518)454-5295.

Graduate School

Graduate study since 1949. Enrollment: full-time 273; part-time 1229. Graduate faculty: full-time 68, part-time 22. Degrees conferred: M.A., M.S., M.S.Ed., M.B.A., M.B.A.-J.D. (with Albany Law School).

ADMISSION REQUIREMENTS. Transcripts, two letters of recommendation, statement of purpose required in support of application. GMAT required for Business Administration and Accounting. TOEFL required for international applicants. Accepts transfer applicants. Apply to Dean of Graduate, Adult, and Continuing Education Admissions at least two months prior to registration. Rolling admissions process. Application fee $30. Phone: (518)454-5136; fax: (518)458-5479.

ADMISSION STANDARDS. Selective. Usual minimum average: 2.75 (A = 4).

FINANCIAL AID. Scholarships, assistantships, internships, grants, Federal W/S, loans. Approved for VA benefits. Apply by March 1 to appropriate Department for internships, scholarships, assistantships; to Financial Aid Office for all other programs. Phone: (518)454-5168. Use FAFSA and institutional FAF. Some aid for part-time students.

DEGREE REQUIREMENTS. For master's: 30 semester hours minimum, at least 24 in residence; thesis/nonthesis option; written comprehensive exam for some departments.

FIELDS OF STUDY.
Accounting. M.S.
Art Education.
Business Administration.
Communication Disorders.
Computer Information Systems.
Counseling.
Education. Includes early childhood, elementary, secondary, educational psychology, educational administration and supervision, special education.
English.
History and Political Science.
Liberal Studies.
Music.

Music Education.
Public Communications.
Reading.
School Psychology.

COLLEGE OF ST. SCHOLASTICA

Duluth, Minnesota 55811-4199
Web site: www.css.edu

Founded 1912. Coed. Private. Church related. Semester system. Library: 137,000 volumes, 828 subscriptions.

Tuition: per credit $565. On-campus housing available for single students. Average academic year housing costs: $7000. Contact the Housing Office for both on- and off-campus housing information. Phone: (218)723-6483. Day-care facilities available.

Graduate Studies

Graduate study since 1972. Enrollment: full-time 232, part-time 323. Faculty: full-time 38, part-time 31. Degrees conferred: M.A., M.Ed.

ADMISSION REQUIREMENTS. Transcripts, GRE (Nursing, Exercise Physiology program only), two letters of recommendations required in support of application. TOEFL required for international applicants. Accepts transfer applicants. Apply to Graduate Office by March 1 for Physical Therapy, January 31 for Occupational Therapy; apply to all other programs at least one month prior to each quarter. Application fee $50. Phone: (800) 447-5444, (218)723-6285; fax: (218)723-5991.

ADMISSION STANDARDS. Selective. Usual minimum average: 3.0 for last two years (A = 4). TOEFL minimum score 575.

FINANCIAL AID. Scholarships, traineeships, Federal W/S, loans. Approved for VA benefits. Apply to Director of Financial Aid; no specified closing date. Phone: (218)723-6047; fax: (218)723-6290. Use FAFSA. Aid available for part-time students.

DEGREE REQUIREMENTS. For M.Ed.: 34 credit program. For M.A. Nursing: 38–47 credit program. For M.A. Management: 39 credit program. For M.A. Physical Therapy: 85 credit program; internship. For M.A. Occupational Therapy: 76 credit program; fieldwork experience. For M.A. Exercise Physiology: 32 credit program; thesis/internship.

FIELDS OF STUDY.
Curriculum and Instruction.
Educational Media and Technology.
Exercise Physiology.
Health Information Management.
Management.
Nursing.
Occupational Therapy.
Physical Therapy.

ST. THOMAS UNIVERSITY

Miami, Florida 33054-6459
Web site: www.stu.edu

Founded 1966. Located about 5 miles NW of Miami. Coed. Private control (Roman Catholic affiliation). Semester system. Library: 190,000 volumes, 990 subscriptions. Total University enrollment at main campus: 2500.

School of Law

Web site: www.stu.edu/lawschool

Established 1984. Located on main campus. ABA approved since 1988. AALS member. Semester system. Full-time, day study only. Law library: 295,000 volumes, 2740 subscriptions; has LEXIS, NEXIS, WESTLAW, DIALOG, TOMCAT.

Annual tuition: $22,816. On-campus housing available for single students only. Annual on-campus housing cost: single students $12,055 (room and board). Housing deadline July 1. Contact University's Housing Office for both on- and off-campus housing information. Phone: (305)628-6692. Law students generally live off-campus. Off-campus housing and personal expenses: approximately $14,855.

Enrollment: first-year class 191; total full-time 472 (men 53%, women 47%); no part-time students. Faculty: full-time 20, part-time 34. Student to faculty ratio 19.7 to 1. Degrees conferred: J.D., J.D.-M.B.A. (Accounting, International Business), J.D.-M.S. (Sports Administration), LL.M. (International Taxation), LL.M.-M.A. (International Human Rights).

ADMISSION REQUIREMENTS. LSDAS Law School report, LSAT (not later that February test date; if more than one LSAT, average is used), bachelor's degree from an accredited institution, personal statement, one recommendation, transcripts (must show all schools attended and at least three years of study) required in support of application. Applicants must have received bachelor's degree prior to enrollment. Interview not required but may be requested by School. Accepts transfer applicants from other ABA-accredited schools on a space-available basis. Apply to Office of Admission after September 30, before April 30. First-year students admitted Fall only. Rolling admissions process. Application fee $40. Phone: (800)254-4569, (305)623-2310; fax: (305)623-2357.

ADMISSION STANDARDS. Selective. Mean LSAT: 148; mean GPA: 2.8 (A = 4). *U.S. News & World Report* ranking is in the fourth tier of all U.S. law schools. Accepts approximately 70% of total annual applicants.

FINANCIAL AID. Scholarships, minority scholarships, Grants-in-Aid, private and institutional loans; Federal loans and Federal W/S offered through Financial Aid Office. For scholarships/grants (selection criteria places heavy reliance on LSAT and Undergraduate GPA) apply to before May 1 (priority deadline). For all other programs apply to Financial Aid Officer. Phone: (305)628-6547. Use FAFSA (School code: 001468), also submit Financial Aid Transcript, Federal Income Tax forms. Approximately 22% of first-year class received scholarships/Grants-in-Aid. Approximately 80% of students receive some form of financial aid. Average scholarships grant $7,826.

DEGREE REQUIREMENTS. For J.D.: 90 (49 required) credits with a GPA of at least a 2.0 (A = 4), plus completion of upper-divisional writing course; three-year program. For LL.M.: 24 credit program.

UNIVERSITY OF ST. THOMAS

Houston, Texas 77006-4694
Web site: www.stthom.edu

Founded 1885. Coed. Private control. Roman Catholic affiliation. Semester system. Library: 226,500 volumes, 2400 subscriptions.

Tuition: per credit $450. On-campus housing for single students only. Average academic year housing costs: $5050 (including board). Contact Director of Residence Life for both on- and off-campus housing information. Phone: (713)525-3836.

Graduate Study

Enrollment: full-time 244, part-time 749. Graduate faculty: full-time 97, part-time 38. Degrees conferred: M.A., M.B.A., M.Ed., M.I.B., M.L.A., M.S.Acc., M.S.I.S., M.Div., M.A.Th., Ph.D.

ADMISSION REQUIREMENTS. Official transcripts, three letters of recommendation, GMAT (for Business), essay required in support of application. TOEFL required for international applicants. Accepts transfer applicants. Graduates of unaccredited colleges not considered. Apply to Director of Admissions at least two months prior to entrance. Rolling admissions process. Application $25. Phone: (713)525-3505; fax: (713)525-3558; e-mail: admissions@stthom.edu.

ADMISSION STANDARDS. Selective. Usual minimum average: 2.75 (A = 4).

FINANCIAL AID. Fellowships, assistantships, tuition waivers, Federal W/S, loans. Apply to the appropriate School for fellowships, assistantships; to the Office of Financial Aid for all other programs. No specified closing dates. Use FAFSA.

DEGREE REQUIREMENTS. For most master's: 32–36 credits minimum final written/oral exam; no thesis or language requirement. For M.B.A.: 36–42 semester credits. For M.Div.: at least two years in residence; thesis; reading knowledge of either Hebrew, Latin, Greek. For Ph.D.: 60 credits minimum beyond the bachelor's degree; qualifying exam; reading knowledge of two foreign languages; dissertation; final oral exam.

FIELDS OF STUDY.

CAMERON SCHOOL OF BUSINESS:
Accounting. M.S. Acc.
Business Administration. M.B.A.
Information Systems. M.S.I.S.
International Business. M.I.B.

CENTER FOR THOMISTIC STUDIES:
Philosophy. M.A., Ph.D.

SCHOOL OF EDUCATION:
Education. M.Ed.

SCHOOL OF THEOLOGY AT ST. MARY'S SEMINARY:
Divinity. M.Div.
Pastoral Studies. M.A.P.S.
Theological Studies. M.A.T.S.

LIBERAL ARTS:
Liberal Arts. M.L.A.

UNIVERSITY OF ST. THOMAS

St. Paul, Minnesota 55105-1089
Web site: www.stthomas.edu

Founded 1885. Coed on the graduate level. Private control. Roman Catholic affiliation. Semester system. Library: 460,000 volumes, 2530 subscriptions. Total University enrollment: 11,000.

Tuition: per credit $389–$683. No on-campus housing available. Contact Director of Residence Life for both on- and off-campus housing information. Phone: (651)962-6150.

Graduate Study

Graduate study since 1950. Enrollment: full-time 655, part-time 4509. Graduate faculty: full-time 367, part-time 159. Degrees conferred: M.A., M.A.T., M.B.A., M.I.M., M.M., M.B.C., M.S.M.S.E., M.S.D.D., M.S.S., M.S.W., Ed.S.

ADMISSION REQUIREMENTS. Official transcripts, three letters of recommendation, GMAT (for Business), essay required in support of application. TOEFL required for international applicants. Accepts transfer applicants. Graduates of unaccredited colleges not considered. Apply to Director of Admissions at least two months prior to entrance. Rolling admissions process. Application $35. Phone: (651)962-6407; fax: (651)962-6410.

ADMISSION STANDARDS. Selective. Usual minimum average: 2.75 (M.A.), 3.0 (M.B.A.), 3.25 (Ed.S.)

FINANCIAL AID. Fellowships, research assistantships, teaching assistantships, grants, Federal W/S, loans. Apply to the Office of Financial Aid; no specified closing dates. Phone: (651)647-5232. Use FAFSA. Aid available for part-time students.

DEGREE REQUIREMENTS. For most master's: 32–36 credits minimum final written/oral exam; no thesis or language requirement. For M.B.A., M.I.M.: 36–42 semester credits. For Ed.S.: 33 credits beyond the master's; final written/oral exams; final project.

FIELDS OF STUDY.

SCHOOL OF APPLIED SCIENCES AND ENGINEERING:
Manufacturing Systems. M.S.
Manufacturing Systems Engineering. M.S.M.S.E.
Software Design and Development. M.S.D.D.
Software Engineering. M.S.
Software Systems. M.S.S.
Technology Management. M.S.

GRADUATE SCHOOL OF ARTS AND SCIENCES:
English. M.A.
History. M.A.
Music Education. M.A.

GRADUATE SCHOOL OF BUSINESS:
Accounting. M.B.A.
Business Administration. M.B.A., E.M.B.A.
Business Communication. M.B.C.
Human Resource Management. M.B.A.
International Management. M.I.M.
Medical Group Management. M.B.A.
Real Estate Appraisal. M.S.

SCHOOL OF DIVINITY:
Divinity. M.Div.
Ministry. D.Min.
Pastoral Studies. M.A.
Religious Education. M.A.
Theology. M.A.

SCHOOL OF EDUCATION:
Athletic Administration. M.A.
Community Education Administration. M.A.
Critical Pedagogy. M.A.
Curriculum and Instruction. M.A.
Educational Leadership. M.A., Ed.S.
Gifted, Talented, and Creative Education. M.A.
Human Resource Development. M.A.
Learning Technology. M.A.
Organization Development. M.A.
Police Leadership. M.A.
Reading. M.A.
Special Education. M.A.
Teacher Education. M.A., M.A.T.

SCHOOL OF SOCIAL WORK:
Social Work. M.S.W. offered jointly with the College of St. Catherine.

GRADUATE DEPARTMENT OF PROFESSIONAL PSYCHOLOGY:
Counseling Psychology. M.A., Psy.D.

ST. XAVIER UNIVERSITY
Chicago, Illinois 60655-3105
Web site: www.sxu.edu

Founded 1847. Coed. Roman Catholic. Semester system. Library: 153,000, 2150 subscriptions.

Annual tuition: $8550; per credit $475. On-campus housing for 285 graduate students. Average academic year housing costs: $5744. Contact the Director of Campus Life for both on- and off-campus housing information. Phone: (773)298-3499.

Graduate Studies

Enrollment: full- and part-time 1800. College faculty teaching graduate students: full-time 85, part-time 6. Degrees conferred: M.A., M.A.C.S., M.S., M.B.A., M.P.H.

ADMISSION REQUIREMENTS. Transcripts, three letters of recommendation, GRE/GMAT/MAT in support of application. On-line application available. TOEFL required for international applicants. Accepts transfer applicants. Apply to Director of Admissions; no specified closing date. Application fee $35. Phone: (773)298-3053; fax: (773)298-3076; e-mail: admission @sxu.edu.

ADMISSION STANDARDS. Selective. Usual minimum average: 3.0 (A = 4).

FINANCIAL AID. Scholarships, research assistantships, internships, Federal W/S, loans. Approved for VA benefits. Apply by July 15 to Director of Financial Aid. Phone: (773)298-7071; fax: (773)298-3076. Use FAFSA. Aid available for part-time students.

DEGREE REQUIREMENTS. For master's: 30 semester hours minimum; research project.

FIELDS OF STUDY.

GRAHAM SCHOOL OF MANAGEMENT:
Business. Includes specialization options in finance, financial trading and practice, health care, generalist/administration, management, management information systems, marketing, or international business. M.B.A., M.S.
Public Health. M.P.H.

SCHOOL OF ARTS AND SCIENCE:
Applied Computer Science. M.A.C.S.
Counseling Psychology. Includes developmental disabilities, geriatric services, individual and family services.
Speech-Language Pathology. M.S.

SCHOOL OF EDUCATION:
Educational Administration and Supervision. M.A.
Curriculum and Instruction. M.A.
Multicategorical Special Education. M.A.
Reading. M.A.

SCHOOL OF NURSING:
Nursing. Includes medical surgical, community health (MS/MBA), psychiatric, mental health. M.S.

SALEM STATE COLLEGE
Salem, Massachusetts 01970–5353
Web site: www.salemstate.edu

Founded 1854. Located 20 miles NE of Boston. Coed. State control. Semester system. Library: 230,500 volumes, 100,000 microforms.

Tuition: per credit resident $140, nonresident $230. No on-campus housing available.

Graduate School

Enrollment: full-time 155, part-time 1210 (men 342, women 1023). Graduate faculty: full-time 13, part-time 77. Degrees conferred: M.A., M.A.T., M.B.A., M.Ed., M.S., M.S.N., M.S.W., M.S.N.-M.B.A.

ADMISSION REQUIREMENTS. Transcripts, three letters of reference, statement of purpose, GRE/GMAT/MAT required in support of School's application. TOEFL required for international applicants. Interview not required. Accepts transfer applicants. Graduates of unaccredited institutions not considered. Apply to Dean of Graduate School by November 1 (Spring), July 1 (Fall) for M.B.A.; by January 1 for M.S.W.; all others on rolling admissions. Application fee $25. Phone: (978)542-6323.

ADMISSION STANDARDS. Selective. Usual minimum average: 2.5 (A = 4) and 2.7 in major field of study.

FINANCIAL AID. Scholarships, graduate assistantships, Federal W/S, loans. Approved for VA benefits. Apply by May 1 to the Dean of Graduate School for assistantships; to Financial Aid Office for all other programs. Phone: (978)542-6112. Use FAFSA.

DEGREE REQUIREMENTS. For M.Ed., M.A.T.: 36–39 semester hours minimum, at least 27 in residence; final written/oral exam. For M.A.: 33 semester hours; one foreign language or computer statistics; final written exam. For M.S. in Geo Information, Science: 40 semester hours. For M.S. in Math: 30 semester hours. For M.S.N.: 39 semester hours. For M.B.A.: 54 semester hours; computer proficiency. For M.S.W.: 60 semester hours.

FIELDS OF STUDY.
Biology. M.A.T.
Business Administration. M.B.A.
Chemistry. M.A.T.
Counseling and Psychological Services. M.S.
Early Childhood Education. M.Ed.
Elementary Education. M.Ed.
English. M.A., M.A.T.
English as a Second Language. M.A.T., M.Ed.
Geography. M.A.T.
Geographic Information Science. M.S.
History. M.A., M.A.T.
Library Media Studies. M.Ed.
Mathematics. M.S.
Nursing. M.S.N.
Physical Education. M.Ed.
Reading. M.Ed.
School Counseling. M.Ed.
Secondary Education. M.Ed.
Social Work. M.S.W.
Special Education. M.Ed.
Technology in Education. M.Ed.

SALISBURY STATE UNIVERSITY

Salisbury, Maryland 21801-6837

Web site: www.ssu.edu

Founded 1925. Located 125 miles SE of Baltimore. Coed, State control. Semester system. Special facilities: Center for Technology in Education, Research Center for Delmarva History and Culture, Small Business Development Center. Library: 249,700 volumes, 1762 subscriptions.

Tuition: per credit resident $184, nonresident $380. No on- or off-campus housing for graduate students.

Graduate Program

Graduate study since 1962. Enrollment: full-time 110, part-time 428. Graduate faculty: full- and part-time 108. Degrees conferred: M.Ed., M.A., M.B.A., M.S., M.S.W.

ADMISSION REQUIREMENTS. Official transcripts, GRE/ GMAT/ MAT/NTE required in support of application. TOEFL required for international applicants. Accepts transfer applicants. Graduates of unaccredited institutions not considered. Apply by August 1 (Fall), January 1 (Spring) to the Graduate Admissions Office. Application fee $30. Phone: (410)546-6161; fax: (410)546-6016; e-mail: admissions@ssu.edu.

ADMISSION STANDARDS. Varies by department.

FINANCIAL AID. Fellowships, graduate assistantships, internships, grants, loans. Approved for VA benefits. Apply to appropriate department chair for assistantships; to the Financial Aid Office for all other programs. Phone: (410)546-6165; fax: (410) 546-6168. Use FAFSA. Aid available for part-time students.

DEGREE REQUIREMENTS. For M.Ed.: 33 semester hours. For M.S.-Nursing: 39 semester hours. For M.A.-English: 33 credits minimum. For M.B.A.: 30 semester hours. For M.S.W.: 60 credit program.

FIELDS OF STUDY.
Applied Health Physiology. M.S.
Business Administration. M.B.A.
Early Childhood Education. M.Ed.
Education. Includes English, history, mathematics, music, science. M.Ed.
Elementary Education. M.Ed.
English. M.A.
History. M.A.
Nursing. Includes family nurse practitioner. M.S.
Post-Secondary Education. M.Ed.
Psychology. M.A.
Reading. M.Ed.
School Administration. M.Ed.
Social Work. M.S.W.
Teaching. M.A.

SAMFORD UNIVERSITY

Birmingham, Alabama 35229-0002

Web site: www.samford.edu

Founded 1941. Coed. Private control. Baptist affiliation. Semester system. Library: 508,000 volumes, 11,000 subscriptions. Total University enrollment: 4366.

Tuition: per credit $410. No on-campus housing available. Monthly housing costs: $400–$550. Contact Director, Residence Life for both on- and off-campus housing information. Phone: (205)870-2932.

Graduate Studies

Graduate study since 1965. Enrollment: full-time 708, part-time 243. Faculty: full-time 87, part-time 15. Degrees conferred: M.S. in Ed., M.S. in Environ. Mgt., M.S.N., M.B.A., M.S., M.Mus., M.Mus.Ed., Ed.S., M.Div., D. Min., M.Mus., Pharm.D.

ADMISSION REQUIREMENTS. Transcripts, photograph required in support of School's application. GRE/NTE required for Education, Liberal Arts majors; GMAT for Business majors; MAT for Music. TOEFL required for international applicants. Interview desirable. Accepts transfer applicants. Graduates of unaccredited institutions not considered. Apply to Graduate Dean at least one month prior to entrance. Application fee $25. Phone: (205)726-2871; fax: (205)726-2171.

ADMISSION STANDARDS. Selective. Usual minimum average: 2.5 (A = 4).

FINANCIAL AID. Annual awards from institutional funds: scholarships, assistantships, tuition waivers, Federal W/S, loans. Approved for VA benefits. Apply by March 1 to the Financial Aid Office. Phone: (205)870-2905; fax: (205)870-2171. Use FAFSA and institutional FAF. About 10% of students receive aid other than loans from University and outside sources.

DEGREE REQUIREMENTS. For M.A.: 33 semester hours minimum including thesis, at least 24 in residence; reading knowledge of one foreign language; comprehensive exam. For M.S. in Ed., M.Mus.: 32–33 hours minimum, at least 24 in residence; no thesis or language requirement; comprehensive exam. For M.B.A.: 36–45 hours, depending upon previous preparation, at least 24 in residence. For M.Mus.Ed.: essentially the same as for M.S. in Ed., except 37 semester hours required. Final written/oral exams for all master's. For Ed.S.: 30 semester hours beyond the master's. For Pharm.D.: 65 credits, plus 139 professional credits.

FIELDS OF STUDY.
Accounting. M.Acc.
Business Administration. M.B.A.
Church Music. M.M.
Comparative Law. M.C.L.
Divinity. M.Div.
Early Childhood Education. M.S.F.
Educational Leadership. Ed.D.
Elementary Education. M.S.E.
Environmental Management. M.S.E.M.
Ministry. D.Min.
Music Education. M.M.E.
Nursing. M.S.N.
Pharmacy. Pharm.D.
Secondary Education. Includes English, history, mathematics, biology. M.S.E.
Theological Studies. M.T.S.

Cumberland School of Law

Web site: www.cumberland.samford.edu

Established 1847. School acquired by Samford University in 1961. ABA approved since 1949. AALS member since 1952. Semester system. Library: 262,282 volumes, 2959 subscriptions; has LEGALTRAC, LEXIS, NEXIS, WESTLAW, OCLC.

Annual tuition: full-time $19,550, part-time $11,880. Limited on-campus housing available. Average annual living expenses: $13,790.

Enrollment: first-year class 173, full-time 541 (men 56%, women 44%). Faculty: full-time 23, part-time 21. Student to faculty ratio 19.6 to 1. Degrees conferred: J.D., J.D.-M.A.E., J.D.-M.B.A., J.D.-M.P.H., J.D.-M.Div., J.D.-M.S. (Environmental Management), M.C.L. (for International Law School graduates).

ADMISSION REQUIREMENTS. LSDAS Law School report, bachelor's degree, transcripts, three references, LSAT degree required in support of application. Interview recommended. Accepts transfer applicants. Graduates of unaccredited colleges usually not considered. Apply to Admission Office after October 1, before May 1 (priority deadline February 28.). Admits Fall only. Application fee $40. Phone: (205)726-2702, (800)888-7213; fax: (205)726-2057.

ADMISSION STANDARDS. Selective. Mean LSAT: 151, mean GPA: 3.09 (A = 4). Gourman rating: 2.70. *U.S. News & World Report* ranking is in the fourth tier of all U.S. law schools. Accepts 50–60% of total annual applicants.

FINANCIAL AID. Scholarships, Federal W/S, loans. Apply to University's Director of Financial Aid by March 1. Use FAFSA (School code: 001036). Approximately 30% of students receive financial assistance from school.

DEGREE REQUIREMENTS. For J.D.: 90 semester hours program. For master's degrees, see Graduate School listing above. *Note:* School has Summer program in England, British Columbia, and Brazil.

SAM HOUSTON STATE UNIVERSITY
Huntsville, Texas 77341-2448
Web site: www.shsu.edu

Founded 1879. Located 70 miles N of Houston. Coed. State control. Semester system. Special facilities: Sam Houston Memorial Museum, Texas Regional Institute for Environmental Studies. Library: 1,800,000 volumes, 3297 subscriptions.

Tuition: per credit resident $42, nonresident $255. On-campus housing for 102 married students, unlimited for single students. Average academic year housing costs: $3672 (including board) for single students; $3500 for married students. Contact Director of Housing for both on- and off-campus housing information. Phone: (936)294-1812.

Graduate Studies

Graduate study since 1938. Enrollment: full-time 305, part-time 879. College faculty teaching graduate students: full- and part-time 220. Degrees conferred: M.A., M.B.A., M.Ed., M.M., M.M.Ed., M.S., M.F.A., M.L.S., Ed.D. Ph.D.

ADMISSION REQUIREMENTS. Two official transcripts, GRE/GMAT/MAT required in support of application. Recommendations, résumés, departmental application, writing samples required by some departments. TOEFL required for international applicants. Accepts transfer applicants. Graduates of unaccredited institutions not considered. Apply to Graduate Office at least two months prior to registration. Rolling admissions process. Application fee $20. Phone: (936)294-1401; fax: (936)294-1598.

ADMISSION STANDARDS. Selective. Usual minimum average: 2.5 (A = 4).

FINANCIAL AID. Annual awards from institutional funds: scholarships, teaching fellowships, research assistantships, internships, internships, Federal W/S, loans. Approved for VA benefits. Apply well in advance of registration to the Graduate Office for assistantships, fellowships; to the Financial Aid Office for all other programs. Use FAFSA. About 10% of students receive aid from College and outside sources. Aid available for part-time students.

DEGREE REQUIREMENTS. For M.A., M.L.S.: 30 semester hours minimum including thesis, at least 24 in residence; candi-

dacy; comprehensive exam. For M.Ed., M.S., M.B.A.: 36 semester hours minimum, at least 30 in residence; candidacy; thesis optional for six credits; comprehensive oral/written exam. For Ph.D.: 90 semester hours beyond the bachelor's, at least 30 in residence; two semesters for supervised teaching; written/oral exam; dissertation.

FIELDS OF STUDY.

COLLEGE OF ARTS AND SCIENCES:
Biology. M.A., M.S.
Ceramic. M.A., M.F.A.
Chemistry. M.S.
Computing and information Science. M.S.
Dance. M.F.A.
English. M.A.
History. M.A.
Mathematics. M.A., M.S.
Music. Includes conducting, Kodaly pedagogy, performance, musicology, theory/composition. M.M.
Music Education. Includes elementary instrumental, Kodaly pedagogy, vocal. M.Ed.
Physics. M.S.
Political Science. M.A.
Sociology. M.A.
Statistics. M.S.

COLLEGE OF BUSINESS ADMINISTRATION:
Business Administration. M.B.A.

COLLEGE OF CRIMINAL JUSTICE:
Criminal Justice. Ph.D.
Criminal Justice and Criminology. M.A.
Criminal Justice Management. M.S.
Forensic Science. M.S.

COLLEGE OF EDUCATION AND APPLIED SCIENCE:
Administration. M.A., M.Ed.
Agriculture. Includes agriculture, agriculture business, agricultural mechanization. M.S.
Agricultural Education. M.Ed.
Counseling. M.A., M.Ed.
Counselor Education. Ph.D.
Early childhood Education. M.Ed.
Educational Leadership. Ed.D.
Elementary Education. M.A., M.Ed.
Family and Consumer Sciences. M.A.
Family and Consumer Sciences Education. M.Ed.
Health. M.A., M.Ed.
Industrial Education. M.A., M.Ed.
Industrial Technology. M.A.
Kinesiology. M.A., M.Ed.
Library Science. M.L.S.
Psychology. Includes clinical (M.A.), school psychology (M.A.), forensic clinical psychology (Ph.D.).
Reading. M.A., M.Ed.
Secondary Education. M.A., M.Ed.
Special Education. M.A., M.Ed.
Supervision. M.A., M.Ed.
Vocational Education. M.Ed.

SAN DIEGO STATE UNIVERSITY
San Diego, California 92182
Web site: www.sdsu.edu

Founded 1897. CGS member. Coed. State control. Semester system. Special facilities: Center on Aging, Lupinski Institute for Judaic Studies, Production Center for Documentary and Drama, Institute for International Security and Conflict Resolution, Mt.

Laguna Observatory, Center for Energy Studies, Molecular Biology Institute, Institute for Public Health. Library: 1,095,000 volumes, 3,554,000 microforms, 5900 current periodicals, 45 PCs in all libraries.

Annual tuition/fees: full-time, resident $1948, nonresident $1948 plus $246 per unit. On-campus housing for 2077 single students; none for married students. Average academic year housing costs: $7000 (including board). Contact the Director of Housing and Residential Life for both on- and off-campus housing information. Phone: (619)594-5742. Day-care facilities available.

Graduate Division and Research

Enrollment: full-time 1872, part-time 3476. Faculty: full- and part-time over 1200. Degrees conferred: M.A., M.S., M.B.A., M.C.P., M.F.A., M.M., M.P.A., M.P.H., M.S.W., Ph.D.

ADMISSION REQUIREMENTS. Two transcripts, GRE required in support of application. TOEFL (minimum score 550) required for international applicants. GRE Subject Test, GMAT, interview required by some departments. Accepts transfer applicants. Graduates of unaccredited colleges not considered. Apply to Admissions Office of the University by July 1 (Fall), December 1 (Spring). Applicants for doctoral programs must be admitted as a regular student at the appropriate campus as well as to San Diego State University. Rolling admissions process. Application fee $55. Phone: (619)594-3761; fax: (619)594-4902.

ADMISSION STANDARDS. Selective. Usual minimum average: 2.75 (A = 4).

FINANCIAL AID. Teaching associates, fellowships, scholarships, graduate/research/student assistantships, Federal W/S, loans. Apply by February 15 to appropriate department chairman for assistantships; to Financial Aid Office for all other programs. Phone: (619)594-6323. Use FAFSA. About 20% of students receive aid other than loans from University and other sources. Aid available for part-time students.

DEGREE REQUIREMENTS. For M.A., M.S., M.M.: 30 units minimum, at least 21 in residence; thesis/comprehensive exam; reading knowledge of one foreign language for some majors. For M.S. (Counseling): 60 units minimum, at least 30 in residence; comprehensive exam. For M.C.P.: 57 units minimum, at least 30 in residence. For M.B.A.: 30–60 units, at least 21 in residence. For M.F.A.: 60 units, at least 30 in residence. For M.P.A.: 36 units, at least 21 in residence. For M.S.W.: 56 units, at least 28 in residence. For M.P.H.: 48–55 units, depending on concentration, at least 39 in residence. For Ph.D. (Biology, Chemistry, Clinical Psychology, Engineering Sciences/Applied Mechanics, Language and Communicative Disorders, Mathematics and Science Education, Public Health): at least two years in full-time residence, one year on the campus of the University of California at San Diego and one year at San Diego State University; preliminary written exam; dissertation; final oral exam. For Ph.D. (Ecology): at least two years in full-time residence, one year at University of California at Davis and one year at San Diego State University; qualifying exam; dissertation; final oral exam. For Ph.D. (Education): 48 semester units of residency, 24 at Claremont Graduate School and 24 at San Diego State University; qualifying exam; dissertation; final oral exam. For Ph.D. (Geography): at least two years in full-time residence, one year at University of California Santa Barbara and one year at San Diego State University; qualifying exam; dissertation; final oral exam.

FIELDS OF STUDY.
Accountancy. M.S.
Aerospace Engineering. M.S.
Anthropology. Thesis, one language, final oral exam for M.A.
Applied Mathematics. Includes mathematical theory of communication systems. M.S.

Art. Includes art history, studio arts; thesis or creative project for M.A., M.F.A.
Asian Studies. Interdepartmental. M.A.
Astronomy. M.S.
Biology. GRE Subject for admission. Includes ecology, evolutionary biology, molecular biology, physiology. Thesis, final oral exam for M.A., M.S.; one foreign language for M.A. M.A., M.S.; joint doctoral (Ph.D.) program with University of California at San Diego.
Business Administration. GMAT for admission. Includes entrepreneurship, finance, financial and tax planning, human resource management, information systems, international business, management, marketing, operations management, real estate, taxation, total quality management (M.S.). Thesis or comprehensive exam for M.S., M.B.A.
Chemistry. Thesis, final oral exam for M.A., M.S. M.A., M.S; joint doctoral (Ph.D.) program with University of California at San Diego.
Child Development. M.S.
City Planning. M.C.P.
Civil Engineering. Includes environmental engineering. M.S.
Clinical Psychology. Joint doctoral (Ph.D.) program with University of California at San Diego.
Communication. M.A.
Communicative Disorders. Includes audiology, communication sciences, education of the deaf, speech-language pathology. M.A.
Computational Science. M.S.
Computer Science. M.S.
Counseling. M.S. Full-time, Fall admission only. Includes marriage, family, and child counseling, school counseling, school psychology.
Creative Writing. M.F.A.
Criminal Justice and Criminology. M.S.
Drama. Thesis for M.A., M.F.A.
Ecology. Joint doctoral (Ph.D.) program with University of California at Davis.
Economics. M.A.
Education. Includes counseling, educational leadership, educational research, educational technology, elementary curriculum and instruction, policy studies in language and cross-cultural education, reading, secondary curriculum and instruction, special education. M.A.; joint doctoral (Ed.D.) program with Claremont Graduate University.
Electrical Engineering. M.S.
Engineering Sciences/Applied Mechanics. Joint doctoral (Ph.D.) program with University of California at San Diego.
English. One foreign language for M.A. M.A.
Exercise Physiology. M.S.
French. M.A.
Geography. Includes natural resources and environmental policy, transportation. M.A.; joint doctoral (Ph.D.) program with University of California at Santa Barbara.
Geological Sciences. M.S.
Gerontology. M.S.
History. One foreign language for M.A.
Interdisciplinary Studies. M.S.
Language and Communicative Disorders. Joint doctoral (Ph.D.) program with University of California at San Diego.
Latin American Studies. Interdepartmental. M.A.
Liberal Arts. Interdepartmental. M.A.
Linguistics. M.A.
Mathematics. M.A.
Mathematics and Science Education. Joint doctoral (Ph.D.) program with University of California at San Diego.
Mechanical Engineering. M.S.
Microbiology. M.S.
Music. Public recital or thesis for M.A., M.M.
Nursing. Includes advanced practice nursing of adults and the elderly, community health nursing, nursing systems administration. M.S.
Nutritional Sciences. M.S.

Philosophy. M.A.

Physical Education. M.A.

Physics. One foreign language for M.A. M.A., M.S.

Political Science. M.A.

Psychology. GRE Subject for admission. Includes applied. Thesis, final exam for M.A., M.S. M.A., M.S.; joint doctoral (Ph.D.) program in clinical psychology with University of California at San Diego.

Public Administration. Includes city planning, criminal justice administration. M.P.A.

Public Health. Includes biometry, environmental health, epidemiology, health promotion, health services administration (M.P.H.); environmental health science, industrial hygiene, toxicology (M.S.). M.S., M.P.H.; joint doctoral (Ph.D.) program with University of California at San Diego.

Radiological Health Physics. Thesis. M.S.

Regulatory Affairs. M.S.

Rehabilitation Counseling. Fall admission only. M.S.

Social Work. Admits Fall only; apply to Director of School of Social Work between November 1 and April 15; interview required for admission. M.S.W.

Sociology. M.A.

Spanish. M.A.

Speech Communication.

Statistics. Includes biostatistics. M.S.

Telecommunication.

Television, Film, and New Media Production. M.A.

Theatre Arts. Includes acting, design and technical theatre, musical theatre. M.A., M.F.A.

Women's Studies. M.A.

UNIVERSITY OF SAN DIEGO

San Diego, California 92110-2492

Web site: www.acusd.edu

Founded 1949. Private control. Roman Catholic. Semester system. Special facilities: Children's Advocacy Institute, Patient Advocacy Clinic, Public Interest Law Center. Library: 825,000 volumes, 2200 subscriptions. Total University enrollment: 6943.

Tuition: per credit master's program $720, per credit doctoral programs $735. On-campus for both single and married graduate students. Average academic year housing costs: $6590 (including board) for single students; $6900 for married students. Contact Director of Graduate Housing for both on- and off-campus housing information. Phone: (619)260-4777.

Graduate Programs

Enrollment: full-time 553, part-time 745. Graduate faculty: full-time 121, part-time 25. Degrees conferred: M.A., M.F.A., M.S. (Tax), M.A.T., M.Ed., M.B.A., M.I.B., M.S.N., D.N.Sci., Ed.D.

ADMISSION REQUIREMENTS. Two official transcripts, GRE/MAT/GMAT, three letters of recommendation required in support of School's application. TOEFL (minimum score 600) and financial information form required for international applicants. Accepts transfer applicants. Graduates of unaccredited colleges not considered. Apply to the Office of Graduate Admissions; for most master's programs May 1 (Fall), November 15 (Spring), March 15 (Summer), other degree programs have specific deadlines consult Graduate Application for those deadlines. Rolling admissions process. Application fee $35 (master's), $40 (doctoral). Phone: (800)248-4873, (619)260-4514; fax: (619)260-2393; e-mail: grads@acusd.edu.

ADMISSION STANDARDS. Selective. Usual minimum average: 3.0 recommended (A= 4); GMAT score minimum of 525; GRE Verbal, Quantitative, and Analytical score minimum of 500.

FINANCIAL AID. Annual awards from institutional funds: assistantships, traineeships, fellowships, Federal W/S, loans. Approved for VA benefits. Apply by May 1 to the Office of Financial Services. Phone: (800)248-4873, (619)260-4514. Use FAFSA. About 37% of students receive aid other than loans from University and outside sources. Aid available to part-time students.

DEGREE REQUIREMENTS. For M.A.: 30 units minimum, at least 24 in residence; reading knowledge of one foreign language; thesis included; final written exam. For M.A.T., M.Ed., M.S.N.: same as for M.A., except no language requirement. For M.B.A., M.I.B.: 60 units minimum; computer proficiency. For M.S.(Tax): 36-unit program. For D.N.Sc.: 54 units minimum, at least 1 semester in full-time study; written exam; dissertation; oral defense. For Ed.D.: 60 units minimum beyond master's degree, at least two semesters in residence; qualifying exam; candidacy; dissertation; final oral exam.

FIELDS OF STUDY.

COLLEGE OF ARTS AND SCIENCES:

Dramatic Arts. In conjunction with The Old Globe Theatre. M.F.A.

History. M.A.

International Relations. M.A

Marine Science. Includes biological, chemical, geological oceanography. M.S.

Pastoral Care and Counseling. M.A.

Practical Theology. M.A.

SCHOOL OF BUSINESS:

Business Administration. Includes emphasis in electronic commerce, finance, management, marketing, project management, supply management, venture management. M.B.A.

Electronic Commerce. M.S.

Executive Leadership. M.S.

Global Leadership. M.S.

International Business. I.M.B.A.

SCHOOL OF EDUCATION:

Counseling. M.A.

Educational Leadership/Administration. M.Ed.

Educational Technology. Joint doctoral (Ed.D.) Program with San Diego State University.

Leadership Studies. M.A., Ed.D.

Learning and Teaching. M.Ed.

Marital and Family Therapy. M.A.

Special Education. M.A.

Teaching and Learning (Literacy). Joint doctoral (Ed.D.) program with San Diego State University.

HAHN SCHOOL OF NURSING AND HEALTH SCIENCE:

Adult Nurse Practitioner. M.S.N.

Case Management of Vulnerable Populations. Includes acute, long-term community, home health. M.S.N.

Family Nurse Practitioner. M.S.N.

Health Care Systems Administration. M.S.N.

Nursing. Ph.D.

Pediatric Nurse Practitioner. M.S.N.

School of Law

Web site: www.acusd.edu/usdlaw

Established 1954. Located on main campus. ABA approved since 1961. AALS member. Semester system. Full-time, part-time study. Special facilities: Center for Public Interest Law, Institute on International and Comparative Law, Pardee Legal Research Center, Children's Advocacy Institute. Law library: 471,914 volumes, 5361 subscriptions; has LEXIS, NEXIS, WESTLAW, LEGALTRAC, CALI, DIALOG.

Annual tuition: full-time $23,510, part-time $16,690.

Enrollment: first-year class full-time 255, part-time 84; total 975 (men 53%, women 47%). Faculty: full-time 43, part-time 39. Student to faculty ratio 17.2 to 1. Degrees conferred: J.D., J.D.-M.B.A., J.D.-I.M.B.A., J.D.-M.A. (International Relations), J.D.-LL.M., LL.M. (General, Tax), LL.M. (international law for persons who have completed a basic legal education and received a university degree in law in another country).

ADMISSION REQUIREMENTS. LSDAS Law School report, bachelor's degree, transcripts, LSAT required in support of application. Photograph required after admittance. Interview not required. Accepts transfer applicants. Graduates of unaccredited colleges not considered. Apply to Admissions Office after September 1, before March 1 (priority deadline February 1); evening students May 1. Admits first-year students Fall and Summer only. Application fee $35. Phone: (619)260-4528, (800)248-4873; e-mail: jdinfo@acusd.edu.

ADMISSION REQUIREMENTS FOR LL.M. APPLICANTS. Must possess a J.D. or an equivalent foreign law degree. Official transcripts with rank-in-class, résumé, personal statement with rational for graduate study required in support of application. In addition, international applicants whose native language is not English must submit a TOEFL report. Admits Fall, Spring, Summer. Apply by May 1 (Fall), November 1 (Spring), April 1 (Summer) to the Office of Graduate Programs. Notification of admission decision normally begins within six weeks of receipt of completed application. Application fee $40. Phone: (619)260-4596.

ADMISSION STANDARDS. Selective. Mean LSAT: full-time 159, part-time 154; mean GPA: full-time 3.26, part-time 3.13 (A = 4). Gourman rating: 3.81. *U.S. News & World Report* ranking is in the second tier of all U.S. law schools. Accepts 20–25% of total annual applicants.

FINANCIAL AID. Scholarships, fellowships, assistantships, Federal W/S, loans. Apply to Office of Financial Aid by March 1. Use FAFSA (School code: G06976). About 32% of students receive aid other than loans from School.

DEGREE REQUIREMENTS. For J.D.: 85 credits minimum, three-year (day), four-year (evening) program, at least 55 in residence. For LL.M.: at least 24 credits minimum beyond the J.D.; one-year of full-time study and research.
Note: Summer study abroad programs in England, France, Ireland, Italy, Russia, and Spain.

SAN FRANCISCO ART INSTITUTE

San Francisco, California 94133-2299
Web site: www.sfai.edu

Founded 1871. Coed. Private control. Library: 35,000 volumes, 210 subscriptions.
Annual tuition: full-time $20,200, per unit $842. No on-campus housing available. Studio space for graduate students. Contact the Student Services Department for off-campus housing information. Phone: (415)749-4525.

Graduate Program

Enrollment: full-time 120, part-time 5. Faculty: full- and part-time 38. Degree conferred: M.F.A.

ADMISSION REQUIREMENTS. Transcripts, portfolio of original artwork, statement of purpose required in support of application. TOEFL, TSE required for international applicants. Accepts transfer applicants, but no credits are transferred. Apply to Graduate Program Committee by February 15 (Fall), November 1

(Spring). Application fee $65. Phone: (800)345-7324; fax: (415)749-4592; e-mail: admissions@sfai.edu.

ADMISSION STANDARDS. Very competitive. Admission based primarily on portfolio and statement of purpose. TOEFL score minimum 500.

FINANCIAL AID. Academic scholarships, fellowships, grants, Federal W/S, loans. Approved for VA benefits. Apply to Director of Financial Aid; recommended deadline July 15. Phone: (415)749-4500, (415)749-4590. Use FAFSA. About 67% of students receive aid other than loans from Institute.

DEGREE REQUIREMENTS. For M.F.A.: 60 semester units; final examination of work and an exhibition. No language or thesis requirements.

FIELDS OF STUDY.
Filmmaking.
New Genres.
Painting.
Photography.
Printmaking.
Sculpture.

SAN FRANCISCO CONSERVATORY OF MUSIC

San Francisco, California 94122-4411
Web site: www.sfcm.edu

Founded 1917. Coed. Private control. Semester system. Library: 36,800 volumes, 80 subscriptions, 6000 individual recordings and tapes.
Annual tuition: $19,300; per credit $860. No on-campus housing. Contact Admission Office for off-campus housing information.

Graduate Division

Graduate study since 1960. Enrollment: full-time 124, part-time 3 (men 41%, women 59%). Faculty: full-time 20, part-time 25, plus private instructors. Degree conferred: M.M.

ADMISSION REQUIREMENTS. Transcripts, two letters of recommendation, audition required in support of application. TOEFL required for international applicants. Accepts transfer applicants. Graduates of unaccredited institutions not considered. Apply to Director of Student Services by February 15 (Fall), November 15 (Spring) for most majors. Admits Fall and Spring. Application fee $70. Phone: (415)759-3431; fax: (415)759-3499.

ADMISSION STANDARDS. Musical proficiency more important than undergraduate GPA.

FINANCIAL AID. Scholarships, fellowships, assistantships, Federal W/S, loans. Apply to Director of Student Services by March 1; preference given to early applicants. Phone: (415)759-3422. Use FAFSA and institutional FAF. About 65% of students receive aid other than loans from School and outside sources. Aid available for part-time students.

DEGREE REQUIREMENTS. For M.M.: 30 semester hours minimum, all in residence; two public recitals.

FIELDS OF STUDY.
Chamber Music.
Classical Guitar.
Composition.

Conducting.
Keyboard Instruments.
Orchestral Instruments.
Piano Accompanying.
Voice.

SAN FRANCISCO STATE UNIVERSITY

San Francisco, California 94132-1722
Web site: www.sfsu.edu

Founded 1899. CGS member. Coed. State control. Semester system. Library: 900,000 volumes, 3800 subscriptions, 200 PCs in all libraries.

Annual fees/tuition: full-time, resident $1982, nonresident and foreign students $1982 plus $246 per unit. Limited on-campus housing for graduate students. Average academic year housing cost: $5500–$7000 for single students. Contact Housing Office for both on- and off-campus housing information. Phone: (415)338-1067.

Graduate Division

Enrollment: full-time 2015, part-time 2408. Faculty: full-time 475, part-time 236. Degrees conferred: M.A., M.S., M.B.A., M.F.A., M.M., M.P.A., M.P.H., M.P.T., M.S.W., Ed.D., Ph.D.

ADMISSION REQUIREMENTS. Two official transcripts required in support of application. Interview, GRE/GMAT/MAT/NTE, letter of intent required for some departments. TOEFL required for international applicants. Accepts transfer applicants. Graduates of unaccredited institutions not considered. Apply to Office of Graduate Admissions at least one month prior to registration. Application fee $55. Phone: (415)338-2233; fax: (415) 338-2514.

ADMISSION STANDARDS. Very selective for several departments, competitive for the others. Usual minimum average: 3.0 (A = 4). TOEFL score required 550.

FINANCIAL AID. Annual awards from institutional funds: Graduate Equity Fellowships, assistantships, Federal W/S, loans. Approved for VA benefits. Apply by March 1 to appropriate department chair for fellowships, assistantships; to Financial Aid Office for all other programs. Phone: (415)338-1581; e-mail: finaid@sfsu.edu. Use FAFSA. About 60% of students receive aid other than loans from University funds. No aid for part-time or foreign students.

DEGREE REQUIREMENTS. For M.A., M.S., M.M.: 30 units minimum, at least 24 in residence; advancement to candidacy; thesis, creative project/final written/oral exam; usually no language requirement. For M.B.A.: 30–54 units minimum, at least 24 in residence; advancement to candidacy; thesis/research project; no language requirement. For M.P.A.: 37–41 units minimum, at least 24 in residence. For M.P.H.: 53 credit program; practicum; internship. For M.P.T.: offered jointly with University of California, San Francisco; 64 units in residence. For M.S.W.: 60 units minimum, at least 30 in residence; advancement to candidacy; fieldwork/thesis; no language requirement. For M.F.A.: 60 units, at least 30 in residence. For Ed.D., Ph.D.: offered jointly in Special Education with University of California, Berkeley; requirements vary with degree program. For D.P.T.S.: offered jointly with University of California, San Francisco; requirements vary based on past experience.

FIELDS OF STUDY.
Accounting.
Anthropology. M.A.
Applied Geosciences. M.S.
Art. M.A., M.F.A.
Asian American Studies. M.A.

Biology. Includes cell and molecular, conservation, ecology and systematic, marine, microbiology, physiology and behavioral biology. M.A.
Biomedical Laboratory Science. M.S.
Business Administration. M.B.A., M.S.
Chemistry. Includes biochemistry. M.S.
Chinese. M.A.
Cinema. M.F.A.
Cinema Studies. M.A.
Classics. M.A.
Clinical Science. M.S.
Communicative Disorders. M.S.
Comparative Literature. M.A.
Computer Science. M.S.
Counseling. Includes marriage, family, and child counseling. M.S.
Creative Arts. M.F.A.
Creative Writing. M.A.
Drama. M.A.
Economics. M.A.
Education. Includes adult education, early childhood education, educational administration, elementary, equity and social justice in education, instructional technologies, language and literacy education, mathematics education, secondary, special-interest program. M.A.
Engineering. M.S.
English. Includes composition, creative writing, linguistics, literature, teaching English as a foreign language. M.A.
Ethnic Studies. M.A.
French. M.A.
Geography. Includes resource management and environmental planning. M.A.
Geoscience.
German. M.A.
Gerontology. M.A.
Health Science.
History. M.A.
Home Economics.
Human Sexuality Studies. M.A.
Humanities. M.A.
Industrial Arts. M.A.
International Relations. M.A.
Italian. M.A.
Japanese. M.A.
Kinesiology. Includes exercise science, movement science, sports science. M.A.
Marine Science. M.S.
Mathematics. M.A.
Museum Studies. M.A.
Music. M.A., M.M.
Nursing. Includes family nurse practitioner. M.S.
Philosophy. M.A.
Physical Education.
Physical Therapy. M.S.
Physical Therapy Science. Joint doctoral (D.P.T.S.) program with University of California, San Francisco.
Physics. M.S.
Political Science. M.A.
Psychology. Includes developmental, physiological, psychological research, social psychology(M.A.); clinical, industrial/organizational, school (M.S.).
Public Administration. M.P.A.
Public Health. M.P.H.
Radio and Television. M.A.
Recreation. M.S.
Rehabilitation Counseling. M.S.
Russian. M.A.
Science. Interdisciplinary.
Social Science. Includes interdisciplinary studies. M.A.
Social Work. M.S.W.
Spanish. M.A.

Special Education. M.A.; joint doctoral (Ed.D., Ph.D.) program with University of California, Berkeley.

Special Major. M.A., M.S.

Speech Communication. M.A.

Taxation.

Theatre Arts. Includes design/technical production. M.F.A.

Women Studies. M.A.

UNIVERSITY OF SAN FRANCISCO

San Francisco, California 94117-1080

Web site: www.usfca.edu

Founded 1855. Coed. Private control. Roman Catholic, Jesuit affiliation. Semester system. Special facilities: Center for Child and Family Development, Center for Latin American Business, Center for Latino Studies in the Americas, Center for the Pacific Rim, Family Business Resource Center, Fromm Institute, Institute for Catholic Educational Leadership, Institute for Nonprofit Organization Management, International Institute of Criminal Justice Leadership, Ricci Institute. Library: 747,000 volumes, 2418 subscriptions. Total University enrollment: 8000.

Tuition: per unit, master's $800, Ed.D. programs $880; off-campus master's in education $570; College of Professional Studies $695. On-campus housing for 1050 men, 580 women, limited number of married students. Average academic year housing costs: $8350–$10,670 (including board) for single students. Apply to Director of Residence Life. Phone: (415)422-6824.

Graduate Programs

Graduate study since 1867. Enrollment: full- and part-time 3400. Faculty: full-time 72, part-time 105. Degrees conferred: M.A., M.S., M.B.A., M.F.A., M.H.R.O.D., M.N.O., M.R.E., M.P.A., M.S.N., M.S.I.S., Ed.D.

ADMISSION REQUIREMENTS. Two transcripts, two letters of recommendation required in support of application. GRE for M.A. programs; GMAT for M.B.A. TOEFL required for international applicants. Interview not required. Accepts transfer applicants. Graduates of unaccredited institutions not considered. Admissions deadlines vary by program, contact Office of Graduate Admission at least three months prior to desired registration period for specific deadlines. Application fee $40, foreign applicants $50. Phone: (800)CALL-USF (outside California), or (415)422-6563; fax: (415)422-2066; e-mail: graduate@usfca.edu.

ADMISSION STANDARDS. Competitive. Usual minimum average: 3.0 (A = 4).

FINANCIAL AID. Merit scholarships, research assistantships, teaching assistantships, tuition grants, Federal W/S, loans. Approved for VA benefits. Apply by March 1 to appropriate departmental chair for fellowships, assistantships; to Financial Aid Office for all other programs. Phone: (415)422-6303. Use FAFSA. About 60% of students receive aid other than loans from University. Loans available for part-time students.

DEGREE REQUIREMENTS. For M.A., M.S., M.S.N, M.S.I.S.: 24–36 units minimum including thesis, at least 20 in residence; reading knowledge of one foreign language for some majors; final written/oral exam. For M.F.A.: 33 credit, two-year program. For M.B.A.: 30–48 units minimum including thesis, at least 25 in residence; additional study may be required depending upon previous preparation; final oral exam; no language requirements. For M.F.A.: 33 credit, two-year program. For M.H.R.O.D., M.N.O., M.P.A.: 48 credits minimum, at least 30 in residence; final exam. For Ed.D.: 60 semester hours of course work beyond master's degree, at least 48 in residence; qualifying exam; dissertation; final oral exam.

FIELDS OF STUDY.

COLLEGE OF ARTS AND SCIENCES:

Asian-Pacific Studies. M.A.

Biology. M.S.

Chemistry. M.S.

Computer Science. M.S.

Economics.

Environmental Management. M.S.

Sport and Fitness Management. Joint degree with the McLaren School of Business.

Theology.

Writing. M.F.A.

COLLEGE OF PROFESSIONAL STUDIES:

Human Resources and Organizational Development. M.H.R.O.D.

Information Systems. Includes emphasis in health service administration, human resources, information systems, nonprofit administration, organization development. M.S.I.S.

Nonprofit Organization. M.N.O.

Public Administration. Includes health services administration. M.P.A.

MCLAREN SCHOOL OF BUSINESS:

Business Administration. Includes emphasis in e-business, finance, international business, management, marketing, telecommunications management and policy. M.B.A.

Management and Disability Services. M.M.D.S.

SCHOOL OF EDUCATION:

Catholic School Leadership. Ed.D.

Counseling Psychology. Includes adult development, marriage and family therapy, educational counseling. M.A.

Education. Includes elementary, secondary, Catholic school leadership, educational technology. M.A.

International and Multicultural Education. M.A., Ed.D.

Learning and Instruction. M.A., Ed.D.

Organizational Leadership. M.A., Ed.D.

Special Education. M.A.

Teaching English as a Second Language. M.A.

SCHOOL OF NURSING:

Adult Health/Advanced Practice Nurse. M.S.N.

Family Nurse Practitioner. M.S.N.

Nursing Administration. M.S.N.

School of Law

Web site: www.law.usfca.edu

Established 1912. Located on main campus. ABA approved since 1935. AALS member. Semester system. Full-time, part-time study. Special facilities: Center for Applied Legal Ethics, Center for Law and Global Justice. Special programs: Asian Pacific Legal Studies Program; summer study abroad at Trinity College, Ireland, Charles University, Czech Republic, Nayana University, Bali. Faculty exchange programs with schools in Ireland, Czech Republic, Indonesia, PRC, Vietnam. Law library: 302,348 volumes, 2757 subscriptions; has LEXIS, NEXIS, WESTLAW, DIALOG, INNOPAC.

Annual tuition: full-time $23,786; part-time $17,000. Law students tend to live off-campus. Off-campus housing and personal expenses: approximately $15,380.

Enrollment: first-year class full-time 171, part-time 48; total full-time 507, part-time 116 (men 41%, women 59%). Faculty: full-time 22, part-time 35. Student to faculty ratio 22.1 to 1. Degrees conferred: J.D., J.D.-M.B.A., LL.M. (International Transactions and Comparative Law, for foreign lawyers who have completed a basic legal education and received a university degree in law in another country; full- and part-time study).

ADMISSION REQUIREMENTS. LSDAS Law School report, bachelor's degree, transcripts, LSAT, two recommendations required in support of application. Accepts transfer applicants. Graduates of unaccredited institutions not considered. Apply to Director of Admissions by March 30, June 1 (evening). Admits first-year students September only. Application fee $50. Phone: (415)422-6586; fax: (415)422-6433.

ADMISSION REQUIREMENTS FOR LL.M. APPLICANTS. Must have a first law degree from a foreign university authorized by the government of the country to confer such a degree and must be fluent in English. Official transcripts with certified translations and evaluations, two letters of recommendation (if not in English they should be accompanied by an English translation), personal statement (no more than two double-spaced typewritten pages), résumé, evidence of financial support required in support of LL.M. application. In addition, TOEFL (minimum score 600) is required for those whose native language is not English. Admits Fall only. Apply by June 1. Application fee $60. Phone: (415)422-6946; fax: (415)422-6433, attn: LL.M. Director; Web site: www.usfca.edu/law/llm. About 25 students admitted each year.

ADMISSION STANDARDS. Selective. Mean LSAT: full-time 155, part-time 153; mean GPA: 3.16, part-time 3.03 (A = 4). Gourman rating: 3.80. *U.S. News & World Report* ranking is in the third tier of all U.S. law schools. Accepts 30–35% of total annual applicants.

FINANCIAL AID. Scholarships, Federal W/S, loans. Apply by February 1 to Financial Aid Office. Use FAFSA. About 40% of students receive aid other than loans from School. Aid available for part-time students.

DEGREE REQUIREMENTS. For J.D.: satisfactory completion of three-year (day), four-year (evening) program; 86 semester hours program. For LL.M.: 25 course unit program, at least two semesters in full-time residence, four semesters in part-time residence.

SAN JOSE STATE UNIVERSITY
San Jose, California 95192-0025
Web site: www.sjsu.edu

Founded 1857. Located 50 miles S of San Francisco. CGS member. Coed. State control. Semester system. Library: 1,100,000 volumes, 2504 subscriptions.

Annual fees/tuition: full-time resident $1506, nonresident $1998 plus $246 per unit. On-campus housing for married and single students. Average academic year housing costs: $6556 (including board). Contact Housing Office for both on- and off-campus housing information. Phone: (408)924-6160. Day-care facilities available.

Graduate Studies and Research

Graduate study since 1946. Enrollment: full-time 2242, part-time 3278. Faculty: 300 full-time, 124 part-time. Degrees conferred: M.A., M.S., M.B.A., M.S.W., M.P.A., M.U.R., M.P.H., M.F.A.

ADMISSION REQUIREMENTS. Transcripts required in support of application. On-line application available. GRE Subject Tests/GMAT/MAT required or recommended for some programs. TOEFL required for international applicants. Interview not required. Accepts transfer applicants. Graduates of unaccredited institutions not considered. Apply to Graduate Studies Office by June 30 (Fall), November 30 (Spring). Applications considered after above dates on a space-available basis. Application fee $59. Phone: (408)924-2480; fax: (408)924-2477.

ADMISSION STANDARDS. Selective for most majors. Usual minimum average: 2.5 for last 60 credits (A = 4).

FINANCIAL AID. Fellowships, scholarships, research/teaching assistantships, internships, tuition waivers, Federal W/S, loans. Approved for VA benefits. Apply to Financial Aid Office; no closing date specified. Phone: (408)924-6100. Use FAFSA. Aid available for part-time students.

DEGREE REQUIREMENTS. For master's: 30 semester units minimum, at least 24 in residence; final written/oral exam; thesis/nonthesis option; creative project; reading knowledge of one foreign language for some departments.

FIELDS OF STUDY.

COLLEGE OF APPLIED SCIENCE AND ARTS:
Administration of Justice. M.S.
Kinesiology. M.A.
Mass Communications. M.S.
Nursing. M.S.
Nutritional Science. M.S.
Occupational Therapy. M.S.
Public Health. M.P.H.
Recreation. M.S.

COLLEGE OF BUSINESS:
Accounting. M.S.
Business Administration. M.B.A.
Taxation. M.S.
Transportation Management. M.S.

COLLEGE OF EDUCATION:
Administration and Supervision. M.A.
Counselor Education. M.A.
Child and Adolescent Development. M.A.
Elementary Education. M.A.
Higher Education. M.A.
Instructional Technology. M.A.
Special Education. M.A.
Speech Pathology. M.A.

COLLEGE OF ENGINEERING:
Aerospace Engineering. M.S.
Chemical Engineering. M.S.
Civil Engineering. M.S.
Computer Engineering. M.S.
Engineering. M.S.
Industrial and Systems Engineering. M.S.
Materials Engineering. M.S.
Mechanical Engineering. M.S.
Quality Assurance. M.S.

COLLEGE OF HUMANITIES AND THE ARTS:
Art. Includes creative, art history, graphic design. M.A., M.F.A.
Creative Writing. M.F.A.
English. GRE Subject for candidacy. Includes creative writing; one foreign language for M.A. M.A.
French. GRE for candidacy; working knowledge of second language for M.A. M.A.
Linguistics. M.A.
Music. Includes performance, literature, theory and composition, education; GRE, Music Subject Tests for candidacy; thesis project, recital or composition for M.A. M.A.
Philosophy. M.A.
Spanish. GRE for candidacy; working knowledge of second language for M.A. M.A.
TESOL. M.A.
Theatre Arts. M.A.

COLLEGE OF SCIENCE:
Biology. M.A., M.S.
Biotechnology. M.S.
Computer Science. M.S.

Chemistry. Includes analytical, inorganic, organic, physical. M.A., M.S.
Geology. M.S.
Marine Science. M.S.
Mathematics. M.S.
Meteorology. M.S.
Physics. M.S.

COLLEGE OF SOCIAL SCIENCES:
Economics. M.A.
Environmental Studies. M.S.
Geography. M.A.
History. M.A.
Psychology. Includes clinical/counseling, industrial/organizational; project or thesis for M.S.
Public Administration. M.P.A.
Sociology. GRE Subject for candidacy; thesis, one foreign language for M.A. M.A.
Speech Communication. GRE/Subject for candidacy; thesis or project for M.A.

COLLEGE OF SOCIAL WORK:
Mexican American Studies. M.A.
Social Work. M.S.W
Urban Planning. Thesis or project for M.U.P.

GRADUATE STUDIES AND RESEARCH:
Human Factors/Ergonomics. M.S.
Interdisciplinary Studies. M.A.
Library and Information Science. M.L.I.S.

SANTA CLARA UNIVERSITY

Santa Clara, California 95053-0001
Web site: www.scu.edu

Founded 1851. Located 45 miles S of San Francisco. CGS member. Coed. Private control, Roman Catholic affiliation. Quarter system. Special facilities: Bannan Center for Jesuit Education, Center for Advanced Study and Practice of Information Assurance, Center for Innovation and Entrepreneurship, Center for Multicultural Learning, Center for Professional Development, Center for Science, Technology, and Society, Civil Society Institute, East San Jose Community Law Center, Environmental Studies Institute, Food and Agribusiness Institute, High Tech Law Institute, Howard Hughes Medical Institute, Institute for Information Storage Technology, Institute of Globalization, Markkula Center for Applied Ethics, Retail Management Institute. Library: 715,000 volumes, 8919 subscriptions. Total University enrollment 8,100.

Tuition: per unit College of A&S $333; Business and Administration $594; Division of Psychology $383; Engineering $568. On-campus housing for graduate students on a space-available basis. Contact Director of Housing for off-campus housing information. Phone: (408)554-4900. Day-care facilities available.

Graduate Programs

Graduate study since 1951. Enrollment: full-time 1274, part-time 1457. Graduate faculty: full-time 135, part-time 108. Degrees conferred: M.A., M.B.A., M.S. (Engineering), Engineer.

ADMISSION REQUIREMENTS. Two transcripts, three letters of recommendation required in support of application. GRE/GMAT required for some programs. TOEFL required for international applicants. Interview usually not required. Accepts transfer applicants. Graduates of unaccredited institutions not considered. Apply to Dean's Office, School of Engineering June 1 (Fall), January 1 (Spring); Graduate Admissions, School of Business, June 1 (Fall) December 1 (Spring); Graduate Admissions, Division of

Counseling Psychology and Education and College of A&S, April 1 (Fall), February 1 (Spring). Application fee $45–$55 (fee varies from division to division), international application fee $75. Phone: College of A&S (408)554-4455; CP&E (408)554-4656; Business (408)554-2752; Engineering (408)554-4313.

ADMISSION STANDARDS. Competitive. Usual minimum average: 2.75 (Engineering), 3.0 (all other departments) (A = 4).

FINANCIAL AID. Scholarships, fellowships, assistantships, Federal W/S, loans. Approved for VA benefits. Apply by February 1 to appropriate Dean's Office for fellowships, assistantships; to Financial Aid Office for all other programs. Phone: (408)554-4505. Use FAFSA.

DEGREE REQUIREMENTS. For M.A.: 45 quarter units minimum; final written/oral exam may also be required. For M.B.A.: minimum of 18 courses beyond basic courses, at least 16 in residence. For Engineer: minimum of 45 units beyond the master's; thesis. For Ph.D. (Engineering, electrical only): 135 units minimum of graduate credit, at least 11 months in full-time residence; 45 units research credit for the master's and doctor's theses; language requirement to be determined; thesis; final oral exam.

FIELDS OF STUDY.

COLLEGE OF ARTS AND SCIENCES:
Catechetics.
Liturgical Music.
Pastoral Liturgy.
Spirtuality.

LEAVEY SCHOOL OF BUSINESS AND ADMINISTRATION:
Agribusiness.
Business Administration.

DIVISION OF COUNSELING PSYCHOLOGY AND EDUCATION:
Counseling Psychology.
Education.
Educational Administration.
Health Psychology.
Marriage, Family and Child Counseling.
Pastoral Counseling.
Pupil Personnel Services.
Special Education.

SCHOOL OF ENGINEERING:
Applied Mathematics.
Civil Engineering.
Computer Sciences and Engineering.
Electrical Engineering.
Engineering Management.
Mechanical Engineering.
Software Engineering.

School of Law

Founded 1912. ABA approved since 1937. AALS member. Semester system. Special facilities: Institute of International and Comparative Law, Center for Trial and Appellate Advocacy. Law library: 293,241 volumes, 3718 subscriptions; has LEXIS, NEXIS, WESTLAW, OSCAR.

Annual tuition: full-time $23,880, part-time $16,716. No on-campus housing available. Total average annual additional expense: $18,400.

Enrollment: first-year class, full-time 239, part-time 67; total full-time 661, part-time 229 (men 45%, women 55%). Faculty: full-time 38, part-time 21. Student to faculty ratio 17.8 to 1. Degrees conferred: J.D., J.D.-M.B.A., LL.M. (International Law, High Technology).

ADMISSION REQUIREMENTS. LSDAS Law School report, bachelor's degree, transcripts, LSAT required in support of application. Accepts transfer applicants. Graduates of unaccredited colleges not considered. Apply to Office of Admissions after September 1, before March 1. Rolling admissions process. Admits beginning students Fall only. Application fee $50. Phone: (408)554-4800; fax: (408)554-7897.

ADMISSION STANDARDS. Selective. Mean LSAT: full-time 155, part-time 156; mean GPA: full-time 3.28, part-time 3.17 (A = 4). Gourman rating: 3.72. *U.S. News & World Report* ranking is in the second tier of all U.S. law schools. Accepts about 30–35% of total annual applicants.

FINANCIAL AID. Scholarships, fellowships, assistantships, Federal W/S, loans. Apply to Office of the Dean for Scholarships by February 1; Director of Financial Aid for loans by March 1 for all other aid. Use FAFSA (School code: 001326). About 32% of students receive aid other than loans from School.

DEGREE REQUIREMENTS. For J.D.: 86 credit hours minimum, at least three years in residence for day students, at least four years in residence for part-time students.
Note: Summer programs in France, Germany, Hungary, Malaysia, Switzerland, England, Hong Kong, Singapore, Korea, Vietnam, Thailand, Japan, and People's Republic of China.

SARAH LAWRENCE COLLEGE
Bronxville, New York 10708
Web site: www.sarahlawrence.edu

Founded 1928. Located 15 miles N of New York City. CGS member. Coed on graduate level. Private control. Semester system. Library: 288,000 volumes, 1135 subscriptions.

Tuition: per credit $667–$759, depending on program. No on-campus housing for graduate students. Average monthly on-campus costs: $300–$500. Contact Student Affairs Office for off-campus housing information. Phone: (914)395-2373.

Graduate Studies

Graduate study since 1950. Enrollment: full-time 212, part-time 88. Faculty: full-time 25, part-time 20. Degrees conferred: M.A., M.F.A., M.S., M.P.S., M.S.Ed.

ADMISSION REQUIREMENTS. Transcripts, two letters of recommendation required in support of application. Interview sometimes requested. TOEFL required for international applicants. Accepts transfer applicants. Graduates of unaccredited colleges not considered. Apply to Committee on Graduate Studies by February 1. Fall admission. Application fee $45. Phone: (914)395-2371.

ADMISSION STANDARDS. Very selective for most departments, competitive for all others. Usual minimum average: 3.0 (A = 4).

FINANCIAL AID. Annual awards from institutional funds: grants, assistantships, loans. Apply by March 1 to Committee on Graduate Studies. Phone: (914)395-2570. Use FAFSA. About 25% of students receive aid other than loans from College and outside sources. Aid sometimes available for part-time students.

DEGREE REQUIREMENTS. For M.F.A. and most M.A.: 36 credits, at least two years in residence; thesis or project. For some M.A.'s: 40 credits, at least two years in residence; fieldwork. For M.S., M.P.S.: 40 credits, at least two years in residence; fieldwork. For M.S.: 38 credits; fieldwork.

FIELDS OF STUDY.
Art of Teaching. M.S.Ed.

Child Development. M.A.
Dance. M.F.A.
Education. Includes early childhood, elementary.
Health Advocacy. M.A., M.P.S.
Human Genetics. Includes genetic counseling. M.P.S., M.S.
Theater. M.A., M.F.A.
Women's History. M.A.
Writing. Includes creative, nonfiction, poetry. M.F.A.

UNIVERSITY OF SCRANTON
Scranton, Pennsylvania 18510-4631
Web site: www.scranton.edu

Founded 1888. CGS member. Coed. Private control. Catholic affiliation. Semester system. Library: 433,900 volumes, 7550 subscriptions. Total University enrollment: 4700.

Tuition: per credit $564 (tuition guarantee program). No on-campus housing available. Average off-campus housing cost per month: $470. Contact Director, Residence Life for off-campus housing information. Phone: (570)941-6226.

Graduate School

Graduate study since 1951. Enrollment: full-time 219, part-time 384. Graduate faculty: full-time 70, part-time 34. Degrees conferred: M.A., M.B.A., M.H.A., M.S.N., M.S.

ADMISSION REQUIREMENTS. Transcripts, letters of recommendation required in support of School's application. GMAT required for business applicants. Software Engineering applicants may submit either the GMAT or GRE. TOEFL required for international applicants. Interview required for some programs. Accepts transfer applicants. Graduates of unaccredited institutions not considered. Apply to School at least thirty days prior to registration date. Foreign applicants should apply at least three months prior to registration date. Rolling admissions process. Application fee $50. Phone: (800)366-4723, (570)941-6304; fax: (570)941-5995.

ADMISSION STANDARDS. Selective for most departments. Usual minimum average: 2.75 (A = 4).

FINANCIAL AID. Annual awards from institutional funds: fellowships, graduate assistantships, internships, Federal W/S, loans. Approved for VA benefits. Apply by March 1 to Graduate Dean. Phone: (570)941-7700. Use FAFSA and University's FAF. Aid available for part-time students.

DEGREE REQUIREMENTS. For master's: 30–48 semester credits; thesis/nonthesis option; final written/oral exam.

FIELDS OF STUDY.
Administration (Principal K–12).
Biochemistry.
Business. GMAT for admission. Includes specializations in accounting, enterprise management technology, finance, international business, management information systems, marketing, operations management. M.B.A. only.
Chemistry.
Clinical Chemistry.
Community Counseling.
Curriculum and Instruction.
Early Childhood Education.
Elementary Education.
English.
Health Administration.
History.
Human Resources Administration.

Nursing. Includes specializations in adult health, family nurse practitioner, nurse anesthesia.

Occupational Therapy. Program is for applicants with an undergraduate degree in occupational therapy. 24 credit master's.

Reading Education.

Rehabilitation Counseling.

School Counseling.

Secondary Education.

Software Engineering.

Special Education.

Supervision.

UNIVERSITY OF THE SCIENCES IN PHILADELPHIA

Philadelphia, Pennsylvania 19104-4495

Web site: www.usip.edu

Founded 1821. Name changed in 1998. Coed. Private control. Semester system. Special facilities: McNeil Research Center, Institute for Pharmaceutical Economics, Pharmacology/Toxicology Research Center. Library: 76,000 volumes, 809 subscriptions.

Tuition: per credit $770. No on-campus housing available for graduate students. Contact Dean of Student Affairs for off-campus housing information. Phone: (215)596-8844.

College of Graduate Studies

Graduate study since 1921. Enrollment: full-time 57, part-time 30. Graduate faculty: full-time 27, part-time 19. Degrees conferred: M.S., Ph.D.

ADMISSION REQUIREMENTS. Official transcripts, GRE, written statement of professional goals, three letters of recommendation required in support of School's application. On-line application available. TOEFL, TWE, and certification of finances required for international applicants. GMAT required for Biomedical Writing, Pharmacy Administration. Interview, GRE Subject Tests recommended. Accepts transfer applicants. Graduates of unaccredited institutions not considered. Apply to Dean of Graduate School. Admits to Fall and Spring. Application fee $25. Phone: (215)596-8937; e-mail: graduate@usip.edu.

ADMISSION STANDARDS. Very selective. Usual minimum average: 3.0 (A = 4).

FINANCIAL AID. Annual awards from institutional funds: fellowships, teaching assistantships, tuition scholarships, tuition waivers, Federal W/S, loans. Apply to appropriate department chair for fellowships, assistantships; to Financial Aid Office for all other programs. No specified closing date. Use FAFSA and PHEAA. Phone: (215)596-8894; fax: (215)895-1100. About 80% of students receive aid other than loans from College and outside sources.

DEGREE REQUIREMENTS. For M.S. (nonthesis): 30 semester hours of didactic credit. For M.S. (thesis): 20 semester hours of didactic credit; 24 semester hours of credit in research; thesis; proficiency exam may be required. For Ph.D.: 20 semester hours of didactic credit; 48 semester hours of credit in research; at least eight months in full-time residence; proficiency exam may be required; dissertation; final oral/written exam.

FIELDS OF STUDY.

Biochemistry.

Bioinformation.

Biomedical Writing.

Cell Biology and Biotechnology.

Chemistry.

Clinical Health Psychology.

Health Policy.

Pharmaceutical Business.

Pharmaceutics.

Pharmacognosy.

Pharmacology and Toxicology.

Pharmacy Administration.

SEATTLE PACIFIC UNIVERSITY

Seattle, Washington 98119-1997

Web site: www.spu.edu

Founded 1891. Coed. Private control. Free Methodist. Quarter system. Library: 200,000 volumes, 1192 subscriptions.

Limited on-campus housing for single and married graduate students. Average academic year housing costs: $5600 (including board) for single students, $7100 for married students. Contact Coordinator of Housing for both on- and off-campus housing information. Phone: (206)281-2779.

Graduate Studies

Tuition: per credit $325; Business, information Systems $482; Education Counseling $338; Educational Administration $387; MFT $389; Nursing $366; Ed.D. $424; Psy.D. $437. Enrollment: full-time 157, part-time 500. Graduate faculty: full-time 51, part-time 54. Degrees conferred: M.Ed., M.A., M.S., M.S.N., M.B.A., Ed.D., Psy.D.

ADMISSION REQUIREMENTS. Transcripts, two letters of reference, GRE or MAT required in support of application. GMAT for M.B.A. program. Interview required for some departments. TOEFL required for foreign applicants. Accepts transfer applicants. Apply to Graduate School at least four weeks prior to registration. Application fee $35. Phone: (206)281-2125; fax: (206)281-2115.

ADMISSION STANDARDS. Competitive. Usual minimum average: 3.0. (A = 4), 3.0 in last 45 credits. TOEFL minimum score 550; for M.B.A., I.S.M. 575; TESOL 600.

FINANCIAL AID. Teaching/research assistantships, traineeships, Federal W/S, loans. Approved for VA benefits. Apply by April 1 to appropriate School for assistantships, fellowships; to Financial Aid Office for all other programs. Phone: (206)281-2046. Use FAFSA.

DEGREE REQUIREMENTS. For master's: 45 quarter hours minimum, last 15 in residence; three credit course in Christian thought; candidacy; comprehensive exam; thesis/nonthesis option/project. For Ed.D., Psy.D.: 90–96 quarter hours beyond master's degree; qualifying exam; comprehensive exam; dissertation; clinical internship for Psy.D.; final oral exam.

FIELDS OF STUDY.

Business Administration. M.B.A.

Clinical Family Psychology. Psy.D.

Curriculum and Instruction. M.Ed.

Educational Leadership. M.Ed., Ed.D.

Information Systems Management. M.S.

Marriage and Family Therapy. M.S.

Nursing. M.S.N.

School Counseling. M.Ed.

School Psychology. M.Ed.

Sport and Exercise Leadership. M.A.

TESOL. M.A.

Teaching—Secondary. M.A.

SEATTLE UNIVERSITY

Seattle, Washington 98122-4340
Web site: www.seattle.edu

Founded 1891. Coed. Private control. Jesuit affiliation. Quarter system. Library: 216,000 volumes, 2500 subscriptions. Total University enrollment: 5800.

Tuition: per credit hour Business $516; Education, Nursing $398; Ed.D. $482; Institute of Public Service, Psychology $430; Ministry, Theology $397; Software Engineering $465. Limited on-campus housing for graduate single students. Average academic year housing costs: $6768–$7422 (including board). Contact Residential Life Office for both on- and off-campus housing information. Phone: (206)296-6274. Day-care facilities available.

Graduate School

Graduate study since 1901. Enrollment: full-time 353, part-time 1261. Faculty: full-time 119, part-time 58. Degrees conferred: M.A., M.A.P.S., M.A.T.S., M.S., M.Ed., M.B.A., M.I.B., M.A. in Ed., Ed.D., M.C., M.S.E., M.Div., M.M., M.N.P.L., M.I.T., M.S.N., M.P.A., M.S.F., M.A.E., Ed.S.

ADMISSION REQUIREMENTS. Transcripts required in support of School's application. GRE/GMAT/NTE, interview required for some programs. Accepts transfer applicants. Graduates of unaccredited institutions not considered. Apply to Graduate Admissions Office at least four weeks prior to registration. Application fee $55. Phone: (206)296-2000; fax: (206)298-5656; e-mail: grad_admissions@seattleu.edu.

ADMISSION STANDARDS. Selective. Usual minimum average: 2.75 (A = 4).

FINANCIAL AID. Scholarships, assistantships, internships, grants, Federal W/S, loans. Approved for VA benefits. Apply to Financial Aid Office; no specified closing date. Phone: (206)296-5840; fax: (206)296-5656. Use FAFSA. Aid available for part-time students.

DEGREE REQUIREMENTS. For master's: 45–60 quarter hours minimum, at least 25 in residence; thesis; final oral/written exam depending upon program. For Ed.D.: 90 quarter hours minimum; preliminary exam; dissertation; final exam.

FIELDS OF STUDY.

ALBERS SCHOOL OF BUSINESS AND ECONOMICS:
Business Administration. M.B.A.
Finance. M.S.F.
International Business. M.I.B.
Professional Accounting. M.P.A.

COLLEGE OF ARTS AND SCIENCES:
Psychology. M.A.
Not-for-Profit Leadership. M.N.P.L.
Public Administration. M.P.A.

SCHOOL OF EDUCATION:
Adult Education and Training. M.A., M.Ed.
Counseling. M.A.
Curriculum and Instruction. M.A., M.Ed.
Educational Administration. M.A., M.Ed., Ed.S.
Educational Leadership. Ed.D.
Literacy for Special Needs. M.A.
School Psychology. Ed.S.
Student Development Administration. M.A., M.Ed.
Teaching English to Speakers of Other Languages. M.A., M.Ed.
Teaching. M.I.T.

SCHOOL OF SCIENCE AND ENGINEERING:
Software Engineering. M.S.E.

SCHOOL OF THEOLOGY AND MINISTRY:
Divinity. M.Div.
Pastoral Studies. M.A.
Transforming Spirituality. M.A.

School of Law

Web site: www.law.seattleu.edu

Established 1972. Formerly Puget Sound School of Law. Acquired by Seattle University in 1994. ABA approved since 1994. AALS member. Semester system. Special facility: Access to Justice Institute. Law library: 325,162 volumes, 3806 subscriptions; has LEXIS, NEXIS, WESTLAW, DIALOG, BRS, VUTEXT, WILSONLINE, DATATIMES.

Annual tuition: full-time $20,236, part-time $13,492. No on-campus housing available. Total average annual additional expense: $13,242.

Enrollment: first-year class full-time 250, part-time 77; total 938 (men 45%, women 55%). Faculty: full-time 34, part-time 35. Student to faculty ratio 21.2 to 1. Degrees conferred: J.D., J.D.-M.B.A., J.D.-M.S.F., J.D.-M.I.B.

ADMISSION REQUIREMENTS. LSDAS Law School report, bachelor's degree, transcripts, LSAT, letters of recommendation required in support of application. Interviews by invitation only. Accepts transfer applicants. Graduates of unaccredited colleges not considered. Apply to the Office of Admissions by April 1. Admits Fall only. Application fee $50. Phone: (206)398-4200; fax: (206)398-4058.

ADMISSION STANDARDS. Selective. Mean LSAT: full-time 153, part-time 154; mean GPA: 3.25, part-time 3.19 (A = 4). Gourman rating: 2.88. *U.S. News & World Report* ranking is in the fourth tier of all U.S. law schools. Accepts 45–50% of total annual applications.

FINANCIAL AID. Scholarships, tuition waivers, assistantships, Federal W/S, loans. Apply to Student Aid Office by April 1. Use FAFSA (School code: E00615). About 36% of students receive aid other than loans from School.

DEGREE REQUIREMENTS. For J.D.: satisfactory completion of 90 semester hour program.

SETON HALL UNIVERSITY

South Orange, New Jersey 07079-2697
Web site: www.shu.edu

Founded 1856. Located 20 miles SW of New York City. CGS member. Coed. Private control. Roman Catholic. Semester system. Walsh Library: 484,500 volumes, 2270 subscriptions. Total University enrollment: 10,000.

Tuition: per credit nonbusiness $601, business $646. Limited on-campus housing for graduate students. Average academic year housing costs: $9180 (including board). Contact Director of Housing for on- and off-campus housing information. Phone: (973)761-9172.

Graduate Division

Graduate study since 1943. Enrollment: full-time 724, part-time 2027. Faculty: full-time 335, part-time 307. Degrees conferred: M.A., M.A.S.C.L., M.B.A., M.H.A., M.S., M.P.A., Ed.S., Ed.D., Ph.D. (Chemistry and Education).

ADMISSION REQUIREMENTS. Two transcripts, three letters of recommendation, statement of purpose or résumé required in support of application. Interview, MAT/GRE/GMAT required by some departments. TOEFL required for international applicants. Accepts transfer applicants. Graduates of unaccredited institutions not considered. Apply to Graduate Office by July 1 (Fall), November 1 (Spring), May 1 (Summer). Some programs have earlier deadlines. Application fee $30. Phone: (973)761-9343.

ADMISSION STANDARDS. Selective for most departments. Usual minimum average: 3.0 (A = 4).

FINANCIAL AID. Annual awards from university funds: academic scholarships, fellowships, administrative assistantships, teaching assistantships, internships, Federal W/S, loans. Approved for VA benefits. Apply by February 1 to appropriate departmental chair for assistantships, fellowships; to Financial Aid Office for all other programs. Phone: (973)761-9350; fax: (973) 761-7954. Use FAFSA. About 30% of students receive aid other than loans from University and outside sources.

DEGREE REQUIREMENTS. For master's: 30 credits minimum; qualifying exam/thesis required in some departments; competency in one foreign language required in some programs in the College of Arts and Sciences; comprehensive exam. For Ed.D., Ph.D.: 70 credits minimum beyond the bachelor's degree; matriculation exam; dissertation; final oral exam.

FIELDS OF STUDY.

COLLEGE OF ARTS AND SCIENCES:
Asian Studies. M.A.
Biology. M.S.
Chemistry. Includes analytical, inorganic, organic, physical. M.S., Ph.D.
Church Administration. M.P.A.
Corporate and Public Communications. M.A.
English. M.A.
Healthcare Administration. M.B.A.
Jewish-Christian Studies. M.A.
Microbiology. M.S.
Museum Professions. M.A.
Public Administration. M.P.A.
Strategic Communication and Leadership. M.A.S.C.L.

COLLEGE OF EDUCATION AND HUMAN SERVICES:
Bilingual/Bicultural Education. Ed.S.
Catholic Leadership. M.A.
Clinical Psychology. Ph.D., Psy.D.
Counseling Psychology. Ph.D.
Counselor Preparation.
Cultural, Humanistic, and Professional Studies. Ed.S.
Educational Administration and Supervision. M.A., Ed.S.
Educational Media.
Elementary Education.
General Administration. Ed.D.
Health Professions Education.
Higher Educational Administration. Ed.D., Ph.D.
Human Resources Training and Development.
Instructional Design. Ed.S.
Marriage and Family Therapy. M.S., Ed.S., Ph.D.
Professional Education.
Psychological Studies.
School and Community Psychology. Ed.S.
School Business Administration. Ed.D.
Secondary Education. M.A., Ed.S.
Student Personnel Services (K–12).

W. PAUL STILLMAN SCHOOL OF BUSINESS:
Accounting. M.B.A., M.S.

Economics.
Finance. M.B.A.
Financial Institutions. M.B.A.
Information Systems. M.B.A.
International Business. M.S.
Management. M.B.A.
Marketing. M.B.A.
Pharmaceutical Operations. M.B.A.
Professional Accounting. M.S.
Sports Management. M.B.A.
Taxation. M.S.
Note: Evening program requires GMAT for admission; M.B.A., M.S. Taxation. Joint M.B.A.-J.D., M.B.A.-M.P.A., M.B.A.-M.S. (Nursing), M.S. (International Business)-M.A. (Diplomacy and International Relations).

COLLEGE OF NURSING:
Advanced Practice Nurse Studies.
Nurse Practitioner Studies. Includes acute care, adult critical care, gerontological, pediatric, school, women's health care.
Nursing Administrator.
Nursing Care Management.
Nursing Education.

SCHOOL OF DIPLOMACY AND INTERNATIONAL RELATIONS:
Diplomacy and International Relations. M.A.

SCHOOL OF GRADUATE MEDICAL EDUCATION:
Audiology. Sc.D.
Health Sciences. Includes movement science. M.S.
Occupational Therapy. M.S.
Physician Assistant. M.S.
Speech Pathology. M.S.

SCHOOL OF THEOLOGY:
Pastoral Ministry. Includes church management, catechetical health care, liturgical, spirituality, youth.
Theology. Include biblical studies, ecclesia history, Judaeo-Christian studies, moral theology, systematic.

School of Law
Web site: www.law.shu.edu

Established 1951. Located 20 minutes from New York City in Newark (07102-5210). ABA approved since 1951. AALS member. Semester system. Full-time, part-time study. Special facilities: Center for Social Justice, Legal Education Opportunities Institute. Special programs: summer study abroad at University of Parma in Parma (Milan, Florence, Genoa), Italy, American University of Cairo, Egypt. Law library: 412,100 volumes, 3562 subscriptions; has LEXIS, NEXIS, WESTLAW, DIALOG.

Annual tuition: full-time $21,890, part-time $15,590. No on-campus housing available. Law students live off-campus. Contact Admissions Officer for off-campus information. Off-campus housing and personal expenses: approximately $13,890.

Enrollment: first-year class 246, part-time 135; total full- and part-time 1129 (men 52%, women 48%). Faculty: full-time 39, part-time 90. Student to faculty ratio 21.5 to 1. Degrees conferred: J.D., J.D.-M.B.A., J.D.-M.A. (Diplomacy and International Relations), J.D.-M.D. (Robert Wood Johnson Medical School of the UMDNJ), LL.M. (Health Law, full- or part-time program), M.S.J. (Health Law for Health Care Professionals, full- or part-time).

ADMISSION REQUIREMENTS. LSDAS Law School report, LSAT (not later that February test date; if more than one LSAT, average is used), bachelor's degree from an accredited institution, personal statement, two recommendations, transcripts (must show all schools attended and at least three years of study) required in support of application. Applicants must have received bachelor's degree prior to enrollment. Interview not required but may be requested by School. In addition, international applicants whose precollege language was not English and they score 150 or less on the LSAT must submit TOEFL (not older that two years), certified copies of all transcripts and evaluations of all foreign credentials. Joint degree applicants must apply to and be accepted by both Schools; GMAT for M.B.A. Apply to Office of Admission after September 30, before April 1. First-year students admitted Fall only. Rolling admissions process, notification starts in January and is finished by early May. Application fee $50. Phone: (888)415-7271, (973)642-8747.

ADMISSION STANDARDS. Selective. Mean LSAT: full-time 155, part-time 151; mean GPA: full-time 3.1, part-time 2.99 (A = 4). Gourman rating: 3.44 *U.S. News & World Report* ranking is in the second tier of all U.S. law schools.

FINANCIAL AID. Centennial Scholarships, need-based merit scholarships, minority scholarships, Grants-in-Aid, private and institutional loans; Federal loans and Federal W/S offered through University's Financial Aid Office. Assistantships may be available for upper-divisional joint degree candidates. All accepted students are automatically considered for scholarships (selection criteria places heavy reliance on LSAT and Undergraduate GPA). For all other programs apply after January 1, before April 15 to Office of Financial Resource Management. Use FAFSA (School code: G09986), also submit Financial Aid Transcript, Federal Income Tax forms. Approximately 66% of first-year class received scholarships/Grants-in-Aid. Approximately 85% of students receive some form of financial assistance.

DEGREE REQUIREMENTS. For J.D.: 85 (46 required) credits with a GPA of at least 2.0 (A = 4), plus completion of upper divisional writing course; three-year program, four-year part-time program. Accelerated J.D. with one summer of course work. For J.D.-M.B.A.: total 118 credits (J.D. 73 credits, M.B.A. 45 credits); four-year full-time program only. For LL.M., M.S.J.: 24 credit program.

SHIPPENSBURG UNIVERSITY OF PENNSYLVANIA

Shippensburg, Pennsylvania 17257-2299
Web site: www.ship.edu

Founded 1871. Located 40 miles SW of Harrisburg. CGS member. Coed. State control. Semester credit hour system. Library: 445,600 volumes, 1443 subscriptions. Total University enrollment: 6000.

Tuition: per credit resident $292, nonresident $467. On-campus housing for graduate men and women. Average annual housing costs: $4864–$6492. Contact Dean of Students Office for both on- and off-campus housing information. Phone: (717)532-1164. Day-care facilities available.

School of Graduate Studies

Graduate studies since 1959. Enrollment: full-time 181, part-time 602. College faculty teaching graduate students: full-time 116, part-time 22. Degrees conferred: M.A., M.Ed., M.S., M.P.A.

ADMISSION REQUIREMENTS. Transcripts, GRE/MAT required in support of School's application. On-line application available. Some departments require interview, goal statement, or letters of recommendation. TOEFL required for international applicants. Accepts transfer applicants. Apply to Dean of Graduate Studies at least eight weeks prior to registration. Rolling admissions process. Application fee $30. Phone: (717)477-1213; fax: (717)477-4016; e-mail: admiss@ship.edu.

ADMISSION STANDARDS. Selective for most departments. Usual minimum average: 2.75 (A = 4).

FINANCIAL AID. Annual awards from institutional funds: assistantships, internships, Federal W/S, loans. Apply by March 1 to Dean of the Graduate Studies for assistantships; to the Financial Aid Office for all other programs. Phone: (717)477-1131. Use FAFSA and University's FAF. Aid available for part-time students.

DEGREE REQUIREMENTS. For master's: 30–48 semester hours minimum, 24 in residence; thesis/nonthesis option.

FIELDS OF STUDY.
Administration of Justice.
Applied History.
Biology.
Communication Study.
Computer Science. GRE required.
Counseling.
Educational Administration.
Elementary Education.
Geoenvironmental Studies.
Information Systems.
Mathematics.
Psychology.
Public Administration.
Reading.
Special Education.

SIENA HEIGHTS UNIVERSITY

Adrian, Michigan 49221-1796
Web site: www.sienahts.edu

Founded 1919. Located 65 miles SW of Detroit. Coed. Private control. Roman Catholic. Semester system. Library: 125,000 volumes, 650 subscriptions. Total University enrollment: 2000.

Tuition: per credit $296. No on-campus housing for graduate students. Contact Director, Residence Life for off-campus housing information. Phone: (517)263-0731.

Graduate Division

Graduate study since 1953. Enrollment: full-time 36, part-time 167. Graduate faculty: full- and part-time 28. Degree conferred: M.A.

ADMISSION REQUIREMENTS. Transcripts, three letters of recommendation required in support of application. On-line application available. TOEFL required for international applicants. Interview recommended. Accepts transfer applicants. Apply to Graduate Office by April 1 (Summer), August 1 (Fall). Application fee $25. Phone: (517)263-0731, ext. 283.

ADMISSION STANDARDS. Selective for most departments. Usual minimum average: 3.0 (A = 4).

FINANCIAL AID. Limited Federal W/S, loans. Approved for VA benefits. Apply to Financial Aid Office; no specified closing date. Use FAFSA. Phone: (517)263-0731, ext. 211.

DEGREE REQUIREMENTS. For M.A.: 36–48 semester hours; thesis/research project.

FIELDS OF STUDY.
Community Counseling.
Counselor Education.
Educational Leadership.

Health Care Administration.
Organizational Leadership.
Teacher Education.

Spanish. M.A.
Special Education. M.S.
Teaching and Liberal Arts. M.A.T.

SIMMONS COLLEGE

Boston, Massachusetts 02115-5898
Web site: www.simmons.edu

Founded 1899. Coed on graduate level. Private control. Semester system. Library: 285,700 volumes, 1861 subscriptions.

Tuition: $637 per semester hour. On-campus housing for graduate students. Average academic year housing costs: on-campus $9384 (including board), off-campus $15,000. Contact the Office of Student Housing for both on- and off-campus housing information. Phone: (617)521-1102.

Graduate Division

Enrollment: full-time 650, part-time 1462. College faculty: full-time 119, part-time 99. Degrees conferred: M.A., M.S., M.S.Ed., M.B.A., M.A.T., M.Phil., M.S.W., Ph.D., D.A.

ADMISSION REQUIREMENTS. Transcripts, references required in support of application. On-line application available. TOEFL required for international applicants. Interview, GRE/GMAT/MAT sometimes necessary. Apply to Director of appropriate program. Call for information regarding deadlines and application fees; they vary by graduate program. Rolling admissions process. Phone: (617)521-2910; fax: (617)521-2910; e-mail: gsa@admissions.edu.

ADMISSION STANDARDS: Selective. Usual minimum average: 2.75 (A = 4).

FINANCIAL AID. Grants, scholarships, assistantships, internships, tuition waivers, Federal W/S, loans. Type and amount of aid varies according to program of study. Apply by March 1 to Director of Financial Aid. Phone: (617)521-2910. Use FAFSA. Aid available for part-time students.

DEGREE REQUIREMENTS. For master's: 32–56 semester hours, dependent upon the program; thesis required in some programs. For Ph.D.: 70 credits minimum beyond bachelor's, at least 32 in residence; competency in 2 foreign languages, or computer tool may be substituted for 1 language; dissertation; final oral exam.

FIELDS OF STUDY.
Assistive/Special Education Technology. M.S.
Behavioral Education. M.S.
Children's Literature. M.A.
Communications Management. M.S.
Elementary Education. M.A.T.
Educational Leadership. M.S.
English. Includes English, American, comparative. M.A., M.Phil.
English As a Second Language. M.A.T.
Foreign Languages and Literatures. Includes Spanish, French. M.A.
Gender/Cultural Studies. M.A.
Health Care Administration. M.S.
History and Archives Management. M.A.
Language and Literacy in Special Education. M.S.
Management. M.B.A.
Middle School Education. M.A.T.
Nursing. M.S.
Nutrition. M.S.
Physical Therapy. M.S.
School Library Media Specialist. M.S.
Secondary Education. M.A.T.
Social Work. Includes urban leadership. M.S., Ph.D.

SLIPPERY ROCK UNIVERSITY OF PENNSYLVANIA

Slippery Rock, Pennsylvania 16057
Web site: www.sru.edu

Established 1889. Located 50 miles N of Pittsburgh. Coed. State control. Library: 774,723 volumes, 4100 subscriptions. Total University enrollment: 7800.

Annual tuition: full-time resident $4138, nonresident $7008; per credit resident $230, nonresident $389. On-campus housing for single students only. Average academic year housing cost: $4814 (including board). Contact Office of Director of Residence Life for both on- and off-campus housing. Phone: (724) 738-2082. Day-care facilities available.

Graduate School

Enrollment: full-time 323, part-time 335. Faculty: full- and part-time 65. Degrees conferred: M.Ed., M.A., M.S., M.S.N., M.P.A., D.P.T.

ADMISSION REQUIREMENTS. Transcripts, GRE, interview (Physical Therapy) required in support of application. TOEFL required for international applicants. Interview not required. Accepts transfer applicants. Graduates of unaccredited institutions not considered. Apply to Graduate School Office at least two months prior to registration. Application fee $25, $35 for D.P.T. Phone: (724)738-2051; fax: (724)738-2908.

ADMISSION STANDARDS. Selective. Usual minimum average: 2.75, some programs required 3.0 (A = 4).

FINANCIAL AID. Annual awards from institutional funds: scholarships, assistantships, internships, grants, tuition waivers, Federal W/S, loans. Apply by May 1 to appropriate department chair for assistantships; to Office of Financial Aid for all other programs. Phone: (724)738-2044; fax: (724)738-2922. Use FAFSA. About 35% of students receive aid other than loans from College and outside sources. Aid available for part-time students.

DEGREE REQUIREMENTS. For master's: 30 credit hours minimum, at least 18 in residence; thesis or final document; final written/oral exam. For D.P.T.: 60 credits beyond the master's degree, at least two years in full-time residence; qualifying exam; dissertation; internship; final oral exam.

FIELDS OF STUDY.
Accounting. M.S.
Community Counseling.
Elementary Education. Includes elementary school math/science, reading.
Elementary Guidance and Counseling.
English.
Exercise and Wellness Promotion.
Health and Physical Education.
History.
Nursing. Includes nurse practitioner studies.
Park and Resource Management.
Physical Science.
Physical Therapy.
Reading.
Public Administration.

Recreation.
Secondary Education. Includes mathematics, science.
Secondary Guidance.
Special Education. Includes mental retardation learning disabilities, social restoration, supervision of special education, the emotionally disturbed.
Sport Management.
Student Personnel.
Sustainable Systems. Includes built environment/energy management, sustainable resource management.

SMITH COLLEGE

Northampton, Massachusetts 01063
Web site: www.smith.edu

Founded 1871. Located 100 miles W of Boston. Coed on graduate level. Private control. Semester system. Special facilities: Fine Arts Center, Center for the Performing Arts, Clarke Science Center. Cooperative M.E.D. program with the Clarke School for the Deaf; cooperative Ph.D. program with Amherst, Hampshire, Mount Holyoke, University of Massachusetts. Library: 1,200,000 volumes, 5119 subscriptions.

Annual tuition: $23,400, per credit $735. On-campus housing for 25 graduate students; none for married students. Average annual housing cost: $7800 (including board). Phone: (413)585-3050.

Graduate Study

Graduate study since 1879. Enrollment: full-time 43, part-time 43 (men 10%, women 90%). College faculty: full-time 98, part-time 38. Degrees conferred: M.A., M.A.T., M.Ed., M.E.D., (Teaching of the Deaf), M.F.A. (Dance), M.S. in Exercise and Sport Studies.

ADMISSION REQUIREMENTS. Transcripts, GRE/MAT, three letters of recommendation required in support of application. TOEFL required for international applicants. Interview not required. Apply to Director of Graduate Study by January 15 M.E.D. (April 15 without financial aid); April 1 M.F.A.; March 1 all other programs. Application fee $50. Phone: (413)585-3051; fax: (413)585-3054; e-mail: gradstdy@smith.edu.

ADMISSION STANDARDS. Competitive for most departments. Usual minimum average: 3.0 (A = 4).

FINANCIAL AID. Scholarships, grants, fellowships, assistantships, Federal W/S, loans. Apply by January 15 to Director of Graduate Study for scholarships, fellowships; to Financial Aid Office for all other programs. Phone: (413)585-3050; fax: (413)858-2075. Use FAFSA and CSS Profile. About 80% of students receive aid from College and outside sources. Aid available for part-time students.

DEGREE REQUIREMENTS. For M.A., Ed.M., M.E.D., M.F.A.: 8 semester courses minimum in residence; thesis or final project. For M.A.T.: 8 semester courses minimum in residence, usually one academic year plus one summer internship. For M.S. in Exercise and Sport Studies: usually two years in full-time residence.

FIELDS OF STUDY.
Art History. M.A.T.
Biological Sciences. Includes botany, microbiology, zoology. M.A., M.A.T. Cooperative. Ph.D. with five-year college program.
Chemistry. M.A.T.
Elementary Education. Ed.M.
Dance. M.F.A.
English. M.A.T.
Exercise and Sport Studies. M.S.
French. M.A., M.A.T.
Geology. M.A.T.
History. M.A.T., M.A.
Italian. M.A.

Mathematics. M.A.T.
Music. M.A., M.A.T.
Philosophy. M.A.
Physics. M.A.T.
Preschool Education. Ed.M.
Religion. M.A.
Spanish. M.A.T.
Teaching of the Deaf. M.E.D.
Theatre. Includes playwriting. M.F.A.

School for Social Work

Since 1918. Semester system. Annual tuition: full-time $13,328. On-campus housing available. Summer session room and board: $2306.

Enrollment: full-time 396. School faculty: full-time 15, part-time 92. Degrees conferred: M.S.W., Ph.D.

ADMISSION REQUIREMENTS. Official transcripts, MAT required in support of School's application. TOEFL required for international applicants. Accepts transfer applicants. Graduates of unaccredited institutions not considered. Apply by February 15 to the Office of Admissions. Application fee $50. Phone: (413)585-7960; fax: (413)585-7994.

ADMISSION STANDARDS. Competitive. Usual minimum average: 3.0 (A = 4).

FINANCIAL AID. Scholarships, tuition waivers, internships, grants, loans. Apply by May 1 to the Financial Aid Office. Use FAFSA. About 50% of students receive aid from the School and outside sources.

DEGREE REQUIREMENTS. For M.S.W.: 4 semesters in full-time residence; field work experience; final project. For Ph.D.: three years minimum beyond bachelor's; at least two years in residence; advancement to candidacy; comprehensive exam; dissertation; final oral exam.

SONOMA STATE UNIVERSITY

Rohnert Park, California 94928-3609
Web site: www.sonoma.edu

Founded 1960. Located 45 miles N of San Francisco. Coed. State control. Semester system. Library: 571,500 volumes, 2400 subscriptions.

Annual fee: full-time resident $2130, nonresident $2130 plus $246 per unit. On-campus housing for single students only. Average academic year housing costs: $4671 (including board). Contact Housing Office for both on- and off-campus housing information. Phone: (707)664-2541. Day-care facilities available.

Graduate Programs

Enrollment: full-time 181, part-time 311. College faculty teaching graduate students: full-time 26, part-time 61. Degrees conferred: M.A., M.S., M.B.A., M.P.A.

ADMISSION REQUIREMENTS. Transcripts, GRE/GMAT/MAT required in support of application. On-line application available. TOEFL required for international applicants. Accepts transfer applicants. Graduates of unaccredited institutions not considered. Apply to Office of Admissions and Records at least two months in advance of registration. Application fee $55. Phone: (707)664-2778; fax: (707)664-2060.

ADMISSION STANDARDS. Varies by department. Usual minimum average: 3.0 (A = 4).

FINANCIAL AID. Fellowships, internships, assistantships, Federal W/S, loans. Apply by April 1 to Financial Aid Office. Phone: (707)664-2389. Use FAFSA. Aid available for part-time students.

DEGREE REQUIREMENTS. For master's: 30–60 units minimum, at least 21 in residence; thesis/nonthesis option; final oral exam/projects.

FIELDS OF STUDY.
Biology. Includes environmental. M.A.
Computer and Engineering. M.S.
Counseling. Concentrations in marriage, family, and child counseling (M.F.C.C.), school counseling (P.P.S.). M.A.
Cultural Resource Management. Includes anthropology. M.A.
Education. Concentrations in curriculum and instruction, early childhood education, educational administration, reading and language, special education. M.A.
English. M.A.
History. M.A.
Interdisciplinary Studies. M.A., M.S.
Kinesiology. M.A.
Nursing. Concentrations in family nurse practitioner, leader/case management. M.S.
Psychology. Includes art therapy, organizational development, special-interest areas. M.A.

UNIVERSITY OF THE SOUTH
Sewanee, Tennessee 37375-1000
Web site: www.sewanee.edu

Founded 1857. Located 50 miles W of Chattanooga. Coed. Private control. Semester system. Library: 457,526 volumes, 6495 subscriptions.
Annual tuition: full-time $10,920, per credit $265. On-campus housing for 50 graduate students in apartments only. Average academic year housing costs for single or married seminary students: $5200–$9000. Day-care facilities available.

School of Theology

Founded 1872. Enrollment: full-time 97, part-time 17 (M.Dir., and M.A.). Faculty: full-time 9, part-time 6. Degrees conferred: M.Div. (S.T.M. and D.Min. are only in Summer), S.T.M., D.Min., M.A.

ADMISSION REQUIREMENTS. Transcripts, letter of recommendation, GRE, interview required in support of application. TOEFL required for international applicants. Accepts transfer applicants. Apply to Admissions Office before April 1 (Fall), November 15 (Spring). Application fee $25. Phone: (931)598-1283; fax: (931)598-1852.

ADMISSION STANDARDS. Competitive. Usual minimum average: 3.0 (A = 4).

FINANCIAL AID. 75 grants which are need-based, institutional work program for M.Div., M.A. students only. Contact Financial Aid Office for application deadlines. Phone: (615)598-1312; fax: (615)598-1667.

DEGREE REQUIREMENTS. For M.Div.: 91 credits minimum, at least 30 in residence and two semesters in full-time study. For M.A.: 48 hours including thesis. For S.T.M.: 30 credits minimum beyond the M.Div., four summers in residence; thesis. For D.Min.: 30 credits minimum beyond the M.Div., normally takes four summers in residence.

FIELD OF STUDY.
Theology.

UNIVERSITY OF SOUTH ALABAMA
Mobile, Alabama 36688-0002
Web site: www.southalabama.edu

Founded 1964. Semester system. CGS member. Coed. Special facilities: Electron Microscopy Center, Mass Spectroscopy Center, Flow Cytometry Center, DBNA-Protein Sequencing and Synthesis Center, Sickle-Cell Center, Cancer Center. The University's NIH ranking is 200th among all U.S. institutions with 39 awards/grants worth $11,995,643. Library: 335,600 volumes, 2800 subscriptions. Total University enrollment: 12,000.
Tuition/fees: basic fee of $127 per semester; per credit, resident $116, nonresident $230. On-campus housing available for 502 married students, 1690 single students. Average academic year housing costs: $2888–$3296 (including board). Contact Director of Housing for both on- and off-campus housing information. Phone: (334)460-6195.

Graduate School.

Created 1968. Enrollment: full-time 1247, part-time 897. Graduate faculty: full-time 231. Degrees conferred: M.A., M.Acct., M.B.A., M.Ed., M.P.A., M.S., M.S.Ch.E., M.S.E.E., M.S.M.E., M.S.N., Ed.S., Ed.D., Ph.D.

ADMISSION REQUIREMENTS. Transcripts required in support of School's application. Standardized test, recommendation required by some programs. TOEFL required for international applicants. Accepts transfer applicants. Graduates of unaccredited institutions considered. Apply to Director of Admissions by August 1 (Fall), December 15 (Spring), May 20 (Summer). Deadlines for all admissions documents for International students is at least three months prior to date of registration. Application fee $25. Phone: (800)872-5247, (334)460-6310.

ADMISSION STANDARDS. Selective. Usual minimum average: 3.0 (provisional 2.5) (A = 4).

FINANCIAL AID. Research assistantships, teaching assistantships, fellowships, stipends, internships, traineeships, Federal W/S, loans. Approved for VA benefits. Apply by April 1 to appropriate department for fellowships, assistantships; to the Office of Financial Aid for all other programs. Use FAFSA and University's FAF. Approximately 30% of graduate students receive aid other than loans from the University or outside sources. Aid available for part-time students.

DEGREE REQUIREMENTS. For master's: 48 quarter hours minimum, at least 3 quarter hours in residence; foreign language may be required by some programs; comprehensive exam; thesis/nonthesis option. For Ed.S.: 45 quarter hours beyond the master's. For doctoral programs: 90 quarter hours minimum, at least 6 quarters in residence; preliminary exam; dissertation; reading knowledge of one language, a research tool or computer technique; final oral exam.

FIELDS OF STUDY.

COLLEGE OF ALLIED HEALTH PROFESSIONS:
Physical Therapy. M.P.T.
Physician Assistant Studies. M.H.S.
Speech and Hearing Science. M.S.

COLLEGE OF ARTS AND SCIENCES:
Basic Medical Sciences. Specialization in biochemistry, microbiology/immunology, pharmacology, physiology, structural and cellular biology. Ph.D.
Biological Sciences. M.S.
Communication. M.A.
Communication Sciences and Disorders. Ph.D.
English. M.A.

History. M.A.
Marine Sciences. M.S., Ph.D.
Mathematics. M.S.
Psychology. M.S.
Public Administration. M.P.A.
Sociology. M.A.

COLLEGE OF BUSINESS:
Accounting. M.Acc.
Business Administration. M.B.A.

SCHOOL OF COMPUTER AND INFORMATION SCIENCES:
Computer and Information Sciences. M.S.

COLLEGE OF EDUCATION:
Alternative Education. M.Ed.
Alternative Secondary Education. M.Ed.
Community Counseling. M.S.
Counselor Education. Ed.S.
Early Childhood Education. M.Ed., Ed.S.
Educational Leadership. M.Ed., Ed.S.
Educational Media. M.Ed., Ed.S.
Elementary Education. M.Ed., Ed.S.
Exercise Technology. M.S.
Health Education. M.Ed., Ed.S.
Instructional Design and Development. M.S., Ph.D.
Physical Education. M.Ed., Ed.S.
Recreation Administration. M.S.
Rehabilitation Counseling. M.S.
School Counseling. M.Ed.
School Psychometry. M.Ed.
Secondary Education. M.Ed., Ed.S.
Special Education. Ed.S.
Therapeutic Recreation. M.S.

COLLEGE OF ENGINEERING:
Chemical Engineering. M.S.
Electrical Engineering. M.S.
Mechanical Engineering. M.S.

COLLEGE OF NURSING:
Adult Health Nursing. M.S.N.
Clinical Nurse Specialist. M.S.N.
Community-Mental Health Nursing. M.S.N.
Executive and Midlevel Nursing Administration. M.S.N.
Nursing Education. M.S.N.
Women and Child Nursing. M.S.N.

College of Medicine (36688-0002)

Established 1967. Annual tuition: resident $7700, nonresident $15,400, student fees $2605.

Enrollment: first-year class 64 (EDP 10), total 254 (men 60%, women 40%). Faculty: full-time 144, part-time 10. Degrees conferred: M.D., M.D.-Ph.D.

ADMISSION REQUIREMENTS. AMCAS report, transcripts, MCAT, recommendations required in support of final application. Interview by invitation. Applicants must have completed at least three years of college study. Has EDP (Alabama residents only); apply between June 1 and August 1. Preference given to state residents. Graduates of unaccredited colleges not considered. Apply after June 1, before November 15. Application fee $50, submitted with supplemental application. Phone: (334)460-7176; fax: (334)460-6278.

ADMISSION STANDARDS. Selective. Mean MCAT: 9.5; mean GPA: 3.70 (A = 4). Admits about 10–15% of total applicants. Approximately 90% are state residents.

FINANCIAL AID. Limited scholarships, medical student summer research program, loans. Apply after acceptance to Office of

Financial Aid. Phone: (334)460-7918. Use FAFSA (College code: 001057). About 5% of students receive some aid from School.

DEGREE REQUIREMENTS. For M.D.: satisfactory completion of four-year program; all students must pass USMLE Step 1 prior to entering the third year and pass USMLE Step 2 prior to awarding of M.D. For Ph.D., see Graduate listing above.

FIELDS OF GRADUATE STUDY.
Anatomy.
Biochemistry.
Cell Biology.
Genetics.
Immunology.
Microbiology.
Molecular Biology.
Neurosciences.
Pharmacology.
Physiology.

MEDICAL UNIVERSITY OF SOUTH CAROLINA

Charleston, South Carolina 29425-0002
Web site: www.musc.edu

Founded 1824. CGS member. Coed. State control. Semester system. Special facilities: Alcohol Research Center, Bone and Joint Center, Center for Appearance, Center for Drug and Alcohol Programs, Center for Health Care Research, Center for Advanced Imaging Research, Center on Aging, Cholesterol Center, Cystic Fibrosis Center, Digestive Disease Center, Gazes Cardiac Research Institute, General Clinical Research Center, Hollings Cancer Center, Institute of Human Values in Health Care, Institute of Psychiatry, Magil Laser Center, National Crime Victims Research and Treatment Center, Pre-Conception Care Resource Center, Resource Centers of Minority Aging Research, Sarcoidosis Center. The University's NIH ranking is 76th among all U.S. institutions with 205 awards/grants worth $58,139,462. Library: 225,000 volumes, 2180 subscriptions. No on-campus housing available.

College of Graduate Studies

Annual tuition/fees: full-time resident $10,514, nonresident $29,740. Enrollment: full-time 227, part-time 35. Degrees conferred: M.S., Ph.D.

ADMISSION REQUIREMENTS. Transcripts, three letters of recommendation, GRE Subject Tests, interview required in support of application. On-line application available. Accepts transfer applicants. Apply by January 15 to Director of Student Programs. Phone: (800)584-2003; fax: (843)792-6590. Application fee $55. Approximately 90% are state residents.

ADMISSION STANDARDS. Selective. Usual minimum average: 3.0 (A = 4) residents.

FINANCIAL AID. Teaching research/fellowships, teaching assistantships, full and partial tuition waivers, Federal W/S, loans. Apply by April 1 to appropriate department chair for fellowships; to Office of Financial Aid for all other aid. Use FAFSA (College code: 003438). Aid available for part-time students.

DEGREE REQUIREMENTS. For M.S.: 30 semester hours minimum, at least 18 in residence; reading knowledge of one foreign language; thesis; final oral exam. For Ph.D.: 60 credits minimum beyond the bachelor's, at least one year in continuous residence; reading knowledge of two foreign languages; written/oral qualifying exam; dissertation; final oral exam.

FIELDS OF STUDY.
Biochemistry and Molecular Biology. Ph.D.
Biometry and Epidemiology. M.S., Ph.D.
Cell and Molecular Pharmacology and Experimental Therapeutics. Ph.D.
Cell Biology and Anatomy. Ph.D.
Clinical Research. M.S.
Marine Biomedicine and Environmental Sciences. Ph.D.
Molecular, Cellular Biology, and Pathobiology. Ph.D.
Microbiology and Immunology. M.S.
Pathology and Laboratory Medicine. M.S., Ph.D.
Pharmaceutical Sciences. Ph.D.
Physiology/Neuroscience. M.S., Ph.D.

College of Dental Medicine

First class admitted Fall 1967. Semester system.

Annual tuition: resident $8020, nonresident $22,784. Limited on-campus housing available. Average academic year off-campus housing costs: $10,500. Total average cost for all other first-year expenses: $6038.

Enrollment: first-year class 54; total 213 (men 65%, women 35%); postgraduates 26. Faculty: full-time 50, part-time 49. Degrees conferred: D.M.D., D.M.D.-Ph.D.

ADMISSION REQUIREMENTS. AADSAS report, transcripts, DAT required in support of College's application. Interview by invitation only. Preference given to state residents. Applicants must have completed at least three years of college study. Apply to Office of Enrollment Services after June 1, before December 1. Application fee $55. Phone: (843)792-5396; fax: (843)792-3764.

ADMISSION STANDARDS. Selective. Mean DAT: Academic 18, PAT 19; mean GPA: 3.28 (A = 4). Gourman rating: 4.21. Accepts about 15–20% of total annual applicants. Approximately 80% are state residents.

FINANCIAL AID. Scholarships, grants, loans. Apply to Director of Financial Aid after acceptance. Phone: (843)792-2536. Use FAFSA (College code: 003438). About 77% of students receive some aid from School and outside sources.

DEGREE REQUIREMENTS. For D.M.D.: satisfactory completion of four-year program. For Ph.D.: see Graduate School listing above.

FIELDS OF GRADUATE STUDY.
General Dentistry.
Oral and Maxillofacial Surgery.
Pediatric Dentistry.
Pedodontics.
Periodontics.

Medical School (P.O. Box 250203)

Established 1824 and is the South's oldest medical school. Semester system. Annual tuition: full-time, resident $3756, nonresident $12,069; student fees resident $8734, nonresident $22,533. Total average figure for all other expenses: $10,300.

Enrollment: first-year class 135 (EDP 20); total 538 (men 55%, women 45%). Faculty: full- and part-time 820. Degrees conferred: M.D., M.D.-Ph.D.

ADMISSION REQUIREMENTS. AMCAS report, transcripts, MCAT, recommendations, interview required in support of application. Interview by invitation only. Has EDP (South Carolina residents only); apply between June 1 and August 1. Applicants must have completed at least three years of college study. Preference given to state residents. Accepts transfer applicants. Apply to Registrar after June 1, before December 1 (Fall). Application fee $25. Phone: (843)792-3281; fax: (843)792-3764.

ADMISSION STANDARDS. Selective. Mean MCAT: 9.0; mean GPA: 3.46 (A = 4). Gourman rating: 3.40. Accepts 8–10% of total annual applicants. Approximately 95% are state residents.

FINANCIAL AID. Scholarships, internships, loans. Apply to Office of the Dean by April 24. Use FAFSA (School code: 003438). About 35% of students receive aid other than loans from School.

DEGREE REQUIREMENTS. For M.D.: successful completion of four-year program; all students must pass USMLE Step 1 prior to beginning third year. For Ph.D.: see Graduate School listing above.

SOUTH CAROLINA STATE UNIVERSITY
Orangeburg, South Carolina 29117
Web site: www.scsu.edu

Founded 1896. Located 50 miles S of Columbia. CGS member. Coed. State control. Semester system. Special facilities: Biology Center of Excellence, Savannah River Field Station, National Summer Transportation Institute, University Transportation Center. Library: 273,000 volumes, 1650 subscriptions.

Tuition: per credit resident $75, nonresident $190; student fees resident $2189, nonresident $4378.

Limited on-campus housing. Average academic year housing costs: $1283. Contact Director of Housing for both on- and off-campus housing information. Phone: (803)536-8560.

School of Graduate Studies

Established 1946. Enrollment: full-time 250, part-time 475. Faculty: full- and part-time 76. Degrees conferred: M.A., M.A.T., M.Ed., M.S., Ed.S., Ed.D.

ADMISSION REQUIREMENTS. Transcripts, GRE or MAT, NTE (for M.Ed.) required in support of School's application. Online application available. Interview not required. Accepts transfer applicants. Apply to Dean of Graduate Studies one month prior to registration. Rolling admissions process. Application fee $15. Phone: (803)536-8809; fax: (803)536-8812.

ADMISSION STANDARDS. Relatively open for master's, selective for all other degrees. Usual minimum for all master's: 2.5 (A = 4), for Ed.S.: 3.25 GPA, GRE total 850, for Ed.D.: 3.25 GPA, GRE total 1000.

FINANCIAL AID. Fellowships, research assistantships, Federal W/S, loans. Approved for VA benefits. Apply to Director of Financial Aid by June 1. Phone: (803)536-7067; fax: (803)536-8420. Use FAFSA.

DEGREE REQUIREMENTS. For master's: 36 semester hours minimum, at least 30 in residence; GRE, English Subject Test, NTE for candidacy (M.Ed.); comprehensive exams; thesis/nonthesis option.

FIELDS OF STUDY.
Agribusiness.
Biology Education.
Business Education.
Counseling.
Educational Administration.
Elementary Education.
English Education.
Home Economics.
Industrial Education.
Mathematics Education.
Nutritional Science.
Reading.

Rehabilitation Counseling.
Science.
Secondary Education.
Social Studies.
Special Education.
Speech Pathology and Audiology.

UNIVERSITY OF SOUTH CAROLINA

Columbia, South Carolina 29208
Web site: www.sc.edu

Founded 1801. State control. Coed. Semester system. Special facilities: Ira and Nancy Koger Center for the Arts, Belle W. Baruch Institute for Marine Biology and Coastal Research, Counseling and Human Development Center, Center for Developmental Disabilities, Earth Sciences and Resources Institute, Center for Economic Education, Center for Fracture Mechanics and Nondestructive Evaluation, Center for Industrial Research, Center for Industry Policy and Strategy, International Center for Public Health Research, Center for Machine Intelligence, Center for Science Education, Southeast Manufacturing Technology Center, Institute for Southern Studies, Center for the Study of Suicide and Life Threatening Behavior, McKissick Museum. The University's NIH ranking is 197th among all U.S. institutions with 46 awards/grants worth $12,231,051. Library: 2,675,000 volumes, 20,400 subscriptions.

Annual tuition: full-time resident $4214, nonresident $9082; per credit resident $209, nonresident $443. On-campus housing for married students, graduate men, graduate women. Average academic year housing costs: $3200–$4000 for married students, $5200–$6200 (including board) for single students. Contact Director of Family, Conference & Summer Housing for on- and off-campus housing information. Phone: (803)777-4571. Day-care facilities available.

Graduate School

Established 1906. Enrollment: full-time 3500, part-time 3769. Faculty: full- and part-time 1300. Degrees conferred: M.A., M.Acc., M.A.T., M.B.A., M.C.J., M.E., M.Ed., M.E.R.M., M.F.A., M.H.A., M.I.B.S., M.L.I.S., M.M., M.M.A., M.M.Ed., M.N., M.P.A., M.P.E.R., M.S., M.S.W., M.Tax., D.M.A., M.N., Ed.D., Dr.Ph., Ph.D.

ADMISSION REQUIREMENTS. Transcripts, two letters of recommendation, GRE Subject Tests/MAT, GMAT (business majors) required in support of School's application. On-line application available. TOEFL required for international applicants. Interview not required. Accepts transfer applicants. Graduates of unaccredited institutions not considered. Apply to Graduate School with complete credentials by July 1 (Fall), November 15 (Spring), May 1 (Summer). Rolling admissions process. Application fee $35. Phone: (803)777-4243; fax: (803)777-2972.

ADMISSION STANDARDS. Selective for most departments. Usual minimum average: 3.0 (A = 4).

FINANCIAL AID. Annual awards from institutional funds: scholarships, fellowships, teaching assistantships, research assistantships, internships, grants, tuition waivers, Federal W/S, loans. Approved for VA benefits. Apply to Dean of Graduate School for scholarships; to appropriate department chairman for assistantships, fellowships; to Financial Aid Office for all other programs; no specified closing date. Use FAFSA. About 55% of students receive aid other than loans from University and outside sources. Aid available to part-time students.

DEGREE REQUIREMENTS. For M.A., M.S.: 30 semester hours minimum, at least 24 in residence; one language for some programs; thesis/nonthesis option; comprehensive exam. For other master's: usually, language requirement is eliminated and course work is allowed in lieu of thesis. For doctoral programs: 72 hours minimum beyond the bachelor's degree, at least two years in residence; reading knowledge of one foreign language varies by department, research tool, or computer technique; qualifying exam; candidacy; dissertation; final oral exam.

FIELDS OF STUDY.
Accountancy.
Administration in Nursing.
Anthropology. M.A. only.
Applied Art History.
Art Education.
Art History.
Art Studio.
Biological Sciences.
Biomedical Science.
Biostatistics.
Business Administration.
Business Education.
Chemical Engineering.
Chemistry.
Civil Engineering.
Clinical and Community Psychology.
Clinical Nursing.
Community and Adult Programs in Education.
Community Mental Health and Psychiatric Nursing.
Comparative Literature.
Computer Science and Engineering.
Computer Software Engineering.
Conducting.
Counselor Education.
Creative Writing.
Criminal Justice.
Curriculum and Instruction.
Early Childhood Education.
Earth and Environmental Resources Management. M.E.R.M.
Economics.
Educational Administration.
Educational Psychology and Research.
Educational Research.
Educational Technology.
Electrical Engineering.
Elementary Education.
English.
Environmental Health Sciences.
Epidemiology.
Exercise Science.
Experimental Psychology.
Foreign Languages.
Foundations of Education.
French.
Genetic Counseling.
Geography.
Geology.
Geophysics.
German.
Health Care Administration.
Health Education.
Health Education Administration.
Health Nursing.
Health Promotion and Education.
Higher Education and Student Affairs.
Higher Education Leadership.
History.
Hotel, Restaurant, and Tourism Management.
Human Resources.
Industrial Statistics.
International Business.
International Studies.

Jazz Studies.
Journalism and Mass Communication.
Language and Literacy.
Library and Information Science.
Linguistics.
Marine Science.
Mass Communication.
Mathematics.
Mechanical Engineering.
Media Arts.
Music Composition.
Music Education.
Music History.
Music Performance.
Music Theory.
Natural Science.
Nursing.
Nursing Science.
Opera Theatre.
Pharmaceutical Science.
Philosophy.
Physical Activity and Public Health.
Physical Education.
Physical Therapy.
Physics.
Piano Pedagogy.
Political Science.
Psychology.
Public Administration.
Public Health.
Public Health Administration.
Public History.
Reading Education.
Rehabilitation Counseling.
Religious Studies.
School Psychology.
Sciences.
Secondary Education.
Social Studies.
Social Work.
Sociology.
Spanish.
Special Education.
Speech-Language Pathology.
Speech Pathology.
Statistics.
Teaching.
Theatre and Speech.

School of Law

Established 1867. ABA approved since 1925. AALS member since 1924. Semester system. Special facility: National Judicial Advocacy Center. Law library: 473,801 volumes, 3812 subscriptions; has LEXIS, NEXIS, WESTLAW, DIALOG, RLIN, OCLC.

Annual tuition: full-time resident $7990, nonresident $16,530. On-campus housing available. Total average annual additional expense: $10,465.

Enrollment: first-year class 223; total 669 (men 56%, women 44%); no part-time students. Faculty: full-time 35, part-time 3. Student to faculty ratio 22 to 1. Degrees conferred: J.D., J.D.-M.A. (Economics), J.D.-M.B.A., J.D.-M.I.B.S., J.D.-M.Acc., J.D.-M.P.A.

ADMISSION REQUIREMENTS. LSDAS Law School report, bachelor's degree, transcripts, LSAT, personal statement, letters of recommendation required in support of application. Interview not required. Accepts transfer applicants. Preference given to state residents. Graduates of unaccredited colleges not considered. Apply to Director of Admissions after September 1, before February 15; transfer application deadline May 1. Admits begin-

ning students Fall only. Application fee: residents $25, nonresidents $35. Phone: (803)777-6605/6606.

ADMISSION STANDARDS. Selective. Mean LSAT: 156; mean GPA: 3.28 (A = 4). Gourman rating: 3.44. *U.S. News & World Report* ranking is in the second tier of all U.S. law schools. Accepts 35–40% of total annual applicants.

FINANCIAL AID. Scholarships, fellowships, Federal W/S, loans. Apply to University's Financial Aid Office after acceptance, before April 15 (priority date February 1). Use FAFSA (School code: 003448). Approximately 28% of all students receive aid from School funds.

DEGREE REQUIREMENTS. For J.D.: 6 semesters minimum, at least two years in residence; 90 semester credit programs. For master's degree, see Graduate School listing above.

School of Medicine
Web site: www.med.sc.edu

Established 1974. Library: 80,000 volumes. Annual tuition: resident $10,350, nonresident $29,890. Enrollment: first-year class 75 (EDP 10); total 270 (men 65%, women 35%). Faculty: full- and part-time 680. Degrees conferred: M.D., M.D.-M.P.H., M.D.-Ph.D.

ADMISSION REQUIREMENTS. AMCAS report, transcripts, MCAT, recommendations required in support of final application. Interview by invitation only. Personal essay may be requested. Has EDP; apply between June 1 and August 1. Preference given to state residents. Accepts transfer applicants on a space-available basis. Graduates of unaccredited colleges not considered. Apply to Associate Dean for Admissions after June 1, before December 1. Application fee $45. Phone: (803)733-3325; fax: (803)733-3328.

ADMISSION STANDARDS. Competitive. Mean MCAT: 9.0; mean GPA: 3.54 (A = 4). Gourman rating: 3.10. Admits about 10–12% of total annual applicants. Approximately 75% are state residents.

FINANCIAL AID. Scholarships, loans. Apply after acceptance to Office of Student Affairs. Use FAFSA (School code: 003448). About 86% of students receive aid from School.

DEGREE REQUIREMENTS. For M.D.: satisfactory completion of four-year program; all students must pass USMLE Step 1 prior to entering the third year and must pass USMLE Step 2 prior to awarding of M.D. For Ph.D.: see Graduate School listing above.

FIELDS OF GRADUATE STUDY.
Anatomy.
Cell Biology.
Immunology.
Microbiology.
Molecular Biology.
Neurosciences.
Pathology.
Pharmacology.
Physiology.

SOUTH DAKOTA SCHOOL OF MINES AND TECHNOLOGY
Rapid City, South Dakota 57701-3995
Web site: www.sdsmt.edu

Founded 1885. CGS member. Coed. State control. Semester system. Special facilities: Institute for the Study of Mineral Deposits, Mining and Mineral Resources Institute, Engineering and

Mining Experiment Station, Institute of Atmospheric Sciences, Museum of Geology. Library: 104,000 volumes, 800 subscriptions. Total School enrollment: 2300.

Tuition: per credit, resident $94.75, nonresident $279.30. On-campus housing for single students only. Average academic year housing cost: $2578–$3884 (including board). Contact Housing Director for both on- and off-campus housing information. Phone: (605)394-2348.

Graduate Division

Graduate study since 1900. Enrollment: full-time 150 (men 74%, women 26%), part-time 108. School faculty: full-time 110, part-time 30. Degrees conferred: M.S., Ph.D.

ADMISSION REQUIREMENTS. Transcripts, three letters of recommendation required in support of application. GRE/GMAT required by some departments. TOEFL (minimum score 520) required for foreign applicants. Interview not required. Accepts transfer applicants. Graduates of unaccredited institutions not considered. Apply to Dean of Graduate Division at least two months prior to registration, at least four months for international applicants. Application fee domestic students $15, foreign students $100. Phone: (605)394-2493; fax: (605)394-5360; e-mail: admissions@sdsmt.edu.

ADMISSION STANDARDS. Selective for most departments. Usual minimum average: 2.75 (A = 4). TOEFL score 560 for admission without tutoring.

FINANCIAL AID. Annual awards from institutional funds: teaching assistantships, research assistantships, fellowships, Federal W/S, loans. Approved for VA benefits. Apply to Dean, Graduate Division at least three months prior to registration. Use FAFSA. About 50% of students receive aid other than loans from School and outside sources. Aid sometimes available for part-time students.

DEGREE REQUIREMENTS. For M.S.: 30 credit hours minimum, at least 18 in residence; thesis; final oral exam; or 32 hours without thesis, at least 18 in residence; final oral exam. For Ph.D.: four years beyond the bachelor's degree, at least 80 credits (includes M.S. allowance); research requirement; foreign language requirement; qualifying exam; comprehensive exams; thesis; final oral exam.

FIELDS OF STUDY.
Atmospheric, Environmental, and Water Resources. GRE for admission. Ph.D. only.
Atmospheric Sciences. M.S. only.
Chemical Engineering. M.S. only.
Civil Engineering. M.S. only.
Computer Science. GRE for admission. M.S. only.
Electrical Engineering. GRE for admission. M.S. only.
Geology/Geological Engineering. GRE Subject for admission.
Materials Engineering and Science. GRE for admission.
Mechanical Engineering. M.S. only.
Metallurgical Engineering. M.S. only.
Meteorology. GRE Subject for international applicants.
Mining Engineering. M.S. only.
Paleontology. GRE Subject for admission. One language for M.S.. M.S. only.
Technology Management. GMAT for admission. M.S. only.

SOUTH DAKOTA STATE UNIVERSITY
Brookings, South Dakota 57007
Web site: www.sdstate.edu

Founded 1881. Coed. State control. Semester system. Library: 525,000 volumes, 3000 subscriptions.

Tuition: per credit resident $98.65, nonresident $290.75. On-campus housing for 88 married students, 1688 men, 1644 women. Average academic year housing costs: on-campus for single students, $1500 (double room), $2800 (including board). Varies for married students because of off-campus costs. Contact Director of Student Housing for both on- and off-campus housing information. Phone: (605)688-5148. Day-care facilities available.

Graduate School

Graduate study since 1891. Enrollment: full-time 280, part-time 796. Graduate faculty: full-time 286, part-time none. Degrees conferred: M.A., M.S., M.Ed., Ph.D.

ADMISSION REQUIREMENTS. Transcripts, two letters of recommendation required in support of School's application. GRE required for some departments. On-line application available. TOEFL required of international students. Interview not required. Accepts transfer applicants. Graduates of unaccredited colleges not considered. Apply to Graduate Office at least one month prior to registration. Application fee $15. Phone: (605)688-4181; fax: (605)688-6167; E-mail: davisd@adm.sdstate.edu.

ADMISSION STANDARDS. Selective for most departments. Usual minimum average: 2.5 (with condition), 3.0 (unconditional) (A = 4).

FINANCIAL AID. Scholarships, fellowships, teaching assistantships, research assistantships. Approved for VA benefits. Apply to appropriate department chair for assistantships, scholarships; to Financial Aid Office for all other programs. Phone: (605)688-4695; fax: (605)688-6384. Use FAFSA.

DEGREE REQUIREMENTS. For M.A.: 30 credit hours minimum, at least 22 in residence; thesis; final oral exam. For M.Ed.: 32 credit hours minimum, at least 22 in resident; final research/design report; final oral exam; or 35 hours minimum, at least 22 in residence; comprehensive written exam; final oral exam. For M.S.: 30 credit hours minimum, 5-7 credits thesis or 32 credits with research/design paper; 48 credits required for M.S. in Counseling and Human Resource Development. For Ph.D.: 90 credit program (may be reduced to 60 with prior master's degree), at least 50 in residence; preliminary exam; dissertation; final oral exam.

FIELDS OF STUDY.
Agricultural Engineering. M.S., Ph.D. offered in conjunction with Iowa State University.
Agronomy. M.S., Ph.D.
Animal Science. Includes animal and range science, dairy science, veterinary science (M.S.); animal science, dairy science (Ph.D.). M.S., Ph.D.
Atmospheric, Environmental, and Water Resources. Ph.D. only.
Biological Sciences. Includes biology and microbiology, dairy manufacturing, food and biomaterial processing, horticulture, human nutrition and food science, pharmaceutical science, veterinary science (M.S.); animal and range sciences, biology and microbiology, dairy science, plant science, veterinary science, wildlife and fisheries sciences (Ph.D.). M.S., Ph.D.
Biology. M.S.
Chemistry. M.S., Ph.D.
Communication Studies and Journalism. M.A.
Counseling and Human Resource Development. M.S.
Curriculum and Instruction. M.Ed.
Economics. M.S.
Educational Administration. M.Ed.
Engineering. Includes agricultural, civil, computer science, electrical, mechanical, physics. M.S.
English. M.A.
Family and Consumer Sciences. M.S.
Family Financial Planning. M.S.
Geography. M.S.

Health, Physical Education, and Recreation. M.S.
Industrial Management. M.S.
Mathematics. M.S.
Nursing. M.S.
Plant Science. Includes horticulture. M.S.
Rural Sociology. M.S.
Sociology. Includes cultural ecology, demography, family studies, social deviance, social organizations. Ph.D.
Wildlife and Fisheries Sciences. Includes a fisheries option, wildlife option. M.S.

UNIVERSITY OF SOUTH DAKOTA

Vermillion, South Dakota 57069-2390
Web site: www.usd.edu

Founded 1882. Located 60 miles S of Sioux Falls. Coed. State control. Semester system. Special facilities: Business Research Center, Government Research Bureau, Historical Preservation Center, Institute of American Indian, Oral History Center, South Dakota Geological Society, W. H. Over Museum. Library: 1,200,000 volumes, 2810 subscriptions. Total University enrollment: 7000.

Annual tuition: full-time resident $3100, nonresident $5700; per credit resident $92, nonresident $270. On-campus housing for 80 married students. Average annual housing cost: $1850 for married students, $2598 (including board) for single students. Contact Resident Services for both on- and off-campus housing information. Phone: (605)677-5663.

Graduate School

Graduate study since 1889. Enrollment: full- and part-time 1946 (men 70%, women 30%). University faculty: full- and part-time 249. Degrees conferred: M.A., M.B.A., M.F.A., M.M., M.N.S., M.P.A., M.S., Ed.S., Ed.D., Ph.D.

ADMISSION REQUIREMENTS. Two official transcripts, GRE Subject Tests/GMAT required in support of School's application. Interview not required. TOEFL, financial statement required for international applicants. Accepts transfer applicants. Graduates of unaccredited institutions not considered. Apply to Dean of Graduate School by July 15. Application fee $15. Phone: (605) 677-6287.

ADMISSION STANDARDS. Selective for most departments. Usual minimum average: 3.0 (A = 4).

FINANCIAL AID. Scholarships, research assistantships, teaching assistantships, internships, Federal W/S, loans. Approved for VA benefits. Apply by March 15 to appropriate department for assistantships; to Financial Aid Office for all other programs. Phone: (605)677-5446. Use FAFSA. About 25% of students receive aid other than loans from School, 40% from all sources. Aid available for part-time students.

DEGREE REQUIREMENTS. For M.A., M.M.: 30–32 semester hours minimum, at least 20 in residence; thesis/nonthesis option; final oral/written exam. For M.N.S.: 30 hours minimum, at least 20 in residence; thesis; final oral/written exam. For M.B.A., M.P.A.: one calendar year in residence; otherwise same as for M.A. For Ed.S.: 64 semester hours minimum; preliminary exam; research project; comprehensive exam; final oral exam. For Ed.D.: 90 hours minimum beyond the bachelor's degree, at least 30 in residence; preliminary written exam; comprehensive exam; dissertation; final oral exam. For Ph.D.: 84 hours minimum beyond the bachelor's degree, at least two years in residence; preliminary exam; dissertation; final oral exam.

FIELDS OF STUDY.
Accounting. M.P.A.
Administrative Studies. M.S.

Adult and Higher Education. M.A., Ed.S., Ed.D.
Anatomy. M.A., Ph.D.
Biochemistry. Thesis for M.A., Ph.D.
Biomedical Science. M.A., Ph.D.
Biology. M.A., M.S., Ph.D.
Business Administration. GMAT for admission. M.B.A.
Chemistry. M.A.
Communication. M.A.
Computer Science. M.A.
Counseling and Guidance. M.A., Ed.S., Ed.D., Ph.D.
Curriculum and Instruction. Ed.S., Ed.D.
Economics. M.A.
Educational Administration. M.A., Ed.S., Ed.D.
Educational Psychology. M.A., Ed.S., Ed.D.
Elementary Education. M.A.
English. M.A., Ph.D.
Health, Physical Education, and Recreation. M.A.
History. M.A.
Interdisciplinary Studies. M.A.
Management Information Systems. M.S., M.B.A.
Mass Communication. M.A.
Mathematics. M.A.
Music. Includes literature, education, applied. M.M.
Natural Sciences. M.N.S.
Occupational Therapy. M.S.
Physical Therapy. M.S.
Political Science. M.A.
Psychology. Thesis for M.A.; M.A., Ph.D.
Public Administration. M.P.A.
Secondary Education. M.A.
Sociology. M.A.
Special Education. M.A.
Speech Communication. M.A.
Technology for Education and Training. M.S., Ed.S.
Theater. M.A., M.F.A.

School of Law (57069-2390)

Web site: www.usd.edu/law

Established 1901. Located on main campus. ABA approved since 1923. AALS member. Semester system. Full-time, day study only. Law library: 185,560 volumes, 1911 subscriptions; has LEXIS, NEXIS, WESTLAW, DIALOG, SDLN.

Annual tuition: resident $5541, nonresident $11,428. On-campus housing available for single students in the Graduate and Professional Dormitory and for married students in University-owned apartments. Annual on-campus living expense: $10,738. Contact Office of Residential Life for both on- and off-campus housing information. Phone: (605)677-5663. Law students tend to live off-campus. Off-campus housing and personal expenses: approximately $11,500.

Enrollment: first-year class 70; total full-time 168 (men 51%, women 49%). Faculty: full-time 11, part-time 1. Student to faculty ratio 12.7 to 1. Degrees conferred: J.D., J.D.-M.Acc., J.D.-M.B.A., J.D.-M.Econ., J.D.-M.P.A., J.D.-M.A. (English, History, Political Science, Psychology).

ADMISSION REQUIREMENTS. LSDAS Law School report, bachelor's degree, transcripts, two letters of recommendation, LSAT, two photos, personal statement required in support of application. Accepts transfer applicants. Preference given to state residents. Graduates of unaccredited institutions not considered. Apply by March 1 to the Admissions Office. Application fee $15. Phone: (605)677-5443.

ADMISSION STANDARDS. Selective. Mean LSAT: 148; mean GPA: 3.14 (A = 4). Gourman rating: 2.48. *U.S. News & World Report* ranking is in the third tier of all U.S. law schools. Accepts 20–25% of total annual applicants.

FINANCIAL AID. Scholarships, assistantships, Federal W/S, loans. Apply to Financial Aid Office by May 1. Phone: (605)677-

5446. Use FAFSA (School code: 003474). About 77% of students receive aid other than loans from school.

DEGREE REQUIREMENTS. For J.D.: 90 semester hour program, at least two years residence.

School of Medicine (57069-2390)

Web site: www.med.usd.edu

Expansion to a degree-granting medical school was approved by the legislature in 1974.

Annual tuition: resident $10,826, nonresident $25,952; student fees $2876. Total average figure for all other expenses: $7500. Enrollment: first-year class 50; total full-time 210 (men 65%, women 35%). Faculty: full-time 153, part-time 258. Degrees conferred: M.D., M.D.-Ph.D.

ADMISSION REQUIREMENTS. AMCAS report, transcripts, letters of recommendation, MCAT, supplemental application, interview required in support of application. Applicants must have completed at least three years of college study. Does not have EDP. Preference given to South Dakota residents. Accepts transfer applicants on a space-available basis. Apply after June 1, before November 15. Application fee $35, fee after screening $15. Phone: (605)677-6886; fax: (605)677-5109.

ADMISSION STANDARDS. Selective. Mean MCAT: 9.0; mean GPA: 3.70 (A = 4). Gourman rating: 3.16. Accepts 10% of total annual applicants. Approximately 85% are state residents.

FINANCIAL AID. Tuition waivers, scholarships, fellowships. Apply after Fall classes begin to Office of Student Affairs. Use FAFSA (School code: 003474). About 88% of students receive some aid from School.

DEGREE REQUIREMENTS. For M.D.: satisfactory completion of four-year program and the passing of Step 1 and Step 2 of the USMLE prior to graduation. For Ph.D. see Graduate School listing above.

FIELDS OF GRADUATE STUDY.
Anatomy.
Biochemistry.
Microbiology.
Molecular Biology.
Pharmacology.
Physiology.

UNIVERSITY OF SOUTH FLORIDA

Tampa, Florida 33620-9951
Web site: www.usf.edu

Founded 1956. CGS member. Coed. State control. Semester system. Special facilities: H. Lee Moffitt Cancer Center and Research Institute, Florida Mental Health Institute, Florida Institute of Oceanography, Gerontology Center, Center for Nearshore Marine Science, Center for Urban Transportation Research, Center of Microelectronics Research, Center for Engineering Development and Research, Institute Biomolecular Science, Institute on Black Life. The University's NIH ranking is 120th among all U.S. institutions with 108 awards/grants worth $28,331,908. Library: 1,800,000 volumes, 5500 subscriptions. Total University enrollment: 36,000.

Tuition: per semester hour resident $154, nonresident $533. On-campus housing available for single students only. Average academic year housing costs: $2404–$3970. Contact Director of University Housing for both on- and off-campus housing information. Phone: (813)974-2764.

Graduate Studies

Enrollment: full-time 2357, part-time 3916. Faculty: full- and part-time 1400. Degrees conferred: M.A., M.Acc., M.Arch., M.B.A., M.Ed., Ed.S., Ed.D., M.C.E., M.E., M.F.A., M.M., M.P.A., M.P.H., M.S.P.H., M.S.C.E., M.S.C.S., M.S.E., M.S.E.E., M.S.E.M., M.S.E.S., M.S.I.E., M.S.M.E., M.S.W., M.S., Ph.D.

ADMISSION REQUIREMENTS. Transcripts, GRE Subject Tests (GMAT for business only). TOEFL (minimum score 550) and TSE required for international applicants. Interview required by some departments. Three letters of recommendation required by Natural Science Division. Accepts transfer applicants. Graduates of unaccredited institutions not considered. Apply at least two months prior to registration. Application fee $35. Phone: (813)974-8800; e-mail: admissions@grad.usf.edu.

ADMISSION STANDARDS. Selective for most departments. Usual minimum average: 2.75 (A = 4).

FINANCIAL AID. Fellowships, assistantships for teaching/research, Federal W/S, loans. Approved for VA benefits. Apply by February 1 to department chair for fellowships, assistantships; to Director of Financial Aid for all other programs. Phone: (813)974-4700. Use FAFSA.

DEGREE REQUIREMENTS. For master's: 30–36 semester hours minimum, at least 18 credits in residence; reading knowledge of one foreign language for some majors; thesis/nonthesis option; final oral/written exam. For Ed.S.: 30 semester hours beyond the master's. For Ed.D.: essentially the same as for the Ph.D., except no foreign language requirement. For Ph.D.: minimum of 90 credits beyond bachelor's degree; preliminary exam; reading knowledge of two foreign languages or equivalent; dissertation; final oral/written exam.

FIELDS OF STUDY.

SCHOOL OF ARCHITECTURE AND COMMUNITY DESIGN:
Architecture. Joint program with Florida Agricultural and Mechanical University. M.Arch.

COLLEGE OF ARTS AND SCIENCES:
Aging Studies.
American Studies.
Anthropology.
Applied Anthropology.
Applied Physics.
Audiology.
Aural Rehabilitation.
Biology.
Botany.
Cellular and Molecular Biology.
Chemistry. Includes analytical, inorganic, organic, physical.
Classics and Classical Languages.
Communication.
Communication Sciences and Disorders.
Criminology.
English.
English as a Second Language.
Environmental Science and Policy.
French.
Geography.
Geology.
Gerontology.
History.
Latin American, Caribbean, and Latino Studies.
Liberal Arts.
Library and Information Science.
Linguistics.
Marine Science.

Mass Communication.
Mathematics.
Microbiology.
Philosophy.
Physics.
Political Science.
Psychology. Includes clinical, clinical-community, industrial, organizational.
Public Administration.
Rehabilitation and Mental Health Counseling.
Religious Studies.
Social Work.
Sociology.
Spanish.
Speech-Language Pathology.
Women's Studies.
Zoology.

COLLEGE OF BUSINESS:
Accountancy.
Business Administration. Includes Saturday M.B.A.
Business Economics.
Executive M.B.A.
Executive M.B.A. for Physicians.
Management.
Management Information Systems.

COLLEGE OF EDUCATION:
Art Education.
Behavior Disorders Education.
Business/Office Education.
College Student Affairs.
Community College Teaching.
Counselor Educator.
Curriculum and Instruction.
Distributive and Marketing Education.
Early Childhood Education.
Educational Leadership.
Educational Measurement, Research, and Evaluation.
Educational Program Development.
Elementary Education.
English Education.
Foreign Language. Includes French, German, Latin, Spanish.
Gifted Education.
Higher Education.
Industrial Arts/Technical Education.
Instructional Technology.
Interdisciplinary Education.
Languages Arts/Reading Education.
Leadership Development.
Mathematics Education.
Mental Retardation Education.
Middle Grades Education.
Music Education.
Physical Education.
Reading Education.
School Psychology.
Science Education. Includes biology, chemistry, physics.
Second Language Acquisition/Instructional Technology.
Secondary Education.
Social Science Education.
Specific Learning Disabilities Education.
Theater Education.
Technology Education.
Varying Exceptionalities Education.
Vocational Education.

COLLEGE OF ENGINEERING:
Biomedical Engineering.
Chemical Engineering.
Civil Engineering.
Computer Engineering.
Computer Science and Engineering.
Electrical Engineering.
Engineering.
Engineering Management.
Engineering Science
Environmental Engineering (five-year program).
Industrial Engineering.
Information Management.
Mechanical Engineering.

COLLEGE OF FINE ARTS.
Art.
Art Education.
Art History.
Music.
Music Education.
Theater.
Theater Education.

COLLEGE OF NURSING:
Nursing. Includes adult health, child health, critical care, family health, gerontological, occupational health, oncology, psychiatric-mental health.

COLLEGE OF PUBLIC HEALTH:
Biostatistics.
Community and Family Health.
Environmental and Occupational Health.
Environmental Health.
Epidemiology.
Health Administration.
Health-Care Organizations and Management.
Health Policies and Programs.
Health Policy and Management.
Industrial Hygiene.
International Health Management.
Maternal and Child Health/Clinical Social Work.
Occupational Health.
Public Health.
Public Health Education.
Safety Management.
Social and Behavioral Science.
Toxicology.
Tropical/Communicable Diseases.

College of Medicine (33612-4799)

Web site: www.med.usf.edu

Established 1965, first class entered 1971. Annual tuition: resident $10,930, nonresident $30,820; student fees resident $1389, nonresident $2419. On-campus housing available. Total average figure for all other expenses $9100.

Enrollment: first-year class 100 (EDP 29); graduate program, first-year class 10; total 420 (men 56%, women 44%). Faculty: full- and part-time 140, graduate, full-time 50. Degrees conferred: M.D., M.D.-M.P.H., M.D.-Ph.D.

ADMISSION REQUIREMENTS. For M.D.: transcripts, MCAT, recommendations required in support of application. Has EDP (Florida residents only); apply between June 1 and August 1. Preference given to Florida residents. Graduates of unaccredited colleges not considered. Apply to Assistant Dean for Admissions after June 1, before December 1. For Graduate Program: transcripts, GRE required in support of application. TOEFL required of foreign students. Accepts transfer applicants. Apply before August 15 to Graduate Office. Application fee $20. Phone: (813)974-2229; fax: (813)974-4990.

ADMISSION STANDARDS. For M.D.: selective. Mean MCAT: 9.8; mean GPA: 3.7 (A = 4). Gourman rating: 3.41. Accepts about 10–15%, of total annual applicants. 100% are state residents. For Graduate Program: accepts about 20% of total annual applicants. Usual minimum average 3.0 (A = 4).

FINANCIAL AID. For M.D.: limited scholarships, loans. Apply to Office of Financial Aid after acceptance. Use FAFSA (College code: E00568). For Graduate Program: fellowships, assistantships. Apply to Financial Aid Office by March 1. Phone: (813)974-2068. Approximately 80% of students receive some form of assistance.

DEGREE REQUIREMENTS. For M.D.: satisfactory completion of three to four-year program. For Ph.D., M.P.H.: see Graduate School listings above.

FIELDS OF GRADUATE STUDY.
Anatomy.
Biochemistry.
Cell and Molecular Biology.
Immunology.
Microbiology.
Pathology.
Physiology.

SOUTH TEXAS COLLEGE OF LAW

1303 San Jacinto
Houston, Texas 77002-7000
Web site: www.stcl.edu

Established 1923. ABA approved since 1959. AALS member. Semester system. Full-time, part-time study. Special facilities: Center for Legal Responsibility, Legal Institute for Medical Studies. Law library: 401,778 volumes, 4439 subscriptions; has LEXIS, NEXIS, WESTLAW, DIALOG, EPIC.

Annual tuition: full-time $16,860, part-time $11,440. No on-campus housing available. Law students live off-campus. Contact Admission Officer for off-campus information. Off-campus housing and personal expenses: approximately $12,872.

Enrollment: first-year class 308, full-time, 138 part-time; total full- and part-time 1231 (men 52%, women 48%). Faculty: full-time 43, part-time 39. Student to faculty ratio 21.4 to 1. Degree conferred: J.D.

ADMISSION REQUIREMENTS. LSDAS Law School report, bachelor's degree, transcripts, LSAT, letters of recommendation, personal statement required in support of application. Graduates of unaccredited colleges not considered. Accepts transfer applicants. Transfers admitted Fall and Spring. Apply to Director of Admission by February 25 (Fall), October 1 (Spring), January 15 (Summer). Application fee $50. Phone: (713)646-1810.

ADMISSION STANDARDS. Selective. Mean LSAT: full-time 150, part-time 150; mean GPA: full-time 3.01, part-time 2.87 (A = 4). *U.S. News & World Report* ranking is in the fourth tier of all U.S. law schools. Accepts 30–35% of total applicants.

FINANCIAL AID. Scholarships, tuition equalization, grants, Federal W/S, loans. Apply to Financial Aid Office before May 1 (Fall), October 1 (Spring). Use FAFSA (College code: G04977). About 31% of students receive aid other than loans from College and outside sources.

DEGREE REQUIREMENTS. For J.D.: 90 semester hours, at least 24 semester hours and last 3 semesters in residence.

SOUTHEAST MISSOURI STATE UNIVERSITY

Cape Girardeau, Missouri 63701-4799
Web site: www.semo.edu

Founded 1873. Located 125 miles S of St. Louis. CGS member. Coed. State control. Semester system. Library: 429,000 volumes, 6200 subscriptions.

Fees: per semester, resident $1549, nonresident $2808; per credit part-time resident $129, nonresident $234. On-campus housing for married and single students. Average academic year housing costs: single students $4718 (including board); married students $4000. Contact Residence Life Office for on- and off-campus housing information. Phone: (573)651-2274.

School of Graduate Studies and Research

Graduate study since 1965. Enrollment: full-time 220, part-time 971. Faculty: full-time 223. Degrees conferred: M.A., M.B.A., M.M.E., M.N.S., M.S.A., M.S.C.J., M.S.I.S., M.S.N., Ed.S.

ADMISSION REQUIREMENTS. Transcripts required in support of application. GRE required for some programs. TOEFL required for international applicants. Accepts transfer applicants. Graduates of unaccredited institutions not considered. Apply to Dean of Graduate Study by April 1 (Fall), November 15 (Spring), February 1 (Summer). Rolling admissions process. Application fee $20, $100 for international applicants. Phone: (573)651-2192; fax: (573)651-2001.

ADMISSION STANDARDS. Selective. Usual minimum average: 2.5 (A = 4), 3.0 GPA for some programs.

FINANCIAL AID. Graduate scholarships, teaching assistantships, research assistantships, internships, Federal W/S, loans. Approved for VA benefits. Apply with admission application to appropriate department head for assistantships; to Financial Aid Office for all other programs. Phone: (573)651-2253. Use FAFSA. About 15% of students receive aid other than loans from University and outside sources. No aid other than loans for part-time students.

DEGREE REQUIREMENTS. For master's: 32 semester hours minimum, at least 24 in residence; thesis or final document. For Ed.S.: one year beyond the master's.

FIELDS OF STUDY.
Accounting. M.B.A.
Athletic Administration. M.S.A.
Biology. M.N.S.
Chemistry. M.N.S.
Communication Disorders. M.A.
Community Counseling. M.A.
Counseling Education. Ed.S.
Criminal Justice. M.S.C.J.
Educational Administration. Ed.S.
Elementary Education. M.A.
English. M.A.
Environmental Management. M.A.
Exceptional Child Education. M.A.
General Management. M.B.A.
Geosciences. M.N.S.
Health Fitness Administration. M.S.A.
Higher Education Administration. M.A.
History. Includes historic preservation, research, teaching. M.A.
Human Environmental Studies Education. M.A.
Industrial Management. M.S.I.S.
International Business. M.A.
Mathematics. M.N.S.
Music Education. M.M.Ed.

Nursing. M.S.N.
Nutrition and Exercise Science. M.S.N.E.S.
Public Administration. M.S.A.
School Administration. M.A.
School Counseling. Includes elementary school counseling, secondary school counseling. M.A.
Science Education. M.N.S.
Secondary Education. Includes art, business, educational studies, educational technology, middle studies, social studies. M.A.
Teaching English to Speakers of Other Languages. M.A.

SOUTHEASTERN LOUISIANA UNIVERSITY

Hammond, Louisiana 70402-0752
Web site: www.selu.edu

Founded 1925. Located 60 miles N of New Orleans. Coed. State control. Semester system. Special facilities: Center for Regional Studies, Biological Turtle Cove Research Station, Agricultural and Educational Research Station, JFK Assassination Resources Center, Institute for Human Development. Library: 554,000 volumes, 2100 subscriptions.

Annual tuition: full-time resident $2436, nonresident $5328; per semester, part-time resident $343.50, nonresident $343.50, plus nonresident fee. On-campus housing for 60 married students, unlimited for single students. Average academic year housing costs: $3006 (including board) for single students; $3500 for married students. Contact Director of Housing for both on- and off-campus housing information. Phone: (985)549-2118.

Graduate School

Graduate study since 1960. Enrollment: full-time 332, part-time 668. Graduate faculty: full-time 114, part-time 5. Degrees conferred: M.A., M.M., M.Ed., M.S.N., M.B.A., Ed.S.

ADMISSION REQUIREMENTS. Official transcripts, GRE required in support of application. Copy of teaching certificate required for Education majors. GMAT required for M.B.A. applicants. GRE Subject required by some programs. TOEFL required for international applicants. Interview not required. Accepts transfer applicants. Graduates of unaccredited institutions not considered. Apply to Office of Graduate Admissions at least 30 days prior to registration. Rolling admissions process. Application fee $10, $25 for international applicants. Phone: (985)549-5620; fax: (985)549-5632.

ADMISSION STANDARDS. Relatively open. Usual minimum average: 2.5, 3.0 for candidacy (A = 4).

FINANCIAL AID. Fellowships, research assistantships, teaching assistantships, internships, Federal W/S, loans. Apply by May 1 to appropriate department head for fellowships, assistantships; to Financial Aid Office for all other programs. Phone: (985)549-2244. Use FAFSA. About 30% of students receive aid from University and outside sources.

DEGREE REQUIREMENTS. For M.Ed.: 30 semester hours minimum, except Secondary Guidance and Counseling 33 hours, at least 21 in residence; final written/oral exams. For Ed.S.: 30 semester hours minimum, at least 21 in residence; thesis or research project. For M.S.: 30 semester hours minimum; thesis. For M.B.A.: one-year program for students with degree in business, two-year for non-degree holders.

FIELDS OF STUDY.

COLLEGE OF ARTS AND SCIENCES:
Applied Sociology. M.A.
Biology. M.S.

English. M.A.
History. M.A.
Integrated Science and Technology. M.S.
Music. M.M.
Organizational Communication. M.A.
Psychology. M.A.

COLLEGE OF BUSINESS AND TECHNOLOGY:
Business Administration. M.B.A.
Integrated Science and Technology. M.S.

COLLEGE OF EDUCATION AND HUMAN DEVELOPMENT:
Administration and Supervision. M.Ed.
Counselor Education. M.Ed.
Curriculum and Instruction. M.Ed.
Special Education. M.Ed.
Teaching. M.A.

COLLEGE OF NURSING AND HEALTH SCIENCES:
Communication Sciences and Disorders. M.S.
Kinesiology, Health Studies, Health Promotion, and Exercise Science. M.A.
Nursing. M.S.N.

SOUTHEASTERN OKLAHOMA STATE UNIVERSITY

Durant, Oklahoma 74701-0609
Web site: www.sosu.edu

Established 1909. Located 90 miles N of Dallas, Texas. Coed. State control. Semester system. Library: 192,000 volumes, 1300 subscriptions.

Annual tuition: full-time resident $972, nonresident $2169. On-campus housing for 36 married students, 125 single men, 100 single women. Average academic year housing costs: single students $5058 (including board), married students $7450. Contact Housing Director for both on- and off-campus housing information. Phone: (580)745-2948.

Graduate School

Graduate study since 1954. Enrollment: full-time 69, part-time 271. Faculty teaching graduate students: full-time 85, part-time 4. Degrees conferred: M.A.S., M.B.S., M.Ed., M.T.

ADMISSION REQUIREMENTS. Transcripts, GRE/GMAT, interview required in support of School's application. TOEFL required for international applicants. Accepts transfer applicants. Graduates of unaccredited colleges not considered. Apply to Dean of Graduate School at least one month prior to date of registration. Application fee: none, $35 for international applicants. Phone: (580)745-2200; fax: (580)745-7474.

ADMISSION STANDARDS. Selective. Usual minimum average: 2.75 (A = 4).

FINANCIAL AID. Scholarships, teaching assistantships, tuition waivers, Federal W/S, loans. Apply by June 15 to the Director of Financial Aid. Phone: (580)745-2186; fax: (580)745-7469. Use FAFSA and institutional FAF. Aid available for part-time students.

DEGREE REQUIREMENTS. For master's: 33 semester hours minimum, at least 24 in semester hours in residence; thesis/nonthesis option.

FIELDS OF STUDY.
Behavioral Studies. Includes counseling.
Business.

Education. Includes secondary education, elementary education, school counseling, educational administration, educational technology.

Technology. Includes electronics, design, manufacturing processes, computer science, safety, sciences.

SOUTHERN CALIFORNIA COLLEGE OF OPTOMETRY

Fullerton, California 92631-1615
Web site: www.scco.edu

Founded 1904. Coed. Private control. Quarter system. Library: 15,823 volumes, 300 subscriptions.

Annual tuition: full-time $19,500. No on-campus housing available.

Graduate Study

Enrollment: full-time 376 (men 132, women 234). Faculty: full-time 43, part-time 37. Degree conferred: O.D.

ADMISSION REQUIREMENTS. Transcripts, bachelor's degree, OAT, three letters of recommendation, interview required in support of application. Accepts transfer applicants. Apply to Admissions Office by March 15. Admits Fall only. Rolling admissions process. Application fee $50. Phone: (714)449-7445; fax: (714)992-7878.

ADMISSION STANDARDS. Selective. Usual minimum average: 2.75 (A = 4).

FINANCIAL AID. Scholarships, internships, Federal W/S, loans. Approved for VA benefits. Apply by June 1 to Financial Aid Office. Phone: (714)449-7447. Use FAFSA. About 89% of students receive aid other than loans from College.

DEGREE REQUIREMENTS. For O.D.: 4 years and 241 quarter units.

UNIVERSITY OF SOUTHERN CALIFORNIA

Los Angeles, California 90089-0913
Web site: www.usc.edu

Founded 1880. CGS and AAU member. Coed. Private control. Semester system. Special facilities: Annenberg Center for Communication, U.S.C.-Atelier Art Gallery, Arnold Schoenberg Institute, East Asian Studies Center, Center for Feminist Research, Fisher Gallery, Signal and Image Processing Institute, Information Science Institute, Hydrocarbon Research Institute, Center for International Business Education and Research, Center for Laser Studies, Alzheimer's Disease Research Center, Gerontology Research Institute, Center for the Management of Engineering Research and Technology, Center for Multiethnic and Transnational Studies, Information Sciences Institute, Pacific Center for Health Policy and Ethics, Social Science Research Institute, Robotics and Intelligent Systems Institute, Center for Future Research, Center for Software Engineering, Center for Urban Affairs, Von Kleinsmid Center for International and Public Affairs, Wrigley Institute for Environmental Studies. The University's NIH ranking is 33rd among all U.S. institutions with 285 awards/grants worth $130,826,876. Library 3,000,000 volumes, 20,000 subscriptions.

Tuition: per unit $891. On-campus housing available. Average monthly housing costs: $370–$400 for a one-bedroom/two-person unit, $265–$490 for a two-bedroom/four-person unit, $670–835 per month for family units. Contact Housing Office for detailed information. Phone: (800)872-4632. Day-care facilities available.

Graduate Studies

Graduate study since 1910. Enrollment: full-time 7088, part-time 3455. Graduate faculty: 1614. Degrees conferred: M.A., M.A.E.D.P., M.F.A., M.P.T., M.P.P., M.P.A.S., M.S., M.S.N., M.S.S., M.S.S.M., M.U.D., Ph.D.

ADMISSION REQUIREMENTS. Official transcripts, an earned bachelor's degree, GRE required in support of School's application. On-line application available. GRE Subject Test required by some departments. TOEFL encouraged for international applicants. Accepts transfer applicants. Graduates of unaccredited institutions not considered. Apply to University Office of Admissions, preferably early in the preceding semester. Application fee $55. Phone: (213)740-1111; fax: (213)740-7577.

ADMISSION STANDARDS. Competitive for most departments, selective or very competitive for the others. Usual minimum average: 3.0 (A = 4).

FINANCIAL AID. Fellowships, research assistantships, teaching assistantships, Federal W/S, loans. Approved for VA benefits. Apply by February 1 to Dean of Graduate School for scholarships and fellowships, to appropriate department chair for assistantships; to Financial Aid Office for all other programs. Phone: (213)740-1111. Use FAFSA. Most full-time students receive some financial support. About 50% of all students receive aid other than loans from University and outside sources. Aid sometimes available for part-time students.

DEGREE REQUIREMENTS. For master's: 24 units minimum, at least 20 in residence; thesis/nonthesis; final written/oral exam; some departments require language, some permit comprehensive exam in lieu of thesis. For Ph.D.: 60 units minimum beyond the bachelor's, at least three years in residence; preliminary exam; reading knowledge of one foreign language for most programs; dissertation; final oral exam.

FIELDS OF STUDY.
Accounting. Includes business taxation.
American Studies and Ethnicity.
Anthropology. Includes social, visual.
Architecture. Includes building science, landscape architecture.
Art History. Includes museum studies.
Biochemistry and Molecular Biology.
Biokinesiology.
Biology. Includes marine biology, molecular biology.
Biostatistics.
Business Administration. Includes information and operations management, international business, medical management.
Chemistry. Includes chemical physics.
Cinema-Television. Includes critical studies, film, video and computer animation, interactive media, motion picture producing, writing for screen and television.
Classics.
Communication. Includes global communication.
Communications Management.
Comparative Literature.
Computational Linguistics.
Computer Science. Includes computer networks, creative and multimedia technology, robotics and software engineering.
Craniofacial Biology.
Dentistry.
Earth Sciences.
East Asian Languages and Cultures. Includes area studies.

Economics. Includes economic development programming (M.A.E.D.P.).

Education. Includes counseling psychology.

Engineering. Includes aerospace, biomedical, chemical, civil, computer, electric (systems and electrophysics), environmental, industrial and systems, materials science, mechanical, petroleum.

English.

Environmental Studies.

Epidemiology.

Fine Arts. Includes public art studies.

French.

Geography.

German.

Gerontology. Includes public policy.

History.

International Relations.

Journalism. Include broadcast, international, print, strategic public relations.

Kinesiology.

Law.

Linguistics.

Mathematical Finance.

Mathematics. Includes applied mathematics, statistics.

Medicine.

Molecular Epidemiology.

Molecular Microbiology and Immunology.

Molecular Pharmacology and Toxicology.

Music. Includes early music performance, education, history and literature, musicology, performance, theory.

Neuroscience.

Nursing.

Occupational Therapy. Includes occupation sciences.

Pathobiology.

Pathology.

Pharmaceutical Economics and Policy.

Pharmaceutical Sciences.

Pharmacy.

Philosophy.

Physical Therapy.

Physician Assistant Practice.

Physics.

Physiology and Biophysics.

Planning. Includes planning and development studies, real estate development.

Political Economy and Public Policy.

Political Science.

Preventive Medicine. Includes health behavior.

Professional Writing.

Psychology.

Public Administration. Includes health administration, public policy (M.P.P.).

Public Health.

Slavic Languages and Literatures.

Social Work.

Sociology. Includes applied demography, criminology.

Spanish.

Theater. Includes acting, directing, theatrical design, playwriting. M.F.A.

School of Architecture

Established 1887. School's library: 60,000 volumes, 200,000 slides.

Tuition: per credit $891. Enrollment: full-time 41. School faculty: full-time 12, part-time 1. Degrees conferred: M.Arch., M.B.S., M.L.A.

ADMISSION REQUIREMENTS. Transcripts, GRE, design portfolio, three letters of reference required in support of application. TOEFL required for foreign applicants. Graduates of unaccredited colleges not considered. Applicants with nonarchitecture degrees not considered for M.Arch. program. Apply to University Office of Admissions by February 1. Application fee $55. Phone: (213)740-1879.

ADMISSION STANDARDS. Competitive. Usual minimum average: 3.0 (A = 4).

FINANCIAL AID. Scholarships, fellowships, teaching assistantships, Federal W/S, loans. Apply by February 15 to Financial Aid Office. Phone: (213)740-2097. Use FAFSA and University's FAF.

DEGREE REQUIREMENTS. For master's: one to three years minimum, at least one to two in residence; thesis.

FIELDS OF STUDY.

Architecture.

Building Science.

Historic Preservation.

Landscape Architecture.

Marshall School of Business

Web site: www.marshall.usc.edu

Established 1960, name changed in 1997. Accredited programs: M.B.A., Accounting; recognized Ph.D. Semester (11-week terms) system. Special facilities: Center for Accounting Research, Center for Effective Organization, SEC and Financial Reporting Institute, Center for Service Excellence, Center for Telecommunications Management, Center for International Business Education and Research, Leadership Institute. Special programs: foreign exchange programs in Argentina, Australia, Austria, Brazil, Chile, China (PRC), Costa Rica, Denmark, France, Germany, Hong Kong, Indonesia, Japan, Korea, Mexico, Philippines, Singapore, Spain, Switzerland, Taiwan. Library: 100,000 volumes, 1000 subscriptions.

Tuition: $916 per credit. EMBA tuition: $32,000. Enrollment: total full-time 1284, part-time 506 (men 60%, women 40%). Faculty: 173 full-time, 43 part-time; 90% with Ph.D./D.B.A. Degrees conferred: M.A. (Econ.), M.Acc., M.B.A. (full-time, part-time; concentrations in Entrepreneurship, Finance, Financial Management, Human Resource Management, Information Systems, International Business, Management, Marketing, Management Information Systems, Operations Management, Real Estate, Strategic Management, Technology Management), E.M.B.A. (weekends only), IBEAR M.B.A. (International Business Education and Research; one-year program International Business, day and evening sessions), M.B.A.P.M. (for Professionals and Managers; concentrations in Business Economics and Public Policy, Business of Entertainment, Business Entrepreneurship, Consulting Services, Finance, General Management, Health Care Advisory Services, Human Resource Management, Information Systems, International Finance and Economics, Marketing, Operations Management, Real Estate, Statistics, Technology Management, Venture Management), M.B.T. (Business Taxation), M.M.M. (Medical Management), M.S.B.A., M.S.I.O.M. (Information and Operations Management), M.B.A.-D.D.S., M.B.A.-J.D., M.B.A.-M.A. (East Asian Studies), M.B.A.-M.PL. (Planning), M.B.A.-Pharm.D., M.B.A.-M.R.E.D. (Real Estate Development), M.B.A.-M.S. (Industrial and Systems Engineering), M.B.A.-M.S.G. (Gerontology), M.B.A.-M.S.N. (Nursing), Ph.D. (Specializations in Accounting, Finance and Business Economics, Information and Operations Management, Management and Organization, Marketing, Operations Management).

ADMISSION REQUIREMENTS. Transcript, GMAT, introduction to calculus prior to enrollment, letters of recommendation required in support of School's application. Two years of professional work experience preferred. TOEFL required for international applicants. Graduates of unaccredited institutions not considered. Apply to the Graduate School of Business: full-time applicants by April 15, part-time applicants by June 1, April 1 (Fall) October 1 (Spring). Application fee $90 domestic, $125 for international applicants. Phone: (213)740-8846; fax: (213)749-8520.

ADMISSION STANDARDS. Selective. Usual minimum average: 3.2 (A = 4), GMAT 626.

FINANCIAL AID. Annual awards from institutional funds: each year qualified full-time M.B.A. students are offered merit-based fellowships ranging from partial to full-tuition, loans. Approved for VA benefits. Apply by February 15 (Fall). Phone: (213)743-1111. Use FAFSA. About 33% receive aid other than loans from School, outside sources, and interested individuals.

DEGREE REQUIREMENTS. For M.B.A., M.S.I.O.M., M.S.B.A.: contact (213)740-8846; for Accounting contact (213)740-4867; for Ph.D.: contact (213)740-0674.

School of Dentistry (90089-0641)

Founded 1897. Trimester system. Annual tuition: $41,244. Limited on-campus housing available. Average academic year housing costs: $14,500. Contact Housing Office in Student Union Building for both on- and off-campus housing information. Total average cost for all other first-year expenses: $12,000.

Enrollment: first-year class 135; total 293 (men 60%, women 40%). Degrees conferred: D.D.S., D.D.S.-M.B.A., D.D.S.-M.S. (Gerontology). The M.S., Ph.D. are offered through the Graduate School.

ADMISSION REQUIREMENTS. AADSAS, official transcripts, three letters of reference, DAT (no later than October) required in support of School's application. Applicants must have at least two years of college study. Interview by invitation only. Accepts transfer applicants from U.S. and Canadian dental schools only. Graduates of unaccredited colleges not considered. Apply to Office of Admissions and Student Affairs after June 1, before March 1. Deadline for transfer applicants March 1. Application fee $55. Phone: (213)740-2841; fax: (213)740-8109.

ADMISSION STANDARDS. Selective. Mean DAT: Academic 19.28, PAT 17.93; mean GPA: 3.55 (A = 4). Gourman rating: 4.51. Accepts about 20–25% of total annual applicants.

FINANCIAL AID. Scholarships, grants, loans. Apply to Office of Admissions and Student Affairs; no specified closing date. Phone: (213)740-2841. Use FAFSA (School code: 001328). About 75% of students receive some form of financial assistance.

DEGREE REQUIREMENTS. For D.D.S.: satisfactory completion of 11 consecutive 15 week trimesters. For M.S., Ph.D.: see Graduate School listing above.

FIELDS OF GRADUATE STUDY.
Cellular and Molecular Biology.
Craniofacial Biology. M.S., Ph.D.
Experimental Pathology.

Rossier School of Education

Doctoral degrees in education awarded since 1927.

Tuition: $891 per unit. Graduate enrollment: full-time 488, part-time 455. Faculty: full-time 48, part-time 100. Degrees conferred: M.Ed., M.S., M.F.C.C., Ed.D. The Ph.D.: is administered by the Graduate School.

ADMISSION REQUIREMENTS. Official transcripts, GRE required in support of Schools application. Interview not required. TOEFL required for international applicants. International students whose first language is English are exempted. Accepts transfer applicants. Graduates of unaccredited institutions not

considered. Apply to University Office of Admissions one month prior to registration. Application fee $55. Phone: (213)743-1111; School of Education Student Services phone: (213)740-2606.

ADMISSION STANDARDS. Competitive for most departments. Usual minimum average: 3.0 (master's), 3.0 (doctorate) (A = 4).

FINANCIAL AID. Scholarships, fellowships, research assistantships, teaching assistantships, training grants, Federal W/S, loans. Approved for VA benefits. Apply by February 15 to Dean of School of Education for fellowships, assistantships; to Financial Aid for all other programs. Use FAFSA. Phone: (213)740-3495. About 50% of students receive aid other than loans from University and outside sources. Aid available for part-time students.

DEGREE REQUIREMENTS. For M.Ed.: 41 unit program; thesis. For M.S.: 28 units minimum, at least 24 in residence; thesis/nonthesis option or master's seminar. For M.F.C.C.: 51 units, at least four semesters in residence; practicum. For Ed.D.: 96 units minimum beyond the bachelor's, at least 66 in residence; preliminary review; qualifying exam; candidacy; dissertation; final oral exam. For Ph.D., see Graduate School listing above.

FIELDS OF STUDY.
Counseling Psychology. M.S. Ed., Ph.D.
Curriculum and Instruction. Ed.D., Ph.D.
Educational Leadership. Ed.D.
Educational Psychology. Ph.D.
Intercultural and International Education. Ph.D.
Learning and Instruction. M.S. Ed., Ed.D.
Marriage, Family, and Child Counseling. M.F.C.C.
Policy and Organization. Ph.D.
Postsecondary Administration and Student Affairs. M.Ed.
Reading and Literacy Education. Ph.D.
Teaching as a Second Language. M.S.

School of Engineering
Web site: www.usc.edu

Graduate study since 1931. Semester system.

Tuition: per credit $915. Graduate enrollment: full-time 1297, part-time 1209. Graduate teaching faculty: full-time 140, part-time 38. Degrees conferred: M.S., Engineer. The Ph.D. is administered by the Graduate School.

ADMISSION REQUIREMENTS. Two transcripts, GRE required in support of School's application. Some majors also require GRE Subject Test. Interview not required. Accepts transfer applicants. Graduates of unaccredited institutions not considered. Apply to University Office of Admissions at least eight weeks prior to beginning of semester for U.S. citizens and permanent residents, at least three months for international applicants. Application fee $55. Phone: (213)740-5686; fax: (213)740-8493.

ADMISSION STANDARDS. Selective for most departments. Usual minimum average: 3.0 (A = 4) for M.S., 3.5 for Ph.D.

FINANCIAL AID. Annual awards from institutional funds: fellowships, scholarships, teaching/research assistantships, Federal W/S, loans. Approved for VA benefits. Apply by February 15 to chair of major department for assistantships; to Financial Aid Office for all other programs. Use FAFSA and University's FAF. Phone: (213)740-5444; fax: (213)740-0680. About 35% of full-time students receive aid other than loans from both School and outside sources. Loans available for part-time students.

DEGREE REQUIREMENTS. For M.S.: 27 units minimum, at least 23 in residence; thesis/nonthesis option. For Engineer: 30 units beyond the master's degree, at least 26 units in residence; Engineer's exam. For Ph.D.: see Graduate School listing above.

FIELDS OF STUDY.

Aerospace Engineering. Includes option in ocean engineering.

Biomedical Engineering. Includes options in biomedical imagining, telemedicine.

Chemical Engineering.

Civil Engineering. Includes options in applied mechanics, construction engineering, construction management.

Computer Engineering.

Computer Science. Includes options in computer networks, multimedia and creative technologies, software engineering, robotics and automation.

Earthquake Engineering.

Electrical Engineering. Includes options in systems, electrophysics VLS design, computer networks, multimedia and creative technologies.

Environmental Engineering.

Industrial and Systems Engineering. Includes options in operations research, engineering management, manufacturing engineering, safety engineering, systems architecture and engineering.

Materials Science. Includes option in materials engineering.

Mechanical Engineering.

Petroleum Engineering.

School of Fine Arts (90089-0292)

Tuition: per credit $891.

Graduate enrollment: full-time 27, part-time 3. School faculty: full-time 12, part-time 14. Degrees conferred: M.A., M.F.A.

ADMISSION REQUIREMENTS. Two transcripts, three letters of reference (GRE required for Public Art Studies), twenty-slide portfolio for studio M.F.A., supplemental application and materials for M.A. TOEFL required for international applicants. Apply to both School of Fine Arts and Graduate School by February 1. Application fee $55. Phone: (213)740-2787 Art Office, (213)743-1111 University Office of Admissions.

ADMISSION STANDARDS. Competitive. Usual minimum average: 3.0 (A = 4).

FINANCIAL AID. Teaching assistantships, internships, grants, Federal W/S, loans. Approved for VA benefits. Apply by February 1 to School's Financial Aid Office. Phone: (213)740-1111; fax: (213)740-0680. Use FAFSA and University's FAF.

DEGREE REQUIREMENTS. For M.A.: 40 units; internships. For M.F.A.: 48 credits; thesis/exhibition.

FIELDS OF STUDY.

Public Art Studies. M.A.

Studio Art. M.F.A.

Law School (90089-0071)

Established 1896. Located on main campus in Law Center. ABA approved since 1924. AALS member since 1907. Semester system. Full-time, day study only. Special programs: Center for Post Conviction Justice Project; faculty exchange programs with Hebrew University, Tel Aviv University, Israel; Oxford University, England; China University of Political Science, People's Republic of China; judicial externships; internships. Law library: 373,488 volumes, 4300 subscriptions; has LEXIS, NEXIS, WESTLAW, DIALOG; is a Federal Government Depository.

Annual tuition: $28,262. On-campus housing available. Total average annual additional expense: $15,000.

Enrollment: first-year class 205; total full-time 611 (men 52%, women 48%). Faculty: full-time 33, part-time 27. Student to faculty ratio 15.4 to 1. Degrees conferred: J.D., J.D.-M.B.A., J.D.-M.B.T., J.D.-M.P.A., J.D.-M.A. (Communications Management, Economics, International Relations, Religion), J.D.-M.R.E.D.,

J.D.-M.S.W., J.D.-Ph.D. (Social Sciences with California Institute of Technology), LL.M., M.L.S.

ADMISSION REQUIREMENTS. LSDAS Law School report, bachelor's degree, transcripts, LSAT (not later than December), letters of recommendation required in support of application. Interview not required. Accepts transfer applicants. Graduates of unaccredited colleges not considered. Apply to Admissions Office after September 1, before February 1. Fall admission only. Application fee $60. Phone: (213)740-7331.

ADMISSION STANDARDS. Selective. Mean LSAT: 163; mean GPA: 3.49 (A = 4). Gourman rating: 4.44. *U.S. News & World Report* ranking is in among the top 18 of all U.S. law schools. Accepts 20% of total annual applicants.

FINANCIAL AID. Scholarships, merit scholarships, minority scholarships, Grants-in-Aid, institutional loans; Federal loans and Federal W/S (for second- and third-year students only) available. Assistantships may be available for upper-divisional joint degree candidates. All accepted students are automatically considered for all scholarships. Apply by February 15 to Director of Financial Aid for all programs. Phone: (213)740-7331; use Law Center's Financial Aid Form. Use FAFSA (School code: 001328), also submit Financial Aid Transcript, Federal Income Tax forms. Approximately 47% of first-year class received scholarships/Grants-in-Aid. Approximately 50% of students receive some form of financial assistance. USC Loan Repayment Assistance Program for public-interest employment available.

DEGREE REQUIREMENTS. For J. D.: 88 (33 required) credits with a GPA of at least 70 (scale: 0–100), plus completion of upper-divisional writing course; three-year program. Accelerated J.D. with summer course work. For J.D.-M.B.A.: 105–121 total credits. For J.D.-M.P.A.: 93 total credits. For J.D.-M.B.T.: 94–110 total credits. For J.D.-M.A.: Communications, 88 total credits; Economic, 89 total credits; International Relations, 94 total credits; Religion, 88 total credits. For J.D.-M.R.E.D.: 108 total credits. For J.D.-M.S.W.: 118 total credits. For LL.M., M.L.S.: at least 24 credits beyond the J.D.; thesis.

Keck School of Medicine (90033)

Organized 1885. Annual tuition: $34,130; student fees $1102. Total average figure for all other expenses: $12,100. Enrollment: first-year class 160 (10 EDP), total 808 (men 60%, women 40%). Faculty: full-time 685, part-time 56. Degrees conferred: M.D., M.D.-M.S., M.D.-Ph.D.

ADMISSION REQUIREMENTS. AMCAS report, letters of recommendation, MCAT supplement application required for admission. Interview by invitation only. Applicants must have completed at least three years of college study. Has EDP; apply between June 1 and August 1. Accepts transfer applicants. Graduates of unaccredited colleges not considered. Apply after June 1, before December 1. Application fee $90. Phone: (323)442-2552.

ADMISSION STANDARDS. Very competitive. Mean MCAT: 10; mean GPA: 3.57 (A = 4). *U.S. News & World Report* ranking is in the top 38 of all U.S. medical schools. Accepts 3–5% of total annual applicants. Approximately 70% are state residents.

FINANCIAL AID. Scholarships, loans. Apply to University Financial Aid Office. Phone: (323)442-1016. Use FAFSA. About 75% of students receive some aid from School.

DEGREE REQUIREMENTS. For M.D.: satisfactory completion of four-year program; transfer students from other medical schools may be admitted to advanced standing in second- or third-year class; all students must pass USMLE Step 1 prior to entering third year, and must pass USMLE Step 2 prior to awarding of M.D. For M.S., Ph.D., see Graduate School listing above.

FIELDS OF GRADUATE STUDY.
Anatomy and Biology.
Biochemistry.
Genetics.
Microbiology.
Pharmacology and Nutrition.
Physiology and Biophysics.
Preventive Medicine.

Thornton School of Music

Observed its centennial in 1984. Semester system.
Tuition: per credit $891.
Graduate enrollment: full-time 234, part-time 189. Faculty: full-time 54, part-time 75. Degrees conferred: M.M., M.M.Ed., D.M.A. The M.A. and Ph.D. are offered through the Graduate School.

ADMISSION REQUIREMENTS. Transcripts, supplementary application required in support of regular University application. Personal or taped performance audition required for all performance majors; original scores for composition majors; research paper or thesis for M.A. or Ph.D. Accepts transfer applicants. Apply to Office of Admission, School of Music preferably well in advance of registration. Application fee $55. Phone: (213)740-8986; fax: (213)740-8995.

ADMISSION STANDARDS. Selective. Talent weighted more heavily than GPA in most programs.

FINANCIAL AID. Tuition awards, scholarships, teaching assistantships, Federal W/S, loans. Apply by February 15 to School's Office of Financial Aid; no specified closing date. Phone: (213)740-5444; fax: (213)740-0680. Use FAFSA. Application details accompany application for admission.

DEGREE REQUIREMENTS. For M.M.: 30 units minimum, at least 26 in residence. For M.M.Ed.: 30 units minimum, at least 26 in residence; Music Graduate Entrance Exam; one or two recitals for performance majors; thesis for music education majors, thesis and recital for composition majors. For D.M.A.: 65 units minimum beyond the bachelor's, at least 35 units in residence and two consecutive semesters in full-time attendance; reading knowledge of one foreign language; qualifying exam; dissertation for composition, music education, and church music majors; two solo recitals and two other appropriate appearances for performance majors; final oral exam. For M.A., Ph.D., see Graduate School listing above.

FIELDS OF STUDY.
Choral Music.
Composition.
Conducting.
Early Music Performance.
Music Education.
Music History.
Musicology. M.A., Ph.D.
Performance. Includes keyboard collaborative arts, classical guitar, studio guitar, early music, jazz studies, orchestral instruments, keyboard (piano, organ, harpsichord), voice, opera.
Sacred Music.
Theory. M.A., Ph.D.

School of Pharmacy

Founded in 1905. Semester system.
Annual tuition: full-time $27,184; per credit $907.

Enrollment: full-time 754, part-time 67. Faculty: full-time 25, part-time and courtesy clinical 300. Degrees conferred: Pharm.D.; M.S. and Ph.D. administered by the Graduate School.

ADMISSION REQUIREMENTS. Pharm.D.: two transcripts documenting completion of required preprofessional courses, written essay; two letters of recommendation, personal interview required in support of School's application. Accepts transfer applicants. Graduates of unaccredited institutions not considered. Apply to Office of Admissions by March 31 (Fall). Graduate program: two official transcripts, three letters of recommendation, GRE required in support of application. Transfer applicants accepted. Apply to Director of Admissions by March 1 (Fall), December 15 (Spring). Application fee $55. Phone: (213)342-2650.

ADMISSION STANDARDS. Selective. Accepts 23% of applicants in professional and graduate programs. Usual minimum average: 2.75 (A = 4).

FINANCIAL AID. Professional program: loans and scholarships based upon financial eligibility and merit. Institutional FAF included with application package. Graduate programs: fellowships, teaching assistantships, Federal W/S, loans. Apply by February 15 to Coordinator, Graduate Programs Committee. Phone: (213)342-1466.

DEGREE REQUIREMENTS. Professional program: four-year curriculum following two years of preprofessional undergraduate college study. For M.S. and Ph.D.: see the Graduate School listing above.

FIELDS OF STUDY.
Molecular Pharmacology and Toxicology. M.S. Ph.D.
Pharmaceutical Economics and Policy. M.S., Ph.D.
Pharmaceutical Sciences. M.S., Ph.D.
Pharmacy. Pharm.D.

School of Policy, Planning, and Development

Established 1929. Semester system. Campuses located in Sacramento, California, Washington, D.C., and its home campus in Los Angeles.
Tuition: per credit $891. Enrollment: full-time 445, part-time 213. Faculty: full-time 28, part-time 70. Degrees conferred: M.P.A., M.H.A., M.H.M., M.Pl., M.P.D.S., D.P.P., D.P.A., Ph.D., M.Pl.-M.Arch., M.Pl.-M.B.A., M.Pl.-M.A. (Economics, International Relations), M.Pl.-M.R.E.D., M.Pl.-M.S.G., M.Pl.-M.L.A., M.Pl.-M.P.A., M.Pl.-M.P.A.S., M.Pl.-M.S.W., M.R.E.D.-J.D., M.P.A.-M.S.G., M.H.A.-M.S.G., M.P.A.-M.A.I.R., M.P.A.-J.D., M.P.P.-J.D., M.P.A.-M.S.W., M.P.A.-M.A. (Jewish Communal Service).

ADMISSION REQUIREMENTS. U.S.C. Graduate Admission Application, School Supplemental Application, two official transcripts, three letters of recommendation, résumé, GRE or GMAT or LSAT test scores required in support of School's application. TOEFL required for international applicants. Interview not required. Accepts transfer applicants (up to 8 units can be transferred). Apply to School by February 1. Application fee $55. Phone: (213)740-1111. The School's Student Affairs Officer: (213)740-6842.

ADMISSION STANDARDS. Selective. Usual minimum GPA of 3.0 (A = 4) in last 60 semester units or 90 quarter units. GRE (or equivalent GMAT or LSAT) score of 1000 on verbal and quantitative sections.

FINANCIAL AID. Awards from institutional funds: partial tuition scholarships, doctoral fellowships, assistantships, graduate internships, tuition waivers, Federal W/S, loans. Approved for VA benefits. Apply to School by February 15 for Fall awards, November 1 for Spring awards. Financial aid application for

Federal programs are due March 10. Use FAFSA and University's FAF.

DEGREE REQUIREMENTS. For M.P.D.S.: 28 unit program. For M.H.M., M.Pl., M.P.A.: 40–41 units of study. For M.P.P., M.H.A.: 48 units, at least 36 in residence; internship, comprehensive exam. For Ph.D., D.P.A., D.P.D.S.: completion of 60 units beyond the bachelor's degree, at least 30 in residence; qualifying exam; dissertation; systems requirement for D.P.A., a foreign language requirement for Ph.D.

FIELDS OF STUDY.
Construction Management. Jointly offered with Department of Civil Engineering. M.C.M.
Health Administration. M.H.A.
Health Care Management. M.H.C.M.
Planning. M.Pl., Ph.D.
Planning and Development Studies. M.P.D.S., D.Pl.D.S.
Public Administration. M.P.A., Ph.D., D.P.A.
Public Policy. M.P.P.
Public Policy and Management. M.P.P.M.
Real Estate Development. M.R.E.D.

School of Social Work

Graduate study since 1920. Semester system.
Tuition: per credit $891.
Graduate enrollment: full-time 371, part-time 144. Faculty: full-time 13, part-time 47. Degrees conferred: M.S.W., Ph.D.

ADMISSION REQUIREMENTS. Two transcripts, references, personal statement required in support of School's application. TOEFL, TSE required for international applicants. Accepts transfer applicants. Apply to Office of Admissions by April 1. Fall admission only. Application fee $55. Phone: (213)740-2013.

ADMISSION STANDARDS. Competitive. Usual minimum average: 3.0 (A = 4).

FINANCIAL AID. Annual awards from institutional funds: scholarships, fellowships, research/teaching assistantshps, internships, Federal W/S, loans. Approved for VA benefits. Apply by February 15 to the University Financial Aid Office. Phone: (213)740-1111. Use FAFSA and University's FAF. About 45% of students receive aid other than loans from School and outside sources. No aid for part-time students.

DEGREE REQUIREMENTS. For M.S.W.: 56 units minimum in residence. For Ph.D.: see Graduate School listing above.

SOUTHERN COLLEGE OF OPTOMETRY

Memphis, Tennessee 38104
Web site: www.sco.edu

Founded 1932. Coed. Accredited by Southern Association of Colleges and Schools and by Council on Optometric Education. Private control. Quarter system. Library: 20,500 volumes, 531 microforms, 25 PCs.
Annual tuition: regional $12,562, nonregional $17,562. No on-campus housing available. Contact the Records and Admissions Office for off-campus housing information. Phone: (800)238-0180.
Enrollment: full-time 400. College faculty: full-time 39, part-time 4. Degree conferred: O.D.

ADMISSION REQUIREMENTS. Transcripts showing satisfactory completion of 90 semester hours of prescribed preoptometry courses (bachelor's degree preferred), two letters of recommendation, interview, OAT required in support of College's application. Apply to Admissions Office by March 1 (priority date). Rolling admissions process. Application fee $50. Phone: (901) 722-3224, (800)238-0180.

ADMISSION STANDARDS. Competitive. Usual minimum average: 2.5 (A = 4).

FINANCIAL AID. Scholarships, awards, Federal W/S, loans. Approved for VA benefits. Apply by April 1 to Financial Aid Office. Phone: (901)722-3207. Use FAFSA.

DEGREE REQUIREMENTS. For O.D.: 220 quarter hours minimum, at least 180 in residence; externship.

SOUTHERN CONNECTICUT STATE UNIVERSITY

New Haven, Connecticut 06515-1355
Web site: www.southernct.edu

Founded 1893. CGS member. Coed. State control. Semester system. Special facilities: Business and Economic Development Center, Child Abuse Center, Center for Communication Disorders, Center for Computing and Society, Center for Environment, Reading Center, Research in Behavioral Science Center, Urban Studies Center. Library: 510,000 volumes, 2800 subscriptions.
Annual tuition: full-time resident $4767, nonresident $10,716; per credit $243. Some on-campus housing in summer for single graduate students. Average academic year housing costs: $6200 (including board). Contact Housing Office for both on- and off-campus housing information. Phone: (203)392-5870.

School of Graduate Studies

Graduate study since 1947. Enrollment: full- and part-time 4000. Graduate faculty: full-time 154, part-time 70. Degrees conferred: M.A., M.M.F.T., M.B.A., M.L.S., M.P.H., M.S., M.S.Ed., M.S.N., M.S.W., Sixth Year Professional Diploma.

ADMISSION REQUIREMENTS. Transcripts, GRE (nursing, library science), GRE Subject Test (biology, foreign language departments), GMAT (business economics), letters of recommendation or departmental form, interview required in support of School's application. TOEFL required for international applicants. Accepts transfer applicants. Graduates of unaccredited institutions not considered. Apply to Dean of Graduate Studies by July 15 (Fall), November 15 (Spring), May 15 (Summer). Application fee $40. Phone: (203)392-5240.

ADMISSION STANDARDS. Usual minimum average: 2.75 (A = 4) and/or 3.3 in graduate major area.

FINANCIAL AID. Fellowships, assistantships for teaching/research, Federal W/S, loans. Approved for VA benefits. Apply to appropriate department chair for fellowships, assistantships; to Financial Aid Office for all other programs. Phone: (203)392-4232. Use FAFSA. About 10% of students receive aid other than loans from College and outside sources. Aid available for part-time students.

DEGREE REQUIREMENTS. For master's: 30 semester hours minimum, at least 21 credits in residence; comprehensive exam; thesis/nonthesis option. For Professional Diploma: 30 semester hours beyond the master's, all in residence; final comprehensive exam.

FIELDS OF STUDY.
Bilingual/Bicultural Education.
Biology.

Business Administration.
Chemistry.
Communications Disorders.
Counseling.
Elementary Education.
English.
Environmental Education.
Exercise Science.
History.
Instructional Technology.
Library Science and Instructional Technology.
Marriage and Family Therapy.
Mathematics.
Nursing.
Psychology.
Reading.
Recreation and Leisure.
Research, Measurement, and Evaluation.
Romance Languages. Includes French, Italian, Spanish.
School Health Education.
School Psychology.
Science Education.
Social Work.
Sociology.
Special Education.
Urban Studies.
Women's Studies.

SOUTHERN ILLINOIS UNIVERSITY
Carbondale, Illinois 62901-6806
Web site: www.siuc.edu

Founded 1869. Located 100 miles SE of St. Louis, Missouri. CGS member. Coed. State control. Semester system. Special facilities: Center for Archaeological Investigation, Coal Extraction and Utilization Center, Center for Dewey Studies, Materials Technology Center. Library: 3,000,000 volumes, 12,400 subscriptions. Total University enrollment: 22,000.

Annual tuition: full-time resident $3964, nonresident $7967; per credit resident $130.60, nonresident $261.20. On-campus housing for married, single graduate students. Average housing costs: $369–$494 per month. Contact University Housing Office for both on- and off-campus housing information. Phone: (618)453-2301. Day-care facilities available.

Graduate School

Graduate study since 1944. Enrollment: full- and part-time 3263. Graduate faculty: full-time 780, part-time 14. Degrees conferred: M.A., M.S., M.F.A., M.B.A., M.Acc., M.S. in Ed., M.M., M.P.A., Ph.D., Rh.D., D.B.A.

ADMISSION REQUIREMENTS. Official transcripts required in support of School's application. GRE/GMAT/MAT, letters of recommendation required by some departments. TOEFL (minimum score 550) required for international applicants. Accepts transfer applicants. Graduates of unaccredited institutions not considered. Contact departments directly for admission material and requirements. Rolling admissions process. Application fee $20–$50. Phone: (618)536-7791; fax: (618)453-4562; e-mail: gradschl@siu.edu.

ADMISSION STANDARDS. Selective for most departments, very selective or competitive for others. Usual minimum average: 2.7 (A = 4).

FINANCIAL AID. Annual awards from institutional funds: scholarships, fellowships, teaching assistantships, research assis-

tantships, other grants, Federal W/S, loans. Approved for VA benefits. Apply by February 1 to appropriate department chair for fellowships, assistantships; to Financial Aid Office for all other programs. Phone: (618)453-4334; fax: (618)453-7305. Use FAFSA. Over 70% of full-time students are given some type of financial assistance.

DEGREE REQUIREMENTS. For M.A., M.S.: 30–45 semester hours minimum, at least half in residence; foreign language optional with some departments; thesis for many majors; final written/oral exam. For M.F.A.: 40–60 hours minimum, at least half in residence; thesis; final exhibit of creative work; final exam. For M.B.A., M.P.A., M.Acc.: 30–36 hours minimum, at least half in residence; final written/oral exam. For M.S. in Ed.: same as for M.A., M.S. For M.M.: same as for M.S. in Ed., except recital required in some fields. For Ph.D., Rh.D., D.B.A.: no set hourly requirements (some departments set hourly minimum); at least two semesters in full-time residence; departments establish research tools; dissertation for 24 hours; final written/oral exam.

FIELDS OF STUDY.
Accountancy. M.Acc.
Administration of Justice. M.S.
Agribusiness Economics. M.S.
Animal Science. M.S.
Anthropology. M.A., Ph.D.
Applied Linguistics. M.A.
Art. M.F.A.
Behavior Analysis and Therapy. M.S.
Biological Sciences. M.S.
Business Administration. M.B.A., D.B.A.
Chemistry. M.S., Ph.D.
Cinema and Photography. M.F.A.
Civil Engineering. M.S.
Communication Disorders and Sciences. M.S.
Computer Science. M.S.
Creative Writing. M.F.A.
Curriculum and Instruction. M.S. in Ed., Ph.D.
Economics. M.A., M.S., Ph.D.
Education. Ph.D. in 8 concentrations.
Educational Administration. M.S. in Ed., Ph.D.
Educational Psychology. M.S. in Ed., Ph.D.
Electrical Engineering. M.S.
Engineering Science. Ph.D.
English. M.A., Ph.D.
English as a Foreign Language. M.A.
Environmental Resources and Policy. Ph.D.
Food and Nutrition. M.S.
Foreign Languages and Literatures. Includes French, German, Spanish. M.A.
Forestry. M.S.
Geography. M.A., Ph.D.
Geology. M.S., Ph.D.
Health Education. M.S. in Ed., Ph.D.
Higher Education. M.S. in Ed., Ph.D.
Historical Studies. Ph.D.
History. M.A.
Manufacturing System. M.S.
Mass Communication and Media Arts. M.A., M.F.A., Ph.D.
Mathematics. M.A., M.S., Ph.D.
Mechanical Engineering. M.S.
Molecular Biology, Microbiology, and Biochemistry. M.S.
Molecular, Cellular, and Systemic Physiology. M.S., Ph.D.
Mining Engineering. M.S.
Music. M.M.
Pharmacology. M.S., Ph.D.
Philosophy. M.A., Ph.D.
Physical Education. M.S. in Ed., Ph.D.
Physics. M.S.
Physiology. Ph.D.

Plant Biology. M.A., M.S., Ph.D.
Plant and Soil Science. M.S.
Political Science. M.A., Ph.D.
Psychology. M.A., M.S., Ph.D.
Public Administration. M.P.A.
Recreation. M.S. in Ed.
Rehabilitation Administration and Services. M.S., Rh.D.
Rehabilitation Counseling. M.S.
Social Work. M.S.W.
Sociology. M.A., Ph.D.
Special Education. M.S., Ed.D., Ph.D.
Speech Communication. M.A., M.S., Ph.D.
Telecommunications. M.A.
TESOL. M.A.
Theater. M.F.A.
Workforce Education and Development. M.S. in Ed., Ph.D.
Zoology. M.A., M.S., Ph.D.

School of Dental Medicine (62002)

Established 1969. Located in Alton, Illinois, near St. Louis, Mo. Annual tuition: resident $9590, nonresident $28,770. On-campus housing available. Average academic year housing costs: $11,182. Total average costs for all other expenses: $5050.

Enrollment: first-year class 50; total 195 (men 65%, women 35%). Faculty: full-time 45, part-time 38. Degree conferred: D.M.D.

ADMISSION REQUIREMENTS. AADSAS, official transcripts, DAT (October test preferred), three letters of recommendation required in support of School's application. Applicants must have completed at least two years of college study, prefer three years of study. Interview by invitation only. Preference is given to state residents. Graduates of unaccredited colleges not considered. Apply after June 1, before March 1. Application fee $20. Phone: (618)474-7120.

ADMISSION STANDARDS. Selective. Usual minimum average: 2.5 (A = 4). Mean DAT: Academic 18.3, PAT 17.2; mean GPA: 3.5. Gourman rating: 4.06. Admits about 25-30% of total annual applicants. Approximately 85% are state residents.

FINANCIAL AID. Limited scholarships, grants, loans. Apply after acceptance to Office of Student Affairs. Phone: (618)474-7175. Use FAFSA (School code: E00606). About 94% of students receive aid from School and outside sources.

DEGREE REQUIREMENTS. For D.M.D.: satisfactory completion of forty-six-month program.

School of Law

Web site: www.law.siu.edu

Established 1973. ABA approved since 1974. AALS member. Semester system. Library: 358,972 volumes, 4218 subscriptions; has LEXIS, NEXIS, WESTLAW, LEGALTRAC.

Annual tuition: resident $6124, nonresident $16,180. On-campus housing available. Apply to Housing Office. Phone: (618)453-2301. Total average annual additional expense: $8375.

Enrollment: first-year class 120; total 369 (men 59%, women 41%). Faculty: full-time 25, part-time 2. Student to faculty ratio 13 to 1. Degrees conferred: J.D., J.D.-M.B.A., J.D.-M.P.A., J.D.-M.Acc., J.D.-M.S.W., J.D.-M.D.

ADMISSION REQUIREMENTS. LSDAS Law School report, bachelor's degree, transcripts, LSAT, recommendations required in support of application. Graduates of unaccredited institutions not considered. Apply by March 1 to Admissions Office. Rolling admissions process. Application fee $40. Phone: (800)739-9187, (618)453-8858.

ADMISSION STANDARDS. Selective. Mean LSAT: 151; mean GPA: 3.15 (A = 4). Gourman rating: 3.16. *U.S. News & World Report* ranking is in the third tier of all U.S. law schools. Admits about 30–35% of total annual applications.

FINANCIAL AID. Scholarships, grants, full and partial tuition waivers, fellowships, assistantships, loans. Apply to Office of Student Work and Financial Assistance by April 1. Phone: (618)453-4334. Use FAFSA (School code: 001758). Approximately 40% of all students receive some form of financial assistance.

DEGREE REQUIREMENTS. For J.D.: satisfactory completion of 90 semester hour program. For combined degree programs: normally requires one additional year; see Graduate School listing above.

School of Medicine (P.O. Box 19624)

Web site: www.siumed.edu

Established 1969. Located at Springfield (62794-9624). Library: 113,000 volumes, 1600 subscriptions. Annual tuition: resident $13,346, nonresident $40,038; student fees $1216. On-campus housing available. Total average figure for all other expenses: $8697.

Enrollment: first-year class 72; total 317 (men 55%, women 45%). Faculty: full-time 254, part-time 22. Degrees conferred: M.D., M.D.-J.D.

ADMISSION REQUIREMENTS. AMCAS report, transcripts, MCAT, recommendations, screening interview required in support of application. Does not have EDP. Graduates of unaccredited colleges not considered. Apply after June 1, before November 15. Application fee $50. Phone: (217)524-6013; fax: (217)545-5538.

ADMISSION STANDARDS. Competitive. Mean MCAT: 9.3; mean GPA: 3.46 (A = 4). Gourman rating: 3.28. *U.S. News & World Report* ranked the School in the top 25 of all U.S. medical schools in Primary Care preparation. Accepts about 8–10% of total annual applicants, 99% are state residents.

FINANCIAL AID. Scholarships, merit scholarships, minority scholarships, Grants-in-Aid, institutional loans, HEAL, alternative loan programs, Federal Perkins Loans, Stafford Subsidized and Unsubsidized Loans, Illinois Health Improvement Associate Loans are available. Financial aid applications and information are generally available at the on-campus by invitation interview. Scholarships and grants limited to students with demonstrated exceptional need. Contact the Financial Aid Office for current information. Phone: (217)785-2224. For most financial assistance and all Federal programs use FAFSA (School code: E00569), also submit Financial Aid Transcript, Federal Income Tax forms. Approximately 88% of students receive some form of financial assistance.

DEGREE REQUIREMENTS. For M.D.: satisfactory completion of four-year program; first year is spent in Carbondale. All students must pass USMLE Step 1 prior to graduation. For M.D.-J.D.: generally a six-year program.

SOUTHERN ILLINOIS UNIVERSITY AT EDWARDSVILLE

Edwardsville, Illinois 62026-1046
Web site: www.siue.edu

Located 20 miles from St. Louis, Missouri. CGS member. Coed. State control. Semester system. Library: 775,000 volumes, 1200 subscriptions.

Annual tuition: full-time resident $2608, nonresident $4642; special part-time tuition reduction program for Missouri residents. On-campus housing available for 248 married students, 1000 single students. Annual academic year housing costs: $2746 single students (room only); $6000 married students. Contact Housing Office for on- and off-campus housing information. Phone: (618)892-3931. Day-care facilities available.

Graduate Studies and Research

Enrollment: full-time 877, part-time 1418. Faculty: full-time 250, part-time 115. Degrees conferred: M.A., M.B.A., M.F.A., M.M., M.M.R., M.P.A., M.S.A., M.S.C.E., M.S., M.S.Ed., M.S.E., M.S.E.E., Specialist, Ed.D.

ADMISSION REQUIREMENTS. Transcripts required in support of School's application. GRE/MAT/GMAT, letters of recommendation required in some programs. TOEFL required for international applicants. Graduates of unaccredited institutions considered. Apply to Graduate Admissions Office (Box 1047) at least two months prior to registration. Application fee $25. Phone: (618)692-3010; fax: (618)650-3523.

ADMISSION STANDARDS. Selective. Usual minimum average: 2.5 (A = 4).

FINANCIAL AID. Annual awards from institutional funds: academic scholarships, fellowships, assistantships, stipends, tuition remission program, internships, grants, Federal W/S, loans. Approved for VA benefits. Apply by March 1 to appropriate department Chair for assistantships; to Office of Financial Aid for all other programs date. Use FAFSA. Aid available for part-time students.

DEGREE REQUIREMENTS. For master's: minimum 32 credit program, at least 27 in residence; thesis/nonthesis option/research project; internships/practicum; exhibitions/recitals; final exam. For Specialist: 30 credits beyond the master's degree. For Ed.D.: 72 credits, at least two years in residence; qualifying exam; dissertation; final oral exam.

FIELDS OF STUDY.
Accountancy. M.S.
Art Education. M.F.A.
Art Studio. Includes ceramic, digital art, drawing, metalsmithing, painting, printmaking, sculpture, textile art. M.F.A.
Art Therapy Counseling. M.A.
Biological Sciences. M.A., M.S.
Business Administration. M.B.A.
Chemistry. M.S.
Civil Engineering. M.S.C.E.
Computer Science. M.S.
Computing and Information Systems. M.S.
Economics. M.A., M.S.
Educational Administration and Supervision. M.S.Ed., Ed.S.
Elementary Education. M.S.Ed.
Electrical Engineering. M.S.E.E.
English. M.A.
Environmental Studies. M.S.
Geographical Studies. M.S.
Health Care and Nursing Administration. M.S.
History. M.A.
Instructional Technology. M.S.Ed.
Kinesiology. M.S.Ed.
Marketing Research. M.M.R.
Mass Communications. M.S.
Mathematics. M.S.
Medical Surgical Nursing. M.S.
Mechanical Engineering. M.S.M.E.
Music Education. M.M.
Music Performance. M.M.

Nurse Anesthesia. M.S.
Nurse Educator. M.S.
Nurse Practitioner Studies. M.S.
Physics. M.S.
Psychiatric-Mental Health Nursing. M.S.
Psychology. M.S.
Public Administration.
Public Health Nursing. M.S.
School Psychology. Ed.S.
Secondary Education. Includes eleven teaching fields. M.S.Ed.
Social Work. M.S.W.
Sociology. M.A.
Special Education. M.S.Ed.
Speech Communication. M.A.
Speech-Language Pathology. M.S.

UNIVERSITY OF SOUTHERN MAINE
Portland, Maine 04103-9300
Web site: www.usm.maine.edu

Founded in 1878 as Gorham State College and in 1970 merged with the University of Maine at Portland to form the University of Southern Maine. Library: 620,000 volumes, 7600 subscriptions.

Tuition: per hour resident $193, nonresident $538. Limited on-campus housing during academic year. On-campus housing available in summer. Contact Resident Life Office for both on- and off-campus housing information. Phone: (207)780-5158. Day-care facilities available.

Graduate Studies and Research

Graduate study authorized in 1964. Enrollment: full-time 700, part-time 1100. Graduate programs are evenings, Saturdays and Summer sessions. Graduate faculty: full- and part-time 140. Degrees conferred: M.A., M.B.A., M.O.T., M.S., M.S.A., M.S.Ad.Ed., M.S.Ed.

ADMISSION REQUIREMENTS. Transcripts, three references, GRE/MAT/MAT required in support of application. Additional materials may be required. Interview recommended. TOEFL required for international applicants. Accepts transfer applicants. Apply to Office of Graduate Affairs by March 1 for priority consideration. Departmental deadlines may vary. Rolling admissions process. Application fee $25. Phone: (207)780-4336; fax: (207) 780-4959.

ADMISSION STANDARDS. Competitive. Usual minimum average: 2.75 (A = 4).

FINANCIAL AID. Graduate assistantships, internships, tuition waivers, Federal W/S, loans. Approved for VA benefits. Apply to Office of Graduate Affairs by February 15. Phone: (207)780-4380. Use FAFSA.

DEGREE REQUIREMENTS. Variable by program; most master's degree require 32–36 credits; thesis/nonthesis option. Nearly all degree programs are offered at the Portland or Gorham campuses, Occupational Therapy offered at Lewiston-Auburn campus.

FIELDS OF STUDY.

COLLEGE OF ARTS AND SCIENCES:
Accounting. M.S.A.
American and New England Studies. M.A.
Applied Immunology and Molecular Biology. M.S.
Biology. M.S.

Business Administration. M.B.A.
Computer Science. M.S.
Community Planning and Development. M.C.P.D.
Creative Writing. M.F.A.
Health Policy and Management. M.S.
Leadership Studies. M.A.
Music. M.M.
Nursing. M.S.
Occupational Therapy. M.O.T.
Public Policy and Management. M.P.P.
Social Work. M.S.W.
Statistics. M.S.

COLLEGE OF EDUCATION AND HUMAN DEVELOPMENT:
Adult Education. M.S.A.Ed.
Counselor Education. Includes school, clinical counseling, rehabilitation counseling, psychosocial rehabilitation counseling. M.S.Ed.
Educational Leadership. Includes teacher leadership administration, special education administration. M.S.Ed.
Industrial Education. M.S.Ed.
Literacy Education. Includes ESL. M.S.Ed.
School Psychology. M.S.Ed.
Special Education. Includes elementary education, gifted child education, secondary education. M.S.Ed.

SOUTHERN METHODIST UNIVERSITY
Dallas, Texas 75275
Web site: www.smu.edu

Founded 1911. CGS member. Located 5 miles N of downtown. Coed. Private control. Methodist affiliation. Semester system. Special facilities: university herbarium, Dallas Seismological Observatory, Statistical Research Laboratory, Shuler Museum of Paleontology, Institute for the Study of Earth and Man, Electron Microscopy Laboratory, Fort Burgwin Research Center, The Meadows Collection of Art, Computing Laboratory, Environmental Engineering Science Center. Library: 3,100,000 volumes, 11,200 subscriptions. Total University enrollment: 10,000.

Annual tuition: per credit $771. On-campus housing for married and single graduate students. Approximate average academic year housing costs: $4500 for married students, $4400 (room only) for single students. Contact Office of Housing for both on- and off-campus housing information. Phone: (214)768-2407. Day-care facilities available.

Dedman College

Enrollment: full-time 160, part-time 455. Faculty: full- and part-time 241. Degrees conferred: M.A., M.B.E., M.S., Ph.D.

ADMISSION REQUIREMENTS. Two transcripts, GRE, two to four letters of recommendation required in support of College's application. GRE Subject Test required for some departments. TOEFL required for international applicants. Interview not required. Accepts transfer applicants. Graduates of unaccredited institutions not considered. Apply to Office of Research and Graduate Studies; no specified closing date. Application fee $50. Phone: (214)768-4345.

ADMISSION STANDARDS. Selective. Minimum average: 3.0 or GRE V + Q score of 1100. TOEFL minimum score 550.

FINANCIAL AID. Annual awards from institutional funds: scholarships, teaching fellowships, research fellowships, full and partial tuition waivers, internships, Federal W/S, loans. Apply by May 1 to appropriate department for fellowships, assistantships; to Financial Aid Office for all other aid. Phone: (214)768-3314.

Use FAFSA. About 60% of students receive aid other than loans from College and outside sources. Aid available for part-time students.

DEGREE REQUIREMENTS. For M.A., M.S.: 30 semester hours minimum, at least one year or its equivalent in residence for most programs; thesis/nonthesis option; comprehensive written/oral exam. For Ph.D.: generally three years beyond the bachelor's degree, at least one year in residence; qualifying exam; reading knowledge of one foreign language for most programs; dissertation; final oral exam.

FIELDS OF STUDY.
Anthropology. Includes medical anthropology. M.A., Ph.D.
Applied Economics. M.A.
Applied Geophysics. M.S.
Bilingual Education. M.B.E.
Biology. GRE Subject Test in biology required for admission. M.A., M.S., Ph.D.
Chemistry. GRE Subject Test in chemistry required for admission. M.S.
Computational and Applied Mathematics. M.A., Ph.D.
Economics. Includes applied, GRE if GPA is below 3.0. M.A., Ph.D.
English. GRE Subject Test in literature required for admission. M.A.
Geology. M.S., Ph.D.
Geophysics. M.S., Ph.D.
History. M.A.
Latin American Studies. M.A. only.
Liberal Arts.
Mathematical Sciences. Includes applied (M.S.), mathematics (M.A.).
Medieval Studies. M.A.
Physics. M.S.
Political Science. GRE for admission. M.A. only.
Psychology. Includes general/experimental (M.A., Ph.D.), clinical and counseling (M.A. only); MMPI release form required for clinical and counseling.
Religious Studies. M.A., Ph.D.
Statistical Sciences. M.S., Ph.D.

Meadows School of the Arts

Tuition: per credit $771.
Enrollment: full-time 91, part-time 83. Graduate faculty: full-time 88, part-time 25. Degrees conferred: M.A., M.F.A., M.M., M.M.T., M.S.M.

ADMISSION REQUIREMENTS. Transcripts, three letters of recommendation, résumé, qualifying audition required in support of School's application. GRE sometimes required. TOEFL required for international applicants. Apply to Director of Admissions and Records by February 1. Application fee $50. Phone: (214)768-3765; fax: (214)768-3272.

ADMISSION STANDARDS. Selective for most departments, competitive for the others. For most programs talent given greater weight than GPA.

FINANCIAL AID. Scholarships, fellowships, assistantships for teaching/research, internships, Federal W/S, loans. Apply to Financial Aid Office by March 1. Phone: (214)768-3314. Use FAFSA. About 60% of students receive aid from School and outside sources. Aid sometimes available for part-time students.

DEGREE REQUIREMENTS. For M.A.: 36-48 semester hours; reading knowledge of foreign language for some departments; thesis/internship. For M.F.A.: 60–66 semester hours; project. For M.M., M.M.T., M.S.M.: 30 semester hours minimum; recital/final project.

FIELDS OF STUDY.

Art. Includes ceramics, drawing, painting, photography, print-making, sculpture. M.F.A.

Art History. M.A.

Choral Conducting. M.M.

Dance. M.F.A.

Instrumental Conducting. M.M.

Music Composition. M.M.

Music Education. M.M.

Music History and Literature. M.M.

Music Performance. M.M.

Music Theory. M.M.

Music Therapy. M.P.T.

Piano Performance and Pedagogy. M.M.

Theatre. Includes acting, design. M.F.A.

TV/Radio. Includes mass communication. M.F.A., M.A.

Edwin L. Cox School of Business— Graduate Division

Graduate study since 1950. Semester system. Special facilities: Maguire Energy Institute, Caruth Institute of Owner-Managed Business, J.C. Penny Center for Retail Exellence.

Annual tuition: full-time M.B.A. $26,090, per credit $826; E.M.B.A. $63,425. Enrollment: full-time 405, part-time 567. Graduate faculty: full- and part-time 71. Degrees conferred: M.B.A., E.M.B.A., M.S.A.

ADMISSION REQUIREMENTS. Official transcripts, recommendation, GMAT, interview required in support of School's application. TOEFL required of international applicants. Accepts transfer applicants. Graduates of unaccredited institutions not considered. Apply by March 30 (Fall), November 30 (Spring) to Graduate Admissions Office. Rolling admissions process. Application fee $50. Phone: (214)768-3012; fax: (214)768-3713.

ADMISSION STANDARDS. Competitive. Usual minimum average: 3.0 (A = 4).

FINANCIAL AID. Merit-based scholarships, fellowships, research assistantships, internships, tuition waivers, Federal W/S, loans. Approved for VA benefits. Apply by March 1 to the Office of the Dean for assistantships; to Office of Financial Aid for all other programs. Phone: (214)768-3417. Use FAFSA (School code: 003613). Aid available for part-time students.

DEGREE REQUIREMENTS. For M.B.A.: 45-60 semester hours, depending upon previous degree program. For M.S.A.: 30 credit program.

FIELDS OF STUDY.

Accounting. M.S.A.

Business Administration. M.B.A.

School of Engineering and Applied Science— Graduate Division

Web site: www.seas.smu.edu

Graduate study since 1949. Semester system.

Tuition: per credit $625. Enrollment: full-time 104, part-time 709. Graduate faculty: full-time 48, part-time 15. Degrees conferred: M.S., D.Eng., Ph.D.

ADMISSION REQUIREMENTS. Official transcripts, GRE required in support of School's application. TOEFL required for international applicants. Interview not required. Accepts transfer applicants with up to 6 hours of transfer credits. Graduates of unaccredited institutions not considered. Apply to Director of Graduate Division, School of Engineering and Applied Science by application deadline on back of form. Application fee $30. Phone: (214)768-1456; fax: (214)768-3845.

ADMISSION STANDARDS. Selective. Usual minimum average: 3.0 (A = 4).

FINANCIAL AID. Annual awards from institutional funds: research/teaching fellowships, research/teaching assistantships, internships, tuition waivers, Federal W/S, loans. Approved for VA benefits. Apply by May 1 to Director of Graduate Division for assistantships, fellowship; to Financial Aid Office for all other programs. Phone: (214)768-3417; fax: (214) 768-3878. Use FAFSA. About 90% of students receive aid other than loans from School and outside sources.

DEGREE REQUIREMENTS. For M.S.: 30 semester hours minimum, 24 in residence; thesis/nonthesis option. For Ph.D.: 78 semester hours minimum, at least 30 in residence; qualifying exam; dissertation; final exam. For D.Eng.: 78 hours required; essentially the same as for Ph.D., praxis required.

FIELDS OF STUDY.

Applied Science. M.S., Ph.D.

Computer Engineering. M.S., Ph.D.

Computer Science. M.S., Ph.D.

Electrical Engineering. M.S., Ph.D.

Engineering Management. M.S., D.Eng.

Environmental Systems Management. M.S.

Hazardous and Waste Materials Management. M.S.

Manufacturing Systems Management. M.S.

Mechanical Engineering. M.S., Ph.D.

Operations Research. M.S., Ph.D.

Software Engineering. M.S.

Systems Engineering. M.S.

Telecommunication. M.S.

School of Law (75275-0110)

Web site: www.law.smu.edu

Established 1925. Graduate program since 1950. ABA approved since 1927. AALS member. Semester system. Primarily full-time, day study; LL.M. both full- and part-time study. Special facilities: Center for Pacific Rim Legal Studies, Center for NAFTA and Latin American Legal Studies. Special programs: Summer study abroad at University College, Oxford University, England. Law library: 541,971 volumes, 5377 subscriptions; has LEXIS, WESTLAW; is a Federal Government Depository.

Annual tuition: $18,902. On-campus housing available for both single and married students. Annual on-campus housing cost: $12,288 single students, married students $14,288. Contact Office of Housing for both on- and off-campus housing information. Phone: (214)768-2407. Law students can live off-campus. Off-campus housing and personal expenses: approximately $12,000.

Enrollment: first-year class 283; total 779 (men 54%, women 46%); very few part-time students. Faculty: full-time 36, part-time 25. Student to faculty ratio 17.7 to 1. Degrees conferred: J.D., J.D.-M.B.A., J.D.-M.A. (Economics), LL.M. (General, Taxation), LL.M. (Comparative and International Law; for persons who have completed a basic legal education and received a university degree in law in another country), S.J.D.

ADMISSION REQUIREMENTS. For J.D. program: LSDAS Law School report, bachelor's degree, transcripts, letters of recommendation, LSAT required in support of application. Accepts transfer applicants. Apply to School of Law by February 15; beginning students admitted Fall only. For graduate program: transcripts, letters of recommendation required in support of application. Interview not required. Graduates of unaccredited colleges not considered. Apply to Secretary, Committee on Graduate Studies, School of Law, by March 1. Application fee $50. Phone: (214)768-2550; fax: (214)768-4390.

ADMISSION REQUIREMENTS FOR LL.M. APPLICANTS (General, Taxation). Must have a J.D. from an ABA-accredited law school; must have graduated in the top half of class. Official transcripts including rank-in-class, two letters of recommendation, a statement of interest in graduate study required in support of application. Admits Fall and Spring, for full- and part-time study. Apply by April 1 (Fall), December 1 (Spring).

ADMISSION REQUIREMENTS FOR LL.M. APPLICANTS. (Comparative and International Law). Must be graduates of a recognized foreign law school. Official U.S. Law School transcripts or certified translation and evaluation of all foreign credentials; TOEFL for all applicants whose native language is not English, short curriculum vitae, two letters of recommendation, evidence of financial ability to pay degree expenses required in support of application. Admits full-time and Fall only.

ADMISSION REQUIREMENTS FOR S.J.D. APPLICANTS. Must have LL.M. degree from any one of the three SMU School of Law Graduate programs and already have selected a research project or an appropriate area for advanced study or extended research.

ADMISSION STANDARDS. For J.D.: selective. Mean LSAT: 158; mean GPA: 3.32 (A = 4). Gourman rating: 4.36. *U.S. News & World Report* ranking is in the top 49 of all U.S. law schools. Accepts about 30–35% of total annual applicants.

FINANCIAL AID. For J.D. program: scholarships, Federal W/S, loans. Apply to Director of Financial Aid by February 15. Phone: (214)768-3417. Use FAFSA. For graduate program: scholarships, fellowships; apply to Chair of Committee on Graduate Studies by May 1. About 56% of students receive aid other than loans from School.

DEGREE REQUIREMENTS. For J.D.: 90 semester hours minimum, at least last 6 semesters in residence. For LL.M.: at least 24 semester hours minimum, one year in full-time residence. For S.J.D.: one year minimum in residence; thesis; oral exam.

UNIVERSITY OF SOUTHERN MISSISSIPPI

Hattiesburg, Mississippi 39406-0066
Web site: www.usm.edu

Founded 1910. Located 90 miles SE of Jackson. CGS member. Coed. State control. Semester system. Special facilities: Automation and Robotics Application Center, Bureau of Educational Research, Gulf Coast Research Laboratory, Health Related Sciences Institute, Institute of Environmental Science, the Mississippi Polymer Institute, Physical Fitness Institute. Library: 872,000 volumes, 4500 subscriptions.

Annual tuition: full-time resident $2970, nonresident $6898. On-campus housing for 296 married and 4700 single students. Average academic year housing cost: $4212 for married students, $2662 for single students. Contact Resident Life Office for both on- and off-campus housing information. Phone: (601)266-4783. Day-care facilities available.

Graduate School

Established 1947. Enrollment: full-time 1242, part-time 1124. Faculty: full-time 654, part-time 73. Degrees conferred: M.A., M.S., M.Ed., M.B.A., M.F.A., M.L.S., M.M., M.M.E., M.P.A., M.S.N., M.S.W., Ed.S., Ed.D., Ph.D.

ADMISSION REQUIREMENTS. Two transcripts, GRE/GMAT/MAT/NTE Test, two recommendations required in support of School's application. Interview may be required. TOEFL required for international applicants. Accepts transfer applicants. Apply by July 15 (Fall), November 15 (Spring) to Director of Graduate Admissions. Rolling admissions process. Application fee $0, $25 for international applicants. Phone: (601)266-5137; fax: (601)266-5138.

ADMISSION STANDARDS. Selective for most departments. Usual minimum average: 2.75 (A = 4).

FINANCIAL AID. Annual awards from institutional funds: scholarships, teaching assistantships, fellowships, internships, tuition waivers, Federal W/S, loans. Apply by March 15 to Dean for assistantships, fellowships; to Financial Aid Office for all other programs. Phone: (601)266-4774. Use FAFSA. About 60% of students receive aid from School and outside sources. Aid available for part-time students.

DEGREE REQUIREMENTS. For master's: 30 semester hours minimum, at least 15 in residence; reading knowledge of one foreign language; thesis required for many majors; final written/oral exam. For M.Ed., M.S. in Teaching: same as above, except no thesis requirement. For Ed.S.: 30 hours minimum beyond the master's, at least one quarter in full-time residence; final written exam. For Ph.D.: 78 hours minimum beyond the bachelor's, at least two consecutive semesters in full-time residence; reading knowledge of two foreign languages or one language and statistics; preliminary exam; dissertation; final written/oral exam. For Ed.D.: essentially same as for Ph.D., except MAT for candidacy, no language requirement; knowledge of statistics required.

FIELDS OF STUDY.

COLLEGE OF THE ARTS:
Art Education.
Church Music.
Conducting.
Design and Technical Theatre.
Drawing and Painting.
Music Education.
Music History and Literature.
Performance.
Performance and Pedagogy.
Theatre.
Theory—Composition.

COLLEGE OF BUSINESS ADMINISTRATION:
Accounting.
Business Administration.

COLLEGE OF EDUCATION AND PSYCHOLOGY:
Adult Education.
Behavior Disorders.
Clinical Psychology.
College Counseling/Personnel.
Counseling Psychology.
Experimental Psychology.
Early Childhood Education.
Educational Administration and Supervision.
Elementary Education.
Gifted.
Higher Education Administration.
Industrial/Organizational Psychology.
Mental Retardation.
Reading.
School Psychology.
Secondary Education. Includes art, biology, chemistry, physics, English, foreign languages, mathematics, music education, physics education, physics, science, social studies, speech communications.

Special Education.
Specific Learning Disabilities.
Supervision of Instruction.
Technology Education.

COLLEGE OF HEALTH AND HUMAN SCIENCES:
Administration and Teaching.
Exercise Physiology.
Exercise Science.
Family and Consumer Studies.
Health Education.
Health Policy and Administration.
Human Nutrition.
Institution Management.
Kinesiology.
Marriage and Family Therapy.
Nutrition and Food Systems.
Occupational and Environmental Health.
Physical Education.
Public Health Nutrition.
Recreation.
Social Work.
Sport Administration.

INTERNATIONAL AND CONTINUING EDUCATION:
Economic Development.
Geography.
International Development.

COLLEGE OF LIBERAL ARTS:
Anthropology.
Audiology.
Communication.
Creative Writing.
Criminal Justice.
Education of the Deaf.
English.
French.
History.
Juvenile Justice.
Library and Information Science.
Library Science.
Philosophy.
Political Science.
Public Administration.
Public Relations.
Spanish.
Speech/Language Pathology.

COLLEGE OF NURSING:
Adult Health Nursing.
Community Health Nursing.
Family Nurse Practitioner.
Nursing Service Administration.
Psychiatric Nursing.

COLLEGE OF SCIENCE AND TECHNOLOGY:
Biochemistry.
Biological Marine Science.
Biology Education.
Botany.
Chemical Marine Science.
Chemistry.
Chemistry Education.
Computational Science.
Computer Science.
Computer Science Education.
Earth Science Education.
Engineering Technology.

Environmental Biology.
Geological Marine Science.
Geology.
Marine Biology.
Mathematics.
Mathematics Education.
Medical Technology.
Microbiology.
Molecular Biology.
Physical Marine Science.
Physics.
Physics Education.
Polymer Science.
Scientific Computing.
Zoology.

SOUTHERN NAZARENE UNIVERSITY

Bethany, Oklahoma 73008-2694
Web site: www.snu.edu

From 1920–1955 was known as Bethany-Peniel College; name changed in 1986. Coed. Semester system. Affiliated with Church of the Nazarene. Library: 105,000 volumes, 325 subscriptions, 10 PCs.

Tuition: per semester hour $352. On-campus housing available for 60 married students, limited for single graduate students. Average academic year housing costs: single students $3320–$4770 (including board); married students $3500. Contact Dean of Student Services for both on- and off-campus housing information. Phone: (405)491-6316.

Graduate Studies

Graduate program began in 1963. Enrollment: full-time 168, part-time 102 (men 132, women 139). Faculty: full-time 25. Degrees conferred: M.A., M.A.M.F.T., M.S.Mgt., M.Min., M.S.C.P.

ADMISSION REQUIREMENTS. Transcripts, MAT/GMAT, three letters of recommendation required in support of College's application. Interview strongly recommended. TOEFL (minimum score 550) required for international applicants. Accepts transfer applicants. Graduates of unaccredited institutions considered on a conditional basis. Apply to Director of Graduate Studies by August 1 (Fall), December 1 (Spring). Application fee $25. International application fee $35. Phone: (405)491-6316, (405)491-6302.

ADMISSION STANDARDS. Selective. Usual minimum average: 3.0 (A = 4) on last 60 hours.

FINANCIAL AID. Limited teaching fellowships, loans. Approved for VA benefits. Apply to the Financial Aid Office. Phone: (405)491-6310; fax: (405)491-6381. Use FAFSA.

DEGREE REQUIREMENTS. For master's: 32 semester hours minimum; thesis optional; comprehensive exam.

FIELDS OF STUDY.
Business. M.B.A.
Counseling Psychology. M.S.C.P., M.A.M.F.T.
Curriculum and Instruction. Includes early childhood, elementary, communication arts, kinesiology, reading. M.A.
Educational Leadership. M.A.
Management. M.S.M.
Religion. M.A., M.Min.

SOUTHERN OREGON UNIVERSITY

Ashland, Oregon 97520

Web site: www.sou.edu

Founded 1926. Located 300 miles S of Portland. Coed. State control. Quarter system. Library: 275,000 volumes, 760,000 microforms, 2137 current periodicals.

Annual tuition: full-time resident $6303, nonresident $11,085. On-campus housing: 60 units for married students, 2000 single students. Average academic year housing costs: $3500 for married students, $5991 for single students (includes board). Apply to Director of Student Services for off-campus housing information. Phone: (541)552-6371 (single students), (541)488-4401 (married students).

Graduate Division

Graduate study since 1952. Enrollment: full-time 163, part-time 162. College faculty: full-time 170, part-time 10. Degrees conferred: M.A., M.S., M.M., M.A.P.

ADMISSION REQUIREMENTS. Transcripts, GRE/GMAT/NTE, three letters of recommendation, goal statement or letter of intent required in support of application. On-line application available. TOEFL (minimum score 540) required for applicants whose native language is not English. Interview may be required for some programs. Accepts transfer applicants. Apply to Admission Office by April 15 (Fall), October 15 (Winter), January 15 (Spring and Summer). Application fee $50. Phone: (541)552-6411.

ADMISSION STANDARDS. Selective. Usual minimum average: 3.0 (A = 4).

FINANCIAL AID. Graduate assistantships, loans. Approved for VA benefits. Apply to Director of Financial Aid. Phone: (541) 482-6181. Use FAFSA.

DEGREE REQUIREMENTS. For master's: 45 quarter hours minimum, at least 30 in residence; thesis or project option; final oral/written comprehensive exam.

FIELDS OF STUDY.
Applied Psychology. M.A.P.
Elementary Education. M.A., M.S.
Environmental Education. M.A., M.S.
Management. M.M.
Teaching. M.A.T.

SOUTHERN UNIVERSITY AND AGRICULTURAL AND MECHANICAL COLLEGE

P.O. Box 9860

Baton Rouge, Louisiana 70813

Web site: www.subr.edu

Founded 1880. CGS member. Coed. State control. Semester system. Special facilities: Health Research Center, Environmental and Energy Institute, Center for Sickle Cell Disease Research, National Plant Data Center, Small Farm Family Resource Development Center, Research Institute of Pure and Applied Sciences, Center for Social Research. Library: 451,000 volumes, 4000 subscriptions. Total University enrollment: 9500.

Annual tuition: full-time resident $2572, nonresident $7738; part-time varies according to course load. On-campus housing available for single students only. Average academic year housing costs: $5700–$6672 (including board). Contact Housing Office for both on- and off-campus housing. Phone: (225)771-3590.

Graduate School

Established 1956. Enrollment: full-time 279, part-time 679. Faculty: full- and part-time 146. Degrees conferred: M.A., M.Ed., M.P.A., M.S., Ph.D.

ADMISSION REQUIREMENTS. Transcripts required in support of School's application. GRE/GMAT recommended. Interview not required. TOEFL required for international applicants. Accepts transfer applicants. Graduates of unaccredited institutions not considered. Apply to Graduate Office by July 1 (Fall), December 1 (Spring), May 1 (Summer). Rolling admissions process. Application fee $5. Phone: (225)771-5390; fax: (225)771-5723.

ADMISSION STANDARDS. Selective for most departments. Usual minimum average: 2.5 (A = 4).

FINANCIAL AID. Annual awards from institutional funds: teaching assistantships, research assistantships, Federal W/S, loans. Approved for VA benefits. Apply at least thirty days prior to registration to Dean of the Graduate School for assistantships; to the Office of Financial Aid for all other programs. Phone: (225)771-2790. Use FAFSA. About 10% of students receive aid other than loans from School. Aid available for part-time students.

DEGREE REQUIREMENTS. For master's: 30–36 semester hours minimum, at least 24 in residence and 18 weeks in full-time attendance; thesis required for M.A., optional for other degrees; final written/oral exam. For Ph.D.: 60 credit minimum beyond bachelor's; foreign language requirement; qualifying exam; candidacy; dissertation; oral defense.

FIELDS OF STUDY.
Accountancy. M.P.A.
Administration and Supervision. M.Ed.
Biochemistry. M.S.
Biology. M.S.
Chemistry. Includes analytical, inorganic, organic, physical. M.S.
Computer Science. Includes operating/information systems, educational computing. M.S.
Counselor Education. M.A.
Elementary Education. M.Ed.
Environmental Sciences. M.S.
Environmental Toxicology. Ph.D.
Information Systems. M.S.
Mass Communication. M.A.
Mathematics. M.S.
Media. M.Ed.
Mental Health Counseling. M.A.
Micro/Minicomputer Architecture. M.S.
Nursing. M.S.N., Ph.D.
Operating Systems. M.S.
Physics. M.S.
Public Policy and Urban Affairs. Ph.D.
Public Administration. M.P.A.
Rehabilitation Counseling. M.S.
Secondary Education. Includes agriculture, biology, business education, chemistry, English, health and physical education, home economics, industrial arts, mathematics, music, social studies. M.Ed.
Science/Mathematics Education. Ph.D.
Social Sciences. Interdisciplinary. Includes history, political science, sociology. M.A.
Special Education. M.Ed., Ph.D.
Therapeutic Recreation. M.S.
Urban Forestry. M.S.

Law Center

P.O. Box 9294

Founded 1947. ABA approved since 1953. AALS member. Semester system. Law library: 426,386 volumes, 4402 subscriptions; has LEXIS, NEXIS, WESTLAW, DIALOG.

Annual tuition: resident $3288, nonresident $7888. On-campus housing available. Total average annual additional expense: $10,775.

Enrollment: first-year class 112; total full-time 316 (men 50%, women 50%). Faculty: full-time 24, part-time 7. Student to faculty ratio 11.9 to 1. Degree conferred: J.D.

ADMISSION REQUIREMENTS. LSDAS Law School report, bachelor's degree, transcripts, LSAT (prior to March test date), two letters of recommendation, narrative on why one selects the field of law required in support of application. Interview may be requested. Accepts transfer applicants. Graduates of unaccredited colleges not considered. Apply to Office of Admissions by March 30. Beginning students admitted Fall only. Application fee $25. Phone: (504)771-5340, (800)537-1135.

ADMISSION STANDARDS. Selective. Mean LSAT: 146; mean GPA: 2.68 (A = 4). Gourman rating: 2.08. *U.S. News & World Report* ranking is in the fourth tier of all U.S. law schools. Accepts 35% of total annual applicants.

FINANCIAL AID. Scholarships, assistantships, Federal W/S, loans. Apply Financial Aid Committee by April 15. Use FAFSA (Law Center code: 002025). About 26% of students receive aid other than loans from School.

DEGREE REQUIREMENTS. For J.D.: 96 semester hours, 6 semesters in residence.

SOUTHWEST MISSOURI STATE UNIVERSITY
Springfield, Missouri 65804-0094
Web site: www.smsu.edu

Founded 1905. CGS member. Semester system. State control. Special facilities: Center for Archaeological Research, Center for Business and Research, Center for Cultural Programs and Development, Center for Economic Research, Center for Gerontological Studies, Center for Ozarks Studies, Center for Human Resources and Service, Center for Resource Planning and Management. Library: 771,300 volumes, 9000 subscriptions. Total University enrollment: 17,000.

Tuition: per credit, resident $121, nonresident $242. On-campus housing available. Average academic year housing costs: $3846 room/suite style (includes 20 meals per week); $318–$424 per month apartment style. Contact Residence Life for both on- and off-campus housing information. Phone: (417)836-5536. Day-care facilities available.

Graduate College

Enrollment: full-time 854, part-time 2150. Faculty: full-time 396, part-time 19. Degrees conferred: M.A., M.B.A., M.P.A., M.M., M.S., M.S.Ed., M.S.N., M.S.W., Ed.S.

ADMISSION REQUIREMENTS. Official transcripts required in support of application. On-line application available. TOEFL required for foreign applicants. GRE/GMAT required for some programs. Accepts transfer applicants. Graduates of unaccredited institutions not considered. Apply to Graduate College at least six weeks prior to registration. Rolling admissions process. Application fee $25. Phone(417)836-5335; fax: (417)836-6888.

ADMISSION STANDARDS. Selective. Usual minimum average: 2.75 (A = 4) or satisfactory GRE or GMAT scores.

FINANCIAL AID. Assistantships, internships, grants, Federal W/S, loans. Apply by April 1 to department head for assistant-

ships; to Financial Aid Office for all other programs. Phone: (417)836-5262; fax: (417)836-8392. Use FAFSA.

DEGREE REQUIREMENTS. For master's: 32-47 semester hours minimum; research project; comprehensive exam. For Ed.S.: 70 semester hours minimum; research project; comprehensive exam.

FIELDS OF STUDY.
Accounting.
Administrative Studies.
Biology.
Business Administration.
Cell and Molecular Biology.
Chemistry.
Communication.
Communication Sciences and Disorders.
Computer Information Systems.
Defense and Strategic Studies.
Educational Administration.
Elementary Education.
English.
Guidance and Counseling.
Health Administration.
Health Promotion and Wellness Management.
History.
Instructional Media Technology.
International Affairs and Administration.
Materials Science.
Mathematics.
Music.
Natural and Applied Science.
Nurse Anesthesia.
Nursing.
Physical Therapy.
Physician Assistant Studies.
Plant Science.
Psychology.
Public Administration.
Public Health.
Reading.
Religious Studies.
Resource Planning.
Secondary Education.
Social Work.
Special Education.
Theater.
Writing.

SOUTHWEST TEXAS STATE UNIVERSITY
San Marcos, Texas 78666-4605
Web site: www.swt.edu

Founded 1899. Located 28 miles SW of Austin. CGS member. Coed. State control. Semester system. Library: 1,200,000 volumes, 6200 subscriptions.

Tuition: per credit resident $80, nonresident $510. On-campus housing for 100 married students, 2000 men, 2250 women. Average annual housing cost: $7000 for married students, $4500 (including board) for single students. Contact Director of Residential Life for both on- and off-campus housing information. Phone: (512)245-2382.

Graduate School

Graduate study since 1935. Enrollment: full-time 1100, part-time 2000. Graduate faculty: full-time 256, part-time 38. Degrees conferred: M.A., M.Acy., M.A.Geo., M.A.I.S., M.A.T., M.B.A., M.Ed., M.F.A., M.H.A., M.M., M.P.A., M.S., M.S.C.D., M.S.C.J., M.S.H.P., M.S.T., M.P.A., M.S.I.S., M.S.P.T., M.S.W., Ph.D.

ADMISSION REQUIREMENTS. Transcripts, GRE/GMAT required in support of School's application. Interview not required for most programs. TOEFL, TSE (for M.B.A., M.P.A., History) required for international applicants. Accepts transfer applicants. Graduates of unaccredited institutions not considered. Apply to Dean of Graduate School by October 15 (Spring), April 15 (Summer), June 15 (Fall). International applicants must submit application at least one month prior to deadlines above. In addition, if applicant is submitting foreign credentials, a $50 evaluation fee accompany application and $25 application fee. Application fee $25. Phone: (512)245-2581; fax: (512)245-8365; e-mail: gradcollege@swt.edu.

ADMISSION STANDARDS. Selective. Usual minimum average (some programs are higher): 2.75 (A = 4) on last 60 hours of bachelor's degree. Minimum GMAT score 400, minimum TOEFL score 550, minimum TSE score 45.

FINANCIAL AID. Annual awards from institutional funds: minority scholarships, fellowships, teaching assistantships, internships, Federal W/S, loans. Approved for VA benefits. Apply by April 1 to Office of Financial Assistance for fellowships, loans; to appropriate department chair for assistantships. Phone: (512) 245-2315. Use FAFSA. About 10% of students receive aid other than loans from University and outside sources. Aid available for part-time students.

DEGREE REQUIREMENTS. For M.A.: 30 semester hours minimum including thesis, at least 24 in residence; final oral/written exams. For M.A.T., M.Ed., M.M.: 36 semester hours minimum, at least 30 in residence; no thesis required. For M.Acc., M.B.A.: 30 semester hours minimum, but usually 36. For M.S.C.J., M.P.A.: 39 semester hours minimum. For M.A.G, M.S.H.P., M.S.I.S., M.S.T.: 39 semester hours minimum; up to 9 hours may be granted for work/life experience in M.S.I.S. program. For Ph.D.: 46 credit program beyond master's; qualifying exam; dissertation; oral defense.

FIELDS OF STUDY.
Accounting.
Agricultural Education.
Aquatic Biology.
Applied Sociology.
Biochemistry.
Biology.
Business Administration.
Chemistry.
Communication Disorders.
Computer Science.
Counseling and Guidance.
Creative Writing.
Criminal Justice.
Developmental and Adult Education.
Education—Adult, Professional, and Community Education.
Education—School Improvement.
Educational Administration.
Elementary Education. Includes bilingual/bicultural, early childhood education.
Family and Child Studies.
Geography. Includes land/area development and management, resource and environmental studies, cartography/geographic information systems, environmental geography.
Health and Physical Education.
Healthcare Administration.
Health Education.
Health Professions. Includes healthcare human resources.
Health Psychology.
Health Services Research.
History.
Industrial Technology.
Interdisciplinary Studies.
International Studies.
Legal Studies. Includes alternative dispute resolution, environmental law, legal administration.
Literature.
Management of Technical Education.
Mass Communication.
Mathematics.
Music.
Music Education.
Physical Education.
Physical Therapy.
Physics.
Political Science.
Professional Counseling.
Public Administration.
Reading Education.
Recreation and Leisure Services. Includes recreation management, therapeutic recreation.
School Psychology.
Secondary Education.
Social Work. Include administration/supervision practice, direct practice.
Sociology.
Software Engineering.
Spanish.
Special Education.
Speech Communication.
Technical Communication.
Theatre Arts.
Wildlife Ecology.

SOUTHWESTERN OKLAHOMA STATE UNIVERSITY
100 Campus Drive
Weatherford, Oklahoma 73096-3098
Web site: www.swosu.edu

Founded in 1903. Located 70 miles west of Oklahoma City. Coed. State control. Semester system. Library: 250,000 bound volumes, 1300 subscriptions.

Tuition: per credit hour, resident 3000–4000 level—$81.30; 5000 level—$99.60, non-resident 3000–4000 level—$191.75; 5000 level—$229.05. On-campus housing for 64 married students, 1547 single students. Average academic year housing costs: $2800 (including board) for single students; $2000 for married students. Contact the Director of Student Housing for both on- and off-campus housing information. Phone: (580)774-3024.

Graduate School

Graduate study since 1953. Enrollment: full-time 307, part-time 296. Faculty: full- and part-time 131. Degrees conferred: M.Ed., M.S.A.P., M.B.A., M.M.

ADMISSION REQUIREMENTS. Official transcripts, GRE/GMAT required in support of School's application. Letters of reference for some programs. TOEFL (minimum score 550) required for international applicants. Interview not required. Accepts transfer applicants (maximum transfer credits: 9 hours.). Graduates of unaccredited institutions not considered. Apply to Dean of the Graduate School; no specified closing date. Application fee $15. Phone: (580)774-3769; fax: (580)774-7101.

ADMISSION STANDARDS. Usual minimum average: 2.5 (A = 4). Applicants must meet minimum formula of undergraduate GPA plus GRE or GMAT score.

FINANCIAL AID. Fellowships, research assistantships, teaching assistantships, internships, tuition waivers, Federal W/S, loans. Approved for VA benefits. Apply to Director of Financial Aid by March 1. Phone: (580)774-3786; fax: (580)774-3795. Use FAFSA and institutional FAF. Aid available for part-time students.

DEGREE REQUIREMENTS. For M.Ed.: 32 semester hours. For M.B.A.: 33 semester hours. For M.S.A.P.: 36 semester hours. For M.M.: 32 semester hours; final comprehensive exam.

FIELDS OF STUDY.
Art.
Business Administration.
Community Counseling.
Early Childhood.
Educational Administration.
Elementary Education.
English.
Health, Physical Education, and Recreation.
Mathematics.
Music Education. Includes choral, instrumental, performance. M.M. only.
Natural Sciences.
School Counseling.
School Psychometry.
Secondary Education. Includes English, mathematics, natural sciences, social sciences, technology.
Social Sciences.
Special Education.
Technology.

SOUTHWESTERN UNIVERSITY SCHOOL OF LAW

675 South Westmoreland Avenue
Los Angeles, California 90005-3992
Web site: www.swlaw.edu

Established 1911. Located in downtown Los Angeles. ABA approved since 1970. AALS member. Private control. Semester system. Full-time, part-time study. Special facility: National Institute of Entertainment and Media Law. Special programs: Southwestern Conceptual Approach to Legal Education (SCALE, a two-year J.D. program), Part-Time Legal Education Alternative at Southwestern (PLEAS, a program designed for students with child care responsibilities); summer study in Entertainment Law; study abroad in Buenos Aires, Argentina, Vancouver, British Columbia, University of Guanajuato, Mexico; externships. Law library: 415,068 volumes, 4611 subscriptions; has LEXIS, NEXIS, WESTLAW, RLIN, LEGALTRAC, WILSONLINE.

Annual tuition: full-time $23,410, part-time $14,863. No on-campus housing available. Law students live off-campus. Contact Admissions Office for off-campus housing information. Off-campus housing and personal expenses: approximately $13,230.

Enrollment: first-year class full-time 253, part-time 89; total full- and part-time 826 (men 46%, women 54%) Faculty: full-time 38, part-time 14. Student to faculty ratio 16.2 to 1. Degree conferred: J.D.

ADMISSION REQUIREMENTS. LSDAS Law School report, bachelor's degree, transcripts, LSAT required in support of application. Interviews required for SCALE. Letters of recommendation and supplementary essay recommended. Accepts transfer applicants from ABA approved law schools. Apply to Office of Admissions by June 30. Application fee $50. Phone: (213)738-6717; fax: (213)383-1688.

ADMISSION STANDARDS. Selective. Mean LSAT: full-time 151, part-time 149; mean GPA: full-time 3.01, part-time 2.92

(A = 4). Gourman rating: 3.47. *U.S. News & World Report* ranking is in the fourth tier of all U.S. law schools. Accepts about 60% of total annual applicants.

FINANCIAL AID. Scholarships, public interest fellowship, tuition waiver, assistantships, Federal W/S, loans. Apply to Financial Aid Office by June 1. Use FAFSA (School code: G01295). About 15-20% of students receive aid other than loans from School or outside sources. Public-Interest Loan Forgiveness Program available.

DEGREE REQUIREMENTS. For J.D.: 87 semester credits in full- or part-time program; completion of two calendar years in SCALE program.

SPALDING UNIVERSITY

Louisville, Kentucky 40203-2188
Web site: www.spalding.edu

Founded 1814. Coed. Private control. Roman Catholic. Semester system. Library: 200,000 volumes, 800 subscriptions.

Tuition: per credit hour $400 (most master's), $470 (Ed.D.), $425 (master's in Psychology), $515 (Psy.D.). On-campus housing 20 single graduate students. Average academic year housing costs: $2300. Contact Director of Housing for both on- and off-campus housing information. Phone: (502)858-7139.

Graduate Study

Enrollment: full- and part-time 520. College faculty teaching graduate students: full-time 27, part-time 8. Degrees conferred: M.A., M.A.T., M.F.A., M.S.N., Specialist, Psy.D., Ed.D.

ADMISSION REQUIREMENTS. Official transcripts, GRE required in support of application. TOEFL required for international applicants. Accepts transfer applicants. Graduates of unaccredited institutions not considered. Apply to Graduate Admissions Office at least four weeks prior to registration. Psychology, Social Work, Ed.D. programs admit Fall only; Occupational Therapy admits Spring only. Application fee $30. Phone: (502)585-7105; fax: (502)585-7158.

ADMISSION STANDARDS. Selective. Usual minimum average: 3.0 (proposed major) (A = 4).

FINANCIAL AID. Scholarships, administrative/research assistantships, Federal W/S, loans. Approved for VA benefits. Apply to the Director of Student Financial Aid. Phone: (502)585-9911, ext. 200. Use FAFSA and institutional FAF.

DEGREE REQUIREMENTS. For M.A.: 30 semester hours minimum, at least 24 in residence; written comprehensive exam; research papers. For M.A.T., M.A.L.S.: 36 semester hours minimum. For M.S.N.: 39 semester hours minimum, written comprehensive exam; thesis. For M.F.A.: 60 semester hour program; special project. For Specialist: 30 semester hours beyond the master's. For Psy.D.: M.A. plus 69 semester hours; internship and dissertation; final oral exam. For Ed.D.: M.A. plus 60 semester hours; dissertation; final oral exam. Limit of eight years to complete doctorate.

FIELDS OF STUDY.
Clinical Psychology. Includes health psychology.
Creative Writing.
Early Childhood Education.
Education.
Elementary Education.
High School Education.
Leadership Education.
Learning Behavior Disorders.

Library Media Specialist Studies.
Media Librarianship.
Middle School Education.
Montessori Education.
Nursing. Includes adult nurse practitioner studies, family nurse practitioner, leadership in nursing and health care, pediatric nurse practitioner.
Occupational Therapy.
Pastoral Ministries. M.A.
Reading and Writing.
Religious Studies.
School Guidance.
School Principalship.
Social Work.
Writing. Includes creative writing, fiction, poetry, writing for children. M.F.A.

SPRINGFIELD COLLEGE

Springfield, Massachusetts 01109-3797
Web site: www.spfldcol.edu

Founded 1885. Located 85 miles W of Boston. Coed. Private control. Semester system. Library: 150,000 volumes, 850 subscriptions.

Tuition: per credit hour $518. On-campus housing for limited number of married, single-students. Average academic year housing costs (room only): $4815 for single students, $6940 for married students. Contact Housing Director for both on- and off-campus housing information. Phone: (413)748-3102. Day-care facilities available.

School of Graduate Studies

Graduate study since 1899. Enrollment: full-time 1048, part-time 290. College faculty: full-time 156, part-time 15. Degrees conferred: M.S., MED., M.P.E., M.S.W., C.A.S., D.P.E.

ADMISSION REQUIREMENTS. Transcripts, letter of recommendation required in support of application. GRE required for M.P.T. and doctoral applicants. TOEFL required for international applicants. Interview sometimes required. Apply to Office of Graduate Admissions, preferably by July 1 (Fall), November 1 (Spring); Occupational Therapy, Physical Therapy January 1 (Fall only), Social Work (March 15). Application fee $35. Phone: (413)748-3225; fax: (413)748-6394.

ADMISSION STANDARDS. Selective for most majors. Usual minimum average: 2.5 (A = 4).

FINANCIAL AID. Scholarships, teaching/research assistantships, fellowships, rehabilitation traineeships, residence hall directorships, internships, tuition waivers, Federal W/S, loans. Approved for VA benefits. Apply by March 1 to director of appropriate graduate program for fellowships, assistantships; to Financial Aid Office for all other programs. Phone: (413)748-3108. Use FAFSA, Financial Aid transcript. About 60% of full-time students receive aid other than loans from College and outside sources. No aid for part-time students.

DEGREE REQUIREMENTS. For master's: 32 semester hours minimum, at least 26 in residence; may include thesis with final oral/written exam. For C.A.S.: 32 semester hours minimum beyond the master's, at least 26 in residence. For D.P.E.: 90 semester hours minimum, at least 45 in residence and 30 in full-time attendance; preliminary exam; dissertation; final oral exam.

FIELDS OF STUDY.
Art Therapy.
Education. Includes early childhood, elementary, secondary, school adjustment, special education.

Healthcare Management.
Health Science. Includes applied exercise science, sports injury prevention and management.
Health Studies. Includes health promotion/wellness management.
Human Service.
Movement Science. Includes biomechanics, clinical exercise physiology, science and research, exercise physiology.
Occupational Therapy.
Physical Education. Interview for D.P.E. Includes adapted physical education, advanced-level coaching, athletic administration, community physical education, sports management, sports psychology, sports studies, supervisor/director studies, teaching and administration.
Physical Therapy.
Psychology. Includes athletic counseling, general counseling, industrial/organization psychology, marriage and family therapy, mental health counseling, school guidance, student personnel in higher education.
Recreation and Tourism Services. Includes outdoor recreational management, recreational management, therapeutic recreational management.
Rehabilitation Services. Includes alcohol rehabilitation/substance abuse, developmental disabilities, general counseling and casework, psychiatric rehabilitation/mental health counseling, special services, vocational evaluation/work adjustment.
Social Work.

STANFORD UNIVERSITY

Stanford, California 94305-9991
Web site: www.stanford.edu

Founded 1891. Graduate study since 1891. Located near Palo Alto, 30 miles SE of San Francisco. CGS and AAU member. Coed. Private control. Quarter system. Special facilities: Center for Chicano Studies, Hopkins Marine Station at Pacific Grove, California, Hoover Institution of War, Revolution, and Peace, Humanities Center, Institute for Energy Studies, Center for International Studies, Institute for Research on Women and Gender, Stanford Medical Center, Computation Center, Center for Materials Research, Stanford Linear Accelerator Center; special laboratories for study in high voltage, electronics, nuclear engineering, physics, biophysics, and microwaves. The University's NIH ranking is 14th among all U.S. institutions with 638 awards/grants worth $224,780,728. Library: 7,000,000 volumes, 44,000 subscriptions. Total University enrollment: 14,000.

Annual tuition: full-time $27,204, Engineering $29,004. On-campus housing for graduate students: 3000 men and women. Average academic year housing costs: $4543 single students, $12,369 married students. Contact the Housing Assignment Services for on-campus housing Phone: (650)725-2810 and Community Housing Service for off-campus housing Phone: (650)723-3906.

Graduate Study

Graduate study since 1891. Enrollment: full-time 6500. Faculty: full-time 1740. Degrees conferred: A.M., M.S., M.A.T., Engineer, M.F.A., Ed.S., D.M.A., Ed.D., Ph.D.

ADMISSION REQUIREMENTS. Two official copies of all transcripts, GRE, three letters of recommendation in duplicate, statement of purpose required in support of application. On-line application available. Interview not required. TOEFL required for international applicants. Accepts transfer applicants. Graduates of unaccredited institutions not considered. Apply to Office of Graduate Admissions by January 1 (Fall). Most programs admit Fall only. Application fee $80, $95 for international applicants. Phone: (650)723-4291; fax: (650)725-8371.

ADMISSION STANDARDS. Very competitive for most departments, competitive for the others.

FINANCIAL AID. Annual awards from institutional funds: scholarships, teaching fellowships, research fellowships, Federal W/S, loans. Most scholarships and fellowships have no teaching or research requirements. Apply to Financial Aid Office by December 15 for art, history, biological sciences, and biophysics. Apply by January 1 for schools of Education, Earth Science, Humanities and Science, Medicine (non-M.D.); and chemical, civil, and electrical engineering, and computer science. Apply by February 15 for all other engineering departments, for scholarships and fellowships; to appropriate department for assistantships. Phone: (650)723-3058 or (888)FAO-3773. Use FAFSA. Contact Financial Aid Office for loans. About 72% of students receive aid other than loans from University and outside sources.

DEGREE REQUIREMENTS. For M.A., M.S.: three quarters (36–45 units) minimum in residence, some departments require more; thesis/nonthesis option; written/oral exams in some departments; reading knowledge of one foreign language for some departments. For M.A.T.: three quarters (45 units) minimum in full-time residence; teaching credential. For Engineer: six quarters (71–90 units) minimum, at least three quarters in residence; thesis. For Ed.D.: nine quarters (108–135 units) minimum beyond the bachelor's degree, at least six quarters in residence and two quarters in consecutive full-time attendance; candidacy; dissertation, final oral exam. For D.M.A.: same as for Ed.D., except final project usually replaces dissertation. For Ph.D.: nine quarters (109–135 units) minimum beyond the bachelor's degree, at least six quarters in residence, full-time attendance requirement for most departments; preliminary/final written exams in most departments; candidacy; dissertation; final oral exams.

FIELDS OF STUDY.

SCHOOL OF EARTH SCIENCES:
Geological and Environmental Sciences. M.S., Ph.D.
Geophysics. M.S., Ph.D.
Petroleum Engineering. M.S., Ph.D., Engr.

SCHOOL OF EDUCATION:
Administration and Policy Analysis. Ph.D., Ed.D.
Anthropology of Education. Ph.D.
Art Education. Ph.D.
Child and Adolescent Development. Ph.D.
Counseling Psychology. Ph.D.
Curriculum and Teacher Education. Includes art, dance, English, literacy, mathematics, science, social studies.
Economics of Education. Ph.D.
Educational Linguistics. Ph.D.
Educational Psychology. Ph.D.
English Education. Ph.D.
Evaluation. A.M.
General Curriculum Studies. Ph.D.
Higher Education. Ph.D.
History of Education. Ph.D.
International Comparative Education. A.M., Ph.D.
International Educational Administration and Policy Analysis. A.M.
Learning, Design, and Technology. A.M.
Mathematics Education. Ph.D.
Philosophy of Education. Ph.D.
Policy Analysis. A.M.
Science Education. Ph.D.
Social Sciences in Education. Includes anthropology, economics, educational interdisciplinary studies, linguistics, history, philosophy, sociology of education. A.M.
Social Studies Education. Ph.D.
Sociology of Education. Ph.D.
Stanford Teacher Education Program (STEP). A.M.

Symbolic Systems in Education. Ph.D.
Teacher Education. Ph.D.

SCHOOL OF ENGINEERING:
Aeronautics and Astronautics. M.S., Ph.D., Engr.
Chemical Engineering. M.S., Ph.D., Engr.
Civil and Environmental Engineering. M.S., Ph.D., Engr.
Computer Science. M.S., Ph.D.
Electrical Engineering. M.S., Ph.D., Engr.
Management Science and Engineering. M.S., Ph.D.
Manufacturing Systems Engineering. M.S.
Materials Science and Engineering. M.S., Ph.D., Engr.
Mechanical Engineering. M.S., Ph.D., Engr.
Scientific Computing and Computational Mathematics. M.S., Ph.D.

SCHOOL OF HUMANITIES AND SCIENCES:
Anthropological Sciences. A.M., M.S., Ph.D.
Applied Physics. M.S., Ph.D.
Art History. Ph.D.
Art Studio. M.F.A.
Asian Languages. A.M., Ph.D.
Biological Sciences. M.S.
Chemistry. Ph.D.
Classics. A.M., Ph.D.
Communication. A.M., Ph.D.
Comparative Literature. Ph.D.
Cultural and Social Anthropology. A.M., Ph.D.
Drama. Ph.D.
East Asian Studies. A.M.
Economics. Ph.D.
English. A.M., Ph.D.
French. A.M., Ph.D.
German Studies. A.M., Ph.D.
History. A.M., Ph.D.
Humanities. A.M.
International Policy Studies. A.M.
Italian. A.M., Ph.D.
Latin American Studies. A.M.
Linguistics. A.M., Ph.D.
Mathematics. Includes financial mathematics. A.M., M.S., Ph.D.
Modern Thought and Literature. Ph.D.
Music. A.M., M.S., Ph.D.
Philosophy. A.M., Ph.D.
Physics. Ph.D.
Political Science. Ph.D.
Psychology. Ph.D.
Religious Studies. A.M., Ph.D.
Russian and East European Studies. A.M.
Slavic Languages and Literature. A.M., Ph.D.
Sociology. Ph.D.
Spanish and Portuguese. A.M., Ph.D.
Statistics. Ph.D.

Graduate School of Business
Web site: www.gsb.stanford.edu

Established 1925. Private control. Accredited programs: M.B.A.; recognized Ph.D. Special facilities: Center for Entrepreneurial Studies, Center for Social Innovation, Global Organization of Business Enterprise, Global Supply Chain Management Forum, Process of Change Laboratory, Stanford Project on Emerging Companies, Rosenberg Corporation Research Center. Special programs: Stanford Integrated Manufacturing Association, foreign exchange programs in Singapore and Hong Kong, Global Management Immersion Experience.

Annual tuition: full-time $33,000. On-campus rooms and apartments available for both single and married students. Enrollment: M.B.A. full-time 730, part-time 15 (men 70%, women 30%); Ph.D. full-time 105 (men 60%, women 40%). Faculty: 120 full- and part-time; all have Ph.D./D.B.A. Degrees conferred: M.B.A., M.S.M. (Stanford Sloan Program—nine-month program for midcareer managers with at least eight years experience), M.B.A.-J.D., M.B.A.-M.S.E. (Engineering), Ph.D.

ADMISSION REQUIREMENTS. All applicants should have a bachelor's degree from a recognized institution of higher education and a strong mathematics background. Students are required to have their own personal computer. Accepts MBA Multi-App electronic application in lieu of institutional application. Early applications are encouraged for both admission and financial aid consideration. Beginning students are admitted Fall only. U.S. citizens and international applicants apply by October 31, for first decision period, by January 8 for second round, and by March 19 for final round. Submit an application, GMAT results, (will accept GMAT test results from the last five years; latest acceptable date is March), official transcripts from each undergraduate/graduate school attended, three letters of reference/ evaluations, two essays, résumé (prefers at least four years of work experience), and an application fee of $180 to the Director of Admission. In addition, international students (whose native language is other than English) should submit a TOEFL score (TWE recommended), certified translations and evaluations of all official transcripts, recommendation should be in English or with certified translations, proof of health/immunization certificate, and proof of sufficient financial resources for two years of academic study. On-campus visits are encouraged. Joint degree applicants must apply to and be accepted to both schools. Contact the admissions office for current information and specific admissions requirements. Rolling admissions process; notification is made within six weeks of receipt of completed application and supporting documents.

ADMISSION REQUIREMENTS FOR DOCTORAL CANDIDATES. Contact Doctoral Programs, Graduate School of Business, at (650)723-2831 for application material and information. Applications and instructions available at www.gsb.stanford.edu/ phd. Beginning students are admitted Fall Only. U.S. citizens and international applicants apply by January 1 (for most years) Submit an application, GMAT, GRE for Organizational Behavior (will accept GMAT/GRE test results from the last five years), official transcripts from each undergraduate/graduate schools attended, three letters of recommendation, résumé, statement of purpose, a confidential Financial Statement, and application fee of $125 to the Office of Graduate Admission. In addition, international students (whose native language is other than English) should submit certified translations and evaluations of all official transcripts (transcripts should show at least 16 years of full-time academic work commencing with elementary school), recommendation should be in English or with certified translations, proof of health/immunization certificate; TOEFL is not required. International students' contact: (650)723-2831. Interviews are not required or encouraged. Notification is made on or about April 1.

ADMISSION STANDARDS. Very competitive. Mean GMAT: 718; mean GPA: 3.58 (A = 4). Gourman rating: MBA 4.92; Ph.D. 4.92. *U.S. News & World Report* ranking is in the top 2 of all U.S. business schools. *Business Week* listed GSB in the top 10 American business schools. Accepts approximately 10% of total annual applicants.

FINANCIAL AID. Scholarships, Partnership for Diversity Fellowship Program, State Grants, fellowships, graduate assistantships, Federal Perkins Loans, Stafford Subsidized and Unsubsidized Loans, Federal W/S available; the Graduate School of Business has a Loan Forgiveness Program. Financial aid is available for international students in the form of fellowships. Assistantships/fellowships may be available for joint degree candidates. Financial aid applications and information are generally included with the application materials; apply by March 1. Request both fellowship and current need-based financial aid information from the Graduate School of Business. Phone:

(650)723-3282. Use FAFSA (School code: G22249), also submit Financial Aid Transcript, Federal Income Tax forms. Approximately 65% of students receive some form of financial assistance. For Ph.D.: fellowships typically cover full tuition and 85% of students' living expenses.

DEGREE REQUIREMENTS. For M.B.A.: 102 quarter hour program including 62 elective credits, two-year program. For M.S.M.: 52 quarter hour program. For Ph.D.: four- to five-year program; annual faculty evaluations; research assistantship; field exam; University oral exam; advancement to candidacy; dissertation; oral defense.

FIELDS OF STUDY.

M.B.A. FIELDS:
Entrepreneurship.
Global Management.
Health Care Management.
Human Resource Management.
Public Management.
Special Interest.

PH.D. FIELDS:
Accounting.
Economic Analysis and Policy.
Finance.
Marketing.
Operations, Information, and Technology Management.
Organizational Behavior.
Political Economics.
Special Field.

Law School (94305-8610)
Web site: www.stanford.edu

Established 1893. Located on main campus. ABA approved since 1923. AALS member. Semester system. Full-time, day study only. Special facilities: John M. Olin Program in Law and Economics, Stanford Center in Conflict and Negotiation, Stanford Law and Technology Policy Center. Special program: Stanford Program in International Legal Studies (SPILS). Law library: 496,103 volumes, 7719 subscriptions; has LEXIS, NEXIS, WESTLAW; is a Federal Government Depository.

Annual tuition: $27,926. On-campus housing available for both single and married students. Law students tend to live off-campus. Off-campus housing and personal expenses: approximately $13,404.

Enrollment: first-year class 178; total full-time 545 (men 54%, women 46%); no part-time students. Faculty: full-time 34, part-time 29. Student to faculty ratio 13.4 to 1.

Degrees conferred: J.D., J.D.-M.B.A., J.D.,-M.A. (Economics, History, Political Science), J.D.-M.I.P.S., J.D.-M.P.A. (Woodrow Wilson School of Public and International Affairs, Princeton University), J.D.-M.A. (Johns Hopkins School of Advanced International Studies), J.S.M. (for persons who have received a university degree in law in another country or have an advanced degree in law from outside the U.S. and will be returning overseas upon completion of degree; emphasis is on international issues), M.L.S. (a nonprofessional degree for those who do not have a law degree but are pursuing a doctoral degree, have earned another advanced degree, or posses exceptional relevant experience), J.S.D.

ADMISSION REQUIREMENTS. LSDAS Law School report, bachelor's degree, transcripts, two recommendations, LSAT required in support of application. Interview not required. Accepts transfer applicants. Graduates of unaccredited colleges not considered. Apply to Director of Admissions and Financial Aid by February 1. Earlier filing strongly advised. Admits Fall only. Application fee $65. Phone: (650)723-4985.

ADMISSIONS REQUIREMENTS FOR J.S.D. APPLICANTS. A J.D. from an approved ABA/AALS Law School or equivalent degree required for consideration. Official transcripts, two or three letters of recommendation, résumé or other evidence of significant professional accomplishment, personal statement, proposed dissertation research project required in support of Graduate application. Admits Fall only. Apply by April 1 to the Office of Graduate programs. Phone: (650)723-4985.

ADMISSION REQUIREMENTS FOR J.S.M., M.L.S. APPLICANTS. Certified translations and evaluation of all foreign credentials, résumé, personal statement, at least two recommendations, copies of research or published works are required in support of Graduate application. Admits Fall only. Apply by April 1 to Stanford Program in International Legal Studies. Phone: (650)723-4985; fax: (650)725-0253. Selection of SPILS fellows announced by June 1.

ADMISSION STANDARDS. Very competitive. Mean LSAT: 168; mean GPA: 3.81 (A = 4). Gourman rating: 4.88. *U.S. News & World Report* ranking is in the top two of all U.S. law schools. Accepts 7–10% of total annual applicants.

FINANCIAL AID. Scholarships, public service fellowships, Federal W/S, loans. Apply by March 15 (scholarships, no closing date for loans) to Director of Admissions and Financial Aid. Use FAFSA. About 73% of students receive aid from School. Miles and Nancy Rubin Loan Forgiveness Program (for graduates who take low-paying public-interest jobs).

DEGREE REQUIREMENTS. For J.D.: 86 (27 required) credits with a GPA of at least 2.0 (A = 4), plus completion of upper-divisional writing course, one course in legal ethics, one interdisciplinary course examining the American Legal System or examining a foreign or international legal system; three-year program. Accelerated J.D. with summer course work. For J.D.-M.B.A.: four-year program rather than five-year program if both degrees are taken consecutively. For J.D.-Master's: individually designed program, four- to four-and-one-half-year program rather than a five- to five-and-one-half-year program if both degrees are taken consecutively. For J.S.M.: one core seminar, three to five advanced courses or seminars, a multidisciplinary research workshop; written research project. For M.L.S.: 30 credits, must be completed within two consecutive academic years; one writing seminar or directed research project resulting in a written paper. For J.S.D.: at least one year in full-time residence; dissertation of publishable quality, oral defense.

School of Medicine (94305-5404)
Web site: www.med.stanford.edu

Incorporated 1908. Medical library 200,000 volumes. Annual tuition: $25,350 (3-quarter academic year).
Enrollment: first-year class 86 (EDP 2), total 456 (men 58%, women 42%). Faculty: full-time 514, part-time and volunteer 1200. Degrees conferred: M.D., M.D.-Ph.D. (Medical Scientist Training Program).

ADMISSION REQUIREMENTS. AMCAS report, transcripts, recommendations, MCAT, interview required in support of application. Applicants must have completed at least three years of college. Has EDP; apply between June 1 and August 1. Will consider transfer applicants. Apply to Director of Admission after June 1, before November 1. Graduate program: transcripts, GRE required in support of a supplementary application. Apply by February 1 to chair of appropriate department. Application fee $75. Phone: (650)725-6861; fax: (650)725-7855.

ADMISSION STANDARDS. For M.D.: very competitive. Mean MCAT: 10.9; mean GPA: 3.68 (A = 4). Gourman rating: 4.85. *U.S. News & World Report* ranking is in the top 11 of all U.S.

medical schools. Accepts 2–4% of total annual applicants. Approximately 55% are state residents.

FINANCIAL AID. Scholarships, research fellowships, teaching/research assistantships, loans. MSTP funded by NIH. Apply to Office of Student Financial Services after admission, as soon as possible after January 1. Phone: (650)724-3181. Use FAFSA (School code: G24552). About 70% of students receive some aid from the School.

DEGREE REQUIREMENTS. For M.D.: satisfactory completion of thirteen quarters of academic work and passing USMLE Step 2. For Ph.D.: nine quarters minimum beyond the bachelor's, some departments require reading knowledge of one or more languages; preliminary written exam; dissertation; final oral exam.

FIELDS OF GRADUATE STUDY.
Biochemistry. Ph.D.
Biological Sciences. Ph.D.
Biomedical Informatics. M.S., Ph.D.
Biophysics. Ph.D.
Cancer Biology. Ph.D.
Developmental Biology. Ph.D.
Epidemiology. M.S., Ph.D.
Genetics. Ph.D.
Health Services Research. M.S.
Immunology. Ph.D.
Microbiology and Immunology. Ph.D.
Molecular and Cellular Physiology. Ph.D.
Neurosciences. Ph.D.
Structural Biology. Ph.D.

THE COLLEGE OF STATEN ISLAND OF THE CITY UNIVERSITY OF NEW YORK
Staten Island, New York 10301
Web site: www.csi.cuny.edu

Founded 1976. Coed. Municipal control. Semester system. Special facilities: Center for Developmental Neurosciences and Developmental Disabilities, Center for Environmental Science, Center for Immigrant and Population Studies. Library: 203,368 volumes, 3000 subscriptions.
Tuition: per credit, city resident $185, nonresident $320. No on-campus housing. Day-care facilities available.

Division of Graduate Studies

Enrollment: full-time 104, part-time 1265. Faculty: full-time 79, part-time 10. Degrees conferred: M.A., M.S., M.S. in Ed., Advanced Certificate.

ADMISSION REQUIREMENTS. Transcripts, GRE (except teacher education), letters of recommendation required in support of divisional application. TOEFL required for international applicants. Accepts transfer applicants. Graduates of unaccredited institutions not considered. Apply to Office of Admissions well in advance of registration. Application fee $40. Phone: (718)982-2010; fax: (718)982-2500.

ADMISSION STANDARDS. Selective. Usual minimum average: 3.0 (A = 4).

FINANCIAL AID. Fellowships, research assistantships, teaching assistantships, internships, traineeships, tuition waivers, Federal W/S, loans. Approved for VA benefits. Apply to Director of Financial Aid; no specified closing date. Phone: (718)982-2030. Use University's FAF. Aid available for part-time students.

DEGREE REQUIREMENTS. For master's: 30 semester hours minimum, at least 24 in residence; thesis/final written exam.

FIELDS OF STUDY.
Adult Health Nursing.
Biology.
Cinema Studies.
Computer Science.
Educational Leadership. Includes elementary, secondary.
Elementary Education.
English.
Environmental Sciences.
History.
Liberal Studies.
Physical Therapy.
Secondary Education. Includes biology, chemistry, English, mathematics, physics, social studies.
Special Education.

STEPHEN F. AUSTIN STATE UNIVERSITY

Nacogdoches, Texas 75962
Web site: www.sfasu.edu

Founded 1921. Located 140 miles NE of Houston. Coed. State control. Semester system. Library: 850,000 volumes, 4000 subscriptions.

Annual tuition: per credit resident $40, nonresident $255. On-campus housing for 416 married students, 1661 men, 2343 women. Average annual housing cost: $4300 (including board). Contact Director of Housing. For both on- and off-campus housing information. Phone: (936)468-2601.

Graduate School

Graduate study since 1937. Enrollment: full-time 431, part-time 807 (men 40%, women 60%). Graduate faculty: full-time 289, part-time 75. Degrees conferred: M.A., M.B.A., M.Ed., M.F., M.F.A., D.F. (Forestry), M.I.S., M.M., M.P.A., M.S., M.S.F., M.S.W., Ph.D. in Forestry (cooperative with Texas A&M University).

ADMISSION REQUIREMENTS. Transcripts, GRE, GMAT (for M.B.A.) required in support of School's application. On-line application available. TOEFL, TWE required for international applicants. Interview not required. Accepts transfer applicants. Graduates of unaccredited institutions not considered. Apply to Graduate School by July 1 (Fall), November 1 (Spring). Application fee $25, $50 for international students. Phone: (936)468-2807; fax: (936)468-1251; e-mail: gschool@titan.sfasu.edu.

ADMISSION STANDARDS. Selective. Usual minimum average: 2.8 (A = 4).

FINANCIAL AID. Annual awards from institutional funds: scholarships, teaching assistantships, research assistantships, internships, Federal W/S, loans. Approved for VA benefits. Apply by March 1 to Director of Scholarships and Loans for scholarships, to head of major department for assistantships, to Financial Aid Office for all other programs. Phone: (936)468-2403. Use FAFSA. About 50% of students receive aid other than loans from College and outside sources. Aid available for part-time students.

DEGREE REQUIREMENTS. For master's: 30 semester hours minimum including thesis, or 36 semester hours minimum without thesis, at least 24 in residence; final oral/written comprehensive exams. For M.F.: 38 semester hour program; final oral, written or both comprehensive exam. For M.F.A.: 60 semester hour program beyond baccalaureate; written and oral compre-

hensive; thesis. For M.S.W.: 63 semester hour, two-year full-time or four-year part-time program. For Ph.D.: 66 semester hour program beyond the master's, at least two consecutive semesters in residence; foreign language competency; candidacy, qualifying exam; dissertation; final exam.

FIELDS OF STUDY.
Accounting.
Agriculture.
Art. Includes applied, design, fine arts.
Biology.
Biotechnology.
Business. GMAT required for admission. Includes general business, management. M.B.A. only.
Chemistry.
Communication. Includes speech communication, journalism, organizational, radio-television-film.
Computer Science.
Counseling.
Early Education.
Elementary Education.
Educational Leadership.
English.
Environmental Science.
Family and Consumer Sciences.
Forestry. Includes forest management, forest economics, forest ecology, forest entomology, recreation management, wildlife management, range management, silviculture, urban forestry, wood science. M.F., M.S.F., D.F.
Geology.
History.
Human Sciences.
Interdisciplinary Studies.
Kinesiology.
Mathematics. Includes teaching.
Music.
Natural Science.
Physical Education.
Physics. Thesis usually required.
Psychology. Thesis usually required for M.A.
Public Administration.
School Psychology.
Secondary Education.
Social Work.
Spatial Science.
Special Education.
Speech Pathology and Audiology.
Statistics.

STETSON UNIVERSITY

De Land, Florida 32720
Web site: www.stetson.edu

Founded 1883. Located 40 miles N of Orlando. Coed. Private control. Semester system. Library: 491,000 volumes, 149,000 microforms, 1400 current periodicals.

Tuition: per semester hour $430. Limited on-campus housing. Average academic year off-campus housing costs: $500 per month. Contact Dean of Students Office for both on- and off-campus housing information. Phone: (386)822-7000.

College of Arts and Sciences Graduate Programs

Graduate study since 1902. Enrollment: full-time 25, part-time 87. Faculty: full-time 10, part-time 5. Degrees conferred: M.A., M.S., M.A.T., M.Ed., Ed.S.

ADMISSION REQUIREMENTS. Official transcripts, three letters of references, GRE/MAT required in support of application.

On-line application available. Interview required for some departments. Accepts transfer applicants. Apply to Office of Graduate Studies by March 1 (Fall), November 1 (Spring). Application fee $25. Phone: (386)822-7075.

ADMISSION STANDARDS. Selective. Usual minimum average: 3.0 (A = 4).

FINANCIAL AID. Scholarships, internships, tuition waivers, Federal W/S, loans. Apply to the Financial Aid Office; no specified closing date. Phone: (386)822-7501. Use FAFSA.

DEGREE REQUIREMENTS. For master's: 30 semester hours minimum, at least 24 in residence; reading knowledge of one foreign language for some majors; thesis or final oral exam. For Ed.S.: 30 semester hours beyond master's.

FIELDS OF STUDY.
Career Teacher. Ed.S.
Counselor Education.
Education. Includes leadership, guidance, elementary education, learning disabilities, exceptional child.
Educational Leadership. Ed.S.
English.
Marital and Family Counseling/Therapy.
Mental Health Counseling.
School Counseling.

School of Business Administration Graduate Programs

Established 1885. Accredited programs: M.B.A., Accounting. Located on main campus, courses offered in St. Petersburg at College of Law. Semester system.

Tuition: $430 per credit. Enrollment: total full-time 38, part-time 132 (men 50%, women 50%). Faculty: 36 full- and part-time; 95% with Ph.D./D.B.A. Degrees conferred: M.B.A. (Concentrations in Finance), M.B.A.-J.D., M.Acc.

ADMISSION REQUIREMENTS. All applicants should have a bachelor's degree from a recognized institution of higher education, a strong mathematics background, and GPA of at least 2.5 (A = 4). Contact Director of Graduate Business at (904)822-7410 for application material and information. On-line application available. Early applications are encouraged for both admission and financial aid consideration. Beginning students are admitted Fall, Spring, and Summer. U.S. citizens apply by July 15 (Fall), December 15 (Spring), April 15 (Summer), International students apply by June 15 (Fall), November 15 (Spring), March 15 (Summer). Submit an application, GMAT results (will accept GMAT test results from the last five years, latest acceptable date is March), two official transcripts from each undergraduate/ graduate school attended, two letters of recommendation, personal statement, résumé (prefers at least two years of work experience), and an application fee of $25 to the Office of Admission. In addition, international students (whose native language is other than English) should submit a TOEFL (minimum score 550), certified translations and evaluations of all official transcripts, recommendation should be in English or with certified translations, proof of health/immunization certificate, and proof of sufficient financial resources for two years of academic study. On-campus visits and interviews are strongly recommended. Admissions Committee may consider applicants with some academic course work deficiencies. Joint degree applicants must apply to and be accepted to both schools; contact the admissions office for current information and specific admissions requirements.

ADMISSION STANDARDS. Selective. Usual minimum average 2.5 (A = 4). Mean GMAT: 540; mean GPA: 3.1 (A = 4).

FINANCIAL AID. Graduate assistantships, Federal Perkins Loans, Stafford Subsidized and Unsubsidized Loans, Federal W/S available. Financial aid is available for part-time study. Assistantships may be available for joint degree candidates. Financial Aid applications and information are generally available at the on-campus visit/interview; apply by March 15. Request assistantship information from the Director of Graduate Business Programs. Contact the University's Student Financial Planning Office for current need-based financial aid information. Phone: (904)822-7120. Use FAFSA (School code: 001531), also submit Financial Aid Transcript, Federal Income Tax forms. Approximately 20% of students receive some form of financial assistance.

DEGREE REQUIREMENTS. For M.B.A.: 30–59 credit program including 10 elective credits, one- to two-year program; degree program must be completed in eight years. For M.Acc.: 30–60 credit program. For M.B.A.-J.D.: four- to five-year program (both programs will accept 12 credits from the other degree program).

College of Law
Web site: www.law.stetson.edu

Founded 1900. Located in St. Petersburg (33707). ABA approved since 1930. AALS member since 1931. Semester system. Law Library: 366,251 volumes, 5583 subscriptions; has LEXIS, NEXIS, WESTLAW.

Annual tuition: $21,815. On-campus housing available. Apply to Director, Stetson Inn. Total average annual additional expense: $14,335. Housing Office phone: (727)562-7886.

Enrollment: first-year class 283; total full-time 671 (men 45%, women 55%); no part-time study. Faculty: full-time 30, part-time 37. Student to faculty ratio 18.5 to 1. Degrees conferred: J.D., J.D.-M.B.A., LL.M. (International Law and Business).

ADMISSION REQUIREMENTS. LSDAS Law School report, bachelor's degree, transcripts, letters of recommendation, LSAT required in support of application. Accepts transfer applicants. Graduates of unaccredited colleges not considered. Apply to Director of Admissions by February 15. Admits new students to Fall, Spring, Summer. Application fee $50. Phone: (727)562-7802.

ADMISSION STANDARDS. Selective. Mean LSAT: 151; mean GPA: 3.19 (A = 4). Gourman rating: 2.56. *U.S. News & World Report* ranking is in the third tier of all U.S. law schools. Accepts 45–50% of total annual applicants.

FINANCIAL AID. Scholarships, grants, research/teaching assistantships, Federal W/S, loans. Apply to Financial Aid Office by February 15. Phone: (727)562-7802. Use FAFSA (College code: E00342). About 16% of students receive aid other than loans from College.

DEGREE REQUIREMENTS. For J.D.: 88 semester hours minimum; advanced standing for work completed at other accredited law schools considered. For LL.M.: 24 credit program. For M.B.A.: see Graduate School of Business listing above.

STEVENS INSTITUTE OF TECHNOLOGY
Hoboken, New Jersey 07030
Web site: www.stevens-tech.edu

Founded 1870. Coed. Private control. Semester system. Special facilities: Automotive Research Laboratory, Davidson Laboratory for Fluids Research, Plastics Institute of America Laboratory, Laboratory of Psychological Studies, Computer Center, Energy Center, Polymer Processing Institute, Center for Surface Engineered Materials, Schacht Management Laboratory, Specialized Department Laboratories. Library: 135,000 volumes, 200 subscriptions. Total Institute enrollment: 4200.

Tuition: per credit $726; School of Technology $605. Average academic year housing costs: $9360 for married students; $3030–$5800 for single students. Contact Director of Residence Halls for both on- and off-campus housing information. Phone: (210)216-5128.

Graduate School

Enrollment: full-time 395, part-time 2175 (men 75%, women 35%). Faculty: full-time 102, part-time 80. Degrees conferred: M.E., M.Eng., M.S., Engineer (chemical, civil, computer, electrical, mechanical), Ph.D.

ADMISSION REQUIREMENTS. Two official transcripts, two letters of recommendation required in support of School's application. On-line application available. GRE/GMAT for management. TOEFL required for international applicants. Interview not required. Transfer applicants accepted. Graduates of unaccredited institutions not considered. Apply to Graduate School at least one month prior to beginning of semester, for international applicants at least two months prior to beginning of semester. Rolling admissions process. Application fee $50. Phone: (201)216-5234; fax: (201)216-8044.

ADMISSION STANDARDS. Selective. Usual minimum average: 2.5 (A = 4).

FINANCIAL AID. Annual awards from institutional funds: fellowships, teaching assistantships, research assistantships, graduate assistantships, internships, tuition waivers, Federal W/S, loans. Approved for VA benefits. Apply to individual department heads for assistantships, fellowships; to Financial Aid Office of all other programs. Use FAFSA. Phone: (201)216-5291. About 30% of full-time students receive aid from Institute.

DEGREE REQUIREMENTS. For master's: 30 credit hours minimum; thesis/nonthesis option. For Ph.D.: equivalent of three years of course work, at least one year in residence; reading knowledge of one foreign language for some departments; preliminary and/or comprehensive exam; dissertation; final oral exam.

FIELDS OF STUDY.

CHARLES V. SCHAEFER SCHOOL OF ENGINEERING:
Chemical Engineering. Includes polymer engineering. M.Eng., Ch.E., Ph.D.
Civil Engineering. Includes geotechnical/geoenvironmental engineering, structural engineering, water resources engineering. M.Eng., C.E., Ph.D.
Computer Engineering. Includes computer systems, data communications and networks, digital systems design, image processing and multimedia, software engineering. M.Eng., C.E., Ph.D.
Construction Management. M.S.
Electrical Engineering. Includes computer architecture and digital system design, microelectronics and photonics science and technology (interdisciplinary). M.Eng., E.E., Ph.D.
Engineering Management. M.Eng., Ph.D.
Environmental Engineering. Includes environmental process, groundwater and soil pollution control, inland and coastal environmental hydrodynamics. M.Eng., Ph.D.
Integrated Product Development. Includes armament engineering, electrical and computer engineering, manufacturing technologies, systems reliability and design. M.Eng.
Maritime Systems. Includes environmental engineering, management, marine transportation, structural engineering. M.S.
Materials Engineering. Includes microelectronics and photonics, science and technology (interdisciplinary). M.Eng., Ph.D.
Mechanical Engineering. Includes manufacturing systems, product design, thermal engineering. M.Eng., M.E., Ph.D.
Networked Information Systems. Includes data communication network, information networks, multimedia information systems, multimedia technologies, networked information systems, secure network systems. M.Eng.
Ocean Engineering. Includes coastal engineering, hydrodynamics, naval architecture, oceanography. M.Eng., Ph.D.
Systems Design and Operational Effectiveness. M.Eng.
Systems Engineering. M.Eng., Ph.D.

ARTHUR E. IMPERATORE SCHOOL OF SCIENCES AND ARTS:
Applied Mathematics. M.S.
Applied Optics. M.Eng.
Chemical Biology. Includes bioinformatics. M.S.
Chemistry. Includes analytical, chemical biology, organic, physical, polymer. M.S., Ph.D.
Computer Science. Includes cybersecurity, quantitative software engineering. M.S., Ph.D.
Engineering Physics. Includes microelectronics and photonics, science and technology (interdisciplinary). M.Eng.
Information Systems (Interdisciplinary). Includes computer science, e-commerce, quantitative software engineering. M.S.
Mathematics. M.S., Ph.D.
Physics. M.S., Ph.D.
Quantitative Software Engineering. M.S.
Stochastic System Analysis and Optimization. M.S.

WESLEY J. HOWE SCHOOL OF TECHNOLOGY MANAGEMENT:
Executive Master of Technology Management. E.M.T.M.
Information Systems. Includes computer science (interdisciplinary), e-commerce, entrepreneurial IT, financial services, global innovation management, human resource management, information management, information security, integrated information architecture (interdisciplinary), pharmaceuticals, project management, quantitative software engineering (interdisciplinary), systems engineering (interdisciplinary), telecommunications management. M.S.
Management. Includes general management, global innovation management, information management (M.S., Ph.D.), project management, technology management (M.S., Ph.D.). M.S.
Telecommunications Management. Includes business track, on-line security technology and business, global innovation management, project management, technical management track. M.S.

STONY BROOK UNIVERSITY, STATE UNIVERSITY OF NEW YORK

Stony Brook, New York 11794-4433
Web site: www.sunysb.edu

Founded 1957. Located 60 miles E of New York City on Long Island's north shore. CGS and AAU member. Coed. State control. Semester system. Special facilities: Humanities Institute, Institute for American Studies, Institute for Decision Sciences, Institute for Mathematical Science, Institute for Theoretical Physics, Nuclear Structure Laboratory, Marine Sciences Research Center, Institute for Pattern Recognition, Health Sciences Center. The University's NIH ranking is 75th among all U.S. institutions with 212 awards/grants worth $60,091,592. Library: 1,900,000 volumes, 14,000 subscriptions. Total campus enrollment: 20,000.

The Graduate School

Web site: www.grad.sunysb.edu

Annual tuition: full-time, resident $5100, nonresident $8416; per credit, resident $213, nonresident $351. On-campus housing available for married and single graduate students. Housing application mailed with acceptance to degree program. Monthly housing cost: $208–$1180 per month, including most utilities.

Enrollment: full-time 1629, part-time 984. Graduate faculty: full-time approximately 714, part-time approximately 59. Degrees conferred: M.A., M.M., M.F.A., M.P.S., M.S., D.M.A., D.A., Ph.D.

ADMISSION REQUIREMENTS. Two transcripts from all undergraduate and graduate programs (Certified English translations of all international transcripts), GRE, three letters of recommendation required in support of School's application. GRE Subject Test required for some programs. TOEFL or TSE required for international applicants. Apply by January 15 (Fall), October 1 (Spring). Application fee $50. Phone: (613)632-4723; fax: (613)632-7243.

ADMISSION STANDARDS. Competitive. Minimum GPA of 2.75 (A = 4), a GPA of 3.0 in the major or related courses. Very competitive programs require higher GPA. For international applicants: minimum TOEFL score 550 or TSE of 240.

FINANCIAL AID. Current awards from institutional funds: tuition scholarships, teaching and graduate assistantships, graduate research assistantships, state-supported fellowships, internships, tuition waivers, Federal W/S, loans. Approved for VA benefits. Apply to the Graduate Office for scholarships, fellowships, assistantships; to Financial Aid Office for all other programs. Use FAFSA and CSS Profile. About 134 students supported on stipends from outside sources. No aid for part-time students.

DEGREE REQUIREMENTS. For master's: 30 credits minimum with a 3.0 GPA, time limit of three years; reading knowledge of one foreign language for some programs; practicum in teaching; thesis/comprehensive exam/written exam varies by program. For doctoral degrees: at least three years in residence, a minimum of two semesters in full-time study, time limit of seven years after completion of the first 24 credits; GPA of 3.0; preliminary exam; reading knowledge of two foreign languages for some programs; advancement to candidacy; dissertation, dissertation defense; practicum in teaching; final oral/written examination varies by program.

FIELDS OF STUDY.
Anatomical Sciences. Ph.D.
Anthropology. Includes anthropological sciences. M.A.
Applied Mathematics and Statistics. M.S., Ph.D.
Art History and Criticism. M.A., Ph.D.
Art, Studio. M.F.A.
Biological Science. M.A.
Biomedical Engineering. M.S., Ph.D.
Biopsychology. Ph.D.
Cellular and Developmental Biology. Ph.D.
Chemistry. M.S., Ph.D.
Clinical Psychology. Ph.D.
Coastal Oceanography. Ph.D.
Computer Science. M.S., Ph.D.
Dramaturgy. M.F.A.
Earth and Space Science. Includes geosciences. M.S., Ph.D.
Ecology and Evolution. Ph.D.
Economics. M.A., Ph.D.
Electrical Engineering. M.S., Ph.D.
English. Includes comparative literature. M.A., Ph.D.
Experimental Psychology. Ph.D.
Foreign Language Instruction. Includes French, German, Italian, Russian, TESOL. D.A.
Genetics. Ph.D.
Germanic Languages and Literature. M.A.
Health Care Polilcy and Management. M.S.
Hispanic Languages and Literature. M.A., Ph.D.
History. M.A., Ph.D.
Human Resources Management. M.P.S.
Linguistics. M.A., Ph.D.
Management and Policy. M.S.
Marine Environmental Science. M.S.
Materials Science and Engineering. M.S., Ph.D.
Mathematics. M.A., Ph.D.
Mechanical Engineering. M.S., Ph.D.
Molecular Biology and Biochemistry. Ph.D.
Molecular and Cellular Biology. Ph.D.

Molecular and Cellular Pharmacology. Ph.D.
Molecular Microbiology. Ph.D.
Music. M.A., Ph.D.
Music Performance. M.M., D.M.A.
Neurobiology and Behavior. Ph.D.
Oral Biology and Pathology. Ph.D.
Philosophy. M.A., Ph.D.
Physics. Includes scientific instrumentation. M.A., M.S., Ph.D.
Physiology and Biophysics. Ph.D.
Political Science. M.A., Ph.D.
Psychology. M.A.
Public Affairs. M.P.S.
Romance Languages and Literature. Includes French, Italian. M.A.
Slavic Languages and Literature. M.A.
Social/Health Psychology. Ph.D.
Sociology. M.A., Ph.D.
Teaching of English to Speakers of Other Languages (TESOL). M.A.
Technological Systems Management. M.S.
Technology Management. M.S.
Theater. M.A., Ph.D.

School of Dental Medicine

Graduate study since 1973. Annual tuition: resident $10,840, nonresident $21,940. On-campus housing available. Average academic year housing cost: $13,417. Total average cost for all other first-year expenses: $3890.

Enrollment: first-year class 40, total 163 (men 48%, women 52%); postgraduates 14. Faculty: full-time 31, part-time 40. Degree conferred: D.D.S., M.S., Ph.D.

ADMISSION REQUIREMENTS. AADSAS, transcripts, DAT (no later than October), three letters of recommendation from science faculty, personal interviews required in support of application. Applicants must have completed at least three years of college work. Preference given to state residents. Accepts transfer applicants from U.S. and Canadian dental schools. Graduates of unaccredited institutions not considered. Apply through AADSAS after July 1, before January 15. Application fee $75. Phone: (631)632-8980.

ADMISSION STANDARDS. Competitive. Mean DAT: Academic. 19.68, PAT 17.93; mean GPA 3.53 (A = 4). Gourman rating: 4.36. Accepts about 15–20% of total annual applicants; 99% are state residents.

FINANCIAL AID. Full and partial scholarships, Federal W/S, loans. Apply to Financial Aid Office after acceptance. Phone: (631)632-3027. Use FAFSA. About 92% of students receive aid from School and outside sources.

DEGREE REQUIREMENTS. For D.D.S.: satisfactory completion of forty-three-month program. For M.S., Ph.D.: see Graduate School listing.

FIELDS OF GRADUATE STUDY.
Dental Care for the Developmentally Disabled. Postdoctoral program.
Endodentics. Postdoctoral program.
General Dentistry. Postdoctoral program.
Oral Biology and Pathology. M.S., Ph.D.
Orthodontics. Advance certificate, postdoctoral program.
Periodontics. Advance certificate, postdoctoral program.

Harrison School for Management and Policy

Graduate study since 1974. Annual tuition: resident $5100, nonresident $8416.

Enrollment: full-time 39, part-time 91; Advanced Certificate part-time 11. Faculty: full-time 45, part-time 2. Degree Conferred: M.S., Advance Certificate.

ADMISSION REQUIREMENTS. Transcripts, GRE or other relevant admission exam, three letters of reference, essay, registration, certification or licensure; at least one year of full-time practice in the professional field required in support of School's application. TOEFL required for international applicants. Accept transfer applicants. Apply to the Office of Student Services by March 1. Application fee $50. Phone: (631)444-3240; fax: (631)444-7621.

ADMISSIONS STANDARDS. Selective. Usual minimum average: 3.0 (A = 4).

FINANCIAL AID. Internships, Federal W/S, loans. Apply by March 15 to the Financial Aid Office with admissions application. Use FAFSA.

DEGREE REQUIREMENTS. For master's: 60 credits minimum with 3.0 GPA; core and track requirement; practicum; thesis. Must maintain minimum 3.0 GPA. For Advanced Certificate: 18 credits minimum with 3.0 GPA; a health care management focus; two generic management courses.

FIELDS OF STUDY.
Health Care Management. Advance Certificate.
Health Care Policy and Management. M.S.
Management and Policy. M.S.

School of Medicine (11794-8434)
Health Science Center
Web site: www.hsc.sunysb.edu/som

Established 1971. Located at Health Science Center. Semester system. Library: 238,000 volumes, 4400 subscriptions. Affiliated hospitals: University Hospital, Nassau County Medical Center, Northport VA Hospital, Winthrop University Hospital. Special programs: M.S.T.P. combines research training at the School of Medicine with research at Cold Spring Harbor Laboratory and Brookhaven National Laboratory.

Annual tuition: resident $12,840, nonresident $24,940. On-campus rooms and apartments available for both single and married students. Total average cost for all other expenses: $13,000. Contact Student Affairs Office for both on- and off-campus housing information. Phone: (631)632-6750. Medical students tend to live off-campus. Off-campus living expenses: approximately $15,900.

Enrollment: first-year class 100 (EDP 5; M.S.T.P. 5–6 each year); total full-time 481 (men 55%, women 45%). Faculty: full-time 500, part-time/volunteers 1600. Degree conferred: M.D., M.D.-Ph.D., M.S.T.P.

ADMISSION REQUIREMENTS. AMCAS report, transcript, MCAT, letter of evaluation, recommendations required in support of application. Interview by invitation only. Has EDP; apply between June 1 and August 1. Apply to Committee on Admissions after June 1, before November 15. Application fee $75. Phone: (631)444-2113; fax: (631)444-2202.

ADMISSION STANDARDS. Competitive. Mean MCAT: 10, mean GPA: 3.55 (A = 4). Gourman rating: 4.15. Admits about 5–8% of total annual applicants. Approximately 92% are state residents.

FINANCIAL AID. Scholarships, fellowships, assistantships, internships, grants, Federal W/S, loans. Apply after acceptance to Office of Student Affairs. Use FAFSA (School code: 002838). About 25% of students receive some aid from school.

DEGREE REQUIREMENTS. For M.D.: satisfactory completion of four-year program. For M.D.-Ph.D.: satisfactory completion of six to eight-year program. For Ph.D.: see Graduate School listing above.

FIELDS OF GRADUATE STUDY.
Anatomy.
Biochemistry.
Biomedical Engineering.
Biophysics.
Cell Structure.
Cellular Immunology.
Computer Graphics and Molecular Modeling.
Developmental Biology and Genetics.
Epidemiology.
Endocrinology.
Genetic Toxicology.
Membrane Biology and Biophysics.
Molecular Biology and Molecular Genetics.
Molecular Virology.
Neuropharmacology.
Pharmacology.
Physiology.
Tumorigenesis.
Structure and Physical Biochemistry.
Vertebrate Morphology.
Virology.

School of Nursing

Graduate study since 1970. Annual tuition: resident $5100, nonresident $8416; per credit $213 resident, nonresident $351.

Enrollment: full-time and part-time 529. Faculty: full-time 25, part-time 27. Degrees conferred: M.P.S., M.S., B.S./M.S., Post Master's Advance Certificate.

ADMISSION REQUIREMENTS. Transcripts, three letters of reference, personal statement, registered professional nurse licensure within one year of admission, CPR certification, B.S. with major in nursing required in support of School's application. Midwives' M.S. completion program applicants must be ACC certified. Neonatal M.S. applicants must have at least two years of full-time nursing experience in the neonatal intensive care setting. Non-nursing bachelor's degree applicants must pass Regents College Examination in Health Restoration I and II, and Health Support I and II within one year of admission. Accepts transfer applicants. Graduates of unaccredited institutions not considered. Apply to Admissions Office by May 1. Application fee $50. Phone: (631)444-3262; fax: (631)444-3136.

ADMISSIONS STANDARDS. Selective. Usual minimum average: 3.0 (A = 4).

FINANCIAL AID. Partial tuition scholarships for full-time study, fellowships, assistantships, internships, Federal W/S, loans. Apply at time of Admissions. Use FAFSA.

DEGREE REQUIREMENTS. For master's: 45 credits in required core courses in clinical specialty; minimum 3.0 GPA. Certificates of Advanced Standing: 18–24 credits in required courses and clinicals; minimum 3.0 GPA.

FIELDS OF STUDY.
Adult Health Nursing.
Family Nurse Practitioner.
Neonatal Nurse Practitioner.
Nurse Midwifery.
Pediatric Nurse Practitioner.
Perinatal/Women's Health.
Psychiatric/Mental Health Nurse Practitioner.

The School of Professional Development and Continuing Studies

Annual tuition: full-time resident $5100, nonresident $8416; per credit resident $213, nonresident $351.

Enrollment: full-time 200, part-time 1117. Faculty: full-time 25, part-time 101. Degrees conferred: M.A., M.A.T., M.P.S., Advance Certificate.

ADMISSION REQUIREMENTS. Transcripts, essay, three letters of recommendation required in support of School's application. GRE and undergraduate major in related field is required for the MAT candidates. TOEFL required for international applicants. Accepts transfer applicants. Apply to Director of Admissions and Advisement by May 1. Application fee $50. Phone: (631)632-7050; fax: (631)632-9046.

ADMISSION STANDARDS. Selective. Usual minimum average: 2.75 (A = 4). TOEFL score of 550 for international applicants.

FINANCIAL AID. Assistantshps, internships, Federal W/S, loans. Apply to the Financial Aid Office with admissions application. Use FAFSA. Aid available for part-time students.

DEGREE REQUIREMENTS. For master's: 30–36 credits minimum with a 3.0 GPA; time limit five years. For certificates: 18–24 credits with a 3.0 GPA; time limit five years.

FIELDS OF STUDY.
Biology 7–12. M.A.T.
Chemistry 7–12. M.A.T.
Coaching. Advance Certificate.
Earth Science 7–12. M.A.T.
Educational Computing. Advance Certificate.
English 7–12. M.A.T.
Environmental and Occupational Health and Safety. Advance Certificate.
French 7–12. M.A.T.
German 7–12. M.A.T.
Human Resource Management. M.P.S.
Italian 7–12. M.A.T.
Liberal Arts. M.A.
Long Island Regional Studies. Advance Certificate.
Physics 7–12. M.A.T.
Russian 7–12. M.A.T.
School Administrator and Supervisor. Advance Certificate.
School District Administration. Advance Certificate.
Social Science and the Professions/Labor Management Studies. M.P.S.
Social Science and the Professions/Public Affairs. M.P.S.
Social Science and the Professions/Waste Management. M.P.S.
Social Studies 7–12. M.A.T.
Waste Management. M.P.S., Advance Certificate.

School of Social Welfare

Graduate study since 1971. Semester system. Annual tuition: resident $5100, nonresident $8416; per credit resident $213, nonresident $351.

Enrollment: full-time 325, part-time 25. Faculty: full-time 16, part-time 18. Degree conferred: M.S.W.

ADMISSION REQUIREMENTS. Transcript, three letters of reference, essays, evidence of commitment to profession and social concern required in support of School's application. Accepts transfer students. Apply to Office of Admissions by March 1. Phone: (631)444-3141; fax: (631)444-7565. Application fee $50.

ADMISSION STANDARDS. Selective. Usual minimum average: 2.5 (A = 4).

FINANCIAL AID. Fellowships, assistantships, internships, Federal W/S, loans. Apply by March 15 to the Office of Financial Aid. Use FAFSA.

DEGREE REQUIREMENTS. For M.S.W.: 64 credits minimum, 16 in field instruction; master's project; 3.0 GPA.

SUFFOLK UNIVERSITY
Boston, Massachusetts 02108
Web site: www.suffolk.edu

Founded 1906. Located on historic Beacon Hill. Coed. Private control. Semester system. Library: 292,000 volumes, 6500 subscriptions.

Annual tuition: full-time $12,800 for M.A., M.S., M.Ed.; $14,900 for M.B.A.; $14,124 for M.P.A., M.H.A.; $16,500 for M.S.A., M.S.F., M.S.T.; $12,840 for M.S.P.S., M.S.I.E.; $17,000 for Ph.D. No on-campus housing for graduate students. Average academic year off-campus housing costs: $600 per month. Contact Dean of Students for off-campus housing information.

College of Arts and Sciences—Graduate Programs

Enrollment: full-time 160, part-time 1465. University faculty: full-time 247, part-time 1254. Degrees conferred: M.S., M.A., M.Ed., M.B.A., M.H.A., M.P.A., M.S.A., M.S.F., M.S.I.E., M.S.C.S., M.S.C.J., M.S.P.S., M.S.T., C.A.G.S., C.A.P.S., Ph.D., J.D.-M.B.A., J.D.-M.S.I.E., J.D.-M.P.A.

ADMISSION REQUIREMENTS. Official transcripts required in support of application. MAT or GRE, two letters of reference for M.A., M.S., M.S. in Ed., M.Ed., M.S.P.S., Ph.D. applicants. GMAT for M.B.A., M.S.F., M.S.A., M.S.T. applicants. GMAT or GRE for M.S.I.E. applicants. TOEFL required for international applicants. Accepts transfer applicants. Apply to Director of Graduate Admissions by June 15 (Fall), November 15 (Spring). Application fee $35. Phone: (617)573-8302; fax: (617)573-0116.

ADMISSION STANDARDS. Very selective. Usual minimum average: 2.7 (A = 4).

FINANCIAL AID. Annual awards from institutional funds: scholarships, fellowships, internships, assistantships, Federal W/S, loans. Approved for VA benefits. Apply by March 15 to Director of Financial Aid. Phone: (617)573-8470. Use FAFSA and University's FAF. About 10% of students receive aid other than loans from University and outside sources. Aid available for part-time study.

DEGREE REQUIREMENTS. For M.A., M.S.Ed., M.S.I.E., M.S.P.S., M.S.C.S., M.S.C.J.: 30–36 hours minimum, at least 24 in residence. For M.B.A.: 30–36 hours, except students without previous training may be required to complete up to 59 hours. For M.P.A.: 36 hours minimum, at least 30 in residence; For M.S.A., M.S.F., M.S.T.: 30 hours beyond M.B.A., 57–60 without master's. For Ph.D.: 60 hours minimum beyond master's degree, at least 45 hours in residence; reading knowledge of two foreign languages for some departments or one language and a research tool; qualifying exam; candidacy; dissertation; final oral exam.

FIELDS OF STUDY.
Administration of Higher Education. M.Ed.
Adult and Organizational Learning. M.S.
Clinical Psychology. Ph.D.
Communication. M.A.
Computer Science. M.S.C.S.
Criminal Justice. M.S.C.J.
Economics. Ph.D.
Economic Policy. M.S.E.P.
Foundations of Education. M.Ed.
Human Resources. M.S.
International Economics. M.S.I.E.
Mental Health Counseling. M.S.
Middle School Teaching. M.S.
School Counseling. M.Ed.
Secondary School Teaching. Usual subject fields. M.S.

Frank Sawyer School of Management

Web site: www.sawyer.suffolk.edu

Established 1937, expanded to include graduate study in 1948. Accredited programs: M.B.A., Accounting. Located on main campus; courses offered at Cape Cod Community College. Semester system. Special Programs: accelerated MBA program; foreign exchange programs (in Czech Republic, France, Ireland, Italy, Spain, United Kingdom); internships.

Tuition: per semester M.B.A., M.S.A., M.S.T. $10,730; M.S.F. $11,735; M.H.A., M.P.A. $8,915. E.M.B.A. tuition: per course $2,664. On-campus rooms and apartments available for both single and married students. Contact Graduate Housing Office for both on- and off-campus housing information. Phone: (617)573-8239.

Enrollment: total full-time 188, part-time 970 (men 55%, women 55%). Faculty: 39 full-time, 45 part-time; 95% with Ph.D./D.B.A. Degrees conferred: M.B.A. (full-time, part-time, day, late afternoons, evenings, and weekends); accelerated programs; M.B.A. for Attorneys, M.B.A. for CPAs, M.B.A. for Berklee College of Music Management majors; E.M.B.A. (weekends only), eM.B.A. (On-line M.B.A.), M.H.A. (Health Administration), M.P.A. (Public Administration), M.S.A. (Accounting), M.S.F. (Finance), M.S.F.S.B. (Financial Services and Banking), M.S.T. (Taxation), M.B.A.-J.D., M.B.A.-M.S.A., M.B.A.-M.S.T., M.B.A.-M.S.F., M.B.A.-M.P.A., M.P.A.-M.S. (Criminal Justice, Mental Health Counseling, Political Science), M.P.A.-J.D.

ADMISSION REQUIREMENTS. All applicants should have a bachelor's degree from a recognized institution of higher education, a strong mathematics background, and GPA 2.6 (A = 4). Contact either the Director of Graduate Admissions at (617) 573-8302, fax: (617)573-0116, or Director MBA Programs at (617)573-8306 for application material and information. On-line application available. Early applications are encouraged for both admission and financial aid consideration. Beginning students are admitted Fall, Spring, and Summer except for M.S.F. and E.M.B.A. (Fall and Spring only). Both U.S. citizens and international applicants apply by June 15 (Fall), November 15 (Spring), April 15 (Summer). Submit an application, GMAT results (will accept GMAT test results from the last five years, latest acceptable date is June), official transcripts from each undergraduate/graduate school attended, two letters of recommendation, a statement of personal goals, résumé (prefers at least four years of work experience), and an application fee of $50 to the Office of Graduate Admission. In addition, international students (whose native language is other than English) should submit a TOEFL (550 minimum score) report, certified translations and evaluations of all official transcripts, recommendation should be in English or with certified translations, proof of health/immunization certificate, and proof of sufficient financial resources for two years of academic study. On-campus visits are encouraged prior to the admissions reviewing completed application. Admissions Committee may consider applicants with some academic course work deficiencies. Joint degree applicants must apply to and be accepted to both schools; contact the admissions office for current information and specific admissions requirements. Rolling admissions process.

ADMISSION STANDARDS. Selective. Mean GMAT: 520, mean GPA: 2.9 (A = 4). Accepts approximately 65% of total annual applicants.

FINANCIAL AID. Scholarships, grants, fellowships, Federal Perkins Loans, Stafford Subsidized and Unsubsidized Loans, Federal W/S available. Financial aid is available for part-time study in the form of Graduate Management part-time Scholarship Grants. Merit-based financial aid available for international applicants. Fellowships may be available for joint degree candidates. Financial aid applications and information are generally included with the admissions materials. Apply by March 15 (Fall). Request merit-based aid, fellowship information from the School of Management. Phone: (617)573-8088. Contact the University's Financial Aid Office for current need-based financial aid information. Phone: (617)573-8470. Use FAFSA (School code: 00218), also submit institutional FAF, a Financial Aid Transcript, Federal Income Tax forms. Approximately 30% of students receive some form of financial assistance.

DEGREE REQUIREMENTS. For M.B.A.: 30–54 credit (19 courses) program including 24 elective credits, two-year program; degree program must be completed in five years. For E.M.B.A.: 54 credit program. For M.S.A., M.S.T.: 30–60 credit programs. For M.S.E.S.: 48 credit program. For M.S.F., M.S.F.S.B.: 30–48 credit programs. For M.B.A.-J.D.: 117 credit programs, four- to five-year program.

FIELDS OF STUDY.

Accounting.

Business Administration. Includes concentrations in accounting, business law, computer information systems, entrepreneurship, finance, financial economics, health management, human resource management, international business, management, marketing, nonprofit management, organizational behavior, public management, quantitative methods, strategic management.

Finance. Includes financial services and banking (M.S.F.S.B.).

Health Administration.

Public Administration. Includes disability studies, finance and human resources, health administration, nonprofit management, state and local government, philanthropy and media.

Taxation.

Law School

Web site: www.law.suffolk.edu

Established 1906. ABA approved since 1953. AALS member. Semester system. Law library: 319,239 volumes, 5931 subscriptions; has LEXIS, NEXIS, WESTLAW, DIALOG.

Annual tuition: day $23,350, evening $17,512. No on-campus housing available. Total average annual additional expense: $15,000.

Enrollment: first-year class 368 (day), 191 (evening); total full-time and part-time 1699 (men 50%, women 50%). Faculty: full-time 53, part-time 61. Student to faculty ratio 23.1 to 1. Degrees conferred: J.D., J.D.-M.B.A., J.D.-M.P.A., J.D.-M.S.F., J.D.-M.S.I.E.

ADMISSION REQUIREMENTS. LSDAS Law School report, bachelor's degree, transcript, LSAT (no later than February), personal statement, two letters of recommendation required in support of application. Interview not required. Accepts limited number of transfer applicants. Graduates of unaccredited institutions not considered. Apply to Director of Admissions by March 1. Application fee $50. Phone: (617)573-8144; fax: (617)523-1367.

ADMISSION STANDARDS. Selective. Mean LSAT: full-time 153, part-time 153; mean GPA: full-time 3.15, part-time 2.45 (A = 4). Gourman rating: 3.12 *U.S. News & World Report* ranking is in the fourth tier of all U.S. law schools. Accepts about 60% of total annual applicants.

FINANCIAL AID. Scholarships, fellowships, assistantships, Federal W/S, loans. Apply to Financial Aid Office by March 1. Use FAFSA (School code: E00517) and institutional FAF. About 38% of students receive University aid other than loans.

DEGREE REQUIREMENTS. For J.D.: 90 semester hours minimum, at least the last year in residence. For master's degrees: see Graduate School listing above.

Note: Summer program abroad in Lund, Sweden.

SUL ROSS STATE UNIVERSITY
Alpine, Texas 79832
Web site: www.sulross.edu

Founded 1917. Located 300 miles W of San Antonio. Coed. State control. Semester system. Library: 275,000 volumes, 1800 subscriptions. Total University enrollment: 2400.

Tuition: per credit resident $68, nonresident $286. On-campus housing for 155 married students, 320 men, 480 women. Average academic year housing costs: $305–$345 per month for married students, $1805–$2375 (room and board) or $850–$1350 (room only) for single students. Contact Housing Officer for both on- and off-campus housing information. Phone: (915)837-8190.

Graduate Division

Graduate study since 1930. Enrollment: full-time 229, part-time 751 (men 55%, women 45%). Graduate faculty: full-time 60, part-time 20. Degrees conferred: M.A., M.B.A., M.Ed., M.S.

ADMISSION REQUIREMENTS. Two official transcripts, GRE, GMAT required in support of application. On-line application available. TOEFL (minimum score 520), interview required for international applicants. Interview not required for domestic applicants. Accepts transfer applicants. Graduates of unaccredited institutions not considered. Apply to Office of Admissions and Record by July 15 (Fall), December 1 (Spring), May 1 (First Summer Session), June 25 (Second Summer Session). Application fee: none for domestic applicants, $50 for international applicants. Phone: (915)837-8052; fax: (915)837-8431.

ADMISSION STANDARDS. Relatively open. Usual minimum average: 2.5 (A = 4); minimum GRE: 850; minimum GMAT: 400.

FINANCIAL AID. Annual awards from institutional funds: twelve scholarships, ten research assistantships, twenty-four administrative assistantships, four internships, Federal W/S, loans. Approved for VA benefits. Apply by June 1 to Dean, Graduate Division. Use FAFSA. About 68% of students receive aid other than loans from University. Aid sometimes available for part-time students.

DEGREE REQUIREMENTS. For M.A., M.S.: 30 semester hours minimum, at least 18 in residence; thesis; comprehensive exam. For M.Ed.: 36 semester hours minimum, at least 24 in residence; thesis/nonthesis option; comprehensive exam. For M.B.A.: 56 semester hours minimum, at least 30 hours in residence; computer proficiency; thesis/nonthesis option; comprehensive exam.

FIELDS OF STUDY.
Accounting.
Animal Science.
Art. Includes applied, design, education, history.
Bilingual Education.
Biology.
Business Administration. Includes business, international trade, management.
Counseling.
Criminal Justice.
Educational Diagnostician.
Elementary Education.
English.
Geology.
History.
Industrial Arts Education.
Physical Education.
Political Science.
Psychology.
Public Administration.
Range and Wildlife Management.
Reading.
School Administration.
Secondary Education.
Supervision.

SYRACUSE UNIVERSITY
Syracuse, New York 13244-0003
Web site: www.syracuse.edu

Founded 1871. CGS and AAU member. Coed. Private control. Semester system. Special facilities: Center for Advanced Technology in Computer Application and Software Engineering, Science and Technology Center, Northeast Parallel Architectures Center, Center for Membrane Engineering and Science, Center for the Study of Citizenship, Institute for Energy Research, Institute for Sensory Research, Interdisciplinary Institute for Literacy, Advance Graphics Research Laboratory, Natural Sciences Computing Center, Centro de Estudios Hispanicos, Gerontology Center, Robert H. Brethen Operations Management Institute, Better Audio Laboratory and Archive, George Arents Research Library. Library: 2,500,000 volumes, 12,000 subscriptions.

Tuition: per credit $613. On-campus housing for both married and single graduate students. Average academic year housing costs: $5500 (room only) for single students, $10,000 (including board) for married students. Apply to Office of South Campus Housing for both on- and off-campus housing information. Phone: (315)443-2567.

Graduate School

Graduate study since 1876. Enrollment: full-time 2392, part-time 2022. Graduate faculty: full-time 830, part-time 565. Degrees conferred: M.Arch.I., M.Arch.II, M.A., M.S., Ph.D., D.A., Ed.D., C.A.S., E.E., C.E., M.L.S., M.B.A., M.P.A., M.S.C., M.P.S., M.S.W., M.F.A., M.I.D., M.Mus. Combined degree programs: J.D.-M.L.S., J.D.-M.B.A., J.D.-M.S., J.D.-Ph.D., J.D.-M.P.A.

ADMISSION REQUIREMENTS. Two official transcripts, three letters of recommendation, interview for some programs, GRE for most programs, GMAT for Management required in support of School's application. TOEFL required for international applicants. Accepts transfer applicants. Graduates of unaccredited institutions not considered. Apply to Graduate School prior to registration. Application fee $50. Phone: (315)443-4492; e-mail: grad@syr.edu.

ADMISSION STANDARDS. Very competitive for some departments, competitive or selective for the others. Usual minimum average: 3.0 (A = 4).

FINANCIAL AID. Scholarships, fellowships, teaching/research assistantships, internships, tuition waivers, Federal W/S, loans. Approved for VA benefits. Apply by January 10 for fellowships, March 1 for assistantships and scholarships to appropriate department; to Financial Aid Office for all other programs. Phone: (315)443-1513. Submit FAFSA by February 28. About 65% of students receive aid other than loans from University. Aid available for part-time students.

DEGREE REQUIREMENTS. For most master's: 30 semester hours minimum, at least 24 in residence; thesis/nonthesis option for some departments; comprehensive oral/written exam. For Ph.D., Ed.D.; D.A.: 48–90 credit hours, 50% of program in residence; one foreign language and other research tool requirement; qualifying exam; dissertation; final oral exam; recital for D.A.

FIELDS OF STUDY.

SCHOOL OF ARCHITECTURE:
Architecture.

COLLEGE OF ARTS AND SCIENCES:
Applied Statistics.
Art History.
Audiology.
Biology.
Chemistry.
Classics.
Clinical Psychology.
College Science Teaching.
Composition and Cultural Rhetoric.
Creative Writing.
English. Includes creative writing.
Experimental Psychology.
French Language, Literature, and Culture.
General Science.
Geology.
German Language, Literature, and Culture.
Greek Language.
Latin American.
Linguistic Studies.
Mathematics.
Philosophy.
Physics.
Religion.
Romance Languages.
School Psychology.
Science Teaching.
Social Psychology.
Spanish Language, Literature, and Culture.
Speech-Language Psychology.
Structural Biology, Biophysics, and Biochemistry.

SCHOOL OF EDUCATION:
Art Education.
Counselor Education.
Cultural Foundations of Education.
Educating Infants and Young Children with Special Needs.
Educational Leadership.
Elementary Education N–6.
English Education.
Exercise Science.
Higher Education.
Instructional Design, Development, and Evaluation.
Learning Disabilities.
Mathematics Education.
Music Education.
Reading.
Rehabilitation Counseling.
Science Education. Includes biology, chemistry, earth science, physics.
Social Studies Education.
Special Education. Includes educating infants and young children with special needs, learning disabilities, mental retardation.
Speech Education.
Teaching and Curriculum.

L. C. SMITH COLLEGE OF ENGINEERING AND COMPUTER SCIENCE:
Aerospace Engineering.
Chemical Engineering.
Civil Engineering.
Computer and Information Science.
Computer Engineering.
Computer Science.
Electrical Engineering.
Engineering Management.
Environmental Engineering.
Environmental Engineering Sciences.
Hydrogeology.
Manufacturing Engineering.
Mechanical and Aerospace Engineering.
Mechanical Systems.

Neuroscience.
Systems Assurance.
System and Information Science.

COLLEGE OF HUMAN SERVICES AND HEALTH PROFESSIONS:
Child and Family Studies.
Marriage and Family Therapy.
Nursing. Includes Nurse practitioner.
Nursing Informatics.
Primary Care Nursing. Includes adult health, family health, pediatrics.
Social Work.
Teaching Nursing.
Nutrition Science.

SCHOOL OF INFORMATION STUDIES:
Information and Library Science.
Information Management.
Information Transfer.
Library Media Specialist.
School Media Specialist.
Telecommunication and Network Management.

SCHOOL OF MANAGEMENT:
Accounting.
Business Administration.
Finance.
Global Entrepreneurship.
International Business.
Marketing Management.
Organization and Management.

THE MAXWELL SCHOOL:
Anthropology.
Economics.
Geography.
History.
International Relations.
Political Science.
Public Administration.
Social Science.
Sociology.

S. I. NEWHOUSE SCHOOL OF PUBLIC COMMUNICATION:
Advertising.
Broadcast Journalism.
Communications Management.
Film.
Magazine, Newspaper, and On-line Journalism.
Mass Communications.
Media Management.
Media Studies.
New Media.
Newspaper.
Photography.
Public Relations.
Television-Radio-Film.

COLLEGE OF VISUAL AND PERFORMING ARTS:
Advertising Design.
Art Photography.
Art Video.
Ceramics.
Computer Graphics.
Environmental Arts.
Fiber Structure and Interlocking.
Film.
Illustration.
Metalsmithing.
Museum Studies.
Music Composition.

Music Theory.
Organ.
Painting.
Percussion.
Piano.
Printmaking.
Sculpture.
Speech Communication.
Strings.
Voice.
Wind Instruments.

College of Law (13244-1030)
Web site: www.law.syr.edu

Established 1895. Located on main campus. ABA approved since 1923. AALS charter member. Semester system. Full-time, day study, limited part-time program. Special facilities: Business Law Center, Family Law and Social Policy Center, Center for Global Law and Practice, Center for Law and Business Enterprise, Center for Law, Technology, and Management. Special program: Law and Economics Program. Law library: 396,234 volumes, 3261 subscriptions; has LEXIS, NEXIS, WESTLAW, DIALOG.

Annual tuition: $24,959. On-campus housing available for both single and married students. Total average annual housing costs: $13,171. Contact Office of South Campus Housing. Phone: (345)443-2567. Off-campus housing and personal expenses: approximately $11,727.

Enrollment: first-year class 281; total full-time 777 (men 52%, women 48%). Faculty: full-time 39, part-time 18. Student to faculty ratio 16.6 to 1. Degrees conferred: J.D., J.D.-M.B.A., J.D.-M.P.A., J.D.-M.A. (Communications, Economics, History, International Relations, Media), J.D.-M.S. (Accounting, Environmental Science, Engineering, Political Science), J.D.-Ph.D.

ADMISSION REQUIREMENTS. LSDAS Law School report, bachelor's degree, transcripts, LSAT (no later than April 1) required in support of application. Interview not required. Accepts transfer applicants. Graduates of unaccredited institutions not considered. Apply to Director of Admissions after September 15, before April 1. Rolling admissions process. Fall admission only. Application fee $50. Phone: (315)443-1962; fax: (315)443-9568.

ADMISSION STANDARDS. Selective. Mean LSAT: 152; mean GPA: 3.32 (A = 4). Gourman rating: 3.03. *U.S. News & World Report* ranking is in the third tier of all U.S. law schools. Accepts 50% of total applicants.

FINANCIAL AID. Scholarships, grants, partial tuition waivers, fellowships, assistantships, Federal W/S, loans. Apply to Office of Admissions and Financial Aid by March 1. Use FAFSA (College code: 002882). Approximately 71% of students receive some aid from School.

DEGREE REQUIREMENTS. For J.D.: 87 (40 required) credits with a GPA of at least 2.0 (A = 4), plus completion of upper-divisional writing course; three-year program, four-year part-time program. Accelerated J.D. with summer course work. For J.D.-M.B.A., J.D.-M.S. Accounting: four-year program rather than five-year program if both degrees are taken consecutively. For J.D.-M.P.A.: three-year program rather than four-year program if both degrees are taken consecutively. For J.D.-M.A.: three-and-one-half-year program rather than four-and-one-half-year program if both degrees are taken consecutively. For J.D.-M.S.: three-year program rather than four-year program if both degrees are taken consecutively. J.D.-Ph. D.: six-year program rather than seven-year program if both degrees are taken consecutively.

TARLETON STATE UNIVERSITY
Stephenville, Texas 76402
Web site: www.tarleton.edu

Founded 1899. Located 65 miles SW of Fort Worth. Tarleton is a member of the Texas A&M University system. Coed. State control. Semester system. Library: 664,500 volumes, 2200 subscriptions.

Tuition: per credit hour, resident $84, nonresident $283. On-campus housing available. Average academic year housing costs: $4180 (including board) single students; $2200 (room only) married students. Contact Dean of Students for both on- and off-campus housing information. Phone: (254)968-9680.

College of Graduate Studies

Graduate study since 1971. Enrollment: full-time 270, part-time 807. Faculty: full-time 104, part-time 20. Degrees conferred: M.A., M.S., M.Ed., M.B.A., M.C.J.

ADMISSION REQUIREMENTS. Official transcripts, GRE/GMAT required in support of School's application. On-line application available. TOEFL required for international applicants. Accepts transfer applicants. Graduates of unaccredited colleges not considered. Apply to Dean by August 1 (Fall), December 1 (Spring). Application fee $25, $100 for international applicants. Phone: (254)968-9104; fax: (254)968-9670.

ADMISSION STANDARDS. Relatively open. Usual minimum average: 2.5 (A = 4).

FINANCIAL AID. Annual awards from institutional funds: scholarship, teaching assistantships, internships, tuition waivers, Federal W/S, loans. Approved for VA benefits. Apply by May 1 to Graduate Dean. Phone: (254)968-9070; fax: (254)968-9670. Use FAFSA and institutional FAF. Aid available for part-time students.

DEGREE REQUIREMENTS. For master's: 36-48 hours minimum; comprehensive exam; thesis/nonthesis; project for some programs.

FIELDS OF STUDY.
Agriculture. M.S.
Agriculture Education. M.S.
Biology. M.S.
Business Administration. M.B.A.
Counseling. M.Ed.
Counseling Psychology. M.S.
Criminal Justice. M.C.J.
Curriculum and Instruction. M.Ed.
Educational Administration. M.Ed.
Educational Psychology. M.S.
Elementary Administration. M.Ed.
Elementary Education. M.Ed.
English. M.A.
Environmental Science. M.S.
Government. M.A.
History. M.A.
Human Resource Management. M.S.
Information Systems. M.S.
Liberal Studies. M.S.
Management. M.S.
Mathematics. M.S.
Physical Education. M.Ed.
Political Science. M.A.
Reading. M.Ed.
Secondary Education. M.Ed.
Special Education. M.Ed.

TEMPLE UNIVERSITY
Philadelphia, Pennsylvania 19122-6096
Web site: www.temple.edu

Founded 1894. CGS member. Coed. State related. Semester system. Special facilities: Center for African American History and Culture, Center for Frontier Sciences, Center for Neurovirology and Cancer Biology, Center for Professional Development in Career and Technical, Center for Public Policy, Center for Social Policy and Community Development, Center for Student Professional Development, Center for Substance Abuse Research, Center for the Study of Federalism, Center for the Study of Force and Diplomacy, Institute on Aging, Institute on Disabilities, Institute for the Study of Literature, Literacy, and Culture, Institute for Survey Research. The University's NIH ranking is 101st among all U.S. institutions with 117 awards/grants worth $38,345,120. Libraries: 2,189,000 volumes, 16,700 subscriptions. Total University enrollment: 30,000.

Tuition: per semester hour, resident $402, nonresident $582; Nursing, Communication Sciences, Occupational and Physical Therapy resident $418, nonresident $607; Tyler School of Art resident $415, nonresident $607; M.B.A./M.S./E-Business resident $417, nonresident $616; Pharmacy resident $550, nonresident $725; per semester, International Master of Business resident and nonresident $10,904; E.M.B.A. resident and nonresident $23,500. On-campus housing available. Average academic year housing cost: $4938 for single students; $9876 for married students. Contact Office of Student Residences for both on- and off-campus housing information. Phone: (215)204-7223.

Graduate School

Enrollment: full-time 4974, part-time 3863. Faculty: full-time 1177, part-time 200. Degrees conferred: M.A., M.B.A., Ed.M. M.F.A., M.J., M.L.A., M.M., M.M.T., M.P.T., M.S., M.S.D., M.S.Ed., M.S.E., M.S.N., M.S.W., D.M.A., Ed.D., Ph.D.

ADMISSION REQUIREMENTS. Transcripts, letters of recommendation, statement of educational objectives required in support of School's application. GRE/Subject Tests/MAT/ GMAT, auditions, performances, portfolio, and/or interview required by some departments. TOEFL required of all international applicants. Accepts transfer applicants. Apply directly to Academic Department; closing dates vary by department, consult Bulletin. Application fee $40. Phone: (215)204-1380; fax: (215) 204-8781.

ADMISSION STANDARDS. Competitive or selective for most departments. Usual minimum average: 3.0 (A = 4).

FINANCIAL AID. Fellowships, research assistantships, teaching assistantships, administrative assistantships, graduate assistant, internships, tuition waivers, Federal W/S, loans. Approved of VA benefits. Apply by March 1 to appropriate department for scholarships, fellowships, teaching/research assistantships; to Director of Financial Aid for all other programs. Use FAFSA and institutional FAF. Phone: (215)204-1405; fax: (215)204-5897. Aid available for part-time students.

DEGREE REQUIREMENTS. For M.A., M.S.: 24 semester hours minimum; thesis for some departments; final oral/written exam usually required. For M.B.A.: 45–60 semester hours minimum, research paper; final oral/written exam. For M.S.E., M.Ed.: 30 semester hours minimum; final written exam; or 24 semester hours minimum; thesis. For M.F.A.: 48–52 semester hours minimum; thesis; final oral exam. For M.L.A.: 30 semester hours minimum; qualifying essay. For M.M.: 30 semester hours minimum, at least 24 in residence; comprehensive exam. For M.J.: 40 semester hours minimum; written exam; written project; oral exam. For M.S.W.: four semesters in full-time residence; field work experience; final project. For D.M.A.: 38 hours minimum beyond the master's; written/oral qualifying exam; final oral exam; dissertation/final project. For Ed.D.: 68 semester hours minimum beyond the bachelor's degree; preliminary written exam; dissertation; final oral/written exam. For Ph.D.: three years minimum beyond the bachelor's; dissertation; final oral exam.

FIELDS OF STUDY.
Accounting. M.B.A.
Accounting and Financial Management. M.S.
Actuarial Science. M.S.
Adult and Organizational Development. Ed.M.
African American Studies. M.A., Ph.D.
Anatomy. Ph.D.
Anthropology. M.A., Ph.D.
Archeology. Ph.D.
Art Education. Ed.M.
Art History. M.A., Ph.D.
Arts Administration. M.A.
Athletic Training. Ed.M.
Audiology. M.A.
Bassoon. M.M., D.M.A.
Biochemistry. M.S., Ph.D.
Biology. M.S., Ph.D.
Broadcast Telecommunication Mass Media. M.A.
Business Administration. Includes accounting (Ph.D.), finance (Ph.D.), general program (M.B.A.), human resource administration (Ph.D), international business (Ph.D.), management information systems, (Ph.D.), marketing (M.S.), risk, insurance and healthcare (Ph.D.), strategic management (Ph.D.), tourism (Ph.D.).
Career and Technical Education. M.S. Ed.
Cell Biology. M.S.
Cello. M.M., D.M.A.
Ceramics and Glass. M.F.A.
Chemistry. M.A., Ph.D.
Choral Conducting. M.S.
Cinema Studies. M.F.A.
Civil Engineering. M.S.E.
Clarinet. M.M., D.M.A.
Clinical Psychology. Ph.D.
Cognitive Psychology. Ph.D.
Communication Sciences. Ph.D.
Community and Regional Planning. M.S.
Community Health. M.P.H.
Community Planning. M.S.
Computer and Information Sciences. M.S., Ph.D.
Costume Design. M.F.A.
Counseling Psychology. Ed.M., Ph.D.
Creative Writing. M.A.
Criminal Justice. M.A., Ph.D.
Cultural Studies. Ph.D.
Curriculum, Instruction, and Technology in Education. Includes mathematics and science education (Ph.D.), language education (Ph.D.). M.S.Ed., Ph.D.
Dance. Ed.M., M.F.A., Ph.D.
Design. M.F.A.
Developmental Psychology. Ph.D.
Double Bass. M.M., D.M.A.
Early Childhood Education. M.S. Ed.
E-Business. M.B.A., M.B.A.-M.S.
Economics. Includes economics/urban studies (Ph.D.). M.A., Ph.D.
Educational Psychology. Ed.M.
Educational Administration. Ed.M., Ed.D.
Educational Psychology. Ed.M., Ph.D.
Electrical Engineering. M.S.E.
Elementary Education. M.S.Ed.
Engineering. Ph.D.
English. Ph.D.
Environmental Health. M.S.
Exercise Physiology. Ed.M.

Fiber and Fabric Design. M.F.A.
Film ad Media Arts. M.F.A.
Finance. M.B.A., M.S.
Flute. M.M., D.M.A.
French Horn. M.M., D.M.A.
General and Strategic Management. M.B.A., Ph.D.
Genetics. Ph.D.
Geography. M.A.
Geology. M.S.
Graphic Arts. M.F.A.
Guitar. M.M.
Harp. M.M., D.M.A.
Harpsichord. M.M.
Health Studies. Ph.D.
Healthcare Financial Management. M.B.A., M.S., Ph.D.
History. M.A., Ph.D.
Hospitality Management. M.T.H.M.
Human Resource Administration. M.B.A., M.S., Ph.D.
Immunology. Ph.D.
Inclusive School Practices. M.S. Ed.
International Business Administration. M.B.A.
Journalism. M.J.
Kinesiology. Ed.M., Ph.D.
Language Education. Ed.M.
Legal Studies. M.B.A.
Leisure Studies. Ed.M.
Liberal Arts. M.L.A.
Lighting Design. M.F.A.
Linguistics. M.A.
Literature. Ph.D.
Management Information Systems. M.B.A., M.S., Ph.D.
Marketing. M.B.A., M.S., Ph.D.
Mass Media and Communication. Ph.D.
Mathematics. M.A., Ph.D.
Mathematics and Science Education. M.S.Ed.
Mechanical Engineering. M.S.E.
Medicinal and Pharmaceutical Chemistry. M.S., Ph.D.
Metalsmithing. M.F.A.
Microbiology and Immunology. M.S., Ph.D.
Molecular Biology Genetics. Ph.D.
Music Composition. M.M., D.M.A.
Music Education. M.M., Ph.D.
Music History. M.M.
Music Theory. M.M., M.M.T.
Music Therapy. Ph.D.
Nursing. M.S.N.
Oboe. M.M., D.M.A.
Occupational Therapy. M.S., M.O.T.
Opera. M.M.
Oral Biology. M.S.
Painting. M.F.A.
Pathology. Ph.D.
Percussion. M.M., D.M.A.
Pharmaceutics. M.S., Ph.D.
Pharmacology. Ph.D.
Philosophy. M.A., Ph.D.
Photography. M.F.A.
Physical Education. Ed.M., Ph.D.
Physical Therapy. D.P.T., Ph.D.
Physics. M.S., Ph.D.
Physiology. M.S., Ph.D.
Piano. M.M., D.M.A.
Piano Accompanying. Includes chamber music, opera coaching.
   M.M.
Piano Pedagogy. M.M.
Political Science. Includes urban studies (Ph.D.). M.A., Ph.D.
Printmaking. M.F.A.
Public Health. Includes community health education (M.P.H.),
   school health education (Ed.M.), environmental health (M.S.).
Quality Assurance and Regulatory Affairs. M.S.
Recreation. Ed.M.

Religion. M.A., Ph.D.
Risk Management and Insurance. M.B.A.
Saxophone. M.M.
School Psychology. Ed.M., Ph.D.
Sculpture. M.F.A.
Second and Foreign Language Education. M.S.Ed.
Social and Organizational Psychology. Ph.D.
Social Work. M.S.W.
Sociology. Includes urban studies. M.A., Ph.D.
Spanish. M.A., Ph.D.
Special Education. M.S. Ed.
Speech Language Hearing. M.A.
Sport and Recreation Administration. Ed.M.
Statistics. M.S., Ph.D.
String Pedagogy. M.M.
TESOL. M.S. Ed.
Technical Theater. M.F.A.
Theater. Includes acting, directing, scenic design. M.F.A.
Therapeutic Recreation. Ed.M.
Tourism and Hospitality Management. M.T.H.M.
Trombone. M.M., D.M.A.
Trumpet. M.M., D.M.A.
Tuba. M.M., D.M.A.
Urban Education. Ed.M, Ph.D.
Urban Planning. M.S.
Urban Studies. M.A.
Viola. M.M., D.M.A.
Violin. M.M., D.M.A.
Visual Anthropology. Ph.D.
Vocational Education. M.S. Ed.
Voice. M.M., D.M.A.

School of Dentistry (19140)

Organized 1863. Annual tuition: resident $21,314, nonresident $29,454. No on-campus housing available. Average academic year off-campus housing costs: $12,500. Contact the Office for Housing and Financial Aid Counseling. Phone: (215)707-7663. Total average cost for all other first-year expenses: $6000.

Enrollment: D.D.S. program, first-year class 125; 500 total (men 65%, women 35%); graduate program 60. Faculty: full-time 79, part-time 79. Degrees conferred: D.D.S., D.D.S.-M.B.A., M.S., Ph.D.

ADMISSION REQUIREMENTS. For D.D.S. program: AAD-SAS, official transcripts, DAT required in support of School's application. Evidence of proficiency in English required of international students. Applicants must have completed at least three years of college study, four years of study preferred. Preference given to state residents. Transfer applicants not considered. Graduates of unaccredited colleges not considered. Apply to Assistant Dean after August 1, before March 1. Application fee $30. Phone: (215)707-7663; fax: (215)707-2802. For graduate program: official transcripts, D.D.S. or D.M.D. degree, interview required in support of School's application. Transfer applicants, graduates of unaccredited institutions not considered. Apply to School by February 1 (Fall). Application fee $30.

ADMISSION STANDARDS. Selective. Mean DAT: Academic 18.4, PAT 17.7; mean GPA: 3.29 (A = 4). Gourman rating: 4.41. Usual minimum average: 2.5 (A = 4). Accepts 15–20% of total annual applicants for D.D.S. program. Approximately 50% are state residents. For graduate programs: usual minimum average: 3.0 (A = 4).

FINANCIAL AID. For D.D.S. program: limited to state and federal aid programs. Apply to Assistant Dean after acceptance. Phone: (215)707-2667. Use FAFSA (School code: E00353). For graduate program: fellowships, assistantships for teaching/ research. Apply by July 1 to Dean of School. Use FAFSA. About 87% of students receive aid other than loans from School and outside sources.

DEGREE REQUIREMENTS. For D.D.S.: satisfactory completion of forty-five-month program. For Postgraduate Certificate Programs: four semesters minimum (two years) in full-time residence. For M.S.: two semesters minimum (one year) in full-time residence; thesis; final exam. For Ph.D.: see Graduate School listing above.

FIELDS OF GRADUATE STUDY.
Endodontology.
General Dentistry.
Informatics.
Oral Biology. M.S.
Oral Surgery.
Orthodontics.
Periodontology.
Physiology. M.S.; Ph.D. from Graduate School.

James E. Beasley School of Law
Web site: www.temple.edu/lawschool

Established 1895. Located on main campus. ABA approved since 1933. AALS member. Semester system. Full-time, part-time study. Special programs: semester abroad in Tokyo, Japan; summer abroad in Athens, Greece, Rome, Italy, Tel Aviv, Israel, Beijing, People's Republic of China. Law library: 523,108 volumes, 2765 subscriptions; has LEXIS, NEXIS, WESTLAW, DIALOG, RLN, INNOPAC, CALI; is a Federal Government Depository.

Tuition: per semester, full-time day resident $11,288, nonresident $19,562; full-time evening resident $9030, nonresident $15,650; part-time per credit resident $436, nonresident $799; LL.M. (Foreign) full-time per semester $16,192, part-time per credit $754; LL.M (Trial Advocacy) per semester resident and nonresident $15,750; LL.M. (Tax) per credit resident $482, nonresident $663. On-campus housing available for single and married LL.M. students (about half of entering LL.M. class live on-campus). Annual on-campus housing cost: $12,500–$14,600. Housing deadline June 1. Contact Office of University Housing for both on- and off-campus housing. Phone: (218)207-7223. J.D. students tend to live off-campus. Off-campus housing and personal expenses: approximately $16,360.

Enrollment: first-year class full-time 260, part-time 86; total full- and part-time 1075 (men 52%, women 48%). Faculty: full-time 46, part-time 86. Student to faculty ratio 15.9 to 1. Degrees conferred: J.D., J.D.-M.B.A., J.D.-LL.M. (Tax, Trial Advocacy), LL.M. (Tax full- and part-time program; Trial Advocacy, evening and weekend program), LL.M. (international graduates who have completed a basic legal education and received a university degree in law in another country).

ADMISSION REQUIREMENTS. LSDAS Law School report, bachelor's degree, transcripts, LSAT (not later than February) required in support of application. Accepts transfer applicants. Graduates of unaccredited colleges not considered. Apply to School Admissions Office, preferably by March 1. Application fee $50. Phone: (800)560-1428; fax: (215)204-1185.

ADMISSION STANDARDS. Selective. Mean LSAT: full-time 157, part-time 154; mean GPA: full-time 3.32, part-time 3.17 (A = 4). Gourman rating: 3.88. *U.S. News & World Report* ranking is in the second tier of all U.S. law schools. Accepts 40% of total annual applicants.

FINANCIAL AID. Scholarships, Federal W/S, loans. Apply to the Office of Financial Aid by March 1. Use FAFSA (School code: E00354). About 42% of students receive aid other than loans from School.

DEGREE REQUIREMENTS. For J.D.: satisfactory completion of three-year day or four-year evening program: 83 unit program. For LL.M.: at least 24 credits beyond the J.D.; one year minimum; final research project.

School of Medicine (19140)

Established 1901. Special facilities: Center for Substance Abuse Research, Fels Institute for Cancer Research, General Clinical Research Center, Sol Sherry Thrombosis Research Center.

Annual tuition: resident $25,740, nonresident $31,378, student fees $350. Total average for all other expenses: $8550.

Enrollment: M.D. program first-year class 210 (5 EDP), total 806 (men 51%, women 49%); postgraduates 300. Faculty: full-time 450, part-time 100, Degrees conferred: M.D., M.D.-M.P.H., M.D.-Ph.D., M.S., Ph.D.

ADMISSION REQUIREMENTS. For M.D. program: AMCAS report, transcripts, letters of recommendation, MCAT, final screening interview required in support of application. Preference given to state residents. Has EDP; apply between June 1 and August 1. Apply to Director of Admissions after June 1, before December 1. Application fee $55. Phone: (215)707-3656; fax: (215)707-6932. For graduate program: transcripts, two letters of Recommendation, GRE Subject Tests, interview required in support of application. Accepts transfer applicants. Graduates of unaccredited colleges not considered. Apply to Associate Dean of Health Sciences Center prior to registration. Application fee $10.

ADMISSION STANDARDS. For M.D. program: very competitive. Mean MCAT: 10; mean GPA: 3.42 (A = 4). Gourman rating: 4.17. Accepts about 5% of total annual applicants. Approximately 65% are state residents. For graduate program: selective.

FINANCIAL AID. For M.D. program: scholarships, loans; apply to Director, Health Sciences Center Financial Aid Office, by April 1. Phone: (215)707-2667. Use FAFSA and GAPSFAS (School code: E00352). About 80% of students receive some type of aid. For graduate program: scholarships, fellowships, assistantships for teaching/research. Apply to Associate Dean of Graduate School for scholarships, fellowships, to appropriate department chair for assistantships; no specified closing date. About 20% of graduate students receive aid other than loans from School.

DEGREE REQUIREMENTS. For M.D.: satisfactory completion of four-year program; all students must pass USMLE Step 1 prior to entering third year, and pass Step 2 prior to awarding of M.D. For M.S., Ph.D.: see Graduate School listing above.

FIELDS OF GRADUATE STUDY
Anatomy and Cell Biology.
Biochemistry.
Microbiology and Immunology.
Molecular Biology and Genetics.
Pathology.
Pharmacology.
Physiology.

TENNESSEE STATE UNIVERSITY
Nashville, Tennessee 37209-1561
Web site: www.tnstate.edu

Founded 1912. CGS member. Coed. State control. Semester system. Special facilities: Center of Excellence in Information Systems and Engineering Management, Center of Excellence in Research and Policy on Basic Skills, Small Business Development Center. Library: 580,650 volumes, 2500 subscriptions.

Annual tuition: full-time resident $3434, nonresident $9062; per credit resident $211, nonresident $453. On-campus housing for single students. Apply to Dean of Women or Dean of Men. Average annual housing expenses $3290, $4,800 (including board). Day-care facilities available.

Graduate School

Graduate study since 1941. Enrollment: full- and part-time 1280. Faculty: full-time 200. Degrees conferred: M.A., M.A.Ed., M.E., M.Ed., M.B.A., M.P.A., M.S., M.S.N., M.C.J., Ed.D.

ADMISSION REQUIREMENTS. Transcripts, GRE required in support of School's application. On-line application available. TOEFL required for international foreign applicants. Accepts transfer applicants. Apply to Dean, Graduate School, at least six weeks prior to registration. Application fee $15. Phone: (615) 963-5901; fax: (615)963-5963.

ADMISSIONS STANDARDS. Relatively open to selective. Usual minimum average: 2.5 (A = 4).

FINANCIAL AID. Fellowships, assistantships, internships, Federal W/S, loans. Approved for VA benefits. Apply to Director of Financial Aid; no specified closing date. Use FAFSA. Aid available for part-time students.

DEGREE REQUIREMENTS. For master's: 30–33 semester hours minimum, at least 27 in residence; thesis in some departments. For Ed.D.: 69 hours maximum beyond the master's; comprehensive exam; advancement to candidacy; dissertation or special project; final oral exam.

FIELDS OF STUDY.

AGRICULTURE AND CONSUMER SCIENCES:
Agricultural Science. Includes agricultural education, agribusiness, animal science, plant science.
Family and Consumer Sciences.

COLLEGE OF ARTS AND SCIENCES:
Biology.
Biological Sciences.
Chemistry.
Criminal Justice.
English.
Mathematical Sciences.
Music.

COLLEGE OF BUSINESS:
Business Administration.

COLLEGE OF EDUCATION:
Administration and Supervision. Includes higher education administration.
Curriculum and Instruction. Includes adult, curriculum planning, educational technology, elementary, history, reading, secondary education, teaching non-English language, special education.
Elementary Education.
Guidance and Counseling.
Health, Physical Education, and Recreation.
Psychology. Includes counseling psychology, school psychology.
Special Education.

COLLEGE OF ENGINEERING, TECHNOLOGY, AND COMPUTER SCIENCE:
Computer and Information Systems Engineering. Includes computer communication and networks, control systems and signal processing, robotics and computer integrated manufacturing.
Engineering. Includes biomedical, civil, electrical, environmental, manufacturing, mechanical.

INSTITUTE OF GOVERNMENT:
Public Administration.

SCHOOL OF ALLIED HEALTH:
Physical Therapy.
Speech and Hearing Sciences.

SCHOOL OF NURSING:
Nursing. Includes family nurse practitioner, holistic nursing.

TENNESSEE TECHNOLOGICAL UNIVERSITY
Cookeville, Tennessee 38505
Web site: www.tntech.edu

Established 1915. Located 80 miles E of Nashville. CGS member. Coed. State control. Semester system. Special facilities: Center for Electric Power, Center for Manufacturing Research, Water Resources Center. Library: 593,400 volumes, 3752 subscriptions.

Annual tuition: full-time resident $3430, nonresident $9058. On-campus housing for 300 married students (2000 men, 1800 women). Average academic year housing costs: $3000 for married students, $5500 (include board) for single students. Contact Director of Housing for both on- and off-campus housing. Phone: (931)372-3414.

Graduate School

Graduate study since 1958. Enrollment: full-time 350, part-time 886 (men 25%, women 75%). Faculty: full-time 315, part-time 40. Degrees conferred: M.A., M.S., M.B.A., Ed.S., Ph.D. (Engineering only).

ADMISSION REQUIREMENTS. Transcripts, letters of recommendation required in support of School's application. MAT required for education majors. GRE required for science and engineering majors. GMAT required for M.B.A. applicants. TOEFL required for international applicants. Accepts transfer applicants. Apply to Dean of Graduate School by March 1 (Fall), August 1 (Spring); international students apply at least six months in advance. Application fee $5, $30 for international applicants. Phone: (931)372-3233; fax: (931)372-3497.

ADMISSION STANDARDS. Selective. Usual minimum average: 2.75 (A = 4).

FINANCIAL AID. Annual awards from institutional funds: scholarships, teaching assistantships, research assistantships, internships, Federal W/S, loans. Approved for VA benefits. Apply by April 1 to appropriate department chair for assistantships, scholarships; to Financial Aid Office for all other programs. Phone: (931)372-3073; fax: (931)372-6335. Use FAFSA and University's FAF. About 50% of students receive aid from University. Aid available for part-time students.

DEGREE REQUIREMENTS. For master's: 30 semester credits minimum, at least 24 in residence; thesis; final oral exam. For M.B.A.: 36 hours. For Ed.S.: 30 credits minimum beyond the master's. For Ph.D.: 60 hours minimum; one year in residence; qualifying exam; advancement to candidacy; dissertation; final oral exam.

FIELDS OF STUDY.

COLLEGE OF ARTS AND SCIENCE:
Biology. Includes fisheries management, general biology.
Chemistry.
Computer Science.
English.
Environmental Sciences.
Mathematics. Includes applied mathematics, statistics.

COLLEGE OF BUSINESS ADMINISTRATION:
Business Administration.
Distance MBA Program.

COLLEGE OF EDUCATION:
Curriculum and Instruction. Includes curriculum, early childhood, elementary, library science, reading, secondary, special.

Health and Physical Education. Includes adapted physical education, elementary and middle school physical education, lifetime wellness.

Educational Psychology and Counselor Education. Includes agency counselor, education psychology, school counselor, school psychology.

Exceptional Learning. Includes applied behavior and learning, literacy, young children and families.

Instructional Leadership. Includes developmental and administrative studies, elementary education, health and physical education/wellness, materials supervision, music performance and music education, reading, secondary education special education technology.

COLLEGE OF ENGINEERING:

Chemical Engineering.

Civil Engineering. Includes environmental, structural, transportation.

Electrical Engineering. Includes electromagnetic fields and physical electronics, communications theory and electronics, networks and control systems, power systems and energy conversion, computers and digital systems, nuclear systems.

Industrial Engineering.

Mechanical Engineering. Includes acoustics, control systems, design/mechanical systems, materials, thermal science/systems.

UNIVERSITY OF TENNESSEE AT CHATTANOOGA

Chattanooga, Tennessee 37403-2504

Web site: www.utc.edu

Founded 1886 as University of Chattanooga, merged July 1969 with the University of Tennessee. CGS member. Coed. State control. Semester system. Special facilities: Center for Economic Education, Cadek Conservatory of Music, Center for Environmental/Energy Education, Institute of Archaeology, Odor Research Center. Library: 479,000 volumes, 2768 subscriptions.

Tuition: per credit resident $190, nonresident $466. On-campus housing for limited number of single graduate students; none for married students (except during Summer). Average academic year housing costs: $2200 (excluding board). Contact Dean of Student Affairs Office for both on- and off-campus housing information. Phone: (423)755-4246. Day-care facilities available.

Graduate Division

Enrollment: full-time 416, part-time 821 (men 44%, women 56%). University faculty teaching graduate students: full-time 119, part-time 38. Degrees conferred: M.A., M.B.A., M.Ed., M.M., M.P.A., M.S., M.S.C.J., M.S.N.

ADMISSION REQUIREMENTS. Transcripts, GRE, MAT for M.Ed., M.S.C.J., M.A., M.M., and M.S. in Psychology; GMAT for M.B.A., three letters of reference, required in support of application. Interview sometimes required. TOEFL required for international applicants. Accepts transfer applicants. Apply to Graduate Office by August 1 (Fall), well in advance of registration for other semesters. Application fee $25. Phone: (423)755-1740; fax: (423)755-5223.

ADMISSION STANDARDS. Relatively open. Usual minimum average: 2.5 (A = 4).

FINANCIAL AID. Fellowships, assistantships, internships, Federal W/S, loans. Approved for VA benefits. Apply to the Financial Aid Office; no specified closing date. Phone: (423)755-4677.

Use FAFSA and University's FAF. Aid available for part-time students.

DEGREE REQUIREMENTS. For M.A., M.S., M.S.N.: 33 semester hours minimum, at least 27 in residence; thesis/nonthesis option. For M.B.A., M.P.A.: 31–36 semester hours minimum, at least 30 in residence. For M.Ed.: 33 semester hours minimum, at least 24 in residence; final comprehensive exam. For M.S.C.J.: 36 semester hours minimum, at least 30 in residence; qualifying exam; thesis optional; internship. For M.M.: 33 semester hours minimum, at least 30 in residence. Additional requirements depend upon major.

FIELDS OF STUDY.

Accounting.

Athletic Training.

Business Administration.

Computer Science.

Criminal Justice.

Educational Technology.

Elementary Education.

Engineering.

Engineering Management.

English.

Environmental Science.

Guidance and Counseling.

Music.

Nursing. Includes anesthesia, family nurse practitioner.

Psychology. Includes industrial, organizational, school.

Public Administration.

School Leadership.

Secondary Education. Includes English, history, mathematics, natural science, physics, social sciences, business, health, physical education.

Special Education.

UNIVERSITY OF TENNESSEE

Knoxville, Tennessee 37996

Web site: www.tennessee.edu

Founded 1794. CGS member. Coed. State control. Semester system. Special facilities: Institute of Agriculture, Center for Business and Economic Research, Energy, Environment and Resources Center, Forensic Anthropology Center, Management Development Center, McClung Museum, Measurement and Control Engineering Center, Social Science Research Institute, Space Institute, Stokey Institute of Liberal Arts, Transportation Center, cooperating University in Oak Ridge Associate Universities Program. The University's NIH ranking is 92nd among all U.S. institutions with 132 awards/grants worth $43,786,866. Library: 2,400,000 volumes, 17,628 subscriptions. Total University enrollment: 25,500.

Tuition: per credit, resident $192, nonresident $545. On-campus housing for 800 married students, 7500 men, 7500 women. Average annual housing cost: $5300 for single students, $6800 for married students. Apply to Office of Residence Halls or Rental Properties. Phone: (865)974-3411. Day-care facilities available.

Graduate School

Graduate study since 1928. Enrollment: full-time 3518, part-time 1771. University faculty: full-time 1238, part-time 62. Degrees conferred: M.A., M.S., M.Arch., M.B.A., M.F.A., M.P.H., M.P.A., M.Acc., M.Math., M.Music., M.S.N., M.S.P., M.S.S.W., Ed.S., Ed.D., Ph.D.

ADMISSION REQUIREMENTS. Official transcripts required in support of School's application. On-line application available.

GRE Subject/GMAT required for many departments. TOEFL required for international applicants. Interview not required. Additional application materials may be required by some schools; please contact individual schools for current information. Accepts transfer applicants. Graduates of unaccredited institution. Apply to Office of Graduate Admissions and Records by February 1 (Fall). Foreign students apply at least six months prior to registration. Application fee $15. Phone: (865) 974-3251; fax: (865)974-6541; e-mail: gsinfo@utk.edu.

ADMISSION STANDARDS. Very selective for most departments, competitive or selective for the others. Usual minimum average: 2.7 (A = 4).

FINANCIAL AID. Scholarships, fellowships, research assistantships, teaching assistantships, administrative assistantships, internships, Federal W/S, loans. Approved for VA benefits. Apply by March 1 to the Graduate School for fellowships, to appropriate department chairman for assistantships; to Financial Aid Office for all other programs. Phone: (865)974-3131. Use FAFSA. About 65% of students receive aid other than loans from School and outside sources. Aid available for part-time students.

DEGREE REQUIREMENTS. For master's: 30 semester hours minimum; thesis/final project; final oral/written exam. For Ed.S.: 60 semester hours minimum; one to two semesters in full-time attendance; qualifying exam may be required; thesis/nonthesis option; final oral/written exam. For Doctorates: 24 hours minimum beyond the master's, at least one year in full-time residence; comprehensive written exam; reading knowledge of one foreign language or proficiency in research techniques; dissertation; final oral exam.

FIELDS OF STUDY.

INTERCOLLEGIATE PROGRAMS:
Aviation Systems. Offered at UT Space Institute. M.S.
Comparative and Experimental Medicine. GRE for admission.

COLLEGE OF AGRICULTURAL SCIENCES AND NATURAL RESOURCES:
Agricultural and Extension Education.
Agricultural Economics. GRE for admission. Includes agribusiness.
Animal Science. GRE for admission. Includes animal genetics, animal health and well-being, animal management, animal nutrition, animal physiology.
Biosystems Engineering. GRE required for international applicants.
Biosystems Engineering Technology. GRE required for international applicants.
Entomology and Plant Pathology. M.S.
Food Science and Technology. GRE for admission.
Forestry. GRE for admission. M.S.
Natural Resources. GRE for admission. Ph.D.
Ornamental Horticulture and Landscape Design. Includes landscape design horticulture, turfgrass, wood ornamentals. M.S.
Plant and Soil Sciences. GRE for admission.
Wildlife and Fisheries Science. GRE for admission. M.S.

COLLEGE OF ARCHITECTURE AND DESIGN:
Architecture. GRE for admission. M.Arch.

COLLEGE OF ARTS AND SCIENCES:
Anthropology. GRE for admission.
Art. Portfolio for admission. M.F.A. only. Includes ceramics, drawing, graphic design, media arts, painting, printmaking, sculpture, watercolor.
Audiology. GRE for admission. Includes aural habilitation. M.A. only.
Biochemistry, Cellular, and Molecular Biology. GRE for admission.

Botany. GRE for admission.
Chemistry. GRE for admission.
Computer Science.
Ecology and Evolutionary Biology. GRE for admission.
English. GRE General/Subject for admission. Includes writing.
French. M.A.
Geography. GRE for admission.
Geology. GRE for admission.
German. M.A.
History. GRE for admission.
Life Sciences. GRE for admission. Includes genome science and technology, plant physiology and genetics.
Mathematics. Includes applied mathematics, mathematical ecology. M.M.
Microbiology. GRE for admission.
Modern Foreign Languages. Ph.D.
Music. Audition required for admission. M.M.
Philosophy. GRE for admission. Includes medical ethics, religious studies.
Physics.
Planning. GRE for admission. M.S.P.
Political Science. GRE for admission.
Psychology. GRE/Subject for admission.
Public Administration. GRE for admission. M.P.A.
Sociology. GRE for admission.
Spanish. M.A.
Speech and Hearing Science. GRE for admission. Ph.D.
Speech Pathology. GRE for admission. M.A.
Theatre. Audition for admission. M.F.A.

COLLEGE OF BUSINESS ADMINISTRATION:
Accounting. GMAT for admission. M.Acc.
Business Administration. GMAT for admission. Includes accounting, finance, logistics and transportation, management, marketing, operations management.
Economics. GRE or GMAT for admission.
Industrial and Organizational Psychology. GRE for admission.
Management Science. GRE or GMAT for admission. M.S., Ph.D.
Statistics. GRE or GMAT for admission. M.S.

COLLEGE OF COMMUNICATIONS:
Communications. GRE for admission.

COLLEGE OF EDUCATION:
College Student Personnel. GRE for Admission. M.S.
Counseling. GRE required for American applicants.
Education. GRE for admission. Includes art education, curriculum, education of the deaf and hard of hearing, elementary education, English education, foreign language/ESL education, instructional technology, mathematics education, modified and comprehensive special education, reading education, science education, social foundations, social science education, special education (early childhood).
Educational Administration and Policy Studies.
Educational Psychology.
Human Performance and Sports Studies. GRE for admission. Includes exercise science, sports management, sports studies.

COLLEGE OF ENGINEERING:
Aerospace Engineering. GRE for international applicants.
Chemical Engineering. GRE for admission.
Civil Engineering. GRE for international applicants.
Electrical Engineering. GRE for Ph.D. candidates.
Engineering Science. GRE for international applicants.
Environmental Engineering. GRE for international applicants. M.S.
Industrial Engineering. GRE for admission. M.S.
Materials Science and Engineering. GRE for international applicants.
Mechanical Engineering. GRE for international applicants.
Nuclear Engineering. GRE for admission.
Polymer Engineering. GRE for international applicants.

COLLEGE OF HUMAN ECOLOGY:

Child and Family Studies. GRE for admission. M.S.

Health Promotion and Health Education. GRE for admission. M.S.

Human Ecology. GRE for admission. Ph.D.

Human Resources and Development. GRE for admission.

Nutrition. GRE for admission. M.S.

Public Health. M.P.H.

Recreation, Tourism, and Hospitality Management. GRE for admission. M.S.

Safety. M.S.

Textiles, Retailing, and Consumer Sciences. GRE for admission. M.S.

COLLEGE OF NURSING:

Nursing. GRE for admission. Includes adult health nursing, family nurse practitioner, mental health nursing, nurse anesthesia, nursing administration, nursing of women and children.

COLLEGE OF SOCIAL WORK:

Social Work. GRE for admission. Includes clinical social work practice, social welfare management, community practice.

SCHOOL OF INFORMATION SCIENCES:

Information Sciences. GRE for admission. M.S.

College of Law

Web site: www.law.utk.edu

Established 1890. ABA approved since 1925. AALS charter member. Semester system. Located in Knoxville (37996-1810). Library: 483,372 volumes, 6363 subscriptions; has LEXIS, WESTLAW, INFOTRAC. Special facilities: Center for Entrepreneurial Law, Center for Advocacy and Dispute Resolution.

Annual tuition: resident $5870, nonresident $15,672.

Enrollment: first-year class 260; total full-time 478 (men 54%, women 46%). Faculty: full-time 29, part-time 27. Student to faculty ratio 13.7 to 1. Degrees conferred: J.D., J.D.-M.B.A., J.D.-M.P.A.

ADMISSION REQUIREMENTS. LSDAS Law School report, bachelor's degree, transcripts, LSAT (not later than December), two letters of recommendation, personal statement required in support of application. Interview not required. Preference given to state residents. Accepts transfer applicants. Graduates of unaccredited colleges not considered. Apply to Admissions Office after October 1, before February 15. Application fee $15. Phone: (865)974-4131; fax: (865)974-1572.

ADMISSION STANDARDS. Selective. Mean LSAT: 157; mean GPA: 3.51 (A = 4). Gourman rating: 2.95. *U.S. News & World Report* ranking is in the second tier of all U.S. law schools. Accepts about 35–40% of total annual applicants. Approximately 80% of students are state residents.

FINANCIAL AID. Scholarships, fellowships, Federal W/S, loans. Apply to Financial Aid Office by March 1. Use FAFSA (College code: 006725). About 25% of students receive aid other than loans from College.

DEGREE REQUIREMENTS. For J.D.: satisfactory completion of three-year program; 89 credit hour program.

College of Social Work

Web site: www.csw.utk.edu

Founded 1942. Centers in Knoxville, Nashville (37203), and Memphis (38103). Dean's offices in Knoxville. On-campus housing at Knoxville only. Enrollment: full-time 305, part-time 110. Faculty: full-time 33, part-time 4. Degrees conferred: M.S.S.W., Ph.D.

ADMISSION REQUIREMENTS. Transcripts, GRE required in support of application. On-line application available. TOEFL required for international applicants. Accepts transfer applicants. Graduates of unaccredited colleges not considered. Apply to Office of Admissions of College by March 1. Fall admission only. Application fee $35. Phone: (865)974-6697 (M.S.S.W.), (865) 974-6481 (Ph.D.); fax (865)974-4803.

ADMISSION STANDARDS. Competitive. Usual minimum average: 2.7 (A = 4), 3.0 during senior year.

FINANCIAL AID. Fellowships, M.S.S.W. assistantships, Ph.D. assistantships, agency internships, Federal W/S, loans. Approved for VA benefits. Apply to Director of Admissions by February 1. Use FAFSA. Phone: (865)974-3131; fax: (865)974-2175.

DEGREE REQUIREMENTS. For M.S.S.W.: 60 semester hours minimum; thesis or elective courses and comprehensive exam. For Ph.D.: 60 semester hours beyond master's degree, including 24 hours of dissertation research; final oral exam.

FIELDS OF STUDY.

Social Work. Concentrations in clinical social work practice, social welfare management, community.

College of Veterinary Medicine (37901-1071)

Web site: www.vet.utk.edu

Annual tuition: resident $7060, nonresident $18,804. Total average cost for all other expenses: $7000–$9000.

Enrollment: first-year class 68, total full-time 257 (men 45%, women 55%); postgraduates 40. Faculty: full-time 83. Degrees conferred: D.V.M., M.S., Ph.D.

ADMISSION REQUIREMENTS. VMCAS report, transcripts, VCAT, recommendations/evaluations, personal essay, animal/veterinary experience required in support of application. Interview by invitation only. Preference given to state residents. Graduates of unaccredited colleges not considered. Apply to the College (P.O. Box 1071) after July 1, before November 1. Application packets distributed in October must be completed and returned by January 15. Application fee $25. Phone: (865)974-7263.

ADMISSION STANDARDS. Selective. Mean GPA: 3.56 (A = 4). Accepts 33–50% of qualified state applicants. Accepts 15–20% "at large" nonresident applicants.

FINANCIAL AID. Scholarships, fellowships, assistantships, internships, loans available. Apply after acceptance to Office of Financial Aid. Use FAFSA.

DEGREE REQUIREMENTS. For D.V.M.: satisfactory completion of four-year, nine-semester program.

FIELD OF GRADUATE STUDY.

Comparative Experimental Medicine. M.S., Ph.D.

UNIVERSITY OF TENNESSEE AT MARTIN

Martin, Tennessee 38238-1000

Web site: www.utm.edu

Traces its origin to Hall-Moody Institute founded in 1900. State controlled since 1927. Located 125 miles NE of Memphis. CGS member. Semester system. Special facilities: Reelfoot Lake Research and Teaching Center, Center for Excellence in Science and Mathematics Education, Center for Environmental and Conservation Education. Library: 436,366 volumes, 2654 subscriptions. Selected by the Humanities Research Corporation as one of the exemplary institutions of higher education with regard to the use of the computer for learning and teaching.

Annual tuition: full-time resident $3460, nonresident $8956; per credit resident $194, nonresident $500. On-campus housing for 226 married students, 1155 men, 1427 women. Average annual housing cost: $3300–$4000 for married students, $3630 (including board) for single students. Contact Director of Housing for both on- and off-campus housing information. Phone: (731)587-7730. Day-care facilities available.

Graduate Studies

Enrollment: full- and part-time 349 (men 35%, women 65%). Graduate faculty: full-time 114, part-time 12. Degrees conferred: M.S., M.Acc., M.B.A.

ADMISSION REQUIREMENTS. Two official transcripts, GMAT(business) required in support of School's application. GRE/MAT/NTE required before the completion of 6 semester hours. TOEFL required for international applicants. Interview not required. Accepts transfer applicants. Apply to Graduate Studies Office at ten working days prior to registration. Application fee $25, $50 for international applicants. Phone: (731)587-7012; fax: (731)587-7019.

ADMISSION STANDARDS. Relatively open. Usual minimum average: 2.5 cumulative, or 3.0 in upper divisional work (A = 4).

FINANCIAL AID. Annual awards from institutional funds: fellowships, scholarships, assistantships, residence hall assistantships, internships, tuition waivers, loans. Approved for VA benefits. Apply by March 1 to Dean of the School for assistantships; to Financial Aid Director for all other programs. Phone: (731)587-7040. Use FAFSA. About 30% of students receive aid other than loans from University and outside sources. Aid available for part-time students.

DEGREE REQUIREMENTS. For master's: 30–48 semester hours minimum, the equivalent of two semesters in residence unless transferring within the University of Tennessee system; thesis optional in Human Environmental Science, education; final written/oral exam.

FIELDS OF STUDY.

COLLEGE OF AGRICULTURE AND APPLIED SCIENCES:
Agriculture Operations Management.
Family and Consumer Sciences.

COLLEGE OF BUSINESS AND PUBLIC AFFAIRS:
Accountancy.
Business Administration.

COLLEGE OF EDUCATION AND BEHAVIORAL SCIENCES:
Administration and Supervision.
Counseling. Includes community/mental health, school.
Teaching. Includes advanced elementary education, advanced secondary education, subject area.

UNIVERSITY OF TENNESSEE HEALTH SCIENCE CENTER

Memphis, Tennessee 38163-0002
Web site: www.utmem.edu

Founded 1911. CGS member. Coed. State control. Semester system. Special facilities: DEC PDP-11/70, 11/34, IBM 370/ 3031; Stout Neuroscience Mass Spectrometry Laboratory, Memo-

rial Research Center, Clinical Research Center, Molecular Resource Center, Center for Neurosciences, Materials Science Toxicology Laboratory. The University's NIH ranking is 92nd among all U.S. institutions with 132 awards/grants worth $43,786,866. Library: 263,000 volumes, 1784 subscriptions.

On-campus housing available for 147 single men, 205 single women. Average academic year housing costs: $7200. Contact the Director of Housing for both on- and off-campus housing information. Phone: (901)448-5609.

College of Allied Health Sciences

Founded 1972. Annual tuition: full-time resident $5854, nonresident $13,802. Enrollment: full-time 140, part-time 0. Faculty: full-time 7, part-time 12. Degrees conferred: M.P.T. (degree completion program for undergraduates: students transfer 90 approved credits, spend an additional three years in full-time study to receive M.P.T.), M.S.P.T., M.S.C.L.S.

ADMISSION REQUIREMENTS. Official transcripts, two recommendations, GRE, interview required in support of College's application. On-line application available. Interview encouraged. TOEFL (minimum score 550) required for international applicants. Graduates of unaccredited colleges not considered. Preference given to Tennessee residents. Apply to the Director of Admissions by January 15 (Fall priority date, M.P.T., M.S.), September 1 (Winter priority date, M.S.), March 1 (Spring priority date, M.S.). Application fee: $50. Phone: (901)448-7772.

ADMISSION STANDARDS. Selective. Usual minimum average: 3.0 (A - 4).

FINANCIAL AID. Scholarships, assistantships, internships, tuition waivers, Federal W/S, loans. Apply by April 1 to the Financial Aid Office.

DEGREE REQUIREMENTS. For M.P.T.: three-year full-time program. For M.S.P.T., M.S.C.L.S.: 36 credit program; admission to candidacy; practicum.

FIELDS OF STUDY.
Clinical Laboratory Science. M.S.C.L.S.
Physical Therapy. M.P.T., M.S.P.T.

College of Graduate Health Sciences

Annual tuition: full-time resident $5544, nonresident $16,152. Enrollment: full-time 264, part-time 0. Faculty: full-time 170, part-time 12. Degrees conferred: M.S., Ph.D.

ADMISSION REQUIREMENTS. Official transcripts, three recommendations, GRE Test required in support of College's applications. On-line application available. Interview encouraged. Four-year bachelor's degree or equivalent required. TOEFL (minimum score 550) required for international applicants. Graduates of unaccredited colleges not considered. Apply to University Office of Admissions, before May 15 (Fall). Application fee: $50. Phone: (901)448-5560; fax: (901)448-7772.

ADMISSION STANDARDS. Selective. Usual minimum average: 3.0 (A = 4).

FINANCIAL AID. Scholarships, teaching assistantships, research assistantships, fellowships, tuition waivers, Federal W/S, loans. Apply by March 1 to the Financial Aid Office. Phone: (901)448-5569. Use FAFSA (School code: 006725). Most full-time students receive aid from School; aid sometimes available for part-time students.

DEGREE REQUIREMENTS. For M.S.: 30 semester hours minimum, at least 18 in residence; thesis; comprehensive oral/written exam for some departments. For Ph.D.: at least one year in residence; oral/written candidacy exam; dissertation; final oral exam.

FIELDS OF STUDY.
Anatomy and Neurobiology. Includes neuroscience.
Biomedical Engineering.
Dental Science. Includes orthodontics, pediatric dentistry, periodontics.
Epidemiology.
Health Sciences Administration. Includes pharmacoeconomics, health policy, health systems pharmacy management.
Molecular and Cellular Basis of Human Disease. Interdisciplinary.
Molecular Sciences. Includes biochemistry, microbiology, immunology.
Nursing.
Pathology.
Pharmaceutical Sciences. Includes medicinal chemistry, pharmaceutics.
Pharmacology.
Physiology.

College of Dentistry

Founded 1878. Annual tuition: resident $7858, nonresident $21,006. On-campus housing available. Average academic year housing costs: $7000–9000. Contact the Housing Office. Phone: (901)448-5609. Total average for all other first-year expenses: $8490.

Enrollment: first-year class 85; 360 total (men 65%, women 35%); graduate study 22. College faculty: full-time 63, part-time 69. Degree conferred: D.D.S.

ADMISSION REQUIREMENTS. For D.D.S. program: official transcripts, DAT, three letters of recommendation required in support of College's application. Interview by invitation only. Applicants must have completed at least three years of college study, four years of study preferred. Preference given to Tennessee and Arkansas residents. Apply to Assistant Dean after June 1, before December 31. Application fee $50. Phone: (901)448-6201; (800)788-0040. For graduate program: official transcripts, D.D.S. or equivalent degree. Interview by invitation. Transfer applicants, graduates of unaccredited institutions not considered. Apply to College by December 1.

ADMISSION STANDARDS. For D.D.S. program: Selective. Mean DAT: Academic 18, PAT 17; mean GPA: 3.27 (A = 4). Gourman rating: 4.24. Usual minimum average: 3.0 (A = 4); DAT score 17 or better. Accepts 50% of total annual applicants. Approximately 75% are residents of Arkansas and Tennessee. For graduate programs: competitive for most programs.

FINANCIAL AID. Scholarships, grants, loans, Federal W/S; fellowships for periodontics program only. Apply to Financial Aid Office within thirty days of acceptance. Phone: (901)488-5568. Use FAFSA (College code: 006725). About 89% of students receive aid from College and outside sources.

DEGREE REQUIREMENTS. For D.D.S.: satisfactory completion of forty-five-month program.

FIELDS OF GRADUATE STUDY.
General Dentistry. Two-year advanced program; no degree conferred.
Oral and Maxillofacial Surgery. Three-year advanced program; no degree conferred.
Orthodontics. Two-year advanced program; no degree conferred.
Pediatric Dentistry. Two-year advanced program; no degree conferred.
Periodontics. Two-year advanced program; no degree conferred.

Prosthodontics. Two-year advanced program; no degree conferred.

College of Medicine

Founded in 1851, moved to Memphis (38163-2166) in 1911. Annual tuition: resident $13,154, nonresident $27,620; student fees $202. Total average figure for all other expenses: $9000.

Enrollment: first-year class 150, total full-time 601 (men 54%, women 46%). College faculty: full-time 693, part-time 97. Degrees conferred: M.D., M.D.-Ph.D.

ADMISSION REQUIREMENTS. AMCAS report, transcripts, letters of recommendation, MCAT, interview required in support of application. Preference given to Tennessee and the eight contiguous state's residents. Does not have EDP. Apply to Director of Admissions after June 1, before November 15. Application fee $50. Phone: (901)448-5559; fax: (901)448-1740.

ADMISSION STANDARDS. Selective. Mean MCAT: 9.3; mean GPA: 3.59 (A = 4). Gourman rating: 3.62. Accepts about 12–15% of total annual applicants. Approximately 90% are state residents.

FINANCIAL AID. Scholarships, loans. Apply to Director of Admissions after acceptance. Phone: (901)448-5568. Use FAFSA (College code: 006725).

DEGREE REQUIREMENTS. For M.D.: satisfactory completion of four-year, 45-month program; pass Step 1 and Step 2 of USMLE.

FIELDS OF GRADUATE STUDY.
Anatomy.
Biochemistry.
Cell Biology.
Immunology.
Microbiology.
Molecular Biology.
Neurosciences.
Pathology.
Pharmacology.
Physiology.

College of Nursing

Graduate study since 1976. Annual tuition: full-time, resident $6262, nonresident $14,599.

Enrollment: full-time 136, part-time 20. Faculty: full-time 20, part-time 2. Degrees conferred: M.S.N., D.N.Sc., Ph.D.

ADMISSIONS REQUIREMENTS. Official transcripts, bachelor's degree, Graduate Program Data Form, three Graduate Rating Forms required in support of College's application. On-line application available. TOEFL, TSE required for international applicants. Accepts transfer applicants. Graduates of unaccredited colleges not considered. Preference given to Tennessee residents. Apply by March 15 (Fall), September 1 (Winter). Application fee $50. Phone: (901)448-5560; fax: (901)448-7272.

ADMISSIONS STANDARDS. Selective. Usual minimum average: 3.0 (A = 4).

FINANCIAL AID. Fellowships, assistantships, traineeships, Federal W/S, loans. Approved for VA benefits. Apply to Financial Aid Office by February 15. Phone: (901)448-5568. Use FAFSA and institutional FAF.

DEGREE REQUIREMENTS. For M.S.: 36 semester hours; thesis. For Ph.D., D.N.Sc.: 42 semester hours beyond master's; qualifying exam; dissertation; final oral exam.

FIELDS OF STUDY.
Critical and Acute Care Nurse Practitioner. M.S., D.N.Sc.
Family Nurse Practitioner. M.S., D.N.Sc.

Neonatal Nurse Practitioner. M.S., D.N.Sc.
Nurse Administration. D.N.Sc.
Nurse Anesthesia. M.S., D.N.Sc.
Psychiatric Family Nurse Practitioner. D.N.Sc.
Public Health Nursing. D.N.Sc.

College of Pharmacy

Established 1928. Located in Memphis (38163).

Annual tuition: resident $7942, nonresident $18,654. On-campus housing at Medical Units campus in Memphis for 195 men, 233 women; none for married students. (Note: There is no separation of graduate from undergraduate students.) Apply to Office of Student Housing for both on- and off-campus housing. Phone: (901)448-5609.

Enrollment: full-time 396 (men 70%, women 30%). College faculty teaching graduate students: full-time 43, part-time 37. Degrees conferred: M.S., Ph.D., Pharm.D.-Ph.D.

ADMISSION REQUIREMENTS. Transcripts, GRE required in support of application. TOEFL required, TSE recommended for international applicants. Accepts transfer applicants. Apply by February 1 to Office of Dean. Application fee $50. Phone: (901)448-5560; fax: (901)448-7772.

ADMISSION STANDARDS. Very selective for most departments. Usual minimum average: 3.0 (A = 4), GRE combined score 1500.

FINANCIAL AID. Annual awards from institutional funds: fellowships, teaching assistantships, research assistantships, internships, tuition waivers, Federal W/S, loans. Approved for VA benefits. Apply by February 15 to Office of Dean for assistantship, to Financial Aid Office for all other programs. Phone: (901)448-5568. Usa FAFSA. All full-time students receive aid other than loans from College and outside sources.

DEGREE REQUIREMENTS. For M.S.: 30 semester hours minimum; thesis/research project; final written/oral exam. For Ph.D.: minimum of six semesters beyond the B.S.; at least one year in full-time residence; proficiency in designated research tools; dissertation; final written/oral exam.

FIELDS OF STUDY.
Health Science Administration.
Pharmaceutical Studies.

UNIVERSITY OF TENNESSEE—OAK RIDGE NATIONAL LABORATORY

Oak Ridge, Tennessee 37830-8026
Web site: www.lsd.ornl.gov/gst

Coed. State control. Graduate study only. Semester system. Special facilities: DEC PDP-10, IBM 3031. Associated with Oak Ridge National Laboratory.

Annual tuition: full-time, all students are supported with either research or teaching stipend. No on-campus housing available.

Graduate School of Genome Science and Technology

Enrollment: full-time 16 (men 65%, women 35%), part-time 1. School faculty: full-time 4, part-time 24. Degrees conferred: M.S., Ph.D.

ADMISSION REQUIREMENTS. Official transcripts, GRE General/Subject Tests, three references required in support of School's application. TOEFL required for foreign applicants. Accepts transfer applicants. Apply by January 15 (Fall), November

1 (Spring) to Director of School. Application fee $35. Phone: (865)574-1227, fax: (865)576-4149.

ADMISSION STANDARDS. Very selective. Usual minimum average: 3.0 (A = 4).

FINANCIAL AID. Annual awards from institutional funds: fellowships, research assistantships, tuition waivers, loans. Apply by April 1 to Director of School. About 95% of students receive aid other than loans from University and outside sources.

DEGREE REQUIREMENTS. For M.S.: one year minimum; thesis. For Ph.D.: four years minimum; residence requirements may be reduced by previous graduate study; preliminary exam; reading knowledge of one foreign language; dissertation; final oral exam and public presentation of dissertation.

FIELDS OF STUDY.
Bioanalytical Technologies.
Computational Biology and Bioinformatics.
Mammalian Genomics.
Proteomics.
Structural Biology.

UNIVERSITY OF TENNESSEE SPACE INSTITUTE

Tullahoma, Tennessee 37388-8897
Web site: www.utsi.edu

Located 100 miles SE of Nashville. Coed. State control. Graduate study only. Semester system. Special facilities: Arnold Engineering Development Center, Aviation Systems Flight Research, Gas Dynamic Facilities, Center for Laser Application, Wind Tunnel, Water Tunnel, E-Beam and Energy Conversion Facilities. Library: 22,000 volumes, 172 subscriptions.

Annual tuition: full-time resident $3454, nonresident $10,596; per credit resident $192, nonresident $545. On-campus housing for single students only. Average academic year on-campus housing costs: $1680; off-campus housing costs: $425 per month. Contact Director of Housing for both on- and off-campus housing information. Phone: (931)393-7218.

Graduate Programs

Enrollment: full-time 62, part-time 159 (men 85%, women 15%). Graduate faculty: full-time 41, part-time 8. Degrees conferred: M.S., Ph.D.

ADMISSION REQUIREMENTS. Two official transcripts, GRE required in support of application. On-line application available. TOEFL required for international applicants. Interview not required. Accepts transfer applicants. Apply to Assistant Dean for Admissions and Student Affairs at least 2 months prior to registration. Rolling admissions process. Application fee $15, $40 for international applicants. Phone: (931)393-7432; fax: (931)393-7346.

ADMISSION STANDARDS. Very selective. Usual minimum average: 3.0 (A = 4).

FINANCIAL AID. Annual awards from institutional funds: fellowships, research assistantships, internships, full and partial tuition waivers, Federal W/S, loans. Approved for VA benefits. Apply to appropriate department for fellowships, assistantships; to Assistant Dean for Admissions and Student Affairs for all other programs. No specified closing date. Use FAFSA. Aid available for part-time students.

DEGREE REQUIREMENTS. For master's: 30–36 semester hours minimum, the equivalent of two semesters in residence unless transferring within the University of Tennessee system; thesis/nonthesis option; written/oral exam. For Ph.D.: 24 credit hours minimum beyond the master's, at one year in full-time residence; comprehensive written exam; reading knowledge of one foreign language or proficiency in research technique; dissertation; final oral exam.

FIELDS OF STUDY.
Aviation Systems.
Chemical Engineering.
Electrical and Computer Engineering.
Industrial Engineering/Engineering Management.
Materials Science and Engineering.
Mathematics.
Mechanical and Aerospace Engineering/Engineering Science.
Physics.

TEXAS A&M UNIVERSITY
College Station, Texas 77843-1244
Web site: www.tamu.edu

Founded 1876. Located 100 miles N of Houston. CGS and AAU member. Coed. Semester system. State control. Special facilities: Center for Advanced Invertebrate Molecular Sciences, Center for Alcohol and Drug Education Studies, Center for Asphalt and Materials Chemistry, Center for Bioacoustics, Center for Chemical Characterization and Analysis, Center for Comparative Animal Genetics, Center for Demographic and Socioeconomic Research and Education, Center for Electronic Materials, Devices and Systems, Center for Food Processing, Center for Fuzzy Logic, Robotics, and Intelligent Systems, Center for Health Systems and Design, Center for Human Resource Management, Center for Marine Geotechnical Engineering, Center for Nanostructure Materials and Quantum Device Fabrication, Center for Natural Resource Information Technology, Center for North American Studies, Center for Space Power, Center for Structural Biology, Center for Telecommunications Technology Management, Institute for Biosciences and Technology, Center for Biotechnology, Policy, and Ethics, Center for International Business Studies, Aerospace Vehicle Systems Institute, Global Petroleum Research Institute, Institute for Equine Science and Technology, Institute for Manufacturing Systems, Institute for Marine Life Sciences, Institute for Oil Spill Technology, Institute for Plant Genomics and Biotechnology, Institute for Scientific Computation, Institute for Nautical Archaeology, Nuclear Science Center, Offshore Technology Research Center, Polymer Technology Center, Wildlife and Exotic Animal Center, Public Policy Research Institute, Race and Ethnic Studies Center, Texas Agricultural Experiment Station, Texas Engineering Station, Texas Institute of Oceanography, Texas Transportation Institute, Texas Water Resources Institute, Runyon Art Collection, Sustainable Enterprise Institute, Space Research Center, Cyclotron Institute. The University's NIH ranking is 145th among all U.S. institutions with 83 awards/grants worth $20,922,052. Total University enrollment: 37,000. Library: 2,200,000 volumes, 17,300 subscriptions.

Tuition: per credit, resident $132, nonresident $350. Limited on-campus housing available. Average academic year housing costs: $2986–$6350. Contact Director of Campus Housing for both on- and off-campus housing information. Phone: (979)862-3158.

Office of Graduate Studies

Graduate study since 1923. Enrollment: full-time 7500, part-time 300. Graduate faculty: full-time 2000, part-time 500. Degrees conferred: M.A., M.S., M.Agr., M.Arch., M.B.A., M.C.S., M.Ed., M.Eng., M.L.A., M.P.A., M.U.P., D.ED., Ph.D., Ed.D., D.Eng.

ADMISSION REQUIREMENTS. Official transcripts, statement of purpose, three letters of recommendation, GRE/GMAT required in support of application. On-line application available. TOEFL (minimum score 550) required non-native English speakers. Interview, portfolio may be required by some departments or schools/colleges. Accepts transfer applicants. Graduates of unaccredited colleges not considered. Apply to Office of Admissions at least six weeks prior to registration; international applicants at least six months prior to registration. Application fee $50, $75 for international applicants. Phone: (979)854-1031; fax: (979) 845-0727.

ADMISSION STANDARDS. Competitive for some departments, very competitive for the others. Usual minimum average: 3.0 (A = 4).

FINANCIAL AID. Annual awards from institutional funds: scholarships, teaching assistantships, nonteaching assistantships, research assistantships, Federal W/S, loans. Approved for VA benefits. Apply to appropriate department for assistantships; to Financial Aid Office for all other programs. No specified closing date. Phone: (979)845-3236. Use FAFSA. About 65% of students receive aid other than loans from College and outside sources. Aid sometimes available for part-time students.

DEGREE REQUIREMENTS. For M.A.: 30 semester hours minimum, 9 credit hours during one semester or two consecutive six-week summer terms in residents; knowledge of one foreign language; thesis; final oral/written exam. For M.S.: 32 semester hours minimum, 9 credit hours during one semester or two consecutive six-week summer terms in residence; thesis; final oral/written exam. For M.Agr.: 36 semester hours minimum, at least 12 hours on Main Campus; balance on-campus to satisfy residence; final project; final oral/written exam. For M.Arch.: 52 hours for nonthesis program, 12 hours on Main Campus; balance on-campus to satisfy residence. For M.B.A.: 36 hours minimum, at least 12 hours on Main Campus; balance on-campus to satisfy residence; final oral/written exam. For M.C.S.: 36 hours minimum, at least 12 hours on Main Campus; balance on-campus to satisfy residence; final comprehensive exam. For M.Ed.: 36 hours minimum, at least 12 hours on Main Campus; balance on-campus to satisfy residence; final oral/written exam. For M.Eng.: 36 hours minimum, at least 16 in residence; written reports; final oral/written exam. For M.L.A.: 40 hours minimum, 12 hours on Main Campus to satisfy residence. For M.P.A.: 36 hours minimum; 12 hours on Main Campus to satisfy residence. For M.U.P.: 48 hours minimum, at least 12 hours on Main Campus; balance on-campus to satisfy residence; comprehensive oral exam. For doctorate (D.ED., Ed.D., D.Eng.): 6 semesters full-time study or its equivalent, at least 9 credit hours during two consecutive semesters or during one semester and one adjacent twelve-week summer session to satisfy residence; reading knowledge of one or two foreign languages depending on department and degree; qualifying exam; dissertation; final oral exam.

FIELDS OF STUDY.

COLLEGE OF AGRICULTURE AND LIFE SCIENCES:
Agricultural Chemistry.
Agricultural Development.
Agricultural Economics.
Agricultural Education.
Agricultural Systems Management.
Agronomy.
Animal Breeding.
Animal Science.
Biochemistry.

Biological and Agricultural Engineering.
Biophysics.
Dairy Science.
Economic Entomology.
Entomology.
Fisheries Science.
Floriculture.
Forestry.
Horticulture.
Natural Resources Development.
Physiology of Reproduction.
Plant Breeding.
Plant Pathology.
Plant Protection.
Plant Sciences.
Poultry Science.
Rangeland Ecology and Management.
Recreation and Resources Development.
Recreation, Park, and Tourism Sciences.
Rural Sociology.
Soil Science.
Wildlife and Fisheries Sciences.
Wildlife Science.

COLLEGE OF ARCHITECTURE:
Architecture.
Construction Management.
Land Development.
Landscape Architecture.
Urban and Regional Planning.
Urban and Regional Science.
Visualization Sciences.

LOWRY MAYS GRADUATE SCHOOL OF BUSINESS:
Accounting.
Business Administration.
Finance.
Information and Operations Management.
Land Economics and Real Estate.
Management.
Management Information Systems.
Marketing.

COLLEGE OF EDUCATION:
Counseling Psychology.
Curriculum and Instruction.
Educational Administration.
Education Human Resource Development.
Educational Psychology.
Educational Technology.
Health Education.
Kinesiology.
Physical Education.
School Psychology.

DWIGHT LOOK COLLEGE OF ENGINEERING:
Aerospace Engineering.
Agricultural Engineering.
Biomedical Engineering.
Chemical Engineering.
Civil Engineering.
Computer Engineering.
Computer Science.
Electrical Engineering.
Engineering.
Health Physics.
Industrial Distribution.
Industrial Engineering.
Industrial Hygiene.
Interdisciplinary Engineering.
Mechanical Engineering.
Nuclear Engineering.

Ocean Engineering.
Petroleum Engineering.
Safety Engineering.

COLLEGE OF GEOSCIENCES:
Atmospheric Sciences.
Geosciences.
Geography.
Geology.
Geophysics.
Oceanography.

COLLEGE OF LIBERAL ARTS:
Anthropology.
Comparative Literature and Cultures.
Economics.
English.
History.
Modern Languages.
Philosophy.
Psychology.
Sciences and Technology Journalism.
Sociology.
Speech Communication.

COLLEGE OF SCIENCE:
Applied Physics.
Biology.
Botany.
Chemistry.
Mathematics.
Microbiology.
Physics.
Statistics.
Zoology.

COLLEGE OF VETERINARY MEDICINE:
Epidemiology.
Laboratory Animal Medicine.
Veterinary Anatomy.
Veterinary Medical Sciences.
Veterinary Medicine and Surgery.
Veterinary Microbiology.
Veterinary Parasitology.
Veterinary Pathology.
Veterinary Physiology.
Veterinary Public Health.

GEORGE BUSH SCHOOL OF GOVERNMENT AND PUBLIC SERVICE:
Public Service and Administration.
International Affairs.

INTERDISCIPLINARY PROGRAMS:
Agribusiness.
Biotechnology.
Engineering Systems Management.
Food Science and Technology.
Genetics.
Molecular and Environmental Plant Sciences.
Nutrition.
Toxicology.

College of Veterinary Medicine (77843-4461)

Annual tuition: resident $8568, nonresident $19,368. Total average cost for all other expenses: $9500.

Enrollment: first year 128; total 500 (men 50%, women 50%). Faculty: full-time 119, part-time 3. Degrees conferred: D.V.M., M.S., Ph.D.

ADMISSION REQUIREMENTS. VMCAS report, transcripts, MCAT or GRE, 64 undergraduate credits minimum, interview, three evaluations/recommendations, animal/veterinary experience required in support of application. Accepts transfer applicants on a space-available basis only. Accepts state residents only. Apply after July 1, before October 1. Application fee $45. Phone: (979)845-5038.

ADMISSION STANDARDS. Selective. Usual minimum average: 2.90 (A = 4). Mean GPA: 3.60 (A = 4). Admits 30% of total annual applicants. Accepts approximately seven nonresident applicants annually.

FINANCIAL AID. Fellowships, assistantships, partial tuition waivers, Federal W/S, loans available. Apply to Director of Student Financial Aid. Use FAFSA.

DEGREE REQUIREMENTS. For D.V.M.: satisfactory completion of three-year program. For M.S., Ph.D.: see Graduate College listings above.

FIELDS OF GRADUATE STUDY.
Epidemiology.
Laboratory Animal Medicine.
Veterinary Anatomy.
Veterinary Medicine and Surgery (Small and Large Animal).
Veterinary Microbiology.
Veterinary Parasitology.
Veterinary Pathology.
Veterinary Physiology.
Veterinary Public Health.

TEXAS A&M UNIVERSITY— COMMERCE

Commerce, Texas 75429
Web site: www.tamu-commerce.edu

Founded 1889. In 1996 East Texas State University entered the Texas A&M University System. Located 65 miles NE of Dallas. Coed. State control. Semester system. Library: 1,500,219 volumes, 422,000 microforms, 48 PCs.

Tuition: per credit, resident $168.50, nonresident $379.50. On-campus housing for 250 married students, 1558 single students. Average academic year housing cost: $2475 for married students, $4055 (including board) for single students. Apply to Director of Housing. Phone: (903)886-5797. Day-care facilities available.

Graduate School

Graduate study since 1936, Enrollment: full-time 584, part-time 1995. Faculty: full-time 200, part-time 15. Degrees conferred: M.A., M.S., M.M., M.F.A., M.Ed., M.B.A., M.S.L.S., Ph.D., Ed.D.

ADMISSION REQUIREMENTS. Transcript, GRE GMAT, four recommendations (Ph.D.) required in support of School's application. TOEFL required for foreign applicants. Interview not required. Accepts transfer applicants. Graduates of unaccredited institutions not considered. Apply to the Graduate School at least one month (90 days for international applicants) prior to registration. Phone: (903)886-5167; fax: (903)886-5165.

ADMISSION STANDARDS. Selective. Usual minimum average 2.75 (A = 4).

FINANCIAL AID. Assistantships for teaching/research, Federal W/S, loans. Approved for VA benefits. Apply to Financial Aid Office at least four months before aid is needed. Phone: (903)886-5096. Use FAFSA and institutional FAF.

DEGREE REQUIREMENTS. For M.A.: 30 semester hours minimum, at least 24 credits in residence; reading knowledge of one foreign language; admission to candidacy; thesis; final comprehensive exam. For M.S., M.M., M.B.A., M.S.L.S.: ten graduate courses minimum, at least eight in residence; thesis and final oral exam; or twelve graduate courses without thesis. For M.Ed.: 36 semester hour program; final comprehensive exam. For M.F.A.: 62 semester hour program; thesis/creative exhibit. For Ph.D.: 90 semester hours minimum beyond the bachelor's, at least one year in residence; reading knowledge of two foreign languages; qualifying exam; dissertation; final oral exam. For Ed.D.: generally the same as for the Ph.D., except proficiency in computer science, statistics or foreign language.

FIELDS OF STUDY.

COLLEGE OF ARTS AND SCIENCES:
Agricultural Sciences.
Agricultural Education.
Art.
Biological Sciences,
Broadfield Science.
Chemistry.
College Teaching of English. Ph.D. only.
Computer Science.
Earth Science.
History.
English.
Mathematics.
Music
Music Composition.
Music Education.
Music Literature.
Music Performance.
Music Theory.
Physics.
Social Sciences.
Social Work.
Sociology.
Spanish.
Theatre.

COLLEGE OF BUSINESS AND TECHNOLOGY:
Business Administration.
Economics.
Industrial Technology.
Marketing.
Management.

COLLEGE OF EDUCATION:
Counseling.
Early Childhood Education.
Educational Administration.
Educational Psychology. Ph.D. only.
Elementary Education.
Health, Kinesiology, and Sport Studies.
Higher Education Administration.
Higher Education Teaching.
Learning Technology and Information Systems. Includes educational computing, library and information science, media and technology.
Psychology.
Reading.
Secondary Education.
Supervision, Curriculum, and Instruction—Elementary Education. Ed.D. only.
Supervision, Curriculum, and Instruction—Higher Education. Ed.D. only.
Training and Development.
Special Education.

TEXAS A&M UNIVERSITY— CORPUS CHRISTI

Corpus Christi, Texas 78412-5503

Web site: www.tamucc.edu

Established 1947. Name changed 1989. Coed. Semester system. State control. Special facilities: Center for Coastal Studies, Environmental Research Consortium, Haite Research Institute for Gulf of Mexico Studies, Conrad Bluche Institute for Surveying and Science, Center for Water Supply Studies, Center for Educational Development, Evaluation, and Research, Center for Business and Economic Research, Natural Resource Center, Social Science Research Center, Wells Gallery. Library: 500,000, 2204 subscriptions. Total University enrollment: 7400.

Tuition: per credit resident $132, nonresident $350. Limited on-campus housing available for single students, none for married students. Average academic year housing costs: $3000–$3500; off-campus housing costs: $450–$550 per month. Contact Director of Housing for both on- and off-campus housing information. Phone: (361)825-2612.

Graduate Division

Enrollment: full-time 262, part-time 977. Graduate faculty: full-time 109, part-time 49. Degrees conferred: M.A., M.Acc., M.B.A., M.P.A., M.S., M.S.N., Ed.D.

ADMISSION REQUIREMENTS. Official transcripts, GRE/GMAT required in support of application. Letters of recommendation, writing samples, portfolio may be required by some degree programs. TOEFL (minimum score 550) required nonnative English speakers. Interview not required. Accepts transfer applicants. Graduates of unaccredited colleges not considered. Apply to Office of Graduate Studies and Research by July 15 (Fall), November 15 (Spring). Application fee $20, $50 for international applicants. Phone: (361)825-2177.

ADMISSION STANDARDS. Selective. Usual minimum average: 2.75 (A = 4).

FINANCIAL AID. Annual awards from institutional funds: scholarships, assistantships, Federal W/S, loans. Approved for VA benefits. Apply by March 15 to Financial Aid Office. Phone: (361)825-2338. Use FAFSA. About 25% of students receive aid other than loans from College and outside sources. Aid available to part-time students.

DEGREE REQUIREMENTS. For M.A., M.S., M.S.N.: 30–36 semester hours minimum, thesis/nonthesis option; final oral/written exam. For M.B.A., M.Acc.: 36 hours minimum, final oral/written exam. For M.P.A.: 36 hours minimum; comprehensive oral exam. For Ed.D.: six semesters full-time study or its equivalent, at least 9 credit hours during two consecutive semesters or during one semester and one adjacent twelve-week summer session to satisfy residence; qualifying exam; dissertation; final oral exam.

FIELDS OF STUDY.
Accountancy.
Biology.
Business Administration.
Computer Science.
Counseling.
Curriculum and Instruction.
Early Childhood Education.
Educational Administration.
Educational Leadership.
Educational Technology.
Elementary Education.
English.
Environmental Sciences.
History.
Interdisciplinary. Includes arts, humanities, social sciences.
Mariculture.
Mathematics.
Nursing.
Occupational Training and Development.
Psychology.
Public Administration.
Reading.
School Counseling.
Secondary Education.
Special Education.
Studio Arts.

TEXAS A&M UNIVERSITY— KINGSVILLE

Kingsville, Texas 78363

Web site: www.tamuk.edu

Founded 1925. Became part of Texas A&M system 1989. Located 40 miles SW of Corpus Christi. Coed. State control. Semester system. Special facilities: Caesar Kleberg Wildlife Research Institute, Citrus Center, Monoclonal Antibody Facility. Library 460,000 volumes, 2300 subscriptions. Total University enrollment: 6000.

Annual tuition: full-time resident $1666, nonresident $5518. On-campus housing for married students. Average academic year housing cost: $450–$550 per month. Contact Campus Housing Office for both on- and off-campus housing information. Phone: (361)593-3419. Day-care facilities available.

College of Graduate Studies

Enrollment: full-time 360, part-time 763. Faculty: full-time 120, part-time 26. Degrees conferred: M.A., M.S., M.M., M.P.A., M.B.A., M.Engineering, M.Ed., Ed.D. (BiLing.Ed., Ed. Admin.), Ph.D. (Wildlife Sciences).

ADMISSION REQUIREMENTS. Transcripts, GRE/GMAT required in support of College's application. TOEFL (minimum score 500) required for international applicants. Accepts transfer applicants. Apply by April 15 (Fall), November 15 (Spring) to Director of Admissions. Application fee $15, $25 for international applicants. Phone: (361)593-3711.

ADMISSION STANDARDS. Selective. Usual minimum average: 3.0 (A = 4).

FINANCIAL AID. Scholarships, fellowships, assistantships, internships, tuition waivers, Federal W/S, loans. Apply by May 15 to Director of Financial Aid. Phone: (361)593-3911. Use FAFSA.

DEGREE REQUIREMENTS. For master's: 30 semester hours minimum, thesis often required; final written/oral exam. For Ed.D.: 60 semester hours minimum beyond master's degree, at least 48 in residence; qualifying exam; candidacy; dissertation; final oral exam.

FIELDS OF STUDY.
Agriculture. Includes agribusiness, agricultural education, animal science, human sciences, plant and soil sciences, range and wildlife management, wildlife science.

COLLEGE OF AGRICULTURE AND HUMAN SCIENCES:
Agribusiness.
Agriculture Education.
Animal Science.
Human Science. M.S.H.S. only.
Plant and Soil Science.
Range and Wildlife Management.
Wildlife Science. Joint Ph.D. program with Texas A&M University, College Station.

COLLEGE OF ARTS AND SCIENCES:
Art.
Biology.
Chemistry.
Communication Science and Disorders.
English.
Geology.
Gerontology.
History and Politics.
Mathematics.
Music Education.
Psychology.
Sociology.
Spanish.

COLLEGE OF BUSINESS ADMINISTRATION:
Accounting.
Business Administration.

COLLEGE OF EDUCATION:
Adult Education.
Bilingual Education.
Counseling and Guidance.
Early Childhood Education.
Educational Administration.
Educational Leadership.
English as a Second Language.
Kinesiology.
Reading.
Special Education.
Supervision.

COLLEGE OF ENGINEERING:
Chemical Engineering.
Civil Engineering.
Computer Science.
Electrical Engineering.
Environmental Engineering.
Industrial Engineering.
Mechanical Engineering.
Natural Gas Engineering.

TEXAS A&M UNIVERSITY SYSTEM HEALTH SCIENCE CENTER

College Station, Texas 77840-7896
Web site: www.tamushsc.edu

Coed. State control. Semester system. Has locations in Dallas, Temple, and Houston. Library: 200,000 volumes, 2000 subscriptions. The Health Science Center's NIH ranking is 180th among all U.S. institutions with 63 awards/grants worth $14,024,629.

The Graduate School of Biomedical Sciences includes the following units: Baylor College of Dentistry (Dallas), College of Medicine (College Station, Temple), Institute of Biosciences and Technology (Houston), School of Rural Public Health (College Station; M.S. and Ph.D. are under development.). On-campus housing available at all locations.

Baylor College of Dentistry
P.O. Box 660677
Dallas, Texas 75266-0677

Founded in 1905. Affiliated with Baylor University from 1918–1971. Became independent corporation in 1971. Joined the Texas A&M System in 1996 and Health Science Center in 1999. Quarter system. Library: 26,800 volumes, 3100 microforms, 500 current periodicals, 16 PCs.

Annual tuition: resident $5400, nonresident $16,200, fees $2100. Off-campus housing available. Average academic year housing costs: $14,150. Contact the Housing Office for housing information. Phone: (214)828-8210. Total average cost for all other expenses in first year: $6800.

Enrollment: D.D.S. program, first-year class 89; full-time 360 (men 65%, women 35%), graduate study 39. Faculty: full-time 99, part-time 130. Degrees conferred: D.D.S., M.S., M.S.D.

ADMISSION REQUIREMENTS. For D.D.S. program: official transcripts, three letters of recommendation, DAT, personal interview required in support of College's application. Out-of-state applicants use AADSAS. Accepts transfer applicants. Applicants must have completed at least three years of college study. Apply through the Texas Medical and Dental Schools Application Service after May 1, before November 1 (flexible). Application fee $35. Phone: (214)828-8230.

For graduate study: official transcripts, three letters of recommendation, GRE, interview required in support of College's application. Accepts transfer applicants. Graduates of unaccredited colleges not considered. Apply to Registrar of the College after May 1, before November 1. Application fee $35.

ADMISSION STANDARDS. For D.D.S. program: competitive. Mean DAT: Academic 19, PAT 17.8; mean GPA: 3.42 (A = 4). Gourman rating: 3.09. Accepts 30% of total annual applicants. Approximately 90% are state residents. For graduate study: competitive. Usual minimum average: 3.0 (A = 4).

FINANCIAL AID. For D.D.S. program: scholarships, grants, tuition waivers, loans. Apply to Office Financial Aid; no specified closing date. Use FAFSA. Phone: (214)828-8236. For graduate study: fellowships, assistantships for teaching/research. Apply as soon as possible to Head of Department. Use FAFSA (College code: 004448). About 88% of students receive aid other than loans from University and outside sources.

DEGREE REQUIREMENTS. For D.D.S.: satisfactory completion of 45-month program. For M.S., M.S.D.: 45 quarter hours minimum (90 for Clinical Dentistry) ; thesis; comprehensive oral exam. For Ph.D.: 117 quarter hours minimum beyond the master's; preliminary exam; reading knowledge of two foreign languages; final written exam; dissertation; final oral exam.

FIELDS OF graduate STUDY.
Biomedical Sciences.
Dental Hygiene. M.S.
Endodontics.
General Dentistry.
Health Professions Education.
Oral and Maxillofacial Pathology.
Oral and Maxillofacial Surgery.
Orthodontics.
Pediatric Dentistry.
Pedodontics.
Periodontics.
Prosthodontics.

College of Medicine (77843-1114)
Web site: www.tamushsc.edu

Established 1973. Joined the Texas A&M University System Health Science Center in 1999. Library 75,000 volumes. Annual tuition: resident $6550, nonresident $19,650; student fees $1290. Enrollment: first-year class 68; total 187 (men 50%, women 50%). Faculty: full- and part-time 674. Degrees conferred: M.D., M.D.-Ph.D.

ADMISSION REQUIREMENTS. AMCAS report, transcripts, MCAT, three letters of recommendation required in support of application. Interview by invitation. Preference given to state residents. Does not have EDP. Apply through the Texas Medical and Dental Schools Application Service after May 1, before November 1. Application fee $45. Phone: (979)845-7743; fax: (979) 845-5533.

ADMISSION STANDARDS. Competitive. Mean MCAT: 9.6; mean GPA: 3.71. Gourman rating: 3.09. Admits about 8–10% of total annual applicants. Approximately 95% are state residents.

FINANCIAL AID. Scholarships, loans. Apply after acceptance to Student Affairs Office. Phone: (979)845-7743. Use FAFSA (School code: 003632). About 90% of students receive some aid from School.

DEGREE REQUIREMENTS. For M.D.: satisfactory completion of four-year program. For Ph.D.: see Graduate College listing above.

FIELDS OF GRADUATE STUDY.
Anatomy.
Biochemistry.
Biomedical Engineering.
Biophysics.
Cell Biology.
Genetics.
Immunology.
Microbiology.
Molecular Biology.
Neurosciences.
Pathology.
Pharmacology.
Physiology.

TEXAS CHRISTIAN UNIVERSITY

Fort Worth, Texas 76129-0002
Web site: www.tcu.edu

Founded 1873. CGS member. Coed. Private control. Semester system. Special facilities: Center for Remote Sensing, Center for Texas Studies, Experimental Mesocosm Facility, Lake Worth Fish Hatchery, Institute of Behavioral Research, cooperative association with Oak Ridge Institute of Nuclear Studies. Library: 1,300,000 volumes, 4700 subscriptions.

Tuition: per credit $420, M.B.A. $455. Campus housing for married students at Brite Divinity School campus housing; none for graduate single students. Contact the Housing Office for both on- and off-campus housing information. Phone: (817)257-7865.

Graduate Studies

Enrollment: full-time 462, part-time 638. Faculty: full-time 217. Degrees conferred: M.A., M.Acc., M.B.A., M.Ed., M.F.A., M.L.A., M.M., M.M.Ed., M.S., M.S.E., Certificate program, D.M., Ph.D.

ADMISSION REQUIREMENTS. Official transcripts, GRE/GMAT required in support of graduate application. On-line application available. TOEFL and International Student and Scholar Form required for international applicants. Interview not required. Accepts transfer applicants. Graduates of unaccredited institu-

tions not considered. Apply to Graduate Office at least six weeks prior to registration. Application fee $50. Phone: (817)257-7515, (800)828-3764; fax: (817)257-7134. For M.B.A.: phone: (817)257-7531; fax: (817)257-7227.

ADMISSION STANDARDS. Very selective for most departments. Usual minimum average: 3.0 (A = 4).

FINANCIAL AID. Annual awards from institutional funds: fellowships, teaching assistantships, research assistantships, internships, traineeships, Federal W/S, loans. Approved for VA benefits. Apply by March 1 to Graduate School for fellowship, assistantships, internships; to Financial Aid Office for all other programs. Use FAFSA and institution FAF. Phone: (817)257-7858; fax: (817)257-7333. About 77% of students receive aid other than loans from School and outside sources. Limited aid for part-time students.

DEGREE REQUIREMENTS. For master's: 30 semester hours minimum, at least 24 in residence; thesis; final oral exam. For Administrator's Certificate: 60 semester hours beyond the bachelor's degree; special project. For D.M., Ph.D.: three years minimum beyond the bachelor's degree, the second year or its equivalent in full-time residence; reading knowledge of one or two foreign languages, depending upon department; qualifying exam; dissertation; final oral exam.

FIELDS OF STUDY.
Accounting. M.Acc.
Art History. Comprehensive exam for candidacy. M.F.A. only.
Ballet. Final artistic project for degree. M.F.A. only.
Biology.
Business. GMAT for admission. Includes management statistics. M.B.A. only.
Chemistry. German proficiency, cumulative exam required for Ph.D.
Communication in Human Relations. M.S.
Counseling.
Economics. M.A. only.
Educational Administration.
Elementary Education.
English. Candidacy exam for M.A.; one modern language, qualifying exam for Ph.D.
Environmental Sciences.
Geology. Preliminary exam for M.S.
History. One modern language, qualifying exam for Ph.D.
Journalism.
Kinesiology.
Liberal Arts. M.L.A. only.
Mathematics.
Media Arts. Final written exam for M.S. M.S. only.
Modern Dance.
Music. Includes performance, musicology, theory. M.M., M.M.Ed. only.
Nursing.
Physics and Astronomy. One language, qualifying exam for Ph.D.
Psychology. One language, other exams for Ph.D.
Secondary Education.
Special Education.
Speech Communication. Final written exam for M.S. M.S. only.
Speech Pathology. Comprehensive exam for M.S.

TEXAS SOUTHERN UNIVERSITY

Houston, Texas 77004-4584
Web site: www.tsu.edu

Founded 1947. CGS member. State control. Semester system. Special facilities: Cancer Prevention Awareness Center, Center for Excellence in Education, Economic Development Center, Center for Excellence in Urban Education, Center for Transportation Training and Research, Mickey Leland Center on World Hunger and Peace, Center on the Family, Research Center for Minority Institutions, Environmental Science Institute, Center for Toxicological Studies, Minority Biomedical Research Support Program, Environmental Research and Technology Transfer Center, Center for Aging for Horizon Intergenerational Wellness, Center for Cardiovascular Research. Library: 473,500 volumes, 1715 subscriptions. Total University enrollment: 8000.

Annual tuition: full-time resident $2600, nonresident $7200. On-campus housing for married and single students. Average academic year housing costs: $4500–$7500 for married students, $4000 (including board) for single students. Off-campus housing costs: $480 per month. Contact Director of Housing for both on- and off-campus housing information. Phone: (713)527-7205.

Graduate School

Established 1947. Enrollment: full- and part-time 900. Faculty: full-time 158, part-time 38. Degrees conferred: M.A., M.S., M.Ed., M.B.A., M.Mus.Ed., M.C.R., M.P.A., Ed.D., Ph.D., D.Pharm.

ADMISSION REQUIREMENTS. Official transcripts, GRE/GMAT required in support of School's application. TOEFL (minimum score 550) required of international applicants. Accepts transfer applicants. Graduates of unaccredited institutions not considered. Apply to the School by July 15 (Fall), November 15 (Spring), May 1 (Summer). Application fee $35, $75 for international applicants. Phone: (713)313-7232; fax: (713)313-1876.

ADMISSION STANDARDS. Selective. Usual minimum average: 2.5, or 3.0 last 60 credits (A = 4); for M.B.A., 2.75 minimum average (undergraduate GPA plus 200) plus GMAT score = 950; for Ed.D., average GPA for the last 60 semester hours times 100 plus the verbal and quantitative must = at least 1000, minimum average must be at least 2.5.; for Ph.D., 2.75 GPA, GRE score at least 950.

FINANCIAL AID. Fellowships, assistantships, internships, grants, Federal W/S, loans. Approved for VA benefits. Apply by April 30 to Graduate School for assistantships; to Financial Aid Office for all other programs. Phone: (713)313-7207. Use FAFSA and University's FAF. About 25% of students receive aid other than loans from University and outside sources.

DEGREE REQUIREMENTS. For master's: 36 semester hours minimum, at least 30 in residence; thesis/nonthesis option. For M.B.A.: 36 semester hours minimum; 27 in residence. For M.P.A. (Accounting): 36 semester hours minimum, 30 in residence. For M.C.P., M.P.A. (Public Administration), M.A. (Psychology): 48 semester hours minimum; 42 in residence; thesis/no thesis option. For Ed.D.: 72 semester hours minimum, 57 in residence; qualifying exam; dissertation; final oral exam. For Ph.D.: 75 semester hours minimum, at least 66 in residence; candidacy; reading knowledge of one or two foreign languages; dissertation; final oral exam.

FIELDS OF STUDY.
Accounting. M.P.A.
Administrative Management Systems.
Biology.
Business Administration.
Chemistry.
City Planning.
Communications.
Counseling.
Counselor Education.
Education. Includes elementary, secondary (usual subject areas), administration and supervision, higher, curriculum and instruction.
English.
Environmental Toxicology.
General Business.
Health and Human Performance.
History.
Human Services and Consumer Sciences.
Industrial Technology.
Mathematics.
Music. Includes applied, education, composition, musicology.
Psychology.
Public Administration.
Sociology.
Transportation Management and Planning.

Thurgood Marshall School of Law (77004)

Web site: www.tsulaw.edu

Established 1947. ABA approved since 1949. AALS member. Semester system. Law library: 147,728 volumes; 2463 subscriptions. Has LEXIS, WESTLAW, DIALOG.

Annual tuition: full-time resident $5450, nonresident $8874. No on-campus housing available. Total average annual expense: $9920.

Enrollment: first-year class 250, total 623 (men 52%, women 48%). Faculty: full-time 22, part-time 12. Student to faculty ratio 23.6 to 1. Degrees conferred: J.D., J.D.-M.A. (History). J.D.-M.B.A., J.D.-M.P.A.

ADMISSION REQUIREMENTS. LSDAS Law School report, bachelor's degree, two transcripts, LSAT, two letters of recommendation required in support of application. Accepts transfer applicants. Interview not required. Graduates of unaccredited colleges not considered. Preference given to state residents. Admits to Fall semester only. Apply to the Office of Admissions by April 1. Application fee $40. Phone: (713)527-7114.

ADMISSION STANDARDS. Selective. Mean LSAT: 142; mean GPA: 2.74 (A = 4). Gourman rating: 2.33. *U.S. News & World Report* ranking is in the fourth tier of all U.S. law schools. Accepts 30–35% of total annual applicants.

FINANCIAL AID. Scholarships, partial tuition waivers, fellowships, assistantships, Federal W/S, loans. Apply to Director of Financial Aid by May 1. Use FAFSA (School code: 003642). About 90% of students receive some of aid.

DEGREE REQUIREMENTS. For J.D.: 90 semester hours minimum, at least 45 in residence. For master's degrees: see Graduate School listing above.

TEXAS TECH UNIVERSITY

Lubbock, Texas 79409
Web site: www.ttu.edu

Founded 1923. CGS member. Coed. State control. Semester system. Special facilities: Center for Agricultural Technology, Center for Applied Research in Industrial/Automation and Robotics, Institute for Banking and Financial Studies, Institute for Communications Research, Community Design Center, Institute for Disaster Research, Institute for Ergonomics Research, Center for Feed and Industry Research and Education, Center for Forensic Studies, Center for Historic Preservation and Technology, Child Development Center, Center for Petroleum Mathematics, International Textile Research Center, International Center for Arid and Semi-Arid Land Studies, Center for the Study of Addiction, Center for Professional Development, Institute of Environmental and Human Health, Plant Stress and Water Conservation Institute, Center for Public Service, Ranching Heritage

Center, Center for the Study of the Vietnam Conflict, Texas Wine Marketing Research Center, Turkish Oral Archives, Wildlife and Fisheries Management Institute. Library: 4,200,000 volumes, 27,000 subscriptions. Total University enrollment: 24,000.

Annual tuition: full-time resident $1854; nonresident $5724; per credit resident $103, nonresident $318. On-campus housing for single students, none for married students. Annual housing costs: $5079 (including board). Apply to Director of Housing Reservation: Phone: (806)742-2261; to Student Association off-campus housing information: Phone: (806)742-3631. Day-care facilities available.

Graduate School

Graduate study since 1927. Enrollment: full-time 2088, part-time 1300 (men 50%, women 50%). Faculty: full-time 740, part-time 44. Degrees conferred: M.A., M.B.A., M.Ed., M.F.A., M.Eng., M.Ag., M.A.Ed., M.P.A., M.M.E., M.S.Ch.E., M.S.C.E., M.S.E.E., M.S.I.E., M.S.M.E., M.S.P.E., M.S.H.E., M.S., Ed.D., Ph.D.

ADMISSION REQUIREMENTS. Official transcripts, GRE/GMAT required in support of School's application. On-line application available. Letters of recommendation required for some departments. TOEFL required for international applicants. Interview not required. Accepts transfer applicants. Graduates of unaccredited institutions not considered. Apply to Office of the Dean of Graduate Admissions by March 1 (Fall), October 1 (Spring). Application fee $40, $50 for international applicants. Phone: (806)742-2787; fax: (806)742-4038; e-mail: gradschool@ttu.edu.

ADMISSION STANDARDS. Selective for most departments. Usual minimum average: 3.0 (A = 4) or 1000 GRE.

FINANCIAL AID. Annual awards from institutional funds: scholarships, fellowships, teaching assistantships, research assistantships, out-of-state tuition waivers, Federal W/S, loans. Approved for VA benefits. Apply by May 1 to appropriate department chairman for assistantships; to Financial Aid Office for all other programs. Phone: (806)742-3681; fax: (806)742-0880. Use FAFSA and University's FAF. About 20% of students receive aid other than loans from College and outside sources. Aid available for part-time students.

DEGREE REQUIREMENTS. For master's: 30–36 semester hours minimum, at least 24 in residence; thesis/nonthesis option; final comprehensive exam; foreign language requirements vary by department. For doctorates: 72 semester hours minimum, at least two consecutive semesters in residence; oral/written preliminary exam; oral/written qualifying exam for candidacy; foreign language requirements vary by department and program; dissertation; final oral exam.

FIELDS OF STUDY.

GRADUATE SCHOOL:
Interdisciplinary Studies. Includes biotechnology, heritage management, multidisciplinary science, museum science, public administration.

COLLEGE OF AGRICULTURAL SCIENCES AND NATURAL RESOURCES:
Agriculture.
Agricultural and Applied Economics.
Agricultural Education.
Agronomy.
Animal Science.
Crop Science.
Fisheries Science.

Food Technology.
Landscape Architecture. M.L.A. only.
Range Science.
Soil Science.
Wildlife Science.

COLLEGE OF ARCHITECTURE:
Architecture. Master's only.
Land Use Planning, Management, and Design.

COLLEGE OF ARTS AND SCIENCES:
Anthropology.
Applied Linguistics.
Applied Physics.
Atmospheric Science.
Biology.
Chemistry.
Classics.
Communication Studies.
Economics.
English.
Environmental Toxicology.
Exercise and Sport Sciences.
French.
Geosciences.
German.
History.
Mass Communication.
Mathematics.
Microbiology.
Philosophy.
Physics.
Political Science.
Psychology. Includes clinical, counseling, experimental.
Sociology.
Spanish.
Sports Health.
Statistics.
Technical Communication and Rhetoric.
Technical Communications.
Zoology.

COLLEGE OF BUSINESS ADMINISTRATION:
Accounting. Includes auditing/financial reporting, information systems assurance, accounting information systems design, controllership, taxation.
Business Administration. Includes accounting, business statistics, finance, management, management information systems, marketing, production and operations management, taxation, telecom technology management.
General Business. Includes health organization management.

COLLEGE OF EDUCATION:
Bilingual Education.
Counselor Education.
Curriculum and Instruction.
Educational Leadership.
Educational Psychology.
Elementary Education.
Higher Education.
Instructional Technology.
Literacy.
Secondary Education.
Special Education.
Supervision.

COLLEGE OF ENGINEERING:
Chemical Engineering.
Civil Engineering.
Computer Science.
Electrical Engineering.

Environmental Engineering.
Environmental Technology Management. Master's only.
Industrial Engineering.
Manufacturing Systems and Engineering.
Mechanical Engineering.
Petroleum Engineering.
Software Engineering.
Systems and Engineering Management.

COLLEGE OF HUMAN SCIENCES:
Environmental Design.
Environmental Design and Consumer Economics.
Family and Consumer Sciences Education.
Family Financial Planning.
Food and Nutrition.
Human Development and Family Studies.
Marriage and Family Therapy.
Restaurant, Hotel, and Institutional Management.

COLLEGE OF VISUAL AND PERFORMING ARTS:
Art.
Art Education.
Fine Arts (Interdisciplinary). Includes arts, music, theatre.
Music. Includes instrument, voice.
Music Composition.
Music Conducting.
Music Education.
Music History and Literature.
Music Performance.
Music Piano Pedagogy.
Music Theory.
Theatre and Dance.
Theatre Arts.

School of Law

Web site: www.law.ttu.edu

Established 1967. ABA approved since 1969. AALS member since 1969. Semester system. Library: 285,294 volumes, 2362 subscriptions; has LEXIS, NEXIS, WESTLAW.

Annual tuition: resident $6973, nonresident $12,043. On and off-campus housing available. Apply to Housing Office. Total average annual additional expense: $10,485.

Enrollment: first-year class 269; total 650 (men 56%, women 44%). Faculty: full-time 18, part-time 14. Student to faculty ratio 30.1 to 1. Degrees conferred: J.D., J.D.-M.B.A., J.D.-M.P.A., J.D.-M.S. (Agricultural Economics, Accounting), J.D.-M.E.T. (Environmental Toxicology).

ADMISSION REQUIREMENTS. LSDAS Law School report, bachelor's degree, transcripts, LSAT, letters of recommendation required in support of application. Accepts transfer applicants. Graduates of unaccredited colleges not considered. Apply to Dean by February 1. Rolling admissions process. Admits Fall only. Application fee $50. Phone: (806)742-3791; fax: (806)742-1629.

ADMISSION STANDARDS. Selective. Mean LSAT: 153; mean GPA: 3.33 (A = 4). Gourman rating: 3.18. *U.S. News & World Report* ranking is in the fourth tier of all U.S. law schools. Accepts about 50% of total annual applicants.

FINANCIAL AID. Scholarships, assistantships, Federal W/S, loans. Apply to Office of the Director of Financial Aid by June 1. Use FAFSA (School code: 003644). Approximately 43% of students receive some form of financial assistance.

DEGREE REQUIREMENTS. For J.D.: satisfactory completion of 90 credit hour program. For master's degree: see Graduate School listing above.

TEXAS TECH UNIVERSITY HEALTH SCIENCES CENTER
Lubbock, Texas 79430
Web site: www.ttuhsc.edu

Founded 1979. Located adjacent to main campus. Schools located at Health Sciences Center are Graduate School of Biomedical Sciences, School of Allied Health, School of Medicine, School of Nursing, School of Pharmacy. Library: 225,00 volumes, 1600 subscriptions.

School of Allied Health Sciences (79430)

Founded 1981. Tuition: per credit, resident $88, nonresident $306. Enrollment: full- and part-time 500. Faculty: full-time 162, part-time 22. Degrees conferred: M.A.T., M.S.O.T., M.S.R.S., M.S.P.A., M.S.M.P., M.V.R., Au.D., Sc.D.

ADMISSION REQUIREMENTS. Official transcripts, two recommendations, GRE, interview required in support of School's application. On-line application available. Interview encouraged, TOEFL required for international applicants. Graduates of unaccredited colleges not considered. Preference given to Texas residents. Apply to the Office of Registrar before February 15. Application fee: $30, $55 for international. Phone: (806)743-3220; fax: (806)473-3249.

ADMISSION STANDARDS. Selective. Usual minimum average: 2.7–3.0 (A = 4).

FINANCIAL AID. Scholarships, assistantships, fellowships, internships, tuition waiver, Federal W/S, loans. Apply by April 1 to the Financial Aid Office. Phone: (806)743-3025. Use FAFSA (School code: 016024).

DEGREE REQUIREMENTS. For M.A.T.: 47 credit program; thesis/nonthesis option. For M.S.O.T.: 102 credit full-time, three-year program; fieldwork experience; thesis/nonthesis. For M.S.M.P.: 42 credit full-time; clinical preceptorship. For M.S.P.A.: 31-month full-time program. For M.S.R.S.: 48 credit program, internships; clinical practice. For M.V.R.: 48 credit program; clinical internship; practicum. For Au.D.: 125 credit four-year program; clinical internship; clinical practicum; dissertation; oral defense. For Sc.D.: 38 credit program with master's (70 credit program with bachelor's); clinical internship; clinical project.

FIELDS OF STUDY.
Athletic Training. M.A.T.
Audiology. Au.D.
Molecular Pathology. M.S.M.P.
Occupational Therapy. M.S.O.T.
Physical Therapy. M.S.P.T., Sc.D.
Physician Assistant Program. M.S.P.A.
Rehabilitation Counseling. M.S.
Rehabilitation Science. Includes management track, gerontology track. M.S.R.S.
Speech-Language Pathology. M.S.
Vocational Rehabilitation. M.V.R.

School of Medicine

Established 1969 and is part of University Health Science Center, Lubbock (79430). Annual tuition: resident $7325, nonresident $20,425; student fees $925. Total average cost for all other expenses: $10,206.

Enrollment: first-year class 125 (EDP 5); total 391 (men 60%, women 40%). Faculty: full- and part-time 314. Degrees conferred: M.D., M.D.-Ph.D., M.D.-M.B.A.

ADMISSION REQUIREMENTS. Applicants from Texas, Southwestern Oklahoma, Eastern New Mexico given preference, U.S. citizens and permanent residents only. Bachelor's degree from an accredited institution required. Has EDP; applicants must apply directly to Office of Admission between June 1 and August 1. Early applications are encouraged. All other applicants request publication forms and procedural information from the Texas Medical and Dental School Application Service and submit application and application fee (resident $55, nonresident $100), MCAT, official transcripts, a personal statement, two recommendations to the Application Service Center. A secondary application and application fee of $40 is required by the TTUHSC School of Medicine. Interviews are by invitation only and generally for final selection. Notification for EDP normally begins October 1. For regular admission apply after June 1, before November 1. Submit MCAT (will accept MCAT test results from the last three years), official transcripts for each school attended (should show at least 90 semester credits/135 quarter credits; submit transcripts by mid-May to AMCAS), an application and application fee of $40, a personal statement, preprofessional committee evaluation and three recommendations from science faculty to Office of Admission. Interviews are by invitation only and generally for final selection. Dual degree applicants must apply to and be accepted to both Schools; contact the Office of Admission for current information and specific admissions requirements. First-year students admitted Fall only. Rolling admissions process; notification starts October 15 and is finished when class is filled. School does maintain an alternate list. Phone: (806)743-2297; fax: (806)743-2725.

ADMISSION STANDARDS. Selective. Mean MCAT: 9.5; mean GPA: 3.58 (A = 4). Accepts about 15–20% of total annual applicants. Approximately 98% are state residents.

FINANCIAL AID. Scholarships, merit scholarships, minority scholarships, Grants-in-Aid, HEAL, loans. Apply to Office of Student Financial Aid after acceptance. Phone: (806)743-3025. Use FAFSA (School code: 016024). About 65% of students receive financial assistance.

DEGREE REQUIREMENTS. For M.D.: satisfactory completion of four-year program; all students spend the first two years in Lubbock then the third and fourth years in Lubbock, Amarillo, or El Paso. For Ph.D.: see Texas Tech University listing above.

FIELDS OF GRADUATE STUDY.
Anatomy.
Cell Biology and Biochemistry.
Genetics.
Microbiology and Immunology.
Molecular Biology.
Pharmacology.
Physiology.

TEXAS WESLEYAN UNIVERSITY
Fort Worth, Texas 76105-1536
Web site: www.txwesleyan.edu

Founded 1890. Coed. Private control, Methodist affiliation. Semester system. Library: 192,044 volumes, 632 subscriptions.

The University's graduate programs include Business Administration, Education, and Health Sciences. Total University enrollment at main campus: 2800.

School of Law (76102)

Established 1989, became part of University in 1992. School of Law moved to current site in 1997. ABA approved since 1994.

AALS member. Semester system. Full-time, part-time study. Special programs: externships. Law library: 173,121 volumes, 4168 subscriptions; has LEXIS, NEXIS, WESTLAW.

Annual tuition: full-time $16,480, part-time $14,200. University housing available for both single and married students. Annual on-campus housing cost: $8504. Contact Director of Housing for University owned housing. Phone: (817)531-4432. Law students generally live off-campus. Contact Admissions Office for off-campus information. Off-campus housing and personal expenses: approximately $9257.

Enrollment: first-year class full-time 124, part-time 98; total full-time 312, part-time 252 (men 50%, women 50%). Faculty: full-time 24, part-time 30. Student to faculty ratio 16.6 to 1. Degree conferred: J.D.

ADMISSION REQUIREMENTS. LSDAS Law School report, bachelor's degree, transcripts, LSAT required in support of application. Letters of recommendation and supplementary essay recommended. Accepts transfer applicants from ABA approved schools. Apply to Office of Admissions by March 31. Application fee $50. Phone: (800)733-9529, (817)212-4000; fax: (817)212-4002.

ADMISSION STANDARDS. Selective. Mean LSAT: full-time 149, part-time 150; mean GPA: full-time 3.06, part-time 2.77 (A = 4). No Gourman rating. *U.S. News & World Report* ranking is in the fourth tier of all U.S. law schools.

FINANCIAL AID. Scholarships, Federal W/S, loans. Apply to Financial Aid Office by March 1. Phone: (817)579-5738. Use FAFSA. About 15–20% of students receive aid other than loans from School or outside sources.

DEGREE REQUIREMENTS. For J.D.: 88 semester cretits in full- or part-time program.

TEXAS WOMAN'S UNIVERSITY
Denton, Texas 76204-0479
Web site: www.twu.edu

Established 1901. Located 35 miles NW of Dallas. CGS member. Coed on graduate level. State control. Special facilities: Animal Care Facility, CompuPASS Learning Laboratory, Food Testing Laboratory, Speech and Hearing Clinic, Textile Research Laboratory, Institute for Clinical Services and Applied Research, Institute for Women's Health, The Stroke Center. Library: 788,000 volumes, 6000 subscriptions. Total University enrollment: 8400.

Tuition: per semester hour, resident $90, nonresident $305. On-campus housing for 2880 graduate women, 70 graduate men, 53 married students. Average academic year housing costs: $4428 (including board) for single students; $5200 for married students. Apply to the Office of University Housing. Phone: (940)898-3676.

Graduate School

Graduate study since 1930. Enrollment: full-time 978, part-time 2950. Faculty: full-time 292, part-time 100. Degrees conferred: M.A., M.B.A., M.F.A., M.S., M.Ed., M.O.T., M.L.S., M.Ed., Ed.D., Ph.D.

ADMISSION REQUIREMENTS. Official transcript, GRE/GMAT required in support of School's application. Some programs require interview, letters of recommendation. TOEFL required for international applicants. Accepts transfer applicants. Graduates of unaccredited schools not considered. Apply to Office of Student Processing at least ninety days prior to registration. Application fee $30. Phone: (940)898-3188; fax: (940)898-3081; e-mail: gradschool@twu.edu.

ADMISSION STANDARDS. Selective for most departments. Usual minimum average: 3.0 (A = 4).

FINANCIAL AID. Scholarships, research assistantships, teaching assistantships, internships, grants, tuition waivers, Federal W/S, loans. Approved for VA benefits. Apply to appropriate departmental chair for assistantships; to Director of Financial Aid for all other programs. No specified closing date. Phone: (940)898-3050. Use FAFSA. Aid available for part-time students.

DEGREE REQUIREMENTS. For master's: 30 semester hours with thesis or 36 semester hours with professional paper or project; additional requirements vary from program to program. For Ph.D.: at least 90 hours beyond the bachelor's; proficiency in two research tools; qualifying exam; dissertation, final oral/written exam. For Ed.D.: essentially the same as Ph.D., but requires a proficiency in statistics as a research tool. Some doctorates require a residency of two consecutive semesters.

FIELDS OF STUDY.

THE COLLEGE OF ARTS AND SCIENCES (M.A., M.B.A., M.F.A., M.S., PH.D.):
Art.
Art Education.
Art History.
Biology.
Biology Teaching.
Business Administration.
Chemistry.
Chemistry Teaching.
Counseling Psychology.
Dance.
Design. Includes advertising, fashion illustrating, medical illustration.
Drama.
English.
Fashion Merchandising.
Fashion and Textiles.
Government.
History.
Mathematics.
Mathematics Teaching.
Molecular Biology.
Music.
Music Education.
Music Pedagogy.
Music Therapy.
Psychology.
Rhetoric.
School Psychology.
Science Teaching.
Sociology.
Studio Art. Includes ceramics, fabric and printed textile, jewelry and metalsmithing, painting, photography, sculpture.
Women's Studies.

COLLEGE OF PROFESSIONAL EDUCATION (M.A., M.S., M.ED., M.L.S., ED.D., PH.D.):
Administration.
Child Development.
Consumer Sciences.
Counseling and Development.
Early Childhood Education.
Elementary Education.
Family Studies.
Family Therapy.
Home and Family Life.
Library Science.
Marriage and Family Counseling.
Reading Education.

Special Education. Includes administration, educational diagnostician, emotionally disturbed, language and/or learning disabilities, mental retardation, physically handicapped.
Supervision.

COLLEGE OF HEALTH SCIENCES (M.A., M.S., ED.D., PH.D.):
Education of the Deaf.
Exercise and Sport Nutrition.
Food Science.
Health Care Administration.
Health Education.
Health Studies.
Institutional Administration.
Kinesiology.
Nutrition,
Speech-Language Pathology.

COLLEGE OF NURSING (M.S., PH.D.):
Adult Health.
Adult Health Nurse Practitioner.
Child Health.
Community Health.
Family Nurse Practitioner.
Health Systems Management.
Nursing.
Pediatric Nurse Practitioner.
Women's Health.
Women's Health Practitioner.

SCHOOL OF OCCUPATIONAL THERAPY (M.A., M.O.T.):
Occupational Therapy.
Rehabilitation Technology.

SCHOOL OF PHYSICAL THERAPY (M.S., PH.D.):
Physical Therapy (Clinical Level).
Physical Therapy (Entry Level).

THE UNIVERSITY OF TEXAS AT ARLINGTON
Arlington, Texas 76019
Web site: www.uta.edu

Founded 1895. Located in the Center of Dallas–Fort Worth. CGS member. Coed. Public control. Semester system. Special facilities: Automation and Robotics Research Institute, Community Services Research Center, Center for Research in Contemporary Art, Energy Systems Research Center, Center for Rhetorical and Critical Theory, Center for Positron Studies, Center for Social Research, Center for Greater Southwestern Studies and History of Cartography. Library: 1,500,000 volumes, 4700 subscriptions. Total University enrollment: 20,000.

Tuition: per credit, resident $44, nonresidents $55. On-campus housing for 330 married students, 800 single students. Annual housing cost: $3500 single students; $5200 for married students. Contact Director of Housing for both on- and off-campus housing information. Phone: (817)272-2791.

Graduate School

Graduate study since 1952. Enrollment: full-time 2000, part-time 2952 (men 48%, women 52%). Faculty: full-time 411, part-time 42. Degrees conferred: M.A., M.Arch., M.B.A., M.Engr., M.C.R.P., M.S.N., M.C.S., M.E.T., M.P.A., M.S., M.S.S.W., D.Sc., Ph.D.

ADMISSION REQUIREMENTS. Official transcripts, GRE/GMAT (M.B.A., M.P.A.) required in support of School's application. Portfolio required for M.Arch. TOEFL required of international applicants. Accepts transfer applicants. Graduates of unaccredited colleges not considered. Apply to Director of Admissions 60 days prior to beginning of semester; international applicants should apply at least 120 days prior to beginning of semester. Application fee $25, $50 for international applicants. Phone: (817)272-2688; e-mail: graduate.school@uta.edu.

ADMISSION STANDARDS. Very selective or selective. Usual minimum average: 3.0 (A = 4).

FINANCIAL AID. Annual awards from institutional funds: fellowships, teaching assistantships, research assistantships (TSE required of those whose primary language is not English), internships, tuition waivers, Federal W/S, loans. Apply by June 1 to Dean for scholarships, to appropriate departmental chair for fellowships/assistantships; to Financial Aid Office for all other programs. Phone: (817)272-3561. Use FAFSA.

DEGREE REQUIREMENTS. For master's: Plan I—30 semester hours minimum; thesis; final oral exam. Plan II—33 semester hours minimum; internship/project; comprehensive exam. Plan III—36 semester hours minimum; comprehensive exam. For Ph.D., D.Sc.: four years beyond the bachelor's degree minimum, at least one year in residence; qualifying exam; dissertation; final oral exam.

FIELDS OF STUDY.

GRADUATE SCHOOL:
Interdisciplinary Studies. M.A., M.S.
Management of Technology. M.S.

COLLEGE OF BUSINESS ADMINISTRATION:
Accounting. Includes flexible M.B.A., professional accounting (M.P.A.), taxation (M.S.), business administration (Ph.D.). M.P.A., M.S., Ph.D.
Economics. Includes flexible M.B.A., business administration (Ph.D.). M.A., Ph.D.
Finance and Real Estate. Includes flexible M.B.A., real estate (M.S.), business administration (Ph.D.). M.S., Ph.D.
Information Systems and Management Science. Includes flexible M.B.A., information systems (M.S.), business administration (Ph.D.), mathematical sciences (Ph.D.). M.S., Ph.D.
Management. Includes flexible M.B.A., human resource management (M.S.), business administration (Ph.D.). M.S., Ph.D.
Marketing. Includes flexible M.B.A., marketing research (M.S.), business administration (Ph.D.).

COLLEGE OF ENGINEERING:
Aerospace Engineering. M.S., M.Engr., Ph.D.
Biomedical Engineering. M.S., Ph.D.
Civil Engineering. M.S., M.Engr., Ph.D.
Computer Science and Engineering. Includes online computer science (M.S.), online computer science and engineering (M.S.), software engineering (M.SW.Engr.). M.S., M.C.S., M.SW.Engr., Ph.D.
Electrical Engineering. Includes online electrical engineering (M.S.). M.S., M.Engr., Ph.D.
Industrial and Manufacturing Engineering. Includes logistics (M.S.), management of technology (M.S.). M.S., M.Engr., Ph.D.
Materials Science and Engineering. M.S., M.Engr., Ph.D.
Mechanical Engineering. M.S., M.Engr., Ph.D.

COLLEGE OF SCIENCE:
Biology. Includes mathematical sciences (Ph.D.), quantitative biology (Ph.D.). M.S., Ph.D.
Chemistry and Biochemistry. Includes applied chemistry (Ph.D.), mathematical sciences (Ph.D.). M.S., Ph.D.
Environmental Science and Engineering. M.S., Ph.D.
Geology. Includes mathematical science (Ph.D.). M.S., Ph.D.
Interdisciplinary Science. M.A.

Mathematics. Includes mathematical sciences (Ph.D.). M.A., M.S., Ph.D.
Physics. Includes physics and applied physics (Ph.D.). M.S., Ph.D.
Psychology. Includes experimental (M.S., Ph.D.), industrial organizational (M.S.), mathematical sciences (Ph.D.). M.S., Ph.D.

SCHOOL OF ARCHITECTURE:
Architecture. M.Arch.
Landscape Architecture. M.L.A.

SCHOOL OF EDUCATION:
Curriculum and Instruction. M.Ed.
Educational Leadership. M.Ed.
Teaching. M.Ed.T.

SCHOOL OF NURSING:
Nursing Administration. M.S.N.
Nurse Practitioner Programs. Includes acute care nursing, adult nursing, emergency nursing, family nursing, gerontological nursing, pediatric nursing, psychiatric-mental health nursing.

SCHOOL OF SOCIAL WORK.
Social Work. M.S.S.W., Ph.D.

SCHOOL OF URBAN AND PUBLIC AFFAIRS:
City and Regional Planning. M.C.R.P.
Public Administration. M.P.A.
Public and Urban Administration. Ph.D.
Urban Affairs. M.A.

THE UNIVERSITY OF TEXAS AT AUSTIN

Austin, Texas 78712-7666
Web site: www.utexas.edu

Founded 1883. CGS and AAU member. Coed. State control. Semester system. Special facilities: Americo Paredes Center for Cultural Studies, Biochemical Institute, Center for African and African American Studies, Center for Asian Studies, Center for Asian American Studies, Center for Mexican American Studies, Center for Middle Eastern Studies, Center for Russian, East European and Eruasian Studies, Computation Center, Drug Dynamics Institute, Bureau of Economic Geology, Bureau of Engineering Research, Harry Huntt Ransom Humanities Research Center, Lyndon B. Johnson Library and Museum, Bureau of Business Research, Institute of Marine Science, Jack S. Blanton Museum of Art, McDonald Observatory, Population Research Center, Speech and Hearing Center, Teresa Lozano Long Institute of Latin American Studies, Texas Memorial Museum. The University's NIH ranking is 104th among all U.S. institutions with 155 awards/grants worth $35,74474,488. Library: 6,680,000 volumes, 50,000 subscriptions.

Tuition: per credit, resident $132, nonresident $350; M.B.A., M.P.A. nonresidents $568. Average academic year housing costs: extremely wide range. Contact Housing and Food Service Division for both on- and off-campus housing information. Phone: (512)471-3136. Day-care facilities available.

Graduate School

Graduate study since 1909. Enrollment: full-time 10,576 (men 50%, women 50%). Faculty: full-time 1774. Degrees conferred: M.A., M.Arch., M.B.A., M.Ed., M.F.A., M.L.I.S., M.M., M.P.A., M.P.Aff., M.S.Appl.Phy., M.S.Arch.St., M.S.C.R.P., M.S.C.A.M., M.S.C.S., M.S.Econom., M.S.E., M.S.Geo.Sci., M.S.Info.Stds.,

M.S.Marine.Sci., M.S.N., M.S.Phr., M.S.S.T.C., M.S.S.W., M.S.Stat., Ed.D., D.M.A., Ph.D.

ADMISSION REQUIREMENTS. Official transcripts, GRE/GMAT required in support of School's application. Interview required by some departments. On-line application available. TOEFL required for international applicants. Graduates of unaccredited colleges not considered. Apply to Graduate and International Admission Center. Departmental deadlines vary, contact appropriate department for this information, or visit the Web site. Application fee $50; $75 for international applicants. Phone: (512)475-7390.

ADMISSION STANDARDS. Selective for most departments. Usual minimum average: 3.0 (A = 4).

FINANCIAL AID. Annual awards from institutional funds: scholarships, fellowships, assistantships, internships, grants, tuition waivers, Federal W/S, loans. Approved for VA benefits. Apply to appropriate Graduate Adviser for scholarships, assistantships; to Financial Services Office for all other aid. No specified closing date. Phone: (512)475-6282. Use FAFSA. "Substantial numbers" of students receive aid other than loans from School and outside sources. Aid available for part-time students.

DEGREE REQUIREMENTS. For most master's: 30 semester hours minimum, at least one year in residence; thesis; comprehensive oral/written exam for some departments. For M.B.A., M.P.A., M.Arch., M.L.I.S, M.S.S.W., M.S.Pharm., M.S.CRP., M.S.C.S.: 30–60 hours depending on previous background, at least 30 hours in residence; thesis/final report. For M.Ed.: 36 hours minimum, at least 30 in residence; final competency exam. For Ph.D.: at least one year in residence; foreign language requirement set by department; oral/written candidacy exam; dissertation; final oral exam. For Ed.D.: comprehensive oral/written exam; other requirements essentially the same as for Ph.D. For D.M.A.: requirements essentially the same as for Ph.D., except original composition/dissertation/performance.

FIELDS OF STUDY.

SCHOOL OF ARCHITECTURE:
Architectural Studies. M.S.Arch.St.
Architecture—First Professional. M.Arch.
Architecture—Post Professional. M.Arch.
Architecture. Ph.D.
Community and Regional Planning. M.S.C.R.P.

RED MCCOMBS GRADUATE SCHOOL OF BUSINESS:
Accounting. Ph.D.
Business Administration. Includes executive M.B.A. in Mexico City, evening option. M.B.A.
Finance. Ph.D.
Management Science and Information Systems. Ph.D.
Management. Ph.D.
Marketing Administration. Ph.D.
Professional Accounting. M.P.A.

COLLEGE OF COMMUNICATION:
Advertising. M.A., Ph.D.
Communication Sciences and Disorders. M.A., Ph.D.
Communication Studies. M.A., Ph.D.
Journalism. M.A., Ph.D.
Radio-Television-Film. M.A., M.F.A., Ph.D.

COLLEGE OF EDUCATION:
Curriculum and Instruction. M.A., M.Ed., Ed.D., Ph.D.
Educational Administration. M.Ed., Ed.D., Ph.D.
Educational Psychology. Includes counseling (Ph.D.), school (Ph.D.). M.A., M.Ed., Ph.D.
Foreign Language Education. M.A., Ph.D.

Health Education. M.A., M.Ed., Ed.D., Ph.D.
Kinesiology. M.A., M.Ed., Ed.D., Ph.D.
Mathematics Education. M.A. M.Ed., Ph.D.
Science Education. M.A., M.Ed., Ph.D.
Special Education. M.A., M.Ed., Ed.D., Ph.D.

COLLEGE OF ENGINEERING:
Aerospace Engineering. M.S.E., Ph.D.
Architectural Engineering. M.S.E.
Biomedical Engineering. M.S.E., Ph.D.
Chemical Engineering. M.S.E., Ph.D.
Civil Engineering. M.S.E., Ph.D.
Electrical and Computer Engineering. Includes biomedical engineering, communications, networks and systems, computer engineering, electromagnetics and acoustics, energy systems, executive software engineering, plasma, quantum electronics and optics, solid-state electronics. M.S.E., Ph.D.
Energy and Mineral Resources. M.A.
Engineering Mechanics. M.S.E., Ph.D.
Environmental and Water Resources. M.S.E.
Executive Engineering Management. M.S.E.
Materials Science and Engineering. M.S.E., Ph.D.
Mechanical Engineering. M.S.E., Ph.D.
Operations Research and Industrial Engineering. M.S., Ph.D.
Petroleum Engineering. M.S.E., Ph.D.

COLLEGE OF FINE ARTS:
Art Education. M.A.
Art History. M.A., Ph.D.
Design. M.F.A.
Music Composition. M.M., D.M.A.
Music Education. M.M., D.M.A., Ph.D.
Music Performance. M.M., D.M.A.
Music Theory. M.M., Ph.D.
Musicology/Ethnomusicology. M.M., Ph.D.
Studio Art. M.F.A.
Theatre. Includes acting, directing, theatrical design. M.F.A.

COLLEGE OF LIBERAL ARTS:
American Civilization. M.A., Ph.D.
Anthropology. Includes folklore and public culture. M.A., Ph.D.
Arabic Studies. M.A., Ph.D.
Asian Culture and Languages. M.A., Ph.D.
Asian Studies. M.A.
Classics. M.A., Ph.D.
Comparative Literature. M.A., Ph.D.
Economics. M.A., M.S.Econ., Ph.D.
English. Includes creative writing (M.A.). M.A., Ph.D.
French. M.A., Ph.D.
Geography. M.A., Ph.D.
Germanic Studies. M.A., Ph.D.
Government. M.A., Ph.D.
Hebrew Studies. M.A., Ph.D.
History. M.A., Ph.D.
Latin American Studies. M.A., Ph.D.
Linguistics. M.A., Ph.D.
Middle Eastern Studies. M.A.
Persian Studies. M.A., Ph.D.
Philosophy. M.A., Ph.D.
Psychology. Includes clinical. Ph.D.
Russian, East European, and Eurasian Studies. M.A.
Slavic Languages. M.A., Ph.D.
Sociology. M.A., Ph.D.
Spanish, Portuguese. M.A., Ph.D.
Women's and Gender Studies. M.A.

LIBRARY AND INFORMATION SCIENCE:
Library and Information Science. M.L.I.S., Ph.D.

COLLEGE OF NATURAL SCIENCES:
Applied Physics. M.A., Ph.D.

Astronomy. M.A., Ph.D.
Biochemistry. M.A., Ph.D.
Cell and Molecular Biology. M.A., Ph.D.
Chemistry. M.A., Ph.D.
Computer Sciences. M.A., M.S.C.S., Ph.D.
Ecology, Evolution, and Behavior. M.A., Ph.D.
Geological Sciences. M.A., Ph.D.
Human Development and Family Sciences. M.A., Ph.D.
Marine Science. M.A., Ph.D.
Mathematics. M.A., Ph.D.
Microbiology. M.A., Ph.D.
Nutrition. M.A.
Nutritional Sciences. Ph.D.
Physics. M.A., Ph.D.
Plant Biology. M.A., Ph.D.
Statistics. M.S. Stat.

SCHOOL OF NURSING:
Nursing. M.S.N., Ph.D.

COLLEGE OF PHARMACY:
Pharmacy. M.S.Phr., Ph.D.

L.B.J. SCHOOL OF PUBLIC AFFAIRS:
Public Affairs. M.P.Aff.
Public Policy. Ph.D.

SCHOOL OF SOCIAL WORK:
Social Work. M.S.S.W., Ph.D.

JOINT DEGREE PROGRAMS:
Asian Studies/Business Administration. M.A.-M.B.A.
Asian Studies/Public Affairs. M.A.-M.P.Aff.
Communication/Business Administration. M.A.-M.B.A.
Community and Regional Planning/Geography. M.S.C.R.P.-Ph.D.
Latin American Studies/Business Administration. M.A.-M.B.A.
Latin American Studies/Communication. M.A.-M.A.
Latin American Studies/Community and Regional Planning. M.A.-M.S.C.R.P.
Latin American Studies/Law. M.A.-J.D.
Latin American Studies/Public Affairs. M.A.-M.P.Aff.
Law/Business Administration. J.D.-M.B.A.
Law/Public Affairs. J.D.-M.P.Aff.
Law/Russian, East European, and Eurasian Studies. J.D.-M.A.
Middle Eastern Studies/Business Administration. M.A.-M.B.A.
Middle Eastern Studies/Communication. M.A.-M.A.
Middle Eastern Studies/Law. M.A.-J.D.
Middle Eastern Studies/Library and Information Science. M.A.-M.L.I.S.
Middle Eastern Studies/Public Affairs. M.A.-M.P.Aff.
Nursing/Business Administration. M.S.N.-M.B.A.
Public Affairs/Business Administration. M.P.Aff.-M.B.A.
Public Affairs/Communication. M.P.Aff.-M.A.
Public Affairs/Engineering. M.P.Aff.-M.S.E.
Russian, East European, and Eurasian Studies/Business Administration. M.A.-M.B.A.
Russian, East European, and Eurasian Studies/Communication. M.A - M.A.
Russian, East European, and Eurasian Studies/Public Affairs. M.A.-M.P.Aff.

School of Law (78714-9105)

Web site: www.utexas.edu/law

Established 1883. Located on main campus. ABA approved since 1923. AALS member since 1907. Semester system. Full-time, day study only. Special facilities: Center for Public Policy Dispute Resolution, Public Interest Law Center. Special programs: summer study abroad at The University of London, England, University of Sao Paulo, Brazil, University of Tokyo,

Japan. Law library: 971,727 volumes, 9905 subscriptions; has LEXIS, NEXIS, WESTLAW, DIALOG, CALI; is a State and Federal Depository.

Annual tuition: resident $7682, nonresident $16,138. Limited on-campus housing available. Law students generally prefer to live off-campus. Contact University of Texas Housing Division for off-campus information. Phone: (512)471-3136. Off-campus housing and personal expenses: approximately $10,084.

Enrollment: first-year class 477; total full-time 1429 (men 53%, women 47%); no part-time students. Faculty: full-time 64, part-time 51. Student to faculty ratio 17.6 to 1. Degrees conferred: J.D., J.D.-M.B.A., J.D.-M.P.A., J.D.-M.A. (Latin American Studies, Russian, East European, and Eurasian Studies, Middle Eastern Studies), J.D.-M.S.C.R.P., J.D.-Ph.D. (History, Philosophy), LL.M. (for foreign law school graduates who have completed a basic legal education and received a university degree in law in another country), M.C.J.

ADMISSION REQUIREMENTS. Bachelor's degree, transcripts, LSAT required in support of application. Interview not required. Accepts transfer applicants. Graduates of unaccredited institutions not considered. Apply to University Director of Admissions by February 1 (Fall). Application fee $65, $75 for international applicants. Phone: (512)471-3207.

ADMISSION STANDARDS. Selective. Mean LSAT: 162, mean GPA: 3.66 (A = 4). Gourman rating: 4.76. *U.S. News & World Report* ranking is in the top 15 of all law schools. Accepts about 20–25% of total annual applications.

FINANCIAL AID. Law School scholarships, Townes-Rice Scholarships, minority scholarships, Texas Grants, Law School and private loans; Federal loans and Federal W/S offered through University's Financial Aid Office. Assistantships may be available for upper-divisional joint degree candidates and second- and third-year law students. For scholarships, apply to Loans and Scholarships office after January 1, before March 31. For all other programs, apply to University's Office of Student Financial Services, Wooldridge Hall, 600 W. 24th Street. Phone: (512)475-6282. Use FAFSA (School code: 003658), also submit Financial Aid Transcript, Federal Income Tax forms. Approximately 90% of first-year class received scholarships/Grants-in-Aid. No aid available for LL.M. students.

DEGREE REQUIREMENTS. For J.D.: 86 (39 required) credits with a GPA of at least 2.0 (A = 4.), plus completion of upper-divisional writing seminar, one course in Professional Responsibility; three-year program. Accelerated J.D. with two summers of course work. For J.D.-Master's: four-year programs rather than five-year programs if both degrees are taken consecutively. For LL.M. (foreign law graduates): 24 credits; at least two semesters in residence; satisfactory completion of "Introduction to U.S. Law and Legal Research"; completion of a substantial paper. For M.C.J.: degree program is currently inactive.

THE UNIVERSITY OF TEXAS AT BROWNSVILLE AND TEXAS SOUTHMOST COLLEGE

Brownsville, Texas 78520-4991
Web site: www.utb.edu

CGS member, Coed. State control. Semester system. Library: 147,200 volumes, 4400 subscriptions.

Tuition: per credit, resident $120, nonresident $265. No on-campus housing available. Day-care facilities available.

Graduate Studies

Graduate Enrollment: full-time 40, part-time 618. Graduate faculty: full- and part-time 131. Degrees Conferred: M.A., M.A.I.S., M.B.A., M.Ed., M.S.P.H.N, M.S.I.S.

ADMISSION REQUIREMENTS. Two official transcripts, GRE/GMAT, two letters of recommendation required in support of application. TOEFL (minimum score 550) required for international applicants. Accepts transfer students. Graduates of unaccredited institutions not considered. Apply to the Director of Admissions and Records by August 1 (Fall), December 15 (Spring) for priority consideration. Rolling admissions process. Application fee: $15. Phone: (800)860-0287, (956)548-6552; fax: (956)983-7279.

ADMISSION STANDARDS. Selective. Usual minimum average: 3.0 (A = 4).

FINANCIAL AID, Scholarships, assistantships, internships, tuition waivers, Federal W/S, loans. Approved for VA benefits. Apply by April 1 to the appropriate department for scholarships and assistantships; to Director of Financial Aid for all other programs. Use FAFSA. Aid available for part-time students.

DEGREE REQUIREMENTS. For M.A., M.S.: 30 semester credits minimum, at least 24 credits in residence; thesis/nonthesis option; comprehensive written/oral exam. For M.Ed.: 36 semester credits minimum, at least 30 credits in residence. For M.B.A.: 36–45 semester credits minimum, at least 30–39 credits in residence; computer proficiency. For M.S.P.H.N.: 36 semester credits minimum, at least 30 credits in residence; practicum; comprehensive exam.

FIELDS OF STUDY.
Biology. M.S.I.S.
Business Administration. M.B.A.
Counseling and Guidance. M.Ed.
Curriculum and Instruction. M.Ed.
Early Childhood Education. M.Ed.
Educational Administration. M.Ed.
Education Technology. M.Ed.
Elementary Education. M.Ed.
English as a Second Language. M.Ed.
English. M.A., M.A.I.S.
Government. M.A.I.S.
History. M.A.I.S.
Public Health Nursing. M.S.P.H.N.
Reading Specialist. M.Ed.
Sociology. M.A.I.S.
Spanish. M.A., M.A.I.S.
Special Education. Includes educational diagnostician option. M.Ed.
Technology. M.S.

THE UNIVERSITY OF TEXAS AT DALLAS

Richardson, Texas 75083-0688
Web site: www.utdallas.edu

Created 1969. CGS member. Coed. State control. Semester system. Special facilities: Callier Center for Communications Disorders, Center for Applied Optics, Center for Lithospheric Studies, Center for Quantum Electronics, Center for Space Sciences, Center for Genetic Technology, Institute for Environmental Sciences, Communications and Learning Center, Center for China and U.S. Management Studies, Center for Research and Teaching, Bruton Center for Development Studies, Morris Hite Center for Product Development and Marketing Science, Center for International Accounting Development, Translation Center. Library: 524,000 volumes, 3800 subscriptions.

Tuition: per credit, resident $80, nonresident $295. On-campus housing available for single and married students. Average academic year housing costs: $5799 (including board); off-campus costs: $375–$700 per month. Day-care facilities available.

Graduate School

Graduate study since 1969. Graduate enrollment: full-time 1454, part-time 1684. Graduate faculty: full-time 275, part-time 57. Degrees conferred: M.A., M.A.T., M.B.A., M.S., M.S.E.E., M.S.E.S., M.P.A., Ph.D., D.Chem.

ADMISSION REQUIREMENTS. Official transcripts, bachelor's degree, GRE, GMAT (School of Management) required in support of School's application. On-line application available. TOEFL required for international applicants. Accepts transfer students. Graduates of unaccredited institutions not considered. Apply to Director of Admissions by July 15 (Fall), November 15 (Spring). Rolling admissions process. Application fee: $25, international students $75. Phone: (214)883-2294; information line: (214)883-2341; fax: (214)883-2599.

ADMISSION STANDARDS. Selective. Usual minimum average: 3.0 (A = 4).

FINANCIAL AID. Scholarships, assistantships, internships, partial tuition waivers, grants, Federal W/S, loans. Approved for VA benefits. Apply by April 30 to the appropriate department for scholarships and assistantships; to Financial Aid Office for all other aid. Phone: (214)883-2941; fax: (214)883-2947. Use FAFSA and Institutional FAF. About 65% of students receive aid from University and outside sources. Aid available for part-time students.

DEGREE REQUIREMENTS. For master's: 36–45 semester credits minimum; at least 30–39 credits in residence; thesis/nonthesis option; comprehensive written/oral exam. For Ph.D., D.Chem.: 60 credits minimum beyond bachelor's, at least one year in full-time study; proficiency in one foreign language for some programs; qualifying exam; advancement to candidacy; dissertation; final oral exam.

FIELDS OF STUDY.
Accounting and Information Management.
Administrative Sciences. Includes management and administrative sciences.
Applied Cognition and Neurosciences.
Applied Economics.
Applied Mathematics.
Applied Sociology.
Biology—Molecular and Cell Biology.
Business Administration.
Chemistry.
Communication Disorders.
Communication Sciences.
Computer Engineering.
Computer Sciences. Includes software engineering.
Early Childhood Disorders.
Education.
Electrical Engineering. Includes telecommunications, microelectronics.
Engineering Mathematics.
Geographic Information Sciences.
Geosciences.
History of Ideas.
Human Development and Communication Sciences.
Human Development and Early Childhood Disorders.
Humanities. Includes aesthetics studies, studies in literature, history of ideas.

Interdisciplinary Studies.
International Management Studies.
Management and Administrative Sciences.
Management Science.
Mathematical Sciences. Includes applied mathematics, engineering, mathematics, statistics.
Mathematics Education.
Physics.
Political Economy.
Public Affairs.
Science Education.
Telecommunications Engineering.

THE UNIVERSITY OF TEXAS AT EL PASO

El Paso, Texas 79968-0001
Web site: www.utep.edu

Established 1913. CGS member. Coed. State control. Semester system. Special facilities: NSF Material Science Center, El Paso Centennial Museum, Center for Environmental Resource Management, Center for Entrepreneurial Development, Advancement Research and Support, El Paso Solar Pond Research Station, Institute for Manufacturing and Materials Management, Center for Environmental Resource Management, the Hemispheric Trade Center, the Inter-American and Border Studies Center, NSF Materials Science Center, Oral History Institute, Center for Public Policy, Bureau of Business and Economics Research. Library: 850,000 volumes, 2499 subscriptions.

Tuition: full-time resident $2118, nonresident $7230; for Business, Nursing, Engineering, Materials Science and Engineering, Environmental Science and Engineering, resident $2790, nonresident $7710; part-time resident $74, nonresident $289. On-campus housing for 60 married students, 328 men, 122 women. Average academic year housing costs: $375 per month for married students, $280–$425 for single students. Contact Housing Office for both on- and off-campus housing information. Phone: (915)747-5352.

Graduate School

Graduate study since 1940. Enrollment: full-time 222, part-time 2047. University faculty teaching graduate students: full-time 341, part-time 330. Degrees conferred: M.A., M.Ed., M.B.A., M.M., M.P.A., M.Acy., M.S., M.S.I.S., M.A.T., M.A.I.S., M.S.N., Ph.D.

ADMISSION REQUIREMENTS. Two official transcripts, GRE/GMAT required in support of School's application. MAT may be required for nursing students. Interview not required. TOEFL required for international applicants. Accepts transfer applicants. Graduates of unaccredited institutions not considered. Apply by July 1 (Fall), November 1 (Spring) to Graduate Student Services Office. Application fee none, $65 for international applicants. Phone: (915)747-5491; fax: (915)747-5788.

ADMISSION STANDARDS. Selective. Usual minimum average: 2.75 (A = 4).

FINANCIAL AID. Scholarships, fellowships, research/teaching assistantships, internships, partial tuition waivers, Federal W/S, loans. Approved for VA benefits. Apply to the appropriate department for fellowships, assistantships; to the Office of Student Financial Aid for all other programs. No specified closing date, although applicants are advised to submit their applications before March 1 for the upcoming academic year. Office of Student Financial Aid. Phone: (915)747-5204. Use FAFSA and institutional FAF. Aid available for part-time students.

DEGREE REQUIREMENTS. For M.A., M.S.: 30 semester hours minimum, at least 24 in residence; thesis; comprehensive oral/written exam. For M.Ed.: 36 semester hours minimum, at least 30 in residence. For M.B.A., M.Acc.: 36 semester hours minimum, at least 30 in residence; computer proficiency. For M.P.A.: 36 semester hours minimum, at least 30 in residence; internship; comprehensive exam. For M.S.N.: 36 semester hours minimum, at least 30 in residence; practicum; comprehensive exam. For M.S.I.S.: 36 semester hours minimum, at least 30 in residence; report. For M.A.T.: 36 semester hours minimum, at least 30 in residence; comprehensive exam. For M.A.I.S.: 36 semester hours minimum, at least 30 in residence; final project; oral examination. For Ph.D.: 30 semester hours minimum beyond the master's; qualifying exam; proficiency in one foreign language for some programs; dissertation; final oral exam.

FIELDS OF STUDY.
Accountancy. M.Acc.
Adult Health. M.S.N.
Art Education. M.A.
Biological Sciences. M.S.
Border History. M.A.
Business Administration. M.B.A.
Chemistry. M.S.
Civil Engineering. M.S.
Clinical Psychology. M.A.
Communication. M.A.
Computer Engineering. M.S., Ph.D.
Computer Science. M.S.
Creative Writing—English. M.F.A.
Creative Writing in Spanish. M.F.A.
Economics. M.S.
Educational Administration. M.Ed.
Educational Diagnostician Studies. M.Ed.
Educational Psychology and Special Services. M.Ed.
Educational Supervision. M.Ed.
Electrical Engineering. M.S.
Engineering. M.S.
English and American Literature. M.A.
Environmental Engineering. M.S.
General Experimental Psychology. M.A.
Geology. M.S.
Geophysics. M.S.
Guidance and Counseling. M.Ed.
Health and Physical Education. M.Ed.
History. M.A.
Industrial Engineering. M.S.
Information Technology. M.I.T.
Instructional Specialist. M.Ed.
Interdisciplinary Studies. M.A.I.S., M.S.I.S.
Kinesiology. M.S.
Linguistics. M.A.
Manufacturing Engineering. M.S.
Mathematical Sciences. M.S.
Mathematics Teaching. M.A.T.
Mechanical Engineering. M.S.
Metallurgical and Materials Engineering. M.S.
Music. Includes music education, performance. M.M.
Nurse Midwifery. M.S.N.
Nursing Administration. M.S.N.
Parent-Child Nursing. M.S.N.
Physical Therapy. M.P.T.
Physics. M.S.
Political Science. M.A.
Psychiatric/Mental Health Nursing. M.S.N.
Public Administration. M.P.A.
Reading Education. M.Ed.
Sociology. M.A.
Spanish. M.A.
Special Education. M.Ed.
Speech Language Pathology. M.S.
Statistics. M.S.
Studio Arts. M.A.

Teacher Education. M.A.
Theatre Arts. M.A.
Womens Health Care/Nurse Practitioner Studies. M.S.N.

THE UNIVERSITY OF TEXAS AT SAN ANTONIO
San Antonio, Texas 78249
Web site: www.utsa.edu

Founded in 1969. CGS member. Coed. State control. Semester system. Special facilities: Institute for Studies in Business, Economics and Human Resources; Center for Archaeological Research; Center for Applied Research and Technology. Library: 521,000 volumes, 2665 subscriptions. Total University enrollment: 22,000.

Annual tuition: full-time resident $3168, nonresident $8400; per credit, resident $132, nonresident $350. On-campus housing for both single and married students. Average academic year housing costs: $5994 (including board) for single students; $4500 for married students. Contact Director of Chisholm Hall, Phone: (210)458-6700; or Director of University Oaks Apartments. Phone: (210)458-8699.

Graduate School

Graduate study since 1973. Graduate enrollment: full-time 668, part-time 2043. Graduate faculty: full-time 376, part-time 60. Degrees conferred: M.A., M.B.A., M.P.Acct., M.F.A., M.M., M.S., M.P.A., Ph.D.

ADMISSION REQUIREMENTS. Official transcripts, GRE/GMAT required in support of School's application. Auditions/portfolio review required for music/art applicants. TOEFL required for international applicants. Accepts transfer students. Graduates of unaccredited institutions not considered. Applications processed on a rolling basis. Apply to the Director of Admissions and Registrar April 1 (Summer), July 1 (Fall), November 1 (Spring) for priority consideration. Application fee $25. Phone: (210)458-4530.

ADMISSION STANDARDS. Selective. Usual minimum average for last 60 credits for unconditional admission: 3.0 (A = 4).

FINANCIAL AID. Scholarships, assistantships, internships, Federal W/S, loans. Approved for VA benefits. Apply to the appropriate department for scholarships and assistantships; to Director of Financial Aid for all other forms of aid. No specified closing date. Phone: (210)458-4154. Use FAFSA. Aid sometimes available for part-time study.

DEGREE REQUIREMENTS. For M.A., M.S.: 30 semester credits minimum, at least 24 credits in residence; thesis/nonthesis option; comprehensive written/oral exam. For M.B.A., M.P.Acct.: 36–45 semester credits, at least 30–39 credits in residence; computer proficiency. For M.P.A.: 36 semester credits minimum, at least 30 credits in residence; comprehensive exam. For M.M.: 30 semester credits minimum, at least 24 in residence; recital; written/oral exam. For M.F.A.: 60 semester credits minimum, at least 48 credits in residence; gallery level exhibition/special project; written/oral exam. For Ph.D.: 60 credits minimum beyond the master's degree, at least 48 in residence; foreign language proficiency set by department; qualifying exam; candidacy; dissertation; final oral exam.

FIELDS OF STUDY.
Accounting. M.S.
Adult and Higher Education. M.A.
Anthropology. M.A.

Architecture. M.Arch.
Art. M.F.A.
Art History. M.A.
Bicultural Bilingual Studies. Includes English as a Second Language. M.A.
Biology. M.S., Ph.D.
Biotechnology. M.S.
Business Administration. Includes business economics, employee relations, finance, health care management, information systems, management accounting, management of technology, management science, marketing management, taxation. M.B.A., Ph.D.
Chemistry. M.S.
Civil Engineering. M.S.
Computer Sciences. M.S., Ph.D.
Counseling. M.A.
Culture, Literacy, and Language. Ph.D.
Economics. M.A.
Education. Includes curriculum and instruction, early childhood and elementary education, educational leadership, educational psychology/special education, instructional technology, reading and literacy, kinesiology and health promotion.
Educational Leadership. Ed.D.
ElectricalEngineering. M.S., Ph.D.
English. M.A., Ph.D.
Environmental Sciences. M.S.
Finance. M.S.
Geology. Includes applied, environmental, water resources (hydrogeology). M.S.
History. M.A.
Information Technology. M.S.
International Business. M.B.A.
Justice Policy. M.S.
Management of Technology. M.O.T.
Mathematics. Includes mathematics education. M.S.
M.B.A. Executive. E.M.B.A.
M.B.A. Online. M.B.A.
M.B.A. Weekend. M.B.A.
Mechanical Engineering. M.S.
Music. Includes conducting, education, performance, piano pedagogy. M.M.
Political Science. M.A.
Psychology. M.S.
Public Administration. M.P.A.
Sociology. M.S.
Spanish. Includes Hispanic culture, Hispanic literature. M.A.
Statistics. M.S.
Taxation. M.T.
Teaching English as a Second Language. M.A.

THE UNIVERSITY OF TEXAS AT TYLER
Tyler, Texas 75799-0001
Web site: www.uttyler.edu

Coed. State control. Semester system. Special facilities: Zuckerman Electron Microscope Laboratory, University of Texas High Speed Computational Center, Center for Policy Studies, Child and Family Abuse Clearinghouse. Library: 216,000 volumes, 1534 subscriptions.

Annual tuition: full-time, residents $2232, nonresident $6592; per credit, resident $221, nonresident $433. No on-campus housing available.

Graduate Studies

Graduate Enrollment: full-time 106, part-time 561. Graduate faculty: full-time 115, part-time 73. Degrees Conferred: M.A., M.B.A., M.Ed., M.P.A., M.S.N., M.S.

ADMISSION REQUIREMENTS. Two official transcripts, GRE/ GMAT required in support of application. TOEFL required for international applicants. Accepts transfer students. Graduates of unaccredited institutions not considered. Apply to the Director of Admissions and Records by April 1 (Summer), July 1 (Fall), November 1 (Spring) for priority consideration. Rolling admissions process. Application fee none. Phone: (903)566-7142; fax: (903)566-7068.

ADMISSION STANDARDS. Selective. Usual minimum average: 2.75 (A = 4).

FINANCIAL AID. Scholarships, fellowships, assistantships, internships, full and partial tuition waivers, Federal W/S, loans. Approved for VA benefits. Apply to the appropriate department for scholarships and assistantships; to Director of Financial Aid for all other programs. No specified closing date. Phone: (903)566-7221. Use FAFSA and Institutional FAF. Aid available for part-time students.

DEGREE REQUIREMENTS. For M.A., M.S.: 30 semester credits minimum, at least 24 credits in residence; thesis/nonthesis option; comprehensive written/oral exam. For M.Ed.: 36 semester credits minimum, at least 30 in residence. For M.B.A., M.P.A.: 36–45 semester minimum, at least 30–39 credits in residence; computer proficiency. For M.S.N.: 36 semester credits minimum, at least 30 credits in residence; practicum; comprehensive exam.

FIELDS OF STUDY.
Accounting.
Applied Arts and Sciences.
Art.
Biology.
Business Administration.
Chemistry.
Clinical Exercise Physiology.
Clinical Psychology.
Computer Information Systems.
Computer Sciences.
Criminal Justice.
Curriculum and Instruction.
Early Childhood Education.
Educational Administration.
Economics.
Electrical Engineering.
Engineering.
English.
Finance.
General Business.
General Studies.
Health and Kinesiology.
Health Professions.
History.
Interdisciplinary Studies.
Journalism.
Kinesiology.
Liberal Studies. Interdisciplinary.
Management.
Marketing.
Mathematics.
Music.
Nursing.
Political Science.
Public Administration.
Reading.
School Counseling.
Sociology.
Special Education.
Teaching.
Technology.

THE UNIVERSITY OF TEXAS HEALTH SCIENCE CENTER AT HOUSTON

Houston, Texas 77225-0036
Web site: www.uthouston.edu

Established 1972. Located 2 miles SW of downtown. Public control. Semester system. The Health Science Center includes the Medical School, the Dental Branch (formerly Texas Dental College), the Graduate School of Biomedical Sciences, the School of Public Health, the School of Allied Health Sciences and the School of Nursing. Special facilities: AIDS Education and Training Center for Texas and Oklahoma, Center on Aging, Center for Health Policy Studies, Center for Health Promotion Research, Center for Infections Diseases, Center for the Prevention of Injury and Violence, Epidemiology Research Center, Health Policy Institute, Houston Center for Bone Research Human Genetics Center, Human Nutrition Center, Neuroscience Research Center, Positron Diagnostic and Research Center, Southwest Center for Occupational and Environmental Health, Southwest Center for Prevention Research, Speech and Hearing Institute, UT Mental Science Institute. The Center's NIH ranking is 59th among all U.S. institutions with 227 awards/grants worth $83,903,275. Library: 268,000 volumes, 2800 subscription. Total Center enrollment: 3100.

On-campus housing available for both single and married students. Phone: (713)500-8444.

Graduate School of Biomedical Sciences

Web site: www.gsbs.gs.uth.tmc.edu

Established 1963. Coed. Tuition: per credit resident $76, nonresident $281. Enrollment: full-time 450, (men 50%, women 50%). Faculty: full-time 479, part-time 11. Degrees conferred: M.S., Ph.D., M.D.-Ph.D.

ADMISSION REQUIREMENTS. Transcripts, GRE, three letters of recommendation, personal statement background, research interests, and professional goals required in support of School's application. On-line application available. GRE Subject Test recommended. TOEFL and TWE required of international students. Interview optional. Apply to Office of the Registrar, UT Health Science Center, P.O. Box 20036, Houston, Texas 77225, eight weeks prior to registration. Priority deadline for Fall admission is January 15 (Fall), November 1 (Spring). Application fee $10. Phone: (800)UTH-GSBS, (713)500-9860; fax: (713)500-9877.

ADMISSION STANDARDS. Competitive. Usual minimum average: 3.0 (A = 4).

FINANCIAL AID. Scholarships, fellowships, research assistantships, teaching assistantships, training grants, loans. Nearly all admitted students are awarded financial aid. Apply to the Office of Student Financial Aid. Phone: (713)500-3860. Use FAFSA for all nonmerit aid. About 95% of students receive aid from School and outside sources.

DEGREE REQUIREMENTS. For M.S.: 24 hours of course work, two semesters of registration for thesis. For Ph.D.: three tutorial laboratory rotations; four area courses, one ethics course; qualifying exam; dissertation; final oral exam.

FIELDS OF STUDY.
Biochemistry.
Biomathematics and Biostatistics.
Biomedical Sciences. Includes medical physics. M.S. only.
Biophysics.
Cancer Biology.
Cell Biology.
Environmental and Molecular Carcinogenesis.
Genes and Development.
Genetics Counseling. M.S. only.

Human and Molecular Genetics.
Immunology.
Integrative Biology.
Medical Physics.
Microbiology and Molecular Genetics.
Molecular Biology.
Molecular Pathology.
Neurosciences.
Oral Biomaterials. M.S. only.
Pharmacology.
Physiology.
Radiation Biology.
Regulatory Biology.
Reproductive Biology.
Toxicology.
Virology and Gene Therapy.

Dental School

Web site: www.db.uth.tmc.edu

Established 1905. Joined University of Texas system in 1972. Located in Houston (77225-0068).

Annual tuition: full-time, resident $7046, nonresident $17,846. No on-campus housing available. Average academic year housing costs: $14,210. For off-campus housing, contact Resident Manager, Texas Medical Center. Total average cost for all other first-year expenses: $6000.

Enrollment: first-year class 62; 242 total (men 55%, women 45%); graduate program 32. Faculty: full-time 232, part-time 21. Degree conferred: D.D.S.

ADMISSION REQUIREMENTS. AADSAS (nonresidents), official transcripts, three letters of recommendation, DAT required in support of School's application. Applicants must have completed at least three years of college study, four years of study preferred. Interview by invitation only. Preference given to state residents. Accepts transfer students. Apply to UT System, Medical and Dental Application Center, Austin, Texas 78701, after April 15, before November 1. Application fee $55 resident, $190 nonresident. Dental School Admissions Office Phone: (713)500-4151.

ADMISSION STANDARDS. Selective. Mean DAT: Academic 19, PAT 17.4; mean GPA: 3.45 (A = 4). Gourman rating: 4.34. Usual minimum average: 3.0 (A = 4). Accepts about 20–25% of total annual applicants. Approximately 90% are state residents.

FINANCIAL AID. Scholarships, grants, loans. Apply to the Health Science Center's Financial Aid Office; no specified closing date. Phone: (713)500-3860. Use FAFSA (School code: 013956). About 84% of students receive some aid from University and outside sources.

DEGREE REQUIREMENTS. For D.D.S.: satisfactory completion of forty-six-month program.

Medical School

Web site: www.med.uth.tmc.edu

Established 1969. Annual tuition: resident $7450, nonresident $20,550; fees $872. Total average cost for all other expenses: $11,000. Enrollment: first-year class 201; total 815 (men 54%, women 46%).

Faculty: full- and part-time and volunteers 2000. Degrees conferred: M.D., M.D.-M.P.H., M.D.-Ph.D.

ADMISSION REQUIREMENTS. Transcripts, MCAT, recommendations required in support of application. Interview by invitation. Preference given to state residents. Graduates of unaccredited colleges not considered. 90% of class must be state residents. Apply to University of Texas System, Medical and Dental Application Center, Austin, Texas 78701, after May 1. be-

fore November 1. Application fee $55 (resident) plus $5 for each additional school, $100 (nonresident) plus $5 for each additional school. Phone: (713)792-4711; fax: (713)792-4238.

ADMISSION STANDARDS. Selective. Mean MCAT: 9.2; mean GPA: 3.57 (A = 4). Gourman rating: 3.46. Admits about 10–15% of total annual applicants. Approximately 92% are state residents.

FINANCIAL AID. A limited number of scholarships from memorial funds and foundations, institutional loans, HEAL, alternative loan programs, NIH stipends, Federal Perkins Loans, Stafford Subsidized and Unsubsidized Loans, Service Commitment Scholarship programs are available. Assistantships/fellowships may be available for combined degree candidates. Most aid is awarded based on demonstrated need. Financial aid applications and information are available by contacting the Office of the Registrar. Phone: (214) 648-3606. Use FAFSA (School code: 013956), also submit Financial Aid Transcript, Federal Income Tax forms. Approximately 80% of students receive some form of financial assistance.

DEGREE REQUIREMENTS. For M.D.: satisfactory completion of four-year program. All students must pass USMLE Step 1 prior to entering fourth year. For M.D.-M.A., -M.S.: generally from four-and-one-half- to five-and-one-half-year programs. For M.D.-Ph.D.: generally a six- to seven-year program.

FIELDS OF GRADUATE STUDY.
Anatomy.
Biochemistry and Molecular Biology.
Cancer Biology.
Genetics.
Immunology.
Microbiology.
Neurosciences.
Pathology.
Pharmacology.
Regulatory Biology.
Reproductive Biology.
Toxicology.
Virology.

School of Public Health

Founded 1967. Coed. Semester system. Special facilities: Center for Health Policy Studies, Center for Health Promotion and Prevention Research, Center for Health Services Research, Center for Infectious Diseases, Center for Society and Population Health, Coordinating Center for Clinical Trials, Human Genetics Center, Human Nutrition Center, Southwest Center for Occupational and Environmental Health.

Tuition: per credit, resident $76, nonresident $281. Enrollment: full-time 292, part-time 482. Faculty: full-time 79, part-time 10. Degrees conferred: M.P.H., M.S., D.P.H., Ph.D.

ADMISSION REQUIREMENTS, Transcripts, two letters of recommendation, written statement of goals, GRE required in support of application. TOEFL (minimum score 565) required for international applicants. Accepts transfer applicants. Graduates of unaccredited institutions considered. Apply to Office of Registration by February 1 (Fall), August 1 (Spring). Application fee $10. Phone: (713)792-4425.

ADMISSION STANDARDS. Very selective. Usual minimum average: 3.0 (A = 4); GRE: 1000 (combined), 1200 (for doctoral programs).

FINANCIAL AID. Scholarships, fellowships, traineeships, grants and contracts, internships, loans. Approved for VA benefits. Apply to the Financial Aid Office; no specified closing date. Phone: (713)500-3860; fax: (713)500-38863. Use FAFSA. About 33% of students receive aid other than loans from School and outside sources.

DEGREE REQUIREMENTS. For master's: satisfactory completion of 36 credit, 18- to 24-month program; thesis. For D.P.H.: at least one academic year in preparation for qualifying exam; research project. For Ph.D.: satisfactory completion of prescribed course of study, at least to semesters in residence; qualifying exam; dissertation; final oral exam.

THE UNIVERSITY OF TEXAS HEALTH SCIENCE CENTER AT SAN ANTONIO

San Antonio, Texas 78284

Web site: www.uthscsa.edu

Formed in 1959. Coed. State control. Semester system. Special facilities: DEC system -20, DEC/VAX 8650, 8700, 11-/785; Center for Research in Reproductive Biology; Scanning Electron Microscope facility. The Center's NIH ranking is 70th among all U.S. institutions with 218 awards/grants worth $65,997,423. Library: 250,000 volumes, 2500 subscriptions. Total University enrollment: 3000.

Graduate School of Biomedical Sciences

Graduate study since 1972. Tuition: per credit resident $76, nonresident $281. Enrollment: full- and part-time 272 (men 55%, women 45%). Faculty: full-time 225, part-time 36. Degrees conferred: M.S., M.S.N., Ph.D.

ADMISSION REQUIREMENTS. Transcripts, GRE, three letters of recommendation, research interests, and professional goals statement required in support of School's application. Online application available. GRE Subject Test recommended. TOEFL and TWE required of international applicants. Interview optional. Graduates of unaccredited institutions not considered. Apply to Office of the Registrar, eight weeks prior to registration. Priority deadline for Fall admission is January 15. Application fee $10. Phone: (210) 567-3709; fax (210) 567-3719.

ADMISSIONS STANDARDS. Selective. Usual minimum average: 3.0 (A = 4).

FINANCIAL AID. Scholarship, assistantships, fellowships for teaching/research, loans. Apply to appropriate department by March 31. Use FAFSA for all nonmerit aid. About 35% of students receive aid from school and outside sources.

DEGREE REQUIREMENTS. For M.S.: 30 semester hours minimum, at least 24 in residence; thesis; comprehensive oral/written exam for some departments. For Ph.D.: at least one year in residence; foreign language requirement set by department; oral written exam for candidacy; dissertation; final oral exam.

FIELDS OF STUDY.
Biochemistry.
Cellular and Structural Biology.
Clinical Investigation.
Clinical Laboratory Sciences.
Dental Hygiene.
Dentistry. M.S.
Microbiology and Immunology.
Molecular Medicine.
Nursing. M.S.N.
Pathology.
Pharmacology. Ph.D. only.
Pharmacy.
Physiology.
Radiology.

Dental School (78284-7702)

Established 1969. Annual tuition: resident $5400, nonresident $16,200. No on-campus housing available. Average academic year off-campus housing costs: $15,000. Contact Dean for Student Affairs for housing information. Phone: (210)567-3181. Total average cost for all other first-year expenses: $7600.

Enrollment: first-year class 90; 413 total (men 65%, women 35%). Faculty: full-time 146, part-time 49. Degree conferred: D.D.S., D.D.S.-Ph.D.

ADMISSION REQUIREMENTS. AADSAS (nonresidents), official transcripts, DAT (not later than October), three letters of recommendation required in support of School's application. Preference given to state residents and veterans. Interview by invitation only. Graduates of unaccredited institutions not considered. Apply to UT System, Medical and Dental Application Center, Austin, Texas 78701, after May 1, before November 1. Application fee: resident $55, nonresident $100; School's fee $40. Dental School's Admissions Office. Phone: (210)567-2674.

ADMISSION STANDARDS. Selective. Mean DAT: Academic 18.4, PAT 17.1; mean GPA: 3.5. (A = 4). Gourman rating: 4.28. Accepts about 30–35% of total annual applicants. Approximately 90% are state residents.

FINANCIAL AID. Limited state, federal scholarships, loans. Apply to Student Financial Aid office after acceptance. Phone: (210)567-2365. Use FAFSA (School code: 010115). About 90% of students receive aid from School and outside sources.

DEGREE REQUIREMENTS. For D.D.S.: satisfactory completion of thirty-nine-month program.

FIELDS OF GRADUATE STUDY.
Dental Diagnostic Sciences.
Dental Public Health.
Endodontics.
General Dentistry.
Oral and Maxillofacial Surgery.
Orthdontics.
Pediatric Dentistry.
Periodontics.
Prosthodontics.

Medical School (78229-7702)

Established 1959. Annual tuition: resident $6500, nonresident $19,650; student fees $1420. On-campus housing for women; none for married students and men. Average annual housing cost: $15,000. Apply to Manager, Dormitories and Apartments.

Enrollment: first-year class 200, total 819 (men 50%, women 50%). Faculty: full-time 823, part-time 111. Degrees conferred: M.D., M.D.-Ph.D.

ADMISSION REQUIREMENTS. Transcripts, letter of recommendation from Premedical Committee, two additional letters of recommendation, MCAT required in support of application. Interview by invitation only. Applicants must have completed at least three years of college study. Accepts transfer applicants. 90% of class must be state residents. Apply to University of Texas System Medical and Dental Application Center at Austin (78701) after May 1, before October 15. Application center fee: residents $55 plus $5 for each additional school, nonresidents $100 plus $10 for each additional school. Medical School phone: (210)567-2665; fax: (210)567-2685.

ADMISSION STANDARDS. Selective. Mean MCAT: 10.0, mean GPA: 3.50 (A = 4). Gourman rating: 3.73. Accepts about

10–15% of total annual applicants. Approximately 96% are state residents.

FINANCIAL AID. Limited scholarships, loans. Apply after acceptance, before July 1 to Office of Student Services. Phone: (210)567-2635. Use FAFSA (School code: 010115). About 45% of students receive some aid from School.

DEGREE REQUIREMENTS. For M.D.: satisfactory completion of four-year program.

FIELDS OF GRADUATE STUDY.
Biochemistry.
Cell Biology.
Immunology.
Microbiology.
Pharmacology.
Physiology.

UNIVERSITY OF TEXAS MEDICAL BRANCH AT GALVESTON
Galveston, Texas 77555
Web site: www.utmb.edu

Established 1891. CGS member. Coed. State control. Semester system. Special facilities: DEC/VAX11/750, IBM 3081, Biomedical Engineering Center, Marine Biomedical Institute, Molecular Science Institute, Institute for Medical Humanities, Shriner's Burn Institute. The Branch's NIH ranking is 74th among all U.S. institutions with 207 awards/grants worth $62,865,760. Library: 270,000 volumes, 1986 subscriptions.

Limited graduate housing available for single students, none for married students. Average academic year housing costs: $195 per month (room only). Phone: (409)772-1898.

Graduate School of Biomedical Science
Web site: www.utmb.edu/gsbs/programs/html

Graduate study since 1969. Annual tuition: full-time resident $1080, nonresident $6885; per credit resident $38, nonresident $254.

Enrollment: full-time 210, part-time 43 (men 50%, women 50%). Faculty: full-time 256, part-time 15. Degrees conferred: M.A., M.M.S., M.S., M.S.N., Ph.D.

ADMISSION REQUIREMENTS. Official transcripts, three recommendations, GRE required in support of School's application. On-line application available. Four-year bachelor's degree or equivalent required. Interview encouraged. TOEFL (minimum score 550) required for all international applicants. Accepts transfer applicants. Graduates of unaccredited institutions given consideration. Apply to Office of the Registrar by March 1 (Fall), October 1 (Spring), February 1 (Summer). Application fee $25, $50 for international applicants. Phone: (409)772-2665; fax: (409)747-0772.

ADMISSION STANDARDS. Selective. Usual minimum average: 3.0 (A = 4).

FINANCIAL AID. Scholarships, fellowships, research assistantships, internships, Federal W/S, loans. Approved for VA benefits. Apply to Financial Aid Office; no specified closing date. Phone: (409)722-4955; fax: (409)722-4466. Use FAFSA. About 35% of students receive aid other than loans from School. Aid available for part-time students.

DEGREE REQUIREMENTS. For master's: 36 semester hours minimum, at least 24 in residence; thesis; comprehensive oral/written exam for some departments. For Ph.D.: at least one year in residence; foreign language requirement set by department; oral/written candidacy exam; dissertation; final oral exam.

FIELDS OF STUDY.
Cell Biology. Ph.D.
Cellular Physiology and Molecular Biophysics. Ph.D.
Experimental Pathology. Ph.D.
Human Biological Chemistry and Genetics. Ph.D.
Medical Humanities. M.A., Ph.D.
Medical Sciences. M.M.S. only.
Microbiology and Immunology. Ph.D.
Neuroscience. Ph.D.
Nursing. Ph.D.
Pharmacology and Toxicology. Ph.D.
Preventive Medicine and Community Health. Ph.D.

School of Medicine (77555-1317)

Established 1891. Annual tuition: resident $6550, nonresident $19,650; student fees $580. On-campus housing for women; none for married students and men. Average annual housing cost: $12,000. Apply to Manager, Dormitories and Apartments. Phone: (409)772-1898.

Enrollment: first-year class 205, total 804 (men 53%, women 47%). Faculty: full-time 251, part-time 111. Degrees conferred: M.D., M.D.-M.A. (Medical Humanities), M.D.-M.S., M.D.-Ph.D.

ADMISSION REQUIREMENTS. Transcripts, letter of recommendation from Premedical Committee, two additional letters of recommendation, MCAT required in support of application. Interview by invitation only. Applicants must have completed at least three years of college study. Accepts transfer applicants. 90% of class must be state residents. Apply to University of Texas System Medical and Dental Application Center at Austin (78701) after May 1, before November 1. Application center fee: residents $55 plus $5 for each additional school, nonresidents $100 plus $10 for each additional school. School's application fee: none. Phone: (409)772-3256.

ADMISSION STANDARDS. Selective. Mean MCAT: 9.0; mean GPA: 3.66 (A = 4). Gourman rating: 3.74. Accepts about 15% of total annual applicants. Approximately 98% are state residents.

FINANCIAL AID. Limited scholarships, loans. Apply after acceptance, before July 1 to Office of Student Affairs. Phone: (409)772-4955. Use FAFSA (School code: 013976). About 45% of students receive some aid from School.

DEGREE REQUIREMENTS. For M.D.: satisfactory completion of four-year program.

FIELDS OF GRADUATE STUDY.
Allied Health.
Biochemistry.
Cell Biology.
Cellular Physiology and Molecular Biophysics.
Community Health.
Human Biological Chemistry and Genetics.
Immunology.
Medical Humanities.
Microbiology.
Neurosciences.
Pathology.
Pharmacology and Toxicology.
Physiology.
Preventive Medicine.

THE UNIVERSITY OF TEXAS OF THE PERMIAN BASIN

Odessa, Texas 79762-0001
Web site: www.utpb.edu

Coed. State control. Semester system. Special facilities: Center for Energy and Economic Diversification, Center for Behavioral Analysis. Library: 270,000 volumes, 1,074,000 microforms, 723 current periodicals.

Tuition: per credit, resident $66, nonresident $270. On-campus housing for single and married students. Average academic year housing costs: single students $2200, married students $3500. Contact Director of Graduate Housing for both on- and off-campus housing information. Phone: (915)552-2743.

Graduate Studies and Research

Enrollment: full-time 61, part-time 256. Faculty: full-time 48, part-time 7. Degrees conferred: M.A., M.B.A., M.S.

ADMISSION REQUIREMENTS. Two transcripts, GRE/GMAT required in support of application. On-line application available. TOEFL (minimum score 550) required for international applicants. Accepts transfer students. Graduates of unaccredited institutions not considered. Applications processed on a rolling basis. Apply to the Registrar at least 60 days prior to the date of registration. Application fee: none. Phone: (915)552-2530; fax: (915)552-2109.

ADMISSION STANDARDS. Selective. Usual minimum average: 2.5 (A = 4).

FINANCIAL AID. Limited to Federal W/S, loans. Approved for VA benefits. Apply to Director of Financial Aid; no specified closing date. Phone: (915)552-2620. Use FAFSA and Institutional FAF. Aid available for part-time students.

DEGREE REQUIREMENTS. For M.A., M.S.: 30 semester credits minimum, at least 24 credits in residence; thesis/nonthesis option; comprehensive written/oral exam. For M.B.A.: 36–45 semester credits, at least 30–39 credits in residence; computer proficiency.

FIELDS OF STUDY.

COLLEGE OF ARTS AND SCIENCES:
Biology.
Criminal Justice Administration.
English.
Geology.
History.
Kinesiology.
Psychology.

SCHOOL OF BUSINESS:
Professional Accountancy.
Business Administration.
M.B.A. Online.

SCHOOL OF EDUCATION:
Counseling.
Early Childhood Education.
Educational Leadership.
Professional Education.
Reading.
Special Education.

THE UNIVERSITY OF TEXAS— PAN AMERICAN

Edinburg, Texas 78539-2999
Web site: www.panam.edu

Founded 1927. CGS member. Coed. State control. Semester system. Special facilities: Speech and Hearing Clinic, Coastal Marine Biology Laboratory, Rio Grande Valley Archives. Library: 418,750 volumes, 2600 subscriptions.

Tuition/fees: per semester, resident $1037, nonresident $2999. On-campus housing for single students only. Annual housing cost: $3367 (including board). Contact Director of Student Services for both on- and off-campus housing information. Phone: (956)381-3439.

Graduate School

Enrollment: full-time 346, part-time 1226. Graduate faculty: full-time 137, part-time 34. Degrees conferred: M.A., M.B.A., M.Ed., M.S., M.S.I.S.

ADMISSION REQUIREMENTS. Two transcripts, GRE/GMAT required in support of application. TOEFL required for international students. Accepts transfer students. Graduates of unaccredited institutions not considered. Applications processed on a rolling basis. Apply to the Director of Admissions and Records by April 1 (Summer), July 1 (Fall), November 1 (Spring) for priority consideration. Application fee none. Phone: (956)381-2206.

ADMISSION STANDARDS. Selective. Usual minimum average: 2.75 (A = 4).

FINANCIAL AID. Scholarships, assistantships, partial tuition waivers, grants, Federal W/S, loans. Approved for VA benefits. Apply by April 15 to the appropriate department for scholarships and assistantships; to Office of Financial Services for all other programs. Use FAFSA (School code: 003599). Aid available for part-time students.

DEGREE REQUIREMENTS. For M.A., M.S., M.S.I.S.: 30 semester credits minimum, at least 24 credits in residence; thesis/nonthesis option; comprehensive written/oral exam. For M.Ed.: 36 semester credits minimum, at least 30 in residence. For M.B.A.: 36–45 semester credits, at least 30–39 credits in residence; computer proficiency.

FIELDS OF STUDY.

COLLEGE OF ARTS AND HUMANITIES:
Art.
English.
English as a Second Language.
History.
Spanish.
Speech Communication.
Theatre.

COLLEGE OF BUSINESS ADMINISTRATION:
Business Administration.
Business Administration. Emphasis in international business.

COLLEGE OF EDUCATION:
Bilingual Education.
Early Childhood Education.
Educational Administration.
Educational Diagnostician.
Elementary Education.
Gifted Education.
Guidance and Counseling.

Kinesiology.
Reading.
School Psychology.
Secondary Education.
Special Education.
Supervision.

COLLEGE OF HEALTH SCIENCES AND HUMAN SERVICES:
Adult Health Nursing.
Communication Disorders. Includes bilingual/bicultural.
Rehabilitation Counseling.

COLLEGE OF SCIENCE AND ENGINEERING:
Biology.
Computer Science.
Mathematics. Includes mathematical science, mathematics teaching.

COLLEGE OF SOCIAL AND BEHAVIORAL SCIENCES:
Psychology. Includes clinical, experimental.
Public Administration.
Sociology.

INTERDISCIPLINARY MASTER'S DEGREES:
Interdisciplinary Studies.

THE UNIVERSITY OF TEXAS SOUTHWESTERN MEDICAL CENTER AT DALLAS

Dallas, Texas 75235-9096
Web site: www.swmed.edu

Established 1943. Coed. State control. Semester system. Special facilities: Howard Hughes Medical Institute; Zale Lipshy Hospital; Cain Center for Biomedical Research; James M. Collins Center for Biomedical Research; Cecil H. and Ida Green Center for Reproductive Biology Sciences; Robert T. Hayes Center for Mineral Metabolism Research; Erik Jonson Center for Research on Molecular Genetics and Human Disease; Kimberly-Clark Center for Breast Cancer Research; Eugene McDermott Center for Human Growth and Development; Eugene McDermott Center for Pain Management; Mobility Foundation Center for Rehabilitation Research; W. A. "Tex" and Deborah Moncrieg, Jr., Center for Cancer Genetics; Harry S. Ross Heart Center; Frank M. Ryburn, Jr., Cardiac Center; Harold C. Simmons Arthritis Research Center; Harold C. Simmons Comprehensive Cancer Center; Kent Waldrep Foundation Center for Basic Neuroscience Research; Cancer Immunobiology Center; Center for Basic Research in Transplantation Immunology; the Nuclear Medicine Center. The Medical Center's NIH ranking is 32nd among all U.S. institutions with 379 awards/grants worth $144,796,898. Library: 257,780 volumes, 2865 subscriptions.

Southwestern Graduate School of Biomedical Sciences

Tuition: per credit, resident $40, nonresident $255; Biomedical Engineering resident $80, nonresident $295.
Enrollment: full-time 450 (men 50%, women 50%). Faculty: full-time 256, part-time 65. Degrees conferred: M.A., M.S., Ph.D.

ADMISSION REQUIREMENTS. Official transcripts, three recommendations, GRE required in support of School's application. On-line application available. Four-year bachelor's degree or equivalent required. Interviews encouraged. TOEFL required for international applicants. Accepts transfer applicants. Graduates of unaccredited colleges not considered. Apply to Registrar, University of Texas Southwestern Medical Center, deadlines vary by program. Application fee none. Phone: (214)648-5617, fax: (214)648-3289.

ADMISSION STANDARDS. Selective. Usual minimum average: 3.0 (A = 4). GRE average score 1150.

FINANCIAL AID. Scholarships, fellowships, teaching/research assistantships, internships, grants, tuition waivers, Federal W/S, loans. Approved for VA benefits. Apply by March 15 to Financial Aid Office; no specified closing date. Phone: (214)648-3611; fax: (214)648-3289. Use FAFSA. Most Ph.D. students receive stipends.

DEGREE REQUIREMENTS. For master's: 30 semester hours minimum, at least 24 in residence; thesis; comprehensive oral/written exam for some departments. For Ph.D.: at least one year in residence; foreign language requirement set by department; oral/written candidacy exam; dissertation; final oral exam.

FIELDS OF STUDY.
Bioinstrumentation.
Biological Chemistry.
Biomaterial and Tissue.
Biomechanics.
Cell Regulation.
Clinical Psychology.
Genetics and Development.
Immunology.
Integrative Biology.
Medical Illustration.
Medical Imaging.
Molecular Biophysics.
Molecular Engineering.
Molecular Microbiology.
Neuroscience.
Orthopaedic Engineering.
Radiological Sciences.
Rehabilitation Counseling and Psychology.

Southwestern Medical School (75390-9162)

Established 1943. Medical library: 270,000 volumes.
Annual tuition: resident $6920, nonresident $20,020; student fees $882. Enrollment: first-year class 200, total 791 (men 65%, women 35%); total full-time 812. Faculty: full-time 823, part-time 111. Degrees conferred: M.D., M.D.-Ph.D., (Medical Scientist Training Program), M.D.-Ph.D. (medical combined degree program with University of Texas at Arlington).

ADMISSION REQUIREMENTS. Transcripts, letter of recommendation from Premedical Committee, two additional letters of recommendation, MCAT required in support of application. Interview by invitation only. Applicants must have completed at least three years of college study. Accepts transfer applicants. 90% of class must be state residents. Apply to University of Texas System Medical and Dental Application Center at Austin (78701) after May 1, before November 1. Application center fee: residents $55 plus $5 for each additional school, nonresidents $100 plus $10 for each additional school. School's application fee $65. Phone: (214)648-5617; fax: (214)648-3289.

ADMISSION STANDARDS. Selective. Mean MCAT: 10.8; mean GPA: 3.74. Gourman rating 3.76. *U.S. News & World Report* ranking is in the top 15 of all U.S. medical schools. Accepts 10–12% of total annual applicants. Approximately 88% are state residents.

FINANCIAL AID. A limited number of scholarships from memorial funds and foundations, institutional loans, HEAL, alternative loan programs, NIH stipends, Federal Perkins Loans,

Stafford Subsidized and Unsubsidized Loans, Service Commitment Scholarship programs are available. Assistantships/fellowships may be available for combined degree candidates. Most aid is awarded based on demonstrated need. Financial aid applications and information are available by contacting the Office of the Registrar. Phone: (214)648-3606. Use FAFSA (School code: 010019), also submit Financial Aid Transcript, Federal Income Tax forms. Approximately 80% of students receive some form of financial assistance.

DEGREE REQUIREMENTS. For M.D.: satisfactory completion of 4-year program. All students must pass USMLE Step 1 prior to entering fourth year. For M.D.-M.A., M.D.-M.S.: generally from four-and-one-half- to five-and-one-half-year programs. For M.D.-Ph.D.: generally a six- to seven-year program.

FIELDS OF GRADUATE STUDY.
Biochemistry and Molecular Biology.
Biomedical Engineering.
Cell Regulation.
Clinical Psychology.
Genetics and Development.
Immunology.
Integrative Biology.
Molecular Biophysics.
Molecular Microbiology.
Neurosciences.
Radiological Sciences.

THOMAS M. COOLEY LAW SCHOOL

P.O. Box 13038
Lansing, Michigan 48901-3038
Web site: www.cooley.edu

Established 1972. ABA approved since 1975. AALS member. Private. Semester system. Morning, afternoon, evening divisions. Special facilities: Sixty Plus Law Center. Library: 416,525 volumes, 4907 subscriptions; has LEXIS, NEXIS, WESTLAW.

Annual tuition: full-time $17,160, part-time $12,590. No on-campus housing available. Total average annual additional expense: $11,473

Enrollment: first-year class day and evening 752; total 1688 (men 53%, women 47%). Faculty: full-time 46, part-time 97. Student to faculty ratio 23 to 1. Degree conferred: J.D.

ADMISSION REQUIREMENTS. LSDAS Law School report, bachelor's degree, transcripts, LSAT required in support of application. Accepts transfer applicants. Apply to Admissions Office at least one month prior to beginning of trimester. Rolling admissions process. Admits September (morning classes), January (afternoon classes), and May (evening classes). Application fee, none. Phone: (517)371-5140, ext. 2244; fax: (517)334-5718.

ADMISSION STANDARDS. Selective. Admission index is GPA x 15 plus LSAT. Mean LSAT: full- and part-time 143; mean GPA: full-time 2.90, part-time 2.91 (A = 4). Gourman rating: 2.90; *U.S. News & World Report* ranking is in the fourth tier of all U.S. law schools. Admits about 60% of total annual applicants.

FINANCIAL AID. Honor scholarships, Federal W/S, loans. Apply to the Financial Aid Office; no specified closing date. Use FAFSA (School code: G12627). About 75% of students receive some aid from School.

DEGREE REQUIREMENTS. For J.D.: satisfactory completion of 90 credit hour program.

THOMAS JEFFERSON SCHOOL OF LAW

2121 San Diego Avenue
San Diego, California 92110
Web site: www.tjsl.edu

Established 1969. Located in historic "Old Town" section of San Diego. ABA approved since 1996. AALS member. Semester system. Full-time (day), part-time (day or evening) study. Special facilities: Center for Law, Technology, and Communication, Center for Global Legal Studies, Center for Law and Social Justice. Special programs: externships. Law library: 223,580 volumes, 3393 subscriptions; has LEXIS, NEXIS, WESTLAW.

Annual tuition: full-time $21,300, part-time $13,290. No on-campus housing available. Law students live off-campus. Contact the Admissions Office for off-campus information. Off-campus housing and personal expenses: approximately $17,099.

Enrollment: first-year class full-time 173, part-time 56; total full- and part-time 557 (men 59%, women 41%). Faculty: full-time 21, part-time 19. Student to faculty ratio 20.3 to 1. Degree conferred: J.D.

ADMISSION REQUIREMENTS. LSDAS Law School report, LSAT (not later that June (Fall), December 1 (Spring) test date; if more than one LSAT, highest is used), bachelor's degree from an accredited institution, résumé, personal statement, two recommendations, transcripts (must show all schools attended and at least three years of study) required in support of application. Applicants must have received bachelor's degree prior to enrollment. Interview not required but telephone and personal interviews are available. In addition, international applicants whose native language is not English must submit TOEFL (not older that two years). First-year students admitted Fall, Spring. Rolling admissions process. Application fee $35. Phone: (800)936-7529, (619)297-9700; fax: (619)294-4713; e-mail: info@tjsl.edu.

ADMISSION REQUIREMENTS FOR TRANSFER APPLICANTS. Accepts transfers from other ABA-accredited schools. Admission limited to space available. At least one year of enrollment, Dean's letter indicating the applicant is in good standing, LSAT, LSDAS, personal statement regarding reason for transfer, undergraduate transcript, current law school transcript required in support of School application. Rolling admissions process. Application fee $35. Will consider visiting students.

ADMISSION STANDARDS. Selective. Mean LSAT: full-time 150, part-time 149; mean GPA: full-time 2.85, part-time 3.04 (A = 4). *U.S. News & World Report* ranking is in the fourth tier of all U.S. law schools. Accepts about 50–60% of total annual applicants.

FINANCIAL AID. Scholarships, merit scholarships, minority scholarships, private loans, State grants, Federal loans and Federal W/S available. All accepted students are consider for scholarships (a student with a LSAT score of 150 or higher automatically receives either a partial or full scholarship). Apply as soon as possible after January 1. Phone: (619)279-9700, ext. 1350. Use FAFSA (School code: 013780), also submit Financial Aid Transcript, Federal Income Tax forms. Approximately 41% (full-time), 30% (part-time) of first year class received scholarships/Grants-in-Aid. Approximately 70% of students receive some form of financial assistance.

DEGREE REQUIREMENTS. For J.D.: 88 (33 required) credits with a GPA of at least a 2.0 (A = 4), plus completion of upper-divisional writing course; three-year program, four-year part-time program. Accelerated J.D. with summer course work.

THOMAS JEFFERSON UNIVERSITY

Philadelphia, Pennsylvania 19107
Web site: www.tju.edu

Founded 1824. CGS member. Private control. Semester system. The University's NIH ranking is 65th among all U.S. institutions with 223 awards/grants worth $75,889,120. Medical library: 192,000 volumes, 2100 subscriptions.

Annual Graduate School tuition: $19,800; per credit $685. On-campus housing available. Average academic year housing costs: apartments $800–$900/month, dormitory $350/month. Contact the Director of University Housing Office for both on- and off-campus housing information. Phone: (215)955-8913. On-campus day-care facilities available.

College of Graduate Studies

Enrollment: full-time 264, part-time 252 (men 35%, women 65%). Faculty: full-time 200, part-time 11. Degrees conferred: M.S., Ph.D.

ADMISSION REQUIREMENTS. Official transcripts, three letters of recommendation, GRE required in support of College's application. TOEFL required for international applicants. Accepts transfer applicants. Graduates of unaccredited institutions not considered. Apply to Director of admission; no specified closing date. Application fee $40. Phone: (215)503-0155; fax: (215)503-3433.

ADMISSION STANDARDS. Competitive. Usual minimum average: 3.0 (A = 4).

FINANCIAL AID. Fellowships, research assistantships, traineeships, grants, Federal W/S, loans. Approved for VA benefits. Apply by May 1 to the Dean for fellowships, assistantships; to Financial Aid Office for all other programs. Phone: (215)955-2867; fax: (215)955-5186. Use FAFSA and institutional FAF. Aid available for part-time students.

DEGREE REQUIREMENTS. For M.S.: minimum 30 credits, maximum 44; final project or thesis. For Ph.D.: minimum of 45 credits beyond the master's, at least one year in full-time residence; qualifying exam; dissertation; final written/oral exam.

FIELDS OF STUDY.
Biochemistry and Molecular Biology.
Biomedical Chemistry. M. S. only.
Cell and Tissue Engineering.
Developmental Biology and Teratology.
Genetics.
Immunology.
Laboratory Sciences. Includes biotechnology, cytotechnology, medical technology. M.S. only.
Microbiology. M.S. only.
Microbiology and Molecular Virology.
Nursing. M.S. only.
Occupational Therapy. M.S. only.
Pathology and Cell Biology.
Pharmacology.
Physical Therapy. M.S. only.
Physiology.
Public Health.

Jefferson Medical College

Established 1824, one of the oldest medical colleges in the nation and is currently the largest. Semester system; the first two years are spent in studying the basic sciences. Affiliated hospitals: Thomas Jefferson University Hospital, Stein Research Center, Wills Eye Hospital, Veterans Administration Hospital. Special facility: Bodine Center for Radiation Therapy. Special programs:

prematriculation summer sessions; a decelerated program available during first two years.

Annual tuition: $30,979; student fees, none. On-campus apartments available for both single and married students. Contact Housing Office for both on- and off-campus housing information. Phone: (215)955-8913. Medical students tend to live off-campus. Off-campus housing and personal expenses: approximately $11,750.

Enrollment: first-year class 223 (EDP 30); total full-time 902 (men 53%, women 47%). Faculty: full-time 689, part-time/volunteers 3000. Degrees conferred: M.D., B.S.-M.D. (with Penn State University), M.D.-M.B.A. (with Widener University), M.D.-M.H.A. (Widener University), M.D.-M.P.H. (in cooperation with Johns Hopkins School of Public Health), M.D.-Ph.D.

ADMISSION REQUIREMENTS. Preference given to U.S. citizens and permanent residents and children of alumni and faculty. Bachelor's degree from an accredited institution required. Has EDP; applicants must apply through AMCAS (official transcripts sent by mid-May) between June 1 and August 1. Early applications are encouraged. Submit secondary/supplemental application, a personal statement, two recommendations to Office of Admission within two weeks of receipt of application. Interviews are by invitation only and generally for final selection. Notification normally begins October 1. Accepts transfer and international (students must have four-year degree from U.S. institution) applicants. All other candidates apply through AMCAS (file after June 1, before November 15), submit MCAT (will accept MCAT test results from the last three years), official transcripts for each school attended (should show at least 90 semester credits/135 quarter credit; submit transcripts by mid-May to AMCAS), service processing fee. Submit an application fee of $65, a supplemental application, a personal statement, pre-professional committee evaluation, and three recommendations from science faculty to Office of Admission within two to three weeks of the receipt of supplemental materials, but no later than January 15. Interviews are by invitation only and generally for final selection. M.D.-Ph.D. applicants must apply to and be accepted to both Schools, contact the Director of Admission and Recruitment of the College of Graduate Studies for current information and specific admissions requirements. Phone: (215) 955-0155. First-year students admitted Fall only. Rolling admissions process; notification starts October 15 and is finished when class is filled; Phone: (215)955-6983; fax: (215)955-5151.

ADMISSION STANDARDS. Competitive. Mean MCAT: 10, Mean GPA: 3.5 (A = 4). Gourman rating: 3.49. *U.S. News & World Report* ranking is in the top 48 of all U.S. medical schools. Accepts about 3–5% of total annual applicants.

FINANCIAL AID. Scholarships, merit scholarships, minority scholarships, Grants-in-Aid, institutional loans, HEAL, alternative loan programs, Federal Perkins Loans, Stafford Subsidized and Unsubsidized Loans, Primary Care Service Commitment Scholarship programs are available. Fellowships, tuition waivers, and stipends may be available for M.D.-Ph.D. candidates. All aid is based on demonstrated need. Financial Aid applications and the Financial Aid Handbook are available after December 18; applications must be completed and returned no later than April 1. For scholarships, the selection criteria places heavy reliance on MCAT and undergraduate GPA. Contact the Office of Student Financial Aid for current information. Phone: (215)955-5855. Use FAFSA (School code: 010021), also submit Financial Aid Transcript, Federal Income Tax forms. Approximately 72% of students receive some form of financial assistance.

DEGREE REQUIREMENTS. For M.D.: satisfactory completion of four-year program; all students must pass USMLE Step 1 prior to entering third year and all students must pass USMLE Step 2 prior to awarding of M.D. For M.D.-M.B.A.: generally a five-year program. For M.D.-M.P.H.: generally a five-year program. For M.D.-Ph.D.: generally a seven-year program.

FIELDS OF GRADUATE STUDY.
Biochemistry.
Cell Biology.
Genetics.
Immunology.
Microbiology and Molecular Virology.
Molecular Biology.
Molecular Pharmacology and Structural Biology.
Pathology.
Physiology.

THUNDERBIRD, THE AMERICAN GRADUATE SCHOOL OF INTERNATIONAL MANAGEMENT
Glendale, Arizona 85306-6000
Web site: www.t-bird.edu

Founded 1946. Located in a suburban area near Phoenix with campuses in Japan and France. Coed. Private control. Module system. Special facilities: International Studies Research Center, Dom Pedro II Research Center on Iberia, Ibero-American and Lusohispanphone Africa Center, International Business Information Center. Library: 72,900 volumes, 1612 subscriptions, 60 PCs.

Annual tuition: full-time $13,200 per module. On-campus housing available for single students only. Average academic year housing costs: $3010 per module (including board). Contact the Housing Office for off-campus housing information. Phone: (602)978-7132.

Graduate Programs

Enrollment: full-time 1335, part-time 0. Graduate faculty: full-time 106, part-time 39. Degrees conferred: M.B.A.I.M., M.I.M.L.A., M.I.M.-M.B.A.

ADMISSION REQUIREMENTS. Official transcripts, GMAT, required in support of School's application. TOEFL required for international applicants. Accepts transfer applicants. Graduates of unaccredited institutions not considered. Apply by January 15 (Fall), July 31 (Spring) to Dean of Admissions. Rolling admissions process. Application fee $100. Phone: (602)978-7210; fax: (602)439-5432.

ADMISSION STANDARDS. Selective. Usual minimum average: 2.75 (A = 4). Ranked number one in International Management by *U.S. News & World Report.*

FINANCIAL AID. Scholarships, fellowships, assistantships, partial tuition waivers, Federal W/S, loans. Approved for VA benefits. Apply by April 1 to appropriate program chair for fellowships, assistantships; to Financial Aid Office for all other programs. Use FAFSA. About 65% of students receive aid from School and outside sources.

DEGREE REQUIREMENTS. For M.B.A.I.M.: 48–60 credit program; language/nonlanguage option. For M.I.M.: 30–42 credits minimum, all in full-time residence, one- to two-year program; language proficiency for some programs; final oral/written exam. For M.I.M.L.A.: 50 credit program.

FIELDS OF STUDY.
Business Administration. Includes international finance, international marketing, international political economy.
International Health Management.
International Management.
International Management—Latin America.
International Management of Technology.

Note: Joint degree programs are with Arizona State University, University of Arizona, Case Western Reserve University, University of Colorado, University of Denver, Drury College, University of Florida, University of Houston, University of Texas at Arlington, ESADE in Barcelona, Spain.

UNIVERSITY OF TOLEDO
Toledo, Ohio 43606-3390
Web site: www.utoledo.edu

Founded 1872, became a state university in 1967. CGS member. Coed. State control. Semester system. Special facilities: VAX-11/785, Humanities Institute, Polymer Institute, Center for International Studies, Center for Institutional Research and Services, Eitel Institute for Silicate Research, Ritter Astrophysical Research, Polymer Institute, Opinion Research Institute, Urban Affairs Center. Library: 1,600,000 volumes, 4500 subscriptions. Total University enrollment: 20,000.

Annual tuition: full-time resident $6664, nonresident $13,412. Off-campus housing only. Average monthly housing costs: $140–$260. Contact Coordinator of Commuter and Off-Campus Housing Services. Phone: (419)530-2941. On-campus day-care facilities available.

Graduate School

Graduate study since 1912. Enrollment: full-time 1064, part-time 1883. Graduate faculty: full-time 408, part-time 50. Degrees conferred: M.A., M.B.A., M.Ed., M.M., M.S., Ed.S., Ed.D., Ph.D.

ADMISSION REQUIREMENTS. Three official transcripts, three letters of recommendation, GMAT/GRE and Subject Tests required in support of School's application. On-line application available. TOEFL required for international applicants. Accepts transfer applicants. Graduates of unaccredited institutions not considered. Apply to Director of Admissions at least one month prior to registration. All requirements must be completed at least 2 weeks prior to registration. Rolling admissions process. Application fee $30. Phone: (800)914-7764, (419)530-4724; e-mail: grdsch@utnet.utoledo.edu.

ADMISSION STANDARDS. Selective. Usual minimum average: 2.7–3.0 (A = 4).

FINANCIAL AID. Annual awards from institutional funds: scholarships, fellowships, stipends, internships, teaching assistantships, research assistantships, Federal W/S, loans. Approved for VA benefits. Apply by March 1 to Graduate School for assistantships; to Financial Aid for all other programs. Phone: (419)530-8700. Use FAFSA. About 25% of students receive aid other than loans from School and outside sources. Aid available for part-time students.

DEGREE REQUIREMENTS. For master's: 30–33 credit hours minimum, at least 24 in residence; thesis/comprehensive exam/one language for some departments. For Ed.D.: 90 credit hours minimum beyond the bachelor's, at least three consecutive Summers in full-time residence; written comprehensive exam; knowledge of statistics; dissertation; final oral exam. For Ph.D.: 90 credit hours minimum beyond the bachelor's, at least two semesters in full-time residence; reading knowledge of one foreign language for some departments; comprehensive exam; dissertation; final exam.

FIELDS OF STUDY.
Accounting.
Biology. Includes cell-molecular biology, ecology.
Bioengineering.

Business Administration.

Chemical Engineering.

Chemistry.

Civil Engineering.

Counseling.

Criminal Justice.

Curriculum and Instruction. Includes early childhood and elementary, educational media, secondary, special.

Economics.

Education in Public Health.

Educational Administration and Supervision.

Electrical Engineering.

Engineering Physics.

Engineering Science.

English. Includes English as a second language, literature.

Exercise Science.

Foreign Language. Includes French, German, Spanish.

Foundations of Education. Includes educational psychology, educational, sociology, history of education, philosophy of education, educational research and measurement.

Geography and Planning.

Geology.

Guidance/Counselor Education.

Health Education.

Higher Education.

History.

Industrial Engineering.

Liberal Studies.

Manufacturing Management.

Mathematics. Includes applied mathematics, statistics.

Mechanical Engineering.

Medicinal Chemistry.

Music. Includes education, performance.

Pharmaceutical Science.

Pharmacy.

Philosophy.

Physical Education.

Physics.

Physics and Astronomy.

Political Science.

Psychology.

Public Administration.

Public Health.

Recreation and Leisure Studies.

School Psychology.

Sociology.

Speech-Language Pathology.

Taxation.

College of Law (43606-3390)

Web site: www.law.utoledo.edu

Organized 1906. ABA approved since 1939. AALS member. Semester system. Special facilities: Legal Institute of the Great Lakes, Cybersecurities Law Institute. Library: 321,650 volumes, 3263 subscriptions; has LEXIS, NEXIS, WESTLAW.

Annual tuition: full-time resident $8314, nonresident $16,085; part-time resident $6809, nonresident $13,284. No on-campus housing available. For off-campus housing contact either the Student Bar Association or the University's Off-Campus Living Office. Total average annual additional expense: $10,997.

Enrollment: first-year class 100 (day), 40 (evening); total 461 (men 54%, women 46%). Faculty: full-time 24, part-time 12. Student to faculty ratio 14.4 to 1. Degrees conferred: J.D., J.D.-M.B.A., J.D.-M.S.E.

ADMISSION REQUIREMENTS. LSDAS Law School report, bachelor's degree, transcripts, LSAT, two letters of recommendation required in support of application. Campus visit encouraged. Evidence of proficiency in English required of foreign students. Interview not required. Accepts transfer applicants. Graduates of unaccredited colleges not considered. Apply to Office of Admissions by July 1. Fall admission only. Application fee $30. Phone: (419)530-4131; fax: (419)530-4345.

ADMISSION STANDARDS. Selective. Mean LSAT: full-time 153, part-time 151; mean GPA: full-time 3.24, part-time 3.07 (A = 4). Gourman rating: 2.49. *U.S. News & World Report* ranking is in the third tier of all U.S. law schools. Accepts 45–50% of total annual applicants.

FINANCIAL AID. Scholarships, grants, assistantships, Federal W/S, loans. Apply to Office of Financial Aid by August 1. Use FAFSA (College code: 003131). About 27% of students receive aid other than loans from College.

DEGREE REQUIREMENTS. For J.D.: successful completion of three-year program (day), four-year program (evening); 87 credit hour program.

TOURO COLLEGE

300 Nassau Road
Huntington, New York 11743

Jacob D. Fuchsberg Law Center

Web site: www.tourolaw.edu

Established 1980. Located on Long Island's north shore approximately 30 miles E of New York City. Private control. Semester system. ABA approved since 1983. AALS member. Semester system, Full-time, part-time study. Special facilities: Institute of Local and Suburban Law, Institute of Jewish Law. Special programs: summer study abroad at Moscow State University, Russia, Shimla, India; international summer internships in London, Cork, Paris, Brussels, Lisbon, Tel Aviv, Jerusalem. Law library: 397,233 volumes, 3249 subscriptions; has LEXIS, NEXIS, WESTLAW, DIALOG, OCLC, DOWJONES, AUTO-LITE.

Annual tuition: full-time $22,000, part-time $17,160. On-campus apartments available for both single and married students. Total average annual additional expenses: $16,976. Law students tend to live off-campus. Contact Admissions Office for both on- and off-campus information.

Enrollment: first-year class full-time 137, part-time 87; total 622 (men 49%, women 51%). Faculty: full-time 26, part-time 14. Student to faculty ratio 16.5 to 1. Degrees conferred: J.D., J.D.-M.B.A. (with Dowling College), J.D.-M.P.A. (Long Island University, C.W. Post College), J.D.-M.S. (Tax), LL.M. (full- or part-time, for foreign lawyers who have completed a basic legal education and received a university degree in law in another country), LL.M. (General).

ADMISSION REQUIREMENTS. LSDAS Law School report, LSAT (not later that December test date; if more than one LSAT, highest is used), bachelor's degree from an accredited institution, personal statement, transcripts (must show all schools attended and at least three years of study) required in support of application. Recommendations are optional. Applicants must have received bachelor's degree prior to enrollment. Campus visits are encouraged. In addition, international applicants whose native language is not English must submit TOEFL (not older that five years), certified translations and evaluations of all foreign credentials. Joint degree applicants must apply to and be accepted to both schools. Apply to Office of Admission after September 30, before July 15 (priority deadline). First-year students admitted Fall only. Rolling admissions process; notification starts within four to six weeks from the time application is complete and continues until class is filled. Application fee $50. Phone: (631)421-2244, ext. 312; fax: (631)421-2675; e-mail: admissions@tourolaw.edu.

ADMISSION REQUIREMENTS FOR LL.M. (Foreign Lawyers). All applicants must have the foreign equivalent of an American J.D. Official transcript with certified translation and evaluations, two letters of recommendation, personal statement required in support of LL.M. application. TOEFL required for those applicants whose native language is not English. Admits Fall only. Full-time day, part-time day, part-time evening study available. Apply to Admissions Office at least three months prior to preferred date of entrance. Application fee $50.

ADMISSION STANDARDS. Selective. Mean LSAT: full-time 148, part-time 148; mean GPA: full-time 2.94, part-time 2.96 (A = 4). Gourman rating: 2.13. *U.S. News & World Report* ranking is in the fourth tier of all U.S. law schools. Admits 45–50% total annual applications.

FINANCIAL AID. Scholarships, Dean's Fellowships, Merit Scholarships and Incentive Awards, private and institutional loans, Summer Public Interest Fellowships, State grants (TAP), Federal loans and Federal W/S available. All accepted students are automatically considered for scholarships. Apply to Admissions Office as soon as possible after January 1 but not later than May 1. Phone: (631)421-2244, ext. 322. Use FAFSA, also submit Financial Aid Transcript, Federal Income Tax forms. Approximately 44% (full-time), 26% (part-time) of first-year class received scholarships/Grants-in-Aid. Approximately 85% of students receive some form of financial assistance. Public Interest Loan Repayment Program available.

DEGREE REQUIREMENTS. For J.D.: 87 (44–46 required) credits program with a GPA of at least 2.0 (A = 4), plus completion of upper-divisional writing course; three-year full-time program, four-year part-time program. Accelerated J.D. with two summers of course work. For J.D.-Master's: four-year programs rather than five-year programs if both degrees are taken consecutively. For LL.M. (Foreign Lawyers): 27 credits, at least two semesters in residence; successful completion of "Introduction to the U.S. Legal System." For LL.M. (General): 24 credit program.

TOWSON UNIVERSITY

Baltimore, Maryland 21204
Web site: www.towson.edu

Founded 1866. CGS member. Coed. State control. Semester system. Special facilities: Center for Mathematics and Sciences Education, Center for Applied Informatoin Technology, Center for Suburban and Regional Studies, Center for the Teaching and Research on Women, Center for the Teaching and Study of Writing. Library: 536,000 volumes, 2000 subscriptions. Total University enrollment: 16,729.

Tuition: per credit, $211 resident, nonresident $435. Limited on-campus housing. Average academic year on-campus housing costs: $5950; off-campus costs: $730 per month. Contact the Director, Residence for both on- and off-campus housing information. Phone: (410)830-2516.

Graduate School

Graduate study since 1957. Enrollment: full-time 665, part-time 2159. Graduate faculty: full-time 136, part-time 19. Degrees conferred: M.A., M.S., M.Ed., M.F.A., M.M., M.A.T.

ADMISSION REQUIREMENTS. Transcripts required in support of application. GRE, interview required for some programs. TOEFL required for international applicants. Apply to the Graduate School; no specified closing date, some programs have deadlines. Rolling admissions process. Application fee $25. Phone: (410)704-2501; fax: (410)704-4675.

ADMISSION STANDARDS. Selective. Usual minimum average: 2.75 (A = 4).

FINANCIAL AID. Annual awards from institutional funds: fellowships, research assistantships, teaching assistantships, internships, Federal W/S, loans. Approved for VA benefits. Apply by April 1 to Dean of Graduate School for assistantships; to Financial Aid Office for all other programs. Phone: (410)704-2098. Use FAFSA and University's FAF. Aid available for part-time students.

DEGREE REQUIREMENTS. For master's: 30–60 semester hours; thesis/nonthesis option; final written/oral exam.

FIELDS OF STUDY.
Applied and Industrial Mathematics.
Applied Gerontology.
Applied Information Technology.
Art Education.
Biology.
Communication Management.
Computer Science.
Early Childhood Education.
Elementary Education.
Geography and Environmental Planning.
Health Science.
Hunan Resource Development.
Instructional Technology.
Liberal and Professional Studies.
Mass Communication.
Mathematics Education.
Music Composition.
Music Education.
Music Performance.
Nursing.
Occupational Therapy.
Physician's Assistant Studies.
Professional Writing.
Psychology. Includes clinical, counseling, experimental, school.
Reading.
Secondary Education.
Speech-Language Pathology.
Studio Arts.
Teaching.
Theater.
Women's Studies.

TRINITY COLLEGE

Hartford, Connecticut 06106
Web site: www.trincoll.edu

Founded 1823. Coed. Private control. Semester system. Library: 962,700 volumes, 3400 subscriptions.

Tuition: per credit $900. No on-campus housing available. Day-care facilities available.

Graduate Program

Graduate study since 1988. Offered in evenings during academic year, and during Summer term. Graduate enrollment: part-time 175. Faculty: full-time 15, part-time 9. Degrees conferred: M.A.

ADMISSION REQUIREMENTS. Transcripts, letters of academic recommendation required in support of application. On-line application available. Accepts transfer applicants. Graduates of unaccredited institutions not considered. Apply to Office of Graduate Studies by April 1 (Fall), November 1 (Spring). Application fee $50. Phone: (860)297-2527; fax: (860)297-2529.

ADMISSION STANDARDS. Relatively open when provisional acceptees are included. Usual minimum average: 3.0 (A = 4).

FINANCIAL AID. Fellowships, grants, loans. Apply by April 1 to Office of Graduate Studies. Use FAFSA and College's FAF. Aid available for part-time students.

DEGREE REQUIREMENTS. For M.A.: ten courses, includes thesis or comprehensive exam.

FIELDS OF STUDY.
American Studies.
Economics.
English.
History.
Public Policy Studies.

TRINITY UNIVERSITY
San Antonio, Texas 78212-7200
Web site: www.trinity.edu

Founded 1869. CGS member. Coed. Private control. Presbyterian affiliation. Semester system. Special facilities: working agreements with Southwest Research Institute, Southwest Foundation for Research and Education, United States Air Force School for Aerospace Medicine, University of Texas Health Science Center. Library: 871,081 volumes, 3450 subscriptions. Total University enrollment: 2500.
Tuition: per credit $562.50. No housing for graduate students.

Graduate School

Graduate study since 1950. Enrollment: full-time 108, part-time 107. University faculty: full-time 15, part-time 23. Degrees conferred: M.A., M.A.T., M.Ed., M.S.

ADMISSION REQUIREMENTS. Transcripts, letters of recommendation, GRE/GMAT required in support of School's application. TOEFL (minimum score 600) required of international applicants. Accepts transfer applicants. Apply to Graduate Admissions Office at least one month prior to registration. Phone: (210)999-7207.

ADMISSION STANDARDS. Selective. Usual minimum average: 3.0 (A = 4).

FINANCIAL AID. Annual awards from institutional funds: thirty-six departmental assistantships, Federal W/S, loans. Approved for VA benefits. Apply to department of choice for assistantships, to Financial Aid Office for all other programs. No specified closing date. Phone: (210)999-7207. Use FAFSA. About 20% of students receive aid other than loans from School and outside sources.

DEGREE REQUIREMENTS. For master's: 30–36 semester hours minimum, at least 80% in residence; thesis for some departments; nonthesis option includes research project/comprehensive exam/internship.

FIELDS OF STUDY.
Accounting.
Health Care Administration. Two-year program includes one-year residency; external degree (three-year program).
School Administration. Two-year program; includes two-semester internship.
School Psychology.
Teaching.

TROY STATE UNIVERSITY
Troy, Alabama 36082
Web site: www.troyst.edu

Founded 1887. Located 55 miles SE of Montgomery. Coed. State control. Quarter system. Library: 245,000 volumes, 1800 subscriptions.
Tuition: per quarter hour resident $147, nonresident per quarter hour $294. On-campus housing for 48 married students, 1500 single students. Average academic year housing costs: $4274 (including board). Contact Director, University Housing for both on- and off-campus housing information. Phone: (334)670-3346. Day-care facilities available.

Graduate School

Graduate study since 1958. Enrollment: full-time 2115, part-time 2813. Graduate faculty: full-time 287, part-time 147. Degrees conferred: M.S., M.B.A., Ed.S.

ADMISSION REQUIREMENTS. Transcripts, GRE Subject Tests, GMAT/MAT/NTE required in support of School's application. On-line application available. TOEFL required for international applicants. Accepts transfer applicants. Graduates of unaccredited institutions not considered. Apply to Dean of Graduate School at least one month prior to registration. Rolling admissions process. Application fee $40. Phone: (334)670-3178; fax: (334)670-3733.

ADMISSION STANDARDS. Selective. Usual minimum average: 2.5, 3.0 for last two years (A = 4).

FINANCIAL AID. Scholarships, fellowships, internships, Federal W/S, loans. Approved for VA benefits. Apply by May 1 to the Financial Aid Office. Phone: (334)670-3186; fax: (334)670-3702. Use FAFSA. Aid available for part-time students.

DEGREE REQUIREMENTS. For M.S.: 45 quarter hours minimum, at least 36 in residence; thesis/nonthesis option; final written exam. For M.B.A.: 60 quarter hours. For Ed.S.: 50 quarter hours minimum beyond the master's.

FIELDS OF STUDY.

COLLEGE OF ARTS AND SCIENCES:
Criminal Justice.
Environmental Analysis and Management.
International Relations.

COLLEGE OF BUSINESS:
Business Administration. Includes accounting, general business, information systems.
Executive Master of Business Administration.

COLLEGE OF COMMUNICATION AND FINE ARTS:
Conducting.

COLLEGE OF EDUCATION:
Counseling and Psychology.
Elementary Education (K–6).
Elementary-Secondary (P–12). Includes instrumental music, vocal/choral music, instructional support.
P–2 Education. Includes music education (instrumental, vocal/choral), physical education.

COLLEGE OF HEALTH AND HUMAN SERVICES:
Nursing.
Sport and Fitness Management.
Secondary Education (6–12). Includes biology, English/language arts, general science, health, history, mathematics, social studies.
Human Resource Management.

International Relations.
Nursing.
Police Administration.
Public Administration.

TROY STATE UNIVERSITY AT DOTHAN

Dothan, Alabama 36304-0368
Web site: www.tsud.edu

Established 1961. Coed. State control. Quarter system. Library: 100,000 volumes, 600 subscriptions.
Tuition: per hour, resident $147; nonresident $294. No on-campus housing available.

Graduate School

Enrollment: full- and part-time 394. Graduate faculty: full- and part-time 62. Degrees conferred: M.S., M.B.A., M.S.Ed., Ed.S.

ADMISSION REQUIREMENTS. Transcripts, GRE/GMAT/MAT/NTE required in support of School's application. On-line application available. Class B Alabama certification or equivalent required for some programs. Accepts transfer applicants. Graduates of unaccredited colleges not considered. Apply to Director of Admissions and Records at least one month prior to registration. Rolling admissions process. Application fee $20. Phone: (334)983-6556, ext. 228; fax: (334)983-6322.

ADMISSION STANDARDS. Selective. Usual minimum average: 2.5, 3.0 for last two years (A = 4).

FINANCIAL AID. Scholarships, grants, Federal W/S, loans. Approved for VA benefits. Apply by May 1 to the Financial Aid Office. Use FAFSA. Aid available for part-time students.

DEGREE REQUIREMENTS. For M.S., M.S.Ed.: 45 quarter hours minimum, at least 36 in residence; thesis/nonthesis option; final written exam. For M.B.A.: 60 quarter hours, at least 45 in residence; final exam. For Ed.S.: 55 quarter hours minimum beyond the master's.

FIELDS OF STUDY.

COLLEGE OF ARTS AND SCIENCES:
International Relations.

COLLEGE OF BUSINESS ADMINISTRATION:
Accounting.
General Business.
Human Resource Management.

COLLEGE OF EDUCATION:
Counseling and Psychology. Includes advanced community counseling, community counseling, corrections, substance abuse counseling.
Early Childhood Education (N–3).
Educational Leadership (N–12).
Elementary Education (1–6).
Instructional Support. Includes educational leadership, school counseling, school psychometry.
School Counseling (N–12).
School Psychology.
Secondary Education. Includes biology, comprehensive general science, comprehensive language arts, comprehensive social science, English, history, mathematics.
Special Education. Includes collaborative teacher K–6, collaborative teacher 6–12.

TROY STATE UNIVERSITY IN MONTGOMERY

Montgomery, Alabama 36103-4419
Web site: www.tsum.edu

Established 1990. Coed. State control. Semester system. Library: 34,800 volumes, 476 subscriptions.
Tuition: per hour, resident $120, nonresident $240. No on-campus housing available.

Graduate School

Enrollment: full-time 131, part-time 316. Graduate faculty: full-time 22, part-time 18. Degrees conferred: M.A., M.S., M.S.M., M.S.P.A., M.B.A., Ed.S.

ADMISSION REQUIREMENTS. Transcripts, GRE/GMAT/MAT required in support of School's application. On-line application available. Class B Alabama certification or equivalent required for some programs. Accepts transfer applicants. Graduates of unaccredited colleges not considered. Apply to Dean of Graduate Studies at least one month prior to registration. Rolling admissions process. Application fee $30. Phone: (334)241-9581; fax: (334)241-9586.

ADMISSION STANDARDS. Selective. Usual minimum average: 2.5, 3.0 for last two years (A = 4).

FINANCIAL AID. Scholarships, grants, Federal W/S, loans. Approved for VA benefits. Apply by May 1 to the Financial Aid Office. Use FAFSA. Aid available for part-time students.

DEGREE REQUIREMENTS. For M.A., M.S., M.S.M., M.S.P.A.: 30 credit hours minimum, at least 24 in residence; candidacy; thesis/nonthesis option; final written exam. For M.B.A.: 33 credit hours; candidacy; research paper; written/oral comprehensive exam. For Ed.S.: 30 credit hours minimum beyond the master's.

FIELDS OF STUDY.
Adult Education. M.S.
Agency Counseling. Ed.S.
Business Administration. M.B.A.
Computer and Information Systems. M.S.
Counseling and Human Development. M.S., Ed.S.
Elementary Education. M.S.
General Education Administration. Ed.S.
Human Resource Management. M.S.
Public Administration. M.S.P.A.
School Counseling. Ed.S.
Teaching. M.A.

TRUMAN STATE UNIVERSITY

Kirksville, Missouri 63501-4221
Web site: www.truman.edu

Founded 1897. Formerly Northeast Missouri State University, name changed in 1996. CGS member. Located 200 miles NW of St. Louis. Coed. State control. Semester system. Library: 427,286 volumes, 3700 subscriptions. Total University enrollment: 6000.
Annual tuition: full-time, resident $3192, nonresident $5784; per credit, resident $133, nonresident $ 241. On-campus housing for 30 married students, 48 men, 48 women. Average academic year housing costs: $4552 (including board); off-campus housing $350–$400 per month. Contact Housing Office for both on- and off-campus housing information. Phone: (660)785-4227.

Graduate Studies

Enrollment: full-time 146, part-time 47. Faculty: full- and part-time 120. Degrees conferred: M.A., M.S., M.Ac., M.A.E.

ADMISSION REQUIREMENTS. Transcripts, GRE/GMAT required in support of application. TOEFL required for international applicants. Accepts transfer applicants. Graduates of unaccredited institutions not considered. Apply by June 15 to Dean for Graduate Studies. Application fee, none. Phone: (660)785-4109; fax: (660)785-7460; e-mail: gradinfo@truman.edu.

ADMISSION STANDARDS. Selective. Usual minimum average: 2.75 (A = 4).

FINANCIAL AID. Annual awards from institutional funds: fellowships, scholarships, research assistantships, teaching assistantships, Federal W/S, loans. Approved for VA benefits. Apply to the Dean for Graduate Studies; no specified closing date. Phone: (660)785-4130. Use FAFSA. About 13% of students receive aid other than loans from University and outside sources. Aid available for part-time students.

DEGREE REQUIREMENTS. For master's: 30–48 credits minimum; thesis or capstone project; final oral/written comprehensive exam.

FIELDS OF STUDY.
Accountancy. GMAT for admission.
Biology. GRE for admission.
Communication Disorders. GRE for admission.
Counseling. GRE for admission.
Education. GRE for admission.
English. GRE for admission.
History. GRE for admission.
Mathematics. GRE for admission.
Music.

TUFTS UNIVERSITY
Medford, Massachusetts 02155
Web site: www.tufts.edu

Founded 1852. Located 5 miles NW of Boston. CGS member. Coed. Private control. Semester system. Special facilities: Center for Applied Child Development, Electro-Optics Technology Center, Center for Environmental Management, Lincoln Filene Center for Science and Math Teaching, Science and Technology Center. The University's NIH ranking is 91st among all U.S. institutions with 154 awards/grants worth $44,338,862. Library: 1,600,000 volumes, 5329 subscriptions. Total University enrollment: 7500.

Annual tuition: full-time (one-year master's and first year of doctoral program) $26,944; (two-year master's) $20,208, (School Psychology) $23,576; part-time, per course $2694. Limited on-campus housing for single students; none for married students. Average academic year housing costs: $900 per month. Contact Campus Housing Office for both on- and off-campus housing information. Phone: (617)627-3248. Day-care facilities available.

Graduate School of Arts and Science
Web site: www.tufts.edu/as/gsas/gsashome.hmtl

Graduate study since 1875. Enrollment: full- and part-time 1289 (men 43%, women 57%). University faculty teaching graduate courses: full-time 304, part-time 216. Degrees conferred: M.A., M.A.T., M.F.A., M.S., Ph.D.

ADMISSION REQUIREMENTS. Official transcripts, three letters of recommendation, GRE Subject Tests, personal statement required in support of School's application. TOEFL (minimum score 550) required for international applicants. Interview sometimes required. Apply to Director of Admission of Graduate School by February 15 (Fall); some departments have other deadlines. Application fee $50. Phone: (617)627-3395; fax: (617)627-3016.

ADMISSION STANDARDS. Very selective for most departments. Usual minimum average: 3.0 (A = 4).

FINANCIAL AID. Annual awards from institutional funds: scholarships, teaching assistantships, research assistantships, fellowships, internships, Federal W/S, loans. Approved for VA benefits. Apply to the Dean by February 15. Phone: (617)627-3528. Use FAFSA. About 65% of students receive aid other than loans from School and outside sources. Aid available for part-time students.

DEGREE REQUIREMENTS. For master's: 8 courses minimum, at least two terms in residence; thesis/nonthesis option; reading knowledge of one foreign language for some majors; final oral exam. For Ph.D.: 30 courses minimum, at least 10 in residence; qualifying exam; reading knowledge of one or more foreign languages, depending upon department; qualifying exam; dissertation; final written/oral exam.

FIELDS OF STUDY.
Art History. M.A.
Art History and Museum Studies. M.A.
Biology. M.S., Ph.D.
Chemistry. M.S., Ph.D.
Child Development. M.A., M.A.T., Ph.D.
Classics. Includes Latin, Greek. M.A. only.
Classical Archaeology. M.A.
Drama. Theater arts majors must have practical knowledge of stagecraft; Ph.D. is academic, does not include performance or technical practice. M.A., Ph.D.
Economics. M.A.
Education. Includes elementary, secondary, early childhood. M.A.T. only.
Engineering Management. M.S.
English. M.A., Ph.D.
Fine Arts. M.F.A.: thesis is creative project with written discussion. M.A., M.F.A.
French. M.A. only.
German. M.A. study offered at Medford and in Germany. M.A. only.
History. M.A., Ph.D.
History and Museum Studies. M.A.
Interdisciplinary Doctorate. Ph.D.
Mathematics. M.A., M.S., Ph.D.
Mechanical Engineering. M.S., Ph.D.
Museum Education. M.A.
Music. Includes musicology, theory and composition. M.A. only.
Occupational Therapy. M.S., M.A.
Philosophy. M.A. only.
Physics. M.S., Ph.D.
Psychology. M.S., Ph.D.
School Psychology. M.A., M.S., Ph.D.
Urban and Environmental Policy. M.A.

School of Dental Medicine

Established 1868 as Boston Dental College, incorporated into Tufts University in 1899. Located in Boston at the Health Science Center. (02111).

Annual tuition: $33,550. Limited on-campus housing available. Average academic year housing costs: $14,300. Total average cost for all other first-year dental related expenses: $8536.

Enrollment: First-year class 147; total 480 (men 65%, women 35%); Postgraduates 60. Faculty: full-time 34, part-time 322. Degrees conferred: B.A.-D.M.D. (Adelphi University), D.M.D.

ADMISSION REQUIREMENTS. AADSAS report, transcripts, three letters of recommendations (one from a biology instructor, one from a chemistry instructor), DAT, interview required in support of School's application. Accepts transfer applicants. Apply to Admissions Office after July 1, before March 1. Application fee $55. Phone: (617)636-6639.

ADMISSION STANDARDS. Selective. Usual minimum average: 3.0 (A = 4). Mean DAT: Academic 17.98, PAT 17.33; mean GPA: 3.24 (A = 4). Gourman rating: 4.85. Accepts 25–30% of total annual applicants. Approximately 25% are state residents.

FINANCIAL AID. Scholarships, loans. Apply by May 1 to Admissions, Financial Aid and Housing Office after acceptance. Use FAFSA (School code: E00519). About 82% of students receive some aid from School.

DEGREE REQUIREMENTS. For D.M.D.: satisfactory completion of forty-four-month program.

The Fletcher School of Law and Diplomacy
Web site: www.tufts.edu/fletcher

Established 1933. Semester system. Special facilities: William L. Clayton Center for International Economic Affairs, Global Development and Environmental Institute, Edward R. Murrow Center, Hitachi Center for Technology and International Affairs, Center for Human Rights and Conflict Resolution, Institute for Human Security. Programs in International Development, International Environment and Resource Policy, International Information and Communication, International Negotiation and Conflict, Southwest Asia and Islamic Civilization.

Annual tuition: $25,477. Enrollment: full-time 368 (men 50%, women 50%), part-time 56. Faculty: full-time 30, part-time 31. Degrees conferred: M.A., M.A.L.D., Ph.D.; J.D.-M.A.L.D. in conjunction with Harvard Law School and U.C. Berkeley-Boalt Hall Law School; M.B.A.-M.A.L.D. in conjunction with Amos Tuck School of Business Administration, Dartmouth College; M.S.J.-M.A.L.D. in conjunction with Medill School of Journalism, Northwestern University.

ADMISSION REQUIREMENTS. Official transcripts, three letters of reference, GRE or GMAT required in support of School's application. On-line application available. Interview recommended. TOEFL required for international applicants. Apply to Director of Admissions of School after September 1, before January 15. Normally admits Fall only. Application fee $65. Phone: (617)627- 3040; fax: (617)627-3712.

ADMISSION STANDARDS. Highly competitive. Usual minimum average: 3.0 (A = 4).

FINANCIAL AID. Scholarships, fellowships, teaching assistantships, internships, grants, Federal W/S, loans. Approved for VA benefits. Apply by January 15 to Director of Admissions of School. Phone: (617)627-3528. Use FAFSA and Fletcher's FAF. About 65% of students receive aid other than loans from School and outside sources.

DEGREE REQUIREMENTS. For M.A.: one year in residence including 8 semester courses; reading and oral competency in one foreign language; final oral exam and application limited to midcareer professionals only. For M.A.L.D.: two years in residence; 16 semester courses, thesis; oral competency in one language; final oral exam. For Ph.D.: two and a half years in residence including 20 semester courses; written and oral comprehensive exam; reading and oral competency in one language; dissertation; final oral exam.

FIELDS OF STUDY.
Comparative and Developmental Political Analysis.
Development Economics.
Europe.
International Business and Economic Law.

International Business Relations.
International Environment and Resource Policy.
International Information and Communication.
International Monetary Theory and Policy.
International Negotiation and Conflict Resolution.
International Organization.
International Political Economy.
International Security Studies.
International Technology Policy and Management.
International Trade and Commercial Policies.
Law and Development.
Pacific Asia.
Political Systems and Theories.
Public International Law.
Southwest Asia and Islamic Civilization.
United States.

School of Medicine
Web site: www.tufts.edu/med

Established 1893. Located in Boston at the Health Science Center (02111). Library 110,000 volumes. Annual tuition $37,875, student fees $430. On-campus housing available. Total average figure for all other expenses: $11,000.

Enrollment: first-year class 168 (EDP 3); total 733 (men 55%, women 45%). Faculty: full-time 258, part-time 942. Degrees conferred: M.D., M.D.-M.B.A., M.D.-M.P.H., M.D.-Ph.D.

ADMISSION REQUIREMENTS. AMCAS report, transcripts, recommendations, MCAT, required in suport of application. A final screening interview may be requested in some cases. Applicants must have completed at least three years of college study. Accepts transfer applicants. Has EDP; apply between June 1 and August 1. Apply to Director of Admissions after June 1, before November 1 (firm). Application fee $95. Phone: (617)636-6571.

ADMISSION STANDARDS. Very competitive. Mean MCAT: 10.0; mean GPA: 3.5 (A = 4). Gourman rating: 4.46. *U.S. News & World Report* ranking is 43rd among all U.S. medical schools. Accepts 3–5% of total annual applicants. Approximately 25% are state residents.

FINANCIAL AID. Limited number of scholarships, loans. Apply to the Committee on Financial Aid after acceptance, before May 1. Phone: (617)636-6574. Use FAFSA (School code: E00520). About 33% of students receive some aid from School.

DEGREE REQUIREMENTS. For M.D.: satisfactory completion of four-year program; all students must pass USMLE Step 1 prior to entering the third year and pass USMLE Step 2 prior to the awarding of the M.D.

FIELDS OF GRADUATE STUDY.
Biochemistry.
Cell Biology.
Genetics.
Immunology.
Microbiology.
Molecular Biology.
Neurosciences.
Pharmacology.
Physiology.
Public Health.

School of Veterinary Medicine
Web site: www.tufts.edu/vet

Located in North Grafton (01536). Special facility: Center for Animal and Public Policy.

Annual tuition: resident $24,136, contract students $16,065, nonresident $28,065. Total average cost for all other expenses: $9550.

Enrollment: first-year class 80, total full-time 260 (men 50%, women 50%), postgraduates 40. Faculty: full-time 82, part-time 148. Degrees conferred: D.V.M., D.V.M.-M.P.H., D.V.M.-M.S., D.V.M.-Ph.D. The M.S. and Ph.D. are offered through the Graduate College.

ADMISSION REQUIREMENTS. Transcripts, GRE, recommendations, personal essay, animal/veterinary experience required in support of application. Interviews by invitation only. Preference given to state residents. School has contractual agreements with Maine (1), New Hampshire (1–2), New Jersey (6). Accepts transfer applicants (apply by June 1 for following September). Graduates of unaccredited colleges not considered. Apply to the School after July 1, before December 1. Application fee $60. Phone: (508)839-7920; fax: (508)839-2953.

ADMISSION STANDARDS. Selective. Mean GRE: verbal 600, quantitative 690, analytical 720; mean GPA: 3.45 (A = 4). Accepts 25–30% of qualified applicants.

FINANCIAL AID. Scholarships, assistantships, Federal W/S, loans available. Apply to Office of Financial Aid by March 1. Use FAFSA.

DEGREE REQUIREMENTS. For D.V.M.: satisfactory completion of four-year program. For M.P.H., M.S., Ph.D.: see Graduate College listing above.

FIELDS OF GRADUATE STUDY.
Animal and Public Policy. D.V.M.-M.A. (with Fletcher School of Law and Diplomacy).
Applied Biotechnology. D.V.M.-M.S. (with Worcester Polytechnic Institute).
Biochemistry. Ph.D.
Cell Biology. Ph.D.
Immunology. Ph.D.
Microbiology. Ph.D.
Molecular Genetics. Ph.D.
Neurosciences. Ph.D.
Pharmacology. Ph.D.
Physiology. Ph.D.
Public Health. D.V.M.-M.P.H. (with Tufts University School of Medicine.)
Note: All Ph.D. programs through Sackler School of Graduate Medical Sciences and the University of Massachusetts Medical Center, Worchester.

TULANE UNIVERSITY
New Orleans, Louisiana 70118-5669
Web site: www.tulane.edu

Founded 1834. CGS and AAU member, Coed. Private control. Semester system. Special facilities: Amistad Research Center, Center for Archaeology, Newcomb College Center for Research on Women, Center for Bioenvironmental Research, Roger Thayer Stone Center for Latin American Studies, Southeastern Architectural Archives, William Ranson Hogan Jazz Archives, Delta Regional Primate Research Center, Lindy Boggs Center for Energy and Biotechnology, Murphy Institute of Political Economy, Middle American Research Institute, Southern Center of the National Institute for Global Environmental Change, Tulane Research and Teaching Center, U.S.-Japan Cooperative Biomedical Research Laboratories. The University's NIH ranking is 110th among all U.S. institutions with 95 awards/grants worth $31,399,386. Library: 2,003,000 volumes, 15,000 subscriptions. Total University enrollment: 9700.

Annual tuition: full-time $25,616, per credit $1423. Limited on-campus housing available. Average academic year housing costs: $7500 for married students, $7128 (including board) for single students. Apply to Housing Office. Phone: (504)865-5724.

Graduate School

Graduate study since 1883. Enrollment: full-time 875, part-time 51. Graduate faculty: full-time 350. Degrees conferred: M.A., M S., M.F.A., M.L.A., Ph.D.

ADMISSION REQUIREMENTS. Official transcripts of all undergraduate and graduate work, three recommendation forms, statement of career objective, GRE required in support of application. GRE Subject for some departments. TSE (minimum score 220) required for international applicants, if not available in applicant's area submit TOEFL (minimum score 600). Application deadlines: July 1 (Fall), December 1 (Spring) May 1 (Summer). Application fee $45. Phone: (504)865-5100; fax: (504)865-5274.

ADMISSION STANDARDS: Competitive for most departments and selective for all others. Usual minimum average: 2.75 to 3.0 (A = 4).

FINANCIAL AID. Fellowships, teaching/research assistantships, scholarships, internships, tuition waivers, Federal W/S, loans. Approved for VA benefits. Apply by February 1 (Fall semester) to Office of Financial Aid. Phone: (504)865-5723. Use FAFSA.

DEGREE REQUIREMENTS. For M.A., M.S.: 24 semester hours plus thesis, 30 hours without thesis; reading knowledge of one foreign language for some programs; final written/oral exam. For M.F.A.: 30 hours minimum; creative project or recital; final essay. For Ph.D.: 48 hours minimum; reading knowledge of two foreign languages; preliminary or general exam; dissertation; final oral exam.

FIELDS OF STUDY.
Anatomy.
Anthropology.
Applied Development.
Art.
Art History.
Biochemistry.
Biology.
Biomedical Engineering.
Biostatistics.
Business Administration.
Cell and Molecular Biology.
Chemical Engineering.
Chemistry.
Civic and Cultural Management.
Civil Engineering.
Classical Languages.
Computer Science.
Earth and Ecosystem Science.
Economics.
Electrical Engineering.
English.
Environmental Statistics.
Epidemiology.
French.
Geology.
German and Slavic Languages.
History.
Human Genetics.
International Development.
International Health and Development.
Italian.
Latin American Studies.
Liberal Arts.
Mathematics.

Mechanical Engineering.
Microbiology and Immunology.
Molecular and Cellular Biology.
Music.
Neuroscience.
Paleontology.
Parasitology.
Pharmacology.
Philosophy.
Physics.
Physiology.
Political Science.
Portuguese.
Psychology.
Social Work.
Sociology.
Spanish.
Theater.

A. B. Freeman School of Business
Web site: www.freeman.tulane.edu

Established 1914. Private control. Accredited programs: M.B.A., Accounting; recognized Ph.D. Graduate study since 1940. E.M.B.A. offered in Taiwan, Mexico, and Chile. Semester system. Special facilities: Burkenroad Institute, Goldring Institute, Levy-Rosenblum Institute for Entrepreneurship, Management Communication Center. Special programs: foreign exchange programs (in Argentina, Austria, Brazil, Chile, Columbia, Czech Republic, Ecuador, Finland, France, Germany, Hong Kong, Hungary, Mexico, People's Republic of China, Spain, Taiwan, United Kingdom), internships. Library: 35,000 volumes, 28,744 microforms, 910 current periodicals/subscriptions.

Annual tuition: full-time $30,912; per credit $916. Enrollment: total full-time 151, part-time 164 (men 60%, women 40%). Faculty: 60 full-time, 16 part-time; 98% with Ph.D./D.B.A. Degrees conferred: M.B.A. (full-time, part-time, day and evening), E.M.B.A. (alternate weekends), Prof. M.B.A., M.Acc., M.Fin., M.B.A.-J.D., M.B.A.-M.A. (Latin American Studies), M.B.A.-M.P.H., Ph.D.

ADMISSION REQUIREMENTS. Official transcripts, two recommendations, GMAT, personal essay, resume of professional experience required in support of School's application. TOEFL required for international applicants. Evaluative interviews required for all applicants living in the U.S. or Canada. Must have baccalaureate degree from an accredited institution. Apply for Fall admission to Director of Admissions by May 1 (domestic), April 1 (international), December 1 (Spring, spring admission for part-time study only). Application fee $40 (domestic), $50 (international). Phone: (504)865-5410 or (800)223-5402; fax: (504)865-6770; e-mail: freeman.admissions@tulane.edu.

ADMISSION STANDARDS. Competitive. Usual minimum average 3.2 (A = 4).

FINANCIAL AID. Fellowships, research assistantships, administrative assistantships, teaching assistantships, internships, tuition waivers, Federal W/S, loans. Approved for VA benefits. Apply by April 15 to Office of Financial Aid. Phone: (504)865-5273; fax: (504)862-8750. FAFSA (School code: 002029) required for Federal W/S, loans. Phone fellowships are merit based and are awarded to approximately half of the entering class. Research/administrative/teaching assistantships are arranged through faculty and staff. Aid available for part-time students.

DEGREE REQUIREMENTS. For M.B.A.: 63 credit (including 30 elective credits), two-year program; degree program must be completed in seven years. For E.M.B.A.: 49 credit, 19-month program. Professional M.B.A.: 55 credit, three- to seven-year program. For M.Acc.: 30 credit program. For M.Fin: 37 credit, 12-month full-time program. For M.B.A.-M.A.: 75 credit program. For M.B.A.-M.P.H.: 93 credit program. For M.B.A.-J.D.: 130 credit program.

FIELDS OF STUDY.
Accounting. M.Acc.
Business Administration. Includes concentrations in accounting, finance, international management, management, management information systems, marketing, operations management, organizational behavior, strategic planning (MBA); accounting, finance, organizational behavior (Ph.D.). M.B.A., E.M.B.A., Ph.D.
Finance. M.Fin.

School of Engineering—Graduate Division

Founded 1894. Special facilities: Center for Bioenvironmental Research, National Institute for Global Environmental Change, U.S.-China Energy and Environmental Technology Center, Livingston Digital Millennium Center for Computational Science, Center for Ballistic Missile Defense, Tulane Institute for Macromolecular Science and Engineering.

Annual tuition: $27,040. Enrollment: full-time 144, part-time 16. Faculty: full-time 50, part-time 7. Degrees conferred: M.Eng., M.S.E., Ph.D., Sc.D.

ADMISSION REQUIREMENTS. Official transcripts, GRE, three letters of recommendation required in support of School's application. On-line application available. Interview sometimes required. TOEFL required for international applicants. Accepts transfer applicants. Graduates of unaccredited institutions not considered. Apply by August 15 (Fall), January 1 (Spring) to Graduate Division, School of Engineering. Application fee $25. Phone: (504)865-5768; fax (504)862-8747; e-mail: gradengr@ tulane.edu.

ADMISSION STANDARDS. Competitive. Usual minimum average: 3.0 (A = 4).

FINANCIAL AID. Scholarships, fellowships, research assistantships, teaching assistantship, Federal W/S, loans. Apply by February 1 to Graduate Division. Use FAFSA.

DEGREE REQUIREMENTS. For M.Eng.: 30 credit program; no thesis. For M.S.E.: 24 credit program plus thesis. For Ph.D., Sc.D.: 48 credit programs, at least one year in full-time residence; qualifying exam; admission to candidacy; dissertation; written/oral exams.

FIELDS OF STUDY.
Biomedical Engineering. M.Eng., M.S.E., Ph.D., Sc.D.
Chemical Engineering. M.Eng., M.S.E., Ph.D., Sc.D.
Civil Engineering. M.Eng., M.S.E., Ph.D., Sc.D.
Computer Science. M.Eng., M.S.E., Ph.D., Sc.D.
Electrical Engineering. M.Eng., M.S.E., Ph.D., Sc.D.
Environmental Engineering. M.Eng., M.S.E., Sc.D.
Mechanical Engineering. M.Eng., M.S.E., Ph.D., Sc.D.

Law School (70118-5670)
Web site: www.law.tulane.edu

Established 1847. Twelfth oldest U.S. law school. ABA approved since 1925. AALS member. Semester system. Full-time, day study only. Special facilities: Maritime Law Center, Eason Weinmann Center for Comparative Law, Institute for Environmental Law. Special programs: summer study abroad at McGill University, Canada; Trinity College Cambridge, England; Tulane Institute of European Legal Studies, Paris, France; Hebrew University, Israel; University of Siena, Italy; Tulane Center for European Union Law, Amsterdam, the Netherlands. Law library: 512,117 volumes, 4932 subscriptions; has LEXIS, NEXIS, WESTLAW, DIALOG, EELS, ORBIT, QUICKLAW, VU/TEXT; is a Federal Government Depository.

Annual tuition: $25,390. On-campus housing available for both single and married students. Total annual on-campus housing cost: $11,960.

Enrollment: first-year class 322; total full-time 958 (men 50%, women 50%). Faculty: full-time 46, part-time 30. Student to faculty ratio 17.2 to 1. Degrees conferred: J.D., J.D.-M.B.A., J.D.-M.H.A., J.D.-M.P.H., J.D.-M.S.P.H., LL.M. (General, Admiralty, Energy and Environmental Law, International and Comparative Law; for persons who have completed a basic legal education and received a university degree in law in another country), LL.M.-M.A. (Latin American Studies, International Affairs), S.J.D.

ADMISSION REQUIREMENTS. LSDAS Law School report, bachelor's degree, transcripts, LSAT, letters of recommendation required in support of application. Interview not required. Accepts transfer applicants. Graduates of unaccredited colleges not considered. Apply to Admissions Office after October 1, before March 15 (February 1 strongly recommended). Rolling admissions process. Application fee $50. Phone: (504)865-5930.

ADMISSION STANDARDS. Selective. Mean LSAT: 158; mean GPA: 3.35 (A = 4). Gourman rating: 4.42. *U.S. News & World Report* ranking is in the top 43 of all U.S. law schools. Accepts about 45–50% of total annual applicants.

FINANCIAL AID. Scholarships, fellowships (advanced students only), Federal W/S, loans. Apply to Director of Financial Aid by February 15; preliminary Financial Aid form due with admissions application. Use FAFSA (School code: 002029). About 70% of students receive aid other than loans from School.

DEGREE REQUIREMENTS. For J.D.: 6 semesters minimum, at least 2 in full-time residence; 88 semester credits; 20-hour community service obligation. For LL.M.: 24 hours minimum beyond the J.D.; one year in full-time residence; thesis; final written exam. For S.J.D.: usually at least two years in full-time resident beyond the J.D.; dissertation; final written exam.

School of Medicine (70112-2699)

Web site: www.md.tulane.edu

Founded 1834. Annual tuition: $31,830, student fees $1750. On-campus housing for married and single students. Total average figure for all other expenses: $11,900. Enrollment: first-year class 150 (EDP 10); total 598 (men 57%, women 43%). Degrees conferred: M.D., M.D.-M.P.H., M.D.-Ph.D. The M.S., M.P.H., and Ph.D. are offered through other Graduate Schools.

ADMISSION REQUIREMENTS. AMCAS report, transcripts, recommendations, MCAT required in suport of application. Interview by invitation only. Applicants must have completed at least three years of college study. Accepts transfer applicants. Has EDP; apply between June 1 and August 1. Apply to Chair of the Committee on Admissions after June 1, before December 1. Application fee $95. Phone: (504)588-5187.

ADMISSION STANDARDS. Very competitive. Mean MCAT: 10; mean GPA: 3.5 (A = 4). Gourman rating: 4.70. Accepts 3–5% of total annual applicants. Approximately 15% are state residents.

FINANCIAL AID. Scholarships, loans. Apply to the Chair, Financial Aid Committee, by April 1. Use FAFSA (School code: 002029). About 90% of students receive some aid from School.

DEGREE REQUIREMENTS. For M.D.: satisfacotry completion of four-year program. For M.S., M.P.H., Ph.D.: see Graduate Schools listings above.

FIELDS OF GRADUATE STUDY.
Anatomy.
Biochemistry.
Biomedical Engineering.
Cell Biology.
Genetics.
Immunology.
Microbiology.
Molecular Biology.
Neuroscience.
Pathology.
Pharmacology.
Physiology.

School of Public Health and Tropical Medicine (70112-2824)

Founded 1912. Special facilities: Center for Applied Environmental Public Health, Center for Bioenvironmental Research, Center for Infectious Diseases, Environmental Diseases Prevention Research Center, International Communication Enhancement Center, South Center for Public Health Preparedness, South Center Public Health Leadership Institute, South Center Public Health Training Center, Tulane/Xavier Center of Excellence in Women's Health.

Tuition: per credit hour $562. Enrollment: full-time 630, part-time 370 (men 45%, women 55%). Faculty: full-and part-time 101. Degrees conferred: M.P.H., M.S.P.H., M.H.A., M.S.W.-M.P.H., M.A.-M.P.H., M.P.H. & T.M., Dr.P.H., Sc.D., M.D.-M.P.H., M.D.-M.P.H. & T.M., M.D.-M.S.P.H., J.D.-M.P.H. The Ph.D. is offered through the Graduate School.

ADMISSION REQUIREMENTS. Transcripts, three recommendations, GRE required in support of School's application. On-line application available. TOEFL required for international applicants. Interview may be required. Accepts transfer applicants. Apply to the Office of Admissions and Students Affairs by April 15 (Fall), October 15 (Spring), March 15 (Summer). Admits both semesters. Application fee $40. Phone: (800)676-5389, (504)588-5387.

ADMISSION STANDARDS. Very selective. Usual minimum average: 3.0 (A = 4).

FINANCIAL AID. Annual awards from institutional funds: scholarships, research fellowships, research assistantships, Federal W/S. loans. Traineeships available to U.S. citizens. Approved for VA benefits. Apply, preferably by February 1, to Director of the School for scholarships, fellowships, assistantships; to Admission Office for all other programs. Phone: (504)588-5387. Use FAFSA (School code: 002029). About 75% of students receive aid other than loans from School and outside sources.

DEGREE REQUIREMENTS. For M.P.H., M.S.P.H., M.H.A.; 36–45 credit hours minimum, at least one year in residence; capstone experience. For M.P.H. & T.M.: essentially same as for M.P.H., except candidates must hold the M.D. or equivalent. For Dr.P.H., Sc.D.: at least one and up to three years in full-time residence (minimum of 72 credits), depending upon previous preparation and accomplishment; comprehensive exam; dissertation; final oral exam.

FIELDS OF STUDY.
Applied Development.
Biostatistics.
Community Health Sciences.
Environmental Health Education.
Environmental Health Sciences. Includes industrial hygiene, environmental health for developing countries, environmental policy, general technical track (midcareer), industrial hygiene (midcareer), natural resource management, sustainable/toxic and waste management, toxicology and risk assessment, water and sustainable resource management, water quality management.
Epidemiology.

Health Administration.

Health Education and Communication.

Health Systems Management.

International Health and Development.

International Health Systems Management.

Maternal and Child Health.

Medical Management.

Nutrition.

Parasitology.

Public Health. Includes environmental health (midcareer), occupational health, occupational health and safety management (midcareer).

Tropical Medicine.

School of Social Work

Founded 1927. Graduate study only. Special facilities: Center for Lifelong Learning, Porter-Cason Institute for the Advancement of Family Practice, Tulane Center on Aging Research, Education, and Services, Elizabeth Wisner Social Welfare Center for Families and Children.

Tuition: per credit $550. Enrollment: full-time 158, part-time 50. Faculty: full-time 19, part-time 37; clinical instructors 100. Degrees conferred: M.S.W., Ph.D., M.S.W.-M.P.H.

ADMISSION REQUIREMENTS. Official transcripts, two academic references and one current or most recent work reference, autobiographical statement or personal essay required in support of School's application. GRE required for Ph.D program. On-line application available. Interview sometimes required. TOEFL required for international applicants. Accepts transfer applicants. Graduates of unaccredited institutions not considered. Apply by March 31 (Fall full-time program), November 15 (Spring part-time program) to Assistant Dean for Admissions and Student Affairs. Application fee $25, $45 for Ph.D. applicant. Phone: (504)865-5314; fax (504)862-8727.

ADMISSION STANDARDS. Competitive. Usual minimum average: 3.0 (A = 4).

FINANCIAL AID. Merit and need-based scholarships, fellowships, grants, teaching assistantships, Federal W/S, loans. Apply by March 31 to office of Student Affairs of the School. Phone: (504)865-5723. Use FAFSA.

DEGREE REQUIREMENTS. For M.S.W.: 60 semester hours minimum, at least 30 in full-time residence (accelerated program available); no language or thesis requirement. For Ph.D.: a minimum of 16 courses (49 credits); qualifying exam; at least one year in full-time residence; dissertation; written/oral exams. For M.S.W.-M.P.H.: M.S.W. awarded after four semesters, M.P.H. after fifth semester.

THE UNIVERSITY OF TULSA

Tulsa, Oklahoma 74104-3126

Web site: www.utulsa.edu

Founded 1894. CGS member. Coed. Private control. Special facilities: Enterprise Development Center, Venture Capital Exchange, anthropological research sites. Library: approximately 900,000 volumes, 8000 subscriptions; special authors collection, U.S. Civil War collection, and American Indian Law Collection. Total University enrollment: 4200.

Annual tuition: full-time $9500, per credit hour $530. On-campus housing for 632 women, 632 men, 200 married students. Average academic year housing cost: $5830 (including board). Contact Director of University Housing for both on- and off-campus housing information. Phone: (918)631-5249. Day-care facilities available.

Graduate School

Established 1933. Enrollment: full-time 401, part-time 324 (men 55%, women 45%). Faculty: full-time 182, part-time 51. Degrees conferred: M.A., M.S., M.B.A., M.Acc., M.Tax., M.Eng., M.Engineering and Technology Management, M.S.M.S.E., M.S.Eng., M.M.E., M.M., M.T.A., M.F.A., M.N.A., Ph.D., M.N.A.-M.B.A., J.D.-M.S. (Biological Sciences, Geosciences), J.D.-M.A. (Anthropology, Clinical Psychology, English Language and Literature, History, Industrial/Organizational Psychology), J.D.-M.B.A.

ADMISSION REQUIREMENTS. Official transcripts required in support of School's application. On-line application available. GRE/GMAT required for most departments. Evidence of English proficiency and TOEFL required for international students. Interview not required. Transfer students accepted. Graduates of unaccredited institutions not considered. Apply to Graduate School at least one month prior to enrollment. Application fee $30. Phone: (800)882-4723 or (918)631-2336; fax: (918)631-2073; e-mail: grad@utulsa.edu.

ADMISSIONS STANDARDS. Selective. Usual minimum average: 3.0 (A = 4).

FINANCIAL AID. Scholarships, fellowships, teaching assistantships, research assistantships, internships, tuition waivers, Federal W/S, loans. Approved for VA benefits. Apply by February 1 for Fall term. Phone: (918)631-2526; fax: (918)631-2073. Use FAFSA. About 63% of graduate students receive aid other than loans from both the University and outside sources. Aid available for part-time students.

DEGREE REQUIREMENTS. For master's: 30 semester hours minimum, at least 24 in residence; thesis/nonthesis option; final oral exam in some departments. For Ph.D.: 60 semester hours minimum beyond the master's; one foreign language and/or computer language may be required; candidacy exam; qualifying exam; dissertation; comprehensive written/oral exam.

FIELDS OF STUDY.

Accounting. M.Acc.

Acounting and Information Systems. M.A.I.S.

Anthropology. M.A.

Art. M.F.A., M.T.A.

Biological Science. Includes environmental science, genetics, organismic biology. M.S., Ph.D.

Business Administration. GMAT for admission. M.B.A.

Chemical Engineering. M.S. in Engineering, M. of Engineering, Ph.D.

Clinical Psychology. M.A., Ph.D.

Computer Science. M.S., Ph.D.

Education. Includes elementary, secondary, school counseling. M.A., M.S.M.S.E., M.T.A.

Electrical Engineering. M.S. in Engineering, M. of Engineering.

Engineering and Technology Management. In cooperation with College of Business Administration. M. of Engineering and Technology Management.

English Language and Literature. Includes rhetoric and writing, writing in the professions, and research in and analysis of literature. M.A., Ph.D.

Finance. M.S.

Fine Arts. M.F.A.

Geosciences. Includes geochemistry, geology, geophysics. M.S., Ph.D.

History. M.A.

Industrial/Organizational Psychology. M.A., Ph.D.

Information Systems. M.S.

Mathematical Sciences. M.S.

Mechanical Engineering. M.S. in Engineering, M.Eng., Ph.D.

Music. Includes composition, applied music. M.M., M.M.E.

Nursing. M.N.A.
Petroleum Engineering. M.Eng., M.S. in Engineering, Ph.D.
Speech/Language Pathology. M.S.
Taxation. M.S.Tax.

College of Law

Web site: www.utulsa.edu/law

Established 1923. ABA approved since 1950. AALS member. Semester system. Full-time, part-time study. Special facilities: National Energy Law and Policy Institute, Native American Law Center, International/Comparative Law Center. Law library: 290,669 volumes, 4059 subscriptions; has LEXIS, NEXIS, WEST-LAW, DIALOG, LegalTrack.

Annual tuition: full-time $17,817, part-time $12,067. On-campus housing available for both single and married students. Total average annual additional expense: $10,000. Contact Director of Housing for both on- and off-campus housing information. Phone: (918)631-2378. Law students tend to live off-campus.

Enrollment: first-year class full-time 172, part-time 36; total full- and part-time 526 (men 58%, women 42%). Faculty: full-time 27, part-time 28. Student to faculty ratio 13.9 to 1. Degrees conferred: J.D., J.D.-M.Acc., J.D.-M.B.A., J.D.-M.A. (Anthropology, Clinical Psychology, English, History, Industrial and Organizational Psychology), J.D.-M.S. (Biological Sciences, Geosciences), J.D.-M.S.Tax.

ADMISSION REQUIREMENTS. LSDAS Law School report, Bachelor's degree, LSAT required in support of application. Interview not required. Accepts transfer applicants in good standing from accredited law schools. Graduates of unaccredited colleges not considered. Apply to Admissions Office after September 1, before May 15 (flexible). Application fee $30. Phone: (918)631-2406; fax: (918)631-3630.

ADMISSION STANDARDS. Selective. Mean LSAT: full-time 148, part-time 149; mean GPA: full-time 3.06, part-time 3.09. (A = 4). Gourman rating: 3.21. *U.S. News & World Report* ranking is in the fourth tier of all U.S. laws schools. Accepts about 65–70% of total annual applicants.

FINANCIAL AID. Scholarships mainly for advanced students, Federal W/S, loans. Apply to Office of Dean by February 1 (flexible). Use FAFSA (School code: 003185). About 36% of students receive aid other than loans from College and outside sources.

DEGREE REQUIREMENTS. For J.D.: 88 credit hours minimum, at least the last 30 in residence. For master's degree: see Graduate School listing above.

TUSKEGEE UNIVERSITY

Tuskegee, Alabama 36088
Web site: www.tusk.edu

Founded 1881. Located 38 miles E of Montgomery. Coed. Private and state-related control. Semester system. Special facilities: George Washington Carver Research Foundation. Library: 623,000 volumes, 3157 subscriptions.

Annual tuition: full-time resident $9928. On-campus housing for 48 married students, 150 men, 150 women. Average academic year housing costs: $4800–$6000 for married students, $5328 (including board) for single students. Apply to Manager of Auxiliary Enterprises by May 1. Phone: (334)727-8915. Daycare facilities available.

Graduate Programs

Graduate study since 1944. Enrollment: full-time 70, part-time 39. University faculty teaching graduate students: full-time 54, part-time 5. Degrees conferred: M.Ed., M.S., M.S.E.E., M.S.M.E., M.S.N.E., Ph.D.

ADMISSION REQUIREMENTS. Official transcripts, GRE required in support of application. TOEFL required for international applicants. Interview not required. Accepts transfer applicants. Apply to Admissions Office by July 15 (Fall), November 15 (Spring), April 15 (Summer). Application fee $25, $35 for international applicants. Phone: (334)727-8500; fax: (334)727-8451.

ADMISSION STANDARDS. Selective. Usual minimum average: 2.7 (A = 4).

FINANCIAL AID. Annual awards from institutional funds: research assistantships, teaching assistantships, graduate assistantships, internships, Federal W/S, loans. Approved for VA benefits. Apply by April 15 to appropriate department chair for assistantships; to Financial Aid Office for all other programs. Use FAFSA. About 35% of students receive aid other than loans from University and outside sources. Aid available for part-time students.

DEGREE REQUIREMENTS. For master's: 30–36 semester hours; thesis/nonthesis option; final oral/written exam. For Ph.D.: three-year, full-time program; qualifying exam; research proposal; dissertation; oral exam.

FIELDS OF STUDY.
Agricultural and Resource Economics.
Animal and Poultry Science.
Biology.
Chemistry.
Counseling and Student Development.
Electrical Engineering.
Environmental Sciences.
Food and Nutritional Science. Includes food science, nutritional science.
Forest Resources. Three plus two program.
General Science Education.
Materials Science and Engineering. Ph.D. only.
Mechanical Engineering.
Plant and Soil Science.

College of Veterinary Medicine, Nursing, and Allied Health

Established 1945. Annual tuition: full-time $12,000. Total average cost for all other expenses: $5000–$7000.

Enrollment: first-year class 60; total full-time 244 (men 40%, women 60%). Faculty: full-time 62. Degrees conferred: D.V.M., D.V.M.-M.S.

ADMISSION REQUIREMENTS. Transcripts, VCAT/MCAT/GRE, recommendations, animal/veterinary experience required in support of application. Interview by invitation only. Applicants must have completed at least two years of college study. Preference given to state and contract state residents (Kentucky; New Jersey, South Carolina, West Virginia). Apply to Dean of School by first Monday in December. Graduate study: Bachelor's degree, transcripts required in support of application. Apply to Dean of School after July 1, before January 7. Application fee $25. Phone: (334)727-8460.

ADMISSION STANDARDS. Selective. Usual minimum average 2.7 (A = 4). Accepts about 35% of total annual applicants, forty to forty-five "at-large" spaces available for nonresidents.

FINANCIAL AID. For information and forms write to the University's Director of Financial Aid. Apply by April 15. Use FAFSA.

DEGREE REQUIREMENTS. For D.V.M.: satisfactory completion of four-year program. Students in combined programs take graduate course during summer only. For M.S. requirements: see Graduate School listing above.

FIELDS OF GRADUATE STUDY.
Tropical Animal Health. M.S.
Veterinary Science. M.S.

UNIFORMED SERVICES UNIVERSITY OF THE HEALTH SCIENCES

4301 Jones Bridge Road
Bethesda, Maryland 20814-4799
Web site: www.usuhs.mil

Founded 1972. Located on the grounds of the Naval Medical Center, Bethesda. Federal control. Semester system. Special affiliations: Armed Forces Institute of Pathology, National Library of Medicine, National Institutes of Health, U.S. Armed Forces Radiobiology Research Institute, Walter Reed Army Institute of Research.

The University's Schools include the Graduate School of Nursing and School of Medicine. Total University enrollment at main campus: 757

F. Edward Hebert School of Medicine
Room A-10411

Admitted charter class 1976. The academic year is 48 weeks. Special programs: 20% of clinical experience may be taken in other areas of the world. Library: 117,700 volumes/microforms, 1345 current periodical/subscriptions, 40 PC workstations.

Annual tuition: none. No on-campus housing available. Annual living expenses are expected to be covered by the student's annual salary.

Enrollment: first-year class 167; total full-time 673 (men 67%, women 33%). Faculty: full-time 1100, part-time 1500. Degree conferred: M.D.

ADMISSION REQUIREMENTS. Preference given to both military and civilian U.S. citizens between the ages of 18 and 30. All military applicant must submit a "Letter of Approval" to apply. Bachelor's degree from an accredited institution required. All applicants have bachelor's degree awarded prior to enrollment. Does not accept transfer applicants. Apply through AMCAS (file after June 1, before November 1), submit MCAT (will accept MCAT test results from the last three years); official transcripts for each school attended (should show at least 90 semester credits/135 quarter credit; submit transcripts by mid-May to AMCAS). Service processing fee: none, nor a supplementary application fee. Submit a supplemental application, a photograph, a personal statement, preprofessional committee evaluation and three recommendations from science faculty to Office of Admission within two to three weeks of receipt of supplemental materials. Phone: (800)772-1743, (301)295-3101; fax: (301)295-3545; e-mail: admissions@usuhs.mil. Interviews are by invitation only and generally for final selection. First-year students admitted Fall only. Rolling admissions process; notification starts November 1 and is finished when class is filled. Applicant's response to offer due within two weeks of receipt of acceptance letter. Prior to enrollment a student can expect to have a background check performed and will have to pass a medical examination.

ADMISSION STANDARDS. Selective. Mean MCAT: 9.7; mean GPA: 3.52 (A = 4). Gourman rating: 3.18. Accepts 15–20% of total annual applicants.

FINANCIAL AID. Upon matriculation the student becomes an active reserve officer in one of the military service branches and receives a full salary, free health benefits for the student and his or her family, a housing allowance, commissary privileges, and 30 days' paid leave.

DEGREE REQUIREMENTS. For M.D.: satisfactory completion of four-year program. All students must pass USMLE Step 1 prior to entering third year and must pass USMLE Step 2 prior to awarding of M.D. Upon graduation there is a military commitment of not less than seven years on active duty and six years of inactive ready reserve.

UNION COLLEGE

Barbourville, Kentucky 40906-1499
Web site: www.unionky.edu

Founded 1879. Located 100 miles S of Lexington. Coed. Private control. Methodist affiliation. Semester system. Library: 105,200 volumes, 2450 subscriptions.

Tuition: per hour $225. Limited on-campus housing for 30 married students, 50 men, 50 women. Average academic year housing costs: $3040 (including board) for single students. Contact Dean of Students. Phone: (606)546-1230.

Graduate School

Enrollment: full-time 5, part-time 250. Graduate faculty: full-time 6, part-time 18. Degree conferred: M.A. in Ed.

ADMISSION REQUIREMENTS. Two official transcripts, GRE/NTE, two letters of recommendation, teaching certificates required in support of School's application. TOEFL required for international applicants. Interview desirable. Accepts transfer applicants. Graduates of unaccredited institutions not considered. Apply to Dean of the Graduate School by August 15 (Fall), December 15 (Spring). Application fee $15. Phone: (606)546-1210; fax: (606)546-1330.

ADMISSION STANDARDS. Selective. Usual minimum average: 2.5 (A = 4).

FINANCIAL AID. Limited to loans. Approved for VA benefits. Apply to Financial Aid Office. Phone: (606)546-1224; fax: (606)546-1217. Use FAFSA.

DEGREE REQUIREMENTS. For M.A. in Ed.: 30 semester hours minimum, at least 24 in residence and one semester or Summer session in full-time attendance; thesis optional for 6 hours; final written exam.

FIELDS OF STUDY.
Elementary Education. Includes language arts, science, social studies.
Middle School Education. Includes language arts, science, social studies.
P–12 Education. Includes health/physical education, music education, principalships, special education.
Secondary Education. Includes language arts, science, social studies.

UNION COLLEGE

Schenectady, New York 12308-3107
Web site: www.union.edu

Founded 1795. Coed. Private control. Trimester system. Library: 496,000 volumes, 6500 subscriptions.

Tuition: per course $1300–$1555, varies by discipline. No on-campus housing available. Contact Housing Office for off- campus housing information. Phone: (518)388-6061. Day-care facilities available near campus.

Graduate School

Graduate study since 1904. Enrollment: full-time 144, part-time 92. Faculty: full-time 9, part-time 19. Degrees conferred: M.A., M.A.T., M.S., M.B.A., M.S.T., Ph.D.

ADMISSION REQUIREMENTS. Official transcripts, three letters of recommendation required in support of application. Interview not required except for M.A.T./M.S.T. program. Accepts transfers with one or two courses (depending on program). GMAT scores required for admission to Graduate Management Institute. Apply to Graduate Studies Office by May 1, April 1 for M.A.T.; part-time applicants may apply throughout year. Part-time students may complete between one and three courses (depending on program) at Union before applying for degree status. Application fee $50. Phone: (518)388-6288; fax: (518)388-6686.

ADMISSION STANDARDS. Selective. Usual minimum average: 3.0 (A = 4).

FINANCIAL AID. Scholarships, fellowships and assistantships available for full-time students in the Graduate Management Institute, occasional assistantship available in engineering departments internships, tuition waivers, loans. Phone: (518)388-6642; fax: (518)388-6686. Use FAFSA and College's FAF. No institutional aid for part-time students.

DEGREE REQUIREMENTS. For M.A., M.A.T., M.S., M.S.T.: 10 full courses (33 credits) required in most departments; thesis for some departments. For M.S. from Graduate Management Institute: 15 full courses; for M.B.A.: 18 full courses; thesis/final oral/written exam. For Ph.D.: 15 courses minimum, one year of residency; dissertation; final oral/written exam.

FIELDS OF STUDY.
Bioethics.
Business Administration.
Computer Science.
Computer Systems.
Educational Studies.
Electrical Engineering.
Health Administration.
Mechanical Engineering.

THE UNION INSTITUTE AND UNIVERSITY

Cincinnati, Ohio 45206-1925
Web site: www.tui.edu

Founded 1964. Coed. Private control. Semester system. External, nonresidential, self-paced, interdisciplinary, independent study program. Master's programs are offered at Vermont College, Montpelier, Vermont, and Dade County, Florida. Library houses Institute's doctoral dissertation only: approximately 3500. Annual tuition: $8944. No on-campus housing available.

Graduate College

Graduate study since 1969. Enrollment: full-time 1432, part-time 0. Graduate faculty: full- and part-time 86. Degrees conferred: M.A., M.Ed., M.F.A., Ph.D. A

ADMISSION REQUIREMENTS. Master's degree, two official transcripts, three letters of recommendation, three detailed nar-

rative essays (autobiography, statement of interests, proposed program overview) required in support of School's application. Interview not required. Apply to the Dean at least two months prior to preferred date of enrollment. Application fee $50. Rolling admissions process. Phone: (800)486-3116 or (513)861-6400; fax (513)861-0779; e-mail: admission@tui.edu.

ADMISSION STANDARDS. Selective. No minimum GPA or test score required. Individualized admission process based on evidence of ability to self-direct, conceptualize, define, and carry out a doctoral-level research program.

FINANCIAL AID. Limited to Federal W/S, loans. Apply by May 1 to the Financial Aid Office. Phone: (800)486-3116. Use FAFSA and institutional FAF.

DEGREE REQUIREMENTS. For M.A.: 12-month individually designed program. For M.Ed.: entry colloquium; four required residencies; three seminars. For M.F.A. 60 credits individually designed program. For Ph.D.: at least six semesters (24 months) in continuous full-time enrollment; attendance at a ten-day entry colloquium and three five-day seminars; internship; dissertation.

FIELDS OF STUDY.
Business.
Clinical Psychology.
Communication.
Creative and Performing Arts.
Educational Administration.
Health and Health Care.
Interdisciplinary Arts and Science.
Literature.
Multicultural Studies.
Peace Studies.
Philanthropy and Leadership.
Philosophy/Religion.
Psychology. Includes general, marital and family therapy, social.
Public Policy.
Racial and Ethnic Studies.
Science/Mathematics.
Social sciences.
Sociology and Social Work.
Women's Studies.
Note: All fields of study are interdisciplinary, and programs are individually designed.

FIELDS OF STUDY—VERMONT COLLEGE.
American Studies. M.A.
Anthropology. M.A.
Art History. M.A.
Education. M.A.
Environmental Education. M.A.
Gerontology. M.A.
History. M.A.
Human Services Leadership. M.A.
International Relations. M.A.
Literature and Writing. M.A.
Military History. M.A.
Organizational Development. M.A.
Poetry Therapy. M.A.
Political Science. M.A.
Psychology. M.A.
Psychology and Counseling. M.A.
Sociology. M.A.
Visual Arts. Interdisciplinary. Includes craft as fine art, drawing, electronic media, painting, performance, photography, printmaking, sculpture, video/film. M.F.A.
Writing. M.F.A.
Writing for Children and Young Adults. M.F.A.
Women's Studies. M.A.

FIELDS OF STUDY—DADE COUNTY.
Curriculum and Instruction. M.Ed.
Educational Leadership. M.Ed.
Elementary Education. M.Ed.
Gifted Education. M.Ed.
Issues in Education. M.Ed.
Learning Disabilities Guidance and Counseling. M.Ed.
Mentally Handicapped. M.Ed.
PreK–Primary Education. M.Ed.
Reading. M.Ed.
School Psychology. M.Ed.
TESOL. M.Ed.
Varying Exceptionalities. M.Ed.

THE UNIVERSITY OF THE ARTS
Philadelphia, Pennsylvania 19102-9762
Web site: www.uarts.edu

Founded 1876. Coed. Private control. Semester system. Special facilities: electronic media laboratory, video editing studios, Oxberry Animation Stand, analog and digital electronic music studios, music calligraphy laboratory, Borowsky Center for Publication Arts, laser scanner laboratory, industrial design computer-aided product design center. Merriam, Drake, and Black Box Theaters. Library: 118,500 volumes, 5321 subscriptions.

Annual tuition: full-time $17,250; per credit hour $870. No on-campus housing available. Contact the Director of Residential Life for off-campus housing information. Phone: (215)717-6046.

Graduate Program

Enrollment: full-time 81, part-time 63. University faculty teaching graduate students: full-time 26, part-time 12. Degrees conferred: M.A., M.F.A., M.A.T., M.I.D.

ADMISSION REQUIREMENTS. Official transcripts, audition, portfolio, interview, statement of purpose required in support of application. TOEFL required for international applicants. Accepts transfer applicants in Music and Art Education. Apply to the Director of Admission at least two month prior to date of registration. Application fee $50, $75 for international applicants. Phone: (800)616-ARTS, (215)717-6049; fax: (215)717-6045.

ADMISSION STANDARDS. Selective. Usual minimum average: 3.0 (A = 4). Talent is usual basis for most admissions decisions.

FINANCIAL AID. Scholarships, assistantships, internships, Grants-in-Aid, Federal W/S, loans. Approved for VA benefits. Apply with application for admission to Director of Admissions by March 15 (priority consideration). Phone: (215) 875-4858. Use FAFSA. About 24–36% of students receive aid other than loans from University and outside sources.

DEGREE REQUIREMENTS. For M.A.: 36 semester hours minimum, at least 24 in residence; thesis; creative project. For M.F.A.: 60 semester hours, all in residence; thesis; four years for completion required. For part-time M.F.A.: 60 semester hours over four six-week summer residencies; eight independent study projects; thesis/exhibition during fifth summer.

FIELDS OF STUDY.
Art Education.
Book Arts/Printmaking.
Ceramics.
Industrial Design.

Jazz Studies.
Museum Communication.
Museum Education.
Museum Exhibition, Planning, and Design.
Music Education.
Painting.
Sculpture.
Teaching Visual Arts.

UTAH STATE UNIVERSITY
Logan, Utah 84322-0900
Web site: www.usu.edu

Founded 1888. Located 80 miles N of Salt Lake City. CGS member. Coed. State control. Semester system. Library: 1,200,000 volumes, 14,000 subscriptions. Total University enrollment: 20,000.

Tuition: per credit resident $252.48, nonresident $884.06, international students $6942. On-campus housing for 670 married students, 1058 men, 1002 women. Average academic year housing costs: $3700 (including board), $5950 for married students. Contact Director, Housing and Residential Life, for both on- and off-campus housing information. Phone: (435)797-3113. Daycare facilities available.

School of Graduate Studies

Graduate study since 1914. Enrollment: full-time 961, part-time 1147 (men 50%, women 50%). Faculty: full-time 574, part-time 106. Degrees conferred: M.A., M.Ac., M.A.I., M.B.A., M.C.E.D., M.E., M.Ed., M.E.S., M.F., M.F.A., M.L.A., M.M.T., M.S., M.S.S., Ed.S., C.E., E.E., Ed.D., Ph.D.

ADMISSION REQUIREMENTS. Two official transcripts from each postsecondary institution attended, three letters of recommendation, GRE/GMAT (Business) required in support of School's application. On-line application available. TOEFL (minimum score 550) required for international applicants. Accepts transfer applicants. Graduates of unaccredited colleges not considered. Apply to Graduate Office by June 15 (Fall), October 15 (Spring), March 15 (Summer). Application fee $40, $45 for international applicants. Phone: (435)797-1190; fax: (435)797-1192.

ADMISSION STANDARDS. Selective. Usual minimum average GPA: 3.0 (A = 4); admission test score in the 40th percentile of above.

FINANCIAL AID. Fellowships, scholarships, teaching assistantships, tuition waivers and nonresident tuition waivers, internships, Federal W/S, loans. Approved for VA benefits. Apply by February 15 to appropriate department head for fellowships, assistantships; to Financial Aid Office for all other programs. Phone: (435)797-0173; fax: (435)797-0654. Use FAFSA. Aid available for part-time students.

DEGREE REQUIREMENTS. For master's: 30–36 credit hours minimum, at least 24 in residence; reading knowledge of one foreign language for M.A.; thesis/final report in some departments; final exam. For M.F.A.: generally two-year program. For M.B.A.: one to two-year program, depending on background of candidate. For M.F. (for holders of Bachelor's in field other than forestry): 60 credit hours minimum. For Ed.S., C.E., E.E.: 30 credit hours beyond the master's; project. For Ed.D.: 60 credits minimum beyond the master's, at least four semesters in residence; dissertation; comprehensive written exam; final oral exam. For Ph.D.: 60 credits minimum beyond the master's, at least four semesters in residence; dissertation; preliminary exam; comprehensive written exam; final oral exam.

FIELDS OF STUDY.

COLLEGE OF AGRICULTURE:
Agricultural Systems Technology. M.A., M.S.
Animal Science. M.A., M.S., Ph.D.
Biometeorology. M.A., M.S., Ph.D.
Bioveterinary Science. M.A., M.S.
Dairy Science. M.A., M.S.
Plant Science. M.A., M.S., Ph.D.
Soil Science. M.S., Ph.D.
Toxicology. M.S., Ph.D.

COLLEGE OF BUSINESS:
Accounting. M.Acc.
Business Administration. M.B.A.
Business Information Systems. M.S.
Economics. M.A., M.S., M.S.S., Ph.D.
Human Resource Administration. M.R.A.
Human Resource Management. M.S.S.

COLLEGE OF EDUCATION:
Communicative Disorders and Deaf Education. M.A., M.Ed., M.S. Ed.S.
Education. Includes business, information systems and education, communicative disorders, elementary education, research and evaluation, educational audiology; Ed.D., Ph.D.
Elementary Education. M.A., M.Ed., M.S.
Health, Physical Education, and Recreation. M.S., M.Ed.
Instructional Technology. M.S., M.Ed., Ed.S.
Psychology. M.S., Ph.D.
Secondary Education. M.A., M.Ed., M.S., Ed.D., Ph.D.
Special Education. M.S., M.Ed., Ed.S., Ed.D., Ph.D.

COLLEGE OF ENGINEERING:
Biological and Agricultural Engineering. M.S., Ph.D.
Civil and Environmental Engineering. M.S., C.E., M.E., Ph.D.
Electrical Engineering. E.E., M.S., M. E., Ph.D.
Industrial Technology. M.S.
Irrigation Engineering. M.S., Ph.D.
Mechanical Engineering. M.S., M.E., Ph.D.

COLLEGE OF FAMILY LIFE:
Family and Human Development. M.S.
Family Life. Ph.D.
Food Microbiology and Safety. M.F.M.S.
Human Environment. M.S.
Nutrition and Food Sciences. M.A., M.S., Ph.D.

COLLEGE OF HUMANITIES, ARTS, AND SOCIAL SCIENCES:
American Studies. M.A., M.S.
Art. M.A., M.F.A.
Communication. M.A., M.S.
English. M.A., M.S.
History. M.A., M.S., M.S.S.
Landscape Architecture. M.S., M.L.A.
Management and Human Resources. M.S., M.S.S.
Political Science. M.A., M.S.
Second Language Teaching. M.S.L.T.
Social Sciences. M.S.S.
Sociology. M.A., M.S., M.S.S., Ph.D.
Theater Arts. M.A., M.F.A.

COLLEGE OF NATURAL RESOURCES:
Fisheries Biology. M.S., Ph.D.
Fisheries and Wildlife. M.S., Ph.D.
Forestry Resources. M.S., Ph.D.
Forest Management. M.F.
Forestry. M.S., Ph.D.
Geography. M.A., M.S.
Natural Resources. M.N.R.

Range Science. M.S., Ph.D.
Recreation Resource Management. M.S., Ph.D.
Watershed Science. M.S., Ph.D.
Wildlife Biology. M.S., Ph.D.

COLLEGE OF SCIENCE:
Biochemistry. M.S., Ph.D.
Biology. M.S., Ph.D.
Biology Ecology. M.S., Ph.D.
Chemistry. M.S., Ph.D.
Computer Science. M.S., M.C.S., Ph.D.
Geology. M.S.
Industrial Mathematics. M.S.
Mathematical Sciences. Ph.D.
Mathematics. M.S., M.Math.
Physics. M.S., Ph.D.
Statistics. M.S.
Toxicology. M.S., Ph.D.

UNIVERSITY OF UTAH
Salt Lake City, Utah 84112
Web site: www.utah.edu

Founded 1850. CGS member. State control. Semester system. Special facilities: Advanced Combustion Engineering Research Center, American West Center, Archaeological Center, Center of Architectural Studies, Center for Atmospheric and Remote Sounding Studies, Institute for Biomedical Engineering, Center for Controlled Chemical Delivery, Cosmic Ray Observatory, Center for Excellence in Nuclear Technology, Engineering, and Research, Center for Health Care, Hinckley institute of Politics, Intermountain Burn Center, Obert C. and Grace A. Tanner Humanities Center, Center for Human Toxicology, Garn Institute for Finance, Gerontology Center, Huntsman Cancer Institute, Jon A. Dixon Laser Institute, Middle East Center, Social Research Center, Utah Museum of Fine Arts, Utah Museum of Natural History. The University's NIH ranking is 42nd among all U.S. institutions with 341 awards/grants worth $112,749,128. Library: 3,300,000 volumes, 21,000 subscriptions. Total University enrollment: 27,100.

Tuition: full-time resident $2564, nonresident $9049; part-time per credit, resident $356.22, nonresident $1265. On-campus housing for 1092 married students, 102 men, 52 women. Average academic year housing costs: $2280 for single students; $3000 for married students. Contact Director of Residential Living for both on- and off-campus housing information. Phone: (801)581-6667. Day-care facilities available.

Graduate School

Enrollment: full-time 3346, part-time 1722. Faculty: full- and part-time 1134. Degrees conferred: M.A., M.Arch., M.A.T., M.B.A., M.E., M.E.A., M.Ed., M.F.A., M.H.R.M., M.Mus., M.Pr.A., M.P.A., M.S., M.S.P.H., M.S.W., M.Phil., M.Stat., Ed.S., Ph.D., Ed.D., Pharm.D., D.S.W., E.E.

ADMISSION REQUIREMENTS. Official transcripts GRE/GMAT/MAT required in support of School's application. On-line application available. GRE Subject required for some programs. TOEFL required for international applicants. Interview may be required. Accepts transfer applicants. Graduates of unaccredited institutions not considered. Apply to the Director of Admissions by May 1 (Fall), November 1 (Spring); some departments may have earlier deadlines. Application fee $45, $60 for international applicants. Phone: (801)581-7281; fax: (801)585-7864.

ADMISSION STANDARDS. Selective to very competitive. Usual minimum average: 3.0 (A = 4).

FINANCIAL AID. Annual awards from institutional funds: teaching/research assistantships, teaching/research fellowships, internships, traineeships, tuition waivers, Federal W/S, loans. Approved for VA benefits. In addition, all departments have established teaching positions for graduate students with stipends. Apply by March 1 to Graduate Fellowship Office for fellowships, to appropriate department chair for assistantships; to Financial Aid Office for all other programs. Phone: (801)581-6211. Use FAFSA. About 20% of students receive aid other than loans from School and outside sources. Aid available for part-time students.

DEGREE REQUIREMENTS. For master's: 30–48 credit hours minimum, at least 24 in residence; foreign language qualifying exam for M.A.; admission to candidacy; thesis; final oral/written exam. For E.E., Ed.S.: 30 credit hours beyond master's. For Ph.D.: 60 credits minimum, at least one year in full-time residence; foreign language requirements vary by department; qualifying exam; thesis; final oral exam. For Ed.D.: language requirements vary from department to department, some have none at all; other requirements essentially the same as for the Ph.D.

FIELDS OF STUDY.

DAVID ECCLES SCHOOL OF BUSINESS:
Accounting. GMAT for admission; includes professional accounting. M.B.A., M.Pr.A., Ph.D.
Business Administration. GMAT for admission. M.B.A., Ph.D.
Finance. GMAT for admission. M.B.A., M.S., Ph.D.
Human Resource Management. GRE for admission. M.B.A., M.H.R.M., Ph.D.
Management. M.S.
Marketing. GMAT for admission. M.B.A., Ph.D.
Statistics. M.Stat.

GRADUATE SCHOOL OF EDUCATION:
Education, Culture, and Society. M.A., M.Ed., M.S., Ph.D.
Educational Leadership and Policy. Includes school administration, supervision. M.Ed., Ed.D., Ph.D.
Educational Psychology. Includes school counseling, school psychology, professional counseling, professional psychology. M.Ed., M.S., Ph.D.
Special Education. M.A., M.Ed., M.S., Ph.D.
Teaching and Learning. Includes early childhood, elementary, secondary, reading and reading specialist. M.A., M.Ed., M.S., Ph.D.

COLLEGE OF ENGINEERING:
Bioengineering. M.E., M.S., Ph.D.
Chemical Engineering. M.E., M.Phil., M.S., Ph.D.
Civil Engineering. M.E., M.S., Ph.D.
Computer Science. M.E., M.Phil., M.S., Ph.D.
Electrical Engineering. M.E., M.S., Ph.D.
Engineering Administration. M.E.A.
Environmental Engineering. M.E., M.S., Ph.D.
Fuels Engineering. M.E., M.S., Ph.D.
Materials Science and Engineering. Interdepartmental. M.E., M.S., Ph.D.
Mechanical Engineering. M.E., M.Phil., M.S., Ph.D.
Nuclear Engineering. M.E., M.S., Ph.D.

COLLEGE OF FINE ARTS:
Art. Includes art teaching, ceramics, drawing and painting, graphic design, illustration, intermedia/sculpture, photography/digital imaging, printmaking. M.A., M.F.A.
Art History. Includes Asian art, Western European art, American art, 20th-century art. M.A.
Ballet. Includes character dance, performance, teaching. M.A., M.F.A.
Film Studies. Includes critical studies, film and video production, screenwriting. M.F.A.
Modern Dance. Includes performance, choreography, education, history, kinesiology. M.F.A., M.A.

Music. Includes conducting, history, instrumental and vocal performance, jazz studies, music composition, music education, theory. M.A., M.Mus., Ph.D.
Theatre. Includes acting and directing, design, history, literature, playwriting, production and stage management, theatre education. M.F.A., Ph.D.

COLLEGE OF HEALTH:
Audiology. M.A., M.S.
Exercise and Sports Science. M.Phil., M.S., Ed.D., Ph.D.
Food and Nutrition. M.S.
Health Promotion and Education. M.Phil., M.S., Ed.D., Ph.D.
Occupational Therapy. M.O.T.
Physical Therapy. M.P.T.
Recreation and Leisure. M.Phil., M.S., Ed.D., Ph.D.
Speech-Language Pathology. M.A., M.S.

COLLEGE OF HUMANITIES:
Communication. M.A., M.Phil., M.S., Ph.D.
Comparative Literature. M.A., Ph.D.
Creative Writing. M.F.A.
English. M.A., Ph.D.
French. M.A.
German. M.A.
History. GRE for admission. M.A., M.S., Ph.D.
Humanities. M.A., M.F.A., M.S., Ph.D.
Language Pedagogy. Includes French, German, Arabic, Hebrew, Persian, Turkish, Spanish. M.A.T.
Linguistics. Interdepartmental; M.A.
Middle East Studies. M.A., Ph.D.
Philosophy. M.A., M.S., Ph.D.
Spanish. M.A., Ph.D.

COLLEGE OF MINES AND EARTH SCIENCES:
Geological Engineering. M.E., M.S., Ph.D.
Geology. M.S., Ph.D.
Geophysics. M.S., Ph.D.
Metallurgical Engineering. M.E., M.S., Ph.D.
Meterology. M.S., Ph.D.
Mines and Earth Sciences. M.E., M.S., Ph.D.
Mining Engineering. M.E., M.S., Ph.D.

COLLEGE OF NURSING:
Nursing. M.S., Ph.D.
Note: Apply to Dean of College of Nursing and Graduate School; NLNGNE, GRE, MAT for admission.

COLLEGE OF PHARMACY:
Medical Chemistry. M.S., Ph.D.
Pharmaceutics and Pharmaceutical Chemistry. M.S., Ph.D.
Pharmacology and Toxicology. M.S., Ph.D.
Pharmacy. Pharm.D.
Pharmacy Practice. M.S.

COLLEGE OF SCIENCE:
Biological Chemistry. Ph.D.
Biology. M.Phil.
Cell Biology. Ph.D.
Chemical Physics. Ph.D.
Chemistry. Ph.D.
Ecology and Evolutionary Biology. M.S., Ph.D.
Genetics. M.S., Ph.D.
Mathematics. M.A., M.Phil., M.S., Ph.D.
Molecular Biology. Ph.D.
Physics. M.A., M.Phil., M.S., Ph.D.
Science. M.S.

COLLEGE OF SOCIAL AND BEHAVIORAL SCIENCE:
Anthropology. M.A., Ph.D.
Economics. M.A., M.Phil., M.S., M.Stat., Ph.D.
Geography. M.A., M.S., Ph.D.

Political Science. M.A., M.S., Ph.D.
Psychogy. GRE/MAT for admission; M.A., M.S., M.Stat., Ph.D.
Public Administration. M.P.A.
Sociology. M.A., M.S., Ph.D.

GRADUATE SCHOOL OF ARCHITECTURE:
Architecture. M.Arch., M.S.

GRADUATE SCHOOL OF SOCIAL WORK:
Social Work. M.S.W., D.S.W.

College of Law

Web site: www.law.utah.edu

Established 1914. ABA approved since 1927. AALS member. Semester system. Full-time, day study only. Special facility: Wallace Stegner Center for Land, Resources, and the Environment. Law library: 311,231 volumes, 4698 subscriptions; has LEXIS, NEXIS, WESTLAW, VUTEXT; is a State Government Depository.

Annual tuition: resident $5603, nonresident $12,207. On-campus housing available for both single and married students. Annual on-campus estimated housing cost: $6,102. Phone: (801)581-6611. Law students tend to live off-campus. Off-campus housing and personal expenses: approximately $12,246.

Enrollment: first-year class 129; total full-time 377 (men 60%, women 40%). Faculty: full-time 24, part-time 17. Student to faculty ratio 13.1 to 1.

Degrees conferred: J.D., J.D.-M.B.A., J.D.-M.P.A., LL.M. (Environmental and Natural Resource Law).

ADMISSION REQUIREMENTS. LSDAS Law School report, Bachelor's degree, transcripts, LSAT, personal statement required in support of application. Accepts transfer applicants. Apply to Office of Dean of College by February 1 (for priority consideration). Rolling admissions process. Admits Fall only. Application fee $50. Phone: (801)581-7479; fax: (801)581-6897.

ADMISSION STANDARDS. Selective. Mean LSAT: 158; mean GPA: 3.49 (A = 4). Gourman rating: 4.40. *U.S. News & World Report* ranking is in the top 45 of all U.S. law schools. Accepts 35–40% of total annual applicants.

FINANCIAL AID. Scholarships, tuition waivers, fellowships, assistantships, Federal W/S, loans. Apply to Financial Aid Office of University by March 15 for priority consideration. Phone: (801)581-6211. Use FAFSA (College code: 003675). About 36% of students receive aid other than loans from College.

DEGREE REQUIREMENTS. For J.D.: 88 semester hours minimum. For LL.M.: at least 24 credit hours beyond the J.D.; one year in full-time residence.
Note: Study-abroad program in London available.

College of Medicine (84132-2101)

Web site: www.med.utah.edu

Founded 1905, expanded to a four-year program in 1942.
Annual tuition: resident and WICHE contract states $6125, nonresident $13,513, student fees $427. Total average figure for all other expenses: $7725.

Enrollment: first-year class 102, total 419 (men 63%, women 37%). Faculty: full- and part-time 800. Degrees conferred: M.D., M.D.-M.P.H., M.D.-M.S.P.H., M.D.-Ph.D. The M.S. and Ph.D. are offered through the Graduate School.

ADMISSION REQUIREMENTS. AMCAS, transcripts, letters of recommendation, MCAT required in support of application. Interviews by invitation only. Applicants must have completed at least three years of college study. Preference given to state residents and residents of Idaho. Nonresidents must apply under EDP; apply between June 1 and August 1. Apply to Admissions Office after June 15, before October 1. Application fee: $75. Phone: (801)581-7498; fax: (801)585-3300.

ADMISSION STANDARDS. Selective. Mean MCAT: 10; mean GPA: 3.6 (A = 4). *U.S. News & World Report* ranking is in the top 38 of all U.S. medical schools. Accepts 30% of total annual applicants. Approximately 75% are state residents.

FINANCIAL AID. Scholarships, Grants-in-Aid, institutional loans, HEAL, alternative loan programs, NIH stipends, Federal Perkins Loans, Stafford Subsidized and Unsubsidized Loans, Service Commitment Scholarship programs are available. Assistantships/fellowships may be available for dual degree candidates. Financial aid applications and information are generally available at the on-campus by-invitation interview. Contact the Financial Aid Office for current information. Phone: (801)581-6474. Use FAFSA (School code: 003675), also submit Financial Aid Transcript, Federal Income Tax forms. Approximately 75% of students receive some form of financial assistance.

DEGREE REQUIREMENTS. For M.D.: satisfactory completion of four-year program. All students must take USMLE Step 1 and Step 2 and record scores. For M.D.-M.S.P.H, M.D.-M.P.H.: generally a four-and-one-half- to five-and-one-half-year programs. For M.D.-Ph.D.: generally a seven- to eight-year program.

FIELDS OF GRADUATE STUDY.
Biochemistry.
Bioengineering.
Cell and Molecular Biology.
Human Genetics.
Immunology.
Neurobiology and Neuroanatomy.
Oncological Sciences.
Pharmacology and Toxicology.
Physiology.

VALDOSTA STATE COLLEGE

Valdosta, Georgia 31698
Web site: www.valdosta.edu

Founded 1906. Located 75 miles NE of Tallahassee, Florida. CGS member. Coed. State control. Semester system. Library: 375,000 volumes, 3262 subscriptions.

Annual tuition: resident $3036, nonresident $10,272; per credit resident $139, nonresident $440. On-campus housing for 601 graduate men, 1082 graduate women; 12 units for married students. Average academic year housing costs: $3950 for single students; $5200 for married students. Contact Director, Housing and Residence Life for both on- and off-campus housing information. Phone: (229)333-5920.

Graduate School

Graduate study since 1968. Enrollment: full-time 428, part-time 881. College faculty teaching graduate students: full-time 217, part-time 10. Degrees conferred: M.A., M.M.E., M.S., M.B.A., M.Ed., M.P.A., Ed.S., Ed.D.

ADMISSION REQUIREMENTS. Two official transcripts, GRE (for education applicants; M.A., M.S. applicants), GRE or GMAT (for M.P.A. applicants), GMAT (for business) required in support of application. On-line application available. TOEFL required for international applicants. Accepts transfer applicants. Graduates of unaccredited institutions not considered. Apply to Director of Graduate Admissions at least sixty days prior to the beginning of the semester of registration. Application fee $20. Phone: (229)333-5694; fax: (229)245-3853.

ADMISSION STANDARDS. Relatively open. Usual minimum average: 2.5 (A = 4).

FINANCIAL AID. Scholarships, research assistantships, teaching assistantships, internships, traineeships, Federal W/S, grants, loans. Approved for VA benefits. Apply by May 1 to Director of Student Aid. Phone: (229) 333-5935; fax: (229)333-5430. Use FAFSA and institutional FAF. About 20% of students receive aid other than loans from College and outside sources. Aid available for part-time students.

DEGREE REQUIREMENTS. For M.A.: 30 credit hours minimum plus thesis, at least 24 in residence; or 33 credit hours minimum without thesis, at least 25 in residence; reading knowledge of one foreign language; comprehensive/oral exam. For M.Ed., M.M.E.: 30 credit hours minimum plus thesis, at least 25 in residence; or 36 credit hours minimum without thesis, at least 30 in residence; comprehensive written/oral exam. For M.S.: 30 credit hours minimum plus thesis, at least 24 in residence; or 30 hours minimum without thesis, at least 30 in residence; comprehensive written/oral exam. For M.B.A., M.P.A.: 45 credit hours minimum, at least 30 in residence; comprehensive written/oral exam. For Ed.S.: 30 credit hours beyond the master's; thesis/nonthesis option. For. Ed.D.: at least 60 credit hours beyond the master's; qualifying exam; candidacy; dissertation; final oral exam.

FIELDS OF STUDY.

GRADUATE SCHOOL:
Library and Information Science. M.L.I.S.

COLLEGE OF ARTS:
Music Education. M.M.E.

COLLEGE OF ARTS AND SCIENCES:
Criminal Justice. M.S.
English. M.A.
History. M.A.
Marriage and Family Therapy. M.S.
Public Administration. M.P.A.
Sociology. M.S.

COLLEGE OF BUSINESS ADMINISTRATION:
Business Administration. M.B.A.

COLLEGE OF EDUCATION:
Adult and Career Education. Includes business education, technical, trade and industrial, training and development. M.Ed., Ed.D.
Business Education. M.Ed.
Career Education. Includes business education, general career education. Ed.S.
Curriculum and Instruction. Ed.D.
Early Childhood Education. M.Ed., Ed.S.
Educational Leadership. Includes public school leadership, higher education leadership. M.Ed., Ed.S., Ed.D.
Instructional Technology. Includes library media technology, technology applications. M.Ed., Ed.S.
Middle Grades. M.Ed., Ed.S.
Physical Education. M.Ed.
Psychology. Includes clinical/counseling, industrial/organizational. M.S.
Reading. M.Ed.
School Counseling. Ed.S.
School Psychology. Ed.S.
Secondary Education. M.Ed., Ed.S.
Special Education. Includes communication disorders, early childhood special education, general, mild disabilities, mental retardation, interrelated. M.Ed., Ed.S.

COLLEGE OF NURSING:
Nursing. M.S.N.

COLLEGE OF SOCIAL WORK:
Social Work. M.S.W.

VALPARAISO UNIVERSITY
Valparaiso, Indiana 46383-6493
Web site: www.valpo.edu

Founded 1959. Coed. Private control. Lutheran affiliation. Semester system. Library: 714,657 volumes, 16,000 subscriptions.

Tuition: per credit hour $335; Nursing $410; M.B.A. $495. No on-campus housing available. For off-campus information contact Director of Housing. Phone: (219)464-5413.

Graduate Division

Graduate study since 1963. Classes offered in evening and Summer session. Enrollment: full-time 56, part-time 114, Faculty: full-time 20, part-time 5. Degrees conferred: M.A., M.A.L.S., M.Ed., M.M., M.S.N., M.S., Ed.S.

ADMISSION REQUIREMENTS. Official transcripts, interview required in support of application. GRE recommended; required for M.A., M.E., M.S., Ed.S. TOEFL required for international applicants. Accepts transfer applicants. Graduates of unaccredited institutions not considered. Apply to Director of Graduate Studies one month prior to registration for Spring, Summer, and Fall. Application fee $30. Phone: (800)349-2611, (219)464-5313; fax: (219)464-5381.

ADMISSION STANDARDS. Selective. Usual minimum average: 3.0 (A = 4).

FINANCIAL AID. Limited to internships, assistantships, Federal W/S, loans. Approved for VA benefits. Apply to the Office of Financial Aid: no specified closing date. Phone: (800) 348-2611. Use FAFSA.

DEGREE REQUIREMENTS. For M.A.: 30 credit program; practicum; internships. For M.Ed., M.M., M.S.: 30–36 semester hours minimum, at least 24 in residence; no thesis or language requirement. For M.A.L.S.: 42 semester hours minimum, at least 30 in residence; research project. For Ed.S.: 30 credit program beyond master's; special project.

FIELDS OF STUDY.
Business Administration. M.B.A.
Church Music. M.M.
Clinical Mental Health. M.A.
Counseling. M.A.
Deaconess. M.A.L.S.
English. M.A.L.S.
Ethics and Values. M.A.L.S.
History. M.A.L.S.
Human Behavior and Society. M.A.L.S.
Individualized. M.A.L.S.
International Commerce and Policy. M.S.
Learning Disabilities. M.S.
Music. M.M., M.A.L.S.
Nursing. M.S.N.
School Psychology. M.Ed., Ed.S.
Sociology. M.A.L.S.
Special Education. Includes mild disabilities. M.S.
Teaching and Learning. M.Ed.
Theology. M.A.L.S.
Theology and Ministry. M.A.L.S.

School of Law

Founded 1879. ABA approved since 1929. Semester system. Library: 292,051 volumes, 2768 subscriptions; library has LEXIS, NEXIS, WESTLAW, DIALOG, VU/TEXT, QL system.

Annual tuition: full-time $19,452, part-time $15,060. Total average annual additional expense: $7350.

Enrollment: first-year class full-time 126, part-time 15; total full-time 434 (men 54%, women 46%). Faculty: full-time 19, part-time 20. Student to faculty ratio 18.2 to 1. Degrees conferred: J.D., J.D.-M.A. (Psychology), LL.M. (international lawyers).

ADMISSION REQUIREMENTS. LSDAS Law School report, Bachelor's degree, transcripts, LSAT required in support of application. Recommendations strongly suggested. Interview sometimes required. Accepts transfer applicants. Graduates of unaccredited institutions not considered. Apply to Dean by April 15 for priority consideration. Application fee $30. Phone: outside Indiana (888)825-7652, (219)465-7829; fax: (219)465-7872.

ADMISSION STANDARDS. Selective. Mean LSAT: full-time 153, part-time 149; mean GPA: full-time 3.2, part-time 2.91 (A = 4). Gourman rating: 3.60. *U.S. News & World Report* ranking is in the fourth tier of all U.S. law schools. Accepts 50–65% of total annual applicants.

FINANCIAL AID. Scholarships, grants, full and partial tuition waivers, assistantships, Federal W/S, loans. Apply to the Financial Aid Office, preferably before March 1. Use FAFSA (School code: 001842). About 35% of students receive aid other than loans from School.

DEGREE REQUIREMENTS. For J.D. 90 hours, at least 30 in residence; final written exam; 20 hours of pro bono work. For LL.M.: 24 credit hour program.
Note: Summer study abroad in Cambridge (England).

VANDERBILT UNIVERSITY
Nashville, Tennessee 37240-1001
Web site: www.vanderbilt.edu

Founded 1873. CGS member. Coed. Private control. Semester system. Special facilities: Arthritis and Joint Replacement Center, Bill Wilkerson Center for Otolaryngology and Communication Sciences, Center for Baudelaire Studies, Center for Child and Family Policy, Center for Crime and Justice Policy, Center for Entrepreneurship Education, Center for Evaluation Research and Methodology, Center for Environmental Management Studies, Center for Health Policy, Center for Health Services, Center for Innovation in Engineering Education, Center for Intelligent Systems, Center for Latin American and Iberian Studies, Center for Mental Health Policy, Center for Molecular Neuroscience, Center for Molecular Toxicology, Center for Psychotherapy Research and Policy, Center for Space Physiology and Medicine, Center for State and Local Policy, Center for Support of Professional Practice in Education, Center for Teaching, Fine Arts Gallery, Robert Penn Warren Center for the Humanities, Free Electron Laser Center, Informatics Center, Institute for Public Policy Studies, Institute for Software Integrated Systems, John F. Kennedy Center for Research on Education and Human Development, Stevenson Center for Natural Sciences, Arthur J. Dyer Observatory, Vanderbilt Institute for Public Policy Studies. The University's NIH ranking is 26th among all U.S. institutions with 475 awards/grants worth $154,953,933. Library: 2,000,000 volumes. Joint libraries (with George Peabody and Scarritt colleges: 2,000,000 volumes, 21,608 subscriptions. Total University enrollment: 10,000.

Tuition: per credit $1,100. On-campus housing for 140 married students, 110 men, 105 women. Annual housing costs: $5260 single students, $6522 married students. Contact Office of Residential Affairs for both on- and off-campus housing information. Phone: (615)322-2591. Day-care facilities available.

Graduate School

Graduate study since 1875. Enrollment: full-time 1534 (men 50%, women 50%), part-time 125. University faculty: full-time 710. Degrees conferred: M.A., M.S., M.A.T., M.L.A.S., Ph.D.

ADMISSION REQUIREMENTS. Two official transcripts, three letters of recommendation, GRE, statement of purpose required in support of School's application. Interview not required. On-line application available. TOEFL (minimum score 550) required for international applicants. TSE recommended for international applicants wanting to be considered for teaching assistantships. Accepts transfer applicants. Graduates of unaccredited institutions not considered. Apply to Dean of Graduate School by January 15 (Fall), November 1 (Spring), May 1 (Summer). Application fee $40. Phone: (615)343-2727; fax: (615)322-9936.

ADMISSION STANDARDS. Competitive for some departments, selective for others. Usual minimum average: 3.0 (A = 4).

FINANCIAL AID. Fellowships, scholarships, assistantships, research fellowships, assistantships, traineeships, tuition waivers, Federal W/S, loans. Approved for VA benefits. Apply by January 15 to Graduate School for fellowships, assistantships; to Financial Aid Office for all other programs. Use FAFSA. About 70% of students receive aid other than loans from University, 75% from all sources. Aid available for part-time students.

DEGREE REQUIREMENTS. For M.A., M.S.: 24 semester hours minimum; reading knowledge of one foreign language in some programs; thesis/nonthesis option for some departments. For M.A.T: 30–36 semester hours minimum. For Ph.D.: 72 semester hours minimum beyond the Bachelor's degree, at least one year in residence; reading knowledge of one foreign language in some programs; qualifying exam; dissertation; final exam.

FIELDS OF STUDY.
Anthropology.
Art History. Master's only.
Biochemistry. Ph.D. only.
Biological Sciences. Ph.D. only.
Biomedical and Health Sciences.
Biomedical Engineering.
Biomedical Informatics.
Cancer Biology.
Cell and Development Biology.
Cell Biology.
Cellular and Molecular Pathology.
Chemical Engineering.
Chemistry.
Classical Studies.
Comparative Literature.
Computer Science.
Economic Development.
Economics.
Electrical Engineering.
English.
Environmental and Water Resources Engineering.
Environmental Engineering.
French.
Geology. Master's only.
German.
Hearing and Speech Sciences.
History.
Interdisciplinary Materials Science.
Latin American Studies.
Leadership and Organizations. Ph.D. only.
Liberal Arts and Science. Master's only.
Management. Ph.D. only.
Management of Technology.
Materials Science and Engineering.

Mathematics.
Mechanical Engineering.
Molecular Physiology and Biophysics. Ph.D. only.
Neurosciences.
Nursing Science. Ph.D. only.
Pharmacology. Ph.D. only.
Philosophy.
Physics and Astronomy. Includes astronomy (M.S. only).
Political Science.
Portuguese. Master's only.
Psychology. Includes clinical.
Psychology and Human Development.
Religion.
Sociology.
Spanish-Portuguese. Ph.D. only.
Special Education.
Teaching and Learning.

Divinity School

Graduate study since 1875. Coed. Semester system.
Tuition: per credit $682. On-campus housing available.
Enrollment: full- and part-time 154. School faculty teaching professions students: full-time 20, part-time 19. Degrees conferred: M.Div., M.T.S.

ADMISSION REQUIREMENTS. Official transcripts, three letters of recommendation, essay required in support of School's application. TOEFL (minimum score 600) required for international applicants. Interview recommended. Accepts transfer applicants. Apply to Director of Admissions by August I (Fall), December 1 (Spring). Application fee $50. Phone: (615)343-3963; fax: (615)343-9957.

ADMISSION STANDARDS. Selective. Minimum acceptable GPA: 2.9 (A = 4).

FINANCIAL AID. Scholarships, tuition grants, internships, tuition waivers, Federal W/S, loans. Approved for VA benefits. Apply by May 1 to Director of Admissions. Use FAFSA plus CSS Profile.

DEGREE REQUIREMENTS. For M.Div.: 84 credits. For M.T.S.: 51 credits. The M.A. and Ph.D. are offered through the Graduate School.

FIELDS OF STUDY.
Divinity. M.Div.
Theological Studies. M.T.S.

Peabody College of Education and Human Development

Merged with Vanderbilt in 1979. Coed. Semester system. Tuition: per credit $692. Enrollment: full-time 200, part-time 109. College faculty: full-time 97, part-time 45. Degrees conferred: M.S., M.P.P., M.Ed., Ed.S., Ed.D., Ph.D.

ADMISSION REQUIREMENTS. Official transcripts, GRE/MAT required in support of College's application. On-line application available. TOEFL required for international applicants. Interviews required for doctoral programs. Apply to Director of Admissions by February 15 (Fall), November 1 (Spring). Application fee $40. Phone: (615)322-8400; fax: (615)322-8401.

ADMISSION STANDARDS. Very selective for most departments. Usual minimum average: 3.0 for last two years (A = 4).

FINANCIAL AID. Annual awards from institutional funds: scholarships, fellowships, research assistantships, teaching assistantships, internships, grants, traineeships, Federal W/S, loans.

Approved for VA benefits. Apply by May 1 to department chair for fellowships, assistantships; to Director of Financial Aid for all other programs. Phone: (615)322-3591. Use FAFSA and CSS Profile. About 60% of students receive aid from College and outside sources. Aid available for part-time students.

DEGREE REQUIREMENTS. For master's: 30 credit hours minimum, at least 24 in residence; final oral/written exam. For Ed.S.: 30 credit hours minimum beyond the master's, at least one semester in residence; final project. For Ph.D.: 72 credit hours minimum beyond the bachelor's, at least two semesters in full-time residence; qualifying exam; dissertation; proficiency in appropriate research methods; final oral exam. For Ed.D.: essentially the same as Ph.D. except 84 credit hours minimum.

FIELDS OF STUDY.
Curriculum and Instruction.
Early Childhood Education.
Elementary Education.
English Education.
Health Promotion and Education.
Higher Education Administration.
Human Development.
Human Resource Development.
Language and Literacy.
Mathematics Education.
Policy Development and Program Evaluation.
Psychology and Human Development.
School Administration.
Science Education.
Secondary School Teaching.
Social Studies Education.
Special Education.

School of Engineering

Graduate study since 1875. Coed. Semester system.
Tuition: per credit $1100.
Enrollment: full-time 357, part-time 25. School faculty teaching graduate students: full-time 127, part-time 12. Degrees conferred: M.S., M.Eng., Ph.D.

ADMISSION REQUIREMENTS. Official transcripts, letters of recommendation, GRE required in support of application. On-line application available. TOEFL required for international applicants. Interview not required. Accepts transfer applicants. Graduates of unaccredited colleges not considered. Apply to Dean of Graduate School by January 15 (Fall), November 1 (Spring). Application fee $40. Phone: (615)343-3773; fax: (615)343-8006.

ADMISSION STANDARDS. Selective. Usual minimum average: 3.0 (A = 4).

FINANCIAL AID. Fellowships, research assistantships, teaching assistantships, internships, traineeships, Federal W/S, loans. Approved for VA benefits. Apply by January 15 to Dean of the School for fellowships, assistantships; to Financial Aid Office for all other programs. Phone: (615)322-3591; fax: (615)343-8512. Use FAFSA and CSS Profile. Aid available for part-time students.

DEGREE REQUIREMENTS. For M.S., M.E.: 30 semester hours minimum, at least 12 in residence; thesis/research project; final oral exam. For Ph.D.: 72 semester hours, at least 24 credits of course work beyond the master's, at least two semesters in residence; comprehensive exam; dissertation; final oral exam.

FIELDS OF STUDY.
Biomedical Engineering.
Chemical Engineering.

Civil Engineering.
Computer Science.
Electrical and Computer Engineering.
Management of Technology.
Materials Science and Engineering.
Mechanical Engineering.

Owen Graduate School of Management
Web site: mba.vanderbilt.edu

Established 1969. Accredited programs: M.B.A.; recognized Ph.D. Located on main campus, some courses offered in Miami, Florida. Half-semester module system. Special programs: foreign exchange programs with Manchester Business School (England), Ecole Superieure de Sciences Economiques et Commerciales (France), Monterrey Institute of Technology (Mexico), Karlsruhe University (Germany), Norwegian School of Economics and Business (Norway), University of Sao Paulo School of Economics, Management, and Accounting (Brazil), INCAE (Costa Rico), IESA (Venezuela), the Universidad Pontificia Catolica (Chile), and the Copenhagen Business School (Denmark). Library: 44,000 volumes, 1100 subscriptions.

Annual tuition: full-time $29,900, EMBA $31,750, Ph.D. $17,000. Enrollment: total full-time 570 (men 65%, women 35%). Faculty: 37 full-time, 22 part-time; all have Ph.D./D.B.A. Degrees conferred: M.B.A. (full-time only), E.M.B.A. (weekends only, alternating Fridays, Saturdays), I.E.M.B.A. (International Executive, in conjunction with University of Florida), M.B.A.-J.D., M.B.A.-M.A. (Latin American Studies), M.B.A.-M.S.N., M.B.A.-M.T., (Technology, with School of Engineering), Ph.D.

ADMISSION REQUIREMENTS. All applicants should have a bachelor's degree from a recognized institution of higher education and a strong mathematics background. Students are required to have their own personal computer. Contact Owen School of Management for application material and information; phone: MBA (615)322-6469; EMBA (615)322-2513; IEMBA (615)343-4087; Ph.D. (615)343-1989). Early applications are encouraged for both admission and financial aid consideration. Beginning students are admitted Fall only. Both U.S. citizens and international applicants apply by November 30 (first round), January 31 (second round), March 15 (third round), April 15 (fourth round). On-line application available. Submit an application, GMAT (will accept GMAT test results from the last five years, latest acceptable date is March), official transcripts from each undergraduate/graduate school attended, two letters of recommendation, two essays, résumé (prefers at least four years of work experience), and an application fee of $100 to Owen School of Management. In addition, international students (whose native language is other than English) should submit a TOEFL report (minimum score 600), certified translations and evaluations of all official transcripts, recommendation should be in English or with certified translations, proof of health/immunization certificate, and proof of sufficient financial resources for two years of academic study. Interviews required prior to the Admissions Committee reviewing completed application. Joint degree applicants must apply to and be accepted to both schools/programs, contact the admissions office for current information and specific admissions requirements. Rolling admissions process; notification is made within four weeks of receipt of completed application and supporting documents.

ADMISSION REQUIREMENTS FOR DOCTORAL CANDIDATES. Contact Ph.D. Program Administrator, Owen School (phone: (615)343-1989) for application material and information. Applications may be downloaded from Graduate School Web site. Beginning students are admitted Fall Only. Both U.S. citizens and international applicants apply by January 15 (Fall). Submit a Graduate School application, a GMAT/GRE (will accept GMAT/GRE test results from the last five years), two official transcripts from each undergraduate/graduate school attended, three letters of recommendation, résumé, statement of purpose, and application fee of $50 to the Graduate School. In addition, international students (whose native language is other than English) should submit a TOEFL report (minimum score 600), certified translations and evaluations of all official transcripts, recommendation should be in English or with certified translations, proof of health/immunization certificate. Interviews are by invitation for final candidates only. Notification is generally made by mid-April.

ADMISSION STANDARDS. Selective. Mean GMAT: 654; mean GPA: 3.21 (A = 4). Gourman rating: the M.B.A. was rated 4.20; the Ph.D. was rated in the top 50, the score was 4.19. *U.S. News & World Report* ranked Owen in the top 25 of all U.S. business schools. *Business Week* listed Owen in the top 25 of all U.S. business schools. Accepts about 40% of total annual applicants.

FINANCIAL AID. Scholarships, scholar awards, fellowships, graduate assistantships, internships, grants, Federal W/S, loans available. Financial aid may be available for international students in the form of merit-based scholarships. Assistantships/fellowships may be available for joint degree candidates. Financial aid applications and information are generally available at the on-campus visit/interview and are also included with the admission materials, apply by May 1. Contact Owen School's Associate Director for Student Services and Admissions for current need-based financial aid information. Phone: (615)322-6469. Use FAFSA (School code: E00528), also submit CSS Profile, a Financial Aid Transcript, Federal Income Tax forms. Approximately 50% of students receive some form of financial assistance.

DEGREE REQUIREMENTS. For M.B.A.: 60 credit program including 36 elective credits, two-year program; degree program must be completed in six years. For E.M.B.A.: 50 credit, 21-month program. For I.E.M.B.A.: 50 credit, 18-month program. For M.B.A.-M.A., M.B.A.-M.T.: 72 credit programs. For M.B.A.-M.S.N.: 69 credit program. For M.B.A.-J.D.: 151 credit, four-and-one-half- to five-and-one-half-year program. For Ph.D.: three- to five-year program, preliminary exam in a basic discipline or minor area; qualifying exam in major area; research paper; teaching assistantship; dissertation proposal and oral defense; dissertation; oral defense.

FIELDS OF STUDY.
Business Administration. Second year concentrations in accounting, e-commerce, finance, human and organizational performance, information technology, marketing, operations, strategy. M.B.A.
Finance. Ph.D.
Marketing. Ph.D.
Operations Management. Ph.D.
Organization Studies. Ph.D.

School of Law
Web site: www.vanderbilt.edu/law

Established 1874. Located on main campus. ABA approved since 1925. AALS member. Semester system. Full-time, day study only. Special facilities: Vanderbilt Institute for Public Policy Studies, Freedom Forum First Amendment Center. Special programs: Transnational Legal Studies Program; clerkships, internships. Law library: 533,645 volumes, 6173 subscriptions; has LEXIS, NEXIS, WESTLAW, INFOTRAC; is a Federal Government Depository.

Annual tuition: $25,794. On-campus housing available. Apply to Office of Residential and Judicial Affairs. Total average annual additional expense: $15,088.

Enrollment: first-year class 182; total full-time 561 (men 53%, women 47%). Faculty: full-time 30, part-time 25. Student to faculty ratio 15.6 to 1. Degree conferred: J.D., J.D.-M.B.A., J.D.-M.T.S., J.D.-M.Div., LL.M. (for persons who have completed a basic legal education and received a university degree in law in another country). A concurrent M.A. and Ph.D. available through the Graduate School.

ADMISSION REQUIREMENTS. LSDAS Law School report, bachelor's degree, transcripts, three letters of recommendation, LSAT required in support of application. Accepts transfer applicants. Graduates of unaccredited institutions not considered. Apply to Director of Admissions by March 1 (flexible); LL.M. deadline March 1. Application fee $50. Phone: (615)322-6452; fax: (615)322-1531.

ADMISSION REQUIREMENTS FOR LL.M. APPLICANTS. All applicants must have obtained a J.D. (or equivalent) from a U.S. law school or the first (basic) law degree from a foreign law school. Official transcripts (a certified translation and evaluation in addition to original international credentials for international applicants), two letters of recommendation, personal statement required in support of Graduate Programs in Law application. In addition, international candidates whose native language is not English and have attended a law school in a non-English-speaking countries must submit TOEFL. The TSE is strongly encouraged although not required. Admits Fall only. Apply by March 1. Application Fee $50. Phone: (615)322-6452.

ADMISSION STANDARDS. Selective. Mean LSAT: 162; mean GPA: 3.62 (A = 4). Gourman rating: 4.71. *U.S. News & World Report* ranking is in the top 17 of all U.S. law schools. Accepts 10% of total annual applicants.

FINANCIAL AID. Scholarships, loans. Apply to the Office of Financial Aid by February 28 for priority consideration. Use FAFSA (School code: E00529). About 53% of students receive aid other than loans from School.

DEGREE REQUIREMENTS. For J.D.: satisfactory completion of three-year program; 88 semester hour program. For LL.M.: 24 credit full-time program. For master's degree: see Graduate School listing above.

School of Medicine (37232-0685)

Founded 1873. Library: 155,000 volumes; has MEDLINE. Annual tuition: $27,325; student fee $1568. On-campus housing available. Total average cost for all other expenses: $11,000.

Enrollment: first-year class 104 (EDP 5); total 393 (men 60%, women 40%); postgraduates 60. Faculty: full-time 887, part-time 700. Degrees conferred: M.D., M.D.-Ph.D. (Medical Scientist Training Program).

ADMISSION REQUIREMENTS. AMCAS report, transcripts, recommendations, MCAT, bachelor's degree required in suport of application. Interview and final application by invitation only. Has EDP; apply between June 1 and August 1. Apply to AMCAS after June 1, before October 15. Application fee $50. Phone: (615)322-2145; fax: (615)343-8397.

ADMISSION STANDARDS. Very competitive. Mean MCAT: 11.1; mean GPA: 3.74 (A = 4). Gourman rating: 4.65. *U.S. News & World Report* ranking is in the top 16 of all U.S. medical schools. Accepts about 4–6% of total annual applicants. Approximately 7% are state residents.

FINANCIAL AID. Scholarships, fellowships, loans. MSTP funded by NIH. Apply to Assistant Dean, Student Services by June 1. Phone: (615)343-6310. Use FAFSA. About 5% of students receive aid other than loans from School.

DEGREE REQUIREMENTS. For M.D.: satisfactory completion of four-year program. For Ph.D.: see Graduate School listing above.

FIELDS OF GRADUATE STUDY.
Biochemistry.
Biomedical Engineering.
Cell Biology.
Microbiology and Immunology.
Molecular Biology.
Molecular Physiology and Biophysics.
Pathology.
Pharmacology.

VASSAR COLLEGE
Poughkeepsie, New York 12601
Web site: www.vassar.edu

Incorporated 1861. Located 75 miles N of New York City. Coed. Private control. Semester system, Library: 803,000 volumes, 3000 subscriptions. Total College enrollment: 2400.

Total tuition for graduate degree: $24,610; per credit $2900. On-campus housing available. Average academic year housing costs: $7340 (including board). Contact Director of Residential Life for both on- and off-campus housing information. Phone: (845)437-5862. Day-care facilities available.

Graduate Program

Graduate study since 1869. Enrollment: full-time 1, part-time 7. College faculty: 221. Degrees conferred: M.A., M.S.

ADMISSION REQUIREMENTS. Official transcripts, letters of recommendation, interview required in support of application. GRE recommended. TOEFL required for international applicants. Accepts transfer applicants. Graduates of unaccredited institutions not considered. Apply to Chair of appropriate department by April 1. Application fee $60. Phone: (845)437-7000.

ADMISSION STANDARDS. Very competitive.

FINANCIAL AID. Limited to Federal W/S, loans. Use FAFSA, institutional FAF, and CSS Profile. Phone: (845)437-5320; fax: (845)437-5325. About 60% of students receive aid other than loans from College and outside sources. Aid available for part-time students.

DEGREE REQUIREMENTS. For M.A., M.S.: 8 units minimum, at least 6 units in residence; thesis; reading kowledge of one foreign language; final oral/written exam may be required.

FIELDS OF STUDY.
Biology.
Chemistry.

VERMONT LAW SCHOOL
Chelsea Street
South Royalton, Vermont 05506-0096
Web site: www.vermontlaw.edu

Established 1972. Located in a national historic district along the White River. ABA approved since 1975. AALS member. Private control. Coed. Semester system. Full-time, day study only. Special facility: Environmental Law Center. Special program: Law School Exchange Program. Law library: 231,720 volumes, 2461 subscriptions; has LEXIS, NEXIS, WESTLAW, DIALOG; is a U.S. Government Selective Depository.

Annual tuition: $21,033. On-campus housing available for single students only. Contact Business Office for both on- and off-campus housing information. Phone: (802)763-8303. Law students tend to live off-campus. Off-campus housing and personal expenses: approximately $13,902.

Enrollment: first-year class 166; total full-time 501 (men 53%, women 47%); new M.S.E.L. students 25. Faculty: full-time 23, part-time 11. Student to faculty ratio 17.8 to 1. Degrees conferred: J. D., M.S.E.L. (Environmental Law), LL.M. (Environmental Law), J.D.-M.E.S.L.

ADMISSION REQUIREMENTS. LSDAS Law School report, bachelor's degree or equivalent, transcripts, LSAT, recommendations, personal statement required in support of application. Graduates of unaccredited colleges not considered. Apply to Admissions Office by February 1 for priority consideration. Application fee $50. Phone: in Vermont (802)763-8303, ext. 2239; (888)-APPLY-VLS.

ADMISSION STANDARDS. Selective. Mean LSAT: 151; mean GPA: 3.07 (A = 4). Accepts about 30–35% of total applications.

FINANCIAL AID. Scholarships, tuition grants, Federal W/S, loans. Apply to Admissions Office by March 1. Use FAFSA. About 85% of students receive some aid from School.

DEGREE REQUIREMENTS. For J.D.: satisfactory completion of 84 semester hour program. For M.S.E.L., LL.M.: at least 24 credits beyond the J.D.: one year of full-time study.

UNIVERSITY OF VERMONT
Burlington, Vermont 05405-0160
Web site: www.uvm.edu

Founded 1791. Located 95 miles S of Montreal, Canada. CGS member. Coed. State control. Semester system. Library: 1,400,000 volumes, 20,200 subscriptions. The University's NIH ranking is 80th among all U.S. institutions with 153 awards/grants worth $55,926,718. Total University enrollment: 9350.

Tuition: per credit, resident $335, nonresident $838. University on-campus housing for married students and for single students. Average academic year housing costs: $10,000 for single students; $14,500 for married students. Contact Director, Than Allen Housing for both on- and off-campus housing information. Phone: (802)655-0661.

Graduate College

Graduate study since 1807. Enrollment: full- and part-time 1159. Faculty: full-and part-time 361, Degrees conferred: M.A., M.S., M.Ed., M.A.T., M.S.T., M.B.A., M.Ext.Ed., M.P.A., M.S.W., Ed.D., Ph.D.

ADMISSION REQUIREMENTS. Official transcripts, GRE/MAT/GMAT (Business), letters of recommendation required in support of College's application. GRE Subject for some programs. Interview required for some departments. Accepts transfer applicants. Graduates of unaccredited institutions not considered. Apply to Graduate College Admissions Office by April 1, except for Anatomy and Neurobiology, Botany, Field Naturalist Studies, Civil and Environmental Engineering, Communication Services, Counseling, Higher Education and Student Affairs, Microbiology and Molecular Genetics, Public Administration, Social Work, February 1; Cell and Molecular Biology, Pharmacology, Physical Therapy, Psychology, January 1; Curriculum and Instruction, Educational Leadership, Educational Studies, French, Interdisciplinary, Reading and Language Arts, Special Education, August 1; Educational Leadership and Policy Study, May 1; Forestry, Geography, Historic Preservation, Natural Resource Planning, Water Resources, Wildlife and Fisheries Biology,

March 1; March 1 if applying for scholarships and fellowships. Application fee $25. Phone: (802)656-3160; fax: (802)656-0519.

ADMISSION STANDARDS. Very competitive for most departments. Usual minimum average: 3.0 (A = 4).

FINANCIAL AID. Annual awards from institutional funds: fellowships, research assistantships, teaching assistantships, internships, tuition waivers, traineeships, Federal W/S, loans. Approved for VA benefits. Apply by March 1 to the appropriate Chair for fellowships, assistantships; to Office of Financial Aid for all other programs. Phone: (802)656-3156; fax: (802)656-4076. Use FAFSA. Aid available for part-time students.

DEGREE REQUIREMENTS. For M.A., M.S., M.S.T., M.Ed., M.Ext.Ed.: 30 semester hours minimum, at least 22 in residence; thesis/nonthesis option; final oral/written exam. For M.A.T.: same as above, except no thesis. For M.B.A.: 48 semester hours; may be reduced depending upon previous preparation; final written/oral exam. For Ph.D.: 75 semester hours minimum beyond the bachelor's, at least 51 in residence; reading knowledge of one foreign language for some programs; comprehensive exam; dissertation; final oral defense

FIELDS OF STUDY.
Agricultural Biochemistry.
Anatomy and Neurobiology.
Animal and Food Sciences.
Biochemistry.
Biology.
Biomedical Engineering. M.S. only.
Biomedical Technology.
Biostatistics. M.S. only.
Botany.
Business Administration. M.B.A. only.
Cell and Molecular Biology.
Chemistry. One language for M.S.
Civil and Environmental Engineering.
Communication Sciences. M.S. only.
Community Development and Applied Economics.
Computer Science. M.S. only.
Counseling. M.S. only.
Curriculum and Instruction.
Educational Administration and Policy Studies. Ed.D.
Educational Studies.
Electrical Engineering.
Engineering Physics. M.S. only.
English. One language for M.A.; M.A., M.A.T. only.
Extension Education. M.Ext.Ed. only.
Field Naturalist Studies. M.S. only.
Forestry. M.S. only.
French. M.A., M.A.T. only.
Geography. M.A., M.A.T. only.
Geology. M.S., M.A.T., M.S.T. only.
German. M.A., M.A.T. only.
Greek and Latin. M.A., M.A.T. only.
Higher Education and Student Affairs. M.Ed. only.
Historic Preservation. M.S. only.
History. Sample research paper for admission to M.A. M.A., M.A.T. only.
Materials Science.
Mathematical Sciences. Ph.D. only.
Mathematics. M.S. only.
Mechanical Engineering.
Medical Laboratory Science.
Microbiology and Molecular Genetics.
Molecular Physiology and Biophysics.
Movement Sciences and Rehabilitation.
Natural Resource Planning. M.S. only.
Natural Resources. Ph.D. only.
Nursing. M.S. only.

Nutrition and Food Sciences. M.S. only.
Pathology. M.S. only.
Pharmacology.
Physical Therapy.
Physics. M.S. only.
Plant and Soil Science.
Psychology.
Public Administration. M.P.A. only.
Reading and Language Arts.
Social Work. M.S.W. only.
Special Education.
Statistics. M.S. only.
Water Resource. M.S. only.
Wildlife and Fisheries Biology. M.S. only.

College of Medicine

Web site: www.med.uvm.edu

Established in 1822, seventh oldest medical school. Library: 100,000 volumes.

Annual tuition: Vermont resident $20,520; others $35,900, student fees $774. Limited housing available. Total average cost for all other expenses: $12,000.

Enrollment: first-year class 97 (EDP 10); full-time 449 (men 50%, women 50%). Faculty: full- and part-time 892. Degrees conferred: M.D., M.D.-Ph.D.

ADMISSION REQUIREMENTS. AMCAS report, transcripts, MCAT, letters of evaluation required in support of application. Interview by invitation only. Has EDP; apply between June 1 and August 1. Preference given to residents of Vermont, Maine. Apply to Associate Dean for Admission after June 1, before November 1. Application fee $80. Phone: (802)656-2154; fax: (802) 656-8577.

ADMISSION STANDARDS. Competitive. Mean MCAT: 9.27; mean GPA: 3.5 (A = 4). Gourman rating: 3.64. Accepts about 4–6% of all annual applicants. Approximately 33% are state residents.

FINANCIAL AID. Scholarships, merit scholarships, minority scholarships, Grants-in-Aid, UVM 21st-Century Loan Program, HEAL, alternative loan programs, Federal Perkins Loans, Stafford Subsidized and Unsubsidized Loans, Service Commitment Scholarship programs are available. Assistantships/fellowships may be available for M.D.-Ph.D. candidates. Financial aid applications and information are generally available at the on-campus by invitation interview. For scholarships assistance, the selection criteria places heavy reliance on MCAT and undergraduate GPA. Contact the Financial Aid Office for current information. Phone: (802)656-8293. Use FAFSA prior to March 1 (School code: 03696), also submit Financial Aid Transcript, Federal Income Tax forms. Approximately 80% of students receive some form of financial assistance.

DEGREE REQUIREMENTS. For M.D.: satisfactory completion of 45-month program. Taking USMLE Step 1 and Step 2 are optional. For M.D.-Ph.D.: generally a six- to seven-year program.

FIELDS OF GRADUATE STUDY.
Anatomy and Neurobiology.
Biochemistry.
Biophysics.
Cell and Molecular Biology.
Genetics.
Molecular Biology.
Molecular Microbiology and Molecular Genetics.
Molecular Physiology and Biophysics.
Neurosciences.
Pathology.
Pharmacology.

VILLANOVA UNIVERSITY
Villanova, Pennsylvania 19085-1688
Web site: www.villanova.edu

Founded 1843. Located 10 miles W of Philadelphia. CGS member. Coed. Private control. Roman Catholic. Semester system. Library: 1,000,000 volumes, 5338 subscriptions. Total University enrollment: 11,000.

Tuition: per credit Arts $460, Science $520, Nursing $520, Engineering $645, M.B.A. $575. No on-campus housing available. For off-campus housing information, contact housing office. Phone: (610)519-4154.

Graduate School of Liberal Arts and Sciences

Graduate study since 1931. Enrollment: full-time 344, part-time 500 (men 50%, women 50%). Faculty: full-time 210, part-time 46. Degrees conferred: M.A., M.S., Ph.D.

ADMISSION REQUIREMENTS. Two official transcripts required in support of School's application. Recommendations, GRE, interview required for program. TOEFL required for international applicants. Deadlines vary by program. Contact Dean's office for deadlines. Rolling admissions process. Application fee $40. Phone: (610)519-7090; fax: (610)519-7096.

ADMISSION STANDARDS. Competitive for some departments, selective for others. Usual minimum average: 3.0 (A = 4).

FINANCIAL AID. From the University, graduate assistantships, scholarships, fellowships, research assistantships, internships, Federal W/S, loans. Deadline for applications for University aid vary by program. Contact Graduate Dean for specific dates with reference to assistantships, fellowships. Contact Financial Aid Office for all other programs. Phone: (610)519-4010. Use FAFSA and Graduate School FAF. Aid available for part-time students.

DEGREE REQUIREMENTS. For master's: 30–48 semester hours; comprehensive exam; reading knowledge of one foreign language for some majors; thesis/nonthesis option; final oral/written exam. For Ph.D.: 60 semester hours beyond the master's, at least two semesters in residence; qualifying exam, candidacy; dissertation; final oral exam.

FIELDS OF STUDY.
Applied Statistics.
Biology.
Chemistry.
Classical Studies.
Computer Science.
Counseling and Human Relations. Includes community, elementary, secondary.
Criminal Justice Administration.
Elementary Education.
English.
History.
Human Resource Development.
Liberal Studies.
Mathematics.
Philosophy.
Political Science.
Psychology.
Public Administration.
Spanish.
Theater.
Theology.

College of Commerce and Finance

Established 1922, graduate studies since 1982. Accredited programs: M.B.A. Semester system.

Tuition: $575 per credit.

Enrollment: total full-time 97, part-time 715 (men 60%, women 40%). Faculty: 69 full-time, 44 part-time; 94% with Ph.D./D.B.A. Degrees conferred: M.B.A. (full-time, part-time, evening only), M.T. (Taxation), M.B.A.-J.D.

ADMISSION REQUIREMENTS. All applicants should have a bachelor's degree from a recognized institution of higher education. Admission is based on the formula 200 × UGPA + GMAT. Contact College of Commerce at (610)519-4336 for application material and information. Beginning students are admitted Fall, Spring, and Summer. Both U.S. citizens and international applicants apply by June 30 (Fall), November 15 (Spring), April 15 (Summer). Submit an application, GMAT (will accept GMAT test results from the last five years, latest acceptable date is June), official transcripts from each undergraduate/graduate school attended, three letters of recommendation, two essays, personal statement, résumé (prefers at least four years of work experience), and an application fee of $25 to the Office of Graduate Admission. In addition, international students (whose native language is other than English) should submit a TOEFL report (minimum score 600), certified translations and evaluations of all official transcripts, recommendation should be in English or with certified translations, proof of health/immunization certificate, and proof of sufficient financial resources for two years of academic study. On-campus visits are encouraged. Admissions Committee may consider applicants with some academic course work deficiencies. Joint degree applicants must apply to and be accepted to both schools, contact the admissions office for current information and specific admissions requirements. Rolling admissions process; notification is made within four-weeks of receipt of completed application and supporting documents.

ADMISSION STANDARDS. Selective. Usual minimum average: 3.0 (A = 4). Mean GMAT: 560; mean GPA: 3.1 (A = 4).

FINANCIAL AID. Graduate assistantships, Federal Perkins Loans, Stafford Subsidized and Unsubsidized Loans, Federal W/S available. Aid is available for part-time study. Financial aid may be available for international students in the form of graduate assistantships. Assistantships/fellowships may be available for joint degree candidates. Financial aid applications and information are generally included with admissions materials; apply by July 1. Request assistantship information from the College of Commerce. Contact the University's Financial Aid Office for current need-based financial aid information. Phone: (610)519-4010. Use FAFSA (School code: 003368) and PHEAA, also submit Financial Aid Transcript, Federal Income Tax forms. Approximately 10% of students receive some form of financial assistance.

DEGREE REQUIREMENTS. For M.B.A.: 33–48 credit program including 12 elective credits, one- to two-year program; degree program must be completed in ten years. For M.T.: 24 credit program. For M.B.A.-Masters: generally a three-and-one-half- to five-year program. For M.B.A.-J.D.: four-and-one-half- to six-year program.

FIELDS OF STUDY.
Business Administration. Includes concentrations in finance, management, marketing. M.B.A.
Taxation. M.T.

College of Engineering

Tuition: per credit $695.

Enrollment: full-time 72, part-time 371. Faculty: full-time 58, part-time 35. Degrees conferred: M.C.E., M.Ch.E., M.S.C.E., M.S.E.E., M.M.E., M.S.T.E.

ADMISSION REQUIREMENTS. Two official transcripts, GRE required in support of College's application. On-line application

available. TOEFL required for international applicants. Accepts transfer applicants. Graduates of unaccredited institutions not considered. Apply to Director of Admissions; no specified closing date. Rolling admissions process. Application fee $25. Phone: (610) 519-4940; fax: (610)519-4941.

ADMISSION STANDARDS. Selective. Usual minimum average: 3.0 (A = 4).

FINANCIAL AID. Scholarships,research assistantships, teaching assistantships, Federal W/S, loans. Approved for VA benefits. Apply to Dean for assistantships, to Financial Aid Office for all other programs. Phone: (610)519-4010. Use FAFSA and institutional FAF.

DEGREE REQUIREMENTS. For master's: 30–36 hours; thesis/nonthesis option; comprehensive exam.

FIELDS OF STUDY.
Chemical Engineering.
Civil Engineering.
Computer Engineering.
Electrical Engineering.
Mechanical Engineering.
Transportation Engineering.
Water Resources and Environmental Engineering.

School of Law

Founded 1953. ABA approved since 1954. AALS member. Semester system. Special facility: Center for Information Law and Policy. Law library: 458,470 volumes, 3322 subscriptions, 139 computer workstations; has LEXIS, NEXIS, WESTLAW, DIALOG.

Annual tuition: $21,230. No on-campus housing available. Contact Student Bar Association in June for current off-campus housing lists. Total average cost for all other expenses: $15,085.

Enrollment: first-year class 251; total full-time 725 (men 54%, women 46%); no part-time, summer, or evening study. Faculty: full-time 30, part-time 33. Student to faculty ratio 20.1 to 1. Degrees conferred: J.D., J.D.-M.B.A., J.D.-Ph.D. (Law and Psychology), LL.M. (Taxation).

ADMISSION REQUIREMENTS. LSDAS Law School report, bachelor's degree, transcripts, LSAT required in support of application. Interview not required. Transfer applicants considered for admission into second-year class; one full year of superior work at another accredited/approved law school is required. Graduates of unaccredited colleges not considered. Apply to Admissions Office after September 1, before March 1. Application fee $75. Phone: (610)519-7010; fax: (610)519-6291.

ADMISSION STANDARDS. Selective. Mean LSAT: 156; mean GPA: 3.34 (A = 4). Gourman rating: 3.70. *U.S. News & World Report* ranking is in the second tier of all U.S. law schools. Accepts 60% of total annual applicants.

FINANCIAL AID. Scholarships, special minority scholarships, partial tuition waivers, resident assistantships, counselorships, Federal W/S, loans. For resident assistantships, apply to Dean of Residence Life. Apply to Financial Aid Office by March 1 for all other programs. Use FAFSA (School code: E00428). About 20% of students receive aid from Law School sources.

DEGREE REQUIREMENTS. For J.D.: satisfactory completion of three-year program; 87 semester hour program. For LL.M.: at least 24 credits beyond the J.D.: one year in full-time residence.

College of Nursing

Tuition: per credit $520.

Enrollment: full-time 43, part-time 97. Faculty: full-time 30, part-time 4. Degree conferred: M.S.N.

ADMISSION REQUIREMENTS. Two official transcripts, GRE required in support of College's application. TOEFL required for international applicants. Accepts transfer applicants. Graduates of unaccredited institutions not considered. Apply to Director of Admissions by July 1 (Fall), December 1 (Spring). Rolling admissions process. Application fee $25. Phone: (610)519-4907; fax: (610)519-7650.

ADMISSION STANDARDS. Selective. Usual minimum average: 3.0 (A = 4).

FINANCIAL AID. Assistantships, scholarships, traineeships, Federal W/S, loans. Approved for VA benefits. Apply by March 1 to Dean for assistantships; to Financial Aid Office for all other programs. Phone: (610)519-4010. Use FAFSA and institutional FAF. Aid available for part-time students.

DEGREE REQUIREMENTS. For master's: 30–36 semester hours; thesis; comprehensive exam.

FIELDS OF STUDY.
Clinical Case Management.
Community Nurse Service Administration.
Nursing Administration.
Staff Administration.
Teaching of Nursing.

VIRGINIA COMMONWEALTH UNIVERSITY

Richmond, Virginia 23284-3051
Web site: www.vcu.edu

Founded 1838. University formed with merger of Richmond Professional Institute and Medical College of Virginia in 1968. Coed. State control. Semester system. Special facilities: Anderson Art Gallery, Burn Trauma Clinic, Institute of Biotechnology, Business Management Center, Massey Cancer Center, Sickle Cell Anemia Center, Institute of Statistics, Virginia Center on Aging, Virginia Center for Public/Private Initiative, Virginia Institute for Developmental Disabilities. The University's NIH ranking is 78th among all U.S. institutions with 205 awards/grants worth $57,041,992. Library: 1,500,000 volumes, 10,000 subscriptions. Total University enrollment: 24,000.

Annual tuition: resident $5254, nonresident $13,327; per credit resident $270, nonresident $719. Limited on-campus housing for graduate students. Average academic year housing costs: $3500–$5000. Contact Director of residence Life for both on- and off-campus hosing information. Phone: (804)828-7666.

School of Graduate Studies

Enrollment: full-time 2332, part-time 3349. Faculty: full-time 775. Degrees conferred: M.A., M.Acc., M.A.E., M.B.A., M.Ed., M.F.A., M.H.A., M.I.S., M.M., M.P.A., M.P.H., M.S., M.S.H.A., M.S.N.A., M.S.O.T., M.S.W., M.Tax., M.T., M.U.R.P., Ph.D., J.D.-M.H.A., J.D.-M.U.R.P., J.D.-M.S.W., M.S.-D.D.S., M.S.-M.D., Pharm.D., Ph.D., Ph.D.-D.D.S., Ph.D.-M.D., Ph.D.-Pharm.D., C.Acc., C.A.S., C.A.S.R., C.C.S., C.C.J.A., C.I.S., C.P.I., C.P.C., C.P.M., C.T.

ADMISSION REQUIREMENTS. Transcripts, GRE/GMAT/MAT required in support of School's application. TOEFL required for international applicants. Accepts transfer applicants. Graduates of unaccredited institutions not considered. Apply to Director of Admissions. Application deadlines vary by program. Application fee $25. Phone: (804)828-6916; fax: (804)828-6949; e-mail: vcu-grad@vcu.edu.

ADMISSION STANDARDS. Selective. Minimum acceptable GPA: 2.7 (A = 4).

FINANCIAL AID. Annual awards from institutional funds: teaching/research assistantships, full and partial tuition waivers, Federal W/S, loans. Approved for VA benefits. Apply to appropriate department chair for assistantships, fellowships; to Financial Aid Office for all other aid; no specified closing dates. Phone: (804)828-6669; fax: (804)828-6187. Use FAFSA. About 15% of students receive aid other than loans from University and outside sources. Aid available for part-time students.

DEGREE REQUIREMENTS. Vary by program.

FIELDS OF STUDY.
Accountancy. M.Acc.
Administration and Supervision. Includes administration, supervision, dual major in administration and supervision. M.Ed.
Administration of Justice. M.S.
Adult Education. M.Ed.
Aging Studies. C.A.S.
Anatomy. M.S., Ph.D. Includes orthopedic physical therapy track in anatomy. Ph.D.
Applied Social Research.
Art Education. M.A.E.
Art History. Includes architectural history, historical studies, museum studies. M.A., Ph.D.
Biochemistry. Includes biotechnology track in biochemistry and molecular biophysics. M.S., Ph.D.
Biology. Includes molecular, cellular, and environmental biology; systematics and evolution; physiology and developmental biology. M.S.
Biomedical Engineering. M.S., Ph.D.
Biostatistics. M.S., Ph.D.
Business. Includes decision sciences, economics, finance, information systems, marketing, human resources management, industrial relations, realestate and urban land development, risk management and insurance. M.S.
Business. Ph.D.
Business Administration. Generalist and specialization. M.B.A.
Chemistry. Includes analytical, inorganic, organic, physical, M.S., Ph.D.; chemical physics track, Ph.D.
Clinical Laboratory Sciences. Advanced master's, C.A.S., M.S.
Computer Science. C.C.S., M.S.
Counselor Education. Includes classroom guidance, guidance/counseling, dual certificate in counselor and visiting teacher. M.Ed.
Crafts. Includes ceramics, furniture design, glassworking, jewelry or metalworking, textiles. M.F.A.
Creative Writing. Includes fiction, poetry. M.F.A.
Curriculum and Instruction. Includes instructional technology, library, media; early, middle, and secondary education. M.Ed.
Design. Interior environments, photography/film, visual communications. M.F.A.
Economics. Includes general, financial. M.A.
English. Includes literature, writing, and rhetoric. M.A.
Genetic Counseling. M.S.
Gerontology. M.S.
Health Administration. Executive master's, M.S.H.A.
Health Services Administration. Includes hospitals/hospital systems, long-term care facilities, health planning and policy/institutional settings, other areas by permission of graduate program director. M.H.A.
Health Services Organization and Research. Major: health services education, management/information systems, organizational behavior, organizational policy/planning; minor: administration problem areas, health specialty areas. Ph.D.
History. M.A.
Human Genetics. M.S., Ph.D.
Information System. C.I.S.
Interdisciplinary Studies. M.I.S.
Mathematical Sciences. Includes applied mathematics, mathematics, operations research, statistics. M.S.
Mathematics Education. M.Ed.

Media Management, Professional Journalism and Advertising. M.S.

Medicinal Chemistry. Includes organic medicinal chemistry, pharmaceutical analysis, physical medicinal chemistry M.S., Ph.D.

Microbiology and Immunology. Includes biotechnology track in biochemistry and microbiology/immunology. M.S., Ph.D.

Music. Includes composition, education, performance, conducting. M.M.

Nurse Anesthesia. M.S.N.A. Also advanced M.S.N.A. for Certified Registered Nurse Anesthetist. M.S.

Nurse Practitioner. Includes adult health (generalist or immunocompetence), child health, family health, women's health. Post Master's Certificate.

Nursing. Includes adult health (generalist or immunocompetence), child health, family health, psychiatric mental health, women's health; M.S. Biology of health and illness, human health and illness, nursing systems; Ph.D.

Nursing Administration. Includes clinical nurse manager, nurse executive, psychiatric mental health, women's health. M.S.

Occupational Therapy Professional. M.S.O.T.

Occupational Therapy Post-Professional. Includes administration, education, gerontology, hand management, pediatrics, physical disabilities, psychosocial dysfunction. M.S.

Painting and Printmaking. M.F.A.

Pathology. M.S., Ph.D.

Patient Counseling.

Pharmacology and Toxicology. M.S., Ph.D.

Pharmacy and Pharmaceutics. Includes Pharmaceutical analysis pharmaceutics, pharmacy administration. M.S., Ph.D.

Physical Education. M.S.

Physical Therapy-Entry Level. (three-year professional) M.S.

Physical Therapy. Includes advanced, orthopedic physical therapy, kinesiology and biomechanics, hand management, neurology, physical therapy, pediatric physical therapy.

Physics. Includes instrumentation, physics of materials, physics research. M.S.

Physiology. M.S., Ph.D.

Planning Information Systems. C.P.I.

Pre-Medical Basic Sciences. Includes anatomy, biochemistry, human genetic, microbiology, pharmacology, physiology. Post Baccalaureate/Graduate Certificate.

Professional Counseling. C.P.C.

Psychology. Includes clinical, counseling, general. Ph.D.

Public Administration. M.P.A., Ph.D.

Public Health. M.P.H.

Public Management. C.P.M.

Reading. M. Ed.

Recreation, Parks, and Tourism. M.S.

Rehabilitation Counseling. Includes alcohol and drug education/rehabilitation program, community resources utilization and development, correctional rehabilitation, individual and group counseling, mental health rehabilitation, services to the severely physically handicapped, vocational evaluation and work adjustment. M.S.

Sculpture. M.F.A.

Social Work. Includes clinical social work practice, social work planning, and administrative practice. M.S.W., Ph.D.

Sociology. M.S.

Special Education. Includes early childhood, emotional disturbance, learning disabilities, mentally retardation, severe/profound disabilities. M. Ed.

Taxation. Includes academic, professional; M.Tax.

Teaching. Five-year program combining undergraduate and graduate study. Includes early education NK-4, middle education 4-8, secondary education 8-12, special education. M.T.

Theater. Acting, costume design, directing, stage design/technical theater, theater education. M.F.A.

Urban and Regional Planning. Includes economic development, environmental planning, housing and community planning, physical land use planning, planning management, urban revitalization. M.U.R.P.

Urban Revitalization Planning Information. C.U.R.P.

Urban Services. Includes adult education and training, educational leadership, instructional leadership, urban services leadership. Ph.D.

Cooperative Program with Presbyterian School of Christian Education. First year spent at PSCE, second year at VCU in the M.S.W. program for M.A. of Christian Education. An additional year at VCU leads to the M.S.W. degree.

Counselor Education. D.Ed. awarded by the College of William & Mary.

Dual Degree Program in Law and Health Administration with the T. C. William Law School of the University of Richmond. J.D.-M.H.A.

Dual Degree Program in Law and Social Work with the T. C. Williams Law School of the University of Richmond. J.D.-M.S.W.

Dual Degree Program in Law and Urban Planning with the T. C. William Law School of the University of Richmond. J.D.-M.U.R.P.

Engineering Program. M.E. awarded by the University of Virginia and either M.S. or M.E. by Virginia Polytechnic Institute and State (University, Old Dominican University, George Mason University, and Mary/Washington College.

Interdisciplinary Studies with Virginia State University. M.I.S.

MEDICAL COLLEGE OF VIRGINIA CAMPUS OF VIRGINIA COMMONWEALTH UNIVERSITY

P.O. Box 980565
Richmond, Virginia 23298-0565

Founded 1838. University formed with merger of Richmond Professional Institute and Medical College of Virginia in 1968. Public control. Semester system. Special facilities: Burn Trauma Clinic, Institute of Biotechnology, Center for Drug and Alcohol Studies, Massey Cancer Center, Sickle Cell Anemia Center, Transplant Center, Virginia Center of Aging. Library: 600,000 volumes, 2200 subscriptions.

On-campus rooms and apartments available for both single and married students. Annual on-campus living, transportation and personal expenses: $16,525. Contact Admissions Office for both on- and off-campus housing information. Medical students may live off-campus. Off-campus housing and personal expenses: approximately $16,000.

Graduate Studies

Graduate study since 1934 and is now under the School of Medicine's administrative authority. Annual tuition/fees: full-time resident $9743, nonresident $18,811; per credit resident $536, nonresident $1040.

Enrollment: full-time 248, part-time 99. Graduate faculty: full-time 190, part-time 0. Degrees conferred: M.P.H., M.S., Ph.D., M.D.-Ph.D., Specialized Master's, Certificates.

ADMISSION REQUIREMENTS. Transcripts, three letters of recommendation, interview (for most departments), GRE Subject Tests required in support of application. On-line application available. TOEFL required of all international applicants. Accepts transfer applicants. Graduates of unaccredited institutions not considered. Apply to the Office of Graduate Education by April 1 (Fall). Admits Fall only. Application fee $30. Phone: (804)828-1023; fax: (804)828-1473.

ADMISSION STANDARDS. Competitive for most departments. Usual minimum average: 2.75 (A = 4).

FINANCIAL AID. Scholarships, NIH traineeships, fellowships, research assistantships, teaching assistantships, internships, Federal W/S, loans. Approved for VA benefits. Apply to Office of Dean for assistantships, fellowships, to Financial Aid Office for all other programs. No specified closing date. Phone: (804)828-0523; fax: (804)828-2703. Use FAFSA. About 75% of students receive aid other than loans from School and outside sources.

DEGREE REQUIREMENTS. For master's: one year minimum in residence; thesis; final exam. For Ph.D.: two years in residence beyond the master's; comprehensive written; advancement to candidacy; dissertation; final oral exam.

FIELDS OF STUDY.
Anatomy.
Biochemistry.
Biostatistics.
Genetic Counseling. M.S.G.C.
Human Genetics.
Immunology.
Microbiology and Immunology.
Molecular Biology and Genetics.
Neuroscience.
Pathology.
Pharmacology.
Physiology.
Public Health. M.P.H.
Structural Biology.

School of Dentistry (23298-0566)

Established 1893. Located at the Health Sciences complex. State supported.

Annual tuition: resident $9385, nonresident $22,756. Total average cost for all other first-year expenses: $7400. On-campus housing for married and single students. Average academic year housing costs: $13,620 Phone: (804)282-7666.

Enrollment: first-year class 83, total 320 (men 65%, women 35%); postgraduates 51. School faculty: full-time 74, part-time 111. Degrees conferred: D.D.S., D.D.S.-M.S., D.D.S.-Ph.D.

ADMISSION REQUIREMENTS. AADSAS report, transcripts, DAT (no later than October), recommendations, interview required in support of School's application. Applicants must have completed at least 90 semester hours of college study, School prefers 120 semester hour applicants. Interview by invitation only. Accepts transfer applicants. Preference given to state residents. Apply to Director of Admissions after June 1, before November 1. Application fee $70. Phone: (804)828-9196.

ADMISSION STANDARDS. Selective. Mean DAT: Academic 18, PAT 17; mean GPA: 3.38 (A = 4). Gourman rating: 4.15. Accepts about 25–30% of total annual applicants. Approximately 85% are state residents.

FINANCIAL AID. Limited. Apply to Financial Aid officer of School; no specified closing date. Phone: (804)828-9196. Use FAFSA (School code: 003735). Approximately 76% of class receives some form of financial assistance.

DEGREE REQUIREMENTS. For D.D.S.: satisfactory completion of four-year program, least two years in residence. For D.D.S.-M.S.: satisfactory completion of four to five year program. For D.D.S.-Ph.D.: satisfactory completion of six to seven year program. Offered jointly with School of Graduate Studies.

FIELDS OF GRADUATE STUDY.
Dental Anesthesia.
Endodontics.
General Dentistry.
Oral and Maxillofacial Surgery.
Oral Pathology.
Orthodontics.
Pediatric Dentistry.
Periodontics.
Prosthodontics.

School of Medicine (23298-0565)

Established 1838 as a medical department at Hampden-Sidney College, became Medical College of Virginia in 1954, a totally independent institution. Located near the financial and governmental areas of downtown. The basic medical sciences are included in the first two years. Special facility: Medical College of Virginia Clinical Research Center.

Annual tuition: resident $11,062, nonresident $28,360; fees $1282.

Enrollment: first-year class 180 (EDP 10); total full-time 682 (men 53%, women 47%). Faculty: full-time 765, part-time/ volunteers 1350. Degrees conferred: M.D., M.D.-M.P.H., M.D.-Ph.D.

ADMISSION REQUIREMENTS. AMCAS report, transcripts, MCAT, recommendations, interview required in support of application. Applicants must have completed at least 90 hours of college study. Interview by invitation only. Preference given to state residents. Accepts transfer applicants. Has EDP; apply between June 1 and August 1. Apply to AMCAS after June 1, before November 15. Application fee $80. Phone: (804)828-9629; fax: (804)828-1246.

ADMISSION STANDARDS. Competitive. Mean MCAT: 9.6; mean GPA: 3.47 (A = 4). Gourman rating: 3.08. Accepts 5–8% of total annual applicants. Approximately 70% are state residents.

FINANCIAL AID. Scholarships, fellowships, loans, Federal W/S. Apply to Financial Aid Office (phone: (804)828-4006) of the School for scholarships, to Dean of the School for fellowships by September 1. Use FAFSA (School code: 003735). About 55% of students receive aid other than loans from school.

DEGREE REQUIREMENTS. For M.D.: satisfactory completion of four-year program, at least final two years in residence; all students must take USMLE Step 1 and Step 2 and record a score. See Graduate Division entry for Ph.D. requirements.

School of Nursing

Master's study since 1968; doctoral study since 1986. Located at the Health Sciences complex.

Annual tuition/fees: full-time resident $9743, nonresident $18,801; per credit, resident $536, nonresident $1040. Enrollment: full-time 104, part-time 134. Graduate faculty: full-time 36, part-time 4; volunteers 65. Degrees conferred: M.S., Ph.D.

ADMISSION REQUIREMENTS. Official transcripts, personal statement, GRE, nursing license, B.S. in nursing from a NLN accredited school, three references required in support of School's application. TOEFL (minimum score 550) required of international applicants. Graduates of foreign nursing schools who are licensed outside the United States are required to pass the Qualifying Exam of the Commission on Graduates of Foreign Nursing Schools prior to application and include the exam report with their application materials. Accepts transfer applicants. Graduates of unaccredited institutions not considered. Apply by February 1 to School of Graduate Studies. Application fee $30. Phone: (804)282-5171; fax (804)282-7743.

ADMISSION STANDARDS. Competitive. Usual minimum average: 3.0 (A = 4).

FINANCIAL AID. Annual awards from institutional funds. Scholarships, fellowships, grants, teaching assistantships, internships, Federal W/S, loans. Apply by May 1 to the Office of Enrollment Services. Phone: (804)828-5171. Use FAFSA and institutional FAF. About 68% of students receive aid other than loans from both School and outside sources.

DEGREE REQUIREMENTS. For M.S.: 36–48 semester credits minimum (up to 12 approved credits may be transferred), qualifying exam; clinical experience; thesis option. For Ph.D.: 60 credits minimum (up to 15 approved credits may be transferred); qualifying exam; dissertation; oral exam.

FIELDS OF STUDY.
Adult Health. Includes acute care, primary care. Post-master's certificate.
Adult Health Nursing. Includes acute care nursing, primary care nursing. M.S.
Child Health. Post-master's certificate.
Child Health Nursing. M.S.
Clinical Nurse Manager. Post-master's certificate.
Family Health. Certificate.
Family Health Nursing. M.S.
Healing. Ph.D.
Immunocompetence. Ph.D.
Nurse Executive. Post-master's certificate.
Nursing Systems—Clinical Nurse Manager. M.S.
Nursing Systems—Nurse Executive. M.S.
Psychiatric Mental Health Nursing. M.S. Post-master's certificate.
Risk and Resilience. Ph.D.
Women's Health. Post-master's certificate.
Women's Health Nursing. M.S.

VIRGINIA POLYTECHNIC INSTITUTE AND STATE UNIVERSITY
Blacksburg, Virginia 24061-0325
Web site: www.vt.edu

Founded 1872. Located 40 miles W of Roanoke. CGS member. Coed. State control. Semester system. Library: 2,000,000 volumes, 18,000 subscriptions.

Annual tuition: full-time resident $5539, nonresident $8774; part-time, per semester minimum resident $923, nonresident $1462. Limited on-campus housing. Average academic year housing costs: $1090 (room only) single students. Contact Manager, Campus Housing, for both on- and off-campus housing information. Phone: (540)231-6204.

Graduate School
Web site: www.grad.vt.edu

Enrollment: full-time 3875, part-time 2272 (men 65%, women 35%). Faculty: full-time 1500. Degrees conferred: M.A., M.Acc., M.B.A., M.F., M.F.A., M.A.Ed., M.S.Ed., M.Arch., M.A.I.S., M.S., M.S.L.F.S., M.Engr., M.P.A., M.I.S., M.L.A., M.U.A., M.U.R.P., C.A.G.S., Ed.D., Ph.D.

ADMISSION REQUIREMENTS. Official transcripts, three letters of recommendation required in support of application. On-line application available. GRE/GMAT, interview required for some departments. GRE/Subject Tests strongly recommended. TOEFL (minimum score 550) and GRE required for international applicants. Accepts transfer applicants. Graduates of unaccredited colleges not considered. Apply to School by January 15 (for Financial Aid consideration), or at least two months prior to registration; May 15 (Fall), October 15 (Spring) for international applicants. Application fee $45. Phone: (540)231-6691; fax: (540)231-3714.

ADMISSION STANDARDS. Very selective for many departments. Usual minimum average: 3.0, 2.7 for provisional (A = 4).

FINANCIAL AID. Annual awards from institutional funds: scholarships, fellowships, teaching/research assistantships, internships, tuition waivers, Federal W/S, loans. Approved for VA benefits. Apply to appropriate department chairman for scholarships, fellowships, assistantships; to Financial Aid Office for all other programs. Phone: (540)231-5179. Use FAFSA. About 60% of students receive aid other than loans from School and outside sources. Aid available for part-time students.

DEGREE REQUIREMENTS. For master's: 30 semester hours minimum, at least 24 in residence; thesis/nonthesis option; final oral/written exam. For C.A.G.S.: 30 semester hours beyond the master's; final written exam. For Ph.D.: 90 semester hours minimum beyond the bachelor's, at least 30 in full-time attendance; reading knowledge of one foreign language in some departments; preliminary exam; dissertation; final oral/written exam. For Ed.D.: essentially the same as for the Ph.D., except no language requirement.

FIELDS OF STUDY.

COLLEGE OF AGRICULTURE AND LIFE SCIENCES:
Agriculture and Applied Economics. M.S.
Animal and Dairy Science. Ph.D.
Animal and Poultry Sciences. M.S., Ph.D.
Biochemistry. M.S.L.F.S., Ph.D.
Crop and Soil Environmental Sciences. M.S., Ph.D.
Dairy Science. M.S.
Economics in Agricultural and Life Sciences. Ph.D.
Entomology. M.S.L.F.S., Ph.D.
Food Science and Technology. M.S.L.F.S., Ph.D.
Horticulture. M.S., Ph.D.
Plant Pathology, Physiology, and Weed Science. M.S.L.F.S., Ph.D.

COLLEGE OF ARCHITECTURE AND URBAN STUDIES:
Architecture. M.Arch., M.S.
Environmental Design and Planning. Ph.D.
Landscape Architecture. M.L.A.
Public Administration and Public Affairs. M.P.A., Ph.D.
Public and International Affairs. M.P.I.A.
Urban and Regional Planning. M.U.R.P., Ph.D.

COLLEGE OF ARTS AND SCIENCES:
Biology. M.S., Ph.D.
Biochemistry. M.S.L.F.S., Ph.D.
Chemistry. M.S., Ph.D.
Computer Science and Applications. M.S., Ph.D.
Economics, Arts, and Science. M.A., Ph.D.
English. M.A.
Geography. M.S.
Geological Sciences. M.S., Ph.D.
History. M.A.
Mathematics. M.S., Ph.D.
Philosophy. M.A.
Physics. M.S., Ph.D.
Political Science. M.A.
Psychology. M.S., Ph.D.
Science and Technology Studies. M.S., Ph.D.
Sociology. M.S., Ph.D.
Statistics. M.S., Ph.D.
Theatre Arts. M.F.A.

PAMPLIN COLLEGE OF BUSINESS:
Accounting and Information Systems. M.A.I.S., Ph.D.
Business Administration. M.B.A., M.S., Ph.D.
Business Management Science. M.S., Ph.D.
Finance, Insurance and Business Law. M.S., Ph.D.
Hospitality and Tourism Management. M.S., Ph.D.
Management. M.S., Ph.D.
Marketing. M.S., Ph.D.

COLLEGE OF ENGINEERING:
Aerospace Engineering. M.S., M.Eng., Ph.D.
Biological Systems Engineering. M.S., M.Eng., Ph.D.
Chemical Engineering. M.S., M.Eng., Ph.D.
Civil Engineering. M.S., M.Eng., Ph.D.
Computer Engineering. M.S., Ph.D.
Electrical Engineering. M.S., Ph.D.
Engineering Mechanics. M.S., M.Eng., Ph.D.
Environmental Engineering. M.S., M.Eng.
Environmental Sciences and Engineering. M.S.
Industrial and Systems Engineering. M.S., M.Eng., Ph.D.
Materials Science and Engineering. M.S., M.Eng., Ph.D.
Mechanical Engineering. M.S., M.Eng., Ph.D.
Mining Engineering. M.S., M.Eng., Ph.D.
Ocean Engineering. M.S., M.Eng.
Systems Engineering. M.S., M.Eng.

COLLEGE OF HUMAN SCIENCES AND EDUCATION:
Clothing and Textiles. M.S., Ph.D.
Education, Career, and Technical Education. M.S.Ed., Ph.D., Ed.D., Ed.S.
Education—Counselor Education. M.A.Ed., Ph.D., Ed.D., Ed.S.
Education—Curriculum and Instruction. M.A.Ed., Ph.D., Ed.D., Ed.S.
Education—Education Research, Evaluation. Ph.D.
Education—Health and Physical Education. M.S.Ed.
Education—Leadership and Policy. M.A.Ed., Ed.D., Ed.S., Ph.D.
Education—Special Education Administration. Ed.S., Ed.D., Ph.D.
Housing, Interior Design, Resource Management. M.S., Ph.D.
Human Development. M.S., Ph.D.
Human Nutrition, Foods, and Exercise. M.S., Ph.D.

COLLEGE OF NATURAL RESOURCES:
Fisheries and Wildlife Sciences. M.S., Ph.D.
Forestry. M.S., M.F., Ph.D.
Forest Products. M.S., M.F., Ph.D.

VIRGINIA—MARYLAND REGIONAL COLLEGE OF VETERINARY MEDICINE:
Veterinary Medical Sciences. M.S., Ph.D.

INTERDISCIPLINARY DEGREES:
Genetics, Bioinformatics, and Computational Biology. Ph.D.
Information Technology. M.I.T., M.S., Ph.D.
Macromolecular Science and Engineering. M.S., Ph.D.

Virginia–Maryland Regional College of Veterinary Medicine (24061-0443)

Web site: www.vetmed.vt.edu

Annual tuition: full-time resident $8912, nonresident $22,136. Annual housing cost: $10,000–$14,000.

Enrollment: first-year class 80; total full-time 300 (men 45%, women 55%). College faculty: full-time 90. Degrees conferred: D.V.M., D.V.M.-M.S., D.V.M.-Ph.D.

ADMISSION REQUIREMENTS. VMCAS report (nonresidents), transcripts, GRE, Advanced Biology, three recommendations, animal/veterinary experience required in support of application. Interview by invitation only. Applicants must have completed at least two years of college study. Preference given to state (50 positions), Maryland (30 positions), and Delaware (3 positions) residents; remaining 7–10 for nonresidents. Apply to the Office of Student Services after September 1, before November 15. Application fee $45. Phone: (540)231-4699; fax: (540) 231-9290.

ADMISSION STANDARDS. Selective. Usual minimum GPA: 2.8 (A = 4). Mean GRE: 1850 (verbal plus quantitative plus analytical). Accepts 25–30% of total annual applicants.

FINANCIAL AID. Scholarships, fellowships, assistantships, loans. Apply to Financial Aid Office before February 1. Use FAFSA.

DEGREE REQUIREMENTS. For D.V.M.: satisfactory completion of four-year program. For M.S. and Ph.D.: see Graduate School listing above.

FIELDS OF STUDY.
Veterinary Medical Sciences. Interdisciplinary. Includes applied physiology, pharmacology and structural biology, biotechnology applications and genetic diseases, environmental medicine and toxicology, epidemiology and public health risk analysis and food safety, immunodulation and endocrinology, molecular biology of disease agents and vectors, nutritional animal growth and well-being, vaccine development for infectious diseases. M.S., Ph.D.

VIRGINIA STATE UNIVERSITY

Petersburg, Virginia 23806-0001
Web site: www.vsu.edu

Founded 1882. Located 25 miles S of Richmond. Coed. State Control. Semester system. Library: 282,500 volumes, 1150 subscriptions.

Annual tuition/fees: full-time resident $4890, nonresident $10,388; per credit resident $143, nonresident $460. On-campus housing available for single students only. Average academic year housing costs: $5694 (including board) for single students. Contact Dean of Students Office for both on- and off-campus housing information. Phone: (804)524-5862.

School of Graduate Studies

Enrollment: full-time 52, part-time 828. College faculty teaching graduate students: full-time 44, part-time 5. Degrees conferred: M.A., M.S., M.Ed., M.I.S., C.A.G.S.

ADMISSION REQUIREMENTS: Two official transcripts, GRE required in support of application. TOEFL required for international applicants. Accepts transfer applications. Apply to Graduate School by August 1 (Fall), November 1 (Spring). Application Fee $25. Phone: (804)524-5984; fax: (804)524-5104.

ADMISSION STANDARDS. Selective. Usual minimum average: 2.6 (A = 4) for unconditional admission.

FINANCIAL AID. Annual awards from institutional funds. Fellowships, asistantships, Federal W/S, loans. Approved for VA benefits. Apply by March 1 to Financial Aid Office. Phone: (804) 524-5990; fax: (804)524-6818. Use FAFSA. About 10% of students receive aid other than from University and outside sources.

DEGREE REQUIREMENTS. For M.A., M.S.: 24–27 semester hours minimum; thesis for 3–6 hours, 21 semester hours in residence. For M.Ed.: 33 hours including project or 36 hours including statistics and research; comprehensive examination. For C.A.C.S.: 30 semester hours beyond the master's.

FIELDS OF STUDY.
Administration and Supervision. Ed.D. only.
Biology.
Counselor Education.
Economics.
Education. Includes elementary education, educational technology, special education.
Educational Administration and Supervision.
English.

History.
Interdisciplinary Studies.
Mathematics.
Physics.
Psychology.
Vocational and Technical Education.

UNIVERSITY OF VIRGINIA

Charlottesville, Virginia 22906-3196
Web site: www.virginia.edu

Established 1819. Located 66 miles W of Richmond, 120 miles S of Washington. CGS and AAU member. Coed. State control. Semester system. Special facilities: Olsson Center for Applied Ethics, Center for Biological Timing, Center for Electrochemical Sciences and Engineering, Institute for Environmental Negotiation, Center for High Temperature Composites, Taylor Murphy International Business Studies Center, Institute for Nuclear and Particle Physics, Center for Russian and East European Studies, Center for South Asian Studies, University Transportation Center. The University's NIH ranking is 38th among all U.S. institutions with 417 awards/grants worth $121,216,469. Library: 3,200,000 volumes, 51,000 subscriptions. Total University enrollment: 19,000.

Annual tuition: full-time resident $6393, nonresident $19,482; part-time per semester minimum, resident $1215.50, nonresident $3397. Average academic year housing costs: $4767 (including board) for single students; $4000 for married students. Contact Office of Housing, Station 1, Page House, University of Virginia 22904, for both on- and off-campus housing information. Phone: (434)924-6873. Day-care facilities available.

Graduate School of Arts and Sciences

Graduate study since 1904. Enrollment: full-time 1577, part-time 75. University faculty teaching graduate students: full-time 613, part-time 78. Degrees conferred: M.A., M.A.T., M.A.P.A., M.F.A, M.S., Ph.D.

ADMISSION REQUIREMENTS. Transcripts, GRE, two letters of recommendation required in support of School's application. On-line application available. TOEFL (minimum score 600) required for international applicants. Accepts transfer applicants. Graduates of unaccredited institutions not considered. Apply to Office of the Graduate School by July 15 (Fall), December 1 (Spring); international applicants apply by April 1. Application fee $40. Phone: (434)924-7184.

ADMISSION STANDARDS. Very selective for most departments, competitive for others. Usual minimum average: 3.0 (A = 4).

FINANCIAL AID. Annual awards from institutional funds: teaching assistantships, research assistantships, fellowships, traineeships, partial tuition waivers, Federal W/S, loans. Approved for VA benefits. Apply by February 1 (December 1 for international applicants) to individual departments for fellowships, assistantships; to the Office of Financial Aid for all other programs. Phone: (434)924-3725. Use FAFSA. About 60% of students receive aid other than loans from School and outside sources.

DEGREE REQUIREMENTS. For master's: 24 semester hours minimum plus thesis, 30–36 credit without thesis; reading knowledge of one foreign language (by completion of two years of college credit or equivalent) for some programs; final oral/written exam. For Ph.D.: a minimum of 72 semester hours (or 50 beyond the master's); proficiency in one or two foreign languages (if applicable); preliminary/qualifying exam; dissertation; final/oral exam.

FIELDS OF STUDY.
Anthropology. M.A., Ph.D.
Asian Studies. M.A.
Astronomy. M.A., Ph.D.
Bioethics. M.A.
Biology. M.A., M.S., Ph.D.
Chemistry. M.S., Ph.D.
Classics. M.A., Ph.D.
Creative Writing. M.F.A.
Digital Humanities. M.A.
Drama. M.F.A.
Economics. M.A., Ph.D.
English. M.A., Ph.D.
Environmental Sciences. M.A., M.S., Ph.D.
Foreign Affairs. M.A., Ph.D.
French. M.A., Ph.D.
German Language and Literature. M.A., Ph.D.
Government. M.A., Ph.D.
History. M.A., Ph.D.
History of Art. M.A., Ph.D.
Italian. M.A.
Linguistics. M.A.
Mathematics. M.A., M.S., Ph.D.
Music. M.A., Ph.D.
Philosophy. M.A., Ph.D.
Physics. M.A., M.A.P.E., M.S., Ph.D.
Psychology. M.A., Ph.D.
Religious Studies. M.A., Ph.D.
Slavic Languages and Literature. M.A., Ph.D.
Sociology. M.A., Ph.D.
Spanish. M.A., Ph.D.
Statistics. M.S., Ph.D.

School of Architecture

Enrollment: full-time 173 (men 48%, women 52%), no part-time students. Faculty: full-time 44, part-time 19. Degrees conferred: M.Arch., M.Arch.H., M.L.A., M.U.E.P., Ph.D.

ADMISSION REQUIREMENTS. Transcripts, GRE required in support of application. On-line application available. TOEFL required for international applicants. Accepts transfer applicants. Graduates of unaccredited institutions not considered. Apply to Dean of School by January 15 for Architecture, Architecture History, Landscape Architecture; February 1 for, M.U.E.P. Application fee $40. Phone: (434)924-6442; fax: (434)982-2678.

ADMISSION STANDARDS. Very selective. Usual minimum average: 3.0 (A = 4).

FINANCIAL AID. Grants and fellowships. Architecture School Financial Aid form should be filed with application. Loans, Federal W/S available through University's Office of Financial Aid, Michie North, Emmet Street, Charlottesville, Virginia 22903. Phone: (434)982-6000. Apply by March 31 for Fall semester. Use FAFSA and School's FAF.

DEGREE REQUIREMENTS. For M.Arch.: Summer session plus 92 semester hours (less for B.S. in Arch. recipients), at least two years in residence. For M.L.A.: Summer session plus 94 semester hours, at least two years in residence. For M.Arch.H.: 36 semester hours, 24 hours in residence; comprehensive exam; one foreign language; thesis; final oral exam. For M.U.E.P.: 50 semester hours, summer internship. For Ph.D.: 48 semester hours plus 18 semester hours of nontopical research; written and oral exam; additional foreign language; dissertation; oral defense.

FIELDS OF STUDY.
Architectural History. M.Arch.H., Ph.D.
Architecture. Includes American urbanism, preservation; M.Arch.
Landscape Architecture. M.L.A.

Urban and Environmental Planning. Includes urban, environmental land use, policy. M.U.E.P.

Note: Study abroad available in Venice.

Colgate Darden Graduate School of Business Administration

PO Box 6550

Web site: www.darden.edu

Established 1954. Public control. Accredited programs: M.B.A.; recognized Ph.D. First year semester system, second year quarter system. Special facilities: Ballen Center for Entrepreneurial Leadership, Olsson Center for Applied Ethics, Taylor Murphy International Business Studies Center. Special programs: foreign exchange programs in Belgium, Hong Kong, Japan. Library: 80,000 volumes, 1110 subscriptions.

Annual MBA tuition: full-time resident $26,507, nonresident $30,507; Ph.D. full-time resident $6393, nonresident $19,482. Limited on-campus rooms and apartments available for single students.

Enrollment: total full-time 515 (men 60%, women 40%). Faculty: 56 full-time, 35 part-time; 96% with Ph.D./D.B.A. Degrees conferred: M.B.A. (full-time only), M.B.A.-J.D., M.B.A.-M.A. (Asian Studies, Government, Foreign Affairs), M.B.A.-M.E., M.B.A.-M.S.N., M.B.A.-Ph.D., Ph.D.

ADMISSION REQUIREMENTS. All applicants should have a bachelor's degree from a recognized institution of higher education. Students are required to have their own personal computer. Contact Darden School of Business (phone: (800)UVA-MBA1; (434)924-7281) for application material and information. Early applications are encouraged for both admission and financial aid consideration. Does not accept transfer applicants. Beginning students are admitted Fall only. There are three application periods. The first ends December 1, the second ends February 1, and the last ends on March 15. Both U.S. citizens and international applicants should apply no later than March 15 (Fall). On-line application available. Submit an application, GMAT results (will accept GMAT test results from the last five years, latest acceptable date is January), two official transcripts from each undergraduate/graduate school attended, two letters of recommendation, four essays, résumé (prefers at least four years of work experience), and an application fee of $100 ($125 for international applicants) to the office of Admission. In addition, international students (whose native language is other than English) should submit a TOEFL report (minimum score 600), TSE score, certified translations and evaluations of all official transcripts, recommendation should be in English or with certified translations, proof of health/immunization certificate, and proof of sufficient financial resources for one year of academic study. Interviews are strongly recommended prior to the Admissions Committee reviewing completed application. All interview requests from applicants are scheduled from August 1 through February; after February 1 interviews are scheduled at the request of Admissions Committee. Joint degree applicants must apply to and be accepted to both schools, contact the admissions office for current information and specific admissions requirements. Rolling admissions process; notification is made within six to eight weeks of receipt of completed application and supporting documents.

ADMISSION REQUIREMENTS FOR DOCTORAL CANDIDATES. Contact Director of Doctoral Program, Darden School of Business at (434)924-7247 (e-mail: dardendoctoral@darden. gbus.virginia.edu) for application material and information. MBA is generally required for all doctoral applicants. Beginning students are admitted Fall Only. Both U.S. citizens and international applicants apply by February 15. On-line application available. Submit a doctoral application, a GMAT score (will accept GMAT test results from the last five years), official transcripts from each undergraduate/graduate school attended, three

letters of recommendation, essays, résumé, statement of purpose, and application fee of $50 to the Director of Doctoral Program. In addition, international students (whose native language is other than English) should submit a TOEFL report (minimum score 600), TSE scores, certified translations and evaluations of all official transcripts, recommendation should be in English or with certified translations, proof of health/immunization certificate. Interviews strongly encouraged. Notification is generally made by mid-April.

ADMISSION STANDARDS. Very selective. Mean GMAT: 681; median GPA: 3.4 (A = 4). Gourman rating: the MBA was rated in the top 10, the score was 4.85; the Ph.D. was rated in the top 16, the score was 4.76. *U.S. News & World Report* ranked Darden in the top 10 of all U.S. business schools. *Business Week* listed Darden in the top 5 of all American business schools. Accepts approximately 15–20% of total annual applicants.

FINANCIAL AID. International scholarships, scholarships (some scholarship programs may require a essay), special minority stipend program, fellowships, graduate assistantships, Federal W/ S, loans available. Financial aid is available for international students. Assistantships/fellowships may be available for joint degree candidates. Financial aid applications and information are generally included with the admission materials; apply by March 15 (for Darden Scholarships apply by February 15). Request Darden scholarship and fellowship information from Darden. Phone: (434)924-7559. Contact the University's Financial Aid Office for need-based financial aid information. Phone: (434) 243-5033. Use FAFSA (School code: 003745), also submit the University's FAF, the Darden Statement of Financial Aid, a Financial Aid Transcript, Federal Income Tax forms. Approximately 65% of students receive some form of financial assistance.

All doctoral candidates are considered for all merit- or need-based awards, stipends, assistantships, and tuition waivers. Some Darden Loans may be canceled if recipient receives the Ph.D. and serves as a full-time faculty member at an accredited school of business for three years.

DEGREE REQUIREMENTS. For M.B.A.: 78 credit program including 21 elective credits, two-year program; degree program must be completed in two years. For M.B.A.-Masters: generally a three- to four-year programs. For M.B.A.-J.D.: four-and-one-half-year program. For M.B.A.-Ph.D.: four year full-time program. For Ph.D.: three- to four-year program, at least two consecutive academic semester in full-time residence; major field exam; major field research paper; dissertation proposal exam; dissertation; oral defense.

FIELDS OF STUDY.

Business Administration. M.B.A.

Finance. Ph.D.

Management. Includes business ethics, entrepreneurship, general management, strategic management. Ph.D.

Marketing. Ph.D.

Operations Management. Ph.D.

The Curry School of Graduate Education

Graduate study since 1905. Semester system.

Annual tuition: full-time resident $6393, nonresident $19,482. Enrollment: full-time 627, part-time 168. Faculty: full-time 100, part-time 5. Degrees conferred: M.Ed., M.T., Ed.S., Ed.D., Ph.D.

ADMISSION REQUIREMENTS. Official transcripts, GRE Subject Tests, three letters of recommendation required in support of School's application. On-line application available. TOEFL required for international applicants. Accepts transfer applicants. Graduates of unaccredited institutions not considered. Apply to Office of School, preferably by March 1 (Fall), November 15 (Spring). Application fee $40. Phone: (434)924-0741, (804)924-0738.

ADMISSION STANDARDS. Selective. Usual minimum average: 3.0 (A = 4).

FINANCIAL AID. Scholarships, fellowships, grants, teaching assistantships, internships, Federal W/S, loans. Approved for VA benefits. Apply to Office of the School by April 1. Phone: (434) 924-6000. Use FAFSA.

DEGREE REQUIREMENTS. For M.Ed., M.T.: 30–48 semester hours minimum, at least 24 in residence; comprehensive exam. For Ed.S.: 30 semester hours beyond the master's; comprehensive exam. For Ed. D.: at least one semester in full-time residence; preliminary exam; comprehensive exam; final dissertation; final oral exam. For Ph.D.: same as for Ed.D., except research project; proficiency in research methodology and statistics, and two years residency.

FIELDS OF STUDY.
Administration and Supervision.
Clinical Psychology.
Communication Disorders.
Counselor Education.
Curriculum and Instruction.
Education.
Educational Policy Studies.
Educational Psychology.
Health and Physical Education.
Higher Education.
Special Education.

School of Engineering and Applied Science— Graduate Division

Graduate study since 1946. Semester system.
Annual tuition: full-time resident $6393, nonresident $19,482.
Enrollment: full-time 507, part-time 16. Faculty teaching graduate students: full-time 161. Degrees conferred: M.S., M.E., Ph.D.

ADMISSION REQUIREMENTS. Official transcripts, three letters of recommendation, GRE required in support of School's application. TOEFL, financial statement certifying $22,000 available for first year of study required for international applicants. Accepts transfer applicants. Interview not required. Apply to Dean of School by August 1 (Fall), December 1 (Spring); international applicants apply by April 1 (Spring); September 1 (Fall). Application fee $40. Phone: (434)924-3879; fax: (434)982-2734.

ADMISSION STANDARDS. Selective. Usual minimum average: 3.0 (A = 4). TOEFL Score: 600.

FINANCIAL AID. Fellowships, teaching assistantships, research assistantships, traineeships, internships, Federal W/S, loans. Approved for VA benefits. Apply by February 1 to Dean for fellowships, assistantship; to Financial Aid Office for all other programs. Phone: (434)924-3897. Use FAFSA. About 85% of students receive aid other than loans from School and outside sources. Aid rarely available to part-time students.

DEGREE REQUIREMENTS. For M.E., M.S.: 24–30 semester hours minimum, at least one semester in residence for M.S.; thesis/research project; final oral thesis exam. For Ph.D.: 48 semester hours, at least 24 credits of research beyond the master's, at least two semesters in residence; comprehensive exam; dissertation; final oral exam.

FIELDS OF STUDY.
Applied Mathematics.
Applied Mechanics.
Biomedical Engineering.
Chemical Engineering.
Civil Engineering.
Computer Engineering.
Computer Science.
Electrical Engineering.
Engineering Physics.
Materials Science and Engineering.
Mechanical and Aerospace Engineering.
System Engineering.

School of Law (22903-1789)
Web site: www.law.virginia.edu

Established 1825. ABA approved since 1923. AALS member. Semester system. Full-time, day study only. Special programs: clerkships. Law library: 813,160 volumes, 13,198 subscriptions; has LEXIS, NEXIS, WESTLAW; is a Federal Government Depository.
Annual tuition: resident $15,803, nonresident $23,684; LL.M. $22,870. Total average annual additional expense: $12,163.
Enrollment: first-year class 336; total full-time 1064 (men 56%, women 44%); no part-time students. Faculty: full-time 64, part-time 50. Student to faculty ratio 14.2 to 1. Degrees conferred: J.D., J.D.-M.S. (Accounting at the Graduate School of Arts and Science of the University of Virginia), J.D.-M.P.A. (Public Affairs in the Woodrow Wilson School of Public and International Affairs at Princeton University), J.D.-M.A. (International Relations and International Economics at Johns Hopkins University School of Advanced International Studies), J.D.-M.A.L.D. (Law and Diplomacy in the Fletcher School of Law and diplomacy at Tufts University), LL.M. (three-quarters of accepted students are foreign lawyers), S.J.D.

ADMISSION REQUIREMENTS. For J.D. program: transcripts, LSAT, two recommendations required in support of application. Applicants must have completed four years of college study. Interview not required. Accepts transfer applicants. Graduates of unaccredited colleges not considered. Apply to Admissions Office of School, preferably by January 15 (Fall), Application fee $65. Phone: (434)924-7354. For graduate program: transcripts, GRE required in support of application. Interview may be required. Graduates of unaccredited colleges not considered. Apply to Admissions Office of the School; closing date varies by school.

ADMISSION REQUIREMENTS FOR LL.M. All applicants must have received the J.D. or equivalent first professional degree in law from an accredited U.S. law school or comparable foreign law school. Official transcripts with rank-in-class, two letters of recommendation required in support of LL.M. application. In addition, international applicants whose native language is not English must submit TOEFL and certified translations and evaluations of all foreign credentials. Personal interviews may be arranged with the Director of LL.M. Program. Admit Fall only. Apply by April 1 to Graduate Studies Office. Application fee $40. Phone: (434)924-3154; e-mail: gradadmit@law.virginia.edu.

ADMISSION REQUIREMENTS FOR S.J.D. Applicants must submit all materials required for LL.M. In addition, a personal statement expressing the rationale for pursuing the S.J.D. and its relevance to the applicant's planned career; submit dissertation proposal and candidate research plan with an endorsement of the proposal by a resident faculty member who has agreed to supervise the research and writing of dissertation; most candidates have completed the Law School's LL.M.

ADMISSION STANDARDS. Selective. Accepts 20–25% of total annual applicants.

FINANCIAL AID. Scholarships, fellowships, assistantships, Federal W/S, federal and law school loans. Apply to Federal Students Aid Center by February 15 for scholarships and Federal programs. Use FAFSA (School code: 003745). Apply to Chair of Graduate Commission for fellowships, assistantships. About 65% of students receive some aid from all sources.

DEGREE REQUIREMENTS. For J.D.: 86 (27 required) credits with a GPA of at least 2.0 (A = 4), plus completion of upper-divisional writing course; six semesters in residence program. For J.D.-M.S. (Accounting): 98 total credits (J.D. up to 12 credits, M.S. up to 6 credits). For J.D.-M.A.L.D., J.D.-M.A., J.D.-M.P.A.: individualized programs at each university; up to 14 credits may be applied to the J.D. and one semester of residence. For LL.M.: 24 credits, at least two semesters in full-time residence; substantial written work, either within a seminar or as supervised research; specialization in Oceans Law and Policy requires 30 credits. For S.J.D.: completion of a LL.M.; at least one year in full-time study; dissertation must make an original contribution to legal literature and be of publishable quality; oral defense.

School of Medicine (22908)

Established 1825. Annual tuition: full-time resident $14,154, nonresident $26,654; student fees $1296. Total average cost for all other expenses: $12,500.

Enrollment: first-year class 139; total 545 (men 52%, women 48%). Faculty: full-time 777, part-time 165. Degrees conferred: M.D. M.D.-Ph.D. (Medical Scientist Training Program).

ADMISSION REQUIREMENTS. AMCAS report, transcripts, letters of recommendation, MCAT, final screening interview required in support of application. Applicants must have completed at least three years of college study. Does not have EDP. Preference given to Virginia residents. Apply to Director of Admissions (P.O. Box 800725) after June 1, before November 1. Application fee $60. Phone: (434)924-5571; fax: (434)982-2586.

ADMISSION STANDARDS. Competitive. Mean MCAT: 10.5; mean GPA: 3.7 (A = 4). Gourman rating: 4.48. *U.S. News & World Report* ranking is in the top 27 of all U.S. medical schools. Accepts about 3–5% of total annual applicants. Approximately 70% are state residents.

FINANCIAL AID. Scholarships, loans. MSTP funded by NIH. Apply to Financial Aid Director by January 1. Phone: (434)924-0033. Use FAFSA (School code: 003745). About 80% of students receive some type of aid.

DEGREE REQUIREMENTS. For M.D.: satisfactory completion of four-year program. Ph.D. is granted through the Graduate School of Arts and Sciences.

FIELDS OF GRADUATE STUDY.
Biochemistry. Ph.D.
Biological and Physical Sciences. M.S.
Biophysics. Ph.D.
Cell Biology. Ph.D.
Health Evaluation Sciences. M.S.
Microbiology. Ph.D.
Physiology and Biological Physics. Ph.D.
Pharmacology. Ph.D.
Physiology. Ph.D.
Surgery. M.S.

WAGNER COLLEGE
Staten Island, New York 10301
Web site: www.wagner.edu

Founded 1883. Coed. Private control. Receives some support from the Lutheran Church of America. Semester system. Library: 310,000 volumes, 1000 subscriptions.

Tuition: per credit $650. On-campus housing for single students only. Average academic year housing cost: $6800 (including board). Contact Director of Residence Life for both on- and off-campus housing information. Phone: (718)390-3412. Daycare facilities available.

Division of Graduate Studies

Graduate study since 1952. Enrollment: full-time 190, part-time 200. College faculty: full-time 27, part-time 28. Degrees conferred: M.B.A., M.S., M.S.Ed., M.S.N.

ADMISSION REQUIREMENTS. Official transcripts, MAT/NTE/GMAT required in support of application. Interview not required. TOEFL required for international applicants. Accepts transfer applicants. Graduates of unaccredited institutions not considered. Apply to Director of Graduate Admissions at least six weeks prior to registration. Rolling admissions process. Application fee $50; $80 for international applicants. Phone: (718)390-3411.

ADMISSION STANDARDS. Selective for most departments. Usual minimum average: 2.75 (A = 4).

FINANCIAL AID. Fellowships, teaching assistantships, tuition waivers, internships, Federal W/S, loans. Approved for VA benefits. Apply by May 1 to Director of Graduate Studies for fellowships, assistantships; to Office of Financial Aid for all other programs. Phone: (718)390-3183. Use FAFSA. About 20% of students receive aid from College. Aid available for part-time students.

DEGREE REQUIREMENTS. For M.S., M.S.N.: 30–42 credits depending upon department; thesis/nonthesis option. For M.B.A.: 45–51 credits, at least 39 in residence; thesis/nonthesis option. For M.S. in Ed.: 34 credit hours minimum; 36 credit hours minimum in special education; thesis/nonthesis option.

FIELDS OF STUDY.
Accounting. M.S.
Adolescent Education/Special Education (7–9). M.S.Ed.
Advanced Physician Assistant Studies. M.S.
Childhood Education/Special Education (1–6). M.S.Ed.
Early Childhood Education/Special Education (B–2). M.S.Ed.
Microbiology. M.S.
Middle Level Education/Special Education (5–9). M.S.Ed.
Nursing. M.S.N.
Teaching Literacy (B–6). M.S.Ed.

WAKE FOREST UNIVERSITY
Winston-Salem, North Carolina 27106
Web site: www.wfu.ed.

Founded 1834. CGS member. Coed. Private control. Baptist affiliation. Semester system. The University's NIH ranking is 52nd among all U.S. institutions with 233 awards/grants worth $91,618,397. Library: 1,600,000 volumes, 7500 subscriptions.

Annual tuition: full-time $22,200; per credit $775. Limited on-campus housing for graduate students. Contact the Director of Residence Life and Housing for both on- and off-campus housing information. Phone: (336)758-5185.

Graduate School

Graduate study since 1866. Enrollment: full-time 275, part-time 136 (men 184, women 227). Faculty: full-time 404. Degrees conferred: M.A.Ed., M.A.L.S., M.S.A., M.S., Ph.D.

ADMISSION REQUIREMENTS. For Arts and Sciences: official transcripts, three letters of evaluation, statement of interest, interview for most departments, GRE/GMAT (accountancy) required in support of School's application. On-line application available. TOEFL required for international applicants. Accepts transfer applicants. Apply to Dean of Graduate School by February 15. Application fee $25. Phone: (800)257-3166; fax: (336)759-6074. For Bowman Gray School of Medicine-Graduate Program: official transcripts, three letters of evaluation, GRE Subject Tests required in support of School's application. TOEFL required for international students. Accepts transfer applicants. Graduates of unaccredited institutions not considered. Apply to Dean of the Graduate School by January 15. Application fee $25. Phone: (336)758-5301 or (800)257-3166; fax: (336)758-6074.

ADMISSION STANDARDS. Very selective for most departments, selective for the others. Usual minimum average: 3.0 (A = 4).

FINANCIAL AID. For Arts and Sciences: annual awards from institutional funds: scholarships, fellowships, assistantships (varies on availability), Federal W/S, loans. Apply at the time of application to Dean of Graduate School. Phone: (336)758-4743; fax: (336)758-4924. Use FAFSA (School code: E00429). About 85% of students receive aid other than loans from School and outside sources. For Bowman Gray School of Medicine-Graduate Program: scholarships, teaching/ research fellowships, research assistantships. Apply at time of application for admission to Dean of Graduate School. About 34% of students receive aid other than loans from School, 90% for all sources. No aid for part-time students.

DEGREE REQUIREMENTS. For master's: 30 semester hours minimum, at least 24 in residence; reading knowledge of one foreign language for some departments, substitution allowed in others; thesis/nonthesis option; final oral/written exam. For Ph.D.: three years minimum beyond the bachelor's, at least one year in residence; reading knowledge of two foreign languages in some departments, with substitutions allowed in others for one or both; preliminary oral/written exam; dissertation; final exam.

FIELDS OF STUDY.
Accountancy.
Biology. Includes cell and molecular biology, ecology/evolution/ systematics, physiology and behavior, plant biology.
Chemistry
Communication.
Computer Science.
Education. Includes counselor education, teaching education.
English.
Health and Exercise Science.
Liberal Studies. M.A.L.S. only.
Mathematics.
Physics.
Psychology.
Religion.

School of Law (P.O. Box 7206)
Web site: www.law.wfu.edu

Established 1984. ABA approved since 1935. AALS member. Semester system. Full-time, day study only. Special programs: Sister School program in Pecs, Hungary; summer study abroad in London, England, and Venice, Italy. Law library: 353,625 volumes, 6000 subscriptions; has LEXIS, NEXIS, WESTLAW, DIALOG, EPIC, ACES.

Annual tuition: $21,950, LL.M. $19,750. No on-campus housing available. Law students live off-campus. Contact the Admissions Office for off-campus housing information. Off-campus housing and personal expenses: approximately $11,600.

Enrollment: first-year class 160; total full-time 464 (men 56%, women 44%); no part-time students. Faculty: full-time 29, part-time 15. Student to faculty ratio 13.1 to 1. Degrees conferred: J.D., J.D.-M.B.A., LL.M. (American Law for foreign lawyers who have completed a basic legal education and received a university degree in law in another country).

ADMISSION REQUIREMENTS. LSDAS Law School report, Bachelor's degree, transcripts, LSAT, one academic recommendation, Dean's Certification required in support of application. Interviews are recommended only. Accepts transfer applicants on a space available basis. Graduates of unaccredited institutions not considered. Apply to Admissions Office after September 1, before March 15. Rolling admissions process. Application fee $60. Phone: (336)758-5437; fax (336)758-4632.

ADMISSION REQUIREMENTS FOR LL.M. APPLICANTS. All applicants must have a law degree from an approved degree-granting institution in the applicant's home country. Official transcripts in the language of the institution and certified English translation), two recommendations (one from a current or former faculty member), documentation of financial resources from bank or sponsor required in support of LL.M. application. In addition, TOEFL (minimum score 550) is required for those whose native language is not English. Admits Fall only. Apply by March 15 to Director LL.M. Program. Phone: (336)758-6116; e-mail: llm-admission@law.wfu.edu.

ADMISSION STANDARDS. Selective. Mean LSAT: 159; mean GPA: 3.39 (A = 4). Gourman rating 3.14. *U.S. News & World Report* ranking is in the top 36 of all U.S. law schools. Accepts 25–30% of total annual applicants.

FINANCIAL AID. Need-based scholarships, merit scholarships, minority scholarships, assistantships, private and institutional loans, Federal loans; Federal W/S available for second- and third-year students only. Assistantships may be available for upper-divisional joint degree candidates. All accepted students are automatically considered for scholarships. For all other programs apply to Admissions and Financial Aid Office after January 1, before May 1. Use FAFSA (School code: E00514), also submit Financial Aid Transcript, Federal Income Tax forms. Approximately 25%, of first-year class receive scholarships/Grants-in-Aid. Approximately 78% of students receive some form of financial assistance.

DEGREE REQUIREMENTS. For J.D.: 89 credits with a GPA of at least 73 (scale: 0–100), plus completion of upper-divisional writing course; three-year program, four-year program. Accelerated J.D. with summer course work. For J.D.-M.B.A.: a four-year program rather than a five-year program if both degrees are taken consecutively. For LL.M. (foreign lawyers): 24 credits, at least two semesters in residence; "Introduction to American Law" course; thesis/seminar paper; a GPA of 73 (scale 0–100) required.

Babcock Graduate School of Management
7659 Reynolda Station
Web site: www.mba.wfu.edu

Established 1969. Private control. Accredited program: M.B.A. Located on main campus, courses offered at Charlotte, North Carolina, and Munich, Germany; suburban environment. Semester system. Special facilities: Angell Center for Entrepreneurship, Center for Economic Studies, Center for Management Communications, Flow Institute of International Studies, Worrell Professional Center for Law and Management. Special Programs: foreign exchange programs; in East Asia, Germany, United Kingdom; International Internships Program. Library: 22,000 volumes, 350 subscriptions.

Annual tuition: full-time $26,500; evening M.B.A. $51,000 (total cost for degree program); fast-track E.M.B.A. $55,000 (total cost for program). No on-campus housing available. Estimated annual off-campus budget for M.B.A. tuition, room and board, and personal expenses: approximately $39,385.

Enrollment: total full-time 226, part-time 416 (men 75%, women 25%). Faculty: full-time 42, part-time 15; 93% with Ph.D./D.B.A. Degrees conferred: M.B.A. (full-time, part-time, day and evening), E.M.B.A. (weekends only, alternating Fridays, Saturdays), M.B.A.-J.D., M.B.A.-M.D.

ADMISSION REQUIREMENTS. All applicants should have a bachelor's degree from a recognized institution of higher education and a strong mathematics background. Students are required to have their own personal computer. Contact Babcock Graduate School of Management for application material and information; phone: full-time M.B.A. (336) 758-5422, E.M.B.A. and evening M.B.A. (336)758-4584, E.M.B.A. and evening M.B.A. at Charlotte (704)365-1717. Early applications are encouraged for both admission and financial aid consideration. Does not accept transfer students. Beginning students are admitted Fall only. Both U.S. citizens and international apply by April 1 (Fall), December 1 (for Early Decision applicants). On-line application available. Submit an application, GMAT (will accept GMAT test results from the last five years, latest acceptable date is June), two official transcripts from each undergraduate/graduate school attended, two letters of recommendation, three essays, résumé (work experience is not required), and an application fee of $75 to the Office of Admission and Financial Aid. In addition, international students (whose native language is other than English) should submit a TOEFL report (minimum score 580), certified translations and evaluations of all official transcripts, recommendation should be in English or with certified translations, proof of health/immunization certificate, and proof of sufficient financial resources for two years of academic study. Interviews are required for applicants lacking postgraduate work experience, for all other applicants an interview is strongly recommend. Joint degree applicants must apply to and be accepted to both schools; contact the Admissions Office for current information and specific admissions requirements. Rolling admissions process; notification is made within four weeks of receipt of completed application and supporting documents.

ADMISSION STANDARDS. Selective. Mean GMAT: 615; mean GPA: 3.2 (A = 4). *U.S. News & World Report* ranking is in the top 46 of all U.S. business schools. *Business Week* listed Babcock in the top 50 of all U.S. business schools. Accepts about 40–50% of total annual applicants.

FINANCIAL AID. Scholarships, minority scholarships, fellowships, graduate assistantships, Federal W/S, loans. Financial aid is available for part-time study. Assistantships/fellowships may be available for joint degree candidates. Financial Aid applications and information are generally available at the on-campus visit/interview and are included with the admission materials; apply by February 15 for the Babcock Scholars (full-tuition scholarships); by March 1 for merit-based scholarships; final deadline April 1. Contact the Assistant Director, Admissions and Financial Aid for current need-based financial aid information. Phone: (336)758-4424. Use FAFSA (School code: E00515), also submit Financial Aid Transcript, Federal Income Tax forms. Approximately 20% of students receive some form of financial assistance.

DEGREE REQUIREMENTS. For M.B.A.: 66 credit program including 22 elective credits, two-year program; degree program must be completed in five years. For part-time evening M.B.A.: 54 credit program. For E.M.B.A.: 51 credit, 22 month program. For M.B.A.-J.D.: 125 credit, four-and-one-half- to five-year program. For M.B.A.-M.D.: 192 credit, five-and-one-half- to six-year program.

FIELDS OF STUDY.
Business Administration. Includes career concentrations in management consulting, entrepreneurship and family business, finance—commercial banking/lending, finance—commercial finance/treasury, finance—security analysis/portfolio management, finance—investment banking, marketing—brand management, marketing—business-to-business marketing, marketing—international marketing, operations manufacturing management, operations—service operations, operations—operations consulting.

Bowman Gray School of Medicine (27157-1090)

Established 1902. Renamed in 1941. Located at Medical Center. Library: 130,000 volumes, 3800 subscriptions.

Annual tuition: $29,640. Total average cost for all other expenses: $8000–$10,000.

Enrollment; first-year class 108 (EDP 2) (men 64%, women 36%); total full-time 539 (men 67%, women 33%); postgraduates 156. Faculty: full-time 700, part-time 542. Degrees conferred: M.D., M.D.-M.B.A., M.D.-M.A. (International Studies, with Southeastern Theological Seminary), M.D.-Ph.D., M.D.-M.S. (Clinical Epidemiology and Health Services Research). The M.S. and Ph.D. are offered through the Graduate School.

ADMISSION REQUIREMENTS. AMCAS report, transcripts, MCAT, recommendations, including premedical advisory committee, required in support of application. Has EDP; apply between June 1 and August 1. Interviews and supplemental application by invitation only. Preference given to state residents. Apply after June 1, before November 1 to Associate Dean for Admissions. Application fee $55. Phone: (336)716-4264, fax: (336)716-5807.

ADMISSION STANDARDS. Very competitive. Mean MCAT: 9.9; mean GPA: 3.40 (A = 4). Gourman rating: 4.32. *U.S. News & World Report* ranking is in the top 39 of all U.S. medical schools in primary care and in medical research. Accepts 2–3% of total annual applicants. Approximately 55% are state residents.

FINANCIAL AID. Scholarships, loan funds. Apply by April 1 to Financial Aid Director. About 85% of students receive some financial aid.

DEGREE REQUIREMENTS. For M.D.: satisfactory completion of four-year program. For M.S., Ph.D.: see Graduate School listing above.

FIELDS OF GRADUATE STUDY.
Biochemistry and Molecular Biology. Ph.D.
Biomedical Engineering. M.S., Ph.D.
Cancer Biology. Ph.D.
Clinical Epidemiology and Health Services. M.S.
Comparative Medicine. M.S.
Microbiology and Immunology. Ph.D.
Molecular and Cellular Pathobiology. Ph.D.
Molecular Genetics. Ph.D.
Molecular Medicine. M.S., Ph.D.
Neurobiology and Anatomy. Ph.D.
Neuroscience. Ph.D.
Pharmacology. Ph.D.
Physiology. Ph.D.

WALLA WALLA COLLEGE
College Place, Washington 99324-3000
Web site: www.wwc.edu

Founded 1892. Located 160 miles SW of Spokane. Coed. Private control. Seventh-Day Adventist. Quarter system. Library: 235,000 volumes, 300 subscriptions.

Tuition: per credit $381. On-campus housing for 1480 single students, 110 units for married students. Average academic year housing costs: $2700 (room only) for a single student; $3690 for married students. Contact Rental Properties for on- and off-campus housing information. Phone: (509)527-2109.

Graduate School

Graduate study since 1900. Enrollment: full-time 170, part-time 42. Graduate faculty: full-time 30, part-time 13. Degrees conferred: M.A., M.Ed., M.S., M.S.W.

ADMISSION REQUIREMENTS. Official transcripts required in support of School's application. On-line application available. Interview not required. GRE and Subject Test for M.S. Biology. TOEFL required for international applicants. Accepts transfer applicants. Apply to Dean of Graduate Studies at least three months prior to registration. Application fee $40. Phone: (509) 527-2421; fax: (509)527-2253.

ADMISSION STANDARDS. Selective. Usual minimum average: 2.75 (A = 4).

FINANCIAL AID. Scholarships, teaching assistantships, internships, tuition waivers, Federal W/S, loans. Approved for VA benefits. Apply by April 1 to the Financial Aid Office for scholarships, to department chair for assistantships. Use FAFSA and institutional FAF. Phone: (509)527-2815; fax: (509)527-2253. About 30% of students receive aid other than loans from College, 35% from all sources. Aid available to part-time students.

DEGREE REQUIREMENTS. For master's: 45 credits minimum, at least 30 in residence; thesis required for M.S., M.A.; final oral/written exams. For M.S.W.: two-year full-time program.

FIELDS OF STUDY.
Biology. M.A.
Counseling Psychology. M.A.
Education. Includes curriculum and instruction, education leadership, literacy instruction, special education, students-at-risk. M.A., M.Ed.
Social Work. Master's program has clinical focus.
Teaching. Includes educational leadership, professional practice, special education. M.A.T.

WASHBURN UNIVERSITY OF TOPEKA
Topeka, Kansas 66621
Web site: www.washburn.edu

Founded 1865. Located 65 miles W of Kansas City. Coed. Municipal control. Semester system. Special facilities: Center for Diversity Studies, Center for Kansas Studies, Center on Violence and Victim Studies, Washburn Leadership Institute. Library: 500,000 volumes, 7000 subscriptions.

Tuition: per hour, resident $145, nonresident $274. On-campus housing for graduate students available. Average academic year housing costs: $4300. Contact Director of Housing for both on- and off-campus housing information. Phone: (785)231-1065. Day-care facilities available.

Graduate Program

Enrollment: full-time 208, part-time 414. Graduate faculty: full-time 32, part-time 9. Degrees conferred: M.A., M.B.A., M.Ed., M.S.W.

ADMISSION REQUIREMENTS. Official transcripts, references, GMAT, interview required in support of application. TOEFL required for international applicants. Accepts transfer applicants. Apply to Director of Graduate Programs at least one month prior to registration. Application fee: none. Phone: (785)231-1010, ext. 1561.

ADMISSION STANDARDS. Selective. Usual minimum average: 3.0 (A = 4).

FINANCIAL AID. Scholarships, research fellowships, research assistantships, teaching assistantships, internships, Federal W/S, loans. Approved for VA benefits. Apply by April 1 to Dean's office for fellowships, assistantships: to Financial Aid Office all

other programs. Phone: (785)231-1010, ext. 1151. Use FAFSA. Aid available for part-time students.

DEGREE REQUIREMENTS. For M.A., M.Ed., M.S.W.: 32 semester hours minimum, at least 24 in residence; final document. For M.B.A.: 30 semester hours minimum; computer proficiency.

FIELDS OF STUDY.

COLLEGE OF ARTS AND SCIENCES:
Education. M.Ed.
Liberal Studies. M.L.S.
Psychology. M.A.

SCHOOL OF APPLIED STUDIES:
Criminal Justice. M.C.J.
Social Work. M.S.A.

SCHOOL OF BUSINESS:
Accounting. M.B.A.
Business Administration. M.B.A.

School of Law
Web site: www.washburnlaw.edu

Organized 1903. ABA approved since 1923. AALS member since 1905. Semester system. Special facility: Rural Law Center. Law library: 332,384 volumes, 3961 subscriptions; has LEXIS, NEXIS, WESTLAW, DIALOG; 30 computer workstations.

Annual tuition: residents $7712, nonresidents $11,996. On-campus housing available. Annual housing cost: $11,704.

Enrollment: first-year class 149; total 407 (men 57%, women 43%). Faculty: full-time 19, part-time 15. Student to faculty ratio 17.9 to 1. Degree conferred: J.D.

ADMISSION REQUIREMENTS. LSDAS Law School report, bachelor's degree, transcripts, LSAT required in support of application. Interview not required. Accepts transfer applicants. Preference given to state residents. Graduates of unaccredited institutions not considered. Admits to both Fall and Spring semesters. Apply to Admissions Office by March 15 (Fall), September 15 (Spring). Later applications considered on space-available basis only. Application fee $30. Phone: (888)927-4529; fax: (785)232-8087.

ADMISSION STANDARDS. Selective. Mean LSAT: 150; mean GPA: 3.16 (A = 4). Gourman rating: 3.2. *U.S. News & World Report* ranking is in the fourth tier of all U.S. law schools. Accepts 40% of total annual applicants.

FINANCIAL AID. Scholarships, Federal W/S, loans. Apply to Financial Aid Office by March 15 (Fall), September 15 (Spring). for priority consideration. Use FAFSA (School code: 001949). About 43% of students receive aid other than loans from School.

DEGREE REQUIREMENTS. For J.D.: 90 credit hours minimum, at least 24 hours and the last year in residence.
Note: Six-week program of international study at Brunel University of West London (Great Britain) available.

WASHINGTON COLLEGE
Chestertown, Maryland 21620-1197
Web site: www.washcoll.edu

Founded 1782. Located 85 miles NE of Washington, D.C., 55 miles SE of Wilmington, Delaware. Coed. Private control. Semester system. Library: 200,000 volumes, 2300 subscriptions. Total College enrollment: 1200.

Tuition: per course $750. No housing available for graduate students. For off-campus housing, contact Business Office of the College.

Graduate Division

Enrollment: approximately 49 (mainly part-time). Faculty: full-time 28, part-time 7. Degree conferred: M.A.

ADMISSION REQUIREMENTS. Transcripts, letters of recommendation, GRE (required for Psychology), appropriate baccalaureate degree required in support of application. On-line application available. Accepts transfer applicants. Apply to Graduate Office at least one month prior to registration. Application fee $40. Phone: (410)778-7131; fax: (410)778-7275.

ADMISSION STANDARDS. Selective. Usual minimum average: 3.0 (A = 4).

FINANCIAL AID. None at this time. Call Student Aid Office for current information. Phone: (410)778-7214.

DEGREE REQUIREMENTS. For M.A.: 30 semester hours; thesis/nonthesis option.

FIELDS OF STUDY.
Education. Courses only.
English.
History-Social Science.
Psychology.

WASHINGTON AND LEE UNIVERSITY
Lexington, Virginia 24450
Web site: www.wlu.edu

Founded 1849. Located 50 miles NE of Roanoke. Private control. Library: 600,000 volumes, 2500 subscriptions.

On-campus housing available. Average annual housing cost: $4300 for single students. Apply to Director of University Services.

School of Law
Web site: www.law.wlu.edu

Established 1849. ABA approved since 1923. AALS member. Semester system. Law library: 382,913 volumes, 4349 subscriptions; has LEXIS, NEXIS, WESTLAW.

Annual tuition: full-time $16,130. Total average annual additional expense: $6500.

Enrollment: first-year class 122, total 363 (men 59%, women 41%). Faculty: full-time 32, part-time 3. Student to faculty ratio 10.6 to 1. Degree conferred: J.D.

ADMISSION REQUIREMENTS. LSDAS Law School report, bachelor's degree, transcripts, two letters of recommendation, LSAT required in support of application. Interview not required. Accepts transfer applicants. Graduates of unaccredited colleges not considered. Apply to office of Dean of School after July 1, before February 1 for priority consideration. Application fee $40. Admits beginning students to Fall only. Phone: (540)463-8504; fax: (540)463-8546.

ADMISSION STANDARDS. Selective. Mean LSAT: 164; mean GPA: 3.33 (A = 4). Gourman rating: 2.93. *U.S. News & World Report* ranking is in the top 18 of all U.S. law schools. Accepts about 20–25% of total applicants.

FINANCIAL AID. Scholarships, grants, fellowships, Federal W/S, loans. Apply to Dean of School by February 15. Use FAFSA (School code: 003768). About 73% of students receive financial assistance.

DEGREE REQUIREMENTS. For J.D.: 85 semester hours minimum, at least final four semesters in residence.

WASHINGTON STATE UNIVERSITY
Pullman, Washington 99164-1068
Web site: www.wsu.edu

Founded 1890. Located 80 miles S of Spokane. CGS member. Coed. State control. Semester system. Special facilities: Humanities Research Center, Small Business Research Center, Social and Economic Sciences Research Center, Computing Center, Nuclear Reactor Center, Electron Microscope Laboratory, Agricultural Research Centers, College of Engineering Research Division, State of Washington Water Research Center, Bioanalytical Research Center, Laboratory Animal Facility, Molecular Biophysics Laboratory. Library: 2,000,000 volumes, 28,120 subscriptions.

Annual tuition: full-time resident $6088, nonresident $14,914; per credit, resident $304, nonresident $746. On-campus housing for 648 married students, unlimited for single students. Average academic year housing costs: $390–$500 per month for married students; $8374 (including board) for single students. Contact Program Coordinator Residence Halls (509)335-9574 for on-campus housing information: Program Coordinator Housing Commission (509)355-4577 for off-campus housing information. Day-care facilities available.

Graduate School

Graduate study since 1902. Enrollment: full-time 1523, part-time 347. Graduate faculty: full-time 721, part-time 49. Degrees conferred: M.A., M.S., M.F.A., M.A.T., Ed.M., M.B.A., M.Nurs., M.R.P., Ed.D., Ph.D.

ADMISSION REQUIREMENTS. Two official transcripts, GRE/GMAT/MAT required in support of School's application. On-line application available. TOEFL required for international applicants. Accepts transfer applicants. Foreign students apply at least six months prior to registration. Apply to the Director of Admissions at least two months prior to registration. Application fee $35. Phone: (509)335-6424; fax: (509)335-1949.

ADMISSION STANDARDS. Very selective for most departments, relatively open to very competitive for others. Usual minimum average: 3.1 (last two years) (A = 4).

FINANCIAL AID. Annual awards from institutional funds: fellowships, teaching assistantships, research assistantships, internships, traineeships, tuition waivers, Federal W/S, loans. Approved for VA benefits. Apply by February 1 to the Dean of Graduate School for assistantships, fellowships; to Financial Aid Office for all other programs. Phone: (509)335-9711. Use FAFSA (School code: 003800). About 70% of students receive aid other than loans from University and outside sources. Aid available for part-time students.

DEGREE REQUIREMENTS. For M.A., M.S.: 30 credits minimum, at least one year in residence; language requirements vary by department; thesis/nonthesis option; final exam in all departments. For M.A.T.: 30 credits minimum, at least 24 in residence; final oral exam. For Ed.M.: qualifying exam; other requirement, same as for M.A.T. For M.B.A., M.R.P.: 30 credits minimum, no thesis; final oral exam. For M.N.: 45 credits, thesis; final oral exam. For Ed.D., Ph.D.: six semesters minimum beyond the bachelor's, at least four semester, in residences language requirements vary by department; oral/written preliminary exam; thesis; final oral exam.

FIELDS OF STUDY

Accounting. M.Acct.
Agribusiness. M.A.
Agriculture. M.S.
Agricultural and Resource Economics. M.A., Ph.D.
American Studies. M.A., Ph.D.
Animal Sciences. M.S., Ph.D.
Anthropology. M.A., Ph.D.
Apparel Merchandising and Textile. M.A.
Architecture. M.S., M.Arch.
Biochemistry. M.S., Ph.D.
Biology. M.S., Ph.D.
Biotechnology. M.S.
Botany. M.S., Ph.D.
Business Administration. M.B.A., Ph.D.
Chemical Engineering. M.S., Ph.D.
Chemistry. Includes analytical, inorganic, organic, physical. M.S., Ph.D.
Civil Engineering. M.S., Ph.D.
Communication. M.A.
Computer Science. M.S., Ph.D.
Criminal Justice. M.A.
Crop Science. M.S., Ph.D.
Economics. M.A., Ph.D.
Education. Includes educational leadership and counseling psychology, teaching and learning. M.A., Ed.M., Ed.D., Ph.D.
Electrical and Computer Engineering. Ph.D.
Electrical Engineering. M.S.
Engineering. M.S.
Engineering Management. M.Eng.Mgt. only.
Engineering Science. Ph.D.
English. M.A., Ph.D.
Entomology. M.S., Ph.D.
Environmental and Natural Resource Sciences. Ph.D.
Environmental Engineering. M.S.
Environmental Science. M.S.
Exercise Science. M.S.
Fine Arts. M.F.A.
Food Science. M.S., Ph.D.
Foreign Languages and Literatures. M.A.
Genetics and Cell Biology. M.S., Ph.D.
Geology. M.S., Ph.D.
Health Policy and Administration. M.H.P.A.
History. M.A., Ph.D.
Horticulture. M.S., Ph.D.
Human Development. M.A.
Human Nutrition. M.S.
Individual Ph.D. Interdisciplinary. Ph.D.
Interior Design. M.A.
Landscape Architecture. M.S.
Materials Science. Ph.D.
Materials Science and Engineering. M.S.
Mathematics. M.S., Ph.D.
Mechanical Engineering. M.S., Ph.D.
Microbiology. M.S., Ph.D.
Music. M.A.
Natural Resource Sciences. M.S.
Natural Resources. M.S.
Neurosciences. M.S., Ph.D.
Nursing. M.Nurs.
Nutrition. Ph.D.
Pharmacology and Toxicology. M.S., Ph.D.
Physics. M.S., Ph.D.
Plant Pathology. M.S., Ph.D.
Plant Physiology. M.S., Ph.D.
Political Science. M.A., Ph.D.
Psychology. Includes clinical, experimental. M.S., Ph.D.
Public Affairs. M.P.A.
Regional Planning. M.R.P.
Sociology. M.A., Ph.D.
Soil Science. M.S., Ph.D.
Speech and Hearing Science. M.A.
Statistics. M.S.
Technology Management. M.T.M.
Veterinary Science. M.S., Ph.D.
Zoology. M.S., Ph.D.

College of Veterinary Medicine (99164-7012)

Founded 1899.

Annual tuition: full-time resident and contract state residents $9260; nonresidents $22,960. Annual housing cost: $3200–$4000.

Enrollment: first-year class 74, total full-time 280 (men 45%, women 55%). College faculty: full-time 90. Degrees conferred: D.V.M. (awarded by Washington State University and University of Oregon), D.V.M.-M.S.

ADMISSION REQUIREMENTS. VMCAS report, transcripts, GRE, three recommendations, animal/veterinary experience required in support of application. Interview by invitation only. Applicants must have completed at least two years of college study. Preference given to state, Idaho, Oregon, and WICHE residents; accepts about 5 students who are nonresidents and not from WICHE. Accepts transfer applicants under special circumstances only. Apply to the Office of Student Services after August 1, before October 1. Application fee $40. Phone: (509)335-1532.

ADMISSION STANDARDS. Selective. Minimum GPA: 3.2 (A = 4). Mean GPA: 3.5 (A = 4); mean combined GRE at 71st percentile. Accepts 10–15% of total annual applicants. Accepted approximately five nonresident "at-large" applicants.

FINANCIAL AID. Scholarships, loans. Use FAFSA before February 1.

DEGREE REQUIREMENTS. For D.V.M.: satisfactory completion of four-year program.

FIELDS OF GRADUATE STUDY.
Anesthesiology. M.S., Ph.D.
Clinical Neurology and Neurosurgery. M.S.
Equine Surgery. M.S.
Field Disease Investigation. M.S., Ph.D.
Infectious Diseases. M.S., Ph.D.
Immunology. M.S., Ph.D.
Neuroscience. M.S., Ph.D.
Pathology. M.S., Ph.D.
Radiology. M.S., Ph.D.
Small Animal Medicine. M.S.
Small Animal Surgery. M.S.
Theriogenology. M.S., Ph.D.
Veterinary Clinical Pathology. M.S., Ph.D.
Veterinary Science. M.S., Ph.D.

WASHINGTON UNIVERSITY
St. Louis, Missouri 63130-4899
Web site: www.wustl.edu

Founded 1853. CGS and AAU member and charter member of Association of Graduate Schools. Coed. Private control. Semester system. Special facilities: Center for Air Pollution and Trend Analysis, Center for the Study of American Business, Center for American Indian Studies, Institute for Biomedical Computing, Business, Law and Economics Center, McDonnell Center for Cellular and Molecular Neurobiology, Center for Computational Mechanics, Computer and Communications Research Center, Construction Management Center, Center for the Study of Data Processing, Carolyne Roehm Electronic Media Center, Center for Engineering Computing, Center for Genetics in Medicine, McDonnell Center for Studies of Higher Brain Function, Center for the History of Freedom, Center for Intelligent Computer Systems, International Writers Center, Center for the Study of Islamic Societies and Civilizations, Management Center, Markey Center for Research in Molecular Biology of Human Disease, Center for Optimization and Semantic Control, Center for Plant Science and Biotechnology, Center for Political Economy, Center for the Study of Public Affairs, Center for Robotics and Automation, Social Work Research Development Center, McDonnell Center for Space Sciences, Center for Technology Assessment and Policy, Center for the Application of Information Technology, Urban Research and Design Center, Central Institute for the Deaf. The University's NIH ranking is fifth among all U.S. institutions with 737 awards/grants worth $306,649,861. Library: 3,000,000 volumes, 18,000 subscriptions. Total University enrollment: 12,088.

Annual tuition: full-time $24,500; per unit $1020. No on-campus housing available. Average academic year housing costs: $450–$950 per month.

Graduate School of Arts and Sciences

Formal graduate study since 1898. Enrollment: full-time 1365, part-time 25. School faculty: full-time 500, part-time 80. Degrees conferred; A.M., M.S., M.L.A., M.A.Ed., M.A.T., M.M., M.F.A.W., M.S.S.H., A.G.C., Ph.D.

ADMISSION REQUIREMENTS. Official transcripts, GRE Subject Test required in support of application. Official TOEFL or TSE required for international applicants. Interview required in some programs. Accepts transfer applicants. Graduates of unaccredited institutions not considered. Apply to Office of the Dean (Campus Box 1187), preferably by January 15 (January 1 for the Division of Biology and Biomedical Sciences, April 1 for Speech and Hearing). Rolling admissions process. Application $35. Phone: (314)935-6880; fax: (314)935-4887.

ADMISSION STANDARDS. Competitive for most departments. Usual minimum average: 3.0 (A = 4).

FINANCIAL AID. Annual awards from institutional funds: 700 scholarships, 120 fellowships, 300 research assistantships, 250 teaching assistantships, 20 internships, grants, Federal W/S, loans. Approved for VA benefits. Apply by January 15 to Dean for scholarships, to appropriate department head for fellowships, internships, assistantships; to the Financial Aid Office for all other programs. Phone: (314)935-6821. Use FAFSA and University's FAF. About 65% of students receive aid other than loans from School and outside sources.

DEGREE REQUIREMENTS. For A.M., M.L.A., M.S.: 24 semester hours plus thesis, or 30 hours plus essay, at least one year in residence; 6 hours maximum in transfer; final written exam. For M.A.Ed., M.A.T., M.S.S.H: 30 hours minimum, at least 27 in residence; final written exam. For M.M.: 33–37 hours minimum, at least 27 in residence; includes graduate recital; reading knowledge of two modern languages. For M.F.A.W.: 39 hours minimum, at least 33 in residence, up to 15 hours in workshops or tutorials of directed writing. For A.G.C. (Education): normally 30 hours minimum beyond the master's, at least 24 in residence; qualifying written exam; final written project; final oral exam. For Ph.D.: 72 hours minimum beyond the bachelor's, at least 48 in residence; reading knowledge of one or two languages may be specified by major department; qualifying exam; candidacy; dissertation; final oral defense.

FIELDS OF STUDY.
American Culture Studies. A.M.
Anthropology. A.M.
Art History and Archaeology. One language for A.M., two for Ph.D.
Asian and Near Eastern Languages and Literature. A.M.
Biochemistry. Ph.D.
Biology. A.M.
Bioorganic Chemistry. Ph.D.

Business Administration. M.S., Ph.D.; M.B.A., E.M.B.A. offered through Graduate School of Business Administration.
Business and East Asian Studies. A.M.
Chemistry. Includes organic, bioorganic, polymer, physical, biophysical, inorganic, organometallic, bioinorganic, nuclear, radiochemistry. A.M., Ph.D.
Chinese and Comparative Literature. Ph.D.
Chinese Language and Literature. A.M.
Classics. A.M.
Comparative Literature. Includes literary theory, European and American literature, Chinese and Japanese literature. A.M.
Computational Biology. Ph.D.
Developmental Biology. Ph.D.
Drama. A.M.
Earth and Planetary Sciences. Includes sedimentary geology, planetary exploration. Ph.D.
East Asian Studies. Includes economic development, law, political, economic, and intellectual history, literature and culture, art history and archaeology. A.M.
Economics. Includes economic history, economic theory, econometrics, industrial organization, monetary economics, political economy, public economics, public finance. A.M., Ph.D.
Education. Includes teacher education (preservice and inservice), educational research. M.A.Ed., M.A.T., Ph.D.
English and American Literature. A.M., Ph.D.
English and Comparative Literature. Ph.D.
European Studies. A.M.
Evolutionary and Population Biology. Ph.D.
French. A.M.
French and Comparative Literature. Ph.D.
French Language and Literature. Ph.D.
German and Comparative Literature. Ph.D.
Germanic Languages and Literatures. GRE for admission; one language in addition to German for A.M., two for Ph.D.
Hispanic Language and Literature. Ph.D.
History. A.M., Ph.D.
Human Resources Management. A.M.
Immunology. Ph.D.
International Affairs. A.M.
Islamic and Near Eastern Studies. A.M.
Japanese and Comparative Literature. Ph.D.
Japanese Language and Literature. A.M.
Jewish Studies. A.M.
Law and East Asian Studies. A.M.
Liberal Arts. M.L.A.
Literature and History. A.M.
Mathematics. Includes analysis, geometry, algebra. M.S., Ph.D.
Molecular Biophysics. Ph.D.
Molecular Cell Biology. Ph.D.
Molecular Genetics. Ph.D.
Molecular Microbiology and Microbial Pathogenesis. Ph.D.
Movement Science. Ph.D.
Music. Includes musicology, theory, composition; entrance exam for Ph.D.; qualifying exam for master's; two languages for Ph.D. M.M., A.M., Ph.D.
Neurosciences. Ph.D.
Performing Arts. Includes dramatic literature, criticism, theory, modern drama, Renaissance Drama, theater. A.M.
Philosophy. Ph.D.
Physics. A.M., Ph.D.
Physics and Electrical Engineering. Ph.D.
Plant Biology. Ph.D.
Political Economy and Public Policy. Includes public choice, international political economy public policy. A.M.
Political Science. A.M., Ph.D.
Psychology. Includes experimental, development and aging, social. Ph.D.
Romance Languages and Literature. French literature, Spanish literature; 2 languages in addition to major for Ph.D. A.M., Ph.D.
Social Work. Ph.D. only. M.S.W. offered through School of Social Work.

Spanish. A.M.
Spanish and Comparative Literature. Ph.D.
Speech and Hearing Sciences. A.M., M.S.S.H., Ph.D.
Technology and Human Affairs. A.M. only.
Writing Program. Includes fiction, poetry, nonfiction, playwriting. Writing samples must be included with application materials. M.F.A.W.

School of Art

Annual tuition: $22,546. Enrollment: full-time 36. School faculty: full-time 17, part-time 5. Degree conferred: M.F.A.

ADMISSION REQUIREMENTS. Transcripts, BFA or equivalent, twenty slide portfolio, three recommendations, statement of purpose required in support of application. On-line application available. TOEFL required for international students. Graduates of unaccredited colleges not considered. Apply to Graduate Office by February 1. Application fee $75. Phone: (314)935-6500; fax: (314)935-6462; e-mail: cbaldwin@art.wustl.edu.

ADMISSION STANDARDS. Competitive. Usual minimum average: 3.0 (A = 4).

FINANCIAL AID. Scholarships, fellowships, teaching assistantships, technical assistantships, internships, Federal W/S, loans. Approved for VA benefits. Apply to Graduate Office; various deadlines in January and February. Phone: (314)935-4761, fax: (315)935-4862. Use FAFSA and University's FAF. Approximately 100% of students receive aid other than loans from both School and outside sources.

DEGREE REQUIREMENTS. For M.F.A.: 60 credit, full-time program; candidacy; thesis; exhibition.

FIELDS OF STUDY.
Ceramics. Includes glass.
Painting.
Photography.
Printmaking/Drawing.
Sculpture.

John M. Olin School of Business (Campus Box 1133)
Web site: www.olin.wustl.edu

Established 1917, added M.B.A. in 1950, E.M.B.A. in 1983, P.M.B.A. in Health Science, and E.M. in Manufacturing Management in 1997. Accredited program: M.B.A.; recognized Ph.D. Semester system. Special facilities: Business Law and Economics Center, Center for Technology Information and Manufacturing, Center for the Study of American Business. Special Programs: foreign exchange programs (in France, Germany, Hong Kong, United Kingdom, Venezuela), internships. Library: 28,700 volumes, 400 subscriptions.

Annual tuition: full-time $29,700; E.M.B.A. $69,000. No on-campus housing available.

Enrollment: total full-time 298, part-time 366 (men 75%, women 25%). Faculty: full-time 73, part-time 15; all have Ph.D./ D.B.A. Degrees conferred: M.B.A. (full-time, part-time, day and evening), P.M.B.A. (part-time, evening), E.M.B.A. (weekends only, alternating Fridays, Saturdays), E.M.B.A. in Health Services, E.M.M.M., M.B.A.-J.D., M.B.A.-M.A. (East Asian Studies), M.B.A.-M.Arch., M.B.A.-M.S.W., Ph.D.

ADMISSION REQUIREMENTS. All applicants should have a bachelor's degree from a recognized institution of higher education and a strong mathematics background. Contact Director of M.B.A. Admissions for application material and information; phone: (314)935-7301; e-mail: mba@olin.sustl.edu.; E.M.B.A. (314)935-4572. Accepts both M.B.A. Multi-App and CollegeEdge electronic applications in lieu of institutional application. On-

line application available. Early applications are encouraged for both admission and financial aid consideration. Beginning students who are full-time students admitted Fall only, part-time admitted Fall and Spring. Both U.S. citizens and international for full-time studies apply by December 14, January 11, February 15 (Spring), March 29, April 30 (final deadline); part-time apply by March 30 (Fall), November 30 (Spring). Submit M.B.A. application, GMAT (will accept GMAT test results from the last five years, latest acceptable date is March), official transcripts from each undergraduate/graduate school attended, two letters of recommendation, four essays, Work History Form (prefers at least three years of work experience), and an application fee of $80 to the Director of M.B.A. Admissions. In addition, international students (whose native language is other than English) should submit a TOEFL report (minimum score 550), certified translations and evaluations of all official transcripts, recommendation should be in English or with certified translations, proof of health/immunization certificate, and proof of sufficient financial resources for two years of academic study. Interviews are encouraged. Joint degree applicants must apply to and be accepted to both schools/programs, contact the admissions office for current information and specific admissions requirements. The full-time admissions process is based on a series of deadlines: applications submitted by December 14 will receive decision by January 22; applications submitted by January 11 will receive decision by February 19; applications submitted by February 15 will receive decision by April 9; applications submitted by March 29 will receive decision by June 4; applications submitted by April 30 will receive decision by July 2.

ADMISSION REQUIREMENTS FOR DOCTORAL CANDIDATES. Contact Director for Business Ph.D. Admissions at (314)935-6340 for application material and information. Beginning students are admitted Fall Only. Both U.S. citizens and international applicants apply by February 15. Submit an application, GMAT (will accept GMAT test results from the last five years), official transcripts from each undergraduate/graduate school attended, three letters of recommendation, résumé, statement of objectives and application fee of $80 to the Director of Business Ph.D. Admissions. In addition, international students (whose native language is other than English) should submit a TOEFL report (minimum score 600), certified translations and evaluations of all official transcripts, recommendation should be in English or with certified translations, proof of health/immunization certificate. Interviews are encouraged. Notification is generally made mid-April.

ADMISSION STANDARDS. Selective. Mean GMAT: 647; mean GPA: 3.2 (A = 4). Gourman rating: the M.B.A. was rated in the top 31, the score was 4.60; the Ph.D. was rated in the top 35, the score was 4.54. *U.S. News & World Report* ranked Olin in the top 40 of all U.S. business schools; the E.M.B.A. in the top 15. *Business Week* listed Olin in the top 16 of all U.S. business schools.

FINANCIAL AID. Scholarships, special minority stipends, Consortium Fellowships, fellowships, graduate assistantships, Federal W/S, loans. Financial aid is available for part-time study. Financial aid for international students may be available in the form of merit awards. Assistantships/fellowships may be available for joint degree candidates. Financial aid applications and information are generally available at the on-campus visit/interview and are included with admissions materials obtained directly from Olin School of Business; apply by March 31. Request both need- and merit-based information from the School of Business. Phone: (314)935-6610. Use FAFSA (School code: 002520); also submit the School's FAF, a Financial Aid Transcript, Federal Income Tax forms. Approximately 65% of students receive some form of financial assistance. Ph.D. applicants for an Olin Fellowship for Women or a Chancellor's Graduate Fellowship apply in early January.

DEGREE REQUIREMENTS. For M.B.A.: 60 credit program including 24 elective credits, two-year program; degree program must be completed in seven years. For P.M.B.A.: 54 credit, part-time evening program. For E.M.B.A.: 21-month program. For E.M.B.A. in Health Services: 60 credit program. For E.M.M.M.: 60 credit program. For M.B.A.-Master's: generally a three- to five-year program. For M.B.A.-J.D.: four-and-one-half- to five-year program. For Ph.D.: four- to five-year program in full-time residence (and M.S.B.A. maybe earned while pursuing the Ph.D.); oral presentation of a research paper; completion of a minor field requirement; comprehensive exam in major; dissertation proposal and oral defense; dissertation; oral defense.

FIELDS OF STUDY.
Accounting. Ph.D.
Business Administration. Includes concentrations in accounting analysis, entrepreneurship, finance, international management, manufacturing and operations, marketing, Organizational leadership, strategy consulting. M.B.A.
Business Economics. Ph.D.
Finance. Ph.D.
Marketing. Ph.D.
Operations and Manufacturing Management. Ph.D.
Organizational Behavior and Strategy. Ph.D.

Sever School of Engineering and Applied Science

Founded 1948. Tuition: per unit $1120. Graduate enrollment: full-time 330, part-time 460. Institute faculty: full-time 80, part-time 20. Degrees conferred: M.S., M.C.E., M.S.C.E., M.E.M., M.I.M., M.T.M., D.Sc.

ADMISSION REQUIREMENTS. Official transcripts, letters of recommendation required in support of School's application. On-line application available. Interview desirable. GRE required for all financial aid applicants. TOEFL (minimum score 550) required for international applicants. Accepts transfer applicants. Graduates of unaccredited institutions not considered. Apply to Chairman of the Department; no specified closing dates. Application fee: paper $40, on-line $20. Phone: (314)935-6166.

ADMISSION STANDARDS. Selective. Usual minimum average: 2.75 (last 2 years) (A = 4).

FINANCIAL AID. Annual awards from institutional funds: scholarships, research assistantships, traineeships, Federal W/S, loans. Apply by February 15 to appropriate department for scholarships, assistantships; to Financial Aid Office for all other programs. Use FAFSA. Phone: (314)935-4761. About 48% of students receive aid other than loans from Institute and outside sources.

DEGREE REQUIREMENTS. For master's: 30 units minimum, at least 24 in residence; thesis/nonthesis option; final written/oral exam. For D.Sc.: 72 units minimum beyond the bachelor's, at least 48 in full-time residence; qualifying exam; dissertation; final written/oral exams.

FIELDS OF STUDY.
Biomedical Engineering.
Chemical Engineering.
Civil Engineering. Includes material science, international project management, structural (advanced design, earthquake, applied mechanics, structures, transportation).
Computer Engineering. M.S.CoE.
Computer Science.
Control Engineering. M.C.E. only.
Economics and Systems Science. D.Sc. only.
Electrical Engineering.
Electrical Engineering/Physics. Ph.D. only.
Engineering Management. M.E.M. only.
Environmental Engineering. Multidisciplinary.

Information Management. M.I.M. only.
Mechanical Engineering.
Silicon Technology. M.S. only.
Systems Science and Mathematics.
Telecommunications Management. M.T.M. only.

School of Law (Box 1120)
Web site: www.law.wustl.edu

Established 1867. Oldest private law school west of Mississippi. Moved to new facilities in 1997. Located on main campus. ABA approved since 1923. AALS member. Semester system. Full-time, day study only. Special facilities: Center for Interdisciplinary Studies and Institute for Global Legal Studies. Special programs: foreign exchange programs with Utrecht University, Utrecht, the Netherlands; Inns of Court School of Law, London, England; The Gerd Bucerius Law School, Hamburg, Germany; Monash University Faculty of Law, Melbourne, Australia; National Law School of India, Bangalore, India; Indian Law Society Law College, Pune, India; National University of Singapore; Tribhuvan University, Kathmandu, Nepal; Kobe University Graduate School of Law, Japan. Law library: 602,918 volumes, 6513 subscriptions; has LEXIS, NEXIS, WESTLAW, LEGI-SLATE, Congressional Information Systems.

Annual tuition: $25,730. No on-campus housing available. Law students live off-campus. Contact University Housing Office for off-campus information, phone: (800)874-4330 or (314)935-5092; for University Apartment Referral Service, phone: (314)935-5092. Off-campus housing and personal expenses: approximately $15,500.

Enrollment: first-year class 233; total full-time 656 (men 56%, women 44%) Faculty: full-time 36, part-time 39. Student to faculty ratio 15.1 to 1. Degrees conferred: J.D., J.D.-M.B.A., J.D.-M.H.A., J.D.-M.A. (East Asian Studies, European Studies, Environmental Policy, Political Science), J.D.-M.S.W., J. D.-M.S. (Engineering and Policy), M.J.S. (limited to five students per year), LL.M. (Tax, Intellectual Property), LL.M. (for international persons who have completed a basic legal education and received a university degree in law in another country), LL.M.-J.S.D.

ADMISSION REQUIREMENTS. LSDAS Law School report, bachelor's degree, transcripts, LSAT, personal statement, resume, letters of recommendation required in support of application. Interview not required. Accepts transfer applicants. Graduates of unaccredited colleges not considered. Apply to Office of Admissions by March 1 for priority consideration. Admits Fall only. Application fee $60. Phone: (314)935-4525; fax: (314)935-8778.

ADMISSION REQUIREMENTS FOR LL.M. APPLICANTS. For LL.M.: all applicants must have received the LL.B. or J.D. from a law school approved by AALS. Official undergraduate transcripts, official law school transcripts with rank-in-class, verification of LSAT, personal statement, résumé required in support of graduate application. Apply to LL.M. program. Application fee $50. Phone: (314)935-4525. For LL.M. (international applicants): all applicants must have the basic law degree recognized in their own country. Official transcripts with certified translations and evaluations, TOEFL (minimum score 600) for those who native language is not English, letter of credit indicating sufficient financial support required in support of graduate application. Personal interviews may be requested. Admits Fall only. Apply to LL.M. program for International Students. Application fee $50. Phone: (314)935-6404.

ADMISSION REQUIREMENTS FOR LL.M.-J.S.D. (RESEARCH DEGREE) APPLICANTS. All applicants must have received the LL.B. or J.D. from a law school approved by AALS. Official undergraduate transcripts, official law school transcripts with rank-in-class, verification of LSAT, personal statement, résumé required in support of graduate application. Admits Fall only. Apply to Graduate program by March 15. Application fee $50. Phone: (314)935-4525.

ADMISSION STANDARDS. Selective. Mean LSAT: 160; mean GPA: 3.35 (A = 4). Gourman rating: 4.30. *U.S. News & World Report* ranking is in the top 25 of all U.S. law schools. Accepts 40–45% of total annual applicants.

FINANCIAL AID. Olin Scholarship, scholarships, grants, Federal W/S, loans. Apply to Office of Financial Aid by April 15. Use FAFSA. About 55% of students receive scholarships from School.

DEGREE REQUIREMENTS. For J.D.: 85 hours minimum, at least two semesters in full-time residence. For M.J.S.: 30 credits, all in residence; thesis of publishable quality; all course work completed in four years; thesis must be completed within one year of completion of course work. For LL.M.: at least 24 credits beyond the J.D.; one year in full-time residence; thesis.

School of Medicine (63110)

Formed 1891. Library: 217,000 volumes; has MEDLINE.
Annual tuition: $34,280. Total average cost for all other expenses $8000–$10,000.
Enrollment: first-year class 120, total 472 (men 60%, women 40%). Faculty: full-time 1100, part-time 1200. Degrees conferred: M.D., M.A.-M.D., M.D.-Ph.D. (Medical Scientist Training Program).

ADMISSION REQUIREMENTS. AMCAS report, transcripts, recommendations, MCAT required in support of application. Interview by invitation only. Applicants must have completed at least three years of college study. Does not have EDP. Apply through AMCAS after June 1, before December 1. Application fee $50. Phone: (314)362-6857; fax: (314)362-4658.

ADMISSION STANDARDS. Very competitive. Mean MCAT: 11.1; mean GPA: 3.83 (A = 4). Gourman rating: 4.76. *U.S. News & World Report* ranking is in the top 3 of all U.S. medical schools and in the top 30 in primary care. Accepts 3–4% of total annual applicants. Approximately 8% are state residents.

FINANCIAL AID. Scholarships. MSTP funded by NIH. About 63% of students receive aid other than loans from School. Apply to Financial Aid Officer following acceptance. Phone: (314)362-6845. Use FAFSA (School code: G24620). About 90% of students receive some form of financial assistance.

DEGREE REQUIREMENTS. For M.D.: satisfactory completion of four-year program; taking the USMLE Step 1 and Step 2 is recommended. For M.A.-M.D.: satisfactory completion of five-year program. For Ph.D.: see Graduate School listing above.

FIELDS OF GRADUATE STUDY.
Biochemistry.
Bioorganic Chemistry.
Developmental Biology.
Immunology.
Microbial Pathogeneses.
Microbiology.
Molecular Biology.
Molecular Biophysics.
Molecular Cell Biology.
Molecular Genetics.
Molecular Microbiology.
Neurosciences.
Pathology.
Pharmacology.
Physiology.

George Warren Brown School of Social Work

Established 1925. Semester system. Special facilities: Buder Center for American Indian Studies, Center for Mental Health Services Research, Center for Social Development, Comorbidity and Addictions Center.
Annual tuition $15,000. Off-campus housing only. Contact Graduate Housing Office for off-campus housing information. Phone: (314)935-5092.
Enrollment: full-time 351, part-time 62. School faculty: full-time 29, part-time 47. Degrees conferred: M.S.W., M.S.W.-J.D., M.S.W.-M.B.A., Ph.D. (awarded by the Graduate school of Arts and Sciences).

ADMISSION REQUIREMENTS. Transcripts, references required in support of application. Interview may be required. MAT/GRE required for Ph.D applicants. On-line application available. TOEFL required for international applicants. Accepts transfer applicants. Graduates of unaccredited institutions not considered. Apply to Director of Admissions and Student Resources at least two months in advance of registration. Earlier application encouraged. Rolling admissions process. Application fee $35, $45 for both doctoral and international applicants. Phone: (314)935-6676; fax (314)935-4859.

ADMISSION STANDARDS. Very selective. Usual minimum average: 3.0 (A = 4).

FINANCIAL AID. Fellowships, teaching assistantships, scholarships, tuition remission grants, internships, tuition waivers, Federal W/S, loans. Approved for VA benefits. Apply by March 1 to Dean's Office for fellowships, assistantships; to Director of Financial Aid for all other programs, Phone: (314) 935-6655. Use FAFSA (School code: 002520) and Institutional FAF. Approximately 80% of students receive some form of financial assistance. Aid available for part-time students.

DEGREE REQUIREMENTS. For M.S.W.: 45–60 credits minimum, depending on previous academic preparation; 10 of 60 credits are in field practicum, normally in two different social work settings. For Ph.D.: 51 credits beyond the M.S.W. or 72 beyond the baccalaureate; at least one year in full-time residence; qualifying exams; dissertation; final oral exam.

FIELDS OF STUDY.
Social Work (Clinical). Includes children, youth and family, gerontology, mental health, social and economic development. M.S.W.
Social Work. Interdisciplinary. Ph.D.

UNIVERSITY OF WASHINGTON
Seattle, Washington 98195
Web site: www.washington.edu

Founded 1861. CGS and AAU member. Coed. State control. Quarter System. Special facilities: arboretum, Bureau of Governmental Research Services, Botanical and Drug Plant Gardens, Burke Memorial Washington State Museum, Center for Advanced Research Technology in the Arts and Humanities, Center for Advanced Study and Research on Intellectual Property, Center for AIDS and Sexually Transmitted Diseases, Center for American Politics and Public Policy, Center for Child Environmental Health Risks Research, Center for Conservation Biology, Center for Cost and Outcomes Research, Center for Disability Policy and Research, Center for Ecogenetics and Environmental Health, Center for Experimental Nuclear Physics and Astrophysics, Center for Expression Arrays, Center for Health Education and Research, Center for Human Development and Disability, Center for Instructional Development and Research, Center for International Business and Research, Center for International Trade in Forest Products, Center for Internet, Center for Labor Studies, Center for Law, Commerce and Technology, Center for Mind, Brain, and Learning, Center for Multicultural Education, Center for Nanotechnology, Center for Process Analytical Chemistry,

Center for Research on Family, Center for Social Science Computation and Research, Center for Spanish Studies, Center for Statistics and Social Sciences, Center for Studies in Demography and Ecology, Center for Technology Entrepreneurship, Center for Urban Horticulture, Center for Urban Water Resources Management, Center for Videoendoscopic Surgery, Center for West European Studies, Center for Women and Democracy, Center for Women's Health Research, Child Health Institute, Fisheries Research Institute, Friday Harbor Laboratories, Henry Art Gallery, Human Services Policy Center, Institute on Aging, Institute for Ethnic Studies in the United States, Institute for International Policy, Institute for Nuclear Theory, Institute for Public Health Genetics, Institute for Risk Analysis and Risk Communication, Institute for the Study of Educational Policy, Institute for Transnational Studies, Laboratory of Radiation Biology, Northwest Center for Research on Women, Regional Primate Research Center, Washington Mining and Mineral Resources Research Institute, oceanographic research vessels. The University's NIH ranking is third among all U.S. institutions with 900 awards/grants worth $356,240,621. Libraries: 5,800,000 volumes, 50,000 subscriptions. Total University enrollment: 35,600.

Annual tuition: full-time resident $5352, nonresident $13,890; part-time, per quarter resident $510, nonresident $1323. On-campus housing for 672 married students, 4400 units for men and women. Average academic year housing cost: $5877 for married students; $3807 for single students. Contact Student Services Office: (206)543-4059 for on-campus housing information; (206)543-8997 for off-campus housing information. Day care facilities available.

Graduate School

Established 1911. Enrollment: full-time 6698 (men 50%, women 50%), part-time 2129. Graduate faculty: full- and part-time 2500. Degrees conferred: M.A., M.Arch., M.A.I.S., M.A.T., M.B.A., M.Comm., M.Ed., M.F.A., M.I.S., M.L.A., M.Lib., M.O.T., M.P.T., M.S.W., M.S.P.A., M.H.A., M.S., M.S.Aero. & Astro., M.S.B.C.M., M.S.Cer.Eng., M.S.Chem.Eng., M.S.Civ.Eng., M.S.D., M.S.E.E., M.For.Res., M.S.Mech.Eng., M.S.Met.Eng., M.M., M.S.Nuc.Eng., M.N., M.P.A., M.P.H., M.S.P.E., M.S.P.H., M.S.Rad.Sci., M.U.P., Ph.D., Ed.D., D.M.A., D.A.

ADMISSION REQUIREMENTS. Two official transcripts, letters of recommendation, GRE Test required in support of School's application. On-line application available. Satisfactory score on TOEFL required for international students. Accepts transfer applicants. Graduates of unaccredited institutions not considered. Apply to Office of Graduate Admissions by May 15 (Summer), July 1 (Fall), November 1 (Winter), February 1 (Spring). Application fee $50. Phone: (206)543-5929 (request school/program); fax: (206)543-8798; e-mail: uwgrad@u.washington.edu.

ADMISSION STANDARDS. Very competitive for some departments, competitive and selective for the others. Minimum average: 3.0 for last two years (A = 4).

FINANCIAL AID. Scholarships, teaching/research assistantships, internships, grants, tuition waivers, Federal W/S, loans. Approved for VA benefits. Apply by February 28 to appropriate department chair/graduate program coordinator. Phone: (206)543-6101. Use FAFSA. About 35% of students receive aid other than loans from School. Aid available for part-time students.

DEGREE REQUIREMENTS. For master's: 36 credits minimum, at least three quarters (27 credits) in residence; foreign language and thesis for some departments; final oral/written exam. For doctorates: three years minimum, at least one year in full-time residence; reading knowledge of two foreign languages in some programs for Ph.D.; candidacy exam; dissertation; final exam.

FIELDS OF STUDY.

Accounting. M.Prof.Acc.
Aeronautics and Astronautics. M.S.A.A., Ph.D.
Anthropology. M.A., Ph.D.
Applied Mathematics. M.S., Ph.D.
Architecture. M.Arch., M.S.Arch.
Art. M.F.A.
Art History. M.A., Ph.D.
Art Studio. M.F.A.
Asian Languages and Literature. M.A., Ph.D.
Astronomy. M.S., Ph.D.
Atmospheric Sciences. M.S., Ph.D.
Biochemistry. Ph.D.
Bioengineering. M.S.E., Ph.D.
Biological Structure. M.S., Ph.D.
Biology Teaching. M.A.T.
Biostatistics. M.P.H., M.S., Ph.D.
Botany. M.S., Ph.D.
Business Administration. M.B.A., Ph.D.
Chemical Engineering. M.S.Ch.E., M.S.E., Ph.D.
Chemistry. Ph.D.
Civil and Environmental Engineering. M.S.Civ.E., M.S.E., Ph.D.
Classics. M.A., Ph.D.
Communication. M.A., M.C., Ph.D.
Communications—Digital Media. M.C.
Comparative Literature. M.A., Ph.D.
Comparative Medicine. M.S.
Computer Science and Engineering. M.S., Ph.D.
Construction Management. M.S.C.M.
Dance. M.F.A.
Dentistry. Includes endodontics, oral biology (M.S., Ph.D.), oral medicine, orthodonotics, periodontics, pediatric dentistry, prosthodontics. M.S.D.
Drama. Includes acting, costume design, directing, history, lighting design, playwriting, scenic design, theater criticism, theater history. M.F.A., Ph.D.
Economics. M.A., Ph.D.
Education. Includes administration, counselor, curriculum and instruction, special, speech. M.Ed., Ed.D., Ph.D.
Electrical Engineering. M.S.E.E., Ph.D.
Engineering. Interengineering graduate studies. M.S.E., M.Engr., M.S.
English. Includes creative writing (M.F.A.). M.A., M.A.T., Ph.D.
English Language and Literature. M.A., Ph.D.
Environmental Health. M.P.H., M.S., Ph.D.
Epidemiology. Includes international health, maternal and child health. M.P.H., M.S., Ph.D.
Fishery Sciences. M.S., Ph.D.
Forest Resources. M.F.R., M.S., Ph.D.
French Studies. M.A., Ph.D.
Genetic Epidemiology. M.S.
Genome Sciences. Ph.D.
Geography. M.A., Ph.D.
Geological Sciences. M.S., Ph.D.
Geophysics. M.S., Ph.D.
Germanics. M.A., Ph.D,
Health Services Administration. M.H.A.
Health Services. M.P.H., M.S., Ph.D.
History. Includes international studies (M.A. only), comparative religion, East Asian studies, Middle Eastern studies, Russian and East European studies, South Asian studies. M.A., Ph.D.
Immunology. M.S., Ph.D.
Individual Ph.D.
Information Management. M.S., Ph.D.
International Studies. Includes China studies, comparative religion, Japan studies, Korea studies, Middle Eastern studies, Russian/East European/Central Asian studies, South Asian studies. M.I.S. only.
Italian Studies. M.A.
Laboratory Medicine. M.S.

Landscape Architecture. M.L.A.

Law. LL.M., Ph.D.

Library and Information Science. M.Libr&I.S.

Linguistics. Includes romances linguistics. M.A., Ph.D.

Marine Affairs. M.M.A.

Materials Science and Engineering. M.S.M.S.&E., Ph.D.

Mathematics. M.A., M.S., Ph. D.

Mechanical Engineering. M.S.M.E., M.S.E., Ph.D.

Medical Engineering. M.M.E.

Medical History and Ethics. M.A.

Medicinal Chemistry. Ph.D.

Microbiology. Ph.D.

Museology. Interdisciplinary. M.A.

Music. M.A., M.M., D.M.A., Ph.D.

Near and Middle Eastern Studies. Interdisciplinary. Ph.D.

Near East Language and Civilization. M.A.

Neurobiology and Behavior. Ph.D.

Nursing. M.N., M.S., Ph.D.

Nutritional Sciences. M.P.H., M.S., Ph.D.

Oceanography. Includes biological, chemical, physical. M.S., Ph.D.

Oral Biology. M.S.

Pathobiology. M.S., Ph.D.

Pathology. Ph.D.

Pharmaceutics. Ph.D.

Pharmacology. M.S., Ph.D.

Philosophy. M.A., Ph.D.

Physics. M.S., Ph.D.

Physiology and Biophysics. Ph.D.

Political Science. Ph.D.

Psychology. Includes clinical, school. Ph.D.

Public Affairs. M.P.A.

Public Health Genetics. M.P.H., Ph.D.

Quantitative Ecology and Resource Management. M.S., Ph.D.

Rehabilitation Medicine. M.R.M., M.S., M.O.T., M.P.T.

Romance Language and Literature. M.A., Ph.D.

Scandinavian Languages and Literature. M.A., Ph.D.

Scandinavian Studies. M.A., Ph.D.

Slavic Languages and Literature. M.A., Ph.D.

Social Work. M.S.W.

Social Welfare. Ph.D.

Sociology. Ph.D.

Speech and Hearing Sciences. M.S., Ph.D.

Statistics. M.S., Ph.D.

Technical Communication. M.S., Ph.D.

Urban Design and Planning. M.U.P., Ph.D.

Women's Studies. Ph.D.

Zoology. M.S., Ph.D.

School of Dentistry (98195-6365)

Established 1945. Special facilities: Comprehensive Oral Health Research Center of Discovery, National Institute of Dental and Craniofacial Research. Annual tuition: resident $9534, nonresident $24,084. Total average cost for all other first-year expenses $5500. On-campus housing available. Annual housing costs: $10,000.

Enrollment: first-year class 52; total 212 (men 70%, women 30%). Faculty: full-time 69, part-time 48. Degrees conferred: D.D.S., M.S.D., M.S., Ph.D., D.D.S.-M.P.H., D.D.S.-Ph.D. (Basic Science).

ADMISSION REQUIREMENTS. AADSAS report, transcripts, DAT, recommendations required in support of application. Applicants must have completed at least three years of college study. Interview by invitation only. Preference given to state and WICHE residents. Apply through AADSAS after June 1, before November 1. Application fee $35. Phone: (206)543-5840; e-mail: askuwsod@u.washington.edu.

ADMISSION STANDARDS. Selective. Accepts 10-15% of total annual applicants. Approximately 80% are state residents.

FINANCIAL AID. Scholarships, grants, loans. About 20% of students receive aid other than loans from School. Apply to Financial Aid Office by March 1. Phone: (206)543-1511. Use FAFSA.

DEGREE REQUIREMENTS. For D.D.S.: satisfactory completion of 12 quarters of study, including summer quarters after year two, and year three. For M.S.D.: satisfactory completion of one-year program. For M.S., Ph.D.: see Graduate School listing above.

FIELDS OF GRADUATE STUDY.

Endodontics. M.S.D. only.

General Practice. Certificate.

Oral Biology. M.S. and Ph.D. only.

Oral and Maxillofacial Surgery. Certificate.

Oral Medicine. M.S.D. only.

Orthodontics. M.S.D. only.

Pediatrics Dentistry. M.S.

Periodontics. M.S.D. only.

Prosthodontics. M.S.D. only.

School of Law (98105-6617)

Web site: www.law.washington.edu

Established 1899. Located on main campus. ABA approved since 1924. AALS member. Quarter system. Full-time, day study only. Special facility: Center for Advanced Study and Research on Intellectual Property. Law library: 592,265 volumes, 5510 subscriptions; has LEXIS, NEXIS, WESTLAW, DIALOG.

Annual tuition: resident $6216, nonresident $15,327. On-campus housing available for both single and married students. Contact Housing Office for both on- and off-campus housing information. Phone: (206)543-4059. Law students tend to live off-campus. Off-campus housing and personal expenses: approximately $12,432.

Enrollment: first-year class 163; total full-time 432 (men 48%, women 52%). Faculty: full-time 37, part-time 19. Student to faculty ratio 11.7 to 1. Degrees conferred: J.D., J.D.-M.B.A., J.D.-M.A. (International Studies), LL.M. (Asian Law, Law and Marine Affairs, International Environmental Law, Law of Sustainable International Development, Taxation).

ADMISSION REQUIREMENTS. LSDAS Law School report, Bachelor's degree, transcripts, LSAT (not later than December) required in support of application. TOEFL required for foreign students. Interview not required. Graduate of unaccredited colleges not considered. Apply to Admission Office after September 15, before January 15. Admits Fall only. Application fee $35. Phone: (206)543-4078; fax: (206)543-5671. For graduate study, apply to Director, Graduate Program, School of Law.

ADMISSION REQUIREMENTS FOR TRANSFER APPLICANTS. Accepts transfers from other AALS-approved schools. Admission limited to space available. At least one year of enrollment, Dean's letter indicating the applicant is in good standing, prefer applicants in the top quarter of first-year class, LSAT, LSDAS, personal statement regarding reason for transfer, undergraduate transcript, current law school transcript required in support of School's application. Apply to Admission Office by July 15 (Fall only). Admission decision made by mid-August. Application fee $50. Will consider visiting students.

ADMISSION REQUIREMENT FOR LL.M. APPLICANTS. All applicants must hold a J.D. or equivalent degree from a law school that is a member of AALS and is approved by ABA. International applicants must have a first law degree or equivalent and must receive permission from Director of Graduate Admission. Original application, one official transcript, and application fee of $45 should be sent to the Office of Graduate Admission (Box 351280). A second official transcript including ranking-in-class, one or two letters of recommendation, a statement of purpose, a résumé and the goldenrod copy of the application should be sent to the Law School Graduate Admission Office. Admits to all quarters. Deadlines: July 1 (Fall, full- and part-time), November 1 (Winter, part-time only), February 1 (Spring, part-time only), May 15 (Summer, part-time only). Phone: (206)616-5964; fax: (206)685-4469.

ADMISSION STANDARDS. Selective. Mean LSAT: 162; mean GPA: 3.50 (A = 4). Gourman rating: 4.45. *U.S. News & World Report* ranking is in the top 25 of all U.S. law schools. Accepts 25% of total annual applicants.

FINANCIAL AID. Scholarships, partial tuition waivers, fellowships, assistantships, Federal W/S, loans. About 42% of students receive aid other than loans from School. Apply to Assistant Dean of School by March 1. Use FAFSA (School code: 003798).

DEGREE REQUIREMENTS. For J.D.: 135 quarter credits with a GPA of at least 2.0 (A = 4), plus completion of upper-divisional writing course; 60 hours of public service; three-year program. Accelerated J.D. with summer course work. For LL.M. (Asian Law): 36 quarter credits; proficiency in either Japanese, Chinese, or Korean; one comparative law seminar, one graduate research course; research project. For LL.M. (International Environmental Law): 40 quarter credits, at least 15 credits earned in law school; seminar on Problems in International Environmental Law; research paper. For LL.M. (Sustainable International Development): 40 quarter credits, at least 15 credits earned in law school; seminar in Legal Problems of Economic Development; research paper. For LL.M. (Law and Marine Affairs): 40 quarter credits, at least 15 credits earned in law school; one course in Marine Affairs (course must be at the 500 level); Ocean Policy and Resource Seminar. For LL.M. (Tax): 36 quarter credits.

School of Medicine

Founded in 1945. Health Sciences Library: 100,000 volumes. Annual tuition: resident $10,143 nonresident $25,668. Total average cost for all other expenses $7500.

Enrollment: first-year class 178 (M.D.-Ph.D. approximately 8–12 each year), total 700 (men 53%, women 47%). Faculty: full- and part-time and volunteers 1100. Degrees conferred: M.D., M.D.-Ph.D. (Medical Scientist Training Program). The M.S. and Ph.D. are offered through the Graduate School.

ADMISSION REQUIREMENTS. AMCAS report, transcripts, three letters of recommendation, MCAT, autobiography, final screening interview required in suport of application. Does not have EDP. Interview and supplemental materials by invitation only. Accepts transfer applicants. Graduates of unaccredited colleges not considered. Preference given to WAMI residents. Apply to Assistant Dean for Admissions after June 1, before November 1. Application fee $35. Phone: (206)543-7212.

ADMISSION STANDARDS. Selective. Mean MCAT: 10.0; mean GPA: 3.64 (A = 4). Gourman rating: 4.39. *U.S. News & World Report* ranking is in the top 10 of all U.S. medical schools. Accepts about 15–20% of total annual applicants. Approximately 90% are WAMI residents.

FINANCIAL AID. Scholarships, research fellowships, loans. MSTP funded by NIH. Apply to School's Financial Aid Office after acceptance, but before February 28. Phone: (206)685-2520. Use FAFSA (School code: 003798). About 83% of students receive some aid from School.

DEGREE REQUIREMENTS. For M.D.: satisfactory completion of four-year program; all students must pass USMLE Step 1 prior to entering third year, and pass Step 2 prior to awarding of M.D. For M.S., Ph.D.: see Graduate School listing above.

FIELDS OF GRADUATE STUDY.
Biochemistry.
Bioengineering.
Biological Structure.
Biomathematics/Biostatictics.
Cancer Research.
Epidemiology.
Environmental Health.
Genetics.
Immunology.
Molecular and Cellular Biology.
Molecular Biotechnology.
Neurobiology.
Pathology.
Pharmacology.
Physiology and Biophysics.

WAYNE STATE COLLEGE
Wayne, Nebraska 68787
Web site: www.wsc.edu

Founded 1891. Located 100 miles NW of Omaha. CGS member. Coed. State control. Semester system. Library: 192,000 volumes, 1200 subscriptions.

Tuition: per credit, resident $96, nonresident $192. On-campus housing available. Average academic year housing costs: $3670 (including board) for single students; $4650 for married students. Contact Housing Office for both on- and off-campus housing information. Phone: (402)375-7318.

Graduate Studies

Enrollment: full-time 31, part-time 247. Faculty teaching graduate students: full-time 0, part-time 73. Degrees conferred: M.S.E., M.B.A., Ed.S.

ADMISSION REQUIREMENTS. Official transcripts, GRE/GMAT, health form required in support of College's application. On-line application available. TOEFL and Financial Resources Certification form required for international applicants. Accepts transfer applicants. Apply to Office of Admissions at least two months prior to date of registration. Rolling admissions process. Application fee $20; $40 for international applicants. Phone: (800)228-9972, (402)375-7234.

ADMISSION STANDARDS. Relatively open. Usual minimum average 2.5 (A = 4).

FINANCIAL AID. Annual awards from institutional funds: scholarships, teaching assistantships, loans. Apply by May 1 to Director of Graduate Studies Office for assistantships; to Financial Aid Office for all other programs. Phone: (402)375-7204. Use FAFSA (College code: 002566). About 10% of students receive aid other than loans from College and outside sources. No aid for part-time students.

DEGREE REQUIREMENTS. For M.S.E.: 30 semester hours minimum; thesis optional; final oral/written exam. For M.B.A.: 36 credit program. For Specialist: 33 semester hours beyond the master's degree; special project.

FIELDS OF STUDY.
Art Education.
Business Administration.
Communication Arts Education.
Curriculum and Instruction. Includes alternative education, art education, business education, communication arts education, education technology, elementary education, English as a second language, family and consumer science, health/physical education/K–12 education, industrial technology education/vocational education, mathematics education, music education, science education, social sciences education.
English Education.

History Education.

Mathematics Education.

Physical Education. Includes exercise science, sport management.

School Administration. Includes P–6, 7–12, P–12.

School Counseling. Includes P–6, 7–12, P–12, community counseling, higher education counseling.

Science Education.

Social Sciences Education.

Special Education/Special Educator.

Special Education/Instructional Manager.

WAYNE STATE UNIVERSITY

Detroit, Michigan 48202

Web site: www.wayne.edu

Founded 1868. CGS member. Coed. State control. Semester system. Special facilities: Addiction Research Center, Bioengineering Center, Center for Automotive Research, Center for Chicano Boricua Studies, Center for Health Research, Center for Healthcare Effectiveness Research, Center for International Business Studies, Center for Legal Studies, Center for Molecular Medicine and Genetics, Center for Peace and Conflict Studies, Center for the Study of Arts and Public Policy, Center for Urban Studies, Institute of Environmental Health Sciences, Institute for Information Technology and Culture, Institute for Learning and Performance Improvement, Institute for Manufacturing Research, Institute for Organizational and Industrial Competitiveness, Institute for Scientific Computing, Ligon Research Center for Vision, Manufacturing Information Systems Center, Merrill-Palmer Institute, Research Institute for Engineering Sciences, Institute of Gerontology, Barbara Ann Karmanos Cancer Institute, Cohn-Haddow Center for Judaic Studies, C.S. Mott Center for Human Growth and Development, Developmental Disabilities Institute, Douglas A. Fraser Center for Workplace Issues, Hilberry Classic Repertory Theatre, Humanities Center, Labor Studies Center, Morris J. Hood Jr. Comprehensive Diabetes Center, National Teachers Corps Center, Charles Grosberg Religious Center, Mass Communications Center (equipped for closed-circuit TV and portable videotaping operation), Skillman Center for Children, State Policy Center. The University's NIH ranking is 66th among all U.S. institutions with 245 awards/grants worth $72,071,296. Library: more than 2,830,000 volumes, 24,000 subscriptions. Total University enrollment: 31,185.

Tuition: per credit, resident $208, nonresident $459. On-campus housing for 800 single students. Average annual housing cost: $850 per semester in dormitory; $450–$550 per month in apartments. Apply to Housing Authority. Phone: (313)577-2116.

Graduate School

Graduate study since 1930. Enrollment: full- and part-time 9208. Graduate faculty: full- and part-time 858. Degrees conferred: M.A., M.S., M.Ed., M.A.I.R., M.A.T., M.S.L.S., M.B.A., M.F.A., M.L.I.S., M.M., M.P.A., M.U.P., M.S.W., Ed.S., Ed.D., Ph.D.

ADMISSION REQUIREMENTS. Official transcripts required in support of School's application. GRE, MAT, GMAT/other entrance exams, letters of recommendation, interviews required by many departments. TOEFL required for international applicants. Accepts transfer applicants. Graduates of unaccredited institutions not considered. Apply to Office of University Admissions by July 1 (Fall), November 1 (Winter), March 1 (Spring), June 1 (Summer). Application fee $20; $30 for international applicants. Phone: (313)577-3577; fax: (313)577-7536; e-mail: admissions@ wayne.edu.

ADMISSION STANDARDS. Selective for most departments. Usual minimum average: 2.6 (A = 4).

FINANCIAL AID. Annual awards from institutional funds: scholarships, graduate fellowships, minority fellowships, graduate assistantships, internships, Federal W/S, loans. Approved for VA benefits. Apply in early Winter to Graduate Dean for scholarships and fellowships, to department chair for assistantships; to Financial Aid Office for all other programs. Phone: (313)577-2172 (scholarships and fellowships), (313)577-3378 (loans). Use FAFSA and University's FAF. About 30% of students receive aid other than loans from University and outside sources. Aid available for part-time students.

DEGREE REQUIREMENTS. For most master's: Plan A—24 semester hours minimum plus thesis; Plan B—28 semester hours minimum plus essay; Plan C—30 semester hours minimum without thesis or essay, at least 24 in residence; final written/oral exam; no language for most majors. For Ed.S.: 30 hours minimum beyond the master's, at least 24 in residence; terminal project or field study. For Ed.D.: 100 hours minimum beyond the bachelor's, at least 30 in residence; preliminary, qualifying, final written/oral exam; dissertation. For Ph.D.: 90 hours minimum beyond the bachelor's, including dissertation, at least 30 in residence; preliminary exam for some majors; written/oral qualifying exams; final oral exam; reading knowledge of one or more foreign languages required in some fields.

FIELDS OF STUDY.

SCHOOL OF BUSINESS ADMINISTRATION:

Business Administration. M.B.A.

Taxation. M.S.

COLLEGE OF EDUCATION:

Administration and Supervision. Ed.D.

Art Education. M.Ed.

Bilingual/Bicultural Education. M.Ed.

Career and Technical Education. M.Ed., Ed.D., Ph.D.

Counseling. M.A., M.Ed., Ed.D., Ph.D.

Curriculum and Instruction. Ed.D., Ph.D.

Education Evaluation and Research. M.Ed., Ed.D., Ph.D.

Educational Leadership. M.Ed.

Educational Leadership and Policy Studies. Ed.D., Ph.D.

Educational Psychology. M.Ed., Ph.D.

Elementary Education. M.A., M.A.T., M.Ed.

English Education (Secondary). M.Ed.

Foreign Language Education. M.Ed.

Health Education. Includes clinical/community health education. M.Ed.

History and Philosophy of Education. M.Ed.

Instructional Technology. M.Ed., Ed.D., Ph.D.

Mathematics Education. M.Ed.

Physical Education. M.Ed.

Pre-School and Parent Education. M.Ed.

Reading. M.Ed., Ed.D.

Reading, Language, and Literature. Ed.D.

Recreation and Park Service. Includes therapeutic recreation. M.A.

Rehabilitation Counseling and Community Inclusion. M.A.

School and Community Psychology. M.A.

Science Education. M.Ed.

Secondary Education. M.A.T.

Social Studies Education (Secondary). M.Ed.

Special Education. M.Ed., Ed.D., Ph.D.

Sports Administration. Includes interscholastic/intercollegiate, professional. M.A.

COLLEGE OF ENGINEERING:

Biomedical Engineering. M.S., Ph.D.

Chemical Engineering. M.S., Ph.D.

Civil and Environmental Engineering. M.S., Ph.D.

Computer Engineering. M.S., Ph.D.

Electrical Engineering. M.S., Ph.D.

Electronic and Computer Control Systems. M.S.
Engineering Management. M.S.
Engineering Technology. M.S.
Environmental Auditing.
Hazardous Materials Management on Public Lands.
Hazardous Waste Control.
Hazardous Waste Management. M.S.
Industrial Engineering. M.S., Ph.D.
Manufacturing Engineering. M.S.
Materials Science and Engineering. M.S., Ph.D.
Mechanical Engineering. M.S., Ph.D.
Operations Research. M.S., Ph.D.
Polymer Engineering.

COLLEGE OF FINE, PERFORMING, AND COMMUNICATION ARTS:
Art. M.A., M.F.A.
Art History. Includes museum practice. M.A.
Communication. Includes communication studies, public relations and organizational communication, radio-TV-film, speech communication. M.A., Ph.D.
Design and Merchandising. M.A.
Music. Includes composition, choral conducting, music education, performance, theory. M.A., M.M.
Theatre. M.A., M.F.A., Ph.D.

GRADUATE SCHOOL:
Alcohol and Drug Abuse Studies.
Archival Administration.
Developmental Disabilities.
Gerontology.
Infant Mental Health.
Individual Interdisciplinary. Ph.D.
Library and Information Science. M.L.I.S.
Molecular and Cellular Toxicology. M.S., Ph.D.

COLLEGE OF LIBERAL ARTS:
Anthropology. M.A., Ph.D.
Art History. M.A.
Classics. M.A.
Comparative Literature. M.A.
Criminal Justice. M.S.
Economics. M.A., Ph.D.
English. One language for M.A. M.A., Ph.D.
French. M.A.
German. M.A.
History. M.A., Ph.D.
Linguistics. M.A.
Modern Languages. Ph.D.
Near Eastern Languages. M.A.
Philosophy. M.A., Ph.D.
Political Science. M.A., Ph.D.
Public Administration. M.P.A.
Sociology. M.A., Ph.D.
Spanish. M.A.

COLLEGE OF LIFELONG LEARNING:
Interdisciplinary Studies. M.I.S.

COLLEGE OF NURSING:
Adult Primary Care Nursing. M.S.
Adult Acute Care Nursing. M.S.
Neonatal Nurse Practitioner.
Nursing. Ph.D.
Nursing Education.
Nursing, Parenting, and Families. M.S.
Psychiatric Mental Health Nurse Practitioner.
Transcultural Nursing. M.S.

COLLEGE OF PHARMACY AND ALLIED HEALTH PROFESSIONS:
Anesthesia. M.S.
Clinical Laboratory Science. M.S.

Clinical Pharmacy. Pharm.D.
Health Systems Pharmacy Management. M.S.
Occupational and Environmental Health Sciences. M.S.
Occupational Therapy. M.S.
Pharmaceutical Sciences. M.S., Ph.D.
Physical Therapy. M.S.
Physician Assistant Studies. M.S.

COLLEGE OF SCIENCE:
Applied Mathematics. M.A.
Audiology. M.S.
Biological Sciences. GRE for admissions. M.S., Ph.D.
Chemistry. One language for M.S.. M.A., M.S., Ph.D.
Communication Disorders and Sciences. M.A., Ph.D.
Computer Science. M.A., M.S., Ph.D.
Geology. M.S.
Human Development. M.A.
Mathematics. M.A., Ph.D.
Mathematical Statistics. M.A.
Molecular Biotechnology. M.S.
Nutrition and Food Science. M.A., M.S., Ph.D.
Physics. M.A., M.S., Ph.D.
Psychology. M.A., Ph.D.
Speech-Language Pathology. M.A., M.S., Ph.D.

SCHOOL OF SOCIAL WORK:
Social Work. Includes administration and community, family, children and youth services, health care services, mental health services. M.S.W.

COLLEGE OF URBAN, LABOR AND, METROPOLITAN AFFAIRS:
Dispute Resolution.
Economic Development.
Geography. M.A.
Industrial Relations. M.A.I.R.
Urban Planning. M.U.P.

Law School

Web site: www.wayne.edu

Established 1927. Located on main campus. ABA approved since 1927. AALS member. Semester system. Full-time, day, part-time (day or evening) study. Special facilities: Intellectual Property Law Institute, Center for Legal Studies. Special programs: summer study abroad at the Academy of International Law, the Hague, the Netherlands; the London Law Programme; exchange program with the School of Law, University of Warwick, England. Law library: 583,446 volumes, 4983 subscriptions; has LEXIS, NEXIS, WESTLAW, CALI.

Annual tuition: full-time resident $8426, nonresident $17,613; part-time resident $6060, nonresident $12,622. University-owned apartments available for both single and married students. Contact University's Housing Office for both on- and off-housing information. Law students tend to live off-campus. Off-campus housing and personal expenses: approximately $15,200.

Enrollment: first-year class full-time 194, part-time 44; total 742 (men 54%, women 46%). Faculty: full-time 24, part-time 26. Student to faculty ratio 23.3 to 1. Degrees conferred: J.D., J.D.-M.B.A., J.D.-M.A. (History, Public Policy), J.D.-M.A.D.R. (Dispute Resolution), LL.M.

ADMISSION REQUIREMENTS. LSDAS Law School report, LSAT (not later than February test date; if more than one LSAT, highest is used), bachelor's degree from an accredited institution, personal statement, one recommendation, transcripts (must show all schools attended and at least three years of study) required in support of application. Applicants must have received bachelor's degree prior to enrollment. Interview not required. In addition, international applicants whose native language is not English must submit TOEFL scores (not older than two years), certified translations and evaluations of all foreign documents. Apply to Office of Admission after October 1, before March 15. First-year students admitted Fall only. Accepts transfer applicants. Rolling admissions process. Application fee $20; $30 for noncitizens. Phone: (313)577-3937; e-mail: inquire@novell.law.wayne.edu.

ADMISSION REQUIREMENTS FOR TRANSFER APPLI-CANTS. Accepts transfers from other ABA accredited schools. Admission limited to space available. At least one year of enroll-ment, Dean's letter indicating the applicant is in good standing, prefer applicants in the top quarter of first year class, LSAT, LSDAS, personal statement regarding reason for transfer, under-graduate transcript, current law school transcript required in sup-port of School's application. Apply to Admission Office by July 1 (Fall). Admission decision made within one month of the re-ceipt of a completed application. Application fee $20. Will con-sider visiting students.

ADMISSION REQUIREMENTS FOR LL.M. APPLICANTS. All applicants must have an equivalent J.D. (LL.B.) degree from a Common Law–based country or have completed a distinguished academic record in legal studies from a non–Common Law coun-try, approved by the Director of Graduate Studies. Official tran-scripts, a personal statement, résumé, recommendations (optional) required in support of the Graduate application. In addition, inter-national students must submit TOEFL scores (if English is not their native language), a special Graduate International Application, and a statement of financial support. Admits Fall, Winter, Spring/Sum-mer. Apply by July 1 (Fall), November 1 (Winter), March 15 (Spring/Summer) to the Office of University Admissions. Contact the Director of Graduate Studies for LL.M. for program informa-tion. Phone (313)577-3947; fax: (313)577-1060. International ap-plicants should contact the Office of University Admissions for specific admissions information. Phone: (313)577-3577.

ADMISSION STANDARDS. Selective. Mean LSAT: full-time 154, part-time 154; mean GPA: full-time 3.4, part-time 3.25 (A = 4). Gourman rating: 3.66. *U.S. News & World Report* rank-ing is in the third tier of all U.S. law schools. Accepts 40–50% of total annual applicants.

FINANCIAL AID. Need-based scholarships, minority (Kenneth Cockrel, Wade McCree) scholarships, law alumni fellowships, Board of Governor's Grants; private and institutional loans, Federal loans and Federal W/S offered through University's Financial Aid Office. Assistantships may be available for upper-divisional joint degree candidates. All accepted student are automatically consid-ered for scholarships. For scholarship information, contact the Law School at (313)577-5142. Apply for Financial Aid after January 1 before April 30. Phone: (313)577-2172. Use FAFSA (School code: E00435), also submit Financial Aid Transcript, Federal Income Tax forms. Approximately 54% of first-year class received scholarships/Grants-in-Aid. Approximately 85% of students receive some form of financial assistance. Aid available for part-time students.

DEGREE REQUIREMENTS. For J.D.: 86 (36 required) credits with a GPA of at least a 2.0 (A = 4), plus completion of upper-divisional writing course; three-year program, four- to six-year part-time program. Accelerated J.D. with summer course work. For J.D.-Master's: three-and-one-half- to four-year programs rather than four- to five-year programs if both degrees are taken consecutively. For LL.M. (Tax): primarily a part-time evening program; 26 credits, at least 16 credits taken at the Law School; 3.0 (A = 4) GPA required; master's essay.

FIELDS OF GRADUATE STUDY.
Corporate and Finance Law. LL.M.
Labor Law. LL.M.
Tax Law. LL.M.

School of Medicine (48201)

Web site: www.med.wayne.edu

Founded 1868. Library: 150,000 volumes. Located at Detroit Medical Center (48201). Annual tuition: resident $14,203, non-

resident $29,557, student fees $771. Total average cost for all other expenses $10,635.

Enrollment: first-year class 256 (EDP 18), total 1044 (men 57%, women 43%). Faculty: full-time 384, part-time 1200, De-gree conferred: M.D. The Ph.D. is offered through the Graduate School.

ADMISSION REQUIREMENTS. AMCAS report, transcripts, recommendations, MCAT (prefer Spring results) required in sup-port of application. Interview required of those candidates under serious consideration. Applicants must have completed at least three years of college study. Has EDP; apply between June 1 and August 1. Accepts transfer applicants. Preference given to state residents. Apply to Office of Admissions after June 1, before No-vember 1. Application fee $40. Phone: (313)577-1466; fax: (313)577-9420.

ADMISSION STANDARDS. Selective, Accepts 10-12% of total annual applicants. Approximately 92% are state residents.

FINANCIAL AID. Scholarships, loans, college work-study. Sum-mer fellowships. Apply to Committee on Financial Aid and Schol-arships after acceptance. Phone: (313)577-1039. Use FAFSA (School code: E00570). About 30% of students receive aid other than loans from School.

DEGREE REQUIREMENTS. For M.D.: satisfactory completion of four-year program; Step 1 of USMLE must be passed prior to entering third year; all students must take USMLE Step 2 and record a score. For Ph.D.: see Graduate Division listing above. Combined M.D.-Ph.D. program is available. Apply during first year in medical school.

FIELDS OF graduate STUDY.
Anatomy. M.S., Ph.D.
Basic Medical Sciences. M.S.
Biochemistry and Molecular Biology. Ph.D.
Community Health Services. M.S.
Genetic Counseling. M.S.
Immunology and Microbiology. M.S., Ph.D.
Medical Physics. Ph.D.
Medical Research. M.S.
Molecular Biology and Genetics. M.S., Ph.D.
Pathology. Ph.D.
Pharmacology. M.S., Ph.D.
Physical Medicine and Rehabilitation. M.S.
Physiology. M.S., Ph.D.
Psychiatry. M.S.
Radiological Physics. M.S.

WEBSTER UNIVERSITY
Webster Groves, Missouri 63119
Web site: www.webster.edu

Founded 1915. Located in St. Louis and 90 locations world-wide. Coed. Private control. Semester system. Special facility (St. Louis): Center for International Education. Library: 250,000 vol-umes, 1400 subscriptions. Total University enrollment: 17,725.

Tuition (St. Louis): per credit hour $415, M.A.T. $360, on-line M.B.A. and on-line M.A. $460. No on-campus housing available.

Graduate Program

Graduate study since 1963. Enrollment: full-time 3626, part-time 8679. Faculty: full-time 76, part-time 1115. Degrees conferred: M.A., M.B.A., M.F.A., M.A.T., M.M., M.S., M.S.N., D.Mgt.

ADMISSION REQUIREMENTS. Official transcripts, bachelor's degree required in support of application. On-line application available. TOEFL required for international applicants. Accepts transfer applicants. Graduates of unaccredited institutions not considered. Application fee $20. Phone: (314)968-7100 or (800)75-ENROL; fax: (314)968-7116.

FINANCIAL AID. Internships, Federal W/S, loans. Approved for VA benefits. Apply by April 1 to the Financial Aid Office. Phone: (314)968-6992; fax: (314)968-7125. Aid available for part-time students.

DEGREE REQUIREMENTS. For M.A., M.S.: 36 credit program; thesis/nonthesis option. For M.B.A.: 36 credit program. For M.A.T.: 33 credit program. For M.M.: 32–34 credit program. For D.Mgt.: 42 credit program.

FIELDS OF STUDY.
Applied Gerontology.
Art.
Business.
Business Administration.
Business and Organizational Security Management.
Communication.
Computer Resources and Information Management.
Computer Science/Distributed Systems.
Counseling.
Environmental Management.
Finance.
Health Care Management.
Health Services Management.
Human Resources Development.
Human Resources Management.
International Business.
International Relations.
Legal Studies.
Management.
Marketing.
Mathematics.
Media Communications.
Multidisciplinary Studies.
Music. Includes composition, conducting, jazz studies, education, performance, pedagogy.
Nurse Anesthesia.
Nursing.
Procurement and Acquisitions Management.
Public Administration.
Quality Management.
Real Estate Management.
Science.
Social Science.
Security Management.
Space Opeartions. Colorado Springs location only.
Space Systems Operations Management.
Telecommunications Management.
Note: Not all programs available at all sites.

WESLEYAN UNIVERSITY
Middletown, Connecticut 06459-0260
Web site: www.wesleyan.edu

Founded 1831. Located 16 miles S of Hartford. CGS member. Coed. Private control. Semester system. Special facilities: Center for the Arts, Davison Art Center, Freeman Athletic Center, Science Center, Van Vleck Observatory. Library: 2,000,000 volumes, 2719 subscriptions.

Annual tuition: full-time $20,190, per course $2525. On-campus housing for married students, 93 graduate men, 65 graduate women. Average academic year housing cost: $550–$825 per month for married students, $515–$650 (room only) for single students. Apply to Graduate Admissions Office in Middletown for both on- and off-campus housing information. Phone: (860)685-3550. Day-care facilities available.

Graduate Program

Graduate study since 1965. Enrollment: full-time 177, part-time 259. University faculty: full-time 97. Degrees conferred: M.A., M.A.L.S., C.A.S., Ph.D.

ADMISSION REQUIREMENTS. Transcripts, three letters of recommendation, GRE required in support of application. On-line application available. GRE Subject Test recommended. TOEFL required for international applicants. Interview often useful. Accepts transfer applicants. Apply to Graduate Admissions Office by April 1 for most programs, by January 15 for music. Application fee $40. Phone: (860)685-1390; fax: (860)685-2001.

ADMISSION STANDARDS. Very competitive for some departments, competitive for others. Usual minimum average: 3.0 (A = 4).

FINANCIAL AID. Annual awards from institutional funds: scholarships, grants, teaching assistantships, Federal W/S, loans. Approved for VA benefits. Apply, normally by March 15, to appropriate department chair for assistantships; to Financial Aid Office for all other programs. Phone: (860)685-2800. Use FAFSA and institutional FAF. About 98% of students receive aid from University and outside sources. Aid available for part-time students.

DEGREE REQUIREMENTS. For M.A.: one year in full-time study or the equivalent, but no more than four years for completion and at least two-thirds of total program in residence; reading knowledge of one foreign language for most majors, more for some programs; thesis or creative project; final written/oral exam. For M.A.L.S.: 30 semester hours, at least 24 in residence; designed for those who want an interdisciplinary education; credit may be earned solely in Summer sessions or in one calendar year of full-time study. For C.A.S. (for those who hold the master's degree): requirements essentially the same as for M.A.L.S. (transfer credits not accepted). For Ph.D.: normally at least 16 semester courses beyond the bachelor's, usually at least three years in residence; reading knowledge of two foreign languages; preliminary/qualifying exams; dissertation; final written/oral exam.

FIELDS OF STUDY.
Astronomy. Qualifying exam, apprenticeships for M.A. M.A. only.
Biochemistry. Ph.D.
Biology. Ph.D.
Chemistry. Ph.D.
Computer Science.
Earth and Environmental Science. M.A. only.
Ethnomusicology. Ph.D.
Mathematics. Apply by March 15.
Molecular Biology.
Molecular Biophysics. Interdepartmental. Ph.D.
Music. Includes choral conducting and composition in Western music.
Physics. Two years for M.A.
Psychology. Apply by March 15. M.A. only.
Note: Special programs leading to the M.A.L.S. and C.A.S. utilize the course offerings of several University departments, with specializations in arts, humanities, mathematics, general studies, science, social science.

UNIVERSITY OF WEST ALABAMA

Livingston, Alabama 35470

Web site: www.uwa.edu

Founded 1835. Name changed from Livingston University in 1995. Located 120 miles SW of Birmingham. Coed. State control. Semester system. Library: 141,700 volumes, 2000 subscriptions.

Tuition: per credit, resident $133, nonresident $266. On-campus housing for both single and married students. Average academic year housing costs: $2055 (including board) for single students; $2650 for married students (including board). Contact Director of Housing for both on- and off-campus housing information. Phone: (205)652-3400.

School of Graduate Studies

Graduate study since 1958. Enrollment: full- and part-time 329. Graduate faculty: full-time 50, part-time 2. Degrees conferred: M.Ed., M.S.C.Ed., M.A.T.

ADMISSION REQUIREMENTS. Transcripts, GRE/MAT/NTE, Alabama Class B certificate, or equivalent required in support of School's application. (Certificate not required for master's in Continuing Education or M.A.T.) TOEFL required for international applicants. Interview not required. Accepts transfer applicants. Apply to Director of Admissions; no specified closing dates. Rolling admissions process. Application fee $20, $50 for international applicants. Phone: (205)652-3647.

ADMISSION STANDARDS. Selective. Usual minimum average: 2.5 (A = 4).

FINANCIAL AID. Scholarships, assistantships, internships, Federal W/S, loans. Apply to Office of Financial Aid by April 1. Phone: (205)652-3400. Use FAFSA and University's FAF. About 10% of students receive aid other than loans from University, 26% from all sources. Aid available for part-time students.

DEGREE REQUIREMENTS. For M.Ed.: 33 credit program, must take 9–12 credit in full-time residence; no thesis; admission to candidacy; final written exam. For M.S.C.Ed.; 33 credit program, must take 9–12 credits in full-time residence; admission to candidacy; final written exam. For M.A.T. 36 credit program, must take 9–12 credits in full-time residence; admission to candidacy; final written exam. No language requirement for any degrees.

FIELDS OF STUDY.
Continuing Education. M.S.C.Ed. only.
Early Childhood Education. M.Ed.
Education Administration. M.Ed.
Elementary Education. M.Ed.
High School Education. M.Ed.
Library Media. M.Ed.
Nursery–Grade 12 Education. M.Ed.
School Counseling. M.Ed.

WEST CHESTER UNIVERSITY OF PENNSYLVANIA

West Chester, Pennsylvania 19383

Web site: www.wcupa.edu

Founded 1871. Located 25 miles W of Philadelphia and 17 miles north of Wilmington. CGS member. Coed. State control. Semester system. Library: 524,976 volumes, 2800 subscriptions. Total University enrollment: 12,274.

Tuition: per credit, resident $230, nonresident $389. Limited on-campus housing for graduate students. Average academic year housing costs: $2996–$3718 (including board). Apply to Director, Residence Life, for on-campus housing information; to the Office of Off-Campus Life for all off-campus housing information. Phone: (610)436-3307.

Graduate Studies

Graduate study since 1959. Enrollment: full-time 337, part-time 1196. Faculty: full- and part-time 232. Degrees conferred: M.Ed., M.A., M.S., M.M., M.B.A., M.S.A.

ADMISSION REQUIREMENTS. Two official transcripts, letters of recommendation required in support of application. Some programs require GRE and Subject Test, MAT, or GMAT scores, interviews. TOEFL required for international applicants. Apply to Office of Graduate Studies by April 15 (Fall), October 15 (Spring). Application fee $25. Phone: (610)436-2943; fax: (610)436-2736; e-mail: gradstudy@wcupa.edu.

ADMISSION STANDARDS. Vary with program. Usual minimum average: 2.75, 3.00 for full degree status (A = 4).

FINANCIAL AID. Scholarships, awards, graduate assistantships, loans. Apply by February 1 to Dean of Graduate Studies and department chair for assistantships, scholarships, awards; to Financial Aid for all other programs. Phone: (610)436-2943. Use FAFSA.

DEGREE REQUIREMENTS. For master's: 30 credits minimum plus thesis, or 36 credits minimum without thesis; final written/oral exam in most programs.

FIELDS OF STUDY.
Administration. M.S. only.
Biology. M.A. only.
Business Administration. Includes economics/finance, general business, management, technology and electronic commerce. M.B.A.
Chemistry. Includes clinical, general. M.S. only.
Communication Studies. M.A. only.
Communicative Disorders. M.A. only.
Computer Science. M.S. only.
Counselor Education. M.Ed., M.S.
Criminal Justice. M.S. only.
Educational Research. M.S. only.
Elementary Education. M.Ed. only.
Elementary School Counseling. M.Ed.
English. M.A. only.
Environmental Health. M.S. only.
French. M.A., M.Ed.
Geography. M.A. only.
German. M.Ed. only.
Health Services. M.S.A. only.
Higher Education Counseling. M.S. only.
History. M.A., M.Ed.
Human Resources Management. M.S.A. only.
Instructional Media. M.Ed., M.S.
Latin. M.Ed. only.
Leadership for Women. M.S.A. only.
Long-Term Care. M.S.A.
Mathematics. M.A. only.
Music Composition. M.M.
Music Education. M.M. only.
Music History. M.A. only.
Music Performance. M.M.
Music Theory. M.M. only.
Nursing. M.S. only.
Philosophy. M.A. only.
Physical Education. M.S. only.
Physical Science. Includes chemistry, earth science. M.A. only.
Psychology. Includes clinical, general, group psychotherapy, industrial/organizational. M.A. only.

Public Administration. M.S.A. only.
Public Health. M.S. only.
Reading. M.Ed. only.
School Health. M.Ed. only.
Secondary Education. M.Ed. only.
Secondary School Counseling. M.Ed. only.
Social Work. M.S.W.
Spanish. M.A., M.Ed.
Special Education. M.Ed. only.
Sport and Athletic Administration. M.S.A. only.
TESL. M.A.
Training and Development. M.S.A. only.
Urban and Regional Planning. M.S.A. only.

STATE UNIVERSITY OF WEST GEORGIA

Carrollton, Georgia 30118
Web site: www.westga.edu

Became a junior college in 1933. Located 48 miles W of Atlanta. CGS member. Coed. State control. Semester system. Library: 314,213 volumes, 2095 subscriptions. Total University enrollment: 9000.

Annual tuition: full-time resident $2412, nonresident $9648; per semester credit, resident $101; nonresident $402. No on-campus housing for married students. Average academic year housing costs: $3854 (including board). Contact Director of Residential Life for off-campus housing information. Phone: (770)836-6426. Day-care facilities available.

Graduate School

Graduate study since 1967. Enrollment: full-time 325, part-time 1525. College faculty teaching graduate students: full-time 230, part-time 17. Degrees conferred: M.A., M.S., M.M., M.Ed., M.B.A., M.P.A., M.P.Acc., Ed.S.

ADMISSION REQUIREMENTS. Official transcripts, NTE, GRE/GMAT, MAT, recommendations required in support of School's application. Interview for psychology majors. TOEFL (minimum score 550) required for international applicants. Accepts transfer applicants. Graduates of unaccredited institutions not considered. Apply to Dean of the Graduate School by August 1 (Fall), December 15 (Winter), March 10 (Spring), June 6 (Summer). All doctoral applicants must apply by February 28 for summer start. Application fee $20. Phone: (770)836-6419; fax: (770)830-2301.

ADMISSION STANDARDS. Selective. Usual minimum average: 2.5 (A = 4).

FINANCIAL AID. Annual awards from institutional funds: graduate assistantships, research assistantships, internships, tuition waivers, Federal W/S, loans; varying number of dormitory hosts and hostesses. Approved for VA benefits. Apply to Dean of the Graduate School; no specified closing date. Phone: (770)836-6421. Use FAFSA. About 20% of students receive aid other than loans from University and outside sources.

DEGREE REQUIREMENTS. For M.A., M.S.: Plan A—30 semester hours, reading knowledge of one foreign language; thesis; oral defense. Plan B—36 semester hours without thesis; reading knowledge of one foreign language; final comprehensive. For M.M.: 36 semester hours; thesis/nonthesis option; admission to candidacy; recital. For M.P.A.: 36 semester hours, professional seminar; research paper; oral defense. For M.Ed.: 36 semester hours (except 48 for Guidance and Counseling); final written/oral exam. For M.B.A.: 30–57 semester hours (depending on previous academic work), at least 30 credits in residence. For M.P.Acc.: 30 semester hours minimum beyond foundation and basic accounting courses; comprehensive exam. For M.S.N.: 36 semester hour program. For Ed.S.: at least 27 semester hours beyond the master's; admission to candidacy; research project. For Ed.D.: 60 semester hour program; school improvement project; admission to candidacy; dissertation; oral defense.

FIELDS OF STUDY.
Administration and Supervision. M.Ed., Ed.S.
Applied Computer Science. M.S.
Art Education. M.Ed.
Biology. M.S.
Business Education. M.Ed., Ed.S.
Business Administration. M.B.A.
Early Childhood Education. M.Ed., Ed.S.
English. M.A.
French. M.Ed.
Gerontology. Includes direct service, administration and supervision, policy and planning. M.A.
Guidance and Counseling. M.Ed., Ed.S.
History. Includes public history. M.A.
Mathematics.
Media. M.Ed., Ed.S.
Middle Grades Education. M.Ed., Ed.S.
Music. Includes music education, performance.
Nursing. Includes nurse education track, health system leadership track. M.S.N.
Physical Education. M.Ed., Ed.S.
Psychology. Includes organizational development. M.A.
Public Administration. M.P.A.
Professional Accounting. M.P.Acc.
Reading Education. M.Ed.
School Improvement. Ed.D.
Secondary Education. Includes English, mathematics, science, social studies. M.Ed., Ed.S.
Spanish. M.Ed.
Special Education. Includes curriculum and instruction, leadership. M.Ed., Ed.S.
Speech-Language Pathology. M.Ed.
Sociology. Includes criminology, resources and methods, women's studies. M.A.
Rural and Small Town Planning. M.S.

WEST TEXAS A&M UNIVERSITY

Canyon, Texas 79016-0001
Web site: www.wtamu.edu

Established 1909. Located 15 miles S of Amarillo. Coed. State control. Semester system. Special facilities: Drylands Agriculture Institute, Equine Center, Killgore Research Center, Pan Handle Plains Historical Museum, Texas Engineering Experiment Station Regional Division. Library: 349,224 volumes, 5900 subscriptions. Total University enrollment: 6650.

Tuition: per credit resident $50, nonresident $265. On-campus housing costs: $3000–$4500 (includes board). Apply to Director of Housing. Phone: (806)651-3300.

Graduate School

Graduate study since 1932. Enrollment: full- and part-time 1250. Graduate faculty: full-time 180, part-time 45. Degrees conferred: M.A., M.B.A., M.Ed., M.S., M.Ag., M.M., M.P.A., M.S.N., M.F.A.

ADMISSION REQUIREMENTS. Official transcripts, MAT/GRE, GMAT (Business) required in support of School's application. Interview required by some departments. TOEFL required for international applicants. Accepts transfer applicants. Graduates of unaccredited institutions not considered. Apply to Director of Admissions. Rolling admissions process. Application fee for international applications $25. Phone: (806)651-2730; fax: (806)651-2733.

ADMISSION STANDARDS. Relatively open. Usual minimum average: 2.60, 2.85 for last two years (A = 4).

FINANCIAL AID. Annual awards from institutional funds: teaching assistantships, research assistantships, internships, grants, Federal W/S, loans. Approved for VA benefits. Apply to appropriate department chair for assistantships; to Financial Aid Office for all other programs. Phone: (806)651-2055; fax: (806)651-2924. Use FAFSA. About 10% of students receive financial assistance. Aid available to part-time students.

DEGREE REQUIREMENTS. For master's: 30 credit hours with thesis or 36 credit hours with nonthesis option (available in most departments); at least 18 hours in residence comprehensive final exam.

FIELDS OF STUDY.

COLLEGE OF AGRICULTURE, NURSING, AND NATURAL SCIENCE:
Agriculture. M.S.
Biology. M.S.
Chemistry. M.S.
Engineering Technology. M.S.
Environmental Science. M.S.
Family Nursing. M.S.N.
Finance and Economics. M.S.
Mathematics. M.S.

COLLEGE OF BUSINESS:
Accounting. M.P.Acc.
Business. M.B.A.
Finance and Economics. M.S.

COLLEGE OF EDUCATION AND SOCIAL SCIENCES:
Administration. M.Ed.
Counseling. M.Ed.
Criminal Justice. M.A.
Education. M.A., M.Ed.
Educational Diagnostician Studies. M.Ed.
Elementary Education. M.A., M.Ed.
Health and Physical Education. M.S.
History. M.A.
Instructional Technology. M.Ed.
Political Science. M.A.
Professional Counseling. M.A.
Psychology. M.A.
Reading Specialist. M.Ed.
Secondary Education. Includes art, biology, chemistry, economics, English, history, mathematics, music, political science, social studies, speech education. M.Ed.

COLLEGE OF FINE ARTS AND HUMANITIES:
Art. M.A.
Communication. M.A.
Communication Disorders. M.S.
English. M.A.
Music. M.M., M.A.
Studio Art. M.F.A.

UNIVERSITY-WIDE PROGRAMS:
Interdisciplinary Studies. M.A., M.S.

WEST VIRGINIA SCHOOL OF OSTEOPATHIC MEDICINE
400 North Lee Street
Lewisburg, West Virginia 24901-1128
Web site: www.wvsom.edu

Founded 1974 as Greenbrier College of Osteopathic Medicine, became part of West Virginia State System of Higher Education in 1976. Located in rural Appalachia. Public control. Three-phase system. Library: 18,660 volumes, 468 subscription; has MEDLINE, CANCERLINE, BIOETHIC, HEALTH, PALINET, TOXLINE, DIALOG, OCLC.

Annual tuition: resident $13,070, nonresident $32,350. No on-campus housing available. Contact Admissions Office for off-campus housing information. Off-campus housing and personal expenses: approximately $15,000.

Enrollment: first-year class 75; total full-time 285 (men 58%, women 42%). Faculty: full-time 38, part-time 94. Degree conferred: D.O.

ADMISSION REQUIREMENTS. Preference given to state residents, then to SREB contract states, and then to residents of the Southern Appalachian states; U.S. citizens and permanent residents only. Bachelor's degree from an accredited institution required. All applicants have bachelor's degree awarded prior to enrollment. Apply through AACOMAS (file after June 1, before January 2), submit MCAT (will accept test results from last three years), official transcripts for each school attended (should show at least 90 semester credits/135 quarter credit), service processing fee. After a review of the AACOMAS application and supporting documents a decision is made concerning which candidates should receive supplemental materials. On-line application available. The supplemental application, an application fee of $35 ($75 for nonresidents), a personal statement, and three recommendations (one from a D.O.) should be returned to the Office of Admissions as soon as possible, no later than March 1. Interviews are by invitation only and generally for final selection. First-year students admitted Fall only. Rolling admissions process; notification starts in November and is finished when class is filled. School does maintain an alternate/waiting list. CPR Certification is required prior to enrollment. Phone: (800)356-7836, (304)645-6270, ext. 373; fax: (304)645-4859; e-mail: admission@wvsom.edu.

ADMISSION REQUIREMENTS FOR TRANSFER APPLICANTS. Accepts transfers from other accredited U.S. osteopathic medical schools. Admission limited to space available. Contact the Office of Admissions for current information and specific requirements.

ADMISSION STANDARDS. Selective. Usual minimum average: 2.75 (A = 4). Mean MCAT: 7.3; median GPA: 3.40 (A = 4). Accepts approximately 7% of total annual applications.

FINANCIAL AID. Tuition fee waivers, scholarships, grants, institutional loans, NOF, HEAL, alternative loan programs, West Virginia Board of Trustees Medical Student Loan Program, Federal W/S, loans. Service Obligation Scholarship programs, Armed Forces and National Health Service programs are available. Financial Aid applications and information are given out at the on-campus, by-invitation interview. Contact the Financial Aid Office for current information. Phone: (304) 645-6270. Apply by April 1 to the Financial Aid Office. Use FAFSA (School code: 011245), also submit Financial Aid Transcript, Federal Income Tax forms. Approximately 85% of students receive some form of financial assistance.

DEGREE REQUIREMENTS. For D.O.: satisfactory completion of four-year program.

WEST VIRGINIA UNIVERSITY
Morgantown, West Virginia 26506-6009
Web site: www.wvu.edu

Established 1867. Located 70 miles S of Pittsburgh, Pennsylvania. CGS member. Coed. State control. Semester system. Special facilities: Agricultural Experiment Station, Center for Black Culture and Research, Bureau of Business Research, Bureau of Government Resource, Energy Research Center, Concurrent Engineering Research Center, Fluidization Center, Engineering Experiment Station, Gerontology Center, Institute for the History of Technology and Industrial Archeology, Institute for Labor Relations, NASA facility, National Research Center for Coal and Energy, Regional Research Institute, Water Research Institute, Westvaco Natural Resource Center. Women Studies Center. Library: 1,877,000 volumes, 7900 subscriptions. Total University enrollment: 20,000.

Annual tuition: full-time resident $3004, nonresident $8640; per credit resident $167, nonresident $480. Limited on-campus housing for single and married students. Annual housing costs: $5152 (including board) for single student; $5600 for married students. Off-campus housing costs: $350–$515 per month. Contact Housing and Residence Life for both on- and off-campus housing information. Phone: (304)293-3621.

Graduate Studies

Enrollment: full-time 2828, part-time 1787. Faculty: full-time 737, part-time 319. Degrees conferred: M.A., M.S., M.Agr., M.M., M.B.A., M.F.A., M.P.A. (Professional Accountancy), M.P.A., M.S.F., M.S.E., M.S.E.E., M.S.A.E., M.S.C.E., M.S.Ch.E., M.S.E.E., M.S.E.M., M.S.F., M.S.I.E., M.S.M.E., M.S.N., M.S.PNGE., M.S.W., M.S.J., M.A.L.S., C.A.S., Ed.D., D.M.A., Ph.D.

ADMISSION REQUIREMENTS. Official transcripts required in support of application. On-line application available. GRE Subject Tests/GMAT, letters of recommendation, interviews required for some departments. TOEFL required for foreign applicants. Accepts transfer applicants. Graduates of unaccredited colleges not considered. Apply to Director of Admissions and Records at least one month prior to general registration. Rolling admissions process. Application fee $50. Phone: (800)344-NWUI; fax: (304) 293-3080.

ADMISSION STANDARDS. Selective for most departments, very selective or competitive for the others. Usual minimum average: 2.75 (A = 4).

FINANCIAL AID. Annual awards from institutional funds: scholarships/fellowships, teaching assistantships, research assistantships, tuition waivers, internships, Federal W/S, loans. Approved for VA benefits. Apply by February 1 to appropriate department chairman for fellowships, assistantships; to the Office of Financial Assistance for all other programs. Phone: (304) 293-5242. Use FAFSA. Aid available for part-time students.

DEGREE REQUIREMENTS. For master's: 30 semester hours minimum, at least 24 in full-time residence; thesis/nonthesis option; final report for many departments; final oral/written exam in many programs. For C.A.S.: 30 hours minimum beyond the master's, at least 24 in residence including one semester or Summer session in full-time study; research report; final oral exam. For Ed.D.: 72 semester hours minimum beyond the bachelor's, at least two consecutive semesters in full-time residence; advancement to candidacy exams; dissertation; final oral exam. For D.M.A.: three years full-time study, at least one year in full-time residence; written research project; reading knowledge of one foreign language. For D.M.A., Performance: same as above except major solo recital. For D.M.A., Composition: major composition project; final oral exam. For Ph.D.: three years minimum beyond the bachelor's, at least two semesters in full-time residence; foreign language competency required by most departments; dissertation; final oral exam.

FIELDS OF GRADUATE STUDY.

DAVIS COLLEGE OF AGRICULTURE, FORESTRY, AND CONSUMER SCIENCES:
Agricultural Resources Economics. M.S.
Agricultural and Environmental Education. M.S.
Agricultural Education. M.S.
Agriculture, Forestry, and Consumer Sciences. M.Agr.
Agronomy. M.S.Agr.
Animal and Food Sciences. Ph.D.
Animal and Veterinary Science. M.S.
Entomology. M.S.
Environmental Microbiology. M.S.
Family and Consumer Sciences. M.S.
Forest Resource Science. Ph.D.
Forestry. M.S.F.
Genetics and Developmental Biology. M.S., Ph.D.
Horticulture. M.S.
Natural Resources Economics. Ph.D.
Plant Pathology. M.S.
Plant and Soil Sciences. Ph.D.
Recreation, Parks, and Tourism Resources. M.S.
Reproductive Physiology. M.S., Ph.D.
Wildlife and Fisheries Resources. M.S.

EBERLY COLLEGE OF ARTS AND SCIENCES:
Biology. M.S., Ph.D.
Chemistry. M.S., Ph.D.
Communication Studies. M.A.
Creative Writing. M.A.
English. M.A., Ph.D.
Foreign Languages. M.A.
Geography. M.A., Ph.D.
Geology. M.S., Ph.D.
History. M.A., Ph.D.
Legal Studies. M.L.S.
Liberal Studies. M.A.L.S.
Mathematics. M.S., Ph.D.
Physics. M.S., Ph.D.
Political Science. M.S., Ph.D.
Psychology. M.A., Ph.D.
Public Administration. M.P.A.
Social Work. M.S.W.
Sociology. M.A.
Statistics. M.S.

COLLEGE OF BUSINESS AND ECONOMICS:
Business Administration. M.B.A.
Economics. M.A., Ph.D.
Industrial Relations. M.S.
Professional Accountancy. M.P.A.

COLLEGE OF CREATIVE ARTS:
Art. M.A.
Music. M.M., D.M.A.
Theatre. M.F.A.
Visual Arts. M.F.A.

COLLEGE OF ENGINEERING:
Aerospace Engineering. M.S.A.E., Ph.D.
Chemical Engineering. M.S.Ch.E., Ph.D.
Civil Engineering. M.S.C.E., Ph.D.
Computer Engineering. Ph.D.
Computer Science. M.S.C.S., Ph.D.
Electrical Engineering. M.S.E.E., Ph.D.
Engineering. M.S.E.
Industrial Engineering. M.S.I.E., Ph.D.

Industrial Hygiene. M.S.
Mechanical Engineering. M.S.M.E., Ph.D.
Mineral Engineering. M.S.E.M., Ph.D.
Occupational Hygiene and Occupational Safety. M.S.
Occupational Safety and Health. Ph.D.
Petroleum and Natural Gas Engineering. M.S.PNGE., Ph.D.
Safety Management. M.S.
Software Engineering. M.S.

COLLEGE OF HUMAN RESOURCES AND EDUCATION:
Counseling. M.A.
Counseling Psychology. Ph.D.
Curriculum and Instruction. Ed.D.
Education Leadership. M.A., Ed.D.
Educational Psychology. M.A., Ed.D.
Elementary Education. Includes multidisciplinary studies. M.A.
Reading. M.A.
Rehabilitation Counseling. M.S.
Secondary Education. Includes English, foreign languages, mathematics, science, social studies. M.A.
Special Education. M.A., Ed.D.
Speech Pathology and Audiology. M.S.
Technology Education. M.A., Ed.D.

PERLEY ISAAC REED SCHOOL OF JOURNALISM:
Journalism. M.S.J.

SCHOOL OF MEDICINE:
Anatomy. M.S., Ph.D.
Applied Exercise Science. Ph.D.
Biochemistry. M.S., Ph.D.
Community Health Education. M.S.
Exercise Physiology. M.S., Ph.D.
Medical Technology. M.S.
Microbiology and Immunology. M.S., Ph.D.
Occupational Therapy. M.O.T.
Pharmacology and Toxicology. M.S., Ph.D.
Physical Therapy. D.P.T.
Physiology. M.S., Ph.D.
Public Health. M.P.H.

SCHOOL OF NURSING:
Nursing. M.S.N., D.S.N.

SCHOOL OF PHARMACY:
Pharmaceutical Sciences. M.S., Ph.D.

SCHOOL OF PHYSICAL EDUCATION:
Athletic Coaching Education. M.S.
Athletic Training. M.S.
Physical Education/Teacher Education. M.S., Ed.D.
Sport Management. M.S.
Sport Psychology. M.S., Ed.D.

School of Dentistry (P.O. Box 9815)

Established 1951, first class began study in 1957. Located at Medical Center.

Annual tuition: resident $9059, nonresident $27,942. Total average cost for all other first-year expenses $8500. Housing available. Contact Director of Housing for both on- and off-campus housing information. Phone: (304)293-4491.

Enrollment: first-year class 39, total full-time 200 (men 60%, women 40%); postgraduates 15. Faculty: full-time 63, part-time 86. Degrees conferred: D.D.S., M.S., D.D.S.-M.S., D.D.S.-Ph.D.

ADMISSION REQUIREMENTS. AADSAS report, transcripts, DAT (not later than November 1) required in support of applica-

tion. Interview by invitation only. Applicants must have completed at least three years of college study for admission. West Virginia residents given preference. Graduates of unaccredited institutions not considered. Apply to Dean of Admissions after June 1, before January 31. Application fee $45. Phone: (304)293-3521.

ADMISSION STANDARDS. Selective. Mean DAT: Academic 17, PAT 16; mean GPA: 3.42 (A = 4). Gourman rating: 4.18. Accepts about 15–20% of total annual applicants. Approximately 50% are state residents.

FINANCIAL AID. Scholarships, loans. Apply to Financial Aid Officer for scholarships and loans; no specified closing date. Phone: (304)293-3706. Use FAFSA (School code: 003827). Approximately 82% of all students receive some form of financial assistance.

DEGREE REQUIREMENTS. For D.D.S.: satisfactory completion of three to four-year program. For M.S.: satisfactory completion of one-year program. For Ph.D.: see Graduate School listing above.

FIELDS OF GRADUATE STUDY.
Dental Hygiene. M S.
Endodontics. M.S.
Oral and Maxillofacial Surgery. Certificate only.
Orthodontics. M.S.
Prosthodentics. M.S.

College of Law (P.O. Box 6130)

Established 1878. Located on main campus. ABA approved since 1923. AALS member since 1914. Semester system. Full-time, day and limited part-time study. Special programs: Appalachian Center for Law and Public Service. Law library: 277,683 volumes, 2925 subscriptions; has LEXIS, WESTLAW, CALI; is a Federal Government Depository.

Annual tuition: resident $5746, nonresident $13,434. On-campus housing available for both single and married students. Contact University's On-campus Housing Office for information. Phone: (304)293-3621. Law students tend to live off-campus. Contact University's Off-campus Housing Office for off-campus information. Phone: (304)293-5613. Off-campus housing and personal expenses: approximately $8,500–$10,400.

Enrollment: first-year class 156; total full-time 433 (men 56%, women 44%); limited part-time study. Faculty: full-time 22, part-time 23. Student to faculty ratio 16.3 to 1. Degrees conferred: J.D., J.D.-M.B.A., J.D.-M.P.A.

ADMISSION REQUIREMENTS. LSDAS Law School report, bachelor's degree, transcripts, LSAT required in support of application. West Virginia residents given preference. Accepts a limited number of transfer applicants. Graduates of unaccredited colleges not considered. Apply to Office of Admission, after September 1, before March 1. Admits beginning students Fall only. Application fee $45. Phone: (304)293-5304; fax: (304)293-6891.

ADMISSION STANDARDS. Selective. Mean LSAT: 152; mean GPA: 3.36 (A = 4). Gourman rating: 3.19. *U.S. News & World Report* ranking is in the third tier of all U.S. law schools. Accepts 25% of total annual applicants.

FINANCIAL AID. Scholarships, Federal W/S, loans. Apply to the Financial Aid Counselor by March 1. Phone: (304)293-5302. Use FAFSA (College code: 003827) and institutional application (due by April 1). About 25% of students receive aid other than loans from College. No aid for part-time students.

DEGREE REQUIREMENTS. For J.D.: 90-credit-hour program, at least 55 in residence.

School of Medicine (P.O. Box 9111)
Web site: www.hoc.wvu.edu/som

Located at Medical Center. Medical training since 1902. Library 84,000 volumes.

Annual tuition: resident $8728 nonresident $20,958; student fees resident $1640, nonresident $4550. Housing available for married and single students. Total average cost for all other expenses $8500.

Enrollment: first-year class 98 (EDP 10), total 374 (men 67%, women 33%); postgraduates 206. Faculty: full-time 482, part-time 34. Degrees conferred: M.D., M.D.-Ph.D., M.D.-M.P.H., The M.S., Ph.D. are offered through the Graduate School.

ADMISSION REQUIREMENTS. AMCAS Report, transcripts, recommendations, MCAT, final screening interview required in support of application. Has EDP (state residents only); apply between June 1 and August 1. Interview by invitation only. Applicants must have completed at least three years of college study for admission. West Virginia residents given preference. Accepts transfer applicants. Graduates of unaccredited colleges not considered. Apply to Chair, Committee on Admissions, after June 1, before December 1. Admits beginning students Fall only. Application fee $30. Phone: (304)293-2408; fax: (301) 293-7814.

ADMISSION STANDARDS. Selective. Mean MCAT: 8.9; mean GPA: 3.64 (A = 4). Gourman rating: 3.47. Accepts about 10–12% of total annual applicants. Approximately 95% are state residents.

FINANCIAL AID. Scholarships, loans; fellowships, assistantships for teaching/research. Apply to Financial Aid Officer for scholarships, loans; to appropriate department chair for fellowships, assistantships; no specified closing date. Use FAFSA (School code: 003827). Approximately 95% of students receive some form of financial assistance.

DEGREE REQUIREMENTS. For M.D.: satisfactory completion of four-year program; all students must pass USMLE Step 1 prior to entering third year, and must pass USMLE Step 2 prior to awarding of M.D. For Ph.D.: see Graduate School listing above.

FIELDS OF graduate STUDY.
Anatomy.
Biochemistry
Immunology.
Microbiology.
Molecular Biology.
Neurosciences. Multidisciplinary.
Pharmacology and Toxicology.
Physiology.

WESTERN CAROLINA UNIVERSITY
Cullowhee, North Carolina 28723-9022
Web site: www.wcu.edu

Founded 1889; college work began 1907. Located 52 miles W of Asheville. CGS member. Coed. State control. Semester system. Special facility: Computer Center with two DEC VAX 4000/700A, Mountain Aquaculture Center, Mountain Heritage Center, Center for Improving Mountain Living. Library: 527,866 volumes, 2900 subscriptions. Total University enrollment: 6500.

Annual tuition full-time resident $1042, nonresident $8354. On-campus housing for 1570 graduate men, 1733 graduate women; 45 units for married students. Average academic year housing costs: single students $3750 (including board), married students $450–$500 per month. Contact Director of Housing for both on- and off-campus housing information. Phone: (828)227-7303.

Graduate School

Graduate study since 1951. Enrollment: full-time 367, part-time 634. Graduate faculty: full-time 273, part-time 20. Degrees conferred: M.A., M.A.Ed., M.H.S., M.I.E., M.B.A., M.M.E., M.P.A., M.P.M., M.S., Ed.S., C.A.S.

ADMISSION REQUIREMENTS. Official transcripts, letters of reference in most programs (GRE for M.A., M.A.Ed., M.H.S., M.I.E., M.M.E., M.P.A., M.S., Ed.S., C.A.S.; GMAT for M.B.A., M.P.M.) required in support of School's application. TOEFL required for international applicants. Accepts transfer applicants. Graduates from unaccredited institutions not considered. Apply to and have all credentials at Graduate School at least two months prior to registration. Application fee $35. Phone: (800)364-9854, (828)227-7398; fax: (828)227-7480.

ADMISSION STANDARDS. Selective. Usual minimum average: 3.0 (A = 4).

FINANCIAL AID. Annual awards from institutional funds: Chancellors' fellowships, teaching/service assistantships, tuition waivers, study grants, Federal W/S, loans. Approved for VA benefits. Apply by March 15 to Dean of Graduate School or department chair for assistantships, fellowships; to the Financial Aid for all other programs. Phone: (828)227-7290. Use FAFSA. About 25% of students receive aid other than loans from University and outside sources. Aid sometimes available for part-time students.

DEGREE REQUIREMENTS. For master's: 30-36 semester hours, at least 24 in residence; comprehensive exam; thesis for M.A., M.H.S., M.S.; some M.A., M.S. programs require one foreign language. For Ed.S.: 30 semester hours beyond the master's; special project.

FIELDS OF STUDY.
Accountancy. M.Acc.
American History. M.A.
Applied Mathematics. M.S.
Art. M.F.A.
Biology. M.S.
Business Administration. M.B.A.
Cherokee Studies. M.A.
Chemistry. M.S.
Communication Disorders. M.S.
Community Counseling. M.S.
Comprehensive Education. Includes art, biology, chemistry, elementary education, English, mathematics, middle grades, music, physical education, reading, social sciences, special education (behavioral disorders, learning disabilities, mental retardation, severe/profound disabilities). M.A.Ed., M.A.T.
Educational Administration. Includes two-year college. M.A.Ed.
Educational Supervision. Includes curriculum and instruction, instructional technology specialist—computers, international studies. M.A.Ed.
English. M.A.
Health Sciences. M.H.S
Human Resource Development. M.S.
Music. Includes applied music. M.A.
Nursing. M.S.N.
Physical Therapy. M.P.T.
Project Management. M.P.M.
Psychology. Includes clinical, school. M.A.
Public Affairs. M.P.A.
School Administration. M.S.A.
School Counseling. M.A.Ed.
Technology. M.S.
Two-Year College Teaching. Includes biology, English, individually approved multidisciplinary studies, mathematics, physical education. M.A.Ed.

WESTERN CONNECTICUT STATE UNIVERSITY

Danbury, Connecticut 06810-6885

Web site: www.wcsu.edu

Established 1903, Located 60 miles N of New York City. Coed. State control. Semester system. Library: 261,328 volumes, 2500 subscriptions.

Tuition: per semester hour, resident $255, nonresident $255. On-campus housing available. Average academic year housing costs: $3950-$4690. Contact Office of Housing for both on- and off-campus housing information. Phone: (203)837-8543.

Graduate Studies

Graduate study since 1955. Enrollment: full-time 22, part-time 611 (men 30%, women 70%). College faculty: full-time 46, part-time 6. Degrees conferred: M.A., M.B.A., M.S., M.H.A., M.S.N.

ADMISSION REQUIREMENTS. Official transcripts, interview required in support of application. GRE/MAT/GMAT required for some programs. TOEFL required for international applicants. Accepts transfer applicants. Graduates of unaccredited colleges not considered. Apply to Dean, Office of Graduate Studies at least 45 days in advance of the beginning of semester of choice. Application fee $40. Phone: (203)837-8244; fax: (203)837-8338.

ADMISSION STANDARDS. Selective for some departments, relatively open for others. Usual minimum average: 2.7 (A = 4).

FINANCIAL AID. Fellowships, assistantships, internships, Federal W/S, loans. Approved for VA benefits. Apply by May 1 to Director of Financial Aid. Phone: (203)837-8580; fax: (203)837-8320. Use FAFSA and University's FAF. About 5% of students receive aid other than loans from outside sources. Aid available for part-time students.

DEGREE REQUIREMENTS. For M.A., M.S.: 30 semester hours minimum, at least 21 in residence; thesis/nonthesis option. For M.S.N.: 40 semester hours. For M.B.A.: 57 semester hours.

FIELDS OF STUDY.
Biological and Environmental Sciences. M.A.
Business Administration. M.B.A.
Counselor Education. M.S.
Earth and Planetary Sciences. M.A.
Education. Includes curriculum, English, instructional technology, mathematics, music education, reading, special education. M.S.
English. M.A.
Health Administration. M.H.A.
History. M.A.
Justice Administration. M.S.
Mathematics. M.A.
Nursing. M.S.N.
School Counseling. M.S.
Visual Arts. M.F.A.

WESTERN ILLINOIS UNIVERSITY

Macomb, Illinois 61455-1390

Web site: www.wiu.edu

Founded 1895. Located 250 miles SW of Chicago. CGS member. Coed. State control. Semester system. Library: 1,000,000 volumes, 3200 subscriptions.

Tuition/fees: per credit, resident $149.18, nonresident $263.93. On-campus housing for 336 married students, 3148 men, 2972 women. Average annual housing cost: $5625 for married students, $4100-$5712 (including board) for single students.

Contact Graduate and Family Housing Office for on-campus (309)298-3331, off-campus (309)298-3285.

School of Graduate Studies

Graduate study since 1945. Enrollment: full-time 689, part-time 1046 (men 30%, women 70%). Graduate faculty: full-time 392, part-time 16. Degrees conferred: M.A., M.S., M.S. in Ed., M.B.A., M.Acc., M.F.A., Ed.S., S.S.P.

ADMISSION REQUIREMENTS. Two official transcripts, GRE Subject Test (Psychology, Political Science only), GMAT (M.B.A. and Accounting only) required in support of School's application. On-line application available. Interview required for some departments. TOEFL (minimum score 550) required for international applicants. Accepts transfer applicants. Graduates of unaccredited institutions not considered. Apply to Graduate Admissions at least three weeks prior to registration. No application fee for domestic applicants, $25 for international applicants. Phone: (309)298-1806; fax: (309)298-2345; e-mail: grad_office@wiu.edu.

ADMISSION STANDARDS. Relatively open. Usual minimum average: 2.5 (A = 4).

FINANCIAL AID. Annual awards from institutional funds: grants, research assistantships, teaching assistantships, internships, Federal W/S, loans. Approved for VA benefits. Apply by March 1 to appropriate chair for assistantships; to Financial Aid Office for all other programs. Phone: (309)298-2446; fax: (309)298-2353. Use FAFSA. About 50% of students receive aid other than loans from University and outside sources.

DEGREE REQUIREMENTS. For master's: 30-36 semester hours minimum, at least 24 in residence; thesis/nonthesis option; final written/oral exam. For Ed.S. (Educational Administration only): 32 hours minimum beyond the master's; 12 credits within a period of three consecutive semesters. For M.F.A. (Theater): 60 hours minimum, two academic years, and one Summer in residence.

FIELDS OF STUDY.
Accountancy.
Biology.
Business Administration.
Chemistry.
College Student Personnel. Interview required for admission.
Communication.
Communication Sciences and Disorders.
Computer Science.
Counseling.
Economics.
Educational Administration and Supervision.
Educational and Interdisciplinary Studies.
Educational Specialist.
Elementary Education.
English.
Geography.
Gerontology.
Health Education.
History.
Instructional Technology and Telecommunications.
Law Enforcement and Justice Administration.
Manufacturing Engineering Systems.
Mathematics.
Music.
Physical Education/Sport Management.
Physics.
Political Science.
Psychology.
Reading.
Recreation, Park, and Tourism Administration.
Secondary Education.

Sociology.
Special Education.
Specialist in School Psychology.
Theater. Interview required for admission.

WESTERN KENTUCKY UNIVERSITY
Bowling Green, Kentucky 42101-3576
Web site: www.wku.edu

Founded 1906. Located 120 miles S of Louisville, 65 miles N of Nashville. CGS member. Coed. State control. Semester system. Library: 875,000 volumes, 5260 subscriptions, 50 PCs in all libraries.

Annual tuition: full-time resident $2350, nonresident $6660; per credit resident $148, nonresident $388. On-campus housing available for single students only. Average academic year housing costs: $1775. Off-campus housing costs: $450–$600 per month. Contact Director of Housing for both on- and off-campus housing information. Phone: (270)745-2100.

Graduate Studies

Graduate study since 1931. Enrollment: full-time 443, part-time 1156 (men 30%, women 70%). Graduate faculty: full-time 312, part-time 37. Degrees conferred: M.A., M.S., M.A.E., M.B.A., M.H.A., M.P.A., M.P.Acc., Ed.S.

ADMISSION REQUIREMENTS. Transcripts, GRE/GMAT (business) required in support of application. TOEFL required for international applicants. Accepts transfer applicants. Graduates of unaccredited institutions not considered. Apply to Office of Graduate Studies by July 1 (Fall), November 1 (Spring). Application fee $30. Phone: (800)896-6960, (270)745-2446; fax: (270)745-5442.

ADMISSION STANDARDS. Selective. Usual minimum average: 2.75 (3.0 for some departments) (A = 4).

FINANCIAL AID. Annual awards from institutional funds: teaching assistantships, research assistantships, internships, tuition waivers, Federal W/S, loans. Approved for VA benefits. Apply by April 1 to Office of Graduate Studies for assistantships; to the Office of Financial Aid for all other programs. Phone: (270)745-2755; fax: (270)745-6586. Use FAFSA. Aid available for part-time students.

DEGREE REQUIREMENTS. For master's: 30 credit hours minimum; thesis/nonthesis option. For Specialist (Ed.S.), S.S.P.: 30 credit hours beyond the master's degree.

FIELDS OF STUDY.
Accountancy.
Agriculture.
Art Education.
Biology.
Business Administration.
Chemistry. Includes coal chemistry.
City and Regional Planning.
Communication.
Communication Disorders.
Computer Science.
Counseling. Includes mental health, school, student affairs in higher education.
Early Childhood Education.
Economics.
Educational Administration.
Elementary Education.
English.
Exceptional Education.

Folklore Studies.
Geoscience.
Health Administration.
History.
Interdisciplinary Administration.
Library Science.
Mathematics.
Nursing.
Physical Education.
Psychology.
Public Administration.
Public Health.
Recreation.
School Administration.
School Psychology.
Secondary Education.
Sociology.

WESTERN MICHIGAN UNIVERSITY
Kalamazoo, Michigan 49008-5242
Web site: www.wmich.edu

Founded 1903. Located 150 miles W of Detroit. CGS member. Coed. State control. Semester system. Special facilities: Applied Mechanics Institute, Behavior Research and Development Center, Business Research and Service Institute, Center for Communications Research, Concurrent Computation Research Center, Design Center, Center for Electron Microscopy, Enabling Technology Center, Center for Research on Educational Accountability and Teacher Evaluation, Geographic Information System Research Center, Medieval Institute, Printing and Research Center, Kercher Center for Social Research, Institute for Water Sciences, Women's Center. Library: 1,649,000 volumes, 600,000 microforms, 540 current periodicals, 288 PCs in all libraries.

Tuition: per semester credit hour, resident $185.62, nonresident $441.83. On-campus housing available for both married and single students. Average academic year housing cost: $5517 (including board) for single students; $467–$717 per month for married students. Contact Housing Director for both on- and off-campus housing information. Phone: (800)882-9819.

The Graduate College

Enrollment: full- and part-time 5900 (men 40%, women 60%). University faculty teaching graduate students: full-time 725, part-time 401. Degrees conferred: M.S., M.A., M.F.A., M.B.A., M.D.A., M.M., M.P.A., M.S., M.S.A., M.S.E., M.S.W, Ed.S., Ed.D., D.P.A., Ph.D.

ADMISSION REQUIREMENTS. Transcripts, GRE Subject (doctoral programs only) required in support of application. Interview required for admission to specialist and doctoral programs. TOEFL or MTELP required for international applicants. Accepts transfer applicants. Graduates of unaccredited institutions not considered. Apply by February 15 to Office of Graduate Admissions and Orientation. Rolling admissions process. Application fee $25. Phone: (616)387-8212; fax: (616)387-8232.

ADMISSION STANDARDS. Selective to relatively open. Usual minimum average: 2.75 (A = 4).

FINANCIAL AID. Annual awards from institutional funds: fellowships, teaching assistantships, research assistantships, tuition grants, Federal W/S, loans. Approved for VA benefits. Apply by February 15 to Graduate College for scholarships, fellowships; to department head for assistantships; to Financial Aid Office for all other programs. Phone: (616)387-6000. Use FAFSA. About 35% of full-time students receive aid from University and outside sources. Aid available for part-time students.

DEGREE REQUIREMENTS. For master's: 30 hours minimum, at least 24 in residence; thesis, one language required for some majors; final written/oral exams; final review. For Ed.S: 30 hours minimum beyond the master's, at least 30 in residence in most cases; final project. For Ph.D.: 90 hours minimum beyond the bachelor's, at least one year in full-time residence, knowledge of two research tools, one of which will normally be a language; qualifying exam; dissertation, for which 15 hours is given; final written/oral exams. For Ed.D., D.P.A.: same as for Ph.D., except only one research tool, which may be a language.

FIELDS OF STUDY.

Accounting. M.S.A.
Anthropology. M.A.
Applied Economics. Ph.D.
Applied Mathematics. M.S.
Art. M.A., M.F.A.
Biological Sciences. M.S., Ph.D.
Biostatistics. M.S.
Business Administration. M.B.A.
Career and Technical Education. M.A.
Chemistry. Includes environmental. M.A., Ph.D.
Communication. M.A.
Comparative Religion. M.A., Ph.D.
Computational Mathematics. M.S.
Computer Engineering. M.S.E.
Computer Science. M.S., Ph.D.
Construction Management. M.S.
Counseling Psychology. M.A., Ed.D.
Counselor Education. M.A., Ed.D.
Creative Writing. M.F.A.
Development Administration. M.D.A.
Earth Science. M.S.
Economics. M.A.
Education and Professional Development. M.A.
Educational Leadership. M.A., Ed.S., Ed.D., Ph.D.
Electrical Engineering. M.S.E.
Engineering Management. M.S.
English. M.A., M.F.A.
Family and Consumer Sciences. M.A.
Fine Arts. 60 credits for M.F.A.
Geography. M.A.
Geology. M.S., Ph.D.
Health Care Administration. M.P.A.
History. M.A., Ph.D.
Home Economics.
Industrial Engineering. M.S.E., Ph.D.
Manufacturing Science. M.S.
Materials Science and Engineering. M.S.E.
Mathematics. M.A., Ph.D.
Mathematics Education. M.A. Ph.D.
Medicine. M.S.
Mechanical Engineering. M.S.E., Ph.D.
Medieval Studies. M.A.
Music. M.M.
Occupational Therapy. M.S.
Operations Research. M.S.
Paper and Imaging Science and Engineering. M.S., Ph.D.
Philosophy. M.A.
Physical Education. M.A.
Physics. M.A., Ph.D.
Political Science. M.A., Ph.D.
Psychology. M.A., Ph.D.
Public Administration. M.P.A., D.P.A.
Rehabilitation Teaching. M.A.
School Psychology. Ed.S., Ph.D.
Science Education. M.A., Ph.D.
Social Work. M.S.W.
Sociology. M.A., Ph.D.
Spanish. M.A.
Special Education. M.A., Ph.D.

Speech Pathology and Audiology. M.A.
Statistics. M.S., Ph.D.
Teaching in the Elementary School. M.A.
Teaching of Geography. M.A.
Teaching in the Middle School. M.A.
Teaching of Music. M.M.

WESTERN NEW ENGLAND COLLEGE

Springfield, Massachusetts 01119-2654
Web site: www.wnec.edu

Founded in 1919. Coed. Semester system. Library: 289,000 volumes, 2900 subscriptions.

Tuition: per credit hour $409. No on-campus housing available for graduate students. For off-campus housing, contact Office of Student Housing.

Graduate Programs

Graduate study since 1978. Enrollment: part-time 1100 (men 65%, women 35%). Faculty: full-time 35, part-time 19. Degrees conferred: M.S., M.B.A., M.S.A., M.S.C.J.A., M.S.E.M., M.S.E.E., M.S.M.E.

ADMISSION REQUIREMENTS. Official transcripts required in support of application. GRE recommended; two letters of recommendation for Engineering applicants, GMAT for Business. Apply to Division of Continuing Education at least one month prior to date of enrollment. Application fee $30. Phone: (413)782-1750; fax: (413)782-1779.

ADMISSION STANDARDS. Selective. Usual minimum average: 2.5 (2.75 Engineering Programs) (A = 4).

FINANCIAL AID. Limited to four assistantships, Federal W/S, loans. Approved for VA benefits. Apply Director of Financial Aid. No specified closing date. Phone: (413)782-1258. Use FAFSA.

DEGREE REQUIREMENTS. For M.S.: 30 semester hours required. For M.B.A.: 30-48 semester hours depending upon undergraduate courses.

FIELDS OF STUDY.

SCHOOL OF BUSINESS:
Accounting.
Business Administration.
Business Administration (weekend).
Criminal Justice Administration.
Finance.
Health Care Management.
Human Resources Management.
Information System.
International Business.
Management of Information System.
Marketing.
Procurement and Contracting.
Systems Management.

SCHOOL OF ENGINEERING:
Electrical Engineering.
Engineering.
Industrial and Manufacturing Engineering.
Mechanical Engineering.

School of Law (01119-2684)
Web site: www.law.wnec.edu

ABA approved since 1974. AALS member. Semester system. Library: 366,378 volumes, 4984 subscriptions; has LEXIS, NEXIS, WESTLAW, DIALOG, MEDIS, OCLC.

Annual tuition: full-time $21,376, part-time $15,789. Limited on-campus housing available. Total average annual additional expense: $11,100.

Enrollment: first-year class full-time 89, part-time 62; total 517 (men 47%, women 53%). Faculty: full-time 22, part-time 20. Student to faculty ratio 16.5 to 1. Degree conferred: J.D.

ADMISSION REQUIREMENTS. LSDAS Law School report, bachelor's degree, transcripts, LSAT, two letters of recommendation, personal statement required in support of application. Apply to Admissions Office by April 1 (full-time program), May 1 (part-time program). Rolling admissions process. Application fee $45. Phone: (800)782-6665; (413)782-1406; fax: (413)796-2067.

ADMISSION STANDARDS. Selective. Mean LSAT: full-time 151, part-time 147; mean GPA: full-time 3.03, part-time 3.03 (A = 4). Gourman rating: 2.68. *U.S. News & World Report* ranking is in the fourth tier of all U.S. law schools. Admits about 50–60% of total annual applicants.

FINANCIAL AID. Scholarships, grants, Federal W/S, loans. Apply to Financial Aid Office by April 1. Use FAFSA (School code: 002226). About 65% of students receive some aid from School.

DEGREE REQUIREMENTS. For J.D.: satisfactory completion of three-year (full-time), four-year (part-time) program; 88 credit hour program.

WESTERN NEW MEXICO UNIVERSITY
Silver City, New Mexico 88061-0680
Web site: www.wnmu.edu

Founded 1893, Located 200 miles SW of Albuquerque. Coed. State control. Semester system. Library: 245,000 volumes, 236 subscriptions.

Tuition: resident $2369, nonresident $8681. On-campus housing for 65 married students, 250 graduate men, 150 graduate women. Average annual housing cost: $3552 (including board) for single students, $2973 for married students. Apply to Director of Residence Life. Phone: (505)538-6629.

Graduate Division

Graduate study since 1950. Enrollment: full- and part-time 368. Graduate faculty: full-time 42, part-time 7. Degrees conferred: M.A., M.A.T., M.B.A.

ADMISSION REQUIREMENTS. Transcripts, GMAT (MBA applicants) required in support of application. On-line application available. GRE required for applicants with a GPA between 2.75 and 3.19. Admission formula for M.B.A. applicants is UGPA × 200 + GMAT score must equal 950 or higher. TOEFL (minimum score 550) required for international applicants. Interview not required. Accepts transfer applicants. Graduates of unaccredited institutions not considered. Apply to Office of Admissions by June 1 (Fall), October 1 (Spring). Application fee $10. Phone: (505)538-6106; fax: (505)538-6127.

ADMISSION STANDARDS. Selective. Usual minimum average: 3.0 (A = 4).

FINANCIAL AID. Annual awards from institutional funds: graduate assistantships, teaching assistantships, internships, tuition waivers, Federal W/S, loans. Approved for VA benefits. Apply to Director of Graduate Division by April 1. Phone: (505)538-6173. Use FAFSA. About 10% of students receive aid other than loans from University and outside sources.

DEGREE REQUIREMENTS. For M.A., M.A.T.: 30–36 semester hours minimum with thesis, at least 30 in residence; or 36 semester hours without thesis, at least 30 in residence. For M.B.A.: 36 semester hours minimum.

FIELDS OF STUDY.
Business Administration.
Counseling. 48 credit M.A. program.
Educational Education.
Elementary Education.
Reading Education.
Secondary Education. Includes art, English, history, mathematics, movement sciences, music.
Special Education (K–12). 39 credit M.A.T.

WESTERN OREGON UNIVERSITY
Monmouth, Oregon 97361-1394
Web site: www.wou.edu

Organized 1882. Located 64 miles SW of Portland. Coed. State control. Semester system. Special facilities: Regional Resource Center on Deafness, Educational Evaluation Center, Teaching Research Center. Library: 257,000 volumes, 1700 subscriptions.

Annual tuition: full-time resident $6372, nonresident $11,169; part-time, resident $502 per semester, nonresident $502. On-campus housing for both single and married students available. Average academic year housing costs: $5724 (including board) for single students; $4200 for married students; off-campus housing costs: $350–$500 per month. Contact Student Affairs Office for both on- and off-campus housing information. Phone: (503)838-8311. Day-care facilities available.

Graduate Programs

Enrollment: full-time 127, part-time 206. Faculty: full-time 111, part-time 25. Degrees conferred: M.A., M.A.T., M.S.Ed.

ADMISSION REQUIREMENTS. Transcripts, GRE/MAT required in support of application. Interview required for some programs. TOEFL required for international applicants. Accepts transfer applicants. Graduates of unaccredited institutions not considered. Apply by May 15 (Fall), January 15 (Spring) to Director of Admission. Rolling admissions process. Application fee $50. Phone: (503)838-8211; fax: (503)838-8067.

ADMISSION STANDARDS. Competitive. Usual minimum average: 2.75 (A = 4).

FINANCIAL AID. Research assistantships, teaching assistantships, full and partial tuition waivers, internshpis, Federal W/S, loans. Approved for VA benefits. Apply by March 1 to Provost for assistantships; to Financial Aid Office for all other programs. Phone: (503)838-8475. Use FAFSA (University code: 003209) and College's FAF. About 5% of students receive aid from College and outside sources. Aid available for part-time students.

DEGREE REQUIREMENTS. For master's: 30–36 semester hours minimum, at least 24–30 in residence; thesis/nonthesis option; final oral/written exam.

FIELDS OF STUDY.
Correctional Administration. M.A., M.S.
Early Intervention/Special Education. M.S.Ed.
Health. M.A.T.
Humanities. M.A.T.
Information Technology. M.S.Ed.
Mathematics. M.A.T.
Rehabilitation Counseling. M.S.Ed.

Secondary Education. Includes humanities, science, social science, socially and educational different. M.A.T., M.S.Ed.

Science. M.A.T.

Social Science. M.A.T.

Special Educator. M.S.Ed.

WESTERN UNIVERSITY OF HEALTH SCIENCES

Pomona, California 91766-1889

Web site: www.westernu.edu

Founded 1977 as the College of Osteopathic Medicine of the Pacific, name changed in 1996 and is a graduate university of medical sciences. Located 35 miles E of Los Angeles. Private control. Semester system. Special facilities: a partner with San Bernardino County's Arrowhead Medical Center in an Academic Center for Excellence in the Health Sciences at San Bernardino County's Arrowhead Medical Center. Library: 22,000 volumes, 350 subscriptions.

Total University enrollment at main campus: 982.

College of Osteopathic Medicine

Established 1977. Curriculum based on a three-phase system. Special program: Summer Anatomy program for underrepresented minorities.

Annual tuition: $28,010. No on-campus housing available. Contact Admissions Office for off-campus housing information. Off-campus housing and personal expenses: approximately $14,936.

Enrollment: first-year class 179; total full-time 699 (men 58%, women 42%). Faculty: full-time 42, part-time/volunteers 1000. Degree conferred: D.O.

ADMISSION REQUIREMENTS. Preference given to state residents, U.S. citizens, and permanent residents only. Bachelor's degree from an accredited institution required. All applicants have bachelor's degree awarded prior to enrollment. Has EDP; applicants must apply through AACOMAS before June 15. Early applications are encouraged. Submit supplemental application, a personal statement, three recommendations to Office of Admission within two weeks of receipt of application, but not later than August 1. For serious consideration an applicant should have at least a 3.30 (A = 4) in both Sciences and overall GPA and a minimum average MCAT of 9.0. Interviews are by invitation only and generally for final selection. Notification normally begins in October. Apply through AACOMAS (file after June 1, before January 1), submit MCAT (will accept test results from last three years), official transcripts for each school attended (should show at least 90 semester credits/135 quarter credit), service processing fee. After a review of the AACOMAS application and supporting documents, a decision is made concerning which candidates should receive supplemental materials. The supplemental application, an application fee of $60, a personal statement, and three recommendations (one from a D.O.) should be returned to Office of Admission as soon as possible, but not later than February 15. Interviews are by invitation only and generally for final selection. Accepts transfer applicants on a space-available basis. First-year students admitted Fall only. Rolling admissions process; notification starts in October and is finished when class is filled. School does maintain an alternate list. Phone: (909)623-6116.

ADMISSION STANDARDS. Selective. Usual minimum average: 2.5 (A = 4). Mean MCAT: 8.33, mean GPA: 3.3 (A = 4); science GPA: 3.2.

FINANCIAL AID. Scholarships, grants, California State Graduate Fellowships, institutional loans, NOF, HEAL, alternative loan programs, Federal Perkins Loans, Stafford Subsidized and Unsubsidized Loans, Service Obligation Scholarship programs, Armed Forces and National Health Service programs are available. Financial aid applications and the Financial Aid Handbook are generally available at the on-campus, by-invitation interview. All financial aid is based on demonstrated need. Contact the Financial Aid Office for current information. Phone: (909)469-5350. Use FAFSA (School code: 024827), also submit Financial Aid Transcript, Federal Income Tax forms. Approximately 75% of students receive some form of financial assistance.

DEGREE REQUIREMENTS. For D.O.: satisfactory completion of four-year program. All students must take the National Board of Osteopathic Medical Examination Part I.

WESTERN WASHINGTON UNIVERSITY

Bellingham, Washington 98225-5996

Web site: www.wwu.edu

Established 1893. Located 85 miles N of Seattle. CGS member. Coed. State control. Quarter system. Library: 600,000 volumes, 4800 subscriptions.

Annual tuition: full-time, resident $4812, nonresident $13,109; per credit resident $151, nonresident $461. On-campus housing for 1460 women, 1164 men; 13 coed units, 1 woman only; 3 apartment buildings, 268 apartment units for single and married students. Average academic year housing costs: $4990 (including board) for single students. Contact Director, University Residences for both on- and off-campus housing information. Phone: (360)650-2950.

Graduate School

Graduate study since 1947. Enrollment: full-time 618, part-time 239. (men 40%, women 60%). Faculty teaching graduate students: full-time 300, part-time 25. Degrees conferred: M.A., M.S., M.Ed., M.B.A., M.Mus.

ADMISSION REQUIREMENTS. Transcripts, letters of recommendation, GRE, GMAT, current résumé required in support of School's application. Interview required for some programs. TOEFL required for non-native English-speaking applicants. Accepts transfer applicants. Graduates of unaccredited colleges not considered. Apply to Dean of Graduate School by June 1 (Fall), October 1 (Winter), February 1 (Spring), May 1 (Summer). Many programs admit Fall Quarter only; some programs have earlier deadlines. Application fee $35. Phone: (360)650-3170; fax: (360)650-6811; e-mail: gradschl@wwu.edu.

ADMISSION STANDARDS. Selective. Required average: 3.0 (A = 4) last 90 quarter credits (60 semester hours).

FINANCIAL AID. Scholarships, fellowships, teaching assistantships, research assistantships, tuition waivers, Federal W/S, loans. Approved for VA benefits. Early application is encouraged. Apply by February 15 to Graduate School for scholarships, fellowships, assistantships, fee waivers; the Student Financial Services Office for all other programs. Phone: (360)650-3470; fax: (360)650-7291. Use FAFSA. About 25% of students receive aid other than loans from College and outside sources. Aid available for part-time students.

DEGREE REQUIREMENTS. For master's: 45 quarter hours minimum with thesis, or 48 quarter hours minimum without thesis and written comprehensive exam; reading knowledge of foreign language required for some departments.

FIELDS OF STUDY.

Adult Education.

Anthropology.

692 Westfield State College

Archives and Records Management.
Art and Art Education.
Biology.
Business Administration.
Chemistry.
Communication Sciences and Disorders.
Computer Science.
Elementary Education.
English.
Environmental Science.
Environmental Studies Education.
Exceptional Children.
Foreign Languages.
Geography.
Geology.
History.
Human Movement and Performance.
Instructional Technology.
Mathematics.
Marine and Estuarine Science.
Music.
Political Science.
Psychology.
Rehabilitation Counseling.
School Administration.
School Counselor.
Science Education.
Secondary Education.
Sociology.
Student Personnel Administration.
Technology.
Theatre.

WESTFIELD STATE COLLEGE

Westfield, Massachusetts 01086
Web site: www.wsc.ma.edu

Founded 1838. Located 12 miles W of Springfield. Coed. State control. Semester system. Library: 166,721 volumes, 819 subscriptions.

Tuition: per semester hour, resident $145, nonresident $155. No on-campus housing available for graduate students. Contact Director, Residential Life, for off-campus housing information. Phone: (413)572-5402.

Division of Graduate and Continuing Education

Graduate study since 1963. Enrollment: full-time 24, part-time 270. Faculty teaching graduate students: 21 full-time, 29 part-time. Degrees conferred: M.A., M.S., M.Ed., C.A.G.S.

ADMISSION REQUIREMENTS. Transcripts required in support of application. TOEFL required for international applicants. GRE, MAT recommended. Interview may be requested. Accepts transfer applicants. Graduates of unaccredited colleges not considered. Apply to Dean, Graduate Studies and Continuing Education prior to registration. Application fee $30. Phone: (413)572-8022; fax: (413)572-5227.

ADMISSION STANDARDS. Selective. Usual minimum average: 2.6 (A = 4).

FINANCIAL AID. Graduate assistantships, grants, New England Regional Student Program, Federal W/S, loans. Apply by April 1 to Dean, Graduate Studies and Continuing Education for assistantships; to Financial Aid Office for all other programs. Phone: (413)572-5407. Use FAFSA. Aid available for part-time students.

DEGREE REQUIREMENTS. For master's: 33 semester hours minimum; comprehensive exam; thesis/nonthesis option in some programs. For C.A.G.S.: 30 semester hours minimum beyond the master's; comprehensive exam.

FIELDS OF STUDY.
Administrator of Special Education. M.Ed., C.A.G.S.
American History. M.Ed.
Biology. M.Ed.
Criminal Justice. M.S.
Educational Administration. M.Ed., C.A.G.S.
Elementary Education. M.Ed.
English. M.A.
History. M.Ed.
Intensive Special Needs. M.Ed.
Mathematics. M.Ed.
Middle School Teacher.
Occupational Education. M.Ed., C.A.G.S.
Physical Education. M.Ed.
Psychology. Includes counseling/clinic, school guidance. M.A.
Secondary Education. M.Ed.
School Principal. Includes elementary, middle, secondary. M.Ed., C.A.G.S.
Social Studies. M.Ed.
Special Education. Includes pre-K–9, 5–12, intensive. M.Ed.
Teaching of Reading. M.Ed.
Technology for Educator. M.Ed.

WESTMINSTER COLLEGE

New Wilmington, Pennsylvania 16142-0001
Web site: www.westminster.edu

Founded 1852. Located 60 miles NE of Pittsburgh. Coed. Private control. Presbyterian affiliation. Semester system. Library: 230,000 volumes, 827 subscriptions.

Annual tuition: $22,300, per course $1239. No on-campus housing available.

Graduate Program

Graduate study since 1944. Enrollment: part-time 147. Graduate faculty: full-time 5. Degree conferred: M.Ed.

ADMISSION REQUIREMENTS. Transcripts required in support of application. MAT occasionally required. Graduates of unaccredited colleges not considered. Accepts transfer applicants. Apply to Director of Admissions by August 30 (Fall), January 15 (Spring). Rolling admissions process. Application fee $20. Phone: (724)946-7186; fax: (724)946-7171.

ADMISSION STANDARDS. Selective. Usual minimum average: 2.75 (A = 4).

FINANCIAL AID. Internships, loans, grants. Apply to Financial Aid Office; no specified closing date. Phone: (724)946-7100. Use FAFSA.

DEGREE REQUIREMENTS. For M.Ed.: 10 courses minimum, at least 8 in residence; final written exam.

FIELDS OF STUDY.
Education.
Educational Administration.
English.
History.
Reading Specialist.
School Counseling.

WHEELOCK COLLEGE

Boston, Massachusetts 02215-4176
Web site: www.wheelock.edu

Founded 1888. Private control. Semester system. Library: 96,000 volumes, 546 subscriptions.

Tuition: per credit $575. On-campus housing available. Apply to Director of Graduate Admissions.

Graduate Division

Graduate study since 1953. Enrollment; full-time 176, part-time 263. Graduate faculty: full-time 36, part-time 32. Degrees conferred: M.S., C.A.G.S.

ADMISSION REQUIREMENTS. Transcripts, three references, essay, interview in support of application. On-line application available. TOEFL required for international applicants. Accepts transfer applicants. Graduates of un accredited institutions not considered. Apply to Director of Graduate Admissions by July 1 (Fall), November 1 (Spring). Application fee $35, international applicants $40. Rolling admissions process. Phone: (617)879-2178; fax: (617)232-7127.

ADMISSION STANDARDS. Selective. Usual minimum average: 3.0 (A = 4).

FINANCIAL AID. Scholarships, grants, assistantships, Federal W/S, loans. Apply by April 1 to Director of Financial Aid, Graduate School. Phone: (617)879-2178. Use FAFSA and institutional graduate FAF. About 50% of students receive aid other than loans from College. Aid available for part-time students.

DEGREE REQUIREMENTS. For M.S.: 32-40 semester hours minimum. For C.A.G.S.: 30 semester hours beyond the master's; thesis required.

FIELDS OF STUDY.
Birth to Three—Development and Intervention.
Child Life and Family Centered Care.
Language and Literacy.
Leadership.
School Principal and Supervisor/Director.
Social Work.
Teaching and Learning.
Teaching Students with Special Needs.
Urban Teaching.

WHITTIER COLLEGE

Whittier, California 90608-0634
Web site: www.whittier.edu

Chartered 1901. Located adjacent to Los Angeles. Coed. Private control. Quaker affiliation. Library: 225,300 volumes, 1357 subscriptions.

Tuition: per credit $350. No on-campus housing available. Day-care facilities available.

Graduate Program

Enrollment: full- and part-time 75. College faculty teaching graduate students: full-time 4, part-time 9. Degree conferred: M.A.

ADMISSION REQUIREMENTS. Transcripts, GRE or MAT required in support of application. TOEFL required for international applicants. Accepts transfer applicants. Apply to the Graduate Program; no specified closing dates. Rolling admissions process. Application fee $60. Phone: (562)907-4200, ext. 4204.

ADMISSION STANDARDS. Selective. Usual minimum average: 3.0 (A = 4).

FINANCIAL AID. Fellowships, assistantships, internships, tuition waivers, loans. Apply to the Office of Financial Aid; no specified closing date. Use FAFSA.

DEGREE REQUIREMENTS. For M.A.: 30–36 credits minimum, at least 18 in residence; thesis.

FIELD OF STUDY.
Educational Designs. All M.A. programs are an individually designed course of study.

School of Law (92626)

3333 Harbor Boulevard
Costa Mesa, California 92626
Web site: www.law.whitter.edu

Founded in 1966 as Beverly Law School, merged with Whittier College in 1975. Now located in Costa Mesa, Orange County, two blocks north of the San Diego Freeway. ABA approved since 1978. AALS member since 1987. Semester system. Full-time, part-time study. Special facilities: Center for Children's Rights, Center for Intellectual Property Law. Law library: 341,631 volumes, 5097 subscriptions; has LEXIS, NEXIS, WESTLAW, DIALOG; is a State and Federal Document Repository.

Annual tuition: full-time $23,014, part-time $13,822. No on-campus housing available. Law students live off-campus. Contact Office of the Assistant Dean for off-campus information. Off-campus housing and personal expenses: approximately $15,495.

Enrollment: first-year class full-time 237, part-time 111; total 712 (men 48%, women 52%). Faculty: full-time 25, part-time 38. Student to faculty ratio 20.5 to 1. Degrees conferred: J.D., LL.M. (U.S. Legal Studies—for foreign lawyers who have completed a basic legal education and received a university degree in law in another country).

ADMISSION REQUIREMENTS. LSDAS law school report, LSAT (not later than February (Fall), June (Spring) test date; if more than one LSAT, highest is used), bachelor's degree from an accredited institution, personal statement (not to exceed three pages), recommendations, transcripts (must show all schools attended and at least three years of study) required in support of application. International applicants whose native language is not English must submit a TOEFL report (minimum score 550 and not older than two years), certified translations and evaluations of all foreign credentials; use the Credential Evaluation Service, 5353 West Third Street, Los Angeles, California 90020. Phone: (310)390-6276. Apply to Office of Admission by March 15 (Fall), November 1 (Spring). First-year students admitted Fall and Spring. Rolling admissions process. Application fee $50. Phone: (800)808-8188, (714)444-4141; fax: (714)444-0250; e-mail: info@law.whittier.edu.

ADMISSION REQUIREMENTS FOR TRANSFER APPLICANTS. Accepts transfers from other ABA-accredited schools. Admission limited to space available. At least one year of enrollment, Dean's letter indicating the applicant is in good standing, LSAT, LSDAS, personal statement regarding reason for transfer, two letters of recommendation, undergraduate transcript, current law school transcript required in support of School's application. Apply to Admission Office by June 1. Admission decision made by late July. Application fee $50. Will consider visiting students.

ADMISSION STANDARDS. Selective. Mean LSAT: full-time 148, part-time 147: mean GPA: full-time 2.89, part-time 2.83 (A = 4). Gourman rating: 2.53. *U.S. News & World Report* ranking is in the fourth tier of all U.S. law schools. Accepts approximately 40–50% of total annual applicants.

FINANCIAL AID. Need-based scholarships, merit scholarships, diversity scholarships, private and institutional loans, state grants, Federal W/S, loans. All accepted students who have signed and returned the preliminary financial aid applications with the admissions application are automatically considered for scholarships. For all other programs apply by April 1 (Fall), November 1 (Spring). Use FAFSA (School code: E00480), also submit Financial Aid Transcript, Federal Income Tax forms. Approximately 26% (full-time), 26% (part-time) of first-year class received scholarships/Grants-in-Aid. Approximately 78% of current students receive some form of financial assistance.

DEGREE REQUIREMENTS. For J.D.: 87 (40 required) credits with a GPA of at least 77 or higher (C = 77–84), plus completion of upper-divisional writing course; three-year program, four-year plus two summer session part-time program. Accelerated J.D. with summer course work. For LL.M. (U.S. Legal Studies): 24 credit, full-time, twelve-month program.

WHITWORTH COLLEGE
Spokane, Washington 99251-0001
Web site: www.whitworth.edu

Founded 1890. Coed. Private control. Presbyterian affiliation. 4-1-4 system. Library: 135,300 volumes, 725 subscriptions.

Tuition: per credit $275. No on-campus housing available for graduate students. Contact Housing Office for both on- and off-campus housing information. Phone: (509)466-3287.

Graduate Study

Enrollment: full- and part-time 205. College faculty teaching graduate students: full-time 16, part-time 35. Degrees conferred: M.A.T., M.Ed., M.I.M., M.I.T.

ADMISSION REQUIREMENTS. Official transcripts, GRE required in support of application. On-line application available. Interview sometimes requested. TOEFL required for international applicants. Accepts transfer applicants. Apply by April 1 (Fall), November 1 (Spring) to Office of Admissions. Rolling admissions process. Application fee $35. Phone: (509)466-1000, ext. 3212.

ADMISSION STANDARDS. Selective. Usual minimum average: 2.75 (A = 4).

FINANCIAL AID. Fellowships, internships, grants, Federal W/S, loans. Apply by March 1 to Office of Financial Aid. Use FAFSA. Aid available for part-time students.

DEGREE REQUIREMENTS. For master's: 30-36 semester credits minimum, thesis/nonthesis option, research paper or internship; comprehensive exam.

FIELDS OF STUDY.
Administration. M.Ed.
Elementary Education. M.Ed.
Gifted and Talented. M.A.T.
Guidance and Counseling. M.Ed.
International Management. M.I.M.
Secondary Education. M.Ed.
Special Education. M.A.T.
Teaching. M.I.T.

WICHITA STATE UNIVERSITY
Wichita, Kansas 67260-0004
Web site: www.wichita.edu

Founded 1895. CGS member. Coed. State control. Semester system. Special facilities: Administrative Assessment Center, National Institute for Aviation Research, Digital Computing Center, Center for Economics Development and Business Research, Center for Energy Studies, Center for Entrepreneurship, Center for Forensic Science, Center for Urban Studies, Rehabilitation Engineering Center, Gerontology Center, Reading Assessment Center, two low-speed and two supersonic-speed wind tunnels, Water Tunnel. Library: 1,100,000 volumes, 12,000 subscriptions. Total University enrollment: 15,000.

Tuition: per credit resident $128.50, nonresident $368.50 On-campus housing available. Average academic year housing costs: $4155 (including board) for single students; $1785–$11,000 for married students. Contact Office of Student Housing for both on- and off-campus housing information. Phone: (316)689-3693.

Graduate School
Web site: www.wichita.edu/gradsch

Graduate study since 1928. Enrollment: full-time 1000, part-time 1873 (men 45%, women 55%). University faculty: full-time 440, part-time 39. Degrees conferred: M.A., M.S., M.A.J., M.B.A., M.Ed., M.S.E., M.F.A., M.M., M.M.Ed., M.C.S., M.S.N., M.P.A., M.P.F., M.P.T., Ed.S., Ed.D., Ph.D.

ADMISSION REQUIREMENTS. Two official transcripts required in support of School's application. On-line application available. GRE/GMAT may be required by some programs. Portfolio required for M.F.A. applicants. TOEFL required for international applicants; TSE required for assistantship consideration. Interview not required. Accepts transfer applicants. Apply to Graduate Office at least four weeks prior to registration. Application fee: $25, $40 for international applicants. Phone: (316)689-3095; fax: (316)689-3253.

ADMISSION STANDARDS. Selective. Usual minimum average: 2.75 for last two years (A = 4).

FINANCIAL AID. Fellowships, assistantships for teaching/research, traineeships, internships, tuition waivers, Federal W/S, loans. Apply by April 1 to appropriate department chair for assistantships and fellowships; to Financial Aid Office for all other programs. Phone: (316)689-3430. Use FAFSA and University's FAF. About 20% of students receive aid other than loans from University and outside sources. Aid available for part-time students.

DEGREE REQUIREMENTS. For M.A., M.S.: 30 credit hours minimum; final written/oral exam; reading knowledge of one language for many departments. For M.A.J., M.P.T.: 33 hours minimum including thesis, internships, or practicum. For M.B.A.: 33-54 hours, depending upon previous academic background. For M.Ed., M.S.N.: 30 hours plus thesis or 36 hours without thesis; final written exam. For M.S.E.: 36 hours without thesis, final oral/written exam. For M.F.A.: 60 hours minimum in art, 48 minimum in creative writing, including final creative project or thesis; final written/oral exam. For M.M.: 30 hours minimum, including thesis or recital; final oral exam. For M.M.Ed.: 30 hours including thesis or recital; or 32 hours, including research seminar, final oral exam. For M.P.A.: 39 hours minimum, including urban affairs core and internships or practicum. For Ed.S.: normally 30 hours beyond the master's; final written/oral exam. For Ph.D., Ed.D.: 90 hours beyond the bachelor's; preliminary written exam; foreign languages or research tools; dissertation; final oral exam.

FIELDS OF STUDY.
Accounting. GMAT for admission. M.P.A., M.B.A. only.
Administration of Justice. M.A.J.

Aerospace Engineering. GRE for admission. M.S., Ph.D.

Anthropology. M.A.

Art Education. Portfolio for admission. M.A.

Biology. GRE Subject Test, three letters of recommendation for admission. M.S. only.

Business. GMAT for admission. M.S. only.

Business Administration. GMAT for admission. M.B.A. only.

Chemistry. GRE Subject Test, two letters of reference, statement for goals and research interest. Apply by second Monday in November (Spring), second Monday in April (Fall). M.S., Ph.D.

Communication. Includes communications, theater/drama. GRE for admissions. M.A.C. only.

Communicative Disorders and Sciences. GRE, three letters of recommendation for admission. Apply by March 1 (Summer and Fall), October 1 (Spring). M.A., Ph.D.

Computer Science. GRE taken during first year. M.S. only.

Counseling. Statement of Goals, three letters of recommendation for admission. M.Ed.

Creative Writing. Includes fiction, poetry. M.F.A.

Criminal Justice. M.A.

Curriculum and Instruction. GRE/MAT, three recommendations for admission. M.Ed.

Economics. GRE taken during first year. M.A.

Educational Administration and Supervision. GRE, three letters of recommendation. M.S., Ed.D.

Educational Psychology. M.Ed.

Electrical Engineering. GRE for admission. M.S., Ph.D.

Engineering Management. M.E.M.

English. M.A.

Environmental Science. M.S.

Fine Arts. Includes ceramics, painting, printmaking, sculpture. Portfolio, three letters of recommendation, statement of goals, résumé for admission. M.F.A. only.

Geology. M.S.

Gerontology. Names of three references for admission. M.S.

History. One language for M.A. M.A. only.

Industrial Engineering. GRE for admission. M.S., Ph.D.

Liberal Studies. Essay, personal interview for admission. M.A. only.

Mathematics. M.S.

Mathematics—Applied. GRE Subject Test for admission. Ph.D.

Mechanical Engineering. GRE for admission. M.S., Ph.D.

Music. Includes history/literature, instrumental conducting, opera performance, performance piano/organ, piano pedagogy, theory/composition. M.M.

Music Education. Includes choral, elementary, instrumental, music in special education, vocal music. M.M.Ed.

Nursing. Includes administration, education. M.S.N.

Physical Education, M.Ed.

Physical Therapy. Departmental application, three references for admission. M.P.T.

Physics. M.S.

Political Science. GRE for admission. M.A.

Psychology. Includes community/clinical, human factors. GRE General/Subject required for admission; one language or research tool for M.A. M.A., Ph.D.

Public Administration. GRE desirable. M.P.A.

Public Health. GRE or equivalent test, program application, one-year professional experience for admission. M.P.H.

School Psychology. GRE, three reference, Statement of Goals and research interest. Ed.S. only.

Social Work. M.S.W.

Sociology. One language depending upon thesis topic. M.A.

Spanish. One language in addition to Spanish. M.A.

Special Education. GRE, one-year teaching experience for admission. M.Ed.

Sport Administration. Three references, personal interview for admission. M.Ed.

Statistics. M.S. only.

Studio Art. Includes ceramics, painting, printmaking, sculpture. M.F.A.

WIDENER UNIVERSITY

Chester, Pennsylvania 19013-5792

Web site: www.widener.edu

Founded 1821. Located 15 miles S of Philadelphia. CGS member. Coed. Independent. Semester system. Special facilities: CDC CYBER 930, Digital VAX-11/750, Prime 9955, Prime 2555, Child Development Center, Engineering Research Center, University Art Museum. Prime-Medusa Computer Aided Design Laboratory, Center for Computer Assisted Instruction, Business Research Center. Library: 300,000 volumes, 2256 subscriptions. Total University enrollment: 7500.

Tuition: per credit M.B.A. $510; Nursing $540; M.P.A., M.L.A. $420; M.Ed. $385; Engineering $560; Social Work $485; D.P.T. per year $20,310; Psy.D. per year $15,800; other doctoral programs per credit $505. No on-campus housing available. Off-campus housing available within walking distance of the campus. Average academic year housing costs $6500 (including board). Contact Director of Housing by May 30 for housing information. Phone: (610)499-4393.

Graduate Studies

Enrollment: full- and part-time 3550. Faculty: full-time 156, part-time 216. Degrees conferred: M.A., M.B.A., M.Ed., M.S., M.S.N., M.E., M.H.P., M.P.A., M.S.W., Psy.D., D.N.Sc., Ed.D., M.E.-M.B.A., J.D.-M.B.A., J.D.-Psy.D., Psy.D.-M.H.A., Psy.D.-M.S. (Human Resource Management), Psy.D.-M.A. (Criminal Justice), Psy.D.-M.P.A.

ADMISSION REQUIREMENTS. Transcripts required in support of application. GRE/GMAT required for some departments. TOEFL required of international applicants. Accepts transfer applicants. Graduates of unaccredited institutions not considered. Apply to Assistant Provost at least one month prior to preferred entrance date. Application fee $25-$40. Phone: (610)499-4372.

ADMISSION STANDARDS. Usual minimum average: 2.5 (A = 4) master's level, 3.0 for doctoral programs.

FINANCIAL AID. Limited to assistantships, loans. Approved for VA benefits. Apply by April 15 to Director of Financial Aid for all programs. Use FAFSA and institutional FAF.

DEGREE REQUIREMENTS. For master's: 30-45 semester hours minimum with or without thesis, at least 24 in residence, final written/oral exam in some programs. For D.N.Sc., 60-63 credits; computer literacy, preliminary exam; dissertation; final written/oral exam. For Ed.D., Psy.D.: 60-65 credits beyond master's; preliminary exam; dissertation/project; final written/oral exam.

FIELDS OF STUDY.

Accounting Information Systems.

Business Administration and Management. Includes health and medical services administration.

Chemical Engineering.

Civil Engineering.

Computer and Software Engineering.

Criminal Justice.

Educational Leadership.

Electrical/Telecommunication Engineering.

Elementary Education.

Engineering.

Engineering Management.

Environmental Engineering Option.

Health Administration.

Health Education.

Health and Medical Services Administration.

Human Resources Management.

Human Sexuality Education.

Information Systems.

Liberal Studies.
Management and Technology.
Mathematics Education.
Mechanical Engineering.
Nursing. Includes adult health, community-based nursing, emergency critical-care nursing, family nurse practitioner studies, nurse education.
Physical Therapy.
Public Administration.
Reading.
Social Work.
Special Education.
Superintendency.
Taxation.

School of Law—Delaware (P.O. Box 7474)
4601 Concord Pike
Wilmington, Delaware 19803-0474
Web site: www.law.widener.edu

Founded 1971, affiliated with Widener in 1975. ABA approved since 1975. AALS member. Semester system. Full-time, part-time day study. Special facilities: Health Law Institute, Trial Advocacy Institute. Special programs: summer study abroad at the International Law Institute, University of Geneva, Switzerland; the International Law Institute, University of Nairobi, Kenya; the International Law Institute, Macquarie University, Sidney Australia. Law library: 416,717 volumes, 5196 subscriptions; has LEXIS, NEXIS, WESTLAW, DIALOG, LEGALTRAC, INFOTRAC.

Annual tuition: full-time $20,250, part-time $15,150. On-campus housing available. Contact Admissions Office for both on- and off-campus information. Off-campus housing and personal expenses: approximately $11,970.

Enrollment: first-year class full-time 284, part-time 120; total 1063 (men 53%, women 47%). Faculty: full-time 39, part-time 38. Student to faculty ratio 19.8 to 1. Degrees conferred: J.D., J.D.-M.B.A., J.D.-Psy.D., J.D.-M.M.P. (with University of Delaware), LL.M. (Corporate Law and Finance, Health Law).

ADMISSION REQUIREMENTS. LSDAS Law School report, bachelor's degree, transcripts, LSAT, letters of recommendation required in support of application. Accepts transfer applicants. Graduates of unaccredited colleges not considered. Apply to Admissions Office by May 15. Rolling admissions process. Application fee $60. Phone: (302)477-2162; fax: (302)477-2224.

ADMISSION STANDARDS. Selective. Mean LSAT: full-time 148, part-time 149; mean GPA: full-time 3.02, part-time 2.96 (A = 4). Gourman rating: 2.07. *U.S. News & World Report* ranking is in the fourth tier of all U.S. law schools. Admits about 50–55% of total annual applications.

FINANCIAL AID. Scholarships, Federal W/S, loans. Apply to Office of Financial Aid by April 15. Use FAFSA (School code: 003313). About 26% of students receive some aid from School.

DEGREE REQUIREMENTS. For J.D.: satisfactory completion of three-year (day) or four-year (evening) program; 87-credit-hour program. For LL.M.: at least 24 credits beyond the J.D.; two semesters in full-time residence.

School of Law (P.O. Box 69381)
Harrisburg, Pennsylvania 17106-9381
Web site: www.law.widener.edu

Established 1989. Located 7 miles from Pennsylvania's State Capital. Students have same access to facilities and programs as those students at Wilmington campus. ABA approved since 1989.

Semester system. Full-time, part-time study. Special programs: summer programs offered in Nairobi, Kenya; Geneva, Switzerland; Sydney, Australia; Venice, Italy. Law library: 188,600 volumes/microforms, 4207 subscriptions, 52 computer workstations; has LEXIS, NEXIS, WESTLAW, DIALOG, LEGALTRAC, INFOTRAC.

Annual tuition: full-time $20,250, part-time $15,150. No on-campus housing available. Law students live Off-campus. Contact Admissions Office for off-campus information. Off-campus housing and personal expenses: approximately $11,970.

Enrollment: first-year class full-time 97, part-time 54; total 397 (men 54%, women 46%). Faculty: full-time 16, part-time 15. Student to faculty ratio 17.9 to 1. Degree conferred: J.D.

ADMISSION REQUIREMENTS. LSDAS Law School report, LSAT (not later than February test date; if more than one LSAT, highest is used), bachelor's degree from an accredited institution, personal statement, two recommendations, transcripts (must show all schools attended and at least three years of study) required in support of application. Applicants must have received bachelor's degree prior to enrollment. Interview not required. Campus visits encouraged. Apply to Office of Admission by May 15 (Fall), March 31 is preferred date, December 1 (Spring). Rolling admissions process. Application fee $60. Phone: (717)541-3903.

ADMISSION REQUIREMENTS FOR TRANSFER APPLICANTS. Accepts transfers from other ABA-accredited schools. Admission limited to space available. At least one year of enrollment, Dean's letter indicating the applicant is in good standing, LSAT, LSDAS, personal statement regarding reason for transfer, personal interview, current law school transcript required in support of School's application. Apply to Admission Office by July 1. Admission decision made within one month of the receipt of completed application. Application fee $60. Will consider visiting students.

ADMISSION STANDARDS. Selective. Mean LSAT: full-time 147, part-time 148; mean GPA: full-time 3.07, part-time 2.93 (A = 4). Gourman rating 2. 07. *U. S. News & World Report* ranking is in the fourth tier of all U.S. law schools. Accepts approximately 70% of total annual application.

FINANCIAL AID. Full and half scholarships, State scholarship, Grants-in-Aid, private and institutional loans, Federal loans and Federal W/S available. All accepted students are automatically considered for scholarships; use School's Institutional Data Form. For all other programs apply as soon as possible after January 1, but not later than April 5. Use FAFSA (School code: E00651), also submit Financial Aid Transcript, Federal Income Tax forms. Approximately 28% of students receive aid other than loans from School. Loan Repayment Assistance Program available.

DEGREE REQUIREMENTS. For J.D.: 87 (44 required) credits with a GPA of at least a 2.3 (A = 4), plus completion of upper-divisional writing course; three-year full-time program, four-year part-time program. Accelerated J.D. with summer course work.

WILKES UNIVERSITY
Wilkes-Barre, Pennsylvania 18766-0002
Web site: www.wilkes.edu

Founded 1933. Located 100 miles NW of Philadelphia. Coed. Private control. Semester system. Library: 210,000 volumes, 4800 subscriptions.

Tuition: per semester hour $569, Education $292. Limited on-campus housing for graduate students.

Graduate Studies

Graduate study since 1959. Enrollment: full-time 295, part-time 1500 (men 35%, women 65%). Faculty: full- and part-time 113. Degrees conferred: M.S., M.B.A., M.H.A.

ADMISSION REQUIREMENTS. Transcripts, GRE/MAT/ GMAT letters of recommendation required in support of School's application. On-line application available. Interview may be required. Accepts transfer applicants. Apply to Dean of Admissions; no specified closing date. Application fee $30. Phone: (570)408-4160; fax: (570)408-7860.

ADMISSION STANDARDS. Selective. Usual minimum average: 2.75 (A = 4).

FINANCIAL AID. Graduate assistantships, counselorships, Federal W/S, loans. Apply to Director of Graduate Studies by March 1; no specified closing date. Phone: (570)408-4345. Use FAFSA and University's form (PHEAA).

DEGREE REQUIREMENTS. For master's: 30-39 credit hours minimum, at least 24 in residence. For Ph.D.: at least 60 credits beyond the bachelor's degree, two years in residence; foreign language requirement varies by department; preliminary exam; candidacy; dissertation; final oral exam.

FIELDS OF STUDY.
Business Administration. GMAT for admission. Concentrations in accounting, e-business, entrepreneurship, finance, human resource management, international business, management, marketing.
Classroom Technology.
Development and Strategies.
Educational Leadership.
Electrical Engineering. GRE for admission. M.S., Ph.D.
Health Administration.
Instructional Technology.
Mathematics.
Nursing. GRE or MAT for admission
Secondary Education. Includes biology, chemistry, English, history, mathematics, physics.
Special Education.

WILLAMETTE UNIVERSITY

Salem, Oregon 97301-3931
Web site: www.willamette.edu

Founded 1842. Located 42 miles S of Portland. The University consists of a College of Liberal Arts, College of Law, and the Atkinson Graduate School of Management. Library: 408,000 volumes, 3100 subscriptions.

Limited on-campus housing available for graduate students. Average academic year housing costs: $7550–$11,350 (including board). Contact Dean of Residence Life for both on- and off-campus housing information. Phone: (503)370-6212.

George H. Atkinson Graduate School of Management

Web site: www.willamette.edu/agsm

Graduate study since 1974. Coed. Semester system. Special facilities: Atkinson School Technology Center (includes 23 PCs), Public Policy Research Center.

Annual tuition: full-time $18,050; per credit $602.
Enrollment: full-time 151, part-time 21. Faculty: full-time 14, part-time 12. Degrees conferred: M.B.A., M.B.A.-J.D.

ADMISSION REQUIREMENTS. Transcripts, GMAT/GRE, letters of reference, application form and essay required in support of School's application. On-line application available. TOEFL required for applicants. Graduates of unaccredited institutions not considered. Apply by April 1 for priority consideration; rolling admissions process after that on a space-available basis only. Application fee $50. Phone: (503)370-6167; fax: (503)370-3011; e-mail: joneill@willamette.edu.

ADMISSION STANDARDS. Selective. Usual minimum average: 3.0 (A = 4).

FINANCIAL AID. Scholarships, research assistantships, internships, Federal W/S, loans. Approved for VA benefits. Apply by July 1. Phone: (503)370-6273. Use FAFSA.

DEGREE REQUIREMENTS. For M.B.A.: 63 semester hours. Joint Law and Management degree requires four years of full-time study.

FIELD OF STUDY.
Business, Government, and Not-for-Profit Management.

College of Law (97301-3922)

Web site: www.willamette.edu/wucl

Established 1883. ABA approved since 1938. AALS member. Semester system. Full-time, day study only. Special facility: Center for Dispute Resolution, Truman Wesley Collins Legal Center. Special programs: summer study abroad in the People's Republic of China and Ecuador. Law library: 286,946 volumes, 3295 subscriptions; has LEXIS, NEXIS, WESTLAW, DIALOG, CALI.

Annual tuition: $19,080. On-campus housing available for single students only. Contact Office of Residential Life for both on- and off-campus housing information. Phone: (503)370-6212. Law students tend to live off-campus. Off-campus housing and personal expenses: approximately $11,456.

Enrollment: first-year class 165; total full-time 434 (men 52%, women 48%); no part-time study available. Faculty: full-time 16, part-time 8. Student to faculty ratio 22.5 to 1. Degrees conferred: J.D., J.D.-M.B.A.

ADMISSION REQUIREMENTS. LSDAS Law School report, bachelor's degree, transcripts, references, LSAT required in support of application. Accepts transfer applicants. Graduates of unaccredited colleges not considered. Apply to Dean after September 1, before April 1 for priority consideration. Rolling admissions process. Application will be accepted as long as space is available. Admits beginning students Fall only. Application fee $50. Phone: (503)370-6282.

ADMISSION STANDARDS. Selective. Mean LSAT: 154; mean GPA: 3.23 (A = 4). Gourman rating: 3.61. *U.S. News & World Report* ranking is in the third tier of all U.S. law schools. Accepts 50% of total annual applicants. Approximately 64% of enrolled students are nonresidents.

FINANCIAL AID. Scholarships, partial tuition waivers, Federal W/S, loans. Apply to the Office of Financial Aid by February 1. Phone: (877)744-3736. Use FAFSA. About 59% of students receive aid other than loans from School and outside sources.

DEGREE REQUIREMENTS. For J.D.: 88 semester hours minimum; writing requirements; final exam.
Note: Study-abroad program in Shanghai (China) available.

THE COLLEGE OF WILLIAM AND MARY

Williamsburg, Virginia 23187-8795
Web site: www.wm.edu

Founded 1693. Located 50 miles SE of Richmond. CGS member. Coed. State control. Semester system. Special facilities: Applied Research Center, Archaeological Conservation Center, Center for Archaeological Research, Center for Conservation Biology, Center for Gifted Education, Center for Public Policy, Institute for the Bill of Rights, Omohundro Institute of Early American History and Culture, National Institute of American History and Democracy, National Planned Giving Institute, Reves Center for International Studies, Roy R. Charles Center, Virginia Institute of Marine Science (VINIS), Writing Resources Center, Millington Life Sciences Hall, Muscarelle Museum, William Small Physical Laboratory; research opportunities at Colonial Williamsburg Foundation, Continuous Electron Beam Accelerator Facility (CEBAF), the Eastern State Hospital, the National Center for State Courts, and the Langley Research Center (LaRC) of the National Aeronautics and Space Administration. Graduate students work at the national laboratories and accelerator installations throughout the world. Libraries of the College are the central Earl Gregg Swem; the chemistry, physics, geology, biology, and music libraries; the Marshall-Wythe Law Library; the School of Marine Science; the Professional Resource Center (School of Business Administration); Learning Resource Center/curriculum Library (School of Education): 1,400,000 volumes, 8000 subscriptions.

Annual tuition: full-time resident $5448, nonresident $16,650. On-campus housing for 122 graduate men and women, and 10 married students' apartments. Average academic year housing costs: $11,878 (including board) single students; $8000 for married students. Contact Office of Residence Life for on-campus information, phone: (757)221-4314; Office of Off-Campus Housing for off-campus information, phone: (757)221-3302.

Graduate Studies

Enrollment: full- and part-time 2010. Graduate faculty: full- and part-time 675. Degrees conferred: M.A., M.A.Ed., M.S., M.Ed., M.B.A., M.L.&T., M.P.P., Ed.D., Psy.D., Ph.D., M.B.A.-J.D., M.B.A.-M.P.P.

ADMISSION REQUIREMENTS. Official transcripts, letters of reference required in support of application. GRE/GMAT, interview required for some departments. TOEFL required for international applicants. Accepts transfer applicants. Apply to appropriate department chair or dean of professional school by May 1 for priority consideration. Application fee varies by school. Phone: (757)221-2467; fax: (757)221-2464.

ADMISSION STANDARDS. Competitive for some departments, selective for all others. Minimum average: 2.5 (A = 4).

FINANCIAL AID. Awards from institutional funds: fellowships, scholarships, research fellowships, teaching assistantships, internships, Federal W/S, loans. Approved for VA benefits. Apply to appropriate department chair for fellowships, assistantships; to Financial Aid Office for all other programs. Phone: (757)221-1220; fax: (757)221-2515. Use FAFSA. About 50% of students receive aid other than loans from College and outside sources.

DEGREE REQUIREMENTS. For M.A.: 24 semester credits, at least one year in residence; reading knowledge of one foreign language for some departments; thesis; final exam. For M.S.: 32 semester credits minimum; thesis not required. Other require-

ments same as for M.A. For M.P.P.: 48 semester credits over two years; ten-week internship in summer between first and second years. For M.Ed., M.A. in Ed. 30 semester credits minimum, at least 18 in residence; thesis/final project (except for Secondary School Teaching); comprehensive exam. For M.B.A.: 60 semester credits minimum; thesis optional. For M.L.&T: one year minimum beyond the J.D. or equivalent. For Ed.D.: 90 semester credits minimum, at least 60 in residence; preliminary exam; dissertation; final oral exam. For Psy.D.: three years minimum, three terms per year, at least two years in residence; one year internship, comprehensive exam; final written or oral exam. For Ph.D.: three years minimum, at least one year in residence; reading knowledge of one or two foreign languages in some departments; comprehensive exam; dissertation; final oral exam.

FIELDS OF STUDY.

ARTS AND SCIENCES:
American Studies. M.A., Ph.D.
Anthropology. Includes historical archaeology. M.A. only.
Applied Sciences. Includes applied mathematics and computer science, chemical physics, atmospheric and plasma science, materials science; thesis optional. M.S., Ph.D.
Biology. M.A.
Chemistry. M.A., M.S.
Computer Science. Includes computational operations research. M.S., Ph.D.
History. Includes M.A. apprenticeship and Ph.D. internship programs in historical archaeology, historical editing, historical libraries. M.A., Ph.D.
Physics. Includes computational science. M.S., Ph.D.
Psychology. M.A. in general psychology, Psy.D. in clinical.
Public Policy. M.P.P.

SCHOOL OF BUSINESS ADMINISTRATION:
Accounting. M.Acc.
Business Administration. M.B.A., E.M.B.A.

SCHOOL OF PSYCHOLOGY AND COUNSELOR EDUCATION:
Counselor Education. Includes community, community and addiction, family, school. M.Ed., Ed.D., Ph.D.
Educational Leadership. Includes K–12 administration and supervision, higher education, gifted education. M.Ed.
Education Policy, Planning, and Leadership. Includes general education administration, gifted education administration, higher education, special education administration. Ed.D., Ph.D.
Elementary School Teaching. M.A.Ed.
Gifted Education. M.A.Ed.
Reading, Language, and Literacy. M.A.Ed.
School Psychology. M.Ed., Ed.S.
Secondary Education. Includes English, mathematics, modern foreign languages, science, social studies. M.A.Ed.
Special Education. M.A.Ed.

SCHOOL OF MARINE SCIENCE:
Marine Science. M.S., Ph.D.

THOMAS JEFFERSON PROGRAM IN PUBLIC POLICY:
Human Resource Policy. M.P.P.
International Policy. M.P.P.
Regulatory Policy. M.P.P.
State and Local Policy. M.P.P.

Marshall-Wythe Law School (P.O. Box 8795)

Web site: www.wm.edu/law

Established 1779. Located on main campus. ABA approved since 1932. AALS member. Semester system. Full-time, day study only. Special facility: Institute of Bill of Rights Law. Special programs: summer study abroad at University of Exeter, Devonshire, England; University of Madrid, Spain; University of Adelaide, Australia. Law library: 364,066 volumes, 5285 subscriptions; has LEXIS, NEXIS, WESTLAW, DIALOG; is a Federal Government Depository.

Annual tuition: resident $9591, nonresident $18,839. On-campus housing available for both single and married students. Contact Resident Life Office for both on- and off-campus housing information. Phone: (757)221-4314. Law students tend to live off-campus. Off-campus housing and personal expenses: approximately $12,878.

Enrollment: first-year class 180; total full-time 520 (men 57%, women 43%); no part-time students. Faculty: full-time 26, part-time 27. Student to faculty ratio 16.7 to 1. Degrees conferred: J.D., J.D.-M.B.A., J.D.-M.P.P., J.D.-M.A. (American Studies), LL.M. (American Legal System—for foreign attorneys who have completed a basic legal education and received a university degree in law in another country).

ADMISSION REQUIREMENTS. LSDAS Law School report, bachelor's degree, transcripts, LSAT, two letters of recommendation required in support of application. TOEFL required for foreign applicants. Accepts transfer applicants. Graduates of unaccredited colleges not considered. Apply to Admissions Office after September 15, before March 1 for priority consideration. Application fee $30. Phone: (757)221-3785; fax: (757)221-3261.

ADMISSION REQUIREMENTS FOR TRANSFER APPLICANTS. Accepts transfers from other ABA-accredited schools. Admission limited to space available. At least one year of enrollment, Dean's letter indicating the applicant is in good standing (prefer applicants in the top quarter of first-year class), LSAT, LSDAS, personal statement regarding reason for transfer, two letters of recommendation, current law school transcript with rank in class required in support of School's application. Apply to Admission Office by July 1. Admission decision made by early August. Application fee $40. Will consider visiting students.

ADMISSION REQUIREMENTS FOR LL.M. APPLICANTS. All applicants must have a basic law degree from a country other than the U.S.; the institution must be fully accredited and recognized by the relevant educational authority of that country; and applicant can not be a permanent resident of U.S. citizen. Original or certified copies of all original official transcripts/academic record, certified English translations of all non-English credentials, two letters of recommendation, personal statement required in support of LL.M. application. Admits Fall only. Apply by February 1 to the School of Law's Admissions Office. Application fee $40.

ADMISSION STANDARDS. Selective. Mean LSAT: 161; mean GPA: 3.34 (A = 4). Gourman rating: 3.45. *U.S. News & World Report* ranking is in the top 32 of all U.S. law schools. Accepts 20–25% of total annual applicants.

FINANCIAL AID. Scholarships, fellowships, assistantships, Federal W/S, loans. Apply to the Office of Financial Aid by February 1. Use FAFSA (School code: 003705). About 40% of students receive aid other than loans from School.

DEGREE REQUIREMENTS. For J.D.: 90 semester credit program, at least final year in residence. For LL.M.: at least 24 credits beyond J.D.; one year in full-time residence.

WILLIAM CAREY COLLEGE
Hattiesburg, Mississippi 39401-5499
Web site: www.wmcarey.edu

Founded 1906. Located 125 miles from New Orleans, Louisiana. Coed. Semester system. Library: 107,000 volumes, 30,000 microforms, 628 subscriptions.

Tuition: per credit hour $245 (M.Ed., M.B.A.), $230 (Psychology). Limited on-campus housing available.

Graduate Division

Founded in 1969. Enrollment: full- and part-time 185 (men 13, women 10). Faculty: full-time 21, part-time 11. Degrees conferred: M.Ed., M.B.A.

ADMISSION REQUIREMENTS. Transcripts, letters of recommendation, teaching certificate (for Education) required in support of application. TOEFL required for international applicants. Accepts transfer applicants. Apply to the Chair Graduate Division; no specified closing date. Rolling admissions process. Application fee $10. Phone: (601)318-6774.

ADMISSION STANDARDS. Selective. Usual minimum average: 2.5 (A = 4).

FINANCIAL AID. Scholarships, Scholar Grants, Federal W/S, loans. Phone: (601)318-6153. Use FAFSA (College code: 002447) and College's FAF. About 10% of students receive aid from College and outside sources. Aid available for part-time students.

DEGREE REQUIREMENTS. For M.B.A., M.Ed.: 30-36 semester hours minimum; evaluation tests; comprehensive exam.

FIELDS OF STUDY.
Business Administration. M.B.A.
Educational Leadership. M.Ed.
Elementary Education. M.Ed.
Secondary Education. M.Ed.

WILLIAM MITCHELL COLLEGE OF LAW
875 Summit Avenue
St. Paul, Minnesota 55105-3076
Web site: www.wmitchell.edu

Established 1900. Located in downtown St. Paul. Private control. ABA approved since 1938. AALS member. Semester system. Full-time, part-time study. Law library: 305,891 volumes, 4738 subscriptions; has LEXIS, WESTLAW.

Annual tuition: full-time (three-year program) $19,030, part-time (four-year program) $13,830. No on-campus housing available. Law students live off-campus. Contact Student Services Office for off-campus information. Off-campus housing and personal expenses: approximately $12,870.

Enrollment: first-year class full-time 193, part-time 121; total 999 (men 46%, women 54%). Faculty: full-time 27, part-time 114. Student to faculty ratio 25.8 to 1. Degree conferred: J.D.

ADMISSION REQUIREMENTS. Bachelor's degree, transcripts, LSAT, writing sample required in support of application. Interview not required. Transfer applicants accepted. Graduates of unaccredited colleges not considered. Apply to Admissions Office by June 29 for priority consideration. Admits Fall only. Application fee $45. Phone: (612)290-6329.

ADMISSION STANDARDS. Selective. Mean LSAT: full-time 154, part-time 150; mean GPA: full-time 3.28, part-time 3.05

(A = 4). Gourman rating: 2.91. *U.S. News & World Report* ranking is in the third tier of all U.S. law schools. Accepts 65% of total annual applicants.

FINANCIAL AID. Scholarships, minority scholarships, Federal W/S, loans. Approved for VA benefits. Apply to Financial Aid Office before March 15. Use FAFSA (College code: G02391). About 50% of students receive aid other than loans from College. Aid available for part-time, third-, and fourth-year students.

DEGREE REQUIREMENTS. For J.D.: 86-semester-hour program; advanced standing considered. For LL.M.: at least 24 credits beyond J.D.

WILLIAM PATERSON UNIVERSITY OF NEW JERSEY
Wayne, New Jersey 07470-8420
Web site: www.wpunj.edu

Founded 1855, Located 20 miles W of New York City. CGS member. Coed. State control. Semester system. Special facility: New Sarah Byrd Askew library. Library: 286,000 volumes, 1950 subscriptions. Total University enrollment: 10,000.

Tuition: per credit resident $278, nonresident $394. On-campus housing available for single graduate students only. Average academic year housing costs: $3315 (including board). Contact Director of Residence Life for both on- and off-campus housing information. Phone: (973)720-2714.

Graduate Programs

Graduate study since 1966. Enrollment: full-time 213, part-time 670. Faculty: full-time 238, part-time 3. Degrees conferred: M.A., M.A.T., M.B.A., M.Ed., M.S., M.S.N.

ADMISSION REQUIREMENTS. Official transcripts, interview, GRE or MAT, GMAT (Business) required in support of application. TOEFL, W.E.S. required for international applicants. Accepts transfer applicants. Apply to Office of Graduate Studies and Research by August 1 (Fall), November 1 (Spring) for most departments. Application fee $35. Phone: (973)720-2237; fax: (973)720-2035.

ADMISSION STANDARDS. Selective. Usual minimum average: 3.0 (A = 4).

FINANCIAL AID. Graduate assistantship, internships, loans. Approved for VA benefits. Apply to the Office of Graduate Studies and Research for assistantships, internships; to the Financial Aid Office for all other programs. Phone: (973)720-2022. Use FAFSA.

DEGREE REQUIREMENTS. For master's: 30-42 credit hours minimum, at least 24 in residence; research thesis; project; comprehensive exam. For M.B.A.: 60 credit hours minimum.

FIELDS OF STUDY.
Applied Clinical Psychology. M.S.
Biological Sciences. M.A., M. S.
Biotechnology and Communication Disorders. Includes speech-language pathology. M.S.
Communication Arts. Includes interpersonal communication, television. M.A. only.
Community-Based Nursing. Includes tracks in educational, administrative, advanced practice. M.S.N.

Counseling Services. Includes agency, school; M. Ed.
Education. Includes bilingual/English as a second language, early childhood, educational leadership, educational media, language arts, learning technologies, teaching children mathematics. M.Ed. only.
Elementary Education. M.A.T.
English. Includes literature, writing. M.A. only.
Finance. M.B.A.
General Business. M.B.A.
Jazz Studies. M.M.
Management. M.B.A.
Marketing. M.B.A.
Music Education. M.M.
Music Management. M.M.
Reading. M.Ed.
Sociology. Includes diversity studies, crime and justice. M.A.
Special Education. Includes development disability, learning disability. M.Ed. only.
Visual Arts. Includes painting, sculpture, ceramics, furniture design, metals, photography, printmaking, textiles. M.A. only.
Note: Certification Programs in Education available.

WILLIAMS COLLEGE
Williamstown, Massachusetts 01267
Web site: www.williams.edu

Founded 1793. Located 50 miles E of Albany, New York. Coed. Private control. Semester system. Special facilities: Center for Development Economics, Center for Foreign Languages, Literature, and Culture, Center for Environmental Studies, Center for the Humanities and Social Sciences, Center for Technology in the Arts and Humanities, art museum, Clark Art Institute, Adams Memorial Theater. Library: 680,000 volumes, 3000 subscriptions.

Annual tuition: full-time $27,500 (Art History), $26,500 (Development Economics). On-campus housing required for single graduate Students. Annual housing cost: $6600. Contact Graduate housing office. Phone: (413)458-2303, ext. 403.

Graduate Study

Enrollment; full-time 40, part-time 0. Faculty: full-time 24. Degree conferred: M.A.

ADMISSION REQUIREMENTS. Transcripts, four letters of recommendation, GRE (for Art History), two essays required in support of application. On-line application available. Interview recommended. Accepts transfer applicants. TOEFL required for international applicants. Apply to Director, Graduate Programs by January 15. Phone: Art History (413) 458-2303, ext. 533; CDE (413) 597-2148. Application fee $35.

ADMISSION STANDARDS. Competitive. Usual minimum average: 3.0 (A = 4).

FINANCIAL AID. Fellowships, full- and partial scholarships, internships, loans. Apply by March 1 to Financial Aid Office. Phone: (413)597-4181. Use FAFSA. Approximately 100% of students receive some aid from College and outside sources.

DEGREE REQUIREMENTS. For M.A.: eleven courses, two winter study periods, one year minimum in resident; reading knowledge of two foreign languages; thesis; final oral exam.

FIELDS OF STUDY.
Art History.
Development Economics.

WINONA STATE UNIVERSITY
Winona, Minnesota 55987-5838
Web site: www.winona.msus.edu

Founded 1858. Located 110 miles SE of Minneapolis. Coed. State control. Quarter system. Library: 244,000 volumes, 1950 subscriptions.

Tuition: per credit, resident $145, nonresident $229. Average academic year housing cost: $3470 (including board). Limited on-campus housing for graduate students. Contact Director of Student Housing for both on- and off-campus housing information. Phone: (507)457-5305. Day-care facilities available.

Graduate Studies

Graduate study since 1953. Enrollment: full-time 114, part-time 258. College faculty teaching graduate students: full-time 66, part-time none. Degrees conferred: M.S., M.A., M.B.A., Specialist Degree in Educational Administration.

ADMISSION REQUIREMENTS. Transcripts GRE/GMAT required in support of application. On-line application available. Interview not required. TOEFL required for international applicants. Accepts transfer applicants. Graduates of unaccredited institutions not considered. Apply to Office of Graduate Studies at least one month prior to registration. Application fee $20. Phone: (507)457-5088; fax: (507)457-5578.

ADMISSION STANDARDS. Selective. Usual minimum average: 2.5 (A = 4).

FINANCIAL AID. Annual awards from institutional funds: assistantships, traineeships, internships, Federal W/S, loans. Approved for VA benefits. Apply at least six months prior to registration to appropriate department chair for assistantships; to Financial Aid Office for all other programs. Phone: (507)457-5090. Use FAFSA. Aid available for part-time students.

DEGREE REQUIREMENTS. Thesis plan: 45 quarter hours minimum; final written/oral exam. Nonthesis plan: 48-72 quarter hours; final written exam. Specialist: 45 quarter hours beyond the master's; special project.

FIELDS OF STUDY.
Advanced Practice Nursing. Includes adult or family nurse practitioner, clinical nurse specialist, nurse administrator, nurse educator. M.S.
Counselor Education. Includes community counseling, chemical dependency, elementary school counseling, professional development, secondary school counseling. M.S.
Education. Includes K–12. M.S.
Educational Leadership. Includes K–12 principal, superintendent. M.S., Ed.S.
English. M.A., M.S.
Nursing. M.S.
Science and Engineering. Includes software technology. M.S.
Special Education. M.S.

WINTHROP UNIVERSITY
Rock Hill, South Carolina 29733
Web site: www.winthrop.edu

Founded 1886. Located 25 miles SW of Charlotte, North Carolina. State control. Semester system. Library: 638,000 volumes, 2706 subscriptions. Total University enrollment: 6400.

Annual tuition: full-time resident $4132, nonresident $7458; per semester hour resident $173, nonresident $312. On-campus housing available for married and single students; 54 married housing units. Average academic year housing costs: $4820 (including board) for single students; $5600 for married students. Contact Director, Residence Life, for housing information. Phone: (803)323-2260.

Graduate Studies

Enrollment: full-time 256, part-time 389. University faculty: full- and part-time 162. Degrees conferred: M.A., M.S., M.F.A., M.Mth., M.A.T., M.L.A., M.M., M.Ed., M.B.A., M.M.E., Ed.S., S.S.P.

ADMISSION REQUIREMENTS. Official transcripts from all postsecondary institutions attended, GMAT (business), GRE/MAT, NTE/Class III Professional Teaching Certificate for certain programs required in support of application. TOEFL or ELS Language Center English proficiency level 109 required for international applicants. Accepts transfer applicants. Graduates of colleges not accredited by a regional accrediting agency must be approved by the Graduate Council. Apply to the Office of Graduate Studies; no specified closing date. Application fee $35, $50 for international applicants. Phone: (800)411-7041; fax: (803)323-2292.

ADMISSION STANDARDS. Selective. Usual minimum average: 3.0 (A = 4).

FINANCIAL AID. Annual awards from institutional funds: scholarships, research assistantships, graduate assistantships, internships, Federal W/S, loans. Approved for VA benefits. Forms for assistantships available in Office of Graduate Services. Apply by February 1 to Financial Aid Office for all federal programs. Phone: (803)323-2189; fax: (803)323-4528. Use FAFSA and institutional FAF. Aid available for part-time students.

DEGREE REQUIREMENTS. For all master's: 30-60 semester hours minimum; M.A., M.S. thesis optional. For Ed.S., S.S.P.: 60-66 semester hours beyond the bachelor's.

FIELDS OF STUDY.

COLLEGE OF ARTS AND SCIENCES:
Biology. M.S.
English. M.A.
History. M.A.
Human Nutrition. M.S.
Liberal Arts. M.L.A.
Mathematics. M.Mth.
School Psychology. M.S., SSP.
Spanish. M.A.

COLLEGE OF BUSINESS ADMINISTRATION:
Business Administration. Includes accounting, international. M.B.A.
Software Development. M.S.

RICHARD W. RILEY COLLEGE OF EDUCATION:
Counseling and Development. Includes community/agency, school. M.Ed.
Curriculum and Instruction. Includes early childhood, elementary, secondary. M.Ed.
Education. Includes art (K–12), biology, business/marketing, dance (K–12), English, French, family and consumer sciences, mathematics, music (K–12), physical (K–12), social studies, Spanish, theater. M.A.T.
Educational Leadership. M.Ed.
Middle Level Education. M.Ed.
Physical Education. M.S.
Reading. M.Ed.
Special Education. M.Ed.

COLLEGE OF VISUAL AND PERFORMING ARTS:
Arts Administration. M.A.
Art and Design. M.F.A.
Art Education. M.A.
Conducting. M.M.
Music Education. M.M.E.
Performance. M.M.

MEDICAL COLLEGE OF WISCONSIN

Milwaukee, Wisconsin 53226-0509
Web site: www.mcw.edu

Founded 1913, became a freestanding school of medicine in 1967. Coed. Public, formerly associated with Marquette University. Semester system. Special facilities: Bioinformatics Research Center, Biostatistics Consulting Center, Cancer Center, Cardiovascular Center, Center for AIDS Intervention Research, Center for Animal Research Imaging, Center for the Study of Bioethics, End of Life Physician Education Resource Center, Foley Center for Aging, Free Radical Research Center, Functional Imaging Research Center, General Clinical Research Center, Health Policy Institute, Human Molecular Genetics Center, Injury Research Center, National EST Center, MRI Center, Blood Research Institute. The College's NIH ranking is 68th among all U.S. institutions with 203 awards/grants worth $71,638,967. Library: 230,000 volumes, 1200 subscriptions. Total College enrollment: 1500.

No on-campus housing available. Total average costs for all other expenses beyond tuition: $10,000.

Graduate School of Biomedical Sciences

Annual tuition: full-time $9,695, per credit $540.

Enrollment: full-time 200. Faculty: full-time 160, part-time 46. Degrees conferred: M.A., M.P.H., M.S., Ph.D.

ADMISSION REQUIREMENTS. Transcripts, GRE, three letters of recommendation, personal statement, interview required in support of application. TOEFL (minimum score 580) required of all foreign applicants. Accepts transfer applicants. Graduates of unaccredited colleges not considered. Apply to Office of Admissions June 1 (Fall), December 1 (Spring). Application fee $40. Phone: (414) 456-8218; e-mail: gradschool@mcw.edu.

ADMISSION STANDARDS. Competitive. Usual minimum average: 3.0 (A = 4)

FINANCIAL AID. Scholarships, stipends, research assistantships, fellowships, Federal W/S, loans. Apply to Director of Financial Aid by February 15. Phone: (414)456-8208. Use FAFSA. About 20% of students receive some aid from College and outside sources.

DEGREE REQUIREMENTS. For M.A.: 30 credit, full-time, two-year program; clinical practicum, teaching practicum; thesis. For M.P.H.: three- to four-year part-time program; research project. For M.S.: 30–36 semester hours minimum; foreign language requirement varies by department; comprehensive exam; thesis. For Ph.D.: six semesters in residence, at least two semesters in full-time study; qualifying exam; dissertation; final oral exam. For M.D.-Ph.D.: satisfactory completion of six- to seven-year program.

FIELDS OF STUDY.
Biochemistry. Ph.D.
Bioethics. M.A.
Bioinformatics. Joint program with Marquette University. M.S.
Biomedical Science. Interdisciplinary. M.S.
Biophysics. M.S., Ph.D.

Biostatistics. Ph.D.
Cell and Development Biology. Ph.D.
Epidemiology. M.S.
Functional Imaging. Joint program with Marquette University. Ph.D.
Healthcare Technologies Management. Joint program with Marquette University. M.S.
Medical Informatics. Joint program with Milwaukee School of Engineering. M.S.
Microbiology and Molecular. Ph.D.
Neurosciences. Interdisciplinary. Ph.D.
Pathology.
Pharmacology and Toxicology. Ph.D.
Physiology. Ph.D.
Preventive Medicine. M.P.H.
Public Health. M.P.H.
Public Health and Occupational Health. M.P.H.

Medical School

Annual tuition: resident $19,604, nonresident $29,695. Total average other expenses: $10,500.

Enrollment: first-year class 204 (EDP 30); total 807 (men 56%, women 44%). Faculty: full-time 758, part-time 68. Degrees conferred: M.D., M.D.-M.S., M.D.-Ph.D. (Medical Scientist Training Program).

ADMISSION REQUIREMENTS. AMCAS report, transcripts, MCAT, two letters of recommendation, personal interview required in support of application. Has EDP; apply between June 1 and August 1. Interview by invitation only. Preference given to state residents. Graduates of unaccredited colleges not considered. Apply to Committee on Admissions after June 1, before November 1. Application fee $60. Phone: (414)456-8246; fax: (414)456-6506.

ADMISSION STANDARDS. Very competitive for nonresidents, selective for residents. Mean MCAT: 9.8; mean GPA: 3.70 (A = 4). Gourman rating: 3.23. *U.S. News & World Report* ranking is in the top 47 of all U.S. medical schools in primary care programs. Accepts about 4–6% of total annual applicants. Approximately 50% are state residents.

FINANCIAL AID. Scholarships, loans. Apply to Director of Financial Aid after acceptance, before April 24. Use FAFSA. About 20% of students receive some aid from College and outside sources.

DEGREE REQUIREMENTS. For M.D.: satisfactory completion of four-year program; all students must pass USMLE Step 1 prior to entering third year; all students must take USMLE Step 2 and record a score. For M.D.-Ph.D.: satisfactory completion of six to seven-year program.

UNIVERSITY OF WISCONSIN— EAU CLAIRE

Eau Claire, Wisconsin 54702-4004
Web site: www.uwec.edu

Founded 1916. Located 85 miles E of St. Paul, Minnesota. CGS member. Coed. State control. Semester system. Special facilities: Foster Art Gallery, Center for Communication Disorders, Human Development Center, Kate Gill Literary Research Center, S. W. Casey Observatory, James Newman Clark Bird Museum, Pigeon Lake Field Station, L. E. Phillips Planetarium. Library: 703,300 volumes, 3376 subscriptions. Total University enrollment: 10,500.

Annual fees: full-time resident $4186, nonresident $13,130; per credits resident $233, nonresident $730. On-campus housing for single graduate students, none for married students. Average academic year housing costs: $3400 (including board). Contact Director of Housing for both on- and off-campus housing information. Phone: (715)836-3674. Day-care facilities available.

Graduate Studies

Graduate study since 1960. Enrollment: full-time 98, part-time 231. Graduate faculty: full-time 36, part-time 21. Degrees conferred: M.A., M.A.T., M.B.A., M.E., M.M., M.S., M.S.N., M.S.T., M.S.E.

ADMISSION REQUIREMENTS. Official transcripts, GRE/GMAT, interview required in support of application. TOEFL required for international applicants. Accepts transfer applicants. Apply to Director of Admissions at least 30 days prior to registration. Application fee $35. Phone: (715)836-2721; fax: (715)836-4892.

ADMISSION STANDARDS. Relatively open. Usual minimum average for probationary admission: 2.25 (A = 4).

FINANCIAL AID. Annual awards from institutional funds: scholarships, fellowships, graduate assistantships, tuition waivers, Federal W/S, loans. Approved for VA benefits. Apply by March 1 to Director of Financial Aid. Phone: (715)836-3733, Fax: (715)836-2380. Use FAFSA. About 40% of full-time students receive aid other than loans from University and outside sources. Aid available for part-time students.

DEGREE REQUIREMENTS. For master's: 30-36 semester hours minimum, at least 21 in residence; thesis/nonthesis option/final paper; final written/oral comprehensive exam.

FIELDS OF STUDY.

COLLEGE OF ARTS AND SCIENCES:
Biology. M.S.
Education. M.S.
English. M.A.
History. M.A.
School Psychology. Ed.S.

COLLEGE OF BUSINESS:
Business Administration. M.B.A.

COLLEGE OF PROFESSIONAL STUDIES:
Biology. M.A.T., M.S.T.
Communication Disorders. M.S.
Elementary Education. M.S.T.
English. M.A.T., M.S.T.
Environmental and Public Health. M.S.
History. M.A.T., M.S.T.
History/Social Science. M.S.T.
Mathematics. M.A.T., M.S.T.
Nursing. M.S.N.
Professional Development. M.Ed.
Reading. M.A.T.
Special Education. M.S.Ed.

UNIVERSITY OF WISCONSIN— LA CROSSE

La Crosse, Wisconsin 54601-3742
Web site: www.uwlax.edu

Founded 1909. Located 125 miles W of Madison. CGS member. Coed. State control. Semester system. Special facilities: Bureau of Business and Economic Research, Center for Education Profession, Rhea Pederson Reading Center, River Studies Cen-

ter. Library: over 550,000 volumes, 2200 subscriptions. Total University enrollment: 9000.

Annual fees: full-time resident (and Minnesota contract) $5012.40, nonresident $15,622.50. Limited on-campus housing for single graduate students only. Average academic year housing costs: $3800 (including board). Contact Director of Campus Housing for both on- and off-campus housing information. Phone: (608)785-8075. Day-care facilities available.

Graduate Studies

Graduate study since 1956. Enrollment: full-time 253, part-time 329. University faculty teaching graduate students: full-time 139, part-time 55. Degrees conferred: M.B.A., M.E.P.D., M.P.H., M.S., M.S.Ed.

ADMISSION REQUIREMENTS. Transcript, GMAT (Business) required in support of application. TOEFL required for international applicants. Accepts transfer applicants. Graduates of unaccredited institutions not considered. Apply to Admissions Office at least one month prior to registration. Rolling admissions process. Application fee $45. Phone: (608)785-8939; fax: (608)785-8940.

ADMISSION STANDARDS. Selective. Required minimum overall GPA of 2.85, or 3.0 (A = 4) in last 60 undergraduate credits.

FINANCIAL AID. Graduate assistantships, tuition waivers, Federal W/S, loans. Approved for VA benefits. Apply by March 15 to Director of Financial Aid. Phone: (608)785-8604. Use FAFSA. About 50% of students receive aid from University and outside sources. Aid available for part-time students.

DEGREE REQUIREMENTS. For master's: 30-48 credit hours minimum, at least 24 in residence; thesis/final document; final oral/written exam.

FIELDS OF STUDY.
Adult Fitness-Cardiac Rehabilitation.
Biology.
Business Administration.
Clinical Microbiology.
College Student Development and Administration.
Community Health Education.
Exercise and Sport Science. Includes human performance, special (adapted) physical education, sport administration, teaching physical education.
Physical Therapy.
Professional Development.
Reading.
Recreation Management.
School Health Education.
School Psychology.
Special Education.
Special Physical Education.
Therapeutic Recreation.

UNIVERSITY OF WISCONSIN

Madison, Wisconsin 53706-1380
Web site: www.wisc.edu

Founded 1848. CGS and AAU member. Coed. State control. Semester system. Special facilities: Aquatic Sciences Center, Sea Grant Institute, Water Resources Institute, Institute on Aging, Biotechnology Center, Center for Demography and Ecology, Developmental and Molecular Toxicology Center, Educational Research and Development Center, Institute for Molecular Virology, Institute for Research in the Humanities, Industrial Relations Research Institute, Institute for Environmental Studies, Space Science and Engineering Center, McArdle Cancer Research Laboratory, Synchrotron Radiation Center, Waisman Center on Mental Retardation and Human Development, Wisconsin Regional Primate Center, Wisconsin Center for Applied Microelectronics, Wisconsin Clinical Cancer Center, Women's Studies Research Center. The University's ranking is 22nd among all U.S. institutions with 583 awards/grants worth $187,013,494. University libraries: 6,100,000 volumes, 66,000 subscriptions. Total University enrollment: 40,300.

Annual tuition: full-time resident: $6879.50, Minnesota compact students $7373.10, nonresident $22,149.90; Business: resident $8335.50, Minnesota Compact $16,163.50, nonresident $23,773.90. Limited on-campus housing available for graduate students. Average academic year housing costs: $6000 for single students, $8500 for married students. Contact Director of Residence Halls, Assignment Office of University Housing for both on- and off-campus housing information. Phone: (608)262-2522. Day-care facilities available.

Graduate School

Established 1904. Enrollment: full- and part-time 8620 (men 55%, women 45%). Faculty: full- and part-time about 2100. Degrees conferred: M.A., M.B.A., M.F.A., M.M., M.Acc., A.Mus.D., Ph.D.

ADMISSION REQUIREMENTS. Official transcripts required in support of School's application. GRE Subject Tests, GMAT required by many departments. Evidence of proficiency in English or TOEFL, or MELAB required for international students. Interview not required. Accepts transfer applicants. Graduates of unaccredited institutions not considered. Apply to Dean of Graduate School at least six weeks prior to registration. Application fee $45. Phone: (608)262-2433; fax: (608)262-5134.

ADMISSION STANDARDS. Very selective for most departments, competitive for others. Usual minimum average: 3.0 (A = 4).

FINANCIAL AID. Scholarships, fellowships, teaching research/project assistantships, internships, grants, tuition waivers, Federal W/S, loans. Approved for VA benefits. Apply by January 15 to appropriate department with completed forms, transcripts, and GRE Subject Test. Phone: (608)262-3060. Use FAFSA. Aid available for part-time students.

DEGREE REQUIREMENTS. For master's: two semesters minimum, at least one in residence. In addition, each department has its own requirements regarding oral/written exams and thesis/nonthesis option. For M.F.A.: 4 semesters minimum, at least two in residence; final oral exam. For Ph.D.: six semesters minimum, at least three semesters in residence, and one year in full-time attendance; comprehensive preliminary exam; thesis; final oral exam. For A.Mus.D.: essentially the same as for the Ph.D.

FIELDS OF STUDY.
Accounting.
Actuarial Science.
African Languages and Literature.
Afro-American Studies.
Agricultural and Applied Economics.
Agricultural Engineering.
Agricultural Journalism.
Agronomy.
Animal Sciences.
Anthropology.
Art.
Art Education.
Art History.
Arts Administration.
Astronomy.
Atmospheric and Oceanic Sciences.
Bacteriology.
Biochemistry.
Biological Systems Engineering.
Biomedical Engineering.
Biometry.
Biomolecular Chemistry.
Biophysics.
Botany.
Business.
Cancer Biology. Includes oncology.
Cartography and Geographic Information Systems.
Cellular and Molecular Biology.
Chemical Engineering.
Chemistry.
Chinese.
Civil and Environmental Engineering.
Classics.
Communication Arts.
Communicative Disorders.
Comparative Literature.
Computer Science.
Conservation Biology and Sustainable Development.
Consumer Science.
Continuing and Vocational Education.
Counseling.
Counseling Psychology.
Creative Writing.
Curriculum and Instruction.
Dairy Science.
Development Studies.
Economics.
Education Administration.
Education and French.
Education and German.
Education and Mathematics.
Education and Spanish.
Educational Administration.
Educational Policy Studies.
Educational Psychology.
Electrical Engineering.
Endocrinology-Reproductive Physiology.
Engineering.
Engineering Mechanics.
English.
Entomology.
Environmental Chemistry and Technology. Includes water chemistry.
Environmental Monitoring.
Family and Consumer Journalism.
Finance, Investments, and Banking.
Food Science.
Forestry.
French.
French Studies.
General Management.
Genetics.
Geography.
Geological Engineering.
Geology.
Geophysics.
German.
Greek.
Hebrew and Semitic Studies.
History.
History of Science.
Horticulture.
Human Ecology. Includes consumer behavior and family economics, design studies.
Industrial Engineering.
Information Systems Analysis and Design.
International Business.
Italian.
Japanese.

Journalism and Mass Communication.
Kinesiology.
Land Resources.
Landscape Architecture.
Languages and Cultures of Asia.
Latin.
Latin American, Caribbean, and Iberian Studies.
Legal Institutions.
Library and Information Studies.
Life Sciences Communication.
Limnology and Marine Science.
Linguistics.
Management and Human Resources.
Manufacturing Systems Engineering.
Marketing.
Mass Communications.
Materials Science.
Mathematics.
Mechanical Engineering.
Medical Genetics.
Medical Microbiology and Immunology.
Medical Physics.
Metallurgical Engineering
Microbiology.
Molecular and Cellular Pharmacology.
Molecular and Environmental Toxicology.
Music. Includes education, ethnomusicology, history, performance, theory.
Neuroscience.
Nuclear Engineering and Engineering Physics.
Nursing.
Nutritional Sciences.
Operations and Information Management.
Pathology.
Pharmaceutical Sciences.
Pharmacy.
Philosophy.
Physics.
Physiology.
Plant Breeding and Plant Genetics.
Plant Pathology.
Political Science.
Population Health.
Portuguese.
Psychology.
Public Affairs. Includes international public affairs.
Real Estate and Urban Land Economics.
Rehabilitation Psychology.
Risk Management and Insurance.
Rural Sociology.
Scandinavian Studies.
Science Education.
Second Language Acquisition.
Slavic Languages and Literature.
Social Welfare.
Social Work.
Social and Administrative Sciences in Pharmacy.
Sociology.
Soil Science.
Spanish.
Special Education.
Statistics.
Supply Chain Management.
Theatre and Drama.
Therapeutic Science.
Urban and Regional Planning.
Veterinary Science.
Water Chemistry.
Water Resources Management.
Wildlife Ecology.
Zoology.

Law School (53706-1399)

Web site: www.law.wisc.edu

Established 1868. Located on main campus. ABA approved since 1923. AALS charter member. Semester system. Full-time, day study. Special facility: Center for Public Representation. Special programs: Criminal Justice Administration Program, Legal Assistance to Institutionalized Persons Program (LAIP). Law library: 502,845 volumes, 4693 subscriptions; has LEXIS, NEXIS, WESTLAW, DIALOG.

Annual tuition: resident $7437, nonresident $20,059; part-time resident $6199, nonresident $16,719. On-campus housing available for both single and married students. Contact Office of University Housing for on-campus housing information. Phone: (608)252-2522. Law students tend to live off-campus. Contact Campus Assistance Center for off-campus information. Phone: (608)262-2400. Contact the Family Housing Office for off-campus married housing information. Phone: (608)262-2789. Off-campus housing and personal expenses: approximately $10,980.

Enrollment: first-year class 270; total full-time 828 (men 51%, women 49%); limited part-time study. Faculty: full-time 44, part-time 5. Student to faculty ratio 15.0 to 1. Degrees conferred: J.D., J.D.-M.B.A., J.D.-M.P.A., J.D.-.M.A. (Ibero-American Studies), J.D.-M.S. (Environmental Studies, Industrial Relation), J.D.-M.I.L., J.D.-M.L.S., J.D.-Ph.D. (Philosophy, Sociology), LL.M., S.J.D.

ADMISSION REQUIREMENTS. For J.D. program: LSDAS Law School report, bachelor's degree, transcripts, LSAT, personal statement required in support of application. Interview not required. Accepts a few transfer applicants on space available basis only. Apply to Admissions Committee of School after October 1, before February 1; for transfer applicants July 1. Fall admission only. Application fee $45. Phone: (608)262-5914.

ADMISSION REQUIREMENTS FOR TRANSFER APPLICANTS. Accepts transfers from other ABA-accredited schools. Admission limited to space available. At least one year of enrollment, Dean's letter indicating the applicant is in good standing, prefer applicants in the top 15% of first-year class, LSAT, LSDAS, personal statement regarding reason for transfer, undergraduate transcript, current law school transcript required in support of School's application. Apply to Admission Office by July 1 (Fall). Preference given to Wisconsin residents. Admission decision made within one month of receipt of application. Application fee $45. Will consider visiting students.

ADMISSION REQUIREMENTS FOR LL.M., S.J.D. APPLICANTS. For LL.M.: all applicants must hold a J.D. or equivalent law degree. Official transcripts, three letters of recommendations, a plan of work (at least four double-spaced, typed pages, including a statement of objective, outline of proposed research and explanation of course/seminar needs), consent of a faculty member of the law school to act as the principal academic adviser required in support of LL.M. application. In addition, holders of law degrees from foreign countries must submit proof of completion of all academic work necessary for entering a law profession in the applicant's home country; TOEFL (minimum score 625) required for all international applicant whose native language is other than English. Apply by March 15 (Fall) , November 15 (Spring) to Committee on Academic Program. Application fee $45. Phone: (608)262-9120.

For S.J.D.: all applicants must hold a J.D. or the equivalent law degree and usually a LL.M. from the University of Wisconsin. Official transcript, three letters of recommendation, LL.M. thesis or equivalent project, at least six double-spaced, typed pages outlining objective, methodology, required materials and timetable, consent of a faculty member of the law school faculty to act as the principal academic adviser required in support of S.J.D. application. In addition, holders of law degrees from foreign countries must submit proof of completion of all academic work necessary for entering the law profession in the applicant's home country; TOEFL (minimum score 625) required for all international applicant whose native language is other than English. Apply by March 15 (Fall), November 15 (Spring) to Committee on Graduate Program. Application fee $45. Phone: (608)262-9120.

ADMISSION STANDARDS. Selective. Mean LSAT: 160; mean GPA: 3.43 (A = 4). Gourman rating: 4.49. *U.S. News & World Report* ranking is in the top 25 of all U.S. law schools. Accepts 35–40% of total annual applicants. Approximately 70–80% of class are state residents.

FINANCIAL AID. For J.D. program: scholarships, Federal W/S, loans. Apply by February 1 to Financial Aid Office. Use FAFSA (School code: 003895). For graduate study: scholarships, research fellowships, teaching assistantships. Apply by March 1 to the Dean (attention: Research Committee). About 17% of students receive aid other than loans from School.

DEGREE REQUIREMENTS. For J.D.: 90-credit-hour program, at least final 30 credits in residence. For LL.M.: at least 24 credits beyond the J.D.; one year in residence; thesis/research project. For S.J.D.: one year minimum in residence; thesis. For master's and doctoral degrees: see Graduate School listing above.

Medical School
Medical Sciences Center, Room 1140
Web site: www.med.wisc.edu

Initiated a two-year program in 1907, expanded to four years in 1924. Located at the Center for Health Sciences. Affiliated hospital: University of Wisconsin Hospital and Clinics. Special facilities: Biotechnology Center, Cardiovascular Research Center, Center for Neuroscience, Center for Tobacco Research and Intervention, Clinical Nutrition Center, Environmental Toxicology Center, General Clinical Research Center, Institute on Aging, Prevention Center, Primate Research Center, UW Comprehensive Cancer Center, Waisman Center on Mental Retardation and Human Development. Library: 165,000 volumes, 2000 subscriptions.

Annual tuition: resident $18,566, nonresident $28,068. On-campus rooms and apartments available for both single and married students. Contact Assignments Office for both on- and off-campus housing information. Phone: (608)262-2522. Medical students tend to live off-campus. Off-campus housing and personal expenses: approximately $10,000.

Enrollment: first-year class 150 (EDP 10); total full-time 607 (men 53%, women 47%). Faculty: full-time 322, part-time 60. Degrees conferred: M.D., M.D.-M.S., M.D.-Ph.D. (M.S.T.P.).

ADMISSION REQUIREMENTS. Preference given to state residents, U.S. citizens, and permanent residents who have taken all their undergraduate work at an accredited U.S. or Canadian institution. Bachelor's degree from an accredited institution required. Has EDP for state residents only; applicants must apply through AMCAS (official transcripts sent by mid-May) between June 1 and August 1. Early applications are encouraged. Submit secondary/supplemental application, a personal statement, two recommendations to Office of Admission within two weeks of receipt of application. Interviews are by invitation only and generally for final selection. Notification normally begins October 1. All other applicants apply through AMCAS (file after June 1, before November 1), submit MCAT scores (will accept MCAT test results from the last three years), official transcripts for each school attended (should show at least 90 semester credits/135 quarter credits; submit transcripts by mid-May to AMCAS), service processing fee. Submit an application fee of $45, a supplemental application, a personal statement, pre-professional committee evaluation, and three recommendations from science faculty to

the Admission Committee within two to three weeks of receipt of supplemental materials, but no later than December 1. Interviews are by invitation only and generally for final selection. In addition, M.D.-Ph.D. integrated degree applicants must submit a supplemental application and there is a separate interview by invitation. GRE is required for fellowship consideration. Contact the Admissions Office or Student Services Coordinator for current information and any additional admissions requirements; phone: (608)262-1348; fax: (608)263-4925). First-year students admitted Fall only. Rolling admissions process, notification starts November 15 and is finished when class is filled.

ADMISSION STANDARDS. Selective. Mean MCAT: 9.8; mean GPA: 3.37 (A = 4). Gourman rating: 4.42. *U.S. News & World Report* ranking is in the top 31 (research) and in the top 18 (primary care) of all U.S. medical schools. Accepts 20–30% of total annual applicants.

FINANCIAL AID. Service Commitment Scholarship Program, grants, institutional loans, HEAL, alternative loan programs, NIH stipends, loans available. Assistantships/fellowships/stipends may be available for M.D.-Ph.D. degree candidates. Financial aid applications and information are generally available at the on-campus, by-invitation interview. All financial aid is based on proven need and generally is in the form of long-term loan programs. Apply by February 15. Contact the Financial Aid Office for current information. Phone: (608)262-3060. Use FAFSA (School code: 003895), also submit Financial Aid Transcript, Federal Income Tax forms. Approximately 90% of students receive some form of financial assistance.

DEGREE REQUIREMENTS. For M.D.: satisfactory completion of four-year program; all students must pass USMLE Step 1 prior to entering third year and must pass USMLE Step 2 prior to awarding of M.D. For M.D.-M.S.: generally a four-and-one-half- to five-and-one-half-year program. For M.D.-Ph.D.: generally a seven-year program.

FIELDS OF GRADUATE STUDY.
Biomolecular Chemistry.
Cellular and Molecular Biology.
History of Medicine and Medical Ethics.
Medical Genetics.
Microbiology Training Program.
Molecular and Cellular Pharmacology.
Neurosciences Training Program.
Oncology.
Pathology and Laboratory Medicine.
Physiology.
Population Health (Preventive Medicine).

School of Veterinary Medicine (53706-1102)

Annual tuition: resident $13,542, nonresident $20,404. Total average cost for all other expenses: $8400.

Enrollment: first-year 80, total 340 (men 45%, women 55%). Faculty: full-time 80. Degrees conferred: D.V.M., D.V.M.-M.S., D.V.M.-Ph.D.

ADMISSION REQUIREMENTS. VMCAS report (nonresident), transcripts, GRE, 60 undergraduate credits minimum, three evaluation/recommendations, animal/veterinary experience support of application. Preference given to state resident. Accepts transfer applicants on a space-available basis only. Apply to Dean of School after September 1, before October 1. Application fee $35. Phone: (608)263-2525.

ADMISSION STANDARDS. Selective. Usual minimum average: 3.51 (A = 4). Mean GRE combined: 1865. Accepts about 10% of total annual applicants. First-year class is approximately 60–70 state residents; 10–20 spaces available for nonresidents.

FINANCIAL AID. Scholarships, assistantships, Federal W/S, loans. Apply to Director of Student Financial Aid. Use FAFSA.

DEGREE REQUIREMENTS. For D.V.M.: satisfactory completion of four-year program. For joint degree programs: see Graduate College listing above.

UNIVERSITY OF WISCONSIN— MILWAUKEE
Milwaukee, Wisconsin 53201-0340
Web site: www.uwm.edu

Founded 1956. CGS member. Coed. State control. Semester system. Special facilities; Center for Architecture and Urban Planning Research, Center for Business Competitiveness, Center for Great Lakes Studies/Great Lakes Research Facility, Center for Latin American, Center for Nursing Research and Evaluation, Center for 21st Century Studies, Field Station, Great Lakes Water Institute, Institute on Race and Ethnicity, Laboratory for Surface Studies, Management Research Center, Marine and Freshwater Biomedical Sciences Center, Center for Urban Initiatives and Research, Center for Urban Transportation Studies, Urban Research Center, Center for Women's Studies. Library: 1,300,000 volumes, 10,000 subscriptions.

Annual tuition: full-time resident $6652, Minnesota Compact students $7420, nonresident $21,016; per credit resident $570.10, Minnesota Compact students $618.10, nonresident $1,467.95. Limited on-campus housing available for single students. Average academic year housing costs: $4396–$4597. Contact Director of Residence Life for both on- and off-campus housing information. Phone: (800)622-0287, (414)229-4065. Day-care facilities available.

Graduate School
Web site: www.uwm.edu/Dept/Grad_Sch

Graduate study since 1965. Enrollment: full-time 1474, part-time 2072 (men 40%, women 60%). Faculty: full-time 735. Degrees conferred: M.A., M.S., M.Arch., M.B.A., M.F.A., M.I.L.R., M.M., M.L.I.S., M.P.A., M.S.W., M.U.P., Ph.D.

ADMISSION REQUIREMENTS. Official transcripts required in support of School's application. GRE/GMAT/MAT recommended. Interview required for some programs. TOEFL required for international applicants. Accepts transfer applicants. Graduates of unaccredited institutions not considered. Apply to Graduate School by January 1 (Fall and Summer), September 1 (Spring). Application fee domestic $45, international applicants $75. Phone: (414)229-4982; e-mail: gradschool@uwm.edu.

ADMISSION STANDARDS. Selective. Usual minimum average: 2.75 (A = 4).

FINANCIAL AID. Scholarships, fellowships, teaching assistantships, research assistantships, teaching assistantships, internships, tuition waivers, Federal W/S, loans. Approved for VA benefits. Apply by mid-January to the Graduate School Fellowship Office for fellowships; to appropriate department for assistantships; to Financial Aid Office by April 15 for all other programs. Phone: (414)229-4541; fax: (414)229-5689. Use FAFSA. Aid available for part-time students.

DEGREE REQUIREMENTS. For master's: 24-48 semester hours; thesis/nonthesis option for many majors; final written/oral exam for some majors. For Ph.D.: 54 credits minimum beyond the bachelor's; foreign language or research skill for most programs; dissertation; final oral defense.

FIELDS OF STUDY.
Administrative Leadership and Supervision in Education. M.S.
Anthropology. M.S., Ph.D.
Architecture. M.Arch., Ph.D.
Art. M.A., M.F.A.
Art Education. M.S.
Art History. M.A.
Biological Sciences. M.S., Ph.D.
Business Administration. M.B.A., E.M.B.A.
Chemistry. M.S., Ph.D.
Clinical Laboratory Sciences. M.S.
Communication. M.A.
Communications Sciences and Disorders.
Computer Science. M.S. Ph.D. offered through Engineering Department.
Criminal Justice. M.S.
Cultural Foundations of Education. M.S.
Curriculum and Instruction. M.S.
Economics. M.A., Ph.D.
Educational Psychology. M.S.
Engineering. M.S., Ph.D.
English. M.A., Ph.D.
Exceptional Education. M.S.
Foreign Language and Literature. M.A.
Geography. M.A., M.S., Ph.D.
Geosciences. M.S., Ph.D.
History. M.A.
Human Resources and Labor Relations. M.H.R.L.R.
Kinesiology. M.L.S.
Liberal Studies. M.L.S.
Library and Information Science. M.L.I.S.
Management Science. Ph.D.
Mass Communication. M.A.
Mathematics. M.S., Ph.D.
Music. M.M.
Nursing. M.S., Ph.D.
Occupational Therapy. M.S.
Performing Arts. Includes dance, film, and theater. M.F.A.
Philosophy. M.A.
Physics. M.S., Ph.D.
Political Science. M.A., Ph.D.
Psychology. M.S., Ph.D.
Public Administration. M.P.A.
Social Work. M.S.W.
Sociology. M.A.
Urban Education. Ph.D.
Urban Planning. M.U.P.
Urban Studies. M.S., Ph.D.

UNIVERSITY OF WISCONSIN— OSHKOSH
Oshkosh, Wisconsin 54901-3551
Web site: www.uwosh.edu

Established 1871. Located 85 miles NW of Milwaukee. Coed. State control. Semester system. Library: 446,700 volumes, 5219 subscriptions.

Annual fees: full-time resident $4186, nonresident $13,130. On-campus housing for 50 graduate men, 50 graduate women; none for married students. Average academic year housing costs: $2570 (single room, two semesters). Apply to Director of Residence Life for both on- and off-campus housing information. Phone: (920)424-3212. Day-care facilities available.

Graduate School

Established 1963. Enrollment: full-time 190, part-time 1012 (men 35%, women 65%). University faculty teaching graduate students: full-time 245, part-time 17. Degrees conferred: M.S., M.S.N., M.S.Ed., M.B.A., M.P.A.

ADMISSION REQUIREMENTS. Official transcripts required in support of School's application. GMAT or GRE, interview required by some programs. TOEFL required for international applicants. Accepts transfer applicants. Graduates of unaccredited institutions not considered. Apply to Dean of Graduate School at least three months prior to registration. International applicant at least 6 months prior to registration. Application fee domestic $45, international $75. Phone: (920)424-1223; fax: (920)424-7317; e-mail: gradschool@uwosh.edu.

ADMISSION STANDARDS. Selective. Usual minimum average: 2.75 (A = 4). Some programs require 3.0 minimum.

FINANCIAL AID. Annual awards from institutional funds: academic scholarships, assistantships, advanced opportunity grants to minority students, internships, Federal W/S, loans. Approved for VA benefits. Apply by March 15 to Graduate Dean. Phone: (920)424-3377. Use FAFSA. About 20% of students receive aid other than loans from University and outside sources. Aid sometimes available to part-time students.

DEGREE REQUIREMENTS. For master's: 30-48 semester hours minimum, at least 21 in residence; admission to candidacy; thesis/research paper; comprehensive oral/written exam.

FIELDS OF STUDY.
Biology/Microbiology. GRE for admission. M.S.
Business Administration. GMAT for admission. M.B.A.
Counselor Education. M.S.Ed.
Curriculum and Instruction. M.S.Ed.
Educational Administration. Cooperative Program with University of Wisconsin, Madison. M.S.
Educational Leadership. M.S.
Elementary Education. M.S.Ed.
English. M.A.
Mathematics Education. M.S.
Nursing. M.S.N.
Physics. M.S.
Psychology. GRE for admission. Includes experimental, industrial/organizational. M.S.
Public Administration. M.P.A.
Reading. M.S.Ed.
Social Work. M.S.W.
Special Education. M.S.Ed.

UNIVERSITY OF WISCONSIN— PLATTEVILLE

Platteville, Wisconsin 53818-3099
Web site: www.uwplatt.edu

Founded 1866. Located 70 miles SW of Madison. Coed. State control. Semester system. Library: 422,000 volumes, 1499 subscriptions.
Annual tuition: full-time resident $4438, nonresident $13,919; per semester (minimum) resident $529, nonresident $1882. On-campus housing for single graduate students. Average academic year housing costs: $1882 (room only). Average summer housing cost: $300–$400. Contact Director of Student Housing for both on- and off-campus housing information. Phone: (608)342-1845; e-mail: egley@uwplatt.edu. Day-care facilities available.

School of Graduate Studies

Graduate study since 1957. Enrollment: full-time 33, part-time 84. Graduate faculty: full-time 5, part-time 10. Degrees conferred: M.S., M.S.Ed.

ADMISSION REQUIREMENTS. Official transcripts required in support of School's application. On-line application available. TOEFL required for international applicants. Interview not required. Accepts transfer students. Apply to the School of Graduate Studies by May 15 (Summer) prior to registration for other semesters. Application fee $45. Phone: (800)362-5515, (608)342-1125; fax: (608)342-1122; E-mail: admit@uwplatt.edu.

ADMISSION STANDARDS. Selective. Usual minimum average: 2.75; 2.9 for last 60 credits (A = 4).

FINANCIAL AID. Assistantships, internships, grants, Federal W/S, loans. Approved for VA benefits. Apply by July 1 to Dean of the School of Graduate Studies. Phone: (608)342-1836; fax: (608)342-1122. Use FAFSA. About 20% of students receive aid other than loans from all sources. Aid available for part-time students.

DEGREE REQUIREMENTS. For master's: 30-36 semester hours minimum, at least 24 residence; thesis; oral exam/research paper; comprehensive exam.

FIELDS OF STUDY.
Agricultural Industries.
Counselor Education.
Criminal Justice.
Education.
Engineering.
Industrial Technology Management.
Project Management.

UNIVERSITY OF WISCONSIN— RIVER FALLS

River Falls, Wisconsin 54022-5013

Founded 1874. Located 30 miles SE of St. Paul, Minnesota. CGS member. Coed. State control. Semester system. Library: 448,000 volumes, 1660 subscriptions.
Annual tuition: full-time, resident $4438, nonresident $13,919. On-campus housing for single students, limited number of married students. Average annual housing cost: $3800 for single students. Apply to Housing Director. Day-care facilities available.

Outreach and Graduate Studies

Graduate study since 1962. Enrollment: full-time 142, part-time 205 (men 35%, women 65%). University faculty: full-time 243, part-time 5. Degrees conferred: M.S.Ed., M.M., M.S.

ADMISSION REQUIREMENTS. Official transcripts, bachelor's degree in support of application. Some programs require interview and letters of recommendation. GRE or MAT for counseling program. TOEFL required for international students. Accepts transfer students. Apply to the Office of Graduate study; deadlines vary by department. Application fee $45. Phone: (715)425-3843; fax: (715)425-0622.

ADMISSION STANDARDS. Relatively open. Minimum average: 2.75 (A = 4).

FINANCIAL AID. Annual awards from institutional funds: assistantships, internships, Federal W/S, loans. Approved for VA benefits. Apply to Dean of Graduate School. Phone: (715)425-3843. Use FAFSA. Aid available for part-time students. About 40% of students receive aid from University and outside sources.

DEGREE REQUIREMENTS. For master's: 30-40 credit hours minimum (no more than 9 credits in transfer); thesis/final document; final oral/written exam.

FIELDS OF STUDY.
Agriculture Education. M.S.
Communicative Disorders. M.S.Ed., M.S.
Counseling. M.S.Ed.
Fine Arts. M.S.Ed.
Language, Communication, and Literature. M.S.Ed.
Management. M.M.
Reading. M.S.Ed.
School Psychology. M.S.Ed., Ed.S.
Science. M.S.Ed.
Social Science. M.S.Ed.

UNIVERSITY OF WISCONSIN— STEVENS POINT

Stevens Point, Wisconsin 54481-3897
Web site: www.uwsp.edu

Founded 1894. Coed. State control. Semester system. Special facilities: Center Wisconsin Environmental Field Station, Forest and Wildlife Research Station, Planetarium, Museum of Natural History. Library: 362,500 volumes, 1800 subscriptions.

Annual tuition: full-time resident $4225, nonresident $13,169. On-campus housing for single students only. Average academic year housing costs: $3616 (including board). Contact Director of Student Housing for both on- and off-campus housing information. Phone: (715)346-3511. Day-care facilities available.

Graduate Studies

Enrollment: full-time 103, part-time 192 (men 20%, women 80%). Full-time faculty teaching graduate students: 262. Degrees conferred: M.A., M.B.A., M.M., M.S.T., M.S., M.S.E., M.M.Ed.

ADMISSION REQUIREMENTS. Official transcripts, GRE required in support of application. TOEFL required for international applicants. Accepts transfer applicants. Graduates of unaccredited institutions not considered. Apply to Dean of Graduate School by March 15 (Fall), November 15 (Spring). Some graduate program may require additional application materials. Rolling admissions process. Application fee $45. Phone: (715)346-2441.

ADMISSION STANDARDS. Selective. Usual minimum average: 2.75 (A = 4). Individual graduate programs may require a higher G.P.A.

FINANCIAL AID. Research assistantships, graduate assistantships, internships, Federal W/S, loans. Approved for VA benefits. Apply May 1 to Dean of Graduate School for assistantships; to Director of Financial Aid for all other programs. Phone: (715)346-4771. Use FAFSA. Aid sometimes available for part-time students.

DEGREE REQUIREMENTS. For master's: 30–36 credits minimum, including culminating experience, at least 24–30 in residence; admission to candidacy; thesis/nonthesis option; final written/oral exam for some programs.

FIELDS OF STUDY.
Business Administration. Cooperative program with University of Wisconsin—Oshkosh. M.B.A.
Communication. M.A.
Corporate Communication. M.A.
Communicative Disorders. M.S.
Education. Includes general, elementary. M.S.E.
Educational Administration. Cooperative program with University of Wisconsin—Superior. M.S.E.
English. M.S.T.
Guidance and Counseling. Cooperative programs with University of Wisconsin—Oshkosh. M.S.E.

Human and Community Resources. MS.
Music Education. M.M.Ed.
Natural Resources. M.S.
Nutritional Sciences. M.S.
Teaching. Includes biology, English, Reading. M.S.T.

UNIVERSITY OF WISCONSIN—STOUT

Menomonie, Wisconsin 54751
Web site: www.uwstout.edu

Chartered 1893. Located 60 miles E of St. Paul. State control. Semester system. Special facilities: Design Research Center, Manufacturing Technology Transfer Center, Center for Innovation and Development, Center for Excellence in Advanced Technology, Center for Vocational, Technological and Adult Education, Center for Excellence in Tourism, Food and Tourism Industries, Social Science Research Center. Library: 218,000 volumes, 1600 subscriptions.

Annual tuition: full-time resident $4480, nonresident $12,344. Off-campus housing only. Average academic year room and board costs: $5000 for married students, $3432 for single students. Contact Stout Student Affairs Office. Phone: (715)232-2100. Day-care facilities available.

Graduate School

Graduate study since 1935. Enrollment: full-time 267, part-time 251 (men 40%, women 60%). Graduate faculty: full-time 194, part-time 0. Degrees conferred: M.S., M.S. Ed., Ed.S.

ADMISSION REQUIREMENTS. Official transcripts required in support of College's application. GRE required for Applied Psychology. Interview required for some programs. TOEFL required for international applicants. Accepts transfer applicants. Apply to Graduate Student Evaluator at least one month prior of registration. Application fee $45. Phone: (715)232-1322; fax: (715)232-2413.

ADMISSION STANDARDS. Selective in some departments, relatively open in others. Usual minimum average: 2.25 (A = 4).

FINANCIAL AID. Annual awards from institutional funds: scholarships, teaching/research assistantships, tuition waivers, Federal W/S, loans. Approved for VA benefits. Apply by April 1 to Financial Aid Director. Phone: (715)232-1363; fax: (715)232-5246. Use FAFSA. About 50% of students receive aid other than loans from University and outside sources. Aid available for part-time students.

DEGREE REQUIREMENTS. For master's: 30-48 semester hours minimum, at least 6 in residence; thesis or final paper. For Ed.S.: 36 semester hours beyond the master's.

FIELDS OF STUDY.
Applied Psychology. Includes health psychology, industrial/organizational psychology, program evaluation. M.S.
Career and Technical Education. Includes administration, marketing education, local vocational education coordinator, special needs, teaching. M.S., Ed.S.
Education.
Food and Nutrition Sciences. Includes food science and technology, human nutritional science, food and nutrition management and marketing. M.S.
Guidance and Counseling. Includes secondary school counseling. M.S.
Home Economics. Include apparel, design manufacturing and retailing, early childhood, family and consumer education, family studies and human development. M.S.

Hospitality and Tourism. Includes global hospitality management (on-line degree program). M.S.

Industrial Technology Education. M.S.

Management Technology. M.S.

Marriage and Family Therapy. M.S.

Mental Health Counseling. Includes community mental health/agency counseling, clinical mental health counseling, alcohol and other drug abuse counseling, career counseling, child and adolescent counseling, eating disorders, gerontological counseling, health psychology counseling, M.S.

Risk Control. M.S.

School Psychology. M.S.Ed., Ed.S.

Technology Management. Program is administered by Indiana State University and is offered through a consortium of seven universities across the U.S. Ph.D.

Training and Development. M.S.

Vocational Rehabilitation. Includes rehabilitation facility administration, rehabilitation counseling, school to work transition, vocation evaluation. M.S.

Vocational Rehabilitation.

UNIVERSITY OF WISCONSIN— SUPERIOR

Superior, Wisconsin 54880-2873

Web site: www.uwsuper.edu

Founded 1893. CGS member. Coed. State control. Semester system. Special facilities: Halden Fine and Applied Arts Center, Lake Superior Research Institute. Library: 285,000 volumes, 1600 subscriptions.

Annual tuition: full-time resident and Minnesota Compact students $4806.51, nonresident $15,416; part-time per credit, resident and Minnesota Compact students $337.25, nonresident $926.70. On-campus housing for single students only. Average academic year housing costs: $2592 (including Board). Off-campus housing costs; $350–$600. Contact Resident Life Center for both on- and off-campus housing information. Phone: (715)394-8438. Day-care facilities available.

Graduate Division

Established 1949. Enrollment: full-time 99, part-time 277. University faculty: full-time 92; part-time 27. Degrees conferred: M.A., M.S.Ed., Ed.S.

ADMISSION REQUIREMENTS. Official transcripts required in support of application. GRE/GMAT required by some departments. Interview required for Ed.S. program. TOEFL required for international applicants. Accepts transfer applicants. Apply to Dean of Graduate Division by April 1 (Fall), October 15 (Spring). Rolling admissions process. Application fee $45; $75 for international applicants. Phone: (715)394-8295; fax: (715)394-8040.

ADMISSION STANDARDS. Selective. Usual minimum average: 2.5 (A = 4).

FINANCIAL AID. Annual awards from institutional funds: scholarships, assistantships, minority fellowships, internships, grants, tuition waivers, Federal W/S, loans. Apply by April 15 to Dean of Graduate Division for assistantships; to the Financial Aid Office for all other programs. Use FAFSA. About 25% of students receive aid other than loans from School and outside sources. Aid available for part-time students.

DEGREE REQUIREMENTS. For M.A., M.S.Ed.: 30–36 credits minimum, at least 24 in residence; MAT for candidacy; thesis/final project; final written/oral exam. For Ed.S.: 30 credits minimum beyond the master's, final written/oral exams; internship may be required.

FIELDS OF STUDY.

Communicating Arts. M.A.

Educational Administration. M.S.Ed., Ed.S.

Guidance and Counseling. M.S.Ed.

Instruction. M.S.Ed.

Reading. M.S.Ed.

Special Education. M.S.Ed.

Visual Arts. M.A.

UNIVERSITY OF WISCONSIN— WHITEWATER

Whitewater, Wisconsin 53190-1790

Web site: www.uww.edu

Established 1868. Located 51 miles W of Milwaukee. CGS member. Coed. State control. Semester system. Library: 436,500 volumes, 2206 subscriptions.

Annual tuition: full-time resident $4870, $5424 (Business); nonresident $15,480, $16,060 (Business); per credit, resident $270, $301 (Business); nonresident $860, $892 (Business). On-campus housing for single students only. Average academic year housing costs: $3284 (including board). Contact Office of Residential Life for both on- and off-campus housing information. Phone: (262)472-1151. Day-care facilities available.

School of Graduate Studies

Enrollment: full- and part-time 1120. Faculty: 307. Degrees conferred: M.A.T., M.S.Ed., M.S., M.B.A., M.E.P.D., M.M.E.

ADMISSION REQUIREMENTS. Official transcripts required in support of School's application. On-line application available. GMAT required for Business. TOEFL required for international applicants. Accepts transfer applicants. Graduates of unaccredited colleges not considered. Apply to School of Graduate Studies by July 15 (Fall), December 1 (Spring). Rolling admissions process. Application fee $45. Phone: (262)472-1006; fax: (262) 472-5210.

ADMISSION STANDARDS. Relatively open. Usual minimum average: 2.5 (A = 4).

FINANCIAL AID. Assistantships, internships, fee waivers, Federal W/S, loans. Approved for VA benefits. Apply by March 15 to Dean, School of Graduate Studies, for assistantships; to the Financial Aid Office for all other programs. Use FAFSA. Aid available for part-time students.

DEGREE REQUIREMENTS. For all master's: 30–36 semester hours minimum; thesis/nonthesis option; internships for some programs; final written or oral comprehensive exam option.

FIELDS OF STUDY.

COLLEGE OF ARTS AND COMMUNICATION:

Communication. M.S.

COLLEGE OF BUSINESS AND ECONOMICS:

Accounting. M.P.A.

Business Administration. Includes accounting, decision support systems, finance management, managerial economics, marketing, international business. M.B.A.

Business Education. M.S.

Computer Information Systems. M.S.

School Business Management. M.S.E.

COLLEGE OF EDUCATION:
Communicative Disorders. M.S.
Counseling. M.S.
Curriculum and Instruction. Includes art education, early childhood, gifted and talented, reading. M.S.
Educational Administration. M.S.
Reading. M.S.E.
Safety. Includes occupational, school, traffic. M.S.
Special Education. Includes MR, EM, learning disabilities, early childhood, severely, profoundly handicapped, transitional needs; M.S.E.

COLLEGE OF LETTERS AND SCIENCE:
Educational Specialist. Ed.S.
Public Administration.
School Psychology. M.S.E.

WORCESTER POLYTECHNIC INSTITUTE

Worcester, Massachusetts 01609-2247
Web site: www.wpi.edu

Founded 1865. Located 35 miles W of Boston. CGS member. Coed. Private control. Semester system. Special facilities: Alden Research Laboratories (fluid mechanics), Aluminum Casting Research Laboratory, Applied Bioengineering Center, Computational Electromagnetics and Ultrasonics Systems Design and Development, Center for Crystal Growth in Space, Center for Holographic Studies and Laser Technology, Catalytic Sciences Laboratory, Electron Microscopy Laboratory, Center for Inorganic Membrane Studies, Center for Intelligent Processing of Materials, Magnetic Imaging Center, Manufacturing Engineering Application Center, Nuclear Reactor (pool type), Powder Metallurgy Center, computation facility, Van de Graaff accelerator, Center for Wireless Information Networks Studies. Library: 340,500 volumes, 1400 subscriptions. Total Institute enrollment: 3650.

Tuition: per credit hour $703. No on-campus housing for single or married graduate students. Contact Residential Services Office for off-campus housing information. Phone: (508)831-5645.

Graduate Program

Enrollment: full-time 441, part-time 334. Graduate faculty: full-time 189, part-time 50. Degrees conferred: M.B.A., M.Eng., M.S., Ph.D.

ADMISSION REQUIREMENTS. Official transcripts, GRE/GMAT (for some departments), three letters of recommendation required in support of application. On-line application available. GRE recommended. Interview not required. TOEFL required for international applicants. Accepts transfer applicants. Graduates of unaccredited institutions not considered. Apply by March 1 to Office of Graduate Admission. Application fee $50. Phone: (508)831-5301; fax: (508)831-5717; e-mail: gao@wpi.edu.

ADMISSION STANDARDS. Selective for most departments. Usual minimum average: 3.0 (A = 4).

FINANCIAL AID. Annual awards from institutional funds: fellowships, scholarships, teaching assistantships, assistantships, internships, grants, tuition waivers, loans. Approved for VA benefits. Apply by February 1 (for priority consideration) to Office of Graduate Admissions. Phone: (508)831-5469; fax: (508)831-5743. Use FAFSA and institutional FAF. About 47% of full-time students receive aid other than loans from Institute and outside sources.

DEGREE REQUIREMENTS. For M S., M.Eng.: 30–36 credit hours minimum, at least 20 in residence; thesis/nonthesis option. For M.B.A.: 45 credits, minimum, at least 30 in residence; computer proficiency. For Ph.D. minimum of three years or about 90 credits beyond the bachelor's, at least 30 credits of research; one year in full-time residence; dissertation; final oral exam.

FIELDS OF STUDY.
Biology and Biotechnology. GRE for admission.
Biomedical/Clinical Engineering. GRE for admission.
Biomedical Science.
Chemical Engineering. GRE for international applicants.
Chemistry and Biochemistry.
Civil and Environmental Engineering.
Computer and Communications Networks. GRE for admission.
Computer Science. GRE for admission.
Electrical and Computer Engineering. GRE for admission.
Fire Protection Engineering.
Management. GMAT for admission. M.B.A., M.S.-M.B.A.
Manufacturing Engineering.
Marketing and Technological Innovation.
Materials Science and Engineering.
Mathematical Sciences.
Mathematics for Educators.
Mechanical Engineering.
Operations and Information Technology.
Physics.

WORCESTER STATE COLLEGE

Worcester, Massachusetts 01602-2597
Web site: www.worcester.edu

Founded 1874. Located 30 miles W of Boston. Coed. State control. Semester system. Special facilities: Center for Effective Instruction, Center for Health Professions, Center for the Study of Human Rights, Center for Business and Industry, Latino Education Institute, Intergenerational Urban Institute. Library: 144,067 volumes, 1000 subscriptions.

Tuition: per credit, resident $112, nonresident $112; Speech-Language Pathology $275; Occupational Therapy $375. No on-campus housing available.

Graduate Studies

Graduate study since 1947. Enrollment: full- and part-time 600. Faculty: full-time 33, part-time 26. Degrees conferred: M.S., M.Ed., Certification Programs.

ADMISSION REQUIREMENTS. Transcripts, two letters of recommendation, GRE or MAT, interview required in support of application. TOEFL required for international applicants. Accepts transfer applicants. Graduates of unaccredited institutions not considered. Apply to Admissions Office at least one month prior to projected date of entrance, except for Speech-Language Pathology and Occupational Therapy (contact department for deadlines). Application fee $10 state residents, $40 for nonresidents. Phone: (508)793-8120; fax (508)793-8100.

ADMISSION STANDARDS. Selective. Usual minimum average: 2.75 (A = 4).

FINANCIAL AID. Assistantships, internships, Federal W/S, loans. Approved for VA benefits. Apply to Financial Aid Office; no specified closing date. Phone: (508)793-8056; fax: (508)793-8194. Use FAFSA.

DEGREE REQUIREMENTS. For master's: 33–36 semester hours minimum, at least 24 in residence; final written/oral exam.

FIELDS OF STUDY.
Biotechnology. M.S.
Community Health Nursing. M.S.
Early Childhood Education. M.Ed.
Elementary Education. M.Ed.
English. M.Ed.
History. M.Ed.
Health. M.Ed.
Health-Care Administration. M.S.
Human Services Management. MS.
Leadership and Administration. M.Ed.
Middle School Education. M.Ed.
Nonprofit Management. M.S.
Occupational Therapy. M.S.
Reading. M.Ed.
Secondary Education. M.Ed.
Speech-Language Pathology. M.S.

WRIGHT STATE UNIVERSITY

Dayton, Ohio 45435
Web site: www.wright.edu

Became independent unit in 1967. CGS member. Coed. State control. Quarter system. Special facilities: Cox Institute, Center for Environmental Quality, Groundwater Management Center, NASA-Lewis Research Center, Intelligent Systems Applications Center, Kettering Research Laboratory, Center for Labor-Management Cooperation, Edison Materials Technology Center, Ohio Aerospace Institute, Center for Urban and Public Affairs. Library: 1,000,000 bound volumes, 5000 subscriptions. Total University enrollment: 15,400.

Tuition: full-time per quarter resident $1949, nonresident $3394; per quarter hour for less than 10.5 hours, resident $184, nonresident $318. On-campus housing available. Average academic year housing costs: $4084 (including board) for single students; $7925 for married students. Contact Office of Residence Services for both on- and off-campus housing information. Phone: (937)775-4172.

School of Graduate Studies

Web site: www.wright.edu/sogs

Graduate study since 1965. Enrollment: full- and part-time 3000 (men 45%, women 55%). University faculty teaching graduate students: full-time 646, part-time 40. Degrees conferred: M.A., M.S., M.Ed., M.B.A., M.S.C.E., M.S.E., M.S.T., M.A.T., M.R.C., M.Hum., M.Mus., M.U.A., Ed.S., Psy.D., Ph.D.

ADMISSION REQUIREMENTS. Transcripts required in support of School's application. On-line application available. TOEFL (minimum score 550), TSE required for international applicants. GRE required for M.S. in Economics, M.A. in Applied Behavioral Science, M.S.C.E. in computer engineering, M.S. in computer science, M.S. in human factors and industrial/organizational psychology, M.U.A. in urban administration and the Psy.D., Ph.D. programs. The GMAT is required for the M.B.A., M.S. in logistics management. GRE/MAT required for College of Education and Human Services programs. Accepts transfer applicants. Apply to Assistant Dean and Director of Graduate Admissions and Records at least one month prior to registration. Application fee $25. Phone: (937)775-2976; fax: (937)775-3781; e-mail: wsugrad@wright.edu.

ADMISSION STANDARDS. Selective. Usual minimum average: 2.7 (A = 4).

FINANCIAL AID. Annual awards from institutional funds: scholarships, research assistantships, teaching assistantships, graduate assistantships, internships, predoctoral and postdoctoral fellowships, Federal W/S, loans. Approved for VA benefits. Ap-

ply to School of Graduate Studies for assistantships, fellowships, internships; to Office of Financial Aid for all other programs. No specified closing date. Phone: (937)775-2321. Use FAFSA. About 50% of full-time students receive aid.

DEGREE REQUIREMENTS. For master's: 45 quarter hours minimum, at least 33 in residence; thesis for most M.A. and M.S. programs; comprehensive exam. For M.B.A.: 51 credit program. For Ph.D.: two-year minimum in residence beyond the master's; reading knowledge of one foreign language; written/oral exam; dissertation; final oral exam. For Psy.D.: essentially the same as for Ph.D., except a research tool in place of the one foreign language.

FIELDS OF STUDY.

RAJ SOIN COLLEGE OF BUSINESS:
Accountancy. M.Acc.
Business Administration. M.B.A.
Business Economics. M.B.A.
E-Commerce. M.B.A.
Finance. M.B.A.
International Business. M.B.A.
Logistics Management. M.B.A., M.S.
Management. M.B.A.
Management Information Systems. M.B.A.
Marketing. M.B.A.
Operations Management. M.B.A.
Project Management. M.B.A.
Social and Applied Economics. M.S.

COLLEGE OF EDUCATION AND HUMAN SERVICES:
Business Education. M.A., M.Ed.
Business, Technology, and Vocational Education. M.A., M.Ed.
Chemical Dependency. M.R.C.
Classroom Teaching. M.A., M.Ed.
Counseling. M.A., M.Ed., Ed.S.
Early Childhood Education. M.A., M.Ed.
Education and Human Services. M.A., M.Ed., M.S.
Education Administrative Specialist. Includes teacher leader, vocational education administration. M.A., M.Ed.
Educational Leadership. M.A., M.Ed.
Gifted Education Needs. M.A., M.Ed.
Health, Physical Education, and Recreation. M.S., M.Ed.
Higher Education/Adult Education. Ed.S.
Intervention Specialist. M.A., M.Ed.
Library/Media. M.A., M.Ed.
Pupil Personnel Services. M.A., M.Ed.
Rehabilitation Counseling. M.R.C.
Teacher Education. Includes math education. M.A., M.Ed.

COLLEGE OF ENGINEERING AND COMPUTER SCIENCE:
Biomedical Engineering. M.S.E.
Computer Engineering. M.S.C.E., Ph.D.
Computer Science. M.S.C.S., Ph.D.
Computer Science and Engineering. Ph.D.
Electrical Engineering. M.S.E.
Engineering. Ph.D.
Human Factors Engineering. M.S.E.
Materials Science and Engineering. M.S.E.
Mechanical Engineering. M.S.E.

COLLEGE OF LIBERAL ARTS:
Applied Behavioral Science. Includes criminal justice and social problems, international relations and comparative politics. M.A.
English. Includes English, English writing and language. M.A.
History. M.A.
Humanities. M.Hum.
Literature. M.A.
Music Education. M.M.
TESOL. M.A.
Urban Administration. M.U.A.

MIAMI VALLEY COLLEGE OF NURSING AND HEALTH:
Acute Care Nurse Practitioner. M.S.
Administration of Nursing and Health-Care Systems. M.S.
Adult Health. M.S.
Child and Adolescent Health. M.S.
Community Health. M.S.
Family Nurse Practitioner. M.S.
Nurse Practitioner. M.S.
Nursing and Health. M.S.
School Nurse. M.S.

COLLEGE OF SCIENCE AND MATHEMATICS:
Anatomy. M.S.
Applied Mathematics. M.S.
Applied Statistics. M.S.
Biochemistry and Molecular Biology. M.S., Ph.D.
Biological Sciences. M.S.
Biomedical Sciences. Ph.D.
Chemistry. M.S.
Earth Science Education. M.S.T.
Environmental Sciences. M.S.
Geological Sciences. M.S.
Geophysics. M.S.
Human Factors and Industrial/Organizational Psychology. M.S.,
   Ph.D.
Mathematics. M.S.
Medical Physics.
Microbiology and Immunology. M.S.
Physic. Includes teaching of physics (M.S.T.). M.S., M.S.T.
Physiology and Biophysics. M.S.

SCHOOL OF PROFESSIONAL PSYCHOLOGY:
Clinical Psychology.

SCHOOL OF GRADUATE STUDIES:
Aerospace Medicine. M.S.
Interdisciplinary Studies. M.A., M.S.

School of Medicine (P.O. Box 1751)
Web site: www.med.wright.edu

Established 1973. Quarter system.
Annual tuition: resident $12,066, nonresident $17,088, student fees $731. Enrollment: first-year class 90 (EDP 5); total 361 (men 46%, women 54%). Faculty: more than 1200. Degrees conferred: M.D., M.D.-Ph.D.

ADMISSION REQUIREMENTS. AMCAS report, transcripts, MCAT, recommendations required in support of application. Interview and supplementary application by invitation only. Preference given to state residents. Has EDP (Ohio residents only); apply between June 1 and August 1. Apply to Office of Student Affairs/Admissions after June 1, before November 15. Application fee $35. Phone: (937)775-2934; fax: (937)775-3322.

ADMISSION STANDARDS. Selective. Mean MCAT: 8.5, mean GPA: 3.49 (A = 4). Gourman rating: 3.07. Admits about 8–10% of total annual applicants. Approximately 91% are state residents.

FINANCIAL AID. Limited scholarships, loans, grants. Apply after acceptance to Office of Student Affairs. Phone: (937)775-2934. Use FAFSA (School code: 003078). About 90% of students receive some aid from School.

DEGREE REQUIREMENTS: For M.D.: satisfactory completion of four-year program.

FIELDS OF GRADUATE STUDY.
Anatomy.
Biochemistry.
Immunology.
Microbiology.
Pathology.
Pharmacology.
Physiology.

UNIVERSITY OF WYOMING
Laramie, Wyoming 82071-3108
Web site: www.uwyo.edu

Founded 1886. CGS member. State control. Semester system. Special facilities: American Heritage Center, Anthropology Museum, Center for Rural Health Research and Education, Elk Mountain Observatory, Enhanced Oil Recovery Institute, Geological Museum, International Archive of Economic Geology, Institute of Business and Management Services, Mineral Research and Reclamation Center, National Park Service Research Center, Laramie Petroleum Research Center, Natural Resources Research Institute, Red Buttes Research Center, Rocky Mountain Herbarium, Small Business Development Center, Survey Research Center, Wyoming Geographic Information Science Center, Wyoming Statistical Analysis Center. Library: more than 1,000,000 volumes, 13,000 subscriptions; is a Federal Document Depository. Total University enrollment: 11,000.

Annual tuition: full-time resident $2988, nonresident $8676; per credit, resident $166, nonresident $482. On-campus housing for 700 married students; limited for single graduate students. Average academic year housing costs: $4500 for married students, $5529 (including board) for single students. Contact Director of Housing for both on- and off-campus housing information. Phone: (307)766-3179. Day-care facilities available.

Graduate School
Web site: grad.uwyo.edu

Graduate study since 1897. Enrollment: full-time 757, part-time 657. University faculty teaching graduate students: full-time 500, part-time 52. Degrees conferred: M.A., M.S., M.A.E., M.A.T., M.M., M.S.E., M.S.T., M.B.A., M.P.A., M.F.A., M.P., I.M.A., I.M.S., Ed.S., Ed.D., Ph.D., Ph.D.E.

ADMISSION REQUIREMENTS. Transcripts, three letters of recommendation, GRE, GMAT (Business) required in support of School's application. On-line application available. GRE Subject required by some departments. TOEFL (minimum score 525) required for international applicants. Interview generally not required. Accepts transfer applicants. Graduates of unaccredited institutions not considered. Apply to Admissions Office by June 1. Application fee $40. Phone: (307)766-2287; fax: (307)766-2374.

ADMISSION STANDARDS. Very selective for most departments, selective for the others. Usual minimum average: 3.0 (A = 4).

FINANCIAL AID. Annual awards from institutional funds: scholarships, research fellowships, teaching assistantships, research assistantships, internships, traineeships, Federal W/S, loans. Approved for VA benefits. Apply by February 15 to appropriate department chair for fellowships, assistantships; to Financial Aid Office for all other programs. Phone: (307)766-2116; fax: (307)766-3800. Use FAFSA. About 75% of students receive aid other than loans from School and outside sources. Aid available for part-time students.

DEGREE REQUIREMENTS. For master's: 30–52 semester hours minimum; thesis/nonthesis option in some departments; final oral/written exam. For Ed.S.: 30 hours minimum beyond the master's, at least two semesters in residence. For Ed.D.: three years minimum beyond the bachelor's, at least 78 semester hours residence including one and a half consecutive semesters; preliminary exam; final project; reading knowledge of one foreign language or competency in research tool often required; final oral/written exam. For Ph.D.: 72 semester hours minimum beyond the bachelor's, at least 18 semester hours in residence; preliminary exam; thesis; final oral/written exam.

FIELDS OF STUDY.

COLLEGE OF AGRICULTURE:

Agricultural Economics. M.S.
Agricultural Economics/Water Resources. Interdisciplinary. M.S.
Agronomy. M.S.
Animal and Veterinary Science. M.S.
Entomology. M.S., Ph.D.
Entomology/Water Resources. Interdisciplinary. M.S.
Family and Consumer Science. M.S. only.
Food Science and Human Nutrition. Interdisciplinary. M.S.
Molecular Biology. M.S., Ph.D.
Rangeland Ecology and Watershed Management. M.S., Ph.D.
Rangeland Ecology and Watershed Management/Water Resources. Interdisciplinary. M.S.
Reproductive Biology. Interdisciplinary. Ph.D.
Soils Science. M.S., Ph.D.
Soils Science/Water Resources. M.S.

COLLEGE OF ARTS AND SCIENCES:

American Studies. Interdepartmental. M.A. only.
Antrhopology. M.A. only.
Botany. M.S., Ph.D.
Botany/Water Resources. Interdisciplinary. M.S.
Chemistry. M.S., M.S.T., Ph.D.
Community and Regional Planning. M.P. only.
Communication. M.A. only.
Computer Science. M.S., Ph.D.
English. M.A. only.
French. M.A.
Geography. M.A., M.S.T.
Geography/Water Resources. Interdisciplinary. M.A.
Geology. M.S., Ph.D.
Geology/Water Resources. Interdisciplinary. M.S.
Geophysics. M.S., Ph.D.
Geophysics/Water Resources. Interdisciplinary. M.S.
German. M.A.
History. GRE Subject for admission; one language for M.A.. M.A., M.S.T.
Interdisciplinary Masters. Self-designed master's with up to three curricula combined. I.M.A., I.M.S.
International Studies. Interdepartmental; one language, thesis for M.A. M.A. only.
Mathematics. M.A.. M.A.T., M.S., M.S.T., Ph.D.
Music. Includes applied music, music history and literature, theory and composition. M.A. only.
Natural Science. M.S., M.S.T.
Neurosciences. Ph.D.
Philosophy. M.A. only.
Physics. GRE Subject for admission. M.S., M.S.T., Ph.D.
Planning. M.P.
Political Science. M.A.
Psychology. Thesis for M.A. M.A., M.S., Ph.D.
Psychology/Early Childhood Development. M.A., M.S.
Public Administration. M.P.A.
Recreation and Park Administration. M.S. only.
Reproductive Biology. Interdisciplinary. M.S., Ph.D.
Sociology. Thesis for M.A.; M.A. only.
Spanish. M.A.
Statistics. M.S., Ph.D.
Zoology and Physiology. M.S., Ph.D.
Zoology and Physiology/Water Resources. M.S.

COLLEGE OF BUSINESS:

Accounting. M.S.

Business Administration. GMAT for admission. M.B.A.
E-Business. M.S.
Economics. M.S., Ph.D.
Finance. M.S.

COLLEGE OF EDUCATION:

Adult and Postsecondary Education. M.A., Ed.S., Ed.D.
Community Counseling. M.S.
Counselor Education. Includes counselor education and supervision (Ph.D.), school counseling (M.S.), student affairs in higher education (M.S.). M.S., Ph.D.
Curriculum and Instruction. M.A., Ed.D., Ph.D.
Distance Education. Ed.D., Ph.D.
Educational Leadership. M.A., Ed.S., Ed.D., Ph.D.
Instructional Technology. M.S., Ed.D.
Special Education. M.A., Ed.S.

COLLEGE OF HEALTH SCIENCES:

Audiology. M.S.
Nursing. M.S.
Kinesiology and Health Education. M.S.
Speech-Language Pathology. M.S.

COLLEGE OF ENGINEERING:

Atmospheric Sciences. M.S., Ph.D.
Bioengineering. Interdisciplinary; thesis for M.S.
Chemical Engineering. Thesis for M.S.. M.S. only.
Civil Engineering. M.S., Ph.D.
Computer Science. M.S., Ph.D.
Electrical Engineering. M.S., Ph.D.
Environmental Engineering. Interdisciplinary. M.S. only.
Mechanical Engineering. M.S., Ph.D.
Petroleum Engineering. M.S., Ph.D.

College of Law (82071-3035)

Established 1920. ABA approved since 1923. AALS member. Semester system. Law library: 273,738 volumes, 2084 subscriptions; has LEXIS, NEXIS, WESTLAW, INFOTRAC.

Annual tuition: resident $4620, nonresident $9701. On-campus housing available. Apply to Director of Housing. Total average cost for all other expenses: $7490.

Enrollment: first-year class 76; full-time 229 (men 56%, women 44%). Faculty: full-time 12, part-time 6. Student to faculty ratio 15.9 to 1. Degrees conferred: J.D., J.D.-M.B.A., J.D.-M.P.A.

ADMISSION REQUIREMENTS. LSDAS Law School report, bachelor's degree, transcripts, LSAT (no later than February) required in support of application. Preference given to state residents. Accepts transfer applicants. Graduates of unaccredited institutions not considered. Apply to Director of Admissions after September 1, before March 15. Rolling admission process. Fall admission only for beginning students. Application fee $35. Phone: (307)766-6416.

ADMISSION STANDARDS. Selective. Mean LSAT: 149; mean GPA: 3.24 (A = 4). Gourman rating: 2.59. *U.S. News & World Report* ranking is in the third tier of all U.S. law schools. Accepts about 25% of total annual applicants.

FINANCIAL AID. Scholarships, fellowships, Federal W/S, loans. Apply to Director of Financial Aids by February 15. Use FAFSA (School code: 003932). About 35% of students receive aid other than loans from College.

DEGREE REQUIREMENTS. For J.D.: satisfactory completion of three-year program, at least two years in residence; 88-semester-hour program.

XAVIER UNIVERSITY
Cincinnati, Ohio 45207-5311
Web site: www.xu.edu

Founded 1831. Coed. Private control. Roman Catholic. Semester system. Library: 307,000 volumes, 1550 subscriptions. Total University enrollment: 6575.

Tuition: per credit $450; for M.Ed. $390, Psy.D. $610. No on-campus housing, except on a space-available basis. Contact Director of Residence Life for off-campus housing information. Phone: (513)745-4894.

Graduate School

Graduate study since 1946. Enrollment: full-time 568, part-time 1426. University faculty: full- and part-time 208. Degrees conferred: M.A., M.B.A., M.Ed., M.S., M.H.S.A.

ADMISSION REQUIREMENTS. Official transcripts required in support of School's application. On-line application available. GRE/MAT/GMAT required for some departments. TOEFL required for international applicants. Accepts transfer applicants. Graduates of unaccredited institutions not considered. Apply to Graduate Services Office at least one month prior to registration. Application fee $35; $45 for M.B.A. applicants. Phone: (800)344-4690, (513)745-3360; fax: (513)745-1048; M.B.A.: (513)745-3525; e-mail: xugrad@xu.edu.

ADMISSION STANDARDS. Selective. Usual minimum average: 2.7 (A = 4), varies by program.

FINANCIAL AID. Annual awards from institutional funds: scholarships, assistantships, tuition waivers, internships, Federal W/S, loans. Approved for VA benefits. Apply by April 1 to Graduate Services Office for scholarships, assistantships; to Financial Aid Office for all other programs. Phone: (513)745-3142; fax: (513)745-2806. Use FAFSA. About 5% of students receive aid other than loans from University and outside sources. Aid available for part-time students.

DEGREE REQUIREMENTS. For M.A.: 30 semester hours minimum, at least 24 in residence; MAT for candidacy; reading knowledge of one foreign language in some programs; thesis; final oral exam. For M.B.A.: 36 semester hours minimum, at least 27 in residence; GMAT for candidacy. For M.Ed.: 30–42 semester hours minimum, at least 24–36 in residence; MAT for candidacy. For M.S.: 30 semester hours minimum, at least 24 in residence; MAT for candidacy; thesis/research paper; final oral/written exam. For M.H.A.: 60 semester hours minimum, at least 45 in residence; GMAT for candidacy; residency requirement.

FIELDS OF STUDY.
Administration. M.Ed.
Business Administration. M.B.A.
Community Counseling. M.A.
Criminal Justice. M.S.
Elementary Education. M.Ed.
English. M.A., M.Ed.
Health Services Administration. Includes long-term care. M.H.S.A.
History. M.A., M.Ed.
Human Resource Development. M.Ed.
Humanities. M.A.
Montessori Education. M.Ed.
Multicultural Literature for Children. M.Ed.
Music. M.Ed.
Nursing. GRE or MAT for admission. Includes nursing administration, education, forensic, school nurse. M.S.
Psychology. M.A., Psy.D.
Reading. M.Ed.
School Counseling. M.Ed.
Secondary Education. M.Ed.
Special Education. M.Ed.
Sport Administration. M.Ed.
Theology. M.A.

XAVIER UNIVERSITY OF LOUISIANA
New Orleans, Louisiana 70125-1098
Web site: www.xula.edu

Founded 1925. CGS member. Coed. Private control. Roman Catholic affiliation. Semester system. Library: 108,000 volumes, 2000 subscriptions.

Tuition: per credit $200. No on-campus housing for graduate students. Day-care facilities available.

Graduate School

Enrollment: full-time 185; part-time 50 (men 35%, women 65%). Graduate faculty: full-time 5, part-time 7. Degrees conferred: M.A., M.Th.

ADMISSION REQUIREMENTS. Transcripts, two letters of recommendation, GRE or MAT required in support of application. TOEFL required for international applicants. Interview not required. Accepts transfer applicants. Graduates of unaccredited colleges not considered. Apply to Dean of School by July 15 (Fall), December 1 (Spring). Application fee $25. Phone: (504)483-7487; fax: (504)485-7921.

ADMISSION STANDARDS. Relatively open. Minimum average: 2.5, 3.0 in major field (A = 4).

FINANCIAL AID. Scholarships, internships, tuition waivers, Federal W/S, loans. Approved for VA benefits. Apply to Financial Aid Office; no specified closing date. Phone: (504)483-3517; fax: (504)482-6258. Use FAFSA. Aid available for part-time students.

DEGREE REQUIREMENTS. For master's: 33 credits minimum; thesis/nonthesis option.

FIELDS OF STUDY.
Educational Administration and Supervision. Includes school principalship, supervisor of education.
Counseling. Includes school counseling, mental health counseling.
Curriculum and Instruction. Includes early childhood, elementary, reading specialist, secondary, workshop way.
Theology.

YALE UNIVERSITY
New Haven, Connecticut 06520
Web site: www.yale.edu

Founded 1701. Located 80 miles NE of New York City. CGS member. Coed. Private control. Semester system. Special facilities: Beinecke Rare Book and Manuscript Library; Peabody Museum of Natural History; Art Gallery; Paul Mellon Center for British Art and British Studies; observatory; computer center; Child Study Center, Kline Geology Laboratory; Kline Chemistry Research Laboratory; Josiah Willard Gibbs Research Laboratories for biology, physics, molecular biology, biophysics; Center for International and Area Study; Nuclear Structure Laboratory for "Emperor" tandem electrostatic Van de Graaff accelerator; Kline Biology Tower for research and graduate training in biological sciences; Electron and Heavy Ion Accelerator Laboratories; Becton Engineering and Applied Science Center; Institute of Sacred Music; Institute for Social and Policy Studies; Social Interaction Laboratory; Political Science Research Laboratory.

The University's NIH ranking is 10th among all U.S. institutions with 733 awards/grants worth $256,664,005. Library: more than 10,500,000 volumes, 55,000 subscriptions. Total University enrollment: 11,000.

Annual tuition: full-time $24,480; modest continuing registration fee after the fourth year. On-campus housing for married students, graduate men and women. Average academic year housing costs: $11,148 single students, $17,270 married students. Contact University Housing Department for both on- and off-campus housing information. Phone: (203)432-2160.

Graduate School of Arts and Science

Graduate School organized in 1847, graduate study since 1732. Enrollment: full- and part-time 2150. University faculty teaching graduate courses: over 500. Degrees conferred: M.A., M.S., M.Phil., Ph.D. (M.A. as a terminal degree only in International and Developmental Economics, International Relations, African Studies Afro-American Studies, American Studies, Archeological Studies, East Asian Studies, English, German, History, History of Medicine and Life Sciences, Medieval Studies Music, Near Eastern Languages and Civilizations, Soviet and East European Studies, Slavic Languages and Literature, and Statistics. M.S. as a terminal degree only in Engineering and Applied Science, Mathematics, Molecular Biophysics and Biochemistry).

ADMISSION REQUIREMENTS. Transcripts, GRE, three letters of recommendation required in support of application. GRE Subject Test required by astronomy, biology, chemistry, computer science, economics, engineering and applied science, English language and literature, genetics, pharmacology, physics, physiology, statistics. Interview required in some cases. TOEFL required for international applicants. Accepts transfer applicants, usually for Ph.D. only. Apply to Coordinator, Graduate Admissions, P.O. Box 1504A, Yale Station, New Haven, Connecticut 06520, preferably one year prior to desired entrance but no later than January 2. Normally admits Fall only. Application fee $70. Phone: (203)432-2770.

APPLICATION STANDARDS. Competitive to very selective. Usual minimum average 3.0 (A = 4).

FINANCIAL AID. Scholarships, fellowships, assistantships, Federal W/S, loans. Apply by January 2 to appropriate department chair for fellowships, assistantships; to Director of Financial Aid for all other programs. Phone: (203)432-2739. Use FAFSA. Support for Graduate School students while they are in residence at Yale comes from a great variety of sources. More than 80% of full-time candidates for the Ph.D. degree receive substantial aid from Yale or from other institutions and agencies interested in graduate education.

DEGREE REQUIREMENTS. For master's en route to Ph.D.: completion of first year of Ph.D. program; one academic year in full-time residence; recommendation by the appropriate department for the award of the degree, subject to final review by the Committee on Degrees. For terminal master's (full- and part-time programs): one or two academic years of full-time residence depending on the program; high-pass average with at least one term grade of Honors in one full-year graduate course or in two full-term graduate courses. foreign language requirements set by department; master's essay required by some departments. For M.Phil.: completion of all requirements for the Ph.D. except those relating directly to the dissertation. For Ph.D.: three academic years in residence; no more than four years to fulfill foreign language and course requirements as set by individual departments; grade of Honors in at least one full-year course or two full-term courses; qualifying written/oral exam; admission to candidacy; prospectus and dissertation; final oral exam.

FIELDS OF STUDY.

African Studies. Two-year M.A. program; proficiency in one African language.

African-American Studies. Two-year M.A. program. M.A., Ph.D.

American Studies. Reading knowledge of two languages or high level of proficiency in one language required. M.A., Ph.D.

Anthropology. Faculty decides with each student individually the particular requirements in respect to languages, statistics, or other research tools. M.A., Ph.D.

Applied Mathematics. GRE Subject Test encouraged. M.A., Ph.D.

Applied Physics. M.S., Ph.D.

Archaeological Studies. No foreign language required. M.A.

Astronomy. Working knowledge of at least two languages; one French, German, or Russian required. M.S., Ph.D.

Atmospheric Science. Interdepartmental.

Biological and Biomedical Sciences. GRE Subject Test recommended; MCAT can be substituted for some programs. Contact BBS department for application. Ph.D.

Biostatistics. M.S.

Cell Biology. No foreign language requirement. Ph.D.

Cellular and Molecular Physiology. Apply through the BBS department. Ph.D.

Chemical Engineering. M.S., Ph.D.

Chemistry. GRE required, a foreign language not required. Ph.D.

Classics. Reading knowledge of French and German, good knowledge of Greek and Latin grammar and ability to read representative passages in both languages at sight required. Ph.D.

Comparative Literature. Reading knowledge of two modern languages plus Latin or Greek required. Ph.D.

Computer Science. No foreign language required. Ph.D.

East Asian Languages and Literature. One European language plus Chinese and Japanese required. Ph.D.

East Asian Studies. Two-year M.A. program; Chinese or Japanese plus French or German proficiency required. M.A.

Ecology and Evolutionary Biology. Ph.D.

Economics. No foreign language required unless connected with dissertation research. Ph.D.

Electrical Engineering. M.S., Ph.D.

Engineering and Applied Sciences. M.S., Ph.D.

English Language and Literature. Ability to read simple prose in three languages or demonstration of the same level of competence in one language and advanced competence in a second language required; one language must be Latin or Greek. Ph.D.

Epidemiology and Public Health. GRE Subject Test optional. Ph.D.

Experimental Pathology. GRE or MCAT for admission. Ph.D.

Film Studies. Ph.D.

Forest and Environmental Studies. GRE required for admission, GRE Subject optional. Ph.D.

French. Reading knowledge of a second Romance language; Latin and non-Romance language (usually German) required. Ph.D.

Genetics. No foreign language required. Ph.D.

Genetics and Development. Apply through the BBS department. Ph.D.

Geology and Geophysics. No foreign language required, but students may be assigned foreign language literature in certain fields of specialization. Ph.D.

Germanic Languages and Literature. Reading knowledge of French and Latin as well as thorough preparation in German required. M.A., Ph.D.

History. Reading knowledge of one foreign language required. M.A., Ph.D.

History of Art. Reading knowledge of German and second language relevant to proposed specialty within the field of art history required. Ph.D.

History of Medicine and Life Sciences. M.S., Ph.D.

Immunobiology. Writing sample required; GRE recommended. Ph.D.

Immunology. Apply through BBS department. Ph.D.

International and Developmental Economics. M.A.

International Relations. Reading knowledge of one foreign language (usually French or German) required for admission; two-year M.A. program. M.A.

Investigation Medicine. Ph.D.

Italian Language and Literature. Reading knowledge of a second Romance language, Latin, and a non-Romance language (usually German) required. Ph.D.

Linguistics. Proficiency in French and German. Ph.D.

Management. Accepts either GRE or GMAT for admission. Ph.D.

Mathematics. GRE/Subject Test for admission; reading knowledge of two foreign languages required. M.S., Ph.D.

Mechanical Engineering. Ph.D.

Medieval Studies. Reading knowledge of simple Latin (medieval prose), French, and German required. M.A., Ph.D.

Microbiology. Apply through BBS department. Ph.D.

Molecular Biophysics and Biochemistry. No foreign language required. Apply through BBS department. Ph.D.

Molecular, Cellular, and Developmental Biology. Apply through BBS department. Ph.D.

Music. Reading knowledge of German and French or Italian required. M.A., Ph.D.

Near Eastern Languages and Civilizations. Includes Arabic and Islamic studies, archaeology of the ancient Near East, Assyriology, Egyptology, coptic, northwest Semitic studies. Reading knowledge of French and German required. M.A., Ph.D.

Neurobiology. No foreign language required. Ph.D.

Neuroscience. No foreign language required. Ph.D.

Pharmacological Sciences and Molecular Medicine. Apply through BBS department. Ph.D.

Pharmacology. Apply through BBS department. Ph.D.

Philosophy. Reading proficiency in French and German required. Ph.D.

Physical Chemistry. Proficiency in French, Russian, or preferably German required. Ph.D.

Physics. Proficiency in one foreign language required. Ph.D.

Political Science. Demonstration of competence in one foreign language required. Ph.D.

Psychology. No language requirement. Ph.D.

Religious Studies. Reading proficiency in French and German required. Ph.D.

Renaissance Studies. Reading exams in Latin prose, Italian, and a third language chosen from French, German, Greek, or Spanish. Ph.D.

Rusian and East European Studies. Reading knowledge of Russian East European language required for admission; two-year M.A. program. M.A.

Slavic Languages and Literature. Adequate command of the Russian language plus a reading knowledge of French and German required. M.A., Ph.D.

Sociology. Proficiency in statistics, methods, and theory; reading knowledge of French, German, or Russian required. Ph.D.

Spanish and Portuguese. Reading knowledge of a second Romance language, Latin, and a non-Romance language (usually German) required. M.A., Ph.D.

Statistics. M.S., Ph.D.

School of Architecture

Visual arts study since 1832. Library 151,300 volumes.

Annual tuition: $26,100, fees $630. On-campus housing available.

Enrollment: full-time 150. Faculty: full-time 4, part-time 37. Degrees conferred: M.Arch. I., M.Arch. II., M.E.D., M.Arch.-M.B.A., M.Arch-M.E.D.

ADMISSION REQUIREMENTS. Transcripts, GRE, portfolio, three letters of reference, personal history required in support of School's application. For M.E.D.: research topics and proposed program of study required. TOEFL required for international applicants. Graduates of unaccredited institutions not considered. Apply by January 4 for postprofessional program, by January 10

for others. Fall admission only. Application fee $70. Phone: (203)432-2296.

ADMISSION STANDARDS. Very competitive. Usual minimum average: 3.5 (A = 4).

FINANCIAL AID. Annual awards from school funds: scholarships, teaching assistantships, Federal W/S, loans. Approved for VA benefits. Apply by February 1 to appropriate department for scholarships, assistantship; to Financial Aid Office for all other programs. Phone: (203)432-2291. Use FAFSA. Some 65% of students receive aid from loan sources and the School.

DEGREE REQUIREMENTS. For M.Arch. I.: B.A. or B.S. required, completion of three-year, full-time program, two years in residence. For M.Arch. II.: a two-year, full-time postprofessional program; in final term an appropriate independent studies thesis may be approved. For M.E.D.: B.A., B.S., B.Arch. or M.Arch. required, completion of two-year program, three semesters in residence; thesis/independent project. For postprofessionals: B.Arch. or equivalent, two-year residence.

FIELDS OF STUDY.
Architecture.
Environmental Design.

School of Art

Tuition: full-time $20,700. Graduate enrollment: full-time 119 (men 45%, women 55%). No part-time students. School faculty: full-time 11, part-time 74. Degree conferred: M.F.A.

ADMISSION REQUIREMENTS. Official transcripts, three letters of recommendation, slide portfolio, one-page statement of intent required in support of School's application. No on-line application available. TOEFL required for international applicants. Interview not required. Admits Fall only. Apply to Admissions Office by January 15. Rolling admissions process. Application fee $75. Phone: (203)432-2600; e-mail artschool.info@yale.edu.

ADMISSION STANDARDS. Selective. Selection based on talent and academic preparation.

FINANCIAL AID. Annual awards from institutional funds: scholarships, assistantships, Federal W/S, loans. Apply by February 28 (priority deadline) to Office of Student Financial Services. Phone: (203)432-2700; fax: (203)432-7557. Use FAFSA (School code: 001426). About 50% of students receive some aid from School and outside sources.

DEGREE REQUIREMENTS. For M.F.A.: 60 credit, two-year program.

FIELDS OF STUDY.
Graphic Design.
Painting.
Painting/Printmaking.
Photography.
Printmaking.
Sculpture.

Divinity School

Yale College was founded in 1701 to train ministers; the religion programs separated from Yale College in 1822, and the Divinity School was established.

Tuition: full-time $15,140; per course $1892.50. Graduate enrollment: full-time 411 (men 50%, Women 50%). No part-time students. School faculty: full-time 33, part-time 10. Degrees conferred: M.A.R. (both a Comprehensive M.A.R. and a Concentrated M.A.R. are offered), M.Div., S.T.M. For doctoral study apply to Department of Religion, Graduate School of Arts and Sciences.

ADMISSION REQUIREMENTS. Official transcripts, three letters of recommendation, personal essays, five-page writing sample required in support of School's application. On-line application available. TOEFL (minimum score 600) required for international applicants. Interview not required. Accepts transfer applicants. Apply to Admissions Office by February 1 (Fall), November 1 (Spring). Rolling admissions process. Application fee $75. Phone: (203)432-5360; fax: (203)432-7475.

ADMISSION STANDARDS. Selective.

FINANCIAL AID. Annual awards from institutional funds: renewable academic scholarships, internships, grants (need-based), Federal W/S, loans. Apply to Director of Admissions by March 1. Phone: (203)432-5026; fax: (203)432-5756. Use FAFSA and CSS Profile. About 75% of students receive some aid from School and outside sources.

DEGREE REQUIREMENTS. For M.Div.: 72 credit units in full-time residence. For M.A.R.: 48 credit units in full-time residence. For S.T.M.: 24 credit unit minimum in full-time residence; thesis. *Note:* Divinity School preschool available; none for infants, toddlers.

School of Drama

Graduate studies in drama since 1925. Annual tuition: $17,800. Graduate enrollment: 193. No part-time students. Limited number of Special Students for one year. School faculty: 69. Degrees conferred: M.F.A., D.F.A., Certificate in Drama, Technical Internship Certificate.

ADMISSION REQUIREMENTS. Statement of purpose, resume, official transcripts, three letters of recommendation required in support of application. Samples of work, GRE required in Dramaturgy and Dramatic Criticism, Stage Management, Sound Design/Engineering, Technical Design and Production, and Theater Management. TOEFL required for international applicants. Apply to the School of Drama by January 15 for Acting and Directing; February 1 for all other departments; February 15 for financial aid applicants. Application fee $60, $20 for Technical Internship Certificate. Phone: (203)432-1507; fax: (203)432-9668.

ADMISSION STANDARDS. Selective to very competitive.

FINANCIAL AID. Scholarships, internships, Federal W/S, loans. Apply by February 15 to Financial Aid Office. Phone: (203)432-1540. Use FAFSA and CSS Profile. About 87% of students receive aid other than loans from School and outside sources.

DEGREE REQUIREMENTS. For M.F.A. and Certificate in Drama: granted upon completion of three years' residency and successful completion of coursework. For D.F.A.: oral qualifying exam; approved written dissertation within two years after completing Yale M.F.A. For Internship Certificate; awarded upon completion with distinction of the one-year internship program.

FIELDS OF STUDY.
Acting. Audition and interview for admission. M.F.A., Certificate in Drama.
Design. Includes scene, costume, lighting; interview, portfolio for admission (no slides). M.F.A., Certificate in Drama.
Directing Session. Interview for admission.
Dramaturgy and Dramatic Criticism. Interview of qualified applicant for admission, two writing samples; GRE.
Playwriting. One original play. M.F.A., Certificate in Drama.
Sound Design. GRE, interview for admission. M.F.A., Certificate in Drama.
Stage Management. GRE, interview for admission. M.F.A.
Technical Design and Production. GRE, interview for admission. M.F.A., Certificate in Drama.
Technical Internship Program. GRE or SAT; interview for admission.
Theater Management. GRE, interview for admission. M.F.A.

School of Forestry and Environmental Studies

Established 1900. Special facilities: Center for Biodiversity and Conservation Science, Center for Coastal and Watershed Systems, Center for Environmental Law and Policy, Center for Industrial Ecology, Global Institute of Sustainable Forestry, Hixon Center for Urban Ecology, Tropical Resources Institute.

Annual tuition: full-time master's $21,990, D.F.E.S. $24,480. Graduate enrollment: full-time 265, part-time 4. School faculty: full-time 28, part-time 4. Degrees conferred: M.F., M.F.S., M.E.S., M.F., D.F.E.S., M.E.M.-M.A. (Economics, International Relation), M.F.M.A. (Economics, International Relation), M.E.M-M.B.A., M.F-M.B.A., M.E.M.-J.D., M.F.-J.D., M.E.M.-M.P.H., M.F.-M.P.H. The Ph.D. is offered through the Graduate School.

ADMISSION REQUIREMENTS. Official transcripts, GRE, three letters of recommendation required in support of School's application. On-line application available. Interview not required but encouraged. Graduates of unaccredited institutions not considered. Apply to Director of Admission by February 1. No application fee. Phone: master's (203)432-5138, doctoral applicants (203)432-5146; fax: (203)432-5942.

ADMISSION STANDARDS. Competitive. Usual minimum average: 3.0 (A = 4).

FINANCIAL AID. Scholarships, grants, teaching assistantships, loans. Approved for VA benefits. Apply to Director of Financial Aid by February 1 for M.F., M.F.S., M.E.S.; by January 1 for Ph.D., D.F.E.S. Phone: (203)432-5105. Use FAFSA (School code: 001426).

DEGREE REQUIREMENTS. For M.E.M.: two years full-time 48 credit program; selection of advanced study program. For M.E.S., M.F.S.: two-year full-time 48 credit program; thesis or major paper. For M.F. (one-year M.F. available for professionals with at least seven years full-time forestry experience); two-year 48 credit multidisciplinary program; internship. For Ph.D.: see Graduate School listing above. For D.F.E.S.: similar to Ph.D. program.

FIELDS OF STUDY.
Environmental Management. Includes ecology, ecosystems and biodiversity, forestry, forest science and the management of forests for conservation and development, global change and polity, health and environment, industrial environmental management, policy economics and law, the social ecology of conservation and development, urban ecology and environmental planning, design, and values, water science, policy and management.
Environmental Science.
Forest Science.
Forestry.
Note: School has special program with Peace Corps, which promotes volunteer service.

Law School (P.O. Box 208329)
Web site: www.law.yale.edu

Established 1801. ABA approved since 1923. AALS member. Semester system. Full-time, day study only. Special facilities: Center For Law Economics and Public Policy, Orville H. Schnell Jr. Center for International Human Rights. Law library: 1,016,551 volumes, 9934 subscriptions; has LEXIS, NEXIS, WESTLAW, DIALOG, OCLC; is a Federal Government Depository.

Annual tuition: for J.D. $28,400; LL.M., M.S.L. $31,400; J.S.D. $5235 per term. On-campus housing available for both single and married students. Annual on-campus living expenses: $11,840. Housing deadline June 1. Contact Housing Department for both on- and off-campus housing information. Phone: (203) 432-9756. Law students tend to live off-campus. Off-campus housing and personal expenses: approximately $11,840.

Enrollment: first-year class 201; total full-time 595 (men 51%, women 49%). Faculty: full-time 52, part-time 25. Student to faculty ratio 9.9 to 1. Degrees conferred: J.D., J.D.-M.A., J.D.-M.B.A., J.D.-M.Div., J.D.-M.E.S., J.D.-M.F.S., J.D.-M.D., J.D.-M.P.A., J.D.-M.P.P.M., J.D.-Ph.D., LL.M. (generally open for those committed to law teaching as a career), LL.M. (for persons who have completed a basic legal education and received a university degree in law in another country), M.S.L. (Master's of Studies in Law, for nonlawyers), J.S.D. (open to LL.M. graduates from Yale only).

ADMISSION REQUIREMENTS. LSDAS Law School report, bachelor's degree, transcripts, two letters of recommendation, LSAT, 250-word essay required in support of application. Accepts transfer applicants. Graduates of unaccredited colleges not considered. Apply by February 15 to Office of Admission for J.D. program; to Graduate Committee for graduate programs. Joint degree applicants must apply to and be accepted by both programs. Beginning students admitted Fall only. Application fee $65. Phone: (203)432-4995.

ADMISSION REQUIREMENTS FOR TRANSFER APPLICANTS. Accepts about 10–12 transfers each year from other ABA-accredited schools. At least one year of enrollment, Dean's letter indicating the applicant is in good standing, applicants must have maintained a weighted B average, LSAT, LSDAS, personal statement regarding reason for transfer, two letters of recommendation, undergraduate transcripts, current law school transcript required in support of School's application. Apply to Director of Admission after May 1, before July 20. Admission decision made by the first week of August. Application fee $65. Will consider visiting students.

ADMISSION REQUIREMENTS FOR LL.M. APPLICANTS. All applicants must have graduated from either an AALS member law school or an ABA-accredited law school with a high rank in class. If from another country, the applicant must have graduated with a high rank from a law school or law faculty with standards substantially equivalent to those of U.S. applicants. Official undergraduate college/university transcripts, official law school transcript, résumé, proposed study plan, personal statement, two letters of recommendation required in support of application. In addition, TOEFL is required for those whose native language is not English; all transcripts and recommendations must be in English or accompanied by an English translation. Admits Fall only. Apply by December 15 to Graduate Programs Office. Application $60. Phone:(203)4332-1693; e-mail: coutrue@mail.law.yale.edu.

ADMISSION STANDARDS. Very competitive. Mean LSAT: 171; mean GPA: 3.91 (A = 4). Gourman rating: 4.91. *U.S. News & World Report* ranking is first among all U.S. law schools. Accepts about 8% of total annual applicants.

FINANCIAL AID. Scholarships, Federal W/S, loans; fellowships, assistantships for graduate law study. Apply to the Office of Financial Aid by March 15. Use FAFSA (School code: E00444). Apply to the Secretary of Graduate Financial Aid Committee for fellowships, assistantships, and certain scholarships. About 75% of students receive aid from School.

DEGREE REQUIREMENTS. For J.D.: 81 credit program, at least three years in full-time residence. For LL.M.: at least 24 credit hours beyond the J.D., two semesters minimum in full-time residence. For M.S.L.: one year in full-time residence. For J.S.D.: two semesters minimum beyond the J.D. in full-time residence; dissertation.

School of Management (P.O. Box 208200)

Web site: www.yale.edu/som

Established 1976 Accredited program: M.B.A. The Master in Public and Private Management degree was changed to M.B.A. on September 1, 1998, by vote of faculty; recognized Ph.D. Located on main campus. Special facilities: Chief Executive Leadership Institute, International Center for Finance, International Institute for Corporate Governance, the Partnership on Nonprofit Ventures.

Annual tuition: full-time M.B.A. $25,250; Ph.D. $24,480. On-campus rooms and apartments available for both single and married students. Average annual on-campus housing cost: $10,580. Contact Graduate Housing Office for both on- and off-campus housing information. Phone: (203)432-9756. Estimated annual M.B.A. budget for tuition, room and board, and personal expenses: approximately $49,790.

Enrollment: M.B.A. full-time 241 (men 67%, women 33%). Faculty:. full-time 47, part-time 49; all have Ph.D./D.B.A. Degrees conferred: M.B.A. (full-time only) joint degree programs can be arranged with the Schools of Architecture, Divinity, Drama, Epidemiology and Public Health, Forestry and Environmental Studies, Law, Nursing and the following programs from the Graduate School Arts and Science: East Asian Studies, International Development Economics, International Relations, Russian and East European Studies, Ph.D. (degree is offered through the Graduate School).

ADMISSION REQUIREMENTS. All applicants should have a bachelor's degree from a recognized institution of higher education and a strong mathematics background. Students are required to have their own personal computer. Contact School of Management at (203)432-5173 for application material and information. Accepts M.B.A. Multi-App electronic application in lieu of institutional application. Applications for downloading are generally available in August; Adobe Acrobat Reader is required. Early applications are encouraged for both admission and financial aid consideration. Beginning students are admitted Fall only. Both U.S. citizens and international applicants apply by November 10 (round 1), January 5 (round 2), March 15 (round 3). Submit School of Management application, GMAT results (will accept GMAT test result from the last five years, latest acceptable date is March), official transcripts from each undergraduate/graduate school attended, three letters of recommendation, three essays, résumé (prefers at least four years of work experience), and an application fee of $175 to the Admission Office, School of Management. In addition, international students (whose native language is other than English) should submit a TOEFL report (minimum score 600), certified translations and evaluations of all official transcripts, recommendations should be in English or with certified translations, proof of health/immunization certificate, and proof of sufficient financial resources for two years of academic study. For current information and/or modification in admission requirements, the international applicant's contact phone number is (203)432-2305. On-campus visits are encouraged. Interviews are by invitation and are generally requested for clarification of application materials. Joint degree applicants must apply to and be accepted by both schools and programs; contact the Admissions Office for current information and specific admission requirements. Admission decisions are made in three rounds. Applications received by November 10 will be notified by January 15; applications received by January 5 will be notified by March 25; applications received by March 15 will be notified by May 20.

ADMISSION REQUIREMENTS FOR DOCTORAL APPLICANTS. Contact Ph.D. Office, School of Management at (203)432-6028 for application material and information. Application can be downloaded from Web site, Adobe Acrobat Reader is required. Beginning students are admitted Fall only. Both U.S. citizens and international applicants apply by January 2. Submit School of Management application, GMAT scores (will accept GMAT test results from the last five years), official transcript from each undergraduate/graduate school attended, three letters of recommendation, four or five essays, résumé, statement of goals and objectives, and application fee of $75 to the Admission Office. In addition, international students (whose native language is other than English) should submit a TOEFL report (minimum score 600), certified translations and evaluations of all official transcripts, recommendations should be in English or with certified translations, proof of health/immunization certificate. International students' contact: (203)432-2305. Interviews are encouraged. Notification is generally made by mid-April.

ADMISSION STANDARDS. Highly selective. For M.B.A.: mean GMAT: 698; mean GPA: 3.5 (A = 4). Gourman rating: for M.B.A. 4.16; for Ph.D. 4.49. *U.S. News & World Report* ranking is in the top 13 of all U.S. business schools. *Business Week* listed the School in the top 25 of all U.S. business schools.

FINANCIAL AID. Scholarships, minority scholarships, fellowships, graduate assistantships, Federal Perkins Loans, Stafford Subsidized and Unsubsidized Loans, Federal W/S available; Public Service Loan Forgiveness Program. Financial aid may be available for international students from the University; submit Financial Aid Application for Foreign Students. Assistantships, fellowships may be available for joint degree candidates. Financial aid applications and information are generally included with admission materials; apply by February 15 (rounds 1 and 2), May 1 (round 3). Request scholarship, fellowship, assistantships and all need-based financial aid information from the School of Management. Use FAFSA (School code: 001426), also submit Financial Aid Transcript, Federal Income Tax forms. Approximately 65% of students receive some form of financial assistance.

DEGREE REQUIREMENTS. For M.B.A.: 18 course, 54 credit full-time program, including 7 elective courses, two-year program; summer internships between first and second year; M.B.A. degree program must completed in two years. For M.B.A.-master's: generally the joint degree program reduces the time required for both degrees taken separately by approximately one year. For Ph.D.: three-to-five year program; general written/oral exam, dissertation proposal, oral defense; dissertation; final oral defense.

FIELDS OF STUDY.
Accounting. Ph.D.
Business Administration. Concentrations in finance, leadership, marketing, operation management, public management, strategy. M.B.A.
Finance. Ph.D.
Marketing. Ph.D.

School of Medicine (06510)

Established 1810. Located at the Medical Center. Semester system. The first two years of study are spent in the basic medical sciences. Library: 360,000 volumes, 2500 subscriptions.

Annual tuition: $30,900; student fees $375; M.P.H. $23,250; per credit $750. On-campus rooms and apartments available for both single and married students at the Medical Center. Contact Housing Department for both on- and off-campus housing information. Phone: (203)432-9756. Off-campus housing and personal expenses: approximately $13,500.

M.D. enrollment: first-year class 100 (EDP 1–3); total full-time 513 (men 46%, women 54%); M.P.H. total 116. Degrees conferred: M.D., M.P.H., M.D.-M.B.A., M.D.-J.D., M.D.-M.Div., M.D.-M.P.H., M.D.-Ph.D., M.S.T.P. The Ph.D. is offered through or in conjunction with the Graduate School.

ADMISSION REQUIREMENTS. For M.D. program: transcripts, two letters of recommendation, MCAT required in support of application. Interviews arranged by invitation only. Applicants must have completed at least three years of college study. Transfer applicants seldom accepted. Has EDP; apply between June 1 and August 1. Graduates of unaccredited colleges not considered. Apply to Assistant Dean for Admissions after June 1, before October 15. Application fee $75. Phone: (203)785-2643; fax: (203)785-3234. For M.P.H. program: transcripts, GRE, three letters of recommendation required in support of application. Applicants must hold either (1) the degree of M.D., D.D.S., Ph.D., or D.V.M. or equivalent, or (2) master's or bachelor's in biological or social sciences plus professional academic qualifications or experience. Graduates of unaccredited colleges not considered. Apply to Department of Epidemiology and Public Health by March 1. Application fee $75. Phone: (203)784-2844.

ADMISSION STANDARDS. Very competitive. Mean MCAT: 11.2; mean GPA: 3.74 (A = 4). Gourman rating: 4.89. *U.S. News & World Report* ranking is in the top nine of all U.S. medical schools. Accepts about 3–5% of total annual applicants. Approximately 12% are state residents.

FINANCIAL AID. For M.D.: Scholarships, merit scholarships, minority scholarships, Service Commitment Scholarships, Grants-in-Aid, institutional loans, HEAL, NIH stipends, Federal Perkins Loans, Stafford Subsidized and Unsubsidized Loan Programs are available. Assistantships, fellowships, stipends may be available for M.D.-Ph.D., combined degree candidates. All financial aid is based on documented need. Financial aid applications and information are generally available at the on-campus, by-invitation interview or they will be sent out to all applicants in January. Contact Financial Aid Office for current information. Phone: (203)785-2645. Use FAFSA (School code: E00450), also submit Financial Aid Transcript, Federal Income Tax forms. Approximately 90% of students receive some form of financial assistance. For M.P.H.: scholarships, grants, loans. Apply by March 1 to Financial Aid Office. Use FAFSA (M.P.H. code: 001426).

DEGREE REQUIREMENTS. For M.D.: satisfactory completion of four-year program; thesis. All students must pass USMLE Step 1 prior to entering third year and USMLE Step 2 prior to awarding of M.D. For M.P.H.: two-year, 60 credit program, at least three terms are spent in full-time residence; internships; thesis. For M.D.-M.P.H.: generally a five- to five-and-one-half-year program. For M.D.-Ph.D., M.D.-J.D.: generally six- to seven-year programs.

FIELDS OF GRADUATE STUDY.
Anthropology.
Biochemistry.
Bioinformatics and Computational Biology.
Biomedical Engineering.
Biostatistics. M.P.H.
Cell Biology.
Cellular and Molecular Physiology.
Chronic Disease. M.P.H.
Environmental Health. M.P.H.
Epidemiology and Public Health. M.P.H.
Experimental Pathology.
Genetics.
Global Health. M.P.H.
Health Policy and Administration. M.P.H.
History of Medicine.
HPA Health Management. M.P.H.
Immunology.
Immunobiology.
Investigative Medicine.
Microbial Diseases. M.P.H.
Microbiology.
Molecular Biophysics and Biochemistry.

Molecular, Cell Biology, Genetics, and Development.
Molecular, Cellular, and Development Biology.
Neurobiology.
Neurosciences.
Pharmacology.
Pharmacology and Molecular Medicine.
Physiology and Integrative Medical Biology.

School of Music

Tuition: $21,300. Graduate enrollment: full-time 214. School faculty; full-time 20, part-time 36. Degrees conferred: M.M., M.M.A., D.M.A. A Certificate program is offered for those who do not hold a bachelor's degree, and an Artist Diploma is offered for those who hold a master's degree.

ADMISSION REQUIREMENTS. Official transcripts, audition tapes, three letters of recommendation, interview, and audition required in support of School's application. Auditions/interviews by invitation and based on audition tape. On-line application available. GRE exams required of composers, conductors, organists, and M.M.A. candidates. TOEFL (minimum score 550) required for international applicants. Apply to Director of Admissions by December 31. Application fee $100. Phone: (203)432-4155; fax: (203)432-7448.

ADMISSION STANDARDS. Highly selective.

FINANCIAL AID. Annual awards from institutional funds: scholarships, fellowships, Federal W/S, loans. Apply to Financial Aid Office by February 28. Phone: (253)432-1962. Use FAFSA and institutional FAF. About 90% of students receive aid other than loans from School and outside sources.

DEGREE REQUIREMENTS. For M.M.: 72 semester hours minimum, at least two years in full-time residence; reading knowledge of a modern European language; public presentation of recital/compositions each year of residency. For M.M.A.: 108 semester hours minimum, at least three years in full-time residence; public presentation of recitals/compositions every year; thesis; comprehensive written and oral examination. For A.D.: two-year full-time program; 14 credits per term; one solo recital/one major ensemble performance/one performance of a worked composed. For D.M.A.: awarded to candidates who have earned the M.M.A. at Yale and whose achievements in the music profession in the following two to five years have reached the level of distinction to merit granting the degree.

FIELDS OF STUDY.
Composition.
Conducting. Includes orchestral and choral.
Performance. Includes vocal and instrumental.
Sacred Music. Interdisciplinary; cooperative program with Divinity School.

School of Nursing

Established in, and graduate study since, 1923. Special facilities: Center for Excellence in Chronic Illness Care, Center for Health Policy and Ethics. Annual tuition: $23,100. On-campus housing available at the Medical Center/Hospital. Three programs of study available: master's program for applicants with R.N. licensure and baccalaureate degree in any discipline; or master's program for non-nurse college graduates.

Graduate enrollment: full-time 184, part-time 65. Teaching faculty: full-time 54, part-time 33. Members of other University faculties also give instruction. Degrees conferred: M.S.N., M.S.N.-M.B.A., M.S.N.-M.P.H., D.N.Sc.

ADMISSION REQUIREMENTS: Transcripts, three personal references, GRE, admission essay, personal interview required in support of School's application. On-line application available. For the R.N. master's program, nursing experience desirable but not required. TOEFL required of international applicants. Interviews are by invitation only and are for final selection. Transfer applicants usually not accepted. Graduates of unaccredited institutions not considered. Apply to Student Affairs Office by November 15 for non-nurse program; January 15 for R.N. master's program; March 1 for D.N.Sc. program. For R.N. applicants there are three admission cycles: apply by January 15, notification is by April 15; apply by April 1, notification by June 15; apply by May 1, notification by July 15. Rolling admissions process. Full-time, scheduled part-time, and nonmatriculated study available. Fall admission only. Application fee $75. Phone: (203)785-2389; fax: (203)737-5409.

ADMISSION STANDARDS. Competitive. Usual minimum average: 3.0 (master's applicants), 3.2 (doctoral applicants) (A = 4).

FINANCIAL AID. Traineeships, scholarships, Federal W/S, loans. Approved for VA benefits. Apply by March 1 to School for traineeships, scholarships; to Financial Aid Office for all other programs. Phone: (203)785-2389; fax: (203)737-5409. Use FAFSA. Doctoral students are awarded two years of tuition, health coverage, and stipend.

DEGREE REQUIREMENTS. For M.S.N.: 40 credits full-time program for R.N. master's program and three-year full-time program for graduate entry non-nurse program; scholarly inquiry praxis; final oral exam. For D.N.Sc.: three-year full-time program; preliminary exam; qualifying exam; satisfactory completion of three areas of study and three areas of research and clinical focus; dissertation; final oral exam.

FIELDS OF STUDY.
Adult Advanced Practice Nursing. Includes acute care nurse practitioner, clinical nurse specialist, oncology nurse practitioner.
Adult, Family, Gerontological, and Women's Health Primary Care.
Nurse-Midwifery.
Nursing Management and Policy.
Pediatric Nurse Practitioner. Includes chronic Illness.
Psychiatric-Mental Health Nursing. Includes psychiatric nurse practitioner.
Note: Once a clinical specialty has been selected, the following concentrations are offered: Diabetes Care, Health Care Ethics, Home Care, Supportive Care, School-Based Health Care.

YESHIVA UNIVERSITY
New York, New York 10033-3201
Web site: www.yu.edu

Founded 1886. CGS member. Coed. Private control. Semester system. Special facilities: Yeshiva University Museum, research centers in various diseases, Center for Research in Cancer, Rose Fitzgerald Kennedy Center for Research in Mental Retardation and Human Development, Jack and Pearl Resnick Gerontology Center, Legal Services Clinic, Center for Psychological Intervention. The University's NIH ranking is 35th among all U.S. institutions with 313 awards/grants worth $122,473,774. University libraries: 1,100,000 volumes, 10,000 subscriptions. Total University enrollment: 6300.

No on-campus housing available.

Bernard Revel Graduate School

Established 1937. Semester system. Tuition: per credit $615.
Enrollment: full-time 8, part-time 88. Harry Fischel School for Higher Jewish Studies (established 1945) is Summer component. Summer enrollment: 21. Faculty: full-time 9, part-time 5. Degrees conferred: M.A., Ph.D.

ADMISSION REQUIREMENTS. Official transcripts, appropriate bachelor's degree, knowledge of Hebrew language, literature, and Judaic studies, GRE required in support of School's application. Interview and entrance exam sometimes required. TOEFL required for international applicants. Accepts transfer applicants. Apply to Office of Admissions at least three months prior to registration. Rolling admissions process. Application fee $35. Phone: (212)960-5254; fax: (212)960-5245.

ADMISSION STANDARDS. Selective. Usual minimum average: 3.0 (A = 4).

FINANCIAL AID. Scholarships, fellowships, tuition waivers, loans. Apply by February 15 to Dean of the Graduate School for scholarships, assistantships; to Financial Aid Office for all other programs. Phone: (212)960-5253. Use FAFSA.

DEGREE REQUIREMENTS. For M.A.: 30 credits minimum; comprehensive exam; thesis/nonthesis option/research project. For Ph.D.: 42 credits beyond the M.A. in Jewish Studies; reading knowledge of Hebrew; qualifying exam; dissertation; final oral exam.

FIELDS OF STUDY.
Bible. M.A., Ph.D.
Jewish Philosophy. M.A.
Medieval Jewish History. M.A., Ph.D.
Modern Jewish Philosophy. M.A., Ph.D.
Talmudic Studies. M.A.

Azrieli Graduate School of Jewish Education and Administration

Established 1983. Semester system. Tuition: per credit $615.
Enrollment: full-time 1, part-time 226. School faculty; full-time 6, part-time 11. Degrees conferred: M.S., Specialist's Certificate, Ed.D.

ADMISSION REQUIREMENTS. Official transcripts, two letters of recommendation, GRE and writing sample, evidence of advanced background in Jewish Studies and competence in Hebrew required in support of School's application. For Specialist and Ed.D. applicants, at least two years of teaching experience in an accredited school is required. On-line application available. TOEFL (minimum score 550) required for international students. Accepts transfer applicants. Graduates of unaccredited institutions not considered. Apply to the Office of the Dean at least three months prior to registration. Application fee $35. Phone: (212)960-0186.

ADMISSION STANDARDS. Selective. Usual minimum average: 2.75 (A = 4).

FINANCIAL AID. Scholarships, loans. Apply by April 1 to Office of Student Finances of the University. Phone: (212)960-5269. Use FAFSA. Aid available for part-time students.

DEGREE REQUIREMENTS. For M.S.: 30 credit program; supervised student teaching. For Specialist's: 30 credit program; supervised administration internships in Jewish education; comprehensive written exam. For Ed.D.: 65 credit program beyond master's; internship in administration and supervision in Jewish education; comprehensive written exam; dissertation; final oral defense.

FIELDS OF STUDY.
Jewish Administration and Supervision.
Jewish Education.

Benjamin N. Cardozo School of Law (10003)
Web site: www.cardozo.yu.edu

Established 1976. Located at the foot of Fifth Avenue in historic Greenwich Village. ABA approved since 1978. AALS member. Semester system. Full-time, day study only. Special facilities: Jacob Burns Institute of Advanced Legal Studies, Samuel and Ronnie Heyman Center for Corporate Governance, Floersheimer Center for Constitutional Democracy. Law library: 450,894 volumes, 6179 subscriptions; has LEXIS, NEXIS, WESTLAW, OCLC.
Annual tuition: $25,433; LL.M. $29,900; per credit $1400. No on-campus housing available. Law students live off-campus. Contact Admissions Office for off-campus information. Off-campus housing and personal expenses: approximately $21,093.
Enrollment: first-year class 332, total full-time 932 (men 50%, women 50%); no part-time students. Faculty: full-time 43, part-time 49. Student to faculty ratio 18.1 to 1. Degrees conferred: J.D., J.D.-M.S.W. (Yeshiva University), J.D.-M.A. (Economics, Philosophy, Political Science, Sociology—New School University), J.D.-M.S. (Management—New School University), LL.M.

ADMISSION REQUIREMENTS. LSDAS Law School report, bachelor's degree, transcripts, LSAT, recommendations, personal statement required in support of application. Accepts transfer applicants. Graduates of unaccredited colleges not considered. Apply by April 1 for priority consideration. Admits September (traditional program), January and May (Accelerated Entry Plan). Application fee $60. Phone: (212)790-0274; fax: (212)790-0482.

ADMISSION STANDARDS. Selective. Mean LSAT: 158; mean GPA: 3.25 (A = 4). Gourman rating: 3.76. *U.S. News & World Report* ranking is in the second tier of all U.S. law schools. Admits about 25–30% of total annual applicants.

FINANCIAL AID. Scholarships, assistantships, Federal W/S, loans. Apply to Financial Aid Office by April 15. Use FAFSA (School code: 002903). Approximately 67% of students receive some form of aid.

DEGREE REQUIREMENTS. For J.D.: satisfactory completion of 84-credit program. For LL.M.: 24 credit program.

Albert Einstein College of Medicine—Sue Golding Graduate Division of Medical Sciences
1300 Morris Park Avenue
Bronx, New York 10461

Establish 1957. Special facilities: Chanin Institute for Cancer Research, Center for Synchrotron Biosciences, Center for Aids Research, Center for Reproductive Biology, Children's Evaluation and Rehabilitation Center, Comprehensive Bone Center, Diabetes Research and Training Center, Gruss Magnetic Resonance Research Center, Institute for Aging Research, Institute for Communicative Disorders, Institute for Community and Collaborative Health, Marion Bessin Liver Research Center, Neuropsychopharmacology Center, Resnick Gerontology Center, Rose Fitzgerald Kennedy Center for Research in Mental Retardation and Human Development, Seaver Foundation for Bioinformatics.
Annual tuition: $24,500. Housing facilities same as for College of Medicine.
Enrollment: full-time 217 (men 55%, women 45%). Faculty full-time 415; no part-time faculty. Degree conferred: Ph.D.

ADMISSION REQUIREMENTS. Transcripts, two or three letters of recommendation, GRE required in support of application. On-line application available. TOEFL required for international applicants. Accepts transfer applicants. Graduates of unaccredited colleges not considered. Apply to Director of Admissions by January 15. Application fee $45. Phone (718)430-2345; fax: (718)430-8655; e-mail: phd@aecom.yu.edu.

ADMISSION STANDARDS. Selective. Accepts about 12% of total annual applicants.

FINANCIAL AID. Tuition scholarships and fellowship stipends available in most departments. Apply to appropriate department chair by February 1; for all other aid, contact the Student Finance Officer. Phone: (718)430-2336. Use FAFSA.

DEGREE REQUIREMENTS. For Ph.D.: three years minimum of full-time study totaling 90 credits, at least two years in residence; written/oral exam in a foreign language; qualifying exam; thesis; oral exam.

FIELDS OF STUDY.
Anatomy and Structural Biology.
Biochemistry.
Cell Biology.
Developmental and Molecular Biology.
Microbiology and Immunology.
Molecular Genetics.
Molecular Pharmacology.
Neuroscience.
Pathology.
Physiology and Biophysics.

Albert Einstein College of Medicine

Web site: www.aecom.yu.edu

Established 1955. Located in the Westchester Heights campus (Bronx 10461), adjacent to Jacobi Medical Center. Special facilities: Allman Research Center, Irwin S. and Sylvia Chanin Institute for Cancer Research, Arthur B. and Diane Belfer Educational Center for Health Sciences, Louis E. and Dora Rousso Center. Special programs: Biomedical Sciences Pathways; International Health Fellowships and programs in Israel, Germany, France, Sweden, and Japan. Library: 200,000 volumes, 2400 subscriptions.

Annual tuition: $32,725; fees $1950. The College operates two apartment complexes for both single and married students. Contact Housing Office for both on- and off-campus housing information. Phone: (718)430-3552. Annual housing, food and personal expenses: approximately $21,000.

Enrollment: first-year class 180; total full-time 720 (men 54%, women 46%). Faculty: full-time 1000, part-time and volunteers 850. Degrees conferred: M.D., M.D.-Ph.D., M.S.T.P.

ADMISSION REQUIREMENTS. AMCAS report, transcripts, letters of recommendation, MCAT required in support of application. Has EDP; apply between June 1 and August 1. Interviews by invitation only. Applicants should have completed four years of college study; in exceptional cases, three years. Graduates of unaccredited colleges not considered. Apply after June 1, before November 1. Application fee $90. Phone: (718)430-2106; fax: (718)430-8825.

ADMISSION STANDARDS. Very competitive. Mean MCAT: 10.6; mean GPA: 3.6 (A = 4). Gourman rating: 4.28. *U.S. News & World Report* ranking is in the top 31 of all U.S. medical schools. Accepts about 2–3% of total annual applicants. Approximately 40% are state residents.

FINANCIAL AID. Scholarships, merit scholarships, minority scholarships, Grants-in-Aid, institutional loans, HEAL, alternative loan programs, NIH stipends, Federal Perkins Loans, Stafford Subsidized and Unsubsidized Loans, Service Commitment Scholarship programs are available. M.S.T.P. carries a full tuition scholarship and a stipend. All financial aid is based on documented need. Financial aid applications and information are generally available at the on-campus, by-invitation interview. Contact the Student Finance Officer for current information. Phone: (718)430-2336. Use FAFSA (School code: G09895), also submit Financial Aid Transcript, Federal Income Tax forms. Approximately 75% of students receive some form of financial assistance.

DEGREE REQUIREMENTS. For M.D.: satisfactory completion of four-year program. All students must pass USMLE Step 1 prior to entering third year and USMLE Step 2 prior to awarding of M.D. For M.D.-Ph.D.: generally a six- to seven-year program.

FIELDS OF GRADUATE STUDY.
Anatomy and Structural Biology.
Biochemistry.
Cell Biology.
Developmental and Molecular Biology.
Microbiology and Immunology.
Molecular Genetics.
Molecular Pharmacology.
Neurosciences.
Pathology.
Physiology and Biophysics.

Ferkauf Graduate School of Psychology

Established 1965. Semester system. Annual tuition: $18,300.

Enrollment: full-time 285, part-time 52 (men 20%, women 80%). School faculty: full-time 28, part-time 70. Degrees conferred: M.A., Psy.D., Ph.D.

ADMISSION REQUIREMENTS. Transcripts, two letters of recommendation, GRE required in support of School's application. GRE Subject Test recommended. On-line application available. TOEFL (minimum score 550) required for international students. Accepts transfer applicants. Graduates of unaccredited institutions not considered. Apply to the Office of Admissions by January 15 (Psy.D., Ph.D.), February 15 (M.A.). Application fee $35. Phone: (718)430-3820; fax: (718)430-3252.

ADMISSION STANDARDS. Competitive for most departments. Usual minimum average: 3.0 (A = 4).

FINANCIAL AID. Scholarships, fellowships, assistantships for teaching/research, internships, grants, Federal W/S, loans. Apply by March 1 to Office of Student Finances of the University. Phone: (212)960-5269. Use FAFSA. Aid available for part-time students.

DEGREE REQUIREMENTS. For M.A.: 36 credits; thesis/nonthesis option; comprehensive exam. For Psy.D., Ph.D.: 78 credits minimum; comprehensive exam, dissertation; final oral exam.

FIELDS OF STUDY.
Clinical Health. Ph.D.
Clinical Psychology. Psy.D.
Developmental Psychology. Ph.D.
General Psychology. Includes experimental, developmental, social-personality. M.A.
School-Child Clinical Psychology. Psy.D.

Wurzweiler School of Social Work

Established 1957. Graduate study only. Annual tuition: full-time $16,000 (M.S.W.); $615 per credit (Ph.D.).

Enrollment: full-time 244, part-time 236. Faculty: full-time 24, part-time 36. Degrees conferred: M.S.W., Ph.D., Certificate in Jewish Communal Services.

ADMISSION REQUIREMENTS. Official transcripts, interview, three letters of recommendation, personal statement required in support of application. Two interviews required for doctoral applicants and an M.S.W. from an accredited college or university. On-line application available. TOEFL (minimum score 550) required for non-English-speaking applicants. Accepts transfer applicants. Graduates of unaccredited colleges not considered. Fall admission only. Rolling admissions process. Application fee $35. Phone: (212)960-0800, (212)960-0840 (doctoral applicants); fax: (212)960-0822.

ADMISSION STANDARDS. Competitive. Usual minimum average: 3.0 (A = 4).

FINANCIAL AID. Scholarships, grants, fellowships, research assistantships, internships, Federal W/S, loans, stipends from private, national, and state agencies. Approved for VA benefits. Apply to School's Admissions Officer by March 15 for Block Plan, May 15 for all programs. Phone: (212)960-5269; fax: (212) 960-0037. Use FAFSA.

DEGREE REQUIREMENTS. For M.S.W.: 60 credits, including prescribed courses; 1200 hours of field instruction; written essay. For Ph.D.: three years beyond the M.S.W.; prescribed and elective seminars; comprehensive exams; field study; dissertation; final oral exam.

FIELDS OF STUDY.
Community Social Work.
Jewish Communal Services. Certificate only.
Social Casework/Clinical Social Work.
Social Group Work.
Note: The M.S.W. is offered in four formats: Concurrent, Plan for Employed Persons (P.E.P.), Block, Clergy.

YOUNGSTOWN STATE UNIVERSITY

Youngstown, Ohio 44555-0002
Web site: www.ysu.edu

Founded 1908. CGS member. Coed. State control. Semester system. Special facilities: Center for Historic Preservation, Center for International Studies and Programs, Ethics Center, Professional Communication Design and Production Center, Public Service Center. Library: 993,314 volumes, 6518 subscriptions.

Tuition: per credit, area resident $189, resident $284, nonresident $384. On-campus housing available for single students only. Average academic year housing costs: $4800 (including board). Contact Housing Office for both on and off-campus housing information. Phone: (330)742-3547. Day-care facilities available.

School of Graduate Studies

Graduate study since 1967. Enrollment: full-time 206, part-time 962 (men 40%, women 60%). Graduate faculty: full-time 246, part-time 41. Degrees conferred: M.A., M.B.A., M.M., M.P.T., M.P.H., M.S., M.S.E., M.S.Ed., Ed.D.

ADMISSION REQUIREMENTS. Official transcripts required in support of application. GRE/MAT/GMAT, interview required for some programs. TOEFL (minimum score 550) required for international applicants. Accepts transfer applicants. Graduates of unaccredited institutions not considered. Apply to Graduate School Admissions Office at least two months prior to registration.

Application fee $30, $75 for international applicants. Phone: (330)742-3091; fax: (330)742-1580.

ADMISSION STANDARDS. Selective in some departments, relatively open in others. Usual minimum average: 2.75 (A = 4).

FINANCIAL AID. Annual awards from institutional funds: scholarships, fellowships, research assistantships, teaching assistantships, internships, Federal W/S, loans. Approved for VA benefits. Apply by March 1 to Office of the Dean for fellowships, assistantships; to Financial Aid Office for all other programs. Use FAFSA. About 35% of students receive aid from University and outside sources. Aid available for part-time students.

DEGREE REQUIREMENTS. For master's: 30–45 semester hours minimum, at least 24–36 in residence; thesis/nonthesis option or final paper. For Ed.S.: 30 semester hours beyond the master's; special project. For Ed.D.: 90 semester hours minimum beyond the master's, at least two years in residence; qualifying exam; research tool; dissertation; final oral exam.

FIELDS OF STUDY.
Accounting. M.B.A.
Biology. Thesis for M.S.. M.S.
Business Administration. M.B.A.
Chemistry. Thesis for M.S.. M.S.
Chemical Engineering. M.S.E.
Civil and Environmental Engineering. M.S.E.
Counseling. M.S.Ed.
Criminal Justice. M.S.
Economics. M.A.
Educational Administration. M.S.Ed.
Educational Leadership. Admits Fall only. Ed.D.
Electrical and Computer Engineering. M.S.E.
English. M.A.
Environmental Studies. M.S.
Finance. M.B.A.
Health and Human Services. M.H.H.S.
History. M.A.
Industrial and Manufacturing Systems Engineering. M.S.E.
Management. M.B.A.
Marketing. M.B.A.
Master Teacher—Elementary. Includes early childhood, middle grade, reading. M.S.Ed.
Master Teacher—Secondary. Includes the usual subjects. M.S.Ed.
Master Teacher—Special Education. Includes early childhood, gifted and talented. M.S.Ed.
Materials Science. M.S.E.
Mathematics. Includes computer science. M.S.
Mechanical Engineering. M.S.E.
Music Education. M.M.
Music History and Literature. M.M.
Music Performance. M.M.
Music Theory and Composition. M.M.
Nursing. Includes chronic illness care, nurse anesthetist. M.S.N.
Physical Therapy. M.P.T.
Public Health. M.P.H.

LOCATION OF INSTITUTIONS, BY STATE

Since the institutional entries in the main body of this book are arranged alphabetically without reference to locations, page numbers are not provided here.

Alabama

Alabama Agricultural and Mechanical
  University
Alabama State University
Alabama, University of
  Birmingham
  Huntsville
  Tuscaloosa
Auburn University
Auburn University (Montgomery)
Jacksonville State University
Montevallo, University of
North Alabama, University of
Samford University
South Alabama, University of
Troy State University
Troy State University (Dothan)
Troy State University (Montgomery)
Tuskegee University
West Alabama, University of

Alaska

Alaska, University of

Arizona

Arizona State University
Arizona State University West
Arizona, The University of
Northern Arizona University
Phoenix, University of
Thunderbird, the American Graduate School
  of International Management

Arkansas

Arkansas State University
Arkansas, University of
  Fayetteville
Central Arkansas, University of
Harding University
Henderson State University

California

Alliant International University
Antioch Los Angeles
Antioch Santa Barbara
Armstrong University

Azusa Pacific University
California College of the Arts
California Institute of Technology
California Institute of the Arts
California Lutheran University
California Polytechnic State University,
  San Luis Obispo
California State Polytechnic University,
  Pomona
California State University
  Bakersfield
  Chico
  Dominguez Hills
  Fresno
  Fullerton
  Hayward
  Long Beach
  Los Angeles
  Northridge
  Sacramento
  San Bernardino
  San Marcos
  Stanislaus
California, University of
  Berkeley
  Davis
  Hastings College of the Law
  Irvine
  Los Angeles
  Riverside
  San Diego
  San Francisco
  Santa Barbara
  Santa Cruz
California Western School of Law
Chapman University
Claremont Graduate University
Dominican University of California
Golden Gate University
Health Sciences College of Osteopathic
  Medicine of the Pacific, University of
Holy Names College
Humboldt State University
La Verne, University of
Loma Linda University
Loyola Marymount University
Mills College
Monterey Institute of International Studies
Mount St. Mary's College

National University
Naval Postgraduate School
Notre Dame de Namur University
Occidental College
Otis College of Art and Design
Pacific Union College
Pacific, University of
Pepperdine University
Pepperdine University—Culver City
Point Loma Nazarene University
Redlands, University of
San Diego State University
San Diego, University of
San Francisco Art Institute
San Francisco Conservatory of Music
San Francisco State University
San Francisco, University of
San Jose State University
Santa Clara University
Sonoma State University
Southern California College of
  Optometry
Southern California, University of
Southwestern University School
  of Law
Stanford University
Thomas Jefferson School of Law
Touro University College of Osteopathic
  Medicine
Western University of Health Sciences
Whittier College

Colorado

Adams State College
Colorado School of Mines
Colorado State University
Colorado, University of
  Boulder
  Colorado Springs
  Denver
  Health Sciences Center
Denver, University of
Northern Colorado, University of

Connecticut

Bridgeport, University of
Central Connecticut State University
Connecticut College

Connecticut, The University of
  Storrs
  Health Center
Eastern Connecticut State University
Fairfield University
Hartford, University of
Health Center, University of
  Connecticut
New Haven, University of
Quinnipiac University
St. Joseph College
Southern Connecticut State University
Trinity College
Wesleyan University
Western Connecticut State University
Yale University

Delaware
Delaware, University of
Widener University

District of Columbia
American University, The
Catholic University of America, The
District of Columbia, University of
Gallaudet University
Georgetown University
George Washington University, The
Howard University

Florida
Barry University
Central Florida, University of
Florida Agricultural and Mechanical
  University
Florida Atlantic University
Florida Institute of Technology
Florida State University
Florida, University of
Jacksonville University
Miami, University of
North Florida, University of
Nova Southeastern University
Rollins College
St. Thomas University
South Florida, University of
Stetson University
West Florida, University of

Georgia
Armstrong Atlantic State University
Augusta State University
Berry College
Clark Atlanta University
Columbus State University
Emory University
Fort Valley State University
Georgia College and State
  University
Georgia Institute of Technology, The
Georgia Medical College of
Georgia Southern University
Georgia State University
Georgia, The University of
Kennesaw State University
La Grange College
Mercer University
Morehouse School of Medicine
Oglethorpe University
Valdosta State College
West Georgia, State University of

Hawaii
Hawaii Pacific University
Hawaii, University of

Idaho
Boise State University
Idaho State University
Idaho, University of

Illinois
Art Institute of Chicago, The School of the
Bradley University
Chicago College of Osteopathic Medicine
Chicago State University
Chicago, The University of
Concordia University
DePaul University
Dominican University
Eastern Illinois University
Finch University of Health Sciences
Governors State University
Illinois Institute of Technology
Illinois State University
Illinois, University at
  Chicago
  Springfield
  Urbana
John Marshall Law School
Loyola University Chicago
Midwestern University—Chicago College of
  Osteopathic Medicine
National Louis University
Northeastern Illinois University
Northern Illinois University
Northwestern University
Olivet Nazarene University
Rockford College
Roosevelt University
Rush Medical College
St. Xavier University
Southern Illinois University
  Carbondale
  Edwardsville
Western Illinois University

Indiana
Ball State University
Butler University
Indiana State University
Indiana University
  Bloomington
  Indianapolis
Indianapolis, University of
Notre Dame, University of
Purdue University
  Calumet
  West Lafayette
Rose-Hulman Institute of Technology
St. Francis, University of
Valparaiso University

Iowa
Clarke College
Des Moines University of Health Sciences
Drake University
Dubuque, University of
Iowa State University of Science and
  Technology
Iowa, The University of
Loras College
Morningside College
Northern Iowa, University of
Osteopathic Medicine and Health Sciences,
  University of

Kansas
Emporia State University
Fort Hays State University
Kansas Medical Center, University of
Kansas State University
Kansas, University of
Pittsburg State University
Washburn University of Topeka
Wichita State University

Kentucky
Eastern Kentucky University
Georgetown College
Kentucky, University of
Louisville, University of

Morehead State University
Murray State University
Pikesville College School of Osteopathic
  Medicine
Salmon P. Chase College of Law of Northern
  Kentucky University
Spalding University
Union College
Western Kentucky University

Louisiana
Louisiana State University and Agricultural
  and Mechanical College
Louisiana State University Health Sciences
  Center
Louisiana State University in Shreveport
Louisiana Tech University
Louisiana at Lafayette, University of
Louisiana at Monroe, University of
Loyola University New Orleans
McNeese State University
New Orleans, University of
Northwestern State University of Louisiana
Southeastern Louisiana University
Southern University and Agricultural and
  Mechanical College
Tulane University
Xavier University of Louisiana

Maine
Maine, University of
Medicine, University of
New England College of Osteopathic
  Medicine, University of
Southern Maine, University of

Maryland
Baltimore, University of
Bowie State University
Frostburg State University
Goucher College
Hood College
Johns Hopkins University, The
Loyola College in Maryland
Maryland at Baltimore, University of
Maryland Institute College of Art
Maryland, University of
Maryland–Baltimore County, University of
McDaniel College
Morgan State University
St. John's College
Salisbury State University
Towson University
Uniformed Services University of the Health
  Sciences
Washington College

Massachusetts
Assumption College
Babson College
Bentley College
Boston College
Boston University
Brandeis University
Bridgewater State College
Clark University
Emerson College
Fitchburg State College
Framingham State College
Harvard University
Hebrew College
Massachusetts College of Art
Massachusetts College of Pharmacy and
  Allied Health Sciences
Massachusetts Institute of Technology
Massachusetts, University of
  Amherst
  Boston
  Dartmouth
  Lowell
Mount Holyoke College

New England Conservatory of Music
New England School of Law
Northeastern University
Salem State College
Simmons College
Smith College
Springfield College
Suffolk University
Tufts University
Western New England College
Westfield State College
Wheelock College
Williams College
Worcester Polytechnic Institute
Worcester State College

Michigan
Andrews University
Central Michigan University
Cranbrook Academy of Art
Detroit College of Law
Detroit Mercy, University of
Eastern Michigan University
Marygrove College
Michigan State University
Michigan Technological University
Michigan, The University of
Northern Michigan University
Oakland University
Saginaw Valley State University
Siena Heights University
Thomas M. Cooley Law School
Wayne State University
Western Michigan University

Minnesota
Bemidji State University
Hamline University
Mayo Medical School
Minnesota State University, Mankato
Minnesota, University of
Minnesota Duluth, University of
Minnesota State University, Moorhead
St. Cloud State University
St. John's University
St. Mary's University of Minnesota
St. Scholastica, College of
St. Thomas, University of
William Mitchell College of Law
Winona State University

Mississippi
Delta State University
Jackson State University
Mississippi College
Mississippi Medical Center, University of
Mississippi State University
Mississippi University for Women
Mississippi, The University of
Southern Mississippi, University of
William Carey College

Missouri
Central Missouri State University
Drury University
Health Sciences, University of
Kirksville College of Osteopathic Medicine
Lincoln University
Maryville University of St. Louis
Missouri, University of
  Columbia
  Kansas City
  Rolla
  St. Louis
Northwest Missouri State University
Saint Louis University
Southeast Missouri State University
Southwest Missouri State University
Truman State University
Washington University
Webster University

Montana
Montana State University
  Billings
  Bozeman
Montana Tech of the University of Montana
Montana, University of

Nebraska
Chadron State College
Concordia University
Creighton University, The
Nebraska, University of
  Kearney
  Lincoln
  Medical Center
  Omaha
Wayne State College

Nevada
Nevada, University of
  Las Vegas
  Reno

New Hampshire
Antioch New England Graduate School
Dartmouth College
Franklin Pierce Law Center
Keene State College
New Hampshire, University of
Plymouth State College
Rivier College

New Jersey
Drew University
Fairleigh Dickinson University
  Madison
  Teaneck
Jersey City University
Kean University
Medicine and Dentistry of New Jersey, University of
Monmouth University
Montclair State University
New Jersey, College of
New Jersey Institute of Technology
Princeton University
Rider University
Rowan University
Rutgers University
  Camden
  Newark
  New Brunswick
Seton Hall University
Stevens Institute of Technology
William Paterson University of New Jersey

New Mexico
Eastern New Mexico University
New Mexico Highlands University
New Mexico Institute of Mining and Technology
New Mexico State University
New Mexico, The University of
St. John's College
Western New Mexico University

New York
Adelphi University
Albany, Law School of Union University
Albany Medical College
Albany, The University at
Alfred University
Bank Street College of Education
Brooklyn Law School
Buffalo, University at
Canisius College
City University of New York, The
  Bernard M. Baruch College
  Brooklyn College

City College, The
Graduate School and University Center
Herbert H. Lehman College
Hunter College
John Jay College of Criminal Justice
Queens College
Staten Island, The College of
Clarkson University
Colgate University
Columbia University
Cornell University
C. W. Post Center of Long Island University
Elmira College
Fordham University
Hofstra University
Insurance, College of
Iona College
Ithaca College
Juilliard School, The
Long Island University (Brooklyn)
Manhattan College
Manhattan School of Music
Manhattanville College
Mount Sinai School of Medicine
New Rochelle, College of
New School University
New York College of Osteopathic Medicine
New York Institute of Technology
New York Law School
New York Medical College
New York, State University of, at
  Binghamton
  Downstate Medical Center (Brooklyn)
  Upstate Medical University (Syracuse)
New York, State University of, College at
  Brockport
  Buffalo
  Cortland
  Environmental Science and Forestry at Syracuse
  Fredonia
  Geneseo
  New Paltz
  Oneonta
  Oswego
  Plattsburg
  Potsdam
New York, State University of, Institute of Technology at Utica/Rome
New York University
Niagara University
Pace University
Polytechnic University
Pratt Institute
Rensselaer Polytechnic Institute
Rochester Institute of Technology
Rochester, University of
Rockefeller University, The
Sage Colleges
St. Bonaventure University
St. John's University
St. Lawrence University
Saint Rose, The College of
Sarah Lawrence College
Stony Brook University
Syracuse University
Touro College—School of Law
Union College
Vassar College
Wagner College
Yeshiva University

North Carolina
Appalachian State University
Campbell University
Duke University
East Carolina University
North Carolina Agricultural and Technical State University
North Carolina Central University
North Carolina State University at Raleigh
North Carolina, The University of
  Chapel Hill

Charlotte
Greensboro
Wilmington
Wake Forest University
Western Carolina University

North Dakota
Minot State University
North Dakota State University
North Dakota, University of

Ohio
Air Force Institute of Technology
Akron, University of
Antioch University McGregor
Bowling Green State University
Capital University
Case Western Reserve University
Cincinnati, University of
Cleveland State University
Dayton, University of
John Carroll University
Kent State University
Medical College of Ohio at Toledo
Miami University
Northeastern Ohio University
Ohio Northern University
Ohio State University, The
Ohio University
Toledo, University of
Union Institute and University
Wright State University
Xavier University
Youngstown State University

Oklahoma
Central Oklahoma, University of
East Central University
Health Science Center, University of
   Oklahoma
Northeastern State University
Northwestern Oklahoma State University
Oklahoma City University
Oklahoma State University
   Stillwater
   Tulsa
Oklahoma, University of
Oral Roberts University
Southeastern Oklahoma State University
Southern Nazarene University
Southwestern Oklahoma State University
Tulsa, The University of

Oregon
Eastern Oregon University
Lewis and Clark College
Oregon Health Sciences University
Oregon State University
Oregon, University of
Pacific University
Portland State University
Portland, University of
Reed College
Southern Oregon University
Western Oregon University
Willamette University

Pennsylvania
Bloomsburg University of Pennsylvania
Bryn Mawr College
Bucknell University
California University of Pennsylvania
Carnegie Mellon University
Clarion University of Pennsylvania
Dickinson School of Law, The
Drexel University
Duquesne University
East Stroudsburg University of Pennsylvania
Edinboro University of Pennsylvania
Gannon College

Indiana University of Pennsylvania
Kutztown University of Pennsylvania
Lake Erie College of Osteopathic Medicine
Lehigh University
Mansfield University of Pennsylvania
Marywood University
Millersville University of Pennsylvania
Pennsylvania College of Optometry
Pennsylvania State University
   University Park
   Harrisburg
   Hershey Medical Center
Pennsylvania, University of
Philadelphia College of Osteopathic Medicine
Pittsburgh, University of
Robert Morris College
St. Francis University
St. Joseph's University
Scranton, University of
Shippensburg University of Pennsylvania
Slippery Rock University of Pennsylvania
Temple University
Thomas Jefferson University
University of the Arts
University of the Sciences in Philadelphia
Villanova University
West Chester University of Pennsylvania
Westminster College
Widener University
Wilkes University

Puerto Rico
Inter American University
Ponce School of Medicine
Pontifical Catholic University of Puerto Rico
Puerto Rico, University of
Puerto Rico Mayaguez, University of

Rhode Island
Brown University
Bryant College
Providence College
Rhode Island College
Rhode Island School of Design
Rhode Island, University of
Roger Williams University

South Carolina
Citadel, The Military College of South
   Carolina
Clemson University
Converse College
Furman University
South Carolina, Medical University of
South Carolina State University
South Carolina, University of
Winthrop University

South Dakota
Augustana College
Black Hills State University
Northern State University
South Dakota School of Mines and
   Technology
South Dakota State University
South Dakota, University of

Tennessee
Austin Peay State University
East Tennessee State University
Fisk University
Meharry Medical College
Memphis, University of
Middle Tennessee State University
South, University of the
Southern College of Optometry
Tennessee State University
Tennessee Technological University
Tennessee, University of
   Chattanooga

Health Science Center
Knoxville
Martin
Oak Ridge
Space Institute
Vanderbilt University

Texas
Abilene Christian University
Angelo State University
Baylor College of Dentistry
Baylor College of Medicine
Baylor University
Dallas, University of
Hardin-Simmons University
Houston, University of
   Houston
   Clear Lake
Incarnate Word, University, of the
Lamar University
Midwestern State University
North Texas, University of
Our Lady of the Lake University
Prairie View A&M University
Rice University
St. Edward's University
St. Mary's University
St. Thomas, University of
Sam Houston State University
Southern Methodist University
South Texas College of Law
Southwest Texas State University
Stephen F. Austin State University
Sul Ross State University
Tarleton State University
Texas A&M University
   College Station
   Commerce
   Corpus Christi
   Kingsville
Texas Christian University
Texas Southern University
Texas Tech University
Texas Wesleyan University
Texas Woman's University
Texas, The University of
   Arlington
   Austin
   Brownsville
   Dallas
   El Paso
   Health Science Center at Houston
   Health Science Center at San Antonio
   Medical Branch Galveston
   Pan American
   Permian Basin
   San Antonio
   Southwestern Health Science Center
   Tyler
Trinity University
West Texas A&M University

Utah
Brigham Young University
Utah State University
Utah, University of

Vermont
Bennington College
Goddard College
Middlebury College
St. Michael's College
Vermont Law School
Vermont, University of

Virginia
Eastern Virginia Medical School
George Mason University
Hampton University
Hollins College
James Madison University

Longwood University
Lynchburg College
Old Dominion University
Radford University
Regent University
Richmond, University of
Virginia Commonwealth University
Virginia Polytechnic Institute and State
  University
Virginia State University
Virginia, University of
Washington and Lee University
William and Mary, The College of

Washington
Antioch University Seattle
Central Washington University
Eastern Washington University
Gonzaga University

Pacific Lutheran University
Puget Sound, University of
Seattle Pacific University
Seattle University
Walla Walla College
Washington State University
Washington, University of
Western Washington University
Whitworth College

West Virginia
Marshall University
West Virginia School of Osteopathic
  Medicine
West Virginia University

Wisconsin
Cardinal Stritch College
Marquette University

Milwaukee School of Engineering
Wisconsin, Medical College of
Wisconsin, University of
  Eau Claire
  La Crosse
  Madison
  Milwaukee
  Oshkosh
  Platteville
  River Falls
  Stevens Point
  Stout
  Superior
  Whitewater

Wyoming
Wyoming, University of

INSTITUTIONAL
ABBREVIATIONS

A.C.U. *Abilene Christian University*
Adams St. C. *Adams State College*
Adelphi U. *Adelphi University*
A.F. Inst. *Air Force Institute of Technology*
Ala. A&M U. *Alabama Agricultural and Mechanical University*
Ala. St. U. *Alabama State University*
Albany Law Sch. *Albany Law School*
Albany Med. C. *Albany Medical College*
Albany, U. *The University at Albany*
Alfred U. *Alfred University*
Alliant Intl. U. *Alliant International University*
Amer. U. *The American University*
Andrews U. *Andrews University*
Angelo St. U. *Angelo State University*
Antioch N. E. Grad. Sch. *Antioch New England Graduate School*
Antioch (L.A.) *Antioch Los Angeles*
Antioch (Santa Barbara) *Antioch Santa Barbara*
Antioch U. (McGregor) *Antioch University McGregor*
Antioch U. (Seattle) *Antioch University Seattle*
Appal. St. U. *Appalachian State University*
Ariz. St. U. *Arizona State University*
Ariz. St. U. (West) *Arizona State University–West*
Ark. St. U. *Arkansas State University*
Armstrong Atlantic St. U. *Armstrong Atlantic State University*
Armstrong U. *Armstrong University*
Sch. Art Inst. Chicago *The School of the Art Institute of Chicago*
Assump. C. *Assumption College*
Auburn U. *Auburn University*
Auburn U. (Montgomery) *Auburn University at Montgomery*
Augustana C. *Augustana College*
Augusta St. U. *Augusta State University*
Austin Peay St. U. *Austin Peay State University*
Azusa Pac. U. *Azusa Pacific University*
Babson C. *Babson College*
Ball St. U. *Ball State University*
Bank St. C. *Bank Street College of Education*
Barry U. *Barry University*
Baruch C. (C.U.N.Y.) *Bernard M. Baruch College of the City University of New York*
Baylor C. Dentistry *Baylor College of Dentistry*
Baylor C. Med. *Baylor College of Medicine*
Baylor U. *Baylor University*
Bemidji St. U. *Bemidji State University*
Bennington C. *Bennington College*
Bentley C. *Bentley College*
Berry C. *Berry College*
Black Hills St. U. *Black Hills State University*
Bloomsburg U. *Bloomsburg University of Pennsylvania*
Boise St. U. *Boise State University*
Boston C. *Boston College*
Boston U. *Boston University*
Bowie St. U. *Bowie State University*

Bowl. Gr. St. U. *Bowling Green State University*
Bradley U. *Bradley University*
Brandeis U. *Brandeis University*
Bridgewater St. C. *Bridgewater State College*
Brooklyn C. (C.U.N.Y.) *Brooklyn College of the City University of New York*
Brooklyn Law *Brooklyn Law School*
Brown U. *Brown University*
Bryant C. *Bryant College*
Bryn Mawr C. *Bryn Mawr College*
Bucknell U. *Bucknell University*
Butler U. *Butler University*
B.Y.U. *Brigham Young University*
Cal. C. Arts *California College of the Arts*
Cal. Inst. Arts *California Insitute of the Arts*
Cal. Luth. U. *California Lutheran University*
Cal. Poly. St. U. (San Luis Obispo) *California Polytechnic State University at San Luis Obispo*
Cal. St. Poly. U. (Pomona) *California State Polytechnic University at Pomona*
Cal. St. U. (Bakersfield) *California State University at Bakersfield*
Cal. St. U. (Chico) *California State University at Chico*
Cal. St. U. (Dominguez Hills) *California State University at Dominguez Hills*
Cal. St. U. (Fresno) *California State University at Fresno*
Cal. St. U. (Fullerton) *California State University at Fullerton*
Cal. St. U. (Hayward) *California State University at Hayward*
Cal. St. U. (Humboldt) *Humboldt State University*
Cal. St. U. (Long Beach) *California State University at Long Beach*
Cal. St. U. (L.A.) *California State University at Los Angeles*
Cal. St. U. (Northridge) *California State University at Northridge*
Cal. St. U. (Sacramento) *California State University at Sacramento*
Cal. St. U. (San Bernardino) *California State University at San Bernardino*
Cal. St. U. (San Francisco) *San Francisco State University*
Cal. St. U. (San Jose) *San Jose State University*
Cal. St. U. (San Marcos) *California State University, San Marcos*
Cal. St. U. (Sonoma) *Sonoma State University*
Cal. St. U. (Stanislaus) *California State University at Stanislaus*
Cal. Tech. *California Institute of Technology*
Cal. U. (Pa.) *California University of Pennsylvania*
Cal. West. Sch. Law *California Western School of Law*
Campbell U. *Campbell University*
Canisius C. *Canisius College*
Capital U. *Capital University*
Card. Stritch C. *Cardinal Stritch College*
Carnegie Mellon U. *Carnegie Mellon University*
Case West. Res. U. *Case Western Reserve University*
Catholic U. *The Catholic University of America*
Catholic U. P.R. *Pontifical Catholic University of Puerto Rico*
C.C.N.Y. (C.U.N.Y.) *City College of the City University of New York*
Cent. Conn. St. U. *Central Connecticut State University*

Cent. Mich. U.   *Central Michigan University*
Cent. Mo. St. U.   *Central Missouri State University*
Cent. Wash. U.   *Central Washington University*
Chadron St. C.   *Chadron State College*
Chapman U.   *Chapman University*
Chase C. Law   *Salmon P. Chase College of Law of Northern Kentucky University*
Chicago St. U.   *Chicago State University*
C. Insurance   *College of Insurance*
Citadel   *The Citadel*
Claremont Grad. U.   *Claremont Graduate University*
Clarion U.   *Clarion University of Pennsylvania*
Clark Atl. U.   *Clark Atlanta University*
Clark U.   *Clark University*
Clarke C.   *Clarke College*
Clarkson U.   *Clarkson University*
Clemson U. Clemson University
Cleve. St. U.   *Cleveland State University*
C. N. Rochelle   *College of New Rochelle*
Colgate U.   *Colgate University*
Colo. Sch. Mines   *Colorado School of Mines*
Colo. St. U.   *Colorado State University*
Columbia U.   *Columbia University*
Columbus St. U.   *Columbus State University*
Concordia U. (Ill.)   *Concordia University*
Concordia U. (Nebr.)   *Concordia University*
Conn. C.   *Connecticut College*
Converse C.   *Converse College*
Cornell U.   *Cornell University*
Cranbrook Acad. Art   *Cranbrook Academy of Art*
Creighton U.   *The Creighton University*
C. St. Rose   *The College of Saint Rose*
C. St. Scholastica   *College of St. Scholastica*
C. Staten Island (C.U.N.Y.)   *The College of Staten Island of the City University of New York*
C.U.N.Y. (Grad. Ctr.)   *The City University of New York*
C. Wm. & Mary   *The College of William and Mary*
C.W. Post (L.I.U.)   *Long Island University, C. W. Post Campus*
Dartmouth C.   *Dartmouth College*
Delta St. U.   *Delta State University*
DePaul U.   *DePaul University*
Des Moines U.   *Des Moines University of Health Sciences*
Detroit C. Law   *Michigan State University—Detroit College of Law*
Dickinson Sch. Law   *The Dickinson School of Law*
Dominican U.   *Dominican University*
Dominican U. (Calif.)   *Dominican University of California*
Drake U.   *Drake University*
Drew U.   *Drew University*
Drexel U.   *Drexel University*
Drury U.   *Drury University*
Duke U.   *Duke University*
Duquesne U.   *Duquesne University*
East Car. U.   *East Carolina University*
East Cent. U.   *East Central University*
East. Conn. St. U.   *Eastern Connecticut State University*
East. Ill. U.   *Eastern Illinois University*
East. Ky. U.   *Eastern Kentucky University*
East. Mich. U.   *Eastern Michigan University*
East. N. Mex. U.   *Eastern New Mexico University*
East. Ore. U.   *Eastern Oregon University*
East Stroudsburg U.   *East Stroudsburg University of Pennsylvania*
East Tenn. St. U.   *East Tennessee State University*
East. Va. Med. Sch.   *Eastern Virginia Medical School of the Medical College of Hampton Roads*
East. Wash. U.   *Eastern Washington University*
Edinboro U.   *Edinboro University of Pennsylvania*
Elmira C.   *Elmira College*
Emerson C.   *Emerson College*
Emory U.   *Emory University*
Emporia St. U.   *Emporia State University*
Fairfield U.   *Fairfield University*
F.D.U. (Madison)   *Fairleigh Dickinson University*
F.D.U. (Teaneck)   *Fairleigh Dickinson University*
Finch U. Health Sci.   *Finch University of Health Sciences of the Chicago Medical School*
Fisk U.   *Fisk University*
Fitchburg St. C.   *Fitchburg State College*
Fla. A&M U.   *Florida Agricultural and Mechanical University*
Fla. Atlantic U.   *Florida Atlantic University*

Fla. Inst. Tech.   *Florida Institute of Technology*
Fla. St. U.   *Florida State University*
Fordham U.   *Fordham University*
Fort Hays St. U.   *Fort Hays State University*
Fort Valley St. U.   *Fort Valley State University*
Framingham St. C.   *Framingham State College*
Franklin Pierce Law Ctr.   *Franklin Pierce Law Center*
Frostburg St. U.   *Frostburg State University*
Furman U.   *Furman University*
Gallaudet U.   *Gallaudet University*
Gannon U.   *Gannon University*
Geo. Mason U.   *George Mason University*
Georgetown C.   *Georgetown College*
Georgetown U.   *Georgetown University*
Geo. Wash. U.   *The George Washington University*
Georgia C. & St. U.   *Georgia College and State University*
Georgia Inst. Tech.   *The Georgia Institute of Technology*
Georgia So. U.   *Georgia Southern University*
Georgia St. U.   *Georgia State University*
Goddard C.   *Goddard College*
Golden Gate U.   *Golden Gate University*
Gonzaga U.   *Gonzaga University*
Goucher C.   *Goucher College*
Gov. St. U.   *Governors State University*
Hamline U.   *Hamline University*
Hampton U.   *Hampton University*
Hardin-Simmons U.   *Hardin-Simmons University*
Harding U.   *Harding University*
Harvard U.   *Harvard University*
Hastings C. Law   *University of California, Hastings College of the Law*
Hawaii Pac. U.   *Hawaii Pacific University*
Hebrew C.   *Hebrew College*
Henderson St. U.   *Henderson State University*
Hofstra U.   *Hofstra University*
Hollins U.   *Hollins University*
Holy Names C.   *Holy Names College*
Hood C.   *Hood College*
Howard U.   *Howard University*
Hunter C. (C.U.N.Y.)   *Hunter College of the City University of New York*
Idaho St. U.   *Idaho State University*
Ill. Inst. Tech.   *Illinois Institute of Technology*
Ill. St. U.   *Illinois State University*
Ind. St. U.   *Indiana State University*
Ind. U.   *Indiana University*
I.U.P.U.I.   *Indiana University Purdue University Indianapolis*
Ind. U. Penn.   *Indiana University of Pennsylvania*
Inter American U.   *Inter American University*
Iona C.   *Iona College*
Iowa St. U.   *Iowa State University of Science and Technology*
Ithaca C.   *Ithaca College*
Jackson St. U.   *Jackson State University*
Jacksonville St. U.   *Jacksonville State University*
Jacksonville U.   *Jacksonville University*
James Madison U.   *James Madison University*
Jersey City St. U.   *Jersey City State University*
John Carroll U.   *John Carroll University*
John Jay C. (C.U.N.Y.)   *John Jay College of Criminal Justice of the City University of New York*
John Marshall Law Sch.   *John Marshall Law School*
Johns Hopkins U.   *The Johns Hopkins University*
Juilliard   *The Juilliard School*
Kans. St. U.   *Kansas State University*
Kean U.   *Kean University*
Keene St. C.   *Keene State College*
Kent St. U.   *Kent State University*
Kirksville C.   *Kirksville College of Osteopathic Medicine*
Kutztown U.   *Kutztown University of Pennsylvania*
LaGrange C.   *Lagrange College*
Lake Erie C.   *Lake Erie College of Osteopathic Medicine*
Lamar U.   *Lamar University*
Lehigh U.   *Lehigh University*
Lehman C. (C.U.N.Y.)   *Herbert H. Lehman College of the City University of New York*
Lewis & Clark C.   *Lewis and Clark College*
Lincoln U.   *Lincoln University*
L.I.U.   *Long Island University, Brooklyn Campus*
L.I.U. (C.W. Post)   *Long Island University, C.W. Post Campus*
Loma Linda U.   *Loma Linda University*

Longwood U.   *Longwood University*
Loras C.   *Loras College*
Loyola C. (Md.)   *Loyola College (Maryland)*
Loyola Marymount U.   *Loyola Marymount University (Los Angeles)*
Loyola U. Chicago   *Loyola University Chicago*
Loyola U. (La.)   *Loyola University New Orleans*
L.S.U.   *Louisiana State University and Agricultural and Mechanical College*
L.S.U. H.S.C.   *Louisiana State University Health Sciences Center*
L.S.U. Shreveport   *Louisiana State University in Shreveport*
La. Tech U.   *Louisiana Tech University*
Lynchburg C.   *Lynchburg College*
Manhattan C.   *Manhattan College*
Manhattan Sch. Music   *Manhattan School of Music*
Manhattanville C.   *Manhattanville College*
Mansfield U.   *Mansfield University of Pennsylvania*
Marquette U.   *Marquette University*
Marshall U.   *Marshall University*
Marygrove C.   *Marygrove College*
Md. Inst. C. Art   *Maryland Institute College of Art*
Maryville U.   *Maryville University of Saint Louis*
Marywood U.   *Marywood University*
Mass. C. Art   *Massachusetts College of Art*
Mass. C. Pharmacy   *Massachusetts College of Pharmacy and Allied Health Sciences*
Mayo Med. Sch.   *Mayo Medical School*
McDaniel C.   *McDaniel College*
McNeese St. U.   *McNeese State University*
Med. C. Georgia   *Medical College of Georgia*
Med. C. Ohio   *Medical College of Ohio at Toledo*
Med. C. Penn.   *Medical College of Pennsylvania and Hahnemann University*
Med. C. Wis.   *Medical College of Wisconsin*
Med. U. So. Car.   *Medical University of South Carolina*
Meharry Med. C.   *Meharry Medical College*
Mercer U.   *Mercer University*
Miami U. (Ohio)   *Miami University (Ohio)*
Mich. St. U.   *Michigan State University*
Mich. Tech. U.   *Michigan Technological University*
Middlebury C.   *Middlebury College*
Mid. Tenn. St. U.   *Middle Tennessee State University*
Midwestern St. U.   *Midwestern State University*
Midwest. U.   *Midwestern University–Chicago College of Osteopathic Medicine*
Millersville U.   *Millersville University of Pennsylvania*
Mills C.   *Mills College*
Milwau. Sch. Eng.   *Milwaukee School of Engineering*
Minn. St. U. (Mankato)   *Minnesota State University Mankato*
Minn. St. U. (Moorhead)   *Minnesota State University Moorhead*
Minot St. U.   *Minot State University*
Miss. C.   *Mississippi College*
Miss. St. U.   *Mississippi State University*
Miss. St. U. Women   *Mississippi University for Women*
M.I.T.   *Massachusetts Institute of Technology*
Monmouth U.   *Monmouth University*
Mont. St. U.   *Montana State University*
Mont. Tech   *Montana Tech of the University of Montana*
Montclair St. U.   *Montclair State University*
Monterey Inst.   *Monterey Institute of International Studies*
Morehead St. U.   *Morehead State University*
Morehouse Sch. Med.   *Morehouse School of Medicine*
Morgan St. U.   *Morgan State University*
Morningside C.   *Morningside College*
Mt. Sinai Sch. Med.   *Mount Sinai School of Medicine*
Mt. St. Mary's C.   *Mount St. Mary's College*
Murray St. U.   *Murray State University*
Natl. Louis U.   *National-Louis University*
Natl. U.   *National University*
Naval P.G. Sch.   *Naval Postgraduate School*
New Eng. Cons. Music   *New England Conservatory of Music*
New Eng. Sch. Law   *New England School of Law*
N.J.I.T.   *New Jersey Institute of Technology*
N. Mex. Highlands U.   *New Mexico Highlands University*
N. Mex. Inst. M&T   *New Mexico Institute of Mining and Technology*
N. Mex. St. U.   *New Mexico State University*
New Sch. U.   *The New School University*
Niagara U.   *Niagara University*
No. Ariz. U.   *Northern Arizona University*

No. Car. A&T   *North Carolina Agricultural and Technical State University*
No. Car. Cent. U.   *North Carolina Central University*
No. Car. St. U. (Raleigh)   *North Carolina State University at Raleigh*
No. Dak. St. U.   *North Dakota State University*
Northeastern Ill. U.   *Northeastern Illinois University*
No. E. Ohio U.   *Northeastern Ohio Universities*
No. E. St. U.   *Northeastern State University*
Northeastern U.   *Northeastern University*
No. Ill. U.   *Northern Illinois University*
No. Kent. U.   *Northern Kentucky University*
No. Mich. U.   *Northern Michigan University*
No. St. U.   *Northern State University*
Northrop U.   *Northrop University*
Northwestern U.   *Northwestern University*
Notre Dame U.   *Notre Dame de Namur University*
Nova S.E. U.   *Nova Southeastern University*
No. W. Mo. St. U.   *Northwest Missouri State University*
No. W. Okla. St. U.   *Northwestern Oklahoma State University*
No. W. St. U. La.   *Northwestern State University of Louisiana*
N.Y.I.T.   *New York Institute of Technology*
N.Y. Law Sch.   *New York Law School*
N.Y. Med. C.   *New York Medical College*
N.Y.U.   *New York University*
Oakland U.   *Oakland University*
Occidental C.   *Occidental College*
Oglethorpe U.   *Oglethorpe University*
Ohio No. U.   *Ohio Northern University*
Ohio St. U.   *The Ohio State University*
Ohio U.   *Ohio University*
Okla. City U.   *Oklahoma City University*
Okla. St. U.   *Oklahoma State University*
Okla. St. U. (Tulsa)   *Oklahoma State University in Tulsa*
Old Dom. U.   *Old Dominion University*
Olivet Naz. U.   *Olivet Nazarene University*
Oral Roberts U.   *Oral Roberts University*
Ore. Health & Sci. U.   *Oregon Health and Science University*
Ore. St. U.   *Oregon State University*
Otis Art Inst.   *Otis College of Art and Design*
Our Lady Lake U.   *Our Lady of the Lake University*
Pace U.   *Pace University*
Pac. Luth. U.   *Pacific Lutheran University*
Pac. Union C.   *Pacific Union College*
Pac. U.   *Pacific University*
Penn. C. Opt.   *Pennsylvania College of Optometry*
Penn. St. U.   *Pennsylvania State University*
Penn. St. U. Harrisburg   *Pennsylvania State University at Harrisburg*
Penn. St. U. Med. Ctr.   *Pennsylvania State University Milton S. Hershey Medical Center*
Pepperdine U.   *Pepperdine University*
Pepperdine U. (Culver City)   *Pepperdine University, Culver City*
Phila. C. Osteo. Med.   *Philadelphia College of Osteopathic Medicine*
Pittsburg St. U.   *Pittsburg State University*
Plymouth St. C.   *Plymouth State College*
Point Loma Nazarene U.   *Point Loma Nazarene University*
Poly. U.   *Polytechnic University*
Ponce Sch. Med.   *Ponce School of Medicine*
Pont. Cath. U. P.R.   *Pontifical Catholic University of Puerto Rico*
Portland St. U.   *Portland State University*
Prairie View A&M U.   *Prairie View Agricultural and Mechanical University*
Pratt Inst.   *Pratt Institute*
Princeton U.   *Princeton University*
Providence C.   *Providence College*
Purdue U.   *Purdue University*
Purdue U. (Calumet)   *Purdue University Calumet*
Queens C. (C.U.N.Y.)   *Queens College of the City University of New York*
Quinnipiac U.   *Quinnipiac University*
Radford U.   *Radford University*
Reed C.   *Reed College*
Regent U.   *Regent University*
Rhode Island C.   *Rhode Island College*
Rhode Island Sch. Design   *Rhode Island School of Design*
Rice U.   *Rice University*
Rider U.   *Rider University*
R.I.T.   *Rochester Institute of Technology*
Rivier C.   *Rivier College*

Robert Morris C.   *Robert Morris College*
Rockefeller U.   *The Rockefeller University*
Rockford C.   *Rockford College*
Roger Williams U.   *Roger Williams University*
Rollins C.   *Rollins College*
Roosevelt U.   *Roosevelt University*
Rosary C.   *Rosary College*
Rose-Hulman Inst. Tech.   *Rose-Hulman Institute of Technology*
Rowan U.   *Rowan University*
R.P.I.   *Rensselaer Polytechnic Institute*
Rush Med. C.   *Rush Medical College of Rush University*
Rutgers U.   *Rutgers University*
Rutgers U. (Camden)   *Rutgers University Camden*
Rutgers U. (Newark)   *Rutgers University Newark*
Sage C.   *The Sage Colleges*
Sag. Val. St. U.   *Saginaw Valley State University*
Salem St. C.   *Salem State College*
Salisbury St. U.   *Salisbury State University*
Samford U.   *Samford University*
Sam Houston St. U.   *Sam Houston State University*
San Fran. Art Inst.   *San Francisco Art Institute*
San Fran. Conserv. Music   *San Francisco Conservatory of Music*
San Fran. St. U.   *San Francisco State University*
Santa Clara U.   *Santa Clara University*
Sarah Lawrence C.   *Sarah Lawrence College*
S.D.S.U.   *San Diego State University*
Seattle Pac. U.   *Seattle Pacific University*
Seattle U.   *Seattle University*
Seton Hall U.   *Seton Hall University*
S. F. Austin St. U.   *Stephen F. Austin State University*
Shippensburg U.   *Shippensburg University of Pennsylvania*
Siena Heights U.   *Siena Heights University*
Simmons C.   *Simmons College*
Slippery Rock U.   *Slippery Rock University of Pennsylvania*
Smith C.   *Smith College*
Southeastern La. U.   *Southeastern Louisiana University*
Southeastern Okla. St. U.   *Southeastern Oklahoma State University*
Southeast Mo. St. U.   *Southeast Missouri State University*
So. Cal. C. Optometry   *Southern California College of Optometry*
So. Car. St. U.   *South Carolina State University*
So. C. Optometry   *Southern College of Optometry*
So. Conn. St. U.   *Southern Connecticut State University*
So. Dak. Sch. M&T   *South Dakota School of Mines and Technology*
So. Dak. St. U.   *South Dakota State University*
So. Ill. U.   *Southern Illinois University*
So. Ill. U. (Edwardsville)   *Southern Illinois University at Edwardsville*
So. Meth. U.   *Southern Methodist University*
So. Nazarene U.   *Southern Nazarene University*
So. Ore. U.   *Southern Oregon University*
So. Tex. C. Law   *South Texas College of Law*
So. U. & A&M C.   *Southern University and Agricultural and Mechanical College*
Southwest Mo. St. U.   *Southwest Missouri State University*
Southwest Tex. St. U.   *Southwest Texas State*
Southwestern Okla. St. U.   *Southwestern Oklahoma State University*
Southwestern U. Law   *Southwestern University School of Law*
Spalding U.   *Spalding University*
Springfield C.   *Springfield College*
St. Bonaventure U.   *St. Bonaventure University*
St. Cloud St. U.   *St. Cloud State University*
St. Edward's U.   *St. Edward's University*
St. Francis U.   *St. Francis University*
St. John's C.   *St. John's College (New Mexico)*
St. John's C. (Md.)   *St. John's College (Maryland)*
St. John's U. (Minn.)   *St. John's University (Minnesota)*
St. John's U. (N.Y.)   *St. John's University (New York)*
St. Joseph C. (Conn.)   *St. Joseph College (Connecticut)*
St. Joseph's U. (Penn.)   *St. Joseph's University (Pennsylvania)*
St. Lawrence U.   *St. Lawrence University*
St. Louis U.   *Saint Louis University*
St. Mary's U. (Minn.)   *St. Mary's University of Minnesota*
St. Mary's U.   *St. Mary's University*
St. Michael's C.   *St. Michael's College*
St. Thomas U.   *St. Thomas University*
St. Xavier U.   *St. Xavier University*
Stanford U.   *Stanford University*
Stetson U.   *Stetson University*
Stevens Inst. Tech.   *Stevens Institute of Technology*

Stony Brook U. (S.U.N.Y).   *Stony Brook University, State University of New York*
Suffolk U.   *Suffolk University*
Sul Ross St. U.   *Sul Ross State University*
S.U.N.Y. (Binghamton)   *State University of New York at Binghamton*
S.U.N.Y. (Oswego)   *State University of New York at Oswego*
S.U.N.Y.C. (Brockport)   *State University of New York College at Brockport*
S.U.N.Y.C. (Buffalo)   *State University of New York College at Buffalo*
S.U.N.Y.C. (Cortland)   *State University of New York College at Cortland*
S.U.N.Y.C. Environ. Sci. & For. (Syracuse)   *State University of New York College of Environmental Science and Forestry at Syracuse*
S.U.N.Y.C. (Fredonia)   *State University of New York College at Fredonia*
S.U.N.Y.C. (Geneseo)   *State University of New York College of Arts and Sciences at Geneseo*
S.U.N.Y.C. (New Paltz)   *State University of New York College at New Paltz*
S.U.N.Y.C. (Oneonta)   *State University of New York College at Oneonta*
S.U.N.Y.C. (Plattsburgh)   *State University of New York College at Plattsburgh*
S.U.N.Y.C. (Potsdam)   *State University of New York College at Potsdam*
S.U.N.Y. Downstate   *State University of New York Downstate Medical Center at Brooklyn*
S.U.N.Y. I.T.   *State University of New York Institute of Technology at Utica/Rome*
S.U.N.Y. Upstate   *State University of New York Upstate Medical University at Syracuse*
Syracuse U.   *Syracuse University*
Tarleton St. U.   *Tarleton State University*
Teachers C.   *Teachers College (Columbia University)*
Temple U.   *Temple University*
Tenn. St. U.   *Tennessee State University*
Tenn. Tech. U.   *Tennessee Technological University*
Tex. A&M U.   *Texas Agricultural and Mechanical University—College Station*
Tex. A&M U. (Commerce)   *Texas A&M University—Commerce*
Tex. A&M U. H.S.C.   *Texas A&M University System Health Science Center*
Tex. A&M U. (Corpus Christi)   *Texas Agricultural and Mechanical University, Corpus Christi*
Tex. A&M U. (Kingsville)   *Texas A&M University—Kingsville*
Tex. Christ. U.   *Texas Christian University*
Tex. So. U.   *Texas Southern University*
Tex. Tech U.   *Texas Tech University*
Tex. Tech U. H.S.C.   *Texas Tech University Health Sciences Center*
Tex. Wesleyan U.   *Texas Wesleyan University*
Tex. Woman's U.   *Texas Woman's University*
Thom. Cooley Law Sch.   *Thomas M. Cooley Law School*
Thom. Jefferson Sch. Law   *Thomas Jefferson School of Law*
Thom. Jefferson U.   *Thomas Jefferson University*
Thunderbird   *Thunderbird American Graduate School of International Management*
Touro C.   *Touro College*
Towson U.   *Towson University*
Trinity C.   *Trinity College*
Trinity U.   *Trinity University*
Troy St. U.   *Troy State University*
Troy St. U. (Dothan)   *Troy State University at Dothan*
Troy St. U. (Mont.)   *Troy State University (Montgomery)*
Truman St. U.   *Truman State University*
Tufts U.   *Tufts University*
Tulane U.   *Tulane University*
Tuskegee U.   *Tuskegee University*
U. Akron   *University of Akron*
U. Ala.   *University of Alabama*
U. Ala. (Birm.)   *University of Alabama at Birmingham*
U. Ala. (Huntsville)   *University of Alabama at Huntsville*
U. Alaska   *University of Alaska*
U. Ariz.   *The University of Arizona*
U. Ark.   *University of Arkansas*
U. Arts   *The University of the Arts*
U. Balt.   *University of Baltimore*
U. Bridgeport   *University of Bridgeport*
U. Buffalo (S.U.N.Y.)   *University at Buffalo, State University of New York*

U. Cal. (Berkeley) *University of California at Berkeley*
U. Cal. (Davis) *University of California at Davis*
U. Cal. (Irvine) *University of California at Irvine*
U. Cal. (Riverside) *University of California at Riverside*
U. Cal. (San Diego) *University of California at San Diego*
U. Cal. (San Fran.) *University of California at San Francisco*
U. Cal. (Santa Barbara) *University of California at Santa Barbara*
U. Cal. (Santa Cruz) *University of California at Santa Cruz*
U. Cent. Ark. *University of Central Arkansas*
U. Cent. Fla. *University of Central Florida*
U. Cent. Okla. *University of Central Oklahoma*
U. Chicago *The University of Chicago*
U. Cincinnati *University of Cincinnati*
U.C.L.A. *University of California, Los Angeles*
U. Colo. *University of Colorado, Boulder*
U. Colo. C.S. *University of Colorado, Colorado Springs*
U. Colo. Denver *University of Colorado, Denver*
U. Colo. Health Sci. Ctr. *University of Colorado Health Science Center*
U. Conn. *The University of Connecticut*
U. Conn. Health Ctr. *University of Connecticut Health Center*
U. Dallas *University of Dallas*
U. Dayton *University of Dayton*
U. Del. *University of Delaware*
U. Denver *University of Denver*
U. Detroit Mercy *University of Detroit Mercy*
U.D.C. *University of the District of Columbia*
U. Dubuque *University of Dubuque*
U. Fla. *University of Florida*
U. Georgia *The University of Georgia*
U. Hartford *University of Hartford*
U. Hawaii *University of Hawaii at Manoa*
U. Health Sci. *University of Health Sciences (Chicago)*
U. Houston *University of Houston*
U. Houston (Clear Lake) *University of Houston, Clear Lake*
U. Idaho *University of Idaho*
U. Ill. *University of Illinois*
U. Ill. (Chicago) *University of Illinois at Chicago*
U. Incarnate Word *University of the Incarnate Word*
U. Indianapolis *University of Indianapolis*
U. Iowa *The University of Iowa*
U. Kans. *University of Kansas*
U. Kans. Med. Ctr. *University of Kansas Medical Center*
U. Ky. *University of Kentucky*
U. La Verne *University of La Verne*
U. La. (Lafayette) *University of Louisiana at Lafayette*
U. La. (Monroe) *University of Louisiana at Monroe*
U. Louisville *University of Louisville*
U. Maine *University of Maine*
U. Maine (Portland-Gorham) *University of Maine at Portland-Gorham*
U. Mass. *University of Massachusetts*
U. Mass. (Boston) *University of Massachusetts Boston*
U. Mass. (Dartmouth) *University of Massachusetts Dartmouth*
U. Mass. (Lowell) *University of Massachusetts Lowell*
U. Md. *University of Maryland*
U. Md. (Baltimore) *University of Maryland at Baltimore*
U. Md. (Baltimore Cnty.) *University of Maryland Baltimore County*
U. Med. & Dent. N.J. *University of Medicine and Dentistry of New Jersey*
U. Memphis *University of Memphis*
U. Miami (Fla.) *University of Miami*
U. Mich. *The University of Michigan*
U. Minn. *University of Minnesota*
U. Minn. (Duluth) *University of Minnesota Duluth*
U. Miss. *The University of Mississippi*
U. Miss. Med. Ctr. *University of Mississippi Medical Center*
U. Mo. (Columbia) *University of Missouri at Columbia*
U. Mo. (K.C.) *University of Missouri at Kansas City*
U. Mo. (Rolla) *University of Missouri—Rolla*
U. Mo. (St. Louis) *University of Missouri at St. Louis*
U. Mont. *University of Montana*
U. Montevallo *University of Montevallo*
U. N.H. *University of New Hampshire*
U. N. Mex. *The University of New Mexico*
U. N. Orleans *University of New Orleans*
U. Neb. *University of Nebraska*
U. Neb. (Kearney) *University of Nebraska at Kearney*
U. Neb. (Med. Ctr.) *University of Nebraska Medical Center*

U. Neb. (Omaha) *University of Nebraska at Omaha*
U. Nev. *University of Nevada, Reno*
U. Nev. (Las Vegas) *University of Nevada, Las Vegas*
U. New Eng. C.O.M. *University of New England College of Osteopathic Medicine*
U. New Haven *University of New Haven*
U. No. Ala. *University of North Alabama*
U. No. Car. (Chapel Hill) *The University of North Carolina at Chapel Hill*
U. No. Car. (Charlotte) *University of North Carolina at Charlotte*
U. No. Car. (Greensboro) *The University of North Carolina at Greensboro*
U. No. Car. (Wilmington) *University of North Carolina at Wilmington*
U. No. Col. *University of Northern Colorado*
U. No. Dak. *University of North Dakota*
U. No. Fla. *University of North Florida*
U. No. Iowa *University of Northern Iowa*
U. No. Tex. *University of North Texas*
U. Notre Dame *University of Notre Dame*
U. Okla. *University of Oklahoma*
U. Okla. Health Sci. Ctr. *University of Oklahoma Health Science Center*
U. Ore. *University of Oregon*
U. Pac. *University of the Pacific*
U. Penn. *University of Pennsylvania*
U. Phoenix *University of Phoenix*
U. Pitt. *University of Pittsburgh*
U. Portland *University of Portland*
U. Puerto Rico *University of Puerto Rico*
U. Puerto Rico, Mayaguez *University of Puerto Rico, Mayaguez*
U. Puget Sound *University of Puget Sound*
U. Redlands *University of Redlands*
U. Rhode Island *University of Rhode Island*
U. Richmond *University of Richmond*
U. Rochester *University of Rochester*
U. San Diego *University of San Diego*
U. San Fran. *University of San Francisco*
U. Sci. Phila. *University of the Sciences in Philadelphia*
U. Scranton *University of Scranton*
U. So. Ala. *University of South Alabama*
U. So. Cal. *University of Southern California*
U. So. Car. *University of South Carolina*
U. So. Dak. *University of South Dakota*
U. So. Fla. *University of South Florida*
U. So. Maine *University of Southern Maine*
U. So. Miss. *University of Southern Mississippi*
U. South *University of the South*
U. St. Francis *University of St. Francis*
U. St. Thomas *University of St. Thomas*
U. St. Thomas (Minn.) *University of St. Thomas*
U. St. Thomas (Tex.) *University of St. Thomas*
U. Tenn. *University of Tennessee*
U. Tenn. (Chattanooga) *University of Tennessee at Chattanooga*
U. Tenn. H.S.C. *University of Tennessee Health Science Center*
U. Tenn. (Martin) *University of Tennessee at Martin*
U. Tenn. (Oak Ridge) *University of Tennessee at Oak Ridge*
U. Tenn. Space Inst. *University of Tennessee Space Institute*
U. Tex. (Arlington) *The University of Texas at Arlington*
U. Tex. (Austin) *The University of Texas at Austin*
U. Tex. (Brownsville) *The University of Texas at Brownsville*
U. Tex. (Dallas) *The University of Texas at Dallas*
U. Tex. (El Paso) *The University of Texas at El Paso*
U. Tex. Health Sci. Ctr. (Houston) *The University of Texas Health Science Center at Houston*
U. Tex. Health Sci. Ctr. (San Antonio) *University of Texas Health Science Center at San Antonio*
U. Tex. Med. Br. (Galveston) *University of Texas Medical Branch at Galveston*
U. Tex. S.W. Med. Ctr. (Dallas) *The University of Texas Southwestern Medical Center at Dallas*
U. Tex. Pan Amer. *The University of Texas—Pan American*
U. Tex. Perm. Basin *The University of Texas of the Permian Basin*
U. Tex. (San Antonio) *The University of Texas at San Antonio*
U. Tex. (Tyler) *The University of Texas at Tyler*
U. Toledo *University of Toledo*
U. Tulsa *The University of Tulsa*
U. Utah *University of Utah*
U. Vt. *University of Vermont*

U. Va.   *University of Virginia*
U. Wash.   *University of Washington*
U. West Ala.   *University of West Alabama*
U. Wis.   *University of Wisconsin*
U. Wis. (Eau Claire)   *University of Wisconsin Eau Claire*
U. Wis. (La Crosse)   *University of Wisconsin La Crosse*
U. Wis. (Milwaukee)   *University of Wisconsin Milwaukee*
U. Wis. (Oshkosh)   *University of Wisconsin Oshkosh*
U. Wis. (Platteville)   *University of Wisconsin Platteville*
U. Wis. (River Falls)   *University of Wisconsin River Falls*
U. Wis. (Stevens Point)   *University of Wisconsin Stevens Point*
U. Wis. (Stout)   *University of Wisconsin Stout*
U. Wis. (Superior)   *University of Wisconsin Superior*
U. Wis. (Whitewater)   *University of Wisconsin Whitewater*
U. Wyo.   *University of Wyoming*
Uniformed Serv. U. Health Sci.   *Uniformed Services University of the Health Sciences*
Union C. (Ky.)   *Union College (Kentucky)*
Union C. (N.Y.)   *Union College (New York)*
Union Inst.   *The Union Institute and University*
Utah St. U.   *Utah State University*
Va. Commonwealth U.   *Virginia Commonwealth University*
Valdosta St. C.   *Valdosta State College*
Valparaiso U.   *Valparaiso University*
Vanderbilt U.   *Vanderbilt University*
Va. Poly. Inst.   *Virginia Polytechnic Institute and State University*
Vassar C.   *Vassar College*
Va. St. U.   *Virginia State University*
Villanova U.   *Villanova University*
Vt. Law   *Vermont Law School*
Wagner C.   *Wagner College*
Wake Forest U.   *Wake Forest University*
Walla Walla C.   *Walla Walla College*
Washburn U.   *Washburn University of Topeka*
Wash. C.   *Washington College*
Wash. & Lee U.   *Washington and Lee University*
Wash. St. U.   *Washington State University*
Wash. U. (Mo.)   *Washington University*
Wayne St. C.   *Wayne State College*
Wayne St. U.   *Wayne State University*

Webster U.   *Webster University*
Wesleyan U.   *Wesleyan University*
West. Car. U.   *Western Carolina University*
West Chester U. Pa.   *West Chester University of Pennsylvania*
West. Conn. St. U.   *Western Connecticut State University*
West Ga. St. U.   *State University of West Georgia*
West. Ill. U.   *Western Illinois University*
West. Ky. U.   *Western Kentucky University*
West. Mich. U.   *Western Michigan University*
West. New Eng. C.   *Western New England College*
West. N. Mex. U.   *Western New Mexico University*
West. Oregon U.   *Western Oregon University*
West Tex. A&M U.   *West Texas A&M University*
West. U. Health Sci.   *Western University of Health Sciences*
West Va. Sch. Osteo. Med.   *West Virginia School of Osteopathic Medicine*
West Va. U.   *West Virginia University*
West. Wash. U.   *Western Washington University*
Westfield St. C.   *Westfield State College*
Westminster C.   *Westminster College*
Wheelock C.   *Wheelock College*
Whittier C.   *Whittier College*
Whitworth C.   *Whitworth College*
Wichita St. U.   *Wichita State University*
Widener U.   *Widener University*
Wilkes U.   *Wilkes University*
Willamette U.   *Willamette University*
Wm. Carey C.   *William Carey College*
Wm. Mitchell C. Law   *William Mitchell College of Law*
Wm. Paterson U.   *William Paterson University of New Jersey*
Williams C.   *Williams College*
Winona St. U.   *Winona State University*
Winthrop U.   *Winthrop University*
Worcester Poly. Inst.   *Worcester Polytechnic Institute*
Worcester St. C.   *Worcester State College*
Wright St. U.   *Wright State University*
Xavier U. (La.)   *Xavier University of Louisiana*
Xavier U. (Ohio)   *Xavier University*
Yale U.   *Yale University*
Yeshiva U.   *Yeshiva University*
Youngstown St. U.   *Youngstown State University*

INDEX TO FIELDS OF STUDY

American colleges and universities offer graduate and professional degree programs in a bewilderingly varied number of disciplines and areas of specialization. An indication of the scope of opportunities for advanced study is found in the index that follows, listing major fields of study and the institutions that provide them.

Before turning to the index, it is *very important* that the user read and understand the following explanatory notes. Without knowledge of these caveats, the reader may overlook available educational opportunities.

1. Major and subfields of study are listed under these headings:

Agriculture
(Typically includes Agribusiness, Agricultural Economics, Agricultural Education, Agricultural Engineering, Agronomy, Animal Behavior, Animal Sciences, Dairy Sciences, Plant Science, Plant Pathology, Plant Physiology, Poultry Science; may include Agricultural Extension, Botany, Crop Science, Soils Sciences)
Architecture
  Naval Architecture
Area Studies
  African/Afro-American Studies
  Asian Studies
  Brazilian Studies
  Canada Area Studies
  Caribbean Studies
  Egyptology
  European Studies
  Hispanic/Iberian Studies
  Indo-European Studies
  Islamic Studies/Literature
  Latin American Studies
  Mediterranean Studies
  Mexican-American Studies
  Near/Middle Eastern Studies
  New York Area Studies
  North American Studies
  Pacific Area Studies
  Russian/East European
    Studies
  Uralic Studies
Basic Medical Sciences
(Typically includes Anatomy, Microbiology, Pathology, Pharmacology, Physiology; often includes Endocrinology, Neurological Sciences, Parasitology, Virology)
  Bacteriology
  Immunology
  Radiological Sciences
  Toxicology
Biological Sciences
(Typically includes Biology, Entomology, Zoology)
  Biochemistry
  Biomathematics/Biostatistics

  Biometry/Biometrics
  Biophysics
  Cancer Biology
  Cell Biology
  Environmental Biology
  Genetic Counseling
  Genetics
  Marine Biology
  Molecular Biology
Business/Business Administration, Commerce/Management
(Typically includes Accounting, Finance, Marketing; often includes Advertising, Industrial Administration, Industrial and Labor Relations, Operations Research, Public Relations; majors in Economics are also common in graduate schools of business as well as in graduate schools of arts and science)
  Actuarial/Insurance Sciences
  Hotel/Hospitality Management
  Human Resource Management
  Information Science/Systems/Studies
  International Business/Economics
  Management Information Systems
  Management of Technology
  Management Strategy and Policy
  Nonprofit Management
  Quantitative Analysis/Studies
  Real Estate
  Taxation
Communications
(Typically includes Mass Communication, Organizational Communication)
  Creative Writing/Writing
  Film/Television (Typically includes Broadcasting, Cinema, Motion Picture)
  Journalism
  Technical Writing
  Telecommunication
Computer Science
(Typically includes Computer Systems, Computer Information Systems, Management Systems)
Criminal Justice/Corrections/Criminology
(May include Law Enforcement, Police Science)
Dentistry

Education
(Typically includes Administration and Supervision, Curriculum and Instruction, Elementary and Secondary Education, Evaluation and Research, Foreign Language Education, Foundations and Philosophy, Guidance and Counseling, Health Education, History and Philosophy of Education, Physical Education, School Psychology, Special Education; often includes Business Education, Early Childhood Education, Extension Education, Middle School Education, Speech Pathology and Audiology, Student Personnel Services, Vocational/Technology Education: offered by more than 500 institutions in all 50 states, so individual institutions are not listed here)
  Adult Education (Typically includes Community Education)
  Art Education
  Audiovisual Education (Typically includes Educational/Instructional Technology and Media)
  Bilingual/Multilingual/Multicultural Education
  Community College Teaching
  Computers in Education
  Drug and Alcohol/Substance Abuse Counseling
  Education of the Gifted
  Education of the Multiple Handicapped
  English as a Second Language
  Learning Disabilities
  Marriage and Family Counseling
  Recreation/Recreational Administration
  Safety Education
  School Librarianship, Library Science, Library Media
  Teaching of Emotionally Disturbed
  Teaching of Mentally Retarded
  Teaching of Physically Handicapped
  Urban Education
Engineering and Technology
(Typically includes Applied Sciences, Chemical Engineering, Civil Engineering, Computer Science/Engineering, Construction Engineering, Electrical Engineering,

Energy Engineering, Engineering and Applied Sciences, Industrial Engineering, Mechanical; often includes Aeronautical/Astronautical Engineering, Material Engineering/Science, Mechanics, Metallurgy/Metallurgical Engineering, Operations Research, Structural Engineering, Systems Engineering/Science)

Architectural Engineering
Bioengineering/Biomedical Engineering
Ceramic Engineering
Engineering Management
Environmental Engineering
Geological, Geosciences, Geotechnical Engineering
Manufacturing Engineering
Marine Science/Engineering, Ocean Engineering, Oceanography
Mineral/Mining Engineering/Technology
Ocean Engineering
Optical Sciences
Paper Engineering/Science/Technology
Petroleum Engineering
Polymer Engineering/Science
Software Engineering
Systems Engineering
Textile Engineering/Science
Transportation/Traffic Engineering

Environmental Sciences
(Typically includes Ecology, Forestry, Forest Science, Wood Science/Technology)
Fish/Wildlife Management
Landscape Architecture
Meteorology/Atmospheric Sciences
Range Management/Science
Water Resources Administration

Fine Arts
(Typically includes Art History, Studio Arts; often includes Commercial Arts, Applied Arts, Crafts, Design, Graphic Design, Industrial Design)
Arts Management
Arts Therapy
Interior Design
Museum Training/Studies/Historic Preservation
Photography
Textile Design

Foreign Languages/Literatures
(Typically includes French, German, Spanish; often includes Italian, Portuguese, Romance Languages)
African Languages
Akkadian
Bengali
Caucasian
Celtic
Chinese/Japanese/Asian Languages
Greek

Hebrew/Arabic/Near and Middle Eastern Languages/Literatures
Hindi
Latin
Russian/Slavic Languages
Sanskrit
Scandinavian Languages/Literatures
Translation and Interpretation
Urdu

Home/Consumer Economics, Food Science, Food Service, Technology, Child and Family Life, Nutrition

Horticulture

Humanities
(Typically includes English and History: offered by nearly 400 institutions in all 50 states, so individual institutions are not listed here)
Classics
Comparative Literature
Folklore
Linguistics
Philosophy

Law

Liberal/Interdisciplinary/Multidisciplinary Studies

Library/Science/Information Studies

Medicine
Medical Illustration
Medical Technology
Tropical Medicine

Music
(Typically includes Composition, Music Education, Music History, Musicology, Performance, Theory; may include Ethnomusicology)
Music Therapy

Nursing and Health Professions
Child Care/Pediatric Nursing
Family Nursing (Typically includes Adult, Geriatric, Maternity, Parent, Child)
Gerontological Nursing
Health Care/Health Services/Hospital Administration/Management
Nurse Anesthesia
Nurse Midwifery
Nursing (Typically includes Advanced Practice Nursing, Administration, Education, Medical Surgical)
Occupational Therapy
Oncology Nursing
Physical Therapy
Prosthetics
Psychiatric Nursing
Public/Community Health Nursing
Rehabilitation Counseling/Services

Optometry/Vision Sciences

Osteopathic Medicine

Pharmacy
(Typically includes Pharmaceutical Chemistry, Pharmaceutical Science, Pharmacognosy; for Pharmacology, see *Basic Medical Sciences* listing above)

Physical Sciences
(Typically includes Chemistry, Mathematics and Physics; often includes Applied Mathematics; offered by nearly 400 institutions, so individual institutions are not listed)
Analytical Chemistry
Applied Physics
Astronomy/Planetary Sciences/Space Science
Geochemistry
Geology
Geophysics

Public Administration
(Typically includes Energy Management and Policy, Public Policy, Public Management, Public Affairs)

Public and Community Health
Environmental and Occupational Health
Epidemiology
International Health

Religion
(Typically includes Bible Studies, Religious Studies, Theology; often includes Religious Education)

Social Sciences
(Typically includes Economics, Political Science, Psychology, Sociology)
Anthropology
Archaeology
Geography
Medieval/Renaissance Studies
Peace Studies/Science, Conflict Resolution
Population Studies
Urban Studies
Women's/Feminists' Studies

Social Work
(Typically includes Human Services, Social Service, Social Welfare)

Theater/Drama/Theater Arts
(Typically includes Acting, Directing, Speech Arts; often includes Criticism, Theater/Costume Design, Technical Production)
Dance
Dance Therapy
Music Theater
Playwriting
Theater for Deaf
Theater Management

Urban Design/City Planning
(Typically includes City Planning, Community Planning, Environmental Design, Urban and Regional Planning, Urban Design)

Veterinary Medicine
(Typically includes Veterinary Sciences)

2. Each major and subfield heading is followed by the abbreviated names of every institution offering study leading to a degree in even one of the subfields customarily associated with the larger area. Thus, if an institution offers *only* fisheries biology, for example, its name is nevertheless included under BIOLOGICAL SCIENCES. The major fields are complete in listing appropriate institutions as of the time of preparation of this manuscript. Inasmuch as the information presented here is only as accurate as that provided by the institutions, and inasmuch as changes occur rapidly in higher education, some programs may not have been properly credited, or may have been discontinued, modified, or added. It bears repeating that this *Guide* is intended only as a first source of information, and certainty in academic planning information can be assured only by contacting the institution in which one is interested.

3. Subfields listed under the major headings are those of special interest or those sufficiently unusual to justify special notice. The student should bear in mind that nomenclature and departmental organization vary substantially from institution to institution. Using the BIOLOGICAL SCIENCES example again, a biology department may offer majors in botany, zoology, entomology, fisheries biology, cellular biology, and others, but this information may not have been made clear or available. Any one of these may have the status of separately constituted academic departments, so that a graduate school with a biology department offering study in botany may have another department, with a different faculty, in zoology. Entomology, a branch of zoology, may be available through still another department. College catalogs can be unilluminating on such points, and seemingly endless combinations can be constructed. The point is, the major listings can be

assumed to be as accurate as possible, but the subfields cannot. A potential student should first determine whether the broad field of study in which he or she is interested is available at a particular institution, *then* look to the subfields for clarification, remembering that the latter may be incomplete.

4. At multidivisional universities, study in a particular field may be offered by two or more divisions. Biochemistry may be a program of the chemistry or biology departments of the graduate school of arts and science and also available in the medical school of the same university. Universities with several campuses may offer the same major at three or more different locations *and* divisions. All divisions of an institution must therefore be checked for a particular program.

5. Since names describing fields of study frequently differ, the most common variations parenthetically follow the labels used in this index. When appropriate, it is noted that certain majors are "typically" or "often" included under any given heading.

6. Historically, a number of areas of study have grown and split, the new parts coming under different jurisdictions within the same institution. The dividing lines often remain vague, however. Home economics and music are examples. Home economics might be offered by a school of agriculture, a school of home economics, and a school of education, all in the same university. For this index, some fields of study have been combined in recognition of this commonality. For instance, although there may be three separate departments providing study in musicology, performance, and music education, in practice it is relatively unusual for an institution to offer one and not the others.

7. The abbreviations used for the institutions are meant to be understandable as they stand. If they are not, the reader can refer to the explanatory table that precedes this index. As a final note, the slash mark means *only* "and/or" in this index, as throughout this book.

Agriculture

(Typically includes Agricultural Economics, Agribusiness, Agricultural Education, Agricultural Engineering, Agronomy, Animal Behavior, Animal Sciences, Dairy Science, Plant Science, Plant Pathology, Plant Physiology, Poultry Science; may include Agricultural Extension, Crop Science, Soils Sciences)

Ala. A&M U.
Angelo St. U.
Ariz. St. U.
U. Ariz.
Ark. St. U.
U. Ark.
Auburn U.
B.Y.U.
Cal. Poly. St. U. (San Luis Obispo)
Cal. St. Poly. U. (Pomona)
Cal. St. U. (Chico)
Cal. St. U. (Fresno)
U. Cal. (Berkeley)
U. Cal. (Davis)
U. Cal. (Riverside)
Cent. Mo. St. U.
Clemson U.
Colo. St. U.
U. Colo.
U. Conn.
Cornell U.
Corpus Christi St. U.
U. Dayton
U. Del.
Drexel U.
East. Ky. U.
Fla. A&M U.
Fla. St. U.
U. Fla.
U. Georgia
U. Hawaii
U. Idaho
Ill. St. U.
U. Ill.
Iowa St. U.
Kans. St. U.

Kent St. U.
U. Ky.
L.S.U.
U. Maine
U. Md.
M.I.T.
U. Mass.
Mich. St. U.
U. Minn.
U. Mo. (Columbia)
U. Mo. (St. Louis)
Miss. St. U.
Miss. St. U. Women
Mont. St. U.
U. Mont.
Murray St. U.
U. Neb.
U. Nev. (Reno)
U. N.H.
S.U.N.Y.C. Environ. Sci. & For. (Syracuse)
N. Mex. St. U.
No. Car. A&T C.
No. Car. St. U. (Raleigh)
No. Dak. St. U.
Northwest Mo. St. U.
Ohio St. U.
Okla. St. U.
Ore. St. U.
Penn. St. U.
Prairie View A&M U.
U. Puerto Rico
Purdue U.
U. Rhode Island
Rutgers U.
Sam Houston St. U.
Santa Clara U.
S. F. Austin St. U.
So. Car. St. U.
So. Dak. St. U.
So. Ill. U. (Carbondale)
Southern U.
Southwest Tex. St. U.
Sul Ross St. U.
Stanford U.
Tarleton St. U.
Tenn. St. U.
U. Tenn.
Tex. A&M U.
Tex. A&M U. (Commerce)
Tex. A&M U. (Kingsville)
Tex. Tech U.
U. Tex. (Austin)

Tuskegee Inst.
Utah St. U.
U. Vt.
Va. Poly. Inst.
Va. St. U.
Wash. St. U.
U. Wash.
Wayne St. U.
West Tex. A&M U.
West Tex. St. U.
W. Va. U.
West. Ill. U.
West. Ky. U.
U. Wis.
U. Wis. (River Falls)
U. Wyo.

Architecture

Ariz. St. U.
U. Ariz.
Auburn U.
Ball St. U.
Buffalo U. (S.U.N.Y.)
Cal. Poly. St. U. (San Luis Obispo)
Cal. St. Poly. U. (Pomona)
U. Cal. (Berkeley)
U.C.L.A.
Carnegie Mellon U.
Catholic U.
C.C.N.Y. (C.U.N.Y.)
U. Cincinnati
Clemson U.
U. Colo. (Denver)
Columbia U.
Cornell U.
Cranbrook Acad. Art
Fla. A&M U.
U. Fla.
Georgia Inst. Tech.
Harvard U.
U. Hawaii
Howard U.
U. Houston
U. Idaho
Ill. Inst. Tech
U. Ill.
U. Ill. (Chicago)
Iowa St. U.
Kans. St. U.
U. Kans.
Kent St. U.
U. Kentucky

L.S.U.
U. Md.
M.I.T.
Miami U. (Ohio)
U. Miami (Fla.)
U. Mich.
U. Minn.
Miss. St. U.
Mont. St. U.
Morgan St. U.
U. Neb.
U. Nev.
N.J.I.T.
U. N. Mex.
N.Y.I.T.
No. Car. St. U. (Raleigh)
U. Notre Dame
Ohio St. U.
Okla. St. U.
U. Okla.
U. Ore.
Penn. St. U.
U. Penn.
Pratt Inst.
Princeton U.
U. Puerto Rico
Rhode Island Sh. D.
R.P.I.
Rice U.
U. So. Cal.
U. So. Fla.
Syracuse U.
Tex. A&M U.
Tex. Tech U.
Tulane U.
U. of Arts
U. Tenn.
U. Tex. (Arlington)
U. Tex. (Austin)
U. Tex. (San Antonio)
U. Utah
Va. Poly. Inst.
U. Va.
Wash. St. U.
Wash. U.
U. Wash.
U. Wis. (Milwaukee)
Yale U.

NAVAL ARCHITECTURE

U. Cal. (Berkeley)
U. Mich.

Area Studies

U. Ala.
U. Albany (S.U.N.Y.)
U. Ariz.
Ball St. U.
Baylor U.
Boston C.
Boston St. U.
Boston U.
Bowl. Gr. St. U.
Brandeis U.
Brown U.
U. Buffalo (S.U.N.Y.)
B.Y.U.
Cal. St. U. (Fullerton)
Cal. St. U. (Long Beach)
Cal. St. U. (L.A.)
U. Cal. (Berkeley)
U.C.L.A.
U. Cal. (San Diego)
Case West. Reserve U.
Catholic U.
U. Chicago
C.C.N.Y. (C.U.N.Y)
Claremont Grad. Sch.
Columbia U.
U. Conn.
U. Dayton
Fairfield U.
Fisk U.
Fla. St. U.
U. Fla.
Georgetown U.
Geo. Wash. U.
Gov. St. U.
Harvard U.
U. Hawaii
Howard U.
Hunter C. (C.U.N.Y.)
U. Ill.
Ind. U.
U. Iowa
John Carroll U.
Johns Hopkins U.
U. Kans.
L.S.U.
U. Md.
U. Miami (Fla.)
Mich. St. U.
U. Mich.
U. Minn.
U. Mo. (Columbia)
Monterey Inst.
N. Mex. Highlands U.

U. N. Mex.
C.U.N.Y.
S.U.N.Y. (Binghamton)
N.Y.U.
Northeastern Ill. U.
No. Ill. U.
No. W. St. U. La.
U. Notre Dame
U. Ore.
Penn. St. U.
U. Penn.
Pepperdine U.
Princeton U.
U. Puerto Rico
Purdue U.
Queens C. (C.U.N.Y.)
St. John's U. (N.Y.)
St. Louis U.
St. Michael's C.
S.D.S.U.
Seton Hall U.
U. So. Cal
So. Meth. U.
Stanford U.
Stetson U.
Syracuse U.
U. Tex. (Austin)
Tulane U.
Union C. (N.Y.)
Utah St. U.
U. Utah
Vanderbilt U.
Vassar C.
Wash. St. U.
Wash. U.
U. Wash.
Wayne St. U.
West. Car. U.
West. Mich. U.
U. Wis.
U. Wyo.
Yale U.
Yeshiva U.

AFRICAN/AFRO-
AMERICAN
STUDIES
U. Albany (S.U.N.Y.)
Boston U.
Brown U.
U. Cal. (Berkeley)
U.C.L.A.
C.C.N.Y. (C.U.N.Y.)
Clark Atlanta U.
Columbia U.
U. Conn.
Cornell U.
Duquesne U.
Emory U.
Fisk U.
U. Fla.
Geo. Wash. U.
Howard U.
Ind. U.
U. Ill.
U. Iowa
Johns Hopkins U.
U. Md. (Baltimore
   Cnty.)
U. Mass.
Morgan St. U.
No. Car. A&T St. U.
Northwestern U.
S.U.N.Y.C. (Brockport)
U. Notre Dame
Ohio St. U.
Ohio U.
Princeton U.
St. John's U. (N.Y.)
Temple U.
U. Tex. (Austin)
U. Wis.
Yale U.

ASIAN LANGUAGES/
STUDIES
U. Ariz.
B.Y.U.
Cal. St. U. (Long Beach)
U. Cal. (Berkeley)
U. Cal. (Irvine)
U.C.L.A.
U. Cal. (San Diego)
U. Cal. (Santa Barbara)
U. Chicago
U. Colo.
Columbia U.
Cornell U.
Duke U.
Fla. St. U.
Geo. Wash. U.
Harvard U.
U. Hawaii
U. Ill.
Ind. U.
U. Iowa
Johns Hopkins U.
U. Kans.
U. Mass.
U. Mich.
U. Minn.
Monterey Inst.
C.U.N.Y. (Grad. Cent.)
U. Notre Dame
N.Y.U.
Ohio U.
U. Ore
U. Penn.
U. Pitt.
Princeton U.
St. John's C. (N.M.)
St. John's U. (N.Y.)
S.D.S.U.
U. San Fran.
U. So. Ca.
Seton Hall U.
Stanford U.
U. Tex. (Austin)
U. Va.
Wash. U. (Mo.)
U. Wash.
U. Wis.
Yale U.

BRAZILIAN
STUDIES
U. Minn.
N.Y.U.

CANADA AREA
STUDIES
Johns Hopkins U.
St. Mary's U.

CARIBBEAN
STUDIES
Fisk U.
S.U.N.Y. (Binghamton)

EGYPTOLOGY
Brown U.
U. Chicago
Johns Hopkins U.

EUROPEAN
STUDIES
Geo. Wash. U.
Ind. U.
Johns Hopkins U.
C.U.N.Y. (Grad. Cent.)
U. Mich.
Princeton U.

HISPANIC/IBERIAN
STUDIES
Brown U.
Cal. St. U. (Los Angeles)

Cal. St. U.
   (Northridge)
U.C.L.A.
U. Cal. (Santa Barbara)
Catholic U.
C.U.N.Y. (Grad. Cent.)
Conn. C.
U. Ill.
Ind. U.
Johns Hopkins U.
U. Minn.
U. N. Mex.
N.Y.U.
U. Notre Dame
U. Pitt.
U. Puerto Rico
San Jose St. U.
So. Meth. U.
U. Wash.
U. Wis.

INDO-EUROPEAN
STUDIES
U.C.L.A.
U. Chicago

ISLAMIC STUDIES/
LITERATURE
U.C.L.A.
Catholic U.
U. Chicago
Johns Hopkins U.

LATIN AMERICAN
STUDIES
U. Ala.
U. Albany (S.U.N.Y.)
American U.
Ariz. St. U.
U. Ariz.
Brown U.
B.Y.U.
Cal. St. U. (L.A.)
U. Cal. (Berkeley)
U.C.L.A
U. Cal. (San Diego)
U. Cal.
   (Santa Barbara)
Catholic U. P.R.
U. Cent. Fla.
U. Chicago
Columbia U.
U. Conn.
Cornell U.
Duke U.
Fla. Intl. U.
U. Fla.
Georgetown U.
Geo. Wash. U.
Ind. U.
U. Ill.
Johns Hopkins U.
U. Kans.
Monterey Inst.
U. N. Mex.
U. No. Car.
   (Chapel Hill)
U. Notre Dame
N.Y.U.
Ohio St. U.
Ohio U.
U. Pac.
U. Pitt.
Princeton U.
Queens C. (C.U.N.Y.)
S.D.S.U.
So. Meth. U.
Stanford U.
U. Tex. (Austin)
Tulane U.
Vanderbilt U.
West Va. U.
U. Wis.

MEDITERRANEAN
STUDIES
Brandeis U.

MEXICAN-
AMERICAN
STUDIES
Cal. St. U. (L.A.)
Cal. St. U.
   (Northridge)
San Jose St. U.

NEAR/MIDDLE
EASTERN STUDIES
U. Ariz.
Brandeis U.
Brown U.
B.Y.U.
U. Cal. (Berkeley)
U.C.L.A.
U. Chicago
Columbia U.
Cornell U.
Georgetown U.
Geo. Wash. U.
Harvard U.
Ind. U.
Johns Hopkins U.
U. Mich.
Monterey Inst.
N.Y.U.
Ohio St. U.
U. Penn.
Princeton U.
U. Tex. (Austin)
U. Utah
U. Va.
Wash. U.
U. Wash.
Wayne St. U.
Yeshiva U.

NEW YORK AREA
STUDIES
C.U.N.Y. (Grad. Ctr.)

NORTH AMERICAN
STUDIES
U. Ala.
U. Alaska
U. Ariz.
Appal. St. U.
Baylor U.
Boston C.
Boston U.
Bowl. Gr. St. U.
Brandeis U.
Buffalo U. (S.U.N.Y)
B.Y.U.
Brown U.
Cal. St. U. (Fullerton)
Cal. St. U. (L.A.)
Cal. St. U. (Northridge)
U. Cal. (Berkeley)
U.C.L.A.
Case West. Res. U.
Columbia U.
U. Del.
East Car. U.
East. Mich. U.
Emory U.
Fla. St. U.
Geo. Wash. U.
Harvard U.
U. Hawaii
Ind. U.
U. Iowa
Johns Hopkins U.
U. Kans.
U. Md.
U. Mass. (Boston)
Mich. St. U.
U. Mich.

U. Minn.
U. Miss.
N. Mex. Highlands U.
U. N. Mex.
S.U.N.Y.C. (Cortland)
N.Y.U.
No. East. St. U.
U. Notre Dame
Penn. St. U.
U. Penn.
Purdue U.
St. Louis
St. Mary's U.
S.D.S.U.
Seton Hall U.
U. So. Maine
Trinity C.
Utah St. U.
Wash. St. U.
C. Wm. & Mary
U. Wyo.
Yale U.

PACIFIC AREA
STUDIES
Geo. Wash. U.
U. Hawaii

RUSSIAN/EAST
EUROPEAN
STUDIES
American U.
Ariz. St. U.
Boston C.
Brown U.
U. Cal. (Davis)
U. Chicago
C.C.N.Y. (C.U.N.Y.)
Columbia U.
Cornell U.
Fla. St. U.
Georgetown U.
Geo. Wash. U.
Harvard U.
Hunter C. (C.U.N.Y.)
U. Ill.
U. Ill. (Chicago)
Ind. U.
U. Iowa
Johns Hopkins U.
U. Kans.
Mich. St. U.
U. Mich.
U. Minn.
Monterey Inst.
Ohio St. U.
Princeton U.
U. So. Cal.
Stanford U.
U. Tex. (Austin)
U. Va.
U. Wash.
Wayne St. U.
U. Wis.
Yale U.

URALIC STUDIES
Columbia U.
Ind. U.

Basic Medical Sciences

(Typically includes
Anatomy, Microbiology,
Pathology, Pharmacology,
Physiology; often in-
cludes Endocrinology,
Neurological Sciences,
Parasitology, Virology)

U. Ala.
U. Ala. (Birm.)

Albany Med. C.
American U.
Angelo St. U.
Ariz. St. U.
U. Ariz.
Ark. St. U.
U. Ark.
Auburn U.
Ball St. U.
Baylor U.
Boston U.
Bowl. Green St. U.
Brandeis U.
B.Y.U.
Brooklyn C. (C.U.N.Y.)
Brown U.
Bryn Mawr C.
Bucknell
U. Buffalo (S.U.N.Y)
Butler U.
Cal. Inst. Tech.
Cal. St. U. (Fresno)
Cal. St. U. (Fullerton)
Cal. St. U. (Long Beach)
Cal. St. U. (L.A.)
U. Cal. (Berkeley)
U. Cal. (Davis)
U. Cal. (Irvine)
U.C.L.A.
U. Cal. (Riverside)
U. Cal. (San Diego)
U. Cal. (San Francisco)
Carnegie Mellon U.
Case West. Res. U.
Catholic U.
U. Cent. Fla.
U. Chicago
U. Cincinnati
C.C.N.Y. (C.U.N.Y.)
Clemson U.
Colo. St. U.
U. Colo.
U. Colo. Health Sci. Ctr.
U. Conn.
U. Conn. Health Ctr.
Columbia U.
Cornell U.
Creighton U.
Dartmouth C.
U. Dayton
U. Del.
DePaul U.
Drexel U.
Duke U.
Duquesne U.
East Car. U.
East Tenn. St. U.
Emory U.
F.D.U.
Finch Univ. Health Sci.
Fla. Inst. Tech.
Fla. St. U.
U. Fla.
Fordham U.
Geo. Mason U.
Georgetown U.
Geo. Wash. U.
Georgia Inst. Tech.
Med. C. Georgia
Georgia St. U.
U. Georgia
Harvard U.
U. Hawaii
U. Health Sci. (Chicago)
Howard U.
Hunter C. (C.U.N.Y.)
Idaho St. U.
U. Idaho
Ill. Inst. Tech.
Ill. St. U.
U. Ill. (Chicago)
Ind. St. U.
Ind. U.

Ind. U.P.U.I.
Iowa St. U.
U. Iowa
James Madison U.
Johns Hopkins U.
Kans. St. U.
U. Kans.
Kent St. U.
U. Ky.
Lehigh U.
Loma Linda U.
L.I.U.
L.S.U. H.S.C.
La. Tech. U.
U. La. (Lafayette)
U. Louisville
Loyola U. Chicago
U. Maine
Marquette U.
Mayo Grad. Sch.
U. Md.
U. Md. (Baltimore)
M.I.T.
U. Mass.
U. Mass. (Worcester)
McNeese St. U.
Meharry Med. C.
Miami U.
U. Miami
Mich. St. U.
Mich. Tech. U.
U. Mich.
U. Minn.
Miss. St. U.
U. Miss. Med. Ctr.
U. Mo. (Columbia)
U. Mo. (K.C.)
Mont. St. U.
U. Mont.
Morehead St. U.
Mt. Sinai Sch. Med.
U. Neb.
U. Neb. Med. Ctr.
U. Nev. (Reno)
U. N.H.
U. Med. & Dent. N.J.
N. Mex. St. U.
U. N. Mex.
U. N. Orleans (Med. Ctr.)
N.Y. Med. C.
S.U.N.Y.C. (Potsdam)
S.U.N.Y. Downstate
S.U.N.Y. Upstate
N.Y.U.
No. Car. Cent. U.
No. Car. St. U. (Raleigh)
U. No. Car. (Chapel Hill)
No. Dak. St. U.
U. No. Dak.
Northeastern U.
No. Ill. U.
U. No. Tex.
No. W. St. U. La.
Northwestern U.
U. Notre Dame
Nova U.
Med. C. Ohio
Ohio St. U.
Ohio U.
Okla. St. U.
U. Okla.
U. Okla. Health Sci. Ctr.
Old Dominion U.
Oregon Health & Sci. U.
Ore. St. U.
U. Ore.
U. Pac.
Penn. St. U.
U. Penn.
Phila. C. Pharm.
U. Pitt.
Princeton U.
U. Puerto Rico

Purdue U.
Queens C. (C.U.N.Y.)
R.P.I.
U. Rhode Island
Rice U.
U. Rochester
Rockefeller U.
Roosevelt U.
Rush U.
Rutgers U.
St. John's U. (N.Y.)
St. Louis U.
S.D.S.U.
San Fran. St. U.
San Jose St. U.
Seton Hall U.
U. So. Ala.
Med. U. So. Car.
So. Dak. St. U.
U. So. Dak.
U. So. Cal.
U. So. Car.
U. So. Fla.
So. Ill. U.
So. Meth. U.
Stanford U.
Stevens Inst. Tech.
Stony Brook U. (S.U.N.Y.)
Syracuse U.
Temple U.
Tenn. St. U.
U. Tenn. (Knoxville)
U. Tenn. (Memphis)
Tex. A&M U.
Tex. A&M U. H.S.C.
Tex. Christian U.
Tex. Tech U. H.S.C.
U. Tex. (Austin)
U. Tex. Health Sci. Ctr. (Houston)
U. Tex. Health Sci. Ctr. (San Antonio)
U. Tex. S.W. Med. Ctr. (Dallas)
U. Tex. Med. Branch (Galveston)
Thom. Jefferson U.
Tufts U.
Tulane U.
U. Tulsa
Uniformed Serv. U. Health Sci.
Utah St. U.
U. Utah
Vanderbilt U.
U. Vt.
Va. Commonwealth U.
Va. Poly. Inst.
Va. St. U.
U. Va.
Villanova U.
Wagner C.
Wake Forest U.
Wash. St. U.
Wash. U.
U. Wash.
Wayne St. U.
W. Va. U.
C. Wm. & Mary
Wayne St. U.
Med. C. Wis.
U. Wis.
Wright St. U.
U. Wyo.
Yale U.
Yeshiva U.

BACTERIOLOGY

U. Iowa
Purdue U.
U. Tenn. (Memphis)
U. Tex. Med. Br. (Galveston)

U. Va.
U. Wis.
W. Va. U.

IMMUNOLOGY

Albany Med. C.
U. Ala.
U. Ariz.
U. Ark. Med Sci.
Baylor C. Med.
Boston U.
Brown U.
U. Buffalo (S.U.N.Y.)
Cal. Inst. Tech.
U. Cal. (Berkeley)
U. Cal. (Davis)
U.C.L.A.
U. Cal. (San Diego)
U. Cal. (San Fran.)
Case West. Res. U.
U. Chicago
Colo. St. U.
U. Colo. Health Sci. Ctr.
U. Conn. Health Ctr.
Cornell U.
Creighton U.
Dartmouth C.
Drexel U.
Duke U.
East Car. U.
Emory U.
Finch U. Health Sci. (Chicago)
Fla. St. U.
U. Fla.
Georgetown U.
Geo. Wash. U.
Harvard U.
U. Ill. (Chicago)
Ind. U.
Iowa St. U.
U. Iowa
Johns Hopkins U.
Kans. St. U.
U. Kans.
U. Ky.
U. Louisville
L.S.U. H.S.C.
Loyola U. (Chicago)
Marquette U.
U. Md. (Baltimore)
M.I.T.
U. Mass.
Mayo Gr. Sch.
U. Med. & Dent. N.J.
U. Miami
Mich. St. U.
U. Mich.
U. Minn.
U. Neb.
N.Y. Med. C.
N.Y.U.
U. No. Car. (Chapel Hill)
U. No. Dak.
U. No. Tex. Health Sci. Ctr.
Northwestern U.
Ohio St. U.
U. Okla. Health Sci. Ctr.
Oregon Health & Sci. U.
Penn. St. U.
U. Penn.
U. Pitt.
Purdue U.
U. Rochester
Rush U.
Rutgers U.
St. Louis U.
U. So. Ala.
U. So. Cal.
Med. U. So. Car.
U. So. Dak.
U. So. Maine
Stanford U.

Stony Brook U. (S.U.N.Y.)
Temple U.
U. Tenn.
Tex. A&M U. H.S.C.
U. Tex. (Austin)
U. Tex. Health Sci. Ctr. (Houston)
U. Tex. Med. Br. (Galveston)
U. Tex. S.W. Med. Ctr. (Dallas)
Thom. Jefferson U.
Tufts U.
Tulane U.
Uniformed Serv. U. Health Sci.
Utah St. U.
U. Utah
Vanderbilt U.
Va. Commonwealth U.
U. Va.
Wake Forest U.
Wash. U.
U. Wash.
Wayne St. U.
W. Va. U.
U. Wis.
Wright St. U.
Yale U.
Yeshiva U.

RADIOLOGICAL SCIENCES

U. Cal. (Irvine)
Colo. St. U.
Georgetown U.
Geo. Wash. U.
U. Iowa
U. Okla.
U. Tex. Health Sci. Ctr. (Houston)
U. Tex. S.W. Med. Ctr. (Dallas)

TOXICOLOGY

U. Ala. (Birmingham)
U. Albany (S.U.N.Y.)
American U.
U. Ariz.
U. Ark.
Brown U.
U. Buffalo (S.U.N.Y.)
U. Cal. (Davis)
U. Cal. (Irvine)
U.C.L.A.
Case West. Res. U.
U. Cincinnati.
U. Colo. Health Sci. Ctr.
Columbia U.
U. Conn.
Cornell U.
Dartmouth C.
Duke U.
Duquesne U.
Fla. A&M U.
U. Fla.
Geo. Wash. U.
Med. C. Georgia
U. Ill. (Chicago)
Ind. U.
Iowa St. U.
Johns Hopkins U.
U. Kans.
U. Ky.
L.I.U.
L.S.U. H.S.C.
U. Louisville
U. Md.
U. Md. (Baltimore)
M.I.T.
U. Mass. Med. Sch. (Worcester)

U. Med. & Dent. N.J.
Mich. St. U.
U. Mich.
U. Minn.
U. Minn. (Duluth)
U. Miss.
U. Miss. Med. Ctr.
U. Mo. (Columbia)
U. Mo. (Kansas City)
U. Neb.
U. N. Mex.
N.Y.U.
No. Car. St. U. (Raleigh)
U. No. Car. (Chapel Hill)
Northeastern U.
Northwestern U.
Ohio St. U.
Oregon St. U.
U. Pac.
U. Pitt.
U. Puerto Rico
Purdue U.
U. Rhode Island
U. Rochester
Rutgers U.
St. John's U. (N.Y.)
S.D.S.U.
U. Sci. Phila.
U. So. Cal.
Stony Brook U.
  (S.U.N.Y.)
U. Tenn.
Tex. A&M U.
Tex. A&M U. H.S.C.
Tex. Tech U.
U. Tex. Health Sci. Ctr.
  (Houston)
U. Tex. Med. Br.
  (Galveston)
Thom. Jeff. U.
Utah St. U.
U. Utah
Vanderbilt U.
Va. Commonwealth U.
Wash. St. U.
U. Wash.
Wayne St. U.
W. Va. U.
Med. C. Wis.
U. Wis.
Wright St. U.

Biological Sciences

(Typically includes Biology, Botany, Zoology/Entomology; often includes Marine Biology, Fisheries Biology; see also *Basic Medical Sciences*)

A.C.U.
Adelphi U.
U. Akron
Ala. A&M U.
Ala. St. U.
U. Ala.
U. Ala. (Birm.)
U. Alaska
Albany Med. C.
U. Albany (S.U.N.Y.)
American U.
Andrews U.
Angelo St. U.
Appal. St. U.
Ariz. St. U.
U. Ariz.
Ark. St. U.
U. Ark.
Auburn U.
Austin Peay St. U.
Ball St. U.
Barry U.

Baylor U.
Bemidji St. U.
Bloomsburg U. Pa.
Boise St. U.
Boston C.
Boston U.
Bowl. Gr. St. U.
Bradley U.
Brandeis U.
U. Bridgeport
Bridgewater St. U.
Buffalo U. (S.U.N.Y.)
B.Y.U.
Brooklyn C. (C.U.N.Y.)
Brown U.
Bryn Mawr C.
Bucknell U.
Cal. Inst. Tech.
Cal. Poly. St. U. (San
  Luis Obispo)
Cal. St. Poly. U.
  (Pomona)
Cal. St. U. (Chico)
Cal. St. U. (Fresno)
Cal. St. U. (Fullerton)
Cal. St. U. (Hayward)
Cal. St. U. (L.A.)
Cal. St. U. (Long Beach)
Cal. St. U. (Northridge)
Cal. St. U. (Sacramento)
Cal. St. U. (San
  Bernardino)
Cal. St. U. (San Marcos)
Cal. St. U. (Stanislaus)
U. Cal. (Berkeley)
U. Cal. (Davis)
U. Cal. (Irvine)
U.C.L.A.
U. Cal. (Riverside)
U. Cal. (San Diego)
U. Cal. (San Francisco)
U. Cal. (Santa Barbara)
U. Cal. (Santa Cruz)
Carnegie Mellon U.
Case West. Res. U.
Catholic U.
U. Cent. Ark.
U. Cent. Fla.
Cent. Mich. U.
Cent. Mo. St. U.
U. Cent. Okla.
Cent. Wash. U.
Chicago St. U.
U. Chicago
U. Cincinnati
C.C.N.Y. (C.U.N.Y)
Clarion U. Pa.
Clark Atlanta U.
Clark U.
Clemson U.
Cleve. St. U.
Colo. St. U.
U. Colo.
U. Colo. Health Sci. Ctr.
Columbia U.
U. Conn.
U. Conn. Health Ctr.
Cornell U.
Creighton U.
Dartmouth C.
U. Dayton
U. Del.
Del. St. U.
Delta St. U.
U. Denver
DePaul U.
U. Detroit Mercy
Drexel U.
Duke U.
Duquesne U.
East Car. U.
East Stroudsburg U. Pa.
East Tenn. St. U.

East. Ill. U.
East. Ky. U.
East. Mich. U.
East. N. Mex. U.
East Tenn. St. U.
East. Va. Med. Sch.
East. Wash. U.
Edinboro U. Pa.
Emory U.
Emporia St. U.
F.D.U. (Madison)
F.D.U. (Teaneck)
Finch U. Health Sci.
Fisk U.
Fla. A&M U.
Fla. Atlantic U.
Fla. Inst. Tech.
Fla. St. U.
U. Fla.
Fordham U.
Fort Hays St. U.
Frostburg St. U.
Geo. Mason U.
Georgetown U.
Geo. Wash. U.
Med. C. Georgia
Georgia C. St. U.
Georgia Inst. Tech.
Georgia So. U.
Georgia St. U.
U. Georgia
Hampton U.
U. Hartford
Harvard U.
U. Hawaii
Hofstra U.
U. Houston
Howard U.
Humboldt St. U.
Hunter C. (C.U.N.Y.)
Idaho St. U.
U. Idaho
Ill. Inst. Tech.
Ill. St. U.
U. Ill.
U. Ill. (Chicago)
Incarnate Word U.
U. Indianapolis
Ind. St. U.
Ind. U.
Ind. U. Penn.
I.U.P.U.I.
Iowa St. U.
U. Iowa
Jackson St. U.
Jacksonville St. U.
James Madison U.
John Carroll U.
Johns Hopkins U.
Kans. St. U.
U. Kans.
Kent St. U.
U. Ky.
Lamar U.
Lehigh U.
Lehman C. (C.U.N.Y.)
Loma Linda U.
L.I.U.
L.S.U.
L.S.U. H.S.C.
La. Tech U.
U La. (Lafayette)
U. La. (Monroe)
U. Louisville
Loyola U. Chicago
Loyola U. (La.)
U. Maine
Marquette U.
Marshall U.
U. Md. (Baltimore)
U. Md. (Baltimore Cnty.)
Marywood U.
M.I.T.

U. Mass.
Mayo Grad. Sch.
McNeese St. U.
Meharry Med. C.
Miami U. (Ohio)
U. Miami (Fla.)
Mich. St. U.
Mich. Tech. U.
U. Mich.
Mid. Tenn. St. U.
Midwest St. U.
Midwest U.
Millersville U. Pa.
Minn. St. U. (Mankato)
U. Minn.
Miss. C.
Miss. St. U.
U. Miss.
U. Mo. (Columbia)
U. Mo. (K.C.)
U. Mo. (St. Louis)
Mont. St. U.
U. Mont.
Montclair U.
Morehead St. U.
Morehouse Sch. Med.
Morgan St. U.
Mt. Sinai Sch. Med.
Murray St. U.
N.J.I.T.
U. Neb. (Kearney)
U. Neb. (Omaha)
U. Nev.
U. Nev. (Reno)
U. N.H.
U. Med. & Dent. N.J.
N. Mex. Highlands U.
N. Mex. St. U.
U. N. Mex.
U. N. Orleans
U. N. Orleans (Med. Ctr.)
New Sch. U.
Pittsburgh St. U.
S.U.N.Y. (Binghamton)
S.U.N.Y.C. (Brockport)
S.U.N.Y.C. (Buffalo)
S.U.N.Y.C. (Cortland)
S.U.N.Y.C. (Fredonia)
S.U.N.Y.C. (Geneseo)
S.U.N.Y.C. (New Paltz)
S.U.N.Y.C. (Oneonta)
S.U.N.Y.C. (Plattsburgh)
S.U.N.Y.C. Environ. Sci.
  & For. (Syracuse)
N.Y. Inst. Tech.
N.Y. Med. C.
N.Y.U.
U. No. Ala.
No. Car. A&T St. U.
No. Car. Cent. U.
No. Car. St. U. (Raleigh)
U. No. Car. (Chapel Hill)
U.N.C. (Charlotte)
U. No. Car. (Greensboro)
U. No. Colo.
No. Dak. St. U.
U. No. Dak.
U. No. Fla.
U. No. Tex.
Northeastern U.
Northeastern Ill. U.
No. E. Mo. St. U.
No. Ariz. U.
U. No. Colo.
No. Ill. U.
U. No. Iowa
No. Mich. U.
Northwest Mo. St. U.
Northwestern U.
U. Notre Dame
Nova U.
Oakland U.
Occidental C.

Med. C. Ohio
Ohio St. U.
Ohio U.
Okla. St. U.
U. Okla.
U. Okla. Health Sci. Ctr.
Old Dom. U.
Ore. Health & Sci. U.
Ore. St. U.
U. Ore.
U. Pac.
Med. C. Penn.
Penn. St. U.
U. Penn.
Pittsburg St. U.
U. Pitt.
Ponce Sch. Med.
Portland St. U.
Prairie View A&M U.
Princeton U.
U. Puerto Rico
Purdue U.
Purdue U. (Calumet)
Queens C. (C.U.N.Y.)
Quinnipiac C.
R.P.I.
Rhode Island C.
U. Rhode Island
Rice U.
U. Richmond
U. Rochester
Rockefeller U.
Rutgers U.
Rush U.
St. Cloud St. U.
St. Francis U.
St. John's U. (N.Y.)
St. Joseph C. (Conn.)
St. Louis U.
St. Mary's U.
Sam Houston St. U.
San Fran. St. U.
U. San Fran.
S.D.S.U.
San Jose St. U.
Seton Hall U.
Shippensburg U. Pa.
Smith C.
Sonoma St. U.
U. So. Ala.
Med. U. So. Car.
So. Car. St. U.
U. So. Car.
So. Dak. St. U.
U. So. Dak.
U. So. Fla.
So. Conn. St. U.
Southeast Mo. St. U.
Southeastern Mass. U.
U. So. Cal.
So. Conn. St. U.
So. Ill. U.
So. Ill. U.
  (Edwardsville)
So. Meth. U.
U. So. Miss.
So. U. A&M C.
Southwest Mo. St. U.
Southwest Tex. St. U.
Stanford U.
S.F. Austin St. U.
Stevens Inst. Tech.
Stony Brook U.
  (S.U.N.Y.)
Sul Ross St. U.
Syracuse U.
Temple U.
Tenn. St. U.
Teachers C. (Columbia
  U.)
Tenn. Tech. U.
U. Tenn.
U. Tenn. (Memphis)

U. Tenn. (Oak Ridge)
Tex. A&M U.
Tex. A&M U.
  (Commerce)
Tex. A&M U. H.S.C.
Tex. Christ. U.
Tex. So. U.
Tex. Tech U.
Tex. Tech U. H.S.C.
Tex. Woman's U.
U. Tex. (Arlington)
U. Tex. (Austin)
U. Tex. (Dallas)
U. Tex. (El Paso)
U. Tex. (San Antonio)
U. Tex. (Southwestern
  Med. Sch. Dallas)
U. Tex. (Tyler)
U. Tex. Health Sci. Ctr.
  (Houston)
U. Tex. Health Sci. Ctr.
  (San Antonio)
Thom. Jeff. U.
U. Toledo
Touro C.
Towson U.
Tufts U.
Tulane U.
U. Tulsa
Tuskegee U.
Uniformed Services U.
Utah St. U.
U. Utah
U. Vt.
Vanderbilt U.
Villanova U.
Va. Commonwealth U.
Va. Poly. Inst.
Va. St. U.
U. Va.
Wake Forest U.
Walla Walla C.
Wash. St. U.
Wash. U. (Mo.)
U. Wash.
Wayne St. U.
Wesleyan U.
West Chester U. Pa.
U. West Fla.
West Tex. St. U.
W. Va. U.
West. Car. U.
West. Conn. St. U.
West. Ill. U.
West. Ky. U.
West. Mich. U.
West N. Mex. U.
West. Wash. U.
Wichita St. U.
Wilkes U.
C. Wm. & Mary
Wm. Patterson U.
Winona St. U.
Med. C. Wis.
U. Wis.
U. Wis. (Eau Claire)
U. Wis. (La Crosse)
U. Wis. (Milwaukee)
U. Wis. (Oshkosh)
U. Wis. (Platteville)
Worcester Poly. Inst.
Worcester St. C.
Wright St. U.
U. Wyo.
Yale U.
Yeshiva U.
Youngstown St. U.

BIOCHEMISTRY

U. Ala. (Birmingham)
U. Alaska
U. Albany (S.U.N.Y.)
U. Ak.

Albany Med. C.
Ariz. St. U.
U. Ariz.
U. Ark.
Baylor C. Med.
Boston C.
Boston U.
Brandeis U.
Buffalo U. (S.U.N.Y.)
B.Y.U.
Brown U.
Bryn Maw C.
Cal. Inst. Tech.
Cal. St. U. (Fullerton)
Cal. St. U. (Hayward)
Cal. St. U. (Long Beach)
Cal. St. U. (L.A.)
U. Cal. (Berkeley)
U. Cal. (Davis)
U. Cal. (Irvine)
U. C. L. A.
U. Cal. (Riverside)
U. Cal. (San Diego)
U. Cal. (San Fran.)
U. Cal. (Santa Barbara)
Carnegie Mellon U.
Case West. Res. U.
C.C.N.Y. (C.U.N.Y.)
U. Chicago
U. Cincinnati
Clemson U.
Colo. St. U.
U. Colo.
Columbia U.
U. Conn. Health Ctr.
Cornell U.
Creighton U.
Dartmouth C.
U. Del.
De Paul U.
Duke U.
Duquesne U.
East. Car. U.
East Tenn. St. U.
Emory U.
Finch U. Health Sci.
Fla. St. U.
U. Fla.
Georgetown U.
George Washington U.
Med. C. Georgia
Georgia Inst. Tech.
Georgia St. U.
U. Georgia
Harvard U.
U. Hawaii
U. Houston
Howard U.
Hunter C. (C.U.N.Y.)
U. Idaho
Ill. Inst. Tech.
U. Ill.
U. Ill. (Chicago)
Ind. U.
I.U.P.U.I.
Iowa St. U.
U. Iowa
Johns Hopkins U.
Kans. St. U.
U. Kans.
Kent St. U.
U. Ky.
Lehigh U.
Loma Linda U.
L.S.U. H.S.C.
U. Louisville
Loyola U. Chicago
U. Maine
U. Md.
U. Md. (Baltimore)
U. Md. (Baltimore
  County)
M.I.T.

U. Mass.
U. Mass. (Lowell)
U. Mass. (Med. C.
  Worcester)
Mayo Grad. Sch.
Meharry Med. C.
Miami U.
U. Miami
Mich. St. U.
U. Mich.
U. Minn.
U. Minn. (Duluth)
Miss. St. U.
U. Miss. Med. C.
U. Mo. (Columbia)
U. Mo. (K.C.)
U. Mo. (St. Louis)
Mont. St. U.
U. Mont.
Mt. Sinai Sch. Med.
U. Neb.
U. Neb. Med. Ctr.
U. Nev. (Reno)
U.N.H.
U. Med. & Dent. N.J.
N. Mex. Inst. M&T
N. Mex. St. U.
U. N. Mex.
S.U.N.Y. Downstate
S.U.N.Y. Upstate
New York Med. C.
N.Y.U.
No. Car. St. U.
U. No. Car. (Chapel Hill)
No. Dak. St. U.
U. N. Dak.
No. Ill. U.
U. No. Tex.
Northwestern U.
U. Notre Dame
Med. C. Ohio
Ohio St. U.
Ohio U.
Okla. St. U.
U. Okla. Health Sci. C.
Old Dom. U.
Ore. Health & Sci. U.
Ore. St. U.
U. Ore.
U. Pac.
Med. C. Penn.
Penn St. U.
U. Penn.
U. Pitt.
U. Puerto Rico
Purdue U.
Queens U. (C.U.N.Y.)
R.P.I.
U. Rhode Island
Rice U.
U. Rochester
Rush U.
Rutgers U.
St. Louis U.
U. San Fran.
San Jose St. U.
U. Scranton
Seton Hall U.
U. So. Ala.
U. So. Cal.
U. So. Car.
Med. U. So. Car.
So. Dak. St. U.
So. Ill. U.
U. So. Miss.
So. U. A&M.C.
Stanford U.
Stevens Inst. Tech.
Stony Brook (S.U.N.Y.)
Syracuse U.
Temple U.
U. Tenn.
U. Tenn. (Memphis)

Tex. A&M U.
Tex. A&M U. H.S.C.
Tex. Tech U. H.S.C.
U. Tex. (Austin)
U. Tex. Health Sci. Ctr.
  (Houston)
U. Tex. Health Sci. Ctr.
  (San Antonio)
U. Tex. Med. Branch
  (Galveston)
U. Tex. S.W. Med. Ctr.
  (Dallas)
Thom. Jefferson U.
U. Toledo
Tufts U.
Tulane U.
Uniformed Services U.
  Health Ctr.
Utah St. U.
U. Utah
Va. Commonwealth U.
Va. Poly. Inst.
U. Va.
Vanderbilt U.
Villanova U.
U. Vt.
Wake Forest U.
Wash. St. U.
Wash. U.
U. Wash.
Wayne St. U.
Wesleyan U.
W. Va. U.
Med. C. Wis.
U. Wis.
Wright St. U.
Yale U.
Yeshiva U.

BIOMATHEMATICS/
BIOSTATISTICS

U. Ala. (Birmingham)
Ariz. St. U.
Boston U.
Brown U.
Buffalo U. (S.U.N.Y.)
U. Cal. (Berkeley)
U.C.L.A.
Case West. Res. U.
U. Cinn.
Columbia U.
Drexel U.
Emory U.
Geo. Mason U.
Georgetown U.
Geo. Wash. U.
Harvard U.
Iowa St. U.
Johns Hopkins U.
U. Ill. (Chicago)
U. Iowa
Loma Linda U.
U. Mass.
U. Mich.
U. Minn.
Mt. Sinai Sch. Med.
N.Y. Med. C.
N.Y.U.
No. Car. St. U. (Raleigh)
U. N.C. (Chapel Hill)
Ohio St. U.
U. Okla. Health Sci. Ctr.
Ore. Health & Sci. U.
U. Penn.
U. Pitt.
Rice U.
U. Rochester
Stony Brook U. (S.U.N.Y.)
S.D.S.U.
Med. U. So. Car.
U. So. Cal.
U. So. Car.
Tulane U.

U. Utah
Vanderbilt U.
Va. Commonwealth U.
U. Vt.
West. Mich. U.
U. Wash.
Med. C. Wis.
Yale U.

BIOMETRY/
BIOMETRICS

U. Ala. (Birmingham)
U. Albany (S.U.N.Y.)
U. Buffalo (S.U.N.Y.)
U.C.L.A.
Case West. Res. U.
U. Colo. Health Sci. Ctr.
Columbia U.
Cornell U.
L.S.U. H.S.C.
U. Minn.
Mt. Sinai Sch. Med.
U. Neb.
No. Car. St. U. (Raleigh)
U. N.C. (Chapel Hill)
Oregon St. U.
U. So. Cal.
Med. U. So. Car.
Temple U.
U. Tex. Health Sci. Ctr.
  (Houston)
Va. Commonwealth U.
U. Wis.

BIOPHYSICS

U. Ala. (Birmingham)
Ariz. St. U.
U. Ark.
Baylor C. Med.
Boston U.
Brandeis U.
U. Buffalo (S.U.N.Y.)
Cal. Inst. Tech.
Carnegie Mellon U.
Case West. Res. U.
U. Cal. (Berkeley)
U. Cal. (Davis)
U. Cal. (Irvine)
U. Cal. (San Diego)
U. Cal. (San Fran.)
U. Chicago
U. Cincinnati
Clemson U.
U. Colo.
Columbia U.
U. Conn.
Cornell U.
Duke U.
East Car. U.
East Tenn. St. U.
Emory U.
Fla. St. U.
Georgetown U.
Harvard U.
U. Hawaii
U. Houston
Howard U.
U. Ill.
U. Ill. (Chicago)
Ind. U.
I.U.P.U.I.
Iowa St. U.
U. Iowa
Johns Hopkins U.
U. Ky.
U. Louisville
L.S.U. H.S.C.
U. Md. (Baltimore)
Mayo Grad. Sch.
U. Miami
Mich. St. U.
U. Mich.
M.I.T.

U. Minn.
U. Miss.
U. Mo. (Kansas City)
Mt. Sinai Sch. Med.
U. Neb.
U. Med. & Dent. N.J.
S.U.N.Y. Downstate
N.Y.U.
Northwestern U.
U. Notre Dame
Med. C. Ohio
Ohio St. U.
U. Okla. Health Sci. Ctr.
Ore. St. U.
U. Penn.
U. Pitt.
Princeton U.
Purdue U.
R.P.I.
U. Rhode Island
U. Rochester
U. So. Cal.
U. So. Fla.
Stanford U.
Stony Brook U. (S.U.N.Y.)
Syracuse U.
U. Tenn. (Memphis)
Tex. A&M U.
U. Tex. (Arlington)
U. Tex. (Austin)
U. Tex. (Houston)
U. Tex. S.W. Med. Ctr.
   (Dallas)
U. Utah
U. Vt.
Va. Commonwealth U.
Va. Poly. Inst.
U. Va.
Vanderbilt U.
Wake Forest U.
Wash. St. U.
Wash. U.
U. Wash.
Wayne St. U.
Med. C. Wis.
U. Wis.
Wright St. U.

BIOTECHNOLOGY
Brown U.
U. Conn.
Dartmouth C.
East Car. U.
Ill. Inst. Tech.
U. Ill. (Chicago)
U. Minn.
No. Car. St. U.
U. No. Tex.
Northwestern U.
Penn. St. U.
U. Penn
Tex. A&M U.
U. Tex. (San Antonio)
Thom. Jefferson U.
Tufts U.
U. Va.
U. Wash.
U. Wis.
Worcester Poly Inst.

CANCER BIOLOGY
U. Ariz.
Harvard U.
Northwestern U.
Stanford U.
Wayne St. U.
Yeshiva U.

CELL BIOLOGY
U. Ala.
Albany Med. C.
U. Albany (S.U.N.Y.)
Ariz. St. U.

U. Ariz.
Baylor C. Med.
Boston U.
Brandeis U.
Brown U.
U. Buffalo (S.U.N.Y.)
Cal. Inst. Tech.
U. Cal. (Berkeley)
U. Cal. (Davis)
U. Cal. (Irvine)
U.C.L.A.
U. Cal. (San Diego)
U. Cal. (San Fran.)
U. Cal. (Santa Barbara)
Carnegie Mellon U.
Case West. Res. U.
Catholic U.
U. Chicago
U. Cincinnati
Colo. St. U.
U. Colo.
U. Colo. Health Sci. Ctr.
Columbia U.
U. Conn.
U. Conn. Health Ctr.
Cornell U.
Creighton U.
Dartmouth C.
U. Del.
Duke U.
East Car. U.
East Tenn. St. U.
Emory U.
Emporia St. U.
Finch U. Health Sci.
Fla. St. U.
U. Fla.
Geo. Mason U.
Geo. Wash. U.
Georgetown U.
Med. C. Ga.
Georgia St. U.
U. Georgia
Harvard U.
U. Hawaii
Ill. Inst. Tech.
U. Ill.
U. Ill. (Chicago)
Ind. U.
I.U.P.U.I.
Iowa State U.
U. Iowa
James Madison U.
Johns Hopkins U.
Kansas St. U.
U. Kans.
Kent St. U.
L.I.U.
L.S.U. H.S.C.
Loyola U. (Chicago)
U. Md.
U. Md. (Baltimore)
U. Md. (Baltimore Cnty.)
Marquette U.
M.I.T.
U. Mass.
U. Mass. Med. Ctr.
   (Worcester)
U. Miami
Mich. St. U.
U. Mich.
U. Minn.
U. Minn. (Duluth)
Mt. Sinai Sch. Med.
U. Mo. (Kansas City)
U. Mo. (St. Louis)
U. Neb.
U. Nev. (Reno)
U. Med. & Dent. N.J.
U. N. Mex.
S.U.N.Y. Downstate
S.U.N.Y. Upstate
N.Y. Med. C.

N.Y.U.
No. Car. St. U.
U. No. Car. (Chapel Hill)
No. Dak. St. U.
Northwestern U.
U. Notre Dame
Oakland U.
Med. C. Ohio
Ohio St. U.
Ohio U.
U. Okla.
Ore. Health & Sci. U.
Ore. St. U.
Penn. St. U.
U. Penn.
U. Pitt.
Princeton U.
Purdue U.
R.P.I.
Rice U.
U. Rochester
Rutgers U.
St. Louis U.
S.D.S.U.
San Fran. St. U.
U. So. Ala.
U. So. Cal.
Med. U. So. Car.
U. So. Car.
U. So. Dak.
U. So. Fla.
So. W. Mo. St. U.
Stanford U.
Stony Brook U. (S.U.N.Y.)
Temple U.
U. Tenn.
U. Tenn. (Memphis)
Tex. A&M U.
Tex Tech U. H.S.C.
U. Tex. (Austin)
U. Tex. (Dallas)
U. Tex. (San Antonio)
U. Tex. Health Sci. Ctr.
   (Houston)
U. Tex. Health Sci. Ctr.
   (San Antonio)
U. Tex. Med. Br.
   (Galveston)
U. Tex. S.W. Med. Ctr.
   (Dallas)
Thom. Jefferson U.
Tufts U.
Tulane U.
Uniformed Serv. U.
   Health Sci.
U. Utah
Vanderbilt U.
U. Vt.
U. Va.
Va. Commonwealth U.
Va. Poly. Inst. & St. U.
Wash. St. U.
Wash. U.
U. Wash.
Wayne St. U.
Wesleyan U.
W. Va. U.
Med. C. Wis.
U. Wis.
Yale U.
Yeshiva U.

**ENVIRONMENTAL
BIOLOGY**
Baylor U.
U. Cal. (Berkeley)
Duquesne U.
U. Colo.
East. Ill. U.
Ga. St. U.
Gov. St. U.
Hood C.
U. La. (Lafayette)

U. Louisville
U. Mass. (Boston)
Mont. St. U.
S.U.N.Y.C. Environ. Sci.
   & For. (Syracuse)
U. Nev.
U. No. Dak.
U. Notre Dame
N.Y.U.
Ohio U.
Rutgers U.
Sonoma St. U.
U. So. Miss.
Tenn. Tech. U.
Tulane U.
Wash. U.
W. Va. U.
U. Wis.

**GENETIC
COUNSELING**
U. Cal. (Berkeley)
U. Cal. (Irvine)
Case West. Res. U.
U. Cinn.
U. Colo.
Johns Hopkins U.
U. Minn.
Northwestern U.
U. Pitt.
U. So. Car.
U. Tex. Health Sci. Ctr.
   (Houston)
Va. Commonwealth U.

GENETICS
U. Ala. (Birmingham)
Albany Med. C.
U. Albany (S.U.N.Y.)
Ariz. St. U.
U. Ariz.
Baylor C. Med.
Brandeis U.
U. Buffalo (S.U.N.Y.)
B.Y.U.
Cal. Inst. Tech.
U. Cal. (Davis)
U. Cal. (Irvine)
U.C.L.A.
U. Cal. (San Diego)
U. Cal. (San Fran.)
Carnegie Mellon U.
Case West. Res. U.
U. Chicago
U. Cincinnati
Clemson U.
Colo. St. U.
U. Colo.
U. Colo. Health Sci. Ctr.
Columbia U.
U. Conn.
U. Conn. Health Ctr.
Cornell U.
Dartmouth C.
U. Del.
Duke U.
Emory U.
Fla. St. U.
U. Fla.
Geo. Wash. U.
Georgia St. U.
U. Georgia
Harvard U.
U. Hawaii
Howard U.
Hunter C. (C.U.N.Y.)
Ill. St. U.
U. Ill. (Chicago)
Ind. U.
Iowa St. U.
I.U.P.U.I.
U. Iowa
Johns Hopkins U.

Kans. St. U.
U. Kans. Med. Ctr.
L.S.U. H.S.C.
U. Md.
U. Md. (Baltimore)
Marquette U.
U. Mass. Med. Ctr.
   (Worcester)
U. Miami
M.I.T.
Mich. St. U.
U. Mich.
U. Minn.
Miss. St. U.
U. Mo. (Columbia)
U. Mo. (St. Louis)
Mont. St. U.
Mt. Sinai Sch. Med.
U. Med. & Dent. N.J.
U. N.H.
N.Y.U.
No. Car. St. U.
U. N. Mex.
U. No. Car. (Chapel Hill)
U. No. Tex.
U. Notre Dame
Northwestern U.
Med. C. Ohio
Ohio St. U.
Okla. St. U.
Ore. Health & Sci. U.
Ore. St. U.
U. Ore.
Penn. St. U.
U. Penn.
U. Pitt.
Purdue U.
U. Rhode Island
U. Rochester
Rockefeller U.
Rutgers U.
U. So. Cal.
Med. U. So. Car.
Stanford U.
Stony Brook U.
   (S.U.N.Y.)
Temple U.
U. Tenn.
Tex. A&M U.
Tex. A&M U. H.S.C.
U. Tex. Health Sci. Ctr.
   (Houston)
U. Tex. Health Sci. Ctr.
   (San Antonio)
U. Tex. S.W. Med. Ctr.
   (Dallas)
Thom. Jefferson U.
Tufts U.
Tulane U.
Uniformed Serv. U.
   Health Sci.
U. Utah
U. Vt.
Va. Commonwealth U.
Va. Poly. Inst.
U. Va.
Wake Forest U.
Wash. St. U.
Wash. U.
U. Wash.
Wayne St. U.
W. Va. U.
Med. C. Wis.
U. Wis.
Yale U.
Yeshiva U.

**MARINE BIOLOGY/
SCIENCE**
U. Alaska
Cal. St. U. (Stanislaus)
U. Cal. (San Diego)
U. Hawaii

U. Houston
U. Maine
U. Md.
U. Miami
U. No. Car. (Wilmington)
Nova U.
U. So. Fla.

MOLECULAR BIOLOGY

U. Ala. (Birmingham)
Albany Med. C.
U. Albany (S.U.N.Y.)
Ariz. St. U.
U. Ariz.
U. Ark.
Baylor C. Med.
Boston U.
Brown U.
U. Buffalo (S.U.N.Y.)
B.Y.U.
Cal. Inst. Tech.
U. Cal. (Berkeley)
U. Cal. (Davis)
U. Cal. (Irvine)
U.C.L.A.
U. Cal. (San Diego)
U. Cal. (San Francisco)
U. Cal. (Santa Barbara)
Carnegie Mellon U.
Case West. Res. U.
U. Chicago
U. Cinn.
Colo. St. U.
U. Colo.
U. Colo. Health Sci. Ctr.
Columbia U.
U. Conn.
U. Conn. Health Ctr.
Cornell U.
Dartmouth C.
U. Del.
Drexel U.
Duke U.
East Car. U.
Emory U.
Fla. St. U.
U. Fla.
Geo. Mason Univ.
Geo. Wash. Univ.
Georgetown U.
Med. C. Georgia
U. Georgia
Harvard U.
U. Hawaii
Howard U.
U. Ill.
U. Ill. (Chicago)
Ind. U.
I.U.P.U.I.
Iowa St. U.
U. Iowa
Johns Hopkins U.
Kans. St. U.
U. Kans.
Kent St. U.
Lehigh U.
L.S.U. H.S.C.
Loyola U. (Chicago)
U. Louisville
U. Md.
U. Md. (Baltimore)
Marquette U.
U. Mass.
U. Mass. Med. Sch. (Worcester)
Mayo Med. Sch.
U. Miami
Mich. St. U.
U. Mich.
U. Minn.
U. Minn. (Duluth)

Miss. St. U.
U. Mo. (K.C.)
Mt. Sinai Sch. Med.
U. Neb.
U. Nev. (Reno)
U. Med. & Dent. N.J.
N. Mex. St. U.
U. N. Mex.
S.U.N.Y. Downstate
S.U.N.Y. Upstate
N.Y. Med. C.
N.Y.U.
U. No. Car. (Chapel Hill)
U. No. Tex. Health Sci. Ctr.
Northwestern U.
U. Notre Dame
Med. C. Ohio
Ohio St. U.
Ohio U.
Okla. St. U.
U. Okla.
Ore. Health & Sci. U.
U. Oregon
Penn. St. U.
U. Penn.
U. Pitt.
Princeton U.
Purdue U.
R.P.I.
U. Rochester
Rutgers U.
St. Louis U.
S.D.S.U.
San Fran. St. U.
U. So. Ala.
U. So. Cal.
Med. U. So. Car.
U. So. Car.
So. Ill. U.
U. So. Miss.
Stanford U.
Stony Brook (S.U.N.Y.)
Temple U.
U. Tenn.
U. Tenn. (Memphis)
Tex. A&M U.
Tex. A&M U. H.S.C.
U. Tex. (Austin)
U. Tex. (Dallas)
U. Tex. (San Antonio)
U. Tex. Health Sci. Ctr. (Houston)
U. Tex. Health Sci. Ctr. (San Antonio)
U. Tex. Med. Br. (Galveston)
Tex. Woman's U.
Thom. Jeff. U.
Tufts U.
Tulane U.
Uniformed Serv. U. Health Sci.
Utah St. U.
U. Utah
Vanderbilt U.
U. Vt.
Va. Commonwealth U.
Va. Poly. Inst.
U. Va.
Wake Forest U.
Wash. St. U.
Washington U.
U. Wash.
Wayne St. U.
West Va. U.
U. Wis.
Wright St. U.
U. Wyo.
Yale U.
Yeshiva U.

Business

(Business Administration, Commerce, Management: typically includes specializations in Accounting, Finance, Marketing; often includes Advertising, Industrial Administration, Industrial and Labor relations, Insurance, Operations Research, Public Relations, Quality Control, Real Estate, Taxation; majors in Economics are also common in graduate schools of business as well as in graduate schools of arts and science)

A.C.U.
Adelphi U.
U. Akron
Ala. A&M U.
Ala. St. U.
U. Ala.
U. Ala. (Birm.)
U. Ala. (Huntsville)
U. Alaska
U. Albany (S.U.N.Y.)
Alfred U.
Alliant Intl. U.
American U.
Andrews U.
Angelo St. U.
Antioch N.E.
Antioch U. (L.A.)
Antioch U. (McGregor)
Appal. St. U.
Ariz. St. U.
Ariz. St. U. (West)
U. Ariz.
Ark. St. U.
U. Ark.
Armstrong U.
Assump. C.
Auburn U.
Auburn U. (Montgomery)
Augusta St. U.
Austin Peay St. U.
Azusa Pac. U.
Babson C.
Ball St. U.
U. Baltimore
Barry U.
Baruch C. (C.U.N.Y.)
Baylor U.
Bentley C.
Berry C.
Black Hills St. U.
Bloomsburg U. of Pa.
Boise St. U.
Boston C.
Boston U.
Bowie St. U.
Bowl. Gr. St. U.
Bradley U.
U. Bridgeport
U. Buffalo (S.U.N.Y.)
B.Y.U.
Brooklyn C. (C.U.N.Y.)
Bucknell U.
Butler U.
Cal. Luth. U.
Cal. Poly. St. U. (San Luis Obispo)
Cal. St. Poly. U. (Pomona)
Cal. St. U. (Bakersfield)
Cal. St. U. (Chico)
Cal. St. U. (Dominguez Hills)
Cal. St. U. (Fresno)

Cal. St. U. (Fullerton)
Cal. St. U. (Hayward)
Cal. St. U. (Long Beach)
Cal. St. U. (L.A.)
Cal. St. U. (Northridge)
Cal St. U. (Sacramento)
Cal. St. U. (San Bernardino)
Cal. St. U. (San Marcos)
Cal. U. (Pa.)
U. Cal. (Berkeley)
U. Cal. (Davis)
U. Cal. (Irvine)
U.C.L.A.
U. Cal. (Riverside)
Campbell U.
Canisius C.
Capital U.
Card. Stritch C.
Carnegie Mellon U.
Case West. Res. U.
Catholic U.
U. Cent. Ark.
Cent. Conn. St. U.
U. Cent. Fla.
Cent. Mich. U.
Cent. Mo. St. U.
U. Cent. Okla.
Cent. St. U.
Chadron St. U.
Chapman U.
U. Chicago
U. Cincinnati
Citadel
Claremont Grad. U.
Clarion U. of Pa.
Clark Atlanta U.
Clark U.
Clarkson U.
Clemson U.
Cleve. St. U.
Colo. St. U.
U. Colo.
Columbia U.
Columbus St. U.
U. Conn.
Cornell U.
Creighton U.
U. Dallas
Dartmouth C.
U. Dayton
Del. St. U.
U. Del.
Delta St. U.
U. Denver
DePaul U.
U. Detroit Mercy
Dominican U.
Dominican U. Calif.
Drake U.
Drexel U.
Drury U.
U. Dubuque
Duke U.
Duquesne U.
East Carolina U.
East Tenn. St. U.
East. Ill. U.
East. Ky. U.
East. Mich. U.
East. N. Mex. U.
East. Wash. U.
Emory U.
Emporia St. U.
Fairfield U.
F.D.U. (Madison)
F.D.U. (Teaneck)
Fitchburg St. C.
Fla. A&M U.
Fla. Atlantic. U.
Fla. Inst. Tech.
Fla. St. U.
U. Fla.

Fordham U.
Fort Hays St. U.
Framingham St. C.
Frostburg St. U.
Gannon U.
Geo. Mason U.
Georgetown U.
Geo. Wash. U.
Georgia C. St. U.
Georgia Inst. Tech.
Georgia So. C.
Georgia St. U.
U. Georgia
Golden Gate U.
Gonzaga U.
Gov. St. U.
Hamline U.
Hampton U.
Hardin-Simmons U.
U. Hartford
Harvard U.
Hawaii Pac. U.
U. Hawaii
Henderson St. U.
Hofstra U.
Holy Names C.
Hood C.
U. Houston
U. Houston (Clear Lake)
Howard U.
Humbolt St. U.
Idaho St. U.
U. Idaho
C. Insurance
Ill. Inst. Tech.
Ill. St. U.
U. Ill.
U. Ill. (Chicago)
Incarnate Word U.
U. Indianapolis
Ind. St. U.
Ind. U.
I.U.P.U.I.
Ind. U. Penn.
Inter American U.
Iona C.
Iowa St. U.
U. Iowa
Jackson St. U.
Jacksonville St. U.
Jacksonville U.
James Madison U.
John Carroll U.
Johns Hopkins U.
Kans. St. U.
U. Kans.
Kent St. U.
Kutztown U. of Pa.
U. Ky.
U. La. (Lafayette)
U. La. (Monroe)
La Grange C.
Lamar U.
U. LaVerne
Lehigh U.
Lincoln U.
L.I.U.
L.I.U. (C.W. Post)
L.S.U.
L.S.U. Shreveport
La. Tech. U.
U. Louisville
Loyola C. (Md.)
Loyola Marymount U.
Loyola U. (Chicago)
Loyola U. (La.)
Lynchburg C.
U. Maine
Manhattan C.
Marquette U.
Marshall U.
U. Md.
Marywood U.

M.I.T.
U. Mass.
U. Mass. (Boston)
U. Mass. (Dartmouth)
U. Mass. (Lowell)
McNeese St. U.
U. Memphis
Mercer U.
Miami U. (Ohio)
U. Miami (Fla.)
Mich. St. U.
Mich. Tech. U.
U. Mich.
Mid. Tenn. St. U.
Midwest St. U.
Minn. St. U. (Mankato)
Minn. St. U. (Moorhead)
U. Minn.
U. Minn. (Duluth)
Miss. C.
Miss. St. U.
U. Miss.
U. Mo. (Columbia)
U. Mo. (K.C.)
U. Mo. (St. Louis)
Monmouth U.
U. Mont.
Montclair U.
U. Mont.
Morehead St. U.
Morgan St. U.
Murray St. U.
Natl. U.
Natl. Louis U.
Naval P.G. Sch.
U. Neb. (Kearney)
U. Neb.
U. Neb. (Omaha)
U. Nev.
U. Nev. (Reno)
U. N.H.
U. New Haven
N.J.I.T.
N. Mex. Highlands U.
N. Mex. St. U.
U. N. Mex.
U. N. Orleans
C. New Rochelle
New Sch. U.
C.U.N.Y. (Grad. Ctr.)
S.U.N.Y. (Binghamton)
S.U.N.Y. (New Paltz)
S.U.N.Y. C. (Oneonta)
S.U.N.Y. (Oswego)
S.U.N.Y. I.T.
N.Y.I.T.
N.Y.U.
Niagara U.
U. No. Ala.
No. Car. Cent. U.
No. Car. St. U.
U. No. Car. (Chapel Hill)
U. No. Car. (Charlotte)
U. No. Car. (Greensboro)
U. No. Car. (Willmington)
No. Dak. St. U.
U. No. Dak.
U. No. Fla.
U. No. Iowa
U. No. Tex.
No. E. Ill. U.
No. E. St. U.
Northeastern U.
No. Ariz. U.
No. Ill. U.
No. Ky. U.
U. No. Iowa
No. W. Mo. St. U.
Northwestern U.
Notre Dame U.
U. Notre Dame
Nova U.

Oakland U.
Ohio St. U.
Ohio U.
Okla. City U.
Okla. St. U.
U. Okla.
Old Dom. U.
Olivet Naz. U.
Oral Roberts U.
Ore. St. U.
U. Ore.
Our Lady Lake U.
Pace U.
Pac. Luth. U.
U. Pac.
Penn. St. U.
U. Penn.
Pepperdine U. (Culver City)
U. Phoenix
Pittsburg St. U.
U. Pitt.
Plymouth St. C.
Point Loma Nazarene U.
Poly U. N.Y.
Pont. Cath. U. P.R.
Portland St. U.
U. Portland
Prairie View A&M U.
Providence C.
U. Puerto Rico
U. Puerto Rico (Mayaguez)
Purdue U.
Purdue U. (Calumet)
Queens C. (C.U.N.Y.)
Quinnipiac U.
Radford U.
U. Redlands
Regent U.
R.P.I.
U. Rhode Island
Rice U.
Rider U.
Rivier C.
U. Richmond
Robert Morris C.
Rochester Inst. Tech.
U. Rochester
Rockford C.
Rollins C.
Roosevelt U.
Rowan U.
Rutgers U.
Sage Grad. Sch.
Saginaw Val. St. U.
St. Bonaventure U.
St. Cloud St. U.
St. Edward's U.
St. Francis U.
U. St. Francis (Ind.)
St. John's U. (N.Y.)
St. Joseph's U.
St. Louis U.
St. Mary's U. (Minn.)
St. Mary's U. (Tex.)
C. St. Rose
C. St. Scholastica
U. St. Thomas
U. St. Thomas (Tex.)
St. Xavier U.
Salem St. U.
Salisbury St. U.
Samford U.
Sam Houston St. U.
S.D.S.U.
San Fran. St. U.
San Jose St. U.
U. San Diego
U. San Fran.
Santa Clara U.
U. Scranton
Seattle Pac. U.

Seattle U.
Seton Hall U.
Sonoma St. U.
U. So. Ala.
U. So. Cal.
So. Car. St. U.
U. So. Car.
U. So. Dak.
U. So. Fla.
So. East. Mo. St. U.
Southeastern Okla. St. U.
So. Ill. U.
So. Ill. U. (Edwardsville)
U. So. Maine
So. Meth. U.
U. So. Miss.
So. Nazarene U.
So. Ore. U.
So. U. & A&M C.
Southwest Mo. St. U.
Southwest Tex. St. U.
Southwestern Okla. St. U.
Stanford U.
S. F. Austin St. U.
Stetson U.
Stevens Inst. Tech.
Stony Brook U. (S.U.N.Y.)
Suffolk U.
Sul Ross St. U.
Syracuse U
Tarleton St. U.
Temple U.
Tenn. St. U.
Tenn. Tech. U.
U. Tenn.
U. Tenn. (Chattanooga)
U. Tenn. (Martin)
Tex. A&M U.
Tex. A&M U. (Commerce)
Tex. A&M U. (Corpus Christi)
Tex. A&M U. (Kingsville)
Tex. Christ. U.
Tex. So. U.
Tex. Tech U.
Tex. Woman's U.
U. Tex. (Arlington)
U. Tex. (Austin)
U. Tex. (Brownsville)
U. Tex. (Dallas)
U. Tex. (El Paso)
U. Tex. (San Antonio)
U. Tex. (Permian Basin)
U. Tex. (Tyler)
Thunderbird
U. Toledo
Towson U.
Trinity U.
Troy St. U.
Troy St. U. (Dorthan)
Troy St. U. (Montgomery)
Tulane U.
U. Tulsa
Union C.
Utah St. U.
U. Utah
Valdosta St. U.
Vanderbilt U.
U. Vt.
Villanova U.
Va. Commonwealth U.
Va. Poly. Inst.
Va. St. U.
U. Va.
Wagner C.
Wake Forest U.
Washburn U.
Wash. St. U.
Wash. U. (Mo.)

U. Wash.
Wayne St. C.
Wayne St. U.
Webster U.
West Chester U. Pa.
West Ga. C.
West Tex. St. U.
W. Va. U.
West. Car. U.
West. Conn. St. U.
West. Ill. U.
West. Ky. U.
West. Mich. U.
West. New Eng. C.
West. N. Mex. U.
West Tex. A&M U.
W. Va. U.
West. Wash. St. U.
Wichita St. U.
Widener U.
Wilkes U.
Williamette U.
C. Wm. & Mary
Wm. Carey C.
Wm. Paterson U.
Winthrop U.
U. Wis.
U. Wis. (Eau Claire)
U. Wis. (La Crosse)
xU. Wis. (Milwaukee)
U. Wis. (Oshkosh)
U. Wis. (Stevens Point)
U. Wis. (Stout)
U. Wis. (Whitewater)
Worcester Poly. Inst.
Wright St. U.
U. Wyo.
Xavier U. (Ohio)
Yale U.
Youngstown St. U.

ACTUARIAL/ INSURANCE SCIENCES

Ball St. U.
Cent. Conn. St. U.
U. Fla.
Georgia St. U.
U. Hartford
C. Insurance
Ind. U.
U. Mich.
U. Minn.
U. Neb.
N.Y.U.
U. No. Tex.
Penn. St. U.
U. Penn.
Roosevelt U.
Temple U.
Va. Commonwealth U.
U. Wis.
Youngstown St. U.

HOTEL/ HOSPITALITY MANAGEMENT

U. Ala.
Black Hills St. U.
Cent. Mich. U.
Colo. St. U.
Cornell U.
U. Denver
F.D.U. (Madison)
F.D.U. (Teaneck)
Geo. Wash. U.
Golden Gate U.
U. Hawaii
U. Houston
Iowa St. U.
Kans. St. U.
U. Md.
U. Mass.
Mich. St. U.
U. Mo. (Columbia)
U. Nev.
U. New Haven
N.Y.U.
U. No. Car. (Greensboro)
U. No. Tex.
Boston U.
Bowie St. U.
U. Bridgeport
Cal. St. U. (Hayward)
Cal. St. U. (Sacramento)
Chapman U.
Claremont Grad. U.
Clemson U.
Cleveland St. U.
U. Conn.
Cornell U.
U. Dallas
DePaul U.
Drexel U.
East. Cent. U.
F.D.U. (Madison)
F.D.U. (Teaneck)
U. Fla.
Framingham St. C.
Geo. Wash. U.
Georgia St. U.
Golden Gate U.
Hawaii Pac. U.
Hofstra U.
U. Houston
Ill. Inst. Tech.
U. Ill. (Chicago)
Ind. St. U.
Ind. U.
Inter American U.
Ohio St. U.
Okla. St. U.
Penn. St. U.
Purdue U.
R.I.T.
Roosevelt U.
U. So. Cal.
U. So. Car.
Temple U.
U. Tenn.
Va. Poly. Inst.
U. Wis. (Stout)

HUMAN RESOURCE MANAGEMENT

(Typically includes Career Development/ Management, Personnel Management, Industrial and Labor Relations)

A.C.U.
Adelphi U.
U. Ala.
U. Albany (S.U.N.Y.)
American U.
Antioch U. (L.A.)
Auburn U.
Auburn U. (Mont.)
Azusa Pac. U.
Baruch C. (C.U.N.Y.)
Boston C.
Iona C.
Iowa St. U.
Johns Hopkins U.
L.I.U.
Loyola U. (Chicago)
Marquette U.
Marshall U.
Marywood U.
U. Memphis
Mich St. U.
Minn. St. U. (Moorhead)
U. Mo. (St. Louis)
Natl. U.
New Sch. U.
No. Car. A&T U.

U. No. Tex.
Nova U.
N.Y.I.T.
N.Y.U.
Oakland U.
Ohio St. U.
U. Ore.
Penn. St. U.
U. Pitt.
Purdue U.
R.I.T.
Rollins C.
Rutgers U.
Sage Grad. Sch.
St. Francis U. (Pa.)
U. St. Thomas
St. Xavier U.
U. Scranton
S.D.S.U.
U. San Fran.
U. So. Cal.
U. So. Car.
So. East Mo. St. U.
Suffolk U.
Temple U.
U. Tenn.
Tex. A&M U.
Towson U.
Troy St. U.
Vanderbilt U.
Villanova U.
Va. Poly. Inst.
Webster U.
Widener U.
U. Wis. (Milwaukee)
U. Wis. (Stout)
Xavier U.

INFORMATION SCIENCE/STUDIES/ SYSTEMS

U. Ala. (Birmingham)
U. Albany (S.U.N.Y.)
American U.
Ariz. St. U.
U. Ark.
U. Baltimore
Ball St. U.
Bradley U.
Brooklyn C. (C.U.N.Y.)
Buffalo U. (S.U.N.Y.)
B.Y.U.
Cal. St. U. (Fresno)
Cal. St. U. (Fullerton)
U. Cal. (Berkeley)
U. Cal. (Irvine)
U.C.L.A.
U. Cal. (San Fran.)
Carnegie Mellon U.
Case West. Res. U.
U. Cent. Okla.
U. Chicago
Claremont Grad. U.
Columbia U.
U. Del.
DePaul U.
Drexel U.
East Car. U.
East Tenn. St. U.
Fla. Inst. Tech.
U. Fla.
Geo. Mason U.
Geo. Wash. U.
Georgia Inst. Tech.
Georgia St. U.
U. Hawaii
Harvard U.
Hood C.
U. Houston
U. Ill.
Ind. U.
Kans. St. U.
Kutztown U. Pa.

Lamar U.
Lehigh U.
L.I.U. (C.W. Post)
U. Louisville
U. Md.
U. Md. (Baltimore Cnty.)
Marquette U.
Marshall U.
U. Mass.
Mercer U.
U. Miami
U. Minn.
U. Mo. (Columbia)
Montclair U.
U. Nev. (Reno)
U. N. Haven
N.J.I.T.
N.Y.U.
N. Car. Cent. U.
U. No. Car. (Chapel Hill)
U. No. Car.
   (Greensboro)
U. No. Fla.
U. No. Tex.
Northeastern U.
Northwestern U.
Nova U.
Ohio St. U.
Okla. St. U.
U. Oregon
Pace U.
Penn St. U.
U. Penn.
U. Phoenix
U. Pitt.
Poly. U.
Pratt Inst.
Princeton U.
R.P.I.
R.I.T.
U. Rochester
Roosevelt U.
Rutgers U.
St. John's U. (N.Y.)
St. Mary's U. (Tex.)
San Jose St. U.
Seton Hall U.
U. So. Ala.
U. So. Cal.
U. So. Car.
U. So. Fla.
So. Ill. U.
So. Meth. U.
S.U.N.Y. I.T.
Syracuse U.
Temple U.
U. Tenn.
U. Tex. (Austin)
U. Toledo
Towson U.
Troy St. U.
U. Utah
Va. Poly. Tech.
Vanderbilt U.
W. Va. U.
U. Wash.
Wichita St. U.
U. Wis.
U. Wis. (Milwaukee)

INTERNATIONAL BUSINESS/ ECONOMICS

U. Akron
Alliant Intl. U.
American U.
Armstrong U.
Azusa Pac. U.
Babson C.
Baruch C. (C.U.N.Y.)
Baylor U.
Bentley C.
Boston U.

Brandeis U.
Cal. St. U. (Fullerton)
Cal. St. U. (Hayward)
Cal. St. U. (L.A.)
U. Cal. (Berkeley)
Catholic U.
Cent. Mich. U.
U. Chicago
U. Cinn.
Claremont Grad. U.
U. Colo. (Denver)
Columbia U.
U. Conn.
U. Dallas
U. Denver
DePaul U.
Dominican U. (Calif.)
Drury U.
East Mich. U.
Fairfield U.
F.D.U. (Madison)
F.D.U. (Teaneck)
U. Fla.
Geo. Wash. U.
Georgia St. U.
Golden St. U.
U. Hartford
Hawaii Pac. U.
U. Hawaii
Hofstra U.
U. Houston
Ind. U.
Kans. St. U.
U. Ky.
L.I.U. (C.W. Post)
U. Md.
U. Memphis
U. Miami
U. Minn.
Montclair U.
Monterey Inst.
Morgan St. U.
Natl. U.
U. N. Haven
U. N. Mex.
New Sch. U.
N.Y.U.
Nova U.
Okla City U.
U. Okla.
Oral Roberts U.
U. Oregon
Pace U.
Penn. St. U.
U. Penn.
Pepperdine U. (Culver City)
U. Phoenix
Portland St. U.
Quinnipiac U.
Rice U.
U. Rhode Island
Roosevelt U.
Rutgers U.
St. John's U. (N.Y.)
St. Joseph U.
St. Louis U.
St. Thomas U.
S.D.S.U.
U. San Diego
U. San Fran.
Seton Hall U.
U. So. Cal.
U. So. Car.
Suffolk U.
Sul Ross St. U.
Syracuse U.
Temple U.
Tex. Tech U.
U. Tex. (Dallas)
Thunderbird
U. Toledo
U. Tulsa

Wash. St. U.
Wash. U.
U. Wash.
Webster U.
Wilkes U.
U. Wis.
Wright St. U.

MANAGEMENT INFORMATION SYSTEMS

American U.
U. Ariz.
Babson C.
U. Baltimore
Barry U.
Boston C.
Boston U.
Bowie St. U.
Buffalo U. (S.U.N.Y.)
U. Cal. (Berkeley)
Cal. St. Poly. U. (Pomona)
Cal. St. U. (Sacramento)
Carnegie Mellon U.
Case West. Res. U.
U. Chicago
U. Colo.
Columbia U.
U. Denver
DePaul U
Duquesne U.
F.D.U. (Madison)
F.D.U. (Teaneck)
Fla. A&M U.
U. Fla.
Geo. Wash. U.
Georgia C. St. U.
Golden Gate U.
U. Hartford
U. Houston
Ind. U.
Iona C.
L.I.U. (C.W. Post)
Marywood U.
M.I.T.
Miami U.
Mich. St. U.
No. Car. St. U.
Northeastern U.
No. Ill. U.
Northwestern U.
Nova U.
N.Y.U.
Okla. City U.
U. Ore.
Pace U.
Penn St. U
U. Penn.
U. Pitt.
Poly. U.
Purdue U.
Rutgers U.
St. Edward's U.
St. John's U. (N.Y.)
U. San Diego
Seattle Pac. U.
Seton Hall U.
U. So. Cal.
U. So. Dak.
So. Ill. U. (Edwardsville)
So. Meth. U.
Stanford U.
Stevens Inst. Tech.
Syracuse U.
Temple U.
U. Tenn.
Tex. A&M U.
Tex. Tech U.
U. Tex. (San Antonio)
Troy St. U.
Tulane U.
Vanderbilt U.
Wake Forest U.

Wash. U.
Webster U.
West. New Eng. C.
U. Wis. (Milwaukee)
Wright St. U.
Yale U.

MANAGEMENT OF TECHNOLOGY

Boston U.
Cal. Poly. St. U. (San Luis Obispo)
Carnegie Mellon U.
U. Colo.
Fla. Inst. Tech.
Georgia St. U.
U. Minn.
Murray St. U.
Natl. U.
U. Neb. (Omaha)
N.Y.U.
Ore. St. U.
U. Penn.
Pepperdine U.
U. Phoenix
Poly. U.
R.P.I.
Stevens Inst. Tech.
Tex. A&M U.
U. Tex. (San Antonio)
Thunderbird
Wash. St. U.
Wash. U.
U. Wis. (Stout)

MANAGEMENT STRATEGY

Alliant Intl. U.
U. Ariz.
Baruch C. (C.U.N.Y.)
Case West. Res. U.
Claremont Grad. U.
Drexel U.
U. Fla.
Mich. St. U.
U. Minn.
U. No. Car. (Chapel Hill)
U. No. Tex.
Purdue U.
Regent U.
Syracuse U.
Temple U.
U. So. Cal
U. Tenn.
U. Tex. (Austin)
U. Wis.

NONPROFIT MANAGEMENT

Boston U.
Case West. Res. U.
Columbia U.
DePaul U.
Ind. U.
I.U.P.U.I
Marywood U.
U. Mo. (St. Louis)
N.Y.U.
Northwestern U.
Pace U.
U. Penn.
St. Mary's U. (Minn.)
U. St. Thomas
Seattle U.
Suffolk U.

QUANTITATIVE ANALYSIS/STUDIES

Cal. St. U. (Hayward)
Clark Atl. U.
DePaul U.
Drexel U.
F.D.U. (Teaneck)

Hofstra U.
L.S.U.
La. Tech. U.
Loyola C.
Montclair U.
U. No. Car. (Chapel Hill)
N.Y.U.
U. Ore.
Purdue U.
R.P.I.
U. Rhode Island
Rutgers U.
St. John's U. (N.Y.)
St. Louis U.
Seton Hall U.
Tex. Tech U.
U. Tex. (Arlington)
Troy State U. (Dothan)
Va. Commonwealth U.

REAL ESTATE
American U.
U. Ariz.
U. Cal. (Berkeley)
U. Cinn.
Columbia U.
Cornell U.
U. Denver
U. Fla.
Geo. Wash. U.
Georgia St. U.
L.I.U.
U. Memphis
N.Y.U.
U. No. Tex.
Northwestern U.
Penn. St. U.
U. Penn.
U. So. Cal.
So. Meth. U.
Tex. A&M U.
U. Tex. (Arlington)
Va. Commonwealth U.
Webster U.
U. Wis.

TAXATION
U. Akron
U. Ala.
Albany U. (S.U.N.Y.)
American U.
Ariz. St. U.
Baruch C. (C.U.N.Y.)
U. Baltimore
Bentley C.
Boston U.
Cal. St. U. (Fullerton)
Cal. St. U. (Hayward)
Cal. St. U. (L.A.)
Capital U.
Case West. Res. U.
U. Cent. Fla.
U. Colo.
U. Denver
DePaul U.
Drake U.
Drexel U.
Duquesne U.
Fairfield U.
F.D.U. (Madison)
F.D.U. (Teaneck)
Fla. Atlantic U.
U. Fla.
Fordham U.
Georgetown U.
Geo. Wash. U.
Georgia St. U.
Golden Gate U.
U. Hartford
Hofstra U.
Ill. Inst. Tech.
Ind. U.
L.I.U.

L.I.U. (C.W. Post)
Loyola Marymount U.
L.S.U.
U. Memphis
U. Miami
U. Minn.
Miss. St. U.
U. Miss.
U. Mo. (Kansas City)
U. Mo. (St. Louis)
U. N. Haven
U. N. Mex.
U. N. Orleans
S.U.N.Y. (Albany)
N.Y.U.
U. No. Tex.
Northeastern U.
U. Okla.
Pace U.
Regent U.
Robert Morris C.
St. John's U. (N.Y.)
St. Thomas U.
St. Xavier U.
U. San Diego
San Jose St. U.
Seton Hall U.
U. So. Cal.
U. So. Car.
So. Meth. U.
Suffolk U.
Temple U.
U. Tenn.
Tex. Tech U.
U. Tex. (Arlington)
U. Tex. (San Antonio)
U. Toledo
U. Tulsa
Va. Commonwealth U.
Villanova U.
U. Wash.
Wayne St. U.
Widener U.

Communications
(Includes Mass
Organizational
Communication)
A.C.U.
U. Akron
U. Ala.
U. Alaska
U. Albany (S.U.N.Y.)
American U.
Andrews U.
Angelo St. U.
Ariz. St. U.
U. Ariz.
Ark. St. U.
U. Ark. (Little Rock)
Art Inst. Chicago
Auburn U.
Austin Peay St. U.
Ball St. U.
U. Baltimore
Barry U.
Baylor U.
Black Hills St. U.
Bloomsburg U. Pa.
Boise St. U.
Boston U.
Bowie St. U.
Bowl. Gr. St. U.
B.Y.U.
Bridgewater St. U.
Brooklyn C. (C.U.N.Y.)
Brown U.
U. Buffalo (S.U.N.Y.)
Butler U.
Cal. Inst. Arts
Cal. St. U. (Chico)
Cal. St. U. (Fresno)

Cal. St. U. (Fullerton)
Cal. St. U. (Hayward)
Cal. St. U. (Long Beach)
Cal. St. U. (L.A.)
Cal. St. U. (Northridge)
Cal. St. U. (Sacramento)
U. Cal. (Berkeley)
U. Cal. (Davis)
U.C.L.A.
U. Cal. (San Diego)
U. Cal. (Santa Barbara)
Canisius C.
Carnegie Mellon U.
Catholic U.
Cent. Conn. St. U.
U. Cent. Fla.
Cent. Mich. U.
Cent. Mo. St. U.
Chapman U.
U. Chicago
U. Cinn.
Clarion U. Pa.
Clark U.
Clemson U.
Cleveland St. U.
Colo. St. U.
U. Colo.
U. Colo. C.S.
U. Colo. Denver
Columbia U.
U. Conn.
Cornell U.
U. Dayton
U. Del.
U. Denver
DePaul U.
Drake U.
Drexel U.
Drury U.
Duquesne U.
East Tenn. St. U.
East. Wash. U.
Edinboro U. Pa.
Emerson C.
Emporia St. U.
F.D.U. (Teaneck)
Fla. Atlantic U.
Fla. Inst. Tech.
Fla. St. U.
U. Fla.
Fordham U.
Fort Hays Kans. St. U.
Gallaudet U.
Georgetown U.
Geo. Wash. U.
Georgia So. U.
Georgia St. U.
U. Georgia
Gov. St. U.
U. Hartford
Harvard U.
U. Hawaii
Howard U.
U. Houston
Idaho St. U.
Ill. Inst. Tech.
Ill. St. U.
U. Ill.
U. Ill. (Chicago)
U. Incarnate Word
Ind. St. U.
Ind. U.
I.U.P.U.I.
Iona C.
Iowa St. U.
U. Iowa
Ithaca C.
Jackson St. U.
Jacksonville St. U.
Kans. St. U.
U. Kans.
Kent St. U.
U. Ky.

U. La. (Lafayette)
U. La. (Monroe)
Lehman C. (C.U.N.Y.)
L.S.U.
La. Tech U.
Loyola Marymount U.
Loyola U.
U. Maine
Marquette U.
Marshall U.
U. Md.
Marywood U.
U. Mass.
U. Memphis
Miami U. (Ohio)
U. Miami
Mich. St. U.
Mich. Tech. U.
U. Mich.
U. Minn.
Minn. St. U. (Mankato)
Minn. St. U. (Moorhead)
Miss. C.
Miss. St. U.
U. Miss.
U. Mo. (Columbia)
U. Mo. (K.C.)
U. Mont.
Monmouth U.
Montclair U.
U. Montevallo
Morehead St. U.
N.J.I.T.
U. Neb. (Kearney)
U. Neb. (Lincoln)
U. Neb. (Omaha)
U. Nev. (Las Vegas)
N. Mex. St. U.
U. N. Mex.
U. N. Orleans
C. N. Rochelle
S.U.N.Y.C. (Brockport)
S.U.N.Y.C. (New Paltz)
New Sch. U.
N.Y.I.T.
N.Y.U.
No. Car. St. U.
U. No. Car. (Chapel Hill)
U. No. Car. (Greensboro)
No. Dak. St. U.
U. No. Dak.
No. E. Ill. U.
Northeastern U.
U. No. Colo.
U. No. Iowa
U. No. Tex.
Northwestern U.
Notre Dame U.
U. Notre Dame
Ohio St. U.
Ohio U.
U. Okla.
U. Ore.
Pace U.
U. Pac.
Penn. St. U.
U. Penn.
Pepperdine U.
Pittsburg St. U.
U. Pitt.
Portland St. U.
U. Portland
U. Puerto Rico
Purdue U.
Purdue U. (Calumet)
Queens C. (C.U.N.Y.)
Quinnipiac U.
Regent U.
R.P.I.
Rhode Island Sch. Design
R.I.T.
Roosevelt U.

Rutgers U.
Sage Grad. U.
St. Cloud St. U.
St. Louis U.
St. Mary's U.
S.D.S.U.
San Fran. Art Inst.
San Fran. St. U.
San Jose St. U.
Seton Hall U.
Shippensburg U. Pa.
Simmons C.
U. So. Cal.
U. So. Car.
So. Dak. St. U.
U. So. Dak.
U. So. Fla.
So. Ill. U.
So. Meth. U.
U. So. Fla.
U. So. Miss.
So. Nazarene U.
Southwest. Mo. St. U.
Southwest Tex. St. U.
Stanford U.
S. F. Austin St. U.
Suffolk U.
Sul Ross St. U.
Syracuse U.
Teachers C. (Columbia U.)
Temple U.
U. Tenn.
Tex. A&M U.
Tex. Christ. U.
Tex. Tech U.
Tex. Woman's U.
U. Tex. (Austin)
U. Tex. (Dallas)
U. Tex. (El Paso)
U. Tex. (Pan American)
U. Tex. (Tyler)
Towson U.
Utah St. U.
U. Utah
U. Vt.
U. Va.
Wake Forest U.
Wash. St. U.
Wash. U.
U. Wash.
Wayne St. C.
Wayne St. U.
Webster U.
W. Va. U.
West Chester U. Pa.
West. Ill. U.
West. Ky. U.
West. Mich. U.
Wichita St. U.
Wm. Paterson U.
U. Wis.
U. Wis. (Milwaukee)
U. Wis. (Stevens Point)
U. Wis. (Superior)
U. Wis. (Whitewater)
U. Wyo.

CREATIVE WRITING/WRITING
A.C.U.
U. Ala.
U. Alaska
American U.
Antioch U. (L.A.)
Antioch U. (McGregor)
Ariz. St. U.
U. Ariz.
U. Ark.
Ball St. U.
Bennington C.
Boise St. U.
Boston U.
Bowl. Gr. St. U.

Brooklyn C. (C.U.N.Y.)
Brown U.
Cal. C. Arts
Cal. St. U. (Chico)
Cal. St. U. (Fresno)
Cal. St. U. (Long Beach)
Cal. St. U. (Sacramento)
Cal. St. U. (San Marcos)
U. Cal. (Davis)
U. Cal. (Irvine)
Carnegie Mellon U.
U. Cent. Fla.
U. Cent. Mich.
U. Cent. Okla.
Chapman U.
U. Chicago
City C. (C.U.N.Y.)
Claremont Grad. U.
Clemson U.
Colo. St. U.
U. Colo.
Columbia U.
Cornell U.
U. Denver
DePaul U.
East. Mich. U.
East. Wash. U.
Emerson C.
Fla. St. U.
Ga. St. U.
Geo. Mason U.
Goddard C.
Hofstra U.
Hollins U.
U. Houston
Hunter C. (C.U.N.Y.)
Ill. St. U.
U. Ill. (Chicago)
Ind. U.
Ind. U. Pa.
U. Iowa
Johns Hopkins U.
L.I.U.
U. La. (Lafayette)
U. Louisville
Loyola Marymount U.
L.S.U.
Manhattanville C.
U. Mass.
U. Mass. (Dartmouth)
U. Md.
U. Memphis
Miami U.
Mich. St. U.
U. Mich.
Mills C.
Minn. St. U. (Mankato)
Minn. St. U. (Moorhead)
Miss. St. U.
U. Mo. (St. Louis)
U. Mont.
Natl. Louis U.
U. N.H.
U. Nev.
N. Mex. St. U.
New Sch. U.
S.U.N.Y. (Binghamton)
N.Y.U.
U. No. Car. (Greensboro)
No. Ariz. U.
No. Mich. U.
Northeastern U.
Northwestern U.
U. Notre Dame
U. Ore.
Penn. St. U.
U. Penn.
Purdue U.
Queens C. (C.U.N.Y.)
R.P.I.
Roosevelt U.
Rowan U.
Rutgers U.

S.D.S.U.
San Fran. St. U.
U. San Fran.
Sarah Lawrence C.
Sonoma St. U.
So. Ill. U.
So. Meth. U.
U. So. Cal.
U. So. Car.
So. W. Tex. St. U.
Syracuse U.
Temple U.
U. Tenn.
Towson U.
U. Tex. (Austin)
U. Tex. (El Paso)
Utah St. U.
U. Utah
U. Va.
Va. Commonwealth U.
Wash. U.
West. Ill. U.
West. Mich. U.
W. Va. U.
Wichita St. U.
Wright St. U.

FILM/TELEVISION
(Broadcasting, Cinema, Motion Pictures)

U. Ala.
American U.
Antioch U. (McGregor)
Art Inst. Chicago
Auburn U.
Boston U.
Brooklyn C. (C.U.N.Y.)
Butler U.
B.Y.U.
Cal. C. Arts
Cal. St. U. (Fullerton)
U.C.L.A.
Carnegie Mellon U.
Catholic U.
Cent. Mich. U.
U. Cinn.
Claremont Grad. U.
U. Colo.
Columbia U.
DePaul U.
Emerson C.
Emory U.
Fla. St. U.
U. Fla.
Geo. Mason U.
Hollins U.
Howard U.
Ind. U.
U. Iowa
Kans. St. U.
U. Kans.
Loyola Marymount U.
Marquette U.
Mass. C. Arts.
U. Md.
U. Memphis
Miami U.
U. Miami (Fla.)
Mich. St. U.
U. Mich.
U. Minn.
Mont. St. U.
U. Mont.
N.Y.U.
U. No. Car. (Chapel Hill)
U. No. Car. (Greensboro)
U. No. Tex.
Northwestern U.
Ohio St. U.
Ohio U.
U. Okla.
U. Ore.
Penn. St. U.

U. Pitt.
Rhode Island Sch. Design
R.I.T.
S.D.S.U.
San Fran. Art. Inst.
San Fran. St. U.
U. So. Cal.
So. Ill. U.
So. Meth. U.
Stanford U.
S. F. Austin St. U.
Syracuse U.
Temple U.
U. Tenn.
U. Tex. (Austin)
Tulane U.
U. Utah
U. Va.
U. Wash.
Wayne St. U.
W. Va. U.
U.Wis. (Milwaukee)

JOURNALISM
U. Ala.
American U.
Ariz. St. U.
U. Ariz.
Ark. St. U.
U. Ark.
Ball St. U.
Baylor U.
Boston U.
Cal. St. U. (Fullerton)
Cal. St. U. (Northridge)
U. Cal. (Berkeley)
Cent. Mich. U.
U. Colo.
Columbia U.
Emerson C.
U. Fla.
Georgia C. & St. U.
U. Georgia
U. Ill.
Ind. U.
Iowa St. U.
U. Iowa
Kans. St. U.
U. Kans.
Kent St. U.
L.S.U.
U. Md.
Marquette U.
Marshall U.
U. Memphis
U. Miami (Fla.)
Mich. St. U.
U. Mich.
U. Miss.
U. Mo. (Columbia)
U. Mont.
Murray St. U.
N.Y.U.
U. Neb.
U. Nev. (Reno)
U. No. Car. (Chapel Hill)
U. No. Tex.
Northeastern U.
Northwestern U.
Ohio St. U.
Ohio U.
U. Okla.
U. Ore.
Penn. St. U.
U. Portland
Quinnipiac U.
Regent U.
Roosevelt U.
U. So. Cal.
U. So. Car.
So. Dak. St. U.
So. Ill. U.
Stanford U.

Syracuse U.
Temple U.
U. Tenn.
Tex. A&M U.
Tex. Christ U.
Tex. So. U.
U. Tex. (Austin)
W. Va. U.
U. Wis.
U. Wis. (Milwaukee)

TECHNICAL WRITING
Boise St. U.
Bowl. Gr. St. U.
Carnegie Mellon U.
U. Cent. Fla.
Colo. St. U.
Drexel U.
Miami U.
Mich. Tech. U.
U. Minn.
No. Car. St. U.
Northeastern U.
Ore. St. U.
R.P.I.
Tex. Tech U.
U. Wash.

TELE-COMMUNICATIONS
U. Ala.
U. Ark.
Azusa Pac. U.
Barry U.
Boston U.
Cal. St. U. (Fresno)
U. Cal. (San Diego)
U. Colo.
Columbia U.
U. Dallas
DePaul U.
Drexel U.
Geo. Mason U.
Geo. Wash. U.
Ill. Inst. Tech.
Ind. U.
Iona C.
U. La. ((Lafayette)
U. Md.
U. Miami (Fla.)
Mich. St. U.
U. Mich.
N.J.I.T.
Northwestern U.
N.Y.U.
Ohio U.
Pace U.
Penn. St. U.
U. Penn.
U. Pitt.
Poly. U.
R.I.T.
Roosevelt U.
U. San Fran.
So. Ill. U.
So. Meth. U.
Syracuse U.
Tex. So. U.
Tex. Tech U.
U. Tex. (Dallas)
Webster U.
West. Ill. U.

Computer Science

(Typically includes Computer Systems, Computer Information Systems)

A.F. Inst.
Ala. A&M U.
U. Ala.

U. Ala. (Birm.)
U. Ala. (Huntsville)
U. Alaska
U. Albany (S.U.N.Y.)
American U.
Andrews U.
Appal. St. U.
Ariz. St. U.
U. Ariz.
Ark. St. U.
U. Ark.
Auburn U.
Azusa Pac. U.
Ball St. U.
Baruch C. (C.U.N.Y.)
Baylor U.
Bemidji St. U.
Boise St. U.
Boston C.
Boston U.
Bowie St. U.
Bowl. Gr. St. U.
Bradley U.
Brandeis U.
B.Y.U.
U. Bridgeport
Bridgewater St. C.
Brooklyn C. (C.U.N.Y.)
Brown U.
U. Buffalo (S.U.N.Y.)
Cal. Inst. Tech.
Cal. Poly. St. U. (San Luis Obispo)
Cal. St. Poly U. (Pomona)
Cal. St. U. (Chico)
Cal. St. U. (Fresno)
Cal. St. U. (Fullerton)
Cal. St. U. (Hayward)
Cal. St. U. (Long Beach)
Cal. St. U. (Northridge)
Cal. St. U. (Sacramento)
Cal. St. U. (San Marcos)
U. Cal. (Berkeley)
U. Cal. (Davis)
U. Cal. (Irvine)
U.C.L.A.
U. Cal. (Riverside)
U. Cal. (San Diego)
U. Cal. (Santa Cruz)
Cal. U. Pa.
Carnegie Mellon U.
Case West. Res. U.
Catholic U.
Cent. Conn. St. U.
U. Cent. Fla.
Cent. Mich. U.
U. Chicago
U. Cinn.
City C. (C.U.N.Y.)
Clark Atl. U.
Clarkson U.
Clemson U.
Cleve. St. U.
Colo. St. U.
U. Colo.
U. Colo. (Denver)
Columbia U.
U. Conn.
Cornell U.
Creighton U.
Dartmouth C.
U. Dayton
U. Del.
U. Denver
DePaul U.
U. Detroit Mercy
Drexel U.
Duke U.
East Stroudsburg U. Pa.
East Tenn. St. U.
East. Wash. U.

Emory U.
F.D.U. (Teaneck)
Fitchburg St. C.
Fla. Atlantic U.
Fla. Inst. Tech.
Fla. St. U.
U. Fla.
Fordham U.
Geo. Mason U.
Geo. Wash. U.
Georgia Inst. Tech.
Georgia St. U.
U. Georgia
Gov. St. U.
U. Hawaii
Hofstra U.
Hollins U.
Hood C.
U. Houston
Howard U.
Hunter C. (C.U.N.Y.)
U. Idaho
Ill. Inst. Tech.
Ill. St. U.
U. Ill.
U. Ill. (Chicago)
Ind. U.
I.U.P.U.I.
Iona C.
Iowa St. U.
U. Iowa
Jackson St. U.
James Madison U.
Johns Hopkins U.
Kansas St. U.
U. Kans.
Kent St. U.
Kutztown U.
U. Ky.
U. La. (Lafayette)
Lamar U.
Lehigh U.
Lehman C. (C.U.N.Y.)
L.I.U.
L.S.U.
La. Tech U.
Loyola Marymount U.
Loyola U. (Chicago)
U. Maine
Marquette U.
U. Md.
U. Md. (Baltimore Cnty.)
M.I.T.
U. Mass.
U. Mass. (Boston)
U. Mass (Lowell)
U. Memphis
Mercer U.
U. Miami
Mich. St. U.
U. Mich.
Mich. Tech. U.
Mid. Tenn. St. U.
Minn. St. U. (Mankato)
Minn. St. U. (Moorhead)
U. Minn.
U. Minn. (Duluth)
Miss. C.
Miss. St. U.
U. Mo.
U. Mo. (K.C.)
U. Mo. (Rolla)
U. Mo. (St. Louis)
Mont. St. U.
U. Mont.
Montclair U.
Naval P.G. Sch.
U. Neb.
U. Nev. (Les Vegas)
U. Nev. (Reno)
N.J.I.T.
U. N.H
N. Mex. Highlands U.

N. Mex. Inst. M&T
N. Mex. St. U.
U. N. Mex.
S.U.N.Y. (New Paltz)
S.U.N.Y. I.T.
N.Y.I.T.
N.Y.U.
No. Car. St. U. (Raleigh)
U. No. Car. (Chapel Hill)
U. No. Car. (Charlotte)
U. No. Car. (Greensboro)
No. Dak. St. U.
U. No. Dak.
U. No. Fla.
U. No. Tex.
Northeastern U.
No. East. Ill.
No. Ill. U.
Northwestern U.
U. Notre Dame
No. West Mo. U.
Oakland U.
Ohio St. U.
Ohio U.
Okla. City U.
Okla. St. U.
U. Okla.
Old Dom. U.
Ore. St. U.
U. Ore.
Pace U.
Pac. Luth. U.
Penn. St. U.
U. Penn.
U. Phoenix
U. Pitt.
Poly. U.
Portland St. U.
Princeton U.
Purdue U.
Queens C. (C.U.N.Y.)
R.P.I.
U. Rhode Island
Rice U.
Rivier C.
R.I.T.
U. Rochester
Roosevelt U.
Rutgers U.
St. Cloud St. U.
St. John's U. (N.Y.)
St. Joseph U.
St. Louis U.
St. Mary's U. (Tex)
Sam Houston St. U.
S.D.S.U.
San Fran. St. U.
U. San Fran.
San Jose St. U.
Santa Clara U.
Shippensburg U.
So. Dak. Sch. M&T
U. So. Cal.
U. So. Car.
U. So. Dak.
So. Ill. U.
U. So. Fla.
U. So. Maine
So. Meth. U.
So. Ore. U.
Southwest Tex. St. U.
Stanford U.
C. Staten Island
    (C.U.N.Y.)
S. F. Austin St. U.
Stevens Inst. Tech.
Stony Brook U.
    (S.U.N.Y.)
Suffolk U.
Syracuse U.
Temple U.
U. Tenn.
U. Tenn. (Chattanooga)

Tex. A&M U.
Tex. A&M U.
    (Commerce)
Tex. A&M U. (Corpus
    Christi)
Tex. A&M U.
    (Kingsville)
Tex. Tech. U.
U. Tex. (Arlington)
U. Tex. (Austin)
U. Tex. (Dallas)
U. Tex. (El Paso)
U. Tex. (San Antonio)
U. Tex. (Tyler)
Troy St. U.
Troy St. U. (Dothan)
Tufts U.
Tulane U.
U. Tulsa
Union C.
Utah St. U.
U. Utah
Vanderbilt U.
U. Vt.
Villanova U.
Va. Commonwealth U.
Va. Poly. Inst.
U. Va.
Wake Forest U.
Wash. St. U.
Wash. U. (Mo.)
U. Wash.
Wayne St. U.
Webster U.
West Chester U. Pa.
W. Va. U.
West. Car. U.
West. Conn. U.
U. West Fla.
West. Ill. U.
West. Ky. U.
West. Mich. U.
West. Wash. U.
Wichita St. U.
C. Wm. & Mary
U. Wis.
U. Wis. (Milwaukee)
Worcester Poly. Inst.
Wright St. U.
U. Wyo.
Yale U.

Criminal Justice/
Corrections/
Criminology

(Includes Law Enforce-
ment, Police Science)

U. Ala.
U. Ala. (Birm.)
U. Albany (S.U.N.Y.)
American U.
Ariz. St. U.
U. Ark.
Armstrong Atlantic St. U.
Auburn U. (Mont.)
U. Baltimore
Boise St. U.
Boston U.
U. Buffalo (S.U.N.Y.)
Cal. St. U. (Fresno)
Cal. St. U. (Long Beach)
Cal. St. U. (L.A.)
Cal. St. U. (Sacramento)
Cal. St. U. (San
    Bernardino)
U. Cal. (Irvine)
U. Cent. Fla.
U. Cent. Okla.
Cent. Conn. St. U.
Cent. Mo. St. U.
Chapman U.

Chicago St. U.
U. Cincinnati
Clark Atl. U.
U. Colo. (Denver)
Columbus St. U.
U. Del.
Delta St. U.
U. Detroit Mercy
East Cent. U.
East. Ky. U.
East. Mich. U.
East Tenn. St. U.
Fitchburg St. U.
Fla. St. U.
Fordham U.
Geo. Wash. U.
Ill. St. U.
U. Ill. (Chicago)
Ind. St. U.
Ind. U.
Ind. U. Penn.
Iona C.
U. Iowa
Jackson St. U.
Jacksonville St. U.
Jersey City St. U.
John Jay C. (C.U.N.Y.)
Kent St. U.
L.I.U. (C.W. Post)
U. La. (Monroe)
U. Louisville
L.S.U.
Loyola U. (Chicago)
Marshall U.
U. Md.
Marywood U.
U. Mass. (Lowell)
U. Memphis
Mich. St. U.
Mid. Tenn. St. U.
U. Minn.
Minot St. U.
U. Mo. (K.C.)
U. Mo. (St. Louis)
Monmouth U.
Natl. U.
U. Neb.
U. Nev.
U. N. Haven
N. Mex. St. U.
C.U.N.Y. (Grad. Ctr.)
S.U.N.Y.C. (Buffalo)
Niagara U.
No. Car. Cent. U.
U. No. Car. (Charlotte)
No. East. St. U.
Northeastern U.
Northwestern U.
No. Ariz. U.
Okla. City U.
Penn. St. U.
U. Pitt.
Portland St. U.
Radford U.
Rutgers U.
Saginaw Val. St. U.
St. Cloud St. U.
St. Joseph U.
St. Mary's U. (Tex.)
Sam Houston St. U.
S.D.S.U.
San Jose St. U.
Seton Hall U.
Shippensburg U. Pa.
So. E. Mo. St. U.
U. So. Car.
So. Ill. U.
U. So. Miss.
Southwest Tex. St. U.
Suffolk U.
Sul Ross St. U.
Temple U.
Tenn. St. U.

U. Tenn.
U. Tenn. (Chattanooga)
U. Tex. (Arlington)
U. Tex. (San Antonio)
Troy St. U.
Valdosta St. U.
Villanova U.
Va. Commonwealth U.
Wash. St. U.
Wayne St. U.
Webster U.
West Chester U. Pa.
West Ill. U.
West. New Eng. C.
West. Ore. U.
Westfield St. U.
Wichita St. U.
Widener U.
U. Wis. (Milwaukee)
Wright St. U.
Xavier U. (Ohio)
Youngstown St. U.

Dentistry

U. Ala. (Birm.)
Boston U.
U. Buffalo (S.U.N.Y.)
U.C.L.A.
U. Cal. (San Francisco)
Case West. Res. U.
U. Colo. Health Sci. Ctr.
Columbia U.
U. Conn. Health Ctr.
Creighton U.
U. Detroit Mercy
U. Fla.
Med. C. Georgia
Harvard U.
Howard U.
U. Ill. (Chicago)
Ind. U.
U. Iowa
U. Ky.
Loma Linda U.
U. Louisville
L.S.U. H.S.C.
Marquette U.
U. Md. (Baltimore)
U. Med. & Dent. N.J.
Meharry Med. C.
U. Mich.
U. Minn.
U. Miss. Med. Ctr.
U. Mo. (K.C.)
U. Neb. Med. Ctr.
N.Y.U.
U. No. Car. (Chapel Hill)
Ohio St. U.
U. Okla. Health Sci. Ctr.
Oregon Health & Sci. U.
U. Pac.
U. Penn.
U. Pitt.
U. Puerto Rico
Med. U. So. Car.
U. So. Cal.
So. Ill. U. (Edwardsville)
Stony Brook U.
    (S.U.N.Y.)
Temple U.
U. Tenn. (Memphis)
Tex. A&M U. H.S.C.
    (Baylor C. Dent.)
U. Tex. Health Sci. Ctr.
    (Houston)
U. Tex. Health Sci. Ctr.
    (San Antonio)
Tufts U.
Va. Commonwealth U.
U. Wash.
W. Va. U.

Education

(Typically includes Administration and Supervision, Curriculum and Instruction, Elementary and Secondary Teaching, Evaluation and Research, Foreign Language Education, Foundations and Philosophy of Education, Guidance and Counseling, Health/Physical Education, History and Philosophy of Education, Home Economics Education, Reading Specialist, Recreation, School Psychology, Special Education, Speech Pathology and Audiology, Vocational/Distributive/Occupational Education; often includes Business Education, Early Childhood Education, Extension Education, Middle School Education, Student Personnel Services; offered by more than 500 institutions in all 50 states, so individual institutions are not listed here)

ADULT EDUCATION (INCLUDES COMMUNITY EDUCATION)
U. Ala.
U. Alaska
U. Ark.
Auburn U.
Ball St. U.
U. Buffalo (S.U.N.Y.)
Cal. St. U. (L.A.)
U. Cent. Okla.
Cent. Mo. St. U.
Cleve. St. U.
U. Conn.
Columbia U. (Teachers C.)
Drake U.
E. Car. U.
East. Wash. U.
Fla. A&M U.
Fla. Atlantic U.
Fla. St. U.
Fordham U.
Georgia So. C.
U. Georgia
U. Ill.
Ind. U.
Ind. U. Penn.
Kans. St. U.
U. Ky.
Loyola U. Chicago
Marshall U.
U. Md.
U. Memphis
Mich. St. U.
U. Minn.
U. Mo. (Columbia)
Mont. St. U.
Morehead St. U.
Natl. Louis U.
Natl. U.
S.U.N.Y.C. (Buffalo)
N.Y.U.
No. Car. A&T
No. Car. St. U. (Raleigh)
U. No. Car. (Chapel Hill)
No. Ill. U.
Northwestern U.
Nova U.

U. Okla.
Ore. St. U.
Penn. St. U.
U. Phoenix
U. Redlands
U. Rhode Island
Rutgers U.
St. Joseph's U.
San Fran. St. U.
Seattle U.
U. So. Fla.
U. So. Maine
U. So Miss.
Suffolk U.
Syracuse U.
Tenn. St. U.
U. Tenn.
Tex. A&M U. (Kingsville)
Tex. Woman's U.
Troy St. U. (Montgomery)
Va. Commonwealth U.
Va. Poly. Inst.
U. West Ala.
West. Wash. U.
U. Wis.
U. Wis. (Platteville)
U. Wyo.

ART EDUCATION
U. Ala. (Birm.)
Alfred U.
U. Ariz.
Sch. Art Inst. Chicago
U. Arts
Ball St. U.
Boise St. U.
Boston U.
Brooklyn C. (C.U.N.Y.)
B.Y.U.
Cal. St. U. (Long Beach)
Cal. St. U. (L.A.)
Case West. Res. U.
Cent Conn. St. U.
U. Cent. Fla.
Cent. Mo. St. U.
U. Cent. Fla.
Cent. M. St. U.
U. Cincinnati
City C. (C.U.N.Y.)
Columbia U. (Teachers C.)
Columbus St. U.
East. Ky. U.
East. Mich. U.
Fla. St. U.
Ga. So. U.
Ga. St. U.
U. Ga.
Hofstra U.
U. Houston
U. Ill.
Ind. U.
I.U.P.U.I.
James Madison U.
Jersey City St. U.
U. Kans.
Kutztown U. Pa.
U. Ky.
L.I.U. (C.W. Post)
Mansfield U. Pa.
Md. Inst. C. Art
Marywood U.
Mass. C. Art
U. Mass. (Dartmouth)
Miami U.
Mich. St. U.
Minn. St. U. (Moorhead)
U. Minn.
Miss. C.
U. Miss.
U. N. Mex.
C. New Rochelle

S.U.N.Y.C. (Buffalo)
S.U.N.Y.C. (New Paltz)
N.Y.U.
No. Car. A&T St. U.
U. No. Car. (Greensboro)
U. No. Iowa
U. No. Tex.
Notre Dame U.
Ohio St. U.
Ohio U.
Penn. St. U.
U. Pitt.
Pratt U.
Purdue U.
Queens C. (C.U.N.Y.)
R.I.T.
Rhode Island Sch. Design
Rutgers U.
Sam Houston St. U.
San Jose St. U.
C. St. Rose
U. So. Miss.
U. So. Fla.
Sul Ross St. U.
Syracuse U.
Temple U.
Tex. Woman's U.
U. Tex. (Austin)
Towson U.
Tulane U.
Va. Commonwealth U.
Wayne St. U.
West Ga. C.
West. Car. U.
West. Ky. U.
Wichita St. U.
Winthrop U.
U. Wis.
U. Wis. (Milwaukee)
U. Wis. (Superior)
Xavier U.

AUDIOVISUAL EDUCATION
(Typically includes Educational/Instructional Technology and Media)
Adelphi U.
Ala. St. U.
U. Albany (S.U.N.Y.)
Alliant I. U.
American U.
Appal. St. U.
Ariz. St. U.
U. Ariz.
U. Ark.
Auburn U.
Azusa Pac. U.
Bank St. C.
Bloomsburg U. Pa.
Boise St. U.
Boston U.
Bowl. Gr. St. U.
Cal. St. U. (Chico)
Cal. St. U. (L.A.)
Cal. St. U. (San Bernadino)
Canisius C.
Cent. Conn. St. U.
Cent. Mich. U.
Cent. Mo. St. U.
U. Cent. Okla.
U. Colo. (Denver)
Columbia U. (Teachers C.)
Clarke C.
U. Conn.
Dak. St. U.
U. Dubuque
Duquesne U.
East Car. U.
East Tenn. St. U.
East. Wash. U.
Fairfield U.

Fla. St. U.
Gallaudet U.
Gannon U.
Geo. Mason U.
Geo. Wash. U.
Georgia So. C.
Georgia St. U.
U. Georgia
Gov. St. U.
Harvard U.
U. Hawaii
U. Houston
Ind. U.
I.U.P.U.I.
Iona C.
Iowa St. U.
Jackson St. U.
Jacksonville St. U.
Jersey City St. U.
U. Ky.
Kent St. U.
L.I.U. (C. W. Post)
L.S.U.
Lehigh U.
U. Md. (Baltimore Cnty.)
U. Mass. (Boston)
Marywood U.
McDaniel C.
McNeese St. U.
Mich. St. U.
Minn. St. U. (Mankato)
Mont. St. U.
Natl. U.
U. Neb.
U. N. Mex.
N.Y.U.
No. Car. A&T St. U.
No. Car. Cent. U.
No. Car. St. U.
U. No. Car. (Chapel Hill)
U. No. Colo.
No. Ill. U.
Nova S.E. U.
Ohio U.
Okla. St. U.
Old Dom. U.
U. Oregon
Penn. St. U.
U. Phoenix
Pittsburg St. U.
U. Pitt.
Portland St. U.
Prairie View A&M U.
Purdue U.
Radford U.
R.I.T.
St. Cloud St. U.
S.D.S.U.
San Fran. St. U.
San Jose St. U.
Seton Hall U.
So. East. Okla. St. U.
U. So. Ala.
U. So. Cal.
U. So. Car.
So. Conn. St. U.
U. So. Fla.
So. Ill. U. (Edwardsville)
U. So. Miss.
Southwest. Okla St. U.
Syracuse U.
Temple U.
U. Tenn.
Tex. A&M U.
Tex. A&M U. (Commerce)
Tex. So. U.
Tex. Tech U.
Towson U.
Troy St. U. (Dothan)
Utah St. U.
Va. Poly. Inst.

Va. St. U.
Wayne St. U.
West Car. U.
West Conn. St. U.
West Ky. U.
Westfield St. U.
U. Wis.
U. Wis. (La Crosse)
U. Wis. (Stout)
U. Wyo.
Xavier U. (Ohio)

BILINGUAL/ MULTILINGUAL/ MULTICULTURAL EDUCATION
Adelphi U.
U. Alaska
Alliant Intl. U.
U. Ariz.
Azusa Pac. U.
Bank St. C.
Bennington C.
Boston U.
Brooklyn C. (C.U.N.Y.)
Cal. St. U. (Bakersfield)
Cal. St. U. (Chico)
Cal. St. U. (Dominguez Hills)
Cal. St. U. (Fullerton)
Cal. St. U. (L.A.)
Cal. St. U. (Sacramento)
Cal. St. U. (San Bernardino)
U. Cal. (Berkeley)
U. Cal. (Irvine)
Chicago St. U.
City C. (C.U.N.Y.)
U. Colo.
Columbia U. (Teachers C.)
U. Conn.
U. Del.
East. Mich. U.
Fairfield U.
F.D.U. (Teaneck)
Fla. St. U.
U. Fla.
Fordham U.
Geo. Mason U.
Georgetown U.
U. Georgia
Hofstra U.
U. Houston
Hunter C. (C.U.N.Y.)
U. Ill.
Iona C.
Jersey City St. U.
Kean U.
Lehman C. (C.U.N.Y.)
L.I.U.
Loyola Marymount U.
U. Md.
U. Mass. (Boston)
Maryville U.
U. Mich.
Minn. St. U. (Mankato)
U. Minn.
Natl. U.
U. N. Mex.
C. N. Rochelle
S.U.N.Y.C. (Brockport)
S.U.N.Y.C. (Buffalo)
N.Y.U.
No. Ariz. U.
U. No. Tex.
Our Lady Lake U.
U. Pac.
Penn. St. U.
U. Penn.
Point Loma U.
U. Puerto Rico
Queens C. (C.U.N.Y.)
Rhode Island C.

Rutgers U.
St. John's U. (N.Y.)
Sam Houston St. U.
U. San Fran.
S.D.S.U.
Seton Hall U.
So. Conn. U.
So. Meth. U.
Stanford U.
Sul Ross St. U.
U. Tenn.
Tex. A&M U.
    (Kingsville)
Tex. Tech U.
U. Tex. (Brownsville)
U. Tex. (San Antonio)
U. Tex. (Pan American)
Utah St. U.
Wash. St. U.
U. Wash.
West. Ore. U.

**COMMUNITY
COLLEGE
TEACHING**
Columbia U. (Teachers C.)
East. Wash. U.
Fla. St. U.
U. Fla.
Geo. Mason U.
Mich. St. U.
No. Ariz. U.
No. Car. St. U.
No. Mich. U.
Ore. St. U.
Pittsburg St. U.
Rowan U.
U. So. Fla.
West. Mich. U.

**COMPUTERS IN
EDUCATION**
Alliant Intl. U.
Azusa Pac. U.
Barry U.
Bank St. C.
U. Bridgeport
Brooklyn C. (C.U.N.Y.)
Cal. Poly. St. U. (San
    Luis Obispo)
Cal. St. U. (Dominguez
    Hills)
Cal. St. U. (L.A.)
Cal. U. Pa.
Canisius C.
Card. Stritch C.
U. Cent. Okla.
Cleveland St. U.
Columbia U. (Teachers C.)
DePaul U.
East Wash. U.
Fairfield U.
Fla. Inst. Tech.
U. Fla.
Gonzaga U.
U. Geogia
Hofstra U.
Jacksonville U.
U. La. (Lafayette)
L.I.U.
L.I.U. (C.W. Post)
U. Mich.
Miss. C.
Natl. Louis U.
N.Y.I.T.
U. No. Iowa
U. No. Tex.
No. West. Mo. St. U.
Nova U.
Oakland U.
Ohio U.
Oka. St. U.
U. Ore.

U. Penn.
U. Phoenix
Providence U.
R.I.T.
Rowan U.
Sam Houston St. U.
Shippensburg U. Pa.
U. Tex. (Austin)
U. Tex. (Tyler)
Union C.
Webster U.
Wilkes U.
Wright St. U.

**DRUG AND
ALCOHOL/
SUBSTANCE ABUSE
COUNSELING**
Antioch N. E. Grad. Sch.
Gov. St. U.
L.I.U.
U. No. Fla.
Sage Grad. Sch.
Springfield C.

**EDUCATION OF
THE GIFTED**
U. Ala.
Ariz. St. U.
Ark. St. U.
U. Ark.
Barry U.
Cal. St. U. (L.A.)
Cal. St. U. (Northridge)
Cal. St. U. (Sacramento)
Chicago St. U.
Clark Atlanta U.
Cleveland St. U.
Columbia U. (Teachers C.)
U. Conn.
Converse C.
Drury U.
Emporia St. U.
Georgia C. & St. U.
U. Georgia
U. Houston
Hunter C. (C.U.N.Y.)
Ind. St. U.
Ind. U. Pa.
Jacksonville U.
U. Kans.
Kent St. U.
U. La. (Lafayette)
Mansfield U. Pa.
Millersville U. Pa.
Minn. St. U. (Mankato)
U. Neb. (Kearney)
C. N. Rochelle
U. No. Colo.
U. No. Iowa
Northeast. Ill. U.
Nova U.
Ohio U.
Okla. City U.
Purdue U.
U. St. Thomas (Minn.)
U. So. Ala.
U. So. Miss.
U. So. Fla.
Stetson U.
Tex. A&M U.
W. Va. U.
C. Wm. & Mary
U. Wis. (Whitewater)
Whitworth C.
Wright St. U.
Xavier U.
Youngstown St. U.

**EDUCATION OF
THE MULTIPLE
HANDICAPPED**
U. Ala.

Ariz. St. U.
Cleveland St. U.
Columbia U. (Teachers C.)
Georgia C. St. U.
Minot St. U.

**ENGLISH AS A
SECOND
LANGUAGE**
Adelphi U.
Alliant Intl. U.
Ariz. St. U.
Azusa Pac. U.
Ball St. U.
Boston U.
U. Buffalo (S.U.N.Y.)
Cal. St. U. (Dominguez
    Hills)
Cal. St. U. (L.A.)
Cal. St. U. (Sacramento)
Cal. St. U. (San
    Bernardino)
U.C.L.A.
Cent. Conn. St. U.
Cent. Mo. St. U.
Columbia U. (Teachers C.)
East. Mich. U.
Fairfield U.
F.D.U. (Teaneck)
Fordham U.
Geo. Mason U.
U. Hawaii
Hunter C. (C.U.N.Y.)
Ind. U.
Inter. American U. (P.R.)
Jersey City St. U.
U. Kans.
Lehman C. (C.U.N.Y.)
L.I.U.
L.I.U. (C.W. Post)
U. Mass. (Boston)
U. Miami
Mich. St. U.
U. Minn.
Monterey Inst.
Murray St. U.
C. N. Rochelle
S.U.N.Y.C. (New Paltz)
N.Y.U.
No. Ariz. U.
Nova U.
Okla. City U.
Oral Roberts U.
Penn. St. U.
U. Penn.
Portland St. U.
U. Puerto Rico
Queens C. (C.U.N.Y.)
Rutgers U.
St. Michael's C.
San Fran. St. U.
U. San Fran.
San Jose St. U.
U. So. Cal.
U. So. Car.
So. Ill. U.
Stony Brook U.
    (S.U.N.Y.)
Temple U.
U. Tex. (San Antonio)
U. Tex. (Pan American)
Whitworth C.
Wm. Paterson U.

**LEARNING
DISABILITIES**
(Includes Multiple
    Handicaps)
Ala. A&M U.
U. Ala.
U. Ala. (Birm.)
U. Ariz.
U. Ark.

Ball St. U.
Bank St. C.
Bloomsburg St. U.
Boston C.
Brooklyn C. (C.U.N.Y.)
Bowl. Gr. St. U.
Cal. St. U. (Chico)
Cal. U. Pa.
Card. Stritch C.
Cent. Mo. St. U.
Cent. St. U.
Chapman U.
Chicago St. U.
Clarke C.
Cleveland St. U.
Columbia U. (Teachers C.)
Columbus C.
DePaul U.
U. Detroit Mercy
East Cent. St. U.
East. Mont. C.
Gallaudet U.
Georgia C. St. U.
Georgia St. U.
U. Georgia
Hampton U.
Hunter C. (C.U.N.Y.)
U. Ill.
Iowa St. U.
James Madison U.
Kent St. U.
U. La Verne
Lehman C. (C.U.N.Y.)
U. Maine
U. Mass. (Lowell)
Memphis St. U.
Minn. St. U. (Mankato)
Minot St. U.
Mont. St. U.
Montclair U.
C. N. Rochelle
U. Neb. (Kearney)
U. Neb. (Omaha)
N.Y.U.
U. No. Car. (Chapel Hill)
Northeastern Ill. U.
Northwestern U.
U. Ore. C. Education
Our Lady Lake U.
U. Pitt.
Radford U.
U. Redlands
U. Richmond
Rockford C.
U. St. Francis (Ind.)
C. St. Rose
St. Xavier U.
U. Santa Clara
Seton Hall U.
U. So. Fla.
U. So. Conn.
Stetson U.
Valdosta St. U.
West. Oregon U.
W. Va. U.
Winona St. U.
U. Wis. (Superior)
Worcester St. U.
Xavier U.

**LIBRARIANSHIP,
LIBRARY SCIENCE,
LIBRARY MEDIA**
U. Ala.
Appal. St. U.
U. Ariz.
Boston U.
U.C.L.A.
Catholic U.
Cent. Mich. U.
Cent. Mo. St. U.
Chicago St. U.
Clarion U. Pa.

Clark Atl. U.
Columbia U. (Teachers C.)
Drexel U.
East Car. U.
Emporia St. U.
Fla. St. U.
U. Hawaii
I.U.P.U.I.
Kutztown U. Pa.
U. Ill.
Ind. U.
L.I.U. (C.W. Post)
L.S.U.
McDaniel C.
U. Md.
N. Car. Cent. U.
U. No. Car. (Greensboro)
U. No. Tex.
U. Okla.
U. Pitt.
Pratt Inst.
Queens C. (C.U.N.Y.)
U. Rhode Island
Rutgers U.
St. John's U. (N.Y.)
Sam Houston St. U.
San Jose St. U.
U. So. Car.
So. Conn. St. U.
U. So. Fla.
U. So. Miss.
Spalding U.
Syracuse U.
U. Tenn.
Tex. Woman's U.
U. Wash.
Wayne St. U.
U. Wis.
U. Wis. (Milwaukee)
Wright St. U.

**MARRIAGE &
FAMILY
COUNSELING/
THERAPY**
A.C.U.
U. Akron
U. Ala. (Birmingham)
Alliant Intl. U.
Antioch N. E. Grad. Sch.
Azusa Pac. U.
B.Y.U.
U. Bridgeport
Cal. Luth. C.
Cal. St. U. (Dominguez
    Hills)
Chapman U.
East Car. U.
Fairfield U.
Fla. St. U.
U. Fla.
Golden Gate U.
Hofstra U.
Ind. St. U.
Iona C.
U. La. (Monroe)
U. La Verne
Loma Linda U.
L.I.U. (C.W. Post)
Loyola Marymount U.
Mich. St. U.
Nova U.
U. Phoenix
U. Pitt.
Purdue U.
U. San Diego
U. San Fran.
Santa Clara U.
Seattle Pac. U.
Seton Hall U.
Sonoma St. U.
U. So. Cal.
Stetson U.

Syracuse U.
Tex. Tech U.
Tex. Woman's U.
U. Wis. (Stout)

RECREATION/PARK/ RECREATIONAL ADMINISTRATION/ LEISURE STUDIES

U. Ala.
Ariz. St. U.
U. Ark.
Baylor U.
Boston U.
Bowl. Gr. St. U.
B.Y.U.
Cal. St. U. (Chico)
Cal. St. U. (Long Beach)
Cal. St. U. (Northridge)
Cal. St. U. (Sacramento)
Cent. Mich. U.
Cent. Wash. U.
Clemson U.
Cleveland St. U.
Colo. St. U.
U. Conn.
Delta St. U.
East Car. U.
East. Ky. U.
Fla. St. U.
U. Fla.
Fort Hays St. U.
Georgia So. U.
Georgia St. U.
U. Georgia
U. Hawaii
Howard U.
U. Idaho
U. Ill.
Ind. U.
U. Iowa
U. Kans.
U. La. (Monroe)
Lehman C. (C.U.N.Y.)
U. Memphis
Mich. St. U.
Mid. Tenn. St. U.
U. Minn.
U. Miss.
U. Mo. (Columbia)
U. Mont.
Morehead St. U.
Murray St. U.
U. Neb.
U. Neb. (Kearney)
U. Nev.
U. N. Mex.
S.U.N.Y.C. (Brockport)
S.U.N.Y.C. (Cortland)
N.Y.U.
No. Car. Cent. U.
No. Car. St. U.
No. Car. St. U. (Raleigh)
U. No. Car. (Chapel Hill)
U. No. Colo.
U. No. Ill.
U. No. Tex.
Okla. St. U.
Penn. St. U.
U. Penn.
Purdue U.
Radford U.
U. Rhode Island
San Fran. St. U.
San Jose St. U.
Slippery Rock U. Pa.
So. Dak. St. U.
U. So. Cal.
U. So. Miss.
So. Conn. St. U.
So. Ill. U.
Springfield C.
Temple U.

Tenn. St. U.
U. Tenn.
Tex. A&M U.
U. Toledo
Utah St. U.
U. Utah
Va. Commonwealth U.
Va. Poly. Inst.
Wayne St. U.
U. West Fla.
West. Ill. U.
West. Ky. U.
W. Va. U.
U. Wash.
U. Wis. (La Crosse)
Wright St. U.

SAFETY EDUCATION

Cent. Mo. St. U.
N.Y.U.
U. Tenn.

TEACHING OF EMOTIONALLY DISTURBED

Ala. A&M U.
U. Ala.
U. Albany (S.U.N.Y.)
U. Ariz.
Ball St. U.
Boston U.
Bowl. Gr. St. U.
Brooklyn C. (C.U.N.Y.)
Cal. U. (Pa.)
Cent. Mo. St. U.
Chicago St. U.
City C. (C.U.N.Y.)
Cleveland St. U.
Columbia U. (Teachers C.)
East. Mich. U.
Hampton U.
Hofstra U.
Kent St. U.
Lehman C. (C.U.N.Y.)
Mich. St. U.
Minn. St. U. (Mankato)
Minot St. U.
C. N. Rochelle
U. Neb. (Omaha)
Northeastern Ill. U.
U. Pitt.
Radford U.
U. St. Francis (Ind.)
Syracuse U.
C. St. Rose
U. So. Fla.
Va. Commonwealth U.
Valdosta St. U.
West Car. U.
U. Wis. (Superior)

TEACHING OF MENTALLY RETARDED

Ala. A&M U.
U. Ala.
Appal. St. U.
U. Ariz.
Ball St. U.
Bloomsburg St. U.
Boston U.
Bowl. Gr. St. U.
Brooklyn C. (C.U.N.Y.)
Cal. U. (Pa.)
Cal. St. U. (Dominguez Hills)
Chicago St. U.
City C. (C.U.N.Y.)
Cleveland St. U.
Columbia U. (Teachers C.)
Duquesne U.
East. Mich. U.

Fort Hays Kans. St. U.
Georgia C. St. U.
Hampton U.
Hofstra U.
Kent St. U.
Lehman C. (C.U.N.Y.)
Marygrove C.
Mich. St. U.
Minn. St. U. (Mankato)
Minot St. U.
U. Mo. (St. Louis)
U. Neb. (Omaha)
C. N. Rochelle
Northeastern U.
Northeastern Ill. U.
U. Pitt.
Radford U.
U. St. Francis (Ind.)
C. St. Rose
U. So. Fla.
Syracuse U.
Va. Commonwealth U.
Valdosta St. U.
West. Car. U.

TEACHING OF PHYSICALLY HANDICAPPED

U. Ala.
U. Ariz.
U. Ark.
Ball St. U.
Boston U.
Cal. U. (Pa.)
Cleveland St. U.
Columbia U. (Teachers C.)
Duquesne U.
East. Mich. U.
Hofstra U.
Kent St. U.
Lehman C. (C.U.N.Y.)
Minn. St. U. (Mankato)
Minot St. U.
U. Pitt.
Valdosta St. U.

URBAN EDUCATION

Cal. St. U. (L.A.)
U. Chicago
City C. (C.U.N.Y.)
Cleveland St. U.
Columbia U. (Teachers C.)
Harvard U.
Jersey City St. U.
Morgan St. U.
U. Mass. (Boston)
U. Neb. (Omaha)
Northeastern Ill. U.
Temple U.
Tex. So. U.
Va. Commonwealth U.
U. Wis. (Milwaukee)

Engineering and Technology

(Typically includes Applied Sciences, Chemical Engineering, Civil Engineering, Computer Science/Engineering, Construction Engineering, Electrical Engineering, Energy Engineering, Engineering and Applied Sciences, Industrial Engineering, Mechanical Engineering; often includes Aeronautical/Astronautical Engineering, Engineering, Materials Engineering/Science, Mechanics, Metallurgy/ Metallurgical Engineering, Nuclear Engineering/ Science, Operations Research, Structural Engineering, Systems Engineering/Science)

A.F. Inst.
U. Akron
Ala. A&M U.
U. Ala.
U. Ala. (Birm.)
U. Ala. (Huntsville)
U. Alaska
Ariz. St. U.
U. Ariz.
U. Ark.
Auburn U.
Boston U.
Bradley U.
U. Bridgeport
Brown U.
Bucknell U.
U. Buffalo (S.U.N.Y.)
B.Y.U.
Cal. Inst. Tech.
Cal. Poly. St. U. (San Luis Obispo)
Cal. St. Poly U. (Pomona)
Cal. St. U. (Chico)
Cal. St. U. (Fresno)
Cal. St. U. (Fullerton)
Cal. St. U. (Long Beach)
Cal. St. U. (L.A.)
Cal. St. U. (Northridge)
Cal. St. U. (Sacramento)
U. Cal. (Berkeley)
U. Cal. (Davis)
U. Cal. (Irvine)
U.C.L.A.
U. Cal. (San Diego)
U. Cal. (Santa Barbara)
Cal. U. Pa.
Carnegie Mellon U.
Case West. Res. U.
Catholic U.
U. Cent. Fla.
Cent. Mo. St. U.
U. Cincinnati
C.C.N.Y. (C.U.N.Y.)
Clarkson U.
Clemson U.
Cleveland St. U.
Colo. Sch. Mines
Colo. St. U.
U. Colo.
U. Colo. (Denver)
Columbia U.
U. Conn.
Cornell U.
Dartmouth C.
U. Dayton
U. Del.
U. Denver
DePaul U.
U. Detroit Mercy
Drexel U.
Duke U.
East Car. U.
East. Ill. U.
East. Tenn. St. U.
F.D.U. (Teaneck)
Fitchburg St. U.
Fla. A&M U.
Fla. Atlantic U.
Fla. Inst. Tech.
Fla. St. U.
U. Fla.
Gannon U.
Geo. Mason U.
Geo. Wash. U.
Georgia Inst. Tech.

Georgia St. U.
U. Georgia
Gonzaga U.
Gov. St. U.
U. Hawaii
Hofstra U.
U. Houston
Howard U.
Idaho St. U.
U. Idaho
Ill. Inst. Tech.
U. Ill.
U. Ill. (Chicago)
Ind. St. U.
I.U.P.U.I.
Iowa St. U.
U. Iowa
Johns Hopkins U.
Kans. St. U.
U. Kans.
Kent St. U.
U. Ky.
Lamar U.
Lehigh U.
L.I.U.
L.S.U.
La. Tech U.
U. La. (Lafayette)
U. Louisville
Loyola C.
Loyola Marymount U.
Loyola U. (Chicago)
U. Maine
Manhattan C.
Marquette U.
U. Md.
U. Md. (Baltimore Cnty.)
M.I.T.
U. Mass.
U. Mass. (Dartmouth)
U. Mass. (Lowell)
McNeese St. U.
U. Memphis
Mercer U.
Miami U.
U. Miami (Fla.)
Mich. St. U.
Mich. Tech. U.
U. Mich.
Mid. Tenn. St. U.
Milwaukee Sch. Eng.
Minn. St. U. (Mankato)
U. Minn.
Miss. St. U.
U. Miss.
U. Mo. (Columbia)
U. Mo. (K.C.)
U. Mo. (Rolla)
Monmouth U.
Mont. Tech
Mont. St. U.
Montclair U.
Morgan St. U.
Natl. U.
Naval P.G. Sch.
U. Neb.
U. Nev.
U. Nev. (Reno)
U. N.H.
U. N. Haven
N.J.I.T.
N. Mex. Inst. M&T
N. Mex. St. U.
U. N. Mex.
U. N. Orleans
C.U.N.Y. (Grad. Ctr.)
N.Y.I.T.
S.U.N.Y. (Binghamton)
S.U.N.Y.C. Environ. Sci. & For. (Syracuse)
S.U.N.Y. I.T.
No. Car. A&T St. U.
No. Car. St. U. (Raleigh)

U. No. Car. (Charlotte)
No. Dak. St. U.
U. No. Dak.
Northeastern U.
N. Ill. U.
U. No. Tex.
Northwestern U.
U. Notre Dame
Nova U.
Oakland U.
Ohio St. U.
Ohio U.
Okla. St. U.
U. Okla.
Old Dom. U.
Ore. St. U.
U. Pac.
Penn. St. U.
U. Penn.
Pittsburg St. U.
U. Pitt.
Poly. U.
Portland St. U.
U. Portland
Prairie View A&M U.
Pratt Inst.
Princeton U.
U. Puerto Rico
Purdue U.
Purdue U. (Calumet)
Queens C. (C.U.N.Y.)
R.P.I.
R.P.I. Hartford
U. Rhode Island
Rice U.
R.I.T.
U. Rochester
Rose-Hulman Inst. Tech.
Rowan U.
Rutgers U.
St. Cloud St. U.
St. Mary's U. (Tex.)
U. St. Thomas (Minn.)
S.D.S.U.
San Fran. St. U.
San Jose St. U.
Santa Clara U.
U. Scranton
Seattle U.
U. So. Ala.
U. So. Cal.
U. So. Car.
So. Dak. Sch. M&T
So. Dak. St. U.
U. So. Fla.
So. Ill. U.
So. Ill. U. (Edwardsville)
So. Meth. U.
U. So. Miss.
Stanford U.
Stevens Inst. Tech.
Stony Brook U. (S.U.N.Y.)
Suffolk U.
Syracuse U.
Temple U.
Tenn. St. U.
Tenn. Tech. U.
U. Tenn.
U. Tenn. (Chattanooga)
U. Tenn. (Space Institute)
Tex. A&M U.
Tex. A&M U. (Kingsville)
Tex. Tech U.
U. Tex. (Arlington)
U. Tex. (Austin)
U. Tex. (Dallas)
U. Tex. (El Paso)
U. Tex. (San Antonio)
U. Tex. (Tyler)
U. Toledo
Tufts U.
Tulane U.

U. Tulsa
Tuskegee U.
Union C. (N.Y.)
Utah St. U.
U. Utah
Vanderbilt U.
U. Vt.
Villanova U.
Va. Commonwealth U.
Va. Poly. Inst.
U. Va.
Wash. St. U.
Wash. U. (Mo.)
U. Wash.
Wayne St. U.
West Chester U. Pa.
West. Ky. U.
W. Va. U.
West. Mich. U.
West. New Eng. C.
Wichita St. U.
Widener U.
Wilkes U.
C. Wm. & Mary
U. Wis.
U. Wis. (Milwaukee)
Worcester Poly. Inst.
Wright St. U.
U. Wyo.
Yale U.
Youngstown St. U.

ARCHITECTURAL ENGINEERING
U. Fla.
Ill. Inst. Tech.
Kans. St. U.
U. Kans.
U. Memphis
U. Miami
No. Car. A&T St. U.
Okla. St. U.
Penn. St. U.
R.P.I.
U. So. Cal.
Tex. A&M U.
U. Tex. (Austin)

BIOENGINEERING/ BIOMEDICAL ENGINEERING
U. Akron
U. Ala. (Birm.)
Ariz. St. U.
Baylor C. Med.
Boston U.
Brown U.
U. Buffalo (S.U.N.Y.)
Cal. St. U. (Northridge)
U. Cal. (Berkeley)
U. Cal. (Davis)
U. Cal. (San Diego)
U. Cal. (San Fran.)
Carnegie Mellon U.
Case West. Res. U.
Clemson U.
Colo. St. U.
Columbia U.
U. Conn.
Cornell U.
Dartmouth C.
Drexel U.
Duke U.
Geo. Wash. U.
Georgia Inst. Tech.
U. Georgia
U. Hawaii
U. Houston
U. Ill.
U. Ill. (Chicago)
Iowa St. U.
U. Iowa
Johns Hopkins U.

Kans. St. U.
U. Ky.
La. Tech. U.
L.S.U.
Marquette U.
M.I.T.
U. Memphis
Mercer U.
U. Miami
U. Mich.
U. Minn.
Miss. St. U.
N.J.I.T.
U. Nev. (Reno)
No. Car. St. U.
U. No. Car. (Chapel Hill)
Northwestern U.
Ohio St. U.
Penn. St. U.
U. Penn.
U. Pitt.
Purdue U.
U. Rochester
R.P.I.
Rice U.
Rose-Hulman Inst.
Rutgers U.
U. So. Cal.
Stanford U.
U. Tenn. (Memphis)
Tex. A&M U.
U. Tex. (Arlington)
U. Tex. S.W. Med. Ctr. (Dallas)
Tulane U.
U. Utah
Vanderbilt U.
Va. Commonwealth U.
Va. Poly. Inst.
U. Va.
U. Vt.
Wash. U.
U. Wash.
Worcester Poly. Inst.
Wright St. U.
U. Wyo.

CERAMIC ENGINEERING
Alfred U.
U. Cal. (Berkeley)
U.C.L.A.
Case West. Res. U.
U. Cincinnati
Clemson U.
U. Fla.
Georgia Inst. Tech.
U. Ill.
U. Mo. (Rolla)
Penn. St. U.
R.P.I.
Rutgers U.

ENGINEERING MANAGEMENT
A.F. Inst.
U. Ala. (Huntsville)
U. Alaska
U. Buffalo (S.U.N.Y.)
B.Y.U.
Cal. Poly. St. U. (San Luis Obispo)
Cal. St. U. (Northridge)
Case West. Res. U.
U. Cent. Fla.
Clarkson U.
Colo. St. U.
U. Colo.
U. Dallas
Dartmouth C.
U. Dayton
U. Detroit Mercy
Drexel U.

Fla. Inst. Tech.
Geo. Wash. U.
Ga. Inst. Tech.
U. Kans.
U. La. (Lafayette)
Lamar U.
Lehigh U.
L.S.U.
Loyola Marymount U.
Marquette U.
U. Md.
U. Md. (Baltimore Cnty.)
M.I.T.
U. Mass.
Mercer U.
U. Mich.
Milwaukee Sch. Eng.
U. Mo. (Rolla)
N.J.I.T.
Northeastern U.
Northwestern U.
Oakland. U.
Old Dom. U.
Penn St. U.
Portland St. U.
Poly. U.
R.I.T.
R.P.I.
St. Mary's U. (Tex.)
Santa Clara U.
U. So. Cal.
U. So. Fla.
S. Meth. U.
Stanford U.
Stevens Inst. Tech.
U. Tenn. (Chattanooga)
U. Tenn (Space Institute)
Tex. A&M U.
Tex. Tech U.
Tufts U.
U. Tulsa
U. Utah
Va. Poly. Inst.
Wash. St. U.
Wash. U.
Wayne St. U.
West. Mich. U.
Widener U.

ENVIRONMENTAL ENGINEERING
U. Ala.
U. Alaska
U. Ariz.
U. Ark.
Auburn U.
U. Buffalo (S.U.N.Y.)
Cal. Inst. Tech.
Cal. Poly. St. U. (San Luis Obispo)
U. Cal. (Berkeley)
U. Cal. (Davis)
U. Cal. (Irvine)
U.C.L.A.
Carnegie Mellon U.
Case West. Res. U.
Catholic U.
U. Cincinnati
Clarkson U.
Clemson U.
Colo. Sch. Mines
Colo. St. U.
U. Colo.
Columbia U.
U. Conn.
Cornell U.
Dartmouth C.
U. Dayton
Drexel U.
Duke U.
Fla. Inst. Tech.
U. Fla.
Geo. Wash. U.

Georgia Inst. Tech.
U. Houston
Humboldt St. U.
Ida St. U.
Ill. Inst. Tech.
U. Ill.
U. Iowa
Johns Hopkins U.
U. Kans.
Lamar U.
L.S.U.
U. Louisville
Loyola Marymount U.
U. Maine
Manhattan C.
Marquette U.
M.I.T.
U. Mass.
U. Mass. (Lowell)
U. Memphis
Mich. St. U.
Mich. Tech. U.
U. Mich.
Milwaukee Sch. Eng.
U. Miss.
U. Mo. (Rolla)
Mont. St. U.
Mont. Tech
U. Nev.
U. N. Haven
N.J.I.T.
S.U.N.Y.C. Environ. Sci. & For. (Syracuse)
N.Y.I.T.
U. N. Car. (Chapel Hill)
No. Dak. St. U.
U. No. Dakota
Northeastern U.
Northwestern U.
Ohio U.
Okla. St. U.
U. Okla.
Old Dom. U.
Ore. St. U.
Penn. St. U.
U. Penn.
Poly. U.
R.P.I.
U. Rhode Island
Rice U.
Rose-Hulman Inst. Tech.
Rutgers U.
U. So. Cal.
So. Dak. St. U.
Stevens Inst. Tech.
Syracuse U.
U. Tenn.
Tex. A&M U.
Tex. A&M U. (Kingsville)
Tex. Tech U.
U. Tex (Austin)
Utah St. U.
Vanderbilt U.
Va. Poly. Inst.
U. Va.
Villanova U.
Wash. St. U.
Wash. U.
U. Wash.
Wayne St. U.
U. Wis.
U. Wyo.
Youngstown St. U.

GEOLOGICAL/ GEOSCIENCES/ GEOTECHNICAL ENGINEERING
U. Alaska
Ariz. St. U.
U. Ariz.
U. Cal. (Berkeley)

U. Cal. (Riverside)
Colorado Sch. Mines
Cornell U.
Drexel U.
U. Idaho
Mich. Tech. U.
U. Minn.
U. Mo. (Rolla)
Mont. Tech
U. Nev. (Reno)
N. Mex. Inst. M&T
So. Dak. Sch. of M&T
U. Utah
Wash. St. U.
U. Wash.

MANUFACTURING ENGINEERING

Boston U.
Bradley U.
B.Y.U.
U.C.L.A.
U. Cent. Fla.
U. Detroit Mercy
Ill. Inst. Tech.
U. Ky.
La. Tech U.
Lehigh U.
U. Mass
U. Mich. (Dearborn)
U. N. Mex.
N.J.I.T.
No. Car. St. U.
Okla. St. U.
Ore St. U.
U. Pitt.
Poly. U.
Portland St. U.
Purdue U.
R.P.I.
U. Rhode Island
So. Meth. U.
Stanford U.
Syracuse U.
U. Tex. (El Paso)
Wayne St. U.
West. Mich. U.
U. Wis.
Worcester Poly. Inst.

MARINE SCIENCE/ ENGINEERING/ OCEAN ENGINEERING/ OCEANOGRAPHY

U. Alaska
Boston C.
Cal. St. U. (Fresno)
Cal. St. U. (Hayward)
Cal. St. U. (Sacramento)
U. Cal. (Berkeley)
U. Cal. (San Diego)
U. Cal. (Santa Cruz)
Columbia U.
U. Conn.
U. Del.
Fla. Atlantic U.
Fla. Inst. Tech.
Fla. St. U.
U. Fla.
U. Hawaii
Johns Hopkins U.
L.S.U.
U. Maine
U. Md.
U. Md. (Baltimore Cnty.)
M.I.T.
U. Miami
U. Mich.
Naval P.G. Sch.
U. N.H.
No. Car. St. U. (Raleigh)
U. No. Car. (Chapel Hill)

Nova U.
Old Dom. U.
Ore. St. U.
Princeton U.
U. Puerto Rico
U. Rhode Island
Rutgers U.
U. San Diego
San Jose St. U.
U. So. Ala.
U. So. Cal.
U. So. Car.
U. So. Fla.
U. So. Miss.
Stony Brook U. (S.U.N.Y.)
Tex. A&M U.
U. Wash.
C. Wm. & Mary
U. Wis.
Yale U.

MINERAL/MINING ENGINEERING TECHNOLOGY

U. Ala.
U. Alaska
U. Ariz.
U. Cal. (Berkeley)
Colo. Sch. Mines
Columbia U.
U. Idaho
U. Ky.
Mich. Tech. U.
U. Minn.
U. Mo. (Rolla)
Mont. Tech
U. Nev. (Reno)
N. Mex. Inst. M&T
U. No. Dak.
Penn. St. U.
So. Dak. Sch. M&T
So. Ill. U.
U. Utah
Va. Poly. Inst.
W. Va. U.

OPTICAL SCIENCES

Ala. A&M U.
U. Ala. (Huntsville)
U. Ariz.
Cleveland St. U.
U. Dayton
U. Houston
U. N. Mex.
Ohio St. U.
R.I.T.
U. Rochester

PAPER ENGINEERING/ SCIENCE/ TECHNOLOGY

Georgia Inst. Tech.
Miami U. (Ohio)
S.U.N.Y.C. Environ. Sci. & For. (Syracuse)
No. Car. St. U.
U. Wash.
West. Mich. U.

PETROLEUM ENGINEERING

U. Alaska
U. Cal. (Berkeley)
Colo. Sch. Mines
U. Houston
U. Kans.
L.S.U.
La. Tech U.
U. La. (Lafayette)
Miss. St. U.
U. Mo. (Rolla)
Mont. Tech

N. Mex. Inst. M&T
U. Okla.
Penn. St. U.
U. Pitt.
U. So. Cal.
Stanford U.
Tex. A&M U.
Tex. Tech U.
U. Tex (Austin)
U. Tulsa
U. Utah
W. Va. U.
U. Wyo.

POLYMER ENGINEERING/ SCIENCE

U. Akron
Carnegie Mellon U.
Case West. Res. U.
U. Cincinnati
Clemson U.
U. Conn.
Cornell U.
U. Detroit Mercy
East Mich. U.
U. Fla.
Georgia Inst. Tech.
Lehigh U.
U. Mass.
U. Mass. (Lowell)
M.I.T.
U. Mo. (K.C.)
No. Dak. St. U.
Penn. St. U.
Poly. U.
Princeton U.
R.P.I.
U. So. Miss.
U. Tenn.
Wayne St. U.

SOFTWARE ENGINEERING

Andrews U.
Cal. St. U. (Sacramento)
Carnegie Mellon U.
U. Conn.
DePaul U.
Geo. Mason U.
Kansas St. U.
Monmouth U.
Natl. U.
U. N. Haven
R.I.T.
San Jose St. U.
U. St. Thomas (Minn.)
Seattle U.
U. Scranton
U. So. Cal.
So. Meth. U.
Stevens Inst. Tech.
U. Tex. (Arlington)
Tex. Christ. U.
Wayne St. U.
Widener U.

SYSTEMS ENGINEERING

A. F. Inst.
U. Ariz.
Boston U.
Cal. Inst. Tech.
Cal. St. U. (Fullerton)
Case West. Res. U.
U. Fla.
Geo. Mason U.
Geo. Wash. U.
Georgia Inst. Tech.
Howard U.
Kans. St. U.
Lehigh U.
U. Md.

U. Memphis
Northeastern U.
U. Neb.
Oakland U.
Ohio U.
Okla. St. U.
U. Penn.
U. Pitt.
Poly. U.
Purdue U.
R.P.I.
Rutgers U.
U. So. Cal.
So. Meth. U.
Temple U.
U. Tenn. (Space Inst.)
Va. Poly. Inst. & St. U.
U. Va.
Wash. U.
W. Va. U.

TEXTILE ENGINEERING/ SCIENCE

Auburn U.
Clemson U.
Cornell U.
Georgia Inst. Tech.
U. Mass. (Dartmouth)
No. Car. St. U. (Raleigh)
Purdue U.

TRANSPORTATION/ TRAFFIC ENGINEERING

U. Cal. (Berkeley)
Cent. Mo. St. U.
U. Dayton
U. Del.
Iowa St. U.
Morgan St. U.
N.J.I.T.
Northeastern U.
Northwestern U.
U. Okla.
Penn. St. U.
U. Penn.
Poly. U.
Princeton U.
R.P.I.
U. So. Cal.
U. Tenn.
Tex. A&M U.
Tex. So. U.
U. Tex. (Austin)
U. Va.
Villanova U.
Wash. U.
U. Wash.

Environmental Health/Sciences/ Studies

(Typically includes Ecology, Forestry, Forest Science, Wood Science/ Technology)

Ala. A&M U.
U. Ala.
U. Alaska
U. Albany (S.U.N.Y.)
American U.
Antioch N.E.
U. Ariz.
Baylor U.
Brown U.
U. Buffalo (S.U.N.Y.)
B.Y.U.
Cal. Inst. Tech.
Cal. Poly. St. U. (San Luis Obispo)

Cal. St. Poly. U. (Pomona)
Cal. St. U. (Fullerton)
U. Cal. (Berkeley)
U. Cal. (Davis)
U. Cal. (Irvine)
U. Cal. (Santa Barbara)
U.C.L.A.
Case West. Res. U.
U. Chicago
U. Cincinnati
City C. (C.U.N.Y.)
Clemson U.
Colo. Sch. Mines
U. Colo. (Denver)
Columbia U.
U. Conn.
Cornell U.
Drexel U.
Duke U.
Duquesne U.
East Tenn. St. U.
Fla. Inst. Tech.
U. Fla.
Geo. Mason U.
Geo. Wash. U.
U. Georgia
U. Hawaii
Harvard U.
Humbolt St. U.
Hunter C. (C.U.N.Y.)
Idaho St. U.
U. Idaho
U. Ill.
Ind. U.
Jackson St. U.
Johns Hopkins U.
U. Kans.
U. Ky.
L.I.U. (C.W. Post)
L.S.U.
Loyola Marymount U.
U. Maine
Marshall U.
U. Md.
U. Md. (Baltimore Cnty.)
M.I.T.
U. Mass.
U. Mass. (Boston)
U. Mass. (Lowell)
McNeese St. U.
Miami U. (Ohio)
U. Miami (Fla.)
Mich. St. U.
Mich. Tech. U.
U. Mich.
Minn. St. U. (Mankato)
U. Minn.
Mont. St. U.
U. Mont.
Montclair U.
U. Neb.
U. Nev. (Reno)
U. N. Haven
N.J.I.T.
N. Mex. Highlands U.
C.U.N.Y. (Grad Ctr.)
S.U.N.Y.C. Environ. Sci. & For. (Syracuse)
No. Car. St. U. (Raleigh)
U. No. Car. (Chapel Hill)
No. Ariz. U.
No. Dak. St. U.
U. No. Iowa
U. No. Tex.
Nova U.
Ohio St. U.
Ohio U.
Okla. St. U.
U. Okla.
Ore. St. U.
Penn. St. U.
U. Penn.

U. Pitt.
Poly. U.
Portland St. U.
Purdue U.
R.P.I.
U. Rhode Island
Rice U.
Rutgers U.
Shippensburg U. Pa.
U. So. Car.
U. So. Conn.
So. Ill. U.
So. Ill. U. (Edwardsville)
S. F. Austin St. U.
Stony Brook U. (S.U.N.Y.)
U. Tenn.
Tex. A&M U. (Corpus
    Christi)
Tex. Christ. U.
U. Tex. (San Antonio)
Tufts U.
Tuskegee U.
Utah St. U.
U. Utah
U. Vt.
Va. Poly. Inst.
U. Va.
Wash. St. U.
U. Wash.
W. Va. U.
West. Tex. A&M U.
West. Wash. U.
Wichita St. U.
C. Wm. & Mary
U. Wis.
U. Wyo.
Yale U.

**FISH/WILDLIFE
MANAGEMENT**
U. Alaska
U. Ariz.
Auburn U.
B.Y.U.
U. Cal. (Berkeley)
Clemson U.
Colo. St. U.
Cornell U.
U. Fla.
Frostburg St. U.
Humboldt St. U.
U. Idaho
Iowa St. U.
L.S.U. A&M C.
U. Maine
U. Md.
U. Mass.
U. Miami (Fla.)
Mich St. U.
U. Minn.
Miss. St. U.
U. Mo. (Columbia)
Mont. St. U.
U. Mont.
U. Neb.
U. N.H.
N. Mex. St. U.
S.U.N.Y.C. Environ. Sci.
    & For. (Syracuse)
No. Car. St. U. (Raleigh)
U. No. Dak.
Ore St. U.
Penn. St. U.
So. Dak. St. U.
Sul Ross St. U.
Tenn. Tech. U.
U. Tenn.
Tex. A&M U.
Tex. A&M U.
    (Kingsville)
Tex. Tech U.
Utah St. U.
Va. Poly. Inst.

U. Vt.
U. Wash.
W. Va. U.

**LANDSCAPE
ARCHITECTURE**
U. Ariz.
Ball St. U.
Cal. St. Poly U.
    (Pomona)
U. Cal. (Berkeley)
Clemson U.
U. Colo.
Cornell U.
U. Fla.
U. Georgia
Harvard U.
U. Ill.
Iowa St. U.
Kans. St. U.
L.S.U.
U. Mass.
Mich. St. U.
U. Mich.
U. Minn.
Morgan St. U.
S.U.N.Y.C. Environ. Sci.
    & For. (Syracuse)
No. Car. St. U. (Raleigh)
Ohio St. U.
Okla. St. U.
U. Okla.
U. Ore.
Penn St. U.
U. Penn.
Rhode Island Sch. Design
U. So. Cal.
Tex A&M U.
Tex. Tech U.
U. Tex. (Arlington)
U. Tenn.
Utah St. U.
U. Va.
Va. Poly. Inst.
Wash. St. U.
U. Wash.
U. Wis.

**METEOROLOGY/
ATMOSPHERE
SCIENCES**
U. Ala. (Huntsville)
U. Alaska
U. Albany (S.U.N.Y.)
U. Ariz.
U. Cal. (Davis)
U.C.L.A.
U. Chicago
City C. (C.U.N.Y.)
Clemson U.
Colo. St. U.
U. Colo.
Columbia U.
Cornell U.
Creighton U.
U. Del.
Drexel U.
Fla. St. U.
Georgia Inst. Tech.
U. Hawaii
U. Ill.
Iowa St. U.
Johns Hopkins U.
U. Kansas
U. Md.
M.I.T.
U. Miami
U. Mich.
U. Mo. (Columbia)
Mont. St. U.
Naval P.G. Sch.
N. Mex. Inst. M&T
No. Car. St. U.

Ohio St. U.
U. Okla.
Ore. St. U.
Penn. St. U.
Princeton U.
Purdue U.
Rutgers U.
St. Louis U.
San Jose St. U.
So. Dak. Sch. M&T
So. Dak. St. U.
Stony Brook U.
    (S.U.N.Y.)
Tex. A&M U.
Tex. Tech U.
U. Utah
U. Wash.
U. Wis.
U. Wyo.
Yale U.

**RANGE
MANAGEMENT/
SCIENCE**
U. Ariz.
B.Y.U.
U. Cal. (Berkeley)
Colo. St. U.
U. Idaho
Mont. St. U.
N. Mex. St. U.
No. Dak. St. U.
Okla. St. U.
Ore. St. U.
Sul Ross St. U.
Tex. A&M U.
Tex. Tech U.
Utah St. U.
U. Wyo.

**WATER
RESOURCES/
ADMINISTRATION**
U. Ariz.
U. Cal. (Berkeley)
U. Cal. (Davis)
Colo. St. U.
U. Del.
Duke U.
Fla. Inst. Tech.
U. Fla.
Geo. Wash. U.
U. Idaho
Iowa St. U.
U. Kans.
U. Mich.
U. Mo. (Rolla)
Mont. Tech
U. Nev.
U. Nev. (Reno)
U. N.H.
U. N. Mex.
U. Okla.
S.U.N.Y.C. Environ. Sci.
    & For. (Syracuse)
Penn. St. U.
Princeton U.
Rutgers U.
So. Dak. Sch. Mines
Utah St. U.
Villanova U.
U. Vt.
U. Wis.
U. Wyo.

Fine Arts

(Typically includes Art
History, Studio Arts; of-
ten includes Commercial
Art, Applied Art, Crafts,
Design, Graphic Design,
Industrial Design)

Adams St. U.
Adelphi U.
U. Ala.
Albany (S.U.N.Y.)
Alfred U.
American U.
Ariz. St. U.
U. Ariz.
Ark. St. U.
U. Ark.
Art. Inst. Chicago
Auburn U.
Ball St. U.
Bennington C.
Bloomsburg U. Pa.
Boise St. U.
Boston U.
Bowl. Gr. St. U.
Bradley U.
B.Y.U.
Brooklyn C. (C.U.N.Y.)
Brown U.
Bryn Mawr C.
U. Buffalo (S.U.N.Y.)
Cal. C. Arts
Cal. Poly. St. U. (San
    Luis Obispo)
Cal. St. U. (Chico)
Cal. St. U. (Fresno)
Cal. St. U. (Fullerton)
Cal. St. U. (Long Beach)
Cal. St. U. (L.A.)
Cal. St. U. (Northridge)
Cal. St. U. (Sacramento)
U. Cal. (Berkeley)
U. Cal. (Davis)
U. Cal. (Irvine)
U.C.L.A.
U. Cal. (Riverside)
U. Cal. (San Diego)
U. Cal. (Santa Barbara)
Carnegie Mellon U.
Case West. Res. U.
Catholic U.
Cent. Conn. St. U.
Cent. Mich. St. U.
Cent. Mo. St. U.
Cent. Wash. U.
U. Chicago
U. Cincinnati
C.C.N.Y. (C.U.N.Y.)
Claremont Grad. U.
Clemson U.
Cleveland St. U.
Colo. St. U.
U. Colo.
Columbia U.
U. Conn.
Cornell U.
Cranbrook Acad. Art
U. Dallas
U. Del.
U. Denver
Drake U.
Drexel U.
Duke U.
East Car. U.
East Tenn. St. U.
East Ill. U.
East. Mich. U.
East. Wash. U.
Edinboro U. Pa.
Emory U.
Fla. Atlantic U.
Fla. St. U.
U. Fla.
Fort Hays St. U.
Geo. Wash. U.
Georgia So. U.
Georgia St. U.
U. Georgia
Gov. St. U.
U. Hartford

Harvard U.
U. Hawaii
U. Houston
Howard U.
Hunter C. (C.U.N.Y.)
Idaho St. U.
U. Idaho
Ill. Inst. Tech.
Ill. St. U.
U. Ill.
U. Ill. (Chicago)
Ind. St. U.
Ind. U.
Ind. U. Pa.
U. Indianapolis
Iowa St. U.
U. Iowa
Jacksonville U.
James Madison U.
Jersey City St. U.
Johns Hopkins U.
Kans. St. U.
U. Kans.
Kent St. U.
U. Ky.
Lamar U.
Lehman C. (C.U.N.Y.)
L.I.U. (C.W. Post)
L.S.U.
La. Tech. U.
U. Louisville
Marshall U.
Md. Inst. C. Art
U. Md.
U. Md. (Baltimore Cnty.)
Marywood U.
Mass. C. Art.
U. Mass.
U. Mass. (Dartmouth)
McDaniel C.
U. Memphis
Miami U. (Ohio)
U. Miami (Fla.)
Mich. St. U.
U. Mich.
Mills C.
Minn. St. U. (Mankato)
Minn. St. U. (Moorhead)
U. Minn.
U. Minn. (Duluth)
Miss. C.
Miss. St. U.
U. Miss.
U. Mo. (Columbia)
U. Mo. (K.C.)
Mont. St. U.
U. Mont.
Montclair U.
Morehead St. U.
U. Neb.
U. Neb. (Kearney)
U. Nev.
N. Mex. St. U.
U. N. Mex.
U. N. Orleans
C. New Rochelle
New School U. (Parsons
    Sch. Design)
C.U.N.Y. (Grad. Ctr.)
S.U.N.Y. (Binghamton)
S.U.N.Y.C. (New Paltz)
S.U.N.Y.C. (Oswego)
N.Y.U.
No. Car. St. U. (Raleigh)
U. No. Car. (Chapel Hill)
U. No. Car. (Greensboro)
U. No. Colo.
U. No. Dak.
U. No. Tex.
No. Ill. U.
U. No. Iowa
No. W. St. U. La.
Northwestern U.

U. Notre Dame
Ohio St. U.
Ohio U.
Okla. St. U.
U. Okla.
Old Dom. U.
U. Ore.
Otis Art Inst. L.A.
Penn. St. U.
U. Penn.
Pittsburg St. U.
U. Pitt.
Portland St. U.
Pratt Inst.
Princeton U.
Purdue U.
Queens C. (C.U.N.Y.)
Radford U.
Rhode Island C.
Rhode Island Sch. Design
Rice U.
R.I.T.
U. Rochester
Rockford C.
Rutgers U.
St. Cloud St. U.
St. Louis U.
Sam Houston St. U.
S.D.S.U.
San Fran. Art. Inst.
San Fran. St. U.
San Jose St. U.
Smith C.
U. So. Cal.
U. So. Car.
So. Conn. St. U.
U. So. Dak.
U. So. Fla.
Southeast Mo. St. U.
So. Ill. U.
So. Ill. U. (Edwardsville)
So. Meth. U.
So. Ore. St. U.
Stanford U.
S. F. Austin St. U.
Stony Brook U.
　(S.U.N.Y.)
Sul Ross St. U.
Syracuse U.
Temple U.
U. Tenn.
Tex. A&M U.
　(Commerce)
Tex. A&M U.
　(Kingsville)
Tex. Christ. U.
Tex. Tech U.
Tex. Woman's U.
U. Tex. (Austin)
U. Tex. (El Paso)
U. Tex. (San Antonio)
U. Tex. (Tyler)
U. Arts
Towson U.
Tufts U.
Tulane U.
U. Tulsa
Utah St. U.
U. Utah
Va. Commonwealth U.
U. Va.
Vanderbilt U.
Wash. St. U.
Wash. U. (Mo.)
U. Wash.
Wayne St. U.
West Tex. A&M U.
W. Va. U.
West. Ky. U.
West. Mich. U.
West. Wash. U.
Wichita St. U.
Wm. Paterson U.

Williams C.
U. Wis.
U. Wis. (Milwaukee)
U. Wis. (Superior)
U. Wyo.
Yale U.

ARTS MANAGEMENT

U. Akron
American U.
Boston U.
Cal. St. U. (Dominguez Hills)
Carnegie Mellon U.
U. Cincinnati
Columbia U. (Teachers C.)
Drexel U.
Fla. St. U.
Golden Gate U.
Ill. St. U.
Ind. U.
U. N. Orleans
New Sch. U. (Parsons Sch. Design)
S.U.N.Y. (Binghamton)
N.Y.U.
Ohio St. U.
Okla. City U.
U. Ore.
Pratt Inst.
St. Mary's U. (Minn.)
Seton Hall U.
U. So. Cal.
So. Meth. U.
Syracuse U.
Temple U.
Tex. Tech U.
U. Wis.

ART THERAPY

Sch. Art Inst. Chicago
U. Arts
U. Bridgeport
Cal. St. U. (L.A.)
Emporia St. U.
Geo. Wash. U.
Hofstra U.
U. Ill. (Chicago)
L.I.U. (C.W. Post)
U. Louisville
Loyola Marymount U.
Marywood U.
U. N. Mex.
C. N. Rochelle
S.U.N.Y.C. (Buffalo)
N.Y.U.
No. Ill. U.
Notre Dame U.
Pratt Inst.
So. Ill. U. (Edwardsville)
Springfield C.
U. Wis. (Superior)

INTERIOR DESIGN

Ariz. St. U.
Sch. Art Inst. Chicago
Chapman U.
U. Cincinnati
Drexel U.
Fla. St. U.
U. Houston
Ind. U.
U. Kans.
U. Ky.
La. Tech U.
U. Mass. (Dartmouth)
Md. Inst. C. Art
New Sch. U. (Parsons Sch. Design)
U. No. Car. (Greensboro)
No. Ill. U.
U. No. Tex.

U. Ore.
Pratt Inst.
Rhode Island Sch. Design
R.I.T.
Syracuse U.
Temple U.
Tex. Woman's U.
Va. Poly. Inst.
Wash. St. U.
Wayne St. U.
U. Wis.

MUSEUM TRAINING/STUDIES HISTORIC PRESERVATION

Sch. Art Inst. Chicago
Bank St. C.
Cal. St. U. (Dominguez Hills)
Case West. Res. U.
U. Cent. Okla.
C.C.N.Y. (C.U.N.Y.)
Colo. St. U.
U. Colo.
Columbia U.
U. Del.
U. Denver
Duquesne U.
East. Mich. U.
Framingham St. C.
Geo. Wash. U.
Hampton U.
U. Mich.
Mid. Tenn. St. U.
U. Mo. (Columbia)
U. Neb.
S.U.N.Y.C. (Buffalo)
S.U.N.Y.C. (Oneonta)
N.Y.U.
U. Ore.
U. Penn.
Rutgers U.
San Fran. St. U.
Seton Hall U.
U. So. Cal.
U. So. Car.
Syracuse U.
Tex. Tech U.
Tufts U.
U. Vt.
Wayne St. U.
C. Wm. & Mary

PHOTOGRAPHY

U. Ala.
Sch. Art Inst. Chicago
Bradley U.
Brooklyn C. (C.U.N.Y.)
Cal. C. Arts
Cal. Inst. Arts
Cal. St. U. (Fullerton)
Cal. St. U. (L.A.)
U. Colo.
Columbia U.
Cornell U.
Cranbrook Acad. Art
Geo. Wash. U.
Georgia St. U.
U. Houston
Ill. St. U.
Ind. U.
James Madison U.
L.S.U.
La. Tech U.
Md. Inst. C. Art
Mass. C. Art
U. Memphis
U. Miami
U. Mich.
Mills C.
U. Mo. (K.C.)
U. N. Orleans

S.U.N.Y.C. (New Paltz)
U. No. Tex.
U. Notre Dame
Ohio U.
Otis Sch. Art & Design
Pratt Inst.
Rhode Island Sch. Design
R.I.T.
San Fran. Art Inst.
San Jose St. U.
U. So. Car.
So. Meth. U.
Syracuse U.
Temple U.
Tex. Woman's U.
Utah St. U.
U. Utah
Va. Commonwealth U.
Wash. U.
Yale U.

TEXTILE DESIGN

Cal. C. Arts
U. Cal. (Davis)
Cornell U.
Cranbrook Acad.
Ind. St. U.
Ind. U.
U. Kans.
Kent St. U.
Mass. C. Arts
U. Mass. (Dartmouth)
U. Minn.
U. No. Tex.
Rhode Island Sch. Design
So. Ill. U. (Edwardsville)
Syracuse U.
Temple U.
Tex. Woman's U.
U. Wis.

FOREIGN LANGUAGES/ LITERATURES

(Typically includes French, German, Spanish; often includes Italian, Portuguese, Romance, Russian/ Slavic Languages)

U. Akron
U. Ala.
U. Albany (S.U.N.Y.)
American U.
Appal. St. U.
Ariz. St. U.
U. Ariz.
U. Ark.
Auburn U.
Ball St. U.
Boston C.
Boston U.
Bowl. Gr. St. U.
Brooklyn C. (C.U.N.Y.)
Brown U.
Bryn Mawr C.
U. Buffalo (S.U.N.Y.)
B.Y.U.
Cal. St. U. (Fullerton)
Cal. St. U. (Long Beach)
Cal. St. U. (L.A.)
Cal. St. U. (Northridge)
Cal. St. U. (Sacramento)
U. Cal. (Berkeley)
U. Cal. (Davis)
U. Cal. (Irvine)
U.C.L.A.
U. Cal. (Riverside)
U. Cal. (San Diego)
U. Cal. (Santa Barbara)
Case West. Res U.
Catholic U.
Cent. Conn. St. U.

U. Chicago
U. Cincinnati.
C.C.N.Y. (C.U.N.Y.)
Colo. St. U.
U. Colo.
Columbia U.
Conn. C.
U. Conn.
Cornell U.
U. Del.
U. Denver
Duke U.
Duquesne U.
East. Mich. U.
Emory U.
F.D.U. (Madison)
F.D.U. (Teaneck)
Fla. Atlantic U.
Fla. St. U.
U. Fla.
Fordham U.
Georgetown U.
Geo. Mason U.
Geo. Wash. U.
Georgia St. U.
U. Georgia
Harvard U.
U. Hawaii
U. Houston
Howard U.
Hunter C. (C.U.N.Y.)
U. Idaho
Ill. St. U.
U. Ill.
U. Ill. (Chicago)
Ind. St. U.
Ind. U.
Iona C.
U. Iowa
Johns Hopkins U.
Kans. St. U.
U. Kans.
Kent St. U.
U. Ky.
L.I.U.
L.S.U.
U. La. (Lafayette)
La. Tech U.
U. Louisville
U. Maine
Marquette U.
U. Md.
U. Mass.
U. Memphis
Miami U. (Ohio)
U. Miami (Fla.)
Mich. St. U.
U. Mich.
Middlebury C.
Millersville U. Pa.
Minn. St. U. (Mankato)
U. Minn.
U. Miss.
U. Mo. (Columbia)
U. Mont.
Montclair U.
Monterey Inst.
U. Neb.
U. Nev.
U. Nev. (Reno)
N. Mex. St. U.
U. N. Mex.
C.U.N.Y. (Grad. Ctr.)
S.U.N.Y. (Binghamton)
N.Y.U.
No. Car. A&T St. U.
No. Car. Cent. U.
U. No. Car. (Chapel Hill)
U. No. Car. (Greensboro)
U. No. Colo.
No. Ill. U.

U. No. Iowa
U. No. Tex.
Northwestern U.
U. Notre Dame
Ohio St. U.
Ohio U.
U. Okla.
U. Ore.
Penn. St. U.
U. Penn.
U. Pitt.
Portland St. U.
Princeton U.
Purdue U.
Queens C. (C.U.N.Y.)
Rhode Island C.
U. Rhode Island
Rice U.
U. Rochester
Rutgers U.
St. John's U. (N.Y.)
St. Joseph's C. (Pa.)
St. Louis U.
S.D.S.U.
San Fran. St. U.
San Jose St. U.
Seton Hall U.
Simmons C.
Smith C.
So. Conn. St. U.
U. So. Fla.
U. So. Cal.
U. So. Car.
So. Ill. U.
Southwest Tex. St. U.
Stanford U.
Stony Brook U.
  (S.U.N.Y.)
Syracuse U.
Temple U.
U. Tenn.
Tex. Tech U.
U. Tex. (Austin)
U. Tex. (El Paso)
U. Tex. (San Antonio)
U. Tex. (Pan
  American)
U. Toledo
Tufts U.
Tulane U.
U. Utah
Vanderbilt U.
U. Vt.
Villanova U.
U. Va.
Wash. St. U.
Wash. U. (Mo.)
U. Wash.
Wayne St. U.
West Chester U. Pa.
W. Va. U.
West Ky. U.
West. Mich. U.
Wichita St. U.
Winthrop U.
U. Wis.
U. Wis. (Milwaukee)
U. Wyo.
Yale U.

**AFRICAN
LANGUAGES**
U. Albany (S.U.N.Y.)
U.C.L.A.
Columbia U.
Cornell U.
Howard U.
U. Ill.
Johns Hopkins U.
N.Y.U.
Northwestern U.
Ohio St. U.
U. Wis.

Yale U.

AKKADIAN
Catholic U.
Columbia U.
Harvard U.

BENGALI
U. Chicago

CAUCASIAN
Columbia U.

CELTIC
Catholic U.
Harvard U.

**CHINESE/
JAPANESE/ASIAN
LANGUAGES**
Boston C.
B.Y.U.
U. Cal. (Berkeley)
U.C.L.A.
U. Cal. (Santa
  Barbara)
U. Chicago
U. Colo.
Columbia U.
Cornell U.
Fla. St. U.
Georgetown U.
Harvard U.
U. Hawaii
Ind. U.
U. Iowa
U. Kans.
U. Mass.
Mich. St. U.
U. Mich.
Middlebury C.
U. Minn.
Monterey Inst.
N.Y.U.
U. No. Car.
  (Chapel Hill)
Northwestern U.
Ohio St. U.
U. Ore.
U. Pitt.
Princeton U.
St. John's (N.M.)
San Fran. St. U.
U. So. Cal.
Stanford U.
U. Tex. (Austin)
Wash. U. (Mo.)
U. Wash.
Wayne St. U.
U. Wis.
Yale U.

GREEK
Boston C.
Bryn Mawr C.
U. Cal. (Berkeley)
U.C.L.A.
Catholic U.
U. Chicago
Columbia U.
Fla. St. U.
U. Ill.
Ind. U.
U. Iowa
John Carroll U.
U. Mich.
U. Minn.
U. Miss.
N.Y.U.
Northwestern U.
Stanford U.
U. Tex. (Austin)
Tufts U.

U. Vt.

**HEBREW/ARABIC/
NEAR AND MIDDLE
EASTERN
LANGUAGES/
LITERATURES**
U. Ariz.
Brandeis U.
Brown U.
B.Y.U.
U. Cal. (Berkeley)
U.C.L.A.
Catholic U.
U. Chicago
Columbia U.
Cornell U.
Georgetown U.
Harvard U.
Ind. U.
Johns Hopkins U.
U. Mich.
Middlebury C.
U. Minn.
N.Y.U.
U. Penn.
Princeton U.
U. Tex. (Austin)
U. Utah
U. Va.
U. Wash.
Wayne St. U.
U. Wis.
Yale U.

HINDI
U. Chicago

LATIN
Ariz. St. U.
Ball St. U.
Boston C.
Bryn Mawr C.
U. Cal. (Berkeley)
U.C.L.A.
Catholic U.
U. Chicago
Columbia U.
Fla. St. U.
Ill. St. U.
U. Ill.
Ind. U.
U. Iowa
John Carroll U.
U. Mich.
U. Minn.
U. Miss.
Northwestern U.
N.Y.U.
Stanford U.
U. Tex. (Austin)
Tufts U.
U. Vt.
West Chester U. Pa.

**RUSSIAN/SLAVIC
LANGUAGES**
U. Ariz.
Boston C.
Brown U.
Bryn Mawr C.
B.Y.U.
U. Cal. (Berkeley)
Columbia U.
Harvard U.
U. Ill.
Ind. U.
U. Iowa
U. Md.
Mich. St. U.
U. Mich.
Middlebury C.
U. Minn.

Monterey Inst.
N.Y.U.
U. No. Car. (Chapel Hill)
U. Ore.
San Fran. St. U.
Stanford U.
U. Wash.

SANSKRIT
U. Chicago
Harvard U.

**SCANDINAVIAN
LANGUAGES/
LITERATURES**
B.Y.U.
U. Cal. (Berkeley)
U.C.L.A.
U. Chicago
Columbia U.
Harvard U.
U. Minn.
U. Wash.
U. Wis.

**TRANSLATION AND
INTERPRETATION**
U. Ark.
Georgia St. U.
Gallaudet U.
Monterey Inst.
U. Puerto Rico

URDU
U. Chicago

**Home/Consumer
Economics, Food
Science, Food
Service,
Technology, Child
and Family Life,
Nutrition**

U. Akron
Ala. A&M U.
U. Ala.
Andrews U.
Appal. St. U.
Ariz. St. U.
U. Ariz.
U. Ark.
Auburn U.
Ball St. U.
Boston U.
Bowl. Gr. St. U.
U. Bridgeport
B.Y.U.
Brooklyn C. (C.U.N.Y)
U. Buffalo (S.U.N.Y.)
Cal. Poly. St. U. (San
  Luis Obispo)
Cal. St. Poly. U.
  (Pomona)
Cal. St. (Chico)
Cal. St. U. (Fresno)
Cal. St. U. (Long Beach)
Cal. St. U. (L.A.)
Cal. St. U. (Northridge)
U. Cal. (Berkeley)
U. Cal. (Davis)
U.C.L.A.
Case West. Res. U.
Cent. Mich. U.
Cent. Mo. St. U.
Cent. Wash. U.
Chapman U.
U. Chicago
U. Cinn.
Colo. St. U.
Columbia U.
U. Conn.
Cornell U.

U. Del.
U. Denver
Drexel U.
East Car. U.
East. Ill. U.
East. Ky. U.
East. Mich. U.
East Tenn. St. U.
F.D.U. (Teaneck)
Fla. St. U.
U. Fla.
Framingham St. U.
Georgia C. & St. U.
Georgia So. U.
U. Georgia
Harvard U.
U. Hawaii
Hood C.
Howard U.
Hunter C. (C.U.N.Y.)
Idaho St. U.
U. Idaho
Ill. St. U.
U. Ill.
Incarnate Word U.
Ind. St. U.
Ind. U. Pa.
Iowa St. U.
Johns Hopkins U.
Kans. St. U.
U. Kans.
Kent St. U.
U. Ky.
U. La. (Lafayette)
Lamar U.
Lehman C. (C.U.N.Y)
Loma Linda U.
L.S.U.
La. Tech U.
U. Maine
Marshall U.
U. Md.
Marywood U.
U. Mass.
U. Memphis
Mercer U.
Miami U. (Ohio)
Mich. St. U.
Minn. St. U. (Mankato)
Minn. St. U.
  (Moorhead)
U. Minn.
Miss St. U.
U. Mo. (Columbia)
Montclair U.
U. Neb.
U. Nev. (Reno)
U. N.H.
N. Mex. St. U.
U. N. Mex.
N.Y.U.
No. Car. A&T St. U.
No. Car. St. U.
  (Raleigh)
U. No. Car.
  (Greensboro)
No. Dak. St. U.
Northeastern U.
No. Ill. U.
U. No. Tex.
Nova U.
Ohio St. U.
Ohio U.
Okla. St. U.
U. Okla.
Ore. St. U.
Penn. St. U.
U. Pitt.
U. Puerto Rico
Purdue U.
U. Rhode Island
Rutgers U.
Sage Grad. Sch.

S.D.S.U.
San Fran. St. U.
San Jose St. U.
U. So. Cal.
So. Car. St. U.
So. Dak. St. U.
So. East. Mo. St. U.
So. Ill. U.
U. So. Miss.
Southern U.
Stanford U.
Syracuse U.
Tenn. St. U.
U. Tenn.
U. Tenn. (Martin)
Texas A&M U.
Tex. So. U.
Tex. Tech U.
Tex. Woman's U.
U. Tex. (Austin)
U. Tex. (Dallas)
Tulane U.
Tuskegee U.
Utah St. U.
U. Utah
Va. Poly. Inst.
U. Vt.
Wash. St. U.
U. Wash.
Wayne St. U.
W. Va. U.
West. Car. U.
West Ky. U.
West. Mich. U.
Winthrop U.
U. Wis.
U. Wis.
　(Stevens Point)
U. Wis. (Stout)
U. Wyo.

Horticulture

U. Ark.
Auburn U.
B.Y.U.
U. Cal. (Davis)
Clemson U.
Colo. St. U.
Cornell U.
U. Del.
U. Fla.
U. Georgia
U. Hawaii
Iowa St. U.
Kans. St. U.
L.S.U.
U. Md.
Mich. St. U.
U. Minn.
Miss. St. U.
U. Mo. (Columbia)
U. Neb.
N. Mex. St. U.

No. Car. St. U. (Raleigh)
No. Dak. St. U.
Ohio St. U.
Okla. St. U.
Oregon St. U.
Penn. St. U.
U. Puerto Rico
Purdue U.
Rutgers U.
So. Ill. U.
U. Tenn.
Tex. A&M U.
Tex. Tech U.
Va. Poly. Inst.
Wash. St. U.
U. Wash.
W. Va. U.
U. Wis.

Humanities

(Typically includes English and History; offered by nearly 400 institutions in all 50 states, so individual institutions are not listed here)

CLASSICS

U. Albany (S.U.N.Y.)
U. Ariz.
Ball St. U.
Boston C.
Boston U.
Brown U.
Bryn Mawr C.
U. Buffalo (S.U.N.Y.)
B.Y.U.
U. Cal. (Berkeley)
U. Cal. (Davis)
U. Cal. (Irvine)
U.C.L.A.
U. Cal. (Santa Barbara)
Catholic U.
U. Chicago
U. Cinn.
U. Colo.
Columbia U.
Conn. C.
U. Conn.
Cornell U.
Duke U.
Fla. St. U.
U. Fla.
Fordham U.
Georgia St. U.
U. Georgia
Harvard U.
U. Hawaii
Hunter C. (C.U.N.Y.)
U. Ill.
Ind. U.
U. Iowa
John Carroll U.
Johns Hopkins U.
U. Kans.
Kent St. U.
U. Ky.
Loyola U. (Chicago)
U. Md.
U. Mass.
U. Mich.
U. Minn.
U. Miss.
U. Mo. (Columbia)
U. Neb.
C.U.N.Y. (Grad. Ctr.)
N.Y.U.
U. No. Car.
　(Chapel Hill)
U. No. Car.
　(Greensboro)
Northwestern U.
Ohio St. U.
U. Ore.
U. Penn.
U. Pitt.
Princeton U.
Rutgers U.
San Fran. St. U.
U. So. Cal.
Stanford U.
Syracuse U.
U. Tex. (Austin)
Tufts U.
Tulane U.
Vanderbilt U.
Villanova U.
U. Va.
U. Vt.
Wash U. (Mo.)
U. Wash.

Wayne St. U.
U. Wis.
Yale U.

COMPARATIVE LITERATURE

American U.
Ariz. St. U.
U. Ariz.
U. Ark.
B.Y.U.
Brown U.
U. Buffalo (S.U.N.Y.)
Cal. St. U. (Fullerton)
U. Cal. (Berkeley)
U. Cal. (Davis)
U. Cal. (Irvine)
U.C.L.A.
U. Cal. (Riverside)
U. Cal. (San Diego)
U. Cal. (Santa Barbara)
U. Cal. (Santa Cruz)
Case West. Res. U.
Catholic U.
U. Chicago
U. Colo.
Columbia U.
U. Conn.
Cornell U.
U. Dallas
Dartmouth C.
Duke U.
Emory U.
F.D.U. (Teaneck)
Fla. Atlantic U.
U. Georgia
Harvard U.
U. Ill.
Ind. U.
U. Iowa
Kent St. U.
L.S.U.
U. Md.
U. Mass.
Mich. St. U.
U. Mich.
U. Minn.
U. N. Mex.
C.U.N.Y. (Grad. Ctr.)
S.U.N.Y.
　(Binghamton)
N.Y.U.
U. No. Car.
　(Chapel Hill)
Northwestern U.
Ohio St. U.
U. Ore.
Penn. St. U.
U. Penn.
Princeton U.
U. Puerto Rico
Purdue U.
U. Rochester
Rutgers U.
San Fran. St. U.
U. So. Cal.
U. So. Car.
Stanford U.
Stony Brook U.
　(S.U.N.Y.)
Tex. Tech U.
U. Tex. (Austin)
U. Tex. (Dallas)
U. Utah
Vanderbilt U.
Wash. U. (Mo.)
U. Wash.
Wayne St. U.
West. Ky. U.
W. Va. U.
U. Wis.
U. Wis. (Milwaukee)
Yale U.

FOLKLORE

U. Cal. (Berkeley)
U.C.L.A.
Ind. U.
U. No. Car. (Chapel Hill)
U. Ore.
U. Penn.
Utah St. U.
West. Ky. U.

LINGUISTICS

U. Ala.
U. Albany (S.U.N.Y.)
Ariz. St. U.
U. Ariz.
Ball St. U.
Boston C.
Boston U.
B.Y.U.
Brown U.
U. Buffalo (S.U.N.Y.)
Cal. St. U. (Fresno)
Cal. St. U. (Fullerton)
Cal. St. U. (Long Beach)
Cal. St. U. (Northridge)
Cal. St. U. (San
　Bernardino)
U. Cal. (Berkeley)
U. Cal. (Davis)
U.C.L.A.
U. Cal. (San Diego)
U. Cal. (Santa Barbara)
U. Cal. (Santa Cruz)
Carnegie Mellon U.
U. Chicago
U. Colo.
U. Conn.
Cornell U.
U. Del.
East. Mich. U.
Fla. Atlantic U.
U. Fla.
Gallaudet U.
Geo. Mason U.
Georgetown U.
U. Georgia
Harvard U.
U. Hawaii
Hofstra U.
U. Houston
U. Ill.
U. Ill. (Chicago)
Ind. U.
U. Iowa
U. Kans.
U. Louisville
L.S.U.
U. Md.
U. Mass.
M.I.T.
Mich. St. U.
U. Mich.
U. Minn.
U. Mont.
U. N. Mex.
C.U.N.Y. (Grad. Ctr.)
N.Y.U.
U. No. Car. (Chapel Hill)
N. East. Ill. U.
U. No. Dak.
Northwestern U.
Oakland U.
Ohio St. U.
Ohio U.
U. Ore.
Penn. St. U.
U. Penn.
U. Pitt.
Purdue U.
U. Puerto Rico
Queens C. (C.U.N.Y.)
Rice U.
Rutgers U.

S.D.S.U.
San Jose St. U.
U. So. Cal.
U. So. Car.
U. So. Fla.
So. Ill. U.
Stanford U.
Syracuse U.
Temple U.
Tex. Tech U.
U. Tex. (Arlington)
U. Tex. (Austin)
U. Tex. (El Paso)
U. Utah
U. Va.
U. Wash.
Wayne St. U.
W. Va. U.
U. Wis.
Yale U.

PHILOSOPHY

U. Albany (S.U.N.Y.)
American U.
Ariz. St. U.
U. Ariz.
U. Ark.
Baylor U.
Boston C.
Boston U.
Bowl. Gr. St. U.
Brooklyn C. (C.U.N.Y.)
Brown U.
U. Buffalo (S.U.N.Y.)
Cal. St. U. (Long Beach)
Cal. St. U. (L.A.)
U. Cal. (Berkeley)
U. Cal. (Davis)
U. Cal. (Irvine)
U.C.L.A.
U. Cal. (Riverside)
U. Cal. (San Diego)
U. Cal. (Santa Barbara)
Carnegie Mellon U.
Catholic U.
Cent. Mich. U.
U. Chicago
U. Cincinnati
Claremont Grad. U.
Cleveland St. U.
Colgate U.
Colo. St. U.
U. Colo.
Columbia U.
U. Conn.
Cornell U.
U. Dallas
U. Denver
DePaul U.
Duke U.
Duquesne U.
Emory U.
Fla. St. U.
U. Fla.
Fordham U.
Georgetown U.
Geo. Wash. U.
Georgia St. U.
U. Georgia
Gonzaga U.
Harvard U.
U. Hawaii
U. Houston
Howard U.
U. Ill.
U. Ill. (Chicago)
Ind. U.
U. Iowa
Johns Hopkins U.
U. Kans.
Kent St. U.
U. Ky.
L.S.U.

U. Louisville
Loyola U. (Chicago)
Marquette U.
U. Md.
M.I.T.
U. Mass.
U. Memphis
Miami U. (Ohio)
U. Miami (Fla.)
Mich. St. U.
U. Mich.
U. Minn.
U. Miss.
U. Mo. (Columbia)
Montclair U.
U. Mont.
U. Neb.
U. Nev. (Reno)
U. N. Mex.
New Sch. U.
C.U.N.Y. (Grad. Ctr.)
S.U.N.Y. (Binghamton)
S.U.N.Y.
N.Y.U.
U. No. Car.
   (Chapel Hill)
No. Ill. U.
Northwestern U.
U. Notre Dame
Ohio St. U.
Ohio U.
Okla. St. U.
U. Okla.
U. Ore.
Penn. St. U.
U. Penn.
U. Pitt.
Princeton U.
U. Puerto Rico
Purdue U.
R.P.I.
U. Rhode Island
Rice U.
U. Rochester
Rutgers U.
St. Louis U.
St. Mary's U.
U. St. Thomas (Tex.)
S.D.S.U.
San Fran. St. U.
San Jose St. U.
U. So. Car.
U. So. Cal.
U. So. Fla.
So. Ill. U.
So. Ill. U.
   (Edwardsville)
U. So. Miss.
Stanford U.
Stony Brook U.
   (S.U.N.Y.)
Syracuse U.
Temple U.
U. Tenn.
Tex. A&M U.
Tex. Tech U.
U. Tex. (Austin)
U. Toledo
Tufts U.
Tulane U.
U. Utah
Vanderbilt U.
Villanova U.
U. Va.
Wash. U. (Mo.)
U. Wash.
Wayne St. U.
West Chester U. Pa.
West. Mich. U.
U. Wis.
U. Wis. (Milwaukee)
U. Wyo.
Yale U.

Law

U. Akron
U. Ala.
Albany Law Sch.
American U.
Ariz. St. U.
U. Ariz.
U. Ark.
U. Ark. (Little Rock)
U. Balt.
Baylor U.
Boston C.
Boston U.
U. Buffalo (S.U.N.Y.)
B.Y.U.
Brooklyn Law Sch.
U. Cal. (Berkeley)
U. Cal. (Davis)
U.C.L.A.
Cal. West. Sch. Law (San
   Diego)
Campbell U.
Capital U.
Case West. Res. U.
Catholic U.
Chapman U.
Chase C. Law
U. Chicago
U. Cinn.
Cleveland St. U.
U. Colo.
Columbia U.
U. Conn.
Cornell U.
Creighton U.
U. Dayton
U. Denver
DePaul U.
Detroit C. Law
U. Detroit Mercy
Dickinson Sch. Law
U. D.C.
Drake U.
Duke U.
Duquesne U.
Emory U.
Fla. St. U.
U. Fla.
Fordham U.
Franklin Pierce Law Ctr.
Geo. Mason U.
Georgetown U.
Geo. Wash. U.
Georgia St. U.
U. Georgia
Golden Gate U.
Gonzaga U.
Hamline U.
Hastings C. Law (U. Cal.)
Harvard U.
U. Hawaii
Hofstra U.
U. Houston
Howard U.
U. Idaho
Ill. Inst. Tech.
U. Ill.
Ind. U.
I.U.P.U.I.
Inter American U.
U. Iowa
John Marshall Law Sch.
U. Kans.
U. Ky.
U. La Verne
Lewis & Clark C.
L.S.U.
U. Louisville
Loyola Marymount U.
Loyola U. (Chicago)
Loyola U. (La.)
Marquette U.

U. Md. (Baltimore)
U. Memphis
Mercer U.
U. Miami (Fla.)
U. Mich.
U. Minn.
Miss. C.
U. Miss.
U. Mo. (Columbia)
U. Mo. (K.C.)
U. Mont.
U. Neb.
U. Nev.
New Eng. Sch. Law
U. N. Mex.
N.Y. Law Sch.
N.Y.U.
No. Car. Cent. U.
U. No. Car. (Chapel Hill)
U. No. Dak.
Northeastern U.
No. Ill. U.
Northwestern U.
U. Notre Dame
Nova U.
Ohio No. U.
Ohio St. U.
Okla. City U.
U. Okla.
U. Ore.
Pace U.
U. Pac.
U. Penn.
Pepperdine U.
Pont. Cath. U. P.R.
U. Pitt.
U. Puerto Rico
Queens C. (C.U.N.Y.)
Quinnipiac C.
Regent U.
U. Richmond
Roger Williams U.
Rutgers U. (Camden)
Rutgers U. (Newark)
St. John's U. (N.Y.)
St. Louis U.
St. Mary's U.
St. Thomas U.
Samford U.
U. San Diego
U. San Fran.
Santa Clara U.
Seattle U.
Seton Hall U.
U. So. Cal.
U. So. Car.
U. So. Dak.
So. Ill. U. (Carbondale)
U. So. Maine
So. Meth. U.
So. Tex. C. Law
So. U. & A&M C.
Southwestern U. Law
Stanford U.
Stetson U.
Suffolk U.
Syracuse U.
Temple U.
U. Tenn.
Tex. So. U.
Tex. Tech U.
Tex. Wesleyan U.
U. Tex. (Austin)
Thom. M. Cooley Law
   Sch.
Thom. Jefferson Sch. Law
Touro C.
U. Toledo
Tulane U.
U. Tulsa
U. Utah
Valparaiso U.
Vanderbilt U.

Vermont Law Sch.
Villanova U.
U. Va.
Wake Forest U.
Washburn U. Topeka
Wash. & Lee U.
Wash. U. (Mo.)
U. Wash.
Wayne St. U.
West. New Eng. C.
W. Va. U.
Whittier C.
Widener U.
Willamette U.
C. Wm. & Mary
Wm. Mitchell C. Law
U. Wis.
U. Wyo.
Yale U.
Yeshiva U.

Liberal/
Interdisciplinary/
Multidisciplinary
Studies

A.C.U.
U. Albany (S.U.N.Y.)
Antioch N. E. Grad Sch.
Auburn U.
Boise St. U.
Boston U.
Bradley U.
Brooklyn C. (C.U.N.Y.)
B.Y.U.
Cal. St. U. (Chico)
Cal. St. U. (Fullerton)
Cal. St. U. (Long Beach)
Cal. St. U. (San
   Bernardino)
U. Cal. (Irvine)
Cent. Wash. U.
Clark U.
Dartmouth C.
U. Del.
DePaul U.
U. Detroit Mercy
Drew U.
Duke U.
Duquesne U.
East. Wash. U.
Emory U.
Fordham U.
Frostburg St. U.
Geo. Mason U.
Georgetown U.
Hamline U.
Harvard U.
Hofstra U.
Hollins U.
U. Idaho
Ind. U.
Jacksonville St. U.
Johns Hopkins U.
Kean U.
Kent St. U.
L.S.U. (Shreveport)
U. Maine
Manhattanville C.
U. Miami
Mills C.
Minn. St. U. (Moorhead)
Miss. C.
Monmouth U.
U. Mont.
N. Mex. St. U.
New Sch. U.
S.U.N.Y.C. (Brockport)
S.U.N.Y.C. (Buffalo)
S.U.N.Y.C. (Plattsburgh)
N.Y.U.
No. Car. St. U.
U. No. Car. U. (Charlotte)

U. No. Car. U.
   (Greensboro)
U. No. Colo.
Northwestern U.
Notre Dame U.
Ohio U.
Okla. City U.
U. Okla.
U. Penn.
Queens C. (C.U.N.Y.)
Reed C.
U. Richmond
Rollins C.
Rutgers U.
St. John's C. (Md.)
St. John's C. (Minn.)
U. St. Thomas (Tex.)
S.D.S.U.
Simmons C.
U. So. Fla.
So. West. Tex. St. U.
Stony Brook U.
   (S.U.N.Y.)
Syracuse U.
Temple U.
Tex. Christ. U.
U. Tex. (Arlington)
U. Tex. (Dallas)
U. Tex. (El Paso)
U. Tex. (Pan American)
U. Tex. (Tyler)
U. Toledo
Towson U.
Va. Commonwealth U.
Vanderbilt U.
Villanova U.
Wesleyan U.
W. Va. U.
Wichita St. U.
Widener U.
Winthrop U.

Library/
Information
Science/Studies

U. Ala.
U. Albany (S.U.N.Y.)
Appal. St. U.
U. Ariz.
U. Buffalo (S.U.N.Y.)
U.C.L.A.
Catholic U.
U. Cent. Ark.
Cent. Mich. St. U.
Cent. Mo. St. U.
Chicago St. U.
Clarion U. Pa.
Clark Atlanta U.
Columbia U.
Drexel U.
East Car. U.
East Tenn. St. U.
Emporia St. U
Fla. St. U.
U. Hawaii
U. Ill.
Ind. St. U.
Ind. U.
Inter American U.
I.U.P.U.I.
U. Iowa
Kent St. U
U. Ky.
Kutztown U. Pa.
L.I.U. (C.W. Post)
L.S.U.
U. Md.
McDaniels C.
U. Mich.
U. Mo. (Columbia)
U. Nev.
No. Car. Cent. U.

U. No. Car. (Chapel Hill)
U. No. Car. (Greensboro)
U. No. Tex.
U. No. Iowa
U. Okla.
U. Pitt.
Pratt Inst.
U. Puerto Rico
Queens C. (C.U.N.Y.)
U. Rhode Island
Rutgers U.
St. John's U. (N.Y.)
Sam Houston St. U.
San Jose St. U.
Simmons C.
U. So. Car.
U. So. Fla.
So. Conn. St. U.
U. So. Miss.
Spalding U.
Syracuse U.
U. Tenn.
U. Tex. (Austin)
Tex. Woman's U.
U. Wash.
Wayne St. U.
West Ky. U.
U. Wis.
U. Wis. (Milwaukee)

Medicine

U. Ala. (Birm.)
Albany Med. Sch.
U. Ariz.
U. Ark.
Baylor C. Med.
Boston U.
Brown U.
U. Buffalo (S.U.N.Y.)
U. Cal. (Davis)
U. Cal. (Irvine)
U.C.L.A.
U. Cal. (San Diego)
U. Cal. (San Fran.)
Case West. Res. U.
U. Chicago
U. Cincinnati
U. Colo. Health Sci. Ctr.
Columbia U.
U. Conn.
Cornell U.
Creighton U.
Dartmouth C.
Drexel U.
Duke U.
E. Car. U.
E. Tenn. St. U.
East. Va. Med. Sch.
Emory U.
Finch U. Health Sci. (Chicago)
U. Fla.
Georgetown U.
Geo. Wash. U.
Med. C. Georgia
Georgia St. U.
Harvard U.
U. Hawaii
Howard U.
U. Ill.
U. Ill. (Chicago)
Ind. U.
U. Iowa
Johns Hopkins U.
U. Kans.
U. Ky.
Loma Linda U.
L.S.U. H.S.C.
L.S.U. Shreveport
U. Louisville
Loyola U. (Chicago)
Marshall U.

U. Md.
U. Mass. (Worcester)
Mayo Med. Sch.
Meharry Med. C.
Mercer U.
U. Miami (Fla.)
Mich. St. U.
U. Mich.
U. Minn. (Duluth)
U. Minn. (Minneapolis)
U. Miss. Med. C.
Morehouse Sch. Med.
U. Mo. (Columbia)
U. Mo. (K.C.)
Mt. Sinai Sch. Med. (N.Y.U.)
U. Neb. Med. C.
U. Nev. Reno
U. Med. & Dent. N.J. (Newark)
U. Med. & Dent. N.J. (Piscataway)
U. N. Mex.
N.Y. Med. C.
S.U.N.Y. Downstate
S.U.N.Y. Upstate
N.Y.U.
U. No. Car. (Chapel Hill)
U. No. Dak.
No. East. Ohio U.
Northwestern U.
Ohio St. U.
Med. C. Ohio (Toledo)
U. Okla.
Ore. Health & Sci. U.
Penn. St. U.
U. Penn.
U. Pitt.
Ponce Sch. Med.
U. Puerto Rico
U. Rochester
Rush U.
St. Louis U.
U. So. Ala.
Med. U. So. Car.
U. So. Car.
U. So. Dak.
U. So. Cal.
U. So. Fla.
So. Ill. U.
Stanford U.
Stony Brook U. (S.U.N.Y.)
Temple U.
U. Tenn. (Memphis)
Tex. A&M U.
Tex. Tech U.
U. Tex. (San Antonio)
U. Tex. Med. Br. (Galveston)
U. Tex. S.W. Med. Ctr. (Dallas)
U. Tex. (Houston)
Thom. Jefferson U.
Tufts U.
Tulane U.
Uniformed Serv. U. Health Sci.
U. Utah
Vanderbilt U.
U. Vt.
Va. Commonwealth U.
U. Va.
Wake Forest U.
Wash. U. (Mo.)
U. Wash.
Wayne St. U.
W. Va. U.
Med. C. Wis.
U. Wis.
Wright St. U.
Yale U.
Yeshiva U.

MEDICAL ILLUSTRATION

Med. C. Georgia
Johns Hopkins U.
U. Mich.
R.I.T.
U. Tex. S.W. Med. Ctr. (Dallas)

MEDICAL TECHNOLOGY

Andrews U.
Ball St. U.
U. Buffalo (S.U.N.Y.)
F.D.U. (Teaneck)
U. Md.
U. No. Dak.
Old Dom. U.
St. John's U. (N.Y.)
U. So. Miss.
U. Wis. (Eau Claire)
U. Wis. (Milwaukee)

TROPICAL MEDICINE

U. Hawaii
Johns Hopkins U.
L.S.U. H.S.C.
U. Puerto Rico
Tulane U.

Music

(Typically includes Composition, Music Education, Musicology, Performance, Theory; may include Ethnomusicology)

U. Akron
Ala. A&M U.
Ala. St. U.
U. Ala.
U. Alaska
Andrews U.
Appal. St. U.
Ariz. St. U.
U. Ariz.
Ark. St. U.
U. Ark.
U. Arts
Auburn U.
Austin Peay St. U.
Azusa Pac. U.
Ball St. U.
Baylor U.
Bennington C.
Boise St. U.
Boston U.
Bowl. Gr. St. U.
Bradley U.
Brandeis U.
B.Y.U.
Brooklyn C. (C.U.N.Y.)
Brown U.
U. Buffalo (S.U.N.Y.)
Butler U.
Cal. St. U. (Chico)
Cal. St. U. (Fresno)
Cal. St. U. (Fullerton)
Cal. St. U. (Hayward)
Cal. St. U. (Long Beach)
Cal. St. U. (L.A.)
Cal. St. U. (Northridge)
Cal. St. U. (Sacramento)
U. Cal. (Berkeley)
U. Cal. (Davis)
U. Cal. (Irvine)
U.C.L.A.
U. Cal. (Riverside)
U. Cal. (San Diego)
U. Cal. (Santa Barbara)

U. Cal. (Santa Cruz)
Carnegie Mellon U.
Case West. Res. U.
Catholic U.
U. Cent. Ark.
Cent. Mich. U.
Cent. Mo. St. U.
U. Cent. Okla.
Cent. Wash. U.
U. Chicago
U. Cincinnati
C.C.N.Y. (C.U.N.Y.)
Claremont Grad. U.
Cleve. St. U.
Colo. St. U.
U. Colo.
Columbia U.
Concordia U. (Ill.)
Conn C.
U. Conn.
Converse C.
Cornell U.
U. Del.
U. Denver
DePaul U.
Drake U.
Duke U.
Duquesne U.
East Car. U.
East Ill. U.
East. Ky. U.
East. Mich. U.
East. N. Mex. U.
East. Wash. U.
Emory U.
Emporia St. U.
Fla. Atlantic U.
Fla. St. U.
U. Fla.
Geo. Mason U.
Georgia So. U.
Georgia St. U.
U. Georgia
Hardin-Simmons U.
U. Hartford
Harvard U.
U. Hawaii
Holy Names C.
U. Houston
Howard U.
Hunter C. (C.U.N.Y.)
U. Idaho
Ill. St. U.
U. Ill.
Ind. St. U.
Ind. U.
I.U.P.U.I.
Ind. U. Pa.
U. Iowa
Ithaca C.
Jacksonville St. U.
Jacksonville U.
James Madison U.
Jersey City St. U.
Johns Hopkins U.
Juilliard Sch.
Kans. St. U.
U. Kans.
Kent St. U.
U. Ky.
Lamar U.
Lehman C. (C.U.N.Y.)
L.I.U. (C.W. Post)
L.S.U.
U. La. (Lafayette)
U. La. (Monroe)
U. Louisville
Loyola U. (La.)
U. Maine
Manhattan Sch. Music
Mansfield U. Pa.
Marshall U.
U. Md.

Marywood U.
U. Mass.
U. Mass. (Lowell)
McDaniels C.
McNeese St. U.
U. Memphis
Miami U. (Ohio)
U. Miami (Fla.)
Mich. St. U.
U. Mich.
Mid. Tenn. St. U.
Mills C.
Minn. St. U. (Mankato)
Minn. St. U. (Moorhead)
U. Minn.
Minot St. U.
Miss. C.
U. Miss.
U. Mo. (Columbia)
U. Mo. (K.C.)
U. Mont.
Montclair U.
U. Montevallo
Morehead St. U.
Morgan St. U.
Murray St. U.
U. Neb.
U. Neb. (Kearney)
U. Neb. (Omaha)
U. Nev.
U. Nev. (Reno)
New Eng. Cons. Music
U. N.H.
N. Mex. St. U.
U. N. Mex.
U. N. Orleans
C.U.N.Y. (Grad. Ctr.)
S.U.N.Y. (Binghamton)
S.U.N.Y. (Fredonia)
S.U.N.Y.C. (Potsdam)
N.Y.U.
N. Car. Cent. U.
U. No. Car. (Chapel Hill)
U. No. Car. (Greensboro)
U. No. Colo.
U. No. Dak.
U. No. Fla.
Northeastern Ill. U.
No. Ariz. U.
No. Ill. U.
U. No. Iowa
U. No. Tex.
No. Wash. U.
Northwestern St. U. La.
Northwestern U.
Notre Dame U.
U. Notre Dame
Oakland U.
Ohio St. U.
Ohio U.
Okla. City U.
U. Okla.
U. Ore.
U. Pac.
Penn. St. U.
U. Penn.
Pittsburg St. U.
U. Pitt.
Portland St. U.
U. Portland
Prairie View A&M U.
Princeton U.
Queens C. (C.U.N.Y.)
Radford U.
U. Redlands
Rhode Island C.
U. Rhode Island
Rice U.
Rider U.
U. Rochester
Roosevelt U.
Rowan U.
Rutgers U.

St. Cloud St. U.
St. John's U. (Minn.)
C. St. Rose
Salisbury St. U.
Samford U.
Sam Houston St. U.
S.D.S.U.
San Fran. Cons. Mus.
San Fran. St. U.
San Jose St. U.
Smith C.
U. So. Cal.
U. So. Car.
U. So. Dak.
U. So. Fla.
Southeast Mo. St. U.
Southeastern La. U.
U. So. Cal.
So. Ill U.
So. Ill. U.
  (Edwardsville)
So. Meth. U.
U. So. Miss.
Southwest Tex. St. U.
Southwestern
  Okla. St. U.
Stanford U.
Stony Brook U.
  (S.U.N.Y.)
S. F. Austin St. U.
Sul Ross St. U.
Syracuse U.
Temple U.
Tenn. St. U.
U. Tenn.
U. Tenn.
  (Chattanooga)
Tex. A&M U.
  (Kingsville)
Tex. Christ. U.
Tex. So. U.
Tex. Tech U.
Tex. Woman's U.
U. Tex. (Austin)
U. Tex. (El Paso)
U. Tex. (San Antonio)
U. Tex. (Tyler)
U. Toledo
Towson U.
Truman St. U.
Tufts U.
Tulane U.
U. Tulsa
U. Utah
Valdosta St. U.
Valparaiso U.
Va. Commonwealth U.
U. Va.
Wash. St. U.
Wash. U. (Mo.)
U. Wash.
Wayne St. U.
Webster U.
Wesleyan U.
West Chester U. Pa.
West Car. U.
West. Ga. St. U.
West Tex. A&M U.
W. Va. U.
West. Ill. U.
West. Ky. U.
West. Mich. U.
W. Va. U.
West. Wash. St. U.
Wichita St. U.
Winthrop U.
U. Wis.
U. Wis. (Eau Claire)
U. Wis. (Milwaukee)
U. Wis. (Stevens Point)
U. Wis. (Whitewater)
Wright St. U.
U. Wyo.

Yale U.
Youngstown St. U.

MUSIC THERAPY
Fla. St. U.
Mich. St. U.
N.Y.U.
So. Meth. U.
Tex. Woman's U.

Nursing and Health Professions

CHILD-CARE/CHILD HEALTH/PEDIATRIC NURSING
U. Buffalo (S.U.N.Y.)
Case West. Res. U.
Catholic U.
U. Cincinnati
Columbia U.
Emory U.
U. Hawaii
U. Ill. (Chicago)
Mich. St. U.
U. Mo. (K.C.)
U. Penn.
Seton Hall U.
Stony Brook U.
  (S.U.N.Y.)
Tex. Woman's U.
Va. Commonwealth U.
Wayne St. U.

FAMILY NURSING
(Typically includes Adult, Geriatric, Maternity, Parent–Child)
Adelphi U.
Ariz. St. U.
Boston C.
U. Buffalo (S.U.N.Y.)
Cal. St. U. (Fresno)
Case West. Res. U.
Catholic U.
U. Colo. Health Sci. Ctr.
Columbia U.
Emory U.
Med. C. Georgia
U. Hawaii
U. Ill. (Chicago)
Ind. U.
Kent St. U.
Loma Linda U.
L.S.U. H.S.C.
U. Miami
U. Mo. (K.C.)
N.Y.U.
Ore. Health & Sci. U.
U. Penn.
U. Pitt.
Seton Hall U.
Stony Brook U.
  (S.U.N.Y.)
U. Tenn. (Memphis)
U. Tex. Health Sci. Ctr.
  (Houston)
U. Tex. Health Sci. Ctr.
  (San Antonio)
Va. Commonwealth U.
Wayne St. U.

GERONTOLOGICAL NURSING
Emory U.
Hunter C. (C.U.N.Y.)
Loma Linda U.
U. Mass. (Lowell)
Mich. St. U.
N.Y.U.
U. Penn.
Seton Hall U.

HEALTH CARE/ HEALTH SERVICES/ HOSPITAL ADMINISTRATION/ MANAGEMENT
U. Ala. (Birm.)
American U.
Ariz. St. U.
Barry U.
Baruch C. (C.U.N.Y.)
Baylor U.
Boston U.
Brooklyn C. (C.U.N.Y.)
U. Buffalo (S.U.N.Y.)
B.Y.U.
Cal. St. U. (Bakersfield)
Cal. St. U. (Chico)
Cal. St. U. (Los Angeles)
Cal. St. U. (San
  Bernardino)
Capital U.
Card. Stritch C.
Case West. Res. U.
Chapman U.
U. Cincinnati
Clark U.
U. Colo.
Columbia U. (Teachers C.)
Columbus St. U.
U. Conn.
Cornell U.
U. Dallas
Drexel U.
U. Detroit Mercy
Duke U.
Duquesne U.
U. Fla.
Framingham St. C.
Gannon U.
Geo. Wash. U.
Georgia St. U.
Golden Gate U.
Gov. St. U.
U. Hartford
U. Hawaii
Harvard U.
Hofstra U.
Hunter C. (C.U.N.Y.)
U. Ill. (Chicago)
Ind. U.
I.U.P.U.I.
Iona C.
U. Iowa
Johns Hopkins U.
U. Kans.
U. Ky.
Kent St. U.
U. La Verne
Loma Linda U.
L.I.U.
L.I.U. (C.W. Post)
Loyola U. (Chicago)
Marywood U.
U. Mass. (Lowell)
U. Memphis
Med. U. So. Car.
U. Miami
U. Mich.
U. Minn.
Miss. C.
U. Mo. (Columbia)
U. Mo. (K.C.)
U. Miss.
Natl. U.
U. N. Haven
Northeastern U.
New Sch. U.
New York Med. C.
N.Y.U.
U. No. Tex.
Northwestern U.
Nova U.
Ohio St. U.

Ohio U.
U. Okla.
Our Lady Lakes U.
Pace U.
Pac. Luth. U.
Penn. St. U.
U. Penn.
U. Pitt.
Quinnipiac U.
R.P.I.
Rutgers U.
Sage Grad. Sch.
St. Joseph's U.
St. Louis U.
St. Mary's U. (Minn.)
St. Xavier U.
Seton Hall U.
Simmons C.
U. So. Cal.
U. So. Car.
U. So. Maine
Southeast Mo. St. U.
Southwest Tex. St. U.
Springfield C.
Stony Brook U.
  (S.U.N.Y.)
Suffolk U.
U. Tenn.
Tex. Tech U.
Tex. Woman's U.
Thunderbird
Towson U.
Union C.
Va. Commonwealth U.
Villanova U.
U. Wash.
Webster U.
Widener U.
Wilkes U.
Wright St. U.
Xavier U. (Ohio)

NURSE ANESTHESIA
U. Ala. (Birm.)
U. Buffalo (S.U.N.Y.)
Cal. St. U. (Long Beach)
U.C.L.A.
Case West. Res. U.
U. Cincinnati
Columbia U.
DePaul U.
U. Detroit Mercy
Drexel U.
Emory U.
Gannon U.
Med. C. Georgia
Gonzaga U.
U. Kans.
U. Mich.
U. No. Car. (Greensboro)
U. Pitt.
Med. U. So. Car.
Southwest Mo. St. U.
U. Tenn. (Chattanooga)
U. Tex. Health Sci. Ctr.
  (Houston)
Va. Commonwealth U.
Wayne St. U.
Xavier U. (La.)

NURSE MIDWIFERY
Case West. Res. U.
U. Cinn.
U. Colo. Health Sci. Ctr.
Columbia U. (Teachers C.)
Emory U.
U. Ill. (Chicago)
U. Miami
N.Y.U.
U. Penn.
Med. U. So. Car.
U. Tex. (El Paso)
Va. Commonwealth U.

NURSING
(Typically includes Nurse Practitioner, Administration, Education, Medical Surgical)

A.C.U.
Adelphi U.
U. Akron
U. Ala. (Birm.)
U. Ala. (Hunt.)
U. Alaska
Andrews U.
Ariz. St. U.
U. Ariz.
Ark. St. U.
U. Ark.
Armstrong Atlantic St. U.
Auburn U. (Mont.)
Augustana C.
Azusa Pac. U.
Ball St. U.
Barry U.
Bloomsburg U. Pa.
Boston C.
Bowie St. U.
Bradley U.
U. Buffalo (S.U.N.Y.)
B.Y.U.
Cal. St. (Bakersfield)
Cal. St. U. (Chico)
Cal. St. U. (Dominguez
  Hills)
Cal. St. U. (Fresno)
Cal. St. U. (Long Beach)
Cal. St. U. (L.A.)
Cal. St. U. (Sacramento)
U.C.L.A.
U. Cal. (San Fran.)
Capital U.
Case West. Res. U.
Catholic U.
U. Cent. Ark.
U. Cincinnati
Clarion U. Pa.
Clemson U.
U. Colo. Health Sci. Ctr.
Columbia U. (Teacher C.)
U. Conn.
Creighton U.
U. Del.
DePaul U.
Delta St. U.
U. Detroit Mercy
Drake U.
Drexel U.
Duke U.
Duquesne U.
East Car. U.
East. Ky. U.
East. Tenn. St.
East. Wash. U.
Edinboro U. Pa.
Emory U.
F.D.U. (Teaneck)
Fla. Atlantic U.
Fla. St. U.
U. Fla.
Fort Hays St. U.
Gannon U.
Geo. Mason U.
Georgetown U.
Georgia C. St. U.
Med. C. Georgia
Georgia St. U.
Gonzaga U.
Gov. St. U.
Hampton U.
U. Hartford
U. Hawaii
Howard U.
Hunter C. (C.U.N.Y.)
Idaho St. U.

U. Ill. (Chicago)
Incarnate Word U.
Ind. St. U.
I.U.P.U.I.
Ind. U. Pa.
U. Iowa
Johns Hopkins U.
Kean U.
Kent St. U.
U. Kans. Med. Ctr.
U. Ky.
Lehman C. (C.U.N.Y.)
Loma Linda U.
L.S.U. H.S.C.
U. Louisville
Loyola U. Chicago
U. Maine
Marquette U.
Marshall U.
U. Md.
U. Md. (Baltimore)
U. Mass.
U. Mass. (Boston)
U. Mass. (Dartmouth)
U. Mass. (Lowell)
U. Miami
Mich. St. U.
U. Mich.
Midwest. St. U.
Minn. St. U. (Mankato)
Miss. St. U. Women
U. Minn.
U. Miss.
U. Mo. (Columbia)
U. Mo. (K.C.)
Monmouth U.
Mont. St. U.
Murray St. U.
U. Neb.
New Jersey City U.
U. Nev. (Las Vegas)
U. Nev. (Reno)
Niagara U.
U.N.H.
U. Med. & Dent. N.J.
U. N. Mex.
U. N. Orleans Med. Ctr.
C. N. Rochelle
S.U.N.Y. (Binghamton)
S.U.N.Y.C. (New Paltz)
S.U.N.Y. Downstate
S.U.N.Y. Upstate
N.Y.U.
No. Ariz. U.
U. No. Car. (Chapel Hill)
U. No. Car. (Charlotte)
U. No. Car. (Greensboro)
U. No. Colo.
U. No. Dak.
No. Ill. U.
No. Mich. U.
Northwestern St. U. La.
Oakland U.
Med. C. Ohio
Ohio St. U.
Old Dom. U.
U. Okla. Health Sci. Ctr.
Ore. Health & Sci. U.
Pace U.
Pac. Luth. U.
Penn. St. U.
U. Penn.
U. Phoenix
Pittsburgh St. U.
U. Pitt.
U. Portland
Purdue U. (Calumet)
Radford U.
U. Rhode Island
Rivier C.
U. Rochester
Rush U.
Rutgers U.

Sage Grad. Sch.
St. Joseph's C.
St. Louis U.
C. St. Scholastica
St. Xavier U.
Salem St. C.
Salisbury St. U.
Sanford U.
S.D.S.U.
U. San Diego
San Fran. St. U.
U. San Fran.
San Jose St. U.
U. Scranton
Seattle Pac. U.
Seattle U.
Seton Hall U.
Slippery Rock U. Pa.
Sonoma St. U.
Southeast Mo. St. U.
U. So. Ala.
U. So. Car.
Med. U. So. Car.
U. So. Cal.
So. Conn. St. U.
So. Dak. St. U.
U. So. Fla.
So. Ill. U. (Edwardsville)
U. So. Maine
Southwest Mo. St.
Spalding U.
Stony Brook U. (S.U.N.Y.)
Syracuse U.
Temple U.
Tenn. St. U.
U. Tenn.
U. Tenn. (Chattanooga)
U. Tenn. (Memphis)
Tex. A&M U. (Corpus Christi)
Tex. Woman's U.
U. Tex. (Arlington)
U. Tex. (El Paso)
U. Tex. Health Sci. Ctr. (Houston)
U. Tex. Health Sci. Ctr. (San Antonio)
U. Tex. (Tyler)
Thom. Jefferson U.
Troy St. U.
U. Tulsa
U. Utah
Valdosta St. U.
Valparaiso U.
Vanderbilt U.
Villanova U.
U. Va.
Va. Commonwealth U.
U. Vt.
Wagner C.
Wash. St. U.
U. Wash.
Wayne St. U.
West Tex. A&M U.
W. Va. U.
West Chester U. Pa.
West. Conn. St. U.
West. Ky. U.
Wheelock C.
Wichita St.
Widener U.
Wilkes U.
Winona St. U.
U. Wis.
U. Wis. (Eau Claire)
U. Wis. (Milwaukee)
U. Wis. (Oshkosh)
Wright St. U.
U. Wyo.
Xavier U.
Xavier U. (La.)
Yale U.

OCCUPATIONAL THERAPY
U. Ala. (Birm.)
Boston U.
U. Buffalo (S.U.N.Y.)
Cal. St. U. (Sacramento)
U. Cent. Ark.
Colo. St. U.
Columbia U. (Teachers C.)
East. Ky. U.
U. Fla.
Med. C. Georgia
U. Ill. (Chicago)
U. Indianapolis
U. Kans. Med. Ctr.
Midwestern U.
U. N.H.
N.Y.U.
U. No. Car. (Chapel Hill)
Nova U.
U. Pitt.
U. Puget Sound
Rush U.
Sage Grad Sch.
C. St. Scholastica
San Jose St. U.
U. So. Cal.
Med. U. So. Car.
U. So. Dak.
U. So. Maine
Springfield C.
Temple U.
Tex. Woman's U.
Thom. Jefferson U.
Towson U.
Tufts U.
Va. Commonwealth U.
Wash. U.
U. Wash.
Wayne St. U.
West. Mich. U.

ONCOLOGY NURSING
Case West. Res. U.
Columbia U.
Duke U.
Emory U.
U. Penn.

PHYSICAL THERAPY
U. Ala. (Birm.)
Andrews U.
Armstrong Atlantic U.
Baylor U.
Boston U.
Buffalo U. (S.U.N.Y.)
Cal. St. U. (Fresno)
U. Cal. (San Fran.)
U. Cent. Ark.
Cent. Mich. U.
Chapman U.
U. Colo.
Columbia U. (Teachers C.)
Drexel U.
Duke U.
East. Wash. U.
Emory U.
U. Fla.
Gannon U.
Med. C. Georgia
Georgia St. U.
Gov. St. U.
Idaho St. U.
I.U.P.U.I.
U. Indianapolis
U. Iowa
U. Kans.
U. Ky.
L.I.U.
L.S.U. H.S.C.
U. Mass. (Lowell)

U. Miami
Midwestern U.
U. Minn.
U. Mont.
U. Med. & Dent. N.J.
N.Y.U.
No. Ariz. U.
U. No. Car. (Chapel Hill)
U. No. Dak.
Northwestern U.
Nova U.
Oakland U.
Ohio U.
Old Dom. U.
Phila. U.
U. Pitt.
U. Puget Sound
Quinnipiac U.
U. Rhode Island
Rutgers U. (Camden)
St. Louis U.
C. St. Scholastica
San Fran. St. U.
Simmons C.
Slippery Rock U. Pa.
U. So. Cal.
Med. U. So. Car.
U. So. Dak.
So. Ill. U.
Southwest Tex. St. U.
Springfield C.
Temple U.
Tex. Woman's U.
Thom. Jefferson U.
Va. Commonwealth U.
U. Vt.
U. Wash.
Wayne St. U.
West. Car. U.
U. Wis. (La Crosse)
Witchita St. U.
Widener U.

PROSTHETICS
N.Y.U.

PSYCHIATRIC NURSING
Adelphi U.
Boston C.
Catholic U.
U. Cincinnati
Columbia U.
Hunter C. (C.U.N.Y.)
U. Ill. (Chicago)
Ind. U.
I.U.P.U.I.
Kent St. U.
L.S.U. H.S.C.
U. Mass. (Lowell)
N.Y.U.
U. Penn.
U. Pitt.
Sage Grad. Sch.
St. Joseph's C. (Conn.)
St. Xavier
U. So. Miss.
Stony Brook U. (S.U.N.Y.)
U. Tex. (El Paso)
Tex. Woman's U.
Va. Commonwealth U.
Wayne St. U.

PUBLIC/ COMMUNITY HEALTH NURSING
Boston C.
Case West. Res. U.
U. Cincinnati
Drexel U.
U. Hawaii
Hunter C. (C.U.N.Y.)

Ind. U.
U. Ill. (Chicago)
I.U.P.U.I.
Johns Hopkins U.
L.S.U. H.S.C.
U. Mass. (Lowell)
Sage Grad. Sch.
U. So. Miss.
St. Xavier
Tex. Woman's U.
Wright St. U.

REHABILITATION COUNSELING/ SERVICES
U. Ala.
U. Albany (S.U.N.Y.)
U. Ariz.
Ark. St. U.
U. Ark.
Assumption C.
Barry U.
Boston U.
Bowl. Gr. St. U.
U. Buffalo (S.U.N.Y.)
Cal. St. U. (Fresno)
Cal. St. U. (L.A.)
Cal. St. U. (San Bernardino)
U. Cincinnati
Columbia U. (Teachers C.)
East Car. U.
East Cent. U.
Edinboro U. Pa.
Emporia St. U.
Fla. St. U.
U. Fla.
Fort Valley St. U.
Geo. Wash. U.
Georgia St. U.
Hofstra U.
Hunter C. (C.U.N.Y.)
Ill. Inst. Tech.
U. Ill.
I.U.P.U.I.
U. Iowa
Jackson St. U.
Kent St. U.
U. Ky.
U. Md.
U. Memphis
Mich. St. U.
Minn. St. U. (Mankato)
U. Nev.
N.Y.U.
U. No. Car. (Chapel Hill)
Northeastern U.
U. No. Colo.
U. No. Tex.
Ohio U.
U. Pitt.
U. Puerto Rico
St. Cloud St. U.
St. John's U. (N.Y.)
S.D.S.U.
San Fran. St. U.
U. Scranton
So. Car. St. U.
U. So. Car.
U. So. Fla.
So. Ill. U.
So. U. & A&M C.
Springfield C.
Syracuse U.
U. Tenn.
U. Tex. S.W. Med. Ctr. (Dallas)
Va. Commonwealth U.
Wayne St. U.
W. Va. U.
West Ore. U.
U. Wis.

U. Wis. (Milwaukee)
Wright St. U.

Optometry/Optical/Vision Sciences

U. Ala. (Birm.)
U. Ala. (Huntsville)
U. Ariz.
U. Cal. (Berkeley)
Cleveland St. U.
U. Houston
Ind. U.
U. N. Mex.
No. Eastern St. U.
Ohio St. U.
Old Dom. U.
Pac. U.
Penn. C. Opt.
U. Rochester
So. C. Opt.
So. Cal. C. Opt.

Osteopathic Medicine

Des Moines U.
U. Health Sci.
Kirksville C. O. Med.
Lake Erie C.
Mich. St. U.
Midwest. U.
U. N. England
U. Med. & Dent. N.J.
N.Y.I.T.
Nova U.
Ohio U.
Okla. St. U.
Phila. C. Osteo. Med.
U. No. Tex.
West. U. Health Sci.
West. Va. Sch. Osteo. Med.

Pharmacy

(Typically includes Pharmaceutical Chemistry, Pharmaceutical Science, Pharmacognosy; for Pharmacology, see *Basic Medical Sciences* listing above)

U. Ala. (Birm.)
U. Ariz.
U. Ark.
Auburn U.
U. Buffalo (S.U.N.Y.)
Butler U.
U. Cal. (San Fran.)
Campbell U.
U. Cincinnati
U. Colo.
Columbia U.
U. Conn.
Creighton U.
Drake U.
Duke U.
Duquesne U.
Finch U. Health Sci.
Fla. A&M U.
U. Fla.
U. Georgia
U. Houston
Howard U.
Idaho St. U.
U. Ill. (Chicago)
U. Iowa
U. Kans.
U. Ky.
U. La. (Monroe)

L.I.U.
U. Md. (Baltimore)
Mass. C. Pharm.
Mercer U.
U. Mich.
U. Minn.
U. Miss.
U. Mo. (K.C.)
U. Mont.
U. Neb.
U. N. Mex.
No. Car. St. U.
U. No. Car. (Chapel Hill)
No. Dak. St. U.
Northeastern St. U.
Northeastern U.
Nova U.
Ohio St. U.
U. Okla.
Ore. St. U.
U. Pac.
U. Pitt.
U. Puerto Rico
Purdue U.
U. Rhode Island
Rutgers U.
St. John's U. (N.Y.)
Samford U.
U. So. Cal.
Med. U. So. Car.
U. So. Car.
U. Sci. Phila.
So. Dak. St. U.
Temple U.
U. Tenn.
Tex. So. U.
U. Tex. (Austin)
U. Tex. Health Sci. Ctr. (Houston)
U. Tex. Health Sci. Ctr. (San Antonio)
U. Tex. S.W. Med. Ctr. (Dallas)
U. Toledo
U. Utah
Va. Commonwealth U.
Wash. St. U.
U. Wash.
Wayne St. U.
W. Va. U.
U. Wis.
Xavier U. (La.)

Physical Sciences

(Typically includes Chemistry, Mathematics, and Physics; offered by nearly 400 institutions, so individual institutions are not listed here; also often includes Statistics, Applied Mathematics)

ANALYTICAL CHEMISTRY

U. Akron
Boston C.
B.Y.U.
Cleveland St. U.
Gov. St. U.
U. Houston
Howard U.
Kent St. U.
Mich. St. U.
Miss. St. U.
U. Mo. (Kansas City)
Northeastern U.
Purdue U.
San Jose St. U.
Seton Hall U.
U. So. Fla.
So. U.

Va. Commonwealth U.
Wash St. U.
U. Wis.

APPLIED PHYSICS

Ala. A&M U.
Appal. St. U.
Brooklyn C. (C.U.N.Y.)
U. Buffalo (S.U.N.Y.)
Cal. Inst. Tech.
U. Cent. Okla.
Colo. Sch. Mines
Columbia U.
Cornell U.
Geo. Mason U.
Harvard U.
U. La. (Lafayette)
U. Mass. (Boston)
U. Mich.
N.J.I.T.
U. New Orleans
U. No. Car. (Charlotte)
U. Puerto Rico
Stanford U.
Tex. Tech U.
Va. Commonwealth U.
U. Wash.
Yale U.

ASTRONOMY/PLANETARY SCIENCES/SPACE SCIENCES

U. Alaska
Ariz. St. U.
U. Ariz.
Boston U.
Bowl. Gr. St. U.
U. Buffalo (S.U.N.Y.)
B.Y.U.
Cal. Inst. Tech.
U. Cal. (Berkeley)
U.C.L.A.
U. Cal. (Santa Cruz)
Case West. Res. U.
U. Chicago
Clemson U.
U. Colo.
Columbia U.
Cornell U.
Creighton U.
Dartmouth C.
U. Del.
Fla. Inst. Tech.
U. Fla.
Georgia St. U.
Harvard U.
U. Hawaii
U. Ill.
Ind. U.
Iowa St. U.
U. Iowa
Johns Hopkins U.
U. Kans.
U. Ky.
L.S.U.
U. Md.
M.I.T.
U. Mass.
Mich. St. U.
U. Mich.
U. Minn.
U. Neb.
N. Mex. St. U.
U. No. Car. (Chapel Hill)
Northwestern U.
Ohio St. U.
Ore. St. U.
Penn. St. U.
U. Penn.
U. Pitt.
Princeton U.
Rice U.

U. Rochester
S.D.S.U.
U. So. Car.
Stony Brook U. (S.U.N.Y.)
U. Tex. (Austin)
Vanderbilt U.
U. Va.
U. Wash.
Wesleyan U.
U. Wis.
U. Wyo.
Yale U.

GEOCHEMISTRY

Cal. Inst. Tech.
U.C.L.A.
Colo. Sch. Mines
Geo. Wash. U.
Ind. U.
Mont. Tech
N. Mex. Inst. M&T
U. Mo. (Rolla)
U. Nev. (Reno)
Penn. St. U.
Purdue U.
U. Tulsa

GEOLOGY

U. Akron
U. Ala.
U. Alaska
U. Albany (S.U.N.Y.)
Ariz. St. U.
U. Ark.
Auburn U.
Ball St. U.
Baylor U.
Boise St. U.
Boston C.
Bowl. Gr. St. U.
B.Y.U.
Brooklyn C. (C.U.N.Y.)
Bryn Mawr C.
U. Buffalo (S.U.N.Y.)
Cal. Inst. Tech.
Cal. St. U. (Bakersfield)
Cal. St. U. (Chico)
Cal. St. U. (Fresno)
Cal. St. U. (Hayward)
Cal. St. U. (Long Beach)
Cal. St. U. (L.A.)
Cal. St. U. (Northridge)
U. Cal. (Berkeley)
U. Cal. (Davis)
U.C.L.A.
U. Cal. (Riverside)
U. Cal. (Santa Barbara)
Case West. Res. U.
Cent. Mich. U.
Cent. Wash. U.
U. Cincinnati
C.C.N.Y. (C.U.N.Y.)
Colo. Sch. Mines
Colo. St. U.
U. Colo.
Columbia U.
U. Conn.
Cornell U.
U. Del.
Duke U.
East Car. U.
East. Ky. U.
East. Wash. U.
Fla. Atlantic U.
Fla. St. U.
U. Fla.
Fort Hays St. U.
Geo. Wash. U.
Georgia St. U.
U. Georgia
Harvard U.
U. Hawaii

U. Houston
Idaho St. U.
U. Idaho
U. Ill.
U. Ill. (Chicago C.)
Ind. St. U.
Ind. U.
I.U.P.U.I.
Iowa St. U.
U. Iowa
Johns Hopkins U.
Kans. St. U.
U. Kans.
Kent St. U.
U. Ky.
U. La. (Lafayette)
Lehigh U.
Loma Linda U.
L.S.U.
U. Maine
U. Md.
M.I.T.
U. Mass.
U. Memphis
Miami U. (Ohio)
U. Miami
Mich. St. U.
Mich. Tech. U.
U. Mich.
U. Minn.
U. Miss.
U. Mo. (Columbia)
U. Mo. (K.C.)
U. Mo. (Rolla)
Mont. Tech
U. Mont.
U. Neb.
U. Nev. (Reno)
U. N.H.
N. Mex. Inst. M&T
N. Mex. St. U.
U. N. Orleans
S.U.N.Y. (Binghamton)
S.U.N.Y.C. (New Paltz)
No. Car. St. U. (Raleigh)
U. No. Car. (Chapel Hill)
U. No. Car. (Wilmington)
U. No. Dak.
No. Ariz. U.
No. Ill. U.
Northwestern U.
Ohio St. U.
Ohio U.
Okla. St. U.
U. Okla.
Old Dom. U.
Ore. St. U.
U. Ore.
Penn. St. U.
U. Penn.
U. Pitt.
Portland St. U.
Princeton U.
Queens C. (C.U.N.Y.)
U. Rhode Island
U. Rochester
Rutgers U.
S.D.S.U.
San Jose St. U.
U. So. Car.
So. Dak. Sch. M&T
U. So. Fla.
So. Ill. U.
So. Meth. U.
U. So. Miss.
Stanford U.
S. F. Austin St. U.
Stony Brook U. (S.U.N.Y.)
Sul Ross St. U.
Syracuse U.
Temple U.
U. Tenn.

Tex. A&M U.
Tex. Christ. U.
U. Tex. (Arlington)
U. Tex. (Austin)
U. Tex. (El Paso)
U. Tex. (Permian Basin)
U. Tex. (San Antonio)
U. Toledo
Tulane U.
U. Tulsa
Utah St. U.
U. Utah
Vanderbilt U.
U. Vt.
Va. Poly. Inst.
Wash. St. U.
Wash. U.
U. Wash.
Wayne St. U.
W. Va. U.
West. Mich. U.
West. Wash. U.
Wichita St. U.
U. Wis.
U. Wis. (Milwaukee)
Wright St. U.
U. Wyo.
Yale U.

GEOPHYSICS

U. Akron
U. Alaska
Boise St. U.
Boston C.
Cal. Inst. Tech.
U. Cal. (Berkeley)
U.C.L.A.
U. Cal. (Santa Barbara)
U. Chicago
Colo. Sch. Mines
U. Colo.
U. Conn.
Fla. St. U.
Georgia Inst. Tech.
U. Georgia
U. Hawaii
U. Houston
Ind. U.
Johns Hopkins U.
U. Idaho
U. Ill. (Chicago)
L.S.U.
M.I.T.
U. Memphis
U. Miami
Mich. Tech. U.
U. Minn.
U. Mo. (Rolla)
N. Mex. Inst. M&T
U. Nev. (Reno)
U. N. Orleans
No. Car. St. U. (Raleigh)
U. Okla.
Ore. St. U.
Penn. St. U.
U. Pitt.
Princeton U.
R.P.I.
Rice U.
St. Louis U.
So. Meth. U.
Stanford U.
Stony Brook U. (S.U.N.Y.)
Tex. A&M U.
U. Tex. (El Paso)
U. Utah
Va. Poly. Inst.
Wash. U.
U. Wash.
U. Wis.
U Wyo.
Yale U.

Public Administration

(Typically includes Energy Management and Policy, Public Policy, Public Management, Public Affairs)

Alfred U.
U. Akron
U. Ala.
U. Ala. (Birm.)
U. Ala. (Huntsville)
U. Alaska
U. Albany (S.U.N.Y.)
American U.
Angelo St. U.
Appal. St. U.
Ariz. St. U.
U. Ariz.
Ark. St. U.
U. Ark.
Auburn U.
Auburn U. (Montgomery)
Ball St. U.
U. Baltimore
Baruch C. (C.U.N.Y.)
Baylor U.
Boise St. U.
Boston C.
Boston U.
Bowie St. U.
Bowl. Gr. St. U.
Brandeis U.
Bridgewater St. C.
Brooklyn C. (C.U.N.Y.)
U. Buffalo (S.U.N.Y.)
B.Y.U.
Cal. Luth. U.
Cal. St. (Bakersfield)
Cal. St. U. (Chico)
Cal. St. U. (Dominguez Hills)
Cal. St. U. (Fresno)
Cal. St. U. (Fullerton)
Cal. St. U. (Hayward)
Cal. St. U. (Long Beach)
Cal. St. U. (L.A.)
Cal. St. U. (Northridge)
Cal. St. U. (Sacramento)
Cal. St. U. (San Bernardino)
Cal. St. U. (Stanislaus)
U. Cal. (Berkeley)
Canisius C.
Carnegie Mellon U.
Cent. Mich. U.
Cent. Mo. St. U.
U. Chicago
U. Cincinnati
Claremont Grad. U.
Clark Atlanta U.
Clark U.
Clemson U.
Cleveland St. U.
Columbia U.
Columbus St. U.
U. Colo.
U. Conn.
Cornell U.
U. Dayton
U. Del.
DePaul U.
U. Detroit Mercy
Drake U.
Duke U.
Duquesne U.
East Car. U.
East Ky. U.
East. Mich. U.
East Tenn. St. U.
East. Wash. U.

F.D.U. (Madison)
F.D.U. (Teaneck)
Fla. Atlantic U.
Fla. St. U.
U. Fla.
Framingham St. C.
Gannon U.
Geo. Mason U.
Georgetown U.
Geo. Wash. U.
Georgia C. & St. U.
Georgia Inst. Tech.
Georgia So. C.
Georgia St. U.
U. Georgia
Golden Gate U.
Gov. St. U.
Hamline U.
U. Hartford
Harvard U.
U. Hawaii
U. Houston
Howard U.
Idaho St. U.
U. Idaho
Ill. Inst. Tech.
U. Ill. (Chicago)
Ind. St. U.
Ind. U.
I.U.P.U.I.
Ind. U. Pa.
Iowa St. U.
Jackson St. U.
Jacksonville St. U.
James Madison U.
John Jay C. (C.U.N.Y.)
Johns Hopkins U.
Kans. St. U.
U. Kans.
Kean U.
Kent St. U.
Kutztown U. Pa.
U. Ky.
Lamar U.
U. La Verne
Lewis & Clark C.
U. Louisville
L.I.U.
L.I.U. (C.W. Post)
L.S.U.
U. Maine
Marywood U.
U. Mass.
U. Mass. (Boston)
U. Md.
U. Md. (Baltimore Cnty.)
U. Memphis
U. Miami
Mich. St. U.
U. Mich.
Minn. St. U. (Mankato)
U. Minn.
Miss. St. U.
U. Miss.
U. Mo. (Columbia)
U. Mo. (K.C.)
U. Mo. (St. Louis)
Mont. St. U.
U. Mont.
Murray St. U.
Natl. U.
U. Neb. (Omaha)
U. Nev. (Las Vegas)
U. Nev. (Reno)
U.N.H.
U. N. Haven
New Mex. Highlands U.
N. Mex. St. U.
U. N. Mex.
U. N. Orleans
New Sch. U.
C.U.N.Y. (Grad. Ctr.)
S.U.N.Y. (Binghamton)

S.U.N.Y.C. (Brockport)
N.Y.U.
No. Ariz. U.
No. Car. Cent. U.
No. Car. St. U. (Raleigh)
Northeastern U.
U. No. Car. (Chapel Hill)
U. No. Car. (Charlotte)
U. No. Car. (Greensboro)
U. No. Dak.
U. No. Fla.
No. Ill. U.
No. Mich. U.
U. No. Tex.
Northwestern U.
Notre Dame U.
Nova U.
Oakland U.
Ohio St. U.
Ohio U.
Okla. City U.
U. Okla.
Old Dom. U.
U. Ore.
Pace U.
Penn. St. U.
U. Penn.
U. Pitt
Portland St. U.
Princeton U.
U. Puerto Rico
Regent U.
U. Rhode Island
U. Rochester
Roosevelt U.
Rosary C.
Rutgers U.
Sage Grad. Sch.
St. Edward's U.
St. Louis U.
St. Mary's U.
S.D.S.U.
San Fran. St. U.
U. San Fran.
San Jose St. U.
Seattle U.
Seton Hall U.
Shippensburg U. Pa.
Sonoma St. U.
U. So. Ala.
U. So. Cal.
U. So. Car.
U. So. Dak.
U. So. Fla.
Southeast Mo. St. U.
So. Ill. U.
U. So. Maine
So. Meth. U.
Southwest Mo. St. U.
Southwest Tex. St. U.
Suffolk U.
Sul Ross St. U.
Syracuse U.
Tenn. St. U.
U. Tenn.
U. Tenn. (Chattanooga)
Tex. A&M U.
Tex. So. U.
Tex. Tech. U.
U. Tex. (Arlington)
U. Tex. (Austin)
U. Tex. (Dallas)
U. Tex. (Pan American)
U. Tex. (San Antonio)
U. Toledo
Troy St. U.
U. Utah
Valdosta St. U.
U. Vt.
Villanova U.
Va. Commonwealth U.
Va. Poly. Inst.
U. Va.

Wash. U.
U. Wash.
Wayne St. U.
Webster U.
West Chester U. Pa.
West. Car. U.
West. Ga. St. U.
West. Ky. U.
West. Mich. U.
W. Va. U.
Wichita St. U.
Widener U.
C. Wm. & Mary
U. Wis.
U. Wis. (Milwaukee)
U. Wis. (Oshkosh)
U. Wyo.

Public and Community Health

U. Ala. (Birm.)
U. Albany (S.U.N.Y.)
Boston U.
Brooklyn C. (C.U.N.Y.)
U. Buffalo (S.U.N.Y.)
Ca. St. U. (Fresno)
Cal. St. U. (Long Beach)
Cal. St. U. (Northridge)
Cal. St. U. (Sacramento)
U. Cal. (Berkeley)
U.C.L.A.
U. Colo. Health Sci. Ctr.
Columbia U.
U. Conn.
U. Denver
East Tenn. St. U.
Emory U.
Geo. Wash. U.
Harvard U.
U. Hawaii
Hunter C. (C.U.N.Y.)
U. Ill.
U. Ill. (Chicago)
Ind. U.
U. Iowa
Johns Hopkins U.
U. Kans.
U. Ky.
L.I.U.
Loma Linda U.
U. Mass.
U. Med. & Dent. N.J.
Meharry Med. C.
U. Miami
U. Mich.
Minn. St. U. (Mankato)
U. Minn.
U. Mo. (Columbia)
U. N. Mex.
N.Y. Med. C.
N.Y.U.
U. No. Car. (Chapel Hill)
No. Ill. U.
U. No. Colo.
U. No. Tex.
Northwestern U.
Nova U.
Med. C. Ohio
Ohio St. U.
U. Okla. Health Sci. Ctr.
Old Dom. U.
Ore. St. U.
U. Ore.
U. Pitt.
U. Puerto Rico
U. Rochester
Rutgers U.
Sage Grad. Sch.
St. Louis U.
S.D.S.U.
San Fran. St. U.
San Jose St. U.

U. So. Cal.
Med. U. So. Car.
U. So. Car.
U. So. Fla.
Temple U.
U. Tenn.
Tex. A&M U.
U. Tex. Health Sci. Ctr.
  (Houston)
U. Tex. Med. Br.
  (Galveston)
U. Toledo
Tufts U.
Tulane U.
U. Utah
Va. Commonwealth U.
U. Wash.
Wayne St. U.
West. Ky. U.
W. Va. U.
Med. C. Wis.
U. Wis.
U. Wis. (La Crosse)

ENVIRONMENTAL/
OCCUPATIONAL
HEALTH
U. Ala. (Birmingham)
U. Cal. (Berkeley)
U.C.L.A.
U. Cincinnati
Colo. St. U.
Columbia U.
East Car. U.
East Tenn. St. U.
Emory U.
Harvard U.
Hunter C. (C.U.N.Y.)
Johns Hopkins U.
U. Mich.
U. Minn.
Montclair U.
Murray St. U.
U. Nev. (Reno)
U. N. Haven
N.Y.U.
Northwestern U.
U. Okla.
Ore. St. U.
U. Pitt.
Poly. U.
U. Puerto Rico
Purdue U.
U. So. Car.
U. So. Fla.
Tulane U.
U. Wash.
Wayne St. U.
West Chester U. Pa.
U. Wis. (Eau Claire)
Yale U.

EPIDEMIOLOGY
U. Ala. (Birm.)
U. Ariz.
Boston U.
U. Buffalo (S.U.N.Y.)
U. Cal. (Berkeley)
U. Cal. (Davis)
U.C.L.A.
U. Cal. (San Diego)
Case West. Res U.
Columbia U.
Cornell U.
Duke U.
Emory U.
Geo. Wash. U.
Harvard U.
U. Hawaii
U. Ill. (Chicago)
U. Iowa
Johns Hopkins U.
Loma Linda U.

U. Md. (Baltimore)
U. Miami
U. Mich.
U. Minn.
N.Y. Med. C.
U. No. Car. (Chapel Hill)
U. Okla.
Ore. Health & Sci. U.
U. Penn.
U. Pitt.
Purdue U.
U. So. Cal.
U. So. Car.
Stanford U.
Tex. A&M U.
U. Tex. Health Sci. Ctr.
  (Houston)
Tulane U.
U. Va.
Wake Forest U.
U. Wash.
Med. C. Wis.
Yale U.

INTERNATIONAL
HEALTH
Emory U.
Harvard U.
Johns Hopkins U.
U. Mich.
Thunderbird
Tulane U.

Religion

(Typically includes Bible
Studies, Religious Stud-
ies, Theology; often in-
cludes Religious
Education)

A.C.U.
Andrews U.
Ariz. St. U.
Assumption C.
Azusa Pac. U.
Barry U.
Baylor U.
Boston C.
Boston U.
Brown U.
U. Cal. (Berkeley)
U. Cal. (Santa Barbara)
Card. Stritch C.
Catholic U.
U. Chicago
Claremont Grad. U.
Colgate U.
U. Colo
Columbia U.
Concordia U. (Ill.)
U. Dallas
U. Dayton
U. Denver
U. Detroit Mercy
Drew U.
Duke U.
Duquesne U.
Emory U.
Fla. St. U.
U. Fla.
Fordham U.
Gannon U.
Geo. Wash. U.
U. Georgia
Gonzaga U.
Hardin-Simmons U.
Harvard U.
U. Hawaii
Hebrew C.
Holy Names C.
U. Incarnate Word
Ind. U.

U. Iowa
John Carroll U.
U. Kans.
Loma Linda U.
Loyola U.
Loyola U. (Chicago)
Loyola U. (La.)
Marquette U.
Marygrove C.
Marywood U.
Miami U. (Ohio)
Mt. St. Mary's C.
N.Y.U.
U. No. Car. (Chapel
  Hill)
Northwestern U.
Notre Dame U.
U. Notre Dame
Okla. City U.
Olivet Naz. U.
Oral Roberts U.
U. Pac.
U. Penn.
Pepperdine U.
U. Pitt.
Point Loma U.
U. Portland
Princeton U.
Providence C.
Rice U.
St. Bonaventure U.
St. John's U. (Minn.)
St. John's U. (N.Y.)
St. Joseph C. (Conn.)
St. Louis U.
St. Mary's U.
St. Mary's U. (Minn.)
St. Michael's C.
U. St. Thomas (Tex.)
Samford U.
U. San Diego
U. San Fran.
Santa Clara U.
Seattle U.
Seton Hall. U.
Smith C.
U. So. Cal.
U. So. Car.
U. So. Fla.
So. Meth. U.
So. Naz. U.
Southwest Mo. St.
Spalding U.
Stanford U.
Syracuse U.
Temple U.
U. Tenn.
Tex. Christ. U.
Vanderbilt U.
Villanova U.
U. Va.
Wake Forest U.
Wash. U.
U. Wash.
Xavier U. (Ohio)
Yale U.
Yeshiva U.

Social Sciences

(Typically includes Eco-
nomics, Political Science,
Psychology, Sociology)

A.C.U.
Adelphi U.
U. Akron
Ala. A&M U.
U. Ala.
U. Ala. (Birm.)
U. Ala. (Huntsville)
U. Alaska
U. Albany (S.U.N.Y.)

Alfred U.
Alliant Intl. U.
American U.
Andrews U.
Angelo St. U.
Antioch N. E. Grad. Sch.
Antioch (L.A.)
Antioch U. (McGregor)
Antioch (Santa Barbara)
Antioch U. (Seattle)
Appal. St. U.
Ariz. St. U.
U. Ariz.
U. Ark.
Assump. C.
Auburn U.
Auburn U. (Montgomery)
Augusta St. U.
Austin Peay St. U.
Azusa Pac. U.
Ball St. U.
U. Baltimore
Baruch C. (C.U.N.Y.)
Barry U.
Baylor U.
Bemidji St. U.
Boston C.
Boston U.
Bowl. Gr. St. U.
Brandeis U.
U. Bridgeport
Bridgewater St. C.
B.Y.U.
Brooklyn C. (C.U.N.Y.)
Brown U.
Bryn Mawr C.
Bucknell U.
U. Buffalo (S.U.N.Y.)
Cal. Inst. Tech.
Cal. Luth. U.
Cal. Poly St. U. (San Luis
  Obispo)
Cal. St. Poly U. (Pomona)
Cal. St. U. (Bakersfield)
Cal. St. U. (Chico)
Cal. St. U. (Dominguez
  Hills)
Cal. St. U. (Fresno)
Cal. St. U. (Fullerton)
Cal. St. U. (Hayward)
Cal. St. U. (Long Beach)
Cal. St. U. (L.A.)
Cal. St. U. (Northridge)
Cal. St. U. (Sacramento)
Cal. St. U. (San
  Bernardino)
Cal. St. U. (San Marcos)
Cal. St. U. (Stanislaus)
Cal. U. Pa.
U. Cal. (Berkeley)
U. Cal. (Davis)
U. Cal. (Irvine)
U.C.L.A.
U. Cal. (Riverside)
U. Cal. (San Diego)
U. Cal. (San Fran.)
U. Cal. (Santa Barbara)
U. Cal. (Santa Cruz)
Carnegie Mellon U.
Case West. Res. U.
Catholic U.
U. Cent. Ark.
Cent. Conn. St. U.
U. Cent. Fla.
Cent. Mich. U.
Cent. Mo. St. U.
U. Cent. Okla.
Cent. Wash. U.
Chapman U.
Chicago St. U.
U. Chicago
U. Cincinnati
Citadel

C.C.N.Y. (C.U.N.Y.)
Claremont Grad. U.
Clark U.
Clark Atlanta U.
Clemson U.
Cleveland St. U.
Colo. St. U.
U. Colo.
Columbia U.
Concordia U.
Conn. C.
U. Conn.
Cornell U.
U. Dallas
Dartmouth C.
U. Dayton
U. Del.
Delta St. U.
U. Denver
DePaul U.
U. Detroit Mercy
Dominican U. (Calif.)
Drake U.
Drew U.
Drexel U.
Duke U.
Duquesne U.
East Car. U.
East Stroudsburg U. Pa.
East Tenn. St. U.
East. Ill. U.
East. Ky. U.
East. Mich. U.
East. N. Mex. U.
East. Wash. U.
Edinboro U. Pa.
Emory U.
Emporia St. U.
Fairfield U.
F.D.U. (Madison)
F.D.U. (Teaneck)
Fisk U.
Fla. A&M U.
Fla. Atlantic U.
Fla. Inst. Tech.
Fla. St. U.
U. Fla.
Fordham U.
Fort Hays St. U.
Framingham St. C.
Frostburg St. U.
Gallaudet U.
Geo. Mason U.
Geo. Wash. U.
Georgetown U.
Georgia C. St. U.
Georgia Inst. Tech.
Georgia So. U.
Georgia St. U.
U. Georgia
Goddard C.
Golden Gate U.
Gonzaga U.
Gov. St. U.
U. Hartford
Harvard U.
U. Hawaii
Henderson St. U.
Hofstra U.
Holy Names C.
Hollins U.
Hood C.
U. Houston
U. Houston (Clear Lake)
Howard U.
Humbolt St. U.
Hunter C. (C.U.N.Y.)
Idaho St. U.
U. Idaho
Ill. Inst. Tech.
Ill. St. U.
U. Ill.
U. Ill. (Chicago)

Ind. St. U.
Ind. U.
I.U.P.U.I.
Ind. U. Penn.
Inter American U.
Iona C.
Iowa St. U.
U. Iowa
Jackson St. U.
Jacksonville St. U.
James Madison U.
Jersey City St. U.
Johns Hopkins U.
John Jay C. (C.U.N.Y.)
Kans. St. U.
U. Kans.
Kean U.
Kent St. U.
U. Ky.
Lamar U.
Lehigh U.
Lewis and Clark C.
Lincoln U.
Loma Linda U.
L.I.U.
L.I.U. (C.W. Post)
Loras C.
L.S.U.
L.S.U. (Shreveport)
La. Tech U.
U. La. (Monroe)
U. Louisville
Loyola C.
Loyola Marymount U.
Loyola U. (Chicago)
U. Maine
Marquette U.
Marshall U.
U. Md.
U. Md. (Baltimore)
Marywood U.
M.I.T.
U. Mass.
U. Mass. (Boston)
McNeese St. U.
U. Memphis
Miami U. (Ohio)
U. Miami (Fla.)
Mich. St. U.
U. Mich.
Mid. Tenn. St. U.
Midwestern U.
Millersville U. Pa.
Minn. St. U. (Mankato)
Minn. St. U. (Moorhead)
U. Minn.
Miss. C.
Miss. St. U.
U. Miss.
U. Mo. (Columbia)
U. Mo. (K.C.)
U. Mo. (St. Louis)
Monmouth U.
Mont. St. U.
U. Mont.
Montclair St. U.
Morehead St. U.
Morgan St. U.
Mount Holyoke C.
Murray St. U.
Natl. Louis U.
Natl. U.
U. Neb.
U. Neb. (Omaha)
U. Nev.
U. Nev. (Las Vegas)
U.N.H.
N. Mex. Highlands U.
N. Mex. St. U.
U. N. Mex.
U. N. Orleans
C. New Rochelle
New Sch. U.

C.U.N.Y. (Grad. Ctr.)
S.U.N.Y. (Binghamton)
S.U.N.Y.C. (Brockport)
S.U.N.Y.C. (New Paltz)
S.U.N.Y.C. (Oswego)
N.Y.U.
No. Car. Cent. U.
No. Car. St. U. (Raleigh)
U. No. Car. (Chapel Hill)
U. No. Car. (Charlotte)
U. No. Car. (Greensboro)
No. Dak. St. U.
U. No. Dak.
U. No. Fla.
Northeastern U.
No. Ill. U.
No. Ariz. U.
U. No. Colo.
No. Ill. U.
U. No. Iowa
U. No. Tex.
U. No. Tex. Health Sci. Ctr.
No. W. Mo. St. U.
No. W. Okla. St. U.
No. W. St. U. La.
Northwestern U.
Notre Dame U.
U. Notre Dame
Nova U.
Ohio St. U.
Ohio U.
Okla. St. U.
U. Okla.
U. Okla. Health Sci. Ctr.
Old Dom. U.
U. Ore.
Our Lady Lake U.
Pace U.
Pac. Luth. U.
Pac. U.
U. Pac.
Penn. St. U.
U. Penn.
Pepperdine U.
U. Phoenix
Pittsburg St. U.
U. Pitt.
Portland St. U.
Prairie View A&M U.
Princeton U.
U. Puerto Rico
Purdue U.
Purdue U. (Calumet)
Queens C. (C.U.N.Y.)
Radford U.
R.P.I.
Rhode Island C.
U. Rhode Island
Rice U.
U. Richmond
Rochester Inst. Tech.
U. Rochester
Rockford C.
Rollins C.
Roosevelt U.
Rowan U.
Rutgers U.
Sage Grad. Sch.
Saginaw Val. St. U.
St. Bonaventure U.
St. Cloud St. U.
U. St. Francis
St. John's U. (N.Y.)
St. Joseph's U. (Penn.)
St. Louis U.
St. Mary's U.
C. St. Rose
Salisbury St. U.
Sam Houston St. U.
S.D.S.U.
San Fran. St. U.
U. San Fran.

San Jose St. U.
U. Scranton
Seattle U.
Seton Hall
Shippensburg U. Pa.
Sonoma St. U.
U. So. Ala.
U. So. Cal.
U. So. Car.
So. Dak. St. U.
U. So. Dak.
U. So. Fla.
Southeastern La. U.
So. Conn. St. U.
So. Ill. U.
So. Ill. U. (Edwardsville)
So. Meth. U.
U. So. Miss.
So. Naz. U.
So. Ore. U.
So. U. & A&M C.
Southwest Mo. St.
Southwest Tex. St. U.
Spalding U.
Stanford U.
S. F. Austin St. U.
Stony Brook U. (S.U.N.Y.)
Sul Ross St. U.
Syracuse U.
Temple U.
Tenn. St. U.
U. Tenn.
U. Tenn. (Chattanooga)
Tex. A&M U.
Tex. A&M U. (Commerce)
Tex. A&M U. (Corpus Christi)
Tex. A&M U. (Kingsville)
Tex. Christ. U.
Tex. So. U.
Tex. Tech U.
Tex. Woman's U.
U. Tex. (Arlington)
U. Tex. (Austin)
U. Tex. (Brownsville)
U. Tex. (El Paso)
U. Tex. (Permian Basin)
U. Tex. (Tyler)
U. Toledo
Towson U.
Trinity C.
Trinity U.
Tufts U.
Tulane U.
U. Tulsa
Union Inst.
Utah St. U.
U. Utah
Valdosta St. U.
Valparaiso U.
Vanderbilt U.
U. Vt.
Villanova U.
Va. Commonwealth U.
Va. Poly. Inst.
Va. St. U.
U. Va.
Wake Forest U.
Washburn U.
Wash. C.
Wash. St. U.
Wash. U. (Mo.)
U. Wash.
Wayne St. U.
Webster U.
Wesleyan U.
West Chester U. Pa.
W. Va. U.
West. Car. U.
West. Ill. U.

West. Ky. U.
West. Mich. U.
West. N. Mex. U.
West Tex. A&M U.
West. Wash. U.
Westfield St. C.
Wichita St. U.
Widener U.
C. Wm. & Mary
Winthrop U.
U. Wis.
U. Wis. (Eau Claire)
U. Wis. (La Crosse)
U. Wis. (Milwaukee)
U. Wis. (Oshkosh)
U. Wis. (River Falls)
U. Wis. (Superior)
U. Wis. (Whitewater)
Wright St. U.
U. Wyo.
Xavier U. (Ohio)
Yale U.
Yeshiva U.
Youngstown St. U.

ANTHROPOLOGY

U. Ala.
U. Ala. (Birmingham)
U. Alaska
U. Albany (S.U.N.Y.)
American U.
Ariz. St. U.
U. Ariz.
U. Ark.
Ball St. U.
Boston U.
Brandeis U.
U. Buffalo (S.U.N.Y.)
B.Y.U.
Brown U.
Cal. St. U. (Bakersfield)
Cal. St. U. (Chico)
Cal. St. U. (Fullerton)
Cal. St. U. (Hayward)
Cal. St. U. (Long Beach)
Cal. St. U. (L.A.)
Cal. St. U. (Northridge)
Cal. St. U. (Sacramento)
U. Cal. (Berkeley)
U. Cal. (Davis)
U. Cal. (Irvine)
U.C.L.A.
U. Cal. (Riverside)
U. Cal. (San Diego)
U. Cal. (San Fran.)
U. Cal. (Santa Barbara)
U. Cal. (Santa Cruz)
Case West. Res. U.
Catholic U.
U. Chicago
U. Cincinnati
Colo. St. U.
U. Colo.
Columbia U.
U. Conn.
Cornell U.
U. Denver
Duke U.
East Car. U.
East. N. Mex. U.
Emory U.
Fla. Atlantic U.
Fla. St. U.
U. Fla.
Geo. Wash. U.
Georgia St. U.
U. Georgia
Harvard U.
U. Hawaii
U. Houston
Hunter C. (C.U.N.Y.)
Idaho St. U.
U. Idaho

U. Ill.
U. Ill. (Chicago)
Ind. U.
Iowa St. U.
U. Iowa
Johns Hopkins U.
U. Kans.
Kent St. U.
U. Ky.
Lehigh U.
L.S.U.
U. Md.
U. Mass.
U. Memphis
Mich. St. U.
U. Mich.
U. Minn.
U. Miss.
U. Mo. (Columbia)
U. Mont.
Montclair U.
U. Neb.
U. Nev.
U. Nev. (Reno)
N. Mex. St. U.
U. N. Mex.
New Sch. U.
C.U.N.Y. (Grad. Ctr.)
S.U.N.Y. (Binghamton)
N.Y.U.
U. No. Car. (Chapel Hill)
No. Ariz. U.
No. Ill. U.
Northwestern U.
Ohio St. U.
U. Okla.
Ore. St. U.
U. Ore.
Penn. St. U.
U. Penn.
U. Pitt.
Portland St. U.
Princeton U.
Purdue U.
Rice U.
Rutgers U.
S.D.S.U.
San Fran. St. U.
U. So. Cal.
U. So. Car.
U. So. Fla.
So. Ill. U.
So. Meth. U.
U. So. Miss.
Stanford U.
Stony Brook U. (S.U.N.Y.)
Syracuse U.
Temple U.
U. Tenn.
Tex. A&M U.
Tex. Tech U.
U. Tex. (Arlington)
U. Tex. (Austin)
U. Tex. (San Antonio)
U. Toledo
Tulane U.
U. Tulsa
U. Utah
Vanderbilt U.
U. Va.
Wake Forest U.
Wash. St. U.
Wash. U. (Mo.)
U. Wash.
Wayne St. U.
West. Mich. U.
West. Wash. U.
W. Va. U.
Wichita St. U.
C. Wm. & Mary
U. Wis.
U. Wis. (Milwaukee)

U. Wyo.
Yale U.

ARCHAEOLOGY
Ariz. St. U.
U. Ariz.
Boston U.
Brown U.
Bryn Mawr C.
U. Cal. (Berkeley)
U.C.L.A.
U. Chicago
Columbia U.
Cornell U.
Fla. St. U.
Harvard U.
Ind. U.
U. Mass. (Boston)
Mich. Tech. U.
U. Mich.
U. Minn.
U. Mo. (Columbia)
C.U.N.Y. (Grad. Ctr.)
N.Y.U.
No. Ariz. U.
U. No. Car. (Chapel Hill)
U. Penn.
Princeton U.
So. Meth. U.
U. Tex. (San Antonio)
Tufts U.
Wash. U.
Yale U.

GEOGRAPHY
U. Akron
U. Ala.
U. Albany (S.U.N.Y.)
Appal. St. U.
Ariz. St. U.
U. Ariz.
U. Ark.
Ball St. U.
Boston U.
U. Buffalo (S.U.N.Y.)
B.Y.U.
Cal. St. U. (Chico)
Cal. St. U. (Fresno)
Cal. St. U. (Fullerton)
Cal. St. U. (Hayward)
Cal. St. U. (Long Beach)
Cal. St. U. (L.A.)
Cal. St. U. (Northridge)
Cal. U. (Pa.)
U. Cal. (Berkeley)
U. Cal. (Davis)
U.C.L.A.
U. Cal. (Riverside)
U. Cal. (Santa Barbara)
Cent. Conn. St. U.
Chicago St. U.
U. Chicago
U. Cinn.
Clark U.
U. Colo.
U. Conn.
U. Del.
U. Denver
East Car. U.
East Tenn. St. U.
East. Ky. U.
East. Mich. U.
Fla. Atlantic U.
Fla. St. U.
U. Fla.
Geo. Mason U.
Geo. Wash. U.
Georgia St. U.
U. Georgia
U. Hawaii
Hunter C. (C.U.N.Y.)
U. Idaho
U. Ill.

U. Ill. (Chicago)
Ind. St. U.
Ind. U.
Ind. U. Penn.
U. Iowa
Johns Hopkins U.
Kans. St. U.
U. Kans.
Kent St. U.
U. Ky.
L.S.U.
Marshall U.
U. Md.
U. Mass.
U. Memphis
Miami U. (Ohio)
Mich. St. U.
Minn. St. U. (Mankato)
U. Minn.
U. Mo. (Columbia)
U. Mont.
Murray St. U.
U. Neb.
U. Neb. (Omaha)
N. Mex. St. U.
U. N. Mex.
U. N. Orleans
S.U.N.Y. (Binghamton)
No. Ariz. U.
U. No. Car. (Chapel Hill)
U. No. Car. (Charlotte)
U. No. Car. (Greensboro)
U. No. Dak.
Northeastern Ill. U.
No. Ill. U.
U. No. Iowa
Northwestern U.
Ohio St. U.
Ohio U.
Okla St. U.
U. Okla.
Ore. St. U.
U. Ore.
Penn. St. U.
Portland St. U.
Rutgers U.
St. Cloud St. U.
S.D.S.U.
San Fran. St. U.
San Jose St. U.
U. So. Cal.
U. So Car.
So. Dak, St. U.
U. So. Fla.
So. Ill. U.
So. Ill. U. (Edwardsville)
U. So. Miss.
Syracuse U.
Temple U.
U. Tenn.
Tex. A&M U.
U. Tex. (Austin)
U. Toledo
Towson U.
U. Utah
Va. Poly. Inst.
U. Vt.
U. Wash.
Wayne St. U.
West Chester U. Pa.
West. Ill. U.
West. Ky. U.
West. Mich. U.
West. Wash. U.
W. Va. U.
U. Wis.
U. Wis. (Milwaukee)
U. Wyo.

MEDIEVAL/
RENAISSANCE
STUDIES
Ariz. St. U.

Boston C.
Catholic U.
U. Conn.
Cornell U.
Duke U.
Fordham U.
Harvard U.
Ind. U.
Marquette U.
U. Mo. (Columbia)
C.U.N.Y. (Grad. Ctr.)
S.U.N.Y. (Binghamton)
U. Notre Dame
Rutgers U.
West. Mich. U.
Yale U.

PEACE STUDIES/
SCIENCE/CONFLICT
RESOLUTION
Alliant Intl. U.
American U.
Antioch U. (McGregor)
Cal. St. U. (Dominguez
   Hills)
Cornell U.
Duquesne U.
Geo. Mason U.
U. Mass (Boston)
Nova U.
U. Notre Dame
U. Penn.
Pepperdine U.
Wayne St. U.

POPULATION
STUDIES
Columbia U.
Georgetown U.
Harvard U.
Johns Hopkins U.
U. Mich.
Penn St. U.
U. Penn.
Princeton U.

URBAN STUDIES
U. Akron
Ala. A&M U.
U. Albany (S.U.N.Y.)
Boston U.
Brooklyn C. (C.U.N.Y.)
Cleveland St. U.
U. Del.
East Tenn. St. U.
Fla. St. U.
Georgia St. U.
Hunter C. (C.U.N.Y.)
Jersey City St. U.
L.I.U.
U. Louisville
M.I.T.
Mich. St. U.
Minn. St. U. (Mankato)
U. Mo. (K.C.)
Montclair U.
U. N. Orleans
New Sch. U.
C.U.N.Y. (Grad. Ctr.)
N.Y.U.
Old Dom. U.
U. Penn.
Portland St. U.
Queens C. (C.U.N.Y.)
R.P.I.
Rutgers U.
So. Conn. St. U.
St. Louis U.
Temple U.
Tex. A&M U.
U. Tex. (Arlington)
Trinity U.
Tufts U.

Va. Commonwealth U.
Va. Poly. Inst.
U. Wash.
U. Wis. (Milwaukee)
Wright St. U.

WOMEN'S/
FEMINIST STUDIES
U. Ala.
U. Buffalo (S.U.N.Y.)
U. Cincinnati
Clark Atl. U.
DePaul U.
Duke U.
East. Mich. U.
Emory U.
Geo. Wash. U.
Georgia St. U.
Goddard C.
U. Mass. (Boston)
Minn. St. U. (Mankato)
New Sch. U.
C.U.N.Y. (Grad. Ctr.)
N.Y.U.
No. Ill. U.
Ohio St. U.
U. Okla.
Rutgers U.
San Fran. St. U.
Sarah Lawrence C.
So. Ill. U. (Edwardsville)

Social Work
(Includes Human Ser-
vices, Social Service, Social Welfare)

Adelphi U.
Ala. A&M U.
U. Ala.
Albany U. (S.U.N.Y.)
Ariz. St. U.
U. Ark.
Barry U.
Boise St. U.
Boston C.
Boston U.
Brandeis U.
B.Y.U.
Bryn Mawr C.
U. Buffalo (S.U.N.Y.)
Cal. St. U. (Fresno)
Cal. St. U. (Long Beach)
Cal. St. U. (Sacramento)
Cal. St. U. (San
   Bernardino)
Cal. St. U. (Stanislaus)
U. Cal. (Berkeley)
U.C.L.A.
Case West. Res. U.
Catholic U.
U. Cent. Fla.
Cent. Mich. U.
U. Chicago
U. Cincinnati
Clark Atl. U.
Cleveland St. U.
Colo. St. U.
Columbia U.
Columbia U. (Teachers C.)
U. Conn.
U. Denver
East Car. U.
East. Mich. U.
East. Wash. U.
Fla. St. U.
Fordham U.
Gallaudet U.
Georgia St. U.
U. Georgia
Gov. St. U.
U. Hawaii

U. Houston
Howard U.
Hunter C. (C.U.N.Y.)
U. Ill.
U. Ill. (Chicago)
I.U.P.U.I.
U. Iowa
Jackson St. U.
U. Kans.
U. Ky.
L.S.U.
U. Louisville
Loma Linda U.
Loyola U. (Chicago)
U. Maine
U. Md.
U. Md. (Baltimore)
Marywood U.
U. Mass (Boston)
Mich. St. U.
U. Mich.
Minn. St. U. (Moorhead)
U. Minn.
U. Mo. (Columbia)
U. Neb. (Omaha)
U. Nev.
U. Nev. (Reno)
U. N.H.
N. Mex. Highlands U.
N. Mex. St. U.
C.U.N.Y. (Grad. Ctr.)
S.U.N.Y.C. (Brockport)
N.Y.U.
No. Car. A&T St. U.
U. No. Car. (Chapel Hill)
U. No. Car. (Charlotte)
U. No. Dak.
Ohio St. U.
Okla. St. U.
U. Okla.
Our Lady Lake U.
U. Penn.
U. Pitt.
Portland St. U.
U. Puerto Rico
Radford U.
Rhode Island C.
Rutgers U.
St. Louis U.
Salem St. U.
S.D.S.U.
San Fran. St. U.
San Jose St. U.
S. F. Austin St. U.
Simmons C.
Smith C.
So. Conn. St. U.
U. So. Cal.
U. So. Car.
U. So. Fla.
So. Ill. U.
U. So. Miss.
Southwest Mo. St.
Southwest Tex. St. U.
Springfield C.
Stony Brook U.
   (S.U.N.Y.)
Syracuse U.
Temple U.
U. Tenn.
U. Tex. (Arlington)
U. Tex. (Austin)
Tulane U.
U. Utah
Valdosta St. U.
Va. Commonwealth U.
U. Vt.
Walla Walla C.
Wash. U. (Mo.)
U. Wash.
Wayne St. U.
W. Va. U.
West. Mich. U.

Widener U.
U. Wis.
U. Wis. (Milwaukee)
Yeshiva U.

Theater/Drama

(Speech/Drama, Speech Arts, Theater Arts; typically includes Acting, Directing; often includes Children's Theater, Criticism, Theater/Costume Design, Technical Production)

U. Akron
U. Ala.
U. Albany (S.U.N.Y.)
Ariz. St. U.
U. Ariz.
Ark. St. U.
U. Ark.
Baylor U.
Bennington C.
Boston U.
Bowl. Gr. St. U.
Brandeis U.
B.Y.U.
Brooklyn C. (C.U.N.Y.)
Butler U.
Cal. Inst. Arts
Cal. St. U. (Fullerton)
Cal. St. U. (Long Beach)
Cal. St. U. (L.A.)
Cal. St. U. (Northridge)
Cal. St. U. (Sacramento)
U. Cal. (Berkeley)
U. Cal. (Davis)
U. Cal. (Irvine)
U.C.L.A.
U. Cal. (San Diego)
U. Cal. (Santa Barbara)
U. Cal. (Santa Cruz)
Carnegie Mellon U.
Case West. Res. U.
Catholic U.
Cent. Mich. U.
Cent. Mo. St. U.
Cent. Wash. U.
U. Cincinnati
U. Colo.
Columbia U.
Conn. C.
U. Conn.
Cornell U.
U. Del.
DePaul U.
East. Mich. U.
Emerson C.
Fla. Atlantic U.
Fla. St. U.
U. Fla.
Geo. Wash. U.
U. Georgia
U. Hawaii
U. Houston
Humboldt St. U.
Hunter C. (C.U.N.Y.)
Idaho St. U.
U. Idaho
Ill. St. U.
U. Ill.
U. Ill. (Chicago)
Ind. St. U.
Ind. U.
U. Iowa
U. Kans.

Kent St. U.
U. Ky.
U. La. (Monroe)
Lamar U.
L.I.U. (C.W. Post)
L.S.U.
U. Louisville
U. Maine
U. Md.
U. Mass.
U. Memphis
Miami U. (Ohio)
U. Miami (Fla.)
Mich. St. U.
U. Mich.
Minn. St. U. (Mankato)
U. Minn
U. Miss.
U. Mo. (Columbia)
U. Mo. (K.C.)
U. Mont.
Montclair U.
U. Neb.
U. Nev.
U. N. Mex.
U. N. Orleans
C.U.N.Y. (Grad. Ctr.)
S.U.N.Y. (Binghamton)
N.Y.U.
U. No. Car. (Chapel Hill)
U. No. Car. (Greensboro)
No. Dak. St. U.
U. No. Dak.
U. No. Tex.
No. Ill. U.
Northwestern U.
Ohio St. U.
Ohio U.
Okla. City U.
Okla. St. U.
U. Okla.
U. Ore.
Penn. St. U.
Pittsburgh St. U.
U. Pitt.
Portland St. U.
U. Portland
Purdue U.
Rhode Island C.
Roosevelt U.
Rowan U.
Rutgers U.
S.D.S.U.
U.S.D.
San Fran. St. U.
San Jose St. U.
Sarah Lawrence C.
Smith C.
U. So. Cal.
U. So. Car.
U. So. Dak.
U. So. Fla.
So. Ill. U.
So. Meth. U.
U. So. Miss.
Southwest Mo. St. U.
Southwest Tex. St. U.
Stanford U.
S. F. Austin St. U.
Stony Brook U. (S.U.N.Y.)
Sul Ross St. U.
Syracuse U.
Temple U.
U. Tenn.
Tex. Christ. U.
Tex. Tech U.
Tex. Woman's U.

U. Tex. (Austin)
U. Tex. (El Paso)
U. Tex. (Pan American)
Tufts U.
Tulane U.
Utah St. U.
U. Utah
Villanova U.
Va. Commonwealth U.
Va. Poly. Inst.
U. Va.
Wash. St. U.
Wash. U.
U. Wash.
Wayne St. U.
W. Va. U.
West. Ill. U.
West. Wash. U.
U. Wis.
U. Wis. (Milwaukee)
U. Wis. (Superior)
Yale U.

DANCE
American U.
Ariz. St. U.
Bennington C.
B.Y.U.
Butler U.
Cal. St. U. (Fullerton)
Cal. St. U. (Long Beach)
U. Cal. (Irvine)
U.C.L.A.
U. Cal. (Riverside)
Case West. Res. U.
U. Cincinnati
U. Colo.
Columbia U. (Teachers C.)
Conn. C.
Fla. St. U.
Geo. Mason U.
U. Hawaii
Hunter C. (C.U.N.Y.)
U. Ill.
Ind. U.
U. Iowa
U. Md.
Mills C.
U. Mich.
U. Minn.
U. Neb.
U. Nev.
S.U.N.Y.C. (Brockport)
U. N. Mex.
N.Y.U.
U. No. Car. (Greensboro)
Ohio St. U.
U. Okla.
U. Ore.
Sam Houston St. U.
Sarah Lawrence C.
Smith C.
So. Meth. U.
Temple U.
Tex. Christ. U.
Tex. Woman's U.
U. Tex. (Austin)
U. Utah
U. Wash.

DANCE THERAPY
Hunter C. (C.U.N.Y.)

MUSIC THEATER
Fla. St. U.
Ind. U.
U. Mich.
N.Y.U.

PLAYWRITING
Catholic U.
N.Y.U.
Temple U.

THEATER FOR THE DEAF
Conn. C.

THEATER MANAGEMENT
Columbia U.
Emerson C.
U. Miami
N.Y.U.
Yale U.

Urban Design/City Planning

(Typically includes Community Planning, City Planning, Environmental Design, Urban and Regional Planning, Urban Design)

U. Akron
Ala. A&M U.
U. Albany (S.U.N.Y.)
American U.
Ariz. St. U.
U. Ariz.
Auburn U.
Ball St. U.
Boston U.
U. Buffalo (S.U.N.Y.)
Cal. Poly. St. U. (San Luis Obispo)
Cal. St. Poly. U. (Pomona)
Cal. St. U. (Chico)
U. Cal. (Berkeley)
U. Cal. (Davis)
U. Cal. (Irvine)
U.C.L.A.
Catholic U.
U. Cincinnati
Clemson U.
Cleveland St. U.
U. Colo.
Columbia U.
Cornell U.
East. Ky. U.
East. Wash. U.
Fla. Atlantic U.
Fla. St. U.
U. Fla.
Georgia Inst. Tech.
Harvard U.
U. Hawaii
Hunter C. (C.U.N.Y.)
Ill. Inst. Tech.
U. Ill.
U. Ill. (Chicago)
Ind. U.
I.U.P.U.I.
Iowa St. U.
U. Iowa
Kans. St. U.
U. Kansas
U. La. (Lafayette)
U. Louisville
U. Md.
M.I.T.
U. Mass.
U. Memphis
Mich. St. U.

U. Mich.
U. Minn.
Morgan St. U.
U. Neb.
U. N. Mex.
U. N. Orleans
N.Y.U.
U. No. Car. (Chapel Hill)
Northeastern Ill. U.
Ohio St. U.
U. Okla.
Old Dom. U.
U. Ore.
Penn. St. U.
U. Penn.
U. Pitt.
Portland St. U.
Pratt Inst.
Princeton U.
U. Puerto Rico
R.P.I.
Rice U.
Rutgers U.
S.D.S.U.
San Jose St. U.
U. So. Cal.
U. Tenn.
Tex. A&M U.
Tex. So. U.
Tex. Tech U.
U. Tex. (Arlington)
U. Tex. (Austin)
U. Toledo
Utah St. U.
Va. Commonwealth U.
Va. Poly. Inst.
U. Va.
Wash. St. U.
U. Wash.
Wash. U. (Mo.)
Wayne St. U.
West Chester U. Pa.
West. Ky. U.
U. Wis.
U. Wis. (Milwaukee)
U. Wyo.
Yale U.

Veterinary Medicine

Auburn U.
U. Cal. (Davis)
Colo. St. U.
Cornell U.
U. Fla.
U. Georgia
U. Ill.
Iowa St. U.
Kans. St. U.
L.S.U.
Mich. St. U.
U. Minn.
Miss. St. U.
U. Mo. (Columbia)
No. Car. St. U. (Raleigh)
Ohio St. U.
Okla. St. U.
Ore. St. U.
U. Penn.
Purdue U.
U. Tenn. (Knoxville)
Tex. A&M U.
Tufts U.
Tuskegee U.
Va. Poly. Tech.
Wash. St. U.
U. Wis.